WITHDRAWN FROM COLLECTION

Lonely Planet

India

Joe Bindloss, Lindsay Brown, Paul Harding, Anirban Mahapatra, Daniel McCrohan, Isabella Noble, John Noble, Michael Benanav, Stuart Butler, Mark Elliott, Trent Holden, Bradley Mayhew, Kevin Raub, Sarina Singh, Iain Stewart

Contents

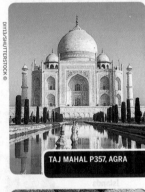

TAJ MAHAL P357, AGRA

DIY13/SHUTTERSTOCK ©

SPICES AT A MARKET STALL

ITSMEJUST/SHUTTERSTOCK ©

ON THE ROAD

Contents

Contents

Welcome to India

With its sumptuous mix of traditions, spiritual beliefs, festivals, architecture and landscapes, your memories of India will blaze bright long after you've left its shores.

India's Great Outdoors

India's landscapes are as fantastically varied as its cultural traditions. From the snow-dusted peaks of the Himalaya to the sun-splashed beaches of the tropical south, the country has a bounty of outdoor attractions. You can scout for big jungle cats on scenic wildlife safaris, paddle in the shimmering waters of coastal retreats, take blood-pumping treks high in the mountains, or simply inhale pine-scented air on meditative forest walks. Among all these natural treasures is a wealth of architectural gems, from serene temples rising out of pancake-flat plains to crumbling forts peering over plunging ravines.

So Delicious

Indian cuisine is a scrumptious smorgasbord of regionally distinct recipes – from the competing flavours of masterfully marinated meats and thalis (plate meals) to the simple splendour of vegetarian curries and deep-sea delights. Spices lie at the heart of Indian cooking, with the crackle of cumin seeds in hot oil a familiar sound in most kitchens. The country is also renowned for its tempting array of street food, with vendors selling everything from spicy samosas and kebabs to cooling *kulfi* (ice cream) and lassi (yoghurt drink).

Expectedly Unexpected

A go-with-the-flow attitude will help keep your sanity intact when traversing the chaotic canvas that is India. With the country's ability to inspire, exasperate, thrill and confound all at once, be prepared for unexpected surprises. This can be challenging, particularly for first-time visitors: despite India's wonders, the poverty is confronting, the bureaucracy can be frustrating and the crush of humanity may turn the simplest task into a frazzling epic. But love it or loathe it – and most visitors see-saw between the two – to embrace India's unpredictability is to embrace its soul.

Soul Warming

Spirituality is the ubiquitous thread in India's richly diverse tapestry, weaving all the way from the snowy mountains of the far north to the tropical shores of the deep south. Hinduism and Islam have the most followers, while Sikhism, Buddhism, Jainism, Christianity and Zoroastrianism are also widely practised. The array of sacred sites and rituals pay testament to the country's long and colourful religious history. And then there are its festivals, from formidable city parades to simple village harvest fairs that pay homage to a locally worshipped deity.

Why I Love India

By Sarina Singh, Writer

The moment I start to think I'm right on the precipice of unravelling one of India's deep mysteries, the country has an uncanny way of reminding me that it would take many lifetimes to do so. Indeed, demystifying India is a perpetual work in progress. And that is precisely what makes the country so alluring: the constant exploration; the playful unpredictability; and knowing that, just when it's least expected, you can find yourself up close and personal with moments that have the power to alter the way you view the world and your place in it.

For more about our writers, see p1256

Above: Holi festival (p29) celebrations

India

External boundaries shown reflect the requirements of the Government of India.

ELEVATION

| 6000m |
| 5000m |
| 4000m |
| 3000m |
| 2000m |
| 1000m |
| 0 |

Ladakh
Snow-capped mountainscapes and thrilling treks (p232)

Delhi
Ancient ruins, magic, mayhem and street food (p60)

Amritsar
Site of the glorious, revered Golden Temple (p214)

Udaipur
This lakeside city is a vision in white (p156)

Jaisalmer
A sandcastle-like fort and desert safaris (p188)

Shimla
India's premier hill station (p287)

Rishikesh
Self-styled yoga capital of the world (p415)

Agra
The Taj Mahal – architectural masterpiece (p355)

Khajuraho
Sex-themed sculptures spice up magnificent temples (p637)

Varanasi
Holy rituals along the sacred Ganges (p380)

Darjeeling
Tasting fine teas in front of epic Himalayan vistas (p498)

The Wild Northeast
Tribal encounters for the adventurous (p558)

500 km
250 miles

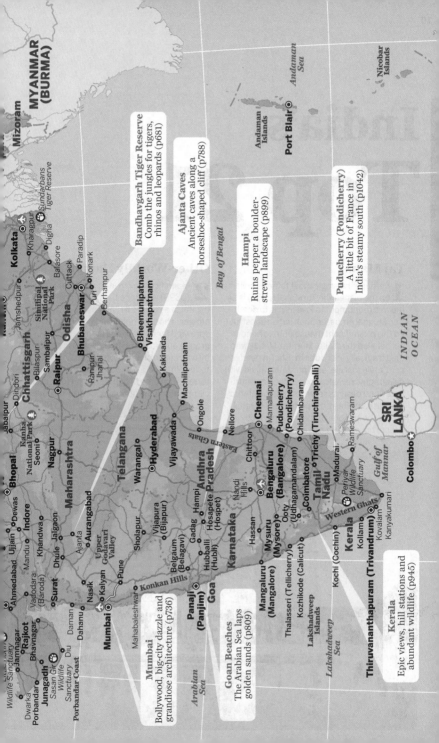

MYANMAR (BURMA)

Mizoram

Andaman Sea

Nicobar Islands

Andaman Islands

Port Blair

Bandhavgarh Tiger Reserve
Comb the jungles for tigers, rhinos and leopards (p681)

Ajanta Caves
Ancient caves along a horseshoe-shaped cliff (p788)

Hampi
Ruins pepper a boulder-strewn landscape (p899)

Puducherry (Pondicherry)
A little bit of France in India's steamy south (p1042)

Sundarbans Tiger Reserve

Kolkata

Kharagpur

Digha

Paradip

Bay of Bengal

Jamshedpur

Bilaspur

Bilaspur

Dindori

Jabalpur

Bhopal

Indore

Ujjain

Dewas

Ahmedabad

Vadodara (Baroda)

Dhule

Khandwa

Jalgaon

Ajanta

Mandu

Seoni

Kanha National Park

Raipur

Chhattisgarh

Sambalpur

Similipal National Park

Odisha

Bhubaneswar

Puri

Konark

Berhampur

Cuttack

Balasore

Rampur-Jharial

Visakhapatnam

Bheemunipatnam

Kakinada

Machilipatnam

Vijayawada

Telangana

Warangal

Hyderabad

Andhra Pradesh

Eastern Ghats

Nagpur

Maharashtra

Aurangabad

Nasik

Kalyan

Mumbai

Pune

Mahabaleshwar

Konkan Hills

Upper Godavari Valley

Sholapur

Vijapura (Bijapur)

Gadag

Hampi

Hosapete (Hospet)

Belgaum (Belagavi)

Hubballi (Hubli)

Karnataka

Hassan

Nandi Hills

Bengaluru (Bangalore)

Mysuru (Mysore)

Ooty (Udhagamandalam)

Coimbatore

Chittoor

Nellore

Ongole

Chennai

Mamallapuram

Puducherry (Pondicherry)

Chidambaram

Tamil Nadu

Trichy (Tiruchirappalli)

Madurai

Rameswaram

Periyar Wildlife Sanctuary

Western Ghats

Kerala

Kochi (Cochin)

Kollam

Kovalam

Thiruvananthapuram (Trivandrum)

Kanyakumari

Gulf of Mannar

SRI LANKA

Colombo

INDIAN OCEAN

Lakshadweep Sea

Lakshadweep Islands

Mangaluru (Mangalore)

Thalasseri (Tellicherry)

Kozhikode (Calicut)

Arabian Sea

Panaji (Panjim)

Goa

Mumbai
Bollywood, big-city dazzle and grandiose architecture (p736)

Goan Beaches
The Arabian Sea laps golden sands (p809)

Kerala
Epic views, hill stations and abundant wildlife (p945)

Dwarka

Porbandar

Porbandar Coast

Wildlife Sanctuary

Jamnagar

Rajkot

Junagadh

Sasan Gir Wildlife Sanctuary

Bhavnagar

Daman

Diu

Dahanu

India's
Top 21

Taj Mahal

1 Perhaps the single most famous building on the planet, the Taj Mahal (p357) is as much a monument to love as it is to death. The Mughal emperor Shah Jahan constructed this magnificent mausoleum to honour his beloved third wife, Mumtaz Mahal, who died tragically in childbirth. Clad in pearlescent while marble, and intricately inlaid with calligraphy, semiprecious stones and intricate floral designs representing the eternal paradise, the Taj is the pinnacle of Mughal creativity, and one of the most perfectly proportioned buildings ever constructed.

Other-Worldly Hampi

2 Magnificent even in ruins, Hampi (p899) was once the cosmopolitan capital of a powerful Hindu empire, Vijayanagar, whose temples and water tanks sprawled for miles over a landscape of granite outcrops and boulders. Ransacked by warring armies, its toppled temples are today almost continuous with the rocky terrain. Traverse the centuries on foot, rock-climb among the outcrops, or drift through the ruins by boat on the Tungabhadra River: however you explore, Hampi will transport you to another world. Virupaksha Temple (p900)

Ladakh's Moonscapes

3 Rolling north from the sun-baked Indian plains, the air grows cooler and crisper and the terrain more rugged as you climb into the high Himalaya. In culture and topography, Ladakh (p232) is closer to Buddhist Tibet than Hindu India, and centuries-old monasteries cling on in its wild desert valleys. Snow closes off this former Buddhist kingdom for half the year, so most visitors come for the brief summer when the snow melts on the mountain passes and patches of greenery appear. Even in a country of superlatives, there's nowhere quite like Ladakh! Phyang Gompa (p259)

Caves of Ajanta

4 They may have lived a life of austere humility, but the 2nd-century-BC monks who created the Ajanta caves (p788) certainly had an eye for the dramatic. Thirty rock-cut grottoes worm through the face of a horseshoe-shaped cliff, protecting some of the finest carvings ever produced. The caverns were originally hollowed out to provide peaceful spaces for meditation and contemplation, but later generations adorned the chambers with exquisite carvings and paintings depicting the Buddha's former lives. Renunciation of the worldly life was never so sophisticated.

PIXOSO.KZ/SHUTTERSTOCK ©

AKELBIRK/SHUTTERSTOCK ©

Wildlife Safaris

5 Spotting India's national animal in the wild takes perseverance and a bit of luck, but if you do spy a tiger burning bright in the Indian jungle, the experience will stay with you for a lifetime. Even if you don't encounter one of Shere Khan's cousins, look out for leopards, bears, monkeys, rhinos, elephants and a host of other wildlife in national parks such as Bandhavgarh (p681; pictured), Kaziranga and Nagarhole. There's hardly a corner of India that doesn't have some kind of natural reserve where you can join a safari in search of adventure.

Boating the Backwaters of Kerala

6 Lazily navigating the radiant backwaters of Kerala (p972) is like floating off into a dream. Probably India's most laid-back state has 900km of interconnected rivers, lakes, canals and lagoons lined with swaying coconut palms and picturesque villages. The most atmospheric way to explore this waterlogged rural heartland is on board a teak-and-palm-thatch houseboat. Spend the days watching village life drift past in a timeless tableau, before feasting on Keralan seafood curries and falling into a restful sleep beneath a canopy of twinkling stars.

Cuppa in a Hill Station

7 India's lowlands are full of wonders, but come summer it can get darn hot down there. Indian royals and imported colonials escaped the heat by heading to cool mountain refuges, such as Darjeeling (p498), Shimla (p287) and Kodaikanal (p1077), tucked into the forested foothills of the Himalaya or crowning the peaks of the Western Ghats down south. Dripping with Raj nostalgia, India's hill stations are places to curl up under a blanket with a steaming cup of locally grown tea, watching mist drift through the tea plantations (pictured) beneath grandstand views of the peaks.

DMITRY RUKHLENKO/SHUTTERSTOCK ©

Risqué Khajuraho

8 Ever fancied being a fly on the wall at an orgy? Where couples intertwine in positions that defy the physically possible? Khajuraho could well be your place. Some say the sensuous carvings on Khajuraho's temples (p637) depict the Kamasutra, or tantric practices for initiates; others claim they're a reminder to the faithful to set lust aside before entering holy places. But pretty much everyone agrees that they're delightfully mischievous. Once the titillation wanes, you'll notice that the skill and delicacy of the carving on these historic temples is even more impressive than the subject matter.

Jaisalmer's Desert Mirage

9 A gigantic golden sandcastle that rises like a mirage from Rajasthan's Thar Desert, the 12th-century citadel of Jaisalmer (p188; pictured) is impossibly romantic and picturesque. With its crenellated ramparts and barrel-shaped towers, this is the very vision of a desert fortress, emerging from and almost continuous with the camel-coloured scrub landscape on all sides. Inside, a royal palace, atmospheric old havelis (merchants' mansions), delicately chiselled Jain temples and maze-like lanes conspire to create one of the country's most atmospheric places.

Mumbai's Architectural Visions

10 Mumbai (p736) is more than just a city. This frenetic, fabulous metropolis is the beating heart of Indian film, fashion and finance, built on the hopes and dreams of its 22 million inhabitant. Sprawling over seven islands, Mumbai is prosperous and desperate, brash but also life-affirming. From the skyscraping towers of north Mumbai to the art deco apartments of Marine Drive (pictured) and the faded Victoriana of Fort, Mumbai wears its history, and its ambitions, on its sleeve – come for the food and culture, and be seduced.

Goan Beaches

11 With swishing palms sandwiched between sugar-white sands and lapping kingfisher-blue waves, the coastline of Goa (p809) has a laid-back, hedonistic charm that's like nowhere else in India. With a string of what could be India's most beautiful beaches, this is no undiscovered escape, but the coastal strip bustles with beachside snack shacks, accommodation for every taste and budget, and markets full of blissed-out tie-dye-clad travellers. It's a slice of paradise that appeals to social animals and fans of creature comforts who like their seafood fresh and their holidays easy.

Holy Varanasi

12 Life, death and all things in-between play out in vivid colour in Varanasi (p380), India's most sacred city. Like the sacred Ganges that traces its eastern edge, centuries of ritual and tradition flow over Varanasi's riverside ghats (pictured), where holy men fill the air with incense, pilgrims bathe in a vast human tide, and devout Hindus pass into the life hereafter on funeral pyres. To be here is to witness India at its most open, so step into the dizzying spiritual whirlwind and get carried away by Varanasi's kaleidoscope of colours.

Amritsar's Golden Temple

13 The holiest Sikh shrine, Amritsar's Golden Temple (p215) is a place where spirituality pushes through into the material world. A continuous chain of pilgrims circles the Saravar, a water tank excavated by the fourth Sikh guru in 1577, while priests chant passages from the Guru Granth Sahib, the Sikh holy book, in the gold-encased chapel at the centre of the pool. To visit is to glimpse the soul of the Sikh religion, characterised by honour, courage and hospitality – best exemplified by the Guru-Ka-Langar, the vast kitchen for pilgrims that feeds 100,000 people daily.

Epic Rail Journeys

14 A train journey across India, passing lime-green rice paddies, jungle-cloaked hills and jutting temple spires, is an epic experience. Sure, you could save time by flying, but it's tricky to mix with the masses and soak up India's dramatically diverse scenery from 35,000ft. Riding the rails is a chance to chit-chat with locals over a hot cup of chai, or gaze out the window at the ever-changing landscape, contemplating India's contradictions. Ramp up the romance on the toy train from Kalka to Shimla (p295; pictured), or one of India's other delightful mountain railways.

DAVID EVISON/SHUTTERSTOCK ©

XANDRA R./SHUTTERSTOCK ©

Historic Delhi

15 India's captivating capital (p60) bears the scars of a string of former empires, from tombs and fortresses left behind by sultans and warlords to the broad streets laid out by British colonials. Delhi may be chaotic today, but it rewards visitors with an abundance of riches: fabulous food and culture; Mughal relics and maze-like markets; New Delhi, with its political monuments and museums; the ancient forts of Tughlaqabad and Purana Qila; and ruined wonders at the Qutab Minar complex (p78; pictured) and Mehrauli. Come and be mesmerised by 3000 years of history.

Tribal Northeast

16 If the crowds wear you down in Rajasthan or Kerala, point your compass northeast to India's rugged tribal states, linked to the rest of India by just a narrow strip of land, and culturally closer to Myanmar, Bhutan and Bangladesh. For decades the region was off-limits due to colonial-era red tape, but visiting is getting easier all the time. If you venture to the mountainous north of Arunachal Pradesh (p573), or former headhunter villages in forested Nagaland (p582), you'll be stepping off the tourist map into a world of tribal customs and untamed scenery.
Apatani woman from the Ziro Valley (p575)

French-Flavoured Puducherry

17 Where else in the world could you start the day with Ashtanga yoga, breakfast on pain au chocolat, wander streets full of French-colonial villas, glean spiritual tips at a legendary ashram, then dine on fabulous Indian fusion food before strolling beside the tropical ocean? In this former French colony (p1042), mustard-coloured houses line cobblestone streets, grand cathedrals overflow with architectural frou-frou, and the croissants are the real deal. But Puducherry (Pondicherry) is also a Tamil town – with all the history, temples and hustle and bustle that go along with that.

Meditative Rishikesh

18 India's self-styled yoga capital (p415) has been a source of enlightenment since long before the Beatles stopped by in full-blown hippie mode. Blessed with a glorious setting in the Himalayan foothills, tracing the banks of the Ganges, Rishikesh is the perfect place to settle for a time to practise your downward dog, try some laughter therapy, ritually bathe in the Ganges or whatever else floats your spiritual boat. Then there's that mountain air, blissfully fresh and clean after the polluted fug of the plains.

Grand Mehrangarh

19 India is awash with magnificent fortresses, but Jodhpur's Mehrangarh (p179) is particularly humbling. A Rajput maharaja raised this mighty bastion to defend his newly founded capital at Jodhpur, and the fortress saw a string of bloody battles as rival powers eyed its magnificence. With its inlaid interiors and gateways big enough to accommodate war elephants, Mehrangarh showcases Rajasthan's grandeur but also its tragedies – handprints of royal wives who immolated themselves on the funeral pyre of Maharaja Man Sing still mark the walls.

Elegant Udaipur

20 An ice-white city (p156) of faded splendours, sitting on the bank of a mirror-like lake, Udaipur is one of India's most romantic locations. As the sun sets over its turreted palaces, reflected in the millpond-calm waters of Lake Pichola, and voices float upwards from its busy bazaars, Udaipur will transport you to the India of fables. Sure, you'll have company on the journey, but as you look out over the Rajput elegance of the graceful Lake Palace or wander Udaipur's backstreet mansions and gardens, you certainly won't mind! City Palace (p157)

The Wild Western Ghats

21 Stretching like an emerald scarf from Maharashtra to Tamil Nadu, the Western Ghats are the south's answer to the Himalaya, here you'll find ridges choked in jungle, nostalgic hill stations, scattered tea and spice plantations, and national parks teeming with elephants, leopards and tigers. There's even a charming, steam-powered miniature train, chugging uphill to Ooty (Udhagamandalam; p1092; pictured) via Coonoor. You'll find plenty of colonial-era bungalows turned hotels, where you can sit with a cup of Indian tea and watch the mists swirl over mountains.

Need to Know

For more information, see Survival Guide (p1189)

Currency
Indian rupee (₹)

Languages
Hindi and English (official)

Visas
Required for most visitors; e-Visa (valid 60 days) available for more than 150 nationalities. Longer trips require a standard six-month tourist visa.

Money
ATMs widely available; carry cash as backup, especially in remote regions. Don't accept damaged banknotes: they won't be accepted by others.

Mobile Phones
India operates on the GSM network at 900MHz, the world's most common standard. Roaming connections excellent in urban areas, poor in the countryside and the Himalaya. Local prepaid SIMs widely available.

Time
India Standard Time (GMT/UTC plus 5½ hours)

When to Go

Leh
GO Jul–Sep

Delhi
GO Nov–Mar

Kolkata
GO Nov–Mar

Mumbai
GO Nov–Feb

Bengaluru (Bangalore)
GO Nov–Mar

Chennai
GO Nov–Mar

Alpine desert (including snow)
Desert, dry climate
Mild to hot summers, cold winters
Tropical climate, rain year-round
Tropical climate, wet & dry seasons
Warm to hot summers, mild winters

High Season
(Dec–Mar)

➡ Pleasant weather – warm days, cool nights. Peak tourists, peak prices.

➡ Cold or freezing conditions from December to February at altitude.

➡ Temperatures climb steadily from February.

Shoulder
(Jun–Nov)

➡ Passes to Ladakh and the high Himalaya open from June to September.

➡ Monsoon rains persist through to September.

➡ The southeastern coast and southern Kerala see heavy rain from October to early December.

Low Season
(Apr–Jun)

➡ April is hot; May and June are scorching. Competitive hotel prices.

➡ From June, the monsoon sweeps from south to north, bringing draining humidity.

➡ Beat the heat (but not the crowds) in the cool hills.

Useful Websites

Incredible India (www.incredibleindia.org) Official India tourism site.

Lonely Planet (www.lonelyplanet.com/india) Destination information, the Thorn Tree travel forum and more.

Templenet (www.templenet.com) Temple talk.

Rediff News (www.rediff.com/news) Portal for India-wide news.

Down to Earth (www.downtoearth.org.in) Focuses on Indian environmental issues often overlooked by the mainstream media.

Important Numbers

From outside India, dial your international access code, India's country code (☏91), then the number (minus the initial '0').

Country code	☏91
International access code	☏00
Emergency (ambulance/ fire/police)	☏112

Exchange Rates

Australia	A$1	₹49
Canada	C$1	₹51
Euro zone	€1	₹80
Japan	¥100	₹64
New Zealand	NZ$1	₹47
UK	UK£1	₹89
US	US$1	₹70

For current exchange rates, see www.xe.com

Daily Costs

Budget: Less than ₹3000

➡ Dorm bed: ₹400–₹600

➡ Double room in a budget hotel: ₹400–₹1000

➡ All-you-can-eat thalis (plate meals): ₹100–₹300

➡ Bus and train tickets: ₹300–₹500

Midrange: ₹4000–₹10,000

➡ Double hotel room: ₹1500–₹5000

➡ Meals in midrange restaurants: ₹600–₹1500

➡ Admission to historic sights and museums: ₹500–₹1500

➡ Local taxis/autorickshaws: ₹500–₹2000

Top End: More than ₹10,000

➡ Deluxe hotel room: ₹5000–₹24,000

➡ Meals at superior restaurants: ₹2000–₹5000

➡ First-class train travel: ₹1000–₹8000

➡ Renting a car and driver: ₹2000 and up per day

Opening Hours

Banks (nationalised) 10am to 2pm/4pm Monday to Friday, to noon/1pm/4pm Saturday; closed second and fourth Saturday

Bars and clubs noon to 12.30am

Markets 10am to 7pm in major cities; rural markets may be weekly, from early morning to lunchtime

Post offices 9.30am to 5pm Monday to Saturday

Restaurants 8am to 10pm, or lunch (noon to 3pm) and dinner (7pm to 10pm or 11pm)

Shops 10am to 7pm or 8pm, some closed Sunday

Sights Museums (& other sights) are often closed on Monday

Arriving in India

Indira Gandhi International Airport (Delhi) Express metro to New Delhi station ₹60. Frequent 24-hour AC buses to Kashmere Gate station ₹50. Taxis from ₹450; Uber and Ola Cabs cheaper (add ₹150 to fares for airport parking/entry).

Chhatrapati Shivaji Maharaj International Airport (Mumbai) Non-AC/AC taxis ₹670/810 to Colaba and Fort, ₹400/480 to Bandra. Train (avoid 6am-to-11am rush hour): autorickshaw (₹18 per km) to Andheri station, then Churchgate or CST train (₹10, 45 minutes). Off-peak UberGo ₹250 to Bandra Kurla Complex, ₹260 to Bandra (W), ₹460 to Fort, ₹560 to Colaba.

Kempegowda International Airport (Bengaluru) AC taxis ₹750 to ₹1000; Uber/Ola ₹550 to ₹650. Frequent AC Vayu Vajra buses ₹170 to ₹260.

Chennai International Airport Metro ₹50 to ₹70. Taxis ₹450 to ₹600; Ola cheaper.

Getting Around

Air Flights are available to most major centres and state capitals; cheap flights are on offer with budget airlines.

Train Frequent services to most destinations; inexpensive tickets are available, even on sleepers.

Bus Buses go everywhere; some destinations are served 24 hours, but longer routes may have just one or two buses a day.

For much more on **getting around**, see p1210

PLAN YOUR TRIP NEED TO KNOW

First Time India

For more information, see Survival Guide (p1189)

Checklist

➡ Ensure your passport has six months' validity past your arrival date and two blank pages

➡ Arrange vaccinations

➡ Apply for an e-Visa (https://indianvisaonline. gov.in), if required, at least four and at most 120 days before your arrival date; carry a copy of your electronic travel authorisation (ETA)

➡ Inform your debit/credit-card company you're heading away

➡ Arrange travel insurance

What to Pack

➡ Well-concealed money belt

➡ Sunscreen and sunglasses

➡ Earplugs – essential for nuisance noise

➡ Mosquito repellent

➡ A reliable padlock for budget hotel doors

➡ Sheet sleeping bag for budget hotel rooms and dorms

➡ An MP3 player to help pass the time while waiting for delayed transport

Top Tips for Your Trip

➡ Make a plan, but don't be over-ambitious, and allow time for for flexible travel.

➡ Alternate between cities and the coast, hills or countryside to recharge.

➡ To stay healthy: use hand sanitiser, eat freshly cooked food and never drink tap water.

➡ Book long-distance train journeys ahead, especially during festival times.

➡ Be ready for hassle in touristy places.

➡ Dress to respect local culture.

➡ Wear thin, covering cotton for the plains, warm-weather gear for the hills.

➡ Bargaining is part of life, but keep a sense of proportion.

What to Wear

Male and female travellers should wear non-revealing clothes as a sign of respect for local social mores. This is essential at holy sites (carry a thin headscarf to cover your hair).

Follow the lead of locals. The *salwar kameez* – a long, flowing shirt with loose-fitting trousers – is practical for women, as is the *kurta* (a long, loose-fitting shirt) for men. Bring comfortable covered shoes/trainers, plus slip-on shoes for sacred sites, and cold-weather clothing for the Himalaya.

Sleeping

In most of India you'll get a cheaper rate as a walk-in guest than if you book ahead, except at higher end places, hostels and chain hotels where online discounts are the norm.

Hostels Good-quality hostels offer clean, well-equipped dorms and a backpacker vibe.

Homestays Usually away from tourist hubs, but a great opportunity to experience ordinary Indian life.

Guesthouses & Hotels India has the whole gamut, from top-end five stars to no-frills cheapies.

Scams

To avoid India's legendary scams, note the following:

➡ Buy train and bus tickets from official outlets where possible; people offering to lead you to the 'ticket desk' may steer you to a commission-paying travel agency.

➡ Find your own way to hotels and guesthouses; arrive with a 'guide' and the rate may be hiked to cover their commission.

➡ Be dubious of detours to shops by rickshaw and taxi drivers; this is usually a ruse to earn a commission.

Bargaining

Bargaining is a way of life in India, including at markets and most shops. Keep things in perspective: / haggle hard, except where fixed prices are displayed, but not without a sense of humour. You'll usually have to agree to a price before hiring a taxi or autorickshaw, or a car and driver for longer trips. Uber or Ola use fixed prices.

Tipping

Restaurants and hotels
Service fees sometimes added automatically; otherwise, 10% is reasonable.

Hotel/train/airport porters
₹10 to ₹20.

Taxis and rickshaws Not expected, but appreciated.

Private drivers ₹200 per day for good service.

Trekking Per day from ₹350/200 for guides/porters.

Tour guides ₹200 to ₹350 per day is fair.

Long-distance motorcycle touring (p1214) is popular in India

Etiquette

Dress Avoid offence by eschewing tight, sheer or skimpy clothes.

Shoes It's polite to remove your shoes before entering homes and places of worship.

Photos It's best to ask before snapping people, sacred sites or ceremonies.

Feet Avoid pointing the soles of your feet towards people or deities, or touching anyone with your feet.

Greetings Saying 'namaste' with your hands together in a prayer gesture is a respectful Hindu greeting; for Muslims, say 'salaam alaikum' ('peace be with you'; the response is 'alaikum salaam').

Hands The right hand is for eating and shaking hands; the left is the 'toilet' hand.

Eating

India's cuisine is a feast for the senses, but consider the following precautions to avoid food-related illness:

➡ Avoid tap water, and food rinsed in it.
➡ Eat only freshly-cooked food.
➡ Avoid shellfish and buffets.
➡ Peel fruit or wash in purified water.
➡ Eat in busy restaurants with a high turnover of customers.

What's New

Handy Hostels

A reaction to rising hotel prices, India's hostel scene is going from strength to strength; Delhi's Madpackers (p87) and GoStops (p82), Jaipur's Jaipur Janta (p118), Beehive (p879) in Mysuru (Mysore), Rishikesh's Live Free (p419) and Shalom Backpackers (p419) and Mumbai's Cohostel (p750) are leading the charge.

Airports Everywhere

Kannur's new international airport (p1007) took off in 2018, while Sikkim's sparkling new airfield at Pakyong (p544) promises one of India's most dramatic mountain flights. Even Hampi (p906) now has domestic links from upgraded Jindal Vijaynagar Airport.

Hassle-Free Andamans

Permit requirements for the Andaman Islands were eased in 2018; genuine luxury accommodation in the form of Exotica (p1107) and Jalakara (p1107) on Swaraj Dweep (Havelock) only adds to the appeal.

Taxi Apps

Uber and Ola Cabs are revolutionising city travel – no more brain-shattering haggling over cab fares! Both are banned in Goa, but Goa Tourism launched its own competitor, Goa Miles (p811) in 2018.

Colossal Statues

At 182m, Gujarat's new Statue of Unity (p706) is the biggest statue on earth, but it may soon be eclipsed by a rival in Mumbai. Over in Sikkim, Pelling's 42m-high statue of Chenrezig (p551) is just the latest in a string of giant deities.

Unravelling Punjab's Secrets

Newly opened in Amritsar, the Golden Temple Interpretation Centre (p215) is doing amazing work demystifying Sikhism's rich history and traditions, while the new Partition Museum (p215) shines a light on Punjab's darkest days.

Easier Northeast

Easing permit restrictions (now just required for Arunachal Pradesh) and improved transport links are opening up the Northeast Region. A 5km-long bridge over the Brahmaputra near Dibrugarh (p571) has shaved hours off the journey from Assam to Arunachal Pradesh, and border crossings (p586) now link Myanmar to Manipur and Mizoram.

Goa's Craft Beer

Goa's love of beer has brought the craft movement to its tropical shores, with several new microbreweries flaunting sophisticated brews.

Metros, Finally!

As Delhi's metro (p107) continues to expand, Hyderabad's new system (p933) offers a speedy, air-conditioned escape from the city's congestion; Kochi's much-anticipated metro (p996) opened in mid-2017, zipping above frenzied Ernakulam.

Heritage Homestays

Homestays are going upmarket; the Keralan capital's fabulous Padmavilasom Palace, reborn in 2018, delights with banana-leaf feasts and boutiquey sleeps in a 150-year-old royal Travancore home. (p950)

Goa Cruises

At last! As of 2018, Angriya Cruises transports travellers in style between Mumbai and Mormugao port, near Vasco da Gama in Goa. (p811)

For more recommendations and reviews, see lonelyplanet.com/india

If You Like...

Forts & Palaces

India's architecture tells a tale of conquest, domination and inordinate riches.

Rajasthan Nowhere matches the Land of Kings for romantic splendour; Jaisalmer, Jodhpur, Amber and Udaipur top the fort and palace stakes. (p108)

Maharashtra The land of warrior king Shivaji prickles with defensive masterpieces, including Daulatabad and island fortress Janjira. (p774)

Hyderabad Royal relics fill the Telangana capital, from time-ravaged Golconda fort to the lavish Falaknuma Palace. (p916)

Delhi This historically strategic city has imperial forts like other places have traffic islands. (p60)

Mysuru (Mysore) The majestic Mysuru Palace once housed one of India's most extravagant maharajas. (p873)

Grand Temples

No one does temples like India – from psychedelic South Indian Hindu towers to serene and silent Buddhist cave temples.

Tamil Nadu Bursting with *gopuram* (gateway) temple towers that climb to the sky in rainbow-coloured tiers of sculpted deities. (p1011)

Golden Temple The greatest of all Sikh temples rises like a treasure box above a sacred pool in Amritsar. (p215)

Rajasthan Jain temples at Jaisalmer, Ranakpur and Mt Abu offer some of India's most mind-blowingly intricate carvings. (p108)

Khajuraho Exquisite carvings of deities, spirits, musicians, regular people, mythological beasts – and sex, lots of sex. (p637)

Ladakh A wealth of Buddhist monasteries in a stunning lunar landscape. (p232)

Ancient Ruins

The ruins left behind by countless cultures and empires lie scattered across cities and countryside.

Hampi Rosy-hued temples and palaces of the mighty capital of Vijayanagar are scattered among other-worldly boulders and hilltops. (p899)

Mandu The tombs, palaces, monuments and mosques on Mandu's green plateau are among India's finest Islamic structures. (p668)

Delhi Conquered and built up repeatedly over 3000 years, Delhi is packed with the monumental ruins of ancient powerhouses. (p60)

Fatehpur Sikri A ghostly abandoned Mughal city, close to Agra and the Taj Mahal. (p372)

Maharashtra Magnificent rock-cut Buddhist temple caves at Ajanta and Ellora. (p774)

City Sophistication

India's cities offer fabulous fine dining, star-studded nightlife, five-star shopping and the cream of the arts.

Mumbai Home of Bollywood, Mumbai has it all: fashion, film stars, elegant dining, ritzy bars and top-notch art galleries. (p736)

Delhi Sophisticated Delhi is famous for its cultural life, with a packed festival calendar, exceptional shopping, stunning museums and fabulous dining. (p60)

Kolkata Renowned for music, poetry, literature and film, Kolkata also offers magical markets, grand colonial-era buildings and delicious seafood-based cuisine. (p453)

Bengaluru (Bangalore) Karnataka's burgeoning IT hub is loved for its nightlife, with microbreweries, gastropubs and music bars packed with partying locals. (p858)

Chennai Towering temples, stylish bars, swish hotels, fabulous shopping and a booming restaurant scene filled with the flavours of the south. (p1013)

Hill Stations

Those with the means have always fled to the hills to escape the hair-dryer heat of summer.

Tamil Nadu Kodaikanal and Ooty serve up misty forests, rolling tea plantations, mountain hikes, and accommodation in colonial-era bungalows. (p1076)

Munnar Kerala's not-too-touristy hill station sits amid rolling tea and spice plantations, where tropical birds give song in the morning mist. (p978)

Shimla Packed with Raj-era relics, Shimla is a great appetite-whetter for the magnificent Himalayan peaks visible from its ridge-top promenade. (p287)

Darjeeling The quintessential summer escape, surrounded by emerald-green plantations, with a backdrop of Himalayan giants. (p498)

Nainital Uttarakhand's favourite hill station, whose once-grand colonial-era hotels lie scattered around a lovely lake. (p445)

Beaches

India has some stunning stretches of coast that more than fulfill the tropical dream.

Kerala Backpacker favourite Varkala is backed by beautiful sea cliffs, Kovalam curls around a golden bay, and more deserted Thottada is shaded by nodding palms. (p945)

Goa Even when overrun with travellers, Goa's beaches are still gorgeous; Mandrem (p890) and

Top: Confluence of the Zanskar and Indus rivers (p259), Ladakh

Bottom: Camels at the Pushkar Camel Fair (p144), Rajasthan

Palolem (p849) are two of the prettiest.

Havelock Island (Swaraj Dweep) In the Andaman Islands, one of the world's most gorgeous beaches, with clear, aquamarine water lapping against white powder. (p1104)

Gokarna Sun seekers and devotees mix on Gokarna's beautiful beaches, which back onto an ancient pilgrimage town. (p895)

Puri Atmosphere lures people to this seaside pilgrim town, with a lively beach festival each November. (p605)

Yoga, Ayurveda & Spiritual Pursuits

India was the birthplace of myriad spiritual traditions from yoga and meditation to plant-based ayurvedic medicine.

Bihar Pilgrims and the spiritually curious flock to Bodhgaya to study and meditate where Buddha attained enlightenment. (p525)

Kerala This lush, green southern state is where ayurveda originated, and there's a herbal-oil-based treatment on almost every corner. (p945)

Rishikesh One of India's most popular places to salute the sun, with lessons for every level. (p415)

Mysuru (Mysore) K Pattabhi Jois developed Ashtanga yoga here, and it's still a great place to join a long or short course. (p873)

Ladakh Leh is packed with places offering meditation courses and yoga, and anyone can join in the real deal at a Buddhist monastery. (p233)

Wildlife Safaris

India's legendary Royal Bengal tigers can be elusive, but leopards, elephants, antelope, bison, one-horned rhinos and deer are often less shy.

Madhya Pradesh & Chhattisgarh This is serious tiger country, and sightings are likely in a string of national parks, including Kanha, Bandhavgarh and Pench Tiger Reserve. (p625)

Assam Kaziranga National Park is the world's rhinoceros capital; you may see dozens on a single safari. (p566)

Kerala Wayanad Wildlife Sanctuary is one of the few places where you have a good chance of spotting wild elephants. (p1003)

Gujarat Gir National Park provides a sanctuary for Asia's only wild lions, along with over 300 species of birds. (p716)

Rajasthan Spot tigers and other signature species amid the jungle and fortress ruins of Ranthambhore National Park. (p145)

Mountains

View the peaks from the comfort of a hill-station bungalow or see the summits up close on a mountain trek.

Ladakh Traverse 5000m passes between saw-tooth crags and sleep in villages that have survived unchanged through the centuries in this desolate moonscape. (p232)

Lahaul & Spiti Green Lahaul and rain-starved Spiti are divided from the rest of Himachal Pradesh by soaring mountain passes; even the drive up here is an epic adventure. (p343)

Darjeeling Overnight in simple lodges on the Singalila Ridge Trek, or sit pretty in one of Darjeeling's historic hotels for incredible views of the eastern Himalaya. (p508)

Sikkim View mighty Khangchendzonga, the world's third-highest mountain, up close from Pelling or the trekking trails to Goecha La and Dzongri. (p551)

Uttarakhand Join the pilgrim crowds bound for the dramatic Char Dam temples, or find true peace in Uttarakhand's mountain meadows. (p413)

Traveller Enclaves

Sometimes you just want to find some like-minded souls to swap stories from the road and discuss life-altering bowel events.

Goa Traveller magnet and beach haven, with Palolem and (cheaper) Arambol as its chief enclaves. (p809)

Rishikesh Yoga practitioners are irresistibly drawn to this self-styled yoga capital at the foot of the Himalaya. (p415)

McLeod Ganj The spiritually minded flock to this Buddhist community near Dharamsala to glean wisdom from the Dalai Lama. (p326)

Pushkar Travellers and pilgrims converge on this holy town for its Camel Fair, but you'll find a lively crowd here year-round. (p140)

Parvati Valley People linger for weeks or months sampling local 'herbs' and enjoying the ethereal beauty of this Himalayan valley. (p306)

Leh In summer half of Goa decamps from the coast to the lofty capital of Ladakh to continue the party. (p233)

Month by Month

January

Post-monsoon cool lingers throughout the country, with downright cold in the mountains. Moderate weather and several festivals make it a popular time to travel (book ahead!), while Delhi hosts big Republic Day celebrations.

✾ Republic Day

Republic Day commemorates the founding of the Republic of India on 26 January 1950; the biggest celebrations are in Delhi, with a vast military parade along Rajpath, and the Beating of the Retreat ceremony three days later. There are pigeon races in Old Delhi.

✾ Sankranti

Sankranti, the Hindu festival marking the sun's passage into Capricorn, takes place on 14 or 15 January, and is celebrated in many ways across India – from banana-giving to decorating sacred cows. But it's the mass kite-flying in Gujarat, Andhra Pradesh, Uttar Pradesh and Maharashtra that's most spectacular.

✾ Pongal

The Tamil festival of Pongal, equivalent to Sankranti, marks the end of the harvest season. Families prepare pots of *pongal* (a mixture of rice, sugar, dhal and milk), symbolic of prosperity and abundance, then feed them to decorated and adorned cows.

✾ Vasant Panchami

Hindus dress in yellow and place books, musical instruments and other educational objects in front of idols of Saraswati, the goddess of learning, to receive her blessing. The holiday sometimes falls in February.

February

This is a good time to be in India, with balmy weather in most non-mountainous areas. It's still peak travel season, and sunbathing and skiing are still on.

✾ Losar (Tibetan New Year)

Losar is celebrated by Tantric Buddhists all over India – particularly in Himachal Pradesh, Sikkim, Ladakh and Zanskar – for 15 days. The event usually falls in February or March, though dates can vary between regions.

✾ Shivaratri

Held in February or March, Shivaratri, a day of Hindu fasting, recalls the *tandava* (cosmic victory dance) of Lord Shiva. Temple processions are followed by the chanting of mantras and the anointing of linga (phallic images of Shiva). Upcoming dates: 21 February 2020, 11 March 2021.

✾ Carnival in Goa

The four-day party kicking off Lent is particularly big in Goa. Sabado Gordo (Fat Saturday) gets the festivities going with elaborate parades, and the revelry continues with street parties, concerts and general merrymaking. Can also fall in March.

March

The last month of high season, March is full-on hot in most of India, with rains starting in the Northeast Region. Wildlife is easier to spot, as animals emerge to find water ahead of the monsoon.

Holi

In February or March, Hindus celebrate the beginning of spring according to the lunar calendar by throwing coloured water and *gulal* (powder) at anyone within range. Bonfires the night before symbolise the demise of demoness Holika. Upcoming dates: 9 March 2020, 28 March 2021.

April

The heat has officially arrived in most places, which means you can get deals and avoid tourist crowds. The Northeast, meanwhile, is wet, but it's peak time for visiting Sikkim and highland West Bengal.

Mahavir Jayanti

Mahavir Jayanti commemorates the birth of Jainism's 24th and most important *tirthankar* (teacher and enlightened being). Temples are decorated and visited, Mahavir statues are given ritual baths, processions are held and offerings are given to the poor. Upcoming dates: 6 April 2020, 25 April 2021.

Rama Navami

During this one- to nine-day festival, Hindus celebrate Rama's birth with processions, music, fasting and feasting, enactments of scenes from the Ramayana and, at some temples, ceremonial weddings of Rama and Sita idols. Upcoming dates: 2 April 2020, 21 April 2021.

Easter

The Christian holiday marking the Crucifixion and Resurrection of Jesus Christ is celebrated simply in Christian communities with prayer and good food, particularly in Goa and Kerala. Upcoming dates for Easter Sunday: 12 April 2020, 4 April 2021.

Ramadan (Ramazan)

Thirty days of dawn-to-dusk fasting mark the ninth month of the Islamic calendar. Muslims traditionally turn their attention to God, with a focus on prayer and ritual purification. Ramadan begins around 24 April 2020 and 13 April 2021.

May

It's hot almost everywhere – incendiary, in fact. Festivals take a back seat as humidity builds up, awaiting the release of the rain. Hill stations are hopping, though, and in the mountains it's premonsoon trekking season.

Buddha Jayanti

The celebration of Buddha's birth, nirvana (enlightenment) and parinirvana (total liberation from the cycle of existence, or passing away) is calm but moving: devotees dress simply, eat vegetarian food, listen to dharma talks and visit monasteries or temples. Upcoming dates: 7 May 2020, 26 May 2021.

Eid al-Fitr

Muslims celebrate the end of Ramadan with three days of festivities. Prayers, shopping, gift-giving and, for women and girls, *mehndi* (henna designs) may all be part of the celebrations. Upcoming dates: 24 May 2020, 13 May 2021.

June

June is low season because of the heat, but it's a good time to trek up north, as the passes open to Ladakh. The rainy season starts just about everywhere else, making national-park access tricky.

Rath Yatra

The Chariot Festival in June or July sees effigies of Lord Jagannath (Vishnu incarnated as Lord of the Universe) and his siblings carried on vast, colourful chariots, most famously in Puri, Odisha (Orissa). Millions come to see the festivities. Upcoming dates: 23 June 2020, 12 July 2021.

July

It should be raining almost everywhere now, but flooding causes problems in many regions. Consider visiting Ladakh, where the weather's surprisingly dry and pleasant, or do a rainy-season meditation retreat, an ancient Indian tradition.

Naag Panchami

Held in July or August, Naag Panchami, particularly vibrant in Pune and

Kolhapur (Maharashtra) and Karnataka, is dedicated to Ananta, the serpent upon whose coils Vishnu rested between universes. Women fast at home, while serpents are venerated as totems. Upcoming dates: 25 July 2020 and 13 August 2021.

Eid al-Adha

Commemorates Ibrahim's readiness to sacrifice his son to God; Muslims slaughter a goat or sheep and share it with family, the community and the poor. Upcoming dates: 31 July 2020, 19 July 2021.

August

Monsoon should be still going strong, but this is the best time to visit Ladakh. Tropical areas such as Kerala and Goa boast lush, green jungle, and it's often raining only a few hours a day.

Independence Day

This public holiday on 15 August celebrates India's independence from Britain in 1947. Celebrations include flag-hoisting ceremonies and parades. The biggest celebrations are in Delhi, where the prime minister addresses the nation from the Red Fort, and there events such as pigeon racing and kite flying in Old Delhi.

Janmastami

Krishna's birthday celebrations can last a week in Krishna's birthplace, Mathura; elsewhere the festivities range from fasting to *puja* (prayers) and offering sweets, to drawing elaborate *rangoli* (rice-paste designs) outside homes. Janmastami is held in August or September. Upcoming dates: 11 August 2020, 30 August 2021. (p388)

Onam

In August or September, Onam is Kerala's biggest cultural celebration. The entire state celebrates the golden age of mythical King Mahabali for 10 days. Upcoming dates: 30 August 2020, 21 August 2021.

Ganesh Chaturthi

The birth of the much-loved elephant-headed god is celebrated over 10 days, particularly in Mumbai, Hyderabad and Chennai. Clay idols of Ganesh are paraded through the streets before being ceremonially immersed in rivers, sacred temple tanks or the sea. Upcoming dates: 22 August 2020, 10 September 2021.

Ashura

Shiite Muslims commemorate the martyrdom of the Prophet's grandson Imam Hussain on the 10th day of Muharram with beautiful processions, especially in Hyderabad. Sunni Muslims commemorate the fast of Moses (Moosa) when Allah saved the Israelites from their enemy in Egypt. Upcoming dates: around 28 August 2020 and 18 August 2021.

September

The rain is petering out (but temperatures are still relatively high), and the monsoon is usually finished in places such as Rajasthan, which can be surprisingly green. Autumn trekking season begins mid-month in the Himalaya.

October

This is when the travel season starts to kick off in earnest. October, also known as shoulder season, brings festivals and mostly good weather, with reasonably comfy temperatures and lots of post-rain greenery.

Gandhi Jayanti

This national holiday is a solemn celebration of Mohandas Gandhi's birth, on 2 October, with prayer meetings at his cremation site in Delhi, Raj Ghat. (p73)

Navratri

The Hindu Festival of Nine Nights preceding Dussehra celebrates Durga in all her incarnations. Festivities, in September or October, are

---

INDIAN LUNAR CALENDARS

Many festivals follow the Indian lunar calendar (a complex system based on astrology) or the Islamic calendar (which shifts 11 days earlier each year relative to the Gregorian calendar). Because of this, the dates of many festivals change annually. Contact local tourist offices for current dates, or see www.india.gov.in/calendar for a list of the year's gazetted government holidays.

particularly vibrant in West Bengal, Maharashtra and Gujarat; in Kolkata, Durga images are ritually immersed in rivers and water tanks. Upcoming dates: 17 October 2020, 7 October 2021. (p695)

✮✮ Dussehra

Colourful Dussehra celebrates the victory of Hindu god Rama over demon-king Ravana and the triumph of good over evil. It's big in Kullu: more than 200 deities are carried into the town on palanquins, and festivities last a week. Upcoming dates: 8 October 2019, 25 October 2020, 14 October 2021.

✮✮ Durga Puja

The conquest of good over evil is exemplified by the goddess Durga's victory over buffalo-headed demon Mahishasura. Celebrations occur around the time of Dussehra in October, particularly in Kolkata, where thousands of images of the goddess are displayed, then ritually immersed in rivers and water tanks.

✮✮ Diwali

In the lunar month of Kartika, in October or November, Hindus celebrate the Festival of Lights for five days. There's massive build-up, and on the day people exchange gifts, let off unbelievable amounts of fireworks, and light lamps to lead Lord Rama home from exile. Upcoming dates: 27 October 2019, 14 November 2020, 4 November 2021.

November

The climate is blissful in most places – still hot, but not uncomfortably so – but the southern monsoon sweeps through Tamil Nadu and Kerala.

✮✮ Eid-Milad-un-Nabi

The Islamic festival of Eid-Milad-un-Nabi celebrates the birth of the Prophet with prayers and processions. Upcoming dates: around 10 November 2019, 29 October 2020, 19 October 2021.

✮✮ Nanak Jayanti

The birthday of Guru Nanak, founder of Sikhism, is celebrated with prayer, *kirtan* (devotional singing) and processions for three days, especially in Punjab and Haryana. Upcoming dates: around 12 November 2019, 30 November 2020 and 19 November 2021, but some mark the festival on 14 April, possibly Nanak's actual 1469 birth date.

✮✮ Pushkar Camel Fair

Held during Kartika (the eighth lunar month, usually falling in October or November), this fair attracts 200,000 people, who bring some 50,000 camels, horses and cattle. It's a swirl of colour, magic and mayhem, thronged with musicians, mystics, tourists, camera crews, traders, devotees and animals. (p144)

☆ International Film Festival of India

Held in Panaji (Panjim) in Goa in late November, India's largest film festival draws Bollywood's finest for premieres, parties, screenings and ceremonies. See www.iffigoa.org for details.

December

December is peak tourist season, and no wonder: you're guaranteed glorious weather (except in the chilly mountains), the humidity's low, the mood's festive and the beaches are blissful.

🏃 Wedding Season

Marriage ceremonies peak in December, and you may see many a *baraat* (bridegroom's procession), featuring white horse, nervous protagonist and fireworks, on your travels. Across the country, loud music and spectacular several-day-long parties abound, with brides adorned with *mehndi* and pure gold regalia.

🏃 Birdwatching

Many of India's 1250-plus bird species perform their winter migration from November to January or February, and excellent birdwatching spots are peppered across the country; www.birding.in is an excellent resource.

✮✮ Christmas Day

Christian Goa, and parts of Kerala and the Northeast Region, come alive in the lead-up to Christmas, Mass is celebrated on 24 December, and Christmas Day is celebrated with feasting and fireworks.

India: Off the Beaten Track

THE K3: KISHTWAR–KILLAR–KEYLONG

Dubbed the world's most dangerous road, the K3 teeters along terrifyingly narrow rock ledges high above the Chenab River in Jammu. (p283)

KUMBHALGARH WILDLIFE SANCTUARY

In dense forests in Rajasthan this wildlife sanctuary provides homes to antelope, gazelle, leopard, wolves and the occasional sloth bear. (p167)

LONAR METEORITE CRATER

Created 50,000 years ago this huge crater in Maharashtra has a shallow green lake at its base and wilderness all around. (p791)

DUDHSAGAR FALLS

Meaning 'Sea of Milk' Dudhsagar is Goa's 300m-high, tiered waterfall, reached by a bumpy, 45-minute 4WD ride through stunning jungle scenery. (p838)

MURUDESHWAR

This beachside pilgrimage town in Karnataka is known for its colossal seashore stature of Lord Shiva overlooking the Arabian Sea. (p897)

DHANUSHKODI

Once a thriving port, now a ghost town standing at the end of a remote promontory in Tamil Nadu. (p1072)

KABUL

K2 (Godwin Austin) (8611m)

Kargil

THE K3: KISHTWAR–KILLAR–KEYLONG

Srinagar

ISLAMABAD

JAMMU

Jammu

Udaipur

Amritsar

Shimla
Nanda Devi (7816m)

Dehra Dun

PAKISTAN

INDIA

HARYANA

DELHI

Bikaner

Gurgaon

RAJASTHAN

Jaisalmer

Jaipur

Agra

Jodhpur

Ajmer

Jhansi

KUMBHALGARH WILDLIFE SANCTUARY

Udaipur

Bhuj

Ahmedabad (Amdavad)

Mandvi Rajkot

Bhopal

GUJARAT

Indore

Saurashtra (Kathiawar Peninsula)

Surat

Tadoba-Andhari Tiger Reserve

Gulf of Khambhat

Ajanta

Aurangabad

LONAR METEORITE CRATER

Mumbai

MAHARASHTRA

Warangal

Hyderabad

Panaji (Panjim)

DUDHSAGAR FALLS

GOA

ANDHRA PRADESH

KARNATAKA

MURUDESHWAR

Bengaluru (Bangalore)

Mangaluru (Mangalore)

Valiyaparamba

Mysuru (Mysore)

TAMIL NADU

Coimbatore

Lakshadweep Sea

Parambikulam Tiger Reserve

Trichy (Tiruchirappalli)

KERALA

DHANUSHKODI

Thiruvananthapuram (Trivandrum)

Gulf of Mannar

COLOMBO

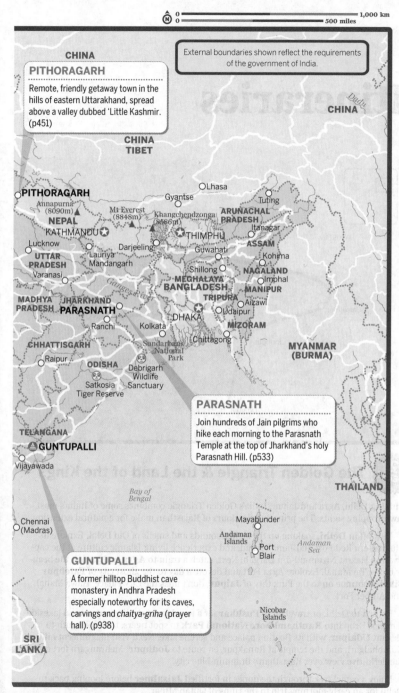

⊛N 0 ____ 1,000 km
0 ____ 500 miles

External boundaries shown reflect the requirements
of the government of India.

PITHORAGARH

Remote, friendly getaway town in the
hills of eastern Uttarakhand, spread
above a valley dubbed 'Little Kashmir.'
(p451)

CHINA

CHINA

CHINA
TIBET

○Lhasa
Gyantse

○Tuting

ARUNACHAL
PRADESH
○Itanagar

○PITHORAGARH
Annapurna
(8090m)▲
NEPAL
KATHMANDU✪

Mt Everest
(8848m)▲

Khangchendzonga
(8586m)▲

☉THIMPHU

ASSAM

Lucknow○
UTTAR
PRADESH
Varanasi○

○Darjeeling
Lauriya
Mandangarh

Guwahati○
Shillong○
MEGHALAYA
BANGLADESH

○Kohima
NAGALAND
○Imphal
MANIPUR

Ganges River

MADHYA
PRADESH

JHARKHAND
PARASNATH○
Ranchi○

TRIPURA
○Udaipur
DHAKA○

○Aizawl

MIZORAM

Kolkata○
Sundarbans
National
Park

Chittagong○

MYANMAR
(BURMA)

CHHATTISGARH
○Raipur

ODISHA
Debrigarh
Wildlife
Sanctuary
Satkosia
Tiger Reserve

PARASNATH

Join hundreds of Jain pilgrims who
hike each morning to the Parasnath
Temple at the top of Jharkhand's holy
Parasnath Hill. (p533)

TELANGANA
⚓GUNTUPALLI
○Vijayawada

THAILAND

Bay of
Bengal

○Chennai
(Madras)

Mayabunder○

Andaman
Islands

○Port
Blair

Andaman
Sea

GUNTUPALLI

A former hilltop Buddhist cave
monastery in Andhra Pradesh
especially noteworthy for its caves,
carvings and *chaitya-griha* (prayer
hall). (p938)

Nicobar
Islands

SRI
LANKA

Itineraries

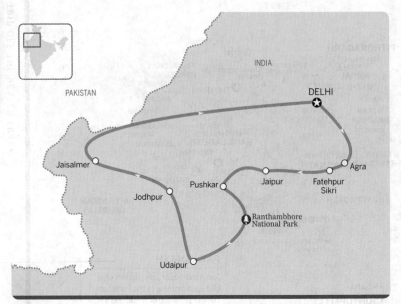

2 WEEKS The Golden Triangle & the Land of the Kings

Linking Delhi, Agra and Jaipur, India's Golden Triangle combines some of India's most jaw-dropping sights. The princely splendours of Rajasthan make for a natural extension.

Kick off in **Delhi**, soaking up the sights, sounds and smells of Old Delhi. Explore its Mughal-era Red Fort and Jama Masjid, and experience living Islamic culture at the captivating Hazrat Nizam-ud-din Dargah. Next, catch a train to **Agra** and gasp at the beauty of the Taj Mahal. Explore Agra Fort and devote a day to the ghost city of **Fatehpur Sikri**. Continue on to the Pink City of **Jaipur**; don't miss the City Palace, Hawa Mahal and Amber Fort.

Return to Delhi, or travel on to **Pushkar** for a few days of chilling out around lakeside temples. Drop into **Ranthambhore National Park** to spot tigers, then roll south to elegant **Udaipur**, with its floating palace and serene lake. Next, visit magnificent hilltop Kumbhalgarh and the temple at Ranakpur, en route to **Jodhpur**; Mehrangarh fort offers the definitive view over Rajasthan's Brahmin-blue city.

Enjoy a camel trek through the dunes in fortified **Jaisalmer** before looping back to Delhi for an early-morning trip to the ruins of Qutab Minar.

North & South

Tourist visas last six months, allowing you to mix famous highlights with detours off the established tourist grid.

Start by exploring **Delhi**, then ride the rails north to **Amritsar** to see Sikhism's glittering Golden Temple. Connect through Chandigarh to lofty **Shimla**; from this classic hill station you can roam northwest to **Dharamsala**, home of the Dalai Lama, before doubling back to adrenalin-charged **Manali**, starting point for the thrilling overland journey to rugged **Ladakh** (June to September). When you've had your fill of mountain air, head south for some yoga in **Rishikesh**, and descend to **Agra** to admire the visionlike Taj Mahal. Next, go south to **Khajuraho**, with its risqué temples, and scan the jungle for tigers in **Bandhavgarh Tiger Reserve**. Continue to **Varanasi** for a mesmerising boat trip along the sacred Ganges.

Roam east to **Kolkata**, bustling capital of West Bengal. Swing north as far as **Darjeeling** or **Sikkim** for sweeping Himalayan views, then drift down the coast to the temple towns of **Konark** and **Puri** in Odisha (Orissa). Continue south to **Chennai** for a big-city view of South India.

From Chennai, detour south to the temple wonders of **Mamallapuram (Mahabalipuram)**, continuing to French-colonial **Puducherry (Pondicherry)**. Rumble on to **Madurai**, with its deity-encrusted temple towers. Enjoy some beach time in **Kerala** before roaming inland to nostalgic **Mysuru (Mysore)** to see how maharajas lived.

Continuing north, head to **Hampi**, where collapsed temples lie strewn among the boulders, then unwind on the sun-stroked coast of **Goa**. Wine, fine-dine and go Bollywood-crazy in **Mumbai**, then admire the glorious cave paintings and carvings at **Ajanta** and **Ellora**.

Finish with Rajasthan's triumvirate of coloured cities – pink **Jaipur**, blue **Jodhpur** and white **Udaipur**. There might just be time to detour to the fascinating temples and nature reserves of **Gujarat** before you take one last train ride to Delhi.

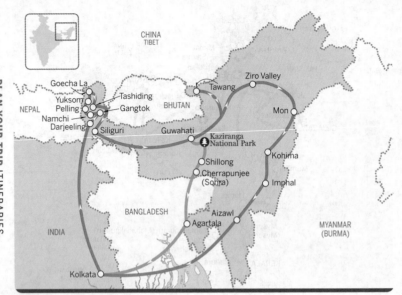

1 MONTH Mountains & Tribal Culture

Sikkim and the Northeast States, with their incredible mountain scenery, are still a well-kept secret for many travellers, but plan ahead as permits and security can be an issue.

Starting in **Kolkata**, make your first stop genteel **Darjeeling** – here you can sample the subcontinent's finest teas and pick up a permit for Sikkim, one of the most serene retreats in the country. Rumble by jeep to **Gangtok**, the Sikkimese capital, for trips to historic Buddhist monasteries and views over epic mountain scenery. Roll on to **Namchi** to see giant statues of Shiva and Padmasambhava, and to **Pelling** for inspiring views of the white-peaked Khangchendzonga and the beautiful Pemayangtse Gompa. Take the weeklong trek from **Yuksom** to **Goecha La**, a 4940m pass with incredible views, then exit Sikkim via **Tashiding**, with more wonderful views and another stunning monastery, before you travel to **Siliguri** for the train journey east.

Arrange tours and permits for the Northeast States in **Guwahati** or online. Then head from Guwahati to Arunachal Pradesh to admire the stunning, city-size Buddhist monastery at **Tawang**, before exploring the fascinating tribal villages around the **Ziro Valley**. A visit to Nagaland opens up fascinating tribal villages around **Mon**, dotted with traditional longhouses and squeezed into remote forested valleys, and the capital, **Kohima**, with its moving WWII relics. Going south, you can encounter Meitei culture in newly accessible **Imphal** in Manipur and Mizo culture in **Aizawl** in Mizoram before you fly back to Kolkata.

As an alternative, you could try this classic loop (for which Arunachal Pradesh permits are not required): from Guwahati, head to **Kaziranga National Park** to spot rare rhinos. Detour to sleepy **Shillong**, and hike to the waterfalls and incredible living root bridges of **Cherrapunjee (Sohra)**. Take the long overland road trip to **Agartala**, dusty capital of Tripura, before you return to Kolkata by air or overland through Bangladesh.

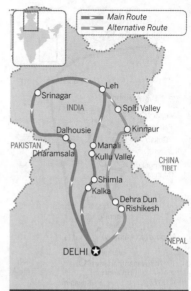

Main Route

Alternative Route

3 WEEKS The Spiritual Centre

India has a wealth of temples, and this trip around the central plains takes in some of the most fabulous.

Start amid the chaos and culture of **Kolkata**, then swap the big-city bustle for the peace of **Bodhgaya**, where the historical Buddha attained enlightenment. Roll across the plains to **Sarnath**, where Buddha later gave his first dharma lesson.

Move on to one of Hinduism's most sacred spots, ancient **Varanasi**, then swap living history for ancient erotica at the Hindu temples of **Khajuraho**. Next, head southwest to **Sanchi**, where Emperor Ashoka first embraced Buddhism, and zip on through Bhopal to the caves of **Ajanta**, filled with timeless Buddhist carvings.

In Rajasthan, stop off in whimsical **Udaipur**, with its lakes and palaces, then explore the milky-marble Jain temples of **Ranakpur** or **Mt Abu**. Continue to **Pushkar**, coiled around its sacred lake, and trip out to nearby **Ajmer**, one of India's key Islamic pilgrimage sites. Swing through atmospheric **Jaipur** to end the trip in **Delhi**, with its magnificent Mughal ruins.

4 WEEKS Himalayan Adventures

The heart-stopping Himalayan views on this mountainous loop will stay with you forever.

Ride the rails from **Delhi** to **Kalka**, to board the narrow-gauge train to colonial-era **Shimla**. Start your mountain exploration with some gentle rambles, then roll north to the **Kullu Valley**, India's adventure sport capital.

From the hill resort of **Manali**, embark on the epic two-day journey to **Leh** in mountainous Ladakh (July to September), to hike to precariously poised Buddhist monasteries, then roll west to Kashmir (checking first that it's safe to travel) and stay on a **Srinagar** houseboat. Next, loop south to elegant **Dalhousie**, and soak up Buddhist culture in nearby **Dharamsala**, before returning to Delhi.

To mix things up, consider heading southeast from Leh into the dramatic **Spiti Valley**, with its own collection of centuries-old monasteries. Ride the rattletrap bus to vertiginous **Kinnaur**, and make stops in **Dehra Dun** and **Rishikesh** to brush up on your yoga, before closing the loop in Delhi.

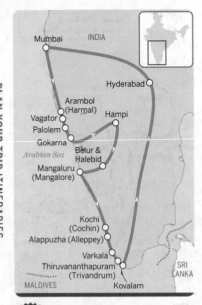

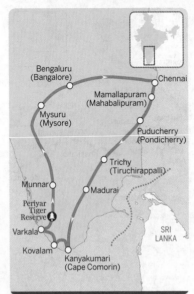

2 WEEKS Beaches & Southern Cities

This laid-back meander takes in some of India's finest coastal retreats.

Start in **Mumbai** and people-watch, amble and feast, then take a boat trip to the temples on Elephanta Island, before travelling south by train to beach-blessed Goa.

Take your pick from tropical sands at **Arambol (Harmal)**, **Vagator** and **Palolem**, then continue along the coast to the sacred town of **Gokarna**. For a change of pace, detour inland to **Hampi**, with its serene Vijayanagar ruins, and more magnificent stone carving at **Belur** and **Halebid**. Return by train to **Mangaluru (Mangalore)** to gorge on spectacular seafood, then chug south to lovely, laid-back **Kochi (Cochin)**.

Cruise Kerala's languorous backwaters from **Alappuzha (Alleppey)**, before dipping your toes in the warm waters around **Varkala** and **Kovalam**. End the journey south at cultured **Thiruvananthapuram (Trivandrum)**, then fly to historic **Hyderabad** for a taste of Islamic India, before one last train ride back to Mumbai.

3 WEEKS A Southern Loop

Chennai, the fast-changing capital of the south, is the easiest starting point for exploring India's southern tip.

Kick off with some fiery thalis in **Chennai**, then drift south to admire the elaborate temple carvings in **Mamallapuram (Mahabalipuram)**.

Amble around French-flavoured **Puducherry (Pondicherry)**, before leaving the coast behind for the temple towns of Tamil Nadu. Essential stops include boulder-covered **Trichy (Tiruchirappalli)** and **Madurai**, with its soaring, deity-covered towers. From here, zip down to **Kanyakumari (Cape Comorin)**, India's southernmost point.

Next, kick back on the sand at beachtastic **Kovalam** or **Varkala**, then trade the palms for jungle vines and wild elephants in steamy **Periyar Tiger Reserve**. Allow time for a trip to **Munnar**, for tranquil rambles though tea plantations.

Heading north, visit colourful **Mysuru (Mysore)**, with its flamboyant maharaja's palace, and stop in at cosmopolitan **Bengaluru (Bangalore)** to sample its craft beers before looping back to Chennai.

Plan Your Trip
Booking Trains

In India, riding the rails has a romance all of its own. The Indian rail network snakes almost all over the country, trains run almost all the time, and there are seats to suit every size of wallet. However, booking can be a hassle – particularly from outside the country.

Train Reservations

Travellers to India have several options when it comes to making reservations. You can book online or with an Indian travel agent from outside India and have the reassurance of knowing that the train you want to travel on won't be booked out on the day you want to travel. Alternatively, you can leave booking till you arrive, and take the chance that a seat might be available.

However you book, you must make a reservation for chair-car, executive-chair-car, sleeper, 1AC, 2AC and 3AC carriages. Book well ahead for overnight journeys or travel during holidays and festivals.

Waiting until the day of travel to book is not recommended, though on short journeys, buying a general 2nd-class ticket for the next available train is a handy, cheap option, though you may have to stand.

Reserved tickets show your seat/berth and carriage number. Carriage numbers are written on the side of the train and a list of names and berths is usually posted on the side of each reserved carriage.

Booking Online

Booking online should be the easiest way to buy tickets – though it still isn't quite as straightforward as you'd expect, and the reservation system is only open from 12.30am to 11.45pm (IST). Bookings open 120 days before departure for long-distance trains, sometimes less for short-haul trips.

Train Classes

Air-Conditioned 1st Class (1AC)

The most expensive class, with two- or four-berth compartments with locking doors and meals included.

Air-Conditioned 2-Tier (2AC)

Two-tier berths arranged in groups of four and two in an open-plan carriage. Bunks convert to seats by day and curtains offer some privacy.

Air-Conditioned 3-Tier (3AC)

Three-tier berths arranged in groups of six in an open-plan carriage with no curtains.

Air-Conditioned Executive Chair (ECC)

Comfortable, reclining chairs and plenty of space; usually on Shatabdi express trains.

Air-Conditioned Chair (CC)

Similar to the executive-chair carriage but with less-fancy seating.

Sleeper Class (SL)

Open-plan carriages with three-tier bunks and no air-con, but the open windows afford great views.

Unreserved/Reserved 2nd Class (II/SS or 2S)

Known as 'general' class; shared, padded bench seats and usually too many people to fill them, but no reservations are necessary.

RAILWAY RAZZLE DAZZLE

You can live like a maharaja on one of India's luxury train tours, with accommodation on board, tours and meals included in the ticket price. As well as the following, consider the Golden Chariot (www.goldenchariottrain.com), a luxurious round-trip journey from Bengaluru (Bangalore); the train was under renovation at time of writing but is due to resume service in 2019.

Palace on Wheels (www.palaceonwheels.net) Eight- to 10-day tours of Rajasthan, departing from Delhi. Trains run on fixed dates from September to April; the fare per person for seven nights in a single/double cabin starts at US$4550/3500. Try to book 10 months in advance.

Royal Rajasthan on Wheels (www.royal-rajasthan-on-wheels.com) Another epic luxury ride from Delhi through Rajasthan. Lavish one-week trips take place from September to April. The fare per single/double cabin for seven nights starts at US$6055/9100, plus taxes.

Deccan Odyssey (www.deccan-odyssey-india.com) Seven-night whirls around Maharashtra, Goa and beyond cost from US$6100/8750 per single/double.

Mahaparinirvan Express (aka Buddhist Circuit Special; www.irctcbuddhisttrain. com) An eight-day trip from Delhi running from September to March and visiting India's key Buddhist sites, plus the Taj Mahal, and Lumbini in Nepal. Rates begin at US$945 per person. Note: you'll need a Nepali visa and a double/multiple-entry Indian visa (not included in the price).

The government-run Indian Railway Catering & Tourism Corp (IRCTC; www. irctc.co.in) takes bookings for regular and luxury trains. Using the site involves a frustrating, complex registration process, and many travellers have reported problems using international cards (though this may change). An IRCTC number may be needed for other booking sites.

An Indian mobile SIM will make life less frustrating when booking online; however, foreigners can verify their IRCTC account from abroad by entering a foreign mobile number, which will trigger an email from IRCTC allowing you to enter a verification code for your mobile (for which there's a small fee) after submitting a registration form. Enquiries should be directed to care@irctc.co.in.

The following are useful for online international bookings, all with user-friendly booking apps.

12Go (www.12go.asia) Handy ticketing agency, though only for India's 1000 most popular routes; accepts international cards.

Cleartrip (www.cleartrip.com) A reliable private agency; accepts international cards but requires an IRCTC registration, linked to your Cleartrip account.

Make My Trip (www.makemytrip.com) Reputable private agency; accepts international credit cards.

Booking on Arrival

If you plan to leave booking trains until you arrive in India, it pays to familiarise yourself with the routes you might travel before you get to the country. Booking in person at train stations is much easier if you have a train number and know the correct station names to list on the reservation form.

On arrival, pick up a copy of *Trains at a Glance*, a booklet sold at station news stands listing most of India's train routes, or check routes on the Indian Railways website (www.indianrailways.gov.in). See (p1216) for the full lowdown on rail travel in India.

Plan Your Trip

Trekking

India has world-class trekking opportunities, particularly in the Himalaya, where staggering snow-clad peaks, traditional tribal villages, sacred Hindu sites, ancient Buddhist monasteries and blazing fields of wildflowers are just some of the features that create extraordinary mountain experiences. Hit the trails for easy half-day jaunts or strenuous multiday expeditions.

Trail Tips

The commercial trekking industry is much less developed in India than in neighbouring Nepal, so some places still feel wild and relatively unspoilt. On most routes, you can hire porters or pack animals to haul your gear. If you go with a trekking company, specify *everything* that's included beforehand, and get it in writing if possible – some trips can be fairly bare-bones.

Wherever you go, make sure you have any permits you may need, and monitor your health – acute mountain sickness (p1223) is a serious risk on trails over 3000m. Beware of herding dogs in the mountains; they're famously aggressive.

Route Planning

Detailed maps of the Indian Himalaya are difficult to buy in-country. Some maps found online are good enough for planning, and even navigating if you're experienced at reading them. For Ladakh, excellent Olizane 1:150,000 maps cover the region in three large sheets, available (at a considerable price) in Leh; some maps from the more schematic 1:200,000 Leomann series are sporadically available in Manali and McLeod Ganj.

On popular pilgrims' trails it's impossible to get lost, but less-travelled tracks can fork or vanish altogether, so hiring a local guide can be wise.

Best Treks

The Himalaya

Jammu & Kashmir Ladakh offers some incredible trails, including routes through the popular Markha Valley and the wildly beautiful Zanskar region (p252), with homestays possible on many routes.

Himachal Pradesh Accessible Alpine adventures, from day walks between Buddhist hamlets on the high-altitude Spiti Homestay Trail, to full-scale adventures like the Pin-Parvati Trek (p310).

Uttarakhand Enjoy the pristine splendour of the Kuari Pass, Milam Glacier and Har-ki-Dun Valley (p440) treks or join pilgrims treks to sacred Kedarnath temple (p435) or Hem Kund (p438).

Sikkim Gaze at Khangchendzonga (8598m), the world's third-highest mountain, on the Goecha La Trek (p555).

South India

Karnataka Explore the serene hills and forests of Kodagu (p887).

Kerala Go in search of tigers, elephants and deer at the Periyar Tiger Reserve (p973).

Peak Bagging

Mountaineers need permission from the **Indian Mountaineering Foundation** (📞011-24111211; www.indmount.org; 6 Benito Juarez Rd, New Delhi; ⊙10am-5pm daily, except 2nd weekend of month; Ⓜ Sir Vishveshwaraiah Moti Bagh) to climb most peaks over 6000m. Expedition fees vary, rising with the height of the peak and the number of people on your team. Fortunately, permits for quite a few high 'trekking' summits cost only US$30 to US$100, particularly in Ladakh, Lahaul, Spiti and Sikkim; among them is Stok Kangri (6120m), an affordable but rewarding taste of high-altitude mountaineering.

Acclimatisation

Throughout the Himalaya, plan for some extra days to acclimatise while en route to high-altitude destinations. These mountains deserve your respect – don't try to trek beyond your physical or technical abilities.

MOST ADVENTUROUS TREKS

For serious mountain adventures, point your compass towards the following:

Har-ki-Dun Valley Trek (p440; Uttarakhand) Seriously remote and a haunt of snow leopards.

Kuari Pass Trek (p440; Uttarakhand) Rugged mountain views around 7816m Nanda Devi, India's second-highest peak.

Ladakh to Zanskar Trek (p268; Kashmir & Ladakh) A camping classic, linking Buddhist villages through arid, high-altitude terrain.

Pin-Parvati Trek (p310; Himachal Pradesh) A breathless, exhilarating climb over the snow-bound Pin-Parvati Pass (5319m).

Pemako (p577; Arunachal Pradesh) A sacred *kora* (ritual circuit) of the mystical lake Danakosha, set among snowy peaks at 3750m.

Packing

➡ Bring gear and clothing that are appropriate for the conditions you expect to encounter.

➡ On well-established trails, heavy hiking boots are overkill, but on remote mountain tracks they can be lifesavers.

➡ First-aid and water-purification supplies are often essential.

➡ Rain gear is a must, and warm layers are crucial for comfort at altitude.

➡ Remember a hat and sunscreen!

Trekking Ethics

➡ Follow low-impact trekking practices (you know the mantra: take only photographs, leave only footprints).

➡ Cook over stoves, since local people rely on limited fuel-wood sources.

➡ Respect local cultural sensibilities by dressing modestly.

➡ Ask permission before snapping photos.

➡ Remember that while locals' hospitality may be endless, their food supply might not be.

➡ Refrain from giving gifts to children.

When to Go

With India's diverse topography, the best trekking times depend on the region.

May and June This is a good time for mountain trekking but also high season for domestic travellers. Trails to holy Hindu sites can be packed.

Mid-July–mid-September During monsoon, trekking in the wrong place can be deadly. Ladakh and Spiti stay pretty dry. Uttarakhand's famous Valley of Flowers National Park (p438) unfurls a dazzling botanical carpet.

Mid-September–mid-November Post-monsoon, searing blue skies usually bless the Himalaya. While nights may dip below freezing, days are usually sunny and warm. Facilities often close for winter, so check in advance to see what will be open.

December–March February is the only month when you can attempt the hazardous Chadar Trek (p268), walking along a frozen river to the Zanskar region.

April Head for the hill stations, as it's ripping hot down low and usually still snow-packed up high.

Plan Your Trip

Yoga, Ayurveda & Spiritual Pursuits

India offers a profound spiritual journey for those so inclined, and all travellers can enjoy the benefits of trips to ayurveda and yoga centres.

Yoga

You can practise yoga almost everywhere, from beach resorts to mountain retreats. In 2014, at India's initiative, the UN adopted a resolution declaring 21 June International Yoga Day.

Destinations with a yoga scene include Anjuna, Arambol, Assagao and Mandrem in Goa; Vashisht, McLeod Ganj and Dharamkot in Himachal Pradesh; Udaipur, Pushkar and Jaipur in Rajasthan; and of course Rishikesh in Uttarakhand.

Andaman Islands

Jalakara (p1107) Poolside yoga plus massage at an exclusive boutique hotel on Havelock Island – for hotel guests only.

Goa

Himalaya Yoga Valley (p840) Popular training school in Mandrem.

Swan Yoga Retreat (p835) Retreat in a soothing jungle location in Assagao.

Himalayan Iyengar Yoga Centre (p841) Courses in Arambol (Harmal).

Bamboo Yoga Retreat (p855) Beachfront yoga in Patnem.

Karnataka

Mysuru (p880) The birthplace of ashtanga yoga; there are centres all over the city.

What to Choose

Ashrams (p45)

India has plentiful ashrams – places of striving organised through communal living and established around the philosophies of a guru (spiritual guide or teacher). You can arrange to stay for an extended period, living by the rules of a particular organisation.

Ayurveda (p44)

Ayurveda is the traditional science of Indian herbal medicine and holistic healing, based on natural plant extracts, massage and therapies to treat body and mind. Treatment centres across the country can introduce you to this ancient healing art.

Meditation (p45)

Many centres in Buddhist areas offer training in *vipassana* (mindfulness meditation) and Buddhist philosophy, particularly at sites associated with the life of the historical Buddha. Note that many require a vow of silence and abstinence from tobacco, alcohol and sex.

Yoga

Yoga's roots lie in India and you'll find hundreds of schools following different disciplines to suit all levels of skill and commitment. Rishikesh (p417) in Uttarakhand and Mysuru (Mysore; p873) in Karnataka are major centres for yoga learning.

Shree Hari Yoga (p897) In Gokana, offers a beachside location for hatha, ashtanga and vinyasa.

Kerala

Kovalam (p952), Varkala (p957) and Kochi (p983) are popular places for yoga.

Sivananda Yoga Vedanta Dhanwantari Ashram (p952) Waterside ashram in Neyyar Dam, near Thiruvananthapuram (Trivandrum); renowned for longer courses.

Soul & Surf (p959) Rooftop yoga, retreats and meditation in Varkala.

Secret Beach Yoga Homestay (p969) Yoga and *kalaripayatt* (ancient South Indian martial art) in Kattoor.

Maharashtra

Kaivalyadhama Yoga Institute & Research Center (p799) Yogic healing in Lonavla.

Mumbai

Yoga Institute (p747) Daily and longer-term programs.

Yogacara (p747) Hatha yoga, plus massages and treatments.

Tamil Nadu

International Centre for Yoga Education & Research (p1045) Has 10-day introductory courses and advanced training in Puducherry (Pondicherry).

Krishnamacharya Yoga Mandiram (p1019) Chennai-based yoga courses, therapy and training.

Isha Yoga Center (p1082) Well-known ashram 30km west of Coimbatore. Visitors are welcome for meditations; if you want to stay or take yoga courses, book ahead.

Uttar Pradesh

DarkLotus (p384) Highly recommended yoga classes are held along the river in Varanasi and at temples around the city.

Uttarakhand

Rishikesh (p417) Take your pick from centres and ashrams offering yoga for all levels.

Ayurveda

Ayurveda – Indian herbal medicine – aims to restore balance in the body.

Delhi

Sivananda Yoga (p80) Excellent centre for all levels. Offers courses and drop-in classes.

Goa

Shanti Ayurvedic Massage Centre (p840) In Mandrem.

Himachal Pradesh

Men-Tsee-Khang (Tibetan Medical & Astrological Institute; p327) The primary authority on Tibetan medicine; has its HQ and two clinics in McLeod Ganj, plus nearly 50 other clinics across India.

Ayuskama Ayurvedic Clinic (p335) In Bhagsu; Dr Arun Sharma gives highly rated treatments and courses for would-be practitioners.

ASHRAMS

As part of their work, many ashrams offer philosophy, yoga or meditation courses, but visitors are usually required to adhere to strict rules and a donation is appropriate to cover your expenses. Be aware that many gurus in recent times have been accused of exploiting their followers, either financially or sexually. Always check the reputation of any ashram you wish to join.

Major ashrams include:

➡ Matha Amrithanandamayi Mission (p964; Amrithapuri, Kerala)
➡ Brahma Vidya Mandir (p793; Sevagram, Maharashtra)
➡ Sevagram Ashram (p793; Sevagram, Maharashtra)
➡ Osho International Meditation Resort (p801; Pune, Maharahstra)
➡ Sri Aurobindo Ashram (p1042; Puducherry, Tamil Nadu)
➡ Sri Ramana Ashram (p1040; Tiruvannamalai, Tamil Nadu)
➡ Belur Math (p463; Kolkata)
➡ Mahabodhi Centre (p238; Leh, Ladakh)

Karnataka

Ayurvedagram (p863) In a garden setting in Bengaluru (Bangalore).

Soukya (p863) Ayurveda and yoga in Bengaluru.

Indus Valley Ayurvedic Centre (p878) Therapies from ancient scriptures in Mysuru (Mysore).

Swaasthya Ayurveda Retreat Village (p888) Retreats and therapies in the Kodagu (Coorg) region.

Kerala

Dr Franklin's Panchakarma Institute (p956) In Chowara, south of Kovalam.

Ayurdara (p985) One- to three-week treatments by the water on Vypeen Island in Kochi (Cochin).

Neeleshwar Hermitage (p1009) Ayurveda, meditation and beachfront yoga in a luxury Bekal setting.

Harivihar (p1006) Yoga, ayurveda and meditation retreats at a 19th-century royal residence in Kozhikode (Calicut).

Madhya Pradesh

Kairali Spa (p635) Ayurvedic massage treatments in Orchha.

Ayur Arogyam (p644) Expert ayurvedic treatments in Khajuraho.

Maharashtra

Yogacara (p747) Ayurveda and massage in Mumbai.

Tamil Nadu

Sita (p1044) Ayurveda and yoga in Puducherry (Pondicherry).

Sivananda Vedanta Yoga Centre (p1069) Classes and training in central Madurai, plus courses and teacher training at its ashram.

Mamallapuram (Mahabalipuram; p1033) Lots of yoga classes (of varying quality). The nearby village of Kovalam (Covelong) has beach yoga and the annual Covelong Point Surf, Music & Yoga Festival.

Uttar Pradesh

Swasthya Vardhak (p384) Varanasi's real-deal ayurvedic pharmacy. Free consultations.

Buddhist Meditation

Whether for an introduction or more advanced study, there are India-wide courses and retreats. McLeod Ganj is the main centre for the study of Tibetan Buddhism; public teachings or audiences are given by both the Dalai Lama and the 17th Karmapa.

Andhra Pradesh

Numerous Burmese-style *vipassana* courses are available, including those at the Vipassana International Meditation Centre (p922) near Hyderabad, and Dhamma Nagajjuna (p937), overlooking Nagarjuna Sagar Dam.

Bihar

Root Institute for Wisdom Culture (p527) Courses from two to 21 days in Bodhgaya.

Tergar Monastery (p527) Courses in Tibetan Buddhism in Bodhgaya.

Delhi

Tushita Mahayana Meditation Centre (p80) Twice weekly sessions in a temple-like meditation space.

Himachal Pradesh

Library of Tibetan Works & Archives (p327) Serious Buddhist philosophy courses in McLeod Ganj.

Tushita Meditation Centre (p335) Ten-day introduction-to-Buddhism tasters as well as retreats and drop-in meditation sessions in Dharamkot.

Deer Park Institute (p1198) Courses and workshops on Buddhist and Indian philosophy, and meditation retreats led by Buddhist masters in Bir.

Jammu & Kashmir

Mahabodhi Centre (p238) Three-day introductory *vipassana* courses and daily drop-in meditation classes near Leh.

Maharashtra

Vipassana International Academy (p780) Holds 10-day *vipassana* courses in Igatpuri.

Mumbai

Global Pagoda (p743) *Vipassana* courses from one to 10 days on Gorai Island.

Plan Your Trip

Volunteering

Rich in culture and history, India may be beautiful, but poverty and hardship are the harsh reality for many of its citizens. Charities and aid organisations across the country welcome committed volunteers.

How to Volunteer

Choosing an Organisation

Choose an organisation that can specifically benefit from your abilities and skills.

Time Required

How much time can you devote to a project? You're more likely to be of help if you can commit for at least a month or two, ideally longer.

Money

Giving your time for free is only part of the story; most organisations expect volunteers to cover their accommodation, food and transport.

Conditions

Make sure you understand what you're signing up for: many organisations expect volunteers to work full-time, five days a week.

Transparency

Ensure that the organisation you choose is reputable and transparent about how it spends its money. Where possible, get feedback from former volunteers.

Aid Programs

It may be possible to find a placement after you arrive in India, but charities and non-government organisations (NGOs) generally prefer volunteers who have applied in advance and been approved for the kind of work involved. Reputable organisations will insist on a background check for volunteers working with children.

As well as international organisations, local charities and NGOs often have opportunities. For listings of local agencies, check www.ngosindia.com or contact the Delhi-based **Concern India Foundation** (☑011-26210998; www.concernindiafoundation. org).

The following programs are just some that may have opportunities for volunteers. Note that Lonely Planet does not endorse any organisations that we do not work with directly, so it is essential that you do your own thorough research before agreeing to any placement.

Caregiving

If you have medical experience, there are numerous opportunities to provide healthcare and support for vulnerable people.

Kolkata

Missionaries of Charity (p465) St Teresa's charity (Mother Theresa's Motherhouse) places volunteers in hospitals and homes for impoverished children and adults.

Calcutta Rescue (Map p458; ☎033-22175675; www.calcuttarescue.org; 4th fl, 85 Collin St) Placements for medical and health professionals in Kolkata and other parts of West Bengal.

Madhya Pradesh & Chhattisgarh

Sambhavna Trust Clinic (p650) In Bhopal; accepts volunteers to help long-term victims of the toxic gas leak of 1984.

Maharashtra

Sadhana Village (☎020-25380792; www.sadhanavillageschool.org; 1, Priyankit, Lokmanya Colony, Paud Rd) Pune residence for adults with disabilities; has a minimum commitment of two months for volunteers.

Rajasthan

Marwar Medical & Relief Society (☎0291-2545210; www.mandore.com; Dadwari Lane, c/o Mandore Guesthouse) NGO running educational, health, environmental and other projects in Jodhpur district.

Community

Many community volunteer projects work to provide healthcare and education to villages.

Bihar & Jharkhand

Root Institute for Wisdom Culture (p527) Heath professionals are welcome to volunteer at Root's charitable health program in Bodhgaya.

Delhi

Hope Project (p81) A broad-based community project welcoming short- or long-term volunteers who can offer childcare, medical, English-language teaching, IT or other skills.

Himachal Pradesh

Lha (p329) Arranges placements at a host of projects with the Tibetan community, including roles for language teachers and healthcare or IT professionals in McLeod Ganj.

Karnataka

Kishkinda Trust (p906) Volunteers are needed to assist with sustainable community development in Hampi.

Madhya Pradesh & Chhattisgarh

Orchha Home-Stay (p636) Offers volunteer placements in varied roles to help rural villagers in Orchha.

Mumbai

Slum Aid (☎in UK +44 0790 896 7375; www.slumaid.org) Works in Mumbai slums to improve lives; placements from two weeks to six months.

Rajasthan

URMUL Trust (☎0151-2523093; www.urmul.org; Ganganagar Rd, Urmul Bhawan, Bikaner; ☉9am-5pm Mon-Fri) Volunteer placements (minimum one month) in English teaching, healthcare and other work in western Rajasthan.

Seva Mandir (☎0294-2451041; www.sevamandir.org; Old Fatehpura, Udaipur) Opportunities on projects including afforestation, water resources, health, education and the empowerment of women in southern Rajasthan.

West Bengal

Human Wave (☎9831387317; www.humanwaveindia.org; 52 Tentultala Lane, Mankundu) Short-term placements on community-development and health schemes around West Bengal.

Makaibari Tea Estate (p497) Kurseong based; volunteers can assist with teaching, and health and community projects.

Teaching

Many Buddhist schools need experienced teachers of English for long-term placements; enquire locally in Sikkim, Himachal Pradesh, West Bengal and Ladakh. Reputable organisations require safety checks for adults working with children.

HELPING TIBETAN REFUGEES

Since 1959 more than 100,000 Tibetan refugees have fled to India to escape persecution. Newly arrived refugees require extensive support and there are often volunteering opportunities in McLeod Ganj and other areas with large Tibetan populations.

Himachal Pradesh

Learning & Ideas for Tibet (p329; LIT) Based in McLeod Ganj; current needs are for teachers of English, French, German, Mandarin, Japanese and computer skills, to work with Tibetan refugees.

Tibet World (p329) Openings for teachers of yoga and languages, especially Mandarin, English and French – both regular and drop-in slots available in McLeod Ganj.

Jammu & Kashmir

Druk Padma Karpo School (Druk White Lotus School; www.dwls.org; Km458, Leh–Karu Hwy; donation appreciated; ⊙9am-1pm & 2-6pm Apr-Aug) ✏ Buddhist monastery school in Ladakh (Shey) with long-term placements (May to September only) for English teachers.

West Bengal & Darjeeling

Hayden Hall (Map p500; www.haydenhall.org; 42 Laden La Rd; ⊙10am-5pm Mon-Sat, 10am-12.30pm Sun) ✏ Offers minimum two-month opportunities for volunteers with medical, teaching and social-work experience in Darjeeling.

Working with Children

Various charities provide support for disadvantaged children, but always investigate what steps organisations are taking to protect children in their care. Be wary of any organisation that does not insist on background checks on volunteers.

Delhi

Salaam Baalak Trust (p81) Volunteer English teachers, doctors, counsellors and computer experts provide education and support for street children at this long-running NGO.

Reality Tours & Travel (p82) Slum education projects; volunteers should have relevant professional or academic qualifications. Minimum three months.

Torch (www.torchdelhi.wixsite.com/torch) Works with homeless children, and looks for volunteers who can help with art activities, music and writing.

Goa

Mango Tree Goa (☑9604654588; www.mango treegoa.org; The Mango House, near Vrundavan Hospital, Karaswada) Opportunities in Mapusa for volunteer nurses and teaching assistants to help impoverished children.

El Shaddai (p833) Placements helping impoverished and homeless children; one-month minimum commitment in Assagao.

Uttar Pradesh

Learn for Life Society (p389) Volunteer opportunities at a small Varanasi school for disadvantaged children. Two months minimum commitment.

Working with Women

India has a range of local charities working to empower and educate women.

Rajasthan

Sambhali Trust (Map p180; ☑0291-2512385; www.sambhali-trust.org; c/o Durag Niwas Guest House, 1st Old Public Park, Raika Bagh, Jodhpur) In Jodhpur; volunteers needed to teach and help organise workshops for disadvantaged women.

Tamil Nadu

RIDE (p1039) Works to empower village women and welcomes volunteers in Kanchipuram.

Environment & Conservation

A range of local organisations work in environmental education and sustainable development.

Andaman Islands

ANET (p1103) Occasional openings for specialised volunteers to assist with environmental activities.

Reef Watch Marine Conservation (p1104) Marine-conservation non-profit organisation accepts volunteers for anything from beach cleanups to fish surveys.

Himachal Pradesh

Ecosphere (p349) This multifaceted sustainable-development NGO in Kaza has a few openings for short- and long-term volunteers, including clean-energy projects and cafe work.

Jammu & Kashmir

Ice Stupa Farmstays (p259) Residential placements on rural farms.

Karnataka

Rainforest Retreat (p888) Placements in organic farming, sustainable agriculture and waste management at this lush hideaway in the Kodagu region.

Top: Mother Teresa's 'Motherhouse' (p457); Kolkata

Bottom: Volunteer at an animal rescue centre in Rajasthan

FILIP JEDRASZAK/SHUTTERSTOCK ©

AGENCIES OVERSEAS

International volunteering agencies abound, and it can be tricky trying to assess which ones are worthwhile. Agencies offering the chance to do whatever you want, wherever you want, are almost always tailoring projects to the volunteer rather than finding the right volunteer for the work. Look for projects that will derive real benefits from your skills. To find agencies in your area, read Lonely Planet's *Volunteer: A Traveller's Guide*.

Himalayan Education Lifeline Programme (HELP; www.help-education.org) British-based charity organising placements for volunteer teachers in Himalayan regions including at Pelling in Sikkim.

Indicorps (www.indicorps.org) Matches volunteers to projects across India, particularly in social development.

Jamyang Foundation (www.jamyang.org) Arranges volunteer placements for experienced teachers in Buddhist nunneries in Zanskar (Jammu and Kashmir) and Spiti (Himachal Pradesh).

Voluntary Service Overseas (VSO; www.vso.org.uk) British organisation offering long-term professional placements in India and worldwide.

Workaway (www.workaway.info) Connects people with guesthouses, organic farms and more, offering free accommodation and food in return for working five day weeks.

Maharashtra

Nimbkar Agricultural Research Institute (Nari; ☎9168937964; www.nariphaltan.org; Phaltan-Lonand Rd, Phaltan) Offers internships in sustainable agriculture lasting two to six months for agriculture, engineering and science graduates in Phaltan.

Tamil Nadu

Keystone Foundation (p1086) Kotagiri based; offers occasional opportunities to help improve environmental conditions, working with indigenous communities.

Working with Animals

Opportunities for animal lovers are plentiful.

Andhra Pradesh

Blue Cross of Hyderabad (☎9642229858; https://bluecrossofhyd.org; Rd No 35, Jubilee Hills; ⊙Tue-Sat 10am-1pm & 2pm-5pm) A shelter with more than 1300 animals; volunteers help care for animals or work in the office.

Goa

International Animal Rescue (p834) Rescues and looks after dogs, cats and other animals; volunteers are welcome but must have evidence of rabies vaccination.

Mumbai

Welfare of Stray Dogs (Map p752; ☎022-64222838; www.wsdindia.org; Yeshwant Chambers, Burjorji Bharucha Marg, Kala Ghoda) Volunteers can work with the animals, manage stores or educate kids in school programs.

Rajasthan

Animal Aid Unlimited (p157) In Udaipur, accepts volunteers to help injured, abandoned or stray animals.

Tamil Nadu

Madras Crocodile Bank (p1032) A reptile-conservation centre in Vadanemmeli with openings for volunteers (minimum two weeks).

Arunachala Animal Sanctuary (p1040) Travellers are welcome to help; just show up. Potential openings for longer-term volunteers based in Tiruvannamalai.

Plan Your Trip
Travel with Children

Fascinating and thrilling India will be even more astounding for children than for their wide-eyed parents. The country's scents, sights and sounds will make for an unforgettable adventure and one that most kids will take in their stride.

India for Kids

Travelling with children in India is usually a delight, though you (and your kids) may have to get used to being treated like a celebrity, including endless photo calls. This may prove disconcerting, but you can always politely decline.

As a parent on the road in India, the key is to remain firm, even if you feel you may offend a well-meaning local by doing so. The attention your children will inevitably receive is almost always good-natured, but it can be invasive and tiring for kids, and being continually touched by an array of strangers.

Hotels will almost always come up with an extra bed (although they rarely have more than one, so you may need to do some bed sharing as a family, or get two rooms), and restaurants can usually find a familiar dish or two for inexperienced tummies.

Children's Highlights
Fairy-Tale Splendour

Jaisalmer, Rajasthan Enjoy playing knights around the world's biggest sandcastle, Jaisalmer's centuries-old fort (p188), and take a camel ride in the Thar Desert.

Best Regions for Kids
Rajasthan

Vibrant festivals, medieval forts, fairy-tale palaces, tiger safaris, camel rides across desert dunes and a well-oiled tourist infrastructure for hassle-free travel.

Goa

Palm-fringed white-sand beaches, seaside activities and inexpensive exotic food; an ideal choice for family holidays, whatever the budget.

Uttar Pradesh

The picture-perfect Taj Mahal and the nearby abandoned city of Fatehpur Sikri will set young imaginations ablaze.

Kerala

Canoe and houseboat adventures, surf beaches, Arabian Sea sunsets, snake-boat races and wildlife spotting.

Himachal Pradesh

Pony and yak rides around colonial-era hill stations, rafting, horse riding, tandem paragliding (kids can do it), walks and, for older kids, canyoning around Manali.

Delhi Run around magnificent forts (p76), explore Lodi Garden (p77) and Mehrauli Archeology Park (p78), or try hands-on exhibits and ride in a toy train at the **National Rail Museum** (Map p72; ☎011-26881816; www.nrmindia.com; Service Rd, Chanakyapuri; adult/child ₹50/10, Sat & Sun ₹100/20; ⏱10am-5pm Tue-Sun; Ⓜ Safdarjung).

Ranthambhore National Park, Rajasthan Hop aboard a jeep (p145) to search for monkeys, peacocks and tigers. Evening safaris are best for young children: morning ones tend to be too early, too long and, before the sun rises properly, too cold.

Udaipur, Rajasthan Go boating on the lake (p159), take a horse-riding excursion and explore enchanting palaces.

Orchha, Madhya Pradesh Wander the crumbling palaces and battlements of little-known Orchha (p632), then go rafting (p634) in the Betwa River.

Madhya Pradesh The land of Kipling's *Jungle Book* has plenty of opportunities for tiger safaris (p678). Again, evening safaris are best for youngsters.

Natural Encounters

Tiger parks, Madhya Pradesh The land of Kipling's *Jungle Book* has plenty of opportunities for tiger safaris. Delve deep into the jungle or roam the plains at the tiger parks of Kanha (p678), Pench (p682) or your best chance for seeing one, Bandhavgarh (p681).

Elephants, Kerala In Wayanad (p1003) kids can spot wild elephants, as well as langurs, chitals (spotted deer), sambars (deer), peacocks and wild boar.

Dolphins, Goa Splash out on a dolphin-spotting boat trip (p822) from almost any Goan beach to see the marine mammals cavorting among the waves.

Hill-station monkeys Head up to Shimla (p292; Himachal Pradesh) or Matheran (p797; Maharashtra) for close encounters with cheeky monkeys (but not too close...they can be vicious!).

Lions, Gujarat Go on safari through Gir National Park (p716) at dusk or dawn and spot the only Asiatic lions in existence.

Keoladeo National Park, Rajasthan Rent bikes for a leisurely cycle around this lakeside bird reserve (p131).

Fun Transport

Autorickshaws, everywhere Bump thrillingly along at top speed in these child-scale vehicles (p1213).

Bikes, Delhi Older children who are competent riders, and toddlers who can fit in a child seat, can enjoy a cycle tour (p81).

Toy train, West Bengal Take a joy ride on the cute-as-a-button steam train (p507) from Darjeeling to Ghum and back.

Hand-pulled rickshaw, Maharashtra From this monkey-infested hill station in Matheran you can continue to the village on horseback or in a hand-pulled rickshaw (p797).

Boating, Kerala Go houseboating, canoeing or kayaking in Alappuzha (Alleppey), on the state's beautiful backwaters (p964), with lots of interesting stops en route. If you hit town on the second Saturday in August, take the kids to see the spectacular Nehru Trophy boat race.

Beachfront Kick-Backs

Palolem, Goa Plump for a beachfront palm-thatched hut and take it easy at beautiful Palolem beach (p849), with Goa's shallowest, safest waters.

Patnem, Goa Kick back at peaceful Patnem (p845), with its appealing beach and cool, calm, child-friendly restaurants.

Kovalam, Kerala Family-friendly beach (p952) area.

Varkala, Kerala Also family-friendly, Papanasham Beach (p957) comes with a stunning cliffside backdrop.

Havelock, Andaman Islands Splash about in the shallows at languid Havelock Island (Swaraj Dweep; p1104), where there's also fabulous snorkelling and diving.

Planning

Before You Go

➡ Look at climate charts; choose your dates to avoid the extremes of temperature that may put younger children at risk.

➡ Visit your doctor to discuss vaccinations, health advisories and other heath-related issues.

➡ For more tips on travel in India, pick up Lonely Planet's *Travel with Children* or visit the Thorn Tree forum at www.lonelyplanet.com/thorntree.

What to Pack

You can also get these items in many parts of India:

➡ Disposable or washable nappies, nappy-rash cream, extra bottles, wet wipes, infant formula and canned, bottled or rehydratable food.

➡ A fold-up baby bed or the lightest travel cot you can find.

➡ Don't take a stroller/pushchair: India's pavements are not up to the job. Bring a baby-carrier backpack, or for older kids, a lightweight scooter.

➡ A few less-precious toys that won't be mourned if lost or damaged.

➡ A swimming jacket, life jacket or water wings for the sea or pool.

➡ Good sturdy footwear.

➡ Books, audiobooks and activity books, for whiling away long journeys.

➡ Insect repellent, mosquito nets, hats and sun lotion.

Accommodation

➡ India offers such an array of accommodation options – from beach huts to five-star bubbles – that you're bound to find something that will appeal to the whole family.

➡ Swish upmarket hotels are almost always child-friendly, but so are many midrange and budget guesthouses and hotels, whose staff will usually bend over backwards to accommodate children, and can normally rustle up extra beds or mattresses.

➡ It's sometimes difficult to find a room with more than one extra bed, but most places are happy for families to share beds in a regular-size double room.

➡ The very best five-star options are equipped with children's pools, games rooms and even children's clubs.

Eating

➡ If you're travelling in regions such as Rajasthan, Himachal Pradesh, Goa or Kerala, or in big cities, there's always a wide range of international cuisine on offer.

➡ Easy portable snacks such as bananas, samosas, *puri* (puffy dough pockets), white-bread sandwiches and packaged biscuits (Parle G brand are always a hit) are available everywhere.

➡ Many children will delight in paneer (unfermented cheese) dishes, simple *dhals* (mild lentil curries), creamy kormas, buttered *naans* (tandoori breads), pilaus (rice dishes) and Tibetan *momos* (steamed or fried dumplings).

➡ Few children, no matter how culinarily unadventurous, can resist the finger-food fun of a vast South Indian *dosa* (paper-thin lentil-flour pancake).

Transport

➡ Public transport is often extremely overcrowded, so plan fun, easy days to follow longer bus or train rides.

➡ Toilets on trains, or at bus rest stops, can be dire; keep wipes and hand sanitiser handy.

➡ Long train rides are generally more comfortable, and more interesting, for children than long bus or car rides.

➡ Pack plenty of diversions (books, travel games, card games, activity books).

➡ Don't forget to join in with the games yourself; family I Spy is always a winner, or see who's first to spot 10 cows/monkeys/camels.

➡ Encouraging your child to keep a holiday journal/scrapbook is a great way to fill time.

➡ If you're hiring a car and driver, and you require safety capsules, child restraints or booster seats, bring these with you or make this requirement absolutely clear to the hiring company as early as possible. Don't be afraid to tell your driver to slow down and drive responsibly.

Health

➡ The standard of healthcare varies widely in India. Talk to your doctor at home about where you'll be travelling to get advice on vaccinations and what to include in your first-aid kit.

➡ Access to healthcare is better in parts of the country with high visitor numbers; most hotels will be able to recommend a reliable doctor.

➡ Prescriptions are quickly and cheaply filled over the counter at the country's plentiful pharmacies, often found near hospitals.

➡ Diarrhoea can be very serious in young children. Seek medical help if it is persistent or accompanied by fever; rehydration is essential. Heat rash, skin complaints such as impetigo, and insect bites or stings can be treated with the help of a local pharmacy.

Regions at a Glance

From 21st-century cities to tribal villages, from palm-fringed backwaters to knife-edge mountain ranges, and from ancient temples to sun-scoured desert fortresses, India's regions are an astounding cocktail of contrasts, colours and experiences.

Delhi

Food
Shopping
Ruins

Delhi will transport you back in time, from the magnificent ruins of medieval empires to the timeless to and fro of Old Delhi's bazaars. In-between, make time to feast on taste bud tingling street food and haggle in Delhi's markets and emporiums.

p60

Rajasthan

Palaces & Forts
Arts & Crafts
Wildlife

Rajasthan's forts and palaces are the crowning glory of this Land of Kings, and former royal hunting reservations have been reborn as national parks. You'll also find princely legacies in Rajasthan's bazaars, from miniature paintings to traditional puppets.

p108

Punjab & Haryana

Architecture
Pageantry
Food

Besides the stunning Golden Temple, the Punjab has forts and palaces to spare, and fabulous cuisine to feast on while you explore. Leave time to pop up to the Attari–Wagah Border crossing for a fabulous piece of transborder pomp.

p204

Kashmir & Ladakh

Landscapes
Trekking
Religion

From alpine Kashmir to the moonscapes of Ladakh and Zanskar, nature's awesome scale will humble you here. Connect with the region's soul through treks to ancient Buddhist villages and respectful visits to Kashmir's papier mâché–lined mosques.

p229

Himachal Pradesh

Adventure
Scenery
Cultures

High Himalayan passes connect plunging valleys, creating a vast natural playground for trekking, climbing, motorcycling, paragliding and skiing. The scenery is consistently awe-inspiring, and people follow Hindu and Buddhist customs that have hardly altered in centuries.

p286

Agra & the Taj Mahal

Architecture
Tombs
Forts

Agra's Mughal architecture is the height of imperial grandeur; the awesome symmetry of the Taj Mahal will simply take your breath away. And don't miss other local masterpieces, such as Akbar's Mausoleum and |the mighty buttresses of Agra Fort.

p355

Uttar Pradesh

Cities
Religion
Ghats

Uttar Pradesh is sublimely religious. Dotted across its plains are ancient Islamic cities, Buddhist pilgrimage centres, and two of the seven sacred cities of Hinduism. Follow the holy Ganges and its tributaries, finishing at Varanasi, India's most spiritual city.

p377

Uttarakhand

Trekking
Yoga
Wildlife

Trekkers can take their pick from timeless temples, sacred lakes, remote glaciers and rolling alpine meadows. Head to Rishikesh for a spiritual tune-up or seek snow leopards, sloth bears and blue sheep in Uttarakhand's national parks.

p413

Kolkata

Culture
Food
Architecture

Once the capital of the British Raj, Kolkata is stuffed full of colonial-era architecture, but the modern city is a very Indian mix of chaos, commerce and sophisticated culture. Food here is renowned across the subcontinent, with the focus on fresh seafood.

p453

West Bengal

Hill Stations
Wildlife
Hotels

Darjeeling is the definitive Indian hill station, offering spectacular Himalayan views, tea tasting and all sorts of nostalgic Raj-era accommodation. At the state's other extreme, drop down to waterlogged Sunderbans Tiger Reserve to spot an awesome Royal Bengal tiger.

p485

Bihar & Jharkhand

Religion
Ruins
Wildlife

Bodhgaya, where Buddha attained enlightenment, is a magnet for Buddhist pilgrims, while Jains flock to sacred Parasnath Hill. Trace Buddha's life at Bodhgaya, Rajgir, Vaishali and Nalanda, or seek wild elephants at Betla (Palamau) National Park.

p516

Sikkim

Views
Monasteries
Trekking

The forested ridges of this former Buddhist kingdom are studded with Tibetan-style Buddhist monasteries, Hindu temples and mega-statues. This is just a warm-up act for Sikkim's Himalayan peaks, with mesmerising Khangchendzonga calling out to trekkers like a beacon.

p535

Northeast States

Culture
Wildlife
Adventure

The Northeast is home to some of India's most enigmatic tribes, who follow ancient customs in villages of grass-thatched, bamboo houses tucked into remote valleys. The one-horned Indian rhino is just one of the exotic animals on this wild frontier.

p558

Odisha

Architecture
Tribal Culture
Wildlife

Odisha's dazzling temples were the work of rulers who spared no expense in their veneration of the divine, while tribal markets offer fascinating opportunities to mingle with Odisha's indigenous inhabitants. Nature-lovers will enjoy the tiger reserves and coastal wetlands.

p595

Madhya Pradesh & Chhattisgarh

Wildlife
Monuments
Culture

A region of eclectic attractions, with India's most famous tiger reserves, erotic carvings on the World Heritage–listed Khajuraho temples, fascinating old forts and palaces, and a wealth of tribal villages, markets and crafts.

p625

Gujarat & Diu

Wildlife
Crafts
Treks

Gujarat's national parks protect Asiatic lions and wild asses, while weavers and embroiderers transform every human settlement into a riot of colour. To feel Gujarat's spiritual pulse, visit Gandhi's ashram at Ahmedabad, or join pilgrims on treks up temple-topped peaks.

p688

Mumbai

Architecture
Food
Nightlife

Blending British grandeur and Indian exuberance, Mumbai's architecture is a fabulous fusion of styles. Global flavours mingle at the city's excellent restaurants, canteens and food stands. After hours, look out for Bollywood stars and sporting celebs in Mumbai's ritzy clubs and bars.

p736

Maharashtra

Caves
Beaches
Wine

Ajanta and Ellora hide exquisite cave paintings and rock sculptures, while the Konkan Coast has some of the most secluded beaches in India. Inland, Nashik is the epicentre of India's burgeoning wine industry, producing exciting vintages that are causing an international stir.

p774

Goa

Beaches
Food
Architecture

Goa's beaches are no secret, but with palm fronds swishing overhead and sugar-sand under your feet, you won't really mind. Add fresh seafood, magical markets and beautiful colonial-era architecture, and it's easy to see what all the fuss is about.

p809

Karnataka

Temples
Wildlife
Food

The temples of Karnataka overflow with deities and demons, while the Nilgiri Biosphere Reserve is home to abundant elephants, plus stalking tigers and leopards. The table is laden, too, with everything from Udupi vegetarian thalis to fresh Mangalorean seafood.

p856

Telangana & Andhra Pradesh

Religion
Food
Beaches

Hyderabad's past splendours and contemporary style make it one of India's most engaging cities. Escape the city rush at peaceful rural Buddhist sites and beach retreats such as Visakhapatnam.

p914

Kerala

Backwaters
Food
Wildlife

Set back from idyllic beaches, the inlets and lakes of
Kerala's backwaters are a
peaceful retreat from the
modern age. Back on land,
you'll find cultural riches,
a lavish, coconut-flavoured
cuisine, and wildlife-filled
national parks in the hills
of the Western Ghats.

p945

Tamil Nadu

Temples
Hill Stations
City Life

Age-old tradition meets
cosmopolitan flair in bustling Chennai, while Tamil
Nadu's intricately carved
temples attract pilgrims
from across India. For a
peaceful escape, retreat to
the Western Ghats' cool
Raj-era hill stations or the
pretty French Quarter of
Puducherry (Pondicherry).

p1011

Andaman Islands

Water Sports
Beaches
Culture

With lush greenery,
pristine waters and a sand-
sprinkled shoreline, the
Andamans are an ideal
place to chill out. There's
excellent snorkelling and
diving offshore, and tribal
people and settlers from
India and Southeast Asia
create a unique cultural mix
inland.

p1095

On the Road

Delhi

⟐ 011 / POP 29 MILLION / ELEV 250M

Best Places to Eat

➡ Karim's (p87)

➡ Darbar (p89)

➡ Andhra Pradesh Bhawan Canteen (p91)

➡ Naivedyam (p93)

➡ Potbelly (p93)

➡ Rajdhani (p92)

Best Places to Stay

➡ Diya Bed & Breakfast (p83)

➡ Madpackers Hostel (p87)

➡ Haveli Dharampura (p82)

➡ Lutyens Bungalow (p86)

➡ Imperial (p85)

Why Go?

You need patience to love Delhi. At first it slaps you in the face – whack! – and you're left to pick yourself up, unsure quite what hit you. It's hectic, noisy, polluted and unfeasibly overcrowded, but give it some time and you soon realise that the chaos that knocked you flying is the very thing that makes this wonderful city tick.

Hugely historic, and in parts intensely spiritual, Delhi bursts with life like few other places on Earth, and is forced by the sheer weight of humanity to dance to its own unique, unpredictable rhythm. Learn to skip to its beat, though, and you'll soon find its charms become irresistible.

Ride a cycle-rickshaw through mesmerising Old Delhi, with its frenetic bazaars and sizzling street food; take an autorickshaw to the suburbs for tumbledown ruins, leafy parks and Raj-era monuments; or hop on the sky train to glitzy Gurgaon (Gurugram) for a peek at the India of the future.

When to Go
Delhi

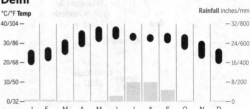

Oct–Mar Delhi at its best: chilly mornings, but warm days. Smog can spoil November.

May–Aug The months to avoid – hot, humid and uncomfortable.

Jun–Sep Monsoon season sees still-high temperatures and frequent downpours.

History

One of the world's oldest continually inhabited major settlements, Delhi is a city of layers; built, destroyed and rebuilt several times. It has had numerous incarnations, some easier to distinguish than others, but it is commonly agreed that there are eight historical cities of Delhi, most of which have left their indelible mark in the city's fascinating array of archaeological remains.

The first city for which clear archaeological evidence remains was Lal Kot, or Qila Rai Pithora, founded by the Hindu king Prithvi Raj Chauhan in the 12th century. The city fell to Afghan invaders in 1191, and for the next 600 years Delhi was ruled by a succession of Muslim sultans and emperors. The first, Qutub-ud-din Aibak, razed the Hindu city and used its stones to construct Mehrauli and the towering Qutab Minar.

Qutub-ud-din Aibak's 'Mamluk' (Slave) dynasty was quickly replaced by the Khilji dynasty, following a coup. The Khiljis constructed a new capital at Siri, northeast of Mehrauli, supplied with water from the royal tank at Hauz Khas. Following another coup, the Tughlaq sultans seized the reins, creating a new fortified capital at Tughlaqabad, and two more cities – Jahanpanah and Firozabad – for good measure.

The Tughlaq dynasty fell after Tamerlane stormed through town in 1398, opening the door for the Sayyid and Lodi dynasties, the last of the Delhi sultanates, whose tombs are scattered around the Lodi Garden. The scene was set for the arrival of the Mughals.

Babur, the first Mughal emperor, seized Delhi in 1526, and a new capital rose at Shergarh (the present-day Purana Qila), presided over by his son, Humayun.

Frantic city building continued throughout the Mughal period. Shah Jahan gained the Peacock Throne in 1627 and raised a new city, Shahjahanabad, centred on the Red Fort. The Mughal city fell in 1739 to the Persian Nadir Shah, and the dynasty went into steep decline. The last Mughal emperor, Bahadur Shah Zafar, was exiled to Burma (Myanmar) by the British for his role in the 1857 First War of Independence; there were some new rulers in town.

Initially Calcutta had been declared the capital of British India but at the Delhi Durbar of 1911, held at the Coronation Park, King George V announced the shifting of the capital back to Delhi. It was time for another bout of construction.

The architect Edwin Lutyens drew up plans for a new city of wide boulevards and stately administrative buildings to accommodate the colonial government – New Delhi was born. Its centrepiece was Rajpath, a vast boulevard leading from Rashtrapati Bhavan (the President's Palace) all the way to India Gate, Delhi's iconic 42m-tall war-memorial arch.

Partition – the devastating division of British India in 1947 that eventually led to the creation of the three independent dominions of Bangladesh, India and Pakistan – saw Delhi ripped apart as hundreds of thousands of Muslim inhabitants fled north while Sikh and Hindu refugees flooded inwards, a trauma from which some say the city has never recovered. The modern metropolis certainly faces other challenges, too – traffic, pollution, overpopulation, crime and the deepening chasm between rich and poor. However, the city continues to flourish, with its new, modern satellite cities spreading Delhi further and further outwards.

DELHI HISTORY

TOP DELHI FESTIVALS

Check online to confirm exact dates, or contact India Tourism Delhi (p103).

Republic Day (⊘26 Jan, Rajpath) A spectacular military parade.

Beating of the Retreat (⊘29 Jan, Rashtrapati Bhavan) More military pageantry in Rajpath.

Independence Day (⊘15 Aug, Red Fort) India celebrates its independence from Britain.

Dussehra (⊘Sep/Oct) Hindu celebration of good over evil with parades of colourful effigies.

Qutab Festival (⊘Oct/Nov, Qutab Minar Complex) Sufi singing and classical music and dance at the Qutab Minar complex.

Diwali (⊘Oct/Nov) Fireworks across the city for the Festival of Light.

Delhi International Arts Festival (⊘Nov/Dec) Exhibitions, performing arts, film, literature and culinary events.

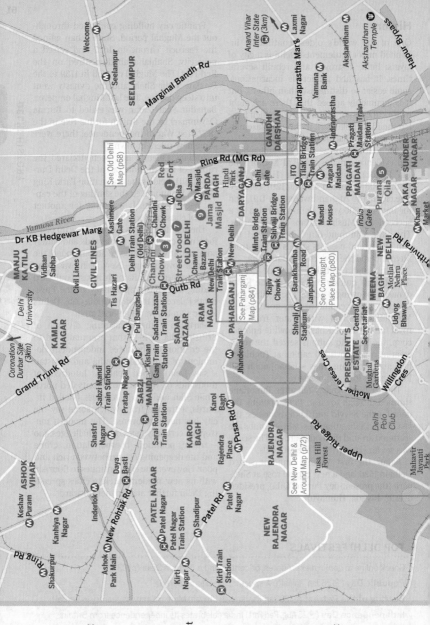

Delhi Highlights

1 Red Fort (p64)

Exploring this Mughal masterpiece, imagining its former traumas and splendours.

2 Qutab Minar Complex (p78)

Visiting Delhi's first Islamic city at sunrise, and gasping at its majestic centrepiece tower, the world's tallest brick minaret.

3 Old Delhi's Bazaars (p99)

Losing yourself in the street-market mayhem of Old Delhi's lost-in-time alleyways around Chandni Chowk.

4 Humayun's Tomb (p76)

Enjoying the architectural virtuosity and mirror-image gardens of Delhi's most spectacular resting place.

5 Purana Qila (p76)

Exploring the tumbledown ruins of Delhi's 'Old Fort'

before picnicking in the gardens.

6 Lodi Garden
(p77) Joining local families as you roam around the lawns, bamboo groves, and tree-shaded pathways of Delhi's loveliest park.

7 Street food
(p87) Sampling Old Delhi's flavour-packed street food from hole-in-the-wall eateries in and around Chandni Chowk.

8 Tughlaqabad
(p79) Marvelling at the immense 14th-century ruined fort that briefly ruled Delhi in its third incarnation.

9 Jama Masjid
(p65) Experiencing the serenity of the 'Friday Mosque,' with its wide open courtyard.

10 Hazrat Nizam-ud-din Dargah (p77)
Drinking in the mystical, magical atmosphere and hearing qawwali (Islamic devotional singing) at this hallowed Sufi shrine.

⊙ Sights

Most sights in Delhi are easily accessible by metro, though to reach some you'll have to take a rickshaw or taxi (or endure a fair walk) from the station, even if it bears the same or a similar name to the sight, eg Qutab Minar and Tughlaqabad. Old Delhi's sights are nicely concentrated so are best visited on foot; it's fascinating to walk the bustling lanes in any case. And if you get tired, just hail a passing cycle-rickshaw. Taking a walking tour is a great way to get accustomed to Old Delhi's frenetic streets. New Delhi's wide, tree-lined avenues are pleasant to walk along, but distances can be vast, so you'll often want to make use of passing autorickshaws. Sights in Delhi's more southerly districts are much more spread out so they're difficult to visit in one hit; plan accordingly.

Note that many tourist sights are closed on Mondays.

◉ Old Delhi

★ Red Fort
FORT

(Map p68; Indian/foreigner ₹50/600, with card payment ₹35/550, video ₹25, audio guide in Hindi/English or Korean ₹69/118; ⊙ dawn-dusk Tue-Sun; Ⓜ Chandni Chowk) Founded by Emperor Shah Jahan and surrounded by a magnificent 18m-high wall, this fort took 10 years to construct (1638–48) and is rumoured to have had the decapitated bodies of prisoners built into the foundations for luck. It once overlooked the Yamuna River, which has now shrunk to some distance away. A tree-lined waterway, known as *nahr-i-bihisht* (river of paradise), once ran out of the fort and along Chandni Chowk, fed by the Yamuna.

Shah Jahan never took up full residence here, after his disloyal son, Aurangzeb, imprisoned him in Agra Fort.

The last Mughal emperor of Delhi, Bahadur Shah Zafar, was flushed from the Red Fort in 1857 and exiled to Burma (Myanmar) for his role in the First War of Independence. The British destroyed buildings and gardens inside the fortress walls and replaced them with barrack blocks for the colonial army.

The audio guide tour, by acclaimed company Narrowcasters, is worthwhile as it brings the site to life.

Controversially, in 2018 the government leased out the job of maintaining the fort to a private firm, the Dalmia Bharat Group, prompting accusations from conservationists that it had sold the country's heritage. Dalmia soon began wholesale renovations, including laying new red-sandstone pathways over some of the existing quartzite stone paths.

At the time of writing, all the Red Fort's museums were closed for renovations. With the exception of the arcades at Chatta Chowk and Diwan-i-Am, it was not possible to enter the interiors of the buildings inside the fort, but the main structures are expected to re-open once renovations are complete. The fort's sound-and-light show was also suspended as part of the revamp.

➡ **Lahore Gate**

The main entrance to the Red Fort is hidden by a defensive bastion built in front by Shah Jahan's son Aurangzeb. During the struggle for independence, nationalists promised to raise the Indian flag over the gate, an ambition that became a reality on 15 August 1947. The Prime Minister makes a speech here every Independence Day.

➡ **Chatta Chowk**

(Covered Bazaar) This imperial bazaar used to cater to royal women and glitter with silk and jewels for sale. Today's wares are rather more mundane souvenirs.

➡ **Diwan-i-Am**

(Hall of Public Audiences) This arcade of sandstone columns was where the emperor greeted guests and dignitaries from a throne on the raised marble platform, which is backed by fine pietra dura (inlaid stone) work that features Orpheus, incongruously, and is thought to be Florentine.

➡ **Diwan-i-Khas**

(Hall of Private Audiences) This hall was used for bowing and scraping to the emperor. Above the corner arches to the north and south is inscribed in Urdu, 'If there is paradise on the earth – it is this, it is this, it is this'. Nadir Shah looted the legendary jewel-studded Peacock Throne from here in 1739. Bahadur Shah Zafar became the last Mughal emperor here in May 1857, but was exiled by the British seven months later.

➡ **Khas Mahal**

(Special Palace) South of the public area of the Diwan-i-Khas is the Khas Mahal, where the emperor lived and slept, shielded from prying eyes by lace-like carved marble screens. A cooling channel of water, the *nahr-i-bihisht* (river of paradise), once flowed through the apartments to the adjacent Rang Mahal (Palace of Colour), home to the emperor's chief wife. The exterior of the palace was once lavishly painted; inside is an elegant lotus-shaped fountain.

MAJNU-KA-TILLA: DELHI'S TIBETAN QUARTER

Majnu-ka-Tilla is an enclave that has served as a base for Tibetan refugees since around 1960, and its traffic-free alleyways are a great place to shop for Tibetan trinkets and Buddhist-based souvenirs; try **Akama** (⊙9.30am-8.30pm) or the market (p100). There are some lovely cafes, too; **Ama** (H40 Tibetan Colony; dishes ₹150-300, coffee from ₹85; ⊙7am-9.45pm; 🛜) is the most popular, though **Kham Coffee** (15A Tibetan Colony, ⊙8.30am-9.30pm) has a more traditional Tibetan feel. **Wongdhen House** (📞011-23816689; 15A New Tibetan Colony, r from ₹700, without bathroom ₹500; 🖳🛜) is a friendly budget guesthouse, with its 4th-floor terrace opening out onto views of the river and Delhi's new, iconic **Signature Bridge** (New Aruna Colony, Wazirabad).

The enclave is 2km from Vidhan Sabha metro station; turn right out of Gate 2, then right at the second set of traffic lights, and cross the busy main road at the end (there's a footbridge). It's ₹30 to ₹40 in an autorickshaw.

➡ Shahi Burj

(Emperor's Tower) This three-storey octagonal tower that was Shah Jahan's favoured workplace. From here he planned the running of his empire. In front of the tower is what remains of an elegant formal garden, centred on the Zafar Mahal, a sandstone pavilion surrounded by a deep, empty water tank. At the time of research, the Shahi Burj could only be viewed from outside.

➡ Salimgarh

(⊙10am-5pm Tue-Sun) Across a bridge from the Red Fort, but part of the same complex, this fort was established by Salim Shah Suri in 1546, so predates its grander neighbour. Salimgarh was later used as a prison, first by Aurangzeb and later by the British; you can visit the ruined mosque and a small prison building.

★ Jama Masjid   MOSQUE

(Friday Mosque; Map p68; camera & video each ₹300, tower ₹100; ⊙non-Muslims 8am-1hr before sunset, minaret 9am-5.30pm; Ⓜ Jama Masjid) A beautiful pocket of calm at the heart of Old Delhi's mayhem, the capital's largest mosque is built on a 10m elevation, towering above the surrounding hubbub. It can hold a mind-blowing 25,000 people. The marble and red-sandstone structure, known also as the 'Friday Mosque', was Shah Jahan's final architectural triumph, built between 1644 and 1658. The four watchtowers were used for security. There are two minarets standing 40m high, one of which can be climbed for amazing views. There are numerous entrance gates, but only Gate 1 (south side), Gate 2 (east), and Gate 3 (north) allow access to the mosque for visitors. The eastern gate was originally for imperial use only. Entrance is free, but you have to buy a ₹300 ticket if you

are carrying any sort of camera (including a camera phone), even if you don't intend to use it. Once inside, you can buy a separate ₹100 ticket to climb the 121 steps up the narrow southern minaret (notices say that unaccompanied women are not permitted). From the top of the minaret, you can see how architect Edwin Lutyens incorporated the mosque into his design of New Delhi – the Jama Masjid, Connaught Place and Sansad Bhavan (Parliament House) are in a direct line.

Visitors should dress conservatively and remove their shoes before entering the mosque, though you can carry your shoes with you inside if you wish to leave from a different gate, or are worried about losing them (many locals do this).

Chandni Chowk   AREA

(Map p68; Ⓜ Chandni Chowk) Old Delhi's main drag is lined by Jain, Hindu and Sikh temples, plus a church, with the Fatehpuri Masjid at one end. Tree-lined and elegant in Mughal times, the thoroughfare is now mind-bendingly chaotic, with tiny little ancient bazaars tentacling off it. In the Mughal era, Chandni Chowk centred on a pool that reflected the moon, hence the name, 'moonlight place'. The main street is almost impossible to cross, full as it is of cars, hawkers, motorcycles, rickshaws and porters.

Digambara Jain Temple   JAIN TEMPLE

(Map p68; Chandni Chowk; ⊙6am-noon & 6-9pm; Ⓜ Lal Qila) Opposite the Red Fort is the red sandstone Digambara Jain Temple, built in 1658. Interestingly, it houses a **bird hospital** (donations appreciated; ⊙10am-5pm) established in 1956 to further the Jain principle of preserving all life, treating 30,000 birds a year. Remove shoes and leather items before entering the temple.

Red Fort

HIGHLIGHTS

The main entrance to the Red Fort is through ❶ Lahore Gate – the bastion in front of it was built by Aurangzeb for increased security. You can still see bullet marks on the gate, dating from 1857, the First War of Independence, when the Indian army rose up against the British.

Walk through the Chatta Chowk (Covered Bazaar), which once sold silks and jewellery to the nobility; beyond it lies Naubat Khana, a part white-plaster, part russet-red building, which houses Hathi Pol (Elephant Gate), so called because visitors used to dismount from their elephants or horses here as a sign of respect. From here it's straight on to the ❷ Diwan-i-Am, the Hall of Public Audiences.

Behind this are the private palaces, the ❸ Khas Mahal and the ❹ Diwan-i-Khas. Entry to this Hall of Private Audiences, the fort's most expensive building, was only permitted to the officials of state. The artificial stream the Nahr-i-Bihisht (Stream of Paradise) used to run a cooling channel of water through all these buildings.

Nearby is the ❺ Moti Masjid (Pearl Mosque) and south is the Mumtaz Mahal, which before renovations housed the Museum of Archaeology, or you can head north, where the Red Fort gardens are dotted by palatial pavilions and old British barracks. Here you'll find the ❻ Baoli, a spookily deserted water tank, though you can no longer climb down into it. Another five minutes' walk – across a road, then a railway bridge – brings you to the island fortress of Salimgarh.

(Note that many of the fort buildings were closed for renovations at the time of research, but the pavilions can be viewed from outside, and most structures are expected to reopen once the renovations are complete.)

TOP TIPS

➡ To avoid crowds, get here early or late in the day; avoid weekends and public holidays.

➡ Bring the fort to life with the excellent audio guide, available at the ticket office.

Baoli
The Red Fort step well is seldom visited and is a hauntingly deserted place, even more so when you consider its chambers were used as cells by the British from August 1942.

Salimgarh

Museum on India's Struggle for Freedom (closed for renovations)

Chatta Chowk

Lahore Gate
Lahore Gate is particularly significant, as it was here that Jawaharlal Nehru raised the first tricolour flag of independent India in 1947.

FEYGINFOTO/SHUTTERSTOCK ©

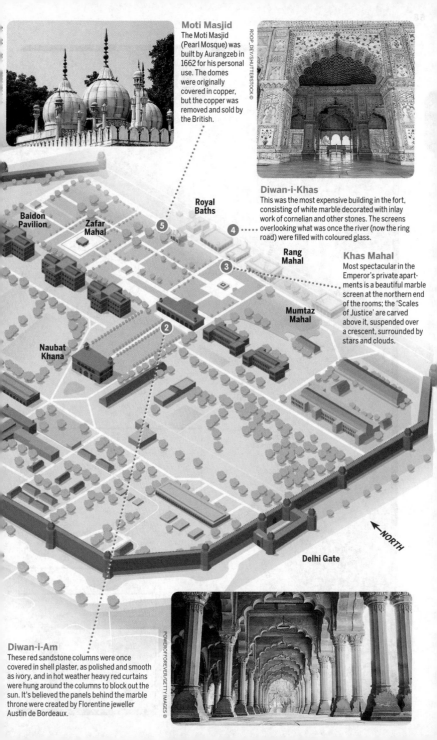

Moti Masjid
The Moti Masjid (Pearl Mosque) was built by Aurangzeb in 1662 for his personal use. The domes were originally covered in copper, but the copper was removed and sold by the British.

ROOP_DEV/SHUTTERSTOCK ©

Diwan-i-Khas
This was the most expensive building in the fort, consisting of white marble decorated with inlay work of cornelian and other stones. The screens overlooking what was once the river (now the ring road) were filled with coloured glass.

Royal Baths

Baidon Pavilion

Zafar Mahal

5

4

Rang Mahal

3

Khas Mahal
Most spectacular in the Emperor's private apartments is a beautiful marble screen at the northern end of the rooms; the 'Scales of Justice' are carved above it, suspended over a crescent, surrounded by stars and clouds.

Mumtaz Mahal

2

Naubat Khana

NORTH

Delhi Gate

Diwan-i-Am
These red sandstone columns were once covered in shell plaster, as polished and smooth as ivory, and in hot weather heavy red curtains were hung around the columns to block out the sun. It's believed the panels behind the marble throne were created by Florentine jeweller Austin de Bordeaux.

POWEROFFOREVER/GETTY IMAGES ©

Old Delhi

DELHI

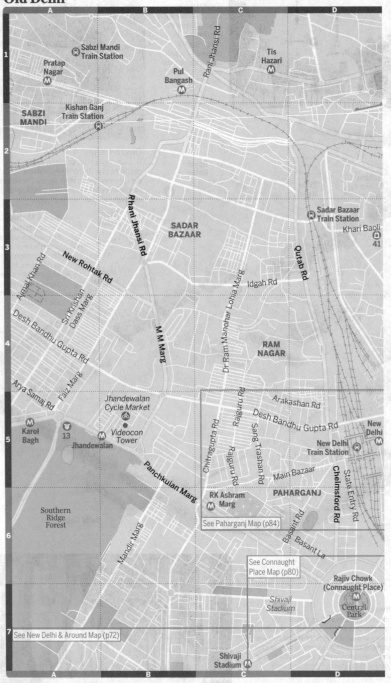

Sabzi Mandi Train Station

Pratap Nagar

Rani Jhansi Rd

Pul Bangash

Tis Hazari

SABZI MANDI

Kishan Ganj Train Station

Sadar Bazaar Train Station

Khari Baoli

41

SADAR BAZAAR

Rhani Jhansi Rd

Qutab Rd

New Rohtak Rd

Afnal Khan Rd

Sri Krishan Dass Marg

Desh Bandhu Gupta Rd

Idgah Rd

M M Marg

Dr-Ram Manohar Lohia Marg

RAM NAGAR

Arya Samaj Rd

Faiz Marg

Jhandewalan Cycle Market

Arakashan Rd

New Delhi

Chitragupta Rd

Rajguru Rd

Desh Bandhu Gupta Rd

Karol Bagh

13

Videocon Tower

Jhandewalan

Rajguru Rd

Sang Trashan Rd

New Delhi Train Station

Panchkuian Marg

Main Bazaar

Chelmsford Rd

State Entry Rd

RK Ashram Marg

PAHARGANJ

See Paharganj Map (p84)

Southern Ridge Forest

Mandir Marg

Basant Rd

Basant La

See Connaught Place Map (p80)

Rajiv Chowk (Connaught Place)

Central Park

Shivaji Stadium

See New Delhi & Around Map (p72)

Shivaji Stadium

DELHI

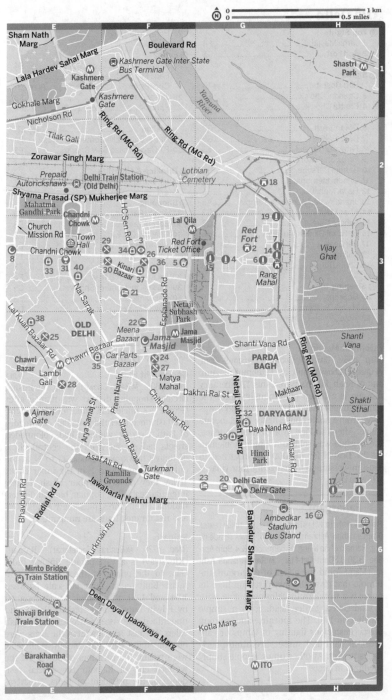

Old Delhi

Fatehpuri Masjid MOSQUE
(Map p68; Chandni Chowk; ⊙5am-9.30pm; Ⓜ Chandni Chowk) Built by Fatehpuri Begum, one of Shah Jahan's wives, this 17th-century mosque is a haven of tranquillity after the frantic streets outside. The central pool was taken from a noble house, hence the elaborate shape. After the First War of Independence, the mosque was sold to a Hindu nobleman by the British for ₹19,000 and returned to Muslim worship in exchange for four villages 20 years later.

◉ Paharganj

Ramakrishna Mission HINDU TEMPLE
(Ramakrishna Ashram; Map p84; www.rkmdelhi. org; Ramakrishna Marg; ⊙5am-noon & 4-9pm Apr-Sep, 3.30-8.30pm Oct-Mar; Ⓜ Ramakrishna Ashram Marg) Amid the chaos of Paharganj, the temple that gives the metro station here its name is a wonderfully calming escape, with a landscaped garden leading to a simple meditation hall. The morning and evening *aarti* (auspicious lighting of lamps or candles), at 5am and sunset, are atmospheric times to visit. At other times, people simply meditate in peace.

◉ New Delhi

Connaught Place AREA
(Map p80; Ⓜ Rajiv Chowk) This confusing circular shopping district was named after George V's uncle, the Duke of Connaught, and fashioned after the Palladian colonnades of Bath. Greying, whitewashed, colonnaded streets radiate out from the central circle of Rajiv Chowk, with blocks G to N in the outer circle and A to F in the inner circle. Today they mainly harbour brash, largely interchangeable but popular, bars, and international chain stores, plus a few good hotels and restaurants. Touts are rampant.

Rajpath AREA
(Map p72; Ⓜ Central Secretariat) Rajpath (Kingsway) is a vast parade linking India Gate to the offices of the Indian government. Built on an imperial scale between 1914 and 1931, this complex was designed by Edwin Lutyens and Herbert Baker, and underlined the ascendance of the British rulers. Yet just 16 years later, the Brits were out on their ear and Indian politicians were pacing the corridors of power. At the western end of Rajpath the official residence of the president of India, **Rashtra-**

pati Bhavan (⌨ 011-23015321; www.rashtrapati sachivalaya.gov.in/rbtour; ₹50; ⊙ 9am-4pm Fri-Sun, online reservation required), now partially open to the public via guided tour, is flanked by the mirror-image, dome-crowned North Secretariat and South Secretariat. These house government ministries and are not open to the public. The Indian parliament meets nearby at the Sansad Bhavan (Map p72), a circular, colonnaded edifice at the end of Sansad Marg, also not open to the public.

At Rajpath's eastern end is mighty India Gate. This 42m-high stone memorial arch, designed by Lutyens, pays tribute to around 90,000 Indian Army soldiers who died in WWI, the Northwest Frontier operations and the 1919 Anglo-Afghan War.

★ **Gurdwara Bangla Sahib** SIKH TEMPLE

(Map p72; Ashoka Rd; ⊙ 4am-9pm; Ⓜ Patel Chowk) This magnificent white-marble gurdwara (Sikh temple), topped by glinting golden onion domes, was constructed at the site where the eighth Sikh guru, Harkrishan Dev, stayed before his 1664 death. Despite his tender years, the six-year-old guru tended to victims of Delhi's cholera and smallpox epidemic, and the waters of the large tank are said to have healing powers. It's full of colour and life, yet tranquil, and live devotional songs waft over the compound. As at all gurdwaras, free meals are served to pilgrims daily. Just inside the entrance to the complex is a small museum, chronicling the history of Sikhism and its gurus and martyrs.

Agrasen ki Baoli MONUMENT

(Map p80; Hailey Lane; ⊙ dawn-dusk; Ⓜ Janpath) This atmospheric 14th-century step-well was once set in the countryside, till the city grew up around it; 103 steps descend to the bottom, flanked by arched niches. It's a remarkable thing to discover among the office towers southeast of Connaught Place. It's garnered more attention since it was used as a shelter by Aamir Khan in the 2015 movie *PK*.

Jantar Mantar HISTORIC SITE

(Map p80; Sansad Marg; Indian/foreigner ₹25/300, video ₹25; ⊙ dawn-dusk; Ⓜ Patel Chowk) This is one of five observatories built by Maharaja Jai Singh II, ruler of Jaipur. Constructed in 1725, Jantar Mantar (derived from the Sanskrit word for 'instrument', but which has also become the Hindi word for 'abracadabra') is a quiet park containing a collection of curving geometric buildings that are carefully calibrated to monitor the movement of the stars and planets.

Jhandewalan Hanuman Temple HINDU TEMPLE

(Map p68; Link Rd, Jhandewalan; ⊙ dawn-dusk; Ⓜ Jhandewalan) This temple is not to be missed (it's actually hard to miss) if you're in Karol Bagh. Take a short detour to see the 34m-tall Hanuman statue that soars above both the roads and the raised metro line. Getting up close, there are passageways through the mouths of demons to a series of atmospheric, deity-filled chambers.

Crafts Museum MUSEUM

(Map p72; ⌨ 011-23371641; Bhairon Marg; Indian/foreigner ₹20/200; ⊙ 10am-5pm Tue-Sun; Ⓜ Pragati Maidan) Much of this lovely museum is outside, including tree-shaded carvings and life-size examples of village huts from various regions of India. Displays celebrate the traditional crafts of India, with some beautiful textiles on display indoors, such as embroidery from Kashmir and cross-stitch from Punjab. Highlights include a huge wooden 18th-century temple chariot from Maharashtra. Artisans sell their products in the rear courtyard. The museum also includes the excellent Cafe Lota (p92) and a very good shop.

National Museum MUSEUM

(Map p72; ⌨ 011-23019272; www.national museumindia.gov.in; Janpath; Indian/foreigner ₹20/650, camera ₹20/300; ⊙ 10am-6pm Tue-Sun, free guided tour 10.30am & 2.30pm Tue-Fri, 10.30am, 11.30am, 2.30pm & 3pm Sat & Sun; Ⓜ Udyog Bhawan) This glorious, if dusty, museum is full of treasures. Mind-bogglingly ancient, sophisticated figurines from the Harappan civilisation, almost 5000 years old, include the remarkable Dancing Girl, and there are also some fine ceramics from the even older Nal civilisation. Other items include Buddha

---

LOCAL KNOWLEDGE

CHANGING OF THE GUARD

Members of the public can make a rare foray into the forecourt of Rashtrapati Bhavan (p70) to witness the twice-weekly Changing of the Guard ceremony. It's held at 8am on Saturdays (10am mid-March to mid-November) and at 4.30pm on Sundays (5.30pm mid-March to mid-November) and lasts around 45 minutes. Entry is via Gate 2 or Gate 37. Numbers are limited. Bring your passport.

New Delhi & Around

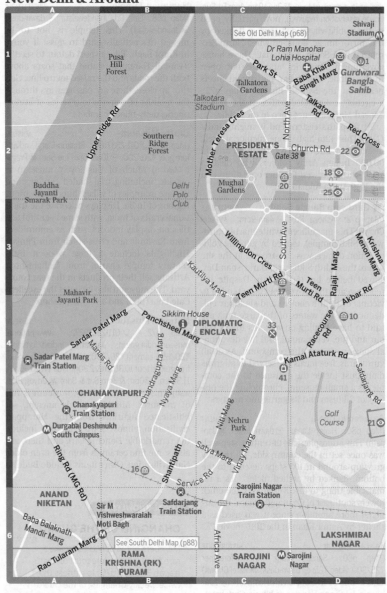

relics, exquisite jewellery, miniature paintings, medieval woodcarvings, textiles and musical instruments. Don't miss the immense, five-tier wooden temple chariot built in South India in the 19th century and now on display just inside the museum gates.

Gandhi Smriti   MUSEUM
(Map p72; ☑011-23012843; 5 Tees Jan Marg; ⊙10am-5pm Tue-Sun, closed 2nd Sat of month; Ⓜ Lok Kalyan Marg) FREE This poignant memorial to Mahatma Gandhi is in Birla House, where he was shot dead on the grounds by a

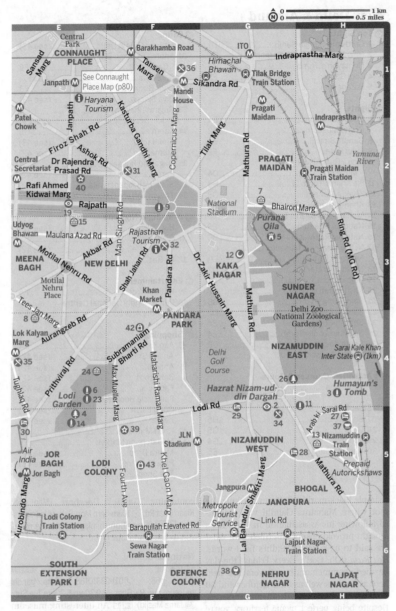

See Connaught Place Map (p80)

Hindu zealot on 30 January 1948, after campaigning against intercommunal violence.

The house itself is where Gandhi spent his last 144 days. The exhibits include film footage, modern art, and rooms preserved just as Gandhi left them. The small clothes shop within the grounds sells garments made from *khadi*, homespun cotton that was championed by Gandhi during the Independence movement.

Raj Ghat
MONUMENT

(Map p68; ☉10am-8pm; Ⓜ Jama Masjid) FREE
This peaceful, well maintained park contains

New Delhi & Around

a simple black-marble platform marking the spot where Mahatma Gandhi was cremated following his assassination in 1948. It's a thought-provoking spot, inscribed with what are said to have been Gandhi's final words, *Hai Ram* ('Oh, God'). Every Friday (the day he died) commemorative prayers are held here at 5pm, as well as on 2 October and 30 January, his birth and death anniversaries. Despite being perfect picnic territory, you're not allowed to bring food into the park, and there's nowhere to buy any once inside. Further north you'll find memorials commemorating where Jawaharlal Nehru, Indira Gandhi and Rajiv Gandhi were cremated. South from Raj Ghat, just across Kisan Ghat Rd, are some equally peaceful landscaped gardens containing **Gandhi Darshan** (Map p68; Kisan Ghat Rd; ⊙10am-5pm Mon-Sat; Ⓜ Indraprastha) FREE, a pavilion displaying photos relating to the Mahatma.

National Gandhi Museum MUSEUM

(Map p68; ☎011-23310168; http://gandhimuseum.org; Raj Ghat; ⊙9.30am-5.30pm Tue-Sun; Ⓜ Jama Masjid) FREE An interesting museum preserving some of Gandhi's personal belongings, including his spectacles and even two of his teeth. You can also listen to his voice on the other end of a telephone receiver. Movingly and somewhat macabrely, also here are the dhoti, shawl and watch he was wearing when he was assassinated, and one of the bullets that killed him.

Indira Gandhi Memorial Museum
MUSEUM

(Map p72; ☑ 011-23010094; 1 Safdarjang Rd; ⊘9.30am-4.45pm Tue-Sun; Ⓜ Lok Kalyan Marg) FREE In the residence of controversial former prime minister Indira Gandhi is this interesting museum devoted to her life and her political-heavyweight family. It displays her personal effects, including the blood-stained sari she was wearing when she was assassinated in 1984; in the back garden a glass-covered pathway traces her final steps before she was shot and killed by two security guards. Many rooms in the house are preserved as they were, providing a window into the family's life.

Nehru Memorial Museum
MUSEUM

(Map p72; ☑ 011-23016734; www.nehrumemorial. nic.in; Teen Murti Rd; ⊘9am-5.30pm Tue-Sun; Ⓜ Udyog Bhawan) FREE Built for the British commander-in-chief and previously called 'Flagstaff House', the stately Teen Murti Bhavan was later the official residence of Jawaharlal Nehru (India's first prime minister). It's now a museum devoted to Nehru's life and work; the bedroom, study and drawing room are preserved as if he'd just popped out.

On the grounds is a 14th-century hunting lodge, built by Feroz Shah, and a more recent **planetarium** (☑ 011-23014504; www.nehru planetarium.org; 40min show adult/child ₹80/50; ⊘shows English 11.30am & 3pm, Hindi 1.30pm & 4pm), which has shows about the stars in Hindi and English.

Feroz Shah Kotla
HISTORIC SITE

(Map p68; Bahadur Shah Zafar Marg; Indian/foreigner ₹75/300, with card payment ₹20/250, video ₹25; ⊘dawn-dusk; Ⓜ ITO) Firozabad, the fifth city of Delhi, was built by Feroz Shah Tughlaq in 1354, the first city here to be built on the river. Only the fortress remains, with crumbling walls protecting the Jama Masjid (Friday mosque), a *baoli* (step-well), and the pyramid-like **Hawa Mahal** (included in Feroz Shah Kotla entry; ⊘dawn-dusk), topped by a 13m-high sandstone Ashoka Pillar inscribed with 3rd-century-BC Buddhist edicts. There's an otherworldly atmosphere to the ruins.

Entrance is free after 2pm every Thursday when crowds gather at the mosque and other points of importance to light candles and incense and leave bowls of milk to appease Delhi's djinns (invisible spirits), who are said to occupy the underground chambers beneath the ruins.

Shoes should be removed when entering the mosque and Hawa Mahal.

◉ South Delhi

★Hauz Khas
AREA

(Map p88; ⊘dawn-dusk; Ⓜ IIT) Built by Sultan Ala-ud-din Khilji in the 13th century, Hauz Khas means 'noble tank', and its reservoir once covered 28 hectares. It collected enough water during the monsoon to last Siri Fort throughout the dry season. Today it's much smaller, but still a beautiful place to be, thronged by birds and surrounded by parkland. Overlooking it are the impressive ruins of Feroz Shah's 14th-century **madrasa** (Map p88; Ⓜ IIT, Green Park, Hauz Khas), or religious school, and his **tomb** (Map p88; Ⓜ Green Park), which he had built before his death in 1388.

To reach the lake shore, either cut through the adjacent Deer Park (p101) during daylight hours, which has more ruined tombs and a well-stocked deer enclosure, or walk past all the Hauz Khas shops, beyond No 50, and enter the grounds of Feroz Shah's madrasa, from where you can look out over the lake before climbing down to the water's edge.

There are numerous Lodi-era tombs scattered along the access road to Hauz Khas Village, and in nearby Green Park.

Bahai House of Worship
TEMPLE

(Lotus Temple; Map p88; ☑ 011-26444029; www. bahaihouseofworship.in; Kalkaji; ⊘9am-7pm Tue-Sun Apr-Sep, to 5.30pm Oct-Mar; Ⓜ Okhla NSIC, Kalkaji Mandir, Nehru Place) Designed for tranquil worship, Delhi's beautiful Lotus Temple offers a rare pocket of calm in the hectic city. This architectural masterpiece was designed by Iranian-Canadian architect Fariburz Sahba in 1986. It is shaped like a lotus flower, with 27 delicate-looking white-marble petals. The temple was created to bring faiths together; visitors are invited to pray or meditate silently according to their own beliefs. The attached visitor centre tells the story of the Bahai faith. Photography is prohibited inside the temple. Bear in mind that it gets very busy at weekends, with long queues and far less tranquillity.

Siri Fort
FORT

(Map p88; Ⓜ Hauz Khas, Green Park) Only some of the walls remain of this 14th-century fort, built by Ala-ud-din Khilji as the second of the seven historical cities of Delhi. They are impressive nonetheless, and it is said that the heads of 8000 Mongols were

SIRI FORT AUDITORIUM

Built within the ruined grounds of the 14th-century Siri Fort (p75), this **venue** (Map p88; https://in.bookmyshow. com; Aug Kranti Marg, Siri Fort Institutional Area, Siri Fort; Ⓜ Green Park) is one of Delhi's premier auditoriums and the headquarters of the Directorate of Film Festivals. The main auditorium has a capacity of 700 and is a great place to take in a concert, a play or a film screening. Check the website for schedules.

buried into the foundations! Within the boundaries of the walls is an auditorium, a sports complex and the village of Shahpur Jat (p101), which contains an interesting collection of boutique shops and cafes hidden amongst its tight network of alleyways.

◉ Sunder Nagar, Nizamuddin & Lodi Colony

★**Purana Qila**   FORT

(Old Fort; Map p72; 📞 011-24353178; Mathura Rd; Indian/foreigner ₹25/300, with card ₹20/250, moat ₹20, video ₹25, sound-and-light show adult/ child ₹100/50; ⊘ dawn-dusk; Ⓜ Pragati Maidan) Shh, whisper it quietly: this place is better than the Red Fort. Delhi's 'Old Fort' isn't as magnificent in size and grandeur, but it's far more pleasant to explore, with tree-shaded landscaped gardens to relax in, crumbling ruins to climb over (and even under, in the case of the tunnels by the mosque) and no uptight guards with whistles telling you not to go here and there.

Ringed by a moat, part of which has been refilled with water, and accessed through the majestically imposing Bada Darwaza gateway, this 16th-century fort is where Mughal Emperor Humayun met his end in 1556, tumbling down the steps of the Sher Mandal, which he used as a library.

The fort had been built by Afghan ruler Sher Shah (1538–45), during his brief ascendancy over Humayun. It's well worth a visit, with its peaceful gardens studded with well-preserved ancient red-stone monuments, including the intricately patterned Qila-i-Kuhran Mosque (Mosque of Sher Shah), behind which are tunnels to explore and parts of the outer walls that can be climbed upon. There's also a small museum (closed on Fridays) set within the walls just inside Bada Darwaza gateway. The sound-and-light show,

which is performed in the evening beside the Humayuni Darwaza gateway, is also non-operational on Fridays.

An elongated lake has been created from the fort's former moat, and in late afternoon is well worth wandering along as the sun lights up the towering walls above it, making for fabulous sunset photos. You'll have to buy an extra ₹20 'moat ticket' along with your main ticket in order to explore it.

Across busy Mathura Rd are more relics from the city of Shergarh, including the beautiful **Khairul Manazil mosque** (Map p72; Mathura Rd; Ⓜ Pragati Maidan), still used by local Muslims and a favoured haunt of flocks of pigeons.

★**Humayun's Tomb**   MONUMENT

(Map p72; Mathura Rd; Indian/foreigner ₹40/600, with car payment ₹35/550, video ₹25; ⊘ dawn-dusk; Ⓜ JLN Stadium, Hazrat Nizamuddin) Humayun's tomb is sublimely well proportioned, seeming to float above its symmetrical gardens. It's thought to have inspired the Taj Mahal, which it predates by 60 years. Constructed for the Mughal emperor in the mid-16th century by Haji Begum, Humayun's Persian-born wife, the tomb marries Persian and Mughal elements, with restrained decoration enhancing the architecture. The arched facade is inlaid with bands of white marble and red sandstone, and the building follows strict rules of Islamic geometry, with an emphasis on the number eight.

The beautiful surrounding gardens contain the tombs of the emperor's favourite barber – an entrusted position given the proximity of the razor to the imperial throat – and Haji Begum. This was where the last Mughal emperor, Bahadur Shah Zafar, took refuge before being captured and exiled by the British in 1857.

To the right as you enter the complex, **Isa Khan's tomb** is a fine example of Lodi-era architecture, constructed in the 16th century. Further south is the monumental **Khan-i-Khanan's tomb** (Rahim Khan Marg; Indian/ foreigner ₹25/300, with card payment ₹20/250; ⊘ dawn-dusk; Ⓜ Hazrat Nizamuddin), plundered in Mughal times to build Safdarjang's tomb.

As part of a huge ongoing restoration project, a new state-of-the-art visitor centre is being built just outside the entrance, and will have underground walkways linking the complex with neighbouring Sunder Nursery and Hazrat Nizam-ud-din Dargah across Mathura Rd.

Sunder Nursery PARK

(Map p72; Mathura Rd; Indian/foreigner ₹35/100; ⊙ dawn-dusk; Ⓜ Hazrat Nizamuddin or JLN Stadium) One of Delhi's newest tourist sights, this wonderful park was an overgrown wasteland until recent renovations brought the 16th-century Mughal gardens back to something approaching their former glory. It's now a vast landscaped heritage park with clipped lawns, delicate waterways and a network of paths dotted with fruit trees, flower beds, tree-shaded benches and numerous 16th-century Mughal tombs and pavilions, some of which still lie in a charming state of ruin, some of which have been lovingly restored.

The central pathway has been created upon the line of the Mughal-era Grand Trunk Road and leads all the way from the entrance to the water gardens at the border with Delhi's zoo. Off the sides are woods to explore, a bonsai garden and more Mughal ruins. The restoration project is a work in progress, but this is already proving to be one of Delhi's standout green spaces.

★ **Hazrat Nizam-
ud-din Dargah** SHRINE

(Map p72; off Lodi Rd; ⊙ 24hr; Ⓜ JLN Stadium) Visiting the marble shrine of Muslim Sufi saint Nizam-ud-din Auliya is Delhi's most mystical, magical experience. The dargah is hidden away in a tangle of bazaars selling rose petals, attars (perfumes) and offerings, and on some evenings you can hear the *qawwali* (Islamic devotional singing of the Sufis), amid crowds of devotees. The ascetic Nizam-ud-din died in 1325 at the ripe old age of 92. His doctrine of tolerance made him popular not only with Muslims, but with adherents of other faiths, too.

Later kings and nobles wanted to be buried close to Nizam-ud-din, hence the number of nearby Mughal tombs. Other tombs in the compound include the graves of Jahanara (daughter of Shah Jahan) and the renowned Urdu poet Amir Khusru. Scattered around the surrounding alleyways are more tombs and a huge *baoli* (step-well). Entry is free, but visitors may be asked to make a donation. You must remove your shoes before entering the shrine, but there's no need to do so whilst wandering the bazaars that approach it, despite pushy shoe keepers telling you otherwise; follow the lead from visiting locals.

A tour with the Hope Project (p81), which ends at the shrine, is recommended for some background.

★ **Lodi Garden** PARK

(Map p72; Lodi Rd; ⊙ 6am-8pm Oct-Mar, 5am-8pm Apr-Sep; Ⓜ Khan Market, Jor Bagh) Delhi's loveliest escape was originally named after the wife of the British Resident, Lady Willingdon, who had two villages cleared in 1936 in order to landscape a park containing the Lodi-era tombs. Today, these lush, tree-shaded gardens – a favoured getaway for Delhi's elite, local joggers and courting couples – help protect more than 100 species of trees and more than 50 species of birds and butterflies as well as half a dozen or so fabulously captivating 15th-century Mughal monuments.

The twin tombs of Bada Gumbad and Sheesh Gumbad, both built 1494, the c 1450 bulbous Mohammed Shah's tomb and the 1518 fortress-like walled complex of Sikander Lodi's tomb, are the park's most notable structures, but also look for Athpula, an eight-piered bridge spanning a small lake, which dates from Emperor Akbar's reign.

MONKEYS AT THE HANUMAN TEMPLE

For some almost guaranteed monkey-watching action, head to the much-revered **Hanuman Temple** (Hanuman Mandir; Map p80; Baba Kharak Singh Rd, Connaught Place; ⊙ dawn-dusk; Ⓜ Rajiv Chowk) near Connaught Place. Dedicated to the Monkey God Hanuman, loyal friend of Rama in the Ramayana, this Hindu temple is always busy with devotees, but particularly so on Tuesdays and Saturdays. Though discouraged by the authorities (and sometimes fined for doing so) devotees like to offer food to the troops of monkeys who hang out in the trees outside the temple. Monkeys are thought to be reincarnations of Hanuman so having one take food from your hand is auspicious.

It's important to note that you shouldn't try to feed the monkeys yourself. Though they spend their lives in the city centre, these are wild animals, and numerous people have been attacked by them outside this temple. Take photos and videos by all means, but don't get too close, particularly if there are baby monkeys in the troop that the adults might be protecting.

★ **Akshardham Temple** HINDU TEMPLE
(☑ 011-43442344; www.akshardham.com; National Hwy 24, Noida turning; temple free, exhibitions & water show ₹250, water show ₹80; ⊙ temple 9.30am-6.30pm Tue-Sun, exhibitions 9.30am-5pm, water show after sunset; Ⓜ Akshardham) Delhi's largest temple, the Gujarati Hindu Swaminarayan Group's Akshardham Temple was built in 2005, and is breathtakingly lavish. Artisans used ancient techniques to carve the pale red sandstone into elaborate reliefs, including 20,000 deities, saints and mythical creatures. The centrepiece is a 3m-high gold statue of Bhagwan Shri Swaminarayan surrounded by more, fabulously intricate carvings.

The 'exhibitions' ticket includes a boat ride through 10,000 years of Indian history, with animatronics telling stories from the life of Swaminarayan.

Visiting the temple is more of a theme-park experience than a spiritual one, such are the tourist crowds and the security, but the architecture of the main buildings, and artisanship of their carvings is exceptional. A shame, then, that you cannot take photographs. Cameras, along with pretty much all other possessions apart from your wallet and passport, must be deposited in the free bag-drop by the entrance. You also cannot bring food and drink inside, but there's an outdoor food court within the complex.

The temple is in Delhi's eastern suburbs, but just 200m walk from Akshardham metro station.

Safdarjang's Tomb MONUMENT
(Map p72; Aurobindo Marg; Indian/foreigner ₹25/300, video ₹25; ⊙ dawn-dusk; Ⓜ Jor Bagh) Built by the Nawab of Avadh for his father, Safdarjang, this grandiose, highly decorative mid-18th-century tomb, set within palm-lined gardens, is an example of late-Mughal architecture. There were insufficient funds for all-over marble, so materials to cover the dome were taken from the nearby mausoleum of Khan-i-Khanan, and it was finished in red sandstone.

◉ **Greater Delhi & Gurgaon (Gurugram)**

★ **Qutab Minar Complex** HISTORIC SITE
(Map p88; ☑ 011-26643856; Indian/foreigner ₹40/600, with card payment ₹35/550; ⊙ dawn-dusk; Ⓜ Qutab Minar) If you only have time to visit one of Delhi's ancient ruins, make it this. The first monuments here were erected by the sultans of Mehrauli, and subsequent rulers expanded on their work, hiring the finest craftspeople and artisans to set in stone the triumph of Muslim rule. The complex is studded with ruined tombs and monuments, the majestic highlight of which is the Qutab Minar, a 73m-tall 12th-century tower, after which this complex is named.

Ala-ud-din's sprawling madrasa (Islamic school) and tomb stand in ruins at the rear of the complex, while Altamish is entombed in a magnificent sandstone and marble mausoleum almost completely covered in Islamic calligraphy.

The **Qutab Festival** (⊙ Nov/Dec) of Indian classical music and dance takes place here.

To reach the complex, turn right out of Qutab Minar metro station, then turn left up the first slip road (after about 500m) and you'll soon reach the entrance.

➡ **Quwwat-ul-Islam Masjid**
(Might of Islam Mosque) At the foot of the Qutab Minar stands the first mosque to be built in India. An inscription over the east gate states that it was built with materials obtained from demolishing '27 idolatrous temples'. As well as intricate carvings that show a clear fusion of Islamic and pre-Islamic styles, the walls of the mosque are studded with sun disks, *shikharas* (rising towers) and other recognisable pieces of Hindu and Jain masonry. This was Delhi's main mosque until 1360.

➡ **Iron Pillar**
In the courtyard of the Quwwat-ul-Islam Masjid is a 6.7m-high iron pillar that is much more ancient than any of the surrounding monuments. It hasn't rusted over the past 1600 years, due to both the dry atmosphere and its incredible purity. A six-line Sanskrit inscription indicates that it was initially erected outside a Vishnu temple, possibly in Bihar, in memory of Chandragupta II, who ruled from AD 375 to 413. Scientists are at a loss as to how the iron was cast using the technology of the time.

★ **Mehrauli Archaeological Park** PARK
(Map p88; ⊙ dawn-dusk; Ⓜ Qutab Minar) **FREE** There are extraordinary riches scattered around Mehrauli, with more than 440 monuments – from the 10th century to the British era – dotting a forest and the village itself behind the forest. In the forest, most impressive are the time-ravaged tombs of Balban and Quli Khan, his son, and the Jamali Khamali mosque, attached to the tomb of the Sufi poet Jamali. To the west is the 16th-

OFF THE BEATEN TRACK

TEMPLE TIME

For an off-beat side-trip in Gurgaon, take time out from your shopping sprees to visit **Sai Ka Angan Temple** (www. saikaangan.com; E-Block, Sushant Lok Phase I, opposite Paras Hospital, Gurgaon; ⊙ dawn-dusk; Ⓜ Sector 53-54), a small, peaceful complex dedicated to the pan-religion spiritual master Sai Baba of Shirdi who is regarded by his many devotees as a saint. A particularly serene time to visit is during the Thursday evening *aarti* (auspicious lighting of lamps and candles). It's 2km from Sector 53-54 metro station.

century Rajon ki Baoli, Delhi's finest stepwell, with a monumental flight of steps.

At the northern end of Mehrauli village is Adham Khan's Mausoleum, which was once used as a British residence, then later as a police station and post office. Leading northwards from the tomb are the pre-Islamic walls of Lal Kot.

To the south of the village are the remains of the Mughal palace, the Zafar Mahal, once in the heart of the jungle. Next door to it is the Sufi shrine, the Dargah of Qutab Sahib. There is a small burial ground with one empty space that was intended for the last king of Delhi, Bahadur Shah Zafar, who died in exile in Burma (Myanmar) in 1862. South of here is a Lodi-era burial ground for *hijras* (transvestites and eunuchs), **Hijron ka Khanqah** (Map p88; Kalka das Marg). The identity of those buried here is unknown, but it's a well-kept, peaceful place, revered by Delhi's *hijra* community. A little further south are Jahaz Mahal ('ship palace', also built by the Mughals) and the Haus i Shamsi tank , off Mehrauli-Gurgaon Rd.

Wild pigs scamper about the forest, while bright-green parakeets and large black kites swoop from tree to tree. Troops of monkeys clamber across the ruins, especially at dusk. Stone pillars with the names of the main sights carved onto them guide you along the maze-like network of dusty forest pathways; don't come here too late in the day, as it can be easy to get lost.

You can reach the forested part of the park by turning right out of Qutab Minar metro station then taking the small gate on your left, just as you reach the slip road that leads up to Qutab Minar. Note, there is no obvious entrance with English signage, but you'll notice the landscaped park-like area from the road.

★ **Tughlaqabad**   FORT
(Indian/foreigner ₹30/300, with card payment ₹25/250; ⊙ dawn-dusk; Ⓜ Govind Puri) This magnificent 14th-century ruined fort, half reclaimed by jungle and gradually being encroached on by villages, was Delhi's third incarnation, built by Ghiyas-ud-din Tughlaq. The sultan poached workers from the Sufi saint Nizam-ud-din, who issued a curse that shepherds would inhabit the fort. However, it's monkeys rather than shepherds that have taken over. There are fantastic emerald-green views. Interlinking underground rooms, which you can explore, were used as storehouses.

The sultan's well-maintained sandstone mausoleum once stood in the middle of a lake, but now is separated from his fallen city by a road. It's included in the entry ticket.

The ruins of the fort are fairly deserted, so it's best to visit them in a group; you could easily spend a couple of hours exploring, so you may not wish to visit them alone. It does get hot out here, so bring plenty of water and snacks – there's nowhere to buy anything.

To reach the fort, take an autorickshaw from the Govind Puri metro station (₹50). Shared autos (₹10) tend only to take you to the end of Guru Ravi Das Marg, leaving you to walk the final 500m to the entrance.

Champa Gali   ARTS CENTRE
(Map p88; Lane 3, West End Marg, Saket; Ⓜ Saket) The small arty enclave known as Champa Gali is hidden away in the lanes behind the fake Dilli Haat handicrafts market ('Delhi Haat') and is one of Greater Delhi's best-kept secrets. It's a favourite for Delhi's young fashionistas, and contains a cluster of craft boutiques and cool cafes, including standout coffee roasters Blue Tokai (p98) and tea specialists Jugmug Thela (p98). It's tough to find; turn left out of Saket metro station, take the first left, then turn left down Lane 3. You'll eventually reach the open courtyard on your right, through an inconspicuous gateway with no sign.

🏃 Activities & Courses

Saffron Palate   COOKING
(Map p88; ☎ 9971389993; www.saffronpalate. com; R21 Hauz Khas Enclave; per person ₹4000;

Connaught Place

M Hauz Khas) These award-winning Indian cookery classes are run by Neha Gupta in her family home and last for around three hours. The classes, which tend to start at 11am, culminate in a full-course Indian lunch.

Traveling Spoon   FOOD
(www.travelingspoon.com) Travelling Spoon connects locals with travellers wishing to experience home-made meals. Foodie travellers can choose from a clutch of hosts happy to cook, teach and serve traditional cuisine from the comfort of their homes. To find hosts, search for New Delhi on the website; prices depend on the host and meal served.

Sivananda Yoga   HEALTH & WELLBEING
(Map p88; ☎011-40591221; www.sivananda. org.in; A41 Kailash Colony; 3-week beginner course ₹4000; ⊗6am-8pm Mon-Fri, 8am-12.30pm Sat, 8am-2.30pm & 5.30-7.30pm Sun; M Kailash Colony) This excellent ashram offers courses and workshops for both beginners and the advanced, plus drop-in classes ranging from one to two hours. On Sunday (12.30pm to 2pm) there is a free introductory drop-in class.

**Tushita Mahayana
Meditation Centre**   MEDITATION
(Map p88; ☎011-26513400; http://tushitadelhi. com; 9 Padmini Enclave; ⊗6.30-7.30pm Mon &

☞ Tours

★ **Street Connections** WALKING
(www.streetconnections.co.uk; 3hr walk ₹750; ⊙9am-noon Mon-Sat) 🖈 This fascinating walk through Old Delhi is guided by former street children who have been helped by Salaam Baalak Trust (p81). It explores the hidden corners of Old Delhi, starting at Jama Masjid and visiting small temples and crumbling *haveli* mansions before an e-rickshaw ride takes you to the sneeze-inducing spice market then to one of SBT's shelter homes.

Salaam Baalak Trust WALKING
(SBT; ☑011-23586416; www.salaambaalaktrust. com; suggested donation ₹400; ⊙10am-noon) 🖈 Founded by the mother of film director Mira Nair, following her 1988 hit film about the life of street children, *Salaam Bombay!*, this 30-year-old charity offers two-hour 'street walks' around Paharganj, guided by former street children, who tell you their own, often-shocking, stories and take you to visit a couple of the trust's 'contact points' near New Delhi train station.

Hope Project WALKING
(☑011-24357081, 011-24356576; www.hope projectindia.org; 1½hr walk suggested donation ₹300) 🖈 The Hope Project guides interesting walks around the Muslim basti (slum) of Nizamuddin, which surrounds Hazrat Nizam-ud-din Dargah. You can specify your preferred time; one good option is to take the walk on a Friday afternoon to end for the *qawwali* (Islamic devotional singing) performed each week at the intimate shrine of Hazrat Inayat Khan. Wear modest clothing.

★ **DelhiByCycle** CYCLING
(☑9811723720; www.delhibycycle.com; per person ₹1850; ⊙6.30-10am) Founded by a Dutch journalist, these cycle tours are the original and the best, and a thrilling way to explore Delhi. Tours focus on specific neighbourhoods – Old Delhi, New Delhi, Nizamuddin, and the banks of the Yamuna – and start early to miss the worst of the traffic. The price includes chai and breakfast. Helmets and child seats are available.

Lalli Singh Tours OUTDOORS
(www.lallisinghadventures.com) Knowledgable and long-standing Delhi-based outfit that rents out Royal Enfield motorcycles, and at the time of research was planning to start offering tailor-made motorcycle tours, including sidecar tours of Delhi.

Thu; M Hauz Khas) **FREE** Twice-weekly, guided, Buddhist meditation sessions in a peaceful, temple-like meditation hall. Sessions are free. Donations are welcomed.

Kerala Ayurveda AYURVEDA
(Map p88; ☑011-41754888; www.ayurvedancr. com; E-2 Green Park Extension, Green Park Market; 1hr full-body massage from ₹1700; ⊙8am-6.30pm; M Green Park) Treatments from *sarvang ksheerdhara* (massage with buttermilk) to *sirodhara* (warm oil poured on the forehead).

Connaught Place

◎ Sights
1 Agrasen ki Baoli F5
2 Connaught Place.............................. D2
3 Hanuman Temple B3
4 Jantar Mantar.................................... C5

🛏 Sleeping
5 Hotel Palace Heights.......................... D2
6 Imperial C5
7 Park Hotel B4
8 Prem Sagar Guest House B2
9 Radisson Blu Marina.......................... C1

🍴 Eating
10 Coffee Home B3
11 Farzi Cafe.. D2
12 Hotel Saravana Bhavan D5
13 Kake-da-Hotel E1
14 Kerala House Canteen B5
15 Naturals... E1
16 Rajdhani D3
17 Véda.. C1
Zaffran... (see 5)

🍷 Drinking & Nightlife
1911.. (see 6)
Aqua .... (see 7)
Atrium, Imperial................................. (see 6)
18 Cha Bar E3
19 Chai Point E3
20 Indian Coffee House......................... B3
21 Lord of the Drinks............................ C2
22 My Bar... D3
23 Unplugged D1

🛍 Shopping
24 Central Cottage Industries
    Emporium....................................... D5
25 Fabindia.. C2
26 Janpath & Tibetan Markets D4
27 Kamala.. A3
28 Khadi Gramodyog Bhawan................ C3
29 Rikhi Ram C1
30 State Emporiums A3
31 The Shop C3

Reality Tours & Travel TOURS
(☏9818227975; http://realitytoursandtravel.com; tour from ₹1000) Long-established in Mumbai, the highly professional Reality Tours is now offering tours of Delhi, including the excellent Sanjay Colony tour – a visit to a slum area of Delhi (no photographs permitted out of respect for locals' privacy). The tour guides are knowledgeable and friendly, and 80% of profits go to supporting development projects in the colony.

Other tours offered are Old Delhi Street Food, bicycle tours and a sightseeing tour.

🛏 Sleeping

Delhi hotels range from wallet-friendly dives to lavish five-stars. India was a latecomer in the hostel game, but there are now finally a decent number of hostels, offering backpacker-friendly services and good-quality dormitory accommodation in Delhi and beyond. It's wise to book ahead if you're staying in midrange or top-end accommodation, but budgeteers will have no problem getting rooms on the fly, and you'll get cheaper rates as a walk-in guest.

🛏 Old Delhi

★GoStops HOSTEL $
(Map p68; ☏011-41056226; www.gostops.com; 4/23B Asaf Ali Rd; dm ₹550-850, d ₹3300; ❄@🛜; Ⓜ Delhi Gate) This is one of the best of Delhi's new breed of hostels, in an interesting location on the fringes of Old Delhi, with young, friendly staff, a brightly tiled kitchen, large lounge areas, and comfortable, clean dorms (with reading lamps and lockers) and smart private rooms. There are regular cookery and yoga classes and tours of the city and beyond.

Hotel Broadway HOTEL $$
(Map p68; ☏011-43663600; www.hotelbroadway delhi.com; 4/15 Asaf Ali Rd; s/d incl breakfast from ₹2500/3800; ❄@🛜; Ⓜ Delhi Gate) Five-storey Hotel Broadway was Delhi's first 'high-rise' when it opened in 1956, with single rooms going for ₹15. Today it's comfortable, charming, quirky, and slightly more expensive. It's worth staying here for the restaurant Chor Bizarre (p88) and Thugs bar. Some rooms have old-fashioned wood panelling, while others have been kitted out by French designer Catherine Lévy.

Hotel Aiwan-e-Shahi HOTEL $$
(Map p68; ☏011-47155106; www.hotelaiwan eshahi.com; 1061 Dariba, near Jama Masjid Gate 3; d ₹2400, with view ₹3000; ❄🛜; Ⓜ Jama Masjid) A new building facing Jama Masjid, this hotel has smart, comfortable rooms, some of which have great views of the mosque. The best views, though, are reserved for the 4th-floor roof-terrace restaurant and coffee shop, which nonguests are welcome to use too.

★Haveli Dharampura HERITAGE HOTEL $$$
(Map p68; ☏011-23263000; www.havelidharam pura.com; 2293 Gali Guliyan; d from ₹14,700; ❄🛜;

Ⓜ Jama Masjid) This is a beautiful restored *haveli*, full of Mughal atmosphere and centred on a courtyard. Rooms have grandiose polished-wood beds, but it's worth paying for a larger room, as the smallest are a little cramped. The excellent restaurant, Lakhori (p88), serves historic Mughal recipes, there's *kathak* dancing Friday and Sunday evenings, and high tea (4pm to 6pm) served daily on the roof terrace.

You can also watch the traditional local pursuits of *kabootar bazi* (pigeon flying) and *patang bazi* (kite flying) from the rooftop.

🗺 Paharganj, Main Bazaar

★ Backpacker Panda   HOSTEL $

(Map p84; ☎ 011-23588237; http://backpacker panda.com; 22/1 Main Bazaar; 6-/8-bed dm ₹449/429, d ₹1000; 🛜; Ⓜ Ramakrishna Ashram Marg) A great alternative to Paharganj's less-than-fancy cheap hotels, Panda offers bright, clean dorms (one is female only) with attached bathrooms, charge points, lockers, windows, clean linen and comfortable mattresses. There's a TV room, a kitchenette, and it's close to the metro.

Hotel Rak International   HOTEL $

(Map p84; ☎ 011-23562478; www.hotelrakinter national.com; 820 Main Bazaar, Chowk Bawli; s/d ₹650/750, with AC ₹850/950; 🌣🛜; Ⓜ Ramakrishna Ashram Marg) Hotel Rak International is off the Main Bazaar (so it's quieter) and overlooks a little square and temple. The modest rooms at this popular place are a good choice in this price range, with marble floors and bathrooms, plus, unusually, twin rooms and...windows! The pricier rooms overlook the square.

Hotel Namaskar   HOTEL $

(Map p84; ☎ 011-23583456; www.namaskar hotel.com; 917 Chandiwalan, Main Bazaar; r from ₹500, with AC from ₹800; 🌣🛜; Ⓜ Ramakrishna Ashram Marg) Up the narrow alley called Chandi Wali Gali, this long-running traveller cheapo is run by two amiable brothers and offers a friendly welcome. It may be humid and noisy, but the rooms get a fresh coat of powder-pink paint annually, which gives it a fresher feel than many of its peers.

Hare Rama Guest House   GUESTHOUSE $

(Map p84; ☎ 011-41698544; T298, just off Main Bazaar; r from ₹700; 🌣; Ⓜ Ramakrishna Ashram Marg) Opposite Ajay Guest House, down the same alley off Main Bazaar, rooms here are clean, simple, tile-floored affairs that im-

prove as you go up each floor, though few have exterior windows. The most endearing feature here, though, is the breezy rooftop restaurant.

★ Diya Bed & Breakfast   B&B $$

(Map p84; ☎ 9811682348; http://stay.street connections.co.uk; top fl, 2413-2415 Tilak St, Paharganj; s/d incl breakfast ₹2000/2750; 🌣🛜; Ⓜ Ramakrishna Ashram Marg) Like a serene South Delhi guesthouse, but on a Paharganj backstreet, this unique place has three lovely, well-cared-for rooms, a shared kitchen and a quiet, leafy roof terrace. It's run by the charity Street Connections (p81), and staff and management are former street kids from the Salaam Baalak Trust. It's ideal for solo women or families. Reservations essential.

Cottage Ganga Inn   HOTEL $$

(Map p84; ☎ 011-23561516; www.cottageganga inn.com; 1532 Bazar Sangtrashan; r ₹1200-1500; 🌣@🛜; Ⓜ Ramakrishna Ashram Marg) Quieter than most Paharganj choices, this place is tucked in a tree-shaded courtyard off the Main Bazaar, next to a nursery school. It's clean, calm, comfortable and good value. Rooms at the front have windows and cost more.

Hotel Relax   HOTEL $$

(Map p84; ☎ 011-23562811; Ramdwara Rd, by Nehru Bazaar, off Main Bazaar; r ₹1200-2000; 🌣🛜; Ⓜ Ramakrishna Ashram Marg) Unusually well decorated for this area and this price range, Relax is housed in an old, but attractive, property with leafy balconies and halls and corridors dotted with antique furniture. Rooms are clean and comfortable, if nothing special, but it's the common areas that make this place stand out from the crowd.

Metropolis Tourist Home   HOTEL $$

(Map p84; ☎ 011-23561794; www.metropolis touristhome.com; 1634-5 Main Bazaar; r from ₹1770; 🌣@🛜; Ⓜ Ramakrishna Ashram Marg) A long-standing favourite in the backpacking district, this hotel has comfortable, renovated rooms decorated in 100 shades of brown. The slightly pricey rooftop restaurant feels almost European, with its greenery, low lights and foreign clientele.

Hotel Hari Piorko   HOTEL $$

(Map p84; ☎ 011-23587888; www.hotelhari piorkodelhi.com; Main Bazaar; r from ₹2500; 🌣🛜; Ⓜ Ramakrishna Ashram Marg) A bit more upmarket than other places on Main Bazaar, this is definitely a hotel rather than

Paharganj

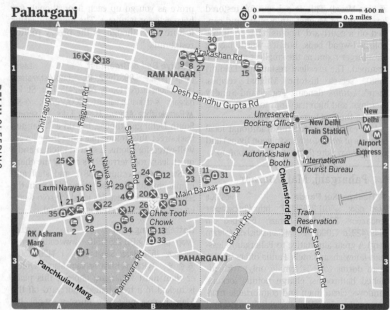

Paharganj

⊚ Sights
1 Ramakrishna Mission	A3

🛏 Sleeping
2 Backpacker Panda	A3
3 Bloom Rooms @ New Delhi	C1
4 Cottage Ganga Inn	B2
5 Diya Bed & Breakfast	A2
6 Hare Rama Guest House	B3
7 Hotel Amax Inn	B1
8 Hotel Godwin Deluxe	B1
9 Hotel Grand Godwin	B1
10 Hotel Hari Piorko	B2
11 Hotel Namaskar	C2
12 Hotel Rak International	B2
13 Hotel Relax	B3
14 Metropolis Tourist Home	A2
15 Zostel	C1

✗ Eating
16 Bikaner Sweet Corner	A1
17 Brown Bread Bakery	B2
18 Darbar	A1
19 Exotic Rooftop Restaurant	B2
20 Krishna Cafe	B2

21 Leo's Restaurant	A2
22 Madan Café	A2
Malhotra	(see 14)
Metropolis Restaurant &	
Bar	(see 14)
23 Satguru Dhaba	B2
24 Shim Tur	B2
25 Sita Ram Dewan Chand	A2
26 Tadka	B3

🍷 Drinking & Nightlife
27 Cafe Brownie	C1
28 My Bar	A3
29 Sam's Bar	B2
30 Voyage Cafe	C1

🛍 Shopping
31 Delhi Foundation of Deaf Women	C2
32 Main Bazaar	C2
33 Paharganj Fruit Market	B3
34 Paharganj Vegetable & Spice Market	B3
35 Yes Helping Hands	A3

a guesthouse, and has well-turned-out, reasonably spacious, modern rooms. There's an OK restaurant upstairs, and a small ayurvedic spa (massage treatments from ₹800).

🛏 Paharganj, Arakashan Road

Zostel　　　　　　　　　　　HOSTEL $
(Map p84; ☎ 011-23540456; www.zostel.com/zostel/Delhi; 5 Arakashan Rd; dm ₹600-650,

d ₹1680-2790; ✳ 🛜; Ⓜ New Delhi) Part of the Zostel chain, this place is shabbier than some of Delhi's other backpacker hostels. However, it's got the obligatory cheerful murals, the dorms are decent (the six-bed dorm is much roomier than the eight-bed), with lockers, reading lamps and charging sockets, and it's a friendly place to meet other backpackers.

Hotel Amax Inn
HOTEL $$

(Map p84; ☎ 011-23543813; www.hotel amax.com; 8145/6 Arakashan Rd; s/d/tr from ₹950/1050/1450; ✳ @ 🛜; Ⓜ Ramakrishna Ashram Marg or New Delhi) In a lane off chaotic Arakashan Rd, the Amax is a long-running traveller favourite, with clean, though occasionally stuffy, budget rooms. Staff are friendly, and clued up about traveller needs, and there's a small greenery-fringed roof terrace that connects to rooms in the slightly cheaper annex opposite. The triple (Room 403) opening onto the rooftop is worth asking for.

Hotel Godwin Deluxe
HOTEL $$

(Map p84; ☎ 011-23613797; www.godwin hotels.com; 8501 Arakashan Rd; s/d incl breakfast ₹3500/4000; ✳ @ 🛜; Ⓜ Ramakrishna Ashram Marg or New Delhi) Run by the same owners as the OK, but less glitzy, **Grand Godwin** (Map p84; ☎ 011-23546891; 8502/41 Arakashan Rd; s/d incl breakfast ₹3000/3500; ✳ @ 🛜) next door, Godwin Deluxe offers similarly good service, and comfortable, spacious, clean rooms that are accessed either via a glass lift with street views or up a striking all-marble, spiral staircase.

Bloom Rooms @ New Delhi
HOTEL $$$

(Map p84; ☎ 011-41225666; www.staybloom. com; 8591 Arakashan Rd; s/d from ₹3500/5000; ✳ @ 🛜; Ⓜ New Delhi) Bloom Rooms' white-and-yellow, pared-down designer aesthetic is unlike anything else in this 'hood, and its IKEA-like rooms surround a pleasant interior courtyard with plenty of seating. Some also have shared balconies overlooking Arakashan Rd. Pillows are soft, beds are comfortable, and there's good wi-fi plus free mineral water and tea and coffee. Check the website for discounted rates.

🛏 New Delhi

Prem Sagar Guest House
GUESTHOUSE $$

(Map p80; ☎ 011-23345263; www.premsagarguest house.com; 1st fl, 11 P-Block, Connaught Place; s/d incl breakfast from ₹3000/4000; ✳ 🛜; Ⓜ Rajiv Chowk) This is an old-school place, with 12 snug rooms that aren't flash but are clean. You'll get better value elsewhere, but for Connaught Place this is about as low budget as it gets. Rooms open onto a narrow, open-air atrium and there's a pot plant–filled rear terrace.

★ Imperial
HOTEL $$$

(Map p80; ☎ 011-23341234; www.theimperial india.com; Janpath; s/d from ₹20,000/22,500; ✳ @ 🛜 🏊; Ⓜ Janpath) Classicism meets art deco at the Imperial, which dates from 1931 and was designed by FB Blomfield, an associate of Lutyens. Rooms have high ceilings, flowing curtains, French linen and marble baths. There's the temple-like Thai restaurant Spice Route; the 1911 bar (p97) is highly recommended; and the cafe Atrium, Imperial (p97) serves the perfect high tea.

The hallways and atriums are lined with the hotel's venerable 18th- and 19th-century art collection.

Hotel Palace Heights
HOTEL $$$

(Map p80; ☎ 011-43582610; www.hotelpalace heights.com; 26-28 D-Block, Connaught Place; s/d from ₹7080/8260; ✳ @ 🛜; Ⓜ Rajiv Chowk) This small-scale boutique hotel offers some of busy Connaught Place's nicest rooms, with gleaming white linen, and caramel and amber tones. There's an excellent restaurant, **Zāffrān** (☎ 011-43582610; mains ₹350-650; ☾ noon-3.30pm & 6.30-11.30pm) also.

Radisson Blu Marina
HOTEL $$$

(Map p80; ☎ 011-46909090; www.radissonblu. com; 59 G-Block, Connaught Place; s/d from ₹10,240/11,520; ✳ @ 🛜; Ⓜ Rajiv Chowk) One of Connaught Place's swisher choices, the Radisson feels pleasingly luxurious, with sleek, stylish, all-mod-cons rooms, the Great Kebab Factory restaurant, and a cool bar, the Connaught, where you can sip drinks under hanging red lamps.

Park Hotel
HOTEL $$$

(Map p80; ☎ 011-23743000, reservations 1800 1027275; www.theparkhotels.com; 15 Sansad Marg; r from ₹10,000; ✳ @ 🛜 🏊; Ⓜ Janpath) Conran-designed, with lots of modern flair, the Park is hip and stylish, and has all the five-star accoutrements you'd expect: a spa, smart eateries and a great poolside bar, **Aqua** (beers/cocktails from ₹445/845; ☾ 11am-midnight; 🛜).

South Delhi

Jugaad Hostel
HOSTEL $

(Map p88; 011-41077677; www.jugaadhostels.com; F-128, 4th fl, Jhandu Mansion, Mohammadpur Rd, RK Puram Sector 1; dm/r from ₹700/3600; ❄@🛜; ⓜBhikaji Cama Place) There's an urban factory feel to this excellent hostel with wooden-crate bed frames and exposed brick walls. Dorms and private rooms all have en suites, and the bunk beds come with reading lamps, charging sockets and lockers. There's also a roof terrace with swing chairs. Staff are friendly and helpful, and there's a women-only dorm.

Bed & Chai
HOSTEL $$

(Map p88; 011-46066054; www.bedandchai.com; R55 Hans Raj Gupta Marg; dm incl breakfast ₹850, d from ₹2700; ⓜNehru Place) For a quiet stay, this French-owned guesthouse has simple rooms, decorated with flashes of colour and some quirky, original design touches. There's a spacious dorm and a roof terrace strewn with Tibetan prayer flags. Rates include breakfast that comes with excellent chai, of course.

Treetops
GUESTHOUSE $$$

(Map p88; 011-26854751, 9899555704; baig.murad@gmail.com; R-8B, Hauz Khas; d from ₹5600; ❄🛜; ⓜHauz Khas) Motor-journalist-novelist-philosopher Murad and his hobby-chef wife Tannie have a gracious home. To stay here feels rather like visiting some upper-crust relatives from another era. There are two large rooms opening onto a leafy rooftop terrace; the smaller room downstairs is cheaper but can feel less private. Evening meals are available.

Scarlette
GUESTHOUSE $$$

(Map p88; 011-41023764; www.scarlettenewdelhi.com; B2/139 Safdarjung Enclave; d from ₹6000; ❄🛜; ⓜBhikaji Cama Place) In serene, leafy Safdarjung Enclave, and not far from Hauz Khas Village and the Deer Park, Scarlette is a *maison d'hôtes* (guesthouse) with four

rooms, plus an apartment, decorated with beautiful artistic flair by the French textile-designer owner. It's a good choice for solo women, but note there's a minimum stay of two days.

Sunder Nagar, Nizamuddin & Lodi Colony

⭐Lutyens Bungalow
GUESTHOUSE $$$

(Map p72; 011-24611341; www.lutyensbungalow.co.in; 39 Prithviraj Rd; s/d incl breakfast from ₹6500/7000; ❄@🛜☒; ⓜLok Kalyan Marg, Jorbagh) A rambling bungalow with a colonial-era feel, surrounded by verandahs and hanging lamps, this family-run guesthouse has a wonderful garden, with lawns, flowers and fluttering parakeets. Rooms are pleasant, with wooden furnishings and an old-fashioned vibe, and it's a particularly good place to stay with kids because of the unusual amount of rambling space, and the lovely swimming pool.

⭐Lodhi
HOTEL $$$

(Map p72; 011-43633333; www.thelodhi.com; Lodi Rd; r from ₹33,280, with pool ₹53,760; ❄🛜☒; ⓜJLN Stadium) The Lodhi is one of Delhi's finest luxury hotels, with huge, lovely rooms and suites. Each room has a balcony, and the enormous deluxe rooms are the only rooms in Delhi with their own private plunge pools. Attention to detail is superb. There's also a top-notch spa (1hr massage from ₹3800), tennis courts, a slimline outdoor pool, two restaurants and a small night club.

G-49
GUESTHOUSE $$$

(Bed & Breakfast; Map p72; 011-47373434; www.bed-breakfast.asia; G-49 Nizamuddin West; r incl breakfast from ₹5000; ❄🛜; ⓜHazrat Nizamuddin) In a green-fringed corner of Nizamuddin, this guesthouse with leafy outlooks is owned by local homeware designers and has stylish, simple rooms – two with a balcony. There's a plant-filled, fairy-lit patio and an attractive dining room.

Bnineteen
GUESTHOUSE $$$

(Map p72; 011-41825500; www.bnineteen.com; B-19 Nizamuddin East; s/d incl breakfast from ₹8000/9000; ❄@🛜; ⓜHazrat Nizamuddin) Architect-owned, Bnineteen is a looker. Big contemporary rooms have large windows. Located in posh, peaceful Nizamuddin East, it has great views over Humayun's Tomb from the rooftop. There's a kitchen on every floor that comes with its own cook.

SLEEPING PRICE RANGES

The following price ranges refer to a double room with private bathroom and are inclusive of tax.

$ less than ₹1000

$$ ₹1000–₹4000

$$$ more than ₹4000

Greater Delhi & Gurgaon (Gurugram)

★**Madpackers Hostel** HOSTEL **$**
(Map p88; ☑ 011-41677410; S-39A 3rd fl,
Panchsheel Park; dm/r from ₹650/2000; ✳@☎;
Ⓜ Hauz Khas) A friendly, relaxed hostel with
a bright and airy sitting room that's one of
the best places in town to hang out and meet
like-minded travellers. It has mixed dorms
(with one female-only) and graffitied walls,
and it's in a leafy area, albeit beside a super-
busy highway.

Cinnamon Stays GUESTHOUSE **$$**
(☑ 7525952362, 011-39654545; www.cinnamon
stays.in; MD 34, Eldeco Mansionz, Sector 48, Sohna
Rd; r incl breakfast from ₹2500; Ⓜ Sector 55-56)
There's a warm welcome at this Gurgaon
homestay run by husband-and-wife team
Shilpi Singh and Manish Sinha, who have
gone on to start their own travel company,
Unhotel (www.unhotel.in). In a peaceful de-
tached house, rooms come with attached
bathrooms, essential amenities and a scat-
tering of kitschy wall-art featuring Bolly-
wood personalities. Contact them for other
homestay locations.

✗ Eating

While Delhiites graze all day on the city's
masterful, taste-tingling *Dilli-ka-Chaat*
(street-food snacks), the city's dining scene is
also becoming increasingly diverse. Creative
cuisine at Delhi's modern Indian restaurants
now sits alongside traditional purveyors of
delicate dhals and meaty Mughal delights.

Reservations are recommended for high-
end restaurants.

✗ Old Delhi

★**Natraj Dahi Balle Corner** STREET FOOD **$**
(Map p68; 1396 Chandni Chowk; plates ₹50;
⊙10.30am-11pm; Ⓜ Chandni Chowk) This tiny
place on the corner of a narrow *gali* (lane) is
famous for its *dahi bhalle* (fried lentil balls
served with yoghurt and garnished with
chutney) and deliciously crispy *aloo tikki*
(spiced potato patties), each of which costs
₹50. You'll have to elbow your way to the
front of the queue to get your share, but it's
worth the effort.

★**PT Gaya Prasad**
Shiv Charan STREET FOOD **$**
(Map p68; 34 Gali Paranthe Wali; parathas ₹60-70;
⊙7am-10pm; Ⓜ Jama Masjid) This winding lane

off Chandni Chowk has been dishing up its
namesake *parathas* (traditional flat bread)
fresh off the *tawa* (hotplate) for generations,
originally serving pilgrims at the time of the
Mughals. Walk down it from Chandni Chowk,
take two turns and you'll find this, the most
popular *paratha* joint of many. Stuffings in-
clude green chilli, almond, banana and more.

Bade Mia Ki Kheer STREET FOOD **$**
(Old Kheer Shop; Map p68; shop 2867, Lal
Kuan Bazaar; kheer ₹30; ⊙11am-late; Ⓜ Chaw-
ri Bazaar) Established in 1880 and still run
by the Siddique family, this friendly place
makes nothing but superdelicious, creamy,
cardamon-scented *kheer* (rice pudding),
usually served cold but if you're lucky and it
has just made a batch, served hot.

Jalebi Wala SWEETS **$**
(Map p68; Dariba Corner, Chandni Chowk; jalebis
₹50, samosa ₹25; ⊙8am-10pm; Ⓜ Lal Qila) Century-
old Jalebi Wala does Delhi's – if not India's
– finest *jalebis* (deep-fried, syrupy dough), so
eat up and worry about the calories tomor-
row. It's ₹50 per 100g-serving (roughly one
piece). It also does a mean samosa.

Kuremal Mohan Lal ICE CREAM **$**
(Kuremal kulfi-walla; Map p68; Kucha Pati Ram, off
Sitaram Bazaar; kulfi ₹60; ⊙noon-11pm; Ⓜ Chawri
Bazaar) The Kuremal family have been mak-
ing *kulfi* (traditional Indian ice cream) since
1906, and serve up delicious options includ-
ing pomegranate and rose from their small
shop in this alluring part of Old Delhi. Lolly-
sized versions cost ₹60. Giant iced fruit balls
are ₹200. Beware pretenders; the original is
at shop No 526.

★**Karim's** MUGHLAI **$$**
(Map p68; Gali Kababyan; mains ₹120-400;
⊙9am-12.30am; Ⓜ Jama Masjid) Down a narrow alley off a lane leading south from Jama
Masjid, Karim's has been delighting carnivores since 1913. Expect meaty Mughlai
treats such as mutton *burrah* (marinated
chops), delicious mutton Mughlai, and the
breakfast mutton and bread combo *nahari*.
There are numerous branches, including at
Nizamuddin West (p93), but this no-frills,
multiroomed courtyard location is the oldest
and best.

Al-Jawahar MUGHLAI **$$**
(Map p68; Matya Mahal; dishes ₹110-400;
⊙7am-midnight; Ⓜ Jama Masjid) Although
overshadowed by its famous neighbour,
Karim's, Al-Jawahar is also fantastic, serving

South Delhi

DELHI EATING

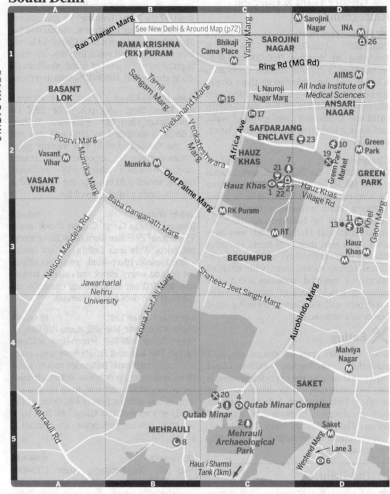

See New Delhi & Around Map (p72)

up tasty Mughlai cuisine at Formica tables in an orderly dining room, and you can watch breads being freshly made at the front. Kebabs and mutton curries dominate the menu, but it also does good butter chicken and korma.

Chor Bizarre
KASHMIRI $$$

(Map p68; ☑ 011-23273821; Hotel Broadway, 4/15 Asaf Ali Rd; mains ₹325-500; ☺ noon-3pm & 7.30-11pm; Ⓜ New Delhi) Hotel Broadway's excellent, if quirky, restaurant has wood-panelling, traditional wooden furniture and fascinating bits of bric-a-brac, including a vintage car. More importantly it offers de-

licious and authentic Kashmiri cuisine, including *wazwan*, the traditional Kashmiri feast.

Lakhori
INDIAN $$$

(Map p68; ☑ 011-23263000; www.havelidhara-mpura.com; Haveli Dharampura, 2293 Gali Guliyan; tasting menus veg/nonveg ₹1800/2200; mains ₹500-900; ☺ noon-10.30pm; ☎; Ⓜ Jama Masjid) This beautifully restored *haveli* is a labour of love by politician Vijay Goel, and it's good to see one of Old Delhi's grand *havelis* finally get some TLC. The restaurant is especially atmospheric in the evening, with tables in the courtyard and Mughlai and local recipes

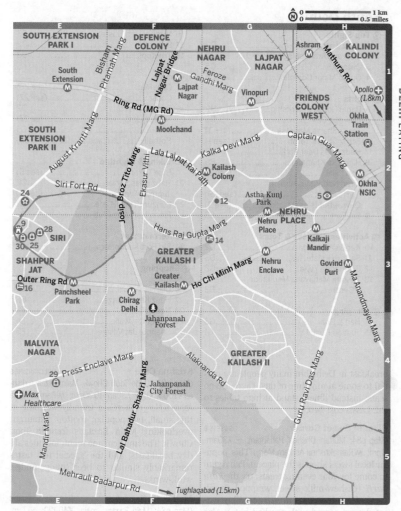

on the menu. Indian high tea (₹1100; 4pm to 6pm) is served daily on the rooftop.

On weekends there is *kathak* dancing on the balcony.

✗ Paharganj

⭐ Darbar
INDIAN $

(Map p84; Multani Dhanda, Paharganj; snacks ₹30-100, dishes ₹125-270, thalis ₹210-260; ⏱8.30am-11.30pm; Ⓜ Ramakrishna Ashram Marg) Considering its gritty Paharganj location and its street-food roots, the interior of this locals' favourite is surprisingly elegant (there's even a chandelier!). Street-food *chaat* (savoury

snacks) are served by the entrance, while the main menu focuses on rich Mughlai curries, delicate South Indian delights such as dosa and *uttapam* (savoury rice pancake), and some outstanding thalis; the 10-piece Shahi thali (₹240) is a feast.

⭐ Sita Ram Dewan Chand
INDIAN $

(Map p84; 2243 Chuna Mandi; half/full plate ₹35/60; ⏱8am-6pm; Ⓜ Ramakrishna Ashram Marg) A family-run hole-in-the-wall serving inexpensive portions of just one dish – *chhole bhature* (spicy chickpeas, accompanied by delicious, freshly made, puffy, fried bread with a light paneer filling). It's a traditional

DELHI EATING

South Delhi

breakfast in Delhi, but many people are partial to some at any time of day. There are no seats; instead diners stand at high tables to eat. Lassis cost ₹40.

Bikaner Sweet Corner   SWEETS $
(Map p84; Multani Dhanda, Paharganj; ⊙7.30am-11pm; ⓂRamakrishna Ashram Marg) This popular local sweet shop is the place in Paharganj to come for your evening treats; try the *kaju barfi* (cashew-milk sweet wrapped in silver leaf) or the *gajar halwa* (crumbly carrot dessert served with crushed nuts). Also sells dried fruit and nuts plus other savoury snacks. Sweets are sold by weight; 100g (₹50 to ₹125) gets you six or seven pieces.

Satguru Dhaba   INDIAN $
(Map p84; 854 Mantola Mohalla, Paharganj; dishes ₹50-250, thalis ₹100; ⊙8am-midnight; ⓂRamakrishna Ashram Marg) Eat like a local rather than a tourist at this popular Paharganj *dhaba* (simple roadside eatery). It's no frills, for sure, but the food is tasty, as are the prices. From Main Bazaar, walk up Chandi Wali Gali, past Hotel Namaskar. Turn left at the end and it's on your left. English menu, but no English sign.

Krishna Cafe   MULTICUISINE $
(Map p84; Chhe Tooti Chowk, Main Bazaar; dishes ₹100-250; ⊙7.30am-10.30pm; ⓂRamakrishna Ashram Marg) There's a friendly welcome at this small, but popular, rooftop restaurant overlooking Main Bazaar's frenetic Tooti Chowk. The multicuisine menu includes all-day breakfasts, and the 'special tea' tastes remarkably similar to beer (nudge-nudge, wink-wink).

Madan Café   MULTICUISINE $
(Map p84; Main Bazaar; mains ₹40-120; ⊙7am-10pm; ⓂRamakrishna Ashram Marg) This friendly, pint-sized, roadside eatery is probably the cheapest place to get a meal on Main Bazaar, and is great for watching the world go by with a steaming cup of chai. The multicuisine menu includes backpacker breakfasts such as pancakes, porridge and omelettes, but there's plenty of local dishes, too.

★Tadka   INDIAN $$
(Map p84; 4986 Ramdwara Rd; mains ₹180-210; ⊙9am-10.30pm; ⚡; ⓂRamakrishna Ashram Marg) Named for everyone's favourite *dhal*, Tadka's no-frills interior and relatively low prices belie its fabulously tasty menu, which

includes delicious dhal (naturally), some rich, creamy paneer dishes and standout roti and naan bread. The *dum aloo* (potato skins stuffed with paneer in a tomato sauce) is divine.

★ Shim Tur
KOREAN $$

(Map p84; 3rd fl, Navrang Guesthouse, Tooti Gali; meals ₹200-500; ⊙10.30am-11pm; Ⓜ Ramakrishna Ashram Marg) The Korean food is fresh and authentic here; try the *bibimbap* (rice bowl with a mix of vegetables, egg and pickles; ₹270). But it takes determination to find this place: take the turning for the Hotel Rak International, opposite which is the grotty, unsigned Navrang Guesthouse. Follow the signs up to its rooftop and you'll find the small, bamboo-lined, softly lit terrace.

Exotic Rooftop Restaurant
MULTICUISINE $$

(Map p84; Tooti Chowk, Main Bazaar, Paharganj; mains ₹200-400; ⊙8am-11.30pm; Ⓜ Ramakrishna Ashram Marg) Currently the most popular of the numerous rooftop restaurants and cafes overlooking frenetic Tooti Chowk, Exotic is a small laid-back place with a breezy perch and a decent please-all backpacker menu (biryani, pizza, falafel, pancakes). There's no lift, so you'll have to climb up four flights of stairs, but there are cold beers (₹180) waiting for you at the top.

Brown Bread Bakery
MULTICUISINE $$

(Map p84; ground fl, Ajay Guest House, 5084A Main Bazaar; mains ₹200-400, buffet breakfast ₹350; ⊙7.30am-10pm; 🛜🍽; Ⓜ Ramakrishna Ashram Marg) Transported to Delhi from its mother ship in Varanasi, this German-owned bakery-cum-cafe-cum-restaurant does standout, largely organic, health-conscious food, including Manali cheese and a fantastic range of bread, baked in a purpose-built bakery just around the corner. It's let down slightly by its gloomy, hotel-lobby location and overly nonchalant staff, but you won't find better bread anywhere around here.

Leo's Restaurant
NORTH INDIAN $$

(Map p84; Main Bazaar, Paharganj; dishes from ₹200; ⊙10am-11pm; 🌐🛜; Ⓜ Ramakrishna Ashram Marg) Leo's is a good choice if you fancy a beer with your curry (you can just come for a drink if you like). It does a range of tasty North Indian dishes, plus a few Chinese offerings, and the small 'combo' meals are perfect for lunch for solo diners.

Metropolis Restaurant & Bar
MULTICUISINE $$

(Map p84; Metropolis Tourist Home, 1634-35 Main Bazaar, Paharganj; mains ₹150-450; ⊙8am-midnight; 🛜; Ⓜ Ramakrishna Ashram Marg) This venerable hotel's leafy, part-shaded, rooftop restaurant offers a calming respite from the noisy streets below. There's beer (Kingfisher ₹144), wine (₹360 per glass) and a food menu consisting mostly of Indian mains (₹150 to ₹450), but also pizza, pasta and Chinese.

Malhotra
NORTH INDIAN $$

(Map p84; 1833 Laxmi Narayan St; mains ₹170-270, thalis from ₹175; ⊙7am-11pm; 🛜; Ⓜ Ramakrishna Ashram Marg) One street back from the Main Bazaar chaos, Malhotra is a reliable choice, popular with locals and foreigners, and with a good menu of set breakfasts and North Indian standards, such as *mattar paneer* (pea and cottage cheese curry).

🍴 New Delhi

★ Andhra Pradesh Bhawan Canteen
SOUTH INDIAN $

(Map p72; 1 Ashoka Rd; dishes ₹150-180, thalis ₹130, breakfast ₹75; ⊙8-10.30am, noon-3pm & 7.30-10pm; Ⓜ Patel Chowk) A hallowed bargain, the canteen at the Andhra Pradesh state house serves cheap and delicious unlimited South Indian thalis to a seemingly unlimited stream of patrons. Come on Sunday for the fabled Hyderabadi chicken biryani (₹235).

★ Triveni Terrace Cafe
CAFE $

(Map p72; 205 Tansen Marg, Mandi House; dishes ₹70-200; ⊙10am-9pm, food to 6.30pm; Ⓜ Mandi House) Located in a peaceful garden-courtyard inside Triveni Art Gallery, this delightful cafe has seating on a plant-filled terrace overlooking a small, grassy amphitheatre, where dance rehearsals sometimes take place while you eat. The small menu includes tasty, good-value Indian meals and snacks (*pakora*, *paratha*, thali) plus toasted sandwiches and French-press coffee (₹120).

★ Naturals
ICE CREAM $

(Map p80; 8 L-Block, Connaught Place; single scoop ₹70; ⊙11am-midnight; Ⓜ Rajiv Chowk) Founder Mr Kamath's dad was a mango vendor in Mangalore, which apparently inspired his love of fruit. He went on to start Naturals, with its wonderfully creamy, fresh flavours, such as watermelon, coconut, (heavenly) mango and roasted almond.

LOCAL KNOWLEDGE

DELHI STREET FOOD

Old Delhi sizzles with the sound of *Dilli-ka-Chaat* (street-food snacks) being fried, boiled, grilled and flipped. *Chaat* to look out for include: *dahi bhalle* (fried lentil balls served with yoghurt and garnished with chutney); *aloo tikki* (spiced potato patties); *shakarkandi* (sweet potato) baked on coals on a flip-out table; and *aloo chaat* (fried pieces of parboiled potato mixed with chickpeas and chopped onions, and garnished with spices and chutney).

Aside from *Dilli-ka-Chaat*, Delhi specialities include breakfast-favourite *chole bhature* (spicy chickpeas, accompanied by puffy, fried bread with a light paneer filling); and *chole kulche*, a healthier version of *chole bhature* made with boiled chickpeas and less-greasy baked bread. *Nihari* (goat curry eaten with roti) is a popular breakfast for Delhi's Muslim population, and the only breakfast item at legendary Karim's (p87).

Kerala House Canteen SOUTH INDIAN **$**
(Map p80; 3 Jantar Mantar Rd; meals ₹50; ⊙8-10am, 12.30-2.30pm & 7-9.45pm; ⓂPatel Chowk) The staff canteen at Kerala House (Kerala Government HQ in Delhi) offers bargain set meals cooked with authentic Keralan spices. Lunchtimes are wildly popular with rice meals (veg, chicken, fish or buffalo) served with pappad and unlimited refills of lentil and bean side dishes. Dinner sees rice replaced with *parathas,* while *appams* (onion and coconut pancakes) are served at breakfast. Diners are sometimes asked to use the back entrance to Kerala House on Janpath Lane.

Kake-da-Hotel MUGHLAI **$**
(Map p80; ☑9136666820; 67 Municipal Market; mains ₹90-300; ⊙noon-11.30pm; ⓂRajiv Chowk) This no-frills, always-busy *dhaba* (snack bar) is a basic hole in the wall that's hugely popular with local workers for its famous butter chicken (₹230) and other Mughlai Punjabi dishes. Staff are rushed off their feet, but the owner is welcoming to the few foreign diners who visit.

Coffee Home INDIAN **$**
(Map p80; Baba Kharak Singh Marg; dishes ₹50-150; ⊙11am-8pm; ⓂShivaji Stadium) Shaded under the wide reaches of an old banyan tree, the garden courtyard at Coffee Home is always busy with office workers lingering over chai and feasting on South Indian snacks such as masala dosa. It is handily located next to the government emporiums.

★**Cafe Lota** MODERN INDIAN **$$**
(Map p72; Crafts Museum; dishes ₹215-415; ⊙8am-9.30pm; ⓂPragati Maidan) Bamboo slices the sunlight into flattering stripes at this outdoor restaurant offering a modern take on delicious Indian cooking from across the regions. Sample its take on fish and (sweet potato) chips, or *palak patta chaat* (crispy spinach, potatoes and chickpeas with spiced yoghurt and chutneys), as well as amazing desserts and breakfasts. It's great for kids.

★**Hotel Saravana Bhavan** SOUTH INDIAN **$$**
(Map p80; 46 Janpath; dishes ₹95-210, thalis ₹210; ⊙8am-11pm; ⓂJanpath) Fabulous dosas, *idlis* and other South Indian delights. With queues coming out the door, this is the biggest and the best of Delhi's Saravana Bhavan branches, and you can see dosas being made in the back. Also offers great South Indian coffee.

★**Rajdhani** INDIAN **$$$**
(Map p80; ☑011-43501200; 18 N-Block, Connaught Place; thalis ₹525; ⊙noon-3.30pm & 7-11pm; ☑; ⓂRajiv Chowk) Thalis fit for a king. Treat yourself with food-of-the-gods vegetarian thalis that encompass a fantastic array of Gujarati and Rajasthani dishes.

Farzi Cafe MODERN INDIAN **$$$**
(Map p80; ☑9599889700; 38 E-Block, Connaught Place; mains ₹360-560; ⊙noon-12.30am; ⓂRajiv Chowk) This buzzy Connaught Place joint signifies the Delhi foodie penchant for quirkiness, with all sorts of 'molecular gastronomy' and unusual fusion dishes such as butter chicken *bao* (in a bun). It's ₹100 for Kingfisher beer, and there are *bunta* (traditional homemade fizzy pop) cocktails. There's live Sufi, Hindi and Bollywood-style pop music on Saturday nights from 9pm.

Véda INDIAN **$$$**
(Map p80; ☑011-41513535; 27 H-Block, Connaught Place; mains ₹500-700; ⊙noon-11.30pm; ⓂRajiv Chowk) Fashion designer Rohit Baal created Véda's sumptuous interior, making for Connaught Place's most dimly lit eatery,

a dark boudoir with swirling neo-Murano chandeliers and shimmering mirror mosaics. The menu proffers tasty classic Mughlai dishes (butter chicken, dhal makhani and the like) and it mixes a mean martini.

Chor Bizarre   KASHMIRI $$$
(Map p72; ☑011-23071574; Bikaner House, Pandara Rd; mains ₹325-500; ⊙noon-3.30pm & 7-11.30pm; Ⓜ Khan Market) In the beautifully restored colonial-era Bikaner House, Chor Bizarre ('Thieves' Market') is a new branch of Hotel Broadway's famous restaurant on the outskirts of Old Delhi. Like the original, the interior here is also full of quirky old-fashioned charm, and the menu includes authentic, delicious dishes such as Kashmiri *haaq* (spinach with chilli).

🗡 South Delhi

Evergreen   CAFE $
(Map p88; S29-30 Green Park Market; dishes ₹100-200, thalis ₹165-240; ⊙9am-9pm; Ⓜ Green Park) Part cafe, part sweet shop, Evergreen has been keeping punters happy since 1963 with its veg snacks, *chaat*, thalis and dosas.

★Naivedyam   SOUTH INDIAN $$
(Map p88; ☑011-26960426; dishes ₹150-200, thalis ₹275-380; ⊙11am-11pm; Ⓜ Green Park) This superb South Indian restaurant feels like a temple, with a woodcarved interior, waiters dressed as devotees, and incense burning on the exterior shrine. Diners receive a complimentary lentil soup-drink and pappadam as they browse the menu, which includes delectable dosas and to-die-for thalis.

★Potbelly   NORTH INDIAN $$
(Map p88; 116C Shahpur Jat Village; dishes ₹150-450, thalis from ₹300; ⊙12.30-11pm; Ⓜ Hauz Khas) It's a rare treat to find a Bihari restaurant in Delhi, and this artsy, shabby-chic place with fabulous views from its 4th-floor perch has authentic Bihari thalis and dishes such as *litti* chicken – whole-wheat balls stuffed with *sattu* (ground pulse) and served with *khada masala* chicken.

Cafe Red   CAFE $$
(Map p88; 5-G Jungi House, Shahpur Jat Village, Siri Fort; mains ₹150-300; ⊙10.30am-8.30pm; 🛜; Ⓜ Hauz Khas) A fun and trendy ground-floor cafe that's hidden down an alley and serves omelettes, sandwiches, soups and pizza as well as espresso coffee and shakes. Has some patio seating, too.

Coast   SOUTH INDIAN $$$
(Map p88; ☑011-41601717; Hauz Khas; dishes ₹360-580; ⊙noon-midnight; Ⓜ Green Park) A light, bright restaurant on several levels, with views over the parklands of Hauz Khas, chic Coast serves light South Indian dishes, such as *avial* (vegetable curry) with *risheri* (pumpkin with black lentils), plus tacos, burgers, salads and hit-the-spot mustard-tossed fries. Decent wine list, too.

🗡 Sunder Nagar, Nizamuddin & Lodi Colony

Nagaland House   INDIAN $
(Map p72; 29 Dr APJ Abdul Kalam Rd; thalis ₹120-200; ⊙7-9am, noon-3pm & 7.30-10pm; Ⓜ Lok Kalyan Marg) The quiet, friendly, Nagaland canteen is a simple room overlooking a tangle of palm trees and is worth seeking out for punchy pork offerings, with dishes such as pork with bamboo shoots and a Naga-style pork thali. Veg, fish and chicken thalis are also available.

Gujarat Bhawan   GUJARATI $
(Map p72; 11 Kautilya Marg, Chanakyapuri; breakfast ₹60, thalis ₹110-140; ⊙7.30-10.30am, 12.30-3pm & 7.30-10pm; ☑; Ⓜ Lok Kalyan Marg) On a street lined with state bhavans (Bihar, Tamil Nadu, Karnataka), many of which have canteens, the Gujarat State–run canteen is typically simple, but serves up nourishing, plentiful, cheap-as-chips vegetarian home-style Gujarati thalis.

Karim's   MUGHLAI $$
(Map p72; 168/2 Jha House Basti; dishes ₹120-400; ⊙1-3pm & 6.30-11pm Tue-Sat; Ⓜ JLN Stadium) Hidden down the buzzing alleys that surround Hazrat Nizamuddin Dargah is this branch of historic Karim's, serving meaty Mughlai delights such as kebabs and rich curries.

★Mamagoto   ASIAN $$$
(Map p72; ☑011-45166060; 53 Middle Lane, Khan Market; mains ₹400-800; ⊙12.30-11.30pm; Ⓜ Khan Market) Fun, friendly and fabulously colourful, this laid-back east-Asian restaurant, with funky manga art and retro Chinese posters on the walls, has an eclectic menu spanning Japan, China and Southeast Asia – including noodles, dumplings and some authentically spicy hawker-style Thai food.

SAIKO3P/SHUTTERSTOCK ©

1. Lodi Garden (p77)
Dotted with 15th century Mughal monuments the gardens are a favourite for Delhi locals

2. Red Fort (p64)
This 380-year-old building allegedly has the decapitated bodies of prisoners built into its foundations.

3. Humayun's Tomb (p76)
Said to be the inspiration for the Taj Mahal in Agra, this tomb follows strict Islamic geometry

4. Jama Masjid (p65)
Holding up to 25,000 people, Delhi's largest mosque still allows space for reflection

FOOD PRICE RANGES

Prices reflect the cost of a standard main meal (unless otherwise indicated). Reviews are listed by author preference within the following price categories.

$ less than ₹150

$$ ₹150–₹300

$$$ more than ₹300

Sodabottleopenerwala PARSI **$$$**
(Map p72; www.sodabottleopenerwala.in; Khan Market; mains ₹325-745; ⊘9am-midnight; Ⓜ Khan Market) The name is like a typical trade-based Parsi surname, the place emulates the Iranian cafes of Mumbai, and the food is authentic Persian, including vegetable berry pilau, mixed-berry trifle and *lagan nu custer* (Parsi wedding custard).

Perch INTERNATIONAL **$$$**
(Map p72; ⌨9728603540; Khan Market; dishes ₹325-975, wine per glass ₹325-800, cocktails ₹500-650; ⊘8am-midnight; 🕾; Ⓜ Khan Market) The coolification of upscale shopping enclave Khan Market continues apace with Perch, a wine bar-cafe that's all pared-down aesthetic, waiters in pencil-grey shirts, soothing music, international wines and pleasing international snacks such as Welsh rarebit and tiger prawn with soba noodles.

★Indian Accent INDIAN **$$$**
(Map p72; ⌨011-26925151; https://indianaccent.com/newdelhi; Lodhi Hotel, Lodi Rd; dishes ₹500-1750, tasting menu veg/nonveg ₹3600/3900; ⊘noon-2.30pm & 7-10.30pm; Ⓜ JLN Stadium) Inside luxury Lodhi (p86) hotel, though privately run, Indian Accent is one of the capital's top dining experiences. Chef Manish Mehrotra works his magic using seasonal ingredients married in surprising and beautifully creative combinations. The tasting menu is astoundingly good, with wow-factor combinations such as tandoori bacon prawns or paper dosa filled with wild mushroom and water chestnuts. Dress smart. Book ahead.

✖ Greater Delhi & Gurgaon (Gurugram)

★DLF Cyber Hub INTERNATIONAL
(www.dlfcyberhub.com; DLF Cyber City, Phase II, NH-8; ⊘most restaurants 11am-11pm, bars to 1am; Ⓜ Cyber City) This is a food court par excellence, and you'll find any type of cuisine you fancy here, from Indian street food and Tibetan *momos* (dumplings) to high-end European and chic cafe bites. Tables spill out onto the large plaza; there's also an indoor 1st-floor food court with some cheaper options.

Standouts include **Burma Burma** (⌨0124-4372997; www.burmaburma.in; dishes ₹300-500; ⊘noon-3pm & 7-11pm), for Southeast Asian food and fine teas; the cool **Cyber Hub Social** (dishes ₹200-500; ⊘11am-11pm), with funky terrace seating and private rooms; **Farzi Cafe** (www.farzicafe.com; dishes ₹400-600; ⊘11am-1am), for upmarket Indian street food; the **People & Co** (p99) for live comedy; **Yum Yum Cha** (dim sum from ₹345, sushi from ₹485; ⊘12.30-11pm) for dim sum and sushi; and Soi 7 (p99) for craft beer brewed on-site. For a cheaper, on-the-hop option, grab a samosa (₹25) and a filter coffee (₹35) from the teeny stairwell takeaway Madras Coffee House.

Olive MEDITERRANEAN **$$$**
(Map p88; ⌨011-29574443; Bhulbhulaiya Rd, behind Qutab Minar, Mehrauli; pizza from ₹950, meze platters from ₹1500; ⊘noon-midnight; Ⓜ Qutab Minar) There are plenty of cafes and fast-food joints near the entrance to Qutab Minar, but if you fancy eating in style after visiting the ruins, follow the road around the back of the complex to beautiful Olive, with its *haveli* courtyard setting and award-winning Mediterranean menu.

🍷 Drinking & Nightlife

Delhi's ever-growing cafe scene has given rise to artisanal coffee, Turkish pastries and the like, while the city's bar and live-music choices are also burgeoning, though licences rarely extend later than 12.30am. For the latest places to go at night, check out Little Black Book (https://lbb.in/delhi) or Brown Paper Bag (http://brownpaperbag.in/delhi).

🍸 Old Delhi

Drinking is frowned upon in much of Muslim-dominated Old Delhi, but there are plenty of bars around the backpacker hub of Paharganj. Most are dark, seedy-looking (though really quite harmless) dive bars that are frequented almost solely by men. But there are a few OK exceptions on Main Bazaar, such as Sam's Bar (p97). Most restaurants on Main Bazaar do not have alcohol licences; some will, though, sell you a can of beer on the sly, served in a coffee mug. In such cases, be sure to drink discreetly so that you don't get them in trouble.

★ **PT Ved Prakash Lemon Wale**   JUICE BAR

(Map p68; ☎ 011-23920931; 5466 Ghantaghar, Chandni Chowk; lemonade ₹10; ⊙ 11.30am-10.30pm; Ⓜ Chandni Chowk) Quenching Chandni Chowk's thirst for over a century now, this stalwart has a menu comprising just one item: homegrown fizzy lemonade that comes from a glass bottle sealed with a marble. Summer days find this hole-in-the-wall place completely engulfed by loyal fans seeking much-needed relief from the heat.

🍷 Paharganj

Cafe Brownie   CAFE

(Map p84; 41 Arakashan Rd; coffee from ₹70; ⊙ 7.30am-11pm; 🛜; Ⓜ New Delhi Railway Station) Cute little cafe for an email catch-up, espresso in one hand, brownie or muffin in the other.

Voyage Cafe   CAFE

(Map p84; 8647 Arakashan Rd; coffee from ₹50; ⊙ 24hr; 🛜; Ⓜ New Delhi Railway Station) Cakes, shakes and very affordable Lavazza coffee, plus floor-to-ceiling windows for that full-on street-view experience.

Sam's Bar   BAR

(Map p84; Main Bazaar; ⊙ 1pm-12.30am; Ⓜ Ramakrishna Ashram Marg) If you can nab one of the two tables by the big window overlooking Main Bazaar this is a fine place to chill with a couple of beers (from ₹115). Sam's Bar is more laid-back than most Paharganj bars, with a mixed crowd of men and women, locals and foreigners. There's a full food menu as well as drinks.

My Bar   BAR

(Map p84; Main Bazaar, Paharganj; ⊙ 11am-12.30pm; Ⓜ Ramakrishna Ashram Marg) A dark but lively bar, this place is loud and fun, with a cheery, mixed crowd of backpackers and locals, who may even start dancing... There are several other branches, in **Connaught Place** (Map p80; 49 N-Block; ⊙ 11am-12.30am; Ⓜ Rajiv Chowk) and Hauz Khas. Cocktails from ₹220. Beer from ₹100.

🍸 New Delhi

Chai Point   CAFE

(Map p80; N-Block, Connaught Place; ⊙ 8am-11pm; 🛜; Ⓜ Rajiv Chowk) This buzzing, split-level cafe specialises in healthy chai infusions

(masala, ginger, cardamom, lemongrass; ₹75 to ₹100) but also serves good lassis (₹119 to ₹129) and fresh coffee alongside banana cake and other sweet treats. Ask for a glass cup; otherwise you'll get your chai in a less-than-satisfying disposable paper cup.

Cha Bar   CAFE

(Map p80; Oxford Bookstore, 81 N-Block, Connaught Place; tea ₹35-100, dishes ₹100-175; ⊙ 9.30am-9.30pm; Ⓜ Rajiv Chowk) Connaught Place's Oxford Bookstore contains the hugely popular cafe Cha Bar, with more than 150 types of tea to choose from, as well as a good-value food menu including a range of tasty biryanis (₹170). At lunchtimes it buzzes with happy, chattering, 20-something locals.

Indian Coffee House   CAFE

(Map p80; 2nd fl, Mohan Singh Place, Baba Kharak Singh Marg; snacks ₹50-100, filter coffee ₹36; ⊙ 9am-9pm; Ⓜ Rajiv Chowk) Up on the 2nd floor of Mohan Singh Place, Indian Coffee House has faded-to-the-point-of-dilapidated charm, with the waiters' plummage-like hats and uniforms giving them a rakish swagger. You can feast on finger chips and South Indian snacks like it's 1952, and the roof terrace is a tranquil spot to linger, although watch out for marauding macaques!

★ **Atrium, Imperial**   CAFE

(Map p80; Imperial Hotel, Janpath; ⊙ 8am-11.30pm; Ⓜ Janpath) Is there anything more genteel than high tea at the Imperial (p85)? Sip tea from bone-china cups and pluck dainty sandwiches and cakes from tiered stands, while discussing the latest goings-on in Shimla and Dalhousie. High tea is served in the Atrium from 3pm to 6pm daily (₹1500 plus tax).

★ **Unplugged**   BAR

(Map p80; ☎ 011-33107701; 23 L-Block, Connaught Place; beers/cocktails from ₹145/400; ⊙ noon-midnight; Ⓜ Rajiv Chowk) There's nowhere else like this in Connaught Place. You could forget you were in CP, in fact, with the big courtyard garden, wrought-iron chairs and tables, and swing seats, all under the shade of a mother of a banyan tree hung with basket-weave lanterns. There's live music on Wednesday, Friday, Saturday and Sunday evenings: anything from alt-rock to electro-fusion.

★ **1911**   BAR

(Map p80; Imperial Hotel, Janpath; ⊙ 11am-12.45am; Ⓜ Janpath) The Imperial, built in the 1930s, resonates with bygone splendour. This bar is a more recent addition, but still riffs on the Raj. Here you can sip the perfect cocktail (₹1000) amid designer-clad clientele, against a backdrop of faded photos and murals of maharajas.

Lord of the Drinks BAR

(Map p80; ☑ 9999827155, 9999827144; G-72, 1st fl, Outer Circle, Connaught Place; beers/cocktails from ₹135/545, mains ₹400-800; ⊙ 11am-1am; ☎; Ⓜ Rajiv Chowk) A cavernous space done up in wood, leather and metal trim, with cosy corners and a huge sports TV screen. Serves trademark oversized drinks, including mugs of Kingfisher for ₹135, while everything goes on the food menu, from *bhurji* (crumbled spiced paneer) to Parmesan tart.

South Delhi

★ Hauz Khas Social BAR

(Map p88; www.socialoffline.in/HauzKhasSocial; 12 Hauz Khas Village; ⊙ 11am-12.30am; Ⓜ Green Park) This chilled-out restaurant-bar-club is a Hauz Khas hub, and has an urban warehouse-like interior with stone walls, high ceilings and huge plate-glass windows overlooking lush greenery and the Hauz Khas lake. There's an extensive food menu (dishes ₹200 to ₹500) plus beers, cocktails and regular live music and DJs in the evenings.

★ Piano Man Jazz Club CLUB

(Map p88; http://thepianoman.in; B-6 Commercial Complex, Safdarjung Enclave; ⊙ noon-3pm & 7.30pm-12.30am; Ⓜ Green Park) The real thing, this popular, atmospheric place with proper musos is a dim-lit speakeasy with some excellent live jazz performances.

★ Ek Bar BAR

(Map p88; D17, 1st fl, Defence Colony; ⊙ 5pm-1am; Ⓜ Lajpat Nagar) On the upper floors of a building in the exclusive area of the Defence Colony, this place has stylish, kooky decor in deep, earth-jewel colours, serious mixology (cocktails from ₹475) showcasing Indian flavours (how about a gin and tonic with turmeric?), modern Indian bar snacks, nightly DJs, and a see-and-be-seen crowd.

Kunzum Travel Cafe CAFE

(Map p88; www.kunzum.com; T49 Hauz Khas Village; ⊙ 11am-7.30pm Tue-Sun; ☎; Ⓜ Green Park) ✐ Quirky Kunzum has a pay-what-you-like policy for the French-press coffee and tea, and sells its own brand of travel guides to Delhi. There's free wi-fi, a few travel books and magazines to browse, and paints and brushes on a table for you to produce your own artwork.

Sunder Nagar, Nizamuddin & Lodi Colony

Big Chill CAFE

(Map p72; Khan Market; ⊙ noon-11.30pm; Ⓜ Khan Market) Popular, film-poster-lined cafe at Khan Market, packed with chattering Delhiites. The menu is a telephone directory of Continental and Indian dishes (₹290 to ₹625). Nearby is its spin-off cakery (for cakes and pastries) and creamery (for ice cream).

Café Turtle CAFE

(Map p72; Khan Market; dishes ₹375-545; ⊙ 8.30am-8.30pm; Ⓜ Khan Market) Allied to the Full Circle Bookstore (p102), this brightly painted boho cafe gets busy with chattering bookish types, and is ideal when you're in the mood for coffee and cake in cosy surroundings, with a leafy outdoor terrace as well. There is also a branch in **Nizamuddin East** (Map p72; 8 Nizamuddin East Market; dishes ₹375-545, coffees from ₹200; ⊙ 8.30am-8.30pm; Ⓜ Jangpura).

Greater Delhi & Gurgaon (Gurugram)

★ Blue Tokai CAFE

(Map p88; www.bluetokaicoffee.com; Champa Gali, Lane 3, West End Marg, Saket; coffee from ₹100, snacks ₹150-300; ⊙ 9am-10pm; ☎; Ⓜ Saket) Found in a magically unexpected art enclave called Champa Gali, down a lane beside the fake Dilli Haat shopping centre ('Delhi Haat'), Blue Tokai is one of a few cool cafes here, but is the one the coffee aficionados come to. They grind their own beans here and you can get serious caffeine hits such as nitrogen-infused cold brew.

★ Jugmug Thela TEAHOUSE

(Map p88; www.jugmugthela.com; Champa Gali, Lane 3, Westend Marg, Saket; teas & coffees ₹70-100, sandwiches ₹120-280; ⊙ 10.30am-8.30pm; ☎; Ⓜ Saket) Another hidden surprise in Champa Gali – the mini art enclave down Lane 3 behind the fake Dilli Haat store – this tea specialist has more than 180 herbs and spices to work with. It serves delicious ayurvedic teas and other blends, plus organic coffee and fabulously unique sandwich combos (spicy potato and pomegranate; almond and banana) that shouldn't work, but do.

Soi 7   BAR
(DLF Cyber Hub; draught beer from ₹325; ☺11am-1am; Ⓜ Cyber City) Up on the top floor of DLF Cyber Hub, this popular bar brews four different beers in-house (₹325 for a half-litre glass), stocks numerous single-malt whiskeys and whips up a range of cocktails. It does food, too.

☆ Entertainment

The type of entertainment common in big Western cities (theatres, concerts, sports events) is somewhat thin on the ground in Delhi, though the city does have a busy cultural scene, especially during the three-week **Delhi International Arts Festival** (DIAF; www.diaf.in; ☺Nov/Dec). October and March also sees annual or one-off shows and concerts (often free) happening nightly.

Kingdom of Dreams   THEATRE
(☑0124-4528000;   www.kingdomofdreams. in; Auditorium Complex, Sector 29, Gurgaon (Gurugram); shows Tue-Fri ₹1199-3199, Sat & Sun ₹1299-4199, refundable entry to Culture Gully ₹600; ☺12.30pm-midnight Tue-Fri, noon-midnight Sat & Sun, showtimes vary; Ⓜ IFFCO Chowk) An entertainment extravaganza, Kingdom of Dreams offers live Bollywood-style shows that are out-and-out sensory assaults. Performances are supported by world-class techno-wizardry, as the cast swing, swoop and sing from the rafters. There's a free shuttle from the metro every 15 minutes, but it's only a 500m walk; come out of Gate 2 and take the first right.

Even if you don't fancy a show, it's worth browsing the food options on Culture Gully – a kitsch but somehow great mock-up of an Indian street that's indoors under a sky dome. The Cultural Gully entrance fee is refundable on purchase of a show ticket.

Next door is the far more modest **open-air theatre** (☺7.30pm Sat; Ⓜ IFFCO Chowk) **FREE**, with free traditional-music performances every Saturday evening.

People & Co   COMEDY
(www.canvaslaughclub.com;   DLF Cyber Hub; ☺nightly; Ⓜ Cyber City) A restaurant and bar with comedy nights every evening, usually from around 7.30pm. Some nights are free. Bigger names bring a cover charge (from ₹500). Check the website for listings.

Indira Gandhi National Centre for the Arts   ARTS CENTRE
(Map p72; ☑011-23388105; www.ignca.gov. in; 11 Mansingh Rd, near Andhra Bhavan; ☺9am-5.30pm Mon-Fri; Ⓜ Janpath, Central Secretariat, Patel Chowk) A hub of cultural and artsy seminars, exhibitions and performances housed in a well-located, landscaped sprawl not far from India Gate. Frequented by culture vultures for a regular fix of classical and vocal recitals, dance performances, film screenings and literary fests. See the website for forthcoming events and activities.

Habitat World   LIVE PERFORMANCE
(Map p72; ☑011-43663333; www.habitatworld. com; India Habitat Centre, Lodi Rd; Ⓜ Jor Bagh) This is an important Delhi cultural address, with art exhibitions, performances and concerts, mostly free. Check the website for events.

🛍 Shopping

Wares from all over India glitter in Delhi's step-back-in-time bazaars, emporiums and markets. The city is also increasingly a centre of contemporary design (especially fashion), with independent boutiques and big shiny malls.

Away from government-run emporiums and fixed-price shops, haggle hard, but with good humour. Many drivers earn a commission by taking travellers to overpriced places – don't fall for it.

🛍 Old Delhi

Chandni Chowk   CLOTHING, ELECTRONICS
(Map p68; ☺approx 10am-7pm; Ⓜ Chandni Chowk) Old Delhi's backbone is an iconic shopping strip, dotted by temples, snarled by traffic and crammed with stores selling everything from street food to saris. Tiny bazaars lead off the main drag, so you can dive off and explore these small lanes, which glitter with jewellery, decorations, paper goods and more.

➡ **Kinari Bazaar**

(☺11am-8pm; Ⓜ Jama Masjid) Kinari means 'hem' in Hindi, and this colour-blazing market sells all the trimmings that finish off an outfit. It's famous for *zardozi* (gold embroidery), temple trim and wedding turbans, and is extremely photogenic.

➡ **Dariba Kalan**

(☺approx 10am-8pm; Ⓜ Lal Qila) For silver (jewellery, ornaments, old coins), head for Dariba Kalan, the alley near the Sisganj Gurdwara, and with the easy-to-spot Jalebi Wala (p87) at its mouth.

➡ Nai Sarak

(☺ approx 10am-8pm; Ⓜ Jama Masjid) Running south from the old Town Hall, Nai Sarak is lined with stalls selling saris, shawls, chiffon and *lehenga* (blouse and skirt combo).

➡ Ballimaran

(☺ 10am-8pm; Ⓜ Chandni Chowk) This area is apparently where Delhi's Yamuna boat operators once lived. Today this market street and the smaller lanes fanning off it specialise in sequined slippers and fancy, curly-toed jootis (traditional slip-on shoes).

★ Spice Market   MARKET

(Gadodia Market; Map p68; Khari Baoli; Ⓜ Chandni Chowk) It feels as if little has changed for centuries in Delhi's fabulously atmospheric, labyrinthine spice market, as labourers hustle through the narrow lanes with huge packages of herbs and spices on their heads whilst sunlight pours down through cracks in the hessian sacks hanging overhead for shade. The colours are wonderful – red chillies, yellow turmeric, green cardamons – and there's so much spice in the air, people walk around unable to suppress their sneezes.

There are eye-catching displays of everything from lentils and rice to giant jars of chutneys, pickles, nuts and tea, and you can buy small packets of items, despite it being a wholesale market.

Majnu-ka-Tilla   TIBETAN MARKET

(Tibetan Colony, Majnu-ka-Tilla; ☺ around 10am-8pm; Ⓜ Vidhan Sabha) Delhi's Tibetan enclave, Majnu-ka-Tilla, is a fascinating tangle of tiny alleys – too narrow for vehicles – that are dotted with cheap guesthouses, Tibetan cafes, and dozens of small shops selling all manner of Tibetan trinkets and souvenirs,

from prayer flags and incense sticks to free-Tibet T-shirts and Buddhist bracelets. It's 2km from Vidhan Sabha metro station (₹30 to ₹40 in an autorickshaw).

Aap Ki Pasand   DRINKS

(San-Cha Tea; Map p68; ☑ 23260373; www.aapkipasandtea.com; 15 Netaji Subhash Marg; ☺ 10am-7pm Mon-Sat; Ⓜ Jama Masjid, Delhi Gate) Specialists in the finest Indian teas, from Darjeeling and Assam to Nilgiri and Kangra. You can try before you buy, and teas come lovingly packaged in drawstring bags. There's another branch at Santushti Shopping Complex (San Cha; Map p72; ☑ 011-264530374; www.sanchatea.com; Santushti Shopping Complex, Racecourse Rd; ☺ 10am-7pm Mon-Sat; Ⓜ Lok Kalyan Marg).

🏠 Paharganj

Main Bazaar   HANDICRAFTS, CLOTHING

(Map p84; Paharganj; ☺ 10am-9pm Tue-Sun; Ⓜ Ramakrishna Ashram Marg) Backpacker Central, this crazy-busy bazaar that runs through Paharganj sells almost everything you want, and a whole lot more. It's great for buying presents, clothes, inexpensive jewellery bits and bobs, and luggage to put everything in as you're leaving India, or for hippy-dippy clothes to wear on your trip. Haggle with purpose.

Beware the street-side henna scam, where mehndi-wallahs will quote a price for a beautiful henna tattoo only later to reveal that the price was per inch.

Just south of Main Bazaar is a street-side fruit market (Map p84; ☺ 8am-10pm; Ⓜ Ramakrishna Ashram Marg), around the corner from which the Vegetable & Spice Market (Map p84; ☺ 8am-10pm; Ⓜ Ramakrishna Ashram Marg) is the best place to shop for spices in Paharganj – you should be able to get 100g bags of cumin or coriander powder for just ₹25.

Yes Helping Hands   CLOTHING

(Map p84; www.yeshelpinghands.org; Main Bazaar, Paharganj; ☺ 9am-9pm; Ⓜ Ramakrishna Ashram Marg) 🖉 With its roots in Pokhara, Nepal, this fair-trade nonprofit organisation sells quality weave and knitwear, including pashmina shawls, cashmere scarfs and hemp bags with an aim to helping provide training and employment opportunities for people with disabilities in Nepal and Ladakh.

OLD DELHI MUSICAL INSTRUMENT SHOPS

As well as the many shops and markets to explore in Old Delhi, it's worth browsing the myriad **musical instrument shops** (Map p68; ☺ approx 10am-8pm Mon-Sat; Ⓜ Delhi Gate, Jama Masjid) along Netaji Subhash Marg for sitars, tabla sets and other beautifully crafted Indian instruments. Expect to pay upwards of ₹20,000 for a decent quality sitar, and around ₹3000 to ₹6000 for a tabla pair.

Delhi Foundation of Deaf Women
ARTS & CRAFTS

(DFDW; Map p84; www.dfdw.net; 1st fl, DDA Community Hall, Mantola Mohalla, near Chandi Wali Gali, Paharganj; ⊙10am-6pm Mon-Sat; ⋒Ramakrishna Ashram Marg) ✐ Beautiful handmade handicrafts (bags, purses, gift cards, bookmarks) made by members of the city's deaf foundation and sold from their community hall. Very hard to find; from Main Bazaar, walk up Chandi Wali Gali, turn right at the end, and it's soon on your right, down a tiny alley.

New Delhi

★ Central Cottage Industries Emporium
ARTS & CRAFTS

(Map p80; ☎011-23326790; Janpath; ⊙10am-7pm; ⋒Janpath) This government-run multilevel store is a wonderful treasure trove of fixed-price, India-wide handicrafts. Prices are higher than in the state emporiums, but the selection of woodcarvings, jewellery, pottery, papier mâché, stationery, brassware, textiles (including shawls), toys, rugs, beauty products and miniature paintings makes it a glorious one-stop shop for beautiful crafts. There's the Smoothie cafe by the entrance.

★ Kamala
ARTS & CRAFTS

(Map p80; Baba Kharak Singh Marg; ⊙10am-7pm Mon-Sat; ⋒Rajiv Chowk) Crafts, curios, textiles and homewares from the Crafts Council of India, designed with flair and using traditional techniques but offering some contemporary, out-of-the-ordinary designs.

State Emporiums
HANDICRAFTS, CLOTHING

(Map p80; Baba Kharak Singh Marg; ⊙11am-1.30pm & 2-6.30pm Mon-Sat; ⋒Shivaji Stadium) Handily in a row are these regional treasure-filled emporiums. They may have the air of torpor that often afflicts governmental enterprises, but shopping here is like travelling around India – top stops include Kashmir, for papier mâché and carpets; Rajasthan, for miniature paintings and puppets; Uttar Pradesh, for marble inlay work; Karnataka, for sandalwood sculptures; and Odisha, for stone carvings.

Khadi Gramodyog Bhawan
CLOTHING

(Map p80; Regal Bldg, 24 Connaught Circus; ⊙11am-7.30pm; ⋒Rajiv Chowk) ✐ Known for its excellent *khadi* (homespun cloth), including good-value shawls, *salwar kameez* and *kurta pyjama,* this three-floor shop also sells handmade paper, incense, spices, henna and lovely natural soaps.

Fabindia
CLOTHING, HOMEWARES

(Map p80; www.fabindia.com; 1 A-Block, Connaught Place; ⊙10am-8.30pm; ⋒Rajiv Chowk) Surprisingly well-priced, high-quality, ready-made clothes in funky Indian fabrics, from elegant kurtas (long collarless shirts) and dupattas (women's scarves) to Western-style shirts, plus stylish homewares.

The Shop
CLOTHING, HOMEWARES

(Map p80; 10 Regal Bldg, Sansad Marg; ⊙9.30am-7.30pm Mon-Sat, 11am-6pm Sun; ⋒Janpath, Rajiv Chowk) Gorgeous little boutique with a calm, no-pressure-to-buy ambience, attractive Indian clothing, and light, bright printed-cotton homewares.

Rikhi Ram
MUSIC

(Map p80; ☎011-23327685; www.rikhiram.com; 8A G-Block, Connaught Place; ⊙11am-8pm Mon-Sat; ⋒Rajiv Chowk) A tiny, but beautiful, old shop selling professional classic and electric sitars, tablas and more. Tablas start at ₹50,000.

Janpath & Tibetan Markets
ARTS & CRAFTS

(Map p80; Janpath; ⊙11.30am-7pm Mon-Sat; ⋒Rajiv Chowk) These twin markets, made up of small shop fronts stretching along Janpath, sell shimmering mirrorwork embroidery, colourful shawls, Tibetan bric-a-brac, brass Oms, dangly earrings and lots of clothing. There are some good finds if you rummage through the junk, and if you haggle you can get some bargains.

South Delhi

★ Hauz Khas Village
HANDICRAFTS, CLOTHING

(Map p88; Hauz Khas Fort Rd; ⊙11am-7pm Mon-Sat; ⋒IIT) This arty little enclave has narrow lanes crammed with boutiques selling designer Indian clothing, handicrafts, contemporary ceramics, handmade furniture and old Bollywood movie posters. Intriguingly, it's located beside numerous 13th- and 14th-century ruins (p75), as well as a forested deer park (⊙5am-8pm; to 7pm winter; ⋒IIT, Green Park) FREE and a lake. Standout eating and drinking options include Naivedyam (p93) and Hauz Khas Social (p98).

Shahpur Jat Village
MARKET

(Map p88; ⊙10am-7pm Mon-Sat; ⋒Hauz Khas, Green Park) Located within the boundaries of the ruined walls of Siri Fort (p75; the second of Delhi's seven historic cities), this urban village contains an artsy collection of high-end clothing boutiques, health-conscious cafes and no-frills eateries, many of which are hidden amongst a network of graffiti-splattered alleyways, making this one of Delhi's more intriguing places to shop.

Standout shops include **Aum** (www. aumdelhi.com; 5G Jungi House, ⊙11am-7pm Mon-Sat; ⓜHauz Khas), for fabulously colourful contemporary Indian women's clothing, and **NeedleDust** (www.needledust.com; 40B, ground fl, Shahpur Jat; ⊙10.30am-7.30pm Mon-Sat; ⓜHauz Khas), for exquisite embroidered jooti (leather slippers). For food, try the excellent Bihari restaurant Potbelly (p93), or hip Cafe Red (p93).

Dilli Haat ARTS & CRAFTS
(Map p88; Aurobindo Marg; Indian/foreigner ₹30/100; ⊙10.30am-10pm Mar-Nov, 11am-9pm Dec-Feb; ⓜINA) Right beside INA metro station, this popular, but somewhat stage-managed, open-air food-and-crafts market is a cavalcade of colour and sells regional handicrafts from all over India; bargain hard. At the far end are lots of regional food stands where you can sample cuisine from every corner of the country. Beware impostors; this is the only real Dilli Haat in Delhi.

Sunder Nagar, Nizamuddin & Lodi Colony

★**Khan Market** MARKET
(Map p72; ⊙approx 10.30am-8pm Mon-Sat; ⓜKhan Market) ⏿ Khan Market is Delhi's most upmarket shopping enclave, the most expensive place to rent a shop in India, and is favoured by the elite and expats. Its boutiques focus on fashion, books and homewares, and it's also a good place to eat and drink.

For handmade paper, check out **Anand Stationers** (⊙10am-8pm Mon-Sat, noon-6pm Sun), or try **Mehra Bros** (⊙10am-8pm) for cool papier-mâché ornaments. Literature lovers should head to **Full Circle Bookstore** (www.fullcirclebooks.in; 23 Khan Market; ⊙8.30am-8.30pm) and **Bahrisons** (www.books atbahri.com; ⊙10.30am-7.30pm Mon-Sat, 11am-7pm Sun). For Indian clothes and homewares, hit **Fabindia** (⊙10.30am-9.30pm), **Anokhi** (www.anokhi.com; 32 Khan Market; ⊙10am-8pm), or **Good Earth** (9 ABC Khan Market; ⊙11am-8pm), and, for elegantly packaged ayurvedic remedies, browse **Kama** (22A Khan Market; ⊙10.30am-8.30pm).

Meharchand Market MARKET
(Map p72; Lodi Colony; ⓜJLN Stadium) Across the road from the government housing of the Lodi Colony, this is a long strip of small boutiques selling homewares and clothes. Quality clothing shops include **Play Clan** (⏿011-24644393; www.theplayclan.com; shop 17-18; ⊙10.30am-7.30pm; ⏿; ⓜJor Bagh) and **The Shop** (⊙10am-8pm Mon-Sat, 11am-7pm Sun; ⓜJor Bagh), while stand-out eateries are the fully organic **Altitude Cafe & Deli** (www. thealtitudecafe.com; mains ₹340-580; ⊙8.30am-7.30pm; ⏿; ⓜJLN Stadium), the Middle Eastern sweets and coffee shop **Kunafa** (sweets per kg from ₹300, coffee ₹250; ⊙10am-10pm; ⓜJLN Stadium) and Asian-tapas restaurant **Diva Spiced** (www.divarestaurants.com; dishes ₹550-1350; ⊙11.30am-11.30pm; ⓜJLN Stadium).

Greater Delhi & Gurgaon (Gurugram)

Select Citywalk MALL
(Map p88; www.selectcitywalk.com; Press Enclave Marg, Saket; ⊙10am-11pm; ⓜMalviya Nagar) Enormous, supermodern shopping complex containing three or four interconnected shopping malls, a handful of five-star hotels and even an art gallery. The central mall – Select Citywalk – has top-end clothing stores, plus restaurants, cafes and a couple of cinemas. Attached DLF Place contains more of the same, while quieter DLF South Court houses the stylish **Kiran Nadar Museum of Art** (Map p88; ⏿011-49160000; www.knma.in; 145 DLF South Court Mall, Select Citywalk, Saket; ⊙10.30am-6.30pm Tue-Sun; ⓜMalviya Nagar) FREE.

ⓘ Information

DANGERS & ANNOYANCES
➡ Delhi is relatively safe in terms of petty crime, though pickpocketing can be a problem in crowded areas so keep your valuables safe.

➡ Roads are notoriously congested; take extreme care when crossing them, or when walking along narrow lanes that don't have footpaths.

➡ Pollution is another real danger in Delhi. Consider wearing a properly fitting face mask.

➡ Women should never walk in lonely, deserted places, even during daylight hours.

➡ Be aware of touts at the airport, train station and around tourist areas.

➡ Beware also of fake tourist offices.

Safety & Women Travellers

Delhi has, unfortunately, a deserved reputation as being unsafe for women. Precautions include never walking around in lonely, deserted places, even during daylight hours, keeping an eye on your route so you don't get lost (download a map that you can use offline) and taking special care after dark – ensure you have a safe means of transport home with, for example, a reputable cab company or driver.

Touts

Taxi-wallahs at the airport and around tourist areas frequently act as touts for hotels, claiming that your hotel is full, poor value, dangerous, burnt down or closed, or that there are riots in Delhi. Any such story is a ruse to steer you to a hotel where they will get a commission. Insist on being taken to where you want to go – making a show of writing down the registration plate number, and phoning the autorickshaw/taxi helpline may help. Men who approach you at Connaught Place run similar scams to direct you to shops and tourist agents, often 'helpfully' informing you that wherever you're headed is closed.

Train Station Hassle

Touts at New Delhi train station endeavour to steer travellers away from the legitimate International Tourist Bureau and into private travel agencies where they earn a commission. Touts often tell people that their tickets are invalid, there's a problem with the trains, or say they're not allowed on the platform. They then 'assist' in booking expensive taxis or 3rd-class tickets passed off as something else. You're particularly vulnerable when arriving tired at night. As a rule of thumb: don't believe anyone who approaches you trying to tell you anything at the train station, even if they're wearing a uniform or have an official-looking pass.

Fake Tourist Offices

Many Delhi travel agencies claim to be tourist offices, even branding themselves with official-looking logos. There is only one India Tourism Delhi office; if you need a travel agent, ask for a list of recommended agents from them. Be wary of booking a multistop trip out of Delhi, particularly to Kashmir. Travellers are often hit for extra charges, or find out they've paid over the odds for the class of travel and accommodation.

INTERNET ACCESS

Pretty much all accommodation and most cafes, bars and restaurants offer free wi-fi access these days. There are some free wi-fi hotspots around the city, in some shopping malls, for example, and in airport buildings. Internet cafes are a thing of the past.

It's easy to gain 3G and 4G access via smartphone data packs bought for local SIM cards.

MEDIA

Newspapers The most respected English-language newspapers in terms of balanced reporting are the *Hindustan Times* (www.hindustantimes.com) and the *Indian Express* (www.indianexpress.com).

Magazines For printed listings see the long-running weekly pamphlet *Delhi Diary* (www.delhidiary.in), which is available at local bookshops. *Motherland* (www.motherlandmagazine.com) is a stylish bi-monthly cultural magazine.

What's On To check out what's on, see the ubercool Little Black Book (https://lbb.in/delhi) or Brown Paper Bag (http://brownpaperbag.in/delhi). And don't miss the Delhi Walla blog (www.thedelhiwalla.com), a wonderful window into Delhi's daily life.

MEDICAL SERVICES

Pharmacies are found on most shopping streets and in most suburban markets. Recommended hospitals include:

All India Institute of Medical Sciences (AIIMS; Map p88; ☑ 011-26589142, 011-65900669; www.aiims.edu; Ansari Nagar; Ⓜ AIIMS)

Apollo Hospital (☑ 011-26925858, 011-29871090; www.apollohospitals.com/locations/india/delhi; Mathura Rd, Sarita Vihar; Ⓜ Jasola Apollo)

Dr Ram Manohar Lohia Hospital (RML Hospital; Map p72; ☑ emergencies 011-23365525, enquiries 011-23404286; www.rmlh.nic.in; Baba Kharak Singh Marg; Ⓜ Patel Chowk)

Max Healthcare (Map p88; ☑ 011-26515050; www.maxhealthcare.in; Press Enclave Rd, Saket; Ⓜ Malviya Nagar)

MOBILE PHONES

You can use your unlocked mobile phone from home on roaming, but it's much cheaper to buy a local SIM card. You'll need your passport to register a local SIM, and the details of your accommodation in Delhi.

It's best to buy a local SIM card with a data package either from the airport when you arrive, or from a genuine branch of one of the main phone providers in the city centre; Vodafone or Airtel are the most reliable. If you go through a local shop or kiosk you may experience delays in getting connected, or be overcharged.

Airtel (Map p80; No 5 M-Block, Radial Rd 5, Connaught Place; ⊘ 10am-8pm Mon-Sat; Ⓜ Rajiv Chowk)

Vodafone (Map p80; D27, Connaught Place; ⊘ 10.30am-7.30pm Mon-Sat; Ⓜ Rajiv Chowk)

TOURIST INFORMATION

India Tourism Delhi (Government of India; Map p80; ☑ 011-23320008, 011-23320005; www.incredibleindia.org; 88 Janpath; ⊘ 9am-6pm Mon-Fri, to 2pm Sat; Ⓜ Janpath) This official tourist office is a useful source of advice on Delhi, getting out of Delhi, and visiting surrounding states. But note, this is the only official tourist information centre outside the airport. Ignore touts who (falsely) claim to be associated with this office. Anyone who 'helpfully' approaches you is definitely not going to take you to the real office.

Regional tourism offices with a base in Delhi include:

Haryana Tourism (Map p72; ☑ 011-23324911; www.haryanatourism.gov.in; 36 Chander Lok Bldg, Janpath; Ⓜ Janpath)

Rajasthan Tourism (Map p72; ☑ 011-23389525, 011-23381884; www.tourism.rajasthan.gov.in; Pandara Rd, room 8, behind Bikaner House; Ⓜ Khan Market)

Sikkim House (Map p72; 011-2688302; www.sikkim.gov.in; 14 Panchsheel Marg, Chanakyapuri; Ⓜ Lok Kalyan Marg)

POST

There are post offices all over Delhi that can handle letters and parcels (most with packing services nearby, usually directly outside the entrance).

Poste restante is available at India Post's New Delhi **General Post Office** (GPO; Map p72; ☑ 011-23743602; Gole Dakhana, Baba Kharak Singh Marg; ☺10am-5pm Mon-Sat; Ⓜ Patel Chowk); it will keep parcels for up to a month before they are sent back to the sender; as well as the addressee's name, ensure mail is addressed to 'Poste Restante, c/o Postmaster, GPO, New Delhi – 110001'.

For ordinary postal services, it's quicker and easier to use smaller Branches of India Post, such as the one at **Connaught Place** (Map p80; 6 A-Block, Connaught Place; ☺8am-7.30pm Mon-Sat; Ⓜ Rajiv Chowk).

Courier services may be arranged through **DHL** (Map p80; ☑ 011-23737587; ground fl, Mercantile Bldg, Tolstoy Marg; ☺9am-9pm Mon-Sat; Ⓜ Janpath) at Connaught Place.

❶ Getting There & Away

AIR

Indira Gandhi International Airport
(☑ 01243376000; www.newdelhiairport.in; Ⓜ IGI Airport) is about 14km southwest of the centre. International and domestic flights use Terminal 3. Ageing Terminal 1 is reserved for low-cost carriers. Free shuttle buses (present your boarding pass and onward ticket) run between the two terminals every 20 minutes, but can take a while. Leave at least three hours between transfers to be safe.

The Arrivals hall at Terminal 3 has 24-hour foreign exchange, ATMs, prepaid taxi and car-hire counters, tourist information, a pharmacy, bookshops, cafes, a **Plaza Premium Lounge**

(☑ 011-61233933; www.plazapremiumlounge.com; T3 departures hall, Indira Gandhi International Airport; s/d 3hr ₹2500/3500; Ⓜ IGI Airport) with short-stay rooms (there's another of these at Terminal 1 arrivals) and sleeping pods under the banner of **Sams Snooze at My Space** (☑ 8800444132; www.snoozeatmyspace.com; Terminal 3 International Departures, Indira Gandhi International Airport; s/tw 3hr from ₹2500/4500; ✸ ☎; Ⓜ IGI Airport).

You'll need to show your aeroplane ticket or boarding pass to enter the Departures building; a digital version on your phone will suffice. If you're meeting someone at the airport, you can pay ₹100 to enter the Arrivals building. Otherwise you'll have to wait outside for them.

Delhi's airport can be prone to thick fog from November to January (often disrupting airline schedules) – it's wise to allow a day between connecting flights during this period.

Airlines include:

Air India (Map p72; ☑ 011-24667100; www.airindia.com; Sri Aurobindo Marg, Safdarjung Airport Area; ☺9.30am-7pm; Ⓜ Jorbagh)

Jagson Airlines (Map p80; ☑ 011-23721593; www.jagsongroup.in; Vandana Bldg, 11 Tolstoy Marg; ☺10am-6pm Mon-Sat; Ⓜ Janpath)

SpiceJet (☑ 9871803333; www.spicejet.com; 319 Udyog Vihar, Phase-IV, Gurgaon (Gurugram); ☺9am-6pm; Ⓜ Cyber City)

BUS

Although train travel is more popular for long distances, buses are a useful option to some closer destinations, or if the trains are booked up.

Practically all state-run services leave from the large **Kashmere Gate Inter State Bus Terminal** (ISBT; Map p68; ☑ 011-23860290; Ⓜ Kashmere Gate) in Old Delhi, accessible by metro (exit gate 7). There are offices representing the states to which buses from here frequently travel to (Haryana, Punjab, Rajasthan, Himachal Pradesh, Uttar Pradesh, Uttarakhand), though they are generally useless, as tickets are instead bought from booths downstairs, beside the individual bus stands. Most destinations are served by both local buses and more comfortable, more expensive AC (air-con) buses. You can't prebook the local buses, and there's no need to anyway; just turn up and buy a ticket on the next available bus. Tickets for AC buses, which are less frequent, can be booked in advance though, either in person a day or two before, or through a travel agent or some hotels.

The **Anand Vihar Inter State Bus Terminal** (Swami Vivekanand Inter State Bus Terminal; Ⓜ Anand Vihar ISBT) has some services to Nainital and Kumaun in Uttarakhand. Some cheaper buses to destinations in Uttar Pradesh, Madhya Pradesh and Rajasthan leave from the Sarai Kale Khan Inter State Bus Terminal (ISBT) on the ring road near Nizamuddin train station. **Himachal Bhawan** (Map p72; 📞 011-23716689; Sikandra Rd; Ⓜ Mandi House) has buses to Manali and Shimla, both in Himachal Pradesh.

There are buses to Agra, but considering the traffic at either end, you're better off taking the train.

Wherever you're going, it's wise to arrive at the bus station at least 30 minutes ahead of your departure time.

Note that some, more expensive, private deluxe buses leave from other locations in central Delhi – enquire at travel agencies or your hotel for details. You can also book tickets or check information on Cleartrip (www.cleartrip.com),

SELECTED TRAINS FROM DELHI

DESTINATION	TRAIN NO & NAME	FARE (₹)	DURA-TION (HR)	FREQUENCY	DEPARTURES & TRAIN STATION
Agra	12280 Taj Exp	105/375 (A)	3	1 daily	6.45am NDLS
	12002 Bhopal Shatabdi	525/1020 (B)	2	1 daily	6am NDLS
Amritsar	12029 Swarna Shatabdi	905/1725 (B)	6½	1 daily	7.20am NDLS
	12013 Amritsar Shatabdi	905/1725 (B)	6	1 daily	4.30pm NDLS
Bengaluru (Bangalore)	22692 Bangalore Rajdhani	3010/4190/6795 (C)	34	4 weekly	8.45pm NZM
Chennai	12434 Chennai Rajdhani	2910/4020/6475 (C)	29	2 weekly	3.55pm NZM
	12622 Tamil Nadu Exp	780/2050/3005 (D)	33	1 daily	10.30pm NDLS
Goa (Madgaon)	12432 Trivandrum Rajdhani	2705/3780/6175 (C)	25½	3 weekly	10.55am NZM
	12780 Goa Exp	775/2040/2990 (D)	38½	1 daily	3pm NZM
Haridwar	12017 Dehradun Shatabdi	610/1200 (B)	5	1 daily	6.45am NDLS
Jaipur	12958 ADI Swarna Jayanti Rajdani	825/1100/1710 (C)	4½	1 daily	7.55pm NDLS
	12916 Ashram Exp	235/595/830 (D)	5	1 daily	3.20pm DLI
	12015 Ajmer Shatabdi	655/1305 (B)	4½	1 daily	6.05am NDLS
Kalka (for Shimla)	12011 Kalka Shatabdi	615/1270 (B)	4	2 daily	7.40am NDLS
Khajuraho	12448 UP Sampark Kranti Exp	365/960/1360 (D)	10½	1 daily	8.10pm NZM
Lucknow	12004 Lucknow Swran Shatabdi	910/1865 (B)	6½	1 daily	6.10am NDLS
Mumbai	12952 Mumbai Rajdhani	2105/2925/4760 (C)	16	1 daily	4.25pm NDLS
	12954 August Kranti Rajdhani	2105/2925/4760 (C)	17	1 daily	4.50pm NZM
Udaipur	12963 Mewar Exp	415/1100/1565 (D)	12½	1 daily	7pm NZM
Varanasi	12560 Shivganga Exp	415/1105//1575 (D)	12	1 daily	6.55pm NDLS

Train stations: NDLS – New Delhi; DLI – Old Delhi; NZM – Hazrat Nizamuddin
Fares: (A) 2nd class/chair car; (B) chair car/1st-class AC; (C) 3AC/2AC/1st-class AC;
(D) sleeper/3AC/2AC

Make My Trip (www.makemytrip.com), Goibibo (www.goibibo.com) or Red Bus (www.redbus.in).

Ambedkar Stadium Bus Stand (Map p68; 011-23318180; Ambedkar Stadium; M Delhi Gate) has international bus services to Kathmandu in Nepal, and Lahore in Pakistan.

TRAIN

There are three main stations in Delhi: (Old) Delhi train station (aka Delhi Junction) in Old Delhi, New Delhi train station near Paharganj, and Nizamuddin train station, south of Sunder Nagar. Make sure you know which station your train is leaving from. All three have metro stations outside them.

New Delhi Railway Station (btwn Ajmeri Gate & Main Bazaar Paharganj; ⊘24hr; M New Delhi) is the largest and best connected of Delhi's train stations, and the best option for foreign travellers wanting to buy train tickets, thanks to its very helpful **International Tourist Bureau** (ITB; Map p84; 011-23405156; 1st fl, New Delhi Train Station; ⊘6am-10pm; M New Delhi), a ticket office reserved solely for the use of foreign travellers (you have to show a foreign passport to even be allowed inside). To find it, walk in the station's main entrance (on the Paharganj side of the train station) then, just before you reach platform 1, walk up the staircase to your right. At the 1st floor turn right and the office is along the corridor on your left. Do *not* believe anyone who tells you this ticket office has shifted, closed or burnt down – this is a scam to divert you elsewhere. Walk with confidence and ignore all 'helpful' or 'official' approaches. The ITB is a large room with about 10 or more computer terminals – don't be fooled by other 'official' offices.

Once inside, first take a queuing number. While you wait for your number, go to the information desk to one side of the room to get details of your journey. Once you know which train you wish to book, fill in one of the passenger booking slips and take it, along with your passport, to the booking desks once your number has come up. You can pay with cash or card.

There's also a public **Train Reservation Office** (Map p84; Chelmsford Rd; ⊘8am-8pm; M New Delhi) a few hundred metres outside the train station, closer towards Connaught Place. Anyone, local or foreign, can buy train tickets here, but for foreigners it makes no sense to come here where queues are longer and English-language skills less prevalent. There's also an **Unreserved Booking Office** (Map p84; New Delhi train station; ⊘24hr; M New Delhi) to your right as you exit the train station (again, at the Paharganj side of the station). This is for buying same-day 'general' tickets to nearby destinations; a very cheap option, but although you'll be allowed to get on the train, you're not guaranteed a seat.

ℹ Getting Around

TO/FROM THE AIRPORT

Metro The easiest and quickest way from the airport to the centre is via the metro's Airport Express line (www.delhimetrorail.com), which runs from 5.15am to 11.40pm and costs ₹60/50 from the international/domestic terminal to New Delhi Railway Station.

Bus AC buses also run from outside Terminal 3 to the centre.

Taxi Use the Delhi Traffic Police Prepaid Taxi counter outside both terminals. A trip to the centre costs ₹350 to ₹450. Many hotels can arrange a pick-up, which will be less hassle, though more expensive than arranging a taxi yourself.

AUTORICKSHAW & E-RICKSHAW

Delhi's signature green-and-yellow autorickshaws are everywhere. You never have to worry about finding one – drivers will find you! They have meters, but they are never used, so ensure you negotiate the fare clearly before you start your journey. As a guide, Paharganj to Connaught Place should cost around ₹30.

Delhi Traffic Police run a network of prepaid autorickshaw booths, where you pay a fixed fare in return for a ticket that you hand over to the driver once you reach your destination. There are 24-hour booths outside the three main train stations; **New Delhi** (Map p84; outside New Delhi Railway Station, Paharganj side; ⊘24hr; M New Delhi), **Old Delhi** (Map p68; outside Old Delhi Railway Station; ⊘24hr; M Chandni Chowk) and **Nizamuddin** (Map p72; outside Nizamuddin Railway Station). Other booths are outside the **India Tourism** (Map p80; 88 Janpath; ⊘11am-8.30pm; M Janpath, Rajiv Chowk) Delhi office and at **Central Park** (Map p80; Central Park, Connaught Place; M Rajiv Chowk), Connaught Place.

Fares with ordinary autos are invariably elevated for foreigners, so haggle hard, and if the fare sounds too outrageous, find another ride.

An auto ride from Connaught Place should be around ₹30 to Paharganj, ₹60 to the Red Fort, ₹70 to Humayun's Tomb and ₹100 to Hauz Khas. However, it will be a struggle to get these prices. From 11pm to 5am there's a 25% surcharge.

To report overcharging, harassment, or other problems take the licence number and call the **Auto Complaint Line** (011-42400400, 25844444).

Delhi's ever-expanding fleet of golf-cart-lookalike e-rickshaws (electric rickshaws) offer a more environmentally friendly alternative to autorickshaws and taxis. Many of them are shared rickshaws, plying fixed routes for very cheap individual fares, but many can also be hired privately. Fares should be roughly the same as autorickshaws.

TAXI APPS & AUTO APPS

Car-sharing services Uber (www.uber.com/in/en) and Ola Cabs (www.olacabs.com) have transformed travel around Delhi. Uber Autos is another option on the Uber app, and helps find you an autorickshaw rather than a taxi. They are even cheaper than the taxis.

Note that drivers will almost always call you en route, asking for directions and clarification of where you want to go (even though this information is in front of them on their phone's app), and will often not be able to speak English, so you'll sometimes have to get a bilingual local to help with communication.

Cabs also tend to take a lot longer to arrive than your app says, and they often arrive at a point that is a short walk from the agreed pick-up.

Given these issues, it's usually much quicker to hail an ordinary autorickshaw or taxi from the roadside. However, Uber and Ola do tend to work out cheaper.

BICYCLE

Bike Rental New Delhi Municipal Council (NDMC) unveiled 250 shiny new smart bikes (www.smartbikemobility.com) in November 2018, hoping to soon expand the fleet to 500. Bikes are docked at 23 stations, mostly around central New Delhi for now, and are unlocked via a mobile app. The first 30 minutes of use is free. Foreigners need a local mobile phone number to register, but can link their account to a foreign bank card (VISA or Mastercard only). And word is, e-scooters are next!

Bike Tours DelhiByCycle (p81) offers recommended cycle tours.

Purchase To buy your own bike, head to the **Jhandewalan Cycle Market** (Map p68; ⊙11am-8pm; M Jhandewalan), near Videocon Tower, five minutes walk from Jhandewalan metro station.

BUS

Foreign travellers rarely use Delhi's public buses, which can get crowded and are difficult to negotiate for non-Hindi-speaking passengers. But there are several useful routes, including the Airport Express bus and Bus GL-23, which connects the Kashmere Gate and Anand Vihar bus stations. Most short hops cost around ₹10.

CYCLE RICKSHAW

Cycle-rickshaws are useful (and great fun) for navigating Old Delhi and the suburbs, but they are banned from many parts of New Delhi, including Connaught Place (though they'll still drop you off there from Paharganj). Negotiate a fare before you set off – expect to pay ₹20 to ₹30 for a short trip. Tip well; it's a tough job, and many rickshaw riders are homeless and spend the nights sleeping on their rickshaws.

METRO

Delhi's **metro** (www.delhimetrorail.com; single journey ₹10-60) is fast and efficient, with signs and arrival/departure announcements in Hindi and English. Trains run from around 6am to 11pm and the first carriage in the direction of travel is reserved for women only. Trains can get insanely busy at peak commuting times (around 9am to 10am and 5pm to 6pm) – avoid travelling with luggage during rush hour if at all possible (however, the Airport Express line is much less busy and has plenty of luggage space).

Tokens (₹10 to ₹60) are sold at metro stations. A metro smart card (₹50 deposit plus ₹100 minimum initial top-up) gets you 10% off all journeys (20% outside the peak hours of 8am to noon and 5pm to 9pm). There are also tourist cards (one-day card ₹200 plus ₹50 deposit; three-day card ₹500 plus ₹50 deposit), but they're really not worth it unless you're planning on taking a lot of metro journeys, as most journeys only cost around ₹20.

Because of security concerns, all bags are X-rayed and passengers must pass through an airport-style scanner.

TAXI

Local taxis (recognisable by their black-and-yellow livery) have meters but, like the ones in autorickshaws, these are effectively ornamental as most drivers refuse to use them; ensure you negotiate a price before you start your trip.

Taxis typically charge twice the autorickshaw fare. Note that fares vary as fuel prices go up and down. From 11pm to 5am there's a 25% surcharge for autorickshaws and taxis.

Kumar Tourist Taxi Service (Map p80; ☏ 011-23415930; www.kumarindiatours.com; 14/1 K-Block, Connaught Place; ⊙8am-9pm) A reliable company; a day of Delhi sightseeing costs from ₹3000 (an eight-hour and 80km limit applies).

Metropole Tourist Service (Map p72; ☏ 011-24310313, 9810277699; www.metrovista.co.in; 224 Defence Colony Flyover Market; ⊙8am-6.30pm; M Jangpura) Another reliable and long-running taxi service, and decent value, too.

Rajasthan

POP 77.1 MILLION

Best Places to Eat

➜ Peacock Rooftop Restaurant (p122)

➜ Jagat Niwas Palace Hotel (p163)

➜ Niro's (p123)

➜ Ambrai (p164)

➜ Shri Mishrilal Hotel (p185)

Best Places to Stay

➜ Hotel Pearl Palace (p118)

➜ Inn Seventh Heaven (p143)

➜ Jagat Niwas Palace Hotel (p162)

➜ Hotel Ranthambhore Regency (p147)

➜ Haveli Braj Bhushanjee (p150)

Why Go?

It is said there is more history in Rajasthan than in the rest of India put together. Welcome to the Land of the Kings – a realm of maharajas, majestic forts and lavish palaces. India is littered with splendid architecture, but nowhere will you find fortresses quite as magnificent as those in Rajasthan, rising up imperiously from the landscape like fairy-tale mirages or epic movie sets.

Enchanting as they are, there is much more to this spectacular state than its architectural wonders. This is also a land of sweeping sand dunes and shaded jungle, of camel trains and wild tigers, of glittering jewels, vivid saris and vibrant culture. There are enough festivals here to fill a calendar, while the shopping and cuisine are nothing short of spectacular. In truth, Rajasthan just about has it all – it is the must-see state of India, brimming with startling, thought-provoking and, ultimately, unforgettable attractions.

When to Go

Jaipur

Dec–Feb Pleasant daytime temperatures, but can get cold at night; peak tourists, peak prices.

Sep–Nov, Feb & Mar Warm nights suit many visitors fleeing colder climes.

Apr–Aug April and June are hot awaiting the monsoon, which brings rain in July and August.

History

Rajasthan is the ancestral home of the Rajputs, warrior clans who claim to originate from the sun, moon and fire, and who have controlled this part of India for more than 1000 years. While they forged marriages of convenience and temporary alliances, pride and independence were always paramount, and this lack of unity led to the Rajputs becoming vassals of the Mughal empire.

Mughal rule of Rajasthan was marked by rebellion, uprisings and tragedy, as whole cities committed *jauhar* (ritual mass suicide) rather than submit to the Mughals. Nevertheless, as the Mughal empire declined, the Rajputs clawed back their independence and signed treaties with the British allowing individual Rajput kingdoms to operate as independent princely states under the umbrella of British rule.

At Independence, Rajasthan's many maharajas were allowed to keep their titles and property holdings and were paid an annual stipend commensurate with their status to secure their participation in the union. However, this favourable arrangement lapsed in the 1970s and Rajasthan submitted fully to central control.

EASTERN RAJASTHAN

The cities and sites of eastern Rajasthan are easily accessible from Jaipur, as well as Agra and Delhi (all stops on the 'Golden Triangle'). For immersion in history, see Alwar and Deeg's evocative palaces, plus the magnificent forts at Bharatpur and Ranthambhore.

Wildlife enthusiasts will relish the opportunities available at Ranthambhore, Keoladeo and Sariska Tiger Reserve. Tiger-spotting is unsurpassed at Ranthambhore, which has provided the tigers to repopulate Sariska, while Keoladeo, India's premier bird sanctuary, hosts an astonishing population of resident and migratory birds in a picturesque wetland setting.

Travellers of all descriptions are drawn to Pushkar, a pastel blue town that hosts an extravagant, internationally renowned camel fair. Pushkar is also a Hindu pilgrimage site and legendary travellers' halt to chill and shop, while nearby Ajmer hosts the extraordinary dargah (shrine or place of burial of a Muslim saint) of Khwaja Muin-ud-din Chishti, India's most important Muslim pilgrimage site.

Jaipur

☐ 0141 / POP 3.1 MILLION

Enthralling, historical Jaipur, Rajasthan's capital, is the gateway to India's most flamboyant state.

The city's colourful, chaotic streets ebb and flow with a heady brew of old and new. Careering buses dodge dawdling camels, leisurely cycle-rickshaws frustrate swarms of motorbikes, and everywhere buzzing autorickshaws watch for easy prey. In the midst of this cacophony and mayhem, the splendours of Jaipur's majestic past are islands of relative calm evoking a different pace and another world.

At the city's heart, the City Palace continues to house the former royal family; the Jantar Mantar, the royal observatory, maintains a heavenly aspect; and the honeycomb Hawa Mahal gazes on the bazaar below. And just out of sight, in the arid hill country surrounding the city, is the fairy-tale grandeur of Amber Fort, Jaipur's star attraction.

History

Jaipur is named after its founder, the great warrior-astronomer Jai Singh II (1688–1743), who came to power at age 11 after the death of his father, Maharaja Bishan Singh. Jai Singh could trace his lineage back to the Rajput clan of Kachhwahas, who consolidated their power in the 12th century. Their capital was at Amber (pronounced 'amer'), about 11km northeast of present-day Jaipur, where they built the impressive Amber Fort.

The kingdom grew wealthier and wealthier, and this, plus the need to accommodate the burgeoning population and a paucity of water at the old capital at Amber, prompted

---

ⓘ COMPOSITE TICKETS

Consider buying a **composite ticket** (Indian/foreigner ₹300/1000), which gives you entry to Amber Fort, Central Museum, Jantar Mantar, Hawa Mahal, Isarlat and Narhargarh and is valid for two days from the time of purchase. It can be bought from any of the listed sites. A separate **ticket** (Indian/foreigner ₹190/500; two days) includes entry to the City Palace, Royal Gaitor, Cenotaphs of the Maharanis and Jaigarh; for foreigners this ticket is included with entry to the City Palace.

Rajasthan Highlights

1 Jaisalmer (p188)
Visiting the 12-century sandstone fort and riding a camel over silky sand dunes.

2 Udaipur (p156)
Kicking back at a lakeside restaurant in Rajasthan's most romantic city.

3 Pushkar (p140)
Attending this extraordinary camel fair, which combines Hindu spiritualism, camel commerce and cultural celebration.

4 Jodhpur (p178)
Viewing the Blue City from the ramparts of Rajasthan's most spectacular fort, Mehrangarh.

5 Ranthambhore National Park (p145)
Exploring this former hunting reserve where your chances of spotting a tiger are excellent.

6 Jaipur (p109)
Wandering the colourful bazaars of the Pink City and exploring the marvellous Amber Fort.

7 Bundi (p148)
Experiencing Rajasthani culture and heritage in a town where tourism remains low key.

8 Shekhawati (p172) Discovering the whimsical murals decorating the once-lavish *havelis* (traditional residences).

9 Chittorgarh (p153)
Immersing yourself in the romanticism of Rajput myth and legend at this enormous, sprawling and tragic fortress.

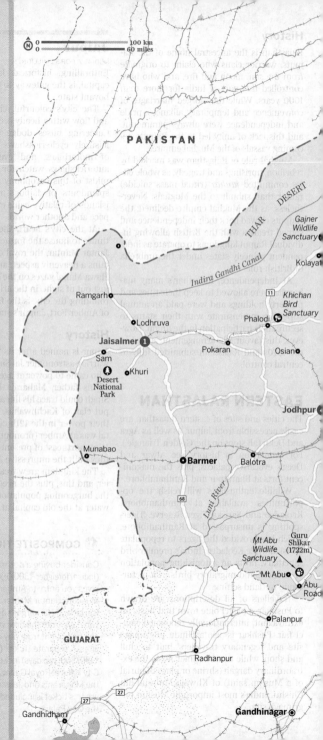

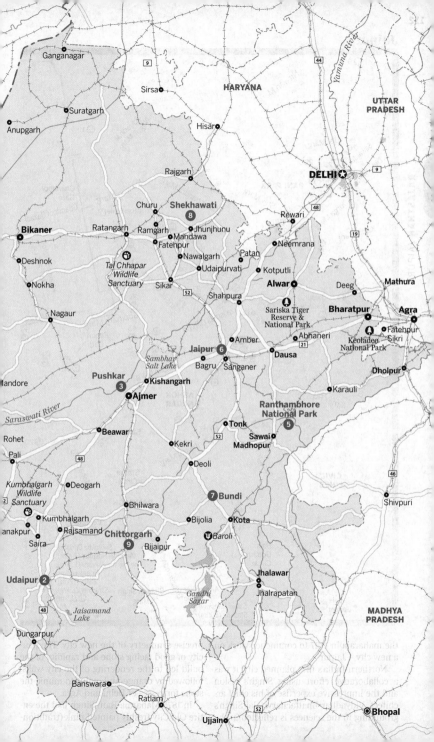

Jaipur

A B C D

🛈 9

Nirwan Marg

1

Vidyadhar
Nagar Marg

🏨 19

Tulsi Marg

26
Sawai Jai Singh Hwy 🏨 21 29
Devi Marg 🏨 10 Chandpol
35 Gate

🏛 24 Chandpol Bazaar

BANI PARK Shiv Marg Kantichandra Marg Nirwan Marg

17 Jai
Singh Chandpole Ⓜ
Chowk

Durga Marg

2

Kabir Marg 🏨 16

Khajane Walon
ka Rasta

🏛 36 59 14
58 Ⓜ Sansar Chandra Marg

Station Rd Ⓜ Sindhi 🏨 18
Camp

55 🛈 Jaipur 45 27 11
Railway 57 💲 15 25 Indra Bazaar
Jaipur 60 Ⓜ 48 Mirza Ismail (MI) Rd Gopinath Marg 39
Palace 56 🛈 12

Khatipura Rd ◉ 5 43 Panch
Batti

3

🏨 32 22 13 38 🍽 41
53 50 42

Jacob Rd Ashoka Marg

Ajmer Rd ASHOK
NAGAR

4

34 🏨 51 37 ❌

Sarojini Marg

Prithviraj Marg 🏨 20

CIVIL
LINES Statue
Circle Mahavir Rd

RAMBAGH

5

46

Central
Park

49

Bais
Godam
Circle Santokba Durlabhji
Memorial Hospital (700m);
Yog Sadhna Ashram (1.5km);
Air India (2km);
Balaji (12km);
Sanganer (12km);
(12km)

Bais
Godam Ambedkar Bhawan Singh
Circle Marg 31 🏨
Sawai Mansingh 🏨 33
Stadium (500m)

6

A B C D

the maharaja in 1727 to commence work on
a new city – Jaipur.

Northern India's first planned city, it was
a collaborative effort using Singh's vision
and the impressive expertise of his chief architect, Vidyadhar Bhattacharya. Jai Singh's
grounding in the sciences is reflected in the

precise symmetry of the new city. The paucity of good facing stone and rapidity of the
build led to the rendering of the city walls,
followed by orange-pink paint to mimic the
stone fortresses of Delhi and Agra.

In 1876 Maharaja Ram Singh had the entire Old City freshly painted pink (tradition-

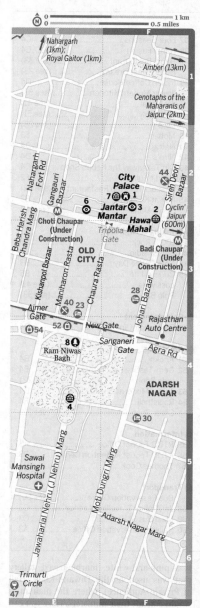

◉ Sights

◉ Old City (Pink City)

The Old City (often referred to as the Pink City) is both a marvel of 18th-century town planning, and a place you could spend days exploring – it's the beating heart of Jaipur.

Avenues divide the Pink City into neat rectangles, each specialising in certain crafts, as ordained in the Shilpa-Shastra (an ancient Hindu treatise on architecture). The main bazaars in the Old City include Johari Bazaar, Tripolia Bazaar, Bapu Bazaar and Chandpol Bazaar. The whole is partially encircled by a crenellated wall punctuated at intervals by grand gateways. The major gates are Chandpol (*pol* means 'gate'), Ajmer Gate and Sanganeri Gate.

★City Palace   PALACE

(☏ 0141-4088888; www.royaljaipur.in; Indian/foreigner incl camera ₹130/500, guide from ₹300, audio guide ₹200, Royal Grandeur tour Indian/foreigner ₹2500/3000; ⊙ 9.30am-5pm) A complex of courtyards, gardens and buildings, the impressive City Palace is right in the centre of the Old City. The outer wall was built by Jai Singh II, but within it the palace has been enlarged and adapted over the centuries. There are palace buildings from different eras, some dating from the early 20th century. It is a striking blend of Rajasthani and Mughal architecture.

The price of admission includes entry to Royal Gaitor and the Cenotaphs of the Maharanis, as well as to Jaigarh, a long climb above Amber Fort (p129). This composite ticket is valid for two days and costs Indians an extra ₹60 on top of City Palace entry (no extra cost for foreigners).

➡ **Mubarak Mahal**

Entering through Virendra Pol, you'll see the Mubarak Mahal (Welcome Palace), built in the late 19th century for Maharaja Madho Singh II as a reception centre for visiting dignitaries. Its multiarched and colonnaded construction was cooked up in an Islamic, Rajput and European stylistic stew by the architect Sir Swinton Jacob. It now forms part of the Maharaja Sawai Mansingh II Museum, containing a collection of royal costumes and superb shawls, including Kashmiri pashmina. One remarkable exhibit is Sawai Madho Singh I's capacious clothing; it's said he was a cuddly 2m tall, 1.2m wide and 250kg.

ally the colour of hospitality) to welcome the Prince of Wales (later King Edward VII), reinforcing the city's tone. Today all residents of the Old City are compelled by law to preserve the salmon-pink facade.

Jaipur

➡ The Armoury

The Anand Mahal Sileg Khana – the Maharani's Palace – houses the Armoury, which has one of the best collections of weapons in the country. Many of the ceremonial items are elegantly engraved and inlaid, belying their grisly purpose.

➡ Diwan-i-Khas (Sarvatobhadra)

Set between the Armoury and the Diwan-i-Am art gallery is an open courtyard known in Sanskrit as Sarvatobhadra. At its centre is a pink-and-white, marble-paved gallery that was used as the Diwan-i-Khas (Hall of Private Audience), where the maharajas would consult their ministers. Here you can see two enormous silver vessels, each 1.6m tall and reputedly the largest silver objects in the world.

➡ Diwan-i-Am Art Gallery

Within the lavish Diwan-i-Am (Hall of Public Audience) is this art gallery. Exhibits include a copy of the entire Bhagavad Gita handwritten in tiny script, and miniature copies of other holy Hindu scriptures, which were small enough to be easily hidden in the event that zealot Mughal armies tried to destroy the sacred texts.

➡ **Pitam Niwas Chowk & Chandra Mahal**

Located towards the palace's inner courtyard is Pitam Niwas Chowk. Here four glorious gates represent the seasons – the Peacock Gate depicts autumn, the Lotus Gate signifies summer, the Green Gate represents spring, and finally the Rose Gate embodies winter.

Beyond this *chowk* (square) is the private palace, the Chandra Mahal, which is still the residence of the descendants of the royal family and where you can take a 45-minute Royal Grandeur guided tour of select areas.

★ **Jantar Mantar** HISTORIC SITE
(Indian/foreigner ₹50/200, guide ₹200, audio guide ₹100; ⊙9am-4.30pm) Adjacent to the City Palace is Jantar Mantar, an observatory begun by Jai Singh II in 1728 that resembles a collection of bizarre giant sculptures. Built for measuring the heavens, the name is derived from the Sanskrit *yanta mantr,* meaning 'instrument of calculation', and in 2010 it was added to India's list of Unesco World Heritage Sites. Paying for a local guide is highly recommended if you wish to learn how each fascinating instrument works.

Jai Singh liked astronomy even more than he liked war and town planning. Before constructing the observatory he sent scholars abroad to study foreign constructs. He built five observatories in total, and this is the largest and best preserved (it was restored in 1901). Others are in Delhi, Varanasi and Ujjain. No traces of the fifth, the Mathura observatory, remain. A valid composite ticket (p109) will also gain you entry.

★ **Hawa Mahal** HISTORIC BUILDING
(Palace of Breeze; Sireh Deori Bazaar; Indian/foreigner incl camera ₹50/200, guide ₹200, audio guide ₹177; ⊙9am-5.30pm) Jaipur's most distinctive landmark, the Hawa Mahal is an extraordinary pink-painted, delicately honeycombed hive that rises a dizzying five storeys. It was constructed in 1799 by Maharaja Sawai Pratap Singh to enable ladies of the royal household to watch the life and processions of the city. The top offers stunning views over Jantar Mantar and the City Palace in one direction and over Sireh Deori Bazaar in the other.

There's a small museum (open Saturday to Thursday), with miniature paintings and some rich relics, such as ceremonial armour, which help evoke the royal past.

Claustrophobes should be aware that the narrow corridors can sometimes get extremely cramped and crowded inside the Hawa Mahal. Entrance is from the back of the complex. To get here, return to the intersection on your left as you face the Hawa Mahal, turn right and then take the first right again through an archway. Shopkeepers can show you another way – past their shops! A valid composite ticket (p109) will also gain you entry.

◉ New City

By the mid-19th century it became obvious that the well-planned city was bulging at the seams. During the reign of Maharaja Ram Singh (1835–80) the seams ruptured and the city burst out beyond its walls. Civic facilities, such as a postal system and piped water, were introduced. This period gave rise to a part of town very different from the bazaars of the Old City, with wide boulevards, landscaped grounds and grand European-influenced buildings. All of this is rather hard to appreciate in today's fuming, beeping, traffic-clogged thoroughfares.

Central Museum MUSEUM
(Albert Hall; J Nehru Marg; Indian/foreigner ₹40/300, audio guide Hindi/English ₹118/177; ⊙9.30am-5pm Tue-Sun) This museum is housed in the spectacularly florid Albert Hall, south of the Old City. The building was designed by Sir Swinton Jacob, and combines elements of English and North Indian architecture, as well as huge friezes celebrating the world's great cultures. It was known as the pride of the new Jaipur when it opened in 1887. The grand old building hosts an eclectic array of tribal dress, dioramas, sculptures, miniature paintings, carpets, musical instruments and even an Egyptian mummy.

Ram Niwas Bagh PARK
(₹20; ⊙8am-8pm) Adjacent to, but a world away from, busy MI Rd is this oasis of green where you can wander through geometric gardens of roses, palms and ferns. Alternatively, find yourself a shady patch of grass to sit and read a book or take to the jogging track.

◉ City Edge

Surrounding the city are several historic sites including forts, temples, palaces and

HEAVEN-PIERCING MINARET

Piercing the skyline near the City Palace is this unusual minaret, Isarlat (Iswari Minar Swarga Sal, Heaven-Piercing Minaret; Indian/foreigner ₹50/200; ⊙9am-4.30pm), erected in the 1740s by Jai Singh II's son and successor Iswari. The entrance is around the back of the row of shops fronting Chandpol Bazaar – take the alley 50m west of the minaret along the bazaar or go via the Atishpol entrance to the City Palace compound, 150m east of the minaret. You can spiral to the top of the 43m minaret for excellent views.

Iswari ignominiously killed himself by snakebite (in the Chandra Mahal) rather than face the advancing Maratha army – his 21 wives and concubines then did the necessary 'noble' thing and committed *jauhar* (ritual mass suicide by immolation) on his funeral pyre. A valid composite ticket (p109) will also gain you entry.

gardens. Some of these can be visited on the way to Amber Fort.

Nahargarh
FORT

(Tiger Fort; Indian/foreigner ₹50/200; ⊙10am-5pm) Built in 1734 and extended in 1868, this sturdy fort overlooks the city from a sheer ridge to the north. The story goes that the fort was named after Nahar Singh, a dead prince whose restless spirit was disrupting construction. Whatever was built in the day crumbled in the night. The prince agreed to leave on condition that the fort was named for him. The views are glorious and there's a restaurant that's perfect for a cold beer.

One way to visit is to climb the steep, winding 2km path to the top, starting from the end of Nahargarh Fort Rd. To drive, you have to detour via the Amber area in a circuitous 8km round trip. A valid composite ticket (p109) will also gain you entry.

Royal Gaitor
HISTORIC SITE

(Gatore ki Chhatriyan; Indian/foreigner ₹20/30; ⊙9am-5pm) The royal cenotaphs, just outside the city walls, beneath Nahargarh, feel remarkably undiscovered and are an appropriately restful place to visit. The stone monuments are beautifully and intricately carved. Maharajas Pratap Singh, Madho Singh II and Jai Singh II, among others, are honoured here. Jai Singh II has the most impressive marble cenotaph, with a dome supported by 20 carved pillars.

Jal Mahal
HISTORIC BUILDING

(Water Palace; ⊙closed to the public) Near the cenotaphs of the maharanis of Jaipur, and beautifully situated in the watery expanse of Man Sagar, is this dreamlike palace. Its origins are uncertain, but it was believed to have been extensively restored if not built by Jai Singh II (1734). It's currently undergoing restoration under the auspices of the Jal Tarang (www.jaltarang.in) project.

Cenotaphs of the Maharanis of Jaipur
HISTORIC SITE

(Maharani ki Chhatri; Amber Rd; Indian/foreigner ₹20/30; ⊙9am-5pm) About 5km from the centre, along the road to Amber, the cenotaphs of the maharanis of Jaipur are worth a visit for a tranquil stroll.

Galta
HINDU TEMPLE

Squeezed between cliffs in a rocky valley, Galta is a desolate, if evocative, place. The temple houses a number of sacred tanks, into which some daring souls jump from the adjacent cliffs. The water is claimed to be several elephants deep and fed from a spring that falls through the mouth of a sculpted cow.

There are some original frescos in reasonable condition in a chamber at the end of the bottom pool, including those depicting athletic feats, the maharaja playing polo, and the exploits of Krishna and the *gopis* (milkmaids). It is also known as the Monkey Temple and you will find hundreds of monkeys living here – bold and aggressive macaques and more graceful and tolerable langurs. You can purchase peanuts at the gate to feed to them, but be prepared to be mobbed by teeth-baring primates.

Although only a few kilometres east of the City Palace, Galta is about 10km by road from central Jaipur. An autorickshaw should charge around ₹500 return with waiting time, a taxi will charge at least ₹800.

On the ridge above Galta is the Surya Mandir (Temple of the Sun God), which rises 100m above Jaipur and can be seen from the eastern side of the city. A 2.5km-long walking trail climbs up to the temple from Suraj Pol, or you can walk up from the Galta side. There are hazy views over the humming city.

🏃 Activities

A few hotels will let you use their pool for a daily fee; try those at Narain Niwas Palace

Hotel (p122) and **Mansingh Hotel** (Sansar Chandra Marg; nonguests ₹350; ⊙7am-8pm).

Kerala Ayurveda Kendra AYURVEDA
(☑0141-4022446; www.keralaayurvedakendra.com; 32 Indra Colony, Bani Park; ⊙9am-9pm) Is Jaipur making your nerves jangle? Get help through ayurvedic massage and therapy. Treatments include *sirodhara* (₹1750/2800 for 50/90 minutes), where medicated oil is steadily streamed over your forehead to reduce stress, tone the brain and help with sleep disorders. Massages (male therapist for male clients and female for female clients) cost from ₹900 for 50 minutes. It offers free transport to/from your hotel.

Jhalana Leopard Safari SAFARI
(☑9929400009; https://jhalanaleopard.business.site; Jhalana Forest Reserve; Indian per 6-seat 4WD ₹4500, foreigner per person ₹2500; ⊙6.45-9.30am & 3-5.50pm winter, 5.45-8.50am & 3.45-6.15pm summer) Jhalana Leopard Safari has the sole contract for running safaris in this city-edge forest reserve. The reserve is only 21 sq km, surrounded by human settlement, and the habitat for more than 20 leopards. The 2¾-hour safaris don't necessarily venture very far from the front gate but we can confirm that leopards can be spotted less than 100m from this gate – and effortlessly jumping over the 2m high fences! The reserve is also home to hyenas, monkeys, deer and nilgai (blue bull), and is a prime birdwatching destination, especially in summer.

The price for foreigners includes hotel transfer to/from Jaipur and a seat in a shared 4WD.

Yog Sadhna Ashram YOGA
(☑9314011884; Bapu Nagar; ⊙closed Tue) Free classes take place among trees off University Rd (near Rajasthan University) and incorporate breathing exercises, yoga asanas (postures) and exercise. Most of the classes are in Hindi, but some English is spoken in the 7.30am to 9.30am class. You can visit for individual classes, or register for longer courses.

Madhavanand Girls College YOGA
(C19 Behari Marg, Bani Park; ⊙6-7am) This college runs free casual yoga classes every day in both Hindi and English. Very convenient if you happen to be lodging in Bani Park – the college is next door to Madhuban hotel.

🍴 Courses

Jaipur Cooking Classes COOKING
(☑9928097288; www.jaipurcookingclasses.com; 33 Gyan Vihar, Nirman Nagar; class veg/nonveg from ₹2100/3800) Popular cooking classes with chef Lokesh Mathur, who has more than 25 years' experience working in the restaurant and hotel business. Classes cover both classic dishes and Rajasthani menus and can be veg or nonveg. After a three-hour lesson, you sit down for a lunch or dinner of what you've prepared. Lokesh's kitchen is outside the western outskirts of Jaipur, near Ajmer Rd. Call ahead for exact directions for your driver.

RAJASTHAN JAIPUR

TOP STATE FESTIVALS

Jaisalmer Desert Festival (⊙Jan/Feb) A chance for moustache twirlers to compete in the Mr Desert contest.

Gangaur (⊙Mar/Apr) A festival honouring Shiva and Parvati's love, celebrated statewide but with fervour in Jaipur.

Mewar Festival (⊙Mar/Apr) Udaipur's version of Gangaur, with free cultural events and a colourful procession down to the lake.

Teej (⊙Jul/Aug) Jaipur and Bundi honour the arrival of the monsoon and Shiva and Parvati's marriage.

Dussehra Mela (⊙Oct/Nov) Commemorates Rama's victory over Ravana (the demon king of Lanka). It's a spectacular time to visit Kota – the huge fair features 22m-tall firecracker-stuffed effigies.

Marwar Festival (⊙Sep/Oct; p182) Celebrates Rajasthani heroes through music and dance; one day is held in Jodhpur, the other in Osian.

Pushkar Camel Fair (⊙Oct/Nov; p144) The most famous festival in the state; it's a massive congregation of camels, horses and cattle, pilgrims and tourists.

Dhamma Thali Vipassana Meditation Centre
HEALTH & WELLBEING

(☑ 0141-2680220; www.thali.dhamma.org; courses by donation) This serene *vipassana* meditation centre is tucked away in the hilly countryside near Galta, a 12km drive east of the city centre. It runs courses in meditation for both beginners and more advanced students throughout the year. Courses are usually for 10 days, during which you must observe noble silence – no communication with others.

👉 Tours

Cyclin' Jaipur
CYCLING

(☑ 7728060956; www.cyclinjaipur.com; 3hr tour ₹2000; ⏱ tour 6.45-9.45am) Get up early to beat the traffic for a tour of the Pink City by bike, exploring the hidden lanes, temples, markets and food stalls of Jaipur. It's a fun way to learn about the workings and culture of the Old City before the gridlock and fumes set in. Breakfast (street food) and refreshments during the tour are included, and helmets are provided on demand.

Tours start at Karnot Mahal, on Ramganj Chaupar in the Old City. Tailor-made walking and food tours are also available.

Vintage Jeep Tour
TOURS

(☑ 0141-2373700, 9829404055; www.pearlpalace heritage.com/exclusive-vintage-jeep-tour-jaipur; Lane 2, 54 Gopal Bari; per person ₹2500; ⏱ 9am-5.30pm) A fun way to explore Jaipur's major sights (including Amber and the City Palace) is by jeep – a genuine US Army 1942 Ford Jeep. With a dedicated driver and a guide on board, you are guaranteed to be part of a small tour group (maximum three guests), giving great flexibility. Admission prices and lunch costs are not included.

RTDC Transport Unit
TOURS

(☑ 0141-2371641; www.rtdctourism.rajasthan. gov.in; RTDC Hotel Gangaur, Sanjay Marg; half-/full-day tour ₹400/500; ⏱ 8am-6.30pm Mon-Sat) Full-day tours take in all the major sights of Jaipur (including Amber Fort), with a lunch break at Nahargarh. The lunch break can be as late as 3pm, so have a big breakfast. Rushed half-day tours (8am to 1pm, 11.30am to 4.30pm, and 1.30pm to 6.30pm) still squeeze in Amber. The tour price doesn't include admission charges.

Departing at 6.30pm, the **Pink City by Night** tour (₹700) explores several well-known sights (outside viewing only) and includes dinner at Nahargarh.

Tours depart from Jaipur train station; the company also picks up and takes bookings from the RTDC Hotel Teej, RTDC Hotel Gangaur and the tourist information office at the Jaipur Railway Station.

🛏 Sleeping

Jaipur accommodation pretty much covers all bases, and travellers are spoiled for choice in all budget categories. From May to September, most midrange and top-end hotels offer bargain rates, dropping prices by 25% to 50%.

🏨 Around MI Road

⭐ Hotel Pearl Palace
HOTEL $

(☑ 0141-2373700, 9414236323; www.hotelpearl palace.com; Hari Kishan Somani Marg, Hathroi Fort; r ₹1310-1240; ❄ 🛜) The legendary Pearl Palace continues to exceed guests' expectations with excellent rooms that defy their tariffs. There's quite a range of rooms to choose from, and all are spotless and stylish, with modern amenities and bathrooms. Services include money changing, city tours and travel arrangements, and the hotel features the excellent Peacock Rooftop Restaurant (p122). Advance booking is recommended.

Karni Niwas
GUESTHOUSE $

(☑ 9929777488, 0141-2365433; www.hotelkarni niwas.com; C5 Motilal Atal Marg; r ₹850-1000, with AC ₹1650; ❄ @ 🛜) This friendly hotel has clean, cool and comfortable rooms, though mattresses may be a bit thin. There's no restaurant, but there is a kitchen and relaxing plant-decked terraces to enjoy room service on. And being so central, restaurants aren't far away. The owner shuns commissions for rickshaw drivers; free pick-up from the train or bus station is available.

Jaipur Janta
HOSTEL $

(☑ 9829040897; www.jaipurjanta.com; 3 Jalupura Scheme, Gopinath Marg; dm ₹350-600; ❄ 🛜) This sparkling, spacious and relaxing hostel comes from the folks at Arya Niwas, and is adjacent to another of their concerns: Jai Niwas. There's a kitchen for guest use, and courses, such as cooking, are available. It has a shoes-off policy inside, but there are lockers – and shoe covers if you want to stay shod. Book direct for a discount.

Roadhouse Hostel Jaipur
HOSTEL $

(☑ 7313301301; www.roadhousehostels.com; D-76 Prithviraj Rd; dm/s/d ₹300/1000/1200; ❄ 🛜)

This bright and friendly hostel is in a quiet residential part of town, but it's not too far from all the restaurants on MI Rd. Six- and eight-bed dorms are spotless and air-conditioned and there are a couple of private rooms. There is a free-use kitchen and games room, and management will help with transport tickets.

There's a handy rickshaw stand at the end of the road.

★ **Atithi Guest House** GUESTHOUSE $$
(☎ 0141-2378679; www.atithijaipur.com; 1 Park House Scheme Rd; s/d ₹1344/1456, with AC ₹1680/1904; ❄@🛜) This nicely presented modern guesthouse, well situated between MI and Station Rds, offers strikingly clean, simple rooms dotted around a quiet courtyard. It's central but peaceful, and the service is friendly and helpful. Vegetarian meals are available (the quality coffee, tea, bakery offerings and thali are particularly recommended), and you can have a drink on the very pleasant rooftop terrace.

★ **Hotel Arya Niwas** HOTEL $$
(☎ 0141-2372456; www.aryaniwas.com; Sansar Chandra Marg; s/d incl breakfast from ₹1700/2350; ❄@🛜) Just off Sansar Chandra Marg, this very popular travellers' haunt has a travel desk, book and gift shop, and a range of in-house activities, from block printing and cooking to yoga lessons. The spotless rooms vary in layout and size so check out a few. Outside, there's an extensive wide verandah facing a soothing expanse of lawn to loll about on.

For a hotel of 125 rooms it is very well run with several eco initiatives, including reducing plastic wherever possible and providing clean drinking water on every floor and a reusable bottle in every room. The vegetarian restaurant also has espresso coffee.

Pearl Palace Heritage HOTEL $$
(☎ 0141-4106599, 9772558855; www.pearlpalaceheritage.com; Lane 2, 54 Gopal Bari; r ₹4720-5900; ❄🛜) The second hotel for the successful Pearl Palace (p118) team is an upper-mid-range property, featuring a lift, 5-star hotel linen and some extraordinary decor. Stone carvings adorn the corridors and each spacious room vibrantly recreates an individual Indian theme, such as a village hut, a Rajput fort, or a mirror-lined palace boudoir. Modern facilities have been carefully integrated into the appealing traditional designs.

The AC top floor restaurant specialises in Indian regional cuisines, but also has some Continental comfort food.

All Seasons Homestay HOMESTAY $$
(☎ 9460387055, 0141-2369443; www.allseasonshomestayjaipur.com; 63 Hathroi Fort; s/d from ₹2128/2240; ❄🛜) Ranjana and her husband Dinesh run this welcoming homestay in their lovely bungalow on a quiet backstreet behind Hathroi Fort. There are 10 pristine guest rooms, two of which have small kitchens for longer stays. There's a pleasant lawn, home-cooked meals and cooking lessons. Advance booking is recommended.

Nana-ki-Haveli HERITAGE HOTEL $$
(☎ 0141-2615502; www.nanakihaveli.com; Fateh Tiba; r ₹1800-3000; ❄🛜) Tucked away off Moti Dungri Marg is this tranquil place with comfortable, simple rooms decorated with a few traditional flourishes. It's hosted by a lovely family, and feels more like a homestay than a hotel, and is a good choice for solo female travellers. It's fronted by a relaxing lawn and offers home-style cooking and discounted rooms in summer.

Alsisar Haveli HERITAGE HOTEL $$$
(☎ 0141-2368290; www.alsisar.com; Sansar Chandra Marg; s/d incl breakfast from ₹7605/10,530; ❄@🛜🏊) This heritage hotel housed in a gracious 19th-century mansion is set in beautiful green gardens, and has a lovely swimming pool and grand dining room. It's a veritable oasis. Its bedrooms don't disappoint either, with elegant Rajput arches and antique furnishings. Perhaps a little impersonal because it hosts many tour groups; occasional discounts can be found by booking directly online.

Hotel Diggi Palace HERITAGE HOTEL $$$
(☎ 0141-2373091; www.hoteldiggipalace.com; off Sawai Ram Singh Rd; s/d/ste incl breakfast from ₹6490/7080/8790; ❄🛜🏊) About 1km south of Ajmer Gate, this former residence of the

---

SLEEPING PRICE RANGES

Accommodation prices refer to a double room with bathroom in Rajasthan and are inclusive of taxes, unless otherwise noted:

$ less than ₹1500

$$ ₹1500–₹5000

$$$ more than ₹5000

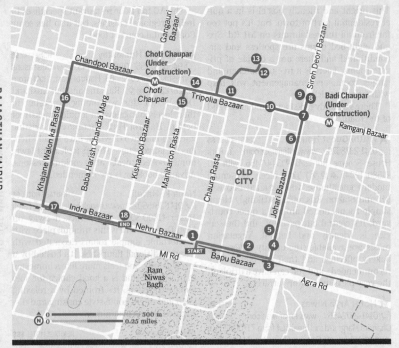

🏃 City Walk
Pink City

START NEW GATE
END AJMER GATE
LENGTH 4.5KM; THREE TO FIVE HOURS

Entering the old city from ❶ **New Gate**, turn right into ❷ **Bapu Bazaar**, inside the city wall. Brightly coloured bolts of fabric, jootis (traditional, pointy-toed, slip-in shoes) and aromatic perfumes make the street a favourite destination for Jaipur's women. At the end of the bazaar you'll come to ❸ **Sanganeri Gate**. Turn left into ❹ **Johari Bazaar**, the jewellery market, where you will find jewellers, goldsmiths and artisans doing glazed meenakari (enamelwork), a speciality of Jaipur.

Continuing north you'll pass the famous ❺ **LMB Hotel**; check out the sweets counter, the ❻ **Jama Masjid**, with its tall minarets, and the bustling ❼ **Badi Chaupar** public square. Be very careful crossing the road here; the works for the underground metro have added to the usual mayhem. To the north is ❽ **Sireh Deori Bazaar**, also known as Hawa Mahal Bazaar. The name is derived from the spectacular ❾ **Hawa Mahal** (p115), a short distance to the

north. Turning left on ❿ **Tripolia Bazaar**, you will see a lane leading to the entrance to the Hawa Mahal. A few hundred metres west is the ⓫ **Tripolia Gate**. This is the main entrance to the ⓬ **Jantar Mantar** (p115) and ⓭ **City Palace** (p113), but only the maharaja's family may enter here. The public entrance is via the less ostentatious Atishpol (Stable Gate), a little further along.

After visiting the City Palace complex, head back to Tripolia Bazaar and resume your walk west past ⓮ **Isarlat** (p116), which is well worth the climb for the view. Cross the bazaar (when safe) at the minaret and head west. The next lane on the left is ⓯ **Maniharon Rasta**, the best place to buy colourful lac (resin) bangles.

Back on Tripolia Bazaar, continue west to cross Choti Chaupar to Chandpol Bazaar until you reach a traffic light. Turn left into ⓰ **Khajane Walon ka Rasta**, where you'll find marble and stoneware carvers at work. Continue south until you reach a broad road just inside the city wall, ⓱ **Indra Bazaar**. Follow the road east towards ⓲ **Ajmer Gate**, which marks the end of the tour.

thakur (nobleman) of Diggi is surrounded by vast, tree-shaded lawns and is refreshingly peaceful. All rooms are spacious with large bathrooms – you don't get significantly more luxury or room size for choosing a more expensive suite. It's a bit faded and well worn but genuinely friendly.

Bani Park

The Bani Park area is relatively peaceful, away from main roads, but only about 2km west of the Old City (northwest of MI Rd).

Vinayak Guest House   HOTEL $
(☑ 0141-2205260, 9829867297; vinayakguesthouse@yahoo.co.in; 4 Kabir Marg, Bani Park; dm ₹299, r ₹500-1100; ❀⏾) This welcoming guesthouse is in a small, quiet street behind busy Kabir Marg, very convenient to the train station. The AC dorm features big lockers and a hot shower. There is a variety of different rooms and tariffs; those with AC also have great renovated bathrooms and are your best option. The vegetarian restaurant on the rooftop gets good reports.

★Madhuban   HOTEL $$
(☑ 0141-2200033; www.madhuban.net; D237 Behari Marg; s/d/ste incl breakfast from ₹2460/2800/4250; ❀@⏾❄) Madhuban has bright, antique-furnished, spotlessly clean rooms, plus a private enclosed garden for alfresco meals. The vibrantly frescoed restaurant serves Rajasthani specialities in addition to continental and North Indian dishes, and sits beside the courtyard plunge pool. The relatively peaceful locale of Bani Park makes this place a comfortable stay. Bus and train station pick-up available.

Dera Rawatsar   HOTEL $$
(☑ 0141-2200770; www.derarawatsar.com; D194 Vijay Path, Bani Park; r incl breakfast ₹4500-5500, ste ₹8000; ❀@⏾❄) Situated in a quiet suburban street and yet close to the bus station, this hotel is managed by three generations of women of a Bikaner noble family. The hotel has a range of lovely decorated rooms, sunny courtyards, and offers home-style Indian meals. It is a relaxing and gracious option for all travellers, and a particularly good choice for families and female travellers.

Hotel Anuraag Villa   HOTEL $$
(☑ 0141-2201679; www.anuraagvilla.com; D249 Devi Marg; r ₹1344, with AC from ₹2352; ❀⏾) This quiet and comfortable option has no

fuss, spacious rooms and an extensive lawn where you can find some quiet respite from the hassles of sightseeing. It has a highly commended vegetarian restaurant with its kitchen on view, and efficient, helpful staff.

Jaipur Inn   HOTEL $$
(☑ 0141-2201121, 9829013660; www.jaipurinn.com; B17 Shiv Marg, Bani Park; r from ₹1250, with AC from ₹1500; ❀⏾) A long-time budget travellers' favourite offering an assortment of eclectic and individual rooms. Inspect a few before settling in. Plus points include the helpful manager and several common areas where travellers can make a coffee, use the wi-fi, or grab a meal. Yoga and Bollywood dance lessons can be had on the rooftop.

Hotel Meghniwas   GUESTHOUSE $$$
(☑ 0141-4060100; www.meghniwas.com; C9 Sawai Jai Singh Hwy; r/ste ₹5900/7670; ❀⏾❄) In a building erected by Brigadier Singh in 1950 and run by his gracious descendants, this very welcoming hotel has comfortable and spotless rooms, with traditional carved-wood furniture and leafy outlooks. The standard rooms are spacious, and although it's on a major road it is set well back behind a leafy garden. There's a first-rate restaurant and an inviting pool.

Jas Vilas   GUESTHOUSE $$$
(☑ 0141-2204902; www.jasvilas.com; C9 Sawai Jai Singh Hwy; s/d incl breakfast from ₹6730/7670; ❀⏾❄) This small but impressive hotel was built in 1950 and is still run by the same charming family. It offers spacious rooms, most of which face the large sparkling pool set in a romantic courtyard. Three garden-facing rooms are wheelchair accessible. In addition to the relaxing courtyard and garden, there is a cosy dining room and helpful management.

Shahpura House   HERITAGE HOTEL $$$
(☑ 0141-4089100; www.shahpura.com; D257 Devi Marg; r/ste from ₹11,520/14,800; ❀⏾❄) Elaborately built and decorated in traditional style, this heritage hotel offers immaculate rooms, some with balconies, featuring murals, coloured-glass lamps, flatscreen TVs, and even ceilings covered in small mirrors (in the suites). This rambling palace has a durbar (royal court) hall with a huge chandelier, and a cosy cocktail bar.

There's also an inviting swimming pool and an elegant rooftop terrace restaurant that stages cultural shows.

Old City

Hotel Sweet Dream
HOTEL $

(☏ 0141-2314409; www.hotelsweetdreamjaipur. in; Nehru Bazaar; s/d ₹1000/1455, with AC from ₹1900/2240; 图 ⚛) Probably the best option right inside the Old City, and one of Jaipur's better budget hotels. Many of the rooms have been renovated and enlarged, so inspect more than one room. There are increasing amenities the higher up the price scale (or the rickety elevator) you go. There's a bar plus an excellent rooftop terrace restaurant.

Hotel Bissau Palace
HERITAGE HOTEL $$

(☏ 0141-2304391; www.bissaupalace.com; outside Chandpol; r ₹3540-7080; 图 ⚛ ⚛) This is a worthy choice if you want to stay in a palace. It's located just outside the city walls, less than 10 minutes' walk from Chandpol (a gateway to the Old City). There's a swimming pool, a handsome wood-panelled library and three restaurants. The hotel has oodles of heritage atmosphere, with antique furnishings and mementos.

Rambagh Environs

Rambagh Palace
HERITAGE HOTEL $$$

(☏ 0141-2385700; www.tajhotels.com; Bhawani Singh Marg; r from ₹57,220; 图 @ ⚛ ⚛) This splendid palace was once the Jaipur pad of Maharaja Man Singh II and his glamorous wife Gayatri Devi. Veiled in hectares of manicured gardens, the hotel – run by the luxury Taj Group brand – has fantastic views across the immaculate lawns. More expensive rooms are naturally the most sumptuous.

Nonguests can join in the magnificence by dining in the lavish restaurants or drinking tea on the gracious verandah. At least treat yourself to a drink at the spiffing Polo Bar (p124).

Narain Niwas Palace Hotel
HERITAGE HOTEL $$$

(☏ 0141-2561291; www.hotelnarainniwas.com; Narain Singh Rd; s/d incl breakfast from ₹8500/8800; P 图 @ ⚛ ⚛) In Kanota Bagh, just south of the city, this genuine heritage hotel has genuine heritage splendour. There's a lavish dining room with liveried staff, an old-fashioned verandah on which to drink tea, and antiques galore. The standard rooms are in a garden wing and aren't as spacious as the high-ceilinged deluxe rooms (₹14,720), which vary in atmosphere and amenities.

A new wing of deluxe rooms features a lift and modern rooms with a few tasteful traditional flourishes. Out back you'll find a large secluded pool (nonguests ₹300 for two hours between 8am and 4pm – after 4pm guests only), a heavenly spa, and sprawling lawns and tree-shaded gardens adorned with strutting peacocks.

✗ Eating

✗ Around MI Road

Indian Coffee House
CAFE $

(MI Rd; coffee ₹27-46, snacks & mains ₹25-60; ⊘ 6am-9pm) Set back from the street, down an easily missed alley, this traditional coffee house (a venerable co-op–owned institution) offers a pleasant cup of filtered coffee in very relaxed surroundings. Aficionados of Indian Coffee Houses will not be disappointed by the fan-cooled, spare, pale-yellow ambience. Inexpensive *pakoras* (deep-fried battered vegetables) and dosas grace the menu.

Old Takeaway the Kebab Shop
KEBAB $

(242 MI Rd; kebabs ₹90-180; ⊘ 6-11pm) One of several similarly named roadside kebab shops on this stretch of MI Rd, this one (next to the mosque) is the original (so we're told) and the best (we agree). It knocks up outstanding tandoori kebabs, including paneer, mutton and tandoori chicken. Like the sign says: a house of delicious nonveg corner.

Jal Mahal
ICE CREAM $

(MI Rd; cups & cones ₹30-120; ⊘ 10am-11pm) This great little ice-cream parlour has been going since 1952. There are around 50 flavours to choose from, but if it's hot outside, it's hard to beat mango. There are also plenty of other ice-cream concoctions, including sundaes and banana splits, many with fanciful names.

Rawat Kachori
SWEETS $

(Station Rd; kachori ₹30, lassi ₹50, sweets per kg ₹350-850; ⊘ 6am-10pm) Head to this popular takeaway with an attached restaurant for delicious Indian sweets and famous *kachori* (potato masala in a fried pastry case), a scrumptious savoury snack. A salty or sweet lassi should fill you up for the afternoon.

★ Peacock Rooftop Restaurant
MULTICUISINE $$

(☏ 0141-2373700; Hotel Pearl Palace, Hari Kishan Somani Marg; mains ₹150-390; ⊘ 7am-11pm) This multilevel rooftop restaurant at the Hotel Pearl Palace gets rave reviews for its excellent yet inexpensive cuisine (Indian, Chinese and continental) and fun ambience. The attentive service, whimsical furnishings and romantic view towards Hathroi Fort make it a first-rate restaurant. In addition to the dinner menu, there are healthy breakfasts and great-value burgers, pizzas and thalis for lunch.

It's wise to make a booking for dinner.

Four Seasons
MULTICUISINE $$

(☑ 0141-2375450; D43A Subhash Marg; mains ₹230-300; ⊙ 11am-10.45pm; ❋ ☑) Four Seasons is one of Jaipur's best vegetarian restaurants. It's a popular place with dining on two levels and a glass wall to the busy kitchens. There's a great range of dishes on offer, including tasty Rajasthani specialities, South Indian dosas, Chinese fare, and a selection of thalis and pizzas. Note that the Italian menu starts at 1pm. No alcohol.

Anokhi Café
INTERNATIONAL $$

(☑ 0141-4007245; 2nd fl, KK Sq, C-11 Prithviraj Marg; mains ₹250-350; ⊙ 10am-7.30pm; ☎ ☑) This serene and cool cafe with a fashionable organic vibe is the perfect place to come if you're craving a crunchy, well-dressed salad, a quiche or a thickly filled sandwich – or just a respite from the hustle with a latte or an iced tea. Whole fresh loaves of organic bread can be also be purchased.

Handi Restaurant
NORTH INDIAN $$

(☑ 0141-4917115; MI Rd; mains ₹240-440; ⊙ noon-11pm) Handi has been satisfying customers since 1967, with scrumptious tandoori and barbecue dishes and rich Mughlai curries. In the evenings it sets up a smoky kebab stall at the entrance to the restaurant. Good vegetarian items are also available. The rooftop section (6pm to 11pm) has a bar.

It's opposite the main post office, tucked at the back of the Maya Mansions.

Surya Mahal
SOUTH INDIAN $$

(☑ 0141-2362811; MI Rd; mains ₹150-320, thali ₹240-350; ⊙ 8am-11pm; ❋ ☑) This popular option near Panch Batti specialises in South Indian vegetarian food; try the tasty *dhal makhani* (black lentils and red kidney beans). There are also Chinese and Italian dishes, and good ice creams, sundaes and cool drinks. No alcohol.

Natraj
INDIAN $$

(☑ 0141-2375804; MI Rd; mains ₹180-250, thali ₹270-550; ⊙ 8.30am-10.45pm; ❋ ☑) Not far from Panch Batti is this classy vegetarian place, which has an extensive menu featuring North Indian, Continental and Chinese cuisine and booth seats. Diners are blown away by the potato-encased 'vegetable bomb' curry. There's a good selection of thalis and South Indian food as well as a great array of Indian sweets.

★ Niro's
INDIAN $$$

(☑ 0141-2374493; www.nirosindia.com; MI Rd; mains ₹400-580; ⊙ 10am-11pm; ❋) Established in 1949, Niro's is a long-standing favourite on MI Rd that, like a good wine, only improves with age. Escape the chaos of the street by ducking into its cool, clean, mirror-ceilinged sanctum to savour veg and nonveg Indian cuisine with professional service. Classic Chinese and Continental food are available, but the Indian menu is definitely the pick.

Even locals rave about the butter chicken and rogan josh. Beer and wine are served.

Handi Fusion
MULTICUISINE $$$

(☑ 0141-4096969; Maya Mansions, MI Rd; mains ₹285-510, thali veg/nonveg ₹560/715; ⊙ noon-11pm; ❋) Handi Fusion is casual, verging on elegant, and welcoming, with an army of attentive waiters and a bar serving cold beer and wine. It offers generous helpings of excellent veg and nonveg Indian cuisine, including aromatic Rajasthani specials such as the Jaisalmeri *laal maas* (mutton curry). Continental and Chinese food is also on offer, but the curry-and-beer combo is hard to beat.

Jaipur Modern Kitchen
MEDITERRANEAN $$$

(☑ 0141-4113000; www.jaipurmodern.com; 51 Sardar Patel Marg, C-Scheme; mains ₹350-600; ⊙ 11am-10.30pm; ❋ ☑) ⊘ Within the eponymous homewares and fashion showroom (p126) is this super Mediterranean cafe showcasing organic ingredients and supporting local sustainable agriculture. The tasty pizzas, pasta and wraps are all made in-house, and gluten-free dishes are available. There's a special emphasis on locally grown quinoa; the Q menu features soups, appetisers, mains and desserts, all containing the versatile seed.

Little Italy
ITALIAN $$$

(☑ 0141-4022444; 3rd fl, KK Sq, Prithviraj Marg; mains ₹320-500; ⊙ noon-10pm; ❋) The best Italian restaurant in Jaipur, Little Italy is part of a national chain that offers excellent vegetarian pasta, risotto and wood-fired pizzas in contemporary surroundings. The menu is extensive and includes some Mexican items, plus first-rate Italian desserts. It's licensed and there's an attached sister concern, Little India, with an Indian and Chinese menu.

RAJASTHAN JAIPUR

✕ Old City

Pandit Kulfi
ICE CREAM $

(10-111 Sireh Dion Mahal (Hawa Mahal Rd), Old City; cone plain/flavoured ₹20/30; ⊙ 11am-11.30pm) Despite the crusty exterior this tiny shop has a delightfully creamy centre. Pandit gets rave reviews for its conical *kulfi* (firm-textured ice cream) on a stick. Flavours include pistachio, chocolate, custard apple, mango and *paan* (betel nut). If you are here around 4pm you can see the *kulfi* being poured into the conical moulds and set in a box of salted ice.

Mohan
INDIAN $

(144-5 Nehru Bazaar; mains ₹30-150, thali ₹85; ⊙ 9am-10.30pm; ✑) Tiny Mohan is easy to miss: it's a few steps down from the footpath on the corner of the street. It's basic, cheap and a bit grubby, but the vegetarian thalis, curries (half-plate and full plate available) and snacks are freshly cooked and very popular.

LMB
INDIAN $$

(✑ 0141-2565844; Johari Bazaar; mains ₹230-390; ⊙ 8am-11pm; ✳✑) Laxmi Misthan Bhandar, LMB to you and me, is a vegetarian restaurant in the Old City that's been going strong since 1954. A welcoming air-conditioned refuge from frenzied Johari Bazaar, LMB is also an institution with its singular decor, attentive waiters and extensive sweet counter. Now it is no longer sattvik (pure vegetarian), you can order meals with onion and garlic.

Hotel Sweet Dream
MULTICUISINE $$

(✑ 0141-2314409; www.hotelsweetdreamjaipur.in; Nehru Bazaar; mains ₹135-290; ✳) This hotel in the Old City has a splendid restaurant on the roof with views down to bustling Nehru Bazaar. It's a great place to break the shopping spree and grab a light lunch or a refreshing *makhania* lassi (a filling, saffron-flavoured lassi). The menu includes pizza and Chinese, but the Indian is best.

🍷 Drinking & Nightlife

★Lassiwala
CAFE

(MI Rd; lassi small/large ₹30/60; ⊙ from 7.30am) This famous, much-imitated institution is a simple place that whips up fabulous, creamy lassis in clay cups. They close when sold out – so get here early to avoid disappointment! Will the real Lassiwala please stand up? It's the one that says 'Shop 312' and 'Since 1944', directly next to the alleyway. Imitators spread to the right as you face it.

★Curious Life
CAFE

(✑ 0141-2229877; www.facebook.com/curiouslife coffeeroasters; P25 Yudhisthira Marg, C-Scheme; coffees from ₹150; ⊙ 9am-10pm; ☏) The latest coffee trends brew away in this showcase of Indian hipsterhood. Single-origin, espresso, French press, AeroPress, V60 pour over – you name it, you'll find it brewing here among the predominantly 20-something crowd. There are also smoothies, shakes, pancakes and muffins. The coffee chemistry going on behind the counter borders on the obsessive – just how the customers like it.

★Bar Palladio
BAR

(✑ 0141-2565556; www.bar-palladio.com; Narain Niwas Palace Hotel, Narain Singh Rd; cocktails from ₹600; ⊙ 6-11pm) This cool bar-restaurant has an extensive drinks list and an Italian food menu (mains ₹360 to ₹420). The vivid blue theme of the romantic Orientalist interior flows through to candlelit outdoor seating, making this a very relaxing place to sip a drink, snack on bruschetta and enjoy a conversation. Il Teatro is an occasional live-music event at the bar – see the website for dates.

Polo Bar
BAR

(Rambagh Palace Hotel, Bhawan Singh Marg; ⊙ noon-midnight) This spiffing watering hole adorned with polo memorabilia boasts arched, scalloped windows framing the neatly clipped lawns. A bottle of beer costs from ₹400, a glass of wine from ₹600, and cocktails from ₹650. Delicious snacks are also available throughout the day.

100% Rock
BAR

(Hotel Shikha, Yudhishthir Marg, C-Scheme; pint of beer/cocktails from ₹220/380; ⊙ 11am-12.30am; ☏) Attached to, but separate from Hotel Shikha, this is the closest thing there is to a beer garden in Jaipur, with plenty of outdoor seating as well as an overly dim air-con room with a small dance floor. Two-for-one beer and cocktail offers last from opening to 10.30pm, understandably making this popular.

Café Coffee Day
CAFE

(Radisson Hotel, MI Rd; coffees ₹80-150; ⊙ 10am-10pm) The India-wide franchise that successfully delivers espresso, plus the occasional creamy concoction and muffin, has several branches in Jaipur. In addition to this one, sniff out the brews at Paris Point on Sawai Jai Singh Hwy (aka Collectorate Rd), at the Central Museum, and near the exit point at Amber Fort.

☆ Entertainment

Jaipur isn't a big late-night party town, though many of its hotels put on some sort of evening music, dance or puppet show. English-language films are occasionally screened at some cinemas – check the cinemas and local press for details.

★ Raj Mandir Cinema   CINEMA

(📞 0141-2379372; www.therajmandir.com; Baghwandas Marg; tickets ₹150-400; ⊘ reservations 10am-6pm, screenings 12.30pm, 3pm, 6.30pm & 10pm) Just off MI Rd, Raj Mandir is *the* place to go to see a Hindi film in India. This opulent cinema looks like a huge pink cream cake, with a meringue auditorium and a circular foyer somewhere between a temple and Disneyland. Bookings can be made one hour to seven days in advance at window 11.

Chokhi Dhani   LIVE PERFORMANCE

(📞 0141-5165000; www.chokhidhani.com; Tonk Rd; adult/child incl Rajasthani thali from ₹700/400; ⊘ 6-11pm) Chokhi Dhani, meaning 'special village', is a mock Rajasthani village 20km south of Jaipur, and is a fun place to take kids. There are open-air restaurants where you can enjoy a tasty Rajasthani thali, plus a bevy of traditional entertainment – dancers, acrobats, snack stalls – and adventure-park-like activities for kids to swing on, slide down and hide in.

Sawai Mansingh Stadium   CRICKET

(SMS Stadium; Bhawan Singh Marg) The home ground for the local cricket team, the Rajasthan Royals, in the Indian Premier League.

🔒 Shopping

Jaipur is a shopper's paradise. Commercial buyers come here from all over the world to stock up on the amazing range of jewellery, gems, textiles and crafts that come from all over Rajasthan. You'll have to bargain hard, particularly around major tourist sights. Many shops can send your parcels home for you – often for less than if you do it yourself.

The city is still loosely divided into traditional artisans' quarters. Bapu Bazaar is lined with saris and fabrics, and is a good place to buy trinkets. Johari Bazaar and Sireh Deori Bazaar are where many jewellery shops are concentrated, selling gold, silver and highly glazed enamelwork known as meenakari, a Jaipur speciality. You may also find better deals for fabrics with the cotton merchants of Johari Bazaar.

Kishanpol Bazaar is famous for textiles, particularly bandhani (tie-dye). Nehru Bazaar also sells fabric, as well as jootis (traditional, often pointy-toed, slip-in shoes), trinkets and perfume. The best place for bangles is Maniharon Rasta.

Plenty of factories and showrooms are strung along the length of the road to Amber, between Zorawar Singh Gate and the Park Regis Hotel, to catch the tourist traffic. Here you'll find huge emporiums selling block prints, blue pottery, carpets and antiques. Note that these shops are used to busloads of tourists swinging in to blow their cash, so you'll need to wear your bargaining hat.

Rickshaw-wallahs, hotels and travel agents will be getting a hefty cut from any shop they steer you towards. Many unwary visitors get talked into buying things for resale at inflated prices, especially gems. Beware of these get-rich-quick scams.

Rajasthali   ARTS & CRAFTS

(MI Rd; ⊘ 11am-7.30pm Mon-Sat) This state-government-run emporium, opposite Ajmer Gate, is packed with quality Rajasthani artefacts and crafts, including enamelwork, embroidery, pottery, woodwork, jewellery, puppets, block-printed sheets, miniatures, brassware, mirrorwork and more. Scout out prices here before launching into the bazaar; items can be cheaper at the markets, but the

SHOPPING FOR GEMS

Jaipur is famous for precious and semi-precious stones. There are many shops offering bargain prices, but you do need to know your gems. The main gem-dealing area is around the Muslim area of Pahar Ganj, in the southeast of the Old City. Here you can see stones being cut and polished in workshops tucked off narrow backstreets.

One of the oldest scams in India is the gem scam, where tourists are fooled into thinking they can buy gems to sell at a profit elsewhere. To receive an authenticity certificate, you can deposit your gems at the **gem-testing laboratory** (📞 0141-2568221; www.gtljaipur.info; Rajasthan Chamber Bhawan, MI Rd; ⊘ Mon-Sat) between 10am and 4pm, then return the following day between 4pm and 5pm to pick up the certificate. The service costs ₹1050 per stone, or ₹1650 for same-day service, if deposited before 1pm.

quality is often higher at the state emporium for not much more money.

Jaipur Modern FASHION & ACCESSORIES
(☑ 0141-4112000; www.jaipurmodern.com; 51 Sardar Patel Marg, C-Scheme; ⊗ 11am-9pm) This contemporary showroom offers local arts and crafts, clothing, homewares, stationery and fashion accessories. The staff are relaxed (no hard sell here) and if you are not in the mood to shop, there's a great cafe serving organic South Indian coffee and Mediterranean snacks.

Inde Rooh CLOTHING
(☑ 9929442022, 9829404055; www.inderooh. com; Hotel Pearl Palace, Hari Kishan Somani Marg; ⊗ 10.30am-10.30pm) This tiny outlet in the Hotel Pearl Palace highlights the talents of Jaipur's traditional block printers blended with contemporary design. Handmade and stitched, the quality and value of the women's and menswear compares well with Jaipur's more famous fashion houses. Homewares are also available.

Anokhi CLOTHING, TEXTILES
(www.anokhi.com; 2nd fl, KK Sq, C-11 Prithviraj Marg; ⊗ 10am-8pm) Anokhi is a classy, upmarket boutique selling stunning high-quality textiles such as block-printed fabrics, tablecloths, bed covers, cosmetic bags and scarves, as well as a range of well-designed, beautifully made clothing that combines Indian and Western influences. There's a wonderful organic cafe on the premises and a decent bookshop in the same building.

Silver Shop JEWELLERY
(Hotel Pearl Palace, Hari Kishan Somani Marg; ⊗ 6-10pm) A trusted jewellery shop backed by the Hotel Pearl Palace, which hosts the store. A money-back guarantee is offered on all items. Find it under the peacock canopy in the hotel's Peacock Rooftop Restaurant.

ⓘ Information

MEDICAL SERVICES
Most hotels can arrange a doctor on-site.

Santokba Durlabhji Memorial Hospital (SDMH; ☑ 0141-2566251; www.sdmh.in; Bhawan Singh Marg) Private hospital, with 24-hour emergency department, helpful staff and clear bilingual signage. Consultancy fee ₹400.

Sawai Mansingh Hospital (SMS Hospital; ☑ 0141-2518597, 0141-2518222; Sawai Ram Singh Rd) State-run, but part of Soni Hospitals Group (www.sonihospitals.com). Before 3pm,

outpatients go to the CT & MRI Centre; after 3pm, go to the adjacent Emergency Department.

MONEY
There are plenty of places to change money, including numerous hotels, and masses of ATMs, most of which accept foreign cards.

Thomas Cook (☑ 0141-2360940; Jaipur Towers, MI Rd; ⊗ 9.30am-6pm) Changes cash and travellers cheques.

POST
DHL Express (☑ 0141-2361159; www.dhl.co.in; G8, Geeta Enclave, Vinobha Marg; ⊗ 10am-8pm) Look for the subbranch on MI Rd then walk down the lane beside it to find DHL Express. For parcels, the first kilogram is expensive, but each 500g thereafter is cheap. All packaging is included in the price. Credit cards and cash accepted.

Main Post Office (☑ 0141-2368740; MI Rd; ⊗ 8am-7.45pm Mon-Fri, 10am-5.45pm Sat) A cost-effective and efficient institution, though the back-and-forth can infuriate. Parcel-packing-wallahs outside the post office must first pack, stitch and wax seal your parcel for a small fee before sending.

TOURIST INFORMATION
Jaipur Vision and *Jaipur City Guide* are two useful, inexpensive booklets available at bookshops and some hotel lobbies (where they are free). They feature up-to-date listings, maps, local adverts and features.

RTDC Tourist Office (☑ 0141-5110598; www. rajasthantourism.gov.in; Paryatan Bhavan, Sanjay Marg; ⊗ 9.30am-6pm Mon-Sat) has maps and brochures on Jaipur and Rajasthan. Additional branches at the **airport** (☑ 0141-2725708; ⊗ 9am-5pm Mon-Fri) and the **train station** (☑ 0141-2315714; Platform 1; ⊗ 24hr).

ⓘ Getting There & Away

AIR
Jaipur International Airport (☑ 0141-2550623; www.jaipurairport.com) is located 12km southeast of the city.

It's possible to arrange flights to Jaipur from Europe, the US and other places, via Delhi. A few direct flights run to/from Bangkok and the Gulf.

Air India (www.airindia.com) Daily flights to/from Delhi and Mumbai.

Alliance Air (www.airindia.in/alliance-air.htm) Weekly flights to/from Agra.

IndiGo (www.goindigo.in) Flights to/from Ahmedabad, Bengaluru (Bangalore), Chennai, Delhi, Hyderabad, Kolkata, Mumbai and Pune.

Jet Airways (www.jetairways.com) Flights to Delhi and Mumbai.

MAIN BUSES FROM JAIPUR

DESTINATION	FARE (₹)	DURATION (HR)	FREQUENCY
Agra	265, AC 563	5½	hourly
Ajmer	150, AC 302	2½	at least hourly
Bharatpur	195, AC 410	4½	at least hourly
Bikaner	361, AC 716	5½-7	hourly
Bundi	240	5	hourly
Chittorgarh	339, AC 574	7	hourly
Delhi	274, AC 900	5½	at least hourly
Jaisalmer	593	14	2 daily
Jhunjhunu	181, AC 320	3½-5	half-hourly
Jodhpur	331, AC 713	5½-7	hourly
Kota	252	5	hourly
Mt Abu	AC 919	10½-13	1 daily
Nawalgarh	145, AC 258	2½-4	hourly
Pushkar	160	3	3 daily
Udaipur	420, AC 767	10	at least hourly

SpiceJet (www.spicejet.com) Daily flights to/from Delhi.

Thai Smile (www.thaismileair.com) Three weekly flights to/from Bangkok.

BUS

Rajasthan State Road Transport Corporation (RSRTC, aka Rajasthan Roadways) buses all leave from the **main bus station** (www.rsrtc.rajasthan.gov.in; Station Rd; left luggage per bag per 24hr ₹20), picking up passengers at Narain Singh Circle (where you can also buy tickets). There's a left-luggage office at the main bus station, as well as a prepaid autorickshaw stand.

Ordinary buses are known as 'express' buses, but there are also 'deluxe' and 'super deluxe' buses (coaches), which vary a lot but are generally more expensive and comfortable (usually with AC) than ordinary express buses. Deluxe buses leave from Platform 3, tucked away in the right-hand corner of the bus station. Unlike ordinary express buses, seats can be booked in advance from the **reservation office** (0141-5116032; Main Bus Station; 8am-6pm).

With the exception of those going to Delhi (half-hourly), deluxe buses are much less frequent than ordinary buses.

There are numerous private bus companies servicing Jaipur from outside the main bus station. A useful service for Pushkar is Jai Ambay Travelling Agency (p145), which has a direct, daily, AC coach (₹350) leaving for Pushkar at 9am arriving at 12.30pm.

CAR & MOTORCYCLE

Most hotels and the RTDC tourist office can arrange a car and driver. Depending on the vehicle, costs are ₹9 to ₹12 per kilometre, with a minimum rental rate equivalent to 250km per day. Also expect to pay a ₹200 overnight charge, and note that you will have to pay for the driver to return to Jaipur even if you are not returning.

You can hire, buy or fix a Royal Enfield Bullet (and lesser motorbikes) at **Rajasthan Auto Centre** (9829188064, 0141-2568074; www.royalenfieldsalim.com; Sanganeri Gate, Sanjay Bazaar; 10am-8pm Mon-Sat, to 2pm Sun), the cleanest little motorcycle workshop in India. To hire a 350cc Bullet costs ₹600 per day (including two helmets) within Jaipur.

TRAIN

The **reservation office** (enquiries 131, reservations 135; 8am-2pm & 3-8pm) is to your left as you enter Jaipur train station. It's open for advance reservations only (more than five hours before departure). Join the queue for 'Freedom Fighters and Foreign Tourists' (counter 769).

For same-day travel, buy your ticket at the northern end of the train station at Platform 1, window 10 (closed 6am to 6.30am, 2pm to 2.30pm and 10pm to 10.30pm).

Station facilities on Platform 1 include an RTDC tourist office, Tourism Assistance Force (police), a cloakroom for left luggage (₹20 per bag per 24 hours), retiring rooms, restaurants and air-conditioned waiting rooms for those with 1st-class and 2AC train tickets.

There's a prepaid autorickshaw stand and local taxis at the road entrance to the train station.

Services include the following:

Agra sleeper ₹205, 3½ to 4½ hours, nine daily
Ahmedabad sleeper from ₹370, nine to 13 hours, seven daily (12.30am, 2.20am, 4.25am, 5.35am, 8.40am, 2.20pm and 8.35pm)

MAJOR TRAINS FROM JAIPUR

DESTINATION	TRAIN	DEPARTURE TIME	ARRIVAL TIME	FARE (₹)
Agra (Cantonment)	19666 Udaipur–Kurj Exp	6.15am	11am	205/540 (A)
Agra (Fort)	22987 All–AF Superfast	8.10am	12.20pm	122/430 (C)
Ahmedabad	12958 Adi Sj Rajdhani	12.30am	9.40am	1230/1680 (B)
Ajmer (for Pushkar)	12195 Ajmer–AF Intercity	9.40am	11.50am	110/345 (C)
Bikaner	12307 Howrah–Jodhpur Exp	12.45am	8.15am	275/705 (A)
Delhi (New Delhi)	12016 Ajmer Shatabdi	5.50pm	10.40pm	750/1395 (D)
Delhi (Sarai Rohilla)	12985 Dee Double Decker	6am	10.30am	505/1205 (D)
Jaisalmer	14659 Delhi–JSM Exp	11.45pm	11.45am	350/935 (A)
Jodhpur	22478 Jaipur–Jodhpur SF Exp	6am	11am	515/625 (E)
Sawai Madhopur	12466 Intercity Exp	11.05am	1.15pm	180/325/560 (F)
Udaipur	19665 Jaipur–Udaipur Exp	11pm	6.35am	270/715 (A)

Fares: (A) sleeper/3AC, (B) 3AC/2AC, (C) 2nd-class seat/AC chair, (D) AC chair/1AC, (E) AC chair/3AC, (F) sleeper/AC chair/3AC

Ajmer (for Pushkar) sleeper from ₹100, two hours, 21 daily

Bikaner sleeper ₹275, 6½ to 7½ hours, four daily (12.05am, 5am, 4.15pm and 9.45pm)

Delhi sleeper ₹135, 4½ to six hours, at least nine daily (1am, 2.50am, 4.40am, 5am, 6am, 2.35pm, 4.25pm, 5.50pm and 11.15pm), more on selected days

Jaisalmer sleeper ₹350, 12 hours, three daily (11.10am, 4.15pm and 11.45pm)

Jodhpur sleeper from ₹250, 4½ to six hours, 10 daily (12.45am, 2.45am, 6am, 9.25am, 11.10am, 11.25am, 12.20pm, 5pm, 10.40pm and 11.45pm)

Ranthambhore NP (Sawai Madhopur) sleeper ₹180, two to three hours, at least nine daily (12.30am, 5.40am, 6.40am, 11.05am, 2pm, 4.50pm, 5.35pm, 7.35pm and 8.25pm), more on selected days

Udaipur sleeper ₹270, seven to eight hours, three daily (6.15am, 2pm and 11pm)

ℹ Getting Around

TO/FROM THE AIRPORT

There are no bus services from the airport. An autorickshaw/taxi costs at least ₹350/450. There's a prepaid taxi booth inside the terminal.

AUTORICKSHAW

Autorickshaw drivers at the bus and train stations might just be the pushiest in Rajasthan. If open use the fixed-rate prepaid autorickshaw stands instead. Keep hold of your docket to give to the driver at the end of the journey. In other cases be prepared to bargain hard – expect to pay at least ₹100 from either station to the Old City.

CYCLE-RICKSHAW

You could do your bit for the environment (but not the poor fellow's lungs) by flagging down a lean-limbed cycle-rickshaw rider. Though it can be uncomfortable watching someone pedalling hard to transport you, this *is* how they make a living. A short trip costs about ₹50.

PUBLIC TRANSPORT

Jaipur Metro (☑ 0141-2385790; www.jaipur metrorail.in; fare ₹6-17, 1-day tour card ₹50) currently operates about 10km of track, known as the Pink Line, and nine stations. The track starts southwest of the Pink City in Mansarovar, travels through Civil Lines, and currently terminates at Chandpole. At the time of writing, the continuation of this track through the Pink City from Chandpole to Badi Chaupar was under construction. Fares are between ₹6 (one to two stations) and ₹17 (six to eight stations), plus there is a one-day tour card for ₹50.

TAXI

If you have the apps, both Uber and Ola operate in Jaipur and both offer cheaper services than autorickshaws, without the need to haggle the price down from an unreasonable starting point.

There are unmetered taxis available, which will require negotiating a fare.

Metro Cabs (☑ 0414-4244444; www.metro cabs.in; flagfall incl 2km ₹50, then per km ₹10-12, plus per min ₹1, night surcharge 10pm-6am 25%; ☺ 24hr) can be hired for sightseeing from ₹999.

Around Jaipur

Jaipur's environs have some fascinating historical sites and interesting towns and villages that make great day trips. A comprehensive network of local buses and the ease of finding a taxi or autorickshaw makes getting to these regions simple (if not always comfortable). It's also possible to join a (rather rushed) tour run by the RTDC that includes a commentary on the various places visited.

Amber

The magnificent, formidable, honey-hued fort of Amber (pronounced 'amer'), an ethereal example of Rajput architecture, rises from a rocky mountainside about 11km northeast of Jaipur, and is the city's must-see sight.

Amber was the former capital of Jaipur state. It was built by the Kachhwaha Rajputs, who hailed from Gwalior, in present day Madhya Pradesh, where they reigned for over 800 years. The construction of the fort, which was begun in 1592 by Maharaja Man Singh, the Rajput commander of Akbar's army, was financed with war booty. It was later extended and completed by the Jai Singhs before they moved to Jaipur on the plains below.

The town of Amber, below the fort, is also worth visiting, especially the Anokhi Museum of Hand Printing. From the museum you can walk around the ancient town to the restored Panna Meena Baori (step-well) and Jagat Siromani Temple (known locally as the Meera Temple).

◉ Sights

★ Amber Fort
FORT

(Indian/foreigner ₹100/500, night entry ₹100, guide ₹200, audio guide ₹200-250; ⊙ 8am-6pm, night entry 7-9pm) This magnificent fort comprises an extensive palace complex, built from pale yellow and pink sandstone, and white marble, and is divided into four main sections, each with its own courtyard. It is possible to visit the fortress on elephant-back, but animal welfare groups have criticised the keeping of elephants at Amber because of reports of abuse, and because carrying passengers can cause lasting injuries to the animals.

As an alternative, you can trudge up to the fort from the road in about 10 minutes, or take a 4WD to the top and back for ₹450 (good for up to five passengers), including a one-hour wait time. For night entry, admission for foreigners drops to the Indian price.

However you arrive, you will enter Amber Fort through the Suraj Pol (Sun Gate), which leads to the Jaleb Chowk (Main Courtyard), where returning armies would display their war booty to the populace – women could view this area from the veiled windows of the palace. The ticket office is directly across the courtyard from the Suraj Pol. If you arrive by car you will enter through the Chand Pol (Moon Gate) on the opposite side of Jaleb Chowk. Hiring a guide or grabbing an audio guide is highly recommended, as there are very few signs and many blind alleys.

From Jaleb Chowk, an imposing stairway leads up to the main palace, but first it's worth taking the steps just to the right, which lead to the small Siladevi Temple, with its gorgeous silver doors featuring repoussé (raised relief) work.

Heading back to the main stairway will take you up to the second courtyard and the Diwan-i-Am (Hall of Public Audience), which has a double row of columns, each topped by a capital in the shape of an elephant, and latticed galleries above.

The maharaja's apartments are located around the third courtyard – you enter through the fabulous Ganesh Pol, decorated with beautiful frescoed arches. The Jai Mandir (Hall of Victory) is noted for its inlaid panels and multimirrored ceiling. Carved marble relief panels around the hall are fascinatingly delicate and quirky, depicting cartoon-like insects and sinuous flowers. Opposite the Jai Mandir is the Sukh Niwas (Hall of Pleasure), with an ivory-inlaid sandalwood door and a channel that once carried cooling water right through the room. From the Jai Mandir you can enjoy fine views from the palace ramparts over picturesque Maota Lake below.

The zenana (secluded women's quarters) surrounds the fourth courtyard. The rooms were designed so that the maharaja could embark on his nocturnal visits to his wives' and concubines' respective chambers without the others knowing, as the chambers are independent but open onto a common corridor.

The **Amber sound-and-light show** (☑ 0141-2530844; Kesar Kiyari complex; Indian/foreigner ₹100/200; ⊙ English 7.30pm, Hindi 8.30pm) takes place below the fort in the complex near Maota Lake.

Jaigarh
FORT

(Indian/foreigner ₹50/100, car ₹50, Hindi/English guide ₹200/300; ⊙ 9am-5pm) A scrubby green hill rises above Amber and is topped by the imposing Jaigarh, built in 1726 by Jai Singh. The stern fort, punctuated by whimsical-hatted lookout towers, was never captured and has survived intact through the centuries. It's an uphill walk (about 1km) from

Amber and offers great views from the Diwa Burj watchtower. The fort has reservoirs, residential areas, a puppet theatre and the world's largest wheeled cannon, Jaya Vana.

During the Mughal empire, Jaipur produced many weapons for the Mughal and Rajput rulers. The cannon, a most spectacular example, was made in the fort foundry, which was constructed in Mughal times. The huge weapon dates from 1720, has a barrel around 6m long, is made from a mix of eight different metals and weighs 50 tonnes. To fire it requires 100kg of gunpowder, and it has a range of 30km. It's debatable how many times this great device was used.

A sophisticated network of drainage channels feeds three large tanks that used to provide water for all the soldiers, residents and livestock living in the fort. The largest tank has a capacity for 22.8 million litres of water. The fort served as the treasury of the Kachhwahas, and for a long time people were convinced that at least part of the royal treasure was still secreted in this large water tank. The Indian government even searched it to check, but found nothing.

Within the fort is an armoury and museum, with the essential deadly weapons collection and some royal knick-knacks, including interesting photographs, maps of Jaigarh, spittoons, and circular 18th-century playing cards. The structure also contains various open halls, including the Shubhat Niwas (Meeting Hall of Warriors), which has some weather-beaten sedan chairs and drums lying about.

Admission is free with a valid ticket from the Jaipur City Palace (p113) that is less than two days old.

Anokhi Museum of Hand Printing
MUSEUM

(☑ 0141-2530226; Anokhi Haveli, Kheri Gate; adult/child ₹80/25; ⏲ 10.30am-4.30pm Tue-Sat, from 11am Sun, closed May–mid-Jul) This interesting museum in a restored *haveli* (traditional, ornately decorated residence) documents the art of hand-block printing, from old traditions to contemporary design. You can watch masters carve unbelievably intricate wooden printing blocks and even have a go at printing your own scarf or T-shirt. There's a cafe and gift shop, too.

Panna Meena Baori
HISTORIC SITE

A pretty *baori* (step-well) with geometrical designs and sharp shadows that has been restored. Pity about the putrid water.

🛏 Sleeping & Eating

★ Mosaics Guesthouse
GUESTHOUSE **$$**

(☑ 0141-2530031, 9950457218; www.mosaicsguesthouse.com; Siyaram Ki Doongri; s/d incl breakfast ₹3400/4000; ❋ 🛜) Get away from it all at this gorgeous arty place (the French owner is a mosaic artist and will show off his workshop) with four lovely rooms, courtyard garden, and a rooftop terrace with beautiful fort views. Set-price Franco-Indian meals cost ₹800/1000 for veg/nonveg. It's about 1km past the fort near Kunda Village – head for Siyaram Ki Doongri, where you'll find signs.

There are discounts in summer.

ℹ Getting There & Away

Frequent buses to Amber depart from near the Hawa Mahal in Jaipur (non-AC/AC ₹14/25, every 15 minutes), which will drop you opposite where you start your climb up to the entrance of Amber Fort.

An autorickshaw/taxi will cost at least ₹400/700 for the return trip from Jaipur. The Vintage Jeep Tour (p118) and RTDC city tours (p118) include Amber Fort.

Bharatpur & Keoladeo National Park
☑ 05644 / POP 254,860

Bharatpur is famous for its wonderful Unesco-listed Keoladeo National Park, a wetland and significant bird sanctuary. Apart from the park, Bharatpur also has a few historic vestiges and a good museum worth visiting, though it wouldn't be worth making the journey here for these sights alone. The old town is busy, noisy and not particularly visitor-friendly. Bharatpur hosts the boisterous and colourful Brij Festival just prior to Holi celebrations.

◎ Sights

Lohagarh
FORT

FREE The still-inhabited, 18th-century Lohagarh, or Iron Fort, was so named because of its sturdy defences. Despite being somewhat forlorn and derelict, it is still impressive, and sits at the centre of town, surrounded by a moat. There's a northern entrance, at Austdhatu (Eight-Metal) Gate – apparently the spikes on the gate are made of eight different metals – and a southern entrance, at Lohiya Gate.

Maharaja Suraj Mahl, constructor of the fort and founder of Bharatpur, built two towers, the Jawahar Burj and the Fateh

ABHANERI

The village of Abhaneri is home to one of Rajasthan's most spectacular sights. With around 11 visible levels (depending on groundwater level) of zigzagging steps, the 10th-century **Chand Baori** (⊙ dawn-dusk) `FREE`, a step-well, is an engineering and geometric wonder. Flanking the cavernous step-well is a small crumbling palace, where royals used to picnic and bathe in private rooms (water was brought up by ox-power).

A three-day festival held in September features local folk musicians, street performances and arts and crafts. The venue is, of course, the magnificent step-well.

Abhaneri village is about 95km east of Jaipur, a 10km detour north off National Hwy 21, the main Agra–Jaipur highway.

From Jaipur catch a bus to Sikandra (₹78, 1½ hours), from where you can hop in a crowded share taxi (₹10) for the 5km trip to Gular. From Gular catch a share taxi or minibus to Abhaneri (another 5km and ₹10). For those with their own transport, Abhaneri and its step-well is a worthwhile stop between Jaipur and Agra/Bharatpur.

Burj, within the ramparts to commemorate his victories over the Mughals and the British. The fort also contains three old palaces within its precincts, one of which contains a museum.

★ Museum
MUSEUM

(Lohargarh; Indian/foreigner ₹20/100; ⊙ noon-8pm Tue-Sun) One of the Lohagarh palaces, centred on a tranquil courtyard, houses this museum, which has royal artefacts, including weaponry, miniature paintings, metalwork and pottery. There are two sculpture galleries flanking the impressive Durbar Hall, which includes some beautiful 7th- to 10th-century pieces. Don't miss the palace's original *hammam* (Turkish bath), which retains some fine carvings and frescos.

⊙ Keoladeo National Park

This tremendous **bird sanctuary and national park** (Indian/foreigner ₹75/500, video ₹600/900, guide per hour ₹250, bike/mountain-bike/binoculars rental per day ₹50/60/100, bicycle rickshaw per hour ₹150; ⊙ 6am-6pm Apr-Sep, 6.30am-5.30pm Oct-Mar) has long been recognised as one of the world's most important bird breeding and feeding grounds. In a good monsoon season over one-third of the park can be submerged, hosting more than 360 species within its 29 sq km. The marshland patchwork is a wintering area for aquatic birds, including visitors from Afghanistan, Turkmenistan, China and Siberia. The park is also home to deer, nilgai (antelope) and boar, which can be readily spotted.

Keoladeo originated as a royal hunting reserve in the 1850s. It continued to supply the tables of the maharajas with fresh game until as late as 1965. In 1982 Keoladeo was declared a national park and it was listed as a World Heritage Site in 1985.

By far the best time to visit this park is October to February, when you should see many migratory birds. At other times it can be dry and relatively bird-free.

Visiting the Park

The best times to visit the park are in the morning and evening, but note that park admission entitles you to only one entrance per day. One narrow road (no motorised vehicles are permitted past checkpoint 2) runs through the park, and a number of tracks and pathways fan out from it and thread their way between the shallow wetlands. Generally speaking, the further away from the main gate you go, the more interesting the scenery, and the more varied the wildlife becomes.

Only the government-authorised cycle-rickshaws (recognisable by the yellow licence plate) are allowed beyond checkpoint 2, and they can only travel along the park's larger tracks. You don't pay an admission fee for the drivers, but they charge ₹150 per hour; some are very knowledgeable.

An excellent way to see the park is by hiring a bicycle at the park entrance. Having a bike is a wonderfully quiet way to travel, and allows you to avoid bottlenecks and take in the serenity on your own. However, we recommend that lone female travellers who wish to cycle do so with a guide (who will cycle alongside you), as we've had more than one report of lone women being harassed by young men inside the park in recent years.

You should get a small map with your entrance ticket, though the park isn't big, so it's difficult to get lost.

Bharatpur

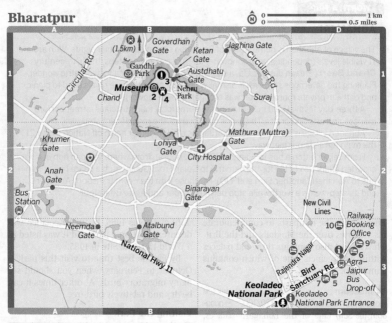

Bharatpur

⊚ Top Sights
1 Keoladeo National Park	C3
2 Museum	B1

⊚ Sights
3 Jawahar Burj	B1
4 Lohagarh	B1

⊜ Sleeping
5 Birder's Inn	D3
6 Falcon Guest House	D3
7 Hotel Sunbird	D3
8 Kiran Guest House	D3
9 New Spoonbill Guesthouse	D3
10 Royal Guest House	D3

🛏 Sleeping & Eating

There are plenty of sleeping options, suiting all budgets, near the park on Bird Sanctuary Rd, so don't feel pressured by touts at Bharatpur's train or bus stations.

Falcon Guest House   GUESTHOUSE $
(☏8619965315, 05644-223815; falconguesthouse@hotmail.com; Gori Shankur Colony; s/d from ₹600/800, r with AC ₹1200-2000; ✳@🕏) The Falcon may well be the pick of a bunch of hotels all in a row and all owned by the same extended family. It's a well-kept, snug place to stay, run by the affable Mrs Rajni Singh.

There is a range of comfortable, good-sized rooms at different prices, including a family room. The best rooms have balconies.

Husband Tej Singh is an ornithologist and is happy to answer any bird-related questions. Flavoursome home-cooked food is served in the garden restaurant.

Kiran Guest House   GUESTHOUSE $
(☏9460912641, 9828269930; www.kiranguesthouse.com; 364 Rajendra Nagar; r ₹400-800, with AC ₹1100; ✳🕏) Managed by eager-to-please brothers, this guesthouse delivers great value, with seven simple, clean and spacious rooms and a pleasant rooftop where you can eat tasty home cooking. It's on a quiet road not far from Keoladeo park. Nature guiding and free pick-up from the Bharatpur train and bus stations are offered.

New Spoonbill Guesthouse   HOTEL $
(☏05644-223571, 7597412553; www.hotelspoonbill.com; Gori Shankur Colony; s/d ₹700/800, with AC ₹1000/1100; ✳@🕏) Owned and run by the same family as the original Spoonbill Hotel down the road, this place has simple but smart rooms, each with a small terrace. The larger rooms are great, with lots of windows. The dining room looks onto the garden, and delicious home-cooked meals, plus milk from the home cow, are available.

Royal Guest House HOTEL $
(☑ 9414315457; www.royalguesthousebharatpur.
com; B-15 New Civil Lines, near Saras Circle; r ₹600-
800, with AC ₹1000; ✴ @ ☎) Rooms at the Royal are all clean and fresh, and the rooftop
restaurant is cosy, making the whole place
feel more like a homestay than a guesthouse.
The ultrakeen management, who live on the
premises, do money changing and run a sister operation, Royal Farm, 3.5km from here.

★**Hotel Sunbird** HOTEL $$
(☑ 05644-225701, 8764943438; www.hotelsunbird.
com; Bird Sanctuary Rd; s/d incl breakfast from
₹1950/2260; ✴ ☎) This popular, well-run
place close to the Keoladeo park entrance
may look modest from the road, but out
back there's a lovely garden (with bar) and
spacious rooms with balconies. Rooms are
clean and comfortable and the restaurant
dishes up a good range of tasty veg and non-
veg dishes. Packed lunches and guided tours
for the park are available.

★**Birder's Inn** HOTEL $$
(☑ 7297991613, 05644-227346; www.birdersinn.
com; Bird Sanctuary Rd; s/d incl breakfast from
₹3500/3900; ✴ @ ☎ ✴) The Birder's Inn is
a popular, long-standing base for exploring
Keoladeo National Park. There is a multicuisine restaurant and a small pool to cool
off in. The rooms are airy, spacious and nicely decorated, and are set far back from the
road in well-tended gardens. Guides from
the hotel are available for Keoladeo.

Royal Farm GUESTHOUSE $$
(☑ 9414315457; www.royalfarmbharatpur.com;
Agra Rd; r ₹1400, with AC ₹1600; ✴ ☎) There
are just six spacious rooms in this quaint
farmhouse set back from the busy Agra Rd.
The rooms have marble floors, solar hot
water, good mattresses and flatscreen TVs.
This farmhouse has an organic farm and a
milking cow and a buffalo to help supply the
ingredients for the vegetarian kitchen.

❶ Information

Main post office (Gandhi Park; ⊘ 10am-1pm &
2-5pm Mon-Sat) Near Gandhi Park.

Tourist office (☑ 05644-222542; Saras Circle;
⊘ 9.30am-6pm) On the crossroads, about
700m from the national park entrance; has a
free map of Bharatpur and Keoladeo National
Park.

❶ Getting There & Away

BUS

Buses running between Agra and Jaipur will drop
you at Saras Circle by the tourist office or outside
the Keoladeo park entrance if you ask.

Services from Bharatpur bus station and
Saras Circle include the following:

Agra with/without AC ₹164/72, 1½ hours, half-
hourly around the clock from Saras Circle

Alwar ₹136, four hours, hourly until 5.30pm
from main bus station

Deeg ₹39, one hour, hourly until 8pm from
main bus station

Delhi ₹201, five hours, four buses daily,
4.30am, 6.11am, 6.30am, 9.30am from main
bus station

Fatehpur Sikri ₹29, 30 minutes, half-hourly
around the clock from Saras Circle

Jaipur ₹195, 4½ hours, half-hourly around the
clock from main bus station

TRAIN

The train station is about 4km from Keoladeo
and the main hotel area; a rickshaw should cost
around ₹70. There is a **railway booking office**
(Saras Circle; ⊘ 8am-2pm Mon-Sat) in the same
building as the tourist office.

Agra 2nd-class seat/sleeper/3AC
₹60/145/500, 1½ to two hours, nine daily
between 4.45am and 8.10pm

Delhi 2nd-class seat/sleeper/3AC
₹110/170/540, three to four hours, 12 trains
daily, plus three other services on selected days

Jaipur 2nd-class seat/sleeper/3AC
₹110/150/510, three to four hours, nine daily
between 2am and 10pm

MAJOR TRAINS FROM BHARATPUR

DESTINATION	TRAIN	DEPARTURE	ARRIVAL	FARE (₹)
Agra (Cantonment)	19666 Udz–Kurj Exp	9.46am	10.55am	145/500 (A)
Delhi (Hazrat Nizamuddin)	12059 Kota–Jan Shatabdi	9.25am	12.30pm	110/410 (B)
Jaipur	19665 Kurj–Udaipur Exp	6.55pm	10.50pm	150/510 (A)
Sawai Madhopur	12904 Golden Temple Mail	10.30am	12.55pm	170/540 (C)

Fares: (A) sleeper/3AC, (B) 2nd-class/AC chair, (C) 2nd class/3AC

WORTH A TRIP

SURAJ MAHL'S PALACE, DEEG

At the centre of Deeg – a small, rarely visited, dusty tumult of a town about 35km north of Bharatpur – stands the incongruously glorious **Suraj Mahl's Palace** (Deeg; Indian/foreigner ₹25/300; ⊙9am-5pm Sat-Thu) edged by stately formal gardens. It's one of India's most beautiful and carefully proportioned palace complexes. Pick up a map and brochure at the entrance; photography is not permitted in some of the bhavans (buildings).

Built in a mixture of Rajput and Mughal architectural styles, the 18th-century Gopal Bhavan is fronted by imposing arches to take full advantage of the early-morning light. Downstairs is a lower storey that becomes submerged during the monsoon as the water level of the adjacent tank, Gopal Sagar, rises. It was used by the maharajas until the early 1950s, and contains many original furnishings, including faded sofas, huge punkas (cloth fans) that are over 200 years old, chaise longues, a stuffed tiger, elephant-foot stands, and fine porcelain from China and France.

In an upstairs room at the rear of the palace is an Indian-style marble dining table – a stretched oval-shaped affair raised just 20cm off the ground. Guests sat around the edge, and the centre was the serving area. In the maharaja's bedroom is an enormous, 3.6m by 2.4m, wooden bed with silver legs.

Two large tanks lie alongside the palace, the aforementioned Gopal Sagar to the east and Rup Sagar to the west. The well-maintained gardens and flower beds, watered by the tanks, continue the extravagant theme with over 2000 fountains. Many of these fountains are in working order and coloured waters pour forth during the monsoon festival in August.

The Keshav Bhavan (Summer or Monsoon Pavilion) is a single-storey edifice with five arches along each side. Tiny jets spray water from the archways and metal balls rumble around in a water channel imitating monsoon thunder. Deeg's massive walls (which are up to 28m high) and 12 vast bastions, some with their cannons still in place, are also worth exploring. You can walk up to the top of the walls from the palace.

Other bhavans (in various states of renovation) include the marble Suraj Bhavan, reputedly taken from Delhi and reassembled here, the Kishan Bhavan and, along the northern side of the palace grounds, the Nand Bhavan.

Deeg is an easy day trip (and there's nowhere good to stay) from Bharatpur or Alwar by car. All the roads to Deeg are rough and the buses crowded. Frequent buses run to and from Alwar (₹60, 2½ hours) and Bharatpur (₹28, one hour).

Ranthambhore NP (Sawai Madhopur) 2nd-class seat/sleeper/3AC ₹135/170/540, two to three hours, 10 daily between 1am and 9.40pm. These trains all continue to Kota (four hours) from where you can catch buses to Bundi.

ⓘ Getting Around

A cycle- or autorickshaw from the bus station to the main hotel area should cost around ₹40 (add an extra ₹40 from the train station).

Alwar

📶 0144 / POP 341,430

Alwar is perhaps the oldest of the Rajasthani kingdoms, forming part of the Matsya territories of Viratnagar in 1500 BC. It became known again in the 18th century under Pratap Singh, who pushed back the rulers of Jaipur to the south and the Jats of Bharatpur to the east, and who successfully resisted the Marathas. It was one of the first Rajput states to ally itself with the fledgling British empire, although British interference in Alwar's internal affairs meant this partnership was not always amicable.

Alwar is the nearest town to Sariska Tiger Reserve & National Park and has a fascinating museum and interesting fort, but it sees relatively few tourists.

◉ Sights

City Palace　　　　　　　　HISTORIC BUILDING
(Vinay Vilas Mahal) Under the gaze of Bala Quila fort sprawls the colourful and convoluted City Palace complex, with massive gates and a tank reflecting a symmetrical series of ghats and pavilions. Today most of the complex is occupied by government offices, overflowing with piles of dusty papers and soiled by pigeons and splatters of *paan* (a mixture of betel nut and leaves for chewing).

★ **Alwar Museum**   MUSEUM

(Government Museum; Indian/foreigner ₹50/100; ⊙9.45am-5.15pm Tue-Sun) Hidden within the City Palace is the excellent Alwar Museum. Its eclectic exhibits evoke the extravagance of the lifestyle of the maharajas: stunning weapons, stuffed Scottish pheasants, royal ivory slippers, miniature paintings, royal vestments, a solid silver table, and stone sculptures, such as an 11th-century carving of Vishnu.

Somewhat difficult to find in the Kafkaesque tangle of government offices, it's on the top floor of the palace, up a ramp from the main courtyard. There should be plenty of people around to point you in the right direction and from there you can follow the signs.

Cenotaph of Maharaja Bakhtawar Singh   HISTORIC BUILDING

(Chhatri of Moosi Rani; City Palace) This double-storey edifice, resting on a platform of sandstone, was built in 1815 by Maharaja Vinay Singh, in memory of his father. To gain access to the cenotaph, take the steps to the far left when facing the palace. The cenotaph is also known as the Chhatri of Moosi Rani, after one of the mistresses of Bakhtawar Singh who performed self-immolation on his funeral pyre – after this act she was promoted to wifely status.

Bala Quila   FORT

(Indian/foreigner ₹10/200, car ₹50, safari gypsy ₹1350; ⊙6am-6pm) This imposing fort stands 300m above Alwar, its fortifications hugging the steep hills that line the eastern edge of the city. Predating the time of Pratap Singh, it's one of the few forts in Rajasthan built before the rise of the Mughals, who used it as a base for attacking Ranthambhore. Mughal emperors Babur and Akbar have stayed overnight here, and Prince Salim (later Emperor Jehangir) was exiled in Salim Mahal for three years.

Now in ruins, the fort houses a radio transmitter station and parts are off limits. The surrounding hills are under the auspices of Sariska Tiger Reserve and subsequently reserve entry fees apply (and heavy fines if you aren't out before sunset). You can walk the very steep couple of kilometres up to the fort entrance or take the road. The **ticket office** (⊙6am–6pm) is at the bottom of the hill west of the city palace.

🛏 Sleeping

RTDC Hotel Meenal   HOTEL $

(☑0144-2347352; meenal@rtdc.in; Topsingh Circle; s/d ₹900/1100, with AC ₹1100/1300; ❄) A respectable option with tidy yet bland and tired rooms typical of the chain. It's located about 1km south of town on the way to Sariska, so it's quiet and leafy, though a long way from the action.

★ **Hotel Aravali**   HOTEL $$

(☑0144-2332883; reservations.alwar@gmail.com; Nehru Rd; r incl breakfast from ₹2950, ste ₹7080; ❄ 🕸 ☰) One of the town's best choices, this conveniently located hotel has been partly refurbished. Cheaper rooms are a little worn and weary but rooms are large and well furnished and have big bathrooms. The multicuisine **Bridge Restaurant** (☑0144-23322316; mains ₹250-500; ⊙7am-11pm; ❄) is one of the best in town, and there's a bar. Turn left out of the train station and it's about 300m down the road.

🍴 Eating & Drinking

Prem Pavitra Bhojnalaya   INDIAN $

(near Hope Circle; mains ₹80-120; ⊙10.30am-4pm & 6.30-10pm; ✑) Alwar's renowned restaurant has been going since 1957. In the heart of the old town, it serves fresh, tasty pure-veg food – try the delicious dhal fry with Desai ghee and *palak paneer* (unfermented cheese chunks in a pureed spinach gravy). The servings are big; half-serves are available. Finish off with its famous 'special *kheer*' (creamy rice pudding).

Turn right out of the bus station, take the first left (towards Hope Circle) and it's on your left after 100m.

Gigil Cafe   CAFE

(Moti Dungri Rd; ⊙7am-11pm; 🕸) Breezy Gigil Cafe has introduced espresso coffee to Alwar. There's also bakery items and a multicuisine veg restaurant kicks of at 10am. The baristas are not yet proficient, but they are keen and by the time you read this the coffees should be great. You can sit under a shady pergola streetside or inside to cool off under the AC.

ℹ Information

State Bank of India (SBI; Company Bagh Rd; ⊙9.30am-4pm Mon-Fri, to 12.30pm Sat) Changes major currencies and has an ATM. Near the bus station.

Tourist Office (☏ 0144-2347348; Nehru Rd; ⏱ 9.30am-6pm Mon-Fri) Can only offer a map of Alwar (if it is open when it should be). Near the train station.

ⓘ Getting There & Around

A cycle-rickshaw between the bus and train stations costs around ₹40. Look out for the shared taxis (₹10 to ₹15) that ply fixed routes around town. They come in the form of white minivans and have the word 'Vahini' printed on their side doors. One handy route goes past Hotel Aravali, the tourist office and the train station before continuing on to the bus station and terminating a short walk from the City Palace complex.

A return taxi to Sariska Tiger Reserve will cost you around ₹1500.

BUS

The Alwar **bus station** (Old Bus Stand Rd) is on Old Bus Stand Rd, near Manu Marg. Services include:

Bharatpur ₹128, four hours, hourly from 7am to 8.30pm

Deeg ₹87, 2½ hours, eight services from 5am to 8.30pm

Delhi ₹177, four hours, every 20 minutes from 5am to 9pm

Jaipur ₹160, four hours, half-hourly from 5am to 5.10pm

Sariska ₹40, one hour, several daily until 10.30pm.

TRAIN

The **train station** (Nehru Rd) is fairly central, on Nehru Rd. Around a dozen daily trains leave for Delhi (sleeper/3AC ₹140/500, three to four hours) throughout the day.

It's also three to four hours to Jaipur (sleeper/3AC ₹170/540) from here. Sixteen trains depart daily and prices are almost identical to those for Delhi.

Sariska Tiger Reserve & National Park

☏ 0144

Enclosed within the dramatic, shadowy folds of the Aravalli Hills, the **Sariska Tiger Reserve & National Park** (☏ 0144-2841333; www.rajasthanwildlife.in; Indian/foreigner ₹105/570, safari vehicle ₹1250, temple-bound vehicle ₹250; ⏱ safaris 7-10.30am & 2-5.30pm Nov-Feb, 6.30-10am & 2.30-6pm Mar-Jun & Oct) is a tangle of remnant semideciduous jungle and craggy canyons sheltering streams and lush greenery. It covers 866 sq km (including a core area of 498 sq km), and is home to pea-

cocks, monkeys, majestic sambars, nilgai, chital, wild boars and jackals.

In 2018 there were 17 tigers roaming the reserve, including five newborn cubs. Poaching, however, by local villagers is an ongoing problem. Although you may not spot a tiger in Sariska, it is still a fascinating wildlife-filled sanctuary. The best time to see wildlife is November to March, and you'll see most activity in the evening. The park is closed to safaris from 1 July to 30 September, though still open for temple pilgrimages.

◉ Sights

Besides wildlife, Sariska has some fantastic sights within the reserve or around its periphery, which are well worth seeking out. If you take a longer tour, you can ask to visit one or more of these. Some are also accessible by public bus.

Hanuman Temple   HINDU TEMPLE

(Sariska Tiger Reserve; ⏱ Tue & Sat 6am-6pm) This small Hanuman temple, deep in the park, has a recumbent idol, adapted from a rock, which is painted orange and shaded by silver parasols. People give offerings of incense and receive tiny parcels of holy ash. From the temple there is a pleasant walk, for more than 1km, to Pandu pol, a gaping natural arch.

Kankwari Fort   FORT

(Sariska Tiger Reserve) Deep inside the sanctuary, this imposing small jungle fort, 22km from Sariska, offers amazing views over the plains of the national park, dotted with red mud-brick villages. A four- to five-hour 4WD safari (one to five passengers plus mandatory guide) to Kankwari Fort from the Forest Reception Office near the reserve entrance will costs ₹5100 with two foreign passengers.

This fort is the inaccessible place that Aurangzeb chose to imprison his brother, Dara Shikoh, Shah Jahan's chosen heir to the Mughal throne, for several years before he was beheaded.

Bhangarh   HISTORIC SITE

Around 55km south from Sariska, beyond the inner park sanctuary and out in open countryside, is this deserted, well-preserved and notoriously haunted city. Founded in 1631 by Madho Singh, it had 10,000 dwellings, but was suddenly and mysteriously deserted about 300 years ago. It's best reached by car (parking ₹50) or taxi but can be reached by a twice-daily bus (₹39) that runs through the sanctuary to nearby Gola-ka village. Check what time the bus returns, otherwise you risk getting stranded.

☞ Tours

Private cars, including taxis, are limited to sealed roads heading to the Hanuman temple and are allowed only on Tuesday and Saturday. The best way to visit the park is by gypsy (open-topped, six-passenger 4WD), which can explore off the main tracks. Gypsy safaris start at the park entrance, and vehicle plus driver hire is ₹3350 (hire and entry) for a three-hour safari; the vehicles can take up to five people (including guide). Guides are mandatory (₹400 for three hours) and you also have to factor in personal entry fees and GST.

Bookings can be made at the **Forest Reception Office** (Safari Booking Office; ☑ 0144-2841333; www.rajasthanwildlife.in; Jaipur Rd; ⊘ 6.55-7.30am & 1-3pm Nov-Jan, 6.25-7am & 12.30-2.30pm Mar-Jun & Oct), where buses will drop you.

🛏 Sleeping & Eating

RTDC Hotel Tiger Den HOTEL $$
(☑ 0144-2841342; tigerden@rtdc.in; r incl 2 meals ₹2724, with AC from ₹3396; ❄ 🛜) Hotel Tiger Den isn't fancy – a cement block fronted by a lawn and backed by a rambling garden. Its best feature is that it is very close to the reserve entrance. On the plus side the management is friendly, there is a bar, and the rooms have balconies with a pleasant outlook. Bring a mosquito net or repellent.

Hotel Sariska Palace HERITAGE HOTEL $$$
(☑ 7340186019; www.thesariskapalace.in; r ₹10,750, ste from ₹13,500; ❄ 🛜 ⛱) Near the reserve entrance is this imposing former hunting lodge of the maharajas of Alwar. There's a driveway leading from opposite the Forest Reception Office. Rooms have soaring ceilings and soft mattresses, and those in the annex by the swimming pool have good views. The Fusion Restaurant here serves expensive Indian and Continental dishes.

Sariska Tiger Heaven HOTEL $$$
(☑ 9251016312; www.sariskatigerheaven.com; Thanagazi; r incl all meals from ₹7500; ❄ ⛱) This isolated place about 3km west of the bus stop at Thanagazi village will pick you up from the village's bus stop (₹200). Rooms are set in stone-and-tile cottages and have big beds and windowed alcoves. It's a tranquil, if overpriced, place to stay. Staff can arrange 4WDs and safaris and guides to the reserve.

ℹ Information

Interpretation Centre (Sariska Tiger Reserve & National Park; ⊘ 8am-7pm) Near the reserve's booking office. Gives an honest and sobering appraisal of Sariska's past, present and ongoing threats. It's worth a look, and there's a small souvenir shop attached.

ℹ Getting There & Away

Sariska is 35km from Alwar, a convenient town from which to approach the reserve. There are crowded buses from Alwar (₹35, one to 1½ hours, hourly) and on to Jaipur (₹129, four hours). Buses stop in front of the Forest Reception Office.

Ajmer

☑ 0145 / POP 542,320

Ajmer is a bustling, chaotic city, 130km southwest of Jaipur and just 13km from the Hindu pilgrimage town of Pushkar. It surrounds the expansive lake of Ana Sagar, and is itself ringed by the rugged Aravalli Hills. Ajmer is Rajasthan's most important site in terms of Islamic history and heritage. It contains one of India's most important Muslim pilgrimage centres, the shrine of Khwaja Muin-ud-din Chishti, who founded the Chishtiya order, the prime Sufi order in India. As well as some superb examples of early Muslim architecture, Ajmer is also a significant centre for the Jain religion, possessing an amazing golden Jain temple. However, with Ajmer's combination of high-voltage crowds and traffic, especially during Ramadan and the anniversary of the saint's death, most travellers choose to use Ajmer as a stepping stone to laid-back Pushkar.

⊙ Sights

Dargah of Khwaja Muin-ud-din Chishti ISLAMIC SHRINE
(www.dargahajmer.com; ⊘ 4am-9pm) This is the tomb of Sufi saint Khwaja Muin-ud-din Chishti, who came to Ajmer from Persia in 1192 and died here in 1236. The tomb gained its significance during the time of the Mughals – many emperors added to the buildings here. Construction of the shrine was completed by Humayun, and the gate was added by the Nizam of Hyderabad. Mughal emperor Akbar used to make the pilgrimage to the dargah from Agra every year.

You have to cover your head in certain parts of the shrine, so remember to take a scarf or cap – there are plenty for sale at the

Ajmer

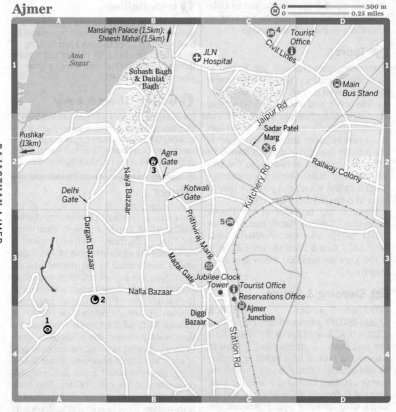

Ajmer

colourful bazaar leading to the dargah, along with floral offerings and delicious toffees.

The main entrance is through Nizam Gate (1915). Inside, the green and white mosque, Akbari Masjid, was constructed in 1571 and is now an Arabic and Persian school for religious education. The next gate is called the Shahjahani Gate, as it was erected by Shah Jahan, although it is also known

as 'Nakkarkhana', because of the two large *nakkharas* (drums) fixed above it.

A third gate, Buland Darwaza (16th century), leads into the dargah courtyard. Flanking the entrance of the courtyard are the *degs* (large iron cauldrons), one donated by Akbar in 1567, the other by Jehangir in 1631, for offerings for the poor.

Inside this courtyard, the saint's domed tomb is surrounded by a silver platform. Pilgrims believe that the saint's spirit will intercede on their behalf in matters of illness, business or personal problems, so the notes and holy string attached to the railings around it are thanks or requests.

Pilgrims and Sufis come from all over the world on the anniversary of the saint's death, the Urs, in the seventh month of the Islamic lunar calendar. Crowds can be suffocating.

Bags must be left in the cloakroom (₹10 each, with camera ₹20) outside the main entrance.

Soniji Ki Nasiyan (Red) Temple JAIN TEMPLE
(Golden Temple; Prithviraj Marg; ₹10; ⊙8.30am-5.30pm) This marvellous Jain temple, built in 1865, is also known as the Golden Temple, due to its amazing golden diorama in the double-storey temple hall. The intricate diorama depicts the Jain concept of the ancient world, with 13 continents and oceans, the golden city of Ayodhya, flying peacock and elephant gondolas, and gilded elephants with many tusks. The hall is also decorated with gold, silver and precious stones. It's unlike any other temple in Rajasthan and is well worth a visit.

Adhai-din-ka-Jhonpra HISTORIC SITE
(Two-and-a-Half-Day Building; ⊙dawn-dusk) Beyond the Dargah of Khwaja Muin-ud-din Chishti, on the town outskirts, are the extraordinary ruins of the Adhai-din-ka-Jhonpra mosque. According to legend, construction in 1153 took only 2½ days. Others say it was named after a festival lasting 2½ days. It was originally built as a Sanskrit college, but in 1198 Mohammed of Ghori seized Ajmer and converted the building into a mosque by adding a seven-arched wall covered with Islamic calligraphy in front of the pillared hall.

🛏️ Sleeping & Eating

Haveli Heritage Inn HOTEL $$
(☑0145-2621607; www.haveliheritageinn.com; Kutchery Rd; r ₹1340-3000; ❋@🛜) Set in a 140-year-old *haveli* (traditional, ornately decorated residence) this welcoming city-centre oasis is arguably Ajmer's best midrange choice. The high-ceilinged rooms are spacious (some are almost suites), sim-

ply decorated, air-cooled and set well back from the busy road. There's a pleasant, paved courtyard and the hotel is infused with a family atmosphere, complete with home-cooked meals.

Badnor House GUESTHOUSE $$
(☑0145-2627579; www.badnorhouse.com; Savitri Girls' College Rd, Civil Lines; s/d incl breakfast ₹2600/3000; ❋🛜) This guesthouse provides an excellent opportunity to stay with a delightful family and receive down-to-earth hospitality. There are five heritage-style doubles with period furnishings and TVs, which are separated from the family's large bungalow.

Mansingh Palace HOTEL $$$
(☑0145-2425702; www.mansinghhotels.com; Circular Rd, Vaishali Nagar; r from ₹4200, ste ₹7000; ❋@🛜⊠) This modern and comfortable option, on the shores of Ana Sagar about 3km from the centre, is rather out of the way. However, the attractive and spacious rooms, some with views and balconies, make this one of Ajmer's best choices. The hotel has a shady garden, a bar and a seriously good restaurant, the Sheesh Mahal.

★**Sheesh Mahal** MULTICUISINE $$
(☑0145-2425702; Circular Rd, Vaishali Nagar; mains ₹180-480; ⊙noon-3pm & 7-10.30pm) This upmarket restaurant, located in Ajmer's top hotel, the Mansingh Palace, offers excellent Indian, Continental and Chinese dishes, as well as a buffet when the tour groups pass through. The service is slick, the AC and beer are on the chilly side, and the food is very good; it also has a bar.

RAJASTHAN AJMER

BUSES FROM AJMER

DESTINATION	FARE (₹)	DURATION (HR)
Agra	392	10
Ahmedabad	556	13
Bharatpur	330	7
Bikaner	267	7
Bundi	184	5
Chittorgarh	195, AC 348	5
Delhi	400, AC 1182	8½
Jaipur	148, AC 300	2½
Jaisalmer	464	11
Jodhpur	205, AC 441	6
Udaipur	301, AC 537	9

Mango Curry/ Mango Masala MULTICUISINE $$

(☑0145-2422100; Sadar Patel Marg; mains ₹160-320; ⊙9am-11pm; ▣) With dim, bar-like lighting and American diner decor, this is a popular Ajmer hang-out. It's divided in two: Mango Masala is no alcohol and vegetarian, while Mango Curry has plenty of good non-veg options. Pizzas, Chinese, and North and South Indian dishes are available throughout, plus there's cakes and ice cream, and a bakery/deli for takeaways.

ℹ Information

Main post office (Prithviraj Marg; ⊙10am-1pm & 1.30-6pm Mon-Sat) Less than 500m from the train station.

Tourist Offices There are two branches – at the **train station** (⊙9am-5pm) and **Hotel Khadim** (☑0145-2627426; ⊙9am-5pm Mon-Fri).

ℹ Getting There & Away

For those pushing on to Pushkar, haggle hard for a private taxi – ₹350 to ₹400 is a good rate.

BUS

Government-run buses leave from the **main bus stand** (Jaipur Rd) in Ajmer, from where buses to Pushkar (₹20, 30 minutes) also leave throughout the day. In addition to these buses, there are less-frequent 'deluxe' coach services running to major destinations such as Delhi and Jaipur. There is a 24-hour cloakroom at the bus stand (₹20 per bag per day).

TRAIN

Ajmer is a busy train junction. To book tickets, go to booth 5 at the train station's **reservations office** (Station Rd; ⊙8am-8pm Mon-Sat, to 2pm Sun). Services include the following:

Agra (Agra Fort Station) sleeper/AC chair ₹265/570, 6½ hours, at least seven daily (1.35am, 2.10am, 3.40am, 6am, 12.50pm, 2.55pm and 11.55pm)

Chittorgarh sleeper/3AC ₹180/560, three hours, at least six daily (1.25am, 2.15am, 1pm, 4.10pm, 8.30pm and 9pm)

Delhi (mostly to Old Delhi or New Delhi stations) 2nd-class seat/sleeper ₹175/290, eight hours, at least 11 daily around the clock

Jaipur 2nd-class seat/sleeper/AC chair ₹100/150/325, two hours, at least 24 throughout the day

Jodhpur sleeper/3AC ₹170/510, four to five hours, two direct daily (1.35pm and 2.25pm)

Mt Abu (Abu Road) sleeper/3AC ₹245/550, five hours, 12 daily

Mumbai sleeper/3AC ₹500/1320, around 19 hours, at least three daily (11.10am, 4.40pm and 7.20pm)

Udaipur sleeper ₹235, five hours, four daily (1.25am, 2.15am, 8.25am and 4.10pm)

Pushkar

☑0145 / POP 21,630

Pushkar has a magnetism all of its own – it's quite unlike anywhere else in Rajasthan. It is world famous for its spectacular Camel Fair, which takes place in the Hindu month of Kartika (October/November). If you are anywhere nearby at the time you would be crazy to miss it.

For the rest of the year Pushkar remains a prominent Hindu pilgrimage town, humming with *puja* (prayers), bells, drums and devotional songs. The town wraps itself around a holy lake featuring 52 bathing ghats and 400 milky-blue temples, including one of the world's few Brahma temples. The main street is one long bazaar, selling anything to tickle a traveller's fancy, from hippy-chic tie-dye to didgeridoos. The result is a muddle of religious and tourist scenes. Yet, despite the commercialism, the town remains enchantingly mystic and relaxed.

Pushkar is only 11km from Ajmer, separated from it by rugged Nag Pahar (Snake Mountain).

MAJOR TRAINS FROM AJMER

DESTINATION	TRAIN	DEPARTURE	ARRIVAL	FARE (₹)
Agra (Agra Fort Station)	12988 Ajmer–SDAH Exp	12.45pm	6.50pm	265/675 (A)
Delhi (New Delhi)	12016 Ajmer Shatabdi	2.05pm	10pm	905/1725 (B)
Jaipur	12991 Udaipur–Jaipur Exp	11.30am	1.30pm	85/325/495 (C)
Jodhpur	15014 Ranighat Express	1.40pm	5.35pm	170/510 (A)
Udaipur	09721 Jaipur–Udaipur SF SPL	8.25am	1.15pm	140/590/995 (C)

Fares: (A) sleeper/3AC, (B) AC chair/1AC, (C) 2nd-class seat/AC chair/3AC

⊙ Sights

Fifty-two bathing ghats surround the lake, where pilgrims bathe in the sacred waters. If you wish to join them, do so with respect. Remember, this is a holy place: remove your shoes and don't smoke, kid around or take photographs.

Some ghats have particular importance: Vishnu appeared at Varah Ghat in the form of a boar, Brahma bathed at Brahma Ghat, and Gandhi's ashes were sprinkled at Gandhi Ghat (Gau Ghat), formerly Gau Ghat.

Pushkar has hundreds of temples, though few are particularly ancient, as they were mostly desecrated by Aurangzeb and subsequently rebuilt.

Old Rangji Temple   HINDU TEMPLE
Old Rangji Temple (c 1844) is close to the bazaar and is alternatively empty and peaceful or alive with chanting worshippers.

Savitri Mata Temple   HINDU TEMPLE
(Saraswati Temple) The ropeway (9.30am to 7.30pm, return trip ₹119) makes the ascent to the hilltop Saraswati Temple a breeze. The temple overlooks the lake and the views are fantastic at any time of day. Alternatively, you could take the one-hour trek up before dawn to beat the heat and capture the best light.

Brahma Temple   HINDU TEMPLE
Pushkar's most famous temple is the Brahma Temple, said to be one of the few such temples in the world as a result of a curse by Brahma's consort, Saraswati. The temple is marked by a red spire, and over the entrance gateway is the *hans* (goose symbol) of Brahma. Inside, the floor and walls are engraved with dedications to the dead.

Pap Mochani (Gayatri) Temple   HINDU TEMPLE
The sunrise views over town from Pap Mochani (Gayatri) Temple, reached by a track behind the Marwar bus stand, are well worth the 30-minute climb.

⮌ Courses

Saraswati Music & Dance School   MUSIC
(☑ 9829333548, 9828297784; www.hemantdevaradance.com; Mainon ka Chowk; dance classes per hour from ₹500, music-class prices on application) Birju teaches tabla (drums), flute, harmonium and singing; brother Hemant teaches dance, including *kathak* (classical dance), Rajasthani folk and Bollywood dance. Birju often conducts evening performances (7pm to 8pm), and also sells instruments.

Cooking Bahar   COOKING
(☑ 0145-2773124; www.cookingbahar.com; Mainon ka Chowk; class ₹1200) Part of the Saraswati Music School family, Deepa conducts cooking classes that cover three vegetarian courses.

🛏 Sleeping

Owing to Pushkar's star status among backpackers, there are far more budget options than midrange, though many budget properties have a selection of midrange-priced rooms. At the time of the camel fair, prices multiply up to three-fold or more, and it's essential to book several weeks ahead.

★ Hotel Everest   HOTEL $
(☑ 0145-2773417, 9414666958; www.pushkarhotel everest.com; off Sadar Bazaar; r ₹300-850, with AC ₹1120-1288; ❄@🛜) This welcoming budget hotel is nestled in the quiet laneways north of Sadar Bazaar. It's run by a friendly father-and-son team who can't do too much for their appreciative guests. The rooms are variable in size, colourful and spotless, and the beds are comfortable. The rooftop is a pleasant retreat for meals or just relaxing with a book.

Ask here about private excursions into Pushkar's hinterland to see temples and the famous Aloo Baba, a potato-eating sadhu.

Hotel Tulsi Palace   HOTEL $
(☑ 8947074663; www.hoteltulsipalacepushkar. co.in; VIP Rd, Holika Chowk; r ₹500-700, with AC ₹1000-1500; 🛜) Tulsi Palace is a great budget choice with a variety of bright and airy rooms around a central courtyard. The attached Little Prince Cafe on the 2nd-floor verandah serves Continental breakfasts and Indian lunch and dinner, and has prime street-life views. The friendly staff will help with your transport needs.

Hotel Kanhaia Haveli   HOTEL $
(☑ 0145-2772146; www.pushkarhotelkanhaia. com; Choti Basti; r ₹400-600, with AC ₹1500-2000; ❄🛜) With a vast range of rooms, from budget digs to suites, you are sure to find a room and price that suits. Rooms get bigger and lighter, with more windows, the more you spend (though all are scrupulously clean). Some rooms have balconies, while all have cable TV. There is a multicuisine restaurant with views on the rooftop.

Hotel White House   GUESTHOUSE $
(☑ 0145-2772147; www.pushkarwhitehouse.com; off Heloj Rd; r ₹350-950, with AC ₹1000-1500; ❄@🛜) This family run place is indeed white, with spotless rooms. Some are decidedly on the

Pushkar

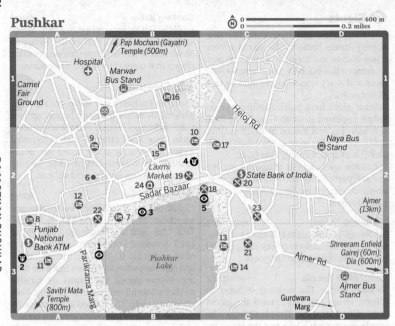

Pushkar

◎ Sights
1 Brahma Ghat	A3
2 Brahma Temple	A3
3 Gandhi Ghat	B2
4 Old Rangji Temple	B2
5 Varah Ghat	C2

◈ Activities, Courses & Tours
Cooking Bahar	(see 6)
6 Saraswati Music & Dance School	A2

◉ Sleeping
7 Bharatpur Palace	B2
8 Hotel Akash	A2
9 Hotel Everest	A2
10 Hotel Kanhaia Haveli	B2
11 Hotel Navaratan Palace	A3
12 Hotel Paramount Palace	A2
13 Hotel Pushkar Palace	C3
14 Hotel Sunset	C3
15 Hotel Tulsi Palace	B2
16 Hotel White House	B1
17 Inn Seventh Heaven	C2

◈ Eating
18 Falafel & Laffa Wrap Stalls	C2
19 Honey & Spice	B2
20 Naryan Café	C2
21 Om Shiva Garden Restaurant	C3
22 Out of the Blue	A2
23 Shri Vankatesh	C2
Sixth Sense	(see 17)
Sunset Café	(see 14)

◎ Shopping
24 Sadar Bazaar	B2

small side, but the nicest are generous and have balconies. It's efficiently run and there is good organic traveller fare and views from the plant-filled rooftop restaurant. Yoga is offered, as is a welcome brew of mango tea for every guest.

Hotel Akash HOTEL $
(☎ 0145-2772498; filterboy21@yahoo.com; Badi Basti; d ₹600, s/d without bathroom ₹300/500; ☎) A simple budget place with keen young management and a large neem tree sprout-ing up from the courtyard to shade the rooftop terrace. Rooms are basic fan-cooled affairs that open out to a balcony restaurant good for spying on the street below.

Bharatpur Palace HOTEL $
(☎ 0145-2772320; www.hotelbharatpurpalace.com; Sadar Bazaar; d ₹1680, without bathroom ₹1344; ❄ ☎) This rambling building occupies one of the best spots in Pushkar, on the upper levels adjacent to Gandhi Ghat. It features aesthetic blue-washed simplicity: bare-

bones rooms with unsurpassed views of the holy lake. The rooftop terrace (with restaurant) has sublime vistas, but respect for bathing pilgrims is paramount for intended guests.

Hotel Paramount Palace
HOTEL $

(☏ 0145-2772428; www.pushkarparamount.com; r ₹400-1500, with AC ₹2000; ✳🛜) Perched on the highest point in Pushkar overlooking an old temple, this welcoming hotel has excellent views of the town and lake (and lots of stairs). The rooms vary widely; the best have lovely balconies, stained-glass windows and are good value. There's a dizzyingly magical rooftop terrace and a small garden with hammocks.

Hotel Navaratan Palace
HOTEL $

(☏ 0145-2772145; www.navratanpalace.com; near Brahma Temple; s/d incl breakfast ₹800/900, with AC ₹1000/1200; ✳🛜⛱) This hotel has a lovely enclosed garden with a fabulous pool (nonguests ₹100), children's playground and pet tortoises. The rooms, crammed with carved wooden furniture, are clean and comfortable but small.

⭐ Inn Seventh Heaven
HERITAGE HOTEL $$

(☏ 0145-5105455; www.inn-seventh-heaven.com; Choti Basti; r ₹1350-3750; ✳🛜) Enter this lovingly converted *haveli* (traditional, ornately decorated residence) through heavy wooden doors into an incense-perfumed courtyard, with a marble fountain in the centre and surrounded by tumbling vines. There are a dozen individually decorated rooms on three levels, all with traditionally crafted furniture and comfortable beds. Rooms vary in size, from the downstairs budget rooms to the spacious Asana suite.

On the roof you'll find the excellent Sixth Sense restaurant (p144), as well as sofas and swing chairs for relaxing with a book. Early booking (two-night minimum, no credit cards) is recommended.

Hotel Sunset
HOTEL $$

(☏ 0145-2772725; Parikrama marg; r ₹1200-1600) Behind the popular Sunset Cafe is a garden and a double storey row of rooms all with TVs, AC and comfortable beds. The quiet location and access to a good atmospheric restaurant make this a good choice.

Dia
B&B $$

(☏ 0145-5105455; www.diahomestay.com; Panch Kund Marg; r incl breakfast ₹3550-4950; ✳@🛜) This beautifully designed B&B by the folks at Inn Seventh Heaven has five very private doubles a short walk from town. The rooms are straight out of a design magazine and will have you swooning (and extending your booking). You can dine here at the cosy rooftop restaurant or head to the Sixth Sense restaurant at Inn Seventh Heaven.

Hotel Pushkar Palace
HERITAGE HOTEL $$$

(☏ 0145-2772001; www.hotelpushkarpalace. com; s/d/ste incl breakfast ₹8260/8730/19,200; ✳@🛜) Once belonging to the maharaja of Kishangarh, the top-end Hotel Pushkar Palace has a romantic lakeside setting. The rooms have carved wooden furniture and beds, and all rooms above the ground floor, and all the suites, look directly out onto the lake: no hotel in Pushkar has better views. A pleasant outdoor dining area overlooks the lake.

✖ Eating

Pushkar has plenty of atmospheric eateries with lake views, and menus reflecting backpacker tastes and preferences. Strict vegetarianism, forbidding even eggs, is the order of the day.

Naryan Café
CAFE $

(Mahadev Chowk, Sadar Bazaar; breakfast from ₹90; ⏱6am-10pm) Busy any time of day, this is particularly popular as a breakfast stop: watch the world go by with a fresh coffee (from ₹40) or juice (from ₹50) and an enormous bowl of homemade muesli, topped with a mountain of fruit.

Shri Vankatesh
INDIAN $

(Choti Basti; mains ₹60-170; ⏱9am-10pm) Head to this no-nonsense local favourite and tuck into some dhal, paneer or kofta, before mopping up the sauce with some freshly baked chapatis and washing it all down with some good old-fashioned chai. The thalis (₹100 to ₹150) are excellent value, too. Watch your food being cooked or head upstairs to people-watch the street below.

Falafel & Laffa Wrap Stalls
MIDDLE EASTERN $

(Sadar Bazaar; wraps ₹100-200; ⏱7.30am-10.30pm) Perfect for quelling a sudden attack of the munchies, and a big hit with Israeli travellers, these adjacent roadside joints knock up a choice selection of filling falafel-and-hummus wraps. Eat them while sitting on stools on the road or devour them on the hoof.

PUSHKAR CAMEL FAIR

Come the month of Kartika, the eighth lunar month of the Hindu calendar and one of the holiest, Thar camel drivers spruce up their ships of the desert and start the long walk to Pushkar in time for Kartik Purnima (Full Moon). Each year around 200,000 people converge on the Pushkar Camel Fair, bringing with them some 50,000 camels, horses and cattle.

The place becomes an extraordinary swirl of colour, sound and movement, thronged with musicians, mystics, tourists, traders, animals, devotees and camera crews.

Trading begins a week before the official fair (a good time to arrive to see the serious business), but by the time the RTDC mela (fair) starts, business takes a back seat and the bizarre sidelines (snake charmers, children balancing on poles etc) jostle onto centre stage. Even the cultural program seems peculiar, with contests for the best moustache, and most beautifully decorated camel. Visitors are encouraged to take part. See if you fancy taking part in the costumed wedding parade, or join a Visitors versus Locals sports contest such as traditional Rajasthani wrestling.

It's hard to believe, but this seething mass is all just a sideshow. Kartik Purnima is when Hindu pilgrims come to bathe in Pushkar's sacred waters. The religious event builds in tandem with the camel fair in a wild, magical crescendo of incense, chanting and processions to dousing day, the last night of the fair, when thousands of devotees wash away their sins and set candles afloat on the holy lake.

Although fantastical, mystical and a one-off, it must be said that it's also crowded, noisy (light sleepers should bring earplugs) and occasionally tacky. Those affected by dust and/ or animal hair should bring appropriate medication. However, it's a grand epic, and not to be missed if you're anywhere within camel-spitting distance. The fair usually takes place in November, but dates change according to the lunar calendar.

Out of the Blue
MULTICUISINE $$

(Sadar Bazaar; mains ₹160-300; ☺8am-11pm; 🛜)
Distinctly a deeper shade of blue in this sky-blue town, Out of the Blue is a reliable restaurant. The menu ranges from noodles and *momos* (Tibetan dumplings) to pizza, pasta, falafel and pancakes. A nice touch for those averse to stairs is the street-level espresso coffee bar (coffees ₹70 to ₹120) and German bakery.

Honey & Spice
MULTICUISINE $$

(Laxmi Market, off Sadar Bazaar; mains ₹90-250; ☺8.15am-6pm; 🖋) 🍃 Run by a friendly family, this tiny wholefood breakfast and lunch place has delicious South Indian coffee and homemade cakes. Even better are the salad bowls and hearty vegetable combo stews served with brown rice – delicious, wholesome and a welcome change from frequently oil-rich Indian food.

Sixth Sense
MULTICUISINE $$

(Inn Seventh Heaven, Choti Basti; mains ₹120-300; ☺8am-2.30pm & 6-10.30pm; 🛜) This chilled rooftop restaurant is a great place to head to even if you didn't score a room in the popular hotel. The pizza and the Indian seasonal vegetables and rice are all very good, as is the filter coffee and fresh juice. Its ambience is immediately relaxing and the pulley apparatus that delivers food from the ground-floor kitchen is a delight.

Save room for the desserts, such as the excellent homemade tarts.

Sunset Café
MULTICUISINE $$

(☎0145-2772725; mains ₹170-390; ☺7.30am-midnight; 🛜) Right on the eastern ghats, this cafe has sublime lake views from its front porch and rooftop. It offers the usual traveller menu, including curries, pizza and pasta, plus there's a German bakery serving reasonable cakes. The lakeside setting is perfect at sunset and gathers a crowd.

Om Shiva Garden Restaurant
MULTICUISINE $$

(☎0145-2772305; www.omshivagardenrestaurant. com; mains ₹150-290; ☺8am-11pm; 🛜) This traveller stalwart near Naya Rangji Temple continues to satisfy, with wood-fired pizzas and espresso coffee featuring on its predominately Italian and North Indian menu. It's hard to pass on the pizzas, but there are also some Mexican and Chinese dishes and 'German bakery' items to try.

 Shopping

Sadar Bazaar
MARKET

Pushkar's Sadar Bazaar is lined with enchanting little shops and is a good place for picking up gifts. Many of the vibrant Rajasthani textiles originate from Barmer, south of Jaisalmer, or Gujarat. There's plenty of silver and beaded jewellery catering both to local and foreign tastes, including some heavy tribal pieces. Expect to haggle.

ℹ Information

The nearest government tourist office is in Ajmer. Your hotel hosts are almost always up to speed with the latest tourist information.

Post office (off Heloj Rd; ⊙ 9.30am-5pm Mon-Fri) Near the Marwar bus stand.

State Bank of India (SBI; Sadar Bazaar; ⊙ 10am-4pm Mon-Fri, to 12.30pm Sat)

DANGERS & ANNOYANCES

Beware of anyone giving you flowers to offer a *puja* (prayer): before you know it you'll be whisked to the ghats in a well-oiled hustle and asked for a personal donation of up to ₹1000. Other priests do genuinely live off the donations of others and this is a tradition that goes back centuries – but walk away if you feel bullied and always agree on a price before taking a red ribbon (a 'Pushkar passport') or flowers.

During the camel fair, Pushkar is besieged by pickpockets working the crowded bazaars. You can avoid the razor gang by not using thin-walled day packs and by carrying your pack in front of you. At any time of year, watch out for rampaging motorbikes ridden by inconsiderate youths in the bazaar.

ℹ Getting There & Away

Pushkar's tiny train station is so badly connected it's not worth bothering with. Use Ajmer junction train station instead.

A private taxi to Ajmer costs ₹300 to ₹400 (note that it's almost always more expensive in the opposite direction). To enter Pushkar by car there is a toll of ₹20.

BUS

Frequent buses to/from Ajmer (₹20, 30 minutes) depart from the Naya Bus Stand, and also from the Ajmer Bus Stand on the road heading eastwards out of town. Most other buses leave from the Naya Bus Stand, though some may still use the old Marwar Bus Stand (but not RSRTC buses).

Local travel agencies sell tickets for private buses – you should shop around. These buses often leave from Ajmer, but the agencies should provide you with free connecting transport. Check whether your bus is direct, as many services from Pushkar aren't. And note, even if they are direct buses they may well stop for some time in Ajmer.

A useful service for getting to Pushkar from Jaipur is **Jai Ambay Travelling Agency** (☑ 0141-2205177; www.jaiambaytravellingagency.com;

2 D Villa Station Rd; ₹350), which has a direct, daily, AC coach (₹350) leaving for Pushkar at 9am arriving at 12.30pm. The return journey waits for some time in Ajmer and is not so useful.

ℹ Getting Around

There are no autorickshaws in central Pushkar, but it's a breeze to get around on foot. If you want to explore the surrounding countryside, you could try hiring a motorbike (₹300 per day) from one of the many places around town. For something more substantial, try **Shreeram Enfield Gairej** (Ajmer Rd; per day ₹800), which hires and sells Enfield Bullets.

Ranthambhore National Park

☑ 07462

This famous **national park** (www.rajasthanwild life.in; ⊙ Oct-Jun) is the best place to spot wild tigers in Rajasthan. It comprises 1334 sq km of wild jungle scrub hemmed in by rocky ridges, and at its centre is the 10th-century Ranthambhore Fort. Scattered around the fort are ancient temples and mosques, hunting pavilions, crocodile-filled lakes and vine-covered *chhatris* (cenotaphs). The park was a maharajas' hunting ground until 1970, a curious 15 years after it had become a sanctuary.

Seeing a tiger (around 60 to 67 in 2018) is partly a matter of luck; leave time for two or three safaris to improve your chances. But remember there's plenty of other wildlife to see, including more than 300 species of birds.

It's 10km from Sawai Madhopur (the gateway town for Ranthambhore) to the first gate of the park, and another 3km to the main gate and Ranthambhore Fort.

◉ Sights

Ranthambhore Fort   FORT

(⊙ 6am-6pm) **FREE** From a distance, the magical 10th-century Ranthambhore Fort is almost indiscernible on its hilltop perch – as you get closer, it seems almost as if it is growing out of the rock. It covers an area of 4.5 sq km, and affords peerless views from the disintegrating walls of the Badal Mahal (Palace of the Clouds), on its northern side. The ramparts stretch for more than 7km, and seven enormous gateways are still intact.

To visit on the cheap, join the locals who go there to visit the temple dedicated to Ganesh. Shared 4WDs (₹40 per person) go from the train station to the park entrance – say 'national park' and they'll know what you want. From there, other shared 4WDs (₹20 per

Ranthambhore National Park

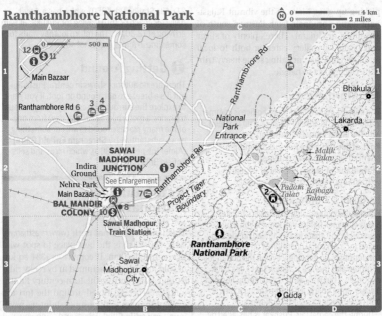

Ranthambhore National Park

person) shuttle to and from the fort, which is inside the park. Alternatively hire your own gypsy (and driver) for about ₹1500 for three hours through your hotel.

🏃 Activities

Safaris take place in the early morning and late afternoon, starting between 6am and 7am or between 2pm and 3.30pm, depending on the time of year. Each safari lasts for around three hours. The mornings can be exceptionally chilly in the open vehicles, so bring warm clothes.

The best option is to travel by gypsy (six-person, open-topped 4WD; Indian/foreigner ₹974/1714). You still have a chance of

seeing a tiger from a canter (20-seat, open-topped truck; ₹617/1357), but other passengers can be very rowdy.

Be aware that the rules for booking safaris (and prices) are prone to change. You can book online through the park's official website (www.rajasthanwildlife.in), or go in person to the safari booking office (p147). And to be sure of bagging a seat in a vehicle, start queuing at least an hour (if not two) before the safaris are due to begin – meaning a very early start for morning safaris! Booking with agencies and hotels is much simpler, but be aware that they add a commission (₹100 to ₹800 per person per safari) to the official rates.

🛏 Sleeping & Eating

Many visitors are on packages that include all meals. In any case, it is usually most convenient to eat in your own hotel.

Hotel Aditya Resort
HOTEL **$**

(☎ 9414728468; www.hoteladityaresort.com; Ranthambhore Rd; r ₹400-700, with AC ₹900; 🅿 @ 🛜) This friendly place is one of the better of the few in the budget category along Ranthambhore Rd. There are just six simple, unadorned rooms (four have AC); try to get one with an outside window. The rooftop restaurant is a simple affair but the food consistently gets good reports.

The staff will help with safari bookings, but be sure to ask how much they are charging for the service.

Vatika Resort
BOUTIQUE HOTEL **$$**

(☎ 07462-222457; www.ranthambhorevatika resort.com; Ranthambhore Rd; s/d incl breakfast ₹1800/2250, with all meals ₹2800/3250; 🅿 @ 🛜) A lovely little hotel with simple but immaculate rooms, each with terrace seating overlooking a beautifully tended, flower-filled garden. It's about 1km beyond the main strip of accommodation on Ranthambhore Rd (although still 5km before the park's main gate), so much quieter than elsewhere. It's 3km from Hammir Circle roundabout.

Tiger Safari Resort
HOTEL **$$**

(☎ 07462-221137; www.tigersafariresort.com; Ranthambhore Rd; r incl breakfast ₹2590; 🅿 @ 🛜 🏊) A reasonable midrange option, with spacious doubles and 'cottages' (larger rooms with bigger bathrooms) facing a garden and small pool. The management is adept at organising safaris and wake-up calls before the morning safari. As per all the other hotels, a commission is added for this service, so ask for a breakdown of the costs.

⭐ Hotel Ranthambhore Regency
HOTEL **$$$**

(☎ 07462-221176; www.ranthambhor.com; Ranthambhore Rd; s/d incl all meals from ₹7670/873022; 🅿 @ 🛜 🏊) A very professional place that caters to tour groups but can still provide great service to independent travellers. It has immaculate, well-appointed rooms (marble floors, flatscreen TVs etc), which would rate as suites in many hotels. The central garden with an inviting pool is a virtual oasis, and there's a plush bar, an efficient restaurant and a pampering spa.

⭐ Khem Villas
BOUTIQUE HOTEL **$$$**

(☎ 07462-252099; www.khemvillas.com; Khem Villas Rd; s/d incl all meals ₹14,000/16,000, tents ₹21,500/27,000, cottages ₹24,500/29,500; ❄ @ 🛜) Set in 9 hectares of organic farmland and reforested jungle, this splendid ecolodge was created by the Singh Rathore family, the driving force behind the conservation of tigers at Ranthambhore. The accommodation ranges from colonial-style bungalow rooms to luxury tents and sumptuous stone cottages. Privacy is guaranteed – you can even bathe under the stars.

ℹ Information

Ranthambore Adventure Tours (☎ 9414 214460; www.ranthambhoreadventuretours. com; Ranthambhore Rd; ⊙ 4am-8.30pm) Safari agency that gets good reviews. At the time of research it was charging ₹2200 per person for a seat in a gypsy and ₹1800 in a canter.

Safari Booking Office (off Ranthambhore Rd, Shilpgram; ⊙ 5-6am & 1-2.30pm) The booking office, which gets chaotic when it opens, is located inside the Shilpgram campus off Ranthambhore Rd. Seats in gypsies and canters can be reserved on the website, though a single gypsy (with a premium price) and five canters are also kept for direct booking at the Forest Office.

State Bank of India (SBI; Hammir Circle; ⊙ 10am–2pm or 4pm Mon-Fri, to 1pm Sat), Has an ATM, and another ATM outside the train station

Tourist Office (☎ 07462-220808; Train Station; ⊙ 9.30am-6pm Mon-Fri, 10am-4pm Sat & Sun) Has maps of Sawai Madhopur, and can offer suggestions on safaris.

ℹ Getting There & Away

There are very few direct buses to anywhere of interest, so it's always preferable to take the train.

TRAIN

Sawai Madhopur junction station is near Hammir Circle, which leads to Ranthambhore Rd.

Agra (Agra Fort Station) sleeper ₹200, six hours, three daily (11.35am, 4.10pm, 11pm)

Delhi 2nd-class/sleeper/3AC ₹140/260/660, 5½ to eight hours, 13 daily

Jaipur 2nd-class seat/sleeper/3AC ₹95/180/560, two hours, 11 to 13 daily

Keoladeo NP (Bharatpur) 2nd-class/sleeper/3AC ₹85/170/540, 2½ hours, 10 to 13 daily

Kota (from where you can catch buses to Bundi) 2nd-class/sleeper/3AC ₹90/170/550, one to two hours, hourly

ℹ Getting Around

Bicycle hire (around ₹40 per day) is available in the main bazaar. Autorickshaws are available at the train station; it's ₹60 to ₹120 for an autorickshaw from the train station to Ranthambhore Rd, depending on where you get off. Many hotels will pick you up from the train station for free if you call ahead.

If you want to walk, turn left out of the train station and follow the road up to the overpass (200m). Turn left and cross the bridge over the railway line to reach a roundabout (200m), known as Hammir Circle. Turn left here on to Ranthambhore Rd to find accommodation.

SOUTHERN RAJASTHAN

Bundi

📋 0747 / POP 103,290

Bundi is a captivating town of narrow lanes of Brahmin-blue houses with a temple at every turn. There are fascinating step-wells, reflective lakes, and colourful bazaars. Dominating Bundi is a fantastical palace of faded parchment cupolas and loggias rising from the hills behind the town. Though an increasingly popular traveller hang-out, Bundi attracts nothing like the tourist crowds of places such as Jaipur or Udaipur. Few places in Rajasthan retain so much of the magical atmosphere of centuries past.

Bundi came into its own in the 12th century when a group of Chauhan nobles from Ajmer was pushed south by Mohammed of Ghori. They wrested the Bundi area from the Mina and Bhil tribes and made Bundi the capital of their kingdom, known as Hadoti. Bundi was generally loyal to the Mughals from the late 16th century on, but it maintained its independent status until incorporated into the state of Rajasthan after 1947.

⊙ Sights

Bundi has around 60 beautiful *baoris* (step-wells), some right in the town centre. The majesty of many of them is unfortunately diminished by their lack of water today – a result of declining groundwater levels – and by the rubbish that collects in them which no one bothers to clean up. The most impressive, **Raniji-ki-Baori** (Queen's Step-Well; Indian/foreigner ₹50/200; ☺9.30am-5pm), is 46m deep and decorated with sinuous carvings, including the avatars of Lord Vishnu. The Nagar Sagar Kund is a pair of matching step-wells just outside the old city's Chogan Gate.

Three sights around town, the Raniji-ki-Baori, **84-Pillared Cenotaph** (Indian/foreigner ₹50/200; ☺9.30am-5pm) and Sukh Mahal (p150), can be visited using a composite ticket (Indian/foreigner ₹75/350) – a great saving if you plan to visit two or more of these sights.

Bundi Palace   PALACE

(Garh Palace; Indian palace/fort/camera ₹80/100/50, foreigner palace, fort & camera ₹500; ☺8am-6pm) This extraordinary, partly decaying edifice – described by Rudyard Kipling as 'the work of goblins rather than of men' – almost seems to grow out of the rock of the hillside it stands on. Though large sections are still closed up and left to the bats, the rooms that are open hold a series of fabulous, fading turquoise-and-gold murals that are the palace's chief treasure. The palace is best explored with a local guide (₹700 half-day plus ₹100 for guide entry).

The palace was constructed during the reign of Rao Raja Ratan Singh (r 1607–31) and added to by his successors. Part of it remained occupied by the Bundi royals until 1948.

If you are going up to Taragarh as well as the palace, get tickets for both at the palace entrance. Once inside the palace's Hathi Pol (Elephant Gate), climb the stairs to the Ratan Daulat or Diwan-i-Am (Hall of Public Audience), with a white marble coronation throne. You then pass into the Chhatra Mahal, added by Rao Raja Chhatra Shabji in 1644, with some fine but rather weathered murals. Stairs lead up to the Phool Mahal (1607), the murals of which include an immense royal procession, and then the Badal Mahal (Cloud Palace; also 1607), with Bundi's very best murals, including a wonderful Chinese-inspired ceiling, divided into petal shapes and decorated with peacocks and Krishnas.

★ Chitrasala   PALACE

(Umaid Mahal; ☺8am-6pm) Within the Bundi Palace complex (p148) is the Chitrasala, a small 18th-century palace built by Rao Ummed Singh. To find it, exit through the palace's Hathi Pol (Elephant Gate) and walk around the corner uphill. Above the palace's garden courtyard are several rooms covered in beautiful paintings. There are some great Krishna images, including a detail of him sitting up a tree playing the flute after stealing the clothes of the *gopis* (milkmaids).

The back room to the right is the Sheesh Mahal, badly damaged but still featuring

Bundi

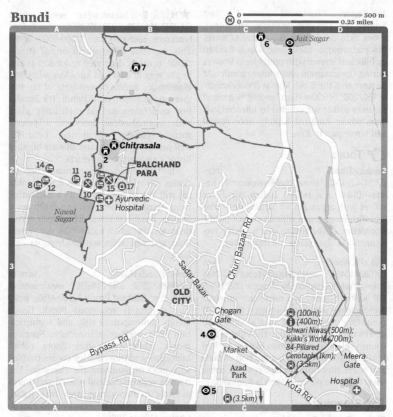

Bundi

⊙ Top Sights

1 Chitrasala B2

⊙ Sights

2 Bundi Palace B2
3 Jait Sagar C1
4 Nagar Sagar Kund C4
5 Raniji-ki-Baori C4
6 Sukh Mahal C1
7 Taragarh B1

🛏 Sleeping

8 Annpurna Haveli A2
9 Bundi Vilas A2

10 Haveli Braj Bhushanjee A2
11 Haveli Katkoun A2
12 Hotel Bundi Haveli A2
13 Kasera Heritage View A2
14 Shivam Tourist Guest House A2

🍴 Eating

Bundi Vilas .... (see 9)
15 Morgan's Place B2
16 Rainbow Cafe A2

🛍 Shopping

17 Yug Art B2

some beautiful inlaid glass, while back in the front room there's an image of 18th-century Bundi itself.

Taragarh   FORT

(Star Fort; ₹100, camera/video ₹50/100; ⊙ 8am–5pm) This ramshackle, partly overgrown 14th-century fort, on the hilltop above

Bundi Palace, is a wonderful place to ramble around – but take a stick to battle the overgrown vegetation, help the knees on the steep climb and provide confidence when surrounded by testosterone-charged macaques. To reach it, just continue on the path up behind the Chitrasala.

Jait Sagar
LAKE

Round the far side of Taragarh (p149), about 2km north from the centre of town, this picturesque, 1.5km-long lake is flanked by hills and strewn with pretty lotus flowers during the monsoon and winter months. At its near end, the **Sukh Mahal** (Indian/foreigner ₹50/200; ◉ 9.30am-5pm Tue-Sun) is a small summer palace surrounded by terraced gardens where Rudyard Kipling once stayed and wrote part of *Kim*.

☞ Tours

Keshav Bhati
TOURS

(☑ 9414394241; bharat_bhati@yahoo.com) Keshav Bhati is a retired Indian Air Force officer with a passion for Bundi. He is also an official tour guide with an encyclopaedic knowledge of the region and is highly recommended. Tour prices are negotiable.

Kukki's World
TOURS

(☑ 9828404527; www.kukkisworld.com; 43 New Colony; half-/full-day tour for 2 people US$58/67) OP 'Kukki' Sharma is a passionate amateur archaeologist who has discovered around 70 prehistoric rock-painting sites around Bundi. His trips get you out into the villages and countryside, which he knows like the back of his hand. You can visit his collection of finds and select sites from his laptop at his house (near the main police station) beforehand.

🛏 Sleeping

Shivam Tourist Guest House
GUESTHOUSE $

(☑ 9460300272, 0747-2447892; Balchand Para; s/d ₹550/700, r with AC ₹1000-1200) This guesthouse is run by two energetic young couples who are keen to help travellers get the most from their stay in Bundi. Rooms are simple but comfortable, brightly painted and spotless; the better rooms are upstairs. There is an all-veg rooftop restaurant with great sunset and palace views.

Cooking and henna-design classes are offered, plus ayurvedic massage and they can help with booking transport.

Annpurna Haveli
GUESTHOUSE $

(☑ 9602605455, 0747-2447055; www.annpurna havelibundi.com; Balchand Para; r ₹800, with breakfast & AC ₹1200; ❀ 🕾) Annpurna is a very peaceful family-run guesthouse of just six rooms opposite Nawal Sagar. The simple and clean rooms are a great budget choice, and the best rooms have lake views. Home-cooked meals are enjoyed either in the dining room or on the roof in fine weather.

★ Haveli Braj Bhushanjee
HERITAGE HOTEL $$

(☑ 0747-2442322, 9783355866; www.kiplings bundi.com; Balchand Para; r ₹1500-6000; ❀ 🕾) This rambling 200-year-old *haveli* (traditional, ornately decorated residence) is run by the very helpful and knowledgeable Braj Bhushanjee family, descendants of the former prime ministers of Bundi. It's Bundi's first guesthouse and an enchanting place with original stone interiors, a private garden, splendid rooftop views, beautiful, well-preserved murals, and all sorts of other historic and valuable artefacts.

The terrific range of accommodation includes some lovely, modernised rooms that are still in traditional style. It's a fascinating living museum where you can really get a feel for Bundi's heritage. The *haveli* serves delicious vegetarian meals with rice, wheat flour and vegetables sourced from its own farm.

Hotel Bundi Haveli
HOTEL $$

(☑ 9929291552, 0747-2446716; www.hotelbundi haveli.com; Balchand Para; r ₹1300-4750; ❀ 🕾) The exquisitely renovated Bundi Haveli blends contemporary style and sophistication with heritage architecture. Spacious rooms, white walls, stone floors, colour highlights and framed artefacts are coupled with modern plumbing and electricity. Yes, it's very comfortable and relaxed and there's a lovely rooftop dining area with palace views and an extensive, mainly Indian menu (mains ₹150 to ₹280).

Haveli Katkoun
GUESTHOUSE $$

(☑ 0747-2444311, 9414539146; www.katkounhaveli bundi.com; s/d ₹700/1200, r with AC ₹1800-2200; ❀ 🕾) Just outside the town's western gate, Katkoun is a completely revamped *haveli* with friendly family management who live downstairs. It has large, spotless rooms offering superb views on both sides, to either the lake or palace, and has an open-sided rooftop restaurant (mains ₹100 to ₹250), known for its Indian nonveg dishes.

Kasera Heritage View
GUESTHOUSE $$

(☑ 0747-2444679, 9983790314; www.kasera heritageview.com; s/d from ₹1200/1500, with AC from ₹1800/2200; ❀ @ 🕾) A revamped *haveli*, Kasera has an incongruously modern lobby, but offers a range of slightly more authentic rooms. The welcome is friendly, it's all cheerfully decorated, the rooftop restaurant has great views, and discounts of 20% to 30% are offered in summer.

The owners' sister *haveli*, Kasera Paradise, just below the palace, has the same contact details and rates.

Ishwari Niwas HERITAGE HOTEL **$$**
(☑0747-2442414; www.ishwariniwas.com; 1 Civil Lines; r ₹3400-4500; ❀🅿🛜) This graceful colonial-era hotel is run by a family with Bundi royal ancestry. Rooms are arranged around a peaceful courtyard garden; those in the old wing are variable and atmospheric, those in the new wing are spacious and modern. All are comfortable and well appointed. The dining hall sports stuffed beasts and a very interesting old map of Bundi.

Bundi Vilas HERITAGE HOTEL **$$$**
(☑0747-2444614, 9214803556; www.bundivilas.com; r incl breakfast from ₹6000; ❀@🛜) This 300-year-old *haveli* up a side alley has been tastefully renovated with golden Jaisalmer sandstone, earth-toned walls and deft interior design. The five deluxe and two suite rooms exude period character yet have excellent bathrooms. Set in the lee of the palace walls, this guesthouse has commanding views of the town below and palace above from the rooftop terrace restaurant.

✖ Eating

★ Bundi Vilas INDIAN **$$**
(☑0747-2444614; www.bundivilas.com; Balchand Para; set dinners ₹800; ⏰7-10pm; 🛜🅿) The most romantic restaurant in Bundi welcomes visitors from other hotels. Dine in the sheltered yet open-sided terrace, or on the rooftop with uninterrupted views of the fort. It's wise to book as spots are limited for the candlelit dinner experience beneath the floodlit palace. The set dinner offers several courses of exquisite food, and beer and wine are available.

Morgan's Place MULTICUISINE **$$**
(☑7833863447; Kasera Paradise Hotel; mains ₹250-400; ⏰9am-10pm; 🛜) Morgan's Place is a relaxed (possibly overly relaxed) rooftop restaurant. If you're in the mood for caffeine (it serves espresso coffee), don't mind climbing lots of stairs, and aren't in a hurry, then it delivers. It also serves fresh juice, respectable wood-fired, thin-crust pizza, pasta, chicken schnitzel and falafel.

Rainbow Cafe MULTICUISINE **$$**
(☑9887210334; mains ₹120-300; thalis ₹250-500; ⏰7am-11pm; 🛜) Bohemian ambience with chill-out tunes, floor-cushion seating, good snacks and 'special' lassis. You need to be patient, but food eventually emerges from the tiny kitchen. Located on the rooftop of the town's western gate and caged off from marauding macaques with a bamboo trellis.

🛍 Shopping

★ Yug Art ART
(www.yugartbundi.com; near Surang Gate; portrait postcard ₹1000-2000, comics from ₹3000; ⏰10am-7.30pm) Many art shops will offer you Rajasthani miniatures, but Yug Art offers to put you into one. Provide a photo and you can be pictured on elephant-back or in any number of classical scenes. Alternatively, Yug will record your India trip in a unique travel comic – you help with the script and he'll provide the artwork.

ℹ Information

Head to Sadar Bazar to find ATMs.

Ayurvedic Hospital (☑0747-2443708; Balchand Para; ⏰9am-1pm & 4-6pm Mon-Sat, 9-11am Sun) This charitable hospital prescribes natural plant-based remedies. There are medicines for all sorts of ailments, from upset tummies to arthritis, and many of them are free.

Tourist Office (☑0747-2443697; Kota Rd; ⏰8.30am-6pm) Offers bus and train schedules and free town maps.

ℹ Getting There & Around

An autorickshaw from town to the train station costs ₹80 by day and ₹120 at night.

BUS

For Ranthambhore, it's quicker to catch the train or a bus to Kota, then hop on a train to Sawai Madhopur. Direct services from **Bundi bus stand** (Kota Rd):

Ajmer ₹186, four hours, hourly

Chittorgarh 163, 4½ hours, two daily

Jaipur ₹236, five hours, hourly

Jodhpur ₹370, eight hours, five daily

Kota ₹39, 40 minutes, every 15 minutes

Pushkar ₹200, 4½ hours, one daily

Sawai Madhoper ₹120, five hours, three daily

TRAIN

Bundi station is 4km south of the old city. There are no daily trains to Jaipur, Ajmer or Jodhpur. It's better to take a bus, or to catch a train from Kota or Chittorgarh.

Agra (Agra Fort Station) sleeper ₹160, 12½ hours, daily (5.30pm)

Chittorgarh sleeper/3AC ₹180/540, 2½ to 3½ hours, three to five daily (2.10am, 2.25am, 7.05am, 9.17am and 11pm)

Delhi (Hazrat Nizamuddin) sleeper ₹315, eight to 12 hours, two daily (5.45pm and 10.38pm)

Sawai Madhopur sleeper ₹180, 2½ to five hours, three daily (5.30pm, 5.45pm and 10.28pm; the last train is the fastest)

Udaipur sleeper/3AC ₹220/540, five hours, daily (12963 Mewar Express; 2.10am)

Varanasi 3AC ₹1325, 23½ hours, Wednesday only (19669 Humsafar; 4.55pm)

Kota

📞 0744 / POP 1 MILLION

An easy day trip from Bundi, Kota is a gritty industrial and commercial city on the Chambal, Rajasthan's only permanent river. You can take boat trips on the river here, for bird- and crocodile-watching, or explore the city's old palace.

Historically a city of strategic importance, Kota still has an army base. It also has a spectacular palace with an excellent museum.

◉ Sights & Activities

City Palace   PALACE, MUSEUM
(Kotah Garh; www.kotahfort.com; Indian/foreigner ₹100/300; ⊙10am-4.30pm) The City Palace, and the fort that surrounds it, make up one of the largest such complexes in Rajasthan. This was the royal residence and centre of power, housing the Kota princedom's treasury, courts, arsenal, armed forces and state offices. The palace, entered through a gateway topped by rampant elephants, contains the offbeat Rao Madho Singh Museum, where you'll find everything for a respectable Raj existence, from silver furniture to weaponry, as well as perhaps India's most depressingly moth-eaten stuffed trophy animals.

The oldest part of the palace dates from 1624. Downstairs is a durbar (royal court) with beautiful mirrorwork, while the elegant, small-scale apartments upstairs contain exquisite, beautifully preserved paintings, particularly the hunting scenes for which Kota is renowned.

To get here, it's around ₹100 in an autorickshaw from the bus stand, and at least ₹150 from the train station.

Boat Trips   BOATING
(per person 5min/1hr ₹60/1300; ⊙10.30am-dusk) Take a hiatus from the city on a Chambal River boat trip. The river upstream of Kota is part of the Darrah National Park and it's beautiful, with lush vegetation and craggy cliffs on either side. Boats start from **Chambal Gardens** (Indian/foreigner ₹2/5), 1.5km south of the fort on the river's east bank. Maximum of six people per boat. Trips provide the opportunity to spot a host of birds, as well as gharials (thin-snouted, fish-eating crocodiles) and muggers (keep-your-limbs-inside-the-boat crocodiles).

🛏 Sleeping

Palkiya Haveli   HERITAGE HOTEL $$
(📞 0744-2387844; www.palkiyahaveli.com; Mokha Para; s/d ₹2580/3300; ❄🛜) This exquisite *haveli* has been in the same family for 200 years. Set in a deliciously peaceful corner of the old city, about 800m east of the City Palace, it's a lovely, relaxing place to stay, with

---

THE MINI MASTERPIECES OF KOTA & BUNDI

Some of Rajasthan's finest miniature and mural painting was produced around Bundi and Kota, the ruling Hada Rajputs being keen artistic patrons. The style combined the dominant features of folk painting – intense colour and bold forms – with the Mughals' concern with naturalism.

The Bundi and Kota schools were initially similar, but developed markedly different styles, though both usually have a background of thick foliage, cloudy skies and scenes lit by the setting sun. When architecture appears it is depicted in loving detail. The willowy women sport round faces, large petal-shaped eyes and small noses – forerunners of Bollywood pin-ups.

The Bundi school is notable for its blue hues, with a palette of turquoise and azure unlike anything seen elsewhere. Bundi Palace in particular hosts some wonderful examples.

In Kota you'll notice a penchant for hunting scenes with fauna and dense foliage – vivid, detailed portrayals of hunting expeditions in Kota's once thickly wooded surrounds. Kota's City Palace has some of the best-preserved wall paintings in the state.

MAJOR TRAINS FROM KOTA

DESTINATION	TRAIN	DEPARTURE	ARRIVAL	FARE (₹)
Agra	19037/19039 Avadh Exp	2.40pm	9.50pm	225/600/850 (A)
Chittorgarh	29020 Dehradun Exp	8.45am	11.35am	170/635/1180 (C)
Delhi (Hazrat Nizamuddin)	12903 Golden Temple Mail	11.05am	6.45pm	315/805/1115/1855 (E)
Jaipur	12955 Mumbai–Jaipur Exp	8.55am	12.40pm	225/580/780/1275 (E)
Mumbai	12904 Golden Temple Mail	2.25pm	5.20am	490/1275/1805/3035 (E)
Sawai Madhopur	12059 Shatabdi	5.55am	7.03am	125/370 (D)
Udaipur	12963 Mewar Exp	1.30am	7.15am	245/580/780/1275 (E)

Fares: (A) sleeper/3AC/2AC, (B) sleeper, (C) sleeper/2AC/1AC, (D) 2nd class/AC chair, (E) sleeper/3AC/2AC/1AC

welcoming hosts, a high-walled garden and a courtyard with a graceful neem tree.

There are impressive murals and appealing heritage rooms, and the food is top-notch.

ⓘ Information

Tourist Office (☑ 0744-2327695; RTDC Hotel Chambal; ☺ 9.30am-6pm Mon-Sat) Has free maps of Kota.

ⓘ Getting There & Around

Minibuses and shared autorickshaws link the train station and main bus stand (₹10 per person). A private autorickshaw costs ₹50 to ₹100.

BUS

Services from the main bus stand (on Bundi Rd, east of the bridge over the Chambal River) include the following:

Ajmer (for Pushkar) ₹230, four to five hours, at least 10 daily

Bundi ₹39, 40 minutes, every 15 minutes throughout the day

Chittorgarh ₹216, four hours, half-hourly from 6am

Jaipur ₹252, five hours, hourly from 5am

Udaipur ₹320 to ₹380, six to seven hours, at least 10 daily

TRAIN

Kota is on the main Mumbai–Delhi train route via Sawai Madhopur, so there are plenty of trains to choose from, though departure times aren't always convenient.

Agra (Fort) sleeper ₹225, five to nine hours, at least four daily (7.30am, 9.50am, 2.40pm and 9pm)

Chittorgarh sleeper ₹170, three to four hours, three to four daily (1.10am, 1.25am, 6.05am and 8.45am)

Delhi (New Delhi or Hazrat Nizamuddin) sleeper ₹315, five to eight hours, almost hourly

Jaipur sleeper ₹225, four hours, six daily (2.55am, 7.40am, 8.55am, 12.35pm, 5.35pm and 11.50pm), plus other trains on selected days

Mumbai sleeper ₹490, 14 hours, five daily fast trains (7.45am, 2.25pm, 5.30pm, 9.05pm and 11.45pm)

Sawai Madhopur 2nd-class seat/sleeper ₹125/180, one to two hours, more than 24 daily

Udaipur sleeper ₹245, six hours, one or two daily (1.10am and 1.30am)

Chittorgarh (Chittor)

☑ 01472 / POP 184,000

Chittorgarh is the largest fort complex in India, nearly 6km long and 500m across, and is a fascinating place to explore. It sits atop a hill that rises abruptly from the plains, its defensive walls augmented on all sides by 150m-plus cliffs.

Chittorgarh's history epitomises Rajput romanticism, chivalry and tragedy, and it holds a special place in the hearts of many Rajputs. Three times (in 1303, 1535 and 1568) Chittorgarh was under attack from a more powerful enemy; each time, its people chose death before dishonour. The men donned saffron martyrs' robes and rode out from the fort to certain death, while the women and children immolated themselves on huge funeral pyres. After the last of the three sackings, Rana Udai Singh II fled to Udaipur, where he established a new capital. In 1616, Jehangir returned Chittor to the Rajputs. There was no attempt at resettlement, though it was restored in 1905.

⊙ Sights

★ **Chittorgarh** FORT
(Indian/foreigner ₹40/600; ☺ dawn-dusk) A zigzag ascent of more than 1km starts at Padal Pol and leads through six gateways to the

Chittorgarh (Chittor)

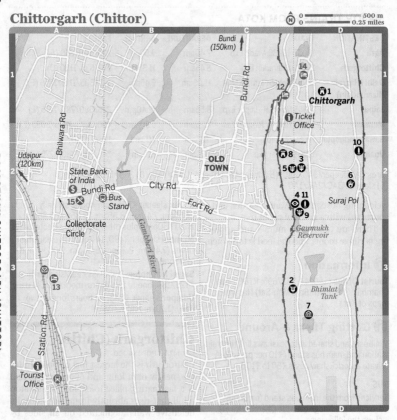

main gate on the western side, the Ram Pol (the former back entrance). Inside Ram Pol is a still-occupied village – turn right here for the **ticket office** (☉dawn-dusk). The rest of the plateau is deserted except for the wonderful palaces, towers and temples that survive from the fort's heyday, along with a few recent temples. A loop road runs around the plateau.

A typical vehicular exploration of the fort takes two to three hours. Licensed guides charging around ₹400 for up to four hours are available for either walking or autorickshaw tours, usually at the ticket office. There's a sound-and-light show at dusk (Hindi/English ₹100/200); the English show is on Fridays.

➤ Meera & Kumbha Shyam Temples

Both of these temples southeast of the Rana Kumbha Palace were built by Rana Kumbha in the ornate Indo-Aryan style, with classic, tall sikharas (spires). The Meera Temple, the smaller of the two, is now associated with the mystic-poetess Meerabai, a 16th-century Mewar royal who was poisoned by her brother-in-law but survived due to the blessings of Krishna. The Kumbha Shyam Temple (Temple of Varah) is dedicated to Vishnu and its carved panels illustrate 15th-century Mewar life.

➤ Tower of Victory

The glorious Tower of Victory (Jaya Stambha), symbol of Chittorgarh, was erected by Rana Kumbha in the 1440s, probably to commemorate a victory over Mahmud Khilji of Malwa. Dedicated to Vishnu, it rises 37m in nine exquisitely carved storeys, and you can climb the 157 narrow stairs (the interior is also carved) to the 8th floor, from where there's a good view of the area.

Below the tower, to the southwest, is the Mahasati area, where there are many *sati* (ritual suicide of widow on husband's funeral pyre) stones – this was the royal cremation ground and was also where 13,000 women committed *jauhar* (ritual mass suicide by immolation) in 1535. The Samidheshwar Temple, built in the 6th century and restored in 1427, is nearby. Notable among its intricate carving is a Trimurti (three-faced) figure of Shiva.

➤ Gaumukh Reservoir

Walk down beyond the Samidheshwar Temple and at the edge of the cliff is a deep tank, the Gaumukh Reservoir, where you can feed the fish. The reservoir takes its name from a spring that feeds the tank from a *gaumukh* (cow's mouth) carved into the cliffside.

➤ Padmini's Palace

Continuing south, you reach the Kalika Mata Temple, an 8th-century sun temple damaged during the first sacking of Chittorgarh and then converted to a temple for the goddess Kali in the 14th century. Padmini's Palace stands about 250m further south, beside a small lake with a central pavilion. The bronze gates to this pavilion were carried off by Akbar and can now be seen in Agra Fort.

➤ Suraj Pol & Tower of Fame

Suraj Pol, on the fort's east side, was the main gate and offers fantastic views across the cultivated plains. Opposite is the Neel-kanth Mahadev Jain Temple. A little further north, the 24m-high Tower of Fame (Kirtti Stambha), dating from 1301, is smaller than the Tower of Victory. Built by a Jain merchant, the tower is dedicated to Adinath, the first Jain *tirthankar* (one of the 24 revered Jain teachers) and is decorated with naked figures of various other *tirthankars*, indicating that it is a monument of the Digambara (sky-clad) order. A narrow stairway leads up the seven storeys to the top. Next door is a 14th-century Jain temple.

🛏 Sleeping & Eating

Chittorgarh Fort Haveli
HOTEL $

(☏9829170190; www.chittorgarhforthaveli.com; Ram Pol, Chittorgarh Fort; r from ₹1200; 🛜) The newest accommodation inside the fort, this refurbished *haveli* provides clean and comfortable rooms at a budget price. Rooms are furnished simply, but in traditional Rajput style, and some have great views. A small range of meals, including breakfast, is available on the pleasant rooftop terrace.

★ Padmini Haveli
HERITAGE HOTEL $$

(☏9414734497, 9414110090; www.thepadmini haveli.com; Annapoorna Temple Rd, Shah Chowk, Village, Chittorgarh Fort; r/ste incl breakfast ₹4200/5200; ❄@🛜) This fabulous guesthouse with charming, enthusiastic and well-informed hosts is the best accommodation within the fort. Stylish rooms have granite bathrooms and traditional decoration, and open onto the communal courtyard of the *haveli*. The hosts are official Chittorgarh guides and they live on-site, providing Italian coffee and delicious homemade meals and jams.

There are only six rooms, four standard and two suites, so booking is advised. This white-washed *haveli* with a large black door can be hard to find in the labyrinthine laneways of the village, so call first.

Hotel Pratap Palace
HOTEL $$

(☏01472-240099; www.hotelpratappalace chittaurgarh.com; off Maharana Pratap Setu Marg; s/d from ₹2650/3140; ❄@🛜) This hotel has a range of rooms, though its business as a lunch stop for bus groups takes precedence over its accommodation enterprise. Even the more expensive rooms can suffer from poor maintenance, and cleanliness standards could be higher. There's a large multicuisine restaurant that produces buffets for tour groups. Try to order à la carte if you can.

The owners also run village tours, horse rides and the upmarket Hotel Castle Bijaipur out of town.

Hotel Castle Bijaipur   HERITAGE HOTEL **$$$**
(☑ 01472-276351; www.castlebijaipur.co.in; Bijaipur; s/d from ₹4500/5000, ste ₹10000; ❄ 🛜 🕾) This fantastically set 16th-century palace is an ideal rural retreat 41km by road east of Chittorgarh. It's a great place to settle down with a good book, compose a fairy-tale fantasy or just laze around. Rooms are romantic and luxurious, and there's a pleasant garden courtyard and an airy restaurant serving Rajasthani food. It's popular with tour groups.

Reservations should be made through the website or through Chittor's Hotel Pratap Palace. The owners can arrange transfer from Chittor as well as horse and 4WD safaris, birdwatching, cooking classes, massage and yoga.

**Chokhi Dhani Garden
Family Restaurant**   INDIAN **$**
(☑ 9413716593; Bundi Rd; mains ₹80-150, thalis ₹120-290; ⊙ 9am-10.30pm; ❄ 🍴) This fancooled roadside *dhaba* (casual eatery, serving snacks and basic meals) with extra seating in the back does a good-value selection of vegetarian dishes, including filling thalis and a variety of North and South Indian dishes.

ⓘ Information

ATMs can be found near Collectorate Circle.

Main post office (Bhilwara Rd; ⊙ 10am-4pm Mon-Fri, to noon Sat)

State Bank of India (SBI; Bundi Rd) Has an ATM.

Tourist office (☑ 01472-241089; Station Rd; ⊙ 10am-1.30pm & 2-5pm Mon-Sat) Friendly and helpful, with a town map and brochure.

ⓘ Getting There & Around

A full tour of the fort by autorickshaw should cost around ₹400 to ₹500 return. You can arrange this yourself in town.

BUS

Services from the Chittorgarh **bus stand** (Bundi Rd) include the following:

Ajmer (for Pushkar) ₹197, AC ₹347, four hours, hourly until midafternoon

Bundi ₹163, four hours, three daily

Jaipur ₹339, AC ₹660, seven hours, around every 1½ hours

Kota ₹198, four hours, hourly

Udaipur ₹120, AC ₹255, 2½ hours, half-hourly

TRAIN

Ajmer (for Pushkar) sleeper ₹135, three hours, five to seven daily (12.30am, 2.50am, 8.20am, 11.20am, 1.55pm, 5.15pm and 10.30pm)

Bundi sleeper ₹200, two to 3½ hours, three daily (2.50pm, 3.45pm and 8.45pm)

Delhi (Delhi Sarai Rohilla or Hazrat Nizamuddin) sleeper ₹530, 10 hours, two fast trains daily (7.30pm and 8.45pm)

Jaipur sleeper ₹195, 5½ hours, four to five daily (12.30am, 2.50am, 8.20am, 8.35am and 4.15pm)

Sawai Madhopur sleeper ₹275, four to nine hours, three daily (2.50pm, 3.45pm and 8.45pm; the latest is the quickest)

Udaipur sleeper ₹200, two hours, six to seven daily (4.25am, 5.05am, 5.35am, 1.55pm, 2.25pm, 4.50pm and 7.25pm)

Udaipur

☑ 0294 / POP 451,100

Udaipur has a romance of setting unmatched in Rajasthan and arguably in all India – snuggling beside tranquil Lake Pichola, with the purple ridges of the Aravalli Range stretching away in every direction. Fantas-

MAJOR TRAINS FROM CHITTORGARH

DESTINATION	TRAIN	DEPARTURE	ARRIVAL	FARE (₹)
Ajmer (for Pushkar)	12991 Udaipur–Jaipur Exp	8.20am	11.25am	135/515/765/715 (A)
Bundi	29019 MDS–Kota Exp	3.35pm	5.45pm	200/1020/1715 (B)
Delhi (Hazrat Nizamuddin)	12964 Mewar Exp	8.50pm	6.35am	530/1425/2030/3430 (C)
Jaipur	12991 Udaipur–Jaipur Exp	8.20am	1.30pm	195/720/885 (D)
Sawai Madhopur	29019 MDS–Kota Exp	3.35pm	9.25pm	275/1020/1715 (B)
Udaipur	19329 Udaipur City Exp	4.50pm	7.15pm	200/720/1020/1715 (C)

Fares: (A) 2nd-class seat/AC chair/3AC/1st-class seat, (B) sleeper/2AC/1AC, (C) sleeper/3AC/2AC/1AC, (D) 2nd-class seat/AC chair/3AC

tical palaces, temples, *havelis* (traditional, ornately decorated residences) and countless narrow, crooked, timeless streets add the human counterpoint to the city's natural charms. For the visitor there's the serenity of boat rides on the lakes, the bustle and colour of bazaars, a lively arts scene, the quaint old-world feel of its heritage hotels, tempting shops and some lovely countryside to explore on wheels, feet or horseback.

Udaipur's tag of 'the most romantic spot on the continent of India' was first applied in 1829 by Colonel James Tod, the East India Company's first political agent in the region. Today the romance is wearing slightly thin as ever-taller hotels compete for the best view and traffic clogs ancient thoroughfares.

History

Udaipur was founded in 1568 by Maharana Udai Singh II following the final sacking of Chittorgarh by the Mughal emperor Akbar. This new capital of Mewar had a much less vulnerable location than Chittorgarh. Mewar still had to contend with repeated invasions by the Mughals and, later, the Marathas, until British intervention in the early 19th century. This resulted in a treaty that protected Udaipur from invaders while allowing Mewar's rulers to remain effectively all-powerful in internal affairs. The ex-royal family remains influential and in recent decades has been the driving force behind the rise of Udaipur as a tourist destination.

⊙ Sights

★**City Palace**   PALACE
(www.eternalmewar.in; adult/child ₹30/15; ⊙9am-11pm) Surmounted by balconies, towers and cupolas towering over the lake, the imposing City Palace is Rajasthan's largest palace, with a facade 244m long and 30.4m high. Construction was begun in 1599 by Maharana Udai Singh II, the city's founder, and it later became a conglomeration of structures (including 11 separate smaller palaces) built and extended by various maharanas, though it still manages to retain a surprising uniformity of design.

You can enter the complex through **Badi Pol** (Great Gate; City Palace Rd) at the northern end, or the Sheetla Mata Gate to the south. Tickets for the City Palace Museum are sold at both entrances. Note: you must pay the ₹30 City Palace entrance ticket in order to pass south through Chandra Chowk Gate, en route to the Crystal Gallery or Rameshwar

Ghat for the Lake Pichola boat rides, even if you have a City Palace Museum ticket.

Inside Badi Pol, eight arches on the left commemorate the eight times maharanas were weighed here and their weight in gold or silver distributed to the lucky locals. You then pass through the three-arched Tripolia Gate into a large courtyard, Manek Chowk. Spot the large tiger-catching cage, which worked rather like an oversized mousetrap, and the smaller one for leopards.

★**City Palace Museum**   MUSEUM
(City Palace; adult/child ₹300/100, guide per hour ₹250, audio guide ₹200; ⊙9.30am-5.30pm, last entry 4.30pm) The main part of the City Palace is open as the City Palace Museum, with rooms extravagantly decorated with mirrors, tiles and paintings, and housing a large and varied collection of artefacts. It's entered from Ganesh Chowk, which you reach from Manek Chowk.

The City Palace Museum begins with the Rai Angan (Royal Courtyard), the very spot where Udai Singh met the sage who told him to build a city here. Rooms along one side contain historical paintings, including several of the Battle of Haldighati (1576), in which Mewar forces under Maharana Pratap, one of the great Rajput heroes, gallantly fought the army of Mughal emperor Akbar to a stalemate.

As you move through the palace, highlights include the Baadi Mahal (1699), where a pretty central garden gives fine views over the city. Kishan (Krishna) Vilas has a remarkable collection of miniatures from the time of Maharana Bhim Singh (r 1778–1828). The story goes that Bhim Singh's daughter

---

ANIMAL AID UNLIMITED

The spacious refuge of **Animal Aid Unlimited** (☑9784005989, 9829843726; www.animalaidunlimited.org; Badi Village) treats around 200 street animals a day (mainly dogs, donkeys and cows) and answers more than 3000 emergency rescue calls a year. The refuge welcomes volunteers and visitors: you can visit between 9am and noon without needing to call first. The refuge is in Badi village, 7km northwest of Udaipur.

A round trip by autorickshaw, including waiting time, costs around ₹500. Call Animal Aid Unlimited if you see an injured or ill street animal in Udaipur.

Udaipur

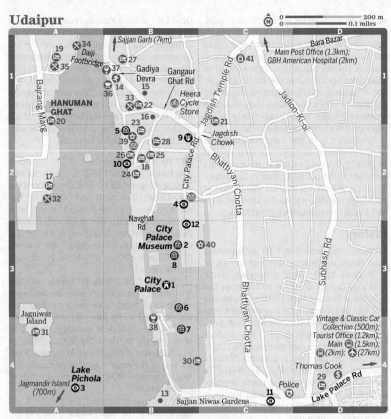

Krishna Kumari drank a fatal cup of poison here to solve the dilemma of rival princely suitors from Jaipur and Jodhpur who were both threatening to invade Mewar if she didn't marry them. The Surya Choupad features a huge, ornamental sun – the symbol of the sun-descended Mewar dynasty – and opens into Mor Chowk (Peacock Courtyard) with its lovely mosaics of peacocks, the favourite Rajasthani bird.

The southern end of the museum comprises the Zenana Mahal, the royal ladies' quarters, built in the 17th century. It now contains a long picture gallery with lots of royal hunting scenes (note the comic strip–style of the action in each painting). The Zenana Mahal's central courtyard, Laxmi Chowk, contains a beautiful white pavilion and a stable of *howdahs*, palanquins and other people-carriers.

Crystal Gallery
GALLERY

(City Palace; adult/child incl audio guide ₹700/450; ☺9am-7pm) Houses rare crystal that Maha-

rana Sajjan Singh (r 1874–84) ordered from F&C Osler & Co in England in 1877. The maharana died before it arrived, and all the items stayed forgotten and packed up in boxes for 110 years. The extraordinary, extravagant collection includes crystal chairs, sofas, tables and even beds. The rather hefty admission fee also includes entry to the grand **Durbar Hall** (City Palace). Tickets are available at the City Palace gates or the Crystal Gallery entrance. Photography is prohibited.

Government Museum
MUSEUM

(Indian/foreigner ₹20/100; ☺10am-5pm Tue-Sun) Entered from Ganesh Chowk, this museum has a splendid collection of jewel-like miniature paintings of the Mewar school and a turban that belonged to Shah Jahan, creator of the Taj Mahal. Stranger exhibits include a stuffed monkey holding a lamp. There are also regal maharana portraits in profile, documenting Mewar's rulers along with the changing fashions of the moustache.

Udaipur

★ **Lake Pichola**   LAKE
Limpid and large, Lake Pichola reflects the grey-blue mountains on its mirror-like surface. It was enlarged by Maharana Udai Singh II, following his foundation of the city, by flooding Picholi village, which gave the lake its name. The lake is now 4km long and 3km wide, but remains shallow and dries up completely during severe droughts. The City Palace complex, including the gardens at its southern end, extends nearly 1km along the lake's eastern shore.

Boat trips (adult/child 10am-2pm ₹400/200, 3-5pm ₹700/400; ⊙10am-5pm) leave roughly hourly from Rameshwar Ghat, within the City Palace complex (note, you have to pay ₹30 to enter). The trips make a stop at Jagmandir Island, where you can stay for as long as you like before taking any boat back. Take your own drinks and snacks, though, as those sold on the island are extortionately expensive. You can also take 25-minute boat rides from **Lal Ghat** (Lal Ghat Rd; ₹250 per person) throughout the day without the need

to enter the City Palace complex: it's worth checking in advance what time the popular sunset departure casts off.

Jagmandir Island   ISLAND
The palace on Jagmandir Island, about 800m south of Jagniwas, was built by Maharana Karan Singh II in 1620, added to by his successor Maharana Jagat Singh, and changed very little until the last few years when it was partly converted into another (smaller) hotel. When lit up at night it has more romantic sparkle to it than the Lake Palace. As well as the seven hotel rooms, the island has a restaurant, bar and spa, which are open to visitors.

With its entrance flanked by a row of enormous stone elephants, the island has an ornate 17th-century tower, the Gol Mahal, carved from bluestone and containing a small exhibit on Jagmandir's history, plus a garden and lovely views across the lake.

Boat trips leave roughly hourly from Rameshwar Ghat, within the City Palace complex (note, you have to pay ₹30 to enter).

The trips make a stop at Jagmandir Island, where you can stay for as long as you like before taking any boat back. You can take your own drinks and snacks to avoid the expensive options on the island.

Jagdish Temple
HINDU TEMPLE

(⊙ 5.30am-2pm & 4-10pm) Reached by a steep, elephant-flanked flight of steps, 150m north of the City Palace's Badi Pol, this busy Indo-Aryan temple was built by Maharana Jagat Singh in 1651. The wonderfully carved main structure enshrines a black stone image of Vishnu as Jagannath, Lord of the Universe. There's also a brass image of the Garuda (Vishnu's man-bird vehicle) in a shrine facing the main structure.

Bagore-ki-Haveli
MUSEUM

(Gangaur Ghat; Indian/foreigner ₹50/100, camera ₹50; ⊙ 9.30am-5.30pm) This gracious 18th-century *haveli*, set on the water's edge at Gangaur Ghat, was built by a Mewar prime minister and has since been carefully restored. There are 138 rooms set around courtyards, some arranged to evoke the period during which the house was inhabited, while others house cultural displays, including – intriguingly enough – the world's biggest turban.

Sajjan Garh
PALACE

(Monsoon Palace) Perched on top of a distant hill like a fairy-tale castle, this melancholy, neglected late-19th-century palace was constructed by Maharana Sajjan Singh. Originally an astronomical centre, it became a monsoon palace and hunting lodge. Now government owned, it's in a sadly dilapidated state, but visitors stream up here for the marvellous views, particularly at sunset. It's 5km west of the old city as the crow flies, about 9km by the winding road.

At the foot of the hill you enter the 5-sq-km **Sajjan Garh Wildlife Sanctuary** (Indian/foreigner ₹50/300, car ₹200). A good way to visit is with the daily sunset excursion in a minivan driven by an enterprising taxi driver who picks up tourists at the entrance to Bagore-ki-Haveli at Gangaur Ghat every day at 5pm. The round trip costs ₹350 per person, including waiting time (but not the sanctuary fees). His minivan has 'Monsoon Palace–Sajjangarh Fort' written across the front of it. Alternatively, autorickshaws charge ₹200 one way to the sanctuary gate, which they are not allowed to pass. Share taxis ferry people the final 4km up to the palace for ₹200 per person.

Vintage & Classic Car Collection
MUSEUM

(Garden Hotel, Lake Palace Rd; adult/child ₹350/200; ⊙ 9am-9pm) The maharanas' car collection makes a fascinating diversion, for what it tells about their elite lifestyle and for the vintage vehicles themselves. Housed within the former state garage are 22 splendid vehicles, including the beautiful 1934 Rolls-Royce Phantom used in the Bond film *Octopussy,* and the Cadillac convertible that whisked Queen Elizabeth II to the airport in 1961. The museum is a 10-minute walk east along Lake Palace Rd.

🏃 Activities & Courses

Krishna Ranch
HORSE RIDING

(⌨ 9828059505; www.krishnaranch.com; full day incl lunch ₹3700) Experienced owner-guide Dinesh Jain leads most trips himself, riding local Marwari horses. The ranch is situated in beautiful countryside near Hawala village, 7km northwest of Udaipur. There are also attractive cottages (p163) at the ranch.

Prakash Yoga
YOGA

(⌨ 0294-2524872; inside Chandpol; by donation; ⊙ classes 8am & 7pm) A friendly hatha yoga centre with hour-long classes. The teacher has more than 20 years' experience. It's tucked inside Chandpol, near the footbridge, but well signed.

Shashi Cooking Classes
COOKING

(⌨ 9929303511; www.shashicookingclasses.blog spot.com; Sunrise Restaurant, 18 Gangaur Ghat Rd; 4hr class ₹1500; ⊙ classes 10.30am & 5.30pm) Readers rave about Shashi's high-spirited classes, teaching many fundamental Indian dishes. Classes go for 3½ to four hours and include a free recipe booklet.

Sushma's Cooking Classes
COOKING

(⌨ 7665852163; www.cookingclassesinudaipur.com; Hotel Krishna Niwas, 35 Lal Ghat; 2hr class ₹1500) A highly recommended cooking class run by the enthusiastic Sushma. Classes offer up anything from traditional Rajasthani dishes and learning how to make spice mixes, through bread-making to the all-important method of making the perfect cup of chai.

Prem Musical Instruments
MUSIC

(⌨ 9414343583; 28 Gadiya Devra; per hour ₹700; ⊙ 9am-8.30pm) Rajesh Prajapati (Bablu) is a successful local musician who gives sitar, tabla and flute lessons. From his tiny shop established in 1997 he also sells and repairs instruments and can arrange performances.

Ashoka Arts   ARTS & CRAFTS
(Hotel Gangaur Palace, Ashoka Haveli, Gangaur Ghat Rd; per hour from ₹200) Learn the basics of classic miniature painting from a local master.

☞ Tours

Art of Bicycle Trips   CYCLING
(☑8769822745; www.artofbicycletrips.com; 27 Gadiya Devra, inside Chandpol; half-day tour ₹2000) This well-run outfit offers a great way to get out of the city. The Lakecity Loop is a 30km half-day tour that quickly leaves Udaipur behind to have you wheeling through villages, farmland and along the shores of Fateh Sagar and Badi Lakes. Other options include a vehicle-supported trip further afield to Kumbhalgarh and Ranakpur. Bikes are well maintained and all come with helmets.

Millets of Mewar   WALKING
(☑8890419048; www.milletsofmewar.org; Hanuman Ghat; per person ₹2000) Health-food specialists Millets of Mewar (p163) organises two-hour city tours (minimum two people) on which you can meet local artisans who live and work in Udaipur. Tours should be booked a day in advance; they leave from the restaurant at 10am.

🛏 Sleeping

Many budget and midrange lodgings cluster close to the lake, especially on its eastern side in Lal Ghat. This area is a tangle of streets and lanes close to the City Palace. It's Udaipur's tourist epicentre and has numerous eateries and shops. Directly across the water from Lal Ghat, Hanuman Ghat has a slightly more local vibe and often better views, though you're certainly not out of the touristic zone.

🛏 Lal Ghat

Lal Ghat Guest House   GUESTHOUSE $
(☑9414812491, 0294-2525301; www.lalghat.com; 33 Lal Ghat; dm ₹250, r ₹750, with AC ₹2000; ❄@🛜) This mellow guesthouse by the lake was one of the first to open in Udaipur, and it's still a sound choice, with an amazing variety of older and newer rooms. Accommodation ranges from a spruce, nonsmoking dorm (with curtained-off beds and lockers under the mattresses) to the best room, which sports a stone wall, a big bed, a big mirror and AC.

Most rooms have lake views and those in the older part of the building generally have more character. There's a small kitchen for self-caterers.

Bunkyard Hostel   HOSTEL $
(☑9166656366; Lal Ghat; dm ₹550, r from ₹1700; ❄🛜) Bright and cheerful, Bunkyard has colourful rooms, helpful staff and a rooftop restaurant with lake views. There's free chai on the roof at sunset.

Note that the dorm is air-conditioned.

Nukkad Guest House   GUESTHOUSE $
(☑0294-2411403; nukkad_raju@yahoo.com; 56 Ganesh Ghati; s without bathroom ₹200, r ₹550-800; 🛜) Nukkad has clean and simple fan-cooled rooms radiating off a vertigo-inspiring central atrium. On the roof there's a sociable restaurant were you can access the hotel's wi-fi. Join afternoon cooking classes and morning yoga sessions (by donation) without stepping outside the door – just don't stay out past curfew or get caught washing your clothes in your bathroom.

Jaiwana Haveli   HOTEL $$
(☑9829005859, 0294-2411103; www.jaiwanahaveli.com; 14 Lal Ghat; r incl breakfast ₹5000; ❄@🛜) Professionally run by two helpful brothers and efficient staff, this smart place has spotless, unfussy rooms with good beds, TVs and attractive block-printed fabrics. Book a corner room for views. The rooftop restaurant has great lake views and Indian food (mains ₹250 to ₹595), plus there's a mod cafe (p164) on the ground floor.

Hotel Baba Palace   HOTEL $$
(☑0294-2427126; www.hotelbabapalace.com; Jagdish Chowk; r incl breakfast from ₹2000; ❄🛜) This central hotel has sparkling rooms with decent beds behind solid doors and there's an elevator. It's eye to eye with the Jagdish Temple, so many of the rooms have interesting views; all have air-conditioning and TVs, some have delightfully canopied beds. On top there's the popular Mayur Rooftop Cafe (p163). Free airport pick-ups available.

Hotel Krishna Niwas   HOTEL $$
(☑9414167341, 0294-2420163; www.hotelkrishnaniwas.com; 35 Lal Ghat; d ₹1750-2499; ❄@🛜) Run by an artist family, Krishna Niwas has smart, clean, AC rooms; those with views are smaller, and some come with balconies. There are splendid vistas from the rooftop, and a decent restaurant. You can also try your own cooking or paint your own miniature after taking an in-house cooking lesson or painting course (₹1200 for three hours).

Pratap Bhawan
HOTEL $$

(☏ 0294-2560566; www.pratapbhawanudaipur.
com; 12 Lal Ghat; r ₹1650-2500; ❄ 🕸) A curving
marble staircase leads up from the wide lob-
by to large rooms with big bathrooms and,
in many cases, cushioned window seats. A
deservedly popular place, with the excellent
rooftop Charcoal restaurant (p163).

Poonam Haveli
HOTEL $$

(☏ 0294-2410303; www.hotelpoonamhaveli.com;
39 Lal Ghat; r incl breakfast ₹3480; ❄ @ 🕸) A
modern place decked out in traditional style,
friendly Poonam has 16 spacious, spotlessly
clean rooms with marble floors, big beds,
TVs and spare but tasteful decor, plus pleasant sitting areas.

None of the rooms enjoy lake views, but
the rooftop Winter garden restaurant does,
and it also makes wood-fired pizzas among
the usual Indian and traveller fare. There is
an elevator.

Hotel Gangaur Palace
HERITAGE HOTEL $$

(☏ 0294-2422303; www.ashokahaveli.com; Asho-
ka Haveli, 339 Gangaur Ghat Rd; s ₹800, d ₹1500-
3000; ❄ ❄ 🕸) This elaborate, faded *haveli* is
set around a stone-pillared courtyard, with a
wide assortment of rooms on several floors.
It's gradually moving upmarket with an ele-
vator and with bright rooms featuring lake
views, wall paintings and window seats.

The hotel also has an in-house palm read-
er, a fixed price art shop, art school (p161),
and a rooftop cafe and restaurant.

★ Jagat Niwas
Palace Hotel
HERITAGE HOTEL $$$

(☏ 0294-2420133, 7073000378; www.jagatniwas
palace.com; 23-25 Lal Ghat; r incl breakfast from
₹5096; ❄ 🕸 🛳) This leading hotel set in
two converted lakeside *havelis* takes the
location cake, and staff are efficient and
always courteous. The lake-view rooms are
charming, with carved wooden furniture,
cushioned window seats and pretty prints.
Rooms without a lake view are as comfortable and attractive, and considerably cheaper, than those with the view.

The white-washed building is full of
character, featuring pleasant sitting areas,
terraces and courtyards, and it makes the
most of its position with a picture-perfect
rooftop restaurant and small pool.

🔎 Hanuman Ghat

Dream Heaven
GUESTHOUSE $

(☏ 9928258222, 0294-2431038; www.dreamheaven.
co.in; Hanuman Ghat; r ₹400-1200; ❄ @ 🕸) This
higgledy-piggledy building boasts clean
rooms with wall hangings and paintings.
Bathrooms are smallish, though some rooms
have a decent balcony and/or views. The
food at the rooftop restaurant (dishes ₹120
to ₹200), which overlooks the lake, is fresh
and tasty; it's the perfect place to chill out on
a pile of cushions.

goStops Udaipur
HOSTEL $

(☏ 1133138155; www.gostops.com; Hanuman Ghat;
dm incl breakfast ₹425-500, r incl breakfast ₹2130,
with AC ₹2660; ❄ 🕸) The attractions of this
buzzing place include the rooftop space to
chill out in, the colourful decor and the sheer
number of activities, walks, yoga, bike rides,
painting courses etc, that are scheduled regularly. The hostel is in Hanuman Ghat so it is
relatively peaceful, too.

Amet Haveli
HERITAGE HOTEL $$

(☏ 0294-2431085; www.amethaveliudaipur.com;
Hanuman Ghat; s/d from ₹3750/4130; ❄ @ 🕸 🛳)
A 350-year-old heritage building on the
lakeshore, with delightful rooms featuring
cushioned window seats, coloured glass and
little shutters. They're set around a pretty
courtyard and pond. Splurge on one with a
balcony or giant bath tub. One of Udaipur's
most romantic restaurants, Ambrai (p164),
is part of the hotel.

🔎 City Palace

Shiv Niwas Palace Hotel
HERITAGE HOTEL $$$

(☏ 0294-2528016; www.hrhhotels.com; City Palace Complex; r ₹14,000-72,000; ❄ 🕸 🛳) This
hotel, in the former palace guest quarters,
has opulent common areas such as its pool
courtyard, bar and lawn garden. Some of the
suites are truly palatial, filled with fountains
and silver, but the standard rooms are poorer
value. Go for a suite, or just for a drink, meal
or massage. Rates drop dramatically from
April to September.

Taj Lake Palace
HERITAGE HOTEL $$$

(☏ 0294-2428800; www.tajhotels.com; r from
₹35,000; ❄ @ 🕸 🛳) The icon of Udaipur,
this romantic white-marble palace seem-
ingly floating on the lake is extraordinary,
with open-air courtyards, lotus ponds and
a small, mango-tree-shaded pool. Rooms

are hung with breezy silks and filled with carved furniture. Some of the cheapest overlook the lily pond rather than the lake; the mural-decked suites will make you truly feel like a maharaja. Access is by boat from the hotel's own jetty in the City Palace gardens. Rates can vary a lot with season and demand: check the website.

Other Areas

Rangniwas Palace Hotel   HERITAGE HOTEL $$
(☏0294-2523890; www.rangniwaspalace.com; Lake Palace Rd; s/d from ₹1460/1760, ste ₹5900; 🌓🛜🌊) This 19th-century palace has plenty of heritage character, though some rooms are rather old fashioned. There's a central garden with a small pool shaded by mature palms. The quaint rooms in the older section are the most appealing, while the suites – featuring terraces with swing seats or balcony window seats overlooking the garden – are a delight.

Krishna Ranch   COTTAGE $$
(☏9828059505, 9828059506; www.krishnaranch.com; s/d incl breakfast from ₹2200/2500; 🌓🛜) 🍃 This delightful countryside retreat has five cottages set around the grounds of a small farm. Each comes with attached bathroom (with solar-heated shower), tasteful decor and farm views. Meals are prepared using organic produce grown on the farm. The ranch is 7km from town, near Badi village, but there's free pick-up from Udaipur.

It's an ideal base for the hikes and horse treks (p160) that the management – a Dutch-Indian couple – organise from here, though you don't have to sign up for the treks to stay here.

✖ Eating

Udaipur has scores of sun-kissed rooftop restaurants, many with mesmerising lake views. The fare is not always that inspiring or varied, but competition keeps most places striving for improvement.

✖ Lal Ghat

Cafe Edelweiss   CAFE $
(73 Gangaur Ghat Rd; sandwiches from ₹180; 🌓8am-8pm; 🛜) This itsy cafe serves tasty baked goods and real coffee. Offerings include sticky cinnamon rolls, chocolate cake and apple crumble. There's muesli or eggs for breakfast, and various sandwiches available all day.

Charcoal   MULTICUISINE $$
(☏9414235252; www.charcoalpb.com; Pratap Bhawan, 12 Lal Ghat; mains ₹180-550; 🌓8am-11pm; 🛜) As the name implies, barbecue, satay and tandoor specials feature at this innovative rooftop restaurant. There are plenty of vegetarian and juicy meat dishes on offer and the homemade soft corn tacos with a variety of fillings are deservedly popular.

Mayur Rooftop Cafe   MULTICUISINE $$
(Hotel Baba Palace, Jagdish Chowk; mains ₹210-380; 🌓7am-10pm; ❄🛜) This delightful rooftop restaurant has a great view of the multihued light show on the Jagdish Temple. Choose between the AC room or the breezy open section. The usual multicuisine themes fill out the menu, and the quality is top-notch. The Rajasthani thali is a great way to introduce yourself to Rajasthani cuisine – quite different to the standard North Indian cuisine.

Vegetarians will love the choice of nine paneer dishes.

★ Jagat Niwas Palace Hotel   INDIAN $$$
(☏0294-2420133; 23-25 Lal Ghat; mains ₹250-500; 🌓7-10am, noon-3pm & 6-10pm) A wonderful, classy, rooftop restaurant with superb views towards the city palace, Pichola Lake and Hanuman Ghat. Choose from an extensive selection of mouthwatering curries (tempered for Western tastes) – mutton, chicken, fish, veg – as well as the tandoori classics. There's a tempting cocktail menu, Indian wine and the beer is icy cold. Book ahead for dinner.

Savage Garden   MEDITERRANEAN $$$
(☏8890627181; 73 Gangaur Ghat Rd; mains ₹280-520; 🌓11am-11pm) Savage Garden does a winning line in soups, chicken, and homemade pasta dishes. Try ravioli with goat ragu, and the signature sweet-savoury chicken breast stuffed with cashew nuts and paneer cheese and served with carrot rice. The splendid rooftop setting (up a narrow set of stairs) is above Cafe Edelweiss (same management).

✖ Hanuman Ghat

Millets of Mewar   INDIAN $
(☏8769348440; www.milletsofmewar.org; Hanuman Ghat; mains ₹130-250, thali ₹250; 🌓8.30am-10.30pm; 🛜) 🍃 Local millet is used where possible instead of wheat and rice at this environmentally aware, slow-food restaurant. There are vegan options, gluten-free dishes, fresh salads, and juices and herbal teas. Also on the menu are multigrain sandwiches and

millet pizzas, plus regular curries, Indian snacks, pasta and pancakes.

Little Prince
MULTICUISINE $$

(Daiji Footbridge; mains ₹180-290, veg thali ₹350; ⊙8.30am-11pm) This lovely open-air eatery looking towards the quaint Daiji Footbridge dishes up delicious veg and nonveg meals. There are plenty of Indian options, along with pizzas, pastas and some variations on the usual multicuisine theme, including Korean and Israeli dishes. The ambience is superrelaxed and the service friendly.

★ Ambrai
NORTH INDIAN $$$

(☑0294-2431085; www.amethaveliudaipur.com; Amet Haveli, Hanuman Ghat; mains ₹320-690; ⊙12.30-3pm & 7.30-10.30pm) Set at lakeshore level, looking across the water to the floodlit City Palace in one direction and Jagniwas in the other, this is one romantic restaurant at night with candlelit, white-linen tables beneath spreading rayan trees. And the service and cuisine do justice to its fabulous position, with terrific tandoor and curries and a bar to complement the dining.

🍷 Drinking & Nightlife

Paps Juices
JUICE BAR

(inside Chandpol; ⊙9am-8pm) This bright-red spot is tiny but very welcoming, and a great place to refuel during the day with a shot of Vitamin C from a wide range of delicious juice mixes. If you want something more substantial, the various muesli mixes are pretty good, too.

Jaiwana Bistro Lounge
CAFE

(☑9829005859; Jaiwana Haveli, 14 Lal Ghat; ⊙7am-10.30pm; 🛜) This modern, cool and clean cafe has espresso coffee and fresh healthy juices to help wash down the tasty bakery items and other main meals.

Jheel's Ginger Coffee Bar & Bakery
CAFE

(Jheel Palace Guest House, 56 Gangaur Ghat Rd; ⊙8am-8pm; 🛜) This small but slick cafe by the water's edge is on the ground floor of Jheel Palace Guest House. Large windows and a waterside sit-out afford good lake views, and the coffee is excellent. It also does a range of cakes and snacks. Note, you can take your coffee up to the open-air rooftop restaurant if you like.

Sunset Terrace
BAR

(Fateh Prakash Palace Hotel; ⊙7am-10.30pm) On a terrace overlooking Lake Pichola, this bar is perfect for a sunset gin and tonic. It's also

a restaurant (mains ₹800 to ₹1500), with live music performed every night.

☆ Entertainment

Dharohar
DANCE

(☑0294-2523858; Bagore-ki-Haveli; Indian/foreigner ₹90/150, camera ₹150; ⊙ticket sales 6.15pm, show 7pm) The beautiful Bagore-ki-Haveli (p160) hosts the best (and most convenient) opportunity to see Rajasthani folk dancing, with nightly shows of colourful, energetic Marwari, Bhil and western Rajasthani dances, as well as traditional Rajasthani puppetry.

Mewar Sound & Light Show
LIVE PERFORMANCE

(Manek Chowk, City Palace; adult/child from ₹250/150; ⊙7pm Sep-Apr, 8pm May-Aug) Fifteen centuries of intriguing Mewar history are squeezed into one atmospheric hour of commentary and light switching – in English from September to April, in Hindi other months. Seating is either on a raised platform (Hathnal ki Chandni) or at ground level (Manmek Chowk).

🛍 Shopping

Tourist-oriented shops – selling miniature paintings, woodcarvings, silver jewellery, bangles, spices, camel-bone boxes, and a large variety of textiles – line the streets radiating from Jagdish Chowk. Udaipur is known for its local crafts, particularly miniature painting in the Rajput-Mughal style, as well as some interesting contemporary art.

The local market area extends east from the old clock tower at the northern end of Jagdish Temple Rd, and buzzes loudest in the evening. It's fascinating as much for browsing and soaking up local atmosphere as it is for buying. Bara Bazar, immediately east of the old clock tower, sells silver and gold, while its narrow side street, Maldas St, specialises in saris and fabric. A little further east, traditional shoes are sold on Mochiwada.

Foodstuffs and spices are mainly found around the new clock tower at the east end of the bazaar area, and Mandi Market, 200m north of the tower.

Sadhna
CLOTHING

(☑0294-2454655; www.sadhna.org; Jagdish Temple Rd; ⊙10.30am-7pm) 🌿 This is the crafts outlet for Seva Mandir, a long-established NGO working with rural and tribal people. The small, hard-to-see shop sells attractive fixed-price textiles; profits go to the artisans and towards community development work.

ℹ Information

EMERGENCY

Police (☑ 0294-2414600, emergency 100; Bhattiyani Chotta, Sheetla Mata Gate) The tourism police office. There are also police posts at Suraj Pol, Hati Pol and Delhi Gate, three of the gates in the old-city wall.

MEDICAL SERVICES

GBH American Hospital (☑ emergency 9352304050, enquiries 0294-2426000; www.gbhamericanhospital.com; Meera Girls College Rd, 101 Kothi Bagh, Bhatt Ji Ki Bari) Modern private hospital with 24-hour emergency service, about 2km northeast of the old city.

MONEY

There are ATMs along Gangaur Ghat Rd, City Palace Rd, near the bus stand and outside the train station.

Thomas Cook (Lake Palace Rd; ⊘ 9.30am-6.30pm Mon-Sat) Changes cash and travellers cheques.

POST

DHL (1 Town Hall Rd; ⊘ 10am-7pm Mon-Sat) Has a free collection service within Udaipur.

DHL Express (☑ 9414812491, 0294-2525301; Lal Ghat Guesthouse, Lal Ghat) Conveniently situated inside Lal Ghat Guesthouse.

Main post office (Chetak Circle; ⊘ 10am-1pm & 1.30-6pm Mon-Sat) North of the old city.

Post office (City Palace Rd; ⊘ 10am-4pm Mon-Sat) Tiny post office that sends parcels (including packaging them up), and there are virtually no queues. Beside the City Palace's Badi Pol ticket office.

TOURIST INFORMATION

The official **tourist office** (☑ 0294-2411535; Fateh Memorial Bldg, Airport Rd; ⊘ 10am-5pm Mon-Fri) is situated near Suraj Pol and is of little use apart from supplying a map. Small tourist offices operate erratically at the train station and airport.

ℹ Getting There & Away

AIR

Udaipur's airport, 25km east of town, is served by flights from Delhi, Mumbai and other hubs. A prepaid taxi from the airport to the Lal Ghat area costs ₹450.

Air India (www.airindia.com) Flies daily to Mumbai and Delhi.

IndiGo (www.goindigo.in) Two direct flights daily to Delhi and one direct flight daily to Mumbai and Jaipur.

Jet Airways (www.jetairways.com) Flies twice daily to Delhi and daily to Mumbai.

SpiceJet (www.spicejet.com) Flies daily to Delhi and Mumbai.

BUS

RSRTC and private buses run from the main bus stand, 1.5km east of the City Palace. Turn left at the end of Lake Palace Rd, take the first right then cross the main road at the end, just after passing through the crumbling old Suraj Pol. It's around ₹50 in an autorickshaw.

If arriving by bus, turn left out of the bus stand, cross the main road, walk through Suraj Pol then turn left at the end of the road before taking the first right into Lake Palace Rd.

Private bus tickets can also be bought at any one of the many travel agencies lining the road leading from Jagdish Temple to Daiji Footbridge.

TRAIN

The train station is about 2.5km southeast of the City Palace, and 1km directly south of the main bus stand. An autorickshaw between the train station and Jagdish Chowk should cost around ₹100 to ₹150.

There are no direct trains to Abu Road, Jodhpur or Jaisalmer.

Agra sleeper ₹530, 13 hours, daily (10.20pm)

Ajmer (for Pushkar) seat/sleeper ₹195/325, five hours, four daily (6am, 3.05pm, 5.15pm

RSRTC BUSES FROM UDAIPUR

DESTINATION	FARE (₹)	DURATION (HR)	FREQUENCY
Ahmedabad	235, AC 580	5	6 daily from 5.30am
Ajmer (for Pushkar)	296	7-10	hourly from 5am
Bundi	328	6	daily (7.45am)
Chittorgarh	120, AC 210	2½	half-hourly from 5.15am
Delhi	672, AC 1766	15	2 or 4 daily
Jaipur	424, AC 767	9	hourly
Jodhpur	273, AC 599	6-8	hourly
Kota	321	7	hourly
Mt Abu (Abu Road)	198	4	daily (8.45am)

MAJOR TRAINS FROM UDAIPUR

DESTINATION	TRAIN	DEPARTURE	ARRIVAL	FARE (₹)
Agra (Cantonment)	19666 Udaipur–Kurj Exp	10.20pm	11am	530/1450 (A)
Ajmer (for Pushkar)	09722 Udaipur–Jaipur SF SPL	3.05pm	8pm	195/840 (B)
Bundi	12964 Mewar Exp	6.15pm	10.35pm	285/765 (A)
Chittorgarh	12982 Chetak Exp	5.15pm	7.10pm	230/765 (A)
Delhi (Hazrat Nizamuddin)	12964 Mewar Exp	5.15pm	5.05am	560/1500 (A)
Jaipur	12991 Udaipur–Jaipur Exp	6am	1.35pm	240/1075 (B)

Fares: (A) sleeper/3AC, (B) 2nd-class seat/AC chair

and 10.20pm), via Chittorgarh (seat/sleeper ₹115/230, two hours)

Bundi sleeper ₹220, 4½ hours, daily (6.15pm)

Delhi sleeper ₹560, 12 hours, two daily (5.15pm and 6.15pm)

Jaipur seat/sleeper ₹240/375, around seven hours, three daily (6am, 3.05pm and 10.20pm)

ⓘ Getting Around

AUTORICKSHAW

These are unmetered, so you should agree on a fare before setting off – the normal fare anywhere in town is around ₹50 to ₹100. You will usually have to go through the rigmarole of haggling, walking away etc to get this fare. Some drivers ask tourists for ₹150 or more. It costs around ₹400 to ₹500 to hire an autorickshaw for a day of local sightseeing.

The commission system is in place, so tenaciously pursue your first choice of accommodation.

BICYCLE & MOTORCYCLE

A cheap and environmentally friendly way to buzz around is by bicycle (around ₹200 per day), although motorcycle traffic and pollution make it very tiresome if not dangerous. Scooters and motorbikes, meanwhile, are great for exploring the surrounding countryside.

Heera Cycle Store (☏9950611973; off Gangaur Ghat Rd; ⊙7.30am-8pm) Hires out bicycles/scooters/Bullets for ₹200/500/800 per day (with a deposit of US$200/400/500); you must show your passport and driver's licence. There are numerous other hire companies in and around Lal Ghat.

Around Udaipur

Kumbhalgarh

☏02954

About 80km north of Udaipur is Kumbhalgarh, a remote historical fort, outwardly fulfilling expectations of the chivalrous and warlike Rajput era. Its associated battlements are said to be second only to the Great Wall of China in extent. However, the poor condition and barren rooms of the palace complex do nothing to evoke the splendour of the past let alone justify the inflated admission price for foreigners.

The rugged Kumbhalgarh Wildlife Sanctuary (p167) can also be visited from Kumbhalgarh.

◉ Sights

Kumbhalgarh   FORT

(Indian/foreigner ₹40/600; ⊙9am-6pm) One of the many forts built by Rana Kumbha (r 1433–68), under whom Mewar reached its greatest extents, this isolated fort with a derelict palace is perched 1100m above sea level, with hazy views melting into the distance. The journey to the fort, along twisting roads through the Aravalli Hills, is a highlight in itself.

Kumbhalgarh was the most important Mewar fort after Chittorgarh, and the rulers, sensibly, used to retreat here in times of danger. Not surprisingly, Kumbhalgarh was only taken once in its entire history. Even then, it took the combined armies of Amber, Marwar and Mughal emperor Akbar to breach its strong defences, and they only managed to hang on to it for two days.

The fort's thick walls stretch about 36km; they're wide enough in some places for eight horses to ride abreast and it's possible to walk right around the circuit (allow two days). They enclose around 360 intact and ruined temples, some of which date back to the Mauryan period in the 2nd century BC, as well as palaces, gardens, step-wells and 700 cannon bunkers.

If you're staying here and want to make an early start on your hike around the wall, you may still get into the fort before 9am, although no one will be around to sell you a ticket. There's a sound-and-light show (in Hindi) at the fort at 6.30pm (Indian/foreigner ₹118/236).

Sleeping & Eating

Kumbhal Castle   HOTEL $$

(☑ 9116616217; www.thekumbhalcastle.com; Fort Rd; r from ₹3130; ❄ ☎ �) The Kumbhal Castle, 2km from the fort, has old-fashioned but pleasant rooms featuring bright bedspreads and window seats, shared balconies and good views. The superdeluxe rooms are considerably bigger and worth considering for the few hundred extra rupees. There's an in-house restaurant.

Aodhi   HOTEL $$$

(☑ 8003722333; www.hrhhotels.com; r from ₹8160; ❄ @ ☎) Just under 2km from the fort is this luxurious and blissfully tranquil hotel with an inviting pool, rambling shady gardens and winter bonfires. The spacious rooms, in different styles of stone cottages, have private terraces, balconies or pavilions, and are decorated with wildlife and botanical art.

Nonguests can dine in the restaurant, where good North Indian fare is the pick of the options on offer, or have a drink in the cosy Chopal Bar. Room rates plummet from April to September.

Getting There & Away

A day-long round trip in a private car from Udaipur to Kumbhalgarh and Ranakpur will cost around ₹3000 per car. This is by far the best way to tackle these sights.

You can get there by bus, but will need to be happy to be sardined into a battered bus

and prepared for cancellations leaving you potentially stranded (don't say we didn't warn you). From Udaipur's main bus stand, catch a Ranakpur-bound bus as far as Saira (₹81, 2¼ hours, hourly), a tiny crossroads town where you can change for a bus to Kumbhalgarh (₹43, one hour, hourly). That bus, which will be bound for Kelwara, will drop you at the start of the approach road to the fort, leaving you with a 1.5km uphill walk to the entrance gate.

The last bus back to Saira swings by at 5.30pm (and is always absolutely jam-packed). The last bus from Saira back to Udaipur leaves at around 8pm. To get to Ranakpur from Kumbhalgarh, head first to Saira then change for Ranakpur (₹23, 40 minutes, at least hourly).

Ranakpur

☑ 02934

On the western slopes of the Aravalli Hills, 75km northwest of Udaipur, and 12km west of Kumbhalgarh as the crow flies (but 50km by road, via Saira), is the village of Ranakpur, which hosts one of India's biggest and most important Jain temple complexes.

Built in the 15th century in milk-white marble, the main temple of Ranakpur, **Chaumukha Mandir** (Ranakpur Jain Temple, Four-Faced Temple; Indian/foreigner free/₹200, camera or mobile phone ₹100; ⊙ Jains 6am-7pm, non-Jains noon-5pm), is dedicated to Adinath, the first *tirthankar* (great Jain teacher), depicted in the many Buddha-like images in the temple. An incredible feat of Jain devotion, the temple is a complicated series of 29 halls, 80 domes and 1444 individually engraved pillars. The interior is completely covered in knotted, lovingly wrought carving, and has a marvellously calming sense of space and harmony. Entry includes audio guide.

OFF THE BEATEN TRACK

KUMBHALGARH WILDLIFE SANCTUARY

Ranakpur is a great base for exploring the hilly, densely forested **Kumbhalgarh Wildlife Sanctuary** (Indian/foreigner ₹50/300, 4WD or car ₹200; ⊙ safaris 6-9am & 3-4.30pm), which extends over some 600 sq km. It's known for its leopards and wolves, although the chances of spotting antelopes, gazelles, deer and possibly sloth bears are higher, especially from March to June. You will certainly see some of the sanctuary's 200-plus bird species.

Beside the park office, near the Ranakpur Jain temples, is the recommended tour company **Evergreen Safari** (☑ 7568830064; 4WD 2½ hour ₹2500). There are also several safari outfits on the road leading up to Kumbhalgarh Fort, including **A-one Tour & Safari** (☑ 8003854293; Pratap Circle; 4WD 2½ hour ₹3500; ⊙ safaris 6-9am & 3-4.30pm). Most hotels will use these or similar outfits to organise your safari.

There's a ticket office for the sanctuary right beside where the bus drops you off for the Jain temples, but the nearest of the sanctuary's four entrances is 2km beyond here.

Shoes, cigarettes, food and all leather articles must be left at the entrance (there are lockers, ₹10); women who are menstruating are asked not to enter.

Also exquisitely carved and well worth inspecting are two other Jain temples, dedicated to Neminath (the 22nd *tirthankar*) and Parasnath (the 23rd *tirthankar*), both within the complex, and a nearby Sun Temple. About 1km from the main complex is the Amba Mata Temple.

The village also makes a great base for exploring the impressive Kumbhalgarh Wildlife Sanctuary (p167) or for taking a day trip to visit the fort at Kumbhalgarh (p166).

🛏 Sleeping & Eating

★ **Aranyawas** HOTEL $$$
(📞02956-293029; www.aranyawas.com; r from ₹6500; ✳@☎) In secluded, tree-shaded grounds off Hwy 32, 12km south of the temple, Aranyawas has 20 attractive rooms in two-storey stone cottages. They aren't fancy, but are spacious, neat and tasteful, with pine furnishings and, in most cases, balconies overlooking a river and jungle-clad hills. There's a large *baori* (step-well)–inspired pool surrounded by trees and a bonfire for evening drinks in winter.

The restaurant (mains ₹250 to ₹350, buffet lunch or dinner ₹550) is a lovely place to stop for a meal and is open to nonguests as well.

Ranakpur Hill Resort HOTEL $$$
(📞9829157303; www.ranakpurhillresort.com; Ranakpur Rd; s/d from ₹5900/6490; ✳@☎☎) This is a well-run hotel with a decent pool and shady gardens, around which are arranged the attractive cottages sporting marble floors, stained glass, floral wall paintings and touches of mirrorwork. There is also a multicuisine restaurant, and horse-riding packages can be arranged. Check for discounts on the website. It's 3.5km north of the temple complex, along Hwy 32.

❶ Getting There & Away

A day-long round trip in a taxi/hired car from Udaipur to Ranakpur and Kumbhalgarh costs around ₹3000.

It's uncomfortable and time-consuming, and therefore not recommended, to travel by local bus. Nevertheless, here are the details. Direct buses to Ranakpur leave roughly hourly from the main bus stands in both Udaipur (₹98, three hours) and Jodhpur (₹197, four to five hours). You'll be dropped outside the temple complex unless you state otherwise. Return buses stop

running around 7pm. Buses departing for Udaipur can drop you at Saira (₹23, 40 minutes, hourly), about 25km south of Ranakpur, to connect with a bus to Kumbhalgarh (₹43, one hour, hourly).

Mt Abu

📞02974 / POP 22,940 / ELEV 1200M

Rajasthan's only hill station nestles among green forests on the state's highest mountain at the southwestern end of the Aravalli Hills and close to the Gujarat border. Quite unlike anywhere else in Rajasthan, Mt Abu provides Rajasthanis, Gujaratis and a small number of foreign tourists with respite from scorching temperatures and arid terrain elsewhere. It's a particular hit with honeymooners and middle-class families from Gujarat.

Mt Abu town sits towards the southwestern end of the plateau-like mountain, which stretches about 19km from end to end and 6km from east to west. The town is surrounded by the 289-sq-km Mt Abu Wildlife Sanctuary, which extends over most of the mountain.

The mountain is of great spiritual importance for both Hindus and Jains and has over 80 temples and shrines, most notably the exquisite Jain temples at Delwara, built between 400 and 1000 years ago.

◉ Sights

The white-clad people you'll see around town are members of the Brahma Kumaris World Spiritual University (www.bkwsu. com), a worldwide organisation that has its headquarters here in Mt Abu. The university's **Universal Peace Hall** (Om Shanti Bhawan; ⏱8am-6pm), just north of Nakki Lake, has free 30-minute tours that include an introduction to the Brahma Kumaris philosophy (be prepared for a bit of proselytising). The organisation also runs the **World Renewal Spiritual Museum** (⏱8am-8pm) FREE in the town centre.

Nakki Lake LAKE
Scenic Nakki Lake, the town's focus, is one of Mt Abu's biggest attractions. It's so named because, according to legend, it was scooped out by a god using his *nakh* (nails). Some Hindus thus consider it a holy lake. It's a pleasant 45-minute stroll around the perimeter – the lake is surrounded by hills, parks and strange rock formations. The best known, Toad Rock, looks like a toad about to hop into the lake. The 14th-century **Raghunath Temple** (⏱dawn-dusk) stands near

DELWARA TEMPLES

The remarkable **Delwara Temples** (donations welcome; ☉ Jains 6am-6pm, non-Jains noon-6pm) are Mt Abu's most remarkable attraction and feature some of India's finest temple decoration. They predate the town of Mt Abu by many centuries and were built when this site was just a remote mountain wilderness. It's said that the artisans were paid according to the amount of dust they collected, encouraging them to carve ever more intricately. Whatever their inducement, there are two temples here in which the marble work is dizzyingly intense.

The older of the two is the Vimal Vasahi, on which work began in 1031 and was financed by a Gujarati chief minister named Vimal. Dedicated to the first tirthankar (great Jain teacher), Adinath, it took 1500 masons and 1200 labourers 14 years to build, and allegedly cost ₹185.3 million. Outside the entrance is the House of Elephants, featuring a procession of stone elephants marching to the temple, some of which were damaged long ago by marauding Mughals. Inside, a forest of beautifully carved pillars surrounds the central shrine, which holds an image of Adinath himself.

The Luna Vasahi Temple is dedicated to Neminath, the 22nd tirthankar, and was built in 1230 by the brothers Tejpal and Vastupal for a mere ₹125.3 million. Like Vimal, the brothers were both Gujarati government ministers. The marble carving here took 2500 workers 15 years to create, and its most notable feature is its intricacy and delicacy, which is so fine that, in places, the marble becomes almost transparent. The many-layered lotus flower that dangles from the centre of the dome is a particularly astonishing piece of work.

As at other Jain temples, leather articles (including belts and shoes), cameras and phones must be left at the entrance, and menstruating women are asked not to enter.

Delwara is about 3km north of Mt Abu town centre: you can walk there in less than an hour, or hop aboard a shared taxi (₹10 per person) from up the street opposite Chacha Cafe. A taxi all to yourself should be ₹200 round trip, with one hour of waiting time.

the lake's southern shore. **Boating** (pedalo per person ₹200, shikara ₹1100) here is popular.

Sunset Point　　　　　　　VIEWPOINT
(Indian/foreigner ₹50/300) Sunset Point is a popular place to watch the brilliant setting sun. Hordes stroll out here every evening to catch the end of the day, the food stalls and all the usual jolly hill-station entertainment. To get there, follow Sunset Point road west of the polo ground out of town.

Mt Abu Wildlife Sanctuary　　WILDLIFE RESERVE
(Indian/foreigner ₹50/300, vehicle ₹200; ☉8am-5pm) This 289-sq-km sanctuary covers much of the mountain plateau and surrounds the town of Mt Abu. It is home to leopards, deer, foxes and bears. Contact Mt Abu Treks to arrange an overnight stay.

Guru Shikhar　　　　　　　MOUNTAIN
At the northeast end of the Mt Abu plateau, 17km by the winding road from the town, rises 1722m-high Guru Shikhar, Rajasthan's highest point. A road goes almost all the way to the summit and the Atri Rishi Temple, complete with a priest and distant, though often hazy, views. A popular spot, it's a highlight of the RSRTC tour; if you decide to go

it alone, a 4WD from Mt Abu will cost ₹800 return.

🌏 Tours

⭐**Mt Abu Treks**　　　　　　TREKKING
(☑9414154854; www.mount-abu-treks.blogspot.com; Hotel Lake Palace; 3-4hr trek per person ₹700, full day incl lunch ₹1500) Mahendra 'Charles' Dan arranges tailor-made treks ranging from gentle village visits to longer, wilder expeditions into Mt Abu Wildlife Sanctuary. He's passionate and knowledgeable about the local flora and fauna. Short treks are available as well as an overnight village trek including all meals (₹3500). Transport to/from trailheads and the sanctuary entrance fee (Indian/foreigner ₹50/300) is extra.

Shri Ganesh Hotel　　　　　TREKKING
(☑02974-237292; http://shri-ganesh.hotels-rajasthan.com; per person 2hr ₹300, 4hr ₹1000) Organises good short hikes, starting at 7am and 4pm.

RSRTC　　　　　　　　　　TOURS
(half-/full-day tours ₹50/110; ☉full-day 9.30am, half-day 1pm) The RSRTC runs bus tours of Mt Abu's main sights, leaving from the bus stand where reservations can be made. Both

Mt Abu

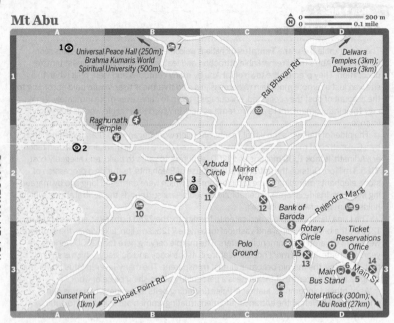

Mt Abu

tours visit Achalgarh, Guru Shikhar and the Delwara temples and end at Sunset Point. The full-day tour also includes Adhar Devi, the Brahma Kumaris Peace Hall and Honeymoon Point. Admission and camera fees and the ₹20 guide fee are extra.

🛏 Sleeping

Room rates can double, or treble, during the peak seasons – mid-May to mid-June, Diwali and Christmas/New Year – but generous discounts are often available at other times at midrange and top-end places. If you intend to come here during Diwali, you'll need to

book way ahead and you won't be able to move for the crowds. Many hotels have an ungenerous 9am checkout time.

★ **Shri Ganesh Hotel**　　　　　HOTEL $
(☏02974-237292;　http://shri-ganesh.hotels-rajasthan.com; dm ₹350, s/d ₹500/600, r with bathroom ₹700-1500; ❄@?) A fairly central and popular budget spot, Shri Ganesh is well set up for travellers, with an inexpensive cafe/restaurant and plenty of helpful travel information. Rooms are very well kept; clean and tidy. Daily forest walks (p169) and cooking lessons are on offer.

Hotel Saraswati
HOTEL $

(☎ 02974-238887; www.hotelsaraswati.co.in; r from ₹1000; ❄ 🛜) Saraswati is a reasonably appealing place in a peaceful setting behind the polo ground. Rooms are big enough and in varied states of repair: see a few before you decide. Hot water is only available from 7am to 11am. The restaurant serves Gujarati thalis.

Hotel Lake Palace
HOTEL $$

(☎ 02974-237154; www.savshantihotels.com; r from ₹3580; ❄ 🛜) The Lake Palace has an excellent location right beside the lake and away from the crowds. There are a couple of terraces overlooking the lake and promenade. Rooms are simple, uncluttered and clean. All have air-conditioning and some have semi-private lake-view balconies. There's a rooftop multicuisine restaurant, too.

Kishangarh House
HERITAGE HOTEL $$$

(☎ 02974-238092; Rajendra Marg; cottages incl breakfast ₹5500, r incl breakfast from ₹6500; ❄ 🛜) The former summer residence of the maharaja of Kishangarh is now an interesting though faded and forlorn heritage hotel. The deluxe rooms in the main building are big, with extravagantly high ceilings. The cottage rooms at the back are smaller and cosier. There's a delightful sun-filled drawing room and lovely terraced gardens.

Hotel Hillock
HOTEL $$$

(☎ 02974-238463; www.hotelhillock.com; Raj Bhavan Rd; r ₹11,800; ❄ 🛜 🏊) Plush and contemporary, with Rajasthani colours and designs, Hillock's rooms are some of the most comfortable in Mt Abu. Add in the fine Mayur restaurant, the On The Rocks bar, and delightful gardens sporting a cool pool and you have one of the hill station's top options.

✖ Eating

Arbuda
INDIAN $

(Arbuda Circle; mains ₹110-250, thali ₹170; ⏱ 8am-10.30pm; 🖬) This big restaurant is set on a sweeping open terrace filled with chrome chairs. It's very popular for its vegetarian Gujarati, Punjabi and South Indian food, and does fine Continental breakfasts and fresh juices.

Chacha Cafe
MULTICUISINE $$

(Main St; mains ₹180-450; ⏱ 11am-11pm; ❄ 🛜) A very neat, bright pure-veg eatery with excellent service and cold beer. Downstairs there's booths and welcome AC, upstairs is outside and ideal in the cool evenings. The presentable fare ranges from dosas and biryanis to pizzas, vegetarian burgers and cashew curry.

It's next to the large Chacha Museum crafts and souvenir shop.

Kanak Dining Hall
INDIAN $$

(Lake Rd; thali Gujarati/Punjabi ₹180/250; ⏱ 8.30am-3.30pm & 7.30-10.30pm) The excellent all-you-can-eat thalis are contenders for Mt Abu's best meals. There's seating indoors in the busy dining hall or outside under a canopy. It's conveniently located near the bus stand for the lunch break during the all-day RSRTC tour.

Tandoori Bites
BARBECUE $$

(Main St; mains ₹130-370; ⏱ 12.30-11.30pm) This bright eatery near the taxi stand sets up a barbecue out the front to entice customers with the delicious smoky smells. It does a good range of vegetarian curries and veg barbecue, though there's no doubt this is an excellent choice for carnivores on a budget.

Mulberry Tree Restaurant
MULTICUISINE $$$

(Hilltone Hotel, Main St; mains ₹250-460; ❄) Mt Abu's Gujarati tourists make veg thalis the order of the day in the town, so if you're craving a bit of nonveg, the smart Mulberry Tree Restaurant at the Hilltone Hotel is a good upmarket place to go. There are plenty of meaty Indian options on the menu and alcohol is available to wash it down.

TREKKING & TWITCHING AROUND MT ABU

Getting off the well-worn tourist trail and out into the forests and hills of Mt Abu is a revelation. This is a world of isolated shrines and lakes, weird rock formations, fantastic panoramas, nomadic villagers, orchids, wild fruits, plants used in ayurvedic medicine, sloth bears (which are fairly common), wild boars, langurs, and even the occasional leopard. There are over 150 bird species recorded including the prized green avadavat and red spurfowl.

A warning from the locals before you set out: it's very unsafe to wander unguided in these hills. Travellers have been mauled by bears and, even more disturbing, have been mugged (and worse) by other people.

RAJASTHAN MT ABU

MAJOR TRAINS FROM ABU ROAD

DESTINATION	TRAIN	DEPARTURE	ARRIVAL	FARE (₹)
Ahmedabad	19224 JAT ADI Exp	10.50am	3pm	140/495/700(A)
Delhi (New Delhi)	12957 Swarna J Raj Exp	8.50pm	7.30am	1845/2725/3155 (B)
Jaipur	19707 Aravali Exp	9.40am	7pm	260/700/1000 (A)
Jodhpur	19223 Ahmedabad–Jammu Tawi Exp	3.30pm	8.05pm	185/495/700 (A)
Mumbai	19708 Aravali Exp	4.50pm	6.35am	355/970/ 1400(A)

Fares: (A) sleeper/3AC/2AC, (B) 3AC/2AC/1A

 Drinking & Nightlife

Café Coffee Day CAFE
(coffee from ₹116; ⊙9am-11pm) A branch of the
popular caffeine-supply chain. The tea and
cakes aren't bad either.

Polo Bar BAR
(☑02974-235176; Jaipur House; beer and cocktails ₹240; ⊙11.30am-3.30pm & 7.30-11pm) The
terrace at the Jaipur Hotel, formerly the
maharaja of Jaipur's summer palace, is a
dreamy place for an evening tipple, with divine views over the hills, lake and the town's
twinkling lights.

ⓘ Information

There are ATMs on Raj Bhavan Rd, including one
outside the tourist office, as well as on Lake Rd.

Bank of Baroda (Main St; ⊙10am-3pm
Mon-Fri, to 12.30pm Sat) Changes currency
and travellers cheques, and does credit-card
advances. Has ATM.

Main Post Office (Raj Bhavan Rd; ⊙9am-5pm
Mon-Sat)

Tourist Office (Main St; ⊙9am-5.30pm Mon-
Fri) Opposite the main bus stand, this centre
distributes free maps of town.

ⓘ Getting There & Away

Access to Mt Abu is by a dramatic 28km-long road
that winds its way up thickly forested hillsides
from the town of Abu Road, where the nearest
train station is located. Many buses from other
cities go all the way up to Mt Abu, some only go
as far as Abu Road. Buses (₹35, one hour) run
between Abu Road and Mt Abu half-hourly from
about 6am to 7pm. Share taxis cost ₹30. A private
taxi from Abu Road to Mt Abu is ₹700 by day or
₹1000 by night. Vehicles are charged when entering Mt Abu (small/large car ₹100/200).

BUS

There are government and private (usually more
comfortable and more expensive) bus services
to various points. **Rajasthan Travels** (www.

rajasthanbus.com; Main St; ₹100 per person;
⊙9.30am-5pm) runs buses to Ahmedabad
(seat/sleeper ₹460/650), Jaipur (seat/sleeper
₹500/600, one daily 7pm) and Udaipur (₹260,
8.30am), among others destinations. It has
several booths around town including one near
the main bus stand. Services from Mt Abu's
main bus stand:

Ahmedabad seat/sleeper ₹460/650, six hours,
several daily

Jaipur seat/sleeper/AC ₹500/600/916, 11
hours, several daily

Jodhpur ₹306, seven hours, three daily
(6.30am, 8.45am, 12.30pm)

Udaipur ₹260, 4½ hours, several daily

TRAIN

Abu Road station is on the line between Delhi and
Mumbai via Ahmedabad. An autorickshaw from
Abu Road train station to Abu Road bus stand
costs ₹20. Mt Abu has a train **reservations office**
(Main St; ⊙8am-2pm Mon-Sat), above the tourist
office, with quotas on most of the express trains.

ⓘ Getting Around

There are no autorickshaws in Mt Abu, but it
is easy to get around on foot. Motorcycles and
scooters are not hired to foreigners in Mt Abu,
forcing foreigners to hire a taxi or walk to the
outlying sights.

To hire a jeep or taxi for sightseeing costs
about ₹700/1500 per half-day/day. There's a
taxi stand down by the polo ground on Main St.
Shared taxis to Delwara leave from a separate
stand beside the market. Alternatively, many
hotels can arrange a vehicle with driver.

NORTHERN RAJASTHAN (SHEKHAWATI)

Far less visited than other parts of Rajasthan, the Shekhawati region is renowned
for its extraordinary painted *havelis* (traditional, ornately decorated residences),
highlighted with dazzling, often whimsical,

Shekhawati

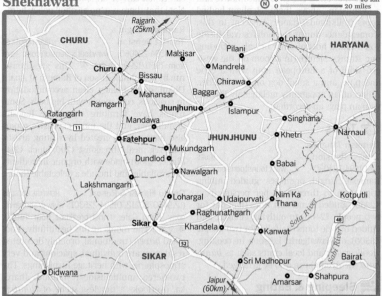

murals. These works of art are found in tiny towns connected by single-track roads that run through desolate countryside north of Jaipur.

Today it seems curious that such attention and money were lavished on these out-of-the-way houses, but these were once the homelands of wealthy traders and merchants.

From the 14th century onwards, Shekhawati's towns were important trading posts on caravan routes from Gujarati ports to the fertile and booming cities of the Ganges plain. The expansion of the British port cities of Calcutta (now Kolkata) and Bombay (Mumbai) in the 19th century could have been the death knell for Shekhawati, but the merchants moved to these cities, prospered, and sent funds home to construct and decorate their extraordinary abodes.

Nawalgarh

01594 / POP 95,350

Nawalgarh is a small town almost at the very centre of the Shekhawati region. With some excellent accommodation options, it makes a great base for exploring the region. It has several fine *havelis* and a colourful and mostly pedestrian-friendly bazaar.

Sights

Dr Ramnath A Podar Haveli Museum
MUSEUM

(www.podarhavelimuseum.org; Indian/foreigner ₹80/100, camera ₹30; ⊙8.30am-6.30pm) Built in 1902 on the eastern side of town, and known locally as 'Podar Haveli', this is one of the region's few buildings to have been thoroughly restored. The paintings of this *haveli* are the most vivid murals in town, although purists point to the fact that they have been simply repainted rather than restored.

On the ground floor are galleries on Rajasthani culture, including costumes, turbans, musical instruments and models of Rajasthan's forts.

Morarka Haveli Museum
MUSEUM

(₹70; ⊙8am-7pm) This museum has well-presented original paintings, preserved for decades behind doorways blocked with cement, plus there is ongoing restoration. The inner courtyard hosts some gorgeous Ramayana scenes; look for the slightly incongruous image of Jesus on the top storey, beneath the eaves in the courtyard's southeast corner.

Bhagton ki Choti Haveli
HISTORIC BUILDING

(Bhagat Haveli; ₹50; ⊙8am-6pm) Under the eaves on the external western wall of

Bhagton ki Choti Haveli is a locomotive and a steamship. Above them, elephant-bodied *gopis* (milkmaids) dance. Adjacent to this, women dance during the Holi festival. Inside you'll find a host of other murals, including one strange picture (in a room on the western side) of a European man with a cane and pipe, and a small dog on his shoulder. Adjacent, an apparently melancholy English woman plays an accordian.

☞ Tours

Ramesh Jangid's
Tourist Pension   TOURS
(📞01594-224060;   www.touristpension.com) Ramesh Jangid organises guided hiking trips (two to three days per person from ₹2250), guided camel-cart rides (half-day for two people ₹2400) to outlying villages, and guided bicycle tours (half-day for two people ₹3500) of Nawalgarh. Lessons in cooking, woodcarving and local crafts such as *bandhani* (tie-dyeing) can also be arranged.

🛏 Sleeping & Eating

Nawalgarh Homestay   HOMESTAY $
(📞9414491281, 7665711416; Chiraniya Mill, off Kothi Rd; 🖥) This homestay under the recommended New Bungli Restaurant is run by the same small group of families. Rooms are simple, spacious, cool and clean and you have the benefits of the excellent home-style food prepared for the restaurant, plus the advantage of having in-house guides to show you the town's *havelis*.

DS Bungalow   HOMESTAY $
(📞9983168916, 9828828116; s/d ₹500/800; 🖥) Run by a friendly, down-to-earth couple, this simple place with clean, air-cooled rooms is a little out of town on the way to Roop Niwas Kothi. It's backed by a garden with a pleasant outdoor mud-walled restaurant serving delicious home cooking. The more energetic can arrange camel tours here.

Apani Dhani   GUESTHOUSE $$
(📞01594-222239; www.apanidhani.com; s/d from ₹990/1670, r with AC from ₹2790; ❋🖥) 🅿 This award-winning ecotourism venture is a relaxing place on the edge of town. Rooms with comfortable beds are in cosy mud-hut, thatched-roof bungalows set around a bougainvillea-shaded courtyard. The adjoining organic farm supplies food, and there are solar lights, water heaters and compost toilets. Tours around the area, via bicycle,

car, camel cart or on foot, can be arranged. Note that there is a 'no alcohol' policy here.

Ramesh Jangid's
Tourist Pension   GUESTHOUSE $$
(📞01594-224060;   www.touristpension.com; s/d from ₹950/1290; @🖥) 🅿 This guesthouse, run by genial Rajesh, son of Ramesh at Apani Dhani, offers homey, clean accommodation in spacious, cool rooms with big beds. Some rooms have furniture carved by Rajesh's grandfather, and the more expensive rooms also have murals created by visiting artists. Pure veg meals (breakfast ₹200, lunch ₹250, dinner ₹300) made with organic ingredients are available, and include a delectable thali.

Grand Haveli & Resort   HERITAGE HOTEL $$
(📞9460780212, 01594-225301; www.grandhaveli. com; Baori Gate; r incl breakfast from ₹4000; ❋🖥🏊) The rooms at this beautifully renovated *haveli* (traditional, ornately decorated residence) are individual, spacious and very atmospheric, with heritage furnishings. The two-tiered, multicuisine restaurant, Jharoka, overlooks a timeless scene of *chhatris* (cenotaphs) through a large window. The hotel has developed more rooms across the road. These are more standard and less atmospheric, but large and comfortable.

★New Bungli Restaurant   NORTH INDIAN $$
(📞9414491281; Chiraniya Mill, off Kothi Rd; mains ₹175-370; ⏰8am-10pm; 🖥) Under billowing sails this breezy, rooftop restaurant delivers high-quality food. The veg and nonveg curries, including rich *laal maas* (mutton curry), creamy *palak paneer* (unfermented cheese chunks in a pureed spinach gravy) and a lovely dish using small local eggplants, are all professionally prepared and served. You can even get a free cooking class by watching your meal being prepared.

❶ Getting There & Away

BUS
The **main bus stand** (State Hwy 8) is little more than a dusty car park accessed through a large yellow double-arched gateway. Services run roughly every hour to Jaipur (₹145 to ₹258, 3½ hours), Jhunjhunu (₹40, one hour) and Mandawa (₹35, 45 minutes).

TRAIN
Nawalgarh is on the route of the Sikar Dee Express. The train departs Dehli Sarai Rohilla station at 6.50am (on Wednesday and Friday) and at 11.25pm (on Tuesday, Thursday and Satur-

SHEKHAWATI'S OUTDOOR GALLERIES

In the 18th and 19th centuries, shrewd Marwari merchants lived frugally and far from home while earning money in India's new commercial centres. They sent the bulk of their vast fortunes back to their families in Shekhawati to construct grand *havelis* (traditional, ornately decorated residences) to show their neighbours how well they were doing and to compensate their families for their long absences. Merchants competed with one another to build ever more grand edifices – homes, temples, step-wells – which were richly decorated, both inside and out, with painted murals.

The artists responsible for these acres of decoration largely belonged to the caste of *kumhars* (potters) and were both the builders and painters of the *havelis*. Known as *chajeras* (masons), many were commissioned from beyond Shekhawati – particularly from Jaipur, where they had been employed decorating the new capital's palaces – and others flooded in from further afield to offer their skills. Soon, there was a cross-pollination of ideas and techniques, with local artists learning from the new arrivals.

The early paintings are strongly influenced by Mughal decoration, with floral arabesques and geometric designs. The Rajput royal courts were the next major influence; scenes from Hindu mythology are prevalent, with Krishna particularly popular.

With the arrival of Europeans, walls were embellished with paintings of the new technological marvels to which the Shekhawati merchants had been exposed in centres such as Calcutta (now Kolkata). Pictures of trains, planes, telephones, gramophones and bicycles featured, often painted direct from the artist's imagination. Krishna and Radha are seen in flying motorcars, while the British are invariably depicted as soldiers, with dogs or holding bottles of booze.

These days most of the *havelis* are still owned by descendants of the original families, but not inhabited by their owners, for whom small-town Rajasthan has lost its charm. Many are occupied just by a single *chowkidar* (caretaker), while others may be home to a local family. Though they are pale reflections of the time when they accommodated the large households of the Marwari merchant families, they remain a fascinating testament to the changing times in which they were created. Only a few *havelis* have been restored; many more lie derelict, slowly crumbling away.

For a full rundown on the history, people, towns and buildings of the area, track down a copy of the excellent *The Painted Towns of Shekhawati* by Ilay Cooper, which can be picked up at bookshops in the region or in Jaipur.

day). It arrives at Nawalgarh station at 12.15pm and 5am (the following day) respectively. The fare is sleeper/3AC ₹195/510; other classes are available. The trains continue to Sikar (arriving 1.10pm and 5.45am) on broad gauge, but beyond Sikar to Jaipur work is ongoing to convert the old metre-gauge track.

In the opposite direction, the trains depart Nawalgarh at 2.46pm (on Wednesday and Friday) and 11.43pm (Wednesday, Friday and Sunday) arriving at Delhi at 8.45pm and 5.40am respectively.

Jhunjhunu

📞 01592 / POP 118,500

Shekhawati's most important commercial centre has a different atmosphere from the region's smaller towns, with lots of traffic and concrete, and the hustle and bustle that befits the district capital. On the other hand, it does have a few appealing *havelis* and a colourful bazaar.

⊙ Sights

Mohanlal Ishwardas Modi Haveli   HISTORIC BUILDING

(Nehru Bazaar; ₹50; ⊙8am-6pm) On the northern side of Nehru Bazaar is Mohanlal Ishwardas Modi Haveli (1896). A train runs merrily across the front facade. Above the entrance to the outer courtyard are scenes from the life of Krishna. On a smaller, adjacent arch are British imperial figures, including monarchs and robed judges. Facing them are Indian rulers, including maharajas and nawabs. Around the archway, between the inner and outer courtyards, there are some glass-covered portrait miniatures, along with some fine mirror-and-glass tilework.

Modi Havelis   HISTORIC BUILDING

(Nehru Bazaar; ₹50; ⊙8am-6pm) The Modi Havelis face each other and house some of Jhunjhunu's best murals and woodcarving. The *haveli* on the eastern side has a painting of a woman in a blue sari sitting before a gramophone; a frieze depicts a train, alongside which soldiers race on horses. The spaces between the brackets above show the Krishna legends. The *haveli* on the western side has some comical pictures, featuring some remarkable facial expressions and moustaches.

Khetri Mahal   HISTORIC BUILDING

(₹50; ⏾ dawn-dusk) A series of small laneways at the western end of Nehru Bazaar (a short rickshaw drive north of the bus station) leads to the imposing Khetri Mahal, a small palace dating from around 1770 and once one of Shekhawati's most sophisticated and beautiful buildings. It's believed to have been built by Bhopal Singh, Sardul Singh's grandson, who founded Khetri. Unfortunately, it now has a desolate, forlorn atmosphere, but the architecture remains a superb open-sided collection of intricate arches and columns.

🛏 Sleeping

Hotel Jamuna Resort   HOTEL $$

(📱8955976348,   01592-232871;   www.hotel jamunaresort.in; Mahavir Path, near Nath Ka Tilla; r incl breakfast ₹750, deluxe ₹2200-2600; ✳🖥🛜🏊) Hotel Jamuna Resort has everything the traveller needs for a bargain price. The rooms in the older wing are either vibrantly painted with murals or decorated with traditional mirrorwork, while the rooms in the newer wing are modern and airy. There's an inviting pool (₹100 for nonguests) set in the garden, plus purpose-built kitchens set up for in-house cooking courses.

The friendly family owning and managing the hotel have a wealth of knowledge on the villages of Shekhawati and tours can be organised here. Free pick-up from the train or bus stations can be arranged.

ℹ Getting There & Away

BUS

There are two bus stands: the **main bus stand** (Paramveer Path) and the **private bus stand** (Khem Shakti Rd). Both have similar services and prices, but the government-run buses from the main bus stand run much more frequently. Shared autorickshaws run between the two (₹10 per person).

Services from the main bus stand:

Bikaner ₹226, five to six hours, hourly

Delhi ₹250, five to six hours, hourly

Fatehpur ₹60, one hour, half-hourly

Jaipur ₹190, four hours, half-hourly

Mandawa ₹25, one hour, half-hourly

Nawalgarh ₹40, one hour, half-hourly

TRAIN

Jhunjhunu is on the route of the Sikar Dee Express. The train departs Delhi Sarai Rohilla station at 6.50am (on Wednesday and Friday) and at 11.25pm (on Tuesday, Thursday and Saturday). It arrives at Jhunjhunu station at 11.30am and 4.12am (the following day) respectively. The fare is sleeper/3AC ₹180/510 (other classes available). The trains continue to Sikar (arriving 1.10pm and 5.45am) via Nawalgarh (2nd class ₹55) on broad gauge, but beyond Sikar to Jaipur work is ongoing to convert the old metre-gauge track.

In the opposite direction, the train departs Jhunjhunu at 3.20pm (on Wednesday and Friday) and 11.27pm (Wednesday, Friday and Sunday) arriving at Delhi at 8.45pm and 5.40am respectively.

Fatehpur

📍 01571 / POP 92,600

Established in 1451 as a capital for nawabs (Muslim ruling princes), Fatehpur was their stronghold for centuries before it was taken over by the Shekhawati Rajputs in the 18th century. The wealth of the merchant community, which included the Poddar, Choudhari and Ganeriwala families, is illustrated by the town's grandiose *havelis*, *chhatris* (cenotaphs), wells and temples. It's a busy little town and many of the *havelis* are in a sad state of disrepair, with a few notable exceptions.

⊙ Sights

Apart from the magnificent Le Prince Haveli, other sights include the nearby Chauhan Well; Jagannath Singhania Haveli; the Mahavir Prasad Goenka Haveli, which is often locked but has superb paintings; the Geori Shankar Haveli, with mirrored mosaics on the antechamber ceiling; and south of the private bus stand, Vishnunath Keria Haveli, and Harikrishnan Das Saraogi Haveli, with a colourful facade and iron lacework.

Le Prince Haveli   HISTORIC BUILDING

(📍01571-233024; www.leprincehaveli.com; incl guided tour ₹250; ⏾9am-5pm) This 1802 *haveli* (traditional, ornately decorated residence) has been stunningly restored by French artist Nadine Le Prince and is one of the most exquisite *havelis* in Shekhawati. Visiting students of art history conduct the detailed guided tours (45 minutes, French or English) on the fresco technique and the history of the *havelis* and the merchants who built them. There's a small gallery and a garden bar in which to relax with a post-tour refreshment. Rooms have been converted into beautifully decorated guest rooms.

The *haveli* is around 2km north of the two main bus stands, down a lane off the main road. Turn right out of the bus stands, and the turnoff will eventually be on your right, or hop into an autorickshaw.

🛏 Sleeping & Eating

⭐ **Le Prince Haveli** BOUTIQUE HOTEL **$$**
(☎ 8094880977,01571-233024;www.leprincehaveli. com; near Chauhan Well; r from ₹990, with bathroom/AC from ₹2800/5310; ⏱ mid-Jul–mid-Apr; ❄🖥🌐) The beautifully restored Le Prince Haveli has 14 highly variable, authentically decorated rooms overlooking a tranquil central courtyard. Run as a European homestay, buffet meals (Indian and French cuisine; breakfast ₹200, lunch ₹400, dinner ₹600) are served on the terrace at fixed times. The alfresco bar and pool area make a great oasis and a perfect place to unwind.

There's a 10% discount for two nights, a 20% discount for three nights or more and an additional 20% discount in mid-July to September. Ask about its stable of classic Royal Enfield Bullets for a unique guided tour around the relatively traffic-free roads of Shekhawati.

ℹ Getting There & Away

At the private bus stand and Churu Bus Stand on the Churu–Sikar road, and the central Mandawa Bus Stand, private buses leave for the following Shekhawati destinations throughout the day, departing as they fill with passengers:

Churu ₹39, one hour
Jhunjhunu ₹45, one hour
Mandawa ₹25, one hour
Nawalgarh ₹50, two hours
Ramgarh ₹25, 45 minutes

From the RSRTC bus stand, further south down the same road, buses leave for the following:

Bikaner ₹195, 3½ hours, hourly
Delhi ₹290, seven hours, five daily
Jaipur ₹165, 3½ hours, two daily

Mandawa

☎ 01592 / POP 23,340

Of all the towns in the Shekhawati region, Mandawa is the one best set up for tourists,

with plenty of places to stay and some decent restaurants. Expect a few touts and begging children, but this small 18th-century settlement is still a pleasant base for your *haveli* explorations.

There is only one main drag, with narrow lanes fanning off it. The easy-to-find Hotel Mandawa Haveli is halfway along this street and makes a handy point of reference. Most buses drop passengers off on the main street as well as by the bus stand.

👁 Sights

Binsidhar
Newatia Haveli HISTORIC BUILDING
This 1920s *haveli* on the northern side of the Fatehpur–Jhunjhunu road houses the State Bank of India. There are fantastically entertaining paintings on the external eastern wall, including a European woman in a chauffeur-driven car, the Wright brothers in flight watched by women in saris, a strongman hauling a car, and a bird-man flying in a winged device.

Murmuria Haveli HISTORIC BUILDING
(₹200; ⏱8am-6pm) The Murmuria Haveli dates back to the 1930s. From the sandy courtyard out front, you can get a good view of the southern external wall of the adjacent double *haveli*: it features a long frieze depicting a train and a railway crossing. Nehru is depicted on horseback holding the Indian flag. Above the arches on the southern side of the courtyard are two paintings of gondolas on the canals of Venice.

Entry fee also includes access to Goenka Double Haveli and Seth Dayaram Dedraj Goenka Haveli.

🛏 Sleeping & Eating

Hotel Shekhawati HOTEL **$**
(☎ 9314698079, 01592-223036; www.hotel shekhawati.com; r ₹400-2800; ❄🖥) Near Mukundgarh Rd, the only real budget choice in town is run by a registered tourist guide. Bright, comically bawdy murals painted by artistic former guests give the rooms a splash of colour. Tasty meals are served on the peaceful rooftop. Competitively priced camel, horse and 4WD tours can also be arranged here, reinforcing it as a good budget option.

Hotel Mandawa Haveli HERITAGE HOTEL **$$**
(☎ 8890841088, 01592-223088; www.hotel mandawahaveli.com; r/ste from ₹3480/7080; ❄🖥) Close to Sonathia Gate, on the main

road, this hotel is set in a glorious, restored 1890s *haveli* with rooms surrounding a painted courtyard. The cheapest rooms are small, so it's worth splashing out on a suite, filled with arches, window seats and countless small windows.

There's a rooftop restaurant serving delicious food; it's especially romantic at dinner time, when the lights of the town twinkle below. A set dinner costs ₹600.

Hotel Radhika Haveli Mandawa
HERITAGE HOTEL $$

(☎01592-223045, 9784673645; www.hotel radhikahavelimandawa.com; s/d/ste incl breakfast ₹2790/2800/4250; ❉⊛) This lovely restored *haveli* sits in a quiet part of town with a small lawn and has comfortable and tasteful rooms that are traditional but without garish murals. There's a good vegetarian restaurant in-house, and it's very close to Monica Rooftop Restaurant should you crave a chicken dish.

Hotel Heritage Mandawa
HERITAGE HOTEL $$

(☎01592-223742, 9414647922; www.hotel heritagemandawa.com; r/ste incl breakfast from ₹1800/4500; ❉⊛) This gracious old *haveli* has traditionally decorated rooms. The eclectic suites have small mezzanine levels either for the bed or the bathroom. Rooms are highly variable, so check a few. Music performances and puppet shows are held in the small garden.

Monica Rooftop Restaurant
INDIAN $$

(☎9928207523, 01592-224178; mains ₹120-400; ⊗8am-10pm; ⊛) This delightful rooftop restaurant, in between the fort gate and main bazaar, serves tasty Indian and Chinese meals and cold beer. It's in a converted *haveli* but only the facade, rather than the restaurant itself, has frescos.

ℹ Information

State Bank of India (SBI; Main Bazaar; ⊗10am-4pm Mon-Fri, to 1pm Sat) In Binsidhar Newatia Haveli; changes cash only. There's a State Bank of India ATM across the road.

ℹ Getting There & Away

The main bus stand, sometimes called Bikaner bus stand, has frequent services (roughly half-hourly), including those listed below. Note, there is also a separate Nawalgarh bus stand, just off the main drag, with services to Nawalgarh only. Both bus stands are so small they are unrecognisable as bus stands unless a bus

is waiting at them. Look for the chai stalls that cluster beside them and you should have the right spot. The main bus stand is at one end of the main street, on your left as the road bears right.

Bikaner ₹233, five hours
Fatehpur ₹35, one hour
Jhunjhunu ₹25, one hour
Nawalgarh ₹35, 45 minutes

WESTERN RAJASTHAN

Jodhpur

☎0291 / POP 1,033,800

Mighty Mehrangarh, the muscular fort that towers over the Blue City of Jodhpur, is a magnificent spectacle and an architectural masterpiece. Around Mehrangarh's base, the old city, a jumble of Brahmin-blue cubes, stretches out to the 10km-long, 16th-century city wall. The Blue City really is blue! Inside is a tangle of winding, glittering, medieval streets, which never seem to lead where you expect them to, scented by incense, roses and sewers, with shops and bazaars selling everything from trumpets and temple decorations to snuff and saris.

Modern Jodhpur stretches well beyond the city walls, but it's the immediacy and buzz of the old Blue City and the larger-than-life fort that capture travellers' imaginations. This crowded, hectic zone is also Jodhpur's main tourist area. Areas of the old city further west, such as Navchokiya, are just as atmospheric, with far less hustling.

History

Driven from their homeland of Kannauj, east of Agra, by Afghans serving Mohammed of Ghori, the Rathore Rajputs fled west around AD 1200 to the region around Pali, 70km southeast of Jodhpur. They prospered to such a degree that in 1381 they managed to oust the Pratiharas of Mandore, 9km north of present-day Jodhpur. In 1459 the Rathore leader Rao Jodha chose a nearby rocky ridge as the site for a new fortress of staggering proportions, Mehrangarh, around which grew Jodha's city: Jodhpur.

Jodhpur lay on the vital trade route between Delhi and Gujarat. The Rathore kingdom grew on the profits of sandalwood, opium, dates and copper, and controlled a large area, which became cheerily known as

Marwar (the Land of Death) due to its harsh topography and climate. It stretched as far west as what's now the India–Pakistan border area, and bordered with Mewar (Udaipur) in the south, Jaisalmer in the northwest, Bikaner in the north, and Jaipur and Ajmer in the east.

Sights & Activities

★ Mehrangarh   FORT
(www.mehrangarh.org) **FREE** Rising perpendicular and impregnable from a rocky hill that itself stands 120m above Jodhpur's skyline, Mehrangarh is one of the most magnificent forts in India. The battlements are 6m to 36m high, and as the building materials were chiselled from the rock on which the fort stands, the structure merges with its base. Still run by the Jodhpur royal family, Mehrangarh is packed with history and legend.

Mehrangarh's main entrance is at the northeast gate, Jai Pol. It's about a 300m walk up from the old city to the entrance, or you can take a winding 5km autorickshaw ride (around ₹120).

Jai Pol was built by Maharaja Man Singh in 1808 following his defeat of invading forces from Jaipur. Past the **museum ticket office** (⊙9am-5pm) and a small cafe, the 16th-century Dodh Kangra Pol was an external gate before Jai Pol was built, and still bears the scars of 1808 cannonball hits. Through here, the main route heads up to the left through the 16th-century Imritia Pol and then Loha Pol, the fort's original entrance, with iron spikes to deter enemy elephants. Just inside the gate are two sets of small hand prints, the sati (ritual suicide of widow on husband's funeral pyre) marks of royal widows – the last to commit sati were Maharaja Man Singh's widows in 1843.

Past Loha Pol you'll find a restaurant and Suraj Pol, which gives access to the museum. Once you've visited the museum, continue on from here to the panoramic ramparts, which are lined with impressive antique artillery. The ramparts were fenced off in 2016 after a fatal selfie accident – hopefully a temporary measure, as the views are spectacular.

Also worth exploring is the right turn from Jai Pol, where a path winds down to the Chokelao Bagh, a restored and gorgeously planted 18th-century Rajput garden (you could lose an afternoon here lolling under shady trees reading a book), and the Fateh Pol (Victory Gate). You can exit here into the old city quarter of Navchokiya.

You don't need a ticket to enter the fort itself, only the museum section. However, the museum guards may not let you walk past the museum entrance, so it's better to enter from Fateh Pol if you wish to just wander about the grounds.

★ Mehrangarh Museum   MUSEUM
(www.mehrangarh.org; Indian/foreigner incl audio guide ₹100/600, camera/video ₹100/200, guide ₹400; ⊙9am-5pm) The fort's museum encompasses its former palace, and is a superb example of Rajput architecture. The network of courtyards and halls features stone-lattice work so finely carved that it often looks more like sandalwood than sandstone. The galleries around Shringar Chowk (Anointment Courtyard) display India's best collection of howdahs (seat for carrying people on an elephant's back) and Jodhpur's royal palanquin collection. The superb audio guide is included with your ticket, but bring ID or a credit card as deposit.

One of the two galleries off Daulat Khana Chowk displays textiles, paintings, manuscripts, headgear and the curved sword of the Mughal emperor Akbar; the other gallery is the armoury. Upstairs is a fabulous gallery of miniature paintings from the sophisticated Marwar school and the beautiful 18th-century Phul Mahal (Flower Palace), with 19th-century wall paintings depicting the 36 moods of classical ragas as well as royal portraits; the artist took 10 years to create them using a curious concoction of gold leaf, glue and cow's urine.

Takhat Vilas was the bedchamber of Maharaja Takhat Singh (r 1843–73), who had just 30 maharanis and numerous concubines. Its beautiful ceiling is covered with Christmas baubles. You then enter the extensive zenana (area in an upper-class home where women are secluded), the lovely latticed windows of which are said to feature over 250 different designs (and through which the women could watch the goings-on in the courtyards). Here you'll find the Cradle Gallery, exhibiting the elaborate cradles of infant princes, and the 17th-century Moti Mahal (Pearl Palace), which was the palace's main durbar hall (royal reception hall) for official meetings and receptions, with gorgeously colourful stained glass.

Note that the museum can be suffocatingly crowded in the holiday period following Diwali.

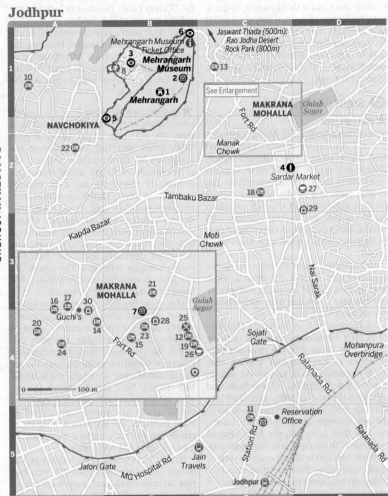

See Enlargement

Rao Jodha Desert Rock Park

PARK

(☏9571271000; www.raojodhapark.com; Mehrangarh; ₹100, guide ₹200; ⊙7am-6.30pm Apr-Sep, 8am-5.30pm Oct-Mar) This 72-hectare park – and model of ecotourism – sits in the lee of Mehrangarh. It has been lovingly restored and planted with native species to show the natural diversity of the region. The park is criss-crossed with walking trails that take you up to the city walls, around Devkund lake, spotting local and migratory birds, butterflies and reptiles. For an extra insight into the area's native flora and fauna, take along one of the excellent local guides.

Walks here are the perfect restorative if the Indian hustle has left you in need of breathing space. Visit in the early morning or late afternoon for the most pleasant temperatures. The visitors centre is thoughtfully put together, and there's a small cafe, too.

Jaswant Thada

HISTORIC BUILDING

(Indian/foreigner ₹30/50, camera/video ₹50, guide ₹100; ⊙9am-5pm) This milky-white marble memorial to Maharaja Jaswant Singh II, sitting above a small lake 1km northeast of Mehrangarh, is an array of whimsical domes. It's a welcome, peaceful spot after the hubbub of the city, and the views across to the

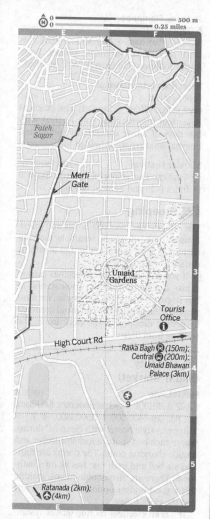

0 — 500 m
0 — 0.25 miles

Jodhpur

fort and over the city are superb. Built in 1899, the cenotaph has some beautiful *jalis* (carved-marble lattice screens) and is hung with portraits of Rathore rulers going back to the 13th century.

Look out for the memorial to a peacock that flew into a funeral pyre.

Umaid Bhawan Palace PALACE
(Umaid Bhawan Rd) Gaj Singh II still lives in part of this hilltop palace, built in 1929 for Maharaja Umaid Singh. It was designed by the British architect Henry Lanchester and took more than 3000 workers 15 years to complete its 365 rooms, at a cost of around ₹11 million.

The museum (9am to 5pm, Indian/foreigner ₹50/100), which includes photos of the elegant art-deco interior plus an eccentric collection of elaborate clocks, is the only part open to casual visitors.

The building is mortarless, and incorporates 100 wagon loads of Makrana marble and Burmese teak in the interior. Apparently its construction began as a royal job-creation program during a time of severe drought. Much of the building has been turned into a suitably grand hotel. Casual visitors are not welcome at either the royal residence or the hotel. Don't miss the maharaja's highly polished classic cars, displayed in front of the museum, by the entrance gate. It's 3km southeast of the old city; take an autorickshaw.

Toorji Ka Jhalra   HISTORIC BUILDING
(Step-well; Stepwell Sq, Makrana Mohalla) `FREE`
This geometrically handsome step-well (also known as a *baori* or *wav*) has been rejuvenated after decades as a rubbish dump. Its clean lines and clear, fish-filled water will leave you mesmerised. It's a great place to just sit and watch, and the attached cafe (p185) adds further incentive for a visit.

Clock Tower   MONUMENT
The century-old clock tower is a city landmark surrounded by the vibrant sounds, sights and smells of Sardar Market. The market is bordered by triple-arched gateways at its northern and southern ends. The narrow, winding lanes of the old city spread out in all directions from here. Westward, you plunge into the old city's commercial heart, with crowded alleys and bazaars selling vegetables, spices, sweets, silver and handicrafts.

Flying Fox   ADVENTURE SPORTS
(www.flyingfox.asia; adult/child ₹1999/1600; ⊙9am-5pm) This circuit of six zip lines flies back and forth over walls, bastions and lakes on the northern side of Mehrangarh. A brief training session is given before you start and safety standards are good: 'awesome' is the verdict of most who dare. Flying Fox has a desk near the main ticket office and its starting point is in the Chokelao Bagh. Tours last up to 1½ hours, depending on the group size. Book online for a discount on the walk-up price.

✦ Festivals & Events

World Sacred Spirit Festival   MUSIC
(www.worldsacredspiritfestival.org; Mehrangarh; ⊙Feb) Jodhpur hosts the World Sacred Spirit Festival, featuring international musicians playing in various settings within Mehrangarh.

Jodhpur Flamenco & Gypsy Festival   MUSIC
(www.jfgfestival.com; ⊙Apr) Mehrangarh, this most spectacular of music venues, hosts April's Jodhpur Flamenco & Gypsy Festival.

Rajasthan International Folk Festival   MUSIC
(www.jodhpurriff.org; ⊙Sep/Oct) The excellent Rajasthan International Folk Festival, with five days of music concerts by Indian and international artists, is held at Mehrangarh.

Marwar Festival   PERFORMING ARTS
(⊙Sep/Oct) The colourful Marwar Festival includes polo and a camel tattoo.

🛏 Sleeping

The old city has over 100 hotels and guesthouses, most of which scramble for your custom as soon as you get within breathing distance of Sardar Market.

If you call ahead, many lodgings can organise a pick-up from the train station or bus stops, even at night. Otherwise, for most places in the old city you can avoid nonsense by getting dropped at the clock tower and walking from there.

🛏 Old City (Sadar Market)

HosteLavie   HOSTEL $
(☏0291-2611001; www.hostelavie.com; Killi Khana, Fort Rd; dm ₹400-500, r ₹1500-1800; ❋ 🛜) A European-style hostel with clean AC dorms, where each bed sports a lockable locker and mobile charging point. The dorms are four- and six-bed and each one has its own bathroom. There are also double rooms, making this a good budget option between the fort and the clock tower.

It has an excellent rooftop terrace restaurant with espresso coffee, Indian veg, and authentic Korean veg and nonveg.

Yogi Guest House   GUESTHOUSE $
(☏0291-2643436; www.yogiguesthouse.com; dm ₹400, r ₹800, with AC ₹2200; ❋ 🛜) Yogi's is a venerable travellers' hang-out, with a clean dorm and budget rooms in a 500-year-old blue-washed *haveli* (traditional, ornately decorated residence) just below the fort walls. It's a friendly place with well-kept, clean rooms. There's also a lovely rooftop restaurant with great views.

Hill View Guest House
GUESTHOUSE $

(☑ 0291-2441763, 9829153196; hill_view2004@yahoo.com; Makrana Mohalla; dm ₹150, r ₹300-700, with AC ₹1500; ❄ ☎) Perched above town and just below the fort walls, this hotel is run by a friendly, enthusiastic Muslim family who'll make you feel right at home. Rooms are basic, clean and simple, all with bathrooms (but not all with decent windows), and the terrace has a great view over the city. Good, home-cooked veg and nonveg food is on offer. Village and camel tours can be arranged here.

Kesar Heritage Hotel
GUESTHOUSE $

(☑ 9983216625; www.kesarheritage.com; Makrana Mohalla; r ₹900-2200; ❄ ☎) A popular budget choice, Kesar plays a good hand with large airy rooms (a few have balconies, AC and flatscreen TVs) and friendly, helpful management. The side-alley location puts noisily sputtering rickshaws out of earshot of light sleepers. The vegetarian rooftop restaurant gets rave reviews for its delicious food and views to Mehrangarh.

Pushp Guest House
GUESTHOUSE $

(☑ 0291-2648494; www.pushpguesthouse.com; Pipli-ki-Gali, Naya Bass, Manak Chowk; r ₹400-600, with AC ₹1000; ❄ ☎) A small family-run guesthouse with five clean, colourful rooms with windows. It's tucked down the narrowest of alleys, but you get an up-close view of Mehrangarh from the rooftop restaurant, where owner Nikhil rustles up great vegetarian fare. Nikhil will send a rickshaw to the railway station to pick you up for ₹100.

★ Krishna Prakash Heritage Haveli
HERITAGE HOTEL $$

(☑ 0291-2633448; www.kpheritage.com; Nayabas; r incl breakfast ₹2015-4720; ❄ @ ☎ ⊠) This multilevel heritage hotel right under the fort walls is great value and a peaceful choice. It has decorated carved furniture and colourful murals, and rooms are well proportioned; the deluxe ones are a bit more spruced up, generally bigger, and set on the upper floors, so airier. There's a shaded swimming pool and a relaxing terrace restaurant.

Free bus and train station pick-ups are offered and there are facilities for drivers.

Haveli Inn Pal
HERITAGE HOTEL $$

(☑ 0291-2612519; www.haveliinnpal.com; Gulab Sagar; r incl breakfast ₹3850-5150; ❄ @ ☎) This smaller sibling of Pal Haveli is accessed through the same grand entrance, but is located around to the right in one wing of the

residence. It's a simpler heritage experience, with comfortable rooms, and lake or fort views from the more expensive ones. It has its own very good rooftop restaurant, Panorama 360° (p184).

Free pick-ups from Jodhpur transport terminals are offered, and discounts are often available for single occupancy.

Jhankar Choti Haveli
HERITAGE HOTEL $$

(☑ 0291-2621390; www.jhankarhaveli.com; Makrana Mohalla; r incl breakfast ₹2500-4500; ❄ ☎) Above the restaurant of the same name are nine delightful and spacious rooms carved out of a beautiful *haveli* (traditional, ornately decorated residence). Rooms feature raw red stone walls and shiny marble floors. Antique furniture decorates the rooms, which aren't cluttered at all. And bathrooms are modern and have baths.

Stepwell House
HOTEL $$

(☑ 0291-2614615; www.stepwellhouse.com; Stepwell Sq, Makrana Mohalla; r incl breakfast standard/superior ₹2960/4130; ❄ @ ☎) This 250-year-old building inside the walled city is a popular, efficient and friendly place. Rooms vary greatly and are individually decorated with colour themes and paintings; many have semibalconies and fort views. The rooftop restaurant, **Jharokha 360°** (mains ₹270-380; ◷ 8am-11pm), has excellent food and views. It's opposite the restored and beautiful Toorji Ka Jhalra step-well.

Guests can take advantage of the swimming pool and spa at the neighbouring (and associated) Raas for an extra payment.

★ Pal Haveli
HERITAGE HOTEL $$$

(☑ 0291-3293328; www.palhaveli.com; Gulab Sagar; r incl breakfast ₹5500-10,500; ❄ @ ☎) This stunning *haveli* one of the best and most attractive in the old city, was built by the Thakur of Pal in 1847. There are 21 charming, spacious rooms, mostly large and elaborately decorated in traditional heritage style, surrounding a central courtyard. The family retain a small museum here. The rooftop restaurant, Indique (p184), is one of the city's finest and has incredible views.

Raas
BOUTIQUE HOTEL $$$

(☑ 0291-2636455; www.raasjodhpur.com; Toorji ka Jhalara; r incl breakfast from ₹26,880; ❄ ☎ ⊠) Developed from a 19th-century city mansion, Jodhpur's first contemporary-style boutique hotel is a splendid oasis of clean, uncluttered style, hidden behind castle-like gates. The red-sandstone-and-terrazzo rooms come with plenty of luxury touches. Most have balconies with great Mehrangarh views – also to be enjoyed from the lovely pool in the garden courtyard. There are two restaurants and a highly indulgent spa.

Old City (Navchokiya)

Cosy Guest House GUESTHOUSE $

(☑0291-2612066, 9829023390; www.cosyguest house.com; Chuna Ki Choki; r ₹400-1000, without bathroom ₹350; ❇☎) A friendly place in an enchanting location, this 500-year-old glowing blue house has several levels of higgledy-piggledy rooftops and a mix of rooms, some monastic, others comfortable with AC and views. There's also a relaxing rooftop restaurant.

Ask the rickshaw driver for Navchokiya Rd, from where the guesthouse is signposted, or call the genial owner Mr Joshi.

★ Singhvi's Haveli GUESTHOUSE $$

(☑9826258920, 0291-2624293; www.singhvi haveli.com; Ramdevji-ka-Chowk; r ₹900-3800; ❇☎) This 500-odd-year-old, family-run, red-sandstone *haveli* is an understated gem. Run by two friendly brothers, Singhvi's has 13 individual rooms, ranging from simple places to lay your head to the magnificent Maharani Suite, with its 10 windows and fort view.

There's two relaxing vegetarian restaurants, one decorated with saris and floor cushions, the other a romantic rooftop with fort views.

Train Station Area

Govind Hotel HOTEL, HOSTEL $

(☑0291-2622758; www.govindhotel.com; Station Rd; dm ₹250, s/d from ₹850/950, with AC from ₹1400/1600; ❇☎) Well set up for travellers, with helpful management and a location very convenient to the Jodhpur train station. All rooms are clean and tiled, with smart bathrooms. There's a rooftop restaurant and a coffee shop with excellent espresso and cakes.

✗ Eating

Panorama 360° INDIAN $$

(☑9414005479; Haveli Inn Pal, Gulab Sagar; mains ₹300-450; ☉8am-10pm) This cosy restaurant on the rooftop of Haveli Inn Pal (p183) features great food, attentive staff and a spectacular view of the fort. It dishes up delicious breakfasts comprising (real) coffee, eggs and pancakes, and it welcomes guests from other hotels. There's great tandoori food and North Indian curries, nonveg and veg, and beer and wine are served.

Nirvana INDIAN $$

(☑0291-2631262; 1st fl, Tija Mata ka Mandir, Tambaku Bazar; mains ₹270-350, thali ₹400-450; ☉9am-10pm) Sharing premises with a Rama temple and a hotel (☑0291-2631262; nirwanahome.jod@gmail.com; s/d from ₹1500/2000, ste ₹4000; ❇☎), Nirvana has both an indoor cafe, covered in ancient Ramayana wall paintings, and a rooftop eating area with panoramic views. The Indian vegetarian food is among the most delicious you'll find in Rajasthan. The special thali is enormous and easily enough for two. Continental and Indian breakfasts are served in the cafe.

KP's Restaurant MULTICUISINE $$

(☑9829241547; Killi Khana; mains ₹140-400, thali ₹260-360; ☉7.30am-10.30pm) The rooftop restaurant at Krishna Prakash Heritage Haveli (p183) welcomes all to sample its delicious food and fort views. There are Chinese and Continental dishes, but the North Indian, including *kaju dakh* (cashew and raisin curry) and the veg or nonveg thali, are delicious. For carnivores who like it spicy, the *laal maas* (mutton curry), is the go-to dish.

Favourites such as butter chicken, dhal makhani and *palak paneer* also feature.

Jhankar Choti Haveli MULTICUISINE $$

(☑9828031291; Makrana Mohalla; mains ₹230-300; ☉8am-10pm; ❇☎☎) Stone walls and big cane chairs in a leafy courtyard, along with prettily painted woodwork and whirring fans, set the scene at this semi-open-air travellers' favourite. It serves up good Indian vegetarian dishes, plus pizzas, burgers and baked-cheese dishes. There's an AC section, a Café Coffee Day franchise and a rooftop for meals with a view.

★ Indique INDIAN $$$

(☑0291-3293328; Pal Haveli Hotel; mains ₹350-600; ☉noon-10.30pm) This candlelit rooftop restaurant at the Pal Haveli hotel (p183) is the perfect place for a romantic dinner, with superb views to the fort, clock tower and Umaid Bhawan. The food covers traditional tandoori, biryanis and North Indian curries, but the Rajasthani *laal maas* (mutton curry) is a delight. Ask the bartender to knock you up a gin and tonic before dinner.

🍷 Drinking & Nightlife

★ Shri Mishrilal Hotel
CAFE

(Sardar Market; ⏰ 8.30am-10pm) Just inside the southern gate of Sardar Market, this place is nothing fancy, but whips up the most superb creamy *makhania* lassis (filling, saffron-flavoured lassis). These are the best in town, probably in all of Rajasthan, possibly in all of India.

★ Cafe Sheesh Mahal
CAFE

(Pal Haveli Hotel; ⏰ 9.30am-9pm) Coffee drinkers will enjoy the precious beans and the care that is bestowed on them at the deliciously air-conditioned Cafe Sheesh Mahal. The beans are of South Indian origin, roasted by Lavazza. And the pancakes (₹150) here deserve their legendary status.

Stepwell Cafe
CAFE

(☎ 0291-2636455; Toorji ka Jhalra; ⏰ 7.30am-10.30pm; 🛜) This delightful modern cafe with espresso coffee, cakes and Italian dishes, as well as wine, spirits and beer, sits to one side of the wonderfully restored stepwell, Toorji ka Jhalra. It's a great place to relax and contemplate the time when stepwells such as these kept the city alive. Or you can just watch the kids jump into the water with an impressive booming splash.

🛍 Shopping

MV Spices
FOOD

(www.mvspices.com; 107 Nai Sarak; ⏰ 9am-9pm) The most famous spice shop in Jodhpur (and believe us, there are lots of pretenders), MV Spices has five small branches around town, including one at Sadar Market, Mehrangarh, that are run by the seven daughters of the founder of the original stall. It will cost around ₹100 to ₹500 for 100g bags of spices, and the owners will email you recipes so you can use your spices correctly when you get home.

Sambhali Boutique
FASHION & ACCESSORIES

(Killi Khana; ⏰ 10am-7pm) 🖉 This small but interesting shop sells goods made by women who have learned craft skills with the Sambhali Trust, which works to empower disadvantaged women and girls. Items include cute stuffed silk or cloth elephants and horses, bracelets made from pottery beads, silk bags, and block-printed muslin curtains and scarves.

Laxmi Niwas
FASHION & ACCESSORIES

(Stepwell Sq; ⏰ 9am-9pm) Several trendy and quality boutique stores with exquisite block-printed clothes, gifts and tableware can be found in this building opposite the Toorji ka Jhalra step-well (p182). There's also a bakery and coffee shop and access

RAJASTHAN JODHPUR

ℹ CROSSING TO PAKISTAN: JODHPUR TO KARACHI

For Karachi (Pakistan), the 14889 Thar Express, alias the Jodhpur–Munabao Link Express, leaves Bhagat Ki Kothi station, 4km south of the Jodhpur train station, at 1am on Saturday only. You need to arrive at the station six hours before departure – the same time it takes to reach Munabao (about 7am) on the border. There you undergo lengthy border procedures before continuing to Karachi (assuming you have a Pakistan visa) in a Pakistani train, arriving about 2am on Sunday. Accommodation is sleeper only, with a total sleeper fare of around ₹800 from Jodhpur to Karachi. In the other direction the Pakistani train leaves Karachi at about 11pm on Friday, and the Indian train 14890 leaves Munabao at 7pm on Saturday, reaching Jodhpur at 11.50pm. It is currently not possible to book this train online; you will need to go to the station.

Border Hours
Visas are not available at the border, which is open only when the trains (from Jodhpur and Karachi) are arriving/departing.

Foreign Exchange
There are no official money changers at the border. However, changing money at the border and on the trains with unofficial money changers is possible.

Onward Transport
The Pakistani train takes you into Karachi Cantonment Railway Station, where taxis are available.

to the rooftop restaurant Jharokha 360° (p183).

Information

There are foreign-card-friendly ATMs dotted around the city, though fewer are in the old city.

Guchi's (☑ 8233002003; Killikhana, Naya Bass, Makrana Mohalla; ⊙ 8am-10pm) This travel agency exchanges currency.

Main post office (Station Rd; ⊙ 9am-4pm Mon-Fri, to 3pm Sat, stamp sales only 10am-3pm Sun)

Tourist office (☑ 0291-2545083; High Court Rd; ⊙ 9am-6pm Mon-Fri) Offers a free map.

ℹ Getting There & Away

AIR

The airport is 5km south of the city centre, about ₹500 by taxi.

Jet Airways (www.jetairways.com), Air India (www.airindia.in) and SpiceJet (www.spicejet.com) fly daily to/from Delhi, Ahmedabad, Indore and Mumbai.

BUS

Government-run buses leave from the **central bus stand** (Raika Bagh), directly opposite Raika Bagh train station. Walk east along High Court Rd, then turn right under the small tunnel. Services include the following:

Ajmer (for Pushkar) ₹227, AC ₹443, five hours, hourly until 6.30pm

Bikaner ₹266, 5½ hours, frequent from 5am to 6pm

Jaipur ₹331, AC ₹713, seven hours, frequent from 4.45am to midnight

Jaisalmer ₹272, 5½ hours, 10 daily

Mt Abu (Abu Road) ₹306, 7½ hours, nine daily until 9.30pm

Osian ₹69, 1½ hours, half-hourly until 10pm

Rohet ₹47, one hour, every 15 minutes

Udaipur ₹273, AC ₹604, seven hours, 10 daily until 6.30pm

For private buses, you can book through your hotel or an agency such as Guchi's. Although it's marginally cheaper to deal directly with the bus operators on the road in front of Jodhpur train station, they have no commercial interest in you and you may find yourself on a bad bus and dropped by the roadside far from your intended destination. **Jain Travels** (☑ 0291-2643832; www.jaintravels.com; MG Hospital Rd; ⊙ 7am-11pm) appears to be reliable. Buses leave from bus stands out of town, but the operator should provide you with free transport (usually a shared autorickshaw) from their ticket office. Example services:

Ajmer (for Pushkar) ₹180, five hours, at least six daily

Bikaner seat/sleeper ₹220/320, five hours, at least five daily

Jaipur seat/sleeper ₹260/380, 7½ hours, five daily

Jaisalmer ₹300, 5½ hours, hourly

Mt Abu (direct) seat/sleeper ₹315/550, 7½ hours, daily

TAXI

You can organise taxis for intercity trips, or longer, through most accommodation places or travel agents such as Guchi's; otherwise, you can deal directly with drivers. There's a taxi stand outside Jodhpur train station. A reasonable price is ₹10 per kilometre, with a minimum of 300km per day. If it is not already in the agreed price, the driver will charge an extra ₹200 for overnight stops and will also charge for his return journey. Guchi's organises one-way fares by coordinating with numerous drivers.

TRAIN

The computerised **reservation office** (Station Rd; ⊙ 8am-8pm Mon-Sat, to 1.45pm Sun) is 300m northeast of Jodhpur train station. Window 786 sells the tourist quota. Services:

Ajmer (for Pushkar) sleeper/3AC ₹185/510, 5½ hours, two daily (6.20am and 7.10am)

Bikaner sleeper/3AC ₹210/530, 5½ to seven hours, five to eight daily (7.25am, 7.45am,

MAJOR TRAINS FROM JODHPUR

DESTINATION	TRAIN	DEPARTURE	ARRIVAL	FARE (₹)
Ajmer (for Pushkar)	54801 Jodhpur–Ajmer Fast Passenger	7.10am	12.35pm	185/510
Bikaner	14708 Ranapur Exp	9.50am	3.30pm	210/530
Delhi	12462 Mandor Exp	7.45pm	6.40am	380/986
Jaipur	14854 Marudhar Exp	9.30am	3.30pm	250/625
Jaisalmer	14810 Jodhpur–Jaisalmer Exp	11.40pm	6.10am	215/565
Mumbai	14707 Ranapur Exp	2.30pm	9.40am	485/1270

Fares: sleeper/3AC

9.50am, 10.25am, 10.55am, 2.25pm and 8.25pm)

Delhi sleeper/3AC ₹380/986, 11 to 14 hours, four daily (6.20am, 11.15am, 7.45pm and 9.25pm)

Jaipur sleeper/3AC ₹250/625, five to six hours, six to 12 daily from 1.45am to 11.25pm

Jaisalmer sleeper/3AC ₹215/565, five to seven hours, three or four daily (5.30am, 7.25am, 6pm and 11.40pm)

Mumbai sleeper/3AC ₹485/1270, 16 to 19 hours, two to six daily (3.20am, 5.10am, 5.30am, 2.30pm, 6.30pm, 6.45pm); all go via Abu Rd for Mt Abu (4½ hours)

Udaipur There are no direct trains; change at Marwar Junction.

ℹ Getting Around

Despite the absurd claims of some autorickshaw drivers, the fare between the clock tower area and the train stations or central bus stand should be around ₹70 to ₹80.

Around Jodhpur

Southern Villages

A number of largely traditional villages are strung along and off the Pali road southeast of Jodhpur. Most hotels and guesthouses in Jodhpur offer tours to these villages, often called Bishnoi village safaris. The Bishnoi are a Hindu sect who follow the 500-year-old teachings of Guru Jambheshwar, who emphasised the importance of protecting the environment. Many visitors are surprised by the density – and fearlessness – of wildlife such as blackbuck, nilgai (antelope), chinkara (gazelle) and desert fox around the Bishnoi villages.

The 1730 sacrifice of 363 villagers to protect khejri trees is commemorated in September at Khejadali village, where there is a memorial to the victims fronted by a small grove of khejri trees.

At Guda Bishnoi, the locals are traditionally engaged in animal husbandry. There's a small **lake** (Indian/foreigner ₹20/80) – full only after a good monsoon – where migratory birds such as demoiselle cranes, and mammals including blackbucks and chinkaras, can be seen, particularly at dusk when they come to drink.

The village of Salawas is a centre for weaving beautiful *dhurries* (rugs), a craft also practised in many other villages. A cooperative of 42 families here runs the **Roopraj Dhurry Udyog** (☑ 9982400416; www.roopraj durry.com; ⊙ dawn-dusk), through which all profits go to the artisans. A 1m by 1.5m *dhurrie* costs a minimum of ₹5000, including shipping. Other families are involved in block-printing.

Other Muslim villages, such as Singhasini, comprise potter families. Using hand-turned (and powered) wheels they produce big earthenware pots known as *matka*, used for storing and cooling water. Bishnoi village tours tend to last four hours in total and cost around ₹800 per person. Those run by Deepak Dhanraj of **Bishnoi Village Safari** (☑ 9829126398; www.bishnoivillagesafari.com; half-day tour per person ₹800) get good feedback, but many other places do them.

Osian

☑ 02922 / POP 12,550

The ancient Thar Desert town of Osian, 65km north of Jodhpur, was an important trading centre between the 8th and 12th centuries. Known as Upkeshpur, it was dominated by the Jains, whose wealth left a legacy of exquisitely sculpted, well-preserved temples. The **Mahavira Temple** (⊙ 6am-8.30pm) surrounds an image of the 24th *tirthankar* (great Jain teacher), formed from sand and milk. **Sachiya Mata Temple** (⊙ 6am-7.15pm) is an impressive walled complex where both Hindus and Jains worship.

Osian, along with Jodhpur, co-hosts the Marwar Festival (p182), a colourful display of Rajasthani folk music, dance and costume held every September/October.

Raju Bhanu Sharma, a personable Brahmin priest, has an echoing **guesthouse** (☑ 9414440479; bhanusharma.osian@gmail.com; s/d without bathroom ₹400/600) geared towards pilgrims near the Mahavira Temple. Rooms are simple, with shared bathroom and bucket hot water. Raju is also a registered guide and can arrange 4WD excursions and camel safaris, and he is very knowledgeable about Osian's temples. You can find him sitting in his sari shop opposite the gateway to the temple.

A native of Bhikamkor village, northwest of Osian, **Gemar Singh** (☑ 9460585154; www. hacra.org; per person per day around ₹3150) arranges popular camel safaris, homestays, camping, desert walks and 4WD trips in the deserts around Osian and its Rajput and Bishnoi villages. The emphasis here is on channelling the benefits of tourism to local people. Pick-up from Osian bus station, or from Jodhpur, can be arranged. Minimum two people per trip.

LOCAL KNOWLEDGE

BHANG FOR YOUR BUCK

Jaisalmer's licensed **Bhang Shop** (Gopa Chowk; lassi from ₹150) is a simple, unpretentious place. The magic ingredient is bhang: cannabis buds and leaves mixed into a paste with milk, ghee and spices. As well as lassi, it also does a range of bhang-laced cookies and cakes – choose either medium or strong. Bhang is legal, but it doesn't agree with everyone, so go easy.

❶ Getting There & Away

Frequent buses depart from Jodhpur to Osian (₹69, 1½ hours). Buses also run from Phalodi (₹90, two hours). Trains between Jodhpur and Jaisalmer also stop here. A return taxi from Jodhpur costs about ₹2000.

Jaisalmer

📲 02992 / POP 65,470

The fort of Jaisalmer is a breathtaking sight: a massive sandcastle rising from the sandy plains like a mirage from a bygone era. No place better evokes exotic camel-train trade routes and desert mystery. Ninety-nine bastions encircle the fort's still-inhabited twisting lanes. Inside are shops swaddled in bright embroideries, a royal palace and numerous businesses looking for your tourist rupee. Despite the rampant commercialism, it's hard not to be enchanted by this desert citadel. Beneath the ramparts, particularly to the north, the narrow streets of the old city conceal magnificent *havelis* (traditional, ornately decorated residences), all carved from the same golden-honey sandstone as the fort – hence Jaisalmer's designation as the Golden City.

A city that has come back almost from the dead in the past half-century, Jaisalmer may be remote, but it's certainly not forgotten – indeed it's one of Rajasthan's biggest tourist destinations.

History

Jaisalmer was founded way back in 1156 by a leader of the Bhati Rajput clan named Jaisal. The Bhatis, who trace their lineage back to Krishna, ruled right through to Independence in 1947.

The city's early centuries were tempestuous, partly because its rulers relied on looting for want of other income, but by the 16th century Jaisalmer was prospering from its strategic position on the camel-train routes between India and Central Asia. It eventually established cordial relations with the Mughal empire. In the mid-17th century, Maharawal Sabal Singh expanded the Jaisalmer princedom to its greatest extents by annexing areas that now fall within the administrative districts of Bikaner and Jodhpur.

Under British rule the rise of sea trade (especially through Mumbai) and railways saw Jaisalmer's importance and population decline. Partition in 1947, with the cutting of trade routes to Pakistan, seemingly sealed the city's fate. But the 1965 and 1971 wars between India and Pakistan gave Jaisalmer new strategic importance, and since the 1960s, the Indira Gandhi Canal to the north has brought revitalising water to the surrounding desert.

Today, tourism, wind-power generation, solar power generation and the area's many military installations are the pillars of the city's economy.

◉ Sights

⭐ **Jaisalmer Fort**   FORT

(Golden Fort) Jaisalmer's fort is a living urban centre, with about 3000 people residing within its walls. It is honeycombed with narrow winding lanes, lined with houses and temples – along with a large number of handicraft shops, guesthouses and restaurants. You enter the fort from the east, near Gopa Chowk, and pass through four massive gates on the zigzagging route to the upper section. The final gate opens into the square that forms the fort's centre, Dashera Chowk.

Founded in 1156 by the Rajput ruler Jaisal and reinforced by subsequent rulers, Jaisalmer Fort was the focus of a number of battles between the Bhatis, the Mughals of Delhi and the Rathores of Jodhpur. In recent years, the fabric of the fort has faced increasing conservation problems due to unrestricted water use caused, in the most part, by high tourist numbers.

⭐ **Fort Palace Museum**   PALACE

(Indian/foreigner incl audio guide ₹100/500, camera ₹100; ⊙8am-6pm, from 9am Nov-Mar) Towering over the fort's main square, and partly built on top of the Hawa Pol (the fourth fort gate), is the former rulers' elegant seven-storey palace. Highlights of the tour include the mirrored and painted Rang Mahal (the bedroom of the 18th-century ruler Mulraj II), a gallery of finely wrought 15th-century sculptures donated to the rulers by the builders of the fort's temples, and the spectacular 360-degree views from the rooftop.

One room contains an intriguing display of stamps from the former Rajput states. On the eastern wall of the palace is a sculpted pavilion-style balcony. Here drummers raised the alarm when the fort was under siege. You can also see numerous round rocks piled on top of the battlements, ready to be rolled onto advancing enemies. Much of the palace is open to the public – floor upon floor of small rooms provide a fascinating sense of how such buildings were designed for spying on the outside world. The doorways connecting the rooms of the palace are quite low. This isn't a reflection on the stature of the Rajputs, but was a means of forcing people to adopt a humble, stooped position in case the room they were entering contained the maharawal.

The last part of the tour moves from the king's palace (Raja-ka-Mahal) into the queen's palace (Rani-ka-Mahal), which contains an interesting section on Jaisalmer's annual Gangaur processions in spring. The worthwhile 1½-hour audio-guide tour (available in six languages) is included with the entry fee, but you must leave a ₹2000 deposit, or your passport, driver's licence or credit card.

Jain Temples   JAIN TEMPLE

(Indian/foreigner ₹50/200; ⊙ Chandraprabhu, Rikhabdev & Gyan Bhandar 8am-noon, other temples 11am-noon) Within the fort walls is a maze-like, interconnecting treasure trove of seven beautiful yellow sandstone Jain temples, dating from the 15th and 16th centuries. Opening times have a habit of changing, so check with the caretakers. The intricate carving rivals that of the marble Jain temples in Ranakpur and Mt Abu, and has an extraordinary quality because of the soft, warm stone. Shoes and all leather items must be removed before entering the temples.

Chandraprabhu is the first temple you come to, and you'll find the ticket stand here. Dedicated to the eighth tirthankar (great Jain teacher), whose symbol is the moon, it was built in 1509 and features fine sculpture in the mandapa (temple forechamber), the intensely sculpted pillars of which form a series of toranas (architraves). To the right of Chandraprabhu is the tranquil Rikhabdev temple, with fine sculptures around the walls, protected by glass cabinets, and pillars beautifully sculpted with apsaras (celestial nymphs) and gods.

Behind Chandraprabhu is Parasnath, which you enter through a beautifully carved torana culminating in an image of the Jain tirthankar at its apex. A door to the south leads to small Shitalnath, dedicated to the 10th tirthankar, whose image is composed of eight precious metals. A door in the northern wall leads to the enchanting, dim chamber of Sambhavanth – in the front courtyard, Jain priests grind sandalwood in mortars for devotional use. Steps lead down to the Gyan Bhandar, a fascinating tiny underground library founded in 1500, which houses priceless ancient illustrated manuscripts. The remaining two temples, Shantinath and Kunthunath, were built in 1536 and feature plenty of sensual carving. Note, the restrictive visiting times are for non-Jains. The temples are open all day for worshippers.

Laxmi Narayan Temple   HINDU TEMPLE

The Hindu Laxmi Narayan Temple, in the centre of the fort, is simpler than the Jain temples here and has a brightly decorated dome. Devotees offer grain, which is distributed before the temple. The inner sanctum has a repoussé silver architrave around its entrance, and a heavily garlanded image enshrined within.

Baa Ri Haveli   MUSEUM

(☑ 02992-252907; Fort; ₹50) This 450-year-old haveli, once belonging to Brahmin priests that advised the maharajah, now houses an interesting museum on its several levels. Artefacts from all aspects of fort life from cooking to clothing are on display.

★ Patwa-ki-Haveli   HISTORIC BUILDING

(Indian/foreigner ₹50/200; ⊙ 9am-6pm) The biggest fish in the haveli pond is Patwa-ki-Haveli, which towers over a narrow lane, its intricate stonework like honey-coloured lace. Divided into five sections, it was built between 1800 and 1860 by five Jain brothers who made their fortunes in brocade and jewellery. It's all very impressive from the outside; however, the first of the five sections, the privately owned Kothari's Patwa-ki-Haveli Museum (Indian/foreigner ₹100/250; ⊙ 9am-6pm), richly evokes 19th-century life and is the only one worth paying entry for.

Jaisalmer

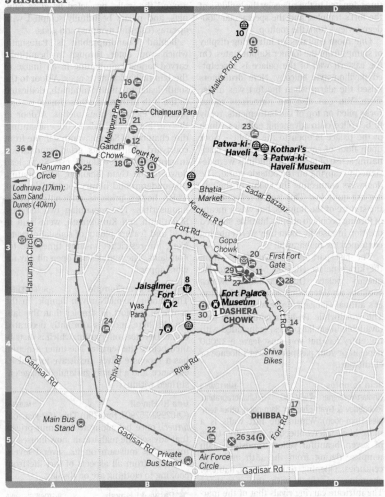

Other sections include two largely empty government-owned 'museums' and two private sections containing shops.

Nathmal-ki-Haveli
HISTORIC BUILDING

(⏰8am-7pm) This late-19th-century *haveli* (traditional, ornately decorated residence), once used as the prime minister's house, is still partly inhabited. It has an extraordinary exterior, dripping with carvings, and the 1st floor has decorative paintings using gold leaf. The left and right wings were the work of two brothers, whose competitive spirits apparently produced this virtuoso work – the two sides are similar, but not identical. Sand-stone elephants guard the entrance to what is effectively a shop.

Desert Cultural Centre & Museum
MUSEUM

(📞02992-253723; Gadi Sagar Rd; museum ₹50, camera ₹50, combined museum & puppet show ₹100; ⏰9am-6pm, puppet shows 6.30-8.30pm) This interesting little museum tells the history of Rajasthan's princely states and has exhibits on traditional Rajasthani culture. Features include Rajasthani music (with video), textiles, a *kavad* (a brightly painted mobile story box/shrine made of wood), and a *phad* (scroll painting) depicting the story

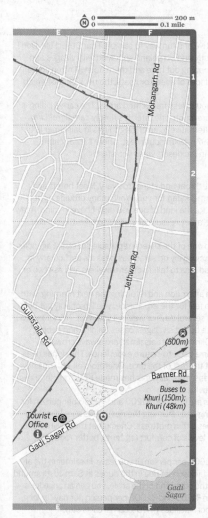

Jaisalmer

of the Rajasthani folk hero Pabuji, used by travelling singers as they recite Pabuji's epic exploits. It also hosts nightly half-hour puppet shows with English commentary. The ticket includes admission to the Jaisalmer Folklore Museum.

Thar Heritage Museum   MUSEUM
(☏ 9414150762; Main Rd, Artists Colony; ₹100; ☺ 10am-8pm) This private museum has an intriguing assortment of Jaisalmer artefacts, from turbans, musical instruments, fossils and kitchen equipment, to displays on birth, marriage, death and opium customs. It's brought alive by the guided tour you'll get from its founder, local historian and folk-lorist LN Khatri. Look for the snakes and ladders game that acts as a teaching guide to Hinduism's spiritual journey. If the door is locked you'll find Mr Khatri at his shop,

JAISALMER CAMEL SAFARIS

Trekking around by camel is the most evocative and fun way to sample Thar Desert life. Don't expect dune seas, however – the Thar is mostly arid scrubland sprinkled with villages and wind turbines, with occasional dune areas popping out here and there. You will often come across fields of millet, and children herding flocks of sheep or goats, the neck bells of which tinkle in the desert silence.

Most trips now include 4WD rides to get you to less frequented areas. The camel riding is then done in two two-hour batches, one before lunch, one after. It's hardly camel *trekking*, but it's a lot of fun nevertheless. A cheaper alternative to arranging things in Jaisalmer is to base yourself in the small village of Khuri (p197), 48km southwest, where similar camel rides are available, but where you're already in the desert when you start.

Before You Go

Competition between safari organisers is cut-throat and standards vary. Most hotels and guesthouses are very happy to organise a camel safari for you. While many provide a good service, some may cut corners and take you for the kind of ride you didn't have in mind. A few low-budget hotels in particular exert considerable pressure on guests to take 'their' safari. Others specifically claim 'no safari hassle'.

You can also organise a safari directly with one of the several reputable specialist agencies in Jaisalmer. Since these agencies depend exclusively on safari business it's particularly in their interest to satisfy their clients. It's a good idea to talk to other travellers and ask two or three operators what they're offering.

A one-night safari, leaving Jaisalmer in the afternoon and returning the next morning, with a night on some dunes, is a minimum to get a feel for the experience: you'll probably get 1½ to two hours of riding each day. You can trek for several days or weeks if you wish. The longer you ride, the more understanding you'll gain of the desert's villages, oases, wildlife and people.

The best-known dunes, at Sam (p197), 40km west of Jaisalmer, are always crowded in the evening and are more of a carnival than a back-to-nature experience. The dunes near Khuri are also quite busy at sunset, but quiet the rest of the time. Operators all sell trips now to 'nontouristy' and 'off-the-beaten-track' areas. Ironically, this has made Khuri quieter again, although Sam still hums with day-tripper activity.

With 4WD transfers included, typical rates are between ₹1200 and ₹2500 per person for a one-day, one-night trip (leaving one morning and returning the next). This should include meals, mineral water, blankets and sometimes a thin mattress. Check that there will be one camel for each rider. You can pay for greater levels of comfort (eg tents, better food), but *always* get it all down in writing.

You should get a cheaper rate (₹1100 to ₹1600 per person) if you leave Jaisalmer in the afternoon and return the following morning. A quick sunset ride in the dunes at Sam costs around ₹800 per person, including 4WD transfer. At the other end of the scale, you can arrange for a 20-day trek to Bikaner. Expect to pay between ₹1200 and ₹2000 per person per day for long, multiday trips, depending on the level of support facilities (4WDs, camel carts etc).

Desert Handicrafts Emporium (p196), on Court Rd.

☞ Tours

The tourist office (p196) runs sunset tours to the Sam Sand Dunes though these are invariably disappointing because of the crowds, litter and harassment. Other tours visit Amar Sagar, Lodhruva and Bada Bagh by car. Your best bet is to find a camel safari operator who can take you away from the noisy crowds.

🛏 Sleeping

While staying in the fort might appear to be Jaisalmer's most atmospheric choice, habitation inside the fort – driven in no small part by tourism – is causing irreparable damage to the monument. As a result, we don't recommend staying inside. Fortunately, there's a wide choice of good places to stay outside the fort. You'll get massive discounts between April and August, when Jaisalmer is hellishly hot.

What to Take

A wide-brimmed hat (or Lawrence of Arabia turban), long trousers, a long-sleeved shirt, insect repellent, toilet paper, a torch (flashlight), sunscreen, a water bottle (with a strap), and some cash (for a tip to the camel men, if nothing else) are recommended. Women should consider wearing a sports bra, as a trotting camel is a bumpy ride. It can get cold at night, so if you have a sleeping bag bring it along, even if you're told that lots of blankets will be supplied. During summer, rain is not unheard of, so come prepared.

Which Safari?

Recommendations shouldn't be a substitute for doing your own research. Whichever agency you go for, insist that all rubbish is carried back to Jaisalmer.

Thar Desert Tours (☑ 9414365333; www.tharcamelsafarijaisalmer.com; Gandhi Chowk; ⊘ 8.30am-7.30pm) This well-run operator charges ₹1300 per person per day including water and meals, adjusting prices depending on trip times. It limits tours to five people maximum, and we also receive good feedback about them. Customers pay 80% upfront.

Sahara Travels (☑ 02992-252609, 9414319921; www.saharatravelsjaisalmer.com; Gopa Chowk; ⊘ 6am-8pm) Run by the son of the late LN Bissa (aka Mr Desert), this place is very professional and transparent. Prices for an overnight trip (9am to 11am the following day) are ₹2100 per person, all inclusive. A cheaper overnight alternative that avoids the midday sun starts at 2pm and finishes at 11am for ₹1650.

Trotters (☑ 9828929974; www.trottersjaisalmer.net; Gopa Chowk; ⊘ 5.30am-9.00pm) This company is transparently run with a clear price list showing everything on offer, including trips to 'off-the-beaten-track' areas as well as cheaper jaunts to Sam or Khuri. Prices for an overnight trip (6.30am to 11am/5.30pm the following day) are ₹2250 to ₹2450 per person, all inclusive.

In the Desert

Camping out at night, huddling around a tiny fire beneath the stars and listening to the camel drivers' songs, is magical.

There's always a long lunch stop during the hottest part of the day. At resting points the camels are unsaddled and hobbled; they'll often have a roll in the sand before limping away to browse on nearby shrubs, while the camel drivers brew chai or prepare food. The whole crew rests in the shade of thorn trees.

Take care of your possessions, particularly on the return journey. Any complaints you do have should be reported, either to the **Superintendent of Police** (☑ 02992-252233), the tourist office (p196) or the intermittently staffed **Tourist Assistance Force** (Gadi Sagar Rd) posts inside the First Fort Gate and on the Gadi Sagar access road.

The camel drivers will expect a tip (up to ₹100 per day is welcomed) at the end of the trip; don't neglect to give them one.

Arya Haveli   GUESTHOUSE $
(☑ 9782585337; www.aryahaveli.com; Mainpura Para; dm incl breakfast ₹275, r fan only ₹350-650, r with AC incl breakfast ₹1500; ❉ 🛜) Helpful staff add to a stay at this spruced-up guesthouse. Rooms are well appointed and looked after; the cheaper ones face an internal courtyard, the best have their own balcony. The top-floor Blues Cafe is a nice place to relax to some good music and tasty food.

Hostel Renuka   HOTEL $
(Renuka Camel Safari; ☑ 9414150291, 02992-252757; www.renukacamelsafari.com; Chainpura Para; dm ₹150, r ₹350-750; ❉ 🛜) Spread over three floors, Hostel Renuka has squeaky-clean rooms – the best have balconies, bathrooms and air-conditioning. It's been warmly accommodating guests since 1988, so management knows its stuff. The roof terrace has great fort views and a good restaurant, and the hotel offers free pick-up from the bus and train stations.

Hotel Tokyo Palace   HOTEL $
(☑ 9414721282, 02992-255483; www.tokyopalace.net; Dhibba Para; dm ₹200, r incl breakfast ₹1500-3000; ❉ 🛜 🛆) Well run by honest,

traveller-friendly management, this hotel has clean midrange rooms, some with lovely window seats, as well as plenty of budget options, including separate basement dorms for men and women (bathrooms are the next level up). A big bonus is the pool and relaxing rooftop restaurant.

Hotel Gorakh Haveli
HOTEL **$**

(☎ 9680020049, 02992-252978; www.hotel gorakhhaveli.com; Dhibba Para; r from ₹900, with breakfast & AC ₹1250-2500; ❊ ☎) A pleasantly low-key spot south of the fort, Gorakh Haveli is a modern place built with traditional sandstone and some attractive carving. Rooms are comfy and spacious, staff are amiable, and there's a reasonable all-veg, multicuisine rooftop restaurant (mains ₹30 to ₹150), with fort views, of course. A 30% discount on rooms is offered in summer.

Hotel Swastika
HOTEL **$**

(☎ 02992-252483; swastikahotel@yahoo.com; Chainpura Para; dm ₹100, s/d/tr ₹200/300/400, r with AC ₹600; ❊ ☎) In this long-running place, the only thing you'll be hassled about is to relax. Rooms are plain, quiet, clean and very good for the price; some have little balconies. There are plenty of restaurants nearby.

Shahi Palace
HOTEL **$**

(☎ 02992-255920, 9660014495; www.shahipalace hotel.com; off Shiv Rd; r ₹550-2550; ❊ ☎) Shahi Palace is a deservedly popular option. It's a modern building in the traditional style with carved sandstone. It has attractive rooms with raw sandstone walls, colourful embroidery, and carved stone or wooden beds. The cheaper rooms are mostly in two annexes along the street, Star Haveli and Oasis Haveli. The rooftop restaurant (mains ₹100 to ₹220) is excellent. Camel safaris can be organised.

Indian veg and nonveg dishes are available, plus some European fare, cold beer and a superb evening fort view. Free pick-up from the train and bus station.

★ Hotel Nachana Haveli
HERITAGE HOTEL **$$**

(☎ 02992-252110; www.nachanahaveli.com; Goverdhan Chowk; s/d/ste incl breakfast ₹4250/4750/5750; ❊ ☎) This 280-year-old royal *haveli*, set around three courtyards – one with a tinkling fountain – is a fascinating hotel with a highly regarded restaurant (p195). The raw sandstone rooms have arched stone ceilings and the ambience of a medieval castle. They are sumptuously and romantically decorated. The common areas come with all the Rajput trimmings, including swing chairs and antiques.

Although centrally located, the hotel is set back from the road and the stone walls ensure a peaceful sleep.

Hotel Shanti Home
BOUTIQUE HOTEL **$$**

(☎ 02992-251474, 9928738269; shantihomejsm@ gmail.com; Dhibba Para; r incl breakfast ₹1200-2500; ❊ ☎) Near the fort gate this unassuming small hotel has just seven delightful, bright, spacious and stylish rooms, all well appointed with comfortable beds. There's a great rooftop restaurant, Flavours, enjoying fort views. And there's a handy ATM on the premises.

Hotel Pleasant Haveli
HOTEL **$$**

(☎ 02992-253253; www.pleasanthaveli.com; Chainpura Para; r from ₹2300; ❊ ☎) This welcoming place has lots of lovely carved stone, a beautiful rooftop (with nonveg restaurant) and just a handful of spacious and attractive colour-themed rooms, all with modern, well-equipped bathrooms, minifridge, and AC, at least one with an over-bed mirror and dual showers. Complimentary water bottle and free pick-ups from transport terminals are available.

Killa Bhawan Lodge
HOTEL **$$**

(☎ 02992-253833; www.killabhawan.com; Patwa-ki-haveli Chowk; r incl breakfast ₹3480-4130; ❊ ☎) Near Patwa-ki-Haveli, this small hotel is a delight. There are only a handful of big and beautifully decorated rooms, a pleasant rooftop restaurant, KB Cafe, that looks up to the fort, and free water bottle, tea and coffee all day.

★ 1st Gate Home Fusion
BOUTIQUE HOTEL **$$$**

(☎ 02992-254462, 9462554462; www.1stgate. in; First Fort Gate; r incl breakfast from ₹8790; ❊ ☎ ⊠) Italian-designed and superslick, this is Jaisalmer's most sophisticated hotel and it is beautiful throughout, with a desert-meets-contemporary-boutique vibe. The location lends it one of the finest fort views in town, especially from its split-level, open-air restaurant-cafe area. Rooms are immaculate with complimentary minibar (soft drinks), fruit basket and bottled water replenished daily.

Breakfast includes espresso coffee, and there is a plunge pool, gym and spa.

★ Suryagarh
HOTEL **$$$**

(☎ 02992-269269; www.suryagarh.com; Kahala Fata, Sam Rd; r/ste incl breakfast from

₹21,760/26,880; ❊@🛜🏊) The undisputed king in this category, Suryagarh rises like a fortress beside the Sam road, 14km west of town. It's a relatively new building in traditional Jaisalmer style centred on a huge palace-like courtyard with beautiful carved stonework. Features include a fabulous indoor pool and a multicuisine restaurant, Nosh (mains ₹650 to ₹800; nonguests welcome). Rooms follow the traditional/contemporary theme.

It's a spectacular place, but it doesn't stop there. A great range of activities and excursions are on offer plus nightly entertainment.

🍴 Eating & Drinking

Chandan Shree Restaurant INDIAN $
(near Hanuman Circle; mains ₹100-200; ⏰7am-11pm; 🍴) An always busy (and rightfully so) vegetarian dining hall serving up a huge range of tasty, spicy South Indian, Gujarati, Rajasthani, Punjabi and Bengali dishes.

★Saffron MULTICUISINE $$
(Hotel Nachana Haveli, Goverdhan Chowk; mains ₹245-385, thali veg/nonveg ₹385/545; ⏰7am-11pm) On the spacious roof terrace of Hotel Nachana Haveli, the veg and nonveg food here is excellent. It's a particularly atmospheric place in the evening, with private and communal lounges and more formal seating arrangements. The Indian food is hard to beat, though the Italian isn't too bad either. Alcohol is served and the thali is generous.

Monica Restaurant MULTICUISINE $$
(📞9414149496; Amar Sagar Pol; mains ₹100-300, veg/nonveg thali ₹225/400; ⏰8.30am-3pm & 6.30-10pm) The airy open-air dining room at Monica just about squeezes in a fort view, but if you end up at a table with no view, console yourself with the excellent veg and nonveg options. Meat from the tandoor is particularly well flavoured and succulent, the thalis varied, and the salads fresh and tasty.

Jaisal Italy ITALIAN $$
(📞02992-253504; www.jaisalitaly.com; First Fort Gate; mains ₹130-330, thali ₹220-350; ⏰7.30am-11pm; ❊🛜) Just inside First Fort Gate, Jaisal Italy has decent vegetarian Italian and Indian dishes, including bruschetta, antipasti, pasta, pizza, salad and desserts, plus Spanish omelettes. All this is served up in an exotically decorated indoor restaurant (cosy in winter, deliciously air-conditioned in summer) or on a delightful terrace atop the lower fort walls, with cinematic views. Alcohol is served.

Desert Boy's Dhani INDIAN $$
(Dhibba Para; mains ₹120-350, thali ₹350-450; ⏰11am-4pm & 7-11pm; ❊🛜🍴) A walled-garden restaurant where tables are spread around a large, stone-paved courtyard shaded by a spreading tree. There's also traditional cushion seating undercover and in an AC room. Rajasthani music and dance is performed from 8pm to 10pm nightly, and it's a very pleasant place to eat excellent, good-value Rajasthani and other Indian veg dishes.

★1st Gate Home Fusion ITALIAN, INDIAN $$$
(📞02992-254462, 9462554462; First Fort Gate; mains ₹360-500; ⏰7.30am-10.30pm; 🛜🍴) Sitting atop the boutique hotel of the same name, this split-level, open-air terrace has dramatic fort views and a mouthwatering menu of authentic vegetarian Italian and Indian dishes. Also on offer are excellent wood-fired pizzas, delicious desserts, and good strong Italian coffee. Wine (by the bottle or glass), beer and cocktails are available.

🛍 Shopping

Jaisalmer is famous for its stunning embroidery, bedspreads, mirrorwork wall hangings, oil lamps, stonework and antiques. Watch out when purchasing silver items: the metal is sometimes adulterated with bronze.

There are several good *khadi* (homespun cloth) shops where you can find fixed-price tablecloths, rugs and clothes, with a variety of patterning techniques including tie-dye, block printing and embroidery. Try **Zila Khadi Gramodan Parishad** (Malka Prol Rd; ⏰10am-6pm Mon-Sat), **Khadi Gramodyog Bhavan** (Dhibba; ⏰10am-6pm Mon-Sat) or **Gandhi Darshan Emporium** (near Hanuman Circle; ⏰11am-7pm Fri-Wed).

Bellissima ARTS & CRAFTS
(Dashera Chowk; ⏰8am-9pm) This small shop near the fort's main square sells beautiful patchworks, embroidery, paintings, bags, rugs, cushion covers and all types of Rajasthani art. Proceeds assist underprivileged women from surrounding villages, including those who have divorced or been widowed.

Jaisalmer Handloom ARTS & CRAFTS
(www.jaisalmerhandloom.com; Court Rd; ⏰9am-10pm) This place has a big array of bedspreads, tapestries, clothing (ready-made and custom-made, including silk) and other textiles, made by its own workers and others. If you need an embroidered camel-saddle-cloth (and who doesn't?), try for one here.

MAJOR TRAINS FROM JAISALMER

DESTINATION	TRAIN	DEPARTURE	ARRIVAL	FARE (₹)
Bikaner	12467 Leelan Exp	11.55pm	5.20am	250/625
Delhi	14660 Jaisalmer–Delhi Exp	4.45pm	11.15am	450/1205
Jaipur	14660 Jaisalmer–Delhi Exp	4.45pm	4.50am	350/935
Jodhpur	14809 Jaisalmer–Jodhpur Exp	7am	1pm	215/565

Fares: sleeper/3AC

Desert Handicrafts Emporium ARTS & CRAFTS (Court Rd; ⊙9.30am-9.30pm) With some unusual jewellery, paintings, and all sorts of textiles, this is one of the most original of numerous craft shops around town.

ⓘ Information

MONEY

There are ATMs near the fort gate, near Hanuman Circle, on Shiv Rd, and outside the train station. Lots of licensed money changers are in and around Gandhi Chowk, east of Hanuman Circle.

POST

Main post office (Hanuman Circle Rd; ⊙10am-5pm Mon-Sat) West of the fort.

Post office (Gopa Chowk; ⊙10am-5pm Mon-Fri, to 1pm Sat) Just outside the fort gate; sells stamps and you can send postcards.

TOURIST INFORMATION

Tourist Office (☏02992-252406; Gadi Sagar Rd; ⊙9.30am-6pm) Free town map.

ⓘ Getting There & Away

AIR

Jaisalmer's new airport, 5km south of town, had been lying mothballed for a few years, but in 2018 SpiceJet (www.spicejet.com) commenced daily flights to/from Ahmedabad, Jaipur, Delhi and Mumbai.

BUS

RSRTC buses leave from the **main bus stand** (Shiv Rd). There are services to Ajmer (₹466, 9½ hours) and Jodhpur (₹272, 5½ hours) throughout the day. Buses to Khuri (₹39, one hour) depart from a stand just off Gadi Sagar Rd on Barmer Rd.

A number of private bus companies have ticket offices at Hanuman Circle. **Hanuman Travels** (☏9413362367) and **Swagat Travels** (☏02992-252557) are typical. The buses themselves leave from the **private bus stand** (Air Force Circle). Typical services:

Ajmer (for Pushkar) seat/sleeper ₹310/480, nine hours, two or three daily

Bikaner seat/sleeper ₹215/430, 5½ hours, three to four daily

Jaipur seat/sleeper ₹420/550, 11 hours, two or three daily

Jodhpur seat/sleeper ₹210/420, five hours, half-hourly from 6am to 10pm

Udaipur sleeper ₹370/480, 12 hours, one or two daily

TAXI

One-way taxis (you pay for the empty return trip) cost about ₹5000 to Jodhpur, ₹5500 to Bikaner or ₹9000 to Udaipur. There's a taxi stand on Hanuman Circle Rd.

TRAIN

The **train station** (⊙ticket office 8am-8pm Mon-Sat, to 1.45pm Sun) is on the eastern edge of town, just off the Jodhpur road. There's a reserved ticket booth for foreigners.

Bikaner sleeper/3AC ₹250/625, around six hours, two or three daily (11.25am, 10.10am and 11.55pm)

Delhi sleeper/3AC ₹450/1205, 18 hours, two or three daily (1am, 1.25am and 4.45pm) via Jaipur (12 hours)

Jaipur sleeper/3AC ₹350/935, 12 hours, three daily (1am, 4.45pm and 11.55pm)

Jodhpur sleeper/3AC ₹215/565, five to six hours, three daily (1am, 7am and 4.45pm)

ⓘ Getting Around

AUTORICKSHAW

It costs around ₹50 from the train station to Gandhi Chowk, north of the fort.

CAR & MOTORCYCLE

It's possible to hire taxis or 4WDs from the stand on Hanuman Circle Rd. To Khuri, the Sam Sand Dunes or Lodhruva, expect to pay from ₹1200 return including a wait of about an hour or so.

Shiva Bikes (☏9461113600; First Fort Gate; motorbike per day ₹500-2000; ⊙8am-9pm) is a licensed hire place with motorbikes (including Royal Enfield Bullets) and scooters for exploring town and nearby sights. Helmets and area maps are included.

Around Jaisalmer

Sam Sand Dunes

The silky **Sam Sand Dunes** (vehicle/camel ₹50/80), 41km west of Jaisalmer along a good sealed road, are one of the most popular excursions from the city. About 2km long the dunes are undeniably among the most picturesque in the region. Some camel safaris camp here, but many more people just roll in for sunset, to be chased across the sands by tenacious camel owners offering short rides. Plenty more people stay overnight in one of the several tent resorts near the dunes.

The place acquires something of a carnival atmosphere from late afternoon till the next morning, making it somewhere to avoid if you're after a solitary desert experience.

If you're organising your own camel ride on the spot, expect to pay ₹300 for a one-hour sunset ride, but beware tricks from camel men such as demanding more money en route.

Khuri

☑ 03014

The village of Khuri, 48km southwest of Jaisalmer, has quite extensive dune areas attracting their share of sunset visitors, and a lot of mostly smallish 'resorts' offering overnight camel safari packages. It also has a number of low-key guesthouses where you can stay in tranquillity in a traditional-style hut with clay-and-dung walls and thatched roof, and venture out on interesting camel trips in the relatively remote and empty surrounding area.

Khuri is within the Desert National Park, which stretches over 3162 sq km southwest of Jaisalmer to protect part of the Thar ecosystem, including wildlife such as the desert fox, desert cat, chinkara (gazelle), nilgai (antelope), and some unusual bird life including the endangered great Indian bustard.

Be aware that the commission system is entrenched in Khuri's larger accommodation options. If you just want a quick camel ride on the sand dunes, expect to pay around ₹150 per person.

🛏 Sleeping

★ **Badal House** HOMESTAY $
(☑ 8107339097; napsakhuri@gmail.com; r/hut per person incl full board ₹400/300) Here you can stay in a family compound in the cen-tre of the village with a few spotlessly clean, mud-walled, thatch-roofed huts and equally spotless rooms (a couple with their own cold shower and squat toilet), and enjoy good home cooking. Former camel driver Badal Singh is a charming, gentle man who charges ₹650 for a camel safari with a night on the dunes.

He doesn't pay commission so don't let touts warn you away.

The Mama's Resort & Camp TENTED CAMP $$
(☑ 03014-274042, 9414205970; www.the mamasjaisalmer.com; cottage/tent ₹7500/8500) A well-regarded tent camp, with gorgeous en suite luxury tents tricked out with Jaisalmer fabrics, as well as small mud-brick cottages with simpler but still comfortable rooms. There's sunset camel safaris, delicious meals and Rajasthani music and dancing in the evening, and it is all included in the package.

❶ Getting There & Away

You can catch local buses from Jaisalmer to Khuri (₹39, one hour) from a road just off Gadi Sagar Rd. Walking from Jaisalmer Fort towards the train station, take the second right after the tourist office, then wait by the tree on the left, with the small shrine beside it. Buses pass here at around 10am, 1.30pm, 3pm and 4pm.

Return buses from Khuri to Jaisalmer leave at roughly 8am, 10am, 11.30am and 3pm.

A taxi from Jaisalmer will cost at least ₹1500. Even if you are staying here you will be paying for the return trip.

Bikaner

☑ 0151 / POP 644,400

Bikaner is a vibrant, dust-swirling desert town with a fabulous fort and an energising outpost feel. It's less dominated by tourism than many other Rajasthan cities, though it has plenty of hotels and a busy camel-safari scene, which attracts plenty of travellers looking to avoid the crowding that occasionally occurs around Jaisalmer-based safaris.

History

The city was founded in 1488 by Rao Bika, a son of Rao Jodha, Jodhpur's founder, though the two Rathore ruling houses later had a serious falling out over who had the right to keep the family heirlooms. Bikaner grew quickly as a staging post on the great caravan trade routes from the late 16th century onwards, and flourished under a friendly relationship with the Mughals, but declined

Bikaner

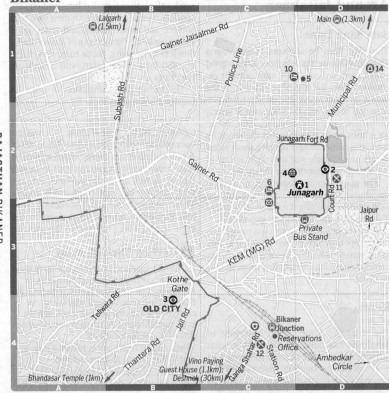

as the Mughals did in the 18th century. By the 19th century the area was markedly backward, but managed to turn its fortunes around by hiring out camels to the British during the First Anglo-Afghan War. In 1886 it was the first desert princely state to install electricity.

⊙ Sights

★ Junagarh

FORT

(Indian/foreigner ₹50/300, video ₹150, audio guide ₹50, personal guide ₹350; ⊙10am-5.30pm, last entry 4.30pm) This most impressive fort was constructed between 1589 and 1593 by Raja Rai Singh, ruler of Bikaner and a general in the army of the Mughal emperor Akbar. You enter through the **Karan Prole** (Court Rd) gate on the east side and pass through three more gates before the ticket office for the palace museum. An audio guide (requiring an identity document as a deposit), is avail-

able in English, French, German and Hindi, and is very informative.

The beautifully decorated Karan Mahal was the palace's Diwan-i-Am (Hall of Public Audience), built in the 17th and 18th centuries. Anup Mahal Chowk has lovely carved jarokhas (balcony windows) and jali (carved lattice screens), and was commissioned in the late 17th century by Maharaja Anup Mahal. Rooms off here include the sumptuous Anup Mahal, a hall of private audience with walls lacquered in red and gold, and the Badal Mahal (Cloud Palace), the walls of which are beautifully painted with blue cloud motifs and red and gold lightning.

The Gaj Mandir, the suite of Maharaja Gaj Singh (r 1745–87) and his two top wives, is a fantastic symphony of gold paint, colourful murals, sandalwood, ivory, mirrors, niches and stained glass. From here you head up to the palace roof to enjoy the views and then down eventually to the superb Ganga Dur-

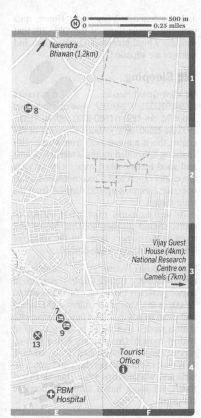

bar Hall of 1896, with its pink stone walls covered in fascinating relief carvings. You then move into Maharaja Ganga Singh's office and finally into the Vikram Vilas Durbar Hall, where pride of place goes to a WWI De Havilland DH-9 biplane bomber: General Maharaja Sir Ganga Singh commanded the Bikaner Camel Corps during WWI and was the only non-white member of Britain's Imperial War Cabinet during the conflict.

Prachina Cultural
Centre & Museum   MUSEUM
(Junagarh; Indian/foreigner ₹30/100; ⊘9am-6pm) Across the fort's main courtyard from the palace entrance, this museum is fascinating and well labelled. It focuses on the Western influence on the Bikaner royals before Independence, including crockery from England and France and menu cards from 1936, as well as some exquisite costumes, jewellery and textiles, and exhibits on contemporary Bikaner crafts.

Old City   AREA
Still with a faint medieval feel despite the fume-belching motorbikes and autorickshaws, this labyrinth of narrow, winding streets conceals a number of fine *havelis*, and a couple of notable Jain temples just inside the southern wall, 1.5km southwest of Bikaner Junction train station. It makes for an interesting wander – we guarantee you'll get lost at least once. It's encircled by a 7km-long, 18th-century wall with five entrance gates, the main entrance being the triple-arched Kothe Gate.

★Bhandasar
Temple   JAIN TEMPLE
(⊘5am-1pm & 5.30-11.30pm) Of Bikaner's two Jain temples, Bhandasar is particularly beautiful, with yellow-stone carving and vibrant paintings. The interior of the temple is stunning. The pillars bear floral arabesques and depictions of the lives of the 24 *tirthankars* (great Jain teachers). It's said that 40,000kg of ghee was used instead of water in the mortar, which locals insist seeps through the floor on hot days. The

RAJASTHAN BIKANER

priest may ask for a donation for entry, although a trust pays for the temple upkeep.

 Tours

Camel Man
TOURS

(☑ 0151-2231244, 9829217331, 9799911117; www.camelman.com; Vijay Guest House, Jaipur Rd; half-/full-/multiday trip per person per day from ₹1000/1400/1800) The standout Bikaner safari operator in terms of quality, reliability and transparency of what's on offer is Vijay Singh Rathore, aka Camel Man, who operates from Vijay Guest House.

Vino Desert Safari
TOURS

(☑ 9414139245, 0151-2270445; www.vinodesertsafari.com; Vino Paying Guest House; overnight per person ₹2500, multiday trek per person per day ₹1500-2000) A popular and long-established outfit, Vino Desert Safari is run by Vinod Bhojak, of Vino Paying Guest House.

Vinayak Desert Safari
TOURS

(☑ 9414430948, 0151-2202634; www.vinayakdesertsafari.com; Vinayak Guest House, Old Ginani; per person from ₹900) Vinayak Desert Safari runs 4WD safaris with zoologist Jitu Solanki. This safari focuses on desert animals and birds including the impressive cinereous vulture, with its 3m wingspan, which visits the area in numbers from November to March. Jitu can organise botanical and birdwatching tours to Bikaner, Tal Chhapar Sanctuary, Gajner Wildlife Sanctuary, Kichan and Desert National Park.

Bikaner by Cycle
CYCLING

(☑ 9799911117; www.bikanerbycycle.com; Vijay Guest House, Jaipur Rd; incl breakfast ₹1500) Hiteshwar Singh Rathore, son of the Camel Man, and also based at Vijay Guest House, runs morning bicycle tours of the Old City that includes a local breakfast. Quality bikes and helmets are supplied.

🛏 Sleeping

★ Vijay Guest House
GUESTHOUSE $

(☑ 9829217331, 9799911117; www.camelman.com; Jaipur Rd; dm ₹150, r ₹600-1000, with AC ₹1200-1500, ste ₹1800; ❄ 🞧) About 4km east of the centre, this is a home away from home, with spacious, light-filled rooms, a warm welcome and good home-cooked meals. Owner Vijay is a camel expert and a recommended safari operator. Free pick-up and drop-off from the train station.

As well as camel trips, 4WD outings to sights around Bikaner, cooking classes and tours to the owner's house in the village of Thelasar, Shekhawati, are offered.

Vinayak Guest House
GUESTHOUSE $

(☑ 9414430948, 0151-2202634; vinayakguesthouse@gmail.com; Old Ginani; r ₹400-800, with AC ₹1000; ❄ 🞧) This place offers eight varied and clean rooms in a quiet family house with a little garden (hot water by bucket only in budget rooms). On offer are a free pick-up service, good home-cooked food, cooking lessons, bicycles (₹50 per day), and camel safaris and wildlife trips with Vinayak Desert Safari. It's about half a kilometre north of Junagarh.

Vino Paying Guest House
GUESTHOUSE $

(☑ 0151-2270445, 9414139245; www.vinodesertsafari.com; Ganga Shahar; s/d ₹350/500; 🞧) This guesthouse, in a family home 3km south of the main train station, is a cosy choice and the base of a good camel-safari

---

BIKANER CAMEL SAFARIS

Bikaner is an excellent alternative to the Jaisalmer camel-safari scene. There are fewer people running safaris here, so the hassle factor is quite low. Camel trips tend to be in the areas east and south of the city and focus on the isolated desert villages of the Jat, Bishnoi, Meghwal and Rajput peoples. Interesting wildlife can be spotted here, such as nilgais (antelope), chinkaras (gazelle), desert foxes, spiny-tailed lizards and plenty of birds including, from September to March, the demoiselle crane.

Three days and two nights is a common camel-safari duration, but half-day, one-day and short overnight trips are all possible. If you're after a serious trip, Kichan is a seven-day trek. The best months to head into the desert are October to February. Avoid mid-April to July, when it's searingly hot.

Typical costs are ₹1800 to ₹2500 per person per day including overnight camping, with tents, mattresses, blankets, meals, mineral water, one camel per person, a camel cart to carry gear (and sometimes tired riders), and a guide in addition to the camel men.

Many trips start at Raisar, about 8km east of Bikaner.

operator. It has six rooms in the house and seven around the garden; all are fan-cooled. Home-cooked food is served and cooking classes are on offer. It's opposite Gopeshwar Temple; free pick-up from train and bus stations are offered.

Chandra Niwas
Guest House
HOTEL $

(☑ 0151-2200796, 9413659711; chandraniwas@yahoo.in; Rangmanch Rd, Civil Lines; r ₹500, with AC ₹800-2000; ✳☎) This small, tidy and welcoming guesthouse is in a relatively quiet location, though still handy to Bikaner's sights. The rooms are very clean and comfortable, and there is a lovely terrace restaurant where you can get a veg/nonveg thali for ₹180/250, plus a downstairs restaurant and a coffee shop next door.

★ Bhairon Vilas
HERITAGE HOTEL $$

(☑ 9928312283, 0151-2544751; www.bhaironvilas.com; s/d from ₹2240/2800; ✳☎⊠) This hotel on the western side of Junagarh is run by a former Bikaner prime minister's great-grandson. Rooms are mostly large and are eclectically and elaborately decorated with antiques, gold-threaded curtains and old family photographs. There's a bar straight out of the *Addams Family*, a garden restaurant, a coffee shop, and a boutique that specialises in beautiful, original wedding saris. Camel safaris and local guides can be arranged here.

Udai Niwas
HOMESTAY $$

(☑ 0151-2223447, 9971795447; Rangmanch Rd, Civil Lines; s/d ₹2240/2800; ✳) This friendly and relaxed homestay is set behind its cheerful associated Café Indra. The six guest rooms are large, spotless and comfortable, and you can choose to eat the delicious home-cooked meals with the family in the dining room or not. There's even a laundry to do your own washing.

Hotel Harasar Haveli
HOTEL $$

(☑ 0151-2209891; www.harasar.com; r ₹1344-3300; ✳☎) At this modern hotel with the frontage of an old sandstone *haveli* you'll find unexpectedly grand accommodation divided into four price points. The decor is stylish: that's not fancy blue and gold wallpaper in your room, but exquisitely hand-painted floral patterns. Old dark-wood furniture continues the classy character. Service is excellent, and the in-house restaurant on the terrace serves alcohol.

Located opposite Karni Singh Stadium, about 1km northeast of Junagarh.

Narendra Bhawan
HOTEL $$$

(☑ 7827151151; www.narendrabhawan.com; Karni Nagar, Gandhi Colony; r from ₹7670; ✳☎⊠) This former residence of the former Maharaja of Bikaner Narendra Singh has been renovated into a fine hotel that pays respect to its previous owner in its tasteful and sometimes eclectic decoration. It is a stately building, yet there is a welcoming, relaxed vibe from the staff. The high-quality food and rooftop pool add to the luxe feel.

✗ Eating & Drinking

Café Indra
CAFE $$

(☑ 8287895446; Rangmanch Rd, Civil Lines; mains ₹130-380; ⊙ 11.30am-10.30pm; ✳☎) This bright and clean cafe is a great place to relax with an espresso coffee or a cool drink, and equally good as a place for veg and nonveg lunch or dinner, with an array (and two sizes) of wood-fired pizzas, burgers and wraps.

★ Gallops
MULTICUISINE $$

(☑ 0151-3200833; www.gallopsbikaner.com; Court Rd; mains ₹225-600; ⊙ 10am-10pm; ✳☎) This contemporary cafe and restaurant close to the Junagarh entrance is known as 'Glops' to rickshaw-wallahs. There are snacks such as pizzas, wraps and sandwiches, and a good range of Indian and Chinese veg and nonveg dishes. You can sit outside or curl up in an armchair in the air-conditioned interior with a cold beer or an espresso coffee.

Shakti Dining
INDIAN $$

(☑ 9928900422; Prithvi Niwas, Civil Lines; mains ₹150-260; ⊙ 11am-11pm; ✳☎) Central and modern, Shakti's serves good Indian classics in a garden setting or in air-conditoned comfort. No alcohol. Also here is the funky **Road Runner Cafe** (☑ 9928900422, 0151-2545033; mains ₹150-260; ⊙ 11am-11pm; ✳☎) for a more casual dining experience.

Heeralal's
MULTICUISINE $$

(☑ 0151-2205551; Station Rd; mains ₹150-210, thali ₹175-270; ⊙ 7.30am-10.30pm; ✳☑) This bright and hugely popular 1st-floor restaurant serves up pretty good veg Indian dishes, plus a few Chinese mains and pizzas (but unfortunately no beer), amid large banks of plastic flowers. It's a good place to sit and relax if waiting for a train. The ground-floor fast-food section is less appealing, but it does have a good sweets counter.

Ganesha Coffee Lounge `CAFE`

(coffee ₹80-120; ☺10am-9pm; ☎) With cool tunes and magical atmosphere inside the compound of Bhairon Vilas, Ganesha has good coffee, organic tea, cold drinks and cakes.

Shopping

Bikaner Miniature Arts `ART`

(☑9829291431; www.bikanerminiturearts.com; Municipal Rd; ☺9am-8pm) The Swami family has been painting miniatures in Bikaner for four generations, and now run this art school and gallery. The quality of work is astounding, and cheaper than you'll find in some of the bigger tourist centres. Art classes can be arranged.

Information

Main post office (☺9am-4pm Mon-Fri, to 2pm Sat) Near Bhairon Vilas hotel.

PBM Hospital (☑0151-2525312; Hospital Rd) One of Rajasthan's best government hospitals, with 24-hour emergency service.

Tourist office (☑0151-2226701; ☺9.30am-6pm Mon-Fri) This friendly office (near Pooran Singh Circle) can answer most tourism-related questions and provide transport schedules and maps.

Getting There & Away

AIR

Alliance Air (www.airindia.in/alliance-air.htm), a subsidiary of Air India, flies to/from Delhi and Jaipur daily.

BUS

There's a private bus stand outside the southern wall of Junagarh with similar services (albeit slightly more expensive and less frequent) to the government-run services from the main bus stand, which is 2km directly north of the fort (autorickshaw ₹20). In addition to those leaving from the main bus stand, there are buses to Deshnok that leave from a stand on National

Hwy 89, 3km south of Bikaner Junction railway station.

Services from the main bus stand:

Ajmer (for Pushkar) ₹269, six hours, half-hourly until 6pm

Delhi ₹445, 11 hours, at least four daily

Deshnok ₹35, one hour, half-hourly until 4.30pm

Jaipur ₹334, with AC ₹716, seven hours, hourly until 5.45pm

Jaisalmer ₹309, 7½ hours, noon daily

Jhunjhunu ₹226, five hours, four daily (7.30am, 8.30am, 12.20pm and 6.30pm)

Jodhpur ₹243, five hours, half-hourly until 6.30pm

Pokaran ₹211, five hours, hourly until 12.45pm

For Jaisalmer, it's sometimes faster to head to Pokaran (which has more departures) and change there.

TRAIN

The main train station is Bikaner Junction, with a computerised **reservations office** (☺8am-10pm Mon-Sat, to 2pm Sun) in a separate building just east of the main station building. The foreigners' window is 2931. A couple of other useful services go from Lalgarh station in the north of the city (autorickshaw ₹60).

Delhi (Delhi Sarai Rohilla) sleeper/3AC ₹300/780, eight to 14 hours, three to six daily (6.30am, 9.30am, 4.45pm, 5.05pm, 7.50pm and 11.30pm)

Jaipur sleeper/3AC ₹275/705, 6½ hours, five or six daily (12.10am, 6am, 10am, 6.45pm, 11.10pm and 11.55pm)

Jaisalmer sleeper/3AC ₹250/625, 5½ hours, two or three daily (7am, 6.30pm and 11.05pm)

Jodhpur sleeper/3AC ₹170/510, five hours, six to seven daily (12.45am, 6.30am, 7.10am, 11am, 1.40pm, 9.40pm and 10.10pm)

No direct trains go to Ajmer for Pushkar.

Getting Around

An autorickshaw from the train station to Junagarh palace should cost less than ₹50, but you'll probably be asked for more.

MAJOR TRAINS FROM BIKANER STATION

DESTINATION	TRAIN	DEPARTURE	ARRIVAL	FARE (₹)
Delhi (Sarai Rohilla)	22471 Dee Intercity SF Exp	9.30am	5.25pm	300/780
Jaipur	12467 Leelan Exp	6am	12.35pm	275/705
Jaisalmer	12468 Leelan Exp	11.05pm	5.45am	250/625
Jodhpur	14887 KLK-BME Exp	11am	4.06pm	170/510

Fares: sleeper/3AC

THE TEMPLE OF RATS

The extraordinary **Karni Mata Temple** (camera/video ₹30/50; ⊘ 4am-10pm) at Deshnok, 30km south of Bikaner, is one of India's stranger attractions. Its resident mass of holy rodents is not for the squeamish, but most visitors to Bikaner brave the potential for ankle-nipping and put a half-day trip here on their itinerary. Frequent buses leave from Bikaner's main bus stand but also from a bus stop south of town on the road to Deshnok and Nagaur. A return autorickshaw/taxi from Bikaner with a one-hour wait costs around ₹600/800.

Karni Mata lived in the 14th century and performed many miracles during her lifetime. When her youngest son, Lakhan, drowned, she ordered Yama (the god of death) to bring him back to life. Yama said he was unable to do so, but that Karni Mata, as an incarnation of Durga, could restore Lakhan's life. This she did, decreeing that members of her family would no longer die but would be reincarnated as *kabas* (rats). Around 600 families in Deshnok claim to be descendants of Karni Mata and believe they will be reincarnated as *kabas*.

The temple isn't, in fact, swarming with rats, but there are a lot of them here, especially in nooks and crannies and in areas where priests and pilgrims leave food for them. And yes, you do have to take your shoes off to enter the temple: it's considered highly auspicious to have a *kaba* run across your feet – you may be graced in this manner whether you want it or not.

You can find food and drinks for yourself at the numerous snack stalls outside.

Around Bikaner

There are some very interesting temples and old cenotaphs dotted around Bikaner, and you can also make a half-day trip to the fascinating National Research Centre on Camels. To experience a safari-style desert night in a luxury tent look at the packages available at **Raisar Camp** (☑ 9829063446; www.raisar camp.com; off National Hwy 11, Raisar Village; per person incl dinner, breakfast & camel safari ₹2900).

The **National Research Centre on Camels** (☑ 0151-2230183; www.nrccamel.res. in; Indian/foreigner ₹50/200, camera ₹100, rides ₹100; ⊘ noon-6pm) is 8km southeast of central Bikaner, beside the Jodhpur–Jaipur Bypass. While here you can visit baby camels, go for a short ride and look around the small museum. There are about 400 camels, of four different breeds. The British Army had a camel corps drawn from Bikaner during WWI. Guides are available from ₹50. The on-site Camel Milk Parlour offers samples to try including *kulfi* (flavoured firm-textured ice cream) and lassi.

The round trip from Bikaner, including a half-hour wait at the camel farm, is around ₹300/₹600 for an autorickshaw/taxi. Don't rely on the fact that there may be an available autorickshaw waiting outside: always organise a round trip.

RAJASTHAN AROUND BIKANER

Punjab & Haryana

Best Places to Eat

➜ Guru-Ka-Langar (p216)

➜ Kesar Da Dhaba (p220)

➜ Bharawan Da Dhaba (p219)

➜ Food Library (p226)

➜ Indian Coffee House (p210)

➜ Cloud 9 (p211)

Best Places to Stay

➜ Baradari Palace (p226)

➜ Mrs Bhandari's Guesthouse (p219)

➜ Tikkar Taal Tourist Complex (p214)

➜ Grand Hotel (p218)

➜ Hotel Icon (p209)

Why Go?

The glittering highlight of this otherwise understated region is Amritsar's unmissable Golden Temple. Punjab is studded with gleaming gurdwaras (Sikh temples), but it's the Golden Temple that everyone comes to see. Visiting it is a spiritual experience that will stay with you long after you leave India.

But this historically turbulent terrain offers plenty more besides. The neighbouring states of Punjab and Haryana were carved from the Indian half of Punjab province following the devastating upheaval that was Partition. Since then, Punjab has grown from strength to strength as the homeland of India's warm and welcoming Sikh community, while Haryana has become a dynamic business hub. The hinterland is dotted with fascinating, rarely visited, historical towns that tell tales of battling empires and playboy maharajas, and hide within their dusty bazaars some of India's most alluring abandoned forts.

When to Go
Chandigarh

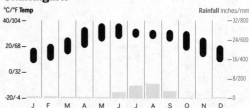

Mar Three days of Sikh celebrations for Holla Mohalla unravel at Anandpur Sahib.

Apr Punjab's largest festival, Baisakhi, marks the Sikh New Year and the founding of the Khalsa.

Oct Diwali means lights, candles and fireworks everywhere; particularly magical at the Golden Temple.

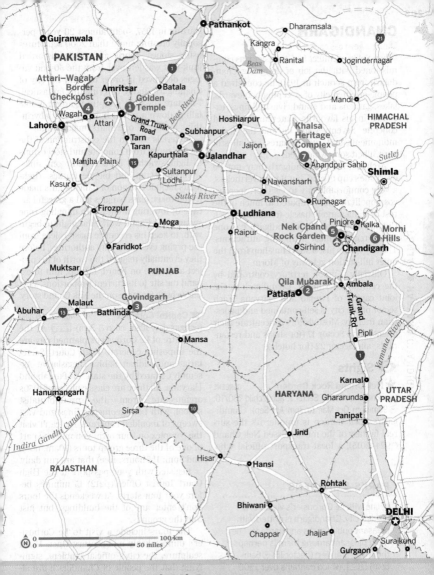

Punjab & Haryana Highlights

1 **Golden Temple** (p215) Feeling the spiritual energy at Sikhism's holiest site in Amristar.

2 **Qila Mubarak** (p225) Diving into the old town of Patiala before sizing up its charming 18th-century fort.

3 **Govindarh** (p224) Climbing the towering walls of Punjab's oldest and most magnificent fort and looking out from its ramparts across little-known Bathinda.

4 **Attari–Wagah Border Checkpost** (p222) Watching the theatre between Indian and Pakistani border guards during the passionate border-closing ceremony.

5 **Nek Chand Rock Garden** (p206) Tumbling into an alternative reality in Chandigarh's unique rock garden.

6 **Morni Hills** (p213) Cooling off at Haryana's only hill station.

7 **Khalsa Heritage Complex** (p227) Visiting Anandpur Sahib's flower-shaped museum of Sikh history.

CHANDIGARH

📞 0172 / POP 1,055,000

When Swiss architect Le Corbusier was commissioned with the job of designing Chandigarh from scratch in 1950, he conceived a people-oriented city of sweeping boulevards, lakes, gardens and grand civic buildings, executed in his favourite material: reinforced concrete. Seventy years on and the parks, monuments and civic squares are all still here, albeit somewhat aged.

Architecturally, Chandigarh may not be everyone's cup of chai, but it is, nevertheless, a very comfortable city to visit: prosperous, cosmopolitan and, compared to much of the rest of India, largely hassle-free. And in Nek Chand's Rock Garden, Chandigarh has one of the region's most intriguing attractions. The city is also just a short bus-hop from the quiet hill-station getaway of Morni.

Officially a union territory controlled by the central government, Chandigarh is the joint capital of Punjab and Haryana. Each sector of the city is self-contained and pedestrian friendly. Most visitors concentrate their attention on Sector 17 (for shops and restaurants) and Sector 22 (for hotels).

◉ Sights

★**Nek Chand Rock Garden**   GARDENS
(www.nekchand.com; Sector 1; adult/child ₹30/10; ⊙9am-6pm Oct-Mar, to 7pm Apr-Sep) Chandigarh's Rock Garden is unique: it's the surreal fantasy of the much-missed Nek Chand (1924–2015), a local transport official who,

starting in 1957, spent almost 20 years personally creating more than 2000 sculptures using stones, debris and other discarded junk that was left over from the 50-odd villages destroyed in order to build the city of Chandigarh. Today, entering this fantastical, 7-hectare (18-acre) sculpture garden is like falling down a rabbit hole into the labyrinthine interior of one man's imagination.

Materials used in the construction of the garden range from concrete and steel drums to light switches, broken bathroom sinks, terracotta scrap and bicycle frames. Highlights include a legion of dancing girls made from broken glass bangles and a graceful arcade of towering arches with dangling rope swings. Nek Chand worked at night to begin with, to keep his eccentric masterpiece from the prying eyes of the city authorities, before they eventually realised the worth of his project and came on board, helping him to expand the site to its current proportions. Visit the website for more on the Nek Chand story.

★**Capitol Complex**   NOTABLE BUILDING
(⊙tours daily 10am, noon & 3pm) FREE At the epicentre of Le Corbusier's planned city are the imposing concrete High Court, Secretariat and Vidhan Sabha (Legislative Assembly), shared by the states of Punjab and Haryana. All three are classic pieces of 1950s architecture from the proto-brutalist school, with bold geometric lines and vast sweeps of moulded concrete. You can't visit the complex on your own; you must be part of one of the three group tours (10am, noon and 3pm; 1½ hours; free) that are run daily.

Register with your passport at the High Court Tourist Office (p212) 15 minutes before your tour starts. At weekends the tours don't enter any of the buildings, but just tour the grounds.

The tours include a visit to Le Corbusier's unmistakably mid-century Open Hand sculpture, the city's official emblem, signifying that the people of Chandigarh are always 'open to give, open to receive'. On the approach road to the High Court, the small **High Court Museum** (⊙10am-5pm Mon-Sat) FREE displays assorted judicial memorabilia including original Le Corbusier sketches, a signed copy of the Indian constitution and several pieces of evidence from notable court cases, including handcuffs worn by Nathuram Godse, Mahatma Gandhi's assassin. Like the sculpture, this can be visited unaccompanied.

PARKS & GARDENS

In line with Le Corbusier's vision of a garden city, Chandigarh is dotted with pleasant public parks and gardens. The most pleasant among them is perhaps the **Rose Garden** (Sector 16; ⊙6am-8pm) FREE, which contains over 1500 rose varieties. Home to an overwhelming population of bougainvilleas, the eponymous **Bougainvillea Garden** (Sector 3; ⊙8am-5pm) FREE has a thought-provoking memorial to Indian soldiers killed in cross-border conflicts since Independence. Less central is the **Terraced Garden** (Sector 33; ⊙6am-8pm) FREE, which draws locals with its seasonal flower shows and musical-fountain sessions in the evenings.

Sukhna Lake
LAKE

(Sector 1) Fulfilling the leisure objective of Le Corbusier's urban master plan, this landmark artificial lake is a popular rest and recreation stop for Chandigarh's resident families. It has ornamental gardens, a children's fairground, places to eat and drink, and pedal boats to hire for leisure rides on the still waters of the lake.

Le Corbusier Centre
MUSEUM

(Madhya Marg, Sector 19-B; ⊙10am-5pm Tue-Sun) FREE One for fans of 20th-century avant-garde architecture and design, this fascinating museum displays documents, sketches and photos of Le Corbusier, along with letters revealing the politics behind the Chandigarh project, including one from Jawaharlal Nehru to the Punjab Chief Minister recommending Corbusier for the project. Also interesting are some sketches, paintings and a model for a proposed Governor's House that was eventually rejected because Nehru found it too extravagant.

Government Museum & Art Gallery
GALLERY

(Jan Marg, Sector 10-C; ₹10, camera ₹5; ⊙10am-4.30pm Tue-Sun) You'll find a fine collection of artworks and treasures at this impressive state museum, including trippy paintings of the Himalaya by Russian artist Nicholas Roerich, elegant carvings from the Buddhist Ghandara civilisation, *phulkari* (embroidery work) and Sobha Singh's much-reproduced portrait of Guru Gobind Singh. At one end, through a separate entrance, is the Child Art Gallery, with colourful artworks from local schoolchildren. The ₹10 ticket covers entrance to Natural History Museum.

Chandigarh Architecture Museum
MUSEUM

(City Museum; Jan Marg, Sector 10-C; ₹10, camera ₹5; ⊙10am-4.30pm Tue-Sun) Using photos, letters, models, newspaper reports and architectural drawings, this museum tells the story of Chandigarh's planning and development, including the abandoned first plan for Chandigarh by Albert Mayer and Matthew Nowicki. It's one of the main buildings within Chandigarh's museum complex, though demands a separate ticket from the other two museums.

Natural History Museum
MUSEUM

(Jan Marg, Sector 10-C; ₹10, camera ₹5; ⊙10am-4.30pm Tue-Sun) This place is a must-visit for those travelling with children, and has exhibits featuring fossils, model dinosaurs, exquisite hand-embroidered pictures of birds and a diorama with a caveman using an electric torch to illuminate his cave art! The ₹10 ticket also covers entrance to the Government Museum & Art Gallery.

Activities

Chandigarh Ayurved Centre
AYURVEDA

(☑0172-2542231; www.chandigarhayurvedcentre.com; 1701, Sector 22-B; treatments from ₹350; ⊙9am-7.30pm Mon-Sat, to 2pm Sun) This small, welcoming ayurvedic treatment centre also does relaxation therapies for walk-in visitors. A 40-minute, full-body massage costs ₹800, including a 20-minute steam-room session afterwards. The *shirodhara* and *takradhara* treatments, where either ayurvedic oil (*shirodhara*) or buttermilk (*takradhara*) are poured continuously over your forehead for 30 minutes, cost the same.

Pedal Boats
BOATING

(Sukhna Lake; 2-/4-seater per 30min ₹200/400; ⊙8.30am-5.30pm) Brightly coloured boats are available through the day for some carefree boating on the still waters of the Sukhna Lake (p207). The ticket counter is on the approach to the quay, across a courtyard from a bunch of snack and juice stalls. You can also take 30-minute round trips on a small cruise boat (₹300 per person).

Tours

Tourist Bus
BUS

(☑0172-2703839; half-day tour ₹50; ⊙9am-3.30pm) Chandigarh Tourism runs a hop-on, hop-off double-decker tourist bus leaving from outside Hotel Shivalikview every day at 9am, 10.30am, noon, 2pm and 3.30pm. Buy a ticket at the time of boarding the vehicle. Stops include the Rose Garden, Government Museum & Art Gallery, Nek Chand Rock Garden and Sukhna Lake.

Sleeping

Hotel Satyadeep
HOTEL $

(☑0172-2703103; hddeepsdeep@yahoo.com; SCO 1102-3, Sector 22-B; s/d from ₹850/900; ❄@) Run by a management comprising courteous Sai Baba devotees, Satyadeep has wood-panelled corridors leading to simple, well-kept, bright and breezy rooms, some of which open out onto shared balconies. It's upstairs from Sai Sweets, which meets your craving for postdinner desserts.

Chandigarh

SECTOR 11

SECTOR 12

Vidya Path

SECTOR 15

Udyan Path

Madhya Marg

SECTOR 16

SECTOR 24

Udyog Path

11

Jan Marg

31

27

22

25

Sector 23 Market Rd

32

SECTOR 23

Dakshin Marg

CMC Rd

Jan Marg

Udyog Path

ISBT 17

Train Reservation Office

RK Taxi Service

Sector 22 Market Rd

Shastri Market Rd

23

24

33

15

30

18

20

CMC Rd

21

29

Himalaya Marg

SECTOR 22

SECTOR 21

Dakshin Marg

17

Udyog Path

SECTOR 35

ISBT 43 Bus
Stand (5km)

Hotel Divyadeep   HOTEL $

(☑ 0172-2705191; hddeepsdeep@yahoo.com; SCO 1090-1, Sector 22-B; s/d from ₹850/900; ❅) Run by a group of Sai Baba devotees, Divyadeep has smart but austere rooms, and welcoming staff. Rooms have small TVs, but no internet or wi-fi.

Hotel Samrat   HOTEL $$

(☑ 0172-2701846; Dakshin Marg, Sector 22-D; s/d from ₹1900/2460; ❅ 🛜) A solid mid-range option with smallish, but clean and comfortable rooms with TV and complimentary wi-fi.

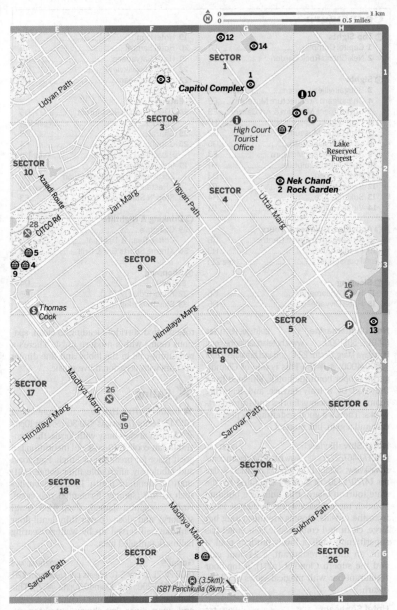

★**Hotel Icon** BOUTIQUE HOTEL **$$$**
(☑ 9501113920; www.iconhotels.asia; SCO 58-61, Madhya Marg, Sector 8-C; s/d incl breakfast from ₹3000/3850; ❋@☎) One of Chandigarh's best boutique addresses, the Icon justifies every penny it charges (though with discounts the rates are very reasonable) in the form of elegant wood-floored, satin-upholstered rooms, a bakery with good coffee and one of the best fine-dining restaurants in town. There are a number of health spas nearby; reception can book you a therapy session.

Chandigarh

Hotel Aquamarine BOUTIQUE HOTEL **$$$**
(☑ 0172-5014000; www.hotelaquamarine.com; Himalaya Marg, Sector 22-C; s/d incl breakfast from ₹3500/4000; ❋@🕸) This is one of Chandigarh's proper boutique hotels, shielded from the road by a leafy terrace and featuring rooms full of luscious fabrics and framed artworks. There's a good restaurant, a pleasant cafe and a gym, but no pool.

Hotel Shivalikview HOTEL **$$$**
(☑ 0172-4672222; www.citcochandigarh.com/shivalikview; Sector 17-E; s/d incl breakfast & dinner ₹4720/5430; ❋@🕸🏊) Operated by the state tourism board, this hulk of a building is much more pleasant inside than it looks from the outside. Rooms are unexciting but large, clean and comfortable. The hotel has superfriendly staff, a lovely outdoor pool, a gym, an Indian restaurant, a 24-hour cafe and the superb Cloud 9 (p211), a top-floor restaurant-bar with magical views of Chandigarh.

Hotel Sunbeam HOTEL **$$$**
(☑ 0172-4505050; www.hotelsunbeam.com; Udyog Path, Sector 22-B; s/d from ₹4130/4720; ❋🕸) The smartest of three hotels standing side by side across the road from ISBT 17 bus station, Hotel Sunbeam (not to be confused with next-door Sunbeam Premium) has an elegant lobby with a trickling waterfall and rose-scented corridors leading to clean, spacious rooms with a modern finish. There's a restaurant-cafe in the lobby and fine dining upstairs with occasional live music.

🍴 Eating

★ Indian Coffee House SOUTH INDIAN **$**
(SCO 12, Sector 17; snacks ₹20-80; ⊘9am-10pm; ☑) Almost always busy with locals, this venerable, fan-cooled, 40-year-old institution is a great place for breakfast or lunch. Egg, toast and fabulously affordable filter coffee (₹31) share a menu of South Indian favourites such as *idli* (spongy, fermented rice cake), *vada* (doughnut-shaped, deep-fried lentil savoury) and dosa (paper-thin lentil-flour pancake), all served up by waiters wearing hallmark fantailed hats.

Gopal's NORTH INDIAN **$**
(SCO 20-21, Sector 8-C; sweets per piece from ₹20, dishes ₹60-200; ⊘8.30am-10.30pm; ❋☑) This popular Punjab restaurant chain is a clean and smart diner that churns out cheap, utterly delicious platters of dosas and *chhole bhature* – deep-fried *puris* (a flat savoury dough that puffs up when deep-fried) served with spicy chickpea curry – for hungry patrons through the day. The fabulous ground-floor sweet shop has a divine selection of Indian desserts to eat in or take away.

Stop 'N Stare
Food Point
CAFE $

(Sector 10; snacks ₹15-80; ⊙8am-7pm; ✒) Perfect for a pit stop after a tour of Chandigarh's museums, this simple cafe with shaded garden seating serves lassi (yoghurt and iced-water drink), tea and instant coffee, as well as Indian snacks such as patties, *paratha* (Indian-style flaky bread) and *kulcha* (soft-leavened bread), eaten with a chickpea masala.

It's behind the Government Museum & Art Gallery.

Sai Sweets &
Bhoj Vegetarian
Restaurant
SWEETS $

(SCO 1102-3, Sector 22-B; sweets ₹30, snacks ₹60-80, thalis ₹185-235; ⊙8am-11pm; ✒) This clean and wholesome sweet shop below Hotel Satyadeep serves tasty *mithai* (Indian sweets), such as *ladoo* (sweet ball made with gram flour and semolina), *gulab jamun* (deepfried balls of dough soaked in rose-flavoured syrup) and *barfi* (a dense, milk-based sweet). They are sold by the kilogram (₹300 to ₹550) or individually (around ₹30).

Having recently merged with Bhoj Vegetarian Restaurant it now also does breakfasts – *paratha* and *channa bhatura* (Indian fried bread with chickpea) – until noon, and thalis, dosa (paper-thin lentil-flour pancake) and the like from then until closing.

★Cloud 9
MULTICUISINE $$

(Hotel Shivalikview, Sector 17-E; mains ₹300-600, beers from ₹200; ⊙food 11am-3pm & 7-11pm, drinks 11am-11pm; ✸) Offering magical panoramic views of the tree-lined city and the distant Shivalik Hills, this smart, newly renovated restaurant and bar has two menus (Chinese and Indian/multicuisine), smiley staff and floor-to-ceiling windows. There's plenty of space, and you can come just for drinks if you don't fancy eating.

Hibachi
MULTICUISINE $$

(SCO 58-61, Madhya Marg, Sector 8-C; mains ₹250-400; ⊙11.30am-11.30pm; ✸🛜) On the ground floor of Hotel Icon, Hibachi is the place to go if you're craving some Japanese or Southeast Asian food. There's some imaginative sushi on offer here, along with Burmese *khao suey*, pad thai, Chinese *kung pao* chicken with peanuts and even Malay-style laksa. There's also a well-stocked bar serving chilled beers (₹250) and premium Scottish malts.

20-20 Punjabi Restaurant
PUNJABI $$

(SCF 15, Shashtri Market Rd, Sector 22-D; mains ₹110-220; ⊙noon-5pm & 7-11pm; ✸) This small, no-frills restaurant in the heart of bustling Shastri Market whips up tasty Indian staples plus Punjabi specialities. The *dhal Punjabi* is for spice fiends, while the *kadhai chicken*, with a thick sauce, is another delicious house special – the half portion is plenty for two to share. The combo meals (₹120 to ₹200) are ideal for solo diners.

★Ghazal
MUGHLAI $$$

(✆0172-2704448; SCO 189-91, Sector 17-C; mains ₹300-800; ⊙11am-11pm; ✸) A Chandigarh stalwart and still going strong, Ghazal has a dignified air and a fine menu of Mughlai classics including chicken and mutton, plus some well-prepared Continental and Chinese dishes. The vegetable *jalfrezi* (₹325) is a fiery sensation. At the back of the restaurant, a suited bartender guards a long line of imported single malts (₹435) and beers (from ₹155).

🍹 Drinking & Nightlife

Coffee Bean & Tea Leaf
CAFE

(Himalaya Marg, Sector 22-C; coffee from ₹150, dishes from ₹200; ⊙9am-1am Sun-Thu, to 3am Fri & Sat; 🛜) The most comfortable cafe in Chandigarh, Coffee Bean & Tea Leaf is attached to the excellent Hotel Aquamarine, and has an air-con-cooled interior, as well as a small shaded patio out front. There's good coffee, a decent menu (sandwiches, pasta, all-day breakfasts), and fast, reliable wi-fi.

Chaiphile
TEA

(www.chaiphile.com; Shastri Market, Sector 22; chai ₹25; ⊙11am-8pm) A chai stall like you've never seen, this modern-day chai-wallah claims to be serving India's only tandoori chai, brewed in a tandoori oven and served with a sizzle by being poured over a fire-heated clay cup. Chai is served all day, but the sizzling chai show is usually performed late on, after about 5pm.

Xtreme Sports Bar & Grill
BAR

(beers from ₹89; ⊙11am-midnight) Local beers go for as little as ₹89 here, but this is no dive; it also does cocktails and mocktails, is dotted with TVs for football fans and has a small table-football table for punters to play with. Does food too.

🛍 Shopping

★1469
GIFTS & SOUVENIRS

(www.1469workshop.com; SCO 81, Sector 17-D; ⊙10.30am-9pm) Named after the birth year of Guru Nanak (the founder of the Sikh faith), this funky independent clothing store sells fabulously colourful scarves, shawls and traditional Punjabi clothing, as well as modern T-shirts (from ₹600) with an irreverent Punjabi twist. It also stocks some lovely jewellery, including the steel *kara* bracelets worn by Sikhs.

Shastri Market MARKET

(off Sector 22 Market Rd; ☺10am-10pm Tue-Sun) This bustling, sprawling street market sells a mind-boggling array of household goods and clothing, and is sprinkled with pop-up street-food stalls selling yummy local treats.

Khadi India (17-E) CLOTHING

(SCO 28, Sector 17-E; ☺11am-8pm Mon-Sat, noon-8pm Sun) This nongovernment operation has good-value, homespun textiles and clothing, and herbal beauty products of premium quality, the sale of which directly supports small community producers in rural India. Also has a range of simple but lovely souvenirs made from wood, leather and various metals.

ⓘ Information

INTERNET ACCESS

Internet cafes are a thing of the past. Most hotels have free wi-fi, but some budget hotels have no internet access, so you may wish to make use of the free wi-fi available at the town's cafes and bars.

MEDICAL SERVICES

Shalby Hospital (📞0172-4907100; www.silveroakshospital.com; Phase 9, Sector 63, Mohali) is a state-of-the-art hospital about 7km southwest of Chandigarh's centre. It is well set up to treat foreign visitors.

MONEY

Most sector markets have ATMs accepting foreign cards. Sector 17 has the highest concentration of ATMs, as well as local bank branches.

Thomas Cook (📞0173-6610901; SCO 17, Sector 9-D; ☺10am-7pm Mon-Fri, to 4pm Sat) can help with foreign exchange.

POST

Chandigarh's **main post office** (Sector 17; ☺10am-4pm Mon-Sat) has international parcel and express post services.

TOURIST INFORMATION

There's no central tourist office, but you can try getting information from the helpful staff at the tourist board–run Hotel Shivalikview (p210).

The **High Court Tourist Office** (High Court Complex; ☺8.30am-5pm) is the place to register for free tours of the Capitol Complex (p206).

ⓘ Getting There & Away

AIR

There are daily domestic flights operated by airlines including Air India, GoAir, IndiGo and Jet Airways to destinations such as Delhi, Mumbai, Bengaluru and Srinagar.

There's also an international flight to Dubai, operated by IndiGo.

BUS

Chandigarh has two main Inter State Bus Terminals (ISBT): **ISBT 17** (Sector 17) and **ISBT 43** (Sector 43). Numerous red air-conditioned (AC) buses (₹20) run between ISBT 17 and 43.

ISBT Panchkulla (Panchkulla) is also of use to tourists for its buses to Morni Hills. Local buses 2F and 2B link ISBT 17 and ISBT Panchkulla (₹20).

Buses from ISBT 43

The following buses leave frequently throughout the day from ISBT 43. AC Volvo and Mercedes buses leave from the far end of the station (platforms 37 to 39) to destinations such as Amritsar, Jammu, Bathinda and Patiala, and cost around twice the price of ordinary buses listed here.

Anandpur Sahib ₹100, two hours

Bathinda ₹280, five hours

Dehra Dun ₹230, five hours

Dharamsala ₹350, eight hours

Jammu ₹320, eight hours

Kalka (for Shimla) ₹32, one hour

Manali ₹450, 11 hours

Pathankot ₹305, five hours

Patiala ₹90, two hours

Shimla ₹300, four hours

Sirhind ₹50, two hours

Buses from ISBT 17

The following buses leave frequently throughout the day from ISBT 17:

Amritsar AC ₹600, four hours

Delhi airport Volvo ₹620, six hours

Delhi (Kashmere Gate) Ordinary/Volvo ₹325/580, five hours

Haridwar Ordinary ₹245, five hours

Jaipur Ordinary/Volvo ₹450/1200, 12 hours

Pipli (for Kurukshetra) Ordinary ₹100, two hours

Rishikesh Ordinary ₹290, eight hours

TRAIN

The train station is 7km southeast of the city centre, though there's a handy **train reservation office** (☺8am-8pm Mon-Sat, to 2pm Sun) on the 1st floor in ISBT 17.

Buses 20 and 28 link ISBT 17 to the train station (₹20). Expect to pay around ₹100 in an autorickshaw.

Several fast trains go to New Delhi daily. The quickest and slickest is the twice-daily Kalka Shatabdi (AC chair ₹575, 3½ hours), which leaves at 6.53am and 6.23pm. To get to Delhi for less, buy an unreserved 'general' ticket (₹65 to ₹105) when you turn up at the station, and then just pile into the 2nd-class carriage of the next available train.

More than half a dozen trains go to Kalka (2nd class ₹45, 35 minutes), from where narrow-gauge trains rattle up the hills to Shimla.

Two daily trains go to Amritsar (2nd class/AC chair ₹120/435, 4½ hours) at 7am and 5.10pm. Unreserved 'general' tickets cost ₹100.

ⓘ Getting Around

RK Taxi Service (☐ 9815832555; www.rk taxiservice.com; ISBT 17; ⊙ 9am-7pm) has an office at the south end of ISBT 17 and charges around ₹1000 for the airport, ₹2500 return for Morni, ₹1800 for a full-day city tour, and ₹3500 for Delhi.

Bicycles are available for rent (half-/full day ₹100/200, ₹500 refundable deposit) from Mermaid Restaurant & Bar, by the entrance to Sukhna Lake (p207), and from Hotel Shivalikview (p210), for the same prices. They're also available for free from the High Court Tourist Office (p212) (though they don't have locks).

Expect to pay about ₹50/20 for a short hop in an auto/cycle rickshaw. Hiring an auto for half a day (up to four hours) to take in sights such as Nek Chand Rock Garden and Sukhna Lake will cost around ₹500 to ₹600.

Frequent local buses link ISBT 17 with sights around town such as the rock garden, High Court and Sukhna Lake (18, 18B and 202 from platform 40; ₹15 to ₹20), as well as the following:

Train Station Nos 22 and 28; ₹20
ISBT 43 bus station ₹20
Panchkulla bus station Nos 2B and 2F; ₹20

Ordinary buses are green. AC buses are red, and are slightly more expensive. If you're planning to take a few trips in one day it's worth buying a day pass (ordinary/AC bus ₹50/60), which you can purchase on any bus.

TO/FROM THE AIRPORT

Chandigarh's new airport is 13km from the centre. Buses 38 and 38A run from ISBT 17 bus station to the airport from 6am to 5.20pm (₹30, one hour). Alternatively, take an autorickshaw for around ₹350 to ₹400, or a taxi for around ₹1000.

AROUND CHANDIGARH

Morni Hills

Perched at 1220m, and set amid monkey-filled forests on a spur running west from the Shivalik Hills, Morni Hills is Haryana's only hill station. Here you'll find a handful of rustic resorts, the village of Morni and, 8km downhill from the village, Tikkar Taal, a pair of pretty lakes with boats for rent (from ₹400) and the bucolic surrounds of farmland rising in terraces up the lower slopes.

PUNJAB & HARYANA MORNI HILLS

TOP STATE FESTIVALS

Kila Raipur Sports Festival (⊙ Feb) Three days of traditional games and contests, including bullock-cart races, kabaddi (traditional game, like tag), strength contests and folk dancing, in Kila Raipur near Ludhiana (www.ruralolympic.net).

Surajkund Crafts Mela (⊙ 1-15 Feb) This two-week fair in February features a splendid congregation of North Indian folk artists, artisans, musicians and dancers in Surajkund, near Delhi.

Holla Mohalla (⊙ Mar) Sikhs celebrate the foundation of the Khalsa (Sikh brotherhood) with martial-arts demonstrations and battle re-enactments in Anandpur Sahib.

Baisakhi (⊙ 13-14 Apr) Sikhs across Punjab head to gurdwaras (Sikh Temples) to celebrate the Punjabi New Year, and revel in colourful celebrations, music, dance and feasting.

Gita Jayanti (⊙ Nov/Dec) One week of cultural events takes place in Kurukshetra to commemorate the anniversary of the Bhagavad Gita sermons as cited in the Mahabharata.

Pinjore Heritage Festival (⊙ late Dec) This two-day cultural bash features music and dance performances, handicrafts and food stalls at Pinjore Gardens, near Chandigarh.

Harballabh Sangeet Sammelan (⊙ late Dec) This 140-year-old music festival in Jalandhar showcases Indian classical music over three days.

With a gorgeous location on the shore of the second lake, **Tikkar Taal Tourist Complex** (☑ 01733-250166; Tikkar Taal; dm/d ₹400/2000; ❀) has clean, comfortable rooms with private bathrooms, and a great-value 16-bed dormitory, also with its own bathroom, and also with views of the lake. There's a restaurant with terraced seating and gardens leading down to the lake. There's nothing much to do here, but it's a wonderfully peaceful place to stay if you want to escape the urban frenzy for a day or two, and hiking around the farmland is a joy.

There are frequent daily buses to Morni (₹35, 1½ hours) from Chandigarh's ISBT Panchkulla (p212) bus station. From Morni village, there are three minibuses to Tikka Taal (₹20; 6.30am, 7.30am and 3.30pm). They return from outside Tikkar Taal Tourist Complex at 7.30am, 8.30am and 4.15pm. The 4.15pm connects with the last bus back to Chandigarh, which leaves Morni village at 5pm.

Private cars from Morni village to Tikka Taal cost about ₹700 return, including waiting time. Alternatively, it's a lovely two-hour, 8km downhill walk along a quiet, largely forest-shaded road; hike back up the same road your Chandigarh bus came from, then turn left as the road bears sharp right (after about 700m).

Pinjore (Yadavindra) Gardens

The beautifully restored, 17th-century Mughal-era **Pinjore Gardens** (☑ 01733-230759; Pinjore; ₹25; ⊙ 7am-10pm), on the edge of the small town of Pinjore, are built on seven levels with water features and serene views of the Shivalik Hills. Hundreds of bats hang from branches outside the entrance. Inside, parakeets flit from tree to tree.

Within the walled grounds there's a **restaurant** (mains ₹80-180; ⊙ 7am-10pm; ❀) in the Rang Mahal pavilion, which has a bar and lovely views of the gardens. Come in December for regional delicacies and cultural performances as part of the Pinjore Heritage Festival (p213).

Should you fancy an overnight stay, there are pleasant rooms with Mughal-style flourishes and views of the gardens at the **Budgerigar Motel** (☑ 01733-231877; pinjore@hry.nic.in; d from ₹2020; ❀). Its main entrance is just outside the garden walls, to the right as you face the entrance, but it can also be accessed from inside the gardens through the restaurant.

Nearby are the scattered ruins of the **Bhima Devi Temple** (⊙ 10am-5pm); once an ornate 10th-century Hindu place of worship, but now a collection of broken pillars, statuettes and friezes (including some Khajuraho-esque erotic carvings) dotted around a pleasant shaded garden. To get here, turn left as you exit the gardens and walk past the water-slide park.

Frequent buses leave from Chandigarh's ISBT 43 to Pinjore (₹40, one hour). The gardens are on your left as you drive into the town. Less frequent services depart from ISBT 17.

PUNJAB (INDIA)

A particularly tourist-friendly region, thanks to its strong expatriate connections with the UK and Canada, Punjab, the homeland of India's Sikh population, provides a wonderful opportunity to go traipsing into the backyards of North India. The Golden Temple in Amritsar is an undoubted highlight, but Punjab hides other small treasures among its agricultural expanses. Rarely visited towns like Patiala, Bathinda and Faridkot contain seemingly lost-in-time marketplaces and crumbling forts that hint at faded grandeur, while welcoming gurdwaras (Sikh temples) are to be found across the state.

Irrigated by mighty Himalayan rivers such as the Beas, the Ravi and the Sutlej, Punjab is also a region of fertile land that supplies the bulk of India's demand for wheat and rice, while also doubling as a nerve centre of India's textile and manufacturing industries.

Amritsar

☑ 0183 / POP 1.13 MILLION

Founded in 1577 by the fourth Sikh guru, Guru Ram Das, Amritsar is home to the spectacular Golden Temple, Sikhism's holiest shrine and one of India's most serene and humbling sights. The hyperactive streets surrounding the temple have been calmed to some extent by recent urban landscaping, including graceful pedestrianised walkways, but duck into any side alley and you'll soon discover Amritsar's fantastically frenetic old-city bazaars, sheltering a sensory overload of sights, sounds and smells.

◉ Sights

Golden Temple Rd, from the Partition Museum to the Golden Temple, has had a recent spruce-up and, unlike the tangle of hectic market lanes fanning off from it, is now a graceful, mostly pedestrianised stretch of road with uniformed shopfronts and a smattering of eye-catching statues.

★ Golden Temple   SIKH TEMPLE

(Golden Temple Complex; ⊘24hr) **FREE** The legendary Golden Temple is actually just a small part of this huge gurdwara complex, known to Sikhs as Harmandir Sahib. Spiritually, the focus of attention is the tank that surrounds the gleaming central shrine – the Amrit Sarovar (Pool of Nectar), from which Amritsar takes its name, excavated by the fourth Sikh guru, Ram Das, in 1577. Ringed by a marble walkway, the tank is said to have healing powers, and pilgrims come from across the world to bathe in its sacred waters.

Floating at the end of a long causeway, the Golden Temple itself is a mesmerising blend of Hindu and Islamic architectural styles, with an elegant marble lower level adorned with flower and animal motifs in pietra dura work (as seen on the Taj Mahal). Above this rises a shimmering second level, encased in intricately engraved gold panels, and topped by a dome gilded with 750kg of gold. In the gleaming inner sanctum (photography prohibited), priests and musicians keep up a continuous chant from the Guru Granth Sahib (the Sikh holy book), adding to the already intense atmosphere. Given the never-ending beeline of devotees, you will likely only get a few minutes within the sanctum before you are gently urged to exit and make way for other devotees. Entry and exit are both via the causeway.

The Guru Granth Sahib is installed in the temple every morning and returned at night to the Akal Takhat (Timeless Throne), the temporal seat of the Khalsa brotherhood. The ceremony takes place at 5am and 9.30pm in winter, and 4am and 10.30pm in summer. Inside the Akal Takhat, you can view a collection of sacred Sikh weapons. The building was heavily damaged when it was stormed by the Indian army during Operation Blue Star in 1984. It was repaired by the government but Sikhs refused to use the tainted building and rebuilt the tower from scratch.

More shrines and monuments are dotted around the edge of the compound. Inside the main entrance clock tower, the **Sikh Museum** (⊘7am-7pm summer, 8am-6pm winter) **FREE** shows the persecution suffered by the Sikhs at the hands of Mughals, the British and Indira Gandhi. At the southeast end of the tank is the Ramgarhia Bunga, a protective fortress topped by two Islamic-style minarets; inside is a stone slab once used for Mughal coronations, but which was seized from Delhi by Sikh forces in 1783.

★ Golden Temple
Interpretation Centre   MUSEUM

(⊘9am-4pm Tue-Sun) **FREE** Hidden beneath the marble square outside the clock-tower entrance to the Golden Temple, this fascinating multimedia museum tells the story of Sikhism and the significance of the Golden Temple through four entertaining 15-minute videos projected onto first an inverted pyramid, then a 180-degree cinema, then a screen above a 3D scale model of the temple and finally on a screen inside a shrine-like room. Showings start every hour, just past the hour. Swap your photo ID for an English-translation headset.

★ Partition Museum   MUSEUM

(⊘8130001947; www.partitionmuseum.org; Golden Temple Rd; Indian/foreigner ₹10/250; ⊘10am-6pm Tue-Sun) Housed in the beautifully restored 19th-century Town Hall, this unique museum (the only one in the world dedicated to Partition) offers a poignant and often-haunting portrayal of the tragic

---

ⓘ GOLDEN TEMPLE ETIQUETTE

Before entering the compound, remove your shoes and socks (there are *chappal* – sandal – stands at the entrances), wash your feet in the shallow foot baths and cover your head; scarves can be borrowed (no charge) or bought from nearby souvenir hawkers for ₹20. Tobacco and alcohol are strictly prohibited within the premises. If you want to sit beside the tank, sit cross-legged and do not dangle your feet in the water. Photography is permitted from the walkway surrounding the pool, but not inside the Golden Temple itself. Staff-wielding, blue-robed temple guards called *jathhedars* patrol the compound around the clock; approach them for any assistance or query regarding etiquette.

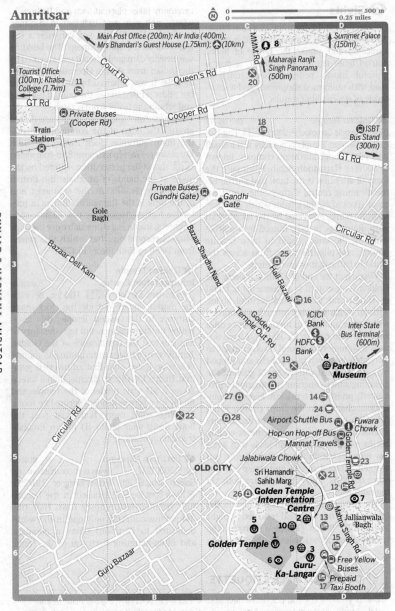

events leading up to, during and following Partition. Newspaper cuttings, photographs (some of which people may find disturbing) and video interviews tell the tumultuous story from the point of view of the survivors of what was the largest migration in human history.

★**Guru-Ka-Langar**   SIKH SITE
(⊙24hr) **FREE** At the southeast end of the Golden Temple Complex is the Guru-Ka-Langar, an enormous dining room where an estimated 100,000 pilgrims come to eat every day after praying at the Golden Temple. There's no charge to eat here, but

Amritsar

a donation is appropriate, and voluntary help with the staggering pile of washing up is always appreciated. Catering equally to everyone from paupers to millionaires, it's a humbling demonstration of the Sikh principles of hospitality, community service and charity.

The meals themselves comprise simple but sumptuous servings of *dhal*, roti and *rajma* (kidney beans), handed out by temple workers to diners who sit cross-legged on the floor and eat off stainless steel plates. There are no seating categories, so you could be sharing dining space with anyone from beggars to corporate bosses. The dining room is open round the clock, and epitomises the popular Sikh saying that no one in Amritsar ever goes to bed on a hungry stomach.

Jallianwala Bagh   HISTORIC SITE
(Golden Temple Rd; ⊘ 6am-9pm summer, 7am-8pm winter) FREE Reached through a narrow gatehouse leading to an enclosed courtyard, this poignant park commemorates the 1500 Indians killed or wounded when a British officer ordered his soldiers to shoot unarmed protesters in 1919. Some of the bullet holes are still visible in the walls, as is the well into which hundreds desperately leapt to avoid the bullets. There's an eternal flame of remembrance, an exhibition telling stories of victims, and a Martyrs' Gallery, with portraits of independence heroes.

Mata Temple   HINDU TEMPLE
(Mata Lal Devi Ji; Rani-ka-Bagh, Model Town; ⊘ dawn-dusk) FREE Credited with fertility-improving powers, this fascinating labyrinthine Hindu temple commemorates the 20th-century female saint Lal Devi. From the main hall, a narrow series of stairways and passages winds past mirrored mosaics, fairground-style carvings and untold deity statues to a semisubmerged mock-up of the Vasihno Devi cave temple. Walking west along GT Rd, turn right after the train station, up Albert Rd, then take the first left and the temple will be to your left at the end of the lane.

Ram Bagh   PARK
(MMM Rd; ⊘ dawn-dusk) FREE Ram Bagh was the former palace grounds of Maharaja Ranjit Singh (1780–1839), who founded the Sikh empire. It now serves as a public park. At its heart, you'll find the summer palace of the former maharaja, in commission between 1818 and 1837. It's a modest structure in comparison to some of India's other palaces but atmospheric nonetheless. In the park's northwest corner is **Maharaja Ranjit Singh Panorama** (₹10; ⊘ 9am-5pm Tue-Sun), a low-tech museum depicting the maharaja's greatest battles

Tours

The Grand Hotel (p218) runs two-hour old-city tours (₹350), day tours of the main sights

THE JALLIANWALA BAGH MASSACRE

Following the introduction of the *Rowlatt Act 1919*, which gave British authorities the power to imprison Indians suspected of sedition without trial, Amritsar became a focal point for the independence movement. After a series of hartals (strikes) in which many protesters and three British bank managers were killed, Brigadier-General Reginald Dyer was called upon to return order to the city.

On 13 April 1919 (Baisakhi Day), more than 5000 Indians convened for a peaceful protest in Jallianwala Bagh (p217), a public courtyard surrounded by high walls on all sides, with only a narrow lane on the northern side for entry and exit. Under orders to make an example of the protesters, Dyer arrived with 150 troops and ordered his soldiers to open fire. When the barrage of bullets ceased, nearly 400 protesters were dead, according to the British authorities, although Indian National Congress placed the figure at more than 1000, and around 1500 were wounded, including many women and children.

Dyer's action was supported by the British establishment but described as 'monstrous' by Winston Churchill, and as 'a savage and inappropriate folly' by Edwin Montagu, the Secretary of State for India. The Nobel Prize–winning poet Rabindranath Tagore renounced his knighthood in protest against the massacre. The incident galvanised Indian nationalism – Gandhi responded with a program of civil disobedience, announcing that 'cooperation in any shape or form with this satanic government is sinful'.

Reginald Dyer died in retirement in England in 1927. Michael O'Dwyer, governor of the Punjab at the time of the massacre, was assassinated by the Sikh revolutionary Udham Singh in London in 1940. Richard Attenborough's acclaimed film *Gandhi* (1982) dramatically re-enacts the events at Jallianwala Bagh.

by taxi (₹1800) and can arrange a taxi to the Attari–Wagah border-closing ceremony (₹1500 round trip).

The tourist office (p221) runs a great-value two-hour Heritage Walk (Indian/foreigner ₹25/75), covering the old-city bazaars. It starts from the Partition Museum at 8am and 4pm daily (9am and 5pm December to February) and finishes outside the Golden Temple. Just turn up at the museum 10 minutes before start time.

The open-top double-decker **Hop-on Hop-off bus** (✆ 7029690001; www.amritsar dekho.com; Fuwara Chowk, Golden Temple Rd) isn't actually 'hop-on hop-off', but it does offer two tours: a trip to see the border-closing ceremony (₹250, five hours, 2pm) at the Attari–Wagah border with Pakistan, and a full-day city tour (₹350, eight hours, 10am), taking in four or five city-centre sights before incorporating the trip to the border ceremony. Tickets are bought from a ticket booth beside where the bus starts and finishes.

🛏 Sleeping

There are dozens of hotels suiting all budgets in and around the old-city lanes of the Golden Temple area, and this is certainly the most atmospheric place to stay. As always in India, it's cheaper to just turn up and negotiate a room rate, rather than book in advance; there are so many options here that there's

really no need to book unless you'll be turning up late at night.

Grand Hotel
HOTEL $

(✆ 0183-2562424; www.hotelgrand.in; Queen's Rd; d from ₹1200; ❈ @ 🖜) Across the road from the train station, but far from grungy, the Grand is an oasis of calm amid an otherwise chaotic location. Rooms are spacious – if not exactly grand – and surround a wonderfully charming courtyard garden. The restaurant, with seating overlooking the garden, and the inviting bar serving chilled beers are also highly recommended. The hotel management organises tours.

Tourist Guesthouse
GUESTHOUSE $

(✆ 9356003219; www.touristguesthouse.com; 1355 GT Rd; dm/d ₹200/600; @ 🖜) This good-value backpacker stalwart offers pocket-friendly prices and humble rooms with high ceilings and fans. There's a small restaurant, a cute little garden (where you can take your meals), rooftop seating and an overall traveller-oriented vibe. The location, between a busy flyover and the railway line, is hardly the quietest, but this is still a solid choice.

Hotel Ishita Inn
HOTEL $

(✆ 0183-5013433; Golden Temple Rd, Town Hall; with/without AC ₹900/700; ❈ 🖜) This compact four-storey hotel has simple but comfortable rooms with TV and small shower room, and a great location on the fringes of the Golden Temple action. The lobby wi-fi extends to the 1st-floor rooms. Good value.

Sri Guru Ram Das Niwas
GUESTHOUSE $

(Golden Temple Complex; dm free but donations appropriate, d with/without AC ₹500/300; ✳@) Inexpensive rooms are available in this *niwas* (pilgrims' hostel) at the southeast end of the Golden Temple Complex. Foreigners are generally accommodated in the dorm at Sri Guru Ram Das Niwas, or at rooms in the other buildings in the vicinity. Check in at the nearby Guru Arjan Dev Niwas to see what is available.

Staying here is a fascinating experience but rooms and dorms are basic, with shared bathrooms, and there's a three-day maximum stay. Each person gets use of a locker in the dorms, but you need your own padlock.

★ Mrs Bhandari's Guesthouse
GUESTHOUSE $$

(☑0183-2228509; http://bhandari_guesthouse.tripod.com; 10 Cantonment; s/d from ₹2600/3000; ✳@☎▣) Founded by the much-missed Mrs Bhandari (1906–2007), this slightly mothballed but friendly guesthouse is set in spacious grounds in Amritsar cantonment, about 2.5km from the train station. The large rooms have a hint of colonial-style charm about them, and the welcome is warm. The well-kept gardens include swings, see-saws, plenty of seating and a small swimming pool.

Budget travellers can camp here for ₹350 per person if they bring their own gear. Pickup is free from the train station and meals are available. It's about ₹70 in a cycle-rickshaw from the old city, and about ₹200 in an autorickshaw from the bus stand. To walk here, go up Court Rd, turn left at the second roundabout, then over two more small roundabouts and it's on your right.

Hotel Indus
HOTEL $$

(☑0183-2535900; www.hotelindus.com; 211/3 Sri Hamandir Sahib Marg; d from ₹2100, with Golden Temple view ₹3000; ✳@☎) The dramatic million-dollar view of the Golden Temple from the rooftop restaurant-of-sorts is reason enough to stay at this modern hotel. Rooms are compact but comfy, and suitably appointed for the price. Book well ahead to secure one of the two rooms with temple vistas.

Hotel Vacation Inn
HOTEL $$

(☑0183-5052878; www.hotelvacationinn.com; 11-12 Brahm Buta Market; r from ₹1650; ✳☎) Brand new in 2018, this modern hotel represents good value in the market lanes surrounding the Golden Temple. Rooms lack character, but are bright with large windows, big TVs, tea-making facilities and wi-fi. No restaurant, but room-service menu available.

Hotel City Heart
HOTEL $$$

(☑9855545151; www.hotelcityheartamritsar.com; Golden Temple Rd; r ₹4700; ✳☎) With a great location on recently renovated Golden Temple Rd, this smart, superclean, old-city hotel has modern, spacious rooms and friendly staff. No restaurant, but room-service menu available.

Ramada Amritsar
HOTEL $$$

(☑0183-5025555; www.ramadaamritsar.com; Hall Bazaar; s/d incl breakfast from ₹7080/7670; ✳@☎▣) This grand-looking hotel is the only top-end option in the old city. The lobby is somewhat chintzy, but rooms are smart and modern, and the service is excellent. It's walking distance from the Golden Temple, and there's a lovely rooftop pool with fabulous views of the old city.

✖ Eating

Amritsar is famous for its *dhabas* (casual eateries serving snacks and basic meals) serving yummy Punjabi treats such as *kulcha* (deep-fried flatbread), stuffed *parathas*, spicy variants of lentils and Amritsari deep-fried fish tikkas garnished with lemon, chilli, garlic and ginger. Also don't miss eating at least once at Guru-Ka-Langar (p216), the enormous pilgrims canteen inside the Golden Temple.

Gurdas Ram
INDIAN $

(Jalebiwala Chowk; jalebi per serving ₹20; ☯9.30am-10.30pm; ☑) Get your fingers sticky at this 60-year-old *jalebi* joint, serving up the delicious Indian dessert consisting of saffron-coloured coils of deep-fried batter dunked in sugar syrup. The place is so famous they even named the street crossing after it (Jalebiwala Chowk).

★ Bharawan Da Dhaba
PUNJABI $$

(Town Hall Chowk; meals ₹150-250, thalis ₹175-230; ☯7.30am-12.30am; ✳☑) Pronounced 'praa-waan', this down-to-earth Amritsar institution has been serving lip-smacking Punjabi treats since 1912. The thalis are delectable platters of dhal, *channa* (chickpea), and/or paneer (soft, unfermented cheese made from milk curd), served with naan, roti or rice (or all of them). The *kulcha* are particularly tasty and for afters, don't miss the *phirni* (cardamon-flavoured rice pudding; ₹35) served in cute clay pots.

★ Kesar Da Dhaba PUNJABI $$

(Shastri Market, Chowk Passian; dishes ₹75-250, thalis ₹195-295; ⊙11am-5pm & 7-11pm; ✔) Originally founded in Pakistan's Punjab province, this 100-year-old eatery relocated to Amritsar after Partition. Since then it has been serving up delicious *paratha* thalis and silver-leaf-topped *firni* (ground rice pudding; ₹20) in small clay bowls, as well as arguably the best lassi in town (₹60) from this hard-to-find old-city location. Just keep asking the way; everyone knows it.

★ Brothers' Dhaba PUNJABI $$

(Bade Bhai Ka; Town Hall Chowk; mains ₹130-260, thalis ₹135-255; ⊙8am-midnight; ✱✔) This fast and friendly upmarket *dhaba* serves some of Amritsar's tastiest *parathas* stuffed with herbs, potato and pomegranate seeds that burst in the mouth as tiny explosions of taste. It also does hot and yummy breakfast platters featuring curried potato and deep-fried *kulcha*.

Crystal Restaurant MULTICUISINE $$$

(Crystal Chowk; mains ₹400-700, beer from ₹250; ⊙11am-11.30pm; ✱) Bossing this corner of Queen's Rd, Crystal has two restaurants here, as well as a kebab stand and a new lounge-bar. The original ground-floor restaurant has a fin de siècle air, with mirror-lined walls and ornate stucco trim, while the excellent menu is dominated by Mughlai favourites – the house speciality is the delicious *murg tawa frontier* (₹450), morsels of chicken in dense onion gravy.

Upstairs is the Crystal Restaurant Plaza, run by a rival branch of the same family and serving the same menu in more modern surroundings. Outside is a no-nonsense takeaway joint where you can enjoy some of the same dishes, plus plenty of tandoori offerings, while standing at high, roadside tables. And just around the corner is a lift leading to Crystal's 3rd-floor lounge-bar; again with the same menu, but the added attraction of bird's-eye street views.

🍷 Drinking & Nightlife

Cafe Green CAFE

(www.cafegreen.co.in; Saragarhi Sarai Building, Town Hall; coffee from ₹40, snacks ₹50-200; ⊙24hr) There's no wi-fi, but this clean, modern, family-friendly cafe does the cheapest proper coffee in town (espresso ₹40, Americano ₹60), as well as sandwiches, pastries, ice creams and other snacks.

Café Coffee Day CAFE

(Golden Temple Rd; coffees from ₹120; ⊙9am-11pm; 📶) An air-conditioned oasis with fresh coffee and free wi-fi, this chain cafe is conveniently located within shouting distance of the Golden Temple area. There are tasty cakes, puffs, wraps and street-view seating to go with your latte or espresso.

Bottoms Up Pub BAR

(Queen's Rd, Grand Hotel; beers ₹130; ⊙11am-11pm) The congenial bar at the Grand Hotel serves icy cold, glycerine-free, draught King-

---

STROLLING AMRITSAR'S BAZAARS

The Golden Temple sits on the edge of a mesmerising maze of crowded market streets, where anything and everything can be found, from ceremonial swords to wedding suits. Start your explorations at the main entrance to the Golden Temple. From here, stroll northwest (so, to your left if you have your back to the Golden Temple) to the end of the temple compound and duck into the atmospheric Kathian Bazaar for blankets, stationery, tin pots and red-and-silver wedding bangles. At the far end, turn right onto bustling Guru Bazaar Rd, past shops full of glittery womenswear, then take the first significant left into Shashtri Bazaar, where dupattas (scarves) give way to fancy woollen shawls. At the end of the bazaar, turn right then right again beside a string of food and fruit stalls, into frenetic Katra Jaimal Singh Bazaar, crammed with tailors and fashion stores. At the T-junction, turn left into narrow Tahali Sahib Bazaar, piled high with glittering satin dupattas, before popping out by Brothers' Dhaba.

Tip: follow this walking tour to get your bearings before doing another circuit, this time exploring the myriad narrow alleyways that branch off these main bazaars. Alternatively, take the excellent Heritage Walk (p217), run twice daily by the tourist office. It also focuses on these bazaars.

fisher beer and some tasty meals from the hotel's common kitchen.

Shopping

Wandering around the winding alleys of the old-city bazaars is a head-spinning assault on the senses. Things to look out for include jooti (embroidered and brocaded leather slippers), dupatta (women's scarves), woollen shawls and bangles (including the steel *kara* bangles worn by Sikhs).

Booklovers Retreat   BOOKS
(Hall Bazaar; ⊙ 9.30am-8pm Mon-Sat) An old-school bookshop laden with interesting tomes spanning diverse genres, including the latest Indian and international English bestsellers, plus guidebooks and Indian cookery books.

Information

INTERNET ACCESS
Free wi-fi is widely available at Amritsar's hotels, and in Café Coffee Day near the Golden Temple. Internet cafes are a thing of the past, although one former **internet cafe** (Shop 208, 1st fl, Clock Tower Market; per hour ₹40; ⊙ 10.30am-7pm; 🕾) near the Golden Temple still opens its doors for wi-fi use.

MEDICAL SERVICES
Fortis Escorts Hospital (⚍ 9915133330, 0183-3012222; www.fortishealthcare.com; Majitha Verka Bypass; ⊙ 24hr) is an international-standard hospital in Amritsar's suburbs, about 7km northeast of the old city.

MONEY
Amritsar has an ever-mushrooming supply of ATMs, including many around the Golden Temple and ones at the airport, the train station and the main bus station. **Mannat Travels** (⚍ 0183-5006006; 5 Dharam Singh Market, Fuwara Chowk; ⊙ 9.30am-8pm Mon-Sat) is a trustworthy money changer in the old city.

Close to the Partition Museum, **HDFC** (ground fl, RS Towers, Hall Bazaar; ⊙ 9.30am-3.30pm Mon-Sat, ATM 24hr) and **ICICI** (ground fl, RS Towers, Hall Bazaar; ⊙ 9.30am-4pm Mon-Sat, ATM 24hr) deal in foreign exchange and have 24-hour ATMs that accept foreign cards.

POST
At the junction of Court Rd with Albert Rd is the **main post office** (Court Rd; ⊙ 10am-4pm Mon-Fri, to 2pm Sat), with fast post and parcel facilities. There is also a handy **post office** (Golden Temple Rd, Fuwara Chowk; ⊙ 10am-4pm Mon-Fri, to 2pm Sat) near the Golden Temple with similar facilities.

TOURIST INFORMATION
By the second entrance to the train station is a **tourist office** (⚍ 0183-2402452; www.punjabtourism.gov.in; Queen's Rd, train station exit; ⊙ 9am-5pm Tue-Sun) with brochures and free maps covering Punjab, including detailed street maps of Amritsar, Patiala, Bathinda, Anandpur Sahib and Kapurthala.

❶ Getting There & Away

AIR
About 11km northwest of the centre, Amritsar's **International Airport** (Sri Guru Ram Dass Jee International Airport; www.amritsarairport.com; Ajnala Rd, Rajasansi) has connections to major Indian cities such as Delhi (from ₹4000) and Mumbai (from ₹9000), courtesy of airlines such as **Air India** (⚍ 0183-2500127; www.airindia.in; B-Block, Ranjit Ave; ⊙ 9am-5pm Mon-Sat), IndiGo and Jet Airways. It also has a few international flights, including ones to Kuala Lumpur, Singapore and Birmingham in the UK.

BUS
Companies running private buses operate from near Gandhi Gate and from Cooper Rd, near the train station. Evening AC buses run to Delhi (seat/sleeper ₹800/1000, eight hours) and Jaipur (sleeper ₹1400, 12 hours), while non-AC ones run to Jammu (seat/sleeper ₹400/500, four hours). Four or five AC buses also run to Chandigarh (₹600, five hours).

The main **Inter State Bus Terminal** (ISBT; GT Rd) is about 3km north of the Golden Temple, near Mahan Singh Gate. There's at least one daily bus to Chamba (₹280, six hours), Dharamsala (₹300, seven hours) and Manali (ordinary/AC ₹700/1600, 12 hours).

Frequent buses also serve Wagah Border (₹40, one hour), Faridkot (₹150, three hours), Pathankot (₹140, three hours) and Patiala (₹300, five hours), Bathinda (₹230, four hours), Chandigarh (ordinary/AC ₹300/610, five hours) and Delhi (ordinary/AC ₹510/1125, nine hours).

TRAIN
The fastest of many trains to Delhi is the twice-daily Amritsar Shatabdi (AC chair ₹810, six hours, 4.55am and 4.50pm). From New Delhi train station, the same trains make the return trip at 7.20am and 4.30pm. There are around a dozen other daily trains to Delhi (sleeper/3AC/2AC ₹290/690/970), taking seven to nine hours.

Two daily trains go to Chandigarh (2nd class/AC chair ₹120/435, five hours) at 5.10am and 5.30pm. Eleven go daily to Pathankot Junction (sleeper/3AC ₹140/495, three hours).

There's one daily train to Patiala (general/sleeper/3AC ₹90/180/495, 5½ hours, 8.30am)

SLEEPING PRICE RANGES

Accommodation price ranges refer to a double room with bathroom and include taxes.

$ less than ₹1500

$$ ₹1500–₹3000

$$$ more than ₹3000

The daily 6.40pm Amritsar–Howrah Mail links Amritsar with Varanasi (sleeper/3AC/2AC ₹500/1355/1975, 22 hours) and Kolkata's Howrah train station (sleeper/3AC/2AC ₹695/1870/2755, 37 hours).

ⓘ Getting Around

To the airport, an autorickshaw costs around ₹350 and a taxi about ₹500 to ₹600. There's also a free **airport shuttle bus** (Fuwara Chowk) that runs between the airport and the Golden Temple three times a day; from the airport at 6.15am, 9.15am and 1.15pm, and from Fuwara Chowk to the airport at 6am and noon.

Free **yellow buses** (Sri Harmandir Sahib Marg) run between the train station and the Golden Temple from 4am to 9pm. Otherwise, from the train station to the Golden Temple, a rickshaw/autorickshaw will cost around ₹50/100, but you'll have to haggle hard for a fair price. Taxis loiter around the station and at the **prepaid taxi booth** (☑ 8360119094; Sri Harmandir Sahib Marg; ⊙ 8.30am-9pm) to the east of Golden Temple, while **Ola Cabs** (☑ 0183-3355335; www.olacabs. com) has smart and swift radio taxis plying Amritsar round the clock.

Taxis taking you to the Golden Temple area will often drop you at Fuwara (Fountain) Chowk or the Town Hall (aka the Partition Museum), from where you can walk the last few hundred metres through a recently renovated pedestrianised tourist corridor and souvenir market, flanked by graceful red-sandstone shopping arcades on both sides.

Around Amritsar

India–Pakistan Border at Attari–Wagah

Because of the tense relations between India and Pakistan, few foreigners actually cross the border between Attari and Wagah, 30km west of Amritsar, though it is possible to do so, providing you have a Pakistan visa, of course. However, plenty of people come to watch the curious border-closing ceremony every evening at the Attari–Wagah Border Checkpost.

◉ Sights

Border-Closing Ceremony   GATE
(Attari–Wagah; ⊙ 5.30pm, 4.30pm winter) FREE
Every afternoon Indian and Pakistani border guards meet at the border post between Attari and Wagah to engage in a 30-minute display of military showmanship that verges on pure theatre. Officially, the purpose of the ceremony is to lower the national flag and close the border for the night, but what actually occurs is a bizarre mix of pseudo-formal and competitive marching, flag-folding, chest beating, forceful stomping and almost comical high-stepping. Bring your passport.

While the participants treat the ceremony with absolute seriousness, the crowds who gather to watch from the grandstands on either side of the border come for the carnival mood. During the build-up to the ceremony, spontaneous anthem chanting, rapturous rounds of applause and Bollywood-style dancing in the street are de rigueur. Then a roar goes up from the crowd as the first soldier from each side marches furiously towards the border, to begin the first round of who-can-high-step-the-highest. It's all highly nationalistic, but considering the tense relations between the two countries, remarkably good-natured. The oiled moustaches and over-the-top dress uniforms (with fanlike flourishes atop each turban) only add to the theatrical mood.

Not everyone gets in, so try to arrive at least one hour before the ceremony begins. It's a mad scrum at the main entrance gate (women must queue on the right; men on the left) as people are let through in sudden bursts, but once you're through, things calm down, and you are channelled into the appropriate stands (foreign tourists are allowed to sit in the second-best seats, just behind the VIPs).

Note, you must drop off all bags (even handbags) at lockers (₹50) in the tourist reception centre by the entrance, although you are allowed to carry things (water bottle, phone, camera etc) in your hands.

ⓘ Getting There & Away

Local buses run every 15 minutes from Amritsar's main bus stand to Wagah Border (₹40, one hour), from where it's a few hundred metres' walk to the customs post (or ₹10 in a shared autorickshaw – it's quicker walking if it's busy). The border ceremony is held a further few hundred metres beyond the customs post.

The bus is the cheapest way to get here by far, but it's also easy to arrange a taxi; ₹1300 return from the prepaid taxi booth by the Golden Temple, or around ₹1500 through your hotel. It's also possible to take the Hop-on Hop-off bus tour (p218) from the Golden Temple (₹250 per person).

Pathankot

📞 0186 / POP 148,500

The dusty frontier town of Pathankot is merely a transport hub for the neighbouring states of Himachal Pradesh and Jammu & Kashmir, and there's little here to make you linger. The train and bus stations are 400m apart. Turn left out of either to reach the other.

Pathankot bus station has a **guesthouse** (dm ₹100, d ₹300-400) featuring very basic rooms and a common shower room. **Hotel Comfort** (📞 0186-2226403; Gurdaspur Rd; d from ₹1580; ❄) is the smartest of a couple of hotels that are just outside the bus station. It has a restaurant and bar.

🛈 Getting There & Away

From Pathankot Junction train station on Gurdaspur Rd there are 12 daily trains to Amritsar (general/sleeper ₹25/140, two to three hours). Ten daily trains leave for New Delhi (sleeper/3AC/2AC ₹305/790/1115, eight hours).

The Kangra Valley Toy Train leaves from Pathankot Junction four times a day (6.45am, 10am, 1.30pm and 3.45pm) and runs along the scenic narrow-gauge line to Kangra Mandir (seat ₹25, four hours), from where it's a one-hour bus ride to Dharamsala.

From Pathankot bus station, there are frequent services throughout the day to Dharamsala (₹164, four hours), Amritsar (₹135, three hours), Chandigarh (₹320, six hours), Dalhousie (₹120, 3½ hours), Delhi (ordinary/Volvo AC ₹550/1200, 11 hours), Jammu (₹110, three hours) and Manali (₹570, 11 hours).

Kapurthala

📞 01822 / POP 100,000

Once the capital of a wealthy independent state, Kapurthala is an unusual place to explore. The resident maharaja, Jagatjit Singh, was a travel junkie – he married Spanish flamenco dancer Anita Delgado and constructed numerous buildings inspired by his travels.

🌀 Sights

The Jagatjit Palace (now the exclusive Sainik School and not open to the public) was modelled on Versailles, while the wonderfully atmospheric Moorish Mosque copies

the Grand Mosque in Marrakesh (Morocco). Other buildings of note include the British-style Jagatjit Club and Jubilee Hall (neither of which can be entered), and the Shalimar Bagh public gardens containing the cenotaphs of the Kapurthala royal dynasty.

You'll pass most of the notable sights on a pleasant 2km walk from the bus stand to the mosque. Turn left (east) out of the bus stand, then right at the end of the road to reach Jagatjit Palace. Turn right for Jagatjit Club, then take the tree-shaded lane opposite it, through Kemret Gardens, to reach the charming 150-year-old Government Guesthouse. Turn right here, then first left to reach Jubilee Hall (now a college). Turn right again then left at the end of the road, past London Hotel, then left at the mini-roundabout to reach the mosque.

Shalimar Bagh is 700m west of the bus stand.

🛏 Sleeping & Eating

There are some OK rooms at **Hotel Royal** (📞 01822-505110; Jalandhar Rd; s/d from ₹1000/2000; ❄), 200m east of the bus stand. The most comfortable place to stay, though, is **London Hotel** (📞 01822-230146; www.londonhotelkpt.com; Sultanpur Rd; s/d from ₹2000/2300; ❄🛜), with clean, cosy rooms, a bar and three small restaurants, including one on the roof terrace. It's about 750m from the bus stand; turn right out of the bus stand, take the first left, left again at the roundabout, then first right.

There are restaurants at both London Hotel (including a rooftop terrace) and Hotel Royal, while **Mehfil-e-Sham** (dishes ₹50-150; ⊙noon-10pm; 🛜) is a tree-shaded garden restaurant inside Shalamar Bagh, serving South Indian and Chinese dishes, as well as tea, coffee and ice cream.

🍷 Drinking & Nightlife

For a good-value cappuccino (₹90), plus tasty cakes and sandwiches, head to **Barista** (Jalandar Rd; coffee/snacks from ₹90/100; ⊙10am-11pm; 🛜), a bright, friendly, wi-fi-enabled cafe 200m east of the bus stand, opposite Hotel Royal. For a beer, head to London Hotel.

🛈 Getting There & Away

To get to Amritsar from Kapurthala, you need to take a bus to Subhanpur (₹15, 30 minutes) then change for Amritsar (₹65, 1½ hours). There are four morning buses to Faridkot (₹140, 2½ hours) between 6am and 10.30am. Otherwise, you'll have to go to Jalandhar (₹25, 45 minutes), then Moga (₹95, two hours), then Faridkot (₹65, one hour).

Faridkot

📞 01639 / POP 87,695

Faridkot was the capital of a once glorious Sikh state that has all but vanished over time. It's one of Punjab's least visited towns, and remains well off the beaten tourist track.

👁 Sights

Today, peacocks stalk the faded battlements of the once mighty Qila Mubarak, a fort protected by 15m-high walls, which was the ancestral home of the maharajas of Faridkot. Nearby, the ever-busy Tilla Baba Farid Ji is a recent rebuild of an age-old gurdwara, dedicated to the 13th-century Sufi poet Baba Sheikh Farid, whose poems were an inspiration for Guru Nanak, founder of Sikhism. Also in town is the Raj Mahal, the current residence of the former royal family, who moved here from the fort in the 1880s. There's also the beautiful, 30m-tall, French-designed Victoria Memorial Clock Tower (c 1902), as well as the attractive pastel-green District Library.

All the sights are within walking distance of each other. To get the fort, turn left out of the bus station, then right at the roundabout, and keep walking, past the Memorial Library, and on through an old green archway. Turn left at the end, then bear right and the fort will be in front of you. You can't enter the fort, but you can complete a circuit around the outside of its formidable walls. Down a side lane to the left of the fort as you face it is Tilla Baba Farid Ji, which you can enter, along with throngs of visiting devotees. Returning from the fort, walk back through the green archway, then turn left to pass the Raj Mahal, before reaching the splendid Victoria Memorial Clock Tower.

🛏 Sleeping & Eating

There's a cluster of hotels about a 750m walk from the bus station. Turn left out of the bus station, left at the roundabout, then first right and you'll soon reach them all.

Hotel Sandhuz HOTEL $$
(📞 01639-250039; Kotkapura Rd; r from ₹2000; ❄🛜) Arguably the smartest of the four hotels within walking distance of the bus stand, Sandhuz promises hot showers, clean

sheets and a popular family restaurant. Also has a bar.

ℹ Getting There & Away

Frequent buses run from Faridkot to Amritsar (₹150, three hours), Bathinda (₹65, 1½ hours), Chandigarh (₹270, five hours) and Patiala (₹230, four hours).

Bathinda

📞 0164 / POP 286,000

Bathinda is a quiet, friendly town that sees few foreign tourists...or even domestic tourists for that matter. However, the bazaars around the bus station are fun to wander through, and the fort is one of Punjab's top-draw sights.

👁 Sights

⭐ **Govindgarh** FORT
(Razia Sultan Fort; ⏰ dawn-dusk) **FREE** Of all the ruined forts in Punjab, Bathinda's Govindgarh is the mightiest and most impressive. It's also the oldest, dating way back to the 7th century, although rebuilt in its current red-brick form during the 12th century. It's an enormous structure, located bang in the middle of the city, and an unexpected highlight of a visit to this region. The fort's 36m-tall, 6m-thick walls tower over the old city bazaars and – best of all – can be freely explored.

Unlike other ancient forts in the region, Govindgarh has two gurdwaras and is thus always open to the public. Besides visiting the gurdwaras themselves, you can wander the lawned gardens within the walls and even climb up to a spot on the ramparts for magnificent views of the city. Don't miss walking around the outside of the fort to the western face, where the immense walls are at their most impressive, towering above dhobi-wallahs (clothes washers) and cotton-loomers working on the dusty streets below.

To get to the fort, turn left out of the bus station, take the first left then keep walking straight through the bazaar for about 700m.

🛏 Sleeping & Eating

Hotel Appreciate HOTEL $
(📞 0164-3201875; d from ₹1000; ❄) Hotel Appreciate promises decent value among a bunch of budget hotels near the bus station. Behind the property's Lego-like facade are simple air-conditioned rooms with hot-water taps (but cold-water showers) and

clean sheets. You can see the hotel's sign from the bus-stand forecourt, and there's a back exit that leads to the lane it's on.

Roadways PUNJABI $
(GT Rd; mains ₹70-160; ⊙8.30am-8pm) Close to the bus stand, this deceptively cavernous roadside *dhaba* (simple eatery) has ceiling fans cooling an unusual art deco interior and a menu of breakfast *parathas*, Punjabi mains (including Amritsar *kulcha*) and an inexpensive veg thali. Turn right out of the bus stand and it's on your right.

Sagar Ratna SOUTH INDIAN $$
(GT Rd; mains ₹150-250, thalis ₹275-340; ⊙11am-10pm; ❀☿) For a pleasant departure from local Punjabi flavours, try one of the many dosas at this authentic South Indian restaurant located on the main drag. There's good South Indian coffee (₹50) to go with your meal too. It's 2.5km from the bus stand. Turn left out of the bus stand and it'll eventually be on your right.

❶ Getting There & Away

Ten daily trains leave for New Delhi (sleeper/3AC ₹200/495, six to eight hours) round the clock. Five daytime trains go to Patiala (2nd class/AC chair ₹80/260, three hours) between 6.30am and 5.50pm.

Frequent buses go to Amritsar (₹220, four hours), Chandigarh (non-AC/AC ₹300/600, five hours), Faridkot (₹65, 1½ hours) and Patiala (₹205, three hours).

Patiala

🗲0175 / POP 405,200
Punjab's best-kept secret, Patiala was once the capital of an independent Sikh state, ruled by an extravagant family of maharajas. As the Mughal empire declined, the rulers of Patiala curried favour with the British and filled their city with lavish palaces and follies. After Independence and the subsequent abolition of privy purses, royal fortunes began to decline, and the once regal city slowly became a shadow of its former self. Today, the grand monuments are all crumbling, but the old city, ringed by 10 historic gates, is still swooningly atmospheric. In mid-January, the skies above Patiala burst into life for the Basant kite festival.

The first thing to do when you get here is grab a free map of the town from the tourist office (p226). Even then, be prepared to get lost in the old-city bazaars.

EXPLORING PATIALA

A self-guided walking tour around Adalat Bazar can help you explore some smaller, but interesting, historic sights tucked away in the nooks and crannies of the old town.

Turn right out of Qila Mubarak, then right again, and follow the road south to the monumental gateway by the Shahi Samadhan, the royal cemetery housing the mortal remains of deceased kings and other royalty. The three-storey tomb of Maharaja Aala Singh Samad (d 1822) is the grandest of all the tombs. The main gate of the compound usually remains closed, but the watchmen on duty will open up and show you around if you turn up any time between dawn and dusk.

If you continue along the same road past Shahi Samadhan and bear left by the Samania Gate, you'll reach Mohindra College Rd and the twin towers of the Mohindra College, a former palace converted into a private school. Continue past here, and turn left at the end to reach Sheesh Mahal.

◉ Sights

★**Qila Mubarak** FORT
(Adalat Bazar) The ancestral home of the maharajas of Patiala, this richly ornamented 18th-century fort is an *Arabian Nights* fantasy of soaring buttresses and latticed balconies. You can't enter the interior of the fort, but you are allowed to walk between the hugely impressive inner and outer walls, surrounded by crumbling masonry and flocks of parakeets. The fort is 2km south of the bus stand, hidden in amongst a web of old-town bazaars; ₹30 in a cycle rickshaw.

Inside the fort entrance, to your right, the 1859 Durbar Hall has a museum that is undergoing wholesale renovations.

Sheesh Mahal MUSEUM
(Sheesh Mahal Rd; ₹10; ⊙10.30am-5pm Tue-Sun) Graced by two wedding-cake towers and an ornamental suspension bridge, Sheesh Mahal is one of Punjab's more striking buildings. Inside the lavishly decorated interior is a gallery displaying royal treasures including paintings, coins and various finely crafted objects of art. The tree-shaded parks fronting the mansion boast exquisite marble statues, including a larger-than-life 1903 sculpture of

DON'T MISS

PUNJAB'S TASTIEST TREATS

Must-try Punjabi dishes include *kulcha* (fried bread), *chhole* (spicy chickpea curry), char-grilled tandoori mutton, *dhal makhani* (black lentils and red kidney beans in a cream and butter gravy), tandoori chicken, *rajma chawal* (kidney bean curry with basmati rice), Amritsari fried fish and the iconic butter chicken, the prototype for chicken tikka masala.

Queen Victoria by British sculptor Francis Derwent Wood. It's 2.5km south of the fort (cycle rickshaw ₹40); 4km south of the bus stand (₹70 to ₹80).

🛏 Sleeping

It's possible to visit on a day trip from Chandigarh, but Patiala's old city deserves more of your time, so it's worth staying over.

Hotel Chinar HOTEL $
(☑ 0175-2225592; r from ₹500; ✴) One of the few cheapies in town that accepts foreigners, Chinar is in a lane right behind the bus stand. The geysers don't work in all the bathrooms, and only some rooms have a TV, so check a few before committing. Also has a popular ground-floor bar.

Hotel Imperial Corner HOTEL $$
(Heritage Corner; ☑ 7307404018; r ₹1800-3000; ✴🖨) Right beside the bus stand, above easy-to-spot Food Library, this recently refurbished hotel has modern and spacious, though slightly spartan, rooms.

★ Baradari Palace HERITAGE HOTEL $$$
(☑ 0175-2304433; www.neemranahotels.com; Baradari Gardens; s/d from ₹5300/6500; ✴🖨) Built as a garden palace for Maharaja Rajinder Singh, this nostalgic heritage hotel is Punjab's most graceful place to spend a night. The enormous, artfully restored rooms are an exercise in luxury and classy aesthetics, while the mansion's stately terraces and grand patios overlook elegant gardens. It's a 15-minute walk west from the bus stand, or a ₹30 cycle-rickshaw ride.

🍴 Eating

The old city is dotted with bakeries and sweet shops, some of which you can have inexpensive meals in too.

Gopal's NORTH INDIAN $
(Lower Mall Rd; dishes ₹80-180; ⊗8am-10pm; ✏) This popular vegetarian eatery prides itself on delicious servings of *channa bhatura* (Indian fried bread with chickpeas), thalis and sweetmeats that are wolfed down by eager diners through the day.

It's 1.5km southwest of the bus stand; turn left down Mall Rd, past the tourist office, and it's on the left at the first big roundabout. Cycle rickshaw: ₹30.

★ Food Library INDIAN $$
(Mall Rd; mains ₹120-320; ⊗11am-11pm; ✴🖨) The speciality *dum-a-dum biryani* (veg, chicken or mutton) in this young, friendly, 1st-floor eatery bursts with flavour, but there are also tasty dhals and tandoori tikkas, plus an oh-so-creamy *Patiala shahi paneer*. The rotis and naans are baked to perfection too. And best of all you can watch everything being kneaded, flipped, fried and baked in the clean, open kitchen.

Floor-to-ceiling windows allow you to watch the street scenes below as you tuck into your meal, and there's wi-fi too. Extra bonus: it's right by the bus stand, so easy to find.

ℹ Information

Tourist office (Mall Rd; ⊗9am-4pm Tue-Sun) Near the bus stand; has free city maps.

ℹ Getting There & Away

Frequent buses run from Patiala to Chandigarh (₹95, two hours), Amritsar (₹300, five hours), Sirhind (₹40, one hour), Anandpur Sahib (₹120, three hours) and Delhi (ordinary/AC ₹260/500, six hours).

Patiala's small train station, with an old steam loco on display outside it, is opposite the bus stand. There are two direct trains to Delhi (general/2nd class/AC chair ₹90/105/395, five to six hours) at 7.40am and 1.53pm; one to Amritsar (sleeper/3AC/2AC ₹180/495/700, six hours) at 10.40am; and six to Bathinda (general/AC chair ₹35/240, three hours).

Anandpur Sahib

☑ 01887 / POP 16,300

The second-most-important pilgrimage site for Sikhs after the Golden Temple in Amritsar, Anandpur Sahib was founded in 1664 by the ninth Sikh guru, Guru Tegh Bahadur, some years before he was beheaded by the Mughal emperor Aurangzeb. To resist the persecution of the Sikhs, his son, Guru Gobind Singh, founded the Khalsa (Sikh brotherhood) here in 1699, an event celebrated during the Holla Mohalla festival (p213).

◉ Sights

Kesgarh Sahib
SIKH TEMPLE

The largest and most dramatic gurdwara in Anandpur Sahib is the Kesgarh Sahib, set back from the main highway on the edge of the old town. An elegant white structure with a domed central spire, it marks the spot where the Khalsa was inaugurated, and enshrines an armoury of sacred Sikh weapons. As with all the main gurdwaras, this one provides visitors (of any faith) with free meals and basic pilgrims' accommodation (donations are appropriate).

Anandpur Sahib Fort
FORT

(Kesgarh; ⊙dawn-dusk) FREE Up to your right as you walk out the back of Kesgarh Sahib gurdwara, a broad paved path climbs the hillside to the small Kesgarh fort, which affords glorious views over a sea of gurdwara domes. Kesgarh is the most prominent of Anandpur Sahib's five forts, all of which were built by Guru Gobind Singh as defensive battlements.

Khalsa Heritage Complex
MUSEUM

(Virasat-e-Khalsa; www.virasat-e-khalsa.net; ⊙10am-4pm Tue-Sun) FREE The striking five-petal form (inspired by the five warrior-saints in the Khalsa) of the Khalsa Heritage Complex, which opened in 2011, is one of India's most impressive modern buildings. This fascinating museum complex uses elaborate murals and friezes to bring Sikh history to life.

⊨ Sleeping & Eating

Grand Hotel
HOTEL $

(☑01887-230144; Main Bazaar, Ravidass Chowk; rooms from ₹1000; ❋⊚) Far from grand (in fact, it's hidden above a row of shops), this hotel does have clean rooms with TV and wi-fi (the only hotel with wi-fi, it seems), and is right in the town centre, beside Pal Restaurant and all the bustling bazaars.

Hotel Holy City Paradise Inn
HOTEL $

(☑9815135800, 01887-232330; Academy Rd; r with/without AC ₹1200/800; ❋⊚) This small but well-run place has clean and comfy rooms, a friendly welcome, a good restaurant serving local food (7am to 10pm) and a quiet location on the road above the walkway linking Kesgarh Sahib Gurdwara and Anandpur Sahib Fort. It's almost too quiet (and dark) walking home in the evening, though.

Pal Restaurant
INDIAN $

(mains ₹70-190, thalis ₹60-150; ⊙6am-midnight) Friendly Pal Restaurant, above Pal Sweetshop, is close to the bus station and serves good-value Indian cuisine, including local thalis. The sweets are tasty too. Turn left out of the bus stand, left again, and it's on your left.

ⓘ Information

About 2km from the centre, **Mata Nanki Charitable Hospital** (☑01887-230284; Ropar Rd; near Khalsa College) is a small but reputable general hospital run by a British-based charity.

ⓘ Getting There & Away

The bus and train stations are 300m apart on the main road outside town. Buses leave frequently for Chandigarh (₹100, two hours), Amritsar (₹190, 4½ hours) and Patiala (₹120, three hours).

Three daily trains go to Chandigarh (2nd class/AC chair ₹95/315, two to three hours) at 5.46am, 8.03am and 3pm. There's a 7.30am train to Amritsar (general ₹95, six hours). The overnight 14554 Himachal Express (sleeper/3AC/2AC ₹215/585/830, 7½ hours, 10.12pm) goes to New Delhi.

HARYANA

Though its creation as a separate state dates to a relatively recent 1966, when it was carved out from the post-Partition Indian state of East Punjab, this burgeoning region was the setting for several pivotal events in the history of northern India. Despite this, modern Haryana is home to very few sights that truly appeal to foreign tourists. Bordering Delhi to the west and northwest, with vast agricultural expanses and booming industrial hotspots, most of the state lies beyond the tourism radar.

Kurukshetra (Thanesar)

☑01744 / POP 964,200

According to Hindu legend, Kurukshetra (formerly Thanesar) was where Lord Brahma created the universe, and where Lord Krishna delivered his Bhagavad Gita sermon before the epic 18-day Mahabharata battle, an event commemorated by the Gita Jayanti (p213) festival. Given its religious and mythological significance, the town is mobbed by pilgrims, sadhus and educational tour groups, who vastly outnumber the few tourists.

English maps of the area are available at the ticket counter of the Sri Krishna Museum and are available for free with every purchased museum ticket. There's also a large map drawn on the wall just outside the museum ticket office.

Sights

Brahmasarovar HISTORIC SITE

FREE The focus of attention at Kurukshetra is the vast, sacred body of water that is Brahmasarovar, India's largest ceremonial tank. According to Hindu holy texts, the ghat-flanked tank was created by Lord Brahma. Sadhus (holy people) and pilgrims often crowd the ghats, particularly at dawn and dusk, while the ashrams lining the tank feature scenes from Hindu epics and walk-through models of sacred sites. There are also giant Hindu statues and small shrines on the central causeway that crosses the water.

Sri Krishna Museum MUSEUM

(Pehowa Rd; ₹30; ⊙10am-5pm) The Sri Krishna Museum features an impressive collection of sculptures, carvings and paintings, and a low-tech multimedia exhibition with dioramas, giant statues, surreal sounds and a walk-through maze. Look out for some rare exhibits, such as palm-leaf etchings from Orissa and excavated artefacts from ancient Indus Valley settlements. There's a simple canteen with alfresco seating in the museum gardens, where you can grab a snack (₹10 to ₹30) and some chai (₹10).

Sleeping & Eating

Yatri Niwas HOTEL $$

(☑01744-291615; Pipli-Jyotisar Rd; d from ₹2000; ❋) Fronted by a grassy lawn, this whitewashed standard-issue government complex has unimaginative but well-appointed rooms assuring adequate value for money, as well as service and security to match. Food (veg thalis ₹125, other mains ₹90 to ₹120) at the in-house restaurant is recommended, and day trippers can also step in for meals. The property is a five-minute walk north of Brahmasarovar.

❶ Getting There & Away

Local buses between Chandigarh (₹100, two hours) and Delhi (local/AC ₹145/255, four hours) stop at Pipli on the national highway, about 6km outside Kurukshetra. From here, shared autorickshaws (₹20) shuttle passengers between the bus stand and Brahmasarovar.

Sultanpur Bird Sanctuary

An easy day trip from Delhi, this small, 360-acre nature reserve (Indian/foreigner ₹5/40, camera/video ₹25/500; ⊙7am-4.30pm Wed-Mon) makes for a relaxing city getaway. It's far from spectacular, but for those who need a break from Delhi's traffic, noise and pollution, Sultanpur offers the chance to go for a gentle lakeside stroll, surrounded by nature, just 15km from Gurgaon.

More than 100 species of migratory birds, including Siberian cranes, greater flamingo and rosy pelican, join a host of resident species (white-throated kingfisher, white ibis, great egret) each year. The park is centred on a marshland lake encircled by a pleasant, largely tree-shaded, 3.5km-long nature trail. You may also spot nilgai (Asia's largest antelope) or the more slimline blackbuck grazing in the shallows.

Adjacent to the park entrance and set in landscaped grounds Rosy Pelican Tourist Complex (☑09873-741060; htcsultanpu1000@gmail.com; Gurugram Rd, d from ₹2020; ❋), operated by Haryana Tourism, features a mix of decent to pleasant rooms and can be a quiet and relaxed place to spend a night. Day trippers can eat at the in-house restaurant.

To get there, take the Delhi metro to Huda City Centre station then, from across the main road, take bus route 321 (labelled on the bus stop) to Gurgaon Bus Stand (₹10, 20 minutes); from there take a Farrukhnagar-bound bus to Sultanpur (₹15, 40 minutes). Alternatively, there's a prepaid autorickshaw stand right outside Huda City Centre metro station which quotes ₹300 for the one-way trip to the park; it's easy to flag down a passing auto for the return trip. Hiring a taxi for a day trip from Delhi will cost around ₹2000.

Kashmir & Ladakh

Best Places to Eat

➜ Alchi Kitchen (p263)

➜ Bon Appetit (p244)

➜ Falak (p285)

➜ Mughal Darbar (p278)

Best Places to Stay

➜ Stok Palace Heritage Hotel (p248)

➜ Young Beauty Star (p277)

➜ Nimmu House (p260)

➜ Nyerma Nunnery Guesthouse (p249)

➜ Hidden North Guest House (p259)

Why Go?

The state of Jammu & Kashmir (J&K) brings together three incredibly different worlds. Hindu Jammu and Katra, in the south, are the state's rail hubs and a major draw for domestic pilgrims. Muslim Kashmir is India's Switzerland, attracting local tourists seeking cool summer air, alpine scenery and Srinagar's romantic houseboat accommodation. And then there's the Himalayan land of Ladakh, which for most foreigners is J&K's greatest attraction. Its friendly, ethnolinguistically Tibetan people are predominantly Buddhist; their monasteries are set between canyons and peaks, while emerald-green villages nestle photogenically in highland deserts.

Kashmir is politically volatile, with July and August often the 'season' for shutdowns, demonstrations and curfews. Indeed, arguments over Kashmir's status caused three 20th-century wars. Ladakh is altogether different, a calm oasis where your main concern will be high-altitude acclimatisation. Note that Ladakh is entirely inaccessible by road outside the summer season.

When to Go
Leh

°C/°F **Temp**   Rainfall inches/mm

Apr–Jun Kashmir is in full bloom but overloaded with domestic tourists. Prices peak.

Jul–Aug Perfect for Ladakh; rain drenches Jammu. Pilgrims flood to Amarnath.

Dec–Mar Ski season at Gulmarg. Ladakh has festivals but no road access or tourists, so fly in.

Kashmir & Ladakh Highlights

① **Thiksey Gompa** (p249)
Visiting one of Ladakh's great gompas (monasteries), especially during a festival.

② **Markha Valley** (p252)
Experiencing the stark

magnificence of Ladakh with a hassle-free (and traffic-free) homestay trek.

③ **Srinagar** (p276)
Enjoying an amusingly caricatured Raj-type

experience relaxing on a deluxe Dal Lake houseboat.

④ **Tso Moriri** (p258)
Gawking at the mountain scenery backing this surreal blue lake.

⑤ Yapola Gorge (p263)
Discovering a thrillingly dramatic canyon en route to the breathtaking Sengge La.

⑥ Leh (p233) Escaping India's humid summer heat in the dusty medieval backstreets and Potala-style palace of this entrancing traveller hub.

⑦ Phuktal Gompa (p270)
Incredibly sited cliff-side monastery only accessible on foot past stunning scenery.

LADAKH

Spectacularly jagged, arid mountains enfold this magical Buddhist ex-kingdom. Picture-perfect gompas (Tibetan Buddhist monasteries) dramatically crown rocky outcrops next to fluttering prayer flags and whitewashed stupas, while prayer wheels spun clockwise release merit-making mantras. Gompa interiors are a riot of golden Buddhas and intricately colourful murals and home to red-robed monks. It's a little corner of Tibet marooned in the furthest reaches of India.

Though threatened by a rapidly increasing number of visitors, Ladakh has much to teach the West regarding ecological sustainability. Most Ladakhis are cash poor yet their traditional mud-brick homesteads are large and virtually self-sufficient in fuel and dairy products, and barley used to make *tsampa* (roast barley flour) and *chhang* (barley beer).

The walls of dramatic mountains that hem in Ladakh make for an unforgettable landscape, but be aware that road access requires crossing tortuous high passes, which close from around October to May.

History

Ladakh's (now-deposed) royal family traces its dynasty back 39 generations to AD 975. They took the name Namgyal (Victorious) in 1470 when their progenitor Lhachen Bhagan, ruling from Basgo, conquered a competing Ladakhi kingdom based at Shey. Although Ladakh had been culturally 'Tibetanised' in the 9th century, Buddhism originally arrived in an Indian form that's visible in ancient temple artisanship at Alchi. Over time, however, different Buddhist schools struggled for prominence, with the Tibetan Gelukpa order eventually becoming the majority philosophy after its introduction in the 14th century by Tibetan pilgrim Tsongkhapa.

Sengge Namgyal (r 1616–42), Ladakh's great 'lion king', gained riches by plundering gold reserves from western Tibet and reestablished a capital at Leh. Ladakh remained an independent kingdom until the 1840s when the region was annexed by the Jammu maharajas. The Namgyals eventually passed Leh Palace to the Indian Archaeological Survey and retired to their summer palace at Stok.

Ladakh is now a pair of subdistricts within Jammu and Kashmir. It's a culturally odd situation for a Tibetan Buddhist society to be under the governership of Muslim Kashmir and political tensions lie not far from the surface.

Over the last two decades the rapid influx of visitors has started to threaten Ladakh's remarkably well-balanced traditional society which, until very recently, was self-sufficient – an incredible achievement given the short growing season and very limited arable land in this upland desert. Ladakh and Zanskar are particularly vulnerable to climate change and dwindling glaciers across the region are threatening the region's water supply and therefore its future.

Climate

Ladakh's short tourist season (July to early September) typically sees mild to hot T-shirt weather by day and pleasant, occasionally chilly nights. Early July is great for flowers but August is better for crossing high passes, which can still be snowbound into mid-July. On higher treks night-time temperatures can dip below 0°C even in midsummer. By September, snow is likely on higher ground

---

TOP STATE FESTIVALS

Western Jammu & Kashmir has numerous Hindu pilgrimages. In Ladakh and Zanskar, Buddhist temple festivals abound; www.reachladakh.com has a detailed festival calendar.

Dosmoche (☉ Feb-early Mar) Buddhist New Year. Masked dances; effigies representing the evil spirits of the old year are burnt or cast into the desert in Leh, Diskit and Likir.

Matho Nagrang (☉ Feb-Mar) Monastery oracles perform blindfolded acrobatics and ritual mutilations at Matho Gompa.

Amarnathji Yatra (☉ Jul–mid-Aug; p281) Hindu pilgrims' mountain trek to Amarnath.

Chandi Mata Yatra (☉ Aug) Tens of thousands make the scenic two-day hike (or seven-minute helicopter ride) to Machail.

Ladakh Festival (☉ 3rd week Sep) Events include a carnivalesque opening parade, Buddhist dances, polo, music and archery, in Leh.

Losar (☉ Dec) Tibetan New Year is celebrated two months earlier in Ladakh.

although major passes usually stay open until October. Access roads close entirely in winter (often from November) when temperatures can fall below -20°C and most tourist infrastructure shuts down.

Ladakh enjoys sunshine an average of 300 days a year, but storms can brew suddenly. Although rare, heavy rain can cause devastating mudslides.

Leh

☑ 01982 / POP 46,300 / ELEV 3520M

Few places in India are at once so traveller friendly and yet so enchanting and hassle-free as mountain-framed Leh. Dotted with stupas and whitewashed houses, the Old Town is dominated by a dagger of steep rocky ridge topped by an imposing Tibetan-style palace and fort. Beneath, the bustling bazaar area is draped in a thick veneer of tour agencies, souvenir shops and tandoori-pizza restaurants, but a web of lanes quickly fans out into a green suburban patchwork of irrigated barley fields. Here, gushing streams and narrow footpaths link traditionally styled Ladakhi garden homes that double as charming, inexpensive guesthouses. Leh's a place that's all too easy to fall in love with – but take things very easy on arrival as the altitude requires a few days' acclimatisation before you can safely start enjoying the area's gamut of adventure activities.

◉ Sights

◉ Central Leh

★ Leh Palace   PALACE
(Map p240; Indian/foreigner ₹25/300; ☺ dawn-dusk) Bearing a passing similarity to the Potala Palace in Lhasa (Tibet), this nine-storey dun-coloured edifice is Leh's dominant structure and architectural icon. It took shape under 17th-century king Singge Namgyal but has been essentially unoccupied since the Ladakhi royals were stripped of power and shuffled off to Stok in 1846. Today the sturdy walls enclose some photo exhibition spaces and a small prayer room, but the most enjoyable part of a visit is venturing to the uppermost rooftops for the view.

Interesting structures ranged around the palace's base include the prominent Namgyal Stupa, the colourfully muralled **Chandazik Gompa** (Chenrezi Lhakhang; Map p240; Palace Ridge; ₹30; ☺ hours vary) and Soma Gompa,

---

❶ ALTITUDE PROBLEMS

Leh's altitude, above 3500m, means that many visitors will suffer from headaches and dizziness on arrival. Mild symptoms can be partly relieved by resting and drinking plenty of fluids. If that doesn't help, or if you have inadvertently overexercised, either breathe oxygen at the **Oxygen Bar** (Map p240; Tourist Office, Ibex Rd; examination ₹10, oxygen per 30min ₹50; ☺ 10.30am-7pm Mon-Sat, to 4pm Sun) or, as long as it's combined with rest, take one Diamox tablet morning and evening for three days. Tablets are available from **Het Ram Vinay Kumar Pharmacy** (Map p240; ☑ 01982-252160; Main Bazaar; ☺ 10am-9pm), among others.

Should symptoms become severe, you risk developing potentially fatal Acute Mountain Sickness (AMS). So don't ignore the signs. The condition is eminently treatable if you act promptly. The best option is to call English-speaking specialist **Dr Morup** (Map p234; ☑ 9419883851; Upper Tukcha Rd; consultation ₹1000; ☺ on call), who can assist you at your hotel and/or help you find appropriate treatment.

---

once home to the monastic printing press. Also nearby is the 1430 **Chamba Lhakhang** (Map p240; Palace Ridge), with its colourful three-storey Buddha and medieval mural fragments. Don't count on any of these being open though.

Leh Old Town   AREA
(Map p240) Behind Leh's central Jamia Masjid (p235), winding alleys and stairways burrow between and beneath a series of old mud-brick Ladakhi houses and eroded chortens. The alleys themselves are a large part of the attraction, but some buildings have been particularly well restored, notably the pair of 17th-century mansions now housing the interesting LAMO (p235) arts centre.

To get a taste, walk past the Dhyani Buddha–fronted building that houses Lala's Art Cafe (p244), turn hard left on an easily missed passageway beside a *rigsum gonbo* (represented by a trio of yellow, white and blue mini-stupas) and tunnel under a building past a magenta door marked 'Chamba Gonba' (normally locked). Wind up a rocky slope to LAMO and beyond to the **Old Town**

Leh

Tisseru
Stupa (900m)

YURTHUNG

Sankar Rd

Khaksal
Tisuru Rd

9

2

SANKAR

4   3

5

Rigsum
Gonbo
Shrine

Upper Karzoo La

Sankar La

21

Shanti Rd

12

1

11

24

16

CHANGSPA

KARZOO

18

Changspa
Pond

6

26   28

7

14

15

Snow Leopard
Conservancy
India Trust

25

Karzoo La

Karzoo
Pond

Upper Tukcha Rd

Gawaling La

22

Leopard La

Changspa Rd

OLD
TOWN

10   Dr Morup

23

Upper Tukcha Rd

19

13

Music School Rd

Main Bazaar

Main Tukcha Rd

27

Ibex Rd

Main Bazaar
(West)

Lower Tukcha Rd

17

8

See Central Leh Map (p240)

Fort Rd

Old Rd

Moti
Market

20

33

35

Men-Tsee-Khang (800m);
Sonam Norbu
Memorial Hospital (800m);
Long-distance
Shared-Taxi Park (1.4km);
Choglamsar (14km)

Friendship
Gate

Skalzangling Shared
Taxi Stand (1.5km);
(3km);
Spituk Gompa (5km);
Hall of Fame (3.5km)

30

31

BSNL   32

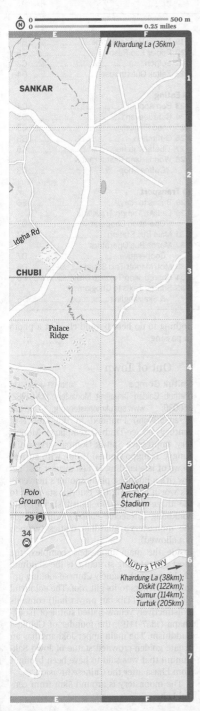

Cafe (Map p240; www.heritagehimalaya.org/cafe; Palace Ridge; tea ₹30-50; ⊙10.30am-5pm Mon-Sat) and the Leh Palace (p233) just above.

Jamia Masjid   MOSQUE
(Map p240; Main Bazaar) In the heart of Leh's market area, the first mosque on this site was built in 1666–67, sealing a political agreement between Ladakh's then ruler Deldan Namgyal and the Mughal emperor Aurangzeb. It was enlarged and rebuilt in 2018. Men only inside.

LAMO   NOTABLE BUILDING
(Ladakh Arts & Media Organisation; Map p240; ☑01982-251554; www.lamo.org.in; Old Town; ₹100; ⊙10am-5pm Mon-Sat) This arts-media trust occupies an adjoining pair of 17th-century Ladakhi mansions, one of which was the home of the *munshi* (king's secretary) and thus one of the finest homes of its era. Beautifully restored since 2006, it provides an interesting backdrop to often-fascinating art exhibitions, film screenings and author talks. A series of guided walking tours is being prepared.

Central Asian Museum   MUSEUM
(Map p240; ☑9419178483; www.tibetheritage fund.org; ₹100; ⊙10am-1pm & 2-6pm) One of Leh's most remarkable buildings, this tapered four-storey stone tower is a modern construction based on a historic Lhasa mansion and built on the site of an old caravan camp. The museum looks at Leh's role in Silk Road trade, with rooms focused on Ladakh, Chinese Turkestan and Tibet.

Tsemo Fort   CASTLE
(Map p240; ₹20; ⊙10am-6pm) Visible from virtually everywhere in Leh, 16th-century Tsemo (Victory) Fort is a defining landmark that crowns the top of Palace Ridge, though there's little to see inside apart from a tiny Buddhist shrine. Directly beneath, **Tsemo Gompa** (Map p240; ₹30; ⊙7.30am-6pm) consists of two little 15th-century temple buildings. One enshrines an 8m-tall gold-faced Maitreya. The other is an atmospheric *gonkhang*, home of protector deities.

◉ Greater Leh

Gomang Stupa   BUDDHIST MONUMENT
(Map p234) This large 9th-century white-washed stupa rises in concentric serrated layers flanked by numerous chortens. The charming, shady setting retains a refreshingly spiritual atmosphere and there are

Leh

several carved stones nearby, including one life-sized Buddha standing beneath a concrete shelter to the north.

Shanti Stupa   BUDDHIST MONUMENT

(Map p234; ◎dawn-9pm) Dominating Leh from a high, rocky ridge, this gigantic white spired pudding of a stupa was built between 1983 and 1991 by Japanese monks to promote world peace. The views over Leh are superb.

Sankar   AREA

(Map p234) For a charming wander, follow canal streams in the captivating yet relatively accessible area around little **Sankar Gompa** (Map p234; ₹30) and the one-room **geological museum** (LRMPS Museum; Map p234; ☑ 9419178704; www.ladakhrocksminerals.com; Sankar; ₹50; ◎10.30am-1pm & 2-7pm May-Aug). From here continue west to the nearby 11th-century Tisseru Stupa, a large, partly restored ruin esembling a stepped pyramid).

Tisseru Stupa   BUDDHIST MONUMENT

(Tisuru Rd, Upper Leh) **FREE** Ladakh's largest stupa is unlike anything else in the region – a giant, bulky mud-brick structure that looks like a half-built ziggurat (stepped pyramid). Were its interior staircases accessible rather than locked behind wooden doors, this 15th-century monument might be one of Leh's bigger attractions, but for now there's

nothing to do here beyond clicking a photo in passing.

◉ Out of Town

Spituk Gompa   BUDDHIST MONASTERY

(Pethub Galdan Targailing Monastery; ☑ 01982-260036; www.spitukmonastery.org; Spituk; ◎7am-6.30pm) Founded in the late 14th century as See-Thub (Exemplary) Monastery, impressive Spituk Gompa surveys the Sengye Tsangpo (Indus) Valley, with surreal views of jets landing at Leh airport just below (it's a Buddhist plane-spotter's heaven!). It's worth climbing the exterior stairway to the three-tiered *latho* (spirit shrine) and gonkhang (protector chapel), which holds the monastery's guardian deities (women not allowed).

Inside the main monastery complex, the most eye-catching structure is the Skudung Lhakhang, with vaguely Chinese-looking upturned corners to its gilt roof. The colourful old *dukhang* (Tibetan prayer hall) contains a distinctively yellow-hatted statue of Tsongkhapa (1357–1419), the founder of Gelukpa Buddhism. The main upper Jokhang has an ornate golden-crowned statue of Jowo Sakyamuni that was said to have been brought from Lhasa after the Chinese invasion.

The monastery is around 5km from central Leh.

Hall of Fame   MUSEUM

(Km428, Leh-Spituk Hwy; Indian/foreigner/camera ₹100/200/20; ⊙9am-1pm & 2-7pm) Two rooms of this extensive, well-presented museum look at Ladakhi history and culture. But mostly it commemorates the Indian Army's role in Ladakh, from helping with cloudburst relief in 2010 to the high-altitude battles fought with Pakistan during the 20th century.

🏃 Activities

Trekking & Jeep Safaris

The range of possible treks is phenomenal. The classic multiday homestay trek follows the delightful roadless Markha Valley (p252), though it's possible to do shorter variations that take in Rumbak, Yurutse and Skiu. Both are perfectly feasible without a guide and carrying only minimal baggage.

The most popular jeep safaris are to the high-altitude mountain lake of Pangong Tso and through the beautiful Nubra Valley (p254). You'll need an agency, if only to organise the permit (p256), which is required by foreign visitors for many border areas in northern Ladakh.

Agencies

Countless agencies offer trekking packages, jeep tours, rafting, biking and permit procurement. Few are systematically bad but many are very inconsistent. A deciding factor is often which agent happens to have a group leaving on the day you need to depart. Ask fellow travellers for recent recommendations and look along Changspa Rd and the eastern end of Upper Tukcha Rd where there is a high concentration of agencies.

We have found small operators **Higher Himalaya** (Map p240; ☏9419333393; www.higherhimalaya.com; Zangsti Rd), **Hidden North Adventures** (Map p240; ☏01982-256007, 9419218055; www.hiddennorth.com; LBA Shopping Complex, Zangsti Rd DB2; ⊙mid-Mar–mid-Oct) and **Shayok** (Map p240; ☏9419342346; www.shayok tours.com; Changspa Rd) to be honest, competitive and helpful with trekking information and as short-notice tour fixers. If you're making advance group bookings, reliable, well-established upper-market options include:

Gesar Travel (Map p240; ☏01982-251684; Hemis Complex 16, Upper Tukcha Rd)

Rimo Expeditions (Map p240; ☏01982-253348; www.rimoexpeditions.com; Zangsti Rd; ⊙5.30am-9pm Jul & Aug, 9am-5pm May, Jun & Sep)

Wild East Adventure (Map p240; ☏01982-257939; www.wildeastadventure.com; Hemis Complex, Upper Tukcha Rd)

Yama Adventures (Map p234; ☏9419178763, 01982-257833; www.yamatreks.com; Fort Rd)

Cycling

An exhilarating yet almost effortless way to enjoy the fabulous scenery around Leh is the Khardung La roll-down, where a jeep takes you and a bicycle up to the 'world's highest road pass' and gravity brings you back down. Potholes and streams in the uppermost 14km (above South Pullu army camp) mean it's a smoother ride to skip the top section and simply whizz down the last 25km to Leh on paved asphalt. Depending on group size, packages cost between ₹1500 and ₹2000 per person including bicycle hire, permits and support vehicle. The trip takes most of the day. Book one day ahead, as a permit is technically required for the upper section of the pass beyond South Pullu.

All agencies also rent mountain bikes (₹700 to ₹1000 per day).

Himalayan Bikers (Map p234; ☏9906989109, 9469049270; www.himalayan-bikers.com; Changspa; ⊙8am-9pm late May–mid-Sep)

Ladakh Cycling (Map p240; ☏9419563761; cyclinginladakh@gmail.com; Zangsti Rd; ⊙Jun-Oct)

Summer Holidays (Map p240; ☏9906985822; www.mtbladakh.com; Zangsti Rd)

Rafting & Kayaking

In summer numerous agencies offer daily rafting (p259) excursions through glorious canyon scenery. Experienced paddlers can follow in a kayak for around 50% extra. Expect to get wet. Relatively easy Phey–Nimmu (grade II, beginners, mid-July to late August) and more exciting Chilling–Nimmu (grade III, late June to early September) runs both cost around ₹1800 per person including equipment and lunch (bring extra drinking water). Reliable companies:

Luna Ladakh (Map p240; ☏9419977732; www.lunaladakh.com; Zangsti Rd; ⊙Jun-Aug)

Rimo Expeditions (Map p240; ☏01982-253348; www.rimoexpeditions.com; Zangsti Rd; ⊙5.30am-9pm Jul & Aug, 9am-5pm May, Jun & Sep)

Splash Adventures (Map p240; ☏9622965941; www.splashladakh.com; Zangsti Parking)

Wet'n'Wild (Map p234; ☏9622967631, 01982-255122; www.wetnwildexplorations.com; Fort Rd; ⊙mid-May–late-Sep)

Luna Ladakh will also add rafting as the finale to a three-day package including mountain biking (Spituk–Zingchen) and trekking (Zingchen–Chilling with homestays) costing ₹7000 per person in a group of five. Given enough interest, Wet'n'wild and Rimo offer group expeditions that descend the Zanskar River from Zangla (accessed via Padum) to Nimmu (three days rafting, three days travel).

Renowned British Himalayan river veteran Darren Clarkson-King runs full Zanskar raft packages with Pureland Expeditions (www.purelandexpeditions.com).

Mountaineering

Ladakh's most popular climb is 6121m Stok Kangri, the triangular snowcapped 'trekking peak' usually visible straight across the valley from Leh. Although accessible to those with minimal climbing experience, scaling its uppermost slopes requires ice axes, ropes, crampons, considerable fitness and an experienced guide. Preclimb acclimatisation is absolutely essential.

Permits are required (Indian/foreigner free/₹3150) and most easily arranged through an agency but you can also normally pick them up at base camp for an extra ₹200.

From Stok, the well-organised agency **Ladakh Mitra** (Map p240; ☏ 9596940169; www.ladakhmitra.com; 1st fl, Unit 17, Hemis Com-

plex, Upper Tukcha Rd; ⊙ 10am-7pm May–mid-Oct) runs a series of three tent camps en route, at Chaglamsar, Manakarmo and base camp, so you can ascend with minimal baggage. Assuming at least four in a group, four-day packages typically start at ₹18,000/22,000 for Indians/foreigners, including permits, food, sleeping, guide, climbing gear and transport. Climbing alone with a personal guide costs ₹27,000/30,000, and not much less for a group of two or three. Bring your own gloves, down jacket, waterproof trek boots, head torch and sunglasses.

Kids can learn to climb at the small bouldering-cafe **GraviT** (Map p240; www.facebook.com/GraviT.Leh; 2nd fl, Raku Complex, Fort Rd; climbing wall per hr ₹150; ⊙ 4-8.30pm), which also organises Sunday expeditions to local climbing spots near Shey plus the annual **Suru Boulder Fest** (www.facebook.com/Suru.boulder; ⊙ late Aug).

Meditation & Yoga

Various yoga, reiki and meditation places pop up each summer: look along Changspa Rd for fliers.

Mahabodhi Centre YOGA, MEDITATION
(Map p234; ☏ 9419542228, 01982-251162; www.mahabodhi-ladakh.org; Changspa Rd; ⊙ Mon-Sat May–mid-Sep) Offers drop-in meditation sessions (₹100 donation) at 6pm; pranayama breathing exercises at 11.15am; and hatha yoga classes (₹300) three times a day for various levels.

⭐ Festivals & Events

Spituk Gustor CULTURAL
(Spituk Gompa; ⊙ Jan) The most colourful traditional festival in the Leh area is held from the 26th to 28th of the 11th Tibetan month. The highlight is a series of *chaam* (masked dances), with the steeply raked steps behind the *dukhang* (Tibetan prayer hall) making a tailor-made amphitheatre.

🛏 Sleeping

Leh has dozens and dozens of charming family-run guesthouses and few options are dire, so don't panic if our suggestions are full. Booking ahead through online agencies is usually a bad idea as you'll likely pay double and room standards can vary significantly within each property. In winter the majority of accommodation closes down.

Try the back alleys either side of Upper Changspa for family-run budget places, Upper Karzoo for garden homestay-guesthouses

---

LEH – WATER & ECO-AWARENESS

Water is precious in Ladakh – those streams you see cascading beside virtually every lane aren't a sign of plenty but an elaborate network of irrigation channels that keep Leh from reverting to a dusty mountain desert. Anything you can do to save water is a positive step. Bucket washes save a lot compared to showers, and a few guesthouses offer traditional water-free Ladakhi long-drop toilets that recycle human waste into compost.

To save Leh from vanishing under a sea of plastic bottles, refills of purified, pressure-boiled water are provided for ₹7 per litre by environmental organisation **Dzomsa** (Map p240; Zangsti Rd; ⊙ 8am-10pm) 🌿. It also has an eco-friendly laundry service (₹95 per kg) and serves locally sourced *tsestalulu* (sea buckthorn) and apricot juices that are free of packaging.

around the ₹800 mark, and Upper Tukcha for slightly plusher family guesthouses costing around ₹1200 with en suite.

Many areas have a rash of new midrange hotels, mostly much alike and catering predominantly to Indian tourist groups. In many cases, other than the spontaneous provision of towels and toilet paper, rooms aren't much better than a good guesthouse.

Sankar and Yurthung areas are often idyllically peaceful but are a fairly long, dark walk home from the centre. Taxis cost ₹150 to ₹200 by day, but disappear quickly at night.

Central Leh

Saiman Guest House
GUESTHOUSE $

(Map p240; ☑01892-253161, 9419987555; off Upper Tukcha Rd; r ₹1000-1300, without bathroom ₹900; 🛜) This outwardly unremarkable family home is a great choice thanks to spacious, sparkling-clean rooms, parasol tables on the flower-edged lawn and a small guest lounge where travellers sit to chat and use the wi-fi over thermos flasks of cardamom tea. English-speaking host Shahida is a mine of local information.

Namgyal Guest House
GUESTHOUSE $

(Map p240; r ₹700, without bathroom ₹300-500) Backing onto the timeless Maney Tsermo stupas, this delightful budget guesthouse is run by ever-laughing Dolkar. She lives in the new annexe, where three en suite rooms have sit-down toilets and geyser showers. Rooms in the traditional Ladakhi main house share bathrooms; upstairs rooms are worth the extra for higher ceilings and more light.

Travellers' House
GUESTHOUSE $

(Map p240; ☑01982-252048; thetravellers house@gmail.com; Karzoo Lane; d ₹900-1400; 🕙May-early Oct; 🛜) Eight well-kept, nononsense guest rooms with geyser-equipped bathrooms and well-chosen art photography face the home of the inspiring, internationally minded family owners and their pet poodle. The nice garden and seating areas are a bonus. Ladakhi breakfasts available (from ₹150).

Kang-Lha-Chen
HOTEL $$

(Map p240; ☑01982-252144; www.hotel kanglhachen.com; Zangsti Rd; s/d ₹2950/4150; 🕙May-end Sep; 🅿🛜) Central, yet set around a peaceful garden-courtyard with seating beneath apricot trees, this longstanding favourite has old-fashioned but well-maintained rooms with excellent box-spring mattresses, Tibetan-style bedside tables and wicker-weave ceilings. The restaurant feels somewhat temple-like, and an oft-missed highlight is the delightful sitting room designed like an antique Ladakhi kitchen.

Almighty Guesthouse
GUESTHOUSE $$

(Map p240; ☑9419179501, 9419345817; Chulung; r ₹2000-2500; 🕙mid-Apr–Oct; 🖥🛜) This luxurious family guesthouse has six capacious rooms with standards better than most hotels (two have balconies). It's slightly hemmed in by bigger buildings but from the rooftop you can glimpse Stok Kangri, the palace and Shanti Stupa. There's patio seating in the small yard. It's next to the Alpine Hotel.

Indus Valley
HOTEL $$$

(Map p240; ☑01982-257575; www.theindusvalleyleh.com; Upper Chulung; s/d ₹10,880/11,520; 🖥🛜) New in 2018 is this top-end place in the centre of Leh combining traditional Ladakhi aesthetics with modern amenities. Rooms are fresh, contemporary and spotless, with glass-walled bathrooms and there's a small garden. Classic rooms are a bit bigger and premier rooms come with a balcony and bathtub. Unexpectedly, a climbing wall is planned.

Greater Leh

★Gangs-Shun
HOMESTAY $

(Map p234; ☑01982-252603, 9419218657; www. gangsshunhomestay.com; Upper Tukcha Rd; r ₹1200-1800, ste ₹1800; 🛜) With box-spring mattresses and modern bathrooms, the experience here is more comfortable than many midmarket hotels but retains a family feel, thanks to the charming English-speaking host Dr Morup (p233). There's a small library of Buddhist books, and oxygen or Diamox is available in case the altitude is getting to you. One family suite has its own kitchenette; two rooms have their own balcony.

Goba Guest House
GUESTHOUSE $

(Map p234; ☑01982-253670; gobaguesthouse@ gmail.com; Goba Lane; r ₹1500, without bathroom ₹500-800; 🅿🛜) There's a great spirit to the traditional main house, open year-round and topped with a prayer room and lovely rooftop panoramas. A more modern hotel-style block (open April to September) has 15 spacious en suite rooms. The garden is a veritable field from which homegrown organic vegetables form the mainstay of family-cooked dinners (book by 4pm).

KASHMIR & LADAKH LEH

Central Leh

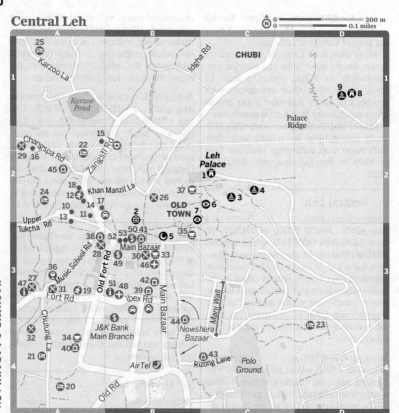

Gyalson Guest House
GUESTHOUSE **$**

(Map p234; ☑ 9622951748; gyalson.guesthouse@gmail.com; Changspa Rd; s/d ₹1300/1500, without bathroom ₹800/1000; ☎) Spick-and-span carpeted rooms in a new but traditionally styled family house with a prime location just behind Wonderland restaurant. The shared family lounge and parasol garden seating make it a sociable place. Great value.

Norzin Holiday Home
HOMESTAY **$**

(Map p234; ☑ 8800238511, 9419178751; Upper Tukcha Rd; d ₹1000, r without bathroom ₹800; ☎) A well-kept modern-traditional family home with views from the roof-shrine terrace, an enclosed garden and an amazing grapevine dominating the glassed-in lounge. Rooms are good quality for the price; room E is coveted for its balcony.

Solpon
GUESTHOUSE **$**

(Map p234; ☑ 9906994466, 01982-253067; tsewangsolpon@yahoo.com; Upper Changspa; d ₹1500, r without bathroom ₹600; ☒ Apr-Oct; ℗☎)

🖉 Even the simplest rooms are appealing, with geyser-heated water in shared bathrooms, while the plush, newer section is almost hotel standard, adorned with still lifes and beautiful landscape photography.

Zaltak Guesthouse
GUESTHOUSE **$**

(Zaltak Cottage; Map p234; ☑ 9797507201, 01982-252593; Gawaling Rd; dm ₹250, d ₹1200, r without bathroom ₹500-600; ℗☎) The old block here is an upgraded standard Ladakhi house with two clean budget rooms. The new back building has excellent-value en suite rooms with sitting areas, large beds and hotel-standard bathrooms.

Both buildings face a very pleasant garden that produces much of the food for family-prepared meals (ask by 4pm for dinner).

Haldupa Guest House
GUESTHOUSE **$**

(Map p234; ☑ 01982-251374; Upper Tukcha Rd; s/d ₹800/1000, r without bathroom ₹300-500; ☎) A couple of cheaper rooms are inside the owners' wonderfully authentic original

Central Leh

house that is dominated by a splendid shrine room. The rest are nicer, modern and spacious with decent bathrooms, hot showers and poplar-willow ceilings in a separate block overlooking the peaceful vegetable garden. Upper-floor rooms are best.

★ **Deskit Villa**   BOUTIQUE HOTEL **$$**
(Map p234; ☑01982-253498, 9419178998, 9622988836; www.deskit-villa.com; Sankar; incl breakfast s/d guesthouse ₹1700/2000, hotel ₹4325/4725; ✵⊗) Hidden behind a family garden guesthouse that's delightful in itself, this 'secret' eight-room boutique hotel is one of the best choices in Leh, with supercomfortable beds, a stupendous rooftop panorama and lots of public and garden space in which to unwind. The dining

room is designed like a traditional Ladakhi kitchen.

Lotus Hotel   HOTEL **$$**
(Map p234; ☑01982-257265; www.lotushotel.in; Upper Karzoo Lane; s/d ₹4000/4400; ⊗Mar-Nov; ⊛) Apart from the parasol tables out the front, you might think you'd arrived at a colourful Tibetan monastery as you enter this photogenic two-storey feast of Ladakhi detail.

The 19 rooms continue the theme, with ornately carved bedheads and *chokse* (low, colourfully painted tables). Mattresses are comfy, but some bathrooms are cramped. A great delight is sipping tea amid the rose bushes and apple trees in the paved garden that has fine views of Tsemo Fort.

Lha-Ri-Mo
HOTEL $$

(Map p234; ☑ 01982-253345, 9419178233; www.
lharimo.com; Fort Rd; s/d ₹2310/3255; ☺ May–
mid-Oct; P ☎) Magenta window frames set
in whitewashed walls create a magical mon-
astery-like aesthetic, enclosed in a delightful
willow-shaded lawn-garden. The restaurant
and neo-Tibetan lounge are also impressive.
The old-school guest rooms aren't quite as
delightful but they're neatly appointed with
brass-effect lamps and the odd wrought-iron
mirror.

Kunzang
BOUTIQUE HOTEL $$

(Map p234; ☑ 9419657123; www.hotelkunzang
leh.com; Western Changspa; r ₹2500; P ☎) The
Kunzang's 12 rooms have an understated
boutique quality, with fresh, pale decor, large
shower heads, excellent beds and fine linens.
Balconies look back across a stream towards
Shanti Stupa or forward to the budget guesthouse annexe, **Kunzang Guest House** (Map
p234; ☑ 962295623; kumzangguesthouse@
yahoo.co.in; d ₹400-700; P ☺).

Poplar Eco-Resort
RESORT $$

(Map p234; ☑ 01982-253518; www.eprladakh.
com; Shenam Rd; s/d ₹2800/3600; ☺ May-early
Oct) Lost in the birdsong of an overgrown or-
chard of apple, apricot and poplar trees, the
resort's 20 rooms come in pairs within well-
spaced bungalows, each sharing a verandah
with wicker chairs.

★Ladakh Residency
HOTEL $$$

(Map p234; ☑ 01982-258111, 9419178039;
www.ladakhresidency.com; Changspa Rd; s/d/ste
₹5900/7600/8785; ☺ mid-Apr–mid-Oct; ☎) Decorated with *thangka* (Tibetan cloth painting)
and Nicholas Roerich prints, this layered col-
lage of wooden balconies and marble floors
has proper king-size beds, bathrooms with
branded toiletries, and Stok Kangri views
from the terrace and many rooms. Furniture
is classily unfussy; kettles are provided; and
there's a working elevator.

★Gomang
Boutique Hotel
BOUTIQUE HOTEL $$$

(Map p234; ☑ 01982-253536; www.gomang
hotelleh.com; Upper Changspa; d/tr ₹8500/11,000;
☺ mid-Mar–mid-Nov; P ☎) ✐ Leh abounds
with new hotels, but the award-winning
Gomang stands out for the loving care of its
management, the gliding service and the at-
tention to detail. Boutique features include
Gomang-branded toiletries, in-room coffee
machines and rooftop sunbeds, but what re-
ally impresses are the swish yet homely pub-
lic spaces, from open terrace to cosy library.

Eating

From June to September, traveller cafes
abound, and European, Israeli and Chinese
options supplement curries, banana pan-
cakes, tandoori pizzas and Tibetan favourites.
Competition keeps standards generally high,
especially in the garden and rooftop restau-
rants of Changspa. Food options around
Main Bazaar get mixed reviews.

Most places close by 11pm in tourist sea-
son. From October to May, it's wise to assume
that almost none will open at all.

Central Leh

Ladakh Women's Café
LADAKHI $

(Map p240; Main Bazaar; mains ₹30-80; ☺ 10am-
6.30pm Tue-Sun) ✐ This tiny little upstairs
place run by a local women's group has a
local vibe and unbeatable rock-bottom pric-
es. Food is limited to a single lunch dish of
the day (*skiu* stew on Wednesdays and Sat-
urdays), so come early before the food runs
out. There are also snacks like cheese toast,
khambir (Ladakhi bread) and buckwheat
pancakes. Tea ₹10.

★Alchi Kitchen
LADAKHI $$

(Map p240; ☑ 01982-227129; Chutey Rantak, Old
Town; mains ₹180-250; ☺ 8am-9pm; ✐) This
branch of the Alchi restaurant offers the same
mix of traditional Ladakhi foods given a modern twist and served in contemporary, stylish
decor (with a fine rooftop). Order a *chutagi*
(traditional Ladakhi pasta stew) or stuffed
khambir (Ladakhi bread), followed by *phat-
ing* (apricots soaked in apricot juice). On Fridays you can get a *mokmok* (*momo*) platter
(including chocolate walnut!) for ₹300.

Unlike the Alchi restaurant, it's open year-
round, making it a good winter option.

Lamayuru Restaurant
MULTICUISINE $$

(Map p240; Fort Rd; mains ₹180-300; ☺ 7am-
10pm; ☎) Well run, reliable and good value,
this trusty standby is one place that we keep
coming back to for everything from Indian
curries (great *kadhai paneer*) and naan to Is-
raeli hummus and a big range of breakfasts.
It also sells Nepali yak cheese (₹1300 per kg).

Il Forno
ITALIAN, INDIAN $$

(Map p240; Zangsti Rd; mains ₹250-350; ☺ 10am-
11pm; ☎) Il Forno's rooftop offers remarkable views of the Leh Palace and Tsemo Fort

across Main Bazaar. Reliable for years, the menu covers many bases from sizzlers to lasagne, but its speciality remains the thin-crust wood-oven pizza (chicken tikka pizza!) simply smothered with cheese. There's also a fairly reliable supply of cold beer (₹250).

Penguin Garden   MULTICUISINE $$
(Map p240; www.penguin.co.in; Chulung; mains ₹160-270, half/whole tandoori chicken ₹300/600; ⊙8am-10.30pm; 🐾) It's well worth seeking out this slightly dusty garden restaurant of apricot trees. If the fresh-cooked tandoori chicken has run out (typical by mid-evening), there is still a world of cuisine to explore, alongside a bakery and cafe.

Tibetan Kitchen   ASIAN $$
(Map p234; ☑8492911940; off Fort Rd; mains ₹150-350) Local families tend to eat at home, but for a special treat this is one of the few tourist-area restaurants they are likely to come to, thanks to ever-reliable Chinese, tandoori (after 6pm), Indian and especially Tibetan cuisine. The chicken *thukpa* (Tibetan noodle soup) is beautifully balanced. Try the *sabagleb*, essentially a crispy circular pie with *momo* stuffing inside.

It's hidden away off a Fort Rd car park and has a dozen outdoor, partly shaded tables (candlelit at night) on a ground of pebbles. Reservations essential.

Chopsticks   ASIAN $$
(Map p240; ☑9622378764; Raku Complex, Fort Rd; mains ₹190-250; ⊙noon-10.30pm) This modern pan-Asian restaurant has built its solid reputation on quality noodle dishes, tasty (but not very spicy) Thai curries and soups. Enter via the outdoor terrace, raised above the melee of Fort Rd. Write your order on the menu.

✴ Changspa

Wonderland Restaurant & Coffee Shop   MULTICUISINE $$
(Map p234; ☑9622972826; pemawangchen67@gmail.com; Changspa Rd; mains ₹150-350; ⊙6.30am-10.30pm) Of several long-established rooftop restaurants on Changspa Rd, ever-popular Wonderland has neither the best view nor the snazziest decor but the food is consistently reliable, especially the Indian and Tibetan dishes (the owners are exiled TIbetans). The coffee and cakes are excellent; and the place opens well before most others, making it ideal when you want an early start.

LADAKHI FOOD

Ladakh's Tibetan favourites:

chhang – Ladakh's barley beer, available at rural homestays but not for general sale

momo – dumplings wrapped ravioli-style in thin pasta

namkin chai (nun chai in Kashmiri) – pink, salted milk tea (nimak chai) with added yak's butter; traditionally the butter is blended into the tea by vigorous use of a plunger in a long cylindrical churning vessel called a gurgur, causing the tea to be commonly nicknamed gurgur chai

namthuk – barley 'soup', like a thin porridge, that sometimes acts as a drink with meals

paba – pea-and-barley meal that is often dunked in tangtur (boiled vegetables in curd)

skyu – vegetable stew containing something like a barley version of Italian *orecchiette* (pasta 'ears')

tingmo (tee-mo) – steamed, unsweetened buns

thukpa – noodle soup

Food Planet   MULTICUISINE $$
(Map p234; ☑9837943385; Changspa Rd; mains ₹170-300; ⊙8am-11pm) A Russian–Indian couple has created a menu that really covers the globe. Expect a lot of the more interesting seasonal dishes to be unavailable (guacamole, Uzbek *shorba* soup) but the chicken breast with mango salsa is excellent. Plus lots of salads and all the usuals.

It's all served in an attractive upstairs room dressed like a lama in maroon and yellow and lit with long-hanging wicker lamps. Rooftop tables have fine views, and the chill-out zone is a popular (if semisecret) hang-out for low-key cocktails, beers and water pipes.

La Piazzetta   MULTICUISINE $$
(Map p240; ☑9419046476; Changspa Rd; mains ₹170-350, pizzas ₹270-380; ⊙9.30am-11.30pm mid-Apr–late Sep; 🐾) Candles, lanterns, muralled walls and an open fire (on colder nights) create a warm, dimly lit appeal that keeps this terrace restaurant buzzing well after most others have closed. The menu includes Indian, Ladakhi, Kashmiri, tandoori

STAKNA

Across the Indus River from the Leh-Manali Hwy, the 17th-century **Stakna Gompa** (₹30; ☺7.30am-6.30pm) rises like an apparition from the Indus Valley floor. Figures of the Bhutanese lama Zhabdrung Rimpoche show that the monastery belongs to the Drukpa school.

A taxi from Leh costs one way/return ₹1040/1350, but Stakna is best included in a multistop visit to Thiksey, Matho and other monasteries along the Leh–Manali Hwy. By public transport, take any vehicle along the Leh–Karu road and get off at Km449 for the road to Stakna Gompa: it leads north, crossing the Indus on a bridge decked with prayer flags.

and European dishes, pizza and a brave if rather un-Thai stab at green curry.

Café Jeevan — MULTICUISINE **$$**
(Map p234; Changspa Rd; mains ₹160-240; ☺8am-10pm Jul-Oct; 🛜🍴) Good for fresh juices, breakfasts, vegetarian Italian food, and especially for interesting, locally grown salads. There's a glass-walled kitchen, a cosy yet gently suave interior, and the covered roof terrace is ideal for catching sunset rays.

★**Bon Appetit** — MULTICUISINE **$$$**
(Map p234; ☎01982-251533; mains ₹280-400; ☺11am-11pm; 🛜) Hidden down unlikely footpaths south of Changspa Rd, classy Bon Appetit has far more finesse than most in Leh, so consider booking. Much on the eclectic menu has an Italian feel, but you'll also find good salads and tandoori grills. It's a great place to bring a date or for a sunset drink (beer ₹250) on the patio.

G-Kitchen — MULTICUISINE **$$$**
(Map p234; Changspa Rd; mains ₹300-470; ☺11am-11pm; 🛜) G-Kitchen is a definite notch above the competition in Changspa thanks to its stylish decor, airy terrace and its ambitious menu. Lamb dishes come with caramelised onion, mashed potato in a port tamarind sauce, or minced with apricot sour cream and harissa sauce.

🍸 Drinking & Nightlife

Leh sleeps early and doesn't have much of a drinking or nightlife culture. There are a couple of legal cocktail places plus a handful of unlicensed restaurants that bend the

rules by serving beer without putting it on the menu. Ask. For takeaway beer, there's the handy **Indus Wine Shop** (Map p240; Ibex Rd; beer ₹135; ☺9am-9.30pm); it closes on 'dry days' (8th, 15th and last days of the Tibetan month) as do all legal bars.

There are dozens of places serving espresso coffee. Top contenders include bookshop-cafe **Lehling** (Map p240; Main Bazaar; ☺9am-10pm; 🛜), old faithful Wonderland Restaurant & Coffee Shop (p243) and the charming but easily missed **Ja Khang** (Map p240; Main Bazaar West; coffee ₹70-110; ☺9.30am-8pm; 🛜), which is quieter than most. For historical ambience, unique Lala's Art Cafe is a delight, while **Brazil Café** (Map p240; Main Bazaar; coffee ₹80-150; ☺9am-7pm) uses fine beans and has hard-to-beat Leh Palace views.

★**Lala's Art Cafe** — CAFE
(Leh Heritage House; Map p240; ☎9596660593; www.tibetheritagefund.org; Old Town; coffee from ₹70; ☺9.30am-7.30pm Mon-Sat, 2.30-7.30pm Sun) Entered beside a 2000-year-old Dhyani Buddha stela, this tiny, traditional temple-like house was saved from demolition and immaculately restored in 2006. Stone steps lead to an atmospheric cafe with floor seating and a small art display; a ladder stairway continues to an open roof terrace. Serves coffee, *khambir* (Ladakhi bread) sandwiches (₹100), cakes (₹80), local juices, and fruit or mint lassis.

Lehchen — BAR
(Map p240; Music School Rd; cocktails ₹400, beer ₹250-300; ☺noon-11pm; 🛜) Leh's first decent cocktail bar also does very good tandoori meals (evenings only) and some semi-gourmet European meals, including lamb strips with potato and yak cheese (₹440) Other mains cost ₹300-450.

🛍 Shopping

Dozens of colourful little shops, street vendors and **Tibetan Refugee Markets** (Map p240; ☺10am-9pm May-Sep) sell wide selections of *thangkas*, Ladakhi hats, recently made 'antiques', heavy turquoise jewellery and Kashmiri shawls. Compare prices in the little family shops of **Nowshera Bazaar** (New Shar Market; Map p240), parallel to Main Bazaar, or the upmarket Tibetan outlet **Norbulingka** (Map p240; www.norbulingkashop.org; Rizong Complex; ☺9am-7.30pm Jul-Sep) 🍃.

Lehling and **Ladakh Bookshop** (Map p240; ☎9868111112; hanishbooks@yahoo.co.in; Main Bazaar; ☺9am-9pm) are particularly well stocked with postcards, novels, spiritual works and books on Ladakh, Kashmir and Tibet. The latter has a cafe.

Main Bazaar has several excellent outdoor-equipment stores. Some, including **Venture Ladakh** (Map p240; ✆9419983077; www.ventureladakh.in; Changspa Rd; ⊙9am-9pm Jun-Sep), rent climbing and trekking gear.

Jigmat Couture　　　CLOTHING
(Map p240; ✆9697000344, 01982-255065; www.jigmatcouture.com; Tsaskan Complex, Main Bazaar West; ⊙10.30am-7.30pm Mon-Sat, 2-7.30pm Sun) Ladakh's first home-grown fashion house uses local design as starting inspiration and sources much of its raw material from nomadic herders. This is the kind of cool ethnic clothing you could actually wear back home.

ⓘ Information

INTERNET ACCESS
Almost every cafe, restaurant and guesthouse in Leh offers free wi-fi but electricity supplies are patchy and connections come and go.

MEDICAL SERVICES
Men-Tsee-Khang (✆01982-253566; www.men-tsee-khang.org; consultation ₹100; ⊙9am-1pm & 2-5pm Mon-Fri, plus 1st & 3rd Sat of month) Charitable foundation with an Amchi (Tibetan herbal medicine) centre and dispensary. Consultations available without appointment.
Sonam Norbu Memorial Hospital (✆01982-253629) Leh's best hospital, with a separate 20-bed tourist ward and ambulance service.

MONEY
There are numerous moneychangers on Changspa Rd, Upper Fort Rd and around Main Bazaar. **Paul Merchant** (Map p240; Main Bazaar; ⊙9.30am-8pm) is open long hours, though rates are better and commissions lower at **J&K Bank** (Map p240; Ibex Rd; ⊙10am-2pm & 2.30-4pm Mon-Fri). ATMs are widespread, with many on Main Bazaar. The **SBI ATM** (Map p240; Main Bazaar; ⊙24hr) has the lowest charges. On rare occasions almost all Leh's ATMs have been known to temporarily stop functioning; it's wise to keep a stock of cash available.

TELEPHONE
Inexpensive SIM cards are available from **AirTel** (Map p240; off Main Bazaar; ⊙10am-5.30pm) and **BSNL** (Map p234; Main Bus Station; ⊙10am-1.30pm & 2.30-5pm Mon-Sat) for use within Jammu and Kashmir, but be aware that coverage in Ladakh outside Leh, Alchi and Lamayuru is minimal on AirTel. Application requires two photographs plus photocopies of both passport and visa, and BSNL also requires photocopy of a local's ID and telephone number (ask your guesthouse owner).

TOURIST INFORMATION
Tourist office (Map p240; ✆01982-257788; Ibex Rd; ⊙9am-7.30pm Mon-Sat, 10am-4pm Sun) Helpful with festival dates and bus timetables.
Mantra Travel Lounge (Map p240; ✆9419219783; www.facebook.com/mantrathetravellounge; Raku Complex, Fort Rd; ⊙10am-9.30pm; 🕾) A youthful cafe-style alternative,

---

THE ELUSIVE SNOW LEOPARD

Much celebrated but rarely seen, the snow leopard is one of Ladakh's most iconic mammals. There are thought to be less than 300 left, and possibly as few as 100.

Tourism-related campaigns to save the animal and its ecosystem have been relatively successful over the last decade, notably by persuading villagers that the leopards can be a boon rather than a threat to their livelihoods.

The **Snow Leopard Conservancy India Trust** (Map p234; ✆01982-257953; www.snowleopardhimalayas.in; Leopard Lane, Leh; ⊙9.30am-5pm Mon-Fri) 🖉 supports around 150 homestays in snow-leopard habitat across Ladakh and Zanskar and is a fantastic resource for travellers heading off the beaten track. The homestays contribute 10% of their income to a community wildlife fund and allow the conservancy to fund an insurance program that repays villagers if one of their yaks is killed by a snow leopard.

Many of the homestays are great bases for leopard-spotting, especially in places such as Rumbak, Phyang, Uley (9km from Yangthang in Sham) and the Rong region (between Upshi and Tso Moriri).

In Leh, snow-leopard-watching tours are operated by the **Ladakhi Women's Travel Company** (Map p240; ✆01982-257973, 9469158137; www.ladakhiwomenstravel.com; Unit 22, Hemis Complex, Upper Tukcha Rd; ⊙10am-6pm), **Snow Leopard Quest** (✆9419344761; www.snowleopardquest.in) 🖉 and Hidden North Adventures (p237) among others. February and March is when the big cats follow their prey (ibex and blue sheep) to lower altitudes, and the snowy terrain at this time makes their tracks easier to spot.

designed as an info and exchange centre; meet fellow travellers or use free wi-fi.

Noticeboards at Mantra, outside Dzomsa (p238), in agencies and pasted over town have adverts for tours, treks and activities.

🛈 Getting There & Away

AIR

Flights into Leh are dramatically scenic (be sure to get a window seat), but can be cancelled at short notice during bad weather. Almost all flights fly early morning as high winds often blow up in the afternoon, making landing difficult in the steep, mountain-sided valley.

Jet Airways, Air India and GoAir fly to Delhi; the former two use Delhi's Terminal 3 which is where international connections leave from, while GoAir uses nearby Terminal 2.

Air India (Map p240; ☑ 01982-258595; www. airindia.in; Main Bazaar; ⊙ 6am-noon) Flies to/ from Srinagar (Wednesdays) and Jammu (thrice weekly).

GoAir (www.goair.in) Flies daily to Jammu and to Srinagar but not back, as part of Mumbai–Leh–Srinagar–Mumbai and Delhi–Leh–Jammu–Delhi loop flights.

Jet Airways (Map p240; ☑ 01982-257444; www.jetairways.com; NAC Complex, Main Bazaar; ⊙ 10.30am-5pm Mon-Sat) Offers one-ticket connections to Kathmandu and London.

BUS

The **main bus station** (Map p234) is 700m south of the town centre via the stairway of Kigu-Tak bazaar from Friendship Gate.

MOTORCYCLE

Touring Ladakh by motorcycle has become a major fad in the last few years. Leh has countless rental companies, especially along Music School Rd and Changspa Rd, with more than 8000 bikes reckoned to be available, yet in June (peak Indian holiday season) there may still be excess demand.

Hiring an Enfield Bullet typically costs ₹1400/1600 per day for a 350/500cc; an Enfield Himalayan is much the same. A 'Scooty' (moped) is much easier to handle for short day trips outside Leh and costs just ₹800.

You'll need to show your licence (though a few agencies will quietly rent to unlicensed riders) and leave some sort of ID.

Carry spare fuel for longer trips: Ladakh's only petrol stations are at Leh, Choglamsar, Serthi (2km from Karu), Diskit (opening unreliable),

BUSES FROM LEH

Unless noted, departures are from the main bus-station area. Some services depart earlier in winter. Durations very approximate.

DESTINATION	FARE (₹)	DURATION (HR)	FREQUENCY
Alchi	107	2¼	8am & 4pm
Hemis Shukpachan (A)	131	4	2pm Mon, Wed & Sat (returns 8.30am)
Kargil (C)	400	8-10	5am
Keylong (D)	485	14	4.15am
Lamayuru	195	5	9am (or use Chiktan, Fokha, Kargil or Srinagar buses)
Likir Gompa	80	2	4pm (returns 7am)
Matho	30	50min	4.40pm
Ney (via Basgo)	95	2	4pm (returns 7.30am)
Phyang	35	45min	7.30am & 2pm
Sakti & Chemrey	50	1¾	8.30am, 2.30pm, 3.30pm & 4.30pm (returns 7.30am, 8am, 9am & 3pm)
Saspol	90	2	3pm (returns 7.30am)
Srinagar (B)	1203	18	2pm
Stakna	41	40min	4.30pm (returns 8.45am)
Thiksey	30	40min	8.30am
Tia & Timishgan (A)	143	4	1pm (returns 8am)

(A) Ladakhi Bus Operators Cooperative (LBOC; ☑ 01982-252792); (B) J&K SRTC (☑ 01982-252085); (C) Kargil Bus Operators Union; departs from the southeast corner of the **polo ground** (Map p234); buy tickets the afternoon before departure from driver; (D) HRTC.

All other services are local minibuses, mostly working with the **Mazda Bus Operators' Cooperative** (Map p234; ☑ 9906995889); no prebooking.

Padum (unreliable), Phyang junction, Khalsi, Wakha and Kargil.

SHARED JEEP & SHARED TAXI

Shared transport leaves from three places.

➡ From the **Long-distance Shared-Taxi Park** (Bamboo Ghat, Leh-Choglamsar Rd), next to a large white stupa, 1.5km southeast of the main petrol pump:

Kargil (per seat ₹1000, front seat ₹1200, seven hours) Departures 7am to 10am.

Manali (front/middle/back seats ₹3000/2500/2000, 19 to 22 hours) Departures 4pm to 6pm.

Srinagar (front/back seats ₹2500/2000, 15 hours) Departures 4pm to 6pm.

➡ From the **stand** (Map p234) at the entrance to the polo ground:

Nubra Valley Most jeeps to Diskit (₹400) and Sumur depart around 6am but we have found cars here as late as 3pm. Book a seat the afternoon before if possible. Remember that foreigners need a permit. Possibly also jeeps for other Nubra destinations.

➡ From the **Old Bus Stand** (Map p234), at the southern end of Moti Market:

Indus Valley Minibuses depart frequently to Choglamsar (₹20). Change there for Thiksey, Shey, Karu, Matho and Stok.

Spituk Take a shared minivan (₹10) to Skalzangling near the airport and change.

TAXI & CHARTER JEEP

Given irregular bus services, chartering a vehicle makes sense for visiting rural Ladakh. Fares are set by the **Ladakh Taxi Operators Cooperative** (Map p240; ☏ 01982-252723; www.ladakhtaxi union.com; Ibex Rd; ☺10am-1pm & 2-4pm), which publishes an annually updated booklet (₹30), sold at its office next to the **Central Taxi Stand** (Map p240; Ibex Rd). The great news is there's no haggling, though booking via a small local agency can sometimes get a minor discount (and a reliable driver).

We quote the lowest standard rates, ie for taxi-vans or Sumo charter jeeps. Prices are 5% higher for Xylo, Scorpio and Qualis vehicles, 10% higher for Innova and Aria. Rates assume reasonable photo and visit stops; longer waits are officially chargeable (per hour/half-day/full day ₹290/1200/2390). Extra overnight stops add a further ₹350.

Requesting unplanned diversions from the agreed route once underway can cause unexpected difficulties, so plan carefully.

Taxi-union regulations mean you can't hire a single vehicle to take you from Leh to Zanskar or Srinagar; you'll have to change vehicles and drivers in Kargil.

DESTINATION	FARE ONE WAY (₹)	FARE RETURN (₹)
Alchi	2013	2616
Chilling	3149	4174
Hemis	2416	3138
Lamayuru	3903	5047
Likir	1703	2214
Phyang	773	1004
Shey	422	548
Thiksey	663	867

Note: Combining destinations reduces the total price, eg Leh–Shey–Thiksey–Hemis–Stok–Leh costs ₹2710.

Longer one-way chartered fares include to Keylong (₹16,650), Kargil (₹7130) and Srinagar (₹14,120). For a total list of fares see www.ladakh taxiunion.com.

❶ Getting Around

Leh airport is 4km south of Leh centre. A taxi transfer costs ₹400.

Leh's little microvan taxis charge from ₹100 per hop. Flagging down rides rarely works; to make arrangements go to a taxi stand, most centrally at **Zangsti** (Map p240; Zangsti Parking), **Moti Market** (Map p234; Old Bus Stand) or the central taxi stand near the tourist office.

Around Leh – Southeast

☏ 01982

The main day trips around Leh are the monastery villages of the Indus Valley. You can combine several of the destinations to make a full-day taxi trip, or visit one or two as part of a longer jeep excursion to Pangong, Tso Moriri or Nubra.

The most popular choices are Shey, Thiksey and Hemis, but you can avoid the crowds by picking lesser-known villages like Matho and Sakti.

❶ Getting There & Away

It's a great idea to charter a taxi (or rent a scooter) and combine a series of villages in a day-trip loop. Taxi prices are fixed, and you can see in two days what might take a week by bus. For example, a Leh–Shey–Thiksey–Hemis–Stok–Leh taxi tour costs ₹2710.

Although a few overcrowded buses still run from Leh to certain Indus Valley villages, timings can make it impossible to return the same day. Many locals take shared taxi-vans from Leh's old bus stand to Choglamsar, switching there for Stok, Thiksey, Shey or Karu.

Stok

POP 1640 / ELEV 3490M

Across the valley from Leh, Stok's main drawcards are its 19th-century royal palace, its collection of traditional Ladakhi houses and its role as a possible starting point for hikes to Rumbak and for climbing Stok Kangri (p238). Stok also makes a quiet alternative to Leh as a Ladakh touring base thanks to its small but excellent choice of accommodation.

Stok's primary attraction is its three-storey **palace** (☑ 01982-242003; ₹70; ⊙ 9am-1pm & 2-6.30pm May-Oct). A smaller and more intimate version of Leh Palace, it is the summer home of Ladakh's former royal family, but it also houses a museum. Cross the village to **Gyab-Thago Heritage House** (☑ 9622966413; Village Rd; donation ₹100; ⊙ 10am-5pm May-Sep), a fabulously maintained historic home with original furnishings and fittings; for entry ask at the homestay next door.

The easiest way to travel between the two is on a 5km loop via the Trekking Point, passing modest Stok Gompa, which sits beneath a gleaming 21m-tall golden Buddha statue that's visible for kilometres.

🛏 Sleeping & Eating

Gyab-Thago Homestay　　　　GUESTHOUSE $
(☑ 9419218421; www.ladakhmitra.com; r without bathroom incl half board per person ₹1100; ⊙ May-Sep) Thoroughly traditional but markedly more comfortable than many homestays, Gyab-Thago's rooms are airy and clean, sharing a spick-and-span bathroom. Meals in the impressive Ladakhi kitchen–dining room are so authentic that groups come here from Leh specially for the experience, though you won't get quite as full a spread if you pay standard homestay rates.

The building is on the east side of the valley, signed 2km north of the Trekking Point. Call ahead as rooms can be booked by climbing groups.

★ **Stok Palace Heritage Hotel**　　　HERITAGE HOTEL $$$
(☑ 9622968709,　　9419279944; www.stok palaceheritage.com; Stok Palace; s/d incl half board from ₹14,000/14,850, cottages per room/cottage ₹13,825/23,960; ⊙ palace rooms May-Sep; ➄ ❄) How often do you get the chance to bed down in a genuine, functioning Himalayan royal palace? The six suites of old rooms here have been stylishly redecorated with modern bathrooms, but maintain plenty of traditional design features, while the remarkable 'Queen's Room' (single/double ₹20,400/23,600) retains brooding 200-year-old original murals. You might even get to have tea or dine with the king during your stay. There's also a trio of exclusive, modern Ladakhi-style cottages in the Chulli Bagh (Apricot Garden) in the village below. Each cottage has two bedrooms with a shared lounge and underfloor-heated bathroom and *bukhari* (wood-fired ovens) for winter heating (open year-round).

ℹ Getting There & Away

From Leh's old bus stand, shared taxis run to Choglamsar, where you can switch to a Stok-bound minivan (₹30 to ₹50 per seat, ₹300 per vehicle). Vans leave Stok for Leh when full – typically once or twice an hour – from the Trekking Point using Main Rd. A taxi from Leh costs ₹575/745 one way/return. Add on Stakna and Matho for a total ₹1890 day trip.

Matho

POP 1240 / ELEV 3485M

Matho's large Sakya Buddhist **monastery** (☑ 01982-246085; www.mathomuseumproject. com) is perched above the bucolic village with dreamy views across the Indus Valley's patchwork of emerald-green fields and desert-mountain horizons. The gompa has a fine museum and an unusual protector chapel whose floor is submerged under 15cm of grain.

During the famous festival, Matho Nagrang (p232), Matho monastery oracles perform daring acrobatics while effectively blindfolded, 'seeing' only through the fearsome 'eyes' painted on their chests. They also engage in ritual acts of self-mutilation and make predictions for the coming year. The festival is on the 14th and 15th days of the first Tibetan lunar month.

Shey

POP 2490 / ELEV 3240M

Shey's primary historical sight is the 17th-century Royal Palace, recently restored but essentially empty except for the palace **temple** (Shey Palace; ₹30; ⊙ 6am-6.30pm) and its stunning 16th-century Buddha statue. Clamber up the extensive castle ruins above the palace ridge for fabulous valley views.

Around 200m back towards Leh from the palace approach lane, five ancient **Buddha carvings** (Km459, Leh-Manali Hwy) hide on a dangerous corner next to the Km459 road marker.

About 1km east of Shey, the unpaved Arya Avaloketashora Monastery Rd leads up for 2km past dozens of ancient, photogenic whitewashed stupas, making a nice detour if you have time.

Although a few public buses run directly from Leh (₹30, 40 minutes), locals generally take shared taxi-vans to Choglamsar (₹20) and switch to a second van there.

From Leh, you can combine a taxi trip to Shey with Thiksey (around ₹800 return).

Thiksey

POP 2490 / ELEV 3260M

Glorious **Thiksey Gompa** (☑ 01982-267011; www.thiksey-monastery.org; admission ₹30, video ₹100; ⊙ 6am-1pm & 1.30-6.30pm, festival Oct/Nov) is one of Ladakh's biggest and most recognisable monasteries, photogenically cascading down a raised rocky promontory. At its heart, the main *dukhang* (prayer hall) oozes atmosphere, and a Maitreya temple contains a giant future Buddha who wears an exquisitely ornate crown. More obviously ancient are the *gonkhang* and the tiny old library up on the rooftop (often closed).

The Thiksey entrance ticket includes entry to a fascinating **museum** (⊙ hours vary) – it's hidden beneath the monastery restaurant so ask the manager for the key.

Dozens of monks gather for chanted prayers in the assembly hall between 6am and 7.30am most days, and visitors are welcome, though the fascinating ceremony can feel overwhelmed by the numbers of onlookers.

🛏 Sleeping & Eating

To be ready for the start of morning prayers, some visitors stay in the plain **monastery guesthouse** (r ₹1200, without bathroom ₹800; 🛜) or the more comfortable monastery-owned **Chamba Hotel** (☑ 01982-267385, 9419178381; www.thiksay.org; Km454, Leh-Karu Hwy; s/d ₹2510/3310; 🛜) at the base of the gompa hill. There are also several homestays in the village.

★ Nyerma Nunnery Guesthouse
GUESTHOUSE $

(The Taras; ☑ 9906985911; www.ladakhnuns.com; Nyerma village; r incl half board per person ₹1100; ⊙ May-Sep; 🛜) 🌱 Run by Buddhist nuns and Dutch volunteers, this wonderful six-room getaway attracts longer-stay guests who want to unwind in a calm, meditative environment. The comfortable and stylish accommodation has a fascinating setting

amid the 1000-year-old chortens of Ringchen Zangpo's ancient university, and there are great walks to the nearby fortlike *latho* (local deity shrine) or to the meditation caves on the hillside behind the guesthouse.

The guesthouse is 2km east of Thiksey, 1.2km north of the Leh-Karu Hwy at Km452 by Lazeez Restaurant (nearly halfway to Stakna). A taxi to/from Leh costs ₹600.

★ Café Cloud
MULTICUISINE $$$

(☑ 9419983021, 01982-267100; Km453, Leh-Karu Hwy; mains ₹250-575; ⊙ 11am-10pm end May-Sep; 🛜) Hidden behind adobe walls, 1km from Thiksey, this upmarket garden restaurant is essentially the only choice for quality European food east of Leh. Dishes include pan-seared basa fish, Thai curry, an Indian combo of the day and Friday- and Saturday-evening tandoori dishes.

ℹ Getting There & Away

To reach Thiksey from Leh, hop on a shared taxi-van to Choglamsar (₹20) and switch there to another eastbound vehicle (₹20, 20 minutes). Steps lead steeply up to the monastery, or those with their own transport can take the paved road that curves 1.5km up to the gompa main entrance.

A taxi from Leh costs around ₹800 return, including a stop at Shey.

Hemis

POP 350 / ELEV 3670M

Unlike most Ladakhi monasteries, the 17th-century **Hemis Gompa** (www.drukpa-hemis.org; ₹100; ⊙ 8am-1pm & 2-6pm) is

Around Leh

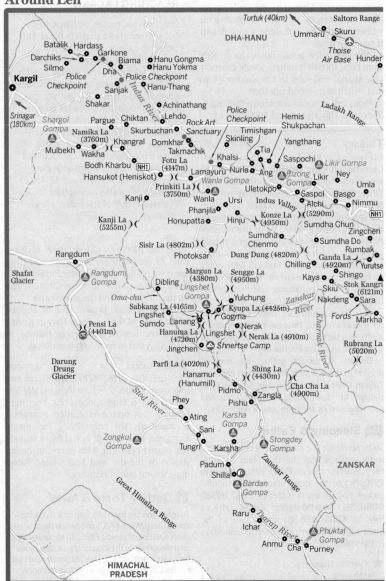

hidden in a cliff-backed valley rather than on top of a crag, meaning it only reveals itself at the last minute. The spiritual centre of Ladakh's Drukpa Buddhists, it's arguably Ladakh's most famous Buddhist monastic complex. The central courtyard and main temple buildings are impressive, the museum is the best in Ladakh, and there's plenty more to explore amid the atmospheric upper shrines. It is also the site of the Hemis Tsechu Festival, a celebration of the birthday of the great Tibetan 'saint' Padmasambhava (Guru Rinpoche). With three days of masked dancing, much of which

concrete stairway up to **Gotsang Hermitage** (⊙ dawn–dusk). Allow nearly an hour for the trip up, half that back. The hermitage's main shrine is the mountain cave in which Tantric master Gyalwang Gotsang (1189–1258) meditated. He was the enlightened Tibetan lama who first charted the pilgrim path around Mt Kailash and to whom Ladakh's Drukpa Buddhists cast back their lineage.

Near the main monastery, the compact and timeless Hemis village is also worth a stroll. An extraordinarily long series of mani walls (Tibetan stone walls with sacred inscriptions) descends further towards Karu, passing an octagonal stupa-shaped building built for the 2016 Hemis Mela festival.

The excellent-quality paved road from Stakna to Hemis makes for a good mountain-bike ride.

Taxis run to Hemis from Leh (one way/ return ₹2416/3140), though you'll get better value as part of a multistop trip.

You can get to Karu by shared taxi from Choglamsar (₹50). From Karu, Hemis is 7km up a desert road (one way/return taxi ₹300/600, including waiting time). If you can find one, shared taxis (or paid hitchhikes) cost ₹70.

Chemrey & Takthog

POP 6920 / ELEV 3660M

Less popular with travellers than Thiksey but every bit as spectacular, **Chemrey Monastery** (Thekchhok Gompa; Km7, Karu-Pangong Rd; museum ₹50; ⊙ museum 8.30am-1pm & 2-6pm) sits high on a dramatic hillock above waving fields of ripening barley. It's the perfect Ladakhi postcard view.

Around 3km further north, past a ruined **dzong** (Km1.5, Wari La Rd, Sakti) FREE and at the third of three junctions, a road leads towards the Wari La pass through Sakti, a charming village of whitewashed chortens and hillside chapels. The most famous pilgrimage site here is the meditation cave of Buddhist saint Padmasambhava at **Takthog (Dakthok) Gompa** (Wari La Rd, Sakti; ₹50; ⊙ festival Jul).

The charming **Solpon Homestay** (☑ 9906304067; Km2, Wari La Rd; s/d incl half board from ₹1000/1500; 🖧), 2km from Takthog Gompa, is an excellent choice with views of Sakti Fort while the area's best hotel is **Sakti Villa** (☑ 01982-251063; www.saktivilla.com; Km4, Wari La Rd; s/d incl half board ₹3000/3500; 🖧), 300m before Takthog. There's no accommodation in Chemrey.

retells the story of Padmasambhava's life, the main event is held on the 10th and 11th days of the fifth lunar month.

To escape the tourist crowds, stroll beyond the new school construction to a group of white chortens, then take the streamside footpath, finally swinging west to take the

TREKKING IN LADAKH & ZANSKAR

Bargain-value, thrillingly scenic treks are the best way to take you into Ladakh's magical road-less villages, through craggy gorges and across stark, breathless mountain passes flapping with prayer flags. When the rest of the Himalaya is drenched in monsoon rains, Ladakh's weather is at its very best.

Seasons

The main trekking season is from late June to early September, though in the Markha and Sham areas routes can be feasible from May to early October. Late August is usually prefera-ble for trails with significant river crossings due to lower water levels. Although you'll need to fly in, February and March are also growing in popularity as a time for ornithologists and espe-cially for those wanting to spot ibex and the rare snow leopard.

Preparation

Most trekking routes start around 3500m, often climbing above 5000m, so proper acclimati-sation is essential to avoid Acute Mountain Sickness (AMS). Other tips:

➡ Consider prebooking a jeep transfer back from your finishing point.

➡ Carry a walking stick and backed sandals for wading rivers.

➡ Bring water-purification supplies.

Horse Treks

At these altitudes, carrying heavy packs is much more exhausting than many walkers antici-pate. For wilder routes, engaging packhorses reduces the load and the accompanying horse-person can often double as a guide. Agencies will very happily arrange all-inclusive packages with horses, guides, food and (often old) camping gear. If you're self-sufficient and patient it's often possible to find your own horseperson from around ₹700 per horse or donkey per day. Note that you will almost always need to engage more than one horse and you'll have to pay for any extra days needed for them to return to the starting point. During harvest season (Au-gust) availability drops and prices rise.

Homestay Treks

Almost all rural villages along well-trodden trekking routes offer very simple but wonderfully authentic homestays. The cost is typically fixed at ₹1000 per person (less in Zanskar), includ-ing simple meals that are often taken in the traditional family kitchen. Mud-brick rooms gen-erally have rugs, blankets and solar-battery electric lamps. Having your own sleeping bag is an advantage but not strictly necessary.

Chemrey and Takthog are short diversions off the Karu–Pangong road and are generally visited as add-ons to a two-day Pangong jeep excursion. Alternatively, you can visit both monasteries as a day trip from Leh by taxi (around ₹2500 return) or as an overnight add-on to a Hemis trip.

Markha Valley

Ladakh's most popular trekking route fol-lows a straightforward and scenically glori-ous route through traditional villages in the roadless Markha Valley before finally climb-ing to cross the Kongmaru La (5260m). A plethora of homestays every hour or two, all charging ₹1000 per person including break-fast, dinner and a packed lunch, means you

don't need to carry much equipment or even food. Having a guide/translator adds to the homestay experience but isn't entirely nec-essary if you have a good map and a decent sense of direction.

Nimaling has no village but a camp of pre-erected tents charges ₹1200 per head including meals. Warm clothes for the night here (at 4850m) are essential. It's worth carrying a spare pair of backed sandals for river crossings, which can be a little over ankle deep. Yurutse, Rumbak and the entire Markha Valley fall within **Hemis National Park** (per person per day ₹20).

Main Trek

Starting from the new bridge 4km south of Chilling, or alternatively at the nearby trail-head village of Skiu, reasonably fit hikers

Smaller villages occasionally run out of homestay beds but homeowners will always find somewhere for you to stay. Bigger villages such as Rumbak, Hinju and Skiu/Kaya work on a rota system, so you don't get to choose where you stay.

You might also find seasonal parachute cafes, so named as they are tents made from old army parachutes. These provide tea and simple snacks, and sometimes offer basic lodging.

Having an experienced local guide is not only useful for route finding but also for making social interactions more meaningful at homestays. With a couple of days' notice you can engage a guide through trekking agencies and even some homestays. Costs average around ₹2000 per day including food.

Which Trek?

Popular options include:

DAYS	ROUTE	HOMESTAYS	HIGH PASSES
2	Zingchen–Rumbak–Stok	plenty	4900m
3	Hinju (p264)–Sumdha Chenmo–Sumdha Chun–Alchi	yes	2
2	Cha–Phuktal (p270)–Purney	yes	no
3	Zingchen (p253)–Yurutse–Skiu–Chilling	yes	4920m
4+	Markha Valley (p252) from Chilling to Shang Sumdo	yes (or tent-camp)	5260m
5 (8)	(Rumtse)–Tso Kar–Tso Moriri (p258)	no	4 (7)
4	Kyupa La–Lingshet–Pidmo (p268)	limited	2

For a relatively easy trek, Zingchen–Rumbak–Yurutse–Zingchen makes a great one- or two-day sampler from Leh.

For a link to Spiti, try the six-night Korzok–Kibber trek, which has just one major pass and a river crossing.

Resources

➡ *Ladakh Zanskar* (http://ladak.free.fr) by Jean Louis Taillefer. Excellent if you read French.

➡ Cicerone's *Trekking in Ladakh* by Radek Kucharski.

➡ Olizane (www.olizane.ch) has three trekking maps (1:150,000) which are the best you can get, generally available in Leh for ₹2500 each.

should budget on four days to reach Shang Sumdo. This involves walking roughly seven-hour days and sleeping at Sara or Nakdeng, Hankar and Nimaling. If you'd prefer to do the trek in shorter sections, take five or six days, stopping instead at Skiu or Kaya, Markha, Umlung or Hankar, and Nimaling plus, perhaps, Chokdo to break up the long descent on the final day.

From Chilling and Kaya as far as Hankar you'll find villages every two or three hours' walk; these contrast very photogenically with the stark, dry, spikily upturned strata all around them. Human-made highlights include tiny Tacha Gompa, lying 25 minutes before Umlung (Umblung), and the shattered fortress ruins at Upper Hankar. Both are perched improbably atop razor-sharp ridges.

As the first two days have only gentle inclines, the Markha Trek helps you acclimatise as you go. Nevertheless, be sure not to start too soon after arrival in Ladakh.

Trekking from Zingchen

If you're well pre-acclimatised, you could add two or three beautiful extra days to the main Markha Valley trek by starting instead from the end of the paved road past Zingchen. From there it's three hours' walk to the single homestay at Yurutse, which has views of Stok Kangri; should that be full you might have to backtrack to charming Rumbak, which has nine homestays.

Start early the next morning; cross the Ganda La (4920m), two hours from Yurutse, and descend to traditional Shingo (six to seven hours), where there are three homestays. If you have the energy, you could continue to Skiu on the Markha Valley main trail in around another three hours, but unlike Shingo, Skiu–Kaya is very spread out, meaning you might have a long further walk to find that night's homestay.

ⓘ Getting There & Away

The most common starting point for visiting the Markha Valley is the Zanskar River crossing 4km south of Chilling; it's a ₹3150 taxi ride from Leh. A bridge reopened here in 2018 and a dirt road now continues to Skyu.

Alternative starting points are Stok and Zingchen. A taxi drop to Zingchen from Leh costs ₹1640. The usual end point of the trek is Shang Sumdo where, in season, taxis generally await arriving hikers at the second parachute tent; these charge ₹2500 per car or ₹600 per person to Leh.

Nubra Valley

☑ 01980

The deep-cut Shayok and Nubra River Valleys offer tremendous scenery on a grand scale, with green oasis villages surrounded by thrillingly stark scree slopes, and harsh arid mountains, strongly reminiscent of Pakistan's Northern Areas. There are sand dunes, monasteries, a ruined palace and – at Turtuk and Bogdang – a whole different culture (Balti) to discover. Permits (p256) are required by foreigners.

ⓘ Getting There & Away

The majority of visitors explore the Nubra Valley using a chartered jeep from Leh. There are many variants. Leh–Diskit–Hunder return in two days costs from ₹7800 per vehicle. A Leh–Turtuk three-day return costs ₹13,870. To add Sumur/Panamik costs around ₹1500/2500 extra.

Alternatively, as long as you have Nubra permits, it's easy enough to travel by shared jeep to Diskit, where there is a taxi stand to organise local excursions and from which Turtuk is reachable by bus (daily except Sundays).

While most visitors access Nubra via 5602m Khardung La, a narrow road across the remote 5308m Wari La has been upgraded and allows an alternative loop returning via Agham and Sakti.

Nubra to Pangong Tso

The wild and remote road between Nubra and Pangong means you don't have to return to Leh to link two of Ladakh's classic excursions. The narrow ribbon of laneway is highly vulnerable to landslides, however, and at three places there are river fords (at Km20.6, Km25.5 and Km28.3 from Agham) that can become dangerously high – especially on July afternoons when melting snows fill the side streams. Ideally use the road in the early mornings.

There is no habitation whatsoever along the 38km between Agham and Shayok village. Shayok village has a small gompa and at least four small homestays. There's more choice in Durbuk, 17km further where you meet the main Leh–Pangong road.

Leh–Diskit–Hunder–Spangmik costs ₹14,130 by chartered jeep for two days, or ₹18,200 for three days with the addition of Turtuk.

Leh to Diskit

The Nubra road zigzags up stark bare-rock mountains for around 1½ hours to **Khardung La** (Km39, Leh-Diskit Rd), which at 5602m is claimed (disputably) to be the world's highest motorable pass. Descending again, look for *dzo* (a cow and yak cross-breed) around the pretty pond known misleadingly as Tsolding Buddha Park. Army posts at south and north Pallu check permits and passports at Km24 and Km53.

After Khardung village (Km72), a good lunch stop, the scenery takes on a stark grandeur, with splendid Shayok Valley views at Km86. Khalsar (Km95) was ravaged in 2015 by floods but there are still a couple of small restaurants; one 2km beyond Khalsar offers **rafting** (☑ 9419300811; rsrkhalsar@gmail.com; Km3.5, Khalsar-Diskit Rd; per person ₹800-1200; ☺ May–mid-Sep) on the Shayok River.

Diskit

POP 1850 / ELEV 3125M

Diskit is the Nubra Valley's transit hub, home to its most appealing monastery (with giant Chamba statue), its only bar and only petrol pump, 1km west of town. Accommodation here is generally better value than at nearby Hunder, and although at first sight the town's central bazaar area can appear off-puttingly bland, the mountain valley setting is beautiful and the Old Town is well worth a wander.

The town's main sight is **Diskit Gompa** (Ganden Tashi Chosling Gompa; ₹30; ☺ 6.30am-7pm), sitting atop a 2km spaghetti of hairpin bends that passes a gigantic (32m) full-colour Chamba (Maitreya Buddha) statue. There are fabulous valley views from the statue. The monastery protector chapel features a six-armed white Mahakala statue that clasps the spookily withered forearm and skull of a Mongol warrior.

In the bazaar area, **Sand Dune Hotel** (☑9469176111, 01980-220022; hotelsanddune@gmail.com; Diskit Bazaar; s/d from ₹1500/1800, deluxe ₹2200/2500; 🖥) has the prettiest garden of six decent options. For bargain deals, look across town near the base of the Diskit Gompa access lane, notably the spacious upstairs rooms at stream-serenaded **Kharyok Deluxe Guest House** (☑01980-220050, 9469176131; Diskit bypass; s/d ₹500/1000; P🖥) or the newest rooms at old faithful **Sunrise Guest House** (☑9469261853; sunrise.guest66@gmail.com; Old Diskit; s/d ₹500/800; ☺May-Sep). There are lots of other good choices in between.

❶ Getting There & Away

Shared jeeps to Leh (₹400, 4½ hours) depart when full from Diskit bus station between 6.30am and 9am. There are also overloaded afternoon minibuses to virtually every main Nubra village (including Panamik 3pm and Turtuk 2.30pm, except Sundays) returning early morning.

For charter jeeps, ask at the **Nubra Taxi Union** (☑9419871626; ☺7am-6pm). Useful fares:

Diskit Gompa ₹200 return

Hunder Direct/via camel point ₹300/400

Leh ₹5500 One way

Pangong Tso Via Agham, stop in Leh, two days ₹12,500

Tegar and Sumur ₹2000 return

Turtuk ₹3474/4500 one way/return (₹7500 overnight)

Hunder

POP 1240 / ELEV 3085M

Lost in greenery and closely backed by soaring valley cliffs, 7km from Diskit, Hunder village is popular with Indian visitors, who settle into one of the dozens of guesthouses and tent camps, and then spend the late afternoon exploring the photogenic sand dunes 3km from town.

Of more interest to most foreigners is the fascinating series of *mani* walls, stupas and shrines that sit underneath a precarious ridgetop fort ruin high above the main road near the modest **gompa** (☺6-8am).

Increasingly, foreign backpackers who don't require the midrange comfort of Hunder's accommodation options tend to make their way to less commercial Turtuk or visit Hunder from nearby Diskit, which has better transport connections.

Most Hunder guesthouses charge ₹1000 to ₹1500, such as the small, family-run **Galaxy Guest House** (☑9419585450, 01980-221054; dm/d/q ₹300/1000/1200, incl half board ₹500/1500/2000; ☺Apr-Nov; P🖥) 🅿.

The best of around a dozen 'luxury' camps are the lushly verdant, occasionally quirky **Nubra Organic Retreat** (☑01980-201070, 9469176076; www.nubraorganicretreat.com; Hunder; s/d ₹4650/6000; ☺mid-Apr–Sep; P🖥) 🅿 and, for great views and better value, the delightful **Kora Valley** (☑01980-221339, 9469517223; www.thakora.in; Umbey Rd; d tent ₹2000, incl full board ₹3000; ☺May-Sep; P🖥) 🅿 set around a 'maypole' of prayer flags in Umbey, a couple of kilometres east of central Hunder.

You really need your own transport to enjoy Hunder. The Diskit–Turtuk bus rolls around the Hunder bypass early afternoon westbound, and late morning on the return. A one-way taxi from Hunder to Diskit costs around ₹300.

Turtuk

POP 3750 / ELEV 2790M

The turbulent Shayok Valley between Hunder and Turtuk is 80km of scenic magnificence marred only by the occasional military convoy or low-flying transport plane. The grand raw-rock valley briefly narrows near tiny Changmar, the western limit of Ladakhi Buddhist culture. Thereafter, the rare green splashes of village are culturally and linguistically Muslim Balti, and a dead ringer for northern Pakistan. Summer sees locals carting huge bundles of barley straw on their backs between the apricot trees.

Upper Turtuk has unforgettable views towards serrated high peaks in Pakistan that mark the Line of Control just 7km away. Indeed Turtuk itself was part of Pakistan until the 1971 war.

Note that while many borderholics find Turtuk a Ladakh highlight, some travellers consider its quiet simplicity doesn't quite justify the long journey.

The village has three distinct sections. The main road passes through the lower part known as Turtuk Chutang, which has a small scattering of shops and government offices. Most guesthouses and homes are in the pretty village area on the raised plateau above, which is divided by a side river into older western Turtuk Youl and more open, green eastern Turtuk Farol. The two upper

---

ⓘ LADAKH PERMITS

To visit Nubra Valley, Pangong Tso, Dha Hanu, Tso Moriri and the Upper Indus (beyond Upshi) foreigners require a Protected Area Permit (Indian citizens simply fill in a self-declaration form). Applications must be processed through an approved travel agency (p237), though it is technically possible to start the process online at www.lahdclehpermit.in. One minor hitch for single travellers is that there must be at least two applicants at the time of application, but agencies can usually fudge this and once you have the permit, travelling alone seems perfectly OK.

Agencies generally need 24 hours to get a permit. Make several extra copies of your permit to please overzealous check posts.

Permits are valid for up to seven days. On top of the variable agency fee (anything up to ₹600), the permit cost is composed of three elements: a ₹100 Red Cross contribution; a ₹20 per day 'wildlife fee'; and a ₹300 environment tax.

---

areas are connected by a suspension footbridge. Neither has roads.

⊙ Sights

The main delight is simply watching Turtuk village life and wandering between the beautiful field-hemmed viewpoints. The old houses of Turtuk Youl are being upgraded rapidly but many retain 'coolers' – stone block mini-buildings through which ice-cold streams are funnelled to form natural refrigerators.

The town's Old Mosque (Turtuk Youl) in the western part of the old village has a distinctive wooden minaret with spiral staircase, and the modest little Yabgo 'Palace' (Pon Khar; ☑ 9419996841; Turtuk Youl; by donation; ☺ 8am-6pm, closed Friday noon-2pm) nearby is still home to a self-proclaimed descendant of the raja, who traces the royal family's once-magnificent dynasty in his one-room museum.

🍴 Sleeping & Eating

The best views are in Turtuk Farol, where the long-term travellers' favourite is Kharmang Guest House (☑ 9469006200, 9596476308; www.kharmangguesthouse.yolasite.com; s/d incl half board ₹1350/1800, without bathroom ₹950/1400). Khan Guest House (☑ 01980-248130, 9469232578; Turtuk Farol; r per person incl half board ₹500-700) is also attractively located. On the main road, Ashoor Guest House (☑ 01980-248153, 9419800776; ashoor.turtuk@yahoo.com; Main Rd, Turtuk Chutang; r ₹800-1200, without bathroom from ₹700; ☺ Apr-Oct; 🅿) is decent value, while nearby Turtuk Holiday (☑ 9906993123; www.turtukholiday.com; Main Rd, Turtuk; s/d tent incl half board from ₹4000/5000; ☺ Apr-Oct; 🅿) 🍴, currently a garden tent camp, is the top place in town.

Both Balti Farm (☑ 01980-248103; www.turtukholiday.com; Turtuk Holiday, Main Rd, Turtuk; mains ₹200; ☺ 7.30-10am, 1-3pm & 7.30-10pm) and the Balti Kitchen (Turtuk Farol; mains ₹200-250; ☺ 7am-11pm; ☑) do imaginative takes on traditional Baltistani cuisine, with a choice of garden or indoor seating.

ⓘ Getting There & Away

Bring spare photocopies of your Protected Area Permit.

Shared jeeps (₹200, three hours) and minibuses (₹150, four hours) leave Turtuk at 6am for Diskit (buses return at 2.30pm, except Sundays). It's 90km on a mostly well-paved road.

Sumur, Tegar & Panamik

POP 3240 / ELEV 3130M

The northern Nubra/Siachen valley is quieter and cheaper than the western Shayok Valley and it also boasts more history as the route of Silk Road caravans which for centuries travelled over the Saser La pass to Yarkand in Central Asia.

If you have your own transport, Sumur-Tegar is worth considering as a laid-back Nubra base.

Most interesting is Tegar (Tiger) village, where the Zimskang Museum (by donation ₹50; ☺ by request) is an unmarked historic house, found by descending a footpath alongside chortens and a *mani* wall from the ancient little Mane Lhakhang Gompa. High above the gompa, the crumbling three-storey shell of Zamskhang Palace (Km25, Khalsar-Panamik Rd) is what's left of Nubra's former royal citadel. An appealing if steep back lane loops back downhill to Sumur via the colourfully rebuilt Samstemling Gompa (by donation; ☺ 8am-noon & 1.30-6pm).

To really get off the beaten track, continue north past lovely Yulkam village and less lovely Panamik, with its clean but uninspiring hot springs. Register at the police checkpost, then cross the Nubra River to the west bank and hook south for 4km to the turn-off to remote Ensa Monastery, high above the road. A lovely *kora* (pilgrim path) takes you past dozens of white chortens to offer fabulous valley views at what feels like the end of the world.

★**AO Guesthouse**   GUESTHOUSE **$**
(☑9469731976; Sumur Link Rd; r ₹500-800; ⊙May-Oct) This friendly place has a pleasant garden courtyard, a shared upper terrace and fine views from the best upstairs rooms. The guesthouse's proximity to the main junction, next to several shops, also makes it better than most Sumur options for public transport. It's excellent value.

Yarab Tso   HOTEL **$**
(☑9419342231, 01980-223661; www.hotelyarabt-so.com; Km24.5, Main Rd, Tegar; d ₹1200, s/d incl half board ₹2100/2800; P☎) This impressive traditional-style Ladakhi building is set in farm-size grounds and boasts its own bakery. Rooms are let down a bit by simple bathrooms but the upper-floor rooms at least are pretty comfortable and there's an appealing family-style sitting room.

Buses to Diskit (₹50) depart between 8am and 8.30am, returning about 3pm. A shared jeep-taxi to Leh (₹400) leaves at 7.30am most mornings.

Pangong Tso

ELEV 4250M

Stretching around 150km (with the eastern two-thirds in Tibet), this mesmerising lake plays artist with a surreal palette of vivid colours – from Caribbean-style turquoise to leaden grey, depending on the light – contrasting magically with the surrounding khakhi swirls of arid, snow-brushed mountains. Visitor activities don't stretch much beyond ogling the ever-changing lake and taking bracing lakeshore walks.

A Leh–Pangong jeep or motorbike safari is a scenically impressive adventure, crossing the 5360m Chang La en route, but it's a trip that is now very popular with domestic Indian tourists, so brace yourself for some crowds. It's a long drive, so plan on sleeping at least one night, preferably in quieter Man. To get here non-Indians need to obtain permits (p256) through an agency in Leh.

🛏 Sleeping

The widest choice of accommodation is in Spangmik (pronounced 'Pangmik'), but Man village, 10km further is a more peaceful option.

Even at the best places you'll only get hot water in a bucket and electricity between 7am and 11pm. All the tented camps close for the season around mid-September.

Prices tend to be 30% lower than rack rates if you arrive without a reservation. Walk-in rates are listed here.

🛌 Spangmik

Scrappy Spangmik is Pangong's busiest accommodation spot, though a 2018 government regulation threatens to forcibly relocate the over 50 tented camps that currently mar the once-peaceful village. If the camps do actually disappear, you'll be left with a handful of simple homestays (typically ₹550 per person including half board) in the upper village.

The best budget places are **Diskit Khangcher Guest House** (☑9419682755; per person incl half board with/without bathroom ₹750/550; ⊙May-Sep) and **Padma Homestay & Tents** (☑9469515696; homestay beds ₹400, d tent incl half board ₹1800; ⊙May-Oct). For a more upscale tented camp, see if well-run **Yak Camp** (☑9797312357; d ₹1500, incl half board ₹3000; ⊙May-Sep) and the lakeshore **Camp Watermark** (☑9760027905; www.ladakhcamps.com; d incl half board ₹6000; ⊙late Apr-Sep) are still operating.

Ser Bhum Tso Resort (☑9469718862, 9419176660; www.serbhumtsoresortpangong.com; s/d incl half board ₹2500/4000; ⊙mid-Apr–late Oct) is the most upscale hotel, though it's still pretty simple.

🛌 Man

A maze of dry-stone walls and trickling brooks, Man is a peaceful rural village. There are several simple homestays, including pleasant **Yokma Homestay** (☑9419529595; r per person incl half board ₹800), in the upper

---

SLEEPING PRICE RANGES

Accommodation price ranges for Kashmir and Ladakh:

$ less than ₹1500

$$ ₹1500–₹5000

$$$ more than ₹5000

village. At the opposite end of the scale, the eight yurt-like tents of **Pangong Hermitage** (☑ 9419863755; www.ladakhsarai.com; d incl full board ₹10,000-15,000; ☺ May-Oct) are luxurious (four-poster beds!) and astoundingly expensive for such a remote place.

ⓘ Getting There & Away

Most people visit Pangong Tso as part of a rented vehicle tour. Karu (the nearest petrol station) to Spangmik is around 120km and takes half a day.

Two-day return jeep tours from Leh cost ₹8100 to Spangmik, or ₹9640 to Man and Merak. Don't even think about a day trip. The road to Spangmik is paved but the 10km onwards to Man is bumpy.

For minimal extra cost you could add side trips to Chemrey (p251) and Takthog (p251) monasteries to your jeep excursion and stop at colourful Tangtse Gompa (Tangtse; by donation) en route, but make these stops on the way back towards Leh, so that outbound you get a wider choice of accommodation on arrival at the lake.

Combining Pangong with the Nubra Valley is possible via the Durbuk–Shayok–Agham–Khalsar road, though the three fords between Shayok and Agham can be tricky to cross in summer. A three-day loop costs from ₹20,480.

The cash-strapped and time-rich could consider the summer bus that runs from Leh to Spangmik, departing at 6.30am on Tuesdays, Thursdays and Saturdays (₹270), returning next morning at 8am.

Tso Moriri Loop

ELEV 4540M

One of Ladakh's great high-altitude lakes, Tso Moriri shimmers with an ever-changing series of reflections in its vivid blue waters.

The 215km drive from Leh takes you past the lovely villages (notably Likche and Himya) of the Indus Valley known as Rong, and returns via the salt lake of Tso Kar, where birdwatchers scan for black-necked cranes between June and late September. You finish off on a section of the Manali–Leh highway, crossing en route the very impressive 5328m Taglang La, one of the world's highest motorable passes.

Far fewer tourists come to Tso Moriri in comparison to Pangong Tso, which is why we like it, and there's more to do, from trekking and climbing routes to encounters with local herders. Most people visit on a two- or three-day loop from Leh, overnighting at Korzok.

To visit Tso Moriri and the Indus Valley, foreigners need three copies of a Protected Area Permit (p256), issued by agencies in Leh. They're checked at Upshi (sometimes), Mahe Bridge and Korzok's Indo-Tibetan Border Police post.

Indian citizens need three self-declaration forms. Permits are not needed for Tso Kar if you visit from the Manali highway.

Tso Moriri to Kibber Trek

An excellent trek is the six-night, seven-day walk from Tso Moriri to Kibber in Spiti (Himachal Pradesh) along an ancient trade route. Most of the hike is in high-altitude rolling valleys but there is one major pass (5500m) with some glacier walking. Day three starts with wading a river that can become uncrossable in the afternoon. Foreigners can only do the trek from north to south, as a Tso Moriri permit is needed from Leh.

Horses (₹450) and guides (₹1000) are available in Korzok given a day or two's warning.

🛏 Sleeping & Eating

The best deals in Korzok are in simple homestay-guesthouses. Our favourites are **Goose Homestay** (☑ 9469591231; s/d incl half board ₹1000/1500), which has lake views from its two best rooms, and **Crane Homestay** (☑ 9469534654; s/d ₹1000/1500, r incl half board ₹2000), which lacks a family vibe but boasts views and helpful English-speaking host Choktup. A step up is a room with en suite booth-bathrooms at **Dolphin Guest House** (☑ 9906995628, 9419856244; r incl half board ₹1300-2500).

Korzok's only 'hotel' is the **Lake View** (☑ 9469457025, 9419345362; www.tsomoririhotellakeview.com; s/d ₹2992/3850; ☺ May–mid-Oct); its rooms are pleasantly appointed, even if the public areas feel like a building site.

Korzok has six bedded-tent camps at prices that are variable according to demand. It's always cheaper to simply turn up rather than prebook in Leh. There are also sheltered stream-side camping spots nearby. At the north end of town, **Tsomoriri Resort & Camp** (☑ Leh 01982-258855; www.ladakhcampsandretreats.com; d incl full board ₹3500-4500; ☺ May-Sep) has good tents and decent views.

Overlooking the crane breeding grounds at end-of-the-world Thukje beside Tso Khar, rooms 107 to 112 of motel-like **Tsokar Eco Resort** (☑ Leh 9906060654; tsokarecoresort@gmail.com; s/d ₹1400/2500) are the area's only en suite rooms, though there are bedded tents with attached bathrooms at next door **Lotus Camp** (☑ 9419819078; chotsering100@

yahoo.com; d incl half board ₹5000; ⊙ Jun–mid-Sep) and at cheaper, simpler two-tent **Tsepal Guest House** (⌨ 9906060654; tent s/d ₹1000/1500, mains ₹100; ⊙ Jun-Sep).

❶ Getting There & Away

A two-day jeep charter looping Leh–Korzok–Thukje then returning to Leh across Taglang La costs ₹12,900 by Sumo and ₹14,300 by Innova jeep. A three-day, one-way excursion doing the same then continuing south to Keylong and Manali costs from ₹26,220 and ₹37,800 respectively. Doing the latter in reverse is not practicable for foreigners, who need permits pre-issued in Leh.

Leh to Kargil

There are many fascinating sights close to the Leh–Srinagar road. You'll need a motorbike or a vehicle to make the most of numerous short diversions, for example to Basgo, Likir and Alchi. The most popular stops en route are at Alchi and Lamayuru. With more time consider side trips to Timishgan and Wanla-Honupatta.

❶ Getting There & Around

Hopping by very limited public transport is slow going: other than daily Leh–Kargil and Leh–Srinagar through buses, the only options west from Khalsi are Leh–Dha buses (daily), Leh–Lamayuru (summer only) and four other weekly services to Chiktan or Fokha. Lamayuru and Khalsi both have a couple of taxis but tracking them down can be difficult.

It makes sense to get a group together in Leh and arrange a shared jeep with side trips, at least as far as Mulbekh or Shargol from where there are buses to Kargil.

Phyang

⌨ 01982 / POP 2160 / ELEV 3580M

Pretty Phyang village is a large, green expanse of layered, tree-hemmed barley fields, 20km from Leh in the next parallel valley west. There's a big 16th-century Drigung-school **gompa** (₹50) that has some fine old murals, while further up the western side of the valley is a fortress ruin and an ancient **Guru Lhakhang** (⌨ Lobsang Chospal 9596834460, Tsering Norboo 9469728179; ⊙ on request) FREE that has some precious Alchi-style murals if you can find the key-holder. Bring a torch (flashlight).

You're most likely stay overnight to unwind at the **Hidden North Guest House** (⌨ 9419218055, 01982-226007; www.hiddennorth.com; d incl full board ₹2800-3600, room only witht/without bathroom ₹1800/1000; ⊙ May-Sep or by arrangement; 🐾), where a Ladakhi-Italian family has created a delightfully relaxing getaway of eight rooms in the north of the valley with panoramic views encompassing Phyang Gompa. Meals, guided treks and animal-watching trips (February and March) are available. Free filtered water and tea. The guesthouse is 1.4km beyond the gompa.

There are also **farmstay** (⌨ 01982-226117; www.icestupa.org/farmstays; per day approx ₹750) 🐾 opportunities in several local homes.

Phyang is an easy day trip from Leh with your own transport. From Leh there are buses to the gompa area at 8am and 2.30pm, returning at 9.30am and 1.30pm. For the Hidden North Guest House ask for Phyang Tsakma. A taxi from Leh costs ₹500/645 one way/return. Without your own transport, getting around the village will involve a considerable amount of walking. Hidden North (p259) rents mountain bikes (₹1200 per day) to its guests.

Nimmu & Chilling

West of Phyang, shortly past the viewpoint above the confluence of the olive-green Indus and the turbid brown Zanskar rivers, you'll reach the pretty village of Nimmu, which has several places to eat, some rafting companies and some appealing accommodation.

Around 30km up the Zanskar from Nimmu, idyllic Chilling is famed for its coppersmiths, but is used mostly as a starting point for rafting back to Nimmu, or as a launchpad for the Markha Valley Trek (p252), which starts by crossing the river bridge 4km south of town.

For an interesting detour en route from Nimmu to Chilling, look for the turn-off at Km19, just south of Sumdha Do village. A newly finished road leads to an atmospheric little Alchi-style temple (p264) and several homestays in the hamlet of Sumdha Chun.

The Zanskar River between Chilling and Nimmu is Ladakh's foremost rafting route between late May and September. Families like the tame 6km float from Tsogtse, while longer trips from Skorpochey (14km) and Chilling (26km) have grade III and above sections.

Most people organise their trip through agencies in Leh, notably Wet'n'Wild (p237) or Splash Adventures (p237), while some trekking agents combine rafting with

LEH TO MANALI

Beautiful but exhausting and occasionally spine-jangling, the Leh–Manali route is one of the Himalaya's great road journeys. The Upshi–Keylong section alone crosses four passes over 4900m, and then there's the infamously unpredictable Rohtang La pass before Manali. Although the road is 'normally' open from June to late September, unseasonable snow or major landslides can close it for days (or weeks). BCM (www.bcmtouring.com), LAHDC (http://leh.nic.in) and High Road (www.vistet.wordpress.com) report the road's current status.

Bus & Minibus

The cheapest option is to take the 5am HRTC bus to Keylong (₹540, 14 hours) and change there. Buy tickets from the driver's assistant at the main bus station the evening before; the incoming bus should arrive around 7pm (look for the HP number plate).

Marginally more comfortable **HPTDC** (Himachal Pradesh Tourism Development Corporation; Map p240; ☎9418078019, 9418691215; http://hptdc.in; Fort Rd, Leh; ⏰10am-1pm & 2-8pm, Jul–mid-Sep) buses (₹2900, two days) leave every second day in July and August plus a couple of times in early September. Departures are at 5am from opposite the tourist office (p245). Prebook tickets upstairs in the small office beside Wet'n'Wild (p237). Fares include basic overnight accommodation in dorms at Keylong, plus one breakfast and dinner.

Faster nonstop 12-seater Tempo minibuses leave around 7pm (₹2000, six hours) from **Ladakh Tempo Travellers Operation Cooperative** (Map p234; ☎01982-253192) near the bus station. Book two days ahead and double-check the departure point. The route will be far quicker once the Rohtang Tunnel opens, hopefully in 2020.

Jeep

HP-registered jeeps at the Long-Distance Shared-Taxi Park (p247) ask ₹2000/2500/3000 back/middle/front seat to Manali; they generally depart between 4pm and 6pm. These folks are sometimes in a hurry to leave, so you may be able to rent the whole vehicle for considerably less than the official charge (₹19,500 including one overnight stop en route).

Car & Motorcycle

There's no petrol station for 365km between Karu and Tandi (8km south of Keylong). Driving northbound, the Rohtang La requires permits (p345), and on Tuesdays after 6am northbound private traffic is not allowed beyond Gulaba. Southbound traffic is unaffected.

Route Highlights

The Manali road heads south at Upshi (Km425) via Miru (Km410), a pretty village with a shattered fortress and numerous stupas. Beyond is a beautiful, narrow valley edged with serrated vertical mineral strata in alternating layers of vivid red-purple and ferrous green.

a Markha Valley or Zingchen–Yurutse–Chilling trek.

Surprisingly, there's a choice of high-quality accommodation in Nimmu, notably the boutique **Nimmu House** (☎8447757518; http://ladakh.nimmu-house.com; off NH1 at Km388; s/d incl full board from ₹11,900/12,800; ⏰late Apr–late Sep; 🅿📶) 🌿, a fabulous three-storey French-run mansion and palace, once belonging to cousins of the Ladakhi royals. It's supercomfortable, with memory-foam beds, a lovely stone terrace and light-touch luxurious interiors, while maintaining the spirit of the old building, with wobbly old floors, antique pillars and an upper-floor shrine room. Four rooms of varying sizes are in the old house, and there are seven immaculate, designer safari tents in the idyllic orchard garden. The fixed menu changes daily using fresh, locally sourced ingredients. Yoga and mountain biking available. The house is 400m up the lane towards Chamba Gompa. More affordable are the good-value roadside properties **Nilza Guest House** (☎9622971571; raftanimo@gmail.com; Km387.4, Kargil-Leh Hwy; r ₹1500, without bathroom ₹500-1200; ⏰Jun–mid-Sep) and midrange **Takshos Hotel** (☎9419815233, 01982-225064; Leh-Srinagar Hwy; r incl breakfast ₹1200-2500; ⏰Jun-Sep; 🅿📶). Nimmu is 30km west of Leh on the Kargil highway.

Basgo & Ney

Basgo (population 1700, elevation 3230m) was once a capital of lower Ladakh, and the shattered remnants of its former **palace** (per

A millennium ago, Gya (Km398) was the capital of King Gyapacho's upper Ladakhi monarchy before he joined forces with Tibetan prince Skiddeyimagon (who shifted the power centre to Shey). Today it's a small, picturesque village; across the river a short drive leads up to the 1000-year-old castle ruin, now partly occupied by a small gompa.

Rumtse (Km394), with its handful of homestays and camping spots, is the last green oasis; there are no further villages for 250km, just tiny seasonal camp-settlements. Numerous hairpin bends climb to Taglang La (Km364), which at 5328m is the highest point on the route (though not the world's second-highest road pass as a road sign claims).

At Km287, 10km beyond Pang, the road rises through a memorable, spiky-edged canyon before crossing Lachlung La (5060m) and Nakila La (4915m), descending the 21 switchbacks of the Gata Loops (Km254 to Km246) and trundling through two very photogenic valleys with glimpses of Cappadocia-style erosion formations approaching Sarchu.

Southbound Advantages

If doing the trip southbound from Leh to Manali you could visit Tso Moriri en route (not possible northbound for permit reasons) and if you choose to break the trip at Sarchu or Pang, you'll be better acclimatised for those high-altitude sleeps.

Overnight Stops

The Leh–Manali trip can take anywhere from 15 to 22 hours. Overnighting in Sarchu breaks the journey into two roughly equal sections, but the altitude (around 4000m) can cause problems (especially if heading northbound, as you're unlikely to be acclimatised). Note that there are essentially two Sarchus: a 500m strip of cheap, ugly metal-shack cafes just north of the Km222 bridge, and a dozen bedded tent-camps mostly dotted between Km214 and Km217 on an attractive raised riverside plateau.

Stopping at Keylong, Jispa (Km138 to Km139) and Gemur (Km134) is more comfortable, with better accommodation at lower altitudes, but Leh–Keylong is a long day's ride.

To make Leh–Manali a three-day ride you might stop in Pang (Km298) and then Keylong. Pang has an altitude of 4634m, so the unacclimatised might need to use the army camp's free oxygen if altitude sickness hits. Pang's parachute cafes and mud-walled hostel rooms are very basic.

Lonely parachute cafes are also available at Debring (Km343 and Km340), Whisky Nallah (Km270), Bharatpur (Km197), Zingzingbar (Km174) and Darcha Bridge (Km143).

temple ₹30) form a remarkable sight above the NH1 Kargil–Leh Hwy. It's worth the 1.6km road detour to the top of the ruins to enjoy the fine views and to visit the three medieval two-storey Maitreya statues, one of bronze, the others of painted clay, dating back to the 15th and 17th centuries.

With your own transport you can also detour 8km north to a giant golden Buddha statue at Ney. It's nearly 26m tall, though that includes the three-storey building that forms his seat.

Sham

☎ 01982

The parallel north–south valleys of Lekir, Yangthang, Hemis Shukpachan and Timish-gan together make up Sham. Long visited by trekkers as part of the three-day Sham 'baby trek', the valleys are now connected by paved roads, offering a fine new option for motorcyclists and mountain bikers.

The triple villages of Timishgan, Ang and Tia are worth visiting in their own right, even if you aren't trekking across Sham. Timishgan is dominated by the historic monastery-palace known as Timishgan Khar. In the 15th century this was the capital of lower Ladakh and in 1684 an important treaty was signed here to facilitate trade between Ladakh and Tibet.

Tia is one of Ladakh's most delightful villages, with traditional homes piled on top of each other on a knoll and linked by a labyrinth of stairways and tunnel passages. All it

KASHMIR & LADAKH LEH TO KARGIL

WORTH A TRIP

SASPOL

On the way to or from Alchi it's worth detouring to see the the roadside **triple chamba statues** (Chamchen Choskorling; Km371.5, NH1) at nearby Saspol (opposite the SBI Bank). Saspol also has some fantastic Zangpo-era **cave paintings** (Gon Nila-Phuk) cut into the cliff beneath its ruined fortress 800m behind the village. Roads lead here from the east and west end of the village but on foot it's easiest to just cut through village paths.

Saspol has three homestays, including the recommended **Thongyok Guest House** (☑9419001904, 9419177523; Km371, NH1; dm/s/d ₹500/1200/1500; ℗𝄢).

lacks is a wizard's hovel at the top. It's 5km northwest of Timishgan.

Sham Trek

The 'Sham baby trek' is popularly used as a three-day acclimatisation warm-up hike. Its big advantages are relatively low altitudes, ample homestays and the fact that you can choose to stop at any stage and still have a relatively painless way to get back to Leh. Downsides include a lack of shade in desert-like conditions and the fact that the route parallels the new road from Likir to Timishgan. There are still plenty of ascents and descents.

Although the trek is typically started from Likir, the longer Likir–Yangthang leg could easily be skipped without great loss. In fact, an interesting alternative is to walk Timishgan–Hemis Shukpachan–Yangthang then descend via **Rizong Gompa** (₹30; ☉7am-1pm & 1.30-6pm), which takes two hours, to the NH1 at Uletokpo.

🛏 Sleeping

Hemis Shukpachan has a dozen widely scattered homestays, the small **Chotak Guest House & Tent Camp** (☑9469526703; Hemischu Rd; per person incl full board ₹1200) and the comfortable midrange **Togocheepa Eco Hotel** (☑9596811940; www.togocheepaecohotel.com; s/d ₹4500/5500), 1.5km south of the centre.

Yangthang has four traditional homestays in its clustered village core and there are homestays in Ang.

If you're in Likir to do the Sham Trek, it's probably worth staying in sprawling lower Likir, which has several homestay-guesthouses.

There are also a few good-value budget options in the scenic area up by the gompa.

There are numerous homestays in Timishgan and on the road to Ang, including the excellent **Yak Guesthouse** (☑9469253646; Ang Rd; per person incl half board ₹1000; 𝄢), which has space for camping. Midrange **Namra Hotel** (☑01982-229033, 9419178324; www.namrahotel.com; Ang Rd; s/d incl half board ₹5350/6100, heritage s/d ₹9000/10,500; 𝄢) is easily the best in town, though overpriced.

★ **Apricot Tree**   BOUTIQUE HOTEL **$$$**
(☑01982-229504, 9419866688; www.theapricottreehotel.com; Km350, NH1 Kargil-Leh Hwy, Nurla; s/d ₹5545/6930, incl half board ₹7680/9070; ☉May-Sep; 𝄢) A little like a Ladakhi hacienda, this understated boutique hotel oozes designer minimalist style. The 21 rooms are brought to life with locally styled balconies from which to contemplate the Indus. It's a great base for visits to Timishgan or Rizong, or a day hike to Tar village across the Indus.

ℹ Getting There & Away

A daily bus runs from Leh to Timishgan and Tia at 1pm, returning at 8am. On alternate days, there's a Leh–Hemis Shukpachan bus on a similar schedule driving via Likir and Yangthang. There's also a daily Leh–Likir bus.

A daily bus runs from Likir Gompa to Leh (₹80) leaving around 7am. Otherwise, walk down to the NH1 (1.5km from lower Likir) and pick up the bus from Lamayuru that passes through between 4pm and 5.30pm.

The Timishgan/Tia–Leh bus service (₹130) departs at 8am and 9am, returning at 1pm and 3pm.

Alchi & Around
POP 2380 (ALCHI) / ELEV 3100M (ALCHI)

◉ Sights

The village of Alchi is unmissable for the murals and carvings of its world-famous temple complex, founded in the early 11th century by 'Great Translator' Lotsava Ringchen Zangpo (p263) and one of the Himalaya's great artistic treasures. The village itself is a charming and relaxing place to be based for a couple of days.

Alchi's star attraction, the **Choskhor Temple Complex** (Indian/foreigner ₹50/20; ☉8am-1pm & 2-6pm), comprises four main temple buildings. Each one is small and unassuming from outside but the stunning millenium-old murals are unmatched highlights of Ladakh's first wave of Indo-Tibetan Buddhist art; a style that would go on to influence western Tibet and beyond. Bring a torch (flashlight). The site was largely abandoned after the 16th century.

Visits (no photography allowed) start with Sumrtsek Temple, fronted by a wooden porch, the carving style of which is very much Indian rather than Tibetan. The murals inside are stunning. Next along, Vairocana Temple is impressive for its inner wall-sized mandalas. The temple founder Ringchen Zangpo himself appears in the Lotsa Temple, while the attached Manjushri Temple enshrines a joyfully colourful four-sided statue of Manjushri (Bodhisattva of Wisdom).

The temple complex is reached by a narrow pedestrian lane lined by mass-produced souvenir stalls. A path circles the temple exterior and leads down to the Indus River.

🛏 Sleeping & Eating

Alchi has around a dozen accommodation options packed around the temple area. In a sizable garden 800m back towards Leh, the friendly **Choskor Guest House** (📞9419826363; mdorjay@yahoo.co.in; s/d ₹800/1200; 🅿🛜) charges reasonable prices for decent, if older, guesthouse rooms.

★**Alchi Kitchen**   LADAKHI **$$**
(📞9419438642; alchikitchen@gmail.com; mains ₹100-280; ⊙8am-10pm May-Sep; 🛜) Alchi Kitchen offers a rare chance to taste traditional Ladakhi foods made with a modern twist. The striking, mod-trad open kitchen runs out flavoursome *skyu* (vegetable stew containing something like a barley version of Italian *orecchiette* – pasta 'ears') and *chutagi* but there are also saffron paneer *momos*, stuffed *khambir* and *kushi pheymar*, a sweet and filling mix of barley and apricot flours with cheese and sugar that makes for a great trekking snack.

ℹ Getting There & Away

Central Alchi is 4km down a dead-end spur lane that leaves the Leh–Kargil road at Km370, immediately crossing a bridge over the Indus. Direct buses to Leh depart daily at 7.30am from both Alchi (₹100, 2¼ hours) and Saspol (₹90, two hours), returning at 4pm and 3pm respectively.

Yapola Valley

The road branching south from Km318 on the NH1 (8km east of Lamayuru) links several fascinating, unspoilt villages, a superb canyon and some of Ladakh's most impressive mountain landscapes. Wanla alone is worth the brief diversion from the Leh–Kargil road to see the stunning Kashmiri-style murals of its medieval **gompa** (www.achi association.org; ₹50; ⊙dawn-dusk) and fort ruins perched on a knife-edge ridge above town.

At minuscule Phanjila, a spur road diverges to appealing Hinju, where homestays provide the launchpad for the wild trek to Sumdha Do (two days) and Alchi.

South of Phanjila, a newly improved but largely unpaved road passes through spectacular Yapola Gorge before reaching traditional Honupatta village, then across the magnificent Sisir La (4800m) and Sengge La (4950m) passes, descending in between to Photoksar, a cliff-knoll village at over 4100m.

Jeeps can now reach just past the 4425m Kyupa La pass, from which Lingshet, trekking base for reaching Zanskar (p268), is a half-day walk.

Wanla has a couple of homestays and guesthouses, of which the most tempting is the **Rongstak** (📞9419982366; Km6, Phanjila Rd; per person incl full board ₹1100; ⊙May-Oct) at the northern edge of town. There are homestays at Phanjila, Ursi, Hinju, Honupatta, Sumdo, Photoksar and Lingshet.

THE GREAT TRANSLATOR

In the 10th century, Kashmir rather than Ladakh was the region's centre of Buddhist scholarship. One of western Tibet's three regional monarchs, Yeshey-Od, decided to send 21 of the kingdom's brightest students to investigate Kashmir's religious scholarship. All but two reputedly died in the process, but one who made it home (after 17 years) was Ringchen Zangpo. He became known as the 'Great Translator', having put more than 100 Buddhist scriptures into Tibetan.

His return to Ladakh in AD 993, accompanied by 32 Kashmiri artists, set off an astonishing flurry of temple building. Remarkably, several original interiors, statues and carvings remain from this period, most famously at the temples in Alchi, Manggyu and Sumdha Chun (p264), along with similar structures at Saspol, Wanla and Kanji. Zangpo also set up a great Buddhist university at Nyerma near Thiksey, of which a few sturdy wall fragments remain.

Trekking to Sumdha Chun & Beyond

Hinju is the starting point of the adventurous two-day homestay trek to Sumdha Chun and beyond. The first day is a long climb over the 4950m Konze La, while the second day features some wild mountain-gorge scenery (route-finding and stream crossing required), and then a final short walk along a road. Homestays and food are available at Hinju, Sumdha Chenmo and Sumdha Chun.

A highlight of Sumdha Chun is its famous but little-visited monastery. From here you can pre-arrange a taxi pickup or walk down the road to Sumdha Do on the Chilling–Nimmu road, from where you can link up with the Markha Valley trek.

An ambitious alternative option is to make the long, steep climb from Sumdha Chun north over the 5300m Stakspi La and then down to Alchi (around 10 hours total, with 1200m ascent and 2000m descent). A village guide would be useful to help you find the best way up the scree-lined pass.

Lamayuru

☑ 01982 / POP 700 / ELEV 3390M

Slow-paced Lamayuru is one of Ladakh's most memorable villages and an ideal place to break the journey from Kargil to Leh. Set among remarkable mountain-backed badland scenery, picturesque homes huddle around a crumbling central hilltop that's a Swiss cheese of caves and erosion pillars topped by a photogenic gompa. It's breathtaking.

Lamayuru's **gompa** (Km310, NH1; ₹50; ⊙7am-1pm & 1.30-6pm) is one of the most photogenic Buddhist monasteries in Ladakh. Behind glass within the gompa's main prayer hall is a tiny cave-niche in which 11th-century mystic Naropa (AD 1016–1100) meditated.

🛏 Sleeping & Eating

★ Dragon Hotel   GUESTHOUSE $
(☑9469294037, 01982-224501; www.dragonhotel
lamayuru.wordpress.com; NH1; s/d ₹1200/1500,
r without bathroom ₹400-600; ⊙hotel May-Sep;
🛜) Accessed through a pleasant garden restaurant (mains ₹120 to ₹150) directly behind the bus stop, the Dragon Hotel's new en suite rooms are clean, spacious and good value, with modern bathrooms. The homestay section is much simpler but clean (hot water by bucket), and the rooftop has great views. Contact manager Tashi.

Tharpaling Guest House   GUESTHOUSE $
(☑01982-224516, 9419343917; Km311, NH1; per person incl half board ₹600; 🛜) Ever-smiling matriarch Tsiring Yandol gives this roadside place a jolly family feel, serving dinners in a particularly homely communal dining room. All but two of the seven rooms have en suite bathrooms.

Hotel Moonland   HOTEL $$
(☑9419888508, 01982-224576; www.hotelmoon
land.in; Km310.5, NH1; old block s/d ₹1500/1900,
annexe ₹2100/2700; ⊙late Apr-Sep; 🛜) Set in a pretty garden at the first hairpin bend, 400m beyond the bus stop, Moonland's old building rooms have seen better days but the garden and restaurant have postcard-perfect views towards the monastery (beer ₹200). Much better rooms are available in the piney new 28-room annexe behind the old hotel, where the very comfortable rooms come with modern bathrooms and balcony views.

🛈 Getting There & Away

Most buses stop only briefly in passing, and times can be plus or minus an hour:

Kargil (₹200, five hours) From Leh, sometime between 9am and 10am.

Leh (₹195, five hours) Departs daily at 2pm in summer. The Kargil–Leh bus passes through between 8.30am and 9.30am daily but is often full.

Srinagar (₹1000, 13 hours) Passes through around 6pm. Hopefully.

Mulbekh, Wakha & Shargol

☑ 01985 / POP 4060 / ELEV 3270M

The Wakha–Mulbekh Valley is the last predominantly Buddhist area on the route west from Leh, a role Mulbekh flaunts with its famous roadside Buddha relief carving and two small but intriguing little monasteries, the cliffside Rgyal Gompa near Wakha and dramatic **Shargol Gompa** (Urgyen Dzong) some 10km to the west, near Km236.

Mulbekh Chamba   BUDDHIST MONUMENT
(Km243, NH1) Mulbekh's foremost sight is a 1000-year-old Maitreya Buddha relief, carved into an 8m fang of rock. It's right by the roadside, rising through the middle of the minuscule Chamba Gompa and it marks the limit of Ladakhi Buddhist influence.

Mulbekh Castle Site   VIEWPOINT
Mulbekh is overlooked by the impregnable site of King Tashi Namgyal's 18th-century castle, high above the road. Burnt during an

1835 raid, the castle has only two tower stubs remaining, but the site sports a small gompa, and a new one is under construction. There are symphonic views across the green valley.

The area's best accommodation is **Horizon Camp** (☑ 9469045459; horizonladakh camp@gmail.com; Km245, NH1; s/d ₹3000/3550, incl half board ₹4000/4550; ☺May-Sep), a bedded tent camp in a beautiful garden, 150m from Wakha's petrol station. Central Mulbekh has several inexpensive, friendly homestay-guesthouses.

Several overloaded Kargil-bound buses pass through between 7am and 8.30am, returning ex Kargil around 3pm. In the afternoon, a J&K SRTC bus leaves Shargol for Kargil at 3pm (returning 7am).

Towards Lamayuru, the Kargil bus passes through Mulbekh between 6am and 7am, usually making a breakfast stop at Wakha.

Kargil & Zanskar

Ladakh's less visited 'second half' comprises remote, sparsely populated Buddhist Zanskar and the slightly greener Suru Valley. Residents of the Suru Valley, and its regional capital, Kargil, predominantly follow Shia Islam. The scenery is truly majestic but remarkably few tourists seem to make it out here.

Kargil

☑ 01985 / POP 18,200 / ELEV 2690M

Arriving from Srinagar, Ladakh's proudly Muslim second city seems quaint, with its vibrant workshops and old merchant stores cramming the packed, ramshackle central bazaar. Coming from Leh, however, Kargil can feel grimy, male-dominated and a tad chaotic. The town became etched into the Indian consciousness in 1999, after Pakistani forces disguised as Kashmiri militants crossed the Line of Control, triggering the 74-day Kargil War.

Kargil's main commercial centre follows the west bank of the powerful Suru Valley. The central junction is Lal Chowk where north–south Main Market intersects with Hospital Rd around 300m south of Poyen Bridge. Heading north up Main Market you'll pass in quick succession the Jamia mosque, Roots Cafe, Ice Berg Guest House and the share taxi stand for Drass. Heading south is Khomeini Chowk, the Tourist Reception Centre, then a dog-leg past the *madrassa* (Islamic religious school) to the main taxi stand. All of these places are within easy walking distance.

◉ Sights & Activities

★ Hundarman Broq   VILLAGE

(without/with guide ₹100/250; ☺10am-5pm or by arrangement) Set in a sharp mountain gully 11km northeast of Kargil, the tumbledown ghost village of Hundarman is a remarkable sight. Rocky crags tower above, a steeply raked arc of stone-walled terraces sits below and virtually all of the low-ceilinged homes are stacked on top of one another, forming a fascinating core that has been (somewhat) preserved as a unique time capsule.

A guided visit organised through Roots Cafe (p265) (₹300 to ₹600 per person plus ₹1000 taxi return) is recommended, as it gets you into a two-room 'museum of memories' displaying aged utensils, touching personal mementos of former residents and projectiles that hit the village in the various Indo-Pakistan wars. The village was part of Pakistan until 1971 and was abandoned a few years after.

The upper village 1km beyond is still populated and is a fascinating place to wander as well, though you'll need your passport and a local guide to get past the army checkpoint.

Munshi Aziz Bhat Serai Museum   MUSEUM

(Central Asian Museum; ☑9469730109; www.kargil museum.org; 147 Munshi Enclave; ₹50, camera ₹50; ☺8am-8pm Apr-Nov) Celebrating Kargil's pre-1947 role as a Silk Route trading centre, this small, intriguing private museum illustrates the caravan trade to Central Asia with coins, clothes, saddles, maps and rare 1931 photos by Rupert Wilmot. Many exhibits were rescued from the now-derelict caravanserai of the owner's grandfather for whom the museum is named. To find the museum, climb the stairway that leads up from Main Bazaar, 100m north of Roots Cafe. It's worth calling ahead.

★ Roots Cafe   TOURS

(☑01985-233009, 9419289275; www.rootsladakh. com; Main Bazaar; ☺10am-10pm) This very friendly venture is Kargil's focal point for travellers. As well as a funky upstairs cafe, Roots is the place to get inspired for visits to the greater Kargil region. The folks here organise excursions to fascinating Hundarman Broq, night photography walks, rafting trips and treks, and can also arrange trekking gear rental, hired mountain bikes (₹1000 to ₹1200 per day), motorbikes (₹1500 per day) and shared rides.

🛏 Sleeping

New International Guest House
GUESTHOUSE $

(📱9419176568, 01985-233044; 73murtaza@gmail.com; Hussaini Park; r ₹600-1200; ⏰May-Oct; 📶) Much better than other Kargil budget dives, this guesthouse has rooms that are unusually airy and well kept, and a block of new rooms and a restaurant is being finished up across the road. Owner Mohammad Murtaza is charming and helpful. It's on the lane leading from the rear, north side of the old bus station towards the river.

⭐ Hotel Jan Palace
HOTEL $$

(📱9419504904, 01985-234135; www.hoteljanpalacekargil.com; r ₹1000-1500; 📶) Jan Palace's spacious rooms remain among the brightest and most reliably clean in central Kargil. Bedrooms offer little decorative style, but modern bathrooms are spotless and come with towels, toiletries and superhot solar showers.

It's down a lane 50m off the main bazaar street so is relatively quiet.

Zojila Residency
HOTEL $$

(📱9419176249, 01985-232281; www.zojilaresidency.com; Bemathang; s/d/ste ₹2760/3680/6540; ⏰Apr-Oct; 📶) A professional lobby leads to fresh rooms that have high ceilings and relatively stylish white, olive and purple colour schemes. The quieter rooms face the river across a waterside terrace. Around 300m beyond Iqbal (Bardo) bridge, it's the best of several choices in the Bemathang neighbourhood, 1.5km south of central Kargil.

⭐ Hotel the Kargil
BOUTIQUE HOTEL $$$

(📱01985-232424; www.hotelthekargil.com; Hospital Rd; s/d ₹5300/6300; ⏰Apr-Oct; P❄📶) Opened in 2017, well-run and locally owned Hotel the Kargil is easily the best place in town, with supercomfortable beds, stylish modern bathrooms, back garden seating and a great restaurant. Look for the Pakistani shell sitting casually in the lobby.

Discounts of 30% are standard. Add ₹1000 per person for breakfast and dinner.

🍴 Eating

Charming little Roots Cafe (p265) is popular for snacks like *kati* rolls (a *paratha* – Indian-style flaky bread – fried with a coating of egg and filled with sliced onions, chilli and your choice of stuffing) and *shawarma* (spit-roasted kebab). Of numerous Main Bazaar options, our favourite is the PC Palace Restaurant (PC Palace Hotel; mains ₹200-300; ⏰7.30am-10pm).

ℹ Information

Tourist Reception Centre (📱01985-232721; ⏰10am-4pm Mon-Sat) This vine-draped sleepy governmental building is the place to book Suru Valley tourist bungalows (p267).

ℹ Getting There & Away

Charter and shared jeeps to Leh, Srinagar and Zanskar and most buses leave from the large local bus station 1km southeast of town.

Leh Private buses (₹400, 10 hours) depart at 6am, passing Mulbekh (two hours) and Lamayuru (five hours). You might find a shared jeep (₹900 to ₹1000) as late as 7am.

Mulbekh Minibuses (₹60) leave at 2pm and 3pm, returning next morning.

Srinagar Private buses (₹400, 10 hours, one to two daily) depart at 10pm, driving overnight to reach the hair-raising Zoji La pass (3529m) before the one-way system for large vehicles reverses. Shared jeeps (₹900, seven hours) leave between 6am and 2pm when full. It's worth hiring your own taxi (₹6000) to experience the scenery, which is especially memorable between Drass and Kangan.

Suru Valley For Sanku and nearer villages, red-and-white Mazda minibuses depart sporadically. A 1pm bus for Parkachik and the 1pm and 2pm services to Barsoo (for Khartse Khar) leave from the local bus station.

Zanskar Kargil–Padum buses are sporadic. Shared jeeps (₹2000, 12 to 14 hours) park in the local bus station and depart at dawn.

J&K SRTC Buses (📱9469530271; Hussaini Park; ⏰9am-4pm) to Panikhar (₹80, 7am) and Parkachik (₹112, 11.30am) run from a small stand hidden away on the east side of Hussaini Park, near the New International Guest House. Purchase tickets from the green ticket booth.

For one-way private jeep or taxi hire, figure on ₹13,000 to Padum, ₹2500 to Panikhar or ₹7100 to Leh. Return trips include to Mukbekh (₹3000) or Khartse Khar (₹2000). Book a day before at the bus station or via Roots Cafe (p265).

ℹ Getting Around

By day, microvans (₹10) shuttle down the riverside from Poyen Bridge via the main bus station to Bemathang and Baroo.

Suru Valley

📱01985 / POP 45,100

Potentially as big an attraction as better-known Zanskar, to which it is the main access route, the Suru Valley's semi-alpine Muslim villages are dotted among wide green valleys with the region's most impressive snow-topped mountainscapes rising above. Views are most dramatic between Purtikchay and Damsna and again from Parkachik.

If you're driving, consider a 5km detour east of busy little Sanku towards Barsoo/Bartoo to see the **Khartse Khar Buddha** (Barsoo Rd, Khartse Khar) carving.

The valley has little tourist infrastructure, but English-speaking guide Gulam Ali is a helpful contact should you want trekking ideas. He runs the homestay-style Hotel Khayoul, hidden away near the tourist bungalow in the upper west area of Panikhar; call ahead as he also works in Kargil.

Options for local trekking include the three- or four-day Sapil Lake and Rushi La trek from Shergole to Sanku, or the six-day Warwan Valley loop from Panikhar over two high passes. Roots Cafe (p265) in Kargil arranges treks here and can help with guides and horses.

A strenuous but satisfying day trek takes you across the 3900m Lago La over a finger of land from Pursa on the Panikhar bypass road to Parkachik (four to six hours' hike), with fabulous Nun glacier views from the pass. Ask the Hotel Khayoul about the easy one-day Bobang Peak–view walk.

From Tangole, you could make one- or two-day forays up towards the Nun base camp.

🛏 Sleeping

Good budget options include the unpretentious but decently maintained J&K Tourist Bungalows at several Suru locations. The best are at Purtikchay, Tangole and Parkachik, but there are also bungalows at Sanku and Panikhar; book at the Tourist Reception Centre in Kargil. There are four guesthouse/homestays between Sanku and Panikhar, of which the most interesting is the **Hotel Khayoul** (☑ 9469192810, 9419864611; khayoulhotel@gmail.com; Panikhar; r without bathroom ₹600); its six attractively furnished rooms share a bathroom that's better than most in rural homes. Much of its appeal is that charming owner Gulam Ali is about the best contact you can find in the Suru Valley for making local discoveries or organising treks.

ℹ Getting There & Away

Private buses run fairly regularly between Kargil and Sanku. J&K SRTC buses to Kargil leave Panikhar around 8am and noon (₹80), and Parkachik (₹112) around 7am.

Share taxis (₹100) are occasionally available on the Panikhar–Kargil route. For Zanskar, onward transport is generally limited to highly uncertain hitching. Panikhar's Hotel Khayoul can organise vehicles with advance notice.

Zanskar

☑ 01983 / POP 15,300

Majestically rugged, the greatest attraction of this mountain-hemmed Ladakhi Buddhist valley is simply getting there, preferably on a trek. As in Ladakh, the main sights are timeless monasteries, notably at Karsha, Stongdey, Sani and Phuktal, the latter only accessible on foot. The area's tiny capital, Padum, is not much more than a village with a few shops. It is not a major attraction in itself but is a key transit point if you want to drive in or out on what remains, for now, the only reliable access route (via Kargil). While days can be scorching hot, come prepared for cold nights, even in summer.

ℹ Getting There & Away

For at least the next couple of years, the only motorable road to Zanskar is from Kargil, initially passing through the Suru Valley, then becoming a rough track to scrappy Rangdum and across the 4401m Pensi La. This is closed in winter when – apart from walking along the frozen Zanskar River on the perilous Chadar Trek (p268) – there is no access to Zanskar whatsoever.

At the time of writing a rough new road was being constructed linking Padum to Manali via Darcha and the Shingo La. A few intrepid motorcyclists are already tackling the route.

RANGDUM

POP 280 / ELEV 3980M

Wind-scoured Rangdum village is where shared jeeps take a meal break on the 11-hour Kargil–Padum ride. There's little to see except the surrounding horizon of Patagonian-style jagged peaks, but if you want to break the drive it's possible to overnight here. **Rangdum Gompa** (₹50) is 5km away next to an army check post and worth a visit. As you move on from Rangdum to Padum be sure to stop at the 4401m Pensi La to get breathtaking views of the Darung Drung Glacier.

The most obvious place to stay is the overpriced **La Himalaya 4100** (☑ 9469735834; r with/without bathroom ₹2000/1500, mains ₹100-150; ⊙ May-Aug), but you'll find much better value at the **Tsewang Khangsar Homestay** (per person incl half board ₹800) 400m to the north.

TREKKING TO ZANSKAR

The Ladakh–Zanskar trek is most often undertaken as an agency-arranged group expedition with packhorses and full camping gear, starting at Photoksar village and being met at the other end by a vehicle at Pidmo Bridge.

If you prefer to organise your trek independently, note that the jeep road now extends as far as Gongma village just after the Kyupa La. Horses or donkeys and local guides are usually available at short notice in Lingshet, a couple of hours' walk away. Reaching the Kyupa La costs around ₹9000 by chartered taxi from Leh.

The main route can be done without camping in midsummer, but homestays and tea tents are very limited, so carrying a tent and especially a sleeping bag is advised in case there is no space.

Day 1 From just past the Kyupa La it's a half-day walk to the sprawling, charming village of Lingshet, whose large, welcoming gompa is at the settlement's upper north edge. Lingshet has plenty of widely dotted homestay options but few are signed, so you'll need to ask around.

Campers can consider continuing three hours further to a campsite at Lanang. A single building here has two small, ultrabasic rooms where you can overnight, assuming the caretaker turns up.

Day 2 Hike 10 hours from Lingshet or seven from Lanang, including three hard, steep hours up the Hanuma La (4720m). Sleep at Shnertse, which has camping and a tea tent with basic accommodation. Or continue around two hours further, descending to the bridge where there's camping and a single hut (often used by groups as a kitchen). More reliable for a homestay bed is Jingchen, a lonely farmhouse 40 minutes' walk up the side valley.

Day 3 and 4 Hike seven hours including over the steep 4020m Parfila La to Hanamur (Hanumil) village (one homestay). Most people sleep here but less attractive Pidmo (with a basic homestay) is just two hours further. A prebooked car can collect you from the far end of the Pidmo suspension bridge. Otherwise, walk on a further two hours to Zangla.

An alternative camping route heading west after Lingshet takes you in a day to Lingshet Sumdo in the valley leading to Dibling village. Heading southeast (away from Dibling) you pass through an area of yak herders and rejoin the main trek after Jingchen.

Winter: The Chadar Trek

In winter snow cuts off Zanskar's tenuous road links altogether. But in February it is possible to walk in from Chilling following an ancient seasonal trade trail that essentially follows the frozen Zanskar River – often on the ice, crossing side streams on precarious snow bridges and camping in caves en route. This hazardous 'Chadar Trek' was once seen as an 'ultimate adventure', but, while it remains hazardous, increased popularity with Indian domestic tourists means that of late the trek can feel oddly overcrowded. Over 3000 Indian trekkers currently walk the route within a 40-day period.

If you attempt the trek, allow around six days each way, and when selecting a support company don't seek out the cheapest (which often have too few guides and porters per client). Climate change has made the ice less stable than in previous decades, so it's essential to have an experienced local guide who can 'read' the ice. Camping en route is in caves or riverside ledges, so you need excellent four-season gear. Carrying easy-to-access spare socks and a towel is essential; if you do put a foot through the ice you'll have to react fast to prevent frostbite. Indian trekkers need a medical certificate from Leh before they are allowed to undertake the trek.

PADUM

☏ 01983 / POP 1710 / ELEV 3570M

Zanskar's dusty little capital village is a useful hub with an impressive mountain backdrop, though it lacks much architectural character. Within a block of the central crossroads you'll find the share taxi stand, shops, an unreliable internet cafe, the majority of Padum's dozen hotel-guesthouses and restaurants plus a helipad. The town is primarily useful as a base to visit local monasteries or to organise or relax after a long trek.

Unlike most of Zanskar, central Padum has mains electricity for much of the day.

The J&K Bank has an ATM (open 10am to 5pm), but you'd be wise to bring all the rupees you need with you.

Sights & Activities

Towards the southern end of Padum past the large mosque, Padum Khar is a small 'old town' area on a boulder-scattered hillock. Nearby, by the police station, Gyalwa Ringna is a rock carved with ancient Buddhist figures.

Other walks include 2km northeast to the more traditional village of Pibiting, with its hilltop Guru Rinpoche Lhakhang. Just behind Padum is Stakrimo Monastery, offering fine valley views. Walk there from Padum Khar.

Further away, Sani Gompa (Turtot Gyat, Sani Khar; Sani), 9km north of Padum, is Zanskar's oldest monastery, with a stupa dating back to King Kanishka (2nd century AD).

Multiday trekking remains a popular way to reach the Yapola Valley (north) for connections to Lamayuru. A couple of agencies in Padum can arrange guides/horses given a day or two.

Spirit of Zanskar   TREKKING
(9419864995; spalgon2000@yahoo.com; Zambala Rd; 8am-9pm) One of the most active Padum agencies, Spirit of Zanskar can – with two days' notice – arrange a donkey/horse for ₹1000/1200 per day (two animals minimum, plus return fee) for treks starting from Pidmo (towards Lingshet) or full-service treks elsewhere. Contact Tashi Falgon.

Sleeping & Eating

Most hotels close from late October to June, except when prebooked for winter trekking groups.

There's a handful of shops, greengrocers and eating places on the main street, most appealingly at the Gaskyit Hotel (Gakyi Hotel; 9469592372; gakihotel77@gmail.com; Main Market; s/d ₹900/1200), Hotel Ibex (9419803731, 01983-245214; ibexpadumzanskar@gmail.com; Main Market; d/tr ₹1000/1500) and Changthang Restaurant (Main Market; mains ₹70-160; 9am-10.30pm), plus more cheaply in the tiny little cafes in the lane between the Gaskyit Hotel and the Zan-Khar (Main Market; mains ₹120-200; 8am-9.30pm) restaurant.

Mont-Blanc Guest House   HOMESTAY $
(9469239376; tenzinpalkit@yahoo.co.in; s/d ₹800/1000, without bathroom ₹600/800) About 800m south of the main market, 200m before the mosque, this friendly four-room guesthouse has some of Padum's most attractively appointed rooms. There are fine views, especially from the rooftop and front-facing windows, and relaxing garden seating.

Zambala Hotel   HOTEL $
(9469629336; Zambala Rd; s/d ₹800/1000) Two minutes' walk northeast of the bazaar, the Zambala has 13 pleasant rooms with bathrooms (hot water by bucket) wrapped around a small, grassy central space. There's no real reception; ask for assistance at the dining room upstairs.

Hotel Rigyal   HOTEL $
(9469224500; www.hotelrigyal.com; s/d ₹1000/1200) Set back peacefully away from the main market beyond the helipad, Rigyal's rooms have small, clean bathrooms with hot-water showers, and the nice garden makes for a pleasant hang-out. Rear-facing windows have views of glacier-topped Ubarak Kangri.

Getting There & Away

Jeeps run to Kargil (per person/vehicle ₹2000/13,400, around 12 hours). Bargaining might be possible with returning Kargil drivers. Contact drivers the evening before – their vehicles are generally parked along Zambala Rd with destination signs and their mobile numbers in the window.

Other one-way/return jeep rates from Padum:

Cha ₹3500/4000
Karsha ₹800/1200
Pidmo Bridge ₹2500/2700
Pishu ₹1800/2700
Rangdum ₹7000/9000
Stongdey Gompa ₹1000/1500
Zangla ₹2000/3000

The only petrol station in Zanskar is at Km3 of the Padum–Karsha road. In summer it usually has supplies but can't be fully relied upon.

KARSHA
POP 1080 / ELEV 3663M

Across the valley from Padum, Karsha is Zanskar's most striking village, full of photogenic old-fashioned homes, barley fields and threshing circles worked by *dzo* (yak-cow cross-breeds).

Rising directly above is a near-vertical red-rock mountainside, sliced in half by a deep chasm. Whitewashed monastic buildings cascading down the north side form Zanskar's biggest Buddhist monastery complex (Jul), with an upper prayer hall

HIKING TO PHUKTAL

The day or overnight hike to Phuktal Gompa is one of the most beautiful in the Himalaya and the monastery itself is one of the most dramatically situated in Ladakh. It's now possible to drive to within a 2½-hour walk of the monastery, meaning you can visit as a day hike, or overnight at the monastery.

The trail starts from near Cha village, a three-hour drive south of Padum, and climbs past a line of mani walls (Tibetan stone walls with sacred inscriptions) to reach a small pass and ruins from where you first catch sight of the turquoise Tsarap-chu river. The trail follows the barren Utah-like northern bank of the river for two incredibly scenic hours.

After passing (but not crossing) a rickety stick bridge the trail climbs for two minutes to reach Phuktal's basic monastery **guesthouse** (per person incl half board ₹1000). Visible impressively ahead, as though tumbling out of the sacred cliff cave, is the 15th-century **Phuktal Gompa** (donation requested; ⊙8am-7pm), a 10-minute stroll away. The main chapel has some fine Alchi-school murals pasted on the walls and there are a couple of atmospheric chapels to the left of the cave entrance.

If you have time, a spectacular 45-minute-long pilgrim path climbs from the monastery guesthouse to the ledge above the monastery and then drops down the far side to enter the back gate of the gompa.

The guesthouse has four very basic rooms and a tent site, and there are also several unsigned homestays in Yogar village on the other side of the river (cross the Tsarap-chu on the earlier rickety bridge and then branch left).

To return you can follow the route you came. Alternatively, take the southern side of the river, after crossing the rickety bridge, for 1½ hours to Purney which has three homestays (per person with half board ₹1000) and a simple teahouse. From here you can meet your vehicle if the Tsarap-chu road bridge has been constructed. If not, directly below lower Purney where two rivers meet, cross the bridge across the main Lungnak River and head north on west-bank trails to Gyalbok and then cross the river on one of two scarily rickety bridges, rejoining the main road north of Cha.

(₹100; ⊙hours vary) whose stupa contains the mummified body of its 14th-century founder.

Climbing the other side of the chasm is a Buddhist nunnery, an ancient citadel and the remarkable yet little-visited Alchi-style **Chukchikjal Temple** (⊙by request) featuring a splendid 11th-century carved Chenresig statue. Ask for the key at the nunnery dining hall.

Accommodation is in several basic but welcoming homestay-guesthouses. **Grand Leopard** (☑9469290976; per person incl full board ₹800) is great for food and for its knowledgeable, hospitable owners; **Theiur** (☑9469407411; r ₹800, mains ₹150) is unusual for its large garden and for having an indoor toilet. Most comfortable is the eight-roomed **Zanskar Eco Lodge** (r incl breakfast ₹1200, s/d incl half board ₹1500/2000), right in the centre of the village.

ZANGLA
POP 1070 / ELEV 3500M

Forming an arc of traditional homes around a wide circle of terraced barley fields, Zangla is the last major road-linked Zanskar village north of Padum. On a bare crag at its southwestern corner is the small hilltop fortress palace, and at the far end of the village, there's a small, friendly Buddhist nunnery from which an alternative trail leads north to Km33 on the road to Pidmo Bridge (5km beyond).

Zangla makes a fine if bumpy half-day jeep excursion from Padum. En route it's worth detouring up to **Stongdey Gompa** (Km13, Padum-Zangla Rd) for superb morning views of the breathtaking valley.

Zangla has several homestays in the upper village near the turn-off for the palace. The well-kept Pami Homestay is easy to spot with its distinctive lavender-pink window frames.

Stongdey Gompa runs a comfortable two-roomed **guesthouse** (by donation) outside its south entrance (no food available) and there are homestays in the village below, notably at the house of **Pasang Lawang** (☑9469226949; per person incl half board ₹1000).

SOUTH OF PADUM

The road south from Padum passes **Bardan Gompa** (Km10, Padum-Raru Rd; ₹50), spectacularly set on a rocky outcrop high above the river. Some 7km further, Muney Gompa is less dramatic despite its own riverside crag setting, but its five-room **Shanti Guesthouse** (www.shanti-house.net; Muney Gompa, Km17, Padum-Raru Rd; r per person incl full board ₹1800; ⊘end Jun–mid-Sep) is managed with Gallic flair as a place to spend a few days unwinding, meditating and soaking up local culture.

Ichar is one of the valley's most intriguing villages, with a looming gompa and, on slightly higher ground, a small reflective pond and a knot of very evocative old-town homes. It's invisible from the main road.

The destination for most is Cha on the north bank, from where the hiking trail to the cliff-face monastery at Phuktal starts.

Jeeps can drive as far as Cha but the bridge across the Tsarap-chu to Purney is still unfinished. Hitch-hiking is possible if you have great patience, but you might wait all day. Most trekkers share a chartered vehicle.

THE KASHMIR VALLEY

Rimmed by layers of alpine peaks, the 140km-long Kashmir Valley opens up as a giant, beautiful bowl of lakes and orchards. Tin-roofed villages guard terraced paddy fields delineated by apple groves and pin-straight poplars. Proudly independent-minded Kashmiris mostly follow a Sufi-based Islamic faith, worshipping in distinctive wooden mosques with central spires, and they are fiercely proud of their homeland. It's a stunningly beautiful place, but one wracked by political violence in recent decades.

History

Geologists and Hindu mystics agree that the Kashmir Valley was once a vast lake. Where they disagree is whether it was drained by a post-ice-age earthquake or by Lord Vishnu and friends as a ploy to kill a water demon.

In the 3rd century BC the Hindu kingdom of Kashmir became a major centre of Buddhist learning under emperor Ashoka. In the 13th and 14th centuries, Islam arrived through the inspiration of peaceable Sufi mystics. Later, some Muslim rulers such as Sultan Sikandar 'Butshikan' (r 1389–1413), set about the destruction of Hindu temples and Buddhist monasteries. However, others such as the great Zain-ul-Abidin (r 1423–74) encouraged such religious and cultural tolerance that medieval visitors reported finding it hard to tell Hindus and Muslims apart. Mughal emperors including Akbar (1556–1605), whose troops took Kashmir in 1586, saw Kashmir as their Xanadu and developed a series of extravagant gardens around Srinagar.

When the British arrived in India, Jammu and Kashmir were a loose affiliation of independent kingdoms, nominally controlled by the Sikh rulers of Jammu. In 1846, after the British defeated the Sikhs, they handed Kashmir to Maharaja of Jammu Gulab Singh in return for a yearly tribute of six shawls, 12 goats and a horse. Singh's autocratic Hindu-Dogra dynasty ruled until Independence, despite rising resentment from the majority Muslim population.

Partition & Conflict

As Partition approached in 1947, Maharaja Hari Singh favoured Kashmiri independence rather than joining either India or Pakistan, but he failed to make a definitive decision. Finally, to force the issue, Pashtun tribespeople backed by the new government in Pakistan attempted to grab the state by force, setting off the first India-Pakistan war. The invaders were pushed out of the Kashmir Valley, but Pakistan retained control of Baltistan, Muzaffarabad and the valley's main access routes. Kashmir has remained divided ever since along a tenuous, UN-demarcated border known as the Line of Control. A proposed referendum to let Kashmir's people decide (for Pakistan or India) never materialised, and Pakistan invaded again in 1965, triggering another protracted conflict.

In the 1970s a generation of visitors rediscovered Indian Kashmir as an idyllic summer getaway. But armed rebellion became intense during the later 1980s, and Kashmir was placed under direct rule from Delhi in 1990. For several bloody years, massacres and bomb attacks were countered by brutal counterinsurgency tactics from the Indian armed forces. Significant human-rights abuses were reported on both sides.

After the brief India-Pakistan 'Kargil War' of 1999, a ceasefire and increasing autonomy for Kashmir were matched by a significant reduction in tensions. Coordinating relief after a tragic 2005 earthquake also helped bring the Indian and Pakistani governments a little closer. Militant attacks dwindled, and domestic tourism blossomed anew despite disturbances in 2008 (over an arcane land dispute at Amarnath) and 2010 (after the shooting of juvenile stone-throwers).

In July 2016 months of unrest were ignited by the army's killing of Burhan Wani, a prominent pro-independence activist and 'commander' of Hizbul Mujahideen, considered to be a terrorist organisation. Dozens of people died and thousands were injured, over 100 blinded by pellet guns, as the valley was put under 50 consecutive days of curfew.

Disturbances continued into 2017, when a by-election was marked by violence and a record low 7% voter turnout. The situation was quieter at the time of writing, but resentment and violence bubbles just under the surface and can boil over without warning.

Srinagar

☑ 0194 / POP 1,405,000 / ELEV 1583M

Ringed by an arc of green mountains, Srinagar's greatest drawcard is mesmerisingly placid Dal Lake, on which a bright array of stationary houseboats and *shikara* (gondola-like boats) add a splash of colour and a unique opportunity for romantic chill-outs. Charming Mughal gardens dot the lake's less urbanised eastern shore; while the old town bustles with fascinating Central Asian–style bazaars and a collection of soulful Sufi shrines, as well as a fortress and many historic wooden mosques. Add in a mild summer climate, feisty Kashmiri cuisine and famous local apples, walnuts and almonds, and you have one of India's top tourist draws.

Except, that is, when communal tensions paralyse the city. Sadly that happens all too regularly, leaving a chance that you'll be stuck in strikes, pro-independence demonstrations and partial curfews. Although foreign tourists themselves have never been seen as targets, you should absolutely check on the latest situation before you visit.

Srinagar's three main areas converge around Dalgate, where the canal-like southwestern nose of Dal Lake passes through a lock gate. Northwest lies the Old City. The busy commercial centre is southwest around Lal Chowk. Looping south and west of the central area is the flood-prone Jhelum River.

◉ Sights

◉ Dal Lake & Around

★ **Dal Lake** LAKE
Over 15km around, Dal Lake is Srinagar's jewel, a vast sheet of water reflecting the carved wooden balconies of the houseboats and the misty peaks of the Pir Panjal mountains. Flotillas of gaily painted *shikaras* (gondola-like taxi boats) skiff around the lake, transporting goods to market, children to school and travellers to delightful houseboats inspired by originals from the Raj era.

If you get up early, you can paddle out to see the floating flower and **vegetable market** (☉ 5-6.30am): a colourful spectacle, but one where you can expect plenty of attention from souvenir vendors.

For a visual portrait of Dal Lake life, watch the prize-winning 2012 movie *Valley of Saints*.

First Row Houseboats LANDMARK
(Dal Lake) For guests, the first-row houseboats can prove noisy and lacking in privacy. However, as an attraction they collectively form Srinagar's signature image.

Mirzabagh Veg Boat Dock HARBOUR
Much of Srinagar's fresh produce is brought in from 'floating gardens' and landed at this tiny dock, making for photogenic scenes.

Shankaracharya Mandir HINDU TEMPLE
On top of thickly forested Shankaracharya Hill, this small Shiva temple is built from hefty blocks of ancient grey stone. Previously known as Takht-i-Sulaiman (Throne of Solomon), it's now named for Hindu sage Adi Shankara who visited here in AD 750, but signs date the octagonal structure as 5th century and the site is even older.

Access is by a winding 5.5km road from a checkpoint near Nehru Park (₹300 return by autorickshaw). Walking up is not recommended as there are bears living in the intermediate forest.

◉ Mughal Gardens

Srinagar's famous gardens date to the Mughal era. Most have a fundamentally similar design, with terraced lawns, fountain pools and carefully manicured flowerbeds interspersed with mighty *chinar* (plane) trees, pavilions and mock fortress facades. The most famous garden is **Shalimar Bagh** (adult/child ₹24/12; ☉ 8.30am-7pm), built for Nur Jahan by her husband, Jehangir. However, **Nishat Bagh** (adult/child ₹24/12; ☉ 9am-dusk) is more immediately impressive, with steeper terracing and a lake-facing panorama.

If you have time, other gardens include **Pari Mahal** (adult/child ₹24/12; ☉ 9am-7.30pm), set amid palace ruins high above the lakeshore. The ensemble looks most intriguing at night from afar. En route to Pari Mahal are the petite **Cheshmashahi Garden** (Pari Mahal Rd; adult/child ₹24/12; ☉ 8.30am-7.30pm) and

KASHMIR & LADAKH SRINAGAR

the extensive, less formal **Botanical Garden** (adult/child ₹24/12; ⊙8.30am-6.30pm), behind which, in March and April, a 12-hectare **Tulip Garden** (adult/child ₹100/50; ⊙Mar & Apr) blooms colourfully.

Figure on ₹1200 for an autorickshaw tour of all the gardens.

⊙ Old City

The main points of interest in Old Srinagar are its distinctive Kashmiri mosques and vibrant Sufi shrines. When visiting, follow normal Islamic formalities (dress modestly, remove shoes), and ask permission before entering or taking interior photos. Women will usually be expected to cover their hair and use a separate entrance and may not be able to enter some inner shrines.

★**Khanqah Shah-i-Hamadan**   MOSQUE
(Khanqah-e-Muala; Khawaja Bazaar area; ⊙4.30am-9pm) This distinctively spired 1730s Muslim pilgrim hall is Srinagar's most beautiful mosque. It was constructed without any nails, and both frontage and interiors are covered in exuberantly painted paper mache reliefs and elaborately coloured *khatamband* (faceted wood panelling). Non-Muslim visitors can peek through the door but may not enter.

Badshah Tomb   ARCHITECTURE
(Old City; ⊙9am-6pm) Looking more Byzantine than Kashmiri, the multidomed 15th-century brick tomb of King Zeinalabdin's mother was built on the plinth of a much older former Buddhist temple. It sits unvisited within an ancient graveyard hidden in Gadu Bazaar's maze of copperware, spice and cloth vendors' shops.

Jama Masjid   MOSQUE
(Nowhatta; ⊙8am-9pm) Looking like the movie set for an imagined Central Asian castle, this mighty 1672 mosque (built on an earlier 1394 construction) forms a quadrangle around a large garden courtyard with fountain and monumental spired gatehouses marking the four cardinal directions. There's room for thousands of devotees among the 378 roof-support columns, each fashioned from the trunk of a single deodar tree.

Pir Dastgir Sahib   ISLAMIC SHRINE
(Nowpora Rd; ⊙5.30am-7.30pm) This large, popular Sufi shrine was ravaged by fire in 2012 but the colourful paper mache interior work for which it was renowned has been restored. The shrine is particularly popular with women and bustles with activity.

⊙ Hari Parbat

Visible from all over Srinagar, this hilltop was once an island in a giant lake. It's now crowned by Hari Parbat Fort (p274), which is entered via a lane starting north of **Badamvaer Gardens** (Badamwari; Hari Parbat Rd; adult/child ₹20/10; ⊙5.30am-8pm).

SAFETY IN KASHMIR

Kashmir's difficult 20th-century history and the delicate relationship between nationalist Muslims and Jammu Hindus create a cauldron of communal tensions, which are contained or exacerbated (according to one's viewpoint) by a very visible Indian army presence. When things are calm, Kashmir is probably safer than most places in India. But cycles of unrest, stone-throwing and curfews can erupt remarkably rapidly.

If troubles should break out while you're there, use common sense, avoid public demonstrations and military installations and consult a wide range of resources to get a feel of the situation. Useful starting points include the forum of www.indiamike.com and local news feeds, including *Kashmir Times* (www.kashmirtimes.com), *Greater Kashmir* (www.greaterkashmir.com), *Kashmir Monitor* (www.kashmirmonitor.in) and *Daily Excelsior* (www.dailyexcelsior.com).

At such times Srinagar's Old City is worth avoiding (and is in fact often sealed off by razor wire), as is Anantnag (and thus trips to Pahalgam), Kishtwar and Ganadrbal, but Dal Lake generally remains trouble-free even during fairly significant disturbances. Foreign tourists have never been targets, but in the worst recent periods (summers of 2008, 2010 and 2016), things were bad enough to paralyse land transport for days or even weeks. At such times, it was often still possible to drive some routes at night and Srinagar airport remained open, for those who could reach it. Internet and mobile-phone networks are also often down during disturbances.

Srinagar

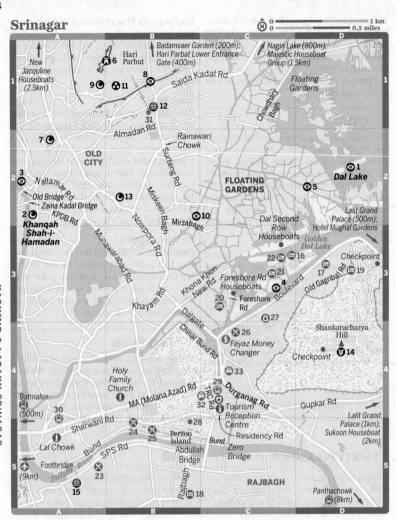

The **Naagar-Nagar Interpretation Centre** (Ropeway Gardens; ☺10am-4pm Sat-Thu) provides historical context to the area. Beside it, a **cable car** (1 way/return ₹70/120; ☺10am-4.30pm) runs to the hill's southern midslopes, near the Akhund Mulla Shah Mosque ruins and the Makhdoom Sahib Shrine. Three stepped routes lead to the same area: the most easterly starts near Kathi Darwaza, a historical gateway close to the white-domed Chetipacha Gurdwara.

Hari Parbat Fort
FORT

(Indian/foreigner ₹50/100; ☺10am-3pm Sat-Thu) On the strategically and spiritually significant Koh-e-Maran hill, north of the city centre, is this powerful *qila* (fort), which dates to the 6th century. The hill was further fortified by Emperor Akbar in 1590, but most of the upper walls date from the 1808 constructions of Pathan governor Atta Mohammad Khan.

Inside the fort walls is the Sri Sharika Temple, home to the city's 18-armed guardian goddess. Local Hindus believe Sharika (a form of Durga) and Vishnu liberated Kashmir by defeating the lake demon, Jalodabhava, on this hill.

Approach the fort from the northeast, not from the south side. The fort access lane starts with a checkpoint; then a sweaty 10-minute

Srinagar

walk along fairly obvious shortcuts brings you to a second sign-in, 15 minutes' walk up steps, to the fort's uppermost tower. Autorickshaws can reach the second checkpost.

⊙ Central Srinagar

Sri Pratap Singh Museum MUSEUM
(☑ 0194-2312859; SPS Rd; Indian/foreigner ₹10/50, photography per gallery Indian/foreigner ₹100/200; ⊗ 10.30am-4pm Tue-Sun) It's worth visiting this richly endowed historical museum for its fine 7th-century Buddhist statues, Mughal paper mache work, 4th-century tiles from the Buddhist site of Harwan, plus the normal weaponry and traditional Kashmiri costumes. The upper-floor halls of the new building were still being assembled during our visit.

🛏 Sleeping

Staying on a houseboat (p276) is one of Srinagar's highlights, but choose carefully.

Budget hotel options are relatively limited (try Dalgate or Old Gagribal Rd), while there are midrange hotels in profusion. Many, however, are unkempt and rely on noisy, large groups. Note that when there's no civil unrest, prices can rise very steeply during Indian holiday seasons (typically May, June and, to a lesser extent, October).

★ Hotel Swiss GUESTHOUSE $
(☑ 0194-2500115, Rouf 9906519745; www.swiss hotelkashmir.com; 172 Old Gagribal Rd; d ₹800-

1000; P 🕾) One of India's friendliest family guesthouses, the Swiss isn't showy but offers high-quality, spacious en suite hotel rooms decorated with plush carpets and set around a sunny lawn. It's handy for the lake, yet far enough to avoid traffic noise in an area that generally stays safe during periods of unrest. Best of all is the invaluable and tirelessly helpful manager Rouf.

**John Friends
Guesthouse** GUESTHOUSE $
(☑ 0194-2458342, 9906475607; Pedestrian Marg, Dalgate; dm ₹200, d with/without bathroom ₹500/300; 🕾) Reached from a lakeshore path by a plank-and-stilt walkway, John Friends' signature attraction is its apple-tree garden and direct access to backwater canals (albeit somewhat stagnant). The 12 bargain-value rooms come with bathrooms and there's a six-mattress dorm and communal sitting areas; upstairs rooms are brighter and fresher. Self-paddled boat hire (₹40 per hour) is a great way to explore the lake.

★ Green Acre HOTEL $$
(☑ 0194-2313848, 9419006638; www.wazirhotels. com; Rajbagh; d ₹5000-7500; P ❄ 🕾) Set amid the manicured lawns of a rose garden, Green Acre's centrepiece is a 1942 classic-Raj mansion with a perfect reading perch on the 1st-floor common balcony. It's a quiet retreat, but inconveniently away from Dal Lake. Singles costs ₹500 less. Discounts of 30% to 40%.

HOUSEBOATS

Srinagar's signature houseboats first appeared in colonial times when the British were prohibited from owning land. The best 'super deluxe' boats are palatial, with chandeliers, carved walnut panels, ceilings of khatamband (walnut wood panelling) and chintzy sitting rooms redolent of the late Raj. Category A boats are comfy but less ornate. Lower categories (C and D) can be pretty ropey and might lack interior sitting areas or private bathrooms.

Be aware that unlike those in Kerala, these boats never move. The Srinagar houseboat experience is more like staying in a romantic, mini-guesthouse complete with cook and waiter. Most are moored in sizeable groups, so you have excellent people-watching on the one hand; on the other, don't expect quiet seclusion unless you pick one way out of the central area. There are rarely views from the rooms, so the shared sitting area is important.

Better houseboats typically have three or four en suite double bedrooms, the back one usually bigger and sometimes better appointed than the rest. The setup is like a spacious sleeper train carriage.

Choosing from 1400 boats is challenging. Some owners are superfriendly families; others are crooks. Ask fellow travellers for recent firsthand recommendations. Outside the busiest seasons (May, June and October) and especially when the political climate drives tourists away, look carefully at a selection and pick one that suits your taste. Many owners will offer a free, no-strings *shikara* (gondola-like boat) ride to come and check out their boat.

Drop-in bargains are possible at all but the priciest boat groups. Contact them directly for the best rates. Most will offer a free transfer from the airport.

Houseboat Tips

For most visitors, staying on a houseboat is a delightful Srinagar highlight. But a few have reported feeling cheated, being held virtual hostage or suffering inappropriate advances from houseboat staff. Some tips:

- Beware of houseboat packages and *never book in Delhi*.
- Check out houseboats in person or via trusted websites before agreeing to anything.
- Get a clear, possibly written, agreement stating what the fees cover (tea? drinking water? *shikara* transfer? canoe usage? second helpings at dinner?).
- Check whether the boat really is the category that the owner claims (certificates should be posted) or risk paying Deluxe prices for a B-grade boat.
- Don't be pressured into giving 'charity' donations or signing up for overpriced treks.
- Don't leave valuables unattended: boat-borne thieves work rapidly.
- Don't leave your passport with the houseboat owner.
- Tell a friend or trusted hotelier where you're staying.
- Bring mosquito spray for dusk.
- It's worth spending a bit more for a nice houseboat; this is one place to splurge.

Choosing the Area

Most options are on Dal and Nagin Lakes. Nagin Lake is generally quieter than Dal Lake, but it's rather far from the city centre. In almost any location, visits from *shikara*-riding souvenir sellers, floating shops, fruit-salad *chaat*-wallahs and others are common.

Be careful with boats that are close to the shore. Boats here are inexpensive (under ₹1000) but often basic. Security is a minor concern, as thieves can easily slip aboard.

Chocolate Box BOUTIQUE HOTEL **$$**
(☎9796577334, 0194-2500298; www.chocolateboxsrinagar.com; Ghat 12, Boulevard; d ₹1600-2400; 📶) Well-chosen elements of designer style make this 13-room boutique hotel one of the Boulevard's most appealing options. Rooms 107 and 108 have private lake-facing balconies and get snapped up quickly.

Lalit Grand Palace HERITAGE HOTEL **$$$**
(☎0194-2501001; www.thelalit.com; Gupkar Rd; r/ste from ₹16,000/20,000; 📶❄) This 1910 former Maharaja's palace is set in hectares of

DAL LAKE OPTIONS:

Dal First Row Facing the noisy Boulevard, easy to-and-fro by *shikara* (gondola-like boat; ₹50 per hop), but busy and with road noise. These boats are better to look at than to stay in. There are plans to eventually relocate all these boats.

Dal Second Row Though only slightly further back, boats here are invisible from the Boulevard and better placed for sunset views. There's plenty of colourful bustle, yet it's only ₹80 to reach here by *shikara* from Ghats 9 or 12. One superdeluxe favourite is **Young Beauty Star** (☑ 9906513764, 9419060790; www.dallakehouseboat-raga.com; s/d incl full board ₹2200/2800; ☎; ⛴ Ghat 9), with a junction location that provides superb views of lake life from its front sun deck, which has parasol seating. It has a comfortable lounge and beds, and sober decor with fine carved wood. Similarly comfortable, **Chicago's** (☑ 0194-2502558, Ajaz Khar 9419061430; www.chicagohouseboats.com; s/d incl half board ₹1800/2700; ☎; ⛴ Ghat 9) three excellent boats have charming English-speaking owners and once hosted Indira Gandhi.

Moon of Kashmir (☑ 9906686454; www.moonofkashmir.com; Boulevard Rd, Gate 7; A-category s/d incl half board ₹2000/2500, B-category s/d incl half board ₹1300/1500; ☎; ⛴ Ghat 7) Low-key and more of a budget option but very welcoming, with two deluxe boats and one budget D-class boat without lake views.

Butts Clermont (☑ 0194-2415325, 9419056761; www.buttsclermonthouseboat.com; Naseem Bagh; d incl full board ₹7400) This lonely gaggle of houseboats, way up above Hazratbal, is moored beside its own private Mughal garden. It's long been a VIP favourite but it's not quite the worth the price.

Sukoon Houseboat (☑ 01942-500450, Delhi 088800920760; www.abchapriretreats.in; Kabootar Khana; s/d incl half board ₹12,400/13,400; ⊙ Mar-Oct; ❄☎; ⛴ Ghat 19a) 🍃 Taking houseboat luxury to a new level, Sukoon is impressive for its levels of service, excellent food, secluded location and fabulous rooftop sunloungers. It's also the most environmentally friendly option on the lake.

NAGIN LAKE OPTIONS:

Nagin East Bank Boats are easily accessible by road and have views of Hari Parbat. **Majestic Houseboat Group** (☑ 9858004462; www.majestichouseboat.com; r incl half board ₹1000-3500; ☎) has a secluded location beside a park and has a range of boats for every budget. To the north the funky **Butterfly** (1002 Nights; ☑ 9596553551, 0194-2429889; www.butterflyhouseboat.com; r ₹3000-5000) has decor that must be seen to be believed.

Nagin West Bank Boats have glorious views with wooded mountain scarps reflected in the lake. They are usually approached by *shikara* from the east bank. Getting into town is a pain, so plan to spend your days relaxing aboard if you pick this area. **New Jacquline** (☑ 9419001785, 0194-2421425; www.newjacqulinehouseboats.com; d incl half board ₹4000-5200; ⛴ Ghat 1), accessed by shikara from Ghat No 1, is a particularly comfortable choice here.

Prices

Officially, prices are 'set' by the Houseboat Owners Association and range from ₹600/800 for a category D single/double to ₹3800/4800 for a Deluxe single/double (or ₹900/1300 to ₹5000/6500 including half board). In reality, however, that's only a vague guide. Some places openly ask more, many ask less, and when occupancy is low, it's often possible to find great bargains.

manicured lawns with many historical heirlooms dotted about the suave interior. Only suites occupy the original palace building, but modern rooms in the long new wing are effortlessly stylish; those on the ground floor have walk-out garden balconies and offer the best value. The Chinar garden restaurant is charming.

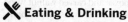 **Eating & Drinking**

Srinagar's Muslim mores mean that alcohol isn't served in restaurants, though a few upmarket hotels have bars. For takeaway alcohol there's an entirely unadvertised **wine shop** (⊙9am-9pm Sat-Thu, closed during Ramadan) hidden down an alley off the Boulevard, just west of the Hotel Heemal.

Stream
MULTICUISINE $$

(Boulevard; mains ₹230-450; ⊙noon-10.30pm; ✱) Comfortably air-conditioned, this reliable, smart eatery is slightly set back from the Boulevard and serves a particularly good range of pan-Indian options, plus shakes and smoothies.

14th Avenue Cafe & Grill
INTERNATIONAL $$

(☑0194-2310472; SPS Rd; mains ₹200-450, pizzas ₹400-500; ⊙10am-10pm; ✱🔊) This fashionable, five-table coffee-cube overlooking the Jhelum River serves a selection of traveller-pleasing European snacks and offers free delivery of its thin-crust pizzas within a 5km radius. Or just drop in for coffee and cake.

★ Ahdoos Restaurant
KASHMIRI $$$

(www.ahdooshotel.com; Residency Rd; mains ₹425; ⊙10.30am-10pm) This historic restaurant (a century old in 2018) is the classiest place in town to try meaty wazwan (traditional Kashmiri multicourse meal) dishes such as *methi maaz* (mutton with fenugreek) and *rista* (minced lamb meatballs in onion sauce), plus there are kebabs from the tandoor. The service and decor are excellent and you can choose from interior or outside seating.

The restaurant started as a bakery and the ground-floor cafe continues that tradition with a range of excellent espresso and cakes.

Mughal Darbar
KASHMIRI $$$

(☑0194-2476998; www.mughal-darbar.com; Residency Rd; mains ₹150-400, 1-/4-person wazwan ₹770/3600; ⊙10.30am-10.30pm; ✱) This upstairs restaurant is a great place to try a full spread of Kashmiri cuisine, though good Indian veg dishes are also served. A special room with carpet floor seating and copper serving dishes is available if booking ahead for a full wazwan (Kashmiri multi-course meal). Oriental murals and pillars in the main dining room give it a vaguely regal air.

🛍 Shopping

The Boulevard's various emporia sell Kashmiri souvenirs including elegantly painted paper mache boxes and carved walnut woodwork, plus cashmere and pashmina shawls. Chain-stitched *gabbas* (Kashmiri rugs with appliqué), crewel embroidery work or floral *namdas* (felted wool carpets) also make good

souvenirs. Saffron, cricket bats and dried fruits are widely sold around Lal Chowk.

ℹ Information

Fayaz Money Changer (1st Lane, Boulevard, Dalgate; ⊙9am-2pm & 2.30-6.30pm) Changes all cash currencies and is reliable. Beware of freelancers on the street offering improbably good rates: you're likely to get forged banknotes.

Tourist Police Station (☑0194-2502276; TRC Rd) Next door to the new TRC building.

Tourist Reception Centre (TRC; ☑0194-2502512; www.jktourism.org; TRC Rd; ⊙24hr, permit applications and gear rental 10am-3pm Mon-Sat) This smart new building is the place for general information, permits (₹200) for trekking the Seven Lakes route, camping- and hiking-equipment rental and to book Gulmarg gondola tickets in advance.

ℹ Getting There & Away

AIR

Served by daily flights from Delhi and Jammu, and twice-weekly flights to Leh, Srinagar's airport is 1.2km behind a security barrier where there can be long queues for baggage and body screening. To get through you'll need to show an air ticket or e-ticket confirmation printout. Allow at least two hours' leeway.

On arrival and departure by air, foreigners must fill a J&K entry/departure form which demands you give the name of your hotel. If you don't know where you'll be staying, write 'TRC' (Tourist Reception Centre).

Air India (☑0194-2450231; www.airindia.in; Linz Lane; ⊙10am-1pm & 2-5pm Mon-Sat) To Delhi (Terminal 3), Jammu and Leh (Wednesday and Thursday).

BUS & JEEP

There are departures for the following locations:

Anantnag (Islamabad) Shared taxi (₹100, 90 minutes) from **Tourist Taxi Stand 7** (Dalgate). Change in Anantnag for Pahalgam and Vailoo.

Delhi The J&K SRTC bus (seat/sleeper/AC ₹1430/1590/1910, around 24 hours) departs at 8.30am.

Jammu The new Srinagar–Jammu highway has cut driving time to around eight hours, unless there are jams. Private buses (mostly overnight) start from inconvenient Panthachowk bus station, 8km south of the centre (₹600 by taxi). Rickety J&K SRTC buses (₹340 to ₹450, 10 hours) depart at 7.30am and (some evenings) 5pm from the far more convenient **J&K SRTC bus station** (☑0194-2455107; TRC Rd). Shared jeeps (per person/vehicle from ₹900/4950) leave from across the road; finding a ride is easiest before 9am.

Kargil Shared jeeps (per person/vehicle ₹900/6400) depart before 9am from **Tourist Taxi Stand 1** (TRC Rd).

Leh The J&K SRTC bus typically departs at 7.30am (₹1170, two days) and makes a night stop en route in Kargil; book one day ahead. From Tourist Taxi Stand 1, most shared jeeps (per person ₹2100, 14 hours) leave before 7am. Book a day ahead to score good seats.

Buses and shared taxis to Kangan, for Sonamarg and Naranag, leave from several places, including the Hazratbal bus stand.

Batmaloo bus station, west of the centre, has services to Tangmarg for Gulmarg, or try the less convenient Palimpura bus stand west of the city.

Dozens of stands offer jeep and taxi rental. Approximate return prices include Pahalgam (₹2500 to ₹2900), Sonamarg (₹2500) and Gulmarg (₹2200); Jammu one way costs ₹7000.

ℹ Getting Around

Autorickshaws cost ₹70 for short hops, around ₹250 per hour for tours.

Shikaras, colourful gondolalike boats, officially charge ₹500 per hour, or ₹50/80 for hops from the shore to front/midrow houseboats. In reality many *shikara*-wallahs accept as little as ₹200 per hour, but the less you pay the more likely you'll be to encounter some alternative sales pressure.

Overcrowded minibuses ply the main routes from Lal Chowk minibus stand, including Lal Chowk–Hazratbal and Lal Chowk–Shalimar Bagh via Dal Lake's south bank.

TO/FROM THE AIRPORT

Prepaid taxis from the airport cost around ₹830; figure on ₹700 in the other direction. Alternatively, walk (1.2km) or take the irregular free shuttle bus to the outer security gate and try to find an autorickshaw from there.

In times of curfew, getting to the airport can cost as much as ₹1000, and you'll probably have to get there at dawn whatever time your flight is. The terminal building only allows passenger access three hours before a scheduled departure, so you may be stuck waiting outside.

Pahalgam & Aru

☑ 01936 (PAHALGAM) / POP 10,300 (PAHALGAM) / ELEV 2150M

Surrounded by alpine peaks, the Lidder and Seshnag Rivers tumble down picturesque, deep-cut mountain valleys covered with giant conifers. The alpine meadows, crisp air and more than 20 lakes here are a hiker's paradise, and it's easy to arrange guides and horses for a multiday trek.

Not quite spoiling this great natural beauty is Pahalgam, sprawling 4km around the river junction. It's a major Indian resort town offering golf and rafting and is a staging point for the midsummer Amarnathji pilgrimage.

The best hiking actually starts 12km away in Aru (elevation 2440m), a mellow mountain village that is a better base for hikers; most backpackers blow straight through Pahalgam with just a change of vehicle.

It's important to check the security situation before heading off on foot into the hills; never trek alone.

Treks

Between June and early October you can make an overnight trek to Tarsar Lake from Aru or continue on to nearby Masar and Sonasar alpine lakes. Longer treks go via Lidderwat to Sikwas and Sanmus to Sumbal near Sonamarg, or to the Kolahoi Glacier; for these you need to have a reliable agency. Always check the security situation as militant activity could potentially affect the area.

From Chandanwari in the East Lidder valley it's an easy day hike to Sheshnag Lake.

Most guesthouses in Aru can find a horse and horseperson for around ₹1000 per day, or can arrange full treks.

🛏 Sleeping

Aru is well set up for backpackers, including the welcoming **Friends Guesthouse** (☑9419458130; www.friendsguesthousepahalgam. com; r ₹600-800); new and clean **Aru Heights** (☑9469218170; r ₹1000); and funky **Rohella Guesthouse** (☑9469391802; s/d ₹500/600; ☺Apr-Oct), the latter a firm favourite with the juggling Israeli crowd. The well-run **Milky Way Hotel** (☑9419638392; www.milkyway kashmir.com; r ₹2500-4000, tr/q ₹3200/6000) has comfortable midrange rooms and a good-value restaurant. All places can offer advice on local treks.

ℹ Getting There & Around

During tourist season, J&K SRTC buses make day-return trips from Srinagar (₹420, 2½ hours), departing Srinagar around 7.30am and departing Pahalgam at 4.30pm. However, the service can be cancelled at short notice.

Alternatively, from Srinagar, head first to Anantnag by shared taxi (₹80, one hour) then swap vehicles at the same stand for Pahalgam (₹80, 90 minutes).

There are two roads to Pahalgam; via Anantnag and a less used but shorter route via Bijbehara (₹90 shared taxi from Pahalgam).

KASHMIRI FOOD

Kashmir has a distinct cuisine. A full wazwan (traditional Kashmiri multicourse meal) can have dozens of courses, notably *goshtaba* (pounded mutton balls in saffron-yoghurt curry), *tabak maaz* (fried lamb's ribs), *mirchi korma* (stewed lamb with chillis) and rogan josh (rich, spicy lamb curry). Kashmiri chefs also serve aromatic cheese-based curries and seasonal *nadir* (lotus stems), typically served in *yakhni* (curd-based sauce with fennel). Kashmiri kahwa is a luxurious tea flavoured with saffron, cinnamon and crushed almonds.

A taxi from Pahalgam to Srinagar costs ₹2100.

The only vehicles permitted to go to Aru (minivan ₹600, 12km) and Chandawari (₹700, 19km) start from the **tourist taxi stand** (☑ 01936-243120), just opposite the Pahalgam **jeep stand & bus station** (Pahalgam Bazaar).

Gulmarg

☑ 01954 / ELEV BASE/TOP STATION 2600M/3750M

If you're looking for extreme skiing in high-altitude powder, Gulmarg might be the dream winter-sports destination you've been looking for. But foreigners who have seen mountaintops and snow before might find Gulmarg's double-shot gondola (www.gulmarggondola.com; cable car first stage/both stages ₹740/1690, ski pass per day/week Indians ₹1210/7130, foreigners ₹1900/9490; ☺ 9am-3pm, last return around 5pm) overrated in summer due to gruelling queues at the cable car.

In winter Gulmarg comes into its own as a ski centre, famed for its perfect high-altitude powder. Although a winter-only chair lift partially paralleling the gondola's second stage offers an easy way up, this is really a venue for extreme skiers. The basin enfolding the gondola is patrolled and blasted for avalanche prevention, but the vast majority of other couloirs and forest tracks are unsecured, so it's essential to be snow-savvy and to check conditions carefully. Gulmarg Avalanche Advisory (www.gulmarg-avalanche-advisory.com) gives detailed updates throughout the season, which runs December to March, with the best conditions usually from mid-January to late February.

GM Ahanger (☑ 9596295371, 9697767268; ahangergm@gmail.com) has been recommended as a ski guide, and outlets such as **Kashmir Alpine** (☑ 01954-254638; www.kashmiralpine.com) rent decent gear. Swiss-based FSH (www.freeskihimalaya.com) and Australia-based Bills Trips (www.billstrips.com) offer complete ski packages, and Kashmir Heli-Ski (www.kashmirheliski.in) can get you further off-piste.

Gulmarg is only 1½ hours' drive from Srinagar, but stay overnight to get a head start onto the pistes. Modest but switched-on **Raja Hut** (☑ 9797297908; rk5536058@gmail.com; s/d from ₹1200/2500) is run by a genial snowboarder and is favoured by many budget-minded international adventure folk. Other decent choices include the cheery if slightly worn, pine-decor **Heevan Retreat** (☑ 01954-254455; www.ahadhotelsandresorts.com; s/d incl breakfast ₹9500/12,500; ☏), plain, family-style **Shaw Inn** (☑ 9596972200; s/d incl breakfast ₹8000/9000) or the dauntingly suave palace-hotel **Khyber Himalayan** (☑ 9596780653; www.khyberhotels.com; Khyber Rd; d ₹13,500-21,500, cottages ₹40,000-150,000; ☏☒).

A day-return jeep hire from Srinagar costs ₹2200 per vehicle (around two hours each way). Alternatively, from Srinagar's Batmaloo bus station, take a shared jeep to Tangmarg (₹80), then change for the last 13km of hairpin bends to Gulmarg (₹70).

In summer a barrier is closed beside the jeep stand, forcing you to walk the last 15 minutes to the gondola.

Naranag & Lake Gangabal

☑ 01942 (NARANG) / POP 450 (NARANG) / ELEV 2280M (NARANG)

Home to seminomadic Gujar people and a pair of enigmatic 8th-century Shiva temple ruins, Naranag village sits in a deep-cut river valley thick with mature conifer forests. For visitors it's best known as the trailhead for multiday treks in Kashmir's 'Great Lakes' uplands. The prime two-day camping destination for trekkers is beautiful Lake Gangabal (3575m), which can be reached in about seven hours of hiking from Naranag, gaining 1200m.

From Gangabal, it's possible to continue in five or six days to Sonamarg via the classic Seven Lakes trek (late July to September). There are several route variations but all require a ₹200 permit from the TRC (p278) in Srinagar; bring a copy of your visa/passport photo page and a planned itinerary. The trekking season is from May to the end of September.

Prospective guides will find you in Naranag, and most guesthouses can arrange guides, packhorses or full-package treks (per person per day ₹2500) but it's a good idea to bring your own equipment. A horse and horseperson cost ₹1500 per day.

There are several basic homestay-lodges near the first temple, where the trail to Gangabal starts. **Khan Guesthouse** (☑ Imtiaz 9469913579; s/d without bathroom ₹200/400) offers three attic rooms with a shared downstairs bathroom. **Ashraf Jagil's Homestay** (☑ 9484274792; r ₹500) has large bare rooms where you can put down your sleeping bag. Ask Srinagar's Hotel Swiss (p275) if its Swiss Retreat has opened yet. When it does, it should be Naranag's most inviting option.

One 8am bus service leaves Naranag for Kangan (₹20, 80 minutes, 16km), returning at 3pm; there are also more frequent shared taxis (₹40). Kangan–Srinagar shared taxis (₹80, one hour) and cheaper buses serve Srinagar's Batmaloo or (less convenient) Palimpura bus stations.

A charter jeep from Srinagar costs ₹2200 (two hours).

Sonamarg

☑ 0194 / POP 800 (SUMMER ONLY) / ELEV 2670M

The name Sonamarg means 'Golden Meadow', suitably enticing for an upland valley surrounded by soaring, sharpened peaks and *Sound of Music* scenery. The main, seasonal settlement, at Km85 of the Srinagar–Leh highway, is an uninteresting strip of hotels and simple restaurants. But that's easy to escape by walking for around an hour into a parallel valley to admire the multiple fingertips of Thajiwas Glacier.

If you want to hike much further, Sonamarg is the end (or possible start) of the Seven Lakes Trek. Summer sees thousands of Hindu pilgrims walk the Amarnathji Yatra that starts just 15km east of Sonamarg at Baltal.

🛏 Sleeping & Eating

Most Sonamarg options are vastly overpriced at high-season rates but you can get good discounts in September. **Hotel Royal** (Sonamarg Bazaar; r ₹1500-1800; ☺May-Oct) is the best of a dreary line of restaurant-hotels in Sonamarg centre; better options across the road include JKTDC-run **Hotel Kongposh** (r ₹2240).

The aging but beautifully located **Tourist Dormitories** (Thajiwas Meadow; dm ₹200) are 15 minutes' walk from Km83 towards Thajiwas Glacier. The best of the dozens of resort hotels are between Km83 and Km84.

For trips between Kargil and Srinagar, Sonamarg is a popular meal stop, less for its culinary reputation than as a way to recover from and prepare for the nerve-jangling 3529m Zoji La. The main bazaar strip has many refuelling-stop *dhabas* (casual eateries) for passing motorists.

ℹ Getting There & Around

Taxis head to Thajiwas car park (₹400) and Baltal (₹720) from the **Sonamarg Jeep Stand** (Sonamarg Bazaar).

Kargil Chartered jeeps ask ₹6000. Kargil- and Leh-bound buses pass through at around 8am and 10.30am, respectively, but are often full on arrival. So, too, are most shared jeeps from

---

THE AMARNATHJI YATRA

Amarnath's unique attraction is a natural stone lingam, seen as symbolising Lord Shiva, in an isolated mountain cave at 3888m, 14km from the nearest road. Joining the scenic *yatra* (pilgrimage) to behold it, in mid-July to mid-August, is an unforgettable experience. But with around 20,000 pilgrims a day, it's certainly not a meditative country hike.

There are two routes. From the vast Baltal Camp, 15km east of Sonamarg, Amarnath is just 14km away (two days, one night). Wealthier pilgrims complete the journey by pony, *dandy* (palanquin) or in part by helicopter. The longer approach starts from Pahalgam with a 16km taxi ride to Chandawari (₹700), then a 36km, three-day/two-night hike via Lake Sheshnag and Panchtarni. Either way, camps en route provide all the essentials, so you don't need to carry much more than spare warm clothes.

Beware that both blizzards and Kashmiri militants have killed pilgrims in the past, and prospective *yatri* (pilgrims) need to be suitably equipped and must apply for a special permit through the **Sri Amarnath Shrine Board** (SASB; ☑ 0194-2313146; www.shriamarnathjishrine.com; ☺mid-Jul–mid-Aug). You can download the form online, but you'll need to present it, along with photos, passport/visa copy, a medical certificate and a ₹150 fee, in either Jammu or at the Tourism Reception Centre in Nowgam, 12km from Srinagar.

Srinagar, but it's worth looking for JK07 number plates at the restaurant strip or bus stand. If space is available, pay ₹600 per person to Kargil. An alternative is to have a friendly hotelier phone-reserve a seat in a jeep ex-Srinagar, but you'll need to pay the full ₹900 fare up front (plus commission).

Srinagar Direct buses at 7am and 8.30am are appallingly slow (₹120, over five hours), so most locals take a shared Sumo to Kangan (₹100, 90 minutes) and another from there to Srinagar (₹80, one hour).

South of Srinagar

If you're driving from Srinagar to Jammu, Kishtwar or Pahalgam, you'll pass some minor curiosities, including saffron fields at Pampore (Km276), cricket-bat makers at Sangam (Km256) and the ancient settlement of **Awantipora** (Indian/foreigner ₹25/300, video ₹25; ☉ sunrise-sunset), where you can easily visit the roadside 9th-century ruins of the huge Avantiswamin and Avantisvara Shiva temples.

If those haven't slaked your thirst for ancient ruins, consider a short diversion from the Pahalgam road to Mattan (Martand), 2.5km above, which are the remnants of a more impressive, 8th-century **sun temple** (☉ dawn-dusk) set in splendidly tended grounds (follow signs to Kehrbal). A few kilometres closer to Pahalgam is the popular Sufi pilgrimage site of **Aishmuqam** (Km23, Anantnag-Pahalgam Rd).

Reached via a separate road south of Srinagar Airport is Char-i-Sharif, the shrine town of Kashmir's 'patron saint' Sheikh Nuraddin-Wali, and 9km beyond is the pine-framed meadow of Yusmarg, where some Muslim scholars claim Jesus came to 'retire' after surviving the crucifixion.

The Mughal Road

The seasonal 'Mughal Road' (open mid-June to October) from Anantnag to Kishtwar is a narrow ribbon of asphalt winding up 32km of almost-constant hairpin bends from picnic village Daksum (10km beyond Vailoo) to the 3800m pass called Sinthan Top, then tumbling back down as a rough track towards Chingam.

Although there are two basic hotels in central Vailoo, it's far nicer to sleep 6km away at the **Hotel Alpine** (☑ Srinagar 0191-2549065; Kokernag; r standard/deluxe ₹700/1500,

r without bathroom ₹500), within the beautiful botanical gardens of Kokernag. The best bungalow rooms are great value, with new bathrooms and appealing garden terraces.

By public transport, take a shared Sumo (₹40) to Vailoo (wai-yil) from the Kokernag stand in Anantnag. Around five shared Sumos per day continue to Kishtwar (per person/vehicle ₹300/3500, six hours), departing between 6am and 10am.

JAMMU & SOUTHERN KASHMIR

Jammu, the hub of J&K's predominantly Hindu southern region, swelters at the edge of the plains. It's mainly a destination for Hindu pilgrims headed to Katra (April to June and October to December), Gulabgarh (August) or Amarnath (July) via Pahalgam.

But the region has several lesser-known attractions, including the launch point, at Kishtwar, for the remarkable K3 route. The road heads via Killar to Keylong in Himachal Pradesh, following the dramatic Chenab River canyons and navigating one section of narrow jeep road that has been dubbed the 'world's most dangerous'.

Jammu

☑ 0191 / POP 560,000 / ELEV 330M

Steaming hot compared to the rest of the state, Jammu is J&K's winter capital. Pre-Independence the city was the seat of the powerful Dogra dynasty, whose palaces remain the city's most appealing sights. Religiously Hindu, Jammu dubs itself as the 'city of temples'. Few of these temples are historically significant, and for foreign tourists there's little pressing need to hang around after making transport connections to Amritsar, Srinagar or Dharamsala.

◉ Sights

Raghunath Mandir HINDU TEMPLE
(Raghunath Bazaar; donations accepted; ☉ 8am-8.30pm) The large, 19th-century Raghunath Mandir marks the heart of older Jammu and features several pavilions containing thousands of what look like grey pebbles set in concrete. In fact, these are *saligrams* (ammonite fossils) symbolically representing the 33 million deities of the Hindu pantheon.

THE K3: KISHTWAR–KILLAR–KEYLONG

On a map it all looks so easy: a road that neatly follows the Chenab, Chandra and Bhaga Rivers from Kishtwar in southern Kashmir to Keylong in Lahaul. But the reality of driving the K3 is so much more: it's a superbly photogenic adrenaline-fix ride. It roller-coasters along terrifyingly narrow ledges barely wide enough for a vehicle to pass, soaring high above the river while daggers of rock dangle from overhead.

Virtually the whole route is gorgeous, but most thrilling is the 5km section between Tayari and the improbably perched village of Ishtiyari, which some have dubbed 'the world's most dangerous road'. Although less toe-curling, another scenic highlight is the beautiful configuration of huge rocks and mature trees in the canyon around 50km east of Kishtwar.

To travel Kishtwar to Keylong, allow at least two full days, with a night's stop in Killar (p345). Ideally add a second in Gulabgarh, where J&K's three religious areas intersect: the town has a Buddhist monastery, a mosque and several Paddari-style Hindu temples, notably the Chandi Mata shrine and Sitlama Temple.

Jeeps ply the Gulabgarh–Killar route (five hours) most days, or hire your own Sumo (₹3000). The nearest petrol stations are in Bhadarwah and Kishtwar. The route is only passable from June to October. Killar has twice-daily buses to Keylong (₹210, 10 hours).

From Jammu bus station there are frequent buses to Kishtwar (₹290, eight hours) and one 4.30am bus to Gulabgarh (₹400, 11 hours). Check the security situation in Kishtwar before travelling there.

Kishtwar

Kishtwar's best viewpoint is the former site of the long disappeared Qila palace-fort, the residence of king Taj Singh. His much celebrated conversion to Islam was inspired by Shah Fariduddin Shaib (1592–1691), now entombed at **Astan Bala** (Durbar-e-Faridia), Kishtwar's foremost spiritual centre.

Around the bus-stand area there's a wide choice of budget crash pads; better options, notably **Blue Sapphire** (☑ 7051038398; www.hotelbluesapphire.in; Km1, Kishtwar-Tayari Rd, Wassar; r ₹1000-2000; ℗), are 2km further east near the big new DC Office.

Most buses fill up on the main road near the bus station, close to the Jamia Mosque. Direct buses to Gulabgarh leave around 11am and 1pm (₹100, three hours), en route from Jammu. Shared jeeps (per seat ₹150) depart when full from the bus stand.

Buses to Jammu (₹290, eight hours) depart hourly until noon.

Gulabgarh

There's a handful of simple guesthouses along the main street leading between the Sitlama Temple and the helipad. The best choice is unmarked **Himalayan Guest House** (☑ 9419953139; r ₹600-700).

Buses to Jammu leaving at 5am and 5.30am (₹400, 12 hours) drive via Kishtwar (₹100, three hours). Shared jeeps to Kishtwar (per seat ₹100 to ₹150, three hours) depart when full.

Mubarak Mandi   PALACE
(Durbagarh Rd) Started in 1710 and vastly expanded after 1824 under the Dogras, this extensive complex of palace buildings is fascinating for both its scale and its startling state of semicollapse. The only part that's accessible is the former durbar hall containing the **Dogra Art Gallery** (☑ 0191-2561846; Mubarak Mandi Complex, Durbagarh Rd; Indian/foreigner admission ₹10/50, photography ₹140/280; ☉ 10am-4.30pm Tue-Sun).

Amar Mahal   PALACE
(standard/special entry ₹20/100, photography ₹50; ☉ 9am-1pm & 2-6pm Tue-Sun Apr-Sep, to 5pm Oct-Mar) In the 1890s the Dogra maharajas moved from the Mubarak Mandi to this European-style brick mansion in the north of town, with castle-style miniturrets and sweeping clifftop views. It's now a museum whose star exhibit is a canopied royal throne made from over 100kg of gold. Other exhibits are limited to royal family photos, but

Jammu

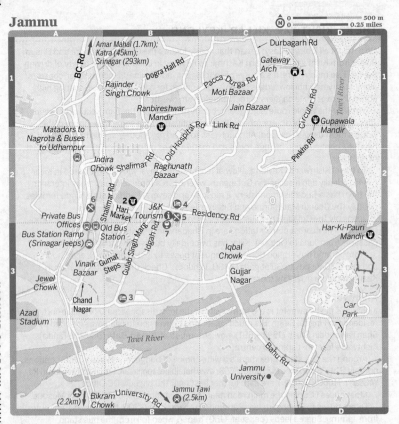

Jammu

◎ Sights
Dogra Art Gallery ....(see 1)
1 Mubarak Mandi D1
2 Raghunath Mandir B2

🛏 Sleeping
3 Fortune Riviera.......................................B3
4 Hotel Natraj B2

✕ Eating
5 Falak B2
6 Lime Tree...A2

🍷 Drinking & Nightlife
7 Saqi Bar...B3

with the 'special' ticket you can visit the up-stairs maharani's chambers, with its looming portrait of Queen Victoria and bathroom complete with royal perfume collection.

Afterwards, have a cocktail at **Polo Bar** (Hari Niwas Hotel; beer/cocktails from ₹150/190;

⊙11am-11pm), which shares the manicured lawns. Buses bound for Nagrota and Udham-pur pass the driveway entrance every few minutes till around 6pm, returning to BC Rd.

🛏 Sleeping

Hotel Natraj   HOTEL $$
(☎0191-2547450; Residency Rd; r ₹1350-1800; ❄🏠) Modern rooms with a hint of style have good air-con and, in the smallish bathrooms, piping-hot showers, plus the central location is perfect. The lackadaisical reception is hidden away in a vegetarian restaurant on Panj Bakhtar Rd. The better rooms face out onto bustling (read: noisy) Residency Rd; others suffer from a lack of windows.

★**Hari Niwas Palace**   HERITAGE HOTEL $$$
(☎0191-2543303; www.hariniwaspalace.in; Palace Rd; s/d incl breakfast from ₹5280/6600; P❄🏠) On the clifftop lawns next to the Amar Mahal and with similarly royal connections, Jammu's most atmospheric and relaxing

property is guarded by bronze ceremonial cannons and a moustachioed doorman. Pick deluxe rooms 207 to 212 for best-value views towards the Tawi River from the shared balcony. Or request elegant 'royal' room 205 for its four-poster bed.

Fortune Riviera HOTEL $$$
(☑ 0191-2561415; www.fortunehotels.in; 9 Gulab Singh Marg; s/d incl breakfast from ₹5310/5900; P❋❐) Central Jammu's most stylish and attentively businesslike hotel has a glass elevator, a fine North Indian restaurant, a 24-hour coffee shop and a bar – all for just 29 soothingly beige rooms. Online rates can be as low as ₹2500 and often include an airport drop.

✖ Eating & Drinking

The Residency Rd area has some great street food, ranging from tandoori chicken to kebabs and fried fish. Start looking outside the Hotel Natraj.

Drinking options are much more plentiful than in Kashmir. **Saqi Bar** (Hotel Jammu Residency, Residency Rd; beer ₹240; ⏲10am-11pm; ❐), behind the tourist office, has more character than most but is dark and male dominated. Women hoping for a quiet drink will feel more comfortable at the classy Polo Bar (p284) or the rotating Falak restaurant (p285). For DJ'd music and a rooftop drink, head to **Lime Tree** (www.lordshotels.com; 4th fl, Lords Inn, BC Rd; mains ₹350-575; ⏲7-11pm; ❋).

★**Falak** INDIAN $$$
(☑ 0191-2520770; www.kcresidency.com; 7th fl, KC Residency Hotel, Residency Rd; mains veg/nonveg from ₹475/575; ⏲noon-11pm; ❋) This smart revolving restaurant serves superb tandoori kebabs and pan-Indian dishes while offering 360-degree views of the crowded Jammu cityscape. Try the Jammu speciality *khatta gosht dhoonidar* (smoked lamb flavoured with pomegranate paste) and finish off with a *kesari phirni* (rice pudding with saffron).

Alcohol is available, but taxes add 31.5% to prices on the drinks menu.

ℹ Getting There & Away

AIR
There are multiple daily flights to Delhi and Srinagar, three weekly flights to Leh and connections to Mumbai.

Air India (☑ 0191-2456086; www.airindia.com; J&K Tourism complex; ⏲10am-1pm & 2-4.30pm Mon-Sat) Delhi, Srinagar and Leh (Sunday, Monday and Friday).

BUS & SHARED TAXI
Most public buses still use the big, rotting concrete **old bus station** (General Bus Stand; BC Rd) complex. A new bus station is under construction just to the north. For the following long-distance destinations dozens of private bus offices line BC Rd across from the old bus station.

Amritsar Many daily buses (AC seat/sleeper ₹400/500, six hours) via Pathankot in Punjab.

Delhi Private services are most comfortable and run overnight (AC seat/sleeper ₹600/800, 11 hours, evening departures).

Dharamsala Direct buses are very hard to find; change in Pathankot.

Manali Multiple private buses (AC ₹900, 12 hours) ply this route in the evening.

Srinagar Private bus companies mostly offer overnight services (seat/sleeper ₹400/500, nine hours). Shared taxis (seat ₹1000) gather along the **bus station ramp** (Shalimar Rd) and several other locations; they're quicker than buses but only leave when full. Last choice is the morning J&K SRTC bus (₹333 to ₹567) from the old bus station. Most services are cancelled when Kashmir experiences turmoil. An air-conditioned taxi to Srinagar costs ₹6500, double the cost of a flight.

TRAIN
Jammu Tawi, Jammu's main train station, is south of the river, 5km from the old bus station. The new northbound railway should one day reach Srinagar.

Amritsar 18310 Jat Tata Sambalpur Express (sleeper/3AC ₹160/495, five hours, 2.20pm).

Delhi 12446 Uttar Sampark Kranti Express (sleeper/3AC/2AC ₹355/930/1315, 10 hours, 8.45pm). The slower 11078 Jhelum Express departs at 9.45pm and continues to Agra (sleeper/3AC/2AC ₹395/1060/1555, 14 hours).

ℹ Getting Around

For transport into town from the airport, turn left on exiting the airport grounds and get a prepaid taxi (₹300) at the Durga Petrol Station. Autorickshaws here ask for just ₹50 less.

Short autorickshaw hops start at ₹50.

Local minibuses called 'matadors' serve the city and outlying areas and charge ₹10. **'Nagrota' matadors** (BC Rd) pass within 300m of the Amar Mahal. Minibuses run between the east side of the bus station and train station.

Himachal Pradesh

Best Places to Eat

➡ Johnson's Cafe (p317)

➡ Alliance Guesthouse (p314)

➡ Raju Bharti's Guest House (p305)

➡ Evergreen (p309)

➡ Vibes (p317)

➡ Hotel Deyzor Restaurant (p348)

Best Places to Stay

➡ Orchard Hut (p341)

➡ Wildflower Hall (p293)

➡ Himalayan Village (p308)

➡ Hotel Deyzor (p348)

➡ Alliance Guesthouse (p314)

➡ Gone Fishing (p305)

Why Go?

With spectacular snowy peaks and plunging river valleys, beautiful Himachal is India's outdoor adventure playground. From trekking and climbing to rafting, paragliding and skiing, if it can be done in the mountains, it can be done here. A convoluted topography of interlocking mountain chains also makes Himachal a spectacular place simply to explore, by bus, car, motorbike, jeep or foot. Every pass crossing into a new valley brings you into a different world, with its own culture, deities and even language. Villages perched on staggering slopes enchant with fairy-tale architecture and their people's easygoing warmth. Hill stations appeal with a holiday atmosphere and colonial echoes, while backpacker magnets lure with chilled-out vibes and mountain beauty. In the Dalai Lama's home-away-from-home, McLeod Ganj, or in remote Lahaul and Spiti with their centuries-old Buddhist cultures, you might wonder whether you've inadvertently stumbled into Tibet.

When to Go
Manali

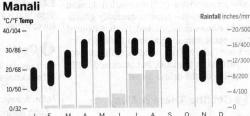

May–Jun & early Sep–Oct Outside the monsoon season; perfect for trekking and other activities.

Mid-Jul–early Sep The monsoon drenches the lower-lying areas but Lahaul and Spiti stay dry.

Nov–Apr Good for snow-lovers, but the high passes to Lahaul and Spiti are blocked.

History

Ancient trade routes dominate the history of Himachal Pradesh. Large parts of northern Himachal came under Tibetan control in the 10th century, and Buddhist culture is still the defining characteristic of the mountain deserts of Lahaul and Spiti. The more accessible areas in the south and west were ruled by hosts of rajas, ranas and *thakurs* (noblemen), creating a patchwork of tiny states, with Kangra, Kullu and Chamba the most important. Sikh rajas conquered large areas in the early 19th century, but lost them with the Anglo-Sikh Wars of the 1840s, which brought most of Himachal under British control.

The British started creating little bits of England in the hills of Dalhousie, Dharamsala and Shimla, the last of which, from 1864, became the British Raj's summer capital. Narrow-gauge railways were later pushed up to Shimla and along the Kangra Valley. The areas under direct British rule were administered as part of the Punjab, while Chamba and the southern princedoms remained nominally independent, known as the Punjab hill states. Himachal Pradesh was formed from these princely states after Independence, liberating many villages from the feudal system. In 1966 the districts administered from Punjab were added, and full statehood was achieved in 1971. Initially neglected by central government, Himachal has been reinvented as the hydropower dynamo for India, with dams producing electricity for half the country.

SOUTHERN HIMACHAL PRADESH

As soon as you cross the state line from Haryana, the landscape starts to crinkle and fold in steep, forest-covered ridges – the foothills that herald the grand Himalayan ranges further north. The main travel destination in the south is the popular hill station Shimla, the former summer capital of British-ruled India.

Shimla

🎵 0177 / POP 170,000 / ELEV 2205M

Strung out along a 12km ridge, with steep forested hillsides falling away in all directions, the Himachal capital is one of India's most popular hill resorts, buzzing with a happy flow of heat-escaping Indian vacationers. For some visitors the attraction is perus-

ing a dwindling series of relics from Shimla's previous incarnation as the summer capital of British India. Traffic is banned from the central part of town, so walking is pleasant – even when huffing and puffing uphill. The long, winding main street, The Mall, runs east and west just below the spine of the hill. South of it, the maze-like alleys and stairways of the bustling bazaar cascade steeply down to traffic-infested Cart Rd.

From mid-July to mid-September Shimla is frequently wreathed in cloud, and from January it often gets a carpeting of snow. November is cold but clear with a distant horizon of Himalayan peaks sometimes visible from The Ridge.

History

Until the British arrived, there was nothing at Shimla but a sleepy forest glade known as Shyamala (a local name for Kali – the Hindu destroyer-of-evil goddess). Then the new British political officer for the Hill States, Charles Kennedy, built a cottage here in 1822 and nothing was ever the same again. In 1864 Simla (its colonial-era name, and still that of its train station) became the official summer capital of the Raj. From then until 1939 the entire government of India fled here for half of every year from the sweltering heat of the lowlands, bringing with them hundreds of muleloads of files, forms and other paraphernalia of government.

When the Kalka–Shimla railway was opened in 1906, Shimla's status as India's premier hill station was assured. The town became a centre not only of government but also of social frolics for the elite of the Raj. Maharajas as well as colonial grandees built mansions here, and the season was filled with grand balls at the Viceroy's lodge, picnics in the woods, amateur dramatics at the Gaiety Theatre and much flirtation and frivolity. Rudyard Kipling, who spent several summers here, used Shimla as the setting for parts of *Kim* and his short-story collection *Plain Tales from the Hills*.

Himachal Pradesh Highlights

1 **Kinnaur-Spiti loop** (p296) Daring the hair-raising passes, gorges and cliff-ledge roads of one of Asia's great road trips.

2 **Trekking** (p324) Choosing from dozens of spectacular mountain crossings – easy, demanding, or moderate such as the Hamta Pass.

3 **McLeod Ganj** (p326) Immersing yourself in Tibetan culture or yoga, volunteering with refugees or just chilling out in the mountains.

4 **Manali** (p314) Skiing, trekking, climbing, paragliding, rafting or just enjoying the traveller scene in Himachal's backpacker playground.

5 **Chehni Kothi** (p304) Walking forest paths to this timeless village with its trio of temple towers, the tallest an astonishing 11 storeys high

6 **Parvati Valley** (p306) Blissing out on the hippie trail in this hauntingly beautiful valley.

7 **Shimla** (p287) Riding the toy train up from the plains and exploring relics of the British Raj in its former summer capital, still one of India's favourite hill stations.

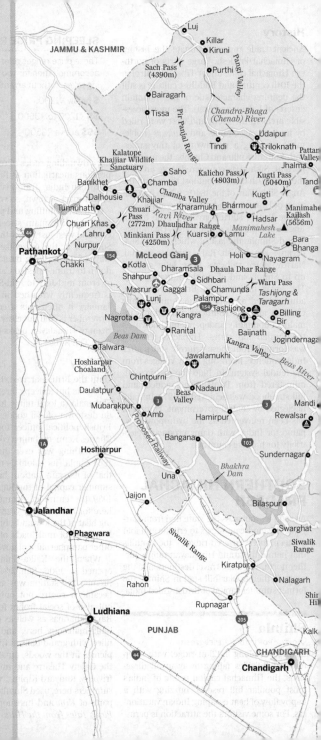

Shimla

◉ Sights

★ The Ridge
STREET

Along the central ridgetop, this broad pedestrian esplanade diverges from The Mall at Scandal Point, guarded by a fancifully hatted policeman. Thronged with strolling locals and visitors, it rises to a triangular parade ground backed by Christ Church and dotted with statues.

Gaiety Theatre
HISTORIC BUILDING

(☏0177-2650173; www.gaiety.in; The Mall; Indian/foreigner ₹10/25, camera ₹15/25; ⊙11am-1.30pm & 2-5.30pm Tue-Sun, to 6.30pm summer) Lovingly restored between 2004 and 2009 and hoping for Unesco status, this remarkable 320-seater theatre opened in 1877, originally as part of a bigger grandiose civic centre. It's long been a focus of Shimla social life, and Rudyard Kipling, Baden-Powell, Shashi Kapoor and Michael Palin are among those who have trodden its Burmese teak boards.

It's worth the entry fee to admire the unusual gilt-patterned interior and to hear the (included) historical commentary by dapper and unstoppably fluent guide Mr R Gautam.

★ Viceregal Lodge
HISTORIC BUILDING

(Indian Institute of Advanced Study; www.iias.org; tour Indian/foreigner ₹40/85, grounds only ₹20; ⊙visits 9.30am-4.45pm Tue-Sun, grounds to 5.30pm, extra visits 5.30pm & 6.15pm mid-May–mid-Jul.) A cross between Harry Potter's Hogwarts and a Scottish baronial castle, this 1888 pile was the official summer residence of the British viceroys until WWII and the scene of two crucial conferences (1945 and 1946) that essentially sealed the partition of India. To look inside join a group (departing every 45 minutes from the cafe/ticket booth) for 20 minutes perusing three rooms of historic photos. Then exit through the superb three-storey entrance hall that looks like an MC Escher design built in Burmese teak.

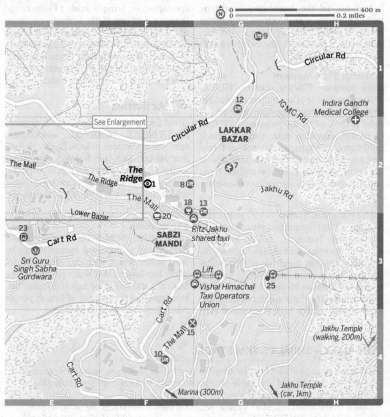

Shimla

◎ Top Sights
1 The Ridge	F2

◎ Sights
2 Bantony	D2
3 Gaiety Theatre	C4
4 Gorton Castle	B2
5 Railway Board Building	C2
6 Town Hall	C4

✪ Activities, Courses & Tours
7 Great Escape Routes	G2

🛏 Sleeping
8 Ballyhack Cottage	F2
9 Chapslee	G1
10 Clarkes Hotel	F4
11 Hotel Amber	B4
12 Hotel White	G1
13 YMCA	G2

✖ Eating
14 Ashiana	C4
15 Café Simla Times	F4
16 Himachali Rasoi	C4
17 Indian Coffee House	B4
Wake & Bake	(see 16)

🍷 Drinking & Nightlife
18 Brew Estate	F2
19 Hide Out Cafe	C4
20 Honey Hut	F3

ℹ Information
21 Additional District Magistrate	B4
22 HPTDC Tourist Office	C4

ℹ Transport
23 Bus stop for Chotta Shimla	E3
24 HPTDC Bus Stop	B2
HRTC booth	(see 26)
25 Jakhu Ropeway	G3
26 Rail Booking Window	C4

HIMACHAL PRADESH

The rest of the huge, grey sandstone building houses a postdoctoral humanities research centre. The well-manicured gardens make a nice stroll. The lodge is 3.5km west of Scandal Point.

Himachal State Museum MUSEUM
(Indian/foreigner ₹30/100, camera ₹50/100; ☺10am-5pm Tue-Sun) On a hilltop some 2.5km west of Scandal Point, the state museum sits right at the base of the prominent TV Tower. Rich if somewhat static displays include miniatures, carvings, traditional costumes and jewellery. More context is available in the revamped archaeology/petroglyph room and the interesting if somewhat out-of-place army section.

Jakhu Hanuman Statue HINDU TEMPLE
A 108ft (33m) vermillion-pink statue of monkey-god Hanuman pokes his head above the treetops on Shimla's highest hilltop. Appropriately, hundreds of rhesus macaques loiter around here hoping for gifts of *prasad* (temple-blessed food offerings) from visitors. They have a habit of snatching loose objects such as hats, phones and even spectacles, so bring a stick to discourage them, or rent one (₹10). Access is by **cable car** (☑0177-2086666; Richmount Rd; adult/child ₹250/200, return ₹450/390; ☺9.30am-6.45pm) or a steep but worthwhile 1.5km hike from beside Christ Church (allow around 40 minutes up, much more if you're unfit).

 Activities

Great Escape Routes OUTDOORS
(☑0177-6533037, 9418012500; www.facebook.com/himalayanescapes; 6 Andhi Bhavan; ☺9am-8pm Apr-Oct, 10am-5pm Nov-Mar) Specialises in trekking and other adventure trips, including mountain-bike, motorcycle and wildlife tours, around Himachal Pradesh and beyond.

Shimla Walks WALKING
(☑9817141099, 9459519620; www.shimlawalks.com) A very professional operation run by local writer Sumit Vashisht, Shimla Walks offers excellent guided walks on and off the beaten track, including tailored family history trips aimed primarily at British people whose forebears lived or died here.

THE MALL – SHIMLA'S 7KM STROLL

Traffic-free for a good part of its winding 7km length, The Mall, along with The Ridge, form the strolling heartbeat of Shimla life, strung with hotels, shops, eateries and colonial-era buildings in assorted states of repair.

Near its southeast end, start an east–west Mall walk at the handsome half-timbered **Clarkes Hotel** (☑0177-2651010; www.clarkesshimla.com; r ₹11,500-13,500, ste ₹16,640; 🛜), dating from the 1890s. The Mall's main shopping strip then leads up past the Gaiety Theatre (p290), opened in 1877; and the recently rebuilt 1910 Town Hall, oddly reminiscent of the mansion in Hammer Horror films. It's almost beside Scandal Point, so named because of an incident in which the Maharajah of Patiala kidnapped a British damsel (in some stories the Viceroy's daughter) to add to his reputedly extensive harem.

West of Scandal Point, just above The Mall, is the **main post office** (☺9.30am-5.30pm Mon-Fri, to 12.30pm Sat), housed in a pretty 19th-century quasi-Tudor folly. A further 200m west, again just above The Mall, is the wonderfully whimsical **Bantony** (Kali Bari Rd), a turreted red-brick mansion from 1880 that was once home to the Maharajah of Sirmaur. Together with its quaint red-brick cottage next door, Bantony is now sadly the epitome of Shimla picturesque decay, though, since 2017, very tentative moves have begun to restore the place.

Another 500m west, the Railway Board Building, built in 1897 with fire-resistant cast iron and steel, now houses government and police offices. Just past here is the austere grey-stone Gorton Castle from 1904, formerly the colonial government secretariat (visitors can walk around the outside but can't go inside). A further 1km brings you to Shimla's most famous luxury hotel, the Oberoi Cecil (p293), founded in 1902 and radically refurbished in the 1990s but with its western end still preserving classic century-old half-timbering. From the Oberoi, it's 1.4km westward to the most splendiferous and important of all Shimla's Raj-era edifices, the Viceregal Lodge (p290), via a peaceable walk passing the state museum and Peterhof, the somewhat underwhelming 1981 hotel-rebuild of a former viceroy's mansion.

🛏 Sleeping

Shimla has countless hotels but many of the better resorts are a long way from the centre. The town's popularity with domestic tourists keeps room rates comparatively high during the peak seasons (approximately mid-April to mid-July, October to mid-November, Christmas/New Year and other major holidays). At other times, discounts of 30% or 40% are often available.

YMCA
HOSTEL $$

(☑0177-2650021; ymcashimla@yahoo.co.in; The Ridge; r ₹2000, without bathroom ₹800; ☎) Shimla's backpacker stalwart, the friendly, bright-red YMCA has been open since 1930 and takes all comers, regardless of age, gender or religion. Rooms are plain budget affairs but neat and pleasant for the price, which includes a basic breakfast in the time-warp dining room.

Spars Lodge
GUESTHOUSE $$

(☑0177-2657908; www.sparslodge.com; Museum Rd; s ₹1900 d ₹2465-3760; ☎) Around 2km west of Scandal Point, on the road up to the State Museum, Spars has a homely feel with just eight clean, unfussy rooms of varying sizes: all but 202 and 203 have views, which are best of all from the appealing top-floor dining and sitting area.

Hotel White
HOTEL $$

(☑0177-2656136; www.hotelwhitesimla.com; Lakkar Bazar; d ₹2350-2950, ste ₹4200-6000; ☎) Northeast of The Ridge through a bustling bazaar, Hotel White is clean, simple and has spacious if rather dated premium rooms (₹2700) with fine valley views from the balconies. Cheaper rooms, facing the road and with limited light, are not recommended.

★ Sunnymead
B&B $$$

(☑0177-2801436, Madhavi 9736584045; www. sunnymeadestate.com; Sunnymead Estate, below Cart Rd, near Hotel Blossom; s/d incl breakfast ₹6000/9500; ☎) 🍴 Some 40 steps down through a barely signed green gate take you from busy Cart Rd into a magical forest-garden wonderland. Here nestles this wonderfully cosy 1890s cottage homestay full of interesting art, books and furnishings. The four rooms are comfy and characterful, the biggest double with four poster bed and balcony. You'll need to like pets.

Booking ahead is essential as the hostess travels widely. Her exacting tastes ensure delicious breakfast and high tea (included, fabulous lemon cake), and dinners are also possible by arrangement (₹2000). It's 3km west of the Old Bus Station.

★ Wildflower Hall
HERITAGE HOTEL $$$

(☑0177-2648585; www.oberoihotels.com; Chharabra; s/d from ₹43,520/44,800; ❀@☎☀) If money was no object, regal Wildflower Hall would be almost anyone's top choice of lodgings in Himachal Pradesh. It looms like a modernist Bavarian Castle on a forested hilltop, 14km east of Shimla. Though built between 1995 and 2000, it exudes the very essence of colonial class, from the highly educated, costumed staff to the teak-panelled lobby-lounge, card-room and full-size snooker table.

The restaurant terrace has spectacular clear-day Himalayan views of its own and a menu that is full of exciting culinary ideas. It is open to nonguests with advance reservations but only when hotel occupancy is low.

★ Chapslee
HERITAGE HOTEL $$$

(☑0177-2658663; www.chapslee.com; Elysium Hill; s/d/ste incl half-board ₹18,560/23,680/32,000; ☎) For the full Raj treatment, you can't beat this exclusive retreat crammed with chandeliers, tapestries, antiques and family portraits. Five supercomfortable bedrooms are available within the lavish family mansion of a raja's grandson who lovingly maintains the aristocratic flavour of bygone days. A huge gold-toned drawing room, monkeys playing on the lawn, impeccable service and fine meals all add to a memorable experience.

Ballyhack Cottage
B&B $$$

(☑8091300076; www.ballyhackcottage.com; Sidhowal Lodge Estate, The Ridge; d incl breakfast ₹4200-4800, f ₹8000; ☎) Completely unsigned, this marvellously located five-room property sits behind the main house in the walled gardens of historic Sidhowal Lodge, just behind Christ Church. New and comfortable in a Nordic-meets-Old Shimla style, guests have the added bonus of a shared lounge upstairs and a second sitting space in a stand-alone garden cottage.

Oberoi Cecil
HOTEL $$$

(☑0177-2804848; www.oberoicecil.com; The Mall, Chaura Maidan; r ₹18,560-21,750, ste from ₹64,000; ℗❀@☎☀) Shimla's glitziest hotel wraps most of its plush rooms around a multistorey piano-bar atrium, yet maintains a discreet sense of colonial-era charm that resonates with its earlier historical incarnation (the original started business in 1903).

✖ Eating

★ Himachali Rasoi
HIMACHAL $

(☑0177-2652386; Middle Bazaar; half-/full thali ₹171/219, tea/water ₹24/25; ⊙1-6pm; ☑) It's just four heavy wooden tables crammed into a bazaar-box shop-unit but the metalcraft lamps add character and the deliciously flavoured thalis (multicurry tray-meals) are a wonderful introduction to local Himachal vegetarian food.

Wake & Bake
MULTICUISINE $$

(34/1 The Mall; dishes ₹100-330; ⊙9.30am-9.30pm; ☎) On two upper floors via an almost invisibly narrow stairway, this loveably cosy coffee shop serves espressos made from organic South Indian beans, but also cakes, sweet and savoury pancakes, hummus, falafel, toasties, veg stir-fry, pasta and *kathi* (a Kolkata street-food dish) rolls. Various breakfast options, too. Wi-fi is free.

Ashiana
INDIAN $$

(☑0177-265864; ashiana@hptdc.in; The Ridge; mains ₹145-295, rice ₹120, tea ₹35; ⊙9am-10pm, main kitchen 1-4pm & 7-10pm) In a distinctive all-window circular building, Ashiana is an almost-elegant restaurant for snacks, Indian and (some) Chinese food plus a few Himachali specialities, including *anardana* (chicken in pomegranate) and *sepu vadi* (lentil balls with spinach). There are fine views in both directions and a delightful sunny terrace.

Café Simla Times
CONTINENTAL $$$

(The Mall; mains ₹350-500; ⊙1-10.30pm, kitchen to 10pm) Fronted by an old Fiat 1100, the enticing Simla Times combines a wonderfully panoramic open terrace area with a casually cosmopolitan indoor section of distressed tables, books, bottles and a distinctive ceiling mural. Dining-wise it's hard to beat for quality international dishes including a surprisingly impressive Thai green curry. Beers (₹450) are well chilled, cocktails are more hit-and-miss.

🍷 Drinking & Nightlife

Honey Hut (The Mall; espresso/cappuccino ₹60/110, cakes ₹40-110; ⊙9am-10.30pm) is cuter than nearby Café Coffee Day for barista-style espressos. **Hide Out Cafe** (The Mall; espresso/cappuccino ₹74/84; ⊙7am-10pm; ☎) and Wake & Bake (p294) are also fine, independent options. **Indian Coffee House** (The Mall; dishes ₹40-95, coffee from ₹29; ⊙8am-8.30pm) is an old-school gem for the atmosphere more than the filter coffee.

★ Brew Estate
MICROBREWERY

(www.facebook.com/brewestateshimla; The Ridge; ⊙11am-11.30pm) Shimla's first brewpub is a large, hip, party space around a central bar-island serving its own trio of well-balanced German- and Belgian-inspired ales (half-litre ₹345) along with Jägerbombs, 'jello-syringe' shots and cocktails made by bottle-spinning mixologists.

ℹ INNER LINE PERMITS IN SHIMLA

Foreigners planning to travel the Kinnaur–Spiti loop need a document known as an inner line permit for the section between Rekong Peo in Kinnaur and Sumdo in Spiti. In Rekong Peo or Kaza (Spiti), the permit is easily obtained in an hour or so, any day except Sunday or the second Saturday of the month. It's more of a palaver to apply in Shimla. There you'll first need to get a sponsorship letter from an authorised travel agency (typically costing ₹200 or so on top of the ₹300 per person permit fee). Two shoe-box sized agents on The Mall in the block west of the Indian Coffee House specialise in this and will likely send someone to show you the ropes. You'll take their letter plus copies of your passport and visa to the nearby office of the **Additional District Magistrate** (ADM; ☑0177-2657005; Room 207/208, New Bazaar; ⊙10am-1.30pm & 3.30-4.30pm Mon-Sat, closed 2nd Sat each month), upstairs in Block B (the cream-coloured concrete building) of the DC Office (aka Collectorate Building). Then, after a cursory meeting, go down two storeys to the ground-floor Sugam Office where they take your photo and the permit should be issued – eventually. Don't be in a hurry. Sometimes it takes all day.

Note that the Shimla office technically demands that there should be at least two people applying together but in reality most agencies can group you with other applicants to get around that.

A few Asian nationalities, including Chinese and Taiwanese, cannot get inner line permits but must apply for a special permit from the Ministry of Home Affairs in Delhi.

Shopping

Himachali and Kashmiri shawls are highlights of the low-key tourist-centric shopping experience along The Mall. For a slice of more traditional commerce, wander the bazaar, a fascinating labyrinth below The Mall. Different zones have different specialities: don't miss Sabzi Mandi for vegetables, or the knife-grinders using penny-farthing-style treadles around 150–160 Lower Bazaar.

Information

HPTDC Tourist Office (Himachal Pradesh Tourist Development Corporation; ☑ 0177-2652561; www.hptdc.gov.in; Scandal Point; ⊘ 9am-7pm) Helpful for local information and advice; also books HPTDC buses, hotels and tours.

Getting There & Away

AIR

Shimla Airport (Jubbarhatti) is a flattened ridgetop, 23km west of town. There's one daily flight connection from Delhi's terminal 3 on Air India's subsidiary Alliance Air using antiquated, unpressurised prop-planes. During the summer monsoon season cancellations are quite common, or you might be diverted last minute to Chandigarh. A taxi to Shimla from the booking counters at Delhi/Chandigarh airports costs ₹8500/3500 taking around 10/4½ hours respectively.

BUS

Himachal Road Transport Corporation (HRTC) buses to most destinations start from **ISBT** (Inter State Bus Terminus, New Bus Station; Bypass Rd, Tutikandi), or 'new bus station', a 7km double-back trip west from the town centre: you'd be advised to make advance reservations at the helpful **HRTC booth** (⊘ 11am-2pm & 3-6pm) at Scandal Point.

HPTDC runs a Volvo AC bus to Delhi (₹900, 10 hours) at 8.30pm, and a non-AC deluxe bus to Manali (₹550, nine hours) at 8.30am, both starting from a stop on Cart Rd west of Victory Tunnel: get tickets at the HPTDC Tourist Office.

Down a series of stairways from The Ridge, **Rivoli Bus Stand** (Lakkar Bazaar Bus Stand; Circular Rd) deals with most destinations north and east, with buses to Rampur (roughly hourly until 7pm, Sarahan (9.50am, 10.20am and 12.10pm) and Rekong Peo (10.40am, 11am and 11.25am) plus various local villages including Naldehra (roughly hourly until 5.40pm). There are two 'ticket booths' but mostly they'll just tell you the number plate of the bus; you then pay on board.

TAXI

The **Kalka-Shimla Himachal Taxi Union** (☑ 0177-2658225; Cart Rd) and **Shimla Prepaid**

Taxi (Old Bus Sation; ⊘ 5.30am-7.30pm) both have representatives near the Old Bus Station, while **Vishal Himachal Taxi Operators Union** (☑ 0177-2805164; Cart Rd) operates from the bottom of the passenger lift. Day trips cost around ₹1600 for up to 80km plus ₹12 to ₹15 for each extra kilometre. Fares include Chandigarh ₹2500, Delhi ₹7200, Amritsar ₹7200 and Manali ₹6000+, all for up to four people. AC costs extra.

Most hotels and travel agencies can also organise transfers and car+driver deals for extended tours (around ₹4000 a day is typical).

TRAIN

One of the little joys of Shimla is getting to it by the narrow-gauge Kalka–Shimla Railway from Kalka, just north of Chandigarh. This 'toy train' has been operating since 1906 and is one of the World Heritage–listed Mountain Railways of India. Although the steam trains are long gone, it's a scenic five-to-six-hour trip, with 102 tunnels and 988 bridges on its winding 96km route. Shimla station is just below Cart Rd, 1.5km west of Scandal Point. Walking uphill into town takes 20 to 30 minutes.

Trains leave seven times daily in each direction, with passengers clapping and whooping on many a tunnel. The most comfortable option is the Shivalik Express (train 52451 from Kalka at 5.20am, train 52452 back from Shimla at 5.50pm). For Delhi connections, the Himalayan Queen uses Delhi Sarai Rohilla (DEE) station (around 600m south of Shastri Nagar Metro) and allows comfortable connection times at Kalka for a total fare of ₹700 (AC chair).

Other trains between Kalka and Shimla have fairly spartan 1st-class coaches (around ₹270) and usually some 2nd-class coaches (₹65).

The **rail booking window** (⊘ 9am-1pm & 2-4pm Mon-Sat) at Scandal Point is central but can be somewhat chaotic.

Himalayan Queen Schedule

DEPART	ARRIVE/ DEPART KALKA (KLK)	ARRIVE	TRAIN NO
Delhi Sarai Rohilla (DEE) 5.35am	11.10am/ 12.10pm	Shimla 5.30pm	14095/ 52455
Shimla (SML) 10.40am	4.10pm/ 4.55pm	Delhi 10.40pm	52456/ 14096

Getting Around

The only way to get around central Shimla is on foot. Vehicles, including taxis, are banned from t he Ridge and much of The Mall, with traffic funnelled along Cart Rd and Circular Rd. A pedestrian

BUSES FROM SHIMLA ISBT

DESTINATION	FARE (₹)	DURATION (HR)	DEPARTURES
Chandigarh	179-250	5	every 15-30min 4am-10pm
Dehra Dun	410-890	8	5.15am, 9.30pm plus 7.50pm Volvo
Delhi (Volvo)	910	10	8.30am, 9.45am, 11.15am, 1.45pm, 8pm, 9pm, 9.30pm, 10.30pm
Dharamsala	360	10	9.40am, 11.15am, 2.30pm
Dharamsala (deluxe)	515	8	9.30pm
Kalpa	375	11	6.45am
Manali	395	8-9	9.15am, 10.30am
Manali (deluxe)	486-541	8-9	8am, 8.20pm, 9pm (AC)
Mandi	240-310	6	15 daily
Rekong Peo	355	10	4am, 5am, 6am, 9am, 10.30am, 6.30pm, 8pm; other services from Rivoli bus stand
Sangla	350	10	7.15am

lift (adult/senior ₹10/7; ⊘ 8am-9pm) connects **Cart Rd** with **The Mall** about 600m east of Scandal Point. Taxis from the train station/ISBT to the bottom of the lift cost ₹200/300.

Buses (₹7) run every few minutes between the ground floor of ISBT and the **Old Bus Station** (☑ 0177-2656326; Cart Rd).

For ₹20 per person, Ride With Pride share-taxis shuttle when full to 'Advanced Studies' (ie the Viceregal Lodge) from both **BSNL** (The Mall) and **Gorton** (The Mall).

KINNAUR

The district of Kinnaur, along with closely linked Bushahr, is blessed with magnificent mountain and valley scenery and a distinctive cultural and ethnic mix that mutates from Aryan Hindu to Tibetan Buddhist as you progress eastward. This is a land of ridge-villages with slate-roofed temples and countless apple orchards separated by plunging gorges and backed by towering snowcapped peaks. Beyond it lies remote Spiti, which visitors can combine with Kinnaur into a Shimla–Keylong loop through unendingly breathtaking scenery.

The Kinnauris are proud but friendly people who mainly survive through farming and apple growing. You can recognise them all over India by their short cylindrical hats (*thapeng* or *basheri*) with a half-round flash of green or red felt on the upturned lappet.

To truly appreciate their land, you need to leave the main road: other than Rampur, most population centres are high up steep mountainsides accessed by seemingly endless hairpin lanes.

NH5 (formerly NH22) threads a spectacular route up the Sutlej (or Satluj) Valley, following or paralleling the course of the historic Hindustan–Tibet Rd, a track constructed by the British in the 19th century in the hope of providing access to Tibet. Lower Kinnaur gets monsoon rains in July and August, but east of Rekong Peo the landscape quickly becomes much more arid as you pass through a gap in the Great Himalayan Range and into the range's rain shadow. Check road conditions before departing as monsoon landslides, floods in the Sutlej Valley or heavy winter snows can block the roads for days or even weeks.

During Kinnaur's peak domestic tourist seasons – mid-April to June and late September to late October – prices climb considerably and popular accommodation gets booked up, but at other times you may well get discounts. At the time of writing there was no internet access in the Sangla Valley or Nako.

Rampur

☑ 01782 / POP 10,300 / ELEV 960M

Changing buses in this bustling valley town gives you more options in travelling between Shimla and Sarahan or Rekong Peo. Handily, right in the centre, is the photogenic palace-hotel of the Bushahr rajas who had their winter capital here from the 18th to mid-20th centuries. In November the town hosts one of Himachal's biggest commercial and cultural fairs, the **Lavi Fair** (www.facebook.com/Lavi.Rampur; ☺ 11-14 Nov).

Padam Palace
PALACE

A fanciful feat of oriental neo-gothic architecture, the handsome Padam Palace is central Rampur's only real 'sight'. Built between 1919 and 1925 for the Raja of Bushahr, the main building is still private, but one section is now the Nau Nabh Hotel, and the garden is open to visitors.

🛏 Sleeping & Eating

Luxurious yet fair-priced, the delightful **Nau Nabh** (☑ 01782-234405; www.hotelnaunabh.com; r ₹2360-7020; [P][❄][🛜]) occupies a totally renovated two-centuries-old adjunct to the Padam Palace. Across the road, 100m to the east, **Hotel Satluj View** (☑ 01782-233924; hotelsatlujview@yahoo.in; r with/without view ₹950/800, AC ₹1650; [❄]) has three fresh if chinzily restored AC rooms along with shabbier if perfectly acceptable standard rooms, the best of which have views across the Sutlej River's pedestrian suspension bridge. The small, multicuisine restaurant at the **Nau Nabh** (mains ₹180-410; ☺ 7am-11pm) has easily the best food, but the Hotel Satluj View's restaurant does decent North Indian fare.

ⓘ Getting There & Away

For Sarahan (₹65, two hours), departures leave frequently until 5pm or later from the old bus stand outside the palace. Most other services with **HRTC** (☑ 01782-233131) use the new bus station, 2km further east and 700m off the main road. It's accessible by autorickshaw shuttle (₹10). Destinations include the following:

Kalpa (₹170, 5½ hours) 5.30am and noon.

Kaza (₹400, overnight) 11.30pm.

Kullu (₹232, 10 hours) Via the Jalori Pass and Banjar (₹155, six hours) at 6.35am, 9.40am and 11am. April to November only, snow permitting.

Rekong Peo (₹160, five hours) At least hourly until 4.30pm.

Sangla (₹160, four hours) At 4am and 12.30pm (or change at Karcham).

Shimla (₹195, five hours) At least hourly until 8.30pm via Old Bus Stand and the steep-terraced apple-growing region of Narkanda.

Sarahan

☑ 01782 / POP 1700 / ELEV 2170M

Little Sarahan was the former summer capital of the Bushahr kingdom and is dominated by one of Himachal's most instantly recognisable monuments, the fabulous **Bhimakali Temple** (☺ 6am-7pm). Set within three courtyards, it features two classic Kinnauri towers with Tibet-meets-Transylvania horror-movie silhouettes, best photographed from behind with a backdrop of distant soaring peaks. Like the three surrounding courtyard buildings, the constructions are of layered stone and timber (to absorb the force of earthquakes), topped with a storey or two of intricately carved wood panelling and heavy slate roofing. One originally 12th-century tower collapsed fairly recently but has been beautifully restored. The other (left) dates from the 1920s, and both contain highly revered shrines to Bhimakali (the local version of Kali) on canopied silver thrones. A guard at the inner courtyard ensures that cameras, mobile phones and leather goods are deposited in little lockers (free) and that male visitors don a requisite cap (provided).

Temple Resthouse
GUESTHOUSE $

(☑ 01782-274248; dm ₹70, back/front/large r ₹350/500/550) Plain, simple but clean and understandably popular, the Resthouse lies right within the ancient temple's outer courtyard (gates locked 9.30pm to 4am), ideally placed to soak up the atmosphere including the full predawn blast of ritual music.

Hotel Srikhand
HOTEL $$

(☑ 01782-274234, 9857385707; www.hptdc.gov.in; small/medium/large r ₹1600/2490/3000) Rooms are rather bland, some with damp-bubbled paint, but the better ones are sizeable and all have super mountain views, which are even better from the **restaurant** (mains ₹90-230, beer ₹250; ☺ 7.30am-9.30pm), which serves unexpectedly good food.

ⓘ Getting There & Away

There are buses to Shimla (₹300, seven hours) at 4am, 6.30am, 8am and noon, but you can also get one of the frequent services to Rampur (₹70, two hours) and change there. Until recently, a blockage on this road meant travellers had to change buses but a new bridge should bypass the problem section.

To head on eastward into Kinnaur, start by taking any bus (₹30, 45 minutes) or taxi (₹500) as far as Jeori. That's 17km of switchbacks below Sarahan on NH5 with passing buses for Rekong Peo, Sangla and beyond a possibility. The last bus back up from Jeori to Sarahan usually leaves around 6.30pm.

Sangla Valley

The Sangla Valley is a deeply carved cleft between burly mountain slopes, where evergreen forests rise to alpine meadows crowned by snowy summits. Village cores here feature temples built in traditional Kinnauri style of timber and stone with heavy slate roofs. The road up the valley leaves the NH5 at Karcham hydroelectric dam. Much of the first 15km to Kupa is cut hair-raisingly high into an almost vertical cliff face. Sangla, the only town, hides its fascinating old section completely out of view from the road. Thereafter, the valley has essentially just three villages, including Batseri across the river, which has won prizes for cleanliness, and Rakchham, which sits in an intriguing chaos of large boulders. After the Mastrang police checkpoint (show your passport), the already beautiful valley gets ever more spectacular with sharp-sculpted snow peaks towering ahead above Chitkul. All main settlements have temples worth perusing.

Sangla & Around

☑ 01786

Though hardly a city, little Sangla is the valley's largest settlement. Its useful main-street bazaar has snack-cafes, taxis, a cybercafe and an ATM. Getting away from the main street emphasises Sangla's majestic setting. In the old, lower town, the highlight to seek out is the multishrine Nag Temple – take the steps leading down from the building containing Sangla Holiday Home restaurant, then fork left. If you've got energy left, a longer walk takes you 2km north (and steeply up) to **Kamru Fort** (⊙ 5am-6pm), a typical local design at the back of Kamru village, the original capital of the Bushahr kingdom.

🛏 Sleeping

Hans Hotel   GUESTHOUSE $
(☑ Ashok 9805119098; Sangla; r ₹500-1500) Nearing completion at the time of research, Hans Hotel's killer feature is the large open terrace with not just mountain panoramas but also glimpses of (distant) Kamru Fort and a birds-eye overview of Old Sangla's rooftops. Lively, English-speaking manager Ashok is a nature-loving trekking guide.

Banjara Camps   TENTED CAMP $$$
(☑ 011-65152334; www.banjaracamps.com; Batseri; incl full board tent ₹9000-11,000, downstairs/upstairs d ₹12,000/13,000, cottage ₹14,000;

⊙ closed mid-Nov–mid-Mar) As well as comparatively luxurious bedded tents, Banjara's very extensive riverside apple orchard also features two cottages and The Retreat, a relaxed, upmarket hotel section with restaurant-lounge and 14 beautifully crafted rooms with excellent beds. The downstairs rooms share between pairs a terrace incorporating hammock and swing from which to ponder the idyllic scene, backed by spiky peaks. You'll need wheels.

It's 2km of hairpins below Km23.4 of the Chitkul road, 6km from Sangla.

ℹ Getting There & Away

Buses from Sangla (times approximate):

Chitkul (₹40, 1½ hours) 7.45am, noon, 2.15pm, 5pm.
Rampur (₹158, four hours) 7am, 7.30am, 11.30am, 12.30pm, 5.30pm.
Rekong Peo (₹65, two hours) 7am, 1pm, 3.30pm.
Shimla (₹355, 10 hours) 7am, 7.30am, 5.30pm (or go to Rampur and change buses there).

Taxis ask ₹800 to Karcham dam, ₹1500/2000 one way/return to Chitkul. Many are parked near the police station 100m southeast of the bridge: ask shopkeepers opposite to call a driver for you. Or contact friendly **Sandeep Negi** (☑ 9805609140), who speaks some English and has a sturdy seven-seater vehicle.

Chitkul

POP 600 / ELEV 3450M

Chitkul is easily the most scenic settlement along the Sangla Valley. Once on a trade route to Tibet, it's at the junction of several trekking routes and attracts a steady flow of international and domestic tourists, but villagers maintain a pretty traditional lifestyle and a somewhat reserved attitude to outsiders.

Despite the encroachment of concrete and tin, a fair number of traditional houses remain in Kinnauri-style, with heavy slate roofs. In the middle of the village lies the Mohatmin Mandir, a temple dedicated to local god Mathi, with some excellent carvings in wood and stone.

🏃 Activities

A short walk up the hillside above the village opens up some marvellous views. To the east, the high white peak of Tholla beckons, but you're only allowed to walk 3km towards it before reaching the Nagasti 'Indo-Tibetan Border Police Post'. In fact Tibet is still about

40km away. For longer day walks you can head up the Baspa River's side valleys.

Chitkul is where the three-day trekking trail circumambulating Kinner Kailash descends into the Sangla Valley. Trekking routes to the Pabbar Valley and Uttarakhand's Garhwal region head over passes on the south side of the valley (it's eight to 10 days to Harsil near Gangotri).

Many guesthouses and camps organise treks: Baablu at **Kinner Heights** (☑ 8988238129; ⊘ closed Dec-Mar) has lots of experience.

🛏 Sleeping & Eating

Several guesthouses, the swish new hostel **Zostel** (☑ Nitish 9459732785; dm ₹350-500, d ₹1600-2000; ⊘ Mar-Nov), and a couple of not very inviting group-oriented hotels are set at the eastern foot of the village. Long-running, wood-framed **Thakur Guest House** (☑ 8988209604; r ₹500-900; ⊘ closed Nov-Mar) has a friendly old-world vibe here. Sitting peaceably at the back of the village, **Wanderer's Nest** (☑ 9463832985; www.wanderersnest.com; dm ₹500-600, r ₹1500-2000; ⊘ closed Dec-Mar) is new and obliging.

ⓘ Getting There & Away

Buses leave for Rekong Peo (₹120, four hours) at 1.30pm and 3.30pm, the latter continuing overnight to Shimla (₹395, 13 hours). Both go via Sangla (₹40, 1½), to which there is an additional morning service at 6am.

Rekong Peo

☑ 01786 / POP 2500 / ELEV 2290M

Rekong Peo is the main administrative and commercial centre for Kinnaur and a useful transport hub. Most visitors use it as a stepping stone to the pretty, hilltop village of Kalpa, and to obtain inner line permits for onward travel to Spiti. Known locally as 'Peo', the town spreads along a looping road about 10km above NH5. Most hotels, and an SBI ATM, are in the main bazaar below the bus stand.

There's no shortage of grotty traders' hotels in the main bazaar; hidden just above, **Hotel Khunu Dhon-Khang** (☑ 9418395687; s/d ₹2000/2500) is the best central choice.

Head to **Little Chef's Restaurant** (☑ 01786-222133; Main Bazaar; mains ₹129-269, breakfast sets ₹139-179; ⊘ 8am-10pm, main kitchen noon-3pm & 7-10pm only) for the most salu-

brious surroundings and a decent range of dishes in various styles.

ⓘ Getting There & Away

The bus station is 2km uphill from the main bazaar by road, or 500m if you take the steps starting next to the police compound at the top of ITBP Rd (which leaves the main bazaar at Little Chef's Restaurant).

Buses to Shimla run roughly hourly, 4.30am to 6.30pm (₹355, 10 hours), with deluxe services (₹615) at 5.30am and 1.30pm. Buses to Sangla (₹65, 2½ hours) and Chitkul (₹100, four hours) leave at 9.30am, noon and 2.30pm.

For Spiti, get up very early for the 5.30am bus to Kaza (₹355, 11 hours) via Nako (₹175, five hours) and Tabo (₹270, eight hours). A second bus heads to Nako at noon. Both of these depart Rekong Peo an hour earlier from November to March.

Taxi rates are ₹3500 to Chitkul, ₹7000 to Shimla and ₹8000 to Kaza.

Kalpa

☑ 01786 / POP 1240 / ELEV 2960M

Little Kalpa sits on a high promontory with absolutely majestic views of the Kinner Kailash massif. At a towering 6473m, the peak of Jorkanden particularly grabs your eyeballs...and won't let go. Kalpa is a far nicer place to stay than Rekong Peo, from which it's reached by 7km of steep, winding zigzags through orchard terraces and pinewoods.

⊙ Sights & Activities

Kalpa's quaint old centre is in danger of losing its antique charm as many of the old timber buildings have fallen into disrepair and are being replaced by newer concrete. Fortunately, a recently rebuilt classic **fortress tower** (Chandika Killa) makes all the difference, giving the ensemble a strong visual focus. Tucked behind that is the Narayan-Nagini complex, an array of wooden Hindu temple buildings featuring a variety of carved details and sculptures.

An ambitious one-day return hike, or more relaxed over two days with camping, the trail up to the meadows and ponds of Chakkha is a charming hike starting from Hotel Kinner Kailash on Roghi Rd. Fluent English speaker Nav at **Pomra Adventures** (📱9805582595; www.thepomraadventures.com; ⏰9am-6.45pm) is a helpful guide and fixer for this and other treks. The management of the Shamba-La can also organise day hikes for its guests.

🛏 Sleeping & Eating

Kalpa has a considerable range of accommodation. Several guesthouses lie in Chini, the main part of the old village. Many of the more modern hotels are up on Roghi Rd, a 500m stair-walk (or far longer drive) above the centre.

Chini Bungalow Guest House GUESTHOUSE $
(📱9805495656; r ₹1200) A minute's climb up stairways from the Blue Lotus crossroads, this friendly little place has just five clean, cosy rooms and fine mountain views across the old town from its flowery garden and the shared balconies of the three best upper-floor rooms.

Hotel Blue Lotus HOTEL $
(📱01786-226001; khokanroy.bluelotus@gmail.com; r ₹800-1200; 📶) Right at Kalpa's central little crossroads, a 70m stumble uphill from the bus stand, the Blue Lotus has fair-value rooms that aren't world-beaters but are better than the wire and sick-green concrete facade might suggest. Showers run hot, towels are clean and wi-fi works, but the biggest pluses are the extensive if unsophisticated mountain-facing terraces: ideal for meals with a view.

★**Grand Shamba-La** HOTEL $$$
(Grand Shangri-La; 📱01786-226134, 9805695423; www.thegrandshambala.com; Roghi Rd; s/d with half-board ₹4500/5000; 📶) Head and shoulders above the Kalpa competition, the sensitively managed Shamba-La comes with numerous extras that turn a stay into a memorable delight. Decor features tastefully restrained Tibetan detailing, there's a meditation-yoga room, bar-cum-projection room for watching local documentaries and an especially delightful top-floor library lounge with locally relevant volumes.

ℹ Getting There & Away

There's a direct bus to Shimla (₹385, 11 hours) at 6.30am. Otherwise use buses from Rekong Peo. Buses run at least hourly from 7am to 7pm to the traffic light in Rekong Peo's main bazaar (₹15, 30 minutes) via the bus station. A taxi costs ₹400/500 from Rekong Peo to central Kalpa/Roghi Rd, but can be hard to find in reverse.

For walkers, a fascinating option is to descend to Rekong Peo from Duni village on a footpath/stairway between timeless dry-stone walls, passing a Buddhist Arts centre and the traditional-style Brelengi temple in a lonely glade of gigantic old trees.

Rekong Peo to Tabo

The NH5/505 road from Kinnaur into Spiti, often clinging precariously to cliff sides, provides a procession of awe-inspiring vistas, the river flashing hundreds of metres below. Foreigners must show their inner line permits at the Akpa checkpoint (17km east of the Rekong Peo turnoff) and again at Sumdo (an army camp 27km before Tabo).

About 7km east of the Akpa checkpoint, notice the fort-like temples across the river at Moorang. North of the Sutlej–Spiti river confluence, the road threads its way through then above the dramatic Spiti gorge to Nako village: an interesting place to break the journey. The road then descends to the river again at Chango. Around 3km beyond Sumdo checkpoint, an 8km each-way side trip on a newly asphalted lane is well worth the diversion if you have your own wheels to see the curious 'mummy temple' at Gue.

Nako

POP 870 / ELEV 3660M

Culturally closer to Buddhist Spiti than Kinnaur, Nako's village centre retains an area of stone and mud-brick houses that has an almost medieval feel. Though backed by steep, arid mountainsides, Nako's remarkable stone-wall terracing allows agriculture to flourish improbably high above the Hangrang Valley (as the lower Spiti Valley is called).

For fine views, walk around 500m up to the unusual wind-aided prayer wheel on the hill above Nako Lake. For even wider vistas, albeit not of the lake, continue for another 45 minutes steeply upward to the 3900m Nako Pass, a noticeable cleft in the rocky ridge to the south.

🏃 Activities

A well-maintained, easy-to-follow pilgrimage and hiking trail takes around four hours from Nako to a remote monastery at Tashigang hamlet. Padmasambhava (also known as Guru Rinpoche) is believed to have meditated and taught here.

After climbing steeply to Nako Pass, the trail is reasonably level albeit undulating, and very high at around 3850m all the way. Around halfway, 10 minutes beyond the stream crossing, a spring provides fresh water. It's possible to sleep and eat at the Tashigang monastery: take a gift for the monks by way of donation (sugar is appreciated). Nako authorities prefer that tourists take a guide, though the path is clear and many people go without one.

From Tashigang, hardcore hikers can continue about two hours to caves and a tiny monastery at Tsomang (or Somang).

🛏 Sleeping & Eating

Nako has lots of simple homestays and guesthouses, though nothing really luxurious. **Delek Guesthouse** (📱9418764338; r ₹1500) is one of the better budget options, with lovely views, clean, new rooms and delightful staff. The recommended **Himalayan Paradise** (📱9459440971; Lake Rd; r up/down ₹1300/2200; ⊙closed Nov-Mar) has better-than-average rooms and a great view from the restaurant terrace. Nako's one upper-market option is **Knaygoh Kinner Camps** (📱9418440767, Ramesh 8988703480; www.knaygohkinnercamps.com; s/d tent incl half-board ₹4000/5000; r ₹2000-3500; ⊙Apr-Oct), with comfortable furnished tents, the best of which form an arc in a flower-filled area of terracing.

Several simple eateries cluster around the central junction. The attractive restaurant of the **Knaygoh Kinner Camps** (mains ₹150-500; ⊙7am-9.30pm) is normally open to nonguests, and offers a remarkably wide range of food styles.

ℹ Getting There & Away

The bus stop is around 400m north of town beside the helipad *dhabas*. All are in transit and delays of an hour or more are common:

Kaza (₹177, 5½ hours) 10.30am
Rampur (₹375, 10 hours) 7.30am
Rekong Peo (₹168, 5½ hours) 9am and noon
Sumdo (₹65, two hours) 4pm
Tabo (₹105, three hours) 10.30am and 2pm

CENTRAL HIMACHAL PRADESH

Central Himachal is focused on the Kullu Valley, a green vale between high mountains, watered by the Beas River flowing south from the Rohtang La pass. Manali, below the Rohtang, is one of Northern India's most popular travel destinations, a centre for all types of Indian and foreign travellers – hippies, hikers, honeymooners, weekenders and adrenaline junkies.

TOP STATE FESTIVALS

Losar (Tibetan New Year; ⊙late Jan, Feb or early Mar) Tibetans across Himachal, including in McLeod Ganj and Spiti, celebrate their New Year with processions, music and *chaams* (ritual masked dances by monks).

Minjar Festival (⊙last Sun Jul-1st Sun Aug) A week of processions, music, dance and markets at Chamba.

Ki Chaam Festival (Guitor Festival; ⊙Jul/Aug) A week of rituals at Ki Gompa in Spiti, culminates in a day of whirling dances by brightly costumed and masked lamas.

Manimahesh Yatra (⊙late Aug/early Sep) Hundreds of thousands of Shaivites trek up to 4200m to bathe in Manimahesh Lake near Bharmour, one of Shiva's mythical abodes.

Phulech Festival (⊙Sep) Villagers in Kalpa and throughout Kinnaur fill temple courtyards with flowers; oracles perform sacrifices and make predictions for the coming year.

Dussehra (⊙Oct; variable dates) Intense and spectacular weeklong celebration of the defeat of the demon Ravana, at Kullu.

The Kullu Valley is known as Dev Bhumi (Valley of Gods) either because of its many sacred sites or simply because of its exceptional beauty. It's also famous for, among other things, its warm woollen shawls and its charas (hashish). Side valleys, such as Parvati and Tirthan, are if anything, even more beautiful. In hundreds of mountain villages, life still goes on in a pretty traditional way, and the chance to get away from the towns amid the spectacular landscape shouldn't be missed.

Mandi

📶 01905 / POP 26,500 / ELEV 800M

True to its name (meaning 'market'), Mandi is a rambunctious bazaar town. Though once a royal city, few tourists stick around, and in summer, Mandi can feel hot and sticky like the Indian plains. However, it's a useful transport junction, a handy launchpoint for Rewalsar Lake, and is dotted with (according to official figures) 81 temples. Many of these are ancient Shaivite shrines, which are fun to track down in the bazaars and along the banks of the River Beas.

◉ Sights

Less than an hour's circular stroll is enough to get a great feel of older Mandi and its finer historical temples. At the entrance to Bhootnath Bazar, 100m northwest of the Indira Market (the central square), is **Bhootnath Mandir** (Gandhi Chowk). This small 16th-century stone structure with attractively naive carvings around the base of its *sikhara* (spire) and sanctum is Mandi's most active historic temple.

Follow the narrow pedestrian alley of Bhootnath Bazar past a colourful series of sari shops down towards the Beas River. To the left, past a small stone Shiva temple, is

the iconic 1877 Victoria Bridge. To the right you'll find the very colourful Ekardash Rudra Mandir above the old cremation ghats. Continue east to spot several more carved sikhara temples. Most impressive of these, at the river junction, are the intricately sculpted, centuries-old Panchvaktra Mandir and, visible across the Beas River directly north, the matching 1520 **Triloknath Mandir** (NH154). To return to Gandhi Chowk you can shortcut back up Chobata Bazar alley through the Bangla Mohala district.

🛏 Sleeping & Eating

Evening Plaza Hotel   HOTEL $
(📶 01905-225123; Indira Market; r ₹860-1110, with AC ₹1650-2120; ❄) Above Malhotra Jewellers, right on the central square, is this consistently popular budget choice.

Raj Mahal Palace   HERITAGE HOTEL $$
(📶 01905-222401, 9817941450; www.rajmahal palace.com; District Court Gate; r ₹1610-4290; ❄ 🛜) The Raj Mahal occupies a century-old palace annex, part of which is still lived in by Mandi's ex-royal family. Especially at night, the garden and entryway is enchanting, and the guest-only upper hall-lounge has a plethora of old family pictures. While the scrappily maintained guest rooms fall well short of regal, they too exude a certain degree of olde-worlde charm.

The hotel's **Copacabana Bar & Restaurant** (mains ₹170-380; ⊗ 12.30-10pm) offers the appealing option of eating out on the large, tree-shaded lawn.

❶ Getting There & Away

The **bus stand** (NH154) is 500m east of the centre across the Suketi Khad bridge. For Dharamsala, if there are no immediate buses, head to Palampur and change there.

BUSES FROM MANDI

DESTINATION	FARE (₹)	DURATION (HR)	DEPARTURES
Delhi	585/1250 (ord/Volvo)	13	6am, 8.30am, 9.10am & 18 services 5.45pm to 11.30pm
Dharamsala	223/545 (ord/Volvo)	6	5 daily
Kullu	123/370 (ord/Volvo)	2½	half-hourly
Manali	195/420 (ord/Volvo)	4	half-hourly
Palampur	171	4	hourly
Rekong Peo	218-295	12	10.30am, 4.30pm
Shimla	263	6	16 daily

Taxis outside the bus station and on the north side of Indira Market ask ₹1500/2500/3000 to Bir/Manali/McLeod Ganj.

Rewalsar

📋 01905 / POP 2100 / ELEV 1350M

Hidden in the hills 24km southwest of Mandi, the sacred lake of Rewalsar is revered by Hindus and Sikhs but especially by Tibetan Buddhists, who know it as Tso-Pema (Lotus Lake). According to legend, the king of Zahor (today's Mandi) tried to burn alive here the revered Buddhist sage Padmasambhava (Guru Rinpoche), to prevent his daughter Mandarava running off with the long-haired Tantric master. But after seven days on the pyre, instead of ashes, the king found him sitting on a lotus in the middle of a newly formed lake. Today a 12m statue of Padmasambhava dramatically surveys the scene, and the lake's 800m perimeter is surrounded by a collection of mostly modern temples, monasteries and monuments, with all three faiths represented. Despite the untidy architectural hodge-podge a spiritual atmosphere remains and Rewalsar attracts a steady flow of visitors for meditation, prayer or just a day trip.

◎ Sights

Raised well up the hillside overlooking the lake's west bank, the giant statue of Padmasambhava was inaugurated by the Dalai Lama in 2012. The sage's gold face sports his trademark fiercely staring eyes, while his right hand strikes the 'warding-off-evil' mudra (gesture).

Many other minor sites can be seen in a half-hour stroll around the lakeshore. Starting directly north of the bus stand at the lake's southeast corner, notice the Fish Feeding Point, where a seething mass of holy carp gobbles up flour balls or puffed rice thrown by visitors. The Tibetan-style **Drikung Kagyu Gompa** (📋 01905-240638; www.dk-petsek.org; DK Monastery), with its academy for Buddhist monks, stands immediately to the right here. Its temple features a large, central Sakyamuni statue, with Padmasambhava to the left.

At the lake's southwest corner, the small but colourful prayer hall of Tso-Pema Ogyen Heruka Nyingmapa Gompa has artful murals and its dharma bell by the waterfront reverberates throughout Rewalsar when rung. Continuing north you pass a small Hindu temple group beneath a giant Shiva trident

and a grassy little lakeside park with a couple of benches where you can enjoy the view and atmosphere.

On the northeast side of the lake is the gold-domed Guru Gobind Singh Gurdwara, a Sikh temple built in the 1930s. Rewalsar is of special significance to Sikhs as the place where, in 1701, Guru Gobind Singh, the 10th Sikh guru, issued an unsuccessful call to the Hindu rajas of the Punjab hills for joint resistance against the Mughals.

The Rewalsar area's other main Buddhist site is a pair of Padmasambhava Caves, where the sage reputedly meditated. Set behind the butter-lamp rooms of a nunnery-hermitage, these are high on the ridge above Rewalsar overlooking a second, undeveloped lake. By road the site is a 10km drive (one way/return taxi ₹500/700) but part of the delight is the 1.5km walk using short-cut steps through terraced fields and the village of Doh: starting from behind the big Padmasambhava statue the walk takes between 60 and 90 minutes up, half that back. Buses depart Rewalsar bus stand at 9am, 10.15am, noon and 1.15pm bound for Naina Devi Temple (₹20), passing the cave steps 1km before the terminus. They return at 10.30am, 12.30pm, 1.30pm and around 2pm.

🛏 Sleeping & Eating

Suman & Vinod's Homestay APARTMENT $
(📋 9418115833, WhatsApp 9816057821; vinod gupta5833@gmail.com; apt ₹500) Climb the red stair-path beside DK Monastery to find these four furnished mini-apartments in the unmarked, three-storey green building just before the Hotel Wangdu. They are superb value for money with basic kitchen and partial views of the lake, but call ahead or enquire at Nitin Tour & Travels near the Nyingma Monastery.

Emaho Bistro CAFE $
(DK Monastery; dishes ₹40-150; ⊙8am-8pm; 🛜) Emaho is Rewalsar's top place for barista-style coffee with picture-perfect lake views from its sunny raised terrace, and a small selection of books to read.

It also serves cakes, juices, veggie burgers and excellent all-day breakfasts.

❶ Getting There & Away

From platform 5 of Mandi Bus Station, buses to Rewalsar (₹44, 1¼ hours) leave two or three times an hour until late afternoon. Some also pick up along the south side of Indira Market. The return

service leaves about 6pm. A taxi costs around
₹600/1000 one way/return.

Tirthan & Banjar Valleys

Exceptional mountain-backed scenery, charming riverside villages, slate-roofed hay barns, great walks and inviting guesthouses all come together in the delightful region known as Inner Seraj. The area divides into two main valleys at the busy hub town of Banjar. Continuing east, the Tirthan Valley is dotted with rural, riverside getaways, many of them aimed at anglers, but also forming a trekking gateway to the World Heritage-listed Great Himalayan National Park, where spectacular peaks reach 6000m and above. South of Banjar, a separate valley climbs eventually to the 3132m Jalori Pass, which links to Rampur in Kinnaur. Halfway to the pass is the delightful, rapidly expanding little traveller village of Jibhi, set amid trees and tumbling streams, with steeply terraced fields leading up to cedar forests that hide timeless ancient hamlets, notably ridgetop Bahu and unforgettable Chehni Kothi with its phenomenal 11-storey temple-tower.

The range of hikes and birdwatching and wildlife-spotting opportunities is phenomenal. Great DIY village walks are easily organised through local homestays, but for longer treks, especially within the national park, it's worth contacting a specialist agency.

Banjar-based **Himalayan Ecotourism** (☑9816423344, Stephan 9816091093; www.himalayanecotourism.in; SN Hospital Bldg, New Bus Stand; ⊙call ahead) offers quality, low-impact programs promoting sustainable employment by working with guides who are members of local cooperatives. Kullu-based **Sunshine Himalayan Adventures** (☑9418102083, 01902-225182; www.sunshineadventure.com; Akhara Bazar) ✆ is also well established and has its own Tirthan Valley lodge. The main seasons are March to June, September and October. From November to February cafes and much accommodation goes into hibernation and snow often covers the Jalori Pass.

◉ Sights

★ Chehni Kothi
FORT

(Chehni village) Unspoilt Chehni village is one of the most magical villages imaginable. Surveying a wide sweep of valley and ridgetops from 2110m, its antique core features the astounding 350-year-old Chehni Kothi fort-towers, between six and 11 storeys high, depending how you count them, and with a distinct Pisa-like lean. There's a shorter tower across the yard and a third, medieval tower-house in front. A tiny cafe serves Maggi and tea when the owner isn't driving the ox-plough in his nearby field. There's a temple inside the main tower and foreigners are not permitted to enter, even if they dare to climb the dizzying tree-trunk plank-steps that are the tower's only access. Although there's a mud road of sorts, reaching Chehni is usually by foot, using about 1km of forest footpaths, starting 100m from Shringa Rishi Temple, which is 3km off the Banjar–Jibhi road.

★ Bahu
VILLAGE

On a clear November day, it's hard to imagine a more perfectly framed view than that of Bahu's remarkably preserved village core, perched on a ridgetop and backed by dreamy views across the valley to a backdrop of snowcapped peaks.

But hasten your visit before collapse or new construction mars the integrity of the tightly huddled three-storey tower-houses with their slate roofs and wraparound upper balconies. Some are said to be 800 years old. Bahu is 9km up a ladder of hairpins that starts with a river bridge 600m south of Jibhi village. Buses run five times daily from Banjar via Jibhi (₹20, 45 minutes).

Jalori Pass
VIEWPOINT

At the top of the Banjar Valley, Hwy 305 climbs over the panoramic 3223m Jalori Pass, marked by a couple of *dhabas* and a Mahakali temple. In calm weather this is a great spot for observing Himalayan griffon vultures, the biggest birds in the Indian Himalaya. From the pass you can walk 6km east (fairly level) to the small, holy Saryolsar Lake, or 3km west (uphill) to the scanty ruins of Raghupur Fort, through evergreen oak forests in both cases.

A taxi round trip from Jibhi to the pass, including time for you to walk to Saryolsar or Raghupur, costs ₹2000. The road over the pass is unpaved for the 16km from Ghiyagi on the north side to Khanag on the south, and the pass is normally closed by snow from approximately mid-December to early March.

⊨ Sleeping & Eating

In the Tirthan Valley accommodation is dotted fairly diffusely over many kilometres, and although some homestays are fairly basic (albeit not inexpensive), there's not yet any real budget option. Gushaini has a

GREAT HIMALAYAN NATIONAL PARK

This 754-sq-km **park** (GHNP; ☎01902-265320; www.greathimalayannationalpark.org) embraces four river valleys, mature forests, alpine meadows and soaring peaks. It's home to a huge variety of fauna and flora including snow leopards, ultra-rare Himalayan blue poppies and over 200 bird species. The park's open buffer area (the 'Ecozone') starts at Gushaini and has some fine walks, including Gushaini–Karongcha (around 8km, easy), Pekhri to Rangthar (two days) and Bathad to Kullu-Sarahan across the 3277m Bashleo Pass (eight hours, fairly strenuous).

To enter the park's core zone requires both permit (Indian/foreigner per day ₹100/400) and a certified local guide. These can be arranged at any of the park's range offices; the easiest option is the office at **Sai Ropa** (☎9459994494; Gushaini Rd Km4.8, Sai Ropa; ⏰10am-4pm), but there's another at **Jiwa Nal** (☎01903-230038; Larji; ⏰10am-5pm) near Larji. Bring passport and visa photocopies. For one-day passes, permits and guides can be organised on the spot, but for a multiday trek such as the Sainj-Tirthan (five days+), Tithat (six days+) or Shrikhand Mahadev Ascent (nine days climbing a 5227m peak) it's easier to use an agency.

small, ugly bazaar-street but no concentration of accommodation.

In contrast there's a convenient knot of midrange and budget choices at Jibhi, along with plenty more under construction: over 60 choices in the 5km to Shoja.

Mudhouse Hostels HOSTEL $
(☎9459895806; www.facebook.com/Mudhouse-hostels; dm/d/q ₹650/3000/6000) Mudhouse is the nearest Jibhi comes to a Delhi hipster vibe. Its six-bed dorms have rustic-effect branches for bunk-supports, there are indulgent yet in-character balcony-doubles and a chill-out cafe, Lazy Hazy.

★**Raju Bharti's Guest House** FARMSTAY $$
(☎9459833124; www.facebook.com/Rajubhartiguesthouse; Gushaini Rd Km9; per person incl full board veg/nonveg ₹1600/1800) The Tirthan Valley's original and best-known guesthouse, Raju's has a perfect, peacefully spacious farm-garden location across the river, 400m downstream from Gushaini bridge. Foliage and the all-timber, low-ceilinged interiors create an artistically ramshackle if slightly spartan feel.

Access is by low-slung log footbridge or, in high water, an exciting basket-on-a-cable affair across the rushing river. Booking well ahead is wise for the April to June season. The kitchen turns out utterly delicious home-style Indian meals, there's a library, and information on local walks and fishing. It's an excellent deal for individual travellers.

Rana Swiss Cottages COTTAGE $$
(☎01903-228234; www.kshatra.com; Bahu Rd, Jibhi; cottage/duplex ₹2460/2740) Four comfortable, rustic cottages along with a cosy cafe space and open-sided yoga 'temple' are layered up a steep, rural hillside just across a footbridge from central Jibhi. Owner BS Rana is a passionate eco-advocate, champion anti-dam campaigner and grows virtually all the produce needed for the cottages.

★**Gone Fishing** BOUTIQUE HOTEL $$$
(☎8988496587; www.gonefishingcottages.com; Deori; d ₹6000) Gone Fishing has seven high-quality rooms in three inventively designed cottages (each with communal lounge) and is remarkable for using recycled wood and even old whiskey bottles as part of the construction materials.

Staff are highly obliging and the owners are evident artists. The location is tucked away 700m off the main Tirthan Valley road (turn at Km4 and cross the Deori bridge), in a tiny hamlet near a gushing stream.

Doli Guest House MULTICUISINE $$
(Kshtara Cafe; ☎9816058290; www.kshatra.com; Jibhi; mains ₹120-400; ⏰7.30am-10pm early Mar–mid-Oct; 🛜) 🍴 Preserving a wonderfully off-beam 60-year-old wooden house, Doli is both Jibhi's oldest guesthouse (double with/without view ₹1345/950) and its best-known traveller cafe, opening into a pretty garden with summer seating and hammocks overlooking the Jibhi Nala stream.

ℹ Getting There & Around

The road up the Tirthan Valley (NH305) leaves the Kullu–Mandi road (NH3) at the south end of the 3km-long Aut Tunnel. Countless buses on Shimla–Mandi–Kullu–Manali routes pass by but getting off in Aut town gives you a better chance

HIMACHAL PRADESH TIRTHAN & BANJAR VALLEYS

of a seat than waiting at the junction. Taxis to Gushaini or Jibhi cost ₹1200. Buses to Banjar (₹45, 1½ hours) leave Aut at least hourly from 8am to 5pm. Aut's bus and taxi stands are one block east of the main road but buses originating from Kullu pick up on the main NH3.

From 7.30am to 4.30pm buses run almost hourly from Banjar to Gushaini (₹15, 30 minutes) and to Jibhi (₹15, 30 minutes). Between March and November, weather permitting, the 7.30am and 11.30am Jibhi buses continue to Rampur (six hours) across the Jalori Pass. Taxis from Banjar cost ₹300 to Jibhi or Gushaini. Keep the driver's number as locally found taxis in the opposite direction can cost double.

Bhuntar

☎ 01902 / POP 4500 / ELEV 1090M

This forgettable market town is useful as the location of the Kullu Manali airport, and the main junction for transport to the Parvati Valley. Its northern suburb, Shamsi, is home to numerous shawl-making workshops. Bajaura, 5km south of Bhuntar, has countless rafting companies but is also worth a quick stop to see the small, 9th-century **Bishweshwar Mahadev Temple** (Basheshwar Temple; Bishweshwar Temple Rd, Bajaura).

This stone *sikhara*, sitting amid young orchards beside a holy peepul tree, is a small but ornately carved natural monument. Niches on the outside contain superb relief carvings of Vishnu (west side), Ganesh (south) and a partly defaced, spindly Durga (north).

The only reason you'd likely stay in dusty Bhuntar is for an early transport connection: as such the best options are **Hotel Malabar** (☎ 01902-266199; www.hotelmalabarkullu.com; Main Bazaar; r ₹2380-3340, walk-in from ₹1400; ❀) near the bus stand, and **Airport Inn Hotel** (☎ 9816058888, 01902-265171; www.airportinnhotel.in; NH3; lower/upper d ₹2000/2500), right beside at the airport access gate. The latter's best rooms (notably 204) overlook the runway.

CHARAS

Many travellers are attracted to the Parvati Valley and the Manali area by the famous local charas (hashish), which is seriously potent stuff. Though it's smoked fairly openly in the Parvati Valley, Old Manali and Vashisht, it's still illegal and police do arrest people for possession (or hit them for hefty bribes).

❶ Getting There & Away

The airport entrance gate is 600m south of the bus stand. Weather permitting, Air India flies to Delhi daily at around 11am. Cancellations are frequent in the monsoon season.

Buses depart frequently to Mandi (₹100, two hours), some from the central bus stand, others from the NH3 nearby where Shimla buses also pick up. Services to Manali (₹70, 2½ hours) halt across the road. Passing Kullu-bound buses tend to be easier to spot 100m further north at Shamshi Chowk where they fork left, running every few minutes until 10pm or so (₹18, 15 minutes).

For the Parvati Valley, buses to Manikaran (₹70, two hours) via Jari (₹40, 1¼ hours) and Kasol (₹60, 1¾ hours) run about half-hourly from about 5.30am to 6pm, around half of them continuing to Barshani (₹100, three hours).

The **taxi cooperative** (☎ 01902-265175; Main Market; ◷ 6am-9pm) is around the corner from the bus stand. Fares for small vehicles are ₹1250 to Kasol, ₹1400 to Banjar, ₹1750 to Barshani and ₹1600 to Manali.

Parvati Valley

This ethereally beautiful valley stretches up through touristy, forest-ringed Kasol and the busy if grubby little pilgrim hot-springs town of Manikaran to a collection of villages around Barshani with glorious views of 5000m Himalayan peaks. Places like Pulga and Kalga here are key stops on the pre-Goa 'hummus trail' for young Israeli travellers, while Kasol and Tosh increasingly draw young Indian travellers and weekenders. The valley has plenty of hippie/backpacker hang-outs, with cheap accommodation, international food and nonstop music. The well-deserved reputation for charas (hashish) is most noted at the very odd village of Malana. Police sometimes make spot checks for drugs.

There are some excellent treks in the area, including the Chandrakani Pass route to/from Naggar, or the far tougher Pin-Parvati Pass to/from Spiti. For safety reasons, solo trekking is not recommended.

Jari

POP 1140 / ELEV 1590

Jari itself is a ramshackle roadside bazaar settlement 20km up the Parvati Valley from Bhuntar. However, for something far lovelier, walk around 15 minutes up from the bus-taxi stand, following several signs to Village Guest House. This route brings you to the contrastingly peaceful ridgetop hamlet of

Kullu, Parvati & Tirthan Valleys

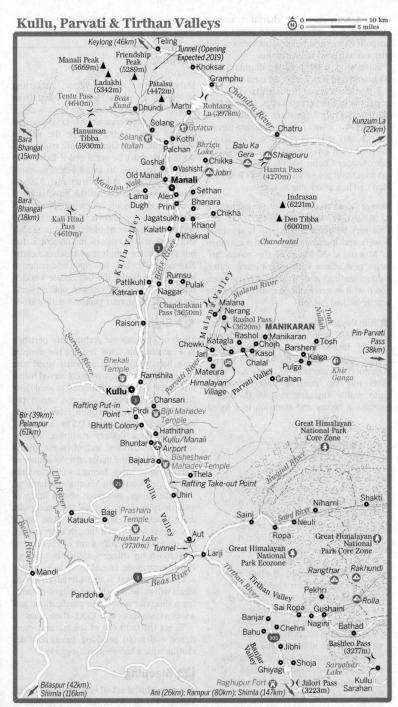

Mateura, with cheap yet charming accommodation, five wood-and-stone temples, an unspoilt charm and remarkable views of the surrounding bowl of mountains.

Buses stop in Jari between Bhuntar (₹40, 1¼ hours) and Kasol (₹20, 30 minutes).

For guide services to Malana or trekking anywhere in the Parvati Valley, contact **Negi's Himalayan Adventure** (☑ 9816081894, 9418281894; www.negis-kasol-malana-parvati.com; Chowki) at Hotel Negi's Nest II, across the river from Jari (around 3km, a ₹150 taxi ride). Owner Chapu Negi is head of the area's mountain rescue team ('India's Toughest Men'), so he's as reliable as it gets.

Village Guest House GUESTHOUSE **$**
(☑ 9816594249; Mateura; s/d ₹500/700; 🛜) This very welcoming property is set amid flowers and fountain pools at the entrance to Mateura Jari. Many of the rooms are large, new affairs with solar-heated water, indoor seating and a semi-private open porch with woven bamboo chairs facing the temple-backed garden.

★ **Himalayan Village** HERITAGE HOTEL **$$$**
(☑ 9805072712, 01902-276266; www.thehimalayanvillage.in; Bhuntar–Kasol Rd Km24.8, Dunkhra; cottage/machan ₹12,800/16,640; 🅿🛜) This magnificent collection of stone-and-wood villas and two 'machan' tower houses is quite unlike anything else in the valley, combining luxury and tradition in a forest

garden, entered via a two-level lobby-lounge house that has a certain 'on safari' feel.

Malana

POP 450 / ELEV 2630M

Malana is one strange village. According to legend, its people are descended from deserters from Alexander the Great's army. They speak their own unique language and operate what's claimed to be the world's oldest democracy. Outsiders are considered unclean so don't be surprised if locals step aside as you pass to avoid being touched. Though it's only 20km from Jari, Malana was for centuries one of the most isolated spots in the region, allowing its famous charas (hashish), known here as 'cream', to become the backbone of its economy. That's still what many visitors mainly come for, but now that a rough road reaches nearby Nareng, the trade is less open and concrete is rapidly replacing the last classic wooden houses. Be ready for random police checkpoints and bring your passport with you.

👁 Sights

Much of Malana's old architecture perished in a catastrophic 2008 fire but the temples have been rebuilt in traditional wood and stone, complete with intricately carved balconies.The key ones are dedicated to local deity Jamadaghni (Jamlu) Rishi, and attract pilgrims from around the region, especially during Malana's main festival (15 to 18 August), which features flowery costumes, processions, music, dancing and, of course, plenty of charas. One of the major temples stands on a central open space, facing a stone platform and stepped seating for Malana's 'parliament'.

In the village, you must obey a litany of esoteric rules. Don't step off the main path, don't touch the temples, don't stray on to any sacred spots (even though there's nothing obvious to identify some of them), and don't touch any villagers or their belongings. If you contravene one of these rules there's a ₹3500 fine. That is considered 'cheap' as locals will subsequently feel obliged to sacrifice a sheep for post-touch purification...and a sheep costs more like ₹5000 these days.

To get the most out of the cultural experience and avoid breaking rules, consider visiting with a knowledgeable guide.

🛏 Sleeping

In a masochistic act of economic self-harm, Malana closed down all its guesthouses and traveller facilities in mid-2017. Newspaper reports claim that the village oracle had decided tourism was a bad thing. The measure was reversed by late 2018. The simple but friendly **Chand View Guest House** (☑ 9805261446; d ₹1500-2000, without bathroom ₹500-700; ⊘ Mar-Nov) near the top, rear section of the village had already reopened at time of writing, and around a dozen more appeared to be under construction.

❶ Getting There & Away

Nerang, 16km north of the Bhuntar–Kasol road, is the nearest village to Malana that has a driveable road. A taxi from Kasol to Nerang costs ₹1800 return with a three-hour wait, or you could save a little by starting from Jari. From the handful of shack-cafes where taxis drop you, walking to Malana takes around 45 minutes on a down-then-up path that is mostly concrete steps. The return walk is slightly quicker.

Before the September 2018 landslides, a daily bus to Kullu (three hours) via Jari left Nerang at 9am, starting back from Kullu about 3pm. It's likely to be reinstated once the road improves.

Kasol

☑ 01902 / POP 750 / ELEV 1620M

Stretched along the lovely Parvati River with forested mountains rising all around, Kasol is the main traveller hub in the valley. Although nominally it's divided into Old (west) and New (east) sections by the central bridge, it's really just one small village, almost overrun with chillum-shops, trinket-sellers and ever-expanding guesthouses. In summertime trance parties are transplanted to the Kasol area from Goa, though things are steadily changing as ultra-budget guesthouses transform themselves into more mainstream hotels. Increasingly the dreadlock crowd is migrating to more offbeat villages, notably around Barshani.

🛏 Sleeping & Eating

Few buildings in town aren't guesthouses! Prices rise in May and June but are negotiable almost everywhere. Some guesthouses close November to March, at which time it's worth trying upper-market hotels, which can offer superb off-season bargains.

Royal Orchard GUESTHOUSE $
(☑ 9459342032; Tushur Lane, New Kasol; r ₹900-2500; ☎) Even the least expensive of the Royal Orchard's 21 rooms are clean, spacious and new, the upper floors enjoying wrap-around balconies.

Taji Place GUESTHOUSE $
(☑ 9816461684; chetanthakurkasol@gmail.com; Tushar Lane, New Kasol; d ₹800-3500, without bathroom ₹500, tr cottage ₹3000; ☎) On a hard-to-beat waterfront lawn with private mini hot spring, Taji has a range of tidy rooms, the cheaper ones accessed off a sunny communal terrace area with lovely river views.

★ **Evergreen** MULTICUISINE $$
(New Kasol; mains ₹200-410; ⊘ 10am-11pm) Low-lit and atmospheric, this perennial favourite is reliable for a whole range of traveller munchies, and often serenaded by a Santana soundtrack.

As well as Israeli specials, pizza, lasagne and homemade tofu, there are Turkish kebabs and sipodium (a generous lamb or chicken barbecue meal with roast veg chips, salad, naan and hummus). It's on the main road in New Kasol, 150m from the bridge.

❶ Getting There & Around

Buses between Bhuntar and Manikaran/Barshani pass through Kasol (₹40, 1¾ hours from Bhuntar) about every half-hour from around 7am to 7.30pm. Direct overnighters ex-Manikaran depart around 6.30pm to Delhi.

Taxi fares from the stand by the central bridge include ₹200 to Manikaran, ₹300 to Jari, ₹800 to Barshani, ₹1250 to Bhuntar, and ₹1200/1800 one way/return to Nerang (for Malana).

Manikaran

☑ 01902 / POP 6100 / ELEV 1730M

Steam continually billows from beneath the otherwise forgettable main Sikh and Hindu temples in Manikaran, 4km east of Kasol. According to legend, a giant snake stole goddess Parvati's earrings while she was bathing (during an 11,000-year meditation session with Shiva), then snorted them out from underground, along with various other jewels. This released the holy hot springs which, along with inexpensive accommodation, are now the minor attractions of this rather glum little pilgrim town straddling filth-strewn river-banks.

The five-storey **Sri Guru Nanak Ji Gurdwara** (Gurdwara Sahib), on the north bank of the foaming river, was built in 1940. Next to the gurdwara is a Shiva temple where pools of boiling hot-spring water are used to cook the rice for the gurdwara. A happy, quite light-hearted atmosphere prevails in both temples.

HIMACHAL PRADESH PARVATI VALLEY

PIN-PARVATI TREK

Only accessible from late June to late September/early October, this strenuous but rewarding six- to nine-day wilderness trek crosses the snowbound Pin-Parvati Pass (5319m) from Barshani in the Parvati Valley to Mudh in Spiti's Pin Valley (p351). July and August can be pretty wet so September is the best month. You'll need to be self-sufficient, and using a reputable trekking agency is wise. Organised treks are relatively pricey because pack animals cannot get across the pass so you need porters (often three per person because of the trek's length) and the crew need to be transported back to their starting point.

From Barshani (or Pulga or Kalga), the route ascends through forest and pasture to Khir Ganga hot springs and Thakur Khan. Two more days through a more arid alpine zone takes you via Pandupul rock bridge (which can be tricky when wet) and Mantalai Lake to High (or Plateau) Camp. A challenging tramp over scree and snow, requiring ropes, leads over the pass then down into the Pin Valley. A day or two extra for acclimatisation, rest or shorter stages on the way up is beneficial. The final stage can be shortened by arranging a pick-up as the last 9km to Mudh is now a driveable track.

Some prefer to do the trek in reverse, giving a rapid ascent and more lingering descent, but you'll need to be better acclimatised.

STAGE	ROUTE	DURATION (HR)	DISTANCE (KM)
1	Barshani to Khir Ganga	3-4	12
2	Khir Ganga to Thakur Khan	6	15
3	Thakur Khan to Mantalai Lake	7	16
4	Mantalai Lake to High Camp	4	12
5	High Camp to Pin Valley Camp via Pin-Parvati Pass	5-6	12
6	Pin Valley Camp to Mudh	8	20

Barshani & Around

POP 1170 (BARSHANI) / ELEV 2170M (BARSHANI)

Part-way up the steep Parvati Valley-side, Barshani has attractive views but is principally the hub from which travellers start the day hike to Khir Ganga hot springs or much shorter strolls to cult hang-out villages Tosh, Kalga and Pulga.

All three have mesmerisingly beautiful panoramic views of craggy peaks in all directions, but each has its own specific character. Popular with Indian tourists, Tosh is the highest (2430m) and the most developed, with lots of new viewguesthouses. Much more architecturally traditional, Pulga has a fine old temple tower and a tightly knit village core of houses roofed in stone slabs, where locals sit at handlooms on old wooden balconies. Yet it's also a major chill-out spot for long-stay travellers, especially Israelis, with party spots nestled into the thick forest behind. Kalga is smaller, its scattered homes charmingly dotted through an orchard with 360-degree mountain views between the trees.

Khir Ganga Hike

Start early for the beautiful Parvati Valley walk from Barshani to the sloping alpine meadow of Khir Ganga, topped at around 3000m by hot springs. The large men's pool has fantastic views, the women's one is enclosed but not covered. Bring bathing clothes. A rapid overload of camps and restaurant tents had been undermining the meadow's peaceful atmosphere until 2017, when most commerce was forcibly ejected. Nonetheless, a couple of shack guesthouses remain (open from Holi to early November) and others are likely to creep back – handy if you arrive too late to get back to Barshani (at least three hours' hike). In mid-winter the meadow lies under deep snow and is completely deserted.

The prettier of two possible walking routes from Barshani leaves the Tosh road just north of the Parvati dam and goes via Nakthan village. This is also the first stage of the Pin-Parvati multiday trek to Spiti.

🛏 Sleeping & Eating

Dozens of places offer cheap accommodation, albeit most of them unsigned: ask! Very basic rooms with/without bathroom generally start at ₹500/250, prices typically rising during May and June. Each village now has at least a couple of higher-quality options; Tosh has plenty. A couple of seasonal shack-shelters are available at Khir Ganga.

Forest View Guesthouse HOTEL **$**
(✆9805338952, 9418184017; Pulga; d/q ₹900/2000) Dominating the rear section of Pulga village, this three-storey white hotel has neat ensuite rooms that each come with semicircular balcony. Views are even more stupendous from the rooftop.

Eyesky Guesthouse GUESTHOUSE **$$**
(Tosh; d ₹600-1200, q ₹1500) Well-run Eyesky is easy to find near the start of Tosh village. The eight rooms are rather bare pink boxes but are good value with geyser-showers and fine views from mountain-facing balconies.

The cafe–lounging area has trippy murals that play with your mind even if you haven't been smoking.

Soul Kitchen INDIAN **$$**
(✆Chandan 9829535930, Tashi 9418003224; Kalga; cakes ₹100-150, 2-/3-course meals ₹400/600; ⊙unpredictable) This very special place occupies a tiny, antique hay barn with splendid views from its equally tiny front terrace at the top of the Kalga to Pulga stairway-path.

Cakes and desserts are Tashi's forte, while Chandan specialises in Rajasthani meals. Or just ask for what you fancy – there's no printed menu. Locally gathered medicinal herbs and essences are also sold.

❶ Getting There & Around

One or two Bhuntar–Kasol–Manikaran buses per hour continue to Barshani (₹30, one hour) from a stop on the road directly above Manikaran bus station. The last buses back leave Barshani at 4pm and 5pm. Taxis to Manikaran cost ₹600.

Tosh is accessible by a rough 3km road (₹300 by taxi) from Barshani. A new road to Pulga is under construction, skirting Kalga's access steps en route, but for now you need to walk; it's around 40 minutes if you find the shortcuts. Walking to Kalga takes around 15 minutes from the Parvati Dam, itself some 800m from Barshani bus stand.

Kullu

✆01902 / POP 18,540 / ELEV 1220M

The bustling administrative capital of the Kullu Valley is a return to Indian normality from the valley's hippie holiday resorts. Few travellers stop here for long but it's a likeable enough place, and in October it stages the area's biggest and most colourful festival, the Kullu Dussehra.

The Beas River's tributary, the Sarvari, cuts Kullu's centre into two halves: Dhalpur (south) has the taxi stand and tourist office, Akhara Bazaar (north) retains just a few archaic wooden buildings around the gilt-domed gurdwara. The bus station lies between, just on the north side of the Sarvari but linked via a footbridge and the pedestrianised main bazaar to Dhalpur.

The Shashtri Nagar suburb, 2km south, is home to a deeply philosophical expat community originally drawn here by the now-deceased guru Swami Shyam (www.swamishyam.com).

⊙ Sights

★Bijli Mahadev Temple HINDU TEMPLE
A popular day trip from Kullu starts with a 20km uphill drive southeast to Chansari followed by a 2.5km uphill hike to the Bijli Mahadev. The temple itself is fairly modest but

---

KULLU DUSSEHRA

Kullu hosts one of the most unusual and colourful Dussehra (p301) festivals in India. Unlike the one-day celebrations common elsewhere, Kullu Dussehra goes on for a week. The opening day is the most exciting, with 200 or more gloriously decorated village *devtas* (deities) from around the valley arriving in town on palanquins, having been carried here on foot.

The *devtas* pay homage to Raghunath Ji at his **temple** (⊙7-11am & 4-8.30pm) in the early afternoon, before moving in a wonderful cavalcade, with trumpets blaring and drums beating and decked in gorgeous garlands and draperies studded with silver masks, down to the Dussehra grounds. Here the tiny image of Raghunath Ji is placed in a large, wheeled, wooden chariot and pulled to its allotted place by teams of rope-hauling devotees amid large, excited crowds, while the village *devtas* 'dance' – tilting from side to side and charging backwards and forwards – before settling down in their own allotted places around the grounds.

it commands spectacular panoramas over the Kullu and Parvati Valleys from its 2460m hilltop location. Beside the temple stands a 20m wooden pole, which attracts occasional divine blessings in the form of lightning.

The surge of power shatters the stone Shiva lingam inside the temple, which is then glued back together with butter. Crowds make a pilgrimage here during the Sawan Kamaina festival from mid-July to mid-August. A few daily buses from Kullu bus station run as far as Chansari (₹30, 1¼ hours). A taxi from Kullu to Chansari costs ₹1500 round trip including a two-hour wait.

🏃 Activities

There is 14km of Grade II and III white water on the Beas River between Pirdi (3km south of Kullu) and Jhiri (2km south of Bajaura). Scores of agencies have roadside sales booths at Jhiri, with prices ranging from ₹700 to ₹1200 per person, generally requiring a minimum of four people. May, June, late September and October are the best seasons. Rafting is banned from 15 July to 15 August because of heavy monsoon waters.

🛏 Sleeping & Eating

Hotel Vikrant HOTEL $
(☑ 9816438299; vikramrashpa@gmail.com; Dhalpur; d ₹700-1600, q ₹1200-1500; ⊛) Backpacker friendly Vikrant lies up a tiny path between the tourist office and giant flag mast in Dhalpur. Its quirky little cafe-lounge features a big Jim Morrison portrait; rooms are more straight-laced but have a simple charm. Those upstairs are bigger and brighter; the most expensive come with kettle and flatscreen TV.

Diamond Vishali Hotel HOTEL $$
(☑ 01902-224225, 9816055802; diamondvishali hotel@gmail.com; Old Kullu Rd, Shastri Nagar; peak season r ₹3500) This smart midrange choice on the main road in Shastri Nagar has a lawn area and 17 balcony rooms all overlooking the river. Beds are remarkably comfortable and bathrooms feature high-powered rainforest showers.

★ Maitre INTERNATIONAL $$
(☑ 9805338824; www.facebook.com/MaitreKullu; Old Kullu Hwy, Shastri Nagar; mains ₹200-400; ⊙ noon-9pm; ☑) Easily missed opposite the petrol station, around 2km south of central Kullu, Maitre is the most appealing Western-centric restaurant for miles around,

with great cakes and coffees supplementing a wide-ranging (non-Indian) vegetarian menu featuring lasagnes, stuffed tacos and Thai salads, soups, cashew-almond sizzlers and a range of Chinese meals.

Gaur Niwas MULTICUISINE $$
(Hot Spice; ☑ 01902-222058, 9816469179, 7807470399; Dhalpur; mains ₹150-290, trout ₹370; ⊙ 9am-9.30pm) Gaur Niwas is a classical if mostly ungentrified heritage house where you can savour meals from tandoori trout to fair-value thalis to penne *alla zingara* sitting at little slate-roofed garden pavilions or on the house's upper wooden balconies.

ℹ Getting There & Away

Buses run about every half-hour to Manali (₹70, 90 minutes), Mandi (₹120, two hours) and Naggar (₹30, one hour) 7am to 6pm or later. For Bhuntar (₹18, 20 minutes) departures are almost nonstop until 7.30pm. Some continue to the Parvati or Tirthan Valleys, but usually you'll have to change in Bhuntar or Aut respectively. Through buses to Amritsar, Chandigarh and Delhi typically originate in Manali, stopping at Kullu Bus Station about 1½ hours after departure.

Naggar

☑ 01902 / POP 550 / ELEV 1710M

High on the east side of the Kullu Valley, little Naggar was once capital of the Kullu kingdom. Russian painter and explorer Nicholas Roerich (Nikolai Rerikh) liked it so much he settled here in the early 20th century and it remains arguably the most charming tourist centre in the valley today. Though easy to visit as a day trip from Manali, interesting sights, fine walks, good food and some excellent guesthouses mean that it's well worth staying overnight. Or longer.

Naggar's main visitor area is around the castle, 1km steeply up from the forgettable bus stand/bazaar area. The road continues another kilometre to the Roerich complex.

◉ Sights

Naggar Castle FORT
(₹30; ⊙ 9am-6pm) Built by the rajas of Kullu around 1500, this fort-cum-mansion is a splendid example of the earthquake-resistant, Kathkuni (alternating stone-and-timber) style of Himachali architecture. Sold to the British assistant commissioner in 1846, the building later became a courthouse and then, in 1976, a hotel (p314). Views from the balconies are a big part of the charm.

SHOPPING FOR SHAWLS

The Kullu Valley is famous for its traditional wool shawls – attractively patterned, lightweight but wonderfully warm. The handloom industry provides an income for thousands of local women. Many are organised into shawl-weaving cooperatives with workshops especially prevalent in Shamshi (northern Bhuntar), but scores of showrooms line the whole Bhuntar–Manali highway. Various different wools are used, resulting in widely varying prices. So while a lambswool shawl might cost, say, ₹700, a similar-sized one using a blend with added angora wool (from rabbits) could be ₹1200 to ₹1600, and those using pure pashmina (from high-altitude goats) could top ₹6000. Pashmina-lambswool blends also exist and there are also convincing 'fake' pashminas that can be hard to distinguish yet cost a fraction of the money.

For reliably high quality without the doubts or the hard sell, visit the nearest branch of **Bhuttico** (www.bhutticoshawl.com; Akhara Bazar, Kullu). Established 1944, it's the biggest weavers' cooperative with showrooms in every town in the valley and several beyond, plus a large **factory showroom** (www.bhutticoshawl.com; Kullu Rd, Bhutti Colony; ⊙9am-7pm or later) 8km south of Kullu where you can see the weavers at work (except Sunday). Bhuttico has fixed, marked prices, so it's a good place to gauge price and quality. It also makes scarves, topis (distinctive local hats), jackets, bags, gloves, *pullas* (slippers made from cannabis stalks) and *pattus*, the wonderfully patterned wraparound wool garments that are Kullu women's traditional clothing.

★ **International Roerich Memorial Trust** MUSEUM
(📞 01902-248590; www.irmtkullu.com; Indian/foreigner/child ₹50/100/30; ⊙10am-1pm & 1.30-5.30pm Apr-Oct, to 4.30pm Nov-Mar) This fascinating complex, set in lovely hillside gardens 1km above the castle, is centred on the former home of Russian painter, writer and explorer Nicholas Roerich and his wife Elena Roerich, a philosopher, writer and translator. They settled here in 1928 and stayed until Nicholas's death in 1947 (Elena moved to Kalimpong). The couple's semi-mystical, aesthetico-orientalist philosophising had an international following in their lifetimes, but it is Nicholas' distinctive painting style that has found enduring appeal.

The house's lower floor displays paintings by both Nicholas (mainly Himalayan mountain scenes) and the couple's second son Svyatoslav (1904–93), along with their 1930 Dodge 6 convertible car. On the upper floor you can peep through windows into some of the family's preserved private rooms. A hut-studio in the lower garden focuses on Svyatoslav and his wife, Indian film star Devika Rani. Across the road, a five-minute stair-climb above the house, the same ticket gets you into the Urusvati Himalayan Research Institute. Here, first son George (aka Yuri, 1902–60) features, along with a collection of Himachali handicrafts and an exhibition on the Roerich Pact, an international agreement on cultural protection which led Nicholas to be nominated for the 1929 Nobel Peace Prize.

Temples

Naggar is home to several intriguing and beautiful small temples. Just 50m down the lane beside the castle is a squat, 11th-century *sikhara*-style **Vishnu Mandir** (Chanalti Lane). Immediately beyond, the road divides outside Poona Lodge. Turn left, descending past the post office and turn left again (the shortcut lane that leads steeply down to Naggar Bazaar) to find the lovely little Gauri Shankar Temple. Or keep right at Poona, pass the brand new but traditionally styled Durga Bhandar tower and after the school you'll find the wooden, pagoda-style **Tripura Sundari Temple** (School Rd), sacred to the local earth/mother goddess. Though its present form dates from 1980, it feels timeless and the site has probably been sacred since pre-Hindu times. Continue up the streamside lane, crossing the asphalt then up zigzagging cobbles to find Murlidhar Krishna Temple (www.yogadham.in/temple; 1.2km by road, half as far using shortcuts). It stands on a hilltop ridge with view terrace, the site of ancient Thawa, a town that predated Naggar by around 1000 years. The temple's 11th-century *sikhara* has been much patched up but includes some intriguing carvings (yogis, musicians and karma sutra postures), while the glowing sanctum enshrines a black-faced Krishna playing the *murli* (flute) – hence the temple's name.

✦ Activities

Naggar is a fine base for walking, whether an hour's return jaunt to the Murlidhar Krishna Temple (p313), a three-hour circuit (gaining 400m) to Rumsu and back or, with a competent guide, the splendid two-day trek across the 3650m Chandrakani Pass to Malana (p308).

Ragini Treks & Tours TREKKING
(☏ 9817076890; www.naggarragini.com; Hotel Ragini) The **Hotel Ragini** (☏ 01902-248185, d ₹1000-2000; 🖘) has an experienced trekking outfit and doubles as Naggar's one licensed money changer.

Chandrakani Pass Trek

Accessible between late May and October or later, the excellent, popular trek from Naggar to Malana crosses the 3650m Chandrakani Pass. It's basically a two-day trek with six to eight hours' actual walking up to the pass, then two to three hours down to Malana. You could save an hour by driving from Naggar to Rumsu and starting there. Reputable agencies in Naggar charge around ₹3000 per person per day for guided and equipped treks with porters. If you want to go more independently, at least take a local guide recommended by your guesthouse (around ₹1000 per day) as the way is not always obvious. Dangerously bad weather can occur at almost any time, so go prepared with food and equipment for overnight camping. The ideal season is mid-September to mid-October, with neither crowds nor (usually) snow. July and August can both see heavy rain.

🛏 Sleeping

⭐ **Alliance Guesthouse** GUESTHOUSE $
(☏ 9418025640, 9817097033; www.alliancenaggar.com; Roerich Marg; d ₹900-1800, tr & q ₹2200, s/d/tr without bathroom ₹550/660/770; 🖘) 🌱 This friendly place, brilliantly run by a French-Indian family, is inconspicuously located on a bend of road between the castle and Roerich Museum. Its warren of spotless rooms range from shared-bathroom cheapies to duplexes perfect for families. Even cheaper rooms have comfy beds and a remarkable range of guest comforts including kettles, tea, coffee, reading lamps, hairdryers, towels and even cotton buds.

Excellent Indian and Continental food is available for guests (pre-order, mains ₹120 to ₹450), including local trout and a few specialities with a French touch. The library has books in numerous languages, there are plentiful sitting areas and staff are super-helpful with bookings and information on local walks.

New Mannat Home GUESTHOUSE $$
(☏ Raju 9816048116, Urmil 9816248116; www.mannathome.com; r ₹1000-2200, per month ₹20,000-35,000; 🖘) Opposite the castle, Mannat offers eight different, clean and mostly spacious rooms, the best with parquet floors and a tasteful beige and wood-tone decor. Many have views, which are especially panoramic from the shared balcony.

The Castle HERITAGE HOTEL $$
(☏ 01902-248316; www.hptdc.gov.in; incl breakfast r ₹1900-3420, ste ₹4720-5550; 🖘) Staying within the castle is a delight if you want to revel in the historical atmosphere. Rooms are better than at many HPTDC-managed properties but can still feel a tad spartan.

✖ Eating & Drinking

There's a decent scattering of cafes around the castle, whose reasonably good **restaurant** (mains ₹130-290, trout ₹500; ⊙ 1-3pm & 8-10pm) stays open year-round (the rest close mid-winter). Guest-only meals at Alliance Guesthouse are hard to beat. For culinary range and great views, the rooftop at Hotel Ragini is a great choice open to all comers.

ⓘ Getting There & Around

Buses run once or twice an hour from Naggar Bazaar to Manali (₹40, one hour, 8am to 6pm), and to Kullu (₹40, one hour, 7.30am to 7pm). A taxi on either route costs ₹800 to ₹900.

An autorickshaw/taxi up to the castle from the Naggar Bazaar bus stop (1km uphill) is ₹70/100.

Manali

☏ 01902 / POP 8100 / ELEV 1900M

With mountain adventures beckoning from all directions, Manali is a year-round magnet. Backpackers are well catered for in parts of Vashisht and Old Manali where numerous agents offer trekking, climbing, rafting and skiing according to season. Meanwhile, so many Indian families and honeymooners come for a first taste of snow that greater Manali now has an estimated 800 to 1000 hotels and guesthouses. Tight-packed resort buildings already fill the town centre and are now steadily devouring former orchard terraces as far

Central Manali

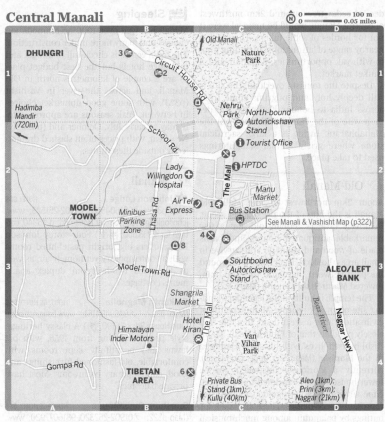

N 0 ———————— 100 m
   0 ———————— 0.05 miles

DHUNGRI

Old Manali

Nature Park

Circuit House Rd

Hadimba Mandir (720m)

School Rd

Nehru Park

North-bound Autorickshaw Stand

Tourist Office

Lady Willingdon Hospital

The Mall

HPTDC

Manu Market

AirTel Express

Bus Station

See Manali & Vashisht Map (p322)

MODEL TOWN

Minibus Parking Zone

Lhasa Rd

Model Town Rd

Southbound Autorickshaw Stand

ALEO/LEFT BANK

Beas River

Naggar Hwy

Shangrila Market

Hotel Kiran

The Mall

Himalayan Inder Motors

Van Vihar Park

Gompa Rd

TIBETAN AREA

Private Bus Stand (1km); Kullu (40km)

Aleo (1km); Prini (3km); Naggar (21km)

HIMACHAL PRADESH MANALI

Central Manali

Activities, Courses & Tours
1 Himalayan Bike Bar	C2

Sleeping
2 Johnson Lodge	B1
3 Johnson's Hotel	B1

Eating
4 Chopsticks	C3
5 Corner House	C2

Johnson's Cafe	(see 3)
6 Vibes	B4

Drinking & Nightlife
Johnson Lodge Bar	(see 2)

Shopping
7 Bhuttico	C1
8 Bookworm	B3

south as once-rustic Prini 'village'. But while the whole area gets jam-packed in season (mid-April to mid-July, mid-September to mid-October, and over Christmas–New Year), it doesn't take too much effort to get off the main tourist trail. And in November, clear skies plus slashed prices make Manali a bargain – if you can handle the cold and the closure of some restaurants.

◉ Sights

Hadimba Mandir HINDU TEMPLE
(Map p322) This much-revered wood-and-stone temple, constructed in 1553, has a three-tier pagoda-style roof plus conical top. The wooden doorway is richly carved with figures of gods, animals and dancers, and the outside walls are adorned with antlers and ibex horns. The setting, amid towering

deodar cedar trees around 2km northwest of central Manali, would be magical were it not for hordes of selfie-takers. They seek a nearby range of 'attractions', including photo-to-with-yak opportunities, a funfair and a trinket market.

Despite the tourism overload, the site is still deeply holy and pilgrims come from across India to honour Hadimba, the demon wife of the Pandava Bhima from the Mahabharata. Inside is a large sacrificial stone where grisly animal slaughterings used to take place.

◎ Old Manali

About 2km northwest of The Mall, Old Manali is the hub of the backpacker scene. Relatively little is actually old, but a few remarkable antiquated houses and barns made of wood and stone do still survive in small areas. Look on Tiger Alley and around the path between there and the 1991-built, towered **Manu Rishi Temple** (Map p322).

The temple is built on the legendary landing site of an ark bearing Manu, creator of civilisation, after a great flood, in a tale that closely parallels that of Biblical Noah. Manu Rishi himself 'lives' with his sister Hadimba in the **Madhar** (Map p322; Upper Old Manali), currently a gloriously unspoiled striped tower-house that is scheduled to be rebuilt. Nine silver masks with golden moustaches represent the co-deities. These are taken for outings by palanquin among much musical fanfare, for festivals or when called upon to bless a new house or business.

⚡ Activities

⭐ **Himalayan Extreme Centre**   OUTDOORS
(Map p322; ☑ 9816174164; www.himalayan-extreme-centre.com; Old Manali; ⊙ 9.30am-10pm high season, 10.30am-7pm off season) Long-running, professional and friendly, HEC is one of just a few tour agencies to open year-round. It can arrange almost any activity you fancy: drop in for informed, unpressured advice and browse a catalogue of options with accompanying videos.

Himalayan Caravan   OUTDOORS
(Map p322; ☑ 9816316348; www.himalayancaravan.com; Manu Temple Rd, Old Manali; ⊙ mid-Mar–mid-Dec) Professional operator for rock climbing, mountaineering and trekking plus winter sports.

🛏 Sleeping

Manali has well over 1000 accommodation choices and many more under construction. The town centre is chock-full of budget and midrange hotels but the best budget places are a couple of kilometres north in Old Manali, and across the river in Vashisht (p323), with some good upmarket choices in between. Peak seasons are approximately May to early July, October and (possibly) New Year, with prices often slashed dramatically outside these times.

🛏 Manali

⭐ **Johnson Lodge**   HOTEL $$$
(Map p315; ☑ 9816045123, 01902-251523; www.johnsonlodge.com; Circuit House Rd; d ₹5940, cottage for 4 ₹13,650; ❋ ⊛ ⓢ) Four-storey Johnson Lodge offers big, bright pastel-hued rooms with a contemporary yet homely air, as well as luxurious two-bedroom duplex apartments ('cottages').

Baikunth Magnolia   HERITAGE HOTEL $$$
(Map p322; ☑ 9459494161; www.baikunth.com; Club House Rd; r ₹6190; ⓢ) A classy heritage-style property dating from 1956, with big lawns and beautifully kept rooms with comfortable, old-fashioned furnishings and good, contemporary bathrooms. Most have private balconies.

Sunshine Guesthouse   HERITAGE HOTEL $$$
(Map p322; ☑ 01902-252320, 9816077920; www.sunshineguesthouse.blogspot.com; Club House Rd; d/ste ₹4500/5200; ⓢ) Authentically colonial without undue luxury, the Sunshine is set in delightfully peaceful, layered lawns off Club House Rd. Four large suites are in the original 1921 wood-and-stone building, with polished walnut-and-pine floors and modernised bathrooms. Four spacious doubles are in a similarly styled if slightly less venerable building next door, all with views straight up the valley.

🛏 Old Manali

The main traveller strip is Manu Temple Rd, which is lined with many a guesthouse, though you can often find somewhat better deals by wandering the various lanes and pathways that lead off it. Many guesthouses close in January and February, some from November to March.

Anand Guest House   GUESTHOUSE $
(Map p322; ☑ 9816174040, 8219882001; Purima Alley; s/d/tr from ₹800/900/1200, top-floor d ₹1000-2000,) A cult backpacker retreat, this large family guesthouse is set in orchards just two minutes' walk off the main Old Manali strip. Rooms set off south-facing balconies aren't luxurious but are very clean and have extra curtained baggage/changing areas. The open yoga terrace has super views. Fluent-English-speaking owner Anand is a former guide who's very traveller-savvy.

Zostel   HOSTEL $
(Map p322; ☑ 9882746334; www.zostel.com; Tiger Alley; dm/r ₹500/2240; ☎) Manali's branch of the reliable hostel chain works its usual backpacker magic with walls you're encouraged to write on, and a lawn whose overhanging trees dangle atmospherically with cubic lanterns.

Apple View Guest House   GUESTHOUSE $
(Map p322; ☑ 9805794113, 9816887844; www.appleviewmanali.com; Peace Plateau; r ₹500-800, s/d without bathroom ₹300/400; ☎) Twelve plain, well-kept rooms with concrete floors share two balcony-terraces with seating areas. Unlike most Manali guesthouses it's still family run, and prices change little by season. If it looks closed, call.

Timberwolves   GUESTHOUSE $$
(Map p322; ☑ 9988876291; www.knowwheretostay.in; Upper Old Manali; ₹1500) Built in 2017, Timberwolves combines a semi-hippie rooftop cafe with 13 contrastingly comfortable, well-built rooms with partial pine-cladding plus, in two, mini-kitchenettes. They all share superb valley views in a very peaceful location at the top of Old Manali.

Tiger Eye Guest House   HOMESTAY $$
(Map p322; ☑ 9816092470; www.tigereyeadventure.com; Tiger Alley; lower/mid/upper r ₹1200/1800/2000; ☎) Fifteen full-comfort rooms in a new but attractive construction built using traditional materials are accessed from L-shaped open balconies with little dining tables gazing out over fine views. It's on a small alley in one of the few really old parts of Old Manali.

Red House   GUESTHOUSE $$
(Map p322; ☑ 9769485664; www.facebook.com/RedHouseManali; Peace Plateau; ☺ dm ₹500 r ₹1700-3500) Up the 'Stairway to Heaven'

from the HPTDC Club House, 'Peace Plateau' is the most unspoilt area of Old Manali's orchard terraces. Here you'll find Red House with a large ground-floor dormitory and four private rooms, each with lovely views in three directions.

✕ Eating

✕ Manali

Vibes   HIMACHALI $$
(Map p315; ☑ 9816245280; www.facebook.com/vibeshimachalicuisine; mains ₹150-200, thali ₹250-430; ☺ 11am-11pm) Upstairs, 250m south of the bus station, Vibes is a great place to try authentic, beautifully presented Himachali food that's rarely available outside local family weddings.

The menu offers helpful explanations, but do note that several dishes, like the *lingdi* (fiddlehead fern-leaves) and *patrodu* (stuffed taro-root), are seasonal and need pre-ordering. There's also a menu of specialist Himalayan teas (₹100 per pot) including first flush with lavender or authentic Tibetan-butter tea.

Chopsticks   ASIAN $$
(Map p315; www.kullu.net/chopsticks; The Mall; mains ₹130-400, trout/prawn dishes ₹500/700; ☺ 9.30am-10.30pm) Tibetan lutes and ornate Chinese lanterns give panel-walled Chopsticks an attractively distinctive if slightly dated feel. It's handily located just across the pedestrianised Mall from the bus station and serves a very wide range of delicious Tibetan, Chinese and pseudo-Japanese dishes that you can accompany with beers (from ₹200) and local fruit wines.

★ Johnson's Cafe   INTERNATIONAL $$$
(Map p315; www.johnsonshotel.com; Circuit House Rd; meals ₹400-650, trout ₹550-700, pizza ₹280-1100; ☺ 8.30am-10.30pm or later; ☎) The relaxed yet stylish garden-fronted restaurant at **Johnson's Hotel** (☑ 8626814404, 01902-253764; r/cottage ₹6000/12,000; ✳ ☎) frames a mountain view through foldaway windows, and its wood-fired pizza oven is cleverly positioned to warm the bar area in winter. Excellent European food includes lamb with mint gravy and plum-sauce spare ribs, but the standout is majestic Manali trout-fillet curry served with rice, salad and delicious *madra-palak* (a spinach-cheese dish).

OUTDOOR ACTIVITIES AROUND MANALI

Manali is the adventure-sports capital of Himachal Pradesh, and all kinds of activities can be organised through operators here.

Mountain Biking

Many agents offer bike hire for ₹400 to ₹800 per day and can give current info on routes. Some will take you on guided rides – ranging from day outings to two-week trips to Ladakh or Spiti with vehicle support. Central Manali's **Himalayan Bike Bar** (Map p315; ☑9418612482; www.facebook.com/himalayanbikebar; The Mall at Mission Rd; ⊙10am-8pm Mon-Sat) is an MTB specialist renting and selling bikes, as well as a good source of information on extreme off-road events.

Mountaineering

Agencies such as Himalayan Caravan (p316) and **Himalayan Yeti** (Map p322; ☑Sunny 9816300789; www.himalayanyeti.in; Manu Temple Rd; ⊙9am-9pm or later) arrange a wide range of expeditions. Given 10 to 14 days, possibilities including peaks around the head of the Solang Valley: Friendship Peak (5289m) and Ladakhi (5342m) are suitable for those with limited experience (training is available), while Hanuman Tibba (5930m) and Manali Peak (5669m) are more difficult. Deo Tibba (6001m), above the east side of the Kullu Valley, is another exciting peak for experienced climbers. Typical prices are around ₹5000 per person per day including instructor/guides, equipment, transport, food and camping. Conditions tend to be best in October and November.

Paragliding

Paragliding is popular at Solang Nullah, Gulaba and Marhi (below the Rohtang La), from April to November – weather permitting. Paragliding is rare during the monsoon. September and October generally have the best thermals, though May and June can be good, too. Tandem flights at Solang Nullah cost around ₹1000 for a one-minute flight above the beginners' ski slope, though that's basically just take-off and land. For ₹3200 you get around 10 minutes (includes the cable-car fare).

Rafting

The region's main rafting takes place near Kullu (p312), but Manali agencies can prove helpful in getting together a group of travellers and organising shared transport.

✗ Old Manali

Countless half-open-air restaurants serve a wide range of backpacker-town suspects, *momos* (Tibetan dumplings), omelettes, banana pancakes, apple pie and the three Is (Italian/Israeli/Indian dishes), plus increasing hints of Thai. The main selection is found by simply turning left at Old Manali Bridge and climbing the hook of Manu Temple Rd. Many of these places close November to March.

Drifters' Inn MULTICUISINE $$
(Map p322; ☑9810978051, 9816005950; www.driftersinncafe.com; Manu Temple Rd; meals ₹230-410, trout ₹440-490; ⊙9.30am-10.30pm Wed-Mon, closed early Jan–mid-Feb; ☎) This loungey restaurant-cafe with a mellow, jazzy soundtrack is good for hearty breakfasts, strong coffee and international dishes, from eggs Florentine to remarkably good Thai green curries.

Rocky's Cafe MULTICUISINE $$
(Map p322; ☑9816491374; www.rockysguesthome.in; Manu Temple Rd; mains ₹120-300, trout ₹400-450; ⊙8am-late peak season, 9am-9pm off season; ☎) Trancey vibes and dangling prayer-catchers set the tone, and there are plenty of chess sets on the wide sunny terrace, but what really makes the climb worthwhile is staring into infinity, contemplating the dazzling panorama.

Cafe 1947 ITALIAN $$$
(Map p322; Manu Temple Rd; 10-inch pizza ₹270-530, trout ₹530; ⊙noon-11pm Thu-Tue, from 7pm Wed) This mood-lit bar-restaurant with a willow-shaded riverside terrace is popular for smoking shisha pipes (₹460) to an insistently upbeat soundtrack. It also serves good lasagne, thin-crust pizza and superb fresh-trout platters: perfectly grilled fish with garlic-coriander sauce, orange and lemon

Skiing & Snowboarding

Solang Nullah is viewed as Manali's main ski resort as it has the region's only cable car, but there's only one piste (around 1.5km) whose lower end is at a mere 2450m. Climate change thus keeps shortening the season, which is basically just January and February (or less). Further skiing options are available in the upper Solang Valley and around Gulaba. For ski packages contact Himalayan Caravan (p316), Himalayan Extreme Centre (p316) or the very experienced family team at Solang Nullah's **Hotel Iceland** (☑9418016008, 9816066508; www.hotelicelandsolang.com; ☎). Heli-skiing packages to high-altitude powder in February and March can be arranged through **Himalayan Heli Adventures** (☑9816025899; www.himachal.com; ☺9am-6pm).

Walking & Trekking

Manali is a popular jumping-off point for organised mountain treks. June, September and October are overall the best months. Popular shorter options include variants on Beas Kund (three days, with the option of extra days hiking up surrounding mountains), the 4250m-high Bhrigu Lake (three days through lovely upland meadows) and the Hamta Pass (p324), which is varied and stunningly beautiful whether crossing into Lahaul (four days) or doing an up-and-back walk. Prices vary incredibly widely by season, group size and facilities offered: a typical range is ₹1600 to ₹3000 per person per day including guides, transport, pack animals, food and camping equipment. More demanding and usually more expensive hikes include the six- to nine-day Pin-Parvati Trek (p310) for which human porters are required, and routes west to the isolated village of Bara Bhangal, continuing to the Chamba or Kangra Valleys (11 days or more).

Plenty of shorter walks are possible from Manali. From Old Manali a very pleasant forest stroll towards Goshal (around an hour, three possible routes) winds through woodlands with occasional views across the valley to the Jogini Waterfalls. You can return along Shanag Lane. A fuller day hike (about five hours up, four hours back) is up to Lama Dugh meadow at 3380m: the way starts along the uphill cobbled path from behind the upper of two **water tanks** (Map p322) above Hotel Delfryn in the Log Huts Area of town. Don't take the mud path that runs almost parallel at first.

garnish, and a whole array of crunchy fresh veggies. Hard to beat.

Casa Bella Vista   MEDITERRANEAN $$$
(Map p322; www.casasdelhimalaya.com/thecafe; Log Huts Rd; mains ₹390-550, 12in pizza ₹420-610, tapas ₹305-370; ☺10am-10.30pm May-Sep; ☎☑) Just across the river from Old Manali, climb a short stairway to enjoy Bella Vista's high-quality vegetarian Spanish and Italian food served in a comfortably spacious setting with a florally feminine touch.

La Plage   FRENCH $$$
(Map p322; ☑9805340977; www.facebook.com/la.plage.manali; Shanag Lane; mains ₹400-700; ☺noon-11pm mid-May–late Aug, closed Mon in Aug) This decadent summer-only outpost of a chic Goan eatery serves French standards, like onion soup or mushroom quiche. You can also try specialities like overnight-cooked lamb, smoked trout, broccoli-and-courgette lasagne

and an indulgent chocolate thali as dessert. Decent Indian and international wines.

🍷 Drinking & Nightlife

While all double as eateries, the most agreeable bar atmospheres are generally at music-oriented riverside places like **Lazy Dog Lounge** (Map p322; Manu Temple Rd; mains ₹220-532, trout ₹706; ☺11am-1am, off-season to 10.30pm; ☎) and Cafe 1947, both with shisha-pipes to smoke, and the suavely fashionable, upper-market cocktail bar at **Johnson Lodge** (Map p315; Circuit House Rd; ☺noon-11pm). For quiet, comfy beers from just ₹180, try **Renaissance** (Map p322; ☑9816096835; Manu Temple Rd; mains ₹150-290).

For barista coffee, top choices are **Corner House** (Map p315; The Mall; mains ₹220-580; ☺9am-11.30pm Apr-Oct, 11am-10pm Nov-Mar) in Manali or seasonal **Dylan's** (Map p322; www.dylanscoffee.com; Manu Temple Rd; ☺9am-10pm

Mon-Sat, closed Nov-Mar; 🕿) in Old Manali, though you'll get plenty of real espressos at riverside Cafe 1947 (p318) and, with a jaw-dropping view, at Rocky's Cafe (p318).

🛍 Shopping

Manali is crammed with shops selling souvenirs from Himachal, Tibet and Ladakh, including turquoise jewellery and lots of brass buddhas. The local speciality is Kullu shawls (p313), for which a good place to start for judging the market is local cooperative **Bhuttico** (Map p315; The Mall; ⊗9am-7pm Mon-Sat), which has several fixed-price shops around town.

Bookworm   BOOKS
(Map p315; 🖉9418542040; near Post Office; ⊗10am-7.30pm Mon-Sat May-Oct, to 6pm Nov, Dec & Apr, closed Jan–mid-Mar) Excellent selection of books including many on the Himalaya. Also stocks strings of authentic prayer flags (from ₹70).

ℹ Information

AirTel Express (Northwest Traders; Map p315; Shop 9, Govinda Complex, Old Mission Rd; ⊗10am-9pm) For a one-/three-month SIM Card (₹300/350) with unlimited Indian calls and 1.4GB per day data, bring one photo plus copies of your passport and visa to this small shop tucked into the little square where SuperBake is far more conspicuous.

Lady Willingdon Hospital (Map p315; 🖉01902-252379; www.manalihospital.com; School Rd) Considered the best hospital in the Kullu Valley; has 24-hour emergency service.

Tourist Office (Map p315; 🖉01902-252175; The Mall; ⊗10am-5pm Mon-Sat, closed 2nd Sat of the month) Answers questions and has a few giveaway booklets plus a highly schematic town map.

ℹ Getting There & Away

Manali's closest airport is 50km south at Bhuntar.

BUS

Government-run Himachal Road Transport Corporation (HRTC) buses along with some private buses (eg to Kullu via Naggar) go from the **bus station** (Map p315; The Mall). Himachal Tourism (HPTDC) runs a few services to Delhi (₹1500) plus seasonally to Leh (late June to mid-September ₹2900, 10am including meals and dorm), Chandigarh (₹600, May and June, 7.30am), Kalka (₹600, May and June, 7.30am) and Shimla (₹550, May and June, 8.30am): these are generally the most comfortable on their routes. They leave from the bus station but tickets are sold at the HPTDC **office** (Map p315; 🖉01902-252116; The Mall; ⊗9am-7pm). Some private buses to other destinations start from the **private bus stand** (Hwy 3), 1.2km south, with tickets presold at travel agencies along The Mall. For the Parvati Valley, take a bus to Bhuntar and change there.

Delhi The HPTDC's comfortable AC Volvo coaches (₹1300, 14 hours) go at 5.30pm and, in busy seasons, 5pm and/or 6pm. Private bus companies run similar overnight services for ₹900 to ₹1800 depending on season. The HRTC runs five AC Volvos (₹1412) each afternoon, plus an AC deluxe (₹1122) at 5.50pm, and seven ordinary or 'semi-deluxe' services daily.

Lahaul & Spiti Seasonal passes link Manali to Lahaul (usually closed November to mid-May) and on to Spiti (usually closed November

HRTC BUSES FROM MANALI

DESTINATION	FARE (₹)	DURATION (HR)	DEPARTURES
Amritsar	659-1563	11-14	1.45pm & 3.30pm; 8pm Volvo
Chandigarh	542-1141	9½-11	5 ordinary, 4 deluxe & many private buses
Dehra Dun	770-1720	15	6.30pm & 8.30pm; 4.30pm Volvo
Delhi	684-1690	14-16	16 daily & 30+ private services
Dharamsala	457-700	10	ordinary 8.20am & 6.40pm, plus seasonal deluxe 7.30pm May-Oct
Haridwar	774-1950	16	12.40pm, 3pm & 8.30pm, Volvo 4.30pm
Jammu	674	14	2.30pm, 4pm
Kaza	300	11	6.30am, approximately mid-Jun–mid-Oct
Keylong	175	7	7 daily, approximately mid-May–early Nov
Kullu	70	1½	every few minutes, 4am-10pm
Mandi	195-420	4	half-hourly, 5am-9pm
Naggar	40	1	at least hourly, 8am-6pm
Shimla	390-650	9	6 daily

to early June) but exact opening dates vary according to weather. A tunnel bypassing the Rohtang La should open up Lahaul to year-round visits from 2019 or 2020. In season, the HRTC runs up to seven daily buses to Keylong (Lahaul) and one to Kaza (Spiti).

Ladakh The bone-shaking, exhausting but spectacular road to Leh is normally open from early June to some time in October (exact dates depend on road conditions). On all journeys to Leh, bring snacks and warm clothing and be alert to the symptoms of Acute Mountain Sickness. Fare-wise the cheapest option is to take a bus to Keylong (Lahaul), sleep there then catch the early morning HRTC bus on to Leh.

From early July to mid-September, a HPTDC bus (₹3000, 34 hours) departs Manali at 9am every second day, with an overnight stop at Keylong, where dormitory accommodation, dinner and breakfast are included in the fare. Throughout the season the Him-aanchal Taxi Operators Union runs minibuses to Leh departing at 10am with overnight halt (₹3200) and nonstop Sumo shared jeeps at 4am (₹3000); no accommodation or food included, pre-book a day ahead. Some travel agencies offer similar services. Generally prices decrease as the season goes on. Some options include accommodation and meals in the two-day package.

The opening of the Rohtang tunnel (expected to be in 2019 or 2020) is likely to radically affect schedules.

Shimla & Dharamsala For Shimla, the HPTDC runs a bus at 8.30am (₹550, nine hours) in May and June; HRTC buses go year-round. For Dharamsala, in addition to HRTC buses (one of which is a Volvo AC), there are usually a couple of evening-departure private buses for around ₹550.

MOTORCYCLE

Many people tackle the mountain passes to Ladakh or Spiti on bought or rented bikes. You can book into a group tour with accommodation, food and backup vehicles included at around ₹5000 per day, or just rent a bike and head off on your own.

For rentals, expect to pay ₹1200 to ₹1500 per day for a 350cc Enfield Classic, ₹1500 to ₹1800 for a 500cc Bullet, and ₹800 to ₹1000 for 220cc bikes. Make sure the deal includes spares, tools, at least third-party insurance, and the registration and pollution certificates needed for your Rohtang La permit where necessary.

Dozens of agencies rent bikes and/or run tours, including the following:

Anu Auto Works (Royal Moto Touring; Map p322; ☑ 9816163378; www.royalmototouring. com; Vashisht Rd; ⊙ office 9am-9pm Jun-Sep) Established, highly regarded and professional outfit that offers Enfield motorbike tours, and rents and repairs Enfields, too.

Bike Rentals Manali (Map p322; ☑ 9816044140; www.bikerentalsmanali.com; Vashisht; ⊙ 9.30am-10pm mid-Mar–Oct, to 7pm Nov & Dec) Enfield rentals and tours.

Enfield Club (Map p322; ☑ 9805146389; Vashisht Rd; ⊙ 9am-9.30pm mid-Apr–Jan) Tiny enthusiasts' workshop doing Enfield rentals and repairs.

Himalayan Inder Motors (Map p315; ☑ 9816113973; Gompa Rd; ⊙ 8am-10pm) Rents Enfields and other makes. The tiny sales window belies a well-established business of nearly three decades' standing.

TAXI & JEEP

The **Him-aanchal Taxi Operators Union** (Map p315; ☑ 01902-252205, 01902-252120; The Mall; ⊙ 8am-10pm May-Oct, to 8pm Nov-Apr) offers fixed-price rides and charters. For the rough but glorious summer-only routes to Spiti and/or Ladakh you'll need a 'jeep', whether a fairly basic high-clearance Sumo or Spacio, or a comfier if less-rugged Innova, Xylo or Tavera. Locals squeeze in up to 10 people, but four or five is better for comfort, and a multiday charter can cost from as little as ₹3500 per vehicle per day. Nonstop Sumo shared jeeps depart at 4am (₹3000).

Alternatively, one-way charters to Leh run ₹18,000/25,000 for a Sumo/Innova. Private travel agencies offer similar deals and some also sell individual seats for around ₹3500 (May to July), dropping to ₹2000 to ₹2500 in August and September.

For Kaza (Spiti), a one-way jeep charter costs around ₹10,000 but predawn public share jeeps are available (₹1000 to ₹1500 per seat); ask the day before at **Hotel Kiran** (Map p315; ☑ 01902-253066), where drivers from Spiti hang out. These run as long as the Rohtang and Kunzum passes are open.

You can organise charters through almost any travel agency. Some of the best in-season prices are available from **Shalom Travels** (Map p322; ☑ 9816746264; Manu Temple Rd; ⊙ 9am-8pm Apr-Sep) and **Nirvana Travels** (Map p322; ☑ 9459544159; School Lane, Old Manali; ⊙ open Apr-Sep) in Old Manali.

Other typical one-way taxi fares:

DESTINATION	FARE (₹)
Bhuntar airport	2200
Dharamsala	5500
Jibhi	4000
Kasol	3000
Keylong	5500
Naggar	1200
Solang Nullah	1200

Manali & Vashisht

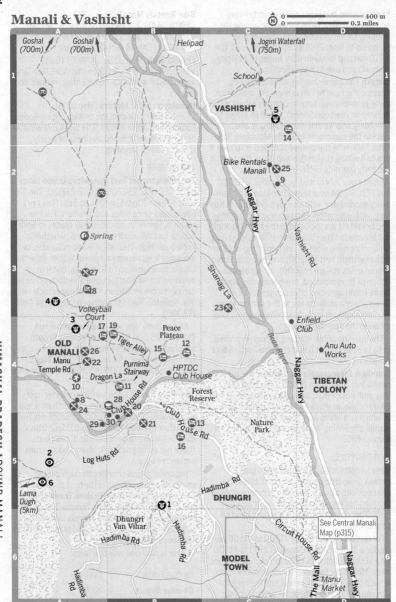

Goshal (700m)

Goshal (700m)

Helipad

Jogini Waterfall (750m)

School

VASHISHT

Bike Rentals Manali

Naggar Hwy

Vashisht Rd

Spring

Shanag La

Enfield Club

Volleyball Court

Peace Plateau

Anu Auto Works

OLD MANALI

Tiger Alley

Manu Temple Rd

Purnima Stairway

HPTDC Club House

TIBETAN COLONY

Dragon La

Club House Rd

Forest Reserve

Nature Park

Club House Rd

Log Huts Rd

Hadimba Rd

DHUNGRI

Lama Dugh (5km)

Dhungri Van Vihar

Hadimba Rd

Hadimba Rd

Circuit House Rd

See Central Manali Map (p315)

MODEL TOWN

Manu Market

The Mall

Naggar Hwy

Hadimba Rd

HIMACHAL PRADESH AROUND MANALI

ⓘ Getting Around

For trips to Old Manali bridge, autorickshaws from **outside the tourist office** (Map p315) should cost around ₹70 after bargaining. Those from the **southbound autorickshaw stand** (Map p315; ☑ 01902-253366; The Mall) near the bus station will charge more.

Around Manali

Vashisht

☑ 01902 / POP 1600 / ELEV 1970M

Vashisht village is a slightly quieter and more compact version of Old Manali, which it faces

Manali & Vashisht

directly across the Beas River, though lack of a nearby bridge means that linking the two can take half an hour by taxi. The village's northern section attracts foreign travellers with cheap accommodation, a chilled atmosphere and charas; Indian tourists come to bathe in the hot springs and tour the temples. Many budget guesthouses and restaurants close down from mid-October to April.

Vashisht Mandir
HINDU TEMPLE
(Map p322; ⊙5am-2pm & 3-9pm) Sulphur-laden hot springs are channelled into small public baths inside the compound of Vashisht Mandir. The three-level wood-and-stone temple within appears to be new but encases a far older carved stone shrine: peer in to catch the silver eye of the time-blackened idol – a statue of the sage Vashisht.

Jogini Waterfalls
WALKING
A pretty walk of about 20 minutes each way from the northern edge of Vashisht brings you to the base of one of Himachal's most impressive accessible waterfalls. Take the path up to the right immediately after the **school** (Map p322) that is built over a stream, then left again after 20m. Follow the clear path (or use a zip line for one part), finishing up through pinewoods at a tiny temple. From there there's a waterfall viewpoint just three minutes' walk up to the right.

To reach the upper fall continue steeply up around 700m further to a holy spot where signs instruct you to remove shoes.

⊨ Sleeping & Eating

Several good midrange hotels lie along the main road, while inexpensive guesthouses and homestays are tucked away along the village alleys and up paths towards the hills.

Hotel Dharma
HOTEL $
(Map p322; ☑9736256074, 9318923151; www.hoteldharmamanali.com; r ₹500-1500; ⊙closed Jan–mid-Mar; @☎) A short, steep walk above the Vashisht Mandir is rewarded with some of the best mountain views from any hotel in the Manali region, and plenty of communal gazing space. The older wing has basic but great-value ensuites (₹500 to ₹700 in season, from ₹300 in November), while the pricier new section has neater carpets, fresher paintwork and private view-balconies.

★ Shri Krishna Palace
BOUTIQUE HOTEL $$
(www.shrikrishnapalace.com; Jogini Lane, Bahang; r ₹3000-4000) Built in 2017 but using traditional construction techniques, this superb family guesthouse sits beside the mellifluously rushing Jogini stream, 10 minutes' walk from Bahang main road but a million miles emotionally. The nine rooms all have terraces or view balconies, top-quality beds, ultraclean floors, and in upper superdeluxe rooms there's also a fridge and local fabric hangings.

The all-veg restaurant (mains ₹130 to ₹190) has a lounge section for (soft) drinks and a light-suffused dining area.

HAMTA PASS TREK

Easily accessible from Manali, this utterly beautiful and very varied camping trek crosses from the Kullu Valley to Chatru on the Keylong–Spiti road in Lahaul's Chandra Valley. Bring spare shoes for a knee-deep stream crossing and be aware that there are two (nontechnical) glacier traverses. Starting from Jobri, where the Hamta and Jobri streams meet, the first two days have a combined ascent of around 800m and are fairly easygoing, helping with acclimatisation. Continuing up and over the 4270m Hamta Pass from the Balu Ka Gera campsite is contrastingly long, steep and tiring, but there are sublime snow-peak views from the top. The best time for this trek is after the monsoon, ie late September and October. Snow on the pass generally lasts until May.

STAGE	ROUTE	DURATION (HR)	DISTANCE (KM)
1	Jobri to Chikka	2	5
2	Chikka to Balu Ka Gera	4	9
3	Balu Ka Gera to Shiagouru via Hamta Pass	8	15
4	Shiagouru to Chatru	4	10

Rasta Cafe　　　　MULTICUISINE **$$**
(Map p322; mains ₹100-280; ☉8am-11pm, closed Nov-late Mar; ☏) Rasta is the top traveller hang-out for, well, practically anything we tried. Service is friendly, and the space is bright and airy with pine tables and cane chairs or low-table cushion seating. And plenty of reggae, too.

❶ Getting There & Away

When full, white Ride With Pride electric minivans shuttle to Vashisht Mandir from the Manali bus station's platform 5 (9am to around 5pm, last return about 6pm).

Autorickshaw fares from Manali start at ₹100 depending on your starting point; don't rely on being able to get one in either direction after 7pm.

Walking between Vashisht and Manali takes about 30 minutes; a footpath down beside Bike Rentals Manali comes out on the main road 300m north of the Vashisht turnoff but from there it's along an unpleasantly busy road.

WESTERN HIMACHAL PRADESH

Western Himachal Pradesh is most famous as the home of the Tibetan government-in-exile and residence of the Dalai Lama at McLeod Ganj, which is a major traveller hub with many opportunities to volunteer or take yoga, meditation or other courses. The Dhauladhar and Pir Panjal ranges make for some excellent trekking, and the Chamba Valley lying between them is beautiful and culturally intriguing. Elsewhere, the Bir-Billing area is attracting growing numbers of adventurers and spiritual seekers with its world-class paragliding and numerous Tibetan monasteries.

Dharamsala

☏01892 / POP 30,800 / ELEV 1380M
Dharamsala (also spelled Dharamshala) is known as the home of the Dalai Lama, though in fact the Tibetan spiritual leader is based 3km up the hill in McLeod Ganj, and that's where most visitors are heading. Dharamsala proper is an untidy market town mostly useful for bus connections.

Museum of Kangra Art　　　MUSEUM
(Map p325; Indian/foreigner ₹20/100; ☉10am-1.30pm & 2-5pm Tue-Sun) The Museum of Kangra Art displays some fine miniature paintings from the Kangra school, along with traditional costumes and photos from the devastating 1905 Kangra earthquake.

❶ Getting There & Away

Dharamsala Airport (DHM) is at Gaggal, 13km southwest. Air India and SpiceJet both fly daily to/from Delhi, though flights are sometimes cancelled in bad weather.

Buses run from **Dharamsala bus station** (Map p325) to McLeod Ganj (₹18, 35 minutes) about every half-hour from 6am to 9pm. For Delhi, the 5.15am and some evening services use the bus station, but numerous other private services between 5.30pm and 7.30pm (₹740 to ₹1550) pick up from an **unmarked junction** (Map p325) 500m southwest on the bypass road.

Dharamsala Taxi Union (Map p325; ☏01892-222105) is up a flight of 185 steps from the bus station's lowest floor. A cab to McLeod Ganj costs ₹250.

Dharamsala

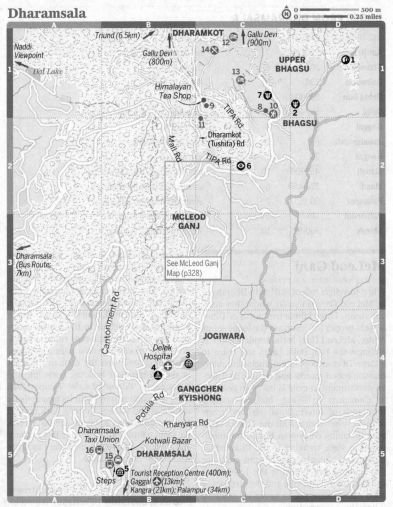

Dharamsala

⊙ Sights

1 Bhagsu Waterfall	D1
2 Bhagsunag Shiva Temple	D1
3 Cultural Museum	B4
Library of Tibetan Works & Archives	(see 3)
4 Men-Tsee-Khang	B4
Men-Tsee-Khang Museum	(see 4)
5 Museum of Kangra Art	B5
6 TIPA	C2
7 Vashnu Mata Temple	C1

✪ Activities, Courses & Tours

8 Ayuskama Ayurvedic Clinic	C1
Buddhist Philosophy Courses	(see 3)
9 Himachal Vipassana Centre	C1
10 Terrestrial Adventures	C1
11 Tushita Meditation Centre	C2

🛏 Sleeping

12 Raj Residency	C1
13 Trimurti Garden Cafe	C1

✗ Eating

14 Bodhi Greens	C1

ℹ Transport

15 Dharamsala Bus Station	B5
16 Long-Distance Bus pick-up point	A5

HIMACHAL PRADESH

BUSES FROM DHARAMSALA

DESTINATION	FARE (₹)	DURATION (HR)	DEPARTURES
Amritsar	295/700	7	ord/Volvo 5am/4.30am
Chamba	364	8	3 daily
Dalhousie	230	5	4 daily
Dehra Dun	535-1045	12	3 daily
Delhi	542-1240	12	5.15am plus many 5.30pm-7.30pm
Gaggal	20	¾	every 15min
Jawalamukhi	65	1½	once or twice hourly
Kangra	30	1	every 20min
Manali	457-700	10	ord 7am & 6pm/Volvo AC 9.30pm
Mandi	220-460	6	various, or change in Palampur
Palampur	60	2	about half-hourly to 8.45pm
Pathankot	136	3½	about hourly, 5am-5.30pm
Shimla	360-515	10	7 daily (morning & evening)

McLeod Ganj

📞 01892 / POP 10,000 / ELEV 1740M

When travellers talk of staying in Dharamsala, McLeod Ganj is usually where they actually mean. Three kilometres north of Dharamsala proper (or 10km via the looping bus route), McLeod Ganj is the residence of His Holiness the 14th Dalai Lama and home to a large Tibetan population, including many maroon-robed monks and nuns. The Tibetan government-in-exile is based in between at Gangchen Kyishong. McLeod attracts thousands of international visitors, many of them volunteering with the Tibetan community, taking courses in Buddhism, meditation or yoga, trekking in the Dhauladhar mountains, shopping for Tibetan crafts, or just hanging out enjoying the low-budget spiritual/alternative vibe and the plethora of good cafes where you're never far from an interesting conversation.

Peak season is April to July, though by late June the monsoon can make things very wet, lasting to early September. Warm clothes are useful between November and March.

◉ Sights

★ **Tsuglagkhang Complex**   BUDDHIST TEMPLE
(Map p328; Temple Rd; ⏰ 5am-8pm Apr-Oct, 6am-6pm Nov-Mar) McLeod's main focus for visiting pilgrims, monks and most tourists is the Tsuglagkhang complex, a custard-coloured concrete monastic village that's home to the Dalai Lama (behind a guarded gateway) along with two colourful temple rooms and the excellent Tibet Museum (p327), whose entrance you'll pass en route.

Don't expect the visual drama of a Ladakhi gompa. The architecture is outwardly functional but there's much inside to intrigue. At 1.30pm (except Sundays) you can watch monks in lively debate in the central courtyard beneath high, expo-style canvas shades. Processing clockwise you'll pass a pilgrims' prostrating area then the door to the right in the westernmost building leads into the **Kalachakra 'Wheel of Life' Temple** (Map p328) (no photography) with its mesmerising mandalas and statues. Coming back around past the monastery kitchens, the last stop is the main temple room featuring fine statuary and the throne on which the Dalai Lama sits when delivering teachings.

**Tsuglagkhang Main
Temple Room**   BUDDHIST TEMPLE
(Map p328) Spiritually (if certainly not architecturally) the Tsuglagkhang's 1969 central temple room is the exiles' concrete equivalent of the Jokhang temple in Lhasa. Behind the Dalai Lama's teaching throne is a softly gilded statue of the historical Buddha flanked by sacred texts.

To the left is a bearded wooden 'starving Buddha' representing his six years of ascetic meditation at Bodhgaya. Behind that are Padmasambhava, the Indian sage believed to have helped spread Buddhism in 8th-century Tibet, and Avalokitesvara (Chenrezig in Tibetan), a replica of the 7th-century image from the Jokhang temple that was destroyed by the Chinese in 1966 during the Cultural

Revolution. It contains relics rescued from the destruction and smuggled out of Tibet. On the right-hand wall, paintings depict the 33rd, 38th and 40th Tibetan kings, credited with bringing Buddhism to their country.

★ Tibet Museum
MUSEUM

(Map p328; www.tibetmuseum.org; ☺9am-1pm & 2-5pm Tue-Sun, closed some Sat) FREE This must-see, two-storey museum sets out to remind visitors of Tibet's history as an independent nation, mourning the Chinese occupation (since 1949) and reporting attempts at Tibetan resistance. This is strikingly presented through sometimes-harrowing photographs and clear English-language explanations.

Library of Tibetan Works & Archives
MUSEUM

(Map p325; ☑9218422467; www.tibetanlibrary.org; Gangchen Kyishong; ☺9am-1pm & 2-5pm Mon-Sat, closed 2nd & 4th Sat of the month) Inside the government-in-exile compound, nearly 2km downhill from the Tsuglagkhang complex, the Library of Tibetan Works & Archives began life as a repository for sacred manuscripts saved from the Cultural Revolution. Today it has over 120,000 manuscripts and books in Tibetan, and more than 15,000 books on Tibet, Buddhism and the Himalayan region in English and other languages.

Upstairs is an interesting cultural museum (Map p325; ₹20; ☺9am-1pm & 2-5pm Mon-Sat, closed 2nd & 4th Sat of the month) with statues, old Tibetan artefacts and books, and a couple of complex 3D mandalas in wood and sand.

Men-Tsee-Khang
BUDDHIST SITE

(Tibetan Medical & Astrological Institute; Map p325; ☑01892-223113; www.men-tsee-khang.org; Gangchen Kyishong; ☺9am-1pm & 2-5pm Mon-Sat, closed 2nd & 4th Sat of the month) Men-Tsee-Khang is an organisation established to preserve the traditional arts of Tibetan medicine and astrology. The Gangchen Kyishong branch includes a college, clinic, research centre and astrological institute plus a well-explained museum (₹20; ☺9am-1pm & 2-5pm Mon-Sat, closed 2nd & 4th Sat).

🏃 Activities

Alternative Therapies, Yoga & Massage

McLeod Ganj has dozens of practitioners of holistic and alternative therapies, some reputable and some making a fast buck at the expense of gullible travellers. Adverts for courses and sessions are posted all over McLeod Ganj and in *Contact* magazine, but talking to other travellers is a better way to find good practitioners.

Several of the best-reputed, longest-established yoga and meditation centres are in Dharamkot and Bhagsu (p335), just outside McLeod.

Holistic Centre of Ayurveda
MASSAGE

(Map p328; ☑9418493871; www.holisticayurveda massage.com; Ladies Venture Hotel, Jogiwara Rd; 1hr ₹800-1000; ☺10.30am-7pm) Resident masseur Shami continues to get rave reviews, so book a day or two ahead for a variety of relaxation, ayurvedic and deep-tissue massages.

Tibetan Medicine

Traditional Tibetan medicine is a centuries-old holistic healing practice and a popular treatment for all kinds of minor and persistent ailments. Its methods include massages, compresses, bath and steam therapies, pills made from plants and minerals, and diet and lifestyle advice. There are several clinics around town, including the Men-Tsee-Khang Therapy Centre (Map p328; ☑01892-221484; www.men-tsee-khang.org; TIPA Rd; ☺9am-1pm & 2-5pm Mon-Sat, closed 2nd & 4th Sat of the month), run by the Tibetan Medical & Astrological Institute.

Trekking

It's possible to trek to the Chamba or Kullu Valleys and even Lahaul. Several agencies in McLeod and in Dharamkot or Bhagsu can make the necessary arrangements for camping, guides and porters or pack animals. Apart from the demanding Indrahar La trek (p330) to the Chamba Valley, the most popular option is the easy three- to five-day loop to Kareri Lake. Guided treks with food, camping and porter(s) can cost anywhere from ₹1500 to ₹3000 per person per day: be sure to check what's included (food? equipment? return transport for the workers?).

Volunteering

McLeod Ganj has more volunteering opportunities than almost anywhere else in India, mostly geared to supporting the Tibetan community in one way or another, often through teaching. Travellers should always investigate any volunteer opportunity themselves to assess the standards and suitability of the project. Lonely Planet cannot vouch for any organisation that we do not work with directly.

Some opportunities are publicised in the free magazine *Contact* (www.contact

McLeod Ganj

Dharamsala
(Bus Route)
(9km)

Dharamkot
(800m)

Dharamkot
(1.5km)

New Bus
Stand

Mall Rd

Dharamkot ('Tushita') Rd

TIPA Rd

Bhagsu Rd

Mithanala Rd

Bhagsu
(1km)

Autorickshaw
Stand

15

22

31

13

21

23

16

HRTC
Ticket
Office

29

8

14

Main
Square

26

20

Nowrojee Rd

Chorten

18

Jogiwara Rd

Dolma
Chowk

7

30

28

Jogiwara Rd

Jogiwara Rd

11

19

27

25

6

24

9

17

Jogiwara Rd

Hotel Bhagsu Rd
(Clubhouse Rd)

10

Temple Rd

5

Temple Rd

12

Temple Rd

Tsuglagkhang
Complex

2

1

3

4

Tibet
Museum

Gangchen Kyishong (1km);
Dharamsala (4km)

0 ___ 100 m
0 ___ 0.05 miles

McLeod Ganj

◉ Top Sights
1 Tibet Museum	B7
2 Tsuglagkhang Complex	B7

◉ Sights
3 Kalachakra Temple	B7
4 Tsuglagkhang Main Temple Room	B7

◔ Activities, Courses & Tours
5 High Point Adventure	B5
6 Holistic Centre of Ayurveda	C4
7 Lha	B3
8 Lhamo's Kitchen	B2
9 LIT	C4
10 Sangye's Kitchen	D5
11 Tibet World	C4

⛉ Sleeping
12 Chonor House	B6
13 Green Hotel	C2
14 Hotel Tibet	B2
15 Kalsang Guest House	B1
16 Kunga Guesthouse	B2
17 Moon Walk Residency	D4

18 Om Hotel	A3
19 Pink House	C4
20 Serkong House	A2

⛝ Eating
21 Clay Oven	B2
22 Common Ground Cafe	B2
Green Hotel Restaurant	(see 13)
23 Jimmy's Italian Kitchen	C2
24 Lung Ta	C4
25 Moonpeak	B4
Nick's Italian Kitchen	(see 16)
26 Shangrila Vegetarian Restaurant	B2

◔ Drinking & Nightlife
27 Café Budan	C4

⛻ Shopping
28 Tibetan Handicraft Center	B3

ⓘ Information
29 Branch Security Office	B2
30 Dr Yeshi Dhonden	B3
31 Men-Tsee-Khang Therapy Centre	B2

magazine.net), or you could approach the following organisations:

Lha (Map p328; ☑ 01892-220992, 9882323455; www.lhasocialwork.org; Temple Rd; ⊙ office upstairs 9am-1pm & 2-5pm Mon-Sat) Arranges placements at a host of community projects.

LIT (Learning & Ideas For Tibet; Map p328; ☑ 7590025915; www.facebook.com/LearningIdeasTibet; Jogiwara Rd; ⊙ office 10am-1pm & 2-5pm Mon-Sat, screenings 6pm) Gives free classes for Tibetan refugees and has a variety of volunteer positions teaching English, French, German, Mandarin or Japanese, and computing skills for beginners. Volunteers can drop in to the 2pm English conversation classes (1½ hours). The office is below Hope Cafe.

Tibet World (Map p328; ☑ 9816999928; http://tibetworld.org; Jogiwara Rd; ⊙ office 9am-5pm Mon-Fri) Teaches hundreds of refugee students, engaging some 200 volunteers, notably for teaching languages and yoga, preferably for one month though drop-in participants are welcomed at one-hour conversation classes (English at 11am and 4pm, French and Mandarin at 4pm).

☙ Courses

There are several places where you can learn to cook your own *momos* and *thukpa*, and get to eat your homework afterwards. Popular, very personal options include **Lhamo's**

Kitchen (Map p328; ☑ 9816468719; www.facebook.com/Lhakpem; Bhagsu Rd; 2hr class ₹300; ⊙ 10am-noon & 5-7pm), beside Kunga Guesthouse, and **Sangye's Kitchen** (Map p328; ☑ 9816164540; Jogiwara Rd; per person ₹250; ⊙ 10am-noon & 4-6pm Thu-Tue), in an unmarked room approximately opposite the upper-market Vaikunth hotel. Call ahead to check what's cooking and book.

The most-established and best-reputed schools of yoga and meditation are mainly found in Dharamkot and Bhagsu (p335). The Library of Tibetan Works & Archives conducts serious **Buddhist philosophy courses** (Map p325; ☑ 9218422467; www.tibetanlibrary.org/study-program; Central Tibetan Secretariat; per month ₹300, registration ₹50; ⊙ classes 9am & 10.30am Mon-Sat) in English lasting from 1½ to four months (1¼ hours daily), plus monthly five-day evening classes (one hour per day), sometimes in Tibetan, sometimes in English.

✦✦ Festivals & Events

Losar (p301), Tibetan New Year, is mainly a family event but sees processions and masked dances at local monasteries. The Dalai Lama often gives public teachings at this time, and again in late September or early October.

The **Shoton Festival** (Tibetan Opera Fest; ⊙ Mar/Apr) brings together a dozen troupes from India and Nepal to perform *Ache Lhamo*, an ancient form of musical dance-theatre often nicknamed Tibetan Opera.

HIMACHAL PRADESH MCLEOD GANJ

Several film festivals liven up McLeod's autumn.

🛏 Sleeping

Popular places fill up quickly; advance bookings are advisable, especially from April to June and in October. Counterintuitively, many of the cheapest options are in the central area (plus in Upper Bhagsu (p335)).

Kalsang Guest House GUESTHOUSE **$**
(Map p328; ☑9736672555, 01892-221709; www.facebook.com/kalsang.guest.house; 423 TIPA Rd; r ₹600-900, s/d without bathroom ₹300/400) One of five guesthouses up a flight of steps off TIPA Rd, Tibetan-run Kalsang has spartan rooms along four pot-planted terraces that get breezier and more panoramic the higher you go. Some have been recently refurbished. Rooftop views are excellent.

Om Hotel HOTEL **$**
(Map p328; ☑9816329985; Nowrojee Rd; r ₹700-800, without bathroom ₹400-450; 🐾) Friendly, family-run Om, down an outwardly unpromising lane from the main square, has simple but pleasing rooms with good views. Its lovely cafe-terrace catches sunset rays with views over the valley.

No reservations are taken so try to go in the morning for a room.

Kunga Guesthouse GUESTHOUSE **$**
(Map p328; ☑9857421180; www.kungaguesthouse.com; Bhagsu Rd; r ₹400-1880; 🐾) Above (and below) Nick's Italian Kitchen (p332), where you check in, Kunga's maze of sub-buildings offers a huge range of rooms from big and bright if sparse, to cheap but basic with a longish walk to the shared toilets.

Pink House GUESTHOUSE **$$**
(Map p328; ☑9805527124; www.pinkhouse.in; off Jogiwara Rd; r from ₹1600; 🐾) This place offers a trippy environment of mural-daubed walls for those who can handle all the steps. The 13 rooms feature 6in mattresses and there are truly splendid views from the Detour Cafe with its beanbags and oil-drum seats.

Moon Walk Residency HOTEL **$$**
(Map p328; ☑9816261717, 9218405453; www.moonwalkresidency.com; Paradise Rd; r ₹2450-3500; 🐾) Hard to beat for views from its better rooms and from the pot-plant 'garden' terrace, Moon Walk's rooms have comfy beds and low-tech furniture that hints at 1940s retro design.

Green Hotel HOTEL **$$**
(Map p328; ☑8352810887, 01892-221200; www.greenhotel.in; Bhagsu Rd; r ₹1200-2500; ❄🐾) An enduring favourite with midrange travellers and small groups, Green Hotel has a diverse

---

INDRAHAR LA TREK

Walking to the Indrahar La (4420m) offers truly spectacular views whether you're crossing to the Chamba Valley (five days) or making an out-and-back trek from McLeod Ganj (four days). The first day's hike climbs three or four hours to the mountain meadow of Triund, which has a couple of basic cafe-guesthouses, or you might continue 90 minutes beyond to camp at Laka Got (aka Snowline, 3350m). Next day from there you could reach the pass and return to Laka the same afternoon, though a second night near the rocky shelter known as Lahesh Cave (3600m) is generally recommended both to help with altitude acclimatisation and to give a good chance of reaching the pass early before clouds obscure the view. Having reached the pass you can scurry back to Triund or, if hiking towards Chamba, descend steeply to the meadow campgrounds at Chata Parao (3rd night), and Kuarsi (4th), from where it's around 5km to Hilling. Hilling has a couple of daily buses that can save you the last 5km to Lamu and a further 3km to 5km (depending on shortcuts) down to the Holi–Kharamukh–Chamba road.

High Point Adventure (Map p328; ☑9816120145; www.highpointadventure.in; Temple Rd; ⏱10am-7pm) offers guide-tent-food packages from ₹8000 per person for the return hike, ₹12,500 for the route to Hilling.

DAY	POSSIBLE ROUTE STAGES	DURATION (HR)	DISTANCE (KM)
1	McLeod Ganj to Triund	3-4	9
2	Triund to Lahesh Cave	3-4	8
3	Lahesh Cave to Chata Parao over Indrahar La	6	10
4	Chata Parao to Kuarsi	5-6	15
5	Kuarsi to Lamu	4	10

MEETING THE DALAI LAMA

Meeting the Dalai Lama is a lifelong dream for many travellers and certainly for Buddhists, but private audiences are rarely granted. Put simply, the Dalai Lama is too busy with spiritual duties to meet everyone who comes to Dharamsala. Tibetan refugees are automatically guaranteed an audience, but travellers must make do with the occasional public teachings held at the Tsuglagkhang (a monastic village that contains, among other things, the residence of the Dalai Lama), normally in September or October and after Losar (Tibetan New Year) in February or March, and on other occasions depending on his schedule. For schedules and just about everything you need to know about His Holiness, visit www.dalailama.com. To attend a teaching, register with your passport at the **Branch Security Office** (Map p328; ☑ 01892-221560; Bhagsu Rd; ☺ 9am-1pm & 2-5pm Mon-Fri & 1st Sat of the month) in the days leading up to the teaching (token fee ₹10, long queues possible). If you don't manage this, registration is usually also possible in the early morning at the temple before the teaching starts. To get the most out of the teachings bring a cushion and an FM radio with headset (sold for around ₹600 in local shops) for simultaneous translation.

range of sunny, superclean rooms in three buildings, most with balconies offering valley and mountain views.

Hotel Tibet
HOTEL $$

(Map p328; ☑ 9736161426; hoteltibetdasa@yahoo.com; Bhagsu Rd; roadside/lower/upper r ₹1120/1650/2240; ☎) Spacious older rooms with parquet floors and functional furniture have been given a good splash of colour and elements of Tibetan design through patterned bedspreads and (in better rooms) colourful painted details.

★Chonor House
BOUTIQUE HOTEL $$$

(Map p328; ☑ 8352816561, 9882976879; www.norbulingka.org; off Temple Rd; r ₹5840-7400, ste ₹8570; ❄@☎) Up a lane near the Tsuglagkhang, Chonor House is an 18-room gem run by the Norbulingka Institute (p334), whose wonderful handmade furnishings and fabrics are widely used. Most rooms have Tibetan themes that run from the carpets to the bedspreads to the murals. All have balconies and there's a tree-shaded garden restaurant.

★Serkong House
HOTEL $$$

(Map p328; ☑ 9857957131; www.norbulingka.org; Nowrojee Rd; s ₹2580-4080, d ₹3320-4750, ste ₹6110; ☎) Unsigned down steps from the top end of Nowrojee Rd, this outwardly unremarkable, three-storey building in magenta and apricot is a delightful surprise with its assiduously cleaned marble floors, silk paintings and pictorial lantern lamps. The 15 large, highly comfortable rooms add low-key, high-quality Tibetan decor touches and many have fine sunset views.

✕ Eating & Drinking

McLeod Ganj is crammed with multicuisine restaurants serving pretty similar menus – omelettes, pancakes, Indian, Tibetan and Chinese staples, pizzas, pasta and assorted other European food. Happily, many of them do a pretty good job. For a quick snack, Tibetans sell takeaway veg *momos* on the upper part of Jogiwara Rd and outside the entrance to the Tsuglagkhang for ₹30 a plate.

Several restaurants double as bars, and there's usually some action on Saturday nights. There are a few small 'wine shops' for takeaway beer and spirits, and caffeine-lovers are spoiled for choice.

Shangrila Vegetarian Restaurant
TIBETAN, INDIAN $

(Map p328; Jogiwara Rd; mains ₹80-100, rice ₹30; ☺ 7.30am-8.30pm; ☎☑) Cheap and cheerful Shangrila provides tasty, well-priced Tibetan staples served up by monks of the Gyudmed monastery.

★Moonpeak
MULTICUISINE $$

(Map p328; www.moonpeak.org; Temple Rd; mains ₹150-300; ☺ 7.30am-8.30pm; ☎) As well as McLeod's best barista coffee, this excellent gallery-cafe serves some very imaginative cuisine including brown-bread open sandwiches (try the roast aubergine with tomato coulis), Himachali thalis, and delicious if gristle-prone mutton-apricot curry.

Clay Oven
MULTICUISINE $$

(Map p328; ☑ 9816116862; TIPA Rd; mains ₹130-360, beer ₹230; ☺ 10.30am-10pm) Upstairs at the start of TIPA Rd, the adobe-and-hardwood interior is made all the more attractive with

HIMACHAL PRADESH MCLEOD GANJ

TIBETAN EXILES

In October 1950, about a year after Mao Zedong declared the founding of the People's Republic of China, Chinese troops invaded Tibet. At the time, Tibet was a de facto independent state led by the Dalai Lama, with a hazy, complicated relationship with China. A year later, in October 1951, Lhasa, the Tibetan capital, fell. Resistance simmered for years in the countryside, and protests against the Chinese occupation broke out in Lhasa in 1959. As the Chinese army moved against the uprising, it fired upon the Norbulingka, the Dalai Lama's summer palace. Believing his life, or at least his freedom, was at risk, the Dalai Lama fled across the Himalaya to India, where he received asylum.

China says its army was sent to Tibet as liberators, to free Tibetans from feudal serfdom and improve life on the vast high plateau. It hasn't worked out that way. While the sometimes-quoted figure of 1.2 million Tibetans killed since 1950 is seriously disputed, no independent observers question the suffering and human-rights abuses, as well as huge losses to Tibet's cultural legacy, that have occurred under Chinese occupation. Many Tibetans still risk the dangerous crossing into India. Today there are around 85,000 Tibetans in India, including those born here. New arrivals come first to the Dharamsala area, where they find support from their community (more than 10,000 strong), their government-in-exile and a legion of NGOs. There are also large Tibetan communities in Karnataka state (p890), where several settlements have been set up since the 1960s.

globe lanterns and flower baskets hanging over the narrow balcony. The menu is specially strong on Tibetan food but adds much more including Nepali, Italian and Thai.

Green Hotel Restaurant   MULTICUISINE $$
(Map p328; Bhagsu Rd; mains ₹110-280; ⊙6.30am-9.30pm; ☎🅿) This traveller-oriented hotel restaurant, with a sunny terrace and comfy couches inside, serves very good vegetarian food that spans a wide range of cuisines.

Nick's Italian Kitchen   ITALIAN $$
(Map p328; Bhagsu Rd; mains ₹110-270; ⊙7am-9pm; ☎🅿) One of McLeod's undisputed traveller hubs, with its shelves of books and very extensive rear terrace, well-run Nick's goes well beyond Italian (though the thin-crust pizzas are good) to cover most veggie culinary bases plus good coffee, great cakes and signature quiche slices (₹110).

Lung Ta   JAPANESE $$
(Map p328; Jogiwara Rd; mains ₹80-130, set meals ₹240; ⊙noon-2.30pm & 5.30-8.30pm Mon-Sat; 🅿) This popular, vegetarian Japanese restaurant is renowned for its daily changing set menus, but also worth visiting for its fairly authentic miso soup (₹50), *okonomiyake* (Japanese veg omelette) and the excellent *kariage-egg-don* (tempura-style veg on rice).

Jimmy's Italian Kitchen   ITALIAN $$
(Map p328; Bhagsu Rd; mains ₹190-300; ⊙9am-10pm; ☎) Spacious and inviting on two levels, with options to sit at gazeworthy-window

bar stools, Jimmy's offers a choice of 18 sauces for its pastas including a tomato-cream-vodka chicken penne.

Common Ground Cafe   ASIAN $$
(Map p328; www.facebook.com/commonground cafe09; Dharamkot Rd; mains ₹90-240; ⊙9am-9pm; ☎) Pleasingly laid-back and sociable, this oasis of peace is pretty central yet faces wooded slopes from its shared tables and floor cushions. The great-value menu offers a sizzling variety of Chinese and Himalayan speciality dishes, from Taiwan-style tofu to Szechuan hotpots to Tibetan *sha tag* (a rich meat-and-veg stir fry). All-day Western-type breakfasts, too, and very good coffee.

Café Budan   CAFE
(Map p328; Jogiwara Rd; coffee ₹50-80, pot-teas ₹60-80; ⊙7.30am-9pm) Relax with good coffee or choose from a dozen varieties of leaf-tea, serenaded by jazzy blues (think Etta James) under low-wattage ball-bulb lights in this enticing mini-cafe.

☆ Entertainment

Irregular live-music nights or jam sessions are advertised around town, mostly between May and July. The **Tibetan Institute of Performing Arts** (Map p325; ☑9418087998; www.tipa.asia; TIPA Rd; ⊙9am-5pm Mon-Sat, closed 2nd & 4th Sat of the month) stages irregular cultural performances, while Tibet World (p329) puts on a Tibetan folk show at 6.30pm on Thursdays (₹200) and screens documentary films (free) at 4pm on Saturdays.

Shopping

Several local cooperatives as well as dozens of shops and stalls sell a very colourful plethora of Tibetan artefacts, including *thangkas,* bronze statues, metal prayer wheels, turquoise necklaces, yak-wool shawls and 'singing' bowls. And book-lovers rejoice! – McLeod surely has the highest bookshop-to-population ratio in India.

Tibetan Handicraft Center   ARTS & CRAFTS
(Map p328;   ✆8350821415;   www.tibetan-handicrafts.com;   Jogiwara Rd;   ◉9am-5pm Mon-Sat) ◢ This women's cooperative employs refugees for the hand weaving of Tibetan wool carpets, a process that you're welcome to watch in action.

There's also a more general gift shop selling souvenirs, quality *thangkas* and resonant bronze meditation gong-bowls. International shipping can be arranged.

ℹ Information

Contact magazine (www.contactmagazine. net) is a useful source of listings as well as news affecting the Tibetan local community.

Delek Hospital (Map p325; ✆01892-222053; www.delekhospital.org/delek; Gangchen Kyishong; outpatient/emergency consultations ₹10/50; ◉outpatient clinic 9am-noon Mon-Sat, emergency 24hr) This small, Tibetan-run hospital practising allopathic medicine has a 24-hour emergency service and ambulance.

ℹ Getting There & Away

AIR
Dharamsala Airport (p324) has flights to/from Delhi.

BUS
Although there are further bus options from Dharamsala, a useful selection start from and arrive at the **New Bus Stand** (Map p328), 150m north of McLeod's main square then two storeys down. Some government buses can be booked at the **HRTC ticket office** (Map p328; ✆01892-220026; Main Sq; ◉10am-5pm), hidden beneath the McLlo Restaurant on the central square. For private overnight services (Delhi, Chandigarh, Rishikesh) book through travel agencies, which abound in the market area, or online with sites such as www.redbus.in.

Buses from McLeod Ganj
Chandigarh ₹800, six hours, 6.30pm
Dalhousie ₹245, seven hours, 6.30am
Dehra Dun 12 hours, 2pm (₹560) and 7pm (₹1200)

Delhi ₹560 to ₹1550, 4am (ordinary), 8.15am and many 5pm to 7pm
Manali ₹400 to ₹600, 11 hours, 8.30pm and 9.30pm
Manikaran via Kasol (Parvati) ₹420, 11 hours, 7pm
Pathankot ₹138, four hours, 10am, 11am, 1.20am, 2.30pm, 4pm
Rishikesh ₹1000, 12 hours, 7.30pm

TAXI
McLeod's **taxi stand** (Map p328; ✆01892-221034; Mall Rd) is just north of the main square. Fares include ₹800 to Dharamsala airport, ₹4000 to Chamba and ₹5500 to Manali. Return day trips cost ₹2000 to Palampur, ₹2500 to Kangra with Masrur.

ℹ Getting Around

Buses to Dharamsala (₹18, 35 minutes) run a couple of times per hour, 4am to 8pm, supplemented with shared jeeps. Taxis charge ₹100 to Gangchen Kyishong, Dharamkot or Bhagsu, ₹150 to the Tibetan Children's Villages (TCV), ₹250 to Dharamsala bus station.

The **autorickshaw stand** (Map p328) is just north of the main square. Fares are around ₹50 to Bhagsu and ₹70 to Dharamkot.

Dozens of central shops have 'Bike on Rent' signs, charging ₹700 to ₹1200 per day for Enfields and ₹500 to ₹800 for scooters. Or ask at your hotel.

Around McLeod Ganj

Bhagsu & Dharamkot
✆01892
Through pine trees north and east of McLeod lie the rapidly developing 'villages' of Upper Bhagsu (officially Bhagsunag) and Dharamkot. More laid-back and alternative than McLeod itself, these settlen–ts attract budget, long-stay travellers with inexpensive digs and classes in tarot, reiki, numerology, crystal healing and varieties of yoga you've never heard of. Learn sitar, tabla, flute or a dozen types of massage, have your hair dreadlocked, dyed or extended, or just lounge in cafes and practise your juggling. Some of the area's best and most serious yoga and meditation schools are here, too.

◉ Sights

Other than along its footpath strip of traveller cafes, crystal shops and yoga options, Dharamkot retains a quiet village vibe, with scattered houses climbing almost to the little

NORBULINGKA INSTITUTE

The wonderful **Norbulingka Institute** (☑ 9418436410; www.norbulingka.org; local & Tibetan ₹50, tourist ₹110, after 5pm free; ⊙ 9am-8pm), 6km southeast of Dharamsala, was established in 1988 to teach and preserve traditional Tibetan art forms. It's a fascinating place to visit.

You can watch artisans at work on woodcarving, metal statue–making, *thangka* painting and embroidery. Set among the institute's delightful Japanese-influenced gardens, the Deden Tsuglakhang temple has a 4m-high gilded Sakyamuni statue. In an arc of buildings facing the temple is a two-room collection of dioramas featuring dolls dressed in traditional costumes to illustrate aspects of traditional Tibetan culture. On Sundays and the second Saturday of each month the workshops are closed, but the rest of the complex is open.

The institute's **shop** (⊙ 9am-5.30pm) sells some of the beautiful craftwork made here, including jewellery, painted boxes and embroidered clothes and cushions. Sales benefit refugee artists, with high prices befitting the great quality.

Visitors can join one of the craft studios to do customised workshops, for any period, at ₹1500/2000 per half-day/day. Book at least two days ahead.

Peaceful and stylish **Norling House** (☑ 8988159349, 9816646423; www.norbulingka.org; d/ste ₹4024/5919; ❈ 🖝), within the institute's gardens, offers comfortable rooms decked out with Buddhist murals and Norbulingka handicrafts. There are several less-alluring alternatives dotted around the institute's perimeter.

Vegetarian meals and snacks, and good coffee, are available at the **Norling Restaurant** (mains ₹170-300, coffee/beer from ₹65/275; ⊙ 7am-9pm; ❈ 🖝 ⊞) and an associated palm-shaded cafe.

A taxi to/from McLeod Ganj costs ₹400/700 one way/return. By bus, catch a Palampur-bound service from Dharamsala and get off at Sacred Heart School, Sidhpur (₹7, 15 minutes), from where it's a 1km gentle uphill walk (or a ₹100 taxi ride).

Gallu Devi Temple from which hikes to Triund and Indrahar La start. Footpaths and a rocky loop road (pending concreting) link to Upper Bhagsu which has a substantial concentration of traveller facilities and activities from yoga to music lessons to meditation and much much more. Part way down the main lane, look into the wonderfully kitschy little **Vashnu Mata Temple** (Map p325): stairs lead up through a concrete lion's mouth and, after being digested in the shrine's claustrophobic 'gut', you emerge again via the jaws of a crocodile.

Descending further, the alternative vibe vanishes as you approach central Bhagsu, which is a mess of concrete hotels, shops and discos. These are aimed squarely at domestic visitors who come for a dip at the open-air pool fronting the small, 16th-century **Shiva temple** (Map p325; Lower Bhagsu) then walk on 1km to the fairly modest **Bhagsu Waterfall** (Map p325).

🏃 Activities

Terrestrial Adventures   TREKKING
(Map p325; ☑ 9418656758, Whatsapp 9882858628; www.terrestrialadventures.in; Main

Sq, Bhagsu; ⊙ 9am-noon) An experienced and well-reputed firm offering a range of serious treks, local rock climbing and rappelling.

Gallu Devi & Triund Hikes
Tiny Gallu Devi temple sits on a viewpoint ridge above Dharamkot, with impressive panoramas both north and south, and a couple of cafes nearby. To walk there from Dharamkot's **Himalayan Tea Shop** (Map p325; items ₹40-100; ⊙ 8am-8pm), head along the track on the left side of the water tank, then after the small school (50m) turn up a rocky path to the diagonal right. This lovely trail winds up through the forest to re-emerge on the jeep track after 1km: turn right and continue 500m to Gallu Devi.

Alternatively, you can walk straight up from upper Dharamkot in around 30 minutes using the stairway beside Raj Regency.

From Gallu Devi a scenic, easy-to-follow path climbs east through rhododendron woods to the panoramic mountain meadow of Triund (2900m), a beautiful walk that gains 800m altitude in a fairly strenuous 2½ to three hours. You pass a couple of tea shops, and Triund has a few *dhabas* offering simple meals, tents, sleeping bags and beds.

Views tend to be best at dawn before clouds gather. Afternoon rain is not uncommon. An overnight stop gives you the best chance of clear weather, and time to hike one hour up to the tea shop and viewpoint at Laka Got meadow (3350m), sometimes called 'Snow-line', before heading back down – or continuing upward if you're on an Indrahar La trek (p330), although a guide is advised for this.

🥾 Courses

Dharamkot and Bhagsu have many of the area's best options for learning yoga, meditation, Buddhist philosophy, reiki, ayurveda, local music, jewellery making and countless other skills. Fliers and posters offer endless suggestions as you walk up the main street towards Upper Bhagsu.

Tushita Meditation Centre   MEDITATION, PHILOSOPHY
(Map p325; www.tushita.info; Dharamkot; 10-day course incl accommodation & meals from ₹6000; ⊙Feb-Nov) Tushita conducts a 10-day 'Introduction to Buddhism' course, other more advanced courses and retreats, nonresidential short courses and drop-in meditation sessions (9.30am daily, except Sunday).

Ayuskama Ayurvedic Clinic   AYURVEDA
(Map p325; ☑9736211210; www.ayuskama.com; Hotel Anand Palace Bldg, Bhagsu; ⊙9am-5pm) Well respected for ayurvedic treatments and courses that range from a week on massage or nutrition to diploma (three months) and practitioner (two years) qualifications.

🛏 Sleeping & Eating

Lower Bhagsu is relatively unappealing; Upper Bhagsu has a somewhat hippie-traveller vibe with lots of inexpensive guesthouses, many unsigned off stairways to the right of the rising road. Long-stayers can get rooms here or in more-spread-out Dharamkot at small family-run places from around ₹7000 a month, often with kitchen use, too.

Trimurti Garden Cafe   GUESTHOUSE $
(Map p325; ☑9816869144; www.trimurtigarden. in; Lower Dharamkot; r ₹900, s/d without bathroom ₹450/500; 🛜) Friendly, secluded Trimurti is rare in maintaining the essence of 'old' Dharamkot. Its eight neat, spotless rooms are centred on a lovely green garden but are often booked out from April to June and mid-September to mid-October for popular yoga-teacher-training courses (www.trimurti yoga.com).

The cafe, open to all (8am to 8.30pm), serves excellent homemade food from muesli to salads to cakes plus a vegetarian thali. You can learn tabla, flute, sitar or vocals from Ashoka, the father of the family.

Raj Residency   GUESTHOUSE $
(Map p325; ☑9736129703, Whatsapp 9418413014; Upper Dharamkot; r ₹800-1000; 🛜) In a peaceful yet accessible spot towards the top of Dharamkot, this great-value, three-storey guesthouse has fine views from its wide front lawn and the balconies of its 12 spacious, clean rooms.

★**Bodhi Greens**   VEGAN $$
(Map p325; Dharamkot; mains ₹140-200; ⊙8.30am-10.30pm; 🛜🥗) For beautifully blended flavours, this all-vegan delight is hard to beat with its imaginative range of stews, delicious 'Buddha-bowls', soups and curries plus smoothies fashioned from non-dairy milks and sweetened with dates rather than sugar.

Kangra

☎01892 / POP 9500 / ELEV 734M
Once capital of its own princely state, bustling Kangra has an imposing ruined fortress, an important Hindu temple and a bargain-value bazaar. Combined with a visit to the rock temples at Masrur, 40km west, the town makes a satisfying taxi-tour day trip from McLeod Ganj (28km) or Dharamsala (18km).

◉ Sights

Kangra Fort   FORT
(www.royalkangra.com; Indian/foreigner ₹25/300, audio guide ₹177/236; ⊙dawn-dusk) At least 1000 years old, Kangra Fort's impregnable stone ramparts impressively buttress a high promontory of land between the Manjhi and Banganga Rivers. Temple and palace buildings within were reduced to rubble by the 1905 earthquake, but the 4km of exterior walls remain, along with a series of stone gateways, restored in 1953. The overall effect gives something of the feel of a Crusader Castle ruin. Climb to the top for especially photogenic viewpoints.

Allow around an hour to explore. The fort is at the south end of town, a ₹100 autorickshaw ride from the bus stand. It was occupied by Hindu rajas, Mughal and Sikh conquerors and, from 1846 until its 1905 destruction, the British.

Maharaja Sansar Chand Museum MUSEUM
(☑ 01892-265866; www.kangragroup.com/
museuminpress.shtml; Indian/foreigner ₹35/100,
audio guide ₹177/236; ⊘ 9am-5.30pm) Up a
curling road, 200m from Kangra Fort ticket
gate, this well-displayed one-room museum
exhibits ornate palanquins, pashmina fly-
whisks and silver-framed beds, giving fine
insights into the lifestyle of the erstwhile
Kangra royal family. The dynasty claims
a lineage of 488 rulers going back to the
Trigarth Rajas who fought Laxman (Ram's
younger brother) in the Ramayana.

Brajeshwari Devi Temple HINDU TEMPLE
(Mandir Bazaar) Rebuilt after the 1905 quake,
this highly revered temple has a centrepiece
that's richly endowed with embossed silver-
work. Four large bronze lions stare towards
the deity, which is veiled in gold filigree and
often submerged beneath votive flowers.

About 1km south of the bus station, the
temple is approached through a long, atmospheric covered bazaar.

The temple is one of the 51 Shakti *peeths*,
marking the sites where body parts from
Shiva's first wife, Sati, fell after she was consumed by flames. Kangra's temple was the
final resting place of Sati's left breast.

🛏 Sleeping & Eating

Easily Kangra's best choice is the fully
air-conditioned **Hotel Grand Raj** (☑ 01892-
260902; www.hotelgrandraj.com; Dharamshala Rd;
s/d from ₹1876/2230; ❄ 🛜), opposite the bus
station, with a pretty grand entrance lobby,
golf-green-style lawn and rooms with good
beds, fridge and wi-fi. It has decent dining,
too. Around 800m south are four dreary
semi-budget options before the main bazaar
turn, and 600m further south are a couple of
slightly better midrange alternatives.

ℹ Getting There & Away

From the big **bus station**, around 1km north of
the bazaar, buses run about every 30 minutes to
Dharamsala (₹25, one hour), Palampur (₹55, 1½
hours) and Pathankot (₹130, three hours).

A return taxi from McLeod Ganj to Kangra Fort
costs ₹1300, including waiting time, or ₹2500
including the Masrur Temples.

Masrur

Pretty, winding lanes through pleasant green
hills lead 31km southwest from Gaggal to
the impressive if severely eroded 8th- to
10th-century **Masrur temple complex**

(Indian/foreigner ₹25/300; ⊘ dawn-dusk).
Though badly damaged by the 1905 earthquake, the elaborately carved sandstone
sikharas are very rare for Northern India
in being hewn directly from living rock. The
complex bears a passing resemblance to the
Hindu temples at Angkor Wat in Cambodia
and to Ellora in Maharashtra and looks especially beautiful reflected across the tank
in front. You can climb three minutes past a
small on-site school to a raised toilet block/
viewpoint for a fine panorama of the mountains behind Dharamsala.

The easiest way to get here is a taxi day
trip costing around ₹2500 from McLeod
Ganj if combined with Kangra Fort (35km
east), or ₹2000 without. By bus it's a fiddle:
from Dharamsala go to Lunj (₹50, 1½ hours),
then take a Nagrota Surian–bound bus 4km
southwest to the junction at Pir Bindli. From
there it's 2.8km: walk or await a roughly
hourly bus to the temples.

Dharamsala to Mandi

The scenery along the wide valley stretching southeast from Dharamsala is dramatic
on clear days, with the Dhauladhar Range
rising to the north, and the valley sweeping
away towards the plains. There are several
interesting places to stop on a journey to
Mandi or Shimla. The Bir-Billing area in
particular is attracting growing visitor numbers, for its world-class paragliding along
with a large number of Tibetan Buddhist
monasteries and institutes.

Palampur

☑ 01894 / POP 3600 / ELEV 1260M

At the foot of the impressive Dhauladhar
mountain range, 35km southeast of Dharamsala, Palampur is surrounded by tea plantations, rice fields, pine woods and a good
scattering of hotels, many of them enticing
upper-market retreats. You can visit tea factories such as the attractive **Wah Tea Estate**
(☑ 9625768273, 9831017629; www.wahtea.com;
Deogran; per person ₹150; ⊘ 9am-5pm Tue-Sun Apr-
Oct, from 8am Mon-Sat Nov-Mar), 7km south (call
ahead), and hike into the hills or use the town
as a comfortable base for regional excursions.

🛏 Sleeping & Eating

The Mansion GUESTHOUSE $
(☑ 9418182828; Main Bazaar; d ₹800) Right at
the town centre above the Book Hive station-

ery shop, The Mansion has eight new, high-ceilinged rooms that are smarter than those of many mid-market hotels. Quality beds, superb value for money.

⭐ **Infinitea** BOUTIQUE HOTEL **$$$**
(☏ 01894-230604; www.clubinfinitea.com; Bundla Tea Estate; d/ste ₹7320/8260; P❄🛜🏊) Few places in rural India exude such a sense of well-judged classic-contemporary taste as this remarkable tea-estate retreat. The centrepiece is a sports club with 20x10m indoor swimming pool and top-quality gym, but there are 10 superb guest rooms, a top-quality multicuisine restaurant (mains ₹240 to ₹790) and a superb bar with views of the tea fields.

🛈 Getting There & Away

From Palampur's bus station, 1km south of the centre, buses leave all day for Dharamsala (₹60, two hours) and Mandi (₹175, 3½ hours). A one-day taxi tour from McLeod Ganj costs around ₹2000.

Palampur to Bir

A taxi tour from Palampur to Bir via narrow, pretty but well-asphalted back lanes, with a few interesting stops, costs around ₹1200.

Don't miss a stop at the **Baijnath Temple** (Vaidyanath Mandir; NH154, Baijnath; ⊙ 4.30am-8.45pm), one of Himachal's most exquisite ancient temples, set high above the Binwa River with a lovely backdrop of mountains. Though small, the 1204 stone structure retains superb carvings of sensual figures reminiscent of those on the Khajuraho temples.

Halfway along the pretty, narrow lane that winds 14km between Baijnath and Bir, the sprawling **Sherabling Monastery** (☏ 01894-209093; www.palpung.org; Bhattu village; ⊙ main hall 8.30am-4.30pm) lies semi-hidden in rolling pine woods. The outwardly staid main monastery building contains an inner quadrangle that reverberates cacophonously in late afternoon with the practice recitations of countless student monks. That in turn contains the main prayer hall, whose dazzling interior features a superb, two-storey golden Maitreya (future Buddha) statue.

Bir & Billing

POP 815 / ELEV 1400M (BIR)
Rapidly developing into a new mini-Dharamsala for outdoors types, little Bir is an attractively compact base for mountain biking and walking but is best known for some of the world's best paragliding. It hosts major competitive flying events most years in October. Experienced solo fliers can reach as far as Dharamsala, Mandi and Manali, while novices can learn the art or make tandem jumps.

Bir is also an important centre of the Tibetan exile community, with several Buddhist monasteries and institutes, some offering courses and retreats. Note that 'tourist Bir' is the area officially called Chowgan (aka Bir Tibetan Colony) while the original village of Bir (now generally called Upper Bir) is around 2km further uphill. It's on the road towards Billing (14km), the ridgetop launch point for paragliding.

Dzongsar Khyentse Chökyi Lodrö Institute BUDDHIST MONASTERY
(www.khyentsefoundation.org/dzongsar-khyentse-chokyi-lodro-college; Chauntra) Inaugurated in 2004, the Dzongsar Khyentse Institute is a Tibetan Buddhist college of higher learning catering for devotees of 300 monasteries covering all subtraditions. Some 500 student-monks attend 11-year courses and there's a temple able to accommodate over 4000 people.

It's 4km southeast of Bir, 1km south of Hwy 154 at Chauntra.

🏃 Activities

As well as paragliding, the Bir-Billing area is good for walking, trekking and mountain biking. There's a very pleasant 7km walk or cycle ride to Sherabling Monastery through woodlands without significant climbs.

Nearly a dozen shops along the main street's western end rent mountain bikes (per hour/day ₹100/700), ideal for cycling the local lanes.

Paragliding
Take-off is from Billing, with the landing zone a large grassy area ringed by view cafes just 10 minutes' stroll northwest of central Bir. October and November have the best flying conditions. Flying is banned during the monsoon from mid-July to mid-September.

Several agencies offer tandem flights of around 30 minutes for ₹1800 to ₹2500 (including transport). Ten-day courses to gain basic certification cost around ₹40,000. The best recommendation of who to fly with is by word of mouth from others who have done it. Reputable operators include **Golden Eagle Paragliding** (☏ 9816577607; www.geparagliding.org) and, for training courses, **PG-Gurukul** (www.paragliding.guru; BTS office complex, Bir Tibetan Colony).

Himalayan Sky Safaris (www.himalayan skysafaris.com), run by top paragliders from the UK, provides guided multiday paragliding tours including high-landing and bivouacking in the mountaintops, but dates are limited.

Courses

Deer Park Institute   ARTS, PHILOSOPHY
(☑ 01894-268508; www.deerpark.in; Tibetan Colony, Bir; course payment by donation; ⊙ office 9am-noon & 2-6pm Mon-Sat) ✎ Deer Park attracts around 5000 students from dozens of countries each year to its plethora of nonacademic, experiential courses and workshops focussed on 'classical Indian wisdom'.

Ranging from two days to a month, these include Buddhist and Indian philosophy, photography, writing, film-making, language learning (Sanskrit, Pali, Tibetan and Chinese) and meditation retreats led by Buddhist masters. Very inexpensive on-site accommodation is available to participants.

☕ Sleeping & Eating

Nyingma Peace Guesthouse   GUESTHOUSE $
(☑ 9816355388, cafe 7807191888; Nyingmaling Lane; r ₹700-1000) Combining clean, no-frills new rooms with a lawn and remarkably inviting coffeeshop-cafe, this monastery guesthouse is a great-value budget choice that's quiet yet very handy for the bus and taxi stands.

Colonel's Resort   HOTEL $$
(☑ 9805534220, 9882377469; www.colonelsresort. com; Chowgan Junction, Bir; r/cabin incl breakfast ₹4400/1100; ✿) Just north of Chowgan junction beside the road to Old Bir, Colonel's is an overgrown boutique homestay-hotel set in spacious south-facing gardens layered down to active stables. The highly comfortable deluxe rooms have big soft beds, large bathrooms with branded toiletries, Tibetan rugs, and well-made wooden furniture. A row of newly built cabin-rooms share a spotless communal bathroom block.

June16   CAFE $$
(www.facebook.com/June16cafe; mains ₹160-230; ⊙ 7am-8pm) Just before the main road curves around to the paragliding landing point, June16 is the cutest of several loveable Bir cafes. Romantically named for the date of the owners' betrothal, there's great coffee and a range of snack-meals including

wraps, mushroom-melt sandwiches, pasta, ratatouille and garlic hummus.

❶ Getting There & Around

From Bir Chowgan Bus Stand, on the eastern side of the tourist area, three direct Volvo buses run to Delhi (₹1100, 12 hours), all departing at around 5.30pm. A bus to Dharamsala (₹170, three hours) leaves at 7.45am, returning 2.25pm.

Around twice an hour there are local buses from Baijnath to Upper Bir; most don't come into Bir Chowgan so you'd need to get off at Chowgan Chowk and walk 600m west for the tourist area.

Longer-distance buses on the Palampur–Mandi route pass frequently by the Bir Rd Bazaar stop on Hwy 154, 1.5km southeast of Chowgan Chowk (₹100 by taxi from Bir Chowgan). Direct taxis cost around ₹1500 to Mandi or ₹600 to Palampur. For the latter, consider paying around double and taking a multistop taxi tour via the smaller lanes and various temples en route. The Bir Chowgan taxi stand is outside Nyingmaling Monastery. **Kapil** (☑ 8679802614) drives very well, speaks good English and charges fair prices.

Chamba Valley

This area was ruled for centuries as the princely state of Chamba, one of the most ancient states in North India. Well off most tourists' radars, it's not only great for temple buffs, but also a delight for scenery addicts and trekkers, the splendidly isolated valley system being separated from the Kangra Valley by the Dhauladhar Range and from Lahaul and Kashmir by the Pir Panjal.

Dalhousie

☑ 01899 / POP 10,600 / ELEV 2050M

With its plunging pine-clad valleys and distant mountain views, ridgetop Dalhousie was founded in the 1850s by the British viceroy whose name it bears. Its heyday came in the 1920s, '30s and '40s when Lahore society flocked here for its hols. The town's star appears to be rising again as a rediscovered escape for honeymooners and families fleeing the heat of the plains. High season is May to June.

There's not much to do in town except go shopping in Gandhi Chowk, check out the two colonial-era churches or stroll the tree-shaded lanes and admire the views. The most uplifting spot around Dalhousie is the upland area Dhainkund (2745m), 4km of hairpins off

Dalhousie

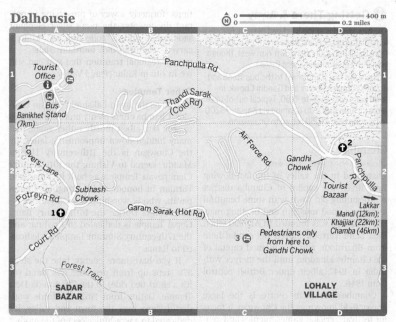

the road to Khajjiar (turn at Lakkar Mandi, 12km east of Dalhousie). Vehicles cannot go beyond a military barrier, from which a 700m stairway-path climbs to a 360-degree viewpoint with superb views of the Pir Pinjal range. Another 1km or so along the ridgetop brings walkers to the Jai Pohlani Mata Temple, with a teahouse and more great views. The scenic trail continues eventually to the Chuari Pass (2772m) on the Chamba–Chuari Khas road.

Dalhousie

⦿ Sights

1 St Francis Church	A2
2 St John Church	D2

🛏 Sleeping

3 Hotel Monal	C3
4 Hotel Mount View	A1

Hotel Monal HOTEL **$$**
(📞9816463388, 9418106230; www.hotelmonal.com; Garam Sarak; r ₹1800-3000) The Monal is the best of a gaggle of midrange hotels tucked down a stairway that descends from Hot Rd (just where the pedestrianised section ends). Room quality varies but maintenance is reasonable and the valley views are superb from the rear terrace.

★ Hotel Mount View HERITAGE HOTEL **$$$**
(📞01899-242120; www.hotelmountview.net; Club Rd; r ₹6850-8850) This 1895 heritage property, in the same family since the 1930s, has been renovated to give top-class comfort while retaining oodles of charm. There's a games room, a gym, billiards, an enticing spa and truly lovely lawns that spread towards a magnificent view.

HIMACHAL PRADESH CHAMBA VALLEY

BUSES FROM DALHOUSIE

DESTINATION	FARE (₹)	DURATION (HR)	DEPARTURES
Chamba via Banikhet	80	2½	7am, 7.30am, 7.45am, 9am, 10.30am, 11.15am
Chamba via Khajjiar	80	2½	9am, 9.30am, 4.30pm
Delhi	390-1400	14	2.55pm, 6.30pm, 7.40pm
Dharamsala	230	5	7.15am, 11.50am, 1.20pm, 2pm
Pathankot	100	3	7 daily

ℹ️ Getting There & Away

The **bus stand** is at the west end of town. For long-distance services, there are more options from Banikhet, a junction town 7km west, though you aren't guaranteed a seat there.

There are taxi stands next to the bus stand and at both Subhash Chowk and Gandhi Chowk. In-town hops cost ₹100 to ₹150. Typical out-of-town fares include ₹1800 to Chamba via Kajjiar, ₹3200 to Dharamsala, ₹1050 return to Dhainkund.

Chamba

📞 01899 / POP 19,950 / ELEV 995M

Ensconced in the valley of the fast-flowing Ravi River, the capital of Chamba district is a beguiling old town with some beautiful temples, a good museum and bustling markets. Chamba was founded in AD 920 when Raja Sahil Varman moved his capital here from Bharmour, and it remained capital of the Chamba kingdom until the merger with India in 1947, albeit under British control from 1846.

Chamba's de facto centre is the large grassy field known as the Chowgan, a focus for festivals, cricket games, picnics and general hanging out.

👁️ Sights

⭐ Lakshmi Narayan Temple Complex HINDU TEMPLE

(⏱️ dawn-dusk) Far and away Chamba's top historical attraction, this temple compound crowning Dogra Bazaar contains a line of six beautifully sculpted stone *sikharas* (10th–19th centuries), festooned with detailed carvings. Enter from a colourful area of metal-beating workshops, past a distinctive Nepali-style stone pillar topped by a statue of the man-bird Garuda, Vishnu's faithful servant.

Within the complex, the largest (and oldest) *sikhara* is dedicated to Lakshmi Narayan (Vishnu). Of the others, three honour versions of Shiva, recognisable by the statues of his 'vehicle', the bull Nandi. The fourth temple's brass images of Gauri and Shankar (Parvati and Shiva) date from the 10th or 11th century.

Bhuri Singh Museum MUSEUM

(📞 01899-222590; Museum Rd; Indian/foreigner ₹30/100, camera ₹50/100; ⏱️ 10am-5pm Tue-Sun) This museum's rich collection is strongest on Pahari (Hill Country) miniature paintings from the Chamba and other schools, but also intriguing are copper-plate inscriptions (formerly a way of preserving important documents), the raja's silver elephant saddle-seat and a collection of ornately carved, centuries-old fountain slabs – a unique regional tradition that you can still see in situ in Killar (Pangi Valley).

Other Temples

As well as the main Lakshmi Narayan complex, Chamba offers plenty more old temples to seek out, albeit mostly rather small, and many hidden down unpromising lanes. By the Chowgan is the 11th-century Harirai Mandir, sacred to Vishnu; the 10th-century Champavati Temple was built by Raja Sahil Varman in honour of his daughter Champavati, who is worshipped locally as an incarnation of Durga; the 16th-century Bansi Gopal Temple is dedicated to Krishna; and the 17th-century Sitaram Temple is dedicated to Rama.

If you have more energy, take the steep 378 steps up from near the bus stand (or it's a short taxi ride) to the Chamunda Devi Temple. Dating from 1762, it affords wonderful views over the town and valley. It's dedicated to a wrathful aspect of the mother goddess Devi, and its front *mandapa* (pavilion) features a forest of bells and rich ceiling carving.

Opposite a medical centre along the road towards the Saal Valley, more steps climb to the exquisite little 12th-century **Bajreshwari Devi Temple**, dedicated to an incarnation of Durga. The very rich carving includes, on the rear *sikhara* wall, an image of Durga slaying the (minuscule-looking) giant Mahisasur and trampling on his buffalo.

🏃 Activities

Mani Mahesh Travels TREKKING

(📞 9418020401, 9816620401; www.orchardhuts. com; outside Lakshmi Narayan Temple Complex; ⏱️ 9am-9pm Mon-Sat) This ecologically minded family outfit offers a range of organic farm experiences, treks (eg Chamba to Dharamsala, five days) and shorter hikes starting from a base at the delightful, co-owned Orchard Hut (p341) and another co-owned mountain retreat four or five hours' walk above.

🛏️ Sleeping & Eating

There are many run-of-the-mill options hidden away in back lanes around the town centre, but a few kilometres out into the countryside are a couple of contrastingly outstanding options.

Chamba

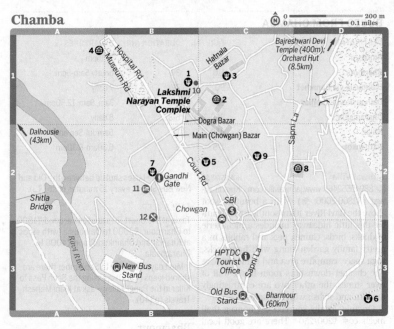

Chamba

◎ Top Sights

1 Lakshmi Narayan Temple Complex B1

◎ Sights

2 Akhand Chandi Palace C1
3 Bansi Gopal Temple................................C1
4 Bhuri Singh Museum A1
5 Champavati Temple C2
6 Chamunda Devi Temple..........................D3
7 Harirai Mandir B2
8 Rang Mahal D2

9 Sitaram Temple C2

◎ Activities, Courses & Tours

10 Mani Mahesh Travels B1

◎ Sleeping

11 Chamba Guesthouse B2

◎ Eating

12 Tasty Tibet..B2

Chamba Guesthouse GUESTHOUSE $

(The Chamba House; ☑ 01899-222564; Gopal Nivas; d ₹800-1150, ste ₹1650; ☎) Chamba's best budget bolthole, the six rooms in this creaky old-school guesthouse have hard beds but hot showers, towels and fine views over the Ravi River from the metal-wired balconies.

★ Orchard Hut HOMESTAY $$

(☑ 9816620401; www.orchardhuts.com; Chaminu village; dm ₹450, r ₹740-2590, apt ₹3500; ☎☒) Unwind amid bucolic views, birdsong and sounds of rushing water, cool off in the plunge pool beneath apricot trees, meditate, learn local cooking and even milk the cow for your breakfast at this perfectly pitched homestay/eco-resort, around 10km north-

east of Chamba. The eight superclean, thoughtfully designed rooms cover all budgets, combining rustic local building materials with quality bathrooms.

Behind safari-lodge-style balconies there's a well-stocked library, and the highly educated hosts know masses about local history. Work off the superb home-cooked meals (organic breakfast/dinner ₹275/450) with a range of hiking options. Don't just show up: it's a 20-minute walk up semi-steep agricultural footpaths from a totally unmarked parking spot beside the Saal River, around 1km beyond Chaminu village: contact Mani Mahesh Travels to coordinate a taxi (₹450 from Chamba) with a guide to show you the way up.

BUSES FROM CHAMBA

DESTINATION	FARE (₹)	DURATION (HR)	DEPARTURES
Amritsar	320	7	11.15pm
Bharmour	110	3½	hourly 5am-5pm
Dalhousie via Banikhet	90	2½	7 daily
Dalhousie via Khajjiar	90	2½	7am, 9am, 12.50pm
Dharamsala	260-365	6-8	5 daily
Killar	450	12	6am Jul-Sep only
Pathankot	175	5	6.30am-6.30pm

Jamwal Villa   HOMESTAY $$
(☏ 8894555246; www.jamwalvilla.com; Kuranh village; r ₹1800-2000; ☎) ✦ In a beautiful spot above the Ravi River 10km southeast of Chamba, this little hideaway includes a menagerie of ducks, birds, Guinea pigs and rabbits in a pretty family garden along with hammocks, yoga space, campfire area and games to play. The cheaper downstairs room has a wall of river stones, the other two are contrastingly modern and stylish with balconies.

Organic, locally sourced veg/nonveg thali meals cost ₹200/250 . There are good local walks or overnight treks.

Tasty Tibet   TIBETAN $
(small/large mains ₹30/60; ⊙ 9am-6.30pm) Above a clothes shop on the motorbike path that links the town and New Bus Stand, this delightful place is cheaper than most *dhabas* yet has almost the style of an urban coffee house. The blackboard menu offers a short selection of tasty Tibetan fare (*thankthuk, thukpa, momos* or chow mein) in generous portions: 'half-size' portions are easily big enough for one.

❶ Getting There & Around

BUS

Most buses start from the New Bus Stand, at the base of town, a 2km drive from the Chowgan but only around 10 minutes' walk using shortcuts. A few buses arriving relatively late in the evening drop passengers conveniently centrally at the Old Bus Stand. For the spectacular trip to Bharmour, sit on the left for the best views. For Dharamsala, if there's no direct bus soon, you can get one to Gaggal (₹240, five to seven hours), where buses leave every few minutes to Dharamsala (₹20, 40 minutes). The best Delhi service is the Volvo AC bus at 6pm. Hourly buses to Pathankot (₹175, five hours, last 6.30pm) pass through Baniket (two hours) where taxis await to shuttle you to Dalhousie, though some services travel direct on each of two different routes.

Turquoise buses shuttle between the Old and New Bus Stands every 15 minutes or so (₹3).

TAXI & JEEP

Taxis at the Court Rd stand ask around ₹1800 to Bharmour, ₹2000 to Dalhousie (with stops at Khajjiar and Dhainkund) and ₹4000 to Dharamsala.

Most days from July to September there are shared jeeps (₹500) crossing the Sach Pass to Killar in the Pangi Valley – ask at Mani Mahesh Travels (p340).

Bharmour

☏ 01895 / POP 2000 / ELEV 2195M

Hovering on the edge of the seemingly bottomless Budil Valley, Bharmour is reached by a mountain road as scenic as it is perilous, winding 60km east of Chamba (it gets really interesting once you leave the Ravi Valley at Kharamukh). This ancient settlement was the area capital until replaced by Chamba in AD 920, and there are some beautiful old temples, though the main reason to come here is for treks to the surrounding valleys and passes. The villages around Bharmour are home to communities of seminomadic Gaddis, pastoralists who move their flocks to alpine pastures during the summer, and return here (or to the Kullu or Kangra Valleys) in winter.

◉ Sights & Activities

The Chaurasi temples, 500m up the street from the bus stand, occupy a wide flagstone courtyard that doubles as an outdoor classroom and cricket practise ground. There are three main Shaivite temples, plus a couple of dozen smaller shrines (*chaurasi* means 84, seemingly an exaggeration). The central **Manimahesh Temple** (⊙ 6am-8.30pm) is a classic stone *sikhara*, built in the 7th century AD. The squat **Lakshna Devi Temple** (⊙ 6am-8.30pm) is of a similar date, with a weathered but wildly carved wooden doorway. For the best valley views, continue up the road from the Chaurasi temples gate to the shabby but panoramic Brahmani Mata Temple, 3km above town. The route passes through the upper village, still full of traditional slate-roofed, wooden houses.

Trekking

The trekking season lasts from May to late October, though July and August see some monsoon rain. Great routes include the following:

➡ Kugti to Jhalma in Lahaul over the 5040m Kugti Pass (five days)

➡ Lamu (Ravi Valley) to McLeod Ganj over the 4420m Indrahar La (five days)

➡ demanding longer treks via the isolated village of Bara Bhangal to Manali or Bir

A popular shorter trek is to the sacred Manimahesh Lake, a two- or three-day return hike (about 13km each way, with an altitude difference of 2100m) starting at Hadsar, 13km east of Bharmour. It can be done without a tent thanks to the many *dhabas* en route. In the two weeks following Janmastami (Krishna's birthday; late August or early September), up to 300,000 pilgrims take this route in the Manimahesh Yatra (p301) pilgrimage in honour of Lord Shiva, climaxing with a freezing dip in the lake. The whole Chamba Valley throngs with people travelling to or from the lake at this time.

Anna Adventures
& Tours   TREKKING
(☑ 9805659622, 8894687758; www.bharmour treks.com; Main Bazaar) Anna Adventures & Tours, with an office on the street between the bus stand and the Chaurasi temples, arranges a full range of treks in the Bharmour region and across the surrounding ranges.

🛏 Sleeping & Eating

As well as hotel restaurants, there are several *dhabas* on the street up to the Chaurasi temples.

Chaurasi Hotel   HOTEL $$
(☑ 9816490969, 9418025004; www.hotelchourasi. com; Main Bazaar; r ₹800-2500; 🛜) You can't miss this red multistorey building up the street towards the Chaurasi temples. Rooms are generous in size and many have soaring views; those in the new block at the side are generally in better condition.

❶ Getting There & Away

Buses leave approximately hourly from 5.30am to 5.30pm for the rugged trip to Chamba (₹110, 3½ hours). The last of these continues overnight to Dharamsala.

A few daily buses head to Hadsar (₹40, one hour); there are also shared jeep-taxis. For buses up the Ravi Valley as far as Holi, take a Chamba-bound bus to Kharamukh and change there.

LAHAUL & SPITI

Lahaul is braced for massive changes. For years, reaching this spectacular if desolate region has involved crossing the seasonal, infamously treacherous Rohtang Pass. However, by 2020 the new Rohtang Tunnel is expected to have opened, making access a breeze from Manali. In its wake, you can expect a rush of new tourism.

Keylong (Lahaul's capital) is on the summer-only mountain highway to Ladakh. To the west, the fascinating, little-visited Pattan and Pangi Valleys are an explorer's delight. To the east, a rough jeep track leads over the soaring Kunzum La into Spiti, Himachal's 'mini-Ladakh'. Riven by deep river chasms, this is a high-altitude desert backed by snow-topped mountains and punctuated by tiny villages set in patches of striking greenery. As in Ladakh, Tibetan Buddhism is the dominant religion in both Spiti and upper Lahaul, though Hinduism is prominent in lower Lahaul. Some curious Lahauli temples encompass both religions.

Climate

Rainfall is minimal, especially in Spiti, and the high altitude ensures low temperatures. Winter temperatures can plummet below –30°C, but summer daytime temperatures often rise into the 20s. When monsoons are soaking the rest of the state (mid-July to mid-September), it's usually dry and sunny here. Whenever you travel, bring some clothing for cold weather.

You must expect the unexpected: in 2018 a mid-September storm lasting for days essentially closed all the passes, leaving Lahaul cut off for around a week. Heavy rain can also cause landslides that block roads for prolonged periods. Watch forecasts carefully.

❶ Getting There & Away

The road north from Manali over the Rohtang La (3978m) is normally open from about mid-May to early November. From the north side of the Rohtang you can head west to Keylong or east to Spiti.

From Keylong, the road to Ladakh continues over the mighty Baralacha La (4950m) and Taglang La (5328m) and is normally open from about early June to some time in October. The road to Spiti over the Kunzum La (4551m) is open from about mid-June to some time in November.

You can cross these passes by minibus, jeep, motorbike or bus, all of which can be arranged in Manali.

When the passes are closed, Lahaul is virtually cut off from the outside world, and Spiti is only accessible from the south by looping through Kinnaur. Check the status of the passes before visiting late in the season – once the snows arrive, you might be stuck for the winter! For updates see www.bcmtouring.com (scroll down, right column). The website www.devilonwheels. com also has lots of useful advice.

Lahaul (but not Spiti or Ladakh) will be open to year-round traffic from Manali with the eventual opening of the 9km tunnel bypassing the Rohtang La (possibly in 2019).

Lahaul

Manali to Keylong

This spectacular trip currently starts with the dramatic crossing of the Rohtang La (3978m), a seemingly endless pass that's usually open from about mid-May to early November. Allow several hours to cross and, if you're driving, be aware that permits are required. Beyond the pass lies Lahaul's awe-inspiring Chandra Valley, which should become accessible year-round once the new Rohtang Tunnel opens.

The name Rohtang literally translates as 'pile of dead bodies' – hundreds of travellers have frozen to death on this pass over the centuries. After heavy rain or snow the pass' closure can be a major logistical headache, but in better weather it's busy with day trippers from Manali enjoying the novelty of a snowball fight. Especially in May and June, the result can be very serious congestion, though pressure has been somewhat relieved by permit requirements. A 9km tunnel avoiding the pass has now been bored and, once finishing work and new access bridges are complete, traffic should bypass the pass altogether.

Until then, the road zigzags up, over and down 14km from the pass to Gramphu, an unsheltered junction (not a town) that marks the turnoff to Spiti. You're now in the Chandra Valley, whose river rages between towering rocky peaks ribboned with waterfalls plunging from raised glaciers. Khoksar, in the valley bottom, has several dhabas and a checkpoint where police note down foreigners' passport details. The new Rohtang Tunnel joins this road 7km further west, 4km before Sissu, which has a few unremarkable tourist guesthouses.

Tandi Bridge, 8km before Keylong, marks the confluence of the Chandra River with the Bhaga (together they become the Chandra-Bhaga and later the Chenab).

Keylong

☏ 01900 / POP 1150 / ELEV 3100M

Keylong's main street, optimistically named The Mall, winds for 1km just below the Manali–Leh road. For many travellers the town is just an overnight stop along that route, seen only briefly and in the dark. However, a longer stay reveals grand mountain views rising above the green Bhaga Valley. There's a laid-back, small-town lifestyle, some scenic walks and a few historic Buddhist monasteries to seek out.

◉ Sights & Activities

Lahaul-Spiti Tribal Museum MUSEUM
(The Mall; ⊙10am-1.30pm & 2.30-5pm Tue-Sun) **FREE** At the west end of town, this semi-interesting museum can give context to what you've seen in local villages, ideas of other places to go and potted histories of the valleys. Traditional artefacts displayed include *chaam* dance masks and a *thod-pa* (part of a skull formerly used by *amchis* or lamas to store healing or sacred liquids).

Shashur Gompa BUDDHIST MONASTERY
Founded in the 17th century by the Zanskari lama Deva Gyatsho, Shashur's original gompa, featuring 5m-high *thangkas*, is now encased within a modern concrete one. By road it's 6km of zigzags from Keylong; on foot allow an hour each way by a series of steep, sometimes-less-than-obvious shortcut paths (harder to find on the return).

Kardang Loop Walk WALKING
To get a better taste of the valley you could walk to Kardang, the now largely modernised village across the valley that was once Lahaul's capital. The walk is only around 1.5km one way (more to the gompa) but it's steep down then up with no flat going, so

take plenty of water and allow a couple of hours.

Descend the footpath-steps between Vikrant Homestay and the boxed prayer wheel at the western end of The Mall. Just before reaching the hospital find the path down (left), cross the River Bhaga on a footbridge, then climb 1km to a road. Khardang is on the right. You could continue 800m further uphill to find the gompa (monastery), or return east along the road for 3km to Lapchang village, where a different path descends 1km to another footbridge, then climbs 1.25km to the main road. Keylong is 1.5km to the west (left).

Brokpa Adventure Tours   TREKKING
(📞9418165176; brokpatrek@yahoo.com; Hotel Dupchen, The Mall; ⊙9am-8pm May & Sep, 7am-10pm Jun-Aug) Talk to Amar for tips on day hikes or to arrange longer treks including the classic routes to Zanskar.

🛏 Sleeping & Eating

Most of Keylong's numerous guesthouses and hotels (typically May–October only) are in two clumps: along the NH3 road high above town around Km115, or above and around the bus station. Some of the latter offer basic dorms for those catching a quick sleep between buses before continuing to Ladakh. Some more-upmarket options in rural locations are impractical without your own wheels.

Nordaling Guest House   HOTEL $
(📞01900-222294, Sonam 9418045394; www.nordalingkeylong.in; lower/upper d ₹1200/1600, q ₹2000-2500; ⊙May-Oct; 🅿🛜) From the bus station, climb 100m northwest then turn right to find this obligingly managed four-storey place. Immaculately clean rooms have sitting spaces and the relatively new versions on the two upper floors are particularly good bets, with fine new bathrooms and lovely balcony views from most.

The appealing garden restaurant offers the best food in town.

Hotel New Gyespa   HOTEL $$
(📞9418136055; www.gyespahotels.webs.com; Snowland Rd; r ₹1000-2000; ⊙May-Oct; 🛜) Only 40m up from the bus station, the large rooms here are some of Keylong's smartest, accessed off polished if starkly bare corridors. The cheapest, hard-floored versions on the ground floor are a fair deal at ₹1000, and prices rise higher up the building where carpets prevail (no view/view ₹1500/2000).

ℹ **ROHTANG PERMITS**

Traffic is limited beyond Gulaba – towards or across the Rohtang pass – to reduce congestion. A permit is required (for cars/motorbikes ₹550/50), for which you apply online from six days before departure (between midday and midnight) on www.rohtangpermits.nic.in or using the Rohtang Permit NIC mobile phone app. You must print out a copy of the receipt, which will have a fixed usage date. Note that vehicles must be less than 10 years old and that the road closes on Tuesdays (and altogether in winter).

ℹ **Getting There & Away**

All services are at the mercy of road conditions and can be cancelled for days after heavy rain or snow. The **bus station** (New Bus Stand) is just above The Mall's eastern end.

From mid-June to mid-September, an HRTC bus departs for Leh (₹550, about 14 hours) at 5am – get tickets at the bus station between 4am and 4.30am. Privately operated Manali–Leh minibuses and shared jeeps continue to run into October, snow conditions allowing, but finding a seat in Keylong is hit and miss unless you're prepared to pay the full Manali–Leh fare and prebook: Amar at Brokpa Adventure Tours (p345) can oblige.

The HRTC also runs six or seven daily buses to Manali (₹173, seven hours, 4.30am to 1.30pm), one to Shimla (₹565, 16 hours, 1.30pm) and two to Delhi (₹850, 23 hours) from about mid-May to early November. Once the Rohtang Tunnel opens (expected 2020), times should shorten and seasons extend.

From about May to mid-November there are buses at 6.30am and 1pm to Chika (₹60, two hours) in the Darcha Valley, on the way up to the Shingo La into Zanskar.

For Kaza (summer only) you could take an early Manali-bound bus and change at Gramphu (₹75, 2½ hours), where the Manali–Kaza bus pulls in around 9am, but Gramphu is an unsheltered road junction and timings aren't coordinated, so the 4.30am bus leaves you waiting ages, but using the 6.30am can be nerve-rackingly close. Once the Rohtang Tunnel opens, it should be much easier to pick up the Kaza bus at Khoksar, where all traffic stops for a police check.

Pattan & Pangi Valleys

At Tandi, 8km southwest of Keylong, a road branches northwest along the beautiful, fertile, little-visited Pattan Valley, carved by the

Chandra-Bhaga (Chenab) River. The river then curves northward into the remote, thinly populated Pangi Valley, the road clinging to cliff ledges between steep, high mountains. In villages here, people have their own language and culture and the whole region is completely cut off from December to March.

Beyond Killar, Pangi's only town, lies probably the scariest of all Himachal's mountain roads, a hair-raising adventure in itself, leading to Kishtwar in Jammu & Kashmir. The other way out of Pangi is similarly dramatic, winding across the Sach Pass over to Chamba. If rain or snow is forecast, think twice about coming this way.

◎ Sights

The main valley starts with numerous agricultural villages and their verdant vegetable terraces perched part way up steep mountainsides. At Km35.7 the road divides, the smaller lane taking an adorable meander between relatively traditional hamlets including Triloknath, a pilgrimage centre thanks to its small but remarkable **temple** (◎6am-7pm), holy to both Hindus and Buddhists. The two roads reconverge near Udaipur, a small town whose **Markula Devi Temple** (Mrikula Mata) is a very distinctive wooden structure with a spiky half-spired roof and an interior containing some of the region's best medieval wood carvings. After Udaipur there are far fewer villages and the road becomes as rough as it is impressive, with several long stretches carved as ledges into cliff faces. If you're continuing on the even more scary K3 (Kishtwar–Killar–Keylong) ledge-road (p283) to Gulabgarh, or crossing the Sach Pass to Chamba, you'll generally need to stop the night in Killar. If so it's well worth walking 750m southeast through the New Bazaar (The Mall) to a small area of pine forest containing the Honsu Nag Mandir, a tiny but classic Pangi-style temple.

⊨ Sleeping & Eating

Triloknath has a pair of basic homestays and Udaipur has three unprepossessing guesthouses. Killar has two hotels, a rest house, a bar with rather dodgy rooms and the **Chandrabhaga Homestay** (☑9418431600; Main Bazaar, Killar; r from ₹700, without bathroom from ₹500, d/q with balcony ₹1000/1500), which looks unfinished but is better than the lot of them. A very basic if superfriendly *dhaba* at **Purthi** has floor-space sleeping areas for ₹200 a head.

❶ Information

Udaipur and Killar have ATMs on their main streets.

❶ Getting There & Away

From Keylong, buses run to Udaipur (₹84, three hours) seven times daily. The 8am, 10am and 3.30pm services divert en route to Triloknath (₹80, two hours). There are also four daily shuttles between Udaipur and Triloknath (₹20, 25 minutes) by eight-seater electric vans, leaving at 8am, 10am, noon and 5pm, returning immediately after arrival.

From about mid-April to mid-November the 6.30am and 11am buses from Keylong continue to Killar (₹210), taking as much as 10 hours to cover the 125km. The second one starts in Manali, so timing is very approximate. Buses back to Keylong leave Killar at 5am (Manali-bound) and 10am.

The route is dusty, bumpy and often as narrow as a ribbon but stunningly beautiful, with the road teetering along a series of precarious ledges high above the fast-flowing river for much of the last 50km into Killar. In rain, sections of road become rivers and the journey can be nail-biting.

From about late June to early October, a bus leaves Killar at 6.30am for Chamba (₹260, about 12 hours) over the Sach Pass (4390m). You might also find shared jeeps (₹500) before 9am.

For Kishtwar in Jammu & Kashmir, you'll usually need to head first from Killar to Gulabgarh (53km) along one of India's most perilous but scenic roads. For the intrepid only! The Luj–Tayari section bumps over bare rocks then along terrifyingly narrow ledges after Ishtiyari, sometimes overhung by daggers of unstable rock. Most days there's likely to be a J&K jeep leaving Killar in mid-morning for Gulabgarh (₹300, four hours). Look around for vehicles with JK number plates. Chartering a jeep should cost ₹3000.

Spiti

Separated from fertile Lahaul by the soaring 4551m Kunzum Pass, the trans-Himalayan region of Spiti is another chunk of Tibet marooned within India, a kind of 'mini-Ladakh' with fewer tourists. The scattered villages in this serrated moonscape arrive like mirages while the turquoise-grey ribbon of the Spiti River is your near-constant companion, albeit sometimes way below in precipitous gorges.

The whole Spiti–Kinnaur loop is scenically spectacular, attracting hordes of summer motorcyclists completing one of India's great road trips.

ℹ Information

Spiti is essentially an internet dark zone, although some Kaza hotels offer just enough bandwidth to message on WhatsApp. Reports suggest that Kaza and Tabo might receive new infrastructure in 2019–2020. Only BSNL has mobile phone coverage, and with minimal internet connectivity.

Gramphu to Kaza

Awe-inspiring for beauty but fiercely rough on the behind, the Spiti-bound route bumps its way up the glacier-carved Chandra Valley with only the tiniest of summer camps en route, notably at tiny Batal, which is just a handful of *dhabas*. A kilometre beyond, a rough but drivable 12km track climbs north towards Chandratal, a 2km-long glacial lake among snow peaks at 4270m.

Meanwhile, the main road switchbacks precipitously up to the Kunzum La, where vehicles perform a respectful circuit of prayer-flag-strewn stupas before continuing down into Spiti through an area of yak meadows. Arguably the views are even more beautiful doing this route in reverse.

The first Spitian village of any size is Losar, where there's a passport check. From here the main valley heads directly for Kaza, while the narrow but asphalted lane marked to Chicham emerges at Kibber after crossing a 2017 suspension bridge with spectacular views.

★ Chandratal   LAKE

(Moon Lake) This gloriously calm glacial lake presents mirror-perfect reflections of the surrounding white-top peaks and geological colour-swirls. At 4270m, the 20-minute walk from the car park gets most visitors breathless enough that they stop at the nearest (southern) end. But it's well worth the 90-minute stroll to go right around the lake's edge, escaping the crowds and appreciating the reflections from ever new angles.

Be aware that sudden snow falls can catch out visitors, so watch weather forecasts carefully. Most visitors come in chartered long-distance taxis, paying an extra ₹1500 to a Kaza–Manali fare to make the Chandratal side trip.

From early June to early October you can stay in bedded tent camps around 3km before the end of the approach track. The idea's nice in principle but the tents have no lake views and most of them are marshalled together into a single meadow.

🛏 Sleeping & Eating

Nomad's Cottage   GUESTHOUSE **$$**

(☑ 9650824268; www.nomadscottage.in; Losar; s/d ₹1300/1900, without bathroom ₹1100/1500; ⊙ May-Oct) Losar has half a dozen OK guesthouses clumped around the bus stand but for something far more atmospheric Nomad's Cottage is well worth the 1.3km detour: 800m towards Kaza then 500m north.

There's wood-beam ceilings, big comfy beds and a Tibetan-styled lounge.

Parasol Camps   TENTED CAMP **$$**

(☑ 9418845817; www.parasolcamps.co.in; Chandratal Camps; d tent with beds & full board ₹3000, with mattress & half-board ₹1600; ⊙ mid-Jun–mid-Oct) One of the best Chandratal camps, Parasol provides cosy tents, good Indian meals, sit-down toilets and buckets of hot water for washing.

Kaza

☑ 01906 / POP 1700 / ELEV 3640M

The capital of Spiti, Kaza is a helpfully compact launch pad for trips to spectacular Ki Gompa and fascinating high-altitude villages including Kibber, Langza and Komic. It's also a good place to organise treks and tours, and for foreigners heading south to procure the necessary inner line permit for the trip into Kinnaur. The town's bazaar and main cafes are in Old Kaza on the east side of often-dry Kaza Nullah stream, across which New Kaza has most of the bureaucratic offices.

ℹ INNER LINE PERMITS IN KAZA

For now at least, applying for the permit to travel between Sumdo (eastern Spiti) and Rekong Peo (Kinnaur) is relatively painless in New Kaza. Collect three photos of yourself and one copy of your passport, visa and entry stamp then go to the Ashoka Photocopy Shop, half a block west of Hotel Deyzor, to buy a set of three application papers (₹10). Take these to room 111 of the nearby **Assistant Deputy Commissioner's Office** (☑ 9459939708; New Kaza; ⊙ 10am-1.30pm & 2.30-4.30pm Mon-Fri & every 2nd Sat), accessed down the next footpath to your left. The process should take around 20 minutes and solo travellers have no problems getting permits here.

🏃 Activities

A few agencies run by highly experienced locals can set you up with treks, jeep safaris, day tours and other travel arrangements.

Incredible Spiti
ADVENTURE SPORTS

(☑ 9650675505; www.incrediblespiti.com; Sakya Abode Hotel) Highly experienced outfit with wide-ranging activities, treks and tours by motorbike and jeep.

Spiti Valley Tours
TREKKING

(☑ 9418537689; www.spitivalleytours.com; Main Bazaar; ⊙ office 8am-7pm Jun-Oct) Lara Tsering's tour agency can offer treks, jeep tours and mountaineering, but its speciality is wildlife and fossil walks from Kibber or from its luxury homestay in Langza.

Well-organised winter wildlife packages (January to March) give you a great chance of spotting rare animals including, quite possibly, snow leopards. The inconspicuous office is above Nimaling Guesthouse on the top floor of the building opposite the SBI ATM.

Spiti Holiday Adventure
TREKKING

(☑ 9418439247; www.spitiholidayadventure.com; Main Bazaar; ⊙ office 8.30am-8pm) Ramesh Lotey's wide-ranging, well-organised outfit organises tours and treks, rents motorbikes (per day ₹1000), changes money and is a good place for travel information generally.

🛏 Sleeping

There are plenty of places to stay in both halves of town. Most close for several months in winter, when only homestays operate.

Travellers Shed
HOMESTAY $

(☑ 8988872791; www.thetravellersshed.com; Khasra 145, New Kaza; dm/d ₹600/1600) With a low-key urban chic that's rare in Kaza, this place is aimed squarely at motorcyclists. There's ample bike parking, a specialist Enfield repair shop, and even the reception lamps are fashioned from old headlights.

Ösel Rooms
GUESTHOUSE $

(☑ 9418215768; off Main Bazaar, Old Kaza; d/tr ₹1000/1500; ⊙ Apr-Nov) Above Taste of Spiti restaurant, seven large rooms with good beds and new bathrooms are made colourful with bright curtains and prayer flags, though the furniture lacks much sophistication.

★ Hotel Deyzor
HOTEL $$

(☑ 9418402660; www.hoteldeyzor.com; behind BSNL office, New Kaza; r ₹1700-3000; ⊙ mid-Apr–mid-Nov; ⊛) 🍴 This inspiring place offers not just comfortable, atmospheric accommodation, solar-power back-up and great food, but also spiritual nourishment and lots of insights into local culture. The owners, a philosophical adventure sportsman and a former national archery champion, are the ultimate Spiti enthusiasts (see www.himalayanshepherd.co for more). It's advisable to book ahead.

They also have a small shop specialising in local Spiti crafts, including yak-wool shawls and rugs and yak-hair ropes.

Sakya Abode
HOTEL $$

(☑ 9418208987; www.sakyaabode.com; New Kaza; r ₹2200-2600; ⊙ late Apr-Nov; @ ⊛) Almost invisible below the U of the main road 100m northeast of Sakya Gompa, Kaza's longest-running hotel has completely renewed the bathrooms in this mud-built structure while maintaining the old log ceilings. Sleeping areas have been spruced up with decorative details and the L-shaped shared balcony-terrace is a lovely place to listen to birds roosting excitedly in the garden at sunset.

The lounge-restaurant is also appealing. They can arrange a whole series of outdoor activities.

🍴 Eating

Sol Cafe
CAFE $

(Main Bazaar; hot drinks ₹50-120, snacks ₹20-140; ⊙ 9am-7.15pm Mon-Sat May-Nov) 🍴 This cool little multicoloured cafe, operated by Ecosphere (p349) volunteers, offers superstrong coffee, herbal and other teas, and light dishes such as French toast, waffles, pancakes and wholewheat baked goods. Vegan options available.

There's a terrace area and a comfy back room with beanbags that hosts movie nights at 6pm (except Sundays). You can fill water bottles with filtered water for free.

★ Hotel Deyzor Restaurant
MULTICUISINE $$

(New Kaza; mains ₹110-440; ⊙ 8am-4pm & 6-10pm mid-Apr–mid-Nov) The Deyzor hotel's restaurant is decked with artistic local photos and offers plenty to read, and there's an eclectic range of dishes, from Thai to *thukpa* to tandoori specials with an emphasis on seasonal local produce. Try the quiches or the grilled honey-lime paneer.

Himalayan Café
MULTICUISINE $$

(off Main Bazaar, Old Kaza; mains ₹140-300; ⊙ 8am-10pm May-Oct) The warm-weather terrace of the Himalayan buzzes with wise-cracking staff, youthful music and a happy graffiti-mural chic that becomes all the more enticing when strung with lights and lanterns at night. Satisfying, well-cooked food covers all bases and beer is available.

ⓘ Getting There & Away

The **bus station** is at the bottom of the bazaar in Old Kaza, with taxi offices opposite.

BUS

Buses depart for Manali (₹350) at 5am, mid-June to mid-October. Currently the trip takes around 10 to 13 hours, depending on the state of the passes, but will get quicker once the Rohtang Tunnel opens (expected 2020). A ticket-buying melee starts around 4.30am. It can be more relaxing to start the journey one night before with the 4.30pm service to Losar (₹90, three hours) then pick up the Manali bus there next morning around 7.30am – but it's a gamble as you can't be assured a seat.

Buses to Rekong Peo (₹360, 11 hours, 7.30am) and Chango (₹123, 4½ hours, 2.30pm) go via Tabo (₹73, 2½ hours). The 7.30am service continues via Nako (₹177, 5½ hours) and eventually, with a driver change, to Shimla.

MOTORCYCLE

A few agents rent motorbikes. If you've arrived on an Enfield, the Travellers Shed offers repairs. If heading for Losar, note that since 2017 there is an appealing alternative route using a winding but newly asphalted lane via Kibber and Chicham, crossing spectacular Chicham Bridge.

TAXI

Lhungta Traveller Union (☏ 9418190083; opposite bus stand, Old Kaza; ⏲ 5.30am-7pm) sells shared-taxi seats (usually more minibus than car) to Manali for ₹1000, departing at 6am daily. It also has fixed-rate taxis everywhere

including to Dhankar (₹1550, 1½ hours), Tabo (₹2000, 1½ hours), Ki (₹750, 45 minutes), Keylong (₹10,500, eight hours) and Manali (₹11,000, nine hours). Prices are per vehicle. For return trips with a one-hour wait, add 20%; for each extra hour's wait, add ₹100 more. Add ₹1500 to a Manali or Keylong fare to visit Chandratal Lake en route. Shared taxis are advertised to Chandratal (₹1000 per seat) but these only usually operate June–July.

Around Kaza

The small, high-altitude villages on the east side of the Spiti Valley (all well above 4000m) have a pristine, desolate beauty all their own, with minimal vegetation except their carefully tended fields of barley and other crops. This is the abode of the Himalayan wolf, snow leopard, blue sheep, golden eagle and griffon vulture. Several of the villages have seasonal guesthouses or homestays and interesting old temples or monasteries. Most travellers visit them as multistop day trips from Kaza but, to get a better sense of the lifestyle of Spiti's amazingly resilient people, you can stay over and trek between several of the villages along the homestay trek route linking Langza, Komic and Demul with Lhalung and Dhankar.

The availability of accommodation means that the homestay trek can be achieved with the minimum of luggage, though beware that the great altitude means you should be well acclimatised. If you want to do just one day, the best option is the Komic–Demul leg with fine views and only 3km of the 16km route using jeep tracks.

SUSTAINABLE SPITI

The much-respected Spiti conservation and development NGO **Ecosphere** (☏ 9418860099; www.spitiecosphere.com; Sol Cafe, Main Bazaar, Old Kaza; ⏲ 10am-7pm Mon-Sat Apr–mid-Dec) 🌿 is behind a whole raft of projects designed to bring a sustainable economy to the region's rural communities. In tourism terms this includes yak safaris, cooking/pottery/yak-rope-twining classes, playing 'nun for a day' in Spiti's Buddhist convents and various homestay-based treks and wildlife-watching experiences. Several high-altitude villages (notably Langza, Komic, Demul, Lhalung and Dhankar) have homestays where, for ₹600 to ₹750 per person per night (including meals), visitors sleep in simple but clean traditional houses, eat home-cooked food and get the chance to experience traditional Spitian village life. Hot water is normally by bucket and squat toilets are prevalent. These villages are linked by the popular 'Homestay Trail' trekking route. The trails are easy enough to find for yourself, but a trained guide (per day ₹1500 to ₹3000, prebooking essential) can add a wealth of detail about the culture, environment and wildlife. Spotting ibex and blue sheep (bharal) is not uncommon in September. However, to catch a glimpse of a snow leopard, you'll need a specialist wildlife sojourn making daily forays from your homestay during deep winter (February is best).

❶ Getting There & Around

A 5pm bus runs daily from Kaza to Ki and Kibber, another runs some days to Komic, other days to Demul. To make interconnections it's foot (the homestay trail), taxi or your own wheels. Two road circuits make for popular taxi excursions, Kaza–Ki–Kibber–Kaza (₹1350) and Kaza–Langza–Komic–Hikkim–Kaza (₹2350). Kaza agencies offer a full day combining the two loops for ₹3000, often adding in a very worthwhile photo stop at Chicham Bridge.

KI
POP 370 / ELEV 3800M

★ Ki Gompa
BUDDHIST MONASTERY
(⊙6am-7pm) Covering a conical hillock with an array of whitewashed monastic buildings, Ki (Kee, Key) is the largest gompa in Spiti. Views of it from the south are particularly photogenic. On request, the monks will open up some of the medieval prayer rooms that survived when the main prayer hall (now rebuilt) was ravaged by fire.

In the Zimshung Lhakhang, the upper library, is the bed that was slept in by the Dalai Lama during his visits in 1960 and 2000. Around 350 monks, including many students from surrounding villages, live here. An atmospheric *puja* is held in the new prayer hall every morning at around 8am. Dance masks are brought out for the annual Ki Chaam Festival (p301) and again for Losar.

KIBBER
☎01906 / POP 370 / ELEV 4200M
Eight kilometres beyond Ki, this relatively large but still traditional village is a good base for local hikes, and the start of the demanding eight- to 10-day trek to Tso Moriri lake in Ladakh over the 5578m Parang La and three-day nontechnical ascents of Khanamo (5964m). Best season is August or early September.

The Kibber area is good for sighting Spiti wildlife including blue sheep, ibex, red fox and Himalayan griffon vulture. In winter it offers better-than-average prospects of sighting the ever-elusive snow leopard (best in February and March).

Norling Adventure Tours
TREKKING
(☎9418556107, 8988471107; www.spitinorling adventure.com; Kibber) The father-and-son team at Norling Home Stay can organise treks and hikes at relatively short notice.

Kanamo Homestay
GUESTHOUSE $
(☎9459053363; www.spitiwanderer.com; per person incl half-board ₹800, in Jun & Jul ₹1000)

Expanded in 2018, Kanamo offers five lovely new rooms, of which three are ensuite for no extra charge. Rates include breakfast and dinner that can be taken in the comfort of your room or at the semitraditional family kitchen-sitting area.

Owner Loam speaks excellent English and organises a range of activities including the Kanamo Trek (approximately ₹10,000 to ₹12,000 per person for three days, inclusive).

Norling Home Stay
GUESTHOUSE $$
(☑Tsering Norphel 8988471107, Tsering Rapten 9418556107; www.spitinorlingadventure.com; Kibber; d ₹1700, without bathroom ₹700) 🖝 Near the bus stand and post office in upper Kibber, this new but very traditionally styled whitewashed home has appealing views across the village and the four 'super-deluxe' ensuite rooms are about the best accommodation available in the upland villages.

❶ Getting There & Away

A bus to Kibber (₹34, 50 minutes) via Ki (₹25, 30 minutes) leaves Kaza at 5pm, starting back from Kibber at 8.30am. Taxis charge ₹1050 one way to Kibber, or ₹1350 for a return trip visiting Ki, too.

LANGZA
POP 135 / ELEV 4325M
Tiny Langza, a switchback 14km drive north of Kaza, sits at 4325m below the modern 6300m peak of Chau Chau. A large modern medicine-Buddha statue stares across the valley from a shoulder of ridge that's just three minutes' climb above the main village. The small temple 250m behind it is around 500 years old. About a 2km walk away is an area rich in ammonite fossils around 100 million years old.

Several of the village's 20 or so houses are homestays. Most charge ₹750 per person including meals and have squat toilets (flushing or dry). Much more comfortable, if essentially unmarked, Lara Homestay costs up to ₹3500 and is run by Kaza's Spiti Valley Tours (p348) as a base for its winter wildlife-watching adventures.

There's no bus service to Langza, though the Komic service gets you much of the way up. Taxis from Kaza cost ₹950/1200 one way/return.

HIKKIM
POP 80 / ELEV 4400M
Hikkim is tiny but, when viewed from above, has the most photogenic setting of all the Kaza area villages. Gaze down across widely layered fields with the start of a can-

yon evident below and a horizon of jagged, saw-edge peaks.

Driving tours stop here primarily to visit what's claimed – disputably – to be the world's highest **post office** (◷10am-4pm Mon-Sat), at an altitude of 4440m. It's virtually indistinguishable from other village houses and, curiously, doesn't actually sell postcards or stamps, though you can buy those across the yard from a small cafe.

Hikkim is around 15km from Kaza, 3km from Komic. It's 8km from Langza via the less-used lower road. Komic–Kaza buses pass by three days a week. A taxi from Kaza would cost ₹950/1200 one way/return or ₹2350 including Komic and Langza. Walking down the steep nullah (ditch or stream) back to Kaza is possible in a couple of hours.

The road descent to Kaza is a terrific drive. After around 4km, look back for a particularly memorable view towards the abandoned mud-walled remnants of Getung Village, sitting atop a canyon junction and looking more like a ruined fortress. Just after this, the road turns into a ladder of hairpin bends with truly splendid valley views.

KOMIC
POP 130 / ELEV 4587M

A sign outside the monastery here proclaims Komic to be the highest motorable village in the world at 4587m. Santa Bárbara in Bolivia (4754m) would disagree, but Komic might well claim the Asian crown. The village comprises about 10 houses and, above them, the Tangyud Gompa, with about 50 lamas. The monastery's history goes back many centuries, but its fort-like main building is relatively new, relocated here after the original near Hikkim was destroyed by a 1975 earthquake. Pujas are offered at 8am to Mahakala, a wrathful emanation of Avalokitesvara. A smaller, older building a short walk up the hill has a stuffed leopard (believed to impart strength to those who touch it) hanging inside the entrance: women are not permitted in its inner prayer room.

Komic village is just 10 homesteads in the bowl of vegetable terraces directly beneath the monastery ridge. Four of them have simple but authentic homestays (May to October, per person ₹600 including meals) with participating families taking turns to take guests. **Spiti Organic Kitchen** (snacks ₹60-180; ◷8am-4pm May-Sep) beside the monastery offers well-cooked local food, including a very tasty *keu* (a dish of local pasta pieces, here written *qu*).

Buses to Komic leave Kaza at 5pm on Monday, Tuesday and Wednesday only, returning next morning at 8am. Taxis from Kaza cost ₹1500/1800 one way/return. From Komic it's about a 16km walk south to Demul, the next village on the 'Homestay Trail', or 26km by jeep track.

Whether you walk or drive, you'll reach an altitude of nearly 4700m a couple of kilometres south of Komic; this is the best leg of the homestay trek for long-distance panoramas. It's also good for sightings of blue sheep.

Pin Valley

Southeast of Kaza, the Spiti River is joined by the Pin River, flowing out of a dramatic, wind-scoured valley from the heights of the Great Himalayan Range. Especially after turning south at Sangam, views are stupendous, with geological strata tilted at all conceivable angles. After a 33km drive you reach little Mudh (3770m), the valley's last settlement and the summer trailhead for the classic multiday treks Pin-Bawa and Pin-Parvati. These set out through the nearby 675-sq-km Pin Valley National Park, where you might spot ibex and blue sheep.

The beautiful if taxing Pin-Bawa trek crosses the 4850m Bhaba (Bawa) Pass coming from Kaphnu in Kinnaur, arriving in Mudh after four days. Unlike the more challenging Pin-Parvati route, Pin-Bawa is possible with pack ponies rather than porters, so is less expensive. Generally it takes a lot of advance planning to do either trek, but if you're lucky and fully equipped (tent, food, warm clothes etc) you just might find an arriving group whose pony-men need to return and who'd be happy to assist.

Be aware that neither route should be attempted between mid-September and late June.

★ **Tara Homestay** GUESTHOUSE $
(☑Kunzang 8988062293, Sonam 8991723015; www.spititaraadventure.com; Mudh; r ₹1000-1200, without bathroom ₹500-800, mains ₹60-110; ◷May-Oct) With solar power, good bathrooms, little *chokse* tables and fresh clean linens, the excellent Tara Homestay remains the pick of Mudh's guesthouses. By day its reliable if unadventurous little restaurant offers rooftop seating with fabulous views.

Owner Sonam speaks functional English and can arrange full treks with porters or horses given around a week's notice.

ℹ Getting There & Away

The road into the Pin Valley branches off the Tabo road at the Attargu Bridge, 15km southeast of Kaza, but traffic is light so hitching is very slow. For years, mudslides at Kirgarang Nullah, 8km along, could block the road, sometimes for weeks during the June–August wet season, but a new higher-level detour road is under construction and expected to be complete by 2020.

Buses to Mudh (₹83, three hours) leave Kaza daily at 4pm, starting back at 6am. The bus makes a 2km detour just south of Gulling to collect passengers from the large Ugyen Sangnak Choling monastery in Kungri. A taxi to Mudh costs ₹2100 from Kaza. It's ₹2500 from Dhankar if you can find a driver.

Dhankar

POP 300 / ELEV 3880M

Dhankar's crag-top fort and old gompa together create one of the most spectacular sights in Spiti. The former capital of the Nono kings who once ruled Spiti, the village is tiny, set high above the confluence of the Spiti and Pin Rivers, up 8km of zigzags from Shichling on the Kaza–Tabo road.

◉ Sights

The spectacular 1200-year-old **Dhankar Gompa** (₹25; ⊙ 8am-dusk) perches precariously between eroded pinnacles on the edge of a cliff. Its top-floor courtyard has a stuffed goat hanging above the stairwell, a room where the Dalai Lama slept, a meditation cave, and a shrine containing ceremonial masks. Another prayer hall, with murals of the Buddha of healing, stands on top of the rock above, accessed by separate concrete steps. The views from these buildings are phenomenal. Dhankar's lamas no longer inhabit the old gompa, having moved to the large, gleaming New Monastery, 800m away, in 2009.

On the hilltop above the gompa are the ruins of the abandoned mud-brick fort-palace that sheltered the valley's population during times of war and gave the village its name (khar means 'citadel' and dhak means 'cliff'). An hour's steep walk up from the village, the small lake Dhankar Tso offers views over the valley and southeast to the twin peaks of Manirang (6593m).

⌷ Sleeping & Eating

Dhankar Monastery Guesthouse GUESTHOUSE $
(☑ 9418646578; dm ₹200, d ₹1500, without bathroom ₹600; ⊙ May-Oct, restaurant 7am-9.30pm)

Beside the New Monastery and dressed in a similar livery, this well-run place has picture-postcard views of the old monastery from the terraces, rooms 4 and 5, and from the five-bed, zero-security dorm. The restaurant prepares Dhankar's widest range of international food (mains ₹130 to ₹380) and decent coffee.

Manirang Home Stay & Cafe HOMESTAY $
(☑ 8988053409; per person incl half-board ₹600; ⊙ cafe 7am-8pm) Around halfway between the new and old monasteries, a descending road doubles back to what's signed as a cafe (international selection) but is also a very archetypal local homestay with superb views of the monastery. Prices are the same whether you sleep in a dorm with floor-mattress or in a private room with bed. The shared dry eco-toilet is indoors.

ℹ Getting There & Away

Tiny Shichling is the nearest main-road town to Dhankar, one hour southeast of Kaza (₹40), 45 minutes west of Tabo (₹35). Here you could ask at the Manerang Food Corner to help you find a local driver to Dhankar monastery (₹500). An official taxi all the way from Kaza to Dhankar costs ₹1550/1860 one way/return, though some Kaza guesthouses can do better, perhaps ₹1500 for the Kaza–Lahlung–Dhankar–Kaza loop.

Lhalung

Hidden up the Lingti Valley, the charming and totally uncommercial village of Lhalung is a series of well-spaced traditional Spitian houses layered up the terraced mountainside. At its upper limit, the outwardly modest medieval monastery contains interior sculptures so remarkable that locals consider them the work of God not man. It's also worth peeping into the side chapel to see a prayer wheel made of painted skin. Across the lawn in the separate even smaller Langkharpo chapel, a unique if unrefined four-sided statue of the white deity sits atop a plinth of snow lions.

Several unmarked homestays charge ₹600 to ₹750 per person including meals.

If you turn east off the main Kaza–Tabo road 16km south of Kaza, Lhalung monastery is reached by 13km of asphalt switchbacks. At Km4.6 of this snake, a 5km unpaved lane cuts across to Dhankar, allowing a two-monastery loop without descending right back to the valley floor.

A daily bus to Lhalung (₹45, two hours; not via Dhankar) leaves Kaza at 5pm, returning next morning at 7am.

Tabo

☑ 01906 / POP 600 / ELEV 3280M

The tiny town of Tabo has a dramatic valley setting, hemmed in by scree slopes 48km southeast of Kaza. Its star attraction, hidden behind uncoloured mud-brick walls, is Tabo Gompa's extraordinary interior featuring some of the finest Indo-Tibetan art found anywhere.

◉ Sights

★ Tabo Gompa
BUDDHIST MONASTERY

(www.tabomonastery.com; donations accepted; ☺ shrines 9am-1pm & 2-4.30pm) Founded in AD 996, and retaining five sub-temples dating back over 900 years, Tabo Gompa is reckoned to be the oldest continuously functioning Buddhist monastery in India. Don't expect the towering, colourful structures of Ladakh: the temples here are low-rise structures whose uncoloured mud exteriors are faintly reminiscent of ancient Malian mosques. Without artificial light, the half-dark intensifies the mystique of the interiors, albeit making it hard to see the detail of many masterpieces of mural and sculpture. No photography inside.

The old gompa's undoubted highlight is the Tsuglkang (main assembly hall) dating back to the monastery's first foundation, possibly by Ringchen Zangpo, the Great Translator. It is entered through the muralled 16th-century Zal-ma antechamber where bags, phones, cameras and torches must be left behind. Two blue protector deities in wonderfully naïve style guard the next doorway, behind which the hall's walls are lined with a remarkable array of near life-size clay sculptures: 28 bodhisattvas plus two more protectors. Murals below depict 10th-century life. The hall's focus is a statue of a four-bodied Vairochana Buddha turning the wheel of law, the whole room being a 3D representation of the Vajradhatu mandala with Vairochana at its centre. Behind, venturing into the unlit inner sanctuary is an eerie experience, with silhouettes of unseen figures suddenly appearing from the gloom as you try to make out the features of a stucco Amitabha Buddha.

To see inside the other smaller sub-temples you might need to ask an attendant to unlock them. Most dramatic of these is the Byams-Pa Chen-po Lha-Khang containing a 3m-high statue of the Maitreya (future Buddha) draped in golden cloth and holding up a reddened palm in a sign of meditation.

Just outside the ancient compound is a sparkling gilded chorten with bulbous midriff, and a brand new monastery, which is where most of the 50 or so monks spend their time. However, despite its partial museumisation, the old gompa still has chanting ceremonies at 6am (one hour) and 4.40pm (20 minutes). You're not allowed in at these times but can enjoy the sounds from outside the building.

Caves
CAVE

A number of small caves, whose openings are easily visible on the hillside just above the main road, were once part of the old monastery complex. Access is a steep 200m walk starting up the steps opposite the Vijay Kumar shop.

🛏 Sleeping & Eating

Tashi Khangsar Hotel
GUESTHOUSE $

(☑ 9418817761, 9418646578; www.spitiyakomyeti.com; r ₹800-1000, camping per tent ₹200; ☺ mid-Mar–Oct) This old-school backpacker favourite has a relaxed, friendly vibe and, though the four rooms are a tad dated, the charm is in sharing the expansive, grassy garden serenaded by rushing water of the nearby river. With books to read and games to play you might want to linger.

From the new monastery's gate, head for the helipad then turn right.

★ Maitreya Regency
BOUTIQUE HOTEL $$

(☑ 8988091566, 9459483103; www.maitreya regencytabo.in; with/without balcony ₹3000/2500) A Buddha figure and local costume displays lead guests into Tabo's most comfortable yet authentic-feeling hotel. Beautifully tiled-floor rooms have excellent beds, fine linens, silky cushions, sitting areas and modern bathrooms supplied with solar-heated water. The good restaurant offers a choice of seating at tables or traditionally on cushions at *chokse* carved benches.

It's next to more-conspicuous Snow Leopard Hotel, just 50m from SBI Bank towards the bus stand.

Cafe Kunzum Top
TIBETAN $

(Sonam Homestay; mains ₹100-350; ☺ 8am-9pm) Shaded by a parachute canopy held high on a prayer pole, Kunzum Top sits amid flowers in the walled yard of the **Sonam Homestay** ([icon]9459481431; www.spitisonamtours.com; r ₹700-1500, d/tr without bathroom ₹500/700; [icon]May-Oct) [icon], which is also a good budget place to stay. It specialises in local and Tibetan food, with a Spiti thali (₹190) giving a beginner's taster of the basics.

Tiger Den   MULTICUISINE $$
(mains ₹120-350; [icon]7am-9pm Apr-Oct) Tabo's most quintessential traveller cafe provides pitas, pizzas, lemon chicken and superb hummus along with Indian and Tibetan fare and so much more. It's set in a yard of hollyhocks and prayer flags, almost next to the new monastery's entrance. Good-value **rooms** ([icon]9459349711; r ₹900-1200; [icon]Apr-Oct) available, too.

[icon] Getting There & Away

Departure times can vary greatly but are approximately as follows:

Kaza (₹70, 2½ hours) 8.30am (ex-Sumdo) and 1pm (ex-Rekong Peo)

Rampur (₹320, 11 hours) 5am

Rekong Peo (₹270, 8½ hours) 5am and 9am, both via Nako (₹105, three hours). The latter originates in Kaza and can be packed.

The bus stand is a yard around 300m west of the monastery gates, just before the town's west gateway-arch. Many waiting passengers sit at the nearby Punjabi Dhaba. However, note that quite commonly the 5am Rekong Peo/Rampur bus actually starts from outside the more central SBI Bank.

There are no official taxis but with some notice hoteliers can often find a driver charging around ₹2000 to Kaza or Dhankar, ₹2500 to Nako or Mudh and ₹6000 to Rekong Peo.

Agra & the Taj Mahal

Best Places to Eat

➡ Pinch of Spice (p368)

➡ Mama Chicken (p368)

➡ Esphahan (p368)

➡ Culinary Junction (p368)

Best Places to Stay

➡ Tourists Rest House (p367)

➡ Bansi Homestay (p366)

➡ Oberoi Amarvilas (p366)

➡ Retreat (p366)

Why Go?

The Taj Mahal rises from Agra's haze as though from a dream. You've seen it in pictures, but experiencing it in person, you'll understand that it's not just a famous monument, but a love poem composed of stone. When you first glimpse it through the arched entryway, you might find yourself breathless with awe. Many hail it as the most beautiful building on the planet.

But Agra, situated along the Yamuna River in the state of Uttar Pradesh, is more than a one-sight town. For 130 years, this was the centre of India's great Mughal empire, and its legacy lives on in beautiful artwork, mouthwatering cuisine and magnificent architecture. The Taj is one of three places here that have been awarded Unesco World Heritage status, along with the immense Agra Fort and the sprawling palace complex of Fatehpur Sikri, which together make a superb trio of top-drawer sights.

When to Go
Agra

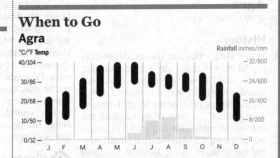

Mid-Sep–Oct The best time to visit: monsoon rains are over and summer temperatures have cooled.

Nov–Feb Daytime temperatures are comfortable but big sights are overcrowded. Evenings are nippy.

Mar Evening chill is gone but raging-hot midsummer temperatures haven't yet materialised.

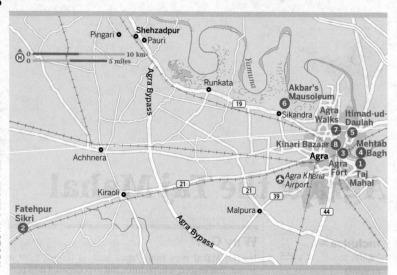

Agra & the Taj Mahal Highlights

1 Taj Mahal (p357) Basking in the beauty of one of the most famous buildings in the world – a must-see!

2 Fatehpur Sikri (p372) Roaming a sprawling palace complex from Mughal times, with an immense and fascinating 450-year-old mosque next door.

3 Agra Fort (p360)

Wandering the many rooms of one of India's most impressive ancient forts.

4 Mehtab Bagh (p363) Relaxing in gardens with perfect sunset views of the Taj.

5 Itimad-ud-Daulah (p363) Marvelling at the marblework of an exquisite tomb nicknamed the Baby Taj.

6 Akbar's Mausoleum (p363) Visiting the impressive resting place of the greatest Mughal emperor.

7 Agra Walks (p364) Strolling deeper into ancient Agra with local guides.

8 Kinari Bazaar (p363) Boggling your senses in one of India's most mesmerising – and hectic – markets.

Agra

☎ 0562 / POP 1.7 MILLION

History

In 1501 Sultan Sikander Lodi established his capital here, but the city fell into Mughal hands in 1526, when Emperor Babur defeated the last Lodi sultan at Panipat, 90km north of Delhi, to found the Mughal dynasty. Agra reached the peak of its magnificence between the mid-16th and mid-17th centuries as the capital of the Mughal empire during the reigns of Akbar, Jehangir and Shah Jahan. During this period, the fort, the Taj Mahal and other major mausoleums were built. In 1638 Shah Jahan built a new city in Delhi, and his son Aurangzeb moved the capital there 10 years later.

In 1761 Agra fell to the Jats, a warrior class who looted its monuments, including the Taj Mahal. The Marathas took over in 1770, but were replaced by the British in 1803. Following the First War of Independence (Indian Uprising) in 1857, the British shifted the administration of the province to Allahabad (now Prayagraj). Deprived of its administrative role, Agra developed as a centre for heavy industry, quickly becoming famous for its chemicals industry and air pollution, before the Taj and tourism became a major source of income.

◉ Sights

The entrance fee for Agra's five main sights – the Taj, Agra Fort, Fatehpur Sikri, Akbar's Tomb and Itimad-ud-Daulah – comprises charges from two different bodies: the Archaeological Survey of India (ASI) and the

Agra Development Association (ADA). Of the ₹1100 basic ticket for the Taj Mahal, ₹500 is a special ADA ticket, which gives you small savings on the other four sights if visited in the same day. You'll save ₹50 at Agra Fort and ₹10 each at Fatehpur Sikri, Akbar's Tomb and Itimad-ud-Daulah. You can buy this ₹500 ADA ticket at any of the five sights – just say you intend to visit the Taj later that day.

All the other sights in Agra are either free or have ASI tickets only, which aren't included in the ADA one-day offer.

Admission to all sights is free for children under 15. On Fridays, many sights offer a modest discount of ₹10 (but note that the Taj is closed on Friday).

★ **Taj Mahal**   HISTORIC BUILDING
(Map p365; 📞0562-2330498; www.tajmahal. gov.in; Indian/foreigner ₹50/1100, mausoleum ₹200, video ₹25; ⊙dawn-dusk Sat-Thu) Poet Rabindranath Tagore described it as 'a teardrop on the cheek of eternity'; Rudyard Kipling as 'the embodiment of all things pure'; while its creator, Emperor Shah Jahan, said it made 'the sun and the moon shed tears from their eyes'. Every year, tourists numbering more than twice the population of Agra pass through its gates to catch a once-in-a-lifetime glimpse of what is widely considered the most beautiful building in the world. Few leave disappointed.

The Taj was built by Shah Jahan as a memorial for his third wife, Mumtaz Mahal, who died giving birth to their 14th child in 1631. The death of Mumtaz left the emperor so heartbroken that his hair is said to have turned grey virtually overnight. Construction of the Taj began the following year; although the main building is thought to have been built in eight years, the whole complex was not completed until 1653. Not long after it was finished, Shah Jahan was overthrown by his son Aurangzeb and imprisoned in Agra Fort, where for the rest of his days he could only gaze out at his creation through a window. Following his death in 1666, Shah Jahan was buried here alongside his beloved Mumtaz.

In total, some 20,000 people from India and Central Asia worked on the building. Specialists were brought in from as far away as Europe to produce the exquisite marble screens and pietra dura (marble inlay work) made with thousands of semiprecious stones.

The Taj was designated a World Heritage Site in 1983 and looks nearly as immacu-

DON'T MISS

TAJ MUSEUM

Within the Taj complex, on the western side of the gardens, is the small but excellent **Taj Museum** (Map p365; ⊙10am-5pm Sat-Thu) `FREE`, housing a number of original Mughal miniature paintings, including a pair of 17th-century ivory portraits of Emperor Shah Jahan and his beloved wife Mumtaz Mahal. It also has some very well preserved gold and silver coins dating from the same period, plus architectural drawings of the Taj and some celadon plates, said to split into pieces or change colour if the food served on them contains poison.

late today as when it was first constructed – though it underwent a huge restoration project in the early 20th century.

Note: the Taj is closed every Friday to anyone not attending prayers at the mosque.

➡ **Entry & Information**
The Taj can be accessed through the west and east gates. The south gate was closed to visitors in 2018 for security concerns but can be used to exit the Taj. The east gate generally has shorter queues. There are separate queues for men and women at both gates. If you are a foreigner, once you get your ticket, you can skip ahead of the lines of Indians waiting to get in – one perk of your pricey entry fee. It's possible to buy your tickets online in advance at https://asi. payumoney.com (you'll get a ₹50 discount for your troubles), but you won't save much time as you still have to join the main security queue. A ticket that includes entrance to the mausoleum itself cost ₹200 extra.

Cameras and videos are permitted, but you can't take photographs inside the mausoleum itself. Tripods are banned.

Remember to retrieve your free 500ml bottle of water and shoe covers (included in Taj ticket price). Bags much bigger than a money pouch are not allowed inside; free bag storage is available. Any food or tobacco will be confiscated when you go through security, as will pens.

➡ **Inside the Grounds**
From both the east and west gates you first enter a monumental inner courtyard with an impressive 30m red-sandstone gateway on the south side.

continued on p360

Taj Mahal

TIMELINE

1631 Emperor Shah Jahan's beloved third wife, Mumtaz Mahal, dies in Buhanpur while giving birth to their 14th child. Her body is initially interred in Buhanpur itself, where Shah Jahan is fighting a military campaign, but is later moved, in a golden casket, to a small building on the banks of the Yamuna River in Agra.

1632 Construction of a permanent mausoleum for Mumtaz Mahal begins.

1633 Mumtaz Mahal is interred in her final resting place, an underground tomb beneath a marble plinth, on top of which the Taj Mahal will be built.

1640 The white-marble mausoleum is completed.

1653 The rest of the Taj Mahal complex is completed.

1658 Emperor Shah Jahan is overthrown by his son Aurangzeb and imprisoned in Agra Fort.

1666 Shah Jahan dies. His body is transported along the Yamuna River and buried underneath the Taj, alongside the tomb of his wife.

1908 Repeatedly damaged and looted after the fall of the Mughal empire, the Taj receives some long-overdue attention as part of a major restoration project ordered by British viceroy Lord Curzon.

1983 The Taj is awarded Unesco World Heritage Site status.

2002 Having been discoloured by pollution in more recent years, the Taj is spruced up with an ancient recipe known as multani mitti – a blend of soil, cereal, milk and lime once used by Indian women to beautify their skin.

Today More than three million tourists visit the Taj Mahal each year. That's more than twice the current population of Agra.

GO BAREFOOT

Help the environment by entering the mausoleum barefoot instead of using the free disposable shoe covers.

Pishtaqs
These huge arched recesses are set into each side of the Taj. They provide depth to the building while their central, latticed marble screens allow patterned light to illuminate the inside of the mausoleum.

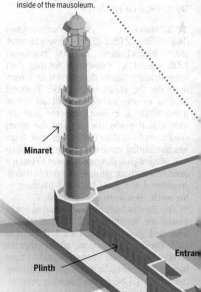

Minaret

Plinth

Entrance

Marble Relief Work
Flowering plants, thought to be representations of paradise, are a common theme among the beautifully decorative panels carved onto the white marble.

LIGHT THE WAY

Use the torch on your smartphone to fully appreciate the translucency of the white marble and semi-precious stones.

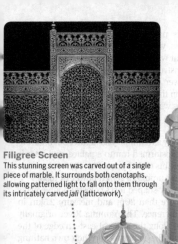

Filigree Screen
This stunning screen was carved out of a single piece of marble. It surrounds both cenotaphs, allowing patterned light to fall onto them through its intricately carved *jali* (latticework).

Central Dome
The Taj's famous central dome, topped by a brass finial, represents the vault of heaven, a stark contrast to the material world, which is represented by the square shape of the main structure.

Yamuna River

NORTH →

Pietra Dura
It's believed that 35 different precious and semi-precious stones were used to create the exquisite pietra dura (marble inlay work) found on the inside and outside of the mausoleum walls. Again, floral designs are common.

Calligraphy
The strips of calligraphy surrounding each of the four pishtaqs get larger as they get higher, giving the impression of uniform size when viewed from the ground. There's also calligraphy inside the mausoleum, including on Mumtaz Mahal's cenotaph.

Cenotaphs
The cenotaphs of Mumtaz Mahal and Shah Jahan, decorated with pietra dura inlay work, are actually fake tombs. The real ones are located in an underground vault closed to the public.

continued from p357

The ornamental gardens are set out along classical Mughal *charbagh* (formal Persian garden) lines – a square quartered by watercourses, with an ornamental marble plinth at its centre. When the fountains are not flowing, the Taj is beautifully reflected in the water.

The Taj Mahal itself stands on a raised marble platform at the northern end of the ornamental gardens, with its back to the Yamuna River. Its raised position means that the backdrop is only sky – a masterstroke of design. Purely decorative 40m-high white minarets grace each corner of the platform. After more than three centuries they are not quite perpendicular, but they may have been designed to lean slightly outwards so that in the event of an earthquake they would fall away from the precious Taj. The red-sandstone mosque to the west is an important gathering place for Agra's Muslims. The identical building to the east, the jawab, was built for symmetry.

The central Taj structure is made of semitranslucent white marble, carved with flowers and inlaid with thousands of semi-precious stones in beautiful patterns. A perfect exercise in symmetry, the four identical faces of the Taj feature impressive vaulted arches embellished with pietra dura scrollwork and quotations from the Quran in a style of calligraphy using inlaid jasper. The whole structure is topped off by four small domes surrounding the famous bulbous central dome.

Directly below the main dome is the Cenotaph of Mumtaz Mahal, an elaborate false tomb surrounded by an exquisite perforated marble screen inlaid with dozens of different types of semiprecious stones. Beside it, offsetting the symmetry of the Taj, is the Cenotaph of Shah Jahan, who was interred here with little ceremony by his usurping son Aurangzeb in 1666. Light is admitted into the central chamber by finely cut marble screens.

The real tombs of Mumtaz Mahal and Shah Jahan are in a basement room below the main chamber.

★ **Agra Fort** FORT
(Lal Qila; Map p361; Indian/foreigner ₹50/650, video ₹25; ⊙ dawn-dusk) With the Taj Mahal overshadowing it, one can easily forget that Agra has one of the finest Mughal forts in India. Walking through courtyard after courtyard of this palatial red-sandstone and marble fortress, your amazement grows as the scale of what was built here begins to sink in.

Construction along the bank of the Yamuna River was begun by Emperor Akbar in 1565 on the site of an earlier fort. Further additions were made, particularly by his grandson Shah Jahan, using his favourite building material – white marble. The fort was built primarily as a military structure, but Shah Jahan transformed it into a palace, and later it became his gilded prison for eight years after his son Aurangzeb seized power in 1658.

The ear-shaped fort's colossal double walls rise more than 20m and measure 2.5km in circumference. The Yamuna River originally flowed along the straight eastern edge of the fort, and the emperors had their own bathing ghats here. It contains a maze of buildings, forming a city within a city, including vast underground sections, though many of the structures were destroyed over the years by Nadir Shah, the Marathas, the Jats and finally the British, who used the fort as a garrison. Even today, much of the fort is used by the military and is off-limits to the general public.

The Amar Singh Gate to the south is the sole entry point to the fort these days and where you buy your entrance ticket. Its dog-leg design was meant to confuse attackers who made it past the first line of defence – the crocodile-infested moat.

Following the plain processional way you reach a gateway and the huge red-sandstone Jehangir's Palace on the right. In front of the palace is Hauz-i-Jehangir, a huge bowl carved out of a single block of stone, which was used for bathing. The palace was probably built by Akbar for his son Jehangir. With tall stone pillars and corner brackets, it blends Indian and Central Asian architectural styles, a reminder of the Mughals' Turkestani cultural roots.

Further along the eastern edge of the fort you'll find the Khas Mahal, a beautiful marble pavilion and pool that formed the living quarters of Shah Jahan. Taj views are framed in the ornate marble grills.

The large courtyard here is Anguri Bagh, a garden that has been brought back to life in recent years. In the courtyard is an innocuous-looking entrance – now locked – that leads down a flight of stairs into a two-storey labyrinth of underground rooms and passageways where Akbar used to keep his 500-strong harem. On the northeast corner of the courtyard you can get a glimpse of the

Agra

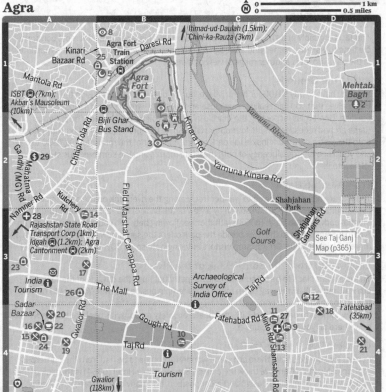

LOCAL KNOWLEDGE

TOP TAJ VIEWS

The Taj is arguably at its most atmospheric at sunrise. This is certainly the most comfortable time to visit in summer, and although it's still popular, there are fewer crowds than later in the day. Sunset is another magical viewing time.

Inside the Grounds

You may have to pay ₹1100 for the privilege, but it's only when you're inside the grounds themselves that you can really get up close and personal with the world's most beautiful building. Don't miss inspecting the marble inlay work (pietra dura) inside the *pishtaqs* (large arched recesses) on the four outer walls. Shine the torch (flashlight) on your phone onto the pietra dura work inside the dark central chamber of the mausoleum (₹200 extra) and you'll see the translucency of both the white marble and the semiprecious stones inlaid into it.

From Mehtab Bagh

Tourists are no longer allowed to wander freely along the riverbank on the opposite side of the Yamuna River, but you can still enjoy a view of the back of the Taj from the 16th-century Mughal park Mehtab Bagh (p363), with the river flowing between you and the mausoleum. A path leading down to the river beside the park offers the same view for free, albeit from a more restricted angle. Guards stop visitors entering both spots 30 minutes before sunset.

Looking Up from the South Bank of the River

This is a great place to be for sunset. Take the path that hugs the outside of the Taj's eastern wall and walk all the way down to the small temple beside the river. You should be able to find boathands down here willing to row you out onto the water for an even more romantic view. Expect to pay around ₹150 per boat. For safety reasons, it's best not to wander down here on your own for sunset.

On a Rooftop Cafe in Taj Ganj

Perfect for sunrise shots: there are some wonderful photos to be had from the numerous rooftop cafes in Taj Ganj. We think the cafe on Saniya Palace Hotel (p364) is the pick of the bunch, with its plant-filled design and great position, but many of them are good. And all offer the bonus of being able to view the Taj with the added comfort of an early-morning cup of coffee.

From Agra Fort

With a decent zoom lens you can capture some fabulous images of the Taj from Agra Fort (p360), especially if you're willing to get up at the crack of dawn to see the sun rising up from behind it (the fort opens 30 minutes before dawn). The best places to snap from are probably the Khas Mahal or Muthamman Burj, the octagonal tower and palace where Shah Jahan was imprisoned for eight years until his death.

Shish Mahal (Mirror Palace), with walls inlaid with tiny mirrors.

Just to the north of the Khas Mahal is the Mathamman (Shah) Burj, the wonderful white-marble octagonal tower and palace where Shah Jahan was imprisoned for eight years until his death in 1666, and from where he could gaze out at the Taj Mahal, the tomb of his wife. When he died, Shah Jahan's body was taken from here by boat to the Taj. The now-closed Mina Masjid served as Shah Jahan's private mosque.

As you enter the large courtyard, along the eastern wall of the fort, is Diwan-i-Khas (Hall of Private Audiences), which was re-

served for important dignitaries or foreign representatives. The hall once housed Shah Jahan's legendary Peacock Throne, which was inset with precious stones – including the famous Koh-i-noor diamond. The throne was taken to Delhi by Aurangzeb, then to Iran in 1739 by Nadir Shah and dismantled after his assassination in 1747. Overlooking the river and the distant Taj Mahal is Takhti-i-Jehangir, a huge slab of black rock with an inscription around the edge. The throne that stood here was made for Jehangir when he was Prince Salim.

Following the north side of the courtyard a side door leads to the tiny but exquisite white-marbled Nagina Masjid (Gem Mosque), built in 1635 by Shah Jahan for the ladies of the court. Down below was the Ladies' Bazaar, where the court ladies bought their goods.

A hidden doorway near the mosque exit leads down to the scallop-shaped arches of the large, open Diwan-i-Am (Hall of Public Audiences), which was used by Shah Jahan for domestic government business, and features a beautifully decorated throne room where the emperor listened to petitioners. In front of it is the small and rather incongruous grave of John Colvin, a lieutenant-governor of the northwest provinces who died of an illness while sheltering in the fort during the 1857 First War of Independence. To the north is the Moti Masjid, currently off limits to visitors. From here head back to the Amar Singh gate.

You can walk to the fort from Taj Ganj via the leafy Shah Jahan Park, or take an autorickshaw for ₹80. Food is not allowed into the fort. The fort opens 30 minutes before sunrise; the ticket office opens 15 minutes before that. Last entry is 30 minutes before sunset.

★**Mehtab Bagh**   PARK
(Map p361; Indian/foreigner ₹25/300, video ₹25; ⊙dawn-dusk) This park, originally built by Emperor Babur as the last in a series of 11 parks on the Yamuna's east bank (long before the Taj was conceived), fell into disrepair until it was little more than a huge mound of sand. To protect the Taj from the erosive effects of the sand blown across the river, the park was reconstructed and is now one the best places from which to view the great mausoleum.

The gardens in the Taj are perfectly aligned with the ones here, and the view of the Taj from the fountain directly in front of the entrance gate is a classic. It's a popular spot at sunset; the ticket office closes 30 minutes before sunset, so don't leave it too late. An autorickshaw here from central Agra costs around ₹150.

★**Itimad-ud-Daulah**   HISTORIC BUILDING
(Indian/foreigner ₹30/310, video ₹25; ⊙dawn-dusk) Nicknamed the Baby Taj, the exquisite tomb of Mizra Ghiyas Beg should not be missed. This Persian nobleman was Mumtaz Mahal's grandfather and Emperor Jehangir's *wazir* (chief minister). His daughter, Nur Jahan, who married Jehangir, built the tomb between 1622 and 1628, in a style similar to the tomb she built for Jehangir near Lahore in Pakistan.

It doesn't have the same awesome beauty as the Taj, but it's arguably more delicate in appearance thanks to its particularly finely carved marble *jalis* (lattice screens). This was the first Mughal structure built completely from marble, the first to make extensive use of pietra dura and the first tomb to be built on the banks of the Yamuna, which until then had been a sequence of beautiful pleasure gardens.

You can combine a trip here with Chini-ka-Rauza (p364) and Mehtab Bagh, all on the east bank. An autorickshaw covering all three should cost about ₹500 return from the Taj, including waiting time.

★**Akbar's Mausoleum**   HISTORIC BUILDING
(Indian/foreigner ₹30/310, video ₹25; ⊙dawn-dusk) This outstanding sandstone and marble tomb commemorates the greatest of the Mughal emperors. The huge courtyard is entered through a stunning gateway decorated with three-storey minarets at each corner and built of red sandstone strikingly inlaid with white-, yellow- and blue-marble geometric and floral patterns. The interior vestibule of the tomb is stunningly decorated with painted alabaster, creating a contrast to the plain inner tomb. The unusual upper pavillions are closed. Look for deer in the surrounding gardens.

The mausoleum is at Sikandra, 10km northwest of Agra Fort. Catch a bus (₹25, 45 minutes) headed to Mathura from Bijli Ghar (p371) bus stand; they go past the mausoleum. Or else take an autorickshaw (₹350 return) or an Ola taxi.

Kinari Bazaar   MARKET
(Map p361; ⊙11am-9pm Wed-Mon) The narrow streets behind Jama Masjid are a crazy maze

---

TOP AGRA FESTIVALS

Taj Mahotsav (www.tajmahotsav.org; ⊙Feb) A 10-day carnival of culture, cuisine and crafts – Agra's biggest party of the year.

Kailash Fair (⊙Aug/Sep) A cultural and religious fair honouring Lord Shiva.

Ram Barat (⊙Sep) An over-the-top dramatic re-creation of the royal wedding procession of Rama and Sita.

of overcrowded lanes bursting with colourful markets. There are a number of different bazaars here, each specialising in different wares, but the area is generally known as Kinari Bazaar as many of the lanes fan out from Kinari Bazaar Rd. You'll find clothing, shoes, fabrics, jewellery, spices, marblework, snack stalls and what seems like 20 million other people.

Amazingly, there is somehow room for buffaloes and even the odd working elephant to squeeze their way through the crowds. Even if you're not buying anything, just walking the streets is an experience in itself.

Chini-ka-Rauza   HISTORIC BUILDING

(⊙dawn-dusk) **FREE** This Persian-style riverside tomb of Afzal Khan, a poet who served as Shah Jahan's chief minister, was built between 1628 and 1639. Rarely visited, it is hidden away down a shady avenue of trees on the east bank of the Yamuna but boasts a fine exterior of coloured tilework and an interior of delicate painted alabaster.

Jama Masjid   MOSQUE

(Map p361; Jama Masjid Rd; ⊙dawn-dusk) This fine mosque, built in the Kinari Bazaar (p363) by Shah Jahan's daughter in 1648 and once connected to Agra Fort, features striking zigzag marble patterning on its domes. The entrance is on the east side.

🏃 Activities & Tours

Hotels allowing nonguests to use their swimming pools include Howard Plaza (p366), ₹1000, and **Amar** (Map p361; ☑0562-4027000; www.hotelamar.com; Fatehabad Rd), ₹650 – with slide.

Agra by Bike   CYCLING

(☑9368112527; www.agrabybike.com; East Gate Rd; per person US$30) John and Moses Rosario get rave reviews for their bike tours of the city and surrounding countryside, most of which end with a boat trip on the Yamuna River behind the Taj. They also offer food walks and Indian cooking classes.

Agra Walks   WALKING

(☑9027711144; www.agrawalks.com; ₹2500) Many folks spend but a day in Agra, taking in the Taj and Agra Fort and sailing off into the sunset. If you're interested in digging a little deeper, this excellent walking/cycle-rickshaw combo tour will show you sides of the city most tourists don't see.

Amin Tours   CULTURAL

(☑9837411144; www.daytourtajmahal.com) If you can't be bothered handling the logistics, look no further than this recommended agency for all-inclusive private Agra day trips from Delhi by car (from US$85 per person, depending on number in group) or express train (from US$90 per person). Caveat: if they try to take you shopping and you're not interested, politely decline.

Taj by Moonlight   TOURS

(Map p365; adult/child Indian ₹510/500, foreigner ₹750/500; ⊙closed Fri & Ramadan) For five nights around the full moon the Taj by Moonlight is open to groups of 50 people in a series of eight 30-minute time slots between 8.30pm and 12.30am. You can only view the Taj from the entry gate viewing area and you only get 30 minutes there, making this an expensive option, but some people love it. The later time slots are best for moonlight views.

Tickets must be bought a day in advance from the **Archaeological Survey of India** (ASI; Map p361; ☑0562-2227261; www.asiagracircle.in; 22 The Mall; ⊙10am-6pm Mon-Fri) office; see its website for details. (Note: this office is known as the Taj Mahal Office by some rickshaw riders.) You need to go through security clearance at the **Shilpgram Tourist Facilitation Centre** (Taj East Gate Rd; ⊙9.30am-5pm Sat-Thu) first, before being taken by security on an electric bus to the eastern gate.

🛌 Sleeping

The main place for budget accommodation is the bustling area of Taj Ganj, immediately south of the Taj, while there's a high concentration of midrange hotels further south, along Fatehabad Rd. Sadar Bazaar, an area boasting good restaurants, offers another option.

🛏 Taj Ganj Area

Saniya Palace Hotel   HOTEL $

(Map p365; ☑8881270199; www.saniyapalace.in; Chowk Kagziyan, Taj South Gate; r with/without AC from ₹1300/600; ❄@🛜) Set back from the main strip down an undesirable alleyway, this isn't the sleekest Taj Ganj option, but it tries to imbue character with marble floors and framed Mughal-style carpet wall hangings. The rooms are clean and large enough, although the bathrooms in the non-AC rooms are minuscule.

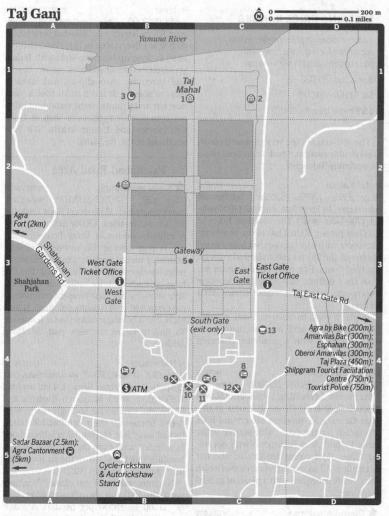

Taj Ganj

Taj Ganj

◉ Top Sights
1 Taj Mahal B1

◉ Sights
2 Jawab C1
3 Mosque B1
4 Taj Museum B2

✪ Activities, Courses & Tours
5 Taj by Moonlight B3

🛏 Sleeping
6 Hotel Kamal C4

7 Hotel Sidhartha B4
8 Saniya Palace Hotel C4

🍽 Eating
9 Joney's Place B4
Saniya Palace Hotel .... (see 8)
10 Shankara Vegis B4
11 Taj Cafe C4
12 Yash Cafe C4

🍷 Drinking & Nightlife
13 Café Coffee Day C4

SLEEPING PRICE RANGES

Accommodation price ranges in this region are for a double room with private bathroom in high season:

$ less than ₹1500

$$ ₹1500–₹4000

$$$ more than ₹4000

The real coup is the very pleasant, plant-filled double rooftop, which trumps its rivals for optimum Taj views.

Hotel Kamal
HOTEL **$**

(Map p365; ☑0562-2330126; hotelkamal@hotmail.com; Taj South Gate; r with AC ₹2000, without ₹700-1400; ✳🛜) The smartest hotel in Taj Ganj proper, Kamal has clean, comfortable rooms with nice touches, such as framed photos of the Taj on the walls and rugs on the tiled floors. Five rooms in the newer annexe are a definite step up, with welcoming woodwork, extra space and stone-walled showers.

It has a cosy, bamboo-enclosed ground-floor restaurant and an underused rooftop restaurant with a somewhat-obscured Taj view.

Hotel Sidhartha
HOTEL **$**

(Map p365; ☑0562-2230901; www.hotelsidhartha.com; Taj West Gate; r with/without AC from ₹1500/950; ✳@🛜) Of the 21 rooms in this West Gate staple, those on the ground floor are stylish for the price, with marble walls, cable TV and clean bathrooms with hot water. Upper-floor rooms are smaller and not as exciting. All rooms surround or overlook a small, leafy courtyard with a pleasant gazebo restaurant.

★ Oberoi Amarvilas
HOTEL **$$$**

(☑0562-2231515; www.oberoihotels.com; Taj East Gate Rd; d with/without balcony ₹95,000/80,500; ✳@🛜⛱) Following Oberoi's iron-clad modus operandi of maharaja-level service, exquisite dining and properties that pack some serious wow factor, Agra's best hotel by far oozes style and luxury. Elegant interior design is suffused with Mughal themes, a composition carried over into the exterior fountain courtyard and stunning swimming pool, both of which are set in a delightful stepped water garden. All rooms (and even some bathtubs) have wonderful Taj views. Online discounts of 30% are common.

Retreat
BOUTIQUE HOTEL **$$$**

(☑8810022200; www.theretreat.co.in; Shilpgram Rd, Taj Nagari; r incl breakfast from ₹4500; ✳@🛜⛱) Everything in this sleek, 51-room hotel is done up boutique-style with Indian sensibilities (lots of soothing mauve, mocha and turquoise throughout), and modern fixtures abound. It has a small pool, a sleek new bar and a multicuisine restaurant offering countrywide specialities such as Goan fish curries and Lahori kebabs. It's 2km southeast of the Taj Mahal.

🛏 Fatehabad Road Area

★ Bansi Homestay
HOMESTAY **$$**

(Map p361; ☑0562-2333033; www.bansihomestayagra.com; 18 Handicraft Nagar, Fatehabad Rd; s/d incl breakfast ₹3000/3500; ✳🛜) 🍃 A retired director of Uttar Pradesh Tourism is your host at this wonderful upscale homestay tucked away in a quiet residential neighbourhood near Fatahabad Rd. The five large rooms boast huge bathrooms with rain-style showers and flank pleasant common areas decorated with Krishna paintings. It feels more like a boutique hotel than a homestay. To find it, follow the alley past the Hotel Atithi.

N Homestay
HOMESTAY **$$**

(Map p361; ☑9690107860; www.nhomestay.com; 15 Ajanta Colony, Vibhav Nagar; s/d incl breakfast ₹1800/2000; ✳🛜) Matriarch Naghma and her helpful sons are the highlight of this wonderful homestay. Their comfortable home, tucked away in a residential neighbourhood 15 minutes' walk from the Taj's West Gate, is blissfully quiet, and two of the six rooms feature spacious balconies (₹2200).

Naghma will cook you dinner (veg/nonveg ₹400/600) and also offers cooking classes (₹1500 to ₹3500 per person). A single dorm (₹800) with four bunk beds and private bathroom offers a budget option.

Howard Plaza
HOTEL **$$$**

(The Fern; Map p361; ☑0562-4048600; www.howardplazaagra.com; Fatehabad Rd; s/d incl breakfast from ₹4500/5500; ✳🛜⛱) Rooms in this very welcoming hotel are decked out in elegant dark-wood furniture and stylish decorative tiling. The slightly pricier Club rooms have nicer decor and bathrooms. You won't find much to fault in either category.

The pool is starting to show its age, but there's a small, well-equipped gym and a very pleasant spa offering a whole range of ayurvedic and massage treatments, including the so-called 'erotic bath' of milk, cinnamon and honey. The breezy, open-air rooftop restaurant doubles as one of the few atmospheric bars in town at night (beer ₹325, cocktails ₹400), with distant Taj views.

Hotel Atithi · HOTEL $$$

(Map p361; ☑0562-2330880; www.hotelatithi agra.com; Fatehabad Rd; s/d from ₹3700/4500; ❋@◉❄◙) Simple but superclean and comfortable rooms here are a decent size – no reason to spring for deluxe rooms. Guests can use the murky swimming pool in the next-door garden wedding venue for free. It's set back from the road and so is quieter than most.

Sadar Bazaar Area

★ Tourists Rest House · HOTEL $

(Map p361; ☑0562-2463961; www.dontworry chickencurry.com; 4/62 Kutchery Rd; s/d with AC ₹800/999, without from ₹500/650; ❋◙◉) If you aren't set on sleeping under the nose of the Taj, this centrally located travellers' hub offers the best-value accommodation in Agra, if not the whole state. It's been under the watchful eye of the same family since 1965, and it's still a great choice.

If you can forgo AC, the fresh and modern cheapies are great value – and things only get better from there. All rooms come with TV, hot water and large windows, and are set around a peaceful plant-filled, palm-shaded courtyard (a real highlight) and a North Indian pure veg restaurant. The bend-over-backwards owners couldn't be more helpful and can solve most of your travel needs. Phone or email ahead for a free pickup. Damn fine masala chai too. Don't let rickshaw drivers confuse you with similarly named but inferior competition.

Clarks Shiraz Hotel · HOTEL $$$

(Map p361; ☑0562-2226121; www.hotelclarksshi raz.com; 54 Taj Rd; r incl breakfast from ₹7670; ❋@◉❄◙) Agra's original five-star hotel, opened in 1961, has done well to keep up with the hotel Joneses. The standard doubles are nothing special for this price range, but the marble-floored premium versions (₹8850) are a pleasant step up, and all bathrooms have been retiled and are spotless.

There are three good restaurants, a rooftop bar, a huge palm-fringed garden and pool area (one of Agra's best) and ayurvedic massages. Some rooms have distant Taj views.

✖ Eating

✖ Taj Ganj Area

Saniya Palace Hotel · MULTICUISINE $

(Map p365; Chowk Kagziyan, Taj South Gate; mains ₹100-200; ◷6am-10pm; ◉) With cute tablecloths, dozens of potted plants and a bamboo pergola for shade, this is the most pleasant rooftop restaurant in Taj Ganj. It also has the best rooftop view of the Taj, bar none. The kitchen is a bit rough and ready, but the Western dishes and Western-friendly Indian dishes are fine and you are really here for the views.

Taj Cafe · MULTICUISINE $

(Map p365; Chowk Kagziyan; mains ₹50-200; ◷7am-11pm; ◉) Up a flight of steps and overlooking Taj Ganj's busy street scene, this friendly, family-run restaurant is a nice choice if you're not fussed about Taj views. There's a good choice of breakfasts, thalis (₹90 to ₹140) and pizza (₹160 to ₹200), and the lassis here won't disappoint.

Joney's Place · MULTICUISINE $

(Map p365; Kutta Park, Taj Ganj; mains ₹70-120; ◷5am-10.30pm) This pocket-sized institution whipped up its first creamy lassi in 1978 and continues to please despite cooking its meals in what must be Agra's smallest kitchen. The cheese and tomato 'jayfelles' (toasted sandwich), the banana lassi (with money-back guarantee) and the *malai* kofta (paneer cooked in a creamy sauce of cashews and tomato) all come recommended, but it's more about crack-of-dawn sustenance than culinary dazzle.

Shankara Vegis · VEGETARIAN $

(Map p365; Chowk Kagziyan; mains ₹90-150; ◷8am-10.30pm; ◉) Most restaurants in Taj Ganj ooze a distinct air of mediocrity – Shankara Vegis is different. This cosy old-timer, with its red tablecloths and straw-lined walls, stands out for great vegetarian thalis (₹140 to ₹250) and, most pleasantly, the genuinely friendly, nonpushy ethos of its hands-on owners. Try the rooftop.

Yash Cafe · MULTICUISINE $$

(Map p365; 3/137 Chowk Kagziyan; mains ₹100-260; ◷7am-10.30pm; ◉) This chilled-out, 1st-floor cafe has wicker chairs, sports channels on TV, DVDs shown in the evening and a good range of meals, from good-value set breakfasts to thalis (₹90), pizza (₹90 to ₹300)

LOCAL KNOWLEDGE

CHAAT GALLI

Fans of street food should make a beeline for the Sadaar Bazaar district . Not only will you find multiple outlets of Mama Chicken, but you can fill up in the nearby *chaat galli* (snack alley), home to a dozen excellent street-food stalls.

First port of call is **Agra Chat House** (Map p361; Chaat Galli, Sadar Bazaar; snacks ₹50-60; ☉1-11pm), the oldest of the street stalls, or the next-door Agarwal Chat House, to invest in a selection of aloo tikki chaat (fried potato croquettes with tamarind sauce, yoghurt, coriander and pomegranate), *dahi bada* (dumplings with yoghurt and tamarind), *chila mong dal* (lentil pancake), *bhalla* (croquette of green bean paste with yoghurt and chutney) or *galgapa* (little *puri* shells filled with flavoured sauce). At around ₹50 a dish you can afford to explore the simple menus.

For dessert, several nearby stalls sell delicious mango or *kaju pista* (cashew and pistachio) *kulfi* (firm-textured ice cream), as well as refreshing *falooda* (cold dessert of rosewater, vermicelli, jelly and milk).

As if that wasn't enough, just round the corner is Panchhi Peta, a tiny branch of Agra's most famous *peitha* shop, offering to-go boxes of Agra's famous sweet (made from pumpkin and glucose, usually flavoured with rosewater, coconut or saffron).

and Indian-style French toast (with coconut – we think they made that up). It also offers a shower and storage space (₹50 for both) to day visitors.

★**Esphahan**　　　NORTH INDIAN $$$
(☎0562-2231515; Taj East Gate Rd, Oberoi Amarvilas Hotel; mains ₹1550-3500; ☉dinner 6.30pm & 9pm; ❈) There are only two sittings each evening at Agra's finest restaurant, so booking ahead is essential, especially as non-hotel-guest tables are limited. The exquisite menu is chock-full of unique delicacies, with the modern fusion tasting menus and Indian thalis offering the best selection.

🍴 Fatehabad Road Area

Culinary Junction　　　INDIAN $$
(www.culinaryjunctionbyudupi.com; 1st fl Arvind Innov8, Fatehabad Rd; mains ₹200-300; ☉noon-11pm; 🍴) It's worth taking a taxi out to this excellent new vegetarian restaurant in the east of town near the Trident Hotel. The tangy and tasty *paneer dhaniya adraki* (soft cheese in ginger and coriander gravy) is a treat, as is the *missi roti* (flatbread) and smoked paprika paneer tikka masala. Service is excellent and it's a modern, classy option.

Dasaprakash Xpress　　　SOUTH INDIAN $$
(Map p361; www.dasaprakashgroup.com; 921 Heritage Villa, Fatehabad Rd; mains ₹115-250; ❈🍴) The fast-food variant of the original Dasaprakash chain from Mysore offers the same great *dosas* (paper-thin lentil-flour pancakes), but in a simpler environment and at prices 40% less than the original.

★**Pinch of Spice**　　　MODERN INDIAN $$$
(Map p361; www.pinchofspice.in; 1076/2 Fatehabad Rd; mains ₹375-450; ☉noon-11.30pm) This modern North Indian superstar is the best spot outside five-star hotels to indulge yourself in rich curries and succulent tandoori kebabs. The *murg boti masala* (chicken tikka swimming in a rich and spicy gravy) and the *paneer lababdar* (unfermented cheese cubes in a spicy red gravy with sauteed onions) are outstanding. Portions are huge. There's also a full bar.

Located opposite the ITC Mughal Hotel. No reservations accepted.

🍴 Sadar Bazaar Area

Brijwasi　　　SWEETS $
(Map p361; Sadar Bazaar; sweets per kg from ₹320; ☉7am-11pm) Sugar-coma-inducing selection of traditional Indian sweets, nuts and biscuits on the ground floor. It's most famous for its *peda* (milk-based sweets), including excellent *rabri* (condensed milk with nuts and spices).

Lakshmi Vilas　　　SOUTH INDIAN $
(Map p361; 50A Taj Rd; mains ₹110-130; ☉11am-10.30pm Wed-Mon; ❈🍴) This no-nonsense, plainly decorated, nonsmoking restaurant is *the* place in Agra to come for affordable South Indian fare. The thali meal (₹160), served from noon to 3.30pm and 7pm to 10.30pm, is good.

★**Mama Chicken**　　　DHABA $$
(Map p361; Stall No 2, Sadar Bazaar; rolls ₹40-190, mains ₹230-290; ☉noon-midnight) This super-

star *dhaba* (casual eatery) is a must: duelling veg and nonveg glorified street stalls employ 24 cooks during the rush, each of whom handles outdoor tandoors, grills or pots. They whip up outrageously good 'franky' rolls (like a flatbread wrap) – including a buttery-soft chicken tikka variety – along with excellent chicken curries, superb naan breads and evening-only chicken tandoori *momos* (Tibetan dumplings).

Eat standing at outside tables or cram into the air-con dining room. Bright lights, obnoxious signage and funky Indian tunes round out the festive atmosphere – a sure-fire Agra must-try.

Dasaprakash
SOUTH INDIAN $$
(Map p361; www.dasaprakashgroup.com; Meher Cinema Complex, Gwailor Rd; mains ₹210-360; ☺noon-10.45pm; ❄️🚻) Fabulously tasty and religiously clean, Dasaprakash whips up consistently great South Indian vegetarian food, including spectacular thalis (₹250 to ₹360), *dosas*, a *rasum* (South Indian soup with a tamarind base) of the day and a few token Continental dishes. The ice-cream desserts (₹100 to ₹295) are another speciality. Comfortable booth seating and wood-lattice screens make for intimate dining.

Other Dasprakash outlets in the city are no longer run by the same owners.

Mughal Room
NORTH INDIAN $$$
(Map p361; 54 Taj Rd; mains ₹900-1500; ☺7.30-11pm Mon-Fri, 12.30-3pm & 7.30-11pm Sat & Sun) The best of three eating options at Clarks Shiraz Hotel, this top-floor restaurant serves up sumptuous Mughlai and regional cuisine. Come for a predinner drink (beer ₹400) at the Sunset Bar for distant views of the Taj and Agra Fort. There's live Indian classical music here every evening at 8.30pm. Book a window table.

🍷 Drinking & Nightlife

A night out in Agra tends to revolve around sitting at a rooftop restaurant with a couple of bottles of beer (₹200). None of the restaurants in Taj Ganj are licensed, but they can find alcohol for you if you ask nicely. They also don't mind if you bring your own drinks, as long as you're discreet.

Café Coffee Day
CAFE
(Map p361; www.cafecoffeeday.com; Sadar Bazaar; coffee ₹110-135; ☺9am-11pm) Probably the trendiest Agra outlet of India's popular cafe chain, this branch near Sadar Bazaar is handy when exploring the market. There's another at the **east gate** (Map p365; www.cafe coffeeday.com; 21/101 Taj East Gate; coffee ₹110-135; ☺6am-8pm) of the Taj.

Amarvilas Bar
BAR
(Taj East Gate Rd, Oberoi Amarvilas Hotel; beer/cocktail ₹500/950; ☺noon-midnight) For a beer or cocktail in sheer opulence, look no further than the bar at Agra's best hotel. Nonguests can wander onto the terrace with its Taj views, but staff often restrict tables to in-house guests if things are busy. Bring your best shirt.

🛍️ Shopping

Agra is well known for its marble items inlaid with coloured stones, similar to the pietra dura work on the Taj. Sadar Bazaar, the old town and the area around the Taj are full of emporiums. Cheaper versions may be made of alabaster or soapstone and are less durable.

Other popular buys include rugs, leather and gemstones, though the latter are imported from Rajasthan and are cheaper in Jaipur.

★Subhash Emporium
ARTS & CRAFTS
(Map p361; ☎9410613616; www.subhashemporium. com; 18/1 Gwalior Rd; ☺9.30am-7pm) Some of the pieces on display at this renowned marble shop are simply stunning (ask to see the 26 masterpieces). While it's more expensive than some shops, you definitely get what you pay for: high-quality marble from Rajasthan and master craftsmanship. Items for sale include tabletops, trays, lamp bases, and candle holders that glow from the flame inside.

Prices are marked, but you can normally get a minimum 15% discount. Credit cards are accepted and shipping can be arranged.

Subhash Bazaar
MARKET
(Map p361; ☺8am-8pm Apr-Sep, 9am-8pm Oct-Mar) Skirts the northern edge of Agra's Jama Masjid and is particularly good for silks and saris.

Modern Book Depot
BOOKS
(Map p361; Sadar Bazaar; ☺10.45am-9.30pm Wed-Mon) Great selection of novels and books on Agra and the Mughals at this friendly, 60-year-old establishment.

Khadi Gramodyog
CLOTHING
(Map p361; MG Rd; ☺11am-7pm Wed-Mon) Stocks simple, good-quality men's Indian clothing made from the homespun *khadi* fabric famously recommended by Mahatma Gandhi. There's no English sign – on Mahatma

THE DANCING BEAR & WORKING ELEPHANT RETIREMENT HOME

For hundreds of years, sloth bear cubs were stolen from their mothers (who were often killed) and forced through painful persuasion to become 'dancing bears', entertaining kings and crowds with their fancy footwork. In 1996 Wildlife SOS (www.wildlifesos.org) – an animal-rescue organisation that is often called around Agra to humanely remove pythons and cobras from local homes – began efforts to emancipate all of India's 1200 or so dancing bears. By 2009, nearly all were freed, and more than 200 of them live at the Agra Bear Rescue Facility (☑9756205080; www.wildlifesos.org; 2hr/full day ₹1500/₹5000; ◷9am-4pm; visiting slots 10am, noon & 3pm), inside Sur Sarovar Bird Sanctuary, 30km outside Agra on the road to Delhi.

Visitors are welcome to tour the parklike grounds and watch the bears enjoying their new, better lives. You'll have to pay the ₹500 entry fee to access the centre through the bird sanctuary.

Wildlife SOS also runs an Elephant Conservation Centre (☑969001182; www. wildlifesos.org; Farah; 2hr/full day ₹1500/₹5000; ◷visiting slots 10am, noon & 3pm; 🖪) 🖉, closer to Mathura, which is more hands-on. You'll get to see the elephants while touring the facility and might be able to help prepare their lunch.

For both locations you should email or phone in advance to arrange one of three daily time slots (10am, noon and 3pm).

Volunteers are welcome here for a day or two weeks. Costs are US$100 per person per day, including accommodation and three meals at a volunteer house 10km away. Email volunteer@wildlifesos.org in advance.

Gandhi (MG) Rd, look for the *khadi* logo of hands clasped around a mud hut.

ℹ Information

DANGERS & ANNOYANCES

As well as the usual commission rackets and ever-present gem-import scam (p1191), some specific methods to relieve Agra tourists of their hard-earned cash include the following.

Rickshaws

When taking an auto- or cycle-rickshaw to the Taj, make sure you are clear which gate you want to go to when negotiating the price. Otherwise, almost without fail, riders will take you to the roundabout at the south end of Shahjahan Gardens Rd – where expensive tongas (horse-drawn carriage) or camels wait to take tour groups to the west gate – and claim that's where they thought you meant. Only nonpolluting autos can go within a 500m radius of the Taj because of pollution rules, but they can get a lot closer than the south end of Shahjahan Gardens Rd.

Fake Marble

Lots of 'marble' souvenirs are actually alabaster, or even just soapstone. So you may be paying marble prices for lower-quality stones. The mini Taj Mahals are always alabaster because they are too intricate to carve quickly in marble.

EMERGENCY

Police Station (Map p361; Mahatma Gandhi (MG) Rd)

Tourist Police (☑0562-2421204; Agra Cantonment Train Station; ◷6.30am-9.30pm) Officers also hang around the East Gate ticket office and the UP Tourism office on Taj Rd, as well as at major sites.

MEDICAL

Amit Jaggi Memorial Hospital (Map p361; ☑9690107860, 0562-2230515; www.ajmh.in; off Minto Rd, Vibhav Nagar) If you're sick, Dr Jaggi, who runs this private clinic, is the man to see. He accepts most health-insurance plans from abroad; otherwise a visit runs ₹1000 (day) or ₹2000 (night). He'll even do house calls.

SR Hospital (Map p361; ☑0562-4025200; Laurie's Complex, Namner Rd) Agra's best private hospital.

MONEY

ATMs are everywhere, including **one** (Map p365) just south of the Hotel Sidhartha in Taj Ganj

SBI (Map p361; Rakabganj Rd; ◷10am-4pm Mon-Fri, to 1pm Sat) Changes cash and travellers cheques and has an ATM.

POST

India Post (Map p361; www.indiapost.gov.in; The Mall; ◷10am-5pm Mon-Fri, to 4pm Sat) Agra's historic eneral Post Office (GPO) dates to 1913 and includes a handy 'facilitation office' for foreigners.

TOURIST INFORMATION

India Tourism (Map p361; ☑0562-2226378; www.incredibleindia.org; 191 The Mall; ◷9am-

5.30pm Mon-Fri) Helpful branch; has brochures on local and India-wide attractions.

UP Tourism (📞 0562-2421204; www.up-tourism.com; Agra Cantonment Train Station; ⏱ 6.30am-9.30pm) The friendly train-station branch inside the Tourist Facilitation Centre on Platform 1 offers helpful advice and is where you can book day-long bus tours of Agra. This branch doubles as the Tourist Police.

UP Tourism (Map p361; 📞 0562-2226431; www.uptourism.gov.in; 64 Taj Rd; ⏱ 10am-5pm Mon-Sat) Office on Taj Rd.

TRAVEL AGENCIES

Bagpacker Travel (Map p361; 📞 9997113228; www.bagpackertravels.com; 4/62 Kutchery Rd; ⏱ 9am-9pm) An honest agency for all your travel and transport needs, including commission-free train and bus tickets, Agra day tours and multiday trips, run by the friendly Anil at Tourists Rest House. English and French spoken.

❶ Getting There & Away

AIR

Air India (p1208) has flights from Agra's Kheria Airport three times a week to Khajuraho (and on to Varanasi), and four flights weekly to Jaipur. There are plans to upgrade the airport, though the long-planned Taj International Airport will likely be constructed closer to Delhi than Agra, and so will be of limited use.

BUS

Luxury air-conditioned Volvo and Scania coaches use the Yamuna Expressway, making them a faster option to Delhi.

Some buses to local desinations operate from **Idgah Bus Stand** (📞 0562-2420324; Idgah Rd):

Bharatpur ₹74, 1½ hours, every 30 minutes, 6am to 6.30pm

Delhi Non-AC ₹228, five hours, every 30 minutes, 5am to 11pm; to Delhi's Sarai Kale Khan bus station

Fatehpur Sikri ₹45, one hour, every 30 minutes, 6am to 6.30pm

Gwalior ₹131, three hours, 3pm, 6pm to 8pm

Jaipur ₹267, six hours, every 30 minutes, 5am to 11pm

Jhansi ₹215, six hours, 11am and 12.30pm

A block east of Idgah, just in front of Hotel Sakura, the tiny booth of the **Rajasthan State Road Transport Corporation** (RSRTC; 📞 0562-2420228; www.rsrtc.rajasthan.gov.in) runs more comfortable coaches to Jaipur throughout the day. Services include non-AC (₹294, 5½ hours, 7.30am, 10am, 1pm and 11.59pm) and luxury Volvo (₹563, 4½ hours, 11.30am and 2.30pm). Women's fares are 30% less.

From the **ISBT Bus Stand** (📞 0562-2603536):

Dehra Dun Luxury Volvo (₹1250, 10 hours, 8.30pm); AC (₹700, 4.30pm); non-AC (₹425, 7pm, 8pm, 9pm and 9.30pm).

Delhi Luxury Scania/Volvo to Sarai Kale Khan stand (₹553 to ₹582, four hours, six daily, 7am, 11am, 1pm, 3.30pm, 5.30pm, 6.30pm); AC Shatabdi to Noida (₹415, four hours, five daily).

Gorakhpur AC bus (₹1099, 16 hours, 1.45pm); non-AC (₹700, 3pm, 5pm, 9pm and 10pm).

Haridwar AC bus (₹992, 10 hours); non-AC (₹400). A few evening buses; change in Haridwar for Rishikesh.

Lucknow Luxury Scania/Volvo (₹860, 10am, 4pm, 6pm, 8.45pm); AC (₹595, 7am, 1.45pm, 6.30pm, 8pm, 8.30pm).

Prayagraj (Allahabad) Luxury Volvo (₹1215, nine hours, 7pm); non-AC (₹550, nine hours, 5pm, 7pm and 7.50pm).

Varanasi Luxury Volvo (₹1500, 11 hours, 7pm); non-AC (₹750, 13 hours, 5pm, 7pm and 7.50pm).

From the **Bijli Ghar Bus Stand** (Agra Fort Bus Stand; Map p361; 📞 0562-2464557):

Mathura ₹76, 90 minutes, every 30 minutes, 6am to 8pm

Tundla train station ₹35, one hour, every 30 minutes, 8am to 6pm; from Tundla you can catch the 12382 Poorva Express train to Varanasi at 8.15pm if the trains from Agra are sold out.

DELHI–AGRA TRAINS FOR DAY TRIPPERS

TRIP	TRAIN NO & NAME	FARE (₹)	TIME (HR)	DEPARTURES
Delhi–Agra	12002 Shatabdi Exp	550/1010 (A)	2	6am
Agra–Delhi	12001 Shatabdi Exp	690/1050 (A)	2	9.15pm
Delhi–Agra	12280 Taj Exp	100/370 (B)	3	7am
Agra–Delhi	12279 Taj Exp	100/370 (B)	3½	6.55pm
Hazrat Nizamuddin–Agra*	12050 Gatimaan Exp	770/1505 (A)	1¾	8.10am
Agra–Hazrat Nizamuddin*	12049 Gatimaan Exp	770/1505 (A)	1¾	5.50pm

Fares: (A) AC chair/ECC, (B) 2nd-class/AC chair; * departs Saturday to Monday

MORE HANDY TRAINS FROM AGRA

DESTINATION	TRAIN NO & NAME	FARE (₹)	TIME (HR)	DEPARTURES
Gorakhpur*	19037/9 Avadh Exp	335/910/1305 (A)	15¾	10pm
Jaipur*	22988 AF All Superfast	120/430 (C)	4	2.50pm
Khajuraho	12448 UP Sampark Kranti	280/720/1010 (A)	7½	11.10pm
Kolkata (Howrah)	13008 UA Toofan Exp	555/1500 (B)	31	12.15pm
Lucknow	12180 LJN Intercity	145/515 (C)	6	5.50am
Mumbai (CST)	12138/7 Punjab Mail	580/1530/2215 (A)	23	8.35am
Varanasi*	14854/64/66 Marudhar Exp	340/930/1335 (A)	14	8.30pm

Fares: (A) sleeper/3AC/2AC, (B) sleeper/3AC only, (C) 2nd-class/AC chair;
* Leaves from Agra Fort station

Shared autos (₹10) run between Idgah and Bijli Ghar bus stands. To get to ISBT, catch an auto-rickshaw (₹200 to ₹250, depending on where your trip starts).

TRAIN

Most trains leave from Agra Cantonment (Cantt) train station, although some services to Varanasi and Jaipur go from Agra Fort station. A few trains, such as Kota PNBE Express, run as slightly different numbers on different days than those listed, but timings remain the same.

Express trains are well set up for day trippers to/from Delhi, but trains run to Delhi all day. If you can't reserve a seat, just buy a 'general ticket' for the next train (about ₹90), find a seat in sleeper class then upgrade when the ticket collector comes along. The fastest service to Delhi is the Gatimaan Express, India's fastest train, hitting speeds of 160km per hour.

For Orchha, catch one of the many daily trains to Jhansi (sleeper from ₹165, three hours), then take a shared auto to the bus stand (₹10), from where shared autos run all day to Orchha (₹20). A private autorickshaw costs ₹200 for the same route.

❶ Getting Around

TO/FROM THE AIRPORT

Kheria Airport is 7km east of central Agra. A taxi here costs around ₹300.

AUTORICKSHAW

Just outside Agra Cantonment train station is the **prepaid autorickshaw booth** (⏳24hr), which gives you a good guide for haggling elsewhere. Usually, trips shorter than 3km should not cost more than ₹50. Always agree on the fare before entering the rickshaw.

For a half-day (four-hour) Agra tour count on ₹400; a full-day (eight-hour) Agra tour costs from ₹600. Note: autorickshaws aren't allowed to go to Fatehpur Sikri.

CYCLE-RICKSHAW

Prices from the Taj Mahal's cycle and auto-rickshaw stand at **South Gate** (Map p365) include Agra Fort ₹40; Bijli Ghar bus stand ₹50; and Fatahabad Rd ₹30.

TAXI

Outside Agra Cantonment train station, the **prepaid taxi booth** (⏳24hr) gives a good idea of what taxis should cost. In general Ola taxis are cheapest.

A taxi to Delhi or Jaipur costs around ₹3500. A half-/full-day Agra tour costs ₹750/1000. Agree with the driver beforehand whether tolls and parking charges are included.

AROUND AGRA

Fatehpur Sikri

📞 05613 / POP 30,000

This magnificent fortified ancient city, 40km west of Agra, was the short-lived capital of the Mughal empire between 1572 and 1585, during the reign of Emperor Akbar. Earlier, Akbar had visited the village of Sikri to consult the Sufi saint Shaikh Salim Chishti, who predicted the birth of an heir to the Mughal throne. When the prophecy came true, Akbar built his new capital here, including a stunning mosque, still in use today, and three palaces, one for each of his favourite wives – one a Hindu, one a Muslim and one a Christian (though Hindu villagers in Sikri dispute these claims).

The city was an Indo-Islamic masterpiece, but was erected in an area that supposedly suffered from water shortages and so was abandoned shortly after Akbar's death. The red-sandstone palace walls are at their most atmospheric and photogenic near sunset.

◉ Sights

Palaces & Pavilions   PALACE

(Indian/foreigner ₹50/610, video ₹25; ☺dawn-dusk) The main sight at Fatehpur Sikri is the stunning imperial complex of pavilions and palaces spread amid a large, abandoned 'city' peppered with Mughal masterpieces: court-yards, intricate carvings, servants quarters, vast gateways and ornamental pools. Budget half a day here.

A large courtyard dominates the northeast entrance at Diwan-i-Am (Hall of Public Audiences). Now a pristinely manicured garden, this is where Akbar presided over the courts – from the middle seat of the five equal seatings along the western wall, flanked by his advisors. It was built to utilise an echo sound system, so Akbar could hear anything at any time from anywhere in the open space. Justice was dealt with swiftly if legends are to be believed, with public executions said to have been carried out here by elephants trampling convicted criminals to death.

The Diwan-i-Khas (Hall of Private Audiences), found at the northern end of the Pachisi Courtyard, looks nothing special from the outside, but the interior is dominated by a magnificently carved stone central column. This pillar flares to create a futuristic flat-topped plinth linked to the four corners of the room by narrow stone bridges. From this plinth Akbar is believed to have debated with scholars and ministers who stood at the ends of the four bridges.

Next to Diwan-i-Khas is the U-shaped Treasury, which houses secret stone safes in some corners (several have been left with their stone lids open for visitors to see). Elephant-headed sea monsters carved on the ceiling struts were there to protect the fabulous wealth once stored here. The so-called Astrologer's Kiosk to the left has roof supports carved in a serpentine Jain style.

Just south of the Astrologer's Kiosk is Pachisi Courtyard, named after the ancient game known in India today as ludo. The large, plus-shaped game board is visible surrounding the block in the middle of the courtyard. In the southeast corner is the most intricately carved structure in the whole complex, the tiny but elegant Rumi Sultana, which was said to be the palace built for Akbar's Turkish Muslim wife. Other theories say it was used by Akbar himself as a rest break during court sessions. Look for the defaced carved birds, animals and flowers in several marble panels.

Just west of the Pachisi Courtyard is the impressive Panch Mahal, a pavilion with five storeys that decrease in size until the top consists of only a tiny kiosk. The lower floor has 84 different columns; in total there are 176 columns.

Continuing anticlockwise will bring you to the Ornamental Pool. Here, singers and musicians would perform on the platform above the water while Akbar watched from the pavilion in his private quarters just behind, known as Daulat Khana (Abode of Fortune). At the back of the pavilion is the Khwabgah (Dream House), a sleeping area with a huge elevated stone bed platform. A water pool below the bed would have acted as a cooler in summer.

Heading west through a doorway from the Ornamental Pool reveals the Palace of Jodh Bai, and the one-time home of Akbar's Hindu wife, said to be his favourite. Set around an enormous courtyard, it blends traditional Indian columns, Islamic cupolas and turquoise-blue Persian roof tiles. Just outside, to the left of Jodh Bai's former kitchen, is the Palace of the Christian Wife. This was used by Akbar's Goan wife Mariam, who gave birth to Jehangir here in 1569. (Some believe Akbar never had a Christian wife and that Mariam was short for Mariam-Ut-Zamani, a title he gave to Jodh Bai meaning 'Beautiful like a Rose', or 'Most Beautiful Woman on Earth'.) Like many of the buildings in the palace complex, it contains elements of different religions, as befitted Akbar's tolerant religious beliefs. The domed ceiling is Islamic in style, while remnants of a wall painting of the Hindu god Shiva can also be found.

Continuing left (west) past the Maryam Garden (with a toilet) will take you west to Birbal Bhavan, ornately carved inside and out, and thought to have been the living quarters of one of Akbar's most senior ministers. The Lower Haramsara, just to the south, housed Akbar's large number of live-in female servants, though some claim it was a stables and that the circular stone loops were use to tether camels and horses.

Jama Masjid   MOSQUE

(Dargah Complex) **FREE** This beautiful, immense mosque was completed in 1571 and contains elements of Persian and Indian design. The main entrance, at the top of a flight of stone steps, is through the spectacular 54m-high Buland Darwaza (Victory Gate), built to commemorate Akbar's military

continued on p376

Fatehpur Sikri

A WALKING TOUR OF FATEHPUR SIKRI

You can enter this fortified ancient city from two entrances, but the northeast entrance at Diwan-i-Am (Hall of Public Audiences) offers the most logical approach to this remarkable Unesco World Heritage Site. This large courtyard (now a garden) is where Emperor Akbar presided over the trials of accused criminals.

Once through the ticket gate, you are in the northern end of the **❶ Pachisi Courtyard.** The first building you see is **❷ Diwan-i-Khas** (Hall of Private Audiences), the interior of which is dominated by a magnificently carved central stone column. Pitch south and enter **❸ Rumi Sultana**, a small but elegant palace built for Akbar's Turkish Muslim wife.

It's hard to miss the **❹ Ornamental Pool** nearby – its southwest corner provides Fatehpur Sikri's most photogenic angle, perfectly framing its most striking building, the five-storey Panch Mahal, one of the gateways to the Imperial Harem Complex, where the **❺ Lower Haramsara** once housed more than 200 female servants.

Wander around the Palace of Jodh Bai and take notice of the towering ode to an elephant, the 21m-high **❻ Hiran Minar**, in the distance to the northwest. Leave the palaces and pavilions area via Shahi Darwaza (King's Gate), which spills into India's second-largest mosque courtyard at **❼ Jama Masjid.** Inside this immense and gorgeous mosque is the sacred **❽ Tomb of Shaikh Salim Chishti.** Exit through the spectacular **❾ Buland Darwaza** (Victory Gate), one of the world's most magnificent gateways.

Buland Darwaza
Most tours end with an exit through Jama Masjid's Victory Gate. Walk out and take a look behind you: Behold! The magnificent 15-storey sandstone gate, 54m high, is a menacing monolith to Akbar's reign.

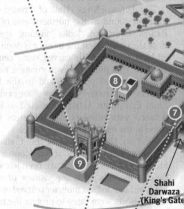

Shahi Darwaza (King's Gate)

Tomb of Shaikh Salim Chishti
Each knot in the strings tied to the 56 carved white marble designs of the interior walls of Shaikh Salim Chishti's tomb represents one wish of a maximum three.

Jama Masjid
The elaborate marble inlay work throughout the Jama Masjid complex is said to have inspired similar work 82 years later at the Taj Mahal in Agra.

Hiran Minar
This bizarre, seldom-visited tower off the north-west corner of Fatehpur Sikri is decorated with hundreds of stone representations of elephant tusks. It is said to be the place where Minar, Akbar's favourite execution elephant, died.

Pachisi Courtyard
Under your feet just past Rumi Sultana is the Pachisi Courtyard where Akbar is said to have played the game *pachisi* (an ancient version of ludo) using slave girls in colourful dress as pieces.

Diwan-i-Khas
Emperor Akbar modified the central stone column inside Diwan-i-Khas to call attention to a new religion he called Din-i-Ilahi (God is One). The intricately carved column features a fusion of Hindu, Muslim, Christian and Buddhist imagery.

Panch Mahal

Diwan-i-Am (Hall of Public Audiences)

Rumi Sultana
Don't miss the headless creatures carved into Rumi Sultana's palace interiors: a lion, deer, an eagle and a few peacocks were beheaded by jewel thieves who swiped the precious jewels that originally formed their heads.

Ornamental Pool
Tansen, said to be the most gifted Indian vocalist of all time and one of Akbar's treasured nine *Navaratnas* (Gems), would be showered with coins during performances from the central platform of the Ornamental Pool.

Lower Haramsara
Akbar reportedly kept more than 5000 concubines, but the 200 or so female servants housed in the Lower Haramsara were strictly business. Knots were tied to these sandstone rings to support partitions between their individual quarters.

continued from p373

victory in Gujarat. Inside is the stunning white marble tomb of Sufi saint Shaikh Salim Chishti, where women hoping to have children come to tie a thread to the *jalis* (carved lattice screens).

The saint's tomb was completed in 1581 and is entered through an original door made of ebony. Inside it are brightly coloured flower murals, while the sandlewood canopy is decorated with mother-of-pearl shell, and the marble *jalis* are among the finest in India. To the right of the tomb lie the gravestones of family members of Shaikh Salim Chishti. Just east of Shaikh Salim Chishti's tomb is the red-sandstone tomb of Islam Khan, the final resting place of Shaikh Salim Chishti's grandson and one-time governor of Bengal.

On the east wall of the courtyard is a smaller entrance to the mosque – the Shahi Darwaza (King's Gate), which leads to the palace complex.

Tours

Official Archaeological Society of India guides can be hired from the Fathehpur Sikri ticket offices at the eastern and southwestern ends of the site for ₹450 (English), but they aren't always the most knowledgeable (some are guides thanks to birthright rather than qualifications). The best guides are available in Agra, and charge ₹750. Our favourite is **Pankaj Bhatnagar** (8126995552; ₹750); he prefers to be messaged on WhatsApp.

Sleeping & Eating

Fatehpur Sikri's culinary specialty is *khataie,* the biscuits you can see piled high in the bazaar. For restaurants, head to one of the hotels.

Hotel Goverdhan HOTEL $
(9412526585; www.hotelfatehpursikriviews.com; Agra Rd; s/d with AC ₹1400/1600, without ₹1000/1200;) Both the air-con and cheaper rooms at this old-time favourite are fresh and spotless, and all are set around a pleasant, well-kept garden. It has a relaxing communal balcony and terrace seating,

new beds in every room, a couple of family suites and a good restaurant (mains ₹150 to ₹220). It's a comfortable place to be based. Discounts of 25% are common.

It's right on the main road by the turn-off to the Jami Masjid.

Hotel Ajay Palace INDIAN $
(9548801213; Agra Rd; mains ₹60-140; 8am-9pm) This friendly, family-run place is a convenient lunch stop before taking the bus back to Agra. Sit on the rooftop at the large, elongated marble table and enjoy a cold beer with a view of the Jama Masjid towering above. Note that it's not 'Ajay Restaurant' inside the bus stand – it's 30m further east.

It also offers four very simple double rooms (₹500) with rock-hard mattresses, hot water by the bucket and sit-down flush toilets.

Information

DANGERS & ANNOYANCES

Take no notice of anyone who gets on the Fatehpur Sikri–Agra bus before the final stop at Idgah Bus Stand and tells you that you have arrived at the city centre or the Taj Mahal. You haven't. You're still a long autorickshaw ride away, and the man trying to tease you off the bus is – surprise surprise – an autorickshaw driver.

Getting There & Away

From the Fatehpur bus stand, buses run to Agra's Idgah Bus Stand (p371) every half-hour (₹45, one hour) until 6pm. If you miss those, walk 1km to the Mughal-style Agra Gate and another 350m to the Bypass Crossing Stop on the main road and wave down an Agra-bound bus. They pass every 30 minutes or so, day and night.

For Bharatpur (₹25, 40 minutes) or Jaipur (₹190, 4½ hours), wave down a westbound bus from the Bypass Crossing Stop.

A return taxi from Agra costs from ₹1500 for a day trip, but clarify that this includes toll and parking charges. A one-way taxi to Delhi or Jaipur costs ₹4000.

Simple passenger trains for Agra leave Fatehpur Sikri at 10.14am, 3.10pm and 3.54pm. Just buy a 'general' ticket at the station and pile in (₹20, one to two hours). The 8.16pm 19037/9 Avadh Express runs to Lucknow and Gorakhpur Junction.

Uttar Pradesh

POP 224 MILLION

Best Places to Eat

➡ Oudhyana (p402)

➡ Darbhanga (p390)

➡ Tunday Kababi (p401)

➡ Brown Bread Bakery (p389)

➡ Eat On (p408)

Best Places to Stay

➡ Brijrama Palace (p387)

➡ Kanchan Villa (p408)

➡ Hotel Ganges View (p388)

➡ MVT Guesthouse (p412)

➡ Ganpati Guesthouse (p385)

Why Go?

There are few states more quintessentially Indian than Uttar Pradesh. The subcontinent's historic and religious roots – Hindu, Buddhist, Islamic and secular – intertwine in this land of sacred rivers and vast plains, manifesting in sights of profound importance.

Aside from iconic Agra, UP is home to Varanasi, India's holiest city, famed for its cremation ghats and vibrant ceremonies along the Ganges River. Stories tell us that Krishna was born in Mathura, while Rama was born in Ayodhya – a place of tragic conflict in modern times that reveals much about the shadow side of the collective Indian psyche. Buddha gave his first sermon in Sarnath and died in Kushinagar, now tranquil pilgrimage destinations. And the Mughals and the Nawabs made their marks as well, leaving behind architectural and gastronomic masterpieces – particularly in Lucknow (and of course Agra). India's most populous state offers more than enough to satisfy the curiosity of any traveller.

When to Go
Varanasi

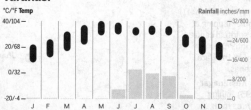

Mid-Sep–Oct Monsoon rains are mostly over and temperatures have cooled...just enough.

Nov–Feb Comfortable winter days and nippy nights mean it's cool but busy.

Mar Some say it's perfect: evening chills subsided and midsummer heat still at bay.

Uttar Pradesh Highlights

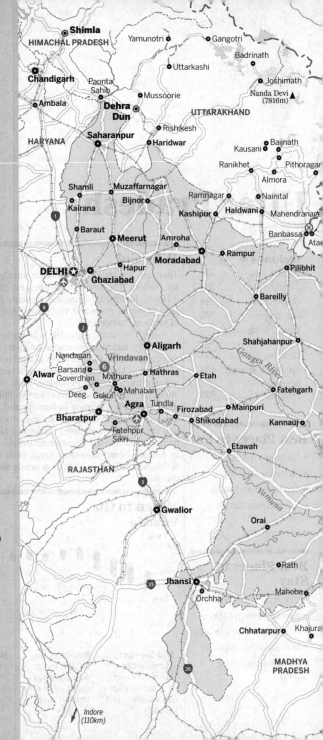

1 Varanasi
(p380) Having your mind blown in India as you've always imagined it, with sacred Ganges ghats and a maze of alleyways with surprises around every corner.

2 Lucknow
(p400) Eating in the kebab capital of India, then strolling among impressively ornamented Nawabi architecture.

3 Sarnath (p393)
Roaming the peaceful park and stupa where Buddha delivered his first sermon.

4 Prayagraj
(Allahabad; p405)
Joining 100 million devotees who converge at the confluence of two (or three) sacred rivers during the Kumbh Mela, and the smaller, annual Magh Mela.

5 Chitrakut
(p405) Experiencing Hindu devotions on a less overwhelming scale at this laid-back riverside pilgrimage town.

6 Vrindavan (p411)
Temple-hopping at this spiritual centre and international home of the Hare Krishnas.

7 Kushinagar
(p395) Joining pilgrims from Myanmar and Thailand in commemorating the spot where Buddha breathed his last.

History

More than 2000 years ago this region was part of Ashoka's great Buddhist empire, remnants of which can be found in the ruins at the pilgrimage centre of Sarnath near Varanasi. Muslim raids from the northwest began in the 11th century, and by the 16th century the region was part of the Mughal empire, with its capital in Agra, then Delhi and, for a brief time, Fatehpur Sikri.

Following the decline of the Mughal empire, Persians stepped in briefly before the Nawabs of Avadh rose to prominence in the central part of the region, notably around the current capital of Lucknow. The Nawabs were responsible for turning Lucknow into a flourishing centre for the arts, culture and culinary delights, which continues to this day. But their empire came to a dramatic end when the British East India Company deposed the last nawab, triggering the First War of Independence (Indian Uprising) in 1857. During the 147-day Siege of Lucknow, British Chief Commissioner Sir Henry Lawrence was killed defending the British Residency, which remains in a remarkable state of preservation in Lucknow.

Agra was later merged with Avadh and the state became known as United Province. It was renamed Uttar Pradesh after Independence and has since been the most dominant state in Indian politics, producing half of the country's prime ministers, most of them from Prayagraj (Allahabad), the locus of the Nehru/Gandhi dynasty.

The people of UP don't seem to have benefited much from this, though, as poor governance, a high birth rate and low literacy have held back the state's economic progress. In 2000 the mountainous northwestern part of the state was carved off to create the new state of Uttaranchal, now called Uttarakhand.

Varanasi

📞0542 / POP 1.4 MILLION

Varanasi is the India of your imagination. This is one of the world's oldest continually inhabited cities, and one of the holiest in Hinduism. Pilgrims come to the Ganges here to wash away sins in the sacred waters, to cremate their loved ones, or simply to die here, hoping for liberation from the cycle of rebirth.

Most visitors agree Varanasi is magical – but not for the faint-hearted. Intimate rituals of life and death take place in public, and the sights, sounds and smells of the mazelike old town – not to mention almost constant attention from touts – can be intense. Still, the so-called City of Light is one of the most colourful and fascinating places on earth. Strolling the ghats or watching sunrise from a boat on the Ganges are a highlight, and confronting the reality and ritual of death can be a powerful experience.

History

Thought to date back to around 1200 BC, and known at various times as Benares and Kashi, the city really rose to prominence in

---

RIVER TRIPS

A dawn rowing boat ride along the Ganges is a quintessential Varanasi experience. The early-morning light is particularly inspiring, and all the colour and clamour of pilgrims bathing and performing *puja* (prayers) unfolds before you. An hour-long trip south from Dashashwamedh Ghat to Harishchandra Ghat and back is popular – be prepared to see a burning corpse at Harishchandra.

Early evening is also a good time to be on the river, when you can light a lotus flower candle (₹10) and set it adrift on the water before watching the nightly *ganga aarti* (river worship ceremony; 7pm) at Dashashwamedh Ghat directly from the boat. The Dashashwamedh ceremony is now very popular, with hundreds of visitors watching from roped-off seating areas (₹100), but there are several quieter ceremonies nearby and further south at Assi Ghat.

The official government price of boats is ₹250 per hour for two to four people, but you'll have to haggle hard to get near that. It's best to organise a boat the day before.

Many guesthouses offer boat trips, and most are good value. Brown Bread Bakery (p385) can arrange a hassle-free ride in its own boats for less than riverside prices (₹150/250 per hour for one/two people, plus ₹800 if you want an English-speaking guide) and you can enjoy pre-ordered coffee and breakfast on the boat.

the 8th century AD, when Shankaracharya, a reformer of Hinduism, established Shiva worship as the principal sect. The Afghans destroyed Varanasi around AD 1300, after laying waste to nearby Sarnath, but the fanatical Mughal emperor Aurangzeb was the most destructive, looting and destroying almost all of the temples. The old city of Varanasi may look antique, but few buildings are more than a couple of hundred years old.

◉ Sights

Vishwanath Temple   HINDU TEMPLE
(Golden Temple; Map p386; ⊙3-11am, 12.30-8pm & 9-11pm) There are temples at almost every turn in Varanasi, but this is the most famous of the lot. It is dedicated to Vishveswara – Shiva as lord of the universe. The current temple was built in 1776 by Ahalya Bai of Indore; the 800kg of gold plating on the tower and dome was supplied by Maharaja Ranjit Singh of Lahore 50 years later.

The area is full of soldiers because of security issues and communal tensions. Bags, cameras, mobile phones, pens and any electronic device must be deposited in lockers (₹20) before you enter the alleyway it's in – or just leave your stuff at your hotel. If you are a foreigner, head to Gate 2, where security will instruct you to walk past the long lines of Indians waiting in the queue, then go through a metal detector and security check. Walk past another line of Indians until you are pointed to a desk, where you must show your passport (not a copy) and leave your shoes. Then enter the temple through a door across the alley.

Once inside, things can be quite intense, with people pushing and tripping over each other for a chance to give an offering and touch the lingam (phallic symbol of Shiva), which absolves one of all sins. Hindus routinely wait in lines for 48 hours to enter on holy days. If you are not fussed about Hindu temples, it's probably not worth the hassle required to visit.

On the northern side of Vishwanath Temple is the Gyan Kupor Well. The faithful believe drinking its water leads to a higher spiritual plane, though they are prevented from doing so by a strong security screen. Non-Hindus are not allowed to enter.

Banares Hindu University   UNIVERSITY, HISTORIC SITE
(BHU; Map p382; www.bhu.ac.in) Long regarded as a centre of learning, Varanasi's tradition of top-quality education continues today at Banares Hindu University, established in 1916. The wide, tree-lined streets and parkland of the 5-sq-km campus offer a peaceful atmosphere a world away from the city outside. On campus is **Bharat Kala Bhavan** (Map p382; Indian/foreigner ₹20/250; ⊙10.30am-4.30pm Mon-Sat), a roomy museum with a wonderful collection of miniature paintings, as well as 12th-century palm-leaf manuscripts, sculptures and local history displays.

Ghats

Spiritually enlightening and fantastically photogenic, Varanasi is at its brilliant best by the ghats, the long stretch of steps leading down to the water on the western bank of the Ganges. Most are used for bathing, but there are also several 'burning ghats' where bodies are cremated in public. The main burning ghat is Manikarnika (p383): you'll often see funeral processions threading their way through the backstreets to this ghat.

The best time to visit the ghats is at dawn, when the river is bathed in a mellow light as pilgrims come to perform *puja* (prayers) to the rising sun, and at sunset when the popular *ganga aarti* (river worship ceremony) takes place at Dashashwamedh Ghat (p383) and others.

About 80 ghats border the river, but the main group extends from Assi Ghat, near the university, northwards to Raj Ghat, near the road and rail bridge.

A boat trip along the river provides the perfect introduction, although for most of the year (October to April) the water level is low enough for you to walk freely along the whole length of the ghats. It's a world-class 'people-watching' stroll as you mingle with the fascinating mixture of people who come to the Ganges not only for a ritual bath but also to wash clothes, do yoga, offer blessings, sell flowers, get a massage, play cricket, wash their buffaloes, improve their karma by giving to beggars or simply stare at the Ganges.

Southern Stretch

★ Assi Ghat   GHAT
(Map p386) The furthest south of the main ghats and one of the biggest, Assi Ghat is particularly important as the River Assi meets the Ganges near here and pilgrims come to worship a Shiva lingam (phallic image of Shiva) beneath a peepul tree. Evenings are particularly lively, as the ghat's vast concreted area fills up with hawkers and entertainers during a small fire ceremony. It also features music and yoga at sunrise. It's a popular starting point for boat trips.

Varanasi

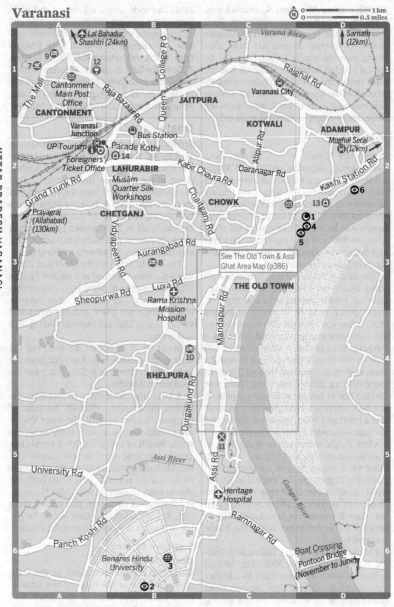

Tulsi Ghat　　　　　　　　　　GHAT
(Map p386) Named after a 16th-century Hindu poet, Tulsi Ghat has fallen down towards the river, but in the month of Kartika (October/November) a festival devoted to Krishna is celebrated here.

Bachraj Ghat　　　　　　　　GHAT
(Map p386) This small ghat is marked by three Jain temples.

Shivala Ghat　　　　　　　　GHAT
(Map p386) A small Shiva temple and a 19th-century mansion built by Nepali royalty

Varanasi

sit back from Shivala Ghat, built by the local maharaja of Benares.

Hanuman Ghat   GHAT
(Map p386) Popular with Rama devotees (Hanuman was Rama's stalwart ally in his quest to rescue Sita from the demon Ravana).

★**Harishchandra Ghat**   GHAT
(Map p386) Harishchandra Ghat is a cremation ghat – smaller and secondary in importance to Manikarnika, but one of the oldest ghats in Varanasi.

Kedar Ghat   GHAT
(Map p386) A colourful ghat with many steps and a small pool, where a fire *aarti* is held every evening at 6.30pm.

Old City Stretch

★**Dashashwamedh Ghat**   GHAT
(Map p386) Varanasi's liveliest and most colourful ghat. The name indicates that Brahma sacrificed *(medh)* 10 *(das)* horses *(aswa)* here. In spite of the persistent boat owners, flower sellers, massage practitioners, and touts trying to drag you off to a silk shop, it's a wonderful place to linger and people-watch while soaking up the atmosphere. Every evening at 7pm an elaborate and popular *ganga aarti* (river worship) ceremony with *puja* (prayers), fire and dance is staged here.

It's easily reached at the end of the main road from Godaulia Crossing.

Man Mandir Ghat   GHAT
(Map p386) Just north of Dashashwamedh Ghat, Man Mandir Ghat was built in 1600 by Raja Man Singh and later housed an observatory. The northern corner of the ghat has a fine stone balcony.

★**Manikarnika Ghat**   GHAT
(Map p386) Manikarnika Ghat, the main burning ghat, is the most auspicious place for a Hindu to be cremated. Dead bodies are handled by outcasts known as *doms,* and are carried through the alleyways of the old town to the holy Ganges on a bamboo stretcher, swathed in cloth. The corpse is doused in the Ganges prior to cremation.

Huge piles of firewood are stacked along the top of the ghat; every log is carefully weighed on giant scales so that the price of cremation can be calculated. Each type of wood has its own price, sandalwood being the most expensive. There is an art to using just enough wood to completely incinerate a corpse. You can watch cremations but always show reverence by behaving respectfully. Photography is strictly prohibited. You're almost guaranteed to be led by a priest, or more likely a guide, to the upper floor of a nearby building from where you can watch cremations taking place, and then asked for a donation (in dollars) towards the cost of wood. If you don't want to make a donation, don't follow them.

Above the steps here is a tank known as the Manikarnika Well. Parvati is said to have dropped her earring here and Shiva dug the tank to recover it, filling the depression with his sweat. The Charanpaduka, a slab of stone between the well and the ghat, bears footprints made by Vishnu. Privileged VIPs are cremated at the Charanpaduka, which also has a temple dedicated to Ganesh.

Dattatreya Ghat   GHAT
(Map p386) Dattatreya takes its name from a Brahmin saint, whose footprint is preserved in a small temple nearby.

ⓘ MORE TIPS FOR VISITING VARANASI

➡ Don't take photos at the 'burning' ghats and resist offers to 'follow me for a better view', where you'll be pressured for money and possibly be placed in an uncomfortable situation.

➡ Do not go to any shop with a guide or autorickshaw driver. Be firm and don't do it. Ever. You will pay 40% to 60% more for your item due to insane commissions, and you'll also be passively encouraging this practice. Do yourself a favour and walk there, or have your ride drop you a block away.

➡ Imposter stores are rampant in Varanasi, usually spelled one letter off or sometimes exactly the same as the original. The shops we have recommended are the real deal. Ask for a visiting card (ie business card) – if the info doesn't match, you have been had.

➡ When negotiating with boaters, confirm the price and currency before setting out. Many just love to say '100!' and then at the end claim they meant dollars or euros.

➡ Do not book guides through your guesthouse, as most of the time the guides will be unofficial. Instead go through UP Tourism (p391) to avoid most of the hassles above. If not, have fun shopping!

➡ Be wary of *bhang lassis* – these are made with hash (degraded cannabis) and can be very strong if that's not what you're looking for (we've heard reports of robberies of intoxicated people).

➡ Beware of fake 'yoga teachers', many of whom are mainly interested in hands-on lessons with young women.

Scindhia Ghat   GHAT
(Map p386) Scindhia Ghat was originally built in 1830, but was so huge and magnificent that it collapsed into the river and had to be rebuilt.

Northern Stretch
Ram Ghat   GHAT
(Map p382) North from Scindhia Ghat, Ram Ghat was built by a maharaja of Jaipur.

Panchganga Ghat   GHAT
(Map p382) Just beyond Ram Ghat, this ghat marks where five holy rivers are supposed to meet.

Alamgir Mosque   MOSQUE
(Map p382) Dominating Panchganga Ghat, this small mosque was built by Aurangzeb on the site of a large Vishnu temple.

Trilochan Ghat   GHAT
(Map p382) At Trilochan, two turrets emerge from the river, and the water between them is especially holy.

🏃 Activities

It's worth an early rise for two of your mornings in Varanasi, one to take in the action on a riverboat trip and another to experience the hubbub of activity on the ghats themselves.

Nonguests can use the outdoor swimming pools at Hotel Surya (p388) for ₹400 and

Hotel Clarks Varanasi (Map p382; The Mall; ⊘8am-7pm) for ₹500.

Siddhartha Yoga Centre   YOGA
(Map p386; ☑9236830966; www.yogasiddharth. com; Manasarowar Ghat) Expats have recommended this yoga centre, perfectly located on the ghats with views across the Ganges. Owner Yogi Siddharth offers 90-minute beginner classes (₹400) in hatha yoga at 9.30am, or private classes (₹1000) at 5pm. Book online. It offers a couple of good-value modern rooms for ₹1500.

DarkLotus   YOGA
(Map p386; ☑7379711888; www.banarasyoga.com; B 1/229 Assi Ghat) Taking yoga out of the studio and around the sacred sites of Varanasi, these highly recommended classes are set along the river and at temples around the city, and there are also yoga-themed walks. Contact through the website for courses and prices.

Swasthya Vardhak   AYURVEDA
(Map p386; ☑0542-2312504; www.swasthya vardhak.in; Assi Crossing; ⊘9am-7pm Mon-Sat, to 5pm Sun) 🖉 Varanasi is full of ayurvedic imposters. Serious seekers should come here, the city's real-deal ayurvedic pharmacy. It's said to be especially effective in combating fever, insomnia, skin problems, IBS, stomach problems and body aches. Consultations with a doctor are free; prescriptions run

from ₹20 to ₹2000. It's on a side street just off the main Shivala Rd.

Courses

Pragati Hindi LANGUAGE
(Map p386; ☑9335376488; www.pragatihindi.com; B-7/176 Harar Bagh) Readers recommend the flexibility of the one-to-one classes taught here by the amiable Rajeswar Mukherjee (Raju). Private classes start from ₹300 per hour. Call ahead, or just drop in to meet Raju and arrange a schedule. Walk up the stairs opposite Chowki Ghat and take the first left, following the 'Hindi' signs.

International Music
Centre Ashram MUSIC
(Map p386; ☑9415987283; tablateeteteete@gmail. com; D33/81 Khalishpura; per class ₹500; ⊙8am-8pm) This family-run centre is hidden in the tangle of backstreets off Bengali Tola. It offers sitar, tabla, flute and classical-dance tuition, and performances are held every Saturday and Wednesday evening at 8pm (₹150). There's a small, easy-to-miss sign on Bengali Tola directing you here.

Yoga Training Centre YOGA
(Map p386; ☑9919857895; www.yogatraining centrevaranasi.in; 5/15 Sakarkand Gali; 2hr class group/private ₹300/800, reiki from ₹800; ⊙8am, 10am & 4pm) Former army clerk and yoga master Sunil Kumar and partners run set classes four times a day on the 2nd and 3rd floors of this small backstreet building near Meer Ghat (but you can drop in anytime for a session).

⚲ Tours

If time is short, UP Tourism (p391) can arrange guided tours by taxi of the major sites, including a 5.30am boat ride and an afternoon trip to Sarnath (p393).

★Varanasi Walks WALKING
(Map p386; ☑7081070222; www.varanasiwalks. com; Assi Ghat; tours ₹1200-2000) The cultural walks on offer from this agency specialising in themed walks explore beyond the most popular ghats and temples, giving eye-opening insight into this holy city. The American founder has lived in Varanasi for years, and most of the guides were born and raised here. Walks are available by reservation; book online or by phone.

🛏 Sleeping

Most of Varanasi's budget hotels – and some midrange gems – are tucked among the narrow streets off the ghats. There's a concentration of midrange places around Assi Ghat; others are clustered between Scindhia and Meer Ghat.

To experience local life, consider one of the city's 150 homestay-style paying guesthouses, costing around ₹500 to ₹900 per night. The UP Tourism (p391) office at the railway station has a full list.

🛏 Old City Area

Brown Bread
Bakery Guesthouse GUESTHOUSE $
(Map p386; ☑0542-2450472, 9838888823; www. brownbreadbakery.com; Bengali Tola, Pandey Ghat; s with AC ₹750, without bathroom or AC ₹450, d with/ without AC ₹1300/800; ※ ⓢ) With the cleanest budget rooms in Varanasi, this simple but well-run guesthouse is one of the best deals in town, despite tiny bathrooms and iffy hot water. Bonus: it shares space with the excellent restaurant (p389) of the same name and offers the best deals around on reliable sunrise boat tours (p380) – you can even arrange for coffee and breakfast on your boat! A two-minute walk from Pandey Ghat.

BunkedUp Hostel HOSTEL $
(Map p386; ☑0542-2450508; www.bunkedup hostels.com; off Bengali Tola; dm incl breakfast ₹400-550, r ₹2000; ※ ⓢ) This hostel, near the ghats and next to a lovely temple, aims to please, with a couple of mixed-gender dorm rooms (with individual fans and electrical outlets) and a women-only dorm, plus two private rooms, all with AC. The rooftop cafe has great views of the river, and there's a movie theatre in the basement. For more private rooms ask about the nearby sister hostel Neela.

Useful extras include cooking classes three times a week, free dawn yoga for beginners at Assi Ghat, a backpacker thali (₹99) and laundry service.

★Ganpati Guesthouse GUESTHOUSE $$
(Map p386; ☑0542-2390057; www.ganpatiguest house.com; 3/24 Meer Ghat; old block r ₹1900, main bldg ₹2800-6490; ※ ⓢ) This old red-brick favourite has a pleasant, shaded courtyard as well as plenty of balcony space dotted around offering fine river views. Rooms are clean, painted with bright, fruity colours and feature tasteful framed wall hangings and modern bathrooms. The best have private Ganges-view balconies.

The least expensive rooms are in an annexed building down the alley, and although

The Old Town & Assi Ghat Area

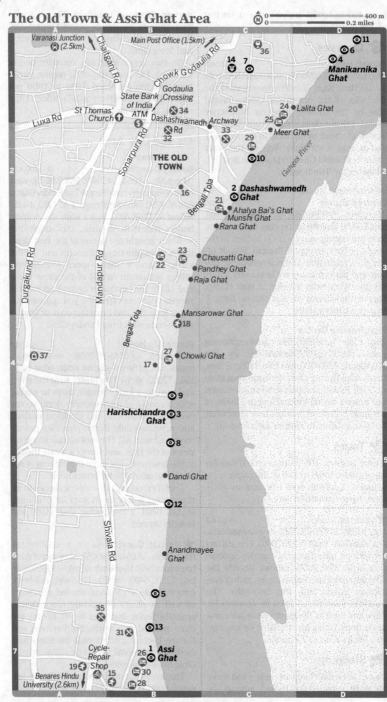

The Old Town & Assi Ghat Area

UTTAR PRADESH VARANASI

this lacks the ambience of the main guesthouse, you can still used the shared common areas and fine restaurant terrace of the main building (serving cold beer).

★ **Homestay**   GUESTHOUSE **$$**
(Map p382; ☏ 9415449348; www.homestayvaranasi.in; D61/16 Sidhgiri Bagh; r incl breakfast ₹2800-3360; ❀❀) This place, in a 1936 colonial home in a residential neighbourhood 1.5km from the old town, is a catch. Good-hearted host Harish, a 37-year veteran of the textile industry – the reputable shop, Paraslakshmi Exports (p391), is on the premises – has six well-maintained rooms that come with antique furniture and are shielded from light, noise and mosquitoes. You'll appreciate it.

Harish can arrange reasonably priced local transport and walking tours, and his wife, Malika, whips up home-cooked meals in the communal dining room. If you don't mind being a bit away from the heart of the ghats action, it's a delightful choice full of family charm. It's also signed 'Malika's Guest House'. It's hard to find the first time, so ring ahead.

Hotel Alka   GUESTHOUSE **$$**
(Map p386; ☏ 0542-2401681; www.hotelalkavns.com; 3/23 Meer Ghat; 'r with AC ₹2500-7000, without AC ₹1200, without AC or bathroom ₹990; ❀@❀) This ghat-side option could use an attentive

eye on its exteriors, but the pretty-much-spotless rooms – either opening onto, or overlooking, a large, plant-filled courtyard over the Ganges – draw the lion's share of care here. In the far corner, room 102 has a terrace that juts out over Meer Ghat for one of the best views in all of Varanasi, a view shared from the balconies of eight of the priciest rooms.

Kedareswar   HOTEL **$$**
(Map p386; ☏ 0542-2455568; www.kedareswarguesthouse.com; B14/1 Chowki Ghat; r without AC & incl breakfast ₹1840, with river view ₹3700; ❀❀) Housed in a brightly painted aquamarine-green building, this friendly six-room place has cramped but immaculate rooms with sparkling bathrooms. Breakfast is served on the rooftop when it's not too hot or rainy. It's popular, so you'll want to book ahead.

★ **Brijrama Palace**   HERITAGE HOTEL **$$$**
(Map p386; ☏ 9129414141; www.brijrama.in; Munshi/Darbhanga Ghat; r ₹21,850-42,550; ❀❀) This meticulously renovated riverfront palace, built in 1812 and known as the Darbhanga Mahal, is simply exquisite. From the period chandeliers to the oriental rugs to the carved stone columns and artwork on the walls, this is the most authentic and luxurious heritage hotel along the ghats. Its Darbhanga restaurant (p390) may well be the best in Varanasi.

Rashmi Guest House

HOTEL $$$

(Palace on River; Map p386; 📞0542-2402778; www.rashmiguesthouse.com; 16/28A Man Mandir Ghat; r incl breakfast ₹3300-7360; ❄@🛜) Incense-scented, white-tile corridors and marble staircases lead to a variety of cramped but smart rooms boasting high marks for cleanliness and style. The more expensive rooms have views of Man Mandir Ghat. Dolphin (p390), the hotel's rooftop restaurant, is a fine place for a beer-chased evening meal and one of the old town's few nonveg options.

🛏 Assi Ghat Area

Stops Hostel

HOSTEL $

(Map p382; 📞9506118023; www.gostops.com; B20/47A2, Vijaya Nagaram Colony; tent Nov-Feb ₹250, dm ₹380-570, d with AC ₹2658, all incl breakfast; ❄@🛜) Varanasi's original hostel is in a four-storey residential building 2km or so from Assi Ghat. Dorms in six-, eight- and 14-bed variations are livened up by colourful lockers, and there are ample hang-out spaces on various floors that cultivate the right vibe – a rare find in UP.

The four private rooms are basic and a bit overpriced; the real draws are the dorms, common areas and the rooftop showers, each uniquely painted by various artistic volunteers. The hostel offers all sorts of tours and activities, from cooking classes and market tours to sunrise river trips, making it easy to get the most out of your stay. It's a solid choice for the socially inclined – the only downside is its distance from the ghats.

Sahi River View Guesthouse

GUESTHOUSE $

(Map p386; 📞0542-2366730; www.sahiriverview.co.in; B1/158 A2 Assi Ghat; s/d incl breakfast ₹400/800, r with AC from ₹1450; ❄@🛜) You'll find a huge variety of rooms at this ramshackle but friendly place, which is better than it looks from its entrance down a scruffy side alley. Most rooms are good and clean, despite the beaten-up furniture, and some have private balconies. Each floor has a pleasant communal seating area with a river view, creating a great feeling of space throughout.

★ Hotel Ganges View

HOTEL $$$

(Map p386; 📞0542-2313218; www.hotelgangesview.co.in; Assi Ghat; ground/upper fl r incl breakfast ₹4500/6500; ❄🛜) Simply gorgeous, this beautifully restored and maintained colonial-style *haveli* (traditional, ornately decorated residence) overlooking Assi Ghat is crammed with books, antiques and classy furniture. Rooms are spacious and immaculate, and there are some charming communal areas in which to relax, including a lovely 1st-floor garden terrace. Book ahead.

Palace on Ganges

HOTEL $$$

(Map p386; 📞0542-2315050; www.palaceonganges.com; B1/158 Assi Ghat; r ₹7450-9950; ❄@🛜) Each room is individually themed on a regional Indian style, using antique furnishings and colourful design themes. The colonial, Rajasthan and Jodhpur rooms are among the best, but look at a few if you can, as the more expensive rooms aren't necessarily better than the less expensive ones. The rooftop restaurant is a highlight.

🛏 Cantonment Area

Hotel Surya

HOTEL $$

(Map p382; 📞0542-2508465; www.hotelsuryavns.com; S-20/51A-5 The Mall Rd; s/d incl breakfast ₹3540/4010, luxury ₹4490/4960; ❄@🛜🖥) Varanasi's cheapest hotel with a swimming pool, Surya has standard three-star Indian rooms, but a modern makeover means the luxury rooms in particular have been tightened up a bit, with stylish new furnishings, upholstery and balconies.

Value here is palpable, as all is built around a huge lawn area that includes a colourful lounge-style bar and cafe flanked

---

TOP STATE FESTIVALS

Magh Mela (☉Jan/Feb; p408) A huge annual religious fair that swells into the Kumbh Mela, a gathering of 30 million people, every 12th year (next held in this state in 2025).

Holi (☉Feb/Mar) Perhaps the world's most colourful festival. Prepare to be powdered!

Purnima (☉Apr or May) Buddha's birthday party.

Janmastami (☉Aug/Sep) Krishna's birthday party.

Dev Diwali (☉Nov) A festival of light in the 'City of Light', Varanasi.

Ram Lila (☉Sep/Oct) The dramatic retelling of Lord Rama's quest to reclaim his wife, Sita, from the demon Ravana; in Varanasi.

BEST LASSI IN ALL VARANASI

Your long, thirsty search for the best lassi in India is over. Look no further than **Blue Lassi** (Map p386; lassi ₹80; ⊙9am-10pm; 🖥), a tiny, hole-in-the-wall yoghurt shop that has been churning out the freshest, creamiest, fruit-filled lassis since 1925. The grandson of the original owner still works here, sitting by his lassi-mixing cauldron in front of a small room with walls plastered with the passport photos of happy drinkers.

There are more than 80 delicious flavour combos, divided by section – plain, banana, apple, pomegranate, mango, papaya, strawberry, blueberry, coconut and saffron. We think banana and apple, the latter flecked with fresh apple shreds, just about top the long list.

The whole scene here is surreal: the lassi takes ages to arrive while a group of thirsty nationalities chats away in a dozen languages; when it does arrive, the lassi is handed off to you in an earthenware pot with the care of a priceless work of art, as the occasional dead body passes by the front of the shop at eye level en route to the Burning Ghat (Manikarnika). It's a classic Varanasi moment, best slotted in between visits to Vishwanath Temple and Manikarnika Ghat.

by a gorgeous, nearly 200-year-old heritage building (the former stomping grounds of a Nepali king), where the excellent **Canton Royale** (mains ₹350-450; ⊙11am-11pm; ▣) is housed. There's also the good (but smoky) Mangi Ferra (p390) bar and the **Aristo Spa** (massage ₹1500-4750; ⊙8am-7.30pm).

🍴 Eating

Varanasi's restaurant scene ranges from backstreet backpacker cafes to opulent palace restaurants serving excellent North Indian cuisine. This is one town where you might want to avoid the street food, as hygiene levels in the old town can be hit-and-miss.

Many eateries in the old town shut in summer due to unbearable humidity and water levels that often flood the ghats and the surrounding area.

🍴 Old City Area

Dosa Cafe SOUTH INDIAN $
(Map p386; 15/49 Man Mandir; dosas ₹40-220; ⊙10am-9pm Thu-Tue) This easy-to-miss three-table cafe woos travellers with Chef Ranjana's out-of-the-box South Indian preparations such as chocolate *idli* (fermented rice cake), and dosa with ratatouille, spinach or dried fruit. It won us over with its choice of oil: pick from refined soybean oil (no), butter (maybe), ghee (maybe) or olive oil (yes!). Creative, progressive and tasty.

Ayyar's Cafe SOUTH INDIAN $
(Map p386; Dashashwamedh Rd; mains ₹45-150; ⊙8am-9pm) Excellent, no-nonsense choice off the tourist path for South Indian masala dosa, and its spicier cousin, the Mysore

dosa. Also one of the few cheapies to serve filtered coffee. The set meals are a great deal. It's tucked away at the end of a short covered alley signed 'New Keshari Readymade' off Dashashwamedh Rd.

★**Brown Bread Bakery** MULTICUISINE $$
(Map p386; ☎9792420450; www.brownbread-bakery.com; Bengali Tola, near Pandey Ghat; mains ₹125-400; ⊙7am-10pm; 🖥) 🍃 This restaurant's fabulous menu includes more than 40 varieties of European-quality cheese and more than 30 types of bread, cookies and cakes – along with excellent pastas, sandwiches and breakfasts. Sit downstairs at street level or upstairs at the casual rooftop cafe, with seating on cushions around low tables and glimpses of the Ganges.

Pop in for the European breakfast buffet (7am to noon; ₹350) or the free, nightly classical-music performances (7.30pm). Part of the profits goes to the Learn for Life (Map p386; ☎0542-2390040; www.learn-for-life.net; D55/147 Aurangabad) school. Warning: don't be fooled by impostors who pretend to be the BBB, and remember: the real BBB will never accept cash donations for Learn for Life.

Keshari Restaurant INDIAN $$
(Map p386; 14/8 Godaulia; mains ₹180-220; ⊙9.30am-10.30pm; 🖉) Known as much for excellent cuisine as for gruff service, this atmospheric spot (carved-wood panelling adorns the walls and ceilings) has been famously at it for nearly a half-century. Indians pack in here for high-quality veg cuisine from all over India. A dizzying array of dishes are on offer (more than 40 paneer curries alone), but they can be a bit oily.

House rules include 'Please keep silence in the hall' and 'Avoid combing of hair'. The restaurant is about 20m down a side street off Dashashwamedh Rd. Do not confuse it with the less desirable Keshari Ruchiker Byanjan around the corner on Dashashwamedh Rd.

★ **Darbhanga**   INDIAN, MULTICUISINE $$$
(Map p386; ☑9129414141; Brijrama Palace Hotel, Munshi/Darbhanga Ghat; mains ₹750-1100, thalis ₹1750; ☺noon-3pm & 7.30-10.30pm; ☒☑) Seriously some of the best Indian food we've ever had. The *palak chaman* (paneer in spinach and spices) is heaven in your mouth and the *aloo chaat* (fried pieces of parboiled potato mixed with chickpeas and chopped onions, and garnished with spices and chutney) is a gourmet-street-food revelation. There's also a good list of Continental and Thai options. For nonguests there's a minimum charge of ₹1000 per person. It's a classy night out that's worth it.

Dolphin Restaurant   INDIAN $$$
(Rashmi Guest House; Map p386; ☑0542-2391768; 16/30 Man Mandir Ghat; mains ₹320-450; ☺7am-10pm; ☒) Atmosphere trumps food at Dolphin (the rooftop restaurant at Rashmi Guest House, p388), which is perched high above Man Mandir Ghat, but it's still a fine place for an evening meal. The breezy balcony offers fine Ganges views, and Dolphin is one of the few places that serves nonveg food and illicit beer.

🍴 Assi Ghat Area

Aum Cafe   CAFE $
(Map p386; ☑9335361122; www.touchoflight.us; B1/201 Assi Ghat; mains ₹70-180; ☺7am-3.30pm Tue-Sun Jul-Apr; ☎☑) 🍽 Run by an American woman who has been coming to India for more than 20 years, this colourful cafe has good lemon pancakes, astounding lemon or organic green-tea lassis and lots of healthy vegetarian options such as *kicharee* (rice, dhal and vegetables with cumin, coriander, fennel, ginger, curd and chutney), alongside a fine bread pudding with lemon.

★ **Open Hand**   CAFE $$
(Map p382; www.openhand.in; 1/128-3 Dumraub Bagh; mains ₹160-280; ☺7am-9pm; ☎) 🍽 This shoes-off cafe-cum–gift shop serves real espresso and French-press coffee alongside breakfast platters featuring pancakes, omelettes and muesli. There's also a range of salads, sandwiches, pastas and baked goods, which are excellent. Sit on the narrow balcony or lounge around the former home, a short walk from Assi Ghat.

Vegan & Raw   VEGAN $$
(Map p386; B-2/224 D1 Shivala Rd; mains ₹170-220; ☺9am-9.30pm; ☎) This casual courtyard restaurant near Tulsi Ghat is an offshoot of Brown Bread Bakery (p389), featuring excellent vegan dishes, including a full page of salads from spinach-radish-walnut to papaya-pomegranate-linseed. Entrees lean towards pizza from the separate Pizzeria Nicoletta kitchen, but it also offers tofu, *momo* (Tibetan dumplings) and couscous. Friday is DJ night and Saturday brings swing dance classes.

🍷 Drinking & Nightlife

Mangi Ferra   CAFE
(Map p382; www.hotelsuryavns.com; S-20/51A-5 The Mall Rd; cocktail ₹310-550; ☺11am-11pm) This colourful, laid-back lounge in the garden at Hotel Surya (p388) is a relaxing place where you can sip an espresso (₹90), a cold one or a cocktail in the large garden, or on waves of couches and armchairs. It's also called Sol Bar. Get 30% off a cocktail between 4pm and 7pm.

Prinsep Bar   BAR
(Map p382; www.tajhotels.com; Gateway Hotel Ganges, Raja Bazaar Rd; beer/cocktail ₹375/650; ☺noon-11pm Mon-Sat, to midnight Sun) For a quiet drink with a dash of history, try this tiny bar named after James Prinsep, who drew wonderful illustrations of Varanasi's ghats and temples (look for an 1830 copy of his *Benares Illustrated* in a glass case here). Stick to beer as the 25ml cocktail pour is weak.

☆ Entertainment

There's nightly live Indian classical music from 7.30pm on the rooftop of the Brown Bread Bakery (p389).

The International Music Centre Ashram (p385) has small performances (₹150) on Wednesday and Saturday evenings.

🛍 Shopping

Varanasi is justifiably famous for silk brocades and beautiful Benares saris, but don't believe much of what the silk salespeople tell you about the relative quality of products, even in government emporiums. Instead, shop around and judge for yourself.

There are loads of musical instrument shops on Bengali Tola (near Rana Ghat), many of which offer lessons.

★ **Baba Blacksheep** FASHION & ACCESSORIES
(Map p386; B12/120 A-9, Bhelpura; ☺ 9.30am-8pm)
If the deluge of traveller enthusiasm is anything to go by, this is one of the most trustworthy, nonpushy shops in India. Indeed it is one of the best places you'll find for silks (scarves/saris from ₹500/4000) and *pashmina* (shawls from ₹1700).

Prices are fixed (though unmarked) and the friendly owner refuses to play the commission game, so autorickshaws and taxis don't like to come here (ignore anyone who says you cannot drive here, and make sure you're in the right place, not an imposter). It's located at Bhelpura crossing under the mosque. It's not the cheapest, but it's a pleasant experience.

Mehrotra Silk Factory FASHION & ACCESSORIES
(Map p382; www.mehrotrasilk.in; 4/8A Lal Ghat; ☺ 10am-8pm) In a labyrinth of alleys behind Lal Ghat, this fixed-price shop, its floor cushioned for seating, offers fine silks for fair prices. Products are as small as a scarf or as big as a bedcover. There's another **branch** (Map p382; 21/72 Englishia Line; ☺ 10am-8pm) near the railway station.

Paraslakshmi Exports FASHION & ACCESSORIES
(Map p382; ☎ 0542-2411496; paraslakhshmi exports@gmail.com; Homestay, D-61/16, Sidhgiri Bagh; ☺ 10am-7pm Mon-Sat, to 2pm Sun) Owner Harish is scrupulously honest in explaining the differing qualities of the silk scarves, handmade Ladakhi pashmina shawls and bedspreads. Prices are fixed, credit cards are accepted and shipping can be arranged. The shop is on the ground floor of his excellent Homestay (p387). Ring ahead and he'll pick you up for free.

ⓘ Information

EMERGENCY
Tourist Police (Map p382; UP Tourism office, Varanasi Junction train station; ☺ 5am-7pm) Officers wear sky-blue uniforms.

MEDICAL SERVICES
Heritage Hospital (Map p382; ☎ 0542-2368888; www.heritagehospitals.in; Lanka) English-speaking staff and doctors; 24-hour pharmacy.
Rama Krishna Mission Hospital (Map p382; ☎ 0542-2451727; www.varanasirkm.org; Luxa Rd, Rm 108; consultation ₹10; ☺ consultation 8.30am-noon) Expat-recommended for cheap consultations and good service.

MONEY
There are many ATMs scattered around town, including State Bank of India in the lobby of the train station and at central **Godaulia Crossing** (Map p386; cnr Dashashwamedh & Sonarpura Rds; ☺ 24hr).

POST
Cantonment Main Post Office (Map p382; ☺ 10am-5pm) The best place to post international parcels.
Main Post Office (GPO; Map p382; www.indiapost.gov.in; off Rabindranath Tagore Rd, Visheshwarganj; ☺ 10am-6pm Mon-Sat) The most central branch.

TOURIST INFORMATION
UP Tourism (Map p382; ☎ 0542-2506670; www.uptourism.gov.in; Varanasi Junction train station; ☺ 10am-6pm) Get the heads-up on autorickshaw prices, the best trains for your

UTTAR PRADESH VARANASI

TRAVELLING TO NEPAL

From Varanasi's bus stand (p392) there are frequent services to Sunauli (₹293, 10 hours, every 30 minutes, 4am to 11pm), where you can easily catch onward buses to Nepal. See p397 for more information.

Travel agents often try to sell tourists 'through' tickets to Kathmandu. In reality only the Nepali-run Shree Manjushree Bus Sewa Samiti (http://manjushreebus.com) has direct overnight AC buses to Kathmandu (₹1300, 17 hours, 10pm), running irregularly when demand warrants it. Book tickets at the bus stand.

It's often better to take a shared taxi or local bus to the border, walk across and take another onward bus (pay the conductor on board).

Travellers have also complained about being pressured into paying extra luggage charges for buses out of Sunauli. You shouldn't have to, so politely decline.

By train, go to Gorakhpur then transfer to a Sunauli shared car just outside the bus station. By air, you'll likely be connecting through Delhi, though there are often direct twice-weekly Varanasi–Kathmandu flights with Buddha Air (www.buddhaair.com).

Nepali visas are available on arrival.

travels, the lay of the land, details on Varanasi's paying-guesthouse program or arrange a guided tour.

ⓘ Getting There & Away

AIR

Varanasi's Lal Bahadur Shashtri Airport has nonstop flights to several cities in India, including Delhi, Mumbai, Benguluru (Bangalore) and Hyderabad. Air India has three flights a week to Agra.

Thai Airways flies directly to Bangkok daily. Nepal's Buddha Air has irregular flights to Kathmandu twice a week.

BUS

The main **bus stand** (Map p382) is opposite Varanasi Junction train station. Get timings and prices for AC buses at www.upsrtconline.co.in.

Delhi AC buses ₹1988, 16 hours, 1pm

Faizabad ₹228, seven hours, frequent service from 5am to 9pm; AC bus ₹299, at 4pm

Gorakhpur ₹232, seven hours, every 30 minutes, 4am to 10pm; also six daily evening AC buses for ₹305

Lucknow Non-AC ₹317, 7½ hours, every 30 minutes, 4am to 11pm; also AC buses ₹480 to ₹900, 7½ hours, 8am, 10.30am, 9pm, 9.30pm and 10.30pm

Prayagraj (Allahabad) ₹137, three hours, every 30 minutes, 4am to 10pm; also eight daily AC buses for ₹177

TRAIN

Varanasi Junction train station is the main station, though a few connections only go through Mughal Serai junction (renamed Deen Dayal Upadyaya in 2017), 18km southeast of the city.

There are several daily trains to Prayagraj (Allahabad), Gorakhpur and Lucknow. A few daily trains leave for Delhi and Kolkata/Howrah

and there is a daily overnight train to Agra Fort. It's easier to get a ticket on trains departing from Varanasi, and they are generally more punctual than long-distance trains.

The direct train to Khajuraho only runs on Monday, Wednesday and Saturday. On other days, go on the same train number to Mahoba Jct, from where you can catch buses to Khajuraho.

Book tourist-quota tickets from the comfortable **foreigners' ticket office** (Map p382; ⊙ 8am-8pm Mon-Sat, to 2pm Sun) and waiting room in the main station lobby.

Luggage theft has been reported on trains to and from Varanasi, so you should take extra care. Reports of drugged food and drink aren't unheard of, so it's probably best to politely decline any offers from strangers.

ⓘ Getting Around

TO/FROM THE AIRPORT

An autorickshaw to the airport in Babatpur, 24km northwest of the city, costs ₹400. A taxi is about ₹850.

BICYCLE

You can hire bikes from a small **cycle-repair shop** (Map p386; ☑ 7237045565; 1/105 Assi-Dham; bike hire per day ₹50; ⊙ 9am-7pm) near Assi Ghat.

CYCLE-RICKSHAW

A small ride – up to 2km – costs ₹50, but be prepared for hard bargaining.

TAXI & AUTORICKSHAW

Prepaid booths for autorickshaws and taxis are directly outside Varanasi Junction train station and give you a good benchmark for prices around town – though it doesn't work as well as some other cities as there are usually no officials policing it, so you'll have to haggle here, too.

HANDY TRAINS FROM VARANASI

DESTINATION	TRAIN NO & NAME	FARE (₹)	DURATION (HR)	DEPARTURE
Agra Fort	14853/63 Marudhar Exp	350/950/1365 (A)	13	5.20pm or 6.15pm
Delhi	12561 Swatantra S Exp	415/1100/1565 (A)	12	12.40am
Delhi	22435 Vande Bharat Exp	1795/3470 (C)	8	3pm**
Gorakhpur	15003 Chaurichaura Exp	170/490/695 (A)	6½	12.35am
Jabalpur	12168 BSB-LTT Sup Exp	315/810/1140 (A)	8½	10.25am
Khajuraho	21108 BSB-Kurj Link E	265/720 (B)	11½	5.45pm*
Kolkata (Howrah)	12334 Vibhuti Exp	415/1100/1565 (A)	13½	6.08pm
Lucknow	14235 BSB-BE Exp	210/570/810 (A)	7¼	11.40pm
Prayagraj	15159 Sarnath Exp	140/490/695 (A)	3	12.25pm

Fares: (A) sleeper/3AC/2AC, (B) sleeper/3AC, (C) chair car/executive class; * Monday, Wednesday, Saturday only, ** Tuesday, Wednesday, Friday, Saturday and Sunday

Note that taxis and autorickshaws cannot access the Dashashwamedh Ghat area between the hours of 9am and 9pm due to high pedestrian traffic. You'll be dropped at Godaulia Crossing and will need to walk the remaining 400m or so to the entrance to the Old City, or 700m or so all the way to Dashashwamedh Ghat. During banned hours, autorickshaws line up near Godaulia Crossing.

Autorickshaws cannot enter the backstreets of the old town, so you'll have to carry your luggage from Mandapur Rd.

Sample fares from the train station:

Assi Ghat Auto/taxi ₹150/300

Godaulia Crossing Auto/taxi ₹100/250

Sarnath Auto/taxi ₹180/400

Mughal Serai Auto/taxi ₹400/750

Shared autorickshaws to Assi Ghat and Lanka Crossing for Banares University leave from Godaulia Crossing and travel down Mandapur/ Shivala Rd. Taxis offer half-/full-day city tours (four/eight hours) for ₹500/1000.

Sarnath

📞 0542

Buddha came to Sarnath to preach his message of the middle way to nirvana after he achieved enlightenment at Bodhgaya, and gave his famous first sermon at the deer park in Isipatana. In the 3rd century BC, Emperor Ashoka erected magnificent stupas and monasteries here, as well as an engraved pillar. When Chinese traveller Xuan Zang dropped by in AD 640, Sarnath boasted a 100m-high stupa and 1500 monks living in large monasteries. However, soon after, Buddhism went into decline, and when Muslim invaders sacked the city in the late 12th century, Sarnath disappeared altogether. It was only 're-discovered' by British archaeologists in 1835.

Today it's one of the four key sites on the Buddhist circuit (p1150) – along with Bodhgaya, Kushinagar and Lumbini in Nepal – and attracts followers from around the world, especially on Purnima (or, informally, Buddha's birthday), when Buddha's life, death and enlightenment are celebrated, usually in April or May.

⊙ Sights

Purchase tickets for Sarnath's sights at the **ticket office** (⊙ dawn-dusk) opposite the Archaeological Museum gardens. In addition to the main sights, check out some of the temples and gardens created by various Buddhist nations.

Dhamekh Stupa & Monastery Ruins   BUDDHIST SITE

(Dharmapala Rd; Indian/foreigner ₹25/300, video ₹25; ⊙ dawn-dusk) Set in a peaceful park containing monastery ruins is this impressive 34m stupa, marking the spot where the Buddha preached his first sermon. The floral and geometric carvings are 5th century AD, but some of the brickwork dates back as far as 200 BC.

Nearby is the 3rd-century-BC Ashoka Pillar, engraved with an edict. It once stood 15m tall and had the famous four-lion capital, now in the museum, perched atop; all that remains are five fragments of its base.

Thai Temple & Monastery   BUDDHIST TEMPLE

(Museum Rd; ⊙ 6.30am-6pm Apr-Sep, 7.15am-5pm Oct-Mar) With its unique, red-walled design, the temple is worth a look, but the real reasons to visit are the peaceful gardens and large standing Buddha that surround it.

Archaeological Museum   MUSEUM

(Museum Rd; ₹5; ⊙ 9am-5pm Sat-Thu) This fully modernised, 100-year-old sandstone museum

Sarnath

⊙ Sights

🛏 Sleeping

✴ Eating

houses wonderfully displayed ancient treasures, such as the very well-preserved, 3rd-century-BC lion capital from the Ashoka Pillar, which has been adopted as India's national emblem, and a huge 2000-year-old stone umbrella, ornately carved with Buddhist symbols.

Mulgandha Kuti Vihar BUDDHIST TEMPLE
(Dharmapala Rd; camera/video ₹20/100; ⏱4am-11.30am & 1.30-7.30pm Feb-Nov, 4am-12.30pm & 1.30-7.30pm Dec & Jan) This turreted temple was completed in 1931 by the Mahabodhi Society, and is noted for its interesting wall frescoes, which depict events from Buddha's life. Buddha's first sermon is chanted daily, starting between 6pm and 7pm, depending on the season. A bodhi tree growing to the east was propagated in 1931 from the tree in Anuradhapura, Sri Lanka, that is said to be the offspring of the original tree in Bodhgaya, under which Buddha gained enlightenment.

🛏 Sleeping & Eating

**Lhaden Chenmo
Tibetan Monastery** GUESTHOUSE $
(☎0542-2595002; monlamtrust@gmail.com; Ashok Marg, Sa 10/83; d with/without AC ₹1000/600, r without bathroom ₹300; ❂🖥) The modest, well-kept Tibetan monastery (the first built by the Dalai Lama in India, in 1955) offers simple but clean rooms with a shared balcony.

Agrawal Paying Guest House GUESTHOUSE $
(☎9839727729, 0542-2595316; agrawalpg@gmail.com; 14/94 Ashok Marg; r ₹1200-1500, with AC ₹1700-2000; ❂🖥) A peaceful place with a refined owner, and spotless marble-floored rooms overlooking a large and very pleasant garden. Upstairs rooms come with AC and hot water and are most spacious.

Vaishali Restaurant INDIAN, CHINESE $
(www.vaishalirestaurant.com; cnr Dharmapala & Station Rds; mains ₹80-250, nonveg ₹350; ⏱8am-9pm) Large and modern, pumpkin-orange 1st-floor restaurant serving mostly Indian dishes, but some Chinese too. It's the best in town.

ℹ Getting There & Away

Local buses to Sarnath (₹20, 40 minutes) pass in front of Varanasi Junction train station, but you may wait a long time for one.

An autorickshaw costs ₹200 one way from Varanasi, or figure on around ₹600 for a return day trip, with waiting time.

If you prefer, you can return to Varanasi in a shared auto or *vikram* (₹15) from a stand outside the Thai temple to Pandeypur, where you'll need to switch to another shared auto to Benia Bagh (₹15), which is just a ₹40 cycle-rickshaw ride from Godaulia Crossing in central Varanasi.

Getting a train to Sarnath is generally more hassle than it's worth, but there are unreserved trains from Varanasi to Sarnath at 6.55am (daily), 9.40am (Monday to Saturday) and 9.50pm (Sunday to Friday); hop on and pay ₹20. From Sarnath to Varanasi, catch train 15159 at 11.35am (Sarnath Express; sleeper/3AC ₹140/490, 45 minutes), or take an unreserved train at 5.43am (Sunday to Friday) or 3.38pm (Monday to Friday).

Gorakhpur

☎0551 / POP 675,000
There's little to see in gritty Gorakhpur, but this well-connected transport hub on the road between Varanasi and Nepal is only a short hop from the pilgrimage centre of Kushinagar (the place where Buddha died), making it a possible stopover.

🛏 Sleeping & Eating

10 Park Street B&B BOUTIQUE HOTEL $$
(☎7618101010; www.10parkstreet.com; BKD Sq, Civil Lines; s/d incl breakfast from ₹3300/3894; ❂🖥) Gorakhpur's hippest choice is this new, fresh and well-run 17-room place decorated with designer touches and colourful pop art. There's little in the way of natural light or communal seating areas, but the smallish rooms are comfortable and have walk-in showers, and the ground-floor restaurant (mains ₹250) is a great refuge for coffee and Western food.

**Chowdhry
Sweet House** MULTICUISINE, DESSERTS $
(cnr Cinema & Bank Rds; mains ₹80-230; ⏱8am-11pm; ☎) This bilevel madhouse is packed with locals taking in an extensive array of delicious Indian and Chinese veg dishes in a diner atmosphere, including ginormous dosas and excellent thalis (₹185 to ₹275). Dinner is served upstairs. Get a cycle-rickshaw ride (₹30) here from the railway station (ask for the Vijay Picture Palace).

Shahanshah INDIAN $$
(Royal Residency Hotel, Golghar Rd; mains ₹180-375; ⏱11am-10.30pm) At the Royal Residency Hotel, this restaurant is a fun homage to Bollywood icon Amitabh Bachhaan, featuring a wall full of headshots and a mural of the star. The atmosphere is modern and pleasant, with tasteful lighting and e-tablet menus. The food is good, too – definitely worth a visit.

ℹ Information

There are State Bank of India ATMs in the train station parking lot and across from Hotel Adarsh Palace.

UP Tourism (☑ 0551-2335450; ⏱10am-5pm Mon-Sat) Inside Gorakhpur's train station.

ℹ Getting There & Away

BUS

Frequent bus services run from the main bus stand, 10 minutes' walk (400m) south of the train station, to Faizabad (₹183, 3½ hours, every 30 minutes), Kushinagar (₹61, 1½ hours, every 30 minutes). Private AC buses to Faizabad (₹261, 3½ hours, hourly) and Lucknow (₹534, six hours) also depart from here throughout the day.

Buses to Sunauli (₹90, three hours, every 30 minutes) leave from just north of the main bus stand. Faster **shared cars** (per person/vehicle ₹300/1500, two hours) to Sunauli leave when full between 5am and 6pm, directly across from the train station.

Buses to Varanasi (₹232 to ₹339, seven hours, hourly, AC bus at 9.30am) and Prayagraj (Allahabad; ₹405, 10 hours, express at 7am, then hourly) should leave from the Kachari bus station, about 3km south of the main bus statnd, but at the time of writing were leaving from a stand at Padleyganj Chauraha junction, so check in advance.

TRAIN

There are three daily trains (four on Tuesday and Thursday, five on Friday and Saturday) from big and bustling Gorakhpur Junction to Varanasi (sleeper/3AC/2AC ₹170/490/695, 5½ hours). A number of daily trains also leave for Lucknow (sleeper/3AC/2AC ₹190/490/695, five hours) and Delhi (sleeper/3AC/2AC ₹395/1080/1555, 14 to 17 hours) and one, the 19038/40 Avadh Express, for Agra Fort (sleeper/3AC/2AC ₹335/910/1305, 14½ hours, 1.20pm).

The **train ticket reservation office** (Railway Station Rd; ⏱ 8am-2pm, 2.15-10pm Mon-Sat, 8am-2pm Sun) is 500m to the right as you exit the station.

Kushinagar

☑ 05564 / POP 23,000

One of the four main pilgrimage sites marking Buddha's life – the others being Lumbini (Nepal), Bodhgaya and Sarnath – Kushinagar is where Buddha died. There are several peaceful, modern temples where you can stay, chat with monks or simply contemplate your place in the world, and there are three main historical sights, including the simple but wonderfully serene stupa where Buddha is said to have been cremated.

◉ Sights

In addition to the main ruins, Kushinagar's one road is lined with elaborate temples run by various Buddhist nations.

★ Mahaparinirvana Temple   BUDDHIST TEMPLE

(Buddha Marg; ⏱6am-dusk) The highlight of this modest temple, rebuilt in 1927 and set among extensive lawns and excavated monastery and stupa ruins with a circumambulatory path, is its serene 5th-century reclining Buddha, unearthed in 1876. Six metres long, it depicts Buddha on his deathbed in the *paranirvana* position; the devotion of pilgrims faced with the image is quite moving. At sunset, monks cover the statue to the shoulders with a long saffron-coloured silk sheet, as though putting Buddha to bed for the night.

Behind the temple is a modern 19m-tall stupa encasing an ancient original, and in the surrounding park is a large bell in honour of the Dalai Lama.

Ramabhar Stupa   BUDDHIST SITE

Architecturally, this half-ruined 15m-high stupa is little more than a dome-shaped clump of red bricks, but there's an unmistakable aura about this place that is hard to ignore. This is where Buddha's body is said to have been cremated, and monks and pilgrims can often be seen offering lotus flowers and meditating by the palm-tree-lined path that leads around the 34m-diameter structure. Nearby is the modern cremation site at **Buddha Ghat** (Buddha Marg).

Mathakuar Temple   BUDDHIST TEMPLE

(Buddha Marg; ⏱dawn-dusk) This small shrine, set among monastery ruins, marks the spot where Buddha is said to have made his final sermon. It now houses a beautiful gilded 3m-tall blue-stone Buddha statue, thought to date from the 10th century AD.

Wat Thai Complex   BUDDHIST TEMPLE

(www.watthaikusinara-th.org; Buddha Marg; ⏱9-11.30am & 1.30-4pm) This large complex, much of it off limits to visitors, features an elaborate temple surrounded by beautifully maintained gardens with bonsai-style trees, and a side stupa containing relics of the Buddha and the late king of Thailand. Accommodation here is reserved for Thai citizens only.

UTTAR PRADESH KUSHINAGAR

Kushinagar

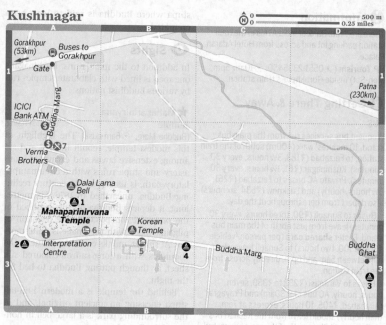

Kushinagar

◎ Top Sights
1 Mahaparinirvana Temple A2

◎ Sights
2 Mathakuar Temple A3
3 Ramabhar Stupa D3
4 Wat Thai Complex B3

⌂ Sleeping
5 Lotus Nikko B3
6 Tibetan Monastery Guesthouse A3

⊗ Eating
7 Yama Cafe A2

🛏 Sleeping & Eating

⭐ **Tibetan Monastery Guesthouse** GUESTHOUSE $
(Phuntsok Choephel Ling Namgyal Monastery; ☑ 9559404571, 9889506590; Buddha Marg; d/tr ₹600/700; ☎) By far the nicest of Kushinagar's pilgrim accommodation offerings, this is a great temple choice. Rooms come with en suite cold-water bathrooms and fans, with relaxing porch sitting areas. Tibetan monks from Dharamsala do a one- to two-year managerial stint here and usually speak good English.

Lotus Nikko HOTEL $$
(☑ 9868877986; www.lotusnikkohotels.com; Buddha Marg; s/d ₹3750/3990; ❄ ☎) Thai and Japanese groups favour this well-run hotel and for good reason: the rooms are simple but spacious and there's a pleasant garden area. The restaurant is probably the best in town and nonguests can often piggyback on the evening Thai buffets.

Yama Cafe MULTICUISINE $
(☑ 9956112749; Buddha Marg; mains ₹60-120; ☺ 8am-8pm) Run by the welcoming Mr Roy, this Kushinagar institution has a simple, traveller-friendly menu that includes toast, omelettes, fried rice and *thukpa* (Tibetan noodle soup).

It's also the best place to come for information about the area, including the guided 13km walk through surrounding farmland to a Gupta-era fort (minimum five people).

ℹ Information

ICICI Bank ATM (Buddha Marg; ☺ 24hr)

Interpretation Centre (Buddha Marg; ☺ 6am-5.30pm) This small room offers background info on Kushinagar, old photos of the 19th-century excavations and a short movie on the main sights.

Verma Brothers (☑ 9935584753; Buddha Marg; ☺ 9am-7pm) Changes a wide range of foreign cash into rupees at good rates.

ℹ Getting There & Away

A new international airport may be open by the time you read this, likely starting with international charter flights for Buddhist groups.

Frequent buses to Gorakhpur (₹61, 1½ hours) can be flagged down along the main road, in the middle lane across from the yellow archway entrance to town.

A return taxi from Gorakhpur costs around ₹2000, including waiting time.

Sunauli & the Nepal Border

♪ 05522 / POP 700

Sunauli (Sonauli) is a dusty town that offers little more than a bus stop, a couple of simple hotels, a few shops and a busy border post. The border is open 24 hours and the crossing is straightforward, so most travellers carry on into Nepal without stopping here, pausing just long enough to get their passport stamped. Some move on to Lumbini via the nearby town of Bhairawa (officially named Siddharthanagar), while others get straight on a bus to Kathmandu or Pokhara.

Buses drop you just a few hundred metres from the Indian Immigration Office (⊙ 24hr) – it's on the main road about 800m from the border post. Don't forget to stamp in or out of India here!

If you need to stay, Hotel Indo-Nepal (☏ 9451273851; r with air-cooler ₹850, r with air-cooler ₹850, with AC ₹1550-2050; ✺ ☎), about 100m north of the Indian Immigration Office and opposite the bus station, is marginally the most comfortable accommodation option in town. The AC rooms have good beds set around a small courtyard, and there's a decent restaurant attached. The manager is helpful. Rooms vary, so have a look at a couple before committing.

ℹ Getting There & Away

Frequent government and private buses run from Sunauli to Gorakhpur (₹112, three hours, 4am to 7pm) from where you can catch trains and buses onwards. One daily AC deluxe Scania bus to Varanasi (₹750, 10 hours) leaves at 7am. Faster shared taxis to Gorakhpur hang out between the bus stand and Indian immigration and leave when full (₹300, two hours). A taxi to Gorakhpur costs around ₹1500.

ℹ CROSSING TO NEPAL: SUNAULI TO BHAIRAWA (SIDDHARTHANAGAR)

Border Hours

The border is open 24 hours but closes to vehicles from 10pm to 6am, and if you arrive in the middle of the night, you may have to wake someone to get stamped out of India.

For further information, head to shop.lonelyplanet.com to purchase a downloadable PDF of the Kathmandu chapter from Lonely Planet's *Nepal* guide.

Foreign Exchange

Money changers on the Nepali side of the border change Indian rupees to Nepali rupees at fixed rates (NRs100:₹60, ₹100:NRs160), as the currencies are pegged. They also change US dollars into Nepali rupees, but not the other way round. Try Najendra Money Changer (Siddhartha Hwy, Belahiya; ⊙ 6.30am-8pm) just over the border on the Nepal side. There are ATMs on both sides of the border, and small denominations of Indian currency (₹100 and under) are accepted for bus fares on the Nepali side.

Onward Transport

Buses to Kathmandu (₹560 to ₹825, 12 hours) leave frequently from the Nepal side of the border. Local buses (₹25) and autorickshaws (₹100) can take you from the border to the Bhairahawa bus station, 3km away, where you can also catch non-AC buses to Kathmandu via Narayangarh; and to Pokhara (₹525, nine hours, last bus 8.30pm).

Local buses for Buddha's birthplace at Lumbini (₹80, one hour) leave from the junction of the Siddhartha Hwy and the road to Lumbini, 5km north of the border.

Buddha Air (www.buddhaair.com) and Yeti Airlines (www.yetiairlines.com) offer flights to Kathmandu from Siddharthanagar (from US$135).

Visas

Multiple-entry visas (15/30/90 days US$25/40/100) are available at the Nepal Immigration Post (⊙ 24hr). You must pay with US cash, not rupees, and you need two passport photos. Visit www.nepalimmigration.gov.np for the latest information on Nepali visas.

Lucknow

📞 0522 / POP 3.4 MILLION

Sprinkled with exceptional Islamic and British Raj–era architecture, stuffed with fascinating bazaars and famed throughout India for its food, the capital of Uttar Pradesh is something of a sleeper: plenty worth seeing, but often overlooked by travellers. Central Lucknow features wide boulevards, epic monuments and several parks and gardens that contribute to an atmosphere of faded grandiosity. Locals tend to be welcoming, and you'll experience little of the hassle of more touristy towns.

The city rose to prominence as the home of the Nawabs of Avadh (Oudh), who were great patrons of the culinary and other arts, particularly dance and music. Lucknow's reputation as a city of culture, gracious living and rich cuisine has continued to this day – the phrase for which conveniently

rhymes in Hindi: *Nawab, aadaab* (respect), *kebab* and *shabab* (beauty).

◉ Sights

★ Residency
HISTORIC SITE

(Indian/foreigner ₹25/300; ⊙ dawn-dusk, museum closed Fri) The large collection of gardens and ruins that makes up the Residency offers a fascinating historical glimpse of the beginning of the end for the British Raj. Built in 1800, the Residency became the stage for the most dramatic events of the 1857 First War of Independence (Indian Uprising): the Siege of Lucknow, a 147-day siege that claimed the lives of thousands. The leafy compound has been left as it was at the time of the final relief and the walls are still pockmarked from bullets and cannon balls.

The focus is the small **museum** (⊙ 9am-5pm, closed Fri) in the main Residency building, which includes a scale model of the original buildings and sketches made just after

Lucknow

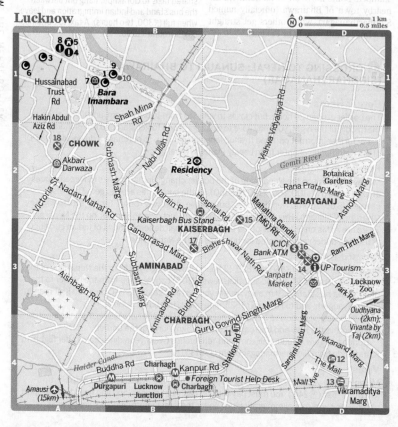

the uprising. The currently closed basement rooms were where many of the British women and children lived throughout the siege.

The cemetery around the ruined St Mary's church is where 2000 of the defenders were buried, including their leader, Sir Henry Lawrence, who – according to the famous inscription on his weathered gravestone – 'tried to do his duty'.

★ **Bara Imambara** ISLAMIC TOMB
(Hussainabad Trust Rd; Indian/foreigner ₹50/500; ⊙6am-6pm) This colossal *imambara* (Shiite tomb complex) is worth seeing in its own right, but the highly unusual labyrinth of corridors inside its upper floors make a visit here particularly special. The ticket price includes entrance to the Chota Imambara and Hussainabad Picture Gallery (p400), both walking distance from here.

The complex is accessed through two enormous gateways that lead into a huge courtyard. On one side is the three-domed Asafri Mosque, on the other a large baoli (step-well), whose multiple levels can be explored – bring a torch (flashlight). At the far end of the courtyard is the huge central hall, one of the world's largest vaulted galleries. Tazia (small replicas of Imam Hussain's tomb in Karbala, Iraq) are stored inside and are paraded around during the Shiite mourning ceremony of Muharram.

But it's what is beyond the small entrance – intriguingly marked 'labyrinth' – to the left of the central hall that steals the show. It leads to the Bhulbhulaiya, a disorienting network of narrow passageways that winds its way inside the upper floors of the tomb's inner structure, eventually leading out to rooftop balconies.

Just beyond the Bara Imambara is the unusual but imposing gateway Rumi Darwaza (Hussainabad Trust Rd), said to be a copy of an entrance gate in Istanbul; 'Rumi' (relating to Rome) is the term Muslims applied to Istanbul when it was still Byzantium, the capital of the Eastern Roman empire. The scalloped western face is the most impressive.

Across the road from the Bara Imambara is the beautiful white mosque Tila Wali Masjid, a deceptively shallow building built in 1680 and most impressive from a distance (it's often locked).

If you are visiting as part of an opposite-sex couple, you will be required to pay for a guide (₹100) to prevent any hanky-panky in the labyrinth (yes, we're serious).

Chota Imambara ISLAMIC TOMB
(Hussainabad Imambara; Hussainabad Trust Rd; Indian/foreigner ₹20/200, incl with Bara Imambara ticket; ⊙8.30am-7pm) This elaborate black-and-white tomb was constructed in 1832 by the third king of Oudh, Mohammed Ali Shah (who is buried here, alongside his mother). Adorned with calligraphy, it has a serene and intimate atmosphere. Mohammed's silver throne and red crown can be seen here, as well as countless chintzy chandeliers and some brightly decorated *tazia*.

In the garden is a water tank and two replicas of the Taj Mahal that are the tombs of Mohammed Ali Shah's daughter and her husband. A traditional hammam is off to one side.

Outside the complex, the decaying salmon-coloured watchtower on the other side of the road is known as Satkhanda (Seven Storey Tower; Hussainabad Trust Rd). It has only four storeys because construction was abandoned in 1840 when Mohammed Ali Shah died.

The nearby 67m red-brick clock tower, the tallest in India, was built in the 1880s. Next to it is the **Hussainabad Picture Gallery** (Baradari; Indian/foreigner ₹20/200, incl with Bara Imambara ticket; ⊙7am-7pm), a run-down red-brick *baradari* (pavilion) built in 1842 that was once a royal summer house. It overlooks an octagonal stepped *talab* (water tank) and houses portraits of Oudh's former nawabs.

Just around the corner is the huge **Jama Masjid** (Friday Mosque; Hussainabad Trust Rd; ⊙dawn-dusk), completed in 1845. Non-Muslims can't enter, but it's worth seeing the impressive three-domed facade.

🗘 Tours

★ UP Tourism Heritage Walking Tour
WALKING

(📞Naved Zia 9415013047; 3hr tour ₹330; ⊙tours 7am Apr-Sep, 8am Oct-Mar) This fabulous tour run by UP Tourism could well turn out to be the best ₹330 you ever spend. Meet your English-speaking guide outside Tila Wali Masjid, then follow the guide first around the mosque and the Bara Imambara before delving in to the architectural delights of the crazy maze of alleyways in the fascinating Chowk district to the south.

You'll sample interesting nibbles such as refreshing *thandai* (made from milk, cardamom, almonds, fennel, saffron etc and – in this case – with or without marijuana!) and get an insider glimpse into various traditions, from indigo block printing to traditional *unani* medicine or *vark* making (edible silver foil). This is an eye-popping way to get your bearings among Lucknow's oldest neighbourhoods. Note: tours are best booked directly by phone and last between 2½ and three hours. If this leaves you wanting more, ask about the new Kaiserbagh heritage walk.

SLEEPING PRICE RANGES

Accommodation price ranges in this region are for a double room with private bathroom in high season:

$ less than ₹1500

$$ ₹1500–₹4000

$$$ more than ₹4000

🛏 Sleeping

Lucknow Homestay
HOMESTAY **$**

(📞9838003590, 0522-2235460; lucknowhomestay@gmail.com; 110D Mall Ave; s/d incl breakfast ₹1000/1200, without bathroom ₹800/1000; ❄🛜) Lucknow's most accommodating budget option is in the leafy neighbourhood home of Naheed and her family, who keep their distance but offer eight spacious, high-ceilinged rooms, four with private bathrooms. Breakfast is served on the cheerful yellow communal dining table. There's a sign in front; enter and go up one flight of stairs. Book ahead – it's popular for long stays.

Rickshaw drivers know Mall Ave, which is actually a neighbourhood (not merely an avenue); the easiest access is from Mahatma Gandhi (MG) Rd. Shared bathrooms are small and offer bucket hot-water showers only and some mattresses are lumpy, but you'll appreciate the quiet and the friendly welcome.

Hotel Ganga Maiya
HOTEL **$$**

(📞0522-4075921, 9335282783; www.hotelgangamaiya.com; 62/9 Station Rd; s/d from ₹1400/1600; ❄🛜) Clean and well run, and even the cheapest rooms have wi-fi, flat-screen TVs and good beds; the higher-priced deluxe rooms (single/double ₹1800/2000) in the colourful back block offer more space and are quieter, making them worth the money.

★ Lebua Lucknow
HISTORIC HOTEL **$$$**

(📞0522-2238333; www.lebua.com; r from ₹7600; ❄@🛜🏊) The 1939 Morris by the entrance sets the tone here, with a classy and stylish collection of courtyards and all-white terraces given colour by original terrazzo flooring, art deco flourishes and lovely bougainvilla. The 41 rooms were once part of a 1936 *haveli* (ornately decorated traditional residence) and boast antique furniture, some with four-poster beds and private terraces.

There's an excellent Italian restaurant (evenings Monday to Friday, lunch and dinner Saturday and Sunday; mains ₹550 to ₹650) with outdoor seating and a pizza oven, and rooftop bar (beer/cocktail ₹300/700; from 7pm), plus a swimming pool with loungers. It's also known as the Saraca Estate after the Ashoka trees in the garden.

🍴 Eating

Lucknow is the undisputed king of UP cuisine. The refined palates of the Nawabs left

LUCKNOW'S KEBABS DECONSTRUCTED

Kakori Kebab

Originates from Kakori, a small town outside Lucknow. Legend has it that the old and tooth-less Nawab of Kakori asked his royal *bawarchi* (chef) to make kebabs that would simply melt in the mouth. So these kebabs are made adding papaya (as a tenderiser) to raw mincemeat and a mix of spices. They are then applied to skewers and barbecued over charcoals.

Galawat

This is the mouth-watering creation that is served up in Lucknow's most famous kebab restaurant, Tunday Kababi. There it is simply referred to as a mutton kebab, and in other restaurants it is often called Tunday. Essentially, they're the same as Kakori kebabs, except that rather than being barbecued they are made into patties and shallow-fried in oil or ghee.

Shami

Raw mincemeat is boiled with spices and black gram lentil. It is then ground on stone before being mixed with finely chopped onions, coriander leaves and green chillies, then shaped into patties and shallow-fried.

the city with a reputation for rich, meaty and impossibly tasty Mughlai cuisine. Restaurants here are famous for mouth-watering kebabs and delicious biryanis.

★ **Tunday Kababi**　　　　NORTH INDIAN $
(Naaz Cinema Rd, off Aminabad Rd; dishes ₹44-220; ⏰11am-11.30pm) This is the cleaner, more tourist-friendly outlet of Lucknow's renowned, 100-year-old, impossible-to-find kebab shop in **Chowk** (near Akbari Darwaza, Chowk; kebab plate ₹20; ⏰10am-11pm), where buffalo-meat kebabs go for ₹20 a plate. Here the prices are higher, but the staff put on quite a show streetside for to-go orders, while the proper restaurant behind dishes up scrumptious plates of mutton biryani, kebabs and tandoori chicken for throngs of carnivores.

The minced-mutton Galawati kebab (₹84 for four) is buttery soft and packs a spicy punch in the gut; eat them with silky *paratha* (Indian-style flaky bread made with ghee and cooked on a hotplate) or a *sheermal* (round bread flavoured with saffron). It's tucked away just off the bustling main Aminabad chowk. You'll find other Tunday kebab restaurants around the city – some of which are franchises, most of which are copies.

Sakhawat　　　　　　NORTH INDIAN $
(www.sakhawatrestaurant.com; 2 Kaiserbagh Ave; kebabs ₹120-160; ⏰4-10.30pm Wed-Mon) This highly recommended hole-in-the-wall doesn't look like much, but the daily-changing kebabs (*galawat* etc) at this locals' haunt are grilled to smoky, crispy perfection – and,

despite appearances, it has won international accolades and doubles as an Awadh cooking institute. Also serves biryanis and several curries.

Naimat Khana　　　　NORTH INDIAN $$
(☑9115004646; www.sanatkada.in/naimat-khana; 130 JC Bose Rd, Kaiserbagh; mains ₹200-425; ⏰noon-10pm Wed-Mon; 🐀) This charming hidden corner at the back of Sanatkada (p402) has a unique concept: persuading Lucknow's oldest households to cook their cherished family recipes for public consumption. Standout dishes include mutton korma, *yaqani pulao* (rice steam-cooked with tender mutton) and *roghani tikiya,* a traditional breakfast of flatbread with *aloo qatli* potato. You won't find these kind of sophisticated, intense favours anywhere else.

Royal Cafe　　　　　MULTICUISINE $$
(51 MG Rd; mains ₹230-490; ⏰11am-11pm; ❄) Even if you don't step inside this classy restaurant, don't miss its exceedingly popular *chaat* (spicy snack) stand at the front. The sweet and savoury mixed-basket *chaat* is served in a crispy *aloo* (potato) basket; eat it on the street for ₹190 or in the restaurant for ₹250. Finish with a foot-long pistachio- and saffron-flavoured *kesar pista kulfi* (ice cream).

Moti Mahal Restaurant　　　INDIAN $$
(75 MG Rd; mains ₹175-210; ⏰7.30am-11pm; ❄🍴) If Mughlai meat country has got you down, seek refuge in this popular veg hideaway on MG Rd. It's perfect for an Indian-style breakfast, a snack or a dessert (try the *rabri* – made from chilled condensed milk

and available in a sugar-free version). Come evening, head upstairs for excellent veg cuisine in the good air-conditioned restaurant.

★**Oudhyana**   MUGHLAI, NORTH INDIAN $$$
(www.vivantabytaj.com; Vivanta by Taj Hotel, Vipin Khand, Gomti Nagar; mains ₹780-900; ⏱12.30-2.45pm & 7.30-11.30pm) If you want to savour the flavours of the Nawabs performing at their culinary best, look no further than Oudhyana, where Chef Nagendra Singh gives Lucknow's famous Awadh cuisine its royal due at this signature restaurant inside the city's **top hotel** (☎0522-6771000; s/d from ₹12,800/15,360; ❋@🖥🏊).

Drinking & Nightlife

EOS Bar & Bistro   BAR
(72 MG Rd; cocktail ₹400-600; ⏱4pm-1am) This chic bar on the rooftop of the Levana Hotel is Lucknow's attempt at a genuinely trendy bar. It draws the young and restless, especially for Saturday night DJ sets and big-screen sports. Otherwise, the breezy, plant- and bamboo-filled spot is pleasant for a cocktail or a full meal (mains ₹500). Happy-hour deals from 4pm to 10pm.

Shopping

Lucknow is famous for *chikan,* an embroidered cloth worn by men and women. It is sold in a number of shops in the labyrinthine bazaars of Chowk (near the Tunday Kebabi there), and in the small, traffic-free Janpath Market, just south of MG Rd in Hazratganj.

Sanatkada   ARTS & CRAFTS
(www.sanatkada.in; 130 JC Bose Rd, Kaiserbagh; ⏱11am-8pm) For the best handicrafts in town head for this collection of fabrics and handmade designer clothes made by NGOs from across India, alongside modern crafts created by Lucknow designers. Handwoven scarves, jute bags and retro Bollywood pillows are fun, and there are twists on the city's famous *chikan* embroidery. Prices are marked; credit cards accepted.

ℹ Information

ICICI Bank ATM (Shalimar Tower, 31/54 MG Rd, Hazratganj; ⏱8am-8pm Mon-Fri, 9am-2pm Sat)
Main Post Office (www.indiapost.gov.in; MG Rd; ⏱10am-4pm Mon-Sat) In a building of Grand Raj–era architecture.
Sahara Hospital (☎0522-6780001; www.saharahospitals.com; Gomti Nagar) The best private hospital in Lucknow.
Tourist Police (MG Rd, Hazratganj; ⏱8am-9pm Mon-Sat) Located at the UP Tourism kiosk.
UP Tourism (☎tourism hotline 0522-3303030; www.uptourism.gov.in; MG Rd, Hazratganj; ⏱8am-9pm Mon-Sat) This small UP Tourism information kiosk conveniently located on MG Rd also houses the Tourist Police.

ℹ Getting There & Away

AIR

The modern **Chaudhary Charan Singh International Airport** (☎0522-2435404; www.lucknowairport.com) is 15km southwest of Lucknow in Amausi, with several airlines offering direct daily service to many domestic cities, including Delhi, Mumbai, Ahmedabad, Kolkata, Jaipur and Benguluru (Bangalore). Nonstop international flights head to several Gulf destinations, as well as Singapore.

BUS

Most long-distance buses leave from modern Alambagh Bus Station. Shared autos (₹10) run

HANDY TRAINS FROM LUCKNOW

DESTINATION	TRAIN NO & NAME	FARE (₹)	DURATION (HR)	DEPARTURE
Agra	12179 LJN AGC INTRCT	145/515 (C)	6	3.55pm
Delhi	12553 Vaishali Exp	335/865/1220 (A)	8	10.25pm
Faizabad	13010 Doon Exp	140/490/695 (A)	2½	8.45am
Gorakhpur	13020 Bagh Exp	190/490/695 (A)	6	6.20am
Jhansi	11016 Kushinagar Exp	195/490/695 (A)	6½	12.40am
Kolkata (Howrah)	13006 ASR-HWH Mail	480/1300/1890 (A)	20½	10.50am
Mumbai (CST)*	12533 Pushpak Exp	626/1627/2337 (A)	24	7.45pm
Prayagraj	14216 Ganga Gomti Exp, 14210 Lucknow-Prayag Intercity	340 (B), 330 (B)	4½, 4	6pm, 7.30am
Varanasi	14236 BE-BSB Exp	210/570/810 (A)	7½	11.25pm

Fares: (A) sleeper/3AC/2AC, (B) AC chair only, (C) 2S/AC chair; * leaves from Lucknow Junction

here from the Charbagh Bus Station, opposite the railway station. Check luxury bus services at www.upsrtconline.co.in. Services offered include the following:

Agra Non-AC (₹400, seven hours, 4.30pm and 8.30pm), regular AC (₹620-₹680, six hours, 8.30am, 6pm and 7pm), Scania AC (₹898, six hours, 10am, noon, 4pm and 10pm).

Delhi Non-AC (₹510, 11 hours), AC (₹805 to ₹1356, nine hours). Departs throughout the day.

Faizabad Non-AC (₹173, four hours, every 30 minutes), Volvo AC (₹386, three hours, 10am).

Gorakhpur Non-AC (₹335, 7½ hours, every 30 minutes), regular AC (₹463 to ₹538, six hours, hourly), Scania-Volvo AC (₹750, six hours, 8.30am, 10am, 11am and 11pm).

Jhansi Regular AC (₹494, eight hours, 4pm and 8pm).

Prayagraj (Allahabad) Non-AC (₹220, five hours, every 30 minutes), regular AC (₹280, five hours, departs throughout day), Volvo AC (₹487, 4½ hours, 10 daily).

Varanasi Non-AC (₹200, eight hours, every 30 minutes), regular AC (₹466 to ₹540, six hours, 9am, 10am, 1pm, 7.40pm, 8.45pm, 9.45pm and 10.20), Volvo AC (₹770, six hours, 8am, 11am, 3pm, 9pm and 10pm).

Kaiserbagh Bus Stand (☑ 0522-2622503; J Narain Rd) also has services to Gorakhpur (₹500) via Faizabad (₹200) every hour or two, as well as hourly buses to Rupaidiha (₹195, five hours), for the little-used Nepal border crossing with Nepalganj.

TRAIN

The two main stations, Lucknow NR (usually called Charbagh) and Lucknow Junction, are side by side about 4.5km or so south of the main sites. Services for most major destinations leave from Charbagh, including several daily to Agra, Varanasi, Faizabad, Gorakhpur and Delhi. Lucknow Junction handles the one daily train to Mumbai and trains to Haldwani. Check your ticket and make sure you go to the right station!

The **Foreign Tourist Help Desk** (◷ 8am-1.50pm & 2-8pm) for booking train tickets is at window 601 inside the Rail Reservation and Booking Centre complex, 150m to your right as you exit Charbagh.

❶ Getting Around

TO/FROM THE AIRPORT

An autorickshaw or Ola taxi to the airport from the train station costs ₹250 and takes about 30 minutes.

LOCAL TRANSPORT

A short cycle-rickshaw ride is ₹30. Dealing with autorickshaws demands serious haggling: from the train station/Charbagh bus stand, pay about ₹90 to Hazratganj, or ₹130 to Bara Imambara.

The cheapest way to get around is by shared autorickshaw – flag one down and tell them the neighbourhood you're headed for (like Hazratganj, for MG Road, or Charbagh, for the railway station) and they'll wave you in if they're going that way. Pay ₹10 to ₹15 depending on the length of the trip.

Ayodhya & Around

☑ 05278 / POP 58,000

As one of Hinduism's seven holy cities, Ayodhya is dominated by religion. The town is revered as the birthplace of Rama, as well as the birthplace of four of Jainism's 24 *tirthankars* (religious teachers). It was also the site of one of modern India's most controversial religious disputes, and you'll see a more robust police presence here than normal, with intense security precautions around the site where Rama is said to have been born.

The slightly larger town of Faizabad, 7km away, is the jumping-off point for Ayodhya and where you'll find more accommodation. As the 18th-century capital of Avadh (Oudh), it's a fascinating town, with some wonderful architecture and plenty of atmospheric bazaars to explore. Best of all, you'll almost certainly have the place to yourself.

⦿ Sights

Bahu Begum Ka Maqbara   HISTORIC BUILDING
(Faizabad; ◷ dawn-dusk) FREE In Faizabad, the so-called 'Taj Mahal of the East' (OK, an overstatement) is a unique 42m-high *maqbara* (mausoleum) built for the queen of Nawab Shuja-ud-Daula. It has three domes built above each other, with wonderfully ornate decoration on the walls and ceilings, and is considered to be a prime example of Awadhi architecture.

Hanumangarhi   HINDU TEMPLE
(◷ dawn-dusk) This is one of the town's most popular temples, and is the closest of Ayodhya's major temples to the main road. Walk up the 76 steps to the ornate carved gateway and the fortresslike outer walls, and join the throng inside offering *prasad* (temple-blessed food) of sweets and marigolds.

Kanak Bhavan   HINDU TEMPLE
(Palace of Gold; www.kanak-bhavan-temple.com; ◷ 8.30-11.30am & 4.30-9.30pm Apr-Sep, 9am-noon & 4-9pm Oct-Mar) This palace converted into a

temple is one of the most impressive in Ayodhya. It was supposedly given to Lord Rama and his wife Sita as a wedding present, and the interior features three shrines dedicated to the holy couple.

Ram Katha Museum   MUSEUM
(Ram Katha Sangrahalay; ☑ 9415328511; ☉ 10am-5pm Mon-Sat) **FREE** Beyond the far northern end of the main road, this museum houses paintings and ancient sculptures. The museum is a short rickshaw ride from Ayodhya's main temples. Take a shared autorickshaw to Tulsi Ghat stand, from where it's a five-minute walk east.

Ram Janam Bhumi   HINDU TEMPLE
(☉ 7-11.30am & 12.30-5pm) This is the highly contentious spot said to be the site of Lord Rama's birth. Security here is staggering (think crossing from West Bank into Israel!). You must first show your passport to a member of the intelligence services, then leave all belongings apart from your passport and money (including sim cards, medicines and pens) in nearby lockers. You are then searched several times before being accompanied through a long, caged corridor that leads to a spot 20m away from a makeshift tent shrine, which marks Rama's birthplace.

🛏 Sleeping & Eating

Hotel Shane Avadh   HOTEL $
(☑ 05278-222075; Civil Lines, Faizabad; 's/d with AC from ₹990/1500, without from ₹450/550; ❄ 🛜) There's a huge range of rooms at this well-run and bustling establishment in Faizabad. The cheapest ones are a bit gritty and have rock-hard beds, but improve rapidly if you pay a little more. The deluxe rooms (single/double ₹1792/2240) offer midrange comfort. Book ahead. Wi-fi only in the lobby; hot water only in the morning. It offers a good restaurant and room service.

Awantika   MULTICUISINE $$
(Chandra Tower, Civil Lines, Faizabad; mains ₹150-250; ☉ 11am-10.30pm; ☑) Clean and hip, this out-of-place restaurant does a seriously good all-veg menu that runs the gamut from Chinese to Italian to Indian. The special thali (₹240) is a real treat, and it's

---

JHANSI: TRANSIT HUB

This nondescript town near the Madhya Pradesh border is famous for its link to Rani Lakshmibai of Jhansi, a key player in the 1857 First War of Independence (Indian Uprising). You might use it as a transit hub for Orchha, Khajuraho and Gwalior, but there's little reason to linger.

Few travellers overnight in Jhansi, as nearby Orchha is much nicer, but **Hotel Samrat** (☑ 0510-2444943; www.hotelsamratjhansi.com; Shivpuri Rd, Civil Lines; s/d with AC from ₹1175/1275, without ₹800/850; ❄ 🛜) near the railway station is an acceptable (if slightly grubby) budget choice if you have a late or early train.

Buses leave from the bus station for Gwalior (₹100, three hours, hourly) and Chhatarpur (₹130, three hours, hourly); from the latter you can switch for Khajuraho (₹50, 1½ hours). For Chitrakut it's easiest to travel on one of the four daily daytime trains or bus-hop via the towns of Rath and Banda.

Tempos (₹20) go between Jhansi bus stand and Orchha all day; private autorickshaws charge ₹150.

Handy trains include the following:

TRAIN & DESTINATION	TRAIN NO	FARES (SLEEPER/3AC/2AC)	DURATION (HR)	DEPARTURE
Punjab Mail to Gwalior	12137	₹170/535/735	1½	2.30pm
Punjab Mail to Agra*	12137	₹195/540/740	3½	2.30pm
Punjab Mail to Mumbai	12138	₹530/1395/2010	19	2.30pm
Grand Trunk Exp to Delhi	12615	₹280/830/1010	7½	11.40pm
Bundelkhand Exp to Varanasi	11107	₹305/720/1190	12½	10.25pm
Udz Kurj Exp to Khajuraho	19666	₹160/490/695	3	3.30pm

* For AC chair car class to Agra (₹370, 3½ hours) take the 12279 Taj Express departing at 3.20pm

CHITRAKUT: VARANASI IN MINIATURE

Known as a mini Varanasi because of its many temples and ghats (but not cremations), this small, peaceful town on the banks of the Mandakini River is the stuff of Hindu legends. It is here that Hinduism's principal trinity – Brahma, Vishnu and Shiva – took on their incarnations. It is also the place where Lord Rama is believed to have spent 11½ years of his 14-year exile after being banished from his birthplace in Ayodhya at the behest of a jealous stepmother.

Today Chitrakut (Chitrakoot) attracts throngs of pilgrims, and the absence of foreign tourists means there's a refreshing lack of hassle here. It's a great choice if you want an authentic Indian experience. Chitrakut is actually in Madhya Pradesh state, but is most easily accessed from Uttar Pradesh.

The Ram Ghat lining the banks on the River Mandakini is the focal point for pilgrims, who make holy dips at dawn before returning at the end of the day for the evening aarti (an auspicious lighting of lamps/candles). It's an interesting place to stroll, with sadhus, dancers and coloured lights lending a carnival atmosphere, and you can take short boat trips up and down the river.

Pilgrims flock to Kamadgiri, a hill revered as the holy embodiment of Lord Rama. A 5km *parikrama* (circuit) around the base of the hill takes you past prostrating pilgrims, bands of monkeys, blind musicians, holy men, tea shops and temples on a fascinating two-hour stroll. It's a fabulous cultural experience. Take a 1.5km shared rickshaw ride (₹10) west of Ram Ghat. Shoes not allowed.

all set to trendy tunes in a funky lounge atmosphere. It's five minutes west of the Hotel Shane Avadh. Indian dishes are unavailable between 3.30pm and 7pm.

ℹ Information

There are a number of ATMs in Faizabad around Hotel Shane Avadh (p404).

ℹ Getting There & Around

From the Faizabad bus stand shared autorickshaws (₹15, 20 minutes) run to Ayodhya. Get off at Hanumangarhi to visit the temples. A private autorickshaw costs ₹200.

From Faizabad bus station, frequent buses run to Lucknow (₹170, three hours), Gorakhpur (₹170, 3½ hours, 5am to 8pm) and Prayagraj (Allahabad; ₹180, five hours, 7am to 10pm).

There are several handy trains from Faizabad (prices given are for sleeper/3AC/2AC):

Delhi 12225 Kaifiyat Express, ₹380/995/1410, 11¼ hours, 7.52pm

Lucknow 13307 Gangasutlej Express, ₹140/485/690, 4½ hours, 11.08am

Varanasi 13010 Doon Express, ₹140/490/695, five hours, 11.10am

One useful service to Varanasi Jct (AC Chair Car ₹325, 4½ hours) is the No 14214 Gonda-Varanasi Intercity, departing from Ayodhya at 9.10am. A cycle-rickshaw from the bus stand to the train station is ₹30; shared autos cost ₹10 per person.

Prayagraj (Allahabad)

☑ 0532 / POP 1.2 MILLION

Brahma, the Hindu god of creation, is believed to have landed on earth in Prayagraj (or Allahabad as it was known until recently), and to have named it the king of all pilgrimage centres. Indeed, Sangam, a river confluence on the outskirts of the city, is the most celebrated of India's four Kumbh Mela festival locations. Prayagraj was also home to the Nehru clan, whose house served as a headquarters for the independence movement against the British Raj.

Yet for all its importance in Hindu mythology, Indian history and modern politics, Prayagraj today is a much humbler place. Though there are a few good places to stay and eat, the main sights are of modest appeal – and the mix of dust, exhaust fumes and traffic make for a gritty stay. The commercial heart of the city is Civil Lines, centred on MG Marg, which has the bulk of the shops, restaurants and hotels.

◉ Sights

★ Sangam   RELIGIOUS SITE

This is the particularly auspicious point (*sangam* means 'river confluence') where two of India's holiest rivers, the Ganges and the Yamuna, meet one of Hinduism's mythological rivers, the Saraswati. All year round,

UTTAR PRADESH

Prayagraj (Allahabad)

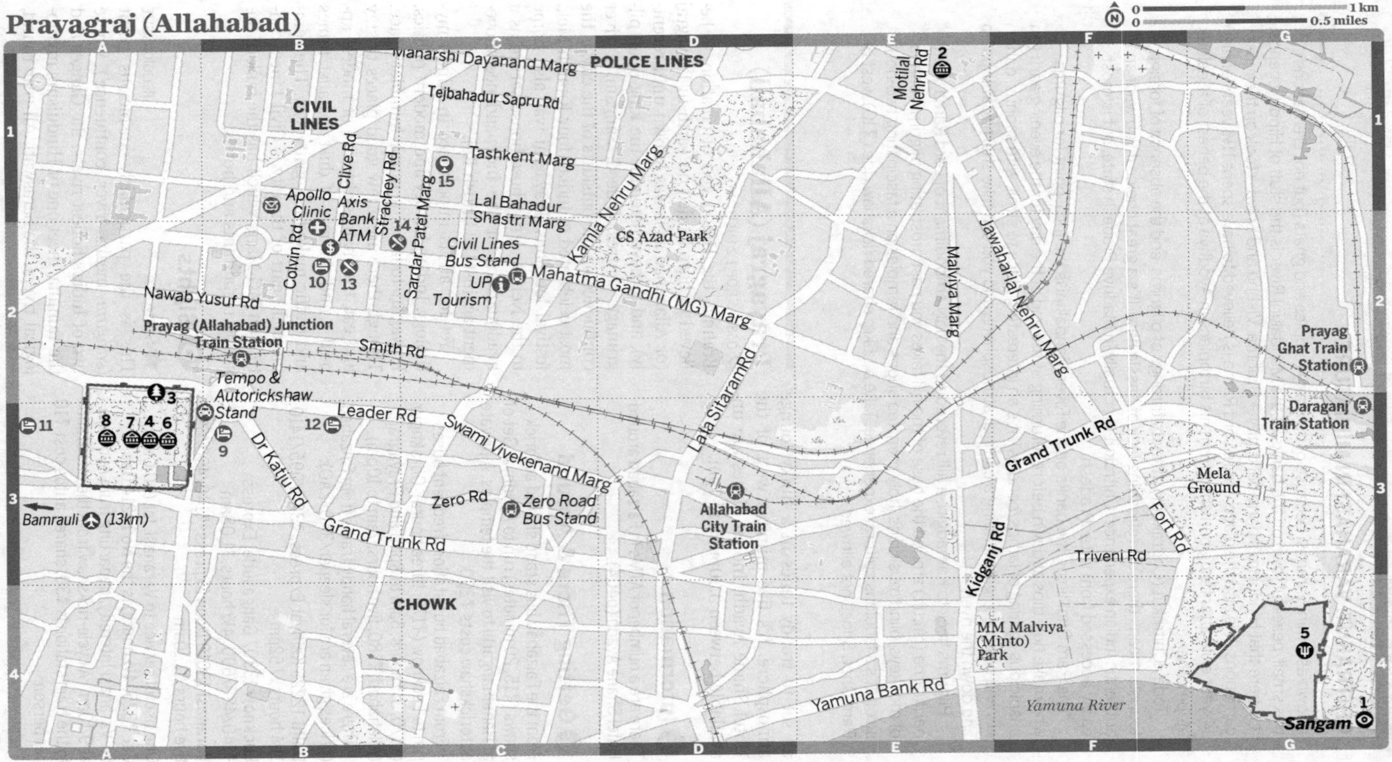

Scale
1 km
0.5 miles

Map labels (by location):

CIVIL LINES

POLICE LINES

CHOWK

Sangam

Yamuna River

Maharshi Dayanand Marg

Tejbahadur Sapru Rd

Tashkent Marg

Lal Bahadur Shastri Marg

Sardar Patel Marg

Kamla Nehru Marg

CS Azad Park

Mahatma Gandhi (MG) Marg

Lala Stiaranrd

Malviya Marg

Motilal Nehru Rd

Jawaharlal Nehru Marg

Grand Trunk Rd

Kidganj Rd

Triveni Rd

Fort Rd

Mela Ground

MM Malviya (Minto) Park

Yamuna Bank Rd

Swami Vivekenand Marg

Zero Road

Zero Rd Bus Stand

Grand Trunk Rd

Leader Rd

Dr Katju Rd

Smith Rd

Civil Lines Bus Stand

UP Tourism

Clive Rd

Strachey Rd

Colvin Rd

Apollo Axis Clinic

Axis Bank

ATM

Nawab Yusuf Rd

Prayag (Allahabad) Train Station

Prayag (Allahabad) Junction Train Station

Prayag Ghat Train Station

Daraganj Train Station

Allahabad City Train Station

Tempo & Autorickshaw Stand

Bamrauli (13km)

Numbered markers: 1, 2, 3, 4, 5, 6, 7, 8, 9, 10, 11, 12, 13, 14, 15

Prayagraj (Allahabad)

pilgrims row boats out to this holy spot, but their numbers increase dramatically during the annual Magh Mela, a six-week festival held between January and March, which culminates in six communal 'holy dips'.

Every 12 years the massive Kumbh Mela takes place here, attracting millions of people, while the Ardh Kumbh Mela (Half Mela) is held here every six years.

In the early 1950s, 350 pilgrims were killed in a stampede trying to get to the soul-cleansing water, an incident re-created vividly in Vikram Seth's essential novel *A Suitable Boy*. The auspicious 2013 Maha (Great) Kumbh Mela, which attracted about 32 million on Mauni Amavasya (the main bathing day) and 100 million across the 55-day festival, is considered to have been earth's largest-ever human gathering. The next Prayagraj Kumbh Mela is in 2025.

Old boathands will row you out to the sacred confluence for around ₹50 per person (hard-bargaining Indian) or ₹100 (hard-bargaining foreigner), or ₹600 to ₹800 per boat, depending on the season.

Khusru Bagh PARK
(⊙ dawn-dusk) FREE This intriguing park, surrounded by huge walls, contains four highly impressive Mughal tombs. One is that of Prince Khusru, the eldest son of Emperor Jehangir, who tried to overthrow his father in 1606, but was instead apprehended, imprisoned and blinded. He was finally murdered in 1622 on the orders of his half-brother, who later took the throne under the name Shah Jahan. If Khusru's coup had succeeded, Shah Jahan would not have become emperor – and the Taj Mahal would not exist.

A three-storey pavilion-shaped tomb belongs to Shah Begum, Khusru's mother (Jehangir's first wife), who committed suicide in 1603 with an opium overdose, distraught over the ongoing feud between her son and his father. Between these two, a third, particularly attractive tomb was constructed by Nesa Begum, Khusru's sister, although it was never actually used as a tomb. A smaller structure, called Tamolon's Tomb, stands to the west of the others, but its origin is unknown.

If you linger around the tombs of Prince Khusru and Shah Begum, someone will appear with keys to let you inside, where you can see a beautiful array of nature paintings and unique, tree-shaped window *jalis* (carved lattices). You'll have to negotiate a price – figure on around ₹100 for all four tombs. Weekends can be busy here.

Anand Bhavan MUSEUM
(Indian/foreigner ₹70/200; ⊙ 10am-5.30pm Tue-Sun) This picturesque two-storey house is a shrine to the Nehru family, which has produced five generations of leading politicians, from Motilal Nehru (Jawaharlal's father) to the latest political figure, Rahul Gandhi. The 1927 stately home is where Mahatma Gandhi, Jawaharlal Nehru and others successfully planned the overthrow of the British Raj. It is full of books, personal effects and photos from those stirring times.

Patalpuri Temple HINDU TEMPLE
(by donation; ⊙ 6am-5.30pm) ✐ Built by the Mughal Emperor Akbar, the 16th-century Allahabad fort on the northern bank of the Yamuna has massive walls with three gateways flanked by towers. Most of it is occupied by the Indian army and cannot be visited, but a small door in the eastern wall by Sangam leads to one part you can enter: the Patalpuri Temple.

This unique underground temple is crowded with idols; pick up some coins from the change dealers outside so you can leave

KUMBH MELA & MAGH MELA

The vast riverbanks at Sangam attract tens of millions of pilgrims every six years in either January or February for either the Kumbh Mela or the Ardh Kumbh Mela (Half Kumbh Mela), but every year there is a smaller Magh Mela. The most recent Ardh Kumbh Mela was in 2019; the next full Kumbh Mela in Prayagraj (Allahabad) is in 2025. For dates and information see www.kumbh.gov.in/en.

The following are auspicious bathing dates during upcoming Magh Melas:

BATHING DAY	2020	2021	2022
Makar Sankranti	15 Jan	14 Jan	14 Jan
Mauni Amavasya	20 Jan	11 Feb	31 Jan
Vasant Panchami	29 Jan	16 Feb	5 Feb
Magh Purnima	9 Feb	27 Feb	16 Feb
Mahashivatri	21 Feb	11 Mar	1 Mar

small offerings as you go. (You may be pressured into giving ₹10 to ₹100 at some shrines, but a few coins are perfectly acceptable.)

Outside the temple is the Undying Banyan Tree. Pilgrims used to leap to their deaths from it, believing this would liberate them from the cycle of rebirth. The tree's roots form one of the shrines in the underground temple.

🛏 Sleeping

Hotel Prayag   HOTEL $
(☑ 0532-2656416; www.prayaggroupofhotels.com; 73 Noorullah Rd; s/d with AC ₹1500/1600, without AC from ₹800/900, without bathroom or AC ₹350/400; ❄🛜) A stone's throw south of the train station, this sprawling, well-organised local flophouse is helpful and boasts wi-fi (lobby only), a State Bank of India ATM and a funky restaurant. There's a wide variety of threadbare, basic rooms in various states of dilapidation (the cheapest ones are for hardened shoestring backpackers only), but staff are friendly and will even help negotiate autorickshaws.

★ Kanchan Villa   HOMESTAY $$
(☑ 9838631111; www.kanchanvilla.com; 64 Lukerganj; s/d from ₹2850/3250, ste from ₹4850, all incl breakfast; ❄@🛜) Ivan – a guitar-playing Indian rum enthusiast – and his wife, Purnima, are your South Indian/Bengali hosts at this fabulous homestay offering a window into a rarely seen side of Christian Indian culture. In a century-old historic home, six rooms are decked out with period furnishings (our fave: Bengali).

The lovely staff will cook for you as well, serving up fresh kebabs from the outdoor tandoor, for example. You'll feel right at home in the living room–bar. Pickups and

drops-offs are available for a fee and useful because the residential address is hard to find; otherwise, it's a short cycle-rickshaw ride (₹70) from the train station.

If you are looking for a rural break, ask about the Lonikot Village Retreat (www.lonikot.com) on the River Tauns at Lonipar, 50km to the south.

Milan Hotel   HOTEL $$
(☑ 0532-2403776; www.hotelmilan.in; 46 Leader Rd; s ₹2020-2500, d ₹2800-3600; ❄🛜) One of the best-value places in Prayagraj (Allahabad) in this price range: rooms are modern and clean, with mellow colour schemes and good beds. Standard rooms lack natural light but are comfortable; deluxe rooms are more spacious but are roadside and noisy. The best standard rooms are at the very back of the building.

Hotel UR   HOTEL $$
(☑ 0532-2427334; mj1874@gmail.com; A/1 MG Marg, Civil Lines; s/d from ₹2800/3140; ❄🛜) This professionally run 20-room midrange hotel is in a good location along MG Marg and offers a slight step up from similarly priced competition. A glass elevator leads to somewhat cramped (due to big beds) but clean rooms, the best of which open onto a plant-lined terrace. Staff are better trained than elsewhere in this price range. Discounts of 20% generally available.

🍴 Eating

★ Eat On   MUGHLAI $
(MG Marg; biryani half/full ₹50/105; ⏱11.30am-10pm Wed-Mon) This standing-room-only food shack does only one thing, but does it so well and so cheaply that queues of hungry punt-

ers spill out into the surrounding streets. The draw is the perfectly spiced chicken biryani, cooked in giant vats and ladled out with a mint raita to an appreciative crowd. Eat standing up or take away.

El Chico Cafe
MULTICUISINE $$

(www.elchico.in; 24 MG Marg; mains ₹220-415; ⊘noon-10.30pm) Cure your homesick hungries in a heartbeat among a forward-thinking Indian crowd. Breakfast for lunch (cinnamon pancakes, waffles, the best coffee in town), sandwiches, wood-fired pizzas and more sophisticated fusion fare fill out the menu. Try the sizzlin' brownie. The cafe is above El Chico. restaurant

El Chico
MULTICUISINE $$$

(www.elchico.in; 24 MG Marg; mains ₹285-450; ⊘10am-10.30pm; ▣) This refined but casual restaurant serves up wonderful Indian (the chicken-chilli-garlic kebab is every bit as delicious as it sounds), tasty-looking Chinese, popular sizzlers and Continental cuisine. It's attached to the modern El Chico Cafe (p409).

🍸 Drinking & Nightlife

Patiyala Peg Bar
BAR

(Grand Continental Hotel, Sardar Patel Marg; beer ₹300; ⊘7-11pm) Prayagraj's (Allahabad's) most interesting bar for tourists has live *ghazal* (Urdu love songs) performed nightly from 7.30pm to 10.30pm. Serves mostly beer and whisky.

❶ Information

ATMs dot the Civil Lines area.

Axis Bank ATM (MG Marg; ⊘24hr)

Apollo Clinic (☑0532-2421132; www. apolloclinic.com; 28B MG Marg; ⊘24hr) A modern private medical facility with a 24-hour pharmacy.

Post Office (www.indiapost.gov.in; Sarojini Naidu Marg; ⊘10am-1.30pm & 2-5pm Mon-Fri, 10am-4pm Sat)

UP Tourism (☑0532-2408873; www.up-tourism.com; 35 MG Marg; ⊘10am-5pm Mon-Sat, closed 2nd Sat of month) At the Rahi Ilawart Tourist Bungalow, next to Civil Lines Bus Stand. Of marginal use.

❶ Getting There & Away

AIR

Prayagraj Airport is 15km west of Prayagraj. Air India (p1208) has one daily flight to Delhi and Jet Airways (p1210) flies three times weekly to Lucknow and Patna.

BUS

From the **Civil Lines Bus Stand** (MG Marg) regular non-AC buses run to the following destinations:

Faizabad ₹195, five hours, every 30 minutes

Gorakhpur ₹308, 10 hours, every 30 minutes

Lucknow ₹220, five hours, hourly, noon to 8pm

Varanasi ₹172, three hours, every 10 minutes

Although none originate in Allahabad, AC buses run to the following destinations:

Agra ₹1216, nine hours, 9.30pmm, overnight deluxe bus

Delhi ₹1721, 13 hours, 5pm

Lucknow ₹310 to ₹500, five hours, throughout the day

Varanasi ₹200, three hours, in the afternoon

To reach Chitrakut go to the Zero Road Bus Stand and hop a bus for Karwi (₹131, 3½ hours, every 30 minutes), from where you can travel the final 10km by shared/private autorickshaw (₹15/200).

TRAIN

Prayag (Allahabad) Junction is the main station. A few daily trains run to Lucknow, Varanasi, Delhi, Agra and Kolkata. Frequent trains also run to Satna or Mahoba from where you can catch buses to Khajuraho. The advance reservation

HANDY TRAINS FROM PRAYAGRAJ (ALLAHABAD)

DESTINATION	TRAIN NO & NAME	FARE (₹)	DURATION (HR)	DEPARTURE
Agra	12403 ALD JP Exp	295/765/1075 (A)	7½	11.30pm
Delhi	12559 Shiv Ganga Exp	375/985/1395 (A)	9¾	10.30pm
Kolkata (Howrah)	12312 Kalka Mail	435/1150/1640 (A)	14½	5.20pm
Lucknow	14209 PRG-LKO Intercity	330 (B)	4	3.40pm
Satna	12428 ANVT REWA Exp	170/540/740 (A)	3	6.55am
Varanasi	15017 Gorakhpur Exp	140/490/695 (A)	4	845am

Fares: (A) sleeper/3AC/2AC, (B) AC chair only

ticket office is on the south side of the station, by platform one.

Note that the 14209/14210 intercity services to/from Lucknow leave from Prayag train station in the east of Prayagraj, not from the main Prayag (Allahabad) Junction.

ℹ Getting Around

An autorickshaw to the airport costs ₹250 and an Ola taxi around ₹350.

Cycle-rickshaws are plentiful; pay ₹30 for a short trip of 1km to 2km, but be prepared to haggle for it.

The stands at the train station and MG Marg are your best bets for autorickshaws. Consider hiring one for a half-day (₹500, four hours) to take in the town's sights, as they are quite spread out.

Vikrams (large shared autos) hang about on the south side of the train station. Destinations include Zero Road Bus Stand (₹10), Civil Lines Bus Stand (₹10) and Sangam (₹15).

Western Uttar Pradesh

Side by side in the west of Uttar Pradesh, on the road from Delhi to Agra, Mathura and Vrindavan are a pair of sacred towns that have played a pivotal role in India's religious history.

Mathura

♪ 0565 / POP 540,000

Famed for being the birthplace of the much-loved Hindu god Krishna, Mathura is one of Hinduism's seven sacred cities and attracts floods of pilgrims, particularly during Janmastami (Krishna's birthday) in August/September and Holi in February/March. The town is dotted with temples from various ages and the stretch of the sacred Yamuna River that flows past here is lined with 25 ghats.

Mathura was once a Kushan capital and a major Buddhist centre with 20 monasteries that housed 3000 monks, but after the rise of Hinduism, and later sackings by Afghan and Mughal rulers, all that's left of the oldest sights are the beautiful sculptures recovered from ruins, now on display in the excellent Archaeological Museum.

◎ Sights

★ Archaeological Museum   MUSEUM

(Museum Rd; Indian/foreigner ₹5/25, camera ₹20; ⊙ 10.30am-4.30pm Tue-Sun, closed every 2nd Sun) This museum, renovated in 2016, houses a

Mathura

superb collection of religious sculptures by the Mathura school, which flourished from the 3rd century BC to the 6th century AD. Good lighting and English text spotlight some 2300-year-old Buddhas, as well as towering Kushan-era royal statues and later Sunga- and Gupta-era Hindu icons. It was Mathuran artists who created some of the earliest images of Buddha.

Kesava Deo Temple   HINDU TEMPLE

(Shri Krishna Janambhoomi; ⊙ 5am-9.30pm summer, 5.30am-8.30pm winter) In the most important temple complex in Mathura, the small, fortresslike room known as Shri Krishna Janambhoomi marks the spot where Krishna is said to have been born in prison more than 5000 years ago. The much larger main temple has a muralled ceiling depicting scenes from Krishna's life, and houses several statues of the flute-playing god and his consort, Radha. Destroyed and rebuilt a number of times over the past thousand years, the current temple was erected in the 1950s.

Vishram Ghat   GHAT

A string of ghats and temples lines the Yamuna River north of the main road bridge. The most central and most popular is Vishram Ghat, where Krishna is said to

Mathura

Top Sights
1 Archaeological Museum................... B2

Sights
  Katra Masjid .... (see 2)
2 Kesava Deo Temple............................A1
3 Vishram Ghat B1

Sleeping
4 Centrum by Brijwasi A2
5 Hotel Brijwasi Royal........................... B2

Eating
  Status Restaurant .... (see 5)

have rested after killing the tyrannical King
Kansa. Boats gather along the banks here
to take tourists along the Yamuna (₹150 per
hour for two people, ₹300 for a full boat).
Take your shoes off when entering the ghats.

Katra Masjid   MOSQUE
This fine sandstone mosque was built by the
Mughal ruler Aurangzeb in 1661. To clear
the site, he ordered the destruction of the
then-standing incarnation of the Kesava
Deo temple, which marked the spot of Krishna's birth. The mosque, which sits directly beside the current version of the Kesava
Deo temple, is now heavily guarded around
the clock by soldiers to prevent a repeat of
the events at Ayodhya in 1992, when rioting Hindus tore down a mosque claiming it
stood on the site of an earlier Rama temple.

Sleeping & Eating

Centrum by Brijwasi   BUSINESS HOTEL **$$**
(☑ 7251017999; www.brijwasihotels.com; Bhute-
shwar Rd; r ₹2240; ✳ � 🖭) This modern budget
business hotel has excellent, spacious rooms
with up-to-date bathrooms, making it both
excellent value for money and superconven-
ient for the next-door bus station. Down-
sides are the fact that you'll probably hear
your neighbour's TV and the slightly un-
predictable hot water. There's no breakfast,
but South Indian snacks are available from the
bright and buzzy ground-floor restaurant.

Status Restaurant   INDIAN **$$**
(SBI Crossing, Station Rd; mains ₹280; ⊙ 7am-
11pm; ☑) At the **Hotel Brijwasi Royal**
(☑ 8191818818; www.brijwasihotels.com; SBI Crossing, Station Rd; s/d incl breakfast from ₹2580/3600;
✳ 🖭 🖸), this classy place serves up some
tasty Indian veg plates, and is deservedly
popular. Go for the tandoori platter (₹375).

Information

State Bank of India ATM (Station Rd, SBI
Crossing; ⊙ 24hr) Next door to Hotel Brijwasi
Royal and not far from the New Bus Stand.

Getting There & Away

Shared autorickshaws and tempos that ply Station and Mathura–Vrindavan Rds charge ₹15 for
the 13km Mathura–Vrindavan run.

The so-called **New Bus Stand** (Bhuteshwar Rd)
has buses to Delhi (₹153, three hours, every 30
minutes, 5am to 7pm) and Agra (₹76, 90 minutes, every 15 minutes, 4am to 9pm).

Frequent trains go to Delhi (sleeper/AC chair
from ₹140/305, two to three hours), Agra
(sleeper/AC chair from ₹140/315, one hour),
and Bharatpur (sleeper/AC chair ₹90/270, 45
minutes). The Bharatpur trains continue to Sawai
Madhopur (for Ranthambhore National Park;
three hours) and Kota (five hours).

Vrindavan

⚏ 0565 / POP 65,000
The town of Vrindavan is where the young
Krishna is said to have grown up. Pilgrims
flock here from all over India and, as it's the
centre of the Hare Krishna community, from
all over the world. Dozens of temples, old and
modern, dot the interesting backstreets and
come in all shapes and sizes, making a visit
here more than just your average temple-hop.

Sights

Many temples are only open in the morning
and from late afternoon, and admission is
free. Among those worth a stop are **Ranga-
ji Temple** (⊙ 5.30-10.30am & 4-9pm summer,
6-11am & 3.30-8.30pm winter), Vrindavan's largest; **Madan Mohan Temple** (⊙ dawn-dusk),
Vrindavan's oldest; **Radha Ballabh Temple**
(⊙ 6am-noon & 4pm-midnight), dedicated to Krishna's consort, Radha; and **Nidhivan Temple** (⊙ dawn-dusk), set in a strange orchard
that Krishna is said to visit every night.

The temples here are spread out and hard
to find, so a cycle-rickshaw tour is a good
way to see them. Expect to pay ₹250 for a
half-day tour (₹400 in an autorickshaw) and
budget some time to explore the backstreets.

**★ Krishna Balaram
Temple Complex**   HINDU TEMPLE
(ISKCON Temple; ⊙ 7.30am-12.45pm & 4-9pm winter, 4.30-9pm summer) The International Society for Krishna Consciousness (www.iskcon.
org), also known as the Hare Krishnas,
is based at the Krishna Balaram temple

Vrindavan

Vrindavan

🏔 0 ━━━━━ 1 km
🏔 0 ━━━━━ 0.5 miles

Vrindavan

complex. Accessed through a beautiful, white marble gate, the temple houses the tomb of Swami Prabhupada (1896–1977), the founder of the Hare Krishna organisation.

Inside, the temple is a whirl of activity, filled with devotees prostrating themselves in prayer, playing drums, chanting and consulting with priests. Several hundred foreigners attend courses and seminars here annually.

Govind Dev Temple   HINDU TEMPLE
(⊙ 8am-12.30pm & 4.30-8pm) This cavernous, red-sandstone temple, built in 1590 by Raja Man Singh of Amber, has 'bells' carved on its pillars. The resident monkeys here are particularly cheeky, so stay alert!

Pagal Baba Temple   HINDU TEMPLE
(⊙ 6am-noon & 3.30-8.30pm winter, 5-11.30am & 3-9pm summer) This 10-storey white marble temple, a fairy-tale-castle lookalike, has an endearingly amateurish collection of animated puppets and dioramas on the ground floor, depicting scenes from the lives of Rama and Krishna.

🛏 Sleeping & Eating

★ **MVT Guesthouse**   GUESTHOUSE $$
(☑ 9997725666; www.mvtindia.com; Bhaktivedanta Swami Marg, Ramanreti; r from ₹2350; ⊕) Run by the Hare Krishna financial endowment and used mostly by followers, but open to all, this relaxing, pleasant guesthouse has the feel of a campus, set around a green lawn and with wicker furniture offering relaxing sitting areas. All rooms are comfortable, though the

deluxe rooms have nicer bathrooms. It has a great restaurant and a licensed money changer on-site.

★ **MVT Restaurant**   MULTICUISINE $$
(mains ₹150-290; ⊙ 8.30am-10am, 12.30-3.30pm & 6.30-9.30pm mid-Aug–mid-Apr; ⊕☑) This mellow, well-run restaurant on the 2nd floor of the MVT Guesthouse is a great place to get a break from Indian food. The menu runs from Thai to Mexican, alongside wraps, salads and good ol' baked potatoes, plus some enticing cakes and a fine granola-banana-date milkshake (but no tea or coffee). The clientele is almost all foreigners.

ℹ Information

There are several ATMs east of the Krishna Balaram Temple complex, as well as several money changers nearby.

Krishna Balaram Welcome Office
(☑ 9557849475; www.iskconvrindavan.com; ⊙ 10am-1pm & 5-8pm) Has lists of places to stay in Vrindavan and can help with booking Gita classes (studies in the Bhagavad Gita, an ancient Hindu scripture) as well as all travel-agency services.

ℹ Getting There & Around

Tempos, shared autos and buses all charge ₹15 between Vrindavan and Mathura; figure on ₹200 for a private autorickshaw. Flag one down anywhere along the main Vrindavan–Mathura road.

Uttarakhand

Best Places to Eat

➜ Prakash Lok (p424)

➜ Chetan Poori Wala (p428)

➜ Little Buddha Cafe (p420)

Best Places to Stay

➜ Mohan's Binsar Retreat (p449)

➜ Gateway Resort (p444)

➜ Haveli Hari Ganga (p424)

➜ Kasmanda Palace Hotel (p431)

➜ Grand Oak Manor (p450)

Why Go?

Uttarakhand is a place of myth and mountains. Hindus think of it as Dev Bhoomi – the Land of Gods – and the dramatic terrain is covered with holy peaks, lakes and rivers. Twisting roads and high-altitude hiking trails lead to spectacular pilgrimage sites where tales from Hindu epics are set. Though the presence of Shiva and Parvati (in a few of her forms) tower over the state, the imprint of the British is equally apparent: the legend of Jim Corbett lives on in the famed tiger reserve that bears his name; popular holiday towns were once Raj-era hill stations; and the Beatles turned Rishikesh into a magnet for spiritual seekers and yoga practitioners worldwide.

Uttarakhand may seem like a silver medallist: it's the state with the second-highest tiger population (after Karnataka) and has India's second-highest peak (Nanda Devi); but its diversity of activities and sheer natural beauty are pure travellers' gold.

When to Go
Rishikesh

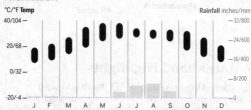

Apr–mid-Jun The best season for tiger spotting at Corbett Tiger Reserve.

Jul–mid-Sep Monsoons may make travel difficult; Valley of Flowers blooms July and August.

Mid-Sep–Nov The perfect time to trek the Himalaya.

Uttarakhand Highlights

1 Gaumukh (p434) Hiking below stunning peaks to the source of the holy Ganges.

2 Har-ki-Pairi Ghat (p422) Floating a candle down the Ganges at the nightly ceremony in Haridwar.

3 Corbett Tiger Reserve (p442) Spotting some stripes at India's first national park.

4 Rishikesh (p415) Pursuing inner peace at the yoga and meditation capital of the universe.

5 Mussoorie (p429) Taking a step back in time to British India at this atmospheric hill-station town with its stately colonial architecture.

6 Valley of Flowers National Park (p439) Strolling among a dazzling display of wildflowers, framed by snowy summits.

7 Kasar Devi (p449) Turning on, tuning in and dropping out in this village famed for its counterculture past and Himalayan backdrop.

History

Over the centuries various dynasties have dominated the region, including the Guptas, Katyuri and Chand rajas. In the 18th century the Nepalese Gurkhas attacked first the kingdom of Kumaon, then Garhwal, prompting the British to step in and take most of the region as part of the Treaty of Sugauli in 1816.

After Independence, the region was merged with Uttar Pradesh, but a vocal separatist movement followed, and the present-day state of Uttaranchal was formed in 2000. In 2007 it was officially renamed Uttarakhand, a traditional name meaning 'northern country'.

Climate

Temperatures are determined by altitude in this state of elevation extremes. Trekking the Himalaya is possible from May to October, but can be dangerous between July and mid-September, during the monsoon, when violent cloudbursts cause landslides. Hill stations offer a welcome escape from summer heat, while low-lying Rishikesh is most comfortable from October to March.

❶ Information

Most towns in the region have an Uttarakhand tourist office. However, the main responsibility for the region's tourism rests with the Garhwal Mandal Vikas Nigam (GMVN; www.gmvnl.in) in the Garhwal district, and Kumaon Mandal Vikas Nigam (KMVN; www.kmvn.gov.in) in the Kumaon district.

❶ Getting Around

Tough old government buses are the main means of travelling around Uttarakhand. In addition, crowded shared jeeps criss-cross the state, linking remote towns and villages to important road junctions. Pay 10 times the share-taxi rate to hire the whole vehicle and travel in comfort. Roads that snake through the hills can be nerve-racking and stomach-churning, and are sometimes blocked by monsoon-season landslides.

Rishikesh

✒ 0135 / POP 102,200 / ELEV 356M

Ever since the Beatles visited the ashram of the Maharishi Mahesh Yogi in the late '60s, Rishikesh has been a magnet for spiritual seekers. Today it styles itself as the 'Yoga Capital of the World', with masses of ashrams and all kinds of yoga and meditation classes. The action is mostly north of the main town, where the exquisite setting on the fast-flowing Ganges River, surrounded by forested hills, is conducive to meditation and mind expansion. In the evening, an almost supernatural breeze blows down the valley, setting temple bells ringing as sadhus ('holy' men), pilgrims and tourists prepare for the nightly *ganga aarti* (river worship ceremony). You can learn to play the sitar or tabla; try Hasya yoga (laughter therapy), practise meditation or take a punt on crystal healing.

Rishikesh is not all spirituality and contorted limbs, it's also a popular white-water rafting centre, backpacker hang-out and Himalayan-trekking gateway.

❶ Orientation

Rishikesh is divided into two main areas: the dusty, crowded, unattractive downtown area (Rishikesh town), where you'll find the bus and train stations as well as the Triveni Ghat (a popular and auspicious bathing ghat and place of prayer on the Ganges); and the riverside communities a few kilometres upstream around Ram Jhula and Lakshman Jhula, where most of the accommodation, ashrams, restaurants and travellers are ensconced. The two *jhula* (suspension bridges) that cross the river are pedestrian-only – though scooters and motorcycles (and cows) freely use them. Swarg Ashram, located on the eastern bank, is the traffic-free 'spiritual centre' of Rishikesh, while High Bank, west of Lakshman Jhula, is a small enclave popular with backpackers.

◉ Sights

◉ Lakshman Jhula

The defining image of Rishikesh is the view across the Lakshman Jhula hanging bridge to the huge, 13-storey wedding-cake temple of Swarg Niwas & Shri Trayanbakshwar. Built by the organisation of the guru Kailashanand, it resembles a fairyland castle and has dozens of shrines to Hindu deities on each level, interspersed with jewellery and textile shops. Sunset is an especially good time to photograph the temple from the bridge itself, and you'll hear the bell-clanging and chanting of devotees in the morning and evening. Shops selling devotional CDs add to the cacophony on this side of the river. Markets, restaurants, ashrams and guesthouses sprawl on both sides of the river; in recent years the area has grown into the busiest and liveliest part of upper Rishikesh.

Rishikesh

Neer Garh
Waterfall (3km);
Neelkantha Mahadev
Temple by road (20km)

Lakshman Jhula

SWARG
ASHRAM

Ganges River

Ram
Jhula

Shivananda
Ashram

HIGH
BANK

Lakshman Jhula Rd

Neelkantha Mahadeva
Temple on foot (7km)

Maharishi
Mahesh Yogi
Ashram

Rajaji Tiger Reserve
(15km)

RISHILOK

Kailash
Gate

MUNI-
KI-RETI

Lakshman Jhula Rd

Chandrabhaga River

Haridwar Rd

Dhalwala Bypass Rd

Dehra Dun Rd

Railway Rd

Train
Station

Uttarakhand
Tourism Office

Haridwar
(19km)

1 km
0.5 miles

Rishikesh

⦿ Swarg Ashram

A pleasant 2km walk south of Lakshman Jhula, along the path skirting the east bank of the Ganges, leads to the spiritual community of Swarg Ashram, made up of temples, ashrams, a crowded bazaar, sadhus and the bathing ghats (steps or landing on a river) where religious ceremonies are performed at sunrise and sunset. The colourful, though rather touristy, *ganga aarti* is held at the riverside temple of the Parmarth Niketan Ashram (p418) every evening around sunset, with singing, chanting, musicians and the lighting of candles.

★ Maharishi Mahesh Yogi Ashram
HISTORIC BUILDING

(Beatles Ashram; Indian/foreigner ₹100/600; ⊙9am-5pm) Just south of Swarg Ashram is what's left of the original Maharishi Mahesh Yogi Ashram, where the Beatles stayed and wrote much of the *White Album* (and a few tracks from *Abbey Road*). After decades of neglect, the Forest Department has reclaimed it from the jungle growth that had nearly consumed it, turning it into a pilgrimage site for fans, plus an evolving graffiti-art museum. Don't miss the meditation hall, with bizarre warrens of rock-lined hallways and striking street-art pieces.

There are numerous abandoned buildings to explore, some downright creepy, including the derelict lodging where the Beatles resided (along with the likes of Mike Love from the Beach Boys, Mia Farrow and her sister Prudence – whom the Beatles song was written after). The meditation domes lost to the jungle also make for a surreal sight. To commemorate the 50-year anniversary of the Beatles' visit, a permanent photograph exhibition was unveiled in 2018 of the snaps taken by Paul Saltzman (www.thebeatlesinindia.com), one of the only photographers permitted inside the ashram, who documented their stay.

✦ Activities

Yoga & Meditation

Yoga and meditation are ubiquitous in India's yoga capital. Teaching and yoga styles vary tremendously, so check out a few classes and ask others about their experiences before committing yourself to a course. Many places also offer ayurvedic massage, and some residential ashrams have strict rules forbidding students from consuming drugs, alcohol, tobacco and meat during their stay.

Omkarananda Ganga Sadan
YOGA

(☑0135-2430763; www.iyengaryoga.in; Lakshman Jhula Rd; r from ₹600, with fan from ₹1700, 3-day

GARHWAL & KUMAON

Uttarakhand is split into two administrative districts: Garhwal and Kumaon. Locals consider the region of Garhwal, covering the western part of Uttarakhand, to be the masculine half of the state due to its exceptionally burly topography. The character of the landscape – and, some say, the people – is largely defined by the four major rivers that flow from Himalayan glaciers and have carved the terrain into a rugged network of ridges and canyons.

Blessed by a landscape that's gentler and sweeter than that of Garhwal, Kumaon is said to be the feminine half of Uttarakhand. With its rolling, terraced hills and graceful Himalayan summits, as well as the strength of its goddess-worshipping culture, there's something incredibly special here that's easy to experience but impossible to define.

minimum) On the Ganges River at Ram Jhula, this ashram has comfortable rooms and specialises in highly recommended Iyengar yoga classes. There are intensive six- to 10-day courses (₹1200 to ₹5850) from October to May; advance reservations recommended. In the gaps between intensives, day classes are offered (beginners/general ₹500/800, beginners 4pm to 5.30pm, general 6pm to 7.30pm, Monday to Saturday).

Anand Prakash Yoga Ashram YOGA
(☑ 0135-2442344; www.anandprakashashram. com; Badrinath Rd, Tapovan; private/share r incl full board ₹1700/1200) About 1km north of Lakshman Jhula is this popular ashram offering morning and afternoon Akhanda yoga classes, included in the price. Silence is the rule from 9pm to 9am. The food is excellent and rooms are simple but comfortable and clean. You should book two to three months in advance. If you're not staying, drop in for classes for ₹200.

Abhayaranya Rishikesh Yogpeeth Yoga Village YOGA
(☑ 9897147590; www.rishikeshyogpeeth.com; Neelkanth Temple Rd, Patna; 40-day course US$2300) With its excellent reputation, this popular yoga-teacher-training school has become something of a local industry. It's 12km from town, close to Patna waterfall.

Parmarth Niketan Ashram YOGA
(☑ 0135-2434301; www.parmarth.com; Swarg Ashram; r with/without AC from ₹1600/180) This ashram, dominating the centre of Swarg Ashram and drawing visitors to its evening *ganga aarti* on the riverbank, has a wonderfully ornate and serene garden courtyard. Daily activities include meditation and yoga, and it offers a range of beginner and intensive yoga courses – apply online. The price includes a room with private bathroom.

Rafting, Kayaking & Trekking

More than 100 operators offer full- and half-day rafting trips, launching upstream and paddling down to Rishikesh. Some also offer multiday rafting trips, with camping along the river. The official rafting season runs from 15 September to 30 June, featuring Grade 3 to 4 rapids. A half-day trip starts at about ₹1200 per person, while a full day costs from ₹2000. Most companies also offer all-inclusive Himalayan treks to places such as Kuari Pass, Har-ki Dun and Gangotri/ Tapovan from around ₹3500 per day.

★ **Red Chilli Adventure** TREKKING, RAFTING
(☑ 0135-2434021, 9412050521; www.redchilli adventure.com; Lakshman Jhula Rd; ⊕9am-8pm) Dependable outfit offering Himalayan trekking and rafting trips throughout Uttarakhand and to Himachal Pradesh and Ladakh. Staff are knowledgeable on the entire area, and can also arrange tours to the nearby national parks, mountain-biking trips and car hire.

GMVN Trekking & Mountaineering Division TREKKING
(☑ 0135-2431793, 0135-2430799; www.gmvnl.in; Lakshman Jhula Rd, Muni-ki-Reti; ⊕10am-5pm) This government operator can arrange high-altitude treks in the Garhwal Himalaya, and hires out trekking equipment, guides and porters. See website for trekking fees.

Walks

An easy, 15-minute walk to two small waterfalls starts 3km north of Lakshman Jhula bridge on the south side of the river. The start is marked by drink stalls and a roadside shrine, and the path is easy to find. 4WD taxis cost ₹150 from Lakshman Jhula.

On the other side of the river, a 20-minute uphill walk (signposted) to **Neer Garh Waterfall** (adult/child ₹50/30) starts about 2km north of Lakshman Jhula.

For a longer hike, follow the dedicated pilgrims who take water from the Ganges to offer at Neelkantha Mahadev Temple, a 7km three-hour walk along a forest path from Swarg Ashram. You can also reach the temple by road (about 20km) from Lakshman Jhula.

✿ Festivals & Events

International Yoga Festival   YOGA
(www.internationalyogafestival.org; ☉ Mar) In the first week of March, swamis and yoga masters from around the world flock to Rishikesh for lectures and training. Most of the action is centred on the Parmarth Niketan Ashram in Swarg Ashram. Check the website for dates.

🛏 Sleeping

🛏 Lakshman Jhula

There are several good budget options on both sides of the river here, the liveliest part of Rishikesh. Some of the best-value places are at the backpacker hostels in the Tapovan area, along the lane that leads to **Divine Ganga Cottage** (☑ 0135-2442175; www.divine gangacottage.com; Lakshman Jhula Rd; r incl breakfast with fan/AC from ₹3000/4100; ✻ @ ☎).

Shalom Backpackers   HOSTEL $
(www.shalombackpackers.com; Paidal Marg, off Lakshman Jhula Rd; dm ₹300-400, r ₹1680-2000; ✻ ☎ ⊠) Modern, vibrant and friendly, this canary-yellow backpacker is rightfully one of Rishikesh's most popular budget choices. It has a spectacular location built overlooking the Ganges, which you can enjoy from its blissful garden hang-out and swimming pool or its upstairs Hoggers Cafe, both good places to meet travellers. Private rooms and dorms are spotless and excellent value.

Live Free Hostel   HOSTEL $
(Lakshman Jhula Rd; dm ₹200-450, r ₹800-1500; ✻ ☎) A multistorey hotel converted into a hostel, Live Free is an arty hub decorated in murals and run by owners who know backpackers' needs. Hammocks are strewn about, and there's a rooftop space overlooking the Ganges and a downstairs lounge with pool table and beanbags. There's complimentary yoga and afternoon chai, as well as free communal dinners every Tuesday.

Blue Jay Hostel   HOSTEL $
(☑ 8057212070, 8279438014; www.facebook.com/bluejayhostels; dm ₹300, r ₹1000-1700; @ ☎) A contemporary alternative to the usual budget offerings is this slick four-storey hostel that features designer touches throughout. Private rooms are spotless and come with balconies, while dorms are modern with air-con and en suite bathrooms and beds have power and USB outlets. Its common room has beanbags, plasma TV, board games and yoga mats for its daily classes.

★**Divine Resort**   HOTEL $$$
(☑ 0135-2442128; www.divineresort.com; Lakshman Jhula Rd; r from ₹7000; ✻ ☎ ⊠) Some rooms in this top-end hotel have stunning river views – but few rival that of the Ganges-facing glass elevator, which could be a tourist attraction all its own. Then there's the infinity pool, perched above the river bank, its two restaurants, modern cafe and cooking classes...we'd say it's the top hotel around Lakshman Jhula.

🛏 High Bank

This small, leafy travellers' enclave is a 20-minute walk up the hill from Lakshman Jhula and has some of the best-value accommodation in Rishikesh.

New Bhandari Swiss Cottage   HOTEL $
(☑ 0135-2435322; www.newbhandariswisscottage. com; High Bank; r with fan/AC from ₹700/1200; ✻ @ ☎) One of the last places on the High Bank lane, this is a large, popular place with rooms ranging from clean and simple to simply impressive. Many have been renovated. There's a good restaurant here, too.

Bhandari Swiss Cottage   HOTEL $
(☑ 0135-2432939; www.bhandariswisscottage rishikesh.com; High Bank; r from ₹600, with AC from ₹1000; ✻ @ ☎) This High Bank favourite has rooms in several budgets – the higher up you stay, the higher the price. Rooms are varying degrees of worn and could use a bit of love, but the big balconies are winners, with expansive views of the green mountains and Ganges. It has a romantic little courtyard **Italian restaurant** (mains ₹150-350; ☉ 7.30am-11pm; ☎) and yoga classes.

SLEEPING PRICE RANGES

The following price ranges refer to a double room with bathroom in this region, and include tax.

$ less than ₹1000

$$ ₹1000–₹3000

$$$ more than ₹3000

Swarg Ashram

If you're serious about yoga and introspection, stay at one of Swarg's numerous ashrams. Otherwise, there's a knot of hotels a block back from the river towards the southern end of Swarg.

★**Vashishth Guest House**   BOUTIQUE HOTEL $$
(☏8979200363, 8171456286; www.vashishthgroup. com; s/d with fan ₹800/990, with AC ₹1410/1990; ❄🕸🛜) This sweet little boutique hotel has colourfully painted walls, comfortable mattresses and a small lending library. A couple of the rooms have good-sized kitchens with cooking utensils, table and chairs. For what you get, this is one of the best deals in Rishikesh.

Eating

Virtually every restaurant in Rishikesh serves only vegetarian food, but there are lots of travellers' restaurants whipping up various interpretations of Continental and Israeli food, as well as Indian and Chinese. High Bank is the only area in town where you'll find meat on the menu.

Lakshman Jhula

Devraj Coffee Corner   CAFE $
(Lakshman Jhula; snacks & mains ₹110-230; ⊙8am-9pm; 🛜) Perched above the bridge and looking across the river to Shri Trayanbakshwar (p415) temple, this cafe is a sublime spot for a break at any time of the day. While it's all about the view, the menu has the likes of brown bread with yak's cheese, pizzas, good coffee, croissants, apple strudel and more.

There's a good **bookshop** (⊙8.30am-9pm) next door.

★**Little Buddha Cafe**   MULTICUISINE $$
(Lakshman Jhula; mains ₹140-280; ⊙8am-11pm; 🛜) This happening tree-house-style restaurant has an ultraloungey top floor, tables overlooking the Ganges and really good international food. Pizzas are big and the mixed vegetable platter is a serious feast. It's

one of the busiest places in Lakshman Jhula, for good reason.

Cafe Delmar/Beatles Cafe   INTERNATIONAL $$
(https://60sbeatlescafe.business.site; Paidal Marg, off Lakshman Jhula Rd, Tapovan; mains ₹150-500; ⊙9.30am-9.30pm) A tribute to the Fab Four's stay in Rishikesh is this swinging Beatles-themed cafe hidden down the bazaar leading into Laxman Jhula. The views of the Ganges are awesome as are its burgers and smoothies. There are plenty of vegan and raw-food dishes, including a tasty eggplant lasagne with cashew cheese.

La-So-Va   BUFFET $$
(www.facebook.com/lasovarishikesh; buffet ₹350; ⊙6.30-10pm) A one-man show run by Eshu who cooks up nightly communal feasts of vegetarian and vegan dishes, all freshly made using local and seasonal ingredients. It's an all-you-can-eat affair with an assortment of healthy Indian dishes, tasty salads and a few international options. It's on the rooftop of **Hotel Surya** (☏0135-2440211, 9410788585; r with fan/AC from ₹500/1000; ❄@🛜), a short stroll from Lakshman Jhula.

High Bank

Swiss Garden   INTERNATIONAL $
(High Bank; ₹130-240; ⊙7am-10.30pm) The current favourite backpacker hang-out in High Bank is this laid-back cafe with outdoor tables under the trees. Here you'll find non-veg on the menu (a rarity in Rishikesh) along with homemade pasta, schnitzel and original brekkie choices such as masala chickpeas served with yoghurt and roti. Watch out for those pesky monkeys loitering in the trees.

Bistro Nirvana   INTERNATIONAL $$
(High Bank; mains ₹90-350; ⊙8.30am-10.30pm) Up the hill on High Bank is this classy little restaurant that's most notable for its menu of nonveg including delicious tandoori-chicken dishes and naans. The burgers, pizzas, salads and cooked and healthy breakfasts are also recommendable.

Shopping

Swarg Ashram is the place to go for bookshops, ayurvedic herbal medicines, clothing, handicrafts and tourist trinkets such as jewellery and Tibetan singing bowls, though there are also plenty of stalls around Lakshman Jhula. If you need outdoor gear, your

---

TOP STATE FESTIVALS

Kumbh Mela (Haridwar; ⊙2022; p422)

International Yoga Festival (Rishikesh; ⊙Mar; p419)

Shivaratri (Dehra Dun; ⊙Mar; p427)

Nanda Devi Fair (Almora; ⊙Sep)

best bet is well-stocked **Adventure Axis** (Badrinath Rd, Lakshman Jhula; ⊙ 10.30am-8pm).

ℹ Information

Himalayan Institute Hospital (☑ 0135-2471200, emergency 0135-2471225; www.hihtindia.org; ⊙ 24hr) The nearest large hospital, 17km along the road to Dehra Dun and 1km beyond Jolly Grant Airport.

Shivananda Ashram (☑ 0135-2430040; www.sivanandaonline.org; Lakshman Jhula Rd) Provides free medical services and has a pharmacy.

DANGERS & ANNOYANCES

Be cautious of befriending sadhus – while some are on genuine spiritual journeys, the orange robes have been used as a disguise by fugitives from the law since medieval times, and people have been robbed and worse.

The current in some parts of the Ganges is very strong and people occasionally drown here. Don't swim beyond your depth.

ℹ Getting There & Away

BUS

There are frequent buses to Haridwar and Dehra Dun; for Mussoorie change at Dehra Dun. Buses run north to Char Dham sites during the yatra (pilgrimage) season (May to October), though direct buses to Gangotri were infrequent at the time of research – to get there, connect in Uttarkashi; likewise, there are no buses to Yamunotri – you'll have to change in Dehra Dun and Barkot.

Private AC and Volvo buses run to Delhi (₹460 to ₹800, seven hours) several times a day.

For Jaipur (seat/AC sleeper 450/550, 11 to 13 hours), Pushkar (seat/sleeper ₹760/850, 14½ to 16 hours) and Agra (seat/AC sleeper/Volvo ₹475/665/1300, 8½ to 12 hours) you'll need to go via Dehra Dun or Haridwar, but tickets can be booked at travel agents in Lakshman Jhula, Swarg Ashram and High Bank.

SHARE JEEP & TAXI

Share jeeps (ISBT Rd) to Uttarkashi (₹350, five hours) and Joshimath (₹600, eight hours) leave when full from Natraj Chowk, near the corner of Dehra Dun Rd and Dhalwala Bypass Rd. It's best to get here between 5am and 7am.

To hire cars for out-of-town destinations, go to the **taxi stand** (☑ 0135-2442097; Lakshman Jhula Rd); the **taxi stand** (ISBT Rd) between the main and yatra (pilgrimage) bus stands; or the **taxi & autorickshaw stand** (Lakshman Jhula Rd) at Ram Jhula. Rates include Haridwar (₹1220, one hour), Dehra Dun (₹1650, 1½ hours), Jolly Grant Airport (₹820, one hour), Ramnagar (for Corbett Tiger Reserve, ₹4590, 4½ hours), Uttarkashi (for Gangotri, ₹4590, seven hours), Nainital (₹6000, 6½ hours), Joshimath (₹6500, nine hours) and Almora (₹8000, 10 hours). For long-distance trips you may find a cheaper rate by asking around at travel agents and guesthouses.

Vikrams (large autorickshaws) charge ₹600 to Haridwar, or ₹90 per person shared.

ℹ Getting Around

Shared vikrams run from the downtown Ghat Rd junction up past Ram Jhula (₹20 per person) and the High Bank turnoff to Lakshman Jhula. To hire a private vikram or autorickshaw from downtown to Lakshman Jhula should cost ₹150 to ₹200 to 'upside' – the top of the hill on which the Lakshman Jhula area sits – and ₹100 to ₹150 to 'downside' – closer to the bridge. Be prepared to haggle, hard.

To get to the eastern bank of the Ganges you either need to walk across one of the suspension bridges or take the **ferry** (one-way/return ₹10/15; ⊙ 7.30am-6.15pm) from Ram Jhula.

BUSES FROM RISHIKESH

The following buses depart from the main bus stand (A) on ISBT Rd or the Yatra/GMOU bus stand (B) also on ISBT Rd. You can buy tickets from a booking stand at **Ram Jhula** (☑ 8932817748; Ram Jhula; ⊙ 9am-8pm), too.

DESTINATION	FARE (₹)	DURATION (HR)	DEPARTURES
Badrinath (B)	425-572	14	5.30am
Dharamsala	617	12	3.30pm
Dehra Dun (A)	52	1	every 20min
Delhi (A)	287/460-770 (ordinary/AC)	7	half-hourly 9.30am-11pm
Gangotri (B)	330	12	5.30am
Haridwar (A)	40	1	half-hourly
Joshimath (B)	360-572	12	half-hourly 3.30-6am, 9am
Kedarnath (B)	300	12	5am
Uttarkashi (B)	240	7	8 buses 3.45am-12.35pm

On the eastern bank of the Ganges, taxis and share jeeps wait to take passengers to waterfalls and Neelkantha Mahadev Temple (p419) (shared/private ₹200/1400). Lakshman Jhula to Swarg Ashram costs ₹400 for the whole vehicle. Find rides at the taxi stand in Swarg Ashram, or the jeep stand in Lakshman Jhula.

Bicycles (per day from ₹300), scooters (per day from ₹400) and motorcycles (per day ₹600 to ₹1800) can be hired around the Lakshman Jhula area from guys on the street, or ask at guesthouses.

Haridwar

☑ 01334 / POP 311,000 / ELEV 314M

Propitiously located at the point where the Ganges River emerges from the Himalaya, Haridwar (also called Hardwar) is Uttarakhand's holiest Hindu city, and pilgrims arrive here in droves to bathe in the fast-flowing Ganges. The sheer number of people gathering around Har-ki-Pairi Ghat give Haridwar a chaotic but reverent feel. Within the religious hierarchy of India, Haridwar is much more significant than Rishikesh, an hour further north, and every evening the river comes alive with flickering flames as floating offerings are released on to the Ganges. It's especially busy during the *yatra* (pilgrimage) season from May to October, in particular during July, when hundreds of thousands of Shiva devotees, known as Kanwarias, descend upon the city.

◉ Sights

★ Har-ki-Pairi Ghat   GHAT

Har-ki-Pairi (The Footstep of God) is where Vishnu is said to have dropped some divine nectar and left behind a footprint. Every evening, hundreds of worshippers gather for the *ganga aarti* (river worship ceremony). Officials in blue uniforms collect donations and, as the sun sets, bells ring out a rhythm, torches are lit, and leaf baskets with flower petals inside and a candle on top (₹10) are lit and placed on the river to drift away downstream.

Someone may claim to be a priest and help you with your *puja* before asking for ₹200 or more. If you want to make a donation, it's best to give to a uniformed collector. To get to Har-ki-Pairi walk the length of the ghats starting from one of the bridges close to the train station. This will allow you to observe the spiritual fervour of pilgrims who've come far and wide to bathe in the Ganges.

Mansa Devi & Chandi Devi Temples

To get to the crowded hilltop temple of Mansa Devi, a wish-fulfilling goddess, take the **cable car** (return ₹100; ⊙6.30am-7pm). The path to the cable car is lined with stalls selling packages of *prasad* (a food offering used in religious ceremonies) to bring to the goddess on the hill. You can walk up (it's a steep 1.5km) but beware of *prasad*-stealing monkeys.

Many visitors and pilgrims combine this with another cable car up Neel Hill, 4km southeast of Haridwar, to **Chandi Devi Temple** (return cable car ₹163; ⊙6.30am-7pm), built by Raja Suchet Singh of Kashmir in 1929.

Pay ₹263 at Mansa Devi to ride both cable cars and take an AC coach (departing every 10 minutes) between the two temples. Photography is forbidden inside the shrines.

☞ Tours

Mohan's Adventure Tours   ADVENTURE

(☑ 9837100215, 9412022966; www.mohans adventure.com; Railway Rd; ⊙9am-9pm) Sanjeev Mehta can organise trekking, fishing, birdwatching, cycling, motorcycling and rafting tours. An accomplished wildlife photographer, he specialises in five-hour safaris within Rajaji Tiger Reserve (p425; ₹2550 per person with two or more, individuals ₹3750); in low season (June to November) trips only visit a small stretch of buffer zone. Sanjeev also runs overnight trips to Corbett Tiger Reserve (from ₹11,950).

✦ Festivals & Events

Kumbh Mela   RELIGIOUS

(⊙2022) The largest religious gathering on earth, drawing millions of worshippers, the Kumbh Mela is an auspicious time to wash away sins in a sacred river. It's celebrated in Haridwar every 12 years, and is next scheduled for 2022. Every sixth year, the Ardh (half) Kumbh Mela is held, also bringing huge crowds to Haridwar.

⌷ Sleeping

Haridwar has loads of hotels catering to Hindu pilgrims. The busiest time of year is the May–October *yatra* season – outside this you'll find rooms discounted by 20% to 50%.

Jassa Ram Rd and other alleys running off Railway Rd have budget hotels, although most are grim. Rishikesh has far superior budget accommodation. Down by the ghats are a number of high-rise hotels that have good views but worse-than-average rooms.

Haridwar

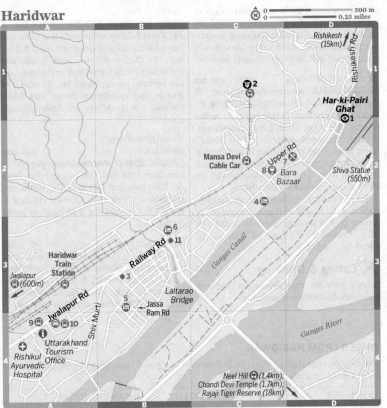

N ⌖ 0 ——————— 500 m
0 ——————— 0.25 miles

Haridwar

◉ Top Sights
1 Har-ki-Pairi Ghat..................................D2

◉ Sights
2 Mansa Devi Temple.............................C1

◉ Activities, Courses & Tours
3 Mohan's Adventure Tours....................B3

◉ Sleeping
4 Haveli Hari Ganga...............................C2
5 Hotel Arjun..B3
6 Hotel La Casa......................................B3

◉ Eating
Haveli Hari Ganga
Restaurant.....................................(see 4)
7 Hoshiyar Puri......................................D2

◉ Drinking & Nightlife
8 Prakash Lok...C2

◉ Transport
9 GMOU Bus Stand.................................A4
10 UK Roadways Bus Stand.....................A4
11 Vikrams to Rishikesh..........................B3

Hotel Arjun HOTEL **$**
(☏ 01334-220409; Jassa Ram Rd; s/d incl breakfast from ₹800/1000; ✸ 🛜) The best of the budget choices, the Arjun beats its neighbours for cleanliness and comfort. Some rooms have balconies that overlook the lively street scenes. Rooms are a mixed bag, though, so

take a look at a few if you can. It's walking distance from the train and bus stations.

Hotel La Casa HOTEL **$$**
(☏ 9639207070; www.lacasahotels.in; Bilkeshwar Rd, opposite Gurdwara; r from ₹1700; ✸ 🛜) One of Haridwar's few solid midrange choices, La

UTTARAKHAND HARIDWAR

Casa has some of the least scuffed rooms in town. They strive for character, with splashes of colour, tasteful furnishings and modern bathrooms. In all, good value (though not quite as nice as it looks on the hotel website).

★ **Haveli Hari Ganga** HERITAGE HOTEL $$$
(☎ 01334-226443; www.havelihariganga.com; 21 Ram Ghat; r/ste incl breakfast ₹9500/12,000; ❀ 🛜) Hidden away in Bara Bazaar, but right on the Ganges, this superb 1918 *haveli* (traditional, ornately decorated residence) is Haridwar's finest hotel. Interior courtyards and marble floors give it a regal charm. It's worth shelling out extra for a Ganges View room, with an airy balcony overlooking the river.

Room rates include breakfast, steam bath, yoga and the hotel's own *ganga aarti* on its private ghat. A rooftop ayurvedic health spa offers treatments. It's hard to find, so call ahead for a pickup.

✖ Eating & Drinking

Being a holy city, only vegetarian food and nonalcoholic drinks are available.

Hoshiyar Puri INDIAN $
(Upper Rd; mains ₹110-250; ⏱ 9am-5pm & 7-10.30pm) Established in 1937, this place still has a loyal (and well-deserved) local following. The *dhal makhani* (black lentils and red kidney beans with cream and butter), *la-cha paratha* (layered fried bread), *aloo gobi* (potato and cauliflower curry) and *kheer* (creamy rice pudding) are lip-smackingly good.

Haveli Hari Ganga Restaurant INDIAN $$$
(☎ 01334-226443; www.havelihariganga.com; 21 Ram Ghat; lunch thali ₹550, dinner buffet ₹950; ⏱ 7-10am, noon-3pm & 7-10pm) The restaurant at this lovely heritage hotel is the classiest in Haridwar. Come for the thali lunch or buffet dinner.

★ **Prakash Lok** LASSI
(Bara Bazaar; ⏱ 10.30am-10.30pm) Don't miss a creamy lassi at this Haridwar institution, famed for its ice-cold, best-you'll-ever-have lassis served in tin cups (₹50). Just about anyone in the Bara Bazaar can point you to it.

BUSES FROM HARIDWAR

The following buses depart from the UK Roadways bus stand. There are also services to Jaipur (from ₹500, 12 hours).

DESTINATION	FARE (₹)	DURATION (HR)	DEPARTURES
Agra	420	12	8.30pm
Chandigarh	240	6	hourly
Dehra Dun	40	2	hourly
Delhi (AC Volvo)	640	6	7am, 1pm, 10.30pm
Delhi (standard)	240	6	half-hourly
Dharamsala (ordinary/AC Volvo)	590/1750	15	2pm, 4pm/5pm
Haldwani	290	8	hourly
Rishikesh	35	1	half-hourly
Shimla	390	11	11am, 12.30pm
Uttarkashi	345	6	6am

In the *yatra* (pilgrimage) season from May to October, the following buses run from the **GMOU bus stand** (☎ 01334-226886; Railway Rd), opposite its ticket office. During monsoon season (July to mid-September), service is occasionally suspended. For Yamunotri, go to Dehra Dun, then take a bus to Barkot. Direct buses to Gangotri were not running at the time of research.

DESTINATION	FARE (₹)	DURATION (HR)	DEPARTURES
Badrinath (via Joshimath)	500	12	5am
Joshimath	420	10	4am, 5am, 6am, 8am
Kedarnath	360	10	4am, 7am
Uttarkashi	250	8	7am, 10am

TRAINS FROM HARIDWAR

DESTINATION	TRAIN NAME & NUMBER	FARE (₹)	DURATION (HR)	DEPARTURE/ARRIVAL
Amritsar	12053 Jan Shatabdi	2nd class/chair car 185/620	7½	2.45pm/10.05pm (Fri-Wed)
	14631 Dehra Dun– Amritsar Exp	sleeper/3AC 250/675	10	9.30pm/7.20am
Delhi (New Delhi Station)	12018 Shatabdi Exp	chair car/executive 880/1270	4½	6.12pm/10.50pm
	12056 Jan Shatabdi Exp	2nd class/chair car 140/475	4¾	6.30am/11.15am
Haldwani (for Nainital & Almora)	14120 Dehra Dun– Kathgodam Exp	sleeper/2AC/1AC 190/700/1165	6½	12.07am/6.48am
Kolkata/Howrah	13010 Doon Exp	sleeper/3AC/2AC 595/1600/2340	32¾	10.15pm/6.55am (2 nights later)
	12370 HW HWH S F Exp	sleeper/3AC/2AC 630/1670/2425	27½	11.50pm/3.20am (Mon, Tue, Thu, Fri & Sun)
Lucknow	13010 Doon Exp	sleeper/3AC/2AC 285/765/1100	10¼	10.20am/8.35am
Varanasi	13010 Doon Exp	sleeper/3AC/2AC 405/1110/1600	17¾	10.20am/4.05pm

❶ Getting There & Away

Haridwar is well connected by bus and train, but book ahead for trains during the pilgrimage season (May to October).

BUS

Government buses run from the **UK Roadways bus stand** (www.utconline.uk.gov.in; Railway Rd) on the main road through town. Private deluxe buses run to Delhi (₹365 to ₹650), Agra (from ₹475, 8½ hours), Jaipur (from ₹550, 10 hours) and Pushkar (from ₹600, 14 hours). Ask the travel agent who makes your booking where to find your bus.

TAXI & VIKRAM

The main **taxi stand** (Railway Rd) is outside the train station. Destinations include Chilla (for Rajaji Tiger Reserve, ₹570), Rishikesh (₹1220, one hour), Mussoorie (₹2620), Dehra Dun (₹1720) and Jolly Grant Airport (₹1420), but it's definitely possible to arrange a taxi for less than these official rates – particularly using the Ola taxi app. You can also hire taxis to go to one or all of the pilgrimage sites on the Char Dham between April and October. One-way rates to single temples range from ₹6750 to ₹8000; a nine-day tour of all four is ₹27,550. Hiring a jeep for the Char Dham costs marginally more, and can be well worth it in monsoon season, or for groups of four or more.

❶ Getting Around

Cycle-rickshaws cost ₹15 for a short distance and around ₹50 for longer hauls, such as from the Haridwar train station to Har-ki-Pairi. Shared electric-motor **vikrams** (off Railway Rd) run up and down Railway Rd (₹20) and all the way to Rishikesh (₹70, one hour) from Upper Rd at Laltarao Bridge, but for that trip buses are more comfortable. Hiring a taxi for three hours to tour the local temples and ashrams costs around ₹800; an autorickshaw costs ₹350. The Ola rideshare app offers the cheapest means of getting around if you have data on your smartphone.

Rajaji Tiger Reserve

ELEV 300-1000M

Unspoilt **Rajaji Tiger Reserve** (Rajaji National Park; ☑ Chilla 0138-2266757, Dehra Dun 0135-2621669, Haridwar 01334-2425193; www.rajajitigerreserve.co.in; Indian/foreigner per day from ₹150/600, vehicle fee ₹250/500, camera ₹50; ⊙ 15 Nov–15 Jun), covering over 1000 sq km in the forested foothills near Haridwar, was declared an official tiger park in 2015, with 34 of the striped cats within its boundaries. It's best known for wild elephants – around 600 at last count – and leopards (about 250). The park's only open mid-November to mid-June.

The thick deciduous forests are also home to chital, sambars, Himalayan Black bear, rarely seen sloth bears and some 300 species of birds. Though your chances of spotting a tiger are slim, you're likely to see some wildlife, and will get a feel for the wilderness.

The village of Chilla, 13km northeast of Haridwar, is the base for visiting the park.

At the Forest Ranger's office, close to the tourist guesthouse (p426) at Chilla, you can organise a jeep tour (₹1800), or you can take your own vehicle (₹500 entry fee) but you'll need to bring a guide (₹200). Safaris run from around 6am to 9.30am (to 10.30am in peak season) and 2pm or 3pm to 5pm or 6pm.

For a more personalised experience, go with Mohan's Adventure Tours (p422), out of Haridwar.

Sleeping & Eating

The park can easily be visited from Rishikesh or Haridwar as a day trip; however, for the full jungle experience you can stay inside the park at a Forest Rest House. There's also the government-run **Chilla Guesthouse** (☑9568006649, 01382-266678; www.gmvnl.in; r from ₹2800; ☒) in Chilla, close to the park gate, with comfortable rooms, a good restaurant and a pleasant garden: for information

and reservations, contact Mohan's Adventure Tours (p422) in Haridwar or the director at the Rajaji National Park Office (p425). The most atmospheric option of all is **Wild Brook Retreat** (☑9314880887, 9982907130; www.wildbrookretreat.com; Bukundi; s/d incl meals ₹3990/6800) ✔, on the far eastern edge of the park.

ⓘ Getting There & Away

Buses to Chilla (₹20, one hour) leave the GMOU bus stand (p424) in Haridwar every hour from 7am to 2pm. The last return trip leaves Chilla at 5.30pm. Taxis charge ₹570 one way for the 13km journey.

Dehra Dun

☑0135 / POP 655,000 / ELEV 652M

Perhaps best known for the institutions the British left behind – the huge Forest Research Institute Museum, the Indian Military Academy, the Wildlife Institute of India and the

Dehra Dun

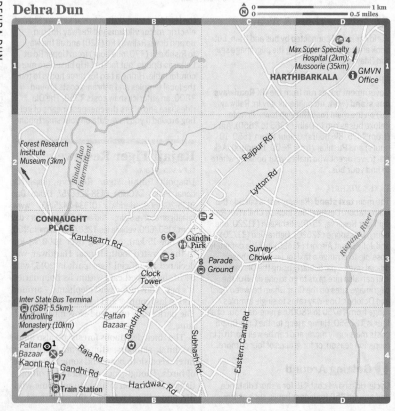

Survey of India – the capital of Uttarakhand is a hectic, congested city sprawling in the Doon Valley between the Himalayan foothills and the Siwalik Range. Most travellers merely pass through on their way to nearby Rishikesh, Haridwar, Mussoorie or Himachal Pradesh, but if you have time, there's enough to do here to make Dehra Dun worth a stop.

◉ Sights

Mindrolling Monastery BUDDHIST MONASTERY
(☑ 0135-2640556; www.mindrolling.org; Budha Temple Rd, Clement Town) The region around Dehra Dun is home to a thriving Tibetan Buddhist community, mainly focused on this attractive monastery, about 10km south of the centre in Clement Town. Everything here is on a grand scale: at more than 60m tall its Great Stupa is believed to be the world's tallest and contains a series of shrine rooms displaying relics, murals and Tibetan art. Presiding over the monastery is the impressive 35m-high gold Sakyamuni Buddha Statue, dedicated to the Dalai Lama.

Take *vikram* 5 from the city centre (₹20). An autorickshaw costs about ₹250.

Forest Research Institute Museum NOTABLE BUILDING
(www.fri.res.in/museum; ₹40, camera ₹50; ⊙ 9am-5.30pm) The prime attraction here is the building itself. Set in a peaceful 5-sq-km park, this grand remnant of the Raj era – where most of India's forest officers are trained – is larger than Buckingham Palace. Built between 1924 and 1929, this redbrick colossus has Mughal towers, perfectly formed arches and porticos, and Roman columns in a series of quadrangles edged by elegant cloisters. Six huge halls have dusty displays on Indian forestry that look like leftovers from a middle-school science fair.

A return autorickshaw from the city centre, including one-hour wait time, costs around ₹350. Or take *vikram* 6 from Connaught Pl and get out at the institute's entry gate.

Ram Rai Darbar MAUSOLEUM
(Paltan Bazaar; ⊙ dawn-dusk) FREE The unique mausoleum of Ram Rai, the errant son of the seventh Sikh guru, Har Rai, is made of white marble, with paintings covering the walls, archways and ceilings. Four smaller tombs in the garden courtyard are those of Ram Rai's four wives. A communal lunch of dhal, rice and chapatis is offered to anyone who wants it, for a donation.

🏃 Activities

Har Ki Dun Protection & Mountaineering Association TREKKING
(☑ 9410134589, 7579143813; www.harkidun.org; Chandrabani Choila) Highly regarded company that offers guided treks in Har-ki-Dun (p440), around the Garhwal Himalaya and beyond.

🎊 Festivals & Events

Shivaratri RELIGIOUS
(Tapkeshwar Temple; ⊙ usually Mar) A festival celebrated in style with carnival rides and stalls at a picturesque riverside cave temple on the outskirts of Dehra Dun.

🛌 Sleeping

There are plenty of grungy cheapies along the Haridwar road outside the train station, some charging as little as ₹400 a double, but the better places can be found along Rajpur Rd.

Moti Mahal Hotel HOTEL $$
(☑ 0135-2651277; www.hotelmotimahal.net; 7 Rajpur Rd; s/d from ₹1700/2000; ❄ 🔌) Centrally located, Moti Mahal offers well-kept rooms, with upholstered furnishings adding a touch of class. Those facing Rajpur Rd suffer from

a bit of street noise, but not badly. Features an excellent restaurant.

Samar Niwas Guest House GUESTHOUSE $$
(☑9837078356; www.samarniwas.com; M-16 Chanderlok Colony; d ₹1500-2500; ✼) This charming four-room guesthouse, in a peaceful residential area just off Rajpur Rd, is as welcoming as it gets. The owners are descendants of the Tehri royal family, but the rulers of the house seem to be the friendly pugs that roam the comfortable lounge-lobby. Rooms are well appointed, but there's no wi-fi.

Hotel President HOTEL $$$
(☑0135-2657082; www.hotelpresidentdehradun. com; Rajpur Rd, 6 Astley Hall; s/d from ₹3300/3500; ✼☏) This Dehra Dun institution is one of the classiest hotels in town, despite being sandwiched within the complex of shops, restaurants and fast-food spots called Astley Hall. Rooms have been renovated and are good value. Staff are professional and helpful, and there's a decent **restaurant** (10 Rajpur Rd, Astley Hall; mains ₹310-675; ☉11am-11pm), and the **Polo Bar** (☉7am-11pm) downstairs.

✕ Eating

★**Chetan Poori Wala** INDIAN $
(Hanuman Chowk, Paltan Bazaar; per puri ₹18; ☉8am-4.30pm) If you're looking for that authentic (and delicious) local dining experience, you've found it. Unlimited thalis are served on plates made of dried leaves in this bustling no-frills joint, and you just pay for the *puri* (deep-fried dough). The sweet *gulab jamun* (deep-fried dough in rose-flavoured syrup) ranks among the best we've ever had.

**Kumar Vegetarian &
South Indian Restaurant** INDIAN $$
(15B Rajpur Rd; mains ₹170-330; ☉11am-4pm & 7-10.30pm) This popular, sparkling-clean restaurant serves what surely comes close to the Platonic form of a *masala dosa* (curried vegetables inside a crisp pancake), which is the main reason locals flock here. Other Indian dishes are also cooked to near perfection and even the Chinese food is quite good. The waitstaff are very attentive.

Moti Mahal SOUTH INDIAN $$
(7 Rajpur Rd; mains ₹110-450; ☉8am-11.30pm; ☏) Locals consistently rate Moti Mahal as one of the best midrange diners along Rajpur Rd. An interesting range of vegetarian and nonvegetarian options include Goan fish curry and Afghani *murg* (chicken),

along with traditional South Indian fare and Chinese food. There's cold beer, too.

ℹ Information

GMVN Office (☑0135-2746847; 74/1 Rajpur Rd; ☉10am-5pm Mon-Sat) For information on trekking in Garhwal, whether booking a GMVN trip or going independently, talk to BS Gusain on the ground floor of the tourism office, or call him on ☑9568006695.

ℹ Getting There & Away

AIR

A few airlines (Jet Airways, SpiceJet, IndiGo and Air India) fly daily between Delhi and Dehra Dun's Jolly Grant Airport – about 20km east of the city on the Haridwar road – with fares starting at around ₹2500 each way. A taxi to/from the airport costs around ₹1100, or take a bus heading to Rishikesh from the Inter State Bus Terminal (p428) and ask to be dropped at the airport (₹40).

BUS

Nearly all long-distance buses arrive and depart from the huge **Inter State Bus Terminal** (ISBT; ☑0135-2640970; www.utconline.uk.gov.in), 5km south of the city centre. Here there are restaurants, ATMs and cyber cafes.

To get there take a local bus (₹5), *vikram* 5 (₹15) or an autorickshaw (₹200). A few buses to Mussoorie leave from here but most depart from the **Mussoorie bus stand** (off Gandhi Rd) (₹60, 1½ hours, half-hourly between 5.30am and 8pm) next to the train station. Most head to Mussoorie's Library bus stand. There are also buses from the Mussoorie bus stand to Barkot – for Yamnotri – (₹240, five hours, 5.30am and 11am); Purola – for Har-ki-Dun – (₹250, seven hours, 6.30am); Uttarkashi (₹280, seven hours, 5.30am) and Joshimath (₹505, 12 hours, 5.30am).

Private buses to Joshimath (₹400, 12 hours, 7am) and Uttarkashi (₹300, eight hours, 7am, 9am and 1.30pm) leave from the **Parade Ground bus stand** (Subhash Rd), where you can show up and get your ticket on the bus.

TAXI

A whole taxi to Mussoorie costs ₹1250, while a share taxi should cost ₹180 per person; both can be found in front of the train station at the **taxi stand** (off Gandhi Rd). Taxis charge ₹1650 to Haridwar or Lakshman Jhula in Rishikesh, and ₹1100 to Jolly Grant Airport.

TRAIN

Dehra Dun is well connected by train to Delhi, and there are a handful of services to Lucknow, Varanasi, Chennai and Kolkata. Of the multiple daily trains from Dehra Dun to Delhi, the best

BUSES FROM DEHRA DUN

The following buses depart from the Inter State Bus Terminal. Head to counter 22 for all enquiries.

DESTINATION	FARE (₹)	DURATION (HR)	DEPARTURES
Chandigarh	260	6	half-hourly 4am-10pm
Delhi (AC/Volvo)	533/754	7	frequent
Delhi (ordinary)	290	7	hourly 4am-10pm
Dharamsala	675	14	5pm
Haldwani (for Nainital & Almora; AC/Volvo)	365/693	10	hourly
Haridwar	75	2	half-hourly
Manali (AC/Volvo)	650/1264	14	6.45am, 3pm, 10.15pm
Ramnagar	295	7	7 daily
Rishikesh	55	1½	half-hourly
Shimla	550	10	5 daily

are the expresses: Shatabdi (train 12018, chair/executive ₹880/1400, six hours, 4.55pm); Janshatabdi (train 12056, 2nd class/chair ₹160/520, six hours, 5.05am); and Nanda Devi Express (train 12206, 3AC/2AC/1st class ₹595/830/1380, six hours, 11.30pm).

The overnight Dehradun–Amritsar Express (train 14631, sleeper/3A class ₹270/735, 12¼ hours) to Amritsar departs nightly at 7.05pm.

🛈 Getting Around

Hundreds of eight-seater *vikrams* (₹10 per trip) race along five fixed routes (look at the front for the number). Most useful is *vikram* 5, which runs between the ISBT stand, the train station and Rajpur Rd, and as far south as the Tibetan colony at Clement Town. *Vikram* 1 runs up and down Rajpur Rd above Gandhi Park, and also to Hathibarkala (check with the driver to see which route he's on). Autorickshaws cost ₹50 for a short distance, ₹180 from ISBT to the city centre or ₹200 per hour for touring around the city.

Mussoorie

📞 0135 / POP 30,200 / ELEV 2000M

Perched on a ridge 2km high, the 'Queen of Hill Stations' vies with Nainital as Uttarakhand's favourite holiday destination. When the mist clears, views of the green Doon Valley and the distant white-capped Himalayan peaks are superb, and in the hot months the cooler temperatures and fresh mountain air make a welcome break from the plains below.

Established by the British in 1823, Mussoorie became hugely popular with the Raj set. The ghosts of that era linger on in the architecture of the churches, libraries, hotels and summer palaces. The town is swamped with affluent Indian tourists between May and July, when it can seem like a tacky holiday camp for families and honeymooners, but at other times many of the 300 hotels have vacancies and their prices drop dramatically. During monsoon, the town is often shrouded in clouds.

◉ Sights

Mussoorie Heritage Centre CULTURAL CENTRE
(📞 0135-2632801; www.facebook.com/mussoorieheritagecentre; Clock Tower, Landour Bazaar; ⊙10am-6pm) FREE Sitting beneath Landour's clock tower is this impressive heritage centre that's set up by dedicated local historian, Surbhi Agarwal. She'll take you through the displays of collectibles and artefacts from Mussoorie, all set in the house she was born in. The small temporary exhibition is always worth checking out, as is its shop selling beautiful artworks, photography and prints, including John Gould's *Birds of Mussoorie*. Ask in advance about arranging heritage walks about town. Next door is Surbhi's father's impressive **antique shop** (⊙10am-6pm) that's been here since the 1960s.

Gun Hill VIEWPOINT
From midway along The Mall, a **cable car** (Upper Mall Rd; return ₹125; ⊙10am-7pm) runs up to Gun Hill (2530m), which, on a clear day, has views of several big peaks. A steep path also winds up to the viewpoint. The most popular time to go up is an hour or so before sunset. There's a minicarnival atmosphere in high season, with kids' rides, food stalls, magic shops and honeymooners having their photos taken in Garhwali costumes.

Mussoorie

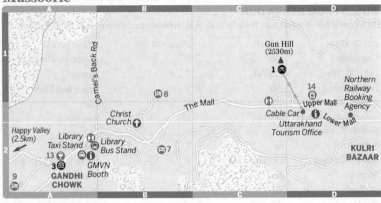

Mussoorie

Sights

1 Gun Hill...C1
2 Mussoorie Heritage Centre...................F1
3 Mussoorie Library..................................A2
4 Picture Palace Cinema...........................E1
5 Union Church...E1

Activities, Courses & Tours

Trek Himalaya............................(see 14)

Sleeping

6 Hotel Broadway.....................................E1
7 Hotel Padmini Nivas..............................B2
8 Kasmanda Palace Hotel........................B1

9 Savoy...A2

Eating

10 Café de Tavern......................................E1
11 Lovely Omelette Centre........................E1
12 Urban Turban..E1

Drinking & Nightlife

13 Imperial Square.....................................A2

Shopping

Vinod Kumar.....................................(see 2)
14 Wildcraft...D1

★ **Happy Valley** BUDDHIST SITE

Only 3km northwest of town, this scenic outlying region of Mussoorie is famous as the site where the Dalai Lama and fellow exiles arrived in 1959, after escaping from Tibet following Chinese occupation. The spiritual leader stayed for one year before relocating the exiled Tibetan government to Dharamsala. It's a beautiful valley with the atmospheric Shedup Choephelling Temple where the local Tibetan community pray, and a nearby hilltop stupa at Dalai Hills with a large Buddha statue, prayer flags and Himalayan views.

**Soham Heritage
& Art Centre** CULTURAL CENTRE

(☑9897241261; off Mall Rd; ₹100; ☉10am-2pm & 3-5pm Thu-Tue) Part museum, part art gallery, Soham Heritage & Art Centre focuses largely on the culture of the Uttarakhand Himalaya. You'll get guided through the displays of cultural artefacts, historical photography and an art gallery featuring paintings by Kavita,

who along with her husband Samer set up this privately run museum. Entry proceeds go towards a local orphanage they run.

🏃 Activities

When the clouds don't get in the way, the walks around Mussoorie offer great views. Camel's Back Rd is a popular 3km promenade from Kulri Bazaar to Gandhi Chowk, and passes a rock formation that looks like a camel. There are a couple of good mountain viewpoints along the way, and you can ride a rickshaw (one way/return ₹250/350) along the trail if you start from the Gandhi Chowk end. An enjoyable, longer walk (5km one way) starts at the Picture Palace Cinema (Mall Rd) and goes past Union Church (Mall Rd) to Landour and the Sisters' Bazaar area.

West of Gandhi Chowk, a more demanding walk is to the Jwalaji Temple on Benog Hill (about 20km return) via Cloud's End Hotel. The route passes through thick forest and offers some fine views. Taking a taxi

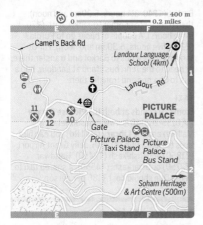

to Cloud's End (one way/return ₹650/1250) cuts the walk by more than half.

Trek Himalaya
TREKKING

(☑9837258589; www.trekhimalaya.com; Upper Mall; ⊗11am-9pm) Trek Himalaya can organise one- to three-day treks in the Mussoorie area, as well as longer customised treks to Har-ki-Dun (p440), Darwa Top and beyond. If weather or road conditions are bad, they don't go. Based out of the Wildcraft (www.wildcraft.in; ⊗11am-9pm) outdoor-gear store.

🏫 Courses

Landour Language School
LANGUAGE

(☑0135-2631487; www.landourlanguageschool.com; Landour; per hour group/private from ₹385/635; ⊗Feb–mid Dec) One of India's leading schools for teaching conversational Hindi at beginner, intermediate and advanced levels. There's an enrolment fee of ₹1000, and course books are an extra ₹2200.

🛏 Sleeping

Mussoorie offers a great opportunity to stay in a heritage hotel – with options in all budgets – allowing you to soak up the town's colonial ambience. Budget places are scarce – you'll find some dives near Picture Palace. But many hotels offer budget rates out of season. Peak season is summer (May to July) when hotel prices shoot up to ridiculous heights.

Hotel Broadway
HOTEL $

(☑0135-2632243; Camel's Back Rd, Kulri Bazaar; d ₹800-1500) The best of the budget places by a mile, this historic 1880s wooden hotel with colourful flower boxes in the windows oozes character. It's in a quiet location (apart from the mosque's early-morning call to prayer) but close to The Mall. Cheaper downstairs rooms could use a refresh, but upstairs rooms are nice; the best has lovely sunlit bay windows.

★Kasmanda Palace Hotel
HERITAGE HOTEL $$$

(☑0135-2632424; www.welcomheritagehotels.in; Mall Rd; r from ₹6500) Located off The Mall, this is Mussoorie's most romantic hotel. The white Romanesque castle was built in 1836 for a British officer and bought by the Maharaja of Kasmanda in 1915. The red-carpeted hall has a superb staircase flanked by moth-eaten hunting trophies. All rooms have charm but the wood-panelled and antique-filled Maharaja Room is the royal best.

There's also a separate cottage with six renovated contemporary-style rooms. An excellent restaurant and pretty garden area – open to nonguests – complete the picture.

Savoy
HERITAGE HOTEL $$$

(☑0135-2637000; www.itchotels.in/destinations/mussoorie.html; behind Gandhi Chowk; r weekday/weekend from ₹15,200/17,150) This famous Mussoorie hotel, built in 1902, underwent a seven-year renovation to restore it to its magnificent former glory, imparting a regal atmosphere with none of the rundown air that often infuses historic properties. Bedrooms, however, feel strangely generic. The restaurant is both an aesthetic and a culinary experience, as is its refined Writers Bar (happy hour 6pm to 8pm).

Hotel Padmini Nivas
HERITAGE HOTEL $$$

(☑0135-2631093, 7310804566; www.hotel-padmininivas.com; Mall Rd; r from ₹3750; @⊚) Built by the British in the 1820s is this former house that's been converted into a sprawling heritage hotel with plenty of old-fashioned charm. Large rooms with quaint sunrooms are beautifully furnished; those in the 'heritage wing' are significantly nicer than those in the side building which feel institutional. The dining room, with antique furniture, is an outstanding feature.

The whole place is set on 2 hectares of landscaped gardens. Genteel management are courteous and professional.

🍴 Eating & Drinking

★Lovely Omelette Centre
FAST FOOD $

(Mall Rd, Kulri Bazaar; mains ₹60-90; ⊗8am-9pm) Mussoorie's most famous eatery is also its smallest – a cubbyhole along The Mall that serves what many say are the best omelettes in India. The speciality is the cheese omelette, with chillies, onions and spices, served over toast, but the maestro at the frying pan will whip up a chocolate omelette on request. On weekends you might have to wait.

Urban Turban
PUNJABI $$

(Mall Rd; mains ₹210-650; ⊙11.30am-11.30pm) This Punjabi bistro packs in the flavour, with perfectly spiced veg and nonveg options: the aromatic Turban Tikka Masala rocked our taste buds to a very happy place. Staff are exceptionally eager to please. If the Hindi power pop on the 1st floor is too loud for you, head up to the quieter 2nd floor. Windows overlook the street.

Café de Tavern
MULTICUISINE $$

(Mall Rd; mains ₹180-450; ⊙11am-10.30pm) Mussoorie's most hip casual eatery is a great spot to drop in for pizzas, deep-fried paneer burgers, all-day greasy breakfasts featuring bacon and a dessert menu to satisfy your sweet tooth. It's a good spot for a drink, too, doing international beers and sangria and mojito cocktails by the jug. Its espresso coffee is quality.

Imperial Square
BAR

(☑0135-2632632; Gandhi Chowk; mains ₹300-700; ⊙8am-11pm; 🎅) With huge windows overlooking Gandhi Chowk, Imperial Square is easily Mussoorie's most scenic spot for a drink. The beer is pricey (₹340) but it's ice cold, and there's a whole menu of meat and vegetarian kebabs to go with it. There's also a bar if you're in the mood for cocktails etc. The newly renovated heritage building dates from 1843.

❶ Information

GMVN Booth (☑0135-2631281; Library bus stand; ⊙8am-5pm) Can book local tours, treks and far-flung rest houses.

❶ Getting There & Away

BUS

Buses depart from Mussoorie's **Library bus stand** (Mall Rd) for Dehra Dun (₹60, 1½ hours) every 30 minutes between 6.30am and 7pm. There's no direct transport from Mussoorie to Rishikesh or Haridwar – change at Dehra Dun. Buses also occasionally use the **Picture Palace Bus Stand** (Mall Rd).

To reach the mountain villages of western Garhwal, grab one of the buses passing through Gandhi Chowk. For Yamunotri, hop on a bus to Barkot (₹240, 3½ hours, 5.30am and noon), then transfer to another to Janki Chatti (₹70, three hours). A couple of buses go to Purola (₹250, five hours, 5.30am and noon). For Uttarkashi, take a bus to Barkot and transfer there, or head to the Tehri bus stand at Landour, hop a bus to Chamba and transfer there.

TAXI

From taxi stands at both the **Picture Palace** (☑0135-2631407; www.mussoorietaxi.in; Mall Rd) and the **Library** (Mall Rd) you can hire taxis to Dehra Dun (₹1250), Jolly Grant Airport (₹1850) and Rishikesh (₹2450), Haridwar (₹2750) or Uttarkashi (₹4550). A shared taxi to Dehra Dun should cost ₹180 per person.

Yamunotri

☑01374 / ELEV 3235M

Yamunotri Temple is tucked in a tight gorge close to the source of the Yamuna, Hinduism's second-most sacred river after the Ganges. Yamunotri is the least visited and therefore least developed of the *char dham* sites, but once you get to the trailhead it's an easy trek.

The 5km, 1½-hour hike to Yamunotri begins at the tiny village of Janki Chatti. At Yamunotri Temple (⊙late Apr–late Oct) there are several hot springs where you can take a dip, and others where pilgrims cook potatoes and rice as *prasad* (food offering used in religious ceremonies). You'll find plenty of priests to help you make *puja* (prayer offerings) for a price. A pony costs ₹800/1320 one way/return, but it's not an overly tough trek.

One kilometre beyond the temple, the Yamuna River spills from a frozen lake of ice and glaciers on the Kalinda Parvat mountain at an altitude of 4421m, but this is a very tough climb that requires mountaineering skills.

Across the river from Janki Chatti is the friendly village of Kharsali, which is worth a stroll if you have the time.

You'll find basic guesthouses in Janki Chatti, the best of which are the two GMVN guesthouses.

❶ Getting There & Away

A 7am bus heads to Dehra Dun (₹220) and Uttarkashi (₹150 to ₹200), and during peak *yatra* season (May to June), there are buses to Mussoorie and Rishikesh, but the most frequent transport services originate in Barkot. There are three or so buses to Barkot (₹70, three hours) departing from Janki Chatti in the morning and usually also early afternoon. Share jeeps also

THE CHAR DHAM

High in the Garhwali Himalaya sit some of the holiest sites in the Hindu religion – Yamunotri, Gangotri (p434), Kedarnath (p435), and Badrinath (p441) – where temples mark the spiritual sources of four sacred rivers: the Yamuna, the Ganges, the Mandakini and the Alaknanda. Together, they make up one of the most important *yatra* (pilgrimage) circuits in all of India, known as the *char dham* (four seats, or abodes). Every year between April and November (they close down over winter), hundreds of thousands of worshippers brave hair-raising mountain roads and high-altitude trails to reach them.

Travelling to one or more of the *char dham* temples is a great way to get a feel for the religious pulse of the subcontinent, amid incredible alpine scenery. Numerous buses, share jeeps, porters, ponies – and now helicopters – are on hand for transport, and there's a well-established network of guesthouses, ashrams and government rest houses. As a result, getting to these temples is easy enough without hiring guides or carrying supplies, and Gangotri and Badrinath temples can be visited without even having to hike. Monsoons in summer, however, can produce dangerous conditions, triggering landslides that block roads and trails for days or weeks.

In June 2013, a torrential cloudburst produced an epic flood that swept away entire villages – and thousands of local people and pilgrims. The official death toll is around 6000, but locals insist the real number was closer to 50,000. Since then the people and government of Uttarakhand have worked to rebuild confidence in the area's safety, in an effort to revive the region's main economic engine. After a few years of decline, the *char dham* has surged back to life. Note that before visiting *char dham* sites, you are supposed to obtain a free photometric ID card (the government's way of tracking people in the event of another natural disaster), which is easily available in many cities and towns around the state. You may never be asked to show yours, but you should get one anyway.

head to Barkot (₹100). A whole taxi costs about ₹2000 each way.

Uttarkashi

☏ 01374 / POP 17,500 / ELEV 1158M

Set along the banks of the holy Bhagirathi, Uttarkashi, 155km from Rishikesh, is the largest town in northern Garhwal and capital of Uttarkashi district. It's an unavoidable stop on the road to both the Gangotri and Yamunotri *char dham* sites. The main bazaar is worth a wander and has all the supplies you might need. A number of outfitters can arrange treks in the region, including to Tapovan (beyond Gangotri/Gaumukh).

The town is home to **Nehru Institute of Mountaineering** (☏ 01374-222123; www.nimindia.net; ☉ 10am-5pm), which trains many of the guides running trekking and mountaineering outfits in India. Uttarkashi also hosts the **Makar Sankranti festival** (☉ Jan).

🛏 Sleeping & Eating

⭐ **Monal Guest House** HOTEL $
(☏ 01374-222270; www.monaluttarkashi.com; Kot Bungalow Rd; s/d from ₹800/900; @ 🛜) This hillside hotel feels like a large, comfortable house, and has clean, tasteful rooms, a big-windowed cafe with espresso machine, books and a peaceful hilltop garden setting. Wing A has a more homely feel than Wing B. Head up to its rooftop for wonderful river views. There are mountain bikes for rent (per day ₹300) and cooking classes (per person ₹2750).

It's off the Gangotri road 3km north of town. Reservations essential.

Hotel Bhandari Annexe HOTEL $
(☏ 01374-222384, 9411147626; www.hotelbhandariannexe.com; s/d from ₹700/800) A step up from the other cheapies near the bus stand is this attractive three-storey guesthouse on the main road close to the Gangotri jeep stand. Rooms are well priced, but cheaper rooms are lacking in natural light. There's a restaurant downstairs.

❶ Getting There & Away

To get to Gangotri, take a shared jeep/taxi (₹230/2300, five hours); they don't leave until full – so head here first thing in the morning. Shared jeeps also leave when full for Rishikesh (₹350), Srinagar (₹300), Haridwar (₹400) and Barkot (₹200).

Buses depart for Rishikesh (₹240, seven hours) and Haridwar (₹250, eight hours) at 5.45am, 6.30am and 7am. Four buses go to Dehra Dun

(₹200, nine hours) between 6am and 2pm. Buses to Srinagar (₹210, eight hours) leave at 5.30am and 8.30pm, and those to Barkot (₹120, five hours) run frequently until 3pm. Buses run directly to Janki Chatti (₹190, seven hours) for Yamunotri temple at 7.30am and 10.30am. Seats may sell out on some routes, so it's a good idea to buy tickets a day in advance.

Whole taxis to Rishikesh cost ₹3500.

Gangotri & Gaumukh Glacier

In a remote setting at an altitude of 3042m, Gangotri is one of the holiest places in India. Not only is it home to one of the four *char dham* temples, but it's the gateway town for the trek to the source of the Ganges.

For a site of such significance, **Gangotri Temple** (☉late Apr–late Oct) is surprisingly underwhelming. Unless you're a devout Hindu, to get a real sense of awe you'll probably have to trek from Gangotri to the true source of the river, at Gaumukh, 18km upstream.

Gangotri village itself is a touristy pedestrianised strip of guesthouses, restaurants and shops selling woollen clothes. The entire town and surrounding treks are closed from November to the end of April.

🏃 Activities

The real reason most foreigners come to Gangotri is for the trek to Gaumukh Glacier – the source of the Ganges River.

Don't be daunted by the trek – the trail rises gradually and is completely solid. Four to six hours (14km) up the trail, at Bhojwasa (Bhojbasa; 3790m), there's a GMVN Tourist Bungalow (p434) and other rudimentary tented dorm lodging; Gaumukh is 4km (1½ hours) past that. On clear days, the best time to visit the source is early to midafternoon, when it's out of the shadows. There, the water flows out of Gangotri Glacier beneath the soaring west face of Bhagirathi Parvat (6856m), with the peak of Shivling (the 6543m 'Indian Matterhorn') towering to the south.

It is possible to do Gaumukh Glacier as a day trip from Gangotri, but you'll have to set out as early as you can (park office is open 6am to 6pm) and it'll be rushed. Your best bet is to take a pony (one way/return ₹1350/2500), which can be hired in Gangotri. Ponies aren't permitted for the last leg from Bhojwasa to Gaumukh, so you'll have to walk that 8km-return trek. A porter is ₹800

to ₹1500 depending on the season, while a guide is ₹1500 to ₹2000.

More ambitious hikers with camping gear often continue to the gorgeous meadow at Tapovan, 6km beyond Gaumukh; tents can be hired from **Real Adventure** (☑9410178414; www.realadventuregangotri.in) or Hotel Mandakini (p434) in Gangotri. As of late 2018 no permits were being issued for overnight stays in Tapovan due to an ongoing court case banning camping in the *bugyal* (meadows).

Before trekking to Gaumukh, you must first get a permit, since access is limited to 150 people per day. This can be obtained from the **permit office** (☉8-10am & 5-7pm) above the bus stand at Gangotri, or from the **District Magistrate Office** (☑9412077500; www.swsuttarkashi.com/permission/gangotrinational park; ☉10am-5pm Mon-Sat) in Uttarkashi. At both places, you'll need to bring a copy of your passport ID page and visa. The permit is valid for two days and costs ₹150/600 per Indian/foreigner (then ₹50/250 for each extra day); camping permits are ₹100 to ₹200, and a cooking permit is ₹200. You can also attempt to arrange a trekking permit online at www.swsuttarkashi.com/permission/gangotrinationalpark. Solo trekkers are required to bring along a guide (a permit won't be issued without one – however, a porter will suffice, a cheaper alternative to a guide).

Before Bhojwasa there's only a tea shop along the trek, 9km into the journey at Chirwasa, so you'll need to bring along enough water.

🛏 Sleeping & Eating

Gangotri village has plenty of guesthouses, ashrams and *dharamsalas* (pilgrim's rest houses) charging ₹300 or less per room. Note that during peak season (May and June) prices double.

Bhojwasa has fewer options, with only grim dorms available at the government-run **GMVN Bhojwasa** (www.gmvnl.in; dm ₹350), and several ashrams that offer tented dorms for ₹350 including meals.

★ Hotel Mandakini   LODGE $$
(☑8279642323, 9458125708; r ₹1200-2000; ☉Apr-Nov) Mandakini is the best place to stay in town, with clean, spacious rooms. Upstairs rooms are the pick with fantastic views (go room C14). Its Nepali manager, Chandar, can be extremely helpful in arranging last-minute permits, particularly for solo trekkers. Bucket hot water is ₹50. It's

UTTARAKHAND'S TOP TREKS

There's no better way to experience the sheer, astonishing beauty and power of the Himalaya than to get up close and trek among this world-famous mountain range. Whether you're seeking a short walk or a full-scale trekking expedition, the Uttarakhand Himalaya offers many fantastic trails.

Gaumukh Glacier Trek among the Land of the Gods along a rocky valley trail to a glacier that's the source of the Ganges.

Valley of Flowers (p439) Experience the kaleidoscopic panoramas of hundreds of flowers at full bloom with a snow-capped mountain backdrop.

Kuari Pass Trek (p440) One of India's finest treks taking you through a mind-blowing Himalayan landscape, including close-ups of Nanda Devi (7816m).

Tungnath & Chandrisilla Trek (p438) Accessible four-hour trek to the highest Shiva temple in the world and unforgettable Himalayan views.

Kedarnath Join the convoy of Hindu pilgrims on a trek up to this holy *char dham* temple sitting below towering Himalayan peaks.

Roopkund Trek (p437) A unique multiday trek through alpine grasslands and forests to a glacial high-altitude lake famed for its mysterious scattering of 9th-century skeletons.

Milam Glacier (p441) One for serious trekkers is this eight-day expedition along an ancient, remote Tibetan trade route leading to an epic glacier.

unsigned, but reached via the stairs just past Hotel Krishna Palace restaurant.

Hotel Krishna Palace　MULTICUISINE $$
(☑9410199108, 8126728108; mains ₹150-350; ⏱8am-10pm) Gangrotri's main traveller hangout and best spot to eat is this ultrafriendly restaurant serving up pizzas topped with mozzarella, along with burgers, grilled sandwiches, sizzlers and a heap of Indian dishes. Its juices, lassis, desserts and breakfasts are also popular choices. It also has budget rooms upstairs (₹300 to ₹1000).

ⓘ Information

There's no ATM in Gangotri, so bring enough cash.

ⓘ Getting There & Away

Bus service to Gangotri is sporadic. The best way to get there is to take a shared jeep (₹230) or whole taxi (one way/return ₹3000/4000) from Uttarkashi, though taxis can also be hired from Rishikesh (₹450 to ₹550) or Haridwar. There are also sporadic bus services from Gangotri to Uttarkashi (₹180) departing at 5am.

Kedarnath

☑ 01364 / ELEV 3583M

Tucked at the base of 6970m peaks, 18km from the nearest road, Kedarnath (⏱late Apr–mid Nov) is the most spectacular of the four *char dham* temples. On a clear day,

you'll see the sky-scraping, snow-covered summits that tower over the temple long before you reach it.

Dedicated to Shiva, Kedarnath temple is revered by Hindus, and pilgrims journey from all over India to take the long trek (or horse ride) up. To get here you'll walk alongside them on the stone-paved pathway etched into the steep slopes of the canyon cut by the Mandakini, following the river upstream. It closes mid-November to late April.

The *puja* offered inside the temple is fervent and can be quite intense, especially around the stone 'hump' which is believed to have been left behind by Shiva when he dove into the ground in the form of a bull.

Kedarnath was at the epicentre of a devastating flood in 2013. Thousands of people including pilgrims, locals, porters and horse guides, perished. Kedarnath village is slowly recovering and life is springing up around the wreckage, with shops, restaurants and hotels reestablishing themselves among the rubble and damaged buildings. Today, nearly as much reverence is paid to a massive boulder that sits behind the temple – which, incredibly, shielded it from the worst of the onslaught and saved it from collapse – as to the temple itself.

The trek up to Kedarnath involves an 18km steep uphill climb from the village of Gaurikund. Expect it to take anywhere from five to seven hours, depending on breaks.

Horse (up/down ₹2300/1500) and helicopter (✓Delhi 011-41649360; www.himalayanheli.com; Guptkashi-Sonprayag Rd, Sersi) are alternatives. There are plenty of stops along the route, where drinks and snacks are available, along with accommodation and medical assistance. Ensure you bring warm clothing (thermals, gloves, beanie) as it gets bitterly cold in Kedarnath.

Prior to hitting the trail, you must get a free photometric ID card in Sonprayag (5am to 6pm), the village 5km before Gaurikund.

Sleeping

Most visitors will spend the evening in Kedarnath village, though there are government-run lodges at several stops along the trail. It's also very likely you'll need to spend a night in Sonprayag or Gaurikund – the gateway towns to begin the trek.

Kedarnath

All accommodation options in Kedarnath village have very basic nonheated rooms, but will provide plenty of thick blankets and hot-water bucket showers (₹50). Note prices skyrocket in May and June.

Punjab Sindh Awas   HOTEL $$
(✓9760203326, 9412915221; from ₹600-2100) Probably the best choice overall is this no-frills hotels in the heart of the action, 200m from the temple. Split over two buildings, pricier rooms get you a geyser and a nicer space. Otherwise it's bucket hot showers and a fairly grubby room – but it's perfectly fine for a night.

Sonprayag, Gaurikund & Guptkashi

At the trailhead for the trek to Kedarnath you will find basic accommodation in Sonprayag and Gaurikund; Gaurikund is much quieter and more atmospheric, making it a better place to stay before or after trekking. Contact **GMVN Gaurikund** (✓9568006656; www.gmvnl.in; Gaurikund; dm from ₹200, r ₹900-2100; ☺late Apr–early Nov) for clean dorms and single rooms in the village. A handful of better hotels can be found about 2km before Sonprayag, at Sitapur – including **Shavalik Valley Resort** (✓8650573796; www.shivalikvalleyresorts.com; r from ₹3800).

If you get stuck in Guptkashi, **Deepak Tourist Lodge** (✓9756899907; r ₹300), a short walk from the bus stand, is a good choice.

ℹ Information

There's a State Bank of India ATM in Sonprayag, but not in Kedarnath – so be sure to carry enough cash.

ℹ Getting There & Away

The main transit hub for the area is Guptkashi, from where you can take a shared/private jeep (₹70/1000) to Sonprayag; last departure around 6pm. Alternatively, take a GMOU bus to Sonprayag from Rishikesh or Haridwar. From Sonprayag, morning buses run to Rishikesh (₹321, seven hours), Haridwar (₹320, eight hours), and Dehra Dun (₹350, nine hours).

From Sonprayag, shared jeeps (₹20) make the trip to the trailhead at Gaurikund.

Going to or from Kedarnath by helicopter is becoming an increasingly popular option for Indians, with numerous operators flying the route that takes a mere seven minutes. It costs from ₹3000 to ₹3650 to fly one way. Several companies fly out of – and have offices in – Phata, between Guptkashi and Sonprayag, while Himalayan Heli Services is based in nearby Sersi. All companies have offices at the Kedarnath helipad. Flights typically end by early afternoon. Weight limits for passengers are 80kg, with around ₹150 per extra kilo; baggage allowance is as little as 2kg. Note that scientists are concerned about the impact of frequent helicopter flights on wildlife in the Kedarnath Wildlife Sanctuary, which surrounds the area.

Joshimath

✓01389 / POP 16.800 / ELEV 1875M

As the gateway to Badrinath Temple and Hem Kund, Joshimath sees a steady stream of Hindu and Sikh pilgrims from May to October. And as the base for the Valley of Flowers and Kuari Pass treks, and Auli ski resort, it attracts adventure travellers year-round.

Reached from Rishikesh by a serpentine mountain road, Joshimath is a thoroughly utilitarian two-street town with erratic power supply and limited places to eat. Although the big mountain views are lost from the town itself, it's only a short cable-car ride (return ₹750; ☺every 20min 8am-5pm) from here to Auli, which has magnificent vistas of Nanda Devi.

🏃 Activities

To trek the Kuari Pass (p440) and other routes in Nanda Devi Sanctuary, you need a permit and a registered guide (per day ₹1000 to ₹1500). There are excellent operators in town who can organise everything,

ROOPKUND TREK: SKELETON LAKE

One of India's more unique treks is the three- to four-day journey up to Roopkund lake, which culminates with the macabre sight of 9th-century skeleton remains that sit at the bottom of the glacial lake. Stumbled upon by a game-reserve ranger in 1942, some 300 bodies were discovered in the shallow lake, perched at the dizzying altitude of 5029m. After decades of debate as to their origins, in 2013 scientists concluded the remains dated from nomadic 9th-century tribespeople, who were believed to have perished in a fatal hail storm.

Today only scatterings of bones and skulls remain; many have been stolen or shifted for research purposes, and they're generally only viewable for a month or so between late June and middle of September; other times they're covered in snow and the trail is inaccessible.

Regardless of the skeletons, it's one of the region's most spectacular treks. While the 2018 camping ban in the *bugyal* (high-altitude meadows) by the Uttarakhand high court has seen it scaled back from what's usually a six- to eight-day trek (check to see if this has been overturned), the trip takes you through the same varied landscapes of oak and rhododendron forests, pristine alpine *bugyal* and life-affirming Himalayan views.

The base camp begins in the village of Wan (2400m) in Chamoli district. It's not a trek for inexperienced hikers, and you'll need to arrange a permit. A guide is highly recommended – best arranged through the trekking companies in Joshimath.

including further-flung and intensely adventurous multiday expeditions.

★ **Himalayan Snow Runner** OUTDOORS
(☑ 9756813236, 9412082247; www.himalayan snowrunner.com; Auli Rd, Main Market) Highly recommended outfit for trekking (from around ₹3000 per person per day), skiing and adventure activities, with camping gear provided. The owner, Ajay, can customise unique trekking routes, and cultural tours to Bhotia and Garhwali villages. The office, on the main road opposite the cable car, also stocks local organic products, handmade clothing and books about Uttarakhand.

★ **Eskimo Adventures** OUTDOORS
(☑ 9412413714, 9756835647; www.eskimo adventure.com) This is the longest-running adventure company in Joshimath. Helpful owner Dinesh offers treks and rock-climbing expeditions (from about ₹3000 per day for five people, from ₹4000 for one to two people), equipment rental (for trekking and skiing) and white-water rafting trips on the Ganges. It also has a recommendable guesthouse 4km from Joshimath on the Auli road (per room ₹2500).

🛏 Sleeping & Eating

Hotel New Kamal HOTEL $
(☑ 9411577880; Auli Rd, Main Market; r ₹500) Small and clean with TVs and hot-water showers. Though the beds are hard, this is one of the better cheapies in Joshimath.

Hotel Mount View Annexy HOTEL $$
(☑ 9573082826, 9634255572; Auli Rd, Main Market; r ₹1000) The rooms at this standard hotel deliver what many others in Joshimath lack: reliable cleanliness, soft mattresses, flatscreen TV, 24-hour hot water and a sense of being well maintained. There's no wi-fi, however. Prices negotiable. It's along the main road, a short walk up from the cable car.

Hotel Malari Inn HOTEL $$
(☑ 9410116094, 01389-222257; www.hotel-malari-inn.weebly.com; Auli Rd, Main Market; r ₹1800-3800; 🛜) On the outskirts of the main market is this renovated large hotel with a range of rooms. Standards are basic but spacious and clean; you pay more for more amenities, a fatter mattress and a balcony with valley views. All rooms have geysers. Discounts are offered outside peak season (May to September).

Auli D's Food Plaza MULTICUISINE $
(Auli Rd, Main Market; mains ₹90-250; ⏱ 9am-10pm) Featuring a full menu of Indian, Chinese and Continental food, including veg and nonveg choices, this 1st-floor restaurant has plastic tablecloths and covered seats, and feels like a banquet hall.

ℹ Getting There & Away

Although the main road up to Joshimath is maintained by the Indian army, and a hydroelectric plant on the way to Badrinath has improved that road, the area around Joshimath is inevitably prone to landslides, particularly in the rainy season from mid-June to mid-September.

TUNGNATH & CHANDRISILLA TREK

One of the best day hikes in Uttarakhand, the trail to Tungnath Mandir (3680m) and Chandrisilla Peak (4000m) features a sacred Panch Kedar temple and a stunning Himalayan panorama.(The Panch Kedar are ficve sacred temples in the Garhwal Himalayan region of Uttarakhand. The others are at Kedarnath, Rudranath, Madhyamaheshwar and Kalpeshwar.)

The trail starts at Chopta, a small village on the winding road between Chamoli (south of Joshimath) and Kund (south of Gaurikund).

A well-paved path from Chopta switchbacks 3.5km uphill, gaining 750m in elevation, to Tungnath Mandir, the highest Shiva temple in the world. There are a number of teahouses from which to enjoy the views.

From here a steep trail continues 1.5km further up the grassy bugyal (high-altitude meadow) trail to the top of Chandrisilla Peak at 4000m. Keep an eye out for icy patches that form along the rocks on the path, which can be slippery. From the summit, the Garhwali and Kumaoni Himalaya stretch out before you, with awesome vistas of major mountains including Nanda Devi, Trishul and the Kedarnath group. There's a small temple up here, too.

From Chopta start early (around 7am) before the clouds move in, or head up in the afternoon; leopards (as well as snow leopards) inhabit the area, so it's best to avoid leaving too early from Chopta. If you want to get to Tungnath for sunrise stay at one of the spartan guesthouses there. There are plenty of teahouses along the trek so you don't need to pack food or water.

The best way to get to Badrinath/Govindghat (for Valley of Flowers and Hem Kund) is by shared jeep (₹100/50), leaving from the Badrinath taxi stand at the far end of Upper Bazaar Rd. Hiring the whole jeep costs ₹1000.

Buses run from Joshimath to Rishikesh and Haridwar (₹500, 11½ hours) at 5am and 6am departing from the tiny **GMOU booth** (Auli Rd, Main Market), where you can also book tickets. From the main jeep stand, private buses leave occasionally for Chamoli (₹100, two hours) and Karanprayag (₹140, four hours), with some continuing to Rishikesh.

To get to the eastern Kumaon region, take any bus or shared taxi to Chamoli then transfer onward to Karanprayag, from where a series of local buses and share jeeps can take you along the beautiful road towards Kausani, Bageshwar and Almora.

Whole taxis are best hired through a travel agency or hotel.

Valley of Flowers & Hem Kund

The two adjoining treks conveniently positioned between Joshimath and Badrinath make it one of Uttarakhand's most scenic destinations. While a steady stream of Sikh pilgrims make the trek to visit Hem Kund, it's the Valley of Flowers that lures most foreign visitors.

British mountaineer Frank Smythe stumbled upon the Valley of Flowers in 1931. The *bugyals* (high-altitude meadows) of tall wildflowers are glorious on a sunny day, rippling in the breeze, and framed by mighty 6000m mountains that have glaciers and snow decorating their peaks all year. The 300 species of flowers make this World Heritage Site a unique and valuable pharmaceutical resource. Unfortunately, most flowers bloom during monsoon season in July and August, when the rains make access difficult and hazardous. There's a misconception that the valley isn't worth visiting outside peak flower season, but even without its technicolour carpet it's ridiculously beautiful. And it's more likely to be sunny.

🏃 Activities

Reaching the Valley of Flowers National Park and Hem Kund first requires a full-day hike from Govindghat to the village of Ghangaria (also called Govinddham), which is just outside the park. The trek to Ghangaria is a scenic but strenuous 14km uphill from Govindghat, which takes five to seven hours – though recent 'improvements' to the route have seen the paving of the first 3km into a drivable road, which many people choose to cover in a shared/private jeep (₹40/400). You can also ease the hike and help the local economy by hiring a pony (₹700) or a porter

Sleeping & Eating

Hotel Neelkanth (☑9456515128, 7500139051; www.neelkanthcampchopta.in; Chopta; r ₹400-1000) Hotel Neelkanth has the best rooms in Chopta, but that's not saying a lot. Rooms are dingy, but beds are comfortable enough and it's well priced. There's a small restaurant and the friendly manager speaks good English.

Moksha (☑8954377279, 8222909200; www.facebook.com/mokshachopta; Chopta; r ₹800-1500; 🖥) Opened by two mates from Delhi (who fittingly met while trekking) is this mellow traveller hang-out decorated in murals and Tibetan prayer flags. The rooms themselves are basic affairs, but its highlight is the rasta cafe where you can chill out with a pizza and game of carom.

Tungeshwar (☑847783331, 9456516665; Tungnath; r ₹1500) If you want to stay up near Tungnath Mandir (p438), then this is your best bet. While the simple rooms with hard beds are overpriced, you're paying for the views.

Getting There & Away

The drive from Chamoli to Chopta is a worthwhile diversion in itself, as it traverses steeply terraced hillsides dotted with rural villages before entering a lushly forested musk-deer sanctuary pierced by dramatic cliffs. A morning bus to Joshimath (₹150, three hours) departs Chopta at 9am, otherwise you'll have to get a private taxi (₹3000). If heading to Kedarnath, your best bet is to get a shared/private jeep to Guptkashi (₹65/1500) from where you can arrange onward transport.

(from ₹800) at the bridge over the Alaknanda River, or at the end of the paved road. There are plenty of tea shops en route selling water, snacks and meals.

The 87-sq-km **Valley of Flowers National Park** (Indian/foreigner up to 3 days ₹150/600, subsequent days ₹50/250; ⏰7am-5pm Jun–early Oct, last entry noon) begins 2km uphill from Ghangaria's ticket office (a 15-minute walk from town) and continues for another 5km. Tracks are easy to follow, but taking a guide in Ghangaria (from ₹1000) is a good idea for both safety in numbers and additional park info. As well as the fabled valley and its astounding scenery, there's a glacier you can walk to, and the grave of botanist Joan Margaret Legge who perished here in 1939. Leopard, bear, blue sheep and deer all inhabit the park.

A tougher hike from Ghangaria involves joining hundreds of Sikh pilgrims toiling up to the 4600m **Hem Kund** (⏰May-Oct), the sacred lake and temple surrounded by seven peaks where Sikh Guru Gobind Singh is believed to have meditated in a previous life. Ponies (from ₹1000) are available if you prefer to ride up the 6km steep zigzag trail. Remarkably, the climb is often undertaken by small children and people with weak legs or lungs – they ride up in a wicker chair hauled on the back of a porter or reclining in a *dandi* (litter), carried on the shoulders of four

men like the royalty of old. There are no tea shops for this leg so pack water and snacks.

You can pick up a walking stick for ₹15 in Govindghat or from the guesthouses in Ghangaria. Top tip: if you have the time, sleep at Badrinath the night before you trek to Ghangaria to acclimatise to the altitude; it'll make the hike easier. Pack plenty of warm clothing as it gets very cold in Ghangaria. Keep an eye out for the enticing electric massage chairs (per 15 minutes ₹50) in Ghangaria.

Note the national park, Hem Kund and all of Ghangaria close from early/mid October until June.

Sleeping & Eating

Overnight stays aren't permitted in the Valley of Flowers or Hem Kund, hence Ghangaria is where trekkers and pilgrims spend the night. Small hotels along Ghangaria's strip cater to trekkers and pilgrims from June to early-/mid-October; outside these months everything closes down. It gets very cold, so bring warm layers.

Hotel Kuber Annex   HOTEL $
(☑8958397949, 7579000833; Ghangaria; r from ₹1000; ⏰late May–early Oct) Reliable hot water, spacious rooms and large beds laden with heavy blankets all make this one of Ghangaria's better options. There's a restaurant

TREKKING THE HIMALAYA

There are many sublime trekking routes in Uttarakhand. For more information, contact GMVN (p428) in Dehra Dun or local trekking outfitters.

In mid-2018 the Uttarakhand High Court issued a ban on all camping in the *bugyals* (alpine meadows), but this is likely to be a temporary measure in order to protect this pristine wilderness from unscrupulous trekking operators. Regardless, all the treks were still running, but be aware some may have slightly shorter, alternative routes to what we've listed (in order to allow camping just off the *bugyals*). Check for the latest updates before setting out.

Har-ki-Dun Valley Trek

The wonderfully remote Har-ki-Dun Valley (3510m), within **Govind Wildlife Sanctuary & National Park** (Indian/foreigner up to 3 days ₹150/600, subsequent days ₹50/250), is a botanical paradise criss-crossed by glacial streams, surrounded by pristine forests and snowy peaks. You might be lucky enough to glimpse the elusive snow leopard above 3500m.

The three-day, 38km trail to Har-ki-Dun begins at Sankri (also called Saur), where the best place to stay is **Wild Orchid Inn** (☑9411500044, 7409500055; www.wildorchidinn.com; d/tr ₹800/1000). There are very basic GMVN tourist bungalows at Sankri and along the way in the villages of Taluka and Osla, but in the valley itself you have to stay in the Forest Rest House or bring a tent. You can cut a day off the hike by taking a share jeep to Taluka and starting from there. A side trip to Jamdar Glacier takes another day. The trek can be busy during June and October.

A couple of reputable guides work out of Sankri – Chain Singh and Bhagat Singh – who run the Har Ki Dun Protection & Mountaineering Association (p427). In addition to outfitting trips to Har-ki-dun, they can take you to the unique villages of the Rupin and Supin Valleys. They also lead treks from Sankri to the Sangla (Baspa) Valley in Himachal Pradesh and along other beautiful routes. Make arrangements in advance by email if possible – these guys are busy!

To get to Sankri, take a direct bus from Gandhi Chowk in Mussoorie or from Dehra Dun's Mussoorie Bus Stand (₹350) – or hop a series of buses and shared or private jeeps until you get there.

Kuari Pass Trek

Also known as the Curzon Trail (though Lord Curzon's party abandoned its attempt on the pass following an attack of wild bees), the trek over the Kuari Pass (3640m) was popular in the Raj era. It's still one of Uttarakhand's finest and most accessible treks, affording breathtaking views of the snow-clad peaks around Nanda Devi – India's second-highest mountain, at 7816m – while passing through the outer sanctuary of Nanda Devi Sanctuary.

on-site and the English-speaking manager can help with arranging guides.

Hotel Priya   HOTEL $$
(☑7409335016, 9412953214; Ghangaria; r ₹500-2500; ☺late May–early Oct) Run by friendly young entrepreneur, Ajay, Hotel Priya has undergone a refit to offer bigger, better quality rooms, but there are still a few cheapies to snag here.

Hotel Bhagat   HOTEL $$
(☑9412936360; www.hotelbhagat.com; Badrinath Rd, Govindghat; r ₹1500-2100) A bit pricier than Govindghat's other guesthouses near the trailhead, but here you'll pay for clean

rooms, river views and hot water. The deluxe rooms especially have superb views.

ⓘ Getting There & Away

All buses and share jeeps between Joshimath and Badrinath (₹40) pass by Govindghat, so you can easily find transport travelling in either direction, though this trickles off later in the day and stops dead at night.

If you want to see the Valley of Flowers but are daunted by the trek, it's possible to get a helicopter from Govindghat to Ghangaria with **Deccan Air** (☑9412051036; www.deccanair.com; one way ₹2875); the booking office is along the Joshimath–Badrinath road, just above Govindghat. Note baggage allowance is only 5kg, and passenger weight limit is 80kg – an additional fee of ₹75 is levied per extra kilo.

The trailhead is at Auli and the 75km trek to Ghat past lakes, waterfalls, forests, meadows and small villages takes five days, though it's possible to do a shorter version that finishes in Tapovan in three days. A tent, guide, permit and your own food supplies are necessary, all of which can be organised easily in Joshimath.

Milam Glacier Trek

This challenging eight-day, 118km trek to the massive Milam Glacier (3450m) is reached along an ancient trade route to Tibet that was closed in 1962 following the war between India and China. It passes through magnificent rugged country to the east of Nanda Devi (7816m) and along the sometimes spectacular gorges of the river, Gori Ganga. You can also take a popular but tough side trip to Nanda Devi East base camp, adding another 32km or three days.

Free permits (passport required) are available from the District Magistrate in Munsyari (p452). You will also need a tent and your own food supplies, as villages on the route may be deserted. The base for this excursion is the spectacularly located village of Munsyari, where a guide, cook and porters can be hired and package treks can be arranged through Nanda Devi Tour N Trek (p452). Otherwise KMVN Parvat Tours (p445) in Nainital can organise all-inclusive eight-day treks (per day from ₹2200). These are best arranged at KMVN but the KMVN Rest House in Munsyari should be able to set you up, too.

Less travelled but equally (or more) stunning treks include the Begini/Dunagiri route north of Joshimath and the Panchachuli East/Chota Kailash route, north of Dharchula.

Pindari Glacier Trek

This six-day, 94km trek passes through truly virgin country that's inhabited by only a few shepherds. It offers wonderful views of Nanda Kot (6860m) and Nanda Khat (6611m) on the southern rim of Nanda Devi Sanctuary. The 3km-long, 365m-wide Pindari Glacier is at 3353m, so take it easy to avoid altitude sickness. Permits aren't needed but bring your passport.

The trek begins and finishes at Loharket (1700m), a village 36km north of Bageshwar. Guides and porters can be organised easily there, or in the preceding village of Song (1400m), or you can organise package treks through companies in Almora. KMVN operates all-inclusive eight-day treks starting from Song for ₹8000 per person, staying at government rest houses. KMVN dorms (mattress on the floor ₹200), basic guesthouses or *dhaba* huts (₹100 to ₹300) are dotted along the route and food is available. KMVN tours are best arranged through KVMN Parvat Tours (p445) in Nainital.

Buses (₹60, two hours) or share jeeps (₹100, 1½ hours) run between Song and Bageshwar. Private taxis between Bageshwar and Song/Loharket cost around ₹2000.

Badrinath & Mana Village

☎ 01381 / POP 850 / ELEV 3133M

Basking in a superb setting in the shadow of snow-topped Nilkantha, **Badrinath Temple** (⊙ 4.30am–noon & 3-8.30pm late Apr–Nov) appears almost lost in the tatty village that surrounds it. Sacred to Lord Vishnu, this vividly painted temple is the most easily accessible and popular of the *char dham* temples. It was founded by Guru Shankara in the 8th century, but the current structure is much more recent.

A scenic 3km walk beyond Badrinath along the Alaknanda River (cross to the temple side for the path), past fields divided by dry-stone walls, leads to tiny but charismatic Mana Village; you can also take a shared jeep (₹50) or taxi (₹250). The village is crammed with stone laneways and traditional houses, some with slate walls and roofs while others are wooden with cute balconies. Wander around and watch villagers at work and play in summer; residents head somewhere warmer and less remote – usually Joshimath – between November and April.

🏃 Activities

Just outside Mana Village in a small cave is the tiny, 5230-year-old Vyas Temple. Nearby is Bhima's Rock, a natural rock arch over a river that is said to have been made by Bhima, strongest of the Pandava brothers, whose tale is told in the Mahabharata.

The 5km hike along the Alaknanda to the 145m Vasudhara Waterfall has a great reward-to-effort ratio, with views up the valley of the Badrinath massif jutting skywards like a giant fang.

A popular trip starting from Mana is the three-day trek to Satopanth Lake. Accessible from June to early October, the 22km trail takes you through ever-changing scenery of birch forest, *bugyal* (meadows) and glacial landscapes before you reach the high-altitude lake at 4600m. It's coloured a striking green and sits among snow-capped Himalaya peaks. For guides and info, get in touch with the trekking companies (p436) in Joshimath.

🛏 Sleeping & Eating

Badrinath can easily be visited in a day from Joshimath if you get an early start, but it's worth staying if you also want to see Mana Village and go hiking. There is a slew of grim budget guesthouses lining the main road into town (₹400 to ₹600 per room); they can be loud with pilgrims. Otherwise hotels here are generally overpriced.

Hotel Urvashi   HOTEL **$**
(📞 9411565459, 8755018300; r ₹1000) One of the few decent budget accommodation options in Badrinath, with friendly staff and a heap of rooms to choose from in a four-storey building.

Badriville Resort   BUNGALOW **$$$**
(📞 9412418725; www.badrivilleresort.in; r from ₹2000-4500) Our favourite hotel in Badrinath, Badriville Resort has clean and comfortable individual bungalow rooms, with the best beds in town. Most have patios with full valley views. The staff are helpful and friendly, and the restaurant serves up delicious fresh food. It's set back about 100m from the main road, just as you enter Badrinath. Major discounts available when slow.

ℹ Information

There's no wi-fi, internet cafes or even phone data in Badrinath, presumably due to its sensitive location close to the Chinese border.

ℹ Getting There & Away

From the large bus station at the entrance to Badrinath, GMOU buses run to Rishikesh (₹430, 10 hours) at 5.30am, 7am, 8am and 9am, but double-check departure times, as these may change. Buses for Joshimath (₹70) are from 5am to 9am, a shared jeep is ₹100. For Valley of Flowers, jump on a bus to Govindghat (₹35).

Corbett Tiger Reserve

📞 05947 / ELEV 385–1100M

World-renowned **Corbett Tiger Reserve** (📞 9759363344, 05947-251489; www.corbettonline. uk.gov.in; day entry Indian/foreigner from ₹200/450, jeep hire from ₹2000, guide ₹600; ⏱ 15 Nov–15 Jun, Jhirna & Dhela zones open year-round, ticket office 5.30-7.30am & 10am-5pm), established in 1936 as India's first national park, covers 1318 sq km of wild forests. It's named for legendary British hunter Jim Corbett (1875–1955), who brought this region international fame with his book *The Man-Eaters of Kumaon*.

As well as being famous for having the most tigers of all India's national parks, Corbett is known for its stunning scenery, including jungle, grasslands, riverine and hilly terrain, home to an abundance of wild elephant, deer, primate, reptile and birdlife, as well as leopard, Himalayan black bear and sloth bear.

The park is divided into six zones that all offer different experiences; most famous is Dhikala, which offers the best chance to spot animals. Take note: the bulk of the park is closed during rainy season (generally mid-November to mid-June), with only a few zones open year-round.

Visiting the Reserve

Though tiger attacks are on the rise in villages around the reserve, tiger sightings on safaris take some luck, as the 215 or so striped cats that roam the reserve are neither baited nor tracked. Your best chance of spotting one is late in the season (April to mid-June), when the forest cover is low and animals come out in search of water.

Notwithstanding tiger sightings, few serious wildlife enthusiasts will leave disappointed, as the park has a variety of wildlife and birdlife in grassland, sal forest and river habitats, and a beautiful location in the foothills of the Himalaya on the river, Ramganga. Commonly seen wildlife include wild elephants (200 to 300 live in the reserve), sloth bears, langur monkeys, rhesus macaques, peacocks, romps of otters and several types of deer. The Ramganga Reservoir attracts large numbers of migrating birds, especially from mid-December to the end of March, and more than 600 species have been spotted here.

Of Corbett's six zones – Bijrani, Dhikala, Dhela, Durga Devi, Jhirna and Sonanadi –

Dhikala is the highlight of the park, 49km northwest of Ramnagar and deep inside the reserve. This is the designated core area, where the highest concentration of the animals you probably hope to see are found. It's open from 15 November to 15 June and only to overnight guests, or as part of a one-day tour available through the park's reception centre (☑ 05947-251489; Ranikhet Rd; ☺ 5.30-7.30am & 10am-5pm), almost opposite Ramnagar's bus stand.

Jhirna and Dhela, in the southern part of the reserve, are the only zones that remain open all year, but your chances of seeing serious megafauna in those areas are iffy. Note that in some years, depending on conditions, the other four zones may open in October, but the only way to find out is to check online.

Be sure to bring binoculars (you can hire them at park gates) and plenty of mosquito repellent and mineral water.

⛟ Tours

The reception centre runs daily bus tours (☑ 05947-251489; Ranikhet Rd; Indian/foreigner ₹1500/2000; ☺ 6am & 11.30am) to Dhikala called Canter Safaris.

Jeeps can be hired at the reception centre, or through your accommodation or a tour agency. Jeep owners have formed a union, so in theory rates are fixed (on a per-jeep basis, carrying up to six people). Half-day safaris (leaving in the morning and afternoon) cost ₹2000 to Bijrani, and ₹2200 for the other zones – not including the entry fees (p443). Check current prices at the reception centre and at your hotel before hiring a jeep. Safaris offered by Karan Singh, who runs Karan's Corbett Motel (p444), are highly recommended.

🛏 Sleeping & Eating

For serious wildlife-viewing, Dhikala – deep inside the reserve – is the prime place to stay, though prices for foreigners are exorbitant. Book through the park's website (www.corbettonline.uk.gov.in) at least one month in advance. Rates listed include taxes and cleaning fees. Ramnagar has accommodation, and is a good base for safaris. Upmarket resorts are found along the road skirting the eastern side of the park between Dhikuli and Dhangarhi Gate.

Most lodges inside the park can arrange food, but it's not a bad idea to stock up on a few basic snacks. Outside the park, there are loads of restaurants in Ramnagar and the Dhikuli area, including within the resorts.

🛏 Dhikala

New Forest Rest House LODGE $$
(☑ 9759363344, 05947-251489; www.corbettonline.uk.gov.in; r Indian/foreigner ₹2150/3740) For high-quality accommodation at Dhikala, the New Forest Rest House can be booked online.

CORBETT PERMITS & FEES

Corbett Tiger Reserve controls tourist impact by limiting the number of vehicles into each zone each day; generally it's limited to 10 cars in the morning and 10 in the evening. You must book your entry permit in advance, via the park's website (www.corbettonline.uk.gov.in) or by signing up for a trip with a safari outfit. If you book online (fee ₹50), which is highly recommended, give your reservation confirmation to your driver, whether you hire one from the reservation centre or use a tour operator. Day trips can be booked 45 days in advance; if you can't plan ahead, you can probably still visit the park – safari operators will ask each other if anyone is running a jeep with open seats that you can fill. Overnight trips to Dhikala are best booked by a safari company.

The visitor entry fee is broken down into several components: the single-day fee (valid for four hours, available for every zone except Dhikala) operates on a sliding scale where the more people the cheaper the cost. For a group of six you'll pay ₹100/450 (Indian/foreigner) per person, whereas for solo travellers a permit will cost ₹600/950. Jeep hire (which fit six people) is from ₹2000 to ₹2200 depending on which gate; a guide (highly recommended) is ₹600; and on top of all of that, there's a ₹250/450 (Indian/foreigner) vehicle entry fee.

How much does this all cost? Add up your jeep hire fee, vehicle entry fee, visitor entry fees, driver's entry fee and empty seat fees, road tax and online booking fee...and that's your total. Taking a safari or hotel tour costs marginally more than arranging everything yourself, but since they provide expert guides fluent in English, they can be well worth the few extra rupees.

UTTARAKHAND CORBETT TIGER RESERVE

Annexe　　　　　　　BUNGALOW **$$**
(☑ 05947-251489, 9759363344; Dhikala; r Indian/foreigner from ₹2150/3700) These private rooms are some of the best at Dhikala, and open onto a verandah.

Old Forest Rest House　　　LODGE **$$$**
(☑ 9759363344, 05947-251489; www.corbettonline.uk.gov.in; r Indian ₹2400-3400, foreigner ₹4230-6240) Good accommodation in Dhikala with river-facing rooms in a historic lodge built by the British during the Raj era. The more expensive rooms are larger and sleep more people.

Elsewhere in the Reserve

Bijrani Rest House　　　　　LODGE **$$**
(☑ 05947-251489, 9759363344; www.corbettonline.uk.gov.in; s/d/q Indian ₹1180/2150/3220, foreigner ₹1830/3740/5580) The first place in from Amdanda Gate at the Corbett Tiger Reserve (p442); meals are available.

Khinnanauli Rest House　　BUNGALOW **$$$**
(☑ 05947-251489, 9759363344; www.corbettonline.uk.gov.in; r Indian/foreigner ₹5000/12,000) VIP lodging near Dhikala, deep in the reserve.

Sarapduli Rest House　　　　HOTEL **$$$**
(☑ 05947-251489, 9759363344; www.corbettonline.uk.gov.in; r Indian/foreigner ₹2900/5240) Clean and simple rooms, set in an area with lots of wildlife, especially birds and crocodiles, but tigers and elephants, too.

Ramnagar

A busy, unappealing town, Ramnagar has plenty of facilities, including internet cafes, ATMs (State Bank of India ATM at the train station and a Bank of Baroda ATM on Ranikhet Rd) and transport connections – mostly along Ranikhet Rd.

Karan's Corbett Motel　　　HOTEL **$$**
(☑ 9837468933; www.karanscorbettmotel.com; Manglar Rd; r from ₹1200; ❋ 🛜) On the fringes of town, surrounded by gardens, mango trees and a recreation oval, this motel has spacious rooms with a terrace, table and chairs. It's the best place to stay in Ramnagar (not to be confused with the Corbett Motel). The owner Karan runs jeep safaris in Corbett.

Hotel Corbett Kingdom　　　HOTEL **$$**
(☑ 7500668883; www.corbettkingdom.com; Bhaghat Singh St; d/tr/q/ste from ₹2500/3500/4500/5000; ❋ 🛜) This straightforward hotel is a comfortable, well-kept option right in the thick of the action in Ramnagar. Marble floors add a touch of class, as does the small pool, gym and on-site restaurant.

North of Ramnagar

A growing number of upmarket African-style safari resorts are strung along the Ramnagar–Ranikhet road that runs along the reserve's eastern boundary. Most are around a settlement called Dhikuli – not to be confused with Dhikala. When most of the reserve is closed (15 June to 15 November), discounts of up to 50% are offered. Most rates are for a room only, but most have packages that include meals and safaris. All places have resident naturalists, recreational facilities, restaurants and bars.

★ **Gateway Resort**　　　　　RESORT **$$$**
(☑ 05947-266600, 7455028252; www.thegateway hotels.com; Dhikuli; r/cottage ₹11,000/16,500; ❋ 🛜 ≋) At the Taj Group's luxury offering, modern rooms and cottages are spread around a verdant garden. There's an outdoor pool and full-service spa and gym, but the real gem is the restaurant, whose outdoor terrace has picture-perfect views of the Kosi River. It's the best place on the resort strip.

Namah　　　　　　　　　　RESORT **$$$**
(☑ 8392914912, 05947-266666; www.namah.in; Dhikuli; r/ste incl meals from ₹15,000/20,000; 🛜 ≋) On the outside, this resort looks and feels like a condo complex. Rooms, however, have personality, with two-toned walls and jungle-themed artwork. The playground, open spaces, pool and rec room make this a good choice for families. Prices fluctuate greatly depending on demand.

🛈 Getting There & Away

Buses run almost hourly from Ramnagar to Delhi (₹290, seven hours), Haridwar (₹220, six hours) and Dehra Dun (₹295, seven hours). Frequent buses run to Haldwani (₹70, two hours), from where you can connect to just about anywhere. For Nainital, take a UK Roadways bus to Haldwani and change there, or hop on a private bus that runs direct to Nainital (₹95) – several depart throughout the morning from outside the main bus stand.

Ramnagar train station is 1.5km south of the main reception centre (p443). The nightly Ranikhet Express-Slip 15013 (sleeper/3AC/2AC ₹175/495/700) leaves Old Delhi at 10.05pm, arriving in Ramnagar at 4.50am. The return trip on train 25014 leaves Ramnagar at 10pm, arriving in Old Delhi at 3.55am. A daytime run from

Old Delhi on train 15035-Slip (2nd class/chair ₹100/375) departs at 4pm, reaching Ramnagar at 8.55pm; the return on train 25036 departs Ramnagar at 9.55am, hitting Delhi at 3.25pm.

Nainital

☑ 05942 / POP 42,000 / ELEV 2084M

Crowded around a deep, green volcanic lake, Nainital is Kumaon's largest town and favourite hill resort. It occupies a steep forested valley around the namesake lake Naini and was founded by homesick Brits reminded of the Cumbrian Lake district.

Plenty of hotels are set on the hillside around the lake. There's a busy bazaar, and a spider's web of walking tracks covers the forested slopes to viewpoints overlooking distant Himalayan peaks. For travellers it's an easy place to kick back and relax, eat well, and ride horses or paddle on the lake. In peak seasons – roughly May to mid-July and October – Nainital is packed to the gills with holidaying families and honeymooners, and hotel prices skyrocket.

◉ Sights & Activities

★ Naini Lake   LAKE

This pretty lake is Nainital's centrepiece and is said to be one of the emerald-green eyes of Shiva's wife, Sati that fell to earth after her act of self-immolation (*naina* is Sanskrit for eye). Boaters will row you around the lake for ₹210 in the brightly painted gondola-like boats, or the **Nainital Boat Club** (Mallital; ⊙10am-4pm) will sail you around for ₹500. **Pedal boats** (₹160 per hour) can also be hired. Naina Devi Temple is on the precise spot where the eye is believed to have fallen. You can walk around the lake in about an hour – the southern side is more peaceful.

Snow View   VIEWPOINT

A **cable car** (return adult/child ₹230/150; ⊙8am-8pm May & Jun, 10.30am-4.30pm Jul-Apr) runs up to popular Snow View at 2270m, which (on clear days) has panoramic Himalayan views, including of Nanda Devi. The ticket office is at the bottom. A highlight of the trip to Snow View is hiking to viewpoints such as Cheena/Naina Peak, 4km away. Local guides may offer to lead you there. If you want to head up for sunrise, recommended if you want snow-capped mountains, taxis charge about ₹500 return. Near the top is **Snowview Heritage Hotel** (☑9411108017; Maldon Cottage Rd, Mallital; ⊙11am-9pm), the only place with a bar in Nainital.

Tiffin Top & Land's End   WALKING, HORSE RIDING

A 4km walk west of the lake brings you to Tiffin Top (2292m), also called Dorothy's Seat. From here it's a lovely 30-minute walk to Land's End (2118m) through a forest of oak, deodar and pine. Mangy horses gather 3km west of town on the road to Ramnagar to take you on rides to these spots for about ₹800.

Agencies

Tranquility Treks   TREKKING

(☑9411196837; www.tranquilitytreks.in) Experienced guide Sunil Kumar leads hikes and focuses on bird- and wildlife-watching. He can take you on day walks (₹1750), overnight hikes (₹5550) or longer where you stay in local villages.

KMVN Parvat Tours   TREKKING

(☑05942-231436; www.kmvn.gov.in; Tallital; ⊙8am-8pm) A helpful office for information and booking KMVN's rest houses and trekking packages.

🛏 Sleeping

Nainital is packed with hotels but they fill up fast at peak times, making it hard to find a bargain at those times. Virtually all hotels offer around 50% discount in low season. The main peak season is generally 1 May to 30 June, and some hotels have a semipeak in October, at Diwali (October/November) and at Christmas.

Traveller's Paradise   HOTEL $$

(☑7830345678; Mallital; r ₹2000-4500; 🛜) A bit north of The Mall, this exceptionally friendly hotel features spacious rooms with flatscreen TVs, couches, faux-wood panelling, wi-fi and quality beds. It's run by the amiable Anu Consul, who spent 10 years living in Mexico, and his wonderful father. Off-season prices start at ₹1800.

Hotel Evelyn   HOTEL $$

(☑05942-235457, 9837360457; www.hotel evelynnainital.in; The Mall, Tallital; d ₹1600-4200; 🛜) This colossal sprawling hotel overlooking the lake is quintessential Nainital – dated, but charming and slightly eccentric. It's big, with stairways and terraces cascading down the hillside, and is a bit old-fashioned, but the well-tended rooms with retro furniture have a nice, cosy feel. Look at a few.

Palace Belvedere   HERITAGE HOTEL $$$

(☑9871587150; www.zeniahotels.com/belvedere palacehotelnainital.htm; off The Mall, Mallital; r from ₹4000; 🛜) Built in 1897, this was the sum-

Nainital

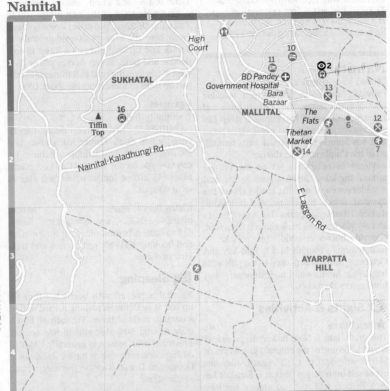

High Court

SUKHATAL

11

10

2

BD Pandey
Government Hospital
Bara
Bazaar

13

16

MALLITAL

The
Flats

12

4

6

Tibetan
Market

7

Tiffin
Top

14

Nainital-Kaladhungi Rd

E Laggan Rd

AYARPATTA
HILL

8

mer palace of the rajas of Awagarh. Animal skins and old prints adorn the walls, lending a faded Raj-era charm. There's a grand staircase and the aged, if worn, rooms are spacious and high-ceilinged. Upstairs gets more light. Downstairs has an elegant dining room (no alcohol), lounge and veranda. Winters can be cold here.

Eating

Sonam Chowmein Corner TIBETAN $
(The Flats, Mallital; half/full plate ₹30/60; ◷ 11am-8pm) In the covered alley of the Tibetan Market, this hole-in-the-wall kitchen whips up fabulous *momos* (dumplings) and chow mein for the best cheap eats in town.

Sakley's Restaurant MULTICUISINE $$
(Mallital; snacks from ₹125, mains ₹250-650; ◷ 9.30am-9.30pm) Going since 1944, this spotless cafe/bakery near the cable car serves up a range of unusual global items such as spicy Sriracha wings, Thai curries, roast lamb and

steaks. The house-made cakes and pastries are great; even if you don't dine here, grab some takeaway dessert (go the banoffee pie) to enjoy by the lake.

Embassy INDIAN $$
(The Mall, Mallital; meals ₹165-345; ◷ 9am-10.30pm) With a wood-lined chalet interior and snappily dressed staff, Embassy has been serving up five pages of menu items since 1964. There's a good terrace for people-watching and tucking into anything from tandoori dishes and creamy curries to grilled sandwiches and pizza. The rosewater lassi is recommended.

Getting There & Away

BUS
Most buses leave from the **Tallital bus stand** (Nainital Rd). Although there are direct buses from Nainital, many more services leave from the transport hubs of Haldwani and Bhowali. From Haldwani, regular buses head to Ramnagar, Delhi,

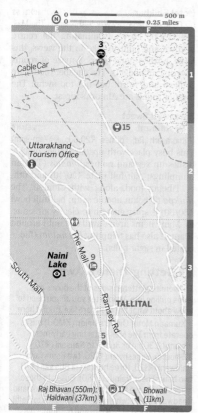

Haridwar and the Nepal border at Banbassa. Haldwani is also a major train terminus. For points north, take a bus or share jeep from Nainital to Bhowali (20 minutes) and catch one of the regular onward buses to Almora, Kausani and Ranikhet.

Seven private buses direct to Ramnagar (₹90, 3½ hours) leave from the **Sukhatal bus stand** (Nainital-Kaladungi Rd), northwest of Mallital, between 8.30am and 4.30pm.

Travel agencies sell tickets for private overnight deluxe coaches (with reclining seats) to Delhi (from ₹600, nine hours), which leave from Tallital around 11am and 10pm.

TAXI & SHARE JEEP

From the Kumaon Taxi Union stand in Tallital, taxis cost ₹500 to Bhowali, ₹100/600 (shared/full) to Kathgodam or Haldwani (1½ hours), and ₹1500 to both Ramnagar and Almora (both three hours).

Share jeeps leave when full. They go to Bhowali (₹10, 20 minutes), where you can get buses and share taxis to Almora and beyond.

TRAIN

Kathgodam (35km south of Nainital) is the nearest train station, but Haldwani, one stop further south, is the regional transport hub. The **train booking agency** (Nainital Rd; ⊙9am-noon & 2-5pm Mon-Fri, 9am-2pm Sat), next to the Tallital bus stand, can book trains to Dehra Dun, Delhi, Moradabad, Lucknow, Gorakhpur and Kolkata. The daily 12039 Kathgodam–New Delhi Shatabdhi (AC chair/exec ₹915/1320) departs Kathgodam at 3.35pm, stops at Haldwani at 3.52pm and reaches New Delhi at 9.10pm. In the other direction, train 12040 departs New Delhi at 6am, arriving at Haldwani at 11.08am and Kathgodam at 11.40am.

Almora

☏ 05962 / POP 35,500 / ELEV 1642M

Set along a steep-sided ridge, Almora is the regional capital of Kumaon, first established as a summer capital by the Chand rajas of Kumaon in 1560. These days you'll find colonial-era buildings, trekking outfits and a couple of community-based weaving enterprises. Don't be put off by the utilitarian main street when you're first deposited at the bus stand – head one block south to pedestrian-only, cobbled Lalal Bazaar, lined with intricately carved and painted traditional wooden shop facades. It's a fascinating place to stroll, people-watch and shop. On clear days, you can see Himalayan snow peaks from various spots around town.

◎ Sights & Activities

Nanda Devi Temple HINDU TEMPLE
(Lalal Bazaar) The stone Nanda Devi Temple dates back to the Chand raja era, and is covered in folk-art carvings, some erotic. Every September the temple hosts the five-day Nanda Devi Fair (p420).

Himadri Hans Handloom FACTORY
(Panchachuli Weavers Factory; ☑ 05962-251053, 05962-230968; www.panchachuli.in; Kasar Devi Rd, Pataldevi Industrial Area; ◎ 10am-5pm Mon-Sat) FREE Himadri Hans employs some 700 women to weave, market and sell woollen shawls. Taxis charge ₹150 return to the factory, or you can walk the 3km – follow the continuation of Mall Rd to the northeast and ask for directions. There's also a factory in Kasar Devi (Panchachuli Weavers Factory; www.panchachuli.in; ◎ 10am-5pm Mon-Sat) you can visit.

High Adventure TREKKING, MOUNTAIN BIKING
(☑ 9412044610; www.trekkinghimalayas.in; Mall Rd) Organises treks around Uttarakhand, and mountain-bike trips near Almora and Nainital. Prices vary depending on route and group size, so call for details.

🛏 Sleeping & Eating

Bansal Guesthouse HOTEL $
(☑ 9557725993, 05962-230864; Lalal Bazaar; r ₹500-900) Almora's best budget choice is in the bustling Bazaar, with small, tidy rooms (some with TV), a rooftop terrace and lovely little cafe. Charming owner Rajul is an artist who paints local landscapes and is an excellent source of local knowledge.

Hotel Shikhar HOTEL $$
(☑ 05962-230253; www.hotelshikhar.in; The Mall; r ₹950-5000; ❋ ⏵) Dominating the centre of town and built to take in the views, this large, boxlike hotel offers a maze of rooms covering all budgets. The cheaper rooms are soulless and worn, but not too awful. The top-tier rooms are Almora's nicest.

Saraswati Sweet & Restaurant TIBETAN $
(Pithoragarh Rd; dishes ₹20-60; ◎ 7am-9pm) This busy place with upstairs tables quickly dishes up veg and nonveg *momos* (Tibetan dumplings; half/full plate ₹20/40) and other Tibetan food, along with Chinese. The *thukpa* (Tibetan noodle soup; half/full bowl ₹30/60) is spicy enough to clear your sinuses. Many items aren't available until around 10am. It also has tempting *bal mithai* (fudge coated in sugar balls).

❶ Getting There & Away

The vomit-splattered sides of the buses and jeeps pulling into Almora tell you all you need to know about what the roads are like around here.

Kumaon Motor Owners Union (KMOU) buses operate from The Mall – starting early morning until 2.30pm or 3pm – to Kausani (₹70, 2½ hours), Bageshwar (₹120, two hours) and Haldwani (₹125, three hours) via Bhowali (₹70, two hours) near Nainital (₹80). Buses to those places also leave from the adjacent Uttarakhand Roadways stand, where you'll find buses to Delhi (₹470, 12 hours) at 5.30pm and 6.30pm – it's best to book Delhi tickets in the morning. For Pithoragarh, head to the Dharanaula bus stand east of the Bazaar on Bypass Rd, where several buses (₹160, five hours) depart between about 8.30am and 11am. For Banbassa on the Nepal border, take a bus to Haldwani and change there.

You can get a taxi or jeep to Kausani (shared/whole taxi ₹150/1200, 2½ hours), Kasar Devi (₹40/400), Jageshwar (₹100/1000, 1½ hours), Pithoragarh (₹250/3500, five hours) and Munsyari (whole taxi only, ₹5500, 10 hours).

BUSES FROM NAINITAL

The following buses leave from the Tallital bus stand (p446). For Kathgodam (₹61), take the Haldwani bus.

DESTINATION	FARE (₹)	DURATION (HR)	DEPARTURES
Almora	100	3	7am, 10am
Dehra Dun	425	10	5.30am, 7.30am, 6pm, 8pm
Delhi (AC/non-AC)	600/390	8	9am, 9.30am, 7.30pm 8.30pm, 9pm (AC)
Haldwani	65	2	half-hourly 5.30am-9pm
Haridwar	355	8	6.30pm

ⓘ CROSSING TO NEPAL: BANBASSA TO MAHENDRANAGAR (BHIMDATTA)

Banbassa is the closest Indian village to the Nepal border post of Mahendranagar (Bhimdatta), 5km away. Check the current situation in western Nepal before crossing here, as roads during the monsoon or immediately after the monsoon season may be impassable due to landslides and washed-out bridges.

Banbassa is easily reached by bus from Haldwani and Pithoragarh. The nearby town of Tanakpur has even more connections.

The border is open 24 hours, but before 6am and after 6pm you're unlikely to find anyone to stamp you out of India and into Nepal. While the border is officially open to vehicles only from 6am to 8am, 10am to noon, 2pm to 4pm and 6pm to 7pm, rickshaws and motorcycles are usually allowed to make the 1km trip across the bridge between the border posts at any time. Otherwise you have to walk it.

Single-entry Nepali visas valid for 15/30/90 days cost US$25/40/100. Bring US dollars.

Onward Transport

From the Nepali border, take an autorickshaw (₹150) or shared taxi to Mahendranagar (Bhimdatta). The bus station is about 1km from the centre on the Mahendra Hwy, from where eight daily buses depart for Kathmandu between 5.30am and 4.30pm (15 hours). There's also a single Pokhara service in the afternoon (16 hours).

All leave from The Mall, except the shared taxis to Pithoragarh, which leave from Dharanaula bus stand. We can recommend Kishan Bisht (☎ 9410915048) as a remarkably sane driver.

Around Almora

Kasar Devi

ELEV 2116M

This peaceful spot about 8km north of Almora has been luring alternative types for close to 100 years. Attracted by the abundance of marijuana that grows wild here, the list of luminaries who've visited, some for extended stays, includes Bob Dylan, Cat Stevens, Timothy Leary, Allen Ginsberg and Swami Vivekananda, who meditated at the hilltop Kasar Devi Temple. Today, the village (known back in the day as Crank's Ridge) is a low-key backpacker destination, with a mellow vibe and clear-day Himalayan views. There's not a lot to do here, but it's a great place to chill. And Mohan's Binsar Retreat can arrange fishing, rafting and trekking trips.

You can get to/from Almora by share jeep (₹40) or private taxi (₹300). You'll need a private taxi for nearby destinations such as Binsar (₹1000) and Jageshwar (₹1500).

HOTs
HOSTEL $

(☎ 9795052484, 9193323331; www.hotshostel.com/kasar-devi; off Binsar Rd; dm/r ₹300/1000)

Slotting in nicely to Kasar Devi's bohemian landscape is this mellow backpacker decorated in psychedelic murals, with friendly staff and a chilled-out restaurant that looks out to the Himalaya. Its dorms are good value while its private rooms are freshened up with pot plants.

★ Freedom Guest House
GUESTHOUSE $$

(☎ 7830355686; Binsar Rd; r ₹1200-1500, f ₹2500; ❊ 🛜) Big, immaculately clean rooms open on to shared terraces with sublime valley and Himalaya views, catching the afternoon and sunset light. Newer rooms on the upper floors have a touch more luxury, but each one is a winner. The owners, Sunder and Gita, go out of their way to please. There's fast wi-fi, reliable hot water and a decent restaurant.

Mohan's Binsar Retreat
GUESTHOUSE $$$

(☎ 9412977968, 05962-251215; www.mohansbinsarretreat.com; Binsar Rd; r incl breakfast from ₹5550; 🛜) Kasar Devi's most luxurious accommodation, Mohan's has huge, beautiful rooms with comfy beds and wooden ceilings and floors. The real draw is the indoor-outdoor terrace restaurant, with great views of the valley below and a shot of distant Himalayan peaks. Local legend has it that Bob Dylan hung out here when it was a humble tea shop in the 1960s.

Binsar

ELEV 2420M

Beyond Kasar Devi, picturesque **Binsar Wildlife Sanctuary** (Indian/foreigner/student ₹150/600/300, plus ₹250-500 vehicle fee; ⏱ 6am-5.30pm), 26km from Almora, was once the hilltop summer capital of the Chand rajas. Now it's a sanctuary protecting 45 sq km. You may spot a leopard or some barking deer, but many people come here for the 200-plus species of birds. On clear days, the Himalayan panorama is breathtaking – from the tower at 'Zero Point', Binsar's summit (2420m), you can see Kedarnath, Trishul, Nanda Devi, Panchachuli and more. Hiking trails wend throughout the lush forest; their main nexus is the **KMVN Tourist Rest House** (☏ 8650002537; www.kmvn.gov.in; r incl breakfast & dinner ₹2500-4300; ☏).

The only downside here is the pricey entry fee. Guides are recommended, especially with the unwanted presence of wild boar (let alone leopard), and can be hired at the sanctuary gate or the Rest House; they charge ₹400 for a 1½-hour hike.

Village Ways (☏ 9920882409; www.villageways.com) and Grand Oak Manor (p450) are two highly recommended outfits running single- and multiday trekking tours between the villages in and around the sanctuary, offering a deeper experience of the natural environment and rural culture of the area.

Most people visit as a day trip from Almora or Kasar Devi, but if your budget allows it's definitely recommended to stay overnight in one of several old manor houses from the days of the British Raj.

A return taxi from Kasar Devi is around ₹1000, or about ₹1300 from Almora. There's no public transport here.

★ **Grand Oak Manor**   HISTORIC HOTEL **$$$**
(☏ 7876806807, 9412094277; www.treeleafhospitality.com/binsar-resorts; r from ₹5000; ☏) Binsar's original Raj-era estate was built in 1856 as the home of British high-commissioner Sir Henry Ramsay. Today it's run by adventure-travel-writer Shikha Tripathi and her husband Sindhu Shah, and has been in the family for just 100 years. The heritage mansion has been lovingly maintained and exudes 19th-century colonial ambience throughout. It blends in beautifully among the forest.

Its restaurant (open to guests only) is another highlight serving set thali meals of Kumaoni speciality dishes – from slow-cooked lamb to deep-fried stinging nettle fritters!

It also customises treks, from day walks to overnight stays in the homes of villagers. Call when you get to **Simba Cafe** (☏ 8126644449; mains ₹200-450; ⏱ 8am-8pm), from where they'll collect you, as it's a steep 4WD track up from there.

Kausani

☏ 05962 / POP 2408 / ELEV 1890M

Perched high on a forest-covered ridge, this tiny, sleepy village has lovely panoramic views of distant snow-capped peaks, mountain-fresh air and a relaxed atmosphere. Mahatma Gandhi found Kausani an inspirational place to write his Bhagavad Gita treatise *Anasakti Yoga* in 1929, and there is still an ashram devoted to him here. Baijnath village, 19km north, has an intriguing complex of 12th-century *sikhara*-style temples in a lovely location shaded by trees, with other shrines in the nearby old village.

Star Gate   PLANETARIUM
(☏ 8126466477; ⏱ 6am-9pm) While this small-scale observatory offers night viewing of distant planets and constellations (₹100) from 6.30pm, it's arguably more interesting to drop by early morning (₹50) to get a close-up look at the spectacular 180-degree Himalayan peaks that are framed beautifully here. It's in town on the road up to Anasakti Ashram.

Anasakti Ashram   HISTORIC SITE
(☏ 05962-258028, 9458094527; Anasakti Ashram Rd; ⏱ 7am-noon & 4-7pm) **FREE** About 1km uphill from the bus stand, Anasakti Ashram is where Mahatma Gandhi spent two weeks in 1929 pondering and writing *Anasakti Yoga*. It has a small museum that tells the story of Gandhi's life through photographs and words. Visit at 6pm to attend nightly prayers in his memory.

You can also stay here overnight from ₹650 in a room with views to the Himalaya.

🛏 Sleeping & Eating

Hotel Uttarakhand   HOTEL **$$**
(☏ 05946-223012, 9012924222; www.uttarakhand-kausani.com; d ₹700-2250; @☏) Just north of the bus stand, but in a quiet location with a panoramic view of the Himalaya from your veranda, this is Kausani's best-value accommodation. The cheaper rooms are small, with bucket hot water, but upper-floor rooms

PITHORAGARH

Spread across the hillsides above a scenic valley that's been dubbed 'Little Kashmir', Pithoragarh (population 56,050; elevation 1514m) is the main town of a little-visited region that borders Tibet and Nepal. Its sights include several Chand-era temples and an old fort, built by Gorkhas in 1791, with wonderful views from its ramparts – but the real reason to come here is to get off the tourist trail. The busy main bazaar is good for a stroll, and townspeople are exceptionally friendly. Picturesque hikes in the area include the rewarding climb up to Chandak (7km) for views of the gorgeous Panchachuli (Five Chimneys) massif.

Hotel Yash (☑ 05964-225066, 9997803429; Naya Bazaar; dm ₹300, r ₹500-3500) The best-value and most traveller-friendly accommodation in Pithoragarh, rooms range from simple with shared bath to large and ornately furnished. The friendly, fusspot owner offers good local info, but be aware that the hotel is locked each evening by 10pm (and it doesn't open until 8am the next day). It's in the main bazaar, close to the bus stand. Rates are negotiable.

Sumeru Resort (☑ 9917025511; www.sumeruresort.in; Pithoragarh–Dharchula Rd; r ₹1000-3000; ❀🛜) If you're looking for somewhere even more chilled than Pithoragarh, head 6km north of town to this stylish resort-style hotel that sits among pine forest and overlooks stunning valley and Himalayan views. It appears to be popular with various Bollywood stars.

Getting There & Away

Buses and shared jeeps leave for Almora (₹250/350, five hours) and Haldwani (₹365/400, 10 hours). Frequent buses go to Delhi until 4pm (₹600, 18 hours); there are hourly services from 5am to 2pm to Banbassa (₹279, six hours), the border crossing town for Nepal. To get to Munsyari, take a share jeep (₹400 to ₹500, seven hours).

are spacious and have hot showers and TVs. The manager is helpful and friendly. The **restaurant** (mains ₹110-350; ⊙7am-10pm) here is the best in town.

Krishna Mountview   HOTEL $$$
(☑ 9927944473, 05942-237550; www.krishnamountview.com; Anasakti Ashram Rd; d ₹2500-3850, ste from ₹5550; 🛜) Just past Anasakti Ashram, this is one of Kausani's smartest hotels, with clipped formal gardens (perfect for mountain views). Try to get a spacious upstairs room; they have balconies, bay windows and rocking chairs.

❶ Getting There & Away

Buses and share jeeps stop in the village centre. Several buses run to Almora (₹125, 2½ hours), but in the afternoon they generally stop at Karbala on the bypass road, from where you need to take a share jeep (₹10). Otherwise a shared jeep to Almora is ₹150.

Heading north, buses run every hour or so to Bageshwar via Baijnath (₹60, 1½ hours). Share jeeps (₹30, 30 minutes) run to Garur, 16km north of Kausani, which is a much more active transport hub, and where you can find share jeeps to Gwaldam for onward buses and jeeps to Garhwal (via Karanprayag).

A taxi to Almora costs around ₹1200; to Nainital or Karanprayag it's about ₹3000.

Bageshwar

☑ 05963 / POP 9100 / ELEV 1004M

Hindu pilgrims visit Bageshwar, at the confluence of the Gomti and Saryu Rivers, for its ancient stone Bagnath Temple. For trekkers it's a base for those returning from the Pindari Glacier trek (p441), and for travellers it serves as a transit town connecting Munsyari and other points east with Kausani, Kasar Devi and Almora. The valley around the town, with fields sculpted above the riverbanks, is strikingly beautiful, and the main market is worth a wander.

Hotel Narendra Palace (☑ 8394953888, 8393999166; Pindari Rd; r with fan ₹500-1140, with AC ₹1848-2520; ❀🛜), about 1km from the bus stand, is the best hotel, with rooms for varying budgets. It also has a great restaurant with a terrace overlooking the river.

❶ Getting There & Away

Several daily buses go to Almora (₹120, three hours) and Kausani (₹50, 1½ hours). Frequent buses run to Song (₹60, two hours), Bhowali

(₹190, six hours) and Haldwani (₹245, 7½ hours). For connections to Garhwal, take a bus to Gwaldam (₹70, two hours) and change there. There are several morning buses to Pithoragarh (₹210, seven hours).

There's a jeep stand near the bus stand, along with a few other spots around town. Share jeeps go to Garur (₹50, 45 minutes), Kausani (₹60, 1½ hours) and Gwaldam (₹80, two hours). A shared/private jeep costs ₹100/2000 to Song (two hours), ₹120/2000 to Loharket (2½ hours), ₹300/5000 to Pithoragarh (six hours) and ₹200/2000 to Almora (two hours); only private jeeps are available to Munsyari (five hours, ₹5000).

Munsyari

Perched on a mountainside surrounded by plunging terraced fields, where the 6000m Panchachuli peaks scrape the sky across the Johar Valley, Munsyari (2290m) is one of the most scenic villages in Uttarakhand. Visited mostly by trekkers heading to the Milam Glacier (p441), the surrounding landscape makes this a worthwhile destination even if you don't plan on lacing up your boots and hitting the trail.

The small **Tribal Heritage Museum** (☏9411337094; Surender Singh Pangtey Rd; ₹10; ☉9am-5pm most days), 2km downhill from the bazaar, has artefacts from the days when Munsyari was an important nexus of trade with Tibet. In town, a Nanda Devi Temple is worth a visit purely for wonderful photo ops with its Himalaya backdrop. Munsyari is also a unique place to experience the Nanda Devi Festival in September.

The main treks that bring travellers to town are Milam Glacier (eight days), Nanda Devi Base Camp (nine to 11 days) and Ralam Glacier (six to seven days). For guides and info, get in touch with Hotel Pandey Lodge (p452) or **Nanda Devi Tour N Trek** (☏9411130330; beerubugyal28@gmail.com).

There are some nice day hikes in the area – ask how to get to Kalya Top (it's a couple of miles off the road that heads uphill, towards Bageshwar) with views of Nanda Devi and Nanda Kot, as well as the Panchachulis. Also ask about walks to nearby lakes, Maheswar Kund or Thamri Kund.

🛏 Sleeping

Several modern hotels have popped up in Munsyari, but we still like **Hotel Pandey Lodge** (☏9411130316; www.munsyarihotel.com; r ₹300-1500), by the bus stand, with its range of good-value rooms, some with amazing views. Across the street, **Snow View Inn** (☏7534881686; Munsyari-Madkot Rd; r ₹400-1200; ☏) is exceptionally friendly.

ℹ Getting There & Away

Share jeeps run to Pithoragarh (₹223, eight hours), Haldwani ₹600, 11 hours), Bageshwar (₹150, six hours), Nainital (₹600, nine hours), Almora (₹450, eight hours) and Thal (₹200, three hours), where you can change for onward transport. If travelling to Munsyari via Thal, get a right-side window seat for the best views along the road. If you came from Thal and are heading to Pithoragarh, consider taking the longer route via Jauljibi for a change of scenery, including some amazing vistas of the Kumaon and Nepali Himalaya.

Kolkata (Calcutta)

☏ 033 / POPULATION 14.5 MILLION

Best Places to Eat

➡ 6 Ballygunge Place (p476)

➡ Kewpies (p472)

➡ Fire and Ice (p472)

➡ Tamarind (p476)

➡ Yauatcha (p472)

Best Places to Stay

➡ Astor (p469)

➡ Calcutta Bungalow (p469)

➡ Elgin Fairlawn (p468)

➡ Oberoi Grand (p468)

➡ Sunflower Guest House (p468)

Why Go?

India's third-largest city is a daily festival of human existence, simultaneously noble and squalid, cultured and desperate, decidedly futuristic while splendid in decay. By its old spelling, Calcutta readily conjures images of human suffering to most Westerners – although that's not a complete picture of this 330-year-old metropolis. Locally, Kolkata is regarded as India's intellectual, artistic and cultural capital. Although poverty is certainly apparent, the self-made middle class drives the city's core machinery, a nascent hipster culture thrives among its millennial residents and its dapper Bengali gentry frequent grand colonial-era clubs.

As the former capital of British India, Kolkata retains a feast of colonial-era architecture contrasting starkly with marginalised urban areas and dynamic new-town suburbs with their air-conditioned shopping malls. Kolkata is the ideal place to experience the mild yet complex tang of Bengali cuisine. Friendlier than India's other metropolises, this is a city you 'feel' more than simply visit.

When to Go
Kolkata

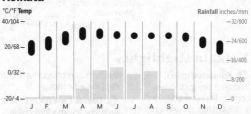

May–Sep Best avoided due to heavy rains that leave the city drenched.

Sep & Oct The city dresses up magnificently for the colourful mayhem of Durga Puja.

Nov–Feb Cool and dry, the winter months are a time for film and music festivals.

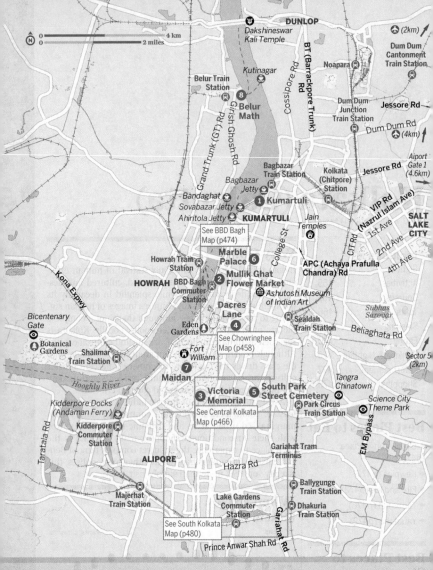

Kolkata Highlights

1 Kumartuli (p463)
Watching clay goddesses come to life in the sculptors' studios of this atmospheric neighbourhood.

2 Mullik Ghat Flower Market (p462) Riding a boat on the Hooghly River to get here.

3 Victoria Memorial (p456) Pondering the architectural brilliance of British Raj's majestic tribute.

4 Dacres Lane (p473) Sampling lip-smacking creole cuisine at street-food stalls.

5 South Park Street Cemetery (p456) Discovering stories from the city's past.

6 Marble Palace (p463) Being intrigued by the idiosyncratic exuberance of Bengal's erstwhile zamindars.

7 Maidan (p457) Hopping onto a tram and enjoying a ride through this colonial-era park.

8 Belur Math (p463) Acquainting yourself with Bengali spirituality at this awe-inspiring institution.

History

Centuries before the advent of Western seafarers, the settlement of Kalikata (site of present-day Kalighat) had been home to a much-revered temple consecrated to the Hindu goddess Kali, which still stands today. That aside, the area was very much a rural backwater, and tales of tigers roaming the impenetrable jungles (where Park St now runs!) are rife in the city's lore. When British merchant Job Charnock showed up in 1690, he considered the site appropriate for a new, defendable colonial settlement, and within a few decades a miniature version of London – christened Calcutta – was sprouting stately buildings and English churches amid wide boulevards and grand formal gardens. The grand European illusion, however, vanished abruptly at the new city's frayed edges, where Indians servicing the Raj mostly lived in cramped, overcrowded slums.

The most notable hiccup in the city's meteoric rise came in 1756, when Siraj-ud-daula, the nawab of nearby Murshidabad, captured the city. Dozens of members of the colonial aristocracy were imprisoned in a cramped room beneath the British military stronghold of Fort William (currently a base of the Indian Army). By dawn, around 40 were dead from suffocation. The British press exaggerated numbers, drumming up moral outrage back home: the legend of the 'Black Hole of Calcutta' was born.

The following year, Lord Robert Clive – then viceroy of India – retook Calcutta for Britain. The nawab sought aid from the French but was defeated at the Battle of Plassey (now Palashi), thanks to the treachery of former allies. A stronger moated 'second' Fort William was constructed in 1758, and Calcutta became British India's official capital, though well into the 18th century leopards were still hunted in the bamboo forests around where Sudder St lies today.

The late-19th-century Bengali Renaissance movement saw a great cultural reawakening among middle-class Calcuttans. This was further galvanised by the massively unpopular 1905 division of Bengal, which sowed the seeds of the Indian independence movement. Bengal was reunited in 1911, but the British promptly transferred their colonial capital to less troublesome New Delhi.

Initially, loss of political power had little effect on Calcutta's economic status. However, the impact of 1947's Partition was devastating. While West Pakistan and Punjab saw a fairly equal (and bloody) exchange of populations, migration in Bengal was largely one way. Around four million Hindu refugees from East Bengal arrived, choking Calcutta's already overpopulated bastis (slums). For a period, people were literally dying of hunger in the streets, creating Calcutta's abiding image of abject poverty. No sooner had these refugees been absorbed

KOLKATA IN...

Three Days

On the first day, admire the Victoria Memorial (p456) and surrounding attractions, then visit India Tourism (p481) to grab a Marble Palace permit (to be used two days hence). Steal an evening boat ride from a pier on the Hooghly Riverbanks (p457), then drink and dine at a Park St institution such as OlyPub (p476) or Peter Cat (p472).

On day two, wander through the colonial-era wonderland of BBD Bagh (p459), experience the fascinating (albeit wistful) alley life of Old Chinatown (p462) and Barabazar (p460), and observe Howrah Bridge (p462) from the colourful Mullik Ghat Flower Market (p462).

Day three is best spent visiting Marble Palace (p463) and nearby Tagore's House (p463), before continuing to Kumartuli (p463) directly or by a vastly longer detour via the spiritual stops of **Dakshineswar** (www.dakshineswarkalitemple.org; Rani Rashmoni Rd; ⊙6am-12.30pm & 3.30-8pm) and Belur Math (p463).

One Week

On day four, experience the contrasts of **South Kolkata**, with its art galleries, textile boutiques, buzzing cafes, green areas, fancy shopping malls, delicious Bengali food and the ritualistic splendour of Kalighat Temple (p464). Then take a short tour to the Sunderbans (p487) in the lower Ganges Delta, where you can spot giant crocodiles and (with some luck) the famed Bengal tigers. Finally, make a daylong excursion to the north of the city to explore the charming former-European outposts located up the Hooghly (p488).

than a second wave arrived during the 1971 India-Pakistan War.

After India's Partition, the port of Calcutta was hit very hard by the loss of its main natural hinterland, which lay behind the closed East Pakistan (later Bangladesh) border. Labour unrest spiralled out of control while the city's dominant party (Communist Party of India) spent most of its efforts attacking the feudal system of land ownership and representing proletarian demands and interests. Despite being well intentioned, many of these moves backfired. Strict rent controls to protect tenants' interests were abused to the extent that even today some long-time tenants pay only a few hundred rupees occupying quarters in the grandest heritage buildings. *Bandhs* (strikes) were called by labour unions almost fortnightly in defence of workers' rights, which severely affected the commercial productivity of the region. Plagued by the routine shutdowns, several corporate firms moved their headquarters from the city to Mumbai or Delhi over the 1980s and 1990s, leaving Calcutta's economy in deep turmoil.

In 2001 Calcutta officially adopted the more phonetic spelling, Kolkata. Around the same time the city administration implemented a new, relatively business-friendly attitude that has encouraged an economic resurgence of sorts. The most visible results are numerous suburban shopping malls and apartment towers, plus the rapid emergence of Salt Lake City's Sector 5 as Kolkata's alternative corporate and entertainment centre (albeit well off tourists' radars). In 2011 the Trinamool Congress Party swept the state elections to end the Communist Party's 34-year reign in West Bengal, and promised to usher in large-scale *paribartan* (change). It's a work in progress that continues to the present day.

Sights

Chowringhee

★ **Victoria Memorial**   HISTORIC BUILDING
(VM; Map p466; ☏ 033-22231890; www.victoria memorial-cal.org; Indian/foreigner incl gardens ₹30/500; ⊙ museum 10am-6pm Tue-Sun, gardens 5.30am-6.30pm) The incredible Victoria Memorial is a vast, beautifully proportioned festival of white marble: think US Capitol meets Taj Mahal. Had it been built for a beautiful Indian princess rather than a colonial queen, this domed beauty flanking the southern end of the Maidan would surely be considered one of India's greatest buildings. Commissioned by Lord Curzon, then Viceroy of India, it was designed to commemorate Queen Victoria's demise in 1901, but construction wasn't completed until 20 years after her death.

Inside, highlights are the soaring central chamber and the Calcutta Gallery, an excellent, even-handed exhibition tracing the city's colonial-era history. Even if you don't want to go in, the building is still worth admiring from afar: there are magnificently photogenic views across reflecting ponds from the northeast and northwest. Or you can get closer by paying your way into the large, well-tended gardens, open from dawn to dusk. Entrance is from the north or south gates (with ticket booths at both). The **east gate** (Map p466) is exit-only by day.

★ **Indian Museum**   MUSEUM
(Map p458; 27 Chowringhee Rd; Indian/foreigner ₹20/500, camera ₹50; ⊙10am-5pm Mar-Nov, 10am-4.30pm Dec-Feb, Tue-Sun) India's biggest and oldest major museum celebrated its bicentenary in February 2014. It's mostly a lovably old-fashioned place that fills a large colonnaded palace ranged around a central lawn. Extensive exhibits in various galleries include fabulous sculptures dating back two millennia (notably the lavishly carved 2nd-century-BC Bharhut Gateway), Egyptian mummies, relics from the ancient Indus Valley civilisation of Harappa and Mohenjodaro, pickled human embryos, dangling whale skeletons and some 37 types of opium in the library-like commercial botany gallery.

St Paul's Cathedral   CHURCH
(Map p466; Cathedral Rd; ⊙9am-noon & 3-6pm) Arguably Kolkata's most iconic Gothic superstructure, decorated with a central crenellated tower, St Paul's would look quite at home in Cambridgeshire but cuts an equally impressive profile against Kolkata's skyline. Built between 1839 and 1847, it has a remarkably wide nave and features a stained-glass west window by Pre-Raphaelite maestro Sir Edward Burne-Jones. Reputedly the first cathedral built outside of the UK, St Paul's takes centre stage on Christmas Eve, when hundreds of people flock in to attend midnight Mass.

South Park Street Cemetery   CEMETERY
(Map p466; Park St; Indian/foreigner ₹20/50, guide booklet ₹100; ⊙10am-5pm) Active from 1767 to about 1840, this historic cemetery re-

mains a wonderful oasis of calm, featuring surreal mossy Raj-era graves from rotundas to soaring pyramids, all jostling for space in an unkempt jungle. Some of the beautiful (though crumbling) graves house mortal remains of eminent citizens from Kolkata's colonial era, including academic Henry Derozio, scholar William Jones and eminent botanist Robert Kyd. Entry is from the north gate on Park St. Photography is not allowed (but mobile-phone snaps are fine).

New Market
MARKET

(Hogg Market; Map p458; Lindsay St; ☉6am-8pm) Marked by a distinctive red-brick clock-tower (Map p458; New Market), this enormous warren of market halls dates to 1874, but was substantially rebuilt after a 1980s fire. By day, handicraft touts can be a minor annoyance, and the crowds can swell in the evenings, especially on weekends. It's more engrossing just after dawn, when there's a harrowing (and a wee morbid) fascination in watching the arrival of animals at the meat market, with its grizzly chopping blocks, blood-splattered floors and pillared high ceilings.

Mother Teresa's
Motherhouse
HISTORIC BUILDING

(Mother Teresa of Calcutta Centre; Map p458; ☏033-22497115; www.motherteresa.org; 54A AJC Bose Rd; ☉8am-noon & 3-6pm Fri-Wed) FREE A regular flow of mostly Christian pilgrims visits the Missionaries of Charity's 'Motherhouse' to pay homage at Mother (and now

Saint) Teresa's large, sober tomb. A small adjacent museum room displays Teresa's worn sandals and battered enamel dinner bowl. Located upstairs is the room where she worked and slept from 1953 to 1997, preserved in all its simplicity. From Sudder St, walk for about 15 minutes along Alimuddin St, then two minutes south. It's in the second alley to the right.

Maidan
PARK

(Map p466) A vast expanse of green in the heart of the city's brick-and-mortar matrix, the Maidan is where Kolkata's residents congregate for walks, spirited cricket and football matches, family outings, dates, ton-ga (horse-drawn carriage) rides and general idling. The grounds are flanked by the Victoria Memorial and St Paul's Cathedral to the south and the Hooghly riverbanks (Map p474) to the west. A tram line cuts through the greens, and hopping onto one of the carriages for a slow ride is great fun.

Historically, the Maidan was created in in 1758, in the aftermath of the 'Black Hole' fiasco. A moated 'second' Fort William, it was shaped in octagonal, Vaubanesque form, and the whole village of Gobindapur was flattened to give the new fort's cannons a clear line of fire. Though sad for then-residents, this created a 3km-long park that is today as fundamental to Kolkata as Central Park is to New York City. Fort William itself remains hidden within a walled military zone to the west of the greens.

KOLKATA (CALCUTTA) SIGHTS

MOTHER TERESA

For many people, Mother Teresa (1910–97) was the living image of human compassion and sacrifice. Born Agnes Gonxha Bojaxhiu to Albanian parents in then-Ottoman Üsküp (now Skopje in Macedonia), she joined the Irish Order of Loreto nuns and worked for more than a decade teaching in Calcutta's St Mary's High School. Horrified by the city's spiralling poverty, she established a new order, the Missionaries of Charity (p465) and founded refuges for the destitute and dying. The first of these, Nirmal Hriday (Map p480; 251 Kalighat Rd), opened in 1952. Although the order swiftly expanded into an international charity, Mother Teresa herself continued to live in simplicity. She was awarded the Nobel Peace Prize in 1979, beatified by the Vatican in 2003 and eventually made a saint in 2016.

However, there are some who detract and question the social worker's call of duty. Feminist author Germaine Greer has accused Mother Teresa of religious imperialism, while journalist Christopher Hitchens' book, *The Missionary Position*, decried donations from dictators and corrupt tycoons. Many have also questioned the order's minimal medical background as well as Teresa's staunch views against contraception. And as recently as in 2018, a Missionaries of Charity home in the neighbouring state of Jharkhand was embroiled in a scandal involving selling babies for adoption.

Regardless, her defenders continue to look up to Mother Teresa for her noble lifelong mission to offer love, care and dignity to the dying and the destitute, while inspiring others to follow in her charitable steps.

Chowringhee

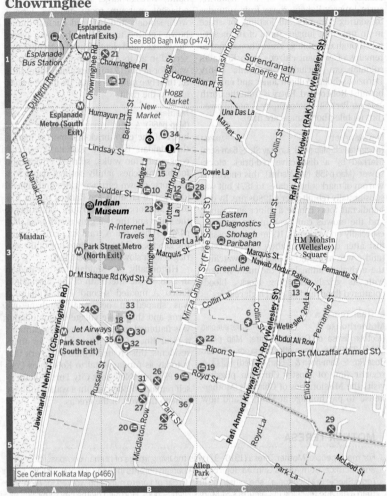

Birla Planetarium

PLANETARIUM

(Map p466; www.mpbirlaplanetarium.org; Chowringhee Rd; ₹80; ⏲program in English 1.30pm & 6.30pm) Loosely styled on Sanchi's iconic Buddhist stupa, this 1962 planetarium presents slow-moving, half-hour audiovisual programs on the wonders of the universe and mysteries of deep space. It's quite convenient as an air-conditioned rest stop in between your day's explorations of nearby sights, and the shows are quite fine in their execution and presentation (the baritone voice-over is particularly dramatic). Recommended for those travelling with children.

Netaji Bhawan

MUSEUM

(Map p466; ☎033-24868139; www.netaji.org; 38/2 Elgin Rd; adult/child ₹5/2; ⏲11am-4.30pm Tue-Sun) Celebrating the life and vision of controversial Bengali leader and pro-Independence radical Subhas Chandra Bose is this house-turned-museum, which also houses an academic research bureau. The yellow limewashed building was Bose's brother's residence, from where he made his famous 'Great Escape' from British-imposed house arrest in January 1941, before eventually joining hands with the Japanese to wage war against British forces. Some rooms re-

KOLKATA (CALCUTTA) SIGHTS

tain a 1940s feel, and the original Wanderer getaway car is parked in the drive.

◉ BBD Bagh

One of Raj-era Calcutta's foremost squares, BBD Bagh (formerly Dalhousie Sq) is centred on a palm-lined central reservoir-lake called Lal Dighi, which once supplied the city's water. Although concrete intrusions detract from the overall spectacle, many a splendid colonial-era edifice remains. Some of them still serve as office buildings and wandering in to them is prohibited, but you're free to admire the structures from outside.

Foremost are the 1780 **Writers' Buildings** (Map p474; BBD Bagh), a twin-block office complex whose glorious south facade looks something like a French provincial city hall. It was originally built as a workplace for clerks ('writers') of the East India Company, and has been under restoration since 2013. Behind, past the repainted **Eastern Railways Building** (Map p474; NS Rd), the former **Chartered Bank Building** (Map p474; India Exchange Pl) has a vaguely Moorish feel with shrubs sprouting from the upper turrets. The 1860s GPO has a soaring rotunda, and the **Standard Life Building** (Map p474; 32 BBD Bagh) sports cherubic details that have been given a fresh lease of life by a new restoration project. Although dilapidated, the ruins of the once-grand **Currency Building** (Map p474; BBD Bagh East; ⊙10am-5pm Mon-Fri) have been stabilised, making an interesting venue for an exhibition–bookshop of the Archaeological Survey of India. Standing proud to the north is **St Andrews Church** (Map p474; 15 Brabourne Rd, BBD Bagh; ⊙7-11am & 3-6pm) with a fine Wren-style spire.

High Court   HISTORIC BUILDING
(Map p474; Esplanade Row West; ⊙10am-5pm Mon-Fri) One of Kolkata's greatest architectural triumphs, the High Court building was built between 1864 and 1872, loosely modelled on the medieval Cloth Hall in Ypres (Belgium). The grand Gothic exterior is best viewed from the south. To enter, you'll have to go to the eastern entrance security desk and apply for an entry pass (carry ID). Once inside, it's fun to explore the endless arches following brigades of lawyers shuffling around in white collar pieces overlaid with flapping black gowns.

St John's Church   CHURCH
(Map p474; Netaji Subhash (NS) Rd; ₹20, car ₹25; ⊙8am-5pm) This circa-1787 stone church is ringed by columns and contains a small, portrait-draped room once used as an office by Warren Hastings, India's first British governor-general. It's on the right as you enter (entry to the main church is via the rear portico). The tree-shaded grounds have several interesting monuments, including the mausoleum of Job Charnock and the relocated Black Hole Memorial. The church is home to an exquisite painting depicting the *Last Supper,* by 18th-century German artist Johann Zoffany.

Old GPO Building   ARCHITECTURE
(Map p474; BBD Bagh) One of the most iconic buildings on BBD Bagh is the old General Post Office, with its central rotunda soaring nearly 40m around a statue of a lance-wielding mail runner. Most postal transactions, however, are in a building 100m further up Koilaghat St. Outside that is a philatelic bureau where you can get commemorative issues or design yourself a sheet of ₹5 stamps incorporating your own photo (₹300). However, these can take up to seven days to be delivered.

Town Hall   MUSEUM
(Kolkata Panorama; Map p474; 4 Esplanade West; weekdays/weekends ₹10/15; ⊙11am-5pm) The imposing colonnaded cube of the former Town Hall Building dates from 1814. It now hosts Kolkata Panorama, an introduction to the city's heritage through a lively collection of working models, videos and interactive exhibits. It's interesting if you have an hour to spare, but as you must be accompanied by a guide it can be hard to 'escape' quickly. Coverage can be historically selective, and many foreigners may struggle to appreciate the detailed sections on Bengali popular culture.

⊙ Barabazar & Howrah

Literally meaning 'Big Market', Barabazar is Kolkata's principal trading hub and deals in literally everything required for the survival of humankind. Located just north of BBD Bagh, Barabazar makes for some great exploring on foot.

A walk through the area links several minor religious sights, but much of the fun comes from exploring the vibrantly chaotic alleys en route that teem with traders, rickshaw couriers, cart pullers and porters (called 'coolies') hauling impossibly huge packages balanced on their heads. Hidden away amid the paper merchants of Old China Bazaar St, the **Armenian Church of Nazareth** (Map p474; Armenian St; ⊙9am-4pm Mon-Sat) was founded in 1707 and is claimed to be Kolkata's oldest place of Christian worship. The larger 1797 Portuguese-Catholic **Holy Rosary Cathedral** (Map p474; Brabourne Rd; ⊙6-11am & 5-6pm) has eye-catching crown-topped side towers and an interior that is festively kitsch.

Kolkata's Jewish community once numbered around 30,000 but these days barely 30 ageing believers turn up at **Maghen David Synagogue** (Map p474; Canning St; ⊙9am-4pm). Around the corner, the **Neveh Shalome Synagogue** (Map p474; Brabourne Rd; ⊙9am-4pm) is almost invisible behind shop stalls. Once you've fought your way across Brabourne St, go down Pollock St between very colourful stalls selling balloons, tinsel and plastic plants to the decrepit Pollock St Post Office, once a grand Jewish school building. Opposite, **BethEl Synagogue** (Map p474; Pollock St; ⊙9am-4pm Mon-Sat) has a facade that looks passingly

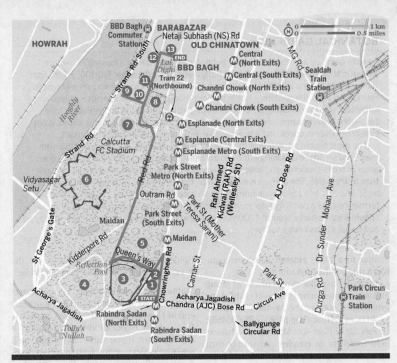

City Walk
Maidan & BBD Bagh

START RABINDRA SADAN METRO STATION
END WRITERS' BUILDINGS
LENGTH 4KM; TWO HOURS

Walk north along Chowringhee Rd (JL Nehru Rd), where to your left you will spot the grand Gothic steeple of ❶ **St Paul's Cathedral** (p456) – reputedly the first cathedral built by the English outside of the UK. Turn left along Queen's Way to spy the dome-shaped ❷ **Birla Planetarium** (p458) on your left. Continue along marvelling at the elegant marble-draped profile of the ❸ **Victoria Memorial** (p456) – Kolkata's most iconic monument from the Raj era. As the manicured expanse of the ❹ **Maidan Racecourse** (p478) reveals itself ahead of you, veer right onto Red Rd and begin a fantastic 2km walk through the ❺ **Maidan** (p457) greens. The shaded route will take you through the grassy, tree-lined grounds where people play, lounge or generally unwind throughout the day. Walking parallel to a tram track, you'll pass the guarded ❻ **Fort William** complex on your left, the skyline of Chowringhee on your right, and several football grounds and sports clubs on both sides

of the road. Once you reach the far north end of the Maidan, stay on Red Rd as it turns left towards ❼ **Eden Gardens** (p478) – Kolkata's legendary cricket battleground – before swerving right onto Netaji Subhash (NS) Rd. Walking northward along this road, you will see the majestic profile of the ❽ **Raj Bhavan** (Map p474; Government Pl) – residence of West Bengal's governor – on your right, and the red steeple of the ❾ **High Court** (p460) as well as the colonnaded facade of the ❿ **Town Hall** (p460) on your left. Continue walking northward along NS Rd for about 200m, and you'll reach the graceful limewashed, stone-spired ⓫ **St John's Church** (p460), where the British governor-general Warren Hastings had his working office. A further 200m along the same road, you'll see the shiny dome of the ⓬ **Old GPO Building** (p460) rise on your left, and the watery expanse of the ⓭ **Lal Dighi** reservoir open up to your right. Staying on NS Rd, walk around the the periphery of Lal Dighi then turn right to arrive at the main facade of the ⓮ **Writers' Buildings** (p459), gleaming in all their glory thanks to an ongoing restoration project.

BOTANICAL GARDENS

Despite being an awkward journey by public transport, Kolkata's lovely 109-hectare **Botanical Gardens** (Botanical Garden Rd, Shibpur; Indian/foreigner ₹10/100; ☉6am-5pm Tue-Sun) makes for a great place to escape from the city's frazzling sounds and smells. Founded in 1786, the gardens – home to more than 12,000 plant species – played an important role in cultivating tea bushes smuggled in from China by the British, long before the drink became a household commodity. Today, there's a cactus house, palm collection, river-overlook and a boating lake with splendid Giant Water Lily pads.

The most touted attraction in the park is the 250-year-old 'world's largest banyan tree'. That's a little misleading – the central trunk rotted away in the 1920s, leaving an array of cross-branches and linked aerial roots that collectively look more like a copse than a single tree. The banyan is a 300m walk from the park's Bicentenary Gate on buses 55 and 213, or a 1.5km walk from the main gate where minibuses as well as bus 55 terminate after a painfully slow journey from Esplanade via Howrah. Taxis from Shakespeare Sarani charge around ₹200 via the elegant Vidyasagar Setu (you'll have to pay an additional ₹10 as bridge toll fee).

similar to a 1930s cinema. The synagogue has a fine colonnaded interior.

If you're travelling as part of a large group and wish to prearrange your visit to the three synagogues, contact the **Jewish Community Affairs Office** (Map p458; ☑9831054669; 63 Park St; ☉10am-4pm Mon-Fri) in advance. Solo travellers or couples can simply turn up at the synagogues within working hours, and present an ID at the gate.

Parallel to Pollock St, wider Ezra St has a brilliant old **perfumerie** (Map p474; 55 Ezra St; ☉10am-7pm Mon-Fri), just before the Shree Cutchi Jain Temple. From there, follow Parsee Church St east to reach Old Chinatown or swing back up the ever-fascinating Rabindra Sarani to find the shop-clad 1926 Nakhoda Mosque (p462) that was loosely modelled on Akbar's Mausoleum at Sikandra.

Howrah Bridge
LANDMARK

(Rabindra Setu; Map p474) Howrah Bridge is a 705m-long abstraction of shiny steel cantilevers and rivets, which serves as a carriageway of nonstop human and motorised traffic across the Hooghly River. Built during WWII, it's one of the world's busiest bridges and a Kolkatan architectural icon. Photography of the bridge is prohibited, but you might sneak a discreet shot while passing through in a taxi, or from one of the various ferries that ply across the river to the vast 1906 Howrah train station.

To lessen traffic load on the bridge and provide easy access to the city's southern districts from Howrah, the newer Vidyasagar Setu bridge was inaugurated in 1992. It can be seen about 3km downstream, cutting a

Golden Gate Bridge–like profile across the river, if you look south from Howrah Bridge.

Mullik Ghat Flower Market
MARKET

(Map p474; off Strand Rd) Near the southeast end of Howrah Bridge, this flower market is fascinatingly colourful virtually 24 hours a day. However, if you visit at daybreak, you'll see wholesalers arrive with huge consignments of flowers that are then auctioned to retailers. Many workers live in makeshift shacks, bathing in the river behind from a ghat with sunset views of Howrah Bridge. At around 7am, local wrestlers practise their art on a small caged area of sand set slightly back from the river.

Nakhoda Mosque
MOSQUE

(Map p474; Zakaria St) Located amid the din and chaos of Rabindra Sarani, the 1926 red-sandstone Nakhoda Mosque rises impressively above the bustling shopfronts of its neighbouring commercial establishments. Its roof, which is adorned with emerald-green domes and minarets, was loosely modelled on Akbar's Mausoleum at Sikandra, while the main entrance gate was inspired by the Buland Darwaza at Fatehpur Sikri. The mosque is Kolkata's largest, and is at the centre of festive action every evening during the holy month of Ramadan.

◎ Old Chinatown

For nearly two centuries, the area around Bentinck St and Phears Lane was Kolkata's Chinatown, populated by Chinese merchants who settled here during Kolkata's maritime heyday. However, dwindling business prospects, relocation to newer suburban colonies and the migration of later generations to the USA and Australia have taken their toll, and today 'old' Chinatown is predominantly Muslim. Just after dawn, there's still a lively market scene that erupts in the tiny square of Tiretta Bazaar, with several stalls selling Chinese breakfast staples such as fishball soup, pork buns and dumplings until about 10am.

Historic shops nearby include musical-instrument makers Mondal & Sons (p479) and the fascinating 1948 gun shop **ML Bhunja** (Map p474; ☑ 9831134146; 301 BB Ganguli St, Lal Bazar; ☉ 11am-6.30pm Mon-Fri), with its musty old cases of rifles, sabres, a flintlock and many an old bayonet laced with snake venom.

Around the once-grand 1924 **Toong On Temple** (Map p474; Blackburn Lane), destitute scavengers sift through rubbish heaps, sleeping in tent-and-box shacks on neighbouring pavements. It's a very humbling experience; take care to respect the dignity of others while walking around the area.

⊙ Rabindra Sarani

The ever-fascinating Rabindra Sarani, a street of densely packed shops and workshops, is threaded through by trams running north from Esplanade via the clay idol-makers' workshops of Kumartuli, before terminating at Galiff Street, the site of Kolkata's curious Sunday-morning pet and bird market. There are a few interesting sights around the Kolkata University building on College St, east of Rabindra Sarani, including the impressive facade of the 1817 Presidency University.

★ Marble Palace   MUSEUM
(46 Muktaram Babu St; ☉ 10am-3pm, closed Mon & Thu) Built in 1835 by a raja from the prosperous Mallick family, this resplendent mansion is as grand as it is curious. Its marble-draped halls are overstuffed with dusty statues of thinkers and dancing girls, much Victoriana, ample Belgian glassware, game trophies and fine paintings, including originals by Murillo, Reynolds and Rubens. To enter, you need prior written permission from West Bengal Tourism (p481) or India Tourism (p481). Entry is technically free, but tips (₹100 per group is fine) are expected by staff guides.

The estate is still maintained by the Mallick family, so it is private property. Photography is not allowed within the palace premises.

Of particular note within the building is the music room, with its lavish floor of marble inlay, where Napoleons beat Wellingtons

three to one. The ballroom retains its vast array of candle chandeliers with globes of silvered glass to spread illumination (original 19th-century disco balls!). There's also a private menagerie on the mansion's grounds, dating back to the early years, which is home to a few monkey and bird species.

To find Marble Palace from MG Rd metro, walk north and turn left at the first traffic light – 171 Chittaranjan (CR) Ave. From the east, it's on the lane that leaves Rabindra Sarani between Nos 198 and 200.

★ Tagore's House   MUSEUM
(Jorasanko Thakurbari; Dwarkanath Tagore Lane, off Rabindra Sarani; Indian/foreigner ₹10/50; ☉ 10.30am-4.30pm Tue-Sun) The stately 1784 family mansion of Rabindranath Tagore has become a shrine-like museum to India's greatest modern poet. Even if his personal effects don't inspire you, some of the well-chosen quotations might spark an interest in Tagore's deeply universalist and modernist philosophy. There's a decent gallery of paintings by his family and contemporaries, and an exhibition on his literary, artistic and philosophical links with Japan. There's also a 1930 photo of Tagore with Einstein shot during a well-publicised meeting.

Tagore's House is maintained and run by Rabindra Bharati University, and the museum is located on the university campus.

⊙ Northern Kolkata

★ Kumartuli Idol-makers   AREA
(Banamali Sarkar St) Countless clay effigies of deities and demons immersed in the Hooghly during Kolkata's colourful *pujas* (offering or prayers) are created in specialist *kumar* (sculptor) workshops in this enthralling district, notably along Banamali Sarkar St, the lane running west from Rabindra Sarani. Craftspeople are busiest from August to October, creating straw frames, adding clay coatings, and painting divine features on idols for Durga and Kali festivals. In November old frameworks wash up on riverbanks and are often repurposed the following year.

★ Belur Math   RELIGIOUS SITE
(☑ 033-26541144; www.belurmath.org; Grand Trunk Rd; ☉ 6.30am-noon & 3.30-5.30pm Oct-Mar, 4-6pm Apr-Sep) Set very attractively amid palms and manicured lawns, this large religious centre is the headquarters of the Ramakrishna Mission, inspired by 19th-century Indian sage Ramakrishna Paramahamsa, who

TOP FESTIVALS

Dover Lane Music Conference (www.doverlanemusicconference.org; Nazrul Mancha, Rabindra Sarovar; ⊙late Jan) Indian classical music and dance at Rabindra Sarovar.

Saraswati Puja (⊙late Jan/early Feb) Prayers for educational success; all dress in yellow.

Kolkata Book Fair (www.kolkatabookfair.net; Milan Mela, EM Bypass; ⊙late Jan/early Feb) Asia's biggest book fair.

Eid-ul-fitr Celebrated after the Islamic holy month of Ramadan.

Rath Yatra (⊙late Jul/early Aug) Major Krishna chariot festival similar to the Puri equivalent.

Durga Puja (⊙late Sep/early Oct) Kolkata's biggest festival.

Kolkata International Film Festival (www.kiff.in; ⊙mid-Nov) Weeklong festival of Indian and foreign movies.

Kolkata Jazzfest (www.jazzfest.in; Fazlul Haque Sarani, Dalhousie Institute; ⊙late Nov/early Dec) Three days of jazz, blues and world music.

Boro Din (⊙25 Dec) Kolkata's version of Christmas.

There is also a wide range of village craft festivals in the area outside the city. Bangla Natak (www.banglanatak.com) is an NGO that helps raise awareness and encourage visitors.

preached the unity of all religions. Its centrepiece is the 1938 **Ramakrishna Mandir** (Belur Math; ⊙6.30am-noon & 3.30-6pm), which somehow manages to look like a cathedral, Indian palace and Istanbul's Aya Sofya all at the same time. Several smaller shrines near the Hooghly riverbank include the **Sri Sarada Devi Temple** (Belur Math; ⊙6.30am-noon & 3.30-6pm) FREE, entombing the spiritual leader's wife, Sarada.

⊙ Kalighat

Kalighat Temple   HINDU TEMPLE
(Map p480; Kali Temple Rd; ⊙5am-10pm, central shrine closed 2-4pm) This ancient Kali temple is Kolkata's holiest spot for Hindus, and possibly the source of the city's name. Today's version is the 1809 rebuild, with floral- and peacock-motif tiles that look more Victorian than Indian. More interesting than the architecture are the jostling pilgrim queues that snake into the main hall to fling hibiscus flowers at a crowned, three-eyed Kali image with a gold-plated tongue. Behind the bell pavilion, goats are ritually beheaded on auspicious days to honour the goddess.

⊙ Ballygunge, Gariahat & Lansdowne

Rabindra Sarovar   PARK
(Map p480; off Southern Ave) The lakes here prettily reflect hazy sunrises, while middle-class Kolkatans jog, row and meditate around the tree-shaded parkland that was

once the site of an Allied Forces medical camp during WWII. Some form circles to do group yoga routines culminating in forced, raucous laugh-ins, engagingly described by Tony Hawks as Laughing Clubs in *The Weekenders: Adventures in Calcutta*. Young lovebirds match the park's avian residents in numbers, and street musicians enthral listeners with soulful tunes, mostly on weekends.

Birla Mandir   HINDU TEMPLE
(Map p480; www.gdbirlasabhagar.com; Ashutosh Chowdhury Ave; ⊙6-11am & 5-9pm) A graceful 20th-century structure built in cream-coloured sandstone, this temple is consecrated to the Hindu gods Narayan (Vishnu) and his wife Lakshmi. The three corn-cob-shaped towers are more impressive for their size than their carvings, and the courtyards are a nice place to sit and spend a few moments in quiet contemplation. There's a state-of-the-art auditorium adjacent to the temple complex called GD Birla Sabaghar (p478) that often hosts musical programs and other performances; see website for upcoming schedules.

CIMA   GALLERY
(Map p480; ☑033-24858717; www.cimaartindia. com; Sunny Towers, 43 Ashutosh Chowdhury Ave; ⊙noon-7pm Tue-Sat, 3-7pm Mon) A cutting-edge contemporary-art gallery located on the 2nd floor of an upmarket South Kolkata building complex, CIMA is a great place to check out works by some of India's top-line contemporary artists as well as old masters. Exhibitions change on a biweekly or monthly basis,

and there are occasionally specially curated shows. There's also a design shop and gift store within the premises, selling an eclectic and highly desirable collection of souvenirs, handicrafts and urban-chic designware.

◉ Alipore

Horticultural Gardens   PARK
(Map p480; Belvedere Rd; ₹20; ◷6-10am & 2-7pm) A hidden island of tranquillity in the heart of Kolkata, this delightful garden complex offers visitors an opportunity to acquaint themselves with tropical plant species, even while feasting their eyes on its placid green surroundings. Hundreds of tropical shrubs and flowering plants blossom around the central lawn, as well as in the themed Japanese Garden and around a cute stony waterfall. There's also an orchard with fruit trees (no picking!), and separate gardens for cacti and orchids.

Alipore Zoo   ZOO
(Map p480; www.kolkatazoo.in; Alipore Rd; entry ₹30, video ₹250; ◷9am-5pm Fri-Wed) Kolkata's 16-hectare zoo opened its doors in 1875 as one of British India's showpiece zoological gardens, but has gradually dropped in stature and standards over the years. The spacious lawns and lakeside promenades are very popular with weekend picnickers (hence all the rubbish). Avoid visiting between Christmas and New Year as the place is swamped by locals. You'll find toilets and stalls selling snacks and bottled water within the premises.

🏃 Activities

Boat Rides   BOATING
(Outram Ghat, Strand Rd) A fantastic way to watch the sun go down over the Hooghly River is by riding a skiff into the waters at dusk. Rowers line up their boats along the pier at Outram Ghat, and offer rides that take you under the Vidyasagar Setu bridge on a round trip from the jetty. Prices are around ₹500 for an hour's ride.

Heritage Tram   TRAM RIDE
(Map p474; tickets ₹100; ◷8.30am Oct-Feb, 7.30am Apr-Sep Sun) The state-owned Calcutta Tramways Company operates a few trams in Kolkata only on select routes. For a special experience of Kolkata's tramways, you could hop onto a renovated air-conditioned heritage tram from the Esplanade tram depot, and embark on a pleasure ride

through the charming northern districts of the city, extending along Rabindra Sarani, passing several notable buildings and neighbourhoods.

Royal Calcutta Golf Club   GOLF
(☎033-24731352; www.rcgc.in; 18 Golf Club Rd; nonmember green fees ₹6500, 9-/18-hole caddy fee ₹225/450) The magnificent Royal Calcutta Golf Club was established in 1829, making it the oldest golf club in the world outside Britain. It's also one of India's few colonial golf clubs where you can tee off as a walk-in nonmember, although for a steep fee. For other facilities (such as swimming or tennis), you'll have to come as a member's guest.

Missionaries of Charity   VOLUNTEERING
(☎033-22497115; www.motherteresa.org) This charitable religious order, founded by Mother (St) Teresa, helps large numbers of the city's destitute sick and dying. Volunteers are universally welcome, with no minimum service period, experience or specific skills required other than a warm heart and patience to listen to and empathise with those whose language they may not understand.

Volunteers need to attend an orientation briefing, held three times weekly at **Sishu Bhavan** (Map p458; 78 AJC Bose Rd; ◷3pm Mon, Wed & Fri), two blocks north of Mother Teresa's Motherhouse (p457). A volunteering 'day' starts at 7am with a bread-and-banana breakfast at the Motherhouse, and is generally over by early afternoon.

📚 Courses

Mystic Yoga Studio   YOGA
(Map p466; www.mysticyoga.in; 2nd fl, 20A Camac St; drop-in sessions ₹700; ◷8am-8pm Mon-Fri, to 5pm Sat & Sun) This mirror-walled commercial studio offers one-hour guided yoga sessions (mostly basic) for drop-in guests. If you're on a long stay, try one of its monthly courses, which are more structured. There's an attached juice bar and organic cafe that plays recorded mantras.

Kali Travel Home   COOKING
(☎033-25550581; www.traveleastindia.com; courses from ₹1200) Enthusiastic entrepreneurs at Kali Travel Home offer personalised Bengali cooking courses with local families. Courses range from basic dishes to special fare (both vegetarian and nonvegetarian), including tossing together a full Bengali lunch platter. Kali also offers guided tours of Kolkata and neighbouring areas.

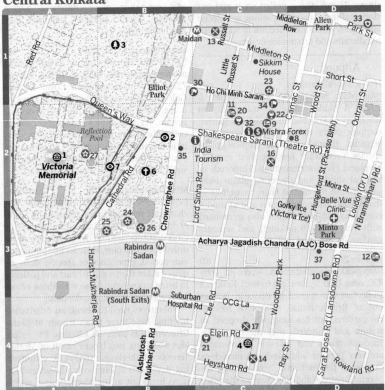

Central Kolkata

☞ Tours

★ Calcutta Walks WALKING

(Map p474; ☎033-40052573, 9830184030; www.
calcuttawalks.com; 9A Khairu Pl; from ₹2000) A
superprofessional outfit run by the knowledgeable conservationist Iftekhar, this organisation offers a wide range of walking, cycling
and motorbike tours. It produces what is arguably the best printed map of Kolkata. Apart
from fixed departure shared walks, you can
also customise a private walk for a higher
price. Calcutta Walks also operates the excellent Calcutta Bungalow (p469) B&B.

Bomti TOURS

(Surajit Iyengar; ☎9831314990; bomtiyengar@
yahoo.com; per group per day ₹8000-10,000, plus
per person meals ₹2500-3000) More than merely a tour guide, Bomti is an art collector and
a veritable well of information on the city's
heritage. Residing in a fascinating heritage
apartment stuffed with art and artisanry
that was once featured in *Elle Decor,* Bomti's

tailor-made personalised tours for up to four
people typically end with a lavish and traditional Bengali meal in his home.

Calcutta Photo Tours PHOTOGRAPHY

(☎9831163482; www.calcuttaphototours.com;
from ₹1750) A range of photography tours on
foot, themed on Kolkata's culture, colonial
heritage and markets, is offered by this professional outfit. Tours start at 6am or 2pm,
and are offered throughout the year.

🛏 Sleeping

Decent accommodation is expensive in Kolkata, and budget places are often dismal.
Midrange and top-end hotels offer significant discounts on rack rates on bookings
through online portals. Midrange hotels
offer better value as walk-ins, while budget
places rarely take bookings. The Salt Lake
area has many business hotels, but it's badly
connected to public transport. Accommodation fills to bursting during Durga Puja

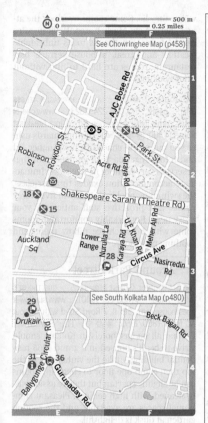

See Chowringhee Map (p458)

AJC Bose Rd

Rowdon St

Robinson St

Acre Rd

Karaya Rd

Park St

Shakespeare Sarani (Theatre Rd)

Auckland Sq

Lower Range

Nurulla La

Karaya Rd

UE Khan Rd

Meher Ali Rd

Circus Ave

Nasirredin Rd

See South Kolkata Map (p480)

Beck Bagan Rd

Drukair

Ballygunge Circular Rd

Gurusaday Rd

0 — 500 m
0 — 0.25 miles

Central Kolkata

KOLKATA (CALCUTTA) SLEEPING

(p471), and demand is high from mid-November to February.

📖 Around Sudder Street

The nearest Kolkata gets to a traveller ghetto is around helpfully located Sudder St. There's a range of backpacker-oriented services, and virtually every second building is a guesthouse or hotel, from charming heritage palaces to ultrabudget dives that represent a whole new league of nastiness.

Afridi International   HOTEL $
(Map p458; ☏ 033-66077525; 3 Cowie Lane; d incl breakfast ₹1900; ❉ 🛜) Possibly the most professionally managed budget hotel in Sudder St, the furniture and fittings here are top-notch, while the entrance is floored in crystalline marble. Some rooms are small and suffer from a trace of damp, but maintenance is regular and the smart upholstery and comfy beds ensure a pleasant stay.

Golden Apple Hotel   GUESTHOUSE $
(Map p458; ☏ 033-66077500; 9 Sudder St; dm cubicle ₹600, d incl breakfast from ₹2850) The

Golden Apple has accommodation that's mostly fresh and tastefully appointed for the price. A handy backpacker feature is the set of 15 top-floor dorm cubicles (doubles), each a lockable bedspace partitioned off by smoked-glass walls and equipped with a storage area beneath the mattress. These, however, can only be booked in person at the reception.

Hotel Aafreen
HOTEL $
(Map p458; ☏033-22654146, 033-32261780; Nawab Abdur Rahman St; d incl breakfast from ₹1400; ✴🛜) Offering midrange value at budget prices, the Aafreen has patterned pink-marble floors and ample-sized rooms that are regularly repainted and boast smart furniture and clean linen. It's close to New Market and Park St areas, and about 800m by foot from Mother Teresa's Motherhouse.

Hotel Galaxy
GUESTHOUSE $
(Map p458; ☏033-22524565; hotelgalaxy.kol@gmail.com; 3 Stuart Lane; d/tr ₹1000/1500; ✴🛜) This quiet, ever-popular guesthouse looks dowdy from outside but the tiny rooms are unexpectedly comfortable and well appointed. Hot water flows freely in the en suite bathrooms and there's free wi-fi (add ₹200 for air-con). There's a small front-porch sitting area, with a minilibrary, where you can leave your hand imprint on a wall that serves as a guestbook.

★ Elgin Fairlawn
HOTEL $$
(Map p458; ☏033-40646300, 033-22269878; www.elginhotels.com; 13A Sudder St; s/d incl breakfast ₹4000/4700; ✴🛜) The elegant Raj-era Fairlawn bungalow dates back to 1783, and the charmingly mothballed hotel that ran here since 1936 has recently been taken over by a luxury hotel group. Renovation is still in progress, and involves retaining all its antiquities and marrying them with requisite touches of modern creature comforts. The tropical greenery fronting the building adds to the appeal.

The hotel counts Patrick Swayze, Sting, Dominique Lapierre and Günter Grass among its celebrity guests – see their photos hanging with countless other precious moments frozen from the past in the central hall.

Hotel Lindsay
HOTEL $$
(Map p458; ☏033-71998866; www.thelindsay.in; 8 Lindsay St; s/d incl breakfast from ₹4150/4750; ✴🛜) A thorough redecoration gives an attractive old-Kolkata 'heritage' ambience to the Lindsay's guest rooms and corridors, belying the 1970s architecture of the tower

where they lie. Some rooms overlook the atmospheric New Market area. Walk-in rates can be lower, but thanks to its unbeatable location and great in-house terrace bar-restaurant, rooms are hard to find without prior bookings.

★ Oberoi Grand
HERITAGE HOTEL $$$
(Map p458; ☏033-22492323; www.oberoihotels.com; 15 Chowringhee Rd; d incl breakfast from ₹14,400; ✴@🛜🏊) Saluting guards usher you out of the chaos of Chowringhee Rd and into a regal oasis of genteel calm that deserves every point of its five stars. Immaculate accommodation exudes timeless class, the swimming pool is ringed with five-storey palms, and proactive staff anticipate your every need. Remarkably comfortable rooms come with a five-choice pillow menu and soothing pool views.

🛏 Around Park Street

★ Sunflower Guest House
GUESTHOUSE $
(Map p458; ☏033-22299401; www.sunflowerguesthouse.com; 5th fl, 7 Royd St; d with/without AC from ₹800/1350; ✴@🛜) The Sunflower is what all budget hotels in Kolkata should strive to be. It's housed in a grand 1865 residential building – take the vintage lift to the top then climb one floor to check in. Rooms can be slightly spartan but they're assiduously cleaned, with high ceilings. Pleasant communal spaces are available, and the rooftop garden at dusk is delightful.

YWCA
HOSTEL $
(Map p458; ☏033-22650392; www.ywcacalcutta.org; 1 Middleton Row; 's/d with AC ₹1000/1300, without AC ₹700/1000, without AC or bathroom ₹450/750; ✴) You don't have to be a woman to get a room in this well-kept, imposing but basic 1925 building. Old high-ceilinged rooms have slatted green doors opening onto a wide arched corridor, whose other open side faces a central tennis court. Large, sparse sitting rooms have a sense of times gone by, without the slightest hint of luxury.

Corporate
HOTEL $$
(Map p458; ☏8981011686, 033-22267551; 4 Royd St; d incl breakfast from ₹4600; ✴🛜) In the suave designer lobby of this slick hotel, the receptionist seems to float in luminous marble. Compact well-maintained rooms in beige and brown tones have comfy thick mattresses with satin sashes and pale polished-stone bathrooms. Suites have small balconies and there's a four-table 'garden' behind the kitch-

en windows. Creature comforts such as kettle, fridge and hairdryer are provided.

★ **Park Hotel** HOTEL **$$$**
(Map p458; ☑ 033-22499000; www.thepark hotels.com; 17 Park St; d incl breakfast from ₹6500; ✴@🛜🏊) A top central choice for hip, up-market accommodation. Modern rooms are snug and feature snazzy decor, while hidden to the rear of the 1st floor is a trio of classy restaurants and a passage past waterfall foliage to Aqua (p477), one of India's coolest poolside bars. Curiously, the hotel's main entrance is through Street, a cafe-deli.

🛌 **Southern Chowringhee**

Central B&B B&B **$$**
(Map p466; ☑ 9836465400; www.centralbnb.com; flat 28, 7th fl, Lansdowne Crt, 5B Sarat Bose Rd; d incl breakfast ₹3550; ✴🛜) Among the best Kolkata apartment-guesthouses to have made its name on the B&B circuit, Central lives up to all its promises. The four rooms are huge and comfortable, with a large shared lounge and communal kitchen. There's fast wi-fi, a basic but sumptuous breakfast, a basket of complimentary snacks, and ever-obliging (if usually invisible) hosts.

★ **Astor** HERITAGE HOTEL **$$$**
(Map p466; ☑ 033-22829950; www.astorkolkata. com; 15 Shakespeare Sarani; d incl breakfast from ₹6500; ✴🛜) Artful evening floodlighting brings out the best of the Astor's solid 1905 architecture, while inside walls are lavished with B&W photos of old Kolkata. A creative palette of chocolate, beige and iridescent butterfly blue brings to life beautifully furnished rooms. Some suites include a four-poster bed. Sizes and shapes vary. There's no lift, however.

Kenilworth HOTEL **$$$**
(Map p466; ☑ 033-22823939; www.kenilworth hotels.com; 1 Little Russel St; d incl breakfast from ₹7150; ✴🛜) The pleasingly bright, fully equipped rooms in this classy Kolkata address have some of the city's most comfortable beds. The deep lobby of marble, dark wood and chandeliers contrasts successfully with a more contemporary cafe that spills out onto an attractive quadrangle of lawn. The Irish-style in-house pub named Big Ben (p476) attracts the city's beautiful people in the evenings.

Park Prime BUSINESS HOTEL **$$$**
(Map p466; ☑ 033-30963096; www.chocolate hotels.in; 226 AJC Bose Rd; d incl breakfast from

₹7100; ✴@🛜🏊) Sleep in an artistic statement with an exterior that looks like a seven-storey computer punch card and rooms that have optical-illusion decor. Headboards carry up across the ceiling and sweep down the wall to emerge as a dagger of desk. It's done without compromising comfort. The foyer is inviting and the rooftop swimming pool nestles beside hip Henry's Lounge Bar.

🛌 **Motherhouse Area**

Monovilla Inn GUESTHOUSE **$**
(Map p458; ☑ 7044091072; www.monovillainn. com; 79/26 B&C AJC Bose Rd; s/d incl breakfast ₹1500/1800; ✴@) Fresh and modern rooms available in a 1940s three-storey building with just two guest rooms per floor. Those located upstairs have better light. There's minimal communal space so you'll be confined to your room most of the time. The toilets are very good for the price. It's located conveniently from Sealdah train station as well as Mother Teresa's Motherhouse.

Georgian Inn GUESTHOUSE **$**
(Map p458; ☑ 9830068355, 9830156625; www. georgianin.com; 1 Doctor Lane; s/d ₹1000/1200, with AC ₹1350/1550; ✴) Very functional, friendly and cheap, this hotel gains in atmosphere thanks to the fascinating melee of Taltala Market that surrounds it. Streetscapes of Doctor Lane to the direct east have architectural hints of old Penang. It's within walking distance of the New Market and Sudder St areas.

🛌 **Northern Kolkata**

★ **Calcutta Bungalow** B&B **$$$**
(☑ 9830184030; www.calcuttabungalow.com; 5 Radha Kanta Jew St; r incl breakfast from ₹7000; ✴🛜) A painstakingly yet meticulously

executed restoration project has seen this once-dilapidated building come alive as the city's most stylish B&B. The charming rooms (full marks for interior decor) are endowed with diverse motifs typical to Kolkata's architecture, such as marble floor tiles engraved with family names, or found objects repurposed into fittings, like lampshades made of giant loudspeaker cones.

The property is managed by leading walking-tour agency Calcutta Walks (p466), and bookings can often be combined with walking tours and other excursions offered by the management.

📖 BBD Bagh

Bengal Buddhist Association GUESTHOUSE $
(Bauddha Dharmankur Sabha; Map p474; ☑033-22117138; dharmankur@gmail.com; 1 Buddhist Temple St; d/tr without bathroom ₹300/400; ❄) While it is meant to house visiting Buddhist scholars, the guesthouse opens its doors to all travellers, as long as they maintain house decorum (the gates are locked from 10.30pm to 5am – and you obviously can't hobble in drunk). The simple rooms share basic common bathrooms with geysers, although there are a few en suite rooms with air-con (₹750).

Broadway Hotel HOTEL $
(Map p474; ☑033-22363930; www.broadway hotel.in; 27A Ganesh Chandra (GC) Ave; s/d/ste with AC 1700/2100/3500, s/d/tr/ste without AC ₹980/1250/1700/2100; ❄🛜) The Broadway is a simple colonial-era hotel that has kept its character without going upmarket. An antiquated lift accesses plain but well-maintained rooms with high ceilings and reupholstered 1950s-style furniture. There's good service, but hot water is by the bucket in cheaper rooms. The in-house bar is delightfully atmospheric.

📖 Southern Kolkata

★**Corner Courtyard** BOUTIQUE HOTEL $$
(Map p480; ☑033-40610145; www.thecorner courtyard.com; 92B Sarat Bose Rd; d incl breakfast ₹5000; ❄🛜) Seven perfectly pitched rooms at this stylish address are named after colours, but they also take photographic subthemes – such as Bengali cinema in 'Charcoal', Kumartuli goddesses in 'Vermilion' and Kolkata's architectural heritage in 'Ivory'. Rooms are on two storeys above a superb little restaurant in a recently restored 1904 townhouse, which includes a charming roof garden drooping with bougainvillea.

Bodhi Tree GUESTHOUSE $$
(Map p480; ☑033-24246534, 8017133921; www. bodhitreekolkata.com; 48/44 Swiss Park; d incl breakfast from ₹3000; ❄🛜) Atmospheric and characterful, a bunch of stone-walled, rustic Buddha-themed guest rooms are attached to this intriguing little 'monastery of art' gallery-cafe, which positions itself as a hippie-chic address for flashpackers. Access is from behind Rabrindra Sarovar metro's southeast exit, walking east for around 300m.

📖 Airport Area

Hotels Balaji & Tirupati HOTEL $
(☑033-25132005, 033-25120065; www.hotel balajiinternational.in; 32 Jessore Rd; d Balaji/Tirupati ₹1700/2400; ❄🛜) Off Jessore Rd between Airport Gates 1 and 2, this smart twin-hotel (named after South Indian divinities) has heavy timber doors, plants on the stairs and good rooms with decent bathrooms, though the mattresses are thin and there's a Donald Duck painted incongruously on some mirrors. Prices include a ride to the airport.

Celesta BOUTIQUE HOTEL $$
(☑033-71000131; www.celesta.in; VIP Rd, Ragunathpur; s/d incl breakfast ₹4600/5200; ❄🛜) Celesta is the suavest of over a dozen hotels in the Raghunathpur area that target travellers in transit (the airport is 15 minutes away by taxi). It makes a style statement with big plate-glass lobby walls and an upper exterior looking like a Mondrian painting. Luxurious beds are piled with pillows in art deco rooms with rain showers.

It's beside the well-signed KFC on the east side of VIP Rd, 4km south of the airport.

Ethnotel HOTEL $$
(☑033-71017000; www.ethnotel.in; 71/1 Jessore Rd, Airport Gate No 2.5; s/d incl breakfast from ₹5000/5500; ❄@🛜) This smart and well-maintained hotel is by far the best mid-range choice for air travellers overnighting in Kolkata on short transit itineraries, as it is located just outside the airport complex. It can organise pickups and drop-offs for guests upon prior request. The rooms are clean and comfortable, and the multicuisine restaurant in the lobby remains open round the clock.

🍴 Eating

Cheaper eateries in Kolkata often serve tapas-sized portions, so order two or three dishes per person along with rice or *luchi* (deep-fried Bengali *puris*). Midrange and top-end restaurants add up to 18% tax to food bills (included in prices quoted). Posher places add a 10% service fee (tips are no longer expected).

Around Sudder Street

Suruchi
MULTICUISINE $

(Map p458; ☏ 033-22290011; 89 Elliot Rd; mains ₹50-150; ⊗ 10.30am-5.30pm) This canteen-style eatery run by an NGO committed to women's empowerment serves fabulous fish, meat and vegetarian dishes redolent with homemade flavours and aromas. The decor is spartan yet ethnic, featuring reed blinds on windows. It's behind an easy-to-spot vermilion-coloured door on Elliot Rd.

Blue Sky Cafe
CAFE $

(Map p458; Chowringhee Lane; mains ₹100-250, juices ₹60-100; ⊗ 8am-10pm) Wise-cracking staff at this travellers' cafe serve up a vast selection of reliable standbys (including great old-style banana pancakes and milkshakes) at long glass tables set close enough to make conversation between strangers a little more likely. The place fills up quickly during meals. The salads are safe to consume as they're washed in bottled water only.

Raj Spanish Cafe
CAFE $$

(Map p458; off Sudder St; mains ₹100-250, pizzas ₹280-450; ⊗ 8.30am-10pm; ☎) Popular as a hang-out for medium-term charity volunteers, this unpretentious place serves good coffee, lassis, pancakes, and a range of Italian, Mexican and Spanish dishes. The pizzas

come out of a wood-fired oven, which is a rarity in town. There's a small outdoor area with some cursory foliage. It's hidden in a lane behind the Roop Shringar fabric shop.

Blue & Beyond
MULTICUISINE $$

(Map p458; 9th fl, Lindsay Hotel, Lindsay St; mains ₹250-350, beer/cocktails from ₹220/300; ⊗ noon-10.30pm) The drawcard here is an open-air rooftop terrace with wide views over New Market, plus a small glass-walled cocktail bar that falls somewhere between 1970s' retro and a space-station acid trip. The globetrotting menu swerves from Caribbean-style calypso fish and Roquefort prawn sizzler to Greek-style chicken and Mexican veg steak.

Around Park Street

Hot Kati Rolls
BENGALI $

(Map p458; Park St; rolls from ₹30; ⊗ 11am-10.30pm) One of Kolkata's best-known hole-in-the-wall places for a *kati* roll. For first-timers, this hit snack is essentially a *paratha* (Indian-style flaky bread), fried one-sided with a coating of egg and then filled with sliced onions, chilli and your choice of stuffing (curried chicken, grilled meat or paneer). Eat it rolled up in a twist of paper as a takeaway.

★ Arsalan
MUGHLAI $$

(Map p458; 119 Ripon St; mains ₹150-300; ⊗ 11.30am-11.30pm) Popular with locals, this central branch of Kolkata's best biryani house is high ceilinged and modern without being fashion-conscious. The main attractions are the celebrated biryanis – aromatic basmati rice, steamed potato and huge

KOLKATA (CALCUTTA) EATING

DURGA PUJA

Much as Carnival transforms cities such as Rio de Janeiro or New Orleans, Durga Puja (p464) brings Kolkata to a fever pitch of colourfully chaotic mayhem: the city's biggest festival celebrates the maternal essence of the divine goddess. For five days in late September or early October, people venerate ornate idols of the 10-armed goddess Durga and her entourage, displayed in *pandals* (temporary shrines) that block roads and dominate yards and little parks.

Over the past 30 years, design competitions and growing corporate sponsorship have seen *pandals* growing ever-more ornate and complex, some with topical or political messages. West Bengal Tourism (p481) tours try to take tourists around a selection of the best *pandals*, but getting anywhere within the city can take hours given the general festive pandemonium. At the festival's climax, myriad Durga idols are thrown into the sacred Hooghly River amid singing, water throwing, fireworks and indescribable traffic congestion. If you just want *pandal* photos without the festival aspect, consider visiting just after Durga Puja when the idols have gone but *pandals* have yet to be deconstructed. Note that the city is virtually in shutdown mode during these five days. Do not schedule any important work during the festival.

chunks of juicy mutton or chicken – that are best paired with melt-in-mouth chicken tikka, skewer-grilled mutton *seekh* kebab and the creamy mutton *galawati* kebab.

Peter Cat
MULTICUISINE $$

(Map p458; ☎033-22298841; Middleton Row; mains ₹250-400; ⊙11am-11pm) This phenomenally popular Kolkata institution is best known for its Iranian-style *chelo* kebabs (barbequed fingers of spiced, minced meat on buttered rice). Other dishes such as the tandoori mixed grill and the chicken sizzler also fly thick and fast. Beer (₹220) comes in pewter tankards and waiters wear Rajasthani costumes. No reservations – just join the queue!

Mamagoto
CHINESE $$

(Map p458; ☎033-33999610; 24 Park St; mains from ₹450; ⊙noon-11.30pm) The decor is stylish, the vibe is laid-back, the service is friendly, and the food is both delicious and comforting. Part of Kolkata's new wave of Chinese eateries, this restaurant is a good spot for cheerful weekend meals. For the best bargain, order yourself a dumpling basket (veg/nonveg ₹695/795), and then put away an unlimited supply of yummy dumplings.

Mocambo
MULTICUISINE $$

(Map p458; Mirza Ghalib St; mains ₹250-450; ⊙11am-11pm) Mocambo dates back to 1956, but with old-fashioned seats in scalloped red leather, it feels more like a mood-lit 1970s steakhouse. A very loyal following comes regularly for its mixed grills, devilled crabs, fish Wellington, chicken Kiev and *bhetki* meunière (barramundi fillets in lemon-butter sauce). An unwritten sartorial admission code applies (no shorts or flip-flops).

⨉ Southern Chowringhee

Kookie Jar
CAFE $

(Map p466; Rowdon St; pastries/savouries from ₹60/80; ⊙8.30am-9pm) This confectionery is a long-time favourite with Kolkata's pastry lovers. Try the myriad forms of chocolate cakes and brownies, or bite into a freshly baked slice of pizza, a meaty puff or a subtly flavoured sandwich. For vegans, there are a few eggless and milkless preparations available.

★Kewpies
BENGALI $$

(Map p466; ☎033-24861600; 2 Elgin Lane; thalis ₹425-800, mains ₹150-450; ⊙12.30-3pm & 7.30-10.30pm Tue-Sun) Kewpie's is a Kolkata gastronomic institution, and dining here feels like a lavish dinner party in a gently old-fashioned home. Reared to perfection by a speciality Bengali chef, this place serves impeccably traditional and authentic Bengali dishes made from the best local ingredients, and though on the pricey side, the food (as well as the experience) is worth every rupee.

★Yauatcha
CHINESE $$

(Map p480; ☎9222222800; 5th fl, Quest Mall; mains ₹250-450; ⊙noon-11pm) Yauatcha has garnered a solid reputation in town for serving Chinese food of the fine-dining variety. There's a vast range of delicious dumplings on the menu, featuring truffle, edamame, scallop and poached Peking duck. The honey-smoked pork ribs and crispy lamb with raw mango are must-eats. Some fine cocktails, chilled beer and pots of jasmine tea also on offer.

Salt House
EUROPEAN $$

(Map p466; ☎9836732154; 6th fl, 40 Shakespeare Sarani; mains ₹425-575; ⊙noon-11.30pm) This stylish new restaurant puts together a delicious menu of European classics (ravioli, risotto, shepherd's pies, and fish and chips, to name a few), often finishing them with a touch of unique local ingredients: leafy microgreens such as *thankuni* and *kolmi*, the aromatic *gondhoraj* lime, robust rooster stock or even a slaw of apple and *kasundi* (mustard relish).

Shiraz Golden Restaurant
MUGHLAI $$

(Map p466; 135 Park St; mains ₹220-300; ⊙noon-11pm) Synonymous with Kolkata's signature biryani (basmati rice with juicy mutton chunks and steamed potatoes, per plate ₹225), Shiraz also offers a range of curries, including a superb ₹190 mutton *kassa* (spiced meat).

Oh! Calcutta
BENGALI $$

(Map p466; ☎033-22837161; 4th fl, Forum Mall, Elgin Rd; mains ₹320-490, beers from ₹230; ⊙12.30-3pm & 7-11pm) Situated within a shopping mall, the shutter-edged mirror 'windows', bookshelves, paintings and B&W photographs create a casually upmarket feel for enjoying some of the city's best Bengali-fusion food. The mild, subtle and creamy *daab chingri* (prawn curry; ₹445) is served in a green coconut, its subtleties brought out particularly well by a side dish of fragrant lime salad.

★Fire and Ice
ITALIAN $$$

(Map p466; ☎033-22884073; www.fireandice pizzeria.com; Kanak Bldg, Middleton St; mains ₹500-700, beer/cocktails from ₹200/450; ⊙noon-11.30pm) Founded and directed by an Italian lady from Naples, Fire and Ice's waiters bring

BENGALI CUISINE

Bengali food is an exceptionally evolved cuisine that is characterised by the astringent aroma of mustard oil, its principal cooking medium. A typical Bengali meal starts with a few preparations of leafy greens and a selection of fried vegetables such as eggplant, bitter gourd or potatoes. The next course comprises a few curries, many of which are accented with the generous use of *posto* (poppy seeds). Other excellent vegetarian choices include *mochar ghonto* (mashed banana flower with potato and coconut), *doi began* (eggplant in curd) and *shukto*, a favourite starter combining at least five different vegetables in a coconut-milk-based sauce, topped with fried bitter gourd and *bori* (crunchy savouries made from mashed dhal paste).

Next comes fish, for which Bengal has earned a legendary reputation. Typical Bengali fish curry types include the light, cumin- or nigella-scented *jhol,* the drier and spicier *jhal* or the richer, ginger- and garlic-based *kalia.* Strong mustard notes feature in *shorshe* curries and *paturi* dishes that come steamed in a banana leaf. Popular fish species include *chingri* (river prawns), meaty *rohu* (white rui), fatty *chital* and the snapper-like *bhetki*. If you can handle the bones, *ilish* (hilsa) is considered the tastiest fish. While it's not de rigueur, meat or *murgi* (chicken) dishes also often feature towards the end of a meal. All of this is polished off with *gobindobhog bhaat* (steamed aromatic rice) or *luchi* (small *puris*).

Mishti (desserts), the final items on the menu, form an important part of Bengali meals. Subtly flavoured *mishti doi* (sweetened yoghurt), *rasgulla* (cream-cheese balls flavoured with rose-water) and *cham-cham* (double-textured curd-based desserts) are the more iconic sweetmeats.

In between meals, Bengal's trademark fast food is the *kati* roll, an oily *paratha* (Indian-style flaky bread) fried with a coating of egg and filled with sliced onions, chilli and your choice of stuffing (curried chicken, grilled meat or paneer). It is generally eaten as a takeaway from hole-in-the-wall serveries. You could also try the spicy *phuchka*, hollow semolina balls stuffed with spicy potato masala dipped in tamarind sauce, or *jhal muri,* a spicy mixture with a base of puffed rice and peanuts.

For a colourful and very affectionate portrait of Kolkata's cuisine, along with a historical record of myriad colonial-era influences and adaptations over centuries, buy a copy of *The Calcutta Cook Book* (₹319), written by Minakshie Dasgupta, Bunny Gupta and Jaya Chaliha, available at leading bookshops.

forth real Italian (al dente!) pastas and Kolkata's best thin-crust pizzas. Old film posters give character to the spacious dining room set behind foliage in a huge heritage building. Few other Kolkata restaurants keep serving as late, or as consistently.

It has a well-stocked cellar, so you can pair a good glass of wine with your food. The proprietor is often around to offer her suggestions.

Monkey Bar — GASTRONOMY $$$

(Map p466; ☎ 033-30990381; Fort Knox Bldg, Camac St; mains ₹350-550, cocktails ₹350-450; ☺ noon-11pm) A fancy address in Kolkata's fine-dining scene, this upscale eatery tosses up an imaginative range of fusion and experimental delicacies within its grunge-modern environs. Pick from items such as Coorg-style pork curry, Kerala-style beef fry and grilled mustard fish. A good list of cocktails – which get cheaper if you order by the pitcher – are also on offer.

✖ BBD Bagh

KC Das — SWEETS $

(Map p474; Lenin Sarani; sweets from ₹20; ☺ 7.30am-9.30pm) This bustling Bengali sweet shop claims to have invented the iconic *rasgulla* (cream-cheese balls flavoured with rose-water) way back in 1868. Also try the *mishti doi* – a Bengali sweet of curd sweetened with jaggery. Seating is available at simple wrought-iron tables and chairs.

Dacres Lane — STREET FOOD $

(Map p474; James Hickey Sarani; mains from ₹30; ☺ 8am-9pm) A series of food stalls selling a unique combination of creole cuisine is interspersed by a few somewhat-dodgy bar-restaurants, whose fairy lights add some warmth to the narrow and dingy lane. Choose from quick-and-easy bites, including *paratha* (Indian-style flaky bread) and curry, toasted bread with mutton, papaya and

BBD Bagh

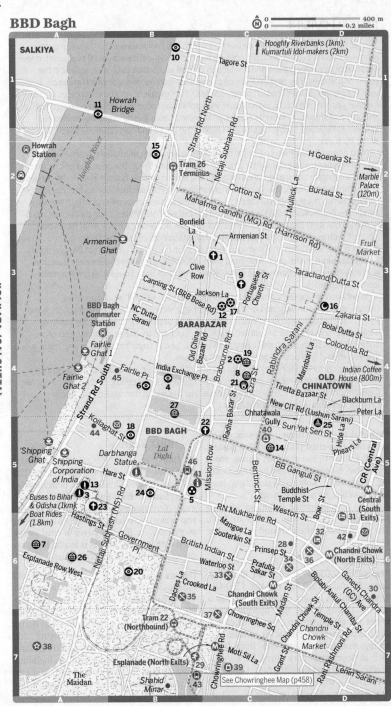

SALKIYA

400 m
0.2 miles

Hooghly Riverbanks (1km);
Kumartuli Idol-makers (2km)

Tagore St

Howrah Bridge

Howrah Station

Tram 26 Terminus

Netaji Subhash Rd

Strand Rd North

Cotton St

Mahatma Gandhi (MG) Rd (Harrison Rd)

H Goenka St

Burtala St

J Mullick La

Marble Palace (120m)

Bonfield La

Armenian St

Armenian Ghat

Clive Row

Canning St (BRB Bose Rd)

Jackson La

Portuguese Church St

Tarachand Dutta St

Fruit Market

Zakaria St

BBD Bagh Commuter Station

NC Dutta Sarani

BARABAZAR

Bolai Dutta St

Coolootola Rd

Fairlie Ghat 1

Fairlie Pl

India Exchange Pl

Old China Bazaar Rd

Brabourne Rd

Rabindra Sarani

Marinbari La

OLD CHINATOWN

Indian Coffee House (800m)

Fairlie Ghat 2

Strand Rd South

Koilaghat St

BBD BAGH

Radha Bazar St

Ezra St

Tiretta Bazaar St

New CIT Rd (Lushun Sarani)

Chhatawala Gully

Sun Yat Sen St

Blackburn La

Peter La

Hide La

Phears La

Shipping Ghat

Shipping Corporation of India

Darbhanga Statue

Hare St

Lal Dighi

Mission Row

BB Ganguli St

Buddhist Temple St

CR (Central Ave)

Buses to Bihar & Odisha (1km); Boat Rides (1.8km)

Hastings St

Government Pl

British Indian St

Bentinck St

Weston St

Bow St

Central (South Exits)

RN Mukherjee Rd

Mangoe La

Sooterkin St

Prinsep St

Chandni Chowk (North Exits)

Esplanade Row West

Waterloo St

Prafulla Sakar St

Madan St

Ganesh Chandra (GC) Ave

Dacres La

Crooked La

Chandni Chowk (South Exits)

Biplabi Ankul Chamba St

Chandni Chowk Temple St

Chandni Chowk Market

The Maidan

Tram 22 (Northbound)

Chowringhee Sq

Chowringhee Rd

Grant St

Rani Rashmoni Rd

Lenin Sarani

Esplanade (North Exits)

Shahid Minar

Moti Sil La

See Chowringhee Map (p458)

BBD Bagh

carrot stew, vegetable fritters, wok-fried noodles and chicken curry with rice.

Anand
SOUTH INDIAN $
(Map p474; 19 CR Ave; dosas ₹80-130, fresh juice ₹70; ⊙11am-10pm, closed Wed) Unbelievably tasty pure-veg dosas are served in this well-kept if stylistically dated family restaurant with octagonal mirror panels and timber strips on the somewhat-low ceiling. It also serves a delicious milky South Indian coffee (₹50) through the day to go with your food of choice.

Amber
INDIAN $$
(Map p474; ☑033-22486520; 11 Waterloo St; mains ₹200-450, beer ₹250; ⊙noon-3pm & 7-11pm) This two-hall middle-class restaurant serves reliable Indian food, though the signature brain curry isn't to everyone's taste. Of the two dining areas, Amber (1st floor) is more family oriented, while Essence (2nd floor) is more dimly lit and predominantly for businesspeople. Menus are essentially the same at both places.

Eau Chew
CHINESE $$
(Map p474; 12 GC Ave; mains ₹180-220; ⊙noon-2.30pm & 6-10pm) This hard-to-find eatery is lodged in a dilapidated building above a petrol station, but city foodies know it as an institution that serves a rare spread of dishes originating from the kitchens of the earliest Chinese settlers in Kolkata. Try the chimney soup, the melt-in-your-mouth roast pork and the signature house noodles, and you'll know what we mean.

Aaheli
BENGALI $$$
(Map p458; ☑033-44003900; 12 JL Nehru Rd, The Peerless Inn; mains from ₹800, meals from ₹1425; ⊙12.30-3pm & 7.30-11pm) Top-notch Bengali cuisine comes to you in traditional brassware amid stylish surroundings at this premium restaurant. The dishes feature authentic flavours from both West Bengal and Bangladesh, and include rare offerings such as *hilsa* (a mackerel-like estuarine fish with a bold flavour) stewed with eggplant and ridge gourd, and mutton cooked the way the bard Rabindranath Tagore reputedly liked it.

REVOLUTIONARY CAFÉ

If you're walking down College St towards Ashutosh Museum of Indian Art from Mahatma Gandhi (MG) Rd, after one block turn left, take the fourth doorway on the left and climb the stairs to the mythic **Indian Coffee House** (1st fl, 15 Bankim Chatterjee St; ⊙9am-9pm Mon-Sat, 9am-12.30pm & 5-9pm Sun). The cheap, dishwater coffee (₹20) can't be recommended, but it's fascinating to look inside this unpretentious high-ceilinged place. It was once a meeting place of freedom fighters in India's pre-Independence era, bohemians during Kolkata's literary, cultural and artistic heydays of the '60s and '70s, as well as revolutionaries owing allegiance to the Naxalite movement of the 1970s.

✖ Southern Kolkata

★6 Ballygunge Place
BENGALI $$
(Map p480; ☑033-24603922; 6 Ballygunge Pl; mains ₹200-300; ⊙noon-3.30pm & 7-10.30pm) Housed in a superbly renovated mid-20th-century mansion, this top-notch restaurant serves some of the best Bengali fare in town. If you're confused about the ingredients, spices and gravies, skip the menu and hit the lunch buffet (vegetarian/non-vegetarian ₹600/700), and you'll be treated to a fantastic sampling of classic and contemporary Bengali cuisine.

★Tamarind
SOUTH INDIAN $$
(Map p480; ☑033-30990434; 177 Sarat Bose Rd; mains ₹280-430; ⊙noon-3.30pm & 7-11pm) This unpretentious restaurant on one of South Kolkata's main thoroughfares serves a melange of traditional and improvised dishes curated from Kerala, Karnataka and Tamil Nadu. Dishes like Coorgi mutton fry, Chettinad chicken, *kottu paratha* (fluffy spicy crumble featuring a *paratha* and eggs) and *appams* (South Indian rice pancake) with mutton stew are unbeatable, probably even by restaurants in South India.

Bhojohori Manna
BENGALI $$
(Map p480; www.bhojohorimanna.com; 18/1 Hindustan Rd; mains ₹80-270, small/large veg thali ₹250/320; ⊙noon-10pm) Each Bhojohori Manna branch in town feels very different, but all feature good-quality Bengali food at sensible prices. The branch on Hindustan Rd

is comparatively spacious, decorated with tribal implements, and the menu allows you to pair a wide selection of fish types with the sauce of your choice. Don't miss the *echorer dalna* (green jackfruit curry) in summer.

★Corner Courtyard
FUSION $$$
(Map p480; ☑9903990597; 92B Sarat Bose Rd; mains ₹350-550, beers/cocktails ₹180/350; ⊙8am-11pm, reduced menu 3-7pm) This reincarnated 1904 mansion has had its walls artistically splattered with doorknobs, locks and old books, complementing its stylish distressed-look decor. The menu is creative and designed to please discerning foodies, from classic Italian dishes such as margherita pizzas and *spaghetti aglio e olio* to Goan chicken curry from India's western shores, and aromatic sambal fish à la Singapore.

🍷 Drinking & Nightlife

Many watering holes in Kolkata remain open until 2am on Friday and Saturday. On other nights, most are half-empty and close by midnight. Many places have a cover fee (charged per couple) that can be recouped in drinks or food to the same value. Women can sometimes enter free but single men (known as stags) are generally kept out.

🍷 Central Kolkata & Chowringhee

OlyPub
BAR
(Map p458; 21 Park St; beers from ₹190; ⊙noon-11pm) This grungy yet oddly convivial watering hole is a low-key Kolkata classic. The upper-floor bar has comfortable sofa seating, although the downstairs lounge with rickety chairs and boisterous drinkers is more atmospheric. Promotional offers on select booze brands are often available. Chateaubriand-style steaks (₹225) are served by the dozens every evening. The loos are stinky, though – we warned you.

Big Ben
PUB
(Map p466; Kenilworth Hotel, Little Russel St; beers ₹250; ⊙noon-11pm) An upscale pub with a 'Britain' theme, this cosy watering hole features a good selection of beers and has live sports on TV. It's a fairly casual setting, but avoid wearing shorts or flip-flops.

Flury's
CAFE
(Map p458; Park St; coffee/tea from ₹160; ⊙7.30am-10pm) Dating back to 1927, Flury's is an enticing art deco palace that's a real

Kolkata institution. The best time to drop by is during breakfast (English breakfast platter ₹670), or in the evenings when you can just drink coffee and eat slices of gooey Sacher-Torte (cake from ₹80). It's surely the only major iconic world cafe to cite beans on toast as a heritage speciality.

Phoenix LOUNGE
(Map p466; Astor Hotel, 15 Shakespeare Sarani; 1.5L beer tower ₹835; ☺5pm-midnight) This stylish yet unthreateningly casual bar is most appealing on Thursday evenings when young local musicians perform jazz, blues and progressive sets (from 9pm). It's also one of the city's few nightlife spots to stock a decent range of sparkling wines. A 'smart casual' dress code applies to all guests.

Aqua LOUNGE
(Map p458; ☑033-22499000; Park Hotel, Park St; cocktails ₹400; ☺7pm-midnight, to 2am weekends) This luxurious yet laid-back open-air lounge allows you to nurse your booze while soothing your eyes on the dreamy waters of the neon-lit central pool. Dress for the evening to be allowed entry (no shorts or flip-flops).

☺ BBD Bagh

Broadway Bar BAR
(Map p474; Broadway Hotel, 27A GC Ave; beers ₹200; ☺noon-10.30pm) Back-street Paris? Chicago in the 1930s? Prague circa 1980s? This cavernous, unpretentious old-men's pub defies easy parallels, but has a compulsive left-bank fascination with cheap booze, heavy ceiling fans, bare walls, marble floors and, thankfully, no music.

☺ Southern Kolkata

Irish House PUB
(Map p480; Quest Mall, Syed Amir Ali Ave; beers from ₹285, cocktails from ₹375; ☺noon-11.30pm) While not really Irish at all, this is as close as Kolkata gets to a fully fledged nonhotel pub-sports bar. There's lots of weekend ambience and a showman holding the fort at the well-stocked bar.

Bikers' Cafe SPORTS BAR
(Map p466; ☑9831151483; 1st fl, 31 Elgin Rd; beers ₹250; ☺7.30am-11pm) A gold-plated low-rider motorbike in the window, helmet lampshades and a Clapton and Led Zep soundtrack set the tone in this youthful pub-diner. Mains include burgers, sandwiches, pizzas, steaks and

sizzlers. There's chilled beer in the fridge and cocktails with names like Harley, Triumph and Enfield. The place opens early for breakfast (platters ₹180–₹230).

Smoke Shack ROOFTOP BAR
(Map p480; Hotel Park Plaza, Dover Pl; cocktails/shots ₹600/500; ☺4-11.30pm) Fancy to the hilt, this open-air terrace bar attracts stylish people and serves a good selection of mojitos and cocktails through the evening. There are tasty kebabs and other assorted finger food to go with your drinks.

Mrs Magpie CAFE
(Map p480; 570 Lake Tce; coffee ₹70-130, snacks ₹100-200; ☺9am-10pm) Cosy, cheerfully lit and adorned with pretty wallpapers, this popular cafe serves cheap and tasty cupcakes (from ₹50) in a wide range of flavours, best paired with fresh espresso. It also serves breakfast platters and afternoon-tea sets.

Dolly's Tea Shop TEAHOUSE
(Map p480; G62 Dakshinapan Shopping Centre; teas ₹100, mocktails ₹100-120; ☺11am-7pm) For sampling authentic Darjeeling teas as well as refreshing mocktails featuring the brew, visit this popular teahouse run by a veteran tea taster. Try the orange–mint julep tea or the lemon-barley tea, with a grilled bacon sandwich on the side.

Hola BAR
(Map p480; Sarat Banerjee Rd; beers/cocktails from ₹325/375; ☺noon-11.30pm) A new gathering spot for South Kolkata's hipster crowd, Hola's main draw is its live-music evenings, which take place several times every month and feature the city's established and upcoming indie bands. The atmosphere is laid-back and cheerful, and there's a good selection of booze at the bar. Occasional food festivals and events are also held.

☆ Entertainment

Kolkata has a smattering of cinemas, performance venues, cultural centres, stadiums, live-music spots and even a colonial-era racecourse. Check the *Telegraph* newspaper's Metro section and various listings brochures. Live music can be sampled in a few garrulous bars in the Esplanade and BBD Bagh area. Those along Waterloo St and Lenin Sarani are popular among the area's office workers.

Jamsteady (www.jamsteady.in) organises the most happening indie concerts and gigs

ARCHITECTURE ACTIVISM

Kolkata is a glorious repository of innumerable architectural beauties, ranging in styles from colonial and art deco to Indo-Saracenic and Gothic, and varying in stature from modest family homes to stately public buildings. However, with several decades (or even centuries) behind them, not all structures have weathered gracefully. Save a handful of the city's splendid facades that have been restored with great precision and care, numerous old buildings across the city now stand in various degrees of disrepair, even as escalating property prices see many of them being razed to make space for modern structures.

Of late, however, a few citizen initiatives have called for the preservation of Kolkata's old houses. In 2015 author Amit Chaudhuri began to raise awareness about Kolkata's architectural legacy and rally for their conservation. A few individuals have gone a step further, by actually investing in old buildings to save them from demolition, then turning them around as successful commercial operations. Calcutta Bungalow (p469) and Sienna Store & Cafe (p479) are two such restorative initiatives that have breathed fresh life into the city's old buildings.

in Kolkata's blues, hip-hop, electronic and funk circuits.

Someplace Else
LIVE MUSIC

(Map p458; Park Hotel, Park St) This nightclub has been steadily promoting live music in Kolkata since the mid-1990s. Acts perform nightly, although you'll have to be lucky to catch some original music. Most are cover bands who belt out regulation rock and blues hits. The ambience is laid-back, and the crowd gets rather raucous on weekends.

Seagull Arts & Media Resource Centre
ARTS CENTRE

(Map p480; ☑ 033-24556942; www.seagullindia. com; Rupchand Mukherjee Lane; ☉ 11am-8pm) Owned by the same management that operates Seagull Bookstore (p479), this acclaimed institution regularly organises art and media exhibitions, film screenings, workshops, panel discussions and a host of other activities, with themes ranging from sociology and philosophy to religion and politics. Most events are free; check the website for details.

ICCR
CULTURAL PROGRAM

(Rabindranath Tagore Centre; Map p466; ☑ 033-22822895; www.tagorecentreiccr.org; 9A Ho Chi Minh Sarani) This state-run cultural melting pot is a large, multilevel operation that regularly hosts exhibitions, dance shows, recitals and lectures in its many galleries and auditoriums. The programs are often free, and snacks (also free!) are usually offered to guests on inauguration days.

GD Birla Sabaghar
PERFORMING ARTS

(Map p480; www.gdbirlasabhagar.com; Queens Park Rd) This state-of-the-art auditorium and performance venue is located within the Birla Mandir (p464) complex, although access is from a side road. It hosts a number of interesting plays, performances, musical concerts and cultural evenings throughout the year. Check the website for details on upcoming programs.

Nandan Complex
CULTURAL PROGRAM

(Map p466; 1/1 AJC Bose Rd) This complex is made up of the auditoriums and theatre halls at Rabindra Sadan, Sisir Mancha and the central Nandan Cinema. Apart from sundry cultural programs through the year, the complex also hosts the popular Kolkata International Film Festival (p464). Tourist information offices and pamphlets give extensive listings of events here.

Maidan Racecourse
SPECTATOR SPORTS

(Royal Calcutta Turf Club; ☑ 033-22312037; www. rctconline.com; AJC Bose Rd; bets from ₹10) The Victoria Memorial provides a magical backdrop to this colonial-era racecourse, from whose 19th-century grandstands you can watch some of India's best horse racing at over 40 annual meets. The New Year Derby is particularly popular, and provides plenty of colourful photo ops featuring horses, jockeys and spectators in flamboyant dresses and hats.

Eden Gardens
SPECTATOR SPORTS

(Ranji Stadium; Map p474; Eden Gardens) The vast Eden Gardens hosts international cricket matches, and is the home ground of the Kolkata Knight Riders IPL team. Until some years ago, when a renovation cut its seating by half, it was billed as the world's largest cricket stadium with an audience capacity of nearly 120,000. Few enthusiasts, however, know the arena by its real name, Ranji Stadium.

🛍 Shopping

★**Byloom** CLOTHING
(Map p480; www.byloom.co.in; 58B Hindusthan Park; ⊙11am-8pm) Some of Kolkata's most exquisite handmade saris are sold at this speciality boutique. There's also a fair smattering of semiprecious jewellery, and an impressive collection of shawls and scarves. Look for pieces that feature the intricate *kantha* embroidery style, or the *khesh* method of weaving employing strips of cloth. A cafe on-site dishes up tasty bites (snacks ₹100).

★**Dakshinapan Shopping Centre** SHOPPING CENTRE
(Map p480; Gariahat Rd; ⊙11am-7pm Mon-Sat) It's worth facing the soul-crushing 1970s architecture for Dakshinapan's wide range of government emporia, which brings together a mind-boggling artisanal diversity from across India under one roof. There's plenty of tack, but many shops offer excellent-value souvenirs, crafts and fabrics. Prices are usually fixed, but buying at an emporium means that authenticity and quality are never called into question.

Sienna Store & Cafe GIFTS & SOUVENIRS
(Map p480; ☎033-40002828; 49/1 Hindustan Park; ⊙11.30am-10pm) Very hipster, very chic, yet unbelievably affordable. Housed in a tastefully renovated mansion, this boutique specialises in a delightful collection of wearables, souvenirs, lifestyle products and tiny bits and bobs that double as great gifts. There's a cosy, buzzy cafe to the rear, which makes light and delicious organic sandwiches, juices, pasta and salads (dishes ₹250).

Dolly's Tea Shop TEA
(Map p480; G62 Dakshinapan Shopping Centre, Gariahat Rd; ⊙11am-7pm Mon-Sat) This tiny tea boutique is one of the best places in Kolkata to pick up some delectable Darjeeling leaves. Dolly, a veteran tea taster who owns the place, is often around to help you with your purchase. The more premium varieties of tea can cost you upward of ₹1000 for a mere 100g! An attached cafe (p477) sells refreshments (tea ₹100).

Weaver's Studio CLOTHING
(Map p480; ☎9831159080; www.weaversstudio.in; 5/1 Ballygunge Pl; ⊙10am-6pm Mon-Sat) Gorgeous handmade textiles and traditional fabrics vie for your attention at this upmarket boutique, run by an organisation that works with artisanal communities. Choose from a plethora of styles, such as exquisite hand-block prints, appliqués, tribal designs, batik and embroidery, and expect to pay a premium price for your unique and indulgent purchase.

Chamba Lama JEWELLRY
(Map p458; New Market; ⊙11am-8pm Mon-Sat) This long-running establishment owned by a Tibetan family is reputed for its collection of intricate silver jewellery and curios, most of them embellished with Tibetan Buddhist motifs. It's a good place to shop for semiprecious stones as well. Discounts are usually offered for sales above a few thousand rupees.

Oxford Bookstore BOOKS
(Map p458; ☎033-22297662; www.oxfordbookstore.com; 17 Park St; ⊙11am-8pm) This is an excellent full-range bookshop that sells a variety of titles, including an impressive catalogue of coffee-table books on India. It stocks Lonely Planet guides and the indispensable *Calcutta Walks Tourist Map* (₹100). Valuable additions come in the form of a stationery section, a DVD section, and a cafe where you can sit and browse titles.

Central Cottage Industries ARTS & CRAFTS
(Map p474; Metropolitan Bldg, Chowringhee Rd; ⊙10am-6pm Mon-Sat) An impressive array of traditional arts and tribal crafts are on sale at this well-stocked government emporium. Service is a bit impersonal and prices can be steeper than some street establishments, but you can rest assured that you're only buying genuine and well-curated merchandise here. There are separate sections for textiles, artefacts, metalwork, woodwork and handmade paper, among others.

Mondal & Sons MUSICAL INSTRUMENTS
(Map p474; ☎9804854213; 8 Rabindra Sarani; ⊙10am-6pm Mon-Fri, to 2pm Sat) For sitars (from ₹5000) or violins (from ₹3000), visit Mondal & Sons, a family-run musical establishment dating to the 1850s. Do not be misled by the modest appearance of the store: the Mondals count Yehudi Menuhin among their satisfied customers.

Seagull Bookstore BOOKS
(Map p480; ☎033-24765869; www.seagullbooks.org; 31A SP Mukherjee Rd; ⊙10.30am-7.30pm) Seagull is a special-interest bookshop with

South Kolkata

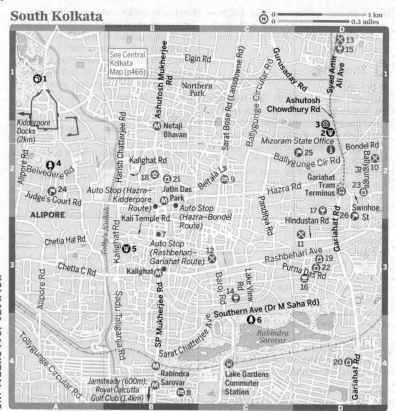

a focus on academia, art, media, humanities, regional politics and social sciences. It also publishes a select catalogue of fiction, nonfiction and coffee-table books by reputed authors and artists.

ℹ️ Information

DANGERS & ANNOYANCES

Kolkata feels remarkably unthreatening, and is usually safe (though stray incidents involving tourists can and do occur).

➡ Predictable beggar-hassle is a minor irritant around Sudder St and Park St areas.

➡ Bandhs occasionally stop all land transport, including suburban trains and taxis to the airport.

➡ Monsoon-season waterlogging can be severe.

INTERNET ACCESS

Inexpensive and widespread 4G/LTE cellular services have slowly begun to phase out internet cafes. Around Sudder St, some back-alley cubbyhole places charge for internet access (per hour ₹20), but it's worth paying a little more for fast connections and more comfortable seating at the travel agency with internet cafe, **R-Internet Travels** (Map p458; Tottee Lane; ⏰9am-10pm).

MEDICAL SERVICES

Medical contacts (including pharmacists, doctors, hospitals and clinics) are widely listed on the popular web portal www.justdial.com/kolkata.

Apollo Gleneagles (📞033-23202122, emergency 033-60601066; www.apollogleneagles.in; off EM Bypass; ⏰24hr) One of Kolkata's top hospitals with round-the-clock emergency service and state-of-the-art diagnostic and treatment facilities.

Belle Vue Clinic (Map p466; 📞9163058000; www.bellevueclinic.com; Dr UN Brahmachari (Loudon) St, Minto Park) A reputable hospital for all kinds of ailments and illnesses, including emergency and critical care.

Eastern Diagnostics (Map p458; 📞033-22178080; www.easterndiagnostics.com; 13C Mirza Ghalib St; ⏰9am-2pm Mon-Sat) A well-known polyclinic for doctors' consultations, with a top-notch diagnostic centre for medical tests.

South Kolkata

◎ Sights
1 Alipore Zoo	A1
2 Birla Mandir	D2
3 CIMA	D2
4 Horticultural Gardens	A2
5 Kalighat Temple	B3
Nirmal Hriday	(see 5)
6 Rabindra Sarovar	C4

◎ Activities, Courses & Tours
7 Help Tourism	B3

🛏 Sleeping
8 Bodhi Tree	B4
9 Corner Courtyard	C2

🍴 Eating
10 6 Ballygunge Place	D2
11 Bhojohori Manna	D3
Corner Courtyard	(see 9)
12 Tamarind	C3
13 Yauatcha	D1

◎ Drinking & Nightlife
Dolly's Tea Shop	(see 20)

14 Hola	C3
15 Irish House	D1
16 Mrs Magpie	D3
17 Smoke Shack	D2

◎ Entertainment
GD Birla Sabaghar	(see 2)
18 Seagull Arts & Media Resource Centre	B2

🛍 Shopping
19 Byloom	D3
20 Dakshinapan Shopping Centre	D4
Dolly's Tea Shop	(see 20)
21 Seagull Bookstore	B2
22 Sienna Store & Cafe	D3
23 Weaver's Studio	D2

❶ Information
24 German Consulate	A2
25 Myanmar Consulate	D2
26 Thai Consulate	D2

MONEY

You won't have to walk far to find ATMs that accept Visa, MasterCard, Cirrus and Maestro cards. International credit cards are widely accepted at stores.

Money Changers

Many private money changers around Sudder St offer commission-free exchange rates that are significantly better than banks. Some will exchange travellers cheques. Shop around and double-check the maths. In the city centre, **Mishra Forex** (Map p466; 11 Shakespeare Sarani; ⊙10am-8pm Mon-Sat, to 4pm Sun) gives reasonable rates and opens daily.

Airport money changers give predictably poor rates and charge up to 5% in commission. There's an ATM in the arrival lounge (booth 22) between exit gates 3B and 4A, and one in the domestic departure lounge (freely accessible from international departures).

POST

CR Ave Post Office (Map p474; CR Ave; ⊙10am-6pm Mon-Sat, to 2pm Sun) Handy for the Chandni Chowk area, and has snail mail, speed post and parcel facilities.

General Post Office (Map p474; 7 Koilaghat St; ⊙7.30am-8.30pm Mon-Sat, 10am-4pm Sun, parcel service 10am-2.30pm, philatelic office 10am-6pm Mon-Fri) The philatelic bureau sells commemorative issues, or can turn your own photos into a sheet of ₹5 stamps (₹300), which can take up to seven days to be ready.

Shakespeare Sarani Post Office (Map p466; Shakespeare Sarani; ⊙10am-6pm Mon-Fri, to 2pm Sat) Minor but helpful, and conveniently located central post office, with general and speed post services.

TELEPHONE

Sudder St agency-shops will readily sell you a SIM card (₹200) once they have a copy of your ID, a passport photo and details of your address/hotel. SIMs are available in micro and nano versions for use with smartphones, but make sure your handset is unlocked. Local/national calls can be made and text messages sent for only a few rupees, while 4G monthly data packs start from around ₹50 per GB.

TOURIST INFORMATION

India Tourism (Map p466; ☏033-22821475; www.incredibleindia.org; 4 Shakespeare Sarani; ⊙10am-6pm Mon-Fri, to 1pm Sat) This office hands out free maps of greater Kolkata, with major sights and stops marked, and also has useful information about travelling to other parts of India.

West Bengal Tourism (Map p474; ☏033-22488271; www.wbtourismgov.in; 3/2 BBD Bagh; ⊙10.30am-1.30pm & 2-5.30pm Mon-Fri, 10.30am-1pm Sat) The office primarily sells its own tours (last sales 4.30pm), and has good free city maps. Its website is useful for local travel information, as well as booking state-operated hotels and lodges across the state.

❶ Getting There & Away

AIR

Rebuilt in 2013, the glassy **Netaji Subhash Chandra Bose International Airport** (NSCBIA (CCU); www.calcuttaairport.com) has an impressive terminal building, although services can get strangely bottlenecked at times, especially in the departure areas. If you're flying out, arrive with ample time and expect long queues at passport control and security check.

Kolkata has a vast selection of domestic connections from early morning to late night. Direct flights run from Kolkata to most regional hubs around India. Sample fares include ₹4400 to Delhi, ₹4600 to Chennai and ₹4850 to Mumbai. It's also a useful hub for regional flights linking Bangladesh (**Air India** (Map p474; ☑ 033-22110730; www.airindia.in; 39 CR Ave; ☉10am-4pm Mon-Sat), Biman, **Jet Airways** (Map p458; ☑ 033-39893333; www. jetairways.com; Park St; ☉10am-7pm Mon-Sat), SpiceJet and Regent Airways), Bhutan (Bhutan Airlines and Druk Air), Myanmar (Air India) and Nepal (Air India). East Asian destinations include Bangkok (Air Asia, IndiGo, Jet Airways, SpiceJet and Thai), Hong Kong (Dragonair), Kuala Lumpur (Air Asia), Kunming (China Eastern Airlines) and Singapore (SilkAir). For long-haul connections to Europe and the USA, there are daily flights via Doha (Qatar Airways) and Dubai (Emirates).

Several international airlines have offices with booking counters in the city.

Air Asia (Map p466; ☑ 033-46004800; www.airasia.com; 46C Chowringhee Rd; ☉10am-8pm Mon-Sat)

Drukair (Map p466; ☑ 033-22805376; www. drukair.com.bt; 1A Ballygunge Circular Rd, 51 Tivoli Crt; ☉10am-5pm Mon-Sat)

Emirates (☑ 9167003333; www.emirates.com; Trinity Tower, 83 Topsia Rd; ☉9.30am-6pm Mon-Sat)

Qatar Airways (☑ 033-40256000; www. qatarairways.com; 31 Topsia Rd, Arcadia Centre; ☉9.30am-5.30pm Mon-Fri)

Thai Airways (Map p466; ☑ 033-22838865; www.thaiairways.com; 229 AJC Bose Rd, 8 fl, Crescent Towers)

BOAT

Shipping Corporation of India (Map p474; ☑ 033-22543427, 033-22543415; www. shipindia.com; Strand Rd; ☉10am-1pm & 2-4pm Mon-Fri) has five ships that depart on scheduled monthly dates to Port Blair (Andaman Islands). The vessels sail from Kidderpore Docks, accessed via Gate 3 opposite Kidderpore commuter train station. Tickets (bunk/cabin/deluxe ₹2776/7101/10,766) go on sale around 10 days prior to the voyage from the 1st floor of the corporation's office.

BUS
Domestic

For Darjeeling or Sikkim, start by taking a bus to Siliguri (12 to 14 hours). These coaches drive overnight departing **Esplanade bus station** (Map p458; Esplanade) between 5pm and 8pm (seat/sleeper from ₹550/650, with AC ₹1200/1400). An NBSTC bus for Cooch Behar leaves at 8pm (₹520, 18 hours).

Buses to Bihar and Odisha (Strand Rd) line up along the road running parallel to the riverbank south of Eden Gardens commuter train station. Most run overnight, departing between 5pm and 8.30pm. Arrive very early if you have baggage. Destinations:

Bhubaneswar Fan/AC ₹400/450, 10 hours

Gaya Seat/sleeper ₹300/450, 13 hours

Puri Seat/sleeper ₹420/480, 12 hours

Ranchi Seat/sleeper from ₹250/350, 10 hours

International

Bangladesh Buses advertised to Bangladesh actually run to Benapol (international checkpost), where you walk across and board another vehicle operated by the same company on to Dhaka.

Shohagh Paribahan (Map p458; ☑ 033-22520757, 033-22520696; 23 Marquis St; ☉6am-10.30pm) has five morning 'Dhaka' services (non-AC/AC ₹900/1550, 14 hours).

Green Line (Map p458; ☑ 7044090042, 7044090041; www.greenlineservices.in; 12 Marquis St; ☉10am-8pm) has three AC buses to Benapol (₹400), all leaving by 7am. Connecting tickets to Dhaka cost Tk1200 (about ₹1000).

Bhutan A Bhutan government-operated bus to Phuentsholing (₹600, 15 hours) leaves at 7pm daily, except Sunday, from the walled northeast yard of Esplanade bus station where there are two special **ticket booths** (Map p474; Esplanade bus station; ☉9.30am-1pm & 2-6pm Mon-Sat). It's faster and more comfortable, however, to take the 13149 Kanchankanya Express (sleeper/3AC/2AC ₹370/1010/1455, 8.30pm, 14 hours) from Sealdah train station to Hasimara, and then travel the last 18km by local bus or taxi to Phuentsholing. Note that you may have to camp a night at this border town for your Bhutanese visa to be processed.

TRAIN
Stations

Long-distance trains depart Kolkata from three major stations. Gigantic Howrah (hao-rah; HWH) has the most connections and is across the river, often best reached by ferry. Sealdah (shey-al-dah; SDAH) is at the eastern end of MG Road. The eponymous Kolkata (or Chitpore; KOAA) is around 5km further north (near Belgachia metro station); it's the newest of the three terminals and has fewer connections compared to the other two stations.

Tickets

To buy long-distance train tickets with 'tourist quota', foreigners should use the **Eastern Railways' International Tourist Bureau** (Map p474; ☑ 033-22224206; 6 Fairlie Pl; ☺10am-4pm Mon-Sat, to 2pm Sun). Bring your passport, as well as a book to read as waits can be very long. On arrival, take and fill in a booking form (forms are numbered and double as queuing chits). Lines form well before opening.

If you're travelling as a group, just one of you can be present, as long as you have everyone else's passports. Note that it's sometimes quicker to use the nearby standard **computerised train booking office** (Map p474; Koilaghat St; ☺8am-8pm Mon-Sat, to 2pm Sun), although that has no tourist quota.

For Dhaka in Bangladesh, the 13108/13109 Maitree Express (AC chair/1AC ₹756/1259, eight hours) departs Kolkata (Chitpore) train station at 7.10am every Monday, Tuesday, Friday and Saturday, returning from Dhaka Cantt at 8.15am Sunday, Wednesday, Friday and Saturday. If you possess a Bangladeshi visa of the rubber-stamped variety (usually the norm at the Bangladesh Deputy High Commission), make sure it clearly mentions entry/exit by train. Buy tickets up to 10 days ahead.

❶ Getting Around

Tickets for buses, trams and the metro on most city transport routes cost ₹5 to ₹20. Men shouldn't sit in clearly assigned 'Ladies' seats.

Note that between 1pm and 9pm, much of the city's one-way road system reverses direction, so bus routes switch and taxis hailed on one-way thoroughfares may be reluctant to make journeys in the other direction.

TO/FROM THE AIRPORT

NSCBI Airport is around 16km northeast of central Kolkata. A dedicated feeder road accesses the new combined terminal from the south (VIP Rd) via Airport Gate 1. Integrated within the arrival lounge of the terminal are several public-transport options into the city, including a **computerised railway reservation centre**

MAJOR TRAINS FROM KOLKATA

DESTINATION	TRAIN NO & NAME	FARE (₹)*	DURATION (HR)	DEPARTURE
Bhubaneswar	18409 Sri Jagannath Exp	260/700/1000	8	7pm (HWH)
Chennai	12841 Coromandel	665/1750/2550	26½	2.50pm (HWH)
	12839 Chennai Mail	665/1750/2550	28	11.45pm (HWH)
Delhi	12303/12381 Poorva	605/1605/2325	22	8am (HWH)
	12313 SDAH Rajdhani	3AC/2AC 2115/2925	17½	4.50pm (SDAH)
Gorakhpur	15047/15049/15051 Purvanchal/KOAA-GKP	430/1170/1690	17¼-19	2.30pm (KOAA)
Guwahati	12345 Saraighat	500/1320/1895	17¾	3.50pm (HWH)
	13173/13175 Kanchanjunga	265/455/1240	21¾	6.35am (SDAH)
Hooghly	Bandel Local	unreserved 10	50min	several hourly (HWH)
Lucknow	13151 Jammu Tawi	470/1275/1850	25	11.45am (KOAA)
	12327/12369 Upasana/Kumbha	505/1340/1920	18¼	1pm (HWH)
Mumbai CST	12810 Mumbai Mail	740/1955/2855	33½	8pm (HWH)
New Jalpaiguri	12343 Darjeeling Mail	350/920/1300	10	10.05pm (SDAH)
	12377 Padatik	350/920/1300	10¼	11.20pm (SDAH)
Patna	13005 Amritsar Mail	310/845/1210	8½	7.10pm (HWH)
	12333 Vibhuti	340/890/1255	8	8pm (HWH)
Puri	18409 Sri Jagannath	300/815/1165	10	7pm (HWH)
	12837 Howrah-Puri	330/860/1215	8¾	10.35pm (HWH)
Varanasi	13005 Amritsar Mail	385/1060/1530	14	7.10pm (HWH)

HWH = ex-Howrah, SDAH = ex-Sealdah, KOAA = ex-Chitpur
* sleeper/3AC/2AC unless otherwise stated

(booth 25, NSCBI Airport; ◷8am-noon, 12.30-5pm & 5.30-8pm Mon-Sat) for trains out of the city.

AC Bus

Volvo airport buses start from a stand that's a minute's walk from Arrivals Gate 1B. Pay on-board. The punctual **AC-39** (NSCBI Airport; ◷24hr) departs hourly for the Esplanade bus station (₹80, one hour) before terminating at Howrah train station (₹100, 1½ hours). Night services depart on the hour between 11pm and 4am.

Taxi

Fixed-price yellow taxis cost ₹350/400 to Sudder St/Howrah train station, taking around one hour when traffic is kind. Prepay at booth 12 or 13 in the arrivals lounge between exits 3B and 4A. App-based Uber and Ola cabs depart from numbered taxi points across the driveway from Gate 1B.

AUTORICKSHAW

Tuk-tuk-style autorickshaws (autos) operate as fixed-route hop-on share taxis with three passengers in the back and one (sometimes two!) beside the driver. Fares are typically ₹7 to ₹10, depending on distance.

Key routes:

Hazra–Bondel (Map p480; Hazra Rd) Runs along Hazra Rd, starting a block east of Jatin Das Park metro station, and goes to Ballygunge.

Hazra–Kiddepore (Map p480; Hazra Rd) Goes west from Jatin Das Park metro station, past the Kalighat idol-makers and on through Alipore.

Loha Pool–Dharamtala (Map p458; Elliot Rd) Starts from Park Circus using Park St (or after 1pm looping via Nasreddin and Karaya roads), goes up AJC Bose Rd (near Mother Teresa's Motherhouse), then along Elliot Rd/Royd St and finally up Mirza Ghalib St/RAK Rd (mornings/afternoons) near Sudder St. Loop reverses after 1pm.

Rashbehari–Gariahat (Map p480; Rashbehari Ave) This is the midsegment of a longer route, and connects the Kalighat metro station to the shopping district of Gariahat along Rashbehari Ave.

BUS & TRAM

Buses in Kolkata come in different forms. The best are a limited fleet of shiny AC buses, but the standard quickly tumbles down to their non-AC variants (which are far greater in number) and crowded red-and-yellow minibuses, mostly run by manic drivers and motormouth conductors. A large selection of minibuses start from the **minibus stand** (Map p474) on the eastern side of BBD Bagh, including a service to Airport Gate 1 via Dum Dum.

Dinky but photogenic trams follow more predictable routes along select city tracks, and are immune to one-way traffic.

FERRY

Crossing the Hooghly River is generally faster and more agreeable by boat than by using the clogged road bridges, especially during rush hour. **River ferries** (tickets ₹5-10; ◷8am-8pm) depart every 10 to 15 minutes from Howrah to jetties in central Kolkata. Convenient dropoff points include:

Chandpal (Strand Rd) For Babughat
Fairlie Ghat 1 and **Fairlie Ghat 2** For BBD Bagh
Bagbazar (Strand Bank Rd) For Kumartuli
Belur For Belur Math and Dakshineswar

METRO

Kolkata's busy and crowded **metro** (www.kmrc. in; tickets ₹5-20; ◷6.45am-9.55pm Mon-Sat, 9.50am-9.55pm Sun) has trains every five to 12 minutes (fewer on Sundays). For Sudder St, use Esplanade or Park St. Some trains are air-con, although you pay the same fare for fan-cooled carriages.

Only one line (running in a north–south direction) is operational so far, but several extensions are planned. Line 2 linking Howrah to Sealdah and Salt Lake, and line 3 linking Esplanade to the southwestern borough of Joka, are due by 2020–21.

Theoretically you may not carry bags over 10kg. If you're staying in the city for a while, consider buying a multiride ticket to save yourself the hassle of queuing every time you ride the service.

TAXI

Kolkata's yellow Ambassador cabs charge ₹25 for up to 2km, and ₹12 per kilometre thereafter. Meters are digital and show the exact fare due. A few air-con taxis (white Suzuki D-Zire cars with a blue stripe) also use the same fare meters, with a 25% air-con surcharge on the displayed fare. Taxis are generally easy to flag down, except during the 5pm to 7pm rush hour and after 10pm when some cabs refuse to use the meter. There is a **prepaid taxi booth** (Map p474; Howrah train station; ◷5am-1am) at Howrah train station, and also at Sealdah train station and the airport.

Clean and cool Uber and Ola cabs currently abound in Kolkata, and can be accessed by updated versions of the apps on your smartphone. The minimum fare is around ₹70. Surge fares during peak hours can be many times the fare of a regular yellow taxi.

West Bengal

Best Places to Eat

➡ Glenary's (p504)

➡ Rustic Flavours (p492)

➡ Chai Country (p498)

➡ Windamere Hotel (p504)

➡ Amber (p495)

Best Places to Stay

➡ Dekeling Resort at Hawk's Nest (p503)

➡ Holumba Haven (p513)

➡ Mitali Homestay (p491)

➡ Glenburn (p503)

➡ Dekeling Hotel (p504)

➡ Windamere Hotel (p504)

Why Go?

A sliver of fertile and densely populated land running from the tea-draped Himalayan foothills to the steamy mangroves of the Bay of Bengal, West Bengal presents a remarkable range of destinations and experiences within a single state. In the tropical southern areas, the wildlife-rich, mangrove-lined waterways of the Sundarbans vie for attention with Bishnupur's ornate terracotta Hindu temples and the cultured, arty vibes of Shantiniketan. Upstream from Kolkata (Calcutta) on the Hooghly River (a branch of the Ganges) you'll reach old European trading towns and three former Bengali capitals at Murshidabad, Gaur and Pandua. The cool northern hills are home not just to quaint British-era hill stations like bustling Darjeeling and more laid-back Kalimpong, but also to fantastic vistas of massive Khangchendzonga, rolling green tea estates, some great hiking and the huffing and puffing 'toy trains' of the almost 140-year-old Darjeeling Himalayan Railway.

When to Go
Darjeeling

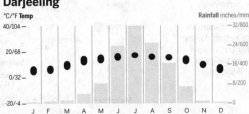

Apr–May & Oct–Nov Best for hill views, trekking and spring blooms up north, but high season in October.

Oct–Mar Dry and relatively cool, the most pleasant time for exploring the lower southern plains.

Dec–Feb Ideal for navigating the dense mangrove forests of the Sundarbans.

West Bengal Highlights

❶ Singalila Ridge Treks
(p508) Gazing at incredible mountain panoramas between ridgetop lodges in a spectacular national park.

❷ Darjeeling
(p498) Visiting a tea estate, sipping a delicate local brew and enjoying fantastic mountain views from this historic hill station.

❸ Shantiniketan
(p490) Soaking up the cultural and arty ambience of this university town amid tranquil rural surroundings.

❹ Toy train (p507) Riding the tiny colonial-era steam-driven train as it puffs and pants its way in and out of Darjeeling.

❺ Bishnupur
(p489) Admiring intricate scenes from the Hindu epics carved on the many medieval terracotta temples.

❻ Sundarbans
(p487) Cruising the waterways of the world's most extensive mangrove forest, to spot darting kingfishers, spotted deer and the elusive Royal Bengal tiger.

History

Historically the name Bengal embraces today's West Bengal, Bangladesh, Tripura and southern Assam's Barak Valley. Referred to as Bongo in the Mahabharata (Great Hindu Vedic epic poem of the Bharata dynasty), Bengal was part of the Mauryan empire in the 3rd century BC, and was later controlled by, among others, the Guptas, the Buddhist Pala empire, Hindu Sena dynasty and the Muslim Delhi Sultanate, these last three all governing from Gaur. Delhi's governors established independence as the Bengal Sultanate in the 14th century, ruling from Pandua, then Gaur. The Mughals invaded in the mid-16th century, and Bengal became one of the richest provinces in their empire, a centre for silk, muslin, pearl, cotton and ships, with its capital at Dhaka, then from 1704 at Murshidabad. Following the death of Aurangzeb in 1707, Bengal became an independent Islamic state under its nawabs.

The British East India Company established a trading post at Calcutta in 1690, which quickly prospered and outshone earlier-established European outposts along the Hooghly River belonging to the Portuguese, Dutch and French. Annoyed by rapid British expansion, Nawab Siraj-ud-daula marched out of Murshidabad and easily took Calcutta in 1756. Robert Clive defeated him the following year at the Battle of Plassey (Palashi), helped by the treachery of Siraj-ud-daula's uncle, Mir Jafar, a commander in the nawab's army. Jafar succeeded his nephew as nawab, but after the Battle of Buxar in 1764 the British took full control of Bengal.

West Bengal was the economic and cultural hub of the British Raj (and Calcutta was its political capital until the British shifted office to Delhi in 1931). It was also the cradle of the 19th/early 20th-century Indian Renaissance and the national freedom movement, and has long been considered India's cultural and intellectual heartland. In 1947 Independence and the Partition of India saw Bengal divided into Hindu-predominant West Bengal (which remained part of India) and Muslim-oriented East Pakistan (now independent Bangladesh), causing the upheaval and migration of millions of Bengalis.

THE GANGES DELTA

Entering West Bengal from the west, the River Ganges splits into the world's biggest delta, myriad smaller (though by no means small) streams that make their way across southern West Bengal or neighbouring Bangladesh into the Bay of Bengal. This heavily populated region of vast alluvial floodplains promises a variety of intriguing experiences well off the common tourist grid: grand palaces, mosques and temples of historic Bengali cultural hubs and capitals; centres of modern artistic excellence; vestiges of European colonial outposts; even some striped Bengal tigers lurking in dense estuarine forests.

ℹ Getting There & Away

Suburban and express trains from Kolkata's Howrah and Sealdah train stations provide access to almost all destinations across the Gangetic Delta. If getting a reservation is problematic, you can almost always just buy an unreserved general 2nd-class ticket at the station and hop on board – the carriages may be crowded but most journeys are a few hours maximum. There are also buses departing in every direction from the Esplanade bus stand in Kolkata.

Sundarbans Tiger Reserve

Home to around 100 Royal Bengal tigers, the 2585-sq-km **Sundarbans Tiger Reserve** (per day Indian ₹50-150, foreigner ₹100-300, boat admission with AC ₹1600- 3500, without AC ₹500-800, guide Indian group ₹600-900, foreign group ₹900-1200) is India's share of the world's largest mangrove forest – a network of channels and semisubmerged mangroves straddling the India–Bangladesh border at the mouth of the Ganges Delta (Bangladesh has the larger share). Parts of this strange, even unearthly, land- and water-scape in both countries are Unesco World Heritage Sites. Tigers lurk in the impenetrable depths of the mangrove forests, and also swim the delta's innumerable channels. Although they do sometimes attack villagers and prey on livestock, tigers are typically shy and sightings are rare. Nevertheless, cruising the waterways of the Sundarbans (also spelt Sunderbans) between the mangrove forests and spotting wildlife, whether it be Gangetic dolphins, water monitors, 5m-long saltwater crocodiles or luminescent kingfishers, is a world away from Kolkata's chaos.

Overall, the best time to visit is between November and February, though warmer March and April are better for tigerspotting.

ⓒ Tours

To explore this tricky and harsh landscape you need a boat. To avoid pitfalls and complications, it's best to travel on an organised trip from Kolkata, not least because all your logistics, permits and paperwork are taken care of.

Tour prices vary widely. They typically include return transport from Kolkata, accommodation (on boats or in lodges, mostly located around the northern fringes of the reserve), food, reserve entry and guide fees, and boat-hire charges. Do check what is and isn't included. On a one-night/two-day trip you normally reach the Sundarbans around lunchtime and do one afternoon boat trip and one morning or full-day boat trip the next day. Boat trips are typically built around visits to various watchtowers dotted around the reserve.

Backpackers   WILDLIFE TOURS
(Map p458; ☑ 9836177140; www.tourdesundar
bans.com; Tottee Lane, Kolkata; Sundarbans tour all-inclusive 1 night ₹4200, 2 nights ₹4725-5500; ⊙ 8am-9pm) Reliable yet laid-back, fun yet spiritual, this knowledgeable 'three brothers' outfit conducts highly recommended tours of the jungle, including birdwatching and local music. Accommodation is either on a cruise boat or in the Backpackers Eco Village; the latter's mud-built cottages have seat toilets and electricity but no AC, with folk music in the evenings. Rates are for a minimum three people.

RIVER CRUISES

If you have pockets deep enough you can explore the Ganges Delta in a most memorable manner on luxury boat cruises from Kolkata along the Hooghly River itself. Cruises usually range from four to 12 days, with fine on-board comforts and stops in places such as Chandannagar, Bandel, Mayapur, Murshidabad and Farakka (for Gaur and Pandua), along with side excursions to some lesser-known places along the way. A few cruises continue up the Ganges as far as Patna and Varanasi. **Bengal Ganga** (☑ 011-26124069; www. bengalganga.com; 7-night cruise all-inclusive s/d from US$5065/7792) and **Assam Bengal Navigation** (☑ 0361-2667871; www.assambengalnavigation.com; per person per day all-inclusive from US$220; ⊙ Aug-Apr) come highly recommended.

Help Tourism   WILDLIFE
(Map p480; ☑ 9733000442; www.helptourism.com; 67A Kali Temple Rd, Kalighat, Kolkata; 1 night all-inclusive per person for 2/4 people ₹16,385/10,740, 2 nights 25,600/17,755; ⊙ office 10.30am-6pm Mon-Sat) Actively involved with local communities, this tour operator takes you up close to rural life in the delta, and provides wonderful access into the forest. Accommodation is in comfortable cottages on Bali island, just outside the tiger reserve, each with two king-size beds, sit-down toilets, verandah and showers. Prices drop as group size increases; enquire directly.

Sunderban Tiger Camp   WILDLIFE
(Map p474; ☑ 8100035749; www.waxpolhotels.com; Waxpol Hotels, 2nd fl, 71 Ganesh Chandra Ave, Kolkata; 1 night all-inclusive s/d from ₹6100/11,290; ⊙ office 10.30am-6pm Mon-Fri) This well-managed outfit provides expert guides and quality accommodation in huts and lovely red-brick cottages with forest-themed wall murals. The huts are the cheapest, but come with a sense of adventure. It offers one-night tours from Kolkata every Sunday, and two-night trips starting Monday, Wednesday and Friday, as well as various private and special theme trips.

Up the Hooghly

The British were not the only Europeans to spot the Hooghly River's potential as a trading nexus as they sought to prosper from shipping Indian produce across the oceans in the 16th to 19th centuries. The Portuguese, Dutch and French all set up trading towns on the Hooghly before the British established Calcutta in 1690, and the Danes came not long afterwards. Seeking out the relics of the old European settlements in what's sometimes called Little Europe, along the banks of the river north of Kolkata, makes for a fascinating outing from the city.

ⓘ Getting There & Away

Very frequent local trains (₹10, one hour) from Kolkata's Howrah station to Bandel Junction (2.5km from Bandel Basilica) stop at Shrirampur (1km from Serampore's Denmark Tavern), Chandan Nagar (2.5km from the Chandannagar riverfront), Chuchura (3km from central Chinsurah) and Hooghly (3km from Hooghly Imambara). Some continue to Bansh Baria station, 1km from the Hanseswari Temple. You can use autorickshaws to move between one town and another without returning to the railway, or hire one for a day for about ₹600. Alternatively, hire a taxi for the day from Kolkata (₹3000).

Serampore

Serampore, 25km north of Kolkata, was a Danish colony under the name Frederiksnagore from 1755 to 1845 (when it was sold to the British East India Company). Here the **Denmark Tavern** (Mahatma Gandhi Rd; mains ₹125-450; ⊙11am-9pm), a riverside colonial inn, has been converted into a cafe-restaurant by Danish organisations and you can enjoy pasta, grilled sandwiches and good coffee as well as curries in smart Indo-Danish surroundings. There's a helpful map of Serampore's Danish monuments in the entrance: seek out especially St Olav's Church (1805) and the grand Serampore College, founded in 1818 by Englishman William Carey and fellow Baptist missionaries (now a further education college). Its library was once one of the largest in India; also here is a one-room Carey Museum.

The Rath Yatra (p493) festival is held in Serampore in June/July.

Chandannagar & Hooghly

About 44km north of Kolkata, Chandannagar was a French colony from 1678 right through to 1950, barring a couple of short British interruptions. The **Institut de Chandernagor** (Dupleix Palace; www.institutede chandernagor.gov.in; Strand Rd, Chandannagar; Indian/foreigner ₹5/20; ⊙11am-5.30pm Sun-Wed & Fri), in the former governor's mansion on the riverfront road, has an interesting museum explaining colonial history on the Hooghly, and contains the four-poster bed of 18th-century governor Joseph Dupleix. Across the road is a kind of mini Arc de Triomphe in honour of Durgacharan Rakshit (1841–98), the first Indian to become a chevalier of the Légion d'Honneur. Moving 150m back from the river, you can visit the Catholic Sacred Heart Church (Église du Sacre Coeur), founded in the 1670s. In mid-November, Chandannagar puts on gorgeous lighting displays for Jagaddhatri Puja, a festival devoted to an incarnation of the Hindu goddess Durga.

Almost no trace remains of the Dutch at their former base of Chinsurah, 5km north of Chandannagar, but 3km further north stands the grand **Hooghly Imambara** (Imambara Rd, Hooghly; ₹10; ⊙8am-5pm Sep-Mar, to 6pm Apr-Aug), a Shiite mosque and assembly hall inaugurated in 1861. Its romantically crumbling

Indo-Saracenic profile offers some very interesting photo ops, and you can climb the lofty clock tower which has breathtaking views of the Hooghly River and houses a giant mechanical clock.

Bandel & Bansberia

The Portuguese were the first Europeans to settle in the Hooghly region, initially in the 1530s at Saptagram, northwest of Chinsurah. The only reminder of their presence now is the **Bandel Basilica** (www.bandelchurch. com; Bandel; ⊙8am-4.50pm), 1.5km north of the Hooghly Imambara. Full of candles and stained glass, this is Bengal's oldest and perhaps most adored church, built in 1599 and often reconstructed since. There are good views from the balcony above its portico, with its statue of Our Lady of Happy Voyage. It's worth continuing 6km north from Bandel to the remarkable **Hanseswari Temple** (⊙dawn-dusk) at Bansberia, built in 1814. Devoted to an avatar of the goddess Kali, it's topped by 13 needle-pointed *sikharas* (Hindu temple-spires), looking like something you'd expect to see in Moscow. Also within the temple premises is the small but elegant Bengali-hut-style Vasudev Temple, with superb terracotta panelling similar to the famous terracotta temples of Bishnupur.

Bishnupur

♪ 03244 / POP 68,000

Known for its beautiful terracotta temples, Bishnupur, 140km northwest of Kolkata, was the capital of the Hindu Malla kings who ruled in this part of western Bengal from the 7th to 18th centuries. Its golden age came in the 16th and 17th centuries when the kings made tribute payments to the Mughals and patronised the arts and crafts. The terracotta temples stand among the finest of Bengali architecture, with their bold mix of Bengali, Islamic and Oriya (Odishan) styles. They're built of brick, with (in most cases) facades covered in hundreds of intricately detailed terracotta panels depicting scenes from the Hindu epics, animals and scenes from contemporary life.

Of the many temples (and other historic structures) scattered around town, the most striking temples are **Rasmancha** (incl Jor Bangla & Shyamrai temples Indian/foreigner ₹25/300; ⊙dawn-dusk), a square structure with three concentric arched galleries surrounding the inner shrine; the elaborate **Shyamrai** (incl

PALATIAL GETAWAYS

Thrown around the countryside not far beyond Kolkata's city limits are a handful of *rajbari* (palaces) built by zamindars (landowners) of past centuries. While most of them stand dilapidated and forlorn, a few have recently made a promising turnaround and joined the top-end tourism bandwagon. Among the palaces offering a luxury experience woven around the bygone lordly life is the **Itachuna Rajbari** (☑ 9674537940, 7003121811; www.itachunarajbari.com; Polba-Khanyan Rd, Itachuna village, Hooghly District; d ₹1680-4960; ❄ 🌐), 95km north of Kolkata. It packs a punch with its renovated stately interiors, fine Bengali food and overall bucolic ambience. The **Rajbari Bawali** (☑ 9073312000; www. therajbari.com; North Bawali village; r incl breakfast ₹7080-8790, full board ₹12,800-14,660; ❄ 🌐), a 30km drive southwest of Kolkata, also makes for a luxurious and atmospheric getaway, with a striking neoclassical courtyard, masterfully restored decor and excellent overall hospitality.

in Rasmancha ticket; ⊙ dawn-dusk) with five *sikhara* domes; **Jor Bangla** (incl in Rasmancha ticket; ⊙ dawn-dusk), twin 'huts' with exquisite carving; Lalji, built in white stone and stucco; and Madan Mohan with fine detailed carving on its south side. You can cover these five in a 2.5km walk (one way), or rent a rickshaw for the tour. A ticket is required for the first three: you need to buy it at Rasmancha and show it at the others.

There's a small **museum** (College Rd; Indian/foreigner ₹5/15; ⊙ 11am-5pm Tue-Sun) that's worth a look for its collection of painted manuscript covers, stone friezes, musical instruments and folk art.

🛏 Sleeping

The cheerfully pink-painted, government-run **Bishnupur Tourist Lodge** (☑ 9732100950; www.wbtdcl.com; College Rd; d ₹750-2020; ❄ 🌐), fronted by grassy lawns, has adequately comfortable, pastel-shaded rooms and a good restaurant, plus a bar. It's close to the Rasmancha temple, and an ₹80 rickshaw ride from the train station. Try to book ahead (the website requires registering but is not impossible to navigate).

Hotel Annapurna (☑ 7407505000; https://annapurnahotel.in; College Rd; d incl breakfast ₹2950-5310; ❄ 🌐), new in 2018, is a step up in comfort, with rooms boasting good mattresses, soft sofas, big showerheads, desks and colourful art. The restaurant serves Continental as well as Indian dishes.

🛍 Shopping

Bishnupur is well known for its Baluchari silk saris, with mythological stories woven into their panels. It is also a sales centre for Bankura horses, stylised terracotta horses made in Panchmura village, 22km southwest, which are among the foremost symbols of Indian folk art. You'll find outlets for both these crafts along Chinnamasta Rd, which heads south off College Rd beside Bishnupur Tourist Lodge.

ℹ Getting There & Away

Two fast daily trains run to Bishnupur from Kolkata (2nd class/chair ₹110/395, 3¼ hours): the 6.25am 12883 Rupasibangla Express from Santragachi Junction station, and the 12827 Howrah Purulia Express at 4.50pm from Howrah. There's an AC bus to Bishnupur from Kolkata's Esplanade bus station at 7.15am (₹230, 4½ hours). To reach Shantiniketan from Bishnupur, you have to change buses in Durgapur (total ₹100, four hours). A taxi day trip from Shantiniketan to Bishnupur costs about ₹3500.

Shantiniketan

☑ 03463 / POP 10,000 APPROX

Shantiniketan (Abode of Peace) is one of the outstanding creations of Rabindranath Tagore (1861–1941), the great writer, artist, songwriter, educationalist, 1913 Nobel literature laureate and central figure of the Bengali Renaissance. It was here in 1901 that Tagore founded a school, and in 1921 a university, the Visva-Bharati. The university became a nerve centre of Bengali culture with a focus on the arts, humanities and contact with nature, along with a revolutionary philosophy of breaking barriers between cultures, religions, castes, the sexes, teachers and students, city and country, east and west. University and school continue largely to follow Tagore's principles today, with around 10,000 Indian and international students, a healthily coeducational atmosphere, and classes still held in the open air under the campus trees.

Around the university is a relaxed small town of leafy lanes, with a cultural/artistic ambience and some charming small-scale lodgings. It's 160km northwest of Kolkata and adjoins the northern side of the run-of-the-mill town of Bolpur, where you'll find the main train and bus stations and other everyday services.

Sights

The Visva-Bharati campus' main area of interest is on the west side of the road heading north from Bolpur, where the university buildings are scattered across spacious, tree-shaded grounds, liberally decorated with a rush of eclectic statues. Apart from the highlight Uttarayan Complex, access to most of the grounds is closed until 1pm, when classes finish. Don't miss the Kala Bhavan, the art school, richly adorned with murals, mosaics and sculptures, many of them done in the 1930s by Nandalal Bose and his students, including the Kalo Bari, a black house adorned with striking sculptural panels in mud, cow dung and tar. The Mandir (Temple), windowed with Belgian stained glass, was built by Rabindranath Tagore's father Debendranath in the 19th century as a prayer hall for the original nondenominational ashram that he founded on what later became part of the university site. (It's normally locked but you can look from outside.)

Uttarayan Complex   MUSEUM
(Rabindra-Bhavana Museum; Visva-Bharati campus; Indian/foreigner ₹50/300; ⏰10am-1pm & 2-5pm Fri-Tue) Ranged around tree-lined avenues, gravelled courtyards and exotic gardens, the Uttarayan Complex, in the heart of the Visva-Bharati campus, includes five architecturally very varied houses, from art deco to rural Bengal, in which Rabindranath Tagore lived at different times and did a lot of his writing. Also here is a museum of Tagore exhibits and memorabilia (including his ancient Humber car).

Festivals & Events

Poush Mela   CULTURAL
(Shantiniketan; ⏰23-28 Dec) The high point of Shantiniketan's festive calendar, Poush Mela fair brings together artists, musicians, artisans and poets from nearby villages and far-flung continents. You can spend time with the *bauls* (the wandering minstrels of Bengal) and listen to their songs about life and love, or roam stalls selling tribal crafts and clothing. Lip-smacking regional fare is served up at the food stalls.

Sleeping & Eating

The choicest places to stay are in the leafy village 'suburbs' on the north side of Shantiniketan. For Poush Mela, book as far ahead as you possibly can: the best places get booked out several months in advance.

Mitali Homestay   HOMESTAY $$
(📞9433075853; www.mitalishantiniketan.com; Phuldanga; d incl breakfast ₹3000-4000; ❉🛜) About 2km north of the university in verdant Phuldanga village, the art-, craft- and book-filled home of a retired diplomat and his chef-and-designer wife promises a delightful experience. Look forward to great company, comfy rooms and delicious home-cooked meals. You can enjoy Bengali meals in the house (veg/nonveg ₹300/400), or dine in the garden restaurant Rustic Flavours (p492) for a wider culinary choice.

You should make contact two weeks ahead (six months ahead for Poush Mela and some other festival periods). As is common practice in Shantiniketan, the hosts normally require 50% advance payment of room costs.

Garden Bungalow   GUESTHOUSE $$
(📞9899760538; www.thegardenbungalow.com; Sonajhuri Pally; r incl breakfast without AC ₹2000, with AC ₹5000-7000; ❉🛜) At the end of a quiet lane right on the northern edge of town, this property offers probably the most comfortable lodgings in Shantiniketan, amid a beautifully designed tropical garden. Four-poster beds, folk art and carved wooden doorways characterise the rooms (air-con in the 19th-century landowner-style main house, no air-con in the 'mud house' built with more traditional local materials).

Park Guest House   GUESTHOUSE $$
(📞9378321552; www.parkguesthouse.in; Deer Park; d incl breakfast ₹1620-2690; ❉🛜) The good-value Park occupies a tranquil, semirural spot a few minutes' walk north of the university campus, with Lal Bandh lake across the road. It's set around a pretty garden courtyard, with snug rooms sporting some tribal decor, tea/coffee makers and bathroom mosaics. The rooftop restaurant serves excellent Bengali and North Indian meals (mains ₹100 to ₹250, thali lunch ₹95).

Nayana's Homestay   HOMESTAY $$
(Chota Kothi; 📞9830044096; www.nayanashomestay.in; off Goalpara Rd, Uttarpally-Phuldanga; r incl breakfast ₹4000; ❉🛜) Nayana's is the abode of a helpful, knowledgeable

member of the Tagore clan, and her two-storey house, on a leafy lane in the north of town, is full of character, crafts and art. The two guest rooms are medium-sized and comfortable without being luxurious, and there's plenty of common space to relax in, including upstairs terraces and a pretty garden.

Rustic Flavours
MULTICUISINE $$$

(☑ 9433898067; Mitali Homestay, Phuldanga; 3-course meals ₹500-800; ⊙ 12.30-2.30pm & 8-10.30pm) ✐ Mitali Homestay's garden restaurant gives everyone the chance to enjoy the wonderful home-style cooking of hostess Sukanya Ray. Her Bengali meals are a delicious journey through a gamut of flavours and textures, and she can do other Indian, Continental, Thai, Chinese or Middle Eastern cuisines with equal talent. Call a day ahead to book and choose what kind of meal you'd like.

🛍 Shopping

The Shantiniketan area has a strong tribal handicrafts tradition and you can find very attractive wares at several outlets in town.

Shonibarer Haat
HANDICRAFTS

(Khoyai Haat; Sonajhuri Forest; ⊙ 2.30-6pm Sat) This open-air market sees local artisans and others selling, among other things, highly colourful textiles, bright tribal jewellery and attractive *dhokra* (lost-wax casting) metalwork, in the bucolic setting of the Sonajhuri eucalyptus woods on the northern edge of town. Some sellers are here every day, but Saturday afternoon, when you'll find food stands and maybe *baul* musicians too, is best.

Tanzil
HANDICRAFTS

(Shyambati; ⊙ 10.30am-9pm) Tanzil stocks a very good range of diverse, mainly tribal, crafts and art from all over India. It's on the main road towards the northern end of town, about 800m past the main turning into the university campus.

ⓘ Getting There & Away

The town of Bolpur, contiguous to Shantiniketan, serves as its transport hub. Numerous daily trains run between Kolkata and Bolpur-Shantiniketan station, 3km south of the university. The best is the 12337 Santiniketan Express (2nd class/chair ₹95/305, 2½ hours) departing at 10.10am from Howrah station. For Siliguri, take the 9.19am Kanchanjunga Express (train 13175 on Monday, Wednesday and Saturday, 13173 other days; sleeper/3AC/2AC ₹250/675/965, nine hours).

Bolpur's Jambuni bus stand, on Tourist Lodge Rd (Pravat Sarani), 100m west of the Geetanjali Cinema, has frequent buses until about 2pm to Suri and Durgapur, where you can change for Berhampore and Bishnupur respectively. It's a total trip of four hours (₹100) to either destination.

Murshidabad & Berhampore

☑ 03482 / POP MURSHIDABAD 44,000; BERHAMPORE 195,000

In Murshidabad, rural Bengali life and the imposing buildings of a historic capital city merge on the verdant shores of the Hooghly River, locally known as the Bhagirathi. Murshidabad replaced Dhaka as capital of the vast Mughal province of Bengal in 1704, became a silk trade centre, and remained Bengal's administrative centre under the British for some decades after Nawab Siraj-ud-daula was defeated by Robert Clive at Plassey (now Palashi) in 1757. The main draw here is the Hazarduari (Indian/foreigner ₹25/300; ⊙ 10am-5pm Sat-Thu), a royal palace famous for its 1000 doors (real and false), built for the nawabs in 1829–37. It houses an astonishing collection of Bengali and European antiquities from the 18th and 19th centuries.

Within the Hazarduari compound are the beautiful Nizamat Imambara (a Shiite ceremonial building), a clock tower, and two elegant Medina Mosques (one between the Hazarduari and Imambara, another inside the Imambara).

Numerous other buildings in varied states of preservation are well worth checking out along Murshidabad's leafy lanes beyond the Hazarduari. Siraj-ud-daula is said to have been assassinated at the Namak Haram Deori (Jafarganj Deorhi; Traitor's Gate; its sign says 'Imambarah & House of Jafar Ali Khan'). The Nasipur Rajbari (Indian/foreigner ₹10/100; ⊙ 10am-4pm) and House of Jagat Seth (Indian/foreigner ₹15/100; ⊙ 6am-6.30pm) were respectively the palaces of a 19th-century tax collector and a Jain family of high influence under both the nawabs and the British.

Murshidabad's founder, Murshid Quli Khan, is buried beneath the eastern staircase of the handsome, pink-brick Katra Mosque (⊙ dawn-dusk), built in 1723, on the east side of Murshidabad.

Within the Kathgola Gardens (Indian/foreigner ₹30/150; ⊙ 7am-5.30pm) is an interesting family mansion of a Jain trading family, dating back to 1873.

TOP STATE FESTIVALS

Gangasagar Mela (Sagar Island; ⊘mid-Jan) Hundreds of thousands of Hindu pilgrims converge on Sagar Island, where the Ganges meets the sea, to bathe en masse in a riotous festival.

Bengali New Year (Nabo Barsho; statewide; ⊘mid-Apr) A holiday celebrating the first day of the Bengali calendar, usually on 14 or 15 April.

Rath Yatra (Chariot Festival; Mahesh, Serampore; ⊘Jun/Jul) Devotees celebrate by dragging the juggernaut chariot of Lord Jagannath between temples in Serampore.

Durga Puja (statewide; ⊘Oct) Celebrations of the 10-armed Hindu goddess Durga take over the state for five or six days, with thousands of Puja *pandals* (temporary, often very grandiose, structures housing Durga images), a great deal of drumming, loud music and coloured lights, even worse traffic jams than usual and a pervasive happy atmosphere. At the end, all the Durgas are paraded to nearby water bodies and pushed in. Celebrated as Dashain in the Himalayan foothills.

Jagaddhatri Puja (Chandannagar; ⊘mid-Nov) Honours the Hindu goddess Jagaddhatri, an incarnation of Durga. An enormous procession carries idols to the Hooghly River in Chandannagar and casts them in.

Poush Mela (Shantiniketan; ⊘Dec; p491) Folk music, dance, regional crafts, food and the songs of *bauls*, Bengal's wandering minstrels, fill the university town of Shantiniketan.

🛏 Sleeping

Hotels in and near Murshidabad itself are few and mostly low on quality. Berhampore, 13km south, has a larger selection and is the area's main transport hub. Good options include **Hotel Sagnik** (📞9434021911; www.hotelsagnik.com; 77 Omrahaganj (Lalbagh); d ₹660-1100; ❄), with well-sized, clean rooms and excellent restaurants, and **Hotel Samrat** (📞9733565555; www.hotelsamrat.net.in; NH34/ new NH12, Panchanantala, Berhampore; without AC s/d ₹525/625, with AC incl breakfast s ₹990, d ₹1190-2110; ❄🛜), with adequate standards and helpful service.

❶ Getting There & Away

The 13113 Hazarduari Express departs Kolkata train station at 6.50am (to Berhampore Court station 2nd class/chair ₹85/320, 3¼ hours; to Murshidabad station ₹90/330, 3½ hours). Trains on to Malda and New Jalpaiguri go from Khagraghat Road station, 4km west of central Berhampore.

Buses leave Berhampore bus station, at a six-way intersection in the town centre:

Kolkata ₹150, six hours, frequent departures
Malda ₹100, four hours, frequent departures
Siliguri Without/with AC ₹300/450, 10 hours, six departures between 7pm and 9.30pm

For Shantiniketan/Bolpur (₹110, five hours) get a bus to Suri from the SBSTC stand about 500m west along Main Rd and change at Suri.

❶ Getting Around

Shared autorickshaws (₹15, 40 minutes) run all day between the eastern corner of the Berhampore bus-station junction and Lalbagh, 2km south of the Hazarduari. Horse buggies and *totos* (battery-powered autorickshaws) offer half-day tours of Murshidabad's spread-out sites for around ₹600.

Gaur & Pandua

Scattered around the paddy fields and tanks of Gaur (Gour), on the Bangladesh border, lies an abandoned city that dominated much of Bengal from the 8th to 14th centuries. A dozen or so mosques and other monuments apart, the capital of the Buddhist Pala and Hindu Sena dynasties and the Muslim Delhi Sultanate's governors is now almost completely disintegrated and overgrown. The Bengal Sultanate moved its capital to Pandua (Adina), 35km north of Gaur, around 1350, and Pandua too has a few impressive monuments. Gaur regained its capital status around 1450, and kept it until it was sacked by the Mughals a century later.

The town of Malda, roughly halfway between Gaur and Pandua, is a convenient base for exploring both places. Malda is also famed for its mangoes. Even if you visit outside summer mango season, you can buy delicious mango pickle and candied mango in the markets.

SLEEPING PRICE RANGES

These price ranges refer to double rooms, with bathroom in high season in this region, with taxes included.

$ less than ₹1500

$$ ₹1500–₹4000

$$$ more than ₹4000

Gaur

Gaur (known historically as Lakhnauti or Gauda), once stretched 30km from north to south (and some of its remaining monuments are across the border in Bangladesh – you'd need a Bangladesh visa to cross the border, and at least a double-entry Indian visa if you want to come back). Its main monuments on the Indian side are mostly built of red brick and are spread along about 2.5km of country lane winding bucolically between trees and tanks. The most impressive are the **Baradwari Mosque** (Barasona Masjid; ☉ dawn-dusk), built in 1526 (the dignified arcade of its 11-domed eastern corridor still intact), and the fortresslike **Dakhil Darwaza** (☉ dawn-dusk) FREE, built in 1425, which was the northern gate to the citadel at the heart of Gaur. South past the Firoz Minar (1486–89), the Qadam Rasul Mosque (1531) enshrines a flat footprint of the Prophet Mohammed, with the Chamkan (Chika) Mosque (1450), the Lukochuri Gate (1655) and Gumti Gate (1512) nearby. The latter, with some blue and white enamel still clinging to its facade, was the southern gate of the citadel.

Pandua

In Pandua are the vast ruins of the 14th-century **Adina Masjid** (☉ dawn-dusk), once India's largest mosque. It originally had nearly 400 small domes and some 90 brick arches. About 2km away is the large, domed **Eklakhi Mausoleum** (☉ dawn-dusk) FREE, so called because it cost ₹1 lakh (₹100,000) to build back in 1431.

🛏 Sleeping & Eating

Continental Lodge BUSINESS HOTEL **$$**
(☎ 03512-252388; www.continentallodge.com; 22/21 KJ Sanyal Rd, Malda; incl breakfast s ₹1140-1890, d ₹1560-2230; ❄ ☎) The Continental has a good central location in Malda and ticks every box with well-kept, mildly contemporary-styled rooms, friendly service, a restaurant

doing Bengali thalis (₹180 to ₹280) as well as North Indian dishes, tour service to Gaur (₹1500) and Pandua (₹1800), and helpful 24-hour checkout.

ℹ Getting There & Around

Several express trains run daily from Kolkata's Howrah train station to Malda Town station, including the 12041 Shatabdi Express (chair ₹780, five hours, 2.15pm) and the 12377 Padatik Express (1AC/2AC/3AC/sleeper ₹1470/880/630/245, 6½ hours, 11.20pm). Both continue to Siliguri (3½ hours), the access point for Darjeeling, departing Malda Town at 7.15pm and 5.45am respectively.

Buses depart regularly for Siliguri (₹200, 7½ hours), Berhampore/Murshidabad (₹100, four hours) and Kolkata (₹260, 10 hours).

For touring the monuments in Gaur and Pandua, you have to hire a taxi for the day (₹2500) in Malda. There's no public transport to the ruins.

WEST BENGAL HILLS

Siliguri & New Jalpaiguri

📋 0353 / POP 513,000 / ELEV 120M

The crowded and noisy transport hub Siliguri is the main jumping-off point for Darjeeling, Kalimpong and Sikkim, and Bhutan, eastern Nepal and India's Northeast States can also be accessed from here. Despite being one of West Bengal's largest cities, Siliguri has very little to detain you except transport connections.

Most of Siliguri's hotels, restaurants and services are spread along riotously noisy Hill Cart Rd (Tenzing Norgay Rd), especially in the vicinity of Siliguri Junction train station and its neighbour, the Tenzing Norgay Central Bus Terminus. The main train station, however, with many more departures than Siliguri Junction, is New Jalpaiguri (NJP), 6km south at the end of NJP Station Rd.

🛏 Sleeping

Hotel Himalayan Regency HOTEL **$**
(☎ 0353-2516624; himalayanhatcheries@gmail.com; Hill Cart Rd, Pradhan Nagar; d with/without AC ₹1300-1200/900; ❄ ☎ ☎) Rooms here are clean and cheerfully colourful, with comfy double beds, and the staff are friendly and cheerful too. You'll find it on the east side of Hill Cart Rd, 500m north of the bus-station intersection.

Mainak Tourist Lodge HOTEL **$$**
(☎ 9733008780, 0353-2513986; www.wbtdcl.com; Hill Cart Rd; incl breakfast s ₹1340-2520, d ₹1950-

3540; ✱ 🛜) State-government-run Mainak is in the (gradual) process of renovating its rooms; the completed ones are pleasantly bright, with splashes of colour, good beds and pine furnishings, and tea/coffee gear. There's a restaurant and a large airy lobby, and it's well set back from the busy road, 800m north of the Central Bus Terminus.

Hotel Sinclairs   HOTEL $$$
(📞 9733462777; www.sinclairshotels.com; Mallaguri; s/d incl breakfast from ₹5780/6140; ✱ 🛜 🏊) Very comfortable Sinclairs, 1km north of the Central Bus Terminus, offers a delicious escape from hectic Hill Cart Rd, with professional, friendly service and fresh, bright, modern rooms with good bathrooms. There's an excellent patio restaurant, a bar, a spa, and a cool clean pool, perfect for escaping the heat of the plains. Generous discounts offered at slower times.

🍴 Eating

Khana Khajana   MULTICUISINE $
(Hill Cart Rd; mains ₹90-210; ⊙8am-10pm) The secluded garden here offers merciful relief from the thunderous Hill Cart Rd chaos. The extensive menu ranges from fine curries and naan (tandoor-cooked flat bread) to Mumbai street snacks, with plenty of hearty vegetarian options and *kulfi* (flavoured, firm-textured ice cream). From the Central Bus Terminus, cross Hill Cart Rd and go 200m along the side lane to the left.

Amber   INDIAN $$
(📞 8130248040; Hill Cart Rd; mains ₹200-400; ⊙10.30am-11pm; ✱) Trusted and air-conditioned Amber, attached to Hotel Saluja Residency, serves mouthwatering dishes, including fluffy naans, lip-smacking curries, tender meat dishes and subtly flavoured biryanis that go down extremely well with the city's food lovers. Plenty of alcoholic drinks too; evenings are especially buzzy here. It's 1.5km south of the Central Bus Terminus.

**Around
the Corner**   CONTINENTAL $$$
(www.facebook.com/aroundthecornersiliguri; Patel Rd By-Lane; mains ₹250-400; ⊙noon-10pm) Around The Corner does Western food as well as any restaurant north of Kolkata. The pasta is European-standard, or you could go for pork steaks, fish and chips, burgers, grilled prawns or apple pie with ice cream. With 10 tables, low lighting and Western rock music, it's also a place you can just come for a drink (beer from ₹150).

It's 'around the corner' behind Hotel Diamond, which you'll spot on Hill Cart Rd 400m north of the Central Bus Terminus.

ℹ Information

Delhi Hotel (Hill Cart Rd; ⊙10am-8pm) Exchanges cash Western currencies and (at poor rates) Nepali rupees. On Hill Cart Rd's eastern side lane, opposite the Central Bus Terminus.

Sikkim Tourist Office (📞 0353-2512646; SNT terminal, Hill Cart Rd side lane; ⊙10am-4pm Mon-Sat) Issues permits for Sikkim on the spot, as does a branch at Bagdogra airport (open 10am to 4pm daily). Bring copies of your passport, visa and one passport-sized photo.

Tourism Centre (📞 0353-2517561; www. wbtourismgov.in; Hill Cart Rd; ⊙10am-5.30pm Mon-Fri, to 2pm Sat) Tourist information office with some helpful staff speaking good English. Can book accommodation at government tourist lodges around West Bengal, including at Jaldapara National Park.

ℹ Getting There & Away

AIR

Bagdogra Airport is 14km west of Siliguri. Seven Indian airlines provide multiple daily flights to Bengaluru (Bangalore), Delhi, Guwahati, Kolkata and Mumbai. Drukair has a couple of weekly flights to Bangkok and Paro (Bhutan).

Five-passenger helicopters (₹3500, 40 minutes) travel daily from Bagdogra to Gangtok at 2.30pm in good weather. Some days there are extra flights. The Sikkim Helicopter Service office at the airport will sell tickets on the day if any are available, but it's much better to book in advance through Sikkim Tourism Development Corporation (p541) in Gangtok.

A prepaid taxi stand at Bagdogra Airport offers fixed fares to many destinations including Darjeeling (₹1860, three hours), Kalimpong (₹1410, three hours), Gangtok (₹2080, five hours), Panitanki (Nepal border; ₹485, 45 minutes) and Jaigaon (Bhutan border; ₹2510, 4½ hours), allowing you to bypass Siliguri entirely. Prices indicated are to the local jeep stand; a hotel drop will cost a little more. The fare to Siliguri Junction station is ₹460 (an autorickshaw is ₹250). Make sure you *prepay* the full fare and are not just given a ticket and left to pay the driver yourself – who will probably try to double the fare.

Wizzride (www.wizzride.com) offers transfers in comfortable five-passenger Innova cars to Kurseong and Darjeeling (per person ₹500 to ₹600), and Gangtok (₹700 to ₹800). You can book and pay online: the site accepts foreign cards.

❶ BORDER CROSSINGS: SILIGURI TO BANGLADESH, BHUTAN & NEPAL

Crossing to Bangladesh: Chengrabandha to Burimari

A number of private bus companies in Siliguri run daily air-con buses direct to Dhaka. **Shyamoli** (☑ 9836937814; Hotel Central Plaza complex, Hill Cart Rd, Malagauri), 1km north of the Tenzing Norgay Central Bus Terminus, has one departing at 1.30pm (₹1200, 18 hours). Book a day or two ahead. You'll need to complete border formalities at Chengrabandha, opposite Burimari, Bangladesh, and you'll need a Bangladesh visa (obtainable in Kolkata or Delhi).

Buses also run about hourly, 5.30am to 5.30pm, from the Central Bus Terminus to Chengrabandha (₹30, 2½ hours).

The border post is open from 8am to 6pm daily.

From near the border post you can catch buses on to Rangpur, Bogra and Dhaka (you may need to take a tempo to Patgram, 13km from the border, first).

Crossing to Bhutan: Jaigaon to Phuentsholing

Bhutan Transport Service runs buses to Phuentsholing inside Bhutan (large/small bus ₹120/150, five to six hours) at 7am, 12.30pm and 2pm from the Howrah Petrol Pump stop on Burdwan Road. You can also take a private bus at 7am, 9am, 1.30pm or 4.30pm from the Central Bus Terminus to Jaigaon (₹170, four hours) on the Indian side of the border, where you clear Indian immigration. A taxi to Jaigaon from Siliguri or Bagdogra airport costs around ₹2500.

Non-Indian nationals need visa clearance from a Bhutanese tour operator to enter Bhutan.

Immigration at the Jaigaon/Phuentsholing border opens from 8am to 9pm.

Frequent minibuses run from Phuentsholing's bus station to Thimphu (Nu 240, six hours), with morning services to Paro (Nu 230, six hours).

Shared taxis (Nu 500 to NU 700 to Thimpu) depart from a stand near the river. A jeep taxi to Thimpu costs Nu 4800.

Crossing to Nepal: Panitanki to Kakarbhitta

For Nepal, local buses to the Indian border town of Panitanki (₹30, 1¼ hours) stop on Hill Cart Rd outside the Central Bus Terminus every few minutes from about 7.30am to 5.30pm. There are also shared jeeps (₹120, one hour, 5am to 6pm) departing when full from the Siliguri Panitanki Kakarvitta Standon the far side of Hill Cart Rd. From the junction where the buses drop you in Panitanki, it's 500m to the Indian immigration post, then a further 1km to the Nepal immigration office in Kakarbhitta (Kakarvitta). For nearly all nationalities, Nepal tourist visas are available on arrival (15/30/90 days US$25/40/100, payable in US$ or Indian rupees); you must provide one passport photo.

Both immigration offices are open 6am to 6pm daily (but note that Nepal time is 15 minutes ahead of India time).

Kakarbhitta bus station, just past Nepal Bank, has buses to numerous destinations. Those to Kathmandu mostly depart between 3pm and 5pm, including about 12 by Mechi Bus (without/with AC NRs 1400/1685, 13 to 17 hours).

Bhadrapur Airport, 23km southwest of Kakarbhitta, has several daily flights to Kathmandu including two (US$142) on Buddha Air (www.buddhaair.com).

BUS

Most North Bengal State Transport Corporation (NBSTC) buses, and some private buses, leave from **Tenzing Norgay Central Bus Terminus** (Hill Cart Rd). Further private bus offices are outside on Hill Cart Rd.

The NBSTC has departures to Darjeeling (₹110, 3½ hours, every 30 or 60 minutes, 6.30am to noon); Kalimpong (₹110, three hours, six daily); Malda (₹200, 7½ hours, frequent); and Kolkata (AC buses ₹650 to ₹900, 15 hours, 6.30pm, 7pm and 7.30pm).

Rayan/Network (☑ 0353-2519251; Hill Cart Rd) runs a daily 4pm bus to Guwahati (₹450, 13 hours) from its office 125m north of the Central Bus Terminus. Deluxe air-con Volvo buses for Kolkata (₹1200, 15 hours) leave between 5.30pm and 7.30pm from **Gupta Travels**

(☏0353-2513451; Hill Cart Rd), just outside the Central Bus Terminus, and other agencies.

Sikkim Nationalised Transport (SNT) runs buses to Gangtok (₹150, 4½ hours, every 30 or 60 minutes 6.30am to 3pm) and other Sikkim destinations from the **SNT terminal** (Hill Cart Rd side lane), 200m southeast of the Central Bus Terminus. You can get your Sikkim permit at the Sikkim Tourist Office (p495) here or at the border at Rangpo.

JEEP & TAXI

An efficient if somewhat cramped way of getting to the hills is by shared jeep, with departures when full until about 4pm. Several jeep stands are dotted along Hill Cart Rd:

Darjeeling (₹150, three hours) Look in front of the petrol station 100m north of the Central Bus Terminus or in front of Hotel Conclave, 300m south of the Central Bus Terminus.

Gangtok (₹400, four hours) There are a couple of stands almost opposite the Central Bus Terminus.

Kalimpong (₹150, three hours) Head to the Panitanki More stand, 700m along Sevoke Rd from Hill Cart Rd (₹30 by autorickshaw from the Central Bus Terminus). Jeeps depart from 7am to 4pm.

Kurseong (₹100, 1½ hours) Depart from in front of Hotel Conclave.

Shared and chartered jeeps for all these destinations also leave from NJP train station.

Chartering a jeep privately costs roughly 10 times the price of a shared ticket. A recommended option for XL-sized travellers is to pay for and occupy the front two or three seats next to the driver.

Wizzride (www.wizzride.com) offers transfers in comfortable Innova cars to Kurseong, Darjeeling and Gangtok from central Siliguri, as well as from Bagdogra airport.

TRAIN

The central Siliguri Junction station has far fewer trains than New Jalpaiguri (NJP), 6km to the southeast. All trains mentioned here except the toy train to Darjeeling depart from NJP only.

Delhi The 1.15pm 12423 Rajdhani Express is your best and quickest bet (3AC/2AC/1AC ₹2255/3105/5015, 21 hours). Alternatively, board the 5.25pm 12505 North East Express (sleeper/3AC/2AC ₹625/1635/2375, 26 hours).

Guwahati The 1.30am 12424 Dibrugarh Town (DBRT) Rajdhani is easily the fastest daily service (3AC/2AC/1AC ₹1010/1345/2110, 6½ hours).

Kolkata The 5.30am 12042 NJP-Howrah Shatabdi is the fastest of many services to Kolkata (chair/executive chair ₹1070/2120, eight hours, Monday to Saturday), via Malda. The 8pm

12344 Darjeeling Mail (sleeper/3AC/2AC/1AC ₹350/920/1300/2180, 10 hours) is an overnight option.

Toy Train

Barring monsoon landslides and other unscheduled stoppages, the historic narrow-gauge Darjeeling Himalayan Railway runs one daily 'toy train' from New Jalpaiguri to Darjeeling, departing at 8.30am and taking seven hours to cover the 88 uphill kilometres (seat ₹1295) – twice as long as the trip by road. It stops at Siliguri Junction (departing 9am, ₹1105 to Darjeeling) and Kurseong en route.

🛈 Getting Around

From the Central Bus Terminus to NJP train station, a taxi/autorickshaw costs ₹250/100. Shared autorickshaws (₹8) run continuously along the length of Tenzing Norgay Rd.

Kurseong

🛈 0354 / POP 14,400 / ELEV 1480M

Kurseong is a tiny but bustling hill town best known for its tea estates and boarding schools founded in the Raj era. Its name derives from the Lepcha word *khorsang*, a reference to a small white orchid prolific in this area. Flanked by hilly slopes draped with manicured tea estates, Kurseong is also a stop for the toy trains of the Darjeeling Himalayan Railway, whose quaint station stands right by Kurseong's central road junction.

Hill Cart Rd – the noisy, traffic-choked main thoroughfare from Siliguri (33km north) to Darjeeling (31km south) – and its remarkably close shadow, the railway line, wind through town.

⊙ Sights & Activities

There are numerous good walks in the area. Eagle's Crag (2km return), south from the station (aim for the TV tower), affords splendid views down to the steamy plains to the south. The walk north to St Mary's Hill (4km) takes you uphill past atmospheric grottos and churches into charming pine forests that lead all the way up to a scenic mountain ridge.

★ **Makaibari**   TEA ESTATE

(☏033-22489091; www.makaibari.com; Pankhabari Rd; factory visit ₹50, day tour ₹800; ⊙5am-5pm Mon-Sat mid-Mar–mid-Nov) If you like tea, you should visit this celebrated organic and biodynamic Darjeeling tea estate. Walk-in visits to the processing factory, with huge sorting

WEST BENGAL KURSEONG

and drying machines, typically last 30 to 45 minutes (mornings before 9am are the best time to see the production process). For a more in-depth experience, reserve a day ahead through Makaibari Homestays (p498) for a day tour, which includes a factory visit, a plantation walk with tea plucking, lunch in a local homestay, and tea tasting.

The estate is 3km southwest of Kurseong station down Pankhabari Rd, and 1km past Cochrane Pl. It's a pleasantish walk down and an uphill walk back. Local vans will take you either way for ₹20 (shared) or ₹200 'reserved' (all to yourself); in town, they wait at St Andrew's Church, 250m down Pankhabari Rd from the station.

A shop at the factory gate sells Makaibari's prized teas (Silver Tips Imperial, the finest, costs ₹3500 per 100g!). Makaibari runs a homestay and volunteer programme from a separate office 150m down the road. Volunteers can find placements in teaching, health and community projects in March, April, May, October and November. A minimum two-week commitment is requested. Ask for Nayan Lama (if he's not in the office, ask at the factory-gate shop).

🛏 Sleeping & Eating

Makaibari Homestays HOMESTAY $$
(📞9832447774; www.makaibari.com; Makaibari tea estate, Pankhabari Rd; per person full board ₹1000) This pioneering programme, active since 2007, aims to harness tourism to empower local women tea pluckers. Twenty family houses on the Makaibari tea estate, within a 10-minute walk of the tea factory, are currently involved in the project. Families speak basic English and the houses are simple but comfortable and cosy, with attached bathrooms for the guest rooms.

The office is 150m down the road from the main tea-factory gate: if no one's there, ask for the programme's manager, Nayan Lama, at the factory-gate shop. Homestay guests get a substantial discount on estate day tours, paying ₹150 instead of ₹800.

Cochrane Place HERITAGE HOTEL $$$
(📞9932035660; www.cochraneplacehotel.com; 132 Pankhabari Rd; s ₹3070-3540; d ₹4130-5310; @🛜) With 360-degree plantation views, this quaint getaway with a century-old main building offers oodles of period furniture and quirky artefacts in its bright and airy rooms. There's a delicious mix of Anglo-Indian, Continental and Indian food, and a fine selection of Darjeeling teas, at the in-house restaurant-cafe Chai Country (mains ₹160-320; ⏰7am-8.30pm). Room rates can go up and down a bit according to season.

It's worth taking an extra day to enjoy an excellent guided village and tea-estate walk or an expert tea-tasting session. Cochrane Place is 2km southwest from Kurseong station on the road to Makaibari (₹10/100 by shared/reserved van from St Andrew's Church).

Margaret's Deck CAFE $
(Hill Cart Rd, Tung; tea pot ₹150-750, light dishes ₹100-350; ⏰8am-7pm) For fine teas and tasty food in contemporarily stylish surroundings, head 8km up the Darjeeling road from Kurseong to this, yes, deck, built out over a steep, panoramic tea-covered slope. Opened in 2017, it has terrace tables and a picture-windowed room with pot plants, flower-print chairs and the tea menu chalked in colours on a blackboard.

ℹ Getting There & Away

Numerous shared jeeps run from beside the train station to Darjeeling (₹80, 1½ hours) and Siliguri (₹80, 1½ hours) until around 4pm, with 8am and 1pm departures for Kalimpong (₹170, 3½ to four hours). Jeeps to Mirik (₹120, 2½ hours) go every couple of hours from 8am to 2pm.

The Darjeeling Himalayan Railway's quaint but slow toy train runs twice daily to Darjeeling: at 6.30am (2nd/1st class ₹60/685, 2½ hours) and 12.55pm (1st class only, ₹685, three hours).

A Bagdogra airport or Siliguri/New Jalpaiguri taxi should be ₹1500 (non-AC).

Darjeeling

📞0354 / POP 119,000 / ELEV 2120M

Spread in ribbons over a steep mountain ridge, surrounded by emerald-green tea plantations and towered over by majestic Khangchendzonga, Darjeeling is the definitive Indian hill station and, for many, West Bengal's premier destination. When you aren't gazing open-mouthed at Khangchendzonga (Great Five-Peaked Sbow Fortress – at 8598m it's the world's third-highest mountain), you can admire colonial-era architecture, visit Buddhist monasteries, and take a ride on the 140-year-old steam-billowing Darjeeling Himalayan Railway. The adventurous can arrange a trek to Singalila Ridge or ride a mountain bike around the hills.

Meanwhile, the steep and winding bazaars at the foot of the town bustle with an array of Himalayan products and faces from across Sikkim, Bhutan, Nepal and Ti-

GORKHALAND

Gorkhas – descendants of tea workers and other Nepalis who began arriving in the West Bengal hills in the mid-19th century – form the bulk of the area's population and in recent decades have become its main political force. Friction with the West Bengal state government led to calls for a separate state of Gorkhaland (within India, but not part of West Bengal) in the 1980s. In 1986 violence, riots and strikes orchestrated by the Gorkha National Liberation Front (GNLF) led to the establishment of the Darjeeling Gorkha Hill Council (DGHC), with a large measure of autonomy from the state government.

Renewed agitation by a GNLF splinter group, the Gorkha Janmukti Morcha (GJM), saw the DGHC replaced in 2012 by the Gorkhaland Territorial Administration (GTA), with greater powers. Periodic agitations continue to break out, characterised by *bandhs* (shutdown strikes), with confrontations between Gorkhaland supporters and police, and all economic activity halted. *Bandhs* lasting six weeks in 2013 and more than three months in 2017 saw offices, shops, hotels, transport, schools, businesses and even the internet shut down throughout the hills. Normally things are calm and life goes on uninterrupted, but it's worth checking the news if you're planning to head to the West Bengal hills.

bet. And when energies start to flag, a good, steaming Darjeeling brew is never far away.

Most tourists visit Darjeeling in autumn (October and November) and spring (mid-March to mid-May) when skies are dry, panoramas are clear and temperatures are pleasant. Winters can be cold here, so bring an extra jumper if visiting from December to February. The rainy months (June to September) can be extremely wet and are best avoided.

ℹ Orientation

Darjeeling sprawls over a west-facing slope in a confusing web of interconnecting roads and steep steps. Expect an uphill hike to your hotel if arriving at the train station or jeep stand. The two main squares – broad, traffic-free Chowrasta, near the top of town, and busy, clogged Clubside junction – are linked by pedestrianised Nehru Rd, which doubles as the main shopping street. The Mall is officially a mainly traffic-free loop road running north from Chowrasta and back to it, but the Mall name is often applied to Chowrasta and Nehru Rd as well. Hill Cart Rd runs the length of the bustling lower bazaar and is Darjeeling's perpetually clogged major vehicle thoroughfare.

History

Darjeeling originally belonged to the Buddhist chogyals (kings) of Sikkim until 1780, when it was annexed by invading Gurkhas from Nepal. The East India Company gained control of the region in 1816, but soon returned most of the lands to Sikkim in exchange for British control over any future border disputes.

During one such dispute in 1828, two British officers stumbled across the Dorje Ling monastery, on a tranquil forested ridge, and passed word to Calcutta (Kolkata) that it would be a perfect site for a sanatorium (they were sure to have also mentioned its strategic military importance in the region). The chogyal of Sikkim (still grateful for the return of his kingdom) agreed to give the sparsely inhabited land to the East India Company, receiving an annual allowance of ₹3000 in return. In 1837 the hill station of Darjeeling was born and the first tea bushes were planted four years later. By 1857, the population of Darjeeling had reached 10,000, mainly because of a massive influx of Nepali tea labourers (known as Gorkhas). The railway arrived in 1881 and Darjeeling's status as a premier hill station of the British Raj was assured.

◉ Sights

◉ North of Chowrasta

Observatory Hill RELIGIOUS SITE
The hill rising above Chowrasta is home to several much-visited temples, approached through a flurry of colourful prayer flags and hanging bells. The main summit temple is sacred to Mahakala, a Buddhist protector deity also worshipped as a wrathful avatar of Shiva. It is staffed by a Hindu priest and Buddhist lama sitting side by side in an admirable display of religious coexistence. A 300m path up to the summit starts about 100m along the eastern Mall road from Chowrasta.

Sadly no mountain panoramas from the top, but if you go back down to the Mall and turn left (north) you'll soon reach a couple of viewpoints with Khangchendzonga-view benches.

Darjeeling

Padmaja Naidu Himalayan
Zoological Park & Himalayan
Mountaineering
Institute (900m)

Jawahar Rd

Tibetan Refugee
Self-Help Centre
(150m)

⚑2

Happy Valley
Tea Estate
(700m)

CR Das Rd

The Mall

The Mall

Lebong Cart Rd

⊙6

🏛34

CR Das Rd

Loch Nagar Rd

Lloyd Botanical
Gardens
Entrance

🏛11

🏦16

Lloyd
Botanic
Garden

Eden
Hospital

Old
Super
Market

Bazaar Cart Rd

Ballem Villa Rd

Gandhi Rd

Bhanu Bhakta
Agharya
Statue
❗

🏛24
27 🍴
28 ℹ   🏛31

🏛38

🍴12

🍴18

Dr Zakir Hussain Rd

32 🍴

CHOWK
BAZAR

Hill Cart Rd

H D Lama Rd

Nehru Rd

21 🍴
🍴22

🍴8
🍴23

✚29

🍴19

🍴7

Dr Zakir Hussain Rd

37 🍴

NB Singh Rd

35 🏛
🍴10

Clubside Junction

Municipality
Offices &
Clock Tower

Tenzing Norgay Rd

Lower Toong Soong Rd

Laden La Rd

HD Sharma Rd

25 🏨
17 🍴
26 🏨
39 🍴
30 🍴

💲5
🏨33

TV
Tower

🍴20

St Mother
Teresa Rd

🏛4
🏨9

🍴36

💲

13

SM Das Rd

Gandhi Rd

🏛40

🏛15

Dr Zakir Hussain Rd

**Darjeeling
Himalayan
Railway**

Darjeeling
Train
Station

🏛1

♨3

🏨14

Hill Cart Rd

Dr Zakir Hussain Rd

N
0 —————— 200 m
0 —————— 0.1 miles

Darjeeling

Padmaja Naidu Himalayan
Zoological Park   ZOO

(📞0354-2253709; www.pnhzp.gov.in; Jawahar Parvat; Indian/foreigner incl Himalayan Mountaineering Institute ₹60/100, camera ₹10; ☉8.30am-4pm Fri-Wed) This zoo, one of India's better ones, was established in 1958 to study, conserve and preserve Himalayan fauna. Housed within its rocky and forested environment are species such as Asiatic black bear, clouded leopard, red panda and Himalayan wolf. The zoo and its snow-leopard breeding centre (closed to the public) are home to the world's largest captive population of snow leopards (currently 11). It's a reasonably pleasant 2km walk, mostly downhill, northwest from Chowrasta.

Himalayan Mountaineering
Institute   MUSEUM

(HMI; 📞0354-2254087; www.hmidarjeeling.com; Jawahar Parvat; Indian/foreigner incl zoo ₹60/100; ☉8.30am-4pm Fri-Wed) Within the zoo precinct, the prestigious HMI was founded in 1954 and has provided training for some of India's leading mountaineers. Its fascinating Mountaineering Museum exhibits evocative memorabilia from the 1922 and 1924 Everest expeditions, which set off from Darjeeling, as well as more-recent summit attempts – including the successful 1953 climb. Just outside the museum are Tenzing Norgay's samadhi (cremation spot) and a Tenzing statue. The intrepid Everest summiteer was a director and adviser at the institute for many years.

Happy Valley Tea Estate   TEA ESTATE

(📞8017700700; Lebong Cart Rd; tour ₹100; ☉9am-4.30pm) This 1854 estate on the northwest edge of town is a good place to learn about tea, especially when plucking and processing are in progress (March to November). An employee guides you through the aromatic factory and its withering, rolling, fermenting and drying processes, explaining how green, black and white teas all come from the same leaf, and you'll get to taste a few varieties. A free shuttle van for visitors runs from **Bhanu Bhawan** (The Mall) in town from 9.30am.

Tibetan Refugee Self-Help Centre COMMUNITY

(☑ 0354-2252552; www.tibetancentredarjeeling. com; Lebong Cart Rd; ⊙ 8am-5pm Mon-Sat) 🖉 Established in 1959, this refugee centre includes a Tibetan Buddhist temple, workshops producing carpets, woodcarvings, wool and woollen items, and a home for the aged, a kindergarten and a clinic. Visitors are welcome to wander through the workshops. There's also an interesting, politically charged photographic exhibition on Tibetan history. The handicrafts are for sale in the showroom, where you can also order a gorgeous Tibetan carpet (US$350 for 6ft by 3ft/1.8m by 0.9m) to be made and shipped to your home. A quick walking approach is to take the lane down beside Hotel Dolphin on The Mall and zigzag downhill about 1.2km (asking directions a few times).

Bhutia Busty Gompa BUDDHIST MONASTERY

This temple originally stood on Observatory Hill, but was rebuilt in its present location in the 19th century. It houses fine murals depicting the life of Buddha, and Khangchendzonga provides a spectacular northern backdrop. Prayers are held at 3pm; the temple is often locked at other times. The monastery is about a 1.2km walk down from Chowrasta: start down CR Das Rd, fork right 200m after the Central Nirvana Resort, and keep asking directions.

◎ South of Chowrasta

Himalayan Tibet Museum MUSEUM

(☑ 0354-2252977; 12 Gandhi Rd; ₹50; ⊙ 10am-5pm Thu-Tue, to 6pm Apr-Oct) This well-thought-out museum (one large room) is a good, colourful introduction to Tibet and its culture. The attractive displays introduce the Dalai Lama, stupas, and Tibetan religion, script, medicine, history and geography with just the right amount of information to avoid overload. Exhibits include fine *thangka* (Tibetan cloth paintings), a 3D map of Tibet and a sand mandala (a visual meditation aid symbolising the universe).

Japanese Peace Pagoda BUDDHIST STUPA

(AJC Bose Rd; ⊙ temple 4.30am-7pm, prayers 4.30-6am & 4.30-6.30pm) Perched on a hillside 2km south of the town centre, the gleaming white, 28m-high Peace Pagoda is one of more than 70 pagodas built around the world by the Japanese Buddhist Nipponzan Myohoji organisation. During the drum-ming *puja* (prayers) sessions in the neighbouring temple, visitors are offered a hand drum and encouraged to join in the rituals. Getting here involves a pleasant walk along Gandhi and AJC Bose Rds, past the curiosity-inspiring Institute for Astroparticle Physics and Space Science.

◎ Out of Town

Tiger Hill VIEWPOINT

To watch the dawn light break over a spectacular 250km stretch of Himalayan horizon, including Everest (8848m), Khangchendzonga (8598m) and two more of the world's five highest peaks, rise very early and take a jeep out to Tiger Hill (2590m), 11km south of Darjeeling, above Ghum. This daily morning spectacle (views are best in autumn and spring) is a major tourist attraction, however, so if you prefer your Himalayan views in peace you might want to try somewhere else.

Hundreds of jeeps leave Darjeeling for Tiger Hill every morning at 4am – traffic snarls en route are quite common. Sunrise trips (usually with stops at Batasia Loop and a Buddhist monastery in Ghum on the way back) can be booked through a travel agency or directly with jeep drivers at the Clubside taxi stand. Return trips cost ₹1200 for a three/four passenger car, ₹1800 for a bigger, comfier Innova, or ₹200 per seat.

🏃 Activities

Senchal Wildlife Sanctuary MOUNTAIN BIKING

(Indian/foreigner ₹50/100; ⊙ mid-Sep–mid-Jun) Mountain bikers can escape all that dirty, noisy motor traffic with a ride on the dedicated mountain-bike trail opened in 2017 through Senchal Wildlife Sanctuary, south of Ghum. The route winds about 14km through pine forests, with gentle gradients and Himalayan viewpoints (total distance from Darjeeling: about 23km one way). Day-trip guides from Darjeeling agencies cost ₹1000 to ₹1500, with bike rental around ₹1000.

Agencies

Adventures Unlimited OUTDOORS

(☑ 9933070013; www.adventuresunlimited.in; 142/1 Dr Zakir Hussain Rd; ⊙ 9am-8.30pm) A well-established firm doing treks to Singalila Ridge (US$65 per person per day) and in Sikkim (US$65 to US$85), plus rental and tours on Enfield and other motorbikes (rental per day from ₹1500) and mountain bikes (₹850 to ₹1500). Ask for Gautam.

Ashmita Trek & Tours
TREKKING

(☎9733106312; www.ashmitatrek.com; 1st fl, Singalila Market bldg, 3A Nehru Rd; ⏰9am-5pm Mon-Sat) A professional, efficient agency with knowledgeable guides, specialising in treks (Sikkim and Nepal as well as Singalila Ridge) and cultural tours. Also offers mountain biking and birdwatching. All-inclusive Singalila treks are ₹4000/3500 per person per day for two/five people.

Himalayan Travels
TREKKING

(☎0354-2256956; www.himalayantravel.co.in; 18 Gandhi Rd; ⏰9am-6pm) Very experienced company that's been arranging treks (US$60 to US$80 per person per day) and mountaineering expeditions in Darjeeling and Sikkim since 1975.

🛏 Sleeping

Darjeeling has several hundred hotels. The main backpacker enclave is Dr Zakir Hussain Rd, which follows the highest ridge in Darjeeling, so be prepared for a hike to the best budget places.

High season (when it's wise to book ahead) is from October to early December and mid-March to mid-May. At other times prices can drop by 50%.

Hotel Tranquility
HOTEL $

(☎0354-2257678; www.darjeelinghotel tranquility.com; 13A Dr Zakir Hussain Rd; d ₹800-1000, tr ₹1200; 🛜) This very good-value place is sparkling clean, with 24-hour hot water, a comfy lobby lounge, views from the rooftop and upper floors, and 16 small but neat white rooms with good mattresses. The helpful owner is a local schoolteacher, and can provide all kinds of info about the area.

Snowlion Homestay
GUESTHOUSE $$

(☎9800869590; www.snowlionhomestay.com; 27A Gandhi Rd; d/ste incl breakfast ₹2690/4720; 🛜) The Snowlion provides a friendly Tibetan welcome and cosy, clean, pine-panelled rooms with soft beds and Tibetan rugs and cushions. The two top-floor suites, each with one double and two single beds, share a panoramic terrace. Enjoy your breakfast in the hosts' family sitting room.

Hotel Seven Seventeen
HOTEL $$

(☎0354-2255099; www.hotel717.com; 26 HD Lama Rd; incl breakfast s ₹3190, d ₹3540-5070; 🛜) This friendly Tibetan-run place on the edge of the bazaar has pleasant wood-skirted rooms with clean bathrooms. Upper-floor rooms

are best; those at the back have great valley views. The excellent-value ground-floor restaurant (mains ₹120 to ₹180) is spacious and civilised, with Indian, Tibetan and Chinese food and alcoholic drinks available.

Revolver
BOUTIQUE HOTEL $$

(☎8371919527; www.revolver.in; 110 Gandhi Rd; d ₹1570-1900; 🛜) This Beatles-themed hotel certainly makes a change from standard hill-station hotel style. It's full of Fab Four memorabilia and the five small but stylish rooms are each named after one of the group (plus Brian Epstein). The downstairs restaurant serves good fresh-ground local coffee and interesting local, Naga and Thai set meals (from ₹150), and there's free filtered water too.

Hotel Aliment
HOTEL $$

(☎0354-2255068; www.facebook.com/hotel alimentdarjeeling; 40 Dr Zakir Hussain Rd; d ₹1800-2500, q ₹2500-3500; 🛜) A dependable choice in a quiet area well above the downtown hubbub, the Aliment has a variety of reasonably priced, wood-lined rooms. The best are on the upper floors with valley views. All have geysers. Staff are helpful and there's a good top-floor Indian restaurant (mains ₹130 to ₹230) and lending library.

★ Dekeling Resort at Hawk's Nest
HERITAGE HOTEL $$$

(☎0354-2253298; www.dekeling.com; 2 Hawk's Nest, AJC Bose Rd; d incl breakfast ₹6140-8730; 🛜) Run by the good people at Dekeling Hotel (p504), this is a great escape from Darjeeling's increasingly noisy centre, situated 1km south en route to the Japanese Pagoda. The four large 140-year-old suites are a perfect conjunction of comfort and authentic colonial ambience, while the modern 'super deluxe' rooms are superbly designed and reposeful with expansive views, parquet floors and solar-heating panels.

★ Glenburn
HERITAGE HOTEL $$$

(☎9830070213; www.glenburnteaestate.com; Darjeeling; s/d full board ₹25,850/43,710; 🛜) About an hour's drive north of Darjeeling, this stylish, uberluxury tea estate is a true indulgence for those looking to splurge. The lovely estate sits pretty amid rolling tea plantations and makes for a perfect hideaway, with elegant colonial-style suites and contemporary comforts. Rates include fine meals of varied cuisines, transport, and sundry activities such as tea-estate tours and hikes.

★**Windamere Hotel** HERITAGE HOTEL **$$$**

(☎0354-2254041; www.windamerehotel.com; Observatory Hill; full board s ₹14,080-20,480, d ₹17,280-21,760; @☎) This quaint, rambling relic of the Raj is one of Darjeeling's most atmospheric digs. The charming Ada Villa, with the tea rooms and bar, was once a boarding house for British tea planters, and the well-tended grounds are spacious with lots of pleasant seating areas. The comfortable rooms, fireplaces and hot-water bottles provide just the right measure of comfort and mothballed charm.

★**Dekeling Hotel** GUESTHOUSE **$$$**

(☎0354-2254159; www.dekeling.com; 51 Gandhi Rd; d ₹2580-4310, without bathroom ₹950; ☎) Spotless Dekeling is full of charming touches such as coloured diamond-pane windows, a wood-fired heater in the sociable lounge-library, wood panelling and sloping attic ceilings, plus superb views. Tibetan owners Sangay and Norbu play perfect hosts and the service is excellent. The central location is also a plus, even if you have to climb a lot of stairs to reach reception!

Elgin Darjeeling HERITAGE HOTEL **$$$**

(☎0354-2257226; www.elginhotels.com; 18 HD Lama Rd; half board s ₹14,460-15,490, d ₹14,850-15,870; @☎) Grand and full of classy ambience, yet friendly and comfortable, the Elgin was once the summer residence of the maharaja of Cooch Behar. The restaurant is elegant and the garden terrace is the perfect place to nurse a beer. For historic charm, ask for an 'attic room' underneath the dripping eaves; for the biggest rooms, try the new, modern wing.

✗ Eating

★**Glenary's** MULTICUISINE **$$**

(Nehru Rd; mains ₹200-375; ☺noon-9.30pm; ☎) Popular Glenary's sits above the famous bakery-cafe of the same name and is a classy Darjeeling staple. Of note are the Continental and Chinese dishes and the tandoori specials; try the beef steak or roast pork or the tasty baked-cheese macaroni. Linen tablecloths, white-and-gold decor and plenty of tables with a view enhance the elegant experience.

Kunga TIBETAN **$$**

(51 Gandhi Rd; mains ₹150-220; ☺7.30am-8.30pm) Kunga is a cosy little wood-panelled place run by a friendly Tibetan family, strong on noodles and *momos* (Tibetan dumplings),

and with excellent *shabhaley* (Tibetan pies), juice, and fruit and muesli with curd. It's always busy and the clientele includes locals, a mark of its culinary authenticity.

Lunar Restaurant INDIAN **$$**

(1st fl, 51 Gandhi Rd; mains ₹150-225; ☺8am-9.30pm) This bright and clean space is perhaps the best vegetarian Indian restaurant in town, with good service and great views from the large windows. The Lunar special masala dosas come with delicious dried fruits, peanuts and cheese. Access is via the same staircase as Hotel Dekeling.

Park INDIAN, THAI **$$**

(☎0354-2255270; 41 Laden La Rd; mains ₹160-400; ☺11am-9pm) The Park is deservedly very popular for its North Indian curries (great chicken-tikka kebab) and authentic Thai dishes, including coconut-chicken soup, spicy green-papaya salad and Thai street noodles. Everything we've had here is good. You can pick from four separate dining rooms, and it has alcoholic drinks, too. Look for the ornate Thai-style entrance.

Dekeva's TIBETAN **$$**

(51 Gandhi Rd; mains ₹120-210; ☺10am-9pm) This cosy place offers generous servings of Tibetan staples and tasty Chinese dishes, and a range of noodles for connoisseurs who can tell their *thenthuk* (Tibetan noodles) from their *gyathuk* (also Tibetan noodles).

Shangri-La INDIAN, TIBETAN **$$**

(Nehru Rd; mains ₹160-320; ☺11.30am-10pm) A classy and modern bar-restaurant near the top of Nehru Rd, Shangri-La specialises in Tibetan, Chinese and Indian offerings in stylish surrounds, with wooden floors, clean tablecloths and roaring fires in winter. There are also three stylish hotel rooms upstairs (doubles ₹2240 to ₹4840 depending on season).

Sonam's Kitchen CONTINENTAL, NEPALI **$$**

(142 Dr Zakir Hussain Rd; mains ₹150-240; ☺8am-2.30pm & 5.30-8.30pm Mon-Sat, 8am-2.30pm Sun; ☎) Friendly little Sonam's serves up strong brewed coffee, authentic French toast, fluffy pancakes (breakfasts until 2.30pm), fresh soups and yummy pasta. The chunky fresh-bread sandwiches can be packed to go for picnics. Book a day ahead for special traditional Nepali dinners.

Windamere Hotel BRITISH **$$$**

(☎0354-2254041; www.windamerehotel.com; Observatory Hill; afternoon tea ₹900; ☺4-6pm)

The authentic afternoon-tea experience at Windamere Hotel is a joy for aficionados of things colonial, with crustless cucumber and tuna sandwiches, shortcake, scones with jam and (albeit synthetic) cream, and brews from the well-reputed Castleton estate, all to be enjoyed while seated on chintz sofas. You need to book in advance and will probably be required to provide a cash advance or bank card details.

Drinking & Nightlife

The top-end hotels all have classy bars: the Windamere is the most atmospheric place to kick back with an early-evening gin and tonic – or a very stiff gimlet (gin and lime juice) – if you are having dinner there.

Gatty's
BAR

(Dr Zakir Hussain Rd; beer/shots from ₹240/100; ☺6-11pm; 🖥) Backpacker-friendly Gatty's is the only place in town that has a pulse after 9pm, with live music at weekends. The food (dishes ₹80 to ₹280) includes house-made lasagne, and pita with hummus or falafel. It brews good espresso and there's cold Kingfisher and Tuborg, too.

Teahouses & Cafes

Glenary's
CAFE

(Nehru Rd; tea pot from ₹80; ☺6.30am-8pm; 🖥) This renowned teahouse has excellent baked goods (cakes, quiches and pies ₹40 to ₹80) as well as tea, and fine views from its outdoor balcony and the indoor conservatory-like area. It's a good place to grab breakfast, from oatmeal to eggs and bacon.

Sunset Lounge
TEAHOUSE

(CR Das Rd, Chowrasta; cup of tea ₹25-400; ☺9.30am-8.30pm; 🖥) This two-floor tearoom run by the Nathmulls tea company offers aficionados a range of quality white, green and black teas by the cup or pot, with in-house baked treats, fine valley views and wi-fi. Ask for the six-cup tasting sample for two people (it's not on the menu).

Himalayan Java
CAFE

(Nehru Rd; coffee ₹70-130; ☺8.30am-8pm; 🖥) 🍃 Branch of the Nepal cafe chain, serving up good organic coffee and desserts, plus breakfast pancakes, waffles and sandwiches (snacks and light dishes ₹90 to ₹250), in a stylish semi-industrial interior – all very popular with a young local crowd. Free filtered-water refills too.

TEA TOURISM

The word Darjeeling means, more than anything the world over, tea – an aromatic muscatel tea, known for its amber colour, tannic astringence and musky, spicy flavour, considered by many to be the world's best. Purists will tell you that Darjeeling teas are best taken alone or with a slice of lemon (and/or a pinch of sugar), but never with milk.

Darjeeling Tea Experiences

While in Darjeeling, two top places to enjoy a pot of this fine brew are Sunset Lounge and House of Tea (Nehru Rd; 2-cup pot of tea ₹100-200; ☺10am-1pm & 2.30-8.30pm), while afternoon tea at the Windamere Hotel provides a complete immersion in the British tea-ceremony experience. For packets of tea to take home, head to Nathmulls Tea Room (p506).

You can learn a lot about tea growing and tea production on a visit to one of the estates that welcome visitors, such as Makaibari (p497) at Kurseong and Happy Valley (p501) in Darjeeling. Spring, monsoon and autumn are the busiest times, when the three respective 'flushes' are harvested. There's normally no plucking on Sunday, which means most of the machinery isn't working on Monday.

If you wish to spend a night amid the plantations, try staying with a tea pickers' family in a homestay (p498) at Makaibari, which also gives you a big discount on day tours of the estate.

Several tea estates offer more luxurious stays. If you're in the mood for splurging, accommodation doesn't get any more exclusive than top-end Glenburn (p503), a working tea estate and resort outside Darjeeling that boasts five members of staff for every guest. A stay at Glenburn is rumoured to have given director Wes Anderson inspiration for his film *The Darjeeling Limited*.

To learn more about the Darjeeling tea story, read Jeff Koehler's 2015 book *Darjeeling: A History of the World's Greatest Tea*.

🛍 Shopping

★ Nathmulls Tea Room
TEA

(www.nathmulltea.com; Laden La Rd; ⊙9am-8pm daily 15 Apr-14 Jun & 15 Sep-14 Nov, Mon-Sat rest of year) The Darjeeling area produces arguably the world's finest teas and Nathmulls is one of the best retailers, with more than 50 varieties. Expect to pay ₹200 to ₹400 per 100g for a decent tea, and up to ₹2500 for the finest flushes. There are also attractive teapots, strainers and cosies as souvenirs. To taste Nathmulls teas, head to Sunset Lounge (p505).

Oxford Book & Stationery Company
BOOKS

(Chowrasta; ⊙10am-7.30pm 15 Apr-14 Jun & 15 Sep-14 Nov, 10am-7.30pm Mon-Fri & 9.30am-2.30pm Sat rest of year) The best bookshop east of Kathmandu, selling a good selection of novels and Himalaya and India titles.

ℹ Information

EMERGENCY

Police Assistance Booth (Chowrasta) A friendly neighbourhood cop is stationed here for quick assistance.

MEDICAL SERVICES

Planter's Hospital (D&DMA Hospital; ☎9332490262; 7 Nehru Rd) The best private hospital in town.

MONEY

Poddar's (☎7001418366; Laden La Rd; ⊙10am-8pm) Changes most currencies at decent rates with no commission.

ℹ CROSSING TO NEPAL: PANITANKI TO KAKARBHITTA

Foreigners can only cross the border into Nepal at Panitanki/Kakarbhitta (p496), not at Pashupatinagar, en route to Mirik. From Darjeeling, you can charter a jeep to Panitanki or catch a shared jeep to Siliguri then local transport to the border.

Samsara Tours, Travels & Treks (p506) can book day and night buses from Kakarbhitta to Kathmandu (₹1000 to ₹1500, 13 to 17 hours, departure 4am and 4pm). Samsara can also book Nepali domestic flights from Bhadrapur to Kathmandu (US$140 to US$180), or you can book online directly with Buddha Air (www.buddhaair.com).

State Bank of India (Laden La Rd; ⊙10am-2pm & 2.30-4pm Mon-Sat, closed 2nd & 4th Sat) Changes major foreign currencies and has an ATM.

TOURIST INFORMATION

Darjeeling Tourism (www.darjeeling-tourism.com) Excellent independent website with heaps of good information about the Bengal hills.

GTA Tourist Information Centre (www.tourismdarjeeling.com; Nehru Rd; ⊙9am-6pm Mon-Sat, to 1pm every other Sat) The staff are friendly, well organised and the best source of information on Darjeeling.

ℹ Getting There & Away

AIR

The nearest airport is 70km south at Bagdogra, 14km from Siliguri. A taxi from Darjeeling costs ₹2200. Allow four hours for the drive, to be safe. Wizzride (www.wizzride.com), launched in 2017 and getting reliable reports, runs several daily trips in comfortable five-passenger Innova cars for ₹500 to ₹600 per person. You can book and pay online; the site accepts foreign cards.

BUS

Samsara Tours, Travels & Treks (☎9733443812; www.samsaratourstravelsandtreks.com; 7 Laden La Rd; ⊙10am-6pm Mon-Sat) can book air-con overnight buses from Siliguri to Kolkata (₹1200 to ₹1700, 15 hours), and ordinary night buses to Guwahati (₹600, 4pm), Patna (₹550 to ₹700, 6pm) and Gaya (₹750, 4pm). Note that these tickets don't include transfers to Siliguri.

JEEP & TAXI

Numerous shared jeeps leave the south end of the crowded **Motor Stand** (Old Super Market, Hill Cart Rd) for Siliguri (₹150, three hours, 6am to 6pm), Kurseong (₹80, 1½ hours, 6am to 4pm or 5pm) and Mane Bhanjang (₹60, 1½ hours, 7am to 5pm). Jeeps for Mirik (₹120, 2½ hours) and Rimbik (₹220, five hours) leave from the northern end. An office inside the ground floor of the Old Super Market building sells tickets for frequent jeeps to Kalimpong (₹150, 2½ hours, 6.30am to 3pm), while two roadside kiosks sell tickets for Gangtok (₹250, four hours, 7am to 3pm). You'll find jeeps to Ghum (₹30) 250m further south on **Hill Cart Rd**.

To New Jalpaiguri or Bagdogra, get a connection in Siliguri, or charter a jeep or taxi from Darjeeling for ₹2200. A chartered jeep to Kalimpong is ₹2000; a taxi to Mane Bhanjang is ₹1500.

Darjeeling Transport Corporation (Laden La Rd) offers chartered jeeps to Panitanki (Nepal border; ₹3500) and Siliguri/Bagdogra airport (₹2200/2500), and round trips for sightseeing to Kalimpong (₹3500), Kurseong (₹2000) and

Around Darjeeling

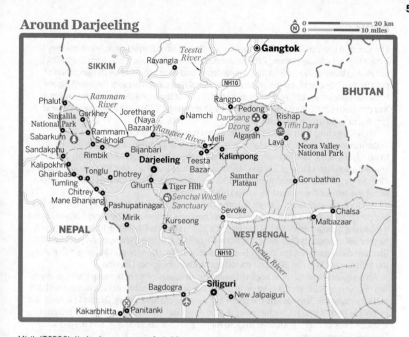

Mirik (₹2500). It also has more comfortable Innova cars for ₹500 to ₹1000 more.

Western Sikkim

The crossing point from West Bengal into Sikkim at Jorethang, north of Darjeeling, has been closed to foreigners since 2016. Unless it reopens, to reach Jorethang you need to take a Gangtok-bound jeep as far as Melli, walk across the bridge into Sikkim and then find a shared jeep (₹150 to ₹200) or a small taxi (₹800 to ₹1000) to Jorethang, or hitch-hike. Fifteen-day Sikkim permits are available free (usually from 8am to 7.30pm) at the checkpost at the west end of the bridge: bring one passport photo and copies of your passport and visa.

TOY TRAIN

The **Darjeeling Himalayan Railway** (DHR; www. dhr.in.net; joy ride ₹805-1405, Darjeeling–Kurseong 2nd-/1st-class ₹60/685, Darjeeling–Siliguri 1st-class ₹1105), known affectionately as the toy train, is one of the few hill railways still operating in India. The panting train made its first journey along its precipice-topping, 2ft-wide tracks in September 1881. Today it passes within metres of local shopfronts as it weaves alongside and across the main road almost the entire 88km from New Jalpaiguri to Darjeeling, bringing traffic to a standstill and tooting its whistle incessantly. The railway climbs 2111m en route from New Jalpaiguri to its highest point at Ghum, and has had Unesco World Heritage listing since 1999.

It's a rare day when the trains run on time and monsoon landslides seem to block sections of track almost every year. However, the short 'joy rides' between Darjeeling and Ghum are relatively reliable.

Only one daily (diesel-powered) train in each direction makes the whole seven-hour(!) trip between New Jalpaiguri and Darjeeling. Train 52541 departs New Jalpaiguri at 8.30am; in the opposite direction, train 52540 departs Darjeeling for New Jalpaiguri at 8am. These trains have 1st-class seating only, costing ₹1295 from New Jalpaiguri to Darjeeling, ₹1105 from Siliguri Junction (6½ hours) and ₹685 from Kurseong (2½ hours). In addition, train 52587 runs just from Kurseong to Darjeeling, departing at 6.30am (2nd/1st class ₹60/685, 2½ hours), and train 52588 leaves Darjeeling for Kurseong at 4pm.

Unless you're a very serious railway buff, the joy-ride trains should satisfy your toy-train urges. These run just from Darjeeling to Ghum and back, a two-hour round trip with a 10-minute stop at the Batasia Loop (where the railway does a full circle to gain height) and half an hour at Ghum, where you can visit the railway museum inside the station. There are normally six steam-powered joy rides daily (₹1310 to ₹1405), pulled by locomotives at least 90 years old, and three diesel-powered runs (₹805).

Book tickets at least a day or two ahead at **Darjeeling train station** (☎ 0354-2252555; Hill Cart Rd; ☺ 8am-5pm Mon-Sat, 8am-2pm Sun).

GHUM

The junction town of Ghum (Ghoom), 6km southwest from Darjeeling, is home not only to India's highest railway station (2258m; the destination of joy-ride trains from Darjeeling), but also to three colourful Buddhist monasteries and what seems to be its own breed of cute fluffy white dogs (you're sure to see several of these if you explore the town). Dawn trips from Darjeeling to Tiger Hill usually stop at one of the monasteries on the way back. You can also reach Ghum from Darjeeling by shared jeep (₹30) from a Hill Cart Rd stand (p506), or by taxi (one way ₹300).

Yiga Choeling Gompa (Old Monastery; www.yigachoeling.com; Ghum; camera ₹100; ⊙ dawn-dusk), the region's most famous monastery, was founded in 1850 and houses up to 40 monks of the Gelugpa school. The serene temple has wonderful old murals and enshrines a 5m-high statue of Jampa (Maitreya or 'Future Buddha') and 300 beautifully bound Tibetan texts. From Ghum station, walk 100m west along the road towards Darjeeling, turn left at the sign for the monastery and go 600m.

The fortress-style **Guru Sakya Gompa** (Hill Cart Rd, Ghum; ⊙ dawn-dusk), with a big new temple consecrated in 2015, conducts prayer sessions between 5.30am and 7.30am (useful if returning from a dawn visit to Tiger Hill). It's 250m towards Darjeeling from the station. A further 350m towards Darjeeling, **Samten Choeling Gompa** (New Monastery; Hill Cart Rd, Ghum; ⊙ dawn-dusk) has the largest Buddha statue in West Bengal, and a chorten containing the ashes of the German Buddhist mystic and author Anagarika Govinda.

An enjoyable walking route back to Darjeeling, deliciously free of honking traffic, is along Tenzing Norgay Rd from the junction at Jorebunglow, 500m east from Ghum station. About half way along the 5km route is the charming, century-old **Mak Dhog Gompa** (Alubari), run by people from Yolmo in Langtang, Nepal, who emigrated here 150 years ago. Its atmospheric upper-floor chapel is dedicated to Guru Rinpoche (Padmasambhava) and the monastery founder Sangay Lama.

If you just want to look at the trains in action, there's plenty of shunting, whistling and steaming at Darjeeling station on and off all day.

ⓘ Getting Around

Darjeeling is quite an enjoyable town to walk around, if you avoid the more traffic-infested roads. Streets leading off Chowrasta are mostly traffic-free. There are several taxi stands, including at Clubside and on Hill Cart Road near the train station, but rates are absurdly high for short hops.

Shared minivans to anywhere north of the town centre (eg North Point) leave from the northern end of the Motor Stand (p506). Free shuttle vans to Happy Valley Tea Estate (p501) start outside the concert hall Bhanu Bhawan (p501) from 9.30am onwards.

Singalila Ridge

The region's outstanding trekking area is the Singalila Ridge, which runs about 50km along the India–Nepal border from Mane Bhanjang to Phalut (and continues into Sikkim, though foreigners aren't allowed to cross the state border here). The ridge offers wonderful views of the Himalayan chain stretching from Nepal, Sikkim and Bhutan. Between Sanda-

kphu (the highest point, 3636m) and Phalut, the panoramas include four of the world's five highest peaks: Everest, Khangchendzonga, Lhotse and Makalu. There are some charming valleys and villages below the ridge, too. Clear skies and warm daytime temperatures in October and November make them ideal months to trek (but be prepared for freezing night-time temperatures at Sandakphu), as do the long days and incredible rhododendron and magnolia blooms of late April and May. **Singalila National Park** (Indian/foreigner ₹100/200, camera/video ₹100/400, vehicle or horse ₹100; ⊙ mid-Sep–mid-Jun) covers the Indian side of the ridge from Tumling to the Sikkim border; the park and access to the ridge are closed from mid-June to mid-September.

Routes

The classic trek heads north along the ridge from Mane Bhanjang (25km west of Darjeeling) to Sandakphu and Phalut (hopping back and forth between India and Nepal), then southeast down via Gorkhey and Rammam to Srikhola or Rimbik. A few intrepid and fit mountain bikers cycle the route in three days: experience is essential and the Kalipokhri–Sandakphu section is generally too steep to ride.

Walkers can shorten some stages (and add days) by sleeping in Kalipokhri (between Tumling and Sandakphu), Molley (2km off the Sandakphu–Phalut stretch) or Gorkhey. You can cut days off the later stages by descending footpaths in one day from Sandakhphu to Srikhola, or from Sabarkum to Rammam.

A recently built concrete road along the 17km stretch from Mane Bhanjang to Ghairibas has significantly reduced the appeal of the early part of the trek. Knowledgeable guides from Darjeeling agencies know off-road alternative paths, but even with them you'll be on the road for about one-third of the way from Mane Bhanjang to Sandakphu.

You can avoid the steep first couple of hours out of Mane Bhanjang by driving to Chitrey, Dhotrey or Tumling. From Dhotrey you join the ridge road at Tonglu.

Another possibility, avoiding jeep-able tracks except the lightly trafficked Sandakphu–Phalut stretch, is a five-to-seven-day northern circuit from Rimbik or Srikhola up to the ridge and down again.

If you just want to do a one-day hike, agencies offer a route from Dhotrey to Tumling (where in clear weather you can glimpse the tip of Everest) and down to Mane Bhanjang.

Singalila Ridge Sample Trek Schedule

DAY	ROUTE	DISTANCE (KM)
1	Mane Bhanjhang (1950m) to Tumling (2980m) via Chitrey & Meghma	13
2	Tumling to Sandakphu (3636m) via Ghairibas & Kalipokhri	17
3	Sandakphu to Phalut (3600m) via Sabarkum	19
4	Phalut to Rammam (2530m) via Gorkhey	16
5	Rammam to Rimbik (2290m) via Srikhola	19

Accommodation

There's accommodation in many of the tiny villages, ranging from government-run trekkers' huts with ₹220 dorms to lodges with simple rooms with private bathroom (hot water by bucket) for ₹1500 to ₹2500. All lodgings offer meals, and bottled and boiled water is available along the route. The better lodges can fill up during peak seasons, but many of them can be booked on the internet. All

have clean bedding and blankets, but warm clothes for dawn peak-viewing are essential. The only place where finding a bed can be a problem is Phalut, which has only one reliable place to stay. Trekkers' huts can be booked at Darjeeling's GTA Tourist Information Centre (p506) but even they will tell you that you're better off at one of the private lodges.

Following are the main lodges for over-night stops, in ascending order of price and quality:

Tumling Mountain Lodge, Siddharta Lodge, Shikhar Lodge

Kalipokhri Chewang Lodge

Sandakphu Trekkers' Huts, View Point Homestay, Namobuddha, Sherpa Chalet, Sunrise Hotel

Molley Trekkers' Hut, Forest Rest House

Phalut Trekkers' Hut, Forest Rest House

Gorkhey Paradise, Eden Lodge

Rammam Dhurba Rai Homestay, Namobuddha Lodge, Sherpa Lodge

Mane Bhanjang has several guesthouses, but **Hawk's Nest** (☑9733081184; Chitrey; dm ₹300, s/d ₹850/1700, half board ₹1000/2000), 2.5km up the hill, is much more pleasant. There are also lodges in Rimbik – best are **Hotel Sherpa** (☑9609790491; s/d incl breakfast ₹800/1000) and **Green Hill** (☑9733069143; s/d/tr ₹1000/1100/1500) – and Srikhola.

For a relaxing end to a trek, consider a stay at **Karmi Farm** (karmifarm@yahoo.co.uk; per person full board ₹2200), a two-hour drive from Rimbik near Bijanbari. The simple but comfortable rooms are decorated with colourful local fabrics, and bathrooms have 24-hour hot water. Singalila treks and other activities can be organised, but it's just as easy to sit with a book and pots of tea, overlooking the bird- and flower-filled gardens and the towering peaks in the distance. Staff can arrange transport given advance notice.

Transport, Guides & Formalities

The cheapest way to trek is to travel by shared jeep from Darjeeling's Motor Stand (p506) to Mane Bhanjang or Rimbik, obtain an obligatory guide or porter there, and find accommodation as you go. Darjeeling trekking agencies offer all-inclusive guided trips with many route options for between ₹3000 and ₹4500 per person per day, including transfers, accommodation and meals. In general you can expect professional agency guides to speak better English than local guides from Mane Bhanjang and they may well have better knowledge of the trails.

Bring your passport as you'll have to register at the Frontier Check Post in Mane Bhanjang and you may have to show it elsewhere too. Opposite the Check Post is the **Highlander Guides & Porters Welfare Association** (☑ 9734056944; www.highlander guidesandporters.com; Mane Bhanjang; ⊙ 6am-6pm mid-Sep–mid-Jun), where everyone going into Singalila National Park from Mane Bhanjang must obtain a local guide (per day per Indian/foreign group ₹1000/1300) or porter (per day ₹1000), unless you come with a Forest Department-authorised guide from Darjeeling. Further along the street is the **Singalila Land Rover Owner's Welfare Association** (☑ 8145822708; Main St, Mane Bhanjang; ⊙ 8am-3pm mid-Sep–mid-Jun), offering jeep-and-driver services to the Singalila Ridge (obligatory for people entering the Singalila National Park – which starts just

after Tumling – by vehicle). Sample one-way fares are ₹1500 to Tumling and ₹4000 to Sandakphu. A further 150m up the street is the Singalila National Park visitors centre, where park entry and camera fees are paid.

From Rimbik, there are shared jeeps back to Darjeeling (₹220, five hours) from 6am to 1pm. Book seats in advance if you can.

Kalimpong

☑ 03552 / POP 49,000 / ELEV 1180M

This bustling bazaar town sprawls along a saddle-shaped mountain ridge overlooking the roaring Teesta River and is lorded over by the summit of Khangchendzonga. Smaller and more laid-back than Darjeeling, Kalimpong boasts Himalayan views, Buddhist monasteries, colonial-era architecture and a fascinating nursery industry, all linked by some fine hikes. You could easily fill three days here.

KALIMPONG WALKS

There's plenty of scope for some great walking around Kalimpong, so allow an extra day or two to stretch your legs. Helpdesk Tourism (p514) and Holumba Haven (p513) offer information on all these walks and can arrange guides (per day ₹1000 to ₹1500) and transport if needed.

Around Town

In Kalimpong itself, Helpdesk can arrange a half-day crafts walk (guide ₹800 to ₹1000), taking in a traditional incense workshop, working silversmiths, noodle makers and a *thangka* (Tibetan cloth painting) studio, all hidden in the backstreet bazaars near Haat Bazaar; a visit to the Himalayan Handmade Paper workshop (p511) can be added too if you like.

One easy half-day walk close to town leads from near Holumba Haven to the villages of Challisey and Chibo Busty and a grand viewpoint over the Teesta River. En route, you can drop by the LK Pradhan Cactus Nursery and a small curd production centre at Tharker Farm, with the option of descending to see two fascinating traditional Lepcha houses at Ngassey village. From Ngassey you can walk five minutes down to 6th Mile on the main road for transport back to Kalimpong.

Pedong Area

Further afield, one potential DIY hike starts at a wide track at 20th Mile, 2km past Algarah on the road to Pedong. The track climbs gently along a forested ridge to the faint 17th-century ruins of Damsang Dzong, site of the last stand of the Lepcha kings against the Bhutanese. Continue along the ridge and then descend to views of Khangchendzonga at Tinchuli Hill, before following the dirt road back from Sillery to the main Algarah–Pedong road. From here you can walk back 4km to Algarah to catch a shared jeep to Kalimpong (last jeep 3pm), or continue 3km to Pedong via the Bhutanese-influenced Sangchen Dorje Gompa in Sakyong Busty, just below Pedong. An NBSTC bus leaves Kalimpong for Algarah (₹30) and Pedong (₹30) at 8.30am, or charter a return taxi for the day (₹1500 to ₹2000). Pedong has several options if you want to stay overnight: the five cottages at the laid-back **Silk Route Retreat** (☑ 9932828753; www.thesilkroute retreat.com; 21st Mile, Pedong; cottage incl breakfast/half board ₹2900/3500; ☎), 1.5km south of town, offer a fine hiking base.

History

Like Darjeeling, the Kalimpong area once belonged to the chogyals of Sikkim, but it fell into the hands of the Bhutanese in the 18th century and then the British in 1865. The British developed it from a tiny hamlet into a hill station and Kalimpong became an important trading centre on the route to the Jelep La pass on the Sikkim–Tibet border, as well as a staging base for Victorian travellers headed into Tibet. Scottish missionaries made great efforts to win over the local Buddhists in the late 19th century and the town remains an important educational centre for the entire eastern Himalaya. China's invasion of Tibet in 1950, and the closure of the Sikkim–Tibet border following the 1962 Sino-Indian War, killed off trade with Tibet through Kalimpong. Tourism is now a mainstay of the local economy.

◉ Sights

Deolo Hill VIEWPOINT
(☉ dawn-dusk) On a clear day, the morning views of Khangchendzonga from this hilltop park, about 500m higher than the town centre, are simply superb. After savouring the views have breakfast (8.30am to 11am) at the Deolo Tourist Lodge here, and then walk down to Kalimpong via Dr Graham's Home. It's a 9km walk or drive from the town centre; a one-way taxi costs around ₹300.

Tharpa Choling Gompa BUDDHIST MONASTERY
(Tripai; ☉ 5.30-11am & 11.30am-5pm) FREE Built from 1912 to 1922, the main temple of this Gelugpa-school Tibetan monastery of 50 monks contains statues of past, present and future Buddhas. Don't miss the fascinating museum just above the main monastery, whose exhibits include a model of the temple made from 28,300 matchsticks. The monastery is about 1.5km northeast (uphill) from the town centre: take the right fork about 800m up the road past Deki Lodge, and you'll find it on your right after 100m.

Himalayan Handmade Paper Industry WORKSHOP
(☑ 9932388321; Panlook Compound, KD Pradhan Rd; ☉ 10am-noon & 1-3pm Mon-Sat) FREE Visitors are welcome to drop into this small workshop to see traditional paper-making processes, from boiling and pulping of the local *argayli* (daphne) bush to sifting, pressing and drying. The resulting insect-resistant paper is used to block-print Buddhist monastic scriptures, but it's also sold here as notebooks and cards. Morning is the best time to see production. It's a 15-minute walk from town, with a partly hidden sign on a 'Private Road' driveway, on the right side of the road.

Durpin Gompa BUDDHIST MONASTERY
FREE Kalimpong's largest monastery, formally known as Zangtok Pelri Phodang, sits atop panoramic Durpin Hill (1372m) and was consecrated by the Dalai Lama in 1976. There are impressive murals in the main prayer room downstairs, presided over by Padmasambhava (the Indian sage credited with spreading Buddhism in Tibet in the 8th century), interesting 3D mandalas (visual meditational aids) on the 2nd floor, and stunning Khangchendzonga views from the terrace. Prayers are held at 6am and 3pm.

The monastery is about 5km south of the town centre, most easily reached by taxi (one way ₹200). It's a pleasant mostly downhill walk back to town, passing the army golf course and canteen. You can stop for a tea at the 1930s English-country-style Morgan House, now a state-government-run hotel.

Lepcha Heritage Museum MUSEUM
(☑ 9933780295; HL Dixit Rd; ☉ 10.30am-4.30pm Mon-Fri) FREE This offbeat collection of Lepcha treasures could be likened to rummaging through the attic of your grandfather's house (if he were a Lepcha elder). A guide explains Lepcha creation myths, while pointing out religious texts, sacred porcupine quill hats and old pangolin skins. It's a 10-minute walk downhill below the Sports Ground. Times vary so call ahead.

Nurseries

Kalimpong is a major flower exporter and produces about 80% of India's gladioli and sundry orchid varieties. Visit **Nurseryman's Haven** (☑ 03552-256936; Holumba Haven, 9th Mile; ☉ 9am-4pm) at Holumba Haven to see some 200-odd species of orchids; **Shanti Kunj** (BL Dixit Rd; ☉ 8.30am-noon & 1-4pm Sun-Fri) to see anthuriums and baby araucarias; and **Pineview Nursery** (☑ 9932201932; Atisha Rd; Indian/foreigner ₹20/50; ☉ 8.30am-4pm Mon-Sat) to gaze at its eminently photographable cactus collection.

🏃 Activities

Gurudongma Tours & Treks OUTDOORS
(☑ 9434062100; www.astonishingindiatours.com; Lobo House, Hill Top) This very experienced local outfit run by 'General Jimmy' Singh

Kalimpong

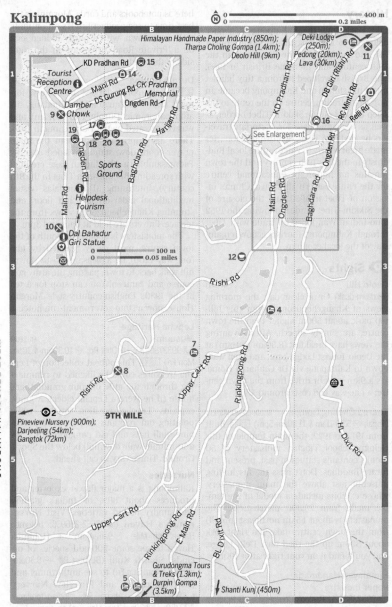

WEST BENGAL KALIMPONG

organises interesting walking trips around Kalimpong area villages and can arrange a wide variety of trips throughout northeastern India. It has comfortable homestays in Kalimpong and in a farmhouse at Samthar, in the hills south of town.

🛏 Sleeping

Manokamana Lodge   GUESTHOUSE $
(📞 03552-257047; manokamanalodge@gmail.com; DB Giri Rd; s/d ₹500/700; @🛜) This simple place run by a friendly family is somewhere between a local hotel and budget backpack-

Kalimpong

ers' digs. Its central location, combined with an internet cafe and an excellent-value restaurant, add to its shoestring appeal, even though the accommodation is fairly basic, characterised by linoleum-floored rooms and bucket hot water in clean attached bathrooms.

Deki Lodge GUESTHOUSE $
(📞 03552-255095; www.dekilodge.yolasite.com; Tripai Rd; s ₹900-1100, d ₹980-2060; 🛜) This friendly Tibetan-owned place is set around a peaceful flower-hemmed family house, and boasts an airy terrace cafe. The rooms are plain but clean and the pricier upper-floor rooms are comfortable, with shared balconies. It's a 10-minute walk northeast of the town centre, just up a side road.

★ **Holumba Haven** BOUTIQUE HOTEL $$
(📞 03552-256936; www.holumba.com; 9th Mile; s ₹2000-2600, d ₹2200-2800, tr ₹2800-3400; 🛜) A unique and utterly charming property combining a nursery and a family-run guesthouse, Holumba is located amid sylvan settings a walkable 1km below town. The spotless, comfy rooms are arranged in cosy cottages spread discreetly around the lush orchid gardens, and good homestyle meals (preorders only) are available in the sociable dining room. Owner Norden is a great source of information on local hikes and trips.

Cloud 9 GUESTHOUSE $$
(📞 9775461366; cloudnine.kpg@gmail.com; Rinkingpong Rd; s ₹1250-1400, d ₹1800-2000; 🛜) The five wood-panelled rooms at this cheerful

property are cosily homey, and the ground-floor restaurant serves interesting Bhutanese, Nepali and Tibetan dishes, plus chilled beer. Binod the owner is a Beatles junkie (note the *Abbey Road* zebra crossing out front) and loves to bond over music in the late evenings.

Kalimpong Park Hotel HERITAGE HOTEL $$
(📞 03552-255304; www.kalimpongparkhotel. com; Rinkingpong Rd; s/d/ste incl breakfast ₹2830/3780/4470; @🛜) This former summer home of the maharajas of Dinajpur is perched on a mountain shelf overlooking the Relli Valley, and packs in oodles of Raj-era charm. Wicker chairs and scarlet blossoms line the verandah and there's a charming lounge bar, along with a restaurant offering British boarding-school staples, such as jelly custard (order in advance).

Elgin Silver Oaks HERITAGE HOTEL $$$
(📞 03552-255296; www.elginhotels.com; Rinkingpong Rd; s/d half board ₹12,160/12,540; @🛜) This 1920s-homestead-turned-heritage-hotel packs plenty of atmosphere and is well run in a professional but friendly way, with a classy restaurant. The wood-floored rooms are plushly furnished in golds, oranges, pinks and blues, and offer grand views down the valley towards the Relli River (ask for a garden-view room). There's a fascinating collection of historical photos on the walls.

Mayfair Himalayan Spa Resort RESORT $$$
(📞 03552-260101; www.mayfairhotels.com; Upper Cart Rd; half board d ₹15,360-25,600; ste ₹32,000-

43,400; ✳ 🛜 ⚋) Kalimpong's historic Himalayan Hotel, acquired by the Mayfair hotel group, has been expanded, glitterised and frillified into a top-drawer Indian luxury resort, with a classy spa, swimming pool, fountains, chandeliers, kids playroom, library, and primary-colour murals and historic black-and-white photos all over the place – all quite tasteful and cheerful and very comfortable in a slightly kitschy way.

The Himalayan Hotel was opened in the first decade of the 20th century and over the years it hosted such Himalayan legends as Charles Bell, Alexandra David-Néel, Heinrich Harrer, Edmund Hillary, Andrew Irvine, George Mallory and Tenzing Norgay.

✕ Eating

Mama-Mia CAFE $
(Mayfair Himalayan Spa Resort, Upper Cart Rd; bakery items ₹70-160; ⏱11am-8pm) The bright and cheerful cafe in the glitzy Mayfair hotel does good coffee and teas and has some very tempting cakes and pastries.

Ni Hao Restaurant CHINESE $$
(DB Giri Rd, 10th Mile; mains ₹150-320; ⏱10am-7.30pm Fri-Wed) This Chinese restaurant with tasty food, amiable staff and a clean, appealing ambience is down a few steps off Rishi Rd in the northeast of the central area. Try the chow mein with handmade noodles or the spicy pepper pork. The combo meals are a good deal for between ₹80 and ₹150.

Gompu's Bar & Restaurant TIBETAN, INDIAN $$
(Gompu's Hotel, Damber Chowk; mains ₹110-200, thalis ₹200-250; ⏱7am-9pm) Gompu's is known for its oversized pork momos (₹110 for four), which have been drawing locals and travellers for as long as anyone can remember. Lunchtime is the best time to find them. It also does filling thalis (all-you-can-eat plate meals), and is a good place for a cold beer (from ₹200) chased by a plate of garlic chilli potatoes.

Cafe Refuel INTERNATIONAL $$
(www.caferefuel.com; Rishi Rd, 9th Mile; dishes ₹120-280; ⏱11.30am-7.30pm; 🛜) Cool place with motorbike-themed decor that uses classic old Vespas for counter seats. The food has a Mexican twist, with homemade nachos, burritos and tostadas alongside burgers, pizza and grilled sandwiches, plus espresso coffee (₹40-₹60) and a foosball table to keep things lively.

🍷 Drinking & Nightlife

Downtown restaurants like Gompu's (p514) and **King Thai** (2nd fl, Maa Super Market, Main Rd; mains ₹180-300; ⏱10am-9pm) double as bars, but even these places are closed by 9pm. Some midrange and most top-end hotels have their own bars.

★ Art Cafe CAFE
(Rishi Rd; coffee ₹50-70; ⏱9.30am-8pm Fri-Wed) Cool cafe with a breezy terrace offering fine views over the hills and valleys to the west and north. It does good coffee, shakes and lemon mint coolers (served in Mason jars) and good things to eat too, from potato wedges to great thin-crust pizzas (mains ₹150–₹230). Very popular with Kalimpong's cool young things.

🛍 Shopping

Haat Bazaar MARKET
(btwn RC Mintri & Relli Rds) On Wednesdays and especially Saturdays, this normally quietish bazaar roars to life with a plethora of merchandise ranging from vegetables and beans to spices, herbs, clothes and plastic garlands.

Lark's Provisions FOOD & DRINKS
(DB Giri Rd; ⏱9am-6.30pm) This is the best place to pick up Edam-like local cheese (per kilogram ₹600), produced in Kalimpong since the Jesuits established a dairy here in the 19th century. It also sells locally made milky lollipops (₹30) and yummy homemade pickles.

ℹ Information

Helpdesk Tourism (📞 8792029913; helpdesk tourism@gmail.com; Sherpa Lodge, Ongden Rd; ⏱9am-5pm) This very helpful private information centre on the ground floor of Sherpa Lodge offers guides (per day ₹1000 to ₹1500) and information on Kalimpong-area hikes, homestays, transport and more. Ask for Raju Sherpa.

ℹ Getting There & Away

All the bus and jeep options and their offices are found next to each other at the crowded Motor Stand.

Himalayan Travellers (📞 9641964277; Motor Stand) This helpful transport company runs shared jeeps to Lava (₹100, 1½ hours, 7am and half-hourly from noon to 3pm). Ask for Vijay.

Kalimpong Mainline Taxi Driver's Welfare Association (KMTDWA; Motor Stand) Shared jeeps to Siliguri (₹160, three hours, about half-hourly 6am to 5pm), Kurseong (₹180, 7.15am and 1pm, 3½ to four hours), Jorethang (₹120, three hours, eight departures 7.30am to 3pm), Gangtok (₹180, three to five hours, 1.20pm and 2.30pm), Mirik (₹250, noon), Panitanki (Nepal border; ₹200, four hours, 12.30pm) and Jaigaon (Bhutan border; ₹250, five hours, 7.30am, 1pm, 1.30pm and 2pm).

Kalimpong Motor Transport (Motor Stand) Shared jeeps to Darjeeling (₹150, three hours) every 30 to 60 minutes 6.30am to 3.30pm, plus charters (₹2000).

Kalimpong Sikkim Syndicate (Motor Stand) Shared jeeps to Gangtok (₹170, three to five hours, half-hourly 6am to 4.30pm), Namchi (₹150, three hours, 8am and 1.30pm) and Ravangla (₹200, 3½ to four hours, 2pm).

NBSTC (Motor Stand) Bengal government buses run to Siliguri (₹110, three hours, at 6.15am, 11.50am, 12.35pm, 3pm and 5.30pm), Pedong (₹30, one hour, 8.30am and 1.30pm), Panitanki (Nepal border; ₹140, four hours, 6.15am and 12.30pm) and Jaigaon (Bhutan border; ₹180, five hours, 8.40am).

Sikkim Nationalised Transport (SNT; Ongden Rd, facing Motor Stand; ☺ counter 11am-1.15pm) A single daily bus to Gangtok (₹105, three to five hours) at 1pm.

Triveni Travels (Motor Stand) Private buses to Siliguri (₹110, three hours, about half-hourly 5.30am to 5pm), Lava (₹70, two hours, 8am), Gangtok (₹110, three to five hours, 7.40am), Panitanki (₹130, four hours, 5.35am and 1.45pm) and Jaigaon (₹200, five hours, 1.50pm).

Tshering Travels (Motor Stand) Private buses to Siliguri (₹110, three hours, half-hourly 5.30am to 5pm), and to New Jalpaiguri station (₹140, 3½ hours) at 1pm. Shared jeeps to Algarah (₹40, 45 minutes) and Pedong (₹50, one hour) leave from in front of this office when full from 7am to 5pm.

ⓘ Getting Around

Taxis (mostly unmarked minivans) can be chartered for local trips from a stand on DB Giri Rd. A half-day rental to see most of the sights costs around ₹1500.

Sporadic shared minivans to Deolo village from **Home Stand** (DB Giri Rd) will drop you at Dr Graham's Home (₹30).

Jaldapara National Park

Jaldapara National Park (☎ 03563-262239; www.jaldapara.com; per person ₹100, vehicle ₹300; ☺ mid-Sep–mid-Jun), a popular destination for domestic tourists but visited by few foreign-ers, protects 216 sq km of lush forests and grasslands along the western floodplain of the Torsa River and is a refuge for about 200 Indian one-horned rhinoceros (*Rhinoceros unicornis*) plus elephants, gaur (Indian bison), several types of deer and over 350 bird species. It's not the easiest place to visit independently and the best accommodation needs to be booked weeks or months in advance, so plan ahead. The best time to visit is mid-November to April, with March and April being best for wildlife-spotting. Bring mosquito repellent.

Madarihat village, on the park's western fringe, 125km east of Siliguri, is the main access point.

Jeep safaris (6-passenger jeep ₹3450) start from Madarihat at 5.30am, 8am, 12.30pm and 3pm. The price includes all park fees as well as jeep and driver. Tickets are sold first-come, first-served at an office in Madarihat (from 6pm the previous day for the two morning safaris, from 10am for later safaris the same day) and can sell out at busy times. Jaldapara and Hollong Tourist Lodges can arrange safaris for their guests, and **Wild Planet Travels** (☎ 9735028733; easthimalayan3@ yahoo.com; opposite Bhanu-Rabindra Park, Madarihat) can make advance bookings.

There's a variety of accommodation options in and around Madarihat village, one of the best being **Jaldapara Tourist Lodge** (☎ 9733008795; www.wbtdcl.com; Madarihat; r with AC ₹2460-3780, without AC ₹1790; ❉ ☎). Book this two weeks ahead if possible, online or at Siliguri Tourism Centre (p495) or other WBTDC properties. Best is **Hollong Tourist Lodge** (☎ 9734116034; www.wbtdcl. com; r ₹2950; ☎), right inside the park, but securing a room is a real challenge. Try to book online one month ahead. Wild Planet Travels (p515) can often book accommodation when no one else can.

Buses run every 30 minutes, 5am to 3.30pm, from Siliguri bus terminal to Madarihat (₹100, four hours). Book at the 'Inter District Minibus Owners Association' counter. Trains from Siliguri Junction station to Madarihat (unreserved seat ₹30 to ₹55, 2¼ to 4¼ hours) depart at 5am, 6.10am, 7.15am, 4.45pm and 6.10pm, returning from Madarihat at 6.15am, 7.10am, 2.20pm, 3.50pm and 5.40pm.

A taxi from Siliguri or Bagdogra Airport should be ₹2500.

Bihar & Jharkhand

Best Places to Eat

➡ Be Happy Cafe (p529)

➡ Mohammad Restaurant (p528)

➡ Pind Balluchi (p521)

➡ Karim's (p519)

➡ Nook (p532)

Best Places to Stay

➡ Rahul Guest House (p527)

➡ Bodhgaya Hotel School (p528)

➡ Hotel Nalanda Regency (p530)

➡ Lemon Tree Premier (p519)

➡ Chanakya BNR Hotel (p532)

Why Go?

Bihar is the birthplace of Buddhism – indeed its very name derives from *vihara*, the Sanskrit word for Buddhist monastery. Thousands of pilgrims from around the world throng its many places of religious significance. Most extraordinary among these spots is Bodhgaya, the site of Buddha's enlightenment, where getting caught up in the spiritual atmosphere is a major draw for travellers. In tribal Jharkhand, holy Parasnath Hill is a revered Jain pilgrimage site, and joining devotees on the hike to the top is a surreal highlight. That apart, the forests of Betla (Palamau) National Park promise a date with elephants and leopards, and maybe even the odd tiger.

Truth be told, this whole region is off the beaten track. Outside Bodhgaya, foreign tourists are almost nonexistent, so if you're looking to sidestep mainstream travel, and especially if you have an interest in Buddhism, this rustic pocket of India could be an unexpected highlight.

When to Go
Patna

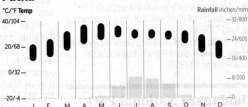

Jan & Feb Temperatures hover between a chilly-to-pleasant 12°C and 25°C.

Jun–Sep Monsoon season. Steer clear – Bihar is India's most flood-prone state.

Oct & Nov Warm days in October and comfortably cool in November.

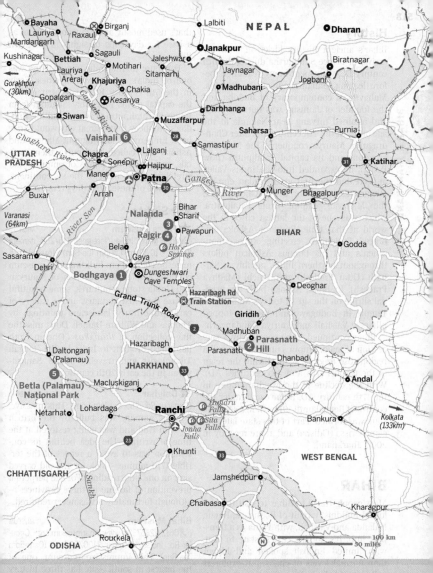

Bihar & Jharkhand Highlights

1 **Bodhgaya** (p525)
Witnessing Buddhists from around the world praying and meditating at the serene site of Buddha's enlightenment.

2 **Parasnath Hill** (p533)
Getting up at 4am for the surreal day-long Jain pilgrimage to the top of Jharkhand's tallest peak.

3 **Nalanda** (p531) Visiting the peaceful ruins of this once-huge ancient university.

4 **Rajgir** (p529) Hiring a tonga (two-wheeled horse-drawn carriage) for the day to explore the myriad Buddhist sites and stupas of this laid-back village.

5 **Betla (Palamau) National** Park (p534) Touring the peaceful forests of this protected area to spot wild elephants, leopards, gaur (wild bison) and spotted deer.

6 **Vaishali** (p522) Walking through northern Bihari villages to the ancient stupas and ruins of this Buddhist pilgrimage spot.

History

Bihar's ancient history kicks off with the arrival of Prince Siddhartha during the 6th century BC, who spent many years here before leaving, enlightened, as the Buddha. Mahavira, a contemporary of Buddha and the founder of Jainism, was born in Bihar and attained nirvana near Nalanda at the age of 72. In the 4th century BC, after Chandragupta Maurya conquered the Magadha kingdom and its capital Pataliputra (now Patna), he expanded into the Indus Valley and created the first great Indian empire. His grandson and successor, Ashoka, ruled the Mauryan empire from Pataliputra, which was one of the largest cities in the world at that time. Emperor Ashoka embraced Buddhism, erecting stupas, monuments and his famous Ashokan pillars throughout northern India, notably at Sarnath (Uttar Pradesh) and Sanchi (Madhya Pradesh). In Bihar, Ashoka built the original shrine on the site of today's Mahabodhi Temple in Bodhgaya and the lion-topped pillars at Vaishali and Lauriya Nandangarh.

Bihar continued to be coveted by a succession of major empires until the Magadha region rose to glory again during the reign of the Guptas (7th and 8th centuries AD). With the decline of the Mughal empire in the 17th century AD, Bihar came under the control of Bengal until 1912, when a separate state was formed. Part of this state later became Orissa (Odisha) and, more recently in 2000, Jharkhand.

BIHAR

Most people travel to Bihar to visit the hallowed Buddhist circuit of Bodhgaya, Rajgir, Nalanda and Vaishali, with Patna as a transport hub. It's not the easiest state to visit, with limited English spoken and higher than normal levels of chaos, but explorers will enjoy tracking down the many fascinating, off-the-beaten track destinations waiting to be discovered.

Patna

☏ 0612 / POP 2,050,000

Bihar's chaotic capital sprawls along the south bank of the Ganges for 15km, just east of the river's confluence with three major tributaries. Patna has a couple of worthwhile sights, but it's a noisy, congested city that's used mostly as a transport hub, or as a base for day trips to sights in northern Bihar.

For more than a millennium, Patna was one of India's most powerful cities. Early in the 5th century BC, Ajatasatru shifted the capital of his Magadha kingdom from Rajgir to Pataliputra (Patna), fulfilling Buddha's prophecy that a great city would arise here. Emperors Chandragupta Maurya and Ashoka also called Pataliputra their capitals, making it the centre of empires that stretched across most of the subcontinent. Little trace of these glory days remains.

◉ Sights

★ Patna Museum   MUSEUM

(Buddha Marg; Indian/foreigner ₹15/250, camera ₹100; ⊙ 10.30am-4.30pm Tue-Sun) Housed in a majestic colonial-era building, this museum contains a splendid collection of Mauryan and Gupta stone sculptures, some beautiful bronze Buddhist statuary, and a gallery of early-19th-century landscape paintings by Thomas and William Daniell. Don't miss the fine collection of *thangkas* (Tibetan cloth paintings) brought to India by the Bengali Tibetologist and traveller Rahul Sankrityayan in the early 20th century.

★ Golghar   HISTORIC BUILDING

(Danapur Rd; ₹5; ⊙ 10am-6pm) This massive, bulbous granary was built by the British army in 1786 and was being restored at the time of writing. The idea behind its construction was to avoid a repeat of the terrible 1770 famine – look for the old carved sign on one side, reading, 'For the perpetual prevention of famine in these provinces' – although fortunately it was never required.

Bihar Museum   MUSEUM

(☏ 0612-2235732; www.biharmuseum.org; Circular Rd; Indian/foreigner ₹100/500; ⊙ 10am-5pm Tue-Sun) This impressive museum, one of the largest in south Asia, has three history galleries, plus displays on contemporary art and ethnic groups of Bihar. It has poached some of the finer pieces of the Patna Museum, including the famous Mauryan-era *Didarganj Yakshi* statue, dating from the 3rd century BC. There's also a children's gallery.

Buddha Smriti Park   PARK

(Muzharal Haque Path (Fraser Rd); park ₹20, museum ₹40; ⊙ 9am-7pm Tue-Sun) This peaceful 9-hectare park, inaugurated by the Dalai

Lama in 2010, is notable for its massive sandblasted charcoal stupa (₹50), which houses a unique, bulletproof relic chamber, and sapling plantings from both the Bodhi Tree in Bodhgaya and Anuradhapura in Sri Lanka. The strikingly modern Buddhist museum is worthwhile, and there is also a library (₹50) and a meditation centre (free).

🛏 Sleeping

Several budget hotels in Patna do not accept foreigners. If you're travelling on the cheap, look for options near the train station, where budget places are usually licensed to accept foreign guests.

Hotel City Centre
HOTEL $

(☏ 9570095985; www.hotelcitycentre.in; Station Rd; d ₹950, with AC ₹2050; ❄ 🖥) This modern glass tower, to your right just as you exit the train station, is temptingly convenient for a transit overnighter. Rooms are simple but decent value (non-AC rooms have squat toilets), staff are helpful and there are several restaurants on the street outside. The upper floors are a bit of a rabbit warren.

Hotel Clark Inn
HOTEL $

(☏ 9939726620; Jamal Rd; r from ₹700) The cheapest hotel we could find that welcomed foreigners, Clark Inn has simple budget rooms with TVs and squat toilets, or bigger and cleaner rooms with air coolers (₹1100). Some have small balconies for the sake of ventilation.

★ Hotel President
HOTEL $$

(☏ 0612-2209203; hotelpresidentpatna@gmail. com; off Fraser Rd; s/d ₹2400/2650; ❄ @ 🖥) This family-run hotel is in a useful and relatively quiet location off Fraser Rd and close to Patna Museum. Rooms – all with air-con – are spacious, stylish and fresh, with TVs, seating areas and hot-water bathrooms. Some have small balconies. It's an excellent midrange choice, especially if you can get a walk-in discount.

Hotel Windsor
HOTEL $$

(☏ 0612-2212428; www.hotelwindsorpatna.com; Exhibition Rd; s/d incl breakfast from ₹2700/3200; ❄ 🖥) This busy, midrange business hotel offers an inventory of well-kept and comfortably appointed rooms. The rooms in the new block are more stylish and spacious, though a bit low on light. There's an in-house travel agency that arranges cars for multiday sightseeing, and a popular restaurant serving North Indian dishes.

Lemon Tree Premier
BUSINESS HOTEL $$$

(☏ 0612-2502700; www.lemontreehotels. com; Exhibition Rd; d incl breakfast from ₹5200; ❄ @ 🖥 🏊) This is Patna's most popular business hotel, standing somewhat in a league of its own by offering the sort of creature comforts and mod cons that most Patna establishments fall short on. The rooms here are spacious and superbly appointed, there's an in-house spa and terrace pool, and the restaurant serves great food, including a sumptuous breakfast spread.

Hotel Maurya Patna
HOTEL $$$

(☏ 0612-2203040; www.maurya.com; Gandhi Maidan; d incl breakfast ₹17,700; ❄ @ 🖥 🏊) Patna's top business hotel has tastefully furnished rooms, a rather barren pool, a couple of nice restaurants and a gym. It all adds up to comfort rather than luxury. Booking online (usually through a booking portal) can bring discounts of up to 50%.

🍴 Eating

Litti Chokha Stall
STREET FOOD $

(opposite Gandhi Maidan; per plate ₹20; ⏱ 7am-8pm) This is one of numerous streetside stalls dotted around the city cooking up Patna's signature snack: *litti chokha* (grilled chickpea-powder-stuffed dough balls served with a side sauce of mashed tomatoes, aubergine and potatoes).

★ Karim's
MUGHLAI $$

(☏ 9294900051; Fraser Rd, Fazal Imam Complex; mains ₹200-350; ⏱ noon-10.30pm) This stylish new outlet – operated by the hallowed kebab house of the same name in New Delhi – has recently begun treating Patna to its legendary menu featuring tikka rolls, chargrilled

TOP STATE FESTIVALS

Chhath Festival (Bihar & Jharkhand; ⏱ Oct or Nov) People perform sunset and sunrise rituals on the banks of rivers and ponds to honour Surya, the Sun God.

Rajgir Mahotsava (Rajgir; ⏱ Dec) A performing-arts gala with dances, devotional songs and instrumental music.

Sonepur Mela (Sonepur; ⏱ Nov or Dec) With 700,000 attendees and countless thousands of animals taking part, this three-week festival is many times the size of Pushkar's Camel Fair (p144).

Patna

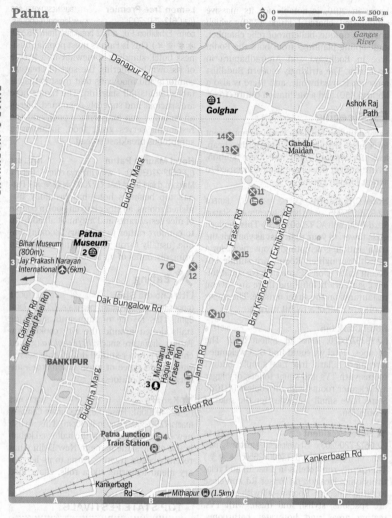

Patna

Top Sights
- **1** Golghar C1
- **2** Patna Museum A3

Sights
- **3** Buddha Smriti Park B4

Sleeping
- **4** Hotel City Centre B5
- **5** Hotel Clark Inn B4
- **6** Hotel Maurya Patna C2
- **7** Hotel President B3

- **8** Hotel Windsor C4
- **9** Lemon Tree Premier C3

Eating
- **10** Baba Hotel C4
- Bellpepper Restaurant .... (see 8)
- **11** Bollywood Treats C2
- **12** Karim's B3
- **13** Litti Chokha Stall C2
- **14** Pind Balluchi C2
- **15** Tandoor Hut C3

mutton *burra* kebab, slow-cooked *qurma* meat stew, a mutton mince-enveloped egg dish called *nargisi kofta*, and fluffy sweet-ened naan-style rotis called *sheermal*.

★ **Pind Balluchi** NORTH INDIAN $$
(☎ 0612-2219101; 16-18 fl, Biscomaun Tower, Gandhi Maidan; mains ₹130-290; ☺ noon-10pm; ❄) For Patna's best food and views, head to this revolving restaurant with ever-shifting vistas over Gandhi Maidan, Golghar and the Ganges beyond. The kebabs are excellent (try the *murgh malai* kebab), and there is a full range of vegetarian dishes such as *kadai paneer*, and fine *kheer* for dessert. Enter on the north side of the building.

Tandoor Hut INDIAN $$
(☎ 9386851333; Fraser Rd; kebabs ₹180-220; ☺ 11am-11pm) This streetside grill serves delicious kebabs and other tandoor offerings, as well as huge biryanis and curries. Eat on-site, take a pack back to your hotel, or call them and ask for a delivery. The chicken *malai* and *reshmi kebabs* are both superb.

Bellpepper Restaurant INDIAN $$
(Exhibition Rd, Hotel Windsor; mains ₹140-320; ☺ 11am-3pm & 7-10.30pm; ❄) Intimate and contemporary, this small restaurant inside Hotel Windsor is particularly popular for its tandoori dishes. The *murg tikka lababdar* (boneless tandoori chicken basted with garlic, ginger, green chillies, and a pistachio and cashew paste) is melt-in-your-mouth sinful. The biryanis are good, too.

Bollywood Treats FAST FOOD $$
(Gandhi Maidan; mains ₹100-200; ☺ noon-9pm) This fast-food place dishes out South Indian snacks, Chinese stir-fries, decent pizza and tempting brownies to Patna's blossoming middle class. There is a Baskin-Robbins ice-cream kiosk, and a corner for cold coffee and milkshakes (₹130). It doesn't start serving food until 1pm.

ℹ Information

MEDICAL SERVICES

Dr Ruban Memorial Hospital (☎ 0612-2271022, 0612-2271020; www.rubanpatliputrahospital.com; Gandhi Maidan; ☺ 24hr) Emergency room, clinic and pharmacy.

MONEY

Axis Bank (Fraser Rd; ☺ 9.30am-3.30pm Mon-Fri, plus 1st & 3rd Sat of month) Exchanges currency and has ATMs.

State Bank of India (Gandhi Maidan; ☺ 10am-4pm Mon-Fri plus 1st & 3rd Sat of month) Exchanges currency and travellers cheques. Has ATMs.

TRAVEL AGENCIES

Thomas Cook (☎ 0612-2221699; www.thomascook.in; Hotel Maurya, Patna Arcade; ☺ 10am-6pm Mon-Sat) Helpful for booking airline tickets and car rental. Also exchanges currency for a commission.

ℹ Getting There & Around

AIR

Patna's Jay Prakash Narayan International Airport is 8km southwest of the city centre. Between them, **Air India** (☎ 044-66921455, 0612-2223199; www.airindia.in; Patna airport), **IndiGo** (☎ 1800 1803838, 9910383838; www.goindigo.in; Patna airport), **Go Air** (☎ 1860-2100999, 0612-2227148; www.goair.in; Patna airport) and **Jet Airways** (☎ 022-39893333, 0612-2223045; www.jetairways.com; Patna airport) fly direct daily to Delhi and Kolkata, with onward connections to other cities.

Autorickshaws/taxis to Patna airport cost ₹180/420 from the prepaid autorickshaw stand by the train station.

BUS

The main bus stand occupies a large, dusty space about 1.5km southwest of the train station – shared autorickshaws (₹10) run here from the back of the train station. It's a noisy, anarchic place, with little English spoken and no booking offices, but if you walk into the chaos telling people where you want to go, you'll eventually get directed to the right bus; buy tickets on-board.

There are frequent services throughout the day to the following destinations:

Gaya ₹100, three hours; there are also a couple of direct buses a day to Bodhgaya (₹120)

Kesariya ₹80, three hours

Motihari ₹150 to ₹170, 4½ hours

Ranchi AC/non-AC ₹380/280, eight hours

Raxaul AC/non-AC ₹250/180, six hours

Vaishali ₹50, two hours

There are also 9pm sleeper buses to Ranchi and Raxaul.

CAR

Hiring a car and driver can be done through Thomas Cook, starting from ₹12 per kilometre (minimum 200km) plus a driver allowance of ₹500 per overnight stay. A taxi from Patna to Bodhgaya costs around ₹3500.

TRAIN

Patna Junction has a **foreign-tourist ticket counter** (window 3; ☺ 8am-8pm Mon-Sat, to

2pm Sun) at the 1st-floor reservation office in the right-hand wing of the train station.

Trains leave roughly hourly for Gaya (2nd class/AC chair ₹50/495, two to three hours), with the 11.15am Patna-Hatiya Express offering air-con sleeper berths. For other trains just buy a 2nd-class 'general' ticket and hop on the next available service.

More than a dozen daily trains leave for New Delhi (sleeper/3AC/2AC ₹500/1320/1895, 12 to 18 hours); the quickest and most convenient time-wise is the RJPB Rajdhani (3AC/2AC/1AC ₹1630/2265/3780), which leaves at 7.25pm and arrives in Delhi at 7.40am.

Seven daily trains go to Kolkata (sleeper/3AC/2AC ₹165/315/855, eight to 14 hours). The best time-wise is probably the Vibhuti Express (10.35pm, nine hours).

At least a dozen daily trains go to Varanasi or nearby Mughal Sarai Junction – renamed Deen Dayal Upadyanya in 2017 – (sleeper/3AC/2AC ₹165/495/700, four to six hours) between 5am and 9pm.

Five fast trains go to Ranchi (sleeper/3AC/2AC ₹340/920/1325, eight to 10 hours). The 6am Ranchi Janshatabdi Express offers air-con chair class (₹630).

The most comfortable option to Rajgir is air-con chair car (₹260, three hours) on the 8.05am 13234 Rajgriha Express.

Note that you may also find trains arriving at Patna's minor stations, such as Rajendra Nagar, 3km east of Patna Junction, or inconvenient Patna Sahib, 11km east.

Patna Area

The Buddhist ruins of Vaishali and Kesariya are linked by public transport from Patna, but you'll have to leave early to visit both in a day. Many people organise a car and driver for a longish day. Motihari can make an overnight base if you're continuing on to Lauriya Nandangarh or the Nepal border.

SLEEPING PRICE RANGES

The following price ranges refer to a double room with bathroom in high season across both Bihar and Jharkhand. Unless otherwise stated tax is included in room rates.

$ less than ₹1500

$$ ₹1500–₹3500

$$$ more than ₹3500

Vaishali

☎ 06224

A quiet, yet significant Buddhist pilgrimage site, Vaishali – 55km northwest of Patna – makes a lovely rural escape from hectic Patna. The small museum here is engaging, while the ruins of Kolhua are wonderfully serene. Simply walking around the surrounding villages and farmland is a treat in itself.

◉ Sights

The bus from Patna will drop you at a junction, from where it's a 1km walk west past monasteries built by Thai, Cambodian and Vietnamese Buddhists to the large ancient coronation water tank known as Abhishek Pushkarini. On the left side of the tank is the modern, whitewashed, Japanese-built **World Peace Pagoda** (⊙ dawn-dusk).

On the opposite side of the tank is the **Buddha Relic Stupa** (⊙ dawn-dusk). The 5th-century stupa, originally 12m tall, is now in ruins, but it was once one of the eight locations in which Buddha's ashes were interred. The soapstone relic casket housing the ashes now resides in Patna Museum (p518). The small **Archaeological Museum** (₹10; ⊙ 9am-5pm Sat-Thu) here contains some fine 1000-year-old Buddhist statuary and an intriguing 1st- to 2nd-century-AD toilet pan.

Between the stupa and the museum, a single-lane road winds its way 5km north through farming villages to the **Kolhua Complex** (Indian/foreigner ₹25/300, video ₹25; ⊙ dawn-dusk). It's worth walking this route, although shared autos also make the trip. Set in a landscaped park, Kolhua comprises a large, hemispherical brick stupa guarded by a lion crouching atop a 2300-year-old Ashoka pillar. The pillar contains none of the Ashokan edicts usually carved onto these pillars (but it does sport graffiti dating from the Raj era). Nearby are the ruins of smaller stupas, monastic buildings where Buddha spent several monsoons, and also one of the first ever Buddhist nunneries. According to legend, Buddha was given a bowl of honey here by monkeys, who also dug out the rainwater tank for his water supply.

ⓘ Getting There & Away

Buses run every hour or so from Patna to Vaishali, and on to Kesariya. The last bus back to Patna swings by the main road at around 4pm.

WORTH A TRIP

KESARIYA

Rising high out of the earth from where the dying Buddha donated his begging bowl, the enormous **Kesariya Stupa** (⊙ dawn-dusk) is an enthralling example of how nature can reclaim a deserted monument. Excavated from under a grassy and wooded veil is what is thought to be the world's tallest (38m) Buddhist stupa, dating from the Pala period (200–750 AD).

Above the 425m-circumference pedestal are five uniquely shaped terraces that form a gargantuan Buddhist tantric mandala. Each terrace has a number of niches containing disfigured Buddha statues, which were destroyed during attacks by foreign invaders in the Middle Ages. The rural setting is a joy, but there is nothing else to see here apart from the stupa and you are not allowed to climb it.

If you don't have your own wheels (recommended), buses from Patna (via Vaishali) can drop you by the stupa, which is visible from the main road. The last bus back swings by at around 3.30pm. Buses from Motihari will drop you at the main crossroads in the village of Kesariya, where there are roadside *dhabas* (casual eateries, serving snacks and basic meals), leaving you with a 2km walk or rickshaw ride south. If you can't find a direct onward bus to Motihari from Kesariya village, take one to the junction of Khajuriya and change there.

Motihari

📞 06252 / POP 120,000

Motihari is a useful base for breaking the long bus ride between Patna and the Nepal border. It's not a particularly pleasant town but there is some historical interest amid the bustle; you can also launch some excursions to a few Buddhist sites in northern Bihar from here.

The town is part of a region from where, in 1917, Mahatma Gandhi founded the civil disobedience movement that ultimately resulted, 30 years later, in the departure of the British from India.

Motihari is also the location of the family home of Eric Arthur Blair, better known by his pen name George Orwell, who was born here in 1903. Orwell's father, Richard W Blair, worked for the opium department, supervising poppy growers and collecting opium for export to China. The family home (2.5km from the bus stand, near Gyan Babu Chowk) has recently been restored and converted into a modest museum.

Accommodation options in Motihari are fairly basic. The best place to stay is the modern and friendly **Hotel Rajeshwari Palace** (📞 06252-222222; Main (Bank) Rd; r with/without AC from ₹2000/1000; ❈ 🖥), which offers fresh and clean rooms 10 minutes' walk west of the bus stand.

❶ Getting There & Away

The bus station is in the east of town, just east of Chautani Chowk. Heading left (west) out of the bus station you pass Chautani Chowk, the Hotel Rajeshwari Palace, a Gandhi statue and, after 2km, Gyan Babu Chowk.

From Motihari there are frequent buses to Patna (₹150 to ₹170, four hours), Raxaul (₹50, two hours) and Kesariya (₹40, two hours), from where you can catch passing buses to Vaishali. Buses to Raxaul sometimes leave from just north of Chautani Chowk.

Raxaul

📞 06255 / POP 55,500

Raxaul is a dusty, congested border town that provides passage into Nepal via a hassle-free border post. Setting out early from Patna, you'll arrive around noon and will probably have no reason to stay the night, unless you encounter some unforeseen roadblock.

Raxaul is no place to linger, but if you must spend the night, **Hotel Kaveri** (📞 06255-221148; Main Rd; r with/without AC ₹1200/500; ❈), on the main road leading to the border (about 1km from the check post), has decent air-con rooms with modern bathrooms, and very basic non-AC rooms with tap-and-bucket showers and shared toilets.

ⓘ Getting There & Away

BUS

The bus stand is 200m down a lane off the main road, about 2km from the border on the right. There are frequent buses, day and night, to Patna (AC/non-AC ₹250/200, seven hours) via Motihari (₹70, two hours). The road to Motihari is dreadfully bumpy so sit near the front of the bus if you can.

TRAIN

The train station is off the main road, 750m from the border, but isn't well connected. The 13022 Mithila Express runs daily to Kolkata (sleeper/3AC/2AC ₹365/1000/1440, 18 hours, 10am). The 15273 Satyagrah Express runs daily to New Delhi (sleeper/3AC/2AC ₹450/1225/1775, 25 hours, 8.30am).

Gaya

🌐 0631 / POP 470,000

The hectic town of Gaya is a religious centre for Hindu pilgrims, who believe that offerings at the town's riverside Vishnupad Temple relieve the recently departed from the cycle of death and rebirth. For foreign tourists, it merely serves as a transit point for Bodhgaya, 13km away.

If you get stuck for the night in Gaya, Ajatsatru Hotel (☏ 0631-2222961; Station Rd; r ₹1100, with AC ₹1600; ❄ ⊕ 🛜) is the best value of a cluster of hotels directly opposite the train station. It has decent-sized but noisy rooms and an OK vegetarian restaurant. There are a few cheaper (and smaller) single rooms.

ⓘ Getting There & Around

AUTORICKSHAW

Shared autos leave when full from Gaya Junction train station for Bodhgaya (₹20), Manpur bus stand (₹10) and Gandhi Maidan bus stand (₹5).

A private auto from Gaya to Bodhgaya usually starts at ₹200 or more.

BUS

Patna (₹100, three hours, hourly) Buses leave from the train station.

Rajgir (₹50, 2½ hours, hourly) Buses leave from Manpur bus stand, across the river to the east.

Ranchi (₹180, seven hours, twice hourly) Buses leave from the Gandhi Maidan bus stand.

TRAIN

Passenger trains with unreserved seating leave every couple of hours for Patna (2nd class ₹25, two to three hours). Express trains (2nd seating/chair/3A ₹90/295/495, two hours) run at 1.20pm and 8.30pm and offer air-conditioned chair-car seats or sleepers.

The fastest overnight trains to New Delhi (sleeper/3AC/2AC from ₹490/1300/1860, 12 to 14 hours) leave at 2.02pm, 2.15pm and 10.54pm.

At least eight trains run daily to Kolkata (sleeper/3AC/2AC ₹270/735/1050, eight to 10 hours), the most convenient being the 9.15pm Doon Express (9½ hours).

ⓘ CROSSING TO NEPAL: RAXAUL TO BIRGANJ

The busy border crossing between Raxual and Birganj is the most direct route to Kathmandu and eastern Nepal.

The border at Raxaul is open from 6am to 10pm.

Onward Transport

On the Nepal side, the town of Birganj is about 3km from the border. You are free to walk across the border to Birganj, or shared autorickshaws charge NRs50 per person from the border to Birganj. A cycle-rickshaw costs about NRs300.

From Birganj, there are frequent buses to Kathmandu (ordinary/deluxe/AC NRs550/600/800, six to seven hours, 5am to 8pm). However, the most comfortable and quickest option is to get a Tata Sumo '4WD' (NRs600 to NRs800, four to five hours, every 20 minutes until 5pm). There are also morning buses to Pokhara (NRs600, eight hours) via Narayangarh (NRs250, four hours) at 5am, 6.30am and 7.30am.

Buddha Air (www.buddhaair.com) has up to five daily flights between Simara (the airport for Birganj) and Kathmandu (US$105, 20 minutes). The airport is 22km from Birganj and a taxi costs around NRs1500.

Visas

Nepali 15-, 30- and 90-day visas (US$25/40/100 and one passport photo) are only available from 6am to 6pm on the Nepal side of the border.

LAURIYA NANDANGARH

Fans of Buddhist history will enjoy the offbeat trip to the huge stupa at Lauriya Nandangarh, 25km northwest of Bettiah. The 2000-year-old, 25m-tall brick stupa consists of five circular and zigzag terraces. The upper section remains covered in foliage and you can climb up for views of the pancake-flat countryside. To get here from the west end of town head 2km south and take a left just past the sugar/ethanol factory, following the factory wall for 1km. An autorickshaw costs around ₹150 return.

Also at the west end of town, 500m north of the main junction, is an 18.5m tall Ashoka pillar, one of only a handful remaining that feature all six of Ashoka's edicts, along with a seated lion carving on top, and the only such pillar still in its original location. Look for the colonial-era graffiti dating from 1873.

To get here from Motihari, take one of the frequent buses to Bettiah (₹40, 90 minutes) and then take a Ramnagar-bound bus to Lauriya Nandangarh (₹30, 45 minutes). On the return you might find a Patna-bound bus direct to Motihari. For Raxaul, take a cramped share jeep to Sagauli (₹30) and change there, or hire an entire jeep to the Nepali border for ₹1200.

If you are travelling in a hired vehicle from Patna and Kesariya, you can stop to visit another Ashoka pillar en route, just west of the village of Lauriya Areraj, 37km southeast of Bettiah.

Almost a dozen daily trains go to Varanasi or nearby Deen Dayal Upadyaya (previously known as Mughal Sarai Junction; sleeper/3AC/2AC ₹190/540/745, three to six hours). The quickest are the 12987 Sealdah Ajmer Express (6.20am) and the 12801 Purushottam Express (2.02pm).

Bodhgaya

📞 0631 / POP 48,100

The crucible of Buddhism, Bodhgaya was where Prince Siddhartha attained enlightenment beneath a bodhi tree 2600 years ago and became Buddha (the 'Awakened One'). In terms of blessedness, this tiny temple town is to Buddhists what Mecca is to Muslims. Unsurprisingly, it attracts thousands of pilgrims from around the world every year, who come for prayer, study and meditation.

The most hallowed spot in town is the bodhi tree that flourishes inside the Mahabodhi Temple complex, amid a beautiful garden setting, its roots embedded in the same soil as its celebrated ancestor.

Additionally, many monasteries and temples dot the town, built in their national style by foreign Buddhist communities. The ambience is a mix of monastic tranquillity, backpacker comforts and small-town hustle, underpinned by an intensity of devotion that makes it endlessly interesting.

◉ Sights

★ Mahabodhi Temple BUDDHIST TEMPLE
(camera ₹100; ⊙5am-9pm) The magnificent Unesco World Heritage-listed Mahabodhi Temple, marking the hallowed ground where Buddha attained enlightenment and formulated his philosophy, forms the spiritual heart of Bodhgaya. Topped by a 50m pyramidal spire, the inner sanctum of the ornate structure houses a 10th-century, 2m-high gilded image of a seated Buddha. Amazingly, four of the original sculpted stone railings surrounding the temple, dating from the Sunga period (184–72 BC), have survived amid the replicas. Cellphones are not allowed within the temple complex.

Built in the 6th century AD atop the site of a temple erected by Emperor Ashoka almost 800 years earlier, the Mahabodhi Temple was razed by foreign invaders in the 11th century, and subsequently underwent several major restorations. Pilgrims and visitors from all walks of life and religions come to worship or just soak up the atmosphere of this sacred place. An enthralling way to start or finish the day is to stroll around the inside of the perimeter of the temple compound (in an auspicious clockwise pattern) and watch a sea of white, maroon and yellow dip and rise, while Tibetan monks perform endless prostrations on their prayer boards. There's a less atmospheric Meditation Park (visitors/meditators ₹25/20; ⊙visitors 10am-5pm,

Bodhgaya

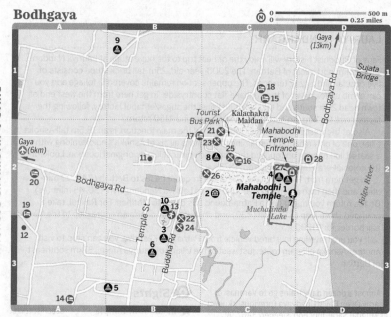

meditators 5-10am & 5-9pm) for those seeking extra solitude within the temple grounds.

Leave your bags and cellphones in the lockers 50m to the west of the entrance. Security has been fairly tight since bombs exploded in the complex in 2013.

Bodhi Tree
BUDDHIST SITE

(Mahabodhi Temple) Undoubtedly, the most sacred fig tree ever to grace the Earth was the Bodhi Tree at Bodhgaya, under which Prince Siddhartha, the founder of Buddhism, achieved enlightenment. Buddha was said to have stared unblinkingly at the tree in an awed gesture of gratitude and wonder after his enlightenment. Today, pilgrims and tourists alike flock here to pray and meditate at the most important of Buddhism's four holiest sites.

Known as Sri Maha Bodhi, the original tree was paid special attention by Ashoka, a mighty Indian emperor who ruled most of the subcontinent from 269 to 232 BC, a century or so after the date the Buddha is believed to have died. Ashoka's jealous wife, Tissarakkhā, felt the emperor should have been directing his devotion towards her, rather than towards a tree and, in a fit of rage, she caused the tree to perish by piercing it with poisonous thorns.

Thankfully, before its death, one of the tree's saplings was carried off to Anuradhapura in Sri Lanka by Sanghamitta (Ashoka's daughter), where it continues to flourish. A cutting was later carried back to Bodhgaya and planted where the original once stood. The red sandstone slab between the tree and the adjacent Mahabodhi Temple was placed by Ashoka to mark the spot of Buddha's enlightenment – it's referred to as the Vajrasan (Lightning Throne).

Great Buddha Statue
BUDDHIST, MONUMENT

(off Temple St; ⊙7am-5.30pm) **FREE** This 80ft-high Japanese-style statue of the Buddha seated in a lotus posture towers above a pleasant garden at the end of Temple St. The impressive monument was unveiled by the Dalai Lama in 1989 and is surrounded by 10 smaller sculptures of Buddha's disciples. The statue is partially hollow and is said to contain some 20,000 bronze Buddhas.

Monasteries & Other Temples

One of Bodhgaya's great joys is its collection of monasteries and temples, each offering visitors a unique opportunity to peek into different Buddhist cultures and compare architectural styles.

The **Indosan Nipponji Temple** (Japanese Temple; Buddha Rd; ⊙6am-noon & 2-6pm) is an exercise in quiet Japanese understatement

Bodhgaya

BIHAR & JHARKHAND BODHGAYA

and has meditation at 5pm. In contrast is the nearby ornate **Bhutanese Monastery** (Buddha Rd; ⊙dawn-noon & 2pm-dusk), which has images of the kings of Bhutan and the bearded Zhabdrung, Bhutan's religious leader, as well as some unusual 3D frescoes. The most impressive of all the modern monasteries is the **Tergar Monastery** (Sujata Bypass Rd; ⊙dawn-noon & 2pm-dusk) of the Karmapa school of Tibetan Buddhism, where the 17th Karmapa is often in residence. It has a small cafe. Another stunner is the sublime **Thai Temple** (Bodhgaya Rd; ⊙6am-noon & 2-6pm), a brightly coloured *wat* with gold leaf shimmering from its arched rooftop and manicured gardens. Meditation is held here mornings and evenings.

The Tibetan Karma Temple (note the double-dragon brass door knockers) and Namgyal Monastery each contain large prayer wheels. The Nyingmapa-school **Shechen Monastery** (off Bodhgaya Rd; ⊙dawn-noon & 2pm-dusk) has a large stupa that contains bone fragments of the Buddha.

Monasteries are open sunrise to sunset, but usually closed from noon to 2pm. A good time to visit is between 4pm and 6pm, as there is often chanting and meditation.

⊘ Courses

**Root Institute for
Wisdom Culture**   MEDITATION
(☑0631-2200714; www.rootinstitute.ngo; ⊙office 9am-noon & 1.15-5pm) Located in a tranquil,

tree-shaded corner of town, this foreign-run institute holds various meditation courses (from two to 21 days) between October and March. Courses cost around ₹1000 per day, including meals and accommodation. The 6.45am meditation session is open to all.

Tergar Monastery   MEDITATION
(☑0631-2201256; www.tergar.org; Sujata Bypass Rd) This monastery offers courses on Tibetan Buddhism and welcomes long-term qualified volunteer English teachers.

⊨ Sleeping

Budget guesthouses are concentrated on the northern side of the Kalachakra Maidan. Note that many places (especially cheaper ones) can be booked out during public prayer sessions or festivities, and room prices can also go up by several notches. It's always best to book in advance.

If there's space, you can stay at the peaceful Root Institute for Wisdom Culture (p527) even if you're not attending any of its courses.

★**Rahul Guest House**   GUESTHOUSE $
(☑0631-2200709; rahul_bodhgaya@yahoo.co.in; near Kalachakra Maidan; s/d ₹600/800, with AC ₹1200-1500; ❋ ♠) Clean and serene, with sociable balcony seating, this family home makes for an excellent stay away from the din, even if the welcome is slightly cool. The rooms upstairs, with whitewashed walls, nice breezes and simple furnishings, are

better than those on the ground floor, but all are good value, particularly the four air-con rooms. Laundry service is available.

Mohammad House
GUESTHOUSE $

(☑ 9934022691; yasmd2002@gmail.com; r from ₹800; ☎) There's an authentic village atmosphere at this hard-to-find, no-frills guesthouse, which is hidden away from the more touristy parts of town. Ducks and chickens scuttle around the narrow lanes that link villagers' colourfully painted homes to the Kalachakra Maidan area. The fan-cooled rooms are simple and spartan, and some have squat toilets.

Gupta House
GUESTHOUSE $

(☑ 7250956999; jyoti_gupta2000in@yahoo.com; beside Kalachakra Maidan; d ₹500-700, with AC ₹1000; ☀ ☎) Rooms at this basic guesthouse are spartan but comfortable enough, with back rooms looking out onto a huge Tibetan monastery. There are a few air-con rooms, too, but the cooling doesn't work when the power is out (which is quite often). The alfresco Hari Om International Cafe out the front is an advantage.

OTHER BUDDHIST SITES

While Bodhgaya comes tops on the list of Buddhist pilgrimages, there are several other hallowed spots in the region (mostly in Bihar and Uttar Pradesh) related to either the Buddha's life or his works. Needless to say, these draw thousands of pilgrims from around the world every year, and are part of India's reputed Buddhist pilgrimage trail. See p1150 for information on the Buddhist Circuit.

Rajgir The Buddha spent some time of his life here.

Nalanda One of the ancient world's greatest universities; a Buddhist centre of excellence.

Sarnath The Buddha taught his first sermon at this site near Varanasi.

Kushinagar The place where Buddha attained *parinirvana*, or release from the cycle of karma and rebirth.

Lumbini (Nepal) The birthplace of Prince Siddhartha, who later became the Buddha.

Sravasti An ancient megacity where the Buddha lived for many years.

★ Shantidevi Ashram's Guesthouse
GUESTHOUSE $$

(☑ 9852053186; www.shantideviashramguesthouse.com; r incl breakfast ₹2250; ☎) This unassuming but tastefully decorated boutique-like guesthouse makes a simple Zen-like retreat from the hustle and bustle of the main drags. Fan-cooled rooms come with artwork, colourful rugs on concrete floors and superhard beds. Bathrooms are small but spotless. There's no restaurant, but guests can use the kitchen and washing machine.

Bodhgaya Hotel School
HOTEL $$

(☑ 0631-2200044; info@bodhgayahotelschool.com; behind Great Buddha Statue; s/d incl breakfast ₹2700/3200; ☀ ☎) This new hotel, located on the fringe of town, offers fabulous value for money. Rooms are simple but excellently appointed, there's 24hr power back-up, and the staff comprises hotel management trainees from the affiliated institute. It's on a quiet unpaved lane behind the Great Buddha Statue.

Kirti Guest House
HOTEL $$

(☑ 0631-2200744; kirtihouse744@yahoo.com; off Bodhgaya Rd; s/d incl breakfast ₹2500/2750; ☀ @ ☎) Run by the Kirti Monastery in Dharamsala, this central hotel offers a quiet atmosphere despite its central location. It's slightly set back from the road and has 60 comfortable, modern rooms. It's often booked out by large groups of visiting monks or pilgrims, so book early if you can.

✗ Eating

★ Mohammad Restaurant
MULTICUISINE $

(mains ₹80-220; ⊙ 7.30am-9.30pm; ☎) Tucked away behind the market stalls at the Tourist Bus Park (take the lane beside Fujiya Green restaurant), Mohammad's whips up a fine array of food from across the Buddhist world – Tibetan, Chinese, Thai, Indian – as well as a strong line in Western favourites, including breakfasts and espresso coffee. The fresh fruit juices are superb and there's covered outdoor seating.

Hari Om International Cafe
MULTICUISINE $

(Kalachakra Maidan; mains ₹80-120; ⊙ 7am-10pm; ☎) This informal, shanty-like, alfresco restaurant on the north side of the Kalachakra maidan has a backpacker-friendly menu, with lots of vegetarian options. Among the banana pancakes you'll find local specialities such as *litti chokha* (a regional snack comprising baked dough balls served with eggplant relish) and *khichdi* (a rice thali with chutneys and mashed potato).

Sewak Hotel
FAST FOOD $

(off Bodhgaya Rd; dishes ₹50-100; ⊙7am-10pm) If you're seeking sustenance at rock-bottom prices, look no further than this *dhaba*-style eatery for excellent snacks (including samosa, dosa and *idli* – a South Indian spongy, round, fermented rice cake), sweets, lassis and basic thalis. There's an adjoining groceries store where you can buy packets of snacks, bars of chocolate and bottled water.

★ Be Happy Cafe
ITALIAN $$

(beside Kalachakra Maidan; mains ₹150-420; ⊙8am-8.30pm; ❄🖥) This quaint and cosy cafe serves aromatic espressos (₹90), herbal teas and healthy Italian cuisine – salads, pastas and freshly baked pizza. This is one place where you can trust the salads and fresh vegetables, and the desserts are the best in town. Reservations are a good idea for lunch, especially during the busy months from November to February.

Nirvana The Veg Cafe
MULTICUISINE $$

(Hotel Maya Heritage; mains ₹100-200; ⊙8am-9pm) 🍴 This new vegetarian restaurant across the street from the Thai Temple plates a good selection of *dosas*, as well as pizzas, sandwiches, burgers and noodles. The service is prompt and friendly, and the split-level decor is stylish, with several best-selling books published over the decades pinned to the ceiling.

Siam Thai
THAI $$

(Bodhgaya Rd; curries ₹200; ⊙8.30am-10pm) Delicious curries made from Thai ingredients, plus interesting starters such as fish cakes and *larb gai* (minced chicken with lemon, lemongrass and mint), are on offer here. The chicken *paenang* is addictive; for something sweeter try the *massaman* curry.

ℹ️ Information

BSTDC Tourist Complex (☑0631-2200672; cnr Bodhgaya Rd & Temple St; ⊙10.30am-5pm Tue-Sat) Basic information available.

State Bank of India (Bodhgaya Rd; ⊙10.30am-4.30pm Mon-Fri, to 1.30pm Sat) Best rates for cash and travellers cheques; has an ATM.

Main Post Office (cnr Bodhgaya & Godam Rds; ⊙10am-3pm Mon-Fri, to 2pm Sat)

Verma Health Care Centre (☑0631-2201101; ⊙8am-9pm) Emergency room and privately

---

ℹ️ DRINKING FACTS

The groundwater in many parts of Bihar is laced with arsenic, the long-term consumption of which can be fatal. While travelling in the state, drink bottled water whenever possible. Be aware that food at cheaper restaurants will possibly be cooked with tap water, so you may be at risk of ingesting small amounts of the chemical if you eat at these places. The best option is to stick to fried or grilled dishes, and avoid gravies and curries as much as possible.

Since 2016, Bihar has been a dry state, so there's no alcohol of any kind for sale.

---

run clinic. A doctor is only on location from around noon to 8pm.

ℹ️ Getting There & Away

Gaya airport is 8km west of Bodhgaya. **Air India** (☑0631-2201155; www.airindia.com) flies daily to Delhi and Varanasi, and twice weekly to Kolkata. Between November and February there are direct international flights from Bangkok (Thailand), Colombo (Sri Lanka), Paro (Bhutan), Yangon (Myanmar) and Ho Chi Minh City (Vietnam).

Shared **autorickshaws** (₹40) leave from north of the Mahabodhi Temple for the 13km trip to Gaya, though not all go as far as the train station. A private autorickshaw to Gaya costs ₹200.

Note, autos occasionally take the back route from Gaya to Bodhgaya, via Sikadia More, and then drop passengers on the approach to Mahabodhi Temple on Bodhgaya Rd.

A few noiseless electric autorickshaws run in Bodhgaya; you can encourage this trend by taking these whenever possible.

Jayjagdamba Travels (☑9472964873; Tourist Bus Park) operates non-AC buses to Varanasi (₹350, seven hours) at 7am, 9am and 5pm, as well as a 2pm bus to Siliguri (₹800, 16 hours), and can arrange a private car to Varanasi (₹4500).

You can buy train tickets from the **Indian Railways Reservation Counter** (Bodhgaya Rd; ⊙8am-noon & 12.30-2pm Mon-Sat), next to the BSTDC Tourist Complex.

Rajgir

☑06112 / POP 41,500

The fascinating surrounds of Rajgir are bound by five semiarid rocky hills, each lined with ancient stone walls – vestiges of the ancient capital of Magadha. As both Buddha and Mahavira spent some serious time here, Rajgir is an important pilgrimage site for Buddhists and Jains, while a mention in the Mahabharata also means that Rajgir sees a large number of Hindu pilgrims, who come to bathe in the hot springs at the Lakshmi Narayan Temple.

Rajgir is littered with historic sites, so bank on spending a couple of days here, including a side trip to Nalanda. It's a lovely part of Bihar; greener and more rural than other places in the region, and relatively hassle-free.

◉ Sights

Vulture Hill
BUDDHIST SITE

(Griddhakuta) Buddha is thought to have preached the Lotus sutra on this rock outcrop. There are some faint remains of a 1500-year-old stupa, some prayer flags and a small shrine where Buddhist pilgrims come to pray. Get here by walking down from the Vishwa Shanti Stupa and detouring for a 10-minute walk uphill along a processional way built by King Bimbisara 2500 years ago.

King Bimbisara's Jail
ARCHAEOLOGICAL SITE

These foundations mark the jail in which King Bimbisara was imprisoned until his death by his son Ajatashatru. Bimbisara was the first king to adopt Buddhism as a state religion.

Saptaparni Cave
BUDDHIST SITE

(⊙ dawn-4pm) A 40-minute uphill hike from the back of the Lakshmi Narayan Temple takes you past Jain and Hindu temples to this atmospheric cave and natural rock platform, where Buddha is said to have meditated. Literally meaning 'seven leaves', Saptaparni cave is the likely location for the First Buddhist Council, held six months after Buddha's death to define the direction of the new faith.

Vishwa Shanti Stupa
BUDDHIST STUPA

(Shanti Stupa Rd; chairlift return ₹60; ⊙ ropeway 8.30am-1pm & 2-5pm) Constructed in 1965, this blazing-white, 40m stupa stands atop Ratnagiri Hill about 5km south of town. Recesses in the stupa feature golden statues of Buddha in four stages of his life – birth, enlightenment, preaching and death. A fun but wobbly single-person chairlift runs to the summit, which affords expansive views of hills and a few Jain shrines dotting the landscape. Next to the stupa, a Japanese-built peace pagoda reverberates to the rhythmic sound of meditative drum beats.

🛏 Sleeping & Eating

Hotel Vijay Niketan
GUESTHOUSE $

(☑ 9835620220; www.hotelvijayniketan.com; Police Station Rd; r with/without AC ₹900/750; ❄ 🛜) The budget rooms here are a bit rough at the edges but are decent for the price (which is often negotiable). It's run by two helpful English-speaking brothers, who can fix any issues with hot water or wi-fi. Upper-floor rooms are best but can be hot, and there are a couple of air-con rooms (₹1680).

Hotel Nalanda Regency
HOTEL $$$

(☑ 7766969099; www.hotelnalandaregency.com; r incl breakfast ₹5400; ❄ 🛜) Perhaps the best-run hotel in town, rooms here are fresh and modern with hot-water bathrooms and an excellent restaurant (mains ₹150 to ₹230), just two minutes' walk north of the bus stand. Walk-in discounts of 40% can make it excellent value.

Indo Hokke Hotel
BOUTIQUE HOTEL $$$

(☑ 06112-255245; www.theroyalresidency.com; Veerayatan Rd; s/d incl breakfast ₹6500/7000; ❄ @ 🛜 🏊) Surrounded by 3 hectares of lovely gardens, this modern, red-brick building features clean, stylish rooms and good service. It's a quiet place with a Buddhist chapel and hot onsen-style baths for groups. The rooms with tiled floors are biggest. It's 500m beyond Veerayatan museum, 3km south and then west of the bus stand.

Green Hotel
INDIAN $

(mains ₹60-150, thali ₹150-250; ⊙ 8am-9.30pm) Diagonally opposite the Lakshmi Narayan Temple complex, this simple restaurant is one of several in a row that offers pleasant alfresco seating, hot tasty food, and prompt and friendly service. The food is good and it's a great place to relax at the end of the day.

❶ Information

The **tourist information centre** (☑ 8292984850; ⊙ 10am-5pm) on the main road between the bus stand and the train station has free maps and literature on Rajgir and the surrounding Buddhist sites.

There are ATMs near the bus stand and one diagonally opposite the Lakshmi Narayan Temple complex.

❶ Getting There & Away

Buses run every 30 minutes to Gaya (₹50 to ₹60, 2½ hours) and Nalanda (₹10, 20 minutes) from the bus stand. For Nalanda take a bus bound for Bihar Sharif.

Two fast trains run daily to Patna (sleeper/AC chair ₹140/260, 2½ hours) at 8am and 4.30pm.

The bus stand is in the centre of town, and the train station 1km to the north. Turn left out of the bus stand and take the third left to reach the train station.

Nalanda

☑ 06112

Founded in the 5th century AD, Nalanda – 15km north of Rajgir – was one of the ancient world's great universities and an important Buddhist centre of academic excellence. When Chinese scholar and traveller Xuan Zang visited sometime between 685 and 762 AD, about 10,000 monks and students lived here, studying theology, astronomy, metaphysics, medicine and philosophy. It's said that Nalanda's three libraries were so extensive they burnt for six months when foreign invaders sacked the university in 1193.

Apart from the ruins, modern Nalanda is merely a tiny village comprising a smattering of houses thrown along dusty lanes. Once you're done exploring the ruins, you could walk around for a bit to take in the sights and sounds of the quaint settlement.

◉ Sights

Allow one to two hours for wandering the extensive monastery **ruins** (Indian/foreigner ₹40/600, video ₹25; ☺9am-5.30pm). They're peaceful and well maintained with a park-like atmosphere of clipped lawns and shrubs. The red-brick ruins consist of 11 monasteries and six temples. Most impressive is the Great Stupa (Number Three), with steps, terraces, monks' residences and a few intact Gupta-era stupas. It is thought that a huge statue of Buddha once crowned the building. Climbing the structures is not allowed.

Unofficial guides (₹150) will approach you and can take you on a planned tour of the vast complex. Each ruin has a signboard including explanatory text in English, but the guides can supplement it with more information.

Across from the entrance to the ruins is the archaeological **museum** (₹5; ☺9am-5pm Sat-Thu), housing the Nalanda University seal and a host of beautiful stone sculptures and bronzes unearthed from Nalanda and Rajgir. Among the many Buddha figures and *kirtimukha* (gargoyles) is a bizarre multiple-spouted pot (probably once used to contain perfumed water).

About 2km from the museum and the ruins (take the first right) is the huge, modern **Xuan Zang Memorial Hall** (Indian/foreigner ₹5/50; ☺8am-5pm), built by the Chinese in honour of the famous Chinese pilgrim who walked to India from China before studying

BIHAR & JHARKHAND NALANDA

❶ TRAVEL SAFE

Bihar has a reputation for lawlessness. Conditions have improved in recent years – bandit activity (such as holding up cars, buses and trains) is only a remote possibility these days, but theft and snatching can and do happen. Besides, incidents such as rioting (incited by communal or political triggers) may occur without any warning, and it always helps to check with hotel owners and travel agents before travelling outside of major towns.

Jharkhand on the other hand has been under the shadow of Maoist insurgency in recent decades, and those planning trips to forest areas such as Betla should always keep an ear to the ground.

➡ Locals will advise you to avoid travelling after dark or hiking in the hills alone, and this is a sensible precaution. Do not flash expensive gadgets or money wallets in public, as these can draw unwanted attention.

➡ It's a good idea to keep up to date with the latest information and developments in the region. Check the newspapers *Bihar Times* (www.bihartimes.in) or the Jharkhand edition of the *Times of India* (www.timesofindia.indiatimes.com/topic/jharkhand) before arrival.

and teaching for several years at Nalanda. A return horse-carriage ride here costs ₹100.

About 1.5km beyond the Nalanda ruins, near Surya Kund pond, you'll find the striking **Nandyavarta Mahal** (⏱5am-9pm) at Kundalpur, believed by the Digambar Jain sect to be the birthplace of Lord Mahavira, the founder of Jainism.

On the pathway leading to the archaeological museum, **Cafeteria Nalanda** (mains ₹150-250; ⏱8am-6pm) makes a pleasant spot for lunch. Otherwise a few simple roadside stalls sell snacks.

❶ Getting There & Away

Buses from Rajgir (₹10) drop you at Nalanda village. From there you can take a shared tonga (per person/cart ₹5/50) for the final 2km to the ruins. Alternately, hire an autorickshaw from Rajgir for a return trip (₹400 including waiting time).

JHARKHAND

Hewn out of neighbouring Bihar in 2000 to meet the autonomy demands of the Adivasi (tribal) population, Jharkhand is a land of immense natural and anthropological wealth. However, despite boasting an incredible 40% of the country's mineral wealth (mostly coal, copper and iron ore), rich forests and cash-rich industrial hubs, it is plagued by poverty, social injustice, corruption, and sporadic outbursts of Maoist and Naxalite violence.

For travellers, Jharkhand's prime attractions are the Jain pilgrimage centre at Parasnath Hill, the unspoilt forests at Betla (Palamau) National Park, and the chance to explore a relatively tourist-free and unspoilt part of India.

Ranchi

☑ 0651 / POP 1.1 MILLION

Set on a plateau at 700m and marginally cooler than the plains, Jharkhand's state capital Ranchi was the summer capital of Bihar under the erstwhile British administration. There's little of interest within the city for travellers, but it acts as a convenient gateway to Betla (Palamau) National Park, as well as the Parasnath Hill.

◉ Sights

State Museum MUSEUM
(☑0651-2270011; www.statemuseumranchi.in; Hotwar, Khelgaon; Indian/foreigner ₹10/200, camera/video ₹25/100; ⏱10.30am-4.30pm Tue-Sun) This surprisingly large state museum has some ethnographic displays, featuring ornate bows and jewellery, but the main draw is the sculpture gallery, with its fine carvings and intriguing photos of remote architectural sites across Jharkhand. It's 8km northeast of the train station; factor in a one-way autorickshaw ride of around ₹200.

🛏 Sleeping & Eating

Hotel AVN Plaza HOTEL $$
(☑0651-2462231; www.hotelavnplaza.com; off Station Rd; s/d incl breakfast from ₹1570/2020, without AC d ₹1070; ✳🛜) This neat, modern hotel has small but clean rooms with TV, wi-fi and modern hot-water showers (some rooms have no windows). There are six standard non-air-con rooms, but these are small and stuffy, with no natural light. It's down a lane, off Station Rd, and is pretty quiet. It has 24hr checkout. Ask for a 15% discount.

⭐ **Chanakya BNR Hotel** HERITAGE HOTEL $$$
(☑0651-2461211; www.chanakyabnrranchi.com; Station Rd; d incl breakfast from ₹4150; ✳@🛜🛏) This charming hotel could be your sole reason for visiting Ranchi. A part-historic railways property located outside the train station, it's a superbly renovated terracotta-roofed Raj relic that oozes vintage and boutique appeal. The property's trees are home to parrots, and it has a small outdoor pool, a fitness centre, two excellent restaurants and a modern bar.

Nook INDIAN $$
(Station Rd; mains ₹100-200; ⏱7.30am-11pm) Arguably the best midrange hotel restaurant in the train-station area, this in-house dining facility at Hotel Kwality Inns is comfortable and the service attentive without being obsequious. The tandoori dishes are excellent, especially the creamy *murgh tikka lababdar*.

❶ Information

There are ATMs at the train station as well as on Station Rd.
Suhana Tour & Travellers (☑9431171394; suhana_jharkhandtour@yahoo.co.in; Gurunanak Market, Station Rd; ⏱8am-8pm Mon-Sat, to 2pm Sun) organises day trips to three nearby waterfalls, and package tours to Betla (Palamau) National Park.

HIKING HOLY PARASNATH

For a fabulously offbeat experience with a spiritual leaning, consider joining the hundreds of Jain pilgrims who hike each morning to the top of holy Parasnath Hill.

Also known as Shikarji (Venerated Peak), Parasnath Hill is the highest mountain in Jharkhand at 1336m, and is a major Jain pilgrimage centre. The ridgetop is studded with 31 tonk (shrines), including the striking white Parasnath Temple, where 20 of the 24 Jain tirthankars (including Parasnath, at the age of 100) are believed to have reached salvation.

The approach to the hill is from the small, but auspicious temple town of Madhuban, 13km northeast of Parasnath train station, at the foot of the mountain. The daily pilgrimage begins from the town at around 4am; it's a 9km hike to the top, gaining 1000m elevation, followed by a 9km clockwise loop around a ridgeline, before reaching the highest peak at Parasnath Temple. To visit in the correct clockwise circuit you need to take the left branch about halfway up the hill, rather than take the right-hand trail straight up to Parasnath Temple. The entire 27km circuit – up, round and back down – takes about nine hours: three hours up, three hours circuiting the peaks, and two hours back down. You could start later in the day and still get back before dark, but hiking while you're half asleep with hundreds of pilgrims as dawn breaks across the mountain is a big part of the experience, and starting early means you avoid the worst of the midday heat. Water, chai and snacks are available along the way. During holidays and major festivals, you could end up walking with as many as 15,000 people, many of whom pay to be carried up in a dholi (litter).

You're likely to spend at least one night in Madhuban. There are three or four hotels in town (plus numerous dharamsalas or pilgrims' rest houses). The best value is the ageing government-run **Tirtha Yatri Kendra** (☑ 9939813270; www.jharkhandtourism.gov. in; tr ₹900, dm per person ₹150) with two spacious three-bed rooms with air-con, as well as several fan-cooled dormitories (with shared bathrooms). It's at the bottom end of the main road leading up to the mountain, next to a creek, just before you reach the museum (there's no English sign). Just before Yatri Nivas, turn left down a lane off the main road, and keep walking for 500m to reach **Shikarji Continental** (☑ 9334294965, 9323360708; r from ₹1200; ❄). This is the best-quality hotel in town, with austere but modern air-con rooms, hot water in the morning and evening, and balconies in the upper floor rooms. **Hotel Sapna & Veg Restaurant** (Main Rd; mains ₹50-130; ◷ 11am-10pm; ✐), towards the top end of the main road at a bend, has a 1st-floor restaurant serving simple South Indian and Punjabi dishes. If you have time to kill in Madhuban, pop into the small **Jain Museum** (₹10; ◷ 8am-6.30pm Mar-Oct, 8.30am-6pm Nov-Feb, closed noon-1pm), on your left at the bottom end of the main road.

Parasnath is most easily reached from Gaya, from where there are frequent trains (two hours). For maximum comfort book an AC chair ticket (₹253) on the 8.15am 12365 Patna–Ranchi Janshatabdi Express (the return train 12366 leaves Parasnath at 5.53pm). Alternatively, just buy a 'general' 2nd-class ticket (₹64) and hop on the next train; you'll usually get a seat, and if not, it's only two hours.

Cramped shared vehicles (jeeps, autos and even the odd bus) wait for passengers to disembark at Parasnath train station to ferry them 13km to Madhuban (per person ₹40). A chartered minivan costs ₹400.

From Parasnath there are frequent trains to Ranchi (2nd/AC chair ₹110/375, four hours) and Varanasi (2nd class/sleeper/3AC ₹136/265/375, six hours), as well as a handful of trains to Kolkata, the most convenient being the 13010 Doon Express (sleeper/3AC/2AC ₹210/560/800, seven hours, 11.56pm).

❶ Getting There & Around

AIR

Ranchi's Birsa Munda Airport is 6km south of the city centre. **Air India** (☑ 1800-1801407; www. airindia.in) and **IndiGo** (☑ 0124-6173838; www. goindigo.in) have daily connections to Kolkata, Delhi and Patna.

A prepaid taxi to Station Rd from the Ranchi airport is ₹300. An autorickshaw in the opposite direction is ₹200.

BUS

From the government bus stand on Station Rd, there are hourly buses to Gaya throughout the day (₹180, six hours) and numerous overnight services to Patna (standard/AC ₹280/450, nine hours), which leave from around 9pm onwards.

Buses to Daltonganj (₹150, five hours) leave from ITI bus stand, 8km northwest of Station Rd (shared/private autorickshaw ₹20/200).

TRAIN

The handy 12366 Janshatabdi Express departs daily at 2.25pm to Patna (2nd class/chair ₹185/630, seven hours), via Parasnath (₹110/375, three hours) and Gaya (₹160/535, 5½ hours).

For Kolkata (chair/executive/3AC/2AC ₹870/1700/675/965, eight to nine hours) the handiest trains are the daytime 12020 Shatabdi Express (1.45pm) and the overnight 18616 Kriya Yoga Express (9.40pm).

The daily 18451 Tapaswini Express goes to Bhubaneswar (sleeper/3AC/2AC ₹340/935/1340, 13 hours, 3.55pm), departing from nearby Hatia station (₹300 by autorickshaw from Station Rd).

Betla (Palamau) National Park

📞 06562

Wild elephants freely roam the virgin forests of this lovely, rarely visited **national park** (📞 06562-222650; ⏰ 6-10am & 2-5pm), spread over the hilly landscape of picturesque Palamau district, some 190km west of Ranchi. Tiger sightings are extremely rare, but a trip to this primeval region of Jharkhand offers a glimpse into the rich tribal heritage of the state. The park covers around 250 sq km, much of which comprises the Palamau Tiger Reserve. Hiding behind dense stands of teak forest, rich evergreens, sal trees and bamboo thickets are about six tigers (going by unofficial 2018 estimates), 52 leopards and 216 elephants. You'll also see plenty of monkeys, spotted deer and possibly some gaur (Indian bison).

🛏 Sleeping & Eating

Tourist Lodge   GUESTHOUSE **$**

(📞 06562-222650; d ₹1250; ❄) This four-room lodge has park views from the balconies. Rooms are clean and have TVs and spacious bathrooms. The nearby canteen (7am to 7pm) arranges a hearty vegetarian thali (₹120) for lunch and dinner. The lodge must

ℹ JEEP SAFARI COSTS

Jeep safaris can be arranged at the Betla (Palamau) National Park gate. The breakdown of the costs for jeep safaris is as follows:

Park entry (per vehicle, per hour) ₹300

Compulsory guide (per vehicle, per hour) ₹100

Jeep hire (per vehicle, per hour) ₹500

Camera fee (per person, per safari) ₹100

So, for example; a two-hour jeep safari for two people, both with cameras, would cost a total of ₹2000. For a single person, it would cost ₹1900. Jeep safaris can last from one hour to up to three or four hours, depending on how long you wish to spend in the park. Jeep rides to Palamau Fort and Kechki River are charged in the same fashion, minus the park fees.

be booked through the Forestry Department in Daltonganj, which can be a hassle.

Van Vihar   HOTEL **$**

(📞 9102403882; www.jharkhandtourism.gov.in; d ₹1456; ❄) The majority of visitors stay overnight at the government-run Van Vihar, 100m before the park entrance. The 25 rooms are comfortable, spacious and clean, with hot-water bathrooms and balconies, though the exuberant groups can be noisy. The in-house restaurant plates up fresh but nondescript fare. Note that the air-con works only when there's power. Book online through the state tourism website.

ℹ Getting There & Away

The nearest town to the park entrance is Daltonganj, about 20km away, which has frequent bus services to Ranchi throughout the day (₹150, five hours). From Daltonganj take a local bus (₹20, roughly hourly until around 4pm) or shared autorickshaw (₹30) to Betla. A private autorickshaw from Daltonganj will cost around ₹400. Buses run from Betla back to Daltonganj and on to Ranchi until around 4pm.

If you don't fancy going it alone, Suhana Tour & Travels (p532), based in Ranchi, does two-day trips to Betla for ₹4800 per person (minimum two people).

Sikkim

Best Places to Eat

→ Nimtho (p542)

→ Wongden Homestay
(p546)

→ Mama's Kitchen (p555)

Best Places to Stay

→ Chumbi Mountain Retreat
(p552)

→ Bamboo Retreat (p545)

→ Lake View Nest (p554)

→ Hotel Garuda (p552)

→ Elgin Mount Pandim
(p552)

Why Go?

Sikkim was its own mountain kingdom till 1975 and still retains a very distinctive personality. The meditative, mural-filled traditional monasteries of Tibetan Buddhism coexist with Hindu shrines of the ever-growing Nepali community, with both religions creating some astonishing latter-day megasculptures to adorn the skyline.

Hassle-free and warm-hearted, it's a state that's all too easy to fall in love with, explaining perhaps why permit regulations prevent foreigners staying too long or going too far. Clean, green and 'all organic' since 2016, Sikkim is mostly a maze of plunging, supersteep valleys thick with lush subtropical woodlands and rhododendron groves, rising in the north to the spectacular white-top peaks of the eastern Himalaya. When clouds clear, an ever-thrilling experience from many a ridge-top perch is spotting the world's third-highest mountain, Khangchendzonga (8598m), on the northwestern dawn horizon.

When to Go
Gangtok

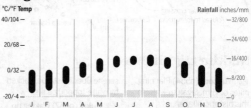

Apr & May Beautiful spring blossoms, partly clear skies, high-season crowds.

Mid-Jun–Sep Monsoon plays spoilsport, but there are great discounts on offer.

Mid-Oct–early Dec Clearest weather for fabulous views but gets cold at altitude.

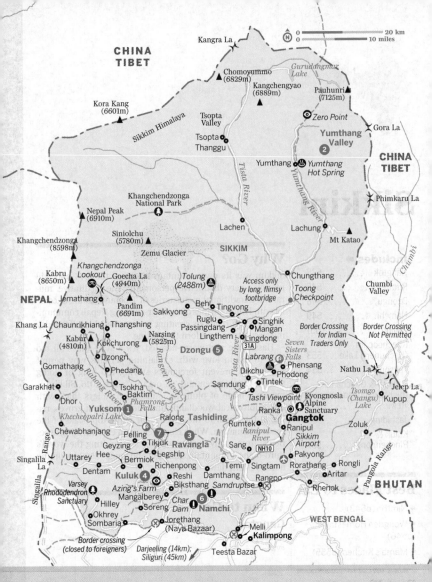

Sikkim Highlights

1 Yuksom (p554) Planning hikes or Himalayan treks from this historic village.

2 Yumthang (p547) Driving through a kaleidoscope of scenery to this picture-perfect valley.

3 Buddha Park (p550) Gazing at Ravangla's giant, serene Buddha statue, backed by white-topped peaks.

4 Kuluk (p557) Waking up to dazzling Khangchendzonga views then exploring Rinchenpong's old monasteries.

5 Dzongu (p546) Spotting rare butterflies and learning about Lepcha culture in an authentic village homestay.

6 Namchi (p549) Finding re-creations of some of India's greatest Hindu temples.

7 Tashiding Gompa (p556) Wandering among prayer flags and ancient chortens (stupas).

History

The Lepcha people, Sikkim's earliest long-term inhabitants, arrived by the 13th century from Assam or Myanmar (Burma). They were followed by Bhutias who struck south from Tibet in the 15th century, having secured a much-celebrated bond of friendship with the Lepchas at Kabi Lunchok. The ascendancy of the Bhutias and their Nyingmapa form of Vajrayana (Tibetan) Buddhism was underlined when three Tibetan lamas met in Yuksom in 1641 to crown Phuntsog Namgyal (a Bhutia) as first chogyal (king) of Sikkim. The capital later moved to Rabdentse (near Pelling), then to Tumlong in North Sikkim, before finally settling in Gangtok.

In their heydays the chogyals ruled parts of what is now eastern Nepal and upper Bengal, but much territory was lost during wars with Bhutan and Nepal. In 1835 the British bamboozled the chogyal into ceding Darjeeling to the East India Company for a nominal rent. Then in 1849 the British annexed the entire area between the present Sikkim border and the Ganges plains, subsequently repulsing an 1886 counterinvasion by Tibet. Large numbers of Nepali-Hindu migrants, encouraged by the British, arrived over subsequent decades, ultimately forming the majority of Sikkim's population.

When India gained independence in 1947, Sikkim's status was nebulous, as there had never been a formal agreement with Britain. The chogyal initially retained formal autonomy for Sikkim, albeit allowing India to direct all foreign policy. However, in 1975 the last chogyal and his American-born queen were deposed when Sikkim became incorporated as an Indian state.

As a state, Sikkim has made great strides at improving rural sanitation, public health and secondary education, though roads need far more work and a September 2011 earthquake devastated many buildings including several historic monasteries. Hydroelectric power is a hot political topic – many new dam projects have been stopped (notably in Dzongu) by activist campaigns; ecological-awareness projects have also stamped out the use of plastic carrier bags. Since 2016 Sikkim has been India's first 'all-organic' farming state.

Activities

Trekking is a high point of any Sikkim sojourn. Mountaineers considering the state's numerous 6000-plus-metre peaks should plan carefully with Namgyal Treks & Tours

(p539) in Gangtok. Paragliding is possible in Gangtok and Pelling. BB Line (p539) arranges motorbike and mountain-bike tours, rafting and kayaking.

 Permits

For almost all permits you'll need photocopies of your passport, visa and inner line permit, plus a passport photo or three. Indeed it's well worth getting plenty of such copies and photos for unforeseen eventualities. Even some hotels expect you to provide them at check-in.

STANDARD PERMITS

Foreigners require an Inner Line Permit (ILP, www.sikkimilp.in) to enter Sikkim (Indians don't). These are free and getting one is a formality. Bring at least one passport-sized photo and photocopies (plus originals) of your passport and visa to one of the following places:

➺ entry checkpoints at Melli or Rangpo (permits issued 8am to 7.30pm only)

➺ Bagdogra Airport's Sikkim Tourism booth (10am to 4pm daily)

➺ Sikkim House in **Kolkata** (Map p466; 4/1 Middleton St; ⊘10am-5pm Mon-Sat) or Delhi (p104).

➺ Sikkim Tourist Office (p495) in Siliguri.

Permits are also available by a more complex process in Darjeeling and, by the time you read this, may be available on arrival at Pakyong Airport (p544).

The lack of a checkpoint at Jorethang is a logistical nuisance meaning no permits are issued and indeed foreigners may not cross to/from West Bengal there.

The standard ILP is valid for 15 days, though longer validity is sometimes provided on request.

Permits can be extended at government offices in **Gangtok** (Foreigners' Registration Office; NH10, Tadong; ⊘10am-4pm Mon-Sat) and 3km below Pelling in **Tikjuk** (3rd fl, West Sikkim District Administrative Centre; ⊘10am-4pm Mon-Sat, closed 2nd Sat of the month), up to a maximum stay of 60 days.

SPECIAL PERMITS

Several areas of Sikkim require specific permits, including the following:

➺ high-altitude trekking routes (p555)

➺ Far North Sikkim (p548)

➺ Dzongu (p546)

➺ Tsomgo Lake (p541).

These permits should be issued through an approved agent and require that there are at least two foreigners (one foreigner plus one Indian isn't enough).

Some other destinations close to the Tibetan border, including Nathu La and Gurudongmar

Lake, are entirely closed to foreigners, though Indian nationals are allowed to visit with approved tours.

High-Altitude Treks

Organised by your trekking agent once you have arranged a guide, permits are issued in Gangtok, though some agents in Yuksom now organise a one-day service by sending your details by WhatsApp.

Far North Sikkim

For travel beyond Singhik up the Lachung and Lachen valleys in North Sikkim, foreigners need restricted-area permits. These allow travel up to the Tsopta and Yumthang valleys. Indian citizens need a police permit to travel north of Singhik but can venture further up the Thanggu valley to Gurudongmar Lake, or to Yume Samdong (Zero Point) past Yumthang. Permits can be procured in Gangtok but are only delivered on the morning of departure and the need for a guide is enforced. Applying in Mangan (p546) is generally a better option.

Dzongu

For Dzongu (the Lepcha area north of Dikchu) you'll need a special permit, usually organised through your prebooked homestay. While the permit is free, homestay owners incur significant costs copying documents and taking taxis to Mangan to make arrangements on your behalf so will normally charge around ₹500 for the service. Alternatively, arrange your own permit in Mangan.

❶ Getting There & Away

Sikkim's new airport (p544) at Pakyong has daily SpiceJet flights to Kolkata and Guwahati. Most travellers, however, still arrive at busy Bagdogra airport near Siliguri in West Bengal. The nearest major train station is at New Jalpaiguri (NJP), also near Siliguri. Although a Gangtok–Siliguri taxi usually takes under five hours, you'd be advised to leave a lot of extra leeway in case of traffic jams and landslides. Or sleep in Darjeeling or Kurseong the night before.

BORDER CROSSINGS

Due to permit-check procedures, foreigners are only allowed to cross between Sikkim and West Bengal at Melli and Rangpo border posts. Not being allowed to cross at Jorethang (p549) precludes linking Darjeeling and West Sikkim by easy public transport.

❶ Getting Around

Apart from a limited bus service, almost all public transport within Sikkim is by shared jeep. Ten passengers squeeze aboard, including two beside the driver: consider booking two seats to avoid claustrophobia.

Distances that look short on a map can be extremely lengthy in reality due to valley crossings on uncountable hairpin bends. Landslides and road building cause regular delays.

EAST SIKKIM

Gangtok

📞 03592 / POP 106,300 / ELEV 1620M

Irreverent, cheerful and pleasantly boisterous, Sikkim's modern capital is layered along a precipitous mountain ridge, descending the hillside in steep tiers. Viewpoints survey plunging green valleys that remain beautiful even when partly shrouded in mist. If the weather plays ball, look for glimpses of snow-topped Khangchendzonga on the distant skyline. More than specific sights, Gangtok is appealing as a place for post-trek R & R or for meeting fellow travellers to organise group tours and permits. The city's mostly pedestrianised social-commercial heart is Mahatma Gandhi (MG) Marg, packed with restaurants, shops, travel agents and a bustling early-evening passeggiata of relaxed wanderers. High above, the contrastingly calm central ridgetop links manicured gardens and an almost jungle-like area around the Chogyal Palace (former royal residence).

◎ Sights

For a satisfying day exploring Gangtok with plenty of walking but almost no uphill sections, try this plan.

Start with a ₹200 taxi ride to the city viewpoint at Ganesh Tok, possibly paying a (considerable) supplement to have the driver whisk you around the zoo (p539). Find the slightly overgrown forest shortcut through the Pinetum down to Enchey Gompa, taking around 15 minutes with a key double-back just before a lower viewpoint.

Take the easily missed stairway opposite the entrance to Hotel Mount Siniolchu and, after descending the lane awhile, take another set of steps that is guarded by a sentry box but OK to use. Emerging near the Tamarind Residency Hotel, continue your descent via Nehru Chowk roundabout to the amusingly naive **Flower Exhibition Centre** (₹20; ⏰9am-5pm). Wander along the attractively wooded Ridge to the gorgeous royal monastery Tsuklakhang (p539), then – assuming that the Upper Ropeway Station is still out of action – find the stairway down to Kazi Rd, emerging outside the Hotel Fair View.

Turn left and continue down to the Namnang Ropeway Station (p545) for a cable-car ride (p545) to Deorali (p545). Visit the Institute of Tibetology and pay ₹10 to return to the city centre by shared taxi.

★ **Tsuklakhang** BUDDHIST TEMPLE
(Bhanu Path; ⊙ dawn-dusk, prayers 6am & 4pm) Gangtok's 'royal' monastery has a very impressive centrepiece temple whose superb interior incorporates a pair of carved dragon columns flanking the main images.

The whole compound is an oasis of calm and, though surrounding monastic quarters are contrastingly neutral, you can get a decent glimpse of the private Chogyal Palace while wandering across the monks' football pitch.

★ **Namgyal Institute of Tibetology** MUSEUM
(NIT; www.tibetology.net; Deorali; ₹20; ⊙ 10am-4pm) The NIT's 1958 core building feels like a Tibetan fantasy palace, with corner towers, colourful mural frontage and a forest-glade setting. The main hall houses a priceless and well-explained collection of culturally Tibetan/ Buddhist iconography and artefacts, including tantric skullcap bowls and trumpets made from human thigh bones. Beautiful Buddhist statuary includes an eight-armed bronze image of victory goddess Namgyalama, who appears to be texting on an invisible phone.

Few tourists venture upstairs to the shrine-like library, whose teak-and-glass cases house mostly wrapped religious scriptures along with the 135-volume *Encyclopaedia Tibetica*.

The institute is six minutes' walk from Deorali Bazaar Ropeway Station (p545) and Deorali taxi stand.

Tashi Viewpoint VIEWPOINT
(Gangtok-Mangan Rd Km1.4) FREE When clouds lift, Gangtok's best glimpses of Khangchendzonga are from this roadside knoll at the junction of routes to Mangan and Nathu La, around 7km northwest of the centre.

Himalayan Zoological Park ZOO
(Gangtok Zoo; Indian/foreigner ₹25/50, motorbike/ car/jeep ₹10/40/100, video ₹500; ⊙ 9.30am-3.30pm Fri-Wed) Among India's best-maintained zoos, this lushly forested park occupies an entire hillside. The star attractions are Sikkim's animal emblems, the red pandas, looking a little like cuddly toy foxes. There are also Himalayan bears and snow leopards roaming enclosures so large that you'll need patience to see them. With a vehicle, allow around two hours to see everything; walks total over 2km from the three parking areas.

TOP STATE FESTIVALS

Losar (⊙ Feb/Mar) Sikkim's biggest *chaam* (masked dance) rings in the Tibetan New Year at Rumtek Gompa (p545).

Bumchu (⊙ Feb/Mar) On the 15th day of the first Tibetan month, lamas open a *bum* (pot) containing *chu* (holy water) to foretell the year's fortunes at Tashiding Gompa (p556).

Saga Dawa (⊙ May/Jun) On the full moon of the fourth Tibetan month, ceremonies and parades commemorate Buddha's birth, enlightenment and death.

Losoong (Namsoong; ⊙ Dec/Jan) The Sikkimese harvest festival is is a period of merrymaking and archery competitions, preceded by flamboyant *chaam* dances, notably at Old Rumtek (p545).

Without wheels, add an extra 1.6km walk each way from/to the ticket booth, which is opposite Ganesh Tok (p538).

Enchey Gompa MONASTERY
(⊙ prayer hall 5am-4pm) On the city's northern outskirts, approached through rustling conifers, Enchey is a small but appealing Nyingma-Buddhist monastery that is, in a sense, Gangtok's raison d'être: it was the site's perceived sanctity that originally attracted people to this once-obscure area. The vibrantly colourful prayer hall features a three-dimensional scene of stacked creatures that offers a curious interpretation of evolution behind the sharp-nosed central Buddha figure.

🏃 **Activities**

Namgyal Treks & Tours OUTDOORS
(☑ 03592-203701, 9434033122; www.namgyaltreks. com; Enchey Compound, Tibet Rd; ⊙ 10am-5pm Mon-Sat) One of Sikkim's best-established agencies for treks and especially mountaineering expeditions, founded in 1991 by Namgyal Sherpa, a highly experienced climber and now president of the local Rotary club.

BB Line Tours & Travels ADVENTURE SPORTS
(☑ 03592-206110, 8170005820; www.toursandtravels.bbline.co.in; 2nd fl, Yama House, MG Marg; ⊙ 9.30am-6.30pm) BB Line is one of Sikkim's most forward-thinking adventure-tourism agencies, developing motorbike and mountain-bike tours, catch-and-release fishing trips, kayaking and rafting.

Gangtok

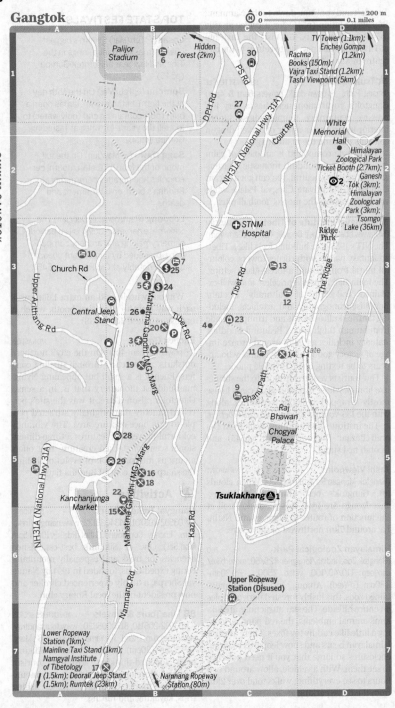

Palijor Stadium

Hidden Forest (2km)

TV Tower (1.1km);
Enchey Gompa (1.2km);
Rachna Books (150m);
Vajra Taxi Stand (1.2km);
Tashi Viewpoint (5km)

PS Rd

DPH Rd

NH31A (National Hwy 31A)

Court Rd

White Memorial Hall

Himalayan Zoological Park Ticket Booth
Ganesh Tok (3km);
Himalayan Zoological Park (3km);
Tsomgo Lake (36km)

STNM Hospital

Ridge Park

The Ridge

Church Rd

Upper Arithang Rd

Central Jeep Stand

Mahatma Gandhi (MG) Marg

Tibet Rd

Bhanu Path

Raj Bhawan

Chogyal Palace

Tsuklakhang

Kanchanjunga Market

Mahatma Gandhi (MG) Marg

Kazi Rd

Namnang Rd

NH31A (National Hwy 31A)

Lower Ropeway Station (1km);
Mainline Taxi Stand (1km);
Namgyal Institute of Tibetology (1.5km); Deorali Jeep Stand (1.5km); Rumtek (23km)

Upper Ropeway Station (Disused)

Namnang Ropeway Station (80m)

0 .... 200 m
0 .... 0.1 miles

Gangtok

Altitude Tours & Travels TREKKING
(📞9733380698; baichungb1@hotmail.com; MG Marg; ⏰approx 6am-9pm Sep-Jun, 9am-5pm Jul & Aug) This popular 'everything' agency, run by very experienced trekking guide Bhaichung Bhutia, has a minuscule office tucked into the doorway beside the tourist office.

STDC SCENIC FLIGHTS
(Sikkim Tourism Development Corporation; 📞03592-203960; www.sikkimstdc.com; MG Marg; ⏰9am-2pm & 3-7pm May, Jun & Sep-Jan, 10am-5pm rest of year) Provides tours, taxi-charters and helicopter flights, including Bagdogra transfers and various pleasure flights. A 15-minute buzz over Gangtok costs ₹9500, a 75-minute Khangchendzonga Ridge fly-past ₹90,000. Price is for four people, book three days ahead.

Tsomgo Lake Excursions SCENIC DRIVE
(per vehicle from ₹4500) Jeep excursions running 60km each way to the Tibetan border post at Nathu La, via small glacial lake Tsomgo (Changu) at 3780m, are wildly popular with Indian tourists getting a first taste of snow. However, permits are required, strict timings enforced and foreigners aren't allowed to go to the border zone at all so cannot join the widely advertised tours.

🛌 Sleeping

⭐ **Hotel Pandim** HOTEL $
(📞03592-207540, 9832080172; www.hotelpandim.com; Bhanu Path; dm/d from ₹500/1500; 📶) This friendly family guesthouse is Gangtok's best budget option, with jaw-dropping mountain panoramas from its top-floor deluxe rooms (₹2000 to ₹2500), from the four-bed dorm, and especially from the delightful Tibetan-styled top-floor cafe-restaurant (guests only, order ahead) where you check in.

Gangtok Lodge GUESTHOUSE $
(📞03592-206562; NH31A; d ₹1500) This neat little eight-room guesthouse has simple rooms with Nepali curtains and hand-painted Sikkimese cabinets adding a little colour.

⭐ **Hidden Forest** GUESTHOUSE $$
(📞9474981367, 9434137409; www.hiddenforestretreat.org; NH10, Middle Sichey; s/d ₹2800/3540; @📶) 🌿 An oasis of birdsong some 2km from central Gangtok, this collection of high-quality, lovingly maintained cottage rooms and houselets is interspersed with countless blooming shrubs and orchids. Gorgeous valley views look towards Rumtek, there's a well-stocked library, a flower nursery and a kitchen garden providing top-quality

organic veg for delicious home-cooked set meals (breakfast/dinner ₹210/315, prebook).

Greendale Residence
HOTEL $$

(☑ 9933009970, 03592-201400; www.greendalesikkim.com; NH31A; d standard/large ₹4500/4900; 🛜) A smart-suited welcome ushers guests into this very well equipped hotel, which adds minor Sikkimese details to oversized, comfortable rooms with rugs on tiled floors, kettle and wi-fi.

Hotel Yavachi
DESIGN HOTEL $$

(☑ 03592-204666; www.hotelyavachi.com; Church Rd; d small/large ₹2800/4000, ste ₹6500; 🛜) Unusually stylish for this price range, Yavachi's comfortably modernist rooms come with ceiling-panel lighting and abstract art, though styles and sizes vary: room 203 is a good bet.

Mintokling Guest House
GUESTHOUSE $$

(☑ 03592-208553; www.mintokling.com; Bhanu Path; s/d/ste ₹3300/3540/4150; 🛜) Nestled amid exotic greenery and set around pretty lawns, this lovely oasis of peace and quiet has a dozen large, well-kept rooms that are partly wood panelled, with embroidered bedspreads and floral detailing.

★ Netuk House
HERITAGE HOTEL $$$

(☑ 03592-206778; www.netukhouse.com; r standard/large ₹6960/8140) Quiet yet central, Netuk House is a luxurious B&B with a dozen rooms in three very different buildings. The most visually exciting is a two-storey temple-esque annex that's a festival of colourful Sikkimery with superb panoramas from upper rooms.

Keepsa Residency
HOTEL $$$

(☑ 03592-203053, 8016099947; Kazi Rd; s/d ₹7434/8260, with view ₹9200/10,000) If you're looking for international-style luxury with quality service and elements of local atmosphere, Keepsa is a great choice – raised above the centre with fine views, carved wooden furniture, green-marble surfaces and lift access to most floors.

Elgin Nor-Khill
HERITAGE HOTEL $$$

(☑ 03592-205637; www.elginhotels.com; s/d incl half board ₹14,980/15,360, ste with/without view ₹22,150/17,025; 🅿🛜) Checking into the Nor-Khill is like time travelling back to the pre-Independence era, when this stately property served as the royal guesthouse. Countless historical photos, splendid period furniture and crystal chandeliers lend a vintage feel to the hallways and the indulgent lobby-lounge. Rooms are spaciously classy too: brighter ones on floor 3.

Eating

Roll House
STREET FOOD $

(kathi rolls ₹30-140; ⊙9am-9pm; 🖋) Small alleyway window serving reliably delicious Kolkata-style wraps plus *momos* (Tibetan dumplings) to take away.

★ Nimtho
SIKKIMESE $$

(☑ 03592-205324; MG Marg; mains ₹120-200; ⊙11am-9pm) Beautifully designed with adobe walls and a mock-up earthen stove, Nimtho gives Sikkimese food a gourmet twist. Sample with a local thali (₹250 to ₹350), or à la carte with modestly sized portions of traditional dishes including *shapta* (wok-fried beef slices), nettle soup, and delicious *ningro churpi* (fiddlehead fern cooked in local cheese).

Local Cafe
CAFE $$

(☑ 6294343002; MG Marg; mains ₹130-370; ⊙9am-8pm) Cosy three-table cafe making excellent coffee (espresso ₹84) and serving wraps, *tsampa* shakes, Tibetan street food, vegetable sushi, pasta and thin-crust pizzas.

Café Royale
CAFE $$

(www.instagram.com/caferoyalegtk; Bhanu Path; cakes ₹50-150, mains ₹220-460; ⊙9.30am-7pm; 🛜) Behind the traditional facade of a former monastery dormitory, this tastefully contemporary cafe displaying guidebooks, bonsai firs and Le Creuset cups, serves barista coffees (₹100–₹140), with peanut-butter cheesecake or excellent hot apple pie. The restaurant section's short menu of well-made, Western-style dishes includes caramelised BBQ ribs, pulled-pork burgers and homemade sausage-and-salsa.

Coffee Shop
INTERNATIONAL $$

(www.facebook.com/thecoffeeshopgangtok; pizzas ₹355-495, mains ₹215-385; ⊙9.30am-9.30pm; 🛜) Ever-popular with the hip local youth crowd, this clean-lined cafe-diner serves far more than just good coffee (₹95–₹135), with all-day breakfasts and a range of international meals including orange-and-beetroot salad, nachos, grilled chops and various thin-crust pizzas. Beer available (₹160–₹240).

OSM
MULTICUISINE $$$

(☑ 03592-202258; MG Marg, Norbuja Complex, 2nd fl; mains ₹220-630; ⊙12.30-10.30pm) Smarter, and open later, than most Gangtok eateries, OSM has a certain contemporary elegance with folded cloth napkins and a vast range of menu options from chilli squid to chicken nuggets via a range of Indian and Chinese options. Beer available ₹180).

> ### SIKKIMESE FOOD
>
> The most common dishes are Tibetan/pan-Himalayan favourites, including *momos* (dumplings) and rich noodle soups including *thentuk/thukpa*, *gyathuk* and *bhathuk*. More archetypically Sikkimese soups use local organic vegetables, whether fermented – such as *gundruk* (spinach) or *sinki* (radishes) – or fresh: *karela* (bitter gourds), *sisnoo* (nettles). Curries might incorporate fried *ningro* (fiddlehead ferns), *bareh* (ground-orchid bud heads) or *fing* (rice-noodle strands). Unusually for India, beef is popular. If ordering pork, be aware that locals like it indulgently fatty.

Mu Kimchi
KOREAN $$$

(☑ 9593340401; www.facebook.com/MuKimchi; 5th fl, Cabin Bldg, Namnang Rd; snacks ₹170-320, meals ₹260-730; ⊙10am-10pm, bar to 11pm) For authentic Korean cuisine, climb the 80 steps to Mu Kimchi, with an interior that balances original bamboo ceilings and woven wicker lamps with a pared-down contemporary minimalism matching the sound system's insistent, bass-heavy mash-ups.

Drinking & Nightlife

For a sunset beer it's hard to beat the large, colourful view-terrace of the **Yak Bar** (Tashi Delek Hotel; shots/beer/cocktails from ₹100/170/200; ⊙10am-9.30pm), hidden away off MG Marg. For more buzz try **Live & Loud** (www.facebook.com/CafeLiveAndLoud; Tibet Rd; tea/coffee/beer/cocktails from ₹54/95/160/350, hookah ₹420; ⊙11am-11pm Sun-Fri, to 1am Sat; 🛜) or **The Square** (MG Marg; beer from ₹160; ⊙10am-9.30pm). Scruffy-chic **Downtown** (MG Marg; shots/wine/beer from ₹40/60/130; ⊙noon-9pm) feels more alternative. On three 'dry days' a month, decided by the Sikkimese lunar calendar, bars close and restaurants won't serve alcohol.

Tea & Coffee

There's no beating the regal setting of the Elgin Nor-Khill for an indulgent, very British Empire–style afternoon tea (₹525) with engraved pewter teapots and scones on doilied stands. To taste locally grown Temi tea in a pleasantly calm setting, head for Golden Tips or the cool little cafe within Rachna Books, which also makes excellent espressos from rare Sikkimese coffee beans. Great barista coffees are also available at Local Cafe and Café Royale.

Shopping

★ Golden Tips
TEA

(☑ 03592-208111; www.goldentipstea.com; MG Marg, 1st fl; ⊙9.30am-8.30pm) This boutique tea store stocks a fine selection of beautifully packaged teas, notably Temi (Sikkimese) and various flushes of premium Darjeeling. A calm, cafe-style tasting area allows you to sip from a choice of over 60 types from ₹50 per cup.

★ Rachna Books
BOOKS

(☑ 03592-204336; www.rachnabooks.com; Jeewan Theeng Marg, Development Area; ⊙9am-7pm Mon-Sat, closed during Dasain) The city's best-stocked bookshop, Rachna doubles as an alternative cultural hub with talks, events, screenings and an excellent cafe (Temi tea ₹50, coffee ₹90–₹150).

Climate Zone
SPORTS & OUTDOORS

(Tibet Rd; ⊙10am-8pm) This reasonably well stocked outdoors shop sells hiking and camping equipment, including trekking sticks, umbrellas and various sizes of backpack.

ℹ Information

MEDICAL SERVICES

STNM Hospital (☑ 03592-222059; NH31A) Government hospital with emergency and out-patient facilities.

MONEY

Gangtok has numerous ATMs and the only official currency-exchange facilities in Sikkim. For better rates than **SBI** (State Bank of India; NH31A; ⊙10am-4pm Mon-Fri), visit **RS Enterprises** (MG Marg; ⊙9.30am-7pm), a back office within the bright Vivo phone shop opposite the Gandhi statue.

TOURIST INFORMATION

STDC (p541) Makes practical arrangements including helicopter and taxi bookings.

Tourist office (☑ 03592-209090; www.sikkimtourism.gov.in; MG Marg; ⊙9am-7pm Jan-Mar & Jun-Aug, to 8pm Sep-Dec & Apr-May) Relatively helpful at answering questions and provides a comprehensive info pamphlet.

ℹ Getting There & Away

AIR
Bagdogra Airport

Bagdogra, near Siliguri in West Bengal, has plentiful flights to Kolkata, Delhi and beyond.

A five-seater helicopter shuttles daily from Gangtok to Bagdogra (₹3500, 40 minutes), departing at 11am and returning at 2.30pm. However, adverse weather or lack of custom can cause last-minute cancellations: nerve-racking if you need to make a flight connection. Also note that all baggage is 'hand baggage' (no knives etc), with a 10kg maximum allowance plus one small carry-on. If you weigh over 80kg you might have to pay two seats. Tickets are available from STDC (p541), which also offers pleasure flights.

Fixed-price taxis from Gangtok to Bagdogra Airport cost ₹3500, but only ₹2500 the other way. Booked online, comfortable airport taxi-transfers cost ₹600 per seat with Metta (www.metta. taxi), ₹712 with WizzRide (www.wizzride.com). Less-comfortable shared jeeps from Siliguri cost ₹300.

The journey should take 4½ hours but can stretch to six or seven in busy periods, longer still after landslides. To reduce uncertainty, consider consider spending a night in Darjeeling en route to the airport.

Pakyong Airport

Inaugurated in October 2018, Sikkim's **airport** (PYG; tmgr_pakyong@aai.aero; Pakyong) is an engineering marvel on a ridgetop at Pakyong, 35km from Gangtok. At the time of research, flights were limited to Guwahati and Kolkata on Spicejet 70-seater prop-planes, but services to Delhi, Bhutan, Nepal and Bangkok were mooted. Sikkim permits may be available on arrival by the time you read this. Buses to Gangtok (₹80, two hours) are timed to depart shortly after each flight arrives.

BUS & SHARED JEEP

For Darjeeling, Kalimpong, Siliguri, Bagdogra, Jaigaon (Bhutan) and Panitanki/Kakarbhitta (Nepal border), private buses and all jeeps start from the **Mainline Taxi Stand** (Deorali Jeep Stand), tucked just off the main road 1.5km south of central Gangtok. However, seven daily government buses to Siliguri (normal/AC ₹160/250) use the more central **SNT Bus Station** (PS Rd; tickets 6am-6pm), along with buses to Pelling (₹190/300, 8am), Namchi (₹105/200, 7am) and Pakyong Airport (AC ₹80, two hours, 7am and 1pm).

For most destinations within Sikkim, jeeps start from the three-layered **Central Jeep Stand** (9475464597; Church Rd): top floor for Rumtek; bottom for Singtam (frequent); middle floor for West and South Sikkim, including 7am and 1pm services to Pelling (₹300, six to seven hours), Ravangla (₹190, four hours), Tashiding (₹250, five to 6½ hours) and Yuksom (₹350, 6½ to eight hours) plus half-hourly jeeps to Namchi (₹190, 2½ to three hours).

Plentiful jeeps for Mangan (₹140, three hours) depart early morning and early afternoon from the **Vajra Taxi Station** (NH31A), 2km north of the centre.

TRAIN

The nearest major train station is about 125km away at New Jalpaiguri (NJP). Tickets can be purchased through the computerised **railway booking counter** (SNT Bus Station; 8am-2pm Mon-Sat, to 11am Sun & public holidays) at the SNT Bus Station or more centrally at **DJ Mandap Tours** (9832373337; MG Marg; 10am-6pm).

THE KARMAPA CONTROVERSY

The 'Black Hat' sect takes its name from the priceless ruby-topped black headgear traditionally worn by the Karmapas (reincarnated spiritual leaders). Said to be woven from the hair of *dakinis* (female spirits who carry the souls of the dead), the hat must be kept locked in a box to prevent it from flying back to the heavens. Nobody, however, has actually seen the hat since 1993, when a bitter controversy arose within the Kagyu sect over the legitimacy of two candidates, with both claiming their right to the throne following the death of the 16th Karmapa in 1981.

The main candidate, recognised by the Dalai Lama, is Ogyen Trinley Dorje (www. kagyuoffice.org), who fled Tibet in 2000. He holds 'temporary' office at the **Gyuto Tantric Monastery** (01892-235307; www.kagyuoffice.org; off SH17, Sidhbari; 9am-6pm) near Dharamsala, but Indian authorities are believed to have prevented him from officially taking up his Rumtek seat for fear of upsetting Chinese-government sensibilities. His rival, Thaye Dorje (www.karmapa.org), operates from the Karmapa International Buddhist Institute in Delhi. Supporters of the two lamas have now been locked in a legal dispute over who can control Rumtek for more than two decades. During 2016, supporters of Ogyen Trinley Dorje launched a renewed series of demonstrations and hunger strikes aimed at persuading the Indian government to allow their candidate to finally take up his Rumtek seat. In an attempt at compromise in March 2018, Delhi promised tentative permission for him to visit Sikkim... but not Rumtek. Only when the dispute is fully resolved and the 17th Karmapa is finally crowned will anyone dare to unlock the box and reveal the sacred black hat. To learn much more about the controversy, read *The Dance of 17 Lives* by Mick Brown.

ℹ️ Getting Around

Central taxi stands are found in Lal Bazaar opposite the Denzong Cinema, beneath the Central Jeep Stand and on **PS Rd** just north of the main post office.

A reliable, highly recommended driver based in the upper part of town is **Tsering Bhutia** (☑9609856738).

Shared taxi fares are usually ₹20 per hop. For Deorali (Tibetology) or Tadong (FRO) start from the signed stands just under the pedestrian bridge on NH31A. For Development Area (Rachna Books etc) the stand is almost vertically above that point, close to Lal Bazaar.

Gangtok Ropeway (adult/child return ₹117/74; ⊘9.45am-12.30pm & 1.30-6pm) takes four minutes to link a lower station on Deorali Chowk at Deorali Bazaar (handy for visitors to the Namgyal Institute of Tibetology) and the Assembly Building on Kazi Rd. All tickets are day-returns. Some visitors come simply for the views, not even getting off. Departures are every 10 minutes.

Rumtek

☑ 03592 / POP 1570 / ELEV 1660M

Facing Gangtok distantly across a plunging green valley, Rumtek's extensive gompa complex is one of Tibetan Buddhism's most venerable institutions as the home-in-exile of the Kagyu (Black Hat) sect. The main access route up starts near Ranipul but you can make Rumtek part of a day-trip loop by including more peaceful and arguably lovelier Lingdum Gompa. Though stretches of road are in dire condition, repairs are slowly progressing and the route is scenically lovely, winding through mossy forests, bamboo groves and terraced paddy fields past many attractive viewpoints. Nearer to Gangtok you'll pass the modest Banjhakri Waterfalls, set in a park of questionable taste full of garish figures that purport to portray pre-Buddhist animist myths.

◉ Sights

Rumtek Gompa MONASTERY

(Rumtek Dharma Chakra Centre; www.rumtek.org; monastery ₹10; ⊘6am-5pm) Rumtek is Sikkim's most spiritually significant monastery complex. It's essentially a self-contained village with a colourful main prayer hall that was built (1961–66) to replace Tibet's Tsurphu Monastery, destroyed during the Chinese Cultural Revolution (though since rebuilt). The interior's centrepiece is a giant yellow throne awaiting the long-overdue coronation of the Kagyu spiritual leader, the (disputed) 17th Karmapa. The main claimant, Ogyen Trinley Dorje, currently resides near Dharamsala due to the Karmapa controversy (p544), sensitivity over which explains all the armed soldiers and why foreigners must show their passport and Sikkim permit on entry.

Behind the monastery, stairs rise beside the distinctively painted Karma Shri Nalanda Institute of Buddhist Studies, leading quickly to a smallish room containing an ornate Golden Stupa (closed approximately 11.30am to 12.30pm). Studded with turquoise and amber gemstones, it's the reliquary of the 16th Karmapa, founder of the current complex and considered almost a saint hereabouts.

Old Rumtek Gompa MONASTERY

(⊘dawn-dusk) 𝗙𝗥𝗘𝗘 Old Rumtek Gompa is an oasis of peace, 1.5km beyond Rumtek proper. Originally founded in 1734 but thoroughly rebuilt, the prayer hall has an intensely colourful interior and picnic areas on the lawns.

Lingdum Gompa MONASTERY

(www.zurmangkagyud.org; Ranka; butter-lamp donation small/medium/large ₹10/20/100; ⊘dawn-dusk) 𝗙𝗥𝗘𝗘 Layered amid peaceful forests, Lingdum Gompa is arguably the most photogenic monastery in the Gangtok area. Its centrepiece is a large, attractive quadrangle leading to a five-storey main prayer hall. Inside, the central gilded-metal statue of Sakyamuni Buddha is flanked by Guru Rinpoche and the 16th Karmapa, plus a library of wrapped scriptures. The tastefully colourful centrepiece dates from 1999 and beside it is a large, new monastic university.

The monastery is 1.5km from Ranka, to which shared taxis (₹40, 40 minutes) leave when full from the PS Rd taxi stand near Gangtok GPO.

🎉 Festivals & Events

In February the Mahakala Dance sees giant figurines of fierce protector deities 'come to life' in the central courtyard. Rumtek also holds impressive masked *chaam* dances during the annual drupchen (group meditation) in May/June, and at Old Rumtek Gompa (p545) two days before Losar (p539).

🛏️ Sleeping

★**Bamboo Retreat** BOUTIQUE HOTEL $$$

(☑03592-252516, 629699377; www.bambooretreat.in; Sajong; incl breakfast with/without view s ₹7080/5550, d ₹8250/7080, apt ₹15,000-19,200; 🅿🛜) This fabulous, low-key resort feels like a pseudo temple and is set gloriously alone amid trees and terraced organic gardens

200m off the Rumtek road (around 1km beyond Sajong). Expect full creature comforts, atmospheric communal spaces, a library, a dining room displaying local artefacts, an incense-wafted temple-room for meditation, and a range of other activities including traditional hot-stone baths, cooking classes and a hike-and-taste day experiencing Lepcha culture.

ⓘ Getting There & Away

Shared jeeps from Gangtok to Rumtek (₹50, 1½ hours) via Ranipul leave from the Central Jeep Stand. Last returns are around 3pm. A charter-taxi loop to Rumtek via Lingdum and Ranka costs ₹1500 to ₹2200.

NORTH SIKKIM

This dramatic, varied and remarkably beautiful area offers enchanting butterflies, traditional Lepcha culture, soaring alpine grandeur and glorious lush forests, but many areas require permits.

Mangan

Mangan is North Sikkim's administrative centre and main commercial hub, ideal as a launching point for visits to Dzongu or Far North Sikkim. The busy bazaar lacks much pizzazz but high above the town reveals its woodland spirit, with occasional tree-framed vistas of soaring white-topped peaks.

Wongden Homestay   GUESTHOUSE $
(☑ 7557042382, 03592-234320, 9434174887; www.wongden.net; Mangan; r with/without balcony ₹1500/1000) This excellent budget option high above Mangan is backed by a lush fruit garden and has dazzling dawn views of Khangchendzonga from the two bright, fresh balcony rooms (the cheaper rooms are contrastingly basic). A great perk of staying here is that you can generally arrange Dzongu/Lachung tours and permits for next-day departure since the hosts are the family of the Subdivisional Magistrate (SDM) who issues them.

Consider paying the extra ₹500 per head to add an excellent home-cooked dinner and very generous breakfast. The homestay is above two small shops on the corner immediately before the government secondary school. That's 1.3km up the diagonal road that starts opposite Hotel Mailling. Keep left before the football pitch.

Planter's Home   HERITAGE HOTEL $$
(☑ 7478181311, 03592-234286; www.theplantershome.com; Pentok Rd, Mangan; r ₹3540-5900, ste ₹7080) Mangan's top option goes for a certain 1930s Raj-era feel, with large framed Sikkim photos to add colour. The location feels semi-rural despite a couple of taller houses nearby that somewhat mar potentially gorgeous valley panoramas across the lawn.

ⓘ Information

Mangan's **DCO** (Mangan; ⊙10am-4pm Mon-Fri) issues permits for Dzongu and Far North Sikkim. Technically you'll need an agency to apply on your behalf but if you're staying at the Wongden Homestay and organising a trip through them, organising permits is a breeze even outside office hours.

ⓘ Getting There & Around

Jeeps to Gangtok (per person/vehicle ₹140/1400, three hours) and Singtam (₹110/1100, 2½ hours), leave between 6am and 8am plus 11am and 1.30pm from a **stand** (☑ 8145856237) that's two floors down in the glass-fronted multistorey car park in Mangan's main bazaar. Paying for the whole vehicle (₹1400) or a charter taxi (₹3000) allows you to stop en route at various impressive waterfalls and river bridges or, with short diversions, at major monastery-temples such as Phensang or Phodong/ Upper Labrang.

Shared taxis shuttle between the jeep stand (road level) in the bazaar and the DCO for ₹20 per head, passing Planter's Home en route.

Dzongu

The protected, linguistically Lepcha area of Dzongu is Sikkim at its most unspoilt. If you value cultural insight over comfort, and butterflies over bus tours, then it's well worth jumping through a few minor bureaucratic hoops to get the permit for a visit.

A good first choice of destination is Passingdang village as it's handily accessible, a hot-spot for butterfly-watching and a good base for further exploration. If you want to stay in the area **Mayallyang Homestay** (☑ 9647872434, 8348332721; www.mayallyang.com; Passingdang, Dzongu; per person incl full board ₹2000) run by youthful host Gyatshe, an energetic antidam campaigner who sees homestays as an important part of sharing his message about ecological and cultural sustainability, is one of Sikkim's most memorable getaways. It's down nearly 100 steps from Passingdang's main street, set amid thick, fruit-filled foliage and ideal for watching butterflies, hiking to Lingthem or just lounging in the enchanting lounge-porch. However, be aware that while the half-timbered homestead has plenty of character, rooms are simple, beds are hard and the shared bathrooms are outside: intentionally so to preserve an authentic village vibe.

Some 7km steeply above Passingdang, by seriously rocky hairpin bends (far less on foot), Lingthem sits amid steeply terraced paddy fields and has an attractive monastery approached through mossy forest steps. Seen from here, snowy peaks appear to hang like a spiky cloud above the round-topped pyramid of Pung Yung Chu.

Villages in upper Tingvong also have fine Khangchendzonga views and getting there has the added excitement of crossing a long suspension footbridge, but thereafter you'll need to have prearranged transport. Cooperative TECS (Tholung Eco-Tourism Cooperative Society; ☑ 8972727072; otpakimu@yahoo.co.in; per person incl full board ₹1000-1500), consistsing of 10 homestays available on a rotating basis to ensure that the benefits of tourism reach more families in the five widely spread hamlets that comprise Tingvong, are unapologetically basic and in a couple of cases rather austere. But they offer some wonderful views and are authentically local. Contact organiser OT Lepcha for details, help with treks and excursions, and to organise pickups from the end of the pedestrian suspension bridge that is Tingvong's access point.

A taxi from Mangan to Lingdong/Passingdang costs around ₹300/500, less to return. There are no ATMs in the Dzongu villages so bring plenty of cash from Mangan or beyond.

Far North Sikkim

Sikkim's Far North is a wonderland of soaring pristine mountainscapes, yak-herding traditions and trekking potential. However, military sensitivities and permit requirements limit the visitor experience to beautiful but often exhausting out-and-back jeep tours with many highlights glimpsed but briefly from a window as you drive by.

With suitable permits, two main valleys are open to visitors. Indian citizens can use over-developed Lachen as a base to admire snowy peaks reflected in the icy waters of Gurudongmar Lake (5150m) and Chomalu (5330m). Foreigners aren't allowed to visit those lakes but can head for Lachung and the glorious Yumthang Valley.

Lachung

Soaring, rock-pinnacled valley walls embroidered with long ribbons of waterfall surround the isolated if widely scattered village/hotel-centre of Lachung. Near the central bridge you can zip-line across the river from tiny Dzongten Cafe (☑ 7478689871, 8967234170; Katao Rd, Lachung; ⊙ approx 6-10am & 4-9.30pm), rent mountain bikes, or stroll uphill for around 20 minutes to find the colourful little Lachung Gompa (Sarchok Gompa; Katao Rd Km1.8, Lachung). However, the main reason anyone comes here is to get a dawn start for day-trip drives to the picture-perfect, peak-rimmed meadow of Yumthang and, permits permitting, 30km further to Zero Point.

Yumthang

The lovely 23km drive from Lachung to Yumthang brings you, after 9km, into an area of mossy rocks and rhododendron bushes that burst forth in riotously colourful blossom between March and early May. Around Km15 a massive landslide has created an opal-blue lake with sandy beaches. Beyond, towering trees are bearded with epiphytes. Occasional views across the valley reveal waterfalls cascading down the cliffs. From a parking area at Km21.9, a footpath to the (utterly forgettable) Yumthang Hot Springs is worth taking as far as the river for very photogenic views of pedestrian bridges festooned in prayer flags.

After series of tourist-centric trinket-stalls and daytime shack cafes, the valley opens out into a lovely open meadow area at Km23. Deep-green forests rise to the east across the ice-blue river, while the valley's western flank soars in sculpted pinnacles. Flowers dot the meadow in spring with gazing *dzo* (yak-cow crossbreeds), providing foreground for picture-perfect landscape photos. Note that it's well worth asking your driver to drop you 500m

---

TONGBA

In homestays, don't miss a chance to taste the classic local speciality known as chhang/tongba/*chee* in Bhutia/Nepali/Lepcha. Typically you'll receive a mini churn-like container filled with fermented millet grains. Add boiling water then sip regularly through a bamboo straw, periodically adding more boiling water to moderate the brew's strength.

beyond the car park to escape the main
day-tripper throng.

Zero Point

Those with prearranged permit dispensation
can drive on past Yumthang via seemingly
endless hairpin bends to Zero Point. Breath-
lessly high (4825m) and brass-monkey cold,
this beautiful alpine upland environment of
trickling streams and boulder fields is distantly ringed by eccentrically shaped crags.
It would be a truly glorious place to explore
further; however, visitors can't wander far.

Seasonal snack-shacks serve Maggi and
shots of Honey Bee brandy, and rent out
Wellington boots for a quick splash in the
streams, but there's not so much as a wom-
en's toilet. The real attraction is the journey,
varied and always spectacular but rough in
parts and overly long for some tastes (nearly
three hours total from Lachung).

🛏 Sleeping & Eating

Tours usually include room and all meals.
Finding a room in Lachung without pre
arrangement is generally easy and good value
outside the April–May peak season, though
many of Lachung's 50-plus hotels close their

reception desks when not expecting reserved
clients. Heating often costs extra (around
₹400 per night). There is no legal visitor accommodation in the Yumthang Valley.

⭐ **Kalden Residency**   GUESTHOUSE $
(☏ 8900085244; Yumthang Rd, Lachung; r ₹1500-
2500) Our favourite budget digs in Lachung,
the Kalden Residency is based around a local-
style timber house, with a couple of newer
buildings around a yard blooming with pot
plants. Rooms are simple but far better than
average for the price, and the family owners
are charming.

Kee-Rong Cottages   GUESTHOUSE $$
(☏ 9475504300, 9474499499; www.keerongcottag
es.com; Lachung; d with/without food ₹3000/2400)
This brand-new, six-room building has large,
modern bathrooms, comfortable beds and
view-balconies from the top three units. It's
good value by Lachung standards but be
careful of protruding nailheads in the some-
what-rough hardwood floors.

Yarlam Resort   RESORT $$$
(☏ 9434330031; www.yarlamresort.com; Yumthang
Rd Km1.3, Lachung; d/ste ₹13,000/15,000) The
most luxurious offering in Lachung, Yarlam
greets new arrivals with tea in the part-
Tibetanised lobby lounge or serene library.
Indulgent rooms have comfy beds overloaded
with pillows and DVD-TVs, and most suites
have spacious balcony seating.

ℹ Getting There & Away

All visits must be organised by tour agencies
using registered jeep-taxis, albeit with occasional
exceptions for motorcycles. Gangtok–Lachung
can take eight hours including assorted stops,
yet tours rarely depart before 10.30am due to
permit-issuing rules. Organising a vehicle from
Mangan makes for a far more relaxed experience,
but finding fellow travellers to share a vehicle is
easier in Gangtok.

SOUTH SIKKIM

South Sikkim's prime attractions are an
unforgettable trio of larger-than-life religious statues. While set back a little further
from the white-top peak than better-known
Pelling, mountain views from this area can
nonetheless be spectacular, in particular
from the Ravangla–Damthang ridge road.

🛏 Sleeping

Namchi, Ravangla and Jorethang all have
ample choice in their respective bazaars for

SLEEPING PRICE RANGES

Accommodation price ranges for Sikkim:

$ less than ₹1500

$$ ₹1500–₹5000

$$$ more than ₹5000

unfussy visitors. However, more interesting rural getaways often require prebooking and a sometimes-significant taxi ride.

ⓘ Getting There & Away

The region's main transport hubs are Jorethang and (less so) Namchi. Shared jeeps are relatively frequent along the Jorethang–Soreng–Kuluk–Dentam and Jorethang–Legship–Geyzing routes. The Singtam–Ravangla road goes scenically via Temi but it's horribly rough, so for comfort consider using the Singtam–Phong–Namchi route and continuing to Ravangla from there.

TRANSIT VIA JORETHANG

To transit between Namchi and Rinchenpong you'll probably need to change vehicles in forgettable Jorethang. Most jeep services use the very central multistorey jeep-station but later in the afternoon, when all transport to West Sikkim appears to have finished, you might still be able to reach Legship on shared jeeps from across the Akar Bridge, just west of town.

A bigger headache for foreigners is that the Sikkim–West Bengal border bridge at Jorethang lacks a permit check post. This means that non-Indians are not permitted to take direct Jorethang–Siliguri or Jorethang–Darjeeling jeeps and are forced to detour to Melli. While it's easy enough to get between Jorethang and Melli, continuing from Melli to Darjeeling or Siliguri is very tough as virtually all vehicles other than public buses will be full. A possible (though time-consuming) tactic to get around this is to take one of the regular jeeps from Jorethang to Kalimpong then backtrack from there. Or for Siliguri, head first to Namchi.

Also note that Jorethang–Gangtok shared jeeps take a route that passes through a stretch of West Bengal between Melli and Rangpo. This presents a different problem for foreigners who are not supposed to reenter Sikkim once stamped out. If you get stuck for the night in Jorethang, there's plenty of budget accommodation, albeit little to recommend.

Namchi

☎ 03595 / POP 12,920 / ELEV 1470M

Two hulking religious superstructures on the jagged horizon are Namchi's great tourist sights. The town itself is a bustling, commercial staging post and a popular place with bikers from Bengal enjoying cheap booze for party weekends. The pedestrianised centre is a pair of interlinked squares, each centred on an ancient tree.

◉ Sights

★ Samdruptse
BUDDHIST MONUMENT

(Padmasambhava Statue; ₹30, parking ₹30; ⊙9am-6pm) Visible for kilometres, this 45m-high statue of Padmasambhava (Guru Rinpoche) is painted in shimmering copper and gilt and sits on a lotus plinth high above Namchi on the forested Samdruptse ridge. Completed in 2004 on a foundation stone laid in 1997 by the Dalai Lama, the statue turns his back on a superlative view of the Khangchendzonga Massif, which is best seen from beside his right haunch. Around the base are some fading historical photos of old Sikkim and within is a prayer room.

From the car park, a 15-minute cable car (return ₹177; ⊙9.30am-5pm) excursion takes you down to a rock garden and back. If all goes to plan, by the time you read this a new extension to the cable car should allow visitors to ride it all the way to the monument from central Namchi.

Samdruptse is 7km from Namchi, 2km off the Damthang–Ravangla road. Taxis from town charge ₹400 return, ₹500 including Ngadak, or ₹1200 for a one-way ride to Ravangla with a Samdruptse side trip en route.

★ Char Dham
HINDU MONUMENT

(Siddesvara Dham; adult/student/senior/parking ₹50/25/25/50; ⊙7am-6pm) This unmissable feast of colour is a remarkable Hindu religious theme park crowning Solophuk hilltop, 5km southwest of Namchi. It brings together replicas of several great Indian pilgrimage sites including Rameswaram, Dwarka and Jagarnath, all set beneath a towering 33m Shiva statue. Whether you find it moving or kitschy, the views and photo opportunities are spectacular.

Ngadak Gompa
BUDDHIST MONASTERY

The Ngadak gompa's large 2014 prayer hall contains some of the richest new monastery paintings in Sikkim. Beside it is the ruinous, unpainted shell of a far older monastery building which gives a hint of antique Sikkim architecture and is reputedly haunted.

It was previously the palace of Pedi Wangmu, the Sikkimese queen who temporarily overthrew her half-brother in 1700 and finally had him killed years later, only to be murdered by his followers. The palace site became a monastery after her death in 1717. The complex is 1km off the Namchi–Ravangla Rd: turn opposite the Kolkata Kolkata hotel-restaurant, 2.8km from central Namchi.

🛏 Sleeping & Eating

Dungmali Heritage Resort GUESTHOUSE $$
(☑ 9734126039; minurai81@yahoo.com; Solophuk Rd; s ₹1300, d rear/front ₹2500/3000, minicottage ₹3000; ☎) Some 4km from Namchi, above the first hairpin bend as you climb to Char Dham, this family guesthouse has seven very clean if unsophisticated rooms. The front-facing ones have superb views of the Khanchenzonga massif.

Summit Sobralia Resort HOTEL $$$
(☑ 9083246084; www.summithotels.in; Chardham Rd; s/d/ste ₹8260/9440/17,700; ☎☀) South-west of Namchi, 1.8km towards Char Dham, Namchi's swankiest option has smart if some-what-formulaic top-end rooms. Some, but by no means all, have framed views of Khang-chendzonga, which is also visible from the little outdoor pool (which could be cleaner).

★ Crumbs n Whips CAFE $$
(www.facebook.com/crumbsnwhipscafebakery; Jorethang Rd; pizzas ₹260-370; ☒9am-9pm) John Wayne, Kurt Cobain and The Beatles are among the cover stars at this internation-al-style coffeehouse-pizzeria that also serves a range of pastas (from ₹230), bakery items, ex-cellent veggie burgers and great barista-style coffee (₹80 to ₹150).

ℹ Getting There & Away

Namchi's multistorey jeep-stand building is directly east of the pedestrianised town centre. From the bottom floor, 8am buses leave for Siliguri, Gangtok and Ravangla, to which there's a second at 11am. One floor up are shared jeeps to Gangtok (₹190, four hours) and Siliguri (₹200, four to five hours), leaving once or twice an hour from 6.30am to 9.30am and noon to 3pm. For Jorethang (₹70, 1¼ hours) vehicles depart when full, mostly mornings. There's a Ravangla jeep (₹80, 1¼ hours) at 9am and one to Geyzing (₹180, three hours) at 7.30am.

Ravangla (Rabongla)

☑ 03595 / POP 2420 / ELEV 2050M

One of Sikkim's most memorable sights is Ravangla's gigantic golden Buddha, sitting serenely with a stunning dawn backdrop of white-topped Himalayan peaks. The village itself, also known as Rabongla or Rabong, is basically a crossroads bazaar with several clusters of hotels from which it's a short (if bumpy) drive to the important monasteries at Ralang.

◉ Sights

★ Buddha Park BUDDHIST MONUMENT
(Tathagata Tsal; www.tathagatatsal.com; Ralang Rd Km2; Indian/foreigner ₹50/200; ☒9am-5.30pm) With a breathtaking backdrop of Himalayan peaks, the 41m-tall Buddha statue is one of Sikkim's most iconic sights. Finished in 2013, it's beautifully set in an area of manicured lawns with piped mantra music adding a meditative atmosphere. Inside the huge plinth, a spiral gallery shows scenes from the Buddha's life, wrapping around an inner cyl-inder of murals containing holy relics from 11 countries. The site is 1.8km along the Ralang road from central Ravangla (₹100 by taxi).

Ralang Monasteries

At Ralang, around 45 minutes' drive below Ravangla, the splendid 1995 **Palchen Choe-ling Monastery** (New Ralang Gompa; ℗) is one of Sikkim's most important Buddhist com-plexes, home to around 300 Kagyu monks. Behind an expansive central courtyard, the main prayer hall has vividly colourful murals and a two-storey, golden Shakyamuni Buddha statue. About 1.5km downhill on the same road, the peaceful (and still active) Old Ralang Gompa was established in 1768. The central temple has been rebuilt since 2012 but has wonderful views from its top-floor balconies, and some modest wood-and-stone cottages around it are now protected examples of old Bhutia architecture.

Chartering a taxi from Ravangla costs around ₹1000 return with an hour's wait. Come in the morning for the best pho-to-friendly light and consider getting dropped off at the Buddha Park on return.

🏃 Activities

A fairly strenuous all-day trek up Maenem Hill (3150m) and back leads through wood-land and the springtime-blooming rhododen-drons and magnolias of the Maenam Wildlife Sanctuary. Continue to Bhaledunga Rock for sweeping views. There's just a chance that you'll encounter red pandas and monal pheasants (Sikkim's state animal and bird re-spectively). Start as early as possible as clouds tend to hide the summit by early afternoon. Find a local to accompany you (for around ₹1000). Bikram Rai (8768442600) has plenty of experience.

🛏 Sleeping

Buddha Retreat BOUTIQUE HOTEL **$$**
(📞9733092588, Gangtok booking office 03592-
202588; www.yangangheritage.com; Ralang Rd; d
from ₹4130; 🅿🛜) Ravangla's most comforta-
ble getaway, the Buddha Retreat's 18 rooms
boast supercomfy beds, ample sitting space,
desk and kettle, with lovely views from some
upper-floor options. Bathrooms are smart
with big-head showers, corridors have Sik-
kimese ceiling motifs and service is under-
statedly professional.

Hotel Zumthang GUESTHOUSE **$$**
(📞9733061311; www.facebook.com/HotelZum
thang; Kewzing Rd; d downstairs/upstairs/balcony
₹1500/2000/2200, ste ₹2500) Family-run with
some Tibetan features to the lobby, this welcoming, clean if somewhat-unsophisticated
hotel has stand-and-gasp oblique mountain
panoramas from the best balcony rooms (notably 301–303 and suite 201).

🍴 Eating

Tathagata Kitchen (📞9933946263; tathagata
kitchen@gmail.com; Ralang Rd; mains ₹100-150,
thalis ₹200-250; ⊙8am-8pm), just below Buddha Park, is hard to beat for comfortable
Sikkimese ambience. Appealing if modest
eateries at the jeep stand include **Kookay**
(Main Bazaar; mains ₹70-180, local wine/beer from
₹60/130; ⊙8.30am-8pm) and slightly more
stylish bar-cafe **Taste of Sikkim** (Main Bazaar;
mains ₹70-190; ⊙8am-8pm), whose melt-in-the-
mouth chicken *momos* are particularly recommended.

ℹ Getting There & Away

For buses to Siliguri (₹170, five hours, 7am),
Gangtok (₹100, five hours, 9am) or Namchi (₹35,
one hour, 7am, 8.30am, 9am and 2.30pm), book
tickets from beneath Hotel 10Zing, at Ravangla's
main junction. Shared jeeps use a multistorey
garage 500m down the Yangyang Rd from there.
Jeeps to Gangtok (₹190) leave at 7am, 7.30am,
8am, 11am and noon. For Pelling take the 9am to
Geyzing (₹120, two hours) or change at Legship
(₹80, frequent till 2pm).

WEST SIKKIM

The world's third-highest mountain, Khangchendzonga, raises its sublime white peak
high above landscapes of lush, forest-draped
ridges. Intriguing monasteries, villages and
waterfalls add appeal, plus there's some fabulous trekking. Yuksom, a historic trailhead
village, is a delight in its own right. Meanwhile, comfort seekers can settle for stupen-

dous mountain views from busy little Pelling
and from quieter, rural Kuluk and Rinchenpong, where you'll also find the lovable yet
forgotten Resum Monastery.

Pelling

📞03595 / POP 900 / ELEV 1930M
Pelling provides countless visitors with
stride-stopping dawn views of white-robed
Khangchendzonga. At first glance the small
town is an architecturally uninteresting cascade of concrete hotels tumbling down an
otherwise-gorgeous woodland ridge. Walk a
little, however, and you'll quickly find yourself
wandering through beautiful natural forest.

Helpful agencies make excursions easy to
organise. Within 3km of Pelling along the
same series of ridgetops are the ruins of an
18th-century palace plus two historic monasteries: busy Pemayangtse Gompa and more
peaceful Sanghak Choeling, now overlooked
by a gigantic Chenrezig Statue which is visible
for kilometres. Around 9km east (6km by a
supersteep shortcut) is the much bigger commercial and transport centre of Geyzing (Gy-
alshing). In between, little Tikjuk hosts West
Sikkim's administrative complex – go there
for permit extensions.

👁 Sights

Chenrezig Statue BUDDHIST MONUMENT
(Sanghak Choeling Rd; Indian/foreigner ₹50/200)
Officially unveiled in November 2018, this
huge, four-armed statue of Chenrezig (Av-
alokiteshvara) sits around 500m beyond the
attractive little **Sanghak Choeling Monastery** (⊙10.30am-1.30pm & 2.30-5.30pm), via a
newly asphalted lane that climbs some very
steep hairpin bends from Upper Pelling
(walking takes around 45 minutes). In front of
the statue is a loop of vertigo-inducing raised
glass walkways, from which around 170 steps
lead to the base of the statue's plinth.

Pemayangtse Gompa BUDDHIST MONASTERY
(📞9932627638; www.sangchenpemayangtse.org;
Indian/foreigner ₹20/50; ⊙6am-6pm) One of Sikkim's oldest and most significant Nyingmapa
monasteries, Pemayangtse (literally 'Perfect
Sublime Lotus') is 500m off the Geyzing road
– turn north 2.2km east of Upper Pelling. It
can get overwhelmed by domestic tourist
groups, but it's atmospherically backed by
traditional wood-and-stone monastic cottages descending from a 2080m hilltop towards
the Rabdentse ruins. There has been a Buddhist shrine on the site since 1647. The oft-
remodelled central temple's most memorable

Pelling

attraction is the top floor's seven-tiered model representing Zangtok Palri (Padmasambhava's heavenly abode), handmade over five laborious years by a single dedicated lama.

Rabdentse
HISTORIC SITE, RUINS

(aviary/ruins ₹50/free; ⊙ 8am-5pm, last entry 4pm) A few partially rebuilt wall stubs are all that remain of the palace complex at Rabdentse, which was Sikkim's royal capital from 1670 until it was sacked by Nepali forces in the 18th century. However, it's worth the 1km forest walk from the main car park to contemplate the fabulous viewpoint on which the ruins are located, best photographed between a trio of small, bare-stone stupas.

Helipad
VIEWPOINT

Just 10 minutes' stroll from Upper Pelling's Zero Point junction, the helipad is about the best viewpoint around, with almost 360-degree views.

🛏 Sleeping

★ Hotel Garuda
HOTEL $

(☑ 9733076484, 9647880728; www.hotelgaruda pelling.com; Main Rd, Upper Pelling; ddm from ₹250, r with/without view from ₹600/1200; 🛜) Great for meeting fellow travellers, Pelling's backpacker classic is very hard to beat across several categories, with great-value rooms, good free wi-fi, travel assistance and excellent food including authentic Sikkimese options. Khangchendzonga views are superb from common terraces and classier upper-room windows.

Rabdentse Residency
HOTEL $

(☑ 7872973447, 9681292163; www.saikripa.in; Lower Pelling; d with/without balcony ₹2000/1500, ste with/without view ₹3500/3000) Quieter and marginally better value than many other group-centric options, the Rabdentse's rooms have *thangkas* (Tibetan cloth paintings), wood panelling and small but functional bathrooms with brilliant views from north-facing versions. It's hidden down a stepped path opposite Hotel Sand & Snow.

Hotel Phamrong
HOTEL $$

(☑ 9732462188; Main Junction, Upper Pelling; s/d/ ste incl breakfast ₹2490/3135/4290, walk-in s/d from ₹1500/2000) This pleasant, well-located mid-range choice throws in curiosities such as a Tibetan-styled reception booth, octagonal four-storey atrium with dangling streamers, and an ethnographic corner on the 2nd-floor landing. Rooms have been cursorily repainted and some upper versions have superb views.

★ Chumbi
Mountain Retreat
HERITAGE HOTEL $$$

(☑ 9933126619; www.thechumbimountainretreat. com; Chumbong Rd; d/ste incl half board ₹19,200/23,040; 🅿🛜) Just a kilometre from Pelling yet with a secluded forest setting, this truly exceptional resort blows visitors away with its artfully understated blend of traditional Sikkimese architecture and 21st-century luxury.

Elgin Mount Pandim
HERITAGE HOTEL $$$

(☑ 03595-250756; www.elginhotels.com; Pemayangtse; s/d/ste incl half board ₹13,950/ 14,465/15,870; 🅿🛜) This erstwhile royal getaway is perched on a hilltop near Pemayangtse Gompa with stupendous views in all directions. Highlights are the manicured lawns and the welcoming lobby; it's everything you'd want in a heritage hotel, busy with uniformed staff and packed with interest but welcomingly unstuffy.

✖ Eating & Drinking

HavMor SOUTH INDIAN $
(Main Rd; mains ₹90-160; ⊙ 7.30am-8pm; 🖉) This bright, budget eatery with hatch servery and souvenir counter is the best place in Pelling for *masala dosas* (curried vegetables inside crisp pancakes).

Newa Grill INDIAN $$
(mains ₹160-320; ⊙ 1-3pm & 6-9.30pm) For a classier meal with richer Indian sauces and more stylish seating than any other of the strip-hotel restaurants in Lower Pelling, head to this tasty choice in the Summit Newa Hotel (rooms ₹5000).

Kabur TIBETAN, CHINESE $$
(📱 9832427723, 9832427723; deepesh83@yahoo.co.in; Geyzing Rd; mains ₹90-250; ⊙ 9am-9pm) This Pelling traveller classic creates a wonderfully cosy atmosphere at night with candles and colourful, half-lit globe lamps; by day the balcony has great views towards the (distant) Chenrezig Statue. The menu has Indian, Chinese and Tibetan selections, with a standout the chicken *taipoo* – a delicious, fist-sized, filled steamed bun.

ⓘ Information

SBI Bank (Dentam Rd) Has an ATM at the Upper Pelling junction but no money-changing facilities.

ⓘ Getting There & Away

FROM PELLING

A very slow SNT bus runs to Siliguri (₹180, around eight hours) via Jorethang and Melli starting at 7am from a layby outside Saredena Hotel; its reception booth sells tickets.

Shared jeeps from Pelling depart at 7am to Gangtok (₹300, six hours) and Siliguri (₹350, six hours); book ahead through **Father Tours** (📱 9733286871, 7797283512; Upper Pelling). Almost all other transport starts from Geyzing's packed jeep stand, which is West Sikkim's de facto transport hub.

Services to Yuksom, Utterey, Khecheopalri and Dentam all pass through Upper Pelling mid-afternoon on their way back from Geyzing. Most will be full but you could also ask your hotelier to phone the driver and request a space be saved. Many tourists simply book a private vehicle through one of the numerous Pelling agencies.

FROM GEYZING

Geyzing, about 9km by road east of Pelling, is West Sikkim's transport hub. Shared-jeep departures include the following:

Gangtok ₹300, seven to nine hours, 7am, 8am, 9am, noon, 12.30pm and 1pm

Jorethang ₹100, two hours, departs when full or change in Legship

Legship ₹50, 45 minutes, frequent departures as full

Namchi ₹180, three hours, 8am, 12.15pm

Ravangla ₹180, one hour, 1.30pm

Siliguri ₹300, 4½ to six hours, 6.45am and 1pm

Singtam ₹220, five hours, 9am, 11am, 1pm

Shared jeeps from Dentam (₹100, 1¼ hours), Darap (₹60, 50 minutes), Khecheopalri (₹100, 1½ hours), Tashiding (₹130, 1½ hours), Utterey (₹120, two hours) and Yuksom (₹130, 2½ hours) all head to Geyzing in the morning then return early afternoon once the passengers (mostly regulars) are ready to come back.

ⓘ Getting Around

Fairly frequent shared taxis shuttle (₹50, 20 minutes) between **Geyzing jeep stand** (Mani Rd) and **Pelling Zero Point** (Upper Pelling), departing when full from around 6.30am through mid-afternoon. They pass close to Pemayangtse, Rabdentse and the Tikjuk district administrative centre gateway en route. A Geyzing–Pelling charter taxi costs ₹250, or ₹500 with stops at each of the above, including an hour at Rabdentse. Doing this trip in reverse from Pelling isn't always as easy, as fewer taxis wait there.

Khecheopalri (Kechuperi) Lake

POP 696 / ELEV 1800M

Pronounced 'ketchup-perry', Khecheopalri Lake is a placid 'holy' reservoir precipitously ringed with thickly forested hills. Tourists rather overwhelm the place on high-season mornings, but by late afternoon peace returns and low light glows beautifully through the trees and multicoloured prayer flags. High above, accessed by a steep, half-hour forest walk, is idyllic Khecheopalri Village, with a wonderfully timeless quality, a 400-year-old Nepali-style 'eyes' stupa, and 360-degree views.

🛏 Sleeping

Sonam's Homestay GUESTHOUSE $
(📱 9735589678; zamyang22@gmail.com; Khecheopalri Village; per person incl meals ₹600) 🍃 Rooms are bare-boards but this wonderful homestay has a magic that entrances, with games to play, great organic food and a library

of books in assorted languages. Endless free tea and biscuits too. The house is easy to find at the top of the major (left-fork) trail up from the Khecheopalri Lake.

★ **Lake View Nest**　　　　　HOMESTAY $$
(☑9593976635, 9735945598; lakeviewnest@gmail. com; Khecheopalri Village; r per person without bathroom incl meals ₹1250-1500) ✎ All alone at the western end of Khecheopalri Village, around 10 minutes' walk from the stupa, this delightful wooden homestay has four attractive rooms with wicker lamps, *thangka* (Tibetan cloth painting) and comfy beds, sharing one remarkably clean bathroom downstairs, with sit-down flush toilet and giant geyser.

ⓘ Getting There & Away

Two or three shared jeeps to Geyzing via Pelling (₹80 to ₹100, 1½ hours) leave the lakeside car park around 6am, returning early afternoon via Pelling. A private taxi from Yuksom or Pelling typically costs around ₹1500/2200 one way/ return with a reasonable wait. Hitching a ride back to Pelling with other tourist vehicles is often possible in the midmorning if you ask nicely.

For now, Khecheopalri Village is only accessible on foot, but there are plans to build a rough access road in the future.

Yuksom

☑03595 / POP 1960 / ELEV 1750M

Though it's tiny, Yuksom was the historical starting point of the Sikkimese nation, its first capital and the coronation place of its first chogyal (king) in 1641. For adventurers Yuksom is the main trailhead for treks towards Khangchendzonga, while if you don't have that kind of energy, it's still an ideal starting point for shorter walks, monastery visits or simply watching local life. Not the views you'll see from Pelling, but some whitetop peaks are visible at dawn, and the lovely forest paths are ample consolations.

◉ Sights

★ **Norbugang Park**　　　　　HISTORIC SITE
(₹20; ☉5am-6pm) All aflutter with prayer flags, the Norbugang 'coronation park' is a historic woodland garden containing a small temple, a huge prayer wheel, a chorten containing earth from each corner of Sikkim, and the simple but deeply significant four-seat Coronation Throne (Norbugang). Standing beneath a vast cedar tree, the 1641 stone throne looks something like an Olympic podium. The park is 1.2km from the bazaar area, 600m off the main road using a turn near Kathok Lake.

Yangthang Rinpoche Statue　　　　　STATUE
Just outside Norbugang's south wall, this giant, seated statue-shrine commemorates Lhatsun Chempo's 20th-century 'reincarnation'. Seen from Tashi Tenka, it's one of Yuksom's most striking structures.

Dubdi Gompa　　　　　BUDDHIST MONASTERY
Said to be Sikkim's oldest still-functioning monastery, this compact, peaceful gompa is beautifully set in tended gardens on the ridge above Yuksom, with dawn views of white peaks between high green folds of forested foothills. Part of the delight of a visit is walking there on a 1.2km footpath of steps and mossy stones, taking nearly an hour from Yuksom's primary health centre (half that back). The path passes water-turned prayer wheels, trumpet lilies and lovely mature forest.

Mani Hall　　　　　BUDDHIST SITE
(Main Rd; ☉24hr) **FREE** Right in the village centre, this unique creation is a glass-walled templelike building enclosing 18 oversized prayer wheels in two close-packed rows.

⚡ Activities

Virtually all Yuksom hotels have in-house agencies to sort out treks and excursions.

Red Panda Tours & Travels　　　　　TREKKING
(☑9002322885, 9733196470; www.redpandatreks. weebly.com; Main Rd; ☉call) With his office beside Gupta Restaurant, former-porter-turned-guide 'Panda' has considerable experience and is once of the busiest trekking agents in town.

Mountain Tours & Treks　　　　　TREKKING
(☑9679225707, 9641352656; www.sherpatreks.in; Main Rd; ☉call) A well-reputed outfit with a good repertoire of high-altitude gear.

🛏 Sleeping

Limboo Homestay　　　　　GUESTHOUSE $
(☑09733084983; www.limboohomestay.com; s/d/ cottages ₹800/1200/1500) ✎ Hidden away opposite the primary health-care centre, Limboo's compact new rooms have little decor but they are unusually clean with good water heaters. The forest is close enough to wake to a full-on dawn chorus of birdsong.

There are fine views from the roof, and the glorious vegetable garden behind produces most of the food for delicious home-cooked meals (for dinner order by 5pm).

Dragon Hotel　　　　　GUESTHOUSE $
(☑9735934578, 9734126208; yukland@ymail.com; Pelling Rd; tw ₹700) Above a family house right

at the start of the village, Dragon has three simple but clean ensuite rooms, two of them with little balconies. There's also a spacious cafe-lounge area (kitchen open to 9pm) with a wide, parasol terrace.

Ejam Residency   HOTEL **$$**

(behind Kathok Lake; ⊙s ₹2100-2800, d ₹2300-3300) Though several storeys high, Ejam feels more like an overgrown home than a hotel. Its great delights are its manicured lawn, a superfriendly welcome and the secluded location that's only accessible by footpath – less than five minutes' walk from Kathok Lake.

Hotel Red Palace   HERITAGE HOTEL **$$**

(☑ 9593668773; www.hotelredpalace.com; Nghadak Monastery Rd; d ₹2000-3100, ste ₹3700; ☎) Like an overgrown Darjeeling mansion but filled with Sikkimese detailing, this charming, very peaceful hotel has partly wood-panelled rooms in four categories (best value ₹2500) and lots of public sofa-spaces, plus a terrace area with bonfire pit and lovely valley views.

✖ Eating

Central **Gupta Restaurant** (Main Rd; mains ₹50-130; ⊙6am-8.30pm) is Yuksom's de facto backpacker meeting point, with a wide range of good-value fare. However, for delicious Sikkimese fare cooked from scratch it's worth prebooking an hour or two ahead at **Mama's Kitchen** (Mangsabung Path; mains ₹70-200; ⊙6am-9pm), tucked down a footpath beside Yak Hotel at the village's southern entrance.

❶ Getting There & Away

At around 6.30am, several shared jeeps leave for Jorethang (₹150, four hours) via Tashiding (₹60, 1½ hours); Geyzing via Pelling (₹130, 2½ hours); and Gangtok (₹350, six hours) – book at Red Panda. There's also a Gangtok service around 2pm, as well as a Geyzing via Tashiding jeep at around 12.30pm.

Dzongri & Goecha La – the Khangchendzonga Trek

For guided groups (couples OK but no lone hikers), Sikkim's classic trek is the multiday epic from Yuksom to the 4940m Goecha La and back. The route showcases more than a dozen massive peaks, typically taking seven or eight days, though possible in five (return) if you're fit and very well preacclimatised. The culmination, after a gruelling, predawn slog, is – weather permitting – an unforgettable view of the awesome Khangchendzonga Massif. With less time, a shorter return to Dzongri still gives superb panoramas of Mt Pandim (6691m); even a two-day return to Tsokha (3050m) is a memorable experience, with waterfalls, hanging bridges and lovely valley views. If you have an extra week, you can cut south at Dzongri and follow the Singalila Ridge to Uttarey, a village west of Dentam.

While none of these routes require technical climbing, the high altitude and long days make it comparatively challenging, especially when the trail is foggy or slippery after rain. Acute Mountain Sickness (AMS) can be a risk, so consider adding rest days.

Late March to mid-May offers the best temperatures but afternoon rain often makes the trails muddy. October and November have high chances of clear skies, though snow and subzero temperatures are possible later in November. Other months are impractical.

Permits and guide must be organised through a registered agency but can generally be arranged within 36 hours in Yuksom, quicker still in Gangtok. Budget from around ₹3000 per person per day in small groups including tents, cook, porter, yaks and all food. Some nights it might be possible to sleep in trekkers' huts but tents are still needed for the night before Goecha-La (camping at Lamuni).

SIKKIM DZONGRI & GOECHA LA – THE KHANGCHENDZONGA TREK

GOECHA LA SAMPLE TREK SCHEDULE

STAGE	ROUTE	DURATION (HR)
1	Yuksom to Baktim/Tsokha	7-8
2	Optional acclimatisation day at Tsokha	
3	Tsokha to Dzongri	4-5
4	Acclimatisation day at Dzongri, or continue to Kokchurong	
5	Dzongri (or Kokchurong) to Lamuni	6-7
6	Lamuni to Goecha La and back (most groups descend further to Thangsing)	9-12 (11-14)
7	Lamuni (Thangsing) to Tsokha	8 (7)
8	Tsokha to Yuksom	5-7

Dzongri & Goecha La

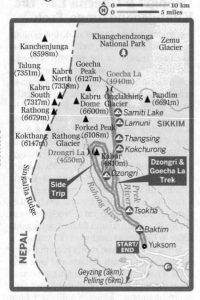

Tashiding

📞 03595 / POP 1870 / ELEV 1240M

Little Tashiding is essentially a low-rise one-street market village sloping up from its jeep stand and briefly bypassed by the Yuksom–Legship road. It's notable as the access point for the Tashiding Gompa, set on an isolated ridgetop 3.5km away. While you don't see many white-top mountains from the village, views over plunging green valleys, forested slopes and occasional stripes of rice terracing more than compensate.

🔘 Sights

Tashiding Gompa   MONASTERY

(⊙ dawn–dusk, main hall closes around 3pm) **FREE**
The ridge between Ralang and Yuksom ends with an upturned promontory (1450m) on which sits the multibuilding complex of Tashiding Gompa, an important Nyingmapa monastery. At its heart, a beautifully proportioned prayer hall has a delicate topknot that contrasts with the two lower stone floors. The murals inside are somewhat time-darkened and the main images are fronted with numerous colourful butter sculptures. Behind the Guru Lakhang building, shaded by two ancient Kashmir cypress trees, is a 'forest' of chorten stupas and mantra stones plus a dharma bell that rings out resonant prayer-

tones. The Bumchu (p539) festival is held here in February/March.

The monastery is 3km down a dead-end lane that starts with a colourful junction gate 400m south of Tashiding village. The last 500m suddenly becomes exceedingly rough and steep. It's better to walk that section using stairway shortcuts.

Phamrong Falls   WATERFALL
(Yuksom–Tashiding Rd Km6) The most dramatic of four waterfalls between Yuksom and Tashiding, the Phamrong's powerful flow fires itself through a high, green notch then crashes down a steep cliff.

🛏 Sleeping & Eating

Sanu Homestay   HOMESTAY $

(📞 9635060062; www.facebook.com/sanu.bhutia.94; Tashiding Gompa Path, Dodam; per person incl meals ₹900) With a minor cult following, Sanu's place has very simple bare floorboard rooms but great food, fine views and it's shaded by papaya trees, halfway up the pedestrians-only 'old road' between lower Tashiding and the gompa.

★ Rabney Residency   HOTEL $$
(📞 9733091760, 8670376362; dm ₹600, r with/without balcony ₹3500/2500, ste ₹4800) Tashiding's smartest rooms and most attractive restaurant (preorder only) are in this unpainted new concrete building tucked behind the central petrol station. There are sparkling clean tiled floors, immaculate bathrooms and stupendous views from the upper balconies

---

TASHIDING TO YUKSOM HIKE

New jeep roads at both ends mean that the once popular Yuksom–Tashiding day hike (19km) is now more commonly reversed and shortened to a few hours. The shortest, still-roadless version starts with a taxi from Tashiding to Pokhari Dara village with its locally famous pea-green pond. From here, a well-trodden, largely self-explanatory route goes through upper Nessa (10 minutes), past lonely, earthquake-damaged Hongri Gompa (one hour), and reaches Tsong less than an hour later. Finding a vehicle from Tsong on to Yuksom can be hit-and-miss. If you fail, walk another 4km to Dubdi Gompa then descend the stairway-path from there. To lengthen the walk further (partly by jeep-road), start further east at attractive Silnon Gompa.

and (unfinished) rooftop area. Hostess Nima Lhamu is a delight.

ℹ️ Getting There & Away

The **jeep stand** (Tashiding Bazaar) is at the south end of the short bazaar street. Departures for Gangtok (₹300, six hours) and Jorethang (₹150, three hours) leave by around 7am. Several Geyzing jeeps (₹130, two hours) leave between 6.30am and 8.30am, with one more around 2pm. For Yuksom (₹60, 2½ hours) there's one jeep at around 9am (usually very full on arrival) and several more between 2pm and 3pm.

Chartering a vehicle to Yuksom (one way/return ₹1200/1500, 1½ hours) costs a lot more but you'll save an hour in travel time.

Kuluk & Rinchenpong

POP 1550 / ELEV 1520M

The small ridgetop settlements of Kuluk and Rinchenpong stare north across a gaping valley, towards a magnificent Himalayan panorama, a view that is arguably even more memorable than from much more developed Pelling. As a bonus, Rinchenpong also has a fine pair of historic monasteries.

👁️ Sights

Rinchenpong Monastery   BUDDHIST MONASTERY
(Sanaienchi Gompa) Built in the 1730s and set on a flat field surrounded by monks' quarters, Sanaienchi Gompa's main three-level prayer house has a real sense of age. Even if you can't find anyone with the key to let you in, there's a peephole in the front door through which you can spy on the central indigo Buddha figure, who's saucily straddled by a tantric damsel. The monastery is 1.2km up a winding lane from Rinchenpong's bazaar, forking right at the only junction.

⭐ **Resum Gompa**   BUDDHIST MONASTERY
(Rinchenpong) This wobbly old temple is a peaceful, half-forgotten delight with appealingly naive paintings and an incredible 360-degree panorama. There's no road so you'll have to walk around 20 minutes up from Rinchenpong gompa, climbing through the forest. En route you'll encounter collapsing stupas and *mani* walls (Tibetan stone walls with sacred inscriptions).

The slightly confusing footpath starts from where the Rinchenpong Monastery road dead-ends at the monastery residence toilet block. Walk to the left then, when the path starts to peter out, cut steeply up through the woodland till you reach the upper water pipe.

Turn left here to bring you to a small clearing and then to Resum Gompa (around 300m).

🛏️ Sleeping

The Rinchenpong-Kuluk area is home to a number of plush farmstays, a couple of semi-luxury resorts, a scattering of hotels and several lodges. Many choices are widely spread out, so better suited to those with independent transport.

⭐ **Ghonday Village Resort**   HOTEL $$
(☑ 9933001127, 9593979695; www.ghondayresort. com; Kuluk; r ₹2500-3300, walk-in ₹1500-2000; 📶) A traditional silk-scarf welcome underlines the high-quality service of this gently luxurious little resort, just 250m steeply down from Kuluk bazaar. There are lovely gardens and jaw-dropping panoramic views of the whole Khanchendzonga range from most of the comfortably well-appointed rooms.

⭐ **Biksthang**   FARMSTAY $$$
(☑ 9593779077; www.biksthang.com; Mangalbarey Rd; incl half board s ₹6600-7950, d ₹8750-12,750; 🅿️ 🎦) 🍃 If you'd like to escape from techno-modernity, yet unwind with highly educated, thoughtful hosts, it's hard to imagine anywhere better than this isolated but very classy farmstay. Eight artistically appointed cottages are tucked between mandarin, cardamon and organic tea groves; the unique dining room is within a photogenic 18th-century farmhouse, and Khangchendzonga reflects grandly in the infinity pool.

The family's historical links are remarkable – as is their specialist library – so there's lots to discuss over delicious home-cooked Sikkimese food and a pot or three of organic tongba (millet beer). Featured in *National Geographic* (February 2016), Biksthang is well off the beaten track: an hour's drive from Jorethang or around 45 minutes from Rinchenpong via the Reshi road. Turn towards Mangalbarey at Km15.8 coming from Rinchenpong (or Km8.2 from Reishi), then after 1.4km you'll see the 300m access lane on the left. Jorethang–Mangalbarey shared jeeps pass by. A taxi from Bagdogra airport/Kuluk costs around ₹4500/1000.

ℹ️ Getting There & Away

Dentam–Jorethang shared jeeps drop off passengers at Kulluk Bazaar, mostly in the morning before 9am southbound, in mid-afternoon on return. Jorethang–Geyzing, Soreng–Geyzing and Rinchenpong–Geyzing vehicles also pass through.

SIKKIM KULUK & RINCHENPONG

Northeast States

Best Places to Eat

➡ Paradise (p562)

➡ Luxmi Kitchen (p585)

➡ Chouka (p567)

➡ Moti Mahal Delux (p571)

➡ Tandoor (p562)

➡ Tawang Food Court (p574)

Best Places to Stay

➡ Diphlu River Lodge (p567)

➡ Aborcountry River Camp (p577)

➡ Ri Kynjai (p592)

➡ Prabhakar Homestay (p561)

➡ Cherrapunjee Holiday Resort (p594)

➡ Razhü Pru (p580)

Why Go?

Sometimes the Seven Sisters of the Northeast (the states of Arunachal Pradesh, Assam, Manipur, Meghalaya, Mizoram, Nagaland and Tripura) hardly seem like India at all. The region's hundreds of tribes and subtribes are slowly embracing modernity, but remain extremely diverse. Cloudy Himalayan valleys near the border of Tibet are dotted with colourful monasteries, echoing with Buddhist chants and clashing cymbals.

The geography is as varied as the culture. While waterfalls thunder down Cherrapunjee's jungle escarpments, blizzards may be blocking the passes to Tawang, and one-horned rhinos go on grazing peacefully in Kaziranga's grasslands beside the mighty Brahmaputra. Northeast travel can be tough, with atrocious roads and long distances. But the destinations are always worth the effort and there'll be a warm welcome that awaits. You are indeed far from the beaten track: only the adventurous need apply.

When to Go
Assam (Guwahati)

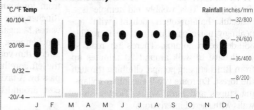

Mar The best season for rhino-spotting in Kaziranga.

Oct A time for dazzling Himalayan vistas and trips to remote outposts.

Dec Fierce Naga warriors in ethnic regalia assemble for Kohima's spectacular Hornbill Festival.

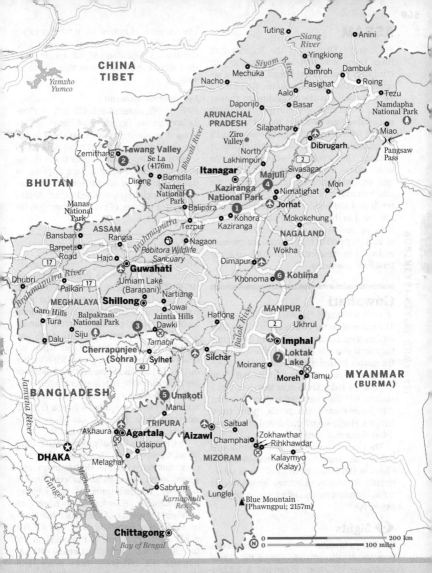

Northeast States Highlights

① **Kaziranga National Park** (p566) Roaming the expansive grasslands in search of rhinos.

② **Tawang Valley** (p572) Touching the clouds at the 4176m Se La pass before descending to the Tibetan Buddhist realm of Tawang.

③ **Cherrapunjee** (p593) Hiking down 2600 steps to the amazing root bridges of Nongriat.

④ **Majuli** (p568) Soaking up the serene atmosphere of India's largest river island.

⑤ **Unakoti** (p590) Staring at massive rock-cut sculptures that are half-hidden in the jungles.

⑥ **Kohima** (p579) Visiting a moving WWII cemetery and climbing to the other-worldly Dzükou Valley.

⑦ **Loktak Lake** (p585) Exploring the lake's unique ecosystem and floating islands.

ASSAM

Stretching 600km along the Brahmaputra River Valley, with a spur down to the hilly southeast, Assam is the largest and most accessible of the Northeast States. Well known for its national parks abounding in rhinoceroses, elephants, deer and primates (with respectable tiger numbers too), it welcomes visitors with a subtly flavoured cuisine and a hospitable population with a vibrant artistic heritage. The archetypal Assamese landscape is a golden-green panorama of rice fields and manicured tea estates, framed by the blue mountains of Arunachal Pradesh in the north and the highlands of Meghalaya and Nagaland to the south. The birthplace of Indian tea, Assam has more than 3000 sq km of land carpeted in bright-green tea gardens, and visits to these estates are high on many travellers' itineraries.

Guwahati

☑ 0361 / POP 962,000

The gateway to the Northeast, and the largest and most cosmopolitan city in the region, Guwahati extends along the south bank of the mighty Brahmaputra. There's a lot of featureless concrete, glass and traffic, but if you explore the older areas near the river, you'll start to feel the character and local flavour that lingers amid the ponds, palm trees, temples, single-storey traditional houses and colonial-era mansions.

The city was a vibrant cultural centre well before the Ahoms arrived from southern China in the 13th century, and it was subsequently the theatre of intense Ahom-Mughal strife, changing hands eight times in 50 years before 1681.

◉ Sights

Kamakhya Mandir HINDU TEMPLE
(www.kamakhyatourism.com; Nilachal Hill; special ticket/queue ₹501/free; ⊗7am-1pm & 2.30pm-dusk) According to Hindu legend, when a distraught Shiva scattered the 108 (or 51) pieces of his deceased wife Sati's body across the land, her *yoni* (vagina) fell on Nilachal Hill, 8km west of central Guwahati. This makes Kamakhya Mandir a specially hallowed shrine for practitioners of *shakti* (tantric worship of female spiritual power). The ₹501 'special ticket' allows you to jump the usual queues to reach the cave-like inner sanctum. Kamakhya is where the huge Ambubachi Mela festival (p564) takes place.

The temple is 5km west from the city along AT Rd then 3km up a spiralling side road. Get any bus west along AT Rd and get off at the foot of the hill, where further transport waits.

Assam State Museum MUSEUM
(GNB Rd; ₹5, camera/video ₹10/100; ⊗10am-3.45pm Tue-Sun Oct-Feb, to 4.30pm Mar-Sep) Housed in an imposing colonial-era building, the state museum has a large medieval sculpture collection and upper floors devoted to informative tribal-culture displays. In the Village Life of Assam section, you can walk through reconstructed tribal homes that give a glimpse of everyday rural life. It's worth a visit.

◉ Old Guwahati

Along the riverbank in the Uzanbazar neighbourhood, **Sati Radhika Prashanti Udyan** (MG Rd; ₹10; ⊗9am-8pm) is a sliver of peaceful, tree-shaded park, particularly popular with courting couples around sunset. South along Lamb Rd, the red-painted **Ugratara Mandir** (Lamb Rd) overlooking Jorpulkuri Ponds was built in 1725 to enshrine the spot where it's believed the goddess Sati's navel fell after her distraught husband Shiva scattered pieces of her body across the subcontinent. A few colonial-era houses survive in this part of town, notably a two-storey **judge's house** (1 JN Borooah Lane) from 1922, now the offices of the Foundation for Social Transformation.

To the west is **Dighalipukhuri Park** (GNB Rd; adult/child ₹10/5; ⊗10am-8pm); its lake was once connected to the Brahmaputra and served as an Ahom naval harbour. Further westward the half-timbered 19th-century **Christ Church** (⊗services 8.30am & 5pm Sun) stands in the middle of the garden-like **Nehru Park** (Hem Baruah Rd; adult/child ₹20/10; ⊗10am-8pm). Past here is Panbazar, one of the city's oldest commercial areas, with interesting silk and book shops along Hem Baruah Road.

🛏 Sleeping

Hotel Suncity HOTEL $
(☑ 7637002177; suncityroom@gmail.com; GS Rd, Paltan Bazar; s/d incl breakfast with AC ₹950/2000, without AC ₹750/1300; ❊🛜) One of the better choices among many cheap hotels just south of Guwahati train station, the Suncity provides clean beds, bathrooms and floors – although some walls could use a wash. Touches of orange, pink and purple cheer up

Guwahati

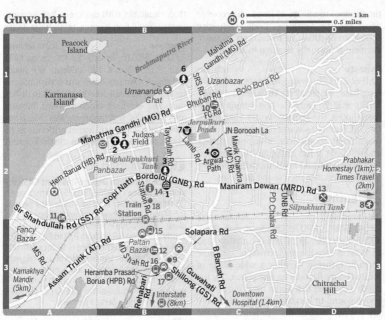

N | 0 ——————— 1 km
0 ——————— 0.5 miles

Guwahati

◉ Sights

1 Assam State Museum	B2
2 Christ Church	B2
3 Dighalipukhuri Park	B2
4 Judge's House	C2
5 Nehru Park	B2
6 Sati Radhika Prasanti Udyan	B1
7 Ugratara Mandir	B2

◔ Activities, Courses & Tours

8 Assam Bengal Navigation	D2
JTI Group	(see 8)
9 Network Travels	B3

◔ Sleeping

10 Baruah Bhavan	C1
11 Dynasty	A2
12 Hotel Suncity	B3

◉ Eating

13 Paradise	D2
Tandoor	(see 11)

ⓘ Information

14 Assam Tourism	B2

ⓘ Transport

15 Assam State Transport Corporation	B3
16 Blue Hill Travels	B3
17 Deep Travels	B3
Network Travels	(see 9)
Paltan Bazar Bus Stand	(see 15)
18 Passenger Reservation System Office	B2

the decor. Reception is on the 1st floor of the building. Non-AC rooms have squat toilets.

★**Baruah Bhavan** GUESTHOUSE **$$**
(☎9954024165; www.baruahbhavan.com; 40 MC Rd, Uzanbazar; r incl breakfast ₹2800-4130; ❉@) This charming 1950s house on Manik Chandra (MC) Rd was built by a celebrated Assamese scholar and has lots of antiques and memorabilia strewn across its living areas. But it's the six individually styled rooms and the attentive service that make it an

exceptional place to stay. Not forgetting the flavourful and generous home-cooked meals (veg/nonveg dinner ₹300/350).

★**Prabhakar Homestay** HOMESTAY **$$$**
(☎9435033222; www.prabhakarhomestay.com; House 2, Bylane No 2, KP Barua Rd, Chandmari; incl breakfast s ₹4620-6050, d ₹5280-6600; ❉❞) In a quiet residential area, this delightful place run by ex-professor Shiela and her husband, Mahesh, is one of the best homestays in India. The property is hemmed by lush gardens,

the spacious rooms are adorned with eco-chic decor and the Assamese meals (₹750) give serious competition to restaurants in town. Payment is normally required in advance.

Dynasty
HOTEL $$$

(☎0361-2516021; www.dynastyhotel.in; SS Rd, Fancy Bazar; incl breakfast s ₹6490-9980, d ₹7080-10,880; ❄@🛜) Once the best among Guwahati's hotels, the Dynasty, on Sir Shahdullah (SS) Rd, retains a sense of nostalgia and offers magnificent rooms with a colonial flavour and soft beds. It has all the facilities you'd expect from a top-end hotel, including a couple of superb restaurants, a sauna and a spa.

✖ Eating

★ Paradise
ASSAMESE $$

(☎9435548812; MRD Rd, Chandmari; mains ₹180-490; ⊗11am-11pm; ❄) The lunch thalis (₹280 to ₹525) at Paradise are archetypal Assamese spreads, bringing together a wide range of local culinary flavours on one platter. Try the subtly flavoured fish *tenga* (sour curry) and you're bound to become a fan for life. There are veg and nonveg thali varieties, with the menu helpfully listing all the items they include.

Majulir Asanj
ASSAMESE $$

(1st fl, Chakradhar Villa, Chandmari U-turn; thalis ₹150-400, mains₹150-300; ⊗11am-10pm) This reliable restaurant, about 200m off MRD Rd, specialises in the food of Majuli Island. Go for fish steamed in banana leaf or an Assamese

---

RIVER CRUISES

To experience the beauty of Assam from a unique perspective (and all of it in style), consider a plush river cruise. Operating from October to May, these multiday luxury rides cover stretches of the Brahmaputra between Guwahati and Majuli Island, dropping anchor at essential stops such as Kaziranga National Park. Activities en route include wildlife tours, cultural excursions and simply lazing on deck with a drink in hand. Guwahati-based **Assam Bengal Navigation** (☎0361-2667871, 9207042330; www.assambengalnavigation.com; 3rd fl, Dirang Arcade, MRD Rd, Chandmari; per person per night all-inclusive US$220-600; ⊗office 10am-6.30pm Mon-Sat, cruises Oct-early May) has all the information.

---

thali (available with duck, chicken, or vegetarian). You'll find it opposite All India Radio.

Tandoor
NORTH INDIAN $$$

(☎0361-2516021; Dynasty, SS Rd; mains ₹470-830; ⊗12.30-3pm & 7.30-10.30pm; ❄) Inside the stately Dynasty hotel, this stylish upscale restaurant has delicious North Indian dishes, including excellent tandoori items, biryanis and plenty of vegetarian choices. Meals are served by waiters in Mughal uniforms as Indian musicians play softly in the background.

❶ Information

Arunachal Pradesh Deputy Resident Commissioner's Office (☎9706790326; Rukminigaon, GS Rd; ⊗9am-5pm Mon-Sat) issues the permits (p574) needed by foreigners and Indians travelling to Arunachal Pradesh. Take any city bus southeast along GS Rd from Paltan Bazar (₹10, 30 to 40 minutes). The office is 100m south off GS Rd, 500m after the large Novotel. Foreigners must bring their passport, photocopies of their passport and tourist visa, fill in a form and pay the rupee equivalent of US$30 per person (US$60 for single-person permits).

❶ Getting There & Away

AIR

The following airlines connect Guwahati to most major Indian cities (often with a transfer in Kolkata or Delhi): IndiGo (www.goindigo.in), SpiceJet (www.spicejet.com), Jet Airways (www.jetairways.com), Air India (www.airindia.com), GoAir (www.goair.in), AirAsia (www.airasia.com) and Vistara (www.airvistara.com).

Indigo, SpiceJet and Jet Airways have the most flights to other Northeast cities. Drukair (www.drukair.com.bt) flies several times weekly to Paro (Thimpu, Bhutan) and twice weekly to Singapore.

Meghalaya Helicopter Service (☎98590 21473; Guwahati Airport; ⊗office open before flights) has flights to Shillong (₹1500, 30 minutes, 9am and 12.30pm Monday to Saturday), weather permitting. Book ahead.

BUS

Long-distance buses within Assam are operated by the quite-efficient **Assam State Transport Corporation** (ASTC; http://astc.assam.gov.in; Paltan Bazar Bus Stand). Various private companies run services within and beyond Assam. Some ASTC services start from the central Paltan Bazar Bus Stand (south side of Guwahati railway station); other ASTC buses and almost all private buses depart from the **Interstate Bus Terminus** (ISBT; NH27, Betkuchi), 9km southwest. Most companies including the ASTC run free shuttles from their city-centre offices to the ISBT.

BUSES FROM GUWAHATI

DESTINATION	FARE (₹)	DURATION (HR)
Agartala	750	21
Aizawl	910	22
Bomdila	700	11
Dibrugarh	480-780	11
Imphal	800	19
Itanagar	600-700	11
Kohima	750	13
Kohora (Kaziranga)	235-300	6
Pasighat	660	14
Shillong	140	3½
Siliguri	550	13
Sivasagar	390-780	9
Tezpur	155-240	4½

Network Travels (☑ 8811079999; www.net worktravels.com; GS Rd, Paltan Bazar; ⊘ 5am-9pm) has one of the most comprehensive and reliable private networks throughout the Northeast (the website has schedules).

See www.redbus.in for schedules and bookings (foreign cards accepted).

For Shillong, there are just two ASTC AC buses at 7am and 8am from Paltan Bazar Bus Stand. Most people travel by shared taxi or jeep.

TAXI, JEEP & CAR

For some destinations the main public transport is shared Sumo jeeps or less cramped people-carriers such as the Mahindra Xylo. The **ASTC Sumo Service** (☑ 8011362131; Paltan Bazar Bus Stand) runs vehicles to Shillong (Sumo/Xylo ₹200/350, three hours, continuous service 5am to 8pm), Bomdila (Sumo ₹600, nine hours, 6.30am), Dirang (Sumo ₹700, 11 hours, 6.30am) and Tawang (Sumo ₹1300, 17 hours, 5.30am).

A taxi for up to four people to Shillong costs ₹1600 from Assam Trunk (AT) Rd outside Paltan Bazar Bus Stand, or ₹2000 (AC ₹2500) from the airport prepaid taxi counter; shared cabs from the airport car park are ₹500 per person.

Many companies hire out cars and jeeps for multiday travel in the Northeast, including Network Travels (p565), **Blue Hill Travels** (☑ 9435547679; HP Brahmachari Rd, Paltan Bazar; ⊘ 7am-8pm) and small but efficient **Times Travel** (☑ 9435110947; timestravel24@gmail.com; 9 Ganesh Mandir Path, New Guwahati). Including driver and fuel, costs range between ₹3200 and ₹6000 per day according to the roads you're travelling and the type of vehicle needed.

TRAIN

Four daily trains connect Guwahati to Delhi; the fastest and most comfortable is the 12423 Dibrugarh Town Rajdhani Express (3AC/2AC ₹2630/3670, 27 hours, 7am). The best daily train to Kolkata (Howrah) is the 12346 Saraighat Express (sleeper/3AC/2AC ₹500/1320/1900, 17 hours, 12.30pm). If travelling to Darjeeling and Sikkim, take either of these, or the 15909 Abadh Assam Express at 10pm, as far as New Jalpaiguri (3AC/2AC from ₹670/950, six to eight hours).

Several daily trains serve Jorhat (2nd seating/sleeper/chair/3AC ₹180/240/540/640, seven to 11 hours), Dibrugarh (sleeper/3AC/2AC ₹320/870/1240, nine to 15 hours) and Dimapur (2nd seating/sleeper/chair/3AC/2AC ₹110/180/430/500/700, 4½ to six hours).

ⓘ Getting Around

Getting into town from Guwahati Airport (23km west) costs ₹550/150/90 for a taxi/shared taxi/airport bus. Going out to the airport, the bus leaves hourly (6am to 5pm) from Paltan Bazar Bus Stand; **taxis** (GS Rd, Paltan Bazar) go from outside Hotel Mahalaxmi on GS Rd.

Autorickshaws charge ₹50 to ₹100 for short hops within the city. You can also book an Uber through their mobile app and enjoy a comfortable air-con ride usually for ₹15 to ₹20 per kilometre (cash payment accepted).

Around Guwahati

A small wildlife sanctuary, **Pobitora Wildlife Sanctuary** (Mayong Village; Indian/foreigner ₹50/500, camera ₹50, jeep rental ₹1000, jeep entry to park ₹300; ⊘ 6.30am-noon & 1-3.30pm Oct-Apr) has a thriving population of some

130 one-horned rhinoceroses, plus around 2000 wild water buffalo and almost 2000 resident and migratory bird species. About 40km northeast of Guwahati, it makes for a good day trip (cabs cost ₹3000 to ₹4000 round trip). Visits are by one-hour jeep safari or early-morning elephant ride. We don't recommend the latter because of the harm that this can cause to the elephants.

Manas National Park

A Unesco World Heritage Site known for its biodiversity and beauty, **Manas National Park** (☑ 9435022920; www.manastigerproject. in; Indian/foreigner ₹100/650, camera Indian/foreigner ₹100/200; ☉ 6am-3pm Oct-May) abuts the Bhutan border about 150km northwest of Guwahati. The park's 500 sq km of grasslands and lowland tropical forest harbour a very impressive list of animals, including around 30 tigers, 30 one-horned rhinos, 100 *barasingha* (swamp deer), 500 wild water buffalo and over 1000 elephants. The Manas (Beki) River flowing out of Bhutan is an additional scenic attraction.

Safaris

The park is divided into three ranges, of which the central Bansbari Range is the most accessible. Standard jeep safaris last around three hours, traversing the Bansbari Range to Mathanguri Forest Lodge close to the Bhutan border. You'd be lucky to sight a tiger, rhino or leopard, but you will almost certainly see a variety of other interesting wildlife. Jeeps are available at the Bansbari gate, where you can also pay your park fees. Costs are normally ₹2600 for jeep hire, driver, obligatory armed guard and vehicle entry to the park, plus ₹100/650 per Indian/foreigner for park entry. Guides are available from ₹300 up to ₹1500 for specialist bird guides. Lodges can arrange everything for you, usually for a few hundred rupees extra.

🛏 Sleeping

Comfortable **Bansbari Lodge** (☑ 9435551297; www.assambengalnavigation.com; Giyatigaon; per person full board ₹4500) is right by the park gate. Jungle packages here (per person ₹9000) cover full board, jeep and elephant-back safaris, a guide and park fees. (You may prefer a second jeep trip instead of the elephant ride because of the associated animal-welfare issues.) **Mathanguri Forest Lodge** (Mathanguri, Manas National Park; dm/r ₹220/1250) is Manas' most in-the-forest lodging experience, sitting almost on the riverbank, deep inside the national park. It has 10 simple medium-sized rooms and an 18-bed dorm. Veg/nonveg meals cost ₹120/240. Book through the **Manas Tiger Project Field Director's office** (☑ 9435022920; fd-manastp@gmail.com; opposite Civil Hospital, Barpeta Road; ☉ 10am-5pm Mon-Fri).

❶ Getting There & Away

Ten daily trains run from Guwahati to the town of Barpeta Road, 20km south of the park's Bansbari gate. From the taxi or bus stands near Barpeta Road station, Tata Magic vans and the occasional bus run to Bansbari (both ₹30, one hour) until about 6pm.

TOP FESTIVALS

Torgya (Tawang Gompa; ☉ Jan) Three days of spectacular masked *chaam* dances by lamas at Tawang Gompa.

Rongali Bihu (☉ mid-Apr) Assamese New Year festivities.

Ambubachi Mela (Guwahati; ☉ late Jun) A melange of tantric fertility rituals at the Kamakhya Mandir.

Ziro Music Festival (Ziro Valley; www.zirofestival.com; ☉ Sep) The Northeast's very own Glastonbury rocks the Ziro Valley.

Wangala (www.wangalafestival.com; Asanang; ☉ Nov) Garo harvest festival with dancing and drumming.

Raas Leela (☉ Nov) Much song and dance in praise of Lord Krishna on Majuli island.

Sangai Festival (www.sangaifestival.gov.in; ☉ 21-30 Nov) Showcase for the arts, crafts, sports and food of Manipur.

Hornbill Festival (Kohima, ☉ Dec; p580) Naga tribes take the stage in full warrior gear just outside Kohima.

Tezpur

☎ 03712 / POP 75,500

Little more than a utilitarian stopover en route to Arunachal Pradesh or upper Assam, Tezpur is a pleasantly laid-back town with some well-kept parks, attractive lakes and beguiling views of the mighty Brahmaputra River as it laps the town's edge.

Central areas have a good number of mid-range and budget options. The large, clean air-conditioned rooms at **Aditya's Hotel Centre Point** (☎03712-232359; hotelcentre point.tez@gmail.com; Main Rd; incl breakfast r with AC ₹1680-2130, without AC AC ₹900; ❅ ⌘) have a modest business-hotel feel; non-air-conditioned rooms lack the accoutrements but are still clean and well maintained. There's a multicuisine restaurant here too.

Best in town is the smart **Hotel KRC Palace** (☎03712-222688; www.hotelkrcpalace.com; JN Rd, Kacharigaon; incl breakfast s ₹3420-6140, d ₹3660-6140, ste ₹11,520; ❅ ⌘), about 1km northwest of the centre. Rooms are modern and very plush, and there are two bright and cheerful restaurants (one multicuisine, one vegetarian), plus a dimly lit bar playing loud Indian pop.

The **ASTC Bus Station** (Jenkins Rd) has frequent buses to Guwahati (non-AC/AC ₹155/240, 4½ hours, 5am to 4.30pm) and Jorhat (₹150, 4½ hours, 5am to 1pm). Jorhat buses will drop you at Kohora (₹100, two hours) for Kaziranga National Park. Inside the bus station, the **ASTC Sumo Counter** (☎9435080318; ASTC Bus Station) operates Sumo jeeps to Bomdila (₹600, four hours, 6am, 11.30am, noon and 1pm), Dirang (₹700, 5½ hours, 6am) and Tawang (₹1050, 12 hours, 6am). Private Sumo operators leaving to the same destinations at 5.30am (same fares) have counters on the street immediately north of the ASTC station. For all Sumos you should book the day before.

Nameri National Park

Beautiful 200-sq-km **Nameri National Park** (www.nameritr.org; Indian/foreigner ₹50/500; ⊙Nov-Apr) lies between the clear Jia Bhorelli River, flowing down from the mountains of Arunachal Pradesh, and the forested hills of Arunachal's Pakke Tiger Reserve. Nameri is very popular with birders (over 370 feathered species, including eight that are globally endangered, have been recorded here), but is an enjoyable visit for anyone, even if you don't

see any breathtaking animals. You get to walk (rather than ride a jeep) through its forests, and you boat across the lovely Jia Bhorelli to reach it. If you want more of the river, 14km gentle rafting trips are easily arranged.

Nameri is a key refuge for the white-winged wood duck, Assam's state bird, and home to some 400 elephants and seven feline species.

Access is from Potasali village, 35km north of Tezpur, just off the road to Bomdila in Arunachal Pradesh. The park closes from May to October.

The standard visit is a 5km walk with an armed guard along a fixed route, which is open from 6am to 11am and 1pm to 4.30pm, partly alongside the river and partly inside the forest. Tickets are sold from 6am to 8am and 1pm to 1.30pm at Nameri National Park Interpretation Centre in Potasali. On top of the park entry fee, you pay ₹100 for the guard,

THE POACHING CONTROVERSY

Kaziranga's success in protecting endangered and vulnerable species is impressive, but the park has attracted some controversy in recent years over the eviction of villagers from fringe areas and for its antipoaching strategy, in which park guards can and do shoot suspected poachers. The poachers come chiefly for rhino horn, which is sold on the black market to those who believe it has miraculous medicinal powers. Media reports and verbal conversations suggest that around 15 to 20 suspected poachers have been shot dead annually in the last few years. Rhinos are still being poached, but rhino deaths dropped from a reported 27 in 2013 to seven or eight in 2017.

and ₹40 per person (round trip) for the river crossing (1km from Potasali). Lodges can provide naturalist guides for around ₹1500.

Stay at Eco-Camp (☑8472800344; www. nameri.co.in; Potasali; dm ₹350, r/f incl breakfast ₹3000/4500) 🐾, which provides accommodation in comfortable tents under thatched roofs in lush gardens. The colourful fabrics, attached bathrooms and sturdy beds make the experience relatively luxurious. Adding to the interest here are breeding centres for the critically endangered pygmy hog and the golden mahseer fish.

You can hire a taxi from Tezpur to Nameri National Park for ₹1000. Or hop into a Tata Magic van to Balipara (₹30, 45 minutes) heading north from Mission Chariali crossroads on Tezpur's northern edge, then take another Tata Magic bound for Bhalukpong from Balipara's central crossroads as far as Nameri Hati Gate (₹30, 30 minutes), the start of the 2km lane leading to Potasali. A taxi from Balipara to Potasali costs around ₹400.

Kaziranga National Park

☑03776

Famed as a haven for the one-horned rhinoceros, one of India's great wildlife emblems, **Kaziranga National Park** (www.kaziranga. assam.gov.in; Indian/foreigner ₹100/650, camera Indian/foreigner ₹100/200; ☉approx mid-Oct–Apr) encompasses grasslands, wetlands and forests for about 60km on the south side of the Brahmaputra River. Its 2400-plus rhinos comprise two-thirds of the world's population and you're highly likely to see some on any safari in the park (usually grazing peacefully). You'll probably also spot some of the park's 1100 elephants, and if you're very lucky, a tiger (over 100 live here). Also commonly seen are two other rare large mammals: the wild water buffalo and eastern swamp deer. The park closes because of the monsoon from about May to mid-October. The ideal wildlife sighting period is from late January (when the tall elephant grass is burnt down) to March.

Safaris

The park is divided into five ranges, four of which can be visited on safaris. Kohora (Central) and Bagori (Western) ranges with their ample grasslands are normally best for overall wildlife sightings and Kohora is the busiest (often too busy), with the best network of jeep tracks. Agoratoli (Eastern) has greater habitat diversity and much less safari traffic and is particularly good for birds (Kaziranga counts over 480 bird species).

Two-to-three-hour **jeep safaris** (jeep rental & safari fees per vehicle ₹1950-2150; ☉7am-noon & 1.30-5pm or sunset, approx mid-Oct–Apr), with up to six passengers per jeep, traverse the ranges looking for interesting wildlife. Each visitable range has its own gate, with park admission and safari-jeep offices adjacent (except that the Kohora gate is 2.5km away from its offices, which are 700m south of the main road in Kohora village). Park entry tickets (not included in safari fees) are sold from 7am to 10am and 1.30pm to 3pm: you need to get your jeep ticket before your entry ticket. Many lodgings will, usually for a few hundred rupees extra, do all the formalities for you and get the jeep to come and pick you up.

An armed guard accompanies most vehicles (and some elephants) entering the park. A ₹100 tip for drivers and guards is customary.

🛏 Sleeping

There's plenty of accommodation close to the park but even so, booking well ahead is recommended in season (November to March). The majority of lodgings are in and around Kohora village on NH715 (old NH37).

Bora's Homestay　　　　GUESTHOUSE $
(☑9864948736; bubulbora87@gmail.com; Krishnapur, Kohora; d/tr ₹1200/1500) Bora's is a

decent and well-established budget option with eight neat pink-and-white rooms. It's 100m along a lane off the highway, 1.2km east of central Kohora. Meals available.

Wild Grass Resort LODGE $$
(☑ 9954416945, 8761833837; wildgrasskaziranga@gmail.com; r incl breakfast Nov-Apr ₹2500, May-Oct ₹950; ☎) Kaziranga's original (1987) resort is slightly ramshackle but retains a cheerful colonial character, especially in the large dining and sitting rooms. The bedrooms look their age style-wise but are still comfortable, with springy mattresses, and overlook trees or gardens. Bookings are essential in December and January. Turn off NH715 (old NH37) 5km east of Kohora opposite the Km373 stone, and go about 600m.

Nature-Hunt Eco Camp LODGE $$
(☑ 9127015502; www.naturehunttours.com; Diring; r incl breakfast ₹2500-2800) Cosy stilt cottages with comfy beds, hot showers and verandahs overlook tea bushes and rice fields. The excellent set dinners include a 'tribal' option (₹600) with rice and fish steamed in banana leaves and chicken cooked inside a bamboo trunk. It's 250m south of the main road, 4km east of Kohora.

Aranya Tourist Lodge HOTEL $$
(☑ 03776-262429; Kohora; d ₹1460-1660; ☎) Conveniently located near the Kohora safari office, the Aranya provides clean rooms, prompt service, decent Indian food (mains ₹150 to ₹300) and a well-stocked bar – not bad for a state-government-run hotel. It's fronted by a colourful flower garden and is popular with Indian groups.

★ Diphlu River Lodge RESORT $$$
(☑ 9435146414, 0361-2667871; www.diphluriverlodge.com; NH715 (old NH37); Nov-Apr jungle plan per person Indian/foreigner ₹14,000/18,000, May-Oct r incl breakfast ₹9975; ☎) Easily the best place to stay in the Kaziranga area, this superb resort 15km west of Kohora near Bagori Police Outpost, combines fine luxuries and top-class service with a rustic look and relaxed atmosphere. The 12 bamboo cottages have soft beds, stylish bathrooms and pleasant verandahs. Oh, and the food is delicious. The November-to-April jungle-plan arrangement includes all meals and two safaris daily.

❶ Getting There & Away

From the bus stop by Kohora's central intersection, buses head to Jorhat (₹90, 2½ hours, about half-hourly 6am to 3pm), Dibrugarh (₹350, five hours, 10am, 10.30am and 11am), Tezpur (₹100, two hours, half-hourly 7am to 3pm) and Guwahati (₹300, four to five hours, hourly 7am to 1pm).

Jorhat

☑ 0376 / POP 127,000
Jorhat is a bustling, green and relatively prosperous town, but has limited interest for travellers except as the main jumping-off point for Majuli Island. The Assam Trunk Rd (AT Rd; NH715; old NH37) runs west–east across town, with MG Rd and, a little further east, Gar-Ali, the main roads heading south off it.

🛏 Sleeping & Eating

Hotel Paradise (☑ 0376-2321521; paradisejorhat@gmail.com; Solicitor Rd; incl breakfast d with AC ₹1790, s/d without AC ₹770/990; ❋ ☎), dating from 1975 but wearing its years very well, is the best value of a string of hotels on Solicitor Rd behind the ASTC Bus Station. It offers clean, reasonably sized rooms, friendly service and a decent restaurant-cum-bar (Indian mains ₹180 to ₹280). **Prism** (☑ 0376-2300050; www.facebook.com/ahamed08; 3rd fl, Big Bazaar Bldg, KB RD; d incl breakfast ₹4720-7080; ❋ ☎), opened in 2017, raises the bar for Jorhat's central hotels with professional service, bright, contemporary rooms and the sleek Red Panda Bistro (Indian and Chinese mains ₹200 to ₹450; no alcohol).

Several tea estates near Jorhat offer you the chance to sample the planter's lifestyle: a highlight is delightful **Puroni Bheti** (☑ 9954150976; puronibheti@gmail.com; Haroocharai Tea Estate; d incl breakfast ₹4000-7000; ❋ ☎), 7km west of the centre and run by a superhospitable planter and his family. Personalised attention, premium accommodation, wonderful homemade food, and music- and laughter-filled evenings with the hosts guarantee a memorable stay.

★ Chouka ASSAMESE $$
(☑ 9864010280; Mithapukuri; mains ₹100-260; ◷ noon-10pm) In a well-spaced dining room

---

SLEEPING PRICE RANGES

The following price ranges refer to a double room with bathroom including taxes in this region.

$ less than ₹1500
$$ ₹1500–₹4000
$$$ more than ₹4000

TRAVELLING SAFELY IN THE NORTHEAST STATES

In recent decades many ethnolinguistic groups in the Northeast have jostled, often violently, to assert themselves in the face of illegal immigration from neighbouring countries, governmental apathy and a heavy-handed security policy. Some want independence from India, others autonomy, but many are fighting what are effectively clan or turf wars. While peace mostly prevails, and unrest and violent insurgency-related incidents have fallen far below their peaks of the 1990s and 2000s, strikes, unrest and violent incidents can flare up suddenly and unpredictably. In 2014 attacks by Bodo groups killed more than 70 people across Assam. Some Naga insurgent groups are still active in Nagaland and neighbouring areas. In Manipur, foreign travellers have at times been restricted for safety reasons to the Imphal area, and in 2016 and '17 the state was ravaged by four months of road blockades, violence and curfews. Manipur has since become much calmer, and at the time of research there were no travel restrictions.

It pays to stay abreast of the situation before travelling. The updating of Assam's National Register of Citizens, a long-drawn-out process aimed chiefly at identifying illegal immigrants from Bangladesh, is one issue to keep an eye on. Regional news media such as Northeast Today (www.northeasttoday.in), Time8 (www.time8.in) and TNT (www.thenortheasttoday.com) are helpful. If you're with a tour company, talk to the operators to make sure your field guide is up to date with the situation.

off MG Rd, Chouka's menu is full of bamboo shoots, banana flowers, elephant apple, mustard greens, poultry in sesame-seed sauce, fish in *tenga* (sour) curry and items steamed in banana leaves. You'll be hard-pressed to find better Assamese cooking anywhere. The thalis, available for lunch and dinner, are superb samplers of owner-chef Dhruva Saikia's talent.

❶ Getting There & Away

Jorhat's small airport is 6km southwest of town. IndiGo (www.goindigo.in) flies daily to Kolkata; Jet Airways (www.jetairways.com) has a few flights per week to Guwahati and Mumbai.

Early-morning Assam State Transport Corporation buses depart from the central **ASTC bus station** (AT Rd), heading to Tezpur (₹140 to ₹180, 4½ hours, half-hourly 5.30am to 8am), Guwahati (₹330, eight hours, 7.40am), Sivasagar (₹50, 1½ hours, 6.45am), and Dibrugarh (₹120, 3½ hours, 6am). Later ASTC buses leave from the **ISBT** (Interstate Bus Terminus; AT Rd), 2km further west: to Tezpur (₹180 to ₹200, 11am and noon), to Guwahati (₹405, 8.15am, 9.30am, 11am and 2.30pm), and to Sivasagar (₹60) and Dibrugarh (₹180) at 7.30am, 8am, 9.30am, noon, 2.30pm, 4pm and 4.30pm. Most buses to Tezpur or Guwahati will drop you at Kohora (2½ hours, ₹90) for Kaziranga National Park.

Jorhat Town railway station is about 1.5km south of AT Rd. The 12068 Jan Shatabdi Express (AC chair ₹590, seven hours, 2.30pm Monday to Saturday) is the most convenient of the three trains to Guwahati.

Majuli Island

☎ 03775 / POP 168,000

Beached amid the mighty Brahmaputra River's ever-shifting puzzle of sandbanks is Majuli, which at around 350 sq km is India's largest river island. Though continually ravaged by the primal forces of nature (much of it disappears under water every monsoon, and it's steadily shrinking due to erosion), Majuli flaunts unparalleled scenic beauty. Coming here is like stepping back to an earlier India of little motor traffic (cycling is a delight), peaceful woodlands and wetlands, and Mishing tribal villages with wooden stilt houses, where the goats, geese, cows and pigs easily outnumber the people. The island's serene atmosphere is enhanced by the influence of its 22 *satras* (Hindu Vaishnavite monasteries and centres for art).

The two main villages are Kamalabari, 4km from the main ferry port, and Garamur, 5km further north. The ideal months to come are November to February.

🛏 Sleeping & Eating

Jyoti Home COTTAGE $$

(☑ 9435657282; jyoti24365@gmail.com; near Faru Satra, Garamur; s/d/tr incl breakfast ₹1000/1500/1800) Five invitingly cosy and clean bamboo and mud-plaster cottages, with semisoft beds and hot showers, are set round a pretty lawn and flower garden. It's run by the helpful Jyoti Narayan Sarma, who also organises **birdwatching outings** (☑ 9435657282; jyoti24365@gmail.com; Jyoti Home, near Faru Satra, Garamur; birdwatching for 2 ₹1000, bicycle hire per day ₹150), cooking classes and cycle hire. Veg/nonveg meals are ₹200/350.

La Maison de Ananda   GUESTHOUSE $$
(☑ 9957186356; www.facebook.com/lamaison deananda; Garamur; d ₹600-3000; ❄) This popular guesthouse has a variety of rooms ranging from an appealing bamboo-stilt cottage decked out in local fabrics to budget rooms where hot water comes by the bucket, plus a newer concrete block with comfortable AC rooms. It's run by a friendly tribal family, and the kitchen cooks up a range of good food including tasty Mishing dinners (₹350).

Mé:Po Okum   COTTAGE $$
(☑ 9435203165; harennarah14@gmail.com; Chitadar Chuk; d ₹1500) Nine basic but decent semi-traditional cottages ranged around a grassy, tree-girt space on the edge of a Mishing tribal village, Mé:Po Okum (Happy Home) is one of Majuli's best overnight options. You can order a tasty local dinner (₹550) that includes chicken cooked inside bamboo and two Mishing fish dishes. It's about 1.5km north of the middle of Garamur.

ℹ Getting There & Around

Crowded ferries to Majuli's Kamalabari Ghat (passenger/bicycle/car or jeep incl driver/goat/buffalo/basket of ducks ₹15/10/706/10/45/3, one hour) leave Nimati Ghat, 15km north of Jorhat, hourly (theoretically) from 7.30am to 3.30pm, and at 4pm. Timetables can vary according to demand, river conditions and season. Return trips (1½ hours) are also supposedly hourly from 7.30am to 2.30pm and at 3pm.

Tightly packed shared vans to Nimati Ghat (₹30, 30 minutes) leave every few minutes from the corner of AT and MG Rds in Jorhat (outside the City Bus Stand). An autorickshaw/taxi from Jorhat to Nimati Ghat should cost ₹250/350.

Vans and jeeps to Kamalabari (₹20, 10 minutes) and Garamur (₹30, 20 minutes) meet arriving ferries at Kamalabari Ghat.

With little traffic and no hills, Majuli is a joy to explore by bicycle. **Majuli Cycle Cafe** (☑ 7575915311; www.majulitourism.org; Garamur; mains ₹100-200; ☺ 8am-9pm) rents good B'Twin mountain bikes and has suggestions for enjoyable routes. Some lodgings also have bikes available.

Sivasagar

☑ 03772 / POP 50,800

Sivasagar (Sivsagar, Sibsagar) holds a special importance in Assam as the heartland of the Ahom kingdom, which was founded in 1228 and ended up ruling up most of Assam from the 16th to 19th centuries. Palaces, temples and other monuments from the Ahom heyday make for a great day's sightseeing in the countryside around Sivasagar, which is also a useful transit point into Nagaland.

◉ Sights

Three typical **Ahom temples** (Sivasagar tank, south side; ☺ dawn-dusk) rise proudly above the partly wooded shore of the graceful Sivasagar tank at the town's heart. The centrepiece is the 33m-high Shivadol, dedicated to Shiva. One of Assam's most important temples, it was built by Ambika, an Ahom queen, in 1734.

About 4km south of central Sivasagar along AT Rd, the two-storey, oval-shaped

---

MAJULI'S SATRAS

A *satra* is a monastery for Vishnu worship, Assam's distinctive form of Hinduism. Formulated by 15th-century Assamese philosopher Sankardev, the faith eschews the caste system and idol worship, focusing on Vishnu as God, especially in his Krishna incarnation. Much of the worship is based on dance, especially the classical Sattriya form, and melodramatic play-acting (known as *bhaona*) of scenes from Hindu mythology. You can see traditional dance masks, and artisans making them, at the small **Samaguri Satra** (☺ studio 9.30am-4.30pm) in the countryside 11km east of Kamalabari.

The most interesting and accessible *satras* include the large, beautifully peaceful Uttar Kamalabari (1km north, then 600m east of Kamalabari) and Auniati (5km west of Kamalabari) another large monastery, where you can visit a small **museum** (Auniati Satra; Indian/foreigner ₹10/50; ☺ 9.30-noon & 1-4pm) of Ahom royal artefacts. The best chances of observing chanting, dances or drama recitations are at the satras around dawn and dusk, or during the big three-night Raas Leela festival, celebrating Krishna, starting on the night of the November full moon.

pavilion **Rang Ghar** (Indian/foreigner ₹25/300; ⊙dawn-dusk) was built by King Pramatta Singha in 1746. Impeccably restored, its gleaming sienna exterior features pretty, mainly floral, carvings. Walk up to the top floor, from where the royalty watched buffalo and elephant fights and other entertainment. On the other side of AT Rd, a short distance further, you can explore the two surviving above-ground levels of **Talatal Ghar palace** (Indian/foreigner ₹25/300; ⊙dawn-dusk), the labyrinthine heart of an Ahom capital complex built in the 1750s. It originally had seven storeys, three of which were underground (including secret escape tunnels).

The somewhat-grandiose complex of **Gauri Sagar** (Indian/foreigner ₹25/300; ⊙dawn-dusk), 13km southwest of Sivasagar on the Jorhat road, comprises an attractive tank and a trio of distinctive 1720s temples built by the Ahom queen Phuleswari.

Southeast of Sivasagar at Garhgaon, climb to the top of the unique, four-storey, brick palace **Kareng Ghar** (Garhgaon; Indian/foreigner ₹25/300; ⊙dawn-dusk), which rises like a stepped pyramid above an attractive trees-and-paddy setting. It was built in 1752 as an addition to the pre-Sivasagar Ahom capital. It's about 15km along the Sivasagar–Sonari highway and down a village road: turn left just before Garhgaon itself.

The first Ahom capital was **Charaideo** (Indian/foreigner ₹25/300; ⊙dawn-dusk), established in 1228 by the dynasty's founder Sukapha after his arrival from Yunnan (southwestern China). The site, 28km east of Sivasagar, comprises a collection of large and small royal funerary mounds – known as *maidams* and still considered sacred – in a picturesque forest setting.

Sleeping & Eating

Reliable **Hotel Brahmaputra** (☎03772-222200; www.hotelbrahmaputra.com; BG Rd; incl breakfast with AC s ₹2130-3300, d ₹3620, s without AC ₹900; ❄📶), about 1.5km east of the centre, features 34 rooms that, despite varying sizes and levels of comfort, all guarantee cleanliness and value for money. Service is professional and helpful, and the in-house restaurant prepares a good complimentary breakfast.

Around 800m south of Sivasagar tank, the appealing **Hotel Shiva Palace** (☎03772-222629; hotelshivapalace.1811@rediffmail.com; AT Rd; incl breakfast s ₹900-3540, d ₹1340-4130; ❄📶) provides smart rooms with comfy beds, clean sheets and good bathrooms. The cheapest are not air-conditioned and are bare but are good budget options, while the pricier rooms easily meet business-hotel standards. Its classy restaurant, **Sky Chef** (mains ₹200-350; ⊙noon-10.30pm; ❄), is a great place for a well-prepared North Indian or Chinese dinner after a long day sightseeing.

Getting There & Around

The **ASTC Bus Station** (cnr AT & GNG Rds) has frequent services to Jorhat (₹40, 1½ hours) and Dibrugarh (₹80, 2½ hours) until 6pm. ASTC buses to Guwahati (non-AC/AC ₹390/470, nine hours) go at 8am, 9am, 8.15pm, 8.30pm and 9pm: these can drop you at Kohora (Kaziranga National Park) en route. ASTC buses to Sonari (₹40 to ₹50, 1½ hours) go at 8am, 2pm and 3pm.

The most convenient and effective way to explore the monuments around Sivasagar is by taxi, or for shorter trips by tempo (large autorickshaw). You can find both on AT Rd opposite the ASTC Bus station, or for cars try nearby **Avijatri Travels** (☎9854775477; www.ajtravelsassam.com; GNG Rd; ⊙8am-10pm). A half-day trip covering Rang Ghar, Talatal Ghar, Gauri Sagar and Kareng Ghar costs around ₹700 by tempo and ₹1500 by taxi. An AC car taking in Chairaideo too should not be more than ₹2300.

Dibrugarh

☎0373 / POP 144,000

The growing, crowded and noisy city of Dibrugarh, on the south shore of the Brahmaputra, is the centre of India's most productive tea-growing district and a useful transport hub for upper Assam, central Arunachal Pradesh and northern Nagaland.

Sleeping & Eating

Hotel Rajawas HOTEL $$

(☎0373-2323307; http://hotelrajawas.com; AT Rd, Chotagola; s/d without AC ₹1000/1680, with AC incl breakfast s ₹2020-3070, d ₹2690-3540; ❄📶) The well-run Rajawas has 30 understated but spotless, comfortable rooms with in-room wi-fi. Staff are on the ball and Moti Mahal Delux (p571), one of Dibrugarh's best restaurants, is right here.

Mancotta Heritage Chang Bungalow BUNGALOW $$$

(☎0373-2301120; www.purvidiscovery.com; Mancotta Rd; incl breakfast s ₹5310, d ₹10,880-12,800; ❄📶) The best place to enjoy a planter-style cuppa, Mancotta has very comfortable rooms in a charming tea-estate bungalow fronted by lawns and lush gardens, 4km south of town. It also arranges tea tours and river cruises on request.

Moti Mahal Delux   NORTH INDIAN $$$
(Hotel Rajawas, AT Rd; mains ₹300-500; ⊘ noon-10.30pm; ✱) Hotel Rajawas boasts the polished Moti Mahal restaurant, popular with the town's gastronomes and serving superb North Indian food, including staples such as chicken tikka masala and *palak paneer* (unfermented cheese chunks in a pureed spinach gravy), as well as several *makhani* specialities (made with butter) including dhal makhani, *paneer makhani* and butter chicken.

ⓘ Getting There & Away

From Mohanbari Airport, 16km northeast of Dibrugarh, IndiGo and Spicejet fly to Guwahati and Kolkata daily. Air India flies to Kolkata five times weekly, and to Guwahati and Delhi twice.

Both ASTC and private buses depart from the **ASTC bus station** (TR Phukan Rd, Chowkidinghee) for Sivasagar (₹90, two hours, frequent 7.30am to 10.30am), Jorhat (₹160, three hours, frequent 7.30am to 10.30am), Tezpur (eight hours; non-AC ₹320, 7.30am; AC ₹395, 8.15am) and Guwahati (₹500 to ₹800, nine to 10 hours, 7.30am, 8am, frequent 7pm to 10pm).

A daily bus service from Dibrugarh to Pasighat in Arunachal Pradesh was launched in 2019 by Arunachal Pradesh State Transport Services, travelling via the new 5km-long Bogibil (Bogibeel) Bridge over the Brahmaputra, 15km downstream from Dibrugarh.

From Dibrugarh Town train station in the town centre, the overnight 12423 Dibrugarh Town Rajdhani Express leaves for Guwahati (3AC/2AC/1AC ₹1195/1625/2600, 8.35pm, 10 hours).

ARUNACHAL PRADESH

Virginal Arunachal Pradesh appears as a giant patch of green on India's map. The country's wildest and least explored state, Arunachal (literally, Land of Dawn-Lit Mountains) rises abruptly from the Assam plains as a mass of improbably steep and densely forested hills, culminating in snow-capped peaks along the Tibetan border. Arunachal lures travellers with the promise of adventurous journeys to remote mountain valleys and encounters with some of its 26 indigenous tribal peoples. Tourism infrastructure – such as hotels or even homestays – has yet to reach many areas; this is travel far beyond standard tourist trails.

China has never formally recognised Indian sovereignty here, and even invaded Arunachal briefly in 1962. Border passes are heavily guarded by the Indian military, but the atmosphere is generally calm. Arunachal has been relatively untouched by political violence, though Naga rebels are active in the state's far southeastern corner.

Western Arunachal Pradesh

A mighty gash in the earth fringed by magnificent mountains and speckled with gold-and-white gompas (Tibetan Buddhist monasteries), the Shangri La–like Tawang Valley awaits at the end of a long, spectacular route up from the Brahmaputra plains. Getting here is an adventure in itself as you zigzag up and down mountainsides where colourful prayer flags and stupas proliferate, while the lush jungle gradually gives way to icy passes and peaks. Most of the population in and en route to Tawang are Monpa, a Buddhist people who historically had their closest links with Tibet.

Climate

October and November are particularly beautiful months to travel this route, with clear weather, waterfalls and the brightly coloured cosmos shrubs along the tarmac. From December to February be prepared for intense cold and snow, while in June through August, views may be hidden by the clouds.

ⓘ Getting There & Away

Budget at least six days for the return trip from Guwahati or Tezpur, including one for breakdowns, unavailable tickets or roads blocked by landslides, mud or snow.

Cramped 10-passenger Sumo jeeps ply the routes to Tawang from Tezpur and Guwahati. It's a scenic but tiring ride from either place and it makes sense to break the journey at Bomdila or Dirang. Those travelling with tour operators will have the luxury of riding in more comfortable vehicles.

Bomdila

☑ 03782 / POP 8300 / ELEV 2430M

About one-third of the journey time from Tezpur to Tawang, Bomdila is a pleasant small town winding lazily up a hillside, with the large Gaden Rabgye Ling (GRL) Buddhist monastery at the top (about 2600m), some 200m higher than the centre. If you're overnighting here, there isn't much to do apart from exploring the market or visiting the colourful monastery.

Just below the monastery, **Doe-Gu-Khil Guest House** (☏03782-223232; Monastery Hill; r ₹900-1750; ☏) provides fabulous views over Bomdila from simply appointed but very clean and well-kept rooms. Meals are fresh and delicious, and staff are charming. Centrally located **Hotel Tsepal Yangjom** (☏03782-223473, 8729881887; www.hoteltse-palyangjom.in; Bazar Line; r ₹3140-5950; ☏) is the most comfortable lodging, with wood-panelled rooms equipped with soft beds, tea and coffee makers, floor rugs and heaters. Its popular restaurant (mains ₹120 to ₹300) serves well-prepared Indian, Chinese and local Arunachal dishes.

Sumo jeeps, and the few bus services, depart from outside the Buddha Stadium on the main road. Book (the day before for Sumos) at counters in the basement of the 'Urban Shopping Complex', opposite. Sumos head to Dirang (₹150, 1½ hours, 9.30am), Tawang (₹500, eight hours, 6am), Tezpur (₹600, four hours, 5.30am and 12.30pm), Guwahati (₹700, nine hours, 6am) and Itanagar (₹900, nine hours, 6am). A Network Travels bus leaves for Guwahati (₹600, nine hours) at 3pm.

Dirang

☑03780 / POP 3750 / ELEV 1620M

Dirang, on the icy-blue Dirang River, is a good stop en route to Tawang, with some interesting spots to visit nearby. Five kilometres south of the main town is the Monpa village of Old Dirang. Steps up from the main road (50m south of the bridge) lead through a stout stone gate into an old citadel, Dirang Dzong, with a huddle of stone-and-wood houses.

The most splendid Buddhist monastery in the area is the Thupsung Dhargyeling Gompa, consecrated by the Dalai Lama in 2017, 20 minutes' walk up from Dirang's central crossroads. Another interesting excursion is to the historic fortified Monpa village of Thembang, 25km east, which also has homestays. Ask at Awoo Resort.

🛏 Sleeping

Hotel Pemaling　　　　　　HOTEL **$$**
(☏8258919962; www.hotelpemaling.com; NH13; d ₹1790-2950, tr/ste ₹3540/4720; ☏) Hotel Pemaling is an excellent family-run hotel with smart rooms, great service, good Indian and Chinese food (mains ₹150 to ₹250) and a pleasant garden where you can enjoy views of the river below and the mountains above. It's 1.5km south of New Dirang, near the petrol pump.

Awoo Resort　　　　　　　RESORT **$$**
(☏9862941109; www.awooresort.com; Busuthang-kha; d ₹1680-4130; ☏) Awoo Resort, on a green hillside site 1km south of New Dirang, has good-value, very clean rooms, some with cosy wood panelling. There's also a decent multicuisine restaurant.

❶ Getting There & Away

Counters on the main street, Bazar Line, sell tickets for shared jeeps to Tawang (₹500, six hours, 7am) and Tezpur (₹700, six hours, 6.30am). For taxis (jeep to Tawang ₹5000) ask at Dirang Valley Tours & Travels. Sonam Galaxy, around the corner at the north end of Bazar Line, sells tickets for jeeps to Guwahati (₹700, 11 hours, 6am) and Itanagar (₹1000, 10 hours, 6.30am).

Dirang to Tawang

Climbing from Dirang, Arunachal's most perilous road is a seemingly endless series of hairpin turns, which pass several army camps and landslide zones to finally top off at the Se La, an icy 4176m pass that breaches the mountains and provides access to Tawang. The pass is sometimes blocked by snow or landslides, so enquire in advance if the road is open, and keep a day or two up your sleeve in case of delays.

From the pass, the road dives down the mountainside into the Tawang Valley. En route, a 1km detour below Jang, the beautiful Nuranang Falls cascade down steep cliffs and continue as a streak of silvery rivulet down the gorge.

There are no sleeping options along the way, so complete the 140km stretch from Dirang to Tawang before sundown. Snacks and tea are available in cafeterias at Se La and the Jaswantgarh War Memorial, 20km down the road.

Tawang Valley

☑03794 / POP 11,200 (TAWANG TOWN) / ELEV 3000M (TAWANG TOWN)

Tawang's setting is more beautiful than the town itself, but murals of auspicious Buddhist emblems and colourful prayer wheels add interest to the central Old Market area.

ARUNACHAL'S TRIBAL GROUPS

An astonishing patchwork of ethnic populations separated by rugged geography, Arunachal is home to 26 main tribal groups, including the Adi (Abor), Nyishi, Tagin, Galo, Apatani and Monpa people. Hindi serves as the lingua franca between the speakers of some 30 different tribal tongues.

Modernity is making inroads into traditional society, with, for example, many new buildings being constructed of concrete instead of wood and thatch, and young people turning their backs on agricultural village life in favour of education and towns. Most ethnic identities remain strong however, and tribes manage to straddle the boundary between old and new – it's not uncommon to see a modern concrete building fitted with a traditional open-hearth kitchen over bamboo flooring.

Christianity is now the state's most popular religion, followed by one-third of residents. The Donyi-Polo (sun and moon worship) religion is an institutionalised form of traditional animist beliefs first developed in the 1970s in response to the spread of Christianity. Donyi-Polo has its own temples and the Donyi-Polo flag, a red sun on a white background, flies on tall poles outside many houses.

Traditional dress is rarely seen today, but for ceremonial occasions, village chiefs typically wear scarlet shawls and a bamboo wicker hat spiked with porcupine quills or hornbill beaks. Women favour handwoven wraparounds like Southeast Asian sarongs, while some of the older men still wear their hair long, with a topknot above their foreheads.

Architecture varies from tribe to tribe – traditional Adi villages are generally the most photogenic, with luxuriant palmyra-leaf thatching on stilted houses and wobbly bamboo suspension bridges strung across river gorges.

◉ Sights

★ Tawang Gompa   BUDDHIST MONASTERY

(⊘ dawn-dusk) The magical Tawang Gompa, founded in 1681 in what was then a Monpa royal palace, overlooks the town from its ridgetop site. Reputedly the world's second-largest Buddhist monastery complex after Drepung Monastery (in Lhasa, Tibet), Tawang has over 400 lamas, whose yellow-roofed living quarters surround the central buildings. It's famed in Buddhist circles for its priceless library, standing next to a magnificently decorated prayer hall that contains an 8m-high Buddha statue. Come at dawn to witness monks performing early-morning prayers.

Across the courtyard from the prayer hall is a **museum** (Tawang Gompa; ₹20; ⊘ 9am-5pm) containing images, robes, trumpets, gongs and ancient masks and manuscripts, along with some personal items of the sixth Dalai Lama and (upstairs) photos of visits by the 14th Dalai Lama and Indian leaders. Three days of spectacular masked *chaam* dances are held in the courtyard during the Torgya festival (p564).

Urgelling Gompa   BUDDHIST MONASTERY

(⊘ vary) **FREE** The ancient if modest Urgelling Gompa, a 3km walk below Tawang town, is where the sixth Dalai Lama, a Monpa, was born in 1683. Before he left for Lhasa, it's said that he stuck his walking stick into the ground just inside the monastery gate and it eventually grew into a giant oak tree. Within the main hall are hand-painted portraits of all the Dalai Lamas, and imprints of the forehead and feet of the sixth Dalai Lama.

Khinmey Gompa   BUDDHIST MONASTERY

(Khinmey Village; ⊘ 9.30am-noon & 2-5pm) This beautiful monastery in a tiny village east of Tawang (9km by vehicle, 6km on foot) is well worth a visit. Its current head, the Thegtse Rinpoche, is the 14th reincarnation of the guru who founded it in 1440. The main prayer hall is covered with fantastic, brightly coloured murals of hundreds of deities and presided over by the fierce-looking Buddhist sage Padmasambhava, flanked by his Indian and Tibetan wives.

🛏 Sleeping

Tawang town has plenty of midrange and budget hotels, guesthouses and homestays. A top budget choice is **Monyul Lodge** (☑ 9402910061; www.monyullodgetawang.in; Old Market; d/tr ₹1000/1200), in the heart of the market area, with fresh sheets, plenty of air and sunlight, and a restaurant serving Indian and Tibetan food.

PERMITS FOR THE NORTHEAST STATES

Rules and regulations about visiting the Northeast States change from time to time, but as of 2019, Arunachal Pradesh was the only Northeast state requiring foreign visitors to obtain a permit – in this case the Protected Area Permit (PAP), without which you cannot enter the state. The PAP is valid for 30 days from its specified starting date and costs the rupee equivalent of US$30 (US$60 for solo-traveller permits), with applications normally processed in two working days or less.

A minimum of two foreigners must apply together for the PAP, except for visits to Tawang (and places en route such as Bomdila and Dirang) and the Ziro Valley, for which solo travellers can obtain permits. In general, permits have to be applied for by registered tour operators: see the list at www.arunachaltourism.com/tour-operators.php. If you are organising your trip with a tour operator, they will normally obtain your PAP for you. Some tour operators will obtain PAPs for tourists who are not using other services from them, usually for a cost of around ₹3000.

Independent travellers can obtain PAPs without tour-operator sponsorship at the Arunachal Pradesh Deputy Resident Commissioner's offices in Guwahati (p562) and Kolkata (☑ 033-23341243; CE-109, Sector 1, Salt Lake City). At research time the Guwahati office was also able to put separate solo travellers together on one group permit, thus enabling them to visit areas beyond Tawang and Ziro.

Indians need an Inner Line Permit (ILP) to visit Arunachal Pradesh, Mizoram or Nagaland. These normally cost ₹100 or less and, depending on the state, can be applied for online, on arrival, or at the state's representatives in some other states.

Whatever permit you get, make several copies of it as you'll often have to hand one in at checkpoints, police stations and hotels.

Sonam Tsomu Homestay GUESTHOUSE $$

(☑ 9436051035; www.facebook.com/anasonamtsomuhomestaytawang; r ₹1600-1950) Sonam's stands in a wonderful position on the monastery ridge with great views in all directions. The seven clean and cosy rooms are equipped with hot-water bathrooms and heaters, and Tibetan, Indian and Chinese meals are available in the panoramic dining room with traditional low seating.

Hotel Gakyi Khang Zhang HOTEL $$

(☑ 9436045064, 03794-224647; www.gkztawang.com; near DC Office; r ₹1680-2910; ☎) A kilometre out of town, just off the road to Tawang Gompa, the GKZ has some of the best rooms around: they're clean and comfortable, many with distant views of the monastery. It has power backup, a decent restaurant and helpful, amiable staff.

Dolma Khangsar GUESTHOUSE $$

(☑ 9436051011; www.dolmahotels.com; Gompa AIR Rd; r ₹1750-3250; ☎) Dolma Khangsar has a great location on the monastery hill, just 300m from Tawang Gompa's entrance arch. Cosy rooms have colourful blankets and rugs, and heaters for cold mountain nights. Potted plants brighten up the balconies and yard, and a panoramic roof terrace makes the most of the position. Meals available.

Eating & Drinking

Tawang Food Court TIBETAN, INDIAN $

(Nehru Market, opposite Mon Paradise; mains ₹80-150; ⊙ 7.30am-11pm) Happily this is not a food court, but a relaxed gathering place where locals and visitors alike can enjoy wine (from ₹80 a glass), whisky or rum alongside tasty preparations like *momos* (Tibetan dumplings), egg *bhujia* (scrambled with onion, chilli and tomato), Bhutanese *dazhi* preparations or a 'Monpa thali', which is actually a good cheese-and-vegie dish served with rice.

★ Dharma Coffee House CAFE

(⊙ 9.30am-7pm) A stunning find on the road to Tawang Gompa, this alpine-style wood-and-brick cafe brews proper cappuccino, a range of teas and delicious cakes (banana-walnut, pineapple upside-down) as well as other comfort foods. With its clean, calm environment, cushioned cane seating and glass-topped tables, it's the kind of place you'd be happy to discover in the Alps or Scandinavia.

❶ Getting There & Around

Leaving Tawang, Sumos depart at 5.30am for Dirang (₹500, six hours), Bomdila (₹500, eight hours), Tezpur (₹1000, 12 hours) and Guwahati

(₹1400, 17 hours). Buy tickets at least one day before at counters in the centre including **Tribal Discovery** (☑ 9436045075; www.tribaldiscovery.org; Old Market; ☺ 4am-8pm), which also has an 11.30am bus to Tezpur (₹710, 13 hours) every two days. On the alternate days, there's a government-run 11.30am Tezpur bus (₹650) from the **APSTC bus stand** (Old Market) down the street.

Taxis will run you to Tawang's outlying monasteries for ₹200 to ₹400 round trip. There's a stand at the east end of Old Market.

Itanagar

☑ 0360 / POP 60,000 / ELEV 300M

Arunachal's capital takes its name from the mysterious Ita Fort, whose 14th- to 15th-century brick ruins crown a hill above the burgeoning mercantile town. Itanagar is a somewhat-characterless concrete creation, but it's quite green and leafy away from the roaring, honking NH415, which runs across town from southwest to northeast. The bustling Ganga Market area is the approximate midpoint and town centre.

**Jawaharlal Nehru
State Museum**   MUSEUM
(Museum Rd; Indian/foreigner ₹10/75, camera ₹20; ☺ 10am-4pm Tue-Sat) With two spacious floors of well-displayed exhibits, the state museum gives a decent representation of Arunachal Pradesh's tribal cultures, especially their crafts, costumes, adornments and tools.

Hotel Arun Subansiri   HOTEL $$
(☑ 0360-2212806; Zero Point Tinali; d with AC ₹2745, s/d without AC ₹1680/1900; ❄☏) With an oversized foyer that would be better suited as a car showroom, the Arun Subansiri won't win any style points. However, it does have comfortable, large rooms with clean bathrooms, firm beds and in-room wi-fi. It's towards the east end of town, within walking distance of the museum.

Hotel SC Continental   HOTEL $$$
(☑ 9436075875; www.hotelsccontinental.com; Vivek Vihar; s/d incl breakfast from ₹3780/4250; ❄@) The SC has very comfortable rooms with tea and coffee makers and reasonably consistent wi-fi in a quiet neighbourhood. The in-house **Fire & Ice restaurant** (mains ₹250-425; ☺ 7am-11pm; ❄) serves good Indian and Chinese fare. To get here, go about 1km southwest down the main road from the Ganga Market, then take the signposted slip road that hairpins to the right.

❶ Getting There & Away

The **APSTS bus stand** (Ganga Market) has services to Guwahati (₹500, 10 hours, 6am and 5pm), Bomdila (₹510, eight hours, 3.30pm), Pasighat (₹330, nine hours, 5.30am and 11am), Aalo (₹500, 14 hours, 2.30pm) and Shillong (₹610, 13 hours, 4pm).

Counters for Sumo jeep services cluster around the bus-stand entrance. Jeeps depart for Bomdila (₹900, nine hours, 6am), Tawang (₹1600, 17 hours, 5.30am), Ziro (₹400, five hours, 5.30am and 10.30pm), Aalo (₹800, 11 hours, 5.30am and 4.30pm) and Pasighat (₹450, nine hours, 5.30am and noon).

The nearest railway station is Naharlagun, 15km east of Itanagar. For Guwahati, the 12087 Shatabdi Express (chair car ₹690, six hours) departs at 5am Tuesday, Thursday and Saturday, and the 15618 Donyi Polo Express (sleeper/3AC/2AC ₹220/600/830, 10 hours) goes daily at 6.45pm.

Central Arunachal Pradesh

For intrepid travellers, central Arunachal Pradesh promises some of the Northeast's most exciting adventures, from tribal encounters in the picturesque Ziro Valley to thrilling excursions in isolated mountain areas like Mechuka or Pemako, all against a never-ending backdrop of spectacular scenery.

In India's tribal heartland, food includes several indigenous species such as mice, tadpoles, silkworm pupae, *mithun* (a semidomesticated bovine native to Northeast India and neighbouring countries), snails and fish such as silver carp. However, you can also find more typical Indian or Tibetan fare in most places.

❶ Getting Around

Roads in the region are mostly in poor to very poor condition and public transport is limited to a few shared jeeps and very few buses, plying routes between the main towns. The route from the Ziro Valley to Aalo via Daporijo is in especially bad shape, and most travel companies currently drive from Ziro to Aalo or Pasighat via North Lakhimpur and Silapathar in Assam.

Ziro Valley

☑ 03788 / POP 42,000 / ELEV 1600M

One of the prettiest landscapes in India, the fertile Ziro Valley is nestled among Arunachal's formidable mountains like a mythical kingdom. The layered landscape of rice fields, bamboo groves, pine forests and villages has been carefully fashioned over many centuries by its Apatani tribal inhabitants (today numbering about 30,000), whose clever use of the available land includes farming fish in the water of the irrigated rice paddies.

The traditional Apatani villages scattered around the valley are tightly packed with wooden stilt houses, though most of their roofs are now tin instead of thatch, and a growing number of people have moved into the valley's more modern two towns: Hapoli (also called New Ziro) in the south and the smaller Old Ziro in the north.

In villages, you may see older Apatani people who still have traditional facial tattoos and (for women) cane plugs that fit into the sides of the nose. The most traditional villages include Hong (the biggest, with around 4000 people), Hija and Bamin. It's best to visit villages with a local guide who can take you into a house or two and explain more about the local customs. Without a guide you may not feel particularly welcome.

Apatani traditions – including tribal dress, processions, communal hospitality, animal sacrifices and a fair amount of drinking – are most in evidence during annual festivals such as Murung (the first half of January) and Myoko (from 20 March to early April). The Ziro Music Festival (p564) takes place in September.

🏃 Activities

With over 300 bird and 170 butterfly species, clear mountain air and a combination of alpine and semitropical vegetation in the surrounding hills, the Ziro Valley has great natural attractions, and hiking and nature observation are growing in popularity here. **Brahmaputra Tours** (☑ 8575248013; www. brahmaputra-tours.com; Circuit House Rd, Hapoli) is a local specialist in birding and nature tours. The Tale Valley, some 32km east of Hapoli and a few hundred metres higher (often snow-covered in winter), has over 300 orchid and 25 rhododendron species.

A fully equipped four- or five-day camping trek with the NGO **NgunuZiro** (☑ 9856209494, 8974954810; www.facebook. com/NgunuZiro) costs around ₹3500 per person per day including guide, porters and wildlife-sanctuary entry fees. There is basic forest-refuge and dormitory accommodation in the valley and at Pange en route.

🛏 Sleeping & Eating

Homestays are the best way to experience Apatani hospitality. There are some 25 registered homestays in and around the valley, although standards vary widely. The best are mostly clustered around Siiro village, 3km southeast of Hapoli. You should call a few days ahead to give hosts time to prepare.

Best value in Hapoli itself is **Hotel Blue Pine** (☑ 8258926562; bluepinehotels@gmail. com; Pai Gate, Hapoli; s ₹1120, d ₹1340-2950), 1.5km from the Sumo stand. Its rooms (squat toilets in the cheapest) are decently maintained, with reasonably comfortable mattresses, and there's a restaurant serving staple Indian and Chinese dishes.

★ NgunuZiro Homestay   HOMESTAY $$

(☑ 9856209494; punyochada@gmail.com; Siiro Village; per person incl half board 1/2/3 or more people ₹1800/1500/1200) Deservedly one of the most popular homestays in the Ziro Valley. Host Punyo Chada speaks excellent English and is a great fount of information and conversation, while his wife Kaka prepares superb meals to be eaten around the communal fireplace. The two spotless, comfy rooms, with soft beds and large windows, are some of the best in the valley.

Hibu Tatu's Homestay   HOMESTAY $$

(☑ 9436224834; hibuatotatu@gmail.com; Siiro Village; per person incl half board 1/2/3 or more people ₹1800/1500/1200) Hibu Tatu's two rooms are big and spotless, with comfy beds and equally good bathrooms. The home cooking is delicious and the location is idyllic, set amid grassy meadows with the valley's only river trickling by out front. It's at the south end of Siiro village.

ⓘ Getting There & Away

Hapoli's Sumo stand is about 800m northeast of the main market. Sumos depart at 5.15am and about every 15 minutes from 9.30am to 11.30am for Naharlagun (₹350, four hours), Itanagar (₹400, five hours) and North Lakhimpur (₹330, six hours). An APSTS bus to Guwahati (₹550, 14 hours) leaves the Sumo stand at noon.

The train station at Naharlagun near Itanagar is a useful stepping stone for reaching the Ziro Valley. The overnight 15617 Donyi-Polo Express from Guwahati (departure 9.20pm) reaches Naharlagun at 5am (sleeper/3AC/2AC ₹200/590/830). A taxi/chartered Sumo from Naharlagun to Ziro costs around ₹5500/4000, but vehicles are not always available on demand. Make arrangements in advance if you can, for

TUTING & PEMAKO

In the far north of Arunachal Pradesh, the isolated town of Tuting sits not far south of the Tibetan border, where the Yarlung Tsangpo River, having crossed the Tibetan Plateau and burrowed through the Himalaya via a series of spectacular gorges, enters the Indian subcontinent and becomes the Siang. Steadily gaining a reputation as a thrilling whitewater-rafting destination, the perilous 180km stretch of the Siang from Tuting to Pasighat is littered with grade IV to V rapids, strong eddies and inaccessible gorges. This is for pros only.

Tuting is also the launch pad for the fabled land of Pemako, known in Buddhist legend as a gateway to the beyond and the earthly representation of the Tibetan goddess Dorje Phangmo (her breasts are two mountain peaks). Most visitors to this isolated and pristine mountain territory are Buddhist pilgrims travelling on foot – though a jeep road now reaches Dewa Kota Monastery, one of the main pilgrimage goals, about 60km up the Yangsang Valley from Tuting. Hardy trekkers (and pilgrims) can reach the mystical lake Danakosha (elevation 3750m) among snowy peaks. Agencies including Abor Country Travels (p565) offer Pemako treks lasting one to two weeks (around US$1500 to US$2500 per person); the best season is from late August to early November. It's also possible to reach Tuting independently by Sumo (there are public services from Pasighat to Yingkiong and from Yingkiong to Tuting, about six hours for each leg), and to find local guides (per day ₹2500) and porters (₹1000) in Tuting.

Two lovely rustic-style but very comfortable places to kick back before or after a Pemako trek are **Yamne Abor** ([phone] 9436053870; www.aborcountrytravels.com; Damroh Village; r incl breakfast ₹2500), near Damroh in the remote Yamne Valley between Pasighat and Yingkiong, and **Aborcountry River Camp** ([phone] 9436053870; www.aborcountrytravels.com; Rane Ghat; r incl breakfast ₹4500; [icon]), beside the Siang just outside Pasighat. Both belong to Abor Country Travels.

example through prebooked accommodation in Ziro.

Aalo

[phone] 03783 / POP 20,700 / ELEV 260M

The scruffy town of Aalo (Along) serves as the jumping-off point for Mechuka and is in the heart of the Adi tribal area. There are several picturesque Adi villages with large palm-thatched houses in the surrounding countryside.

Just off the road to Pasighat are two wobbly, cable-trussed bamboo-decked suspension bridges strung dramatically about 200m across the Siang River. One is 30km from Aalo, just upstream on the Siang from its confluence with the Siyom (a 2km detour off NH13); the other is a further 29km towards Pasighat and less than 100m off the highway.

With spacious and comfortable rooms, good service, a decent air-conditioned restaurant (Indian and Chinese mains ₹150 to ₹400) and a central location, **Hotel West** ([phone] 03783-222566; borahdebajit83@gmail.com; Medical Rd; d ₹600-1700; [icon]) is easily the best place in town to retire to after your day-

long journey. Alternatively, **Reyi Homestay** ([phone] 8794021061; eteliduk@gmail.com; SFS Nagar; s/d incl breakfast ₹1000/1500) has straightforward, clean and well maintained rooms with hot showers. What's special is the beautiful pine-and-bamboo house with spacious verandahs – it all overlooks the lush garden, orchards, fish ponds, forests and the owner's rice fields. It's 4km south of Aalo and a great stop if you're touring by car. It fills up during the peak season (October to February): book ahead.

Kiosks on Main Rd, Nehru Chowk, in the town centre sell tickets for Sumos to Mechuka (₹600, nine hours, 5.30am), Pasighat (₹400, five hours, 5.30am and 11.30am), North Lakhimpur (₹750, nine hours, 5.30am and 4.30pm) and Itanagar (₹800, 12 hours, 5.30am). Renting a Sumo to Mechuka costs ₹5500 one way or ₹14,000 for a three-day return trip.

Mechuka

[phone] 03793 / POP 2000 / ELEV 1920M

The remote valley of Mechuka (Menchukha) makes a wonderful excursion into the Arunachal uplands if you like road trips, hiking and pristine mountain country, and have at least three days to spare. At the end of a nine-hour drive climbing up through forested valleys from Aalo – a road which has only existed since 2007 – you emerge into a different world: a broad grassy valley between snow-capped mountains, watered by the swift Yargyap Chhu (Siyom River), dotted with Buddhist monasteries and precarious hanging bridges, with the colourfully painted wooden cottages of little Mechuka in its midst. Most of the population here is Memba, a Tibetan Buddhist people who are now divided by the international border between India and China.

The main visitor season here is the drier months of October through February. There's often snow in town from January through March.

Two good hikes from Mechuka are up Menchukha La, the treeless hill rising on the north side of the valley opposite town (five to six hours round trip), and over to Dorjiling village (about 1¼ hours one way). Both hikes start from the Bumjipanga vehicle bridge at the east end of Mechuka.

For guides (per day ₹1000) or multiday fully equipped and guided camping treks (per person per day ₹3500 to ₹4000) contact Gebu Sona of Menchukha Tours & Travels.

Thought to be about 400 years old, the charming wooden Samten Yongcha Gompa (Old Gompa) stands on a breezy hilltop 6km (as the crow flies) west of Mechuka, fronted by a forest of prayer flags and with wonderful panoramas over the valley, river and surrounding mountains. The caretaker will probably appear to show you round the two-storey temple with its colourful imagery, including some genuinely scary guardian deities.

🛏 Sleeping & Eating

Mechuka has at least six homestays, all offering reasonably priced meals (usually Tibetan or Indian) as well as lodging.

Gayboo's Traditional Lodge   GUESTHOUSE $
(☑ 9436074877; www.gtlhomestay.com; r ₹500-2000) Mechuka's longest-running guesthouse has 12 wood-panelled rooms with hard beds and varying levels of comfort according to price (shared bathrooms for the cheapest). It serves up satisfying meals (dinner veg/nonveg ₹200/300, breakfast ₹150) and owner Gebu Sona also runs Menchukha Tours & Travels (☑ 9436074877;

menchukhatravels@gmail.com; Gayboo's Traditional Lodge), organising tours and treks.

It's about 750m west of the town centre, on the south side of the airfield.

Yargyap Chhu Home Stay   HOMESTAY $
(☑ 9402663192; lakpasona1981@gmail.com; r ₹1000-1200) This excellent place sits in the countryside just 150m from the Bumjipanga bridge over the Yargyap Chhu. It has large, bright, pine-lined rooms with spotless bathrooms (buckets not showers). The three rooms in the newer building (2018) are particularly appealing. Tibetan and Indian food is available in the communal sitting and dining room, and guests can also cook for themselves if they wish.

ℹ Information

SBI ATM A couple of doors south of the town's central crossroads.

ℹ Getting There & Away

Sumo counters by the central crossroads sell tickets for Sumos departing for Aalo at 5am (₹600, nine hours).

Pasighat

☑ 0368 / POP 25,000 / ELEV 150M

This is where the Siang River surges out of the hills and starts its winding path across the plains, soon to become the Brahmaputra. Pasighat, which sits just next to the Siang, feels more like Assam than Arunachal Pradesh. In September the town hosts the Adi festival of **Solung** (⊙ Sep), but the rest of the year the most interesting sight is the sunrise over the gorgeous river.

In the town **Hotel Aane** (☑ 0368-2222777; MG Rd; d ₹1470-2470, s without bathroom ₹500; ❋) and **Hotel Serene Abode** (☑ 0368-2222382; www.thesereneabodehotel.com; NH515; incl breakfast d ₹2950-5310, s non-AC ₹1680; ❋ ☎) both provide good value for your money.

Aborcountry River Camp (p577) is a wonderful retreat with a handful of cosy rooms set in the forest just above the surging Siang River, across the bridge north of Pasighat. Great meals and drinks are served in an outdoor pavilion (lunch or dinner ₹500), and the camp has top-quality rafts designed specially for the Siang.

From the Sumo stand on the NH515 (old NH52) in the town centre, jeeps head to Aalo (₹400, five hours, 5.30am and 11.30am), Itanagar (₹450, eight hours, 6am and noon), Damroh (₹350, four hours, 6am and noon), Yingkiong (₹500, six hours, 6am and 12.30pm) and Dibrugarh (₹350, four hours, 5am). Bus services to Dibrugarh began in 2019 following the opening of the 5km-long Bogibil Bridge over the Brahmaputra near Dibrugarh.

NAGALAND

Long considered the 'wild east' of India, Nagaland abounds in primeval beauty and tribal culture. Its dazzling hills and valleys, reaching right up to the India–Myanmar border, are other-worldly places where, until not long ago, headhunting Naga tribes fought off intruders and each other. Today Nagas have abandoned headhunting and turned to Christianity. Traditional lifestyles linger strongest in the north, where many people live in thatched longhouses and follow farming and hunting lifestyles. The sense of Naga identity among the 16 or 17 main tribal groups, with multiple languages but cultural similarities, is strong. Traditional attire comes out in full feather-and-spear colour at the many tribal festivals, above all December's Hornbill Festival near Kohima.

🛈 Information

Foreigners are supposed to register at the district Superintendent of Police's office within 24 hours of arrival. In practice this almost always happens automatically as part of the check-in procedure at your hotel.

Dimapur

✒ 03862 / POP 123,000 / ELEV 150M

The flat, uninspiring commercial centre of Nagaland, Dimapur has little to detain visitors, but thanks to possessing Nagaland's only airport and railway station, it's a key access point for Kohima and much of the rest of the state.

Six hotels for a variety of budgets are found along the main drag running east from the railway station.

Just a 10-minute autorickshaw ride (₹200) from Dimapur's airport, **Longchen Homestay** (✒ 8638803298; www.facebook.com/longchenhomestay; House 75B, Lane 2, Ao Yimti Village; d incl breakfast ₹2900; ❄ 🛜) is a great spot to relax, with charmingly welcoming hosts. Four spacious, spotless rooms with broad verandahs overlook the family's rice paddies, and two separate-sex three-bed dorms with

bathrooms should be operational by the time you read this. The dinners (₹300 to ₹350, including a spicy Naga option) are delicious.

Ao Yimti village is entered from the 4km junction on the Kohima road, 3km east of central Dimapur.

🛈 Getting There & Away

From Dimapur's tiny airport, 1km off the Kohima road and 5km from the town centre, Air India (www.airindia.com) and IndiGo (www.goindigo.in) fly daily to Kolkata, with the IndiGo flight continuing to Delhi.

Seven-passenger vans depart when full for Kohima (₹300, 3½ hours, 6am to 5pm) from the yard in front of the railway station. Fourteen-passenger Winger minibuses to Imphal (₹700, nine hours) leave at 6.30am, 10.30am and 8.30pm from the **Blue Hill Stand** (Golaghat Rd), 250m north from the west end of the railway station's northern footbridge.

Several daily trains go to Guwahati, including the 15670 Nagaland Express at 6am (2nd-class seat/3AC/2AC ₹105/495/700, 5¼ hours), and to Dibrugarh.

Kohima

✒ 0370 / POP 115,000 / ELEV 1450M

Scattered across a series of forested ridges and hilltops, Nagaland's capital might on first appearance seem drab and uninspiring, but on closer acquaintance you'll find it's a relatively prosperous place with warm and helpful people, and without the excessive crowds and noise of many other cities. You'll also find that almost everyone has a working knowledge of English, thanks to it being the language of instruction in Nagaland schools. The festive Christmas week is a particularly beautiful time to be in Kohima. On Sundays nearly all businesses and many sights are shut, but it's a delightfully tranquil day to wander round town.

⊙ Sights

★ **Kohima War Cemetery**   CEMETERY
(TCP Junction; ⊙ 8.30am-3.30pm Mar-Oct, to 3pm Nov-Feb) The immaculately maintained war cemetery contains the graves of over 1400 British, Indian and other Allied soldiers, killed in or around Kohima in 1944 as they resisted a Japanese invasion of India from Burma in one of the fiercest battles of WWII. The cemetery is laid out on what were the terraced lawns of the British Deputy Commissioner's bungalow. Some of the most savage fighting took place across the tennis

court near the top, where the white marker lines are still in place.

A disabled tank from the battle remains in situ among trees just above the Imphal road, 550m further up from the cemetery gate, with a sign explaining its dramatic story.

State Museum
MUSEUM

(Bayavu Hill; ₹10, camera/video ₹50/100; ⊙9.30am-3.30pm Mon-Sat) This well-presented government museum, 2km north of Kohima's centre, has galleries on two floors featuring tribal costumes, weapons, musical instruments, sports and jewellery. It's a good place to acquaint yourself with the diverse customs, cultures and crafts of the different Naga tribes – but a map of who's where would be helpful.

Central Market
MARKET

(Super Market; UBC Church Rd; ⊙6am-4pm Mon-Sat) This small but fascinating market outside the Kohima Local Ground stadium, off Razhü Junction, is a compendium of exotic Naga tribal foods with such delicacies as *mefi* (wriggling hornet grubs), frogs, silkworms, snails, crabs in small bamboo baskets, dried fish, dog meat, exotic condiments such as dried and fermented bamboo shoots, fiery Raja (King) chillies and plenty of vegetables.

⭐ Festivals & Events

⭐ Hornbill Festival
CULTURAL

(www.hornbillfestival.com; ⊙1-10 Dec) Nagaland's biggest annual jamboree, the Hornbill Festival is celebrated at the Naga Heritage Village, 10km south of Kohima. Naga tribes converge for a 10-day cultural, dance and sporting bash, much of it in full warrior costume. Of all the Northeast's festivals, this is the most spectacular and photogenic. Some events including night markets and parades take place in Kohima itself.

🛏 Sleeping

Some places multiply their rates threefold during the Hornbill Festival (early December) when everything fills up, so book well in advance. Some hotels open reservations a year ahead.

⭐ Razhü Pru
GUESTHOUSE $$

(☑9402900718; www.razhupru.com; Mission Compound; r incl breakfast ₹2500-4000; ❋🐾) A 1940s family home thoughtfully converted into a guesthouse, Razhü Pru packs a diverse array of Naga heirlooms and artefacts into its wood-panelled living areas. The nine rooms are equipped with comfortable beds, elegant cane furniture and ethnic fabrics, and management is superhelpful. The kitchen serves excellent food including a superb Naga meal (₹550).

Morung Lodge
GUESTHOUSE $$

(☑9862528288; Upper Midland; dm ₹600-1000, d ₹2500) A rare economical option in the centre, with good standards of cleanliness, homey Morung has two small dorms and two doubles with attached bathrooms, plus a plant-decked rear terrace with expansive city views. It's 70m down the first lane to the left as you go south from the central Dzüdou Junction.

Blue Bayou
HOTEL $$

(☑0370-2292008; thebluebayoukohima@gmail.com; opposite War Cemetery entrance; r incl breakfast with AC ₹4720-6490, without AC ₹2950-3540; ❋🐾) Professionally run and central, Blue Bayou provides well-kept rooms, many with gorgeous valley views. There's a good restaurant (mains ₹120 to ₹200) and the hotel's popularity means it's booked out at least nine months ahead for December's Hornbill Festival.

de Oriental Grand
HOTEL $$$

(☑0370-2260052; www.deorientalgrand.com; High School Rd, Themezie; s/d incl breakfast ₹4480/5070; ❋🐾) De Oriental Grand's wood-panelled rooms live up to the promise of the glittering lobby, with deep mattresses, spotless linen and modern bathrooms. The restaurant does an unusually good range of pan-Asian and Continental dishes (mains ₹300 to ₹450). It's about 2km north of the centre.

🍴 Eating & Drinking

Hotels often have multicuisine restaurants where you can eat Indian, Chinese and international dishes as well as Naga specialities. Kohima also has a good selection of cafes. Nagaland is a dry state, but guests can get alcoholic drinks in some hotels.

Ozone Cafe
CAFE $$

(Razhü Junction; mains ₹110-250; ⊙11am-5pm Mon-Sat; 🐾) This central cafe has a sprawling gymnasium-style dining area, where all types of Kohima citizens come to catch up over a variety of dishes including *momos* (Tibetan dumplings), fried rice, burgers, chocolate brownies and drinks such as blueberry green tea or milkshakes.

DZÜKOU VALLEY

This 'hidden valley' at an altitude of around 2500m in the mountains south of Kohima makes a wonderful nature trip if you're prepared for a bit of steep uphill hiking. Dzükou is famed for its monsoon wildflowers (orchids, lilies, rhododendrons) but it has a magical, other-worldly atmosphere any time of year.

Kohima agencies offer guided trips but it's quite feasible to visit Dzükou independently. The trails can be hiked at any time of year and the routes are mostly obvious. Bring warm clothing and, if staying over, preferably a sleeping bag.

The valley is accessible from both Zakhama (Jakhama) and Viswema villages, respectively 16km and 21km south of Kohima on NH2 (old NH39). Shared jeeps leave for Zakhama (₹50, 35 minutes) and Viswema (₹60, 45 minutes) from about 6am to 4pm from outside **Network Travels** (☑ 9436001229; NH2, AOC) in southern Kohima.

A good plan is to go up from Viswema (the less steep approach) and then descend to Zakhama. From Viswema you can hire a jeep to cover the first 8km up the hill for around ₹1500, leaving you with only about one hour's steep uphill walking to the lip of the valley.

At the end of the jeep track up from Viswema, an obvious track leads ahead into the forest from the small parking area. Go 20m along this, then turn right up a narrow path with rough stone steps. The steps lead steeply up through eerily silent cloud forest to reach the edge of the Dzükou Valley after 1.1km. From here follow the path across the hillside to the right: you'll soon see the **Dzükou Valley Guesthouse** (Dzükou Valley; dm/r per person ₹50/150; ☉ year-round) ahead of you. It takes about 1¼ hours to reach it. At the guesthouse you pay your one-time valley entrance fee (Indian/foreigner ₹50/100). It has two large dorms, where you sleep on the floor, and five very basic private rooms with boards to sleep on and private squat toilets. You can also get basic meals and hot drinks here, and they have a limited number of blankets (₹50), foam mats (₹50) and sleeping bags (₹100) to rent.

Various trails weaving around the valley make for a fine day's vagabonding. One good goal is a cross-topped hill, about three hours' round-trip walk from the guesthouse.

To descend to Zakhama, retrace your steps from the guesthouse for nearly 1km and fork left at an 'Alternate Trek Route' sign. From here it's 15 minutes up to the edge of the valley, then about three hours down through the forest to NH2. When you hit the main road, walk 1.5km to the left to the Zakhama jeep stand. The last jeep to Kohima normally leaves around 5pm, but some days it's earlier.

D/Café CAFE
(1st fl, KF Complex, Jail Colony; ☉ 9.30am-8.30pm Mon-Sat) An artsy gathering place with sofas in one corner, D/Café brews freshly roasted organic coffee (including French press, mocha and Turkish) and tasty nibbles including omelettes, waffles, salads and chicken kebabs. There's live music on Wednesday afternoons or evenings (any time from 3.30pm).

ⓘ Information

Ara Travels (☑ 9436000759; yiese_neitho@ rediffmail.com; A Angami, VK Complex, Science College Rd, Jail Colony; guides per day ₹2500; ☉ 10am-4pm Mon-Sat) Guiding services and travel info about Nagaland.

ⓘ Getting There & Arond

The **NST bus station** (Main Town) has one daily bus to Imphal (₹200, six hours, 7.30am). There's no advance booking so get there early. Another option for Imphal is to get a Dimapur–Imphal minibus to pick you up at TCP Junction as they pass through Kohima (normally around 9.30am, 1.30pm and 11.30pm). Call the **Dimapur Winger counter** (☑ 9615847331). You may have to pay the full Dimapur–Imphal fare (₹700) or even more.

Seven-passenger vans depart for Dimapur (₹300, 3½ hours, from 5am) when full, from the street corner at the south end of the NST bus station.

City Stationery (☑ 7085553325; Main Town), opposite IDBI Bank, has comfortable seven-passenger Innova cars departing for Shillong (₹1200, 10 hours) at 6am Monday to Saturday.

A car and driver for a day out to Kisama and Khonoma costs about ₹2500.

Taxis charge ₹100 for anything up to about 3km, and ₹150 to the city outskirts. City buses (₹10) run up and down the main road through town, all terminating at Razhü Junction in the centre. However, it's best to explore on foot.

HEADHUNTING

Long feared for their ferocity in war and their sense of independence, Naga tribes considered headhunting a sign of strength and machismo. Every intervillage conflict saw the victors lopping off the heads of the vanquished and instantly rising in social stature (as well as in the eyes of women). Among certain tribes such as the Konyaks of the Mon district, men who claimed heads were adorned with face tattoos and V-shaped marks on their torsos, in addition to being allowed to wear brass pendants called *yanra* denoting the number of heads they had taken.

Headhunting was outlawed in 1953 (the last recorded occurrence was in 1963). Much of the credit for the change goes to Christian missionaries in the region who preached nonviolence and peaceful coexistence over decades. Some 90% of the Nagas now consider themselves Christian, their unshakeable faith marked by behemoth-like churches that are a prominent landmark in any settlement. Most hamlets removed their grisly human trophies, which are now seen as immoral possessions.

Hiring a cab could mean wasting precious time waiting for traffic to move.

Around Kohima

A trip out to a Naga village in the Kohima countryside is a fascinating way to spend a day – it's most enlightening if you go with a guide or local contact. You can stay overnight in homestays in Khonoma and Kigwema. Contact **Explore Nagaland** (☑ 8132062853; www.explorenagaland.com; Morung Lodge, Upper Midland; homestays incl breakfast dm/d ₹1000/2500) or Alder Tours & Travels (p565).

Khonoma

The Angami village of Khonoma, perched on a ridge among high forested hills 20km west of Kohima, is a neat place of stone-paved pathways and pretty flower gardens, with rice fields picturesquely carpeting the valleys far below. Khonoma was a centre of Naga opposition to the British in the 19th century and to Nagaland's incorporation into independent India in the 20th century. 'Nagas are not Indians' declares one memorial on the road approaching to the village. Three stone forts in the village recall conflicts with the British, as do a monument to British dead at the village's highest point (considered the site of the Nagas' last stand in 1879) and another to local warrior Jüdelie Hiekha beside a plaza below.

Dovipie Inn (☑ 7085896732; www.dovipieinn. com; Khonoma Village; dm ₹800, d ₹2500-3500) at the northern tip of the village provides excellent-quality, panoramic accommodation, plus good food. There are also several homestays, charging around ₹1500 per person including meals, which you can book through travel firms in Kohima.

A bus to Khonoma (₹30, 1¾ hours) leaves Kohima's NST Bus Station at 1.30pm Monday to Saturday, returning early morning the same day.

Naga Heritage Village

The **Naga Heritage Village** (Kisama; ⊙ 9am-4pm Oct-Mar, 9.30am-4.30pm Apr-Sep) has a representative selection of traditional Naga houses and *morungs* (young people's dormitories) with full-size log drums and architectural ornamentation specific to each of Nagaland's tribes. Nagaland's biggest annual jamboree, the Hornbill Festival (p580), is celebrated here. Within the village is the **WWII Museum** (₹10; ⊙ 10am-4pm Mon-Sat), with a collection of memorabilia from the WWII battles fought around Kohima. It's 10km south of Kohima along the Imphal road.

Northern Nagaland

The most unspoiled part of the state, northern Nagaland is rugged and divinely beautiful country. Antiquity survives here in tribal villages composed of thatched longhouses, many of whose inhabitants continue to live a hunting and farming lifestyle. The most accessible villages are the Konyak settlements around Mon, where traditional houses abound. Some villages still have *morungs* (community hall-dormitories) and religious relics from pre-Christian times. Village elders may wear tribal costume, and Konyaks of all ages carry the fearsome-looking *dao* (a machete originally used for headhunting) as a standard accessory.

Visiting a Naga village without a local guide can be frustratingly unproductive. You'd also benefit from having your own sturdy vehicle, as there's very limited public transport and roads are often in atrocious condition.

Mon & Around

The humble hill town of Mon serves as an access point for the many Konyak villages in the area.

KONYAK VILLAGES

The most visited village is Longwa, about 40km from Mon, where the headman's longhouse (rebuilt with an untraditional red tin roof in 2016) spectacularly straddles the India–Myanmar border and contains a fascinating range of weapons, animal horns, gongs, dinosaur-like totems and a WWII metal aircraft seat salvaged from debris scattered in nearby jungles. Several tattooed former headhunters can usually be photographed for a fairly standard ₹100 fee. Tribal jewellery, carved masks and other collectibles (₹200 to ₹1000) are sold by many households. Many Longwa men have a serious opium habit.

Other villages that can be visited from Mon include Old Mon (Mon Village; 6km), with countless animal skulls adorning the outer walls of the headman's house; Shiangha Chingnyu (25km), which has a huge longhouse decorated with animal skulls and three stuffed tigers; and Shangnyu (20km), with a wooden shrine full of fertility references.

🛏 Sleeping

Guesthouses within Mon are mostly prosaic affairs. One or two villages now have homestays where you can sit around the communal fireplace and get an inside track on Konyak life. Longwa has several homestays.

Helsa Cottage   GUESTHOUSE $
(✆ 9862876283; Mon; r ₹1000-1500) Helsa Cottage, about a 600m walk from the private bus stand, provides bare but clean decent-sized rooms, with mosquito nets and buckets of hot water available. It's quite efficiently run, with tasty food too (dinner around ₹200, breakfast ₹120). Electricity comes and goes. The family may be able to

arrange transport tickets and accommodation in Longwa.

Konyak Tea Retreat   FARMSTAY $$$
(www.konyaktearetreat.com; Shiyong Village; per person full board ₹2500) This fantastic homestay is run by the friendly Phejin, the descendant of a legendary Konyak headhunter, and she does an excellent job familiarising guests with her tribal roots. Accommodation is in eco-chic rooms overlooking a tea garden, and the Naga meals are delicious to the last morsel. It's located in the small village of Shiyong, about 30km west of Mon.

❶ Getting There & Away

No public transport leaves Mon on Sundays, so schedule your trip accordingly. On other days gruelling overnight buses leave Mon's private bus stand between 2.30pm and 4.30pm for Dimapur (₹600, 14 hours), Kohima (₹850, 18 hours) and Guwahati (₹700, 13 hours). Sumos depart at 6am to Mokokchung (₹650, 10 hours), and at 6am and 7am to Sonari (₹230, three hours) in Assam, where you can pick up transport to Sivasagar or Jorhat. You can also reach Sonari by taking a Sumo to Namsa (₹200, 2½ hours, about hourly from 7am to 1pm), then an autorickshaw (around ₹250) for the remaining 13km. Coming up to Mon, Sumos leave Namsa about hourly from 6.30am to 2.30pm. All vehicles for Mokokchung, Dimapur and Kohima take routes through Sonari, not via Longleng in Nagaland, and those for Kohima go via Dimapur, not Mokokchung.

Sumos to Longwa (₹170, two hours) depart around 7am and 1pm from a stand on the Sonari road, about 500m from the private bus stand. Returning from Longwa, there is normally a jeep around 6 or 7am and sometimes another around 10am or 1pm.

MANIPUR

A breeding ground for graceful classical-dance traditions, sumptuous cuisine and (it's said) the sport of polo, Manipur (Jewelled Land) sits amid rolling hills stretching to India's border with Myanmar. It's a place of great geographical and cultural variety. The capital, Imphal, and the beautiful, ecologically unique Loktak Lake sit in a fertile, bowl-like valley in the centre of the state. Most of the valley's residents are Meitei (or Manipuri) people, who today largely adhere to a Vaishnavite strand of Hinduism. The forested hill country rising up to 2500m outside the central valley is populated predominantly by now-Christian tribal peoples such as the Nagas and Kukis.

Imphal

📞 0385 / POP 268,000 / ELEV 780M

Manipur's capital and only city is an interesting, relatively orderly place, with a temperate climate and traffic that moves freely and without much honking. The central Kangla Fort is arguably the most impressive and enjoyable historic monument in the Northeast, the vibrant Ima Keithel is reckoned to be the world's largest women-vendors-only market, the two war cemeteries are moving memorials to one of WWII's fiercest battles, and the attractions of Loktak Lake are roughly an hour away. The Sangai Festival (p564) is held in Imphal in late November. A collection of good midrange hotels adds to the appeal of staying here.

◎ Sights

★ Kangla Fort
FORT

(Kangla Pan Rd; Indian/foreigner ₹10/50; ⊙9am-4pm Thu-Tue, to 5pm Mar-Oct) The vast, low-walled fort at the heart of Imphal was, with a few interruptions, the political and religious heart of Manipur for many centuries until taken over by the British after the 1891 Anglo-Manipuri War. Today it's a tranquil, beautifully maintained, parklike space of lawns, moats, ponds and big trees, containing, among many interesting features, several temples, two large white Kangla Sha (protective dragons), a pavilion with spectacular royal longboats, the world's oldest polo field, a historical museum and a pleasant cafe.

The only entrance and exit is through an ornate, exceedingly tall gate on the west side.

ⓘ REGISTERING ON ARRIVAL IN MANIPUR

On arrival at Imphal airport, all foreigners must register at the Foreigners Check Post in the arrivals hall. If travelling by land from Kohima (Nagaland) or Silchar (Assam), foreigners must register at police posts at the state borders at Mao or Jiribam respectively. Foreigners are supposed to register again with the police in Imphal, but in practice your hotel almost always takes care of these formalities.

★ Ima Keithel
MARKET

(Mothers' Market, Khwairamband Bazar; Bir Tikendrajit Rd; ⊙5am-7pm) Housed in three big colonnaded buildings with pagoda-style roofs, this huge bazaar with over 4000 all-women vendors is reckoned to be the largest of its kind in the world. Only married women are allowed to be stallholders. Two buildings focus mainly on clothes and fabrics (look for traditional tribal shawls at good prices), the third deals chiefly in vegetables, fruit, fish and other foods. It's a fascinating place, with some great photo ops (ask first).

War Cemeteries

Two impeccably maintained cemeteries honour many who lost their lives during the Battle of Imphal (March to July 1944), one of the most intense battles of WWII, in which Allied forces repulsed a Japanese attack on eastern India. The Imphal War Cemetery (Imphal-Kohima Rd, Kabo Leika; ⊙9am-4pm Oct-Feb, to 4.30pm Mar-Sep), along a lane off the Imphal–Kohima Rd, 400m north of Hotel Imphal, is the last resting place of more than 1600 mainly British soldiers and airmen. The Imphal Indian Army War Cemetery (Minuthong Hafiz Hatta; ⊙9am-4pm Oct-Feb, to 4.30pm Mar-Sep), 1km east of North AOC junction, contains 820 graves of Indian and African soldiers and two graceful marble cenotaphs engraved with the names of 860 Indians who were cremated.

🛏 Sleeping & Eating

Hotel Nirmala
HOTEL $$

(📞0385-2459014; nirmalahotel@gmail.com; Thangal Bazar; incl breakfast s ₹800-3300, d ₹900-3660; ❋⌨🖥) No-frills Nirmala, in the heart of Imphal's main market area, has a genuine sense of belonging, and staff go about their tasks with quiet dedication. Rooms, ranging from small non-air-con 'ordinary' up to air-con executive suites, are unfussy but clean and provide the necessities.

Sangai Continental
HOTEL $$

(📞8258056325; www.thesangaicontinental.com; Thangal Bazar; incl breakfast s ₹2230-5310, d ₹2680-5900; ❋🖥) The centrally located Sangai Continental provides just what you'd hope for in a midrange business and family hotel. Good-sized contemporary rooms in white and gold with glassed-in showers, plus impeccable cleanliness, efficient staff and one of Imphal's best restaurants, Wild Rice (mains ₹200-580; ⊙7am-10.30pm), all add up to a fine place to stay.

Hotel Imphal HOTEL $$
([☎]8131962190; www.hotelimphal.com; Imphal-Kohima Rd, North AOC; s/d incl breakfast non-AC ₹2950/3570, AC from ₹3960/4510; [❄][@][☎]) This huge hotel (four storeys high and over 100m long) appeals with its manicured lawns, bright rooms with snug beds and fresh white linen, and good restaurant and coffee shop (the latter dispensing fresh filter coffee). Public events are big here, so it could get a bit noisy during one of these galas.

★ Luxmi Kitchen ADIVASI $$
(Jiribam Rd, Wahengbam Leikai; thalis ₹160; [☉]10.30am-3pm Mon-Sat, to 1.30pm Sun) The last word in Manipuri lunch platters, ultrapopular Luxmi does a fabulous *chakluk* (thali) comprising more than a dozen local delicacies such as tangy fish stew, fried fish, leafy greens, *sinju* (a salad with cabbage, lotus stems and chillies), local dhals, *iromba* (fermented fish chutney) and *ngapi* (fermented shrimp paste). A meal here could well be one of the highlights of your Manipur trip.

ⓘ Information

Seven Sisters Holidays ([☎]0385-2443977; www.sevensistersholidays.com; MG Ave; [☉]10am-5.30pm Mon-Sat) This efficient agency can provide guides and cars with drivers for trips in Manipur. Daily rates are ₹3500 for Imphal and Loktak Lake and ₹5000 to ₹6000 for outstation trips. The office is on the 2nd floor of the building on the east side of the hard-to-miss OK restaurant.

ⓘ Getting There & Away

The airport is 9km southwest of Imphal (taxi ₹400). IndiGo (www.goindigo.in), AirAsia (www.airasia.com), Air India (www.airindia.com) and Jet Airways (www.jetairways.com) fly to Guwahati, Kolkata and Delhi; Air India also flies to Aizawl and Dimapur, and IndiGo to Agartala.

Fourteen-passenger Winger minibuses to Kohima (₹600, 5½ hours) and Dimapur (₹700, nine hours) leave about hourly, 5.30am to 2.30pm, from **North AOC junction** (North AOC), between the Classic and Imphal hotels.

Loktak Lake

All the hills around the Imphal Valley drain their waters into picturesque, shimmering blue Loktak Lake, south of Imphal. The 250-sq-km lake is dotted with hundreds of clumps of matted floating vegetation called *phumdis*. Large circular *phumdis* are created as fishing ponds, and fisherfolk build

huts on the floating 'islands' and paddle about in dugout canoes. **Boat rides** (Sendra Island; 10-person boat ½/1/2hr ₹600/1200/2000; [☉]7am-5.30pm) on the lake, and views over it from **Sendra Island** (₹15; [☉]7am-5pm) in the middle, are highly photogenic. In the southern part an enormous 26-sq-km *phumdi* forms the heart of **Keibul Lamjao National Park** (Indian/foreigner ₹30/200, camera ₹50/250, light vehicle ₹100; [☉]7.30am-5.30pm), touted as the world's only floating national park and home to the last surviving wild population of sangai deer.

At the southwestern corner of the lake, Moirang village's **INA Museum** (INA Memorial Complex; Indian/foreigner ₹10/50; [☉]10am-4pm Tue-Sun) commemorates the unfurling of the Azad Hind (Free India) flag here in 1944 by the anticolonial Indian National Army advancing with Japanese WWII forces against British-held Imphal.

The attractive six-bed **Sendra Park hotel** ([☎]0385-2443967; www.classicgroupofhotels.com/sendra; Sendra Island; s/d ₹4120/4720; [❄]) and a few homestays, including **Maipakchao Homestay** ([☎]9856356993; www.loktaksweethomestay.com; Thanga Island; per person full board ₹1200), mean you can stay a night or two.

Sangai Café (Sendra Island; mains ₹120-175; [☉]7am-5pm) provides good meals and coffee plus panoramic lake views. There are a few 'rice hotels' around Moirang bazaar.

Buses (₹50) and 'Winger' minibuses (₹60) to Moirang (1½ hours, 44km) leave two or three times an hour from the Wahengbam Leikai bus stand on the south side of the busy intersection just west of Imphal's Ima Keithel market. Last vehicles back from Moirang leave around 4.30pm or 5pm. Jampacked vans (₹10 to ₹15) run along the road from Moirang to Sendra and Thanga islands. Autorickshaws from Moirang to Keibul Lamjao National Park cost around ₹300 round trip including waiting time.

MIZORAM

Seated along rows of north–south-running mountain ridges, isolated and pristine Mizoram sees few tourists, which makes the verdant, hilly countryside beyond the capital Aizawl a tempting target for off-the-beaten-track adventurers. The predominant ethnic Mizo population, formerly animist headhunters, were converted by Christian missionaries between the 1890s and 1930s.

ⓘ CROSSING TO MYANMAR (BURMA)

There are border-crossing points to Myanmar at Moreh (Manipur), 110km southeast of Imphal, and Zokhawthar (Mizoram), 215km southeast of Aizawl. Travellers must obtain a Myanmar visa in advance (28-day tourist evisas are available through www.evisa.moip. gov.mm).

Moreh to Tamu

The border is open from 7am to 3.30pm daily, Indian time.

Shared taxis to Moreh (₹500 to ₹700, four hours) leave until 1.30pm from near the old Manipur State Road Transport Corporation office in Imphal's Moirangkhom neighbourhood, about 800m south of Kangra Fort.

From Tamu on the Myanmar side of the border, buses and minivans run at least as far as Kalaymyo (Kalay; three hours), 130km south along the road to Mandalay.

Zokhawthar to Rihkawdar

The border is open from 6am to 5pm daily (Indian time). Sumos travel daily except Sunday from Aizawl's **Power House** (Lower Zarkawt, Electric Veng) along the bumpy road to Champhai (₹600, nine hours) and Zokhawthar (10 hours). It makes sense to spend a night in Champhai (which has several hotels), then continue to the border in the morning.

From Rihkhawdar uncomfortable jeeps leave in the morning (except Sunday) to Tiddim (four hours) and Kalaymyo (Kalay; nine hours).

Mizo culture today is liberated from caste and gender distinctions. People of both sexes wear Western-style clothing except on special occasions, such as Sunday, when women don the colourful traditional *puan* wraparound skirt for church services (men wear shirts and ties).

Free of political unrest since becoming a separate state in 1987, Mizoram runs at its own rhythm. Most businesses shut by 6pm and virtually everything closes entirely on Sunday.

Within 24 hours of arrival, foreigners should register at the **Foreigners Registration Office** (📞0389-2333094; CID Complex, Bungkawn; ⏰9am-5pm Mon-Fri, 10am-3pm Sat & Sun) in Aizawl.

Aizawl

📞0389 / POP 293,000 / ELEV 1050M

Clinging to a set of near-vertical ridges by its fingernails, Aizawl (eye-zole) is the most languid and unhurried of Indian state capitals. There's not much to do here apart from soaking up its relaxed feel, gazing at the large number of large churches, and organising a trip into the Mizoram countryside. The predominantly Christian people don't drink, go to bed early and – hard to believe until you actually hear it – don't honk their horns! According to India's 2011 census, the Aizawl and neighbouring Serchhip districts have the highest literacy rates in India, nearly 98%. The area around Chanmari, the heart of Aizawl's low-key hotel and shopping district, is the most interesting, and most tourism-related establishments are located here or near it.

Aizawl has a lot of large churches, but **Solomon's Temple** (www.kohhranthianghlim. org; Chawlhhmun; ⏰10am-4.30pm) outdoes them all. Intended as a re-creation of the Temple of Solomon in Jerusalem, it's a white-marble square with towering facades on each of its 37m sides and steeples at each corner, accommodating 2000 people in its undivided interior. It's 5km northwest of the city centre, with fine valley panoramas from the surrounding garden. A round-trip taxi from town costs ₹450.

🛏 Sleeping & Eating

Aizawl has a mixed bag of semibudget lodgings. Rooms at **Hotel Ritz** (📞0389-2323358; hotelritzazl@gmail.com; Bara Bazar, Dawrpui; s ₹950-1850, d ₹1560-2410, s/d ste from ₹1900/2460; 📶) are good for the price, all with exterior windows (squat toilets in the cheapest). Staff are welcoming and there's complimentary breakfast for all except the cheapest rooms.

Hotel Regency (📞0389-2349334; www. regencyaizawl.com; Zarkawt Main St; incl breakfast s ₹2200-4420, d ₹2800-4800, ste from ₹5090; ❋📶) is much classier, with inviting, spotless rooms off white-tiled corridors, and the excellent **Magnolia Restaurant** (mains ₹210-470; ⏰11am-9.30pm) overlooking the main street, serving tasty Mizo, Chinese and Continental fare. Best of all is the bright, spacious, contemporary **Hotel Floria** (☎0389-2329555, 7627993685; www.hotelfloria.in; Bara Bazar, Dawrpui; incl breakfast s ₹4250-6490, d ₹4720-6960, ste ₹8730; ❈ 🤶), with young, professional staff, tile-and-marble bathrooms, comfy beds and expansive views in the 'luxury' rooms. Its cheerful **Zamzo** (mains ₹250-650; ⊙7am-9.30pm) restaurant does good steaks, pasta and Thai curries as well as Mizo and North Indian dishes.

On Sunday only the better hotel restaurants will save you from starving, as other eating options remain shut.

❶ Information

Tourist Information Centre (☎0389-2333475; http://tourism.mizoram.gov.in; Directorate of Tourism, New Capital Complex Rd, Khatla; ⊙9am-5pm Mon-Fri) This government office (3km south of Chanmari) has some information and leaflets on travel in Mizoram.

❶ Getting There & Around

Lengpui Airport is 32km northwest of Aizawl; a taxi costs ₹1000. Jet Airways (www.jetairways.com) flies nonstop to Guwahati daily and to Delhi three or four times weekly. Air India (www.airindia.com) goes daily to Kolkata and once a week to Imphal.

The principal road access to Aizawl is NH306 from Silchar in southern Assam – a rough drive of eight or nine hours. In Aizawl, long-distance Sumo counters cluster conveniently around Zarkawt Traffic Point (Sumkhuma Point) in the middle of town. Sumos head to Silchar (₹450, eight hours, five daily Monday to Saturday, 6am and 6pm Sunday), and to Shillong (₹1100, 18 hours) and Guwahati (₹1400, 22 hours) at 6pm Monday to Saturday.

Rural Mizoram

Mizoram's green hills get higher as you head east or south towards the Myanmar border. It can be a challenge getting out there but there's some spectacular hill country to explore and rural life to discover.

At 2157m, Blue Mountain in southeast Mizoram is the state's highest peak. It's considered by Mizos to be the abode of gods, but its cliffs are also said to be the abode of ghosts as well as mountain goats. A three-day all-inclusive camping trip to climb Blue Mountain costs around ₹35,000 for two people, round trip from Aizawl, with **Evergreen Tours & Travels** (☎9612080159; www.evergreenmz.

com; B16/2 K Rosiamliana Bldg, Khatla Main Rd; ⊙9.30am-4.30pm Mon-Sat).

Reiek & Hmuifang

Two good destinations for day or overnight trips from Aizawl are Hmuifang, 52km south, and Reiek, 25km west. Both have government tourist resorts (superior tourist lodges), easily summited local peaks – Mt Reiek and Mt Hmuifang – and unspoiled local forests. This is a good opportunity to get a feel for Mizoram rural life.

Sumo services run until about noon, Monday to Saturday, from stands in the Bungkawn Vaiveng neighbourhood for Reiek and in the Ngaizel neighbourhood (southern Aizawl) for Hmuifang. For Hmuifang take a Sialsuk-bound Sumo.

TRIPURA

Far from India's popular tourist circuits and on the way to nowhere else except Bangladesh (which surrounds it on three sides), Tripura sees very few foreign travellers. However, it has a likeable, easy-going capital in Agartala and a handful of palaces, temples and archaeological sites to provide visitors with interesting days. All can be reached in day trips from Agartala, though the outstanding northern archaeological site of Unakoti is also a possible overnight or a stop en route to or from Assam.

Agartala

☎0381 / POP 400,000

Tripura's only 'city', low-key Agartala feels like an India of yore. It's a congested but relaxed place, and in many ways seems more like a small town than a state capital. The pace of life is unhurried and the people are extremely friendly.

Its centrepiece is **Ujjayanta Palace** (Indian/foreigner ₹20/150; ⊙11am-1.30pm & 2-6pm Tue-Sun, closed 2nd & 4th Sat), a striking, dome-capped palace, fronted by two reflecting lakes, housing the large, outstanding Tripura State Museum. The museum's colourful, well-displayed galleries exhibit the arts, crafts, cultures, history and monuments of Tripura and the rest of the Northeast, with some interesting historical features such as a room on the Bangladesh War of Independence in 1971.

Agartala

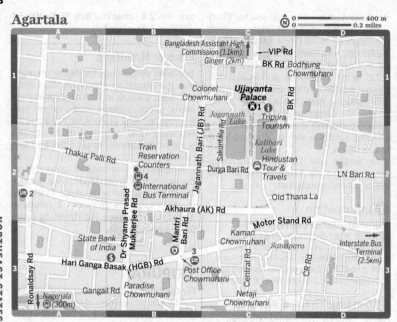

Agartala

🛏 Sleeping & Eating

Ginger HOTEL $$
(📞 0381-2411333; www.gingerhotels.com; Airport Rd, Khejur Bhagan; s/d ₹3430/4000; 🌐@🛜) Part of the Tata-owned Ginger hotel chain, this well-managed, low-cost business hotel has smart rooms in pastel shades – not fancy, but comfortable and very functional. There's a restaurant with excellent buffets, a travel desk, a cafe and SBI ATM in the building. Coming from the airport, the hotel is on your right 2km before town.

Hotel Welcome Palace HOTEL $$
(📞 0381-2384940; www.hotelwelcomepalace.co.in; HGB Rd; d ₹1340-2240, ste ₹2940-4900; 🌐🛜)

This hotel on Hari Ganga Basak (HGB) Rd, in the heart of Agartala's main commercial area, has helpful staff, reasonable rates and the good **Restaurant Kurry Klub** (mains ₹120-220; ⏱ noon-10.30pm; 🌐). Rooms are neat, although some may not have external windows, and those that do may suffer from street noise.

Hotel Sonar Tori HOTEL $$$
(📞 7085052709; www.hotelsonartoriagartala.com; Ronaldsay Rd, near Fire Brigade Chowmuhani; s ₹4720-5900, d ₹5900-7080, ste ₹8260; 🌐🛜) The Sonar Tori has raised the game for Agartala's in-town hotels. The stylish, comfortable rooms in black and cream feature modern bathrooms, and the superior **restaurant** (mains ₹220-340; ⏱ 12.30-3.30pm & 7-10.45pm) serves Thai and Indian curries, Continental dishes and a reasonable choice of vegetarian dishes. Room rates vary according to demand: the website lists current deals.

ℹ Information

Bangladesh Assistant High Commission
(📞 0381-2324807; www.bahcagt.org; off VIP Rd, near Circuit House, Kunjaban; ⏱ application 9.30am-12.30pm Mon-Fri) This office, 1.5km north of the Ujjayanta Palace, issues visas for Bangladesh. You have to apply online (www.visa.gov.bd), bring a printout of your

❶ CROSSING TO BANGLADESH: AGARTALA TO AKHAURA

From central Agartala, the Bangladesh border (open 6am to 6pm) is just 3.5km along Akhaura Rd (₹60 by autorickshaw). You can get a visa through the Bangladesh Assistant High Commission (p588).

Akhaura in Bangladesh is 5km beyond the border and reached by 'CNG' (autorickshaw). From there, trains head to Dhaka, Comilla, Chittagong and Sylhet, and buses run to Chandura (20km), where you can change for Dhaka, Sylhet or Srimangal.

From Agartala's **International Bus Terminal** (Dr Shyama Prasad Mukherjee Rd), behind the TRTC local bus station, **Bangladesh Road Transport Corporation** (BRTC; ☑ 9863730658) runs an AC bus to Dhaka (₹300, six hours) at 1pm Monday, Friday and Saturday.

application to the office and pay your fee at **State Bank of India** (SBI; ☑ 0381-2311364; HGB Rd, Melar Math; ◷10am-4pm Mon-Sat, closed 2nd & 4th Sat). Processing takes one or two working days. Fees, listed on the application website, vary with your nationality and how many entries you want.

❶ Getting There & Around

AIR

Agartala's airport is 12km north of town; a taxi costs ₹300. IndiGo (www.indigo.in) flies five times daily to Kolkata and three times to Guwahati; the flights continue to destinations such as Bengaluru (Bangalore), Delhi, Chennai and Hyderabad. IndiGo also flies three times a week direct to Imphal. Air India (www.airindia.com) has two daily flights to Kolkata.

BUS, TAXI & JEEP

Transport to Udaipur and Melaghar (to either place bus ₹40, shared taxi or jeep ₹60, 1½ hours) departs frequently until at least 4pm from the Nagerjala Bus Stand, just south of the Johar Bridge, 2km southwest of Ujjayanta Palace.

From the Interstate Bus Terminus, 3km east of central Agartala in Chandrapur (autorickshaw ₹50), buses depart at noon for Shillong (₹800, 20 hours) and Guwahati (₹800, 23 hours).

Taxis can be hired for sightseeing in and around Agartala. Efficient **Hindustan Tour & Travels** (☑ 9436463808; www.hindustantourtravels.com; 7 LN Bari Rd; ◷7am-10pm) charges ₹1500 for a day trip to Melaghar and Udaipur.

TRAIN

Agartala's station is 6km south of the centre (₹150 by taxi), off the Udaipur road. The 13174 Kanchanjunga Express at 5.30am Tuesday, Thursday, Saturday and Sunday travels all the way to Kolkata's Sealdah station (sleeper/3AC/2AC ₹600/1630/2380, 38 hours) via Guwahati (₹330/890/1270, 17 hours) and New Jalpaiguri (₹460/1240/1800, 26 hours).

Neermahal & Melaghar

☑ 0381 / POP 12,400

Sleepy Melaghar is home to one of Tripura's most celebrated buildings, the island-set Neermahal palace, reached by boat from a ghat 1km from the centre of town. A day trip here also gives you a pleasant insight into rural Tripura. It's 48km south of Agartala.

A multidomed red-and-white water palace, **Neermahal** (Rudra Sagar; person/camera ₹10/20, boat round trip ₹30; ◷8.30am-4pm) lies empty but shimmering on its own boggy island in Rudra Sagar Lake. Like its counterpart in Rajasthan's Udaipur, this was a princely exercise in aesthetics, in which craftsmen built a summer palace of luxury for the Tripura royals in a blend of Hindu and Islamic styles. Neermahal was inaugurated by the Bengali Nobel laureate Rabindranath Tagore in 1930. The waterborne approach by slow motor-boat is a delightful part of visiting.

Udaipur

☑ 03821 / POP 33,000

Udaipur was capital of the Tripura kingdom before Agartala and remains dotted with ancient temples and tanks. According to Hindu legend, when Shiva, blinded by sorrow and rage, divided the corpse of his beloved wife Sati into 108 pieces, her right leg fell to earth at Matabari, the site of Udaipur's most famous drawcard: the vivid **Tripura Sundari Mandir** (www.matabaritemple.in; ◷4.30am-1.30pm & 3.30-9.30pm), 4km south of town Udaipur is 51km southeast of Agartala and 25km east of Melaghar, and easily combined with Neermahal in a taxi day trip from Agartala, costing around ₹1500.

Several handsome mid-17th-century Bengali-style temples in town (now protected monuments rather than living temples) demonstrate the Tripura kingdom's close ties to Bengal. At the east end of Central Rd, the Chaturdasa Devata Temple and the Lakshmi-Narayan Temple are beautifully proportioned structures with stupa-like finials crowning their roofs and porches. Both are dedicated to various forms of Vishnu. Fork left 75m southeast of here and in another 300m you reach the Teen Mandir, a group of three temples built by Queen Gunavati in 1668. Continuing southeast, fork left after 150m to cross a bridge over the Gomati River, then take the first left turn and you'll find the roofless remains of the old Rajbari Palace (900m from the Teen Mandir) with the elegantly restored Bhubaneswari Temple, and a lookout tower over the river, nearby.

Unakoti

In a hilly jungle setting 160km northeast of Agartala, the archaeological site of **Unakoti** (⏱6am-6pm) FREE is one of Northeast India's little-known jewels. Massive rock-cut sculptures of Hindu gods and goddesses (some dating back to the 7th century) adorn rock faces at the site, including a 10m-tall face of Shiva sculpted on a monolithic rock and a trio of Ganeshas hewn beside a waterfall. Well-paved (though sometimes slippery) paths and steps lead to the main carvings, and unpaved paths lead to various Shiva linga in the forest.

The best nearby sleeping option is **Unakoti Tourist Lodge** (☎9089235098; Kailasahar; r ₹800-950; ❄), 12km from the site; its antiquated but large and relatively clean rooms have hot showers and sit-down toilets. It can provide simple meals too.

Unakoti is 1km north of the road between Kailasahar and Dharmanagar, 9km east of Kailasahar and 19km west of Dharmanagar. You can hire a taxi for a day trip from Agartala or Silchar in southern Assam, each about 4½ hours away (₹4000/4500 one way/return from either place).

Buses depart Agartala's Interstate Bus Terminus (p589) for Kailasahar (₹120, 4½ hours) at 9.30am and noon. Shared taxis, shared autorickshaws, Sumo jeeps and buses ply the Kailasahar-Dharmanagar road (₹20 from Kailasahar to the Unakoti turn-off).

There's also daily train service from Agartala and Silchar to Dharmanagar and Ku-

marghat, which is 24km south of Kailasahar and connected to it by local transport.

MEGHALAYA

Separating the Assam valley from the plains of Bangladesh, hilly Meghalaya (Abode of Clouds) is a cool, pine-fresh mountain state set on dramatic horseshoes of rocky cliffs. Cherrapunjee and Mawsynram are among the wettest places on earth; most of the rain falls between June and September, creating very impressive waterfalls and carving out some of Asia's longest caves.

The state's population predominantly comprises the Jaintia, Khasi and Garo tribal groups, who live in the eastern, central and western parts respectively. Though mostly Christian since the 19th century, these peoples still maintain elements of their old animist culture, including fierce clan loyalties, sacred forests where chickens and goats are still sacrificed and lively harvest festivals with mass dances in colourful traditional dress.

Shillong

📞 0364 / POP 355,000 / ELEV 1500M

Irreverent Shillong was the capital of colonial and post-Independence Assam (which embraced almost the whole Northeast) until 1972, when it became capital of the newly carved-out state of Meghalaya. Since then it has developed some accoutrements of a typical modern Indian town, including urban sprawl, a lot of concrete, and snarled-up traffic along its winding streets. However, it retains some old-time charm in certain pockets – and a strong sense of individuality and difference, with its many Christian churches and its residents' tastes for hanging out in cafes, playing and watching rock music and football, driving around in spruced-up automobiles and gambling on archery.

The heart of town is Police Bazar (PB to locals) where seven roads meet at a hectic roundabout.

◎ Sights & Activities

★ **Don Bosco Museum of Indigenous Cultures** MUSEUM
(☎0364-2550260; www.dbcic.org; Mawlai; Indian/foreigner ₹100/200, mobile/other camera ₹100/200; ⏱9am-5.30pm Mon-Sat, to 4.30pm Dec & Jan) This well-displayed museum is a

Shillong

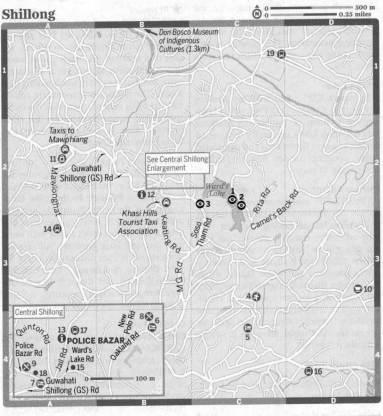

Shillong

⦿ Sights
1 Ward's Lake	C2
2 Ward's Lake Gate No 1	C2
3 Ward's Lake Gate No 2	C2

◆ Activities, Courses & Tours
4 Pioneer Adventure	C3

⌂ Sleeping
5 Café Shillong Bed & Breakfast	C4
6 Earle Holiday Home	B4
7 Hotel Centre Point	A4

✖ Eating
8 City Hut Dhaba	B4
La Galerie	(see 7)
9 Trattoria	A4

⊙ Drinking & Nightlife
10 Café Shillong	D3
Cloud 9	(see 7)

⌂ Shopping
11 Iew Duh	A2

ℹ Information
12 India Tourism	B2
13 Meghalaya Tourism	A4

ℹ Transport
14 Anjeli Bus Station	A3
15 Blue Hill Travels	A4
16 Dhanketi Bus Stand	D4
Meghalaya Helicopter Service	(see 17)
17 MTC Bus Station	A4
18 Network Travels	A4
19 Polo Bus Stand	C1

fabulous repository of tribal artefacts interspersed with exhibits on Christian missionary work. The self-guided visit takes about 1½ hours. The 17 galleries exhibit tribal basketry, musical instruments, weapons, objects of daily life, costumes and jewellery, along with dioramas, charts, maps, photos and videos documenting Northeast life. Afterwards, you can walk up on the roof for expansive panoramas. The museum is 3km north of the city centre; a return taxi costs about ₹400.

Ward's Lake
LAKE

(₹10, camera ₹20; ☉8.30am-4.30pm Wed-Mon Nov-Feb, to 6.30pm Mar-Oct) The central landscaping element of colonial-era Shillong, this attractive lake has a pretty ornamental bridge, adjacent flower beds and manicured lawns, courting couples, boating facilities and gaggles of geese.

Pioneer Adventure
ADVENTURE SPORTS

(☑9856006437; www.pioneeradventuretour.com; Jarman Villa, Hopkinson Rd, Lower Lachumiere; ☉10am-5pm Mon-Sat Oct-May) Leading Shillong adventure company Pioneer can take you diving in the hills! Open-water dives (per person ₹3500) are available at its Shnongpdeng adventure camp near Dawki, where the Umngot River offers up to 10m visibility. Other activities include snorkelling, climbing, rafting, canyoning, cliff jumping and kayaking. Overnight camping packages (per person around ₹10,000) allow you to sample a bit of everything.

🛏 Sleeping

Rooms in Shillong are expensive by Northeast standards.

Earle Holiday Home
HOTEL $

(☑9863302149; earlehh@rediffmail.com; Oakland Rd; r ₹600-2950; ☎) This hotel has character even if it's a little disorganised. The cheaper rooms are original half-timbered affairs in a classic 1920 Shillong hill house adorned with turrets. Rooms in the concrete annex are less atmospheric but generally more comfortable.

Maple Pine Farm
B&B $$

(www.culturalpursuits.com; Lyngkien, Mawphlang; r incl breakfast ₹1560-2450) 🌱 A great off-the-grid place to kick back, Canadian-and-Khasi-owned Maple Pine Farm sits in a peaceful green valley below Mawphlang village, about 28km southwest of Shillong. There are four cosy wooden cabins, all electricity is solar- or wind-powered, and the good meal options (₹250 to ₹375) include Khasi and roast-chicken dinners. Check the website and contact them by email.

★ Ri Kynjai
RESORT $$$

(☑9862420300; www.rikynjai.com; Umiam Lake; r incl breakfast ₹12,160-18,560; ☎) This superbly designed resort among lush woodlands is a gem of a getaway. Abundant use of wood, thatch and earth tones gives a soothingly rustic feel, but the luxury touches don't miss a beat. The multicuisine restaurant (mains ₹300 to ₹470) features numerous Northeast specialities; nonguests can come for lunch by reservation. It overlooks Umiam Lake, 21km north of Shillong.

Hotel Centre Point
HOTEL $$$

(☑0364-2220480; www.shillongcentrepoint. com; Police Bazar; incl breakfast s ₹4720-8790, d ₹5190-8790; ✳☎) Right by the Police Bazar roundabout, the Centre Point is the best centrally located hotel. Run by professional and helpful staff, it has smart rooms with wood panelling and large windows. All creature comforts are at your disposal, including the good **Galerie restaurant** (mains ₹250-500; ☉noon-10.30pm) and **Cloud 9 lounge bar** (www.facebook.com/cloud9.restolounge; ☉1pm-12.30am) for evening drinks and music.

Café Shillong Bed & Breakfast
GUESTHOUSE $$$

(☑8974066089; www.cafeshillongbnb.com; 31 Upper Lachumiere; incl breakfast s ₹4130-5900, d ₹4510-6490; ☎) A typically quaint 'Old Shillong' bungalow has been expertly modernised to provide seven mostly large rooms (some in a newer building) with a bygone-days feel but also up-to-date bathrooms and fittings. Excellent breakfasts, helpful staff and tables out in the front garden all make for an enjoyable stay. It's 1.3km southeast of Police Bazar.

🍴 Eating & Drinking

Trattoria
ADIVASI $

(Police Bazar Rd; mains ₹100-120; ☉11.30am-7.30pm Mon-Sat) There's no better way to sample local Khasi flavours than by dropping in for lunch at this busy place. *Jadoh* (sticky rice stewed in pig blood) and curried pig innards are favourites here, but for the best variety try the immensely popular lunch platter (₹170). An adjacent stall sells packs of exotic pickles, squashes and condiments.

City Hut Dhaba
MULTICUISINE $$

(Oakland Rd; mains ₹210-470; ☉11am-9.30pm) City Hut's smart, efficient waiters serve generous portions of varied Indian, Chinese and barbecue dishes in four clean and agreeable rooms, including a family-only room and an attractive, flower-decked straw pavilion. The quality of food is commendable and the place sees plenty of locals.

Café Shillong CAFE
(☑ 0364-2505759; www.facebook.com/cafeshillong; 1st fl, LP Bldg, Laitumkhrah Main Rd; ◐ noon-9.30pm; 🔊) This fashionable hang-out in bustling Laitumkhrah ('lai-muk-rah' or just 'laimu') has good coffee, yummy steaks and other dishes (₹250 to ₹500), plus live music on Sundays from about 6pm to 8.30pm. The decor features a Les Paul guitar signed by performing musicians. If local legends Lou Majaw or Soulmate happen to be playing, you're in luck.

🛍 Shopping

Iew Duh MARKET
(Bara Bazar; ◐ dawn-dusk Mon-Sat) The vast, crowded public market area (*bara bazar* means 'big market') is one of the most animated shopping areas in the Northeast. You'll reach it about 1.75km west of the big Police Bazar roundabout along GS Rd. Thousands of Khasi tribespeople flock in from their villages, selling everything from baskets and handcrafted arrows to bamboo fish traps and edible frogs.

❶ Getting There & Away

AIR

Air India (www.airindia.com) flies daily from Kolkata to Shillong's small airport, 30km north of town; a taxi into town costs around ₹1000 and takes at least an hour. Guwahati airport, three hours away, has many more flights; taxis from there to Shillong cost ₹2000 (AC ₹2500, shared ₹500).

The **Meghalaya Helicopter Service** (☑ 9436116759; 1st fl, MTC Bus Station, Jail Rd; ◐ 11am-4.15pm Mon-Fri) flies to Guwahati (₹1500, 30 minutes) at 9.30am and 1pm Monday to Saturday, with the Monday, Wednesday and Friday 9.30am flights continuing to Tura (₹1900, 1½ hours from Shillong). Book a week ahead if possible. Flights depart from the Eastern Air Command Headquarters, 12km southwest of Shillong. Maximum baggage allowance is 10kg.

BUS & TAXI

The centrally located **Khasi Hills Tourist Taxi Association** (☑ 0364-2223895; Soso Tham Rd) asks ₹3000 for a day trip to Cherrapunjee and ₹4000 for a ride to the Bangladesh border near Dawki. For Guwahati, a full/shared taxi costs

₹1600/400. **Meghalaya Tourism** (☑ 0364-2226220; www.megtourism.gov.in; Jail Rd; ◐ 7.30am-7pm) has similar rates. A one-way cab to Cherrapunjee should be around ₹1500.

There's cheaper transport from the chaotic **Anjeli Bus Station** (Iew Duh) about 1.2km west of the centre. Frequent shared taxis (₹350) and Sumo jeeps (₹200) to Guwahati (three hours), and Sumos to Dawki (₹120, three hours), go from the main Anjeli building; shared taxis (₹100) and Sumos (₹70) to Cherrapunjee (two hours) go from the upper floor of another building 200m north down the street.

Private buses to more distant destinations, including Agartala, Aizawl, Imphal, Kohima and Siliguri, depart from stands around the city's periphery. Book tickets at counters around the central Police Bazar, including **Network Travels** (☑ 0364-2502559; www.networktravels.com; Shop 44, MUDA Complex, Police Bazar Rd) and **Blue Hill Travels** (Ward's Lake Rd; ◐ 7am-7pm).

The central **MTC bus station** (Jail Rd) has a train reservation counter (the nearest station is in Guwahati) and a handful of government buses including to Guwahati (₹140, three hours, 9am, 1pm and 2pm).

Cherrapunjee (Sohra)
📞 03637 / POP 12,000 / ELEV 1440M

The undulating Meghalaya uplands give way abruptly on the state's southern fringe to deep, jungle-clothed, waterfall-ribboned valleys plunging precipitously to the plains of Bangladesh. Cherrapunjee (also called Sohra), sitting near the lip of the escarpments, is the obvious base for exploring this spectacular landscape. Thanks to the prodigious monsoon rainfall produced by this geography, Cherrapunjee was once feted as the wettest place on earth, though nearby Mawsynram is nowadays reckoned to be a few drops damper. Domestic tourists flock here during the monsoon for the cool air, the celebrated rain and the waterfalls, meaning that Cherrapunjee's peak season runs from about May to August.

Some of the many waterfalls are popular tourist attractions. During the monsoon their volume can increase 20-fold. **Nohkalikai Falls** (viewpoint ₹10, camera ₹50, parking car/motorcycle ₹20/10; ◐ 6am-6pm), at 340m, is said to be the highest single-drop waterfall in India. You can see it from above at a viewpoint 4.4km from Cherrapunjee's market. Local taxis (₹150 each way) shuttle passengers to the viewpoint.

WORTH A TRIP

NONGRIAT ROOT BRIDGES

The most fascinating sights around Cherrapunjee are the incredible living bridges – formed from rubber-fig roots that ingenious Khasi villagers have, over decades, trained across streams as natural pathways. Over 40 of these are said to be scattered around the Meghalaya hills and several of them (including an amazing 'double-decker') are near the jungle valley hamlet of Nongriat – a steep hike down 2600 steps (and up 500) from Tyrna village, 12km southwest of Cherrapunjee.

The descent takes about 1½ hours, including a short detour to the first root bridge (signposted 'Long Root Bridge') about 40 minutes down from Tyrna. You then cross two metal suspension bridges before reaching the second root bridge, just before Nongriat. The double-decker (for which there's a ₹20 entry charge) is five minutes past Nongriat, along with some popular bathing pools in the river. There are several drink and snack stalls en route, but you should carry water too.

Expect the climb back up to Tyrna to take around two hours, with plenty of rest stops on the way.

There's a handful of basic homestays in Nongriat and Tyrna. **Serene Homestay** (☑ 9615252655, 9436739655; byronnongbri@gmail.com; Nongriat; dm/d/q ₹300/800/1200) provides sheets, blankets, mosquito nets, fans and inexpensive food, and is a good budget place to stop a night or two if you want to soak up the jungle atmosphere or explore more trails.

A taxi from Cherrapunjee to Tyrna costs ₹300 to ₹400 and it's a good idea to arrange for the driver to pick you up for the return trip.

🛏 Sleeping & Eating

Cherrapunjee has dozens of homestays and small guesthouses with rooms from about ₹800 to ₹3000, plus a few upmarket places.

Sa-i-Mika Resort RESORT $$
(☑ 9862221718; www.saimikaresort.com; r ₹3000-4800) Two groups of rustic but comfortable stone-walled, tin-roofed cottages are scattered across a hillside 2km west of Cherrapunjee (3km by road). On first impression it seems rather haphazardly managed, but Sa-i-Mika runs fine in its own way. Chirpy local lads cook up noodle dishes, grilled sandwiches and all-day breakfasts – and proffer beer, wine and spirits to the needy.

There's also an extremely bare-bones dorm where you could lay your head if your budget's at rock bottom.

★ **Cherrapunjee
Holiday Resort** RESORT $$$
(☑ 8794803833; www.cherrapunjee.com; Laitkynsew Village; d half board ₹4650-6400; 🕸) Run by an affable Khasi woman, this delightful resort is 15km southwest of Cherrapunjee but only 4km from Tyrna. It has inviting rooms in the main building and more deluxe abodes in a newer block. The home-style meals are simply fantastic, and the resort can provide helpful information and guides for other nearby hikes and canyoning trips.

A bus leaves nearby Laitkynsew village for Shillong (₹70, 6am Monday to Saturday). Coming the other way, it leaves the ground floor of the Cherrapunjee taxi building at Anjeli in Shillong at 1pm. A taxi from Cherrapunjee costs ₹300 to ₹400.

ℹ Getting There & Away

Although straggling for several kilometres, Cherrapunjee has a compact centre. Huddled beside the marketplace is the taxi and jeep stand, with shared taxis (₹100) and Sumos (₹70) to Shillong (two hours).

Odisha

Best Places to Eat

➜ Wildgrass Restaurant (p608)

➜ Kila Dalijoda (p621)

➜ Kanika (p602)

➜ Odisha Hotel (p602)

Best Places to Stay

➜ Kila Dalijoda (p621)

➜ Chandoori Sai (p619)

➜ Desia (p619)

➜ Gajlaxmi Palace (p621)

➜ Garh Dhenkanal Palace (p621)

Why Go?

A favourite destination for adventurous travellers, Odisha (Orissa) rewards those who make the effort to stray off the beaten track with an intricate patchwork of archaeological wonders, fascinating tribal culture, and natural beauty, along with an old-fashioned sprinkling of sun and sand.

The forested hills of the southwest keep Adivasi (tribal) groups largely hidden from mainstream tourism, but it is still possible to visit their weekly markets and interact with villagers leading traditional lives. Forests elsewhere – both inland and along the coast – are home to some of Odisha's wonderful nature reserves, where you might spy 6m-long crocs, rare dolphins, endangered sea turtles and thousands of nesting birds.

Foodies will relish a whole new set of regional flavours cooked up in Odishan kitchens, while history buffs will be left contemplating long-lost Buddhist universities, ancient Jain rock carvings and centuries-old Hindu relics, including Konark's unparalleled Sun Temple.

When to Go
Bhubaneswar

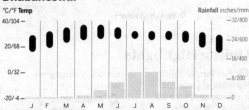

Nov–Feb Warm and dry; best time for the beach and wildlife-spotting in nature reserves.

Jun & Jul It's either baking hot or pouring rain, but Puri's Rath Yatra is Odisha's biggest festival.

Dec The Sun Temple is the magnificent backdrop for the Konark Festival.

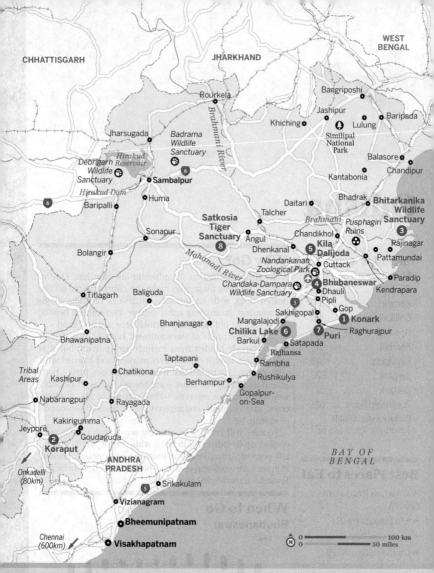

Odisha Highlights

1 **Sun Temple** (p610)
Marvelling at the artistic
magnificence of Konark's
800-year-old edifice.

2 **Koraput** (p616)
Venturing deep into the hills
of Odisha's tribal country for
markets and villages.

3 **Bhitarkanika Wildlife
Sanctuary** (p623) Cruising
past enormous estuarine

crocodiles in mangrove
swamps.

4 **Bhubaneswar** (p597)
Touring some of the ancient
temples that remain hidden in
Odisha's capital city.

5 **Kila Dalijoda** (p621)
Cycling through pristine
villages and immersing yourself
in traditional culture.

6 **Chilika Lake** (p611)
Spotting rare Irrawaddy
dolphins and a wealth of
migratory birdlife.

7 **Puri** (p605) Tapping into
the traveller vibe in Odisha's
most appealing town.

8 **Satkosia Tiger Sanctuary**
(p620) Stepping out of your
camp and gazing across the
sands of the Mahanadi River.

History

Formerly known as Kalinga, Utkala and more recently Orissa, Odisha (per a long-standing name-change campaign that finally received government approval in 2010) was once a formidable maritime empire that had trading routes leading down into Indonesia. Its history is somewhat hazy until the demise of the Kalinga dynasty in 260 BC at the hands of the great emperor Ashoka. Appalled at the carnage he had caused, Ashoka forswore violence and converted to Buddhism. Around the 1st century BC, Buddhism declined and Jainism was restored as the faith of the people. During this period the monastery caves of Udayagiri and Khandagiri (in Bhubaneswar) were excavated as important Jain centres.

By the 7th century AD, Hinduism had supplanted Jainism. Under the Kesari and Ganga kings, trade and commerce increased and Odishan culture flourished – countless temples from that classical period still stand. The Odishans defied the Muslim rulers in Delhi until finally falling to the Mughals during the 16th century, when many of Bhubaneswar's temples were destroyed. Thereafter, until Independence, Odisha was ruled by Afghans, Marathas and subsequently the British.

In recent times (notably the 1990s), a Hindu fundamentalist group called Bajrang Dal undertook a violent campaign against Christians in Odisha in response to missionary activity. The often illiterate and dispossessed tribal people suffered the most from the resulting communal violence, which was as much about power, politics and land as religious belief.

Some of Odisha's western districts – with a significant tribal population – lie along India's Maoist corridor, and insurgency flares up from time to time in these rural areas. The creation of the neighbouring states of Jharkhand, Chhattisgarh and Telangana has prompted recent calls for the formation of a separate tribal-oriented state, Kosal, carved out of western Odisha with Sambalpur as the capital. A separatist political party, the Kosal Kranti Dal (KKD), fielded candidates in the 2009 state election and took to disruptive transport protests in 2010.

ℹ Information

DANGERS & ANNOYANCES

Mosquitoes in some parts of Odisha have a reputation for being dengue and malaria vectors. Arm yourself with repellent and cover up while travelling in forest areas.

The presence of armed insurgency means there can be skirmishes and flare-ups in the tribal regions of Odisha, particularly southwestern districts such as Koraput, Rayagada and Malkangiri. To avoid getting caught in tricky situations, it is best to travel to these districts with a reputed tour operator.

TOURIST INFORMATION

Odisha Tourism (www.odishatourism.gov.in) has a presence in most towns, with offices for information and tour/hotel bookings. Odisha Tourism Development Corporation (www.panthanivas.com), the commercial arm of Odisha Tourism, runs tours and hotels throughout the state.

ℹ Getting There & Away

Air routes connect Bhubaneswar with Bengaluru, Delhi, Hyderabad, Mumbai, Kolkata and Chennai. Major road and rail routes between Kolkata and Chennai pass through coastal Odisha and Bhubaneswar with spur connections to Puri. Road and rail connect Sambalpur with Kolkata, Chhattisgarh and Madhya Pradesh, while Koraput and Rayagada are connected to Bhubaneswar by overnight trains.

BHUBANESWAR

📞 0674 / POP 838,000

Once dubbed the 'Temple City', chaotic Bhubaneswar is a worthwhile pit stop for a day or two. This will allow you to take in the old city's holy centre, which surrounds the ceremonial tank called Bindu Sagar. Thousands of medieval stone temples once stood here; around 50 currently remain. Temples aside, there are a couple of worthwhile museums, an ancient cave complex and the most varied dining scene in Odisha, along with a smattering of decent hotels.

◉ Sights

★ Lingaraj Mandir   HINDU TEMPLE

(Lingaraj Temple Rd; ◷ dawn-dusk) The 54m-high Lingaraj Mandir dedicated to Shiva dates from 1090 to 1104 – though some parts are more than 1400 years old – and is surrounded by several smaller temples and shrines. The granite block within, representing Tribhubaneswar (Lord of Three Worlds), is bathed daily with water, milk and *bhang* (marijuana). The main gate, guarded by two mustachioed yellow lions, is a spectacle in itself as lines of pilgrims approach with offerings in hand. The temple is closed to non-Hindus.

Given the high compound wall, foreigners can view the temple's interiors only from a

Bhubaneswar

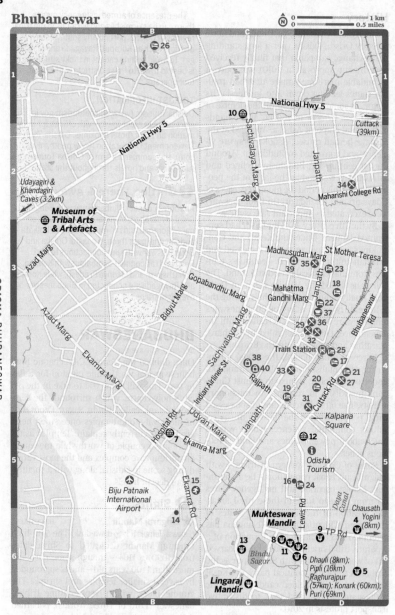

viewing platform (this may also include Hindu foreigners). Face the main entrance, walk right, then follow the wall around to the left and find the viewing platform on your left, just before you reach Chitrakarini Temple. There is occasional aggressive hassling for 'donations' at the viewing platform. The mon-

ey will not go to the temple, so stand your ground and do not pay. Take bus 333 here from Master Canteen bus stand.

★ **Mukteswar Mandir** HINDU TEMPLE
(Kedar Gouri Lane; ⊙ dawn-dusk) This small but beautiful 10th-century structure is one of the

Bhubaneswar

most ornate temples in Bhubaneswar; you'll see reproductions of it on posters across Odisha. Intricate carvings show a mixture of Buddhist, Jain and Hindu styles – look for Nagarani (the Snake Queen), easily mistaken for a mermaid, whom you'll also see at the nearby Rajarani Mandir. The ceiling carvings and stone arch are particularly striking, as is the *torana* (archway) at the front, clearly showing Buddhist sculptural influence.

★ **Museum of Tribal**
Arts & Artefacts   MUSEUM
(off NH16; ⊙10am-5pm Tue-Sun) FREE This superb museum is a must for visitors interested in Odisha's 62 tribes or considering a visit to the state's tribal areas. Complete with interactive elements such as augmented reality glasses, its galleries display traditional dress, bead ornaments, silver collars, coin necklaces, elaborate headdresses, ornate wind pipes and musical instruments. One gallery is dedicated entirely to weaponry, fishing, hunting and agricultural equipment. Behind the museum are replicas of traditional houses from the Gadaba, Kandha, Santal, Saora and other tribes.

Bus 801 goes to nearby Azad Marg, from where the museum is a five-minute walk. Alternately, an autorickshaw from the Master Canteen area will cost you about ₹80.

Udayagiri & Khandagiri Caves   HISTORIC SITE
(off NH16; both sites Indian/foreigner ₹25/300, video ₹50; ⊙dawn-dusk) Six kilometres west of the city centre are two hills riddled with rock-cut shelters. Khandagiri is topped with a fine temple. Many of the caves are ornately carved and thought to have been chiselled out for Jain ascetics in the 1st century BC.

Ascending the ramp at Udayagiri (Sunrise Hill), note Swargapuri (Cave 9) to the right with its devotional figures. Hathi Gumpha (Elephant Cave; Cave 14) at the top has a 117-line inscription relating the exploits of its builder, King Kharavela of Kalinga, who ruled from 168 to 153 BC.

Around the left you'll see Bagh Gumpha (Tiger Cave; Cave 12), with its entrance carved as a tiger mouth. Nearby are Pavana Gumpha (Cave of Wind) and small Sarpa Gumpha (Serpent Cave), where the tiny door is surmounted by a three-headed cobra. On the summit are the remains of a defensive position. Around to the southeast is the single-storey elephant-guarded Ganesh Gumpha (Cave 10), almost directly above the two-storey Rani ka Naur (Queen's Palace Cave; Cave 1), carved with Jain symbols and battle scenes.

Continue back to the entrance via Chota Hathi Gumpha (Lesser Elephant Cave; Cave

3), with its carvings of elephants, and the double-storey Jaya Vijaya Cave (Victory Cave; Cave 5), with a bodhi tree carved in the central area.

Across the road, Khandagiri offers fine views over Bhubaneswar from its summit. The steep path splits about one-third of the way up the hill. The right path goes to Ananta Cave (Eternity Cave; Cave 3), with its carved figures of athletes, women, elephants and geese carrying flowers. Further along is a series of Jain temples; at the top is another (18th-century) Jain temple.

Buses don't go to the caves, but bus 801 runs to the nearby Baramunda bus stand. A return autorickshaw ride from Master Canteen bus stand shouldn't cost much more than ₹350, including waiting time.

State Museum   MUSEUM
(www.odishamuseum.nic.in; Lewis Rd; Indian/foreigner ₹10/100, camera ₹10/100, video ₹200/2000; ⊘10am-4.30pm Tue-Sun) This museum houses Odisha's best collection of rare palm-leaf manuscripts, as well as *patachitra* (scroll paintings), traditional musical instruments, Bronze Age tools, an armoury, and an impressive collection of Buddhist, Jain and Brahmanical sculptures (look for the haunting 8th-century sculpture of Chamunda).

Parsurameswar Mandir   HINDU TEMPLE
(Kedar Gouri Ln; ⊘dawn-dusk) This is an ornate Shiva temple built around AD 650. It has

---

TOP STATE FESTIVALS

Adivasi Mela Features art, dance and handicrafts of Odisha's tribal groups in Bhubaneswar.

Rath Yatra (p607) Immense chariots containing Lord Jagannath, brother Balbhadra and sister Subhadra are hauled from Jagannath Mandir to Gundicha Mandir.

Puri Beach Festival (p607) Song, dance, food and cultural activities on the beach in Puri.

Bali Yatra (⊘Nov/Dec) Immense state fair in Cuttack, with fine silver filigree, *ikat* (fabric made with thread which is tie-dyed before weaving) and other crafts for sale.

Konark Festival (p611) Features traditional music and dance and a seductive temple ritual.

---

lively bas-reliefs of elephant and horse processions, panels of musicians and dancers, and delicately sculpted Shiva images. The temple can be accessed by a pathway leading west through the gardens within the Mukteswar Mandir complex.

Rajarani Mandir   HINDU TEMPLE
(TP Rd; Indian/foreigner ₹15/200, camera ₹25; ⊘dawn-dusk) Built around AD 1100, this temple surrounded by manicured gardens is famous for its ornate *deul* (temple spire). Around the compass points are pairs of statues representing eight *dikpalas* (temple guardians). Between them, nymphs, embracing couples, elephants and lions peer from niches and decorate the temple's pillars.

☞ Tours

Odisha Tourism Development Corporation   CULTURAL
(OTDC; ☑0674-2431515; www.otdc.in; Lewis Rd; ⊘7am-8pm) Daily bus tours by OTDC include city tours (₹335, 9am) to Nandankanan Zoo, Dhauli, the Lingaraj and Mukteswar temples, State Museum, and Udayagiri and Khandagiri Caves. Another tour visits Pipli, Konark and Puri (₹440, 9am), while a third takes in Puri and Satapada on Chilika Lake (₹465, 8am). Book the day before. Tour prices exclude entry fees at sites.

Alternative Tours   TOURS
(☑0674-2593463; www.alternativetoursindia. com; off Ekamra Rd, Palashpalli Market Complex; ⊘10am-6pm Mon-Sat) 🖉 A veteran for tribal tours in Odisha, Nagaland and Arunachal Pradesh, this company's prices start at around ₹9000 per person per day, all-inclusive. It also runs multiday wildlife and heritage tours of Odisha and organises private day tours to Puri and Konark.

✯ Festivals & Events

Adivasi Mela   CULTURAL
(⊘26-31 Jan) Bhubaneswar goes tribal for the annual Adivasi Mela festival, celebrating the art, dance and handicrafts of Odisha's indigenous communities.

🛏 Sleeping

Many hotels have 24-hour checkout. The cheapest and less salubrious hotels are clustered around the train station. There are several midrange places along Janpath and Cuttack Rds, while the city's plushest offerings are found just north of NH 16, which circles the city, in BDA Colony.

Hotel Upasana
HOTEL $

([☑] 9439865225,0674-2310044; www.hotelupasana.
com; 2282 Laxmisagar, off Cuttack Rd; d with AC
from ₹1225, without AC from ₹999; [❋][@][☎]) This
family-run place has shabby rooms with hot
showers and small balconies. There are a
couple of computer terminals in the lobby
for internet, and the wi-fi is mostly limited to
the reception area. No restaurant.

Hotel Grand Central
HOTEL $$

([☑] 9937439074, 9437001152; www.hotelgrand
central.com; Old Station Bazaar; s/d incl breakfast
₹3150/3500; [❋][☎]) Whitewashed corridors
and marble floors lead to smart, well-fitted
rooms at this business-class hotel, located
just behind the train station. There's a res-
taurant, bar, newspaper in the mornings, toi-
letries, complimentary airport pickup (upon
advance notice) and car rental. If there was
an award for India's nicest station-side hotels,
this place would be a serious contender.

Mango Hotel
HOTEL $$

([☑] 0674-7119000; www.staymango.com; Cuttack Rd; d incl breakfast from ₹2425; [❋][☎]) With
friendly front-desk staff, a decent restaurant
serving a mix of North Indian and Odishan
dishes, a pleasant bar (recommended for solo
and women travellers), and spotless rooms
with comfy beds and decent wi-fi, this is the
best midrange choice along Cuttack Rd. The
train station is a five-minute walk away.

Panthanivas Hotel
HOTEL $$

([☑] 0674-2432314; www.panthanivas.com; Lewis
Rd; d incl breakfast from ₹1900; [❋]) A tad over-
priced, this government-run establishment
is conveniently located in front of the OTDC
office (p600) and has a string of well-kept,
air-conditioned rooms. The in-house res-
taurant has decent food, and the reception
coordinates with OTDC to book sightseeing
tours for guests.

Maurya Inn
HOTEL $$

([☑] 0674-2535894; 59 Janpath Rd; d from ₹1680;
[❋]) This is a simple, straightforward midrange hotel with clean, spacious rooms, hot
showers and cable TV. There's no internet or
restaurant, but it's located on one of the city's
main thoroughfares so you have enough
meal options as well as an internet cafe within walking distance.

Hotel Hindustan International
HOTEL $$$

([☑] 0674-6677000, 9937290558; www.hhi
bhubaneswar.com; 112A Kharvel Nagar, Janpath;
s/d incl breakfast from ₹9500/10,000; [❋][@][☎][⛱]))

Although slightly dated, this business hotel
can be a fantastic deal if you secure an on-
line discount, sometimes slashing rates in
half. Rooms are spacious, the lapis-hued pool
beckons after a long day of sightseeing and
the complimentary breakfast is sumptuous.

★ Trident Hotel
RESORT $$$

([☑] 0674-3010000; www.tridenthotels.com; CB1
Nayapalli; d incl breakfast ₹16,000; [❋][☎][⛱]) The
spacious, stylish rooms at the Trident, decorated with fine examples of Odishan stonework, textiles and metalwork, look out onto
the peaceful gardens. There's a private jogging track, luxurious pool and one of the best
restaurants in town. It's located 6km north of
the train station.

New Marrion
HOTEL $$$

([☑] 0674-2380850; www.hotelnewmarrion.com;
6 Janpath Rd; d incl breakfast from ₹8000;
[❋][@][☎][⛱]) A central top-end hotel, Marrion
has rooms with a contemporary, classy de-
sign: LCD TVs, dark-wood panelling and a
small sofa space. Restaurants include South
Indian, an Italian-Mexican combo, Chinese
and a great kebab house; there's also a Café
Coffee Day out front, a contemporary bar and
a spa. Rates can be significantly cheaper if
you book online.

✗ Eating

Truptee
SOUTH INDIAN $

(Cuttack Rd; mains ₹70-160; ⊙7am-10.30pm) A
great choice for South Indian breakfasts, this
clean, family-friendly restaurant does a fine
line in dosas (paper-thin lentil-flour pan-
cakes), *vadas* (doughnut-shaped deep-fried
lentil savoury) and *idlis* (spongy, fermented
rice cakes) before bringing out the curries
and tandoor flatbreads later in the day. Also
prepares thalis (₹100 to ₹150).

Sri Ram Mandir Tiffin Centre
STREET FOOD $

(Janpath Rd; dishes ₹15-40; ⊙6.30am-9pm) *Dahi
vada* (*vada* in flavoured yoghurt sauce) is a
popular Odishan breakfast dish, and locals
flock to this street-side stall beside Sri Ram
Mandir to have their fill, along with other
tasty offerings such as samosas, *aloo chops*
(deep-fried potato patties) and small portions
of veg curry. Simply point at what you want,
pay up and tuck in.

Khana Khazana
INDIAN $

(Kalpana Sq; mains ₹50-170; ⊙5.30-10.30pm) This
long-standing evening-only street stall – with
plastic chairs and tables spread across the
pavement – does a bang-up job with tandoori

ODIA CUISINE

Mustard is the staple condiment in Odishan kitchens, used ubiquitously in seed, paste and oil forms, giving many Odishan dishes a distinct sharp flavour. A typical meal consists of *bhata* (rice) served alongside a variety of tasty side dishes such as *kaharu phula bhaja* (fried pumpkin flower); *dalma* (dhal cooked with pumpkin, potato, green plantain and eggplant, fried in a five-spice oil of fenugreek, cumin, black cumin, anise and mustard, and then topped with grated coconut); and *besara* (vegetables or river fish in mustard-paste gravy). *Saga bhaja* (leafy greens lightly fried with garlic paste and a five-seed mixture called *pancha phutan* (cumin, mustard, anise, black cumin and chilli) is also a treat here. On the coast, fish and prawns are omnipresent: *sarisa machha* is a superb favourite fish dish cooked in a mustard-based curry. *Chhena poda*, made from baked, caramelised cottage cheese, is a dessert that shouldn't be missed.

chicken, delicious noodles and tasty biryanis. The *chicken dum biryani* (₹100) is particularly popular with the locals, as are the great-value rolls (roti wraps that come with various fillings, priced ₹40 to ₹60).

Narula's NORTH INDIAN $$
(Hotel Basera, Janpath; mains ₹170-310; ☉noon-3pm & 7-11pm) Among the best North Indian kitchens in town, this stylish, air-conditioned restaurant serves perfectly cooked tandoori chicken, as well as other classics including butter chicken, dhal makhani (black lentils and red kidney beans with cream and butter), *rajma chawal* (kidney bean curry with basmati rice) and fluffy naan. It's accessed by a narrow staircase leading up between two sporting goods stores.

Odisha Hotel ODISHAN $$
(Market Bldg, Sahid Nagar; thali veg/nonveg ₹165/225; ☉12.30-10.30pm) This simple restaurant is one of the best spots to try authentic Odishan cuisine, served in huge thali-style proportions. There's an English menu available, which also lists a long line of nonveg preps (mutton, chicken and prawn). It's on the second street on the left if heading east along Maharishi College Rd, past Bhawani Mall.

★**Dalma** ODISHAN $$
(Unit IV Madhusudan Nagar; mains ₹80-180, thali ₹180-240; ☉11am-4pm & 7-10.30pm) This outlet of the small Bhubaneswar chain is widely regarded by locals as the best place in town to sample authentic Odishan cuisine, including *aloo bharta* (a delicious mashed potato and aubergine combination), *dalma* (the restaurant's speciality dhal dish, cooked with coconut), *chhena poda* (a yummy baked cottage-cheese dessert) and numerous Odishan thalis.

Hare Krishna Restaurant INDIAN $$
(Lalchand Shopping Complex, Janpath Rd; mains ₹140-280; ☉11.30am-3.30pm & 7-10.45pm; ✐) The beautifully lacquered Gujarati *sankheda* furniture stands out at this stylish but unpretentious vegetarian restaurant where you can enjoy delicious curries, biryanis and tandoor-baked flatbreads in a soothing atmosphere. Enter through Lalchand Shopping Complex.

★**Kanika** ODISHAN $$$
(☎9238413009; www.mayfairhotels.com; Mayfair Lagoon, Jaydev Vihar; mains ₹445-995; ☉noon-3pm & 7.30-11pm) Located at the Mayfair Lagoon hotel, tiny Kanika does a fabulous job with regional Odishan recipes, particularly excelling with local seafood. Specialities include *kankada yarkari* (crab curry); slow-cooked, spiced pomfret; mustard-based dishes; and Odisha's most traditional dessert, the seriously addictive *chhena poda* (literally 'burnt cheese', cooked with sugar, cashew nuts and raisins). Excellent veg and nonveg thalis too.

🍷 Drinking & Nightlife

BNC CAFE
(Brown n Cream; Janpath Rd; ☉8am-11pm) An aircon-cooled cafe with good-value coffee (₹90), plus sandwiches, muffins and ice cream.

🔒 Shopping

Boyanika TEXTILES
(Unit 2, Ashok Nagar; ☉10am-8.30pm) An excellent selection of Odishan textiles, including *ikat* fabric (featuring tie-dyed thread) and *bomkai* saris (known for their intricate needlework), are available at this showroom.

Utkalika ARTS & CRAFTS
(Odisha State Handloom Cooperative; Eastern Tower, Market Bldg, Ashok Nagar; ☉10am-8.30pm)

Located in the busy all-day market streets known as Market Building, Utkalika features Odishan textiles, including appliqué and *ikat* (tie-dyed thread), as well as traditional palm-leaf paintings, fine stone carvings, silver filigree from Cuttack, brasswork and tribal jewellery.

Ekamra Haat   MARKET
(Madhusudan Marg; ⊙11am-9pm) A wide-ranging exposition of Odishan handicrafts (and snack stalls) can be found at the 50 or so stalls at this permanent market, located within pleasant, well-tended gardens.

❶ Information

MEDICAL SERVICES

Apollo Hospital (☑ 0674-7150382, 0674-6661016; www.apollohospitals.com; Plot No 251, Old Sainik School Rd; ⊙24hr) Private medical facility with a 24-hour trauma centre and pharmacy.

MONEY

ATMs are plentiful along Janpath, Cuttack Rd and Lewis Rd. There are also a couple at the train station.

State Bank of India (Lewis Rd; ⊙10am-4pm Mon-Fri, to noon Sat) Exchanges foreign currencies.

POST

Post office (www.indiapost.gov.in; cnr Mahatma Gandhi & Sachivajaya Margs; ⊙9am-7pm Mon-Sat, 3-7pm Sun) Main post office.

TOURIST INFORMATION

India Tourism (☑ 0674-2432203; www.incredibleindia.org; 2nd fl, Paryatan Bhavan, Lewis Rd; ⊙9am-5pm Mon-Fri, to 1pm Sat) Info on nationwide attractions; in the same building as the main Odisha Tourism office.

Odisha Tourism (☑ 0674-2432177; www.odishatourism.gov.in; 2nd fl, Paryatan Bhavan, Museum Campus, Lewis Rd; ⊙10am-5pm Mon-Sat, closed 2nd Sat of the month) The main branch of the government tourist office, with maps and lists of recommended guides. Other branches are at the **airport** (Biju Patnaik International Airport; ⊙10am-5pm) and **train station** (⊙6am-10pm).

❶ Getting There & Away

AIR

Bhubaneswar's **Biju Patnaik International Airport** is 2km south of the city. There are frequent daily flights operated by IndiGo, GoAir and SpiceJet to Delhi, Kolkata (Calcutta), Mumbai, Bengaluru (Bangalore) and Hyderabad. AirAsia also connects the city to Kuala Lumpur and Bangkok, four and three times per week respectively.

TRAIN

Foreigners queue at window 3 at the **computerised reservation office** (⊙8am-8pm Mon-Sat, to 2pm Sun), in a separate building in front of the train station. Destinations are as follows:

Berhampur (Brahmapur) 2nd class/sleeper ₹70/140, two to three hours, more than a dozen, 5am to 7.35pm

BUSES FROM BHUBANESWAR

For destinations northeast of Bhubaneswar, it's quicker to catch a bus to Cuttack's Badambari bus stand and then catch onward services from there; jump on any of these buses heading east along Cuttack Rd. Puri-bound buses from Baramunda bus stand spend ages going around the city and picking up passengers; catch them outside the State Museum (p600) to save time, though they'll be pretty full by then.

Baramunda bus stand is reachable by bus 801 from Master Canteen bus stand (₹10, 20 minutes) or autorickshaw/Uber (around ₹100/150 from the centre).

Services from **Baramunda bus stand** (NH16) are as follows:

DESTINATION	FARE (₹)	DURATION (HR)	DEPARTURES
Baripada	320	6	hourly 9am-11pm
Berhampur	180	4	every 2 hours
Cuttack	30	40min	frequent
Jeypore	non-AC/AC 550/620	13-16	5 daily
Kolkata	non-AC seat/sleeper 400/700, AC seat/sleeper 600/800	9	frequent 7.30am-9pm
Konark	40	2	hourly
Koraput	non-AC seat 460	14	five daily
Puri	40	2	hourly

Kolkata (Calcutta) sleeper/3AC ₹260/700, seven to nine hours, at least 10 daily, 6.10am to 11.50pm

Puri 2nd class/sleeper ₹40/140, two hours, more than a dozen, 6am to 9.10pm

ⓘ Getting Around

AUTORICKSHAW

An autorickshaw to the airport, if hailed on the street, costs around ₹200; an autorickshaw summoned with the Ola app costs around ₹100. Shared autorickshaws ply main routes around the city and charge locals ₹10 for most rides, but foreigners could be asked for up to ₹20 (if this is the case, simply pay what others are paying and hop out).

BUS

Bhubaneswar has a numbered city-bus system that runs between 7am and 9pm from the bus stand known as **Master Canteen**, by the train station. Double-check your bus is going where you want it to, as some bus numbers run along more than one route.

City buses leaving from Master Canteen bus stand:

Airport Bus 207A, ₹10, 15 minutes

Baramunda Bus Stand Bus 801, ₹10, 20 minutes

Dhauli Bus 225, ₹10, 30 minutes

Lingaraj Mandir Bus 333, ₹10, 20 minutes

Mayfair Hotel Bus 207N, ₹10, 20 minutes

Mukteswar Mandir Bus 225, ₹10, 15 minutes

Pipli Bus 701, ₹50, 50 minutes

Puri Bus 701, ₹100, two hours

Udayagiri Caves Bus 801 or 405, ₹10, 30 minutes

CAR & TAXI

Uber and Ola trips across the city usually cost around ₹100 or less. Ola also gives you the option of hiring autorickshaws (at a cheaper rate) and organising a one-way drop-off (to Puri or Konark).

Odisha Tourism Development Corporation (p600) offers car-and-driver services for tours around the area. Local sightseeing trips totalling less than 80km or eight hours cost around ₹1500. For trips over 200km, the charges are ₹12 per kilometre for an AC D-Zire car. Book in person at least a day in advance.

There's a prepaid taxi stand at the airport; taxis to the centre cost ₹350.

In 2018 a city-based voluntary organisation called SOCH began an initiative to train under-privileged women to become taxi drivers; SOCH is expected to grow in terms of commercial operations over time.

Around Bhubaneswar

Scattered around the countryside in all directions from the capital, several worthwhile sites make easy half-day trips from Bhubaneswar. These include a zoo, craft village, tantric temple and centuries-old rock edicts.

◉ Sights

Nandankanan Zoological Park ZOO
(www.nandankanan.org; Indian/foreigner ₹50/100, video camera ₹100; ◷ 7.30am-5.30pm Tue-Sun Apr-Sep, 8am-5pm Tue-Sun Oct-Mar) Famous for its white tigers, Odisha's premier zoological park was founded in 1960 and is known to run India's best captive-breeding program for the big cats. Spread over 4 sq km, the zoo also houses Asiatic lions, Himalayan bears, hippos, several species of crocs, a variety of snakes and a sizeable bird aviary. Forty-five-minute safaris to see some of the lions and tigers roaming a fenced forest area cost ₹30 per person. An autorickshaw/car drop-off costs around ₹200/250.

Dhauli BUDDHIST MONUMENT
(Ashoka Rock Edicts; ◷ dawn-dusk) In about 260 BC, 11 of of Ashoka's 14 famous edicts were

---

TRAINS FROM BHUBANESWAR

DESTINATION	TRAIN NO & NAME	FARE (₹)	DURATION (HR)	DEPARTURE
Chennai	12841 Coromandal Exp	550/1455/2100	19½	9.35pm
Kolkata (Howrah)	18410 Sri Jagannath Exp	260/700/1000	8¼	11.50pm
Koraput	18447 Hirakhand Exp	360/980/1410	14	7.35pm
Mumbai	12880 BBS LTT SF Exp	695/1835/2675	30½	7.10am
New Delhi	12801 Purushottam Exp	695/1835/2675	29¼	11.07pm
Ranchi	12832 BKSC Garib Rath	675 (3AC only)	11	8.15pm
Rayagada	18447 Hirakhand Exp	300/815/1165	9¼	7.35pm

Fares: sleeper/3AC/2AC

carved onto a rock at Dhauli, 8km south of Bhubaneswar. Above the edicts, the earliest Buddhist sculpture in Odisha – a carved elephant representing Buddha – emerges from a rock. From the Dhauli turn-off, accessed by Bhubaneswar-Puri buses (₹15, 30 minutes), it's a tree-shaded 3km walk or shared/private autorickshaw ride (₹10/100) to the rock edicts and then a short, steep walk to the stupa. Uber drop-off costs around ₹180.

Just beyond the rock edicts, each translated into English, is the huge, white Shanti Stupa (Peace Pagoda), built by Japanese monks in 1972 on a hill to the right. Older Buddhist reliefs are set into the modern structure, and there are great views of the surrounding countryside from the top.

Pipli
VILLAGE

This colourful village, 16km southeast of Bhubaneswar, is notable for its locally made brilliant appliqué craft, which incorporates small mirrors and is used for door and wall hangings and the traditional canopies hung over Jagannath and family during festivals. Inexpensive lampshades and parasols hanging outside the shops turn the main road into an avenue of rainbow colours. During Diwali the place is particularly vibrant. Take any Bhubaneswar–Puri bus (₹15) and hop off en route.

Chausath Yogini
HINDU MONUMENT

(⊘ dawn-dusk) Hidden among rice fields 15km south of Bhubaneswar, this small but serene 9th-century open-roofed temple is dedicated to *yoginis* (female tantric mystics) and is one of only four in India. No larger than a village hut, the temple contains intricate rock carvings of 64 *(chausath) yoginis,* each shown standing on top of her *vahana* (vehicle; often in animal form). No buses go here; a return trip from the city by autorickshaw/ Uber costs around ₹500/600.

ℹ Getting There & Away

Pipli and Dhauli are easily accessible via frequent bus connections from Bhubaneswar. To visit the other attractions, you have to go as part of an organised tour, take an Uber/autorickshaw or hire a car with driver (half-/full day ₹800/1500).

SOUTHEASTERN ODISHA

Southeastern Odisha hugs the coast of the Bay of Bengal and is home to the state's most visited spots, including the backpacker outpost of Puri and the Unesco-protected Sun Temple at Konark. Tiny Raghurajpur is craft central, Chilika Lake provides ample birding and dolphin-watching opportunities, and there's a rustic beach at Golpalpur-on-Sea.

Puri

✔ 06752 / POP 200,500

Hindu pilgrims, Bengali holidaymakers and foreign travellers all make their way to Puri. For Hindus, Puri is one of the holiest pilgrimage places in India, with religious life revolving around the great Jagannath Mandir and its famous Rath Yatra (Chariot Festival). The town's other attraction is its long sandy beach, which is much better for strolling than swimming.

In the 1970s the sea and copious supply of *bhang* (marijuana) attracted travellers on the hippie trail here. There's little trace of that scene today, but visitors from around the world still come to chill out and visit the Sun Temple in nearby Konark.

All the action is along a few kilometres of coastline. The backpacker part of town is bunched up towards the eastern end of Chakra Tirtha (CT) Rd, while local tourists flock to busy New Marine Drive in the west, along an extended and bustling esplanade.

⊙ Sights

★ Jagannath Mandir
HINDU TEMPLE

(Swargadwar Rd) This mighty temple is home to Jagannath (Lord of the Universe), an incarnation of Vishnu. Built in its present form in 1198, the temple – closed to non-Hindus – is surrounded by two walls, its 58m-high flag-draped *sikhara* (spire) topped by Vishnu's wheel. Non-Hindus can get a rooftop view and take photos from the Raghunandan Library terrace (cnr Temple & Swargadwar Rds; ⊘ 9am-1.30pm & 4-6pm Mon-Sat) across the street for a 'donation' (₹100 is fine). Cameras and mobile phones are not allowed within the temple.

Model Beach
BEACH

🏊 Puri is no palm-fringed paradise – the beach is wide, shelves quickly with a nasty shore break and is shadeless. But Model Beach, part of a sustainable, community-run beach-tourism initiative, offers a 700m stretch of sand that's easily Puri's finest and cleanest. Palm umbrellas provide shade, and a team of cabana boys and lifeguards known as Sea Riders hawk fixed-price beach chairs

Puri

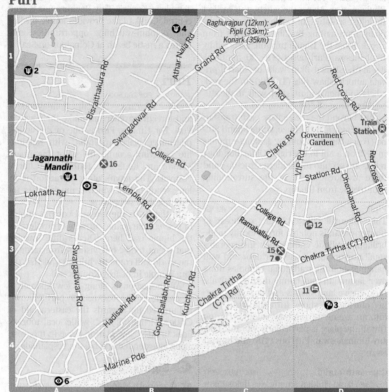

Raghurajpur (12km); Pipli (33km); Konark (35km)

Jagannath Mandir

ODISHA PURI

(per hour ₹20) and massages (₹100 to ₹200); they are also responsible for keeping the beach clean.

Swargdwar   RELIGIOUS SITE
(off New Marine Rd) These hallowed cremation grounds are the final earthly stop for some 40 deceased Hindus who are cremated here daily. You can watch or walk among the open-air ceremonies as long as you behave in a respectful manner and avoid taking photos. It's an obviously solemn affair, but a fascinating glimpse into Puri's role as one of India's holiest cities.

Activities

Barefoot   VOLUNTEERING
(www.heritagetoursorissa.com) This small local NGO, started by Heritage Tours, works to improve community lifestyles through sustainable tourism development. Volunteers must commit to a two-week minimum pe-riod, which can involve teaching English, beach maintenance supervision and train-ing in tourism. From ₹1500 per week includ-ing lodging and meals.

Tours

Grass Routes   CULTURAL
(☑ 9437029698, 9437022663; www.grassroutes journeys.com) ✎ Grass Routes' Indian-Australian husband-and-wife team has a stellar reputation for sensitive, all-inclusive multiday tours of tribal Odisha as well as history and nature tours. Pulak and Claire organise excellent overnight island stays at a private tented camp at Chilika Lake and day trips by bicycle into the picturesque coun-tryside around Puri.

Contact them in advance to discuss and book a tour. Also note that they do not main-tain a physical office in Puri, so you'll have to schedule a meeting by calling or emailing them first.

Heritage Tours CULTURAL
(☏ 06752-255656, 9437023656; www.heritage toursorissa.com; CT Rd, Mayfair Heritage Hotel; ⊕ 8am-8pm) 🖉 Bubu is a tribal and cultural-tourism veteran whose tour company focuses on rural and special-interest ethnic tourism. In addition to Puri walking tours and multiday tribal tours, Heritage also offers bicycle tours covering Puri, Konark, Bhubaneswar and Chilika Lake. The agency's latest venture is a homestay experience in the proprietor's family home in Puri.

OTDC CULTURAL
(☏ 06752-223664; www.otdc.in; CT Rd; ⊕ 10am-10pm Mon-Sat) Runs two-day trips from Puri. Tour 1 (₹450, 6.30am Tuesday to Sunday) calls at Konark, Dhauli, Bhubaneswar's temples, the Udayagiri and Khandagiri caves plus Nandankanan Zoo. Tour 2 (₹300, 6.30am daily) goes for a boat jaunt on Chilika Lake. Admission fees are not included.

🎊 Festivals & Events

Rath Yatra RELIGIOUS
(Chariot Festival; ⊕ Jul/Aug) Immense wooden chariots containing Lord Jagannath, brother Balbhadra and sister Subhadra are hauled from Jagannath Mandir to Gundicha Mandir, beside Puri's main bus stand. The Ulta Rath Yatra (return trip of the chariots) takes place about 10 days later. The English word juggernaut supposedly derives from the sight of Jagannath's massive chariot rolling unstoppably down the road during the procession.

Puri Beach Festival CULTURAL
(⊕ late Nov) A festival featuring song, dance, food and cultural activities, including installations on the beach by sand artists from across India.

🛏 Sleeping

Lodgings accommodating foreigners are found east of VIP Rd, along CT Rd, while hotels catering to domestic tourists front Marine Drive. Book well in advance if your trip coincides with Rath Yatra, Durga Puja (Dussehra) or Diwali. Many hotels have 9am checkout times.

Travellers Inn
GUESTHOUSE $

(☏8280168993, 06752-223592; CT Rd; r ₹850) Accommodation is very basic at this simple CT Rd guesthouse, but the prices are hard to beat. The rooms have some natural light as they open out onto a small, tatty garden courtyard, which leads down to the beach. There are a few dirt-cheap rooms as well (d ₹400), but they offer precious little to write home about.

Puri Home Stay
HOSTEL $

(☏8895353960; www.purihomestays.com; off VIP Rd; s/d ₹1000/1500; ❄🛜) Heritage Tours runs this welcome budget address, hidden on a quiet street off VIP Rd. There are common areas for mingling, including the tree-shaded courtyard and the fantastic roof terrace – ideal for sunset-gazing. Solo travellers can reserve a bed in a shared twin-bed room.

Hotel Lotus
HOTEL $

(☏06752-227033, 9438684302; www.hotellotuspuri.com; CT Rd; r with/without AC ₹1680/780; ❄🛜) Friendly and efficient, Lotus is probably the most popular budget choice among foreign backpackers, offering a range of inexpensive rooms that are clean and comfortable. The fan-cooled rooms, with small balconies, are great value. They fill up quickly, so book ahead.

Hotel Gandhara
HERITAGE HOTEL $$

(☏06752-224117, 06752-224623; www.hotelgandhara.com; CT Rd; incl breakfast d with/without AC ₹3050/1950'; ❄🛜🏊) Gandhara continues to steamroll the competition with its friendliness and amazing value. The 200-year-old pillared heritage building has three wonderfully atmospheric fan-cooled rooms. Pricier and modern AC rooms are in a new block at the back of the garden, overlooking a mango-tree-shaded swimming pool that wins full marks for cuteness.

Z Hotel
HERITAGE HOTEL $$

(☏06752-222554; www.zhotelindia.com; CT Rd; r from ₹2750; ❄🛜) This charming yet understated heritage hotel (pronounced 'jed') was a former royal home and remains one of Puri's most atmospheric choices. Rooms are large and airy, and come with high ceilings, chunky wooden furniture and spotless bathrooms. There's a restaurant, evening films shown in the TV room and wi-fi in common areas.

Chanakya BNR Hotel
HERITAGE HOTEL $$$

(☏9778373373, 06752-223006; www.chanakyabnrpuri.com; CT Rd; r incl breakfast ₹4400; ❄🛜🏊) Conjuring up images of the Raj, this splendid 150-year-old railway hotel features beautiful bygone touches throughout, including 90-year-old mural panels in the lobby stairwell and restaurant. Inside the enormous rooms, there's period furniture and old framed Indian Railways photographs. The 1st-floor rooms open out onto a large shared verandah, but sea views are somewhat impeded by construction across the road.

🍴 Eating

Puri has a decent dining scene that ranges from excellent Odishan specialities and delicious seafood to Indo-Chinese and Western food. Many restaurants are clustered along CT Rd and VIP Rd, and there are plenty of cheap options in the labyrinthine old town.

Puri Cheesecake
SWEETS $

(Temple Rd, Dolamandap Sahi; per piece ₹25; ⊙8am-11pm) Bikram Sahoo and his six brothers have been churning out the unique Odishan delight known as *chhena poda* (made from cottage cheese, sugar and cardamom, and cooked in an iron pan over an open flame, it's a cross between a cheesecake and a flan) for more than 45 years from their sweet shop in Puri's holy quarters. A real treat.

★ Wildgrass Restaurant
ODISHAN $$

(☏9437023656; VIP Rd; mains ₹150-300, thali veg/nonveg ₹200/250; ⊙noon-11pm) Grab yourself a table at this tranquil restaurant, either in one of the thatched pavilions or the air-con dining room, and tuck into excellent house specialities served by supercourteous waiters. The tandoori pomfret is stellar, as is the Chilika crab curry. The seasonal vegetable specialities (best sampled as part of the thali) are not to be missed either.

Chung Wah
CHINESE $$

(VIP Rd; mains ₹250-380; ⊙11.30am-3pm & 7-11pm) Inside the Lee Garden Hotel, this place certainly has the look of a classic Chinese restaurant: dark-wood booths, lattice screens and lots of red and gold and dragon imagery. The food is excellent Indo-Chinese – we particularly liked the hot garlic prawns.

Peace Restaurant MULTICUISINE $$
(off CT Rd; mains ₹80-260; ⊙7am-4pm & 7-11pm) A Puri stalwart that relocated to a quieter location off the main road, the Peace is a pleasant budget option. It does nice work with Western breakfasts and pasta dishes, but excels at simple local thalis and seafood. Save some room for house desserts, including a fried empanada-like banana or apple turnover laced with sugar, cinnamon and honey.

Honey Bee Bakery & Pizzeria CAFE $$
(CT Rd; pizzas ₹250-350, mains ₹150-350; ⊙8.30am-2pm & 6-10pm) Decent pizzas and pancakes, espresso-machine coffee (₹80), toasted sandwiches and breakfast fry-ups (including bacon) are all here at this cute cafe-restaurant with rooftop seating. It's a popular spot for breakfast.

Two States INDIAN $$$
(off CT Rd, Mayfair Heritage; mains ₹280-550; ⊙12.30-3pm & 7.30-10.30pm) This excellent restaurant inside the Mayfair Heritage hotel specialises in two cuisines: Odishan and Bengali. Seafood is the star here and all items on the succinct menu are well executed. Try the prawn cutlet or the prawn *malai* curry (prawns simmered in coconut-milk gravy).

ℹ️ Information

DANGERS & ANNOYANCES

Muggings and attacks on women have been reported along isolated stretches of Puri's beach, even during the day, so take care. Ocean currents can become treacherous in Puri, and drownings are not uncommon, so don't venture out beyond your depth. Ask one of the *noolias* (fisher-lifeguards), identifiable by their white conical wicker hats and yellow shirts, for the best spots (though they're not always around).

MEDICAL SERVICES

District Headquarter Hospital (☑06752-223742; Grand Rd; ⊙24hr) Has 24-hour emergency treatment and outpatient facilities.

MONEY

There are several ATMs along CT Rd.

POST

Post office (www.indiapost.gov.in; cnr Kutchery & Temple Rds; ⊙9.30am-5pm Mon-Sat) Main post office.

TOURIST INFORMATION

Odisha Tourism (☑06752-222740; www.odisha tourism.gov.in; cnr VIP & CT Rds; ⊙10am-5pm Mon-Sat, closed 2nd Sat of the month) Has some info on local attractions.

TRAVEL AGENCIES

Gandhara Travel Agents (www.hotelgandhara. com; Hotel Gandhara, CT Rd; internet per hour ₹30; ⊙8am-7pm Mon-Sat, to 1pm Sun) All-in-one internet cafe, car organiser, ticket agent and money changer.

ℹ️ Getting There & Away

BUS

Frequent buses to Konark (₹30, 45 minutes) leave from the **Konark bus stand** (off Grand Rd). The last bus back is at 6.30pm. Next to the Konark bus stand is the sprawling **main bus stand** (off Grand Rd), where frequent buses head to Bhubaneswar (₹40, two hours) and Satapada (₹40, two hours), as well as Kolkata (Calcutta): AC buses ₹1050, 11 hours, 6pm to 6.30pm, two daily; non-AC buses ₹450, 13 hours, from 3pm. Buses to Bhubaneswar can also be taken from Grand Road.

For Pipli as well as the Raghurajpur turn-off, take a Bhubaneswar-bound bus.

CAR

Heritage Tours (p607) and Gandhara Travel Agents can arrange cars and drivers for round trips to Konark (₹1750) and Satapada (₹2100).

TRAINS FROM PURI

DESTINATION	TRAIN NO & NAME	FARE (₹)	DURATION (HR)	DEPARTURES
Berhampur (Brahmapur)	12843 Puri Ahmedabad Exp	170/540/745	3½	5.30pm
Delhi	12801 Purushottam Exp	715/1885/2755	30¾	9.45pm
Kolkata	18410 Sri Jagannath Exp	300/815/1165	9	10.25pm
Varanasi	12875 Neelachal Exp	515/1375/1970	20¾	10.55am Tue, Fri & Sun

Fares: sleeper/3AC/2AC

RAGHURAJPUR

The fascinating artists' village of Raghurajpur, 12km north of Puri, consists of a single street lined with thatched brick houses, adorned with murals of geometric patterns and figures known as Saora art, a traditional practice that has almost died out elsewhere in Odisha.

Most houses here double as workshops, selling a mix of crafts from palm-leaf etchings (*talpatra*) to colourful cloth paintings (*patachitra*). The former is much more intricate, with artists marking out out animals, flowers, deities and demons with eye-aching detail and combining a mixture of inking and etching on scrolls made of double-ply palm leaves. The cloth paintings, in contrast, feature bright colours and bolder patterns. Most themes centre around mythological tales as well as the kind of murals that decorate temple walls.

There is considerable competition for your business. Compare all available stock to find the best pieces, many of which are several decades old and therefore buried deep in the inventories. Palm-leaf etchings are the pricier of the two forms – prices range from ₹1000 for a recent A4-size piece to upward of ₹12,000 for a vintage piece a metre or so in length.

To get here, take the Bhubaneswar bus from Puri and look for the blue 'Raghurajpur Craft Village' signpost 11km north of Puri, then walk the last 1km.

TRAIN

At least a dozen daily trains with unreserved 2nd-class seating run to Bhubaneswar (₹15 to ₹55, two hours, from 5.45am to 1.50pm).

❶ Getting Around

A few places along CT Rd rent bicycles (per day ₹50), mopeds (per day ₹250) and motorbikes (per day ₹350). From CT Rd, cycle-rickshaws charge ₹50 to the train station and ₹80 to the bus stands or Jagannath Mandir. Autorickshaws charge marginally more.

Konark

📞 06758 / POP 16,800

The iconic Sun Temple at Konark – a Unesco World Heritage Site – is one of India's signature buildings and Odisha's raison d'être. Most visitors are day trippers from Bhubaneswar or Puri, which makes sense, as the temple is Konark's sole attraction.

Originally nearer the coast (the shore has receded almost 3km), Konark was once visible from far out at sea and known as the 'Black Pagoda' by European sailors, in contrast to Puri's whitewashed Jagannath Temple. The inland lighthouse near Chandrabhaga Beach is an odd testament to that fact.

◉ Sights

⭐ **Sun Temple**   HINDU TEMPLE

(Indian/foreigner ₹40/600, camera ₹50; ⊙ dawn-8pm) Conceived as the cosmic chariot of the sun god Surya, this massive, breathtaking-ly splendid temple was constructed in the mid-13th century, probably by Odishan king Narashimhadev I to celebrate his military victory over the Muslims. Around the base, seven rearing horses (representing the days of the week) move the stone leviathan on 24 stone cartwheels (representing the hours of the day). The temple was positioned so that dawn light would illuminate the *deul* (temple sanctuary) interior and the presiding deity.

The temple was in use for maybe only three centuries. In the late 16th century the 40m-high *sikhara* (spire) partially collapsed: speculation about causes ranges from marauding Mughals removing the copper over the cupola to a ransacking Kalapahad displacing the Dadhinauti (arch stone), to simple wear and tear from recurring cyclones. The presiding deity may have been moved to Jagannath Temple in Puri in the 17th century; the interior of the temple was filled in with stone in 1903 by the British.

The temple has been under constant and careful restoration for years now, and its gradual weathering continues to this day. Every year, crumbling sections of ornate wall panels are replaced by new blocks (featuring unremarkable motifs sculpted by modern hands), and the structure slowly sheds the sculptural brilliance that made it so special in the first place.

The *gajasimha* (main entrance) is guarded by two stone lions crushing elephants and leads to the intricately carved *nritya mandapa* (dancing hall). Steps, flanked by straining horses, rise to the still-standing *jagamohan* (assembly hall). Behind is the spireless *deul,* with its three impressive chlorite images of Surya aligned to catch the sun at dawn, noon and sunset. The chariot concept of the temple harks back to a stylistic trend in Indian architecture, reflected in the stone chariot at the Vittala Temple in Hampi and the Pancha Rathas complex (featuring five stone chariots devoted to the Pandavas from the Mahabharata) in Mahabalipuram.

The base and walls present a chronicle in stone of Kalinga life; you'll see women cooking and men hunting. Many are in the erotic style for which Konark is famous and include entwined couples as well as solitary exhibitionists.

Persistent guides (₹150) will approach you at the entrance. The temple's history is a complicated amalgam of fact and legend, and religious and secular imagery, and the guides' explanations can be thought-provoking. But make sure you get a government-approved one; all licensed guides wear their official ID on them and should be easy to spot.

Archaeological Museum MUSEUM
(₹50; ⊙10am-5pm Sat-Thu) This museum contains many impressive sculptures and carvings found during excavations of the Sun Temple.

There are also replicas, models, photographs and site plans of temples across Odisha, and an hourly audiovisual presentation on the history and archaeological importance of the Sun Temple.

✦ Festivals & Events

Konark Festival DANCE
(⊙1-5 Dec) Steeped in traditional music and dance, the Konark Festival takes place in an open-air auditorium with the gorgeous Sun Temple as a backdrop.

ⓘ Information

There's an ATM in the passage leading to the Sun Temple.
Odisha Tourism Development Corporation
(☑ 06758-236821; www.odishatourism.gov.in; Yatrinivas Hotel; ⊙10am-5pm Mon-Sat) This tourist office can line up a registered guide to meet you at the Sun Temple. The temple can also be visited as part of an OTDC day tour from Bhubaneswar or Puri.

ⓘ Getting There & Away

The bus stand is set back from the main road, 200m further away from the temple complex. Hourly buses ply the 33km road between Konark and Puri (₹35, one hour); a return trip from Puri by autorickshaw/car costs around ₹900/1750. There are also frequent buses to Bhubaneswar (₹50, two hours).

Chilika Lake

Chilika Lake is Asia's largest brackish lagoon. Swelling from 600 sq km in the summer months of April and May to 1100 sq km during the monsoons (June to August), the shallow lake is separated from the Bay of Bengal by a 60km-long sandbar called Rajhansa.

DON'T MISS

COASTAL HIDEAWAYS NEAR KONARK

Lotus Resorts (☑ 9090093464; www.lotusresorthotels.com; Puri-Konark Marine Dr; cottage incl breakfast from ₹4200; ❄) About 6km from Konark, on pretty Ramchandi Beach, this collection of weathered Canadian-pine cottages is a beautiful getaway. It's situated off a swimmable cove, and is popular with tour groups. Amenities include a small ayurvedic spa (November to February) and a sand-side restaurant (mains ₹120 to ₹350). Take any bus between Puri (₹25) and Konark (₹10) and look for the sign.

Bookings must be made in advance.

Nature Camp, Konark Retreat (☑ 9337505022, 8908621654; www.naturecampindia. com; tent incl breakfast ₹3000) Plopped down on the banks of the Ramchandi River, just across from a sandy Bay of Bengal beach 10km south of Konark, this friendly, laid-back camp has fan-cooled, comfortable tented rooms dotted around a slightly unkempt forest clearing. The camp is 500m off the main Puri–Konark road; jump off the bus when you see the sign.

Tents come with cute attached shower rooms with sit-down flush toilets. The food consists of two sumptuous Odishan thalis, cooked in a traditional charcoal-fired *chulha* (stove) and served on a banana leaf. You must book ahead.

IMAGESOFINDIA/SHUTTERSTOCK ©

SUMIT_KUMAR.99/SHUTTERSTOCK ©

ANNIE OWEN/ROBERTHARDING/ALAMY STOCK PHOTO

1. Mukteswar Mandir (p598), Bhubaneswar
This 10th century temple is covered in Buddhist, Jain and Hindu carvings

2. Chilika Lake (p611)
Asia's largest lagoon is a haven for birds and wildlife, and home to isolated fishing villages

3. Mali woman, near Koraput (p618)
In this remote part of India traditional tribal cultures are showcased at several markets

4. Sun Temple (p610), Konark
An 800-year-old temple conceived as the cosmic chariot of the sun god Surya

The lake is noted for the million-plus migratory birds – including grey-legged geese, herons, cranes and pink flamingos – that flock here in winter (November to mid-January) from as far away as Siberia and Iran and concentrate in a 3-sq-km area within the bird sanctuary on Nalabana Island.

Other attractions are rare Irrawaddy dolphins near Satapada, the pristine beach along Rajhansa, and Kalijai Island temple, where Hindu pilgrims flock for the Makar Mela festival in January.

Satapada

Little more than a bus stand, a hotel, and a cluster of roadside restaurants beside a long jetty, the tiny village of Satapada – on a headland jutting southwestwards into Chilika Lake – is the starting point for boat trips. These range from short dolphin-spotting excursions to day-long boat outings that take in several islands and limited birdwatching. The boats are noisy, so serious birdwatching is out. Also, they tend to get too close to the dolphins, so make it clear this isn't what you want. In spite of this, it's a tranquil experience being out on this great watery expanse, watching fishers pull in their catch, as their boats move through the labyrinthine reeds.

In the village, you can see a 12m-long baleen whale skeleton at the small **Chilika Ecopark** (Satapada Jetty) `FREE`.

OTDC BOATING
(📞 06752-262077; Yatrinivas Hotel; per person ₹160-400, private boat per hour ₹700-1100) This office arranges a three-hour dolphin-sighting tour on Chilika Lake from Satapada. The tour departs between 9.30am and 10am daily, on a shared basis. If you reserve a boat all to yourself on a per-hour basis, the timings can be flexible. You must book your tickets in advance.

Dolphin Motor Boat Association BOATING
(📞 9337506053; Satapada Jetty; 1/3/7hr trips per boat ₹900/1800/3000) This cooperative of local boat owners has set-price trips that include dolphin-watching (one hour), and dolphin-watching plus visiting the river mouth and Kalijai Island Temple (three hours). Longer tours taking in Nalabana Island bird sanctuary (seven hours) can also be arranged.

Yatrinivas HOTEL $
(📞 06752-262077; d with/without AC ₹1680/650; ✳) Considering the potential storybook lakeside setting, Yatrinivas is surprisingly uninspired. Its three ageing non-AC rooms have seen better days, though they are very spacious and, like the more modern AC rooms, have balconies with lake views. The restaurant (mains ₹80 to ₹150) is pretty much your only eating option.

ℹ Getting There & Away

Frequent ferries (pedestrians/bicycles/motorbikes/cars ₹10/10/20/350, 30 minutes) travel between Satapada and the Janhikuda jetty on the lake's western shore, from where vehicles can then head west and around to the north side of the lake. It's a wonderfully scenic route. Daily departures are at 7.30am, 10am, 1pm and 4pm, returning at 8am, 10.30am, 1.30pm and 4.30pm.

A bus to Berhampur (₹150, 3½ hours), near Gopalpur-on-Sea, starts off from Puri's main bus stand at 6am and travels on the 7.30am ferry before following the beautiful countryside road for two hours until it meets up with the main highway. Wait for the bus on the ferry, then jump on as it drives off. It will already be full of villagers by the time it reaches Satapada so don't expect a seat. The bus will drop you at the turn-off for Gopalpur-on-Sea (ask the attendant in advance), from where you can wave down any passing bus (₹20, 20 minutes). The return bus leaves Berhampur at 12.40pm and crosses Chilika Lake on the 4.30pm ferry to Satapada.

Pretty much every hotel and travel agent in Puri does day trips to Chilika Lake (around ₹2100 return by car), but it's easy to come here independently by local bus (₹40, two to three hours). The last bus back to Puri leaves Satapada at around 5.30pm.

Mangalajodi

On Chilika's north shore, 60km southwest of Bhubaneswar, this small fishing village is the jumping-off point for the bird haven of Chilika Lake, an ecotourism success story virtually unknown to the outside world until 2006. Six years prior, a programme called Wild Orissa (www.wildorissa.org) was started here – a waterfowl safeguard committee that converted bird poachers into protectors. In just over a decade, the waterfowl population has climbed from 5000 to an estimated 300,000, spread among some 160 species.

A packed-earth levee leads out into the lake for around 1.5km, with fishing boats sheltering to one side and animal herders taking their buffalo to pasture across shallow waters, and a forest of reeds sheltering birds on the other side. Towards the end of the levee is a birdwatching tower and the dock from which birding trips depart, with guides slowly propelling their narrow boats through reed tunnels using poles, Venetian-gondola style.

Mangalajodi Eco Tourism   BIRDWATCHING
(☑8895288955, 9776696800; www.mangalajodiecotourism.com) ✈ The Mangalajodi village community – an ecological success story – offers sensitive birdwatching trips to see the dozens of wading and migratory bird species on Chilika Lake. Birding packages including cottage accommodation with full board cost ₹5700/6300 for one/two people. Multiday birding and photography packages are also available.

Boat Trips   BIRDWATCHING
(☑7894699699; two hours ₹900) Bird-poachers-turned-guides punt birdwatchers out onto Chilika Lake on their narrow boats. Guides are well versed in the names and behavioural traits of resident waterfowl and migratory birds.

Godwit Eco Cottage   GUESTHOUSE **$$**
(☑8455075534; www.odishaecotourism.com; s/d ₹1100/2200) Overpriced for what they are, these four dingy yet reasonably clean rooms with bucket showers surround a leafy courtyard on the outskirts of Mangalajodi village. Chilika Lake is about 1km away.

❶ Getting There & Away

Mangalajodi is 10km south of the main highway between Bhubaneswar and Berhampur. Buses (₹40, one hour) run from Bubaneswar to Tangi, the nearest village to Mangalajodi. You'll have to catch an autorickshaw (₹20, 30 minutes) the rest of the way. Grass Routes (p606) in Puri runs birdwatching trips to Mangalajodi.

Barkul

On the northern shore of Chilika Lake, Barkul is just a scattering of houses, small guesthouses and food stalls on a lane that runs from the main highway down to the government-run hotel property Panthanivas Barkul. From here, boats make trips to Nalabana Island (full of nesting birds in December and January) and Kalijai Island (which has a temple on it). You could also charter your own boat to anywhere; deal directly with the boathands.

Panthanivas Barkul hotel runs two-hour round trips to Kalijai Island Temple for ₹4000 per speedboat (up to seven passengers), including some time on the island. Alternately, you could also buy a ticket (per person ₹250) on the mass ferry tour that takes up to 50 passengers.

Panthanivas Barkul (☑06756-227488; d with AC ₹2450, without AC from ₹1000; ✴) has a great setting and is one of the best government-run hotels in Odisha, with comfortable rooms overlooking the lake. The AC rooms and cottages are newer and cleaner, but all rooms are good here. The restaurant does decent Indian and Chinese food (mains ₹80 to ₹200), including some seafood. The dingy bar sells bottles of Kingfisher (₹200).

Frequent buses dash along National Hwy 5 between Bhubaneswar (₹90, 1½ hours) and Berhampur (₹70, 1½ hours). From the Barkul turn-off on the main highway, where the bus will drop you off, Panthanivas Barkul is around 2km. If you don't have much luggage it's a lovely, signposted walk past village homes. Alternatively, hop in a passing autorickshaw (shared/private ₹20/100).

Rambha

The village of Rambha, on the northwestern shore of Chilika Lake, is the nearest place to stay for turtle-watching on Rushikulya beach, but many tourists come for boat trips on the lake in general. Tours of the lake by seven-person speedboats (per hour ₹2000) or 10-person motorboats (per person ₹300) are bookable at the government-run Panthanivas Rambha hotel.

The Panthanivas (p622) features good-value non-AC rooms with balconies and lake views. The AC rooms are more modern, but not quite worth the extra money. The restaurant (mains ₹80 to ₹200) is par for the course, and there's also a bar.

The hotel is a 2km walk from the main highway if you're entering the village from the west end, and around 3km from the east end. Alternatively, hop in a passing autorickshaw (₹20).

From the highway you can easily wave down buses to Barkul (₹40, 30 minutes), Berhampur (₹30, one hour) and Bhubaneswar (₹140, two hours).

Gopalpur-on-Sea
☑0680 / POP 7300

If you enjoy nosing about seaside resorts past their prime, Gopalpur-on-Sea could be just your thing. A port the British left to slide into history, this tiny hamlet was rediscovered by Bengali holidaymakers in the 1980s. Gopalpur has a noble history as a seaport that had connections to Southeast Asia, the evidence of which is still scattered through the town in the form of romantically deteriorating old buildings and a lofty lighthouse rising above the settlement.

The waves here are too rough for swimming, but the relatively clean beach is great for a stroll or a paddle, and it is oddly charismatic in its own strange, antiquated way. The main village is a couple of hundred metres back from the beach, along the road to Berhampur.

🛏 Sleeping

Hotel Sea Pearl HOTEL $
(☑ 9883244245; www.hotelseapearlgopalpur.com; d with AC from ₹1470, without AC ₹900; ❄) Right on the beach, the Sea Pearl is a passable option. Rooms are small, though they feature a sea view of some sort (except the cheapest ones).

Swosti Palm Resort RESORT $$
(☑ 7731061655, 9861269153; www.swostihotels. com; d incl breakfast ₹3300; ❄ 🛜) Set back from the beach by about 200m, this cheerful mid-range resort boasts comfortable and well-appointed rooms; the upstairs units have sea views. There's great multicuisine food (mains ₹120 to ₹340) and chilled beer (₹210) on offer. It's located right next door to Mayfair Palm Beach, on a quiet and leafy plot.

Mayfair Palm Beach HOTEL $$$
(☑ 0680-2227500; www.mayfairhotels.com; r incl breakfast from ₹8300; ❄ 🛜 ☷) This renovated 1914 historic property is Golpalpur-on-Sea's most luxurious, though the service doesn't live up to expectations. The grounds contain winding walkways, a beautiful pool, spa and immaculate terraced gardens leading down to the beach. It's worth paying the extra ₹2000 for the deluxe-category rooms, which have fabulous beach-facing balconies. There's also an excellent restaurant and a striking teak-wood bar.

🍴 Eating & Drinking

Sea Shell Fast Food FAST FOOD $
(mains ₹80-150; ⊙ 8am-10.30pm) This shack features cheap and cheerful alfresco dining on the esplanade overlooking the beach. Noodles, biriyanis and seafood preps seem to strike a chord with its patrons.

Krishna Restaurant INDIAN $$
(mains ₹80-150; ⊙ 9am-10pm) In a lane branching off the main street leading up to the beach, this small restaurant plates up local

faves such as paneer (cottage cheese) in spicy gravy, fish curry, chicken curry, seafood, noodles and fried rice. It's located across the entrance to Hotel Sea Pearl.

Foreign Liquor Off Shop BAR
(⊙ 11am-10pm) Sells big bottles of chilled Kingfisher for ₹150.

❶ Information

The main village has a couple of internet cafes (per hour ₹30).

For cash, there are several ATMs along the main street.

❶ Getting There & Away

Between 7am and 7pm, comfortable half-hourly buses shuttle between the beachfront and Berhampur (₹25, 30 minutes), from where you can catch onward transport by rail or bus.

From Berhampur's new bus stand, there are frequent buses throughout the day to Bhubaneswar (₹180, three hours, frequent), via Rambha (₹40, one hour) and Barkul (₹70, 1½ hours). There are two buses to Rayagada (₹180, eight hours, 9.30am and 1.30pm), and one daily bus to Satapada (₹90, three hours, 12.30pm) via the scenic route along the southeast shore of Chilika Lake and then on the ferry.

SOUTHWESTERN ODISHA

Southwestern Odisha is one of the richest regions in India when it comes to traditional tribal culture. Of the 62 tribes that inhabit Odisha, the majority – including the Bonda, Koya, Paraja, Kondh, Mali and Didayi – reside in villages around Koraput, Jeypore and Rayagada. Most continue to lead lives that have remained largely unchanged for centuries, revolving primarily around subsistence farming. For visitors, the highlight of travel in this part of Odisha involves using the main towns of Koraput and Rayagada as springboards for visiting the colourful tribal markets and witnessing traditional village life.

Koraput

☑ 06852 / POP 48,000
Up in the cool, forested hills, the small market town of Koraput is by far the nicest place from which to launch yourself into this region's tribal country. There's a hill-station feel to the settlement, which features a weekly tribal market on Sundays. The main

ODISHA'S INDIGENOUS TRIBES

Sixty-two Adivasi (tribal) groups live in an area that encompasses Odisha, Chhattisgarh and Andhra Pradesh. In Odisha they account for one-quarter of the state's population and mostly inhabit the jungles and hilly regions of the west and southwest. Their distinctive cultures are expressed in music, dance and arts.

Of the more populous tribes, the Kondh number about one million and are based around Koraput in the southwest, and Rayagada and Kandhamal districts in the west. The 500,000-plus Santal live around Baripada and Khiching areas of the north. The 300,000 Saura live near Gunupur near the border with Andhra Pradesh. The Bonda, known as the 'naked people' for wearing minimal clothing but incredibly colourful and intricate accessories, such as beadwork, have a population of about 5000 and live in the hills near Koraput.

In 2012 permission from the District Collector was required to visit specific areas designated as home to Particularly Vulnerable Tribal Groups (PVTGs) and bans on overnight lodging and private home visits were put in place. This has since changed, and it is now possible to visit tribal regions independently. But owing to access issues as well as the odd Maoist flare-up, most travellers choose to go as part of a customised tour, best organised through reputable private tour agencies in Puri or through the two retreats (p619) in Odisha's tribal country.

Jagannath Temple, which allows admission to non-Hindus, is fascinating, especially for those who can't enter the deity's bigger shrine in Puri.

◉ Sights

Jagannath Temple   HINDU TEMPLE
(☉dawn-dusk) Jagannath Temple, whose whitewashed *sikhara* (temple spire) overlooks Koraput town, is well worth visiting. The courtyard around the *sikhara* contains numerous colourful statues of the wide-eyed Jagannath, the state deity of Odisha, which you'll see painted on homes everywhere. Below the *sikhara*, in a side hall, you'll walk past more than two dozen lingams (the auspicious phallic symbol representing Shiva), before reaching some attractive displays of local *ossa* (traditional patterns made with coloured powders on doorsteps).

Koraput Market   MARKET
(☉8am-5pm) There's a smaller market here every day, but it's Koraput's big Sunday Market that's worth exploring. Tribespeople and local traders alike buy and sell food produce and handmade goods in the lanes around the bus stand and behind the police station; buying stuff here is a rare opportunity to interact with tribespeople on your own.

⌖ Sleeping & Eating

Maa Mangala Residency   HOTEL $
(☎06852-251228; Jeypore Rd; d with/without AC ₹999/699; ✦⏥) The pick of Koraput's rather lacklustre offerings, this hotel on the out-

skirts of town has wi-fi in its spotless rooms and there's a travel desk and a good restaurant. It's a bit of a trek, though, if you're hoofing it from the bus or train station.

Raj Residency   HOTEL $
(☎06852-251591; Post Office Rd; s/d with AC from ₹1250/1500, without AC ₹750/950; ✦⏥) Raj Residency has some of the best digs in town, offering clean, modern rooms with TVs, friendly service and wi-fi. The Indian-Chinese restaurant is also one of the best places for food in Koraput. To get here, turn left up Post Office Rd, walk past the post office and keep going straight for about 400m.

❶ Information

You'll find a few internet cafes in Koraput, charging around ₹30 per hour.

There are ATMs along Koraput's main street.

Odisha Tourism (p603) in Bhubaneswar and Heritage Tours (p607) in Puri have the lowdown on the region.

❶ Getting There & Away

BUS

From the Koraput bus stand, there are half-hourly buses to Jeypore (₹25, 40 minutes) between 6am and 8.30pm. Seven buses make the scenic trip to Rayagada (₹120, four hours) between 6am and 7pm. And at least four evening buses leave for Bhubaneswar (₹430, 12 hours) between 5pm and 7pm.

To get a bus to Onkadelli Market, you'll have to first catch a bus to the scruffy town of Jeypore and then the 7.30am or 9.30am bus to Onkadelli

(₹45, three hours). The Onkadelli buses leave from Jeypore's private bus stand, which is located in front of Jeypore's government bus stand. From Jeypore's government bus stand, there are frequent buses to Visakhapatnam (₹270, six hours, 5am to 11pm) in Andhra Pradesh.

TRAIN

The train station is 3km from the centre; it costs around ₹20/100 in a shared/private autorickshaw to get here from the bus stand.

Bhubaneswar 18448 Hirakhand Express (sleeper/3AC/2AC ₹360/980/1410, 15½ hours, 5.20pm)

Howrah (Kolkata) 18006 Koraput Howrah Express (sleeper/3AC/2AC ₹480/1310/1900, 23¼ hours, 7.05am)

Jagdalpur (Chhattisgarh) 18447 Hirakhand Express (sleeper/3AC/2AC ₹140/495/710, 3½ hours, 10.10am)

Visakhapatnam (Andhra Pradesh) 58502 (2nd class/sleeper ₹60/110, seven hours, 1.15pm)

The journey to Jagdalpur is particularly scenic.

Around Koraput

While Koraput is not a destination in its own right, the countryside around the town certainly is. This unique, remote part of India is particularly rich in traditional tribal culture. Most of the tribespeople are subsistence farmers and you'll see the villagers planting and harvesting in a traditional fashion and carrying heavy loads on their heads to sell at the region's many markets, often walking long distances as transport is scarce. The gentle rhythm of rural life entices visitors to linger longer and explore.

⊙ Sights

The biggest attractions around Koraput are the colourful tribal markets and villages. Originally, foreigners had to submit an itinerary to the local police station and be accompanied by a government-approved guide to visit any of the tribal areas where the markets are held, though this wasn't strictly enforced. The guides themselves processed the 'prior permission' required for foreigners to visit these markets. All you needed to do was give them a copy of your passport and visa, and tell them where you wished to visit. This may still be the case, but since there is no longer a tourist office in Koraput, the exact procedure can be ambiguous and unsystematic. Furthermore, there have been plenty of complaints over time about many government-approved guides: that they would take

their customers' money and abandon them at the market, for instance.

In practical terms, though, it's worth noting that there is nothing to stop travellers from getting on a public bus or chartering a car and driver in Koraput or Rayagada, and then getting to their market of choice under their own steam. Alternatively, one could also simply choose to arrange a tour through a reputable tour operator and avoid all logistical and procedural hassles.

An important point to bear in mind when meeting with a tribe's community is the degree of respect in your interactions. In the past, some guides have been called out for allegedly treating Adivasi people as curious creatures in an anthropological zoo, and their intrusive actions (such as invading the privacy of tribal homes or asking people to perform stereotypical acts) have bordered on cultural exploitation. Keep your interactions with tribes respectful, responsible and sensitive. If you're hiring a guide or tour operator, make sure they are on the same page.

★**Onkadelli Market**   MARKET
(⊙10am-6pm Thu) Onkadelli is a particularly popular tribal produce market, with Bonda, Mali, Kondh and Paraja people attending to buy and sell fruit, vegetables, dried fish, condiments, utensils, objects of daily life as well as handicrafts fashioned by the *dokra* (lost-wax) method of metal casting.

Kundli Market   MARKET
(⊙6pm Thu-5pm Fri) This is the region's largest produce market, taking place from Thursday afternoon until Friday afternoon. Homemade alcohol brewed from the *mahua* flower is sold near the cattle section.

Laxmipur Market   MARKET
(⊙5am-5pm Sat) A produce market attended by Kondh and Paraja people, Laxmipur is located 56km northeast of Koraput and is reachable on any Rayagada-bound bus.

Kotapad Market   MARKET
(⊙5am-5pm Tue) This is a tribal textile market, featuring yarn coloured with natural dyes, located 63km northwest of Koraput.

❶ Getting There & Around

Some of the markets, including Laxmipur, Onkadelli, Koraput and Chatikona, can be reached by public transport, but for the rest you have to hire a car. Consider the locals, many of whom walk for hours to get to the markets!

COUNTRYSIDE RETREATS IN THE TRIBAL SOUTHWEST

Nestled in the village-dotted hills near Koraput, these two rustic hideaways are an excellent way to experience life in this remote region.

On the scenic road between Koraput and Rayagada, in a village called Goudaguda, **Chandoori Sai** (☑ 9443342241; www.chandoorisai.com; per person incl full board ₹4000; ❀ ☎) ✿ is a beautiful retreat that could easily be one of Odisha's most stylish getaways. Run by Leon, who's lived in India for many years, this sustainable earthen-walled refuge has beautiful terracotta flooring and bamboo-sheeted ceilings. The food is fabulous, and it's a real pleasure to interact with tribal women, who act as cultural ambassadors on the property. Sensitive outings are offered to nearby markets, as well as guided walks through the countryside and around the surrounding villages. Independent travellers are welcome; though most come as part of tribal tour packages with Grass Routes (p606).

To reach Chandoori Sai, take any bus between Koraput (40km) and Rayagada (70km) and get off at Kakirigumma; staff will then pick you up from there.

Desia (☑ 9437023656, 9437677188; www.desiakoraput.com; Bantalabiri Village, Lamptaput; s/d incl full board Apr-Sep ₹3000/4000, Oct-Mar ₹3500/5500) ✿ is a gorgeous four-room retreat run by the Puri-based Heritage Tours (p607). Guests can take part in local market trips, hiking and biking excursions around the countryside, cooking and craftwork. Desia invests in nearby villages by running a nursery and primary school for village children. Independent guests are welcome; others come as part of the all-inclusive multiday 'tribal tour' packages.

Desia is located down a lonely country road near the village of Machkund, around 70km southwest of Koraput. Getting here by public transport is difficult; call ahead for pickup from Koraput.

Rayagada

☑ 06856 / POP 73,500

The only reason for staying in the industrial town of Rayagada is to use it as the base for visiting the weekly Wednesday **Chatikona market** (⊙ 5am-4pm Wed) at Bissamcuttack (about 40km north). Here, highly ornamented Dongria Kondh and Desia Kondh villagers from the surrounding Niayamgiri Hills bring their produce and wares to sell. Alongside piles of chillies and dried fish are bronze animal sculptures made locally using the lost-wax method called *dokra*. The market is considered tourist-friendly.

Rayagada's own daily **market** (Sastri Nagar; ⊙ 7am-5pm), between the train station and the bus stand (turn right out of the bus stand, take the second right and it's on your left), is where colourfully dressed tribespeople weave bamboo baskets alongside local traders selling fruit, vegetables, spices, dried fish and the like.

🛏 Sleeping

Hotel Rajbhavan HOTEL $
(☑ 06856-223777; Main Rd; s/d with AC ₹1350/1550, without AC ₹790/990; ❀) Friendly Hotel Rajbhavan is a decent option and has a good multicuisine restaurant (mains ₹80

to ₹200). It's located across the main road from the train station – don't confuse it with the nearby Hotel Raj, which is a step down.

Tejasvi International BUSINESS HOTEL $$
(☑ 7077012814; www.hoteltejasvi.in; Collector Residence Rd, Gandhi Nagar; s/d incl breakfast from ₹1680/2020; ❀ ☎) Tejasvi International is an odd-looking business hotel with good service, comfortable rooms and complimentary wi-fi. To get here, take a right out of the train station, then take the first left and keep walking for about 500m.

ⓘ Getting There & Away

The bus stand is a 1km walk from the train station; turn right out of the train station, walk over the railway line and it's on your left; both are on Main Rd.

From Rayagada bus stand, there are three early-morning local buses to Chatikona (₹40, two hours, 4.45am, 6.30am and 9.30am). Buses to Jeypore (₹120, five hours, five daily) all go via Koraput (₹100, four hours); the route over the forested hills is fabulously scenic. There are frequent evening buses to Bhubaneswar (non-AC ₹400, 12 hours) between 4pm and 7pm.

Of the three trains between Bhubaneswar and Rayagada, the 18447 Hirakhand Express (sleeper/3AC/2AC ₹300/815/1165) departs Bhubaneswar daily at 7.35pm, reaching Rayagada

SATKOSIA TIGER SANCTUARY

Made up of the Satkosia and Baisipalli Wildlife Sanctuaries, the **Satkosia Tiger Sanctuary** (📞06764-230941; www.satkosia.org; per day Indian/foreigner ₹40/1000; ⏰6am-6pm Oct-Jun) is a 964-sq-km forested tiger reserve, 125km northwest of Bhubaneswar, straddled by a breathtaking gorge, cut by the mighty Mahanadi River. It is one of the most beautiful natural spots in Odisha. However, tourists are not allowed inside the park's core zone, where most of the wildlife is found, and 4WD safaris are not on offer. The main appeal of coming here is to spend some time amid the stunning natural scenery.

Nature Camp Tikarpada (📞06764-230941; www.satkosia.org; d incl full board ₹2000) has a spectacular setting, perched above the beaches of the Mahanadi River with the gorge as a scenic backdrop. Tented accommodation here is basic – even the 'deluxe' tents have outhouse bathrooms (albeit private ones), and the standard tents have no showers. Rates include meals and a nature hike that visits the nearby crocodile breeding centre.

Get your permit at **Satkosia Wildlife Division** (📞06764-230941; www.satkosia.org; Hakimpada), 1km from the Angul train station.

Four buses go from Angul bus stand to Tikarpada (₹45, 2½ hours, 6am, 9.30am, 3.30pm and 5pm), via the park gate at Pampasar, where you're supposed to pay your park fees (you may wind up not paying if travelling by bus). Return buses leave Tikarpada at 6.30am, 10.30am and 1pm.

From Angul bus stand, there are frequent buses to Bhubaneswar (non-AC/AC ₹130/170, four hours) and Cuttack (non-AC/AC ₹120/150, three hours) between 6am and 6pm.

Of the seven or so daily trains, the quickest way to get to Angul from Bhubaneswar is on either the 12893 Bhubaneswar–Balangir Express (2nd class/AC chair ₹85/305, 2½ hours, 6.30am) or the 22840 Bhubaneswar–Rourkela Express (2nd class/AC chair ₹85/305, 2¼ hours, 2.10pm). Returning, the handy 22839 Rourkela–Bhubaneswar Express leaves Angul for Bhubaneswar at 10.07am.

at 4.50am – good timing for catching the market bus. The return (18448) leaves Rayagada at 10.30pm.

Jeypore

📞06854 / POP 84,900

Other than the 27km head start, there is little reason to choose the chaotic commercial centre of Jeypore over Koraput as your base for visiting the amazingly colourful Onkadelli market. Better still, stay at Desia (p619), an appealing lodge that's even closer to Onkadelli.

The best place to stay in Jeypore is **Hotel Hello Jeypore** (📞06854-230900; NH43; s/d incl breakfast from ₹1695/2195; ❄🛜⊗). It's just outside the bustle of the city, with a forest looming behind and a cineplex across the road. Rates include yoga classes and there's a good multicuisine restaurant.

Departures from the **government bus stand** (Sardar Patel Marg) include Koraput (₹25, one hour, every 30 minutes), Berhampur (₹420, 12 hours, four daily), Bhubaneswar (non-AC/AC ₹550/620, 13 to 16 hours,

five daily) and Rayagada (₹120, five hours, six daily).

To reach Onkadelli market (₹45, three hours) there are morning buses at 7.30am and 9am from the Ghoroi Bus Union's office on Bypass Rd. A private taxi including waiting time charges ₹3000 for up to four passengers.

The daily 18447 Hirakhand Express runs from Bhubaneswar to Jeypore via Rayagada and Koraput at 7.35pm (sleeper/3AC/2AC ₹380/1035/1485, 16 hours). The 18448 Hirakhand Express makes the return journey at 3.52pm.

NORTHERN & NORTHEASTERN ODISHA

Northeastern Odisha is best known for its nature sanctuaries, notably Bhitarkanika Wildlife Sanctuary and Similipal National Park, and the excellent Buddhist ruins at Ratnagiri, Udayagiri and Lalitgiri. To the north of Bhubaneswar you can stay in heritage palaces and explore the peaceful countryside by foot and by bicycle. Kila Dalijoda arranges pick-up from Bhubaneswar or Cuttack. It's easy to combine a visit to both. From Kila Dalijoda, Bhitarkanika Wildlife Sanctuary is a viable day trip, while Dhenkanal is within easy reach of Satkosia Tiger Reserve.

It's easy to combine a visit to Bhubaneswar and Kila Dalijoda. From Kila Dalijoda, Bhitarkanika Wildlife Sanctuary is a viable day trip, while Dhenkanal is within easy reach of Satkosia Tiger Reserve.

Cuttack

While Cuttack is not a particularly attractive city, it's worth stopping here to check out the **Odisha State Maritime Museum** (www.odishastatemaritimemuseum.org; Jobra; ₹40; ⊙10am-4.30pm Tue-Sun), which puts Odisha's history into context. Overlooking the Mahanadi River, the museum focuses on Odisha's centuries-old maritime history of boatbuilding and trade (particularly with Bali, Indonesia). The displays walk you through the Kalingas' maritime activities, rituals and tools, while the boat shed features river-boat, raft and coracle models from different parts of India. The Jobra workshop gallery introduces the world of sluice gates and boat repair, and an aquarium entertains visitors with marine life from Odisha and the Amazon River.

In November/December the Bali Yatra (p600), a week of festivities commemorating past trading links with Indonesia, is celebrated and you can shop for anything from cattle to fine textiles and silver filigree.

Dhenkanal

The mighty 19th-century **Garh Dhenkanal Palace** (Dhenkanal Palace; ☑9437292448; www.dhenkanalpalace.com; d incl full board ₹9200) built for the raja of Dhenkanal, is set against the foothills of the Eastern Ghats, overlooking the quaint town. The 13 sumptuous, well-restored rooms have en suite bathrooms, period furniture and colourful upholstery, and guests have access to the present raja's library. Trips to surrounding villages can be arranged.

Charmingly set amid dense forest 10km outside of Dhenkanal, **Gajlaxmi Palace** (☑9861011221, 9337411020; www.gajlaxmipalace.com; Borapada; d incl full board & nature walk ₹6500; ✱) is an elegant heritage palace dating back to 1935, and belonging to one of the families of the Dhenkanal royals. The current head of the house, the affable JP Singh Deo, and his wife, Navneeta, have opened up four rooms inside their tranquil mansion for guests.

The village of Dhenkanal and its palaces are easily reachable by train from Bhubaneswar.

Mangarajpur

An hour's drive north from Bhubaneswar, Debjit and his family welcome visitors into their ancestral home, **Kila Dalijoda** (☑9438667086; www.kiladalijoda.com; d incl breakfast ₹5500; ☎) ✐, a rambling mansion set in the peaceful countryside. The home-cooked food is among the best we've had in Odisha, and Debjit takes his guests on walks and bicycle rides through tribal villages. Visits to tribal markets and nearby temples can also be arranged. Kila Dalijoda arranges pick-up from Bhubaneswar or Cuttack.

Pusphagiri Ruins

These fascinating Buddhist ruins, the oldest of which date back to around 200 BC, are the remnants of one of India's earliest *mahaviharas* (Buddhist monasteries that were effectively leading universities of their day). Pusphagiri Mahavihara had three campuses (Ratnagiri, Udayagiri and Lalitgiri) each built upon a small hilltop in the low-lying Langudi Hills. The Kelua River provided a scenic backdrop to the site, and these days supports small farming communities and their mud-and-thatch villages that dot the rural landscape.

If you start early, it's possible to visit the area as a day trip by bus from Bhubaneswar, but having your own wheels or staying overnight in one of the villages gives you the chance to explore each of the three sites properly. Stop by the excellent museum (p622) at Ratnagiri first, as it puts the three sites into context.

◉ Sights

★**Udayagiri**   ARCHAEOLOGICAL SITE
(⊙dawn-dusk) **FREE** Udayagiri's two monastery complexes were active between the 10th and 12th centuries AD. At the first one, there's a large pyramidal brick stupa with a seated Buddha image on each of the four sides. Beyond, a large Buddha statue is locked away behind some fine doorjamb carvings. The second site, marred by graffiti, features an exquisite deity carving, a seated Buddha statue

ODISHA'S OLIVE RIDLEY MARINE TURTLES

One of the smallest sea turtles and a threatened species, the olive ridley marine turtle swims up from deeper waters beyond Sri Lanka to mate and lay eggs on Odisha's beaches. The main nesting sites are Gahirmatha (in Bhitarkanika Wildlife Sanctuary), the Devi River mouth near Konark, and the Rushikulya River mouth by Chilika Lake.

Turtle deaths due to fishing practices are unfortunately common. Although there are regulations, such as requiring the use of turtle exclusion devices (TEDs) on trawl nets and banning fishing from certain prohibited congregation and breeding areas, these laws are routinely flouted in Odisha.

Casuarina trees have been planted to help preserve Devi beach, but they occupy areas of soft sand that are necessary for a turtle hatchery. Other potential threats include an upcoming port and thermal power plant project in Astaranga on the Devi River, and the proposed Palur port, which is planned right next to the Rushikulya River mouth nesting site.

In January and February the turtles congregate near nesting beaches and – if conditions are right – come ashore. If conditions aren't right, they reabsorb their eggs and leave without nesting. Hatchlings emerge 50 to 55 days later and are guided to the sea by the luminescence of the ocean and stars. They can be easily distracted by bright lights; unfortunately NH5 runs within 2km of Rushikulya's beach. Members of local turtle clubs in Gokharkuda, Podampeta and Purunabandha villages often gather up disoriented turtles and take them back to the sea. It's best to visit the nesting beach at dawn when lights are not necessary.

The best place to see nesting and hatching is on the northern side of Rushikulya River, near the villages of Purunabandha and Gokharkuda, 20km from the nearest accommodation in Rambha. Nesting and hatching activities take place throughout the night, so don't use lights.

For updated seasonal information, ask staff at **Panthanivas Rambha** (✆ 06810-278346; d with/without AC ₹1700/900; ﷯) or contact the Wildlife Society of Odisha (p624). Rickshaws between Rambha and Rushikulya cost around ₹600 return for a half-day trip and ₹1200 for the full day.

and monastic cells. The ruins are a 2km walk from the main road.

★ Ratnagiri
ARCHAEOLOGICAL SITE

(Indian/foreigner ₹25/300; ☉ dawn-dusk) Ratnagiri is the most interesting and extensive among the three Pusphagiri sites. Two large monasteries flourished here from the 5th to 13th centuries. Noteworthy are an exquisitely carved doorway inside the first monastery complex, opening onto an expansive courtyard that leads to a shrine housing an intact Buddha statue. Up on the small hillock are the remains of a 10m-high stupa, surrounded by smaller votive stupas. Sadly, all are covered in graffiti in spite of a security guard presence.

Ratnagiri Museum
MUSEUM

(₹10; ☉ 9am-5pm) The four galleries at this fine museum tell the story of the Pusphagiri ruins. Two of them display beautifully preserved sculpture from all three Pusphagiri sites, while the other two galleries are devoted to terracotta plaques, copper plates engraved with Sanskrit, sacred bronzes and other objects found on-site.

Lalitgiri
ARCHAEOLOGICAL SITE

(Indian/foreigner ₹25/300; ☉ dawn-dusk) Several monastery ruins (some dating back to 200 BC) consisting of brick foundations line a gentle incline on Lalitgiri hill. One is surrounded by several dozen small votive stupas. Next to a small museum housing some fine carvings from the site, steps lead up a hillock crowned with a shallow stupa. During excavations in the 1970s, a casket containing gold and silver relics was found here. A bigger museum at the site was nearing completion at the time of writing.

🛏 Sleeping & Eating

Toshali Ratnagiri Resort
HOTEL $$

(✆ 9937023791; www.toshaliratnagiri.com; d incl breakfast ₹3000; ﷯) Featuring tastefully decorated rooms flanking an interior courtyard, this resort is located opposite the Ratnagiri Museum at the far end of Ratnagiri village. It overlooks rice fields and a peaceful village pond. There's a restaurant (mains ₹100 to ₹250) and – considering its remoteness – a well-stocked bar. Reserve in advance.

ℹ️ Getting There & Away

Udayagiri is 23km from Chandikhol. Ratnagiri is 9km past Udayagiri. Lalitgiri is 22km from Chandikhol, but down a different lane, 8km beyond the Ratnagiri/Udayagiri turn-off.

If you opt for public transport from Bhubaneswar, catch a bus to Cuttack (₹25, one hour, frequent) then change for a bus to Chandikhol (₹35, one hour, frequent). Here, from the road leading right, you can catch shared minivans to Ratnagiri (₹30, 45 minutes) via Udayagiri (₹25, 30 minutes), or to Lalitgiri (₹25, 30 minutes) via Hotel Toshali Pusphagiri. Minivans start drying up at around 3.30pm.

A day trip to the three sites with a car and driver from Bhubaneswar costs around ₹3500.

Bhitarkanika Wildlife Sanctuary

Spanning lush mangrove forests, vast wetlands, and the estuaries of three rivers flowing into the Bay of Bengal, Bhitarkanika Wildlife Sanctuary is an immensely wildlife-rich ecosystem. Known within the local tourism circle as India's 'mini Amazon', the 672-sq-km delta is the country's premier crocodile sanctuary, home to diverse birdlife and a preferred nesting site for endangered turtles.

👁 Sights

⭐ Bhitarkanika Wildlife Sanctuary NATURE RESERVE

(per day ₹40, camera/video ₹200/2000; ⊘7am-4pm Aug-Apr) Three rivers flow out to sea at Bhitarkanika, forming a tidal maze of muddy creeks and mangroves. This is India's second-largest mangrove region, and most of the 672-sq-km delta that forms this wonderful sanctuary is a significant biodiversity hot spot. The only way to get around most of the sanctuary is by boat, and the main reason to come is to spot crocodiles and birds (particularly at the heronry site of Bagagahana).

Long-snouted gharials, short squat muggers, and enormous estuarine crocodiles (or 'salties') bask on mud flats here through the day, diving into the water for cover as your boat chugs past. One particular 7m beast even made the Guinness World Records some years ago. It's also worth knowing that this area has the highest concentration of king cobras found anywhere in India, as well as half a dozen other potentially deadly viper species.

The best time to visit is from December to February (note that the sanctuary remains shut for a week in January for the annual crocodile census). You'll see crocs throughout the year, and may also see monitor lizards, spotted deer, wild boar and all sorts of birds, including eight species of brilliantly coloured kingfishers. Herons arrive in early June and nest until early December, when they move on to Chilika Lake, while raucous open-billed storks have set up a permanent rookery here. A short walk through the mangroves from one of the docks inside the sanctuary leads to a birding tower. There is also a 5km nature walk along one of the islands, though that's best done on weekdays when there are fewer visitors.

The park entrance is hidden within the mud-hut village of Dangamal. Tour boats depart from the pier at Dangamal for 3½-hour safaris in the early morning and then at midday. A single ticket costs ₹250, or you can charter the entire boat for ₹3000.

🛏 Sleeping & Eating

⭐ Killa Aul Palace HERITAGE HOTEL $$$

(Rajbati; ☑9437690565; www.killaaulpalace.com; r incl breakfast ₹4500; ❋) In the village of Aul (also pronounced 'aa-li'), this centuries-old former royal palace has been converted into an intimate retreat. The rooms are splendidly furnished with antique furniture, the tranquil grounds and riverfront location add oodles of charm, and meals (per person ₹500) may include giant river prawns. Half-/full-day boat trips (₹4000/6000) into Bhitarkanika are arranged upon request.

Several direct buses serve Aul from Cuttack (₹70, three hours). The raja splits his time between Cuttack and Aul, and it's particularly interesting to stay here when he's around to host you.

⭐ Nature Camp Bhitarkanika CAMPGROUND $$$

(☑9437016054, 9337505022; www.bhitarkanika tour.com; per person incl meals & transfer from Bhubaneswar ₹8340; ⊘Oct-Apr) 🍃 A special experience awaits at this small, sustainable and privately run tented camp at the heart of Dangamal village, built with the help of villagers and just 200m before the sanctuary gate. The stylish Swiss Cottage tents are a tad musty but fully equipped with electricity, fans, sit-down flush toilets and pleasant terraces, and the rustic Odisha cuisine is excellent.

DEBRIGARH WILDLIFE SANCTUARY

In northeastern Odisha, 40km west of Sambalpur, the 347-sq-km **Debrigarh Wildlife Sanctuary** (Indian/foreigner ₹40/1000, camera ₹50; ⏱6am-4pm) is a good location for wildlife-spotting. It comprises the Barapahad Hills, covered with dry deciduous forest, and the vast Hirakud Reservoir, home to mugger crocodiles. Wildlife here includes deer, antelopes, sloth bears, langur monkeys, a few tigers and leopards, as well as 234 bird species.

Access to the jungle usually requires a 4WD, which can be arranged through your hotel in Sambalpur for ₹1300 to ₹1500 plus mileage charges.

Sheela Towers (📞0663-2403111; www.sheelatowers.com; VSS Marg; s/d incl breakfast from ₹2140/2580; ✦🛜) is Sambalpur's top hotel, with a range of comfortable rooms, good wi-fi and in-room complimentary breakfast. The modern art deco restaurant (mains ₹120 to ₹340) does Indian, Chinese and Western dishes, and there's chilled beer (₹220) readily available.

The camp within the sanctuary, **Debrigarh Nature Camp** (www.ecotourodisha.com; d incl full board from ₹5840), offers a selection of well-maintained rooms with clean bathrooms and tasty home-style meals. An additional ₹40 per person per day is billed as the park entry fee.

The **Government Bus Stand** (VSS Marg), in the centre of Sambalpur, has buses running to Jeypore (₹320, 12 hours, 5.50am and 5pm), Koraput (₹350, 13 hours, 5.50am and 5pm), Berhampur (₹300, 12 hours, 6pm, 6.30pm and 9pm) and Bhubaneswar (₹260, eight hours, 10pm).

Of the six trains running to Bhubaneswar, the handy 18451 Tapaswini Express departs at 10.35pm and continues to Puri (sleeper/3AC/2AC ₹235/630/900, nine hours) via Bhubaneswar (sleeper/3AC/2AC ₹210/560/800, seven hours). From Bhubaneswar to Sambalpur, the fastest option is the 12893 Balangir Express, departing at 6.30am (2nd class/AC chair ₹125/460, 4¾ hours).

Dangamal Nature Camp   LODGE **$$$**
(www.ecotourodisha.com; d incl full board ₹4540-5840) The Forestry Department–run Nature Camp is located just inside the sanctuary's main gate. Reservations can be made online through the official website.

ℹ Information

PERMITS

The powers that be at the Bhitarkanika Wildlife Sanctuary are prone to changing the rules regarding permits. Advance registration of foreign visitors may be required, so get in touch with Nature Camp Bhitarkanika (p623) or Aul Palace (p623) in advance if you're interested in going on a boat tour.

TOURIST INFORMATION

Wildlife Society of Odisha (📞9437024265; kachhapa@gmail.com; Shantikunj, Link Rd, Cuttack; ⏱calls 10am-5pm) Has information on the plight of Odisha's olive ridley marine turtles.

ℹ Getting There & Away

The easiest way to visit the Bhitarkanika Wildlife Sanctuary is via an organised trip with Nature Camp Bhitarkanika (p623), which includes pickup from Bhubaneswar and visits to the Pusphagiri ruins en route.

Getting here by public transport is a bit of a mission. Two or three direct buses to Dangamal leave from Cuttack between noon and 1pm. Otherwise, buses go from Cuttack to Pattamundai (₹70, three hours), from where you can catch onward buses to Dangamal (₹45, 2½ hours, last bus 5pm), passing Rajnagar en route.

There are three early-morning buses from Dangamal. The 5am and 7am both go as far as Kendrapara (a small town just past Pattamundai), from where you can catch onward transport to Cuttack or Chandikhol (for the Pusphagiri ruins). The 6am bus goes all the way to Cuttack. Returning later in the day, you'll have to catch an autorickshaw from Dangamal to Rajnagar (around ₹600), from where the last bus to Cuttack leaves at 2pm. You can also take one of the 10 or so trains (2¼ to three hours) from Bhubaneswar to Bhadrak (60km away from Bhitarkanika) and request to be picked up by Nature Camp Bhitarkanika.

ℹ Getting Around

The only way to get around the sanctuary is by boat.

Madhya Pradesh & Chhattisgarh

POP 106.1 MILLION

Best Places to Eat

➜ Under the Mango Tree (p651)

➜ Mr Beans (p664)

➜ Sarafa Bazar (p661)

➜ Salban (p680)

➜ Silver Saloon (p631)

Best Places to Stay

➜ Kings Lodge (p682)

➜ Orchha Home-Stay (p636)

➜ Hotel Isabel Palace (p645)

➜ Shergharh (p680)

➜ Hotel Shreemaya (p664)

➜ Salban (p680)

Why Go?

The spotlight doesn't hit Madhya Pradesh (MP) with quite the same brilliance as it shines on more celebrated neighbouring states, so you can experience travel riches ranking with the best without that feeling of just following a tourist trail.

Khajuraho's temples bristle with some of the finest stone carving in India, their exquisite erotic sculptures a mere slice of the architectural wonders of a region exceedingly well endowed with palaces, forts, temples, mosques and stupas, most gloriously in the villages of Orchha and Mandu. Tigers are the other big news here, and your chances of spotting a wild Royal Bengal in MP are as good as anywhere in India.

Pilgrimage-cum-traveller havens such as Maheshwar and Omkareshwar on the Narmada River are infused with the spiritual and chill-out vibes for which India is renowned, while the adventurous can foray into the tribal zones of Chhattisgarh, fascinatingly far removed from mainstream India.

When to Go
Bhopal

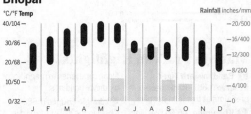

Nov–Feb The most pleasant time to visit central India, despite chilly mornings.

Apr–Jun Hot, but best chance of spotting tigers; thin vegetation and few water sources.

Jul–Sep Monsoon time, but places such as Chhattisgarh are at their most beautiful.

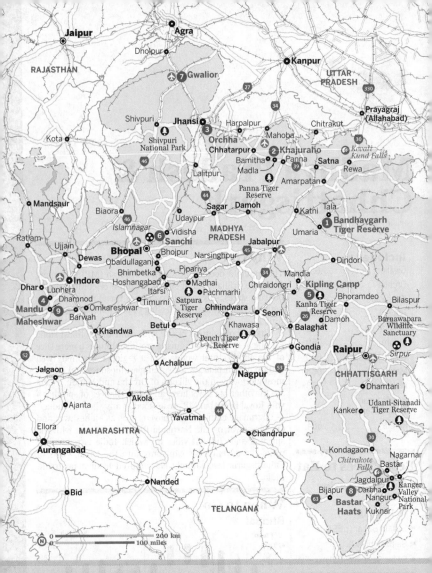

Madhya Pradesh Highlights

1 Bandhavgarh Tiger Reserve (p681) Tracking apex predators at this top tiger park.

2 Khajuraho (p637) Blushing at the carvings on the Chandela dynasty's exquisite temples.

3 Orchha (p632) Bedding down in a village homestay at this beautiful, laid-back town.

4 Mandu (p668) Cycling

along rural lanes to magnificent medieval buildings.

5 Jungle Lodges (p680) Obeying the call of the wild in comfort and style at top-class lodges, such as Kipling Camp.

6 Sanchi (p653) Travelling back two millennia to the golden age of Indian Buddhism.

7 Gwalior (p629) Exploring

the palaces and rock sculptures of the city's historic fort.

8 Bastar Haats (p686) Experiencing tribal culture at Chhattisgarh's fascinating markets.

9 Maheshwar (p673) Absorbing the atmosphere of a pilgrimage centre.

History

Plum in the centre of India, Madhya Pradesh and Chhattisgarh have been subject to a mind-boggling array of empires, kingdoms, sultanates and competing local dynasties. Both the Mauryan empire (4th to 2nd centuries BC) and the Gupta empire (4th to 6th centuries AD) had their capital at Patna (Bihar) and a second capital in Ujjain in western MP. The great Mauryan Buddhist emperor Ashoka chose Sanchi for the site of his Great Stupa. Gupta emperor Chandragupta II had a series of remarkable Hindu cave shrines cut from the rock at nearby Udaigiri six centuries later.

By the 11th century the Paramaras, a Rajput dynasty, established a powerful kingdom in Malwa (western MP and southeastern Rajasthan), with capitals variously at Ujjain, Mandu and Dhar. Around the same time another Rajput dynasty, the Chandelas, established themselves in Bundelkhand (northern MP and southern Uttar Pradesh) and their nimble-fingered sculptors enlivened some 85 temples at Khajuraho with now-famous erotic scenes.

Between the 12th and 16th centuries, the region experienced continuing struggles between Hindu rulers and Muslim rivals from the north, with the tribal Gond kingdom coming to the fore in the east. Much of Madhya's monumental architecture was erected during these centuries by local rulers such as the Muslim Ghuris and Khiljis of Mandu, and the Hindu Bundelas of Orchha and Tomars of Gwalior.

The Delhi-based Mughals won out in the 16th century and stayed in control until they were expelled by the Marathas, the rising Hindu power in central India, after a 27-year war (1681–1707). Powerful Maratha clans like the Holkars of Maheshwar and Indore (several of whose palaces can be visited) and the Scindias of Gwalior ruled most of the region until the Marathas' 1818 defeat by the British, for whom the Scindias became powerful allies.

Madhya Pradesh took on its modern identity in 1956, when several smaller states were combined into one. Chhattisgarh was separated as an independent state in 2000.

NORTHERN MADHYA PRADESH

Gwalior

0751 / POP 1.16 MILLION

Famous for its dramatic and dominant hilltop fort, which Mughal emperor Babur reputedly described as the pearl of Indian fortresses, Gwalior makes an interesting stop en route to some of the better-known destinations in this part of India. The city houses the elaborate Jai Vilas Palace, the historic seat of the Scindia family, who have been playing important roles in Indian history for more than two centuries.

History

The legend of Gwalior's beginning goes that a 6th- or 8th-century hermit named Gwalipa

MADHYA PRADESH & CHHATTISGARH GWALIOR

TOP STATE FESTIVALS

Festival of Dance (Khajuraho; late Feb; (p644) The cream of Indian classical dancers perform amid floodlit temples.

Shivaratri Mela (Pachmarhi; Feb/Mar) Up to 100,000 Shaivite pilgrims, sadhus (holy people) and Adivasis (tribal people) attend celebrations at Pachmarhi's Mahadeo Cave then make a pilgrimage up Chauragarh hill to plant tridents by the Shiva shrine.

Kumbh Mela (Ujjain; Apr/May; p667) Ujjain is one of the four cities where India's biggest religious festival happens once every 12 years, attracting tens of millions of pilgrims. Next in 2028.

Ahilyabai Holkar Jayanti Mahotsav (Maheshwar; May/Jun) The birthday Ahilyabai, the revered Holkar queen, is celebrated with particular fervour in Maheshwar.

Navratri (Festival of Nine Nights; Ujjain; Sep/Oct) Lamps are lit at Harsiddhi Mandir.

Bastar Dussehra (Jagdalpur; Sep/Oct; p685) Dedicated to local goddess Danteshwari, this 75-day festival culminates in a week and a half of (immense) chariot-pulling.

Tansen Music Festival (Tansen Samaroh; http://tansensamaroh.com; Gwalior; last week Dec) Music festival featuring classical musicians and singers from all over India.

Gwalior

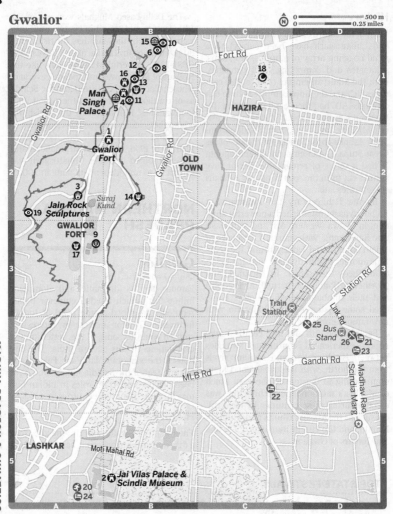

cured a Rajput chieftain, Suraj Sen, of leprosy using water from Suraj Kund tank (which remains in Gwalior Fort). Renaming the chieftain Suhan Pal, Gwalipa foretold that Suhan's descendants would remain in power as long as they retained the name Pal. Suhan's first 83 descendants did just that, but number 84 changed his name to Tej Karan and, naturally, lost his kingdom.

Gwalior owes its importance to its much coveted hilltop fort, in existence since at least the 9th century, which commands important north–south trade routes and changed hands many times before the Tomar dynasty was founded here by Bir Singh Deo in 1398. The dynasty reached its ascendancy under Raja Man Singh (r 1486–1516) but ended in 1526 to be followed by two centuries of Mughal rule. The Scindia clan of Marathas took over in 1765 and made Gwalior their capital in 1810, though it became a British tributary after the Third Anglo-Maratha War of 1818.

During the First War of Independence (Indian Uprising) in 1857, Maharaja Jayajirao remained loyal to the British but his troops rebelled. The British reconquest of Gwalior Fort a year later marked the effective end of the uprising, and it was in the final British assault that the famous rebel leader, the Rani (Queen) of Jhansi, was killed.

Gwalior

⊙ Sights

★ Gwalior Fort   FORT

(⊙dawn-dusk) Stretched majestically along the top of a 3km-long plateau overlooking Gwalior, the fort is a dominant, unmissable sight, full of fascinating palaces, temples, museums and other buildings. Much of the fort is now occupied by the prestigious private Scindia School, established by Maharaja Madho Rao Scindia in 1897 for the education of Indian nobility.

There are two approaches to the fort, both uphill treks. Vehicles can drive up the west side through the Urvai Gate, but this approach is an anticlimax compared with the formidable view of the fort from the eastern approach, which is well worth the walk. Don't, however, miss the rock sculptures part way down the western side.

➡ **Eastern Approach**

From the east a series of five gates punctuates the worn path up to Gwalior Fort (two of the former seven gates have disappeared). You enter by the Gwalior Gate (Alamgiri Gate), dating from 1660, which is followed quickly by the Badalgarh Gate (Hindola Gate), named after Badal Singh, Man Singh's uncle. The State Archaeological Museum (p629) is on the right immediately after this.

Further up is the 15th-century Ganesh Gate, and then a small four-pillared Hindu temple to the hermit Gwalipa, after whom both fort and city are supposedly named. You pass a 9th-century rock-cut Vishnu shrine, the Chaturbhuj Mandir (Temple of the Four-Armed God), before the Lakshman

Gate, probably dating from the 14th century. Finally, you enter the palace area through the two-towered Hathi Gate (Elephant Gate), built in 1516.

➡ **State Archaeological Museum**

(GujariMahal;Indian/foreigner ₹20/250,camera/video ₹50/200; ⊙10am-5pm Tue-Sun) This museum is housed in the 15th-century Gujari Mahal palace, built by Man Singh for his favourite rani (queen), next to the Badalgarh Gate. The entrance is flanked by two 14th-century *sardulas* (mythological man-lion creatures) from the town of Sihoniya. Inside is a large collection of Hindu, Jain and Buddhist sculptures, including the famed Shal Bhanjika, a small but exceptionally well-carved 10th-century female figure from Gyaraspur (if this room is locked ask in the curator's office for the key).

➡ **Man Singh Palace**

(Indian/foreigner ₹25/300, video ₹25; ⊙dawn-dusk) This imperial-style palace, built by Tomar ruler Man Singh between 1486 and 1516, is definitely one of India's more quirkily decorated monuments: its colourful exterior tilework includes a frieze of yellow ducks and mosaics of elephants, crocodiles and tigers in blue, yellow and green! Hence its alternative identity of Chit Mandir (Painted Palace). Man Singh, a connoisseur of the arts, would surely be delighted to know that his creation is now considered the only intact pre-Mughal palace in India.

It's a labyrinth of a building on four levels. Two circular, columned halls on the lower levels were designed for hot weather and connected by 'speaking tubes' built into the

MADHYA PRADESH & CHHATTISGARH GWALIOR

SHIVPURI & MADHAV NATIONAL PARK

A possible day trip from Gwalior is to the old Scindia summer capital of Shivpuri, 117km southwest.

The **Scindia Chhatris** (Shivpuri; ₹50, camera ₹30; ☉ 8am-6pm), 2.5km east of the bus stand (autorickshaw ₹30 to ₹40), are the magnificent cenotaphs of maharajas and maharanis gone by – walk-in marble structures the size of large houses, with Mughal-style pavilions and *sikharas* (Hindu temple-spires) facing each other across a pool with a criss-cross of walkways. The *chhatri* to Madhorao Scindia, built between 1926 and 1932, is exquisitely decorated with intricate pietra dura (precious- and semi-precious-stone inlay work). The patterns and detail of the decoration have a passing resemblance to those on some other rather famous marble building elsewhere in India...

Two kilometres past the *chhatris* is the entrance to **Madhav National Park** (☎ 07492-223379; per vehicle incl guide ₹1110, 6-passenger 4WD rental ₹1600; ☉ dawn-dusk), 355 sq km of very degraded forest as well as lakes and grassland, just east of Shivpuri. It's scattered with relics from the Scindias' hunting days – a shooting box, hunting lodge and sailing club – and is home to antelopes, deer, sloth bears, langurs and a few leopards. A 20km 4WD tour from the park gate on the edge of town takes two to 2½ hours. Don't expect to see a massive amount of wildlife.

Buses leave frequently from the Shivpuri bus stand for Gwalior (₹130, 2½ hours), and also for Jhansi (₹100, three hours), where you can make connections for Orchha and Khajuraho.

walls – and later used by the Mughals as cells for high-ranking prisoners. Some of the darker passageways are now full of roosting bats!

The ticket counter is opposite the palace. You can also hire official guides here for ₹470 for up to four hours. To the north are the ruins of the Vikram Mahal, Karan Mahal and other dilapidated palaces in the north of the fort, grouped under the name **State Protected Monuments** (Indian/foreigner ₹10/250, photography ₹25; ☉ 9am-5pm). Just south is the small **Archaeological Survey of India museum** (ASI; ₹5; ☉ 9am-5pm Sat-Thu), housing a ho-hum collection of Gwalior-area antiquities. Ticket also covers admission to Sasbahu Temple and Teli ka Mandir.

➡ Sasbahu Temples

(Mother-in-Law & Daughter-in-Law Temples; incl in Man Singh Palace ticket; ☉ 6am-6pm) The Sasbahu, dating from the 9th to 11th centuries, are reminiscent of Central American Maya temples, with their dome- and pillar-covered roofs looking like miniature cities. Mother-in-Law, dedicated to Vishnu, has four gigantic and many smaller pillars supporting its heavy roof, layered with carvings.

➡ Teli ka Mandir

(Indian/foreigner ₹25/300, video ₹25; ☉ 6am-6pm) Used as a drinks factory and coffee shop by the British after the First War of Independence (Indian Uprising) of 1857, this 30m-high, 9th-century temple is the oldest

monument in the compound. The modern, gold-topped gurdwara nearby is dedicated to Sikh Guru Hargobind Singh, who was imprisoned in Man Singh Palace from 1617 to 1619. (You have to walk around past Suraj Kund to reach it.)

➡ Jain Rock Sculptures

While there are sculptures carved into the rock at a few points around the fort, including on the way up from the Gwalior Gate, the most impressive is the upper set on the western approach, between Urvai Gate and the inner fort walls. Mostly carved from the cliff-face in the mid-15th century, they represent nude figures of *tirthankars* (the 24 great Jain teachers). They were defaced by Babur's Muslim army in 1527 but have been more recently repaired. There are nine large and many smaller images, including a splendid 17m-high standing sculpture of the first *tirthankar*, Adinath.

⭐ Jai Vilas Palace
& Scindia Museum   PALACE, MUSEUM
(http://jaivilasmuseum.org; Indian/foreigner ₹140/800, camera ₹100; ☉ 10am-5pm Tue-Sun Nov-Feb, to 6pm Tue-Sun Mar-Oct) The museum occupies some 35 rooms of the Scindias' opulent Jai Vilas Palace, built by Maharaja Jayajirao in 1874 using prisoners from the fort. The convicts were rewarded with the 12-year job of weaving the hall carpet, one of the largest in Asia.

Supposedly, eight elephants were suspended from the ceiling of the durbar (royal court) hall to check it could cope with two 12.5m-high, 3.5-tonne chandeliers, said to be the largest pair in the world.

Bizarre items fill the rooms: cut-glass furniture, stuffed tigers and a ladies-only swimming pool with its own boat. The cavernous dining room displays the pièce de résistance, a model railway with a silver train that carried after-dinner brandy and cigars around the table.

Although the palace is undeniably impressive, more than a few people complain about the cost of admission. If money is tight then give it a miss.

Note: only the northern entrance to the palace grounds is open for visitors and it has to be approached from the west (no entry from Moti Mahal Rd).

Tomb of Tansen   ISLAMIC TOMB
(☉ dawn-dusk) Tucked away in a lawned compound in the Hazira neighbourhood, just off the southwest corner of the resplendent tomb of the Sufi saint Mohammed Ghaus, is the smaller, simpler tomb of Tansen, a singer much admired by the Mughal emperor Akbar and held to be the father of Hindustani classical music. Chewing the leaves from the tamarind tree here supposedly enriches your voice. Both men lived in the 16th century.

🛏 Sleeping

Hotel DM   HOTEL $
(☑ 0751-2416660; Link Rd; s ₹500-1200, d ₹600-1800; ❄) Rooms are a bit cramped but they're slightly better than other budget options, and the square garden at the back of the hotel is an unexpected patch of greenery. Best rooms have air-con and sit-down toilets; the cheapest have coolers and squat toilets. All have an old TV locked inside a cabinet. (When did you last steal a hotel TV?)

Hotel Grace   HOTEL $$
(☑ 0751-2340111; www.hotelgrace.in; 40 Manik Vilas Colony; incl breakfast s/d with AC from ₹1700/1850, r without AC ₹999; ❄ 🛜) There's solid value for money at this small hotel with compact, tidy rooms, and bedding that is better than at many much more expensive hotels. Most rooms have bathtubs to luxuriate in. Staff are helpful and speak good English. The only drawback is that there's no in-house restaurant, so breakfast is just served on a tray in your room.

Tansen Residency   HOTEL $$
(☑ 0751-2340370; www.mptourism.com; 6A Gandhi Rd; s/d incl breakfast from ₹2940/3420; ❄ 🛜 🛒) Not bad at all for a government-run hotel, this MP Tourism offering has large-ish rooms with comfy beds...though we're not sure about the cushioned leather panels around the beds in some rooms! Rooms also have updated bathrooms and there's a 1st-floor bar (with a mostly male clientele), a satisfactory buffet breakfast and even a good rooftop pool. It's close to the train and bus stations.

★**Usha Kiran Palace**   HERITAGE HOTEL $$$
(☑ 0751-2444000; www.tajhotels.com; Jayendraganj; s/d incl breakfast from ₹10,280/11,450; ❄ @ 🛒) Live like royalty in this grand 1880 building with expansive gardens that was built as a guesthouse for the Prince of Wales (later King George V). Every room has its unique touches, including different handmade tiles, but all feature understated heritage luxury. The cheapest rooms ('superior' category) can be smaller than you'd hope.

Room prices veer around: you may strike a better offer than the mid-January rates given here. The hotel boasts a gorgeous outdoor pool with separate kids pool, the soothing **Jiva Spa** (☑ 0751-2444000; massage treatments from ₹2500; ☉ 8am-8pm), and the excellent Silver Saloon restaurant. The spiffing Bada Bar, with its century-old, 4-tonne, Italian-slate snooker table, is a fine place for predinner drinks.

🍴 Eating

Indian Coffee House   SOUTH INDIAN $
(Station Rd; mains ₹70-300; ☉ 7am-10.30pm) Hugely popular branch that does all the breakfast favourites – real coffee, dosas, scrambled eggs – but also has a main-course menu, including excellent thalis (₹140 to ₹250).

Moti Mahal Delux   NORTH INDIAN $$
(☑ 0751-4050888; Link Rd; mains ₹225-395; ☉ noon-5pm & 7-11pm) Flavours pop on anything coming out of the tandoor at this jazzy nonveg Delhi transplant. It works magic with northwest frontier cuisine, especially the chicken tikka biryani, mutton rogan josh, and the green-coloured *murg hariyali tikka* (tandoor-baked chicken marinated in spices, yoghurt and herbs, such as coriander and mint). It's next to the bus stand.

★**Silver Saloon**   INDIAN $$$
(Jayendraganj, Usha Kiran Palace; mains ₹520-1390; ☉ 7am-10am, noon-3pm & 7-10.30pm; ❄)

HANDY TRAINS FROM GWALIOR

DESTINATION	TRAIN NO & NAME	FARE (₹)	DURATION (HR)	DEPARTURE
Agra	12617 Mangala Lakshadweep	170/495/680 (A)	2	8.10am
Bhopal	12002 Bhopal Shatabdi	from 765/1525 (B)	4¼	9.33am
Delhi	12625 Kerala Exp	240/605/845 (A)	5½	8.25am
Indore	12920 Malwa Exp	385/1010/1430 (A)	12	12.35am
Jaipur	19665 Udaipur-Khajuraho Exp	225/605/865 (A)	7	3.45pm
Jhansi	12002 Bhopal Shatabdi	from 315/650 (B)	1¼	9.33am
Khajuraho	19666 Udaipur-Khajuraho Exp	120/495/700 (A)	5	1.40pm

Fares: (A) sleeper/3AC/2AC, (B) chair/1AC

High-quality Indian and continental dishes, as well as some Thai, Nepali and Marathi specialities, are served in the air-con restaurant or on the palm-shaded verandah of this exquisite heritage hotel. It offers easily the most upmarket dining in Gwalior.

ⓘ Information

MP Tourism (☎ 0751-2234557; Tansen Residency, 6A Gandhi Rd; ⊙10.30am-5.30pm Mon-Sat) The helpful tourist office is outside Tansen Residency hotel.

ⓘ Getting There & Away

AIR

The **airport** is 10km northeast of the centre. Air India (www.airindia.in) flies three times weekly to/from Delhi.

BUS

Services from the **bus stand** (Link Rd):

Agra ₹130, three hours, half-hourly from 4.30am to 10pm

Delhi ₹350, eight hours, seven daily

Jhansi ₹100, three hours, half-hourly from 5.30am to 11pm

Shivpuri ₹130, 2½ hours, half-hourly from 5am to 10pm

TRAIN

The main station, Gwalior Junction, is centrally located, 2.5km southeast of the fort's eastern entrance. More than 30 daily trains go to Agra's Cantonment station and Delhi, and to Jhansi (for Orchha). More than 20 go to Bhopal, but for Khajuraho and Jaipur there's just one each. For Khajuraho you can also go to Jhansi and get a bus from there.

Orchha

☑ 07680 / POP 11,500

Orchha could make towns many times its size green with jealousy. At heart, Orchha is nothing but a tiny, agricultural village that shouldn't really be of much interest to anyone, but it was blessed by history: for nearly 300 years it was one of the most important urban areas in this part of India. This has left the small town with a supreme display of Mughal-influenced Rajput architecture in the shape of spectacular palaces, temples and royal *chhatris* (cenotaphs). And thanks to an important temple dedicated to Rama, it's also a major pilgrimage and spiritual centre. Combine these with a laid-back atmosphere, some fabulous accommodation options, as well as opportunities to enjoy the surrounding pastoral countryside, with walking, cycling and rafting all on the agenda, and you'll understand why Orchha can be considered one of the highlights of Madhya Pradesh.

History

Orchha owes its glories to the Bundela clan of Rajputs, who set up their headquarters here in 1531 and ruled over the Bundelkhand region (from Jhansi in the west, to Panna in the east, and Narsinghpur in the south) from Orchha till 1783. Orchha reached its zenith under Bir Singh Deo (r 1605–27), who was on good terms with the Mughal emperor Jehangir. In the 1630s Bir Singh Deo's son Jhujar Singh unwisely rebelled against Jehangir's son Shah Jahan, whose armies trashed the Orchha kingdom and damaged some of the town's fine buildings.

⊙ Sights

The combined ticket (Indian/foreigner ₹10/250, camera/video ₹25/200) for Orchha's sights covers seven monuments – the Jehangir Mahal, Raj Mahal, Rai Praveen Mahal, camel stables, *chhatris,* Chaturbhuj Temple and Lakshmi Narayan Temple – and is only sold at the **ticket office** (⊙7.30am-5.30pm at the Raj Mahal. You can walk around the grounds here for free. Also available here are official guides charging ₹470 for up to five people for four hours.

◉ Palace Area

Crossing the granite bridge from the village centre over the often-dry water channel brings you to a fortified complex created by the Bundelas and dominated by two wonderful palaces – the Raj Mahal and Jehangir Mahal.

In several rooms of the 16th-century **Raj Mahal** (◷ dawn-dusk), deities such as Brahma, Vishnu, Rama, Krishna and Sita, plus Orchha royalty, wrestle, hunt, fight and dance their way across walls and ceilings in vivid, colourful murals. The upper floors have great views across the town through their pretty *jali* (carved lattice) windows. A **sound-and-light show** (Indian adult/child ₹130/60, foreigner adult/child ₹300/200; ◷ English 6.30pm, Hindi 7.45pm Oct-Mar, all timings 1hr later Apr-Sep) that's more sound than light, and is only likely to enthuse those interested in Orchha's history, takes place outside the Raj Mahal each evening.

The massive **Jehangir Mahal** (◷ dawn-dusk), an assault course of steep staircases and precipitous walkways, represents a zenith of Indo-Islamic architecture. More decorative than the Raj Mahal, it was built, or at least completed, in the early 17th century by Bir Singh Deo, possibly for a visit by emperor Jehangir. Its walls are crowned by eight domed turrets and eight slender domed pavilions, and superbly devised sightlines carry your gaze through successive arches and doorways to *jali* screens with views over the countryside or town around.

Behind the palace, the **'camel stables'** (Ount Khana; ◷ dawn-dusk) – maybe actually a royal pleasure pavilion – overlook a green landscape dotted with monuments. Downhill from here are the **Khana Hammam** (Royal Bathhouse; ◷ dawn-dusk), with fine vaulted ceilings, and the **Rai Praveen Mahal** (◷ 9am-5pm), a pavilion built for a famous 16th-century courtesan, with a semi-well-kept formal Mughal garden. Murals inside the building immortalise Praveen, dancing, and her lover, Raja Indrajit, on horseback.

◉ Town Centre

★ **Ram Raja Temple** HINDU TEMPLE
(◷ 9am-12.30pm & 7-10.30pm Oct-Mar, 8am-12.30pm & 8-10.30pm Apr-Sep) At the west end of a lively square is the pink- and tangerine-domed Ram Raja Temple, the only temple where Rama is worshipped as a king and busy with crowds of devotees every day. Built as a palace for Madhukar Shah's wife in the 16th century, it became a temple when an image of Rama, temporarily installed by the rani, proved impossible to move. Groups of saddhus gather here, and on weekends and holidays the place buzzes with pilgrims.

★ **Chaturbhuj Temple** HINDU TEMPLE
(◷ 9am-5pm) The spectacular soaring spires of the 16th-century Chaturbhuj Temple are visible from all over town. The Chaturbhuj has never been used for its intended purpose of housing the Rama idol that remains in the Ram Raja Temple next door. You can climb a steep, dark staircase, from the door at the northwest corner of its central interior space, to emerge among the mossy roof pinnacles for the best views in town. Look out for vultures nesting on the roof spires.

Warning 1: no guardrails! Warning 2: devious characters hanging around in the temple might try to make you believe the staircase door is locked, in the hope of a tip for 'unlocking' it.

Phool Bagh GARDENS
(◷ 8am-8pm) Prince Dinman Hardol is venerated as a hero in Bundelkhand for committing suicide to 'prove his innocence' over a supposed affair with his brother's wife. His memorial is in the Phool Bagh, a traditional *charbagh* (formal Persian garden, divided into quarters) adjacent to his palace, the Palaki Mahal. It's an animated scene here with women singing songs about him, tying threads onto the memorial's *jali* (carved lattice screen) and walking around it five times, making wishes they hope he'll grant.

◉ Other Areas

★ **Chhatris** ISLAMIC TOMB
(◷ 9am-5pm) Funerary monuments to Orchha royalty, the huge and serene *chhatris* rise beside the Betwa River at the south end of town. They're best seen at dusk, when birds reel above the children splashing at the river ghats and cinematic sunsets drop across the river. Bir Singh Deo's *chhatri* is set slightly apart, right on the riverbank.

Lakshmi Narayan Temple HINDU TEMPLE
(◷ 9am-5pm) This soaring temple-cum-fort, on the road out to Ganj village, has fine

Orchha

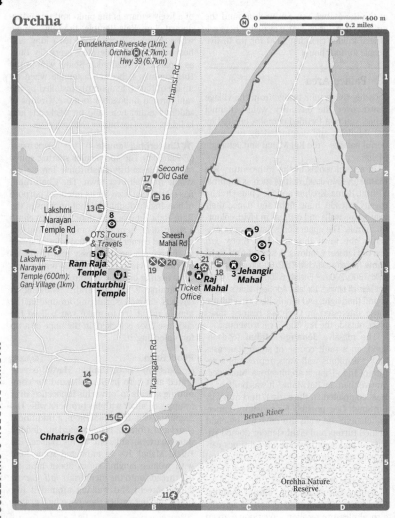

rooftop views and well-preserved murals on the ceilings of its domed towers.

🏃 Activities

If your hotel lacks a pool, you could just cool off in the Betwa – it's one of India's cleanest rivers.

Orchha Nature Reserve　CYCLING, WALKING
(Indian/foreigner ₹40/150, bicycle ₹50; ⏰ dawn-dusk) This 44-sq-km sliver of wooded island between the Betwa and the rock-strewn Jamni River makes an enjoyable few hours' cycling or (in temperate weather) walking. The ticket office is 250m after the causeway

at the south end of Orchha. You can follow a route of about 8km starting from the entry gate 1km past the ticket office, visiting the riverside Pachmariya and two lookout towers, before emerging on the road again 2km south of where you entered.

River-Rafting　RAFTING
(per raft per 1½hr ₹1950) There are some minor rapids upstream from the *chhatris* (cenotaphs) and below the causeway, but this is really just an enjoyable scenic float. Buy tickets at the Betwa Retreat (p635): trips start from the boat club just in front. Rafts take up to six people. There's no minimum number.

Orchha

◉ Top Sights
1 Chaturbhuj Temple	B3
2 Chhatris	A5
3 Jehangir Mahal	C3
4 Raj Mahal	B3
5 Ram Raja Temple	A3

◎ Sights
6 Camel Stables	C3
7 Khana Hammam	C3
8 Phool Bagh	B3
9 Rai Praveen Mahal	C3

⊕ Activities, Courses & Tours
10 Kairali Spa	A5
11 Orchha Nature Reserve	B5
12 Raju Bike	A3
River-Rafting	(see 15)

⊟ Sleeping
13 Aditya Hotel	A2
14 Amar Mahal	A4
15 Betwa Retreat	B5
16 Hotel Fort View	B2
17 Hotel Monarch Rama	B2
18 Hotel Sheesh Mahal	C3

⊗ Eating
Amar Mahal Restaurant	(see 14)
Bundela Restaurant	(see 15)
19 Laxmi Betwa Tarang	B3
20 RamRaja Restaurant	B3

⊕ Entertainment
21 Sound-and-Light Show	C3

Kairali Spa AYURVEDA
(☏ 07680-252222; www.orchharesort.com; treatments ₹900-2500; ◷ 8.30am-8.30pm) Orchha Resort offers good-quality ayurvedic massage treatments with professional masseurs. It also runs yoga and meditation workshops.

Raju Bike CYCLING
(Lakshmi Narayan Temple Rd; per hour/day ₹10/50; ◷ 7am-9pm) Hires out rickety bicycles at unbeatable prices.

🛏 Sleeping

Aditya Hotel HOTEL $
(☏ 07680-252027; adityahotelorchha@gmail.com; r with/without AC ₹1500/700; ❋ ◪) Just behind Phool Bagh, Aditya provides clean, medium-sized, all-white rooms. Room prices vary depending on whether they're upstairs or down and are or aren't air-conditioned. Some upstairs rooms have temple and palace views, and you can have breakfast on a nice little roof terrace up there. Very little English is spoken.

Hotel Monarch Rama HOTEL $
(☏ 07680-252727; hotelmonarchrama@gmail.com; Jhansi Rd; r with/without AC ₹1000/650; ❋ ◪) Rooms here are cleaner and more appealing than at most of the budget competition, and staff are friendly too. Sheets are clean, the bathrooms don't smell, and there are even Indian miniature prints on the walls. No natural light, however, except a little in the two air-con rooms, upstairs, where there's also a small restaurant.

Hotel Fort View HOTEL $
(☏ 07680-252701, 7869370614; fortvieworchha@rediffmail.com; Jhansi Rd; r with/without AC ₹1200/600; ❋ ◪) This hotel might be less than one star (quite a lot less!), but the views over the Raj Mahal from some of the rooms (rooms 108, 111 and 112 are best) are definitely five star. And back to those rooms. Well, they have clean sheets on hardish beds and all the bathrooms have bathtubs...so really not so bad after all.

★ Hotel Sheesh Mahal HERITAGE HOTEL $$
(☏ 07680-252624; www.mptourism.com; incl breakfast r ₹3530, ste ₹6600-7780; ❋ ◪) Literally palatial and like sleeping with history, this hotel occupies an 18th-century former royal guesthouse adjoining the Jehangir Mahal. The eight different rooms are all gorgeous, with colourful traditional-style paintings, thick, pelmeted curtains, cute alcoves and bathrooms that could give you agoraphobia. If you can afford it, go for a suite and pretend to be a king for a day.

Betwa Retreat HOTEL $$
(☏ 07680-252618; www.mptourism.com; cottages/r ₹2590/2990; ❋ ◪) MP Tourism's main Orchha property is a pretty good choice.

SLEEPING PRICE RANGES

Price ranges are for a double room with bath, including taxes in these regions:

$ less than ₹1500

$$ ₹1500–₹3500

$$$ more than ₹3500

VILLAGE LIFE: HOMESTAYS IN GANJ

Thanks to **Orchha Home-Stay** (☑ 8109882335, 9981749660; www.orchha.org; s ₹750, d ₹950-1200, meals ₹60-250; ☎) 🖉, a successful and popular homestay program run by the nonprofit organisation Friends of Orchha, travellers have a wonderful opportunity to stay with local people and experience village life in Ganj, 1km west of central Orchha. You'll be staying in simple village homes and eating simple village meals, and you can rent bikes (₹60 per day) to explore Orchha and the surrounding area.

Don't expect luxury – you'll be sleeping on charpoys (rope beds) in most cases – but the eight rooms, in six homes in the small village, are better and more charming than a lot of budget hotels. Rooms have insulated walls and tiled roofs and are equipped with fans and mosquito nets. Most houses have sit-down toilets, while others have dry-composting squat toilets or a squat toilet linked to a biogas digester.

The interaction with villagers and immersion into village life is priceless (so you probably won't want the wi-fi; ₹100 per day) and guests are provided with a helpful information folder, which includes ideas about what to do and where to go around Ganj and Orchha.

If you want to stay one night only, you can, but room rates will be slightly higher than for longer stays. In any case, the slow pace of life in Ganj is something to be savoured and most guests stay several nights.

Friends of Orchha has an office, open from 3pm, on the right-hand side of the road as you enter Ganj, but it's easy to book directly online through their website, or make arrangements through the program's manager, Romi Samele, at OTS Tours & Travels (p637) in Orchha.

Friends of Orchha also runs an after-school youth club for village children. Options to donate are available.

Accommodation and a good pool are set amid well-kept gardens with views to the river and the *chhatris* (cenotaphs). The 'cottages' are large safari-style tents with solid floors and half-walls, plus bathrooms, good beds, air-con and minibars. Rooms, in vaguely traditional style, are similarly comfy and have tea/coffee equipment.

★ **Amar Mahal** HOTEL $$$
(☑ 07680-252202; www.amarmahal.com; s/d from ₹5460/6650, ste ₹11,760; ❄ @ ☎ ☀) Live the life of a maharaja in this oriental fantasy hotel with its glittering courtyards, pillars and ponds, as well as luxurious rooms with wood-carved four-poster beds. Despite the royal-palace aspirations, the building is less than 20 years old.

Great facilities include a beautiful pool, the Kerala Ayurvedic Centre and the town's best restaurant (p637). Be aware that at weekends it often hosts wedding parties.

Bundelkhand Riverside HOTEL $$$
(☑ 9009749630, 07680-252612; www.bundelkhand riverside.com; s/d incl breakfast ₹4450/5000; ❄ ☎ ☀) Owned by the grandson of Orchha's last king, this hotel feels authentically heritage, although the main building is less than 20 years old. Antique-style furniture abounds and some of the maharaja's personal art collection is displayed in the corridors. Attractive rooms overlook either the river or the graceful gardens, which contain four 16th-century temples, as well as a swimming pool.

✗ Eating

RamRaja Restaurant MULTICUISINE $
(Sheesh Mahal Rd; mains ₹75-395; ⊙ 7am-10.30pm; ☎) This friendly, family-run streetside restaurant offers the best 'traveller' menu in town, with eggy breakfasts, muesli, pancakes, tasty vegetarian fare and real espresso – all under the shade of a large tree. Can also scare up a beer.

Laxmi Betwa Tarang INDIAN $
(Sheesh Mahal Rd; mains ₹80-180; ⊙ 7am-10pm; ☎ 🖉) This place, with an air-conditioned dining room, does the best veg food of any of Orchha's budget restaurants – the thalis (₹130 to ₹350) are particularly good. It also has a rooftop terrace, where you can sit with stupendous views of the Raj Mahal. Beers are off menu but available.

Bundela Restaurant MULTICUISINE $$
(Betwa Retreat; mains ₹140-350; ⊙ 8am-10.30pm) Continental and Chinese dishes are on offer, as well as reliably good Indian fare at this licensed hotel restaurant – and the live tra-

ditional Bundelkhandi music by a trio and singer on the terrace makes evenings a bit special.

Amar Mahal Restaurant NORTH INDIAN $$$
(✆7680252102; www.amrmahal.com; Amar Mahal; mains ₹300-450; ⏱7-10am, noon-3pm & 7.30-10.30pm; ❄) The elegant dining room at the Amar Mahal hotel has an elaborately painted roof complete with real gold-leaf filigree. Needless to say, with such a backdrop the food itself is refined North Indian and the best you'll get in town. There are also a few token Chinese and Continental dishes.

ℹ Information

OTS Tours & Travels (OTS; ✆9981749660; www.facebook.com/otstours; ⏱8.30am-9.30pm) This agency, run by Romi Samele, is the representative in town for Orchha Home-Stay (p636) at Ganj, and is also good for all kinds of travel bookings. It's behind Ram Raja Temple.

ℹ Getting There & Away

Getting to or from Orchha by public transport almost always involves getting to the larger town of Jhansi, 18km northwest, first. Jhansi is on the Delhi–Agra–Gwalior–Bhopal rail route, with more than 30 daily trains in each direction. From Jhansi train station, an autorickshaw to Orchha (45 minutes) costs ₹250 to ₹300; a taxi (30 minutes) is ₹600. Or get a tempo (₹15) from the train station to the bus station, 4km east, then one of the hourly buses to Orchha (₹35, 45 minutes).

TO/FROM KHAJURAHO

Buses from Jhansi go to Chhatarpur (₹100, three hours, hourly 5am to 10pm), where you can switch for Khajuraho (₹50, 1½ hours). Coming from Khajuraho, you can ask the bus driver to drop you at the Orchha turn-off on Hwy 39, where you should be able to wave down a vehicle to take you to Orchha. You could also get a bus bound for Panna and get out at Bamitha (₹120) and then take a tempo or shared 4WD (both ₹10) or autorickshaw (₹150) straight to Khajuraho.

Train 19666, the Udaipur–Khajuraho Express, departs Jhansi at 3.30pm, reaching Khajuraho (sleeper/3AC/2AC ₹160/495/700) at 7.50pm. Another option is train 54159, which leaves Orchha's tiny train station, 5km north of town on the Jhansi road, at 7.25am for Mahoba (₹30, 2¾ hours), but on average it runs over an hour late. From Mahoba train 51821 departs at 10.45am, reaching Khajuraho (₹15) at noon. These trains are slow, with unreserved 2nd-class seating only, and are often very crowded. If you miss the connection at Mahoba (quite likely) the next train to Khajuraho isn't till 6.05pm.

If just reading that lot made you exhausted, simply take a taxi (around ₹2700, four hours).

Khajuraho

☎07686 / POP 24,500

One of India's most fascinating towns, Khajuraho is famed far and wide for the erotic stone carvings that swathe three groups of World Heritage–listed temples. The Western Group of temples, in particular, are superb examples of North Indian architecture, but it's the liberally embellished carvings that have made Khajuraho famous. Embracing the temples are bands of exceedingly artistic stonework showing a storyboard of life a millennium ago – gods, goddesses, warriors, dancers and real and mythological animals.

The temples carvings are renowned for two elements in particular – women and sex. Sensuous *surasundaris* and *apsaras* (heavenly nymphs) and *nayikas* (heroines) have been carved with a half-twist and slight sideways lean that make the playful figures dance and swirl out from the temple. The *mithunas* (pairs, threesomes etc of men and women depicted in erotic poses) display the great skill of the sculptors – and the dexterity of the Chandelas. However, sex isn't the be all and end all of Khajuraho temple art and the majority of carvings focus on more mundane aspects of life, but needless to say, most visitors ignore these!

Khajuraho is fully on the tour-bus map, but despite this and a handful of low-key touts, it's a delightful, quiet little village, where it's easy to while away several days walking and cycling between stunning temples and enjoying the easy-going traveller vibe. The town also makes a reasonable base for nearby Panna Tiger Reserve (p647) .

History

Legend has it that Khajuraho was founded by Chandravarman, son of the moon god Chandra, who descended and saw a beautiful maiden, Hemavati, as she bathed in a stream. Historians tell us that most of the 85 original temples (of which 25 remain) were built between AD 930 and 1050 during the zenith of the Chandela dynasty, a Rajput clan who ruled varying amounts of Bundelkhand (straddling northern Madhya Pradesh and southern Uttar Pradesh) between the 9th and 16th centuries. It's not clear whether Khajuraho was the

Continued on p641

MADHYA PRADESH & CHHATTISGARH KHAJURAHO

Khajuraho Temples

WESTERN-GROUP TOUR

The sheer volume of artwork at Khajuraho's best-preserved temples can be overwhelming. Initiate yourself with this introductory tour, which highlights some of those easy-to-miss details.

First, admire the **1 sandstone boar** in the Varaha shrine before heading to the **2 Lakshmana Temple** to study the south side of the temple's base, which has some of the raunchiest artwork in Khajuraho: first up, a nine-person orgy; further along, a guy getting very friendly with a horse. Up on the temple platform see a superb dancing Ganesh carved into a niche (south side), before walking to the west end for graceful *surasundaris* (nymphs): removing a thorn from a foot (northwest corner) or looking into a mirror (southwest corner).

Next is Khajuraho's largest temple, **3 Kandariya-Mahadev**. Carvings to look for here include the famous headstand position (south side), but the most impressive thing about this temple is the scale of it, particularly its soaring rooftops.

4 Mahadeva and **5 Devi Jagadamba** share the same stone plinth as Kandariya-Mahadev, as do four beautifully carved *sardulas* (part-lion, part-human mythical beasts), each caressing a nymph – one is at the entrance to Mahadeva; the other three stand alone on the plinth.

Walk north from here to the **6 Chitragupta Temple**, with miniature elephants and hunting scenes among its lowest band of reliefs. Inside, spot the tiny sculpture of the seven horses pulling sun god Surya's chariot.

Continue east to the **7 Vishvanath Temple** for more fabulous carvings before admiring the impressive statue of Shiva's bull in the **8 Nandi shrine** opposite.

BODOM/SHUTTERSTOCK ©

Headstand Position

Perhaps Khajur most famous carving, this fle flirtation is abo you as you star the south side o awesome Kand Mahadev.

Sikharas

Despite its many fine statues, perhaps the most impressive thing about Kandariya-Mahadev is its soaring *sikharas* (temple rooftops), said to represent the Himalayan abode of the gods.

Devi Jaga Temp

Kandariya-Mahadev Temple

Maha Temp

NORTH →

Toi

Sardula Statue

There are four nymph-caressing *sardulas* on this huge stone plinth, but this one, guarding the entrance to Mahadeva, is our favourite.

ELENA MIRAGE/SHUTTERSTOCK ©

Surasunda

Beautifully gra depictions of nymphs are fou on a number of Khajuraho tem And despite all depictions of g nastic orgies, t seductive *suras dari* draped in a sari is arguably most erotic of a

WORD OF MOUTH

Government-licensed guides, who gather near the ticket office, may embellish the history a bit but they do help bring the old stones to life.

6 Chitragupta Temple

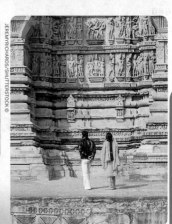

JUST THE TICKET

For an extra-close look at Khajuraho artwork, use your ticket for entrance to the town's Archaeological Museum.

Toilets

7 Vishvanath Temple

Parvati Temple

Lakshmana Temple 2

8 Nandi Shrine

Pratapeswar Temple

Lakshmi Shrine

1 Varaha Shrine

Entrance

Matangesvara Temple

Kama Sutra Carvings
Often referred to as Kama Sutra carvings, Khajuraho's erotic artwork does not properly illustrate Vatsyayana's famous sutra. Debate continues as to its significance: as fertility symbolism, or implying rulers here were virile, thus powerful? Interestingly, the erotic carvings are never located close to the temple deity.

Nandi Statue
This massive 2.2m-long statue of Nandi, the bull-vehicle of Shiva, is enshrined in a pavilion facing Vishvanath Temple.

Vishnu's Boar
This 9th-/10th-century statue of Varaha, the boar incarnation of Vishnu, is carved all over with figures of Brahmanical gods and goddesses. At Varaha's feet notice the serpent Seshanaga in a devotional posture, and the feet of a goddess, now missing.

Khajuraho

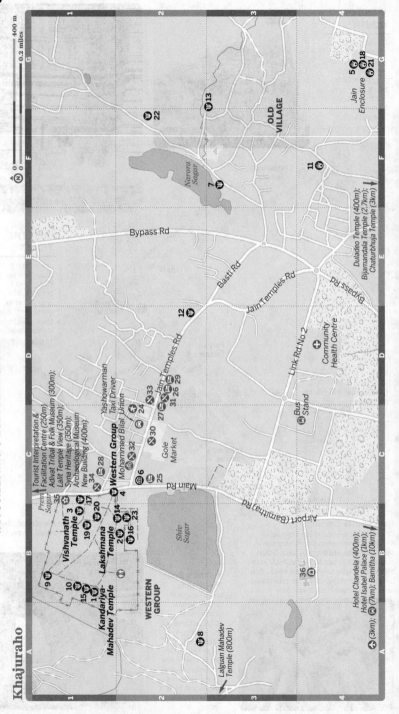

400 m
0.2 miles

Tourist Interpretation &
Facilitation Centre (250m);
Adivat Tribal & Folk Museum (300m);
Lalit Temple View (350m);
Syna Heritage (350m);
Archaeological Museum
New Building (400m)

Prem Sagar

Vishvanath
Temple

Lakshmana
Temple

Kandariya-
Mahadev Temple

WESTERN
GROUP

Western Group

Mohammed Bilal

Yashowarman
Taxi Driver
Union

Gole
Market

Shiv Sagar

Bypass Rd

Basti Rd

Jain Temples Rd

Jain Temples Rd

Link Rd No 2

Main Rd

Narora
Sagar

OLD
VILLAGE

Jain
Enclosure

Community
Health Centre

Bus
Stand

Bypass Rd

Lalguan Mahadev
Temple (800m)

Airport (Bamitha) Rd

Hotel Chandela (400m);
Hotel Isabel Palace (1km);
(7km); Bamitha (10km)

(3km);

Duladeo Temple (400m);
Bijamandala Temple (2.7km);
Chaturbhuja Temple (3km)

Khajuraho

⊙ Top Sights
1 Kandariya-Mahadev Temple.................B1
2 Lakshmana Temple.............................B2
3 Vishvanath Temple.............................B1
4 Western Group....................................C1

⊙ Sights
5 Adinath Temple...................................G4
6 Archaeological Museum.......................C2
7 Brahma Temple...................................F3
8 Chausath Yogini Temple.....................A2
9 Chitragupta Temple............................B1
10 Devi Jagadamba Temple......................B1
11 Ghantai Temple...................................F4
12 Hanuman Temple.................................D2
13 Javari Temple......................................G3
14 Lakshmi Shrine...................................B2
15 Mahadeva Temple................................B1
16 Matangesvara Temple..........................B2
17 Nandi Shrine..C1
18 Parsvanath Temple..............................G4
19 Parvati Temple.....................................B1
20 Pratapeswar Temple............................B1
21 Shantinath Temple...............................G4
22 Vamana Temple....................................F2

23 Varaha Shrine......................................B2

⊙ Activities, Courses & Tours
24 Ayur Arogyam......................................C2

⊙ Sleeping
25 Headquarters Khajuraho......................C2
26 Hotel Harmony.....................................D2
27 Hotel Surya..C2
28 Hotel Yogi Lodge.................................C1
29 Hotel Zen...D2

⊙ Eating
30 Evening Food Stalls.............................C2
31 Guru Kripa Restaurant.........................D2
32 Lassi Corner..C2
33 Mediterraneo.......................................D2
34 Raja Cafe...C1

⊙ Entertainment
Folk Dance Show.............................(see 36)
35 Sound-&-Light Show.............................C1

⊙ Shopping
36 Kandariya..B4

Continued from p637

Continued from p637

Chandelas' capital or more of a sacred ceremonial centre. Mahoba, 50km north, was certainly their capital from some time in the 11th century, though the Khajuraho temples remained active long after this.

Khajuraho's isolation may well have helped preserve it from the desecration Muslim invaders inflicted on temples elsewhere. Perhaps for the same reason the area was slowly abandoned and overtaken by jungle, with many buildings falling into ruin. The wider world remained largely ignorant until British officer TS Burt was apparently guided to the ruins by his palanquin bearers in 1838.

⊙ Sights

⊙ Western Temple Group – Inside the Fenced Enclosure

Khajuraho's most striking and best-preserved temples are those within the fenced-off section of the **Western Group** (Indian/foreigner ₹40/600; ⊙ dawn-dusk). An Archaeological Survey of India (ASI) guidebook to Khajuraho (₹60) may be available at the ticket office. Officially licensed guides, available from beside the ticket office, cost ₹1368. They'll do much to bring the temples to life and explain every sordid detail of the sexual images.

A nightly **sound-and-light show** (Indian/foreigner adult ₹250/700, child ₹120/300; ⊙ English 6.30pm Oct-Feb, 7.30pm Mar-Sep, Hindi 7.40pm Oct-Feb, 8.40pm Mar-Sep) sees technicolour floodlights sweep across the temples of the Western Group as Indian classical music accompanies a potted history of Khajuraho narrated by the 'master sculptor'. Photography is prohibited.

★**Lakshmana Temple**   HINDU TEMPLE
The large Lakshmana Temple took 20 years to build and was completed in about AD 954 during the reign of Dhanga, according to an inscription in its *mandapa* (pillared front pavilion). It's arguably the best preserved of all the Khajuraho temples. On the southern side of its base are some of Khajuraho's most orgiastic carvings, including one gentleman and a horse, with a shocked figure peeping out from behind her hands.

You'll see carvings of battalions of soldiers on the frieze around the base – the Chandelas were generally at war when they weren't inventing new sexual positions – as well as musicians, hunters and plenty of elephants, horses and camels. Some superb carvings can also be found around the *garbhagriha* (inner sanctum). The temple is dedicated to Vishnu, although it's similar in design to the Shiva temples Vishvanath (p642) and Kandariya-Mahadev (p642).

MADHYA PRADESH & CHHATTISGARH KHAJURAHO

The two small shrines facing Lakshmana's east end are the Lakshmi Temple (usually locked) and the Varaha Temple, containing a wonderful, 1.5m-high sandstone carving of Vishnu as his boar avatar, dating from AD 900 and meticulously carved with a pantheon of gods.

★ **Kandariya-Mahadev Temple** HINDU TEMPLE
The 30.5m-long Kandariya-Mahadev, built between 1025 and 1050, is the largest Western Group temple and represents the high point of Chandela architecture. It also has the most representations of female beauty and sexual acrobatics of any Khajuraho temple. There are 872 statues, most nearly 1m high – taller than those at the other temples. One frequently photographed sculpture on the south side illustrates the feasibility of the headstand position.

The 31m-high *sikhara* (temple spire) here is, like a lingam, a phallic Shiva symbol, worshipped by Hindus hoping to seek deliverance from the cycle of reincarnation. It and the *mandapa* (pillared pavilion) are decorated with 84 subsidiary spires, which make up a mountain-like rooftop scene reminiscent of the Himalayan abode of the gods.

Mahadeva Temple HINDU TEMPLE
Mahadeva, a small, partly ruined temple on the same platform as Kandariya-Mahadev and Devi Jagadamba, is dedicated to Shiva, who is carved on the lintel of its doorway. It houses one of Khajuraho's finest sculptures – a *sardula* (mythical beast that's part lion, part other animal – possibly human) engaged in a mutual caress with a kneeling woman.

Devi Jagadamba Temple HINDU TEMPLE
Devi Jagadamba was originally dedicated to Vishnu, but later to Parvati and then Kali. The carvings include *sardulas* accompanied by Vishnu, *surasundaris* (heavenly nymphs), and *mithunas* (pairs of men and women) frolicking in the third band up. Its three-part design is simpler than that of the Kandariya-Mahadev and Chitragupta temples. It has more in common with Chitragupta, but is less embellished with carvings so is thought to be a little older.

Chitragupta Temple HINDU TEMPLE
The Chitragupta Temple (1000–25) is unique in Khajuraho – and rare among North Indian temples – in being dedicated to the sun god Surya. While its condition is not as good as the other Western Group temples, it has

some fine carvings of *apsaras* and *surasundaris*, elephant fights and hunting scenes, *mithunas* and a procession of stone-carriers.

In the dark inner sanctum, at the base of the statue, you can make out the seven horses that pull Surya's chariot, while in the lower of the two main niches beneath the *sikhara* on the south side is an 11-headed carving of Vishnu, representing the god and 10 of his 22 incarnations.

Parvati Temple HINDU TEMPLE
Walking around the Western Group enclosure from the Chitragupta Temple you come to the closed-up Parvati Temple on your right, a small temple originally dedicated to Vishnu and now with an image of Gauri (Parvati) riding a giant lizard.

★ **Vishvanath Temple** HINDU TEMPLE
Believed to have been built in 1002, the Vishvanath Temple anticipates the plan and style of the Kandariya-Mahadev Temple. Dedicated to Shiva, it's a superlative example of Chandela architecture, with a riot of carved figures continuing up to the highest levels of the *sikharas*. Sculptures include a female doing a headstand in the north-side recess; sensuous *surasundaris* writing letters, cuddling babies, looking in mirrors and scratching their backs; and miniature camels, horses, musicians, elephants, warriors and dancers in the lowest frieze.

At the east end of the platform, a 2.2m-long statue of Nandi, Shiva's bull vehicle, faces the temple. The basement of this 12-pillared shrine is decorated with an elephant frieze that recalls similar work on the Lakshmana Temple's facade.

Pratapeswar Temple HINDU TEMPLE
Near the Vishvanath Temple, the white Pratapeswar is a much more recent bricks-and-mortar structure built around 200 years ago.

⊙ Western Temple Group – Outside the Fenced Enclosure

Matangesvara Temple HINDU TEMPLE
(☉dawn-dusk) Right next to the Lakshmana Temple but separated from it by the enclosure fence, Matangesvara is the only temple in the Western Group still in everyday use and lots of Indian tourists come here to make *puja* (offerings or prayers). It may be the plainest temple here (suggesting an early construction), but inside it sports a polished 2.5m-high lingam (phallic symbol of Shiva).

Chausath Yogini Temple
HINDU TEMPLE

The ruins of Chausath Yogini, beyond Shiv Sagar lake, date from the late 9th century and are probably the oldest at Khajuraho. You may find it locked up. Constructed entirely of granite, this is the only temple not aligned east–west. *Chausath* means '64' – the temple once had 64 cells for statues of the *yoginis* (female attendants) of Kali, while the 65th sheltered the goddess herself. It's reputedly India's oldest *yogini* temple.

Lalguan Mahadev Temple
TEMPLE

About 800m west from the Chausath Yogini Temple, down a track and across a couple of fields (just ask the locals), is the sandstone-and-granite Lalguan Mahadev Temple (AD 900), a small ruined shrine to Shiva.

Archaeological Museum
MUSEUM

(Main Rd; ☉9am-5pm Sat-Thu) The town's original Archaeological Museum, opposite the Western Group of temples, has a good collection of sculptures from around Khajuraho, starting in the entrance hall with a wonderful 11th-century statue of Ganesh dancing remarkably sensuously for an elephant-headed deity, with a tiny mouse (his vehicle) at his feet. Admission is only with a same-day ticket for the Western Group (p641). There is also a new archaeological museum in the northern part of town.

Archaeological Museum
New Building
MUSEUM

(incl in ticket to Western Group temples; ☉9am-5pm Sat-Thu) The bright, purpose-built, new building of the Archaeological Museum, north of the Western Group temples, opened in 2016. It contains a collection of Khajuraho sculptures in several galleries and two courtyards, plus information panels on Chandela history and art.

◉ Eastern Temple Group

The Eastern Group includes three Hindu temples scattered around the old village and four Jain temples further south, three of which are in a walled enclosure.

Hanuman Temple
HINDU TEMPLE

(Basti Rd) The small, white Hanuman Temple contains a 2.5m-tall orangepainted statue of the Hindu monkey god. It's most interesting for the pedestal inscription from AD 922, the oldest dateable inscription in Khajuraho.

Brahma Temple
HINDU TEMPLE

The granite Brahma Temple, with its sandstone *sikhara* (temple spire) overlooking Narora Sagar, is one of the oldest in Khajuraho, dating from about AD 900. Inside is an unusual Shiva lingam with four faces (which led to the temple being incorrectly named after the four-faced Brahma) – but the image of Vishnu above the sanctum doorway reveals its original dedication to Vishnu.

Javari Temple
HINDU TEMPLE

(☉dawn-dusk) Resembling the Chaturbhuja Temple (p644) in the Southern Group, the Javari Temple (1075–1100) stands just north of the old village. It's dedicated to Vishnu and is a good example of small-scale Khajuraho architecture for its crocodile-covered entrance arch and slender *sikhara*.

Vamana Temple
HINDU TEMPLE

(☉dawn-dusk) The Vamana Temple (1050–75), 300m north of the old village, is dedicated to the dwarf incarnation of Vishnu. It has quirky touches such as elephants protruding from the walls, but its *sikhara* is devoid of subsidiary spires and there are few erotic scenes.

Ghantai Temple
JAIN TEMPLE

Located between the old village and the Jain Enclosure, the small Jain Ghantai Temple is named after the *ghanta* (chain and bell) decorations on its pillars. It was once similar to the nearby Parsvanath Temple, but only the pillared shell of its porch and *mandapa* (pillared pavilion) remain, and it's normally locked.

Shantinath Temple
JAIN TEMPLE

(with Adinath & Parsvanath temples ₹10; ☉7am-6pm) Shantinath, a mixture of old and modern construction, is the main place of worship in the Jain group. It has a collection of components from older temples, including a 4.5m-high Adinath statue with a plastered-over inscription on the pedestal dating to about 1028.

Parsvanath Temple
JAIN TEMPLE

(with Adinath & Shantinath temples ₹10; ☉7am-6pm) While not competing in size or erotica with the Western Group temples, this largest of the Jain temples in the walled enclosure is notable for the exceptional precision of its construction, as well as for its sculptural beauty. Some of the best preserved examples of Khajuraho's most famous images can be seen here, including the woman removing a thorn from her foot and another applying eye make-up, both on the southern side.

Adinath Temple
JAIN TEMPLE

(with Parsvanath & Shantinath temples ₹10; ⏰7am-6pm) The late-11th-century Adinath has been partially restored over the centuries. With fine carvings on its three bands of sculptures, it's similar to Khajuraho's Hindu temples, particularly Vamana. Only the striking black image in the inner sanctum triggers a Jain reminder.

◉ Southern Temple Group

A paved road running south from near the Jain enclosure leads to three temples that are not Khajuraho's most spectacular, but make for a pleasant cycle into the countryside.

Duladeo Temple
HINDU TEMPLE

(⏰dawn-dusk) The Duladeo Temple, dedicated to Shiva and set among well-tended gardens just above a small river, is Khajuraho's youngest temple, dating to 1100–50. Its relatively wooden, repetitive carvings suggest that Khajuraho's sculptors had passed their artistic peak by this point, although they had certainly lost none of their zeal for eroticism.

Chaturbhuja Temple
HINDU TEMPLE

(⏰dawn-dusk) The small Chaturbhuja Temple (c 1100) anticipates Duladeo and its flaws, but has a fine 2.7m-high, four-armed statue of Vishnu in the sanctum. It is Khajuraho's only developed temple without erotic sculptures.

It's 1.7km past Duladeo: go through Jatkara village and turn left at the T-junction 350m later.

Bijamandala Temple
HINDU TEMPLE

(⏰dawn-dusk) The 700m track to Bijamandala veers left (signposted) 200m before you reach Chaturbhuja Temple. This is the excavated mound of an 11th-century temple, dedicated to Shiva (judging by the white marble lingam at the apex of the mound).

There are remnants of a small-scale frieze with elephants and dancers, but unfinished carvings were also excavated, suggesting what would have been Khajuraho's largest temple was abandoned as resources flagged.

🏃 Activities

Many budget hotels offer cheap ayurvedic massage treatments of varying levels of authenticity. Top-end hotels offer more luxurious versions.

Ayur Arogyam
MASSAGE

(☑07686-272572; www.ayurarogyam.in; Jain Temples Rd; treatments ₹1000-1900) For real-deal ayurvedic treatments, head to Ayur Arogyam, run by a lovely, professionally qualified and experienced Keralan couple.

✦ Festivals & Events

Festival of Dance
DANCE, CRAFTS

(⏰late Feb) Free nightly Indian dance performances amid the Western Group temples are the focus of this week-long festival, which packs Khajuraho with visitors.

🛏 Sleeping

Khajuraho has a superb array of accommodation with something to suit all budgets. Hefty discounts (20% to 50%) are available out of season (approximately April to September). Hotel staff are more than happy to organise tours and travel.

★ Headquarters Khajuraho
HOSTEL $

(☑8085687248; Main Rd; dm ₹400, d from ₹1200; 🖥) This bright hostel painted with murals of cold penguins in woolly scarfs and a tie-dyed Jimmy Hendrix is perfectly positioned overlooking Shiv Sagar lake. It offers well-kept accommodation in two six-bunk dorms with large luggage lockers, and colourful, spacious doubles. There's a great rooftop cafe doing inexpensive breakfasts and thalis, and everything is good and clean, including the guest kitchen.

It offers the full array of budget travel services including onward travel arrangements, tours to Panna National Park and more. One of the best budget options in central India.

Hotel Harmony
HOTEL $

(☑07686-274135; www.hotelharmonyonline.com; Jain Temples Rd; r ₹800-3000; ❈🖥) Cosy rooms off marble corridors are tastefully decorated and come with mostly effective mosquito screens and cable TV. The cheapest rooms are equipped with 1960s wooden furnishings and have a certain retro style. Pricier rooms are pleasingly bright and have views over the courtyard garden. The best-value rooms are those costing ₹1500.

Hotel Surya
HOTEL $

(☑9425146203; Jain Temples Rd; r ₹1000, with AC ₹1200-1500; ❈🖥) There's quite a range of rooms in this sprawling, well-run, decently kept hotel with whitewashed corridors, marble staircases, replica Khajuraho statues (only the erotic ones, of course) and a lovely courtyard and garden out the back. Some rooms have balconies. Yoga and massage are available and there's a book swap.

Hotel Yogi Lodge
HOTEL $

(☑ 97686274158; yogi_sharm@yahoo.com; off Main Rd; s ₹300, d ₹500-600; ☀ 🕸) Rooms at this backpacker-favourite cheapie are simple, but they're reasonably neat and well kept, the sheets do seem to have been laundered and the showers have hot water. The small courtyards, free morning rooftop yoga, and the upstairs patio restaurant with cute stone tables and an eclectic menu (mains ₹100 to ₹260), all give this place character and value.

Hotel Zen
HOTEL $

(☑ 9337871243, 07686-274228; www.hotelzen khajuraho.co.in; Jain Temples Rd; incl breakfast s/d with AC ₹1100/1300, without AC ₹900/1100; ☀ 🕸) Plain rooms on four floors overlook a lush garden with small lotus ponds. Italian and Indian food is available, and the owner is a friendly fellow. There's hot water from 5am to 9am, and massages are available, as well as all the other standard backpacker travel services.

★ Hotel Isabel Palace
HOTEL $$

(☑ 07686-274770; www.hotelisabelpalace.com; off Airport Rd; dm ₹300, incl breakfast r with AC ₹1800-3500, without AC ₹1500; ☀ 🕸) This fantastic hotel, along a quiet dirt road 1.5km south of town, is perfect for flashpackers and backpackers. The sparkling-clean rooms vary according to view (garden or sunrise), decor and furnishings, but all are spacious and very comfortable and have a terrace or balcony. There are nice homely touches such as framed textiles on the walls and colourful, tiled wardrobes.

Lalit Temple View
HOTEL $$$

(☑ 9993092600; www.thelalit.com; Main Rd; budget r ₹5000, d incl breakfast from ₹14,000; ☀ 🕸 🏊) Sweeps aside all other five-star pretenders with immaculate rooms, impeccable service and high prices. Rooms have marble bathrooms, carved-wood furniture and tasteful artwork, though considering how much the hotel charges the 'wow' factor is a bit lacking. There's a beautiful pool area with temple views and a spa.

🍴 Eating & Drinking

For cheap eats, **evening food stalls** (dishes ₹20-60; ⏰ approximately 7-11pm) selling omelettes, *momos* (Tibetan dumplings), South Indian items and paneer patties open up af-

ter sunset towards the west end of Jain Temple Rd. You can get a beer at several of the rooftop restaurants in town, and the more expensive hotels all have bars or licensed restaurants.

Guru Kripa Restaurant
NORTH INDIAN $

(Jain Temples Rd; mains ₹60-120, thalis ₹90; ⏰ 8am-10pm) A change from the town's numerous 'traveller cafes', this solidly local place serves tasty thalis and a range of North Indian dishes. There's a small, modern and clean dining room downstairs and a larger one with views over the street upstairs.

Lassi Corner
INDIAN $

(Jain Temples Rd; dishes ₹15-60, lassis ₹15-80; ⏰ 7.30am-10pm) This tin-and-brick shack is a great place for a quick chai break, lazy lassi (including 'special', which actually means a bhang lassi), breakfast or simple Indian fare. It also serves pancakes and other snacks.

★ Raja Cafe
MULTICUISINE $$

(www.rajacafe.com; Main Rd; mains ₹170-370; ⏰ 8am-10pm; 🕸) Raja's has been on top of its game for nearly 40 years, with espresso coffee, English breakfasts, wood-fired pizzas, superb Indian (including tandoori), Italian and Chinese dishes, and an otherwise-eclectic menu full of things you might miss, depending on your passport (rösti, fish and chips, Belgian waffles...).

The temple-view terrace is great, as is the courtyard shaded by a 170-year-old neem tree. But it's the food that steals the show.

Mediterraneo
ITALIAN $$$

(☑ 07686-272246; Jain Temples Rd; mains ₹215-475, pizzas ₹375-525; ⏰ 7.30am-10pm; 🕸) Mediterraneo manages decent Italian fare including the town's best pasta dishes, and pizzas cooked in a genuine pizza oven. The food is served on a lovely terrace overlooking the street or a smart indoor dining room with black-and-white photos decorating the walls. Beer and Indian Sula wine are also available, and it has real espresso coffee.

🔒 Shopping

Kandariya
ARTS & CRAFTS

(☑ 958442319; Airport Rd; ⏰ 9am-8pm) Huge emporium where full-size replicas of some of Khajuraho's temple carvings can be bought – if you have a spare ₹10,000 to ₹1,000,000! Smaller, more affordable versions, along with textiles, brassware, wood carvings and marble inlay, can be found indoors.

Nightly one-hour folk-dancing **performances** (₹650; ⊙7.30pm) take place in the comfortable indoor theatre here.

❶ Information

State Bank of India (Main Rd; ⊙10.30am-2.30pm & 3-4.30pm Mon-Sat, closed 2nd & 4th Sat of the month) Exchanges foreign cash.

Tourist Interpretation & Facilitation Centre (☑07686-274051; khajuraho@mptourism.com; Main Rd; ⊙10am-6pm Mon-Sat, closed 2nd & 3rd Sat of the month) Has guidebooks and free leaflets on statewide tourist destinations. It's near Circuit House, but also has stands at the airport and train station.

Tourist Police (☑07686-274690; Main Rd; ⊙24hr) Handy booth near the western temples, although not all the officers on duty speak English.

❶ Getting There & Away

AIR

Khajuraho airport (Airport Rd), with a new terminal opened in 2016, is 5km south of town. Jet Airways (www.jetairways.com) flies from Delhi to Khajuraho and back, via Varanasi in both directions, daily from October to April. Air India flies three times weekly from Delhi to Khajuraho via Varanasi and Agra, then back to Delhi via Varanasi year-round.

---

❶ CONNECTIONS AT SATNA

The town of Satna, 120km east of Khajuraho on Hwy 39, is a hub for transport between Khajuraho, eastern Madhya Pradesh and Varanasi.

From Khajuraho, there's one daily bus to Satna (₹130, 4½ hours, 3pm). In the other direction, the Satna–Khajuraho bus leaves at 2.30pm. Much more frequent buses travelling between Chhatarpur and Satna along Hwy 39 pass through Bamitha, 11km south of Khajuraho, and Madla (for Panna Tiger Reserve). You may have to change at Panna town, 19km east of Madla.

Satna's bus and train stations are 2.5km apart (autorickshaw ₹50). There are about 20 daily trains to Jabalpur (sleeper/3AC/2AC ₹170/540/745, three hours), 12 to Varanasi (₹210/600/800, six to eight hours), and several trains to Umaria (for Bandhavgarh Tiger Reserve; ₹170/540/745, 3½ to 4½ hours).

BUS

Khajuraho is out on a bit of limb as far as main bus services are concerned. Plenty of touts hang around the bus station and they're normally pretty helpful when it comes to departing travellers looking for bus info. They're best avoided when arriving and setting out in search of a place to stay.

For Orchha, Jhansi and Gwalior, you have to catch a bus to Chhatarpur (₹50, 1½ hours, every 30 or 60 minutes from 7.30am to 7.30pm) and switch there. Jhansi-bound buses from Chhatarpur can drop you at the Orchha turn-off on Hwy 39, where you can wave down a tempo (₹20) to Orchha.

Numerous buses also run to Madla (for Panna Tiger Reserve; ₹40, one hour), and there's a bus to Jabalpur (seat/sleeper ₹300/350, eight hours) at 7.30pm.

Much more frequent buses can be caught at Bamitha, 11km south on Hwy 39, where buses between Gwalior, Jhansi and Satna shuttle through all day. You can reach Bamitha by tempo or shared 4WD (both ₹10) or autorickshaw (₹150) from the bus stand or as they drive down Airport Rd.

TAXI

Yashowarman Taxi Driver Union (Jain Temples Rd) Fares in non-AC cabs including all taxes and tolls: Satna ₹2500, Orchha ₹3200, Bandhavgarh ₹6000, Varanasi ₹8000, Agra ₹8000. Air-con cabs cost 15% to 25% more.

TRAIN

Three useful long-distance trains leave from Khajuraho station, 8km south of town:

Delhi 22447 Uttar Pradesh Sampark Kranti Express (sleeper/3AC/2AC ₹365/960/1360, 11 hours, 6.20pm daily), via Jhansi (₹190/540/745, five hours) and Agra (₹280/725/1015, eight hours).

Udaipur 19665 Khajuraho Udaipur Express (sleeper/3AC/2AC ₹485/1325/1925, 21 hours, 9.25am daily), via Jhansi (₹160/495/700, four hours), Gwalior, Jaipur and Ajmer.

Varanasi 21107 Bundelkhand Link Express (sleeper/3AC ₹265/725, 11 hours, 11.50pm Tuesday, Friday and Sunday).

For Orchha you can take train 19665 to Jhansi and then local transport (p637) for the final 18km (total travel time about five hours).

The station's **reservation office** (⊙8am-noon & 1-4pm Mon-Sat, 8am-2pm Sun) makes bookings for all reservable trains in India.

Coming to Khajuraho, train 21108 leaves Varanasi Junction on Monday, Wednesday and Saturday at 5.45pm, reaching Khajuraho at 5.15am. The 12448 UP Sampark Kranti leaves Delhi's Hazrat Nizamuddin station daily at 8.10pm and passes Agra (11.05pm) before reaching Mahoba

(5.08am), where part of the train continues to Khajuraho (6.35am). If you book a seat through from Nizamuddin to Khajuraho, you'll automatically be seated in the right carriages. From Jhansi, the 19666 Udaipur Khajuraho Express theoretically departs at 3.30pm and arrives in Khajuraho at 6.30pm, but is often an hour or two late.

ℹ️ Getting Around

Taxis to or from the airport cost ₹300; autorickshaws are ₹80. If you don't have too much luggage, it's easy enough to wave down a bus, tempo or shared 4WD (₹10) as they head along Airport Rd into or out of town.

An autorickshaw to or from the train station costs ₹100. Taxis charge ₹350/450 non-AC/AC.

Bicycle is a great way to get around. **Mohammed Bilal** (☑ 9893240074; Jain Temples Rd; per day ₹100-150; ⏰ 8.30am-6pm) has been in the bike business since 1982. He rents bikes and mountain bikes in varying conditions.

Yashowarman Taxi Driver Union (p646) will take you to **Raneh Falls** (entry per person ₹50, plus motorcycle ₹100, car or 4WD ₹250, compulsory guide ₹75) (round trip) for ₹1000 and Panna Tiger Reserve (p647) (round trip in 4WD, which can be used for safari) for ₹4000. AC cabs cost 15% to 25% more.

Panna Tiger Reserve

☑ 07732

Tigers are making a comeback after being reintroduced in 2009 to **Panna Tiger Reserve** (www.pannatigerreserve.in; reserve entry per 6-passenger 4WD ₹1550, obligatory guide ₹360, 4WD rental ₹1800; ⏰ daily except Wed afternoon Oct-Jun) from other Madhya Pradesh reserves; there are now thought to be more than 35 tigers here. There's a fair chance of seeing leopards, sloth bears or tigers while on safari, but what this park really excels at is birdlife, with over 200 species recorded, including many waterbirds not easily seen in other parks. You can also enjoy a more diverse safari offering than in the region's bigger tiger parks and escape the confines of the safari 4WD to head out in a small boat on the crocodile-inhabited Ken (Karnavati) River. You can visit on an excursion from Khajuraho, or stay in one of the lodges near the reserve's main gate at Madla, 26km southeast of Khajuraho.

Panna is less visited than Bandhavgarh, Kanha or Pench, and safaris here are rarely booked out. Eighteen seats in six-passenger 4WDs are available on a walk-up basis for morning safaris at Madla; 12 for afternoon safaris. Tickets are sold at **Karnavati Interpretation Centre** (☑ 07732-252135; ⏰ 6am-6pm) FREE, 1km from Madla gate, where you can also hire a park-registered safari 4WD (₹1800).

Tickets for up to a further 24 4WDs are sold online (http://forest.mponline.gov.in), but the website doesn't accept foreign cards for payment. Most people get their hotel or a travel agency to organise everything, typically for a total ₹4500 to ₹6000 for up to six people.

🛏️ Sleeping & Eating

Jungle Camp TENTED CAMP $$
(☑ 07732-275275; www.mptourism.com; Madla; r incl breakfast ₹3530; ❄️ 🖧) Right by Madla gate, MP Tourism's Jungle Camp had just been renovated when we passed by and the results are impressive. Accommodation is in large, timber-lined jungle lodges splayed with tiger murals. The rooms feature exposed stone walls and wooden flourishes, have comfortable beds and sofas, and great bathrooms.

⭐ **Sarai at Toria** LODGE $$$
(☑ 9891796671, 9685293130; www.saraiattoria.com; Toria; s/d incl full board ₹19,700/24,900; ⏰ Oct-mid-Apr; 🖧) 🍴 This riverside lodge 2km from Madla gate is a superb base. Eight large, very comfortable cottages are spread around the grounds, with thick, cooling mud walls and a wonderful rustic-chic aesthetic. Everything including the attractive wooden furniture is created from local materials, and the excellent meals include homemade bread and vegetables from the Sarai's organic garden.

It's run by a pair of passionate conservationists, one of whom is a tiger biologist (and author of the fascinating book *Rise and Fall of the Emerald Tigers*) and the other a former wildlife film-maker. This is the perfect base not just for Panna, but also for visiting Khajuraho (a half-hour drive away) and the little-known, but spectacular Chandela forts of Ajaigarh and Kalinjar to the northeast. Boating on the Ken River and a walk to nearby Toria village are included in rates. Most guests stay three or four days. If you feel like just unwinding, pick a book from the library and relax by the riverside or in the open-air dining and lounge area.

ℹ️ Getting There & Away

Four daily buses run between Madla and Khajuraho (₹40, one hour) and there are many more between Madla and Bamitha, 11km south of Khajuraho. There's also frequent service between Madla and Satna (₹120, three hours), although for Satna you sometimes have to change at the nearby town of Panna.

Note that agencies in hotels in Khajuraho will often try to get you to rent a vehicle and guide through them. It's better to organise these through the park directly, or at accommodation in Toria, as this ensures more money makes it to the villagers who live alongside the wildlife.

CENTRAL MADHYA PRADESH

Bhopal

☑ 0755 / POP 1.80 MILLION

Split by a pair of lakes, the capital of Madhya Pradesh offers two starkly contrasting cityscapes. North of the lakes is Bhopal's Muslim-dominated old city, a labyrinthine area of mosques and crowded bazaars. About a quarter of Bhopal's population is Muslim, and the women in black *niqabs* (veils) are reminders of the four female Islamic rulers, known as the Begums of Bhopal, who developed the city in the 19th and early 20th centuries. North of the old city is a reminder of a more recent, tragic history – the Union Carbide chemical plant, site of the world's worst industrial disaster.

South of the lakes, Bhopal is more modern, with wide roads, some excellent museums, and upmarket hotels and restaurants nestled comfortably in the Arera and Shyamla Hills. The central district here is known as New Market.

Bhopal was founded by Raja Bhoj, a king of Malwa (western Madhya Pradesh and southeast Rajasthan) in the 11th century. Conquests and plunder by the Delhi Sultanate, Mandu and the Mughals sank it into oblivion after the 13th century. It was reborn in the 1720s when Dost Mohammed Khan of nearby Islamnagar built a fort here and then made Bhopal his capital.

⊙ Sights

★ Tribal Museum   MUSEUM
(http://mptribalmuseum.com; Shyamla Hills; Indian/foreigner ₹10/250, camera ₹50; ⊙noon-8pm Feb-Oct, 11am-7pm Nov-Jan) Step through the looking glass into what feels like an enchanted forest at this surreal place that is unlike any museum you will have visited before. Dedicated to the tribal peoples who make up more than 10 million of Madhya's population, the exhibits were created by 1500 Adivasis using only materials from their own villages. The results are divided into five large galleries featuring replica tribal houses, ritual sites and stunning artisan pieces including trees carved into elaborate wedding pillars.

★ State Museum   MUSEUM
(Shyamla Hills; Indian/foreigner ₹20/200, camera/video ₹100/200; ⊙10.30am-5.30pm Tue-Sun) This first-class archaeological museum spread over numerous galleries includes some wonderful temple sculptures as well as 87 10th- and 11th-century Jain bronzes unearthed by a surprised farmer in western Madhya Pradesh.

★ Taj-ul-Masjid   MOSQUE
(⊙closed to non-Muslims noon-3pm Fri) Bhopal's third female ruler, Shah Jahan Begum, wanted to create the largest mosque in the world, so in 1877 she set about building the Taj-ul-Masjid. Incomplete at the time of her death in 1901, it was finally finished in the 1980s. Fortresslike pink walls surround a 99-sq-metre courtyard and a prayer hall with 27 scalloped ceiling domes and three gleaming eggshell-like domes on top, all overlooked by two towering minarets.

Gauhar Mahal   PALACE
(VIP Rd; ⊙10am-6pm Mon-Sat) FREE This early 19th-century royal palace, chiefly associated with Qudsia Begum (r 1819–37), now stands empty, but its pretty courtyards, balconies and hallways, in a confection of Mughal, Rajput and other styles, are worth a wander. The guardian will often give you a quick tour (a tip of ₹50 is reasonable).

Jama Masjid   MOSQUE
The gold spikes crowning the squat minarets of the Jama Masjid Mosque, built in the 1830s by Qudsia Begum, glint serenely above the skull caps and veils swirling through the bazaar below.

🛏 Sleeping

Hotel RnB   HOTEL $
(Hotel Sonali Residency; ☑0755-2740880; www.1589hotels.com; Plot 3, Hamidia Rd; s/d from ₹750/1500; ❋🖻) Excellent-value hotel with cheery, bright rooms decorated with explosively loud wall murals and pictures. Rooms come with thoughtful extras such as decent shower gel and puffed up, fluffy towels. It's in a quiet yet central location. On a more

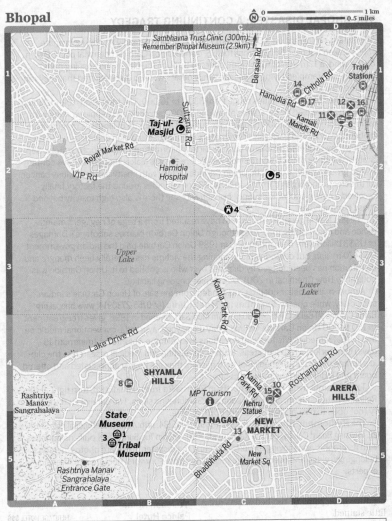

Bhopal

Bhopal

⊚ Top Sights
1 State Museum	B5
2 Taj-ul-Masjid	B2
3 Tribal Museum	B5

⊚ Sights
4 Gauhar Mahal	C2
5 Jama Masjid	C2

⊟ Sleeping
6 Hotel Ranjeet	D1
7 Hotel RnB	D2
8 Jehan Numa Palace Hotel	B4
9 Ten Suites	C4

⊗ Eating
10 Bapu Ki Kutia	C4
11 Manohar	D1
Under the Mango Tree	(see 8)
12 Zam Zam	D1

ⓘ Transport
13 Air India	C5
14 Bhopal Travels	D1
Chartered Bus	(see 16)
15 Minibuses to Hamidia Rd	C4
16 Minibuses to New Market	D1
17 Nadra Bus Stand	D1

THE BHOPAL DISASTER: A CONTINUING TRAGEDY

Shortly after midnight on 3 December 1984, 27 tonnes of deadly methyl isocyanate (MIC) leaked out over Bhopal from the US-owned Union Carbide chemical plant. Blown by the wind, a 12m wall of toxic cloud coursed through the city. In the ensuing panic, people were trampled trying to escape, while others were so disorientated that they ran into the gas.

Estimates of initial fatalities range from 3800 to 16,000. The total death toll, including those who have died since, stands at around 25,000 according to people working with victims. More than 400,000 people have suffered a catalogue of illnesses ranging from diabetes, cancer and paralysis to premature menopause and skin disorders, while their children have suffered problems such as birth malformations and reduced stature. Separately, dumping of toxic waste since well before the gas leak is thought to have contaminated groundwater around the Union Carbide factory with chemicals that cause cancer, birth defects and organ damage. In 2014, 22 communities around the factory finally received a new, piped water supply, but activists say there is also high toxicity beyond these communities.

The gas leak is generally thought to have resulted from a saga of negligent maintenance and cost-cutting measures (though Union Carbide blames sabotage). Damages of US$3 billion were demanded, and in 1989 Union Carbide paid the Indian government US$470 million, but compensation reaching the victims has generally been meagre and distribution has been dogged by disputes over who is entitled to it. Union Carbide was bought by Dow Chemical in 2001. Dow denies ongoing liability.

A multi-million-dollar hospital was funded from the sale of Union Carbide's Indian subsidiary, while charity **Sambhavna Trust Clinic** (☑0755-2730914; www.bhopal.org; Bafna Colony, off Berasia Rd; ⊘8.30am-3pm Mon-Sat), opened in 1996, gives free treatment to 150 to 200 Union Carbide victims a day using yoga, ayurveda, conventional medicine and herbal remedies. Visitors and donations are welcome. Volunteers (minimum 15 days) can work in a range of areas, from water testing and medical research to the clinic's library, pharmacy or medicinal herb garden; they are hugely appreciated and offered board and lodgings in the medical centre.

To find Sambhavna, head 1km north up Berasia Rd from Hamidia Rd, turn right at the Reliance petrol station, and you'll soon see Sambhavna signs. The derelict Carbide factory (not open to casual visitors) is 1km north of here.

The **Remember Bhopal Museum** (☑9589345134; http://rememberbhopal.net; Sr HIG 22, Housing Board Colony, Berasia Rd, Karond; ⊘10am-5pm Tue-Sun) **FREE** pulls no punches with its graphic and moving exhibits depicting the disaster. There are photos, personal belongings, video and over 50 audio recordings from survivors, doctors and forensic experts.

negative note, some of the bed sheets are a little stained.

Many people still know it by its old name of Sonali Residency. From Hamidia Rd, go down the lane alongside Hotel Ranjit and continue round to the right; it's near Radha Talkies Rd.

Hotel Ranjeet
HOTEL $$
(☑0755-2740500; www.ranjeethotels.com; 3 Hamidia Rd; s/d incl breakfast from ₹1590/2020; ❈🛜❄) Despite the roadside location, the Ranjeet has fairly quiet, air-con rooms with moderne rectangular washbasins and toilets, kettles and a slight attempt at artful decor. Beds are soft though.

★ Jehan Numa Palace Hotel
HERITAGE HOTEL $$$
(☑0755-2661100; www.jehannuma.com; 157 Shyamla Hills; incl breakfast r ₹6250-7800, ste from ₹21,250; ❈@🛜❄) This former 19th-century palace lost none of its colonial-era charm through conversion into a top-class hotel. Pillared walkways and immaculate lawns lead you to beautifully decorated rooms. The fact that you can sleep in a patio room – perfectly great – for US$100 in a five-star hotel is ridiculous. Worth a splurge.

The hotel has a palm-lined pool and excellent spa, plus three restaurants, two bars and a coffee shop that are all among the very best in town.

★ **Ten Suites** BOUTIQUE HOTEL $$$
(☎076-11110971, 0755-2665588; www.theten
suites.com; 10 Civil Lines, Professors Colony; r incl
breakfast from ₹4200; ❄ 🛜) Blurring the line
between a small boutique hotel and an up-
market homestay, the elegant Ten Suites has
huge rooms with dark wood furnishings,
tasteful decoration and semi-open-air show-
ers surrounded by potted plants. There's a
superb cafe-bakery on-site and it has a plum
location in a leafy neighbourhood not far
from the lake and city centre.

✕ Eating & Drinking

Zam Zam INDIAN $
(Hamidia Rd; mains ₹80-250; ⏰5am-11pm)
Crowds pack this fast-food hot spot day and
night for some of Bhopal's best biryani, but
it's the rich, thick chunks of chicken tikka
(₹110), grilled over hot coals outside the door
and dipped in green-chilli yoghurt sauce,
that's the true showstopper.

Manohar INDIAN $
(6 Hamidia Rd; mains ₹90-160, thali ₹140-190;
⏰6am-11pm) Bright, clean, canteen-style
Manohar does a brisk business in South In-
dian breakfasts, thalis, snacks, shakes and
polished versions of many Indian street-food
favourites. Also has an impressive range of
sweets at a side counter, including the house
special, *mawa* fruit cake, which is actually a
milk-based sweet (₹540 per kilogram).

Bapu Ki Kutia INDIAN $$
(Roshanpura Rd, TT Nagar; mains ₹150-200, thali
from ₹175; ⏰10.30am-11pm; ✎) Papa's Shack
has been serving up delicious Indian vegetarian dishes since 1964. Prepare to get cosy
with the locals – it's so popular you'll often
share a table. There's an English menu, but
no English sign. Look for the picture of a
beach hut and palm tree above the door.

★ **Under the Mango Tree** MUGHLAI $$$
(☎0755-2661100; Jehan Numa Palace Hotel, 157
Shyamla Hills; mains ₹400-750; ⏰7-11pm) Jehan
Numa Palace's best restaurant specialises in
barbecue kebabs and tandoor dishes (includ-
ing vegetarian options). Most things on the
menu are top-class, but the sampler platter of
varied kebabs (from ₹1000) may well be the
best meal you have in Madhya Pradesh.

Great food, wine, draft beer (Woodpecker,
a local swill) and cocktails all combine un-
der a romantic white pavilion and the heavy
boughs of a venerable centenarian mango
tree. Take note that a couple of days a week
are considered 'dry' days and alcohol isn't
served.

ℹ Information

State Bank of India (TT Nagar Sq; ⏰10.30am-
4pm Mon-Sat) The International Division,
upstairs, changes foreign cash. Has an ATM too.

ℹ Getting There & Away

AIR
Air India (☎0755-2770480; www.airindia.in;
Bhadbhada Rd; ⏰10am-1pm & 2-7pm Mon-Sat)
and Jet Airways fly daily to Delhi and Mumbai.
Indigo and SpiceJet fly to Hyderabad and Spice-
Jet also flies to Ahmedabad and Jaipur.

BUS
Bhopal has two main bus stations: **Nadra Bus
Stand** (Old Bus Stand; Chhola Rd), just off
Hamidia Rd, and the **ISBT** (Inter State Bus Ter-
minus; Habibganj), 5km east of New Market. For
superior comfort to Indore, several companies
run Volvo AC buses including **Chartered Bus**
(☎9993288888; www.charteredbus.in; ISBT)
from the ISBT (₹378, 4½ hours, two or three

MADHYA PRADESH & CHHATTISGARH BHOPAL

HANDY TRAINS FROM BHOPAL

DESTINATION	TRAIN NO & NAME	FARE (₹)	DURATION (HR)	DEPARTURE
Agra	12627 Karnataka Exp	330/860/1215	7	11.40pm
Delhi	12621 Tamil Nadu Exp	400/1060/1505	11	8.25pm
Gwalior	11077 Jhelum Exp	235/640/915	6	9.10am
Indore	12920 Malwa Exp	215/540/745	5	7.40am
Jabalpur	18233 Narmada Exp	215/585/830	7	11.25pm
Mumbai (CST)	12138 Punjab Mail	445/1180/1685	15	4.55pm
Raipur	18238 Chhattisgarh Exp	365/995/1425	15	6.55pm
Ujjain	12920 Malwa Exp	170/540/745	3½	7.40am

Fares: sleeper/3AC/2AC

BEYOND BHOPAL

Several attractive sites in villages or countryside outside Bhopal make good day trips. A taxi for a day should cost between ₹1400 (eight hours, 80km) and ₹2000 (12 hours, 120km).

Islamnagar

This now-ruined fortified town 13km north of central Bhopal was the first capital of the Bhopal princely state, established by Dost Mohammed Khan in the early 18th century. The still-standing walls enclose two small villages as well as two palaces with gardens: the **Chaman Mahal** (Indian/foreigner ₹10/200; ⊘8am-6pm) and **Rani Mahal** (Indian/foreigner ₹10/200; ⊘8am-6pm).

Bhojpur

Built by Bhopal's 11th-century founder, Raja Bhoj, Bhojpur originally stood beside a 400-sq-km artificial lake, which was emptied in the 15th century by the dam-busting Mandu ruler Hoshang Shah. Thankfully, the magnificent Bhojeshwar Temple survived the attack. It's 23km southeast of the city.

Bhimbetka

In forests on craggy hills 45km south of Bhopal are the World Heritage–listed **Bhimbetka rock shelters** (Indian/foreigner ₹50/100; ⊘7am-7pm), containing thousands of paintings of animals, people and other subjects from the Stone Age to medieval times.

hourly, 5am to 9.30pm); tickets can also be booked at its **city ticket office** (☏7389921709; Shop No 3, Shalimar Trade Centre, Hamidia Rd; ⊘7am-10pm), which is close to the train station.

Services from Nadra Bus Stand:

Gwalior Seat/sleeper ₹300/350, 10 hours, 9pm (Bhopal Travels)

Indore ₹188, five hours, every 15 minutes from 4am to 11pm

Pachmarhi ₹300; AC seat/sleeper ₹370/480, seven hours, 11.55pm (Verma Travels)

Sanchi ₹50, 1½ hours, half-hourly from 5am to 10pm

Services from the ISBT:

Jabalpur Non-AC ₹399, AC from ₹500, nine hours, 4.55am, 5.45am, 9.25am, 7.15pm, sleeper 9.25pm.

Khajuraho For Khajuraho you normally have to take a bus to Bamitha (seat/sleeper ₹430/530, 11 hours), 11km south of Khajuraho, then change to a local bus there. The Om Sai Ram company is a good bet.

Pachmarhi ₹300, seven hours, 6.15am, 8am, 10.15am; AC sleeper 12.45am (seat/sleeper ₹370/480); non-AC sleeper 11.55pm (₹300); sleeper buses are by Verma Travels.

The **Bhopal Travels** (☏0755-4083544; 35 JK Bldg, Chhola Rd) office is across the road from Nadra Bus Stand.

TRAIN

There are around 30 daily trains to Gwalior, Agra and Delhi, at least nine to Ujjain and eight to Jabalpur and Mumbai.

ⓘ Getting Around

The modern **airport** (☏0755-26 6001) is 11km northwest of central Bhopal – at least ₹200 by autorickshaw or around ₹500 by taxi.

Minibuses and buses (both ₹10) shuttle between New Market and Hamidia Rd all day and all evening. Catch ones to New Market at the eastern end of Hamidia Rd. Returning from New Market, they leave from near the Nehru Statue. Autorickshaws cost about ₹60 for the same journey. Uber and Ola taxi services are easy to find in Bhopal.

Sanchi

☏07482 / POP 7305

Rising from the dry plains is a rounded hill topped with some of India's oldest Buddhist structures.

In 262 BC, repentant of the horrors he had inflicted on Kalinga (Odisha), the Mauryan emperor Ashoka embraced Buddhism. As a penance he built the Great Stupa at Sanchi, a domed edifice to house religious relics, near the home town (Vidisha) of his wife Devi. Sanchi became an important Buddhist monastic centre and over the following centuries further stupas and other monuments were added. After about the 13th century it was abandoned and forgotten, until rediscovered in 1818 by a British army officer.

Today, the remarkably preserved Great Stupa is the centrepiece of Sanchi's World Heritage–listed Buddhist monuments.

Although you can visit Sanchi in a day trip from Bhopal (46km southwest), the village is a relaxing spot to spend the night, and a number of side trips can be taken from here.

◎ Sights

The hilltop **Buddhist monuments** (Indian/foreigner ₹40/600, video ₹25; ◎ dawn-dusk) stand at the top of Monuments Rd, a continuation of the road that leaves the train station. The **ticket office** (◎ 6am-6pm) is near the beginning of Monuments Rd, in front of the Archaeological Museum (p656). If you don't want to do the short walk up the hill, autorickshaws will deposit you at the top for ₹30. The **Publication Sales Counter** (◎ 8am-6pm) beside the monuments entrance sells the Archaeological Survey of India's good *Sanchi* guide for ₹60 (assuming stocks haven't run out). If you are interested in a human guide, licensed government guides mill about here and charge ₹475/750 for four/eight people for three or four hours.

Remember, it's auspicious to walk clockwise around Buddhist monuments.

Great Stupa
BUDDHIST STUPA

(Stupa 1) Beautifully proportioned, the Great Stupa is the centrepiece of the monumental area, directly ahead as you enter the complex from the north. Originally constructed by Ashoka, it was enlarged a century later and the original brick stupa enclosed within a stone one. Today it stands 16m high and 37m in diameter. Encircling the stupa is a wall with four magnificently carved *toranas* (gateways) that have few rivals as the finest Buddhist works of art in India.

Toranas

The Great Stupa's four *toranas* (gateways) were erected around 35 BC, more than two centuries after the stupa itself. They had all fallen down by 1818, but have since been put back up. The wonderful carvings on their pillars and triple architraves mainly depict scenes from the Buddha's life, the history of Buddhism and the Jatakas, episodes from the Buddha's earlier lives.

At this stage in Buddhist art, the Buddha himself was never represented directly – only his presence was alluded to through symbols. The lotus stands for his birth, the bodhi tree for his enlightenment, the wheel for his teachings, and the footprint and throne for his presence. The stupa itself also symbolises the Buddha.

Northern Gateway
BUDDHIST MONUMENT

The Northern Gateway, topped by a broken wheel of law, is the best preserved of the *toranas*. Elephants support the architraves above the columns, while delicately carved *yakshis* (mythical fairylike beings) hang nonchalantly on each side. Scenes include a monkey offering a bowl of honey to the Buddha, who is represented by a bodhi tree (western pillar, east face, second panel down).

Eastern Gateway
BUDDHIST MONUMENT

The breathtakingly carved figure of a *yakshi* (mythical fairylike beings), hanging from an architrave on the Eastern Gateway, is one of Sanchi's best-known images. The middle architrave depicts the Great Departure, when the Buddha (shown four times as a riderless horse) renounced the sensual life and set out to find enlightenment. On the bottom architrave is Ashoka's visit to the bodhi tree: the emperor is seen dismounting from an elephant then approaching the tree with clasped hands.

The rear of the middle architrave shows the Buddha being worshipped by lions, buffalo and other animals. On the south face of the northern pillar (second panel down) is shown the dream of an elephant standing on the moon, dreamt by the Buddha's mother Maya when he was conceived.

A Buddhist Monuments ticket from the ticket office (p653) is required for access.

Southern Gateway
BUDDHIST MONUMENT

The back-to-back lions on the pillars of the monuments compound's Southern Gateway (the oldest) were a favourite Ashokan motif and now form the state emblem of India, which can be seen on every banknote. The gateway narrates Ashoka's life as a Buddhist, with a representation of the Great Departure (rear of top architrave, east end).

Western Gateway
BUDDHIST MONUMENT

Pot-bellied dwarves support the architraves of the Western Gateway, which has some of the site's most interesting scenes. The back of the bottom architrave and the south pillar's north-face top panel both show the Buddha resisting the temptation and assault by Mara (the Buddhist personification of evil), while demons flee and angels cheer.

The front of the top architrave shows the Buddha along with six Manushi-Buddhas (Buddhas who preceded him), all represented as stupas or trees. On the back of the middle architrave we see the siege of Kushinagar by seven cities that wanted a portion

Sanchi

Train Station

Star Communication

Market

Health Centre

Ticket Office

Bhopal–Vidisha Rd

Monuments Rd

Bhopal (46km)

Vidisha (8km);
Heliodorus Pillar (11km);
Udaigiri Caves (13km)

25

24

26

23

2

Gate

Tank

14

7

27

1
Buddhist Monuments

3

16
15

12 8
22 5 4
13 9
17
20
11
10

6

18
19

21

0 ____ 200 m
0 ____ 0.1 miles

Sanchi

of the Buddha's bone relics after his death, and above the transport of the relics after the agreement to divide them into eight shares.

Other Stupas

You pass Stupa 3 on your left as you approach the Great Stupa from the main entrance. It's similar in design to the Great Stupa, but smaller, with a single, rather fine gateway. One of Sanchi's earliest monuments after the Great Stupa, it dates from the 2nd century BC and once contained relics of two important disciples of the Buddha: Sariputta and Moggallana. These were moved to London in the 19th century but relics thought to be the same ones were returned in 1952 to the modern vihara (resting place) outside the monuments compound.

Only the base is left of the 2nd-century-BC Stupa 4, behind Stupa 3. Between Stupa 3 and the Great Stupa is the small Stupa 5, unusual in that it once contained a statue of Buddha, now displayed in the Archaeological Museum.

Stupa 2 is halfway down the hill to the west from the Great Stupa. You can walk back down to the village via Stupa 2 (but be prepared for some fence-hopping at the bottom). Instead of gateways, 'medallions' decorate its surrounding wall – naive in design, but full of energy and imagination. Flowers, animals and people – some mythological – ring the stupa.

Temples

The rectangular Temple 31, beside Stupa 5, was built in the 6th or 7th century, but reconstructed in the 10th or 11th century.

It contains a well-executed image of the Buddha.

Temple 18, behind the Great Stupa, is a chaitya (prayer room or assembly hall) remarkably similar in appearance to classical-Greek columned buildings. It dates from around the 7th century AD, but traces of earlier wooden buildings have been discovered beneath it. To its left is the small, also Greek-like Temple 17. Beyond both of them, the large Temple 40 dates back in part to the Ashokan period.

Monasteries

The earliest of Sanchi's monasteries were made of wood and are long gone. The usual plan was of a central courtyard surrounded by monastic cells. These days only the courtyards and stone foundations remain. Monasteries 45 and 47, standing on the ridge east of the Great Stupa, date from the 7th to 10th centuries, and have strong Hindu elements in their design. The former has two sitting Buddhas. The one housed inside is exceptional.

The remains of Monastery 51 sit a short distance downhill west of the Great Stupa. Outside its west gate is the Great Bowl, carved from a boulder, into which food and offerings were placed for distribution to the monks.

Pillars

Of the scattered pillar remains, the most important is Pillar 10, erected by Ashoka but later broken. Two upper sections of this beautifully proportioned and executed shaft lie side by side behind the Great Stupa; its superb lions-on-lotus capital is in the Archaeological

MADHYA PRADESH & CHHATTISGARH SANCHI

UDAIGIRI CAVE SHRINES

Cut into a sandstone hill 5km northwest of Vidisha are the **Udaigiri Cave Shrines** (⊙ dawn-dusk) `FREE`, some 20 remarkable, mostly Hindu, cave shrines from the 4th century AD (Gupta period). The first cave you'll reach is Cave 19, dedicated to Shiva, with a finely carved portal. The main group of caves is 400m further along: especially remarkable is Cave 5 with its superb, large-scale image of Vishnu as Varaha, his boar incarnation, rescuing the earth goddess Bhudevi (or Prithvi) from the ocean of chaos with his tusk.

Cave 4 contains an unusual Shiva lingam with Shiva's face (complete with third eye) carved on it and the River Ganges flowing from the top of his head. Cave 13 shows Vishnu sleeping on a bed of cobras. From here you can walk up on the hilltop, with ruins of a 6th-century Gupta temple dedicated to the sun god. Cave 1, on the hillside 350m south of the main group, is one of the two Jain shrines: it contains an image of the *tirthankar* (one of the 24 great Jain teachers) Parasnath, but you can only look through the fence as it's closed for safety reasons.

The caves are frequently locked, but a site guardian can normally be found to open them up for you.

To get here by bike from Sanchi, fork left following a sign for Udaigiri as you enter Vidisha. Continue across the Betwa River, take the first road to the left and follow it for 3km. An autorickshaw from Sanchi costs ₹350 return, or ₹450 with the Heliodorus Pillar and Vidisha thrown in. Or take a bus to Vidisha then a rickshaw (₹150 return). You'll need at least an hour to explore the caves fully.

Museum. Pillars 25 and 26, east of the Great Stupa, and Pillar 35, to its northwest, are less impressive but their capitals (lions from 25 and 26, a figure of the Bodhisattva Vajrapani from 35) can also be seen in the museum.

Other Sights

Archaeological Museum
MUSEUM

(Monuments Rd; ⊙ 9am-5pm Sat-Thu) This fine museum has a small collection of sculptures from the site. The centrepiece is the 3rd-century-BC lions-on-lotus capital from the Ashoka-era Pillar 10. Other highlights include a *yakshi* (mythical fairylike being) hanging from a mango tree, and beautifully serene Buddha figures in red sandstone. There are also some interesting photos showing the site pre-restoration. Admission is included with a ticket for the monuments compound (p653).

Next door is the preserved Gothic-style 'bungalow' of Sir John Marshall, the director of the Archaeological Survey of India who led the excavation and restoration of Sanchi from 1912 to 1919.

Chetiyagiri Vihara
BUDDHIST TEMPLE

(⊙ 9am-5pm) The *vihara* (literally 'resting place'), just outside the monuments compound, was built to house relics of the Buddha's disciples Sariputta and Moggallana, following their return from Britain in 1952. The relics are brought out for public viewing for the Chetiyagiri Vihara festival on the last Sunday of November, an event that attracts tens of thousands of Buddhist monks and pilgrims.

🛏 Sleeping & Eating

Mahabodhi Society of Sri Lanka
GUESTHOUSE, HOSTEL $

(☑ 07482-266699; wimalatissasanchi@yahoo.co.in; Monuments Rd; dm ₹100-200, r with/without AC ₹1500/1000; ☎) This friendly, well-run place is primarily geared to Sri Lankan Buddhist pilgrims but also welcomes international travellers unless it's full (most likely around the late-November Chetiyagiri Vihara festival). The rear building has good, clean, carpeted air-conditioned rooms with big bathrooms, and wearier but still clean non-air-con rooms. Dorms around the shady front courtyard share clean squat toilets and unheated showers.

New Jaiswal Lodge
GUESTHOUSE $

(☑ 9713758366; pranjaljaiswal@gmail.com; Monuments Rd; r ₹600) This friendly place has four basic, but colourful rooms with ceiling fans and small private bathrooms with sit-down toilets and hot bucket showers. Does basic meals and air-coolers can be provided.

Gateway Retreat
HOTEL $$

(☑ 07482-266723; www.mptourism.com; Bhopal-Vidisha Rd; dm ₹300, s/d incl breakfast from ₹2290/2590; ❄ ☎ ☎) This MP Tourism hotel is Sanchi's most comfortable lodging, with average, air-conditioned rooms and bungalows set among well-kept gardens. At the time of research extensive renovations were underway so hopefully in the future it will be better. The **restaurant** (mains ₹170-360; ⊙8am-10.30pm; 🛜) is Sanchi's best, and there's a small bar tucked into its corner.

Gateway Cafeteria   INDIAN $
(Monuments Rd; mains ₹120-175; ⊙8am-10.30pm) This simple but clean MP Tourism place has a very basic Indian menu and coffee.

ℹ Information

Health Centre (📞 07482-266724; Monuments Rd; ⊙8am-1pm & 5-6pm Mon-Sat) Basic health centre. Head to Bhopal for anything more serious.

Star Communication (internet per hour ₹40; ⊙8am-10pm) A couple of computers with internet connections. Perhaps more usefully, it also books bus and train tickets.

ℹ Getting There & Away

BUS
Every half-hour buses connect Sanchi with Bhopal (₹50, 1½ hours, 5am to 10pm) and Vidisha (₹10, 20 minutes, 6am to 11pm). Catch them at the village crossroads.

TRAIN
Train is a decent option for getting to Sanchi from Bhopal. It takes less than an hour so you can just turn up in time to queue for a 'general' ticket (₹10 to ₹30) and then squeeze on. There are at least six trains a day from Bhopal to Sanchi (8am, 10.35am, 3.05pm, 4.10pm, 6.15pm and 10.55pm), and from Sanchi to Bhopal (4.15am, 8am, 10.30am, 4.30pm, 6.15pm and 7.35pm).

For longer trips, there are far more trains from Vidisha, 8km northeast of Sanchi.

Pachmarhi

📞 07578 / POP 13,700 / ELEV 1067M
Madhya Pradesh's only hill station is surrounded by waterfalls, canyons, natural pools, cave temples and the forested ranges of the Satpura Tiger Reserve, and offers a refreshing escape from steamy central India. It's popular with Indians, but few foreign travellers get here.

The most popular tourist activity is touring a selection of places of interest, beauty spots and natural pools by 4WD (with a few walks from parking places). It's also possible to reach some places by foot or bicycle.

Pachmarhi is also the gateway to Satpura Tiger Reserve: the town and some surrounding countryside constitute an island of buffer zone, surrounded by the reserve's core zone. Few people come here exclusively to go on safari but those who do are normally richly rewarded. Sightseeing tours run into the reserve from Pachmarhi, but you'll see more wildlife on a jeep safari from Madhai, 84km northwest.

British army Captain James Forsyth came across Pachmarhi in 1857 and set up India's first Forestry Department at Bison Lodge in 1862. Soon after, the British army set up regional headquarters here, starting an association with the military that remains today.

◉ Sights & Activities

Buffer Zone Sights
Sights in the buffer zone can be visited freely: these include the Pandav Caves, Jata Shankar, Handi Khoh, Priyadarshini Point (Forsyth Point) and Mahadeo Cave, all accessible by paved road (the last three are along the same road). You can rent bicycles or 4WDs in the town's market area to visit these places.

Core-Zone Sights Near Pachmarhi
Chauragarh is in the core zone but can be accessed freely by a five-hour return hike from Mahadeo Cave. Chauragarh apart, entry to the core zone requires a permit, available at Bison Lodge (p660) for a fee that depends on your mode of transport, and in most cases a guide is obligatory. Some guides speak English. The most-visited core-zone sights are Apsara Vihar, the Rajat Prapat viewpoint, Bee Falls, Reechgarh and Dhoopgarh. Most people rent a 4WD with driver (₹2375 per day for up to six passengers, plus ₹1200 for the core-zone entry permit and ₹360 for a guide) at Bison Lodge for this tour. Core-zone entry on foot or bicycle costs ₹70, and by motorcycle ₹190. Bison Lodge can also provide guides for day hikes (₹310 for the entry permit and ₹700 for the guide, for up to six people).

★ **Dhoopgarh**   VIEWPOINT
(Sunset Point) An almost mandatory final stop on 4WD tours, Dhoopgarh looks west over endless valleys, hills and forests and has a broad stepped terrace for everyone to do their sunset selfies on. Dhoopgarh mountain, just behind, is the highest point in Madhya Pradesh (1352m).

MADHYA PRADESH & CHHATTISGARH

Pachmarhi

Pachmarhi

Piparriya (51km);
Madhai (84km)

Satpura Tiger
Reserve Core Zone

Rajat
Prapat
Viewpoint

Apsara Vihar

See Enlargement

Satpura Tiger
Reserve Core Zone

Priyadarshini Point (1.8km);
Mahadeo Cave (7km)

MP
Tourism

Bison Lodge

Mahadeo Rd

Dhoopgarh

Dhoopgarh

PACHMARHI TOWN

MP Tourism
Kiosk

Bus Stand

Arvindar Marg

Baba
Cycles

Subhash Rd

Patel Rd

Railway
Booking
Office

1 km
0.5 miles

N

0   1
0   1
0   2
0   3
0   4

Pachmarhi

★ Apsara Vihar RIVER
(Fairy Pool) A pool underneath a small waterfall, above a canyon southeast of town, this is the best of Pachmarhi's natural pools for swimming. It's a drive of about 1.5km past Pandav Caves, followed by a walk of about 700m.

★ Rajat Prapat Viewpoint VIEWPOINT
A short distance downstream from the Apsara Vihar pools, the stream plunges off the cliff in central India's highest single-drop fall (107m), Rajat Prapat (Silver Fall or Big Fall). Steps up from Apsara Vihar lead to a point with magnificent views of the fall and gorge. It's at its best during or just after the monsoon.

Bee Falls WATERFALL
(Jamuna Prapat) The pretty waterfall and pools at Bee Falls can almost be reached by bike (you have to walk the last quarter-kilometre or so).

Chauragarh MOUNTAIN, TEMPLE
Chauragarh (1308m), Madhya Pradesh's third-highest peak, is topped by a sizeable and panoramic Shiva temple that attracts tens of thousands of pilgrims during the Shivaratri Mela (p627). It's a return hike of about five hours from Mahadeo Cave – 3.5km each way, with 1365 steps to climb and descend.

☞ Tours

Jungle Safaris SAFARI
(reserve entry per 6-passenger vehicle ₹1200, obligatory guide ₹360, 4WD rental approximately ₹2375; ☉Oct-Jun) Four-wheel-drive safaris (2½ to five hours) from Madhai, on the northern edge of

Satpura Tiger Reserve, are an entirely different experience from the beauty-spot-focused tours starting from Pachmarhi. You travel through dense, pristine forests in search of wildlife. Don't expect to see any of the tiger reserve's 20-odd tigers, but there are decent prospects of spotting sloth bears (especially in winter) and leopards.

Up to 12 six-passenger 4WDs are allowed in each session, but only one of these is available for walk-up customers. The rest are sold online (http://forest.mponline.gov.in) – but the website doesn't accept foreign credit or debit cards for payment, so it's best to organise things through a travel agency or one of the hotels or lodges near Madhai (they typically charge around ₹1000 for doing this). Boat safaris can also be organised at Madhai.

Taxis to Madhai from Pachmarhi cost ₹2000 (2½ to three hours), or you can get a bus to Sohagpur (₹80, 2½ hours, 12 daily), then a shared 4WD (₹25, one hour) 20km south to Madhai.

☞ Sleeping & Eating

Pachmarhi

A number of colonial-era bungalows and houses in the Jai Stambh area have been converted into delightful guesthouses and hotels, no less than 14 of them run by MP Tourism. Places fill up and room rates may rise during high season (May to July, national holidays and major festivals).

Hotel Saket HOTEL $$
(☎07578-252165; www.sakethotel.in; Patel Rd; r with/without AC from ₹2600/1600; ❇☞) The wide range of warmly decorated rooms, comfy beds (the circular beds in some rooms are certainly an unusual talking point), bright lobby and dining area, and friendly welcome make this one of the best of many similar-looking hotels in town. Prices drop by half outside high season. The **restaurant** (mains ₹80-180; ☉8am-11pm) does good, cheap Gujarati, North and South Indian, and Chinese dishes.

Hotel Highlands HOTEL $$
(☎07578-252099; www.mptourism.com; Pipariya Rd; r incl breakfast ₹2790; ❇☞) This MP Tourism property at the north end of town has great-value rooms with high ceilings, dressing rooms, modern bathrooms and verandahs, dotted around well-tended gardens. There's a children's play area and a bar-restaurant.

★ **Rock-End Manor** HERITAGE HOTEL $$$
(✆ 07578-252079; www.mptourism.com; s/d incl full board ₹5420/6360; ❄️🛜) A gorgeous colonial-era building, whitewashed Rock-End overlooks the fairways of the army golf course. It's well managed and the six spacious rooms have high ceilings, luxurious furnishings with quality upholstery, framed paintings and full-body massage showers.

Rasoi DHABA $
(Company Garden; mains ₹80-200; ⏰9am-11.30pm) Not your average roadside *dhaba* (casual eatery)! A scrumptious, long-winded, South Indian, nonveg and Chinese menu is served here in several open or partially open-air seating areas. Our waiter's recommendation – veg *tawa* (hotplate; ₹150) – was downright delicious.

🛏️ Madhai

Options in the Madhai area include a few midrange hotels, a forest rest house and a few luxurious top-end jungle lodges.

Madhai Forest Rest House REST HOUSE $
(✆ 07574-254838, bookings 07574-254394; Madhai; r from ₹1000) On the south bank of the Denwa River, where jungle safaris start, this Forest Department–run rest house has six bare, but quite comfortable rooms with sit-down toilets. The canteen serves simple Indian meals. Access is by boat from the north bank. The deer and wild boar strolling through the grounds in the evening are an added bonus.There's no air-con and no coolers, something to bear in mind in the premonsoon months, when temperatures can get into the 40s. It's best to reserve ahead by phone or email.

★ **Denwa Backwater Escape** LODGE $$$
(✆ 011-40146400; www.denwabackwaterescape.com; Madhai; incl full board cottage s/d ₹17,000/19,000, treehouse s/d ₹19,000/21,000; ❄️🛜♿) 🍽 Rolling across 10 acres of green, forested riverside land, this sublime wildlife lodge is easily the best place to stay in the Madhai area. The eight cottages and two tree houses are built in a traditional mud-brick style, but with a crisp and modern safari design, and there are vintage iron and recycled wooden furnishings throughout.

ℹ️ Information

Bison Lodge (✆ 07574-254394; near Jai Stambh; ⏰9am-5pm Thu-Tue, to 11.30am Wed) The lodge was built by Captain Forsyth for his own use in 1862, and also housed the region's Forest Department for more than half a century. This is where you must come for permits and 4WDs to visit sites in the Pachmarhi area that fall within the Satpura Tiger Reserve's core zone – it's usually pretty busy around opening time in the morning.

The lodge building houses a bright, colourful **Wildlife & Cultural Interpretation Centre** (admission ₹10), with displays on the tiger reserve and its flora, fauna and people.

The main office of **MP Tourism** (✆ 07578-252100; Amaltas Complex; ⏰10am-5pm) near the Jai Stambh. Also has a **kiosk** (✆ 07578-252029; ⏰10am-5pm) at the bus stand.

ℹ️ Getting There & Away

From the bus stand in Pachmarhi town, six daily buses go to Bhopal (₹300, AC seat/sleeper ₹370/480, seven hours). There are overnight buses to Indore (AC sleeper ₹525, non-AC ₹450 to ₹500, 12 hours). Buses to Nagpur (₹280 to ₹300, seven hours) leave at 3.30am and 5pm.

Buses run at least hourly to Pipariya (₹65, 1½ hours), where you can catch trains to destinations such as Jabalpur and Varanasi without having to go all the way to Bhopal. Train tickets are sold at the **railway booking office** (Army Area Main Gate; ⏰8.30am-2pm & 4-7.30pm Mon-Sat) and by agencies in the town.

If you're coming from Pipariya, shared 4WDs to Pachmarhi (₹60 to ₹100 per person) leave from the bus stand far more often than buses.

ℹ️ Getting Around

The standard rate for a 4WD and driver for a day, from Bison Lodge or from the bus stand/market area, is ₹2375.

Most Pachmarhi sights can be reached by bicycle, although in many cases you have to walk the last part. The roads are mostly flat except for the last stretches to Dhoopgarh and Mahadeo Cave. You can rent bikes from **Baba Cycles** (Subhash Rd; per hour/day ₹20/100; ⏰10am-9pm) and other shops in the market area.

WESTERN MADHYA PRADESH

Indore

✆ 0731 / POP 1.95 MILLION

Madhya Pradesh's biggest city and commercial powerhouse has much more of a cosmopolitan buzz than anywhere else in the state. Apart from some splendid buildings created by the Holkar dynasty, there's a shortage of outstanding sights, and Indore's traffic and crowds are as hectic as in any Indian city of this size, so for most tourists this is little more than a gateway to Mandu, Maheshwar or Omkareshwar. But with its bustling bazaars, good eating scene and a better-than-average crop of hotels, Indore is a place you may well grow to like if you spend a couple of nights here.

The city feels notably richer and cleaner than most other towns and cities in central India. Indeed, locals like to tell visitors how in India-wide surveys held in 2017 and 2018, Indore was ranked as the cleanest city in India.

◎ Sights

Lal Bagh Palace
PALACE

(Lal Bagh Rd; Indian/foreigner ₹10/250; ⊙10am-5pm Tue-Sun) Built between 1886 and 1921, Lal Bagh is the finest building left by the Holkar dynasty. As was the fashion among many of the late-Raj-era Indian nobility, the lavish interior is dominated by European styles: striated Italian marble pillars, lots of chandeliers and classical columns, murals of Greek deities, a baroque-cum-rococo dining room, an English-library-style office with leather armchairs, a Renaissance sitting room and a Palladian queen's bedroom (with sadly ripped furnishings in some rooms). An autorickshaw from the city centre costs about ₹50.

Rajwada
PALACE, TEMPLE

(Rajwada Chowk; ⊙temple 7am-9pm) The Holkars' original Indore palace, begun in 1749, is currently undergoing major renovations and is closed to the public. The temple in its rear, however, has already been restored and is a lovely little refuge from the hectic city, with a charming wood-pillared courtyard (enter from the north side of the building) and an impressive Shiva lingam. And, on the upper floor, a small museum dedicated to the Holkar dynasty. It contains a few photos, but that's about all.

Central Museum
MUSEUM

(AB Rd; Indian/foreigner ₹20/200, camera/video ₹100/400; ⊙10am-5pm Tue-Sun) This museum has a good (despite its utterly uninspiring presentation) collection of medieval (and earlier) Hindu sculptures, along with tools, weaponry and copper-engraved land titles. Skirmishes took place here during the First War of Independence (Indian Uprising) – the well in the garden was poisoned during the struggle.

🛏 Sleeping

Hotel Neelam
HOTEL $

(☑0731-2466001; 33/2 Patel Bridge Corner; s/d with AC ₹900/1150, without AC from from ₹675/875; ❄🛜) One of the few budget places near the train and bus stations that happily accepts foreigners. Neelam is well run and if you can close your eyes to the slightly stained sheets, then the simple rooms, which are set around a central atrium, are unexpectedly clean. It's tucked down a side alley just beside Patel Bridge.

Hotel Chanakya
HOTEL $$

(☑0731-2707242; 57-58 RNT Marg, Chhawni Chowk; s/d from ₹1210/1540; ❄🛜) Rooms here aren't as flashy as the disco-lit Shiva mini-waterfall in the entrance hallway would suggest, but they are functional and have a bit of classic charm thanks to old wooden

---

SARAFA BAZAR

Many Indoreans consider this **street-food market** (snacks ₹20-70; ⊙9pm-midnight) to be the most exciting thing about their city. It's a great experience, not just for the taste sensations of the local snacks but also for the friendly atmosphere among the nightly crowds. The street is lined with jewellers' shops and after they close, the snack stalls set up in front. The most famous spot is Joshi Dahi Vada which doles out hundreds of serves of *dahi vada* (lentil dumplings in yoghurt with chutney) nightly. It's about halfway along the strip on the south side – easily identified by the crowds in front. Mr Joshi likes to toss dishes of yoghurt into the air to show off its consistency.

The best plan is simply to come hungry and wander along and try what takes your fancy, but two top local favourites definitely worth asking for are *bhutte ka kees* (grated maize sautéed with spices and herbs) and *sabudana khichdi* (soaked sago tossed with spices, herbs and crushed peanuts).

Follow the street along the south side of the Rajwada palace and you'll hit the food stalls within 200m.

MADHYA PRADESH & CHHATTISGARH

Devi Ahilya Marg

Nehru Park Rd

Mahatma Gandhi (MG) Rd

Maharani Rd

Shastri Bridge

Railway Station Rd

1 🏠

⊗ 5

🚌 Gangwal (4.2km)

Jawahar Rd

🚉 Train Station

Patel Bridge

🚌 9

🚩 Lal Bagh
Palace (200m)

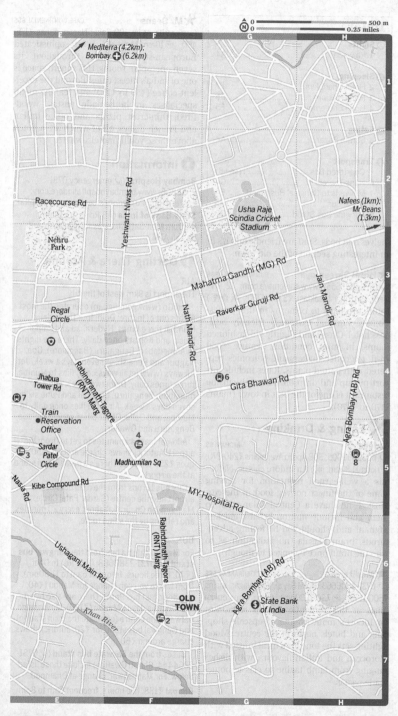

Indore

shelves and beds. Staff are friendly and it's in an interesting section of the old town.

★ Hotel Shreemaya BUSINESS HOTEL **$$$**
(☎ 0731-2515555; www.shreemaya.com; 12 RNT Marg; s/d incl breakfast ₹3720/4720; ❄ @ 🛜) Faults are hard to come by in this professionally run and extremely friendly business hotel. Classy and slightly old-fashioned rooms, in mint condition, feature good wi-fi, tea/coffee makers and balconies peppered with potted plants. Rates include airport pickup and drop off. The multicuisine restaurant is one of the best in town (mains ₹170 to ₹370).

🍴 Eating & Drinking

Nafees AFGHANI **$$**
(☎ 9039090005; 30B Apollo Ave; mains ₹240-270; ⊙ noon-11.30pm; ❄) An Indore classic, Nafees has a well-earned reputation for serving some of the finest nonveg food in the city. Most dishes have a Central Asian twist to them and include mutton kebabs, chicken Afghani and, should you be feeling adventurous, brain masala (no indication as to who the brain once belonged to though).

★ Mediterra MEDITERRANEAN **$$$**
(☎ 0731-4006666; Hotel Sayaji, Vijay Nagar; mains ₹500-1150; ⊙ 7.30-11.30pm) Cure the curry blues at this romantic rooftop restaurant on Indore's main avenue of upscale shopping and hotels north of the centre. Mood lighting sets the tone for a meal infused with Moroccan and Italian flavours, with dishes ranging from lamb tagine to classic homemade pastas.

★ Mr Beans CAFE, CONTINENTAL **$$$**
(www.mrbeans.in; 100 Saket Nagar; dishes ₹175-460; ⊙ 10am-11pm; 🛜) With sophisticated European-style interiors throughout its seven open-plan rooms, this superb space is one of India's nicest cafes. Beyond the excellent coffee (₹50 to ₹150) and tea, the menu specialises in homemade pastas, wood-fired, thin-crust pizzas and other Italian and French dishes, all of which are a notch above those you'll find elsewhere.

🛈 Information

Bombay Hospital (☎ emergency 0731-2558866; www.bombayhospitalindore.com; Eastern Ring Rd) Indore's best general hospital.
State Bank of India (AB Rd; ⊙ 10.30am-4.30pm Mon-Sat) Changes foreign cash and has an ATM.

🛈 Getting There & Around

AIR

The airport is 9km west of the city.

IndiGo (www.goindigo.in) operates the most flights out of Indore: Delhi four times daily, Mumbai three times, Hyderabad and Raipur twice, and Kolkata once daily. There are flights to Ahmedabad, Bengaluru (Bangalore), Goa, Nagpur and Pune six or seven days a week. Jet Airways (www.jetairways.com) flies to Mumbai three times daily, Delhi two times, and Ahmedabad, Bengaluru, Chennai and Pune six or seven days a week. Air India flies once daily to Mumbai and Delhi. Other cities served include Bengaluru and Gwalior.

Allow at least 45 minutes to get to/from the airport. Autorickshaws charge around ₹150, taxis ₹250 to ₹300. There's a prepaid taxi stand at the airport.

City bus 11 runs from the road outside the airport into the centre (Sardar Patel Circle, Madhumilan Chauraha) about every 20 minutes, and returns by the same route.

BUS

For Mandu, catch a bus from the **Gangwal bus stand** (☎ 0731-2380688; Dhar Rd) to Dhar (₹70, three hours, frequent 6am to 11.30pm), from where you can change for Mandu (₹40, one hour, last bus 9pm). There are also two direct buses a day to Mandu (₹120). Minivans go between the centre (opposite the train station) and Gangwal bus stand for ₹20; autorickshaws charge around ₹60.

Buses from the **Sarwate bus stand** (☎ 0731-2364444; Chhoti Gwaltoli) include those listed below. For Maheshwar, change at Dhamnod.

Bhopal ₹188, five hours, frequent 6am to 8pm

HANDY TRAINS FROM INDORE

DESTINATION	TRAIN NO & NAME	FARE (₹)	DURATION (HR)	DEPARTURE
Bhopal	12919 Malwa Exp	215/540/745	5	12.25pm
Delhi	12415 Indore-Delhi Sarai Rohilla Intercity Exp	440/1160/1655	14½	4.35pm
Mumbai (Central station)	12962 Avantika Exp	440/1165/1660	14	4.25pm
Ujjain	12919 Malwa Exp	170/540/745	1½	12.25pm

Fares: sleeper/3AC/2AC

Dhamnod ₹80, 2½ hours, frequent 6am to 8pm

Maheshwar ₹85, 2½ hours, frequent 5am to 10.30pm

Omkareshwar ₹90, three hours, about hourly 6am to 6.30pm

Pachmarhi AC bus sleeper ₹525, 12 hours, 8pm; non-AC ₹450 to ₹500, 9.40pm; Verma Travels

Ujjain ₹60, two hours, frequent 24 hours

For more comfort, **Chartered Bus** (☑ 0731-4288888; http://charteredbus.in; AICTSL Campus, AB Rd) runs AC Volvo coaches to Bhopal (₹378, four hours) two or three times hourly from 5am to 9.30pm, and every hour or two through the night. It also has two daily AC services to Ahmedabad (₹709) and Pune (₹1500), and daily services to Jabalpur (₹1296), Jaipur (₹857) and Udaipur (₹709). From the same terminal, **Royal Bus** (☑ 0731-4088456; www.royalbus.net; AICTSL Campus, AB Rd) has AC buses to Ujjain (₹70, two hours) every 45 minutes from 7.30am to 8.15pm.

Hans Travels (☑ 0731-2510007; www.hans travel.in; Dhakkanwala Kua, South Tukoganj) runs nine daily Volvo AC buses to Bhopal (from ₹333, four hours), and a host of sleeper buses departing between 5pm and 10pm, including the following:

Agra Non-AC/AC ₹600/1010, 16 hours, two daily

Ahmedabad Non-AC/AC ₹500/610, 11 hours, two daily

Gwalior Non-AC/AC ₹450/610, 12 hours, four daily

Jaipur Non-AC/AC ₹500/710, 13 to 15 hours, three daily

Jalgaon (for Ajanta) Non-AC ₹400 to ₹500, eight hours, 9pm and 10pm

Mumbai Non-AC/AC/Volvo AC ₹700/910/1360, 12 to 15 hours, five daily

Nagpur Non-AC/AC/Volvo AC ₹650/810/1010, 10 to 13 hours, four daily

Pune Non-AC/AC/Volvo AC ₹700/900/1360, 12 to 15 hours, eight daily

TAXI

Taxis organised through the better hotels cost ₹2000 one way to Mandu or Omkareshwar, and ₹2500 to Maheshwar. Day hire up to 12 hours and 250km is ₹2500.

TRAIN

There are seven daily trains to Bhopal and 12 to Ujjain. The **train reservation office** (⊙ 8am-10pm Mon-Sat, to 2pm Sun) is 200m east of the station.

Ujjain

☑ 0734 / POP 570,800

Weave your way between pilgrims along the river ghats, make an offering at some of Ujjain's famous temples, and get lost in the old city's maze of alleyways, and you'll see why the holy town of Ujjain has been attracting traders and pilgrims for hundreds of years. An undeniable energy pulses through the sacred sites here – not surprising given this is one of Hinduism's seven sacred cities and also one of the four cities that hosts the gigantic Kumbh Mela pilgrimage festival every 12 years. An estimated 75 million people crowded into Ujjain during the month of its most recent Kumbh Mela in 2016.

⊙ Sights

★ **Mahakaleshwar Mandir**   HINDU TEMPLE
(VIP ticket ₹250; ⊙ 4am-11pm) While this is not visually the most stunning temple, tagging along behind a conga-line through the underground chambers can be magical. At nonfestival times, the marble walkways are a peaceful preamble to the subterranean chamber containing one of India's 12 *jyoti linga* – naturally occurring, especially sacred Shiva linga believed to derive currents of *shakti* (creative energies perceived as female deities) from within themselves rather than being ritually invested with *mantra-shakti* by priests. During festivals it can be oppressively busy.

The temple was destroyed by the Delhi sultan Iltutmish in 1235 and restored by the Scindias in the 19th century. Foreign visitors will generally be encouraged to pay ₹250 for a 'VIP' entry ticket. There's no obligation to buy one of these but it does allow you to skip any entry queues.

MADHYA PRADESH & CHHATTISGARH UJJAIN

Ujjain

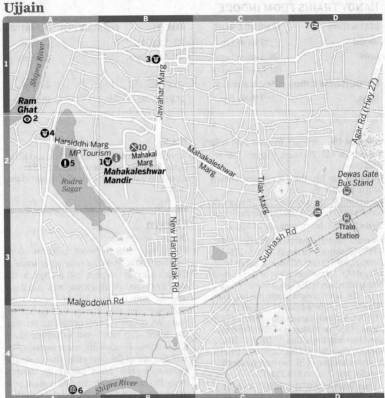

★ Ram Ghat   GHAT

The most central and popular of Ujjain's river ghats, strung with orange- and pink-roofed shrines, is busy all day with people bathing and presenting gifts of milk or flowers to the Shipra River. It's most atmospheric at dawn or dusk when the devout chime cymbals and light candles at the water's edge. During festival times, waves of people sweep to and from the river in a thrilling example of religious devotion.

Harsiddhi Mandir   HINDU TEMPLE

Built during the Maratha period, this temple enshrines a famous vermilion-painted image of goddess Annapurna. At the entrance, two tall blackened stone towers bristling with lamps are a special feature of Maratha art. They add to the spectacle of Navratri (p627) when filled with oil and ignited.

Sinhasan Battisi   MONUMENT

Vikram Teela, a small island in Rudra Sagar lake, is covered with statuary (installed in 2016) that re-creates the magical throne and court of the legendary Ujjain king Vikram-

five structures (for tracking celestial bodies and recording time) has quite detailed explanations in English, but you'd need to be an astronomer to understand them!

🎎 Festivals & Events

⭐ Kumbh Mela
RELIGIOUS

(Simhastha; ☉ Apr/May) Ujjain is one of four sites in India that hosts the incredible Kumbh Mela, during which millions bathe in the Shipra River. It takes place here every 12 years, normally during April and May. The next one is due in 2028.

🛏 Sleeping & Eating

Hotel Ramakrishna
HOTEL $

(☎ 0734-2557012; www.hotelramakrishna.co.in; Subhash Rd; s/d from ₹1000/1210; ❄🖵) This cleaner-than-average Subhash Rd hotel has a wide variety of air-conditioned rooms. Smaller, cheaper rooms are old and faded with bucket-only showers and squat toilets. Throw a couple of hundred extra rupees at the problem though, and you get a big, clean room with a shower. All rooms have wooden window shutters.

The adjoining New Sudama restaurant does inexpensive vegetarian food (mains ₹75 to ₹150).

Hotel Abika Elite
BUSINESS HOTEL $$

(☎ 0734-4010000; www.abikahotels.com; 4 Nasar Ali Marg, Street 2; r from ₹3360) Ujjain's newest – and best – hotel is a great-value treat. Rooms are palatial in size and painted in pleasing whites and lime greens. All rooms have swish bathrooms, plus there are sofas and desks. The in-house restaurant (mains around ₹250) serves Ujjan's best North Indian cuisine.

Hotel Shipra Residency
HOTEL $$

(☎ 0734-2551495; www.mptourism.com; Dewas Rd; incl breakfast r ₹4240; ❄🖵) This decent MP Tourism hotel has attractive rooms with a certain old-fashioned class, comfy beds, tea/coffee equipment and toiletry kits. There's also a small garden and the management are knowledgeable. There's also a stylish restaurant, the Meghdoot (mains ₹150-400; ☉ 11am-3pm & 7-10.30pm).

Damaru Wala
INDIAN $

(138 Mahakal Marg; thali ₹100-140; ☉ 9.30am-midnight) It only does thalis (all-you-can-eat meals) but they're tasty, ones, and served up in a bright, clean, purpose-designed space with white-top tables and black chairs.

aditya. The enthroned king sits surrounded by his circle of nine scholars, the *nava-ratna*, which includes the great (historical) Sanskrit poet Kalidas.

Gopal Mandir
HINDU TEMPLE

(☉ 7am-noon & 4-10pm) The Scindias built this marble-spired temple, a fine example of Maratha architecture, in the 19th century. The sanctum's silver-plated doors originated at the Somnath Temple in Gujarat, but were taken from there to Ghazni, Afghanistan, by Muslim raiders. Ahmad Shah Durani later took them to Lahore (present-day Pakistan), before Mahadji Scindia brought them here.

Vedh Shala
HISTORIC BUILDING

(Observatory, Jantar Mantar; Indian/foreigner ₹10/100; ☉ 8am-6pm) Ujjain has been India's Greenwich since the 4th century BC, and this simple-looking but surprisingly complicated observatory was built by Maharaja Jai Singh between 1725 and 1730. Each of its

HANDY TRAINS FROM UJJAIN

DESTINATION	TRAIN NO & NAME	FARE (₹)	DURATION (HR)	DEPARTURE
Bhopal	12919 Malwa Exp	170/540/745 (A)	3½	2.10pm
Delhi	12415 Nizamuddin Exp	415/1100/1565 (A)	12½	6pm
Indore	18234 Narmada Exp Passenger	100/495/700 (A)	2½	8.30am
Jaipur	12465 Ranthambore Exp	185/335/705/870 (B)	9	7.45am
Mumbai (Central)	12962 Avantika Exp	415/1100/1565 (A)	12½	5.45pm

Fares: (A) sleeper/3AC/2AC, (B) 2nd class/sleeper/chair car/3AC

The restaurant is up a flight of stairs, with a big black, red and white sign in Hindi only.

Shree Ganga

SWEETS $

(50 Amarsingh Marg; sweets per kg from ₹360, mains ₹70-120; ⊙8am-10.30pm) Since 1949, this epic sweet shop has been satiating Ujjaini sugar cravings. There's no English sign or menu, but staff can steer you in the right direction. One speciality is their milk cake, another the *caju barfi* (a fudge-like cashew sweet; ₹940 per kilogram). They also do thirst-quenching freshly squeezed juices, such as pomegranate and pineapple.

Upstairs, there's a great savoury menu from 11am that includes creative South Indian (green chutney masala dosa) and Chinese. It's just to the right of Baker's Lounge.

ℹ Information

MP Tourism (☑0734-2552263; www.mp tourism.com; ⊙10am-6pm Mon-Sat) In the grounds of the Mahakaleshwar Mandi, this tourist information office can provide pretty basic information.

ℹ Getting There & Away

BUS

The main bus station is the **Nanakheda Bus Stand** (Sanwer Rd), 4km south of the centre. From here services run to:

Indore ₹60, two hours, frequently from 5am to 11pm

Bhopal ₹250, five hours, frequently from 6am to 9pm

For Dhar, Maheshwar, Mandu or Omkareshwar, change at Indore.

Local buses (₹9) link the city centre **Dewas Gate Bus Stand** (State Hwy 27) with the Nanakheda Bus Stand. An autorickshaw costs ₹30.

TRAIN

There are about 10 daily trains to Bhopal and 15 to Indore, both of which have many more trains than Ujjain. The only train going every day to

Gwalior and Agra is the Delhi-bound 12919 Malwa Express at 2.10pm; otherwise you can take any train to Bhopal and change there.

ℹ Getting Around

Prepaid autorickshaws from the booth outside the train station charge ₹50 to Ram Ghat and ₹400 for a four-hour tour around Ujjain.

Mandu

☑07292 / POP 10,300 / ELEV 590M

Perched on a pleasantly green, thinly forested 25-sq-km plateau, picturesque Mandu is home to some of India's finest examples of Afghan architecture as well as impressive baobab trees, originally from Africa and carried here on ancient trade routes. The plateau is littered with World Heritage–listed palaces, tombs, monuments and mosques. Some cling to the edge of ravines, others stand beside lakes, while Rupmati's Pavilion, the most romantic of them all, sits serenely on the edge of the plateau, overlooking the vast plains below. Little more than a one-street village, Mandu is a great place to spend a couple of days exploring grand and beautiful architecture in a relaxed rural setting, easily toured by bicycle – and pondering the mutation of the capital of a once-powerful kingdom into just another Indian village.

History

Mandu came to prominence in the 10th century as a fort-capital of the Hindu Paramara dynasty that ruled Malwa (western Madhya Pradesh and southeastern Rajasthan) at the time. Malwa was conquered by the Muslim Delhi sultanate in 1305. After Timur sacked Delhi in 1401, the sultanate's governor in Malwa, the Afghan Dilawar Khan, set up his own kingdom and Mandu's golden age began. His son Hoshang Shah shifted the capital from Dhar to Mandu and raised the place to its greatest splendour. Their Ghuri dynasty was short-lived, however. Hoshang's son was poisoned by a rival, Mahmud Khilji (or Khalji), whose Khilji dynasty ruled Malwa from 1436 until Bahadur Shah of Gujarat conquered it in 1526.

Mandu and Malwa then fell in quick succession to the Mughal emperor Humayun (1534), Mallu Khan, an officer from the Khilji dynasty (1536), and Humayun's North Indian rival Sher Shah (1542). In 1555 Baz Bahadur, a son of Sher Shah's local governor, crowned himself sultan. Baz, however, fled Mandu in 1561 as the Mughal emperor Akbar's troops invaded.

Akbar's successors, Jehangir and Shah Jahan, enjoyed visiting Mandu but its importance had waned. When the Holkar clan of Marathas defeated the Mughals near Dhar in 1732, Mandu came under Maratha control from Dhar and the slide in its fortunes that had begun with the absconding of Baz Bahadur became a plummet.

⊙ Sights

There are three main groups of ruins: the Royal Enclave, the Village Group and the Rewa Kund Group. Each requires its own separate ticket. All other sights are free.

Royal Enclave   HISTORIC BUILDING
The **Royal Enclave monuments** (Indian/foreigner ₹25/300, camera ₹25; ⊙ dawn-dusk) are the only ones fenced off into a single (large) compound. There's a **Publication Sales Counter** (⊙ 9am-5pm) selling guidebooks beside the ticket office.

➜ **Jahaz Mahal**
(Ship Palace) Dating from the 15th century, this is the most famous building in Mandu. Built on a narrow strip of land between Munja and Kapoor tanks, with an upper terrace like a ship's bridge (use your imagination), it's far longer (120m) than it is wide (15m). The pleasure-loving sultan Ghiyas-ud-din Khilji, who is said to have had a harem of 15,000 maidens, constructed its lookouts, scalloped arches, airy rooms and beautiful pleasure pools.

➜ **Hindola Mahal**
(Swing Palace) Just north of Ghiyas' stately pleasure dome is the Hindola Mahal, so-called because the slope of its walls sort of resembles that of the ropes of a swing. Thought to have been a royal reception hall, it's often ascribed to Hoshang Shah, though

some writers attribute it to Ghiyas-ud-Din. Either way it's an impressive and eye-catching design.

➜ **Dilawar Khan's Mosque**
Built by Dilawar Khan in 1405, this is Mandu's earliest Islamic building. It was built mainly with material from earlier Hindu temples – particularly obvious in the pillars and ceilings of the roofed western end.

➜ **Champa Baodi**
So-called because its water supposedly smelled as sweet as the champak flower, the Champa Baodi is a circular step-well with vaulted side-niches. It was accessed by a series of vaulted passages and chambers, called the Tahkhana, some of which you can explore from nearby entrances, though you can't actually reach the well. You can, however, look down into it from above.

➜ **Turkish Bath**
Stars and octagons perforate the domed roofs of this tiny bathhouse, which had hot and cold water and a hypocaust (underfloor-heated) sauna.

➜ **Jal Mahal**
(Water Palace) This palace on an island-like spit of land at the corner of Munja Tank is thought to have been a private retreat for noble couples. It has several step-wells and pools in which they could disport.

Village Group

The **Village Group** (Indian/foreigner ₹25/300, camera ₹25; ⊙ dawn-dusk), set either side of the main road in the village centre, contains three monuments. The ticket office is at the entrance to the Jama Masjid; one ticket covers all three sights.

Jama Masjid   MOSQUE
Entered by a flight of steps leading to a 17m-high domed porch, this disused redstone mosque dominates Mandu village centre. Hoshang Shah begun its construction around 1406, basing it on the great Omayyad Mosque in Damascus, Syria, and Mahmud Khilji completed it in 1454. It's a relatively austere but harmonious building, and reckoned to be the finest and largest example of Afghan architecture in India.

Hoshang Shah's Tomb   ISLAMIC TOMB
Reputed to be India's oldest marble mausoleum, this imposing tomb is crowned with a tiny crescent thought to have been imported from Persia or Mesopotamia. Light filters into the echoing, domed interior through

MADHYA PRADESH & CHHATTISGARH MANDU

Mandu

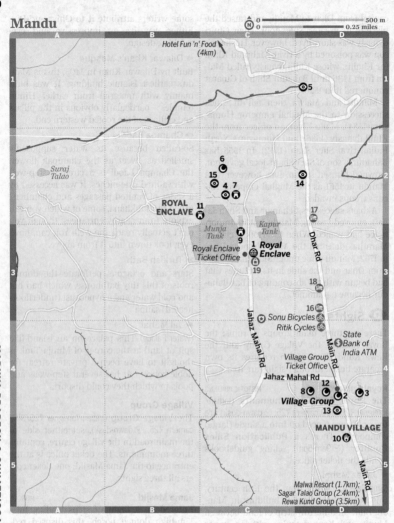

stone *jalis* (carved lattice screens), intended to cast an appropriately subdued light on the tombs. An inscription records Shah Jahan sending his architects – including Ustad Hamid, who worked on the Taj Mahal – here in 1659 to pay their respects to the tomb's builders of two centuries before.

Ashrafi Mahal
ISLAMIC SITE

The Ashrafi Mahal was built as a madrasa (Islamic college) by Hoshang Shah between 1405 and 1422. It was a quadrangle with rows of cells and arcaded corridors on the outside, and four corner towers. Mahmud

Khilji of the following dynasty converted the northwest tower into a seven-storey victory tower, and roofed the courtyard as a platform for his own grand marble tomb. Tomb and tower have vanished but you can climb a grand staircase and walk around the roof.

Rewa Kund Group

A pleasant 4km cycle south from Mandu village, past Sagar Talao, brings you to the Rewa Kund (Indian/foreigner ₹25/300, camera ₹25; ⊙ dawn–dusk) tank and its two nearby monuments. The ticket office is opposite the tank, just before Baz Bahadur's Palace.

Mandu

Baz Bahadur's Palace
PALACE

Baz Bahadur (r 1555–61) was the last independent ruler of Mandu. His palace, a curious mix of Rajasthani and Mughal styles, was built in 1508–09 by the Khilji sultan Nasir-ud-Din. Baz Bahadur supposedly took a liking to it because of his infatuation with the singing shepherdess Rupmati who, according to legend, used to frequent the nearby Rewa Kund.

Rupmati's Pavilion
NOTABLE BUILDING

Standing at the top of an escarpment falling 366m to the plains, Rupmati's Pavilion has a delicacy of design and beauty of location unmatched by Mandu's other monuments. According to Malwa legends, the music-loving Baz Bahadur built it to persuade his golden-voiced shepherdess beloved, Rupmati, to move here from her home on the plains. From its terrace and domed pavilions, Rupmati could gaze at the distant glint of the sacred Narmada River.

In fact, the pavilion probably began life as a watchtower a century or more before Rupmati's time. Nonetheless, the love story is a subject of Malwa folk songs – not least because of its tragic ending. Lured by tales of Rupmati's beauty, Akbar's general Adham Khan marched on Mandu and Baz Bahadur fled, leaving his lover to poison herself rather than fall into the invader's hands.

This place is simply gorgeous at sunset.

Other Sights

Shop of Gada Shah
NOTABLE BUILDING

Almost resembling a Gothic cathedral, this looks more like an emporium than a mere shop. It was a warehouse for saffron and musk, imported and sold at a handsome profit when there were enough wealthy people to buy. Its owner's name, meaning 'beggar master', is thought to identify him as Rajput chief Medini Ray, a powerful subject of the early-16th-century Khilji sultan Mahmud II.

Delhi Gate
GATE

It's worth wandering up to the north end of town to the Delhi Gate, which was the main entrance to Mandu. You can walk up on top of it and along a short stretch of the walls for fine views over the country beyond.

Saturday Haat
MARKET

(⊙10am-dusk Sat) This colourful weekly *haat* (market), behind the Jama Masjid, is similar to ones held in many central Indian areas with a tribal population. Adivasis (tribal people) walk kilometres to buy and sell goods ranging from mountains of red chillies to dried *mahua* (a flower used to make a potent liquor of the same name).

Jain Temple
JAIN TEMPLE

Entered through a kaleidoscopic potpourri of a gate, this complex is a splash of kitsch among the Islamic monuments. The temples feature marble, silver and gold *tirthankars* (the 24 great Jain teachers) with jade eyes, and at the far right-hand end is a theme-park-like museum with a walk-on model of the Shatrunjaya hilltop temple complex in Gujarat. In its colourful murals, bears devour sinners' arms, demons poke out their eyes, and men and women are tied together and burnt.

Nil Kanth Palace
HINDU TEMPLE

If you're looking for a great reason to cycle out into the countryside, consider visiting this unusual former palace turned temple. It stands at the head of a ravine, on the site of an earlier Shiva shrine – its name means God with Blue Throat – and is now again used as a place of worship. A stream built by one of Akbar's governors trickles through a delightful spiral channel and is usually filled with sweet-scented water.

To get here cycle south from the Jama Masjid for 850m and turn right at a large water tower. Follow the road as it twists and turns past outlying houses all the way to Nil Kanth (2.2km). You can continue from here, past more remote settlements, for just over 1km to reach the still-standing gateway of the now-ruined, Maratha-built Songarh Fort, from where there are more great views.

Sagar Talao Group
ISLAMIC SITE

If you have time, this group of handsome buildings is worth a detour between Mandu village and Rewa Kund. The main ones are Malik Mughith's Mosque, built by Mahmud Khilji's father in 1432 using carvings from earlier Hindu buildings; a large, courtyarded caravanserai (1437); the Dai-ki-Chhoti Bahen-ka-Mahal (Wetnurse's Younger Sister's Palace), actually a striking octagonal domed tomb on a raised platform; and the Dai-ka-Mahal (Wetnurse's Palace), another domed tomb, on an arcaded platform that also supports a mosque.

If coming from the village, turn left 200m after the Malwa Resort hotel and the buildings soon appear on the right.

🛏 Sleeping & Eating

Hotel Gurukripa Villa
HOTEL $

(☑ 07292-263243; Dhar Rd; r with/without AC ₹1500/700) Has reasonably clean, but stuffy rooms with the occasional blue, yellow or pink wall, but no natural light. It's one of the only places in Mandu that doesn't seem overpriced.

Mandu Sarai
HOTEL $$

(☑ 7000247329; Dhar Rd; r with/without AC ₹2500/1500; ❄🛜) Right in the heart of the village, some of the rooms at this new, multistory place have views out over the ruins. For the moment, it's all very clean and sparkling. At night, it's lit up with fairy lights like an extravagant Christmas tree.

Malwa Retreat
HOTEL $$

(☑ 07292-263221; www.mptourism.com; Dhar Rd; r/tents incl breakfast from ₹1780/2790; ❄🛜) The

cheaper of MP Tourism's two Mandu properties, with damp-stained air-cooled rooms and bigger, brighter air-con safari tents that are in serious need of renovation. It has wi-fi, the Yatrika restaurant, and reception doubles as the Tourist Interpretation Centre.

Malwa Resort
HOTEL $$$

(☑ 07292-263235; www.mptourism.com; Main Rd; r incl breakfast from ₹3800; ❄🛜⛱) One of the better options in Mandu, this MP Tourism property, 2km south of the village, has large, lake-side gardens containing comfortable rooms in cottages, children's play areas and a pool. The hotel has the town's best restaurant and a bar. Don't miss having morning chai in the lakeside gazebo while watching fishers cast their nets over Sagar Talao.

Restaurant Gurukripa
INDIAN $

(Dhar Rd; thalis ₹140-160; ◷9am-10.30pm) The best place to eat in the village centre is this small and slightly ramshackle place that dishes up a delicious thali. Try the Mandu Special (₹160), which comes with the local speciality, *Mandu dhal bafta*, which is a ball-like lump of crushed lentils fried with ghee.

Yatrika
INDIAN $

(Malwa Retreat, Dhar Rd; mains ₹130-320; ◷8-10am, noon-3pm & 7-10pm; 🛜) The cafe-restaurant at Malwa Retreat dishes out veg and nonveg Indian meals in a relatively flash contemporary premises with an open kitchen. It has wi-fi, but if you want a cold beer, you'll need to head to the sister property, the Malwa Resort.

🛍 Shopping

Roopayan
TEXTILES

(Main Rd; ◷8am-9pm) Next to Malwa Resort, this small shop sells good-quality scarves, shawls, bedspreads and clothing made from material (mostly cotton) that has been block-printed, usually with natural dyes, in the nearby village of Bagh.

ℹ Information

State Bank of India ATM (Dhar Rd) The only ATM in the village and it's not super-reliable so come prepared.

Tourist Interpretation Centre (☑ 07292-263221; Malwa Retreat, Dhar Rd; ◷9am-6pm) It has perfunctory information boards but can answer questions and arrange government-certified guides (per half-day/day ₹470/660).

ℹ️ Getting There & Away

Buses stop at various spots around the central intersection by the Jama Masjid. There are four buses to Indore (₹130, 3½ hours, 8.15am, 9am, 1.30pm and 3.30pm) and one to Ujjain (₹150, six hours, 6am). Buses leave every half hour for Dhar (₹40, one hour, 6am to 7pm), where you can change for Dhamnod (₹50, two hours), then, in turn, for Maheshwar (₹20, 30 minutes) or for Barwah (₹70, two hours), where you can catch another bus or a tempo on to Omkareshwar (₹20, 30 minutes). In fact, it's quicker to get off 22km before Dhar at the junction at Lunhera (₹20, 30 minutes), where you can flag down Dhamnod-bound buses (₹50, 1½ hours). You should leave Mandu no later than 3pm if heading to Maheshwar and by 1pm for Omkareshwar.

Taxis cost about ₹1000 to Maheshwar and ₹1500 to Indore. Ask around the market area in front of the Jama Masjid.

ℹ️ Getting Around

Cycling is the best way to get around, as the terrain is flat, the air clear and the countryside beautiful. Mandu doesn't appear to have any autorickshaws. Neighbours **Ritik Cycles** (☑ 9000157920; Dhar Rd; per day ₹100) and **Sonu Bicycles** (Dhar Rd; per day ₹100) both rent reasonable bikes near the village centre.

Maheshwar

☑ 07283 / POP 30,000

The peaceful riverside town of Maheshwar has long held spiritual significance – it's mentioned in the Mahabharata and Ramayana under its old name, Mahishmati, and still draws sadhus and *yatris* (pilgrims) to its ancient ghats and temples on the holy Narmada River. Away from the ghats and historic buildings, Maheshwar's colourful streets display some brightly painted wooden houses with overhanging balconies.

The ghats are a whirl of colour and interest and the compact old quarter is a pleasure to explore. In many ways, Maheshwar is a sort of refined, spit-shone Varanasi in miniature and the fact that it's well off the beaten tourist path means that the many smiles you'll receive are genuine. If you want to encounter old India at its best, then Maheshwar fits the bill.

👁️ Sights

★ Ghats   GHAT

Running along the banks of the holy Narmada River and shadowed by the daunting walls of the fort, the ghats are the life and spiritual soul of the town. At dawn and dusk locals and pilgrims alike light candles and make *puja* (offerings) to the river and the atmosphere can be magical. During festivals thousands of pilgrims come here for *puja*.

Boat rides along the river are available (from ₹200 per boat).

★ Chhatris   HINDU SHRINE

(Cenotaphs) Down to the right of the ramp descending towards the ghats are the *chhatris* (cenotaphs) of Ahilyabai and Vithoji Rao, a Holkar prince who was trampled to death by elephants in 1801 on orders of his enemies during an inter-Maratha conflict. Ahilyabai's *chhatri,* the larger and more elaborate of the two, with fine stone carving, is known as the Ahilyeshwar Temple. It contains a small statue of the queen, wearing a sari, with a Shiva lingam in front of her.

Maheshwar Palace   PALACE

Maheshwar is dominated by its fort, whose huge ramparts, towering above the river ghats, were built by Emperor Akbar. The Maheshwar Palace and several temples within the fort were added by Queen Ahilyabai in the 18th century. The palace is part public courtyards, part posh hotel.

During daylight hours small parts of the complex (the gardens and a tiny one-room museum dedicated to the queen) are open to the public, but come sunset the imposing wooden gates are closed.

Rehwa Society   WORKSHOP

(☑ 8120001388, 9594025260; www.rehwasociety.org; ⊙ 10am-6pm Wed-Mon, shop daily) On the way down from the palace to the ghats, a small doorway announces the NGO Rehwa Society, a craft cooperative where profits are ploughed back into the education, housing and welfare of the weavers and their families. A local school, run entirely by Rehwa, is behind the workshop. Maheshwar saris, which have recently been trademarked to the town, are famous for their unique weave and simple, geometric patterns.

You can watch the weavers at work – it's a hypnotic experience – and buy shawls (from ₹2100), saris (₹4000 to ₹13,000), scarves (₹1100 to ₹2500) and fabrics made from silk, cotton and wool. There are also volunteer possibilities here.

🛏 Sleeping & Eating

⭐ Hansa Heritage
HOTEL **$**

(📞 07283-273296; http://hansaheritage.in; Fort Rd; r with/without AC ₹950/750, ste ₹1450; ❄ 🛜) Offering exceptional value for money, the Hansa Heritage is a budget boutique hotel with mud-and-grass-daubed walls stencilled in bright colours, antique-looking wooden furniture and attractive coloured-glass window panes. There are bright tiled bathrooms, a downstairs cafe and a megafriendly, English-speaking owner. The location, just 150m from the fort, is is ideal.

Narmada Retreat
HOTEL **$$**

(📞 8349994784; www.mptourism.com; r incl breakfast from ₹3290, ste ₹5420; ❄ 🛜 🏊) This well-managed, MP Tourism–run hotel stands on the riverbank 900m west of the fort (a path links the two), and is a dependable choice with large, tastefully decorated rooms and air-con safari tents set around pampered green gardens with a good pool.

There's also a reliable restaurant, with tandoori and other Indian veg and nonveg dishes (mains ₹140 to ₹350).

Laboo's Café & Lodge
GUESTHOUSE **$$**

(📞 7771004818; info@ahilyafort.com; Fort Gate; s/d incl breakfast ₹1600/1900, mains ₹140-250; ⊙ cafe 7am-8pm; ❄ 🛜) Laboo's is not only a delightful cafe in a tree-shaded courtyard, but also has six wonderful air-conditioned rooms. Each is different, being part of the fort gate and walls, but is decorated with care and attention. The biggest and brightest features its own fort-wall verandah. It's worth reserving a room in advance.

The open-to-all courtyard cafe is the nicest place to eat in town. It has a wide assortment of snacks and light meals, including pancakes and a delicious, unlimited thali (₹250).

⭐ Ahilya Fort
HERITAGE HOTEL **$$$**

(📞 011-41551575; www.ahilyafort.com; d incl full board ₹38,530; ❄ @ 🛜 🏊) Mick Jagger, Demi Moore and Sting have all indulged in this heritage hotel in Maheshwar Palace owned by Prince Shivaji Rao (Richard) Holkar, an Indian-American directly descended from the palace's founder, Queen Ahilyabai. The best rooms are indeed palatial and some come with fabulous river views, while lush gardens house exotic fruit trees, organic vegetable patches and history at every turn.

Rates include all meals as well as sunset boat trips. Booking ahead is essential.

ℹ Information

There's an SBI ATM at the junction of the main road and the start of the old town.

ℹ Getting There & Away

There's no bus station and buses stop on the main road by the junction of the road leading to the old town. There are buses to Indore (₹85, 2½ hours, about every 30 minutes from 6am to 5pm). For Mandu, first head west to Dhamnod (₹20, 30 minutes, buses about every 15 minutes from 6am to 9pm) then take a Dhar-bound bus as far as the junction at Lunhera (₹50, 1½ hours, about half-hourly). From there flag down a bus or tempo (both ₹15, 30 minutes) for the final 14km to Mandu.

For Omkareshwar take a bus to Barwah (₹50, 1½ hours, about half-hourly) and then another bus or a tempo to Omkareshwar (₹20, 30 minutes).

Omkareshwar

🕿 07280 / POP 10,060

This Om-shaped island in the holy Narmada River attracts pilgrims in large numbers and has become a spiritual chill-out destination for some travellers. A controversial dam just upstream has changed the look of Omkareshwar considerably, but the island has retained its spiritual vibe and remains a pleasant and authentic – if typically commercialised – pilgrimage point.

Much activity takes place off the island, in the town on the south side of the river. Two footbridges 400m apart link town and island: the western old bridge crosses from the market square called Getti Chowk, and the eastern new bridge crosses from a large parking area. Halfway between the bridges you'll find the ghats, where you can cross the river on boats for ₹10 per person.

⊙ Sights

Tourists can rub shoulders with pilgrims and sadhus in the island's narrow lanes; browse the colourful stalls selling souvenir linga, piles of orange and yellow powder for tikka marks and flower offerings for the temples; or join pilgrims attending the thrice-daily *puja* (prayer) at the Shri Omkar Mandhata. This salmon-pink, cave-like temple, towering above the island ghats just east of the old bridge, houses the only shapeless jyoti lingam (the jyoti linga are 12 especially important Shiva linga dotted around India). It's one of many Hindu and Jain monuments on the island.

Most Hindu pilgrims make a 7km parikrama (ritual circumnavigation) along a clearly marked path around the island. From the old bridge, the route heads to Sangam Ghat at the western tip of the island, where sadhus bathe in the holy Narmada. It then climbs east to the 11th-century Gaudi Somnath Temple on the highest point, with a mighty 2m-high Shiva lingam inside. (You can go directly to the Gaudi Somnath by turning right 150m from the old bridge and climbing 287 steps.)

From the Gaudi Somnath the path continues east, passing in front of a modern, 30m-high, golden Shiva statue, then loops round, down and up hills, passing a number of temple ruins, to the Shri Omkar Mandata. Don't miss the beautifully sculpted Siddhanath Temple with marvellous elephant carvings around its base.

🛏️ Sleeping & Eating

Manu Guest House   GUESTHOUSE $
(📱9826749004; s/d without bathroom ₹300/400) This welcoming island guesthouse with inspiring views is the best budget base in town. English-speaking Manu and his family will treat you like one of their own and, if asked in advance, can whip up a delicious thali (from ₹100). The six rooms are very simple, yet well looked after, and the shared bathrooms (cold showers) are kept clean.

This is pretty much the only place to stay on the island that isn't a *dharamsala* (pilgrims' rest house). It's a bit hard to find: cross the old bridge from Getti Chowk, come around and down the stairs and turn left. After 15m, turn left into a narrow alley with a painted blue wall saying 'Kalyan Bhattacharya', and head up a steep set of steps. Continue to the left and it's at the rear of the yellow building facing you.

Ganesh Guest House   GUESTHOUSE $
(📱9993735449; sumitbhoi1137@gmail.com; r from ₹300) Follow the signs zigzagging off the path down to the ghats from Mamaleshwar Rd to reach Ganesh, with its decidedly budget rooms and thin mattresses. Upstairs rooms are airier and brighter, while the shaded garden restaurant (mains ₹60 to ₹160; advance notice needed), overlooking the ghats, has a small multicuisine menu (including Western breakfasts) and a peaceful ambience.

Narmada Resort   HOTEL $$$
(📱07280-271455; www.mptourism.com; r incl breakfast ₹3530; ❄️🛜) High up on the hill overlooking the river and the island, this MP Tourism property has rooms in two separate blocks. Those in the older block are well past their best but still better than anywhere else in town. Those in the new block (same price) are very smart, with dark wood furniture and starched white sheets.

The restaurant (7am to 10am, 11.30am to 3pm, 7pm to 10.30pm) is also the best in town with a big choice of Indian and continental dishes.

ℹ️ Information

SBI ATM (Mamaleshwar Rd) Located 200m towards town from the old bus stand.

ℹ️ Getting There & Away

The new bus station is 1.5km southwest from Getti Chowk along Mamaleshwar Rd, and the old bus station is 1km nearer town along the same road. Buses arriving from nearby tourist towns will normally – but not always – drop you at the new bus station. The old bus station is used more by rickety local buses headed to small rural villages and by organised Indian pilgrim groups. The following buses listed generally all start from the new bus station.

Indore ₹90, 2½ hours; depart half-hourly from 5.30am to 10am, then every one to two hours from 10am to 7pm

Maheshwar There's a direct bus (₹70, two hours) at 6am and 10am; or take a bus or tempo to Barwah (₹20, 30 minutes, every 30 to 60 minutes), where Maheshwar buses (₹50, 1½ hours) leave about half-hourly till 5pm

Ujjain ₹150, four hours, 5.45am, 9.30am, 2pm, 3.30pm

For Mandu, first take a bus or tempo to Barwah (₹20, 30 minutes, every 30 to 60 minutes). At Barwah you might just find a bus all the way to Mandu (₹100, four hours), but more likely you'll have to change at Dhamnod and Lunhera en route.

If you're heading for Ajanta (Maharashtra), take a bus to Khandwa (₹80, two hours, about half-hourly) from the new bus stand. From Khandwa there are about 15 daily trains to Jalgaon (2½ hours), which has frequent buses to Ajanta.

EASTERN MADHYA PRADESH

Jabalpur

📱0761 / POP 1.27 MILLION

Domestic tourists mostly come here to visit Marble Rocks, an attractive river gorge

Jabalpur

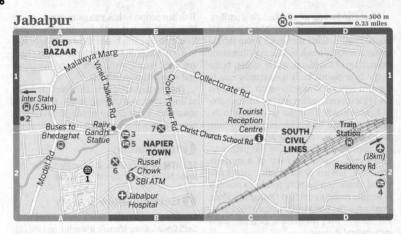

Jabalpur

nearby, but for foreigners this industrial city of *chowks* (market areas) and working-men's taverns is mainly useful as a launch pad for Madhya Pradesh's famous tiger parks: Kanha, Bandhavgarh and Pench.

◉ Sights

Rani Durgawati Museum   MUSEUM
(Napier Town; Indian/foreigner ₹10/100, camera/video ₹50/200; ⊙10am-6pm Tue-Sun) Displays a dusty collection of 10th- and 11th-century sculpture from local sites, while upstairs are galleries for stone and copper inscriptions, ancient coins and a photograph exhibition of Bhedaghat's Chausath Yogini Temple.

☞ Tours

Tiger Safari   WILDLIFE
(☑8120445454; www.thetigersafari.com) 🏍 This very well organised and efficient agency, inherently involved in tiger conservation, can customise safari tours throughout eastern

MP and other major Indian tiger reserves. Photography wildlife tours are a speciality, but it handles birding and cultural itineraries as well.

Expect to pay ₹13,500 (budget) to ₹66,000 (top end) per day for all-inclusive custom safari tours for two people, depending on a variety of factors (type of vehicle, accommodation, number of safaris, number of days etc). Prices come down for groups of more than two people. You can also just rent a quality vehicle and safe driver from the agency (for around ₹4150 per day).

🛏 Sleeping & Eating

Lodge Shivalaya   HOTEL **$**
(☑0761-2625188; Napier Town; r with AC ₹1200-1400, without AC s ₹550-600, d ₹650-750; ❊⊚) Rooms are basic, but clean enough for one night and come with TVs and small bathrooms. Non-air-conditioned rooms open onto shared terraces overlooking the bustling (and noisy) street below; air-con rooms are interior, without natural light, but a little quieter.

Hotel Rahul   HOTEL **$$**
(☑0761-2625525; www.hotelrahuljabalpur.com; Naudra Bridge; incl breakfast s ₹1430-1930, d ₹1780-2130; ⊚) Good-value, simple, small but clean 20-room hotel. Rooms come with tea/coffee equipment and minifridges. One of Jabalpur's better eateries, **Olives Restaurant** (☑9644007660; mains ₹160-300; ⊙7am-10pm), is in the basement.

★Kalchuri Residency   HOTEL **$$$**
(☑0761-2678492; www.mptourism.com; South Civil Lines; s/d incl breakfast ₹4235/4700;

✽ @ 🛜 🖳) One of MP Tourism's nicest properties, the Kalchuri is located in the quieter Civil Lines area just south of the train station. Rooms are large and modern in soothing earth tones, and have TVs, kettles and spacious bathrooms. The rooftop pool is heavenly on a hot day. There's a decent restaurant (mains ₹240 to ₹420) and a spacious pub (beer from ₹250).

Saheb's Food Junction
MUGHLAI $$

(Russel Chowk; meals ₹150-200; ⏰11am-11pm) The best nonveg in Russel Chowk is better than it looks from outside (the dining room is upstairs and air-conditioned), and it isn't afraid to spice things up in its fiery gravies (mutton curry, *kadhai* chicken).

Yellow Chilli
MODERN INDIAN $$$

(📞7400689898; www.theyellowchilli.com; Dixit Pride, Napier Town; mains ₹330-500; ⏰11am-11.30pm) This higher-end Indian chain, the domain of celeb chef Sanjeev Kapoor, is a gastro-godsend in Jabalpur. Creative takes on gourmet Indian fare rule here and everything is a flavour bomb. The coconut saffron *shorba* soup is a fine way to start and you're spoilt for choice among the chicken and lamb dishes and veg and nonveg curries that follow.

🛈 Information

SBI ATM (Russel Chowk)

Tourist Reception Centre (📞0761-2677290; www.mptourism.com; Christ Church School Rd; ⏰10.30am-7.30pm) Has tourist information and makes bookings for MP Tourism hotels. There's also a tourist information counter at the airport.

🛈 Getting There & Away

AIR

The airport is 15km east of the centre. Air India subsidiary Alliance Air flies to Delhi daily. SpiceJet flies to Ahmedabad, Delhi, Mumbai and Hyderabad. Indigo also flies to Hyderabad.

BUS

The **ISBT** (Inter State Bus Terminus; Damoh Rd) is 6km northwest of the centre. Departures (sleeper places available on night buses only):

Bhopal Seat/sleeper ₹450/610, eight hours, nine daily

Khajuraho Seat/sleeper ₹300/350, eight hours, 6.30pm

Nagpur Seat/sleeper ₹369/485, eight hours, half-hourly 5.30am to 12.30am; Volvo AC ₹450, 9.30am, 11am, 2.30pm, 11pm

Raipur Seat/sleeper ₹370/450, 10 hours, 4pm, 7.30pm, 8pm

To the Tiger Reserves

Bandhavgarh Tiger Reserve It's best to take a train direct to Umaria, but you can also take a bus to Katni (₹110, three hours, half-hourly 7am to 8.30pm), from where there are trains and buses to Umaria.

Kanha Tiger Reserve There are buses to Mandla (₹100, 3½ hours, every 15 to 20 minutes from 5.30am to 7pm), from where there are eight buses daily to Khatia (₹60, 2½ hours).

Pench Tiger Reserve Take a Nagpur bus as far as Khawasa (₹180 to ₹200, six hours, half-hourly from 5.30am to 12.30am), then take a shared 4WD (₹20) for the final 12km to Turia.

TRAIN

About 20 daily trains (sleeper/3AC/2AC ₹140/495/700, three hours) leave for Satna, where you can take buses to Khajuraho (usually

MADHYA PRADESH & CHHATTISGARH JABALPUR

HANDY TRAINS FROM JABALPUR

DESTINATION	TRAIN NO & NAME	FARE (₹)	DURATION (HR)	DEPARTURE
Agra	12189 Mahakaushal Exp	425/1125/1600	14	6.10pm
Bhopal	11472 Jabalpur-Indore Exp	250/645/895	6½	11.30pm
Delhi	12192 Shridham SF Exp	505/1340/1920	19	5.30pm
Kolkata (Howrah)	12322 Kolkata Mail	535/1420/2050	23	1.20pm
Mumbai (CST)	12321 Howrah-Mumbai Mail	490/1305/1870	17½	5.55pm
Raipur	12854 Amarkantak Exp	335/870/1230	9½	9.25pm
Satna	Different trains each day	140/495/700	3	8.50am
Umaria	18233 Narmada Exp	90/450/635	4	6.35am
Varanasi	12165 Lokmanya Tilak Exp	330/860/1215	10	8.50pm (Mon, Thu & Fri)
Varanasi	12669 Ganga Kaveri Exp	330/860/1215	10	8.50pm (Tue & Sun)

Fares: sleeper/3AC/2AC

MARBLE ROCKS

Known locally as Bhedaghat, the magnesium-limestone cliffs at this gorge on the holy Narmada River, 20km west of Jabalpur, change colours in different lights, from pink to black. They're particularly impressive by moonlight, and parts are floodlit at night.

More pleasant than awe-inspiring (during the day, anyway), the trip up the 2km-long gorge is made in a shared **motorboat** (per person 30-50min ₹50, entire boat ₹800; ☻ dawn-dusk, closed during monsoon approximately mid-Jun–mid-Oct) from the jetty at Panchvati Ghat. Sticking around? The Dhuandhar (Smoke Cascade) waterfall is a worthwhile 1.5km walk uphill from the ghat. Along the way is the much-revered Chausath Yogini, a circular 10th-century temple dedicated to the Hindu goddess Durga, accessed via a steep flight of steps on the right-hand side of the road. Once at the falls, you can take a short cable-car ride (₹75 return) across the gorge.

Local city bus 7 or 9 leaves about every 15 minutes from 6.15am to 9pm for **Bhedaghat** (Model Rd; ₹20, 45 minutes to one hour). It drops you at a junction 100m from Panchvati Ghat. To return, you can also squeeze into Jabalpur-bound shared autorickshaws (₹20).

with a change at Panna and/or Bamitha). For Bandhavgarh Tiger Reserve, take a train to Umaria, then a 1½-hour bus ride.

ℹ Getting Around

Autorickshaws charge around ₹50 from the train station to Russel Chowk, or ₹100 from the ISBT.

Kanha Tiger Reserve

Madhya Pradesh is one of the kings of the Indian jungle when it comes to tiger parks, and the *Jungle Book* forests of **Kanha Tiger Reserve** (www.kanhatigerreserve.com; core-zone entry per 6-passenger 4WD/seat ₹1550/260, obligatory guide ₹360, 4WD rental ₹2375; ☻ daily except Wed afternoon mid-Oct–Jun) are its most famous. The forests are vast, and while your chances of seeing a tiger are slightly lower than at nearby Bandhavgarh, this is still one of India's best parks for tiger encounters. Here you can really go deep into the forest for a more complete safari experience.

Recent surveys indicate that Kanha's sal forests and meadows contain a growing population of around 125 tigers. There are also around 100 leopards and huge populations of deer and antelopes, including some 400 southern swamp deer *(barasingha)* which exist nowhere else in the world. You'll see plenty of langurs, the odd gaur (Indian bison), wild boar and jackal or two. Over 260 bird species have been recorded here too.

🏃 Activities

Jeep Safaris

The tiger reserve covers 2059 sq km including the 940-sq-km Kanha National Park,

which is the reserve's core zone. Safaris venture into four zones within the core zone; Kisli and Mukki zones have the best reputations for tiger sightings, followed by Kanha zone then Sarhi zone. Kisli and Kanha zones are best accessed from the Khatia gate in Khatia village on the western edge of the core zone. Mukki zone is best accessed from the Mukki gate on the south side, a 54km, 1½-hour drive from Khatia.

Up to 140 six-passenger 4WDs (known as gypsies, because most of them are the Suzuki gypsy make) are allowed into the reserve per day, but most of these can only be booked online (http://forest.mponline.gov.in, up to 120 days in advance) and the website does not accept foreign cards for payment. Save yourself immense hassle by booking through a hotel/agency (usually an additional ₹1000) – and make arrangements as far ahead as possible, because popular zones sell out months ahead.

Many of the more upmarket lodges and hotels block-book a number of safari tickets under the manager's name. This guarantees that their guests can always get a safari slot, but on the flip side, it dramatically reduces the number of tickets available to independent travellers. Even die-hard budget travellers might have to accept that if they want to go on safari, they will have to splash out on top-end accommodation. On the plus side this will invariably result in a better safari experience anyway.

Tickets for 15 4WDs per day (90 seats, divided between the four zones and morning and afternoon safaris) can be purchased in person at the park gates between 6.30pm and 7.30pm for the next morning, and 11am to noon for the same afternoon. But queues can form as early as the previous evening.

There are two safari slots each day: morning (roughly 6am to 11am) and afternoon (roughly 3pm to 6pm). Morning safaris are longer and tend to produce more tiger sightings. Note that the exact timing of safaris does vary a little over the course of the year according to sunrise/sunset times.

Other Options

If you just can't get seats in regular 4WD safaris, you can book a ride in a **canter** (₹530), lumbering 18-seat open 'minibuses' operating from Khatia and Mukki gates. Or you can opt for a **buffer zone safari** (per 4WD ₹4000; ⊙ dawn-11am & 3pm or 4pm-dusk) from Khatia gate. Tickets for both are sold early the previous evening for morning rides, and in the late morning for afternoon sessions.

🌱 Tours

★ Nature Trail
WALKING

(₹250, guide ₹500; ⊙ dawn-11am & 3pm or 4pm-dusk) Almost any experienced safari-goer will tell you that while a 4WD safari is wonderfully exciting and allows you to get close to the big-name creatures, nothing beats the drama of a walking safari, which allows you to touch, smell and hear the jungle in a way that is impossible in a 4WD. A good guide will bring the environment to life and point out the little things that keep the ecosystem ticking over.

A 4km trail starts from Khatia gate and skirts the edge of the reserve's core zone before looping back to the village. Mostly you'll see monkeys and birds, but tigers do venture into this area on occasions and an accompanying guide is obligatory.

Many top-end accommodation options also organise buffer-zone nature walks, normally complimentary for guests.

🛏 Sleeping & Eating

Plenty of midrange and top-end lodges and resorts are dotted around the countryside within about 10km of the Khatia and Mukki gates. Nearly all can organise safaris for you, often in their own park-registered 4WDs. In general Mukki offers a quieter safari and more upmarket accommodation.

🛏 Near Khatia Gate

Motel Chandan HOTEL **$$**
(☑ 9009345333, 9424989289; www.motel chandan.com; Khatia; incl full board dm ₹1200, r with/without AC ₹2000/1800; ❄ 🛜) Superb, well-priced hotel that's just 200m from Khatia gate, Chandan has modernish rooms set around a courtyard garden, and the eight-bed dorm is the area's best budget bet. The friendly owner is a smooth guy with four of his own 4WDs and two resident naturalists for safaris, and he can put travellers together to share safari costs.

A new street-side restaurant (open to all) and more luxurious rooms were under construction at the time of research.

Baghira Jungle Resort HOTEL **$$**
(☑ 07649-277244; www.mptourism.com; Mocha; incl full board s/d ₹5250/5890; ❄ 🛜 🏊) This MP Tourism hotel on the bank of the Banjar River, 5km west of Khatia, is a solid choice. Accommodation comprises large villas each with three rooms on two floors. All rooms have air-con and river views of varying scope, and are comfy and reasonably tasteful in tigerish golds and browns, with tiger-stripe rugs and tiger-pug pillowcases.

A bar and a good restaurant with mainly Indian fare complete the package. With a children's playground, pool and plenty of space, this is a good bet for family travellers.

Pugmark Resort LODGE **$$**
(☑ 07649-277291; www.pugmarkresort.com; Khatia; r incl full board ₹3200; ❄ 🛜) Great-value, spacious, primrose-coloured cottages, 700m off the main road in Khatia, are bright, airy and decorated with dry branches and tiger images and set around a pleasant, albeit slightly overgrown, garden. It's a well-oiled, family-run operation. Rahul, the owner/manager, is very knowledgeable and nails five-star service for three-star prices (in addition to being resident naturalist and artist).

From breakfast on up, the food is outstanding – they even use milk from their own two Holsteins. Wi-fi throughout.

AMERICAN/JUNGLE PLAN

Many of the resorts at the tiger reserves have part- and all-inclusive packages rather than straight accommodation prices. The so-called American Plan includes accommodation and all meals, while the Jungle Plan includes accommodation and meals plus safaris (often two a day).

★**Kipling Camp**   LODGE $$$

(☑ 07649-277218, 9811015221; www.kiplingcamp. com; Mocha; incl full board Indian s ₹12,000-13,100, d ₹16,600-18,800, foreigner s ₹16,400-22,000, d ₹22,000-26,400; ⊗ mid-Oct–early May; ❄ 🐾) 🐾 A wonderful, laid-back wildlife lodge owned by one of India's most dedicated tiger campaigners: film-maker, photographer and writer Belinda Wright. It's as informative as it is relaxing to stay in this jungle setting just 3km from Khatia gate, where wildlife discussions follow excellent communal meals and guests retire to delightful rustic-chic cottages slightly scented with the essence of colonial days.

Nature abounds in the fenceless grounds where langurs and chitals make regular appearances, only to be outshone by an occasional tiger or leopard (ask to look at the on-site camera-trap pictures). Expert, professional and charming staff can guide you on varied walks and excursions, and you can also swim in the river with Tara, the camp's memorable sexagenarian elephant, a truly extraordinary experience. Founded back in 1982, this was India's first-ever wildlife lodge and is run on an ecosensitive, not-for-profit basis, with profits channelled to numerous local community causes.

🛏 Near Mukki Gate

Kanha Safari Lodge   HOTEL $$

(☑ 07636-290715, 9329908054; www.mptourism. com; Mukki; incl full board s ₹3920-4900, d ₹5000-5440; ❄ 🐾) Decent, but generally unimaginative rooms (the air-con deluxe rooms are a bit jazzier) with firm beds are set in one- and two-storey villas around a central garden equipped with a rope bridge and several climbing devices for children. With a bar and reliable restaurant, this MP Tourism hotel is a dependable choice, well positioned just 1km from Mukki gate.

There's a 1600m nature trail on the edge of the property.

★**Salban**   HOMESTAY $$$

(☑ 7692835206, 8510839333; www.salbankanha. com; Baherakhar village, Mukki gate; s/d incl full board ₹7000/10,000; @) 🐾 This award-winning, luxury homestay, the beautiful, spacious home of a couple who are experts in wildlife and travel, makes a great base for the park's southern sector. Between safaris you can sip a G&T and spot birds from the verandah, enjoy great home cooking (the owners have written cookbooks), dip into

their fabulous library or wander around their acres of forest and organic garden.

★**Shergarh**   TENTED CAMP $$$

(☑ 07567953074, 09098187346; www.shergarh. com; Mukki gate; s/d incl full board ₹11,500/16,000; 🐾) 🐾 It's hard to top this intimate safari camp for bush-chic luxury. The setting, beside a swampy lake surrounded by forest, is perfect and the six well-spaced safari tents have solid, wooden beds and inviting bathrooms. The main, terracotta-roofed dining room has an open fire for winter nights and meals are hosted by a team of naturalists and natural raconteurs.

The camp is daringly unfenced, which means deer, wild boar and, occasionally, more toothy creatures stroll through camp at night. Excellent safari vehicles with an in-house naturalist accompanying all guests. All up, this is the camp of choice for the safari aficionado.

ℹ Information

There's an SBI ATM in Khatia, but it wasn't working at the time of research and nor had it for some time. A more reliable ICIC ATM can be found in Mocha. There are no banks or ATMs close to the Mukki gate.

ℹ Getting There & Away

BUS

There are six daily buses from Khatia to Mandla (₹60, 2½ hours, 6.30am, 8am, 8.30am, 12.45pm, 2.15pm, 5.30pm). For Jabalpur (₹100, 5½ hours) you have to change in Mandla, but it's hoped a direct bus will start operating shortly. For Raipur, there's one daily bus from Mocha (₹250, six hours, 8am).

Services from Mandla bus stand:

Jabalpur ₹100, 3½ hours, every 20 or 30 minutes from 5am to 6pm, hourly from 6pm to 11pm

Khatia ₹60, 2½ hours, 9.30am, 10am, 11.30am, 12.15pm, 1.50pm, 2.30pm, 4.15pm, 5.20pm

Nagpur No direct buses; take a bus to Chirai-dongri (₹30) and change there

Raipur seat/sleeper ₹400/450, eight hours, 9.30pm and 10.30pm

Travelling by bus from Kanha to the Bandhavgarh Tiger Reserve involves changes at Mandla, Shahpura and Umaria.

TAXI

Taxis from Khatia should cost ₹3200 to Jabalpur station, ₹3500 to its airport, and ₹4500 to ₹5000 to Nagpur or Raipur.

TRAIN

The nearest train station is Chiraidongri, 32km northwest of Khatia. Local trains run from here to Jabalpur (₹35). At the time of writing, the narrow-gauge line was being converted to a broad-gauge line, which will increase train services in this area.

Bandhavgarh Tiger Reserve

☑ 07627

If your sole reason for visiting an Indian tiger reserve is to see a tiger, look no further. Two or three days at Bandhavgarh (☑ 9424794315; www.bandhavgarh-national-park.com; core-zone entry per 6-passenger 4WD ₹1550, guide ₹360, 4WD rental ₹2500; ⊘ 4WD safaris daily except Wed afternoon mid-Oct–May) should net you a tiger sighting. India's 2014 tiger census counted 68 tigers here, the great majority of them in the relatively small (453 sq km) territory of Bandhavgarh National Park, which forms part of the reserve's core zone. Apart from tigers the park has a diverse range of other wildlife including plenty of, albeit rarely seen, leopards and more commonly sighted animals such as growing populations of wild boar and gaur, as well as lots of spotted deer and langurs.

The main base for visits is the small, laid-back village of Tala, 32km northeast of Umaria, the nearest train station. February to June are generally the best months for tiger sightings, but from April to June it's very hot, with temperatures often climbing above 40°C.

◉ Sights

Interpretation Centre   MUSEUM

(Tala; ⊘ 11am-2pm & 6-8pm, closed Wed evening) FREE Interesting exhibits detailing the history and legends of Bandhavgarh, plus some superb tiger photos on the 1st floor. It's behind the safari ticket office by the main road in Tala.

🏃 Activities

Jeep Safaris

All safaris start from Tala and head into one of three zones of Bandhavgarh National Park. Tala zone is entered from the village itself; the entrances to Khitauli and Maghdi (or Magadhi) zones are about 5.5km and 6km southwest of Tala along the Umaria road.

Up to 170 six-passenger safari 4WDs (known as gypsies) are allowed into the park per day, but most of these can only be booked online (http://forest.mponline.gov.in, up to 120 days in advance) and the website does not accept foreign cards for payment. Save yourself immense hassle by getting your hotel or agency to book your safari (typically an additional ₹1000) – and make arrangements as far ahead as possible, as safaris can sell out months in advance. Many of the more upmarket lodges and hotels block-book a number of safari tickets under the manager's name. This guarantees their guests will get a safari slot, but dramatically reduces the number of tickets available to independent travellers.

Just 12 4WDs per day (72 seats) can be purchased in person at the ticket office in Tala village half an hour before safari starting times, but queues can start forming as early as the night before. Morning safaris, starting between 5.30am and 6.45am (depending on the season) are longer than afternoon safaris (starting at 3pm) and tend to produce more tiger sightings.

You can usually arrange pickup and drop off at your hotel for an additional ₹300 to ₹400. Top-end and some midrange places often use their own safari 4WDs.

Other Options

If all else fails, you can book a ride in a canter (per person ₹550), lumbering 18-seat open 'minibuses' traversing the Maghdi and Khitauli zones. Tickets go on sale at the Tala ticket office half an hour before regular safari start times.

🛏 Sleeping & Eating

Tala Camp   GUESTHOUSE $$

(☑ 9424378258; www.talacamp.com; s/d incl full board ₹3000/3900; 🖥) 🎐 This friendly, family-run place in a rural setting just outside Tala village has clean, tiled rooms for an unbeatable price. More than that, a stay here also comes with the warm, fuzzy feeling of knowing that your money is helping the animals and people of the area.

The money generated by this guesthouse has contributed to building waterholes and supporting anti-poaching projects in the buffer zone.

Nature Heritage Resort   HOTEL $$

(☑ 07627-265351; www.natureheritageresort.com; Tala; s/d incl full board from ₹4000/5000; ❄🖥🐾) A decent choice for a good price. The adobe-toned rooms verge on jungle kitsch, but are pleasant and comfortable, and set in cottages around a shady bamboo grove. It has a couple of its own safari vehicles and an in-house naturalist who will accompany guests. The buffet meals (mainly Indian) are satisfying.

Tigergarh
LODGE $$

(☎ 9922820103, 7489826868; www.tigergarh. com; Ranchha Rd; incl full board s/d ₹4000/4500, cottage s/d ₹5000/5500; ☺ Oct-Jun; 🌫️🌀) 🅿 This stylish 11-room lodge sits under the nose of the surrounding hills in a peaceful spot 3.5km northwest of downtown Tala. The rustic-chic cottages (earthy tones with splashes of brighter colours and bits of folk art) provide considerable comfort, including four-poster beds and rain-style showers. A sustainability mantra permeates the property and the well-kept gardens have a natural feel.

The resident naturalist looks after guests in-house as well as on safaris.

★ Kings Lodge
LODGE $$$

(☎ 011-40146400, 9424642231; www.kingslodge. in; s/d incl full board & safaris ₹28,500/32,000; ☺ mid-Oct–May; 🌫️📶🌀) 🅿 It's as if the designers of this exemplary place read a handy guide to creating the ultimate bush-chic safari lodge and complied exactly. Superplush cottages on stilts are hidden among dense foliage in a quiet buffer-zone setting. Rooms are luxurious, without being over the top, and the Indian meals are generous and delicious.

Every evening there are drinks around a campfire and either a talk or film on an aspect of the park and wildlife. There's a superb swimming pool, quality safari 4WDs, and very experienced and knowledgeable naturalists accompany guests on safari. The company behind it supports numerous community and conservation projects. Check out the on-site butterfly garden and organic veggie patch.

★ Malaya Cafe
CAFE $$

(Main Rd, Tala; dishes ₹80-150, breakfast ₹375; ☺ 9am-8pm Oct-Jun; 📶) This welcoming cafe run by an extroverted escapee from the marketing business in Ahmedabad does fabulous pure-veg breakfast/brunches that are the perfect finish to a morning safari. Real filter coffee or homemade lemonade, fresh and dried fruit, porridge, and lentil pancakes with salad or mashed potatoes typically find their way to your plate. Bookings the previous day advisable.

❶ Information

All of Tala's services are located along a 100m stretch on the main street, including the post office, internet cafes (per hour ₹50), restaurants and a State Bank of India ATM.

❶ Getting There & Away

A cycle-rickshaw between Umaria's train station and bus stand costs ₹10 (10 minutes). Buses to Tala (₹40, one hour) run about half-hourly from 8am to 7pm. Outside those hours, you'll have to take an autorickshaw from the train station (₹600 to ₹700) or arrange a taxi in advance (from ₹1800 to ₹2500).

The last bus from Tala back to Umaria bus stand is at 7pm. There are no autorickshaws in Tala.

TRAIN

Trains from Umaria include the 18477 Utkal Express at 8.55pm to Delhi (Nizamuddin Station; sleeper/3AC/2AC ₹425/1160/1675, 18 hours) via Gwalior (₹320/875/1255, 11 hours), Agra (₹365/995/1425, 14 hours) and Mathura (₹380/1040/1500, 15 hours), and the 18234 Narmada Express at 4.36pm to Jabalpur (sleeper/3AC/2AC ₹90/450/635, 4½ hours), Bhopal (₹285/765/1100, 12 hours), Ujjain (₹360/980/1415, 16 hours) and Indore (₹385/1060/1530, 18½ hours).

The best daily train to Varanasi is the 15160 Sarnath Express (sleeper/3AC/2AC ₹275/745/1070, 12 hours, 4.19am). There are also a number of other fast trains running on different days of the week. Many stop at Satna, where you can catch buses to Khajuraho.

For Raipur (Chhattisgarh), there are three daily trains including the 15159 Sarnath Express (sleeper/3AC/2AC ₹230/620/885, eight hours, 10.16pm)

An alternative to Umaria is Katni, a busier railway junction with direct trains to places like Jabalpur, Satna and Varanasi. You can get to Katni by bus from Umaria (₹60, 2½ hours, 7.30am and half-hourly from 9am to 6pm).

Pench Tiger Reserve

☎ 07695

The third of Madhya Pradesh's trio of well-known tiger reserves, **Pench** (☎ 07692-223794; www.penchtiger.co.in; core-zone entry per 6-passenger 4WD ₹1550, obligatory guide ₹360, 4WD rental ₹2500; ☺ daily except Wed afternoon Oct-Jun) is made up mostly of teak-tree forest rather than sal, and so it has a different flavour from nearby Kanha or Bandhavgarh. It also sees fewer tourists (and fewer tigers); you'll often feel like you have the whole forest to yourself. Even if no tigers appear, there'll be a variety of other wildlife, and the forests are beautiful in their own right.

Pench Tiger Reserve has a total area of 1921 sq km – 60% in Madhya Pradesh, the rest in Maharashtra. The majority of its tigers are on the MP side, specifically in Pench National Park (part of the tiger reserve's core area), which has around 50 of the big stripeys. By far the easiest reached and most used of the park's three entry points is Turia gate, 12km west of Khawasa on the Jabalpur–Nagpur Hwy 44.

🏃 Activities

Jeep Safaris From Turia Gate

Up to 34 six-passenger safari 4WDs (gypsies) are allowed into the national park at the Turia gate for each morning and evening safari slot. But most of these are sold online (http://forest.mponline.gov.in, up to 120 days in advance) and the website doesn't accept foreign cards for payment. It's best to get hotels or agencies to make your safari bookings (generally an additional ₹1000). Do this as far ahead as possible, as safaris often sell out weeks – and even months – in advance.

Tickets for three 4WDs (18 seats) per safari can be purchased in person at the Turia gate from one hour before the safaris begin.

Morning safaris tend to produce more tiger sightings. The smaller number of tigers here means there are generally fewer visitors, so the park can feel less busy and there's (slightly) less emphasis on tigers and tigers alone. For a dedicated wildlife-watcher interested in the bigger picture, this makes this park especially enjoyable.

You can usually arrange for pickup and drop-off at your hotel for an extra few hundred rupees on top of the vehicle-and-driver rental.

Other Safaris

If you just can't get seats in regular 4WD safaris, you can book a ride in a **canter** (₹530), lumbering 18-seat open 'minibuses' operating from Khatia and Mukki gates. Or you can opt for a **buffer zone safari** (per 4WD ₹4000; ⏰dawn-11am & 3pm or 4pm-dusk) from Khatia gate. Tickets for both are sold early the previous evening for morning rides, and in the late morning for afternoon sessions.

🛏 Sleeping & Eating

Kipling's Court
HOTEL $$
(☎07695-232830; www.mptourism.com; incl full board dm ₹1780, r ₹5420-5900; ❄@🛜🏊) This

government-run property, 2km from Turia gate, wins in both the budget category and the family category (it boasts the best playground in Turia). Considering prices include all meals, the two well-kept, six-bed dorms are fine value, though staff can be reluctant to rent them to foreigners. The rooms, in cottages around dutifully manicured gardens, are only average though.

★Baghvan
RESORT $$$
(☎022-66011825; www.tajsafaris.com; r incl full board from ₹24,500; ❄🛜🏊) 🍃 Taj Hotels has luxury properties at all of MP's major tiger parks, but this discerning choice is the most jungly and jaw-dropping. Twelve massive bamboo, sal and concrete cottages are hidden amid the forest and feature exquisite artwork and furniture, indoor/outdoor showers and massive elevated machans (open-air patios).

The common areas follow suit, pleasantly offset by some whimsical art and artefacts. Food is predictably divine. It's 1km from Turia gate and reservations are required. Rates vary wildly with season and demand; B&B and jungle plan (full board plus safaris) are also available.

Tiger 'N' Woods
LODGE $$$
(☎8888399166; http://tigernwoods.com; r incl full board ₹6000; ❄🛜🏊) Friendly young staff lend this place a relaxed, informal atmosphere and the rooms, in wooden stilt houses, are plain but pleasing, with forest-view bathrooms and verandahs. The in-house naturalist leads nature walks. You can have a massage while you're here too.

Mowgli's Den
LODGE $$$
(☎07695-232832; www.mowglisdenpench.com; r incl full board ₹6500; ❄) Mowgli's, 2.5km from Turia gate, has 10 large, comfortable, circular cottages in verdant gardens, all with bamboo furnishings and big bathrooms. The welcoming owners are real wildlife enthusiasts, with plenty of Pench information, and sometimes accompany guests on safaris.

ℹ Information

A Bank of Maharashtra ATM in Khawasa accepts foreign cards.

ℹ Getting There & Away

Frequent buses link Khawasa with Nagpur (₹100, two hours, every half hour) and Jabalpur (₹180 to ₹200, six hours, every half hour). Shared 4WDs (₹20) run between Khawasa and

Turia when full. The national-park gate is 3km beyond Turia village. The nearest airport and major train station are at Nagpur (₹2000 to ₹2500 by taxi).

You can go to Kanha Tiger Reserve from Khawasa without going all the way to Jabalpur or Mandla. Flag down any northbound bus to Seoni (₹55, one hour, every half hour), then take a Mandla-bound bus to Chiraidongri (₹95, three hours, about hourly from 6.40am to 10.40pm), where there are nine daily buses to Khatia gate (₹30, one hour, 11am to 6pm).

CHHATTISGARH

Chhattisgarh is remote, short on major 'sights' and limited in tourist infrastructure, but for the adventurous traveller, time spent here may well prove to be a highlight of your trip to this part of India. The country's most densely forested state (44%) is blessed with considerable natural beauty – waterfalls and unspoilt nature reserves abound. More interestingly, it's home to 42 different tribes whose pointillist paintings and spindly sculptures are as vivid as the colourful haats (p686) that take place across the region, particularly around Jagdalpur in the southern Bastar region.

Raipur

📞 0771 / POP 1.01 MILLION

Chhattisgarh's ugly, busy capital is a centre for the state's steel and other industries and, apart from the ruins at Sirpur, a day trip away, has little to detain you. The Chhattisgarh Tourism Board office here is worth visiting, though. The state government, as well as new educational institutions, hospitals, offices, a technology park and an international cricket stadium, are located in the new city of Naya Raipur, 20km southeast. The city airport is also the closest airport to the southern Mukki-gate entrance of Kanha Tiger Reserve (p678).

🛏 Sleeping

★ **Hareli Eco Resort**   HOTEL **$$**
(📞 9111009064, 0771-4066415; www.tourism.cg.gov.in; Mohda village; r ₹2500; 🅿) 🏊 The best Chhattisgarh Tourism property in the state. There are 12 well-kept stilt-cottage rooms beside a small lake on the south side of **Barnawapara Wildlife Sanctuary** (🌙 Nov–Jun). The wood-lined rooms are big and bright, and have small terraces overlooking the bird-

filled waters. At night, staff light a campfire and the whole place runs off solar power.

★ **Hotel Le Roi**   HOTEL **$$**
(📞 0771-2971354; www.leroihotels.com; MFC Bldg, beside Raipur Junction station; r ₹2100-2600; 🅿 🎏) If you're in this price bracket, don't waste time looking any further than the bright, friendly, efficient Le Roi, right beside the station. Spotless, good-sized, pine-accented rooms have good wi-fi, good air-con, tea/coffee facilities and up-to-date bathrooms where it's a delight to step into the shower.

There's a 24-hour restaurant and coffee shop too. Airport transfers ₹500.

ℹ Information

Chhattisgarh Tourism Board (📞 9926781331, 0771-6453336; tic.rypstation@visitcg.in; Raipur Junction station; 🕖 7am-10pm) Gives statewide advice and can help organise tribal visits, transport, accommodation and guides. Also has a booth at the airport.

ℹ Getting There & Away

AIR

Raipur's Swami Vivekananda Airport is 14km southeast of the centre.

Air India flies to Delhi, Mumbai, Nagpur and Visakhapatnam once or twice daily, and, through its subsidiary Alliance Air, to Bhopal, Jaipur and Kolkata.

IndiGo flies to Delhi and Hyderabad daily and Bengaluru (Bangalore), Chennai, Goa, Indore, Kolkat and Mumbai, and Patna less frequently.

BUS

The main terminal is the somewhat-chaotic **Pandri Bus Stand** (LIC Rd), 2.5km southeast of the train station. An autorickshaw from the prepaid stand outside the train station to the bus station costs ₹50.

Mahendra Travels (📞 0771-4054444; www.mahendrabus.in) is a reliable company with buses to Jagdalpur (seat ₹395, sleeper ₹425 to ₹600, eight hours, every 15 minutes from 5.15am to midnight) and Nagpur (seat/sleeper non-AC ₹300/400, AC ₹600/800, eight hours, eight buses daily).

Dolphin (www.dolphinbusservice.com) runs to Bhubaneswar (Odisha; AC, ₹710/780, 12 hours, 7.15pm).

TRAIN

Useful trains include the 18237 Chhattisgarh Express to Delhi (Nizamuddin station; sleeper/3AC/2AC ₹565/1525/2225, 28 hours, 4.20pm) via Nagpur (5½ hours), Bhopal (14 hours), Jhansi (21 hours), Gwalior (22 hours) and Agra

SIRPUR & AROUND

A possible day or overnight trip from Raipur, the village of Sirpur, 80km east, is dotted with the remains of dozens of Buddhist and Jain monasteries and Hindu temples from the 6th and 7th centuries AD. Many of the excavations are works in progress. The pineapple-shaped 7th-century **Laxman Temple** (Indian/foreigner ₹15/200; ⊙ dawn-dusk) is mostly intact and is one of the oldest brick temples in India. The other main highlights (free to enter, normally open 8am to 6pm) are Teevardwo Buddhist Monastery, with very fine sculptures; the Surang Tila, a highly unusual, pyramid-like Shiva temple faced in white stone; the Anand Prabhu Kuti Vihara (another Buddhist monastery); and the 18th-century Gandeshwar Temple on the bank of the Mahanadi River, still very much a living shrine to Shiva.

The **Tourism Information Centre** (⊙ 10am-5pm), beside the hotel gate at the entrance to the village, has a useful sketch map.

Hiuen Tsiang Tourist Resort (☑ 0771-4066415; s/d ₹1600/2310; ❋) provides big, white air-conditioned rooms with comfy beds and large bathrooms with small bathtubs. Simple Indian meals (mains ₹90 to ₹170) are available. Little English spoken. It can do meals for nonguests but needs a couple of hours' notice.

Buses from Raipur's Pandri Bus Stand go to Mahasamund (₹45, 1½ hours, half-hourly), from where there are buses to Sirpur (₹35, one hour) every hour. A taxi day trip from Raipur should cost around ₹1600.

(24 hours), and the 12859 Gitanjali Express to Kolkata (Howrah station; sleeper/3AC/2AC ₹440/1170/1665, 13 hours, 11.35pm). Other daily trains head to Bhubaneswar, Visakhapatnam, Jabalpur and Varanasi.

Jagdalpur

☑ 07782 / POP 125,000

The capital of the southern Bastar region is an ideal base for exploring tribal Chhattisgarh. The town itself hosts a *haat* (market) every Sunday where you'll see Adivasis (tribal people) buying, selling and bartering alongside town traders, but it's in the surrounding villages that Adivasi life can be fully appreciated. Some villages are extremely remote, and only really accessible with a guide. Others, though, are just a bus ride away and, particularly on market days, can be explored independently.

Sanjay Market, which bursts the Sunday *haat*, is the heartbeat of Jagdalpur. The gaily painted maharaja's palace, 500m north at the end of Palace Rd, is the town's main landmark.

◉ Sights

Anthropological Museum   MUSEUM
(Chitrakote Rd; ⊙ 10.30am-5.30pm Mon-Fri) FREE
Jagdalpur's old-fashioned-looking museum, 3km west of the centre, has illuminating exhibits on tribal customs and culture, as well as many artefacts collected from tribal villag-

es in the 1970s and 1980s. The outdoor sections include re-creations of village houses.

✸✸ Festivals & Events

★ **Bastar Dussehra**   CULTURAL
(⊙ Sep/Oct) In Bastar, the Dussehra date (usually in early October) is just the last of 75 days of rituals and preparations that give Bastar Dussehra claim to be one of the world's longest festivals. Things climax in the final 10 days, and especially the last two nights, with a gigantic wooden chariot *(rath)* being tugged around Jagdalpur by teams of rope-pullers.

⏝ Sleeping & Eating

There are some cheap and mostly grungy hotels near the bus stand and a handful of better places around the centre. The top place in the area, though not actually luxurious, is **Dandami Luxury Resort** (☑ 0771-4224999, 18001026415; s/d incl breakfast from ₹2000/2500; ❋) out at Chitrakote Falls.

Devansh Residency   HOTEL $$
(☑ 07782-221199; www.devanshresidency.com; Collectorate Rd; r incl breakfast from ₹2200; ❋ ☎) A standard, small-town Indian business hotel offering large, but utterly forgettable rooms that are moderately well kept and come equipped with wi-fi and good toiletry kits. The in-house pure-veg **Vaishnavi** (Devansh Residency, Collectorate Rd; mains ₹140-250; ⊙ 7.30am-10.30pm; ☎) restaurant is one of the best in town.

ℹ Information

Tourism Information Centre (☑ 07782-2008001; ctbbastar@rediffmail.com; beside Shahid Park; ⏰ 10am-7pm Mon-Sat) Can help with arrangements for visiting tribal villages, and also sells Bastar handicrafts. It's just off Main Rd, 1km east of the centre.

ℹ Getting There & Around

BUS

The bus stand is about 1.5km south of the centre (₹20 by autorickshaw). Mahendra Travels (p684) and **Kanker Roadways** (☑ 9981199101; www.kankerroadways.in) run buses to Raipur (non-AC from ₹390, AC sleeper ₹500, eight hours) every 15 or 30 minutes from 5am to midnight.

TRAIN

India's highest broad-gauge line heads over the Eastern Ghats to Vizianagram near the Andhra Pradesh coast. The 18448 Hirakhand Express leaves at 2.30pm for Bhubaneswar (sleeper/3AC/2AC ₹395/1085/1565, 18 hours). The 58502 Kirandul–Visakhapatnam Passenger leaves at 9.55am for Visakhapatnam (sleeper ₹140, 10½ hours). Both trains stop at Koraput, Odisha (Orissa), about three hours from Jagdalpur.

The **reservation office** (⏰ 8am-noon & 2-4pm Mon-Sat, 8am-noon Sun) is at the station, 2.5km south of the centre, past the bus stand.

BASTAR HAATS & ADIVASI VILLAGES

There are eight main tribes in Bastar spread among more than 3500 villages, ranging from the Ghadwa (specialists in bell metal) to the Doria in the far southern forests, the only tribe to make their homes from tree branches and leaves (instead of mud thatch). One of the most fascinating ways to get a taste of Bastar's vibrant Adivasi culture is the colourful *haats* (markets). These are the lifeblood of tribal Chhattisgarh. Tribal people walk up to 20km to trade (often barter) everything from their distinctive, almost fluorescent, saris to live red ants.

You'll find all kinds of fascination here, including bell-metal craftwork (a mix of bronze and brass), a skill passed down through generations for some 300 years in some cases. The large piles of what look like squashed dates are in fact dried *mahuwa* flowers, either eaten fresh, or dried then boiled to create steam, which is fermented to produce a potent liquor, the favourite tipple of many Bastar Adivasis.

You can get to many local Adivasi villages by bus from Jagdalpur (most start from Sanjay Market) and this is certainly an option on market days – but some are pretty inaccessible, and if you want to actually meet tribal people, rather than just look at them, a guide is essential as a translator if nothing else. They can also help you arrange homestays. A day with **Awesh Ali** (☑ 9425244925; aweshali@gmail.com; per day from ₹1500) is a truly enlightening experience. He's a highly experienced guide who speaks nine languages (four of which are tribal). Contact him directly, or through Jagdalpur's Tourism Information Centre. A car and driver (which the tourist office can organise) will cost from ₹1400 to ₹1800 per day including fuel.

Most *haats* run from around noon to 5pm. There are many of them – the following are just some of the more popular ones. Ask at Jagdalpur's Tourism Information Centre for details. Shared 4WDs normally hang around markets to take people back to Jagdalpur.

WHEN	WHERE	DISTANCE FROM JAGDALPUR	BUS FROM JAGDALPUR (FARE, DURATION)	FEATURES
Mon	Tokapal	16km	₹25, 30min	bell-metal craftwork from Ghadwa Adivasis
Wed	Darbha	35km	₹45, 1hr	attended by Dhurwa Adivasis
Thu	Bastar	20km	₹30, 30min	easy to reach from Jagdalpur
Fri	Lohandiguda	36km	₹45, 1¼hr	Halba, Muria and Maria tribes; 1km off Chitrakote road
Fri	Nangur	22km	no direct bus	attended by distant forest Adivasis
Fri	Nagarnar	24km	no direct bus	colourful Bhatra Adivasis
Sat	Kuknar	70km	₹65, 2hr	Bison-Horn Maria stronghold
Sun	Jagdalpur	-	-	city location, open late into the evening
Sun	Pamela	12km	₹10, 20min	animated crowds

Around Jagdalpur

Kondagaon

Just off the Raipur road, 77km north of Jagdalpur, the admirable NGO **Saathi** (☎9425259152, 9993861686; www.facebook.com/saathikondagaon; ⊙8am-5.30pm Mon-Sat) ✈ provides crafts training and marketing help (through fair-trade organisations), and assistance in fields like health, education and hygiene, to more than 300 villages. It has workshops and a sales showroom on-site (with some fine bell-metal and wrought-iron pieces, from as little as ₹150) and can provide guides to visit area artisans (₹500 to ₹1000 per day) as well as tuition for one week or longer in bell metal, wrought iron, terracotta or woodcarving.

Head west along Hwy 130D about 3km north of Kondagaon, and within 1km you'll see the Saathi Samaj Sevi Sanstha sign. There's a clean basic guesthouse here with rooms for ₹500 to ₹600 and three vegetarian meals a day available for ₹250.

Chitrakote Falls

Calling the 300m wide and 32m high Chitrakote Falls the 'Indian Niagara' is actually not too far off the mark. Spectacular at any time, India's widest waterfall is at its roaring best after rains. The falls are on the Indravati River, 40km northwest of Jagdalpur. Buses (₹45, 1½ hours, 9am, 11am and 2pm) leave from Anupama Chowk, on Chitrakote Rd 500m from Sanjay Market. The last one back to Jagdalpur is at 4pm. A taxi round trip costs around ₹1500 ₹1800.

Buses to Tirathgarh village (₹45, one hour), leaving Sanjay Market in Jagdalpur several times a day, will drop you at this intersection or at the start of the 1km access track to the falls. A taxi round trip from Jagdalpur is ₹1400 to either the falls or the caves, or ₹1800 for both.

Kanger Valley National Park

An enjoyable outing from Jagdalpur, this park covers 200 sq km in a thickly forested valley south of Jagdalpur, with a number of waterfalls and caves. Visitors head to two main sites. One is Tirathgarh Falls, tumbling 35m in several sections down a canyon formed by the Mugabahar River, a Kanger River tributary. The other is **Kutumsar Cave** (guide ₹250; ⊙8am-3pm Nov-Jun), where guides lead you through up to 300m of narrow passages, concrete steps and large chambers with many stalactites and stalagmites. A taxi round trip from Jagdalpur is ₹1400 to either the falls or the caves, or ₹1800 for both.

Gujarat & Diu

Includes ➜

Best Places to Eat

➜ Vishalla (p697)

➜ Nilambag Palace Restaurant (p707)

➜ Peshawri (p704)

➜ Bhatiyar Gali (p697)

➜ Toran Dining Room (p697)

Best Places to Stay

➜ House of MG (p695)

➜ Diwan's Bungalow (p696)

➜ Bhuj House (p729)

➜ Kathiwada Raaj Mahal (p705)

➜ Orchard Palace (p722)

➜ Royal Oasis (p726)

➜ Desert Coursers Eco Lodge (p734)

Why Go?

Unfairly overlooked by many travellers scurrying between Mumbai and Rajasthan, Gujarat is an easy, and highly rewarding, sidestep off the tourist trail. While its major city Ahmedabad can draw you in with its deep sense of culture and remarkable architecture, the countryside holds most of the state's many treasures. Artisans in tribal villages weave, embroider, dye and print some of India's finest textiles, and excellent parks harbour unique wildlife, including migratory birds, wild asses and growling prides of Asiatic lions. Sacred Jain and Hindu pilgrimage sites sit atop mountains that rise dramatically from vast flatlands. For lovers of sand and sea, the chilled-out, former Portuguese island enclave of Diu lies just off the state's southeastern coast.

Gujarat also claims a special relationship to Mahatma Gandhi – he was born here, he ignited the satyagraha movement from here, he made his Salt March here – and his legacy remains visible in many places.

When to Go
Ahmedabad

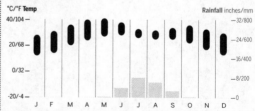

Sep & Oct The Navratri festival brings music and dancing to every town and village.

Nov & Dec It's custard-apple milkshake time in Junagadh.

Nov–Mar Best for Gujarat's national parks and wildlife sanctuaries.

Gujarat & Diu Highlights

1 Kachchh (p727) Exploring tribal villages to admire and acquire some of India's best textiles.

2 Gir National Park & Wildlife Sanctuary (p716) Taking a forest safari in search of Asia's only wild lions.

3 Ahmedabad (p690) Tackling a thali, exploring the old-city mosques, and paying homage to Mahatma Gandhi.

4 Junagadh (p718) Exploring this little-visited town with its extraordinary pilgrimage sites, towering fortress and old quarter.

5 Wild Ass Sanctuary (p734) Looking for Indian wild asses, wolves, hyenas and nilgai antelopes amid the salt plains of Little Rann of Kachchh.

6 Diu (p709) Letting loose in this former Portuguese enclave and scootering around its near-empty roads.

7 Shatrunjaya (p709) Undertaking a dawn pilgrimage to the hilltop Jain temple near Palitana.

History

It's said that Gujarat's Temple of Somnath witnessed the creation of the universe; sometime later, the state became Krishna's stomping ground. On a firmer historical footing, Lothal and Dholavira (Kachchh) were important sites of the Indus Valley civilisation more than 4000 years ago. Gujarat featured in the exploits of the mighty Buddhist emperor Ashoka, and Jainism first took root under a grandson of Ashoka who governed Saurashtra.

The rule of the Hindu Solanki dynasty from the 10th to 13th centuries, with its capital at Patan, is considered Gujarat's cultural golden age. Solanki rule was ended when Ala-ud-din Khilji brought Gujarat into the Delhi sultanate after several campaigns around 1300. A century later the Muslim Gujarat sultanate broke free of Delhi rule and established a new capital at Ahmedabad. The Mughal empire conquered Gujarat in the 1570s and held it until the Hindu Marathas from central India occupied eastern and central Gujarat in the 18th century. The British set up their first Indian trading base at Surat on Gujarat's coast in about 1614, and replaced Maratha power in the early 19th century.

It was from Gujarat that Gandhi launched his program of nonviolent resistance against British rule, beginning with protests and fasting, and culminating with the 390km Salt March, which drew the attention of the world and galvanised anti-British sentiment across India. After Independence, eastern Gujarat became part of Bombay state. Saurashtra and Kachchh, initially separate states, were incorporated into Bombay state in 1956. In 1960 Bombay state was divided along linguistic lines into Gujarati-speaking Gujarat and Marathi-speaking Maharashtra. The capital was shifted to the planned city of Gandhinagar in 1970.

The Congress Party of India largely controlled Gujarat until 1991, when the Bharatiya Janata Party (BJP) came to power. In 2002 communal violence erupted after a Muslim mob was blamed for an arson attack on a train at Godhra that killed 59 Hindu activists. Hindu gangs set upon Muslims in revenge. In three days an estimated 2000 people were killed (official figures are lower) – most of them Muslims – and tens of thousands were left homeless. The BJP-led state government was widely accused of tacitly, and sometimes actively, supporting some of the worst attacks on Muslim neighbourhoods for political gain. Later that year Gujarat's then chief minister Narendra Modi won a landslide re-election victory. A decade hence, in 2012, a former BJP minister was convicted of criminal conspiracy and murder in the Naroda Patiya massacre during the Godhra riots, but Modi has thus far been cleared of all charges related to the violence. Since the 2002 riots, Gujarat has been peaceful, and it enjoys a reputation as one of India's most prosperous and businesslike states. And Modi, of course, became India's prime minister in 2014.

EASTERN GUJARAT

Ahmedabad (Amdavad)

📳 079 / POP 6.36 MILLION

Ahmedabad (also called Amdavad, Ahmadabad or Ahemdavad), Gujarat's major city, will bowl you over – in good ways and bad. Yes, with traffic, noise, and air so thick you can chew it, the place can be a little overwhelming, but the city quickly wins you over with its incredible architecture, ranging from centuries-old mosques and mausoleums to cutting-edge contemporary design. Then there's the old quarter, where the narrow streets hide excitement around every twisting corner. Throw in some excellent museums, fine restaurants and a bustling street-food scene and you end up with a city

TOP STATE FESTIVALS

Uttarayan (☉Jan; p695) Skies swarm with kites in Ahmedabad and other cities.

Modhera Dance Festival (☉around 20 Jan) Indian classical-dance jamboree.

Bhavnath Mela (Bhavnath Fair; ☉Feb/Mar) Hindu festival at the foot of sacred Girnar Hill near Junagadh.

Mahakali Festival (☉Mar/Apr) Pilgrims pay tribute to Kali at Pavagadh Hill.

Navratri (☉Sep/Oct; p695) Nine nights of dancing all around Gujarat.

Kartik Purnima (☉Nov/Dec) A multifaceted holy day for Hindus, Jains, and Sikhs (who celebrate it as Guru Nanak Jayanti). There's a large fair at Somnath (p714) and Jain pilgrims flock to Shatrunjaya Hill (p709).

that rightly deserves its place as India's first Unesco Urban World Heritage Site.

The old city, on the east side of the Sabarmati River, was once surrounded by a 10km-long wall, of which little remains except 15 gates. The new city, on the west side of the river, has several major universities and many middle-class neighbourhoods.

History

Ahmedabad was founded in 1411 by Gujarati sultan Ahmed Shah at the spot where, legend tells, he saw a hare chasing a dog and was impressed by its bravery. The city quickly spread beyond his citadel on the east bank of the Sabarmati, and by the 17th century it was considered one of the finest cities in India, a prospering trade nexus adorned with an array of fine Islamic architecture. Its influence waned, but from the second half of the 19th century Ahmedabad rose again as a huge textile centre (the 'Manchester of the East'). By the late 20th century many of the mills had closed and the subsequent economic hardship may have been a contributing factor to the communal violence that split the city in 2002, when about 2000 people, mostly Muslims, were killed. Today Ahmedabad is booming again as a centre for IT, education and chemical production on top of its traditional textiles and commerce, and it has been officially dubbed a 'megacity'.

◉ Sights

The most interesting part of Ahmedabad is the old city, east of the Sabarmati River – particularly the areas of Lal Darwaja, Bhadra Fort and Teen Darwaja, and the market streets that radiate from them.

★ Calico Museum of Textiles
MUSEUM

(☏079-22868172; www.calicomuseum.org; Sarabhai Foundation; ☺tours 10.30am-1pm Thu-Tue) FREE This museum contains one of the world's finest collections of antique and modern Indian textiles, all handmade and up to 500 years old. There are some astoundingly beautiful pieces, displaying incredible virtuosity and extravagance. You'll see Kashmiri shawls that took three years to make, and double-*ikat* cloths whose 100,000 threads were each individually dyed before weaving. A single tour is offered each day the museum is open; booking weeks in advance is absolutely essential as spaces are limited to 20.

★ Hutheesingh Temple
JAIN TEMPLE

(Balvantrai Mehta Rd; ☺6am-8pm) Outside Delhi Gate, this Jain temple is one of 300 *derasars* in Ahmedabad. Even if you've already seen some, this one will make your jaw drop in wonder at its delicate carvings of deities, flowers and celestial damsels in white marble. Built in 1848, it's dedicated to Dharamanath, the 15th Jain *tirthankar* (great teacher), and each of the 52 sub-shrines in the courtyard is home to his likeness, with bejewelled eyes. The caretaker may let you go on the roof.

No photos are allowed within the temple.

★ Sabarmati Ashram
HISTORIC SITE

(www.gandhiashramsabarmati.org; Ashram Rd; ☺8.30am-6.30pm) FREE In peaceful, shady grounds on the Sabarmati River's west bank, this ashram was Gandhi's headquarters from 1917 to 1930 during the long struggle for Indian independence. It's said he chose this site because it lay between a jail and a cemetery, and any *satyagrahi* (nonviolent resister) was bound to end up in one or the other. Gandhi's poignant, spartan living quarters are preserved, and there's a museum that presents a moving and informative record of his life and teachings.

It was from here, on 12 March 1930, that Gandhi and 78 companions set out on the famous Salt March to Dandi, on the Gulf of Cambay, in a symbolic protest, with Gandhi vowing not to return to the ashram until India had gained independence. The ashram was disbanded in 1933, later becoming a centre for Dalit welfare activities and cottage industries. After Gandhi's death some of his ashes were immersed in the river in front of the ashram.

It's about 5km north of Lal Darwaja. An autorickshaw from the city centre is about ₹50.

★ Sarkhej Roza
HISTORIC BUILDING

(☺9am-dusk) This mosque, tomb and palace complex is dedicated to the memory of Ahmed Shah I's spiritual adviser, Ahmed Khattu Ganj Baksh. The elegant, dilapidated buildings cluster around a great (often dry) tank, constructed by Sultan Mahmud Begada in the mid-15th century. It's an atmospheric place once used as a retreat by Ahmedabad's rulers. It's located in the Sarkhej area, 8km southwest of the old centre; a return autorickshaw from the city centre will cost around ₹150.

Ahmedabad (Amdavad)

Lalbhai Dalpatbhai Museum MUSEUM
(LD Museum; www.ldmuseum.co.in; University
Rd; ⏱10.30am-5.30pm Tue-Sun) FREE Part of
the LD Institute of Indology, this museum
houses a gorgeous collection of ancient and
medieval Indian art treasures, including
Buddhist, Hindu and Jain deities in stone,
marble and bronze, 75,000 Jain manuscripts
and some priceless miniature paintings. A
6th-century sandstone carving from Madhya
Pradesh is the oldest-known carved image of
the god Rama.

Lokayatan Folk Museum MUSEUM
(www.shreyasfoundation.in; ⏱3-5.30pm Tue-Sat,
10.30am-1pm & 3-5.30pm Sun) FREE This museum, 3km west of the river in Bhudarpura,
displays a fascinating range of Gujarati folk
arts – particularly from Kachchh – including
woodcarvings, metalwork, and some wonderful embroidered textiles and amazing
tie-dyed quilts. Look out for elaborate headdresses, beadwork, dowry boxes, household

utensils, camel and horse ornaments made
by the Rabari people and more. The curator
can give you a free tour. An autorickshaw
from the centre costs around ₹50; say you
want to go to the Shreyas Foundation.

Bhadra Fort FORT
(Lal Darwaja; ⏱dawn-dusk) Built immediately
after the founding of Ahmedabad in 1411,
Bhadra Fort houses government offices and
a Kali temple. Its mighty gate formed the
eastern entrance of the Ahmedabad citadel,
which stretched west to the river. Between
the fort and the **Teen Darwaja** (Triple Gateway;
Lal Darwaja) to its east was the Maidan Shahi
(Royal Sq), now a marketplace, where royal
processions and polo games took place. The
evenings are abuzz with food vendors, crushing crowds and sellers of all things bright,
plastic and glittery.

Swaminarayan Temple HINDU TEMPLE
(Kalupur; ⏱dawn-dusk) The glorious, multicoloured, carved-wood Swaminarayan Tem-

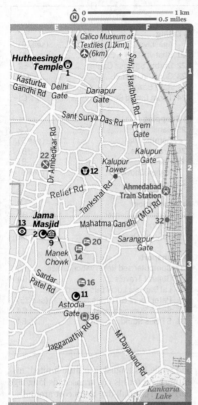

If you wish to photograph the building, you need to seek permission first.

City Museum
MUSEUM

(Sanskar Kendra, Bhagtacharya Rd; ⊙10am-6pm Tue-Sun) **FREE** Inside one of four city buildings designed by Le Corbusier, this museum covers Ahmedabad's history, craft, art, architecture and literature. It includes sections on religious communities, Gandhi and the Independence struggle, as well as a photography gallery and works by Gujarat's notable artists. On the ground floor there's a collection of 100 colourful kites, along with an exploration of the history of kite-flying (the Chinese were the first to do so, in 200 BC).

NC Mehta Gallery
MUSEUM

(University Rd; ⊙10.30am-5.30pm Tue-Sun) **FREE** This gallery has an important collection of jewel-like illustrated manuscripts and miniature paintings. Best known is *Chaurapanchasika* (Fifty Love Lyrics of a Thief), written by Vilhana, an 11th-century Kashmiri poet sentenced to be hanged for loving the king's daughter. Before his execution he was granted one final wish: he chose to recite these 50 poems, which so impressed the king that he gave Vilhana his daughter in marriage.

Vechaar Utensil Museum
MUSEUM

(☑079-26602422; www.vishalla.com; By-Pass Rd; ₹10; ⊙3-10.30pm Tue-Sun) At Vishalla restaurant (p697), this museum displays the graceful practicality of pots and utensils, with more than 4500 items from all over India, some 1000 years old. Look out for enormous oil containers, nutcrackers shaped like buxom women and a prototype samovar. It's around 7km southwest of the centre.

Toilet Garden
MUSEUM

(Safai Vidyalaya, Ashram Rd; ⊙10am-6pm Mon-Sat) **FREE** Who knew that the humble toilet could be so interesting? Part of the Sanitation Institute, the Toilet Garden displays designs for new ecofriendly toilet models. There are lots of diagrams explaining how to use each toilet, and someone from the institute is likely to give you a quick guided tour, during which you're guaranteed to learn something new about the room we all secretly love.

The institute was established by Ishwardada Patel (also known as Mr Toilet), who made it his life's work to promote sanitation across India, where around 40% of the population still don't have access to clean latrines. His other aim was to free human scavengers, belonging to the Dalit caste,

ple, in the old city, was built in 1822 as the first temple of the Swaminarayan Hindu sect. Followers believe that the sect's founder, Swaminarayan (1781–1830), was the supreme being. The daily **Heritage Walk** (☑9824032866; Indian/foreigner ₹30/50; ⊙8am) usually coincides with worship at the temple, with chanting and music on full display.

Mill Owners' Association Building
ARCHITECTURE

(www.atmaahd.com; Ashram Rd; ⊙10.30am-4.30pm Mon-Fri, to 12.30pm Sat) **FREE** One of four buildings in Ahmedabad designed by legendary Swiss-French architect Le Corbusier, this one is the most striking. A dramatic ramp rises up the building, with slanted concrete brise-soleil (sun breakers) that make up the eastern and western facades allowing air to circulate while blocking out the harsh sunlight. The mezzanine hosts temporary art exhibitions. Visits are only possible if requested 15 days in advance by email.

Ahmedabad (Amdavad)

◉ Top Sights
1	Hutheesingh Temple	E1
2	Jama Masjid	E3
3	Siddi Sayid's Mosque	A1

◉ Sights
4	Ahmed Shah's Mosque	D3
5	Bhadra Fort	D3
6	City Museum	C4
7	Lalbhai Dalpatbhai Museum	A2
8	Lokayatan Folk Museum	A4
9	Mausoleum of Ahmed Shah	E3
10	Mill Owners' Association Building	C2
	NC Mehta Gallery	(see 7)
11	Rani Sipri's Mosque	E3
12	Swaminarayan Temple	E2
13	Teen Darwaja	E3

◎ Activities, Courses & Tours
	Heritage Walk	(see 12)

◎ Sleeping
14	Deewanji Ni Haveli	E3
15	Diwan's Bungalow	D3
16	French Haveli	E3
17	Hotel Cadillac	A1
	Hotel Good Night	(see 19)
18	Hotel Volga	A1
19	House of MG	A1
20	Mangaldas Ni Haveli	E3

◎ Eating
	Agashiye	(see 19)
21	Bhatiyar Gali	A1
22	Darbar Samosa Center	E2
23	Gopi Dining Hall	C3
	Ratri Bazaar	(see 9)
24	Toran Dining Room	C1

◎ Shopping
25	Bandhej	C2
	Gamthiwala	(see 9)
26	Gramshree	B1
27	Hansiba	B1
	Manek Chowk	(see 9)
28	nidus	C4

ℹ Information
29	Apollo City Center	B3
30	Gujarat Tourism	C1
31	Tourism Desk	B2

ℹ Transport
32	Computerised Reservation Office	F3
33	Gujarat Travels	C4
34	Lal Darwaja Local Bus Stand	A1
	Patel Tours & Travels	(see 35)
35	Shree Swaminarayan	C4
36	ST Bus Stand	E4

from their degrading and dangerous job of cleaning dry latrines by hand.

Tours

With history woven tightly into its design and architecture, Ahmedabad can be a complex city to understand. To get the most out of a visit, it pays to hire a guide. The following are tried, tested and trusted. Some of them can also act as guides/drivers on longer tours around Gujarat.

Johnny (Shaikh Mukarran; ☑ 9824361058; ahmedabadtravels@gmail.com) You won't find a better, more helpful and friendlier guide to Ahmedabad and beyond than 'Johnny' (that's his nickname). He speaks fluent English and is an expert on art, textiles and architecture (he's the go-to man for visiting textile dealers) and he seems to know anyone and everyone in Gujarat. He can also drive you (safely) throughout the state.

Mohammed Malik (☑ 9825945393; nirupanchal @yahoo.co.in) Mohammed is a reliable, hard-working autorickshaw driver who's available to take you around Ahmedabad. He has a particular interest in architecture,

and while his English is a little limited, his enthusiasm for his city transcends language barriers. Half-/full-day tours cost around ₹600/1200.

Nirav Panchal (☑ 9825626387; nirupanchal@ yahoo.co.in) One of Gujarat's most knowledgeable guides, the charming Nirav leads customised tours, from single-day experiences in Ahmedabad to multiday trips across all parts of the state. He speaks perfect English, and his French isn't bad either. Call or email him for details and prices for tours based on your interests.

Saiyed Badrudin (☑ 7622884557 or 9510225587; easywaysaiyed@gmail.com) A very knowledgeable local guide, Ahmedabad native Saiyed is a fluent English speaker who's happy to arrange tailor-made city sightseeing excursions.

Salim A Chhipa (☑ 9979324103; salim madhupurwala@yahoo.com) A trustworthy and very fairly priced English-speaking guide and rickshaw driver, Salim is a self-taught expert on architecture and is used by many architecture students. Tours with rickshaw cost ₹160 per hour.

✳ Festivals

Uttarayan
CULTURAL

(Makar Sakranti; ⊙ 2nd week Jan) This tradition-al kite festival attracts international partic-ipants and is well worth the stiff neck, as visitors flood the city and kites fill the sky.

Navratri
HINDU FESTIVAL

(Festival of Nine Nights; ⊙ Sep/Oct) Navratri is celebrated India wide, but Gujarat has made it its own. This nine-night-long festival cele-brates feminine divinity in the forms of the goddesses Durga, Lakshmi and Saraswati – particularly Durga's slaying of the demon Mahishasura. Celebrations centre on special shrines at junctions, marketplaces and, in-creasingly, large venues that can accommo-date thousands.

People dress up in sparkling finery to whirl the night away in entrancing *garba* or *dandiya rasa* circle dances until the early hours. Celebrated in every town and village in Gujarat, Navratri is a festival where you may well find yourself joining in.

The night after Navratri is Dussehra, which celebrates the victory of Rama over Ravana, with more nocturnal dancing and fireworks, plus the burning of giant effigies of the defeated demon king.

🛏 Sleeping

Budget hotels are mostly clustered in the noisy, traffic-infested Lal Darwaja area, while the majority of midrange and top-end places are found on Khanpur Rd (paralleling the eastern bank of the Sabarmati), a more con-genial environment but further from most of the interesting sights. There are also sever-al beautiful heritage properties right in the heart of the old city.

Hotel Cadillac
HOTEL $

(☑ 079-25507558; Advance Cinema Rd, Lal Darwaja; r ₹600-700) If you're counting every last ru-pee, you could do worse than this option – an old-timer from 1934 that has kept its wooden balustrade. Mattresses are lumpy and small-er rooms are cell-like; larger rooms are OK, though, and it's kept fairly clean.

Hotel Volga
HOTEL $$

(☑ 079-25509497; www.hotelvolga.in; Hanuman Lane, Lal Darwaja; s/d ₹1345/1590; ※ 🛈) This surprisingly good option tucked down a nar-row street off Relief Rd, behind the House of MG, is worth searching out. Rooms are smart and clean, with many recently upgrad-ed and decorated with curved or padded headboards and accent lighting. Reception is efficient and you can order decent multi-cuisine food to your room. Avoid rooms below the 3rd-floor kitchen.

Hotel Good Night
HOTEL $$

(☑ 079-25506866; www.hotelgoodnight.co.in; Lal Darwaja; s/d from ₹1345/1570; ※ 🛈) One of the best cheapies around, the Hotel Good Night might actually live up to its name. The rooms are spotless and some are surprising-ly arty, while the shirt-and-tie-wearing staff lend a little class to the place.

★ House of MG
HERITAGE HOTEL $$$

(☑ 079-25506946; www.houseofmg.com; Lal Dar-waja; incl breakfast r from ₹6000, ste from ₹9000; ※ 🛈 🍽) Easily Gujarat's best hotel, this 1920s building – once the home of textile magnate Sheth Mangaldas Girdhardas – was convert-ed into a heritage hotel by his great-grandson. The rooms are vast, verandah edged and masterfully decorated, with a traditional yet luxurious ambience. Service is first rate, there

GUJARAT & DIU AHMEDABAD (AMDAVAD)

MOSQUES & MAUSOLEUMS

Under the Gujarati sultanate in the 15th and 16th centuries, and especially under Ahmed Shah I (1411–42) and Mahmud Begada (1459–1511), Ahmedabad was endowed with a remarkable collection of stone mosques in a unique style incorporating elements of Hindu and Jain design. Note that women are not allowed into the actual prayer halls, and at some mosques are restricted to the periphery.

Jama Masjid (Friday Mosque; MG Rd; ⊙6am-6pm) Built by Ahmed Shah in 1423, the massive Jama Masjid ranks as one of India's most beautiful mosques. Demolished Hindu and Jain temples provided the building materials, and the mosque displays some architectural fusion with these religions, notably in the lotus-like carving of some domes, which are supported by the prayer hall's 260 columns. The two 'shaking' minarets lost half their height in the great earthquake of 1819; their lower portions still flank the prayer hall's central portico.

Siddi Sayid's Mosque (Lal Darwaja; ⊙dawn-dusk) One of Ahmedabad's most stunning buildings, this mosque is famed for its exquisite *jali* windows, spiderweb fine, two of them depicting the intricate intertwining branches of the 'tree of life'. Built in the year the Mughals conquered Gujarat (1573) by an Abyssinian in the Gujarati army, it was once part of the old citadel wall.

Mausoleum of Ahmed Shah (Badshah-na-Hazira; MG Rd; ⊙dawn-dusk) This atmospheric mausoleum, outside the east gate of the Jama Masjid (p696), may have been constructed by Ahmed Shah himself before his death in 1442. His cenotaph is the central one under the main dome. An 11pm drumming session in the mausoleum's eastern gateway used to signal the closing of the city gates and still happens nightly, carrying on a nearly 600-year-old tradition. No women are allowed inside.

Ahmed Shah's Mosque (Swami Vivekananda Rd; ⊙dawn-dusk) Southwest of Bhadra Fort and dating from 1414, this is one of the city's earliest mosques, built for the sultan and nobles within Ahmedabad's original citadel. The prayer hall is a forest of beautifully carved stone pillars and *jali* (carved lattice) screens, and the elaborately carved insides of its cupolas have a circular symmetry reminiscent of Hindu and Jain temples.

Rani Sipri's Mosque (Astodia Gate Circle; ⊙dawn-dusk) This small mosque near the ST bus stand is also known as the Masjid-e-Nagira (Jewel of a Mosque) because of its graceful construction, with delicately carved minarets and a domed tomb with fine *jali* screens. It was commissioned in 1514 by Rani Sipri, the Hindu wife of Sultan Mahmud Begada; after her death, she was buried here. Ask the caretaker to unlock the dark and dusty room containing the queen's tomb.

are two excellent restaurants, and the indoor swimming pool is divine (the gym less so).

★**Diwan's Bungalow** HERITAGE HOTEL $$$
(☏079-25355428; MB Kadri Rd; r from ₹5000; ❉⊛) Tucked away in a lively neighbourhood a 10-minute walk from Badra Fort, this glorious restored 19th-century mansion has an air of casual elegance. The lobby and dining room are hung with period chandeliers and an interior terrace opens onto a garden courtyard. Every room is different, but each is large and tastefully appointed, blending modern amenities with historic touches.

Deewanji Ni Haveli HERITAGE HOTEL $$$
(☏079-22140830; www.cityhc.org; Sankadi Sheri, Manek Chowk; r incl breakfast from ₹5000; ⊜❉⊛) Part of the movement to regenerate heritage buildings in Ahmedabad, this striking 250-year-old *haveli* (traditional, ornately decorated residence) has been painstakingly restored. Surrounding a tranquil courtyard, its comfortable rooms – with stuccoed walls, heavy wooden beams and antique furnishings – are very atmospheric. Excellent breakfast included. It's opposite the neighbourhood of Ganga Dhiya ni Pol.

French Haveli HOMESTAY $$$
(☏9016430430, 9978910730; www.french haveli.com; Khida Sheri, Dhal-ni-pol, Astodia Chakra; incl breakfast s/d from ₹2500/3700, ste ₹5000; ⊜❉⊛) In the heart of one of the old city's *pols* (micro-neighbourhoods), this beautifully restored 150-year-old Gujarati heritage home opposite a Jain temple has five

individually decorated rooms. Agaashi, on the 2nd floor, has its own open-air terrace, whereas the Mahajan Suite is the most spacious. Terrific breakfast included. Not suitable for those with mobility difficulties, due to steep stairs. It's vital to book ahead and provide an estimated time of arrival. You'll also likely need them to give you directions, as it's very hard to find.

Mangaldas Ni Haveli　　BOUTIQUE HOTEL **$$$**
(☑079-25506946; www.houseofmg.com; Sankadi Sheri, Manek Chowk; r from ₹5740; ☎) Owned by the House of MG (p695), this intimate hotel has six rooms facing a tranquil courtyard and a mezzanine patio with traditional Gujarati swings. The animal-themed rooms are uniquely decorated using local stencil art; the cow rooms are the most spacious. There are enviable views of the *pol* (neighbourhood) from the upstairs terrace and the restaurant serves Gujarati fast food.

Just around the corner is a second house with two giant, suite-like rooms (₹6740) featuring marvellous carved woodwork. However, meals are served at the main building and you might feel a little lonely staying here on your own.

✗ Eating

Ahmedabad has the best range of restaurants in Gujarat, serving anything from Gujarati thalis and Mughlai curries to international cuisine. There are excellent food stalls and no-frills eateries in the old city, night markets at Manek Chowk and Law Garden, and more upmarket restaurants in the western half of the city and inside hotels.

Bhatiyar Gali　　INDIAN **$**
(Khaas Bazaar, Lal Darwaja; dishes from ₹30; ☺noon-1am) The narrow 'Cook's Lane' and adjoining alleyways really come into their own in the evenings, with no-frills eateries and stalls preparing meaty delights. Bera Samosa serves tiny, delicious, spicy meat samosas and deep-fried meatballs, while Bari Handa is the place for stews simmered in clay ovens overnight. Spicy skewers charcoal-grilled are good, too. It's just east of Teen Darwaza.

★ Ratri Bazaar　　MARKET **$**
(Manek Chowk; dishes from ₹40; ☺7.30pm-1.30am) This is by far the most popular night market in the city, and it heaves with hungry locals. Favourites include the dosa stall that dishes out the South Indian crispy pancake with myriad fillings, the biryani stalls, *kulfi*

(ice cream) from Asharfi Kulfi and Cadbury pizza (a crisp base with melted chocolate and cheese).

Darbar Samosa Center　　GUJARATI **$**
(Gheekanta Rd, Vishwa Karma Bhuwan; 12 samosas ₹60; ☺9am-9pm) The best known of several samosa shops on Gheekanta Rd, this family-run, hole-in-the-wall place has been producing Ahmedabad's tastiest samosas for around 60 years. It specialises in *navtad ni samosa* – small vegetable samosas stuffed with pulses, potato or peas and served with a sweet-and-sour wood-apple sauce with chilli and jaggery or a spicy chickpea gravy.

★ Toran Dining Room　　GUJARATI **$$**
(☑079-27542197; Ashram Rd; thali ₹250; ☺11am-3pm & 7-10pm; ❄) With almost 30 years' experience, bright and modern Toran serves Gujarati thalis of exceptional quality. Around 10 curries and pickles, plus an assortment of breads, will be piled onto your plate. Tuck in and enjoy one of Ahmedabad's best meals. It's busiest at lunchtime, when you might need to queue for a table.

Gopi Dining Hall　　GUJARATI **$$**
(☑9879514277; thali ₹250-330; ☺10.30am-3.30pm & 6.30-10.30pm; ❄) This little restaurant, which first swung open its doors 40 years ago, is a much-loved thali institution, with a small garden and an air-conditioned dining room. You can choose from 'fix', 'full' (unlimited) and 'with one sweet' options depending on how hungry you are. It's near the western end of Ellis Bridge, off Paldi Rd.

★ Vishalla　　INDIAN **$$$**
(☑079-26602422; www.vishalla.com; By-Pass Rd; dinner adult/child ₹689/377; ☺7.30-11pm) On the southwestern outskirts of town, Vishalla is a magical experience in an open-air, lantern-lit, rural fantasy setting complete with live cows! An endless thali of Gujarati dishes you won't find elsewhere is served on leaf plates, at low wooden tables under open-air awnings. Dinner includes excellent folk music, dance and puppet shows.

★ Agashiye　　GUJARATI **$$$**
(☑079-25506946; www.houseofmg.com; House of MG, Lal Darwaja; set meal regular/deluxe ₹990/1200; ☺noon-3.30pm & 7-10.30pm) On the rooftop terrace of the city's finest heritage hotel (p695), Agashiye's daily-changing, all-veg menu begins with a traditional welcome drink and is a cultural journey around the uniquely sweet Gujarati thali, with a multitude of diverse

dishes delivered to your plate. It finishes with hand-churned ice cream. For dinner, book ahead.

🔒 Shopping

★ Hansiba
ARTS & CRAFTS

(☎ 079-26405784; 8 Chandan Complex, CG Rd; ⊙ 11am-7.30pm Mon-Sat) 🍃 The retail outlet of the Self-Employed Women's Association (SEWA), Hansiba sells colourful woven and embroidered shawls, saris, beautifully embroidered ladies' tunics and wall hangings.

Manek Chowk
HANDICRAFTS

(Manek Chowk; ⊙ dawn-dusk) This busy space and the surrounding narrow streets are the commercial heart of the old city. Weave your way through the crowds to soak up the atmosphere and browse the vegetable and sweet stalls and silver and textile shops.

Gamthiwala
TEXTILES

(Manek Chowk; ⊙ 10.30am-7pm Mon-Sat) Gamthiwala, by the entrance to the Mausoleum of Ahmed Shah (p696) in the old city, sells quality block-printed and tie-dyed textiles.

Bandhej
FASHION & ACCESSORIES

(☎ 079-26422181; www.bandhej.com; Shree Krishna Centre, Netaji Rd; ⊙ 10am-8pm) 🍃 Traditional and contemporary saris, embroidered tunics, accessories and gifts – all handcrafted by expert craftspeople from around the country

using eco-friendly materials. There's beautiful glassware made in Ahmedabad, too.

nidus
GIFTS & SOUVENIRS

(☎ 079-26623692; National Insititute of Design, Paldi; ⊙ 11am-7pm Mon-Sat) This gift shop on the NID (National Institute of Design) campus stocks an excellent range of independent designs by the institute's alumni and students. Choose between funky jewellery, unconventional crockery, beautiful stainless-steel dining implements, toys, clothing, leather bags and fun stationery.

Gramshree
ARTS & CRAFTS

(☎ 079-22146530; www.gramshree.org; 4th fl, Shopper's Plaza, CG Rd; ⊙ 8am-8pm) 🍃 Beautiful handcrafted gifts – from embroidered pillowcases and traditional leather sandals to clothing, accessories, stationery and more. Gramshree is a grassroots organisation that supports and empowers more than 500 rural women and women living in slums and invests in various community programs.

ℹ Information

Apollo City Center (☎ 079-66305800; www. apolloahd.com; 1 Tulsibaug Society) is a small but recommended private hospital opposite Doctor House, near Parimal Garden.

All listed hotels have wi-fi, as do many of the more upmarket restaurants and cafes, other-

---

MAJOR TRAINS FROM AHMEDABAD

The most convenient train services are listed below.

DESTINATION	TRAIN NO & NAME	FARE (₹)	DURATION (HR)	DEPARTURE
Bhavnagar	12971 Bandra–Bhavnagar Exp	240/560/760 (A)	5½	5.15am
Bhuj	19115 Sayaji Nagari Exp	235/625/880 (A)	7¼	11.59pm
Delhi (NDLS–New Delhi)	12957 Rajdhani	N/A/2049/1445 (B)	14	5.40pm
Delhi (DLI–Old Delhi)	12915 Ashram Exp	485/1270/1810/3060 (C)	15¾	6.30pm
Jaipur	14312 Ala Hazrat Exp	350/950/1355 (A)	12¼	8.20pm
Jamnagar	22945 Saurashtra Mail	225/600/850/1405 (C)	6½	5.55am
Junagadh	22957 Somnath Exp	230/615/865 (A)	6¼	10.10pm
Mumbai	12010 Shatabdi	780/1655 (D)	6¾	2.40pm (Mon-Sat)
Mumbai	12902 Gujarat Mail	325/830/1160/1950 (C)	8½	10pm
Vadodara (Baroda)	12010 Shatabdi	330/670 (D)	1¾	2.40pm (Mon-Sat)

Fares: (A) sleeper/3AC/2AC, (B) 3AC/2AC/1AC, (C) sleeper/3AC/2AC/1AC, (D) AC chair/executive

wise **Relief Cyber Café** (Relief Rd; per hour ₹20; ⊙10am-midnight) has air-con.

There are numerous ATMs, including HDFC ones, in **Lal Darwaja** (Relief Rd) and slightly south of **Gandhi Bridge** (Ashram Rd).

HDFC Bank (Netaji Rd), near Shree Krishna Centre, changes currency, while **ICICI Bank** (2/1 Popular House, Ashram Rd; ⊙9am-6pm Mon-Fri) and **State Bank of India** (Lal Darwaja; ⊙11am-4pm Mon-Fri, to 1pm Sat) change both travellers cheques and currency. The **main post office** (⊙10am-7.30pm Mon-Sat, to 1pm Sun) is on Ramanlal Sheth Rd.

The very helpful **Gujarat Tourism** (☑079-26578044; www.gujarattourism.com; HK House; ⊙10.30am-6pm Mon-Sat, closed 2nd & 4th Sat of month) has all sorts of information at its fingertips and you can hire cars with drivers here. There's also an office at Ahmedabad train station.

Ahmedabad Municipal Corporation's office (**Tourism Desk** (☑079-32520878; Law Garden; ⊙10.30am-6pm Mon-Sat, closed 2nd & 4th Sat of month) has city maps and puts effort into answering questions.

The Uexplore (www.uexplore.in) website has very useful information, particularly for DIY walking tours.

Getting There & Away

AIR

Ahmedabad's **international airport** (☑079-22869211; www.ahmedabadairport.com) is 9km north of central Ahmedabad. Air India, IndiGo, Jet Airways, SpiceJet and GoAir have frequent flights to Bengaluru, Chennai, Delhi, Goa, Hyderabad, Jaipur, Kolkata and Mumbai.

TRAIN

There's a **computerised reservation office** (⊙8am-8pm Mon-Sat, to 2pm Sun) just outside the main Ahmedabad train station, which is the most convenient for departures. Window 3 handles the foreign-tourist quota. There are numerous daily services (especially to Mumbai).

Getting Around

The airport is 9km north of the centre; a prepaid taxi to the city should cost around ₹600, depending on your destination. An autorickshaw to the old city costs about ₹250.

Autorickshaw drivers are supposed to turn their meter to zero at the start of a trip and then calculate the fare using a conversion chart at the end, but few are willing to use them at all for foreigners, so negotiate before setting off. Short hops around the city should be around ₹40, and

---

BUSES FROM AHMEDABAD

Private buses coming from the north may drop you on Naroda Rd, about 7km northeast of the city centre – an autorickshaw will complete the journey for ₹70 to ₹80.

From the main **ST bus stand** (Gita Mandir Rd), also known as Gita Mandir or Astodia, around 1km southeast of Lal Darwaja, destinations served by state buses include the following.

DESTINATION	COST (₹)	TIME (HR)	FREQUENCY
Bhavnagar	ordinary/AC 130/250	3¾	17 daily
Bhuj	188	6¾	28 daily, mostly evening
Diu	230	9	daily at 8am
Jamnagar	169-182	7	hourly
Jodhpur	400	8½	5 daily
Junagadh	176	7½	26 daily
Rajkot	137	5½	half-hourly
Udaipur	300	5½	10 daily
Vadodara	ordinary/AC 89/180	2½	half-hourly

For long distances, private buses are more comfortable and quicker; most offices are close to Paldi Char Rasta bus station. **Patel Tours & Travels** (☑8866155888; www.pateltoursandtravels.com; Paldi Char Rasta Bus Stand, Paldi Rd) has Volvo AC buses to Rajkot (₹476, four hours, hourly), Jamnagar (₹600, six hours, hourly) and Mumbai (sleeper ₹1000, 11 hours), plus non-AC buses to Mumbai (seat/sleeper ₹810/962, 3pm to 10pm) and six daily buses to Bhuj (non-AC seat/sleeper ₹300/450, AC seat/sleeper ₹533/629). **Shree Swaminarayan** (☑079-26576544; www.sstbus.in; 22 Anilkunj Complex) runs to Diu in non-AC buses (seat/sleeper ₹400/450, 10 hours, 11pm), while **Gujarat Travels** (☑079-26575951; www.gujarattravels.co.in; Paldi Char Rasta Bus Stand, Paldi Rd) has departures to Mt Abu (seat/sleeper ₹600/900, seven hours, 5.30am, 7am, 3pm and 5.30pm).

Lal Darwaja Local Bus Stand has buses running to various destinations around the city and beyond; the most useful for visitors are the buses to Gandhinagar.

from Ahmedabad train station to Lal Darwaja no more than ₹50.

A metro system is under construction. Authorities are aiming for a 2020 completion date, but construction work has already been under way for years, so it's anyone's guess if it will really be ready by then.

Around Ahmedabad

Gandhinagar

✓ 079 / POP 292,795

With greenery and broad avenues, Gandhinagar forms a striking contrast to its neighbour Ahmedabad. This is where state politicians live, in large, fortified houses. Although Ahmedabad became Gujarat's capital when the old state of Bombay was split, this new capital was planned 28km north on the west bank of the Sabarmati River. Named Gandhinagar after Mahatma Gandhi, it's India's second planned city after Chandigarh. The secretariat was moved here in 1970.

Gandhinagar's only real tourist attraction is **Akshardham** (www.akshardham.com/gujarat; J Rd, Sector 20; ◷ 9.30am-6.30pm Tue-Sun), a spectacular temple belonging to the wealthy Hindu Swaminarayan group. Ornately carved and built by nearly 1000 artisans, it's constructed of 6000 tonnes of pink sandstone and surrounded by manicured gardens, and promises to reveal the secret

---

WORTH A TRIP

ADALAJ VAV STEP-WELL

The **Adalaj Vav** (Adalaj Vav; ◷ dawn-dusk) **FREE**, 19km north of Ahmedabad, is among the finest of the Gujarati step-wells. Built by Queen Rudabai in 1498, it has three entrances, leading to a huge platform that rests on 16 pillars, with corners marked by shrines. The octagonal well is five storeys deep and is decorated with exquisite stone carvings; subjects range from eroticism to buttermilk.

From Ahmedabad an autorickshaw costs around ₹600 return. Alternatively, take bus 85 from Lal Darwaja to Chandkheda, transfer to bus 501 towards Sarkej, and ask the driver to let you off at the Adalaj Vav turnoff, from where you can walk or take an autorickshaw about 1km.

---

of life after death. Elaborate underground exhibition areas (admission ₹200) feature high- (and low-) tech multimedia displays on the Swaminarayan movement and the Hindu epics. Note that cameras, mobile phones and bags must be left for safekeeping.

ⓘ Getting There & Away

Buses from Ahmedabad to Gandhinagar (₹26, 45 minutes, every 15 to 30 minutes) depart from the back northwest corner of Lal Darwaja, from the ST bus stand, and from numerous stops along Ashram Rd.

Lothal

About 80km southwest of Ahmedabad lie the remains of one of the most prominent cities of the ancient Indus Valley civilisation. Access to the site is difficult if you don't have your own wheels and you'll need a strong imagination to make the ruins come to life.

Lothal Archaeological Site   HISTORIC SITE
(◷ dawn-dusk) **FREE** Today a hot, dry wind whistles through the trees and over the broken bones of a city that 4500 years ago was one of the most important of the Indus Valley civilisation, which extended into what is now Pakistan. Excavations have revealed the world's oldest known artificial dock, which was connected to an old course of the Sabarmati River. Artefacts suggest that trade may have been conducted with Mesopotamia, Egypt and Persia.

ⓘ Getting There & Away

Lothal is a long day trip from Ahmedabad, and a taxi (around ₹4500 return) is the easiest bet. Five daily trains run from Ahmedabad's Gandhigram station to Lothal-Bhurkhi station (2nd class ₹20, 1½ to 2½ hours), 6km from the site, from where you can catch one of the infrequent buses or walk. Take water with you.

Modhera

The small village of Modhera is home to one of Gujarat's most splendid and important temples.

★ **Sun Temple**   HINDU TEMPLE
(Indian/foreigner ₹25/300; ◷ 9am-5pm) Built in 1027 by Bhimdev I, this is one of the greatest monuments of the Solanki dynasty, whose rulers were believed to be descended from the sun. Like the better-known Sun Temple (p610) at Konark in Odisha, which it predates by 200 years, the Modhera temple was

designed so that the dawn sun shone on the image of Surya, the sun god, during the equinox. Surya Kund, an extraordinary rectangular step-well inside the complex, contains more than 100 shrines, resembling a sunken art gallery.

The exterior of the temple is intricately carved with demons and deities, and the main hall and shrine are reached through a pillared pavilion. Inside, 52 sculpted pillars depict scenes from the Ramayana and the Mahabharata, and a hall with 12 niches represents the different monthly manifestations of Surya. Erotic sculpture panels complete the sensual decoration.

A small archaeological museum features stone panel sections and stone carvings of deities dating from the 8th to the 19th centuries.

Around 20 January the temple is the scene of a three-day classical-dance festival (p690) featuring dancers from all over India.

ℹ Getting There & Away

Modhera is 100km northwest of Ahmedabad. You can take a bus (₹76, two hours, half-hourly) from Ahmedabad's ST bus stand to Mahesana (Mehsana), and then another bus 26km west to Modhera (₹20, one hour). There are also trains from Ahmedabad to Mahesana. A taxi from Ahmedabad is much easier and will cost about ₹3800 return, including a visit to nearby Patan.

Patan

About 130km northwest of Ahmedabad, Patan was Gujarat's capital for six centuries before Ahmedabad was founded in 1411. It was ruined by the armies of Ala-ud-Din Khilji around 1300, and today it's a dusty little town with narrow streets, lined, in the oldest quarters, by elaborate wooden houses.

Patan is famed for its beautiful Patola silk textiles, produced by the laborious double-*ikat* method. Both the warp (lengthways) and weft (transverse) threads are painstakingly tie-dyed to create the pattern before the weaving process begins. It takes about six months to make one sari, which might cost ₹180,000.

The other reason for visiting Patan is for its huge, spectacular step-well, Rani-ki-Vav, easily the most impressive in Gujarat.

◎ Sights

★ Rani-ki-Vav   HISTORIC SITE
(Indian/foreigner ₹40/600; ◷ 9am-5pm) The only real sign of Patan's former glory is this

NALSAROVAR

The 121-sq-km **Nalsarovar Bird Sanctuary** (www.nalsarovar.com; Indian/foreigner ₹40/800, car ₹20, camera/video ₹100/2500; ◷ 6am-6pm), 60km southwest of Ahmedabad, protects Nalsarovar Lake, a flood of island-dotted blue dissolving into the sky and iron-flat plains, and its surrounding wetlands. Between November and February the sanctuary sees flocks of indigenous and migratory birds, with as many as 250 species passing through. To see the birds it's best to hire a boat (around ₹1320 for the entire boat per hour, but boat operators will try to get you to pay more than this official rate).

Ducks, geese, eagles, spoonbills, cranes, pelicans and flamingos are best seen at daybreak and dusk, so it's worth staying in the **luxury tents** (☑ 9427725090; s/d without bathroom ₹1300/1800; ✹) run by Gujarat Tourism, 1.5km from the lake. The sanctuary is busiest at weekends and on holidays, and best avoided then.

A taxi from Ahmedabad costs around ₹4500 for a day trip; combine the sanctuary with a visit to Lothal (p700; 40km south).

astoundingly beautiful step-well. Built in 1063 by Rani Udayamati to commemorate her husband, Bhimdev I, the step-well is the oldest and finest in Gujarat and is remarkably preserved. Steps lead down through multiple levels, with lines of carved pillars and more than 800 sculptures, mostly on Vishnu-avatar themes, as well as striking geometric patterns.

You can only descend the steps of one half of the step-well.

★ Patan Patola
Heritage Museum   WORKSHOP
(☑ 02766-232274; www.patanpatola.com; Patola House, Kalika Rd; Indian/foreigner ₹10/100; ◷ 10am-1.30pm & 3-6pm) Run by the award-winning Salvi family, this museum is an excellent place to see Patola silk weaving in action. The family has specialised in double-*ikat* weaving (a process that their ancestors brought from Southeast Asia) since the 11th century – yes, you've read this correctly! – and you can get a demonstration

ALCOHOL PERMITS

Gujarat is, officially, a dry state, because Gandhi disapproved of the evils of alcohol, but alcohol permits for foreign visitors are easy to get. They're free upon arrival at the airport, or they can be picked up – usually for a small charge – at the 'wine shops' found in many large hotels. Just show your passport to receive a one-month permit. The permit allows you two units over the month, which equates to 20 bottles of standard beer or two 750mL bottles of liquor, which you must drink in private. Cheers!

on the loom and compare the family's craft, including an elephant-motif sari that is considered the family masterpiece, with beautifully displayed single-*ikat* textiles from around the world.

The family mostly uses natural dyes, such as indigo and turmeric. Their handwoven silk saris start at around ₹180,000 (US$2600) and can cost triple that amount, depending on the design. There's a three-year waiting list. They can also execute single-*ikat* weavings, which are considerably more affordable and quicker to make.

The museum is just down the road from the Rani-ki-Vav (p701) step-well.

Panchasara Parshvanath JAIN TEMPLE
(Hemchandracharya Rd) Among more than 100 Jain temples around Patan, this is the largest, with all the domes and sacred carvings your eyes can absorb.

Sleeping & Eating

Apple Residency HOTEL $$
(☑ 8153988851, 02766-297033; www.apple residency.co.in; Panchvati Complex; incl breakfast s/d from ₹950/1400; ❋ ☎) Patan's best hotel isn't far from the railway station and lures travellers with its spick-and-span rooms decked out in neutral creams and browns, all with modern bathrooms. Breakfast is served on a tray in your room.

Food Zone INDIAN $
(mains ₹100-170; ⊙ 11am-3pm & 7-11pm; ❋) This place near the railway tracks has modern booth seating, great thalis and a mix of Gujarati and Indo-Chinese dishes.

Getting There & Away

Patan is 40km northwest of Mahesana. The **bus station** is just east of the centre. Buses leave Ahmedabad's ST bus stand about every hour (₹105, three to 3½ hours). There are also buses to/from Zainabad (₹85, 2½ hours, four daily), via Modhera. A day trip in a private taxi from Ahmedabad costs about ₹3800; combine this with a visit to the Sun Temple (p700) in Modhera.

Vadodara (Baroda)

☑ 0265 / POP 1.72 MILLION

Vadodara (often known as Baroda) lies 106km southeast of Ahmedabad, a little over an hour's drive along National Expressway 1. Vadodara has some interesting sights, but the main reason for coming here is to use the city as a base for a day trip to the nearby World Heritage Site of Champaner and Pavagadh. The city is far less hectic than Ahmedabad, and parts of the Sayajigunj area near the university have a college-town feel.

After the Marathas expelled the Mughals from Gujarat in the 18th century, their local lieutenants, the Gaekwad clan, made Vadodara their capital. Vadodara retained a high degree of autonomy, even under the British, right up to Independence in 1947. Maharaja Sayajirao III (1875–1939) was a great moderniser and laid the foundations of Vadodara's modern reputation as Gujarat's cultural capital, and the city's main attraction – the palace – is part of his legacy.

Sights

★ **Laxmi Vilas Palace** PALACE
(Nehru Rd; Indian/foreigner ₹225/400; ⊙ 10am-5pm Tue-Sun) Still the residence of Vadodara's royal family, Laxmi Vilas was built in full-throttle 19th-century Indo-Saracenic flourish at a cost of ₹6 million – an enormous sum back then. The most impressive Raj-era palace in Gujarat, its elaborate interiors feature well-maintained mosaics, chandeliers and artworks, as well as a highly impressive collection of weaponry. It's set in expansive park-like grounds that include a golf course. An audio guide is included with admission. Allow at least two hours for a visit. Photography is prohibited within the palace.

Baroda Museum & Picture Gallery MUSEUM
(Sayaji Bagh; Indian/foreigner ₹10/200; ⊙ 10.30am-5pm) Within Sayaji Bagh park, this

Vadodara (Baroda)

Vadodara (Baroda)

⊚ Top Sights
1	Laxmi Vilas Palace	C3

⊚ Sights
2	Baroda Museum & Picture Gallery	B1

🛏 Sleeping
3	Hotel Valiant	B2
4	Lemon Tree	B2
5	Oasis Hotel	B2

⊗ Eating
6	Aamantran	A2
7	Kalyan	B2

🛍 Shopping
8	Baroda Prints	A1
9	Baroda Prints & Workshop	C2

🛈 Information
10	Bank of Baroda ATM	A2
11	HDFC ATM	A2
12	ICICI Bank	B2
13	State Bank of India ATM	A2

🛈 Transport
14	ST Bus Stand	A1
15	Sweta Travels	A1

museum houses a diverse collection, much of it gathered by Maharaja Sayajirao III, including statues and carvings from several Asian regions, fine ivory carvings from India, Japan and China, a modest Egyptian room with a mummy, and an entire floor of stuffed and pickled wildlife specimens. The gallery has lovely Mughal miniatures and a motley crew of unsympathetically lit European masters; check out the small contemporary-art gallery instead.

🛏 Sleeping

Most accommodation is in the conveniently central Sayajigunj area; there are a number of very cheap hotels (₹400 to ₹600) there, as well as decent, if cookie-cutter, midrange places. Vadodara also has some very comfortable – and affordable – top-end business hotels.

Hotel Valiant   HOTEL **$$**
(☑0265-2363480; www.hotelvaliant.com; 7th fl, BBC Tower, Sayajigunj; with/without AC s ₹700/1000, d ₹1000/1450; ❉⟨🛜⟩) The Valiant offers surprisingly fresh digs on the upper floors of a high-rise building. Take the lift from the street entrance to find reception in a spacious lobby on the 7th floor. The large and clean, if bland, rooms are some of the best value in town. It's even fairly quiet.

Oasis Hotel   HOTEL **$$**
(☎0265-22225054; www.theoasishotel.net; Sayajigunj; r from ₹3300; ✳🛜🏊) For a touch of comfort, the Oasis delivers. Rooms are aged but have polished-wood floors, wraparound floor-to-ceiling windows and – for a change from the standard hotel showers – bathtubs. Plus, there's a swimming pool on the roof!

Lemon Tree   BUSINESS HOTEL **$$$**
(☎0265-2602000; www.lemontreehotels.com; Sayajigunj; r incl breakfast from ₹3740; ✳🛜) With mellow decor, blackout curtains, work desks with comfy chairs, and floral paintings adorning the walls, the Lemon Tree is a great-value deal. The in-house restaurant serves a decent array of international dishes. Book online for the best rates.

✖ Eating

Kalyan   SOUTH INDIAN **$**
(Sayajigunj; dishes ₹100-210; ⏲7am-11pm; ✎) Kalyan is a breezy student hang-out serving healthy portions of South Indian food and less healthy attempts at Western fast food (though all dishes are vegetarian).

Aamantran   INDIAN **$$**
(☎0265-2321050; Sampatrao Colony; mains ₹150-330, thalis from ₹315; ⏲11am-3pm & 7-10.30pm; ✳) Hailed by many as the best thali in Vadodara, Aamantran's is an all-you-can-eat taste of Gujarat with up to 10 dishes and several breads piled onto the plate. À la carte dishes include a variety of veg tandoor selections, along with North Indian and Jain specialities. Look for the yellow sign in Gujarati.

★Peshawri   NORTH INDIAN **$$$**
(☎0265-2330033; WelcomHotel Vadodara, RC Dutt Rd; mains around ₹800; ⏲7.30-11pm; ✳) Rough stone walls, heavy wooden beams and hanging copper vessels conjure a northwest frontier feel at Vadodara's best restaurant, with loyal customers coming all the way from Ahmedabad and beyond. North Indian and clay-oven dishes are the speciality here; standouts include tandoori *jhinga* (prawns) and *murgh malai* (marinated chicken) kebabs, as well as imaginative stuffed naans. Book ahead.

🔒 Shopping

Baroda Prints   ARTS & CRAFTS
(☎0265-2320392; www.barodaprints.com; 3 Aires Complex, Productivity Rd; ⏲9am-9pm Mon-Sat, 8am-6pm Sun) Gorgeous hand-printed dress materials in original, colourful and attractive designs.

Baroda Prints & Workshop   ARTS & CRAFTS
(www.barodaprints.com; Salatwada Rd; ⏲10am-8pm Mon-Sat, 11am-5pm Sun) At this Baroda Prints (p704) branch you can see printers at work upstairs, then buy the finished product downstairs.

❶ Information

There are ATMs at the train station, on RC Dutt Rd and in Sayajigunj.

ICICI Bank (Sayajigunj; ⏲10am-4pm Mon-Fri, to 1pm Sat) Has an ATM and changes cash in major currencies.

Gujarat Tourism (www.gujarattourism.com; ⏲10am-6pm Mon-Sat, closed 2nd & 4th Sat of month) Located inside the VED Transcube Mall next to the ST bus stand. Staff are friendly, but don't expect much.

❶ Getting There & Away

AIR

Vadodara International Airport (☎0265-2485356) is 4km northeast of the centre and

---

BUSES FROM VADODARA

The **ST bus stand** (Old Chhani Rd), integrated with a shopping mall, is just north of the train station. Frequent buses run to numerous destinations.

DESTINATION	COST (₹)	TIME (HR)	DEPARTURES
Ahmedabad	ordinary/AC 89/180	2	at least hourly
Bhavnagar	137	5½	12 daily
Diu	from 224	10	1.30am & 6am
Mumbai	367-383	9	7.30pm
Udaipur	from 251	8½	3.15am & 6am

Across from the train station, **Sweta Travels** (☎0265-2786917) sends AC Volvo buses to Mumbai (seat/sleeper ₹1500/1800, eight hours, two nightly). Many other companies have private buses to other destinations in Gujarat and Rajasthan from the plethora of offices at Pandya Bridge, 2km north of the train station.

has numerous daily departures to Delhi and Mumbai with Jet Airways, IndiGo and Air India and a lesser number of flights to Indore, Bengaluru, Hyderabad and Jaipur.

TRAIN

Around 40 trains a day run to Ahmedabad, including the 12009 Shatabdi (AC chair/executive ₹330/670, two hours, 11.07am Monday to Saturday). The 44 daily trains to Mumbai include the 12010 Shatabdi (AC chair/executive ₹670/1415, 5¼ hours, 4.19pm Monday to Saturday).

Around Vadodara

Champaner & Pavagadh

This spectacular Unesco World Heritage Site, 47km northeast of Vadodara, combines a sacred, temple-freckled 762m volcanic hill (Pavagadh) that rises dramatically from the plains, and a ruined Gujarati capital with beautiful mosque architecture (Champaner). The whole area is referred to as Pavagadh.

Unlike so many other hilltop Gujarati temple sites, Pavagadh is pilgrimage made easy, thanks to a cable car that sails up the side of the mountain. It makes a good day trip from Vadodara.

◉ Sights

Champaner   HISTORIC SITE
(Indian/foreigner ₹40/600; ⊙8am-6pm) The evocative ruins of the one-time capital of Sultan Mahmud Begada today stand as testament to Champaner's brief period of 15th-century glory. When Champaner was captured by Mughal emperor Humayun in 1535, the Gujarati capital reverted to Ahmedabad, and Champaner fell into ruin. The heart of this historic site is the citadel, whose most impressive features are its 16th-century monumental mosques (no longer used for worship), with their beautiful blend of Islamic and Hindu architecture.

The huge Jami Masjid, just outside the citadel's east gate, has a wonderful carved entrance porch that leads into a lovely courtyard surrounded by a pillared corridor. The prayer hall has two tall central minarets, further superb stone carving, multiple domes, finely latticed windows, and seven mihrabs (prayer niches) along the back wall.

Other beautiful mosques include the Saher ki Masjid, behind the ticket office inside the citadel, which was probably the private royal mosque, and the Kevda Masjid, 300m north of the citadel and about 600m west of the Jami Masjid. Here you can climb narrow stairs to the roof, and higher up the minarets, to spot other mosques even further out in the countryside – Nagina Masjid, 500m north, with no minarets but exquisite geometric carving, particularly on the tomb next to it, and Lila Gumbaj ki Masjid, 800m east, on a high platform and with a fluted central dome. The twin minarets resembling factory chimneys, about 1km west, adorn the Brick Minar ki Masjid, a rare brick tomb.

★ **Pavagadh**   HISTORIC SITE
This scenic hilltop may have been fortified as early as the 8th century. Today, throngs of pilgrims ascend Pavagadh to worship at the important Kalikamata Temple, dedicated to the evil-destroying goddess Kali, who sits atop the summit. You can walk up the pilgrim trail (two to three hours), or take a shuttle (₹20) halfway up the hill from along the Champaner citadel's south wall, from where a **cable car** (return ₹116; ⊙6am-8pm) glides you to within a 700m walk of the temple.

Pavagadh became the capital of the Chauhan Rajputs around 1300 but in 1484 was taken by the Gujarat sultan Mahmud Begada after a 20-month siege; the Rajputs committed *jauhar* (ritual mass suicide) in the face of defeat.

Near the top of the hill are Pavagadh's oldest surviving monument, the 10th- to 11th-century Hindu Lakulisha Temple, and several Jain temples. The views are fantastic and so, if you're lucky, are the cooling breezes. At weekends the usual flow of pilgrims can become a flood and it can take half a day to reach the Lakulisha Temple. But if you think that's chaotic, just try coming over the nine days of Navratri (p695) or during the Mahakali festival (p690).

🛏 Sleeping & Eating

★ **Kathiwada Raaj Mahal**   HERITAGE HOTEL $$$
(☑8698458877, Mumbai 022-23697043; www.kathiwada.com; Kathiwada, Madhya Pradesh; incl breakfast cottages ₹8960, s/d from ₹23,000/28,150; 🕸🌊) Nestling next to the village of Kathiwada in Madhya Pradesh, just near the Gujarat border, this breathtaking 19th-century mansion was once the hunting lodge of the Kathiwada royal family. It's been immaculately restored and today offers one of the best heritage-hotel experiences in India. The whole place is rich in stately character, with treasures apparently filling every corner.

WORTH A TRIP

SOUTH OF VADODARA

Gujarat stretches some 240km south from Vadodara to the border of Maharashtra, 150km short of Mumbai. Surat, 140km south of Vadodara, is where the British established their first Indian settlement in 1614, and today it's Gujarat's second-biggest city and a busy commercial centre for textiles and diamonds. Around 40km south of Surat is Dandi, the destination of Gandhi's epic Salt March in 1930, with several Gandhi monuments by its strikingly empty beach. Just before the Maharashtra border is the former Portuguese enclave of Daman. Though it retains a little of the piquancy of old Portugal, Daman is far less attractive than its counterpart, Diu. In the southeast, the hilly Dangs district is the northern extremity of the Western Ghats, with a large tribal population and little tourist infrastructure. The Dangs Darbar, held the week before Holi, is a spectacular, largely tourist-free, tribal festival.

Regular buses connect Vadodara and Surat. To reach Daman, take a bus from Vadodara to Vapi, 13km from Daman, and then change to a local bus.

The 182m (240m including the base) statue of Indian statesman and independence activist Sardar Vallabhbhai Patel (1875–1950) was the world's tallest statue when it was unveiled in late 2018. The **Statue of Unity** (www.statueofunity.in; adult/child ₹120/60, observation deck ₹350; ⊘9am-6pm Tue-Sun) was built in 15 months by some 3000 workers, and at a cost of around US$420 million, the statue utilises 210,000 cu metres of cement, 6500 tonnes of structural steel and 18,500 tonnes of reinforced steel, as well as 1700 tonnes of bronze plates and 1850 tonnes of bronze cladding.

The government hopes that the statue will inspire pride in India and bring tourist money to an otherwise undeveloped part of Gujarat. Indeed, in the first 11 days after the statue opened to the public 128,000 tourists visited the site.

The nearest town is Kevadia (3km from the statue and 85km from Vadodara), but it's not yet well served by public transport. A few buses go from Vadodara, or you could take one from Vadodara to Rajpipla and change there.

Meals are vegetarian and delicious. It's 1½ hours' drive from Champaner. Advance reservations are vital.

ⓘ Getting There & Around

Buses to Pavagadh run at least once hourly from Vadodara (₹50, 1¼ hours); a return taxi costs around ₹1200. Most buses from Pavagadh to Vadodara continue to Ahmedabad (₹128, four hours).

SAURASHTRA

Before Independence, Saurashtra, also known as the Kathiawar Peninsula, was a jumble of more than 200 princely states. Today it has a number of hectic industrial cities, but most of them retain a core of narrow old streets. Outside the cities it's still villages, fields, forests and a timeless, almost feudal feel, with farmers and *maldhari* herders dressed head to toe in white, and rural women as colourful as their neighbours in Rajasthan.

Saurashtra is mainly flat and its rare hills are often sacred, including the spectacular, temple-topped Shatrunjaya and Girnar. The peninsula is liberally endowed with wildlife sanctuaries, notably Sasan Gir, where Asia's last wild lions roam. Saurashtra is also where Gandhi was born and raised; you can visit several sites associated with his life.

Bhavnagar

☏0278 / POP 593,368

Bhavnagar is a hectic, sprawling industrial centre with a colourful old core. It makes a reasonable base for journeys to Shatrunjaya and Velavadar Blackbuck National Park, though both are at least an hour's drive away.

ⓞ Sights

Old City AREA

North of Ganga Jalia Tank, Bhavnagar's old city is well worth a wander, especially in the early evening – it's busy with small shops and cluttered with elaborate, dilapidated wooden buildings leaning over the colourful, crowded bazaars. Don't miss the vegetable market!

Takhteshwar Temple HINDU TEMPLE

(Takhteshwar Tarheti Rd; ⊘dawn-dusk) Perched atop a small hillock, this temple is up high enough to provide splendid views over the city and out to the Gulf of Cambay.

🛌 Sleeping

Hotel Sun 'n' Shine   HOTEL $$
(☑ 0278-2516131; Panwadi Chowk, ST Rd; s/d incl breakfast from ₹2500/2690; ❄️📶) This well-run hotel has small rooms that are fresh and clean, with comfortable beds and soft pillows; the more you pay, the more windows you get. The atrium's giant wall sculpture of a seminaked woman with a pharaonic look is certainly memorable. Breakfast is substantial, and free airport transfers are offered.

Nilambag Palace Hotel   HERITAGE HOTEL $$
(☑ 0278-2424241; www.nilambagpalace.com; cottage r ₹2950, palace r from ₹4720; ❄️📶🏊) Set in stately gardens with a retinue of peacocks, this former maharaja's palace dating from 1859 is now a wildly atmospheric heritage hotel. The lobby looks like an understated regal living room, with a beautiful mosaic floor and grand portraits adorning the walls. The sizeable palace rooms retain a dusty and faded early-20th-century feel; the 'cottage' rooms are mediocre.

Look out for stuffed heads of various animals, including a cheetah (the maharaja used to have a pet cheetah). Guests have use of a circular swimming pool (nonguests pay ₹100) in the Vijay Mahal in the extensive grounds, plus there's a gym and tennis facilities.

It's located beside the Ahmedabad road, 600m southwest of the bus station.

🍴 Eating

Sankalp   SOUTH INDIAN $$
(www.sankalponline.com; 1st fl, Eva Surbhi Mall, Waghawadi Rd; mains ₹150-300; ☉11am-3pm & 6-11pm) First-class South Indian vegetarian dishes served in clean, contemporary surroundings on the 1st floor of one of the town's biggest malls.

Nilambag Palace Restaurant   NORTH INDIAN $$$
(☑ 0278-2424241; www.nilambagpalace.com; Nilambag Palace Hotel; mains ₹250-650; ☉1-3pm & 7.30-10.30pm) With a stunningly large and royal dining room, complete with old portraits and a stuffed tiger head, this is by far the city's best restaurant. It's particularly atmospheric at night, when the palace-garden seating area is lit with tiny fairy lights. Dishes lean towards North Indian, with plenty of nonveg options and a succulent chicken kebab.

If you're not a guest of the hotel it's wise to call ahead to reserve for dinner.

ℹ️ Information

State Bank of India (Darbargadh; ☉10.30am-4.30pm Mon-Fri) changes cash and travellers cheques and has a 24-hour **ATM**. **HDFC** also has a handy ATM just south of Pill Garden.

Post Office (Navapara Rd; ☉9am-5pm Mon-Fri)

Forest Office (☑ 0278-2426425; Bahumali Bhavan, Annexe, ST Rd; ☉10.30am-6.30pm Mon-Sat, closed 2nd & 4th Sat of month) Book accommodation for Velavadar Blackbuck National Park here. It's near the ST bus stand.

ℹ️ Getting There & Away

AIR

Bhavnagar Airport (☑ 0278-2203113) is about 3.5km from town and has four weekly flights to Mumbai with Air India. A taxi/rickshaw between the airport and city costs around ₹170/110.

BUS

From the **ST bus stand** (ST Rd) there are frequent services to Rajkot (seat/sleeper ₹124/225, four hours, 11 daily), Ahmedabad (AC/non-AC ₹250/130, 4½ hours, at least once hourly), Vadodara (seat/sleeper ₹147/247, 5½ hours, hourly) and Palitana (₹33, 1½ hours, three daily).

Private bus companies include **Tanna Travels** (☑ 0278-2425218; www.tannabus.in; Waghawadi Rd), with air-con buses to Ahmedabad (₹267, four hours, 14 daily).

GUJARATI CUISINE

Gujarat is strong on vegetarian cuisine, partly thanks to the Jain influence here, and the quintessential Gujarati meal is the all-veg thali. It's sweeter, lighter and less spicy and oily than Punjabi thali, and locals – who are famously particular about food – have no doubt it's the best thali in the world. It begins with a large stainless-steel dish, onto which teams of waiters will serve most or all of the following: curries, chutneys, pickles, dhal, *kadhi* (a yoghurt and gram-flour preparation), raita, rotis, rice, *khichdi* (a blend of lightly spiced rice and lentils), *farsan* (savoury nibbles), salad and one or two sweet items – to be eaten concurrently with the rest. Buttermilk is the traditional accompanying drink. Normally the rice and/or *khichdi* don't come until you've finished with the rotis. In most thali restaurants the waiters will keep coming back until you can only say, 'No more'.

Bhavnagar

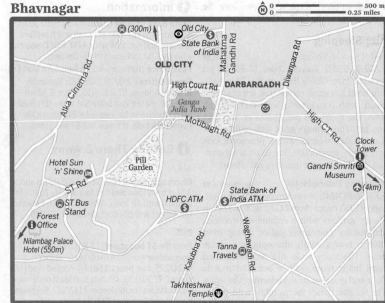

TRAIN

There aren't many trains between Bhavnagar and Ahmedabad, but the one with the most civilised timing is the daily 12972 Bhavnagar–Bandra Express, which departs at 8.30pm and arrives in Ahmedabad (sleeper/3AC/2AC ₹240/560/760) at 1.52am.

Velavadar Blackbuck National Park

Beautiful **Velavadar Blackbuck National Park** (Velavadar NP; Mon-Fri Indian/foreigner car ₹400/US$40, Sat & Sun ₹500/US$50, 4hr guide ₹400/US$20, camera Indian/foreigner ₹200/US$20; ⊙6am-6pm 16 Oct-15 Jun) is famous for its namesake antelope, which sport elegant spiralling horns as long as 65cm in mature males. In 2015 an estimated 14,000 blackbuck inhabited the park (a significant decease on the 25,000 of 2001), alongside nilgais (India's largest antelope) and a wide range of bird species. If you're lucky, you may even spot wolves, which are increasing in number.

A taxi day trip from Bhavnagar costs about ₹3000.

★ **Blackbuck Lodge** HOTEL $$$
(🗋9099912375; www.theblackbucklodge.com; s/d incl full board from ₹17,800/21,400) This cluster of comfortable, grassland-yellow, tastefully decorated stone villas just outside the western entrance of Blackbuck National Park is a wonderfully relaxed place to while away a few days. Packages with safaris are also offered, and blackbuck are easily spotted on the grounds.

Kaliyar Bhavan Forest Lodge HOTEL $$$
(🗋0278-2426425; Indian/foreigner d ₹1000/US$55, with AC ₹3000/US$80) Near the reception centre of Blackbuck National Park, this basic lodge is run by the Forest Office (p707) in Bhavnagar. Choose between two 13-bed dorms, an air-con room and a non-AC room. Good vegetarian meals are served. It's hideously overpriced for foreigners, but the location within the park is amazing for animal spotters.

Palitana

🗋02848 / POP 64,100

Roaring up out of the dust of the bustling little pilgrimage town of Palitana (51km southwest of Bhavnagar) is a high, table-topped hill crowned with the magnificent Jain temples of Shatrunjaya. During the Kartik Purnima festival (p690), accommodation around town floods with pilgrims and is best booked in advance.

◉ Sights & Activities

★ Shatrunjaya
RELIGIOUS SITE

(⊙ temples 6.30am-6pm) One of Jainism's holiest pilgrimage sites, Shatrunjaya is an incredible hill studded with temples, some of which are over 900 years old. It's said that Adinath (also known as Rishabha), the founder of Jainism, meditated beneath the rayan tree at the summit. The temples are grouped into *tunks* (enclosures), each with a central temple flanked by minor ones. The 500m climb up 3300 steps (1½ hours) to the temples adds to the extraordinary experience.

Most days, hundreds of pilgrims make the climb; crowds swell into the thousands around Kartik Purnima (p690), which marks the end of Chaturmas, a four-month period of spiritual retreat and material self-denial that coincides with the monsoon season.

As you near the top of the hill, the track forks. The main entrance, Ram Pole, is reached by bearing left, though the best views are to the right, where on a clear day you can see the Gulf of Cambay. Inside the Nav Tonk Gate, one path leads left to the Muslim shrine of Angar Pir – a Muslim saint who protected the temples from a Mughal attack; women who want children come here and make offerings of miniature cradles. To the right, the second tunk you reach is the Chaumukhji Tunk, containing the Chaumukh (Four-Faced Shrine), built in 1618 by a wealthy Jain merchant. Images of Adinath (believed to have attained enlightenment here) face the four cardinal directions.

You can easily spend a couple of hours wandering among the hundreds of temples up here. The biggest and one of the most splendid and important, with a wealth of fantastic, detailed carving, is the Adinath Temple, on the highest point on the far (south) side.

Shri Vishal Jain Museum
MUSEUM

(₹20; ⊙ 8.30am-12.30pm & 3.30-8.30pm) This dark and dusty museum features model recreations of the Jain stories, Jain artwork and artefacts up to 500 years old, and beautiful ivory carvings. In the basement is a surprising circular temple with mirror walls and centuries-old images of four *tirthankars* (great Jain teachers).

It's 500m down the street from the foot of the Shatrunjaya steps.

🛏 Sleeping & Eating

Takhatgadh Mangal Bhuvan
GUESTHOUSE $

(r ₹400) This pilgrim rest house, with very basic rooms, will let foreign couples (and only couples – no single travellers of either sex) stay if it's not too busy. It's opposite Shri Vishal Jain Museum, just a short walk from the steps up the mountain.

Hotel Sumeru Palitana
HOTEL $$

(☑ 02848-252327; Station Rd; s/d ₹750/1120, with AC ₹1120/1680; ❄ 🛜) Recently overhauled, this once-terrible Gujarat-tourist-board offering now has reasonably decent and clean rooms with leather bedheads, glass tables, and bathrooms that could have stood a bit more renovation. It's a couple of hundred metres from the bus station.

Sankalp Restaurant
SOUTH INDIAN $$

(☑ 02482-242070; Taleti Rd; mains ₹200-300; ⊙ 11am-11pm) Unexpectedly stylish Sankalp has mirrored walls and rows of tables set up canteen style. It serves mainly South Indian dishes, though it seems to have a little of everything.

ℹ Getting There & Away

ST buses run to/from Bhavnagar (₹33, 1½ hours, three daily) and Ahmedabad (₹150, five hours, seven daily). Take a bus to Talaja (₹37, one hour, hourly), where you can change for Diu (₹125, 5¾ hours, five daily). The **bus station** is in the northern part of town.

Four passenger trains run daily to/from Bhavnagar (2nd class ₹15, 1½ hours). The **train station** is in the northern part of town.

Diu

☑ 02875 / POP 52,074

Once governed by Portugal, tiny Diu island, linked by a bridge to Gujarat's southern coast, is still infused with Portuguese history and architecture, and even some remnants of Portuguese culture. The streets of the main town are clean, colourful and

SLEEPING PRICE RANGES

The following price ranges refer to a double room with private bathroom and are inclusive of tax across the regions:

$ less than ₹1000

$$ ₹1000–₹3500

$$$ more than ₹3500

quiet once you get off the tourist-packed waterfront strip, and there are numerous crumbling Portuguese villas and churches. Although it's often thought of as being part of Gujarat, this is incorrect. With Daman it's actually a separate union territory known as Daman and Diu, and it has its own rules and government.

Diu town sits at the eastern end of the island. The northern side of the island, facing Gujarat, is tidal marsh and salt pans, while the southern coast alternates between limestone cliffs, rocky coves and sandy beaches, better for people-watching than sun worshipping.

History

Diu was a major port between the 14th and 16th centuries, when it was the trading post and naval base from which the Ottomans controlled the northern Arabian Sea shipping routes.

The Portuguese secured control of Diu in 1535 and kept it until India launched Operation Vijay in 1961. Diu, Daman and Goa were administered as a single union territory of India until 1987, when Goa became a state. Many Diu families have joint Indian-Portuguese citizenship.

With Daman, Diu is still governed from Delhi as part of the Union Territory of Daman and Diu and is not part of Gujarat. Diu includes Diu island, separated from the mainland by a narrow channel, and two tiny mainland enclaves. One of these, housing the village of Ghoghla, is the entry point to Diu from Una.

⊙ Sights & Activities

⊙ Diu Town

The town is sandwiched between the massive fort at its eastern end and a huge city wall in the west. The Portuguese-descended population mostly lives in the church-studded southern part of Diu town, still called Farangiwada (Foreigners' Quarter). The western part of town is a maze of narrow, winding streets and many houses are brightly painted; the streets are a joy to wander.

★ St Paul's Church   CHURCH
(⊙8am-6pm) Cavernous St Paul's is a wedding cake of a church, founded by Jesuits in 1600 and then rebuilt in 1807. Its neoclassical facade is the most elaborate of any Portuguese-era church in India. Inside, it's a great barn, with a small cloister next door, above which is a school. Daily Mass is held here.

Church of St Francis of Assisi   CHURCH
(Hospital) A surprise awaits at this church, founded in 1593, and previously used as a hospital. The whitewashed exterior is all flaking paint and sea-spray decay, but the interior has recently been faithfully restored to its Portuguese-era beauty. There are blue-and-white arches and a giant carved wooden altar complete with images of the Virgin. Sadly, it's often locked, but even if it is you can normally peek through the wire-mesh doorway in order to ogle the interior.

Zampa Gateway   GATE
Painted bright red, this main town gateway in the huge city wall that hems in the western side of Diu has carvings of lions, angels and a priest, while just inside it is a chapel with an image of the Virgin and Child dating from 1702.

Diu Museum   MUSEUM
(St Thomas' Church; ⊙9am-6pm) **FREE** St Thomas' Church is a lovely, simple building with walls decaying in genteel fashion. It now houses the Diu Museum, with a spooky, evocative collection of wooden saints going back to the 16th century and particularly creepy armless angels. Once a year, on All Saints' Day (1 November), this is used for a packed-out Mass.

Nagar Sheth Haveli   HISTORIC BUILDING
The most impressive and elaborate buildings in Diu town's western maze of tiny streets are found in the Panchwati area. Nagar Sheth Haveli, an old merchant's house, is particularly notable for its stucco scrolls and copious fruit carvings.

⊙ Around the Island

★ Diu Fort   FORT
(Fort Rd; ⊙8am-6pm) **FREE** Built in 1535, with additions made in 1541, this massive, well-preserved Portuguese fort with its double moat (one tidal) was one of the most important Portuguese forts in Asia. Today sea erosion and neglect are leading to a slow collapse. Cannonballs litter the place, and the ramparts have a superb array of cannons. The lighthouse is Diu's highest point, with a beam that reaches 32km. There are a cou-

Diu Town

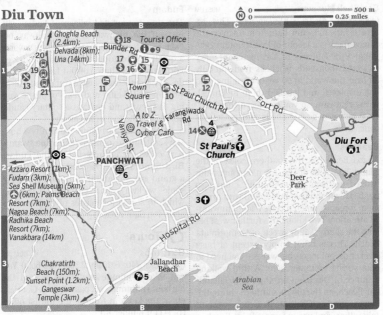

Diu Town

⊙ Top Sights
1 Diu Fort	D2
2 St Paul's Church	C2

⊙ Sights
3 Church of St Francis of Assisi	C2
4 Diu Museum	C2
5 Jallandhar Beach	B3
6 Nagar Sheth Haveli	B2
7 Vegetable Market	B1
8 Zampa Gateway	A2

◯ Activities, Courses & Tours
9 Boat Trips	B1

⊜ Sleeping
10 Hotel Samrat	B1
11 Hotel The Grand Highness	B1
12 Palácio de Diu	C1

⊗ Eating
13 Fish Market	A1
14 O'Coqueiro	C2
15 Ram Vijay	B1

⊜ Drinking & Nightlife
16 Casaluxo Bar	B1

ⓘ Information
ICICI Bank ATM	(see 16)
Post Office	(see 16)
17 State Bank of India	B1
18 State Bank of India ATM	B1

ⓘ Transport
19 Ekta Travels	A1
20 Jethibai Bus Stand	A1
21 JK Travels	A1

ple of small chapels, one holding engraved tombstone fragments.

★ Vanakbara
VILLAGE

At the extreme west of the island, Vanakbara is a fascinating little fishing village and one of the highlights of Diu. It's great to wander around the port, packed with colourful fishing boats and bustling activity – best from 7am to 8am, when the fishing fleet returns and sells off its catch.

Gangeswar Temple
HINDU TEMPLE

Gangeswar Temple, on the south coast 3km west of town, just past Fudam village, is a small coastal cave where five Shiva linga (phallic symbols) are washed by the waves. The most scenic way to approach it is by the good, virtually empty coastal road that starts from near Sunset Point.

Sea Shell Museum   MUSEUM

(adult/child ₹20/10; ⊙10.30am-5pm) This eccentric little museum, 6km from town on the Nagoa road, is a labour of love. Captain Devjibhai Vira Fulbaria of the merchant navy collected thousands of shells from literally all over the world in 50 years of sailing, and has displayed and labelled them in English with great care, so you can learn the difference between cowrie shells and poisonous cone shells.

Beaches

Nagoa Beach, on the southern coast of the island 7km west of Diu Town, is long, palm fringed and safe for swimming – but also trash strewn and very busy, often with drunk men: foreign women receive a lot of unwanted attention. Two kilometres further west begins the sandy 2.5km sweep of Gomptimata Beach. This is often empty, except at busy weekends, but it gets big waves – you need to be a strong swimmer here. Within walking distance of Diu town are the rocky Jalландhar Beach, on the town's southern shore; the longer, sandier Chakratirth Beach, west of Jallandhar; and pretty Sunset Point Beach, a small, gentle curve beyond Chakratirth that's popular for swimming and relatively hassle free. Sunset Point itself is a small headland at the southern end of the beach, topped by the INS Khukhri Memorial, commemorating an Indian Navy frigate sunk off Diu during the 1971 India–Pakistan War. Unfortunately, the region around Sunset Point is also a dumping ground, and any early-morning excursion will reveal that the tidal zone here is a popular toilet venue.

The best beach is Ghoghla Beach, north of Diu. A long stretch of sand, it has less trash and fewer people than the others, along with gentle waves and some decent restaurants.

> ### ℹ BOOZE ALERT
>
> More an annoyance than a danger, drunk men can be tiresome, particularly for women, and particularly around Nagoa Beach. Also, beware of broken glass in the sand and water. Many of the bars aren't likely to be very relaxing for women. If you want a drink have one at a restaurant.
>
> It's illegal to take alcohol from Diu back into Gujarat and police do check departing vehicles.

Fudam

The tiny, untouristed village of Fudam sits just off the highway roughly halfway between Diu town and Nagoa Beach. It's worth a quick stop to admire the white, mildewed Portuguese-era Church of Our Lady of Remedes. If it's not locked, inside you'll find a large wood-panelled altar and years of dust covering the pews (and perhaps a solitary candle burning at the foot of the altar).

Opposite the turnoff for Fudam is a horizon-scratching expanse of estuarine swamp, part of which is protected as the **Fudam Bird Sanctuary** (⊙7am-6pm) `FREE`. There's a grand gateway and then not much except some walkways and viewing areas from which to search for masses of waders, gulls and even flamingos.

☞ Tours

Boat Trips   BOATING

(per person ₹40; ⊙10am-12.30pm & 3-6pm) You can take 15-minute boat trips around the harbour (minimum six passengers). Get tickets at the kiosk in front of the tourist office (p714) on Bunder Rd.

🛏 Sleeping

Diu town has plenty of cheap hotels, but many are pretty unappealing and are patronised by hard-drinking Gujarati men. There is, however, one backpacker place. A good selection of much more upmarket choices can be found within the town and on the beaches; these are generally aimed at holidaying Indian families. Rates are extremely flexible, with discounts of up to 60% available at the more expensive places in quiet periods.

🛏 Diu Town

Hotel Samrat   HOTEL $$

(📞02875-252354; www.hotelsamratdiu.com; Old Collectorate Rd; r ₹2020; ❄ 🕸 🏊) Hotel Samrat is a good midrange choice downtown, with comfortable and well-maintained rooms, some with street-facing balconies. There's even a swimming pool tucked away around the back, plus a decent Indian-Chinese restaurant. All up it's a good deal.

Palácio de Diu   HOTEL $$

(📞02875-254007; www.hotelpalaciodediu.com; r from ₹2000; ❄ 🕸) Not at all like a palace, but a great-value find just the same, this compact and modern four-storey hotel has small rooms with desks, spotted curtains and glitter-splotched walls. The shirt-and-tie-wearing staff are helpful, and the location, right at the point where the most atmospheric part of town starts, couldn't be better.

Azzaro Resort
HOTEL $$$

(☑ 02875-255421; www.azzarodiu.com; Fudam Rd; incl breakfast r ₹7090, ste ₹10,850; ❄ @ 🛜 🏊) A kilometre outside town, this is Diu's most luxurious hotel. It features tasteful rooms with high-tech lighting controls and glass-walled bathrooms (make sure the curtains on the floor-to-ceiling windows are closed before using this so as to avoid giving anyone outside a shock!). All rooms look onto the garden surrounding the bubble-shaped pool.

There's a spa, a gym, two decent restaurants and a 24-hour cafe.

Hotel The
Grand Highness
BUSINESS HOTEL $$$

(☑ 02875-254000; www.thegrandhighness.com; Main Bazaar; r incl breakfast from ₹4300; ❄ 🛜) By far the grandest place in Diu town, this hotel, which is popular with holidaying Indian families, comes with spotless rooms, rain showers, plasma-screen TVs and comfortable beds. The atrium is decorated with contemporary sculptures of graceful high jumpers, and bubble lamps tumble from the ceiling.

🏖 Nagoa Beach

★ Radhika Beach Resort
HOTEL $$$

(☑ 02875-275551; www.radhikaresort.com; Nagoa; d/ste incl breakfast from ₹5550/7450; ❄ 🛜 🏊) Immaculate and unexpectedly creative, with comfortable, condo-like villas set around a figure-eight pool in grassy grounds, Radhika is just steps from Nagoa Beach. The cool rooms have silver and lime-green colour schemes, and desks, bedheads and wardrobes made out of the polished heads of coconuts.

Palms Beach Resort
HOTEL $$$

(☑ 02875-275301; www.thepalmsbeachresort. com; Nagoa; r incl breakfast ₹6600; ❄ 🛜 🏊) The Palms is colourful and clean, with cool rooms in a small, palm-shaded complex with a swimming pool. Some rooms have terraces over the palm trees. However, despite all these strong points it's a tad overpriced. On the main road, pass the turn into Nagoa Beach, and you'll see it on the left after 150m.

✗ Eating

Diu's delicious fresh fish and seafood features heavily on restaurant menus, and most guesthouses will cook anything you buy; there's a daily **fish market** (⊙ 7am-5pm) opposite Jethibai bus stand. A couple of places serve Portuguese-Indian dishes.

Ram Vijay
ICE CREAM $

(scoops from ₹40; ⊙ 9am-9pm) For a rare treat, head to this small, squeaky-clean, old-fashioned ice-cream parlour near the town square for delicious handmade ice cream and milkshakes. Going since 1933, this family enterprise started with soft drinks, and still makes its own brand (Dew) in Fudam village – try a ginger-lemon soda and then all the ice creams! It also does (average) sandwiches.

O'Coqueiro
MULTICUISINE $$

(breakfast ₹80-140, lunch & dinner mains ₹170-380; ⊙ 8am-9pm; 🍴) Here the dedicated Kailash Pandey has developed a soul-infused garden restaurant celebrating freshness and quality. The menu offers uncomplicated but very tasty pasta, chicken and seafood, plus a handful of Portuguese dishes, such as prawns in coconut gravy, learnt from a Diu matriarch. There's also good coffee, cold beer, a book swap and friendly service.

Pride of the Island
MULTICUISINE $$

(☑ 02875-275301; Palms Beach Resort, Nagoa Beach; mains ₹165-395; ⊙ 7am-10.30pm; 🛜 🍴) The open-air restaurant at Palms Beach Resort has excellent food, with inviting breakfasts and delicious choices such as penne with tuna and tomato, fish and chips, and prawn-coconut curry. It's relaxed, pleasant and brightened up by contemporary art pieces.

Sea View Restaurant
SEAFOOD $$

(Ghoghla Beach; meals ₹150-250; ⊙ 8am-11pm) Fronting Ghoghla Beach, next to the eponymous hotel, the open-air Sea View has a full menu of Indian dishes and seafood, with the sand a stone's throw away. The Goan prawn curry (₹180) is big and spicy. Except at holiday time, the clientele is mostly men.

🍷 Drinking & Nightlife

Apart from the restaurants (most of which serve beer), there are a number of bars around town, some on the seedy side. Drinks are blissfully cheap – around ₹70 for a Kingfisher lager. It's rare to see women in any of the bars.

Casaluxo Bar
BAR

(⊙ 9am-1pm & 4-9pm Tue-Sun) Most Diu bars are wholly unappealing places full of Gu-

BUSES FROM DIU

Visitors arriving in Diu by private car or taxi will be charged a border tax of ₹40 per vehicle.

From Jethibai bus stand there are buses to numerous destinations.

DESTINATION	COST (₹)	TIME (HR)	FREQUENCY
Bhavnagar	125	5½	4 daily
Junagadh	150	4½	3 daily
Rajkot	200	5½	3 daily
Veraval	100	2½	3 daily

More frequent departures go from Una, 14km north of Diu. Buses run between Una bus stand and Diu (₹20, 40 minutes, half-hourly) between 6.30am and 8pm. Outside these hours, shared autorickshaws go to Ghoghla or Diu from Tower Chowk in Una (1km from the bus stand), for ₹15. An autorickshaw costs ₹200. Una rickshaw-wallahs are unable to proceed further than the bus station in Diu, so they cannot take you all the way to Nagoa Beach (an additional ₹100).

JK Travels (☑ Una 02875-222212; http://jkbus.in) runs private buses from the Diu bus stand to Ahmedabad at 7.30pm (non-AC sleeper ₹700, 10 hours). **Ekta Travels** (☑ 02875-253474) is another decent option.

jarati men downing whisky and falling over, but at the almost pub-like Casaluxo Bar, facing the town square, there's a (slightly) more salubrious air. It opened in 1963 and, except for some swimsuit posters in the back room, might not have updated its decor since.

ⓘ Information

A to Z (Vaniya St, Panchwati; per hour ₹40; ☺9am-8pm Mon-Fri, to midnight Sat & Sun) Diu town's best internet cafe, near Panchwati Rd.

State Bank of India (Main Bazaar; ☺10am-4pm Mon-Fri) Changes cash and travellers cheques and has an ATM; there's another **SBI ATM** (Goldmoon Complex) on the north side of Bunder Rd, and a handy ICICI Bank ATM near the town square. Many shops around town change money.

Post Office (☺9am-5pm Mon-Sat) Upstairs, facing the town square.

Tourist Office (☑ 02875-252653; Bunder Rd; ☺9.30am-1.30pm & 3-7pm Mon-Sat) Has maps, bus schedules and hotel prices.

ⓘ Getting There & Away

AIR

Alliance Air (www.airindia.com/alliance-air.htm), a budget subsidiary of Air India, flies to/from Mumbai four times weekly from **Diu Airport** (☑ 02875-254743; North Beach Rd). The airport is 6km west of town, just before Nagoa Beach.

TRAIN

Delvada is the nearest railhead, 8km from Diu on the Una road. The 52951 MG Passenger at 2.25pm runs to Sasan Gir (2nd class ₹25, 3½ hours) and Junagadh (₹35, 6¼ hours), while the 52950 Passenger at 8.05am heads to Veraval (₹25, 3¼ hours). Half-hourly Diu–Una buses stop at Delvada (₹23, 20 minutes).

ⓘ Getting Around

Travelling by autorickshaw anywhere in Diu town should cost no more than ₹40. From the bus stand into town is ₹50. To Nagoa Beach and beyond you'll pay ₹120 and to Sunset Point ₹60.

Scooters are a perfect option for exploring the island – the roads are deserted and in good condition. The going rate is ₹350 per day (not including fuel), and motorcycles can be had for ₹400. Most hotels can arrange rentals, but quality varies. You'll normally have to show your driving licence and leave a deposit of ₹1500.

Local buses from Diu town to Nagoa and Vanakbara (both ₹12) leave Jethibai bus stand at 7am, 11am and 4pm. From Nagoa, they depart for Diu town from near the police post at 1pm, 5.30pm and 7pm.

Somnath

☑ 02876

One of India's 12 Shiva *jyoti linga* (devotional representation of Shiva) shrines, Somnath's famous, phoenix-like temple stands in neat gardens above the beach, 6km southeast of the large town of Veraval. Every day thousands of pilgrims pour through the narrow market streets (with no car traffic!), heading with excited anticipation to the temple in order to perform *puja* (offerings or prayers). Somnath celebrates Kartik Purnima (p690), marking Shiva's killing of the demon Tripurasura, with a large, colourful fair.

⊙ Sights

Temple of Somnath HINDU TEMPLE

(⊙ 6am-9pm) It's said that Somraj (the moon god) first built a temple in Somnath, made of gold; this was rebuilt by Ravana in silver, by Krishna in wood and by Bhimdev in stone. The current serene, symmetrical structure was built to traditional designs on the original coastal site; it's painted a creamy colour and has a little fine sculpture. The large, black Shiva lingam at its heart is one of the 12 most sacred Shiva shrines, known as *jyoti linga*.

A description of the temple by Al-Biruni, an 11th century Arab traveller, was so glowing that it prompted a visit in 1024 by a most unwelcome tourist: the legendary looter Mahmud of Ghazni, from Afghanistan. At that time the temple was so wealthy that it had 300 musicians, 500 dancing girls and even 300 barbers. Mahmud of Ghazni took the town and temple after a two-day battle in which it's said 70,000 Hindu defenders died. Having stripped the temple of its fabulous wealth, Mahmud destroyed it. So began a pattern of Muslim destruction and Hindu rebuilding that continued for centuries. The temple was again razed in 1297, in 1394 and finally in 1706 by Aurangzeb, the notorious Mughal ruler. After that, the temple wasn't rebuilt until 1950.

There's a very heavy security presence around the temple compound. Cameras, mobile phones and bags must be left at the cloakroom before you enter. You'll have to pass through a couple of metal detectors and will be physically searched to ensure that you've complied with these rules.

Colourful dioramas of the Shiva story line the north side of the temple garden, though it's hard to see them through the hazy glass. A 35-minute sound-and-light show (₹20; 8pm and 8.45pm) highlights the temple nightly.

🛏 Sleeping & Eating

Hotel Swagat HOTEL **$**

(☑ 02876-233839; www.hotelswagatsomnath.elisting.in; r from ₹600, with AC from ₹1000; ❇) This hotel, diagonally across from Somnath Temple (p715) on the market street, is the best option close to the temple and markets, and one of the few cheapies happy to accept foreigners. Rooms are in reasonable shape, and have modern air-con units and TVs.

New Bhabha Restaurant INDIAN, CHINESE **$**

(mains ₹100-140; ⊙ 11.30am-2pm & 7-10pm; ❇) The pick of a poor bunch of eateries, vegetarian New Bhabha sits 50m north of the ST bus stand, which is one block east of Somnath Temple. You can eat in a small air-con room or outside, open to the street.

ℹ Getting There & Away

From the ST bus station one block east of the temple, buses run to Veraval (₹20, 15 minutes, every half-hour), Diu (₹90, 2½ hours, daily at 5.50pm), Junagadh (₹90, 2½ hours, half-hourly)

ⅅ **TRANSIT HUB: VERAVAL**

Cluttered and chaotic, Veraval is one of India's major fishing ports; its busy harbour is full of bustle and boat building. It was also the major seaport for Mecca pilgrims before the rise of Surat. The main reason to come here now is to visit the Temple of Somnath (p715), 6km southeast; while the town of Somnath is a nicer place to stay, Veraval is more convenient to public transport.

From the centrally located **bus stand** (ST Bus Stand Rd) buses go to Ahmedabad (from ₹215, 9½ hours, eight daily), Junagadh (₹79 to ₹102, two hours, half-hourly), Rajkot (₹123, five hours, half-hourly), Una (for Diu, ₹74, 2¼ hours, hourly), Diu (₹93, 2¾ hours, nine daily) and Sasan Gir (₹47, one hour, daily at 3pm).

Patel Tours & Travels (☑ 0281-6198030; www.pateltoursandtravels.com; ST Bus Stand Rd), opposite the ST bus stand, offers three nightly non-AC buses to Ahmedabad (₹530) and one full-AC luxury sleeper at 10.10pm (₹660).

Four trains daily run to Junagadh, including the 11463 Jabalpur Express, departing at 9.50am (sleeper/3AC/2AC ₹150/510/750, 1¾ hours). The 11463, the 59460 at 1.20pm and the 22958 at 9.35pm continue to Rajkot (₹150/510/715, 4¼ hours) and Ahmedabad (₹270/715/1015, 8¾ hours). Second-class-only trains with unreserved seating head to Sasan Gir (₹10) at 9.45am (two hours) and 1.55pm (1¼ hours). There's a **computerised reservation office** (⊙ 8am-10pm Mon-Sat, to 2pm Sun) at the station.

The quickest way to get to Somnath is by autorickshaw, which costs around ₹15/150 for a shared/private vehicle.

and Ahmedabad (₹215 to ₹340, 10 hours, six daily).

The offices of several private bus companies line the road just next to the ST bus stand. All offer buses to Ahmedabad (AC/non-AC ₹600/480, 10 hours).

Gir National Park & Wildlife Sanctuary

📞 02877

The last refuge of the Asiatic lion (*Panthera leo persica*) is this forested, hilly, 1412-sq-km national park, where visitors may go lion-spotting between mid-October and mid-June (December to April is best). Taking a safari through the dry teak woodlands interspersed with tawny grasslands is a joy – even without the added excitement of searching for big cats, deer and myriad bird species.

Access to the park is only by safari permit, which has to be booked online in advance. Tickets cannot be bought at the park. If you miss out on a permit, your other option for lion encounters is at Devalia Safari Park, a fenced-off part of the park where sightings are guaranteed but very stage managed.

The gateway to Gir National Park is Sasan Gir village, on a minor road and railway between Veraval and Junagadh (about 40km from each).

◉ Sights

★ **Gir National Park**   NATIONAL PARK
(📱 8826678881, 9971231439, 0287-7285541; www.girnationalpark.in; ⊘ Safari tours daily 6.30am, 9.30am & 3.30pm; closed 15 Jun-15 Sep) Early-morning sunlight filters through the leaves and shadows skittle through the undergrowth. Suddenly, the silence is broken by the high-pitched alarm call of a spotted deer: danger is at hand. Somewhere out there the king of the jungle is hunting.

This is Gir National Park, the last home of the Asiatic lion, and Gujarat's most applauded wildlife park. Coming here on a safari is an unforgettable experience. The best time to visit is December to April.

The park was set up in 1965, and a 259-sq-km core area was declared a national park in 1975. Since the late 1960s, lion numbers have increased from under 200 to over 650 (not all of these lions live within the park). The sanctuary's 37 other mammal species, most of which have also increased in numbers, include dainty chitals (spotted deer), sambars (large deer), nilgais (large antelopes), chousinghas (four-horned antelopes), chinkaras (gazelles), crocodiles and rarely seen leopards. The park is a great destination for birders, too, with more than 300 species, most of them resident.

While the wildlife has been lucky, more than half the sanctuary's human community of distinctively dressed *maldhari* (herders) have been resettled elsewhere, ostensibly because their cattle and buffalo were competing for food resources with the antelopes, deer and gazelles while also being preyed upon by the lions and leopards. About 1000 people still live in the park, however, and their livestock accounts for about a quarter of the lions' diet.

Devalia Safari Park   NATURE RESERVE
(bus safari Indian/foreigner Mon-Fri ₹150/US$40, Sat & Sun ₹190/US$50, jeep safari Mon-Fri ₹800/US$80, Sat & Sun ₹1000/US$100; ⊘ 8-11am & 3-5pm) Twelve kilometres west of Sasan Gir village at Devalia, within the Gir National Park precincts, is the Gir Interpretation Zone, better known as simply Devalia. The 4.12-sq-km fenced-off compound is home to a cross-section of Gir wildlife. Lion sightings are basically guaranteed, but it all feels very stage managed and is no substitute for the real park. You may see foxes, mongooses and spotted deer. There's also a leopard in a cage.

The 45-minute bus or jeep tours depart along the trails hourly. An autorickshaw/taxi return trip to Devalia from Sasan Gir village costs around ₹150/350, but if you sign up for the jeep safari, transport is included from the park office in Sasan Gir.

🏃 Activities

★ **Safaris**   WILDLIFE WATCHING
(www.girlion.in; permit Indian/foreigner ₹800/5600, jeep hire ₹1700, guide per 3hr ₹400, camera Indian/foreigner ₹200/1400) Lion safaris are done in 4WDs (gypsys) and only 30 vehicles are allowed in the park at any time. Your best bet for seeing wildlife is early in the morning or a bit before sunset. Permits must be booked online in advance; it's wise to do this as far ahead as possible, as demand often exceeds supply.

Most hotels and guesthouses in and around Sasan Gir have gypsys and drivers, or will arrange them for you, charging ₹3000 or more per vehicle for up to six passengers. Alternatively, you can hire an open 4WD and driver for ₹1700 outside the sanctuary reception centre, in Sasan Gir village. Once you have a vehicle, you must queue at the reception centre to collect your permit and a guide, and pay photography fees. Your driver will usually help with this.

A guide is compulsory and quality varies hugely. Many guides don't speak much English and some don't know quite as much about the forest as they should (visitors have heard them misidentifying the most obvious of birds). Others, by contrast, are superb; a good guide, who can regale you with information on the wildlife and plants of the forest and the conservation issues being faced, can do much to turn an average safari into an extraordinary experience. If you make a special request for an English-speaking and knowledgeable guide, staff at the park office will normally try to help.

Safaris follow set routes: park staff will automatically select a route for you, which you cannot veer off.

About one in two safaris has a lion sighting, so if you're determined to see lions, allow for a couple of trips. To get the most out of a safari, though, it's important not to fixate on lions. Take your time, stop the vehicle, switch off the engine and listen to the forest – search for the little creatures who don't get much safari glory, and just relax and enjoy the whole package.

🍴 Sleeping & Eating

⭐ Nitin Ratanghayara

Family Rooms GUESTHOUSE $
(📞 9979024670, 02877-285686; SBI Bank St, Sasan Gir; r with/without AC ₹1200/800; ❄️ 🛜) At his family's courtyard-style home, friendly, golden-toothed Nitin Ratanghayara has several very good rooms for travellers. They're spotlessly clean, well kept, and much better value than any of the budget joints on the main street. Plus, you get to eat his sister-in-law's home cooking, and you can help her in the kitchen if you like.

Hotel Umang HOTEL $$
(📞 02877-285728; http://hotelumanggir.com; Rameshwar Society, SBS Rd, Sasan Gir; r with/without AC ₹2500/1500; ❄️ 🛜) While it doesn't

THE LAST WILD ASIATIC LIONS

The Asiatic lion (*Panthera leo persica*) once roared as far west as Syria and as far east as India's Bihar. Widespread hunting decimated the population, with the last sightings recorded near Delhi in 1834, in Bihar in 1840 and in Rajasthan in 1870. In Gujarat, too, they were almost hunted to extinction, with as few as 12 remaining in the 1870s. It was not until one of their erstwhile pursuers, the enlightened Nawab of Junagadh, decided to set up a protection zone at the beginning of the 20th century that the lions began slowly to recover. This zone now survives as the Gir Wildlife Sanctuary and the population of lions is growing, with surveys in August 2017 showing a population of around 650.

Gir is nowhere near big enough for the number of lions that currently live there and lions are increasingly leaving the park and attempting (with some success) to set up new populations elsewhere. Some of these new populations are living in very close proximity to people. There's even a group of beach-babe lions doing quite well for itself in the coastal scrubland near Veraval and early-morning beach walkers there will often see more than just seagull footprints in the sand. There is talk of introducing some lions to tiger country in Madhya Pradesh and a large swath of (tiger-free – the two species won't co-exist) land with a dense herbivore population has even been set aside and prepared for them. However, the Gujarat government opposes the notion and refused to go ahead with the project, vying to remain the sole home of India's lions and citing unsuitable habitat, though many big-cat experts dispute this. While it makes sense from a tourism perspective for Gujarat to keep all the lions, from a conservation perspective this is not a good idea. The Gir lions have narrow genetic diversity and a major disease outbreak or similar calamity could devastate the population. As if to underline this, in September and October 2018 at least 23 lions were found dead over a period of three weeks. Postmortems revealed the canine distemper virus as the cause of death in at least five cases. Tests on other lions within the park showed that at least 21 more lions were also carrying the virus.

Separated from their African counterpart (*Panthera leo leo*) for centuries, Asiatic lions have developed unique characteristics. Their mane is less luxuriant and doesn't cover the top of the head or ears, while a prominent fold of skin runs the length of the abdomen. They are also purely predatory, unlike African lions, which sometimes feed off carrion.

have the glamour (or price tag!) of the luxury safari lodges, this is a respectable and quiet budget option with perfectly good rooms, helpful management and decent meals. Discounts are available when business is slow. It's 200m south of the main road, near the town centre; follow the signs.

★ **Asiatic Lion Lodge** LODGE $$$
(☑ 9099077502, 02877-281101; www.asiaticlionlodge.com; Sasan Gir–Bhalchhel–Haripur Rd; r incl full board from ₹7700; ❄️ 🛜) Set in large grounds with lots of trees and birds, this peaceful lodge is around 6km west of Sasan Gir and far enough away from any village to be deliciously quiet. Accommodation consists of bungalow-style, tastefully decorated rooms with thatched roofs. Food is excellent vegetarian and in the evenings there are open-air screenings of an interesting documentary on the lions of Gir (p716).

Fern Gir Forest Resort BOUTIQUE HOTEL $$$
(☑ 02877-285999; www.fernhotels.com; Rte 100A; r incl full board ₹9000; ❄️ 🛜) The two-storey cottages here are so well integrated into the gardens that creepers and vines are slowly threatening to swallow them up. Once you go through the door, though, you'll find supersmart rooms with plush touches and the best bathrooms in lion country. Daily nature walks are available, and there's brilliant birding right in the resort's gardens.

Gateway Hotel HOTEL $$$
(☑ 02877-285551; www.thegatewayhotels.com; r incl full board from ₹17,700; ❄️ 🛜 🏊) 🎏 The remodelling of an old government property by the Taj Group is the finest – and greenest – choice near Gir National Park (p716). The rooms and huge suites are lush with comforts – they even come with yoga mats! All overlook a river where buffaloes wade and lions have been spotted.

Gir Birding Lodge HOTEL $$$
(☑ 9723971842; www.girbirdinglodge.com; Rte 100A; r or cottages incl full board from ₹6400; ❄️ 🛜) This peaceful place, situated in a mango grove that borders a forest, has six simple, sweet cottages with a few nice touches, such as handmade wooden beds. The 16 hotel rooms are modern, if a bit plain. It's particularly good for birders, plus there are complimentary nature walks. Located 2.5km from the village, off the Junagadh road.

❶ Information

Gir Orientation Centre (⊘ 8am-6pm) Next to the reception centre at Devalia (p716), this has an informative exhibition on the sanctuary and its wildlife and a small shop.

❶ Getting There & Away

Buses run from Sasan Gir village to both Veraval (₹41, one hour) and Junagadh (₹62, two hours) throughout the day.

Second-class, unreserved-seating trains run to Junagadh (₹30, 2¾ hours, 5.58pm) and to Veraval (₹25, 1½ hours, 11.58am and 4.27pm).

Junagadh

☑ 0285 / POP 319,460

Reached by few tourists, the ancient, fortified city of Junagadh (its name means 'old fort') has a history stretching back 2300 years. Its modern incarnation is fun to explore, with loud, brash markets, glorious architecture, interesting sights and a population who extend a very warm welcome. Junagadh also makes a good jumping-off point for seeing the lions at Gir National Park. When the Partition of India came in 1947, the nawab of Junagadh opted to take his tiny state into Pakistan. It was a wildly unpopular decision as the inhabitants were predominantly Hindu, so the nawab departed on his own.

❍ Sights & Activities

★ **Girnar Hill** RELIGIOUS SITE
This sacred mountain, rising dramatically from the plains, is covered with Jain and Hindu temples and is a major pilgrimage site. However, as with any good pilgrimage, getting to the temples isn't easy. Pilgrims are faced with a long, steep climb up 10,000 stone steps to the summit. If you want to join them, be prepared to spend a full day walking to get to the uppermost temples.

The Jain temples, a cluster of mosaic-decorated domes interspersed with elaborate stupas, are about two-thirds of the way up. The largest and oldest is the 12th-century Temple of Neminath, dedicated to the 22nd tirthankar (Jain teacher): go through the first left-hand doorway after the first gate. Many temples are locked from around 11am to 3pm, but this one is open all day. The nearby triple Temple of Mallinath, dedicated to the ninth *tirthankar,* was erected in 1177 by two brothers. During festivals this temple is a sadhu (ascetic) magnet.

Junagadh

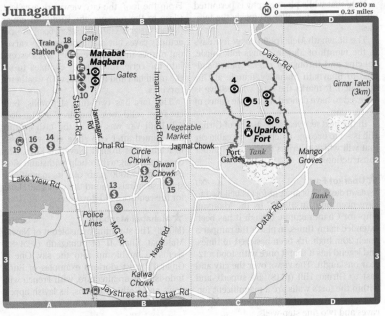

Junagadh

◉ Top Sights
1 Mahabat Maqbara	A1
2 Uparkot Fort	C2

◉ Sights
3 Adi Kadi Vav	C1
4 Buddhist Caves	C1
5 Jama Masjid	C1
6 Navghan Kuvo	C2
7 Vazir's Mausoleum	A1

⌂ Sleeping
8 Click Hotel	A1
9 Lotus Hotel	A1

✕ Eating
10 Geeta Lodge	A1
11 Petals	A1

ℹ Information
12 Axis Bank ATM	B2
13 Bank of Baroda	B2
14 State Bank of India	A2
15 State Bank of India	B2
16 State Bank of India ATM	A2

ℹ Transport
17 Mahasagar Travels	A3
18 Railway Station Reservation Office	A1
19 ST Bus Stand	A2

Further up are various Hindu temples. The first peak is topped by the Temple of Amba Mata, where newlyweds worship to ensure a happy marriage. Beyond here there's quite a lot of down as well as up to reach the other four peaks and further temples. The Temple of Gorakhnath is perched on Gujarat's highest peak at 1117m. The steep peak Dattatraya is topped by a shrine to a three-faced incarnation of Vishnu. Atop the final outcrop, Kalika, is a shrine to the goddess Kali.

The trail begins 4km east of the city at Girnar Taleti; an autorickshaw from town

costs ₹100. Refreshment stalls on the ascent sell chalk, so that you can graffiti your name on the rocks. If you can't face the walk, *dholis* (chairs) carried by porters cost ₹4000 (return) if you weigh between 50kg and 70kg, and ₹4500 for heavier passengers. If your weight range isn't obvious, you'll suffer the indignity of being weighed on a huge beam scale before setting off. (The majority of people milling around at the bottom of the hill have no intention of walking all the way to the top, and many just walk a few hundred metres before returning.)

Note that while photography is permitted on the trail, it's not allowed inside the temples.

The Bhavnath Mela (p690), over five days in the month of Magha, brings folk music, dancing and throngs of *nagas* (naked sadhus) to Bhavnath Mahadev Temple at Girnar Taleti. It marks the time when Shiva is believed to have danced his cosmic dance of destruction.

In the next few years the ascent of Girnar Hill is set to become much easier: a cable car that will whisk pilgrims to the top is under construction.

★ Uparkot Fort   FORT

(☉ dawn-dusk) This ancient fort is believed to have been built in 319 BC by the Mauryan emperor Chandragupta, though it has been extended many times. In places the ramparts reach 20m high. It's been besieged 16 times, and legend has it that it once withstood a 12-year onslaught. The views over the city and east to Girnar Hill (p718) are superb, and within the fort's walls are a magnificent former mosque, a set of millennia-old Buddhist caves and two fine step-wells.

Jama Masjid, the disused mosque, was converted from a palace in the 15th century by Gujarat sultan Mahmud Begada. It has a rare roofed courtyard with three octagonal openings that may once have been covered by domes. It's a shame about the graffiti, but the delicate mihrab (niche) stonework and the forest of columns are still stunning.

From the roof, the city views are excellent. Close to the mosque, the **Buddhist caves** (Indian/foreigner ₹15/200; ☉ 8am-6pm) are not actually caves but monastic quarters carved out of rock in the 2nd century AD. Descend into the eerie, three-storey complex to see the main hall and its pillars, with weathered carvings.

The fort has two fine step-wells, both cut from solid rock. The circular, 41m-deep Adi Kadi Vav was cut in the 15th century and named after two slave girls who used to fetch water from it. Navghan Kuvo, 52m deep and designed to help withstand sieges, is almost 1000 years old. Its magnificent staircase spirals around the well shaft. Look for the centuries-old dovecotes.

★ Mahabat Maqbara   MAUSOLEUM

(MG Rd) The stunning mausoleum of Nawab Mahabat Khan II of Junagadh (1851–82) seems to bubble up into the sky. One of Gujarat's most glorious examples of Euro-Indo-Islamic architecture, with French windows and Gothic columns, its lavish appeal is topped off by its silver inner doors.

Vazir's Mausoleum   MAUSOLEUM

(MG Rd) With almost as much flourish as the neighbouring Mahabat Maqbara mausoleum, the 1896 mausoleum of Vazir Sahib Baka-ud-din Bhar sports four storybook minarets encircled by spiralling stairways. It's not always open, but you can still gaze at it from beyond the gate.

BUSES FROM JUNAGADH

Buses leave the ST bus stand for the following destinations:

DESTINATION	COST (₹)	TIME (HR)	FREQUENCY
Ahmedabad	176	8	half-hourly
Bhuj	188-199	7	10 daily
Diu	117-135	5	4 daily
Jamnagar	102	4	10 daily
Rajkot	86-131	2¾	half-hourly
Sasan Gir	62	2	hourly
Una (for Diu)	110-113	4	10 daily
Veraval	76-102	2½	half-hourly

Various private bus offices, including **Mahasagar Travels** (☎ 0285-2629199; Jayshree Rd), with an office south of the city centre, offer more comfortable buses:

DESTINATION	COST (₹)	TIME (HR)	FREQUENCY
Ahmedabad	non-AC/AC/Volvo 430/490/550	8	half-hourly
Mumbai	sleeper AC 1510	17	5 daily

🛏 Sleeping

Lotus Hotel
HOTEL $$

(☑0285-2658500; www.thelotushotel.com; Station Rd; s/d from ₹2000/2500; ❄❂✿) This luxurious and comfortable option occupies the totally renovated top floor of a former *dharamsala* (pilgrim rest house). Pilgrims never had it so good, with split-system air-con and LCD TVs. Rooms are beautifully bright, spacious and pristine, the beds are great, and everything works – incredible value for such quality. If you want a quiet room at the back it'll cost you an extra ₹1000.

★Click Hotel
HOTEL $$$

(☑02832-244 077; www.theclickhotels.com; Station Rd; r incl breakfast ₹3600; ❂❄✿) Conveniently located next to the train station, this excellent chain hotel is the most comfortable place to stay in town. Rooms are absolutely spotless and come with comfy beds and plasma-screen TVs, the wi-fi is reliable, and though the food choices at the on-site vegetarian restaurant are limited, staff members are eager to please.

🍴 Eating

Geeta Lodge
GUJARATI $

(Station Rd; thalis ₹140; ⊙10am-3.30pm & 6.30-10pm; ✐) Geeta's army of waiters is constantly on the move serving up top-class, all-you-can-eat veg Gujarati thalis at a bargain price. Finish off with sweets, such as fruit salad or puréed mango.

★Petals
MULTICUISINE $$

(www.thelotushotel.com/dining/petals; Lotus Hotel, Station Rd; mains ₹130-250, thalis ₹200; ⊙7-10am, 11am-3pm & 7-11pm) Great food. Great atmosphere. The restaurant next to, and part of, the Lotus Hotel (p721) delivers a sleek first impression, with a modern – and very white – design. The vegetarian menu ranges from Punjabi to sizzlers to Chinese dishes to pasta, but it's the delicious lunchtime Gujarati thalis that can have queues forming out the door.

ℹ Information

State Bank of India (Nagar Rd; ⊙11am-2pm Mon-Fri) changes travellers cheques and cash and has an ATM; there's also a handy **ATM** (Prism Complex) and another branch near the bus station.

Bank of Baroda (cnr MG & Post Office Rds; ⊙8.30am-4.30pm Mon-Fri) has a useful branch on MG Rd and **Axis Bank** (Diwan Chowk) has an ATM. The **Post Office** (⊙10am-3pm) is located off MG Rd, near the local bus stand.

ℹ Getting There & Away

TRAIN
There's a computerised **reservation office** (⊙8am-10pm Mon-Sat, to 2pm Sun) at the railway station.

The Jabalpur Express (train 11463/5) departs at 11.10am for Gondal (sleeper/3AC/2AC ₹140/495/700, one hour), Rajkot (₹140/495/700, 2¾ hours) and Ahmedabad (₹220/595/850, 7¼ hours). The Somnath Express (train 22958) overnighter to Ahmedabad (sleeper/3AC/2AC ₹220/595/850, 6½ hours) departs at 11.02pm.

Second-class train 52952 heads to Sasan Gir (₹30, 2¾ hours).

Gondal

☑ 02825 / POP 112,195

Compact, leafy Gondal, 38km south of Rajkot, sports a string of palaces and a gentle river. Its small scale and relative tranquillity compared to other Gujarati cities make an overnight stay here worthwhile. It was once capital of a 1000-sq-km princely state ruled by Jadeja Rajputs who believe they are descendants of Krishna.

◉ Sights

★Naulakha Museum
MUSEUM

(www.heritagepalacesgondal.com; Naulakha Palace, DCR Pandeya Marg; all museums ₹280, per museum ₹50; ⊙9am-noon & 3-6pm) This eclectic collection of museums is housed in a beautiful 260-year-old riverside palace that was built in a mixture of styles, with striking gargoyles and delicate stone carvings. A full ticket includes entry to the palace itself as well as several museums, including a horse-carriage museum, an eggcup (!) and toy museum, a doll museum and (one that can't help but make you smile) a teapot museum.

Royal Vintage & Classic Car Collection
MUSEUM

(Orchard Palace Hotel, Palace Rd; Indian/foreigner ₹120/250; ⊙9am-noon & 3-6pm) This is the royal collection of cars – 32 impressive vehicles, from a 1907 model made by the New Engine Company Acton and a 1935 vintage Mercedes saloon to racing cars driven by the present maharaja. Most are still in working condition, but sadly you're unlikely to be invited to go for a spin in a Cadillac.

Shri Bhuvaneshwari
Aushadhashram
HISTORIC BUILDING

(www.bhuvaneshwaripith.com; Ghanshyam Bhuvan; ⊙9am-noon & 3-5pm Tue-Sat) Founded in 1910 by Gondal's royal physician, this pharmacy manufactures ayurvedic medicines and it's possible to see all the quirky machinery involved, as well as buy treatments for hair loss, vertigo and insomnia. The founding physician, Brahmaleen Acharyashree, is said to have coined the title 'Mahatma' (Great Soul) for Gandhi. Also here is a temple to the goddess Bhuvaneshwari.

Udyog Bharti
Khadi Gramodyog
WORKSHOP

(✐02825-220177; www.udyogbharti.org; Udyog Bharti Chowk; ⊙9am-noon & 3-5pm Mon-Sat) Women spin cotton upstairs at this large *khadi* (homespun cloth) workshop, while downstairs embroidered *salwar kameez* (traditional dress-like tunic and trouser combination for women) and saris are on sale.

🛏 Sleeping & Eating

★Orchard Palace
HERITAGE HOTEL $$$

(✐02825-220002, 02825-24550; www.heritagepalacesgondal.com; Palace Rd; s/d incl breakfast ₹5710/7140; ❄🛜) This small palace, once the royal guesthouse, is now one of the best heritage hotels in Gujarat. Awash in regal character, its reception rooms, drawing rooms and bedrooms are crammed with antiques, royal portraits, drink decanters and mounted zebra skins and stuffed leopards. There's even a writing desk with a bust of Churchill.

Riverside Palace
HERITAGE HOTEL $$$

(✐02825-221950, 02825-220002; www.heritagepalacesgondal.com; Ashapura Rd; s/d incl breakfast ₹5710/7140; ❄) This is the erstwhile ruling family's main palace and is used as a back-up hotel when the Orchard Palace is full. Built in the 1880s and formerly the crown prince's abode, it's deliciously well worn and adorned with antiques and hunting trophies. Its 11 rooms are like a royal time machine you can sleep in, with river views.

ℹ Getting There & Around

Buses run frequently from the ST stand on Gundana Rd, 500m south of Orchard Palace (p722), to/from Rajkot (normal/express ₹30/44, one hour) and Junagadh (normal/express ₹60/80, two hours).

Slow passenger trains between Rajkot (₹10, one hour, 14 daily) and Junagadh (₹25, 1¾ to three hours, 11 daily) also stop at Gondal.

Hiring an autorickshaw to take you to all the sights and wait while you see them costs about ₹150 per hour.

Jamnagar
📞 0288 / POP 600,945

Jamnagar is a little-touristed but interesting city that centres on a beautiful lake with a promenade that buzzes with life each evening, and an absorbing old core brimming with ornate, decaying buildings and colourful bazaars. The city is also a good jumping-off point for visiting nearby Khijadiya Bird Sanctuary (p725) and Narara Marine National Park (p725).

When exploring the town, look out for examples of Jamnagar's famous, brilliant-coloured *bandhani* (tie-dye) – produced through a laborious 500-year-old process involving thousands of tiny knots in a piece of folded fabric.

Before Independence, Jamnagar was capital of the Nawanagar princely state. Today, Jamnagar is quite a boom town, with the world's biggest oil refinery, belonging to Reliance Petroleum, not far west of the city. The central area is one big commercial zone, with more brightly lit shops and stalls at night than you'll find in many a larger city.

◉ Sights

Khambhaliya Gate
GATE

(Central Bank Rd; ₹5; ⊙photo galley 4-8pm) Built in the 17th century by Wazir Meraman Khawa, and one of two remaining city gates from that period, this elegantly decaying landmark has been restored. After dark the gate is lit up in gaudy colours. There's a small photo gallery on its upper level.

★Shantinath Mandir
JAIN TEMPLE

(Chandi Bazaar Rd; ⊙dawn-dusk) One of the largest Jain temples in the old town, Shantinath Mandir dates to the mid-17th century. Although the outside is classic white, the interior is a fairground of bright colours and recently restored, cartoon-like murals. It's one of the more memorable Jain temples in Gujarat.

Adinath Mandir
JAIN TEMPLE

(Chandi Bazaar Rd; ⊙dawn-dusk) Adinath Mandir, one of the two largest and most elaborate Jain temples in the old town, is dedicated to

Jamnagar

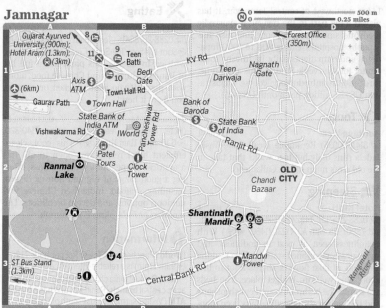

Jamnagar

◎ Top Sights
1 Ranmal Lake	A2
2 Shantinath Mandir	C3

◎ Sights
3 Adinath Mandir	C3
4 Bala Hanuman Temple	B3
5 Bhujiyo Kotho	A3
6 Khambhaliya Gate	B3
7 Lakhota Palace	A2

⊕ Activities, Courses & Tours
Mustak Mepani	(see 10)

⊜ Sleeping
8 Hotel Kalatit	A1
9 Hotel Kiriti	B1
10 Hotel President	B1

⊗ Eating
7 Seas Restaurant	(see 10)
11 Hotel Kalpana	B1

the 16th and first *tirthankars* (great Jain teachers) and explodes with fine murals, mirrored domes and elaborate chandeliers.

★ Ranmal Lake
LAKE

(₹10; ⊙dawn-10.30pm) Every evening it seems as though half the city has descended onto the well-kept, tree-lined promenades running around Ranmal Lake. There's a bona fide astroturf running track and the diminutive mid-19th-century **Lakhota Palace** (₹100, camera ₹100; ⊙8am-8pm), an island fort in the middle of the lake, housing a museum. However, most people skip the culture and just eat ice cream while strolling around chatting with friends. Access is via one of the entrance gates.

Bala Hanuman Temple
HINDU TEMPLE

(www.shribalahanuman.org; Shri Premhikshuji Marg; ⊙dawn-dusk) This temple on the southeastern side of Ranmal Lake has been the scene of continuous chanting of the prayer *Shri Ram, Jai Ram, Jai Jai Ram* since 31 July 1964, earning the temple a place in an Indian favourite, the *Guinness World Records*. Early evening is a good time to visit, as the temple and lakeside area are busiest and most fun at this time.

⊋ Courses

Gujarat Ayurved University
HEALTH & WELLBEING

(☎0288-2664866; www.ayurveduniversity.com; Chanakya Bhavan, Hospital Rd) The world's first ayurvedic university, founded in 1967, is

1.5km northwest of central Jamnagar. It has played a big part in the revival of ayurvedic medicine since Independence and also has a public hospital treating 800 to 1000 inpatients and outpatients daily. Its International Center for Ayurvedic Studies runs a full-time, three-month introductory course (registration US$25, tuition per month US$475).

☞ Tours

Heritage Walk CULTURAL
(☑8141600036) Reputable local guide Yashi Jadela runs daily heritage walks that take in the old city's main sights. Call ahead.

🛏 Sleeping

Hotel Kiriti HOTEL $
(☑0288-2557121; http://hotelkiriti.com; Teen Batti; s/d ₹800/975, with AC ₹1230/1460; ❋ 🛜) With cleanliness seen as next to godliness, and strategically positioned statues of the Buddha and pots of fake flowers, there's a lot to like about this well-run budget place. The beds are comfy, the bathrooms are kept shipshape and the high-powered ceiling fans even manage to drown out the road noise.

Hotel President HOTEL $$
(☑0288-2557491; www.hotelpresident.in; Teen Batti; r ₹990, with AC from ₹2240; ❋ 🛜) This hotel has exceptionally helpful management and a range of reasonable rooms, many with balconies. The air-con rooms have street views and are bigger and generally better than the non-AC, which are at the rear.

Hotel Kalatit HOTEL $$
(☑0288-2771000; www.hotelkalatit.com; Teen Batti; s/d from ₹2070/2465; ❋ 🛜) A step above anything else in the city centre, the Kalatit offers carefully designed and decorated rooms with touches of art. The real highlight, though, is the roof garden, with palm trees and leafy plants.

Hotel Aram HERITAGE HOTEL $$$
(☑0288-2551701; www.hotelaram.com; Pandit Nehru Marg; incl breakfast r ₹2230-3960, ste ₹4320-6500; ❋ 🛜) This former royal property has had an upgrade, creating an interesting mix of historical and contemporary. Rooms vary widely, from simple standards to luxurious superdeluxe rooms and suites, some of which can't decide on a style. Still, it's the nicest place around. There's a very popular multicuisine veg restaurant with garden seating. It's 1.5km northwest of the city centre

✖ Eating

Hotel Kalpana MULTICUISINE $$
(☑0288-2678541; Teen Batti; mains ₹90-170; ◷9am-10.45pm Tue-Sun) Clean and modern, with cushy booths, this place has a full list of Punjabi, Gujarati and Chinese food, along with pizza. If you want chicken or mutton, you'll get it here!

7 Seas Restaurant MULTICUISINE $$
(Hotel President, Teen Batti; mains ₹140-320; ◷6-10am & 11am-11pm; 🛜) This cool, clean, efficient hotel restaurant (open to all) has a nautical theme and a touch of class, offering a good range of veg and nonveg dishes, including seafood, Indianised Chinese and tandoori options, and decent breakfasts. The tandoori *bhindi* (okra) is a triumph.

ℹ Information

IWorld (Pancheshwar Tower Rd; per hour ₹12; ◷9am-11pm) is a reliable internet cafe.

State Bank of India changes foreign currency at its central **branch** (Ranjit Rd) and has a handy **ATM** (Vishwakarma Rd) just south of the town hall. There's also an **Axis ATM** (Bhid Bhanjan Rd) north of the town hall, and a **Bank of Baroda** (Ranjit Rd) branch and ATM on Ranjit Rd. The **post office** is on Chandi Bazaar Rd (◷9am-5pm).

The city's website (www.jamnagar.org) is full of useful information for visitors. It's particularly strong on info for birdwatchers.

ℹ Getting There & Away

AIR
Jamnagar Airport (☑0288-2712187) is located 6km west of the city. Air India has daily flights to Mumbai.

BUS
ST buses run to/from the **ST bus stand** (Government Colony) to Rajkot (₹81, two hours, half-hourly), Junagadh (₹102, four hours, about hourly) and Ahmedabad (₹169 to ₹182, 7¼ hours, about hourly). There are also three morning and evening buses to Bhuj (₹162, 6½ hours).

Private companies based along Vishwakarma Rd include the reliable **Patel Tours** (☑0288-2660243), which has 23 daily Volvo AC buses to Ahmedabad (₹630, seven hours), 34 buses to Rajkot (₹130, two hours) and five non-AC buses to Bhuj (seat/sleeper ₹350/400, six hours), mostly overnighters.

TRAIN
One of the most useful trains is the 22946 Saurashtra Mail, which departs at 4.05pm for Rajkot (sleeper/3AC/2AC/1AC ₹150/510/715/1180, 1¾

WESTERN SAURASHTRA

Mahatma Gandhi was born in 1869 in the port town of Porbandar, 130km southwest of Jamnagar. You can visit **Gandhi's birthplace** (Kasturba Rd; ☉9am-noon & 3-6pm) **FREE** – a 22-room, 220-year-old house with photographic exhibitions of his family's life – and a memorial next door, **Kirti Mandir** (☉7.30am-7pm) **FREE**. En route to Porbandar, the wild, remote and very rarely visited **Barda Wildlife Sanctuary** (Rte 27; ☉6.30am-6pm) **FREE** is a hilly, forested area with stone-built villages, old temples and good hiking. Tourist facilities are minimal.

Dwarka, 104km northwest of Porbandar at the western tip of the Kathiawar Peninsula, is one of the four holiest Hindu pilgrimage sites in India. Its **Dwarkadhish Temple** (☉6.30am-1pm & 5-9.30pm) is believed to have been founded more than 2500 years ago, and has a fantastically carved, 78m-high spire. Dwarka's **lighthouse** (₹10; ☉5-6.30pm) affords a beautiful panoramic view, though photography is not allowed (and neither are mobile phones). The town swells to breaking point for Janmastami in celebration of Krishna's birthday in August/September. There are some good beaches, including the beautiful, long, clean Okhamadhi, 22km south of Dwarka.

A good contact for arranging visits to western Saurashtra is **Mustak Mepani** (☎9824227786) at Jamnagar's Hotel President (p724).

Regular buses connect Porbandar with Dwarka and Jamnagar; Dwarka is also reachable by train from Jamnagar. For the beaches and wildlife reserve, it's best to have your own wheels.

hours) via Wankaner, continuing to Ahmedabad (₹225/600/850/1405, 6¾ hours) and Mumbai (₹420/1135/1625/2745, 16 hours).

ⓘ Getting Around

An autorickshaw from the airport, 6km west, should be around ₹150, and a taxi ₹300 to ₹350. An autorickshaw from the ST bus stand to Bedi Gate costs around ₹30; autorickshaws to the railway station from the centre cost the same.

Around Jamnagar

Khijadiya Bird Sanctuary   BIRD SANCTUARY
(Mon-Fri US$10, vehicle with up to 6 people US$40, Sat & Sun US$12.50, vehicle with up to 6 people US$50, camera US$20; ☉6.30am-6pm) This small, 6-sq-km sanctuary, 12km northeast of Jamnagar, encompasses salt- and freshwater marshlands and hosts more than 200 bird species, including the Dalmatian pelican, painted stork and crab plover. It's best visited in the early morning or late afternoon between October and March, when migratory birds are in residence. The evening arrival of cranes for roosting can be spectacular and there are six towers for birdwatching. Hiring a car from Jamnagar to drive you around the sanctuary costs around ₹1500.

You'll have to show your passport at the interpretation centre before going in. Staff often show up late in the morning, so if you're keen to get in at first light it might be

worth going over the evening before and letting them know that you're intending to be there at the official opening time.

Narara Marine National Park   NATIONAL PARK
(₹400, camera ₹450) Consisting of three parts, this national park and the adjoining marine sanctuary encompass the intertidal zone and 42 small islands along some 120km of coast east and west of Jamnagar – an area rich in wildlife that faces growing challenges from industrialisation. Coral, octopus, anemones, pufferfish, sea horses, lobsters and crabs are among the marine life you may see in shallow water at low tide. Mustak Mepani at Jamnagar's Hotel President arranges tours, cars, drivers and permits.

Rajkot

☎0281 / POP 1.4 MILLION

Rajkot is a large, hectic commercial and industrial city that isn't easy to love, with its heavy traffic, lack of open spaces, and scant worthwhile sights. But the old city, east of the newer centre, still has plenty of character, with narrow streets, markets, and farmers selling ghee on street corners. It's worth a day's visit.

Rajkot was founded in 1612 by the Jadeja Rajputs, and in colonial times it became the headquarters of the Western India States Agency, Britain's administrative centre for

WORTH A TRIP

WANKANER'S PALACES

Wankaner is a quiet, appealing small town 60km northeast of Rajkot, famous for its two highly flamboyant palaces and its scenic setting on the banks of the River Machchhu ('*wanka*' means 'bend' and '*ner*' means 'river'). With a quality place to stay and a slow tempo compared to many bigger Gujarati towns, this is a delightful place to stop for a night.

Ranjit Villas Palace (☏02828-220000; ₹200/Royal Oasis guests free) This grand 1907 palace – an architectural melange of Victorian Gothic arches, splendid stained-glass windows and chandeliers, Mughal domes and Doric columns – was the official residence of the maharajah of Wankaner until 2012, when the family decamped to a smaller place. The palace isn't officially open to the public, but guided tours are often possible if arranged in advance. Even if you can't get inside it's still an arresting sight.

Royal Oasis (☏02828-222002; www.wankanerheritagehotels.com; r from ₹5840; ❋☀) This daffodil-yellow 1937 palace used to be the summer residence of the maharajah of Wankaner and has now been converted into an intimate hotel. The rooms are vast and individually decorated; the French Suite is particularly appealing. Common areas are full of overstuffed armchairs. Delicious vegetarian cooking is served and the art deco pool is sublime.

Buses run from Rajkot (₹24, one hour, half-hourly) to Wankaner's bus stand in the southeast of town.

Wankaner is on the main train line between Rajkot and Ahmedabad and 11 trains pass through daily in each direction.

some 400 princely states in Saurashtra, Kachchh and northern Gujarat. After Independence, Rajkot was capital of the short-lived state of Saurashtra.

◉ Sights

Kaba Gandhi No Delo　　HISTORIC BUILDING
(Ghee Kanta Rd; ☉9am-6pm) FREE This is the house where Gandhi lived from the age of six (while his father was diwan of Rajkot), and it features many photos of the family and lots of interesting information on Gandhi's life. The mahatma's passion for the hand loom is preserved in the form of a small weaving school.

Mayur Patola Art　　WORKSHOP
(☏0281-2464519; www.facebook.com/mayurpatola 56; Sarvoday Society; ☉10am-9pm) Rajkot has quickly developed a Patola-weaving industry. This skill comes from Patan, and is a tortuous process that involves dyeing each thread before it's woven. However, in Patan both the warp and weft threads are dyed (double *ikat*), whereas in Rajkot only the weft is dyed (single *ikat*), so the product is more affordable.

⌁ Sleeping & Eating

Hotel Grand Thakar　　BUSINESS HOTEL $$
(☏0281-2230091; http://hotelthakar.com; Jawahar Rd; s/d incl breakfast from ₹2170/2720; ❋☎) The

excellent Grand Thakar has spotless rooms (the Executive comes with a larger TV and slightly more space than the Superior), marble bathrooms, blackout curtains and a decent multicuisine restaurant that does particularly good Gujarati thalis. Free pick-up/drop-off at the railway station or airport.

**★Heritage
Khirasara Palace**　　HERITAGE HOTEL $$$
(☏02827-234440; www.khirasarapalace.in; Kalawad Rd, Khirasara; r from ₹4500, ste ₹8000-27,000; ❋☎☀) This romantic 16th-century heritage palace has been painstakingly rebuilt at its lofty hillock location. Inside are manicured lawns, a mosaic-tiled pool and spacious, luxurious rooms. The Maharajah Suite comes with antique furniture, though the Maharani Suite has a better ambience. Fantastic restaurant and cafe on-site. Regular buses connect Rajkot to Khirasara (₹17, 30 minutes).

Senso　　MULTICUISINE $$
(☏0281-2480000; mains ₹140-420; ☉24hr; ❋☀) The very good, round-the-clock coffee shop at the **Imperial Palace** (☏0281-2480000; www.theimperialpalace.biz; Dr Yagnik Rd; s/d from ₹6350/6850, ste from ₹13,500; ❋☎☀) does everything from Mediterranean and lasagne to sizzlers and South Indian – all without meat.

ⓘ Getting There & Away

AIR

The airport is 2.5km northwest of the town centre. Air India and Jet Airways fly daily to Mumbai and Air India also has direct daily flights to Delhi.

BUS

Services leaving from the **ST bus stand** (Dhebar Rd) connect Rajkot with Jamnagar (₹81, two hours, half-hourly), Junagadh (₹131, 2¾ hours, half-hourly) and Bhuj (₹151, seven hours, about hourly). Ahmedabad is served by frequent ordinary buses (₹137, 4½ hours, half-hourly) as well as AC Volvos (₹397, three hours). At the time of research the bus station was closed for rebuilding and buses were just stopping on the road outside the station. This makes finding your bus – and someone to buy a ticket from – even more complicated than usual. Be sure to double confirm with everyone that you're getting on the right bus. Private buses operate to Ahmedabad, Bhavnagar, Una (for Diu), Mt Abu, Udaipur and Mumbai. Several offices are on Limda Chowk. Head to **Jay Somnath Travels** (☑ 0281-2222630; www. somnathbus.com; Kasturba Rd) for buses to Bhuj (regular/AC/Volvo ₹253/330/410, five hours).

TRAIN

Among numerous trains, the 22946 Saurashtra Mail leaves at 6.20pm and arrives in Ahmedabad (sleeper/3AC/2AC/1AC ₹190/510/715/1180) at 10.25pm and Mumbai (₹390/1055/1510/2555) at 7.10am. The 22945 departs at 10.35am, runs via Wankaner and arrives at Jamnagar (₹150/510/715/1180) at 12.12pm. An autorickshaw to the station from the centre costs about ₹40.

KACHCHH (KUTCH)

Kachchh, India's wild west, is a geographic phenomenon. The flat, tortoise-shaped land, edged by the Gulf of Kachchh and Great and Little Ranns, is a seasonal island. During the dry season, the Ranns are vast expanses of dried mud and blinding-white salt. Come the monsoon, they're flooded first by seawater, then by fresh river water. The salt in the soil makes the low-lying marsh area almost completely barren. Only on scattered 'islands' above the salt level is there coarse grass, which provides fodder for the region's wildlife.

The villages dotted across Kachchh's arid landscape are home to a jigsaw of tribal groups and subcastes who produce some of India's finest handicrafts – above all, textiles that glitter with exquisite embroidery and mirror work. In spite of the mammoth earthquake in 2001 that destroyed several villages, the residents of this harsh land have determinedly rebuilt their lives and welcome visitors.

Bhuj

☑ 02832 / POP 188,240

The most entrancing city in Gujarat, Bhuj has creaky old palaces full of twinkling treasures and grand dining rooms, and an old town that's an effervescent network of narrow, noisy streets. There are also a couple of interesting museums and lots of shops selling top-quality local textiles.

Bhuj is also an ideal springboard for visits to the surrounding villages and to places of superb natural beauty in the Great Rann, and textile tourism is attracting visitors from around the world.

The Jadeja Rajputs who took control of Kachchh in 1510 made Bhuj their capital 29 years later, and it has remained Kachchh's most important town ever since (it's still the region's capital). In 2001 a massive earthquake left Bhuj almost completely destroyed. Today the city has been largely rebuilt, though it lost much of its historic architecture and some of the palaces retain the scars of that fateful day.

⊙ Sights

★ Aina Mahal

PALACE

(Old Palace; adult/child ₹20/10, camera ₹30; ⊙9.30am-12.15pm & 3-5.45pm) This beautiful palace, built in 1752 and part of the Darbargadh palace complex, lost its top storey in the 2001 earthquake, but the lower floor is open, with a fantastic 15.2m scroll showing a Kachchh state procession. The 18th-century, elaborately mirrored interior is a demonstration of the fascination with all things European – an inversion of European Orientalism – with blue-and-white Delft-style tiling, a candelabra with Venetian-glass shades, and the Hogarth lithograph series *The Rake's Progress*. There are lofty views of Rani Mahal (p728) from atop the tower.

The palace was built for Maharao Lakhpatji by Ramsingh Malam, a sailor from Dwarka who had learnt European arts and crafts on his travels. In the bedroom is a bed with solid-gold legs (the king apparently auctioned his bed annually). In the Fuvara Mahal room, fountains played around the ruler while he sat watching dancers or composing poems.

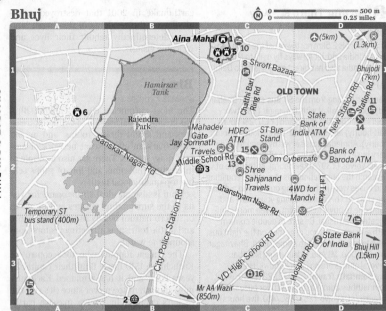

Aina Mahal

Hamirsar
Tank

Rajendra
Park

Shroff Bazaar

OLD TOWN

Chatthi Bari
Ring Rd

State
Bank of
India ATM

Bank of
Baroda ATM

Mahadev
Gate

HDFC
ATM

ST Bus
Stand

Jay Somnath
Travels

Middle School Rd

Om Cybercafe

Shree
Sahjanand
Travels

Ghanshyam Nagar Rd

4WD for
Mandvi

Lal Tekari

Sanskar Nagar Rd

City Police Station Rd

Temporary ST
bus stand (400m)

Hospital Rd

State Bank
of India

Bhuj Hill
(1.5km)

VD High School Rd

Mr AA Wazir
(850m)

Bhujodi
(7km)

New Station Rd

Station Rd

Prag Mahal PALACE
(New Palace; adult/child ₹30/10, camera/video ₹50/500; ⏰9.30am-12.15pm & 3-5.45pm) The largest of the three palaces within the Darbargadh walled complex, 19th-century Prag Mahal is in a forlorn state, damaged by the 2001 earthquake, but the ghostly yet exuberant Durbar Hall, with its vast chandeliers, remains very impressive. The maharajah's taxidermy collection, and some gold-skirted classical statues that wouldn't look out of place decorating a nightclub, are also memorable. Several scenes from *Lagaan,* the acclaimed Bollywood cricket blockbuster, were filmed here.

Rani Mahal PALACE
The 17th-century Rani Mahal, the former main royal residence, was almost completely destroyed in the 2001 earthquake, though you can still admire the latticed windows of its *zenana* (women's quarters). It's particularly beautiful around sunset.

Kachchh Museum MUSEUM
(City Police Station Rd; Indian/foreigner ₹5/50, camera/video ₹100/500; ⏰9am-1.30pm & 2.30-6pm, closed 2nd & 4th Sat of month) Opposite Hamirsar Tank, Gujarat's oldest museum has eclectic and dusty displays spanning textiles, weapons, silverware, sculpture, wildlife, geography and dioramas of Kachchh

tribal costumes and artefacts. Labelling, in English and Gujarati, is minimal.

Folk Art Museum MUSEUM
(Bhartiya Sanskriti Darshan; ₹100, camera ₹200; ⏰10am-noon & 3-6pm Tue-Sun, closed 2nd & 4th Sat of month) This museum, near City Police Station Rd, has displays on traditional Kachchh culture, including reconstructed Rabari *bhungas* (mud-and-mirrorwork huts), musical instruments, numerous wood and stone carvings and much more. The vintage Kachchh textiles are particularly worthwhile. The majority of the museum's collection comes from a single local collector. A guide will likely show you around.

Sharad Baug Palace PALACE
(₹20; ⏰9am-noon & 3-6pm Sat-Thu) This graceful 1867 Italianate palace, set among shade trees full of crows and bats, was the abode of the last maharao of Kachchh, Madansingh, until his death in 1991. It lost most of its 3rd floor in the 2001 earthquake, and the remaining lower floors are closed. However, the adjacent former dining hall now houses the palace's eclectic museum collection, including plenty of taxidermied specimens. The maharao's coffin lies in pride of place in the centre of the building.

Photography is forbidden.

GUJARAT & DIU BHUJ

Bhuj Hill HILL
(Bhujiyo Dungar) On the eastern outskirts of the city, this hill is crowned with a Hindu temple and is a terrific place to watch the sunset. For years there have been plans to build a memorial to the 2001 earthquake victims atop the hill, but the project seems to be progressing very slowly. Autorickshaws to the bottom of the steps from central Bhuj should cost around ₹80.

🛌 Sleeping

City Guest House GUESTHOUSE $
(☑ 9913922669; www.cityguesthousebhuj.com; Langa St; d ₹500, s/d without bathroom from ₹300/400; ❄🛜) Just off Shroff Bazaar, this place has been hosting passing travellers for years and it's unusually bright and cheery for a budget guesthouse. It has clean, basic rooms with colourful bedspreads. Bathrooms have squat toilets or the hybrid variety. Breakfast is available, there are two airy rooftop terraces, and manager Latif rents motorbikes for ₹600 per day.

Hotel Mangalam HOTEL $$
(☑ 02832-220303; www.mangalamhotels.com; Mangalam Cross Rd; s/d from ₹1680/2800; ❄🛜) Towards the southern edge of town, the Mangalam has big, bright rooms with comfy furnishings. The superdeluxe rooms (singles/doubles ₹3540/4130), with their strange half-sunken baths, are the best choice. It's a great hotel, but its distance from, well, anything makes it less appealing. Free airport transfers are offered, and there's an excellent restaurant.

Hotel Gangaram HOTEL $$
(☑ 9429377131; www.hotelgangaram.com; s/d ₹1000/1200; ❄🛜) In the old city, off Shroff

Bazaar, near the Darbargadh, this is a good, if weary-looking, place run by a kindly manager and well away from the din of Bhuj's main thoroughfares. The rooms vary, so look at a few. All the bathrooms are microscopic. Meals are pretty decent.

Click Hotel BUSINESS HOTEL $$$
(☑ 02832-694077; New Railway Station Compound; r incl breakfast ₹4600; ❄🛜) With its spotless if somewhat bland rooms, plasma-screen TVs and reliable wi-fi, this Click outpost is the most comfortable accommodation right by the train station. Even so, it's not one of the chain's better hotels and it's a long way from the city centre.

Hotel Ilark HOTEL $$$
(☑ 02832-258999; www.hotelilark.com; Station Rd; s/d from ₹3250/3550, ste from ₹5240; ❄🛜) One of Bhuj's better hotels, the Ilark has old-fashioned, wood-panelled, wood-furnished rooms that live up to the promise of the flash glass-and-red-paint exterior. Service is professional and there's a good restaurant.

★ Bhuj House HOMESTAY $$$
(☑ 9098187346, 02832-223426; www.thebhuj house.com; Camp Area; r incl breakfast ₹5100-6100; ❄🛜) Run by a delightful Indian-British couple, Jehan and Katie, this lovingly restored 19th-century traditional Parsi heritage house – Jehan's ancestral home – surrounds a secret courtyard garden that's a world away from the traffic chaos outside. The four rooms feature Kachchh embroidery and antique furnishings. Delicious meals are available on request (₹400). It's opposite Camp Police Chowki.

Your hosts can help you arrange your travels around the villages of Kachchh.

✖ Eating

★ **Shankar Vadapav** STREET FOOD **$**
(Middle School Rd; snacks from ₹20) Just a small step up from a food stall, this grimy-walled place is a local legend. Try a *vadapav* (a spiced fried potato with chutney in a sandwich) or go big and get the *mirchvada* (fluffy fried dough covering a whole chilli pepper that's stuffed with a paste of spices and served on bread).

The sign is in Gujarati; it's right next to the Gopi Gola Ghar ice-cream shop.

★ **Toral** VEGETARIAN **$$**
(Comfort Inn Prince, Station Rd; thalis ₹299; ⊙11.30am-3pm & 7.30-11pm; ✤) If you're growing weary of an endless succession of so-so thalis then this upmarket restaurant inside the **Comfort Inn Prince** (☑02832-220370; www.comfortinnprince.com; Station Rd; s/d incl breakfast from ₹3470/4060; ✤✤⊛) will restore your faith. It gets packed at lunchtime as locals and visitors alike pile in for the excellent, bottomless Gujarati thali.

Jesal NORTH INDIAN **$$**
(☑02832-220370; www.comfortinnprince.com; Comfort Inn Prince, Station Rd; mains from ₹200; ⊙7am-3pm & 7-11pm; ✤) Jesal serves up a good mix of North Indian dishes (particularly all things tandoori), along with an extensive menu of Indo-Chinese dishes and a few Western ones.

Green Rock MULTICUISINE **$$**
(Middle School Rd; mains ₹100-210, thalis ₹240; ⊙11am-3pm & 7-10.30pm; ✤) This 1st-floor, air-conditioned place serves up tasty lunchtime thalis, as well as an extensive all-veg menu including many Punjabi and South Indian favourites.

ℹ Information

Om Cybercafe (Middle School Rd; per hour ₹30; ⊙8am-8pm) Across from the bus stand.
State Bank of India (Hospital Rd; ⊙10am-4pm Mon-Fri, to 1pm Sat) Changes major currencies.

ATMs are readily accessible: **HDFC** (Middle School Rd) has one on Middle School Rd; **Bank of Baroda** (Station Rd) has one on Station Rd; and **SBI** has one at the southern end of Station Rd.
Post Office (Dadavadi Rd; ⊙9am-5pm Mon-Fri)

There's no longer an official tourist office, but former tourism director Pramod Jethi (p735) has a small office space at the Prag Mahal from which he provides tourist information.

ℹ Getting There & Away

AIR
Bhuj Airport, 4km north of the centre, has daily flights to Delhi and Mumbai with Air India.

BUS
At the time of research the main town-centre ST bus stand was closed for renovations. It's not known when it will reopen. In the meantime buses are departing from a station a short way southwest of the centre (a seat in a shared autorickshaw is ₹10. They run from around the site of the town-centre bus stand).

Numerous buses run to Ahmedabad (₹188, eight hours, hourly), Rajkot (₹151, seven hours), Jamnagar (₹159 to ₹194, six hours, hourly) and Mandvi (₹67, 1½ hours). Book private buses with **Patel Tours & Travels** (☑02832-224477; www.pateltoursandtravels.com), just a short way along the main highway running east out of town, for Ahmedabad (AC sleeper ₹550, nine hours), or the Volvo AC sleeper (₹750, 7am, 12.30pm and 10pm) with **Shree Sahjanand Travels** (☑9825804773; www.shreesahjanandtravels.com). Patel Tours & Travel also runs non-AC sleepers to Jamnagar (seat/sleeper ₹350/450, seven hours, 9pm, 9.30pm and 10.30pm), while **Jay Somnath Travels** (☑9979869670; Middle School Rd; ⊙8am-9pm) has departures to Rajkot (from ₹270). The quickest way to get to Mandvi is by shared **jeep** (₹50), which run throughout the day.

TRAIN
Bhuj station is 1.5km north of the centre and has a **reservations office** (⊙8am-8pm Mon-Sat, to 2pm Sun). Of the four to five Ahmedabad-bound trains, the 14312 Ala Hazrat Express leaves at 12.40pm (Tuesday, Thursday, Sunday) and arrives at Ahmedabad (sleeper/3AC/2AC ₹235/625/880) at 7.45pm, continuing to Abu Road, Jaipur and Delhi. The 19116 Bhuj BDTS Express leaves at 12.15pm daily and hits Ahmedabad (sleeper/3AC/2AC/1AC ₹235/625/880/1465) at 5.05am and Mumbai's Bandra Station (₹425/1140/1640/2765) at 2.05pm.

ℹ Getting Around

The airport is 5km north of town – a taxi will cost around ₹300, an autorickshaw ₹150. Autorickshaws from the centre to the train station cost around ₹50.

Around Bhuj

Bhuj is an excellent jumping-off point for visiting the local Jat, Ahir, Meghwal, Harijan, nomadic Rabari and other communities that have distinct, colourful craft traditions. The best of the crafts are found in the villag-

MANDVI

Boats are Mandvi's raison d'être. This little town, an hour down the road from Bhuj, is a major shipbuilding yard – but the boats being built here aren't modern metal creations. Instead, hundreds of men construct, by hand, giant wooden *dhows* for faraway Arab merchants, and watching the creation process, with its rhythmic sawing, sanding and cutting, is fascinating.

The town itself is also quite attractive. Mandvi suffered far less destruction than Bhuj in the 2001 earthquake, so the heart of town (around Mochi Bazaar) is lined with beautiful old buildings in faded pastel hues and temples with wildly sculpted, cartoon-like facades. There are also some sweeping beaches, including the glorious, long, clean private beach near Vijay Vilas Palace, and public Kashivishvanath Beach, with food stalls and camel rides, 2km from the centre just east of the Rukmavati River.

Beach at Mandvi Palace (☏ 9879013118, 02834-277597; www.mandvibeach.com; tents incl meals ₹7500; ✳) is a small tent resort set in a peaceful location on a superb swath of clean beach that stretches from **Vijay Vilas Palace** (☏ 02834-277700; Mon-Sat ₹30, Sun ₹40, vehicle ₹50, camera/video ₹50/200; ☉ 7am-7pm). The luxurious air-cooled tents have big beds, white-tiled bathrooms and solid wooden furniture. Nonguests may come for an excellent lunch (₹550, 10am to 3pm) or dinner (₹650, 7pm to 9pm) – all-day access to the private beach is included.

Regular buses to/from Bhuj (₹48) take 1½ to two hours. Faster shared 4WD taxis (₹50) depart from the street south of Bhuj's main vegetable market. **Patel Tours & Travels** (☏ 02834-231460; www.pateltoursandtravels.com; Jain Dharmsala Rd) offers comfortable long-distance services to Ahmedabad (₹580, 8½ hours, 8.30pm).

es on the road north to Khavda, as well as southeast of Bhuj. Other attractions include an important, remote archaeological site, a ghostly monastery and the stark landscape of the Great Rann of Kachchh.

◉ Sights

★ Living & Learning Design Centre (LLDC) Crafts Museum   MUSEUM
(☏ 02832-229090; www.shrujanlldc.org; Bhuj–Bhachau Rd, Ajrakhpur; adult/child ₹50/20; ☉ 10am-6pm Tue-Sun) Fifteen kilometres east of Bhuj, this superb NGO-run museum is a must for anyone interested in the crafts practised by Kachchh artisans. The well-designed and laid-out galleries showcase the 42 embroidery styles of the Ahir, Maghwal, Rabari and others. There are also exhibitions on block printing, plus a demonstration gallery (weekends only) where you can see the magic that goes into creating some of these pieces. Multimedia features let you learn about individual exhibits in greater depth.

★ White Desert   NATURE RESERVE
(permit adult/child/car ₹100/50/50) The name White Desert probably conjures up images of vast, silent expanses of searing salt desert where you can meditate on life from the viewing tower overlooking the great salt expanse. Well, you can rub that image right out. Yes, the desert itself is magnificent, but in season thousands of domestic tourists descend on the place each day, bringing with them everything you didn't expect to find in this remote corner of India.

A permit is needed to visit, and this is paid for and processed in the village of Bhirandiyara. You'll need a photocopy of your passport and visa.

★ Than   MONASTERY
In the hills about 60km northwest of Bhuj is the eerie 12th-century monastery at Than. This is a laid-back place, with architecture ranging from crumbling mud brick to Portuguese-style blue stucco and whitewashed bell towers. It attracts a few sadhus (ascetics) and the main shrine contains a scared fire said to have been burning since the monastery was founded.

Dholavira   ARCHAEOLOGICAL SITE
(₹20; ☉ 8am-6pm) A long drive northeast from Bhuj is the fascinating and remote archaeological site of Dholavira, on a seasonal island in the Great Rann. Excavations have revealed a complex town of stone buildings 1 sq km in area, inhabited by the Harappan civilisation from around 2900

HANDICRAFTS OF KACHCHH

Kachchh is one of India's richest areas for handicrafts and is particularly famed for its beautiful, colourful embroidery work (of which there are 16 distinct styles), but it also has many artisans specialising in weaving, tie-dying, block printing, woodcarving, pottery, bell making and other crafts. The diversity of Kachchh crafts reflects the differing traditions of its many communities. Numerous local cooperatives invest in social projects and help artisans produce work that is marketable yet still preserves their artistic heritage. For those interested in embroidery, a visit to the Living & Learning Design Centre (LLDC) Crafts Museum (p731) in Ajrakhpur, 15km from Bhuj, is an absolute must. It's worth trying to get hold of the Craft Map, printed by the Somaiya Kala Vidya (www.somaiya-kalavidya.org) organisation, which works with individual artisans across Kachchh in a bid to preserve and enhance traditional craft.

To explore the many artisan enterprises in the region, the best option is to hire an experienced guide (p735) for a day or so, as they can explain what each village is known for and steer you towards the best places to buy. You can purchase items of superb quality at the locations below; the cooperatives take cards, but individual craftspeople generally don't, so bring plenty of cash.

Local Handicrafts Cooperatives

Kutch Mahila Vikas Sangathan (☑ 02832-256281; www.kmvs.org.in; 21 Nootan Colony, Dr Urmila Mehta Hospital Lane; ⊙ 10am-6pm) ◢ This grassroots organisation comprises 12,000 rural women, and pays members a dividend of the profits and invests money to meet social needs. The embroidery and patchwork are exquisite, employing the distinctive styles of several communities. Products go under the brand name Qasab and range from bags and bedspreads to cushion covers and wall hangings. Visit the Qasab outlet at Comfort Inn Prince (p730), or Khavda, a village about 80km north of Bhuj. (With Khavda, call Qasab well ahead if you want to arrange a textiles demonstration.)

Kala Raksha (☑ 09427759701, 02832-277237; www.kala-raksha.org; ⊙ 10am-2pm & 3-6pm Mon-Sat) Based at Sumrasar Sheikh, 25km north of Bhuj, Kala Raksha is a nonprofit trust working to preserve and promote Kachchh arts. It works with about 1000 embroiderers and patchwork and appliqué artisans from six communities in some 26 villages. The trust has a small museum and shop, and can help arrange visits to villages to meet artisans. Up to 80% of the sale price goes to the artisans, who also help design and price the goods.

Vankar Vishram Valji (☑ 7046586621; Bhujodi; ⊙ 9am-8pm) A family operation and one of the leading weavers in Bhujodi; it sells beautiful blankets, shawls, stoles and rugs.

---

to 1500 BC. Visitors can explore a series of walls and buildings that have half sunk into the sandy soils.

It's best to organise your own transport (₹5000 one way or return): the only bus to Dholavira leaves Bhuj at 2pm (₹89, six hours) and starts back at 5am.

Bhujodi   VILLAGE
Bhujodi, about 7km southeast of Bhuj, is a village of weavers, mostly using pit looms, operated by both feet and hands. You can look into many workshops, which produce attractive shawls, blankets and other products.

The village is 1km off Hwy 42. You can take a bus towards Ahmedabad and ask the driver to drop you at the turnoff for Bhujo-

di (₹14). A return rickshaw from Bhuj costs around ₹350.

🏃 Activities

Centre for Desert & Ocean   BIRDWATCHING
(CEDO; ☑ 8511981245, 9825248135, 02835-221284; www.cedobirding.com; Moti Virani) ◢ Around 53km northwest of Bhuj, this well regarded company, run by passionate environmentalist Jugal Tiwari and his son Shivam, runs birding trips focusing on the wildlife-rich Banni grasslands. Accommodation (singles/doubles including meals ₹3500/4500) is in well-kept rooms with 24-hour solar-heated water; meals are Gujarati vegetarian. Safaris cost ₹4000 for a car and driver plus an expert naturalist and birder guide.

Shrujan (☏ 02832-240272; www.shrujan.org; Bhujodi; ⊙ 10am-7.30pm) Just past the Bhujodi turnoff, behind the GEB Substation, Shrujan is a nonprofit trust working with more than 3000 women embroiderers of nine communities in 114 villages. Its showroom sells top-class shawls, saris, cushion covers and more. The embroiderers' other wares are on display at the LLDC Crafts Museum in Ajrakhpur.

Dr Ismail Mohammad Khatri (☏ 9427719313, 02832-299786; dr.ismail2005@gmail.com; Ajrakhpur; ⊙ 9am-5pm) In Ajrakhpur, 6km east of Bhujodi along the Bhachau road, Dr Khatri heads a 10-generation-old block-printing business of real quality, using all natural dyes in bold geometric designs. Go in the morning if you want to see a demonstration of the fascinating, highly skilled process. You can buy tablecloths, shawls, skirts, saris and other attractive products.

Parmarth (☏ 9712411959, 9909643903; 106 Ramkrushn Nagar, New Dhaneti; ⊙ 8.30am-9pm) Run by a delightful family whose work has won national awards, Parmarth specialises in Ahir embroidery. The workshop is in New Dhaneti, 17km east of Bhujodi, on the Bhachau road.

Khamir (☏ 02832-271272; www.khamir.org; Kukma Rd, Lakhond Crossroad, Kukma; ⊙ 10am-5.30pm) 🖉 This umbrella organisation is dedicated to preserving and encouraging Kachchh crafts in all their diversity. At its Kukma centre you can see demonstrations and buy some of the artisans' products. It's about 4km beyond Bhujodi, in the Anjar direction.

Traditional Rogan Art (☏ 9825753955, 9662550599; www.roganartnirona.com; Nirona) The village of Nirona, 40km northwest of Bhuj, features several distinctive crafts (lacquerwork, bell making), but none more so than the award-winning ancient art of rogan painting, brought over from Iran 300 years ago and until recently practised by just one extended family in India in this village. Today, though, the family has started training others in the craft. These delicate, detailed cloth paintings take months of work. Narendra Modi famously presented one fine piece to Barack Obama during the former American president's visit.

Textile Dealers

In Bhuj, textile dealers line Shroff Bazaar, just east of the Darbargadh. However, plenty of so-called block-printed fabric is in fact screen-printed.

Mr AA Wazir (☏ 02832-224187; awazir1@rediffmail.com; Plot 107B, Lotus Colony) If you're interested in antique embroidery, contact Mr AA Wazir, opposite the General Hospital in Bhuj. He has a stunning collection of more than 3000 pieces, about half of which are for sale, and is happy to talk about his abiding passion. His pieces are mostly from Kachchh but also from other parts of India and even Pakistan.

🍴 Sleeping & Eating

Toran Tourist Complex HOTEL $
(☏ 9825026813; huts with/without AC ₹1000/700; ❄) The only place to stay right by the archaeological site at Dholavira (p731), Toran consists of rundown circular *bhunga* huts with attached bathrooms, some with AC. Mediocre Gujarati thalis are served in the adjoining cafeteria.

★ **Devpur Homestay** HOMESTAY $$$
(☏ 02835-283065, 9825711852; www.devpur homestay.in; Devpur; incl breakfast d ₹3500-4500; ❄) In the village of Devpur, 40km northwest of Bhuj, this 1905 sandstone manor is the ancestral home of friendly host Krutarthsinh, who is related to the Bhuj royal family. The five rooms are so crammed with character

that there's barely enough room for your own. The Sorthambha Suite with its numerous sky-blue columns is particularly appealing.

Kutch Wilderness Kamp RESORT $$$
(☏ 9726016882, 0706 9068886; www.kutch wildernesskamp.com; r ₹6000; ❄ 🐾) Around 20km north of Bhuj, on the road to Khavda, this resort consists of two-storey circular cottages with terraces overlooking a swimming pool and the far bigger pool that's otherwise known as Rudramata Lake. There's a so-so restaurant, and trips to the surrounding craft villages are arranged at extra cost.

Shaam-e-Sarhad
Village Resort HOTEL $$$
(☏ 02803-296222; Hodka; incl meals tent s/d ₹2800/3400, bhunga s/d ₹3800/5700; ⊙ Oct-

Mar) 🏊 Set in the beautiful Banni grasslands just outside Hodka, 70km north of Bhuj, this safari camp consists of three *bhungas* (traditional mud huts) and six luxurious tents with private bathrooms. Owned and operated by the Halepotra people, it's a fascinating opportunity to witness the daily life of an indigenous community and the positive impact of thoughtful tourism. Superb meals are available.

ⓘ Getting There & Away

Buses that serve the villages of Khavda and Dholavira are few and sporadic. Most visitors organise multiday tours of the region with a car and a knowledgeable guide; there are several excellent guides (p735) in Bhuj that you can contact in advance. A day's driving in a 4WD with a guide costs around ₹5000.

Little Rann of Kachchh (Kutch)

The barren, salt-tinted land of the Little Rann is nature at its harshest and most compelling. The big attraction here is the Wild Ass Sanctuary. Covering a large part of the Rann, the sanctuary is a place of heat-haze mirages and barren vistas where the last remaining population of the cappuccino-coloured Indian wild ass (khur) plods through the dust. Alongside the wild asses can be found foxes, wolves and masses of birdlife. This is one of India's best birding areas.

The Little Rann is punctuated by desolate, illegal salt farms, where people eke out a meagre living by pumping up groundwater and extracting the salt.

Rain turns the desert into a sea of mud, and even during the dry season the solid-looking crust is often deceptive, so it's essential to take a local guide with you when exploring the area.

◉ Sights

★ **Wild Ass Sanctuary** NATURE RESERVE
(4WD safari with up to 6 passengers Indian/foreigner Mon-Fri ₹400/2800, Sat & Sun ₹500/3500, camera Indian/foreigner ₹200/1200; ⊙6am-6pm) This 4953-sq-km sanctuary covers a chunk of the parched land of the Little Rann and is the home of the only remaining population of the Indian wild ass (khur), as well as wolves, blackbuck and chinkara. There's also a huge bird population from October to March (this is one of the few areas in India where flamingos breed in the wild). Guides will arrange

your permits for the reserve; the cost of these is normally additional to safari prices.

About 2500 khurs live in the sanctuary, surviving off the flat, grass-covered expanses or islands, known as *bets,* which rise up to around 3m. These remarkable, notoriously untamable creatures are capable of running at an average speed of 50km/h for long distances.

Easily accessible from Ahmedabad, the sanctuary can be visited in a combined trip with Nalsarovar Bird Sanctuary (p701), Modhera and Patan.

🏃 Activities

★ **Desert Coursers** WILDLIFE WATCHING
(📱9426372113, 9998305501; www.desertcoursers. net; Desert Coursers Eco Lodge) Excellent safari outfit with expert guides, based out of Desert Coursers Eco Lodge. The guides are especially strong on bird life.

🛏 Sleeping & Eating

Eco Tour Camp HOTEL $$
(📱9825548090; www.littlerann.com; Jogad; s/d incl full board from ₹1500/2000; ⊙Oct-Apr) This simple camp, situated right at the edge of the Wild Ass Sanctuary, near Kidi village, is run by the personable Devjibhai Dhamecha; his son Ajay runs 4WD safaris (₹2000 to ₹3000 per 4WD). Accommodation is in basic cement huts, plusher rooms and atmospheric *koobas* (thatch-roofed huts), which are decorated in traditional style and even have bedspreads to match.

Pick-ups (autorickshaw/taxi ₹700/1200) can be arranged from Dhrangadhra, 45km away, en route between Ahmedabad (three hours) and Bhuj (5½ hours).

★ **Rann Riders** COTTAGE $$$
(📱02757-280257; www.rannriders.com; Dasada; r incl all meals ₹10,030; ❄🗔🏊) 🏊 Luxurious Rann Riders, near Dasada, offers accommodation in mirror-pattern-studded *bhungas* (circular huts) or *koobas* (square huts) with rain showers and mosaic-tiled outdoor bathrooms, surrounded by lush gardens with a swimming pool. The price includes excellent 4WD and camel safaris. Horseback safaris cost ₹3500 for two hours; visits to nearby tribal villages can also be arranged.

★ **Desert Coursers Eco Lodge** HOTEL $$$
(Zainabad Camp; 📱02757-241333, 9426372113; www.desertcoursers.net; Zainabad; s/d incl full

EXPLORING KACHCHH

It's possible to get out to some of Kachchh's villages by public transport – for example, there are three buses a day to Khavda (₹55, two hours). You can also take autorickshaws to villages not too far from the city. But you'll have many more options and more flexibility if you hire a car and driver; most Bhuj hotels can organise this for you.

The three following guides can arrange single and multiday tours around the region; guide services per day tend to be ₹1500 to ₹2000, with another ₹3000 for a car/4WD.

Pramod Jethi (☏9374235379; pramodjethi2013@gmail.com; ⊙9.30am-noon & 3.30-6pm) Former curator at the Aina Mahal and expert on everything Kachchhi, arranges thoughtfully themed and customised autorickshaw tours (half-/full day ₹800/1400) to villages outside Bhuj. However, there has been some negative traveller feedback regarding some of the rickshaw drivers he uses.

Salim Wazir (☏9825715504, 02832-224187; salimwazir@gmail.com) An excellent guide who organises trips to the villages of Kachchh, is a textiles expert, so he can explain the processes involved, from different embroidery styles to weaving. He can even take you to nontouristy villages if you're interested in interacting with local shepherds. Call or email ahead, as he tends to get snapped up.

Kuldip Gadhvi (☏9327054172; www.kutchadventuresindia.com) A knowledgeable guide who will take you around the craft villages of Kachchh. His spontaneous, flamboyant style is a hit with many travellers.

board & safari ₹3800/5600; ⊙Oct-Mar; ❉☏) ✈ Run by infectiously enthusiastic naturalist Dhanraj Malik, Desert Coursers Eco Lodge is a supremely relaxed place to hole up in for a few days and get into desert rhythms. The camp has air-conditioned *koobas* (thatch-roofed huts) decorated with mirrors. Very good meals are available and the price includes excellent safaris. Advance bookings advised.

It's 10km from the eastern edge of the Little Rann, just outside Zainabad, 105km northwest of Ahmedabad.

Bell Guest House   HERITAGE HOTEL $$$
(☏9724678145; www.bellguesthouse.com; Sayla; r incl breakfast ₹5750; ❉) Presided over by the erstwhile ruling family of Sayla, Bell is an ageing yet pristine heritage-hotel retreat down a lane off the Sayla roundabout on Hwy 8A. Rooms have dusty antiques and modern en-suite bathrooms. Look for nilgai (antelope) in the surrounding countryside or take trips further afield to meet artisans in nearby villages, or see wild asses or blackbuck.

❶ Getting There & Away

To get to Zainabad from Ahmedabad it's easiest to hire a private car, but you can also take a bus from Ahmedabad's ST bus stand to Dasada, 10km away (₹120, 2½ hours, about hourly), from where Desert Coursers (p734) and Rann Rider (p734)s offer free pick-up. There are direct buses between Zainabad and Patan (₹85, 2½ hours, four daily) via Modhera.

Mumbai (Bombay)

022 / POPULATION 21.1 MILLION

Best Places to Eat

➡ Peshawri (p760)

➡ Bastian (p760)

➡ Bohri Kitchen (p755)

➡ Bombay Canteen (p761)

➡ Pancham Puriwala (p757)

➡ Trishna (p759)

Best Places to Stay

➡ Taj Mahal Palace, Mumbai (p749)

➡ Abode Bombay (p749)

➡ Residency Hotel (p750)

➡ Sea Shore Hotel (p749)

➡ Juhu Residency (p750)

Why Go?

Mumbai, formerly Bombay, is big. It's full of dreamers and hard-labourers, starlets and gangsters, stray dogs and exotic birds, artists and servants, fisherfolk and *crorepatis* (millionaires), and lots and lots of people. It has India's most prolific film industry, some of Asia's biggest slums (as well as the world's most expensive home) and the largest tropical forest in an urban zone. Mumbai is India's financial powerhouse, fashion epicentre and a pulse point of religious tension.

If Mumbai is your introduction to India, prepare yourself. The city isn't a threatening place but its furious energy, limited (but improving) public transport and punishing pollution make it challenging for visitors. The heart of the city contains some of the grandest colonial-era architecture on the planet, but explore a little more and you'll uncover unique bazaars, hidden temples, hipster enclaves and India's premier restaurants and nightlife.

When to Go
Mumbai

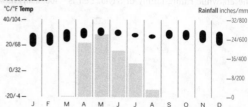

Dec & Jan The very best, least-sticky weather.

Aug & Sep Mumbai goes Ganesh-crazy during its most exciting festival, Ganesh Chaturthi.

Oct–Apr There's very little rain, postmonsoon; the best time of year for festivals.

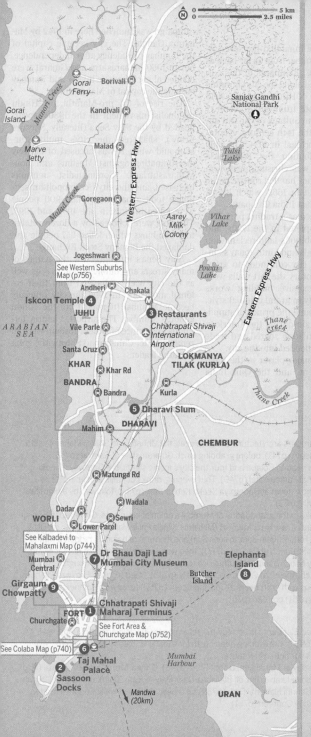

Mumbai Highlights

1 Chhatrapati Shivaji Maharaj Terminus (p741) Marvelling at the magnificent Unesco-listed colonial-era architecture, including this monumental train station.

2 Sassoon Docks (p741) Waging war on your senses at Mumbai's cinematic fishing docks.

3 Restaurants (p760) Dining like a maharaja at one of India's best restaurants, such as Peshawri.

4 Iskcon Temple (p743) Feeling the love with the Krishna crowd at this unique temple.

5 Dharavi Slum (p748) Touring through the self-sufficient world of Asia's largest shanty town.

6 Taj Mahal Palace (p739) Staying at one of the world's most iconic hotels, or dropping in for a drink at its bar, Mumbai's first.

7 Dr Bhau Daji Lad Mumbai City Museum (p742) Ogling this museum's gorgeous Renaissance-revival interiors.

8 Elephanta Island (p746) Beholding the commanding triple-headed Shiva on this Mumbai Harbour island.

9 Girgaum Chowpatty (p743) Snacking on *bhelpuri* (puffed rice and spices) among playing kids, big balloons and a hot-pink sunset.

History

Koli fisherfolk have inhabited the seven islands that form Mumbai from as far back as the 2nd century BC. Remnants of this culture remain huddled along the city shoreline today. A succession of Hindu dynasties held sway over the islands from the 6th century AD until the Muslim Sultans of Gujarat annexed the area in the 14th century, eventually ceding it to Portugal in 1534. The only memorable contribution the Portuguese made to the area was christening it Bom Baia (Good Bay). They handed control to the English government in 1665, which leased the islands to the East India Company.

Bombay flourished as a trading port. The city's fort was completed in the 1720s, and a century later ambitious land-reclamation projects joined the islands into today's single landmass. The city continued to grow, and in the 19th century the fort walls were dismantled and massive building works transformed the city in grand colonial style. When Bombay became the principal supplier of cotton to Britain during the American Civil War, the population soared and trade boomed as money flooded into the city.

Bombay was a major player in the independence movement, and the Quit India campaign was launched here in 1942 by Mahatma Gandhi. The city became capital of the Bombay presidency after Independence, but in 1960 Maharashtra and Gujarat were divided along linguistic lines – and Bombay became the capital of Maharashtra.

The rise of the pro-Marathi, pro-Hindu regionalist movement in the 1980s, spearheaded by the Shiv Sena (literally 'Shivaji's Army'), shattered the city's multicultural mould when it was accused of actively discriminating against Muslims and non-Maharashtrians. Communalist tensions increased, and the city's cosmopolitan self-image took a battering when 900 people were killed in riots in late 1992 and 1993. The riots were followed by a dozen retaliatory bombings which killed 257 people and damaged the Bombay Stock Exchange.

Shiv Sena's influence saw the names of many streets and public buildings – as well as the city itself – changed from their colonial monikers. In 1996 the city officially became Mumbai (derived from the Hindu goddess Mumba). The airport, Victoria Terminus and Prince of Wales Museum were all renamed after Chhatrapati Shivaji, the great Maratha leader.

MUMBAI IN...

Two Days

Begin at one of Mumbai's architectural masterpieces, the Chhatrapati Shivaji Maharaj Vastu Sangrahalaya museum (p741), before grabbing lunch Gujarati-style at Samrat (p758).

In the afternoon head to Colaba and tour the city's iconic sights, the Gateway of India (p740) and Taj Mahal Palace hotel (p749). That evening, drink cocktails and fine-dine at Miss T (p757) or chow down at Bademiya Seekh Kebab Stall (p754), followed by a nightcap at hip Colaba Social (p763).

The next day, take in the granddaddy of Mumbai's colonial-era giants, Chhatrapati Shivaji Terminus (p741), and **Crawford Market** (Mahatma Jyotiba Phule Mandai; Map p744; cnr DN & Lokmanya Tilak Rds, Fort; ☉10am-8pm, to noon Sun) and its maze of bazaars, hidden temples and unique street life. Lunch at Revival (p760), then wander the tiny lanes of Khotachiwadi (p743), followed by beach *bhelpuri* (puffed rice tossed with fried rounds of dough, lentils, onions, herbs and chutneys) at Girgaum Chowpatty (p743). Need a drink? Hip nightlife hub Lower Parel beckons with craft beers at Toit Tap Room (p762) followed by dinner at sceney Bombay Canteen (p761) or Koko (p761).

Four Days

Sail to Unesco-listed Elephanta Island (p746), returning for lunch in artsy Kala Ghoda at Burma Burma (p759). In the evening head north for exquisite seafood at Bastian (p760), followed by serious bar action in Bandra.

Spend your last day at Mahalaxmi Dhobi Ghat (p743), **Shree Mahalaxmi Temple** (Map p744; www.mahalakshmi-temple.com; off Bhulabhai Desai Marg; ☉6am-10pm) and Haji Ali Dargah (p742); or Sanjay Gandhi National Park (p769) for a peaceful forest walk. End with modern Indian fare at Bombay Canteen (p761).

Religious tensions deepened and became intertwined with national religious conflicts and India's relations with Pakistan. A series of bomb attacks on trains killed over 200 in July 2006. Then, in November 2008, a co-ordinated series of devastating attacks (by Pakistani gunmen) targeted landmark buildings across the city, as the Taj Mahal Palace hotel burned, passengers were gunned down inside the Chhatrapati Shivaji railway station and 10 people were killed inside the Leopold Cafe backpacker haunt.

In late 2012, when the Sena's charismatic founder Bal Thackeray died (500,000 attended his funeral), the Shiv Sena mission begin to falter, and in the 2014 assembly elections, President Modi's Bharatiya Janata Party (BJP) became the largest party in Mumbai.

Mumbaikars are a resilient bunch. Increased security is very much part of everyday life today and the city's status as the engine room of the Indian economy remains unchallenged. However, Mumbai politicians certainly have their work cut out, with the megacity's feeble public transport, gridlocked streets, pollution and housing crisis all in desperate need of attention.

◉ Sights

Mumbai is an island – originally seven before land reclaiming sewed them together – connected by bridges to the mainland. The city's commercial and cultural centre is at the southern, claw-shaped end of the island known as South Mumbai. The southernmost peninsula is Colaba, traditionally the travellers' nerve centre, with many of the major attractions.

North of Colaba is the busy commercial area known as Fort, where the British fort once stood. This part of the city is bordered on the west by a series of interconnected grassy areas known as maidans (may-*dahns*).

Continuing north you enter 'the suburbs', which contain the airport and many of Mumbai's best restaurants, shops and nightspots. The upmarket districts of Bandra, Juhu and Lower Parel are key areas (the bohemians and hippies that used to claim Bandra have now moved further north to Andheri West and Vesova).

◉ Colaba

Along the city's southernmost peninsula, Colaba is a bustling district packed with elegant art deco and colonial-era mansions, budget-to-midrange lodgings, bars and res-

TOP FESTIVALS

Mumbai Sanskruti (www.asiaticsociety. org.in; ◔ Jan) This free, two-day celebration of Hindustani classical music is held on the steps of the gorgeous Asiatic Society Library in the Fort area.

Kala Ghoda Arts Festival (www. kalaghodaassociation.com; ◔ Feb) Getting bigger and more sophisticated each year, this two-week-long art fest held in Kala Ghoda and the Fort area sees tons of performances and exhibitions.

Elephanta Festival (www.maharashtra tourism.gov.in; Elephanta Island; ◔ Feb) Unesco-listed Elephanta Island comes to life with dancers, musicians and dramatists over the two-day classical-music and dance festival, usually in February.

Nariyal Poornima (◔ Aug) This Koli celebration in Colaba marks the start of the fishing season and the retreat of monsoon winds.

Ganesh Chaturthi (www.ganesh chaturthi.com; ◔ Aug/Sep) Mumbai gets totally swept up by this 10- to 12-day celebration of the elephant-headed Hindu god Ganesh. On the festival's first, third, fifth, seventh and 11th days, families and communities take their Ganesh statues to the seashore at Chowpatty and Juhu beaches and auspiciously submerge them.

Jio Mami Mumbai Film Festival (MFF; www.mumbaifilmfestival.com; ◔ Oct/ Nov) New films from the subcontinent and beyond are screened at the weeklong MFF at cinemas across Mumbai.

taurants, street stalls and a fisherfolk quarter. Colaba Causeway (Shahid Bhagat Singh Marg) dissects the district. If you're here in August, look out for the Koli festival Nariyal Poornima.

★**Taj Mahal Palace, Mumbai**   LANDMARK (Map p740; https://taj.tajhotels.com; Apollo Bunder) Mumbai's most famous landmark, this stunning hotel is a fairy-tale blend of Islamic and Renaissance styles, and India's second-most-photographed monument. It was built in 1903 by the Parsi industrialist JN Tata, supposedly after he was refused entry to nearby European hotels on account of

Colaba

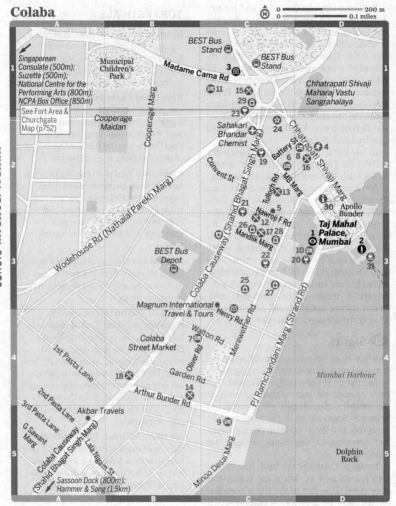

being 'a native'. Dozens were killed inside the hotel when it was targeted during the 2008 terrorist attacks, and images of its burning facade were beamed worldwide. The fully restored hotel reopened on Independence Day 2010.

Much more than an iconic building, the Taj's history is intrinsically linked with the nation: it was the first hotel in India to employ women, the first to have electricity (and fans), and it also housed freedom fighters (for no charge) during the struggle for independence.

Today the Taj fronts the harbour and Gateway of India, but it was originally designed to face the city (the entrance has been changed).

Gateway of India   MONUMENT

(Map p740; Apollo Bunder) This bold basalt arch of colonial triumph faces out to Mumbai Harbour from the tip of Apollo Bunder. Incorporating Islamic styles of 16th-century Gujarat, it was built to commemorate the 1911 royal visit of King George V, but wasn't completed until 1924. Ironically, the British builders of the gateway used it just 24 years later to parade the last British regiment as India marched towards independence.

Colaba

★**Sassoon Docks**   WATERFRONT
(Sassoon Dock Rd; ⊙24hr) No sense is left unaffected at Mumbai's incredibly atmospheric fishing docks, dating to 1875, the oldest and largest wholesale fish market in Mumbai. A scene of intense and pungent activity begins around 5am, when colourfully clad Koli fisherfolk sort the catch unloaded from fishing trawlers at the quay, and carries on throughout the morning.

⊙ Fort Area & Churchgate

Lined up in a row and vying for your attention with aristocratic pomp, many of Mumbai's majestic Victorian buildings pose on the edge of Oval Maidan. This land, and the Cross and Azad Maidans immediately to the north, were all on the oceanfront in those days, and this series of grandiose structures faced west directly to the Arabian Sea.

Kala Ghoda (Black Horse) is a hip, atmospheric subneighbourhood of Fort just north of Colaba (see the neighbourhood's new Spirit of Kala Ghoda monument, erected in 2017, which might strike some as notable for being a riderless horse). It contains many of Mumbai's museums, galleries and design boutiques alongside a wealth of colonial-era buildings and some of the city's best restaurants and cafes.

★**Chhatrapati Shivaji Maharaj Terminus**   HISTORIC BUILDING
(Victoria Terminus (VT); Map p752; Chhatrapati Shivaji Terminus Area, Fort) Imposing, exuberant and overflowing with people, this monumental train station is the city's most extravagant Gothic building and an aphorism of colonial-era India. It's a meringue of Victorian, Hindu and Islamic styles whipped into an imposing Dalí-esque structure of buttresses, domes, turrets, spires and stained glass. It's also known as CSMT.

★**Chhatrapati Shivaji Maharaj Vastu Sangrahalaya**   MUSEUM
(Prince of Wales Museum; Map p752; www.csmvs.in; 159-161 MG Rd, Fort; Indian/foreigner ₹83/500, mobile/camera ₹50/100; ⊙10.15am-6pm) Mumbai's biggest and best museum displays a mix of India-wide exhibits. The domed behemoth, an intriguing hodgepodge of Islamic, Hindu and British architecture, is a flamboyant Indo-Saracenic design by George Wittet (who also designed the Gateway of India). Its vast collection includes impressive Hindu and Buddhist sculpture, terracotta figurines from the Indus Valley, Indian miniature paintings and some particularly vicious-looking weaponry.

Keneseth Eliyahoo Synagogue
SYNAGOGUE

(Map p752; Dr VB Gandhi Marg, Kala Ghoda; ⊙11am-6pm Sun-Thu) Built in 1884, and tenderly maintained by the city's dwindling Jewish community, this white and indigo-trimmed synagogue emerged from under years of scaffolding in 2019, restored to its original 19th-century color scheme. It now dazzles inside with neoclassical splendour, awash in Burmese teak furnishings and Victorian stained glass. Staff are friendly, but it's protected by very heavy security – bring a copy of your passport to gain entry.

Marine Dr
WATERFRONT

(Map p752; Netaji Subhashchandra Bose Rd; ⊙24hr) Built on reclaimed land in 1920 and a part of Mumbai's recently crowned Victorian Gothic and Art Deco Ensembles Unesco World Heritage Site, Marine Dr arcs along the shore of the Arabian Sea from Nariman Point past Girgaum Chowpatty and continues to the foot of Malabar Hill. Lined with flaking art deco apartments, it's one of Mumbai's most popular promenades and sunset-watching spots. Its twinkling nighttime lights have earned it the nickname 'the Queen's Necklace'.

University of Mumbai
HISTORIC BUILDING

(Bombay University; Map p752; www.mu.ac.in; Bhaurao Patil Marg) Looking like a 15th-century French-Gothic mansion plopped incongruously among Mumbai's palm trees, this structure was designed by Gilbert Scott of London's St Pancras station fame. There's an exquisite University Library and Convocation Hall, as well as the 84m-high Rajabai Clock Tower, decorated with detailed carvings. Since the 2008 terror attacks there has been no public access to the grounds, though pressure is beginning to be put on the vice chancellor to open the campus (check ahead).

Jehangir Art Gallery
GALLERY

(Map p752; www.jehangirartgallery.com; 161B MG Rd, Kala Ghoda; ⊙11am-7pm) FREE Renovated in recent years, this excellent gallery hosts exhibitions across several galleries of all types of visual arts by Mumbaikar, national and international artists.

National Gallery of Modern Art
MUSEUM

(NGMA; Map p740; www.ngmaindia.gov.in; MG Rd; Indian/foreigner ₹20/500; ⊙11am-6pm Tue-Sun) Well-curated shows of Indian and international artists in a bright and spacious five-floor exhibition space.

DAG
GALLERY

(Delhi Art Gallery; Map p752; www.discoverdag.com; 58 Dr VB Gandhi Marg, Kala Ghoda; ⊙10.30am-7pm Mon-Sat) FREE This top gallery is spread over three floors of a beautifully restored cream-coloured colonial-era structure. Its quarterly-changing exhibitions are curated from the largest collection of 20th-century modern Indian art in the world and its wares are showcased in museums throughout India as well as additional galleries in New Delhi and New York.

St Thomas' Cathedral
CHURCH

(Map p752; 3 Veer Nariman Rd, Churchgate; ⊙7am-6pm) This charming cathedral, begun in 1672 and finished in 1718, is the oldest British-era building standing in Mumbai and the city's first Anglican church: it was once the eastern gateway of the East India Company's fort (the 'Churchgate' itself). The cathedral is a marriage of Byzantine and colonial-era architecture, and its airy interior is full of grandiose colonial memorials.

◉ Kalbadevi to Mahalaxmi

★ Dr Bhau Daji Lad Mumbai City Museum
MUSEUM

(Map p744; www.bdlmuseum.org; Dr Babasaheb Ambedkar Rd; Indian/foreigner ₹10/100, audio guides ₹30/50; ⊙10am-6pm Thu-Tue) This gorgeous museum, built in Renaissance revival style in 1872 as the Victoria & Albert Museum, contains 3500-plus objects centring on Mumbai's history – photography, maps, textiles, books, manuscripts, *bidriware* (Bidar's metalwork), lacquerware, weaponry and exquisite pottery. The landmark building was renovated in 2008, with its Minton-tile floors, gilded ceiling mouldings, ornate columns, chandeliers and staircases all gloriously restored.

Haji Ali Dargah
MOSQUE

(Map p744; www.hajialidargah.in; off V Desai Chowk; ⊙5.30am-10pm) FREE Floating like a sacred mirage off the coast, this Indo-Islamic shrine located on an offshore inlet is a striking sight. Built in the 19th century, it contains the tomb of the Muslim saint Pir Haji Ali Shah Bukhari. Legend has it that Haji Ali died while on a pilgrimage to Mecca and his casket miraculously floated back to this spot.

It's only possible to visit the shrine at low tide, via a long causeway (check tide times locally). Thousands of pilgrims, especially on Thursday and Friday (when there may be *qawwali;* devotional singing), cross it daily, many donating to beggars who line the

KHOTACHIWADI

This storied *wadi* (hamlet), **Khotachiwadi** (Map p744) is a heritage village nearly 180 years old, is clinging onto Mumbai life as it was before high-rises. A Christian enclave of elegant two-storey Portuguese-style wooden mansions (of which only 23 out of 65 have survived), it's 500m northeast of Girgaum Chowpatty, lying amid Mumbai's predominantly Hindu and Muslim neighbourhoods. The winding lanes allow a wonderful glimpse into a quiet(ish) life away from noisier Mumbai.

It's not large, but you can spend a while wandering the alleyways and admiring the old homes and, around Christmas, their decorations. You can also plan an East Indian feast in advance or sleep at the home of celebrated fashion designer, Khotachiwadi activist and amateur chef James Ferreira (www.jamesferreira.co.in – find his rooms on Airbnb).

To find Khotachiwadi, head for **St Teresa's Church** (Map p744; cnr Jagannath Shankarsheth (JSS) Marg & Rajarammohan Roy (RR) Marg), on the corner of Jagannath Shankarsheth Marg (JSS Marg) and Rajarammohan Roy Marg (RR Rd/Charni Rd), then head directly opposite the church on JSS Marg and duck down the third lane on your left (look for the faded Khotachiwadi wall stencil map that says 'Khotachiwadi Imaginaries').

way. Sadly, parts of the shrine are in a poor state, damaged by storms and the saline air, though a renovation plan exists. It's visited by people of all faiths.

Mahalaxmi Dhobi Ghat   GHAT

(Map p744; Bapurao Jagtap Marg, Mahalaxmi; ☉4.30am-dusk) This 140-year-old dhobi ghat (place where clothes are washed) is Mumbai's biggest human-powered washing machine: every day hundreds of people beat the dirt out of thousands of kilograms of soiled Mumbai clothes and linen in 1026 open-air troughs. The best view is from the bridge across the railway tracks near Mahalaxmi train station.

Girgaum Chowpatty   BEACH

(Map p744) This city beach is a favourite evening spot for courting couples, families, political rallies and anyone out to enjoy what passes for fresh air. Evening *bhelpuri* (puffed rice tossed with fried rounds of dough, lentils, onions, herbs and chutneys) at the throng of stalls at the beach's southern end is an essential part of the Mumbai experience. Forget about taking a dip: the water's toxic. On the 10th day of the Ganesh Chaturthi festival (p739) millions flock here to submerge huge Ganesh statues: it's joyful mayhem.

◉ Western Suburbs

★ Iskcon Temple   HINDU TEMPLE

(Map p756; www.iskconmumbai.com; Hare Krishna Land, Sri Mukteshwar Devalaya Rd, Juhu; ☉4.30am-1pm & 4-9pm) Iskcon Juhu plays a key part in the Hare Krishna story, as founder AC Bhaktivedanta Swami Prabhupada

spent extended periods here (you can visit his modest living quarters-cum-museum in the adjacent building; 10.30am to 12.30pm and 5.30pm to 8.30pm). The temple compound comes alive during prayer time as the faithful whip themselves into a devotional frenzy of joy, with *kirtan* dancing accompanied by crashing hand symbols and drumbeats.

Juhu Beach   BEACH

(Map p756; Juhu Tara Rd, Juhu) This sprawling suburban beach draws legions of Indian families and courting couples frolicking in the Arabian Sea for 6km all the way to Versova. As far as beaches go, it's no sun-toasted Caribbean dream, but it's a fun place to have a drink or try some Mumbai street food from the nearby stalls. It's particularly vibrant during Ganesh Chaturthi (p739).

Gilbert Hill   MOUNTAIN

(Map p756; Sagar City, Andheri West; ☉24hr) Smack dab among the residential apartment blocks of Andheri West sits this 61m-tall black basalt mountain that resembles a chocolate molten cake (unsurprisingly, as it was formed as result of Mesozoic era molten lava squeeze – it's 66 million years old. Climb the steep rock-carved staircase for panoramic views and the two Hindu temples set around a garden.

◉ Gorai Island

Global Vipassana Pagoda   BUDDHIST TEMPLE

(✆022-62427500; www.globalpagoda.org; Global Pagoda Rd, Borivali West; ☉9am-7pm, meditation classes 9.30am-6.30pm) Rising up like a

Kalbadevi to Mahalaxmi

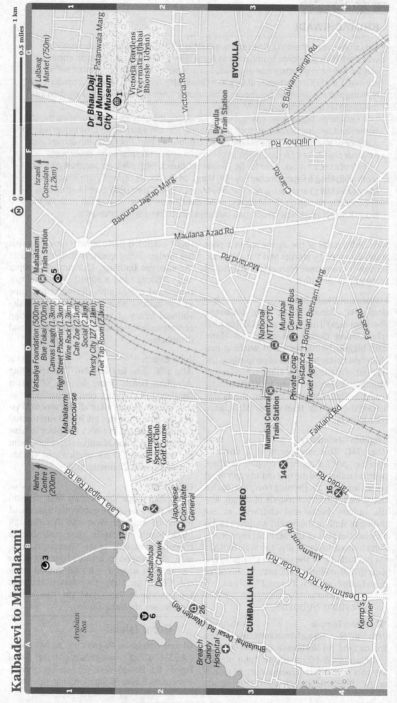

MUMBAI (BOMBAY)

1 km
0.5 miles

Arabian Sea

Nehru Centre (200m)

Lala Lajpat Rai Rd

Mahalaxmi Racecourse

Vatsalya Foundation (500m);
Blue Tokai (700m);
Canvas Laugh (1.3km);
High Street Phoenix (1.3km);
Wine Rack (1.3km);
Cafe Zoe (2.1km);
Social (2.1km);
Thirsty City 127 (2.1km);
Toit Tap Room (2.1km)

Mahalaxmi Train Station

Willingdon Sports Club Golf Course

Japanese Consulate General

Vatsalabai Desai Chowk

Breach Candy Hospital

Bhulabhai Desai Rd (Warden Rd)

CUMBALLA HILL

Deshmukh Rd (Peddar Rd)

Altamount Rd

Kemp's Corner

TARDEO

Mumbai Central Train Station

Private Long-Distance Ticket Agents

National NTT/CTC

Mumbai Central Bus Terminal

J Bonian Behram Marg

Foras Rd

Falkland Rd

Tardeo Rd

Maulana Azad Rd

Morland Rd

Bapurao Jagtap Marg

Israeli Consulate (1.2km)

Dr Bhau Daji Lad Mumbai City Museum

Victoria Gardens (Veermata Jijabai Bhonsle Udyan)

Patanwala Marg

Lalbaug Market (750m)

Victoria Rd

Byculla Train Station

BYCULLA

J Jijibhoy Rd

Clare Rd

S Balwant Singh Rd

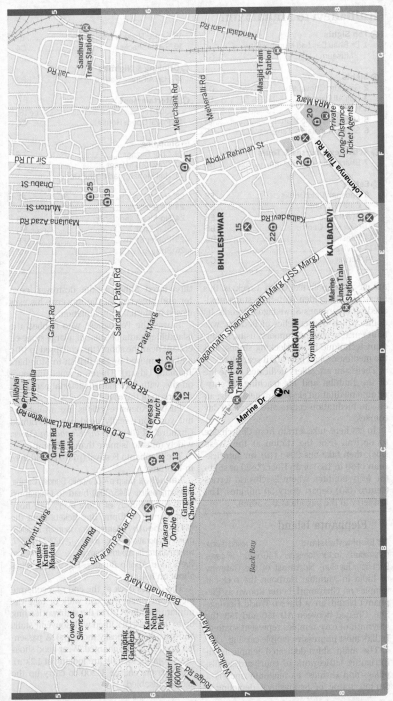

Kalbadevi to Mahalaxmi

mirage from polluted Gorai Creek is this breathtaking, golden 96m-high stupa modelled on Myanmar's Shwedagon Pagoda. Its dome, which houses relics of Buddha, was built entirely without supports using an ancient technique of interlocking stones, and the meditation hall beneath it seats 8000.

There's an art gallery dedicated to the life of the Buddha and his teaching. Twenty-minute meditation classes are held daily; an on-site meditation centre also offers 10-day courses.

To get here, take a train from Churchgate to Borivali (exit the station at the 'West' side), then take bus 294 (₹10), an autorickshaw (₹60 to ₹65) or an Uber (₹420 or so) to the ferry landing, where Esselworld ferries (return ₹50) depart every 30 minutes. The last ferry to the pagoda is at 5.30pm.

⊙ Elephanta Island

★ **Elephanta Island**   HINDU TEMPLE
(Gharapuri; Indian/foreigner ₹40/600; ⊙caves 9am-5pm Tue-Sun) Northeast of the Gateway of India in Mumbai Harbour, the rock-cut temples on Gharapuri, better known as Elephanta Island, are a Unesco World Heritage Site. Created between AD 450 and 750, the labyrinth of cave temples represent some of India's most impressive temple carving.

The main Shiva-dedicated temple is an intriguing latticework of courtyards, halls, pillars and shrines; its magnum opus is a 6m-tall statue of Sadhashiva, depicting a three-faced Shiva as the destroyer, creator and preserver of the universe, his eyes closed in eternal contemplation.

It was the Portuguese who dubbed the island Elephanta because of a large stone elephant near the shore (this collapsed in 1814 and was moved by the British to Mumbai's Jijamata Udyan). There's a small museum on-site, with informative pictorial panels on the origin of the caves.

Pushy, expensive guides are available – but you don't really need one as Pramod Chandra's *A Guide to the Elephanta Caves*, widely for sale, is more than sufficient.

The Elephanta Festival (p739) is held here in February.

Launches (Map p740; Apollo Bunder, Colaba; economy/deluxe ₹145/200) head to Gharapuri from the Gateway of India every half hour from 9am to 3.30pm. Buy tickets from the **MTDC booth** (Maharashtra Tourism Development Corporation; Map p740; ☑022-22841877; www.maharashtratourism.gov.in; ⊙9am-3pm Tue-Sun) at Apollo Bunder. The voyage takes about an hour.

The ferries dock at the end of a concrete pier, from where you can walk or take the miniature train (₹10) to the stairway leading up to the caves (it's lined with souvenir stalls and patrolled by pesky monkeys). A passenger tax (₹5) is also charged. Wear good shoes (those opting to walk are looking at 1.2km). *Doli*-carriers charge ₹1200 to carry up the aged or disabled.

Activities

Mumbai has surprisingly good butterfly- and birdwatching opportunities. Sanjay Gandhi National Park (p769) is popular for woodland birds, while the mangroves of Godrej (13km east of Bandra) are rich in waders. The **Bombay Natural History Society** (BNHS; Map p752; ☑ 022-22821811; www. bnhs.org; Hornbill House, Colaba Causeway, Fort; ☺ 9.30am-5.30pm Mon-Fri) runs excellent trips every weekend.

Outbound Adventure OUTDOORS
(☑ 9820195115; www.outboundadventure.com) Runs one-day rafting trips on the Ulhas River from July to early September (₹2300 per person). After a good rain, rapids can get up to Grade III+, though usually the rafting is calmer. Also organises guided nature walks, birdwatching, camping (from ₹2000 per person per day) and canoeing trips in the Western Ghats.

Antara Day Spa SPA
(☑ 022-66117777; https://theclubmumbai.com/room/antara-spa; 197 DN Nagar, Andheri West; 1hr massage from ₹2500; ☺ 10am-7.30pm) Midrange day spa on private club grounds with skilled therapists offering a range of therapies and treatments, including Swedish, Thai and hot-stone massages. Nonguests must pay a ₹100/120 (week/weekend) entry fee.

Weekdays between 10.30am and 4pm nets a 30% discount on massages.

Palms Spa SPA
(Map p740; ☑ 022-66349898; www.thepalmsspaindia.com; ground fl, Dhanraj Mahal, Chhatrapati Shivaji Marg, Colaba; 1hr massage from ₹3400; ☺ 10am-10pm) Indulge in a rub, scrub or tub at this long-standing Colaba spa. The exfoliating lemongrass and green-tea scrub is ₹2500.

Vatsalya Foundation VOLUNTEERING
(☑ 022-24962115; www.thevatsalyafoundation. org; Anand Niketan, King George V Memorial, off Dr E Moses Rd, Mahalaxmi) Works with Mumbai's street children; there are long- and short-term opportunities in teaching English, computer skills and sports.

Lok Seva Sangam VOLUNTEERING
(☑ 022-24070718; http://loksevasangam.org; D/1 Everard Nagar Eastern Express Hwy, Sion) Lok Seva Sangam has been working to improve lives in the city's slums since 1976. Medical staff who can speak Hindi/Marathi or those with fundraising skills are needed.

Yogacara YOGA
(Map p756; ☑ 022-26511464; www.yogacara. in; 1st fl, SBI Bldg, 18A New Kant Wadi Rd, Bandra West; ☺ yoga per class ₹700, massage 1hr from ₹1850, unlimited per week/month ₹1900/5600) Classic hatha and Iyengar yoga institute, with excellent massages and treatments; the Abhyangam rejuvenating massage is recommended. Ayurvedic cooking, meditation and chakra-healing classes are also offered sporadically.

Courses

★ Flavour Diaries FOOD & DRINK
(Map p756; ☑ 9820143404; www.flavourdiaries. com; 3rd fl, Rohan Plaza, 5th Rd, Khar West; session from ₹4000; ☺ 11am-6pm) If you fancy some good food and a chance to make friends with local Mumbaikars, head to Flavour Diaries in Khar. This interactive cooking studio is spearheaded by renowned UK-born international chef Anjali Pathak, and courses cover everything from Asian and Indian cuisine to American, European and Mediterranean specialities.

★ Yoga Institute YOGA
(Map p756; ☑ 022-26122185; www.theyoga institute.org; Shri Yogendra Marg, Prabhat Colony, Santa Cruz East; courses per 1st/2nd month from ₹700/500) At its peaceful leafy campus near Santa Cruz, the respected Yoga Institute has daily classes as well as weekend and week-long programs, and longer residential courses including teacher training (with the seven-day course a prerequisite).

Tours

★ Khaki Tours OUTDOORS
(Map p752; ☑ 8828100111; www.khakitours.com; 3rd fl, Hari Chambers, 58/64 Shadid Bhagat Singh Marg, Fort; walks from ₹4000, jeep rides from ₹10,000; ☺ 9am-5pm) The best way to get under the skin of Mumbai is to meet and strike up a conversation with a true Mumbaikar. The tours developed by Bharat Gothoskar (and led by city ambassadors with regular day jobs) – city walks, food tours, sailing outings, 'urban safaris' by private jeep – showcase an unseen side of Mumbai in the name of awesomely coined 'heritage evangelism'.

★ Reality Tours & Travel TOURS
(Map p740; ☑ 9820822253; www.realitytours andtravel.com; 1/26 Unique Business Service Centre, Akber House, Nowroji Fardonji Rd, Colaba; most tours ₹750-1700; ☺ 8am-9pm) ⚘ Compelling

DHARAVI SLUM

Mumbaikars were ambivalent about the stereotypes in 2008's *Slumdog Millionaire*, but slums are very much a part of – some would say the foundation of – Mumbai city life. An astonishing 60% of Mumbai's population lives in slums, and one of the city's largest slums is Dharavi, originally inhabited by fisherfolk when the area was still creeks, swamps and islands. It became attractive to migrant workers from South Mumbai and beyond when the swamp began to fill in due to natural and artificial causes. It now incorporates 2.2 sq km of land sandwiched between Mumbai's two major railway lines, and is home to perhaps as many as a million people.

While it may look a bit shambolic from the outside, the maze of dusty alleys and sewer-lined streets of this city-within-a-city is actually a collection of abutting settlements. Some parts of Dharavi have mixed populations, but in other parts inhabitants from different regions of India, and with different trades, have set up homes and tiny factories. Potters from Saurashtra (Gujarat) live in one area, Muslim tanners in another; embroidery workers from Uttar Pradesh work alongside metalsmiths; while other workers recycle plastics as women dry pappadams in the searing sun. Some of these thriving industries, as many as 20,000 in all, export their wares, and the annual turnover of business from Dharavi is thought to exceed US$700 million.

Up close, life in the slums is fascinating to witness. Residents pay rent, most houses have kitchens and electricity, and building materials range from flimsy corrugated-iron shacks to permanent multistorey concrete structures. Perhaps the biggest issue facing Dharavi residents is sanitation, as water supply is irregular – every household has a 200L drum for water storage. Very few dwellings have a private toilet or bathroom, so some neighbourhoods have constructed their own (to which every resident must contribute financially) while other residents are forced to use run-down public facilities.

Many families have been here for generations, and education achievements are higher than in many rural areas: around 15% of children complete higher education and find white-collar jobs. Many choose to stay, though, in the neighbourhood they grew up in.

Slum tourism is a polarising subject, so you'll have to decide for yourself. If you opt to visit, the award-winning Reality Tours & Travel (p747) has an illuminating tour (from ₹900), and puts 80% of profits back into Dharavi social programs. They can also now arrange a meal with a local family for further insight. Photography is strictly forbidden.

Some tourists opt to visit on their own, which is OK as well – just don't take photos. Take the train from Churchgate station to Mahim, exit on the west side and cross the bridge into Dharavi.

To learn more about Mumbai's slums, check out Katherine Boo's 2012 book *Behind the Beautiful Forevers*, about life in Annawadi, a slum near the airport, and *Rediscovering Dharavi* (2000), Kalpana Sharma's sensitive and engrossing history of Dharavi's people, culture and industry.

tours of the Dharavi slum, with 80% of post-tax profits going to the agency's own NGO, Reality Gives (www.realitygives.org). Streetfood, pottery, market, bicycle and sightseeing tours are also excellent.

Bombay Heritage Walks WALKING
(✆9821887321; www.bombayheritagewalks.com; per 2hr tour (up to 5 people) from ₹3750) Started by two enthusiastic architects and operating with a slew of architects, journalists and art historians, BHW has terrific tours of heritage neighbourhoods.

Mumbai Magic Tours TOURS
(✆9867707414; www.mumbaimagic.com; 2hr tour per 2/4 people from ₹1750/1500; ⊙10am-5pm Mon-Fri, to 2pm Sat) Designed by the authors of the fabulous blog Mumbai Magic (www.mumbai-magic.blogspot.com), these city tours focus on Mumbai's quirks, culture, community, food, bazaars, festivals, Jewish heritage and more.

🛏 Sleeping

Mumbai has the most expensive accommodation in India and you'll never quite feel like you're getting your money's worth.

Colaba is compact, has the liveliest tourist scene and many budget and midrange options, but hassles are greater there (hash dealers, beggars). The neighbouring Fort area is convenient for the main train stations and hip dining and shopping epicentre. Most top-end places are along Marine Dr and in the western suburbs.

Colaba

Backpacker Panda HOSTEL $

(Map p740; ☎9607900991; www.backpacker panda.com; 15 Walton Rd; dm ₹800-1200, d with AC ₹2600-4200; ﹡@⊙) Mumbai's best hostel fills four floors of a crusty, can't-miss-it grey-and-pastel-rosé residential building in Colaba, with tiled stairwells and other heritage accents. Four-, six- and eight-bed dorm configurations are spacious and boast air-con and lockers; private rooms are disappointingly simple, but all have fantastic modern bathrooms, a trend seen in the common bathrooms as well.

There's a rooftop lounge and game room as well as a smoking area, plus filtered water on every floor. No breakfast is served. The huge Garage Inc. Public House is in the same building. Also in **Andheri** (Map p756; ☎022-28367141; Shaheed Bhagat Singh Society; dm with AC ₹650-750; ﹡⊙).

Sea Shore Hotel GUESTHOUSE $

(Map p740; ☎022-22874237; 4th fl, 1/49 Kamal Mansion, Arthur Bunder Rd; s/d without bathroom ₹700/1230; ⊙) This place is really making an effort, with small but immaculately clean and inviting rooms, all with flat-screen TVs, set off a railway-carriage-style corridor. Half the rooms even have harbour views (the others don't have a window). The modish communal bathrooms are well scrubbed and have a little gleam and sparkle. Wi-fi in the reception and *some* rooms.

★YWCA GUESTHOUSE $$

(Map p740; ☎022-22025053; www.ywcaic.info; 18 Madame Cama Rd; s/d/tr with AC incl breakfast & dinner ₹2678/4457/6478; ﹡⊙) Efficiently managed, and within walking distance of all the sights in Colaba and Fort, the YWCA is a good deal and justifiably popular. The spacious, well-maintained rooms boast desks, wardrobes and multichannel TVs. Tariffs include a buffet breakfast, dinner, a daily newspaper and bed tea. In addition to the room rates there's a one-time ₹59 membership fee.

★ Abode Bombay BOUTIQUE HOTEL $$$

(Map p740; ☎8080234066; www.abodeboutique hotels.com; 1st fl, Lansdowne House, MB Marg; d with AC incl breakfast ₹5310-14,975; ﹡⊙) A terrific 20-room boutique hotel, stylishly designed with colonial-style and art deco furniture, reclaimed teak flooring and original artwork; the luxury rooms have glorious free-standing bathtubs. Staff are very switched on to travellers' needs, and breakfast is excellent, with fresh juice and delicious local and international choices. A little tricky to find, it's located behind the Regal Cinema.

★ Taj Mahal Palace, Mumbai HERITAGE HOTEL $$$

(Map p740; ☎022-66653366; https://taj.taj hotels.com; Apollo Bunder; s/d tower from ₹13,000/15,000, palace from ₹25,000/27,000; ﹡@⊙⊠) The grande dame of Mumbai is one of the world's most iconic hotels and has hosted a roster of presidents and royalty. Sweeping arches, staircases and domes, and a glorious garden and pool ensure an unforgettable stay. Rooms in the adjacent tower lack the period details of the palace itself, but many have spectacular, full-frontal Gateway of India views. With a myriad of excellent in-house eating and drinking options, plus spa and leisure facilities, it can be a wrench to leave the hotel premises. There's even a small but discernibly curated art gallery. Heritage walks at 3.30pm daily (for guests) provide illuminating context about the hotel's role in the city's history.

Hotel Suba Palace HOTEL $$$

(Map p740; ☎022-22020636; www.subahotels. com/hotel/suba-palace; Battery St; s/d with AC incl breakfast from ₹5900/7320; ﹡⊙) 'Palace' is pushing it slightly, but this modern, brilliantly located little place is certainly a comfortable choice with its contemporary decor: neutral tones from a 2015 upgrade keep the tasteful rooms teetering on modern. There's a good in-house restaurant, and foodie destination the Table (p755) shares the same location.

Fort Area & Churchgate

Traveller's Inn
HOTEL $

(Map p752; ☑ 022-22644685; www.hoteltravellers inn.co; 26 Adi Marzban Path, Fort; dm with/without AC ₹700/600, d with/without AC ₹2300/1800; ❄️@🛜) On a quiet, tree-lined street, this small hotel is a very sound choice. It has clean, if tiny, rooms with cable TV and king-sized beds that represent good value. The two dorms are cramped (the non-AC one Hades-hot in summer; the AC one requires a minimum of three people) but are a steal for Mumbai. A new mosaic-floored hang-out space catches a nice breeze.

The location's excellent and staff are helpful. Breakfast is ₹100.

★ Residency Hotel
HOTEL $$

(Map p752; ☑ 022-22625525; www.residencyhotel. com; 26 Rustom Sidhwa Marg, Fort; s/d with AC incl breakfast from ₹5080/5550; ❄️@🛜) The Residency is the kind of dependable place where you can breathe a sigh of relief after a long journey and be certain you'll be looked after well. It's fine value, too, with contemporary rooms, some boasting mood lighting, mini-bars, flat-screen TVs and hip en suite bathrooms. Best of all, staff are friendly, polite and understand the nuance of unforced hospitality. Its Fort location is also excellent, though noise is will be an issue through 2022 due to metro-station construction right outside its door. The best-run midranger in Mumbai.

Western & Northern Suburbs

Cohostel
HOSTEL $

(Map p756; ☑ 9856564545; bandra@cohostels. com; 43 Chapel Rd, Bandra West; dm incl breakfast ₹800-1000; ❄️🛜) Village-like Ranwar along Chapel Rd leads to Bandra's first note-worthy hostel, which occupies the top floor of a pre-Partition bungalow. Six six-bed dorms feature Australian-pine dorm beds, lockers, air-con and private baths, one of which is female-only. But it's the airy, spacious rooftop and kitchen (induction stove-tops!) where you'll want to hang out. Coffee and tea are made to order.

★ Juhu Residency
BOUTIQUE HOTEL $$

(Map p756; ☑ 022-67834949; www.facebook.com/ JuhuResidency; 148B Juhu Tara Rd, Juhu; d with AC incl breakfast from ₹5900; ❄️@🛜) The aroma of sweet lemongrass greets you in the lobby at this excellent 18-room boutique hotel with an inviting atmosphere – and a fine location, five minutes' walk from Juhu beach.

The chocolate-and-coffee colour scheme in the modish rooms works well, each room boasting marble floors, dark woods, artful bedspreads and flat-screen TVs. To top it all off, free airport pickups are included.

Iskcon
GUESTHOUSE $$

(Map p756; ☑ 022-26206860; www.iskcon mumbai.com/guest-house; Hare Krishna Land, Sri Mukteshwar Devalaya Rd, Juhu; s/d with AC ₹3550/4050, without AC ₹3150/3450; ❄️🛜) An intriguing place to stay inside Juhu's lively Iskcon complex. Though the hotel building is a slightly soulless concrete block, some rooms enjoy vistas over the Hare Krishna temple compound. Spartan decor is offset by the odd decorative flourish such as Gujarati *sankheda* (lacquered country wood) furniture, and staff are very welcoming.

Anand Hotel
HOTEL $$

(Map p756; ☑ 022-26203372; anandpremises @gmail.com; Gandhigram Rd, Juhu; s/d with AC from ₹2464/4130; ❄️🛜) Yes, the decor's in 50 shades of beige but the Anand's rooms are comfortable, spacious and represent decent value, considering the prime location on a quiet street next to Juhu beach. The excellent in-house Dakshinayan restaurant (p760) scores highly for authentic, inexpensive meals, too. It's a particularly good deal for solo travellers.

★ ITC Maratha
HOTEL $$$

(Map p756; ☑ 022-28303030; www.itchotels. in; Sahar Rd, Andheri East; s/d incl breakfast from ₹15,360/17,900; ❄️@🛜🏊) 🏊 This five-star, Leadership in Energy and Environmental Design (LEED) Platinum-certified hotel channels the most luxurious local character. The details are extraordinary: Muhammed Ali Rd–inspired *jharokas* (lattice windows) around the atrium, Maratha-influenced Resident's Bar (a guest-only level overlooking public areas), Warli painting–inspired tower rooms with fiery orange marble. The rooms, awash in lush colour schemes, exude Indian opulence. Peshawri (p760), Mumbai's most memorable Northwest Frontier restaurant, is located here.

★ Taj Santacruz
BOUTIQUE HOTEL $$$

(Map p756; ☑ 022-62115211; https://taj.tajhotels. com/en-in/taj-santacruz-mumbai; Chhatrapati Shivaji International Airport (T1), Airport Rd, Santa Cruz East; s/d from ₹12,000/14,000; ❄️@🛜🏊) Forget the 3500 hand-blown chandelier bulbs or the 75-species aquarium in the lobby of this newer hotel connected to the domestic airport

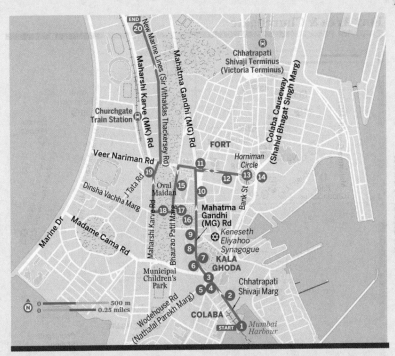

City Walk
Architectural Mumbai

START GATEWAY OF INDIA
END LIBERTY CINEMA
LENGTH 3.5KM; 1¾ HOURS

Mumbai's defining feature is its mix of colonial-era and art deco architecture. Starting from the **1 Gateway of India** (p740), walk up Chhatrapati Shivaji Marg past the art deco residential-commercial complex **2 Dhunraj Mahal**, towards **3 Regal Circle**. Walk the circle for views of the surrounding buildings, including the art deco **4 Regal Cinema** and **5 Majestic Hotel**, now the Sahakari Bhandar cooperative store. Continue up Mahatma Gandhi (MG) Rd, past the beautifully restored facade of the **6 National Gallery of Modern Art** (p742). Opposite is landmark **7 Chhatrapati Shivaji Maharaj Vastu Sangrahalaya** (p741), built in glorious Indo-Saracenic style. Back across the road is the 'Romanesque Transitional' **8 Elphinstone College** and the **9 David Sassoon Library & Reading Room** where members escape the afternoon heat lazing on planters' chairs on the upper balcony. Continue north to admire the vertical deco stylings of the **10 New India Assurance Company Building**. On an

island ahead lies **11 Flora Fountain**, depicting the Roman goddess of flowers. Turn east down Veer Nariman Rd, walking towards **12 St Thomas' Cathedral** (p742). Ahead lies the stately **13 Horniman Circle**, an arcaded ring of buildings laid out in the 1860s around a beautifully kept botanical garden. It's overlooked by the neoclassical **14 Town Hall**, home to the Asiatic Society library. Backtrack to Flora Fountain, continuing west and turning south onto Bhaurao Patil Marg to see the august **15 High Court** (Map p752; www.bombayhighcourt.nic.in; Eldon Rd; ⊙ 10.30am-5.30pm) and ornate **16 University of Mumbai** (p742). The university's 84m-high **17 Rajabai Clock Tower** (p742) is off limits for visitors, but is best observed from within the **18 Oval Maidan**. Turn around to compare the colonial edifices with the row of art deco beauties lining Maharshi Karve (MK) Rd — notably the wedding-cake tower of the **19 Eros cinema** (Map p752; www.eroscinema.co.in; Maharshi Karve Rd, Churchgate). Divert east to New Marine Lines and head 1km north to the **20 Liberty Cinema**, a dazzling, 1200-capacity single-screen art deco gem opened in 1949.

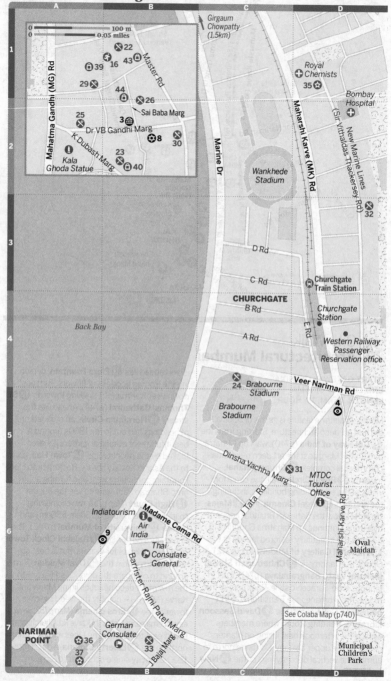

MUMBAI (BOMBAY)

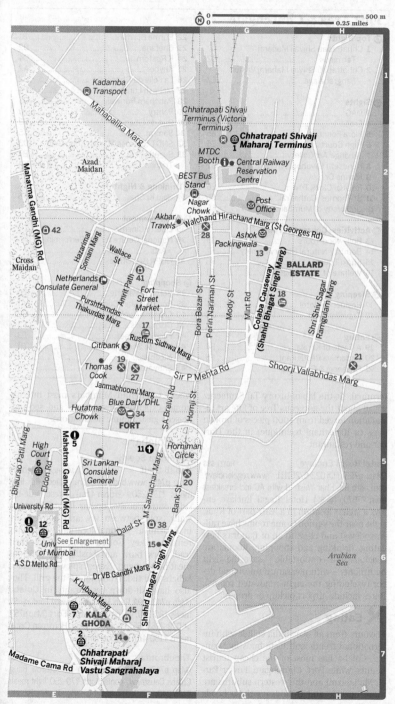

0   500 m
0   0.25 miles

Kadamba Transport

Chhatrapati Shivaji Terminus (Victoria Terminus)

Chhatrapati Shivaji Maharaj Terminus 1

MTDC Booth

Central Railway Reservation Centre

Azad Maidan

Mahapalika Marg

BEST Bus Stand

Nagar Chowk

Post Office

Akbar Travels

Walchand Hirachand Marg (St Georges Rd)

28

42

Ashok Packingwala

13

BALLARD ESTATE

Hazarimal Somani Marg

Wallace St

Netherlands Consulate General

Amrit Path

41

Cross Maidan

Mahatma Gandhi (MG) Rd

Fort Street Market

Bora Bazar St

Perin Nariman St

Mody St

Mint Rd

Colaba Causeway (Shahid Bhagat Singh Marg)

Shri Shiv Sagar Ramgulam Marg

18

Purshttamdas Thakurdas Marg

17

Rustom Sidhwa Marg

Citibank

21

19

Thomas Cook

27

Sir P Mehta Rd

Shoorji Vallabhdas Marg

Janmabhoomi Marg

Blue Dart/DHL

34

SA Brelvi Rd

Homji St

Hutatma Chowk

FORT

High Court

5

6

Sri Lankan Consulate General

11

Horniman Circle

M Samachar Marg

Bank St

Bhaurao Patil Marg

Eldon Rd

20

University Rd

10 12

Univ of Mumbai

Dalal St

38

See Enlargement

15

Arabian Sea

A S D Mello Rd

Dr VB Gandhi Marg

Shahid Bhagat Singh Marg

K Dubash Marg

45

7 **KALA GHODA**

2

14

Chhatrapati Shivaji Maharaj Vastu Sangrahalaya

Madame Cama Rd

754

Fort Area & Churchgate

terminal. At the lap-of-luxury Taj Santacruz it's all about the gorgeous Tree of Life art installation forged from 4000 pieces of broken glass (a Rajasthani technique) in the Tiqri bar and restaurant.

Hotel Regal Enclave HOTEL $$$
(Map p756; ☏022-67261111; www.regalenclave.com; 4th Rd, Khar West; d with AC incl breakfast from ₹7670; ❉☎) Hotel Regal Enclave enjoys a stellar location in a leafy part of Khar, right near the station (some rooms have railway views) and close to all of Bandra's best eating, drinking and shopping. Rooms are spacious and comfortable – save the tight bathrooms – with pleasant if unoriginal decor (excluding the eight renovated rooms). Rates include airport pickup or drop-off.

✗ Eating

Flavours from all over India collide with international trends and taste buds in Mumbai. Colaba has most of the cheap tourist haunts, while Fort, Churchgate, Lower Parel, Mahalaxmi and the western suburbs are more upscale and trendy; it's these hoods where you'll find Mumbai's most international, expensive restaurants and see-and-be-seen gastronomic destinations.

✗ Colaba

Bademiya Seekh Kebab Stall MUGHLAI, FAST FOOD $
(Map p740; www.bademiya.com; Tulloch Rd; light meals ₹130-250; ☺5pm-4am) These side-by-side, outrageously popular late-night street stalls (split between veg and nonveg) are in Bademiya's original location, where they remain a key Colaba hang-out for their trademark buzz and bustle and delicious meat-heavy menu. Expect spicy, fresh-grilled kebabs and tikka rolls hot off the grill. They also have sit-down restaurants in **Colaba** (Map p740; 19A Ram Mention, Nawroji Furdunji St; meals ₹80-370; ☺1pm-2am) and **Fort** (Map p752; ☏022-22655657; Botawala Bldg, Horniman Circle; mains ₹180-410; ☺noon-1am).

Theobroma CAFE $$
(Map p740; www.theobroma.in; 24 Cusrow Baug, Colaba Causeway; confections ₹70-250, light meals ₹125-240; ☺9am-midnight; ☎) Perfectly ex-

ecuted cakes, tarts and brownies go well with the coffee at this staple Mumbai patisserie. The pastries change regularly; if you're lucky, you'll find popular decadence like the chocolate-opium pastry, but it's all great. For brunch have the *akoori* (Parsi-style scrambled eggs) with green mango. The **Bandra branch** (Map p756; 33rd Rd, near Linking Rd; confections ₹70-250; ⏱8am-midnight; 🛜) is big and airy, though with a smaller menu.

Bombay Vintage   INDIAN $$
(Map p740; ☑022-22880017; www.facebook.com/bombayvintage; Regal Circle, Oriental Mansion Bldg, Madame Cama Rd; mains ₹350-970; ⏱noon-midnight; 🛜) Brought to you by the same hospitality team as Woodside Inn (p762), **Pantry** (Map p752; www.thepantry.in; ground fl, Yashwanth Chambers, Military Square Ln, B Bharucha Marg, Kala Ghoda; breakfast ₹1275-345, mains ₹320-600; ⏱8.30am-11pm; 🛜) 🍽 and Miss T (p757), this cool throwback restaurant resurrects Bombay recipes of yore, often elevated versions of back-alley street food and dive-bar grub. Either way, you don't see a lot of options on this menu that pop up elsewhere, which is a refreshing change of pace for Colaba.

⭐**Bohri Kitchen**   BOHRI $$$
(☑9819447438; www.thebohrikitchen.com; ₹1500; ⏱12.30pm Fri & Sat) Served up in a family home, this weekend-only pop-up dining experience was cooked up by former Google employee Munaf Kapadia. It showcases both the spectacular home cooking of his mother, Nafisa, and the unique cuisine of the Bohra Muslim community, which draws on influ-ences from as far afield as Yemen and Gujarat. The concept was so successful that the Maharashtra Government even lifted the idea for an initiative to empower local communities and increase tourism through visitors' bellies! Predictably, the seven-course, home-dining experience is easily one of Mumbai's most magical. Nafisa's smoked mutton *kheema* samosas and 48-hour *raan* are always included in the weekly-changing menu, which is announced on Facebook.

You must book ahead and pay a deposit – this is not a traditional restaurant! – and the address is revealed 24 hours in advance. Then settle in for a special afternoon with the Kapadia family.

Indigo Delicatessen   CAFE $$$
(Map p740; www.indigodeli.com; Pheroze Bldg, Chhatrapati Shivaji Marg; mains ₹665-710; ⏱8.30am-12.30am; 🛜) A bustling and fash-ionable cafe-restaurant with cool tunes and wooden tables. The menu includes all-day breakfasts (₹300 to ₹710) and straightfor-ward international classics like pork ribs, thin-crust pizza and inventive sandwiches. It's always busy, so service can get stretched.

Table   FUSION $$$
(Map p740; ☑022-22825000; www.thetable.in; Kalapesi Trust Bldg, Apollo Bunder Marg; small plates ₹575-1200, mains ₹700-1375; ⏱noon-4pm & 11.30pm-1am, tea 4.30-6.30pm Mon-Sat, noon-4pm Sun; 🛜) The market-fresh, globally inspired fusion menu, most of which was designed by former San Francisco chef Alex Sanchez, changes daily and does everything

MUMBAI (BOMBAY) EATING

THE PARSIS

Mumbai is home to the world's largest surviving community of Parsis, people of the ancient Zoroastrian faith, who fled Iran in the 10th century to escape religious persecution by the new Muslim rulers of Persia. 'Parsi' literally means Persian. Zoroastrians believe in a single deity, Ahura Mazda, who is worshipped at *agiari* (fire temples) across Mumbai, which non-Parsis are forbidden to enter. Parsi funeral rites are unique: the dead are laid out on open-air platforms to be picked over by vultures. The most renowned of these, the Tower of Silence, is located below the Hanging Gardens in Malabar Hill, yet screened by trees and hidden from public view.

The Mumbai Parsi community is extremely influential and successful, with a 98.6% literacy rate (the highest in the city). Famous Parsis include the Tata family (India's foremost industrialists), author Rohinton Mistry and Freddie Mercury. The best way for travellers to dig into the culture is by visiting one of the city's Parsi cafes. These atmospheric time capsules of a bygone era are a dying breed, but several sail on, including the excellent Britannia & Co. (p758) restaurant, **Kyani and Co** (Map p744; 657 JSS Marg, Jer Mahal Estate, Marine Lines; snacks ₹10-180; ⏱7am-8.30pm Mon-Sat, to 6pm Sun) and tourist hotbed Cafe Mondegar (p762).

Western Suburbs

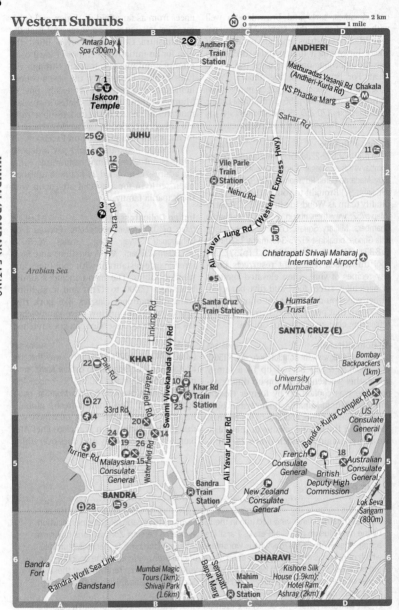

in its power to satisfy your cravings for a curry-free evening out. There's a lot to love: a crunchy kale salad with Iranian dates and toasted pistachios, zucchini spaghetti with almonds and Parmesan, and house-made black-truffle *taglierini*.

Basilico MEDITERRANEAN $$$

(Map p740; www.cafebasilico.com; Sentinel House, Arthur Bunder Rd; mains ₹320-680; ☉9am-12.30am; ☎) Euro-style Basilico does decadent sweets and especially creative fare when it comes to vegans and vegetarians. There are exquisite salads (from ₹330) like

Western Suburbs

quinoa, organic avocado and papaya, and numerous other interesting options like veg Moroccan tagine. It draws a top-end Indian crowd. If you can walk past that hazelnut chocolate crunch cake without biting, you're better than us.

Miss T   SOUTHEAST ASIAN $$$
(Map p740; ☎ 022-22801144; www.miss-t.in; 4 Mandalik Marg, Apollo Bunder; mains for 2 ₹700-2500; ☺ noon-3pm & 7.30pm-1am, bar from 6pm; 🛜) The Colaba Cartel, an impressive team of Mumbai foodies with a proven culinary track record including Pantry (p755), Woodside Inn (p762) and Table (p755), is the mind and manner behind Mumbai's coolest new restaurant. In a historic Mandalik Rd bungalow, Miss T's kitchen magicians include an executive chef from Hoi An (Vietnam) who draws menu inspiration equally from his neighbours (Thailand, Myanmar, Laos).

🍴 Fort Area & Churchgate

K Rustom   SWEETS $
(Map p752; 87 Stadium House, Veer Nariman Rd, Churchgate; desserts ₹40-70; ☺ 9.30am-11pm Mon-Sat, 3-7pm Sun) K Rustom has nothing but a few metal freezers, but the ice-cream sandwiches here have been pleasing Mumbaikar palates since 1953. Pick from 50 flavours; roasted almond crunch is the bestseller.

Pancham Puriwala   NORTH INDIAN $
(Map p752; 8/10 Perin Nariman St, Ballard Estate; mains ₹40-150; ☺ 8.30am-midnight) Located just outside CSMT, this budget eatery is a heritage icon, serving *puri bhaji* (puffed-up bread with a potato-and-pea curry) for over a century. The interiors are not fancy – there's no AC and diners sit on plain stainless benches – but the fun lies in listening to the stories of its owners, who set up this restaurant before the first train services started in India.

SNDT to Cross
Maiden Khao Gali   STREET FOOD $
(Map p752; Vitthaldas Thackersey Marg, Marine Lines; mains from ₹20-120; ☺ 11am-11pm) A heaven for food lovers, Mumbai's famous *khau galis* (literally 'eat lanes') pack in some tantalising street treats, serving up a potpourri of cuisines and historic influences. Students and office workers are lured to the *khau galli* running from SNDT to Cross Maidan by the popular Bombay Sandwich (a toastie made with cheese, chutney and masala spices) and Frankie (a roti rolled with vegetables).

★ Shree Thakkar Bhojanalay   INDIAN $$
(Map p744; ☎ 022-22011232; www.facebook.com/shreethaker1945; 31 Dadisheth Agyari Ln, Marine Lines; thali week/weekend ₹500/600; ☺ 11.30am-3pm & 7-10.30pm Mon-Sat, 11.30am-3.30pm Sun) With a cult following and festive lavender

STREET EATS

Mumbai's street cuisine is vaster than many Western culinary traditions. Stalls tend to get started in late afternoon, when chai complements much of the fried deliciousness; items are ₹10 to ₹80.

Most street food is vegetarian. Chowpatty Beach is a great place to try Mumbai's famous *bhelpuri* (puffed rice tossed with fried rounds of dough, lentils, onions, herbs and chutneys). Stalls offering samosas, *pav bhaji* (spiced vegetables and bread), *vada pav* (deep-fried spiced lentil-ball sandwich), *bhurji pav* (scrambled eggs and bread) and *dabeli* (a mixture of potatoes, spices, peanuts and pomegranate, also on bread) are spread through the city.

For a meaty meal, Mohammed Ali and Merchant Rds in Kalbadevi are famous for kebabs. In Colaba, Bademiya Seekh Kebab Stall (p754) is a late-night Mumbai rite of passage, renowned for its chicken tikka rolls.

The office workers' district on the north side of Kala Ghoda is another good hunting ground for street snacks.

tables to boot, this thali mainstay – one of the oldest in the city – puts on the full-court flavour with its never-ending Gujarati/Rajasthani set meals, full of *farsans* (bite-size snacks) and scrumptious veg curries. The air-con environs are a welcome retreat from the busy congestion below. It has been open since 1945.

La Folie du Chocolate CAFE $$

(Map p752; www.lafolie.in; 16 Commerce House, Rope Walk Ln, Kala Ghoda; cakes ₹240-300; ⏱9am-11.30pm) Chocoholics and cake fetishists look no further – this minuscule Kala Ghoda place will seduce and hook you. Owner Sanjana Patel spent seven years in France studying the art of pastry- and chocolate-making, which was obviously time well spent. Try the Intense Caramel with Haitian chocolate mousse, burnt caramel crème brûlée and butterscotch praline. Koinonia coffee is served – even in keto-butter style.

Samrat GUJARATI $$

(Map p752; www.prashantcaterers.com/samrat; Prem Court bldg, J Tata Rd, Churchgate; thali lunch/dinner ₹345/450; ⏱noon-11pm) Samrat has an à la carte menu but most rightly opt for the famous Gujarati thali – a cavalcade of taste and texture, sweetness and spice that includes numerous curries and chutneys, curd, rotis and other bits and pieces. Samrat is air-conditioned and beer is available.

A Taste of Kerala KERALAN $$

(Map p752; Prospect Chambers Annex, Pitha St, Fort; mains ₹105-455, thali from ₹120-160; ⏱9am-midnight) An inexpensive Keralan eatery with lots of coconut and southern goodness on the menu. Try one of the epic thalis, served on a banana leaf and priced higher at ₹250 on Sundays. There are also seafood specials like prawn-pepper masala. Don't skip the *payasam* (rice pudding with jaggery and coconut milk) for dessert.

Britannia & Co. PARSI $$

(Map p752; Wakefield House, 11 Sport Rd, Ballard Estate; mains ₹200-950; ⏱noon-4pm Mon-Fri, to 10pm Sat) This Parsi institution is the domain of 97-year-old Boman Kohinoor, who will warm your heart with his stories (and he still takes the orders!). The signature dishes are the *dhansak* (meat with curried lentils and rice) and the berry *pulao* – spiced and boneless mutton or chicken, veg or egg, buried in basmati rice and tart barberries imported from Iran. Cash only.

Rue du Liban LEBANESE $$

(Map p752; ☎022-30151205; 43, Sasoon Bldg, VB Gandhi Marg, Kala Ghoda; small plates ₹550-800, mains ₹850-950; ⏱noon-4pm & 7pm-midnight) Moodily lit, art deco-era Beirut-inspired interiors complement the hyperauthentic dishes of the Levant in this sexy Kala Ghoda newcomer. The hummus? Texture-perfect, a precedent followed with lovely *moutabel* (charred eggplant puree with pomegranate, spring onion and sumac), the crunchy, Middle Eastern–authentic falafel, and a long list of excellent hot and cold meze.

Suzette FRENCH $$

(Map p752; www.facebook.com/suzette.cafe; Atlanta Bldg, Vinayak K Shah Marg, Nariman Point; meals ₹390-700; ⏱9am-10.30pm Mon-Sat, 11am-5.30pm Sun; 🛜) 🌱 Relaxed Parisian-style place steeped where possible in organically sourced ingredients. Delectable crêpes, croques, salads, juices and soothing lounge music attract flocks of foreigners in need of a curry recess. On the crêpe front, sweet tooths should try the organic jaggery (₹120); for a savoury flavour, order a croque feta with tomato, mozzarella, creamed spinach and feta (₹490).

The **Bandra West branch** (Map p756; www.facebook.com/suzette.cafe; St John St, Pali Naka; mains 120-760; ⊙9am-10.30pm) 🍴 has outdoor seating and is open daily.

⭐**Khyber** MUGHLAI, INDIAN $$$
(Map p752; 🖋022-40396666; www.khyber restaurant.com; 145 MG Rd; mains ₹590-1110; ⊙12.30-4pm & 7.30-11.30pm) The much-acclaimed Khyber has a Northwest Frontier–themed design that incorporates murals depicting turbaned Mughal royalty, lots of exposed brickwork and oil lanterns – just the sort of place an Afghan warlord might feel at home. The meat-centric menu features gloriously tender kebabs, rich curries and lots of tandoori favourites roasted in the Khyber's famous red-masala sauce.

⭐**Trishna** SEAFOOD $$$
(Map p752; 🖋022-22703214; Ropewalk Ln, Kala Ghoda; mains ₹460-1830; ⊙noon-3.30pm & 6.30pm-midnight) Behind a modest entrance on a quiet Kala Ghoda lane is this often-lauded, intimate South Indian seafood restaurant. It's not a trendy place – the decor is old school, the seating a little cramped and the menu perhaps too long – but the cooking is superb. Witness the Hyderabadi fish tikka, jumbo prawns with green-pepper sauce, and the outstanding king crab and lobster dishes.

Burma Burma BURMESE $$$
(Map p752; 🖋022-40040600; www.burma burma.in; Oak Ln, off MG Rd, Kala Ghoda; meals ₹360-490; ⊙noon-2.45pm & 7-11pm; ☎) A sleek, stylish restaurant that marries contemporary design with a few traditional artefacts (prayer wheels line one wall), providing a beautiful setting for the cuisine of Myanmar (Burma). The menu is well priced, intricate and ambitious, with inventive salads (the pickled tea leaf is extraordinary), curries and soups: *Oh No Khow Suey* is a glorious coconut-enriched noodle broth. No alcohol.

Mahesh Lunch Home SEAFOOD $$$
(Map p752; 🖋022-22023965; www.mahesh lunchhome.com; 8B Cowasji Patel Rd, Fort; mains ₹200-750; ⊙11.30am-4pm & 6-11pm) A great place to try Mangalorean or Chinese-style seafood in Mumbai. It's renowned for its ladyfish, pomfret, lobster, crab (try it with butter garlic pepper sauce) and anything else out of the sea.

There's also a bigger **Juhu branch** (Map p756; 🖋022-66955554; Juhu Tara Rd; mains ₹275-1475; ⊙12-3.30pm & 7pm-12.30am; ☎) with an extended menu.

🍴 Kalbadevi to Mahalaxmi

Badshah Cold Drinks INDIAN $
(Map p744; www.badshahcolddrinks.com; 52/156 Umrigar Bldg, Lokmanya Tilak Marg, Lohar Chawl; snacks & drinks ₹38-240; ⊙7am-12.30am) Opposite Crawford Market, Badshah has been serving snacks, fruit juices and its famous *falooda* (rose-flavoured drink of milk, cream, nuts and vermicelli), *kulfi falooda* (with ice cream) and *kesar pista falooda* (with saffron and pistachios) to hungry bargain hunters since 1905. A must.

New Kulfi Centre ICE CREAM $
(Map p744; 556 Marina Mansion, Sukh Sagar, Sardar V Patel Rd, Girgaon; kulfi per 100g ₹50-100; ⊙9.30am-1am) Serves 36 flavours of the best *kulfi* (Indian firm-textured ice cream) you'll have anywhere. Killer flavours include pistachio, *malai* (cream) and mango.

Swati Snacks FAST FOOD $
(Map p744; www.swatisnacks.com; 248, Karai Estate, Tardeo Rd, Tardeo; snacks ₹20-310, mains ₹135-315; ⊙noon-10.45pm) Get in line for the upscale street food at this Mumbaikar classic, dishing up mostly Gujarati specialities since 1963. Amid minimalist, industrial aluminium diner-like tables offset by wooden banquettes, tasty treats like *panki chatni* (banana leaf–steamed savoury-rice pancakes), *mung dal chilla* (mung-dal pancakes) and *sabudana khichdi* (soaked sago cooked with coconut, green chilli and spices) are worth the wait.

Sardar STREET FOOD $
(Map p744; 166A Tardeo Rd Junction, Tulsiwadi; pav bhaji from ₹140; ⊙noon-2am) If you're spooked about Indian street food, try one of the city's most beloved street staples, *pav bhaji*, at this Mumbai institution. The curried-veg mix is cooked to death on a series of scalding *tawas* (hotplates) and served with a butter floater the size of a Bollywood ego. Get in line; the entire restaurant turns over at once.

Panshikar INDIAN $
(Map p744; www.panshikarfoods.com; Mohan Bldg, Jagannath Shankar Sheth Rd, Girgaon; snacks ₹40-80; ⊙9am-9pm-Sat) This clean and wonderful cheapie near Khotachiwadi is an excellent spot for snacks any time of day, but it all goes down especially well at breakfast. *Subudani wadi* (fried pearl-tapioca balls), *misal pav* (spicy bean sprouts and pulses), *potato wada* (mashed-potato patty), *kothimbir vadi* (crispy gram flour, coriander leaves and spices) – it's all excellent.

Wash it down with a masala chai or *kokum sharbat* (kokum juice).

★Revival
INDIAN $$

(Map p744; 39B Chowpatty Seaface, Chowpatty; thali ₹450; ☺noon-3.30pm & 7-11.30pm; ☎) Waiters at this thali mecca saunter around Chowpatty sea-view digs in silken dhotis, filling your plates with dozens of delectable (veg-only) curries, sides, chutneys, rotis and rice dishes in an all-you-can-eat gastronomic onslaught. The dishes change daily and, all said and done, is probably Mumbai's best thali.

Cafe Noorani
MUGHLAI $$

(Map p744; www.cafenoorani.com; Tardeo Rd, Haji Ali Circle; mains ₹80-575; ☺8am-midnight) Inexpensive, old-school eatery that's a requisite stop before or after visiting Haji Ali Dargah (p742). Mughlai and Punjabi staples dominate, with kebabs chargrilled to perfection and great biryani; try the chicken tikka biryani (₹330).

✗ Western Suburbs

★Hotel Ram Ashraya
SOUTH INDIAN $

(Bhandarkar Rd, King's Circle, Matunga East; light meals ₹40-90; ☺5am-9.30pm) In the Tamil enclave of King's Circle, 80-year-old Ram Ashraya is beloved by southern families for its spectacular dosas, *idli* (spongy, round, fermented rice cake) and *uttapa* (pancake with toppings). Filter coffee is strong and flavoursome. The menu changes daily. It's just outside Matunga Rd train station's east exit and draws Mumbaikars of all persuasions.

Hoppumm
SRI LANKAN $

(Map p756; 8, Rafi Mansion, 28th Rd, Bandra West; mains ₹180-300; ☺11.30-3.30pm & 7.30-11.30pm) 🍽 Mumbai's best new budget eats are served up in this tiny – four tables and a counter – hipsterised Sri Lankan joint. It does absolutely delicious prawn *moilee* (seafood curry) and Ceylon roasted-chicken curries, served in hoppers (bowl-shaped, *appam* pancakes made from fermented rice flour and coconut milk) served alongside Keralan chutney-and-onion sambal. Portions aren't huge, so don't be afraid to order two items.

★Dakshinayan
SOUTH INDIAN $$

(Map p756; Anand Hotel, Gandhi Gram Rd, Juhu; mains ₹100-280; ☺11am-11pm Mon-Fri, from 8am Sat & Sun) With *rangoli* (elaborate designs) on the walls, servers in lungis, and sari-clad women lunching (*chappals* – sandals – off

under the table), Dakshinayan channels Tamil Nadu. There are delicately textured dosas, *idli* and *uttapam*, village-fresh chutneys and perhaps the best *rasam* (tomato soup with spices and tamarind) in Mumbai. Finish off with a South Indian filter coffee, served in a stainless-steel set.

Chilli-heads should order *molagapudi idli*, a dozen *idli* coated in 'gunpowder' (potent spices).

★Kitchen Garden by Suzette
CAFE $$

(Map p756; www.facebook.com/KitchenGarden bySuzette; 9 Gasper Enclave, St John's St, Bandra West; light meals ₹360-770; ☺9am-11pm; ☎) 🍽 From the same French trio that brought us Suzette (p758) comes this superb organic cafe, a haven of health and homesick-remedying salads, sandwiches, cold-press juices and coffee sourced from local cooperatives and organic farms around Maharashtra and worldwide. The burrata, made by an American Indian Hare Krishna in Gujarat, is outstanding, but then again, so is everything.

O Pedro
GOAN $$$

(Map p756; ☑022-26534700; www.opedro mumbai.com; BKC Bldg, No 2, Bandra Kurla Complex, Bandra East; mains ₹295-1400; ☎) The first restaurant that makes it worth venturing into the Bandra Kurla Complex just to eat. The elevated Goan dishes are fantastic: spicy chorizo *bhakri* tacos, creamy seabass ceviche with tamarind, stir-fried prawn *sukhhe* with fresh coconut, Goa chillies and tamarind, fried *rawas* stuffed with green chilli-coconut chutney – it's all an explosion of flavour and spice and everything nice.

★Peshawri
NORTH INDIAN $$$

(Map p756; ☑022-28303030; www.itchotels.in; ITC Maratha, Sahar Rd, Andheri East; mains ₹1600-3225; ☺12.45-2.45pm & 7-11.45pm) Make this Northwest Frontier restaurant, outside the international airport, your first or last stop in Mumbai. It's a carbon copy of Delhi's famous **Bukhara** (☑011-26112233; ITC Maurya, Sardar Patel Marg; mains ₹1500-3000; ☺12.30-2.45pm & 7-11.30pm; Ⓜ Durgabai Deshmukh South Campus), with the same menu and decor. Folks flock here for the buttery dhal *bukhara*, a 24-hour simmered black dhal (₹945), but don't miss kebabs. Try the Murgh Malai (marinated tandoor-grilled chicken) and *raan* (impossibly succulent slow-roasted lamb hock).

★Bastian
SEAFOOD $$$

(Map p756; www.facebook.com/bastianmumbai; B/1, New Kamal Bldg, Linking Rd, Bandra West;

DABBA-WALLAHS

A small miracle of logistics, Mumbai's 5000 *dabba-wallahs* (literally 'food-container person'; also called tiffin wallahs) work tirelessly to deliver hot lunches to office workers throughout the city (and to the poor later on in the evenings, a 2015 initiative).

Lunch boxes are picked up each day from restaurants and homes and carried on heads, bicycles and trains to a centralised sorting station. A sophisticated system of numbers and colours (many wallahs don't read) identifies the destination of each lunch. More than 200,000 meals are delivered – always on time, come (monsoon) rain or (searing) shine.

This system has been used for over a century and there's only about one mistake per six million deliveries. (In a 2002 analysis, *Forbes Magazine* found that the *dabba-wallahs* had a six-sigma, or 99.999999%, reliability rating.) The system was also the subject of a Harvard Business School study in 2010 and a hit feature film in 2013 (*The Lunchbox*).

Look for these master messengers midmorning at Churchgate and Chhatrapati Shivaji Maharaj Terminus (CSMT) stations.

mains for 2 ₹1100-3200; ⏰noon-3pm & 7pm-midnight; 🛜) All the praise bestowed upon this trendy seafooder is indisputably warranted. Chinese-Canadian chef Boo Kwang Kim and his culinary sidekick, American-Korean Kelvin Cheung, have forged an East-meets-West gastronomic dream. Go with the market-fresh side menu: choose your catch (prawns, fish, mud crab or lobster) then pick from an insanely difficult list of impossibly tasty pan-Asian sauces.

⭐**Bombay Canteen**   INDIAN $$$
(📞022-49666666; www.thebombaycanteen.com; Process House, Kamala Mills, SB Marg, Lower Parel; small plates ₹225-650, mains ₹450-975; ⏰noon-1am; 🛜) Bombay Canteen is one of Mumbai's hottest restaurants, courtesy of former New York chef and *Top Chef Masters* winner Floyd Cardoz, and executive chef Thomas Zacharias, who spent time at New York's three-Michelin-star Le Bernardin. India-wide regional dishes and traditional flavours dominate – Kejriwal toast, Goan pulled-pork-vindaloo tacos, mustard chicken curry – each dish an explosion of texture and flavour.

Koko   SUSHI $$$
(📞8451011124; www.facebook.com/KOKOAsian Gastropub; C2, Trade World, ground fl, Kamala Mills, SB Rd, Lower Parel; sushi rolls ₹900-1350, mains ₹590-3100; ⏰12.30-4.30pm & 7pm-12.30am Mon-Thu, to 1am Fri & Sat; 🛜) Creative cocktails at this hot Asian gastrobar include the Tom Yum Cup (basically a tom yam soup laced with vodka), mixed by genuinely talented and friendly bartenders at the lengthy Burmese teak bar. Fantastic sushi – try the wild Japanese salmon truffle roll – and pan-Asian

dishes come from Eric Sifu, a Chinese chef from Malaysia with Michelin on his resume. Reservations essential; style recommended.

Masala Library   MODERN INDIAN $$$
(Map p756; 📞022-66424142; www.masalalibrary. co.in; ground fl, First International Financial Centre, G Block, BKC Rd, Bandra East; mains ₹575-1250, tasting menu ₹2500-2700, with wine ₹4250-4450; ⏰noon-2.15pm & 7-11pm) Daring and imaginative Masala Library dangles the contemporary Indian carrot to foodies and gastronauts, challenging them to rethink their notions of subcontinent cuisine. The tasting menus are an exotic culinary journey – think wild-dehydrated-mushroom chai with truffle-oil crumbs; langoustine *moilee* (seafood curry) with gunpowder mash; and a betel-leaf fairy floss to finish. Reservations essential.

🍷 Drinking & Nightlife

Colaba is rich in unpretentious pub-like joints (but also has some very classy places), while Bandra, Juhu and Andheri are home turf for the film and model set. Lower Parel has become a gourmet-dining hub, while the best craft-beer places are now way the hell up in Andheri. Wednesday and Thursday are big nights at some clubs, as well as the traditional Friday and Saturday; there's usually a cover charge. Dress codes apply, so don't rock up in shorts and sandals. Many places deny entry to men on their own. The trend in Mumbai is towards resto-lounges as opposed to full-on nightclubs. You're also technically supposed to have a licence to drink in Maharashtra; some bars require you to buy a temporary one, for a nominal fee, though we've never been asked.

MUMBAI (BOMBAY) DRINKING & NIGHTLIFE

CRAFT BREW MUMBAI

Few visitors to India would argue that an ice-cold Kingfisher in a dingy, smoke-filled bar isn't a quintessential Indian experience, but craft-beer connoisseurs might also add that India's ubiquitous native lager gets old pretty quick. And then there's those distinctly disgusting YouTube videos of oily, urine-coloured *something* being drained from beer bottles before drinking (it's usually glycerine, widely used in Indian beers as a preservative). Cheers? Not really.

While certainly late to the craft-brew boozefest, Mumbai has finally embraced hop-heavy IPAs, roasty, chocolatey porters and refreshing saisons, thanks to the city's very own craft-beer wallah, American expat Greg Kroitzsh. Kroitzsh opened Mumbai's first microbrewery, the now-shuttered Barking Deer, in 2013, and the taps began flowing in Mumbai as they already had been for some time in craftier Indian cities like Pune, Bangalore and Gurgaon.

Fancy a pint? Hoptimists now head north. In Andheri West, Independence Brewing Company (p763) and **Brewbot** (www.brewbot.in; Morya Landmark 1, off New Link Rd; pint ₹295; ⏰4pm-1am Mon-Fri, noon-1am Sat; 🛜), and the 16-tap **Woodside Inn** (Map p740; www.facebook.com/Woodsideinn; Indian Mercantile Mansion, Wodehouse Rd; ⏰11am-1.30am; 🛜) in Colaba, are within pub-crawl range of each other and are worth the journey, as is the good-time Doolally Taproom (p763) in Khar (also in Andheri and Kemps Corner) and the **Gateway Taproom** (Map p756; www.gatewaybrewery.com; BKC Bldg, No 3, G Block Bandra Kurla Complex; ⏰noon-1.30am; 🛜) in Bandra East. In Lower Parel, **Toit Tap Room** (www.toit.in; Zeba Centre, Mathuradas Mill Compound, Senapati Bapat Marg; ⏰noon-1.30am; 🛜) – a Bangalore transplant – is one of Mumbai's liveliest beer destinations; and Thirsty City 127 (p763) does tasty work next door in a more upscale ambience with the ex-Barking Deer brewer and a Sheffielder master brewer.

It's only a matter of time before taps start flowing in Fort and Colaba as well. The best of the production-only craft beer includes Pune's Great State Ale Works (www.facebook.com/greatstate.aleworks), which often holds tap takeovers in Mumbai (its salted kokum ale is one of India's best craft brews). White Owl (www.whiteowl.in), which has closed its excellent taproom to concentrate on bottling, is also worth seeking out.

The city's signature brew has quickly become Belgian Wit – citrusy and refreshing, it's a perfect accompaniment for hot and humid Mumbai.

🍷 Colaba

Cafe Mondegar
PUB

(Map p740; www.facebook.com/cafemondegar; Metro House, 5A Colaba Causeway; ⏰7.30am-11.30pm) Iranian-founded 'Mondy's' has been drawing a heady mix of foreigners and locals since 1871. It's first and foremost a rowdy bar serving ice-cold mugs of Kingfisher (₹220), but don't discount its wide range of American, English and Parsi breakfast choices (₹130 to ₹350).

Harbour Bar
BAR

(Map p740; www.tajhotels.com/en-in/taj/taj-mahal-palace-mumbai/restaurants; Taj Mahal Palace, Apollo Bunder; ⏰11am-11.45pm) With unmatched views of the Gateway of India and harbour, this timeless bar inside the Taj Mahal Palace is an essential visit. Drinks aren't uberexpensive (from ₹500/700/750 for a beer/wine/cocktail) given the surrounds and the fact that they come with very generous portions of nibbles, including jumbo cashews.

Leopold Café
BAR

(Map p740; www.leopoldcafe.com; cnr Colaba Causeway & Nawroji F Rd; ⏰7.30am-1am) Love it or hate it, most tourists end up at this clichéd Mumbai travellers' institution at one time or another. Around since 1871, Leopold's has wobbly ceiling fans, a rambunctious atmosphere conducive to swapping tales with strangers, and an upstairs DJ most nights from 8pm.

Hammer & Song
COCKTAIL BAR

(www.flamboyante.in; Shop 10, The Arcade, World Trade Centre, Cuffe Parade; ⏰noon-1.30am; 🛜) Off the tourist trail and full of Mumbai's beautiful set, this new bar tucked away inside Cuffe Parade's World Trade Centre is a fun night out, with an emphasis on craft beer and craft cocktails (barrel-aged old-fashioneds, for example) set to a DJ/live saxophonist tag team most nights. The crowd skews upscale and the seats are notably comfy – settle in.

Mixologist Ayush Arora trained at the European Bartender School in Australia.

★ **Social** BAR
(Map p740; www.socialoffline.in; ground fl, Glen Rose Bldg, BK Boman Behram Marg, Apollo Bunder; ⊙ 9am-1.30am; 🛜) Colaba is the best of the locations of the hip Social chain, which combines a restaurant/bar with a collaborative work space. The happening bar nails the cocktails (from ₹295) – the Acharroska is the perfect marriage of Indian pungency and Brazilian sweetness.

The food (mains ₹190 to ₹490) spans everything from Bollywoodised fish and chips and *poutine* (French fries and cheese curds topped with gravy) to Thai thalis and great Parsi dishes for breakfast. There are also Social locations at **Todi Mill** (www.social offline.in; 242 Mathuradas Mill Compound, ⊙ 9am-1am; 🛜) in Lower Parel and **Khar** (Map p756; www.socialoffline.in; Rohan Plaza, 5th Rd, Ram Krishna Nagar; cocktails from ₹295; ⊙ 9am-1am; 🛜).

🍵 Fort Area & Churchgate

Raju Ki Chai TEAHOUSE
(Map p752; www.facebook.com/rajukichai; Shop 4, Kamar Bldg, Cowasji Patel Rd, Kala Ghoda; ⊙ 9am-midnight Mon-Sat, from 2pm Sun) It's nearly impossible to saunter past this tiny brick-and-mortar chai joint – its colourful facade and vibrant interiors lure you in like an industrial-strength magnetic kaleidoscope. Taking street chai to a welcoming new level without disregarding tradition, the concoctions here (₹35 to ₹50) are served in customary clay cups, but not discarded on the pavement as at street stalls.

🍷 Kalbadevi to Mahalaxmi

★ **Haji Ali Juice Centre** JUICE BAR
(Map p744; www.hajialijuicecentre.in; Lala Lajpat Rai Rd, Haji Ali Circle; ⊙ 5am-1.30am) Serves fresh juices and milkshakes (₹50 to ₹400), mighty fine *falooda* and fruit salads. Strategically placed at the entrance to Haji Ali mosque, it's a great place to cool off after a visit. Try the Triveni, a gorgeous trifecta of mango, strawberry and kiwi (₹270).

Blue Tokai COFFEE
(www.bluetokaicoffee.com; Unit 20-22, Laxmi Woollen Mill, Dr E Moses Marg, Mahalaxmi; ⊙ 9am-9pm; 🛜) 🌿 Coffee's Third Wave has finally arrived in India. This speciality coffeehouse,

one of four Mumbai locations, roasts its 100% Indian, traceable single-estate Arabica beans from farms like Vethilaikodaikanal (Tamil Nadu) and Thogarihunkal (Karnataka). It then brews them into espresso (from ₹100), cortados and flat whites (on the hot side) and pourovers and nitro (on the cold side). Coffee connoisseurs unite!

🍸 Western Suburbs

★ **Independence Brewing Company** CRAFT BEER
(www.independencebrewco.com; Boolani Estate Owners Premises Co-Op, New Link Rd, Andheri West; pints ₹400; ⊙ 1pm-1am Mon-Sat, noon-1am Sun; 🛜) A California-trained Indian master brewer oversees the craft at this trendy new Andheri West taproom from Pune-based Independence Brewing Company. Nine of the 10 taps are devoted to IBC brews, like four-grain saison, juicy Indian Pale Ales (IPAs), occasional sours and one of India's only double IPAs. There's Bollywoodised bar food to go along with it (grilled pickled paneer sandwiches, hot paprika wings).

★ **Doolally Taproom** CRAFT BEER
(Map p756; www.doolally.in; Rajkutir 10A, E854, 3rd Rd, Khar West; pints ₹300; ⊙ 7am-1am; 🛜) This Pune transplant, the vision of German brewmaster Oliver Schauf, was India's craft-beer pioneer. The fresh IPA, tangy Belgian Wit and apple cider are staples among the weekly changing 11 taps; and there are gourmet burgers and fat, hand-cut fries. It's steps from Khar station.

Wine Rack WINE BAR
(www.facebook.com/TheWineRackMumbai; ground fl, High Street Phoenix,Tulsi Pipe Rd, Lower Parel; ⊙ noon-1am; 🛜) Sorely needed and refreshingly well done, Mumbai's first take on a serious wine bar should please connoisseurs. Part shop (over 300 bottles), part bar (48 wines by the glass, 21 of which are Indian; ₹325 to ₹995), it draws a sophisticated crowd, though not quite as sexy as the backdrop bar mural would suggest. Impressively stocked bar as well.

★ **Thirsty City 127** BAR
(www.facebook.com/pg/thirstycity127; Todi Mills, Mathuradas Mill Compound, Tulsi Pipe Rd, Lower Parel; ⊙ 6pm-1.30am Tue-Sun; 🛜) The former space of Mumbai's first microbrewery has been revamped into a slick craft beer and cocktail destination under the direction of Indian beer maven/visual artist Vir Kotak.

The striking space catches attention with copper-plated fermentation tanks, velvet and turquoise banquettes, but the swill reigns: eight taps (solid Neipa, Kölsch, Hefeweizen, etc served in Teku glassware) and cocktails (₹800) themed by beer ingredients.

★ Cafe Zoe
BAR

(www.cafezoe.in; Mathurdas Mills Compound, NM Joshi Marg, Lower Parel; ⏰7.30am-1.30am; 🛜) Exposed brick and railing dominate the bilevel hipster hideaway inside a redeveloped cotton mill at Mathurdas Mills Compound. Forty wines by the glass, along with strong, well-mixed cocktails (₹700 to ₹1200) – like black grape caipiroskas and sage and lime martinis – ensure a lively crowd, who mingle alongside the old B&W photos of the space's former life dotting the walls.

Live jazz on Wednesdays at 9pm.

★ Toto's Garage
BAR

(Map p756; ☎022-26005494; 30th Rd, Bandra West; ⏰6pm-1am) A highly sociable, down-to-earth local dive done up in a car-mechanic theme, where you can go in your dirty clothes, drink draught beer (₹200 a glass) and listen to classic rock. Check out the up-ended VW Beetle above the bar. It's always busy and caters to all kinds.

★ Bonobo
BAR

(Map p756; www.facebook.com/Bonobo Bandra; Kenilworth Mall, 33rd Rd, off Linking Rd, Bandra West; ⏰6pm-1am) This bar champions underground and alternative music. DJs spin drum and bass and electronica, big beats and funky tech-house, and musicians play folk and blues. There's a great rooftop terrace and better-than-average craft beer on tap (Gateway and Brewbot). It's always a fun night out with a wildly eclectic crowd.

★ Koinonia Coffee Roasters
COFFEE

(Map p756; www.koinoniacoffeeroasters.com; 66 Chuim Village Rd, Chuim Village, Khar West; ⏰7am-10pm; 🛜) Mumbai's best speciality coffee is served in this tiny Third Wave coffeehouse in atmospheric Chium Village. Single-origin Indian estate coffee is roasted in-house with a top-end Probat roaster. It comes cold-brewed, via Clever and Aeropress methods, as exquisite espresso (₹140), or with a dollop of ice cream from the affogato bar. Selections include salted caramel, Pondicherry vanilla or dark chocolate Italian truffle oil.

☆ Entertainment

Mumbai has an exciting live-music scene, some terrific theatres, an emerging network of comedy clubs and, of course, cinemas and sporting action.

Consult Time Out Mumbai (www.timeout.com/mumbai) and Insider (https://insider.in/mumbai) for events and/or live-music listings. Unfortunately, Hindi films aren't shown with English subtitles. You can book movies, theatre and sporting events online with Book My Show (https://in.bookmyshow.com).

★ Royal Opera House
OPERA

(Map p744; ☎022-23668888; www.royaloperahouse.in; Mama Parmanand Marg, Girgaon; ⏰10am-6pm) India's only surviving opera house reopened to suitably dramatic fanfare with a 2016 performance by Mumbai-born British soprano Patricia Rozario, after a meticulous six-year restoration project that saw the regal address returned to full British-rule glory. Architect Abha Narain Lambah combed through old photographs of gilded ceilings, stained-glass windows and a baroque Indo-European foyer to restore the three-level auditorium.

Quarter
LIVE MUSIC

(Map p744; ☎8329110638; www.thequarter.in; Mathew Rd, Royal Opera House, Girgaon; ⏰10pm-1am) The Royal Opera House's signature entertainment venue (besides the Opera House itself, that is), the Quarter counts unique spaces like an airy, glass-fronted cafe and mozzarella bar, a Creole-cuisine-inspired restaurant and, most interestingly, a live-music venue evocative of a 1950s art deco jazz bar.

Canvas Laugh
COMEDY

(www.canvaslaughclub.com; 3rd fl, Palladium Mall, High Street Phoenix, Lower Parel; tickets ₹200-750) A popular comedy club that hosts around 50 shows per month, with twice-nightly programs on weekends (most comedians use English). It's 900m west of Lower Parel train station inside the High Street Phoenix shopping complex. Book tickets online.

National Centre for the Performing Arts
THEATRE, LIVE MUSIC

(NCPA; Map p752; www.ncpamumbai.com; NCPA Marg, Nariman Point) This vast cultural centre is the hub of Mumbai's highbrow music, theatre and dance scene. In any given week, it might host experimental plays, poetry readings, photography exhibitions, a jazz band

QUEER MUMBAI

Although homosexuality was decriminalised by India's highest court in 2018, Mumbai's LGBTIQ scene is still quite underground, especially for women, but it's gaining momentum. No dedicated LGBTIQ bars/clubs have opened yet, but gay-friendly 'safe house' venues often host private gay parties (announced on Gay Bombay, www.gaybombay.org).

Gay Bombay is a great place to start, with event listings including meetups in Bandra, GB-hosted bar and film nights (including somewhat-regular gay Saturday nights at Liquid Lounge in Girgaum Chowpatty), plus hiking trips, picnics and other queer-community info. Following are some other useful resources.

Gaylaxy (www.gaylaxymag.com) India's best gay e-zine; well worth consulting and has lots of Mumbai content.

Gaysi (www.gaysifamily.com) Mumbai-based lifestyle e-zine.

Humsafar Trust (Map p756; ☑ 022-26673800; www.humsafar.org; 3rd fl, Manthan Plaza Nehru Rd, Vakola Santa Cruz East; ◷ 10am-6.30pm Mon-Fri) Mumbai's most well-known LGBTIQ community organisation. It's also closely connected to the erratically published but pioneering magazine Bombay Dost (www.bombaydost.co.in).

Kashish Mumbai International Queer Film Festival (☑ 022-28618239; www.mumbai queerfest.com; ◷ May) Excellent annual event with a mix of Indian and foreign films; in 2018, 140 films from 45 countries were featured, including 33 LGBTIQ films from India.

LABIA (Lesbian & Bisexuals in Action; www.sites.google.com/site/labiacollective/home) Lesbian and bi support group based in Mumbai; provides a counselling service for women.

Queer Azaadi Mumbai (www.facebook.com/qam.mumbaipride) Organises Mumbai's Pride Parade (www.mumbaipride.in), which is usually held in early February.

Queer Ink (www.queer-ink.com) Online publisher with excellent books, DVDs and merchandise. Also hosts a monthly arts event with speakers, workshops, poetry, comedy, music and a marketplace.

RAGE-by D'kloset Gay parties and events organised via Instagram (www.instagram.com/ragebydkloset).

Salvation Star Community on Facebook (www.facebook.com/SalvationStar) and Twitter (@SalvationStar) that organises and promotes queer events and parties.

from Chicago or Indian classical music. Many performances are free. The **box office** (Map p752; ☑ 022-66223724; ◷ 9am-7pm) is at the end of NCPA Marg.

Prithvi Theatre THEATRE
(Map p756; ☑ 022-26149546; www.prithvitheatre. org; Juhu Church Rd, Juhu) A Juhu institution that's a great place to see both Hindi- and English-language theatre or an art-house film, with the **Prithvi Cafe** (light meals ₹40-180; ◷ 10am-10.30pm) for drinks. Its excellent theatre festival in November showcases contemporary Indian theatre and includes international productions.

Regal Cinema CINEMA
(Map p740; ☑ 022-22021017; www.regalcinema. in; Colaba Causeway, Regal Circle, Apollo Bunder, Colaba; tickets ₹80-250) A faded art deco masterpiece – Mumbai's oldest – that's good for Hollywood and Indian blockbust-

ers. Dating to 1933, it was the first centrally air-conditioned theatre in Asia.

Liberty Cinema CINEMA
(Map p752; ☑ 022-22084521; www.facebook.com/ TheLibertyCinema; 41/42 New Marine Lines, Fort; ◷ tickets ₹100-200) The stunning art deco Liberty was once the queen of Hindi film – think red-carpet openings with Dev Anand. It fell on hard times in recent years, but is on the rebound and is now hosting films again. It's near Bombay Hospital.

🔒 Shopping

Mumbai is India's great marketplace, with some of the country's best shopping. Spend a day at the markets north of CSMT for the classic Mumbai shopping experience. Booksellers set up daily on the footpaths along the main thoroughfare between Colaba and Fort. Snap up a bargain backpacking wardrobe at **Fashion Street** (Map p752; MG Rd, Marine Lines;

⊙hours vary). Kemp's Corner and Kala Ghoda have good shops for designer threads.

Colaba

Cottonworld CLOTHING
(Map p740; www.cottonworld.net; Mandlik Marg; ⊙10.30am-8pm) A great shop for stylish Indian-Western-hybrid goods made from cotton, linen and natural materials. Think Indian Gap, but cooler.

Phillips ANTIQUES
(Map p740; www.phillipsantiques.com; Wodehouse Rd; ⊙10am-7pm Mon-Sat) Art deco and colonial-era furniture, wooden ceremonial masks, silver, Victorian glass, plus high-quality reproductions of old photos, maps and paintings.

Clove CONCEPT STORE
(Map p740; www.clovethestore.com; Churchill Chambers, JA Allana Marg; ⊙11am-8pm) Under the discerning eye of gourmet entrepreneur Samyukta Nair, this Colaba concept store occupies a late-19th-century art deco building chock-full of homegrown designer homewares (gorgeous coffee mugs, copper and clay dishware), jewellery, small-batch body scrubs and top-end designer *chappals* (sandals), *anarkali* (umbrella-flared dresses) and tunics for women, plus sleepwear for both sexes and children.

Nappa Dori DESIGN
(Map p740; www.nappadori.com; Shop 2, Sunny House, Merewether Rd; ⊙10.30am-9pm) This very hip designer-leather shop from Delhi features a near-all-India lineup of carefully curated wallets, passport holders, truck-style travel cases, notebooks and other stylish writing and travel essentials (only the Novesta shoes aren't Indian, they hail from Slovakia). Discerning travellers and writers – take a look.

Fort Area & Churchgate

★**Sabyasachi** CLOTHING
(Map p752; www.sabyasachi.com; Ador House, 6 K Dubash Marg, Fort; ⊙11am-7pm Mon-Sat) It's worth popping in to this high-end traditional garment shop to see the space itself, a gorgeous, cavernous, rose-oil-scented stunner chock-full of owner and designer Sabyasachi Mukherjee's collection of chandeliers, antiques, ceramics, paintings and carpets. As far as retail goes, it's unlike anything you have ever seen.

★**Kulture Shop** DESIGN
(Map p752; www.kultureshop.in; 9 Examiner Press, 115 Nagindas Master Rd, Kala Ghoda; ⊙11am-8pm) Mumbai's coolest design shop has thankfully arrived in South Mumbai! Fittingly, the Pop Art cool kid from **Bandra** (Map p756; 241 Hill Rd, Bandra West; ⊙11am-8pm) has set up shop in Kala Ghoda, where its thought-provoking and conceptually daring art prints, notebooks, coffee mugs, stationery, T-shirts and other immensely desirable objets d'art from a cutting-edge collective of Indian artists will leave your head spinning.

Chimanlals ARTS & CRAFTS
(Map p752; www.chimanlals.com; A2 Taj Bldg, Wallace St, Fort; ⊙9.30am-6pm Mon-Fri, to 5.30pm Sat) The beautiful traditional printed papers here will make you start writing letters.

Nicobar HOMEWARES, CLOTHING
(Map p752; www.nicobar.com; 10 Ropewalk Ln, Kala Ghoda; ⊙11am-8pm) This new and excellent high-end boutique from the same folks who brought us **Good Earth** (Map p740; www.goodearth.in; 2 Reay House, Colaba; ⊙11am-8pm) is a great spot to pick up carefully curated homewares, travel totes and select Indian hipsterware.

MUMBAI FOR CHILDREN

Kidzania (www.kidzania.in; 3rd fl, R City, LBS Marg, Ghatkopar West; child/adult from ₹1000/500; ⊙10am-8pm Tue-Fri, 10am-3pm & 4-9pm Sat & Sun) Kidzania is predictably one of Mumbai's kid-tastic attractions, an educational activity centre where kids can learn all about piloting a plane, fighting fires, policing and get stuck into lots of art- and craft-making. It's on the outskirts on the city, 10km northeast of the Bandra Kurla Complex.

Esselworld (☎022-61589888; www.esselworld.in; Global Pagoda Rd, Borivali West; adult/child from ₹1050/750, with Water Kingdom ₹1390/950; ⊙11am-6pm Mon-Thu, to 7pm Fri & Sat) This Gorai Island amusement park is well maintained and has lots of rides, slides and shade. Ferries leave every 15 minutes (₹50) from Borivali jetty at Gorai Creek, best reached by bus 294 from Borivali Station.

Bombay Shirt Company CLOTHING
(Map p752; ☑ 022-40043455; www.bombayshirts.
com; ground fl, 3 Sassoon Bldg, Fabindia Ln, Kala
Ghoda; shirts from ₹2000; ⏰10.30am-9pm) A
trendy, bespoke shirt tailor for men and
women. You can customise everything – collars, buttons, cuffs and twill tapes. The results are stunning and the prices a fraction of
those back home (unless home is Vietnam).
Shirts take two weeks, and the business
will deliver or ship internationally. It's also
in **Bandra** (Map p756; ☑ 022-26056125; www.
bombayshirts.com; ground fl, Kamal Vishrantee Ku-
tir, 24th Rd;; shirts from ₹2000; ⏰10.30am-9pm).

Bombay Paperie ARTS & CRAFTS
(Map p752; ☑ 022-66358171; www.bombay
paperie.com; 63 Bombay Samachar Marg, Fort;
⏰10.30am-6pm Mon-Sat) Championing a dying
art, this fascinating shop sells handmade,
cotton-based paper crafted into charming
cards, sculptures and lampshades.

Chetana Book Centre BOOKS
(Map p752; www.chetana.com; 34 K Dubash Marg,
Kala Ghoda; ⏰10.30am-7.30pm Mon-Sat, 11.30-7pm
Sun) This great spirituality bookshop has lots
of books on Hinduism, yoga and philosophy,
and the attached **restaurant** (thalis ₹500-635;
⏰12.30-3pm, 4-7pm & 7.30 to 11pm) does excellent
Gujarati and Rajasthani thalis (₹499 to ₹635).

Kalbadevi to Mahalaxmi

★**Chor Bazaar** ANTIQUES
(Map p744; Mutton St, Kumbharwada; ⏰10am-
9pm) Chor Bazaar is known for antiques,
though be wary of reproductions. The main
area of activity is Mutton St, where shops
specialise in these 'antiques' and miscellane-
ous junk. Dhabu St, to the east, is lined with
fine leather goods. It's an atmospheric spot
for an afternoon browse, especially if you
are looking for household trinkets and other
nontouristy bric-a-brac.

★**Haji Mohammad
Bashir Oil Shop** HEALTH & WELLNESS
(Map p744; 426A Hamidiya Masjid, Bapu Khote Rd,
Bhuleshwar; ⏰10am-10.30pm Mon-Sat, 9am-9pm
Sun) Worth a visit as much for the spectacle
if not to buy, this near-century-old traditional oil shop still hand-presses its medicinal,
cooking and massage oils (often to order)
with a sesame wood and metal press. The
menu reaches long and wide (turmeric, avocado, sandalwood, neem, tulsi, almond,
jojoba, cardamom – the list goes on and on,
priced per kilo from ₹400 to ₹25,000).

BOLLYWOOD DREAMS

Mumbai is the glittering epicentre of India's gargantuan Hindi-language film industry. The Lumière brothers screened
the first film ever shown in India at the
Watson Hotel in Mumbai in 1896, and
beginning with the 1913 silent epic *Raja
Harishchandra* (with an all-male cast,
some in drag) and the first talkie, *Alam
Ara* (1931), Bollywood now churns out
more than 1000 films a year – doubling
Hollywood's output, and not surprising
considering it has a captive audience of
one-sixth of the world's population.

Every part of India has its regional
film industry, but Bollywood continues
to entrance the nation with its escapist
formula in which all-singing, all-dancing
lovers fight and conquer the forces
keeping them apart. These days,
Hollywood-inspired thrillers and action
extravaganzas vie for moviegoers' attention alongside the more family-
oriented saccharine formulas.

Bollywood stars can attain near-god-
like status in India and star-spotting is
a favourite pastime in Mumbai's posher
establishments. You can also see the
stars' homes as well as a film/TV studio
with **Bollywood Tours** (Map p752;
☑ 9820255202; www.bollywoodtours.in; 8
Lucky House, Goa St, Fort; per person half-/
full-day tour ₹8140/12,580; ⏰9am-6pm
Mon-Fri, to 5pm Sat), but you're not guaranteed to see a dance number and you
may spend much of the tour in traffic.

It's attached to the lovely Hamidiyah Masjid (mosque).

★**Play Clan** GIFTS & SOUVENIRS
(Map p744; www.theplayclan.com; Shop 1 & 2, Royal
Opera House, Parmanand Marg, Girguam; ⏰11am-
7pm) Kitschy, design-y goods such as stylish
embroidered T-shirts, funky coffee mugs and
coasters, and superhip graphic art, including beaded embroidered art and illustrative
wood prints that are pricey but unique.

M/S KN Ajani HOMEWARES
(Map p744; Shop 102, Krishna Galli, Swadeshi Market, Kalbadevi Rd, Kalbadevi; ⏰noon-7pm Mon-Sat)
One of Mumbai's oldest shops and born
of a dying breed, this family-run retailer
kicked off in 1918. Today, friendly grandson
Paresh still hawks the family jewels: brass,

carbon-steel and aluminium scissors, nut-crackers, locks and knives inside the otherwise textile-driven Swadeshi Market. It's certainly not a conventional souvenir, but it's immensely satisfying to not buy your scissors at an office-supply shop.

No-Mad Fabric Shop
HOMEWARES

(Map p744; ☑ 022-22091787; www.no-mad.in; 3C-209, 1st fl, Mangaldas Market bldg, Kitchen Garden Ln; ⊙ 11am-7pm Mon-Sat) One of Mumbai's hottest new brands, this small showroom, overseen by Nandi the Holy Cow in logo, art and design, is an interior-design oasis in Mangaldas Market. Pick up colourful, India-inspired cocktail napkins, handbags, pillow covers, throws, candles, incense, and copper and brass serving trays, among other stylish items.

No Borders
CLOTHING

(Map p744; www.facebook.com/noborderssshop; 47G, 1st fl, Khotachi Wadi Ln, Kotachiwadi; ⊙ 11am-7pm Tue-Sun) This top-end shop occupies the former studio of fashion designer James Ferreira, located inside his 200-year-old Kotachiwadi bungalow. It curates designer threads from ethnic South Asian tastemakers as well as contemporary Indian, Norwegian and Israeli fashion designers, among others.

Lalbaug Market
SPICES

(Putibal Chawl, Dr Baba Saheb Ambedkar Rd, Lalbaug; ⊙ 11am-4.30pm Mon, 9am-7pm Tue-Sun) You could buy your packaged-for-tourists spices at hassle-y Crawford Market; or, go where Mumbaikars go, which is this fragrant market in Dadar that's considered top-rate for fresh, unadulterated hand-ground powdered goodness, fresh chillies and other chef essentials.

Shrujan
ARTS & CRAFTS

(Map p744; ☑ 022-23521693; www.shrujan.org; Krishnabad Bldg, 43 Bhulabhai Desai Marg, Breach Candy; ⊙ 10am-7.30pm Mon-Sat) 🖋 Selling the intricate embroidery work of women in villages across Kutch, Gujarat, the nonprofit Shrujan aims to help women earn a livelihood while preserving the spectacular embroidery of the area. The sophisticated clothing, wall hangings and purses make great gifts.

Poster Stuff
ART

(Map p744; ☑ 8976605743; 113 Mutton St, Kumbharwada; ⊙ 11am-9pm) Haji Abu's small Chor Bazaar shop offers a cornucopia of vintage Bollywood posters, lobby cards and show cards dating to the 1930s (originals and reprints), some 500,000 in total curated from his grandfather's much larger collection. Pric-

es start at ₹400 on up to ₹400,000. For Bollywood art buffs, this is your Holy Grail.

🛍 Western Suburbs

★ Indian Hippy
ART

(Map p756; ☑ 8080822022; www.hippy.in; 17C Sherly Rajan Rd, off Carter Rd, Bandra West; portraits ₹7500-15,000; ⊙ by appointment) Indian Hippy will put your name in lights, with custom-designed Bollywood posters hand-painted on canvas by the original studio artists (a dying breed since the advent of digital illustrating). Bring or email a photo and your imagination (or let staff guide you). Also sells vinyl LP record clocks, vintage posters and all manner of frankly bizarre Bollywood-themed products. Ships worldwide.

Kishore Silk House
CLOTHING, HANDICRAFTS

(Dedhia Estate, 5/353 Bhandarkar Rd, Matunga East; ⊙ 10am-8.30pm Tue-Sun) Handwoven saris (from ₹300) and dhotis (from ₹250) from Tamil Nadu and Kerala.

High Street Phoenix
MALL

(www.highstreetphoenix.com; 462 Senapati Bapat Marg, Lower Parel; ⊙ 11am-10pm) High Street Phoenix, one of India's first and largest shopping malls, and its mall-within-a-mall, luxury-oriented Palladium, is an indoor/outdoor retail orgy that hosts top shops, great restaurants, fun bars and clubs, a 20-lane bowling alley and an IMAX cineplex. It's also where you go when you want a few horn-free hours.

ℹ Information

DANGERS & ANNOYANCES

For a city of its size, Mumbai affords few serious dangers and annoyances. However, it's worth being mindful of the following points:

➡ The city has a well-documented history of terrorism. Be vigilant – if you notice something off, or tell-tale signs like unattended bags, tell the police as soon as possible.

➡ Be alert for pickpocketing in crowded areas like Crawford Market, Mahalaxmi Temple, the Gateway of India and on crowded trains.

INTERNET ACCESS

While cybercafes are increasingly scarce, all but the simplest hotels, restaurants, cafes and bars now have wi-fi. Commercial establishments generally require a connection via social-media accounts or via a mobile-phone number, to which a unique one-time password (OPT) is sent.

The Maharashtra government also supports a wide network of over 500 public hot spots known as Aaple Sarkar Mumbai Wi-Fi. Check out www.

SANJAY GANDHI NATIONAL PARK

It's hard to believe that within 1½ hours of the teeming metropolis you can be surrounded by this 104-sq-km protected tropical **forest** (☑022-28868686; https://sgnp.maharashtra.gov. in; Borivali; adult/child ₹53/28, vehicle ₹177-266; ☻7.30am-6pm Tue-Sun, last entry 4pm). Here, bright flora, birds, butterflies and elusive wild leopards replace pollution and concrete, all surrounded by forested hills on the city's northern edge. Urban development has muscled in on the fringes of the park, but its heart is very peaceful.

The park's most intriguing option, the **Kanheri Caves** (https://sgnp.maharashtra.gov.in; Borivali; Indian/foreigner ₹25/300; ☻9am-5pm Tue-Sun) is a set of 109 dwellings and monastic structures for Buddhist monks 6km inside the park. The caves, not all of which are accessible, were developed over 1000 years, beginning in the 1st century BC, as part of a sprawling monastic university complex. Avoid the zoo-like lion and tiger 'safari' as the animals are in cages and enclosures.

Inside the park's main northern entrance is an information centre with a small exhibition on the park's wildlife. The best time to see birds is October to April and butterflies from August to November. Activities can now also be booked online.

The nearest station is Borivali, served by trains on the Western Railway line from Churchgate station (₹15 to ₹165, 30 minutes, frequent).

aaplesarkar.maharashtra.gov.in/file/Mumbai-Wifi-hotspots.pdf to locate the one nearest you. **RailWire** (www.railwire.co.in) also offers a signal at select train stations, part of an over 700-station initiative throughout India.

MEDICAL SERVICES

Bombay Hospital (Map p752; ☑022-22067676; www.bombayhospital.com; 12 New Marine Lines, Marine Lines; ☻24hr) A private hospital with the latest medical technology and equipment.

Breach Candy Hospital (Map p744; ☑022-23672888, emergency 022-23667809; www.breachcandyhospital.org; 60A, Bhulabhai Desai Marg, Breach Candy) The best hospital in Mumbai, if not India. It's 2km northwest of Girgaum Chowpatty.

Royal Chemists (Map p752; www.royalchemists.com; 89A Queen's Chambers, Maharshi Karve Rd, Marine Lines; ☻8.30am-8.30pm Mon-Sat) Has delivery services.

Sahakari Bhandar Chemist (Map p740; Colaba Chamber, ground fl, Colaba Causeway, Colaba; ☻10am-8.30pm)

MONEY

ATMs are everywhere, and foreign-exchange offices are also plentiful. There are numerous Citibank branches, including a handy **Fort branch** (Map p752; Bombay Mutual Bldg, 293 Dr Dadabhai Naoroji Rd, Fort), which is handy for its larger, ₹20,000 withdrawal limits. Thomas Cook (p770) has a branch in the Fort area with foreign exchange.

POST

Post office (GPO; Map p752; www.indiapost.gov.in; Walchand Hirachand Marg, Fort; ☻9am-8pm Mon-Sat, to 4pm Sun) The main post office is an imposing building beside CSMT. Opposite gate 4 of the post office in front of Marine Supply is **Ashok Packingwala** (Map p752; ☑9323693870; opp GPO, Gate 4, Walchand Hirachand Marg, Fort) – parcel-wallahs who will stitch up your parcel (for between ₹60 and ₹300). There's also a convenient branch in **Colaba** (Map p740; www.indiapost.gov.in; Henry Rd; ☻10am-5pm Mon-Fri, to 1pm Sat).

Blue Dart/DHL (Map p752; ☑022-22049333; www.bluedart.com; ground fl, Shri Mahavir Chamber, Cawasji Patel St, Fort; ☻9am-9pm Mon-Sat) International courier services.

TOURIST INFORMATION

Indiatourism (Government of India Tourist Office; Map p752; ☑022-22074333; www.incredibleindia.com; ground fl, Air India Bldg, Vidhan Bhavan Marg, Narimen Point; ☻8.30am-6pm Mon-Fri, to 2pm Sat) Provides information for the entire country, as well as contacts for Mumbai guides and homestays.

MTDC Tourist Office (Maharashtra Tourism Development Corporation; Map p752; ☑022-22845678; www.maharashtratourism.gov.in; 4th fl, Apeejay House, 3 Dinsha Vachha Marg, Churchgate; ☻9am-5.30pm Mon-Sat, closed 2nd & 4th Sat of month) The MTDC's head office has helpful staff and lots of pamphlets and information on Maharashtra, as well as bookings for MTDC hotels. It's also the only MTDC office of note that accepts credit cards. There are additional booths at Apollo Bunder (p746) and **Chhatrapati Shivaji Maharaj Terminus** (Maharashtra Tourism Development Corporation; Map p752; ☑022-22622859; www.maharashtratourism.gov.in; Chhatrapati Shivaji Maharaj Terminus, Fort; ☻10am-5.30pm Mon-Sat, closed 2nd & 4th Sat of month).

TRAVEL AGENCIES

Akbar Travels (Map p740; ☑ 022-22823434; www.akbartravels.com; 30 Alipur Trust Bldg, Colaba Causeway, Colaba; ⊙10am-10pm) Extremely helpful and can long-distance book car/drivers and buses. There's another branch in **Fort** (Map p752; ☑ 022-22633434; www.akbartravels.com; 167/169 Dr Dadabhai Naoroji Rd, Fort; ⊙10am-7pm Mon-Sat).

Magnum International Travel & Tours (Map p740; ☑ 022-61559700; www.magnum international.com; 10 Henry Rd, Colaba; ⊙10am-6pm Mon-Fri, to 1pm Sat) Handy Colaba travel agency.

Thomas Cook (Map p752; ☑ 022-48795009; www.thomascook.in; 324 Dr Dadabhai Naoroji Rd, Fort; ⊙9.30am-6pm Mon-Sat) Flight and hotel bookings, plus foreign exchange.

❶ Getting There & Away

AIR

Mumbai's carbon-neutral **Chhatrapati Shivaji Maharaj International Airport** (Map p756; ☑ 022-66851010; www.csia.in; Santa Cruz East), about 30km from the city centre, was recently modernised to the tune of US$2 billion. Now handling all international arrivals is the impressive, remodelled international Terminal 2 (T2), which includes India's largest public-art program (a skylighted, 3.2km multistorey Art Wall along moving walkways, boasting over 5000 pieces of art from every corner of India). The international terminal has its own app (Android/iPhone; Mumbai T2 App).

Domestic flights operate out of both the new T2 and the older Terminal 1 (T1), also known locally as Santa Cruz Airport, 5km away. An interterminal fixed-rate taxi service (non-AC/AC ₹230/260 from T1 to T2, ₹230/250 from T2 to T1) operates between the terminals. Both terminals have ATMs and foreign-exchange counters, and T2 also houses the luxurious **Niranta Transit Hotel** (☑ 022-67296729; www.nirantahotels.com; s/d 4 hrs ₹5510/5900, 7 hrs ₹7080/7670, 24 hrs 11,529/13,800; @ ☎). There's left luggage near the hotel.

Air India (Map p752; ☑ 1800-1801407, 022-22023031; www.airindia.com; Air India Bldg, cnr Marine Dr & Madame Cama Rd, Nariman Point; ⊙9.15am-6.30pm Mon-Thu, 9.15am-6.15pm Fri, 9.15am-1pm & 1.45-5pm Sat), Jet Airways (www.jetairways.com) and Vistara (www.airvistara.com) operate out of T2, while GoAir (www.goair.in), IndiGo (www.goindigo.in) and SpiceJet (www.spicejet.com), among others, operate out of T1 – be sure to check ahead for any changes on the ground. Travel agencies and the airlines' websites are usually best for booking flights.

BUS

Numerous private operators and state governments run long-distance buses to and from Mumbai.

Long-distance government-run buses depart from the **Mumbai Central bus terminal** (Map p744; ☑ 1800-221250, enquiries 022-23024076; Jehangir Boman Behram Marg, RBI Staff Colony) right by Mumbai Central train station. They're cheaper and more frequent than private services, but standards are usually lower with the exception of semiluxury ShivShahi and luxury Shivneri services (always look for those first). The website of the **Maharashtra State Road Transport Corporation** (MSRTC; ☑ 022-23023900; www.msrtc.gov.in) has online schedules and booking at https://public.msrtcors.com/ticket_booking/index.php, though you'll need a resident to book for you if you don't have an Indian credit card.

Private buses are usually more comfortable and simpler to book (if a bit more costly). Many normally depart from Dr Anadrao Nair Rd near Mumbai Central train station, but that has stopped due to metro construction without any timeline for ever returning. If you are in that area, **National NTT/CTC** (Map p744; ☑ 022-23015652; Dr Anadrao Nair Rd, RBI Staff Colony; ⊙6am-11pm)

MAJOR LONG-DISTANCE BUS ROUTES

DESTINATION	PRIVATE NON-AC/AC SLEEPER (₹)	GOVERNMENT NON-AC (₹)	DURATION (HR)
Ahmedabad	500-2000/670-2500	N/A	7-12
Aurangabad	650-1100/550-2500	from 560 (four daily)	9-11
Hyderabad	1200-2000/1310-3000	N/A	16
Mahabaleshwar	1550/450-1349	from 300 (four daily)	7-8
Murud	2500 (seats only)	from 210 (eight daily)	8-10
Nashik	350-1500/400-2510	from 240 (12 per day, 6am-10.45pm)	13-16
Panaji (Panjim)	475-1500/1430-2500	N/A	14-16
Pune	600-2000/350-3000	from 210 (half-hourly, 6.35am-12.30am)	3-5
Udaipur	600-1400/1210-1810	N/A	14-17

remains open behind the metro construction and is a reliable ticketing agent.

The most centralised place to catch private buses these days is around Dadar TT Circle (Dadar East) under the flyover of the same name (free transport is usually provided to both by ticketing agents), but with the exception of the **MSRTC Shivneri buses to Pune** (www.msrtc.org.in; Dadar TT Flyover, Dadar East), you are going to need help to find your bus. The flyover is lined on both sides with private ticketing agents – make sure you arrive early and get specific indications from them where to find your bus. **Neeta Tours & Travels** (☑ 022-24162565; www.neetabus.in; Shop 9, opp Dadar Post Office, Dr Ambedkar Rd, Dadar East) is a good place to start.

Internet ticketing resources such as redBus (www.redbus.in) are in play, though some sites still require Indian mobile numbers and/or domestic payment options – most foreigners will still need to visit the ticketing agents (or have an Indian friend buy your ticket). Be sure to check your departure point (often called 'pickup point') as the reality is that private bus companies depart from numerous points around the city.

In addition to **Dr Anadrao Nair Road** (Map p744; RBI Staff Colony) near Mumbai Central bus station and along both sides of Dr Baba Saheb Ambedkar Rd near the **Dadar TT Flyover** (Dr Baba Saheb Ambedkar Rd) in Dadar East, you'll also find private long-distance ticket agents near **Paltan Road** (Map p744; Sitaram Bldg, F-Block, opp Paltan Rd) in Fort.

Private buses to Goa are more convenient; these vary in price from as little as ₹760 (a bad choice) to ₹3000. Many leave from way out in the suburbs, but government-run **Kadamba Transport** (Map p752; ☑ 9969561146; www.goakadamba.com; 5 Mahapalika Marg, Fort; ☺7.30am-5.30pm Mon-Sat) is convenient for the centre, leaving from in front of Azad Maidan. The trip takes 14 hours.

Fares to popular destinations (like Goa) are up to 75% higher during holiday periods.

TRAIN

Three train systems operate out of Mumbai, but the most important services for travellers are Central Railway and Western Railway. Tickets for either system can be bought from any station that has computerised ticketing.

Central Railway (www.cr.indianrailways.gov.in) – handling services to the east, south, plus a few trains to the north – operates from CSMT (also known as 'VT'). Foreign-tourist-quota tickets and Indrail passes can be bought at Counter 4 of the **reservation centre** (Map p752; ☑ 139; www.cr.indianrailways.gov.in; Chhatrapati Shivaji Maharaj Terminus Area, Fort; ☺8am-8pm Mon-Sat, to 2pm Sun). There is a prepaid taxi scheme near the MTDC tourist information booth (p769). It's ₹160 to Colaba, ₹360 to Bandra, ₹430 to the domestic terminal and ₹500 to the international terminal.

Some Central Railway trains depart from Dadar (D), a few stations north of CSMT, or Lokmanya Tilak (LTT), 16km north of CSMT.

Western Railway (www.wr.indianrailways.gov.in) has services to the north from Mumbai Central train station, usually called Bombay Central (BCT). The **passenger reservation office** (Map p752; ☑ 139; www.wr.indianrailways.gov.in; Station Bldg, Vithaldas Thackersey Marg, Churchgate; ☺8am-8pm Mon-Sat, to 2pm Sun), opposite Churchgate station, has foreign-tourist-quota tickets.

Mumbai's local rail infrastructure has come under fire in recent years. The collapse of Andheri's Gokhale overbridge connecting Andheri West and East stations in 2018 killed two, a stampede killed 23 at Prabhadevi station in 2017, and there was a skywalk cave-in at Charni Road, also in 2017. A system-wide structural audit was underway at the time of writing – and for good reason, as 18,847 people have died riding the rails since 2013!

ⓘ Getting Around

M-Indicator (http://m-indicator.soft112.com) is an invaluable app for Mumbai public transit – from train schedules to rickshaw fares it covers the whole shebang.

TO/FROM THE AIRPORT
Terminal 1

Autorickshaw If it's not rush hour (7am to 11am and 4pm to 8pm), catch an autorickshaw (between ₹25 and ₹48) to Vile Parle station, where you can get a train to Churchgate (from ₹10, 45 minutes).

Ride-share An off-peak UberGo from the airport runs ₹220 to Bandra Kurla Complex or Bandra West, ₹400 to Fort and ₹425 to Colaba. The Uber and Ola pickup point is a straight shot out the arrivals door to sections Z1–7 in the parking lot (Uber can hot-spot those without a connection from their information booth).

Taxi There's a prepaid taxi counter in the arrivals hall. A non-AC/AC taxi with one bag costs ₹570/695 to Colaba or Fort and ₹295/350 to Bandra (a bit more at night).

Terminal 2

Autorickshaw Although available, they only go as far south as Bandra; walk out of the terminal and follow the signs. Prices are ₹50 to ₹60 to Vila Parle, ₹50 to ₹70 to Andheri (a traffic warden *should* keep them honest).

Prepaid taxi Set-fare taxis cost ₹670/810 (non-AC/AC; including one piece of luggage) to Colaba and Fort and ₹400/480 to Bandra. The journey to Colaba takes about an hour at night (via the Sea Link) and 1½ to two hours during the day.

Ride-share Uber and Ola have specific pickup points at the P7 West and East levels respectively; and information booths can hot-spot those without a connection on arrival in order to get you on the road. An off-peak UberGo from the airport runs ₹250 to Bandra Kurla Complex, ₹260 to Bandra West, ₹460 to Fort and ₹560 to Colaba. A ₹105 pickup fee is automatically embedded into the fare.

Train If you arrive during the day (but not during rush hour, and are not weighed down with luggage), consider the train: take an autorickshaw to Andheri train station and then the Churchgate or CSMT train (from ₹10, 45 minutes).

Taxi The trip from South Mumbai to the international airport in an AC taxi should cost from ₹700 to ₹750, plus the ₹70 toll if you take the time-saving Sea Link Bridge. Allow two hours for the trip if you travel between 4pm and 8pm; 45 minutes to 1½ hours otherwise.

BOAT

PNP (Map p740; ☑ 022-22885220; Apollo Bunder, Colaba) and **Maldar Catamarans** (Map p740; ☑ 022-23734841; Apollo Bunder, Colaba) run regular ferries to Mandwa (one way ₹135 to ₹185), useful for access to Murud-Janjira and other parts of the Konkan Coast, avoiding the long bus trip out of Mumbai. Buy tickets at their Taj Gateway Plaza offices.

Launches to Elephanta Island (p746) head to Gharapuri from the Gateway of India every 30 minutes from 9am to 3.30pm (one hour). Buy tickets from the MTDC booth (p746) at the Taj Gateway Plaza. Launches also run to **Mandwa** (Map p740; Apollo Bunder, Colaba). Buy tickets with PNP and Maldar Catamarans.

An overnight luxury cruise liner – the country's first such domestic operation – set sail in late 2018. **Angriya Cruises** (☑ 8314810440; www. angriyacruises.com; Victoria Docks 15, Purple Gate, off Ferry Wharf, Mazagão; d with/without window from ₹6800/5300), connecting Mumbai with Goa, departs Monday, Wednesday and Friday at 4pm from Victoria Docks just north of Fort, arriving by 10am the following day in Mormugao, 30km south of Panaji.

BUS

M-Indicator has a useful 'search bus routes' facility for hardcore shoestringers and masochists – you'll also need to read the buses' Devanagari numerals on older buses and beware of pickpockets. Fares start at ₹8. Check routes and timetables at http://routenetwork. bestundertaking.com.

BEST (www.bestundertaking.com) bus stands are numerous but include the **east** (Map p740; MG Rd, Colaba) and **west** (Map p740; MG Rd, Colaba) sides of Mahatma Gandhi (MG) Rd and at **CSMT** (Map p752; Chhatrapati Shivaji Maharaj Terminus Area, Fort); as well as **Colaba depot** (Map p740; Colaba Causeway).

METRO

Line 1 of the Mumbai Metro (www.reliance mumbaimetro.com) opened in 2014, the first of a long-phase project expected to finish by 2025. It connects 12 stations in the far northern suburbs to Ghatkopar Station in the east, mostly well away from anywhere of interest to visitors save the growing nightlife hubs of Andheri West and Versova, accessed by DN Nagar and Versova stations respectively. However, Line 1 of the monorail should have been extended south as far as Jacob Circle (5km north of CSMT) by the time you read this (after missing years of deadlines), bringing it past nightlife hub Lower Parel.

Single fares are based on distance and cost between ₹10 and ₹40, with monthly Trip Passes (₹750 to ₹1350) also available. Access to stations is by escalator, carriages are air-conditioned, and there are seats reserved for women and the disabled.

Line 3 (aka Colaba–Bandra–SEEPZ) will be a 33.5km, 27-station underground line connecting Cuffe Parade south of Colaba, Fort, all the main railway terminals, Dadar, Bandra Kurla Complex, Bandra, both airport terminals and on to Andheri. It will be of most interest to tourists but won't open until at least 2021. Station construction is currently wreaking havoc on main thoroughfares around all of these areas, causing major traffic issues and other navigation problems.

TAXI & AUTORICKSHAW

Mumbai's black-and-yellow taxis are very inexpensive and the most convenient way to get around southern Mumbai; drivers *almost* always use the meter without prompting. The minimum fare is ₹22 (for up to 1.5km); a 5km trip costs about ₹80. Meru Cabs (www.meru.in) is a reliable taxi service in Mumbai. Book online or via app, including outstation (long-distance) trips.

Ride-share apps in play include Uber (www. uber.com) and Ola (www.olacabs.com); the latter is good for booking autorickshaws as well – no more rickshaw-wallah price gouging (bear in mind with Ola, you will need to give the driver a one-time password – OTP – set when booking in order to commence the ride).

Autorickshaws are the name of the game north of Bandra. The minimum fare is ₹18, up to 1.5km; a 3km trip is about ₹36 during daylight hours.

Both taxis and autorickshaws tack 50% onto the fare between midnight and 5am; and a possible ₹2 fare hike for both was being bandied about at the time of research. Tip: Mumbaikars tend to navigate by landmarks, not street names (especially new names), so have some details before heading out.

MAJOR TRAINS FROM MUMBAI

DESTINATION	TRAIN NO & NAME	SAMPLE FARE (₹)	DURA-TION (HR)	DEPARTURE
Agra	12137 Punjab Mail	585/1555/2250/3855 (A)	22	7.35pm CSMT
Ahmedabad	12901 Gujarat Mail	315/815/1150/1940 (A)	8½	10.05pm BCT
	12009 Shatabdi Exp	1030/1885 East	6½	6.25am BCT
Aurangabad	11401 Nandigram Exp	235/630/900/1510 (A)	7	4.35pm CSMT
	17617 Tapovan Exp	140/505 (C)	7	6.15am CSMT
Bengaluru	11301 Udyan Exp	500/1355/1975/3370 (A)	24	8.10am CSMT
Chennai	12163 Chennai Exp	570/1505/2175/3720 (A)	23½	8.30am CSMT
Delhi	12951 Mumbai Rajdhani	2725/4075/4730 (D)	15¾	5pm BCT
Hyderabad	12701 Hussainsagar Exp	425/1075/1555/2625 (A)	14½	9.50pm CSMT
Indore	12961 Avantika Exp	440/1165/1660/2815 (A)	14	7.10pm BCT
Jaipur	12955 Mumbai Central Jaipur Superfast Exp (MMCT JP SF)	535/1420/2050/3495 (A)	18	6.50pm BCT
Kochi	16345 Netravati Exp	615/1655/2430 (B)	27	11.40am LTT
Madgaon (Goa)	10103 Mandovi Exp	390/1070/1540/2610 (A)	13	7.10am CSMT
	12133 Mangalore Exp	420/1150/1590 (B)	10¾	10.02pm CSMT
	11085 Mao Doubledecker	840 (F)	12	5.33am Wed, Fri & Sun LTT
Pune	11301 Udyan Exp	140/495/700/1165 (A)	3½	8.10am CSMT

Station abbreviations: CSMT (Chhatrapati Shivaji Maharaj Terminus); BCT (Mumbai Central); LTT (Lokmanya Tilak)

Fares: (A) sleeper/3AC/2AC/1AC; (B) sleeper/3AC/2AC; (C) second class/CC; (D) 3AC/2AC/1AC; East CC/Exec CC; (F) CC

TRAIN

Mumbai's suburban train network is one of the world's busiest; forget travelling during rush hours (7am to 11am and 4pm to 8pm). Trains run from 4.15am to 1am and there are two main lines of most interest to travellers: Western Line and Central Line.

Western Line The most useful; operates out of Churchgate north to Charni Rd (for Girgaum Chowpatty), Mumbai Central, Mahalaxmi (for the Dhobi Ghat), Bandra, Vile Parle (for the domestic airport), Andheri (for the international airport) and Borivali (for Sanjay Gandhi National Park), among others. Make sure you don't catch an express train when you need a slow train – the screens dictate this by an 'S' (Slow) or 'F' (Fast) under 'Mode'.

Mumbai's first AC local train was also introduced on this line in late 2017, running at least five times per day Monday through Friday (8.54am, 11.50am, 2.55pm & 7.49pm to Virar plus an additional 5.49pm departure as far as Borivali).

Central Line Runs from CSMT to Byculla (for Veermata Jijabai Bhonsle Udyan, formerly Victoria Gardens), Dadar and as far as Neral (for Matheran).

From Churchgate 2nd-/1st-class fares are ₹5/50 to Mumbai Central, ₹10/105 to Vile Parle and ₹15/140 to Borivali. 'Tourist tickets' permit unlimited travel in 2nd/1st class for one (₹75/275), two (₹115/445) or five (₹135/510) days. AC fares from Churchgate are ₹60 to Mumbai Central, ₹85 to Bandra, ₹125 to Andheri and ₹165 to Borivali.

To avoid the queues, buy a rechargeable **SmartCard** (₹100, ₹50 of which is retained in credit, ₹50 of which is a refundable deposit), good for use on either train line, then print out your tickets at the numerous automatic ticket vending machines (ATVMs) before boarding. (Place your card on the reader, touch the zone of your station, pick the specific station, choose the amount of tickets, choose 'Buy Ticket' and then 'Print'.) Mobile ticketing is also available via the UTS app (Android; www.utsonmobile. indianrail.gov.in) but set-up is more trouble than its worth for nonresidents.

Watch your valuables, and women, stick to the ladies-only carriages except late at night, when it's more important to avoid empty cars.

Maharashtra

Includes ➜

Best Places to Eat

Best Places to Stay

Why Go?

India's third-largest and second-most populous state, Maharashtra is showcase of many of India's iconic attractions. There are palm-fringed beaches; lofty, cool-green mountains; Unesco World Heritage Sites; and bustling cosmopolitan cities (and gorgeous vineyards in which to escape them). In the far east of the state are some of the nation's most impressive national parks, including Tadoba-Andhari Tiger Reserve.

Inland lie the extraordinary cave temples of Ellora and Ajanta, undoubtedly Maharashtra's greatest monuments, hewn by hand from solid rock. Matheran, a colonial-era hill station served by a toy train, has a certain allure, while pilgrims and inquisitive souls are drawn to cosmopolitan Pune, a city famous for its 'sex guru' and alternative spiritualism. Westwards, the romantic Konkan Coast, fringing the Arabian Sea, is lined with spectacular, crumbling forts and sandy beaches; some of the best are around pretty Malvan, which is fast becoming one of India's premier diving centres.

When to Go

Nasik

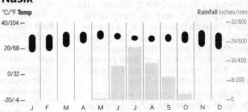

Jan It's party time at Nashik's wineries, marked by grape harvesting and crushing galas.

Sep The frenzied, energetic Ganesh Chaturthi celebrations reach fever pitch.

Dec Clear skies, mild temperatures; the secluded beaches of Murud, Ganpatipule and Tarkali are lovely.

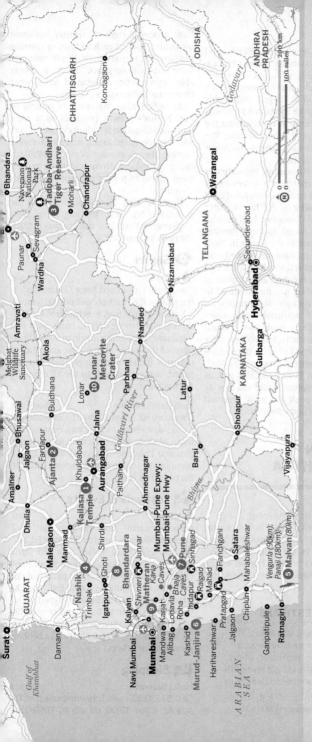

Maharashtra Highlights

1 Kailasa Temple (p785) Being amazed by the intricate beauty in the Ellora temples.

2 Ajanta (p788) Wandering through ancient cave galleries and admiring sublime ancient Buddhist art.

3 Tadoba-Andhari Tiger Reserve (p792) Searching for big cats inside this tiger reserve.

4 Nashik (p776) Sipping on a glass of Chenin Blanc or Cab-Shiraz in this gorgeous wine country.

5 Malvan (p796) Diving or snorkelling in the big blue.

6 Murud-Janjira (p793) Wondering at the might of a lost civilisation at the colossal over-water Janjira Fort.

7 Pune (p800) Delving into new-age spiritualism and modern Indian cuisine.

8 Bhandardara (p780) Riding out a monsoon amid dramatic mountain scenery.

9 Matheran (p797) Exploring the spectacular hill station viewpoints.

10 Lonar Meteorite Crater (p791) Contemplating Mother Nature's wrath at a quirky, primordial crater.

History

Maharashtra was given its political and ethnic identity by Maratha leader Chhatrapati Shivaji (1627–80), who lorded over the Deccan plateau and much of western India from his stronghold at Raigad. Still highly respected today, Shivaji is credited for instilling a strong, independent spirit among the region's people, as well as establishing Maharashtra as a dominant player in the power relations of medieval India.

From the early 18th century, the state was under the administration of a succession of ministers called the Peshwas, who ruled until 1819, ceding thereafter to the British. After Independence in 1947, western Maharashtra and Gujarat were joined to form Bombay state. But it was back to the future in 1960, when modern Maharashtra was formed with the exclusion of Gujarati-speaking areas and with Mumbai (then Bombay) as its capital.

Since then the state has forged ahead to become one of the nation's most prosperous, with India's largest industrial sector, mainly thanks to agriculture, coal-based thermal energy, nuclear electricity, technology parks and software exports. But poor rains in recent years have hampered crop yields, leading to a number of farmer suicides and, as a byproduct, widespread caste violence as Maratha activists push for more reserved jobs in government and education.

NORTHERN MAHARASHTRA

Nashik

📞 0253 / POP 1.57 MILLION / ELEV 565M

Located on the banks of the holy Godavari River, Nashik (or Nasik) gets its name from the episode in the Ramayana where Lakshmana, Rama's brother, hacked off the *nasika* (nose) of Ravana's sister. Today this large provincial city's old quarter has some intriguing wooden architecture, interesting temples that reference the Hindu epic and some huge bathing ghats. The city is noticeably cleaner, better maintained and greener than many Indian cities of its size.

As Indian wine continues its coming of age, Nashik's growth potential as a wine tourism destination is wide open. India's best wines are produced locally and an afternoon touring the gorgeous vineyards (p778) in the countryside surrounding the city is a great reason to point your nose in Nashik's direction.

Every 12 years Nashik plays host to the grand Kumbh Mela, the largest religious gathering on Earth (the last was in 2015, the next one is in 2027).

◉ Sights

★ **Ramkund** GHAT
(Panchavati) This sacred River Godavari bathing ghat in the heart of Nashik's old quarter, a Kumbh Mela venue, sees hundreds of Hindu pilgrims arriving daily to bathe, pray and – because the waters provide moksha (liberation of the soul) – to immerse the ashes of departed friends and family. There's an adjacent market that adds to the alluring and fascinating scene.

Kala Rama Temple HINDU TEMPLE
(Panchavati Rd; ⊗5am-10pm) The city's holiest shrine dates back to 1794 and contains unusual black stone representations of Rama, Sita and Lakshmana. Legend has it that it occupies the site where Lakshmana sliced off Surpanakha's nose.

✦ Festivals & Events

SulaFest WINE
(www.sulafest.com; Sula Vineyards, Gat 36/2, Govardhan Village, off Gangapur-Savargaon Rd; 1-/2-day pass ₹2600/4300; ⊗Feb) Sula Vineyard's SulaFest, which takes place the first weekend of February, is Nashik's biggest party and one of India's best boutique music festivals. The winery swarms with revellers, hyped up on juice and partying to the sound of over 120 live bands and internationally acclaimed DJs on three stages. Check https://in.bookmyshow.com for tickets.

⏟ Sleeping

Hotel Samrat HOTEL $
(📞0253-2306100; www.hotelsamratnasik.com; Old Agra Rd; d from ₹1000, s/d with AC ₹1790/2130;

TOP STATE FESTIVALS

Dussehra (⊗Sep & Oct) A Hindu festival, but it also marks the Buddhist celebration of the anniversary of the famous humanist and Dalit leader BR Ambedkar's conversion to Buddhism.

Naag Panchami (⊗Jul/Aug) A traditional snake-worshipping festival.

Nashik

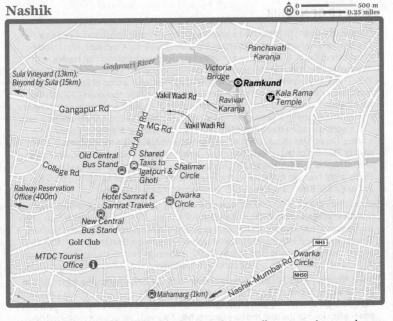

⊛🛜) Its veg restaurant has fallen out of favour as a local hotspot, but Samrat's hotel still offers superb value, with comfortable rooms, some of which have large windows and pine furniture. Located right next to the bus stand, with a private bus agent on its doorstep, it's a sensible choice. Wi-fi is speedy but requires maddening hoop jumping to connect.

Ginger
HOTEL **$$**

(☑0253-6616333; www.gingerhotels.com; Plot P20, Satpur MIDC, Trimbak Rd; s/d ₹2580/3130; ⊛🛜) Primarily a business hotel, this hip Indian chain hotel features DIY services, but there are conveniences aplenty. Though the hotel itself is less lively than some other Ginger hotels in India, the 92 fresh and inviting rooms have blonde wood, high cleanliness standards and swish en suites. It's around 4.5km west of the central district.

★The Source at Sula
BOUTIQUE HOTEL **$$$**

(☑7875555735; www.sulawines.com; Gat 36/2, off Gangapur-Savargaon Rd, Govardhan Village; d/ste from ₹9140/11,750; ⊛🛜🛁) 🍃 Sula's new 31-room, Tuscan-inspired resort occupies the converted facilities of the brand's original winery. Extremely comfortable rooms are decked out in French countryside chic with unobtrusive Indian touches (many with vineyard, pool or cobblestone courtyard views) and spacious bathrooms. Four acacia-wood

tree houses offer extra privacy and more rustic-chic decor. There is also a spa (grapeseed oil massage ₹3100).

★Beyond by Sula
RESORT **$$$**

(☑7875555725; www.sulawines.com; Gangavarhe; d incl breakfast ₹10,240; ⊛🛜🛁) Sula Vineyard's seven-room flagship resort sits a few kilometres from the winery (hence the name: Beyond) near the edges of the beautiful Gangapur Dam backwaters. Uber-contemporary rooms feature polished concrete flooring and huge windows framing the picturesque setting, which culminates in the massive three-bedroom Sky Villa (₹38,400), a modern, architecturally fascinating space evoking the modernist luxury resorts of Patagonia.

★Vallonné Vineyards
GUESTHOUSE **$$$**

(☑9819129455; www.vallonnevineyards.com; Gat 504, Kavnai Shivar; d lawn/vineyard view incl breakfast ₹6500/7500) First and foremost a boutique winery known for its Cabernet Sauvignon and Vin de Passerillage dessert wine (tastings ₹400; 11am to 4.30pm), not to mention the fantastic Malaka Spice (p779) restaurant, Valloné also has two vineyard-view rooms that offer the most extraordinary vistas of any Nashik wine country hotel. Don't expect hotel services, however – though the views make up for this.

GRAPES OF NASHIK

From wimpy raisins to full-bodied wines, the grapes of Nashik have come a long way. The surrounding region had been producing table grapes since ancient times; however, it was only in the early 1990s that a couple of entrepreneurs realised that Nashik, with its fertile soils and temperate climate, harboured good conditions for wine cultivation. In 1997 industry pioneer Sula Vineyards fearlessly invested in a crop of Sauvignon Blanc and Chenin Blanc and the first batch of domestic wines hit the shelves in 2000. Nashik hasn't looked back. These days the wine list in most of Nashik's wineries has stretched to include Shiraz, Merlot, Cabernet, Semillon and Zinfandel as well as a few sparkling wines.

It's worth sampling these drops first-hand by visiting one of the region's beautiful estates. Oenophiles should enlist **Wine Friend** (📞9822439051; www.winefriend.in; full-day tour ₹6000, plus tasting fees), the only experienced guide doing wine speciality tours around Nashik's vineyards (₹6000 plus tasting fees). Alternatively, cars can be hired on Ola for eight hours at ₹1450; or try the friendly and English-speaking Sanil at **SCK Rent-A-Car** (📞8888080525; scktravels2015@gmail.com) for a horn-free ride.

Sula Vineyards (📞9970090010; www.sulawines.com; Gat 36/2, off Gangapur-Savargaon Rd, Govardhan Village; tastings ₹400; ⊙11am-11pm) 🍃 Located 15km west of Nashik, Sula offers a professional tour (around 45 minutes) of its impressive estate and high-tech facilities. This is rounded off with themed six wine-tasting sessions like Beat the Heat (₹400; all whites and sparkling) and Best of Sula (₹400; features its best drops, including two from its top-end Rasa line). The tasting patio here has commanding views of the countryside.

York Winery (📞0253-2230701; www.yorkwinery.com; Gat 15/2, Gangapur-Savargaon Rd, Gangavarhe Village; 5/7 wines ₹150/250; ⊙noon-10pm) A further kilometre from Sula Vineyards, family-owned York Winery offers tours and wine-tasting sessions in a top-floor room that has scenic views of the lake and surrounding hills. Four reds, including its flagship barrel-aged Cab Shiraz, three whites, a rosé and two sparklings are produced. There's a large garden where Western snacks (olives, cheeses) are offered.

Soma Vine Village (📞7028066016; www.somavinevillage.com; Gat 1, Gangavarhe; 5 wines ₹350; ⊙11.30am-6.30pm) One of Nashik's newer wineries, Soma Vine Village, 17km west of the city centre on the same road as Sula and York, offers 45-minute tours that end in a sampling plucked from its 11-wine portfolio, including its award-winning Chenin Blanc Gold and its rosé dessert wine, both excellent.

Chandon (📞9561065030; www.chandon.co.in; Gat 652/653, Taluka-Dindori Village; tastings ₹500; ⊙10am-6pm Mon-Fri) Nashik's newest winery is a world-class facility on meticulously manicured grounds that easily rank as Nashik's most peaceful and beautiful. Tastings (₹500, recoupable with purchase) feature India's leading sparkling wines, Chandon Brut (Chenin Blanc/Chardonnay/Pinot Noir) and Brut Rosé (Shiraz/Pinot Noir). Sip your bubbly in the upscale contemporary lounge, wine gallery or on the tremendously picturesque terrace. It's 26km north of Nashik.

Grover Zampa (📞02553-204379; www.groverzampa.in; Gat 967/1026, Village Sanjegaon, Tallgatpuri; 5/7 wines ₹500/650; ⊙10am-5.30pm, tours 10.30am, 2.30pm & 4pm) It first produced juice with imported French vines at its Karnataka estate in 1992. Today, it's India's oldest surviving winery and easily its most lauded (74 international awards between 2014 and 2016 alone). Tours and tastings at its Nashik estate, 53km southwest of the city, take place in its cinematic cave. The Soireé Brut Rosé and the top-end Chêne Grand Réserve Tempranillo-Shiraz are fantastic. If you come out this way, do dine at nearby Malaka Spice (p779), Nashik's best and most scenic wine-country restaurant, and crash overnight at Valloné Vineyards (p777).

The Vern at BLVD   BOUTIQUE HOTEL **$$$**
(📞0253-6644000; www.blvdnashik.com; 1st Level, BLVD, P20, Trimbak Rd, MIDC; s/d from ₹5900/7080; ❊⊛🤶) Nashik's newest digs are part of an entertainment complex featuring restaurants, bars and banquet halls. An elevator shaft complete with vertical garden leads to carpeted hallways and extremely comfortable and modern rooms, sleekly outfitted with flat-screen TVs and grey marble

bathrooms. For Nashik city proper, it's a step up from the mostly mundane, business-oriented offerings elsewhere.

✕ Eating & Drinking

★ **Sadhana**   BREAKFAST $
(www.sadhanamisal.com; Hardev Baug, Gangapur-Satpur Link Rd, Barden Phata; meals ₹90-100; ☺8am-3pm) This rustic institution on the edge of town serves Nashik's best breakfast of champions, *misal pav* – an unusual Maharashtrian dish prepared with bean sprouts and pulses, topped with flattened puffed rice, crunchy chickpea flour noodles, onions, lemon and coriander and served with a buttered bun – to the tune of up to 5000 people on weekends. Cash only. Unmissable.

Grab an Uber (₹125 or so) to get here.

★ **Divtya Budhlya Wada**   MAHARASHTRIAN $$
(Anadwali, Gangapur Rd; mains ₹160-310, thalis ₹210-350; ☺11am-3.30pm & 7-11pm) If you're looking for a spicy kick in the gut, this local hotspot is the place to come for authentic Maharashtrian food that'll make your nose run. Under an atmospheric, lantern-lit bamboo canopy, locals devour the special mutton thali (₹290; could be more generous) and rustic à la carte countryside dishes bone-in, grease, fat and all. Tasty stuff.

It's located 5km northwest of the centre – order an Uber for ₹85 or so. Signed in Marathi only.

★ **Malaka Spice**   ASIAN $$$
(www.malakaspice.com; Vallonné Vineyard, Gat 504, Kavnai Shiver; mains ₹360-660; ☺11.30am-11.30pm) This excellent branch of Pune's best restaurant is hands-down the most scenic spot to dine in Nashik wine country, with postcard-perfect views across Vallonné Vineyard, Lake Mukane and the dramatic Sahyadris mountains beyond. Tack on a cavalcade of Southeast Asian flavors and a Slow Food, stay-local philosophy and it all adds up to a dining destination worth travelling for.

The Foundry   CLUB
(www.blvdnashik.com; 2nd level, BLVD, P20, Trimbak Rd, MIDC; ☺7.30pm-midnight Sat) Nightlife is scarce in Nashik – it's primarily a spiritual city, despite the surrounding vineyards – but this new, small club inside multipurpose BLVD (pronounce the letters, not 'boulevard') is the hotspot of choice. Pounding techno ricochets off the unfinished concrete dance floor and across a bevy of Bollywood

and international movie posters, exposed air ducts and other industrial-savvy design touches.

ℹ Information

MTDC Tourist Office (Maharashtra Tourism Development Corporation; ☏0253-2570059; www.maharashtratourism.gov.in; T/I, Golf Club, Old Agra Rd, Matoshree Nagar; ☺9.45am-6.45pm Mon-Sat, closed 2nd & 4th Sat)

ℹ Getting There & Away

BUS

The **New Central Bus Stand** (New CBS; ☏0253-2309308; Thakkar Bazar) has services to Aurangabad (non-AC/AC ₹250/425, 4½ hours, hourly, 5am to 12.15am) and Pune (non-AC/AC ₹300/410, 4½ hours, hourly, 4.30am to 1am).

Nashik's **Old Central Bus Stand** (Old CBS; ☏0253-2309310; Police Staff Colony) has buses to Ghoti (₹120, one hour, every two hours, 5am to 10pm), Igatpuri (₹140, one hour, every two hours, 5am to 10pm) and Trimbak (₹40, 45 minutes, every 30 minutes, 4.15am to 11pm). South of town, the **Mahamarg Bus Stand** (Gaikwad Nagar) has services to Mumbai (non-AC/AC ₹220/365, 4½ hours, hourly, 6am to 8pm) and Shirdi (non-AC/AC ₹150/200, 2½ hours, hourly, 6am to 7.30pm).

Private buses head to Ahmedabad (non-AC/AC sleeper from ₹1000/1200, 12 hours, 10 to 15 per day), Kolhapur (AC sleeper from ₹600, 10 hours, 10 daily, 7.30pm to 9pm), Mumbai (from ₹500, four hours, hourly), Pune (from ₹300/450, six hours, hourly) and Nagpur (AC sleeper ₹2200, 12 hours, five daily, 5pm to 7pm). Handy private bus agent **Samrat Travels** (☏92604484820; Hotel Samrat, Old Agra Rd) sits just outside Hotel Samrat.

Many private buses depart from **Dwarka Circle** (Dwarka Circle) and most Mumbai-bound buses terminate at Dadar TT Circle in Mumbai.

TRAIN

The **Nashik Rd train station** (NK; Iali Gaon) is 8km southeast of the town centre, but a useful **railway reservation office** (1st fl, Palika Bazaar, Sharanpur Rd; ☺8am-8pm Mon-Sat, to 2pm Sun) is 500m west of the Old Central Bus Stand. There are over 25 daily trains to Mumbai so you won't have to wait long; these include the daily Pushpak Express (1st/2AC/sleeper ₹1245/745/170, 4½ hours, 3.15pm). Connections to Aurangabad are not good, with only four daily departures; try the Tapovan Express (2nd class/chair ₹85/325, 3½ hours, 9.50am). An Uber to/from the station to Panchavati costs around ₹175.

Around Nashik

Bhandardara

The picturesque village of Bhandardara is nestled deep in the folds of the Sahyadris, about 70km from Nashik. A surprisingly undiscovered place surrounded by craggy mountains, it is one of Maharashtra's best escapes from the bustle of urban India and one of its most cinematic and bucolic retreats. The lush mountain scenery, especially during the monsoon, is extraordinary.

Most of Bhandardara's habitation is set around Arthur Lake, a loosely horseshoe-shaped reservoir fed by the waters of the Pravara River, which is one of India's largest. The lake is barraged on one side by the imposing Wilson Dam, a colonial-era structure dating back to 1910. Hikers should consider a trek to the summit of Mt Kalsubai, which at 1646m was once used as an observation point by the Marathas. Alternatively, you could hike to the ruins of the Ratangad Fort, another of Shivaji's erstwhile strongholds; or to several Bollywood-preferred waterfalls like Randha or Umbrella falls. Guided highlight tours cost ₹700 – guides usually congregate outside **Anandvan Resort** (☑02424-257320; www.anandvanresorts.com; Ghatghar Rd, Village Shendi; ✻☎).

Bhandardara can be accessed by taking a local bus from Nashik's Old Central Bus Stand (p779) to Ghoti (₹120, one hour, every two hours, 5am to 10pm), from where **shared taxis** (Bhandardara Rd) carry on the remaining kilometres to Bhandardara (₹50, 45 minutes, 7am to 5.30pm). An outstation Mini Ola from Nashik runs around ₹1650. You can also grab a seat in a **shared taxi** (CBS Rd, Shalimar) (per person ₹50, 30 minutes, 8am to 10pm) to Ghoti from next door to Hotel Priya in Nashik.

From Mumbai, take a local fast Central Line train from CST to the end of the line at Kasara (₹30, 2¼ hours), from where buses to Sherdi village (Bhandardara) coordinate with the train (₹60, two hours).

Igatpuri

Located about 44km south of Nashik, Igatpuri is home to the headquarters of the world's largest *vipassana* meditation institution, the **Vipassana International Academy** (☑02553-244076; www.giri.dhamma.org; Dhamma Giri, Igatpuri; donations accepted; ☺visitors centre 9.30am-4.30pm). Ten-day residential courses (advance bookings compulsory) are held throughout the year, though teachers warn that it requires rigorous discipline. Visitors can watch a 20-minute intro video or take part in a 10-minute mini Anapana meditation session.

Basic accommodation, food and meditation instruction are provided free of charge, but donations upon completion are accepted.

This strict form of meditation was first taught by Gautama Buddha in the 6th century BC and was reintroduced to India by teacher SN Goenka in the 1960s.

Buses (₹140, one hour, every two hours, 5am to 10.30pm) and shared taxis (p780) (per person ₹60, one hour, 6am to 10pm) for Igatpuri depart next door to Hotel Priya in Nashik. Numerous daily trains call at Igatpuri from Nashik Rd station and Mumbai's CST.

Aurangabad

☑0240 / POP 1.28 MILLION / ELEV 515M

Aurangabad laid low through most of the tumultuous history of medieval India and only hit the spotlight when the last Mughal emperor, Aurangzeb, made the city his capital from 1653 to 1707. With the emperor's death came the city's rapid decline, but the brief period of glory saw the building of some fascinating monuments, including Bibi-qa-Maqbara (p781), a Taj Mahal replica, and these continue to draw a steady trickle of visitors. Alongside other historic relics, such as a group of ancient Buddhist caves (p782), these Mughal relics make Aurangabad a good choice for a weekend excursion from Mumbai. But the real reason for traipsing here is because the town is an excellent base for exploring the World Heritage Sites of Ellora and Ajanta.

Silk fabrics were once Aurangabad's chief revenue generator and the town is still

Aurangabad

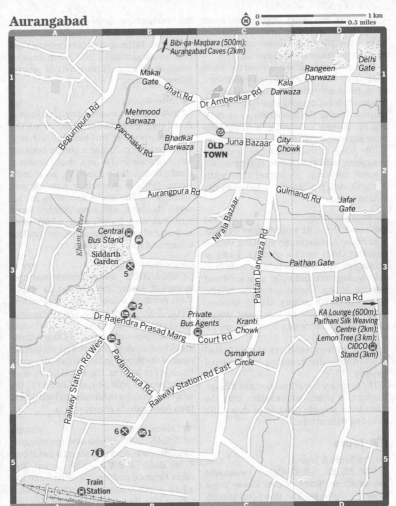

known across the world for its hand-woven Himroo and Paithani saris.

◉ Sights

★ Bibi-qa-Maqbara
MONUMENT

(Begumpura; Indian/foreigner ₹40/300; ⊙ 6am-8pm) Built by Aurangzeb's son Azam Khan in 1679 as a mausoleum for his mother Rabia-ud-Daurani, Bibi-qa-Maqbara is widely known as the poor man's Taj. With its four minarets flanking a central onion-domed mausoleum, the white structure certainly does bear a striking resemblance to Agra's Taj Mahal.

Aurangabad

⊕ Activities, Courses & Tours
Ashoka Tours & Travels .... (see 3)

⊜ Sleeping
1 Ginger Hotel	....	B5
2 Hotel Green Olive	....	B3
3 Hotel Panchavati	....	B4
4 Hotel Raviraj	....	B3

⊗ Eating
| 5 Bhoj | .... | B3 |
| 6 Tandoor | .... | B5 |

⊕ Information
| 7 Indiatourism | .... | A5 |
| MTDC Tourist Office | .... | (see 7) |

It is much less grand, however, and apart from having a few marble adornments, namely the plinth and dome, much of the structure is finished in lime mortar.

Apparently the prince conceived the entire mausoleum in white marble, but was thwarted by his frugal father who opposed his extravagant idea of draining state coffers for the purpose. Despite the use of cheaper material and the obvious weathering, it's a sight far more impressive than the average gravestone.

The Bibi's formal gardens are a delight to explore, with the Deccan hills providing a scenic backdrop. It's located 3km north of the Central Bus Stand – a ₹50 or so Ola rickshaw ride.

Aurangabad Caves

CAVE

(Grishneswar Temple Rd; Indian/foreigner ₹40/300; ☺6am-6pm) Architecturally speaking, the Aurangabad Caves aren't a patch on Ellora or Ajanta, but they do shed light on early Buddhist architecture and make for a quiet and peaceful outing. Carved out of the hillside in the 6th or 7th century AD, the 10 caves, comprising two groups 1km apart (retain your ticket for entry into both sets), are all Buddhist.

Cave 7, with its sculptures of scantily clad lovers in suggestive positions, is a perennial favourite.

The caves are about 2km north of Bibi-qa-Maqbara. A return autorickshaw from the mausoleum shouldn't cost more than ₹250, including waiting time.

👉 Tours

Ashoka Tours & Travels

TOURS

(☑0240-2359102, 9890340816; www.tourist aurangabad.com; Hotel Panchavati, Railway Station Rd West; ☺7am-9pm) The stand-out Aurangabad agency, with excellent city and regional tours and decent car hire at fair rates. Prices for an air-con car with up to four people are ₹1550 for Ellora and ₹2550 for Ajanta. Run by Ashok T Kadam, a knowledgeable former–autorickshaw driver.

🛏 Sleeping

★ Hotel Panchavati

HOTEL $

(☑0240-2328755; www.hotelpanchavati.com; Railway Station Rd West; s/d ₹1000/1260, d with AC ₹1400; ❄@🛜) A traveller-oriented budget hotel, the Panchavati is run by ever-helpful, switched-on management who understand travellers' needs. Rooms are compact but thoughtfully appointed, with crown mould-

ing, comfortable beds (with paisley-style bedspreads), thick bath towels and newly renovated bathrooms. There are two decent restaurants and a 'bar' (read: drinking room) and it's a great place to hook up with fellow travellers.

★ Hotel Raviraj

HOTEL $

(☑0240-2352124; www.hotelraviraj.in; Rajendra Prasad Marg; d with AC from ₹1680; ❄🛜) The standard rooms at this pleasant midrange option masquerading as a budget hotel are easily Aurangabad's best deal. Spacious, comfy linens, flat-screen TVs, good bathrooms (with motion-sensor lighting) and (weak) wi-fi. The pricier executives are basically the same, with more polished furniture. Tack on a friendly staff, a leafy foyer, restaurant/bar and beer-friendly 1st-floor terrace and it's tough to beat.

Ginger Hotel

HOTEL $$

(☑0240-6713300; www.gingerhotels.com/ginger-aurangabad; Railway Station Rd East (Dr Bhapkar Marg), Venkateshwar Colony; s/d incl breakfast from ₹3000/3500; ❄🌐🛜) This 2018 newcomer has upped the stakes in Aurangabad's budget hotel offerings with upgraded Ginger attributes: clean, modern, attractive rooms that are some of the biggest in the nationwide chain's inventory at 30 sq m. Hardwood floors, modern bathrooms, split air-con units and all the mod cons ensure a minimalist and hip retreat from Aurangabad's chaotic streets.

★ Lemon Tree

HOTEL $$$

(☑0240-6603030; www.lemontreehotels.com; R7/2 Chikalthana, Airport Rd; s/d incl breakfast from ₹7780/10,140; ❄🌐🛜🏊) The Lemon Tree offers elegance and class, looking more like a billionaire's luxury whitewashed Mediterranean villa than an Indian hotel. It's well designed, too: all rooms face inwards, overlooking perhaps the best pool on the Decca plateau – all 50m of it. The artsy standard rooms, though not large, are brightened by vivid tropical tones offset against snow-white walls.

Located near the airport, 6km from the centre. You'll find good dining choices here, too, from local cuisine to an Asian noodle bar, and a nice bar with pool, foosball and *carom* (similar to billiards) games.

Hotel Green Olive

HOTEL $$$

(☑0240-2329490; www.hotelgreenolive.com; 13/3 Bhagya Nagar, CBS Rd; s/d from ₹4130/5310; ❄🛜) Cramped bathrooms aside, this boutique-ish business hotel offers stylish, well-equipped and well-maintained rooms. The friendly staff here look after guests commendably and can organise transport and tours; there's a good bar and restaurant on the premises serving Maharashtrian thalis.

✖ Eating & Drinking

★ Green Leaf
INDIAN $$

(www.greenleafpureveg.com; Shop 6-9, Fame Tapadiya Multiplex, Town Centre; mains ₹160-330; ⊙noon-11pm; 🛜) Aurangabad's favourite modern vegetarian is loved for delectable pure-veg dishes that really pop with flavour (try the veg handi or off-menu paneer Hyderabadi) and come with spice level indicators (one chilli pepper equals medium – they don't offer an explanation for the four chilli pepper offerings...). It's 400m north of CIDCO Bus Stand.

★ Bhoj
INDIAN $$

(Railway Station Rd West; thali ₹260; ⊙11am-3pm & 7-11pm) Rightly famous for its delicious, unlimited Rajasthani and Gujarati thalis, Bhoj is a wonderful place to refuel and relax after a hard day on the road (or rails). It's on the 1st floor of a somewhat scruffy little shopping arcade, but the decor, ambience, service and presentation are all first-rate. Arguably the best thali in Maharashtra outside Mumbai.

Tandoor
NORTH INDIAN $$

(Railway Station Rd East, Shyam Chambers; mains ₹130-470; ⊙11am-11pm) Offers fine tandoori dishes, flavoursome North Indian veg and nonveg options, and an extensive beer list (for Aurangabad) in a weirdly Pharaonic atmosphere. Try the wonderful sizzler kebabs. A few Chinese dishes are also on offer, but patrons clearly prefer the dishes coming out of...well...the tandoor. Fully licensed.

HIMROO WEAVING

Himroo material is a traditional Aurangabad speciality made from cotton, silk and metallic threads. Most of today's Himroo shawls and saris are produced using power looms, but some showrooms still stock hand-loomed cloth.

Himroo saris start at around ₹1500 for a cotton and silk blend. Paithani saris, which are of superior quality, range from ₹9000 to ₹20,000 – but some of them take more than a year to make. If you're buying, make sure you get authentic Himroo, not 'Aurangabad silk'.

KA Lounge
BAR

(Satya Dharam Complex, Akashwari Cir, Jalna Rd; ⊙10am-11.30pm; 🛜) Aurangabad's one and only trendy bar-restaurant caters to the city's upwardly hip who knock back cocktails (₹350 to ₹450) – like the cool burning basil and green chilli mojito – from cosy lounge seating amid exposed brick walls. You can easily make an evening of it; the modern fusion menu (mains ₹150 to ₹690) features interesting Indian/Asian/Continental-hybrid cuisine.

🛍 Shopping

Paithani Silk Weaving Centre
TEXTILES

(📞9970092700; www.paithanisilk.com; 54, P-1, Town Centre, Lokmat Nagar; ⊙9.30am-9pm) One of the best places to come and watch weavers at work is the Paithani Silk Weaving Centre where you'll find good-quality products for sale. It's about 6km east of Kranti Chowk (opposite MGM Medical College), so take a taxi.

ℹ Information

Indiatourism (Government of India Tourism; 📞0240-2364999; www.incredibleindia.org; MTDC Holiday Resort, Railway Station Rd East; ⊙10.30am-5.30pm Mon-Fri)

MTDC Tourist Office (Maharashtra Tourism Development Corporation; 📞0240-2343169; www.maharashtratourism.gov.in; MTDC Holiday Resort, Railway Station Rd East; ⊙10am-5.30pm Mon-Sat, closed 2nd & 4th Sat)

Post Office (www.indiapost.gov.in; Buddi Ln, Naralibag; ⊙10am-5pm Mon-Fri, to 1pm Sat)

ℹ Getting There & Away

BUS

Buses leave about every half-hour from the **Central Bus Stand** (📞0240-2242164; Railway Station Rd West) to Pune (non-AC/AC ₹400/775, 5½ hours, 5am to 6pm) and hourly to Nashik (non-AC/AC ₹350/425, 4½ hours, 5am to 10pm). **Private bus agents** (Dr Rajendra Prasad Marg) are clustered on Dr Rajendra Prasad Marg and Court Rd; a few sit closer to the bus stand. Deluxe overnight bus destinations include Mumbai (AC sleeper ₹800 to ₹1450, 7½ to 9½ hours), Ahmedabad (non-AC/AC sleeper from ₹850/1200, 13 to 15 hours) and Nagpur (AC sleeper ₹1000 to ₹2900, non-AC from ₹1100, 8½ to 10 hours). Buses depart from three locations around town, including opposite Hotel Panchavati and next to DMart.

Ordinary buses head to Ellora from the Central Bus Stand every half-hour (non-AC/AC ₹37/345, 30 minutes, 5.30am to 8pm) and to Jalgaon (non-AC ₹200, four hours, 5.45am to 8pm) via

DON'T MISS

DAULATABAD FORT

No trip to Aurangabad is complete without a pit stop at the ruined but truly magnificent hilltop fortress of **Daulatabad Fort** (NH52; Indian/foreigner ₹25/300; ◷6am-6pm), about 15km away from town en route to Ellora, which sits atop a 200m-high craggy outcrop known as Devagiri (Hill of the Gods). A 5km battlement surrounds this ancient fort, a most beguiling structure built by the Yadava kings through the 12th century and originally conceived as an impregnable fort.

In 1328, it was renamed Daulatabad, the City of Fortune, by Delhi sultan Mohammed Tughlaq, who decided to shift his kingdom's capital to this citadel from Delhi. Known for his eccentric ways, Tughlaq even marched the entire population of Delhi 1100km south to populate it. Ironically, Daulatabad – despite being better positioned strategically than Delhi – soon proved untenable as a capital due to an acute water crisis and Tughlaq forced its weary inhabitants to slope all the way back to Delhi, which had by then been reduced to a ghost town.

The climb to the summit takes about an hour, and leads past an ingenious series of defences, including multiple doorways designed with odd angles and spike-studded doors to prevent elephant charges. A tower of victory, known as the Chand Minar (Tower of the Moon), built in 1435, soars 60m above the ground to the right; it's closed to visitors. Higher up, you can walk into the Chini Mahal, where Abul Hasan Tana Shah, king of Golconda, was held captive for 12 years before his death in 1699. Nearby, there's a 6m cannon, cast from five different metals and engraved with Aurangzeb's name.

Part of the ascent goes through a pitch-black, bat-infested, water-seeping, spiralling tunnel. Guides (₹1600 up to five people) are available near the ticket counter to show you around and their torch-bearing assistants will lead you through the dark passageway for a small tip. On the way down you'll be left to your own devices, so carry a torch.

As the fort is in ruins (with crumbling staircases and sheer drops) and involves a steep ascent, the elderly, children and those suffering from vertigo or claustrophobia will find it a tough challenge. Bring water and allow 2½ hours to explore the structure.

There is little in the way of accommodation at Daulatabad – people bed down in Aurangabad or Ellora. For meals, the entrance to the fort is swarming with *dhabas* (casual eateries) and fresh fruit and flavoured crushed-ice stalls.

Ellora-bound buses departing the MSRTC bus stand every half-hour (non-AC ₹20, 30 minutes, 5.30am to 8pm) can drop you at the entrance. The stop for buses back to Aurangabad is 500m south of the Fort entrance on the NH52. Rickshaws charge ₹30 (sharing) or ₹100 back to Aurangabad.

Fardapur (₹180, three hours), which is the drop-off point for Ajanta.

From the **CIDCO Bus Stand** (☏0240-2240149; Airport Rd), by the Lemon Tree hotel junction, 12 direct buses leave for the Lonar meteorite crater every 45 minutes to one hour (₹200, 4½ hours) between 4.45am and 4.45pm.

TRAIN

Aurangabad's **train station** (AWB; Railway Station Rd East) is not on a main line, but it has four daily direct trains to/from Mumbai. The Tapovan Express (2nd class/chair ₹235/505, 7½ hours) departs Aurangabad at 2.35pm. The Janshatabdi Express (2nd class/chair ₹170/585, 6½ hours) departs Aurangabad at 6am. For Hyderabad, trains include the Ajanta Express (sleeper/2AC ₹300/1165, 10 hours, 10.45pm). To reach northern or eastern India, take a bus to Jalgaon and board a train there.

Ellora

☏02437

Give a man a hammer and chisel and he'll create art for posterity. Come to the Unesco World Heritage Site **Ellora cave temples** (Ellora Cave Rd; Indian/foreigner ₹40/600; ◷6am-6pm Wed-Mon), located 30km from Aurangabad, and you'll know exactly what we mean. The epitome of ancient Indian rock-cut architecture, these caves were chipped out laboriously over five centuries by generations of Buddhist, Hindu and Jain monks. Monasteries, chapels, temples – the caves served every purpose and they were stylishly embellished with a profusion of remarkably detailed sculptures.

Undoubtedly Ellora's shining moment is the awesome Kailasa Temple (Cave 16), the world's largest monolithic sculpture, hewn top to bottom against a rocky slope by 7000 labourers over a period of 150 years. Dedicated to Lord Shiva, it is clearly among the best that ancient Indian architecture has to offer.

◉ Sights

Ellora has 34 caves in all: 12 Buddhist (AD 600–800), 17 Hindu (AD 600–900) and five Jain (AD 800–1000) – though the exact time scales of these caves' construction is the subject of academic debate.

Unlike the caves at Ajanta, which are carved into a sheer rock face, the Ellora caves line a 2km-long escarpment, the gentle slope of which allowed architects to build elaborate courtyards in front of the shrines and render them with sculptures of a surreal quality.

The established academic theory is that Ellora represents the renaissance of Hinduism under the Chalukya and Rashtrakuta dynasties, the subsequent decline of Indian Buddhism and a brief resurgence of Jainism under official patronage. However, due to the absence of inscriptional evidence, it's been impossible to accurately date most of Ellora's monuments – some scholars argue that some Hindu temples predate those in the Buddhist group. What is certain is that their coexistence at one site indicates a lengthy period of religious tolerance.

Official guides can be hired at the ticket office in front of the Kailasa Temple for ₹1370 (up to five people). Guides have an extensive knowledge of cave architecture so are worth the investment. If your tight itinerary forces you to choose between Ellora or Ajanta, Ellora wins hands down in terms of architecture (though Ajanta's setting is more beautiful and more of a pleasure to explore).

Ellora is very popular with domestic tourists; if you can visit on a weekday, it's far less crowded. Worth visiting if open for its impressive displays (it was closed during research) is the **Ellora Visitor Centre** (NH211; ⊙ 9am-5pm Wed-Mon).

★ **Kailasa Temple**   HINDU TEMPLE

One of India's greatest monuments, this astonishing temple, carved from solid rock, was built by King Krishna I in AD 760 to represent Mt Kailasa (Kailash), Shiva's Himalayan abode. To say that the assignment was daring would be an understatement. Three huge trenches were bored into the sheer cliff face, a process that entailed removing 200,000 tonnes of rock by hammer and chisel, before the temple could begin to take shape and its remarkable sculptural decoration could be added.

Covering twice the area of the Parthenon in Athens and being half as high again, Kailasa is an engineering marvel that was executed straight from the head with zero margin for error. Modern draughtspeople might have a lesson or two to learn here.

The temple houses several intricately carved panels, depicting scenes from the Ramayana, the Mahabharata and the adventures of Krishna. Also worth admiring are the immense monolithic pillars that stand in the courtyard, flanking the entrance on both sides, and the southeastern gallery that has 10 giant and fabulous panels depicting

MAHARASHTRA ELLORA

CANNABIS CONSERVATION

The remarkable preservation of Ellora's caves and paintings could be attributed to many things, but perhaps none more surprising than a healthy dose of hemp. While the jury is still out on whether the Buddhist, Hindu and Jain monks that called Ellora home over the centuries had a proclivity for smoking cannabis, archaeologists are sure they knew a thing or two about its preservation effects.

An 11-year study released in 2016 revealed that hemp, a variety of the *Cannabis sativa* plant (believed to be one of the world's oldest domesticated crops), has been discovered mixed in with the clay and lime plaster used at Ellora and is credited with being the secret ingredient that has slowed degradation at the Unesco World Heritage Site over the course of 1500 years.

Using electron microscopes, Fourier transforms, infrared spectroscopy and stereomicroscopic studies, chemists from the Archaeological Survey of India found that samples from Ellora contained 10% *Cannabis sativa*, which resulted in reduced levels of insect activity at Ellora – around 25% of the paintings at Ajanta have been destroyed, where hemp was not used. In addition to Ellora, hemp was also implemented by the Yadavas, who built Daulatabad Fort near Aurangabad in the 12th century.

Talk about high and mighty monuments!

Ellora Caves

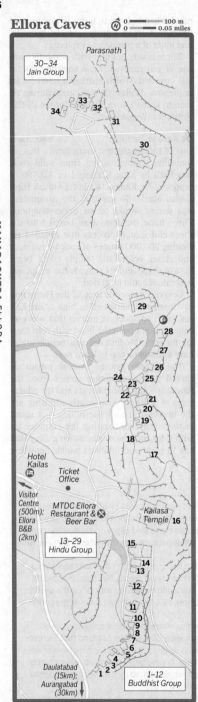

0 — 100 m
0 — 0.05 miles

Parasnath

30–34 Jain Group

33 32
34
31

30

29

28
27
26
24 25
23
22 21
20
19
18
17

Hotel Kailas

Ticket Office

Visitor Centre (500m); Ellora B&B (2km)

MTDC Ellora Restaurant & Beer Bar

Kailasa Temple 16

13–29 Hindu Group

15
14
13
12
11
10 9
8
7
6
4 5
1 2 3

Daulatabad (15km); Aurangabad (30km)

1–12 Buddhist Group

the different avatars (incarnations of a deity) of Lord Vishnu.

After you're done with the main enclosure, bypass the hordes of snack-munching day trippers to explore the temple's many dank, bat urine–soaked corners with their numerous forgotten carvings. Afterwards, hike the sturdier path up to the south of the complex (past the scaffolding) that takes you to the top perimeter of the 'cave', from where you can get a bird's-eye view of the entire temple complex.

Buddhist Caves
CAVE

Calm and contemplation infuse the 12 Buddhist caves, which stretch to the south of Kailasa. All are Buddhist *viharas* (monasteries) used for study and worship, but these multistoreyed structures also included cooking, living and sleeping areas. The one exception is Cave 10, which is a *chaitya* (assembly hall). While the earliest caves are simple, Caves 11 and 12 are more ambitious; both comprise three storeys and are on par with the more impressive Hindu temples.

Cave 1, the simplest vihara, may have been a granary. Cave 2 is notable for its ornate pillars and the imposing seated Buddha that faces the setting sun. Cave 3 and Cave 4 are unfinished and not well preserved.

Cave 5 is the largest vihara in this group at 18m wide and 36m long; the rows of stone benches hint that it may once have been an assembly hall.

Cave 6 is an ornate vihara with wonderful images of Tara, consort of the Bodhisattva Avalokitesvara, and of the Buddhist goddess of learning, Mahamayuri, looking remarkably similar to Saraswati, her Hindu equivalent. Cave 7 is an unadorned hall. Cave 8 is the first cave in which the sanctum is detached from the rear wall. Cave 9, located above Cave 8, is notable for its wonderfully carved fascia.

Cave 10 is the only chaitya in the Buddhist group and one of the finest in India. Its ceiling features ribs carved into the stonework; the grooves were once fitted with wooden panels. The balcony and upper gallery offer a closer view of the ceiling and a frieze depicting amorous couples. A decorative window gently illuminates an enormous figure of the teaching Buddha.

Cave 11, the Do Thal (Two Storey) Cave, is entered through its third basement level, not discovered until 1876. Like Cave 12, it possibly owes its size to competition with Hindu caves of the same period.

Cave 12, the huge Tin Thal (Three Storey) Cave, is entered through a courtyard. The locked shrine on the top floor contains a large Buddha figure flanked by his seven previous incarnations. The walls are carved with relief pictures. Note that the temples are closed on Tuesday.

Jain Caves
CAVE

The five Jain caves, the last created at Ellora, may lack the ambitious size of the best Hindu temples, but they are exceptionally detailed, with some remarkable paintings and carvings.

The caves are 1km north of the last Hindu temple (Cave 29) at the end of the bitumen road; an MSRTC bus departs from in front of Kailasa Temple and runs back and forth (₹20 return; 9.15am to 6pm).

🛏 Sleeping & Eating

Ellora B&B
GUESTHOUSE $

(☑ 9960589867, 9822534157; ellorabedandbreakfast@gmail.com; Ellora Village; s/d incl breakfast from ₹800/1000; 🛜) For a bit of rustic cultural immersion, good-hearted man about town Sadeek and his uncle Rafiq have four simple rooms in their village home, 2km from the caves (and the crowds). The three best rooms open out onto a breezy terrace with farmland and mountain views and feature renovated en suite bathrooms with sit-down flush toilets and 24-hour hot water.

Hotel Kailas
HOTEL $$

(☑ 02437-244446; www.hotelkailas.com; NH211; d with/without AC ₹4130/2570; ❄🛜) The sole decent hotel near the site, with attractive air-con stone cottages set in leafy grounds. The restaurant (mains ₹70 to ₹280) is excellent, with a blackboard menu chalked up that includes sandwiches, breakfasts, curries and tandoori favourites. Wi-fi, however, sold in increments of three hours for ₹100, is ridiculous, though guests get one three-hour slot free.

MTDC Ellora Restaurant & Beer Bar
INDIAN $

(www.maharashtratourism.gov.in; Ellora Cave Rd; mains/thali from ₹80/150; ⊙9am-5pm) Located within the temple complex, this is an easy place for lunch or a cold Kingfisher.

❶ Getting There & Away

Buses depart Aurangabad Central Bus Stand every half-hour (non-AC/AC ₹37/345, 30 minutes, 5.30am to 8pm); the last return bus departs from Ellora at 7pm. Share 4WDs are also an option, but get packed; they leave when full and stop outside the bus stand in Aurangabad (₹30). A full-day tour to Ellora, with stops en route, costs ₹1550 in an air-con car; try Ashoka Tours & Travels (p782). Autorickshaws ask for ₹800.

Ajanta
☑ 02438

Superbly set in a remote river valley 105km northeast of Aurangabad, the remarkable cave temples of Ajanta are this region's second World Heritage Site. Much older than Ellora, these secluded caves date from around the 2nd century BC to the 6th century AD and were among the earliest monastic institutions to be constructed in the country. Ironically, it was Ellora's rise that brought about Ajanta's downfall and historians believe the site was abandoned once the focus shifted to Ellora.

As the Deccan forest claimed and shielded the caves, with roots and shoots choking the sculptures, Ajanta remained deserted for about a millennium, until 1819 when a British hunting party led by officer John Smith stumbled upon it purely by chance.

◎ Sights

One of the primary reasons to visit Ajanta is to admire its renowned 'frescoes', actually temperas, which adorn many of the caves' interiors. With few other examples from ancient times matching their artistic excellence and fine execution, these paintings are of unfathomable heritage value.

Despite their age, the paintings in most caves remain finely preserved and many attribute it to their relative isolation from humanity for centuries. However, it would be a tad optimistic to say that decay hasn't set in.

It's believed that the natural pigments for these paintings were mixed with animal glue and vegetable gum to bind them to the dry surface. Many caves have small, crater-

---

❶ PHOTO RULES

Flash photography is strictly prohibited within the caves, due to its adverse effect on the natural dyes used in the paintings. Authorities have installed rows of tiny pigment-friendly lights, which cast a faint glow within the caves, as additional lighting is required for glimpsing minute details, but you'll have to rely on long exposures for photographs.

Ajanta Caves

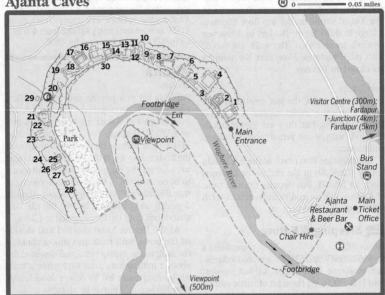

like holes in their floors, which acted as palettes during paint jobs.

Two lookouts offer picture-perfect views of the whole horseshoe-shaped gorge. The first is a short walk beyond the river, crossed via a bridge below Cave 8. A further 40-minute uphill walk (not to be attempted during the monsoons) leads to the lookout from where the British party first spotted the caves.

Most buses ferrying tour groups don't arrive until noon. To avoid the crowds, stay locally in Fardapur or make an early start from Aurangabad.

While closed at time of research, the **Ajanta Visitor Centre** (Aurangabad-Jalgaon Hwy; ☺9am-5.30pm Tue-Sun) is worth visiting if open for its displays, audio guides and cafe.

★ **Ajanta Caves** CAVE
(Indian/foreigner ₹40/600, video ₹25, authorised guide ₹1600; ☺9am-5.30pm Tue-Sun) Ajanta's caves line a steep face of a horseshoe-shaped gorge bordering the Waghore River. Five of the caves are *chaityas* (assembly or prayer halls) while others are *viharas* (monasteries with attached residential cells). Caves 8, 9, 10, 12, 13 and part of 15 are early Buddhist caves, while the others date from around the 5th century AD (Mahayana period). In the austere early Buddhist school, the Buddha was never represented directly but always alluded to by a symbol such as the footprint or wheel of law.

Cave 1 CAVE
Cave 1, a Mahayana *vihara*, was one of the last to be excavated and is the most beautifully decorated. This is where you'll find a rendition of the *Bodhisattva Padmapani*, the most famous and iconic of the Ajanta artworks. A verandah in front leads to a large congregation hall housing sculptures and narrative murals known for their splendid perspective and elaborate detailing of dress, daily life and facial expressions.

Cave 2 CAVE
Cave 2 is a late Mahayana *vihara* with deliriously ornamented columns and capitals and some fine paintings. The ceiling is decorated with geometric and floral patterns. The murals depict scenes from the Jataka tales, including Buddha's mother's dream of a six-tusked elephant, which heralded his conception.

Cave 4 CAVE
Cave 4 is the largest *vihara* at Ajanta and is supported by 28 pillars. Although never completed, the cave has some impressive sculptures, such as the four statues surrounding a huge central Buddha. There

are also scenes of people fleeing from the 'eight great dangers' to the protection of Avalokitesvara.

Cave 6 CAVE

Cave 6 is the only two-storey *vihara* at Ajanta, but parts of the lower storey have collapsed. Inside is a seated Buddha figure and an intricately carved door to the shrine. Upstairs the hall is surrounded by cells with fine paintings on the doorways.

Cave 7 CAVE

Cave 7 has an atypical design, with porches before the verandah leading directly to the four cells and the elaborately sculptured shrine.

Cave 9 CAVE

Cave 9 is one of the earliest *chaityas* at Ajanta. Although it dates from the early Buddhist period, the two figures flanking the entrance door were probably later Mahayana additions. Columns run down both sides of the cave and around the 3m-high dagoba (pagoda) at the far end.

Cave 10 CAVE

Cave 10 is thought to be the oldest cave (200 BC) and was the first one to be spotted by the British hunting party. Similar in design to Cave 9, it is the largest *chaitya*. The facade has collapsed and the paintings inside have been damaged, in some cases by graffiti dating from soon after their rediscovery. One of the pillars to the right bears the engraved name of Smith, who left his mark here for posterity.

Cave 16 CAVE

Cave 16, a *vihara*, contains some of Ajanta's finest paintings and is thought to have been the original entrance to the entire complex. The best known of these paintings is of the 'dying princess', Sundari, wife of the Buddha's half-brother Nanda, who is said to have fainted at the news her husband was renouncing the material life (and her) in order to become a monk.

Cave 17 CAVE

With carved dwarfs supporting the pillars, cave 17 has Ajanta's best-preserved and most varied paintings. Famous images include a princess applying make-up, a seductive prince using the old trick of plying his lover with wine, and the Buddha returning home from his enlightenment to beg from his wife and astonished son.

Cave 19 CAVE

Cave 19, a magnificent *chaitya*, has a remarkably detailed facade; its dominant feature is an impressive horseshoe-shaped window. Two fine, standing Buddha figures flank the entrance. Inside is a three-tiered dagoba with a figure of the Buddha on the front. Outside the cave, to the west, sits a striking image of the Naga king with seven cobra hoods around his head. His wife, hooded by a single cobra, sits by his side.

Cave 26 CAVE

A largely ruined *chaitya*, cave 26 is now dramatically lit and contains some fine sculptures that shouldn't be missed. On the left wall is a huge figure of the reclining Buddha, lying back in preparation for nirvana. Other scenes include a lengthy depiction of the Buddha's temptation by Maya.

🛏 Sleeping & Eating

MTDC Ajanta Tourist Resort HOTEL $$
(☎ 02438-244230; www.maharashtratourism. gov.in; Aurangabad-Jalgaon Hwy, Fardapur; d with/without AC ₹2130/1790; ❄) This government hotel is pricey but the best option at Ajanta, set amid lawns in a peaceful location off the main road in Fardapur, 5km from the caves. Air-con rooms, in apple green structures, are spacious; non-AC rooms are less interesting but fine. There's a garden and restaurant with veg thalis (₹150 to ₹250).

★ Hotel Radhe Krishna DHABA $
(Aurangabad-Jalgaon Hwy, Fardapur; mains ₹70-180, thalis from ₹180; ⊙ 24hr) The best of Fardapur's streetside *dhabas* (casual eatery serving basic meals), this excellent spot is fresh, cheap and satisfying. The famous cook, Babu, and his team get a big kick out of foreigners dropping in, and just watching these guys whip up various curries, thalis and a fry or two is pure entertainment.

ℹ Getting There & Away

Buses from Aurangabad or Jalgaon will drop you at the Fardapur T-junction (where the highway meets the road to the caves), 4km from the site. From here, after paying an 'amenities' fee (₹10), walk to the departure point for the **buses** (with/without AC ₹30/20; ⊙ 9am-6pm), which zoom up to the caves. Buses return half-hourly to the T-junction; the last bus is at 6pm. Note that the caves are closed on Monday.

All **MSRTC** (www.msrtc.gov.in) buses passing through Fardapur stop at the T-junction. After the caves close you can board buses to either

Aurangabad or Jalgaon outside the MTDC Holiday Resort in Fardapur, 1km down the main road towards Jalgaon. Taxis are available in Fardapur; ₹2000/3000 should get you to Jalgaon/Aurangabad.

The Aurangabad–Jalgaon Hwy was being expanded to four lanes at time of writing – expect faster drive times between the two and to Ajanta from either city in the near future.

Jalgaon

📞 0257 / POP 468.300 / ELEV 208M

Apart from being a handy base for exploring Ajanta 60km away, the industrial city of Jalgaon is really nothing more than a convenient transit town. It has rail connections to all major cities across India.

🛏 Sleeping & Eating

★ Hotel Plaza   HOTEL $

(📞 0257-2227354, 9370027354; hotelplaza_jal@yahoo.com; Station Rd; dm ₹300, s/d from ₹650/950, d with AC ₹1500-2000; ❄@🛜) This extremely well-managed and well-presented hotel is only a short hop from the station. Rooms vary in size and layout, but with whitewashed walls, a minimalist feel and bathrooms cleaner than a Jain temple, it's modestly boutique and brilliant value. Everything from the hospitality to the bed linens exceeds expectations.

Hotel Arya   INDIAN $

(Old Mamurabad Rd; mains ₹40-150; ⊙11am-10.30pm) Delicious vegetarian food, particularly Punjabi cuisine, though a few Chinese and South Indian dishes are also offered. It's a short walk south along Station Rd, left at MG Rd and left at the clock tower. You may have to queue for a table at lunchtime.

ℹ Getting There & Away

Jalgaon's **train station** (JL; Station Rd) and **bus stand** (📞 0257-2229774; Mahatma Gandhi Rd) are about 2km apart (₹30 by autorickshaw).

Several express trains connecting Mumbai (sleeper/2AC ₹280/1017, eight hours), Delhi (₹550/2020, 18 hours), Ahmedabad (₹340/1255, 10 hours) and Varanasi (₹485/1970, 20 hours) stop at Jalgaon Junction train station. Ten daily trains head for Nagpur (₹215/1015, five to nine hours).

Non-AC buses to Fardapur T-junction (₹82, 1½ hours), for access to Ajanta, depart every 30 minutes from the bus stand between 5am and 10pm, continuing to Aurangabad (₹235, four hours). There is also one daily AC departure to Nagpur (₹1200, nine hours, 1am).

Private bus companies on Station Rd offer AC sleeper services to Mumbai (₹800, 9½ hours) and Nagpur (₹750, nine hours). Try Durga Travels or Mahalaxmi Travels.

Nagpur

📞 0712 / POP 2.43 MILLION / ELEV 305M

Way off the main tourist routes, the isolated city of Nagpur holds the distinction of being the dead geographical centre of India. It lacks must-see sights but is an important gateway to several reserves and parks including Tadoba-Andhari Tiger Reserve and Pench National Park. It's also close to the temples of Ramtek and the ashrams of Sevagram. Summer is the best time to taste the city's famous oranges, but the trade-off is unbearable heat.

🛏 Sleeping

Legend Inn   HOTEL $$

(📞 0712-6658666; www.thelegendinn.com; 14 Modern Society, Wardha Rd; s/d incl breakfast from ₹4130/4720; ❄@🛜) On the main highway for the Tadoba-Andhari Tiger Reserve, this is an efficiently run hotel, owned by an Indian mountaineering legend, with well-appointed rooms, a good restaurant, smoky bar and smiley staff (which might make up for the low water pressure). Free pick-ups from the airport, 1km away, are included, but the metro will eventually stop right outside its door.

Hotel Hardeo   HOTEL $$$

(📞 0712-6684888; www.hardeohotel.com; Munje Marg, Sitabuldi; s/d incl breakfast from ₹3540/4130; ❄🛜) The best hotel nearest the train station, this upper midrange, professionally run business hotel is 1.3km from the rails. The modern bathrooms, flat-screen LED TVs, lacquer-accented woods and soothing earth tones might just hit the spot after a long haul in sleeper class (as do the large dosas at breakfast). Prices include airport/railway station transfers.

🍴 Eating

★ Varadi That   MAHARASHTRIAN $

(Ganesh Chamber, Mehadiya Chowk, Dhantoli; mains ₹80-200; ⊙11am-4pm & 7.30-11pm) No English inside or out, but this simple but super Maharashtrian stalwart is absolutely excellent for the state's fiery regional cuisine. Try *jhunka* (chickpea flour porridge with chillies and spices) and *kacha bharit* (a fire-roasted aubergine dish with chillies and spices similar to baba ghanoush, served

LONAR METEORITE CRATER

If you like offbeat adventures, travel to Lonar to explore a prehistoric natural wonder. About 50,000 years ago, a meteorite slammed into the earth here, leaving behind a massive crater 2km across and 170m deep (it's said to be the world's third largest). In scientific jargon, it's the only hypervelocity natural-impact crater in basaltic rock in the world. In lay terms, it's as tranquil and relaxing a spot as you could hope to find, with a shallow green lake at its base and wilderness all around, including aquatic birds. The lake water is supposedly alkaline and excellent for the skin. Scientists think the meteorite is still embedded about 600m below the southeastern rim of the crater.

The crater's edge is home to several Hindu temples as well as wildlife, including langurs, peacocks, deer and numerous birds.

The **MTDC Tourist Complex** (☑8806363498; rathod.dilip95@gmail.com; dm ₹250, d with AC ₹2015; ❄ ☎) has a prime location just across the road from the crater and offers deluxe rooms that are in excellent shape, with stylish en suite bathrooms.

There are direct buses every 45 minutes to one hour between Lonar and the CIDCO bus stand in Aurangabad (₹200, 4½ hours, 4.45am to 4.45pm), but you'll need to catch the 7.30am departure at the latest unless you plan on spending the night. The last bus back from Lonar departs at 2pm.

It's also possible to visit Lonar on a day trip from Aurangabad or Jalgaon if you hire a car and driver and don't mind dishing out about ₹3060 (AC).

cold). Both can be scooped up with the house *bhakri* (sorghum bread). Cash only.

★ **Breakfast Story** CAFE **$$**
(www.facebook.com/thebreakfastorynagpur; Sai Sagar Apt, Hingna Rd; mains ₹110-345; ☉8am-2.30pm & 3.30-7pm Mon & Tue, Thu-Sat, 8am-3pm Sun; ☎) This stylish all-day breakfast-only hotspot in a residential building 7km south-west of the centre is worth a diversion. English, American and Belgian breakfast combos, sandwiches, pancakes and waffles,

along with daily chalkboard specials, are served up on artsy wooden tables covered in comics. Cassette tapes, newspapers and other pop art line the walls, completing the cosy, trendy atmosphere.

★ **Majestic Masala** NORTH INDIAN **$$$**
(☑0712-6653666; www.tulihotels.com/tuli-imperial.html; Hotel Tuli Imperial, 37 Central Bazar Rd; mains ₹350-900; ☉noon-3pm & 7pm-midnight) Inside one of Nagpur's most regal hotels, this equally austere, incredibly atmospheric restaurant serves the delectable recipes of India's noble class, including rich Amritsari paneer dishes and tempting meat preparations not commonly seen (slow-fired lamb shanks, smoked mutton, Hyderbadi chicken with fenugreek), served on brass plateware. It's one of the city's top spots.

ℹ Information

MTDC Tourist Office (Maharashtra Tourism Development Corporation; ☑0712-2533325; www.maharashtratourism.gov.in; West High Court Rd, Civil Lines; ☉10am-5pm Mon-Sat, closed 2nd & 4th Sat) Staff here can help with getting to national parks near Nagpur. There is also a **booth** (Maharashtra Tourism Development Corporation; www.maharashtratourism.gov.in; Arrivals Hall, Dr Babasaheb Ambedkar International Airport; ☉9am-6pm Mon-Sat) at the airport.

ℹ Getting There & Away

AIR

Dr Babasaheb Ambedkar International Airport (☑0712-2807501; Sonegaon) is 8km southwest of the centre. Domestic airlines, including Air India (www.airindia.in), IndiGo (www.goindigo.in), Jet Airways (www.jetairways.com) and GoAir (www.goair.in), fly direct to Prayagraj (Allahabad), Delhi, Mumbai, Kolkata, Hyderabad, Bengaluru, Indore, Chennai and Pune. Internationally, Qatar and Air Arabia fly to Doha and Sharjah, respectively.

BUS

The main **MSRTC/Ganesh Peth Bus Stand** (☑0712-2726221; Chopkar Rd) is 2km south of the train station. Ordinary buses head for Aurangabad (non-AC/ShivShahi ₹566/840, 17 daily, 4am to 8pm), Pune (non-AC/ShivShahi ₹1250/1370, 1pm, 4pm, 5pm and 6pm), Ramtek (₹60, 1½ hours, every 30 minutes, 6am to 10pm), Jalgaon (non-AC/ShivShahi sleeper ₹410/1210, nine hours, 7pm and 8.45pm) and Wardha (non-AC/ShivShahi ₹150/200, three hours, every 30 minutes, 5am to 4.30pm and 10.15pm).

TADOBA-ANDHARI TIGER RESERVE

The seldom-visited **Tadoba-Andhari Tiger Reserve** (Chandrapur; per entry week/weekend ₹4000/8000; ⊙ 6am-10am & 3-6pm with seasonal variations), 150km south of Nagpur, is one of the best places to see tigers in India. Seeing fewer visitors than most other Indian forest reserves – it gets around 60% fewer visitors than neighbouring parks in Madhya Pradesh – this is a place where you can get up close to wildlife without having to jostle past truckloads of shutter-happy tourists. Rather than restrict access to certain zones of the park like other tiger parks in India, Tadoba-Andhari opted to limit the number of gypsy safaris per day instead (48) but give them free reign throughout the park. The results are excellent for wildlife-sighting opportunities. The park also remains open throughout the year, unlike many in India.

There are 15 legal lodges around Tadoba-Andhari Tiger Reserve, the majority of them in Moharli, ranging from resort homestays to more upscale options. For the best wildlife experience, however, it's tough to beat **Tiger Trails Jungle Lodge** (☑ 0712-6627649, 9763168010; www.tigertrails.in; Khutwanda Gate; s/d incl all meals from ₹9500/15,000; ✱⊛✉) 𝒫, located at Khutwanda with its own private gate.

Most visitors reach the park by private vehicle. The round trip from Nagpur can cost as much as ₹13,000 with a private driver, but an Ola Outstation in a prime sedan runs just ₹10 per kilometre, so ₹2620.

That said, to reach Khutwanda Gate on public transport, catch a bright and early Chandrapur-bound bus from Nagpur to Warora (non-AC/ShivShahi ₹150/200, three hours, every 30 minutes, 5am to 10pm), where you can catch the sole bus (10.45am) for the remaining 42km to Khuthwanda gate (₹70, 1½ hours). The same bus returns the following day at 6am.

For Moharli, stay on the bus to Chandrapur (non-AC/ShvShahi ₹190/250, four hours) and catch a second bus on to Moharli (₹35, one hour, 6am, 8am, 10am, 2.30pm and 5.30pm). Returning to Chandrapur, buses depart Moharli at 7am, 10.30am, 1pm and 5.30pm.

There are government buses to Madhya Pradesh from the **MP Bus Stand** (☑ 0712-2533695; Sitabuldi), 350m south of the train station, to Khawasa (for access to Pench Tiger Reserve; ₹100, 1¾ hours, every 30 minutes, 6am to 10pm) that continue on to Jabalpur (₹300, six hours) but you'd be better off on private buses to the latter. **Saini Travels** (☑ 0712-6654321; www.sainitravels.com; 1149 Central Ave, Prem Bhawan; ⊙ 8am-10pm) heads out at 8.30am and 11pm from Central Rd (AC seat/sleeper from ₹475/520, six hours).

Private buses leave from the Bhole Petrol Pump, 3km southwest of the train station. **Sanjay Travels** (☑ 0712-2528925; www.sanjaytravels.in; near Bhole Petrol Pump, Nagpur-Aurangabad Hwy; ⊙ 7.30am-10pm) books air-con seats and sleepers with the best companies, such as Purple (www.purplebus.in), to Mumbai (AC from ₹1210, 16 to 20 hours, 3pm, 4pm, 4.30pm and 5pm), Pune (AC from ₹1100, 15 hours, 12 daily, 3pm to 10.30pm), Aurangabad (non-AC/AC from ₹600/625, nine to 13 hours, hourly, 3pm to 10pm), Jalgaon (non-AC/AC from ₹720/900, nine hours, hourly, 4.30pm to 9.45pm) and Hyderabad (₹750 to ₹1000, 9pm and 10.30pm). For Jabalpur, **Nandan Bus** (☑ 0712-6641724; www.nandanbus.com;

Central Rd, Gitanjali Cinema Sq) goes daily at 2.30pm, 6pm, 6.30pm, 9.30pm and 11pm (non-AC/AC from ₹320/551, six to eight hours) from Central Ave.

TRAIN

From Mumbai's CST railway station, the CSMT NGP Duronto runs daily to **Nagpur Junction** (NGP; Sitabuldi) (sleeper/2AC ₹705/2785, 11 hours, 8.15pm). From Nagpur it departs at 8.40pm and arrives at 8.05am the following morning. Heading north to Kolkata is the Gitanjali Express (sleeper/2AC ₹530/2020, 17½ hours, 7pm). Several expresses bound for Delhi and Mumbai stop at Jalgaon (sleeper/2AC ₹280/1015, eight hours) for the Ajanta Caves.

Around Nagpur

Ramtek

About 40km northeast of Nagpur, Ramtek is believed to be the place where Lord Rama, of the epic Ramayana, spent some time during his exile with his wife, Sita, and brother Lakshmana. The place is marked by a cluster of 10 or so ancient **temples** (⊙ 6am-9pm), which sit atop the Hill of Rama and have their own population of resident langur monkeys.

Ramtek is beginning to fancy itself as a burgeoning adventure sports destination and Khindsi Lake is indeed a beautiful spot for kayaking, paragliding or hot-air ballooning. Mansar, 7km west of Ramtek, is an important archaeological site believed to be the 5th-century remains of Pravarapura, the capital ruled by the Vakataka King Pravarasena II.

Buses run between Ramtek and the Ganesh Peth Bus Stand (p791) in Nagpur (₹60, 1½ hours, every 30 minutes, 6am to 9pm).

Sevagram

About 85km from Nagpur, Sevagram (Village of Service) was chosen by Mahatma Gandhi as his base during the Indian Independence Movement. Throughout the freedom struggle, the village played host to several nationalist leaders, who would regularly come to visit the Mahatma at his **Sevagram Ashram** (☑ 07152-284754; www.gandhiashramsevagram. org; ☉ 6am-5.30pm). The overseers of this peaceful ashram, which is built on 40 hectares of farmland, have carefully restored the original huts where Gandhi lived and worked and which now house some of his personal effects. There is a small **museum** (Sevagram Ashram; ☉ 10am-6pm) as well.

In nearby Paunar village, just 3km from Sevagram, you'll find **Brahma Vidya Mandir** (☑ 07152-288388; Paunar; dm incl meals ₹250; ☉ 6am-noon & 2-7pm) founded by nationalist and Gandhi disciple Vinoba Bhave and run almost entirely by women. An experience here is steeped in *swarajya* (self-sufficiency) and is operated on a social system of consensus, with no central management.

Sevagram can be reached by taking a bus from Nagpur to Wardha (non-AC/AC ₹125/1100, three hours, every 30 minutes, 4.30am to 10.15pm), where you'll need to switch to a Sevagram-bound bus (₹10, 10 minutes), which drops you at Medical Sq, 1km from the ashram; or catch a shared autorickshaw (₹20).

SOUTHERN MAHARASHTRA

Konkan Coast

A little-developed shoreline running south from Mumbai all the way to Goa, this picturesque strip of coast is peppered with picture-postcard beaches, fishing villages and magnificent ruined forts. Travelling through this tropical backwater can be sheer bliss, whether you're off to dabble in the sands with Mumbaikars in Ganpatipule, visiting the stunning Janjira Fort at Murud-Janjira or heading into the blue at Malvan, the last beach town of significance before the sands give way to Goa.

Murud-Janjira
☑ 02144

The sleepy fishing hamlet of Murud-Janjira – 165km from Mumbai – should be on any itinerary of the Konkan Coast. The relaxed pace of life, fresh seafood, stupendous offshore Janjira Fort (and the chance to feel the warm surf rush past your feet) make the trip here well worthwhile.

Murud-Janjira's beach is fun for a run or game of cricket with locals and it comes alive with street stalls and beach tomfoolery nightly. Alternatively, you could peer through the gates of the off-limits Ahmedganj Palace, estate of the Siddi Nawab of Murud, or scramble around the decaying mosque and tombs on the south side of town.

⊙ Sights

★ **Janjira Fort**   FORT
(Rajpuri; ☉ 7am-dusk) **FREE** The commanding, brooding fortress of Janjira, built on an island 500m offshore, is the most magnificent of the string of forts that line the Konkan coastline. This citadel was completed in 1571 by the Siddis, descendants of slaves from the Horn of Africa, and was the capital of a princely state.

Over the centuries Siddi alignment with Mughals provoked conflict with local kings, including Shivaji and his son Sambhaji, who attempted to scale the walls and tunnel to it, respectively. However, no outsider (including British, French and Portuguese colonists) ever made it past the fort's 12m-high granite walls which, when seen during high tide, seem to rise straight from the sea. Unconquered through history, the fort is finally falling to forces of nature as its mighty walls slowly crumble and wilderness reclaims its innards.

Still, there's a lot to see today, including the remarkable close-fitting stonework that's protected the citadel against centuries of attack by storms, colonists and gunpowder. You approach the fort via a brooding grey-stone gateway and can then explore its ramparts (complete with giant cannons) and 19 bastions, large parts of which are intact. Its inner keep, palaces and mosque are in ruins, though the fort's huge twin reservoirs remain. As many of the surviving walls and structures are in poor shape, tread carefully while you explore the site, which is unfortunately littered with rubbish.

The only way to reach Janjira is by boat (₹61 return, 20 minutes) from Rajpuri port. Boats depart with a minimum 20 people from 9am to 5pm Saturday to Thursday and 9am to noon and 2pm to 5pm Friday, and allow you 45 minutes to explore the fort. To get to Rajpuri from Murud-Janjira, take an autorickshaw (₹60 to ₹100) or hire a bicycle (warning: it involves quite an uphill slog).

🛏 Sleeping & Eating

Sea Shell Resort
HOTEL $$
(☑ 9833667985; www.seashellmurud.com; Darbar Rd; d with/without AC from ₹3190/2020; ❄ ⊛) Set back from the coastal road across from the improvised beach cricket grounds, this cheery place has glistening, spacious and breezy sea-facing rooms with hot-water bathrooms (including rain-style showers and thick bath towels). There's a tiny pool as well. The owner's son, Zaid, works weekends and is incredibly friendly and helpful. Wi-fi frustratingly remains lobby only.

Golden Swan Beach Resort
HOTEL $$$
(☑ 9225591131; www.goldenswan.com; Darbar Rd; d incl breakfast from ₹5190; ❄ 🐾) Cute seafront cottages and rear rooms, soundtracked by a cacophony of resident swans, occupy fine beach real estate and afford distant views of Ahmedganj Palace and Kasa Fort. Some rooms feature loft beds and small patios ideal for sea-view beers, and all feature newly tiled bathrooms. A charming old bungalow houses rooms nearby, too. Rates increase on weekends.

Hotel Vinayak
SEAFOOD $$
(Darbar Rd; mains ₹75-450; ⊙ 7am-10pm) Its sea-facing terrace is the perfect place to tuck into a delicious and fiery Konkani thali (₹110 to ₹450), with fish curry, *tawa* (hotplate) fish fry, *sol kadhi* (pink-coloured, slightly sour digestive made from coconut milk and kokum fruit) and more. Fresh fish, prawn dishes and good breakfasts are also available.

ℹ Getting There & Around

Ferries and catamarans (₹125 to ₹165) from the Gateway of India in Mumbai cruise to Mandwa pier between 8.15am and 8.15pm. The ticket includes a free shuttle bus to Alibag (30 minutes). Rickety local buses from Alibag head down the coast to Murud-Janjira (₹70, two hours, every 30 minutes to two hours). Alternatively, eight buses depart Mumbai Central bus stand between 6am and 1am and take almost six hours to reach Murud-Janjira (non-AC from ₹220). There are five buses a day to Pune from Murud-Janjira (non-AC from ₹180, seven hours, 7am, 8.45am, 9am, 2.15pm and 4pm).

In the other direction, buses depart Murud-Janjira's **bus stand** (☑ 02144-274044; Revdanda Murud Rd) for Alibag (₹70, two hours, every two hours, 5am to 11pm) – those at 6.30am, 10am, noon, 1pm and 7.30pm are express buses (1½ hours). Bear in mind if you are going to south Mumbai, the bus/ferry combo is the better option; for the western suburbs, airport etc, the bus is better.

The nearest railhead is at Roha, two hours away and poorly connected; and trying to reach Murud from the south (say, Ganpatipule) is equally frustrating (it can be done with a vicious combination of buses and ferries but it's not worth the effort – better to go from Mumbai!).

Bicycles (per hour ₹90) and cars (from ₹14 per kilometre) can be hired at the Golden Swan Beach Resort (p794).

Raigad Fort

Alone on a high and remote hilltop, 24km off Hwy 66, the enthralling **Raigad Fort** (Raigad; Indian/foreigner ₹25/300; ⊙ 6am-7pm) served as Shivaji's capital from 1648 until his death in 1680. The fort was later sacked by the British and some colonial structures added, but monuments such as the royal court, plinths of royal chambers, the main marketplace and Shivaji's tomb still remain – it's worth an excursion.

You can hike a crazy 1475 steps to the top, but for a more 'levitating' experience, take the vertigo-inducing **ropeway** (www.raigad ropeway.com; Lower Station, Hirkaniwadi, Mahad; return ₹300; ⊙ 8am-6pm) – actually a cable car – which climbs up the cliff and offers a bird's-eye view of the deep gorges below. Be warned this is a very popular attraction with domestic tourists and you may have to wait up to an hour for a ride during holiday times. Guides (₹400) are available within the fort complex.

ℹ Getting There & Away

Autorickshaws shuttle up to the ropeway from the town of Mahad on Hwy 66 (look out for the 'Raigad Ropeway' sign) for ₹800 return including wait time. Mahad is 158km south of Mumbai and 88km from Murud-Janjira. The Mahad–Raigad road

ALL ABOARD THE KONKAN RAILWAY!

One in a long list of storied Indian train rides, the Konkan Railway hugs the southwest Indian coast along a 738km journey between Maharashtra, Goa and Karnataka. The line, which has hosted passenger trains since 1998, is considered the biggest and most expansive infrastructure project the country has undertaken (and completed) since Independence. So much so, the very idea was dismissed outright in the early 20th century by the British, who deemed the whole adventure an impossible task of construction and engineering, leaving it to the locals to finish the job over the course of several decades (10 of whom lost their lives in the disaster-plagued process).

Today, the ridiculously scenic route, chock-full of picturesque paddy fields, rolling green hills, craggy mountaintops, storybook sea views and numerous tunnels, waterfalls, viaducts and jungly landscapes, is made possible by 92 tunnels and 2000 bridges, including Panval Viaduct, India's highest (and Asia's third) viaduct at 64m tall.

Most travellers enjoy the Konkan ride on the Mandovi Express from Mumbai to Goa, but train enthusiasts can take in the whole shebang on the Mangalore Express, a 14-hour journey from Mumbai to Mangalore.

is paved and in good condition. Car and drivers charge from non-AC/AC ₹8/10 per km for a day trip (prices go up depending on type of car) here from Murud-Janjira. There is one AC bus from Mahad to Mahabaleshwar (₹110, two hours, 7am).

Ganpatipule

📞 02357

The tiny beach resort of Ganpatipule has been luring a steady stream of beach lovers over the years with its warm waters and wonderful stretches of sand. Located about 375km from Mumbai, it's a village that snoozes through much of the year, except during holidays such as Diwali or Ganesh Chaturthi. These are times when hordes of boisterous tourists turn up to visit the seaside **Shree Ganpatipule Mandir** (www.ganpatipule.co.in; Ganpatipule Beach; ⊙ 6am-9pm), which houses a monolithic Ganesh (painted a bright orange). For more solitude, the sands just south of the main beach (such as Neware Beach) are both more spectacular than Ganpatipule and less crowded – have an autorickshaw take you there.

To reach Ganpatipule, you'll pass through the transport hub of Ratnagiri, home to the crumbling **Thibaw Palace** (Thibaw Palace Rd, Ratnagiri; adult/child ₹3/1; ⊙ 10am-5pm Tue-Sun) FREE, where the last Burmese king, Thibaw, was interned by the British.

🛏 Sleeping & Eating

MTDC Resort   HOTEL **$$**
(📞 02357-235248; www.maharashtratourism.gov.in; d with/without AC from ₹2750/2240; ❄ 🤖) Spread over prime beachfront, this huge operation is something of a holiday camp for Mumbaikar families. Its concrete rooms and cottages would benefit from a little updating, but all have magnificent full-frontal ocean views. It also packs in a decent restaurant that serves cold beer.

⭐ **Bhau Joshi Bhojanalay**   MAHARASHTRIAN **$**
(mains ₹55-135; ⊙ 11.30am-3pm & 7.30-10.30pm) It's not the easiest place to eat (no English sign, nearly no English spoken and no napkins – so bring some baby wipes), but the delicious Maharashtrian food in this clean, orderly restaurant inland from the beach makes up for the struggles. Try the fantastic *baingan masala* (eggplant curry; ₹90). Jain and Punjabi dishes also on offer.

ℹ Getting There & Away

From the small, unstaffed bus stand, there is one ordinary government bus to Pune daily (₹470, 8¼ hours, 6.45am). Regular buses head to Ratnagiri (₹33, 1¼ hours, every 30 minutes, 10am to 8pm). From there, you can pick up buses for destinations further afield such as Pune (non-AC/AC from ₹450/610, 9¼ hours, 6am, 7.45am, 11am, 7.15pm, 9.30pm and 10pm), Mumbai (non-AC/AC from ₹440/590, nine hours, 9.30am, 9pm and 10pm) and Kolhapur (non-AC/AC from ₹172/230, four hours, nine daily, 5.30am to 10.30pm).

There are also private buses to Mumbai (Volvo non-AC seat/AC sleeper from ₹600/900, 10 hours, 6.30pm, 7pm and 7.45pm) and Pune (Volvo AC sleeper from ₹800, nine hours, 6.45pm and 7pm).

From Ratnagiri's old bus stand, buses leave for Goa (semideluxe ₹380, six hours, 5.30am) and Kolhapur (non-AC/AC from ₹172/255, four hours, every 30 minutes, 5.30am to 7.30pm).

Ratnagiri train station is on the Konkan Railway line. From Ratnagiri, the Mandovi Express goes daily to Mumbai (2nd class/sleeper/2AC ₹155/260/1000, 7¾ hours, 2.05pm). The return train heading for Goa (₹130/215/830, 5½ hours) is at 1.15pm.

Malvan

☑ 02365

A government tourism promo compares the emerging Malvan region to Tahiti, which is a tad ambitious, but it does have near-white sands, sparkling seas and jungle-fringed backwaters. Offshore there are coral reefs, sea caves and vibrant marine life that attracts divers, along with a world-class diving school.

Malvan town is one of the prettiest on the Konkan Coast. It's a mellow, bike-friendly place with a good stock of old wooden buildings, a busy little harbour and bazaar and a slow, tropical pace of life. Stretching directly south of the centre is lovely Tarkali Beach, home to many hotels and guesthouses.

◉ Sights & Activities

Tarkali Beach BEACH

A golden arc south of Malvan, this crescent-shaped sandy beach is a vision of tropical India, fringed by coconut palms and casuarina trees, plus the odd cow and camel. At dusk (between October and February) fisherfolk work together to haul in huge, kilometre-long nets that are impressively packed with thousands of *bangda* (mackerel), *tarli* (sardines), pomfret and/or *zinga* (prawns).

A rickshaw here from Malvan town is ₹150.

Sindhudurg Fort FORT

(₹5; ⊙ 8am-5.30pm) Built by Shivaji and dating from 1664, this monstrous fort lies on an off-shore island and can be reached by frequent ferries (adult/child ₹90/50, 8am to 5.30pm), which depart with a minimum 20 people from Malvan's harbour. It's not as impressive as Janjira up the coast, and today lies mostly in ruins, but it remains a powerful presence. You can explore its ramparts and the coastal views are impressive. Boat operators allow you one hour on the island.

★ IISDA DIVING

(Indian Institute of Scuba Diving & Aquatic Sports; ☑ 02365-248790; www.maharashtratourism.gov. in; Tarkali Beach; 1-/2-tank dive ₹4130/8260, PADI Open Water course ₹25,960; ⊙ 9am-6pm) This state-of-the-art PADI 5-Star diving centre, an initiative of Maharashtra Tourism, is India's finest, run by marine biologist and diving pro Dr Sarang Kulkarni. It offers professional instruction, a 20m-long pool for training, air-conditioned classrooms and comfortable sleeping quarters for students. IISDA is also a marine conservation centre. It's located 7km south of Malvan.

🛏 Sleeping & Eating

Vicky's Guest House GUESTHOUSE $

(☑ 9823423046; vickyfernandes11@gmail.com; near Heravi Batti, Dandi Beach; d with/without AC from ₹1500/1000; ❄ 🛜) Down a quiet residential lane surrounded by lush palms 400m from Dandi Beach and steps form Malvan town, cool and mellow Vicky has five (more on the way) purpose-built rooms that don't look like much on arrival but are actually spacious, well equipped and extremely comfortable for the price. Vicky himself is super helpful and hospitable.

Visava Beach Resort RESORT $$

(☑ 9423304304; www.visavaresorttarkarli.com; Tarkali Beach; d ₹2500-3500; ❄ 🛜) It's distinctly rustic, but this laid-back, family-run resort will charm a certain type of beach bum. The 11 rooms (12 more to come) aren't flashy but offer hot water, modern touches and idyllic porches with seating areas and swinging chairs. The sandy grounds are strewn with vegetation and coconut palms and it sits on a quieter, prettier stretch of Tarkali.

★ Hotel Chaitanya KONKAN $$

(502 Dr Vallabh Marg; thalis ₹100-220, mains ₹70-450; ⊙ 11am-11pm) On Malvan's main drag, this great, family-run place specialises in Konkan cuisine including *bangda tikhale* (fish in thick coconut sauce), prawns *malvani* and very flavoursome crab masala; portions won't thrill you, but it's first-rate seafood. Its vegetarian dishes are also excellent. It's always packed with locals and has an air-con section.

ⓘ Getting There & Away

The closest **train station** (KUDL; Railway Station Rd) is Kudal, 38km away. Frequent buses (₹35, one hour, 4.50am to 7.45pm) cover the route from **Malvan Bus Stand** (☑ 02365-252034; Shri Babi Hadkar Marg); alternatively, an autorickshaw is about ₹600. Malvan has ordinary buses to Kolhapur (non-AC from ₹210, five hours, 7am, 2.15pm and 3.15pm), Mumbai (AC ₹840, 12 hours, 8am), Panaji (AC from ₹150, four hours, 6.45am, 7.45am, 2.30pm and 3.15pm) and Ratnagiri (non-AC from ₹225, five hours, 6am, 7.45am and 11.15am). Slightly quicker to Goa are the blue-and-white Kadamba Goan government buses (₹200 to ₹250, 3½ hours, 7.45am, 2.15pm and 3pm) to Panaji, Margao and Vasco.

MALVAN MARINE NATIONAL PARK

The shoreline around Malvan is incredibly diverse, with rich wetlands, sandy and rocky beaches, mangroves and backwaters. But underwater it's arguably even more compelling, with coral patches and caves that shelter abundant marine life and extensive forests of *sargassum* seaweed that acts as a nursery for juvenile fish. Rocky offshore islands attract schools of snapper and large grouper, butterfly fish, yellow-striped fusiliers, manta and sting rays and lobster. Pods of dolphins are regularly seen between October to May and the world's largest fish, the whale shark, even puts in an appearance every now and then.

Presently only a small section is protected as the Malvan Marine Sanctuary, which encompasses the Sindhudurg Fort; yet such is its rich diversity that marine biologists, including the director of the Indian Institute of Scuba Diving & Aquatic Sports (IISDA), Dr Sarang Kulkarni, feel it's essential that the boundaries are extended. A submerged plateau, the Angria Bank, exists 72 nautical miles off Malvan and clocks in at 40km long and 20km wide, with healthy coral and an abundance of sealife. It has been described as India's Great Barrier Reef. The Government of Maharashtra through IISDA has big plans to create world-class infrastructure to provide day trips and live-aboard excursions to Angria.

Plans are also in place for India's first tourism venture by submarine. Based in Vengurla, 51km north of Malvan, it is expected to offer underwater tours of the sanctuary by the end of 2019.

There are private bus agents on Dr Vallabh Marg selling more comfortable seats on Volvo buses to Mumbai and Pune, but these depart 33km inland from Malvan in Kasal and transport is not provided.

Malvan is only 80km from northern Goa; private drivers charge ₹3000 (non-AC) to ₹3500 (AC) for the two-hour trip. Heading north, it's ₹3500 to Ratnagiri and ₹4500 to Ganpatipule.

The region's new airport, Sindhudurg Chipi Airport, 16km southeast of Malvan at Parule-Chipi, was about to open at the time of research. Sitting just 62km northwest of Aswem Beach, it's also useful for Northern Goa.

Matheran

☎ 02148 / POP 5750 / ELEV 803M

Matheran, literally 'Jungle Above', is a tiny patch of peace and quiet capping a craggy Sahyadri summit within spitting distance of Mumbai's heat and grime. Endowed with shady forests criss-crossed with foot trails and breathtaking lookouts, it still retains an elegance and colonial-era ambience, though creeping commercialism and illegal construction are marring its appeal (it could do without the Ferris wheel and wax museum, for example).

In the past, getting to Matheran was really half the fun. While speedier options were available by road, nothing beat arriving in town on the narrow-gauge toy train that chugged up to the heart of the settlement. However, derailment woes caused the suspension of the train in 2016, and it now mainly runs for just a 2km-stretch from Aman Lodge.

Motor vehicles are banned within Matheran, making it an ideal place to give your ears and lungs a rest and your feet some exercise.

◉ Sights & Activities

You can walk along shady forest paths to most of Matheran's viewpoints in a matter of hours; it's a place well suited to stress-free ambling. To catch the sunrise, head to Panorama Point, while Porcupine Point (also known as Sunset Point) is the most popular (read: packed) as the sun drops. Louisa Point and Little Chouk Point also have stunning views of the Sahyadris.

If you're here on a weekend or public holiday you might want to avoid the most crowded section around Echo Point, Charlotte Lake and Honeymoon Point, which get rammed with day trippers.

You can reach the valley below One Tree Hill down the path known as Shivaji's Ladder, supposedly trod upon by the Maratha leader himself.

⌂ Sleeping & Eating

Hope Hall Hotel   HOTEL $
(☎ 7066715973; www.hopehallmatheran.com; MG Rd; d from ₹1200) Run by a very hospitable family, this long-running place has been hosting happy travellers for years (though slow internet often derails their ability to register – and therefore accept – foreigners); the house dates back to 1875. Spacious rooms

with high ceilings and arty touches are in two blocks at the rear of the leafy garden. Good breakfasts and drinks are available.

MTDC Resort LODGE $$
(☑ 02148-230277; www.maharashtratourism.gov.in; d ₹1680, with AC from ₹2576; ❄ 🛜) This government-run place offers functional, economy rooms, disappointing family rooms and very attractive modern air-conditioned rooms in the Shruti Heritage Villa (₹3546). The downside is it's located next to the Dasturi car park, so you're away from the midtown action. There's a restaurant on-site.

★ Dune Barr House HERITAGE HOTEL $$$
(Verandah in the Forest; ☑ 9152519989; www.dunewellnessgroup.com; Barr House; d incl breakfast ₹6000-8000; 🛜) This deliciously preserved 150-year-old bungalow exudes undiluted nostalgia, with quaintly luxurious rooms. Reminisce about bygone times in the company of ornate candelabras, oriental rugs, antique teak furniture, Victorian canvases and grandfather clocks. The verandah has a lovely aspect over Matheran's wooded hillsides.

Shabbir Bhai INDIAN $
(Merry Rd; mains ₹130-290; ⏱ 9am-10.30pm) Known locally as the 'Byrianiwala', this funky joint has a full North Indian menu, but it's all about the spicy biryanis: spiced steamed rice with chicken, mutton and veg. To find it, take the footpath uphill beside the Jama Masjid on MG Rd and follow your nose.

❶ Information

Entry to Matheran costs ₹50 (₹25 for children), which you pay at the Dasturi car park.

❶ Getting There & Away

TAXI

Shared taxis (Neral Matheran Rd; ₹80) run from just outside the western entrance of Neral train station to Matheran's **Dasturi car park** (Neral-Matheran Rd; 30 minutes). Horses (₹350 to all hotels except Verandah in the Forest, which is ₹550) and hand-pulled rickshaws (₹700) wait here to whisk you (relatively speaking) to Matheran's main bazaar. The horse-wallahs are unionised and their prices are officially posted, but do not agree on a price until you have seen the board, which is located 50m *after* the Matheran ticket counter (hotel fares bottom-right in smaller font than the rest of the board). You can also walk this stretch (a somewhat inclined 2km) and your luggage can be hauled for around ₹250.

TRAIN

Matheran's toy train was suspended in 2016 after two derailments, but service was partially reinstated in early 2018. It now chugs between Matheran and **Neral Junction** (Ratnadeep Colony, Neral; 1st/2nd class ₹300/75) once daily, departing Neral at 6.40am, returning at 3.40pm (2.20pm on Mondays). Throughout the rest of the day, it merely ambles the 2km between Aman Lodge Station, located a few metres beyond Dasturi car park, and Matheran Station (1st/2nd class ₹300/45), serving little purpose – though it is helpful if you are lugging heavy bags. The first train departs at 9.02am (8.40am on weekends), and subsequent trains depart every 45 minutes to an hour until 3.05pm (6.05pm on weekends). From Matheran, departures start at 9.30am (8.15am on weekends) and run until 2.40pm (5.40pm on weekends).

From Mumbai's CST station there are two daily express trains stopping at Neral Junction at 7am and 8.40am, but they cannot be booked online as Neral and Mumbai are considered the same metropolitan area by IRCTC. You must book a further destination (Lonavla, for example; 2nd class/chair ₹75/260) and then hop down at Neral (1½ hours). Alternatively, numerous local trains ply the route between Mumbai CST and Dadar.

Lonavla

☑ 02114 / POP 57,400 / ELEV 625M

Lonavla is a raucous resort town about 106km southeast of Mumbai. Its main drag consists almost exclusively of garishly lit shops flogging *chikki*, the rock-hard, brittle sweet made in the area, and you get fun-for-the-whole-family kind of stuff like wax museums, go-karts and India's largest water park. But there are some pleasant side streets, serene residential areas and destination yoga places along with the pastoral surrounding countryside that means you can choose your own path here.

The main reason you'd want to come here is to visit the nearby Karla and Bhaja caves which, after those at Ellora and Ajanta, are the best in Maharashtra.

Hotels, restaurants and the main road to the caves lie north of the train station. Most of the Lonavla township and its markets are located south of the station.

❍ Sights & Activities

★ Lion Point VIEWPOINT
(Lonavla-Aamby Valley Rd, Hudco Colony; ⏱ 24hr) This wildly panoramic viewpoint 12km south of Lonavla is one of the resort town's best non-kitschy sights. On a clear day, small

waterfalls are visible among the lush green conical hills and the deep, cinematic valley, along with views across the Western Ghats. Locals flock here, many of whom climb over the railings for on-the-edge selfies (not recommended) when they are not munching on roasted corn and onion fritters from lines of vendors. Sunset and sunrise are, unsurprisingly, popular. Rickshaws charge ₹600 return from Lonavla with a bit of waiting to enjoy the view.

Nirvana Adventures
PARAGLIDING

(☑ 022-26053724; www.flynirvana.com; 2-day learner course per person incl full board ₹12,000, tandem flights from ₹2500) Mumbai-based Nirvana Adventures offers paragliding courses and short tandem flights from its base camp in a charming rural setting near the town of Kamshet, 25km from Lonavla.

You'll need to hire your own transport to reach the base camp.

Kaivalyadhama Yoga Institute & Research Center
YOGA

(☑ 8551092986, 02114-273039; www.kdham.com; Kaivalyadhama Ashram Kaivalyadhama; 40-day course incl full board US$1200) This progressive yoga centre is located in neatly kept grounds about 2km from Lonavla, en route to the Karla and Bhaja caves. Founded in 1924 by Swami Kuvalayananda, it combines yoga courses with naturopathic therapies. Courses cover full board, yoga classes, activities and lectures.

🛏 Sleeping

⭐ Ferreira Resort
HOTEL $$

(☑ 02114-272689; www.ferreiraresort.in; DT Shahani Rd; s/d Mon-Thu ₹1680/2015, Fri-Sun ₹2015/2465, with AC Mon-Thu ₹1790/2240, Fri-Sun ₹2240/2465; ❄ 🛜) It's certainly not a resort, but it is something of a rarity in Lonavla: a well-priced, family-run place in a quiet residential location that's close to the train station. Ten of the 15 clean but worn air-con rooms have a balcony and there's a little garden as well as room service.

⭐ The Machan
BOUTIQUE HOTEL $$$

(☑ 7666622426; www.themachan.com; Private Rd, Atvan; tree houses Mon-Thu ₹11,520-38,400, Fri-Sun ₹44,800; ❄ 🛜 🏊) 🌿 This astonishing choice hidden away in forested mountains 16km south of Lonavla buries the competition for the state's best hotel. The 28 pine and red meranti wood tree houses rising 10 to 13m above the forest come in all shapes and sizes, but every one is a postcard-perfect getaway from which you will probably need to be dragged at checkout.

The two-bedroom Starlight Villas are the stuff dreams are made of, with a fully retractable roof for stargazing, Victorian deep soaking bathtubs and hammocks on the patio with mountain views – not to mention a sizeable private pool in the forest and two bedrooms connected by a spiral staircase that's perfect for two couples (recycled woods and solar power where possible). Wonderful, home-style meals are taken outdoors and there's yoga, nature walks, bonfires and a spa. You are in the thick of it here with the scorpions, snakes and adorable Malabar giant squirrels. Book well in advance.

🍴 Eating & Drinking

⭐ Kinara Dhaba Village
NORTH INDIAN, CHINESE $$$

(www.thekinaravillage.com; Vaksai Naka, Old Mumbai-Pune Hwy; mains ₹310-600; ⊙ 11am-11.30pm; 🅿) A bit of a *dhaba* Disneyland, but therein lies the fun. About 5km east of Lonavla, near Karla and Bhaja caves, is this fun-for-all restaurant/entertainment venue. Dine under traditional *shamiana* huts amid festival lighting, camel and donkey rides, *jalebi* (deep-fried batter dunked in sugar syrup) carts, fish pedicure pools and Rajasthani astrologers. Live *ghazal* (Urdu love songs) nightly (7pm).

German Bakery Wunderbar
CAFE

(Mumbai-Pune Rd, opposite Kumar Resort; ⊙ 7am-11pm) A youngish and hip crowd flocks to this Pune transplant for cocktails (₹190 to ₹310) and pitchers of Bira draught beer (₹630), as well as an expanded cafe menu (mains ₹220 to ₹450), all taken on a large, semi-open patio with wrought-iron deck furniture and milk-can bar stools..

ℹ Getting There & Away

Neeta Tours & Travels (☑ 8652222640; www.neetabus.in; Valvan Dam, Old Mumbai Pune Hwy) offers numerous luxury air-con buses day and night to Mumbai (from ₹400, two hours, hourly, 7am to 1am) and Pune (from ₹250, two hours, hourly, 8.15am to 11.30pm) to its fancy station 3km northeast of the train station at Hotel Neeta's Inn.

All express trains from Mumbai's CST to Pune stop at **Lonavla** (LNL; Siddharth Nagar) (2nd class ₹65 to ₹90, chair ₹260 to ₹305, 2½ to three hours).

MAHARASHTRA LONAVLA

KARLA & BHAJA CAVES

Karla Caves (Indian/foreigner ₹30/300, video ₹25; ⏱9am-5pm) Karla Cave, the largest early *chaitya* (Buddhist temple) in India, is reached by a 20-minute climb from a mini bazaar at the base of a hill. Completed in 80 BC, the *chaitya* is around 40m long and 15m high and sports a vaulted interior and intricately executed sculptures of Buddha, human and animal figures.

Bhaja Caves (Bhaja Caves Rd; Indian/foreigner ₹30/300, video ₹25; ⏱9am-5.30pm) On the other side of the expressway from Karla Caves in a lush setting 3km off the main road, Bhaja Caves is the greener and quieter of the region's caves. Thought to date from around 200 BC, 10 of the 18 caves here are *viharas* (Buddhist monasteries), while Cave 12 is an open *chaitya* containing a simple dagoba.

Karla is 11km east of Lonavla, and Bhaja 9km. Both can be visited on a local bus to the access point, from where it's about a 6km return walk on each side to the two sites – but that would be exhausting and hot. Autorickshaws charge around ₹1200 (depending on the day of the week) from Lonavla for the tour, including waiting time, but many refuse to go. Local cars go for ₹1200 to ₹1500 depending on your negotiation skills.

Pune

📞020 / POP 5.14 MILLION / ELEV 535M

A thriving, vibrant metropolis, Pune is a centre of academia and business that epitomises 'New India' with its baffling mix of capitalism and spiritualism (ancient and modern). It's also globally famous, or notorious, for an ashram, the Osho International Meditation Resort (p801), founded by the late guru Bhagwan Shree Rajneesh.

Pune was initially given pride of place by Shivaji and the ruling Peshwas, who made it their capital. The British took the city in 1817 and, thanks to its cool and dry climate, soon made it the Bombay Presidency's monsoon capital. Globalisation knocked on Pune's doors in the 1990s, following which it went in for an image overhaul. However, some colonial-era charm was retained in a few old buildings and residential areas, bringing about a pleasant coexistence of the old and new, which (despite the pollution and hectic traffic) makes Pune a worthwhile place to explore.

⊙ Sights

★Raja Dinkar Kelkar Museum
MUSEUM
(www.facebook.com/rajakelkarmuseum; 1377/78 Kamal Kunj, Bajirao Rd, Shukrawar Peth; Indian/foreigner ₹50/200, mobile/camera ₹100/200; ⏱10am-6pm) An oddball of a museum that's one of Pune's true delights, housing only a fraction of the 20,000-odd objects of Indian daily life painstakingly collected by Dinkar Kelkar (who died in 1990). The quirky pan-Indian collection includes hundreds of hookah pipes, writing instruments, lamps, textiles, toys, entire doors and windows, kitchen utensils, furniture, puppets, ivory playing cards and betel-nut cutters.

★Joshi's Museum of Miniature Railway
MUSEUM
(www.minirailways.com; 17/1 B/2 GA Kulkarni Rd, Kothrud; ₹90, minimum 4 people for 25min show; ⏱9am-5pm Mon-Wed & Fri, 9.30am-1pm Thu, 9am-4pm Sat, 5-8pm Sat & Sun) Inside the small Soudamini Instruments factory in eastern Pune is what is claimed to be India's only miniature city, the lifelong obsession of model train enthusiast Bhau Joshi. In short, it's one of the world's great model train layouts, a detailed, fully functional and passionate display of mechanical and engineering wow.

Aga Khan Palace
PALACE
(Pune Nagar Rd, Kalyani Nagar; Indian/foreigner ₹25/300; ⏱9am-5.30pm) The grand Aga Khan Palace is set in a peaceful wooded 6.5-hectare plot northeast of the centre. Built in 1892 by Sultan Aga Khan III, this graceful building was where Mahatma Gandhi and other prominent nationalist leaders were interned by the British following Gandhi's Quit India campaign in 1942.

The main palace now houses the **Gandhi National Memorial** (www.mkgandhi.org/museum/pune.htm; Aga Khan Palace, Pune Nagar Rd, Kalyani Nagar; ⏱9am-5.30pm) where you can peek into the room where the Mahatma used to stay. Photos and paintings exhibit moments in his extraordinary life. Both Kasturba Gandhi, the Mahatma's wife, and Mahadeobhai Desai, his secretary for 35 years, died here in confinement. You'll find their shrines (containing their ashes) in a quiet garden to the rear.

Osho Teerth Gardens
GARDENS

(www.osho.com; DH Dhunjibhoy Rd, Koregaon Park; ⊗6-9am & 3-6pm) The 5-hectare Osho Teerth Gardens are a verdant escape from urban living with giant bamboo, jogging trails, a gurgling brook and smooching couples. You don't have to be an Osho member – they're accessible to all.

Shaniwar Wada
FORT

(Shivaji Rd; Indian/foreigner ₹25/300; ⊗9am-5.30pm) The remains of this fortressed palace of the Peshwa rulers are located in the old part of the city. Built in 1732, Shaniwar Wada was destroyed by a fire in 1828, but the massive walls and ramparts remain, as does a mighty fortified gateway.

On Wednesday to Monday evenings there's a 40-minute sound-and-light show at 7pm (Marathi) and 8pm (Hindi), but not in English.

🏃 Activities

Osho International Meditation Resort
MEDITATION

(☑020-66019999; www.osho.com; 17 Koregaon Park) Indelibly linked with Pune's identity, this iconic ashram-resort, located in a leafy, upscale northern suburb, has been drawing thousands of *sanyasins* (seekers) since the death of Osho in 1990. With its swimming pool, sauna and spa, 'zennis' and boutique guesthouse, it is, to some, the ultimate place to indulge in some luxe meditation.

🛏️ Sleeping

Bombay Backpackers
HOSTEL $

(☑7028826713; www.bombaybackpackers.com; 40B, Lane C, Ragvilas Society, Koregaon Park; dm with/without AC ₹600/500, d ₹2200, all incl breakfast; ❄️🛜) In a quiet residential location in Koregaon Park, Pune's edition of Bombay Backpackers features six- and 10-bed dorms, a basement common area and kitchen, and somewhat indifferent staff. The Osho-themed private rooms are quite spacious, with bamboo tables and chairs on hardwood floors, and are good value for the city.

Hotel Surya Villa
HOTEL $

(☑020-26124501; www.hotelsuryavilla.com; 294/1 German Bakery Ln, Koregaon Park; d with/without AC from ₹2240/1680; ❄️🛜) The Surya's functional, tiled rooms are well kept and generously proportioned and, though a little spartan, they do have bathrooms with hot water, plus wi-fi and cable TV. It enjoys a good location on a quiet street in Koregaon Park, close to popular cafes.

The Samrat Hotel
HOTEL $$

(☑020-26137964; www.thesamrathotel.com; 17 Wilson Garden; s/d incl breakfast from ₹2020/2470, with AC from ₹2800/3420; ❄️🛜) It's not quite as grand as its fancy reception area would indicate, but with a central location just a few steps from the train station and spacious, well-maintained rooms, the 49-room Samrat represents good value. The staff are courteous and eager to please.

Hotel Lotus
HOTEL $$

(☑020-26139701; www.hotelsuryavilla.com; Lane 5, Koregaon Park; s/d with AC incl breakfast ₹2130/2690; ❄️🛜) Hotel Lotus is good value for its quiet, Koregaon Park location and though the rooms are not that spacious, they are light and airy, and all but four have balconies. There's no restaurant, but it offers room service and there are plenty of good eating options close by.

⭐ Sunderban Resort & Spa
HOTEL $$$

(☑020-26124949; www.tghotels.com; 19 Koregaon Park; s/d incl breakfast from ₹4720/5900; ❄️🛜) Set around a manicured lawn right next to the Osho resort, this renovated Art Deco bungalow effortlessly combines colonial-era class with boutique appeal. Deluxe rooms in the main building sport antique furniture, while even the cheapest options are beautifully presented and spacious. The best-value rooms are the lawn-facing studios, recently given a modern upgrade.

Osho Meditation Resort Guesthouse
GUESTHOUSE $$$

(☑020-66019900; www.osho.com; Osho International Meditation Resort, 17 Koregaon Park; s/d ₹5310/5900; ❄️🛜) This uber-chic, 60-room place will only allow you in if you come to meditate at the Osho International Meditation Resort. The rooms and common spaces are an elegant exercise in modern minimalist aesthetics with several very luxurious features – including purified fresh air supplied in all rooms.

🍴 Eating

German Bakery
BAKERY $$

(www.germanbakerypune.in; 292 North Main Rd, Koregaon Park; cakes ₹115-230, mains ₹180-440; ⊗7.45am-11.45pm; 🛜) A Pune institution famous for its traveller-geared grub and fusion food (such as vindaloo pork chops with garlic mash), including omelettes, cooked

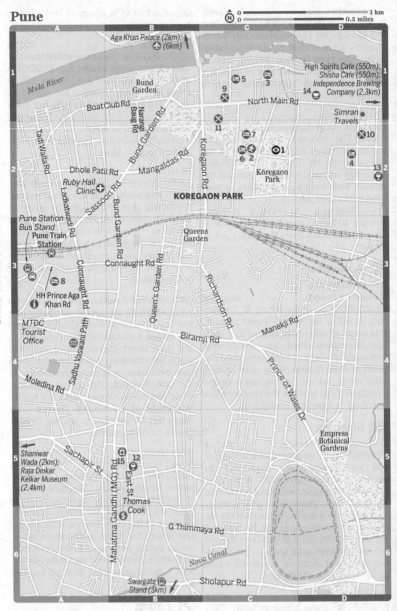

breakfasts, Greek salads, espresso and lots of sweet treats (try the mango cheesecake). Located on a traffic-plagued corner.

★ **Savya Rasa**　　　　　SOUTH INDIAN **$$$**
(☑ 9130095522; www.savyarasa.com; Gera Serenity Bldg, CTS No 15, Koregaon Park; mains ₹400-

800; ☺ noon-3pm & 7-11pm; ☎) This modern, fiercely regional South Indian restaurant champions the best of India's bottom half and isn't afraid to tell you if you are ordering the wrong bread with the wrong curry. Listen to the staff and you'll have one of the region's best meals.

Pune

★ **Malaka Spice**   ASIAN $$$
(www.malakaspice.com; Lane 5, North Main Rd, Koregaon Park; mains ₹340-710; ⊙11.30am-12.30am; ❀🖥) ✐ Maharashtra's shining culinary moment is a fury of Southeast Asian fantasticness; trying to choose one dish among the delectable stir-fries, noodles and curries – all strong on seafood, vegetarian options, chicken, duck and mutton – is futile. Dine alfresco under colourful tree lights and relish the spicy and intricate flavour cavalcade from star chefs reared on a Slow Food, stay-local philosophy.

★ **Le Plaisir**   BISTRO $$$
(☑020-25650106; www.facebook.com/pg/leplaisirpune; Rajkamal Survey No 759/125, Prabhat Rd, Deccan Gymkhana; mains ₹290-420; ⊙9am-9.45pm; 🖥) Foodies in the know often tout this modern bistro on Pune's upscale west side as the city's best place to eat. Sydney-trained chef Siddarth Mahadik keeps it real – nothing flashy, nothing fake is his mantra – and his wholesome fusions creations are well executed, artfully presented and taste great. Worth a trip.

★ **Dario's**   ITALIAN $$$
(www.darios.in; Hotel Sunderban, Koregaon Park; pasta ₹470-550, pizza ₹390-650; ⊙8am-11.30pm) At the rear of Hotel Sunderban, this Italian-run veg paradise is one of Pune's most elegant dining experiences, providing you plant yourself in the gorgeous and intimate courtyard for an alfresco meal. Homemade pastas, very good pizzas and fine salads (try the Bosco; ₹490), including wholewheat, vegan and gluten-free options, fill the extensive menu of delectable remedies for homesickness.

◉ Drinking & Nightlife

★ **Independence Brewing Company**   CRAFT BEER
(☑020-66448308; www.independencebrewco.com; Zero One, 79/1, Pingle Vasti, Mundhwa Rd, Mundhwa; ⊙1pm-1.30am Mon-Sat, from noon Sun) Reserve a table in the outstanding beer garden at this industrially hip craft brewery – Pune's finest – and you'll swear you're in California. The eight taps change often – look out for the Four Grain *saison* (a highly carbonatred pale ale), Juicy IPA, sours, the chocolate-bomb Ixcacao porter and Maharashtra's best (only?) Double IPA.

Badshah   JUICE BAR
(1 East St, Camp; juices ₹90-200; ⊙8am-11.30pm) This institution for *faloodas* (rose-flavoured drinks), *sharbats* (a chilled drink) and fresh juices may have been born in Bombay, but it's been at it in Pune for four decades as well. It's tough to beat its signature *falooda* (with cream and dry fruits) or a fresh *anar* (pomegranate) enjoyed on its pleasant patio on a hot day. Serves heftier Indian meals as well.

Botequim Cervejaria   BAR
(302 Power Plaza, Lane No 7, Koregaon Park; ⊙6.30pm-12.30am) The open-air rooftop at this Brazilian-themed Koregaon Park newcomer is a supreme drinking den, offering 10 craft beer options on draught, including Pune's own excellent Great State Ale Works (who do a fine, creamy Brazilian *chope* – draught beer – and a New England IPA, among others).

Third Wave Coffee Roasters   COFFEE
(www.thirdwavecoffee.in; 1 Vimal Kunj, North Main Rd, Lane E, Koregaon Park; ⊙9am-11pm; 🖥) ✐ This Bengaluru transplant has Punekars

OSHO: THE GURU OF SEX

Ever tried mixing spirituality with primal instincts and garnishing with oodles of expensive trinkets? Well, Bhagwan Shree Rajneesh (1931–90) certainly did. Osho, as he preferred to be called, was one of India's most flamboyant 'export gurus' to market the mystic East to the world and undoubtedly the most controversial.

Initially based in Pune, he followed no particular religion or philosophy and outraged many across the world with his advocacy of sex as a path to enlightenment. A darling of the international media, he quickly earned himself the epithet 'sex guru'. In 1981, Rajneesh took his curious blend of Californian pop psychology and Indian mysticism to the USA, where he set up an agricultural commune in Oregon. There, his ashram's notoriety, as well as its fleet of (material and thus valueless!) Rolls Royces grew, until raging local opposition following a bizarre, infamous food poisoning incident (designed to manipulate local elections) moved the authorities to charge Osho with immigration fraud. He was fined US$400,000 and deported.

An epic journey then began, during which Osho and his followers, in their search for a new base, were either deported from or denied entry into 21 countries. By 1987, he was back at his Pune ashram, where thousands of foreigners soon flocked for his nightly discourses and meditation sessions.

They still come from across the globe. Such is the demand for the resort's facilities that prices are continually on the rise, with luxury being redefined every day. Interestingly, despite Osho's discourse on how nobody should be poor, no money generated by the resort goes into helping the disadvantaged.

In recent years the Osho institute has embraced the digital age, with its online iOsho portal offering iMeditate programs, Osho radio and Osho library; subscriptions are required.

The whole wild ride was laid bare in 2018's *Wild Wild Country*, a six-episode Netflix documentary.

ditching traditional filter coffee for single origin, 100% Arabica Indian specialty espressos (₹110) and other now-ubiquitous Third Wave preparations (Aeropress, Chemex, Syphone etc). It's a big, modern space in Koregaon Park, conducive to working while enjoying creative lattes (Nutella & salted butter) or cold brews (guava chilli).

🛍 Shopping

★ Studio Coppre   HOMEWARES
(📞 9168908484; www.studiocoppre.com; Beverly Estates, 852/4 Bhandarkar Rd, Lane No 12, Deccan Gymkhana; ⊙ 10am-6pm Mon-Sat) 🍴 This craft revival project cofounded by four women champions the dying Indian art of hand-crafted metalware from artisans in Pune, the Konkan Coast and Rajasthan. You'll want an extra suitcase for the gorgeous copper *mathar* bowls (with hand-beaten indentations), carafes, mugs, votives and vases, not to mention the hand-etched bronze thalis and trays, and beautiful decorative inlay boxes.

Bombay Store   GIFTS & SOUVENIRS
(www.thebombaystore.com; 322 MG Rd, Camp; ⊙ 10am-9pm) Stocks quality handicrafts, souvenirs, quirky bags, cool accessories and contemporary furnishings, including Khadi cosmetics and kitschy Elephant Company clocks.

ℹ Information

Ruby Hall Clinic (📞 020-66455100; www.rubyhall.com; 40 Sasoon Rd) One of Pune's best private hospitals, handily located near the train station.

For exchange services, there is a **Thomas Cook** (📞 020-66007903; www.thomascook. in; Thakar House, 2418 General Thimmaya Rd, Camp; ⊙ 9.30am-6.30pm Mon-Sat) branch on General Thimmaya Rd. ATMs are everywhere in Pune, including **Citibank** (www.citibank.com; Ground Onyx, North Main Rd, Tower 37, Koregoan Park), which allows a higher withdrawal limit than Indian banks (₹20,000).

Main Post Office (G.P.O Pune; www.indiapost. gov.in; Sadhu Vaswani Path; ⊙ 10am-8pm Mon-Sat)

MTDC Tourist Office (Maharashtra Tourism Development Corporation; 📞 020-26128169; www.maharashtratourism.gov.in; I Block, Central Bldg, Dr Annie Besant Rd; ⊙ 10am-5pm Mon-Sat, closed 2nd & 4th Sat)

ℹ️ Getting There & Away

AIR

The flashy new Chattrapati Sambhaji International Airport is currently under proposal at Purandar, 36km southeast of Pune. Until its fruition and completion, airlines including Air India (www.airindia.in), GoAir (www.goair.in), IndiGo (www.goindigo.in), Jet Airways (www.jetairways.com) and Spicejet (www.spicejet.com) fly daily from **Pune International Airport** (PNQ; New Airport Rd, Lohgaon), 11km northeast of Koragaon Park, to Mumbai, Delhi, Jaipur, Bengaluru (Bangalore), Nagpur, Goa, Patna, and Chennai, among others. International destinations include Abu Dhabi and Dubai.

BUS

Pune has three bus stands. Maharashtra government buses leave the **Pune Station Bus Stand** (☏ 020-26126218; Agarkar Nagar) for Goa (AC ₹900, 10 hours, 5am, 5.45am, 4.30pm, 7.30pm and 9pm), while Goa government buses (Kadamba Transport) depart at 6.30pm, 7pm and 7.30pm (₹600 to ₹1000). Buses also head to Mumbai's Dadar TT Circle station (₹300 to ₹520, four hours, every 15 minutes, 5.30am to 10.30pm), all of which can drop you in Lonavla (₹70).

From the **Shivaji Nagar Bus Stand** (☏ 020-25536970; Shivajinagar Railway Station Rd), buses go to Aurangabad (non-AC/AC from ₹400/800, five to six hours, every 30 minutes, 5am to 11pm) and Nashik (non-AC/AC from ₹250/410, every 30 minutes, 3.30pm to 11pm). A few semiluxury AC buses also go to Mahabaleshwar (₹265, four hours, 6.15am, 7.45am and 9.30am).

From **Swargate Bus Stand** (☏ 020-24441591; Satara Rd), government buses head to Kolhapur (₹300 to ₹450, six hours, every 30 minutes, 4.30am to 11.30pm) and Mahabaleshwar (₹175 to ₹250, four hours, hourly, 5.40am to 7.20pm). To Donje (Golewadi), for access to Sinhagad Fort, bus 50 or 52 runs frequently from a bus stop (p806) on Shankar Sheth Rd just outside Swargate (₹30, 45 minutes, every 30 minutes, 5.20am to 9.30pm).

Ticket agents selling private long-distance bus tickets are across the street from Shivaji Nagar station – try **Sana Travels** (☏ 8888808984; www.sanakonduskarbus.com; 2 Sita Park, Shivajinagar). Destinations (all AC sleepers) include Bengaluru (from ₹1200, 14 hours, 10 daily, 2.30pm to 10pm), Hyderabad (from ₹1000, 10 hours, 15 daily, 6.30pm to midnight), Goa (from ₹1600, 10 hours, 81 per day, 6.30pm to 1.45am), Mangalore (from ₹1700, 14 hours, 13 daily, 4pm to 11pm) and Nagpur (₹1000, 14 hours, 86 daily, 3.30pm to 10.30pm). Buses for Bengaluru, Goa and Mangalore leave from Swargate; those to Hyderabad from Pune Station; and to Nagpur from Shivaji Nagar.

TAXI

Shared taxis (up to four passengers) link Pune with Mumbai airport around the clock. They leave from the **taxi stand** (☏ 020-26121090; Sanjay Ghandi Rd) in front of Pune Station Bus Stand (per seat ₹400 to ₹475, 2½ hours). There is also an Uber pick-up point just outside the train station exit.

To rent a car and driver try **Simran Travels** (☏ 020-26153222; www.mumbaiairportcab.com; 1st fl, Madhuban Bldg, Lane No 5, Koregaon Park; ⊙ 24hr).

TRAIN

Pune Junction train station (Agarkar Nagar) is in the heart of the city on HH Prince Aga Khan Rd. There are very regular, roughly hourly services to Mumbai and good links to cities including Delhi, Chennai and Hyderabad.

Around Pune

Sinhagad

The ruined **Sinhagad** (Lion Fort; Sinhagad Ghat Rd; ⊙ dawn-dusk) `FREE`, about 24km southwest of Pune, was wrested by Maratha leader Shivaji from the Bijapur kings in 1670. In the epic battle (where he lost his son Sambhaji), Shivaji is said to have used monitor lizards yoked with ropes to scale the fort's craggy walls.

MAJOR TRAINS FROM PUNE

DESTINATION	TRAIN NO & NAME	FARE (₹)	DURATION (HR)	DEPARTURE
Bengaluru	11301 Udyan Express	450/1775	20½	11.45am
Chennai	12163 Chennai Express	515/1970	19½	12.10am
Delhi	11077 Jhelum Express	620/2455	27¾	5.20pm
Hyderabad	17031 Hyderabad Express	330/1295	13½	4.35pm
Mumbai CST	12124 Deccan Queen	105/375	3¼	7.15am

Express fares are sleeper/2AC; Deccan Queen fares are 2nd class/AC chair.

Today, it's in a poor state, but worth visiting for the sweeping views and opportunity to hike in the hills.

Sinhagad is an easy day trip from Pune so there is little reason to eat or sleep here. That said, there are a good deal of hotels and resorts (with restaurants) in the surrounding areas and near Lake Khadakwasla, though the road to the fort itself is virtually empty.

Bus 50 or 52 (Shankar Sheth Rd) runs frequently to Donje (Golewadi) village from Shankar Sheth Rd near Swargate bus stand i9n Pune (₹30, 45 minutes, every 30 minutes, 5.20am to 9.30pm), from where it's a 4km hike if you want to walk or catch a shared 4WD (₹60) that can cart you 10km to the base of the summit.

Shivneri

Situated 90km northwest of Pune, above the village of Junnar, **Shivneri Fort** (Imam Raza Nagar, Junnar; ⊙ dawn-dusk) `FREE` holds the distinction of being the birthplace of Shivaji. Within the ramparts of this ruined fort are the old royal stables, a mosque dating back to the Mughal era and several rock-cut reservoirs. The most important structure is Shivkunj, the pavilion in which Shivaji was born.

About 8km from Shivneri, on the other side of Junnar, is an interesting group of Hinayana Buddhist caves called **Lenyadri** (Lenyadri Ganapati Rd, Junnar; Indian/foreigner ₹25/300; ⊙ 8am-6pm). Of the 27 caves, cave 7 is the most impressive and, interestingly, houses an image of the Hindu god Ganesh.

Views from both monuments are spectacular. There are buses (₹130, two hours, 5am to 4pm) hourly or so connecting Pune's Shivaji Nagar bus stand with Junnar (an Ola outstation day cab from Pune starts from about ₹2026 return). From Junnar's bus stand, a return rickshaw including one hour's wait time runs ₹300 to Shivneri and ₹400 to Lenyadri.

Kolhapur

♪ 0231 / POP 561.300 / ELEV 550M

A little-visited city, Kolhapur is the perfect place to get intimate with the flamboyant side of India. Only a few hours from Goa, this historic settlement has an intensely fascinating temple complex. In August Kolhapur is at its vibrant best when Naag Panchami (p776), a snake-worshipping festival, is held in tandem with one at Pune. Gastro-nomes take note: the town is also the birthplace of the famed, spicy Kolhapuri cuisine, especially chicken and mutton dishes.

◉ Sights

★ Shree Chhatrapati
Shahu Museum   MUSEUM

(New Palace; Indian/foreigner ₹35/80; ⊙ 9.15am-5.30pm) 'Bizarre' takes on a whole new meaning at this 'new' palace, an Indo-Saracenic behemoth designed by British architect 'Mad' Charles Mant for the Kolhapur kings in 1884. The madcap museum is a maze of countless trophies from the kings' trigger-happy jungle safaris, including walking sticks made from leopard vertebrae and ashtrays fashioned out of tiger skulls and rhino feet.

★ Mahalaxmi Mandir   HINDU TEMPLE

(Mahadwar Rd; ⊙ 3am-11pm) One of Maharashtra's most important and vibrant places of worship, the Mahalaxmi Temple is dedicated to Amba Bai (Mother Goddess). The temple's origins date back to AD 10, but much of the present structure is from the 18th century. It draws an unceasing tide of humanity, as pilgrims press to enter the holy inner sanctuary and bands of musicians and worshippers chant devotions. Non-Hindus are welcome and it's a fantastic place for people-watching.

Motibag Talim Mandal   TRAINING CENTRE

(Guru Maharaj Gali, Mangalwar Peth, C Ward; ⊙ 4am-4pm) Kolhapur is famed for the calibre of its Kushti wrestlers and at the Motibag Thalim you can watch young athletes train in an earthen pit. The *akhara* (training ground) is reached through a low doorway and passage to the left of the entrance to Bhavani Mandap (ask for directions). You are free to walk in and watch, as long as you don't mind the sight of sweaty, seminaked men and the stench of urine emanating from the loos.

⌸ Sleeping & Eating

Hotel K Tree   HOTEL $$

(☑ 0231-2526990; www.hotelktree.com; 517E, Plot 65, Shivaji Park; s/d incl breakfast from ₹3660/4010; ❊ ☎) With high service standards and 26 very inviting modish rooms, this newer hotel is starting to show some age, but it's fine value and wildly popular with Indians for its good buffet breakfast (which includes the spicy curry *misal*). It's a toss up between the clandestine bathrooms in deluxe rooms or elevated Asian-style beds in executive rooms.

Hotel Pavillion HOTEL $$
(📞 0231-2652751; www.hotelpavillion.co.in; 392E Assembly Rd, Shaupuri; s/d incl breakfast ₹2130/2350, with AC from ₹2520/2740; ❋ 🛜) Located at the far end of a leafy park-cum-office-area, this hotel guarantees a peaceful stay, occasionally uninspired bathrooms aside. Its large, well-equipped rooms are perhaps a little dated, but many have windows that open out to delightful views of seasonal blossoms.

★ **Dehaati** INDIAN $$
(Ayodha Park, Old Pune-Bangalore Hwy, Nimbalkar Colony; thalis ₹220-530; ⊙ 12.30-3.30pm & 7.30-10.30pm) The city's Kolhapuri thali specialist. Meals come in a number of mutton variations as well as chicken and veg. The vibrant curries, the spiced-up dhal, the rich *aakkha masoor* (Kolhapuri-style whole lentil curry), the intricate *tambda rassa* (spicy red mutton curry), the perfectly flaky chapatis – it's all delicious.

ℹ Information

MTDC Tourist Booth (📞 0231-2652935; www.maharashtratourism.gov.in; Near Mahalaxmi Mandir)

MTDC Tourist Office (Maharashtra Tourism Development Corporation; 📞 0231-2665816; www.maharashtratourism.gov.in; 254B Udyog Bhavan, Assembly Rd; ⊙ 10am-6pm Mon-Sat, closed 2nd & 4th Sat)

ℹ Getting There & Away

BUS

From the **bus stand** (CBS; 📞 0231-2650620; Benadikar Path, Shahupur), services head regularly to Pune (ShivShahi AC ₹420, five hours, every 30 minutes, 5am to 11.30pm), Ratnagiri (ordinary/ShivShahi ₹172/255, 4½ hours, every 30 minutes, 1am and 5.30am to 6.30pm), three ordinary buses to Malvan (₹210, five hours, 5.15am, 6.15am and 12.30pm) and 11 daily buses to Mumbai (ordinary express/ShivShahi ₹485/710, 10 hours, 6.30am to 10pm). There is a reservation counter for all buses.

The best private bus agents gather at the Royal Plaza building at Dabholkar Corner, 300m north of the bus stand. **Paulo Travels** (📞 9326012763; www.paulotravels.com; B/22, Royal Plaza, Dhabolkar Cnr) heads to Goa (Volvo AC seat/sleeper from ₹1300/1600, eight hours, 10 per day, 2.30am to midnight). **Neeta Tours & Travels** (📞 0231-3290061; www.neetabus.in; B/16, Royal Plaza, Dabholkar Cnr) is a good bet for overnight AC services heading to Mumbai (Volvo AC sleeper from ₹1200, nine hours, 9am, 3pm, 5pm and 10.45pm) and Pune (Volvo AC seat from ₹550,

five hours, 7am, 9am, 3pm, 4pm, 5pm, 8pm and 11.30pm).

TRAIN

The **train station** (KOP; Railway Colony, New Shahupuri), known as Chattrapati Shahu Maharaj Terminus, is 10 minutes' walk west of the bus stand. Three daily expresses, including the 10.50pm Sahyadri Express, go to Mumbai (sleeper/2AC ₹305/1180, 13 hours) via Pune (₹210/815, eight hours). The Rani Chennama Express makes the long journey to Bengaluru (₹400/1575, 16½ hours, 2.05pm). There are no direct trains to Goa.

Mahabaleshwar

📞 02168 / POP 12,750 / ELEV 1372M

Once a summer capital under the British, today the best thing about the hill station of Mahabaleshwar (1327m) is the jaw-dropping mountain scenery on the road to get here. It's an overdeveloped mess, tainted by an ugly building boom and traffic chaos as tourists attempt a mad dash to tick off its viewpoints and falls. There's no compelling reason to visit – it's basically one big bustling bazaar surrounded by resorts and views – though the town can be used as a base to visit the impressive Pratapgad Fort (p808) or Kass Pleateau of Flowers, both nearby.

Forget about coming during the monsoon when the whole town virtually shuts down (and an unbelievable 6m of rain falls). If you have an hour or so to kill between buses, budget-friendly **Nature Care Spa** (📞 9168816683; Hotel Shreyas, Main Rd; massages from ₹1500; ⊙ 9am-8pm), across the street from the bus stand at Hotel Shreyas, hits the spot.

🛏 Sleeping & Eating

Glenogle BUNGALOW $$$
(📞 8888999018; www.glenogle.in; Sasoon Rd; 5-bedroom bungalow ₹15,000-30,000; ❋ 🛜) This 1840s tin-roof heritage bungalow sits just as it did when it was built by the British government for one of its captains. Nestled in its own forest just 1.3km from the main bazaar, it feels a world away from the town, with five beautifully appointed bedrooms teeming with arts and antiques.

★ **Grapevine** MULTICUISINE $$$
(📞 02168-261100; Masjid Rd; mains ₹170-950; ⊙ 9.30am-3pm & 5-10pm) Way too hip for Mahabaleshwar, this classy restaurant/wine bar is unmissable. Chef/owner Raio's

WORTH A TRIP

PRATAPGAD FORT

Pratapgad Fort (Poladpur-Mahabaleshwar Rd; ⊙9am-dusk), built by Shivaji in 1656 (and still owned by his descendants), straddles a high mountain ridge 24km northwest of the town of Mahabaleshwar. In 1659, Shivaji agreed to meet Bijapuri General Afzal Khan here in an attempt to end a stalemate. Despite a no-arms agreement, Shivaji, upon greeting Khan, disembowelled his enemy with a set of iron *baghnakh* (tiger's claws). Khan's tomb (out of bounds) marks the site of this painful encounter at the base of the fort.

Pratapgad is reached by a 500-step climb that affords brilliant views. Fresh fruit, juice, snacks and simple restaurants are scattered about the staircase to the fort.

From the bus stand in Mahabaleshwar, a state bus tour (₹150 return, one hour, 9.30am) does a daily shuttle to the fort, with a waiting time of around one hour. Taxi drivers in Mahabaleshwar charge a fixed ₹1000 for the return trip, including one hour's waiting time.

culinary pedigree includes Taj Hotels and his creative takes on Parsi and fresh seafood are divine. The monstrous Mediterranean lamb burger (with feta and harissa mayo) and the soft-shell crab burger are worth the trip here alone, but there's also spicy tiger prawns, lamb shanks and lobster.

ⓘ Getting There & Away

From **Mahabaleshwar bus stand** (Hwy 72), state buses leave regularly for Pune (non-AC/ShivShahi ₹190/210, four hours, every 30 minutes, 5.30am to 6.30pm), Kohlapur (non-AC/ShivShahi ₹365/475, 5½ hours, 6.30am, 8am and 12.30pm) and Satara (non-AC ₹75, two hours, every 30 minutes, 7am to 6.30pm), where you can more often connect to Kolhapur (non-AC ₹175, every 30 minutes). Four daily buses head

to Mumbai between 9am and 9.30pm (non-AC ₹450, seven hours) and one ordinary bus to Goa (non-AC ₹780, 12 hours, 8am).

RB Travels (☑9422405772, 02168-260251; 49 Dr Sabne Rd; ⊙8am-11pm), located on a corner between an alley shortcut to Masjid Rd and the bazaar (across from Meghdoot restaurant), books luxury coaches to Goa (non-AC seat/Volvo AC sleeper ₹1100/1400, 12 hours). You will depart from the bazaar in a car at 7.30pm to Surur Phata junction, 42km away, to wait for the bus on the way from Pune. Transport to Mumbai (Volvo AC sleeper ₹800, six hours, 9.30am, 10.30am, noon, 4pm and 9.30pm) is also available.

For the Pratapgad Fort, a state bus (₹150 return, one hour, 9.30am) does a daily round trip, with a waiting time of around one hour; taxi drivers charge a fixed ₹1000 return.

Goa

⌨ 0832 / POP 1.82 MILLION

Best Places to Eat

➡ Black Sheep Bistro (p816)

➡ Go With the Flow (p828)

➡ Baba Au Rhum (p832)

➡ Bomra's (p823)

➡ Ourem 88 (p853)

Best Places to Stay

➡ Mandala (p840)

➡ Dreams Hostel (p835)

➡ Panjim Inn (p815)

➡ Ciarans (p852)

➡ Vaayu Waterman's Village (p839)

Why Go?

Pint-sized Goa is much more than beaches and trance parties. A kaleidoscopic blend of Indian and Portuguese cultures, sweetened with sun, sea, sand, seafood and spirituality, there's nowhere in India quite like it.

The central region is Goa's historic and cultural heart, home to capital Panaji, Old Goa's glorious churches, inland islands, bird sanctuaries, spice plantations and the wild Western Ghats. North Goa draws the crowds with busy beaches, upbeat nightlife, Goan trance, great food, hippie markets and yoga retreats. South Goa is the state's more serene half, with cleaner, whiter, quieter beaches ranging from village-feel Benaulim to beach-hut bliss at Palolem, Patnem and Agonda.

Goa's rapidly increasing popularity with domestic tourists has put a strain on this tiny state, but most travellers will still find a place and a space to chill out and unwind from the rest of India.

When to Go
Panaji

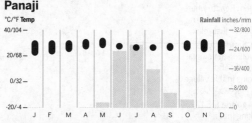

Sep–Nov Some shack restaurants close up, but prices are lower and crowds fewer.

Nov–Mar Wonderful weather; festivals in full swing; peak prices and crowds mid-Dec to early Jan.

Mar–Apr Carnival and Easter celebrations as the season winds down.

Goa Highlights

1 Panaji (p812)
Exploring the historic Latin Quarter, shopping and eating well in India's most laid-back state capital.

2 Assagao (p833) Dropping in to a yoga or cooking class at Assagao, Anjuna, Arambol or Mandrem.

3 Anjuna Flea Market (p832) Haggling for a bargain at this touristy but fun Wednesday market.

4 Old Goa (p820) Standing in silence and taking in the extraordinary churches and cathedrals of Old Goa.

5 Cola Beach (p846) Trekking down to secluded Cola, one of Goa's prettiest beaches.

6 Mandrem (p840) Sleeping in style and stretching out with a good book at this peaceful beach.

7 Palolem (p849) Checking into a beach hut on beautiful Palolem Beach, where you can kayak, learn to cook or just relax.

8 Chandor (p483) Marvelling at colonial mansions and palacios in this village near Margao.

9 Agonda (p847) Booking into a luxurious beachfront hut on this wild beach and learning to surf.

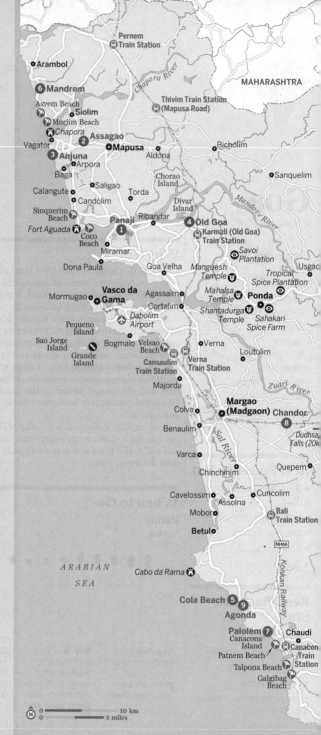

History

Goa went through a dizzying array of rulers from Ashoka's Mauryan empire in the 3rd century BC to the long-ruling Kadamba from the 3rd century AD. Subsequent conflict saw rival sultanates fighting the Hindu Vijayanagar empire for control, before the Adil Shahs of Bijapur created the capital we now call Old Goa in the 15th century.

The Portuguese arrived in 1510 and steadily extended their power from their grand capital at Old Goa out into the provinces, zealously converting the locals to Christianity. Their 400-year reign came to an end in 1961, when Goa was annexed to India after a three-day siege by the Indian Army, but the Portuguese legacy lives on in the state's colonial-era mansions, its cuisine, churches and even in its language.

Goa's hippie heyday began in the late 1960s and it has been a stalwart on the overland trail since, but these days the beaches are packed not so much with backpackers but with an increasing influx of interstate Indian tourists.

ⓘ Information

Goa Tourism Development Corporation (GTDC; ☑ 0832-2437132; www.goa-tourism. com; Paryatan Bhavan, Dr Alvaro Costa Rd, Panaji; ⊙ 9.30am-5.45pm Mon-Fri), usually called Goa Tourism these days, is the state government tourism body and it's a surprisingly progressive government organisation, acting more like a commercial business with numerous hotels and operating a host of tours and even a taxi smartphone app.

ⓘ Getting There & Away

AIR

Goa's airport, **Dabolim** (Goa International Airport; ☑ 0832-2540806; NH566), is served directly by domestic flights, a handful of international flights from the Middle East, and seasonal package-holiday charters (mostly from Russia, Europe and the UK).

Unless you're on a charter, you'll generally have to fly into a major city such as Mumbai or Delhi and change to a domestic flight with Jet Airways, Air India, SpiceJet or IndiGo.

A new greenfield airport at Mopa in North Goa is expected to be completed by 2020.

LAND
Bus

Private and state-run long-distance buses run to and from Goa daily. Tickets can be booked in advance online, at ticket agents located near the bus stands or through travel agents or tourist accommodation. Note that travel into and out of Mumbai by road is interminably slow; the train is faster and more comfortable.

Kadamba (www.goakadamba.com), the state government bus company, operates across the state and to neighbouring regions. For private or state buses you can book online with www.redbus.in.

Train

The 760km-long Konkan Railway (www.konkanrailway.com), completed in 1998, is the main train line running through the state, connecting Goa with Mumbai to the north and Mangalore to the south. The biggest station in Goa is Margao's Madgaon station (p845), and many trains also pass through Karmali station near Old Goa, 12km from Panaji. Smaller stations on the line include Pernem for Arambol, Thivim for Mapusa and the northern beaches, and Canacona for Palolem.

SEA

Cruise ships, mostly from UAE or travelling between Mumbai and the Maldives, call in at Goa's Mormugao cruise ship terminal as part of their itineraries.

In 2018 a Mumbai to Goa ferry began operating three times a week.

Angriya Cruises (☑ 8314810440; www.angriyacruises.com; Mormugao Cruise Terminal; ⊙ 4pm Tue, Thu, Sun Oct-May) is an overnight cruise. Onboard accommodation ranges from dormitory bunks (₹4300) and luxury single pods (₹4650) to spacious double rooms (₹8950 per person) and family rooms (₹5700 per person). Meals are an additional ₹2000/1000 adult/child.

ⓘ Getting Around

Car & Motorcycle Many travellers hire a scooter or motorbike for their trip (₹250 to ₹500 per day). An international driving permit is required for foreigners. Self-drive cars are less common but car and driver services are affordable for groups.

GOA MILES

Ridesharing services such as Uber and Ola are currently banned in Goa, but Goa Tourism has started its own service called Goa Miles (www.goamiles.com), a taxi smartphone app that works much like Uber. The subsidised fares are roughly half what you would pay a taxi driver off the street (closer to the fares charged at the airport prepaid counter), though the success of the service will rely on how many drivers are on the road.

Taxi & autorickshaw Good for short hops around and between towns and beach resorts. Taxis will also take you on longer trips – agree on a fare beforehand.

Bus Extremely cheap, slow but fun local way of getting between towns and villages.

Train There are two rail lines in the state but it's not a particularly quick or convenient way of getting around.

PANAJI & CENTRAL GOA

Some travellers see Goa as one big beach resort, but the central region – with few beaches of note – is the state's historic and cultural heart and soul.

Panaji

📞 0832 / POP 241,000

One of India's most relaxed state capitals, Panaji (Panjim) crowds around the peninsula overlooking the broad Mandovi River, where cruise boats and floating casinos ply the waters, and advertising signs cast neon reflections in the night.

But it's the tangle of narrow streets in the old Latin Quarter of Fontainhas that really steals the show. Nowhere is the Portuguese influence felt more openly than here, where the late afternoon sun lights up yellow houses with purple doors, and around each corner you'll find restored ochre-coloured mansions with terracotta-tiled roofs, wrought-iron balconies and arched oyster-shell windows.

A day or two in Panaji really is an essential part of the Goan experience.

◉ Sights

Some of Panaji's great pleasures are leisurely strolls through the sleepy Portuguese-era Latin Quarter of Fontainhas and Sao Tomé and Altinho Hill. Riverside Campal Gardens, west of the centre, and Miramar Beach, 4km southwest of the city, are also popular spots.

★ **Church of Our Lady of the Immaculate Conception**   CHURCH
(cnr Emilio Gracia & Jose Falcao Rds; ⊙9am-12.30pm & 3-7.30pm Mon-Sat, 11am-12.30pm & 3.30-5pm Sun, English Mass 8am daily) Panaji's spiritual, as well as geographical, centre is this elevated, pearly white church, built in 1619 over an older, smaller 1540 chapel, and stacked like a fancy white wedding cake. When Panaji was little more than a sleepy fishing village, this church was the first port of call for sailors from Lisbon, who would give thanks for a safe crossing, before continuing to Ela (Old Goa) further east up the river. The church is beautifully illuminated at night.

Goa State Museum & Secretariat Building   MUSEUM
(📞0832-2438006; www.goamuseum.gov.in; Avenida Dom Joao Castro; ⊙9.30am-5.30pm Mon-Fri) **FREE** Currently housed in the Secretariat, the oldest colonial building in Goa, the state museum features an eclectic, if not extensive, collection of items tracing aspects of Goan history. As well as some beautiful Hindu and Jain sculptures and bronzes, there are nice examples of Portuguese-era furniture, coins, an intricately carved chariot and a pair of quirky antique rotary lottery machines.

TOP STATE FESTIVALS

Feast of the Three Kings (⊙6 Jan) Boys re-enact the story of the three kings bearing gifts for Christ.

Shigmotsav of Holi (Shigmo; ⊙Feb/Mar) Goa's version of the Hindu festival Holi sees coloured powders thrown about and parades in most towns.

Sabado Gordo (Panaji; ⊙Feb/Mar) A procession of floats and street parties on the Saturday before Lent.

Carnival (⊙Mar) A four-day festival kicking off Lent; the party's particularly jubilant in Panaji.

Feast of the Menino Jesus (Colva; ⊙2nd Mon in Oct) Statue of the baby Jesus is paraded through the streets of Colva.

Feast of St Francis Xavier (Old Goa; ⊙3 Dec) A 10-day celebration of Goa's patron saint.

Feast of Our Lady of the Immaculate Conception (Margao, Panaji; ⊙8 Dec) Fairs and concerts around Panaji's famous church.

PONDA'S TEMPLES & SPICES

The Ponda region, around 30km southeast of Panaji, makes a worthwhile day trip for its Hindu temple complexes and nearby spice plantations.

For nearly 250 years after the arrival of the Portuguese in 1510, Ponda taluk (district) remained under the control of Muslim or Hindu rulers, and many of its temples came into existence when Hindus were forced to escape Portuguese persecution by fleeing across its district border, bringing their sacred temple deities with them as centuries-old edifices were destroyed by the new colonial regime. These 17th and 18th-century temples remain today. If you're short on time, the most appealing and accessible are Shri Manguesh and Shri Mahalsa near the village of Mardol. The Ponda region is also the centre of commercial spice farms in Goa and several have opened their doors as tourist operations, offering a guided tour of the plantation, buffet thali-style lunch and perhaps a cultural show. Farms include:

Pascoal Spice Farm (☑ 0832-2344268; farm tour & lunch ₹400; ☺ 9am-4.30pm)

Sahakari Spice Farm (☑ 0832-2312394; www.sahakarifarms.com; admission & lunch ₹400; ☺ 8am-4.30pm)

Savoi Plantation (☑ 9423888899, 0832-2340272; www.savoiplantations.com; adult/child ₹700/350; ☺ 9am-4.30pm)

Tropical Spice Plantation (☑ 0832-2340329; www.tropicalspiceplantation.com; Keri; tour & lunch ₹400; ☺ 9am-4pm)

Goa State Central Library　LIBRARY
(Sanskruti Bhavan, Patto; ☺ 9am-7.30pm Mon-Fri, 9.30am-5.45pm Sat & Sun) FREE Panaji's modern state library has six floors of reading material, a bookshop and gallery. The 2nd floor features a children's book section and internet browsing (free, but technically only for academic research). The 4th floor has Goan history books and the 6th a large collection of Portuguese books.

Mario Gallery　GALLERY
(☑ 0832-2421776; www.mariodemiranda.com; Duarte Pacheco Rd; ☺ 10am-5.30pm Mon-Fri, to 1pm Sat) FREE This gallery and shop showcases work by India's favourite cartoonist, Loutolim local Mario de Miranda, who died in 2011 at the age of 85. Along with prints, books and drawings, there are printed T-shirts, mugs and bags. His works are so popular that there are similar galleries in Calangute, Margao and Porvorim.

🏃 Activities

One-hour evening boat cruises run by Goa Tourism and private operators leave from the Tourism Jetty near Mandovi Bridge and are a popular way to see the river.

GTDC River Cruise　CRUISE
(Avenida Dom Joao Castro, Tourism Jetty; sunset cruise ₹300; ☺ 6pm) Goa Tourism operates an entertaining hour-long cruise along the Mandovi River aboard the *Santa Monica*, with a live band and/or performances of Goan folk songs and dances. There are also twice-weekly, two-hour dinner cruises. Departs from the Santa Monica Jetty next to the Mandovi Bridge.

Make It Happen　WALKING
(www.makeithappen.co.in; 1/143 Dr Cunha Gonsalves Rd; walking tours from ₹700) For a local insight into Goan history and culture, this Panaji-based outfit of local tour guides leads a number of walks and tours, including Fontainhas and Old Goa heritage walks and tours of Divar Island, Chandor and Saligao. The Fontainhas walk includes access to heritage homes and a performance of *fado* (a melancholic form of Portuguese singing). Book online.

🛏 Sleeping

Panaji has its fair share of accommodation for all budgets but it's not saturated like the beach resorts.

★ Old Quarter Hostel　HOSTEL $
(☑ 7410069108; www.thehostelcrowd.com; 5/146 31st January Rd; dm ₹600-650, s/d with AC from ₹1100/1700; ❇ 🌐) In an old Portuguese house in historic Fontainhas, this flamboyant hostel is a beacon for budget travellers to Panaji. Slick four-bed dorms with lockers as well as private doubles in a separate building, along with the excellent Bombay Roasters Cafe, arty murals, good wi-fi and bikes for hire. Noon checkout.

Panaji

GOA

Campal Gardens (300m); Kala Academy (700m)

Betim (2km); Torda (4km); Mapusa (13km)

Old Goa (9km); Karmali (12km); Ponda (34km)

Mandovi Bridge

Mandovi River

Dabolim (29km); Vasco da Gama (32km); Margao (34km)

PATTO

Amberdkar Park

New Patto Bridge

Old Patto Bridge

Ourem Creek

Dr Alvaro Costa Rd

Panaji Jetty

Avenida Dom João Castro

MG Rd

Footbridge

Ourem Rd

SAO TOMÉ

31st January Rd

GP Rd

CA Rd

St Sebastian Rd

Rua de Natal

Emilio Gracia Rd

Jose Falcao Rd

FONTAINHAS

31st January Rd

MALA

Dabolim (29km (34km)

Margao (34km)

Church of Our Lady of the Immaculate Conception

Dr RS Rd

Cunha Rivara Rd

Avenida Pe Agnelo

Ormuz Rd

Malaca Rd

Azad Maidan

Dayanand Bandodkar Marg

Ferry to Betim

Dr Dada Vaidya Rd

ALTINHO

Dr Pisurlekar Rd

Menezes Braganza Rd

Dr P Shirgaonkar Rd

Swami Vivekanand Rd

18th June Rd

Gen Costa Alvares Rd

Dr Atmaram Borkar Rd

MG Rd

Heliodoro Salgado Rd

Municipal Market

General Bernardo Guedes Rd

Kala Academy (400m)

Caculo Mall (800m)

Panaji

A Pousada Guest House GUESTHOUSE $
(☑ 0832-2422618, 9850998213; sabrinateles@
yahoo.com; Luis de Menezes Rd; s/d from
₹950/1200, d with AC ₹1800; ❀☎) The five
rooms in this bright-yellow place are simple
but clean and come with comfy spring-mat-
tress beds and TV. Owner Sabrina is friendly
and no-nonsense, and it's one of the better
budget guesthouses in Fountainhas.

★ **Panjim Inn** HERITAGE HOTEL $$
(☑ 9823025748, 0832-2226523; www.panjiminn.
com; 31st January Rd; s/d from ₹5900/6500;
superior ₹8200/8700; ❀☎) One of the original
heritage hotels in Fontainhas, the Panjim
Inn has been a long-standing favourite for its
character and charm. Run by the lovely Sukh-
ija family and overseen by helpful staff, this
beautiful 19th-century mansion has 12 char-
ismatic rooms in the original house, along
with newer rooms with modern touches to
complement four-poster beds, colonial-era
furniture and artworks.

Afonso Guesthouse GUESTHOUSE $$
(☑ 0832-2222359, 9764300165; www.afonsoguest
house.com; St Sebastian Rd; d ₹2500-3250; ❀☎)
Run by the friendly Jeanette, this pretty Portuguese townhouse offers eight spacious,
well-kept rooms with timber ceilings. The
little rooftop terrace makes for sunny break-

fasting (not included) with Fontainhas views.
It's a simple, serene stay in the heart of the
most atmospheric part of town. Checkout is
9am and bookings are accepted online but
not by phone.

La Maison BOUTIQUE HOTEL $$
(☑ 0832-2235555; www.lamaisongoa.com; 31st
January Rd; r incl breakfast ₹4700-5300; ❀☎)
One of the growing range of boutique herit-
age hotels in Fontainhas, La Maison is histor-
ic on the outside but thoroughly modern and
swanky within, with a Euro-meets-Orient
vibe. The eight rooms are deceptively simple
and homey but five-star comfortable with
soft beds, cloud-like pillows, writing desks
and flat-screen TVs. Breakfast is included
and attached is the French fusion Desbue
restaurant.

✕ Eating

You'll never go hungry in Panaji, where food
is enjoyed fully and frequently. The Latin
Quarter has a developing foodie scene, where
you can dine on traditional Goan specialities.

Anandashram GOAN $
(31st January Rd; thalis ₹90-140, mains ₹100-350;
☉ noon-3.30pm & 7.30-10.30pm Mon-Sat, noon-
3pm Sun) This little place is renowned locally
for seafood, serving up simple but tasty fish

curries, as well as veg and nonveg thalis for lunch and dinner.

⭐ **Viva Panjim**　　　　　　GOAN $$
(☑ 0832-2422405; 31st January Rd; mains ₹160-300; ☺ 11.30am-3.30pm & 7-11pm Mon-Sat, 7-11pm Sun) Well-known to tourists, this little side-street eatery, in an old Portuguese house and with a few tables out on the laneway, delivers tasty Goan classics at reasonable prices. There's a whole page devoted to pork dishes, along with tasty *xacuti* (a spicy chicken or meat dish cooked in red coconut sauce) and *cafreal* (a marinated chicken dish) meals.

⭐ **Cafe Bodega**　　　　　　CAFE $$
(☑ 0832-2421315; www.cafebodegagoa.in; Altinho; mains ₹170-340; ☺ 10am-7pm Mon-Sat, to 4pm Sun; 🛜) It's well worth a trip up to Altinho Hill to visit this serene inner courtyard cafe-gallery in an azure-and-white Portuguese mansion in the grounds of Sunaparanta Centre for the Arts. Enjoy good coffee, juices and freshly baked cakes around the inner courtyard or lunch on super pizzas and sandwiches.

⭐ **Hotel Venite**　　　　　　GOAN $$$
(31st January Rd; mains ₹320-440; ☺ 9am-10.30pm) With its cute rickety balcony tables overhanging the cobbled street, Venite has long been among the most atmospheric of Panaji's Goan restaurants. The menu is traditional, with spicy sausages, fish curry rice, pepper steak and *bebinca* (Goan 16-layer cake), but Venite is popular with tourists and prices are consequently inflated. Drop in for a beer or shot of feni (Goan liquor) before deciding.

⭐ **Black Sheep Bistro**　　　EUROPEAN $$$
(☑ 0832-2222901; www.blacksheepbistro.in; Swami Vivekanand Rd; tapas ₹250-400, mains ₹350-600; ☺ noon-4pm & 7pm-midnight) Among the best of Panaji's burgeoning boutique restaurants, Black Sheep's impressive pale-yellow facade gives way to a sexy dark-wood bar and loungy dining room. The tapas dishes are light, fresh and expertly prepared in keeping with their farm-to-table philosophy. Salads, pasta, seafood and dishes like lamb osso buco grace the menu, while an internationally trained sommelier matches food to wine.

Route 66　　　　　　　　DINER $$$
(☑ 9623922796; Ourem Rd; mains ₹200-850; ☺ noon-11.30pm; ❄ 🛜) Styled on an American diner, this roomy restaurant across from Ourem Creek specialises in burgers such as the SOB or Wolverine, but also excels at hot dogs, cheese chilli fries, hickory barbecue ribs and New York–style pizzas. For comfort fast food it's hard to beat and there's live music on Thursday, Friday and Saturday nights.

🍷 Drinking & Nightlife

⭐ **Cafe Mojo**　　　　　　　BAR
(☑ 0832-2431973; www.cafemojo.in; Menezes Braganza Rd; ☺ 10am-5am Mon-Thu, to 6am Fri-Sun) The decor is a dark cosy English pub, the clientele young and up for a late party, and the novelty is the e-beer system. Each table has its own beer tap and LCD screen: you buy a card (₹500), swipe it at your table and start pouring – it automatically deducts what you drink (use the card for spirits, cocktails and food, too).

Joseph Bar　　　　　　　BAR
(Gomes Pereira Rd, Sao Tomé; ☺ 6-11.30pm) This hole-in-the-wall bar is a place where locals and tourists gather streetside to chat and drink at tiny tables or perched on scooters. It's a warm and welcoming place with Goan craft beer available.

Riverfront & Down the Road　　　BAR
(cnr MG & Ourem Rds; ☺ 11am-1am) The balcony of this restaurant-bar overlooking the creek and Old Patto Bridge makes for a cosy beer or cocktail spot with carved barrels for furniture. The ground-floor bar (from 6pm) is an old-school nightspot with occasional live music.

☆ Entertainment

Panaji's most visible form of entertainment are the casino boats anchored out in the Mandovi River.

Deltin Royale　　　　　　CASINO
(☑ 9819698196; www.deltingroup.com/deltin-royale; Noah's Ark, RND Jetty, Dayanand Bandodkar Marg; weekday/weekend ₹2500/3500; ☺ 24hr,

---

SLEEPING PRICE RANGES

The following price ranges refer to a double room with bathroom across the state:

$ less than ₹1500

$$ ₹1500–₹7500

$$$ more than ₹7500

Accommodation prices in Goa vary considerably depending on the season and demand.

entertainment 9pm-1am) Goa's biggest and best luxury floating casino, Deltin Royal has 123 tables, the Vegas Restaurant, a Whisky Bar and a creche. Entry includes gaming chips worth ₹1500/2000 (weekday/weekend). Unlimited food and drinks included.

INOX Cinema
CINEMA

(☑ 0832-2420900; www.inoxmovies.com; Old GMC Heritage Precinct; tickets ₹210-240) This comfortable, plush multiplex cinema shows Hollywood and Bollywood blockbusters. Book online to choose your seats in advance.

Kala Academy
PERFORMING ARTS

(☑ 0832-2420452; www.kalaacademygoa.co.in; Dayanand Bandodkar Marg) On the west side of the city, in Campal, is Goa's premier cultural centre, which features a program of dance, theatre, music and art exhibitions throughout the year. Many shows are in Konkani, but there are occasional English-language productions. The website usually has an up-to-date calendar of events.

🛍 Shopping

Municipal Market
MARKET

(Heliogordo Salgado Rd; ⊙ from 7.30am) This atmospheric place, where narrow streets have been converted into covered markets, makes for a nice wander, offering fresh produce, clothing stalls and some tiny, enticing eateries. The fish market is a particularly interesting strip of activity.

Singbal's Book House
BOOKS

(☑ 0832-2425747; Church Sq; ⊙ 9.30am-1pm & 3.30-7.30pm Mon-Sat) On the corner opposite Panaji's main church, Singbal's is a local landmark with an excellent selection of international magazines and newspapers, and lots of books on Goa and travel.

Caculo Mall
MALL

(☑ 0832-2222068; www.caculomall.in; 16 Shanta, St Inez; ⊙ 10am-9pm) Goa's biggest mall is four levels of air-conditioned family shopping heaven with brand-name stores, food court, kids' toys, bowling alley and arcade games.

ℹ Information

MEDICAL SERVICES

Goa Medical College Hospital (☑ 0832-2458700; www.gmc.goa.gov.in; NH66, Bambolim; ⊙ 24hr) This 1000-bed hospital is 9km south of Panaji on NH66 in Bambolim.

TOURIST INFORMATION

Goa Tourism (p811) The GTDC office is in the large Paryatan Bhavan building across the Ourem Creek and near the bus stand. However, it's more marketing office than tourist office and is of little use to casual visitors, unless you want to book one of GTDC's host of tours.

Government of India Tourist Office (☑ 0832-2438812; www.incredibleindia.com; Paryatan Bhavan, Dr Alvaro Costa Rd; ⊙ 9.30am-1.30pm & 2.30-6pm Mon-Fri, 10am-1pm Sat) is in the same building, staff at this tourist office can be helpful, especially for information outside Goa.

ℹ Getting There & Away

AIR

Dabolim Airport (p811) is around 30km south of Panaji. A new airport bus (www.goakadamba.com) between Dabolim and Calangute stops at Panaji on request. Some higher-end hotels offer a minibus service, often included in the room tariff.

BOAT

Taking the rusty but free passenger/vehicle ferry across the Mandovi River to the fishing village of Betim makes a fun shortcut en route to the northern beaches. It departs the jetty on Dayanand Bandodkar Marg. From Betim there are regular buses onwards to Calangute and Candolim.

BUS

All local buses depart from Panaji's **Kadamba bus stand** (☑ interstate 0832-2438035, local 0832-2438034; www.goakadamba.com; Patto Centre; ⊙ reservations 8am-8pm), with frequent local services (running to no apparent timetable) heading out every few minutes; major destinations are Mapusa (₹30, 30 minutes) in the north, Margao (₹40, one hour) to the south and Ponda (₹25, one hour) to the east. Most bus services run from 6am to 10pm. Ask at the bus stand to be directed to the right bus, or check the signs on the bus windscreens.

To get to the beaches in South Goa, take an express bus to Margao and change there; to get to beaches north of Baga, it's best to head to Mapusa and change there. There are direct buses to Candolim (₹20, 35 minutes), Calangute (₹25, 25 minutes) and Baga (₹30, 30 minutes).

State-run long-distance services also depart from the Kadamba bus stand, but prices offered by private operators are similar and they offer greater choice in type of bus and departure times. Many private operators have **booths** (Patto Place) outside the entrance to the bus stand (go there to compare prices and times). At the time of writing all interstate buses were operating from the Kadamba stand but there are plans to move them to a new stand on the Ponda bypass road.

1. Cola Beach (p846)
Difficult to find, but worth the search, this beach is enclosed by forested cliffs

2. Church of Our Lady of the Immaculate Conception (p812)
Panaji's spiritual and geographical centre.

3. Saturday Night Market (p829)
Arpora's evening market is as much about the food and entertainment as the shopping

4. Panaji (p812)
Colonial-era architecture in the state capital shows the Portuguese influence

TRAIN

The closest train station to Panaji is Karmali, 12km to the east near Old Goa. A number of long-distance services stop here, including services to and from Mumbai, and many trains coming from Margao also stop – but check in advance. Panaji's **Konkan Railway Reservation Office** (www.konkanrailway.com; Patto Place; ⊘ 8am-8pm Mon-Sat) is on the 1st floor of the Kadamba bus stand – not at the train station. You can also check times, prices and routes online at www.konkanrailway.com and www.indianrail.gov.in.

ℹ️ Getting Around

It's easy enough to get around central Panaji and Fontainhas on foot, which is just as well because taxis and autorickshaws charge extortionately for short trips (minimum ₹100). Autorickshaws and motorcycle taxis can also be found in front of the post office, on 18th June Rd, and just south of the church. A taxi from Panaji to the airport should cost ₹900 and takes about 45 minutes, but allow an hour for traffic.

Locals buses run to Miramar (₹5, 10 minutes), Dona Paula (₹8, 15 minutes) and to Old Goa (₹10, 20 minutes).

Goa Tourism's **Hop on Hop off bus** (☑ 7447473495; www.hohogoa.com; 1/2 route pass ₹400/700) plies a recurring route along the riverfront taking in the state museum, Kala Academy, Miramar Beach and Dona Paula, then returning and heading out to Old Goa and back.

Old Goa

From the 16th to the 18th centuries, when Old Goa's population exceeded that of Lisbon or London, Goa's former capital was considered the 'Rome of the East'. You can still sense that grandeur as you wander what's left of the city, with its towering churches and cathedrals and majestic convents. Its rise under the Portuguese, from 1510, was meteoric, but cholera and malaria outbreaks forced the abandonment of the city in the 17th century. In 1843 the capital was officially shifted to Panaji. Some of the most imposing churches and cathedrals are still in use and are remarkably well preserved, while other historical buildings have become museums or simply ruins. It's a fascinating day trip, but it can get crowded: consider visiting on a weekday morning.

◉ Sights

★ Basilica de Bom Jesus   CHURCH

(⊘ 7.30am-6.30pm) Famous throughout the Roman Catholic world, the imposing Basilica de Bom Jesus contains the tomb and mortal remains of St Francis Xavier, the so-called Apostle of the Indies. St Francis Xavier's missionary voyages throughout the East became legendary. His 'incorrupt' body is in the mausoleum to the right, in a glass-sided coffin amid a shower of gilt stars. Freelance guides at the entrance will show you around for ₹100.

★ Sé Cathedral   CATHEDRAL

(⊘ 8am-6pm, Mass 7am & 6pm Mon-Sat, 7.15am, 10am & 4pm Sun) At over 76m long and 55m wide, the cavernous Sé Cathedral is the largest church in Asia. Building commenced in 1562, on the orders of King Dom Sebastiao of Portugal, and the finishing touches were finally made some 90 years later. The exterior is notable for its plain style, in the Tuscan tradition. Also of note is its rather lopsided look resulting from the loss of one of its bell

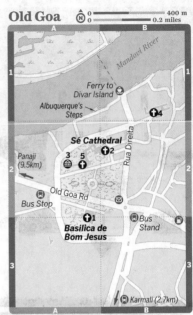

Old Goa

towers, which collapsed in 1776 after being struck by lightning.

Church of St Francis of Assisi   CHURCH
(⊙9am-5pm) West of the Sé Cathedral, the Church of St Francis of Assisi is no longer in use for worship, and consequently exudes a more mournful air than its neighbours.

Church of St Cajetan   CHURCH
(⊙9am-5.30pm) Modelled on the original design of St Peter's in Rome, the Church of St Cajetan was built by Italian friars of the Order of Theatines, who were sent by Pope Urban III to preach Christianity in the kingdom of Golconda (near Hyderabad). The friars were not permitted to work in Golconda, so settled at Old Goa in 1640. The construction of the church began in 1655.

Archaeological Museum   MUSEUM
(adult/child ₹10/free; ⊙9am-5pm) The archaeological museum houses some lovely fragments of sculpture from Hindu temple sites in Goa, and some sati stones, which once marked the spot where a Hindu widow committed suicide by flinging herself onto her husband's funeral pyre.

Other Sights
There are plenty of other monuments, churches and ruins in Old Goa to explore, including the Viceroy's Arch, Adil Shah Palace Gateway, the Chapel of St Anthony, the Chapel of St Catherine, the Church & Convent of St Monica (open from 8am to 5pm), the Convent & Church of St John, the Sisters' Convent, the Church of Our Lady of the Rosary (open from 8am to 5pm), the Monastery of St Augustine and, 2km east of the centre, the Church of Our Lady of the Mount.

ⓘ Getting There & Away
There are frequent buses to Old Goa (₹10, 20 minutes) from the Kadamba bus stand in Panaji to Old Goa's **bus stand** (Old Goa Rd) by the main roundabout. Buses to Panaji or Ponda from Old Goa leave when full (around every 10 minutes) from either the main roundabout bus stand or the bus stop (Old Goa Rd)/ATM at the western end of Old Goa Rd.

From the waterfront near the Viceroy's Arch, a free **ferry** runs to Divar Island. There's a petrol station near the main roundabout.

NORTH GOA

North Goa is the Goa you might have heard all about: crowded beaches, upbeat nightlife, Goan trance, cosmopolitan cuisine, hippie markets and yoga retreats. If you like a fast pace and plenty of things to do, this is the place.

Mapusa
POP 40,500

Mapusa (pronounced 'Mapsa') is the largest town in northern Goa, and is most often visited for its busy Friday **market** (⊙8am-6.30pm Mon-Sat), which attracts scores of buyers and sellers from neighbouring towns and villages. It's a good place to pick up the usual range of embroidered bed sheets and the like, at prices far lower than in the beach resorts. Many travellers pass through Mapusa anyway as it's the major transport hub for northern Goa buses. Most amenities are arranged around the Municipal Gardens, just north of the Kadamba bus station and main market site.

The once budget **Hotel Vilena** (☑0832-2263115; hotelvilena@gmail.com; Feira Baixa Rd; ₹1700-2000; ❇☏) has had a refurb and all rooms are now air-conditioned with bathroom, but it's still good value and the rooms are well kept. There's a restaurant and bar on the 1st floor and a rooftop restaurant called Goan & Grills.

There are food stalls and cafes around the market area. For good people watching and a cold beer, head upstairs to the **Pub** (Market Rd; ⊙10am-4.30pm & 6.30-11pm Mon-Sat), opposite the market.

ⓘ Getting There & Away
BUS

If you're coming to Goa by bus from Mumbai, Mapusa's **Kadamba bus stand** (☑0832-2232161; Calangute-Mapusa Rd) is the jumping-off point for the northern beaches. Local bus services run every few minutes; just look for the correct destination on the sign in the bus windshield. For buses to the southern beaches, take one of the frequent buses to Panaji, then Margao, and change there.

Long-distance services are run by both government and private bus companies. Private operators have booking offices outside the bus stand (opposite the Municipal Gardens). You can check fares and timings for government buses at www.goakadamba.com.

Most long-distance buses depart in the late afternoon or evening. Sample fares include: Bengaluru (₹900, with AC ₹1200; 13 to 14 hours, Hampi (sleeper ₹1000; 9½ hours), Mumbai (₹850, with AC ₹900; 12 to 15 hours) and Pune (₹700, with AC ₹900, 11 to 13 hours).

TAXI

There's a prepaid taxi stand in the town square with a signboard of fixed prices. Cabs to Anjuna or Calangute cost ₹300; Candolim ₹400; Panaji ₹350; Arambol ₹700; Margao ₹1100; Dabolim Airport ₹1150. An autorickshaw to Anjuna or Calangute should cost ₹200.

TRAIN

Thivim, about 12km northeast of town, is the nearest train station on the Konkan Railway. An autorickshaw to or from Thivim station costs around ₹250.

Candolim

POP 8600

Candolim's long and languid beach, which curves to join smaller Sinquerim Beach to the south, is largely the preserve of charter tourists from the UK, Russia and, more than ever, elsewhere in India. It's fringed with a line of beach shacks, all offering sunbeds and shade in exchange for your custom.

⊙ Sights & Activities

Fort Aguada   FORT

(⊙ 8.30am-5.30pm) FREE Standing on the headland overlooking the mouth of the Mandovi River, Fort Aguada occupies a magnificent and successful position, confirmed by the fact it was never taken by force. A highly popular spot to watch the sunset, with uninterrupted views both north and south, the fort was built in 1612, following the increasing threat to Goa's Portuguese overlords by the Dutch, among others.

John's Boat Tours   TOURS

(☑ 9822182814, 0832-6520190; www.johnboattours. com; Fort Aguada Rd; ⊙ 10am-9pm) A respected and well-organised Candolim-based operator offering a wide variety of boat and jeep excursions, as well as overnight houseboat cruises (₹6500 per person including meals). The standard half-day dolphin-watching cruise is ₹1200 (no dolphins, no pay) or join the renowned 'Crocodile Dundee' river trip (₹1400), to catch a glimpse of the Mandovi's mugger crocodile. Boat to Anjuna market is ₹1000.

Sinquerim Dolphin Trips   BOATING

(per person ₹300; ⊙ 8.30am-5.30pm) The boat operators on the Nerul River below Fort Aguada have banded together, so trips are fixed price. A one-hour dolphin-spotting and sightseeing trip costs ₹300 per person with a minimum of 10 passengers. Trips pass Nerul (Coco) Beach, Fort Aguada Jail and the fort.

🛏 Sleeping

Backpacker Panda   HOSTEL $

(☑ 9172313995; www.backpackerpanda.com; 1116, Anna Vaddo; dm from ₹500; 🌫🛜) Down a winding lane and very close to the beach, this is Candolim's best bet for backpackers. Clean four- to eight-bed air-con dorms (some mixed, one female-only) have attached bathrooms and there's an open-sided cafe with loungy seating. Bike hire is available. Follow sign to Sonesta Inns and take the lane to the north.

Shanu's Seaside Inn   GUESTHOUSE $

(☑ 9823016187; www.shanu.in; Escrivao Vaddo; d ₹1000, with AC ₹1500-3400; 🌫🛜) Shanu is one of several large guesthouses in this little grove just behind the dunes of Candolim Beach and it's a fine choice. The 18 rooms vary from basic but comfortable to deluxe rooms with sea views, air-con, king-sized beds and fridge. The owners also run the popular Pete's Shack on the beach.

★ Bougainvillea Guest House   GUESTHOUSE $$

(☑ 9822151969, 0832-2479842; www.bougainvillea goa.com; Sinquerim; r incl breakfast ₹4200-5400, penthouse ₹7800; 🌫🛜) A lush, plant-filled garden leads the way to this gorgeous family-run guesthouse, located off Fort Aguada Rd. The eight light-filled suite rooms are spacious and spotless, with fridge, flat-screen TV and either balcony or private sit-out; the top-floor penthouse has its own rooftop terrace. This is the kind of place guests come back to year after year. Book ahead.

★ Marbella Guest House   BOUTIQUE HOTEL $$

(☑ 0832-2479551, 9822100811; www.marbellagoa. com; Sinquerim; r ₹4200-4900, ste ₹6100-7800; 🌫🛜) This beautiful Portuguese villa, filled with antiques and enveloped in a peaceful courtyard garden, is a romantic and sophisticated old-world remnant. Rooms are individually themed, including Moghul, Rajasthani and Bougainvillea. The penthouse suite is a dream of polished tiles, four-poster bed with separate living room, dining room and terrace. The kitchen serves up some imaginative dishes. No kids under 12.

D'Hibiscus   BOUTIQUE HOTEL $$

(☑ 0832-2479842; www.dehibiscus.com; 83 Sinquerim; d ₹4200, penthouse ₹6600; 🌫🛜) Huge modern rooms with balconies are the draw at this Portuguese home off Sinquerim Beach. The top-floor penthouse rooms, with spa bath, big-screen TV and balcony sunbeds, are worth a splurge.

D'Mello's Sea View Home
HOTEL **$$**

(☏ 0832-2489395; www.dmellos.com; Monteiro's Rd, Escrivao Vaddo; d with/without AC ₹3500/2500, sea view ₹4750/4150; ❄ ☏) D'Mello's has grown up from small beginnings, but is still family-run and occupies four buildings around a lovely garden just back from the beach. The front building has the premium seaview rooms so check out a few, but all are clean and well maintained with balconies, four-poster beds and shuttered windows. Wifi is available in the central area.

✖ Eating

Newton's
SUPERMARKET **$**

(Fort Aguada Rd; ⏰ 9.30am-1am) If you're desperately missing Edam cheese or Marmite, or just want to do some self-catering, Newton's is Goa's biggest supermarket. There's a good line in toiletries, wines, children's toys and luxury food items. The downside is that it's often packed and security guards won't allow bags inside.

Viva Goa!
GOAN **$**

(Fort Aguada Rd; mains ₹100-210; ⏰ 11am-midnight) This inexpensive, locals-oriented little place, also popular with in-the-know tourists, serves fresh fish and Goan seafood specialities such as a spicy mussel fry. Check the market price of seafood before ordering.

★ Café Chocolatti
CAFE **$$**

(409A Fort Aguada Rd; sweets ₹50-200, mains ₹250-450; ⏰ 9am-5pm Mon-Sat; ☏) The lovely garden tearoom at Café Chocolatti may be on the main Fort Aguada Rd, but it's a peaceful retreat where chocolate brownies, waffles and banoffee pie with a strong cup of coffee or organic green tea taste like heaven. Also has a great range of salads, paninis, crepes and quiches for lunch. Take away a bag of chocolate truffles, homemade by the in-house chocolatier.

Stone House
STEAK **$$**

(Fort Aguada Rd; mains ₹200-800; ⏰ 11am-3pm & 7pm-midnight) Surf 'n' turf's the thing at this venerable old Candolim venue, inhabiting a stone house and its leafy front courtyard, with the improbable-sounding 'Swedish Lobster' topping the list, along with some Goan dishes. It's also a popular blues bar with live music most nights of the week in season.

Fisherman's Cove
SEAFOOD **$$**

(☏ 9822143376; Fort Aguada Rd; mains ₹160-350; ⏰ 9am-4.30pm & 6-11.30pm) The corner streetside Fisherman's Cove is always busy thanks to a strong reputation for its seafood and Indian dishes. The food is good but this popularity can mean slow service or a wait for a table. Regular live music and a good bar area.

★ Bomra's
BURMESE **$$$**

(☏ 9767591056; www.bomras.com; 247 Fort Aguada Rd; mains ₹520-650; ⏰ noon-2pm & 7-11pm) Wonderfully unusual food is on offer at this sleek little place serving interesting modern Burmese cuisine with a fusion twist. Aromatic dishes include Bomra's mussel curry, chicken pho or Burmese rice and noodle salad. Decor is palm-thatch style huts in a lovely courtyard garden.

🍷 Drinking & Nightlife

Bob's Inn
BAR

(Fort Aguada Rd; ⏰ noon-4pm & 7pm-midnight) The African wall hangings, palm-thatch, communal tables and terracotta sculptures are a nice backdrop to the *rava* (semolina) fried mussels, but this Candolim institution is really just a great place to drop in for a drink.

LPK Waterfront
CLUB

(couples ₹1700; ⏰ 9.30pm-4am) The initials stand for Love, Peace and Karma: the whimsical, sculpted waterfront LPK across the Nerul River from Candolim is the biggest club in the area, attracting mainly Indian party-goers from all over with huge indoor

Candolim, Sinquerim & Fort Aguada

N 0 —————— 400 m
0 —————— 0.2 miles

See Calangute & Baga Map (p826)

Calangute (500m);
Baga (2km)

17

5

Monteiro's Rd   16

8
10

CANDOLIM

2

14

13
3

Central
Bus Stop

Candolim
Beach

Candolim Beach Rd   12

*Beach
Shacks*

Fort Aguada Rd

15

11

SINQUERIM

19

ARABIAN SEA

Nerul River

18

Betim (8km);
Panaji (11km)

Sinquerim
Beach

7   Fort Aguada
Bus Stop

9   6

4

1

*Fort
Aguada*

GOA

Candolim, Sinquerim & Fort Aguada

and outdoor dance areas. Most popular on Thursday, Friday and Saturday nights, when cover prices vary and include drink coupons.

SinQ CLUB
(☑ 8308000080; www.sinq.co.in; Fort Aguada Rd; couples ₹1500, women ₹500; ⊙ 10pm-3am) The SinQ entertainment scene, almost directly opposite Taj Holiday Village, is one for the cool people but it has expanded to include the Showbar gastropub as well as the beach lounge-bar with cabanas by the pool and a nightclub, so there's something for everyone. Events vary but Wednesday is usually ladies' night.

❶ Getting There & Away

Buses run about every 10 minutes to and from Panaji (₹20, 35 minutes), and stop at the **central bus stop** (Fort Aguada Rd) near John's Boat Tours. Some continue south to the **Fort Aguada bus stop** (Fort Aguada Rd) at the bottom of Fort Aguada Rd, then head back to Panaji along the Mandovi River road, via the villages of Verem and Betim.

Frequent buses also run from Candolim to Calangute (₹10, 15 minutes) and can be flagged down on Fort Aguada Rd.

Calangute & Baga
POP 16,000

For many visitors, particularly cashed-up young Indian tourists from Bengaluru (Bangalore) and Mumbai plus Europeans on package holidays, this is Goa's party strip, where the raves and hippies have made way for modern thumping nightclubs and wall-to-wall drinking. The Calangute market area and the main Baga road can get very busy but everything you could ask for – from a Thai massage to a tattoo – is in close prox-

imity and the beach is lined with an excellent selection of increasingly sophisticated restaurant shacks with sunbeds, wi-fi and attentive service.

◉ Sights & Activities

Yoga classes pop up around Calangute and Baga each season, though it's not as organised as it is in the resorts and retreats further north. Look out for up-to-date flyers and noticeboards for the latest.

You don't have to go far to find beach water sports along the Calangute–Baga strip.

Museum of Goa ARTS CENTRE
(☑ 7722089666; www.museumofgoa.com; 79, Pilerne Industrial Estate, Calangute; Indian/foreigner ₹100/300; ⊙ 10am-6pm) Not so much a museum as a gallery for contemporary art, MOG features artworks, sculptures, exhibitions, workshops, courses, sitar concerts and an excellent cafe and shop. It's the brainchild of well-known local artist and sculptor Dr Subodh Kerkar, with the philosophy of making art accessible to all.

Benz Celebrity Wax Museum AMUSEMENT PARK
(Calangute-Anjuna Rd, Baga; ₹200) This quirky attraction features a wax museum with reasonably accurate figures of Hollywood and Bollywood celebrities, action heroes and sports stars. There's also a 9D cinema (₹200) and bumper cars (₹150). Good for kids or a rainy day.

Baga Snow Park SNOW SPORTS
(☑ 9595420781; www.snowparkgoa.com; Tito's Lane 2, Baga; ₹495; ⊙ 11am-7pm; ▣) This giant fridge is a mini wonderland of snowmen, igloos, slides and ice sculptures. You get kitted out with parka, pants and gloves (included) – it's novel being this cold in India! Good for kids.

GOA CALANGUTE & BAGA

Calangute & Baga

N

0 ——————————— 1 km
0 ——————————— 0.5 miles

Arpora (2km);
Anjuna (4km)

22

See Anjuna Map (p830)

Baga River Rd

Baga River

6

9

15   14

Baga
Bus
Stand

1

BAGA

Calangute-Baga Rd

5

Beach
Shacks

2

11   Tito's   19
Lane

20

Baga
Beach   18   21

Baga
Market

7

Calangute-Baga Rd

8

Calangute-Anjuna Rd

16   Temple   Calangute
Bus Stand

São João   17
Batista
Church   Market   13

4

CALANGUTE

**ARABIAN
SEA**

Dr Afonso Rd

Saligao
(2.5km)

St Anthony's
Chapel

10

**SOUTH
CALANGUTE**

12   3   Holiday St

See Candolim, Sinquerim &
Fort Aguada Map (p824)

GOA

Calangute & Baga

⊙ Sights
1 Benz Celebrity Wax Museum D2

⊕ Activities, Courses & Tours
2 Baga Snow Park B3
3 Goa Aquatics C7

⊜ Sleeping
4 Aerostel D5
5 Alidia Beach Cottages B2
6 Beach Box A2
7 Indian Kitchen C4
8 Johnny's Hotel B5
9 Melissa Guest House A2
10 Ospey's Shelter C7
11 Resort Fiesta B3

⊗ Eating
12 A Reverie C7
13 Cafe Sussegado Souza D5
14 Cliff's Beach Restaurant A2
15 Go With the Flow A2
16 Infantaria C5
17 Plantain Leaf C5

⊙ Drinking & Nightlife
18 Café Mambo B3
19 Cape Town Cafe B3
20 Keventers B3
21 Tito's B3

⊜ Shopping
22 Saturday Night Market D1

Goa Aquatics   DIVING
(☑ 9822685025; www.goaaquatics.com; 136/1 Gaura Vaddo, Calangute; dive trip/course from ₹5000/22,000) This professional dive resort offers a range of PADI courses and boat dives to Grande and Netrani Islands. An introductory dive for beginners is ₹5000 and a four-day PADI Open Water course is ₹22,000.

Barracuda Diving   DIVING
(☑ 0832-2279409, 9822182402; www.barracuda diving.com; Sun Village Resort, Baga; dive trip/course from ₹5000/18,000) This long-standing school offers a range of PADI and SSI classes, dives and courses, including a 'Bubblemakers' introduction to scuba class of 1½ hours for children eight years and older (₹1500), Discover Scuba for ₹6500 and PADI Open Water for ₹22,000. For qualified divers a two-tank dive to Grande Island is ₹5000 (snorkellers ₹1500).

🛏 Sleeping

Calangute and Baga's sleeping options are broad and varied, though it's not a particularly budget-friendly destination, except in the off-season. Quite a few places here remain open year-round.

★ Indian Kitchen   GUESTHOUSE $
(☑ 0832-2277555, 9822149615; www.indiankitchen-goa.com; off Calangute-Baga Rd, Baga; s/d from ₹770/880, AC chalet/apt ₹2100/3500; 🌀🛜🐾) Don't be fooled by the name – there's no longer a restaurant here but there is a great little budget guesthouse. Family-run Indian Kitchen has a range of rooms from basic to more spacious, comfy apartments and wooden chalets by the pool. There's a neat central courtyard and well-stocked library. Each room has its own terrace.

Johnny's Hotel   HOTEL $
(☑ 0832-2277458; www.johnnyshotel.com; Khobra Vaddo, Calangute; s ₹800, d ₹1000-1500, with AC ₹1600-2000; 🌀🛜) The 12 simple rooms at this backpacker-popular place make for a sociable stay, with a downstairs restaurant-bar and regular yoga and reiki classes. A range of apartments and houses are available for longer stays. It's down a lane lined with unremarkable midrange hotels and is just a short walk to the beach.

Aerostel   HOSTEL $
(☑ 9833345744; 2/201 Naikawaddo, Calangute; dm ₹500-750) This basic backpackers' hostel is a welcome budget addition to Calangute in a super-central location behind the main market (it's actually down a quiet lane opposite KFC). The six-/eight-/10-bed dorms are air-conditioned with en suite and there's a basic kitchen.

Ospey's Shelter   GUESTHOUSE $
(☑ 7798100981, 0832-2279505; ospeys.shelter@ gmail.com; Calangute; d ₹1000) Tucked away between the beach and St Anthony's Chapel, in a quiet, lush little area full of palms and sandy paths, Ospey's is a traveller favourite and only a two-minute walk from the beach. Spotless upstairs rooms have fridges and balconies and the whole place has a cosy family feel. Take the road directly west of the chapel – but it's tough to find, so call ahead.

Melissa Guest House   GUESTHOUSE $
(☑ 9822180095; Baga River Rd, Baga; d ₹1000; 🛜) Across the Baga River, Melissa Guest House has just four neat little rooms, all with attached bathrooms and hot-water showers, in a tatty garden. Good value for the location.

★ **Alidia Beach Cottages** GUESTHOUSE $$
(☑ 9822876867, 0832-2279014; Calangute-Baga Rd, Saunta Waddo; d ₹2400, with AC from ₹3900; ❈ ⿻ ⊠) Set back behind a whitewashed chapel off busy Baga Rd, this convivial but quiet place has beautifully kept Mediterranean-style rooms orbiting a gorgeous pool. The cheaper non-AC rooms at the back are not as good, but all are in good condition, staff are eager to please, and there's a path leading directly to Baga Beach.

Beach Box BOUTIQUE HOTEL $$
(☑ 9607473627; http://boxhotels.in; Baga River Rd, Baga; d ₹4200-5400; ❈ ⿻ ⊠) About time someone in Goa thought of recycling old shipping containers. The rooms here are pretty cosy but they're a bit of a novelty in fully equipped half or full-size shipping containers with en suite and air-con. The in-ground pool is also a shipping container and the restaurant-bar is made up of various recycled materials.

Resort Fiesta BOUTIQUE HOTEL $$$
(☑ 9822104512; www.fiestagoa.com; Tito's Lane, Baga; d & ste incl breakfast ₹8000-10,200; ❈ ⿻ ⊠) Large, light-filled rooms are the signature at this beautifully designed boutique resort behind the beachfront restaurant of the same name. The labour of love by owner Yellow Mehta is stylishly appointed with a lovely garden and pool, large verandas and modern touches like TV, minibar and dual wash basins.

✕ Eating

The beach shacks are an obvious go-to, but there are some interesting gems along the 'Strip' and a few excellent upmarket offerings on the north side of the Baga River.

Plantain Leaf INDIAN $
(☑ 0832-2279860; Calangute Beach Rd, Calangute; veg thali ₹150, mains ₹130-270; ⊙ 11am-5pm & 7-11.45pm) In the heart of Calangute's busy market area, 1st-floor Plantain Leaf has consistently been the area's best pure veg restaurant for many years, with classic South Indian banana leaf thalis and dosas, along with more North Indian flavours. Most dishes sneak into the budget category.

Infantaria ITALIAN $$
(Calangute-Baga Rd, Calangute; pastries ₹80-200, mains ₹200-780; ⊙ 7.30am-midnight; ⿻) Once Calangute's best bakery, Infantaria is still a popular Italian-Indian, fondue-meets-curry restaurant. The bakery roots are still there, though, with homemade cakes, croissants,

little flaky pastries and real coffee. Get in early for breakfast before the good stuff runs out. Regular live music in season and it's a popular bar in the evening.

Cliff's Beach Restaurant INDIAN $$
(Baga; mains ₹180-400; ⊙ 9am-11pm; ⿻) The best way to get away from the Baga beach crowd is to walk around the cliff edge north of the Baga River to secluded Cliff's. The menu is typical beach shack but it's just a great location for a cold beer and a swim in the calm waters off the beach. After dark, staff will help walk you back around the cliff.

Cafe Sussegado Souza GOAN $$
(☑ 09850141007; Calangute-Anjuna Rd, Calangute; mains ₹230-480; ⊙ noon-11pm) In a little yellow Portuguese house just south of the Calangute market area, Cafe Sussegado is the place to come for Goan food such as fish curry rice, chicken *xacuti* and pork *sorpotel* (a vinegary stew made from liver, heart and kidneys), with a shot of feni to follow. Authentic, busy and good atmosphere.

★ **Go With the Flow** INTERNATIONAL $$$
(☑ 7507771556; www.gowiththeflowgoa.com; 614 Baga River Rd, Baga; small plates ₹180-420, mains ₹430-840; ⊙ noon-10.30pm; ⿻) Stepping into the fantasy neon-lit garden of white-wicker furniture is impressive and the food is consistently good. With a global menu leaning towards European, African and Asian flavours, this remains one of Baga's best dining experiences. Try some of the small bites (ask about a tasting plate) or go straight for the signature pork belly or African inspired spicy prawn rice.

★ **A Reverie** INTERNATIONAL $$$
(☑ 8380095732; www.areverie.com; Holiday St, Calangute; mains ₹450-800; ⊙ 7pm-late; ⿻) A gorgeous lounge bar, all armchairs, cool jazz and whimsical outdoor space, this is the place to spoil yourself, with the likes of Spanish tapas, truffle bombs, grilled asparagus, French wines and Italian cheeses. A Reverie likes to style itself as 'fun dining' and doesn't take itself too seriously. Though it takes its cocktails seriously.

☕ Drinking & Nightlife

★ **Keventers** MILKSHAKES
(Tito's Lane, Baga; milkshakes ₹80-230; ⊙ 11am-3am) Had enough of the Kingfisher? Keventers, the famous Delhi milkshake maker, has set up in Goa and on Tito's Lane no

There are two well-established evening markets, **Saturday Night Market** (Calangute-Anjuna Rd; ⊙ from 6pm Sat late Nov-Mar) in Arpora and **Mackie's** (Baga River Rd; ⊙ from 6pm Sat Dec-Apr) in Baga, that make an interesting evening alternative to the Anjuna flea market.

The attractions here are as much about food stalls and entertainment as shopping, but there's a big range of so-so stalls, flashing jewellery, spices, clothing and textiles.

less. The hole-in-wall joint serves up classic milkshakes in its signature glass bottles, or sample the more exotic Oreo, bubblegum or salted caramel. It's the perfect antidote to a big night out.

Café Mambo CLUB
(☑ 7507333003; Tito's Lane, Baga; cover charge couples ₹1000; ⊙ 6pm-3am) Part of the Tito's empire, Mambo is one of Baga's busiest clubs with an indoor/outdoor beachfront location and nightly DJs pumping out house, hip hop and Latino tunes. Couples or women only; Friday is the popular Bollywood night.

Tito's CLUB
(☑ 9822765002; www.titos.in; Tito's Lane, Baga; cover charge varies; ⊙ 8pm-3am) The long-running titan of Goa's clubbing scene, Tito's has done its best to clean up its act and organises regular event nights that take on a distinctly Indian club scene. Saturday is Bollywood night. It's generally couples or ladies only – solo men (stags) get in on certain nights at an inflated cover charge, depending on the mood of door staff.

Cape Town Cafe BAR
(www.capetowncafe.com; Tito's Lane, Baga; ⊙ 6pm-1am; 🛜) The most laid-back of the Tito's venues, Cape Town has a street-front lounge bar with wi-fi and live sports on big screens, while inside international DJs play until late. Goan food, bar snacks and hookah pipes available.

ⓘ Getting There & Away

Frequent buses go to Panaji (₹20, 45 minutes) and Mapusa (₹15, 30 minutes) from both the **Calangute** (Calangute Beach Rd) and Baga bus stands.

Kadamba runs a shuttle bus between Calangute bus stand and the airport four times a day (₹150, 1½ hours).

A taxi from Calangute or Baga to Panaji costs around ₹600 and takes about half an hour. A prepaid taxi from the airport to Calangute costs ₹1200.

ⓘ Getting Around

Motorcycle and scooter hire is easy to arrange in Calangute and Baga (ask at your accommodation). Prices are fairly steady at around ₹300 for a gearless Honda Kinetic and ₹350 to ₹400 for an Enfield, but high demand means you might have to pay much more in peak season. Definitely try bargaining in quieter times or for rentals of more than a week.

A local bus runs between the Calangute and Baga stands every few minutes (₹5); catch it anywhere along the way, though when traffic is bad it might be quicker to walk.

Taxis between Calangute and northern Baga beach charge an extortionate ₹100.

Anjuna
POP 9640

Anjuna has been a stalwart of the hippie scene since the 1960s and still drags out the sarongs and sandalwood each Wednesday (in season) for its famous flea market. Though it continues to pull in droves of backpackers, midrange and domestic tourists are increasingly making their way here for a dose of hippie-chic. Anjuna is continuing to evolve, with a heady beach party scene and a constant flowering of new restaurants, bars and backpacker hostels. If anything, Anjuna is having a renaissance.

The village itself is a bit ragged around the edges and is spread out over a wide area, but that's part of the charm. Do as most do: hire a scooter or motorbike and explore the back lanes and southern beach area and you'll find a place that suits. Anjuna will grow on you.

ⓞ Sights & Activities

Anjuna's charismatic, narrow beach runs for almost 2km from the rocky, low-slung cliffs at the northern village area right down beyond the flea market in the south. In season there are water sports here, including jet skis, banana boats and parasailing.

Lots of yoga (p835), ayurveda and other alternative therapies and regimes are on offer in season; look out for noticeboards at popular cafes such as Artjuna Cafe (p832).

Brahmani Yoga YOGA
(☑ 9545620578; www.brahmaniyoga.com; Tito's White House, Aguada-Siolim Rd; class ₹700, 10-class

GOA ANJUNA

Anjuna

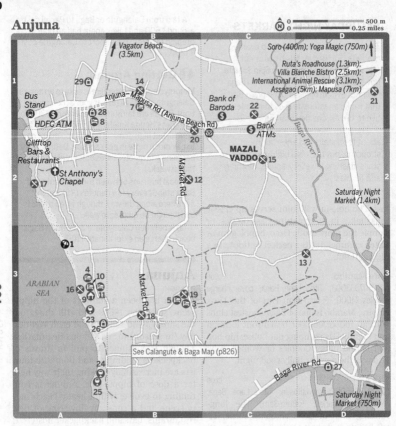

Anjuna

⊙ Sights
1 Anjuna Beach...................................A3

✛ Activities, Courses & Tours
2 Barracuda Diving..............................D4
  Brahmani Yoga............................(see 21)
  Goa Muay Thai............................(see 21)

⛱ Sleeping
3 Banyan Soul.....................................B3
4 Florinda's..A3
5 Headquarters...................................B3
6 Lazy Lama.......................................A2
7 Paradise..B1
8 Red Door Hostel..............................A1
9 Sea Horse.......................................A3
10 The Village.....................................A3
11 Wonderland Hostel.........................A3

⊗ Eating
12 Artjuna Cafe...................................B2

13 Baba Au Rhum................................D3
14 Burger Factory...............................B1
15 Choco Cream Gelati........................C2
16 Elephant Art Cafe...........................A3
17 Eva Cafe..A2
18 FlourPower Bakeria.........................B3
19 German Bakery...............................B3
20 Goa's Ark......................................B2
21 Lila Café..D1
22 Oltremarino....................................C1

🍷 Drinking & Nightlife
23 Cafe Lilliput...................................A3
24 Curlies...A4
25 Shiva Valley....................................A4

🛍 Shopping
26 Anjuna Flea Market.........................A4
27 Mackie's Saturday Nite Bazaar.........D4
28 Manali Guest House.........................A1
29 Oxford Arcade................................A1

pass ₹5000; ⊙classes 9.30am) This friendly drop-in centre offers daily classes from late November to April in ashtanga, vinyasa, hatha and dynamic yoga, as well as pranayama meditation. No need to book: just turn up 15 minutes before the beginning of class.

Goa Muay Thai ***MARTIAL ARTS***
(☑9767479486; www.goamuaythai.com; Tito's White House, Aguada-Siolim Rd; class ₹500, weekly pass ₹2000; ⊙9-10.30am & 5-6.45pm Mon-Fri) These morning and afternoon classes are designed with fitness and technique in mind rather than full-on sparring, so are good for beginners. The boxing ring and gym at Tito's White House sets up in November.

🛏 Sleeping

Wonderland Hostel ***HOSTEL $***
(☑8692993770; www.wonderlandhostel.com; 69/6, Govekar Vaddo; dm ₹500-600, d ₹2000-2500, without bathroom ₹1200-1500; ❊🛜) Superchilled Wonderland, off the path behind Anjuna Beach near Lilliput, has a lineup of cabins comprising en-suite dorms and a few private rooms (some with AC), as well as a couple of old-school basic bamboo tree houses and space for tents. Owner Sandeep welcomes travellers into his loungy chill-out area with a small kitchen and cafe. Free yoga classes daily at 9am.

Red Door Hostel ***HOSTEL $***
(☑0832-2274423; reddoorhostels@gmail.com; dm with/without AC from ₹500/400, d with/without AC ₹2200/1900; ❊🛜) Red Door is a welcoming backpacker place close to Anjuna's central crossroads with clean four- and six-bed dorms plus a few private rooms. Facilities include lockers, free wi-fi, a garden, good communal areas – including a well-equipped kitchen – and a sociable cafe-bar.

Florinda's ***GUESTHOUSE $***
(☑9890216520; s/d ₹800/1000, with AC ₹1500; ❊🛜) One of the better budget places near the beach and a bit hidden next to Janet & John's, Florinda's has clean rooms, with 24-hour hot water, window screens and mosquito nets, set around a pretty garden. The few air-con rooms fill up fast.

Headquarters ***HOSTEL $***
(☑0832-2274510; dm with/without AC ₹500/400; ❊🛜) Near the German Bakery, Headquarters ticks all the budget boxes for cleanliness and comfort with upstairs dorms, kitchen and common areas downstairs and a garden with some potential out back.

Lazy Lama ***HOSTEL $***
(☑9717000955; lazylamagoa@gmail.com; dm ₹300-500) A laid-back hostel down a quiet lane in Anjuna village, Lazy Lama offers six- and 10-bed dorms in a partly converted Portuguese house. Attracts a chilled crowd.

Paradise ***GUESTHOUSE $***
(☑9922541714; janet_965@hotmail.com; Anjuna-Mapusa Rd; d ₹1000-1200, with AC ₹1500-2000; ❊@🛜) This friendly place is fronted by an old Portuguese home and offers neat, clean rooms with well-decorated options in the newer annex. The better rooms have TVs, fridges and hammocks on the balcony. Friendly owner Janet and family also run the pharmacy, general store, restaurant, internet cafe, Connexions travel agency and money exchange!

Banyan Soul ***BOUTIQUE HOTEL $$***
(☑9820707283; www.thebanyansoul.com; d ₹3000; ❊🛜) A slinky 12-room option, tucked down the lane off Market Rd, and lovingly conceived and run by Sumit, a young Mumbai escapee. Rooms are chic and well equipped with AC and TV, and there's a lovely library and shady seating area beneath a banyan tree.

Sea Horse ***HUT $$***
(☑9764465078; www.vistapraiaanjuna.com; ⊙hut with/without AC ₹3500/2000; ❊🛜) A lineup of timber cabins behind the beach restaurant of the same name, Sea Horse offers a good location and decent value. The huts are small and get a little hot – ask for the air-con remote control if it's uncomfortably humid. Staff are friendly and accommodating. The same owners have a pricier beachfront setup nearby called Vista Praia Anjuna.

The Village ***COTTAGE $$***
(☑9988882021; d ₹3800-4500) The solid timber and rendered concrete cottages here are some of the best-designed on the beachfront. Set in a pleasant garden they feature large beds and bathrooms, and air-con to justify the price. It's behind Elephant Art Cafe (p832).

🍴 Eating

★Choco Cream Gelati ***ICE CREAM $***
(Mazal Vaddo; ice cream & gelato ₹120-180; ⊙9am-midnight) This may well be the best Italian-style gelato and ice cream in Goa and regulars know it. Scoops in a cup or waffle cone, shakes, juices and espresso coffee are all available and there's a regular parade of flavours from lemon cheesecake to salted

ANJUNA FLEA MARKET

Anjuna's weekly Wednesday **flea market** (⏲8am-sunset Wed Nov-Apr) is as much part of the Goan experience as a day on the beach. More than three decades ago, it was conceived and created by hippies smoking jumbo joints, convening to compare experiences on the heady Indian circuit and selling pairs of Levi jeans or handmade jewellery to help fund the rest of their stay. These days it's almost entirely made up of traders from Kashmir, Gujarat, Karnataka and elsewhere selling a fairly standard line of spices, T-shirts, bejewelled bedspreads, saris and bags. It's still good fun, with live music in the afternoon and plenty of colour. The best time to visit is early (from 8am) or late afternoon (around 4pm till close just after sunset). The first market of the season is around mid-November, continuing until the end of April.

caramel and tiramisu. There's al fresco eating out front.

FlourPower Bakeria   BAKERY $

(☑9867276541; Market Rd; bread & baked goods from ₹80; ⏲11am-8pm Wed, 7-11pm Fri-Sun) This artisanal bakery produces fresh sourdough bread loaves with loads of love, along with croissants, cakes, cookies and fabulous pizzas.

★ Artjuna Cafe   CAFE $$

(☑0832-2274794; www.artjuna.com; Market Rd; mains ₹130-480; ⏲7.30am-10.30pm; 🛜) Artjuna is right up there with our favourite cafes in Anjuna. Along with all-day breakfast, outstanding espresso coffee, salads, smoothies, sandwiches and Middle Eastern surprises like baba ganoush, tahini and falafel, this sweet garden cafe has an excellent craft and lifestyle shop, yoga classes, movie nights and a useful noticeboard. Great meeting place.

German Bakery   MULTICUISINE $$

(www.german-bakery.in; breakfast ₹60-240, mains ₹190-570; ⏲8.30am-11pm; 🛜🐾) Leafy and adorned with lanterns, cushioned seating, occasional live music and garden lights, German Bakery is a long-standing favourite for hearty and healthy breakfasts, fresh-baked bread, organic food and tofu balls, but the menu also runs to Indian dishes, pasta, burgers and seafood. Has healthy juices (for example wheatgrass and kombuchas) and espresso coffee.

Elephant Art Cafe   CAFE $$

(☑9970668845; mains ₹250-450; ⏲8am-10pm; 🛜) A standout among the many restaurants lining Anjuna's beach, Elephant Art Cafe does a thoughtful range of tapas, sandwiches, fish and chips and pasta. Breakfasts are a highlight, with fruit bruschetta or shakshuka potato pesto eggs among the offerings.

Goa's Ark   MIDDLE EASTERN $$

(☑9145050494; www.goas-ark.com; Anjuna Beach Rd; mains ₹150-670, meze from ₹50; ⏲10am-11pm; 🛜) Set in a pleasant garden, Goa's Ark breaks the mould of most same-same restaurants, specialising in Middle Eastern and Mediterranean cuisine with meze, barbecued meat and falafel. Chargrilled steaks and fish and chips contribute to a meat-heavy menu but vegetarians are not overlooked with baba ganoush, veg burgers and lentil salads.

Eva Cafe   CAFE $$

(☑7350055717; Cliff Walk; mains ₹210-350; ⏲9am-8pm; 🛜) Oceanfront Eva Cafe is a small but cosy place for healthy sandwiches, salads and sublime breakfasts featuring fresh-baked bread and good coffee. The evening menu includes nachos and a cheese platter with wine. Great sunset spot.

Lila Café   CAFE $$

(www.lilacafegoa.com; Tito's White House, Aguada-Siolim Rd; mains ₹100-290; ⏲8.30am-6pm) This German cafe has been a traveller favourite for many years, first in Baga and now at Tito's White House. It serves great home-baked breads, croissants, rösti and perfect frothy cappuccinos, and specialises in buffalo cheese and smoked ham.

★ Baba Au Rhum   FRENCH $$$

(☑9657210468; Anjuna-Baga Rd; baguettes ₹210-300, mains ₹480-550) It's tucked away on the back road between Anjuna and Baga but Baba Au Rhum's reputation (it was previously in Arpora) means it's always busy. Part bakery, part French cafe, this is the place for filled baguettes, croissants, crostini or quiche, as well as creamy pastas or a filet mignon. Craft beer on tap and a relaxed, open garden–restaurant vibe.

Burger Factory   BURGERS $$$

(Anjuna-Mapusa Rd; burgers ₹300-500; ⏲11.30am-3.30pm & 6.30-10.30pm Thu-Tue) There's no mistaking what's on offer at this little open-sided diner. The straightforward menu of burgers isn't cheap, but the buns are big and they are interesting and well crafted. Choose between beef or chicken burgers and toppings such as blue cheese, bacon and avocado.

Oltremarino ITALIAN $$$
(☑ 8412967105; Anjuna Beach Rd; mains ₹450-800; ☺ 1pm-midnight; 🛜) It's high-end Italian dining but the homemade pasta and speciality wood-fired pizzas are worth the splurge at this sweet garden restaurant in the grounds of a fine Portuguese mansion. Helpful staff will walk you through the lengthy menu and will insist you finish your meal with a complimentary shot of homemade Baileys.

🍷 Drinking & Nightlife

Curlies BAR
(www.curliesgoa.com; ☺ 9am-3am) Holding sway at South Anjuna Beach, Curlies mixes laid-back beach-bar vibe with sophisticated nightspot – the party nights here are notorious, legendary and loud. There's a rooftop lounge bar and an enclosed late-night dance club. Thursday and Saturday are big nights, as are full-moon nights.

Cafe Lilliput CLUB
(☑ 0832-2274648; www.cafelilliput.com; ☺ 8am-1am, to 4am on party nights; 🛜) Hovering over the beach near the flea-market site, Lilliput has built itself a reputation as one of the go-to nightspots, but it also has a good all-day restaurant and some interesting accommodation at the back.

Shiva Valley CLUB
(☑ 9689628008; ☺ 8am-3am) At the very southern end of Anjuna Beach, past Curlies,

Shiva Valley has grown from small beach shack to fully fledged trance club, with Tuesday the main party all-nighter.

🛍 Shopping

Oxford Arcade SHOPPING CENTRE
(Anjuna-Vagator Rd; ☺ 9am-9pm) Oxford Arcade, 100m from the Starco crossroads on the road to Vagator, is a fully fledged two-storey supermarket, complete with shopping trolleys and checkout scanners. It's an awesome place to stock up on toiletries, cheap booze and all those little international luxuries.

Manali Guest House BOOKS
(☺ 9.30am-8.30pm) Long-running bookshop and travel agency.

ℹ Getting There & Away

Buses to Mapusa (₹15, 30 minutes) depart every half-hour or so from the main bus stand at the end of the Anjuna–Mapusa Rd near the beach; some buses coming from Mapusa continue on to Vagator and Chapora.

A couple of direct daily buses head south to Calangute; otherwise, take a bus to Mapusa and change there.

Plenty of motorcycle taxis and autorickshaws gather at the main crossroads and you can also easily hire scooters and motorcycles here from ₹250 to ₹400 – most Anjuna-based travellers get around on two wheels.

Assagao

Snuggled in the countryside between Mapusa and Anjuna or Vagator, Assagao is one of North Goa's prettiest villages, with almost traffic-free country lanes passing old Portuguese mansions and whitewashed churches. The area is inspiringly peaceful enough to be home to some of North Goa's best yoga retreats and a growing number of excellent restaurants.

Local organisation **El Shaddai** (☑ 0832-2461068, 0832-6513286; www.childrescue.net; El Shaddai House, Socol Vaddo), a child protection charity, has several schools based here.

🏃 Activities

Spicy Mama's COOKING
(☑ 9623348958; www.spicymamasgoa.com; 517, Bouta Vaddo; 1-day course veg/nonveg ₹2000/3000, 3-day ₹5000/7000, 5-day ₹10,000/12,000) For cooking enthusiasts, Spicy Mama's specialises in spicy North Indian cuisine, from butter chicken to *aloo gobi* (cauliflower and potato

---

ℹ **DRUGS & THEFT**

Despite regular crackdowns and party restrictions, Anjuna and Vagator are still well-known places for procuring illicit substances, though they're not quite so freely available as in Goa's trance-party heyday. Participate at your peril – the police Anti-Narcotics Cell has been known to carry out checks on foreigners and Goa's central jail is not a place you want to spend a 10-year drug-related stretch. Even bribes might not get you out of trouble.

Take great care of your wallet, camera and the like on market day, when pickpocketing can be a problem.

curry) and *palak paneer* (cheese in a puréed spinach gravy), prepared at the country home of Suchi. The standard one-day course is four hours; book online for in-depth multi-day masterclasses and for directions.

International Animal Rescue
VOLUNTEERING

(AnimalTracks; ☑ 0832-2268272; www.international animalrescuegoa.org.in; Madungo Vaddo; ⊙ 9am-4pm) The well-established International Animal Rescue collects and cares for stray dogs, cats and other four-legged animals in distress, carrying out sterilisations and vaccinations. Volunteers are welcome to help with dog walking and playing with puppies and kittens, but must have evidence of rabies vaccination.

🛏 Sleeping & Eating

Namaste Jungle Garden
GUESTHOUSE $$

(☑ 9850466105; 138/3 Bairo Alto; cottage & apt incl breakfast ₹3500; ❄ 🛜) There's a real feeling of communing with nature in these slick and spacious timber cottages set back in a jungly Assagao garden. It also has two apartment-style rooms with kitchen in the main building and massage and yoga available.

Gunpowder
MULTICUISINE $$

(mains ₹200-475; ⊙ 8-10.30am, noon-3.30pm & 7-10.30pm Tue-Sun; 🛜) This garden restaurant behind the People Tree boutique exemplifies the Assagao trend in quality countryside dining, efficient service and wholesome, fresh food. Classic curries and stir-fries, both veg and nonveg, are the stars of the menu, along with tempting desserts (walnut, rum and raisin brownie) and cocktails.

Ruta's Roadhouse
INTERNATIONAL $$

(☑ 8380025757; www.rutas.in; Mapusa Rd; breakfast ₹300, small/big plates ₹200/300; ⊙ 8.30am-6.30pm Mon-Sat) Ruta's has made a home in an old Portuguese house in Assagao, serving up excellent set breakfasts and global culinary offerings from jambalaya to spicy laksa.

★ Villa Blanche Bistro
CAFE $$$

(www.villablanche-goa.com; 283 Badem Church Rd; breakfast ₹100-380, mains ₹350-480; ⊙ 9am-11pm Thu-Tue Nov-May; 🛜🅿) This lovely, German-run chilled garden cafe draws diners to the back lanes of Assagao. Salads, sandwiches, filled bagels and cakes are specialities, but you'll also find Thai curry and German sausages, as well as lots of vegetarian and vegan options. For an indulgent breakfast or brunch try the waffles and pancakes. Sunday brunch (from 10am) is legendary.

🍷 Drinking & Nightlife

Soro
PUB

(☑ 9881934440; Siolim Rd, Badem junction; ⊙ 6pm-2am) The 'village pub' is a welcome addition to the back lanes of sleepy Assagao, with pumping live music on weekends, salsa dancing on Sunday and a fun atmosphere whenever there's a crowd. Decor is part English pub, part American bar, with exposed brick walls, barrel tables and a pool table. There's bar food but this is more for drinking and dancing.

ⓘ Getting There & Away

Local buses between Mapusa and Anjuna (about 15 minutes from each) or Siolim pass through Assagao, but the village is best explored on a rented scooter or by taxi from your beach resort.

Vagator & Chapora

Dramatic red stone cliffs, thick palm groves and a crumbling 17th-century Portuguese fort give Vagator and its diminutive village neighbour Chapora one of the prettiest settings on the North Goan coast. Once known for their wild trance parties and heady, hippie lifestyles, things have slowed down considerably these days and upmarket restaurants are more the style, though Vagator has some of Goa's best clubs. Chapora – reminiscent of the Mos Eisley Cantina from *Star Wars* – remains a favourite for hippies and long-staying smokers, with the smell of charas (resin of the marijuana plant) clinging heavily to the light sea breeze.

◉ Sights & Activities

Chapora is a working fishing harbour nestled at the broad mouth of the Chapora River – the main sight here is the hilltop fort. Vagator has three small, charismatic beach coves below some dramatic cliffs.

Chapora Fort
FORT

FREE Chapora's old laterite fort, standing guard over the mouth of the Chapora River, was built by the Portuguese in 1617, to protect Bardez taluk (district), in Portuguese hands from 1543 onwards. Today it is a crumble of picturesque ruins with only the outer walls remaining, though you can still pick out the mouths of two escape tunnels. The main reason to make the climb up the hill is for the

INLAND YOGA RETREATS

The Anjuna/Vagator/Assagao area has a number of yoga retreats where you can immerse yourself in courses, classes and a Zen vibe during the October to March season.

Purple Valley Yoga Retreat (☑0832-2268363; www.yogagoa.com; 142 Bairo Alto; dm/s 1 week £770/850, 2 weeks £1150/1400) Popular yoga resort in Assagao.

Swan Yoga Retreat (☑8007360677, 0832-2268024; www.swan-yoga-goa.com; drop-in classes ₹500, 1 week s/d from ₹42,000/52,000) In a peaceful jungle corner of Assagao, Swan Retreat is a very Zen yoga experience.

Yoga Magic (☑0832-6523796; www.yogamagic.net; Mapusa-Chapora Rd; share/single ₹7700/11,600; ☎✉) 🍃 Solar lighting, vegetable farming and compost toilets are just some of the worthy initiatives practised in this luxurious yoga resort in Anjuna.

sensational views along the coast from atop the fort walls.

Mukti Kitchen COOKING

(☑8007359170; www.muktikitchen.com; off Vagator Beach Rd, Vagator; veg/nonveg/Goan class ₹2000/2500/3000; ⊙11am-2pm & 6-9pm) Mukti shares her cooking skills twice daily at these recommended classes. Courses include around five dishes that can be tailored – veg or nonveg, Goan, Indian or ayurvedic. Minimum four people, maximum six; book one day ahead. You'll find Mukti's opposite Leoney Resort in Vagator.

🛌 Sleeping

Budget accommodation, much of it in private rooms, ranges along Ozran Beach Rd and Vagator Beach Rd; you'll see lots of signs for 'rooms to let'. Head down the road to the harbour at Chapora and you'll find lots of rooms – and whole homes – for rent, mainly for long-term stays from around ₹15,000 per month. Vagator also has a range of backpacker hostels and more upmarket accommodation.

★ Dreams Hostel HOSTEL $

(☑9920651760; www.dreams-hostel.goa-india-hotels-resorts.com; off Vagator Beach Rd, Vagator; dm ₹400-550, AC cabins ₹2400; ☎☎) With a philosophy of 'art, music, wellness', former backpacker and local DJ Ravi has established a great little creative space for like-minded travellers with a spacious garden, clean dorms, deluxe timber cabins and chilled common areas. The hostel also acts as an artistic residency – the murals and artworks are all done by guests.

★ Jungle Hostel HOSTEL $

(☑0832-2273006; www.thehostelcrowd.com; Vagator Beach Rd, Vagator; dm with/without AC ₹650/550, s/d from ₹1100/1800; ☎☎) One of the original backpacker hostels in North Goa, Jungle brought the dorm experience and an international vibe to Vagator and has expanded to three properties. It's still among the best around and offers cheap transfers to its other properties in Panaji and Palolem. There are clean and bright four- to six-bed dorms and private rooms. Lockers, wi-fi, breakfast and communal kitchen.

Pappi Chulo HOSTEL $

(☑9075135343; pappichulohostel@gmail.com; Ozran Beach Rd, Vagator; dm with/without AC ₹550/450, d ₹2000) Unashamedly Vagator's party hostel, Pappi's has a bar in the garden, movie nights and an international vibe of travellers just hanging out. Themed dorms have lockers and bunk beds.

Baba Guesthouse & Villa GUESTHOUSE $

(☑9822161142; babavilla11@yahoo.in; Main St, Chapora; d with/without AC ₹1000/700; ☎) With its laid-back Chapora location, Baba is often full with long-stayers but you might be lucky as a walk-in. The 14 rooms are clean and simple but serviceable.

Casa de Olga GUESTHOUSE $

(☑9822157145, 0832-2274355; eadsouza@yahoo.co.in; Harbour Rd, Chapora; r ₹800-1350, without bathroom from ₹500) This welcoming family-run homestay, set around a nice garden on the way to Chapora harbour, offers spotless rooms of varying sizes in a three-storey building. The best are the top-floor rooms with swanky bathrooms, TV and balcony.

Shalom GUESTHOUSE $

(☑919881578459, 0832-2273166; www.shalom guesthousegoa.com; Ozran Beach Rd, Vagator; d ₹900-1500, with AC ₹2000; ☎☎) Arranged around a placid garden not far from the

Vagator & Chapora

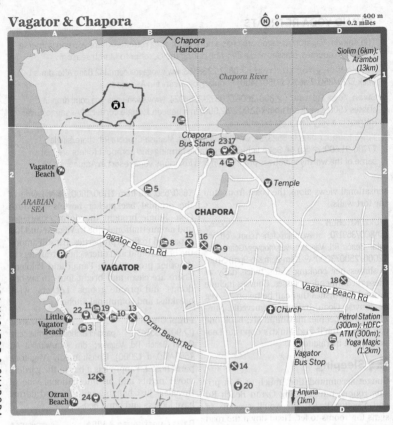

Vagator & Chapora

path down to Little Vagator Beach, this established place is run by a friendly family and offers a variety of extremely well-kept rooms and a two-bedroom apartment for long-stayers.

Bean Me Up Guest House

GUESTHOUSE $$

(☐ 7769095356; www.beanmeup.in; 1639/2 Deulvaddo, Vagator; d incl breakfast ₹1500-2500; ❄️ 🛜) Set around a leafy, shaded courtyard that's home to Vagator's best vegan restaurant Bean Me Up (p837), rooms here look simple but are themed with individual exotic decor, earthy shades, mosquito nets and shared verandas. The mellow yoga-friendly vibe matches the clientele and the included breakfast is decadent. Morning yoga classes.

Baba Place

GUESTHOUSE $$

(☐ 9822156511; babaplace11@yahoo.com; Chapora Fort Rd, Chapora; d ₹2500; ❄️ 🛜 🏊) Baba Place, in the shadow of Chapora Fort, continues to improve with immaculate, decent-sized rooms with verandah, a small pool and a bar-restaurant.

Alcove Resort

HOTEL $$

(☐ 0832-2274491; www.alcovegoa.com; Little Vagator Beach; d ₹5400-8500; ❄️ 🛜 🏊) The location overlooking Little Vagator Beach is hard to beat at this price. Attractively furnished rooms, slightly larger cottages, and four suites surrounding a decent central pool, restaurant and bar, make this a good place for those who want a touch of affordable luxury near the beach. Add ₹500 for air-con.

🍴 Eating

Jaws

INDIAN $

(Vagator Beach Rd, Vagator; mains ₹50-300; ⏰ 9am-9.30pm) With a bakery counter and inexpensive dosas and South Indian thalis, unassuming Jaws is an old-timer but one of the best-value eateries in Vagator. Good for a lazy breakfast or afternoon beer.

⭐ Bean Me Up

VEGAN $$

(www.beanmeup.in; 1639/2 Deulvaddo, Vagator; mains ₹200-400; ⏰ 8am-11pm; 🛜) Bean Me Up is vegan, but even nonveg travellers will be blown away by the taste, variety and filling plates on offer in this relaxed garden restaurant. The extensive menu includes vegan pizzas, ice creams, housemade tofu curry and innovative salads. Ingredients are as diverse as coconut, cashew milk and cashew cheese, quinoa, tempeh and lentil dhal.

Bluebird

GOAN $$

(www.bluebirdgoa.com; Ozran Beach Rd, Vagator; mains ₹280-480; ⏰ 8.30am-11pm; 🛜) Bluebird specialises in Goan cuisine, with genuine vindaloos, chicken *cafreal* (marinated in a sauce of chillies, garlic and ginger), fish curry rice and Goan sausages among the temptations, as well as some delicately spiced seafood dishes. Dine in the lovely open garden cafe.

Mango Tree Bar & Cafe

MULTICUISINE $$

(Vagator Beach Rd, Vagator; mains ₹190-510; ⏰ 24hr; 🛜) With loud reggae, crappy service, darkwood furniture, a sometimes rambunctious bar scene, ancient expats leaning over the bar, draught beer and an overall great vibe, the Mango Tree is a classic Vagator meeting place. It's open late (allegedly 24 hours if it's busy enough) with a menu from Goan to European, pizza and Mexican.

Piccolo Roma

ITALIAN $$

(☐ 7507806821; Anjuna-Chapora Rd, Vagator; pizza & pasta ₹210-520; ⏰ 10am-11pm; 🛜) With an Italian chef in the kitchen, some say the wood-fired pizzas and house-made pasta is the best in Vagator and there's an undeniably pleasant atmosphere in the garden cafe, with its cushions and fairy lights. Starters of antipasto, crostini, soups and salads also grace the menu.

Yangkhor Moonlight

TIBETAN $$

(Ozran Beach Rd, Vagator; mains ₹170-400; ⏰ 8am-11pm; 🛜) Well known locally for its fresh Tibetan food such as *momos* (Tibetan dumplings), *thukpa* (soup) and the rarely seen Tibetan thali (₹250), as well as pasta dishes and even sushi. The decor is simple but most travellers enjoy the food and the ambience.

Food Chord

DINER $$

(☐ 0832-6745000; 544/2, Ozran Beach Rd, Vagator; mains ₹175-550; ⏰ 7am-11.30pm; ❄️ 🛜) At the crazy retro I Love Bellbottoms hotel, this American-style diner has booth seating, Arctic air-con and a menu of club sandwiches, burgers, hot dogs and pizzas. The inner window looks out to the violin-shaped pool (nonguests can swim for ₹1500, redeemable on food and drinks). Full bar with draught beer. Vagator or Vegas?

Midnight Toker

MULTICUISINE $$

(Main St, Chapora; mains ₹140-240; ⏰ 9am-1am; 🛜) The usual array of Indian, Chinese and Russian food is on the menu but this welcoming open-fronted restaurant is also a good place to watch the Chapora scene over a cold beer.

⭐ Thalassa

GREEK $$$

(☐ 9850033537; www.thalassaindia.com; Teso Waterfront; mains ₹300-750; ⏰ 4pm-midnight)

OFF THE BEATEN TRACK

DUDHSAGAR FALLS

Goa's most impressive **waterfall** (entry/camera ₹50/300) splashes 603m down on the eastern border with Karnataka, in the far southeastern corner of the Bhagwan Mahavir Wildlife Sanctuary. The falls are best visited as soon after monsoon as possible (October is perfect), when water levels are highest. Get here via Colem village, 7km south of Molem, by car or by the scenic 8.15am local train from Margao (return train times vary seasonally). From Colem, pick up a shared jeep (₹500 per person for six people) for the bumpy remaining 45-minute journey. An easier option is a taxi or a full-day Goa Tourism Dudhsagar Special' tour (₹2300), starting at 6.30am from Calangute or Panaji.

North Goa's most famous Greek restaurant was forced out of its long-running Vagator location in 2018 but has found a new waterfront home at Teso in Siolim. Still authentic and awesomely good Greek food is served al fresco overlooking the Chapora River.

Antares INDIAN $$$
(☑ 7350011528; www.antaresgoa.com; Ozran Beach Rd, Vagator; mains ₹395-1295; ☺ 11.30am-midnight) Perched on Vagator's southern clifftop, Antares is known as the project of Australian Masterchef contestant Sarah Todd. The atmosphere is beachfront chic meets nightclub and the food pricey Modern Australian meets Indian, with some Goan dishes such as crab *xacuti*.

🍷 Drinking & Nightlife

Hilltop CLUB
(www.hilltopgoa.in; Vagator; ☺ sunset-3am) Hilltop is a long-serving Vagator trance and party venue that's deserted by day but comes alive from sunset. Its edge-of-town neon-lit coconut grove location allows it, on occasion, to bypass noise regulations to host indoor and outdoor concerts, parties and international DJs. Sunday sessions (5pm to 10pm) are legendary.

Nine Bar BAR
(Little Vagator Beach; ☺ 5pm-4am) Once the hallowed epicentre of Goa's trance scene, the open-air Nine Bar terrace, on the clifftop overlooking Little Vagator Beach, is fading

but stills pumps out beats in its soundproof indoor space. It generally doesn't start until December; look out for flyers and local advice to see when the big party nights are on.

Paulo's Antique Bar BAR
(Main St, Chapora; ☺ 3pm-11pm) In season this hole-in-the-wall bar on Chapora's main street overflows with good music and cold beer. In late afternoon the few tables on the veranda are a fine spot to watch the world in miniature go by.

Waters Beach Lounge CLUB
(☑ 9767200012; Ozran Beach, Vagator; ☺ noon-4am) Terracing down the hillside on the Vagator cliffs, this restaurant, bar and club is known for its loud party nights, with open-air dance floors overlooking the Arabian Sea and a soundproof room for late at night – as late as 5am. Top DJs come to play.

Jai Ganesh Fruit Juice Centre JUICE BAR
(Main St, Chapora; ☺ 8.30am-midnight) Thanks to its corner location, with views up and down Chapora's main street, this may be the most popular juice bar in Goa. It's a prime meeting spot and, once parked, most people are reluctant to give up their seat. Juices ₹60 to ₹80.

❶ Information

There's a **HDFC ATM** at the petrol station on the back road to Anjuna.

❶ Getting There & Away

Fairly frequent buses run to both Chapora and Vagator from Mapusa (₹15, 30 minutes) throughout the day, many via Anjuna. There are bus stops in **Chapora** (Main St, Chapora) and on Vagator Beach Rd and **Anjuna-Vagator Rd** (Anjuna-Vagator, Vagator). Practically anyone with legs will rent you a scooter/motorcycle from ₹300/500 per day.

Vagator has North Goa's most popular **petrol station** (Mapusa-Chapora Rd).

Morjim

Morjim Beach was once very low-key – almost deserted – and the southern end is still protected due to the presence of rare olive ridley marine turtles, which come to lay their annual clutches of eggs between November and February.

These days Morjim is super popular with Russian tourists – it's locally known as 'Little Russia' – and consequently there's a bit of a clubbing scene in season and a growing number of restaurants and beach shacks. Though there are lovely views down the headland to Chapora Fort, the southern beach is more black sand than golden due to river runoff.

Based at Marbela Beach Resort, **Banana Surf School** (☏ 7218063571; www.goasurf.com; Marbela Beach; 2-hour surf lesson US$70, 3-day course US$180, board hire per hour/day US$25/60) rents boards and offers beginner lessons, from two hours to five days.

🛏 Sleeping & Eating

⭐ Wanderers Hostel
HOSTEL **$**

(☏ 9619235302; www.wanderershostel.com; Morjim Beach Rd; dm with fan/AC ₹400/500, shared tents ₹300, luxury tents d ₹1500; ❄ 🖥 🐕) About five minutes' walk back from Morjim Beach, Wanderers is a real find for budget travellers. The main building, decorated with original travellers' murals, has spotless dorms with lockers, bed lights and wi-fi, full kitchen, cosy communal areas and a pool table. In the garden next door is a tent village with swimming pool, yoga retreat centre and outdoor cinema.

Goan Café & Resort
RESORT **$**

(☏ 0832-2244394; www.goancafe.com; apt & cottages from ₹1800, with AC ₹2200, tree houses ₹2200, without bathroom ₹1200; ❄ 🖥) Fronting Morjim Beach, this excellent family-run resort has a fine array of beachfront stilted 'tree house' huts and more solid rooms (some with AC) at the back. The beachfront restaurant is good and breakfast is included.

Bora Bora
MULTICUISINE **$$$**

(☏ 8888558614; mains ₹270-550; ⊙ 24hr) Part restaurant, part club, part beach bar, Bora Bora is the only place in this area open 24 hours. Food runs to everything from pizza to Russian, Thai and Indian with seafood nights, but most people come here to chill out and enjoy a drink or one of the DJ nights. It's at the start of Morjim's little 'eat street'.

ℹ Getting There & Away

Occasional local buses run between Siolim and Morjim village (₹10, 15 minutes), but most travellers taxi to their chosen accommodation, then either hire a scooter/motorbike or use taxis from there.

Asvem

Asven is a wide stretch of beach, growing busier each year but still a little overshadowed by Mandrem to the north. Beach-hut accommodation and beach-shack restaurants spring up each season on a very broad stretch of clean, white-sand with few hawkers. The main Morjim–Mandrem road is set some way back from the sands.

🏃 Activities

⭐ Vaayu Waterman's Village
SURFING

(☏ 9850050403; www.vaayuvision.com; surfboard hire per hour/day ₹500/1500, lessons ₹2500) Goa's premier surf shop is also an activity and art centre where you can arrange lessons and hire equipment for surfing, kiteboarding, stand-up paddleboarding (SUP), kayaking and wakeboarding. A highlight is the full-day SUP tour to Paradise Lagoon in Maharashtra. The enthusiastic young owners also run an art gallery, cafe and accommodation across the road from Asvem Beach.

Arti Spa
AYURVEDA

(☏ 9049209597; www.artifabulousbodycare.com; massage & ayurvedic treatments ₹500-2000; ⊙ 8am-9pm) Arti and Dinesh run this well-regarded ayurvedic spa in Asvem (on the main road behind Sea View Resort). Treatments include Keralan massage, aromatherapy and *shirodhara* (an ayurvedic massage treatment where liquids are poured over the forehead).

🛏 Sleeping & Eating

Beachside by Bombay Backpackers
HOSTEL **$**

(☏ 9781040244; Asvem Beach Rd; dm ₹400-450, d ₹1650; 🖥) Down a lane off the main road opposite the beach, this backpackers in a converted house makes a decent budget stay with four- to six-bed dorms with individual fans and lockers. There's a lack of traveller vibe compared with some of north Goa's hostels but the location and price are good.

Vaayu Waterman's Village
BOUTIQUE HOTEL **$$**

(☏ 9850050403; www.vaayuvision.com; hut ₹2500-4400, d with AC ₹4500; ❄ 🖥) The excellent boutique rooms at this water-sports outfit are stylish with the sort of artistic and soulful vibe that goes with the attached gallery, wholefood Prana Cafe, yoga *shala* (studio) and surf shop. Across the road, facing the beach, are beautifully designed Keralan-style bamboo and thatch huts.

Wellness Inn
GUESTHOUSE $$

(☑ 9075006776; www.wellnessinn.in; d/f from ₹3200/4800; ❄ 🛜) This 13-room guesthouse will suit yoga practitioners with daily drop-in classes, yoga training on the rooftop terrace and a health-conscious veg restaurant. Rooms are spacious, airy and all have air-con. It's often busy with travellers on yoga retreats so book ahead.

Yab Yum
HUT $$$

(☑ 0832-6510392; www.yabyumresorts.com; hut/cottage from ₹10,600/12,050; ❄ 🛜) 🌿 This top-notch choice has unusual, stylish, dome-shaped huts – some look like giant hairy coconuts – made of a combination of all-natural local materials, including mud, stone and mango wood, as well as more traditional AC cottages. A host of yoga and massage options is available, and it's set in one of the most secluded beachfront jungle gardens you'll find in Goa.

🛈 Getting There & Away

Buses run between Siolim and Asvem, but it's easier to get a taxi straight to your chosen accommodation, then either hire a scooter/motorbike or use taxis from there.

Mandrem

Mellow Mandrem is something akin to beach bliss, with its miles of clean, white sand separated from the village by a shallow creek. The beach and village has developed in recent years from an in-the-know bolthole for those seeking respite from the relentless traveller scene of Arambol and Anjuna to a fairly mainstream but still very lovely beach hang-out. There's plenty of yoga, meditation and ayurveda on offer here, plus a growing dining scene and plenty of space to lay down with a good book. Many believe there's no better place in North Goa.

🏃 Activities

Kite Guru
WATER SPORTS

(☑ 8788314974; www.kiteguru.co.uk; 2/6/8hr course ₹7000/14,000/21,000, SUP lessons ₹2000) Based at Riverside in Mandrem, this is the best place in Goa to learn to kitesurf. Professional instructors offer group or solo IKO certified lessons and provide all the gear. Also stand-up paddleboard lessons and tours. Board hire for independent SUPers is ₹1000 an hour.

Shanti Ayurvedic Massage Centre
AYURVEDA

(☑ 8806205264; 1hr massage from ₹1000; ⊘ 9am-9pm) Ayurvedic massage is provided here by the delightful Shanti. Try the rejuvenating 75-minute massage and facial package, or go for an unusual 'Poulti' massage, using a poultice-like cloth bundle containing 12 herbal powders. You'll find her place on the right-hand side as you head down the beach road.

Ashiyana Retreat Centre
YOGA

(☑ 9850401714; www.ashiyana-yoga-goa.com; Junas Waddo; drop-in class ₹600) This 'tropical retreat centre' fronting Mandrem Beach and stretching back to the jungle has a long list of classes and courses available from October to April, from retreats and yoga holidays to spa, massage and 'massage camp'. Accommodation (includes free yoga) is in one of its gorgeous, heritage-styled rooms and huts.

Himalaya Yoga Valley
YOGA

(☑ 9960657852; www.yogagoaindia.com; Mandrem Beach) HYV specialises in hatha and ashtanga residential 200-hour teacher-training courses (€1475) in Goa, Dharamsala and Ireland.

🛌 Sleeping & Eating

Riverside
HUT $

(☑ 9049503605; www.riversidemandrem.com; Junas Waddo; huts ₹800-1200; 🛜) At the southern end of Mandrem Beach, overlooking the creek, Riverside is an excellent two-level open-sided restaurant with a collection of well-designed but affordable palm-thatch and timber huts at the back and side. These are some of the best-value beachfront huts in Mandrem and there's a kitesurfing school here and stand-up paddleboards for rent.

★ Dunes Holiday Village
HUT $$

(☑ 0832-2247219; www.dunesgoa.com; huts ₹1500-1750, d with AC ₹2200; ❄ 🛜) The pretty huts here are peppered around a palm-filled lane leading to the beach; at night, lamps light up the place like a palm-tree dreamland. Huts range from basic to more sturdy 'tree houses' (huts on stilts) and there are some guesthouse rooms with air-con. It's a friendly, good-value place with a decent beach restaurant, yoga classes and a marked absence of trance.

★ Mandala
RESORT $$

(☑ 9158266093; www.themandalagoa.com; r & huts ₹1600-7000; ❄ 🛜) Mandala is a very peaceful and beautifully designed eco-village with a range of huts and a couple of quirky air-con rooms in the 'Art House'. Pride of place goes to the barn-sized two-storey villas inspired by the design of a Keralan houseboat. The location, overlooking the tidal lagoon, is serene, with a large garden, daily yoga sessions, an organic restaurant and juice bar.

Beach Street
RESORT $$

(Lazy Dog; ☑ 9403410679; Mandrem Beach; huts ₹4300-6900, chalets ₹8600-11,800; 🛜 🖼) The beachfront huts are adorable at Beach Street, where the adjacent building encloses an inviting pool. Well-designed huts range from simple with bathroom and veranda to two-storey palm-thatch family 'chalets' sleeping five. The Lazy Dog beachfront restaurant here has five-star aspirations with waiters dressed in cruise uniforms.

Riva Beach Resort
RESORT $$

(☑ 0832-2247612; www.rivaresorts.com; d ₹5000-9500; 🖼 🛜 🖼) This sprawling complex of seasonal cottages and hotel-style rooms tumbles down from the main road to the inlet, where bamboo bridges provide access to the beach. Spring mattresses, ocean-view balconies, a good restaurant and on-site yoga retreats. It's a bit of a party spot – Sunday is the pool party.

Karma Kitchen
MULTICUISINE $$

(☑ 8894204735; Junas Waddo; mains ₹220-650; ⊗ 9am-10pm; 🛜) This cruisey courtyard cafe offers a bit of everything but specialises in thalis, tandoor kebabs and seafood, or a combination such as the seafood souvlaki kebab. It's also a good place to come for a drink, with wine by the glass and regular live music, including Sunday sessions.

Bed Rock
MULTICUISINE $$

(Junos Vaddo; mains ₹150-400; ⊗ 8am-11pm; 🛜) Bed Rock is a welcome change from the beach shacks with a reliable menu of Indian and continental faves (pizza, pasta etc), a cosy chill-out lounge upstairs, welcoming staff and a loyal following of regulars. Look out for live music in season.

🛍 Shopping

Arambol Hammocks
HOMEWARES

(☑ 7798906816, 9619175722; www.arambol.com; 327, Junas Waddo) Now in Mandrem, Arambol Hammocks designs and sells hammocks, including their 'flying carpets' and 'flying chairs'.

ℹ Getting There & Around

Buses run between Siolim and Mandrem village (₹10, 20 minutes) hourly, but it's hard work trying to get anywhere in a hurry on public trans-port. Most travellers taxi to their chosen accommodation, then either hire a scooter/motorbike or use taxis from there.

Arambol (Harmal)
POP 5320

Arambol (also known as Harmal) is the most northerly of Goa's developed beach resorts and is still considered the beach of choice for many long-staying budget-minded travellers in the north.

Arambol first emerged in the 1960s as a mellow paradise for long-haired long-stayers escaping the scene at Calangute. Today things are still cheap and cheerful, with budget accommodation in little huts and rooms clinging to the cliffsides, though the main beach is now an uninterrupted string of beach shacks, many with accommodation operations stacked behind.

🏃 Activities

Arambol Paragliding
PARAGLIDING

(10min flight ₹2000; ⊗ 11am-6pm) The headland above Kalacha Beach (Sweetwater Lake) is an ideal launching point for paragliding. There are a number of independent paragliders: ask around at the shack restaurants on the beach, arrange a pilot, then make the short hike to the top of the headland. Most flights are around 10 minutes, but if conditions are right you can stay up longer.

Himalayan Iyengar Yoga Centre
YOGA

(www.hiyogacentre.com; Madhlo Vaddo; 5-day yoga course ₹5500; ⊗ 9am-6pm Nov-Mar) Arambol's reputable Himalayan Iyengar Yoga Centre, which runs five-day courses in hatha yoga from mid-November to mid-March, is the winter centre of the Iyengar yoga school in Dharamkot, near Dharamsala in north India. First-time students must take the introductory five-day course, and can then continue with more advanced five-day courses at a reduced rate.

Surf Wala
SURFING

(☑ 9011993147; www.surfwala.com; Arambol Beach; 1½hr lesson from ₹2500, 3-/5-day course ₹7000/11,500) If you're a beginner looking to get up on a board, join the international team of surfers based at Arambol's Surf Club. Prices include board hire, wax and rashie. Check the website for instructor contact details – between them they speak English, Russian, Hindi, Konkani and Japanese! Board-only rental is ₹500/1500 per hour/day.

GOA ARAMBOL (HARMAL)

🛏 Sleeping

Accommodation in Arambol has expanded from basic huts along the clifftop and guest-houses in the village to a mini-Palolem of beach huts along the main beach and a selection of backpacker hostels. Enter at the 'Glastonbury St' entrance and walk north to find plenty of places clinging to the headland between here and Kalacha Beach, or enter at the south end and ask at any of the beach shacks.

★Happy Panda   HOSTEL $

(☑9619741681; www.happypanda.in; dm ₹500-650, tent from ₹400; ❄🛜) Traveller-painted murals cover the walls in this very chilled backpacker place near the main village. Young owners have worked hard making the dorms, neon common area, bar and garden a well-equipped and welcoming budget place to crash. Artists, cooks and other skilled travellers are encouraged to lend a hand. Bikes for hire and tent accommodation available.

Om Ganesh   GUESTHOUSE $

(☑9404313206; r ₹600-800; 🛜) Halfway along the cliff, Om Ganesh has been around for a while and has solid rooms in a building on the hillside, and seasonal huts-with-a-view on the rooftop.

Pitruchaya Cottages   COTTAGE $

(☑9404454596; r ₹700-800; 🛜) The sea-facing timber cottages here are among the best on the cliffs, with attached bathrooms, fans and verandahs.

Chilli's   HOTEL $

(☑9921882424; Glastonbury St; d ₹700, apt with AC ₹1200; ❄🛜) Near the beach entrance on Glastonbury St, this friendly canary-yellow place is one of Arambol's better nonbeach-front bargains. There are 10 decent, no-frills rooms, all with attached bathroom, fan and a hot-water shower. The top-floor apartment with AC and TV is good value. Motorbikes and scooters available for hire.

Surf Club   GUESTHOUSE $

(www.thesurfclubgoa.com; d ₹1000-1800; 🛜) In a quiet space at the end of a lane, on the southern end of Arambol Beach, the Surf Club is one of those cool little hang-outs that offer a bit of everything: simple but clean rooms, a fun bar with live music and surf lessons and board hire.

Lotus Sutra   RESORT $$

(☑9146096940; www.lotussutragoa.com; d & cottages ₹4000-5500; ❄🛜) The fanciest place on

Arambol's beachfront has a series of bright rooms in a quirky two-storey building and cute individual timber cottages facing a garden-lawn setting or towards the seafront. The Zen Oasis restaurant-bar is a popular spot and features live music.

🍴 Eating

Dylan's Toasted & Roasted   CAFE $

(☑9604780316; www.dylanscoffee.com; coffee & desserts ₹80-200; ⊙9am-11pm late Nov-Apr; 🛜) The Goa (winter) incarnation of a Manali institution, Dylan's is a fine place for an espresso, chocolate chip cookies and old-school dessert. It's a nice hang-out, just back from the southern beach entrance, with occasional live music and open-mic nights.

German Bakery   BAKERY $

(☑9822159699; Welcome Inn, Glastonbury St; pastries ₹30-100; ⊙8am-midnight) This popular little cafe bakes a good line in cakes and pastries, including lemon cheese pie and chocolate biscuit cake, as well as coffee and breakfast. It's a cool meeting spot close to the beach but away from the beach shacks.

★Shimon   MIDDLE EASTERN $$

(☑9011113576; Glastonbury St; mains ₹160-250; ⊙9am-11pm; 🛜) Just back from the beach, and understandably popular with Israeli backpackers, Shimon is the place to fill up on exceptional falafel or *sabich* (crisp slices of eggplant stuffed into pita bread along with boiled egg, boiled potato and salad). The East-meets-Middle-East thali (₹450) comprises a little bit of almost everything on the menu. Follow up with a strong Turkish coffee or its signature iced coffee. No alcohol.

This Is It   MULTICUISINE $$

(☑7775078620; mains ₹160-370; ⊙8am-11pm; 🛜) Many travellers rate this the coolest place on the northern beachfront. A big menu of well-prepared Indian staples, Goan dishes, Chinese, seafood, *momos* and pasta is complemented by a laid-back, traveller-friendly vibe, generous happy hours and regular live music. Popular Holy Cow Backpackers is behind.

Fellini   ITALIAN $$

(☑9881461224; Glastonbury St; mains ₹200-450; ⊙from 6.30pm) On the left-hand side just before the beach, this long-standing evening-only Italian joint is perfect if you're craving a carbonara or calzone. More than 40 wood-fired, thin-crust pizza varieties are on

THE PORTUGUESE LEGACY

The Portuguese departed Goa in 1961 after more than 400 years of colonial rule but they left behind a rich legacy of culture, architecture, churches, schools and medical colleges.

Religion & Festivals

Around one quarter of the Goan population is Christian (largely Roman Catholic), mostly as a result of religious conversion during Portuguese rule. Today this legacy is most obvious in the many whitewashed parish churches across the state but also in the Christian festivals such as Christmas, Easter, Carnival and the Feast of St Francis Xavier.

Food

Goan cuisine is distinct from its South Indian neighbours with its liberal use of pork and uniquely spiced sauces such as *xacuti, cafreal* and *recheado. Vindaloo* is a Goan derivative of Portuguese port stew steeped in wine vinegar and garlic. Seafood is still king though and fish-curry-rice was a staple here long before colonisation. The Portuguese also introduced cashews to Goa, providing the basis for the national alcoholic drink, feni.

Architecture

You don't have to look far to see the fine architecture left behind by the Portuguese in residential mansions and palacios. Your first stop should be Panaji's Latin Quarter of Fontainhas and Sao Thome, where many Portuguese homes have been converted into boutique heritage hotels. In the countryside, South Goan villages such as Chandor, Loutolim and Quepem are awash with grand mansions but if you look past the tourist tat you'll see many well-preserved examples of Portuguese architecture in the backstreets of beach resorts such as Candolim and Calangute.

Susegad

This one is a little less tangible but you'll find it in everyday life during your time in Goa. Derived from the Portuguese *sossegado* ('quiet'), *susegad* is a uniquely Goan term that describes a laid-back attitude and contentment with life. Life might not look very relaxed during peak season in downtown Calangute but the concept of *susegad* lives on in the people of Goa.

the menu, but save space for a very decent rendition of tiramisu. Live music in season.

Double Dutch   MULTICUISINE $$
(mains ₹120-450, steaks ₹420-500; ☺8am-10pm)
In a peaceful garden set back from the main road to the Glastonbury St beach entrance, Double Dutch has long been popular for its steaks, salads, Thai and Indonesian dishes, and famous apple pies. It's a relaxed meeting place with secondhand books, newspapers and a useful noticeboard for current Arambolic affairs.

Rice Bowl   ASIAN $$
(☎9822748451; mains ₹110-290; ☺8am-11pm;
☎) Rice Bowl specialises in Chinese and Japanese cuisine and does it well. With a good view down to Arambol Beach, this is a great place to settle in with a plate of gyoza and a beer, or play a game of pool.

❶ Information

There's an ATM on the main highway in Arambol's village, about 1.5km back from the beach.

If it's not working there's another about 3km north in Paliyem or about the same distance south in Mandrem.

❶ Getting There & Away

Frequent buses to and from Mapusa (₹40, one hour) stop on the main road at the 'backside' (as locals are fond of saying) of Arambol village, where there's a church, a school and a few local shops. From here, it's a 1.5km trek down through the village to the main beach drag (head straight for the southern beach entrance or bear right for the northern 'Glastonbury St' entrance another 500m further on). An autorickshaw will charge at least ₹50 for the trip. Plenty of places in the village advertise scooters and motorbikes for hire (per day scooter/motorbike ₹300/400).

A prepaid taxi from Mapusa to Arambol costs ₹700 but taxis on the street between Arambol and Mapusa or Anjuna/Vagator will ask closer to ₹1000. If you're heading north to Mumbai, travel agents can book bus tickets.

SOUTH GOA

South Goa is the more serene half of the state, and for many travellers that's the attraction. There are fewer activities and not as many bars, clubs or restaurants, but overall the beaches of the south are cleaner, whiter and not as crowded as those in the north.

Margao

POP 122,500

Margao (also known as Madgaon) is the capital of South Goa, a busy – at times traffic-clogged – market town of a manageable size for getting things done. As the major transport hub of the south, lots of travellers pass through Margao's train station or Kadamba bus stand; fewer choose to overnight here, but it's a useful place for market shopping, catching a local sporting event or simply enjoying the busy energy of big-city India in small-town form.

🛏 Sleeping & Eating

Unlike Panaji, Margao doesn't have the range of accommodation that you'd expect in a town of this size. But with the beaches of the south so close, there's really no pressing reason to stay here.

Nanutel Margao
HOTEL $$

(☑0832-6722222; www.nanuhotels.in; Padre Miranda Rd; s/d incl breakfast ₹5300/5900; ❄🖥🌊) Margao's best business-class hotel by some margin, Nanutel is modern and slick with a lovely pool, good restaurant, bar and coffee shop, and clean air-con rooms. The location, between the Municipal Gardens and Largo de Igreja district, is convenient for everything.

Hotel Tanish
HOTEL $$

(☑0832-2735858; www.hoteltanishgoa.com; Reliance Trade Centre, Valaulikar Rd; s/d ₹1200/1700, with AC ₹1500/2000; ❄🖥) Oddly situated inside a modern mall, this top-floor hotel offers good views of the surrounding countryside, with stylish, well-equipped rooms. Try for an outside-facing room, as some overlook the mall interior.

Café Tato
INDIAN $

(Valaulikar Rd; thalis ₹100; ⏱7am-10pm Mon-Sat) A favourite local lunch spot: tasty vegetarian fare in a bustling backstreet canteen, and delicious all-you-can-eat thalis.

★ Longhuino's
GOAN $$

(☑0832-2739908; Luis Miranda Rd; mains ₹180-320; ⏱8.30am-10pm) A local institution since 1950, quaint old Longhuino's serves up tasty Indian, Goan and Chinese dishes, popular with locals and tourists alike. Go for a Goan dish like *ambot tik* (a slightly sour but fiery curry dish), and leave room for the retro desserts such as rum balls and tiramisu.

Chikoo Tree Project
MULTICUISINE $$

(☑9920064597; 85 Dr Miranda Rd; mains ₹150-300; ⏱9am-10pm Tue-Sun) Breakfast on masala dosas and lunch on chicken *momos* or giant *kathi* wraps at this arty, eclectic but casual cafe that's made a welcome addition to Margao's dining scene. Good coffee and fresh-made juices.

Viva Goa
GOAN $$

(mains ₹150-400; ⏱11am-3pm & 7-11pm) Upstairs in Clube Harmonia, South Goa's oldest cultural club venue, Viva Goa is a new iteration of the long-running Colva restaurant, serving genuine Goan cuisine, seafood and a full bar.

MAJOR TRAINS FROM MARGAO

DESTINATION	TRAIN NO & NAME	FARE (₹)	DURATION (HRS)	DEPARTURES
Bengaluru (Bangalore)	02779 Vasco da Gama-SBC Link (D)	380/1025	15	3.50pm
Chennai; via Yesvantpur	17312 Vasco da Gama-Chennai Express (C)	495/1325/1905	21	3.20pm Thu
Delhi	22633 Nizamuddin Exp (A)	2040/2965	30	8.25am
Ernakulam (Kochi)	12618 Lakshadweep Express (C)	465/1215/1715	15	7.40pm
Mangaluru (Mangalore)	12133 Mangalore Express (C)	310/785/1085	6	7.15am
Mumbai	10112 Konkan Kanya Express (C)	410/1105/1575	12	6pm
Pune	12779 Goa Express (C)	375/975/1365	12	3.50pm

Fares: (A) 3AC/2AC, (B) 2S/CC, (C) sleeper/3AC/2AC, (D) sleeper/3AC

🛍 Shopping

MMC New Market
MARKET

(Rua F de Loiola; ⊙8.30am-9pm Mon-Sat) Margao's crowded, covered canopy of colourful stalls is a fun but busy place to wander around, sniffing spices, sampling soaps and browsing the household merchandise.

Golden Heart Emporium
BOOKS

(Confidant House, Abade Faria Rd; ⊙10am-2pm & 4-7.30pm Mon-Sat) One of Goa's best bookshops, Golden Heart is crammed from floor to ceiling with fiction, nonfiction, children's books, and illustrated volumes on the state's food, architecture and history. It also stocks otherwise hard-to-get titles by local Goan authors. It's down a little lane off Abade Faria Rd.

❶ Getting There & Away

BUS

Local and long-distance buses use the Kadamba bus stand, on the highway about 2km north of the Municipal Gardens. Buses to Palolem (₹40, one hour), Colva (₹15, 20 minutes), Benaulim (₹15, 20 minutes) and Betul (₹25, 40 minutes) stop both at the Kadamba bus stand and at informal bus stops on the east and west sides of the Municipal Gardens. For Panaji, take any local bus to the Kadamba bus stand and change to a frequent express bus (₹40, one hour). From there you can change for buses to Mapusa and the northern beaches.

Daily AC state-run buses go to Mumbai (₹900, 16 hours), Pune (₹735, 13 hours) and Bengaluru (₹660 to ₹1200, 12 hours), which can be booked online at www.goakadamba.com. Non-AC buses are about one-third cheaper but are becoming rare on long distance routes. For greater choice and flexibility but similar prices, private long-distance buses depart from the stand opposite Kadamba. You'll find booking offices all over town; **Paulo Travels** (☑0832-2702405; www.paulobus.com; NH66) is among the best, and also has the only buses to Hampi (seat/sleeper ₹900/1500, 11 hours), but the best booking site is Red Bus (www.redbus.in).

TAXI

Taxis are plentiful around the Municipal Gardens and Kadamba bus stand, and are a quick and comfortable way to reach any of Goa's beaches. Prepaid taxi stands are at the train station and main bus stand. Fares include the following: Panaji (₹1050), Palolem (₹1050), Calangute (₹1355), Anjuna (₹1500) and Arambol (₹2000), though you'll pay up to double these fares by hiring a taxi off the street.

For Colva and Benaulim, autorickshaws should do the trip for around ₹150 but taxis ask an inflated ₹500. Motorcycle taxis are still common in Margao and are good for short trips.

TRAIN

Margao's well-organised train station (known as Madgaon on train timetables), about 2km south of town, serves both the Konkan Railway and local South Central Railways routes, and is the main hub for trains from Mumbai to Goa and south to Kochi and beyond. Its **reservation hall** (☑0832-2712790; Train Station; ⊙8am-2pm & 2.15-8pm Mon-Sat, 8am-2pm Sun) is on the 1st floor and there's a foreign tourist quota counter upstairs.

Outside the station you'll find a useful prepaid taxi stand; use this to get to your beachside destination and you'll be assured a fair price. Alternatively, a taxi or autorickshaw to or from the town centre to the station should cost around ₹100.

Colva

POP 3140

Once a sleepy fishing village, and in the sixties a hang-out for hippies escaping the scene up at Anjuna, Colva is still the main townresort along this stretch of coast, but these days it has lost any semblance of the beach paradise vibe. Travel a little way north or south, though, and you'll find some of the peace missing in central Colva.

The **Goa Animal Welfare Trust shop** (☑0832-2653677; www.gawt.org; ⊙9.30am-1pm & 4-7pm Mon-Sat), next door to Leda Lounge, is a charity shop with secondhand books and souvenirs. All proceeds go toward helping out Goa's four-legged friends and the staff are happy to chat about the work of the GAWT, based in Curchorem.

🛏 Sleeping & Eating

Colva has a few budget guesthouses hidden in the wards north of the beach road, but overall good-value pickings are a little slim. Numerous beach shacks line the Colvan sands between November and April, offering the extensive standard range of fare and fresh seafood

Sam's Guesthouse
HOTEL $

(☑0832-2788753; r ₹800; 🖎) Away from the fray, north of Colva's main drag on the road running parallel to the beach, Sam's is a big, cheerful place with friendly owners and spacious rooms that are a steal at this price. Rooms are around a pleasant garden courtyard and there's a good restaurant and whacky 'cosy cave'. Wi-fi in the restaurant only.

★Skylark Resort
HOTEL $$

(☑0832-2788052; www.skylarkresortgoa.com; d with AC ₹3350-4500, f ₹5000; ❄🖎🏊) A serious step up from the budget places, Skylark's

WORTH A TRIP

COLA BEACH

Cola Beach is one of those hidden gems of the south coast – a relatively hard-to-reach crescent of sand enclosed by forested cliffs and with a gorgeous emerald lagoon stretching back from the beach.

It has been discovered of course and between November and April several hut and tent villages such as **Blue Lagoon Resort** (9673277756; www.bluelagoon-cola.com; cottages ₹3800-5400;) set up here, but it's still a beautiful, low-key place and popular with day trippers from Agonda and Palolem.

Further north around the headland is an even more remote beach known as Khancola Beach, or Kakolem, with one small resort reached via a steep set of jungly steps from the clifftop above.

clean, fresh rooms are graced with bits and pieces of locally made teak furniture and block-print bedspreads, while the lovely pool makes a pleasant place to lounge. The best (and more expensive) rooms are those facing the pool.

La Ben   HOTEL $$
(0832-2788040; www.laben.net; Colva Beach Rd; r with/without AC ₹1800/1650;) Neat, clean and not entirely devoid of atmosphere, La Ben is a traveller hang-out in the middle of the action with decent, good-value rooms and has been around for ages. There's a rooftop bar and, at street level, the very good **Garden Restaurant** (mains ₹170-370; 7.30am-11.30pm;).

Soul Vacation   HOTEL $$$
(0832-2788147; www.soulvacation.in; 4th Ward; d incl breakfast ₹6300-8300; f villas from ₹10,400;) Thirty sleek, white rooms arranged around nice gardens and a neat pool are the trademarks of Soul Vacation, set 400m back from Colva Beach. This is central Colva's most upmarket choice and, though pricey, there's a nice air of exclusivity about it. There's an ayurvedic spa, garden cafe and bar.

Sagar Kinara   INDIAN $
(Colva Beach Rd; mains ₹70-190; 7am-10.30pm) A pure-veg restaurant upstairs (nonveg is separate, downstairs) with tastes to please even committed carnivores, Sagar Kinara

is clean, efficient and offers cheap and delicious North and South Indian cuisine all day.

Leda Lounge & Restaurant   BAR
(noon-3pm & 7-11pm) Part sports bar, part music venue, part cocktail bar, Leda is Colva's best nightspot, though it operates as much as a restaurant and even the bar closes in the afternoon. There's live music from Thursday to Sunday, fancy drinks (mojitos, Long Island iced teas) and good food at lunch and dinner.

❶ Getting There & Away

Buses from Colva to Margao run roughly every 15 minutes (₹15, 20 minutes) from 7.30am to about 7pm, departing from the **parking area** (Colva Beach Rd) at the end of the beach road. A taxi/autorickshaw to Margao is ₹500/150.

Scooters can be hired around the bus stand (with some difficulty) for ₹300 per day.

Benaulim

A long stretch of largely empty sand peppered with a few beach shacks and water-sports enthusiasts, the beaches of Benaulim and nearby Sernabatim to the north are much quieter than Colva, partly because the village is a good kilometre back from the beach.

◉ Sights

★ **Goa Chitra**   MUSEUM
(0832-2772910; www.goachitra.com; St John the Baptist Rd, Mondo Vaddo; ₹300; 9am-6pm Tue-Sun) Artist and restorer Victor Hugo Gomes first noticed the slow extinction of traditional objects – from farming tools to kitchen utensils to altarpieces – as a child in Benaulim. He created this ethnographic museum from the more than 4000 cast-off objects that he collected from across the state over 20 years. Admission is via a one-hour guided tour, held on the hour. Goa Chitra is 3km east of Maria Hall – ask locally for directions.

San Thome Museum   MUSEUM
(9822363917; www.goamuseum.com; Colva Rd; ₹200; 9am-6pm) This quirky museum at the Varca (southern) end of Benaulim, dubbed 'Back in Time', has three floors of carefully presented technology through the ages, from old cameras and typewriters to gramophones, clocks and projectors. Highlights include a Scheidmayer grand piano,

Raleigh bicycle and an anchor cast from the same pattern as the *Titanic*'s.

🛏 Sleeping & Eating

★**Blue Corner**   HUT $
(☑9850455770; www.bluecornergoa.com; huts ₹1300; 🛜) It's rare to find good old-fashioned palm-thatch cocohuts on this stretch of beachfront but the 11 sturdy thatched huts at Blue Corner are the best in Benaulim. Each one has a veranda, fan and wi-fi. The beachfront restaurant at the front gets rave reviews from guests.

Anthy's Guesthouse   GUESTHOUSE $
(☑0832-2771680,9922854566; www.anthysguest housegoa.com; Sernabatim Beach; d with/without AC ₹1900/1600; ❈🛜) One of a handful of places lining Sernabatim Beach, Anthy's is a standout favourite with travellers for its good restaurant, book exchange and well-kept cottage-style garden rooms, which stretch back from the beach, surrounded by a garden. There are also a few comfortable wooden cabins.

Rosario's Inn   GUESTHOUSE $
(☑0832-2770636; rosariosinn@ymail.com; r with/ without AC ₹900/600; ❈🛜) Across a football field flitting with young players and dragonflies, family-run Rosario's is a large establishment with very clean, simple rooms and a restaurant. Excellent value for long-stayers.

Palm Grove Cottages   HOTEL $$
(☑0832-2770059;   www.palmgrovegoa.com; Vaswado; d incl breakfast ₹3800-4250; ❈🛜) Old-fashioned, secluded charm and Benaulim's leafiest garden welcomes you at Palm Grove Cottages, a fine midrange choice. The quiet AC rooms, some with balcony, all have a nice feel but the best are the spacious deluxe rooms in a separate Portuguese-style building. The Palm Garden Restaurant here is exceptionally good.

Cafe Malibu   INDIAN $
(mains ₹120-200; ⊙8am-11pm) This unpretentious little family-run cafe offers a nice dining experience in its roadside garden setting on a back lane a short walk back from the beach. It does a good job of Goan specialities as well as Indian and continental dishes.

Farm House   GOAN $$
(☑9822130430, 0832-2770534; Ascona; mains ₹180-340; ⊙11.30am-3pm & 7.30pm-midnight Tue-Sun; 🛜) Beneath a large palapa-style shelter overlooking a well-stocked fish pond beside the Sal River, the Farm House is renowned locally for its Goan dishes, seafood and steaks. Weekends are enormously popular for live music and the opportunity for a spot of fishing (11am to 3pm). It's off the main road at the southern end of Benaulim village.

Johncy Restaurant   MULTICUISINE $$
(Vasvaddo Beach Rd; mains ₹150-450; ⊙7am-midnight) Not so much a shack as a beachfront restaurant, Johncy has been around forever, dispensing standard Goan, Indian and Western favourites – and cold beer – from its location just back from the sand. Live music on weekends.

Pedro's Bar & Restaurant   MULTICUISINE $$
(Vasvaddo Beach Rd; mains ₹120-500; ⊙7am-midnight; 🛜) Set amid a large, shady garden at the beachfront car park and popular with local and international travellers, long-running Pedro's offers standard Indian, Chinese and Italian dishes, as well as Goan choices and 'sizzlers'. Regular live music in season.

Goodfellas   ITALIAN $$$
(☑9657531631;   pizzas & pasta ₹400-650; ⊙6pm-midnight; 🛜) Authentic wood-fired pizza is the standout at this corner bistro where Italians run the kitchen with aplomb. Fresh pasta, lasagne and ravioli also grace the menu with imported cheeses, porcini mushrooms and deli meats. Occasional live music and Sunday lunch.

❶ Getting There & Away

Buses from Margao to Benaulim are frequent (₹15, 20 minutes); some continue on south to Varca and Cavelossim. Buses stop at the Maria Hall crossroads, or at the junctions to Sernabatim or Taj Exotica – just ask to be let off. From Maria Hall an autorickshaw should cost around ₹60 for the five-minute ride to the sea.

If you're staying in Benaulim you'll appreciate having your own transport: look out for 'bike for rent' signs in the village or down at the beach shacks. Rental costs around ₹300 per day.

Agonda
POP 3800

Travellers have been drifting to Agonda for years and seasonal hut villages – some very luxurious – now occupy almost all available beachfront space in season, but it's still more low-key than Palolem and a good choice if

GOA AGONDA

you're after some beachy relaxation. The coast road between Betul and Palolem passes through Agonda village, while the main traveller centre is a single lane running parallel to the beach.

Agonda's beach is wide, quiet and picturesque, though the surf can be rough and swimming treacherous. A forestry department–staffed turtle centre at the northern end protects precious olive ridley sea turtle eggs.

The first surf school in Goa's deep south, **Aloha Surf India** (⏍8605476576; 1hr/2hr/full day board rental ₹400/700/1500, group/private lesson from ₹1500/2500; ◷8am-6pm Oct-May) is run by a passionate local crew. Learn to surf on Agonda's gentle 'green' waves or hire a board. Also stand-up paddleboard lessons and surf tours.

🛏 Sleeping

Fatima Guesthouse GUESTHOUSE $
(⏍0832-2647477; www.fatimasguesthouse.com; d ₹1000-1500, with AC ₹1500-2500; ❄🛜) An ever-popular budget guesthouse set back from the beach, with clean rooms, a good restaurant and obliging staff. Rooftop yoga classes in season.

Abba's Gloryland GUESTHOUSE $
(⏍0832-2647822, 9423412795; www.abbasgloryland.com; Agonda Beach Rd; huts ₹1200, r with AC ₹1900; 🛜) Back from the beach, Abba's is a decent budget choice with timber cottages at the side and air-con rooms in a separate building, all in a pleasant garden.

★ Agonda White Sand HUT $$
(⏍9823548277; www.agondawhitesand.com; Agonda Beach; huts from ₹4600-5200; ❄🛜) Beautifully designed and constructed cottages with open-air bathrooms and spring mattresses surround a central bar and beachfront restaurant. Some have air-con.

H2O Agonda HUT $$
(⏍9921836730; www.h2oagonda.com; Agonda Beach; d incl breakfast from ₹5700-9300; ❄🛜) With its purple and mauve muslin curtains and Arabian nights ambience, H2O is among the most impressive of Agonda's luxury cottage setups. From the hotel-style reception, walk through a leafy garden to the spacious cottages with air-con and enormous open-air bathrooms. The more expensive sea-facing cottages with king-size beds may be worth paying extra for.

🍴 Eating & Drinking

Mandala Cafe CAFE $
(⏍8554091819; Agonda Beach Rd; chai ₹15, dishes ₹100-250; ◷8am-11pm; 🛜) Feeling like a glass of masala chai or a vegan pancake? Slip into a cushioned alcove at this shanti little travellers' cafe for a down-to-earth antithesis to Agonda's over-the-top beach bars.

Kopi Desa EUROPEAN $$
(⏍7767831487; small plates ₹150-295, mains ₹350-695; ◷8am-11pm; 🛜) The name translates from Indonesian as 'coffee village' but this al fresco restaurant and cocktail bar has become firmly established for its imaginative Euro-centric menu, tapas-style plates from pork belly bites to crab and lobster tortellini, sourdough pizzas and burgers. Regular live music in season.

La Dolce Vita ITALIAN $$
(⏍90799911; mains ₹250-500; ◷from 9am-10pm; 🛜) Excellent Italian food is dished out at Dolce Vita, with gingham tablecloths, a long, sprawling blackboard menu, and plenty of passionate yelling and gesturing when the place gets busy. Wood-fired pizzas are authentic.

Zest Cafe VEGETARIAN $$
(⏍8806607919; Agonda Beach Rd; mains ₹190-360; ◷8am-10pm; 🛜) The Agonda branch of Zest has a lush and loungy garden setting to complement the vegan and vegetarian menu of Mexican or teriyaki bowls, pizza, Balinese tofu and raw-food desserts. Great breakfast spot.

Blue Planet Cafe VEGETARIAN $$
(⏍0832-2647448; mains ₹140-250; ◷9am-3pm & 6-9.30pm; 🛜) Scrambled tofu and vegan pancakes grace the menu of soul food at mostly vegan Blue Planet, a welcoming detox removed from the beach scene. You'll find salads, smoothies and innovative veg dishes and a bucolic vibe. It's in an off-track jungle location about 2km from Agonda village (follow the signs off the main Agonda–Palolem road).

Riverside Bar & Restaurant BAR
(⏍7517634728; Agonda Beach Rd; ◷9am-midnight; 🛜) Head on down to the north end of the beach, but on the river side of the road, for a friendly, rustic bamboo-bar hang-out with regular live music, open mic nights and fire dances.

❶ Getting There & Away

Scooters and motorbikes can be rented from places on the beach road for around ₹300 to ₹400. Autorickshaws depart from the main T-junction near Agonda's church to Palolem (₹300) and Patnem (₹300). Taxis are around ₹50 more.

Local buses run from Chaudi sporadically throughout the day (₹15), but ask for Agonda Beach, otherwise you'll be let off in the village about 1km away.

Palolem

POP 12,440

Palolem is undoubtedly one of Goa's most postcard-perfect beaches: a gentle curve of palm-fringed sand facing a calm bay. But in season the beachfront is transformed into a toy town of colourful and increasingly sophisticated timber and bamboo huts fronted by palm-thatch restaurants. It's still a great place to be and is popular with backpackers, long-stayers and families. The protected bay is one of the safest swimming spots in Goa and you can comfortably kayak and paddleboard for hours here.

Just around the headland at the southern end of the beach, Colomb Bay – reached by foot or by road – is another little hideaway with several low-key resorts and restaurants.

Away from the beach you can learn to cook, drop in to yoga classes or hire a motorbike and cruise to surrounding beaches, waterfalls and wildlife parks.

🏃 Activities

Palolem offers no shortage of yoga, reiki and meditation classes in season. Locations and teachers change seasonally – ask around locally to see whose hands-on healing powers are hot this season.

Palolem's calm waters are perfect for kayaking and stand-up paddleboarding. Kayaks are available for hire for around ₹200 per hour, paddleboards for ₹500. Mountain bikes (₹150 per day) can be hired from **Seema Bike Hire** (Ourem Rd).

You'll find plenty of local fishers keen to take you out on dolphin-spotting and fishing expeditions on their outrigger boats. They generally charge a minimum ₹2000 for a one-hour trip but bargaining is possible. They also do trips to nearby Butterfly and Honeymoon Beaches, or up to Agonda and Cola Beaches.

★ **Goa Jungle Adventure** OUTDOORS

(📱9850485641; www.goajungle.com; trekking & canyoning trips ₹2390-3990; ☉Oct-May) This adventure company, run by experienced French guide Manu, will take you out for thrilling trekking and canyoning trips in the Netravali area at the base of the Western Ghats, where you can climb, jump and abseil into remote water-filled plunges. Trips, including jungle survival and sea-cliff jumping, run from half-day to several days. Meeting and registration is in Palolem.

Shoes can be rented for ₹200 per day. Call to arrange a meeting with Manu.

★ **Tanshikar Spice Farm** FOOD & DRINK

(📱9421184114, 0832-2608358; www.tanshikar spicefarm.com; Netravali; tours incl lunch ₹500; ☉10am-4pm) Tanshikar Spice Farm is a working, family-run organic spice farm with crops including vanilla, cashews, pepper, nutmeg and chillies, as well as beekeeping. There are no tour buses out here and the amiable young owner Chinmay gives a personalised tour of the plantation and nearby bubble lake. It can also offer cooking classes and guided jungle treks to nearby waterfalls.

If you really want to feel the serenity, book into one of the excellent mud-walled eco-cottages (₹2000) with bamboo sit-outs, a lovely elevated stilt tree house (₹3000) or a room in the Hindu-style house.

Anand Yoga Village YOGA

(📱7066454773; www.anandyogavillage.com; off Ourem Rd; drop-in classes ₹400, five-pass ₹1500) An international team of yoga instructors runs three daily drop-in classes in hatha, vinyasa and ashtanga disciplines at this inclusive new yoga village. Week-long yoga holidays (€330 per person) including accommodation in comfy timber cabins, breakfast and lunch and unlimited yoga and meditation. Teacher training courses (200 hours) also available.

Aranya Yoga YOGA

(www.aranyayogaashram.com; off Palolem Beach Rd; ₹400; ☉drop-in classes 8am, 10am & 4pm Sep-Mar) Highly regarded daily drop-in yoga classes in hatha, ashtanga and beginners, as well as five-day intensive courses (₹7500) and teacher training courses.

Rahul's Cooking Class COOKING

(📱07875990647; www.rahulcookingclass.com; Palolem Beach Rd; per person ₹1500; ☉11.30am-2.30pm & 6-9pm) Rahul's is one of the original

Palolem

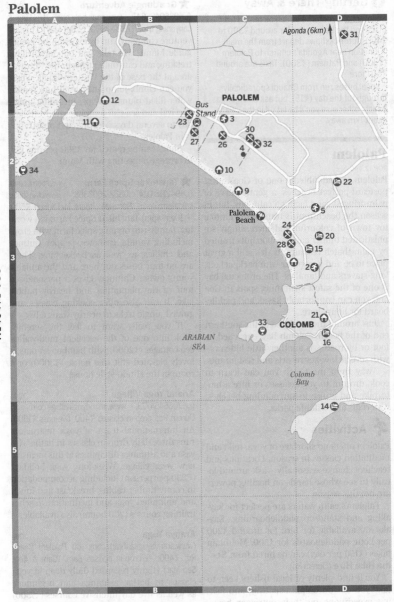

Agonda (6km)

PALOLEM

Bus Stand

Palolem
Beach

ARABIAN
SEA

Colomb
Bay

COLOMB

GOA PALOLEM

cooking schools, with three-hour morning and afternoon classes each day. Prepare five dishes including chapati and coconut curry. Minimum two people; book at least one day in advance.

Masala Kitchen   COOKING
(☎8390060421;   www.aranyayogaashram.com/
cooking-classes; Palolem Beach Rd; per person ₹1300) Established cooking classes at Aranya Yoga just off Palolem Beach Rd; book a day in advance. Includes South Indian thalis served on banana leaf and sattvic cooking.

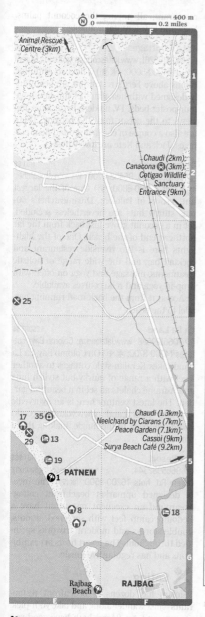

GOA PALOLEM

🛏 Sleeping

Most of Palolem's accommodation is of the seasonal beach-hut variety, though there are plenty of old-fashioned guesthouses or family homes with rooms to rent back from the beach.

Rainbow Lining HOSTEL $
(☎8390248102; 76 Ourem Rd; dm ₹450-600, d ₹2500; ❄🛜) This refurbished house is a good deal for backpackers with four- to 10-bed air-con dorms (bunks are curtained off) and a few private rooms. Friendly owners, rooftop yoga and breakfast available. At the

time of writing, a new restaurant-bar MOG (Mad Over Goa) was about to open.

Camp San Francisco HUT $

(📞 9158057201; www.campsanfrancisco.com; huts & r ₹800-3500) This hut village and associated guesthouse (Casa San Francisco) runs all the way from the beach to Palolem Beach Rd, offering a room or hut to suit most travellers. It's a good deal in mid-season as it has some of the cheaper huts along this stretch of beach. Naturally, there's a restaurant at the front.

Summer HOSTEL $

(📞 0832-2643406; www.thehostelcrowd.com/summerhostel; 99/1 Ourem Rd; dm with/without AC ₹550/450, d ₹1500-1900; ❋ 🛜) The latest offering from the Hostel Crowd is minimalist in design but all the facilities are there, with free breakfast, lockers, communal kitchen and lounge, and the popular Bombay Roasters cafe.

Sevas HUT $

(📞 9422065437; www.sevaspalolemgoa.com; Colomb Bay; d huts ₹800-1500; 🛜) Hidden in the jungle on the Colomb Bay side of Palolem, Sevas has some of the more basic palm-thatch huts around, reflected in the price. But it's a very peaceful place set in a lovely shaded garden area.

★Ciarans HUT $$

(📞 0832-2643477; www.ciarans.com; huts incl breakfast ₹4200-6300, r with AC ₹5500; ❋ 🛜) 🌿 Ciarans has some of the most impressive huts on the beachfront. Affable owner John has worked hard over two decades to maintain a high standard and his beautifully designed cottages around a plant-filled garden are top-notch. There's a popular multicuisine restaurant with nightly live music, tapas restaurant and quality massage and **spa centre** (1hr massage from ₹1900; ⊙9am-8pm).

Eco-credentials are also good here. Ciarans has a sewerage treatment plant, solar hot water and solar lighting. Ciarans also has fine hut resorts at Talpona and Galgibag beaches.

★Cozy Nook HUT $$

(📞 9822584760, 9822382799; www.cozynookgoa.com; huts ₹2500-4000) At the northern end of the beach, long-running Cozy Nook is one of Palolem's originals and still builds well-designed cottages including two-storey bamboo pads with Rajasthani touches, chill-out decks, more pedestrian rooms and a bar and

restaurant, all among the coconut palms. Yoga and kayak rental available.

Kate's Cottages GUESTHOUSE $$

(📞 9822165261; www.katescottagesgoa.com; Ourem Rd; d ₹4000-5000; ❋ 🛜) The two stunning rooms above Fern's restaurant are beautifully designed with heavy timber finishes, huge four-poster beds, TV, modern bathrooms and views to the ocean from the balcony. There are also a couple of cheaper ground-floor cottages. Jack and Kate are lovely hosts.

Dreamcatcher HUT $$

(📞 9878550550, 9646872700; www.dreamcatcher.in; d huts ₹2500-6800; 🛜) One of the largest hut resorts in Palolem, Dreamcatcher's 60-plus sturdy huts are nevertheless secluded, set in a coconut grove just back from the far northern end of the beach. One of the highlights here is the riverside restaurant and cocktail bar, and the wide range of holistic treatments, massage and yoga on offer, with drop-in yoga and reiki courses available.

Access it from the back road running parallel to the beach.

La La Land RESORT $$

(📞 7066129588; www.lalaland.in; Colomb Bay; cottages ₹4200-8700; ❋ 🛜) On Colomb Bay, La La Land takes Keralan-style cottages to another level with a range of quirky but stylish huts and A-frame chalets all set in a beautiful garden. The latest venture here is an ayurvedic spa and Yoga Land (www.yokoyoga.co.uk) *shalas* set back in the jungle, making this a true retreat.

Art Resort HUT $$$

(📞 9665982344; www.art-resort-goa.com; Ourem Rd; huts ₹6200-9500; ❋ 🛜) The nicely designed upmarket beachfront cottages around an excellent restaurant have a Bedouin camp feel with screened sit-outs, double storeys and modern artworks sprinkled throughout. The resort hosts art exhibitions and has regular live music.

✕ Eating

Palolem has dozens of beachfront restaurants – just wander along and take your pick. Ciarans and Art Resort both have good restaurants with regular live music.

Shiv Sai INDIAN $

(thalis ₹100, mains ₹100-200; ⊙9am-11pm) A thoroughly local lunch joint on the parallel beach road, Shiv Sai serves tasty thalis of the veggie, fish and Gujarati kinds, as well as Goan dishes.

★ Magic Italy
ITALIAN $$

(☑ 8805767705; 260 Palolem Beach Rd; mains ₹260-500; ☺ 1-11pm; ☎) On the main beach road, Magic Italy has been around since 1999 and the quality of its pizza and pasta remains high, with imported Italian ingredients like ham, salami, cheese and olive oil, imaginative 13-inch wood-fired pizzas and homemade pasta. Sit at tables, or Arabian-style on floor cushions. The atmosphere is busy but chilled.

German Bakery
BAKERY $$

(Ourem Rd; pastries ₹30-80, mains ₹100-300; ☺ 7am-10pm; ☎) Tasty baked treats are the stars at the established Nepali-run German Bakery, but there is also an excellent range of set breakfasts and yummy stuff like yak-cheese croissants, along with Israeli, Chinese, Italian and Indian options. It's set in a peaceful garden festooned with flags.

Fern's By Kate's
GOAN $$

(☑ 9822165261; Ourem Rd; mains ₹250-450; ☺ 8.30am-10.30pm; ☎) On the road running behind the southern beach entrance, this solid timber family-run place serves up excellent authentic Goan food such as local sausages, fish curry rice and shark *amok tik*, along with a wide range of Indian, continental and sizzler dishes. Pizzas are a new addition – one features Goan sausage.

Little World
VEGETARIAN $$

(☑ 9887956810; Palolem Beach Rd; mains ₹200-400; ☺ 8am-11pm; ☎) Little World is a sweet little vegetarian and vegan cafe with a wholefood philosophy, quirky decor and an inventive menu. Buckwheat pancakes, waffles and scrambled tofu for breakfast, homemade bread and filling salad bowls.

Space Goa
CAFE $$

(☑ 7066067642; www.thespacegoa.com; 261 Devabag; mains ₹180-350; ☺ 8.30am-5.30pm; ☎) On the Agonda road, the Space Goa combines an excellent organic whole-food cafe with a gourmet deli, craft shop and a wellness centre offering meditation, acupuncture and other healing treatments. The food is fresh and delicious and the desserts – such as chocolate-beetroot cake – are divine. Drop-in morning yoga classes are ₹500.

Zest Cafe
VEGETARIAN $$

(☑ 8806607919; www.zestgoa.com; Palolem Beach Rd; mains ₹190-360; ☺ 8am-9pm; ☎🖊) Bowls of pad Thai, plates of meze, vegan platters, raw food cakes and soy or almond milkshakes, all freshly prepared, make Zest a popular hang-out among the vegan, health-conscious crowd. There's an almost identical branch in Agonda.

Café Inn
CAFE $$

(☑ 7507322799; Palolem Beach Rd; mains ₹100-450; ☺ 8am-11pm; ☎) If you're craving a strong latte or a rum-infused slushie, Café Inn, which grinds its own blend of coffee beans, is one of Palolem's more popular hang-outs off the beach. Breakfasts are filling, and comfort-food burgers and panini sandwiches hit the spot. Regular live music and party nights.

★ Ourem 88
EUROPEAN $$$

(☑ 8698827679; mains ₹550-800; ☺ 6-10pm Tue-Sun) British-run Ourem 88 is a gastronomic sensation. It has just a handful of tables and a small but masterful menu, with changing specials chalked up on the blackboard. Try baked brie, tender calamari stuffed with Goan sausage, braised lamb shank or fluffy soufflé. English roast dinner on Sunday. Worth a splurge.

🍷 Drinking & Nightlife

Palolem doesn't party like the northern beaches but it's certainly not devoid of nightlife. Some of the beach bars stay open 24 hours in season, there are silent headphone parties at least once a week and other DJ club nights are organised seasonally. Several beach bars such as Ciarans have live music so you'll find someone playing every night of the week in season.

Leopard Valley
CLUB

(www.facebook.com/leopardvalley; Palolem-Agonda Rd; entry from ₹600; ☺ 9pm-4am Fri) South Goa's biggest outdoor dance club is a sight (and sound) to behold, with 3D laser light shows, pyrotechnics and state-of-the-art sound systems blasting local and international DJs on Friday nights. It's in an isolated but easily reached (by taxi) location between Palolem and Agonda. Check the Facebook page to see what's on.

Neptunes
CLUB

(www.facebook.com/neptunesgoa; Neptune Point, Colomb Bay; ₹800; ☺ 9pm-4am Sat Nov-Apr) On a rocky headland just south of Palolem Beach, this was Palolem's only remaining silent disco at the time of writing. Don your

WORTH A TRIP

GALGIBAG & TALPONA

Galgibag and Talpona form another of South Goa's beach gems – a broad stretch of barely touched sand framed by the Talpona River in the north and the Galgibag River to the south, all backed by swaying pines and palms. The only disruption to this peace is the construction of the new highway bypass, though it's far enough back from the beach to be ignored. Near the southern end, 'Turtle Beach' is where rare, long-lived olive ridley sea turtles come to nest on the beach between November and March. This is a protected area: a Forest Department information hut here should be staffed during nesting season. Food and accommodation options include:

Neelchand by Ciarans (☑ 7796783663, 0832-2632082; www.neelchand.com; cottages ₹4000; ✸ ☎) Absolute beachfront location on near-deserted Talpona Beach. Just seven lovely timber cottages in a sweet little garden.

Peace Garden (☑ 9168520727; www.peacegardengoa.com; huts ₹2100-4800; ☎) Well-constructed hut village on Talpona Beach with a focus on yoga, wellness and relaxation.

Cassoi (☑ 7796456453; www.cassoibyciarans.com; huts & tents ₹3000-5000; ✸ ☎) Woven into the palms on peaceful Galgibag Beach, this hut village has something for everyone.

Surya Beach Café (☑ 9923155396; Galgibag Beach; mains ₹200-350; ☺ 9am-10pm) Specialises in fresh oysters, clams, mussels and crabs caught from the Galgibag River.

headphones and tune into three DJ channels. No entry unless you're dancing.

Sundowner BAR
(www.sundowner-palolem.com; ☺ 9am-midnight; ☎) At the far northern end of the beach, across the narrow estuary (easy to cross at low tide), Sundowner is indeed a cool place to watch the sunset. The seasonal bar is nicely isolated with views across the rocks to forested (and inaccessible) Canacona (Monkey) Island. Also serves pizzas and has a few cottages.

ⓘ Getting There & Away

Frequent buses run to nearby Chaudi (₹8) from the **bus stand** (Palolem Beach Rd) on the corner of the road down to the beach. Hourly buses to Margao (₹40, one hour) depart from the same place, though these usually go via Chaudi anyway. From Chaudi you can pick up regular buses to Margao, from where you can change for Panaji, or south to Polem Beach and Karwar in Karnataka.

The closest train station is Canacona, 2km from Palolem's beach entrance.

An autorickshaw from Palolem to Patnem should cost ₹100, or ₹150 to Chaudi. A taxi to Dabolim Airport is around ₹2500, or ₹2000 to Margao.

Patnem

Smaller and less crowded than neighbouring Palolem, pretty Patnem makes a much quieter and more family-friendly alternative. The waters aren't as calm and protected as at Palolem, but Patnem Beach is patrolled by lifeguards and it's safe for paddling.

The beach is, naturally, lined with shack restaurants and beach-hut operations in season but it has an altogether relaxed vibe where lazing on the sand or sipping a cocktail is the order of the day. It's easy enough to walk around the northern headland to Colomb Bay and on to Palolem.

⏿ Sleeping & Eating

Patnem has a fairly consistent range of a dozen or so seasonal beach huts and a few hotels back from the beach. Long-stayers will revel in Patnem's choice of village homes and apartments available for rent from ₹15,000 to ₹50,000 per month.

Micky's HUT $$
(☑ 9850484884; www.mickyhuts.com; d ₹1500-2000; ☎) Micky's is an old-timer at the north end of Patnem Beach with a range of simple budget huts and rooms. It's run by a friendly family and open for most of the year. There's a cruisey beachfront bar and cafe among the palms.

Kala Bahia
GUESTHOUSE **$$**

(☎9764863073; www.kalabahia.com; r ₹3100-4300; ◷restaurant 8am-10pm Mon-Sat, to 4pm Sun; ☎) At the northern end of Patnem Beach (reached by road via Colomb), Kala Bahia is a sweet guesthouse, veg restaurant and something of an event centre, with yoga, music and movie nights. Cocktails and sunset views looking back down on Patnem Beach are fabulous. Rooms are secure and comfortable and there are a few cabins.

Papaya's
COTTAGE **$$**

(☎9923079447; www.papayasgoa.com; huts ₹2000-3000, cottages with AC ₹4500; ❄☎) Solid huts constructed with natural materials head back into the palm grove from Papaya's popular restaurant. These are easily some of the best cabins and rooms on Patnem Beach: each hut is lovingly built, with lots of wood, four-poster beds and floating muslin, while the one and two-bedroom air-con brick cottages are fitted out like apartments.

Palm Trees
Ayurvedic Heritage
RESORT **$$**

(☎9673178731; www.thepalmtreesayurvedagoa.com; huts ₹5300-6800; ☎) This ayurvedic resort has an exquisite riverside location in a thick palm grove at the southern end of Patnem village (access from Patnem–Rajbag road).

Home
GUESTHOUSE **$$**

(☎9923944676; www.homebeachresort.com; r ₹2000-3500; ◷8am-10pm; ☎) Home is a lovely family-owned guesthouse-style resort with a popular beachfront restaurant serving awesome dessert – chocolate brownies, apple tarts and cheesecake. No beach huts here but eight neatly decorated, light-filled rooms behind the restaurant and some larger family rooms around the garden at the street entrance. Minimum two-night stay.

Bougainvillea Patnem
HUT **$$**

(☎9822189913; www.bougainvilleapatnem.com; huts ₹2000-3500; ☎) Simple but clean and good value rooms behind the restaurant as well as the few premium sea-facing huts at the front. Yoga retreats and drop-in classes and ayurvedic treatments available.

Bamboo Yoga Retreat
HUT **$$$**

(☎9637567730; www.bamboo-yoga-retreat.com; cottages per person €82-92; ☎) This laid-back yoga retreat, exclusive to guests, has a wonderful open-sided *shala* facing the ocean at the southern end of Patnem Beach, and three more *shalas* among the village of beautifully designed timber and thatched huts. Yoga holiday rates include brunch, meditation and two daily yoga classes, but there are also training courses and ayurvedic treatments.

★ Karma Cafe & Bakery
CAFE **$**

(☎9764504253; Patnem Rd, Colomb; baked goods from ₹60, mains ₹120-230; ◷6.30am-9.30pm; ☎) Pull up a cushion at this chilled cafe and bakery opposite the Colomb road and delve into a superb range of freshly baked breads, croissants and pastries as well as coffee and smoothies. Delve further for *momos*, Nepali thalis and even Vietnamese rice paper rolls.

★ Jaali Cafe
CAFE **$$**

(☎8007712248; small plates ₹180-220; ◷9am-6pm Tue, to 11pm Wed-Sun) The menu at this lovely garden cafe is something special with a delicious range of tapas-style Middle Eastern and Mediterranean plates – choose two or three dishes each and share. Sunday brunch is a stellar event popular with local expats. There's also an excellent **boutique** (☎8007712248; ◷9.30am-6.30pm Nov-Apr) and a highly regarded massage therapist on hand.

Salida del Sol
MULTICUISINE **$$**

(☎7507404102; www.salida-patnembeach.com; mains ₹180-390; ◷8am-11pm; ☎) Patnem's beachfront restaurants all have their own qualities and followings and Salida del Sol works on many fronts, from the friendly and attentive staff to fresh food and Arabian Nights atmosphere. A standouts are the *momos* and Nepali set meals but of course there's Indian and Western food including pizza and pasta. Nice huts in the garden at the back, too.

❶ Getting There & Away

The main entrance to Patnem Beach is reached from the country lane running south from Palolem, then turning right at the Hotel Sea View. Alternatively, walk about 20 minutes along the path from Palolem via Colomb Bay, or catch a bus heading south (₹5). An autorickshaw charges around ₹80 from Palolem.

GOA PATNEM

Karnataka

POP 68.3 MILLION

Includes ➡

Best Places to Eat

➡ Karavalli (p867)

➡ Mavalli Tiffin Rooms (p865)

➡ Girimanja's (p893)

➡ SodaBottleOpenerWala (p867)

➡ Raintree (p888)

Best Places to Stay

➡ Dhole's Den (p886)

➡ Electric Cats B&B (p864)

➡ Uramma Cottage (p906)

➡ Heritage Resort (p909)

➡ Waterwoods Lodge (p886)

Why Go?

A stunning introduction to southern India, Karnataka is a prosperous, compelling state loaded with a winning blend of urban cool, glittering palaces, national parks, ancient ruins, beaches, yoga centres and legendary travellers' hang-outs.

At its nerve centre is the capital, Bengaluru (Bangalore), a progressive cybercity famous for its craft-beer and restaurant scene. Heading out of town you'll encounter the evergreen rolling hills of Kodagu, dotted with spice and coffee plantations, the regal splendour of Mysuru (Mysore), and jungles teeming with monkeys, tigers and Asia's biggest population of elephants.

If that all sounds too mainstream, head to the counter-cultural enclave of tranquil Hampi, with hammocks, psychedelic sunsets and boulder-strewn ruins. Or the blissful, virtually untouched coastline around Gokarna, blessed with beautiful coves and empty sands.

When to Go

Bengaluru

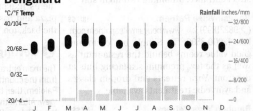

Mar–May The best season to watch tigers and elephants in Karnataka's pristine national parks.	**Oct** Mysuru's Dussehra (Dasara) carnival brings night-long celebrations and a jumbo parade.	**Dec & Jan** The coolest time to explore Hampi and the northern forts, palaces, caves and temples.

Karnataka Highlights

1 **Hampi** (p899) Soaking up the surreal landscapes, sociable travellers' scene and epic ruins in this magical destination.

2 **Mysuru** (Mysore; p873) Touring this civilised city's remarkable palace, then exploring its famous bazaar district.

3 **Gokarna** (p895) Searching for the perfect beach cove in a low-key coastal hideaway, then touring its atmospheric temples.

4 **Bengaluru** (Bangalore; p858) Sampling craft beers or sipping coffee, and enjoying the museums and sights of Karnataka's most cosmopolitan city.

5 **Badami** (p907) Exploring stunning cave temples, rich in sculpture and carvings, that overlook a lovely lake.

6 **Kodagu Region** (p887) Hiking lonely trails past spice plantations in these temperate, evergreen highlands.

7 **Nagarhole National Park** (p886) Spying on lazy tuskers in the forests bordering serene Kabini Lake.

8 **Vijapura** (Bijapur; p910) Strolling the peaceful, manicured grounds of exquisite 16th-century Islamic monuments.

History

A playing field of religions, cultures and kingdoms, the Karnataka region has had a string of charismatic rulers. India's first great emperor, Chandragupta Maurya, made the Karnataka area his retreat when he embraced Jainism at Sravanabelagola in the 3rd century BC. From the 6th to the 14th centuries the land was under a series of dynasties, such as the Chalukyas, Cholas, Gangas and Hoysalas, who left a lasting mark in the form of stunning cave shrines and temples across the state.

In 1327 Mohammed Tughlaq's army sacked Halebid. In 1347 Hasan Gangu, a Persian general in Tughlaq's army, led a rebellion to establish the Bahmani kingdom, which was later subdivided into five Deccan sultanates. Meanwhile, the Hindu kingdom of Vijayanagar, with its capital in Hampi, rose to prominence. Having peaked in the early 1550s, it fell in 1565 to a combined effort of the sultanates.

In subsequent years the Hindu Wodeyars of Mysuru grew in stature and extended their rule over a large part of southern India. They remained largely unchallenged until 1761, when Hyder Ali (one of their generals) deposed them. Backed by the French, Hyder Ali and his son Tipu Sultan set up capital in Srirangapatna and consolidated their rule. However, in 1799 the British defeated Tipu Sultan and reinstated the Wodeyars. Historically, this battle consolidated British territorial expansion in southern India.

Mysuru remained under the Wodeyars until Independence – post-1947, the reigning maharaja became the first governor. The state boundaries were redrawn along linguistic lines in 1956 and the extended Kannada-speaking state of Mysore was born. It was renamed Karnataka in 1972, with Bangalore (now Bengaluru) as the capital.

BENGALURU (BANGALORE)

🖉 080 / POP 11.7 MILLION / ELEV 920M

Cosmopolitan Bengaluru (formerly Bangalore) is one of India's most progressive and developed cities, blessed with a benevolent climate, a modern metro system, and a burgeoning drinking, dining and shopping scene. Its creature comforts are a godsend to the weary traveller who has done the hard yards, and it's a great city for mixing with locals in craft-beer joints or quirky independent cafes. Though there are no world-class sights, you'll find lovely parks and striking Victorian-era architecture.

The past decade or so has seen a mad surge of development, coupled with traffic

TOP STATE FESTIVALS

Udupi Paryaya (☉ Jan/Feb) Held in even-numbered years, with a procession and ritual marking the handover of swamis at Udupi's Krishna Temple.

Classical Dance Festival (☉ Jan/Feb) Some of India's best classical-dance performances take place in Pattadakal.

Vijaya Utsav (p902) A three-day extravaganza of culture, heritage and the arts in Hampi.

Tibetan New Year (☉ Jan/Feb) Lamas in Tibetan refugee settlements in Bylakuppe take shifts leading nonstop prayers that span the week-long celebrations.

Vairamudi Festival (☉ Mar/Apr) At Melkote's Cheluvanarayana Temple, Lord Vishnu is adorned with jewels, including a diamond-studded crown belonging to Mysuru's former maharajas, in a festival attracting 400,000 pilgrims.

Bengaluru Poetry Festival (p864) Draws a roster of international and local poets and writers.

Ganesh Chaturthi (☉ Sep) Families march their Ganesh idols to the sea in Gokarna at sunset.

Dussehra (p879) Mysuru Palace is lit up in the evenings and a vibrant procession hits town, to the delight of thousands.

Lakshadeepotsava (☉ Nov) Thousands and thousands of lamps light up the Jain pilgrimage town of Dharmasthala, offering spectacular photo ops.

Huthri (Nov/Dec) The Kodava community in Madikeri celebrates the start of the harvesting season with ceremony, music, traditional dances and much feasting for a week.

congestion and rising pollution levels. But the central district (dating back to the British Raj years) remains little changed, and the landmark corporate headquarters and business parks of the city's booming IT industry are mostly in the outer suburbs.

History

Literally meaning 'Town of Boiled Beans', Bengaluru supposedly derived its name from an ancient incident involving an old village woman who served cooked pulses to a lost and hungry Hoysala king. Kempegowda, a feudal lord, was the first person to mark out Bengaluru's extents, by building a mud fort in 1537. The town remained obscure until 1759, when it was gifted to Hyder Ali by the Mysuru maharaja. The British arrived in 1809 and made the city their regional administrative base in 1831, renaming it Bangalore. During the Raj era the city played host to many a British officer, including Winston Churchill, who enjoyed life here during his greener years and famously left a debt (still on the books) of ₹13 at the Bangalore Club.

Now home to countless software, electronics and business-outsourcing firms, Bengaluru's knack for technology developed early. In 1905 it was the first Indian city to have electric street lighting. Since the 1940s it has been home to Hindustan Aeronautics Ltd (HAL), India's largest aerospace company. The city's name was changed back to Bengaluru in November 2006, though few use it in practice.

⊙ Sights

★ National Gallery of Modern Art
GALLERY

(NGMA; ☑ 080-22342338; www.ngmaindia.gov.in/ngma_bangaluru.asp; 49 Palace Rd; Indian/foreigner ₹20/500; ⊙ 11am-6.30pm Tue-Sun) Housed in a century-old mansion – the former vacation home of the raja of Mysuru – this world-class art museum showcases an impressive permanent collection (and exhibitions). The Old Wing exhibits works from pre-Independence, including paintings by Raja Ravi Varma and Abanindranath Tagore. Connected by a pedestrian bridge, the sleek New Wing focuses on contemporary post-Independence works by artists including Sudhir Patwardhan and Vivan Sundaram. Guided walks (11.30am Wednesday, 3pm Saturday) are a great way to learn about the museum's highlights.

There's a great art-reference library, a cafe and a museum shop here, too.

★ Cubbon Park
GARDENS

(www.horticulture.kar.nic.in/cubbon.htm; Kasturba Rd; Ⓜ Cubbon Park) In the heart of Bengaluru's business district is Cubbon Park, a well-maintained 120-hectare garden where Bengaluru's residents converge to steal a moment from the rat race that rages outside. The gardens encompass the red-painted Gothic-style State Central Library. Unfortunately, Cubbon is not completely closed to traffic, except on Sundays, when there are concerts, fun runs, yoga and even a small farmers market.

Other wonderful colonial-era architecture around the park includes the colossal neo-Dravidian-style **Vidhana Soudha** (Dr Ambedkar Rd; Ⓜ Vidhana Soudha), built in 1954, which serves as the legislative chambers of the state government, and neoclassical Attara Kacheri, built in 1864 and housing the High Court. The latter two are closed to the public.

Opera House
HISTORIC BUILDING

(☑ 9513899866; 57 Brigade Rd; ⊙ 11am-10pm; Ⓜ MG Rd) FREE Recently restored to its former glory thanks to the financial might of Samsung, the British-era Opera House has been transformed into a temple of tech, complete with virtual-reality experiences and gleaming displays of smartphones and notebooks. Commendably, the original structure has been sensitively renovated, its beautiful interior combining twin colonnades, an elegant curved balcony and a stage framed by classical columns. There's a cafe, and you can book the home-theatre zone to watch a film.

HAL Aerospace Museum & Heritage Centre
MUSEUM

(www.hal-india.com; Airport-Varthur Rd; admission ₹50, mobile/camera/video ₹20/50/75; ⊙ 9am-5pm Tue-Sun) For a peek into India's aeronautical history, visit this wonderful museum past the old airport, where you can see some of the indigenous aircraft models designed by HAL. Interesting exhibits include a MIG-21, home-grown models such as the Marut and Kiran, and a vintage Canberra bomber.

Karnataka Chitrakala Parishath
GALLERY

(www.karnatakachitrakalaparishath.com; Kumarakrupa Rd; ₹50; ⊙ 10am-5.30pm Mon-Sat; Ⓜ Mantri Sq Sampige Rd) A superb gallery with a wide range of Indian and international contemporary art, as well as permanent displays of Mysuru-style paintings and folk and tribal pieces from across Asia. A section is devoted to the works of Russian master Nicholas Roerich, known for his vivid paintings of the Himalaya. The Pan Indian Panorama

KARNATAKA BENGALURU (BANGALORE)

Bengaluru (Bangalore)

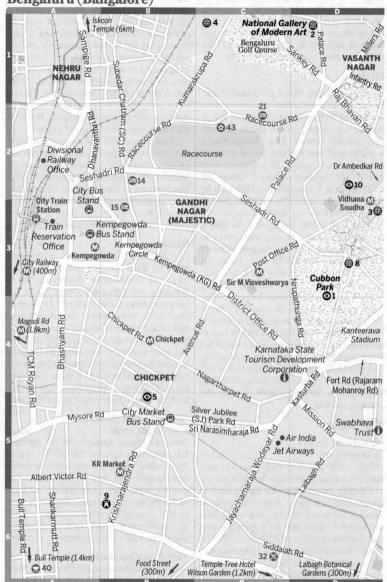

Iskcon Temple (6km)

NEHRU NAGAR

National Gallery of Modern Art 2

Bengaluru Golf Course

VASANTH NAGAR

Infantry Rd

Divisional Railway Office

Racecourse

GANDHI NAGAR (MAJESTIC)

Dr Ambedkar Rd

10

Vidhana Soudha 3

City Train Station

City Bus Stand

Train Reservation Office

Kempegowda Bus Stand

Kempegowda Circle

Kempegowda

8

Cubbon Park 1

City Railway (400km)

Magadi Rd (1.8km)

Chickpet Rd

Chickpet

Sir M Visveshwarya

Kanteerava Stadium

Karnataka State Tourism Development Corporation

Fort Rd (Rajaram Mohanroy Rd)

CHICKPET

Nagartharpet Rd

5

City Market Bus Stand

Silver Jubilee (SJ) Park Rd

Sri Narasimharaja Rd

Swabhava Trust

Mysore Rd

Air India Jet Airways

KR Market

Albert Victor Rd

9

Bull Temple Rd

40

Bull Temple (1.4km)

Food Street (300m)

Temple Tree Hotel Wilson Garden (1.2km)

Siddaiah Rd

32

Lalbagh Botanical Gardens (300m)

collection includes progressive art from SG Vasudev and Yusuf Arakkal.

Krishnarajendra Market   MARKET
(City Market; Silver Jubilee Park Rd; ⊙6am-10pm; Ⓜ Chickpet) For a taste of traditional urban

India, dive into the bustling, gritty Krishnarajendra Market and the dense grid of streets that surround it. Weave your way around the lively, colourful stalls, past fresh produce, piles of vibrant dyes, spices and copper ware. The vibrant flower market is a highlight.

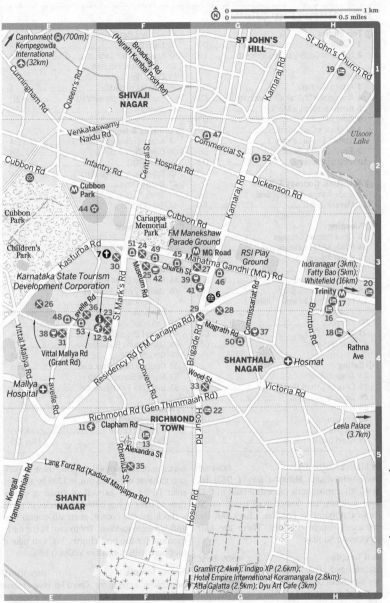

Wonderla　AMUSEMENT PARK

(☎080-22010333; www.wonderla.com; Mysuru-Bengaluru Rd; adult/child Mon-Fri ₹908/725, Sat & Sun ₹1168/932; ☺11am-6pm Mon-Fri, to 7pm Sat & Sun) Adrenaline seekers should look no further than this huge amusement park, which has more than 60 well-maintained rides, a wave pool, water slides and a 'rain disco'. It's just off the Mysuru–Bengaluru highway, 28km from the centre of Bengaluru, and connected by BMTC buses.

Bengaluru (Bangalore)

St Mark's Cathedral CATHEDRAL
(www.saintmarks.in; Mahatma Gandhi (MG) Rd; Ⓜ MG Rd) Atmospheric cathedral built in 1812 with a distinctive domed roof based on St Paul's Cathedral in London. Check out the entrance's ornate carvings. There are four services on Sunday.

Bull Temple HINDU TEMPLE
(Basavanagudi; Bull Temple Rd.; ⊘ 7am-8.30pm; ☒; Ⓜ National College) Built by Kempegowda in the 16th-century Dravidian style, the Bull Temple contains a huge stone monolith of Nandi (Shiva's bull), which is always embellished with lavish flower garlands. This is one of Bengaluru's most atmospheric temples, set in a small park and accessed via a shady path.

Lalbagh Botanical Gardens GARDENS
(www.horticulture.kar.nic.in/lalbagh.htm; Lalbagh Rd; ₹20; ⊘ 6am-7pm; Ⓜ Lalbagh) Spread over 98 hectares of landscaped terrain, these expansive gardens were laid out in 1760 by famous ruler Hyder Ali. As well as amazing centuries-old trees, it has a diverse species of plant – check out the bonsai, giant silk-cotton tree and Japanese gardens. Try to visit in the early morning for the bird chorus. You can take a tour here with Bangalore Walks (p863).

Iskcon Temple HINDU TEMPLE
(www.iskconbangalore.org; Chord Rd, Hare Krishna Hill; ⊘ 7.15am-1pm & 4.15-8.20pm Mon-Fri, 7.15am-8.30pm Sat & Sun; Ⓜ Mahalakshmi) Built by the Hare Krishnas, this impressive hilltop temple, inaugurated in 1997, is lavishly decorated in a mix of ultra-contemporary and traditional styles. There are many food stalls here, so bring an appetite, and concerts and lectures are regularly held. It's around 8km northwest of the centre of town.

Tipu Sultan's Palace   PALACE

(Albert Victor Rd; Indian/foreigner ₹25/300, video ₹25; ⊙8.30am-5.30pm) The elegant Indo-Islamic summer residence of ruler Tipu Sultan is notable for its teak pillars and ornamental frescos.

🏃 Activities

Meraki   SPA

(☑7619613118; www.merakispa.in; 8 Papanna St; 1hr massage from ₹3000; ⊙11.30am-9.30pm) Upmarket spa and wellness centre offering fine massages and treatments, body scrubs and reflexology. During happy hour (11.30am to 1.30pm) a full-body massage is a reasonable ₹2500. It's off St Marks Rd. Also has a **branch** (777,100 Feet Rd; ⊙11am-10pm) in Indiranagar.

Bangalore
Mountaineering Club   TREKKING

(☑7406319666; www.bmcadventures.com; 778 9th A Main Rd, Indiranagar; 3-day treks from ₹5666; ⊙10am-6pm Mon-Thu & Sat, to 10pm Fri; ⓜIndiranagar) Organises guided treks throughout southern India, including to Pushpagiri in the Western Ghats of Karnataka, and the hills of Kodagu. Trips to Himachal Pradesh (from ₹8900) and the Himalayas are also offered.

Equilibrium   CLIMBING

(☑8861684444; http://equilibriumclimbing.com; 3rd fl, 546 Chinmaya Mission Hospital Rd, Indiranagar; day pass ₹399; ⊙6.30am-10pm Mon-Fri, 8am-10pm Sat & Sun; ⓜIndiranagar) A premier climbing centre offering excellent facilities, and instruction including lead climbing and speed climbing. Also arranges weekend and multiday climbing excursions to Badami and Hampi.

Soukya   YOGA

(☑080-28017000; www.soukya.com; Soukya Rd, Samethanahalli, Whitefield; per day incl treatments, meals & accommodation from ₹10,500; ⊙6am-8.30pm) Very upmarket, internationally renowned retreat on a picture-perfect 12-hectare organic farm running programs in ayurvedic therapy and yoga, as well as medical and therapeutic skin treatments.

Body Raaga Wellness Spa   SPA

(☑7829995050; www.bodyraaga.com; 93 Richmond Rd; 45min massage from ₹1250) Centrally located spa with professional masseurs and therapists; rates are moderate. Try a deep-tissue massage, which is perfect if you've just endured a long journey. Also has a branch in **Indiranagar** (☑080-50002828; www.body raaga.com; 1096 12th A Main Rd, Indirangar; 45min massage from ₹1250).

Total Yoga Oneness Centre   YOGA

(☑9740980200; http://total-yoga.org; 872/A 80 Feet Rd, Indiranagar; ⊙7am-9pm Mon-Sat; ⓜIndiranagar) A large, professional studio offering vinyasa flow, classic hatha and power yoga. Classes include 15 minutes of pranayama and meditation.

Ayurvedagram   AYURVEDA

(☑080-65651090; www.ayurvedagram.com; Hemmandanhalli, Whitefield; day packages from ₹4000) Set over 3 hectares of tranquil gardens, with heritage homes transplanted from Kerala, this retreat has tailored ayurvedic treatments, yoga and rejuvenation programs. It's in the outer suburb of Whitefield, around 25km from central Bengaluru.

👉 Tours

⭐Unhurried Tours   WALKING

(☑919880565446; www.unhurried.in; half-day tours ₹2500) Led by Poornima Dasharathi, an author and history enthusiast, these excellent walking tours explore backstreets, temples, street life and local cuisine. Tour duration is two to three hours. Monthly 'open walks' (you join others), cycling and walking tours, and trips to Mysuru are also offered.

⭐Bangalore Walks   WALKING

(☑9845512345; www.bangalorewalks.com; walks ₹600-900; ⊙7-10am Sat & Sun) Runs highly recommended tours, including guided walks through Cubbon Park, a medieval old-city history walk and a 19th-century Victorian walk. Most walks include a delicious breakfast. Customised tours are also possible.

Bus Tours   BUS

(https://kstdc.co; city day tour ₹485) The government's tourism department runs city bus tours that are worth considering (though they do cover a lot of places in a short space of time).

Day trips around Bengaluru are also offered, including a daily departure to Srirangapatna and Mysuru (₹950) that takes in several temples, palaces and gardens.

SLEEPING PRICE RANGES

The following price ranges are for a double room with bathroom and include tax within the state:

$ less than ₹1750

$$ ₹1750–₹5000

$$$ more than ₹5000

✨ Festivals & Events

Bengaluru Poetry Festival   LITERATURE
(☏ 080-41600677; www.facebook.com/bengaluru poetryfestival; ⊙ early Aug) This annual poetry festival features local and international writers and musicians. In 2018 it was held over two days at the Leela Palace hotel (p865).

🛏 Sleeping

Decent budget rooms are in short supply. Most hostels are not centrally located, but you'll find a stack of dive lodges on Subedar Chatram (SC) Rd, east of the bus stands and around the train station.

★ Electric Cats B&B   HOSTEL $
(☏ 080-41104143; www.facebook.com/electric catshostel; 1794 6th Cross Rd; ⊙ dm ₹500-600; ❄ ☏; Ⓜ Indiranagar) Well-organised, sociable Electric Cats, close to the buzzing Indiranagar area, has good dorms (including one female-only dorm) with a shared bathroom. All beds have quality linen, private reading lamps and charging facilities. Drinking water and wi-fi are free, there's no curfew, and staff members are very switched on to travellers' needs, even organising Christmas dinners, pub crawls, barbecues and (free) yoga.

Cuckoo Hostel   HOSTEL $
(☏ 7204156880; www.facebook.com/cuckoohostel; 561 17th A Main Rd, Koramangala; dm/s ₹399/1100; ❄ @ ☏) Run by and attracting a creative crowd, the Cuckoo has regular craft, art and music sessions and occasional debates about the environment and global issues. There are bicycles for hire, laundry facilities and clean, well-presented dorms. It's about 6km southwest of the centre.

Hotel Adora   HOTEL $$
(☏ 080-22200024; www.facebook.com/hotel adora; 47 Subedar Chatram Rd; s/d ₹650/890, with AC ₹1150/1780; ❄ ☏; Ⓜ Kempegowda) A seven-story budget option (there's a lift) with decent, if functional, rooms near the train station and Kempegowda bus stand. Staff members are friendly and helpful, and there's a good veg restaurant on the ground floor.

★ Casa Piccola Cottage   HERITAGE HOTEL $$
(☏ 080-22990337; www.casacottage.com; 2 Clapham Rd; r incl breakfast from ₹4500; ❄ ☏) Tastefully renovated, Casa Piccola has a personalised brand of hospitality that has garnered it a solid reputation. Its atmospheric rooms, with tiled floors and traditional bedspreads, offer a tranquil sanctuary. The

garden features papaya and avocado trees. Book via the website for the best rates.

Laika Boutique Stay   B&B $$
(☏ 9482806630; www.laikabangalore.in; Rathna Rd; r from ₹4235; ❄ ☏; Ⓜ Trinity) Hidden down a leafy side street, this welcoming guesthouse is a wonderful choice for those seeking a more local experience combined with style and comfort. Extra touches, including thoughtful service and home-cooked breakfasts, make it a great choice.

JüSTa MG Road   BOUTIQUE HOTEL $$
(☏ 080-41135555; www.justahotels.com/mg-road-bangalore; 21/14 Craig Park Layout, MG Rd; r/ste incl breakfast ₹3810/5120; ❄ ☏; Ⓜ Trinity) This intimate, arty hotel has slick and spacious rooms with Japanese-inspired motifs throughout. It's very well located, with a metro station and shopping malls close by. The helpful, professional staff members are eager to please.

Tom's Hotel   HOTEL $$
(☏ 080-25575875; http://tomshotelbangalore. com; 1/5 Hosur Rd; s/d incl breakfast with fan ₹2300/2500, with AC ₹2480/2610; ❄ ☏ ⊟) An excellent place with high cleanliness standards and bright, cheerful rooms, Tom's allows you to stay in a central location – it's a 15-minute walk from Mahatma Gandhi (MG) Rd – and has a friendly staff and free wi-fi. There's a fine Mangaluru restaurant here, too, serving well-priced seafood dishes.

Purple Cloud Hotel   HOTEL $$
(☏ 080-48091100; www.purplecloudhotels.com; Down Town Park 2, Sadahalli Gate; r from ₹3850; ❄ ☏) A smart hotel that's well worth considering as an affordable base handy for Kempegowda airport (15km away). Rooms are modern and contemporary, and the in-house Fiery Indian Kitchen is recommended for North and South Indian food.

Hotel ABM International   HOTEL $$
(☏ 080-41742030; www.hotelabminternational. com; 232 Subedar Chatram Rd; r with fan from ₹1650, with AC ₹1900-2650; ❄ ☏; Ⓜ Kempegowda) This well-run modern hotel, near Anand Rao Circle, has neat, simple, well-presented accommodation, room service and fast wi-fi. There's a popular juice bar and restaurant downstairs, and it's walking distance from the Kempegowda Bus Stand and metro.

Temple Tree Hotel Wilson Garden   HOTEL $$
(☏ 080-46622000; http://templetreehotel.com; 9th Cross Rd, Mavalli; r ₹3860-4600; ❄ ☏) A

short stroll from Lalbagh Botanical Gardens (p862), this hip hotel has sleek bathrooms and modish design touches. Garden-view rooms have great balconies, and the rooftop restaurant is superb for breakfast.

Mass Residency

GUESTHOUSE $$

(☑ 9945091735; massresidency@yahoo.com; 18 2nd Main Rd, 11th Cross, JP Nagar; r incl breakfast with fan/AC ₹1600/2000; ❄ 🕾) Run by very hospitable brothers (who are world travellers themselves), this guesthouse has comfortable-enough rooms and a great roof terrace ideal for socialising. It's in a relatively quiet location, 8km south of the centre.

Hotel Empire International Koramangala

HOTEL $$

(☑ 080-40222777; www.hotelempire.in; 103 Industrial Area, Koramangala; s/d ₹2160/2620; ❄ @ 🕾) Located in the trendy Koramangala area, this hotel is a good choice for party people as the area's thick with bars and restaurants. Rooms are decent value, though bathrooms are small, and there's room service from the good in-house restaurant.

Hotel Ajantha

HOTEL $$

(☑ 080-25584321; www.hotelajantha.com; 22A MG Rd; s/d incl breakfast with fan ₹1450/1950, with AC from ₹2370; ❄ 🕾; Ⓜ Trinity) Dependable, affordable budget favourite Ajantha is very close to Trinity metro station and has decent, well-maintained rooms with cable TV. There's a well-regarded restaurant in the compound and the complimentary breakfast is generous.

★ Oberoi

HOTEL $$$

(☑ 080-41358222; www.oberoihotels.com; 39 MG Rd; s/d from ₹12,900/13,800; ❄ @ 🕾 ❄; Ⓜ Trinity) The uber-opulent Oberoi is set in lush gardens around an enchanting 120-year-old tree, yet its central location could not be more convenient. It mixes colonial-era ambience with modern touches like tablet-controlled in-room devices and TVs in the bathrooms. Rooms all have balconies with garden views, and the spa and restaurants are superb.

★ Taj West End

HERITAGE HOTEL $$$

(☑ 080-66605660; www.tajhotels.com; Racecourse Rd; s/d incl breakfast from ₹13,400/14,500; ❄ 🕾 ❄) Expect superb service at this very fine hotel, spread over 8 hectares of stunning tropical gardens. The West End dates to 1887, when it was established as a base for British officers, and it still oozes colonial-era class.

Some of the city's best dining options lie within, include the Blue Ginger (Vietnamese cuisine) and the Masala Klub (Indian).

Lemon Tree Premier Ulsoor Lake

HOTEL $$$

(☑ 080-44802000; www.lemontreehotels.com; 2/1 St Johns Rd; s/d incl breakfast ₹6340/6620; ❄ 🕾 ❄) This well-run hotel is 2km north of MG Rd, so it's close to the city's main shopping and entertainment district. Rooms are equipped with all mod cons, and there's an elegant restaurant where guests can tuck into a lavish breakfast buffet.

Leela Palace

HOTEL $$$

(☑ 080-25211234; www.theleela.com; 23 HAL Airport Rd; s/d from ₹12,700/13,600; ❄ @ 🕾 ❄) Swanky Leela isn't actually a palace (it was built in 2003), but in terms of comfort it's fit for royalty, and golfers (it's next to a course). Gleaming marble, lush carpets, regal balconies and period features are done superbly, as are its beautiful gardens, restaurants, bars and boutiques. Located within the Leela Galleria complex, 5km east of MG Rd.

✖ Eating

Bengaluru's adventurous food scene includes high-end dining, gastropubs and cheap local favourites. Key areas in the centre are around MG Rd and neighbouring Lavelle Rd, while the more distant districts of Indiranagar and Koramangala also have a wide choice of restaurants and cafes.

★ Food Street

STREET FOOD $

(Dev Sagar; Sajjan Rao Circle, VV Puram; meals from ₹100; ⊘ from 5.30pm) For a local eating experience, head to VV Puram, aka Food Street, with its strip of hole-in-the-wall eateries cooking up classic street-food dishes from across India. It's quite a spectacle, with rotis being handmade and spun in the air and *bhajia* (vegetable fritters) dunked into hot oil before packed crowds.

★ Mavalli Tiffin Rooms

SOUTH INDIAN $

(MTR; ☑ 080-22220022; www.mavallitiffinrooms.com; 14 Lalbagh Rd, Mavalli; snacks from ₹52, meals from ₹90; ⊘ 6.30-11am & 12.30-9pm Tue-Sun) A legendary name in South Indian comfort food, this eatery has had Bengaluru eating out of its hand since 1924. Head to the dining room upstairs, queue for a table, and then enjoy as waiters bring you delicious *idli* (fermented rice cakes) and dosa (savoury crepes), capped by frothing filter coffee served in silverware.

Samosa Party INDIAN $
(www.samosaparty.co.in; 11 10th Main Rd, Indiranagar; samosas ₹25-70; ⊙ 8am-9pm) This inexpensive samosa hotspot is perfect for a quick bite on the southwestern side of the Indiranagar area. There's a wide range of trad (and twisted) samosas – mac and cheese, anyone? Wash it all down with a delicious *adrak* (ginger) chai.

Khan Saheb INDIAN $
(www.khansaheb.co; 9A Block, Brigade Rd; rolls from ₹50; ⊙ noon-11.30pm; M MG Rd) Famous for its terrific rolls (wholewheat chapatis), filled with anything from charcoal-grilled meats and tandoori prawns to paneer and sweet-corn tikka.

Gramin INDIAN $
(☑ 080-41104104; 20, 7th Block, Raheja Arcade, Koramangala; mains ₹136-180; ⊙ noon-3.30pm & 7-11pm Mon-Thu, to 11pm Fri-Sun) Gramin offers an affordable, wide choice of flavourful, rural, all-veg North Indian fare in cosy surrounds. Try the excellent range of lentils and curries with oven-fresh rotis, accompanied by sweet rose-flavoured lassi served in a copper vessel. The lunchtime thali (₹155) is always a good bet and includes two veg dishes, roti and some dhal (curry made from pulses).

Funjabi NORTH INDIAN $
(6A Church St; mains ₹95-250; ⊙ 11am-11pm) Accessed via a side alley and a dingy rear staircase, this simple place doesn't have a great location or much atmosphere, but the tasty North Indian *dhaba* (roadside) style grub is satisfyingly rich and authentic. Try the tandoori roti and a butter murg (rich chicken curry) or *malai kofta* (creamy curry with paneer cheese).

Anna Kuteera SOUTH INDIAN $$
(14 St Marks Rd; snacks from ₹35, mains ₹160-220) For a quick bite that's easy on the pocket, join the throngs at this pure-veg eatery; it's very busy indeed at lunchtimes, when there's usually standing room only. Snacks include flavoursome *ravi dosa* (crispy semolina crepes) and good *idli* (spongy, round, fermented rice cakes) and *vada* (doughnut-shaped, deep-fried lentil savouries). North Indian and Chinese dishes are also on the menu.

Smoor Chocolates Signature Lounge CAFE $$
(www.smoorchocolates.com; 1131, 100 Feet Rd; snacks & mains ₹190-625; ⊙ 8am-11pm Sun-Thu, to 1am Fri & Sat; 🛜) The city's finest *chocolaterie* has a lovely, air-conditioned and spacious interior where you can indulge in exquisite gateaux and cakes, and of course a chocolate or two. Also offers good breakfasts, wraps, sandwiches, burgers, tea and espresso coffee.

SlimSins Cafe INTERNATIONAL $$
(☑ 9535582766; www.facebook.com/slimsins; 34/1 36th Cross Rd, 4th Block, Jayanagar; mains ₹190-450; ⊙ 11am-9.30pm Mon-Sat, 9am-9.45pm Sun; M Rashtreeya Vidyalaya Rd) SlimSins lives up to its name, with an interesting menu of sinful-looking food actually made with wholesome ingredients. The open kitchen offers a peek into the culinary action: *ragi* (millet) buns being prepped for burgers, ketogenic-diet favourites like eggplant parmesan, and sweet-potato fries with fresh, healthy dips. It's the perfect place to binge after a workout.

Chinita Real Mexican Food MEXICAN $$
(www.chinita.in; 218 Double Rd, Indiranagar II Stage, Hoysala Nagar; mains ₹275-325; ⊙ 12.30am-3.30pm & 7.30-11pm; M Indiranagar) For authentic Mexican flavours in South India, look no further. The tempting menu features tasty tostadas (crispy tortillas with toppings), braised-pork burritos, and chicken or tofu smeared with a fine *mole* (rich, spicy very Mexican sauce). *Olé!* No tequila, mescal (or even cerveza), though.

Lady Baga GOAN $$
(☑ 080-49652751; www.facebook.com/ladybagablr; 24/5 Lavelle Rd; mains from ₹200; ⊙ noon-midnight Mon-Thu, to 1am Fri-Sun; 🛜) Hot out of the oven, Lady Baga brings its seafood specialities, Goan delicacies and chilled-out vibe to Bengaluru. The food is divine (try the mud crab in garlic sauce) and the retro hippie branding ('Baga' is a nod to a beach in Goa). Right on, maaan.

Koshy's Bar & Restaurant INDIAN $$
(39 St Mark's Rd; mains ₹95-400; ⊙ 9am-11.30pm; M MG Rd) This decidedly old-school resto-pub is an institution for the city's chattering classes: here you can put away tasty North Indian dishes in between mugs of beer and fervent discussions. The decor is all creaky ceiling fans, dusty wooden shuttered windows and lashings of nostalgia. Between lunch and dinner it's 'short eats' only (British-style snacks like baked beans on toast).

Enerjuvate Studio & Café INTERNATIONAL $$
(www.facebook.com/enerjuvatestudio; 82 7th Main Rd, 4th B Block, Koramangala; mains ₹190-450; ⊙ 11.30am-10pm Mon-Fri, 8.30am-10pm Sat & Sun; 🛜) How do you appeal to Bengaluru's young

and hip? Healthy food plus a healthy dose of fast wi-fi is the winning formula at Enerjuvate. The bright dining spaces, partly alfresco, are ideal to work in, with a constant supply of juices and light eats such as millet and red-rice dosa (thin lentil-flour pancakes; ₹180) and great platters (₹150 to ₹350).

Tippler – On the Roof   RUSSIAN $$

(276, 100 Feet Rd, HAL 2nd Stage, Indiranagar; mains from ₹165; ☉noon-12.30am; ☎) Thinking of a big night out? Now there's more than just vodka in Bengaluru. Tippler dishes up a full menu of Russian-inspired food and drinks. Order the platter and you can gorge on Siberian fried potatoes and pickled cabbage with a beaker of rocket-fuel-strong vodka to share. On 'Molotov Mondays' there are all kinds of bar and food specials.

Carrots   VEGAN $$

(☑080-41172812; www.carrots-india.com; 607, 80 Feet Rd, 6th Block, Koramangala; dishes & mains ₹150-375; ☉noon-3.30pm & 7-10.30pm Mon, 11am-4pm & 7-10.30pm Wed-Fri, 11.30am-11pm Sat & Sun; ☎) This 100% vegan restaurant offers organic, gluten-free, largely sugar-free dishes cooked with minimal oil. Savour the veg enchiladas (₹220), lentil pancakes (₹150), Thai peanut salad and desserts such as vegan ice cream. The premises are light and spacious, with rattan seating and a relaxed vibe.

Empire   NORTH INDIAN $$

(www.facebook.com/hotelempire; 36 Church St; mains ₹120-250; ☉11am-11pm; Ⓜ MG Rd) Empire is all about authentic, inexpensive tandoori and meat dishes in unpretentious surrounds (plastic banquette seating and fake wood); try the butter chicken, the kebabs or a mutton biryani. It's busy day and night, and its street-side kitchen dishes out tasty *shawarma* (spit-roasted kebabs) to time-pushed peeps on the go. There are numerous other branches around the city.

★ SodaBottleOpenerWala   INDIAN $$$

(☑7022255299; www.sodabottleopenerwala.in; 25/4 Lavelle Rd; snacks from ₹55, meals ₹300-500; ☉8.30am-midnight; ☎) This terrific new place, with its brilliant comfort-food menu of Persian soups and Parsi specials like *salli boti* (mutton served with matchstick potatoes), is a kooky spin on a Bombay Irani cafe. The decor is semi-wacky, with mismatched seating, clashing colours and quirky ornaments. Definitely order a rich, creamy and foamy Phateli coffee or Irani chai to finish your meal.

★ Sly Granny   INTERNATIONAL $$$

(☑080-48536712; www.facebook.com/slygranny; 618 12th Main Rd, Indiranagar; mains from ₹369; ☉noon-11.30pm Mon-Thu, to 1am Fri, 9am-1am Sat, 9am-11.30pm Sun; ☎) Sly Granny is a fresh breath of flavours, serving up European-meets-Asian cuisine. Tables are on two levels, with a formal restaurant zone and a more casual roof terrace. Try the udon noodles, quinoa salad, walnut tart and massaman curry, and stay for the live gigs.

★ Fatty Bao   ASIAN $$$

(☑080-44114499; www.facebook.com/thefattybao; 610 12th Main Rd, Indiranagar; mains ₹380-650; ☉noon-3pm & 7-10.30pm Sun-Thu, to 11.30pm Fri & Sat; ☎; Ⓜ Indiranagar) This hip rooftop restaurant serves up Asian hawker food to a crowd of fashionable young foodies in a vibrant setting with colourful chairs and wooden bench tables. There's sushi, dim sum, Thai curries and Malaysian street food, as well as Asian-inspired cocktails such as lemongrass mojitos. Presentation of both food and drink is superb.

★ Karavalli   SEAFOOD $$$

(☑080-66604545; Gateway Hotel, 66 Residency Rd; mains ₹525-1575; ☉12.30-3pm & 6.30-11.30pm; Ⓜ MG Rd) Superior seafood restaurant with a wonderfully atmospheric interior that takes in a traditional thatched roof, vintage woodwork and beaten brassware – though the garden seating is equally appealing. Choose from fiery Mangalorean fish dishes, prawns cooked with coriander and saffron (₹1100) or crab Milagu in a pepper masala (₹1575). Meat and veg dishes are also available.

★ Olive Bar & Kitchen   MEDITERRANEAN $$$

(☑080-41128400; www.olivebarandkitchen.com; 16 Wood St, Ashoknagar; mains ₹525-795; ☉noon-3.30pm & 7-11pm; ☎) A whitewashed villa straight from the coast of Santorini, Olive Beach has a menu that evokes wistful memories of sunny Mediterranean getaways. Things change seasonally, but expect Thessaloniki salad, prawns *pil pil* (with garlic and hot peppers) and plenty of veg choices. Round things off with a dessert (all ₹390) like hazelnut chocolate cake or *tres leches* (sponge cake soaked in milk and cream).

Church Street Social   GASTROPUB $$$

(http://socialoffline.in; 46/1 Church St; mains ₹195-700; ☉9am-1am; ☎; Ⓜ MG Rd) This warehouse-style bar-resto, drawing a cool urban crowd, serves cocktails in beakers and

KARNATAKA BENGALURU (BANGALORE)

offers napkins toilet-paper style (on a roll). The menu takes in fine breakfasts, meze platters, ghee roast chicken (₹500) and tikka tacos (₹250).

Fava   MEDITERRANEAN $$$

(www.fava.in; UB City, 24 Vittal Mallya Rd; mains ₹325-850; ⊙11am-11pm; 🕿; Ⓜ Cubbon Park) Dine alfresco on Fava's canopy-covered decking, feasting on large plates of delectable dishes like Middle Eastern meze, minced-lamb kebabs or black-sesame deep-sea tiger prawns. There's a good happy hour (5pm to 8pm) when cocktails are discounted, too.

Ciclo Cafe   CAFE $$$

(12th Main Rd, Indiranagar; mains ₹250-550; ⊙11am-midnight Mon-Thu, to 1pm Fri, 7.30am-1am Sat & Sun; 🕿) This cycle shop and cafe offers a great pit stop in the throbbing Indiranagar area. With food, alcohol, vintage cycles to ogle, and cycle parts and accessories to buy, Ciclo's quite a venue for a meal: try the kaffir-lime chicken tikka (₹350) or Goa pork sausage (₹450).

Siam Trading Company   THAI $$$

(🗷7619415931; www.facebook.com/siambangalore; 1079 12th Main Rd, HAL 2nd Stage, Indiranagar; mains ₹258-438; ⊙noon-1am Wed-Sat, to 11pm Sun-Tue) An extension of the popular One Night in Bangkok pub, pub-like Siam Trading Company has deliberately dingy lighting but fresh and excellent Thai food. The chicken with young peppercorns and basil takes you to the streets of the Thai capital with the first bite.

Open Box   INTERNATIONAL $$$

(🗷080-41290055; www.facebook.com/theopen boxblr; 4th fl, Halcyon Complex, St Mark's Rd; mains ₹250-425; ⊙noon-11.30pm Sun-Thu, to 1am Fri & Sat; 🕿) For a place to unwind, good food and unlimited-drinks deals, look no further than Open Box. (The special that includes three hours of unlimited sangria and beer is particularly popular.) A lot of effort has been put into the menu, which is full of puns and cheesy tag lines.

Plan B Loaded   GASTROPUB $$$

(https://holycowhospitality.com; 13 Rhenius St, Richmond Town; mains ₹275-475; ⊙noon-1am; 🕿) Industrial-chic gastropub that's great for Indian-style pub-grub classics like Coorg pork, really meaty burgers and spinach-and-corn bake, as well as all-day breakfasts. Pitchers of beer are ₹345.

Sunny's   ITALIAN $$$

(🗷080-41329366; 50 Lavelle Rd; mains ₹350-750; ⊙12.30-11.30pm; 🕿) A fixture on Bengaluru's restaurant scene, classy Sunny's has a lovely terrace for alfresco dining. On the menu you'll find authentic thin-crust pizza, Greek salad, homemade pasta, imported cheese and some of the best desserts in the city.

🍷 Drinking & Nightlife

Bengaluru's rock-steady reputation and wide choice of chic watering holes make it the place to indulge in a spirited session of pub-hopping in what is the original Indian beer town. Many microbreweries produce quality ales; all serve food, too.

The trendiest nightclubs typically charge a cover of around ₹1000 per couple, often it's redeemable against drinks or food.

★Third Wave Coffee Roasters   CAFE

(https://thirdwavecoffee.in; 984, 80 Feet Rd, Koramangala; ⊙9am-11pm; 🕿) A mecca for hardcore java heads, this temple to the arabica bean has a multitude of gourmet-coffee combos, including espresso classics, quirky cold brews like coffee colada (with coconut water and the sweetener jaggery) and seasonal specials. Coffee culture is a serious business here. The Third Wave scene is young freelancers on Macbooks, polished-concrete floors and acoustic tunes on the stereo.

★Brahmin's Coffee Bar   CAFE, SOUTH INDIAN

(Ranga Rao Rd, Basavanagudi; snacks ₹16-22; ⊙6am-noon & 3-7pm Mon-Sat; Ⓜ National College) This terrific *darshini* (South Indian cafe) is famous for its filter coffee (₹16). There are only four food items on the menu: *idli* (fermented rice cakes), *vada* (deep-fried lentil savouries), *khara bath* (semolina and cashew snack) and *kesari bath* (sweet made with ghee). It makes a good pit stop between the centre of town and the Bull Temple.

Tata Cha   TEAHOUSE

(www.tatacha.com; 2985 12th Main Rd, HAL 2nd Stage, Indiranagar; ⊙10am-11pm; 🕿) Classic and new flavours of tea, along with tasty food combos like butter chicken and *khichdi* (pureed lentils), make Tata Cha a big hit with Bengaluru tea-lovers. Great energy and atmosphere make this place better than more expensive options close by. There are other branches in the city, including one on **Church St.** (www.tatacha.com; 28 Church St; ⊙10am-11pm; 🕿; Ⓜ MG Rd)

COFFEE CULTURE

Tea may be the national drink, and Bengaluru is considered the birthplace of India's craft-brewing revolution, but the city also has the nation's most ingrained coffee culture. Arabica and robusta beans have been cultivated in Karnataka's evergreen hills for centuries and filter coffee consumed in Bengaluru *darshini* (South Indian cafes) for decades. In the best of these traditional places, like Brahmin's Coffee Bar (p868) customers often eat and drink breakfast standing up, munching on *idli* (South Indian spongy, round, fermented rice cakes) and *vada* (South Indian doughnut-shaped, deep-fried lentil savouries) and slugging filter coffee from glass or stainless-steel beakers.

In 1996 the city was the site of India's very first Café Coffee Day (on Brigade Rd), the founding stone of an espresso empire that now numbers more than 1500 branches across the subcontinent and beyond – though its HQ remains in Bengaluru.

In recent years young guns like Third Wave Coffee Roasters (p868) have introduced a fresh (even boffinish) approach to coffee making by offering syphon, chemex and cold-brew coffee to the city. Want the richest, most luxurious coffee in town? Head to SodaBottleOpenerWala (p867) and order a Phateli coffee.

blueFROG   CLUB
(http://bengalurublufrog.club; 3 Church St; ⊘noon-11.30pm Sun-Thu, to 1am Fri & Sat; Ⓜ MG Rd) Upmarket club and live-music venue that draws a hip, lively crowd with its fine roster of house, techno and trance DJs, and bands (everything from jazz to hip hop). Entrance is free to ₹500 depending on the night.

Atta Galatta   CAFE
(☑080-41600677; www.attagalatta.com; 134 KHB Colony, 5th Block, Koramangala; ⊘11am-8.30pm; ☎) This fine cafe and bakery offers good sandwiches on nutritious bread, cookies and snacks (₹40 to ₹80), and doubles as a bookshop and art venue, hosting readings and performances.

Straight Up Pub   PUB
(www.straightuppub.com; 37 Hennur Bagalur Rd, Kuvempu Layout, Kothanur; ⊘11.30am-1am; ☎) This octopus-themed pub (yes, you read that right) offers a fun, freewheeling night out, with Jocose Juleps (a cocktail of Bourbon and crème de menthe) on the menu and plenty of octopus-related quotes and trivia. Tree trunks for stools and suspended tables add to the vibe. The pub hosts a Ladies Night on Wednesday, live bands on Saturday and DJs.

Barebones   BAR
(www.barebonesbar.com; 303 Ashok Terrace, 100 Feet Rd, Indiranagar; ⊘11.30-1am; ☎; Ⓜ Indiranagar) Sometimes value for money trumps swanky ambience. Barebones lies in the belly of the nightlife area of Bengaluru and the cafe-like interior is a great place to drink and dine. There's plenty on the menu for veg and non-veg folks, but regulars swear by the ghee roast, a much-loved Bengaluru classic.

Bartin's Restobar   BAR
(1211 Milestone, 100 Feet Rd, Indiranagar; ⊘11-1am) Nothing beats the combination of spicy Andhra chilli chicken, cold beer and Bengaluru's evening breezes at this rooftop bar in the buzzy Indiranagar district. Weekends are all about notching up the volume and getting people on their feet.

What's in a Name?   BAR
(☎9591941003; www.facebook.com/whatsinanameblr; 146 5th Block, Koramangala; ⊘11am-1am; ☎) Located above 1st Cross Rd, and adding to the clutch of bars that are tilting the balance of nightlife towards Koramangala, this is a great place to relax. The cocktails don't burn a hole in the pocket and there's good food, from pub-grub combos to specials such as the 'All Day and Night Breakfast'.

Dyu Art Cafe   CAFE
(www.dyuartcafe.yolasite.com; 23 MIG, KHB Colony, Koramangala; ⊘10am-10.30pm Tue-Sun, noon-10.30pm Mon; ☎) Popular cafe-gallery in a leafy neighbourhood with a peaceful courtyard reminiscent of a Zen temple. It has coffee beans from Kerala and does good French press, espresso and iced coffee, along with breakfasts (₹120 to ₹320), homemade cakes, sandwiches and mains.

Pecos Classic   BAR
(www.pecospub.com; Rest House Rd; ⊘10.30am-11.30pm; Ⓜ MG Rd) A kind of non-corporate, locally owned Hard Rock Cafe that's all about classic rock – Hendrix, Grateful Dead and Frank Zappa posters adorn the walls – though it also mixes in some jazz, blues and reggae from time to time. Beer costs from ₹105 a glass, or ₹525 a pitcher.

KARNATAKA BENGALURU (BANGALORE)

Shiro
BAR

(www.facebook.com/experienceshiro; UB City, 24 Vittal Mallya Rd; ⊙12.30pm-midnight Sun-Thu, to 1am Fri & Sat; 🕾) Shiro is a hip lounge bar with elegant interiors complemented by monumental Buddha busts and *apsara* (celestial nymph) figurines. There's also outdoor deck seating. Has good Japanese and Southeast Asian food, and its 'Special Shiro' cocktails are the bomb.

Microbreweries

★ Biere Club
PUB

(www.facebook.com/thebiereclub; 20/2 Vittal Mallya Rd; ⊙11am-11pm Sun-Thu, to midnight Fri & Sat; 🕾) There's a continual buzz about this multistorey temple to craft beer, which always has a guest beer or two on the blackboard. You'll find plenty on the menu (platters, burgers) to nibble while you sup.

Prost
MICROBREWERY

(www.prost.in; 811 5th Cross Rd, Koramangala; ⊙noon-11.30pm Sun-Thu, to 1am Fri & Sat; 🕾) Prost has eclectic industrial decor, a rooftop with several quality craft beers on tap and a tempting food menu. There's live magic on Wednesday, comedy on Thursday, and weekend evenings go off with house DJs and dancing.

Brewsky
MICROBREWERY

(4th & 5th fl, Goenka Chambers, 19th Main Rd, JP Nagar; ⊙noon-12.30am; 🕾) With sweeping city views from its fine roof terrace, a mezzanine zone and a funky restaurant with vintage decor, Brewsky is a fine night out. It brews six beers on site, including a golden ale, a wheat beer and a stout. Tasty 'small bites' and substantial sharing platters are good value.

Barleyz
MICROBREWERY

(www.barleyz.com; 80 Feet Rd, Koramangala; ⊙11am-11.30pm Sun-Thu, to 1am Fri & Sat; 🕾) A suave rooftop beer garden with potted plants, artificial grass and tables with built-in BBQ grills. Offers free tastings of its six beers, as well as rotating seasonal brews. There's also excellent wood-fired pizza, Indian snacks and Western food. Happy hour is 5pm to 7pm daily.

Vapour
BAR

(www.vapour.in; 773, 100 Feet Rd, Indiranagar; ⊙noon-1am; 🕾) Multilevel complex divided into several bars and restaurants, though the highlight is the rooftop with big screen, where you can sample its six microbrews, including a rice beer and a guest ale. Weekend nights are very lively, with DJs and dancing.

Toit Brewpub
MICROBREWERY

(www.toit.in; 298, 100 Feet Rd, Indiranagar; ⊙noon-11.30pm Mon & Tue, to 12.30am Wed, Thu & Sun, to 1am Fri & Sat; 🕾; Ⓜ Indiranagar) A brick-walled gastropub split over three levels where you can sample quality beers brewed on site, including two seasonals and a wheat beer on tap. Try a glass of Bittersweet Symphony, a delicious, citrusy IPA.

Arbor Brewing Company
MICROBREWERY

(www.arborbrewing.in; 8 Magrath Rd; ⊙noon-12.30am; 🕾; Ⓜ Trinity) This classic brewpub was one of the first microbreweries to get the craft-beer barrel rolling in Bengaluru. Choose from stout, porter, IPA, Belgian beers, spiced, sour and fruit beers. It also serves pub grub (pizza, tacos), artisan coffee and gourmet teas.

☆ Entertainment

Humming Tree
LIVE MUSIC

(🗹9945532828; www.facebook.com/thehumming tree; 12th Main Rd, Indiranagar; ⊙11am-11.30pm Sun-Thu, to 1am Fri & Sat; 🕾; Ⓜ Indiranagar) This popular warehouse-style venue has bands (starting around 9pm), DJs and a rooftop terrace. The cover charge is anything from zero to ₹300. There's a good finger-food menu and happy hour until 7pm.

M Chinnaswamy Stadium
CRICKET

(www.ksca.cricket; MG Rd; Ⓜ Cubbon Park) A mecca for cricket-lovers, hosting many matches per year. Check online for the schedule of tests, one-dayers and Twenty20s.

Indigo XP
LIVE MUSIC

(🗹080-25535330; www.facebook.com/indigo xpblr; 5/6th fl, Elite Bldg, Jyoti Nivas College Rd, Koramangala; ⊙4pm-1am; 🕾) Always buzzing, this huge venue hosts bands, DJs, acoustic musicians and stand-up comedy. On the upper floor there's a large terrace for dining and lounging. Also a good place to catch the cricket or footy.

B Flat
LIVE MUSIC

(🗹9591126639; www.facebook.com/bflatindira nagar; 776, 100 Feet Rd, Indiranagar; entry ₹300-500; ⊙noon-midnight; 🕾; Ⓜ Indiranagar) Popular pub and performance venue that features some of India's best blues and jazz acts, alternative and indie bands, comedy, and even experimental theatre.

Ranga Shankara
THEATRE

(🗹080-26592777; www.rangashankara.org; 36/2 8th Cross, JP Nagar) All kinds of interesting theatre (in a variety of languages and spanning various genres) and dance are staged at this cultural centre. Hosts an annual mini-festival in late October/early November.

Bangalore Turf Club HORSE RACING
(☎ 080-22262391; www.bangaloreraces.com; Racecourse Rd) Horse racing is big in Bengaluru. Races are generally held on Friday and Saturday afternoons.

🛍 Shopping

Bengaluru's shopping options are abundant, ranging from teeming bazaars to glitzy malls. Some good shopping areas include Commercial St, Vittal Mallya Rd and the MG Rd area.

★**Goobe's Book Republic** BOOKS
(www.goobes.wordpress.com; 11 Church St; ⊙10.30am-9pm Mon-Sat, noon-9pm Sun; Ⓜ MG Rd) Great little bookshop selling new and secondhand, cult and mainstream books and comics. Good for titles on southern India and run by informed, helpful staff.

★**Mysore Saree Udyog** CLOTHING
(www.mysoresareeudyog.com; 1st fl, 316 Kamaraj Rd; ⊙10.30am-8.30pm) A great choice for top-quality silk saris, blouses, fabrics and men's shirts, this fine store has been in business for over 70 years and has something to suit all budgets. Most garments are made with Mysuru silk. Also stocks 100% *pashmina* (fine cashmere) shawls.

San-Cha Tea Boutique TEA
(☎ 080-22272028; www.sanchatea.com; 54 Lavelle Rd; ⊙11.30am-8.30pm) Tea-lovers, rejoice: this wonderful store has more than 70 varieties of tea, from grand crus to humble teabags, many personally curated by master tea taster Sanjay Kapur. Prices start at ₹240.

Forest Essentials COSMETICS
(www.forestessentialsindia.com; 4/1 Lavelle Junction Bldg, Vittal Mallya Rd; ⊙10am-9pm) High-end natural beauty products, including potions and lotions for hair, face and body as well as all-organic ayurvedic essential oils.

Gangarams Book Bureau BOOKS
(www.facebook.com/gangaramsbookbureau; 3rd fl, 48 Church St; ⊙10am-8pm Mon-Sat; Ⓜ MG Rd) Excellent selection of Indian titles, guidebooks and Penguin classics. Has a knowledgeable staff and author-signing sessions.

Fabindia CLOTHING, HOMEWARES
(www.fabindia.com; Garuda Mall, Magrath Rd; ⊙10am-8pm) Hugely successful chain with a range of stylish traditional clothing, homewares and accessories in traditional cotton prints and silks. Quality skincare products, too. Branches on **Commercial St** (152 Commercial St; ⊙10am-8.30pm), in **Koramangala** (54 17th Main Rd; ⊙10am-8pm) and at the **Lido Mall** (1 MG Rd-Lido Mall, Kensington Rd; ⊙10.30am-9pm; Ⓜ Trinity).

Cauvery Arts & Crafts Emporium GIFTS & SOUVENIRS
(45 MG Rd; ⊙10am-8pm; Ⓜ MG Rd) Government-run store famous for its expansive collection of quality sandalwood and rosewood products as well as handmade weavings, silks and *bidriware* (metallic handicrafts). Fixed prices.

Blossom Book House BOOKS
(84/6 Church St; ⊙10.30am-9.30pm; Ⓜ MG Rd) Great deals on new and secondhand books.

Garuda Mall MALL
(www.garudamall.in; Magrath Rd; ⊙10am-10pm Sun-Thu, to 10.30pm Fri & Sat; Ⓜ Trinity) Modern mall in central Bengaluru with a wide selection of clothing chains and an Inox multiplex cinema.

ℹ Information

Explocity (https://bangalore.explocity.com) has the latest on restaurant openings, cultural events, nightlife and shopping in the city.

MEDICAL SERVICES

Hosmat (☎ 080-25593796; https://hosmat hospitals.com; 45 Magrath Rd; ⊙24hr) Hospital for critical injuries and general illnesses.

Mallya Hospital (☎ 080-22277979; www.mallyahospital.net; 2 Vittal Mallya Rd) Emergency services and 24-hour pharmacy.

POST

Main Post Office (Cubbon Rd; ⊙10am-7pm Mon-Sat, to 1pm Sun; Ⓜ Cubbon Park) On the north side of Cubbon Park.

TOURIST INFORMATION

These well-informed offices offer useful tourist information:

Government of India Tourist Office (GITO; ☎ 080-25583030; indiatourismbengaluru@gmail.com; 2nd fl, Triumph Towers, 48 Church St; ⊙9.30am-5.30pm Mon-Fri, to noon Sat; Ⓜ MG Rd)

Karnataka State Tourism Development Corporation (KSTDC; ☎ 080-41329211; www.kstdc.co; Karnataka Tourism House, 8 Papanna Lane, St Mark's Rd; ⊙10am-7pm Mon-Sat; Ⓜ MG Rd)

Karnataka State Tourism Development Corporation (KSTDC; ☎ 080-43344334; https://

KARNATAKA BENGALURU (BANGALORE)

kstdc.co; Badami House, Kasturba Rd; ⊘10am-7pm Mon-Sat)

TRAVEL AGENCIES

Skyway (☑080-22111401; www.skywaytour. com; 8 Papanna Lane, St Mark's Rd; ⊘9am-6pm Mon-Sat) is a professional and reliable outfit for booking long-distance taxis, air tickets and tours.

ⓘ Getting There & Away

AIR

International and domestic flights arrive at and depart from Bengaluru's **Kempegowda International Airport** (☑1800 4254425; www. bengaluruairport.com), about 35km north of the MG Rd area. There are connections to more than 25 Indian cities. Sample fares include ₹3350 to Mumbai, ₹4000 to Delhi and ₹4800 to Kolkata. Carriers include the following:

Air India (☑080-22978427; www.airindia.com; Unity Bldg, JC Rd; ⊘10am-5pm Mon-Sat)

GoAir (☑080-47406091; www.goair.in; Bengaluru airport)

IndiGo (☑9910383838; www.goindigo.in)

Jet Airways (☑080-39893333; www.jetair ways.com; Unity Bldg, JC Rd; ⊘9.30am-6pm Mon-Sat)

BUS

Bengaluru's huge, well-organised **Kempegowda bus stand** (Majestic; Gubbi Thotadappa Rd; Ⓜ Kempegowda), also commonly known as both Majestic and Central, is directly in front of the City train station. Karnataka State Road Transport Corporation (KSRTC; www.ksrtc.in) buses run to destinations in Karnataka and neighbouring states. **Mysuru Road Satellite Bus Stand** (Mysuru Rd), 8km southwest of the centre, is another important terminal: most KSRTC buses

to Mysuru, Mangaluru and other destinations southwest of Bengaluru leave from here, as does the Flybus to Bengaluru airport.

The KSRTC website lists current schedules and fares. Booking online isn't always possible using international credit cards, but travel agents can assist here. It's wise to book long-distance journeys in advance.

Private bus operators line the street facing Kempegowda bus stand.

TRAIN

Bengaluru's **City train station** (Gubbi Thotadappa Rd; Ⓜ Kempegowda) is the main train hub. There's also **Cantonment train station** (Station Rd), a sensible spot to disembark if you're arriving and headed for the MG Rd area. **Yeshvantpur train station** (Rahman Khan Rd), 8km northwest of downtown, is the starting point for trains to Goa.

The computerised **reservation office** (☑139; City Train Station; ⊘8am-8pm Mon-Sat, to 2pm Sun; Ⓜ Kempegowda) has separate counters for credit-card purchases, for women and for foreigners. Head to the **Divisional Railway Office** (Gubbi Thotadappa Rd) for last-minute reservations. Luggage can be left at the 24-hour cloakroom on Platform 1 at the City train station.

ⓘ Getting Around

TO/FROM THE AIRPORT

Metered AC taxis from the airport to the centre cost between ₹750 and ₹1000, while Uber/Ola cab rates are usually around ₹550 to ₹650; these rates include the ₹120 airport toll. Airconditioned **Vayu Vajra** (☑1800 4251663; www. mybmtc.com) buses run regularly from the airport to destinations around the city and cost ₹170 to ₹260. Flybus (www.ksrtc.in) offers very regular service from the airport to Mysuru and other destinations including Tirupati.

MAJOR BUS SERVICES FROM BENGALURU

DESTINATION	FARE (₹)	DURATION (HR)	DEPARTURES
Chennai	549-955	6½-8	47 daily; 5.30am-11.45pm
Ernakulam	703-1265	10-11	7 daily; 4.10-10pm
Hampi	650-779	7½	11pm, 11.30pm
Hosapete (Hospet)	338-751	6-9	17 daily; 8.45am-11.45pm
Hyderabad	686-1210	8-11	28 daily; 7.15am-11.45pm
Mangaluru (Mangalore)	366-908	6½-9	32 daily; 6.05am-11.50pm
Mumbai	1575	18	3.05pm, 5.05pm, 8pm
Mysuru* (Mysore)	129-326	2½-4	33 daily; 1.30am-10.30pm
Ooty (Udhagamandalam)*	600-840	7-9½	8 daily; 6.15am-11.15pm
Panaji (Panjim)	619-1050	11-13½	3 daily; 7-8.30pm
Gokarna	518-843	9-12	3 daily; 8.30-10.15pm

*Also services from Mysuru Road Satellite Bus Stand

MAJOR TRAINS FROM BENGALURU

DESTINATION	TRAIN NO & NAME	FARE (₹)	DURATION (HR)	DEPARTURES
Chennai	12658 Chennai Mail	260/930	6	10.40pm
Chennai	12028 Shatabdi	790/1050	5	6am & 4.25pm Wed-Mon
Hosapete (Hospet)	16592 Hampi Exp	240/935	9	10.05pm
Hubballi (Hubli)	16589 Rani Chennamma Exp	270/1050	8½	9.15pm
Margao (Madgaon; Goa)	17311 Mas Vasco Exp	360/1420	16	8.10pm Fri
Mysuru (Mysore)	12007 Shatabdi	295/835	2	11am Thu-Tue
Mysuru (Mysore)	12614 Tippu Exp	90/315	2½	3.15pm
Thiruvananthapuram (Trivandrum)	16526 Kanyakumari Exp	410/1620	16½	8pm

Shatabdi fares are AC chair/AC executive chair; express (Exp/Mail) fares are 2nd class/AC chair for day trains and sleeper/2AC for night trains.

AUTORICKSHAW
Very few autorickshaw drivers use meters, but if yours does 50% is added to the metered rate after 10pm.

BUS
Bengaluru has a comprehensive local bus network, operated by the Bangalore Metropolitan Transport Corporation (BMTC; www.mybmtc.com), with a useful website for timetables and fares. However, very few travellers use them these days, preferring the speed of the metro and the convenience of Uber/Ola.

Nevertheless, red AC Vajra buses criss-cross the city, while green Big10 deluxe buses connect the suburbs. Ordinary buses run from the **City bus stand** (Sayyali Rao Rd), next to Kempegowda bus stand; a few operate from the **City Market bus stand** (M Chickpet) further south.

METRO
Bengaluru's shiny new AC metro service, known as **Namma Metro** (toll-free 1800-42512345; http://english.bmrc.co.in), now has two lines operating, connecting at Kempegowda/Majestic (for the bus terminal). It's by far the cheapest and quickest way to get between, say, the central MG Rd area and the nightlife hub of Indiranagar, using the Purple Line. Trains run about every 15 minutes from 6am to 10pm, and fares are ₹10 to ₹22 for most journeys. Travel cards (₹50) and single-journey tokens are available. See the website for the latest updates.

TAXI
There are thousands of Uber and Ola drivers in Bengaluru. To hire a conventional cab for a day, reckon on around ₹2000 for eight hours.

Olacabs (080-33553355; www.olacabs.com) Professional, efficient company with modern air-con cars. Online and phone bookings.

Meru Cabs (080-44224422; www.meru.in) Another good operator.

SOUTHERN KARNATAKA

Hesaraghatta
080 / POP 9250

Located 30km northwest of Bengaluru (Bangalore), the small town of Hesaraghatta is home to **Nrityagram** (080-28466313; www.nrityagram.org; self-guided tour ₹100, children under 12yr free; 10am-2pm Tue-Sun), a leading dance academy established in 1990 to revive and popularise Indian classical dance. The brainchild and living legacy of celebrated dancer Protima Gauri Bedi (1948–98), the complex was designed like a village by Goa-based architect Gerard da Cunha. Long-term courses in classical dance are offered to deserving students, while local children are taught for free on Sunday. Check the website for upcoming performances (₹1000 per person).

From Bengaluru's City Market, buses 266, 253 and 253E run to Hesaraghatta (₹30, one hour), with bus 266 continuing to Nrityagram (p873). From Hesaraghatta an autorickshaw will cost around ₹80 to Nrityagram.

Mysuru (Mysore)
0821 / POP 1,036,000 / ELEV 707M

The historic settlement of Mysuru (which changed its name from Mysore in 2014) is one of South India's most enchanting cities, famed for its glittering royal heritage and magnificent monuments and buildings. Its

WINE & WHISKY IN NANDI HILLS

In a country not known for fine wines and liquors, Bengaluru is very much an exception to the rule. It has not only developed a thirst for craft beer but has on its doorstep one of India's premier wine-growing regions in the **Nandi Hills** (per person/car ₹10/150; ⊙6am-6pm). While wine making is an emerging industry, it's fast gaining a reputation internationally, with many wineries in the area. A few clicks out of town is India's first single-malt whisky distillery.

Grover Wineries (☑080-27622826; www.groverzampa.in; 1½hr tour Mon-Fri ₹850, Sat & Sun ₹1000) At an altitude of 920m, this winery produces quality white and red varietals. Tours include tastings of five wines in the cellar rooms accompanied by cheese and crackers, followed by lunch. From February to May you'll also see grape crushing and can visit the vineyards. It's located on the approach to the Nandi Hills, around 40km north of Bengaluru.

Amrut (☑080-23100402; www.amrutdistilleries.com; Mysuru Rd; tours ₹750) Established in 1948, Amrut, India's first producer of single-malt whisky, offers free distillery tours run by knowledgeable guides. You'll be taken through the entire process before tasting the world-class single malts and blends. It's 20km outside Bengaluru on the road to Mysuru (Mysore); prebookings essential.

Buses head to the Nandi Hills (₹70, two hours) from Bengaluru's Kempegowda (Majestic/Central) bus stand.

World Heritage–listed palace brings most travellers here, but Mysuru is also rich in tradition, with a deeply atmospheric bazaar district replete with spice stores and incense stalls. Ashtanga yoga (p880) is another drawcard and there are several acclaimed schools that attract visitors from across the globe.

History

Mysuru owes its name to the mythical Mahisuru, a place where the demon Mahishasura was slain by the goddess Chamundi. Its regal history began in 1399, when the Wodeyar dynasty of Mysuru was founded, though it remained in service of the Vijayanagar empire until the mid-16th century. With the fall of Vijayanagar in 1565, the Wodeyars declared their sovereignty, which – save for a brief period of Hyder Ali and Tipu Sultan's supremacy in the late 18th century – remained unscathed until Independence in 1947. A new maharaja, Yaduveera Krishnadatta Chamaraja Wadiyar, was crowned in 2015, at the age of 23. He presided over his first Dussehra festival in September of that year.

⊙ Sights

Mysuru isn't known as the City of Palaces for nothing: it's home to a total of seven, as well as an abundance of majestic heritage architecture (p875) dating from the Wodeyar dynasty and British rule. The majority of grand buildings are owned by the state and used as anything from hospitals, colleges and government buildings to heritage hotels. Visit www.karnatakatourism.org/mysore/en for a list of notable buildings.

★**Mysuru Palace** PALACE
(Maharaja's Palace; http://mysorepalace.gov.in; Purandara Dasa Rd; adult/child ₹50/free; ⊙10am-5.30pm) The second-most-visited sight in India (after the Taj Mahal), this palace is among the very grandest of India's royal buildings and was the seat of the Wodeyar maharajas. The original palace was gutted by fire in 1897; today's structure was completed in 1912. The lavish Indo-Saracenic interior – a kaleidoscope of stained glass, mirrors and gaudy colours – is undoubtedly over the top. It's further embellished by carved wooden doors, mosaic floors and a series of paintings depicting life here during the Raj.

English architect Henry Irwin designed the palace and construction cost ₹4.5 million. On the way in you'll pass a fine collection of sculptures and artefacts. Don't forget to check out the armoury, with an intriguing collection of 700-plus weapons. From 7pm to 8pm every Sunday and national holiday, the palace is illuminated by nearly 100,000 light bulbs that accentuate its majestic profile against the night. Entrance to the grounds is at the South Gate ticket office. While you're allowed to snap the palace's exterior, photography within is strictly prohibited. Note that many visitors have been unable to download the palace-information app (promoted at the ticket office).

Devaraja Market
MARKET

(Sayyaji Rao Rd; ⏰6am-8.30pm) Dating from Tipu Sultan's reign, this huge and very lively bazaar has local traders selling traditional items such as flower garlands, incense, spices and conical piles of *kumkum* (coloured powder used for bindi dots), all of which makes for some great photo ops. There's a large fruit and veg section on the western side, too. Gully Tours (p879) offers good guided walks here.

Jaganmohan Palace
PALACE

(Jaganmohan Palace Rd) Built in 1861 as the royal auditorium, this stunning palace just west of Mysuru Palace houses the Jayachamarajendra Art Gallery. Set over three floors, it has a huge collection of Indian paintings, including works by noted artist Raja Ravi Varma, traditional Japanese art and some rare musical instruments. At the time of research it was closed for long-overdue renovations.

Chamundi Hill
VIEWPOINT

This 1062m hill is crowned with the Sri Chamundeswari Temple (⏰7am-2pm, 3.30-6pm & 7.30-9pm). It's a fine half-day excursion, offering spectacular views of the city below. Queues are long at weekends, so visit during the week. From Central bus stand take bus 201 (₹28; AC); a return autorickshaw/Uber trip is around ₹450/700.

Rail Museum
MUSEUM

(KRS Rd; Indian adult/child ₹20/10, foreigner adult/child ₹80/40, camera/video ₹20/30; ⏰9.30am-6pm Thu-Tue) This open-air museum's main exhibit is the Mysuru maharani's saloon, an 1899 wood-panelled beauty with gilded ceilings and chandeliers that provides an insight into the stylish way the royals once rode the rails. There are also steam engines, locomotives and carriages to investigate, many of which were manufactured in the UK. A toy train rides the track around the museum 16 times daily.

Indira Gandhi Rashtriya Manav Sangrahalaya
MUSEUM

(National Museum of Mankind; http://igrms.gov.in; Wellington Lodge, Irwin Rd; ⏰9.30am-5.30pm Tue-Sun) FREE This unassuming colonial building, known as Wellington Lodge, was the residence of Colonel Arthur Wellesley from 1799 to 1801. He later become the duke of Wellington, and defeated Napoleon at Waterloo. Today the building houses ageing exhibits, including textiles and handicrafts and some impressive terracotta sculptures from Rajasthan.

🏃 Activities & Courses

Turiya Wellness
SPA

(📞0821-2971123; http://turiya-wellness.com; 354/B 4th Main Rd, Gokulam; 45min massage from ₹1500; ⏰6am-8pm) A fine ayurvedic spa offering treatments and therapies. Ayurvedic cooking classes and massage courses are also recommended, and there's daily hatha and Ashtanga yoga.

Emerge Spa
SPA

(📞0821-2522500; www.thewindflower.com; Windflower Spa & Resort, Maharanapratap Rd, Nazarbad; massages from ₹2350; ⏰7am-9pm) Wonderful resort spa offering dozens of ayurvedic treatments, including hot-stone massages and pampering rituals. Day packages include access to the hotel's natural pool. Located 3km southeast of Mysuru Palace.

KARNATAKA MYSURU (MYSORE)

COLONIAL-ERA ARCHITECTURE

Mysuru's colonial heritage is considerable, with numerous grand edifices and quirky reminders of the past to investigate. Dating from 1805, Government House (Irwin Rd), formerly the British Residency, is a Tuscan Doric building set in 20 hectares of gardens. Facing the north gate of Mysuru Palace is the 1927 Silver Jubilee Clock Tower (Dodda Gadiara; Ashoka Rd). The beauty of towering St Philomena's Cathedral (St Philomena St; ⏰8am-5pm), built between 1933 and 1941 in neo-Gothic style, is emphasised by its elegant stained-glass windows. Wellington Lodge is an early colonial-era landmark that once housed Colonel Arthur Wellesley (later known as the duke of Wellington); today it's a museum: Indira Gandhi Rashtriya Manav Sangrahalaya (p875). Other notable colonial-era structures include the neoclassical Lalitha Mahal Palace (📞0821-2526100; www.lalithamahalpalace.co.in; r incl breakfast ₹3170-6420, ste from ₹13,680; ❄@🛜☰), designed by British architect EW Fritchley, its white dome perhaps a nod to London's St Paul's Cathedral; it's now a heritage hotel.

Mysuru Palace

A HALF-DAY TOUR

The interior of Mysuru Palace houses opulent halls, royal paintings, intricate decorative details, as well as sculptures and ceremonial objects.

There is a lot of hidden detail and much to take in, so be sure to allow yourself at least a few hours for the experience. A guide can also be invaluable.

After entering the palace the first exhibit is the ❶ **Dolls' Pavilion**, which showcases the maharaja's fine collection of traditional dolls and sculptures acquired from around the world Opposite the ❷ **Elephant Gate** you'll see the seven cannons that were used for special occasions, such as the birthdays of the maharajas. Today the cannons are still fired as part of Dussehra festivities.

At the end of the Dolls' Pavilion you'll find the ❸ **Golden Howdah**. Note the fly whisks on

Private Durbar Hall
Rosewood doors lead into this hall, which is richly decorated with stained-glass ceilings, steel grill work and chandeliers. It houses the Golden Throne, only on display to the public during Dussehra.

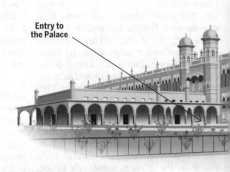

Entry to the Palace

Public Durbar Hall
The open-air hall contains a priceless collection of painting by Raja Ravi Varma and opens onto an expansive balcony supported by massiv pillars with an ornate painted ceiling of 10 incarnations of Vishn

either side; the bristles are made from fine ivory.

Make sure you check out the paintings depicting the Dussehra procession in the halls on your way to the **4 Marriage Pavilion** and look into the courtyard to see what was once the wrestling arena. It's now used during Dussehra only. In the Marriage Pavilion, take a few minutes to scan the entire space. You can see the influence of three religions in the design of the hall: the glass ceiling represents Christianity, stone carvings along the hallway ceilings are Hindu design and the top-floor balcony roof (the traditional women's gallery) has Islamic-style arches.

When you move through to the **5 Private Durbar Hall**, take note of the intricate ivory-inlay motifs depicting Krishna in the rosewood doors. The **6 Public Durbar Hall** is usually the last stop, where you can admire the panoramic views of the gardens through the Islamic arches.

Dolls' Pavilion
The first exhibit, the Dolls' Pavilion, displays the gift collection of 19th- and early-20th-century dolls, statues and Hindu idols that were given to the maharaja by dignitaries from around the world.

Elephant Gate
Next to the Dolls' Pavilion, this brass gate has four bronze elephants inlaid at the bottom, an intricate double-headed eagle up the top and a hybrid lion-elephant creature (the state emblem of Karnataka) in the centre.

Marriage Pavilion
This lavish hall used for royal weddings features themes of Christianity, Hinduism and Islam in its design. The highlights are the octagonal painted-glass ceiling featuring peacock motifs, the bronze chandelier and the colonnaded turquoise pillars.

Golden Howdah
At the far end of the Dolls' Pavilion, a wooden elephant howdah decorated with 80kg of gold was used to carry the maharaja in the Dussehra festival. It now carries an idol of goddess Chamundeshwari.

SINGH_LENS/SHUTTERSTOCK ©

Mysuru (Mysore)

Mysuru (Mysore)

Indus Valley Ayurvedic Centre   AYURVEDA
(☏ 0821-2473263; www.ayurindus.com; Lalithadri-

pura) Set in 10 hectares of gardens and 6km from the city centre, this classy retreat de-

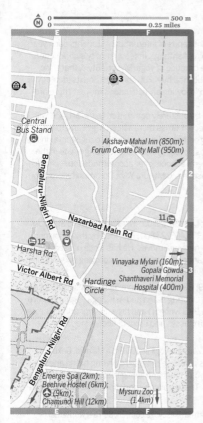

KSTDC Transport Office BUS
(☏ 0821-2423652; www.kstdc.co; city tour ₹400) KSTDC runs a daily Mysuru tour, taking in city sights (excluding the palace), Chamundi Hill, Srirangapatna and Brindavan Gardens. It starts at 8.30am, ends at 8.30pm and is likely to leave you breathless! Other tours go to Belur, Halebid and Sravanabelagola and the Kodagu region (₹890).

★ Festivals & Events

Dussehra CULTURAL
(Dasara; ⊙ Sep/Oct) Mysuru is at its carnivalesque best during the 10-day Dussehra (locally spelt 'Dasara') festival. During this time Mysuru Palace (p874) is dramatically lit up every evening, while the town is transformed into a gigantic fairground, with concerts, dance performances, sporting demonstrations and cultural events running to packed houses. An Open Street Festival is also held, featuring festive food stalls and live music.

🛏 Sleeping

Mysuru has a decent selection of hotels and guesthouses. The city attracts tourists throughout the year and can fill up very quickly during Dussehra (when booking early is highly recommended).

★ Beehive Hostel HOSTEL $
(☏ 9916967853; https://beehivemysore.business. site; 12th Main Rd, JP Nagar; dm/r ₹600/1300; ※🛜) A near-serene location in huge lawned grounds makes this great new hostel a very tranquil base for travellers weary of urban India. The grand yellow villa has excellent facilities, with four private rooms, three dorms, a small library, a guests' kitchen and ample space to socialise. Located 6km south of the city centre.

★ Mansion 1907 HOSTEL $
(☏ 9886523472; www.facebook.com/themansion 1907; 36 Shalivahana Rd; dm with fan/AC ₹500/600, r with fan/AC ₹1400/1800; ※🛜) Excellent hostel in a historic house that shows Indian and British architectural influences. It's very well set up, with spacious dorms and private rooms, cool communal areas decorated with murals and LP covers, a kitchen and speedy wi-fi. There's (free) rooftop yoga for guests, too.

Sonder HOSTEL $
(☏ 8971793193; www.sonderhostel.com; 6, Vivekananda Rd; dm incl breakfast ₹500; ※🛜) Fine backpackers' hostel in a tranquil, leafy

rives its therapies from ancient scriptures and prescriptions. Aromatherapy, *basti* detox treatments and all manner of ayurvedic treats are offered. The overnight package including full board, ayurveda treatment, yoga session and beauty therapy starts at US$212.

Shruthi Musical Works MUSIC
(☏ 9845249518; 1189 3rd Cross, Irwin Rd; per hour ₹450; ⊙ 10.30am-9pm Mon-Sat, to 2pm Sun) Music teacher Jayashankar gets good reviews for his tabla (drum) instruction.

🌀 Tours

★ Gully Tours WALKING
(☏ 9632044188; https://gully.tours; walks from ₹1100) Formerly Royal Mysore Walks, these excellent guided tours are the perfect way to familiarise yourself with Mysuru's epic history and heritage. Offers a range of walks (themes include royal history and food) as well as cycle and jeep tours.

YOGA IN MYSURU

This world-famous centre for yoga attracts thousands of international students each year to learn, practise or become certified in teaching Ashtanga. Indeed, the city's connection with yoga is so profound that it is linked with a practice of yoga, Mysore Style, that's recognised around the world. This style was established by K Pattabhi Jois, and its ideology is more about developing Ashtanga asanas than following an instructor's moves. There are more than 20 established yoga schools in the city.

For the most part, students are required to be austerely committed to the art, and will need to stay at least a month. While in more recent times there's been a growing trend for drop-in classes or week-long courses, long-term students will need to register far in advance, as courses are often booked out. Most foreign yoga students congregate in the upmarket residential suburb of Gokulam. Several schools offer accommodation – check Facebook groups Ashtanga Community in Mysore and Mysore Yoga Community for accommodation rentals.

Yoga Centres

Ashtanga Yoga Research Institute (AYRI; ☑ 9880185500; www.kpjayi.org; 235 8th Cross Rd, 3rd Stage, Gokulam; 1st/2nd month excl taxes ₹35,400/23,800) Founded by the renowned teacher K Pattabhi Jois, who taught Madonna her yoga moves. He has since passed away and the reins have been handed over to his grandson Sharath, who is proving very popular. You need to register at least two months in advance.

IndeaYoga (Ananda Yoga India; ☑ 0821-2416779; www.indeayoga.com; 144E 7th Main Rd, Gokulam; 1 month classes incl food & lodging ₹25,000) Offering hatha and Ashtanga yoga with guru Bharath Shetty (who practised under the late BKS Iyengar) and his wife, Archana. Courses include anatomy and yoga philosophy. Drop-in classes and student accommodation are also offered.

Nirvana Yoga Shala (☑ 0821-4288490; http://mysoreyoga.in; 100 3rd A Main Rd, Gokulam; drop-in/1-month yoga classes ₹500/7500) Offers a diverse program covering hatha and Asthanga, meditation and lectures. Suspension-yoga teacher training is also available. Suitable for short- and long-term students at all levels. There's accommodation (studios with kitchenettes), a sauna, a plunge pool and a cafe.

Atmavikasa Centre (☑ 0821-2341978; www.atmavikasayoga.com; 18, 80 Feet Rd, Ramakrishnanagar; 1 month intensive course ₹42,500) Classical hatha yoga school set up by Acharya Venkatesh and Acharye Hema offering training, therapy and workshops. Enjoys a garden setting in a peaceful suburb 5km southwest of the palace.

Ramesh Shetty's Yoga Shala (☑ 7795977565; http://mysoreashtanga.net; 451/4 Vanivilas Double Rd, Chamarajapura) The Ashtanga vinyasa and hatha yoga teacher training here gets good feedback; courses are linked to Yoga Alliance for accreditation.

Yogadarshanam (☑ 9901760846; http://yogadarshanam.org; 77/A 4th Main Rd, 3rd Stage, Gokulam; courses ₹6200-30,500) Classical Indian yoga centre offering classes, teacher training, workshops and retreats. The one-month foundation course covers yoga fundamentals and is perfect for beginners. Meditation classes are also offered.

Yoga Bharata (☑ 0821-4242342; www.yogabharata.com; 1st fl, 810 Contour Rd, Gokulam; daily class for 1/4 weeks ₹2000/10,000) Ashtanga vinyasa and hatha yoga classes with experienced teachers. Linked to IndeaYoga. Drop-in classes (₹300) are available.

suburb close to many yoga schools. It's a well-designed space with comfy dorms, lockers, board games and books, a kitchen and a friendly vibe. There are regular events such as movie nights and cooking classes.

Hotel Maurya — HOTEL $
(☑ 0821-2426677; www.hotelmauryamysore. com; 9/5 Hanumantha Rao St; s/d/tr from ₹200/375/500; ❄️ 🗑️) A good choice, with helpful management who are eager to help you make the most of Mysuru. There's a wide range of large, unremarkable but inexpensive rooms; you pay extra for AC. It's in the thick of things in the city centre, so expect some traffic noise, and hustle and bustle.

Anokhi Garden Guest House GUESTHOUSE **$$**
(☎0821-4288923; www.anokhigarden.com;
408 Contour Rd, 3rd Stage, Gokulam; s/d from
₹2200/3200; 🖥) Very popular with yoga stu-
dents and young travellers, this cosy French-
run guesthouse offers tidy rooms in a prop-
erty that boasts a lovely garden cafe. Rooms
are spacious, with a splash of colour from
throws and local textiles.

Parklane Hotel HOTEL **$$**
(☎0821-4003500; www.parklanemysore.com;
2720 Harsha Rd; r ₹1680-3190; 🅿@🖥❄) Right
in the heart of the city, with most attractions
within walking distance, this hotel represents fine value. Decor is over-the-top kitsch,
but with its spacious, clean rooms the place
is hard to dislike – though the bathrooms
need upgrading. The lively open-air restaurant is always buzzing, and there's a small
rooftop pool.

Southern Star HOTEL **$$**
(☎0821-2426426; www.hotelsouthernstar.com;
Vinoba Rd; r incl breakfast from ₹4880; 🅿🖥❄)
Offering good value, this large hotel has
many advantages, including a very inviting
pool, lovely leafy grounds and a handy loca-
tion less than a kilometre from the train sta-
tion. Rooms are quite elegant, with wooden
floors, art on the walls and generously sized
bathrooms.

Akshaya Mahal Inn HOTEL **$$**
(☎0821-2447675; www.akshayamahalinn.com; 5/A
Hydarali Rd; r incl breakfast from ₹2460; 🅿🖥) A
couple of kilometres from the heart of town,
this well-run hotel enjoys a convenient location, with a large mall on its doorstep.
Rooms are spacious and represent fine value; all have flatscreen TVs (with cable) and
tea- and coffee-making facilities.

Green Hotel GUESTHOUSE **$$**
(☎0821-4255000; www.greenhotelindia.com;
2270 Vinoba Rd, Jayalakshmipuram; s/d incl break-
fast from ₹3820/4460; 🖥) The maharaja built
the Green Hotel in the 1920s as a palace for
his daughters. Today it's a heritage hotel set
among charming gardens. Rooms in the old
wing have plenty of period character, though
some fixtures are looking a tad tired and
there's no AC. There's a good **cafe** (cakes from
₹40, snacks from ₹70; ⏱10am-7pm; 🖥) 🌿, a res-
taurant and a travel agent.

★**Grand Mercure Mysore** HOTEL **$$$**
(☎0821-4021212; www.accorhotels.com; Nelson
Mandela Circle, New Sayyaji Rao Rd; r from ₹5160;
🅿@🖥❄) The Mercure is a very well-run

hotel, with attentive, friendly staff members
and sleek, well-equipped rooms. There's a
large rooftop swimming pool (big enough for
laps), a gym with city views, a small spa and
a choice of restaurants. Located 4km north
of the city centre.

Royal Orchid Metropole HERITAGE HOTEL **$$$**
(☎0821-4255566; www.royalorchidhotels.com;
5 Jhansi Lakshmi Bai Rd; s/d incl breakfast from
₹6880/7250; 🅿🖥❄) Recently renovated,
this heritage property once served as the
residence for the maharaja's British guests.
It has spectacular grounds and a choice of
atmospheric dining areas, including a shel-
tered courtyard. Rooms ooze character and
boast all mod cons; there are four comfort
levels to choose from. The fitness centre and
very classy bar round things off in style.

Georgia Sunshine Village BUNGALOW **$$$**
(☎0821-247646; https://georgiasunshine.com;
Shimshapura Rd, Hebbani; d/ste incl full board
₹7780/9250; 🅿🖥❄) The affable Hatherell
couple runs this relaxing place, a fine family
getaway with a sparkling swimming pool,
delicious homemade food and accommodation in cosy bungalows. Treks (guides ₹300),
birding walks and fishing trips can be arranged. It's 64km east of Mysuru.

🍴 Eating

Mysuru has a good number of Indian restaurants and casual places for snacking. There
are several healthy-eating cafes thanks to the
sheer number of yogis in town.

★**Vinayaka Mylari** SOUTH INDIAN **$**
(769 Nazarbad Main Rd; dosa ₹30-50; ⏱6am-
1.30pm & 3-8.30pm) This tiny, no-nonsense
place is one of the best spots in town to try
the South Indian classic masala dosa (a large
savoury crepe stuffed with spiced potatoes).
Here they're beautifully light and fluffy and
served on banana leaves. Locals eat them
with coconut chutney and a coffee.

**Madhushahi
Samosa Centre** STREET FOOD **$**
(1518 Vinoba Rd; samosas ₹15-30; ⏱4-9pm Mon-
Sat) This hole-in-the-wall takeaway samosa
place is only open limited hours, but it's well
worth checking out. There's always a queue,
such is its popularity, and of course the samosas are delicious.

Dosa Point SOUTH INDIAN **$**
(1350 Devaraj Urs Rd; dosa ₹40-70; ⏱8am-10pm)
This wildly popular dosa joint is so popular that people munch them on the street

KARNATAKA MYSURU (MYSORE)

outside when the cramped interior is full. Try a rava onion dosa or ghee dosa.

Cafe Aramane SOUTH INDIAN $

(Sayyaji Rao Rd; mains ₹90-120; ⏲8am-10pm) 🍽 This atmospheric and authentic South Indian eatery rolls out steaming breakfast platters for Mysuru's office-goers, serves up thalis for lunch (from ₹80), and welcomes everyone back in the evenings with aromatic filter coffee and a convoy of delicious snacks. There are speciality dosa each day of the week.

Depth 'n' Green VEGETARIAN $

(www.facebook.com/depthngreen; 228/3 1st Main Rd, Gokulam; mains ₹120-200; ⏲8.30am-9.30pm; 🖥) A small, simple but ever-popular all-veg cafe offering a menu of all-day breakfasts (try the 'hearty oats') and satisfying Indian and Western dishes, including great salads. The green smoothies and lassis are also superb. Occasionally hosts evening musical events.

Hotel RRR SOUTH INDIAN $

(Gandhi Sq; mains ₹125-175; ⏲noon-4.30pm & 7-11pm) Classic Andhra-style food is ladled out at this ever-busy eatery, and you may have to queue for a table during lunch. Try its famous chicken or mutton biryanis (served on a banana leaf), too. There's a small AC section.

Anu's Bamboo Hut HEALTH FOOD $$

(📞9900909428; www.facebook.com/cafeingokulam; 367 2nd Main Rd, 3rd Stage, Gokulam; lunch buffet ₹250; ⏲1-3pm & 5-7pm Mon-Sat; 🖥) Rooftop cafe reminiscent of a shack that caters mainly to yoga students, with healthy vegetarian lunch buffets (at 1pm sharp; don't arrive at 2pm or many dishes many be gone) and evening smoothies. Chef-owner Anu is a great source of info and offers cooking classes (₹700, lunch included).

Parklane Hotel MULTICUISINE $$

(Parklane Hotel, 2720 Harsha Rd; mains ₹110-175; 🖥) Mysuru's most social restaurant, with outdoor tables moodily lit by countless lanterns. There's often live traditional music, too. The menu offers delicious regional dishes from across India, as well as Chinese and Continental options and cold beers.

Rasa Dhatu HEALTH FOOD $$

(www.dhatuorganics.com; 2826 10th Cross Rd, Gokulam; snacks/meals from ₹120/140; ⏲10am-10pm Mon-Fri, 8am-10pm Sat & Sun; 🖥) Organic cafe off Adipampa Rd serving up healthy specials such as dosa and roti made from millet grains, and salads, curries and North

or South Indian lunchtime thalis (₹199 to ₹299). Service can be a tad slow at times.

Old House ITALIAN $$

(📞0821-2333255; 451 Jhansi Lakshmi Bai Rd; mains from ₹215; ⏲7.30am-9.45pm; 🖥) Classy Italian place with a delightful terrace where you can enjoy tasty salads, pasta, risotto and pizzas (baked in a wood-fired oven). Also a good bet for breakfast (with everything from croissants to Spanish omelettes). It serves a full range of mocktails and coffees but no alcohol.

Tiger Trail INDIAN $$$

(📞0821-4255566; Royal Orchid Metropole, 5 Jhansi Lakshmi Bai Rd; mains ₹249-799; ⏲7.30-10am, 12.30-3.30pm & 7.30-11pm; 🖥) This hotel's grand dining room (with portraits, chandeliers and Murano-glass mirrors) makes quite a setting for delectable Indian cuisine, or opt for the courtyard, which twinkles with fairy lights at night. Try a Peshwari boti kebab (₹475), a Malabar fish curry (₹399) or any of the excellent North Indian dishes and be sure to have a tipple in the adjacent bar.

🍷 Drinking & Nightlife

⭐ **Frosting** CAFE

(www.frosting.in; 2649 2nd Main Rd, Gokulam; mains ₹185-395; ⏲11am-11.30pm; 🖥) One of the city's most attractive cafes, occupying an elegant villa in an upmarket corner of town. It's a relaxing spot for an espresso or a glass of wine, with an attractive AC interior, a garden and a menu of Italian classics.

Infinit Doora BAR

(www.facebook.com/Infinitmysore; Hotel Roopa, 2724/C Bengaluru-Nilgiri Rd; ⏲noon-11pm; 🖥) The nearest thing to a lounge in Mysuru, this rooftop bar has a classy ambience, a comprehensive drinks selection, smoking and nonsmoking zones and fine city views. Cocktails start at ₹250, and there's a full menu of North and South Indian grub.

Pelican Pub PUB

(25 Hunsur Rd; mains ₹95-245; ⏲11am-11pm; 🖥) A venerable, still-popular watering hole located at the fringes of upmarket Gokulam. Serves draught beer (pitchers are ₹450) and food (try the chilli pork) at bargain-basement rates in the classic pub interior or the alfresco-style garden setting out the back. There's live music some nights.

🛍 Shopping

The bazaar area around Devaraja Market (p875) is a real highlight for those in search of spices, sandalwood products, incense and essential oils (and photographs).

Silk saris are another good buy. Look for the butterfly-esque 'Silk Mark' on your purchase; it's an endorsement indicating quality silk.

Dhatu Organics & Naturals
HEALTH & WELLNESS
(www.dhatuorganics.com; 2826 10th Cross Rd; ⊙8am-9.30pm) Simply outstanding selection of natural products (priced from ₹80), many of them organic, including essential oils and natural cosmetics, fruit and veg, pulses and seeds. Check out its cafe (p882) next door while you're here. Located off Adipampa Rd.

Government Silk-Weaving Factory
CLOTHING
(☑8025586550; www.ksicsilk.com; Mananthody Rd, Ashokapuram; ⊙8.30am-4pm Mon-Sat, outlet 10.30am-7pm daily) Given that Mysuru's prized silk is made under its very sheds, this government-run outlet, set up in 1912, is the best and cheapest place to shop for the exclusive textile. Behind the showroom is the factory, where you can drop by to see how the fabric is made. It's around 2km south of town.

Forum Centre City Mall
MALL
(http://forummalls.in/forum-centre-city; Hyder Ali Rd; ⊙10am-10pm) When you need a dose of air-con and some retail time, this mall fits the bill. Offers a wide range of clothing stores (including H&M and Levi's), cafes and restaurants.

Sumangali Silks
CLOTHING
(⊙10am-9pm) Exceptionally popular with Indian women, and usually very crowded, this multilevel store sells fine silk saris, with quality of varying degrees depending on how much you want to spend (prices start at ₹150). It's off Gandhi Sq.

Sandalwood Oil Factory
GIFTS & SOUVENIRS
(Mananthody Rd, Ashokapuram; ⊙outlet 9.30am-6.30pm, factory closed Sun) A quality-assured place for sandalwood products including incense, soap, cosmetics and the prohibitively expensive pure sandalwood oil (if in stock). Guided tours are available to show you around the factory.

ℹ Information

MEDICAL SERVICES
Government Hospital (☑0821-4269806; Dhanvanthri Rd; ⊙24hr) Centrally located and has a 24-hour pharmacy.
Gopala Gowda Shanthaveri Memorial Hospital (☑0821-4001600; www.gopalagowdahospital.com; T Narasipura Main Rd; ⊙24hr) Best intensive care in Mysuru.

POST
Main Post Office (cnr Irwin & Ashoka Rds; ⊙10am-6pm Mon-Sat)

TOURIST INFORMATION
Karnataka Tourism (☑0821-2422096; www.karnatakatourism.org; 1st fl, Hotel Mayura Hoysala, 2 Jhansi Lakshmi Bai Rd; ⊙10am-5pm Mon-Sat) Helpful and has plenty of brochures.
KSTDC Transport Office (☑0821-2423652; https://kstdc.co; Yatri Navas Bldg, 2 Jhansi Lakshmi Bai Rd; ⊙8.30am-8.30pm) Main office; provides a useful map.

ℹ Getting There & Away

AIR
Mysuru's airport only has one daily connection: Trujet flies to/from Chennai. During Dussehra (p879) there are special Air India flights to Bengaluru.

TRAINS FROM MYSURU

Train tickets can be bought from Mysuru's **railway reservation office** (☑131; ⊙8am-8pm Mon-Sat, to 2pm Sun).

DESTINATION	TRAIN NO & NAME	FARE (₹)	DURATION (HR)	DEPARTURES
Bengaluru (Bangalore)	12613 Tippu Exp	2nd class/AC chair 90/305	2½	11.30am
Bengaluru	12008 Shatabdi Exp	AC chair/AC executive chair 305/775	2	2.15pm Thu-Tue
Chennai	12008 Shatabdi Exp	AC chair/AC executive chair 1140/1840	7½	2.15pm Thu-Tue
Hosapete (Hospet)	16592 Hampi Exp	3AC/2AC sleeper 845/1210	12	7pm
Hubballi (Hubli)	17301 Mysuru Dharwad Exp	sleeper/2AC 275/1070	8½	10.30pm

BUSES FROM MYSURU

DESTINATION	FARE (₹)	DURATION (HR)	DEPARTURES
Bandipur	79	2	10 daily via Ooty
Bengaluru (Bangalore)	129-326	2½-4	33 daily midnight to 10pm
Bengaluru airport	800	3½-4	21 daily
Channarayapatna	88-175	2	17 daily
Chennai	674-1020	9-12½	6 daily from 4pm
Ernakulam	735-846	8½-10	3 daily from 6.05pm
Gokarna	504	12	1 daily at 6.05am
Hassan	118	2½-3	18 daily
Hospete (Hospet)	362-782	9-12½	9 daily
Mangaluru (Mangalore)	256-676	6-7	20 daily
Ooty (Udhagamandalam)	157-567	4-5	12 daily

Fares: (O) Ordinary, (R) Rajahamsa Semideluxe, (V) Airavath AC Volvo

BUS

The **Central bus stand** (Bengaluru-Nilgiri Rd) handles all KSRTC long-distance buses. The **City bus stand** (Sayyaji Rao Rd) is for city, Srirangapatna and Chamundi Hill buses. The **private bus stand** (Sayyaji Rao Rd) services Hubballi, Vijapura (Bijapur), Mangaluru, Ooty and Ernakulam. You'll find several ticketing agents around the stand.

ⓘ Getting Around

Uber and Ola cabs are everywhere in Mysuru. Agencies at hotels can organise drivers for around ₹2000 per day in town, or from ₹2500 per day for out-of-town trips.

Count on around ₹1000 for a day's sightseeing in an autorickshaw.

Mysuru airport is 9km south of the centre. It's not served by public transport; taxis charge around ₹350.

Around Mysuru

Consider a KSTDC tour (p879) for visiting sights around Mysuru.

Venugopala Swamy Temple   HINDU TEMPLE
(◷8am-6pm) Back from the dead, this stunning 12th-century Hoysala temple was submerged when the Kaveri River was dammed in 1930. However, villagers had tantalising glimpses of the ancient structure during drought years when the reservoir waters dropped. Liquor baron and philanthropist Sri Hari Khoday vowed to rebuilt the temple in 2003, and architects photographed and numbered each slab and stone, which were removed block by block and reconstructed by 200 workers at a cost of ₹25,000,000. The project took eight years.

It's 28km northwest of Mysuru, near Hosa Kannambadi village.

Brindavan Gardens   GARDENS
(adult/child ₹40/20, camera/video ₹50/100; ◷6.30am-9pm) If you're familiar with Bollywood, these ornamental gardens might just give you a sense of déjà vu – they've been the backdrop to many a shimmying musical number. The best time to visit is in the evening, when the fountains are illuminated (at 6.30pm) and made to dance to the accompaniment of popular film tunes.

The gardens are 19km northwest of Mysuru. One of the KSTDC tours (p879) stops here, and bus 301 departs from Mysuru's City bus stand hourly (₹23, 45 minutes).

Srirangapatna (Srirangapatnam)

☑ 08236 / POP 27,100

Steeped in bloody history, the fort town of Srirangapatna (Srirangapatnam), 16km from Mysuru, is built on an island straddling the Cauvery River. The seat of Hyder Ali and Tipu Sultan's power, this town was the de facto capital of much of southern India during the 18th century. The ramparts, battlements and some of the gates of the fort still stand, as do a clutch of monuments.

◉ Sights

★**Daria Daulat Bagh**   PALACE
(Summer Palace; Indian/foreigner ₹25/300; ◷8.30am-5.30pm) Set within lovely manicured grounds 1km east of the fort, Tipu's summer palace is Srirangapatna's star attraction. Built from teak and rosewood, it has impressively lavish decoration covering

every inch of its interiors. The ceilings are embellished with floral designs, while the walls bear murals depicting courtly life and Tipu's campaigns against the British. A small museum within displays artefacts and interesting paintings. Audio guides are available.

Colonel Bailey's Dungeon   HISTORIC SITE

FREE North of the island, on the banks of the Cauvery, is this well-preserved 18th-century white-walled dungeon used to hold British prisoners of war, including Colonel Bailey, who died here in 1780. Jutting out from the walls are stone fixtures used to chain the naked prisoners, who were immersed in water up to their necks.

Gumbaz   MAUSOLEUM

(⊙8am-6.30pm) **FREE** In a serene garden, the historically significant Persian-style Gumbaz is the resting place of the legendary Tipu Sultan, his equally famed father, Hyder Ali and his mother Fakr-Un-Nisa. Many other relatives of the sultan are buried in the mausoleum's grounds. The interior of the onion-domed mausoleum is impressive, painted in a tiger-like motif as a tribute to the sultan.

Ranganathittu
Bird Sanctuary   BIRD SANCTUARY

(Indian/foreigner incl 15min boat ride ₹70/140, long-lens camera or video ₹500; ⊙8.30am-5.45pm) The sanctuary includes six islets and the banks of the Cauvery River. Storks, ibises, egrets, spoonbills and cormorants are best seen in the early morning or late afternoon on an extended boat ride (₹1500 per hour). There are also plenty of crocodiles, which are quite easy to spot. There's a restaurant on-site.

❶ Getting There & Away

Hourly buses (₹22 to ₹32, 45 minutes) depart from Mysuru's City bus stand. Passenger trains travelling from Mysuru to Bengaluru also stop here. Bus 301 (₹18, 30 minutes) heading from Mysuru to Brindavan Gardens stops just across from Srirangapatna's main bus stand. A return autorickshaw from Mysuru is about ₹700, and a taxi around ₹1100.

Melukote

Life in the devout Hindu town of Melukote (also called Melkote), 51km north of Mysuru, revolves around the atmospheric 12th-century **Cheluvanarayana Temple** (Raja St; ⊙8am-1pm & 5-8pm), with its rose-coloured *gopuram* (gateway tower) and ornately carved pillars. Get a workout on the hike up

to the hilltop Yoganarasimha Temple, which offers fine views of the surrounding hills.

Three KSRTC buses shuttle daily between Mysuru and Melukote (₹108, 1½ hours).

Somnathpur

Small in scale but masterly in detail, the astonishingly beautiful **Keshava Temple** (Indian/foreigner ₹25/300; ⊙8.30am-5.30pm) is one of the finest examples of Hoysala architecture, on par with the masterpieces of Belur and Halebid. Built in 1268, this star-shaped temple, 33km from Mysuru, is adorned with superb stone sculptures depicting various scenes from the Ramayana and Mahabharata, and the life and times of the Hoysala kings.

Somnathpur is 8km south of Bannur. Take one of the half-hourly buses from Mysuru to Bannur (₹55, 50 minutes) and catch an autorickshaw (around ₹130 one way) from there. A half-day return trip by car from Mysuru should cost around ₹1200.

Bandipur National Park

📋 08229

Part of the Nilgiri Biosphere Reserve, **Bandipur National Park** (http://bandipurtigerreserve.in; Indian/foreigner ₹75/1000, video ₹1000; ⊙6am-9.30am & 4-6pm) is one of South India's most famous wilderness areas. Covering 880 sq km, it was once the Mysuru maharajas' private wildlife reserve, and is now a protected zone for more than 100 species of mammal, including tigers, elephants, leopards, gaurs (Indian bison), chitals (spotted deer), sambars, sloth bears, dholes, mongooses and langurs. It's also home to an impressive 350 bird species. It's only 72km south of Mysuru on the Ooty road.

The **forest department** (📋08229-236043; https://bandipurtigerreserve.in; 1½hr safari per person bus/Gypsy ₹350/3250; ⊙6.30-9.30am & 3.30-6.30pm) has rushed drives on buses (capacity 20) and gypsy jeeps (capacity six), arranged at park headquarters. **Bandipur Safari Lodge** (📋08229-233001; www.junglelodges.com; 2hr safari per person ₹2800; ⊙6am & 4pm) has open-air 4WDs and minibuses, accompanied by knowledgeable guides.

🛏 Sleeping & Eating

Tiger Ranch   LODGE $$

(📋8095408505; http://tigerranch.net; Mangala Village; per person incl full board ₹1670) The very rustic Tiger Ranch has basic cottages, a thatched-roof dining hall and fine home-cooked food. There's good walking in the surrounding forest, and you're sure to encounter wildlife. Evenings can be enjoyed around a bonfire (extra charge). It's located 10km from the park entrance; call ahead to arrange pick-up (₹300). Note that the access road is very rough.

★ Dhole's Den
LODGE $$$

(☑9444468376; www.dholesden.com; Kaniyanapura Village; camping/s/d incl full board from ₹3000/12,900/14,300; ☎) ✦ Dhole's Den offers contemporary design in lovely pastoral surrounds. Stylish rooms and bungalows are decked out with art and colourful fabrics, plus couches and deckchairs. It's environmentally conscious, with solar power, tank water and organic vegies. Camping is available for those on a budget. Located a 20-minute drive from park headquarters; rates include a guided nature walk.

Serai
RESORT $$$

(☑08229-236075; www.theserai.in; Kaniyanapura Village; r incl full board from ₹21,700; ✴☎✳) Set in a coffee plantation that backs onto the park, this luxurious resort has gorgeous Mediterranean-inspired villas (some with private pool) that are in harmony with the natural surroundings. Thatched-roof rooms feature elegant touches such as copper bathroom fixtures, stone-wall showers and wildlife photography on the walls. Its glassed-in restaurant and infinity pool both maximise outlooks to the Nilgiri Hills.

MC Resort
HOTEL $$$

(☑9019954162; www.mcresorts.in; Bengaluru-Ooty Rd, Melukamanahally; s/d incl full board from ₹5310/6490; ☎✳) Decent, resort-style MC has 23 spacious, well-equipped rooms, a large swimming pool, a kids' pool, a multi-cuisine restaurant and a convenient location near the park. Rates include meals. Jungle safaris cost ₹1600 per person and are a step up in quality from the Forest Department's.

❶ Getting There & Away

Buses between Mysuru and Ooty can drop you at Bandipur (₹92, 2½ hours). A taxi from Mysuru costs about ₹2200.

Nagarhole National Park

Rich in jungle and boasting a scenic lake, this **national park** (Rajiv Gandhi National Park; Indian/foreigner ₹200/1000, video ₹1000; ◷6am-6pm) is one of Karnataka's best wildlife getaways. It's home to good numbers of animals, including tigers and elephants. Flanking the Kabini River, it forms an important protected region that includes the neighbouring Bandipur National Park and several other reserves.

The Kabini River empties into the Kabini Reservoir, creating a vast watering hole for Nagarhole's wildlife. Herds of wild elephants and other animals gather on the banks to drink, and the high concentration of wildlife has made this one of the best spotting locations in Karnataka. The traditional inhabitants of the land, the hunter-gatherer Jenu Kuruba people, still live in the park, despite government efforts to relocate them.

Kabini was once a private hunting reserve for the maharaja of Mysuru, and today it hosts some of the top wildlife lodges in southern India. The best time to view wildlife is during summer (April to May), though winter (November to February) is more comfortable.

Government-run safaris (Kabini River Lodge; Indian/foreigner 4WD safari ₹350/1300, bus safari ₹100/300, camera ₹200-400; ◷6am-6pm) in both jeeps (capacity nine) and safari buses (capacity 25) leave at 7am and 3pm when conditions allow in the dry season. Organised by the Kabini River Lodge, **20-seater motorboat** (Kabini River Lodge; per person ₹2000) rides allow for relaxed wildlife viewing and are excellent for birders.

🛏 Sleeping & Eating

Kabini Lake makes a wonderful base and is home to most lodges, but there are no real budget hotels here. For inexpensive places, head to the park HQ.

Karapur Hotel
GUESTHOUSE $

(☑9945904840; Karapura; r ₹1250) The only budget option close to Kabini is this simple lodge with a few rooms above a shop in the township of Karapura, 3km from the park.

★ Waterwoods Lodge
GUESTHOUSE $$$

(☑082-28264421; www.waterwoods.in; d incl full board from ₹15,300; ✴☎✳) On a grassy embankment overlooking scenic Kabini Lake, Waterwoods is a stunning lodge. Most rooms have balconies with wonderful lake views, swing chairs, hardwood floors and designer flair. It's kid friendly, with a trampoline, an infinity pool, free canoe hire and wood-fired pizzas. Pamper yourself in the spa, which has massage rooms, a Jacuzzi and a steam bath.

KAAV Safari Lodge
LODGE $$$

(☑08228-264492; www.kaav.com; Mallali Cross, Kabini; r or luxury tents incl full board from ₹17,800;

✳☂✣) KAAV has open-plan rooms with polished-concrete floors, hip bathrooms and spacious balconies that open directly to the national park. The attention to detail is superb. Head up to the viewing tower to lounge on plush day beds, or take a dip in the infinity pool. No children under 10.

Bison Resort   LODGE $$$
(☑080-41278708; www.thebisonresort.com; Gundathur Village; camping per person from ₹2650, s/d incl full board from US$335/390; ☂✣) Inspired by luxury safari lodges in Africa, Bison succeeds in replicating the classic wilderness experience with a stunning waterfront location and a choice between canvas-walled cottages, stilted bungalows or bush camping. It offers a wide selection of activities, including treks to local tribal villages and sunset boat rides. Service standards are top notch and there are expert naturalists on hand.

Kabini River Lodge   LODGE $$$
(☑08228-264405; www.junglelodges.com/kabini-river-lodge; per person incl full board & activities dm ₹5900, r from ₹11,200; ✣) These attractive bungalows have a prime location beside the lake with a choice between large tented cottages and bungalows. You can enjoy a sundowner in the atmospheric colonial-style bar. Those in the dorm only get a boat (not jeep) safari included.

❶ Getting There & Away

Buses between Mysuru and Ooty can drop you at Bandipur (₹92, 2½ hours). A taxi from Mysuru costs about ₹2200.

Kodagu (Coorg) Region

Nestled amid evergreen hills that line the southernmost edge of Karnataka is the luscious Kodagu (Coorg) region, gifted with emerald landscapes and hectares of plantations. A major centre for coffee and spice production, this rural expanse is also home to the Kodava people, who are divided into 1000 clans. The uneven terrain and cool climate make it a fantastic area for trekking, birdwatching or lazily ambling down little-trodden paths winding around carpeted hills. All in all, Kodagu is rejuvenation guaranteed.

Kodagu was a state in its own right until 1956, when it merged with Karnataka. The region's chief town and transport hub is Madikeri, but for an authentic Kodagu experience you have to venture into the countryside. Avoid weekends if you can, when places can quickly get filled up by weekenders from Bengaluru.

Exploring the region on foot is a highlight for many visitors. Treks are part cultural experience, part nature encounter, involving hill climbs, plantation visits, forest walks and homestays. Several local and Bengaluru-based tour operators offer walks. Popular peaks to trek to include Tadiyendamol (1745m), Pushpagiri (1712m) and Kotebetta (1620m). Plenty of day hikes are possible; a trekking guide is essential for navigating the labyrinth of forest tracks.

Madikeri (Mercara)

☑08272 / POP 35,700 / ELEV 1525M
Madikeri (also known as Mercara) is a congested market town spread out along a series of ridges. The only reason for coming here is to organise treks or sort out the practicalities of travel.

◉ Sights & Activities

Popular local sights include Abbi Falls, the viewpoint at **Raja's Seat** (Mahatma Gandhi Rd; ₹5; ⊙5.30am-7pm) and **Raja's Tombs** (Gaddige) FREE, 7km from Madikeri.

Madikeri Fort   HISTORIC SITE
There are good views from this hilltop fort, built by Tipu Sultan in the 16th century, though today it's the less glamorous site of the municipal headquarters. You can walk a short section of ramparts, and within the fort's walls are the hexagonal palace (now the dusty district-commissioner's office) and a colonial-era church, which houses a quirky **museum** (free entry; ⊙10am-5.30pm Sun-Fri).

Ayurjeevan   AYURVEDA
(☑944974779; Kohinoor Rd; 1hr from ₹1400; ⊙7am-7pm) An ayurvedic 'hospital' that offers a whole range of intriguing and rejuvenating techniques, including rice-ball massages and oil baths. It's a short walk from the State Bank of India.

⬛ Sleeping & Eating

With fantastic guesthouses in the surrounding plantations, there's no real reason to stay in Madikeri, unless you arrive very late.

Hotel Chitra   HOTEL $
(☑08272-225372; www.hotelchitra.co.in; School Rd; d ₹950-1500; ✣) A dependable hotel close to Madikeri's main intersection (so expect some background traffic noise). Provides low-cost, no-frills rooms with cable TV and reliable hot water.

KARNATAKA KODAGU (COORG) REGION

Hotel Mayura Valley View
HOTEL $$

(☑ 08272-228387; www.kstdc.co/hotels/hotel-mayura-valley-view-madikeri; Stuart Hill; d/ste incl breakfast from ₹2400/3300; ❄ 🤶) This government hotel is one of Madikeri's best, with large, bright rooms, a peaceful ambience and fantastic valley views. You pay extra for AC. Its restaurant-bar with a terrace overlooking the valley is a great spot for a tipple.

Coorg Cuisine
INDIAN $

(Main Rd; mains ₹100-195; ⊙ noon-4pm & 7-10pm) Specialising in Kodagu specialities such as *pandhi barthadh* (pork dry fry) and *koli nallamolu barthad* (chicken-pepper fry), this restaurant is well worth trying. It's not exactly atmospheric, located above a shop on the main road, but the seating is comfy and prices reasonable.

★ Raintree
INDIAN $$

(www.raintree.in; 13-14 Pension Lane; meals ₹160-300; ⊙ 11.30am-10pm) This cute converted bungalow makes a cosy place for a delicious meal, with solid wooden furniture and tribal art. The food doesn't disappoint, either, with local specialities and dishes from the coast. It also sells wine and great Kodagu coffee. Located just behind Madikeri Town Hall.

🍷 Drinking & Nightlife

Beans 'n' Brews Cafe
CAFE

(Bus Stand Rd; drinks ₹60-150; ⊙ 9am-10pm; 🤶) A welcoming sight on a cool Coorg morning, this cafe offers a terrific range of steaming gourmet teas (try the Darjeeling Orange Summer tips) and great coffee, including Vietnamese drip.

🛍 Shopping

Choci Coorg
CHOCOLATE

(www.facebook.com/chocicoorgmadikeri; Bus Stand Rd; ⊙ 9am-9pm) Opposite the bus stand, Choci Coorg does many varieties of chocolate, lots of fruity and nut combos and a unique betel-nut flavour.

ℹ Getting There & Away

Madikeri is the main transport hub of the region, with very regular connections to Mysuru, Bengaluru and Mangaluru. There's near-zero public transport to the rural lodges and homestays, but autorickshaws are freely available in Madikeri.

Around Madikeri

The highlands around Madikeri offer some of Kodagu's most enchanting countryside with spice and coffee plantations and excellent accommodation.

🏃 Activities

★ Jiva Spa
SPA

(☑ 08272-2665900; jivaspa.coorg@tajhotels.com; 1st Monnangeri, Galibeedu Post; treatments from ₹2700; ⊙ 9am-9pm) Based at the stunning Taj Madikeri Resort & Spa (p889), this is an excellent place to indulge in a rejuvenating ayurvedic treatment. With soak tubs, a relaxation lounge, a beauty salon and a yoga-and-meditation zone, it's one of the best spas in South India. Appointments essential.

Swaasthya Ayurveda Retreat Village
AYURVEDA

(www.swaasthya.com; Bekkesodlur Village; per person per day incl full board & yoga class from ₹7200) For an exceptionally peaceful and refreshing ayurvedic vacation, head to south Coorg to soothe your soul among the lush greenery on 1.6 hectares of coffee and spice plantations. Prices include treatments.

🛏 Sleeping & Eating

★ Rainforest Retreat
GUESTHOUSE $$

(☑ 08272-265639, 08272-265638; www.rainforestours.com; Galibeedu; s/d tent ₹1500/2000, cottages from ₹2000/3000; 🤶) 🌿 A great place to socialise with eco-minded Indians, this nature-soaked refuge is immersed within forest and plantations, and has an organic, sustainable set-up. Accommodation is lazy camping (prepitched tents with beds) or cottages with solar power. Rates include plantation tours and treks. Check the website for volunteering opportunities. An autorickshaw from Madikeri is ₹250.

Golden Mist
HOMESTAY $$

(☑ 9448903670, 08272-265629; Galibeedu; s/d incl full board ₹2500/4000) An incredibly peaceful, very rustic Indian-German-managed tea-, coffee- and rice-growing farm. The cottages have character, though they're basic and best suited to outdoor types rather than those who prize their creature comforts. Meals are tasty local dishes made from the farm's organic produce. Staff members are very hospitable. It's tricky to find and not signposted; an autorickshaw from Madikeri costs ₹250.

River Edge Valley Homestay
HOMESTAY $$

(☑ 9481759099, 9482422739; www.facebook.com/riveredgevalley; Mukkodlu; per person incl breakfast & dinner weekday/weekend ₹1500/1750) Owned by a hospitable couple, this rustic homestay boasts a hillside location and stunning valley views. It's just the spot to enjoy nature and perhaps do some birdwatching. Rooms are well presented and the home-cooked food is delicious. Located 21km north of Madikeri; the access road can be tough to tackle after heavy rain.

Victorian Verandaz
B&B $$

(☑ 9448059850; http://victorianverandaz.com; Modur Estate, Kadagadal Village; d self-catering ₹2500-6000, B&B ₹2950; 🖱) Fine family-owned lodgings on a huge estate that grows coffee, pepper, cardamom and rice. There's a choice of accommodation: two rental cottages with kitchens that are available on a self-catering basis, and two rooms in a cottage that operate on a B&B basis. There's good birding and trail walking on the estate.

★ Taj Madikeri Resort & Spa
LUXURY HOTEL $$$

(Vivanta; ☑ 08272-265900; www.tajhotels.com; 1st Monnangeri, Galibeedu Post; r from ₹19,200; @🖱🏊) Nestling in misty rainforest, this supremely stylish hotel incorporates principles of space and minimalism, and effectively blends into its environment. Old cattle tracks lead to rooms, with pricier ones featuring private indoor pools, fireplaces and butlers. There are astonishing highland views from the lobby and infinity pool, and a top-class ayurvedic spa.

Kakkabe

☑ 08272 / POP 588

Surrounded by forested hills, this tranquil village and hiking hotspot is an ideal base for an assault on Kodagu's highest peak, Tadiyendamol (1745m), or just for enjoying a wander along scenic highland trails.

🛏 Sleeping & Eating

Most hotels operate on a full-board basis. There are very few other eating options in the area.

★ Honey Valley Estate
GUESTHOUSE $

(☑ 08272-238339; www.honeyvalleyindia.in; d ₹600-1900, f from ₹2400; 🖱) The friendly owners market their delightful homestay as 'perfect for the pleasure of doing nothing at all', but if you do want to shake a leg you'll find 18 local trekking routes. The lodge is at 1250m, so expect cool, fresh mornings. There are 10 accommodation options; meals are ₹150 to ₹200. Accessible by 4WD only (₹200; book via hotel) from Kakkabe.

Chingaara
GUESTHOUSE $$

(☑ 08272-238633; www.chingaara.com; Kabbinakad; r incl half board ₹1750-2700; 🖱) This delightful farmhouse is surrounded by verdant coffee plantations, with good birding in the vicinity. Its nine rooms are spacious, and most have good views. Good home-style cooking is served and staff members will light a bonfire at night. It's 2.5km up a rocky steep hill (4WD only); call ahead and Chingaara's 4WD will pick you up from Kabbinakad junction.

Palace Estate Home Stay
HOMESTAY $

(http://palaceestate.co.in; s/d from ₹1400/3600; 🖱) In the foothills of the Western Ghats, 4.5km southwest of Kakkabe, this lodge is located on a farm where coffee, cardamom, fruit and avocado are cultivated. There's good trekking and a guests' library, and you can take a natural shower in the estate's waterfall if the climate is agreeable. Cash only.

Misty Woods
LODGE $$$

(☑ 08272-238561; www.coorgmisty.com; cottages ₹7000-12,000; 🖱🏊) The name Misty Woods aptly sums up the landscape that surrounds this mountain lodge. The *vastu shastra* (ancient science similar to feng shui) style cottages are both comfortable and stylish, and the games room (with pool table, ping pong, table football and chessboard) is great for rainy days.

❶ Getting There & Away

Regular buses run to Kakkabe from Madikeri (₹52, 1½ hours). Most lodges will pick you up from either Kakkabe or Kabbinakad, 3km beyond Kakkabe.

Hassan

☑ 08172 / POP 142,000

This sprawling, congested city has minimal appeal for the traveller other than as a base for visiting nearby Belur, Halebid or Sravanabelagola. It's something of a transport hub, with good bus and train connections, and has a decent range of accommodation.

The helpful **tourist office** (☑ 08172-268862; AVK College Rd; ⊙ 10am-5.30pm Mon-Fri) can advise on transport options.

🛏 Sleeping & Eating

Jewel Rock Hotel
HOTEL $

(☑ 08172-261048; www.jewelrockhotels.com; BM Rd; d from ₹1000, with air-con ₹1700; ❄🖱) This place is good value, with 36 spacious if somewhat dated rooms. There's a decent

BYLAKUPPE – TIBETAN VILLAGE

Tiny Bylakuppe was among the first refugee camps set up in South India to house thousands of Tibetans who fled from Tibet following the 1959 Chinese invasion. Over 10,000 Tibetans (including some 3300 monks) live around the town, forming South India's largest Tibetan community, but foreigners need a permit to stop overnight.

The area's highlight is the atmospheric **Namdroling Monastery** (www.namdroling.org; ⊙7am-6pm), home to the spectacular **Golden Temple** (Padmasambhava Buddhist Vihara; ⊙7am-6pm), presided over by three 18m-high gold-plated Buddha statues. The temple is at its dramatic best when prayers are in session and it rings out with gongs, drums and the drone of hundreds of young monks chanting. You're welcome to sit and meditate. The **Zangdogpalri Temple** (⊙7am-6pm), a similarly ornate affair, is next door.

While day-trippers are welcome to visit, foreigners are not allowed to stay overnight in Bylakuppe without a Protected Area Permit (PAP) from the Ministry of Home Affairs in Delhi, which can take months to process. Contact the Tibet Bueau Office (www.tibet bureau.in) for details. If you have a permit, the simple **Paljor Dhargey Ling Guest House** (☑08223-258686; pdguesthouse@yahoo.com; r ₹300-500) is opposite the Golden Temple. For delicious *momos* (Tibetan dumplings) or *thukpa* (noodle soup), pop into the Tibetan-run **Malaya Restaurant** (momos ₹60-90; ⊙7am-9pm). Otherwise there are many hotels in nearby Kushalnagar and in the countryside around the village.

Autorickshaws (shared/solo ₹15/30) run to Bylakuppe from Kushalnagar, 5km away. Buses frequently do the 34km run to Kushalnagar from Madikeri (₹40, 45 minutes) and Hassan (₹82, 2½ hours). Most buses on the Mysuru–Madikeri route stop at Kushalnagar.

in-house vegetarian restaurant and bar, plus 24-hour room service. It's 700m west of the train station, just off the busy highway to Bengaluru.

Mallige Residency
HOTEL $$
(☑08172-260333; www.malligeresidency.com; 266 High School Field Rd; r incl breakfast ₹1600-2400, ste ₹2600; ❇☏) Almost a boutique hotel, the fine Malige offers rooms (there are four classes) that are spotless, contemporary and comfortable. It's also home to one of the best restaurants (p890) in town.

Hoysala Village
HOTEL $$$
(☑9591077400; http://hoysalavillageresorts.com; Belur Rd; cottages incl full board from ₹11,130; ❇☏☏) A fine upmarket lodge in leafy grounds with pretty cottages and suites, and a good ayurvedic spa. Lots of activities are offered, from guided birding walks to volleyball, and guests can enjoy traditional dance and music performances. Very relaxing and family friendly.

Parijata Restaurant
VEGETARIAN $$
(Mallige Residency, High School Field Rd; mains ₹80-220; ⊙11am-10pm; ☏) This popular, pure-veg hotel restaurant with inviting modern decor serves both North and South Indian cuisine, but it's the latter that stands out. Prices are moderate.

Swaad
INDIAN $$
(Hotel Raama, BM Rd; mains ₹120-240; ⊙8am-10pm) This inviting air-conditioned all-veg hotel restaurant makes a relaxed place for a meal, serving tasty North and South Indian classics.

❶ Getting There & Away

From the **New Bus Stand** (Hwy 71), 500m south of the town centre, buses depart to Mysuru (₹120, three hours), Bengaluru (₹198 to ₹484, 3½ to 4½ hours) and Mangaluru (₹166 to ₹380, 3½ to 4½ hours). A day tour of Belur and Halebid or Sravanabelagola in a car will cost you about ₹2000.

From Hassan's well-organised train station there's a daily service at 7.45pm to Mysuru (AC chair class ₹260, 2½ hours) and another in the dead of night. For Bengaluru there are three to four daily trains, including the 11312 Solapur Express (sleeper/2AC ₹170/745, five hours).

Belur
☑08177 / POP 9580 / ELEV 968M

The 12th-century Hoysala temples at Belur (also called Beluru) are the apex of one of the most artistically exuberant periods of ancient Hindu cultural development. The main temple, dedicated to Vishnu, has been a place of worship for over 900 years.

Commissioned in 1116 to commemorate the Hoysalas' victory over the neighbouring

Cholas, **Channakeshava Temple** (Temple Rd; guide ₹250; ⊘ 7am-7.30pm) took more than a century to build, and is currently the only one of the three major Hoysala sites still in daily use – try to be there for one of the *puja* (offering or prayer) ceremonies, held at 9am, 3pm and 7.30pm.

Inviting, renovated, state-run **Mayura Velapuri** (✍ 0817-7222209, 8970650026; www. kstdc.co/hotels; Temple Rd; d with fan/AC from ₹1350/1460, ste ₹2240; ❄🛜), 700m from Channakeshava Temple, has comfortable, spacious rooms dotted around shady grounds. It's set back from the road and has a good restaurant-bar serving a variety of Indian dishes (from ₹80) to go with beer.

There are frequent buses to/from Hassan (₹42 to ₹92, 45 minutes), 38km away, and Halebid (₹25, 30 minutes). Tours taking in Belur and nearby Halebid can be easily set up in Hassan.

Halebid

✍ 08177 / POP 9450

Halebid (also called Halibidu or Halebeedu) is a small town that's home to a stunning Hoysala temple and some other minor Jain sites. Most travellers visit on a day trip from Belur or Hassan.

Construction of the **Hoysaleswara Temple** (⊘ dawn-dusk), Halebid's claim to fame, began around 1121 and went on for more than 80 years. It was never completed but nonetheless stands today as a masterpiece of Hoysala architecture. The interior of its inner sanctum, chiselled out of black stone, is marvellous. On the outside, the temple's richly sculpted walls are covered with a flurry of Hindu deities, sages, stylised animals, and friezes depicting the life of the Hoysala rulers.

Set in a leafy garden right opposite the temple complex, **Hotel Mayura Shanthala** (✍ 08177-273224; www.kstdc.co/hotels; r/q incl breakfast from ₹1450/1680; ❄🛜) is the town's best sleeping option.

Regular buses depart for Hassan (₹38, one hour); buses to Belur (15km, ₹25) are also quite frequent.

Sravanabelagola

✍ 08176 / POP 5660

Atop the bare, rocky summit of Vindhyagiri Hill, the 17.5m-high statue of the Jain deity Gomateshvara (Bahubali) is visible long before you reach the pilgrimage town of Sravanabelagola (also spelt Shravanabelagola).

Viewing the statue close up is the main reason for heading to this sedate town, whose name means 'Monk of the White Pond'.

◉ Sights

Apart from the Gomateshvara statue, there are several interesting Jain temples in town. The **Chandragupta Basti** (Chandragupta Community; ⊘ 6am-6pm), on Chandragiri Hill opposite Vindhyagiri, is believed to have been built by Emperor Ashoka. The **Bhandari Basti** (Bhandari Community; ⊘ 6am-6pm), in the southeastern corner of town, is Sravanabelagola's largest temple. Nearby, **Chandranatha Basti** (Chandranatha Community; ⊘ 6am-6pm) has well-preserved paintings depicting Jain tales.

Gomateshvara Statue   JAIN SITE
(Bahubali; ⊘ 6.30am-6.30pm) A steep climb up 614 steps takes you to the top of Vindhyagiri Hill, the summit of which is lorded over by a towering naked statue of Jain deity Gomateshvara (Bahubali). Commissioned by a military commander in the service of the Ganga king Rachamalla and carved out of a single piece of granite by sculptor Aristenemi in AD 98, it is said to be the world's tallest monolithic statue. Leave your shoes at the foot of the hill.

Bahubali was the son of emperor Vrishabhadeva, who later became the first Jain *tirthankar* (revered teacher), Adinath. Embroiled in fierce competition with his brother Bharatha to succeed his father, Bahubali realised the futility of material gains and renounced his kingdom. As a recluse, he meditated in complete stillness in the forest until he attained enlightenment. His lengthy meditative spell is denoted by vines curling around his legs and an anthill at his feet.

Every 12 years, millions flock here to attend the **Mastakabhisheka** (⊘ Feb) ceremony, when the statue is doused in holy water, pastes, powders, precious metals and stones. The next ceremony is slated for 2030.

🛏 Sleeping & Eating

The local Jain organisation **SDJMI** (✍ 08176-257258; d/tr ₹260/330) handles bookings for its 15 guesthouses. Otherwise, options are few.

Hotel Raghu   HOTEL $
(✍ 08176-257238; s/d from ₹500/600, d with AC ₹1000; ❄) Offers very basic rooms that are something of a last resort. However, the vegetarian restaurant downstairs serves an awesome thali (₹90).

Getting There & Away

There are no direct buses from Sravanabelagola to Hassan or Belur – you must go to Channarayapatna (₹28, 25 minutes) and catch an onward connection there. One daily bus runs direct to Mysuru (₹110, two hours).

KARNATAKA COAST

Mangaluru (Mangalore)

🕿 0824 / POP 498,600

Alternating between relaxed coastal town and hectic nightmare, Mangaluru (more commonly known as Mangalore) has a Jekyll-and-Hyde thing going, but it's a useful gateway for the Konkan coast and the inland Kodagu region. While there's not a lot to do here, it has an appealing off-the-beaten-path feel, and the spicy seafood dishes are sensational. Mangaluru sits at the estuaries of the picturesque Netravathi and Gurupur Rivers on the Arabian Sea and has been a major port on international trade routes since the 6th century.

Sights

Sights are thin on the ground in Mangaluru, though there are some curious old Catholic structures that show a distinct European architectural influence.

Pilikula Nisarga Dhama THEME PARK
(🕿 0824-2263565; www.pilikula.com; adult/child ₹120/60, camera ₹150; ⊗9am-5.30pm) A kind of eco-educational theme park, Pilikula is spread over 149 hectares and includes a tropical forest, an arboretum, a herb garden full of rare medicinal plants, an artisan village with craft-making demonstrations, a zoo, a science centre and a lake. The 3D Planetarium (films in English at noon and 4pm daily) is certainly worth taking in. It's 8km east of central Mangaluru. Buses 3A, 3B and 3C head here from Mangaluru, or an Ola/Uber is around ₹200.

Mangaluru (Mangalore)

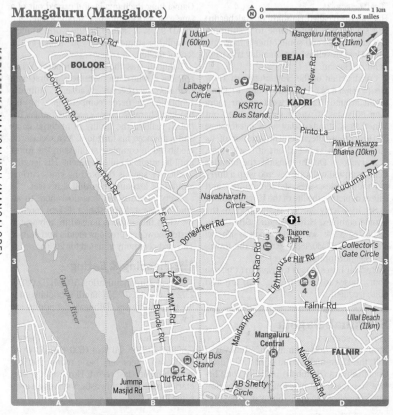

St Aloysius College Chapel CHURCH
(Lighthouse Hill; ⊘9am-6pm) Catholicism's roots in Mangaluru date back to the arrival of the Portuguese in the early 1500s. One impressive legacy is the 1880 Sistine Chapel–like St Aloysius chapel, its walls and ceilings painted with brilliant frescos. No photography is permitted.

🛏 Sleeping & Eating

Hotel Manorama HOTEL $
(✆0824-2440306; www.hotelmanorama.in; KS Rao Rd; r from ₹990; ❉@🛜) Offering fine value, the Manorama has clean rooms and a lobby that provides a memorable first impression with its display of Hindu statues and artefacts. It's close to the City Center mall, which has a food court.

Phalguni River Lodge LODGE $$
(✆0821-2444444; www.phalguniriverlodge.in; Mooodushedde Rd; r incl breakfast from ₹3000; ❉🛜) Next to the Pilikula Nisarga Dhama park, with views of the Gurupur River and coconut groves, this lodge offers a tranquil natural environment for those stressed by Indian city life. Rooms are spacious and there's good grub, including local seafood, available in the restaurant. Managed by the Jungle Lodge chain. Around 8km west of the centre of town.

Hotel Roopa HOTEL $$
(✆0824-2421272; www.roopahotel.com; Balmatta Rd; r incl breakfast from ₹1600; ❉🛜) Close to the KSRTC bus stand, this hotel is professionally managed and has well-presented, spacious rooms. Its restaurant serves authentic Mangalorean cuisine, and there's a bar.

Gateway Hotel HOTEL $$$
(✆0824-6660420; www.tajhotels.com; Old Port Rd; s/d incl breakfast from ₹5720/6280; ❉@🛜🏊) At this well-managed hotel (part of the Taj group) in the heart of the city the spacious rooms have a touch of class, though some retain very dated bathrooms. The lovely 20m swimming pool at the rear is surrounded by lawn and loungers, and there's a small spa and a fine restaurant. Rates are a tad steep, however.

★**Girimanja's** MANGALOREAN $$
(GKT Rd; meals ₹150-280; ⊘11.30am-3.30pm) Terrific, authentic Mangalorean food in very simple, no-nonsense surrounds and very fairly priced. Try the fish fry or prawn fry; sauces are incredibly rich and loaded with local chilli. Lunch only, and be prepared to wait.

Kadal SOUTH INDIAN $$
(Nalapad Residency, Lighthouse Hill Rd; mains ₹120-300; ⊘11am-3.30pm & 6.30-11pm; 🛜) This high-rise restaurant has wonderful city views and elegant, warmly lit interiors. Try the fish thali. Prices are moderate for the quality and experience.

Gajalee SEAFOOD $$$
(✆0824-2221900; Circuit House, Kadri Hills; mains ₹170-1280; ⊘10am-11pm; 🛜) One of Mangaluru's premier seafood restaurants, with a hillside location, sweeping views and a choice of indoor or outdoor seating. Try the clam *koshimbir*, cooked in a rich green masala, or a crab dish. Wine and beer are available, and vegetarians will also dine happily.

🍷 Drinking & Nightlife

★**Spindrift** MICROBREWERY
(https://spindrift.in; 5th fl, Bharath Mall, Lalbagh; ⊘11am-11pm; 🛜) The city's premier microbrewery is a big space with indoor and outdoor seating; the acoustic artists, indie bands and DJs create quite a vibe on weekend nights. Beers on tap (from ₹230) include wheat beer, pilsner and IPA, and there's good finger food, too.

Liquid Lounge PUB
(Balmatta Rd; ⊘10am-11.30pm; 🛜) Much more pub than lounge, this long-running place is your best bet for a beer and a chat. Expect loud rock music on the stereo. Popular with young locals and serves good comfort grub.

TRAINS FROM MANGALURU (MANGLORE)

The main train station, Mangaluru Central, is south of the city centre.

DESTINATION	TRAIN NO & NAME	FARE (₹)	DURATION (HR)	DEPARTURES
Bengaluru (Bangalore)	16512 & 16514 Bangalore Express	sleeper/2AC 255/985	10½	8.55pm
Chennai	12686 Chennai Express	sleeper/2AC 460/1735	16	4.15pm
Gokarna	16523 Karwar Express	sleeper/2AC 205/780	5	8.35pm
Gokarna	12620 Matsyaganda Express	sleeper/2AC 235/830	4	2.25pm
Thiruvananthapuram (Trivandrum)	16630 Malabar Express	sleeper/2AC 345/1355	15	6.15pm

ⓘ Getting There & Away

AIR

Mangaluru International Airport (☎ 0824-2254252; www.mangaloreairport.com) is about 15km northeast of town. There are daily flights to Mumbai, Delhi, Bengaluru, Hubballi, Hyderabad and Chennai, and international connections to Gulf locations including Abu Dhabi, Bahrain, Doha, Dubai and Muscat.

BUS

The **KSRTC bus stand** (☎ 0824-2211243; Bejai Main Rd) is 3km from the city centre. Deluxe buses depart half-hourly to Bengaluru (₹410 to ₹835, seven to nine hours) via Mysuru (₹250 to ₹520, five to six hours).

Dharmasthala

☎ 08256 / POP 10,560

Inland from Mangaluru is a string of Jain-temple towns, such as Venur, Mudabidri and Karkal. The most interesting among them is Dharmasthala village, by the Netravathi River. Tens of thousands of pilgrims pass through this tiny settlement every day. During holidays and major festivals, such as the five-day pilgrim festival of Lakshadeepotsava (p858), the footfall can go up tenfold.

◉ Sights

Manjunatha Temple HINDU TEMPLE
(⊘ 6.30am-2.30pm & 5-8.45pm) A striking Kerala-style temple with meticulously renovated woodcarvings and a pyramidal roof of gold-plated copper plates. Three elephants trunk out blessings to pilgrims outside; men have to enter bare-chested, with legs covered. You can fast-track the queue if you pay ₹200.

Car Museum MUSEUM
(₹5; ⊘ 8.30am-1pm & 2-7pm) The fantastic Car Museum is home to 48 vintage autos, including a 1903 Renault and 1920s Studebaker President used by Mahatma Gandhi, plus classic Mercedes Benz, Chevrolet and Rolls-Royce models. No photos are allowed.

Manjusha Museum MUSEUM
(₹5; ⊘ 10am-1pm & 4.30-9pm) Houses an eclectic collection of Indian stone and metal sculptures, jewellery, local craft products, cameras and stamps. It's opposite the Manjunatha temple.

🛏 Sleeping & Eating

The **temple office** (☎ 08256-277121; www.shridharmasthala.org; r from ₹500) can help you find lodging.

Rajathadri Guest House LODGE $
(www.shridharmasthala.org/accomodation; r with fan/AC ₹500/990) About 700m north of the main temple, this clean guesthouse is used by pilgrims and can be booked online. Rooms sleep up to three.

Manjunatha Temple Kitchen INDIAN
(⊘ 11.30am-2.15pm & 7.30-10pm) FREE Attached to a hall that can seat up to 3000, this place offers simple free meals. It's very efficiently managed.

ⓘ Getting There & Away

There are frequent buses to Dharmasthala from Mangaluru (₹88, 2½ hours).

Udupi

☎ 0820 / POP 184,300

Udupi is home to the atmospheric 13th-century **Krishna Temple** (www.udupisrikrishnamatha.org; Car St; ⊘ 3.30am-10pm), which draws thousands of Hindu pilgrims through the year. Surrounded by eight maths (monasteries), it's a hive of activity, with musicians playing at the entrance, elephants on hand for *puja* and pilgrims constantly coming and

KARNATAKA DHARMASTHALA

going. Non-Hindus are welcome inside the temple; men must enter bare-chested. Elaborate rituals are also performed in the temple during the Udupi Paryaya festival (p858).

Sleeping & Eating

Shri Vidyasamuda Choultry HOTEL $
(☑ 0820-2520820; Car St; r ₹180-380) This simple place has views looking over the ghat.

Hotel Sriram Residency HOTEL $
(☑ 0820-2530761; www.hotelsriramresidency.in; Head Post Office Rd; r with fan/AC from ₹1600/2400; ✳☎) A well-run place with good choice of rooms; some on the upper floors overlook the Krishna Temple. There are two bars and a good seafood restaurant here.

Samanvay Boutique Hotel HOTEL $$
(☑ 0820-6600300; www.samanvayudupi.com; s/d from ₹2000/2500; ✳☎) 'Boutique' is pushing it a tad, but this likeable hotel certainly has a modern feel, with elegant rooms and quality furnishings, including desks and flatscreen TVs. There's a cafe and two restaurants. It's fine value considering the pretty modest rates asked. It's 150m south of the town's Mahatma Gandhi stadium.

Woodlands INDIAN $
(Dr UR Rao Complex; dosa from ₹60, meals from ₹110; ☉8am-3.15pm & 5.30-10.30pm) Woodlands is regarded as the best vegetarian place in town and has an air-con dining room where you can escape the heat. Serves both South and North Indian food. It's a short walk south of Krishna Temple.

Mitra Samaja INDIAN $
(Car St; meals from ₹80; ☉8am-9pm) A famous old establishment that serves delicious snacks, dosa (lentil-flour pancakes) and coffee. Can get crowded. It's just south of the Krishna temple.

❶ Getting There & Away

Udupi is 58km north of Mangaluru along the coast; very regular buses ply the route (₹42 to ₹68, 1½ hours). There's a daily bus to Gokarna (₹184, four hours) at 2pm and many services (mostly at night) to Bengaluru (₹440 to ₹890, eight to 10 hours). Regular buses head to Malpe (₹11, 30 minutes).

Malpe
☑ 0820 / POP 2100

A laid-back fishing harbour on the west coast 4km from Udupi, Malpe has nice beaches ideal for splashing about in the surf. During weekends and holidays jet skis, banana boats and quad bikes taint the scene, however.

From Malpe pier you can take a ferry to tiny St Mary's Island, where Portuguese explorer Vasco da Gama supposedly landed in 1498. Locals sell coconuts (its nickname is Coconut Island), but otherwise there's little to eat or drink. You can take a ferry (₹250 return, 45 minutes, departing from 9am when demand is sufficient) from Malpe pier or charter a private boat from nearby Malpe Beach.

Beachfront **Paradise Isle Beach Resort** (☑ 0820-2538777; http://udupibeaches.com; r ₹3700-6700; ✳@☎☲) has comfortable rooms, many with sea views. **Houseboat** (per couple ₹4000; ☉Oct-Mar) trips around the backwaters of Hoode nearby can also be organised.

Gokarna
☑ 08386 / POP 29,200

A regular nominee among travellers' favourite beaches in India, Gokarna attracts a low-key, chilled-out beach holiday crowd, not for full-scale party people. Most accommodation is in thatched bamboo huts along the town's several stretches of blissful coast.

SURFING SWAMIS

While there's always been a spiritual bond between surfer and Mother Ocean, the **Surfing Ashram** (Mantra Surf Club; ☑ 9663141146; www.surfingindia.net; 6-64 Kolachikambla; board hire/3-day course ₹700/6600) ✎ at Mulki, 30km north of Mangaluru, takes things to a whole new plane. At this Hare Krishna ashram – established by its American guru, who's been surfing since 1963 – devotees follow a daily ritual of *puja* (prayers), chanting, meditation and vegetarian food in between catching barrels. There's surf year-round, but the best waves are May to June and September to October. If there are no waves there are SUP boards for the river or ocean, sea kayaks, and a jet ski for wakeboarding. Snorkelling trips to offshore islands are also possible. The swamis can also assist with information on surfing across India.

In fact there are two Gokarnas. For most Indian visitors Gokarna is a sacred pilgrimage town of ancient temples that are the focus of important festivals such as **Shivaratri** (⊙Feb/Mar) and Ganesh Chaturthi (p858). International travellers flock to the 'other' Gokarna: a succession of ravishing sandy beaches south of town.

◉ Sights

Temples

This is a deeply holy town and foreigners should be respectful in and around its many temples: do not try to enter their inner sanctums, which are reserved for Hindus only. It's customary for pilgrims to bathe in the sea and fast, and many shave their heads, before entering Gokarna's holy places.

★**Mahaganapati Temple**   HINDU TEMPLE
(Car St; ⊙6am-8.30pm) FREE Deeply atmospheric temple complex, encircled by lanes but peaceful inside. Here there's a (rare) stone statue of an upright, standing Ganesh, said to be over 1500 years old, who is depicted with a flat head – said to mark the spot where the demon Ravana struck him. This is the second most holy site in Gokarna and it's customary for pilgrims to visit here first before heading to the neighbouring Mahabaleshwara Temple. Foreigners are not allowed inside the inner sanctum.

★**Mahabaleshwara Temple**   HINDU TEMPLE
(Car St; ⊙6am-8.30pm) This is a profoundly spiritual temple, built of granite by Mayurasharma of the Kadamba dynasty and said to date to the 4th century. It's dedicated to Lord Shiva. Hindus believe it brings blessings to pilgrims who even glimpse it, and rituals are performed for the deceased. A *gopuram* (gateway tower) dominates the complex, while inside a stone statue of Nandi (Shiva's bull) faces the inner chamber, home to Shiva's lingam. Foreigners may enter the complex but not the inner sanctum.

Beaches

The best beaches are due south of Gokarna town: first, Kudle Beach (5km by road from Gokarna), then Om Beach (6km by road). Well hidden away south of Om Beach lie the small, sandy coves of Half Moon Bay and Paradise Beach, which don't have road access. A lovely coastal trail links all the beaches, but as there have been (very occasional) reports of muggings, it's probably best not to walk it alone.

Kudle Beach   BEACH
This lovely wide cove, backed by wooded headlands, offers plenty of room to stretch out on along its attractive sands. Restaurants, guesthouses and yoga camps are dotted around the rear of the beach, but they're well spaced and development remains peaceful and attractive.

★**Om Beach**   BEACH
One of Karnataka's best beaches, Gokarna has a famous stretch of sand that twists and turns over several kilometres to resemble the outline of an Om symbol. The beach comprises several gorgeous coves, with wide stretches interspersed with smaller patches of sand, perfect for sunbathing and swimming. There's fine swimming most of the season when the sea's not choppy, though signs officially ban it (local tourists have drowned here in rough seas). It's 6km from Gokarna town; autorickshaws cost ₹130.

Paradise Beach   BEACH
Lovely, isolated Paradise Beach is a mix of sand and rocks, and a haven for the long-term 'turn on, tune in, drop out' crowd. It's around a 45-minute walk from the southern end of Om Beach (the coastal path here passes Half Moon Bay on the way); there's no road

---

FORMULA BUFFALO

Call it an indigenous take on the Grand Prix: Kambla (traditional buffalo racing) is a hugely popular pastime for villagers along the southern Karnataka coast. Popularised in the early 20th century and born out of local farmers habitually racing their buffaloes home after a day in the fields, the races have now hit the big time. Thousands of spectators attend each edition, and racing buffaloes are pampered and prepared like thoroughbreds.

Kambla events are held between November and March, usually at weekends. Parallel tracks are laid out in a paddy field, and buffaloes hurtle along them towards the finish line. In most cases the rider travels on a board fixed to a ploughshare, literally surfing his way down the track behind the beasts. The faster creatures can cover the 120m-odd distance through water and mud in around 14 seconds!

access. Every season local entrepreneurs rig up huts (around ₹300), but the local government routinely tears them down, so it's pot luck whether you'll find a place to stay.

🏃 Activities

Cocopelli Surf School　　　　　　SURFING
(☎8105764969; www.cocopelli.org; Gokarna Beach; lessons per person ₹2000, board rental per 2hr ₹750; ⊙mid-Oct–May) This reputable surf school offers lessons by internationally certified instructors. It also rents boards and kayaks.

Shankar Prasad　　　　　　　　YOGA
(☎08386-256971;　　www.shankarprasad.org.in; Bankikodla Village) A beautiful ashram in a century-old heritage house, set in huge grounds dotted with coconut palms. Weekly and monthly courses of yoga are well structured and good value; teacher training (200 hours costs from ₹59,000 including full board) is also offered. Accommodation is in dorms or private rooms. It's 5km north of Gokarna town.

Shree Hari Yoga　　　　　　　YOGA
(☎8351068174; www.shreehariyoga.in; Kudle Beach; 90min classes ₹300; ⊙6am-6.30pm Mon-Fri, to 1pm Sat Nov-May) Inland from the beach, this well-regarded yoga school offers excellent classes (hatha, Ashtanga vinyasa and occasionally Mysore style) and teacher training. Drop-ins are available four times a day, and there's evening meditation.

🛏 Sleeping

For most foreigners Gokarna means sleeping right on the beach in a simple shack. However, there's a growing number of more upmarket lodges and hotels, so if you don't want to rough it you don't have to. Note that most places are only open from November to April and prices are very flexible depending on demand.

Zostel Gokarna　　　　　　　HOSTEL $
(☎in Dehli 011-39589002; www.zostel.com; Kudle Beach Rd; dm/cottages ₹800/2600; ❇🛜) Some of the best dorms in Karnataka, with AC, lockers and sea views, await at this efficiently managed hostel. The cottages are also very inviting, perfect for couples, and there are cool common rooms and a restaurant. Located a 10-minute walk from Gokarna town, or a bit further away from Kudle Beach.

Nirvana Café　　　　　　　GUESTHOUSE $
(☎9742466481, 8386257401; suresh.nirvana@gmail.com; Om Beach; cottages ₹750-1200; 🛜) These attractive cottages, towards the eastern

---

OFF THE BEATEN TRACK

MURUDESHWAR

A worthwhile stopover for those taking the coastal route from Gokarna to Mangaluru, Murudeshwar is a beachside pilgrimage town. It's most notable for its colossal seashore statue of Lord Shiva, which sits directly on the shore overlooking the Arabian Sea, making for spectacular photo ops. For the best views, take the lift 18 storeys to the top of the skyscraper-like **Shri Murudeshwar temple** (lift ₹10; ⊙lift 7.45am-12.30pm & 3.15-6.45pm).

Around 500m from Murudeshwar beach, **Hotel Kawari's Palm Grove** (☎08385-260178; r with fan/AC from ₹700/1250; ❇) has basic but clean and spacious rooms. **Mavalli Beach Heritage Home** (☎9901767993; http://mavalli beachheritage.com; r incl breakfast ₹4300; ❇🛜) is a beachfront homestay with four stylish rooms and a warm ambience courtesy of the genial owners.

Murudeshwar is 3km off the main highway. It's accessed by trains and buses passing up and down the coast.

---

end of the beach, are some of Om's best, all with front porches that face a slim central garden. You'll find a good beachfront restaurant, a laundry and a travel agency.

Half Moon Garden Cafe　　　BUNGALOW $
(☎9743615820; Half Moon Bay; huts from ₹400; ⊙Nov-Apr) 🌿 A throwback to the hippie days, this hideaway has a blissful beach and pretty decent, well-kept huts in a coconut grove. It runs on solar power.

Strawberry Farmhouse　　　GUESTHOUSE $
(☎7829367584; Kudle Beach; r ₹800-1300; ❇🛜) Right on the sands at the northern section of Kudle, these spacious cottages (some with AC) all have verandahs, 24-hour hot water and prime water views.

Greenland Guesthouse　　　GUESTHOUSE $
(☎9019651420; r from ₹500; 🛜) Hidden down a jungle path at the edge of town, this mellow, family-run guesthouse has clean rooms in vibrant colours and a lovely verdant garden to enjoy.

White Elephant　　　　　GUESTHOUSE $$
(Arnav Cottages; ☎7090332555; http://white elephanthampi.com; cottages ₹2000-3000; ❇🛜) Well-constructed, spacious cottages and fine

RANI ABBAKKA

The legendary exploits of Rani Abbakka, one of India's first freedom fighters, get little attention outside the Mangaluru region. Her inspiring story is just waiting to be picked up by a Bollywood/Hollywood screenwriter.

As the Portuguese consolidated power along India's western coastline in the 16th century, seizing towns across Goa and down to Mangalore, their attempts to take Ullal proved less successful. This was thanks to its queen, who proved to be a major thorn in their grand plans to control the lucrative spice trade. Her continual efforts to repel their advances is the stuff of local legend.

Well trained in the art of war, in both strategy and combat, Rani Abbakka knew how to brandish a sword. And while she was eventually defeated, this wasn't from a loss on the battlefield but due to her treacherous ex-husband, who conspired against her by leaking intelligence to the enemy.

Her efforts to rally her people to defeat the powerful Portuguese is not forgotten by locals: Rani Abbakka is immortalised in a bronze statue on horseback at the roundabout on the road to Ullal beach, and an annual festival is dedicated to her.

The shore temple that looks over the beautiful Someshwara beach a few kilometres south of Ullal marks the site of her fort, but only sections of its wall remain intact.

sea views are the main draws at this established place (previously called Arnav) above Kudle Beach. It's run by hospitable folk and there's an elevated deck perfect for yoga.

Arya Ayurvedic
Panchakarma Centre SPA HOTEL $$
(☑9611062468; www.ayurvedainindien.com; Kudle Beach; r from ₹1900; ❄☎) At the southern end of Kudle (p896), this ayurvedic centre has some of the best rooms on the beach. It offers simple yet elegant accommodation with quality furnishings a few steps from the shore. Priority is given to those booking ayurvedic packages. There's a fine in-house cafe (p899).

Kudle Beach View Resort & Spa HOTEL $$
(☑8130967666; http://kudlebeachview.com; r ₹4500-6000; ❄☎☀) There are mesmerising views of the ocean from this hotel's restaurant, high above Kudle Beach. Rooms, all modern and well equipped, are located well below, accessed by numerous steps. A new accommodation block was nearing completion at the time of research.

★ SwaSwara HOTEL $$$
(☑08386-257132; www.swaswara.com; s/d 5 nights from €1780/2390; ❄@☎☀) 'Journeying into the self' is the mantra at SwaSwara and you certainly have the infrastructure to achieve that here, as this is one of South India's finest retreats. Yoga, ayurvedic treatments, a meditation dome, and elegant private villas with open-sky showers and lovely sitting areas await. No short stays are possible. It's inland from Om Beach.

Namaste Yoga Farm BUNGALOW $$$
(☑9739600407; www.spiritualland.com; Kudle Beach; incl breakfast & 2 yoga classes r €69-88; ☎) Cottages and rooms are scattered around a shady hillside plot in this Kudle institution, located above the beach and owned by a very amiable German yoga instructor. The accommodation is a little prosaic and perhaps a tad overpriced, but the yoga and breakfast (cooked to order) are exceptional and the vibe is very welcoming.

✕ Eating

★ Prema INDIAN $
(Gokarna Beach Rd; mains ₹100-200; ⊗8am-10pm) Always packed, this humble-looking place has a prime location just before the town beach. It offers Western food, but it's best to stick to the South or North Indian classics. Finish your meal with a rose or coconut ice cream (₹15).

Sunset Point INDIAN $
(Om Beach; mains ₹120-200; ⊗7.30am-10pm) Family-run place at the eastern end of Om Beach with a great perch overlooking the waves. The long menu takes in breakfasts, sandwiches, and Indian and Chinese dishes; grilled prawns are around ₹200.

Chez Christophe FRENCH $$
(☑9901459736; www.facebook.com/chezchristoff; Gokarna Town Beach; mains from ₹150; ⊗Nov-May; ☎) For a very different vibe, stroll up the shore to this chilled French place, a 10-minute walk north from the main section of beach. You'll find authentic salads, fresh pasta, French desserts and wine by the glass.

KARNATAKA GOKARNA

There's low seating, beach swings, and live music some nights.

Arya Ayurvedic
Panchakarma Centre   INDIAN $$
(www.ayurvedainindien.com; Kudle Beach; mains ₹130-220; ☺ 8am-10pm; ☎) Modish beachfront restaurant that boasts an open kitchen and a fine menu of vegetarian dishes freshly prepared using ayurvedic principles.

Namaste Cafe   MULTICUISINE $$
(Om Beach; mains ₹115-450; ☺ 8.30am-4pm & 6-11pm; ☎) This attractive double-deck affair on Om Beach has dreamy, romantic ocean views (you can watch sea eagles soaring over the waves from your table), cold beer, and good seafood, pasta and Indian dishes.

🔒 Shopping

Organic & Herbals   HEALTH & WELLNESS
(Car St; ☺ 10am-9pm) A fine selection of natural beauty products, including handmade soaps, health foods, tea and spices. Prices are very fair.

Shree Radhakrishna Bookstore   BOOKS
(Car St; ☺ 10am-8pm) Postcards, maps and secondhand novels.

ℹ Information

MONEY
There are several ATMs in Gokarna town, including a SBI ATM (Main St).

POST
Post Office (Main St; ☺ 10am-4.30pm Mon-Sat)

ℹ Getting There & Away

BUS
Local and private buses depart daily to Bengaluru (₹510 to ₹724, 12 hours) and Mysuru (from ₹578, 12 hours), as well as Mangaluru (from ₹266, 6½ hours) and Hubballi (₹198, four hours).

For Hampi, Paulo Travels (p907) is a popular choice (November to April only); its buses head via Hosapete (fan/AC ₹1400/1650, nine hours). Note that if you're coming from Hampi, you'll be dropped at Ankola, from where there's a free transfer for the 26km journey to Gokarna.

There are also regular buses to Panaji (Panjim; ₹135, three hours) and Mumbai (₹768 to ₹1035, 12 hours).

TRAIN
Many express trains stop at Gokarna Rd station, 9km from town. There are other options from Ankola, 26km away. Hotels and travel agencies in Gokarna can book tickets.

Of the three daily trains to Mangaluru the 3.12pm Bengaluru Express (sleeper/2AC ₹235/780, 5½ hours) is the most convenient. Heading to Margoa (Madgaon) there are three daily trains; the 8.42am (sleeper/2AC ₹170/745, 2½ hours) continues on to Mumbai (sleeper/2AC ₹460/1750, 12 hours).

Autorickshaws charge ₹230 to go to Gokarna Rd station (₹450 to Ankola); a bus from Gokarna town charges ₹30 and leaves every 30 minutes.

CENTRAL KARNATAKA

Hampi
☑ 08394 / POP 3600

The magnificent ruins of Hampi dot an unearthly landscape that has captivated travellers for centuries. Heaps of giant boulders perch precariously over kilometres of undulating terrain, the rusty hues offset by jade-green palm groves, banana plantations and paddy fields. While it's possible to see this World Heritage Site in a day or two, plan on lingering for a while.

The main travellers' ghetto has traditionally been Hampi Bazaar, a village crammed with budget lodges, shops and restaurants, and towered over by the majestic Virupaksha Temple. Tranquil Virupapur Gaddi, across the river, has become a popular hang-out. However, recent demolitions (p900) in both areas have seen businesses closed.

Direct daily flights to Jindal Vijaynagar Airport, 35km south of the ruins, mean that Hampi has never been more accessible.

History
Hampi and its neighbouring areas are mentioned in the Hindu epic Ramayana as Kishkinda, the realm of the monkey gods. In 1336 Telugu prince Harihararaya chose Hampi as the site for his new capital Vijayanagar, which – over the next couple of centuries – grew into one of the largest Hindu empires in Indian history. By the 16th century it was a thriving metropolis of about 500,000 people, its busy bazaars dabbling in international commerce and brimming with precious

---

ℹ HAMPI RUINS TICKET

Your ticket for Vittala Temple entitles you to same-day admission to most of the paid sites across the ruins (including around the Royal Centre and the Archaeological Museum), so don't lose it.

stones and merchants from faraway lands. All this, however, ended at a stroke in 1565, when a confederacy of Deccan sultanates razed Vijayanagar to the ground, striking it a blow from which it never recovered.

◉ Sights

Set over 36 sq km, the Hampi area has some 3700 monuments to explore – it would take months if you were to do it all justice. The ruins are divided into two main areas: the Sacred Centre around Hampi Bazaar with its temples, and the Royal Centre towards Kamalapuram, where the Vijayanagara royalty lived and governed.

◉ Sacred Centre

★ **Vittala Temple**   HINDU TEMPLE
(Map p904; Indian/foreigner/child under 15yr ₹40/500/free; ⊙8.30am-5.30pm) Hampi's most exquisite structure, the 16th-century Vittala Temple stands amid boulders 2.5km from Hampi Bazaar. Work possibly started here during the reign of Krishnadevaraya (r 1509–29). The structure was never finished or consecrated, yet its incredible sculptural work remains the pinnacle of Vijayanagar art. The courtyard's ornate stone chariot (illustrated on the ₹50 note) is the temple's showpiece and represents Vishnu's vehicle with an image of Garuda within. Its wheels were once capable of turning.

The outer 'musical' pillars, supposedly designed to replicate 81 different Indian instruments, reverberate when tapped. To protect them, authorities have placed them out of bounds. As well as the main temple, whose sanctum was illuminated using a design of reflective waters, you'll find the marriage hall and the prayer hall, to the left and right, respectively, as you enter.

★ **Virupaksha Temple**   HINDU TEMPLE
(Map p902; ₹2, camera/video ₹50/500; ⊙dawn-dusk) The focal point of Hampi Bazaar is this temple, one of the city's oldest structures, and Hampi's only remaining working temple. The main *gopuram* (gateway), almost 50m high, was built in 1442; a smaller one was added in 1510. The main shrine is dedicated to Virupaksha, an incarnation of Shiva.

An elephant called Lakshmi blesses devotees as they enter, in exchange for donations; she gets time off for a morning bath down by the river **ghats** (Map p902).

HAMPI BAZAAR DEMOLITIONS

While in 1565 it was the Deccan sultanates who levelled Vijayanagar, today a different battle rages in Hampi, between conservationists bent on protecting Hampi's architectural heritage and the locals who have settled there.

In 1999 Unesco placed Hampi on its list of World Heritage Sites in danger because of 'haphazard informal urbanisation' around the temples, particularly the ancient bazaar area near Virupaksha Temple. The government consequently produced a master plan that aimed to classify all of Hampi's ruins as protected monuments. After years of inaction this plan was dramatically and forcefully executed in July 2011. Shops, hotels and homes in the ancient bazaar were bulldozed overnight, reducing the atmospheric main strip to rubble in hours; 1500 villagers who'd made the site a living monument were evicted.

Business owners were compensated with small plots of land, some as far away as the village of Kaddirampur, 18km from the bazaar. There was talk of new guesthouses opening up there, but due to its distance from Hampi few bothered to build. Meanwhile, the displaced still await their payouts.

Then in May 2016 history repeated itself: homes, guesthouses and shops in the old village of Virupapur Gaddi were demolished. Larger establishments avoided the clearance by contesting eviction orders in court. Angry locals blame the Hampi World Heritage Area Management Authority (HWHAMA) and the Archaeological Survey of India (ASI) for the demolitions and argue that the master plan is causing a lifeless 'museumification' of what was a vibrant cultural monument.

The main temple road today is devoid of buildings and bustle, and legendary hang-outs like the (original) Mango Tree have been knocked down. By late 2018 things seemed to have stabilised: Hampi Bazaar still exists as an enclave of guesthouses and restaurants north of Virupaksha Temple and businesses were also open over the river in Virupapur Gaddi. But the future for both areas remains uncertain.

Lakshimi Narasmiha · HINDU TEMPLE
(Map p904) An interesting stop along the road to Virupaksha Temple is the 6.7m monolithic statue of the bulging-eyed Lakshimi Narasmiha in a cross-legged lotus position and topped by a hood of seven snakes.

Sule Bazaar · HISTORIC SITE
(Map p904) Halfway along the path from Hampi Bazaar to Vittala Temple, a track to the right leads over the rocks to deserted Sule Bazaar, one of ancient Hampi's principal centres of commerce and reputedly its red-light district. A near-kilometre-long stone colonnade flanking its eastern side is very well preserved. At the southern end of this area is the beautiful 16th-century Achyutaraya Temple.

★ Achyutaraya Temple · HINDU TEMPLE
(Tiruvengalanatha Temple; Map p904) At the southern end of Sule Bazaar is the beautiful Achyutaraya Temple, dating from 1534, one of the last great monuments constructed before the fall of Hampi. You approach the temple via two partly ruined *gopuram* (gateways). The central hall boasts elaborately carved pillars and sculptures, including Krishna dancing with a snake. Its isolated location at the foot of Matanga Hill makes it quietly atmospheric – doubly so since it's rarely visited.

Hemakuta Hill · HISTORIC SITE
(Map p904) To the south, overlooking Virupaksha Temple, Hemakuta Hill has a scattering of early ruins, including monolithic sculptures of Narasimha (Vishnu in his man-lion incarnation) and Ganesh. It's worth the short walk up for the view.

Nandi Statue · STATUE
(Map p904) At the eastern end of Hampi Bazaar is a Nandi statue, around which stand some of the colonnaded blocks of the ancient marketplace. This is the main location for Vijaya Utsav (p902), the Hampi arts festival.

◉ Royal Centre & Around

While it can be accessed by a 2km foot trail from the Achyutaraya Temple, the Royal Centre is best reached via the Hampi–Kamalapuram road. A number of Hampi's major sites stand here.

Zenana Enclosure · RUINS
(Map p904; Indian/foreigner ₹40/500; ⊗8.30am-5.30pm) Northeast of the Royal Centre, within the walled ladies' quarters, is the Zenana Enclosure. Its peaceful grounds and manicured lawns feel like an oasis in the arid surrounds. The Lotus Mahal and Elephant Stables are found here.

Queen's Bath · RUINS
(Map p904; ⊗8.30am-5.30pm) South of the Royal Centre you'll find various temples and waterworks, including the Queen's Bath, deceptively plain on the outside but amazing within, featuring Indo-Islamic architecture.

Archaeological Museum · MUSEUM
(Map p904; Kamalapuram; ⊗10am-5pm Sat-Thu) Boasts a fine collection of sculpture from local sites, plus neolithic tools, 16th-century weaponry and a large floor model of the Vijayanagar ruins. Don't miss the information panels: one details the king's daily rituals, which included drinking 400ml of sesame oil, followed by a wrestling match and then a horse ride, all before daybreak!

Hazarama Temple · HINDU TEMPLE
(Map p904) Features exquisite carvings that depict scenes from the Ramayana, and polished black-granite pillars.

Mahanavami-diiba · RUINS
(Map p904) The Mahanavami-diiba is a 12m-high, three-tiered platform with intricate carvings and panoramic vistas of the walled complex of ruined temples, stepped tanks and the king's audience hall. The platform was used as a royal viewing area for festivities, allowing the Vijayanagar royals (and visiting nobility from other regions) to preside over military parades, sporting contests and musical performances in a show of power, tradition and celebration.

🏃 Activities

Hampi Waterfalls · WATERFALL
About a 2km walk west of Hampi Bazaar, past shady banana plantations, you can scramble over the boulders to reach the attractive Hampi 'waterfalls', a series of small whirlpools among the rocks amid superb scenery.

Bouldering
Hampi is the undisputed bouldering capital of India. The entire landscape is a climber's adventure playground made of granite crags and boulders, some bearing the marks of ancient stonemasons. *Golden Boulders* (2013), by Gerald Krug and Christiane Hupe, has a tonne of info on bouldering in Hampi.

Hampi Bazaar

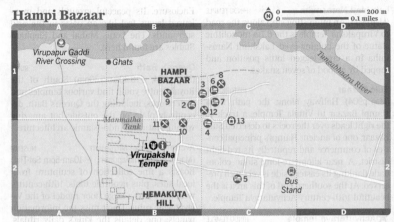

Thimmaclimb
CLIMBING

(Map p904; ☑ 8762776498; www.thimmclimb.
wix.com/hampi-bouldering; Virupapur Gaddi;
classes from ₹500) Established operation run
by local pro Thimma, who guides, runs lessons and stocks professional equipment for
hire and sale. He also runs three-day trips
(₹5000) to Badami for sandstone climbing.

Tom & Jerry
CLIMBING

(Map p904; ☑ 8277792588, 9482746697; http://
climbingshop.hampivillage.com; Virupapur Gaddi;
2½hr classes ₹600) Two local lads who are
doing great work in catering to climbers'
needs, providing quality mats, shoes and
regional knowledge, and running climbing
sessions. They also offer rappelling and
slacklining classes (each ₹500).

Birdwatching

Get in touch with the Kishkinda Trust
(p906) in Anegundi for info on birdwatching in the area, which has over 230 species,
including the greater flamingo. *The Birds of
Hampi* (2014), by Samad Kottur, is the definitive guide.

✼ Festivals & Events

Golden Boulders
SPORTS

(☑ 9482746697; http://goldenbouldersfestival.
hampivillage.com; ☺ Jan) Golden Boulders is
a non-competitive 10-day outdoor climbing
festival. Organised by local climbers Tom &
Jerry (p902), it also features yoga, bouldering on new routes and slacklining.

Vijaya Utsav
CULTURAL

(Hampi Festival; ☺ Jan) Hampi's three-day extravaganza of culture, heritage and the arts.

Virupaksha Car Festival
RELIGIOUS

(☺ Mar/Apr) This big event features a colourful procession characterised by a giant
wooden chariot (the temple car from Virupaksha Temple) being pulled along the main
strip of Hampi Bazaar.

🛏 Sleeping

Most guesthouses are cosy, family-run digs,
perfect for the budget traveller. Walk-in
rates are usually much better than those found
online. More upmarket places are located
further from the centre. Some tour operators
base their clients in Hosapete, a grim town
that's a world away from Hampi in terms of
ambience. Nearby Anegundi (p906) also has
good accommodation.

🛏 Hampi Bazaar

This little enclave is a classic travellers' ghetto. However, its existence is under threat as
there are plans to demolish it.

★ Manash Guesthouse
GUESTHOUSE $

(Map p902; ☑ 9448877420; manashhampi@gmail.
com; r with fan/AC ₹1350/1600; ❄ ☎) This place
consists of just two rooms set off a little yard,
but they're the best in Hampi Bazaar, each
with quality mattresses, attractive decorative
touches and free, fast wi-fi. It's owned by the
Mango Tree (p905) people just along the lane,
so if no one is around ask in the restaurant.

Thilak Homestay
GUESTHOUSE $

(Map p902; ☑ 9449900964; www.facebook.com/
thilak.homestay; r with fan/AC ₹1300/2000; ❄ ☎)
A step up from most places in the bazaar,
this clean, orderly place has eight well-
presented rooms (and more in another

Hampi Bazaar

◉ Top Sights
1 Virupaksha Temple B2

🛏 Sleeping
2 Ganesh Guesthouse............................. B1
3 Gopi Guest House................................ C1
4 Manash Guesthouse C2
5 Padma Guest House............................. C2
6 Pushpa Guest House............................ C1
7 Thilak Homestay.................................. C1

🍴 Eating
8 Chill Out C1
9 Gopi Roof Restaurant B1
10 Mango Tree B2
11 Moonlight... B2
12 Ravi's Rose C1

🛍 Shopping
13 Akash Art Gallery &
Bookstore...C2

block) that have spring mattresses and hot water. Owner Kish is very helpful and can arrange a reliable autorickshaw driver or make other transport arrangements.

Pushpa Guest House GUESTHOUSE $
(Map p902; ☏ 9448795120; pushpaguesthouse99@ yahoo.in; d from ₹1000, with AC from ₹1700; ❋🛜) A decent all-rounder with comfortable, attractive and well-presented rooms that have mosquito nets. It has a lovely roof terrace and a reliable travel agency.

Ganesh Guesthouse GUESTHOUSE $
(Map p902; vishnuhampi@gmail.com; r ₹600-900, with AC from ₹1500; ❋🛜) The small, welcoming, family-run Ganesh has been around for over 20 years and has four tidy rooms. Also has a nice rooftop restaurant.

Padma Guest House GUESTHOUSE $
(Map p902; ☏ 08394-241331; padmaguesthouse@ gmail.com; d ₹900-2000; ❋🛜) Slightly more upmarket than many guesthouses in the bazaar area, this place has a choice of basic, decent rooms, many with views of Virupaksha Temple, though facilities and bathrooms could do with an upgrade. Still, the owners are helpful and can arrange autorickshaw drivers, bikes and onward transport.

Gopi Guest House GUESTHOUSE $$
(Map p902; ☏ 08394-241695; www.facebook. com/gopiguesthouse; r with fan/AC ₹2000/2500; ❋@🛜) A dependable, welcoming place split over two properties on the same street. Gopi offers friendly service and has good-quality rooms that are almost upscale by Hampi standards. There are fine views from its rooftop cafe.

🏠 Virupapur Gaddi & Around

The rural tranquillity of village-like Virupapur Gaddi, across the river from Hampi Bazaar, has real appeal for long-term travellers. Its many nicknames include 'The Island', 'Hippy Island', and 'Little Jerusalem' as it's particularly popular with Israelis.

Sunny Guesthouse GUESTHOUSE $
(Map p904; ☏ 9448566368; www.sunny guesthouse.com; Virupapur Gaddi; r ₹600-1500; @🛜) Sunny both in name and disposition, this popular guesthouse is a hit among backpackers for its characterful huts, very well-maintained tropical garden, hammocks and chilled-out restaurant.

Shanthi GUESTHOUSE $
(Map p904; ☏ 8533287038; http://shanthi hampi.com; Virupapur Gaddi; cottages ₹1300-1850; 🛜) Shanthi offers attractive, earth-themed thatched cottages with couch swings dangling in their front porches. The location is stunning, with a row of cottages directly overlooking rice fields. The only drawback is that the restaurant's food is below par, but with many alternatives on your doorstep that's not a huge concern.

Hampi's Boulders LODGE $$$
(☏ 9448034202, 9480904202; www.hampis boulders.com; Narayanpet; r incl full board from ₹7100; ❋🛜❄) This 'eco-wilderness' resort is 10km west of Virupapur Gaddi by the Tungabhadra River. It's an isolated but supremely relaxed place to escape, with a choice of cottages that have elegant furnishings and river views. There's a stunning natural pool for chlorine-free swims. Rates include a guided walk, and the restaurant's food uses ingredients from its organic farm. Limited wi-fi.

🏠 Kamalapuram & Around

★ Shankar Homestay HOMESTAY $$
(Map p904; ☏ 9482169619; hanumayana@ gmail.com; Ballari; r incl breakfast with fan/ AC ₹2000/2300; ❋🛜) Lovely family-run homestay in a tranquil rural location around 2km west of the Royal Centre (bikes are available). The five spacious rooms are

Hampi & Anegundi

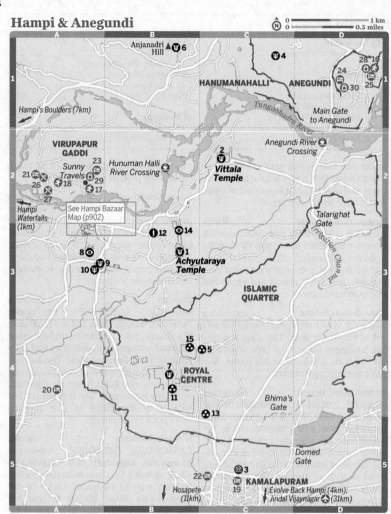

furnished with handmade textiles and crafts, and the ever-helpful, welcoming hosts' cooking is superb: be sure to try dinner here.

Clarks Inn
HOTEL $$

(Map p904; ☎08394-241245; www.clarksinn.in; HCP Rd, Kamalapuram; r ₹3300-4500; ❄️🛜🏊) A tempting new option in Kamalapuram, this modern hotel has inviting, very clean rooms with contemporary decor and flatscreen TVs. The pool is a small indoor affair. It's right opposite the Archaeological Museum (p901).

Sri Sai Baba Lodge
GUESTHOUSE $$

(Map p904; ☎8050144139; www.facebook.com/sri-sai-baba-lodgehomestay-209949712953731; Kamalapuram; r ₹1800-2400; ❄️🛜) A new lodge with neat, clean and orderly rooms, some with four beds, and a welcoming staff. Located on the south side of the ruins in Kamalapuram, close to the museum.

Evolve Back Hampi
LUXURY HOTEL $$$

(www.evolveback.com/hampi; Hallikeri Village; ste from ₹23,000; ❄️🛜🏊) Seriously stylish new place with stunning accommodation. Book a terrace suite for maharaja-size space, in-

Hampi & Anegundi

cluding your own hot tub. The grounds are gorgeous, the staff kindly and efficient, and the facilities good. As it's isolated, around 6km from the Royal Centre, consider a half-board package. Book via the resort's website for the best deal.

✕ Eating

Gouthami   MULTICUISINE $
(Map p904; mains ₹80-250; ☺8am-11pm) A well-run place with cushion seating (or dining tables) and an excess of psychedelic wall hangings. Serves tasty Indian, Israeli and Western classics. There's an espresso machine (cappuccinos ₹120), and it also offers good Turkish coffee and cardamom tea.

Moonlight   MULTICUISINE $
(Map p902; mains ₹80-160; ☺7.30am-10pm) A family-owned place right behind Virupaksha Temple that serves good breakfasts, pancakes, curries and espresso coffee.

Chill Out   MULTICUISINE $
(Map p902; mains ₹90-300; ☺8am-10.30pm; 🛜) Atmospheric rooftop restaurant with cushion seating and lantern lighting, and a menu of curries and Western favourites, including good pizza.

Laughing Buddha   MULTICUISINE $
(Map p904; Virupapur Gaddi; mains from ₹80; ☺8am-10pm; 🛜) Down a lane off the main drag in Virupapur Gaddi, this well-regarded place has serene river views that stretch over to Hampi's temples. Its menu includes curries, burgers and pizzas; you dine on low tables and cushions. Cash only.

Ravi's Rose   MULTICUISINE $
(Map p902; mains from ₹100; ☺8am-10.30pm; 🛜) A social hang-out, with a good selection of dosa and thalis, but most folks are here for the, erm, special lassis (cough).

★Mango Tree   MULTICUISINE $$
(Map p902; mains ₹130-310; ☺7.30am-9.30pm) Hampi's most famous restaurant has relocated to an atmospheric tented restaurant in the bazaar but is still run by three generations of the same local family. It's an efficiently managed place with good service and delicious Indian cuisines served on banana leaves. Try a thali.

Gopi Roof Restaurant   MULTICUISINE $$
(Map p902; www.facebook.com/gopiguesthouse; mains ₹130-300; ☺8am-10pm; 🛜) Serves up flavoursome Indian, Chinese and Israeli food, and even the Mexican grub (try the veg enchiladas) is quite tasty. Sip a lassi (₹60) or masala chai (₹30) while you're waiting for your meal.

🔒 Shopping

Gali Djembe Music Shop   MUSICAL INSTRUMENTS
(Map p904; ☎9449982586; www.facebook.com/pg/galidurugappa; Virupapur Gaddi; ☺10am-7pm) Run by an amiable musician who teaches djembe (drums) and didgeridoo, this store sells Indian and Western musical instruments at fair prices.

KARNATAKA HAMPI

Akash Art Gallery & Bookstore

BOOKS

(Map p902; ⏰7am-9pm) Excellent selection of books on Hampi and India, plus secondhand fiction. The owner offers a free Hampi map and sells postcards, too.

ℹ️ Information

DANGERS & ANNOYANCES

Hampi is generally a safe, peaceful place. However, exercise standard precautions and don't wander around the ruins after dark. Women should avoid being alone in the more remote parts of the site. Note that alcohol and narcotics are illegal in Hampi, and possession can get you into trouble.

MONEY

There's no ATM in Hampi or Virupapur Gaddi, but both have moneychangers. You'll find three ATMs in Kamalapuram (3km away) and one in Anegundi, on the other side of the river.

ℹ️ Getting There & Around

Hosapete is the gateway to Hampi. There's only one daily direct (very slow) bus from Hampi Bazaar to Goa (₹725, 11 hours, 7pm). Travel agents can book bus tickets to Bengaluru (from ₹600, seven hours, several at 11pm), Hyderabad (from ₹820, nine hours, four nightly), Mumbai (from ₹950, 14 hours, many nightly), Mysuru (₹750, 12 hours, 9.30pm) and other destinations; many of these include a minibus transfer from Hampi to Hosapete.

Local buses departing from the **stand** (Map p902) connect Hampi with Hosapete (₹18, 30 minutes, half-hourly) between 5.45am and 7.30pm. An autorickshaw costs around ₹180. For Badami, travel via Hosapete.

Hosapete is Hampi's nearest train station. **Sunny Travels** (Map p904; ☎9448969809; hampisunnytravels@gmail.com; ⏰9.30am-7pm) can help with bookings.

Jindal Vijaynagar Airport, 35km south of Hampi, has recently been upgraded and has daily TruJet flights to Bengaluru and Hyderabad.

Anegundi

☎08394 / POP 5300

Anegundi is an ancient fortified village that's part of the Hampi World Heritage Site, but it predates Hampi by way of human habitation. The settlement has been spared the blight of commercialisation, and retains a delightfully rustic feel: the seasons dictate the cycle of change and craft traditions endure. It's accessed by a river crossing or via a long loop from Virupapur Gaddi.

👁 Sights & Activities

Hanuman Temple

HINDU TEMPLE

(Anjaneya Hill Temple; Map p904; ⏰dawn-dusk) Whitewashed Hanuman Temple, accessible by a 570-step climb up Anjanadri Hill, has fine views of the surrounding rugged terrain. Many believe that this is the birthplace of Hanuman, the Hindu monkey god who was Rama's devotee and helped him in his mission against Ravana. The hike up is pleasant, though you'll be courted by impish monkeys. At the temple you may encounter chillum-puffing sadhus (ascetics). It's a very popular sunset spot, with panoramic views over the Hampi region.

Durga Temple

HINDU TEMPLE

(Map p904; ⏰dawn-dusk) An ancient shrine close to Anegundi village that's worth a visit. The journey from Anegundi is very beautiful, through classic Hampi terrain of ochre boulders and rice paddies.

Kishkinda Trust

VOLUNTEERING

(TKT; Map p904; ☎08533-267777; http://tkt kishkinda.org; Main Rd) 🖉 For cultural events, activities and volunteering opportunities, get in touch with Kishkinda Trust, an NGO based in Anegundi that works with local people.

🛏 Sleeping

Peshegaar Guest House

GUESTHOUSE $

(Map p904; ☎9449972230; www.uramma heritagehomes.com; Hanumanahalli; d ₹1344; 🖥) This heritage house has five simple yet stylish rooms decorated with tribal textiles around a pleasant common area with a courtyard garden. Bathrooms are shared, but there are four.

⭐Uramma Cottage

COTTAGE $$$

(Map p904; ☎9448284658; www.uramma heritagehomes.com; s/d incl breakfast ₹2688/5310; 🖥) A wonderfully atmospheric lodge with rustic-chic cottages scattered around a large, grassy plot. The attention to detail is evident in the chunky wooden furniture, lovely bed linen and handmade textiles that add a splash of colour. Staff members couldn't be more helpful, and the restaurant serves very fine food (meals ₹400) and beer. Rates drop in low season.

Uramma House

GUESTHOUSE $$$

(Map p904; ☎9449972230; www.uramma heritagehomes.com; s/d per person ₹2688/5310; 🖥) This 4th-century heritage house is a gem, with traditional-style rooms featuring exposed beams and boutique touches. It has two bedrooms and a dining room, and is ideal for a family or small group.

Shopping

Kishkinda   ARTS & CRAFTS
(Map p904; http://tktkishkinda.org; Uramma Cottage; 9am-5pm) Fair-trade shop selling handwoven textiles, banana-fibre products and other crafts made in and around Anegundi village.

**Banana Fibre
Craft Workshop**   ARTS & CRAFTS
(Map p904; 10am-1pm & 2-5pm Mon-Sat) Look on at this small workshop as artisans make a range of handicrafts and accessories using the bark of a banana tree and recycled materials. It's all for sale, too.

Getting There & Away

Anegundi is 7km from Hampi, and reached by crossing the river on a boat (₹10) from the pier east of the Vittala Temple (p900). From Hampi, get here by moped or bicycle (if you're feeling energetic). An autorickshaw to the Anegundi crossing costs ₹100 from Hampi.

Hosapete (Hospet)

08394 / POP 171,200

A hectic, dusty regional city, Hosapete (still called Hospet by many) is a transport hub for Hampi. There's no reason to stay here but if you get stuck try **Hotel Malligi** (08394-228101; www.malligihotels.com; Jabunatha Rd; r ₹2400-4200, ste from ₹5000;).

Getting There & Away

Hosapete's bus stand has services to Hampi every half-hour (₹15, 30 minutes). Overnight private sleeper buses run to/from Goa (₹1000 to ₹1450, eight to 10 hours), Gokarna (₹700, 8½ hours), Bengaluru (₹540 to ₹740, seven hours), Mysuru (₹410 to ₹655, 8½ hours) and Hyderabad (₹880 to ₹1210, eight hours). Overnight buses run by **Paulo Travels** (08394-225867; www.paulobus.com) go to Gokarna and Goa.

Hosapete's train station is a ₹30 autorickshaw ride from the town centre. The 18047 Amaravathi Express heads to Margao (Madgaon), Goa (sleeper/2AC ₹225/865, 7½ hours), four times a week at 6.20am. The 16591 Hampi Express departs nightly at 9.15pm for Bengaluru (2AC/1AC ₹935/1570, nine hours) and Mysuru (₹1210/2025, 12 hours). For Hyderabad there are two to three trains per day; the 7pm service is daily (sleeper/2AC ₹305/1195, 12 hours).

Hubballi (Hubli)

0836 / POP 1,051,000

Industrial Hubballi (still called by its old name, Hubli, by many) is a hub for rail routes for Mumbai, Bengaluru, Goa and northern Karnataka. The airport also has good connections. There's no other reason to visit.

If you need to stay overnight, try the budget **Hotel Ajanta** (0836-2362216; Koppikar Rd; s/d from ₹475/600;) or the more upmarket **Hotel Metropolis** (0836-4266666; www.hotelmetropolishubli.com; Koppikar Rd; r with fan/AC from ₹1500/2500;), both near the train station.

Getting There & Away

The recently upgraded airport is 6km west of the centre of town. Four airlines offer daily flights to Ahmedabad, Bengaluru, Chennai, Goa, Kochi and Mumbai. NWKRTC air-conditioned buses connect the airport with the city's train station. A taxi is ₹230.

There are very regular services to Bengaluru, most overnight (₹430 to ₹680, seven to 8½ hours). Plenty of buses travel daily to Vijapura (₹200 to ₹276, five to six hours) and mainly night-time buses go to Hosapete (₹142 to ₹210, four hours). There are also regular connections to Mangaluru (₹480 to ₹654, seven to eight hours), Mumbai (₹725 to ₹1400, 11 to 14 hours), Mysuru (₹439 to ₹835, nine hours) and Panaji (Goa; ₹180 to ₹364, five to six hours).

From the train station, plenty of services head to Hosapete (sleeper/2AC ₹140/700, 2½ hours, six to eight daily), Bengaluru (sleeper/2AC ₹270/1050, eight to nine hours, eight daily), Mumbai (sleeper/2AC ₹380/1485, 15½ hours, one to two daily) and Goa (sleeper/3AC ₹160/700, five to six hours, one to three daily).

NORTHERN KARNATAKA

Badami

08357 / POP 32,200

Once the capital of the mighty Chalukya empire, today Badami is famous for its magnificent rock-cut cave temples, and red-sandstone cliffs that resemble the American Wild West. The scenery is stunning, once you're away from the horrible, dusty, traffic-plagued main road that cuts through town.

Badami's backstreets are fascinating to explore, with old houses, carved wooden doorways and even the occasional Chalukyan ruin.

DANDELI

Located in the jungles of the Western Ghats about 100km from Goa, emerging Dandeli is a wildlife getaway that promises close encounters with diverse exotic animals such as elephants, leopards, sloth bears, gaur, wild dogs and flying squirrels. It's a chosen birding destination, too, with resident hornbills, golden-backed woodpeckers, serpent eagles and white-breasted kingfishers. Also on offer are a slew of adventure activities ranging from kayaking to bowel-churning white-water rafting on the swirling Kali River.

Kali Adventure camp (☑08284-230266; www.junglelodges.com/kali-adventure-camp; Dandeli; per person incl full board dm/tent/r from ₹2006/4142/4994; 🔊) is a forest lodge adhering to ecofriendly principles with good accommodation in rooms or tented cottages. The camp organises white-water rafting on the Kali (possible for most of the year), guided canoe adventures, canyoning and mountain-biking trips. Rates include a jeep safari into Dandeli Wildlife Sanctuary, a coracle trip, a guided walk and all meals.

Frequent buses connect Dandeli to both Hubballi (₹60, two hours) and Dharwad (₹46, 1½ hours), with onward connections to Goa, Gokarna, Hosapete and Bengaluru.

◉ Sights

★ Cave Temples
CAVE

(Indian/foreigner incl North Fort ₹25/300, child under 15yr free, camera ₹25, tour guide ₹300; ◷9am-5.30pm) Badami's highlights are its beautiful cave temples, three Hindu and one Jain, which display exquisite sculptures and intricate carvings. They're a magnificent example of Chalukya architecture and date to the 6th century. All have a columned verandah, an interior hall and a shrine at the rear.

Cave one, just above the entrance to the complex, is dedicated to Shiva. It's the oldest of the four caves, probably carved in the latter half of the 6th century. On the wall to the right of the porch is a captivating image of Nataraja striking 18 dance moves in the one pose, backed by a cobra head. On the right of the porch area is a huge figure of Ardhanarishvara. On the opposite wall is a large image of Harihara, half Shiva and half Vishnu.

Dedicated to Vishnu, cave two is simpler in design. As with caves one and three, the front edge of the platform is decorated with images of pot-bellied dwarfs in various poses. Four pillars support the verandah, their tops carved with a bracket in the shape of a yali (mythical lion creature). On the left wall of the porch is the bull-headed figure of Varaha, the emblem of the Chalukya empire. To his left is Naga, a snake with a human face. On the right wall is a large sculpture of Trivikrama, another incarnation of Vishnu.

Cave three, carved in 578, is the largest and most impressive. On the left wall is a carving of Vishnu, to whom the cave is dedicated, sitting on a snake. Nearby is an image of Varaha with four hands. The pillars have carved brackets in the shape of yalis. The ceiling panels contain images including Indra riding an elephant, Shiva on a bull and Brahma on a swan. Keep an eye out for the image of drunken revellers, in particular one woman being propped up by her husband. There's also original colour on the ceiling; the divots on the floor at the cave's entrance were used as paint palettes. There's a sublime view from cave three over the Agastyatirtha Tank far below, and you can often hear the echoes of women thrashing clothes on its steps reverberating around the hills.

Dedicated to Jainism, cave four is the smallest of the set and dates to between the 7th and 8th centuries. The right wall has an image of Suparshvanatha, the seventh Jain *tirthankar* (teacher), surrounded by 24 Jain *tirthankars*. The inner sanctum contains an image of Adinath, the first Jain *tirthankar*.

North Fort
RUINS

(with cave temples free; ◷9am-5.30pm) High above Badami and Agastyatirtha Tank (p908), the ruins of the North Fort are worth exploring. Only the foundations remain of most of the site, but there are fortifications to investigate and restored granary towers. Of the three temples, the well-preserved 7th-century Malegitti Shivalaya temple is thought to be one of the earliest surviving examples of the Dravidian style in early Chalukya architecture. Entry included with cave-temple admission.

Archaeological Museum
MUSEUM

(₹5; ◷9am-5pm Sat-Thu) The archaeological museum houses superb examples of local sculpture, including a tremendous 12th-century *makara tokarna* (entrance decoration) that has detailed carvings on both sides and a remarkably explicit Lajja-Gauri image of a fertility cult that once flourished in the area. There are many sculptures of Shiva in different forms and there's a diorama of the Shidlaphadi cave. No photography permitted.

🏃 Activities

The bluffs and horseshoe-shaped red-sandstone cliff of Badami offer some great low-altitude climbing. **Climbing Badami** (☑ 8494809253; http://climbingbadami.in; climbing from ₹1000) organises climbs and treks in the region, as do operators in Hampi (p901).

🛏 Sleeping & Eating

Mookambika Deluxe　　　　　　HOTEL $
(☑ 08357-220067; hotelmookambika@yahoo.com; Station Rd; d with fan/AC from ₹1300/1800; ❄️🖥) For 'deluxe' read 'decent' – this hotel offers fair value, with rooms done up in matte orange and green. Staff members are a good source of travel info. It's opposite the bus stand. There's an adjoining bar-restaurant.

★ **Heritage Resort**　　　　　　HOTEL $$
(http://theheritage.co.in; Station Rd; incl breakfast r with fan/AC ₹2400/3000, cottages ₹3900; ❄️🖥) Set back from the highway, the wonderfully peaceful Heritage Resort has 14 tasteful, airy and spacious rooms and cottages with all mod cons (kettle, flatscreen TV, minibar), attractive wooden furniture and a dash of contemporary style. Management is courteous and helpful, the grounds are leafy and the **restaurant** (Heritage Resort, Station Rd; mains from ₹110; 🖥) food is very tasty. It's 2km north of the centre.

Golden Caves Cuisine　　　MULTICUISINE $
(Station Rd; mains ₹80-170; ⏱8.30am-11pm) Worth trying for North and South Indian food, though service can be a bit distracted. There's a pleasant outdoor yard at the back that's perfect for enjoying a beer.

Bridge Restaurant　　　MULTICUISINE $$
(Clarks Inn, Veerpulakeshi Circle; mains ₹195-595; ⏱6.30am-10.30pm; 🖥) Just the place when you need some AC relief, this business hotel's restaurant takes a good stab at Western dishes such as pasta and pizza, as well as Chinese and North Indian fare. South Indian breakfast items like *idli* (spongy, round, fermented rice cakes) and *vada* (doughnut-shaped deep-fried lentil savouries) with chutney and sambal are tasty, too.

ℹ️ Getting There & Away

Badami doesn't have many direct bus services. From the bus stand on Station Rd there's one direct bus to both Vijapura (₹162, four hours, 5pm) and Hubballi (₹195, five hours, 3.15pm). Three daily buses run to Bengaluru (₹388 to ₹435, 10 hours, 7am, 7.30am and 7pm); both morning services go via Hospete (₹156, four hours). Otherwise, take one of the regular buses to Kerur (₹28, 45 minutes), 23km away, which has many more connections.

Around Badami

Pattadakal
☑ 08357 / POP 1680

A secondary capital of the Badami Chalukyas, Pattadakal is known for its finely carved Hindu and Jain temples, which are collectively a World Heritage Site. The surrounding village of Pattadakal is tiny; most travellers visit the site from nearby Badami.

Barring a few that date to the 3rd century, most of Pattadakal's World Heritage-listed temples were built during the 7th and 8th centuries. The main **Virupaksha temple** (⏱6am-6pm) is a massive structure, its columns covered with intricate carvings depicting episodes from the Ramayana and Mahabharata. A giant stone sculpture of Nandi (Shiva's bull) sits to the temple's east. The Mallikarjuna temple, next to the Virupaksha temple, is almost identical in design.

Pattadakal is 20km from Badami, with buses (₹26, 45 minutes) departing every 30 minutes until about 5pm. There's a morning and an afternoon bus to Aihole (₹20), 13km away.

Aihole
☑ 08351 / POP 3200

Some 100 temples, built between the 4th and 6th centuries AD, speck the ancient Chalukyan regional capital of Aihole (*ay*-ho-leh). Most, however, are either in ruins or engulfed by the modern village. Aihole documents the embryonic stage of South Indian Hindu architecture, from the earliest simple shrines, such as the most ancient Ladkhan Temple, to later and more complex buildings, such as the Meguti Temple.

Aihole is 35km from Badami and 13km from Pattadakal.

The impressive 7th-century **Durga Temple** (Indian/foreigner ₹30/200, camera ₹25; ⏱6am-6pm) is notable for its semicircular

KARNATAKA AROUND BADAMI

apse (inspired by Buddhist architecture) and the remains of the curvilinear *sikhara* (temple spire). It's said to be the inspiration for the Parliament of India building in New Delhi. The interiors house intricate stone carvings.

Vijapura (Bijapur)

📞 08352 / POP 343,800 / ELEV 593M

A historic city epitomising the Deccan's Islamic era, Vijapura (renamed in 2014 but still widely called Bijapur) tells a glorious tale dating back some 600 years. Blessed with a heap of mosques, mausoleums, palaces and fortifications, it was the capital of the Adil Shahi kings from 1489 to 1686, and one of the five splinter states formed after the Islamic Bahmani kingdom broke up in 1482. Despite its strong Islamic character, Vijapura is also a centre for the Lingayat brand of Shaivism, which emphasises a single personalised god. The Lingayat Siddeshwara Festival (⊙ Jan/Feb) runs for eight days.

Until recently the city was somewhat lacking in tourist facilities and perhaps consequently few travellers dropped by. But new hotels have recently opened and there's now a decent selection of places to stay.

◉ Sights

★ **Golgumbaz** MONUMENT
(Indian/foreigner ₹25/300; ⊙ 6am-6pm) Set in tranquil gardens, the magnificent Golgumbaz houses the tombs of emperor Mohammed Adil Shah (r 1627–56), his two wives, his mistress (Rambha), one of his daughters and a grandson. Octagonal seven-storey towers stand at each corner of the monument, which is capped by an enormous dome. Once you're inside the sheer scale of the structure becomes apparent: its cavernous interior has a powerful, austere beauty. Climb the steep, narrow steps up one of the towers to reach the 'whispering gallery'.

Archaeological Museum MUSEUM
(₹5; ⊙ 9am-5pm Sat-Thu) A well-presented archaeological museum set in the Golgumbaz lawns. Skip the ground floor and head upstairs; there you'll find an excellent collection of artefacts, such as oriental carpets, china crockery, weapons, armour and scrolls.

★ **Ibrahim Rouza** MONUMENT
(Indian/foreigner ₹15/200; ⊙ 6am-6pm) The beautiful Ibrahim Rouza is among the most elegant and finely proportioned Islamic monuments in India. Its 24m-high minarets are said to have inspired those of the Taj Mahal, and its tale is similarly poignant: built by emperor Ibrahim Adil Shah II (r 1580–1627) as a future mausoleum for his queen, Taj Sultana. Ironically, he died before her and was thus the first person to be laid to rest here. Also interred are the emperor's queen, children and mother.

Citadel FORT
FREE Surrounded by fortified walls and a moat, the citadel once contained the palaces, pleasure gardens and durbar (royal court) of the Adil Shahi kings. Now mainly in ruins, its remaining structures are in need of urgent maintenance. The most impressive of the remaining fragments are the colossal arches of the Gagan Mahal, built by Ali Adil Shah I around 1561. The gates here are locked, but someone will be on hand to let you in.

Vijapura (Bijapur)

The ruins of Mohammed Adil Shah's seven-storey palace, the Sat Manzil, are nearby. Across the road stands the delicate Jala Manzil, once a water pavilion surrounded by secluded courts and gardens. On the other side of Station Rd (MG Rd) are the graceful arches of Bara Kaman, the ruined mausoleum of Ali Adil Shah II (Ali Roza).

Malik-e-Maidan
HISTORIC SITE

(Monarch of the Plains) Perched upon a platform is this beast of a cannon – over 4m long, almost 1.5m in diameter and estimated to weigh 55 tonnes. Cast in 1549, it was supposedly brought to Vijapura as a war trophy thanks to the efforts of 10 elephants, 400 oxen and hundreds of men!

Asar Mahal
HISTORIC BUILDING

(⊙6am-8.30pm) FREE Built by Mohammed Adil Shah in about 1646 to serve as a hall of justice, the graceful Asar Mahal once housed two hairs from Prophet Mohammed's beard. The rooms on the upper storey are decorated with frescoes and a square tank graces the front. It's out of bounds for women.

Jama Masjid
MOSQUE

(Jama Masjid Rd; ⊙9am-5.30pm) Constructed by Ali Adil Shah I (r 1557–80), the finely proportioned Jama Masjid has graceful arches, a fine dome and a vast inner courtyard with room for thousands of more worshippers. It is a sign of respect for women to cover their hair and men and women should wear modest clothing, preferably with long sleeves.

Upli Buruj
HISTORIC SITE

FREE Upli Buruj is a 16th-century, 24m-high watchtower near the western walls of the city. An external flight of stairs leads to the top, where you'll find two hefty cannons and good views of other monuments around town.

🛏 Sleeping & Eating

Hotel Madhuvan International
HOTEL $

(☑08352-255571; Station Rd; r with fan/AC from ₹1300/1800; ❊☎) Located on a quiet side street, this excellent hotel has smart rooms with cable TV, marble floors and attractive furnishings (most with desk and wardrobe). There's a courtyard garden at the front and a good restaurant.

Hotel Shubhashree Comfort
HOTEL $

(☑08352-260505; Solapur Rd; r with fan/AC from ₹1000/1300; ❊☎) On the north side of the city, this hotel offers a comfortable and affordable base. Its well-kept rooms have beds with deep mattresses and good linen. There's a decent all-veg restaurant, too.

★ Kyriad Hotel
HOTEL $$

(☑08352-254242; www.kyriadindia.com; Station Rd; incl breakfast r ₹2400-2800, ste from ₹4800; ❊☎) This fine business hotel has modern rooms equipped with flat-screen TVs (with cable) and modish furniture. Staff members are very helpful and attentive, and there's a lift and 24-hour room service. You'll enjoy the two restaurants; a bar and a gym are planned.

★ Sabala Heritage Home
HERITAGE HOTEL $$

(☑9448118204; www.sabalaheritagehome.org; Bijapur Bypass, NH-13; r incl breakfast & dinner ₹1500, with AC from ₹2500; ❊☎) ☞ At the edge of the city, this hotel has attractive, artistically decorated rooms overlooking farmland. Food is home cooked, flavoursome and inventive. The hotel is linked to an NGO that empowers women and trades fine handicrafts (there's a store here, too). It's 4.5km southeast of the centre.

Hotel Madhuvan International
INDIAN $

(Station Rd; mains ₹80-220; ⊙9-11am, noon-4pm & 7-11pm; ☎) There's a choice of indoor or

KARNATAKA VIJAPURA (BIJAPUR)

BUSES FROM VIJAPURA (BIJAPUR)

The following services leave from the **bus stand** (☑ 08352-0251344; Meenakshi Chowk Rd; ⊙24hr):

DESTINATION	FARE (₹)	DURATION (HR)	FREQUENCY
Bengaluru (Bangalore)	ordinary/sleeper 530/795	9½-11	6 daily
Bidar	270	6	5 daily
Kalaburgi (Gulbarga)	168	4	3 daily
Hosapete (Hospet)	248	5	6 daily
Hubballi (Hubli)	198-242	5	3 daily
Hyderabad	388-740	8-10	5 daily
Mumbai	660	11-13	5 daily
Panaji (Panjim; Goa)	335-455	9	2 daily

The service to Mumbai runs via Pune (₹438, eight hours).

outdoor garden seating at this fine hotel restaurant, which does fantastic vegetarian dishes, including 13 kinds of dosa (thin lentil-flour pancakes) and lots of paneer and korma dishes. Sandwiches and burgers are also available. No booze.

Haritam VEGETARIAN $$
(www.kyriadindia.com; Kyriad Hotel, Station Rd; mains ₹149-199; ⊙7am-10pm; ❈☎) Excellent South and North Indian dishes are on offer here at very fair rates; try a *paneer kadai* (cottage cheese cooked in thick tomato gravy). The premises are modern and air-conditioned, and there's an espresso machine and very warm service.

Qaswa Hills MULTICUISINE $$
(Hotel Pearl, Station Rd; mains ₹85-390; ⊙7am-4pm & 7-10pm; ☎) This basement hotel restaurant buzzes day and night with contented diners. It's renowned for its meat dishes; try a chicken or mutton biryani.

🛍 Shopping

Sabala Handicrafts ARTS & CRAFTS
(http://sabalahandicrafts.com; Bijapur Bypass, NH13; ⊙8am-5.30pm) Fair-trade store selling beautiful handmade textiles, bags, saris, kurtas and accessories. Prices start at ₹800. Profits benefit an NGO that empowers village women. It's 4km southeast of the centre.

ℹ Information

Tourist Office (☑ 08352-250359; Hotel Mayura Adil Shahi Annexe, Station Rd; ⊙10am-5.30pm Mon-Sat) With friendly staff.

ℹ Getting There & Away

There are many additional services from private-bus-company offices to Bengaluru, Hyderabad and Mumbai.

ℹ Getting Around

Given the amount to see and the distances to cover, ₹800 is a fair price to hire an autorickshaw for a full day of sightseeing. Short hops around town cost ₹50.

TRAINS FROM VIJAPURA (BIJAPUR)

The following services depart from Vijapura station.

DESTINATION	TRAIN NO & NAME	FARE (₹)	DURATION (HR)	DEPARTURES
Badami	17320 Hubli-Secunderabad Exp	sleeper/2AC 140/700	2½	1.10am & 2 other daily trains
Bengaluru (Bangalore)	16536 Golgumbaz Exp	sleeper/2AC 375/1470	15	4.55pm & 1 other daily train
Hyderabad	17319 Secunderabad Exp	sleeper/2AC 250/965	12	2.10am
Mumbai	1140 Gadag-Mumbai Exp	sleeper/2AC 350/1300	11½	6 weekly at 5.45pm, via Pune

Bidar

📞 08482 / POP 223,800 / ELEV 664M

Despite being home to amazing ruins and monuments, Bidar, hidden away in Karnataka's far-northeastern corner, gets very little tourist traffic. Drenched in Islamic Indian history, this old-walled town was first the capital of the Bahmani kingdom (1428–87) and later the capital of the Barid Shahi dynasty. This is one of the least Westernised parts of Karnataka, with many niqab-wearing women and turbaned Sikh pilgrims, and though locals are welcoming to visitors, conservative values predominate.

◎ Sights

★ Bidar Fort   FORT
(⊘ 6am-6pm) FREE The remnants of this magnificent 15th-century fort, the largest in South India – and once the administrative capital of much of the region – constitute Bidar's most famous historic site. Surrounded by a triple moat hewn out of solid red rock and many kilometres of defensive walls, the fort has a fairy-tale entrance that twists in an elaborate chicane through three gateways. Bidar Fort once had 37 bastions, several wells and a vast magazine. Reckon on a couple of hours to explore it properly.

Bahmani Tombs   HISTORIC SITE
(⊘ dawn-dusk) FREE The huge domed tombs of the Bahmani kings in Ashtur, 3km east of Bidar, were built to house the remains of the sultans, of which the stunning painted interior of 15th-century Ahmad Shah al Wali's tomb is the most impressive. Sadly, the paintings are in a very poor state today, with years of bird and bat excrement smearing the walls and virtually no internal lighting. A caretaker will likely appear and use a mirror to illuminate the art.

Khwaja Mahmud Gawan Madrasa   RUIN
(⊘ dawn-dusk) FREE Dominating the heart of the old town are the ruins of Khwaja Mahmud Gawan Madrasa, a college for advanced learning built in 1472. To get an idea of its former grandeur, check out the remnants of exquisite coloured tiles on the front gate and one of the minarets, which still stands intact. Tens of thousands of scholars from across the Islamic world once studied here.

Guru Nanak Jhira Sahib   SIKH TEMPLE
(Shiva Nagar; ⊘ 24hr) This large Sikh temple on the northwestern side of town is dedicated to the Guru Nanak and was built in 1948. It's centred on the Amrit Kund (a water tank), where pilgrims cleanse their souls.

🛏 Sleeping & Eating

Hotel Sapna Continental   HOTEL $
(📞 08482-22081; www.hotelsapnacontinental.com; Udgir Rd; r from ₹1100; ❈ 🐾) Offers good value, with spacious rooms and helpful staff. There's no restaurant, but it's right above the popular Kamat Hotel, and under the same management.

Kamat Hotel   SOUTH INDIAN $
(Udgir Rd; meals ₹60-160; ⊘ 7.30am-10pm) Scores highly for Indian staples at very affordable rates – a dhal fry is just ₹68. It's busy through the day. There's an AC room upstairs.

❶ Getting There & Away

From the bus stand, frequent buses run to Kalaburgi (Gulbarga; ₹128, three hours) and there are two evening buses to Vijapura (₹320, seven hours). There are also regular buses to Hyderabad (₹148, four hours, seven daily) and Bengaluru (semideluxe/AC ₹760/925, 13 hours, five daily).

Four daily trains head to Hyderabad, though times are not convenient; the 7.25pm service is your best bet (sleeper/2AC ₹170/745, three hours). For Bengaluru there's a daily train at 12.15pm (sleeper/1AC ₹385/2560, 17 hours).

Telangana & Andhra Pradesh

POP 89.4 MILLION

Best Places to Eat

➡ Firdaus (p927)

➡ SO – The Sky Kitchen (p927)

➡ Hotel Mayura (p944)

➡ Dhaba By Claridges (p927)

➡ TFL (p936)

Best Places to Stay

➡ Taj Falaknuma Palace (p924)

➡ Hotel Marasa Sarovar Premiere Tirupati (p943)

➡ Novotel Visakhapatnam Varun Beach (p939)

➡ Ruby Pride Luxury Hotel (p923)

➡ Taj Krishna (p924)

Why Go?

Hyderabad, one of Islamic India's greatest cities, is reason enough on its own to visit this region. Its skyline is a sight to behold, defined by the great domes and minarets of ancient mosques, mausoleums and palaces of once-mighty dynasties. Delve inside the city's fabled old quarter for fascinating street markets, Sufi shrines, teahouses and biryani restaurants. Meanwhile, Hyderabad's newer districts are awash with the upmarket restaurants of IT-fuelled economic advancement.

The other attractions of these two states (which were one entity until 2014) are less brazen, but there are hidden gems like the wonderful temple sculptures of Ramappa and ancient Buddhist sites at Sankaram and Guntupalli. Coastal Visakhapatnam has a cheery vibe, while joining the pilgrim crowds on the hike up to Tirumala's temple is an unforgettable experience.

When to Go
Hyderabad

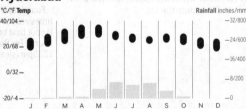

Apr–May Join locals digging into *haleem*, a Ramzan (Ramadam) favourite.

Nov–Feb Explore Hyderabad's sights in balmy 22–28°C weather.

Dec–Apr Best time to enjoy the coastal attractions – there's little rain and it's not *too* hot.

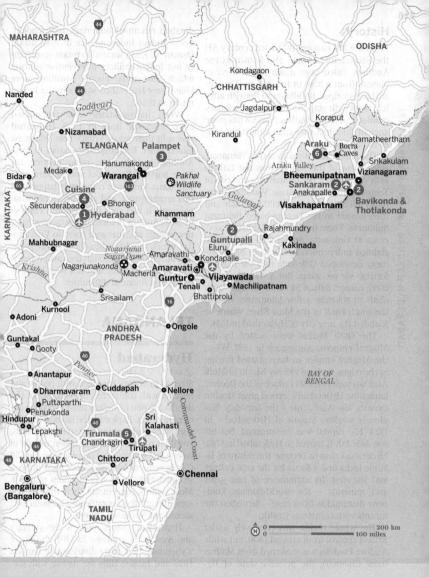

Telangana & Andhra Pradesh Highlights

1 Hyderabad (p916)
Exploring the Old City and its unique markets, architectural marvels and hidden shrines.

2 Monastic trail (p941)
Absorbing the meditative ambience at beautiful Sankaram, as well as Bavikonda, Thotlakonda and Guntupalli, all destinations on this 2300-year-old trail.

3 Palampet (p934)
Revelling in the genius of Kakatiya sculptors at the temple near this village.

4 Cuisine (p926) Feasting on fiery Andhra curries and indulging in memorable biryanis and street snacks.

5 Tirumala (p942) Going with the crowd and finding a spiritual calling with Hindu pilgrims.

6 Araku (p941) Enjoying the delightful train ride here through the lush forests and wide green valleys of the Eastern Ghats.

History

From the 3rd century BC to 3rd century AD the Satavahana empire, also known as the Andhras, ruled over much of the Deccan plateau from a base in this region. The Satavahanas helped Buddhism to flourish after it arrived with emperor Ashoka's missionary monks, and today Andhra Pradesh has more ancient Buddhist sites than almost any other Indian state.

The Hindu Kakatiyas, based at Warangal, ruled most of the region from the 12th to 14th centuries, a period that saw the rise of Telugu culture and language. Warangal eventually fell to the Muslim Delhi Sultanate and then passed to the Deccan-based Bahmani Sultanate. Then, in 1518, the Bahmanis' governor at Golconda, Sultan Quli Qutb Shah, claimed independence. His Qutb Shahi dynasty developed Golconda into the massive fortress we see today. But a water shortage there caused Sultan Mohammed Quli Qutb Shah to relocate a few kilometres east to the south bank of the Musi River, where he founded the new city of Hyderabad in 1591.

The Qutb Shahis were ousted by the Mughal emperor Aurangzeb in 1687. When the Mughal empire in turn started fraying at the edges, its local viceroy Nizam ul-Mulk Asaf Jah took control of much of the Deccan, launching Hyderabad's second great Muslim dynasty, the Asaf Jahis – the famously fabulously wealthy nizams of Hyderabad – in 1724. His capital was Aurangabad, but his son Asaf Jah II moved to Hyderabad in 1763. Hyderabad rose to become the centre of Islamic India and a focus for the arts, culture and learning. Its abundance of rare gems and minerals – the world-famous Kohinoor diamond is from here – furnished the nizams with enormous wealth.

The whole region was effectively under British control from around 1800, but while Andhra Pradesh was governed from Madras (now Chennai), the princely state of Hyderabad remained nominally independent. Come Indian Independence in 1947, nizam Osman Ali Khan wanted to retain sovereignty, but Indian military intervention (during which thousands, mainly Muslims, were killed) saw Hyderabad state join the Indian union in 1948.

When Indian states were reorganised along linguistic lines in 1956, Hyderabad was split three ways. What's now Telangana joined other Telugu-speaking areas to form Andhra Pradesh state; other districts became parts of Karnataka and Maharashtra. Telangana was never completely happy with this arrangement, and after prolonged campaigning, it was split from Andhra Pradesh in 2014. Andhra Pradesh officially now has a new capital at Amaravati (next to Vijayawada), which should eventually be smart, green and ultramodern – though the vast project is way behind schedule and has been beset by delays and financial difficulties.

TELANGANA

Hyderabad

📞 040 / POP 11.5 MILLION / ELEV 600M

Steeped in history, thronged with people and buzzing with commerce, the Old City of Hyderabad is one of India's most evocative ancient quarters. Exploring the lanes of this district, with its chai shops and spice merchants, you'll encounter a teeming urban masala of colour and commerce. Looming over the Old City is some of Islamic India's most impressive architecture, in varying states of repair. Most visitors concentrate their time in this area, though the magnificent Golconda Fort should not be missed either.

Hyderabad's other pole is far younger and west of the centre – its Hi-Tech City, or 'Cyberabad', and other districts like Banjara Hills and Jubilee Hills are replete with glit-

---

TOP STATE FESTIVALS

Sankranti (☉ Jan) This important regionwide Telugu festival marks the end of harvest season. Kite-flying abounds, doorsteps are decorated with colourful *kolams* (rice-flour designs) and men adorn cattle with bells and fresh horn paint.

Brahmotsavam (☉ Sep/Oct) This nine-day festival sees the Venkateshwara Temple at Tirumala awash in vast crowds of worshippers. Special *pujas* (offerings) and chariot processions are held, and it's an auspicious time for *darshan* (deity-viewing).

Muharram (☉ Aug/Sep) Commemorates the martyrdom of Mohammed's grandson Hussain. A huge procession throngs the Old City in Hyderabad.

Hyderabad

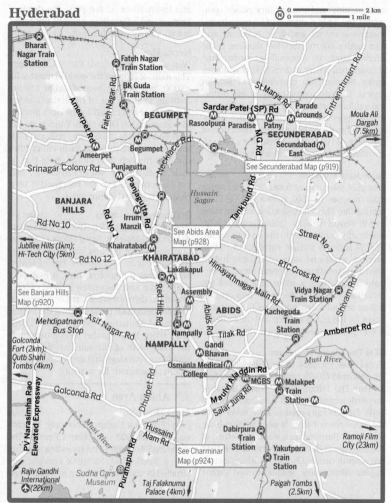

tery malls, multiplexes, clubs, pubs and sleek restaurants.

Hyderabad traffic is appalling, though with the opening of a new metro rail rapid-transit system things should ease somewhat in the coming years.

◉ Sights

◉ Old City

★Charminar   MONUMENT
(Map p924; Charminar Rd; Indian/foreigner ₹5/100; ⊙9am-5.30pm) Hyderabad's principal landmark and city symbol was built by Mohammed Quli Qutb Shah in 1591 to commemorate the founding of Hyderabad and the end of epidemics caused by Golconda's water shortage. The gargantuan four-column, 56m-high structure has four arches facing the cardinal points, with minarets atop each column (hence the name Charminar, 'four minarets'). It's certainly an impressive sight, though the relentless traffic that swirls around the structure, crowds and queues make it somewhat less rewarding to visit.

★Chowmahalla Palace   PALACE
(Map p924; off Charimar Rd; Indian/foreigner ₹50/200, camera ₹50; ⊙10am-5pm Sat-Thu) This

opulent 18th- and 19th-century palace compound, the main residence of several nizams, comprises several grandiose buildings and four garden courtyards. Most dazzling is the Khilwat Mubarak, a magnificent durbar (royal court) hall where nizams held ceremonies under 19 enormous chandeliers of Belgian crystal. Its side rooms today house historical exhibits, arts and crafts, and exhibits of nizams' personal possessions. In the southernmost courtyard is a priceless collection of carriages and vintage cars including a 1911 yellow Rolls-Royce and 1937 Buick convertible.

Salar Jung Museum   MUSEUM

(Map p924; www.salarjungmuseum.in; Salar Jung Rd; Indian/foreigner ₹20/500, camera ₹50; ☺10am-5pm Sat-Thu) This vast collection was amassed by Mir Yousuf Ali Khan (Salar Jung III), who was briefly grand vizier to the seventh nizam. The 39 galleries include early South Indian bronzes, wood and stone sculptures, Indian miniature paintings, European fine art, historic manuscripts, a room of jade and the remarkable *Veiled Rebecca* by 19th-century Italian sculptor Benzoni. Note the entrance ticket for foreigners is steep and the museum is very popular (near bedlam on Sundays).

HEH The Nizam's Museum   MUSEUM

(Purani Haveli; Map p924; off Dur-e-Sharwah Hospital Rd; adult/child ₹80/15, camera ₹150; ☺10am-5pm Sat-Thu) The Purani Haveli was a home of the sixth nizam, Mahbub Ali Khan (r 1869–1911). He was rumoured to have never worn the same thing twice: hence the 54m-long, two-storey Burmese teak wardrobe. Much of the museum is devoted to personal effects of the seventh nizam, Osman Ali Khan, including his silver cradle, gold-burnished throne

and lavish Silver Jubilee gifts. The displays, lighting and information could be improved, but it's still a worthwhile visit.

Mecca Masjid   MOSQUE

(Map p924; Shah Ali Banda Rd; ☺4.30am-9pm) This mosque is one of the world's largest, with 10,000 men praying here at major Muslim festivals, and also one of Hyderabad's oldest buildings, begun in 1617 by the city's founder Mohammed Quli Qutb Shah. Women are not allowed inside the main prayer hall, and male tourists are unlikely to be let in either (they can look through the railings). Note that female tourists, even with headscarves, may not be permitted into the courtyard if their clothing is judged inappropriate.

Badshahi Ashurkhana   ISLAMIC SITE

(Map p924; High Court Rd) The 1594 Badshahi Ashurkhana (literally Royal House of Mourning) was one of the first structures built by the Qutb Shahs in their new city of Hyderabad. Facing a huge courtyard, it is in poor shape today and desperately in need of renovation but there are some terrific tile mosaics. The Ashurkhana is packed during the Islamic festival of Muharram, as well as on Thursdays, when Shiites gather to commemorate the martyrdom of Hussain Ibn Ali. Visitors should remove shoes and dress modestly (including a headscarf for women).

☺ Abids Area

State Museum   MUSEUM

(Map p928; Public Gardens Rd, Nampally; ₹10, camera/video ₹100/500; ☺10.30am-4.30pm Sat-Thu, closed 2nd Sat of month) This sprawling museum is in a fanciful Indo-Saracenic building constructed by the seventh nizam as a playhouse

---

ROYAL HYDERABAD

Founded by the Qutb Shahi dynasty in the late sixteenth century, the city of Hyderabad boasts a unique royal heritage of palaces and tombs, monuments and mosques. With fabulous wealth generated from nearby diamond mines and pearl trading, the city's rulers amassed an astonishing collection of art and antiques, and many pieces are showcased in former royal residences.

Palaces such as the spectacular Chowmahalla Palace (p917) and Purani Haveli, now HEH The Nizam's Museum, harbour priceless objects gathered from across the globe. South of the city centre, the former home of the last nizam of the princely state of Hyderabad Deccan has been expertly restored to become the Taj Falaknuma Palace (p924). It's well worth dropping by for 'high tea' or dinner so you can take in the splendour of its staterooms, halls and grounds.

On the western fringes of the city lies the greatest of all royal residences, Golconda Fort (p920), which predates Hyderabad by centuries. One of India's most impressive fortified monuments, it's in ruins today, though its scale is tremendous.

Secunderabad

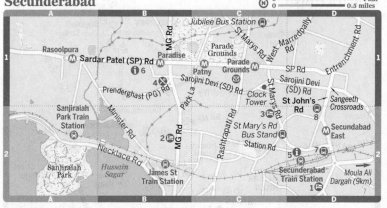

Secunderabad

🛏 Sleeping
1 OYO 984 GN International D2
2 Raj Classic Inn B2
3 Ruby Pride Luxury Hotel C2

✖ Eating
4 Paradise B1

ℹ Information
5 Telangana Tourism D2
6 Telangana Tourism B1

ℹ Transport
7 Rathifile Bus Stand D2
8 Secunderabad Bus Stop
  (Pushpak) D2
  Secunderabad Junction
  Bus Stop .... (see 5)
  Secunderabad Reservation
  Complex .... (see 7)

---

for one of his daughters. It hosts a collection of important archaeological finds as well as an exhibit on the region's Buddhist history. There's an interesting decorative arts gallery, where you can learn about the art of *bidri-ware,* or inlaid metalwork, and *kalamkari* textile painting, plus a bronze-sculpture gallery and a 4500-year-old Egyptian mummy.

British Residency HISTORIC BUILDING
(Koti Women's College; Map p928; Koti Main Rd) This palatial Palladian residence, built in 1803–06 by James Achilles Kirkpatrick, the British Resident (official East India Company representative) in Hyderabad, features in William Dalrymple's brilliant love story *White Mughals.* Work is ongoing to restore the building to its former glory, a project that will take many years to accomplish. There's no official access but Detours (p922) can usually gain entry for those booking one of its fascinating White Mughal tours.

Birla Mandir HINDU TEMPLE
(Map p920; Hill Fort Rd; ⊙ 7am-noon & 2-9pm) The ethereal Birla Mandir, constructed of white

Rajasthani marble in 1976, graces Kalapa-had (Black Mountain), one of two rocky hills overlooking the lake of Hussain Sagar. Dedicated to Venkateshwara, it's a popular Hindu worship centre, with a relaxed atmosphere, and affords magnificent views over the city, especially at sunset. There are several imposing statues including a huge granite image of Venkateshwara. Disabled access is good: there's a lift in the curious clock tower.

◉ Banjara Hills

★ Lamakaan CULTURAL CENTRE
(Map p920; ☎ 9642731329; www.lamakaan.com; next to JVR Park, Banjara Hills; ⊙ 10am-10pm Tue-Sun) This noncommercial 'inclusive cultural space' is an open centre that hosts plays, films, musical events, exhibitions, organic markets and lectures; some events are free. It also has a great Irani cafe, with cheap tea and snacks and free wi-fi. On a lane off Rd No 1.

Kalakriti Art Gallery GALLERY
(Map p920; www.kalakritiartgallery.com; Rd No 10, Banjara Hills; ⊙ 11am-7pm) **FREE** One of the city's

Banjara Hills

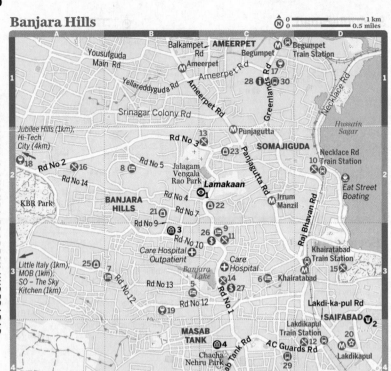

best contemporary galleries, Kalakriti hosts excellent exhibitions by some of India's leading artists, and collaborative programme's with the Alliance Française and Goethe Zentrum. There's a good cafe here too.

Other Areas

★ Golconda Fort
FORT

(Indian/foreigner ₹20/200, 1hr sound-and-light show ₹140; ⊙ 9am-5.30pm, English-language sound-and-light show 6.30pm Nov-Feb, 7pm Mar-Oct) Hyderabad's most impressive sight, this monumental fort lies on the western edge of town. In the 16th century the Qutb Shahs made Golconda a fortified citadel, built atop a 120m-high granite hill surrounded by mighty ramparts, all ringed by further necklaces of crenellated fortifications, 11km in perimeter. From the summit there are stunning vistas across dusty Deccan foothills and the crumbling outer ramparts, over the domed tombs of Qutb Shahs, past distant shanty towns to the horizon haze of the inner city.

By the time of the Qutb Shahs, Golconda Fort had already existed for at least three centuries under the Kakatiyas and Bahmani sultanate, and was already famed for its diamonds, which were mostly mined in the Krishna River valley, but cut and traded here. The Qutb Shahs moved to their new city of Hyderabad in 1591, but maintained Golconda as a citadel until the Mughal emperor Aurangzeb took it in 1687 after a year-long siege, ending Qutb Shahi rule.

Golconda's massive gates were studded with iron spikes to obstruct war elephants. Within the fort, a series of concealed glazed earthenware pipes ensured a reliable water supply, while the ingenious acoustics guaranteed that even the smallest sound from the entrance would echo across the fort complex.

Allow at least a couple of hours to explore the site. Guides charge around ₹600 per

90-minute tour. Small ₹20 guide booklets are also available. Inside the citadel gate, an anticlockwise circuit leads through gardens and up past mostly minor buildings to the top of the hill, where you'll find the functioning Hindu Jagadamba Mahakali Temple and the three-storey durbar hall, with fine panoramas. You then descend to the old palace buildings in the southeastern part of the fort and return to the entrance, passing the elegant three-arched Taramati Mosque.

Golconda is about 10km west from Abids or Charminar: an Uber cab or auto is around ₹270 one way. Buses 65G and 66G run from Charminar to Golconda via GPO Abids hourly; the journey takes about an hour.

★ **Qutb Shahi Tombs** HISTORIC SITE
(Tolichowki; Indian/foreigner ₹15/100, camera or smartphone/video ₹50/100; ◎ 9.30am-5pm Sat-Thu) The subject of one of India's most ambitious heritage projects, these magnificent domed granite tombs form part of a huge archaeological park that is steadily being renovated by the Aga Khan Development Network. All in all there are 40 mausoleums, 23 mosques, a hammam and several pavilions located in landscaped gardens. Seven of the eight Qutb Shahi rulers were buried here under great domes mounted on cubical bases, many of which have beautiful colonnades and delicate lime stucco ornamentation.

★ **Paigah Tombs** HISTORIC SITE
(Santoshnagar; ◎ Sat-Thu 10am-5pm) FREE The aristocratic Paigah family, purportedly descendants of the second Caliph of Islam, were fierce loyalists of the nizams, serving as statespeople, philanthropists and generals. The Paigahs' necropolis, in a quiet neighbourhood 4km southeast of Charminar, is a small compound of exquisite mausoleums made of marble and lime stucco. It's signposted down a small lane opposite Owaisi Hospital on the Inner Ring Rd.

Moula Ali Dargah ISLAMIC SITE
Out on the city's northeastern fringes, the dramatic rock mound of Moula Ali hill has long-distance views, cool breezes and at the top, up 500 steps, a dargah (shrine to a Sufi saint) containing what's believed to be a handprint of Ali, the son-in-law of the Prophet Mohammed. The dargah's reputed healing properties make it a pilgrimage site for the sick.

Buddha Statue
& Hussain Sagar BUDDHIST MONUMENT
(Map p928; boats adult/child ₹55/35; ◎ boats 9am-9pm) Set magnificently on a plinth in the

Hussain Sagar, a lake created by the Qutb Shahs, is a colossal stone statue of the Buddha (18m tall). The Dalai Lama consecrated the monument in 2006, which is evocatively illuminated at night. Frequent boats make the 30-minute return trip to the statue from both Eat Street (p933) and popular Lumbini Park (p933). The Tankbund Rd promenade, on the eastern shore of Hussain Sagar, has great views of the statue.

Nehru Centenary Tribal Museum
MUSEUM

(Map p920; DSS Bhavan, Owaisipura Rd, Masab Tank; Indian/foreigner ₹10/100; ⊙ Mon-Sat 10.30am-5pm) This museum exhibits photographs, dioramas of village life, musical instruments and some exquisite Naikpod masks. It's basic, but you'll get a glimpse into tribal cultures (there are 33 tribal groups in the region, comprising several million people). No photos permitted.

Activities

Travelling Spoon
FOOD

(www.travelingspoon.com; from US$22) Ever wanted to eat real home cooking in India? Travelling Spoon hooks you up with a Hyderabadi family so you can eat their food in their home. Cooking lessons and market visits are also offered.

Vipassana International Meditation Centre
HEALTH & WELLBEING

(Dhamma Khetta; ☑ 040-24240290; www.khetta. dhamma.org; Nagarjuna Sagar Rd, Km12.6) Silent meditation (two-, three-,and 10-day courses) in peaceful grounds 20km outside the city. Apply online. There's no official charge; you donate according to your means.

Tours

Detours
TOURS

(☑ 9000850505; www.detoursindia.com; per person 3hr walk ₹2500) Outstanding cultural tours led by the enthusiastic, knowledgable Jonty Rajagopalan and her small team. Options cover off-the-beaten-track corners of Hyderabad plus markets, food (including cooking lessons and eating) and religion. The crafts tour educates about the use of wood and coconut shells in toy making, as well as tribal art.

Heritage Walks
WALKING

(Map p924; ☑ 9849728841; www.telanganatourism. gov.in/heritagewalks; per person ₹50; ⊙ 7.30-9am Sun & every 2nd Sat) Starting at Charminar and ending at the Chowmahalla Palace, these highly informative (and incredibly inexpensive) walks were designed, and are sometimes led, by architect and historian Madhu Vottery. The price includes breakfast.

SIA Photo Walks
WALKING

(☑ 8008633354; http://siaphotography.in/tours; group walks from ₹300) Excellent street-photography tours of the city curated by Saurabh Chatterjee, who is a knowledgable guide and experienced photographer. Smartphone users will also benefit from his expertise.

Telangana Tourism
TOURS

(☑ 1800 42546464; www.telanganatourism.gov.in) Offers fine weekend tours, such as a 'Nizam Palace' trip that includes the Chowmahalla Palace, Falaknuma Palace and the Golconda Fort (for the sound-and-light show) for ₹3100/2000 with/without high tea at Falaknuma. Also has daily bus tours of city sights (from ₹250 plus admission tickets) and evening Golconda sound-and-light trips. Book at any Telangana Tourism office.

Festivals & Events

Hyderabad Literary Festival
LITERATURE

(www.hydlitfest.org; ⊙ lateJan) A well-established three-day annual event that celebrates literature and the local tradition of *mushaira* (poetry recital). Held at locations including Lamakaan (p919).

Pandit Motiram– Maniram Sangeet Samaroh
MUSIC

(⊙ Nov/Dec) This four-day music festival, named for two renowned classical musicians, celebrates Hindustani music. It's held in the Chowmahalla Palace.

Mahankali Jatra
RELIGIOUS

(⊙ Jun/Jul) A statewide festival honouring Kali, with colourful processions in which devotees convey *bonalu* (pots of food offerings) to the deity. Secunderabad's Mahankali Temple goes wild.

Deccan Festival
MUSIC

(⊙ Feb/Mar) Held in Hyderabad, this five-day festival pays tribute to Deccan culture. Urdu *mushairas* (poetry readings) are held, along with *qawwali* (Sufi devotional music) and other local music and dance performances.

Sleeping

The inner-city Abids area is convenient for Nampally station and the Old City, though it is congested and polluted. For more space

KITSCHABAD

Mixed in with Hyderabad's world-class sights are some attractions on the quirkier side.

Ramoji Film City (www.ramojifilmcity.com; adult/child from ₹1150/950; ⊙9am-5.30pm) The Telangana/Andhra Pradesh film industry, 'Tollywood', is massive, and so is the 6.7-sq-km Film City, where films and TV shows in Telugu, Tamil and Hindi, among others, are made. The day-visit ticket includes a bus tour, funfair rides and shows. Telangana Tourism (p922) runs tours here.

Sudha Cars Museum (19-5-15/1/D, Bahadurpura; Indian/foreigner ₹50/200, camera ₹50; ⊙9.30am-6pm) The eccentric creations of auto-enthusiast K Sudhakar include cars and bikes in the shape of a snooker table, golf ball and lipstick, among other wacky designs. And they all work. The museum is 3km west of Charminar.

National Fisheries Development Board (PV Narasimha Rao Expressway) You'll pass this curious fish-shaped building on your way to or from the city's airport. Its eyes are two circular windows, and it boasts impressive fins.

and greenery head to middle-class Banjara Hills, about 4km northwest of Abids.

Elysium Inn Backpackers Hostel HOSTEL $
(Map p920; ☑8897751857; www.facebook.com/elysiumInnbackpackershostel; 6-3-609/147/A, Anand Nagar Colony, Khairatabad; dm ₹500-585, r ₹1300; ❀❄☎; ⓜKhairatabad) A small hostel in a quiet location with helpful management, a guests' lounge and small kitchen. There are two dorms (one female-only) and a private room: note only the mixed dorm has air-con. It's an 800m walk west of Khairatabad Metro station.

Beehive Hostel HOSTEL $
(Map p920; ☑951995858; https://beehive-hostel.business.site; Rd No.12, Banjara Hills; dm ₹650; ❀❄☎) This bright new hostel is a great choice with its kitchen-diner and spacious lounge. Dorms (mixed and female-only) are well-presented with good bunks, lockers and en-suites. Cleanliness is very good throughout the property.

OYO 984 GN International HOTEL $
(Map p919; ☑070-65067406; www.oyorooms.com; Bhoiguda Road, Railway Officer Colony, Secunderabad; s/d from ₹1380/1480; ❄☎) Rooms here give more than a nod to contemporary style, and wi-fi is reliable. There's no in-house restaurant facility but lots close by as the location is near Secunderabad station. Breakfast is available for ₹50, but it's very basic.

Golden Glory Guesthouse GUESTHOUSE $
(Map p920; ☑040-23554765; www.goldenglory-guesthouse.com; off Rd No 3, Banjara Hills; s/d incl breakfast ₹1100/1300, with AC ₹1300/1700; ❄☎) Offering fine value for the upmarket Banjara Hills location, with ample cafes and eateries

close by, this modestly priced place has clean simple rooms, some with balconies. There's free wi-fi throughout and staff are eager to please.

★ **Ruby Pride Luxury Hotel** HOTEL $$
(Map p919; ☑040-49527844; www.rubypride.com; 167-169 Turner Street, Secunderabad; r incl breakfast ₹2800; ❄☎; ⓜParade Grounds) A well-managed mid-range hotel with modern furnishings; rooms are all air-conditioned and have attractive furniture, minifridge and flatscreen TV. Staff are very switched on and helpful. It's a short walk from Secunderabad station and a kilometre from a metro stop.

Raj Classic Inn HOTEL $$
(Map p919; ☑040-27815291; rajclassicinn@gmail.com; 50 MG Rd, Secunderabad; s/d incl breakfast from ₹1792/2128; ❄☎; ⓜParadise) A pocket-friendly hotel that has been recently renovated, with well-maintained and spacious rooms and friendly, courteous staff. Expect some traffic noise due to its busy location. In-house Chilly's restaurant is recommended for veg food.

Royalton Hotel HOTEL $$
(Map p928; ☑040-67122000; www.royaltonhotel.in; Fateh Sultan Lane, Abids; s/d incl breakfast from ₹2875/3150; ❄☎; ⓜNampally) In a relatively quiet part of Abids, Royalton's gargantuan black lobby chandelier and mirrored lifts give off a slight Manhattan vibe. Rooms have tasteful textiles, glass showers and tea/coffee makers. The hotel is vegetarian and alcohol-free.

Taj Mahal Hotel Abids HOTEL $$
(Map p928; ☑040-24758250; www.hoteltajmahalindia.com; Abids Rd, Abids; incl breakfast s/d

Charminar

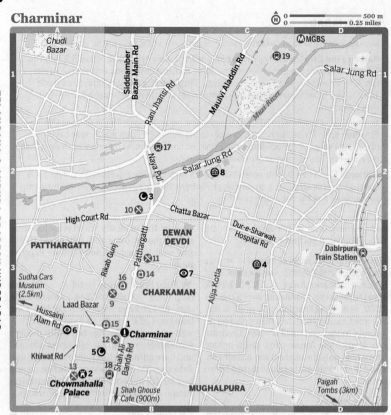

from ₹3066/4210; 🌐🖥️) Not part of the up-market Taj group, this 1924 building never-theless has a classy, if slightly faded colonial ambience. 'Heritage' rooms have character, but most rooms are modern and located in a functional modern block to the side. It's very convenient for sightseeing and the in-house restaurant is excellent for vegetarian food.

⭐ **Taj Falaknuma Palace**   HERITAGE HOTEL **$$$**
(📞 040-66298585; www.tajhotels.com; Engine Bowli, Falaknuma; s/d from ₹39,850/42,600; 🌐@🖥️) The former residence of the sixth nizam, this 1884 neoclassical palace now run by the Taj group oozes class and grandeur with its embossed-leather wallpaper and 24-karat-gold ceiling trim. The rooms are stunning, facilities marvellous and you'll love the views over the city from its hilltop location. In-house restaurants (Adaa for Indian cuisine and Celeste for international) are exceptional too.

⭐ **Taj Krishna**   HOTEL **$$$**
(Map p920; 📞 040-66662323; www.tajhotels.com; Rd No 1, Banjara Hills; s/d from ₹8680/9450; 🌐@🖥️) On the fringe of the Banjara Hills district this landmark hotel has exceptionally lush tropical gardens and one of the nation's nicest hotel pools, 40m in length. Its commodious rooms are being steadily upgraded – those at the rear are quieter. Staff here really go the extra mile to make guests feel at home, and restaurants are superb for authentic Hyderabadi cuisine.

Fortune Park Vallabha   HOTEL **$$$**
(Map p920; 📞 040-39884444; www.fortunehotels.in; Rd No 12, Banjara Hills; s/d incl breakfast from ₹5230/6520; 🌐@🖥️) Enjoys a good location and has large contemporary rooms with stained-glass panels, many with balconies. Room service is available at reasonable prices and the South Indian food and breakfast buffet are excellent.

Eating

The one dish you must try is biryani, which Hyderabadis claim as their own.

In the early evenings, look out for *mirchi bhajji* (chilli fritters), served at street stalls with tea. The Hyderabadi style is famous: chillis are stripped of their seeds, stuffed with tamarind, sesame and spices, dipped in chickpea batter and fried.

Local usage refers to 'thalis' as 'meals'.

Nimrah   CAFE $
(Map p924; Charminar; baked goods ₹3-12; ⊙5.30am-11pm) This classic Irani cafe, always packed to the rafters, is located almost underneath the Charminar's arches. It offers a particularly tasty range of Irani baked goods to accompany your chai pick-me-up. The classic dunk is Osmania biscuits (melt-in-the-mouth shortbreads) but there are many other options including sponge breads and plum slices.

Karachi Bakery   BAKERY $
(Map p920; www.karachibakery.com; Rd Number 1, Banjara Hills; snacks from ₹25; ⊙10am-10pm) Established in 1953 and famous for its cakes, biscuits and bread. Try the traditional *dilkhush* (a pie stuffed with grated coconut, nuts and dry fruit). Has over 20 branches across the city. They also serve meals, including sandwiches and pizza.

Meerut Hotel   INDIAN $
(Map p924; Mir Alam Mandi Rd; mains ₹50-55; ⊙8am-10pm) Offers filling meat and veg curries, delicious tandoor roti (which is baked on the street in front of you) and a mean mutton korma.

Govind Dosa   STREET FOOD $
(Map p924; Charkaman; snacks ₹40-100; ⊙6am-noon) A famous breakfast spot, cheery Govind's street-corner stand is permanently surrounded by happy Hyderabadis savouring his delicious dosa (South Indian savoury crepe; try the butter masala) and *idli* (South Indian spongy, round, fermented rice cakes); the *tawa idli* topped with chilli powder and spices is a great way to kick-start the day.

Kamat Hotel   SOUTH INDIAN $
(Map p928; Nampally Station Rd, Nampally; meals ₹130-270; ⊙7am-10pm; ⓜNampally) Cheap and reliably good for tasty South Indian fare. It's a good option for breakfast or a speedy lunch – try their *idli* or *masala vada* (spicy, deep-fried lentil savoury). There's also a larger AC branch in Saifabad, and two in Secunderabad.

★ Shah Ghouse Cafe   HYDERABADI $$
(Shah Ali Banda Rd; mains ₹80-310; ⊙5am-1am) During Ramadan, Hyderabadis line up for Shah Ghouse's famous *haleem* (a thick soup of pounded spiced wheat, with goat, chicken or beef, and lentils) and at any time of year the mutton biryani is near-perfect. Don't expect ambience: just good traditional food, in a no-frills upstairs dining hall. Wash it down with a delicious lassi (₹60).

Cafe Bahar   HYDERABADI $$
(Map p928; 3-5-815/A, Avanti Nagar, Basheer Bagh; biryanis ₹90-290; ⊙11am-1am) Consistently recommended by locals for authentic Hyderabadi cuisine, this AC place serves generous portions of flavoursome biryanis at modest prices (veg is just ₹90, while a mutton biryani costs ₹150). Kebabs are also good. It's usually crowded so be prepared for a wait.

Chutneys
SOUTH INDIAN **$$**

(Map p920; ☑040-66778484; Shilpa Arcade, Rd No 3, Banjara Hills; meals ₹260-340; ⊙7am-11pm; 🛜; Ⓜ Panjagutta) Chutneys is famous for its South Indian meals and all-day dosa, *idli* and *uttapams* (thick, savoury rice pancake with finely chopped onions, green chillies, coriander and coconut). Try a *pesarattu* (dosa made with green mung beans). Its dishes are moderate on chilli, and Chinese food and North Indian thalis are also available. No booze served.

Paradise
HYDERABADI **$$**

(Persis; Map p919; www.paradisefoodcourt.in; cnr SD & MG Rds; biryani ₹239-319; ⊙11.30am-11pm; Ⓜ Paradise) Paradise is synonymous with biryani in these parts. The main Secunderabad location has five different dining areas: head to the attractive 'roof garden', complete with whirring fans, or pay an AC surcharge to eat inside. Also serves lots of (less pleasing) Chinese dishes. There are over a dozen Paradise restaurants across the city including a large, modern branch at **Khairatabad** (Map p920; ☑040-67408400; NTR Gardens, Khairatabad; mains ₹211-377; ⊙11am-11pm; Ⓜ Khairatabad) close to Abids and Banjara Hills.

Roastery
CAFE **$$**

(Map p920; 418 Rd 14, Banjara Hills; mains ₹188-388; ⊙8am-11.30pm) Located in a converted villa, this is one of west Hyderabad's most popular cafes. Banjara Hills' bright young things flock here for the Western food: salads (try the grilled chicken), bruschettas, burgers, pasta dishes and sandwiches. As the name indicates, Roastery is also famous for its coffee, including nitro cold brew, French press and hot black options.

Chicha's
HYDERABADI **$$**

(Map p920; ☑9959911100; www.facebook.com/chichashyderabad; AC Guards Rd, Lakdikapul; mains ₹219-349; ⊙noon–1.45am; Ⓜ Lakdikapul) Hip hang-out where you can feast on delicious, authentic Hyderabadi dishes and street food in quirky, air-conditioned surrounds. Price are moderate with biryanis starting at ₹219 and every Friday there's a special mutton *haleem* (₹179). Curries are also excellent. No booze.

HYDERABADI CUISINE

Hyderabad has a food culture all of its own and Hyderabadis take great pride and pleasure in it. It was the Mughals who brought the tasty biryanis, skewer kebabs and special Ramadan dishes like *haleem*, so many dishes have a hint of Persia about them.

Biryani is the definitive local meal. In Hyderabad it's often prepared in layers, with uncooked meat at the bottom of the pan (the highest temperature), topped with rice, then another layer of half-cooked spiced meat so that the ingredients are ready at the same time. Hyderabadi biryanis are spicy, but not fancy or fragrant like the biryanis of Lucknow, another town synonymous with the dish. Biryanis in Hyderabad are always served with *mirchi ka slan* (a richly spiced gravy) and *dahi ki* (raita, often called chutney locally). Mutton (goat or lamb) is the classic biryani base, though chicken, egg, fish and vegetable biryanis are plentiful too. Biryanis come in vast quantities and one serve may satisfy two people. Good places to order a biryani include Hotel Shadab in the Old City, Cafe Bahar (p925), Shah Ghouse Cafe (p925) and Paradise, which has several branches across Hyderabad.

To experience the other classic Hyderabad dish, *haleem* (a thick soup of pounded, spiced wheat with goat, chicken or beef, and lentils) you really need to be in the city during Ramadan (known locally as Ramzan). Come nightfall at this time, the serious business of eating begins, as thousands of stalls are set up across the city and locals go *haleem*-hopping to assess the best. Look out for the clay ovens called *bhattis*; you'll probably hear them before you see them. Men gather around, taking turns to vigorously pound *haleem* and the crowds are quite something. Outside Ramzan, *haleem* is rare on local menus. Chicha's serves up the dish each Friday, while hotel restaurants Firdaus and Aish offer fine versions of the dish all year round.

Look out too for *pesarattu* (a pancake-like dosa made with green mung beans), which are stuffed with *upma* (semolina seasoned with cumin, onion, ginger and green chilli) and served with chutney. It's a popular breakfast dish, which you can find at Chutneys.

Taj Restaurant   HYDERABADI **$$**

(Map p924; Khilwat Rd; mains ₹100-210; ⏱10am-9pm) A bustling, no-nonsense place that specialises in biryani and delicious chicken and mutton curries, located just around the corner from the Chowmahalla Palace. There's an AC room on the upper floor.

Hotel Shadab   HYDERABADI **$$**

(Map p924; High Court Rd, north of Charminar; mains ₹180-340; ⏱noon-11.30pm) The time-warp decor looks like it's been based on a 1970s disco but the cuisine is great at this hopping Hyderabadi restaurant. Great for biryanis (veg/non-veg starting at ₹190/270), kebabs and mutton in all configurations and, during Ramadan, *haleem*. Downstairs it's very solo-male; head upstairs to the AC room for more of a family vibe.

Dakshina Mandapa   SOUTH INDIAN **$$$**

(Map p928; Taj Mahal Hotel, Abids Rd, Abids; meals ₹330-425; ⏱7am-10.30pm) Highly regarded spot for South Indian vegetarian food. You may have to wait for a lunch table, but order the South Indian thali and you'll be brought heap after heap of rice and refills of authentic dishes. The AC room upstairs does a superb lunch buffet (noon to 3.30pm).

★**Olive Bistro**   MEDITERRANEAN **$$$**

(⏰9248912347; www.olivebarandkitchen.com; Rd No 46, Jubilee Hills, Durgam Cheruvu; mains ₹540-815; ⏱Mon-Fri 7-11pm, Sat & Sun noon-3.30pm & 7pm-1am; 🛜) Located in a secluded leafy location with lake views from its terrace, this atmospheric restaurant is one of the hottest places in town for Italian and Mediterranean food. Choose from pasta, risottos, meat (like lamb ribs with roasted cous cous) or great seafood; try the *gambas pil pil* (prawns cooked in a garlic and hot pepper sauce).

★**Dhaba By Claridges**   MODERN INDIAN **$$$**

(⏰040-29706704; www.dhababyclaridges.com; Western Pearl Bldg, Survey 13, Kondapur; mains ₹265-445; ⏱noon-11.30pm; 🛜) A good reason to head out west to Hi-Tech City, this hip hang-out offers a contemporary take on North Indian street food (minus the fumes and traffic of course). Dhaba's decor is kooky, with Bollywood-style murals and bold colours to the fore. House cocktails and mocktails are wonderful too.

★**Firdaus**   INDIAN **$$$**

(Map p920; ⏰040-66662323; Taj Krishna hotel, Rd No 1, Banjara Hills; mains ₹550-1650; ⏱Sun-Thu 7.30-11.45pm, Fri & Sat noon-2:45pm & 7.30-11.45pm; 🛜) A classy hotel restaurant, Firdaus offers great Hyderabadi (and also North Indian) dishes to the strains of live *ghazals* (classical Urdu love songs, accompanied by harmonium and tabla). They even serve *haleem* outside Ramadan and superb meat dishes – try the *raan-e-firdaus* (pot roasted lamb).

★**SO – The Sky Kitchen**   MULTICUISINE **$$$**

(⏰040-23558004; www.notjustso.com; Rd No 92, near Apollo Hospital, Jubilee Hills; mains ₹340-530; ⏱noon-midnight; 🛜) Jubilee Hills rooftop restaurant, with candles and loungey playlists, which makes a highly atmospheric eating spot. The superb menu has been crafted carefully, mixing pan-Asian and Mediterranean dishes, with a nod to healthy eating: most dishes are grilled, baked or stir-fried. Indian dishes are also excellent, try the *nizami takari biryani* (rice and vegetables cooked in a terracotta pot).

Aish   HYDERABADI **$$$**

(Map p920; www.theparkhotels.com; The Park, 22 Raj Bhavan Rd; mains ₹485-1225; ⏱12.30-2.45pm, 7-11.30pm; 🛜; Ⓜ Irrum Manzil) Renowned for its Hyderabadi dishes, this elegant hotel restaurant serves fine biryanis, kebabs and wonderful *haleem*, including a veg version (₹675) of this classic dish.

Southern Spice   SOUTH INDIAN **$$$**

(Rd No 10, Jubilee Hills; meals ₹180-479; ⏱noon-3.30pm & 7-10.30pm) Southern Spice offers sublime Andhra-style cooking and specialities from across the South. Try a special veg thali (₹299), which features an unlimited flow of delectable dishes, or the *royala eguru* (prawns in rich gravy). The premises are spacious and air-conditioned, but always busy; book ahead.

Barbeque Nation   INDIAN **$$$**

(Map p920; ⏰040-64806060; www.barbeque nation.com; ANR Centre, Rd No 1, Banjara Hills; veg/non-veg buffet from ₹640/765, dinner from ₹970/1140; ⏱noon-11.30pm; 🛜) All-you-can-eat kebabs, curries, salads and desserts, with many veg and non-veg options. A great-value place to come when you're hungry! Prices fluctuate a little depending on the day and time. Slurp on one of their excellent Indian wines while you dine.

🍷 Drinking & Nightlife

Hyderabad does not have a big drinking scene, and due to local licensing laws many of the liveliest lounges serve nothing stronger than mocktails. Some of the hottest new

TELANGANA & ANDHRA PRADESH HYDERABAD

Abids Area

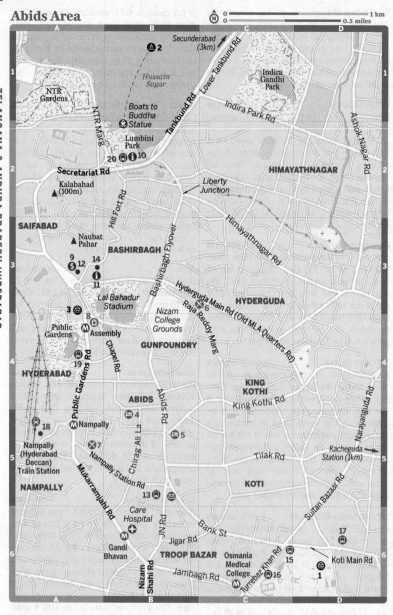

places are west of the centre in leafy Banjara Hills and Jubilee Hills, where you'll find a slew of good rooftop venues.

★ Prost Brewpub · MICROBREWERY

(📱040-33194195; www.prost.in; 882/A Rd No 45, Jubilee Hills; bites from ₹260; ⏱noon-midnight; 🚇) A highly popular, cavernous brewhouse with five tap beers, including an English ale and a stout, plus cider. There are several zones, all stylishly lit, including ample outdoor space and an extensive East-meets-West pub-grub menu (egg fritters, Cajun potatoes, Jeera coriander prawns). Also

Abids Area

◎ Sights
1 British Residency D6
2 Buddha Statue & Hussain Sagar B1
3 State Museum A3

⌓ Sleeping
4 Royalton Hotel B5
5 Taj Mahal Hotel Abids B5

✖ Eating
6 Cafe Bahar C3
   Dakshina Mandapa .... (see 5)
7 Kamat Hotel A5

🔒 Shopping
8 Fabindia A4

ℹ Information
9 State Bank of India A3
10 Telangana Tourism B2
11 Telangana Tourism A3

ℹ Transport
12 Air India A3
13 GPO Abids Bus Stop B5
14 Jet Airways A3
15 Koti Bus Stand C6
16 Koti Bus Stop C6
17 Koti Women's College Bus Stand D6
18 Nampally Reservation Complex A5
19 Public Gardens Bus Stop A4
20 Secretariat Bus Stop (Pushpak) B2

hosts comedy (every Thursday), DJs and live music.

★ **Coffee Cup** CAFE
(☑ 040-40037571; www.facebook.com/the coffeecupp; E 89, off 5th Crescent Rd, Sainikpuri, Secunderabad; ⊙ 9am-11.30pm; ☎) Excellent neighbourhood cafe and creative hub that's a magnet for East Hyderabad's arty crew. Offers a fine selection of interesting coffees, teas, snacks and meals (try a loaded jacket potato). There's stand-up comedy here most Fridays. It's above Canara Bank.

★ **MOB** BAR
(www.facebook.com/itismob; Aryan's, Rd No 92, near Apollo Hospital, Jubilee Hills; ⊙ noon-midnight; ☎) A stylish, sociable Belgium beer house that draws a refreshingly mixed-gender, mixed-age crowd. Try a 'beer platter' for a sample of four choice brews, while on the menu you'll find good fish satay (₹350), fiery prawns (₹445) and other pan-Asian bites. There's live music on Saturday nights. It's 4km west of Banjara Hills' Rd No 1.

Vapour MICROBREWERY
(☑ 040-33165132; www.facebook.com/Vapour Hyderabad; 753 Rd 36, Jubilee Hills; ⊙ 11am-1am; ☎) Buzzing most nights, Vapour is one of the most happening pubs in Hyderabad; book a table ahead on weekends. Brews include apple cider beer, lager, stout and wheat beers. There's a stunning terrace framed by tropical foliage, live music and regular DJ events – check their Facebook page for regular drink and menu promos.

Autumn Leaf Cafe CAFE
(www.facebook.com/autumnleafcafe; 823, Rd No 41, Jubilee Hills; ⊙ Mon-Fri noon-10.30pm, Sat &

Sun from 9am; ☎) Tucked away on a quiet side street, this green oasis has a superb garden where you can nurse a latte or enjoy a juice or milkshake. The menu (dishes ₹200-350) features all-day breakfasts, pasta, pancakes, salads and soups. Look out for 'Chill and Grill' evenings with mellow electronic vibes.

Kismet CLUB
(Map p920; ☑ 040-23456789; www.thepark hotels.com; The Park, Raj Bhavan Rd, Somajiguda; admission per couple ₹700-2000; ⊙ 8pm-midnight or later Wed-Sun; Ⓜ Irrum Manzi) A sleek, upmarket nightclub, with loungey booth seating and a pumping bass-driven sound system. Men won't get past the ranks of bouncers without female companions. Drinks are pricey (cocktails around ₹600), not that the wealthy crowd are too bothered. Musically things range from EDM to Bollywood.

Vertigo BAR
(Map p920; www.facebook.com/vertigothehigh life; 5th fl, Shiv Shakti Tower, Rd No 12, Banjara Hills; ⊙ 11am-midnight) A rooftop bar that boasts a great terrace, with elegant seating and interior rooms for live music and DJs. The eating 'zone' serves North Indian, Chinese and Western food while cocktails start at ₹375. It's opposite Ratnadeep supermarket.

10 Downing Street BAR
(Map p920; http://10ds.in; Lifestyle Bldg, Greenlands Rd, My Home Tycoon department store rear yard; ⊙ 11am-11pm; ☎; Ⓜ Begumpet) With its classic decor of wood panelling and leather sofas, this place is just the ticket for a relaxed drinking session (check out the terrific daytime cocktail prices) and some pub grub. Things rev up as the evening progresses,

CHARMINAR MARKETS

Hyderabadis and visitors of every stripe flock to the Charminar area's labyrinthine lanes to browse, buy and wander. Patthargatti, the broad avenue leading in from the Musi River, is lined with shops selling clothes (especially wedding outfits), perfumes and Hyderabad's famous pearls. **Laad Bazar** (Map p924; ⊙10am-8.30pm), running west from the Charminar, is famed for its sparkling bangle shops: lac bangles, made from a resinous insect secretion and encrusted with colourful beads or stones, are a Hyderabad speciality. In Laad Bazar you'll also find perfumers, wedding goods and fabrics.

Laad Bazar opens into **Mehboob Chowk** (Map p924), a square with shops selling antiquarian books and antiques, a livestock market on its south side, and a market in exotic birds, Chiddi Bazar, just southwest. A short distance north, the **Patel Market** (Map p924; ⊙approximately 11am-8pm) sells cloth fabrics and cranks into action from around 11am in the back lanes between Patthargatti and Rikab Gunj. Further north again and on the other side of Patthargatti, the wholesale vegetable market **Mir Alam Mandi** (Map p924; Patthargatti Rd; ⊙5am-6.30pm) trades in all kinds of fresh stuff from 6.30am to 6.30pm daily.

with different music nightly – club Saturday, Bollywood Sunday and so on.

Coco's Bar & Grill   BAR
(Map p920; ☑040-65542730; 217 Rd No 2, Jubilee Hills; ⊙noon-midnight; 🛜) The rooftop setting, with rustic bamboo couches and thatch roofs, makes Coco's perfect for a cold drink on a balmy evening (beer/mocktails from ₹175/170). There's live blues and soft rock nightly, and decent Indian and Continental food. Happy hour runs between noon and 6pm. Enter down a lane beside Café Coffee Day.

☆ Entertainment

Ravindra Bharathi Theatre   THEATRE
(Map p920; ☑040-23233672; www.ravindrabharathi.org; Ladki-ka-pul Rd, Saifabad; Ⓜ Lakdikapul) Well-curated music, dance and drama performances, and cinema.

🛍 Shopping

Charminar is the most exciting place to shop: you'll find exquisite pearls, slippers, gold and fabrics alongside billions of bangles. Upmarket boutiques and malls are scattered around Banjara Hills and the western suburbs. Patthargatti has dozens of pearl vendors.

GVK One   MALL
(Map p920; www.gvkone.com; Rd No 1, Banjara Hills; ⊙11am-11pm) An upmarket mall with a good selection of clothes shops including M&S and Levi's, ATMs, a small food court, cafes and a cinema.

Kalanjali   CLOTHING
(www.kalanjali.com; 237 Rd No 16, Jubilee Hills; ⊙10.30am-8pm) Fine quality saris, kurtas

(long collarless shirts), *salwar kameez* (dresslike tunic and loose, long pants for women) sets (from ₹2545) and other traditional clothing. They also sell exquisite silver, stone and wooden handicrafts.

Malkha   CLOTHING
(Map p920; www.malkha.in; 4th Floor, 10-3-76, Mehdipatnam, Humayun Nagar; ⊙10am-7pm Mon-Sat) 🍃 Malkha cloth is made near the cotton fields, by hand and with natural dyes, reducing strain on the environment and putting primary producers in control. The result is gorgeous; here you can pick up fabric, saris, dupattas (long scarves; from ₹1200) and kurtas at fair prices.

Suvasa   CLOTHING
(Map p920; www.suvasa.in; Rd No 12, Banjara Hills; ⊙11am-7.30pm) Suvasa's block-printed kurtas are priced from around ₹1200 in cotton, and they also have high-quality *salwar* and dupattas. Homeware, including gorgeous bed and table linen, is worth looking at too.

Hyderabad Perfumers   PERFUME
(Map p924; Patthargatti; ⊙10am-8.30pm Mon-Sat) This fourth-generation family business can conjure something aromatic up for you on the spot. They specialise in *ittar,* natural perfume oils from flowers and herbs; prices start as low as ₹200 and rise to over ₹7000 per bottle.

Fabindia   CLOTHING
(Map p920; www.fabindia.com; Rd No 9, Banjara Hills; ⊙11am-9.30pm) 🍃 Lovely women's (and some men's) clothes in artisanal fabrics with contemporary prints and colours. It also sells homeware including bed linen, cushions and *dhurries* (rugs). Prices are fair. Or visit its

other branch at **Fateh Maidan** (Map p928; ⊙10.30am-8.30pm; Ⓜ Assembly).

Himalaya Book World BOOKS
(Map p920; Panjagutta Circle, Banjara Hills; ⊙10.30am-10.30pm) A fine selection of English-language fiction and nonfiction by Indian and international authors. It has several other branches in town.

ℹ Information

MEDICAL SERVICES

Reputable Care Hospitals are on **Mukarramjahi Road** (Map p928; ☑040-30417777; www.carehospitals.com; Mukarramjahi Rd; Ⓜ Gandhi Bhavan) and **Road No 1** (Map p920; ☑040-30418888; www.carehospitals.com; Rd No 1, Banjara Hills). There's also an outpatient hospital on **Road No 10** (Map p920; ☑040-39310444; 4th Lane, Rd No 10, Banjara Hills).

MONEY

ATMs are everywhere. Citibank ATMs allow large withdrawals: these are at **Banjara Hills** (Map p920; Prashanthi Mansion, Rd No 1, Banjara Hills), **City Center Mall** (Map p920; City Center Mall, Rd No 1, Banjara Hills) and **GVK One Mall** (Map p920; GVK One Mall, Rd No 1, Banjara Hills).

State Bank of India (Map p928; HACA Bhavan, Saifabad; ⊙10.30am-4pm Mon-Fri;

Ⓜ Assembly) Has currency exchange; banks generally offer the best rates.

POST

General Post Office (Map p928; Abids Circle, Troop Bazar; ⊙8am-7pm Mon-Sat, 10am-1pm Sun; Ⓜ Gandhi Bhavan)

Secunderabad Post Office (Map p919; Rashtrapati Rd, Secunderabad; ⊙8am-7pm Mon-Sat; Ⓜ Parade Grounds)

TOURIST INFORMATION

Indiatourism (Map p920; ☑040-23409199; www.incredibleindia.org; Tourism Plaza, Greenlands Rd; ⊙9am-6pm Mon-Fri, 9.30am-1pm Sat; Ⓜ Begumpet) A useful office, with good information on Hyderabad, Telangana and beyond.

Telangana Tourism (www.telanganatourism.gov.in) Has information offices with bookings desks for state-government-run tours, heritage walks and hotels in Telangana. Branches at **Shakar Bhavan** (Map p928; ☑040-66745986; ⊙9.30am-6pm Mon-Fri 9am-noon Sat; Ⓜ Assembly), **Tank Bund Road** (Map p928; ☑040-65581555; ⊙9.30am-6pm Mon-Fri, 9am-noon Sat), **Greenlands Road** (Map p920; ☑040-23414334; Tourism Plaza; ⊙9.30am-6pm Mon-Fri, 9am-noon Sat; Ⓜ Begumpet), **Rajiv Gandhi International Airport** (☑040-24253215; ⊙7am-8pm), **Secunderabad** (Map p919; ☑040-27893100; Yatri Nivas Hotel, SP Rd; ⊙9.30am-6pm Mon-Fri, 9am-noon Sat; Ⓜ Paradise) and **Secunderabad train station**

QAWWALI AND SUFISM IN HYDERABAD

Emerging in the subcontinent in the 13th century, Qawwali music is closely linked with Sufism. Hyderabad is a hotbed of Qawwali singing, and it's not uncommon to hear people softly practicing on trains and buses as they ride about the city. The music of mystical Islam, Qawwali performances usually last for many hours, with the aim of achieving a state of spiritual ecstasy. Improvisation is key, with a lead vocalist alternating with supporting singers. To the untrained ear the singing almost sounds erotic, though the songs are purely religious in their devotion. Musicians accompany the singers with tablas and instruments.

Qawwali is frequently performed at the hundreds of *dargahs* (Sufi shrines) in Hyderabad, including two famous *dargahs* in the Nampally area. There's no formal timetable for events, but performances at **Dargah Yousufain Sharifain** (Nampally Dargah; Nampally Darga Rd; ⊙singing 10pm-1am Thu & Fri; Ⓜ Nampally), the resting place of two Sufi saints, are almost always held on Thursdays and Fridays (10pm-1am). **Dargah Hazrat Shah Khamosh** (Darussalam Rd; Ⓜ Nampally) is another shrine close by where Qawwali sessions are regularly performed. It's the resting place of Sufi saint Hazrat Shah Khamosh, who legend has it, took a vow of silence for 25 years. This large *dargah* dates from the late 19th century and is an unusual blend of Islamic and Gothic styles. Diners at the Taj Falaknuma Palace (p924) are accompanied by Qawwali singing on Sundays. Look out too for festive *urs* (the veneration of the anniversary of death of a Sufi saint; 'urs' means 'marriage' in Arabic and symbolises the union of the saint with God).These are held at shrines across the city, which always feature Qawwalli music.

Perhaps the most famous Qawwali singer of recent times was Nusrat Fateh Ali Khan who released six albums on Real World records (the English band Massive Attack once unofficially remixed a track of his). Leading female Qawwali singers today include the Nooran Sisters from Jalandhar.

(Map p919; ☑ 040-27801614; ☻10am-8pm; Ⓜ Secunderabad East).

ℹ Getting There & Away

AIR

Hyderabad's massive, modern, efficient **Rajiv Gandhi International Airport** (☑ 040-66546370; http://hyderabad.aero; Shamshabad) is 25km southwest of the city centre. It has direct daily flights, including with **Air India** (Map p928; ☑ 040-23389711; www.airindia. com; HACA Bhavan, Saifabad; ☻9.30am-6pm Mon-Sat; Ⓜ Assembly) and **Jet Airways** (Map p928; ☑ 020-39893333; www.jetairways.com; Summit Apartments, Hill Fort Rd; ☻10am-6pm Mon-Sat; Ⓜ Assembly), to over 25 Indian cities plus international cities including Chicago, London, Hong Kong and many Southeast Asian and Gulf destinations.

BUS

The main terminal is the vast **Mahatma Gandhi Bus Station** (MGBS; Imlibun Bus Station; Map p924; ☑ 040-24614406; off Salar Jung Rd; ☻advance booking offices 8am-10.30pm) near Abids. Air-con services by the **Telangana State Road Transport Corporation** (Telangana State Road Transport Corporation; ☑ 1800 2004599; http:// tsrtcbus.in) are quite good. Buses run to many destinations in Madhya Pradesh, Maharashtra and Tamil Nadu too. Nearly all long-distance services depart in the evening. When booking ahead, women should request seats up front as these are reserved for female passengers.

Secunderabad's **Jubilee bus station** (JBS; Map p919; ☑ 040-27802203; Gandhi Nagar, Secunderabad; Ⓜ Parade Grounds) is smaller, with buses to cities including Chennai, Mumbai and these routes:

Bengaluru (Bangalore) ordinary/Volvo AC/ sleeper ₹655/from 844/1280, eight to 11 hours, 20 daily

Vijayawada non-AC/AC ₹326/448, four to six hours, 18 daily

Other useful bus stops include the **bus stand** (Map p919; St Mary's Rd, Secunderabad) on St Mary's Rd, the **Charminar bus stop** (Map p924; Shah Ali Banda Rd) for the Old City, **Koti bus stand** (Map p928; Turrebaz Khan Rd), **Koti Women's College bus stand** (Map p928; Koti Main Rd) and **Rathifile bus stand** (Map p919; Station Rd, Secunderabad) for Secunderabad.

There are also many other private bus companies offering long-distance services. These tend to use their own terminals; check www.make mytrip.com for information and bookings.

TRAIN

Secunderabad, Nampally (officially called Hyderabad Deccan) and Kacheguda are Hyderabad's three major train stations. Most through trains stop at Kacheguda.

The reservation complexes at **Nampally** (Map p928; ☑ 040-27829999; Public Gardens Rd; ☻8am-8pm Mon-Sat, to 2pm Sun; Ⓜ Nampally) and **Secunderabad** (Rathifile; Map p919; St John's Rd; ☻8am-8pm Mon-Sat, 8am-2pm Sun), both in separate buildings away from the stations, have foreign-tourist-quota counters (bring your passport and visa photocopies, along with originals).

ℹ Getting Around

TO/FROM THE AIRPORT

The airport is about a 45-minute drive from town.

Bus

The TSRTC's Pushpak air-conditioned bus service runs between 4am, or 5am and 11pm to/from various stops in the city including:

AC Guards (Map p920; AC Guards Rd; ₹212, two or three hourly) About 1.5km from Abids.

Paryatak Bhavan (Map p920; Greenlands Rd; ₹265, about hourly)

Secretariat (Map p928; NTR Marg) (₹265, about hourly) About 1.5km from Abids.

Secunderabad (Map p919; Rail Nilayam Rd, Secunderabad; ₹265, twice hourly)

BUSES FROM HYDERABAD

DESTINATION	FARE (₹)	DURATION (HR)	FREQUENCY
Bengaluru (Bangalore)	680-1210	8-11	29 buses 5.45am-11.40pm
Chennai	688-1191	11-14	18 buses 6-10.20pm
Hosapete (Hospet)	760-1000	8-10	5 buses daily
Mumbai	999-2235	12-16	49 buses 4.30am-11.50pm
Mysuru (Mysore)	1050-1733	11-13	10 buses 5.30-9pm
Tirupati	652-1991	9-13	36 buses 8am-10pm
Vijayawada	317-497	4-5	every 15-30min 3am-11.59pm
Visakhapatnam	676-1630	11-13	8 buses 4-11pm
Warangal	147-230	2-4	half-hourly

MAJOR TRAINS FROM HYDERABAD & SECUNDERABAD

DESTINATION	TRAIN NO & NAME	FARE (₹)	DURATION (HR)	DEPARTURE TIME & STATION
Bengaluru (Bangalore)	Rajdhani (Nos 22692/4), 12785 Bangalore Exp	1785/2630(B), 370/1390(A)	12, 11½	6.40pm Secunderabad, 7.05pm Kacheguda
Chennai	12604 Chennai Express, 12760 Charminar Exp	405/1520(A), 425/1610(A)	13, 14	4.50pm Nampally, 6.30pm Nampally
Delhi	12723 Telangana Exp, Rajdhani (Nos 22691/3)	670/2575(A), 3110/4645(B)	27, 22	6.25am Nampally, 7.50am Secunderabad
Hosapete (for Hampi)	17603 Exp	275/1070(A)	9	9.05pm Kacheguda
Kolkata	18646 East Coast Exp	615/2430(A)	30	9.50am Nampally
Mumbai	12702 Hussainsagar Exp	425/1610(A)	14	2.45pm Nampally
Tirupati	12734 Narayanadri Exp	395/1475(A	12	6.05pm Nampally
Visakhapatnam	12728 Godavari Exp	400/1505(A)	12½	5.15pm Nampally

Fares: (A) – sleeper/2AC; (B) – 3AC/2AC

The trip takes around one hour. Contact TSRTC or check http://hyderabad.aero for exact timings.

Taxi

The prepaid taxi booth is on the lowest level of the terminal. Fares to Abids or Banjara Hills are ₹600 to ₹750. **Meru Cabs** (☏ 040-44224422) and **Sky Cabs** (☏ 040-49494949) charge similar rates. Uber and Ola are cheaper, around ₹400 to ₹550, and they both have designated pick-up points in Parking Zone C.

AUTORICKSHAW

Expect to pay ₹30 to ₹50 for a short ride, and around ₹120 for 4km. Few drivers use meters.

BOAT

Frequent boats make the 30-minute return trip to the Buddha Statue from both **Eat Street** (Map p920; child/adult ₹35/55; ⊙3-8pm) and popular **Lumbini Park** (Map p928; off NTR Marg; child/adult ₹35/55; ⊙10.30am-8pm).

BUS

Few travellers bother with local buses (₹6 to ₹12 for most rides) but there are some useful routes. Try www.hyderabadcitybus.com (although it can be inaccurate).

City stops include **Afzalgunj** (Map p924; Afzalgunj), **GPO Abids** (Map p928; JN Rd, Abids), **Koti** (Map p928; Turrebaz Khan Rd), **Mehdipatnam** (Mehdipatnam Rd), **Public Gardens** (Map p928; Public Gardens Rd) and **Secunderabad Junction** (Map p919; Station Rd, Secunderabad).

CAR

The going rate for a small AC car with a driver is from ₹1600 per day for city sightseeing,

and ₹2800 to ₹3700 per day for out-of-town trips (including fuel, tolls and driver expenses). **Golkonda Tours** (☏ 9441294987; www. golkondatours.com) are recommended.

METRO RAIL

Hyderabad modern air-conditioned **Metro Rail** (☏ 040-23332555; www.ltmetro.com) runs on elevated tracks above Hyderabad's streets. Lines 1 and 3 commenced service in 2018. The metro stop at MG Bus Station provides a useful link for travellers, and will be a major interchange when future lines are completed. Eventually five lines are planned, covering over 100km, and including links to the airport and Hi-Tec City.

Passengers can choose a smart card (complicated registration necessary and a ₹20 charge) or a token for travelling. Single trips cost ₹10 to ₹60. You can check routes and project updates on the website.

TAXI

There are thousands of Uber and Ola drivers in Hyderabad and fares are very fair indeed (often cheaper than those quoted by autorickshaw drivers). A 3km ride will be around ₹80 to ₹120. Reliable taxi companies include Meru Cabs (p933) and Sky Cabs (p933).

TRAIN

The suburban **MMTS trains** (Multi-Modal Transport System; www.mmtstraintimings.in; fares ₹5-10) are not very useful for travellers, but infrequent trains (every 30 to 45 minutes) run between Hyderabad (Nampally) and Lingampalli via Necklace Rd, Begumpet and Hi-Tech City. There's also a route between Falaknuma (south of Old City) and Lingampalli via Kacheguda and Secunderabad stations.

Bhongir

Most Hyderabad–Warangal buses and trains stop at the town of Bhongir, 60km from Hyderabad. It's worth stopping to climb the impressive **Chalukyan hill fort** (off DVK Rd; Indian/foreigner ₹5/100, camera ₹10; ⊙9am-5pm) on the eastern side of town. You can leave backpacks at the ticket office.

The ramparts and ruined remains of this fantastical-looking 12th-century fort sit on what resembles a gargantuan stone egg on the eastern side of town. Access is via many hundreds of steps that have been cut into the rocky hillside; the climb takes around 40 minutes. Sadly there's a fair bit of trash to guide your way.

Warangal

☑0870 / POP 637,000

Warangal was the capital of the Kakatiya kingdom, which ruled most of present-day Telangana and Andhra Pradesh from the 12th to early 14th centuries. The city merges with the town of Hanumakonda, which has many temples.

◉ Sights

Ancient temples in Hanumakonda include the lakeside **Bhadrakali Temple** (Bhadrakali Temple Rd), 2km southeast of the 1000-Pillared Temple, whose idol of the mother goddess Kali sits with a weapon in each of her eight hands, and the small **Siddeshwara Temple** (Hanumakonda Hill) on the south side of Hanumakonda Hill.

Fort   FORT
(Fort Rd) Warangal's fort, on the southern edge of town, was a massive construction with three circles of walls (the outermost 7km in circumference). Most of it now is either fields or buildings, but at the centre is a huge, partly reassembled Shaivite **Svayambhu Temple** (off Fort Rd; Indian/foreigner ₹25/200, camera ₹25; ⊙9am-8pm), with handsome, large *torana* (architrave) gateways at its cardinal points. An autorickshaw from Warangal station costs around ₹300 return.

1000-Pillared Temple   HINDU TEMPLE
(south of NH163, Hanumakonda; ⊙6am-6pm) The 1000-Pillared Temple, constructed in the 12th century, is in a leafy setting and is a fine example of Kakatiya architecture and sculpture. Unusually, the cross-shaped building has shrines to the sun god Surya (to the

right as you enter), Vishnu (centre) and Shiva (left). Despite the name, it certainly does not have 1000 pillars. Behind rises Hanumakonda Hill, site of the original Kakatiya capital.

⏟ Sleeping & Eating

Hotel Shreya   HOTEL $
(☑0870-2547788; www.hotelshreyawarangal.com; New Bus Stand Rd, Hanumakonda; r incl breakfast ₹1600-2200, ste ₹3200; ❈⊛) Great value, with well-presented rooms that have flatscreen TVs and minifridges. Book a suite for extra space. There's a restaurant for tasty veg dishes and room service. It's steps from Hanumakonda bus stand (p934).

Oyo Hotel Ashoka 3420   HOTEL $$
(☑0870-2578491; www.oyorooms.com; Main Rd, Hanumakonda; r incl breakfast ₹1710-2850; ❈⊛) Near the Hanumakonda bus stand and 1000-Pillared Temple, this large hotel is now managed by Oyo and has a selection of AC rooms in several price categories. Also here is the good veg restaurant **Kanishka** (mains ₹135-260; ⊙6.30am-10.30pm), plus a non-veg restaurant, and a bar and small gym.

Sri Geetha Bhavan   ANDHRA $
(Market Rd, Hanumakonda; mains ₹90-130; ⊙6am-11pm) Good South Indian meals in pleasant AC surroundings. Follow the Supreme Hotels sign.

ⓘ Information

Telangana Tourism (☑0870-2571339; www.telanganatourism.gov.in; opposite Indian Oil, Nakkalagutta, Hanumakonda; ⊙10.30am-5pm Mon-Sat) Helpful staff.

ⓘ Getting There & Away

Buses to Hyderabad (₹138 to ₹280, four hours) leave about three times hourly from **Hanumakonda bus stand** (New Bus Stand Rd), and seven times daily (express/deluxe ₹135/196) from **Warangal bus stand** (☑0870-2565595; Station Rd) opposite the train station.

From Warangal several trains run daily to Hyderabad (sleeper/2AC ₹170/700, three hours), Vijayawada (₹190/745, three hours) and Chennai (₹375/1400, 10½ to 12 hours).

Shared autorickshaws (₹15) ply fixed routes around Warangal and Hanumakonda.

Palampet

About 70km northeast of Warangal, the stunning **Ramappa Temple** (camera ₹25; ⊙6am-6pm) is near the village of Palampet. Built in the early 13th century, it's the outstanding gem of Kakatiya architecture, covered in wonderfully detailed carvings of animals, lovers, wrestlers, musicians, dancers, deities and Hindu legends. Brackets on its external pillars support superb black-basalt carvings of mythical creatures and sinuous women twined with snakes. The large temple tank, Ramappa Cheruvu, 1km south, is popular with migrating birds.

There is one government-run **lodge** (☎0871-5200200, 9848036622; www.telanganatourism.gov.in; Ramappa Cheruvu; cottage ₹1750-3100; ❄) nearby but nothing else. Many travellers base themselves in nearby Warangal.

The easiest way to get here is by chartered taxi (around ₹2200 return from Warangal), but buses also run half-hourly from Hanumakonda (sister town of Warangal) to Mulugu (₹34, one hour), then a further 13km to Palampet (₹18), or ₹200 in an auto.

ANDHRA PRADESH

The state of Andhra Pradesh stretches 972km along the Bay of Bengal between Tamil Nadu and Odisha (Orissa), and inland up into the picturesque Eastern Ghats. Its the epicentre of Telugu language and culture. Explorers will discover one of India's most visited temples (at Tirumala), some fascinating and remote ancient sites from the earliest days of Buddhism and one of the nicest stretches of India's east coast, north of Visakhapatnam – plus you'll be able to enjoy the spicily delicious Andhra cuisine everywhere.

Andhra's tourism website is www.aptourism.gov.in.

Vijayawada

☎0866 / POP 1.19 MILLION

This commercial and industrial city, on the north bank of the Krishna River, forms Andhra's new state capital, with its emerging sister settlement of Amaravati, a showpiece capital complex located on the south bank. Politicians have declared Vijayawada-Amaravati will eventually have 2.5 million inhabitants.

Though the construction of Amaravati has been delayed, there are big changes afoot in and around Vijayawada. Work on new highways continues apace and the city's airport has now been designated international status. Right now there's not much of interest for travellers in the city itself, and nothing at all to see in Amaravati, but Vijayawada makes a logical base for visiting some fascinating historic sites in the lush and green surrounding area.

Sights

★Undavalli Cave Temples HINDU TEMPLE
(Indian/foreigner ₹25/300; ⌚9am-5.30pm) This stunning four-storey cave temple was probably originally carved out of the hillside for Buddhist monks in the 2nd century AD, then converted to Hindu use in the 7th century. The shrines are now largely empty, except those on the third level, one of which houses a huge reclining Vishnu. A row of gnome-like stone Vaishnavaite gurus/preachers gaze out over the rice paddies from the terrace. It's 9km southwest of downtown Vijayawada: autorickshaws or Ola/Uber cabs here cost ₹150 one way.

Kanaka Durga Temple HINDU TEMPLE
(www.kanakadurgatemple.org; Durga Temple Ghat Rd, Indrakeeladri Hill; ⌚4am-9pm) Dating back to the 12th century, this important temple is located on Indrakeeladri Hill, close to the Krishna River, and draws many pilgrims.

Kondapalli Fort FORT
(₹10, camera Indian/foreigner ₹20/100; ⌚10am-5pm) This ruined fortress, 25km northwest of Vijayawada, was built around 1360 by the Reddy kings, and passed through a succession of later rulers, including the Qutb Shahis of Golconda in the 16th century, before becoming a British military camp in 1767. You can wander round several half-ruined halls and courtyards and step into the old royal prison. The structure is currently the subject of a renovation program.

Sleeping & Eating

Hotel Sripada HOTEL $
(☎0866-2579641; hotelsripada@rediffmail.com; Gandhi Nagar; s ₹900-1460, d ₹1010-1690; ❄📶) A short walk from the train station, this is one of the few decent budget hotels in Vijayawada. Offers small AC rooms in reasonable condition, and helpful staff. However, there's no in-house restaurant.

★Minerva Hotel HOTEL $$
(☎0866-6678888; www.minervahotels.in; MG Rd; s/d ₹3500/4000, ste ₹7500; ❄📶) This hotel has rooms with a pleasing contemporary touch, large flatscreen TVs, wooden floors, safe and minibar. The Blue Fox restaurant here is good, there's a coffee shop, and you'll find a cinema and ample shopping close by.

SLEEPING PRICE RANGES

The following price ranges refer to a double room with bathroom in Telangana and Andhra Pradesh:

$ less than ₹1750

$$ ₹1750–₹5000

$$$ more than ₹5000

Hotel Southern Grand HOTEL **$$**
(☎0866-6677777; www.hotelsoutherngrand.com; Papaiah St, Gandhi Nagar; incl breakfast s/d from ₹2200/2600; ❄📶) Offers inviting, contemporary rooms and located just 600m from the train station. The hotel also has an excellent veg restaurant, Arya Bhavan (p936), and a useful travel desk, **Southern Travels** (☎0866-6677777). Book in advance for the best deals.

★**Minerva Coffee Shop** INDIAN **$$**
(Museum Rd; mains ₹160-280; ⏰7am-11pm) Great North and South Indian veg cuisine in bright, spotless AC premises. Meals (thalis) are only available from 11.30am to 3.30pm but top-notch dosa, *idli* and *uttapam* (₹35 to ₹75) are served all day and the biryanis are also good. There's another **branch** (Minerva Hotel, mains ₹160-280; ⏰7am-11pm) in airy, sophisticated surrounds on MG Rd.

Avista INDIAN **$$**
(Hotel Aria, 40 Benz Circle; mains ₹170-350; ⏰7.30am-10.30pm; 📶) Offering comfortable AC surrounds, this hotel restaurant has an eclectic menu, including Western and Chinese dishes, but it's the North Indian food that stands out; try the *malai kofta* (cottage cheese in cardamom gravy, ₹200) or *murgh makhani* (chicken tikka in tomato sauce, ₹300)

Arya Bhavan INDIAN **$$**
(Hotel Southern Grand, Papaiah St, Gandhi Nagar; mains ₹130-170, thalis ₹120-180; ⏰7am-11pm) Pure-veg food in a bright, clean, busy environment, with dosa and other South Indian breakfast items available all day. Good ice cream too!

★**TFL** MULTICUISINE **$$$**
(www.facebook.com/tflvijayawada; Santhi Nagar First Lane; mains ₹180-360; ⏰10am-11.45pm; 📶) A stylish cafe-resto in a converted suburban bungalow with a great covered terrace. Offers Italian, Mexican, American, European and East Asian dishes, including risotto, good pizza and excellent Western breakfasts. Don't skip on their desserts, which are perfect for chocoholics.

ℹ Information

Department of Tourism (☎0866-2578880; Vijayawada Junction station; ⏰10am-5pm) Has helpful staff and can assist with travel planning.

ℹ Getting There & Away

AIR

Vijayawada Airport (http://vijayawadaairport.in) is 17km northeast of the city centre. There are daily flights to Indian cities including Bengaluru, Chennai, Delhi, Hyderabad, Mumbai, Tirupati and Visakhapatnam. Airlines include Air India, Alliance Air, IndiGo, SpiceJet and TruJet.

An IndiGo international connection started flying to Singapore in 2018.

There are 14 daily buses (non-AC/AC ₹50/100, 30 minutes) between the airport and **Pandit Nehru bus station** (Arjuna St; ⏰24hr). Taxis from the official airport rank charge a steep ₹700 to central Vijayawada.

BUS

Services from the large Pandit Nehru bus station (p936) include the following:

Chennai non-AC/AC/semi-sleeper ₹518/777/1170, eight to ten hours, nine daily

Eluru non-AC/AC ₹72/122, 1½ hours, half-hourly

Hyderabad non-AC/AC ₹317/467, four to six hours, half-hourly

Tirupati non-AC/AC ₹474/812, nine hours, half-hourly

Visakhapatnam non-AC/AC ₹430/737, eight to nine hours, half-hourly

Many private bus companies depart from stops around Benz Circle, 4km east of the centre.

TRAIN

Vijayawada Junction station is on the main Chennai–Kolkata and Chennai–Delhi railway lines. The 12841/12842 Coromandel Express between Chennai and Kolkata is quick for journeys up and down the coast. Typical journey times and frequencies, for sleeper/2AC fares:

Bengaluru (Bangalore) ₹780/2750, 12 to 15 hours, five to six daily

Chennai ₹290/1050, 6 to 8 hours, 13 daily

Hyderabad ₹240/800, 5½ to 7 hours, 15 daily

Kolkata ₹555/2125, 18 to 21 hours, five to six daily

Tirupati ₹265/965, six to eight hours, 11-13 daily

Warangal ₹190/745, three hours, 15 daily

Amaravathi

📞 08645 / POP 4800

The historic Buddhist site of Amaravathi (not to be confused with the new state capital, Amaravati) is 43km west of Vijayawada. This was the earliest centre of Buddhism in the southern half of India, with the nation's biggest **stupa** (Indian/foreigner ₹25/300; ⏰ 9am-5.30pm, to 6pm Apr-Nov), 27m high and 49m across, constructed here from the 3rd century BC. Amaravathi flourished as a capital of the Satavahana kingdom, which ruled from Andhra across the Deccan for four or five centuries, becoming a fountainhead of Buddhist art. All that remains onsite of the stupa ruins now are its circular base and a few parts of the surrounding stone railing. (Museums worldwide hold pieces from the ruin, including the British Museum with a collection of 120 marble sculptures and inscriptions.) The great hemispherical dome is gone – but the neighbouring **museum** (₹5; ⏰ 9am-5pm Sat-Thu) has a model of the stupa and some of the intricate marble carvings, depicting the Buddha's life, with which the Satavahanas covered and surrounded it. The giant modern **Dhyana Buddha statue** (₹20; ⏰ 8am-8pm) of a seated Buddha overlooks the Krishna River nearby.

Bus 301 from Vijayawada bus station runs to Amaravathi (₹56, 1½ hours) every 20 minutes, via Unduvalli. Drivers charge around ₹1800 for a half-day excursion from Vijayawada.

Nagarjunakonda

📞 08680

The unique island of Nagarjunakonda is peppered with ancient Buddhist structures. The Ikshvaku dynasty had its capital here in the 3rd and 4th centuries AD, when the area was probably the most important Buddhist centre in South India. There's a huge dam here that is a tourist attraction for domestic tourists.

👁 Sights

Nagarjuna Sagar Dam   DAM

This vast structure, which dams the river Krishna, is 180m in height from its deepest foundation and 1.6km long. The adjacent hydroelectric plant has a power generation capacity of 815.6 MW.

Sri Parvata Arama   BUDDHIST SITE

(Buddhavanam; ⏰ 9.30am-6pm) **FREE** This Buddhism heritage park, featuring a recre-

ation of the huge Amaravathi stupa, is 8km north of the dam. It's been under construction by the state tourism authorities for many years and is still far from complete. The 9m replica of the Avukana Buddha statue was donated by Sri Lanka. There's also an attractive meditation area, Dhyanavanam, with fine lake views. Alight at Buddha Park when coming by bus from Hyderabad.

Nagarjunakonda Museum   MUSEUM

(Indian/foreigner incl monuments ₹20/120; ⏰ 9am-4pm Sat-Thu) The thoughtfully laid-out Nagarjunakonda Museum has Buddha statues and some superbly detailed carvings depicting local contemporary life and the Buddha's lives. The reassembled remains of several buildings, including stupa bases, walls of monastery complexes and pits for horse sacrifice, are arranged on a 1km path running along the island. The largest stupa, in the Chamtasri Chaitya Griha group, contained a bone fragment thought to be from the Buddha himself.

🎓 Courses

Dhamma Nagajjuna   HEALTH & WELLBEING

(📞 9440139329, 9348456780; www.nagajjuna. dhamma.org; Hill Colony) Keeping the Buddha's teachings alive in the region, this centre offers 10-day silent meditation courses in charming flower-filled grounds overlooking Nagarjuna Sagar. Apply in advance; payment is by donation. Alight at Buddha Park when coming by bus from Hyderabad.

🛏 Sleeping & Eating

Nagarjuna Resort   HOTEL $

(📞 08642-242471; Vijayapuri South; r without/with AC ₹900/1600; ❄) Offers spacious though drab rooms, while the balconies enjoy good views. It's conveniently located across the road from the boat launch.

Haritha Vijaya Vihar   HOTEL $$

(📞 08680-277362; www.telanganatourism.gov.in; r with AC incl breakfast Mon-Thu ₹1400-1870, Fri-Sun ₹2400-2970; ❄ 🌐 🏊) This government hotel is 6km north of the dam, with decent rooms, nice gardens, a good pool (nonguests ₹50) and lovely lake views. It's a little overpriced, but the location is exceptional, the restaurant is quite decent and there's a bar.

Hotel Siddhartha   INDIAN $$

(Buddhavanam, Hill Colony; mains ₹125-260; ⏰ 6am-11pm) Beside Sri Parvata Arama, with

GUNTUPALLI

Well off the beaten path, the Buddhist site of **Guntupalli** (Indian/foreigner ₹5/200; ⊙10am-5pm) makes a very scenic adventure. This former hilltop monastery is especially noteworthy for its caves, carvings and *chaitya-griha* (prayer hall). Guntupalli was active from the 2nd century BC to the 3rd century AD.

The cave's domed ceiling is carved with 'wooden beams' designed to look like those in a hut. The *chaitya-griha* has a well-preserved stupa and, like the monks' dwellings that line the same cliff, a gorgeous arched facade also designed to look like wood.

From Eluru, on the Vijayawada–Visakhapatnam road and railway, take a bus 35km north to Kamavarapukota (₹44, 1½ hours, half-hourly), then an autorickshaw 10km west to Guntupalli. A taxi from Eluru costs around ₹1800 return.

tasty curries, biryanis, fish dishes and lots of snacks served in a pleasant, airy pavilion.

❶ Getting There & Away

The easiest way to visit Nagarjunakonda, other than with a private vehicle, is on a bus tour (₹550) from Hyderabad with Telangana Tourism (p922), running on weekends only. It's a very long (15 hours!) day trip, however, on a non-AC bus.

Public buses from Hyderabad's Mahatma Gandhi Bus Station run hourly to Hill Colony/ Nagarjuna Sagar (₹230, four hours): alight at Pylon and catch an autorickshaw (shared/ private ₹20/120) 8km to Vijayapuri South.

Boats (₹150 return) depart for the island from Vijayapuri South, 7km south of the dam, theoretically at 9.30am, 11.30am and 1.30pm (but they invariably leave late), and stay for one to two hours. The first two boats may not go if not enough people turn up, but the 1.30pm boat goes every day (barring high winds) and starts back from the island around 4.30pm.

Visakhapatnam

📞 0891 / POP 1.79 MILLION

Visakhapatnam – also called Vizag (*vie*-zag) – is Andhra Pradesh's largest city, famous for steel and its big port, but also doubling as a beach resort for sea-breeze-seeking domestic tourists. During the main December–February holiday season there's a distinctly kitschy vibe, with camel rides and thousands of bathers (though no swimmers).

The pedestrian promenade along **Ramakrishna Beach** (Beach Rd) is pleasant for a stroll, and nearby Rushikonda Beach is perhaps Andhra's best. Every year the city hosts **Visakha Utsav** (⊙mid-Jan), a festival with food stalls on Ramakrishna Beach, exhibitions and cultural events.

With international connections to the Far East from its increasingly busy airport, more international travellers are passing through now.

◉ Sights

★ **Submarine Museum**   MUSEUM

(Beach Rd; adult/child ₹40/20, camera ₹50; ⊙2pm-8.30pm Tue-Sat, 10am-12.30pm & 2pm-8.30pm Sun) A fantastic attraction located towards the north end of Ramakrishna Beach, the 91m-long, Soviet-built, Indian navy submarine *Kursura* is now a fascinating museum. You're given about 15 minutes to explore the incredibly confined quarters and check out the torpedoes, kitchens and sleeping areas. Some staff speak a little English.

★ **Aircraft Museum**   MUSEUM

(Beach Rd; adult/child ₹70/40; ⊙2pm-8.30pm Mon-Fri, 10am-8.30pm Sat & Sun) Opened in 2017, this museum showcases a Soviet-era TU-142M aircraft that was used by the Indian military for 29 years (and 30,000 hours of accident-free flying). There's excellent information about the history of the plane and Indian aviation. You can enter the aircraft (though access to the cockpit may not be possible due to crowds) and your ticket includes an audio guide. You'll also find a VR gaming zone and cafe here.

Simhachalam Temple   HINDU TEMPLE

(http://simhachalamdevasthanam.net; ⊙4am-10pm) Andhra's second-most visited temple (after Tirumala) is a 16km drive northwest of town. It's dedicated to Varahalakshmi Narasimha, a combination of Vishnu's boar and lion-man avatars, and can get crowded. A ₹100 ticket will get you to the deity (and a sip of holy water) much quicker than a ₹20 one. Buses 6A and 28 go here from the RTC Complex and train station.

🏃 Activities

Andhra Pradesh Tourism (Andhra Pradesh Tourism Development Corporation; ☑0891-2788820; http://aptdc.gov.in; RTC Complex; ⊙8am-8pm Mon-Fri, 9am-1pm Sat) does all-day city tours (₹475 to ₹650), temple visits and trips to Araku Valley, from its RTC Complex (p940) and train station (p940) offices.

Surfers and kayakers can rent decent boards and kayaks from local surf pioneer **Melville Smythe** (☑9848561052; melsmythe@gmail.com; per hr surfboard ₹400-600, 2-person kayak ₹300, surf tuition ₹300), by the jet-ski hut at the south end of Rushikonda Beach.

🛏 Sleeping

Hotels are scattered around town. Beach Rd is the best place to stay, but it's low on inexpensive hotels. There were no hostels in town at the time of research.

Hotel Morya HOTEL $
(☑0891-2731112; www.hotelmorya.com; Bowdara Rd; r ₹990, r with AC from ₹1490; ❄🛜) A good choice, the Morya's standard rooms are small and lack ventilation, but their better AC options are quite spacious, bright and relatively smart. There's a lift, but no restaurant.

SKML Beach Guest House GUESTHOUSE $
(☑9848355131; ramkisg.1074@gmail.com; Beach Rd, Varun Beach; r ₹1200-1300, with AC ₹1850-2300; ❄🛜) SKML is towards the less select southern end of Ramakrishna Beach, but its 12 rooms are clean and decent. Best are the two top-floor 'suites' with sea views, a terrace and a bit of art.

Ambica Sea Green HOTEL $$
(☑0891-2821818; www.ambicaseagreen.com; Beach Rd; r incl breakfast from ₹4680; ❄🛜) A good choice, the contemporary, well-equipped rooms here all have sea views. Breakfast is an excellent buffet spread and staff go the extra mile to help.

Dolphin Hotel HOTEL $$
(☑0891-2567000; http://dolphinhotelsvizag.com; Dabagardens; r/ste incl breakfast from ₹3510/6340; ❄🛜🏊) A large concrete hotel in the centre with quite spacious rooms and an attractive restaurant. Its trump card is the 20m pool, and there's also an excellent gym, one of the best in the city.

Haritha Beach Resort HOTEL $$
(☑0891-2788826; http://aptdc.gov.in; Rushikonda Beach; r with AC incl breakfast ₹2100-3200; ❄🛜) This government-run place has a fine hillside location facing Rushikonda Beach. Rooms are a little old-fashioned, but the executive and luxury categories are large; all have views overlooking the ocean. Just below, and with beach access, **Vihar** (Rushikonda; ⊙11am-10.30pm; 🛜) is great for a beer or meal.

★ Novotel Visakhapatnam Varun Beach HOTEL $$$
(☑0891-2822222; www.accorhotels.com; Beach Rd; r incl breakfast ₹9620; ❄@🛜🏊) A modernist landmark that boasts a commanding position on Beach Rd facing the Bay of Bengal. Rooms are very well-appointed and immaculately presented, all with direct sea views. Dining options are first class, the bar is great for a tipple, the spa is excellent and the pool big enough for laps.

🍴 Eating

The snack stalls on Ramakrishna Beach are hopping at night.

Hotel V Parlour INDIAN $
(https://v-parlour.business.site; Rama Talkies Rd; mains ₹90-270; ⊙noon-10:30pm) A pure-veg place with simple surrounds and generous portions that's always popular. Choose from North or South Indian, or Chinese-style dishes. The stall at the front sells Irani chai too.

★ Sea Inn ANDHRA $$
(Raju Ka Dhaba; ☑9989012102; http://seainn.info; Beach Rd, Rushikonda; mains ₹100-240; ⊙noon-4pm Tue-Sun) Chef Devi cooks Andhra-style curries the way her mum did. Biryanis are spicy-delicious and filling, and you'll also find a short menu of local fish, seafood, chicken and veg dishes. All are served up in a simple, semi-open-air dining room with bench seating, 300m north of the Haritha Beach Resort turn-off. Be prepared to wait for a table; cash only.

★ Dharani INDIAN $$
(Daspalla Hotel, off Town Main Rd, Suryabagh; thalis & mains ₹100-240; ⊙6am-10.30pm) One of the city's best-regarded restaurants, with simply superb veg thalis – order a 'Special' for an authentic taste of the South (₹240). The hotel has several other restaurants too, including Andhra non-veg and North Indian veg options.

WORTH A TRIP

BHEEMUNIPATNAM

This former Dutch settlement, 25km north of Vizag, is the oldest municipality in mainland India, with bizarre sculptures on the beach, an 1861 lighthouse, an interesting Dutch cemetery, and Bheemli Beach, where local grommets surf not-very-clean waters on crude homemade boards. Buses (₹32, one hour, every 30min) trundle up the coast road from Vizag beach, or a one-way Uber/Ola is around ₹375.

Little Italy   ITALIAN $$

(http://littleitaly.in; 1st fl, South Wing, ATR Towers, Vutagedda Rd, Paandurangapuram; mains ₹240-450; ⊙11.30am-11pm; 🛜) This Italian restaurant does fine thin-crust pizza, pasta and reasonable salads in stylish surrounds. No alcohol, but good fruit mocktails. It's behind Ramakrishna Beach.

Bamboo Bay   ANDHRA $$$

(The Park, Beach Rd; mains ₹485-990; ⊙7.30-11pm; 🛜) Excellent Andhra, Chettinad and Mughlai food in the Park hotel's beachside gardens, including lots of seafood. There's a good choice for vegetarians and you can dine on the terrace by candlelight in the evening.

🍷 Drinking & Nightlife

★ Moksha Restocafé   CAFE

(www.facebook.com/moksha.restocafe; Ootagadda Rd, Daspalla Hills; ⊙8am-midnight; 🛜) Community cafe popular with a hip young Vizag crowd, with distant sea views from its terrace. There's fine coffee, including espresso options, and good juices (try the minty lemon). On the menu you'll find Western, Thai, Tibetan and Indian dishes (plus treats like Nutella crepes). Also hosts talks and events.

Tribe   CLUB

(www.facebook.com/tribevizag; The Park, Beach Rd; ⊙Fri & Sat 8pm-1am or later) One of Vizag's busiest and most fashionable clubs, with DJs playing house, R'n'B and Bollywood to a lively crowd; there are also live bands. It opens some Sundays for chill-out sessions. Smart dress required.

ℹ Getting There & Away

AIR

Vizag airport has direct daily flights to over 20 Indian cities including Bengaluru, Bhubaneswar, Chennai, Delhi, Hyderabad, Kolkata, Mumbai, Port Blair and Vijayawada. There are also international connections to Bangkok, Dubai, Kuala Lumpur and Singapore.

BOAT

Boats depart roughly once a month for Port Blair in the Andaman Islands. Call or email for schedules, or check www.andamanbeacon.com. Book for the 56-hour journey (bunk ₹2500, cabin berth from ₹4960) at **AV Bhanoji Rao, Garuda Pattabhiramayya & Co** (☑0891-2562661, 0891-2565597; ops@avbgpr.com; Harbour Approach Rd, next to NMDC, port area; ⊙9am-5pm Mon-Sat). Tickets go on sale around a week before departure. Bring your passport, two photocopies of its data page, and two passport photos.

BUS

Services from Vizag's well-organised **RTC Complex** (☑0891-2746400; RTC Complex Inner Rd) include the following:

Hyderabad non-AC/AC ₹746/1352, 12-15 hours, 12 daily

Jagdalpur non-AC ₹342, nine hours, one daily

Vijayawada general/superluxury/AC ₹408/430/593-808, seven to nine hours, every 30min

CAR

English-speaking **Srinivasa 'Srinu' Rao** (☑7382468137) is a reliable, friendly driver for out-of-town trips. He charges around ₹3300 for an Araku Valley day trip and ₹1700 to Sankaram and back.

TRAIN

Visakhapatnam station (Station Rd), on the western edge of town, is on the main Kolkata–Chennai line. Destinations travelling sleeper/2AC include the following:

Bhubaneswar ₹290/1065, seven hours, 11 daily

Chennai ₹425/1600, 13-16 hours, three to four daily

Hyderabad ₹380/1485, 12-15 hours, eight daily

Kolkata ₹460/1735, 13-16 hours, six to seven daily

Vijayawada ₹255/850, six hours, 16 to 18 daily

The **railway reservation centre** (Station Approach Rd; ⊙8am-10pm Mon-Sat, to 2pm Sun) is 300m south of the main station building.

ℹ️ Getting Around

There are over 2000 Uber (and a similar number of Ola) drivers in Visakhapatnam, so you won't have to wait long for a ride.

For the airport, 12km west of downtown, app-cabs or autorickshaws charge about ₹260. Or take bus 38 from the RTC Complex (₹20, 30 minutes). The airport's arrivals hall has a prepaid taxi booth.

The train station has a prepaid autorickshaw booth. Shared autorickshaws run along Beach Rd from the port at the south end of town to Rushikonda, 10km north of Vizag, charging ₹10 for a short hop.

Around Visakhapatnam

Sankaram

Located 40km west of Vizag, the stunning seldom-visited Buddhist complex of **Sankaram** (⊙8am-6pm) is also known by the names of its two parts, Bojjannakonda and Lingalakonda. Bojjannakonda, the eastern part, has a pair of rock-cut shrines with several gorgeous carvings of the Buddha inside and outside. Above sit the ruins of a huge stupa and a monastery. Lingalakonda, at the western end, is piled with tiers of rock-cut stupas, some of them enormous.

A car from Vizag costs around ₹1700. Or take a bus (₹46, 1½ hours, every half-hour from the RTC Complex) or train (₹38, one hour) to Anakapalle, 3km away, and then an autorickshaw (around ₹140 return including waiting).

Bavikonda & Thotlakonda

Bavikonda (⊙9am-5pm) and **Thotlakonda** (car ₹30; ⊙8am-5.30pm) were Buddhist monasteries on scenic hilltop sites north of Vizag that each hosted up to 150 monks, with the help of massive rainwater tanks. Their remains were unearthed in the 1980s and 1990s.

The monasteries flourished from around the 3rd century BC to the 3rd century AD, and had votive stupas, congregation halls, *chaitya-grihas* (prayer halls), *viharas* (refuges for monks) and refectories. Thotlakonda has sea views, and Bavikonda has special importance because a relic vessel found in its Mahachaitya stupa contained a piece of bone believed to be from the Buddha himself.

Bavikonda and Thotlakonda are reached from turn-offs 14km and 15km, respectively, from Vizag on the Bheemunipatnam road:

Bavikonda is 3km off the main road and Thotlakonda 1.25km. Vizag autorickshaw or Ola/Uber drivers charge around ₹700 return to see both.

Araku Valley

🚃 08936 / ELEV 975M

Andhra's best train ride is through the beautiful, lushly forested Eastern Ghats to the Araku Valley, centred on Araku town, 115km north of Visakhapatnam. The area is home to isolated tribal communities and known for its tasty organic coffee and lovely green countryside. En route you can visit the impressive Borra Caves.

◉ Sights

Borra Caves CAVE

(adult/child ₹60/45, camera/mobile camera ₹100/25; ⊙10am-1pm & 2-5pm) Illuminated with fancy lighting, the huge million-year-old limestone Borra Caves are 38km before Araku town and can be combined with a visit to the Araku Valley. Stairways penetrate the caves, but they can get very crowded, especially on Sundays. Watch out for monkeys. You'll find snack stands close to the entrance; try the bamboo chicken.

Museum of Habitat MUSEUM

(₹40; ⊙8am-1.30pm & 2.30-8pm) This museum has extensive exhibits on the tribal peoples of eastern Andhra Pradesh, including full-scale mock-ups of hunting, ceremonial and other scenes, and a few craft stalls. Worthwhile, but displays and information could be better. Located next to the bus station and 2km east of the train station.

🛏️ Sleeping & Eating

The main drag in Araku has several eateries. The local speciality is *bongulo* chicken, which is spiced chicken cooked in a section of bamboo cane. Do try the local coffee while you're here.

Dream Valley Residency GUESTHOUSE $

(📞9398803229; https://dream-valley-residency. business.site; r₹1300; 🛜) A pocket-friendly motel-tyle place on the south side of the railway tracks. Rooms are in decent shape and have cable TV and en-suites with reliable hot water. The management are helpful and can advise travellers about local attractions.

Hotel Rajadhani HOTEL $

(📞08936-249580; r without/with AC ₹900/1400; ❄️🛜) Reasonable budget hotel with over

30 rooms. They could all be better presented, and service can be lacking, but rooms on the upper floor enjoy valley views from their balconies. There's an **in-house restaurant** (mains ₹120-260; ⊘7am-10pm).

Haritha Valley Resort
HOTEL $$

(☑08936-249202; http://aptdc.gov.in/aptdc; r incl breakfast ₹1900, with AC from ₹2260; ✳🕲🛋) The best place to stay in Araku, with a pool and landscaped grounds. It's a government-run hotel and rooms are maintained quite well, though service is very leisurely. Favoured by Tollywood film crews.

Star Annapurna
INDIAN $

(mains ₹110-250; ⊘7.30am-10pm) Offers a wide choice of flavoursome dishes including a good chicken biryani, fish dishes and lots of well-spiced vegetable curries.

Araku Valley Coffee House
CAFE $

(coffee ₹25-100; ⊘8.30am-9pm) You can sample and buy local coffee and all kinds of chocolatey goods (brownies, chocolate-covered coffee beans) at Araku Valley Coffee House, which also has a tiny **coffee museum** (₹25; ⊘8.30am-9pm). A trampoline will keep the kids entertained and there are often tribal dancing performances too.

❶ Getting There & Away

From Visakhapatnam a train (₹100, four hours) leaves daily at 6.50am, returning from Araku at 3.40pm. Get to Visakhapatnam early to secure a seat and be aware that the return train often leaves late. A special AC 'vistadome' (glass roof) carriage has been added to this service; you need to book 'Executive Chair' class on the IRCTC website (www.irctc.co.in) and tickets cost ₹665.

Buses (roughly hourly) from Visakhapatnam (from ₹130) take 4½ hours. A taxi day trip costs ₹3300 to ₹4000. The APTDC (Andhra Pradesh Tourism Development Corporation; http://aptdc.gov.in) runs tours that all include the Borra Caves; however its day trips are very rushed.

Tirumala & Tirupati
☑0877 / POP 7900 (TIRUMALA) / 296,000 (TIRUPATI)

One of the globe's largest pilgrimage destinations, the holy hill of Tirumala is, on any given day, thronged with thousands of devotees who've journeyed to venerate Lord Venkateshwara here, at his home. Around 60,000 pilgrims come each day, and *darshan* runs 24/7. The **Tirumala Tirupathi Devasthanams** (TTD; ☑0877-2277777, 0877-2233333; www.tirumala.org; KT Rd; ⊘9am-5.30pm Mon-Fri, to 1pm Sat) efficiently administers the multitudes, employing 20,000 people to do so. Despite the crowds, a sense of order, serenity and ease mostly prevails, and a trip to the Holy Hill can be fulfilling even if you're not a pilgrim. Queues during the annual nine-day Brahmotsavam festival (p916) can stretch for kilometres.

Tirupati, the humdrum town at the bottom of the hill, is the functional gateway to Tirumala.

◉ Sights & Activities

Venkateshwara Temple
HINDU TEMPLE

(www.tirumala.org; ⊘24hr) Legends about the hill itself and the surrounding area appear in the Puranas, and the temple's history may date back 2000 years. Devotees flock to Tirumala to see Venkateshwara, an avatar of Vishnu. Among the many powers attributed to Venkateshwara is the granting of any wish made at this holy site. Foreigners (with passport) are able to gain fast-entry (₹300) at the Supatham Gate and avoid the worst of the scrum, though expect jostling.

The main temple is an atmospheric place, though you'll be pressed between hundreds of devotees when you see it. Venkateshwara inspires bliss and love among his visitors from the back of the dark and magical inner sanctum; it smells of incense and resonates with chanting. You'll have a moment to say a prayer and then you'll be shoved out again. Don't forget to collect your delicious *ladoo* from the counter: Tirumala *ladoos* (sweet balls made with chickpea flour, cardamom and dried fruits) are famous across India.

Many pilgrims donate their hair to the deity – in gratitude for a wish fulfilled, or to renounce ego – so hundreds of barbers attend to devotees. Tirumala and Tirupati are filled with tonsured men, women and children.

Upon entry, you'll have to sign a form declaring your faith in Lord Venkateshwara.

Pity the locals queuing for 'ordinary darshan', a wait of anywhere from three to eight hours in claustrophobic metal cages ringing the temple. Special-entry darshan tickets are also bookable online and allow quicker access.

🛏 Sleeping

Avoid weekends if you can, when Tirupati is uber-rammed. There's a fair selection of hotels in town, though standards are not that high.

HIKING THE HOLY HILL

There are two pilgrims' paths from Tirupati to Tirumala's temple. The shorter (9km) Srivari Metlu heads straight up the mountain, taking a relentlessly steep route up. The second option, the 12km Alipiri Metlu, is an ancient pilgrims' path that begins at Alipiri, some 3.5km northwest of the centre of Tirupati, and is the preferred walk for most. Chartered buses from distant Deccan villages line the road leading to the start of the hike, disgorging hundreds of barefoot pilgrims intent on darshan (deity-viewing).

If you want to walk with the pilgrims, try to get as early a start as possible to avoid the heat of the day (the paths and temple are open 24 hours). You don't need to take supplies as there are ample food stalls and drink vendors (and WCs) en route. Most of the hike consists of concrete stairways (each individual step smeared with scarlet and orange dyes, blessings left by the faithful) and paved paths. The route is (mostly) covered with protective roofing, so the pilgrimage is possible no matter what the weather, rain or shine.

Villagers and urbanites, sadhus and techies, children and grannies march together up the holy hill. Cries of encouragement – 'Ola!' – ring across the valley to aid progress. The first, distinctly tough, half of the trek is not particularly scenic as concrete roofing and dense forest hides views back down the mountain. After 2100 or so incredibly steep steps there's the Gali Goporum (temple gateway), the ideal spot for a break. Then the forest clears to reveal a statue of Hanuman, a medical centre and a clutch of food stalls.

The next section is easier, a steady incline along a covered path for 3km or so, passing a deer reserve, before the route then follows a road for around 2km, that enjoys fine mountain vistas. You then reach the Mokala Parvatham temple from where many pilgrims ascend a final flight of steps on their knees, in an act of extreme devotion. The summit is not far from here, some 3550 steps from the starting point, and 980m above sea level. It represents a return to the realities of India complete with honking traffic, hustle and bustle, with the main temple a short walk beyond. Shouts of 'Jai Shri Ram' ('Hail Lord Rama') ensue, as the faithful approach their final destination.

Virtually all Hindu pilgrims perform the entire hike barefoot (though you won't be chastised for wearing footwear). Foreigners (with passport) are able to gain fast-entry (₹300) at the Supatham Gate for entry to Venkateshwara Temple (p942) and darshan.

The Tirumala Tirupathi Devasthanams runs vast **dormitories** (Tirumala; beds free) and **guesthouses** (Tirumala; r ₹50-3000; ❄️) near the temple in Tirumala, intended for pilgrims. To stay here, check in at the Central Reception Office.

Athidhi Residency　　　　HOTEL $
(☑ 0877-2281222; Peddakapu Layout, Tirupati; r ₹1000-1600; ❄️🛜) Keenly priced, this is a deservedly popular place with well-presented rooms that have flat-screen TVs, ceiling fans and attractive en suites. It's a short drive from the train station or walkable from the bus stand.

★**Hotel Marasa**
Sarovar Premiere Tirupati　BOUTIQUE HOTEL $$
(☑ 0877-6660000; www.sarovarhotels.com; 12th Cross Karakambadi Rd, Tirupati; r incl breakfast from ₹3300; ❄️🛜🏊) Really raising the bar in terms of quality in Tirupati, this sleek contemporary hotel is the best in town by

some distance and represents fine value. It's beautifully styled, with modish furnishings throughout and boasts a lovely pool area, two fine **restaurants** (mains ₹250-500; ⏰ 7.30-10am, noon-3.30pm & 7-11pm; 📞), cafe-bar and spa. Rooms are supremely comfortable, and the location on the edge of town is very tranquil.

Hotel Regalia　　　　HOTEL $$
(☑ 0877-2238699; www.regaliahotels.com; Ramanuja Circle, Tirupati; r/ste incl breakfast ₹2999/4999; ❄️🛜) The Regalia provides inviting, contemporary rooms with sleek en suites. There's a pure veg restaurant for Indian cuisine while Flavours scores for global grub and meat dishes. On the east side of town, 1.5km from the train station.

Minerva Grand　　　　HOTEL $$
(☑ 0877-6688888; http://minervahotels.in; Renigunta Rd, Tirupati; s/d with AC from ₹2900/3500; ❄️🛜) In the heart of town, this well-run

establishment has business-style rooms equipped with desks, plump pillows and good mattresses. Its two restaurants, both with icy AC, are great too and there's a bar and small gym.

✖ Eating & Drinking

Tirupati is well-endowed with restaurants. Huge **dining halls** (Tirumala; meals free; ⊙hours vary) on the hill feed thousands of pilgrims daily; veg restaurants also serve meals for ₹25.

Kafe Tirumala   SOUTH INDIAN $
(Lakshmipuram Circle, Tirupati; light meals ₹80-130; ⊙8am-10pm) A kind of modern take on a traditional *darshini* (South Indian breakfast joint) this small likeable place serves up snacks like *idli* and dosa at very reasonable rates. It's standing room only.

★ Hotel Mayura   INDIAN $$
(209 TP Area, Tirupati; meals ₹99-280; ⊙7am-10pm) One of the best places in town for South Indian thalis (₹220), with delicious dishes and lots of chutneys neatly arranged on a banana leaf. Ten kinds of dosa (from ₹99) are available and North Indian dishes are also offered. It's opposite the bus station.

★ Minerva Coffee Shop   INDIAN $$
(Minerva Grand, Renigunta Rd, Tirupati; thalis ₹185-240; ⊙7am-11.30pm; 🛜) The veg-only Minerva does superb Andhra and North Indian thalis (with free refills) and fine filter coffee. Staff are efficient and the ambience is family orientated. It's also a good choice for a local breakfast buffet (₹195).

Maya   INDIAN $$
(Bhimas Deluxe Hotel, 34-38 G Car St, Tirupati; mains ₹120-220; ⊙6am-10pm; 🛜) Great veg meals in the basement of the Bhimas Deluxe, near the train station. Don't confuse it with the Bhimas Hotel next door.

❶ Getting There & Away

From Visakhapatnam a train (₹100, four hours) leaves daily at 6.50am, returning from Araku at 3.40pm. Get to Visakhapatnam early to secure a seat and be aware that the return train often leaves late. A special AC 'vistadome' (glass roof) carriage has been added to this service; you need to book 'Executive Chair' class on the IRCTC website (www.irctc.co.in) and tickets cost ₹665.

Buses (roughly hourly) from Visakhapatnam (from ₹130) take 4½ hours. A taxi day trip costs ₹3300 to ₹4000. The APTDC (Andhra Pradesh Tourism Development Corporation; http://ap tdc.gov.in) runs tours that all include the Borra Caves; however its day trips are very rushed.

Around Tirumala & Tirupati

Chandragiri Fort

This fort complex, 15km west of Tirupati, dates back 1000 years but its heyday came in the late 16th century when the rulers of the declining Vijayanagar empire, having fled from Hampi, made it their capital. The upper fort on the hillside is (frustratingly) out of bounds.

The **palace area** (Chandragiri Fort; Indian/foreigner ₹25/200; ⊙9am-5pm Sat-Thu) contains nice gardens and the Raja Mahal, a heavily restored Vijayanagar palace reminiscent of Hampi buildings. It's at the heart of a 1.5km-long stout-walled enclosure at the foot of a rocky hill.

There's a reasonably interesting museum of bronze and stone sculptures here, which is worth a visit even though it's somewhat lacking in information and context.

Buses for Chandragiri (₹12) leave Tirupati hourly. Cabs charge around ₹600 return.

Kerala

Best Places to Eat

➜ Kashi Art Cafe (p991)

➜ Villa Maya (p951)

➜ Malabar Junction (p992)

➜ Bait (p956)

➜ Dal Roti (p991)

➜ Paragon Restaurant (p1002)

Best Places to Stay

➜ Neeleshwar Hermitage (p1009)

➜ Varnam Homestay (p1004)

➜ Rosegardens (p980)

➜ Old Harbour Hotel (p987)

➜ Reds Residency (p987)

➜ Marari Villas (p970)

Why Go?

For many travellers, Kerala is South India's most serenely beautiful state. This slender coastal strip is defined by its landscape: almost 600km of glorious Arabian Sea coast and beaches; a languid network of glistening backwaters; and the spice- and tea-covered hills of the Western Ghats, dotted with protected wildlife reserves and cool hill stations. Just setting foot on this swathe of soul-soothing, palm-shaded green will slow your subcontinental stride to a blissed-out amble. Kerala is a world away from the frenzy of the rest of India, its long, fascinating backstory illuminated by historically evocative cities like Kochi (Cochin) and Thiruvananthapuram (Trivandrum).

Besides the backwaters, elegant houseboats, ayurvedic treatments and delicately spiced, taste-bud-tingling cuisine, Kerala is home to wild elephants, exotic birds and the odd tiger, while vibrant traditions such as Kathakali, *theyyam* (a trance-induced ritual), festivals and snake-boat races frequently bring even the smallest villages to life.

When to Go
Thiruvananthapuram

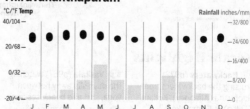

Dec–Feb Perfect beach, backwater and national-park weather; peak-season prices.

Mar–Apr Kathakali at Kottayam and Kollam festivals; high season eases off.

Aug–Oct End of the monsoon period: Onam festival, snake-boat races.

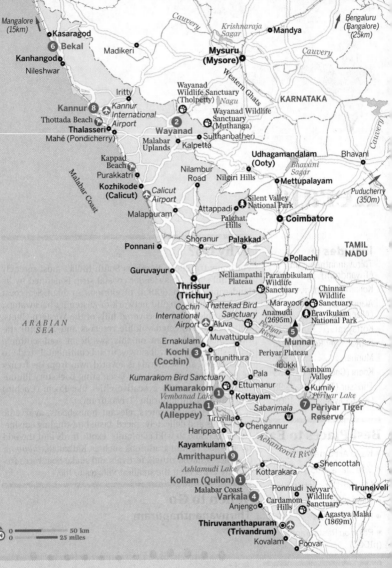

Kerala Highlights

1 Backwaters (p972)
Cruising the backwaters from Alappuzha (Alleppey), Kollam (Quilon) or Kumarakom.

2 Wayanad (p1003) Spotting wild elephants, walking the spice-carpeted hills.

3 Fort Cochin (p983)
Unravelling the history of Kochi (Cochin), while lazing in art-filled cafes.

4 Varkala (p957) Watching the days slip away between yoga, surf and beach sessions.

5 Munnar (p978) Sleeping in a secluded homestay and trekking through tea plantations.

6 Bekal (p1008) Wandering Kerala's unexplored, white-gold northernmost beaches.

7 Periyar Tiger Reserve (p973) Hiking, rafting or boating this protected space.

8 Kannur (p1006) Seeking unspoilt beaches and *theyyam* (a trance-induced ritual).

9 Amrithapuri (p964) Experiencing ashram life at Matha Amrithanandamayi Mission.

History

Traders have been drawn to Kerala's spices for more than 3000 years. The coast was known to the Phoenicians, the Romans, the Arabs and the Chinese, and was a transit point for spices from the Moluccas (eastern Indonesia).

The Cheras ruled much of Kerala until the early Middle Ages, competing with kingdoms and small fiefdoms for territory and trade, but were defeated by the Cholas in the 12th century. St Thomas the Apostle is said to have landed in Kerala in AD 52, bringing Christianity to the subcontinent. Vasco da Gama's arrival at Kappad, just north of Kozhikode (Calicut), in 1498 opened the floodgates to European colonialism as Portuguese, Dutch and English interests fought Arab traders, and then each other, for control of the lucrative spice trade.

The present-day state of Kerala was created in 1956 from the former states of Travancore, Cochin and Malabar (the first two remained independent during British rule). A tradition of valuing the arts and education resulted in a post-Independence state that is one of the most progressive in India, with the nation's highest literacy rate.

In 1957 Kerala voted in the first freely elected communist government in the world, which has gone on to hold power regularly since; the Congress-led United Democratic Front (UDF) governed from 2006 to 2011, but was replaced by the Communist Party of India-led Left Democratic Front in 2016. Many Malayalis (speakers of Malayalam, the state's official language) work in the Middle East and their remittances play a significant part in the economy. A big hope for the state's future is the relatively recent boom in tourism, with Kerala emerging in the past two decades as one of India's most popular tourist hot spots.

SOUTHERN KERALA

Thiruvananthapuram (Trivandrum)

☑ 0471 / POP 743,690

Thiruvananthapuram, Kerala's capital – still usually referred to by its colonial-era name, Trivandrum – is a relatively compact but energetic city spread across low-lying hills and is an easy-going introduction to urban life down south. Most travellers merely springboard from here to the nearby beaches of Kovalam and Varkala, but Trivandrum (once capital of the princely state of Travancore) has enough good food and intriguing sights to justify a stay.

The ancient core of the city, home to the Shri Padmanabhaswamy Temple (closed to non-Hindus), is the southern Fort area, 1km southwest of the main bus and train stations. Around 3km north of Fort along Mahatma Gandhi (MG Rd) lie the museums and Zoological Gardens.

◉ Sights

★ **Museum of History & Heritage** MUSEUM
(KeralaM; www.museumkeralam.org; Park View, Museum Rd; adult/child Indian ₹20/10, foreigner

KERALA THIRUVANANTHAPURAM (TRIVANDRUM)

TOP STATE FESTIVALS

As well as the major state festivals, Kerala has hundreds of annual temple festivals, *theyyam* (a trance-induced ritual), boat-race regattas and street parades.

Ernakulathappan Utsavam (p986; Kochi; ☺ Jan/Feb) Eight days of festivities that peak with music and fireworks; features elephant parades.

Thrissur Pooram (p998; Thrissur; ☺ Apr/May) Kerala's biggest and most vibrant festival; features elephant processions.

Nehru Trophy Boat Race (p965; Alleppey; ☺ Aug) The most celebrated of Kerala's boat races.

Onam (statewide; ☺ Aug/Sep) The entire state celebrates the golden age of mythical King Mahabali for 10 days.

Cochin Carnival (p986; Kochi; ☺ Dec) Ten days of parades, costumes and the arts in Fort Cochin.

Kochi–Muziris Biennale (p986); Kochi; ☺ Dec–Mar) One of Asia's major biennial contemporary-art festivals sweeps through Fort Cochin.

Thiruvananthapuram (Trivandrum)

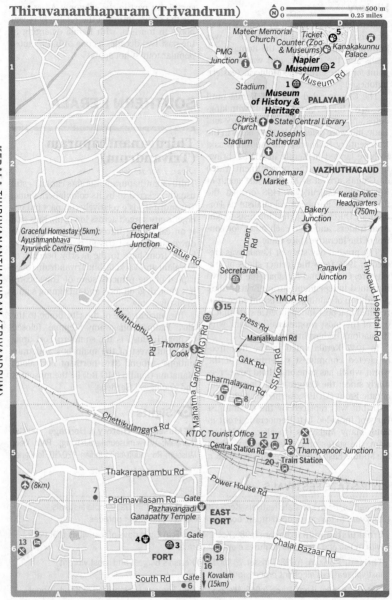

₹200/50, camera ₹25; ☺10am-5.30pm Tue-Sun) Occupying a handsome 120-year-old heritage building within the Kerala Tourism complex, this intelligently presented museum traces Kerala's history and culture through superb static and multimedia displays. Exhibits range from Iron Age implements to bronze, wood and terracotta sculptures, murals, *dhulichitra* (floor paintings), Roman-era coins, re-creations of traditional Keralite homes and replicas of engravings at Wayanad's Edakkal Caves (p1004).

Thiruvananthapuram (Trivandrum)

★**Napier Museum**   MUSEUM
(Art Museum; off Museum Rd; adult/child Indian ₹20/10, foreigner ₹200/100; ⊙10am-4.45pm Tue & Thu-Sun, 1-4.45pm Wed) Housed in an 1880 wooden building designed by Robert Chisholm (a British architect whose Fair Isle–style version of the Keralite vernacular shows his enthusiasm for local craft), this museum holds an eclectic display of bronzes, Buddhist sculptures, temple carts, ivory carvings and a wood-carved model of Kerala's famous Guruvayur temple. The architectural style fuses neo-Gothic and Keralan elements, and the carnivalesque interior is worth a look in its own right.

Zoological Gardens   ZOO
(off Museum Rd; adult/child Indian ₹30/10, foreigner ₹200/100, camera/video ₹50/200; ⊙9am-5.15pm Tue-Sun) Yann Martel famously based the animals in his novel *Life of Pi* on those he observed in Trivandrum's Zoological Gardens. Shaded paths meander through woodland, lakes and a native forest, where tigers, macaques, hippos, peacocks, deer, leopards and other creatures gather, though some live in small, not very open enclosures.

Shri Padmanabhaswamy Temple   HINDU TEMPLE
(Fort; ⊙3.30am-7.30pm) Trivandrum's spiritual heart is this 18th-century temple (closed to non-Hindus) in the Fort area, which fuses Keralan and Dravidian architecture and whose origins go back to at least the 8th century. The main entrance is through the 30m-tall, seven-tier eastern *gopuram* (gateway tower), in Tamil Nadu style.

Puthe Maliga Palace Museum   MUSEUM
(Fort; adult/child Indian ₹70/25, foreigner ₹200/70, phone camera ₹20; ⊙9am-12.45pm & 2-4.45pm Tue-Sun) Overlooking the Shri Padmanabhaswamy Temple tank, the opulent 18th-century palace of the Travancore maharajas is a classically Keralan world of beautifully carved wooden ceilings, tiled roofs, marble sculptures and imported Belgian glass. Inside you'll find Kathakali images, an armoury, portraits of maharajas, ornate thrones and other artefacts. Admission is by informative one-hour tour, though you can just visit the outside of the palace grounds (free).

🏃 Activities

An excellent way to get under the skin of the city is with a **Storytrails** (☑9061222267; www.storytrails.in; tour per person ₹1100) walking tour. The KTDC runs several bus day **tours** (☑0471-2316736; www.ktdc.com; Mascot Hotel, Mascot Sq), including a Glorious Thiruvananthapuram itinerary (₹680) and a Mesmerising Kanyakumari trip (₹990), from its office (p951) at Mascot Hotel (600m west of the Zoological Gardens).

Margi Kathakali School   CULTURAL PROGRAM
(☑0471-2478806; www.margitheatre.org; Fort; admission by donation) Conducts courses in Kathakali and Kootiattam (traditional Sanskrit drama) for beginner and advanced students (enquire directly for rates), and occasionally puts on Kathakali performances. Visitors can peek at uncostumed practise sessions, usually held from 10am to noon Monday

THE INDIAN COFFEE HOUSE STORY

Founded by the Coffee Board in the 1940s, under British rule, the Indian Coffee House is a place stuck in time. Its 400-odd India-wide branches feature old-India prices and waiters dressed in starched white with peacock-style headdresses. In the 1950s the Board began to close down cafes across India, making employees redundant. At this point, Kerala-born communist leader Ayillyath Kuttiari Gopalan Nambiar began to support the workers and founded with them the India Coffee Board Workers' Co-operative Society. The Coffee House has remained ever since, always atmospheric, and still run by its employees, all of whom share ownership.

to Friday. It's behind the Fort School, 200m west of the fort.

CVN Kalari Sangham MARTIAL ARTS
(📞0471-2474182; www.cvnkalari.in; South Rd; 15-day/1-month course ₹1000/2000) Three- to six-month courses in *kalarippayat* for serious students (aged under 30) with some experience in martial arts. Visitors are welcome to watch training sessions from 6.30am to 7.30am Monday to Saturday.

🛌 Sleeping

There are decent-value budget and midrange hotels along Manjalikulam Rd, north of the main train and bus stations.

Princess Inn HOTEL $
(📞0471-2339150; princess_inn@yahoo.com; Manjalikulam Rd; with AC s ₹990-1450, d ₹1290-1620, without AC s ₹580-900, d ₹780-1400; ❋🛜) In a glass-fronted building, the Princess Inn promises a relatively quiet no-frills sleep in a central side-street location. It's comfortable, with TVs, immaculate bathrooms, 24-hour checkout and friendly staff. Worth paying slightly extra for the more spacious 'deluxe' rooms.

Hotel Regency HOTEL $
(📞0471-2330377; www.hotelregency.com; Manjalikulam Cross Rd; with AC s ₹1080-1300, d ₹1550-1700, without AC s ₹750-950, d ₹1080-1150; ❋🛜) Around 600m northwest of the bus and train stations, this tidy, popular place

offers small but spotless rooms with TV; the deluxe rooms are more spacious and there's wi-fi in the lobby, as well as a rooftop garden.

★ Graceful Homestay HOMESTAY $$
(📞9847249556, 0471-2444358; www.gracefulhomestay.com; Pothujanam Rd, Philip's Hill; downstairs s/d ₹1800/2000, upstairs & ste s/d ₹2750/3000, all incl breakfast; 🛜) In the leafy western suburbs of Trivandrum, this lovely, serene family house amid sprawling gardens has four fan-cooled rooms, neatly furnished with individual character and access to kitchen, living areas and balconies. The top-floor double comes with a covered terrace overlooking a sea of palms. Call ahead for directions from the attentive hosts, who prepare fresh Keralan breakfasts.

★ Padmavilasom Palace HOMESTAY $$$
(📞8086080286, 7902203111; http://padmavilasompalace.com; TC29/1769 Perumthanni, Airport Rd, Injakkal; r incl breakfast ₹5000-10,000; ❋🛜) The brainchild (and former family home) of local entrepreneur Archana Mohan, Padmavilasom tactfully reimagines a 150-year-old royal palace into a luxury homestay with a tangible old-Travancore atmosphere. The two upper-floor suites have chequered floors, four-poster beds, desks and sweeping bathrooms. Victorian-era tiles carpet the lobby, beyond which the fabulous **restaurant** (breakfast ₹370, lunch ₹530; ⏰7.30-10.30am & 12.30-3pm; 🛜) serves Keralan-style vegetarian meals around a traditional *naalukettu* (homestead courtyard).

🍴 Eating

★ Ariya Nivaas SOUTH INDIAN $
(Manorama Rd; mains ₹40-150, thalis ₹120; ⏰7am-10pm) Trivandrum's best all-you-can-eat South Indian veg thalis mean long-running Ariya Nivaas is always busy (especially at lunchtime), but service is snappy and the food fresh. There's an air-con dining room upstairs.

Indian Coffee House INDIAN $
(Maveli Cafe; http://indiancoffeehouse.com; Central Station Rd; snacks ₹15-70; ⏰6.30am-10pm) Right beside Trivandrum's main bus stand, this branch of the famous Indian Coffee House serves its strong coffee and wallet-friendly snacks (biryanis, omelettes, masala dosa; savoury crepe stuffed with spiced potatoes) in a red-brick tower that looks like a cross be-

tween a lighthouse and a pigeon coop, and has a spiralling interior lined with concrete benches and tables.

★ **Villa Maya** KERALAN $$$
(☑ 0471-2578901; www.villamaya.in; 120 Airport Rd, Injakkal; mains ₹600-1600; ⊗ noon-11pm; ☎) Villa Maya is more an experience than a mere restaurant. Dining is either in the magnificent 18th-century Dutch-built mansion or in private curtained niches in the tranquil courtyard garden. The Keralan cuisine is expertly crafted, delicately spiced and beautifully presented. Seafood is a speciality, with dishes like stuffed crab with lobster butter, though there are some tantalising vegetarian offerings, too.

❶ Information

KIMS (Kerala Institute of Medical Sciences; ☑ 0471-2941144, emergency 0471-2941400; http://trivandrum.kimsglobal.com; Anayara; ⊗ 24hr) Hospital around 6km northwest of Trivandrum Central train station.

KTDC Central Reservation Centre (☑ 0471-2316736; www.ktdc.com; Mascot Hotel, Mascot Sq; ⊗ 10.15am-1.15pm & 2-5.15pm)

KTDC Tourist Office (www.ktdc.com; KTDC Hotel Chaithram, Central Station Rd; ⊗ 9.30am-7pm)

Tourist Office (☑ 0471-2321132; Museum Rd; ⊗ 24hr)

❶ Getting There & Away

AIR

Trivandrum International Airport (www.trivandrumairport.com), 4km west of the city centre, has direct flights to/from Colombo in Sri Lanka, Malé in the Maldives, and Gulf destinations.

Within India, Air India (p1208), Jet Airways (p1210), IndiGo (p1210) and/or SpiceJet (p1210) fly to/from Mumbai, Kochi (Cochin), Calicut, Bengaluru (Bangalore), Chennai, Delhi, Goa and Hyderabad.

BUS

State-run and private buses use Trivandrum's giant but orderly enough **KSRTC Bus Station Complex** (☑ 0471-2462290; www.keralartc.com; Central Station Rd, Thampanoor), opposite Trivandrum Central train station.

Buses leave for Kovalam (₹17, 30 minutes) every 20 minutes between 6am and 6.30pm from the southern end of the **East Fort bus stand** (MG Rd), next to the **Municipal bus stand** (Chalai Bazaar Rd). For Varkala, it's easier to take the train.

TRAIN

Trains are often heavily booked; reserve ahead online or visit the upstairs **reservation office** (1st fl, Trivandrum Central; ⊗ 8am-2pm & 2.15-5.30pm) just north of Platform 1 on the north side of Trivandrum Central train station. While most major trains arrive into Trivandrum Central in the city centre, some express services

BUSES FROM TRIVANDRUM KSRTC BUS STATION COMPLEX

DESTINATION	FARE (₹)	DURATION (HR)	FREQUENCY
Alleppey	150-240	3½	every 10min
Bengaluru	920-1450	16	2pm, 2.30pm, 3.15pm, 5pm, 7.30pm
Chennai	830	12-16	8 daily 9.45am-7.30pm
Ernakulam (Kochi)	230-390	5½	every 20min (AC hourly)
Kanyakumari	80	3	2.30am, 4.30am, 5.30am
Kollam	80-150	2	every 15min (AC hourly)
Kumily (for Periyar)	250	8	8.15pm
Madurai	370	8	13 daily 8am-9.30pm
Munnar	400	8	6.45am, 1pm, 10.30pm, 11.15pm, 11.45pm
Mysuru	1050	14	5pm, 7.30pm, 8pm
Neyyar Dam	40	1½	every 30-60min 5.05am-7.50pm, 10.55pm
Ooty	695	15	3pm
Puducherry	720	14	1.15pm
Thrissur	350-400	7½	every 20min

MAJOR INTERSTATE TRAINS FROM TRIVANDRUM CENTRAL

DESTINATION	TRAIN NAME & NO	FARE (₹; SLEEPER/3AC/2AC)	DURATION (HR)	DEPARTURES (DAILY)
Bengaluru	16525 Bangalore Exp	420/1145/1650	18¾	12.45pm
Chennai	12696 Chennai Exp	470/1245/1785	16¾	5.15pm
Coimbatore	17229 Sabari Exp	255/685/985	9½	7.15am
Mangaluru	16604 Maveli Exp	370/980/1325	13¾	6.45pm
Mumbai	16346 Netravathi Exp	670/1805/2655	31	9.30am

terminate at Kochuveli train station, 7km northwest of the centre – check in advance.

Within Kerala there are frequent express trains to Varkala (2nd class/sleeper/3AC ₹45/140/495, one hour), Kollam (Quilon; ₹55/170/540, 50 minutes to two hours) and Ernakulam (Kochi; ₹95/165/495, 3¾ to five hours), via Alleppey (₹80/140/495, 2¼ to 3¼ hours) or Kottayam (₹80/140/495, three hours). There are also numerous daily services to Kanyakumari (2nd class/sleeper/3AC ₹60/140/490, 1½ to three hours).

ⓘ Getting Around

Buses run between Trivandrum's East Fort bus stand (p951) and the airport (₹12, 10 minutes) every 20 minutes from 6am to 8.30pm, including several daily orange FlyBus air-con services. Prepaid taxis from the airport cost ₹350 to the city and ₹500 to Kovalam.

Taxi apps Ola Cabs and Uber are the easiest way to get around town. Autorickshaw drivers will *sometimes* use their meters; short hops cost ₹20 to ₹50. There are prepaid autorickshaw stands outside the bus (Central Station Rd) and train (Thampanoor Junction) stations.

Around Trivandrum

On the western fringes of Neyyar Dam, 30km east of Trivandrum, the superbly located 1978 **Sivananda Yoga Vedanta Dhanwantari Ashram** (☑ 9495630951, 9446580764; www.sivananda.org.in/neyyardam; Neyyar Dam; dm & tents ₹830, tw with AC ₹1940, without AC ₹1050-1310) is renowned for its hatha yoga courses, starting on the 1st and 16th of each month. Courses run for a minimum of two weeks and include accommodation and vegetarian meals; one-month yoga-teacher training is also offered. Bookings essential.

From Neyyar Dam, buses run to Trivandrum's KSRTC Bus Station Complex (p951; ₹35, one to two hours) every 30 minutes from 4.30am to 8.15pm, returning every

30 to 60 minutes from 5.05am to 7.50pm, then 10.55pm.

Kovalam

☑ 0471 / POP 25,700

Once a calm fishing village clustered around its crescent beaches and backed by a sea of cascading palms, Kovalam now competes with Varkala as Kerala's most developed resort. The touristed main stretch, Lighthouse Beach, is flanked by hotels and restaurants stretching back into the hillside from the shore; just north, Hawa Beach is usually crowded with day trippers. Neither beach could be described as pristine, but, at under 15km southeast from Trivandrum, Kovalam remains an immensely popular place for fun by the sea; there are promising waves (and a surf club), as well as charming guesthouses and a flourishing ayurveda and yoga scene.

About 2km further north, more peaceful Samudra Beach hosts several upmarket resorts.

⊙ Sights & Activities

Vizhinjam Lighthouse　　　　　LIGHTHOUSE
(Lighthouse Rd; Indian/foreigner ₹20/50, camera ₹10; ⊙10am-1pm & 2-6pm Tue-Sun) Kovalam's most distinguishing feature is the working candy-striped lighthouse at the southern end of Lighthouse Beach. Climb the spiral staircase – or zip up in the lift – for vertigo-inducing, palm-drenched views sweeping up and down the coast.

Rock-Cut Temple　　　　　HINDU TEMPLE
(Vinzhinjam; ⊙dawn-dusk) Amid neatly tended, banyan-shaded grounds 500m north of Vizhinjam harbour, this small shrine is one of Kerala's most ancient rock-cut temples. A sculpture of Dakshinamurthy is flanked by unfinished reliefs of Shiva as Nataraja (with Parvati) and Tripurantaka (carrying a bow

and arrow), all believed to date from the 8th century.

Padmakarma
YOGA

(☑ 9895882915; www.padmakarma.com; Lighthouse Beach; classes ₹500; ⊙ classes 8.15am & 4pm) Has twice-daily drop-in yoga and meditation sessions (morning Iyengar-based, afternoon hatha) with a Sivananda-trained teacher, in a leafy setting tucked back from the southern end of Lighthouse Beach (near Hotel Peacock). Also does 200-hour teacher training.

Kovalam Surf Club
SURFING

(☑ 9847347367; www.kovalamsurfclub.com; Lighthouse Beach; 1½hr group lesson ₹1000) ⬥ This established, multilingual surf shop and club with a community focus, just back from Lighthouse Beach, offers introductory lessons (group or private), board rental (three hours ₹600) and customised surfing tours. The team runs free weekend surf classes for disadvantaged local kids and encourages education.

Cool Divers & Bond Safari
DIVING

(☑ 9946550073, 7560906575; www.bondsafari kovalam.com; Suseela Tower, Kovalam Beach Rd; introductory dive ₹6000; ⊙ 8.30am-5.30pm) An efficient dive outfit providing state-of-the-art equipment, PADI courses (four-day Open Water Diver ₹25,000) and guided trips to local dive sites.

🛌 Sleeping

Look for smaller, better-value picks behind Lighthouse Beach. There are few true budget places, especially during the December-to-January peak season (when advance bookings are essential). Expect excellent discounts outside high season.

Lost Hostel
HOSTEL **$**

(www.thelosthostels.com; near Avaduthura Temple; dm ₹500-600, r ₹1100-1700; 🖥) A fresh budget-traveller bolthole hidden in a yellow house 500m inland from Lighthouse Beach,

> ### DON'T MISS
> ## PADMANABHAPURAM PALACE
>
> Around 50km southeast of Kovalam, just over the border in Tamil Nadu, beautiful Padmanabhapuram Palace (p1073) is considered India's finest surviving example of traditional Keralan architecture. This feast of polished and carved wood is accessible by bus or taxi from Kovalam, Thiruvananthapuram (Trivandrum) or Kanyakumari, via the village of Thuckalay. Kovalam taxis charge ₹3500 for a return trip including waiting time.

providing neat, simple six-bed dorms with fans, personal lockers and modern bathrooms, plus plain en suite twin rooms, communal areas and a shared kitchen.

Paradesh Inn
GUESTHOUSE **$$**

(☑ 9995362952; inn.paradesh@yahoo.com; Avaduthura; incl breakfast s ₹2600-3500, d ₹2900-3800; ⊙ mid-Oct–Mar; 🖥) Overlooking palms from its hillside perch, a five-minute climb inland from Lighthouse Beach, tranquil, Italian-operated, adults-only Paradesh Inn resembles a Greek-island home, with its whitewashed walls, sky-blue accents and Mediterranean charm. Each of the six fan-cooled rooms has a hanging chair outside and there are rooftop views, tasty breakfasts and vegetarian *satya* cooking ('yoga food').

Beach Hotel II
HOTEL **$$**

(www.thebeachhotel-kovalam.com; Lighthouse Beach; r ₹5310-5900, with AC ₹6490-7080; ❋🖥☷) Tucked into the southern curl of Lighthouse Beach, the 14 elegant and refreshingly spacious rooms at this stylish pad gaze out on the beach from private balconies beyond sliding French doors. Wooden furniture, terracotta-tiled floors and earthy patterned textiles create a simple-chic look, while the terrace hosts the excellent restaurant Fusion (p955) and there's a brand-new pool.

Treetops
GUESTHOUSE **$$**

(☑ 9847912398; treetopsofkovalam@yahoo.in; r ₹2000; 🖥) Indeed amid palms and colourful gardens high above Lighthouse Beach (but only a five-minute walk away), British-run Treetops is a warm, calming and easy-going escape from the action below. The four bright, impeccable rooms come with colour and character, plus incense sticks

Kovalam

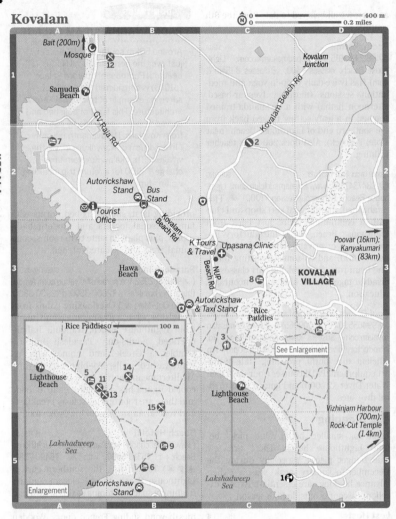

Kovalam

◎ Sights

✦ Activities, Courses & Tours

🛏 Sleeping

🍽 Eating

and their own balconies, and there's a roof-top terrace with sweeping views. Call ahead for bookings and directions.

Beach Hotel
HOTEL $$

(www.thebeachhotel-kovalam.com; Lighthouse Beach; r ₹2800; 🛜) All calming ochre tones, terracotta tiling and minimalist flair, this intimate German-owned seafront pick has eight ground-floor rooms finished with printed throws, modern bathrooms and smart, arty touches, topped by the forever popular Waves Restaurant & Germany Bakery. Each room has its own terrace and staff are helpful and welcoming.

Maharaju Palace
GUESTHOUSE $$

(☑ 9946854270; www.maharajupalace.com; Lighthouse Beach; incl breakfast r ₹2500, with AC ₹2850, cottage room ₹2500-3500; ▣🛜) More peaceful retreat than palace, long-running Dutch-owned Maharaju lies pocketed away down a lane at the southern end of Lighthouse Beach. Timber furnishings, vibrant linens and the odd mural and four-poster mean it's styled with more character than its competition. There's a sweet wood-walled two-room cottage in the garden and chintzy chandeliers adorn the breezy breakfast terrace.

Ganesh House Homestay
HOMESTAY $$

(☑ 9995012627, 0471-2584212; www.theganesh house.com; TC 64/2048 Nedumom, Country Spa Rd, Samudra Beach; incl breakfast r ₹1500, with AC ₹2300-2500; ▣🛜) Seek out a family-style stay at this peach-orange, efficiently run modern home surrounded by greenery, down a dirt path just five minutes' walk inland from quiet Samudra Beach. 'Budget' fan rooms dot the ground floor, while larger air-con rooms sit upstairs beside a small terrace – all bright, clean and comfortable. Days begin with traditional Keralan breakfasts.

Leela
LUXURY HOTEL $$$

(☑ 0471-3051234; www.theleela.com; Samudra Beach; r from ₹13,800, ste from ₹40,880; ▣@🛜🏊) Scented by frangipanis, the sumptuous Leela sprawls across the headland separating Hawa and Samudra beaches. Spacious, smartly designed rooms have colourful textiles, Keralan artwork and sea or garden views. The sophisticated Terrace Restaurant (p957) sits beside the show-stealing clifftop infinity pool, and there's an ayurvedic spa as well as a gym, a 'private' beach, yoga and dance performances.

Taj Green Cove
LUXURY HOTEL $$$

(☑ 0471-6613000; https://taj.tajhotels.com; GV Raja Vattapara Rd, Samudra Beach; r/ste incl breakfast from ₹14,200/21,890; ▣🛜🏊) The Kovalam branch of this glitzy Indian group is nuzzled into lush grounds with direct seafront access. Individual thatched cottages come tastefully adorned, some with private gardens, others with primo sea views. Top-end dining offerings include poolside breakfasts and the magical, seafood-focused waterfront Bait (p956). The signature **Jiva Spa** (☑ 0471-6613048; massage or treatment ₹2100-4000; ⊘8am-9pm) delivers yoga, ayurveda and massage in a luxe setting.

🍴 Eating & Drinking

Each evening the restaurants along the Lighthouse Beach promenade display the catch of the day; costs are around ₹90 per 100g of snapper. There are good restaurants in the tangle of lanes behind, and on quieter Samudra Beach.

★Varsha
SOUTH INDIAN $$

(☑ 9995100301; dishes ₹150-225; ⊘8am-10pm; 🛜) In the lanes behind southern Lighthouse Beach, this little restaurant plates up some of Kovalam's best vegetarian food at reasonable prices, in a simple garden-like space with sandy floors, plastic chairs and a few potted plants. Dishes are fresh and carefully prepared, including spicy masala dosa and a deliciously light off-menu pumpkin-and-spinach curry.

Fusion
MULTICUISINE $$

(www.thebeachhotel-kovalam.com; Beach Hotel II, Lighthouse Beach; mains ₹220-550; ⊘7.30am-10.30pm; 🛜) With its imaginative East-meets-West menu and stylish terrace vibe, the restaurant at Beach Hotel II (p953) is one of Lighthouse Beach's top dining experiences, rustling up Continental favourites, Asian fusion such as chilli-pesto pasta, and interesting seafood numbers like lobster steamed in vodka. It's also good for breakfast: French-press coffee, herbal teas and muesli-and-fruit bowls overlooking beach-front palms.

Waves Restaurant & German Bakery
INTERNATIONAL $$

(www.thebeachhotel-kovalam.com; Beach Hotel, Lighthouse Beach; mains ₹220-550; ⊘7.30am-11pm; 🛜) The burnt-orange balcony, ambient soundtrack, sea views and a wide-roaming, well-executed menu keep Waves – atop

WORTH A TRIP

AYURVEDIC RESORTS NEAR KOVALAM

Between Kovalam and Poovar, amid seemingly endless swaying palms, laid-back village life and some empty golden-sand beaches, are a string of upmarket ayurvedic resorts designed for those serious about fully immersing themselves in ayurveda. They're all 6km to 10km southeast of Kovalam; taxis cost ₹250 to ₹450.

Niraamaya Retreats Surya Samudra (✆0471-2267333, 8045104510; www.niraamaya. in; Pulinkudi; r incl breakfast ₹18,990-40,700; ❄ 🐾 🕿) Built into natural groves of mango, banana and banyan trees and offering A-list-style seclusion, glammed-up traditional Keralan homes, a beachside infinity pool and a renowned ayurvedic spa.

Dr Franklin's Panchakarma Institute (✆0471-2480870; www.dr-franklin.com; Chowara; incl meals & treatments with AC s ₹9620-10,260, d ₹17,230-17,630, without AC s ₹8330-9620, d ₹14,660-17,230; 🕿 🐾) A friendly, reputable, more affordable alternative, with yoga, personalised ayurveda packages and tidy rooms and cottages.

Bethsaida Hermitage (✆0471-2267554; www.bethsaidahermitage.com; Mulloor, Pulinkudi; s/d incl meals with AC from ₹10,280/11,310, without AC from ₹6240/7580; ❄ 🐾 🕿) Charitable Bethsaida is a smart beachside escape with sculpted gardens, hammocks, two sea-view pools, yoga and professional ayurvedic treatments.

Somatheeram (✆0471-2268101; https://somatheeram.in; Chowara; with AC s ₹17,900-20,550, d ₹19,900-22,950, without AC s ₹6820-15,330, d ₹7540-17,000; ❄ 🐾 🕿) 🍃 One of the area's original retreats, award-winning Somatheeram provides ayurveda, yoga, and comfortable red-brick or wooden rooms and cottages.

Beach Hotel (p955) – busy with foreigners. It doubles as the German Bakery, a great spot for breakfast with fresh bread, croissants, pastries and French-press coffee, while dinner turns up Thai curries, German sausages, Indian snacks, pizza, pasta and seafood. There's a small bookshop attached.

Suprabhatham KERALAN $$
(✆9947209756; meals ₹120-250; ⏰7am-11pm; 🕿) It doesn't look like much, but this rustic pure-veg courtyard restaurant hidden back from Lighthouse Beach dishes up excellent Keralan-style cooking, vegetarian thalis and fresh fruit juices. It's all fresh and full of flavour, and local breakfasts of masala dosa, *puttu* and coconut *uttapam* (rice pancake) are available too.

Malabar Cafe INDIAN $$
(Lighthouse Beach; mains ₹110-450; ⏰7.30am-11pm; 🕿) The busy red-cloth tables tell a story: attentive service, candlelight at night and views through pot plants to the crashing waves set the tone for Malabar's tasty India-wide cooking, including nightly fresh-seafood displays and tandoori faves such as paneer tikka. One of the more popular spots along the Lighthouse Beach strip.

Curry Leaf MULTICUISINE $$
(✆9746430087; Samudra Beach; mains ₹100-600; ⏰8am-11pm) On a gently sloping hillside above Samudra Beach, this two-storey restaurant boasts enviable ocean and sunset views beyond slender palms, while keen staff deliver fresh seafood, Continental dishes and tandoori deliciousness. It's well signposted from the beach, up a few stairs, and the uncrowded location is part of the charm.

A Beach Cafe INTERNATIONAL $$
(Lighthouse Beach; mains ₹150-450; ⏰8am-10pm; 🕿) An easy-going balcony restaurant overlooking Lighthouse Beach, the Indian-Swedish-operated ABC does a wide-ranging global menu of omelettes, soups, veg curries, fresh seafood and coconut-pomegranate pancakes, using local organic produce wherever possible, as well as good coffee infused with Kerala-sourced beans.

★**Bait** SEAFOOD $$$
(✆0471-6613000; https://taj.tajhotels.com; Taj Green Cove, GV Raja Vattapara Rd, Samudra Beach; mains ₹360-990; ⏰12.30-10.30pm) Designed as an upmarket alfresco beach shack, the fabulous seafood restaurant at the Taj Green Cove (p955) fronts the sea, with waves and palms on one side and chefs in a semi-open kitchen on the other. Seafood and spicy preparations are as glorious as the blazing sunsets, including delicious fresh fish or tofu steak soaked in 'Kerala coast' spices, with Maharashtrian Sula wines.

Terrace Restaurant
INTERNATIONAL $$$

(☎ 0471-3051234; www.theleela.com; Leela, Samudra Beach; mains ₹550-850; ⊙ 7-10.30am, 12.30-3pm & 7-11pm) One of Kovalam's most scenic (and expensive) restaurants, overlooking the turquoise-tinted infinity pool at the top-end clifftop Leela (p955). The elegant menu plays with Indian and international flavours; tempting bites range from chilli-infused pasta to Keralan specialities like Malabar prawn curry or coconut-laced *pachakkari* (vegetable stew). Or just drop in for a spiced cocktail (₹450 to ₹800) as the sun sets.

ⓘ Information

ATMs cluster along Kovalam Beach Rd.

Tourist office (☎ 0471-2480085; Kovalam Beach Rd; ⊙ 9.30am-5pm Mon-Sat)

Upasana Clinic (☎ 0471-2480632)

ⓘ Getting There & Around

BUS

Buses use the unofficial bus stand outside the entrance to the Leela resort; all buses pass through Kovalam Junction, 2km north of Lighthouse Beach. Buses run to Trivandrum (₹16, 30 minutes) every 15 minutes from 6am to 9pm, with air-con buses (₹40) hourly.

For northbound onward travel, including to Varkala, and (illogically) for Kanyakumari, change in Trivandrum.

MOTORCYCLE, TAXI & AUTORICKSHAW

Taxis between Trivandrum and Kovalam cost ₹500; autorickshaws charge ₹350. Taxis to Kanyakumari are ₹4000 and to Varkala ₹2800. Short autorickshaw hops cost ₹50.

K Tours & Travel (☎ 8089493376; peter sheeba@yahoo.com; NUP Beach Rd; per day scooters/Enfields from ₹400/600; ⊙ 9am-late Mon-Sat, reduced hours Sun) rents out scooters and Enfields.

Varkala

☎ 0470 / POP 40,050

Perched almost perilously along the edge of majestic 15m-high red laterite cliffs, 50km northwest of Trivandrum, Varkala has a naturally beautiful setting that has allowed it to steadily grow into Kerala's most popular backpacker hang-out. A small strand of golden beach nuzzles Varkala's North Cliff area, where restaurants play innocuous world music and shops sell elephant-stamped trousers, silver jewellery and cotton yoga-mat bags. While it's certainly on the beaten track and the sales pitch can

be tiring, it's is still a great place to watch days slowly turn into weeks, and it's easy to escape the crowds further north or south where beaches are cleaner and quieter.

And despite its traveller vibe, Varkala remains essentially an important temple town: the main Papanasham Beach is a holy Hindu spot, overlooked by the ancient Janardhana Temple. About 2km east of here is busy Varkala town.

◉ Sights

Janardhana Temple
HINDU TEMPLE

(Temple Junction; ⊙ 4am-noon & 5-8pm) Varkala is a temple town and the Janardhana Temple, dedicated to Vishnu, is the main event – with its roots dating back to the 13th century, this technicolour Hindu spectacle hovers above Beach Rd, reached by steep stone staircases. Though the main shrine is closed to non-Hindus, visitors are welcome to wander the grounds, home to a huge banyan tree, a Tamil-style *mandapa* (pillared pavilion) with granite columns, and shrines to Ayyappan, Hanuman and other Hindu deities.

Papanasham Beach
BEACH

Ringed by rust-red cliffs, Varkala's main beach is a holy spot for Hindus, who for centuries have made offerings for passed loves ones and washed away worldly sins (assisted by priests) near the junction with Beach Rd. Swimmers and sunbathers congregate towards its northern end.

Black Beach
BEACH

(Thiruvambady Beach) A sandy little blonde-and-black beach just north of Varkala's North Cliff.

Odayam Beach
BEACH

This gold-hued stretch of sand, around 1km north of the North Cliff, makes a peaceful alternative to Varkala's main beach.

Kappil Beach
BEACH

About 8km north of Varkala, this long, beautiful and (so far) undeveloped stretch of golden sand is the beginning of a mini network of backwaters. A two-hour seaside walk leads here along a gently undulating path from Varkala's North Cliff, passing a subtly changing beach landscape, including Odayam Beach and the fishing village of Edava.

Sivagiri Mutt
ASHRAM

(☎ 0470-2602807; ⊙ dawn-dusk) Just east of central Varkala, Sivagiri Mutt is the headquarters of the Shri Narayana Dharma

KERALA VARKALA

Varkala

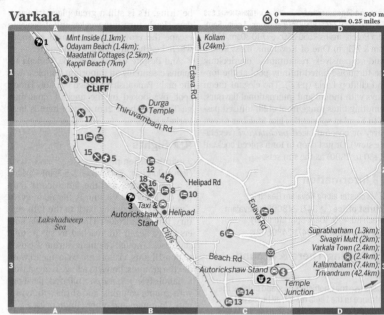

Varkala

Sights
- 1 Black Beach...A1
- 2 Janardhana Temple.............................C3
- 3 Papanasham Beach.............................B2

Activities, Courses & Tours
- 4 AyurSoul...B2
- 5 Haridas Yoga...B2
-   Soul & Surf.....................................(see 13)

Sleeping
- 6 Gateway Hotel Janardhanapuram.......C3
- 7 InDa Hotel..A2
- 8 Jicky's Nest...B2

- 9 Kaiya House..C2
- 10 Lost Hostel..B2
- 11 Mad About Coco..................................A2
- 12 Mango Villa..B2
- 13 Soul & Surf...C3
- 14 Villa Jacaranda...................................C3

Eating
- 15 ABBA...A2
- 16 Coffee Temple.....................................B2
- 17 Darjeeling Cafe....................................A1
- 18 God's Own Country Kitchen................B2
-   Soul Food Cafe.............................(see 13)
- 19 Trattorias...A1

Sanghom Trust, devoted to Shri Narayana Guru (1855–1928), Kerala's most prominent guru and a leading social reformer. It's a major pilgrimage site, with devotees recognisable by their distinctive yellow clothing.

Ponnumthuruthu (Golden) Island
ISLAND

(boat ride 2/3/4 people ₹600/700/800, island admission per person ₹50; ⏰6am-6pm) Around 10km south of Varkala, this acacia-filled island in the middle of a backwater lake conceals a Shiva-Parvati Hindu temple also known as the Golden Temple. The vibrantly coloured, century-old shrine is usually closed to non-Hindus, but the main reason to venture here is the scenic punt-powered boat ride to and around the island. Allow 1½ hours round trip; autorickshaws from Varkala cost ₹600 with waiting time.

🏃 Activities

Yoga (₹350 to ₹550) is offered *everywhere*; reliable options include **Haridas Yoga** (📞9846743231; www.pranayogavidya.com; Hotel Green Palace, North Cliff; classes ₹350; ⏰8am & 4.30pm late Aug–mid-May), Soul & Surf and Mad About Coco.

Surfboards (from ₹250) and boogie boards (₹300) can be hired along the beach and cliffs; be wary of strong currents. Surfing, kayaking, stand-up paddleboarding and SUP yoga sessions are also popular.

Soul & Surf
SURFING, YOGA

(☑9961711099; www.soulandsurf.com; South Cliff; surf lessons ₹2500, board rental half/full day ₹900/1700, yoga ₹550-1000; ⏱Oct-Apr) 🏄 This UK-based outfit organises surfing trips and yoga retreats in season, with stylish accommodation (p960) and a wonderful, laid-back garden cafe (p961) gracing its South Cliff grounds. The on-the-ball international team also offers 1½-hour surf lessons (though nonguest spaces are limited) and board rental, while drop-in rooftop yoga sessions range from vinyasa to candlelight yin meditation.

AyurSoul
MASSAGE

(☑9946645599; www.ayursoulindia.com; Helipad Rd, North Cliff; massage ₹1000-3000; ⏱7.30am-7.30pm) A professional, in-demand ayurveda centre, 300m inland from the helipad. Following a doctor consultation, choose from ayurvedic classics or Western-style spa treatments, all using oils made in-house. Also offers extended packages and accommodation.

Can Fly
PARAGLIDING, WATERSPORTS

(☑9048795781; www.canflyadventure.com; 20min flight ₹3800) This experienced adventure operator offers tandem paragliding from the North Cliff helipad, as well as stand-up paddleboarding and kayaking trips (₹1900 to ₹2200). Activities run from October to May, though you may be able to rent kayaks and paddleboards (₹600) throughout the low season.

🛏 Sleeping

Most places to stay are along and just back from Varkala's North Cliff, around the southern cliffs and on tranquil, less-developed Odayam Beach. Prices skyrocket from mid-December to mid-January, when you'll want to book ahead.

Jicky's Nest
GUESTHOUSE $

(☑0470-2606994, 9846179325; jickys2002@yahoo.co.in; off Helipad Rd; r ₹750-1500, AC cottage ₹2500-3000; ❄🏠) In the palm groves just back from the cliffs, friendly family-run Jicky's has blossomed into several buildings offering plenty of choice for travellers. Rooms in the main whitewashed building are fresh, with sit-out spaces; nearby are a few charming octagonal cottages and some larger air-con rooms. The most char-

acterful rooms are adorned with colourful hand-painted murals of birds and flowers.

Lost Hostel
HOSTEL $

(☑7012416343; www.thelosthostels.com; off Helipad Rd; dm with AC ₹600-900, without AC ₹500-700, r ₹1100-2200; ❄🏠) Six-person, locker-equipped en suite dorms (some are air-conditioned) and smartish private doubles with simple murals are the draw at this social budget hang-out hidden (but well signposted!) down a lane just inland from the helipad. Hammocks dot the front garden, there's a communal kitchen plus a lounge with books and games, and enthusiastic staff provide local information and rent out bikes (₹100).

★ Kaiya House
GUESTHOUSE $$

(☑9746126909; www.kaiyahouse.com; Edava Rd; incl breakfast r with/without AC ₹3300/2800; ❄🏠) 🏄 Not your typical Varkala address, this gorgeously original hideaway is packed with art and antiques and topped by a breezy roof terrace. The five rooms are thoughtfully themed (African, Indian, Chinese, Japanese, English): four-poster beds, wooden carvings, embroidered wall hangings. American owner Debra organises beach clean-ups and welcomes guests with tea, tips, water refills, yoga mats and free walking tours.

InDa Hotel
GUESTHOUSE $$

(☑7025029861; https://inda-in.book.direct; North Cliff, Kurakkanni; incl breakfast s ₹2070-4810, d ₹2130-5020; 🏠) Tucked away behind the North Cliff, this warm, highly regarded guesthouse throws boutique style into its impeccably kept gleaming-white rooms and six individual cottages, scattered across a garden with a leafy lounge area. Open-brick walls meet rattan chairs, floral-print sheets and the odd mural, and the health-oriented cafe specialises in salads, wraps and Buddha bowls (dishes ₹180 to ₹350).

Mad About Coco
GUESTHOUSE $$

(☑9061932651; www.madaboutcocovarkala.com; North Cliff; r with AC ₹3000-5000, without AC

SLEEPING PRICE RANGES

The following price ranges refer to a double room with bathroom in Kerala:

$ less than ₹1200

$$ ₹1200–₹5000

$$$ more than ₹5000

₹2000-3000; ❄☏) 🏊 Comprising two re-vamped houses huddled back from the North Cliff, German-run MAC fuses a so-ciable traveller/yogi vibe with uncluttered rooms jazzed up by colour feature walls and terraces with lounge corners or swing chairs. The boutique-inspired cafe serves healthy bites (overnight oats, fruit bowls, wholemeal French toast) and free water re-fills, and there's twice-daily rooftop yoga in season.

Mango Villa
GUESTHOUSE $$

(☏ 9995040610; www.facebook.com/mangovilla varkala; North Cliff; r with AC ₹3000, without AC ₹900-1200; ❄☏) Hidden just inland from the southern end of the North Cliff, the Belgian-Indian-run Mango Villa lives up to its alluring name with six airy, spotless, contemporary rooms decked out with bam-boo furniture, smart desks, original artwork and, for some, private balconies. There's also a handful of comfy, similarly styled, cold-water 'budget' rooms.

Maadathil Cottages
COTTAGE $$

(☏ 9746113495; www.maadathilcottages.com; Man-thara Temple Rd, Odayam Beach; r incl breakfast ₹1900-5000; ❄☏) With an excellent location on tranquil Odayam Beach, this cluster of delightful beachfront cottages is designed in traditional Kerala style, flaunting heritage furniture, tiled roofs and wood-carved doors alongside large beds and modern bathrooms. All rooms enjoy sea views from spacious pri-vate balconies and some are enlivened by vi-brant hand-painted exterior murals.

Villa Jacaranda
GUESTHOUSE $$$

(☏ 0470-2610296; www.villa-jacaranda.biz; Temple Rd West; r incl breakfast ₹7900-10,000; ❄☏) This intimate, romantic and elegantly understat-ed boutiquey retreat just inland from south-ern Papanasham Beach revolves around four bright, spacious rooms in a beautiful two-storey house wrapped in greenery. Each room has a terrace (where delicious home-cooked breakfasts are served) and is styled with a chic blend of minimalist modern de-sign and antique touches.

Soul & Surf
GUESTHOUSE $$$

(☏ 9961711099; www.soulandsurf.com; South Cliff; incl breakfast s ₹4320-6760, d ₹7320-12,200; ⊙ Oct-Apr; ❄☏) 🏊 Bold pink and turquoise design meets a homely, social feel at this boutiqueified British-run yoga and surf re-treat (p959) spread across lush gardens atop the South Cliff, where rooms, yoga class-

es and the wonderful cafe are open to all. Along with the main guesthouse (which has contemporary top-tier rooms with sea-view terraces), there are smaller rooms in a tradi-tional 150-year-old house opposite.

Mint Inside
GUESTHOUSE $$$

(☏ Whatsapp 7356979929; www.mint-inside. com; Odayam Beach; incl breakfast s ₹800-1600, d ₹2450-5500; ❄☏) Chicly stripped-back rooms and cottages, sharp service and hanging chairs and hammocks greet you at this fresh and welcome arrival on Varkala's growing boutique-guesthouse scene. Expect tasteful grey-and-white styling, concrete bed frames, polished bathrooms, touches of bamboo and a roof terrace. The four sea-facing rooms have air-con and private ter-races, and Odayam Beach is a few minutes' walk away.

Gateway Hotel Janardhanapuram
HOTEL $$$

(☏ 0470-6673300; https://gateway.tajhotels.com; r incl breakfast from ₹11,520; ❄☏) Varka-la's flashiest hotel, the hillside Taj-Group Gateway is all gleaming linen and mocha cushions in smart contemporary rooms overlooking manicured gardens; the best boudoirs have sea views and private balco-nies. There's a fantastic pool overlooking the beach beyond a sea of palms, along with a bar and a restaurant (though overall it feels a little tired).

🍴 Eating & Drinking

Some of the clifftop 'shacks' are now impres-sive multilevel hang-outs with a growing health and environmental awareness.

Suprabhatham
SOUTH INDIAN $

(☏ 0470-2606697; www.suprabhathamrestaurant. com; Maithanam, Varkala Town; dishes ₹30-95; ⊙ 7am-9.30pm) Keralan-style meals, masala dosa and uttapam topped with onion, coco-nut or tomato are the expertly spiced stars at this bustling pure-veg South Indian eat-ery squirrelled away in Varkala town.

Darjeeling Cafe
INTERNATIONAL $$

(www.facebook.com/darjeelingcafevarkala; North Cliff; mains ₹140-450; ⊙ 7am-11pm) With gi-ant dreamcatchers and tiered candlelit ta-bles strewn with flower petals, Darjeeling is always packed with travellers. Snappy, cheerful service complements cocktails (₹250; with metallic straws), fresh juices, good coffee and an alluring global menu: chapati rolls, smoothie bowls, masala dosa,

KERALA'S DRY EXPERIMENT

In 2017 Kerala's left-wing coalition government reversed the controversial 2014 alcohol ban implemented by the then Congress-led government, which was at the time the first step in a 10-year move towards total prohibition. The 2014 ruling saw more than 700 bars promptly shut down (though most eventually reopened as beer and wine parlours); only five-star hotels could have bars and spirits were only available from government liquor shops.

At the time of writing, however, bars can now stay open until 11pm, three- and four-star hotels can serve liquor, two-star hotels can have beer parlours and new bars are able to apply for liquor licenses, though the first day of each month remains a dry day across the state.

Kerala's per capita alcohol consumption is estimated at 8.3L – double the national average, and the highest in the country.

pan-Indian curries, banana-leaf fish, and enormous platters of paneer or fish tikka with chips and salad.

Coffee Temple   INTERNATIONAL $$
(North Cliff; mains ₹100-450; ⏲6.30am-10pm; 🛜) 🍴 At the southern end of the North Cliff trail, this leafy terrace cafe-restaurant remains a firm favourite for your morning coffee fix. Freshly ground beans accompany free water refills and breakfasts of muesli bowls, French toast, smashed avocado, just-squeezed juices and fresh brown bread. The globetrotting menu also features crepes, pastas and Mexican burritos, plus an excellent vegan selection.

ABBA   INTERNATIONAL $$
(www.abbarestaurant.tk; Hotel Green Palace, North Cliff; mains ₹150-400; ⏲7am-11pm; 🛜) Halfway along the North Cliff, this relaxed and welcoming terrace spot with a handy book exchange remains firmly popular for its inventive salads (perhaps carrot, beetroot and mint, or with lashings of halloumi) and world-roaming breakfasts centred on just-baked bread from the attached bakery, but also whips up pastas, pizzas, momos (Tibetan dumplings), burgers, curries, fresh seafood and cocktails (₹220 to ₹300).

God's Own Country Kitchen   MULTICUISINE $$
(North Cliff; mains ₹150-450; ⏲8am-11pm; 🛜) This fun place doesn't really need to play on the Kerala Tourism tagline – the Indian-international food is good (including spiced fish wrapped in banana leaf), there's a great little upper-floor deck and live music sometimes happens in season.

Trattorias   MULTICUISINE $$
(North Cliff; mains ₹130-450; ⏲7am-10.30pm; 🛜) Trattorias sounds Italian and does indeed rustle up decent pastas, pizzas and European breakfasts, but the menu is equally pan-Asian and Indian (with seafood platters and Keralan fish dishes) and the food consistently good. This was one of the original places in Varkala with an Italian coffee machine; the sea-facing terrace is cosy and the team attentive.

★ Soul Food Cafe   INTERNATIONAL $$$
(📱9961711099; www.soulandsurf.com; Soul & Surf, South Cliff; mains ₹300-480; ⏲9-11am, 1-4pm & 6.30-9pm Mon-Sat, 9-11am & 1-4pm Sun Oct-Apr; 🛜) 🍴 Fresh local ingredients fuel inspired, artfully prepared dishes at the beautifully located clifftop garden cafe at Soul & Surf (p959). Here zingy mezze platters arrive with mini pappadams and slithers of chapati, coffee is sourced from South India's Western Ghats, and Kerala favourites on the short-but-sweet menu include *meen pollichathu* (steamed banana-leaf fish). It's usually busy with yogis and surfers. Free water refills.

❶ Information

DANGERS & ANNOYANCES
Varkala's beaches have strong currents; during the monsoon the beach all but disappears, and the cliffs are slowly being eroded. Take care walking on the cliff path, especially at night – some of it is unfenced and slippery.

The commission racket is alive and well – ensure your driver takes you to the accommodation you've asked for.

Many female travellers wear bikinis and swimsuits on the beaches here, though bear in mind that you may feel uncomfortably exposed to stares. Wearing a sarong when out of the water helps avoid offending local sensibilities. Dress conservatively if going into Varkala town or to the Janardhana Temple.

ⓘ Getting There & Away

Varkala's main bus stand is buried in Varkala town, opposite the train station; a handful of daily buses run to/from Trivandrum (₹65, 1½ to two hours) and Kollam (₹45, one hour), a few of them via Temple Junction. Schedules are erratic, so it's usually easier to take the train.

Taxis go to Kollam (₹1200), Trivandrum (₹1500) and Kovalam (₹1900); autorickshaws charge ₹800, ₹1100 and ₹1400 respectively.

There are frequent local and express trains to Trivandrum (2nd class/sleeper/3AC ₹45/140/495, one to 1½ hours) and Kollam (₹45/140/495, 25 minutes to 1¼ hours), plus six daily services to Alleppey (₹65/140/495, two hours).

ⓘ Getting Around

Varkala beach is 3km west of Varkala Sivagiri train station; autorickshaws run to/from Temple Junction for ₹80 and North Cliff for ₹100. Local buses travel regularly between the train station and Temple Junction (₹8 to ₹10) from 6am to 7.30pm.

A few places along the cliff hire out scooters and motorbikes for ₹300 to ₹450 per day.

Kollam (Quilon)

☑ 0474 / POP 348,660

One of the oldest ports in the Arabian Sea, Kollam was once a major commercial hub that saw Roman, Arab, Chinese and later Portuguese, Dutch and British traders jostle into town – eager to get their hands on spices and the region's cashew crops. Today the town marks the southern approach to Kerala's backwaters and one end of the popular backwater ferry trip to Alleppey. Its centre and bazaar are hectic, but surrounding them are the calm waterways of Ashtamudi Lake, fringed with coconut palms, cashew plantations and traditional villages – making Kollam a great place to get a feel for the backwaters (with fewer crowds than Alleppey) and, along with nearby Munroe Island, an increasingly popular overnight stop for travellers.

⊙ Sights & Activities

Kollam Beach is 2km south of town but there are better stretches of sand further south at Eravipuram and Mayyanad. There's a rowdy fish market and harbour north of Kollam's beach.

Thangassery   AREA

Flanking the north end of the harbour, west of Kollam centre, Thangassery was once an important Portuguese, then Dutch and finally British trading post. You can still see the remains of the 1519 Portuguese-era Fort Thomas, next to the early-20th-century lighthouse (Indian/foreigner ₹20/50, camera ₹10; ⊙ 10am-1pm & 2-6pm Tue-Sun).

★ Munroe Island Cruise   BOATING

(tours per person ₹600-750) Excellent tours through the canals of quiet Munroe Island are organised by Kollam's DTPC (p964) and a number of private local operators, including Ashtamudi Villas and Munroe Island Backwaters Homestay. Usually starting at 9am or 2pm, the popular trips begin 15km north of Kollam, from where you take a leisurely three-hour punted canoe ride through a network of canals.

On the canals you can observe daily village life, see *kettuvallam* (rice barge) construction, toddy (palm beer) tapping, coir-making and prawn and fish farming, and do some birdwatching on spice-garden visits. Development and tourism have increased on Munroe Island in recent years, but it's still a pleasant place to explore.

Houseboat Cruises   BOATING

(day/overnight cruise from ₹6490/7090) Kollam has far fewer houseboats than Alleppey, which means its surrounding waters remain slightly less touristed. The DTPC (p964) organises various houseboat day-cruise packages, along with overnight stays and trips from Kollam to Alleppey (from ₹32,000). A couple of private operators, also based at the jetty, offer similar itineraries.

✸ Festivals & Events

Kollam Pooram   CULTURAL

(Asramam Shri Krishna Swami Temple; ⊙ Apr) A 10-day Kollam festival with nightly Kathakali performances and a procession of 30 to 40 ornamented elephants.

President's Trophy Boat Race   SPORTS

(⊙ 1 Nov) The most prestigious boat regatta in the Kollam region, on Ashtamudi Lake.

🛏 Sleeping & Eating

Munroe Island Backwaters Homestay   HOMESTAY $

(☑ 9048176186; www.facebook.com/Munroe IslandBackwatersHomestay; Chittamula Rd, Munroe

Kollam (Quilon)

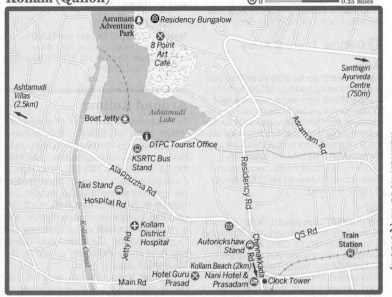

Island; r incl breakfast ₹1200-1500; ⎙) Hidden away in the backwaters of Munroe Island, 16km north of Kollam, this cheery hammock-strewn homestay is popular with travellers for its low-key village setting and warm family feel. There are three colourful cottages in Kerala style, plus three contemporary rooms upstairs overlooking a loungey terrace. Owner Vijeesh runs canoe tours (₹450 to ₹500) and has kayaks and bicycles to borrow.

⭐**Ashtamudi Villas**　　　　GUESTHOUSE **$$**
(☎9847132449, 0474-2706090; www.ashtamudi villas.com; near Kadavoor Church, Mathilil; r ₹1000-3000; ⎙) ⌀ These charming lakeside cottages are easily the best choice for a relaxing, affordable stay in Kollam. Host Prabhath Joseph offers a warm welcome, with ecofriendly architectural design (solar power, rainwater harvesting), colourful decor, gleaming bathrooms, hammocks swinging between palms, a library of Kerala books, tasty meals, and free kayaks and yoga mats. Munroe Island tours are also available.

Nani Hotel　　　　BUSINESS HOTEL **$$**
(☎9207736707; www.hotelnani.com; Chinnakkada Rd; incl breakfast r ₹2520-3840, ste ₹4480; ❋@⎙) Built by a cashew magnate and with on-the-ball staff, this boutique-inspired business hotel is a welcome surprise in Kollam's chaotic centre. The sleek architecture mixes traditional Keralan elements and modern lines. Even the standard rooms come with TV, feathery pillows and sumptuous bathrooms, and there's an elegant multicuisine restaurant, **Prasadam** (☎920773670; mains ₹160-280; ⏲7-10am, noon-3pm & 7-10pm).

8 Point Art Cafe 　　　　CAFE **$**
(☎0474-2970256; www.facebook.com/8pointart cafe; Asramam; mains ₹90-130; ⏲11am-9.30pm) On the fun side of Ashtamudi Lake, 1km north of the jetty, this creative cafe in a restored heritage building with a breezy verandah and a leafy garden is part local art gallery, part fashionable hang-out. Come for the changing free exhibitions, good coffee, small library, and short but thoughtfully prepped menu of sandwiches, burgers and cakes.

Hotel Guru Prasad 　　　　SOUTH INDIAN **$**
(Main Rd; dishes ₹12-45; ⏲7am-9pm) Tucked into a neatly repurposed red-and-white colonial-style building, in the heart of town, this busy all-veg spot draws the crowds with its cheap thalis, dosa (savoury crepe), *vada* (doughnut-shaped deep-fried lentil savoury), *idli* (spongy, round, fermented rice cake) and other snacks.

ⓘ Information

DTPC Tourist Office (☏ 0474-2745625; www.dtpckollam.com; Link Rd; ⊙ 8am-5pm)

ⓘ Getting There & Away

BOAT

Many travellers take the State Water Transport (www.swtd.kerala.gov.in) canal boat to/from Alleppey (₹400, eight hours), which leaves at 10.30am daily from July to March and every second day at other times. Services may be further reduced during the May-to-September low season. It's not necessary to book ahead, but be at the **main boat jetty** (Link Rd) by 9.30am.

From the jetty there are also frequent public ferries across Ashtamudi Lake to Kureepuzha (₹3 to ₹6, one hour).

BUS

From the **KSRTC bus stand** (Link Rd), opposite the boat jetty, buses run every 20 or 30 minutes to Trivandrum (₹68, 1½ hours), Alleppey (₹80, two hours) and Ernakulam (Kochi; standard/AC ₹140/258, four hours). There are two daily direct services to Varkala (₹90 to ₹130, 1½ hours, 7am and 9.30am), though trains are best for Varkala, and a 5am bus to Kumily (₹165, five hours).

TRAIN

There are frequent express trains to Ernakulam (sleeper/3AC ₹140/495, 2½ to 3½ hours, 23 daily), some via Alleppey (₹140/495, 1½ hours), and Trivandrum (₹140/495, 1½ to 2½ hours, 25 daily), via Varkala (₹140/495, 30 minutes). Trains also run four times daily to/from Madurai in Tamil Nadu (sleeper/3AC/2AC ₹315/620/885, eight to 13 hours).

TAXI & AUTORICKSHAW

Taxis cost ₹2200 to Alleppey and ₹1200 to Varkala. For Varkala, you can also take an **autorickshaw** (Chinnakkada Rd) (₹800) along the scenic coastal road.

Around Kollam

Two kilometres south of Kayamkulam (35km north of Kollam), this restored mid-18th-century palace, **Krishnapuram Palace Museum** (Kayamkulam; adult/child ₹20/12, camera/video ₹40/400; ⊙ 9am-1pm & 2-4.30pm Tue-Sun), is one of the finest remaining examples of royal Keralan architecture. Beneath its gabled red-tiled roofs, you'll find paintings, antique furniture, sculptures and a renowned 3m-high mural depicting the Gajendra Moksha (the liberation of Gajendra, chief of the elephants) as told in the Bhagavata Puraṇa.

Frequent buses (₹50, 45 minutes) run from Kollam to Kayamkulam; ask to hop off on the main road near the palace.

Alappuzha (Alleppey)

☏ 0477 / POP 174,180

Alappuzha – most still call it Alleppey – is the hub of Kerala's backwaters, home to a vast network of waterways, over a thousand houseboats and an important coir industry.

MATHA AMRITHANANDAMAYI MISSION

The incongruously salmon-pink **Matha Amrithanandamayi Mission** (☏ 0476-2897578, 9072580923; www.amritapuri.org; Amrithapuri), 30km northwest of Kollam (Quilon), is the famous ashram of one of India's few female gurus, Amrithanandamayi, also known as Amma (Mother) or 'The Hugging Mother' because of the *darshan* (audience) she offers, often hugging thousands of people in marathon all-night sessions. The ashram runs official tours at 5pm daily (check details online or download the Amma app).

It's a huge complex, with about 3500 people living here permanently – monks, nuns, students and families, both Indian and foreign. It offers food, ayurvedic treatments, and a daily schedule of yoga, meditation and *darshan*. Amma herself travels for much of the year (her schedule is online); a busy time of year at the ashram is around Amma's birthday on 27 September.

Visitors should dress conservatively and there is a strict code of behaviour. With prior arrangement – register online – you can stay at the ashram in a triple room for ₹250 per person or a single for ₹500 (including simple vegetarian meals).

Since the ashram is on the main canal between Kollam and Alappuzha (Alleppey), many travellers break the popular ferry ride (p972) by getting off here, staying a day or two, then picking up another cruise. Alternatively, cross the canal via pedestrian bridge to Vallickavu and grab a rickshaw 10km south to Karunagappally or 12km north to Kayamkulam (around ₹200), from where you can catch onward buses or trains.

Wandering around the small but chaotic city centre, with its modest grid of canals, you'd be hard-pressed to agree with the 'Venice of the East' tag, and, sadly, at research time a hulking new highway flyover was marring the beauty of Alleppey's popular beach. But head out towards the backwaters and Alleppey becomes graceful and greenery-fringed, disappearing into a watery world of villages, punted canoes, toddy shops and, of course, houseboats. Floating along and gazing over paddy fields of succulent green, curvaceous rice barges and village life along the banks is one of Kerala's most mesmerisingly beautiful and relaxing experiences.

Kerala's main backwaters stretch north, east and south of Alleppey, while Vembanad Lake, Kerala's largest, reaches all the way north to Kochi.

Sights & Activities

RKK Memorial Museum
MUSEUM
(0477-2242923; www.rkkmuseum.com; NH47; Indian/foreigner ₹150/350; ⏱9am-5pm Tue-Sun) In a grand building fronted by Greco-Roman columns, this intriguing museum houses a priceless, astonishing collection of crystal, porcelain, South Indian antiques, furniture, artworks and (sadly) ivory from the personal family collection of wealthy local businessman Revi Karuna Karan. It was created by his wife Betty as a memorial after he passed away in 2003.

Alleppey Beach
BEACH
Alleppey's main beach is 2km west of the city centre; swimming is fraught due to strong currents, but the sunsets are good and there are a few places for a drink or a snack. Unfortunately, at research time, the setting was being slightly ruined by the construction of an enormous flyover road right by the beach.

Alleppey Lighthouse
LIGHTHOUSE
(Indian/foreigner ₹20/50, camera ₹10; ⏱9-11.45am & 2-5.30pm Tue-Sun) A few blocks back from the beach, the candy-striped 1862 lighthouse contains a small museum with an original oil lamp, but is best visited for the 360-degree views of a surprisingly green Alleppey from the top of its spiralling staircase.

Kerala Kayaking
KAYAKING
(9846585674, 8547487701; www.keralakayak ing.com; Vazhicherry Bridge, VCNB Rd; per person 4/7/10hr ₹1500/3000/4500) Alleppey's orig-

inal and best kayaking outfit. The young crew offers excellent guided kayaking trips through narrow backwater canals. Paddles in single or double kayaks include a support boat and motorboat transport to your starting point. There are four-hour morning and afternoon trips and seven- or 10-hour day trips, as well as multiday village tours (from ₹13,000 per two people).

Houseboat Dock
BOATING
(9400051796; dtpcalpy@yahoo.com; off Punnamada Rd; ⏱prepaid counter 9.30am-4.30pm) Dozens of houseboats gather at Alleppey's main dock. There's a government-run prepaid counter with 'official' posted prices, starting at ₹7000 for two people and up to ₹34,000 for a seven-berth boat (reduced rates June to October), though even these fluctuate with demand. Note that some houseboats dock elsewhere and the most reputable ones often get booked up in advance.

Tours

Any guesthouse, hotel or travel agent, plus the DTPC (p969), can and will arrange canoe or houseboat tours of the backwaters.

Kashmiri-style *shikaras* (covered boats) gather along the North Canal on the road to the houseboat dock; they charge around ₹400 per hour for motorised canal and backwater trips. Punt-powered dugout canoes are slower but more ecofriendly; most tours require four to five hours, with village visits, walks and a stop at a toddy bar; full-day tours cost around ₹700 to ₹900.

Festivals & Events

Nehru Trophy Boat Race
SPORTS
(www.nehrutrophy.nic.in; tickets ₹100-3000; ⏱Aug) The most renowned and fiercely contested of Kerala's boat-race regattas, held annually on the second Saturday of August since 1954. Thousands of people, many aboard houseboats, gather around the starting and finishing points on Alleppey's Punnamada Lake to watch snake boats with up to 100 rowers battle it out.

Sleeping

Alleppey has some of Kerala's most charming and best-value accommodation, particularly when it comes to homestays and backpacker hostels. Homestays are also mushrooming along the coast north of Alleppey and around the remote backwaters.

Alappuzha (Alleppey)

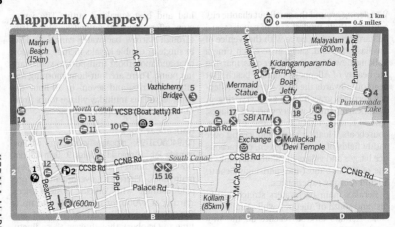

The rickshaw-commission racketeers are at work here; ask to be dropped at a landmark close to your destination, or contact your hotel for a pickup.

Zostel
HOSTEL **$**

(☑ 011-39589008; www.zostel.com; Beach Rd; dm ₹500-550, r ₹1200-2220; ❋ ◎) ◢ Just steps from the sand, Alleppey's lively, contemporary-style branch of India's favourite hostel chain is adorned with colourful shutters and murals – including Indiana Jones on the wall in one of the spacious upper-floor, sea-glimpse private rooms. Six-bunk en suite air-con dorms (mixed or women-only) come with individual lockers, and there's a laid-back lounge. Free water refills.

Artpackers.Life
HOSTEL **$**

(☑ 8281486865; www.artpackers.life; Cullan Rd; incl breakfast dm with/without AC ₹600/490, r ₹1570-1790; ❋ ◎) Overlooking leafy gardens, 400m from the beach, this beautiful old whitewashed building with sky-blue shutters – once a radio station – now doubles as a creative hostel and a resident-artist studio. The two eight-bed dorms have personal lockers, lights and plugs, private bathrooms, soaring ceilings, polished-concrete decor and bunks at mismatched levels; the two private rooms are comfily stylish (though with ceilingless bathrooms).

Nanni Backpackers Hostel
HOSTEL **$**

(☑ 9895039767; www.nannitours.com; Cullan Rd; dm ₹300, r with/without AC ₹1400/700) A very good deal, this easy-going, homely and colourful backpacker hang-out sits 500m inland from the beach and 2km north of the train station. The two neat dorms sleep four or six,

and there are spacious private rooms plus the popular patio Le Coffee Time (p968) cafe and a rooftop terrace. Keen owner Shibu is an excellent source of local information and offers scooter hire (p969).

Dream Nest
GUESTHOUSE **$**

(☑ 9895860716; http://thedreamnest.com; Cullan Rd; dm ₹250, d ₹500-900, r with AC ₹1400-1600; ❋ ◎) The colourfully themed modern rooms and three-bed dorm set back from the road are a good-value find at this budget town-centre guesthouse, with a social communal lounge, a shared kitchen, a book exchange and a youthful traveller vibe. Houseboats, canoe tours and kayaking trips available.

Malayalam
GUESTHOUSE **$$**

(☑ 0477-2234591, 9496829424; www.facebook.com/MalayalamLakeResorts; East Thottathodu Bridge, Punnamada; r ₹1500-2500; ◎) Fringed by gardens of orchids, family-run Malayalam revolves around a pair of spacious two-storey four-room houses facing the lake near the Nehru Trophy Boat Race starting point. Views are sweet and the style is charmingly traditional yet comfortable, with deck chairs on verandahs and glossy woods. It's 2.5km north of town on the canal bank, signposted off Punnamada Rd.

Cherukara Nest
GUESTHOUSE **$$**

(☑ 0477-2251509, 9947059628; www.cherukara nest.com; incl breakfast r with/without AC ₹1800/1400; ❋ ◎) Set in well-tended gardens, this lovely heritage home reveals four large, character-filled rooms with high ceilings, lots of polished-wood touches, and antediluvian doors with ornate locks. There's also a more modern cottage attached. Owner

Alappuzha (Alleppey)

Tony has a good-value houseboat (two/four people ₹6000/8000) and organises full-day canoe or village tours (₹900). It's just east of the bus stand.

Alasr Heritage HOMESTAY **$$**
(☑9947066699; www.facebook.com/alasr-heritage-home-1050461414981804; CCNB Rd; r incl breakfast with/without AC ₹2300/1500; 🛜) A beautiful family house with its roots in the 17th century, canalside Alasr is strung riad-style around a wood-banistered patio. There are seven impeccable rooms with tall ceilings, antique furniture, heritage touches, colourful bedding and modern bathrooms, and the charming family owners rustle up home-cooked breakfasts and organise houseboats, canoe trips and bike hire.

Canoe Ville COTTAGE **$$**
(☑9895213162, 0477-2232535; www.facebook.com/CanoeVilleResort; Choolakkadav Rd, Punnamada; incl breakfast tent per person ₹500, r ₹2000, cottages ₹3000; 🌀🛜) In a peaceful lakefront setting 4km north of Alleppey, this welcoming, creative operation amid natural canals sleeps guests on a floating mini houseboat cottage for a 'houseboat on land' experience (complete with air-con, private bathroom and a large verandah). Owner Jijo also has two lakeside rooms and some budget safari tents, and books kayak, canoe and bike jaunts.

The same family runs the nearby heritage-style **Punnamada Homestay** (☑Whatsapp 9895213162; Kayaloram Resort Rd, Punnamada; r incl breakfast ₹1500; 🛜), with two comfortable rooms and delicious home cooking.

Tharavad GUESTHOUSE **$$**
(☑9349440406, 0477-2244599; alleppeytharavad@gmail.com; west of North Police Station; r incl breakfast ₹2500-3500; 🌀🛜) Glossy teak and antiques, shuttered windows, five characterful rooms, cordial service and well-maintained gardens set the tone at charming, 118-year-old ancestral home Tharavad. It's in a fairly hushed canalside location between Alleppey's town centre and beach, a little back from the road. Premium rooms are most spacious.

Johnson's GUESTHOUSE **$$**
(☑0477-2245825, 9846466399; http://johnsonskerala.com; Cullan Rd; r incl breakfast r with/without AC ₹2500/1300; 🌀🛜) This quirky longtime favourite, run by the gregarious Johnson Gilbert, is a rambling two-storey family residence with themed rooms, old-school furniture, hanging chairs, outdoor bathtubs and hydromassage showers, overlooking a garden with an open-air barbecue and a pet horse. Johnson also has an excellent 'eco-houseboat' (http://ecohouseboat.com; for two people ₹9000 to ₹14,000).

Raheem Residency HERITAGE HOTEL **$$$**
(☑0477-2239767; www.raheemresidency.com; Beach Rd; s ₹9220-11,980; d ₹10,240-13,310; 🌀🛜🏊) Across the road from the beach, this thoughtfully renovated 1860s heritage home offers Alleppey's most character-filled accommodation. The 10 rooms have been restored to their former glory by Irish personality Bibi Baskin and have bathtubs, antique furniture and period fixtures. Common areas include indoor courtyards, a private pool and two excellent restaurants,

Chakara and Harbour, and there's yoga and ayurveda.

Unfortunately, the new flyover on Alleppey Beach detracts from the otherwise charming setting.

Purity LUXURY HOTEL $$$
(☑0478-2862862; www.purityresort.com; east of Muhamma; r incl breakfast €210-340; ▦☏) Fronting Vembanad Lake, 16km north of Alleppey, this Spanish-German-run jewel blends heritage style and Indian antiques with bold contemporary design and a soothing position. Hot pinks, reds and aquamarines wash the 14 boutique-chic rooms with statement bathrooms; some have in-room tubs, others jazzy Tamil Nadu tiles. There's a professional ayurvedic spa, plus yoga, boat rides and a sleek Kerala-inspired restaurant.

✕ Eating & Drinking

Mushroom ARABIC, INDIAN $
(☑9633085702; www.facebook.com/Mushroom Restaurant; CCSB Rd; mains ₹90-170; ☺noon-midnight) A breezy open-air town-centre restaurant embellished with fairy lights and greenery, specialising in cheap, spicy halal meals like chicken *kali mirch,* fish tandoori and chilli mushrooms, plus peppery noodle and rice stir-fries. Lots of locals and travellers give it a fun, relaxed vibe. Also does takeaway.

Le Coffee Time CAFE $
(☑9895039767; www.nannitours.com; Nanni Backpackers Hostel, Cullan Rd; snacks ₹70-150; ☺8am-9pm; ☏) A friendly, tucked-away courtyard cafe at Nanni Backpackers Hostel (p966), 500m west of the beach, with a genuine Italian espresso machine, where you can tuck into pancakes, masala omelettes and other lovingly prepared breakfasts amid hot-pink walls and a stack of books for borrowing.

Cafe Katamaran INTERNATIONAL $$
(☑9746402340; www.facebook.com/cafecatama ran; Beach Rd; mains ₹180-350; ☺8am-midnight) Loved by both visitors and locals, mellow, welcoming Katamaran brings a traveller-style menu to its elevated, low-seating deck looking right out on the beach – *momos,* grilled sandwiches, pastas, curries and seafood specials like grilled garlic-butter fish. There are deliciously fresh juices, lassis and smoothies (including vegan versions), along with breakfasts of pancakes, omelettes or granola, and regular live music.

Halais INDIAN, ARABIC $$
(☑9446053338; www.facebook.com/haneefsaithal ais; CCSB Rd; mains ₹60-400; ☺9.30am-11.30pm) Locally famous for its chicken and mutton biryanis, busy Halais is a clean restaurant hidden behind a street-front sweet shop. It's also popular for Arabian and Yemeni dishes such as shawarma, and does a few dosa, masalas and thalis too.

Royale Chimney INDIAN $$
(☑0477-2237828; www.hotelroyalepark.com; Hotel Royale Park, YMCA Rd; mains ₹160-350; ☺7am-10pm, bar noon-10pm; ☏) There's an extensive menu at this always-busy air-con hotel restaurant, and the food – including biryanis, tandoori, Keralan fish curry and veg and fish thalis – is consistently delicious. You can order from the same menu in the surprisingly smart upstairs beer parlour and wash down

---

KERALA'S 2018 FLOODS

The worst in a century, the devastating floods that swept through Kerala in July and August 2018 killed more than 400 people, displaced over a million more and caused an estimated US$2.5 billion of damage. The exceptionally high rainfall and flooding also had serious knock-on effects, including fatal landslides (which some claim were worsened by deforestation) and a huge drop in tourism (which accounts for 10% of Kerala's GDP).

As a result of climate change, severe flooding is becoming increasingly common across South India; Kerala is one of the country's most vulnerable-to-flooding states, but also, says a 2018 government report, one of its least adept at water management. Many experts claim that the Kerala government should have been better prepared for a natural disaster of this kind.

Idukki district (including Munnar) was one of worst affected areas; others included Alappuzha (Alleppey), Wayanad, Thrissur, Kozhikode (Calicut), Kannur, Chennamangalam (p997) and Kochi (Cochin; though not Fort Cochin), where the airport was closed for two weeks. At the time of writing, Kerala is open, working hard to get back on its feet and in need of strong support from the tourism industry, and tourism services are expected to be back on track by late 2019.

your meal with a cold Kingfisher, while breakfasts wander from omelettes to dosa.

Chakara
MULTICUISINE $$$

(☑ 0477-2239767; www.raheemresidency.com; Beach Rd; mains ₹350-550; ⏱ 7.30-10am, 12.30-3pm & 7-10pm) Opposite the beach, this elegant restaurant at the 1860s heritage-style Raheem Residency hotel (p967) is Alleppey's finest. It has seating on a bijou open-sided terrace reached via a spiral staircase (though the sea views are now mostly blocked by a flyover). The menu creatively combines Keralan and European cuisine, specialising in local seafood; try the Alleppey fish curry or paneer-cashew curry.

Indian wines, Goan port and beer are all served, too, as are mini Keralan meals (₹350). In the fairy-lit garden below is the equally popular **Harbour Restaurant** (☑ 0477-2239767; mains ₹170-500; ⏱ 11am-10pm), with a similar menu and deliciously cool beers.

ℹ Information

DTPC Tourist Office (☑ 9400051796, 0477-2251796; www.dtpcalappuzha.com; Boat Jetty Rd; ⏱ 9.30am-5.30pm)

ℹ Getting There & Away

BOAT

From Alleppey's **boat jetty** (VCSB Rd), State Water Transport (www.swtd.gov.in) ferries are *scheduled* for Kottayam (₹15, 2½ hours) at 7.30am, 9.30am, 11.30am, 2.30pm and 5.15pm, returning at 6.45am, 11.30am, 1pm, 3.30pm and 5.15pm; at the time of writing, ongoing renovation works meant only the 11.30am ferry (returning at 1pm) was operating. Ferries leave for Kollam (₹400, eight hours) daily at 10.30am (every other day April to June).

BUS

From the **KSRTC bus stand** (VCSB Rd), buses head every 30 minutes to Trivandrum (₹150, four hours), Kollam (₹90, 2½ hours) and Ernakulam (Kochi; ₹100, 1½ hours). Buses to Kottayam (₹50, 1½ hours, every 30 minutes 5.40am to 7.30pm) are faster than the ferry. Buses leave for Kumily (Periyar; ₹150, six hours) at 6.40am, 7.50am and 1.10pm; for Munnar (₹150, six hours) at 2am, 4.30am, 8.45am (AC) and 2pm; and for Varkala (₹90, three hours) at 8am, 8.50am and 5.30pm.

TRAIN

Alleppey's train station is 4km southwest of the town centre, with numerous daily trains to Ernakulam (2nd class/sleeper/3AC ₹50/140/495, 1½ hours) and Trivandrum (₹80/140/495, three

GREEN PALM HOMES

Around 12km southeast of Alappuzha (Alleppey), long-running **Green Palm Homes** (☑ 9496956665, 0477-2725865; www.greenpalmhomes.com; Chennamkary; incl full board r ₹2800-5000, cottages ₹6000-8000; ❄) is a series of homestays in a picturesque village on a backwater island, where you sleep in simple rooms in villagers' homes among rice paddies (though 'premium' rooms with bathroom and air-con are available). Take a guided walk (₹500), hire bicycles or kayaks (from ₹300), or join a cooking class (₹250).

The cheapest rooms have shared bathroom; some others have an air-con option (₹500 extra). There's a 30% discount for solo guests.

hours) via Kollam (₹60/140/495, 1½ to 2½ hours). Six daily trains go to Varkala (2nd class/AC chair ₹65/315, two to three hours).

ℹ Getting Around

Autorickshaws from the town centre or bus stand to the beach cost around ₹60. Guesthouses hire out scooters for ₹300 to ₹400 per day, including reliable **Nanni Tours & Travel** (☑ 9895039767; www.nannitours.com; Cullan Rd; ⏱ 8am-9pm).

Marari & Kattoor

☑ 0478

The increasingly popular white-gold beaches at Kattoor and Marari, 10km and 14km north of Alleppey respectively, are gorgeous beachside alternatives to the region's backwaters. Marari, the flashier of the two, is transforming into a fully fledged (yet still naturally beautiful) beach resort, with some exclusive five-star seafront accommodation. Kattoor, sometimes known as 'Secret Beach', is more of a fishing village, where development remains at a minimum and sandy back lanes lead down to near-deserted sands.

🛏 Sleeping & Eating

★ **Secret Beach**
Yoga Homestay
HOMESTAY $$

(☑ 9447786931; www.secretbeach.in; Kattoor; r ₹1000-2500; ❄ 🖥) The location is sublime at this peaceful three-room homestay, separated from a quiet piece of Kattoor Beach by a small lagoon (cross in a borrowed canoe!).

CHURCHES IN NORTHWESTERN KOTTAYAM

Next to the Meenachil River, 2km northwest of Kottayam's centre, lie a couple of ancient churches well worth exploring. The whitewashed, hilltop **St Mary's Syrian Knanaya Church** (Valiyapally; off River Bank Rd; ⊘ hours vary) was founded in 1550 by Syrian Knanaya Christians, though the existing building is from 1588; it's decorated with two granite-carved crosses dated to least as far back as the 7th century with Pahalavi inscriptions. Just 200m south, the elegant, Portuguese-built 1579 **St Mary's Orthodox Church** (Cheriapally; off Kottayam–Kumarakom Rd; ⊘ dawn-dusk) is famous for its blend of European baroque and Keralan temple architecture, as well as for the Portuguese-style vegetable-dye paintings that festoon its altar.

Talented, welcoming young owner Vimal is an accredited yoga and *kalari* instructor (classes ₹300) and, with his family, also offers free bikes and home-cooked meals. Ask locally for 'Akkichen's house'.

★ **Marari Villas** LUXURY HOTEL **$$$**
(☏ 9947948868; www.mararivillas.com; Kattoor; incl breakfast r ₹14,000-19,500, 1-room villa ₹18,500-22,000; ❋ ⊜ ⊠) ✦ Marari stays don't get better than this: four intimate, independent boutique villas dotted along or near the beachfront, washed in dusty reds, whites and turquoises, serving wonderful Keralan cooking and with honey-coloured sand gracing front gardens. Two-room Lotus shares its back-garden pool, yoga deck and ayurvedic massage rooms with Palm (three rooms) and one-room, private-pool Hibiscus and Orchid. Book ahead.

A Beach Symphony COTTAGE **$$$**
(☏ 9947107150; www.abeachsymphony.com; Marari; cottage ₹9900-22,960; ⊘ Sep-May; ❋ ⊜ ⊠) These four individually designed cottages at the main beach entrance shine as one of Marari's most exclusive seafront resorts. Amid breezy gardens, the Keralan-inspired cottages are plush and private, with a luxurious, earthy feel. Khombu and Nagaswaram enjoy beach views; Violin has its own plunge pool. Yoga, bicycle tours, boat trips and meals on your verandah can all be arranged.

ℹ Getting There & Away

Frequent buses head north from Alleppey's KSRTC bus stand (p969) towards Cherthala from 5am to 9pm, stopping along the main NH66 2km inland from Marari beach. Taxis to/from Alleppey cost around ₹700.

Kottayam

☏ 0481 / POP 357,300

Poised between the backwaters and the Western Ghats, 60km southeast of Kochi, Kottayam is renowned for being the centre of Kerala's spice and rubber trade, rather than for its aesthetic appeal. It was also the first town in India to achieve 100% literacy, in 1989. For most travellers it's a hub town, well connected to the mountains and the backwaters, with many travellers taking the public canal cruise to or from Alleppey before heading east to Kumily, west to Kumarakom or north to Kochi. The city has a traffic-clogged centre, but there are a couple of intriguing sights in its northwestern suburbs.

🛌 Sleeping & Eating

Homestead Hotel HOTEL **$**
(☏ 0481-2560467; KK Rd; s ₹600, d ₹990-1400, r with AC ₹2010; ❋ ⊜) In a handy little compound tucked back from busy KK Rd, super-central Homestead has a variety of well-maintained budget rooms, the best of them with prettily patterned sheets and the odd feature wall (ask to view a few). Air-con rooms come with hot water; for others, it's by the bucket.

Windsor Castle & Lake Village Resort HOTEL **$$**
(☏ 0481-2363637; www.thewindsorcastle.co.in; MC Rd, Kodimatha; s ₹3540-4720, d ₹4130-5310, cottages ₹8790; ❋ ⊜ ⊠) Some of Kottayam's comfiest rooms inhabit this grandiose white box, 3km south of the town centre, though the more impressive accommodation is in the Lake Village behind. Smart deluxe cottages, some with a houseboat-like atmosphere, are strewn between private backwaters, manicured gardens and two pools, and there's an upmarket multi-cuisine restaurant.

Thali SOUTH INDIAN **$**
(KK Rd; dishes ₹30-200; ⊘ 8am-8.30pm) This lovely, spotlessly kept 1st-floor dining room with slatted blinds is a swankier version of Kerala's typical set-meals restaurants. The South Indian food here is great, including Malabar fish curry, thalis, masala dosa and

lightly spiced *pachakkari* mopped up with fluffy *appam* (rice pancakes).

Upstairs is equally popular **Meenachil** (dishes ₹60-180; ◔noon-3pm & 6-9.30pm), turning out tasty Chinese and Indian cooking in a warm family setting.

ℹ Information

DTPC Tourist Office (☑ 0481-2560479; www.dtpckottayam.com; Kodimatha; ◔10am-5pm Mon-Sat) At the boat jetty.

ℹ Getting There & Around

Autorickshaws charge ₹40 from the bus stand to the jetty or the train station.

BOAT

State Water Transport (www.swtd.gov.in) ferries *usually* leave Kottayam's **boat jetty** (Kodimatha), 1.5km south of the town centre, for Alleppey (₹15, 2½ hours) at 6.45am, 11.30am, 1pm, 3.30pm and 5.15pm, returning at 7.30am, 9.30am, 11.30am, 2.30pm and 5.15pm. At research time, only the 1pm (returning 11.30am) service was operating due to ongoing restoration work; full services may well have resumed by the time you read this.

BUS

The **KSRTC bus stand** (NH183) is 600m south of the town centre.

TRAIN

Kottayam's train station, 1.5km northeast of the town centre, is served by frequent trains running between Trivandrum (2nd class/sleeper/3AC ₹80/140/495, 3½ to 4½ hours) and Ernakulam (Kochi; ₹50/140/495, 1½ hours).

Kumarakom

☑ 0481

Kumarakom, 15km west of Kottayam on the shores of vast, beautiful Vembanad Lake – Kerala's largest lake – is an unhurried back-water village with a smattering of dazzling top-end resorts, a renowned bird sanctuary and less-crowded canals than Alleppey.

Arundhati Roy, author of the 1997 Booker Prize–winning *The God of Small Things,* was raised in the nearby village of Aymanam.

◉ Sights

Kumarakom Bird Sanctuary   NATURE RESERVE
(☑ 0481-2525864, 9400008620; Kumarakom; Indian/foreigner ₹50/150; ◔6am-5pm) This reserve on the 5-hectare site of a former rubber plantation on Vembanad Lake is the haunt of a variety of domestic and migratory birds. October to February is the time for travelling birds like the garganey teal, osprey, marsh harrier and steppey eagle; May to July is the breeding season for local species such as the Indian shag, pond herons, egrets and darters. Guides cost ₹300 for a two-hour tour; there are also motorboat (₹650) and speedboat trips (₹1200).

⊨ Sleeping

Cruise 'N Lake   GUESTHOUSE $$
(☑ 9447126784, 9846036375; puthenpurajose@gmail.com; Puthenpura Tourist Enclave, Cheerpunkal; r with/without AC ₹2000/1500; ❄ 🛜) Surrounded by backwaters on one side and a lawn of rice paddies on the other, this is the affordable Kumarakom getaway. The eight rooms are plain but modern, with verandahs facing the water, and there's a low-key on-site restaurant gazing out on the lake. It's 3km northwest of Kumarakom Bird Sanctuary; the final 1.5km is down a rugged dirt road.

Kumarakom Lake Resort   RESORT $$$
(☑ 0481-2524900;   www.kumarakomlakeresort.in; Kumarakom North; r/ste incl breakfast from

KERALA KUMARAKOM

BUSES FROM KOTTAYAM

DESTINATION	FARE (₹)	DURATION (HR)	FREQUENCY
Alleppey	47	1½	every 20-40min 6am-5.40pm
Ernakulam (Kochi)	76-236	1-2	every 15min 4.20am-12.30am
Kollam	100	3½	4.30am, 6.45am, 7.30am, 9.40am, 2.20pm
Kumarakom	30	30min	5.30am, every 20min 6.40am-9.30pm
Kumily (for Periyar)	100	3½	3am, 3.40am, 4.40am, every 20min 6am-7pm, hourly 7pm-midnight
Munnar	100	4	3am, 7.50am, 9am, 10.30am, 12.40pm, 2pm, 5pm
Trivandrum	186	4	every 20-30min
Varkala	150	4	6.45am

BOATING KERALA'S BACKWATERS

The undisputed highlight of a trip to Kerala is travelling through the 900km network of waterways that fringe the coast and trickle inland. Long before the advent of roads, these waters were the slippery highways of Kerala, and many villagers still use paddle power as their main form of transport. Trips through the backwaters traverse palm-fringed lakes studded with cantilevered Chinese fishing nets, and wind their way along narrow, shady canals where coir (coconut fibre), copra (dried coconut kernels) and cashews are loaded onto boats. Along the way are remote villages where farming life continues as it has for aeons.

Tourist Cruises

The popular State Water Transport (www.swtd.kerala.gov.in) tourist cruise between Kollam (Quilon) and Alappuzha (Alleppey; ₹400) departs from either end at 10.30am, arriving at 6.30pm, usually daily from July to March and every second day at other times, though it may start running later in the season. Generally, there's a 1pm lunch stop and a brief afternoon chai stop. It's a scenic and leisurely eight-hour journey, though the boat travels along only the major canals, so you won't get many close-up views of the village life that makes the backwaters so special. Some travellers take the trip halfway (₹140 to ₹270) and hop off at the Matha Amrithanandamayi Mission (p964).

Houseboats

If the stars align, renting a houseboat designed like a *kettuvallam* (rice barge) could well be one of the highlights of your trip to India. It can be an expensive experience (depending on your budget) but for a couple on a romantic overnight jaunt or split between a group of travellers, it's usually worth every rupee.

Houseboats cater for couples (one or two double bedrooms) and groups (up to seven bedrooms!). Food (and an onboard chef) is generally included in the quoted cost, as is a driver/captain. Houseboats can be chartered through a multitude of private operators in Alleppey, Kollam, Kottayam and, to a lesser extent, the Valiyaparamba area (p1008) in northern Kerala. The quality of boats varies widely, from ageing boats to floating palaces.

Travel-agency reps will be pushing you to book a boat as soon as you set foot in Kerala, though many travellers prefer to wait until they reach a backwaters hub. The choice is greatest in Alleppey; you're more likely to be able to bargain down a price if you turn up and see what's on offer. That said, many of the most professionally run houseboats now take online bookings and can get snapped up in advance (and may not even dock at the main jetties). Talk to other travellers and choose a houseboat based on a strong local recommendation (whether that's from a friend, a locally based contact or a reputable guesthouse) and book directly with the owner (online or by phone) or through your guesthouse.

In the busy high season or during domestic holidays (such as Pooja, Onam or Diwali) when prices peak, you're likely to get caught in backwater-gridlock – some travellers are disappointed by the number of boats on the water. Expect a boat for two people for 24

₹19,350/60,300; ❄🛜🛟) The queen of Kumarakom's luxury accommodation is this 67-room Keralan-inspired beauty fronting Vembanad Lake, complete with ayurvedic spa, yoga, two restaurants, its own houseboats and idyllic tropical gardens. Most rooms open onto interconnecting palm-fringed pools or have their own plunge pools. Even the standard rooms are spacious, stylish and gloriously comfortable, with hot tubs in the bathroom.

❶ Getting There & Away

Kumarakom is served by buses from Kottayam (₹30, 30 minutes) at 5.30am then every 20 minutes from 6.40am to 9.30pm.

KERALA'S WESTERN GHATS

The Unesco-listed Western Ghats – one of the world's key biodiversity hotspots – are thick with wildlife sanctuaries, outstanding trekking, and fragrant spice, coffee and tea plantations. Kerala's far northern Ghats are

hours to cost ₹6000 to ₹8000 at the budget level; for four people ₹10,000 to ₹12,000; for larger boats or for air-conditioning expect to pay ₹15,000 to ₹35,000. Prices triple from around 20 December to 5 January.

Village Tours, Canoe Boats & Kayaks

Village tours are an excellent way to see the backwaters by day at a slow pace, and usually involve small groups of five to six visitors, a knowledgeable guide and an open canoe or covered *kettuvallam*. The tours (from Kochi, Kollam or Alleppey) last three to 10 hours and cost around ₹500 to ₹1000 per person. They include visits to watch coir-making, boat-building, toddy (palm beer) tapping and fish farming. The Munroe Island trip (p962) from Kollam is a particularly scenic tour of this type; Kochi's Tourist Desk (p994) also organises recommended tours. Kayaking backwaters trips, making similar village stops at similar prices, are becoming a popular alternative.

Public Ferries

For the local backwater transport experience at just a few rupees, there are State Water Transport (www.swtd.gov.in) boats from Alleppey to Kottayam (₹15, 2½ hours) at 7.30am, 9.30am, 11.30am, 2.30pm and 5.15pm, returning at 6.45am, 11.30am, 1pm, 3.30pm and 5.15pm (though only the 11.30am service, returning at 1pm, was operating at research time). The trip crosses Vembanad Lake and has a more varied landscape than the Kollam–Alleppey cruise. Other ageing boats operate from the jetties at Alleppey and Kollam, ferrying locals to backwater villages.

Environmental Issues

Pollution from houseboats is becoming a major problem as boat numbers continue to rise. They were only introduced in the 1990s, and there are now thought to be 1200 to 1400 houseboats plying Kerala's inland waterways – with around 400 to 500 of them believed to be unregistered. Sadly, the backwaters are facing increasing contamination from spilled houseboat fuel, as well as plastic, food and even human waste from houseboats (despite the existence of designated sewage-treatment plants for cleaning houseboat bio-toilets). This translates into water shortages and potential health hazards for local villagers, as well as declining bird populations and fish stocks (which in turn impacts the livelihoods of local fishers). Noise pollution from some of the larger 'party-style' houseboats that have become popular in recent years is also a growing concern. That said, most houseboats do now have bio-toilets, and India's first solar-powered ferry was even successfully introduced on Lake Vembanad in 2017.

Consider choosing one of the few remaining punting, rather than motorised, boats if possible, though these only operate in shallow water – or explore the backwaters with an environmentally responsible kayaking operator instead.

KERALA PERIYAR TIGER RESERVE

home to the serene Wayanad region (p1003), usually accessed from Calicut.

Periyar Tiger Reserve

📞 04869 / POP 30,300 (KUMILY) / ELEV 880M (KUMILY)

South India's most popular wildlife reserve, **Periyar** (Thekkady Tiger Reserve; 📞 04869-224571, 8547603066; www.periyartigerreserve. org; Indian ₹40, adult/child foreigner ₹475/170; ⊗ 6.30am-5.30pm, last entry 4.30pm), encompasses 777 sq km, including a 26-sq-km 1895 artificial lake created by the British. This vast expanse – which became Kerala's first

tiger reserve in 1978 (though founded as a sanctuary in 1934) – shelters wild boar, sambar, bison, langur, 2000 elephants and 35 to 40 hard-to-spot tigers. It's firmly established on both the Indian and foreigner tourist trails and known for its scenic lake cruise (p974). But if you dig deeper, perhaps on a trek with a tribal villager or former poacher, Periyar's hilly jungle scenery takes on a wild, magical feel. Bring warm, waterproof clothing.

Kumily is the closest town, and has hotels, restaurants and Kashmiri emporiums. Thekkady, 4km south of Kumily, is the park centre, with the KTDC hotels and boat jetty.

Confusingly, when people refer to the reserve they use Thekkady, Kumily and Periyar interchangeably. The best wildlife-spotting months are December to April.

◉ Sights & Activities

The Forest Department's Ecotourism Centre (p977) handles all trips accessing the reserve. For the November-to-March high season, book well ahead (online or through your guesthouse). Reservations are *theoretically* via www.periyarfoundation.online, though it wasn't accepting foreign cards at research time. Last resort: try for tickets in person after 7.30pm the day before.

The main way to tour the reserve without taking a guided walk is by 1½-hour KTDC boat trips with the **Periyar Lake Cruise** (Periyar Lake; adult/child ₹240/80; ⊙departures 7.30am, 9.30am, 11.15am, 1.45pm & 3.30pm). You might see deer, boar, otters and birdlife, but it's generally more cruise than wildlife-spotting experience. If you haven't prebooked (at www.periyarfoundation.online), buy tickets from the office above the boat jetty or the boating counter at Kumily's shuttle-bus (p978) car park.

Hiking & Rafting

The Ecotourism Centre (p977) arranges full-day border hikes (₹1800 per person), 2½-hour nature walks (₹350 per person), bamboo rafting (half/full day ₹1800/2400 per person) and three-hour night 'jungle scouts' (₹1200 per person), accompanied by trained tribal guides, as well as overnight 'tiger trail' camping treks (one-night trail ₹6000 per person; minimum charge ₹9000), covering 20km to 30km and led by former poachers retrained as guides. Trips usually require a minimum of two or four people; solo travellers may be able to join other groups. Children must be 12 years or over for most hikes.

Jeep Safaris

The Forest Department runs 40km **jeep safaris** (☑8289821306, 8547123789; per jeep ₹2200, incl boating, trekking & lunch adult/child ₹1500/750) in the reserve's Gavi buffer zone, with the first 20km along main roads. Jeeps depart at 6am, returning at 3pm or 4pm, and kids can join. Book through your guesthouse (admission costs extra).

Cooking Classes

Many local homestays, including Green View (p975) and El-Paradiso (p976), offer cooking classes (₹300 to ₹600 per person). There are also recommended two-hour classes (followed by a feast) at well-established **Bar-B-Que** (☑9895613036; KK Rd; class per person veg/nonveg ₹400/500; ⊙6.30pm), 1km west of the bazaar.

Spice & Tea Plantation Tours

These hills are known for their production of spices (cardamom, vanilla, pepper, cinnamon) and ayurvedic herbs. Several local spice plantations offer guided tours (₹100), including the long-established **Abraham's Spice Garden** (☑9746129050; www.abrahamspice.com; NH183, Spring Valley; tours ₹100; ⊙6am-6pm), 3km west of Kumily. The four-decade-old working **Connemara Tea Factory** (☑8075715496; NH183, Vandiperiyar; tours ₹150; ⊙tours hourly 9am-4pm Mon-Sat), 14km southwest of Kumily, runs one-hour guided tours; buses run from Kumily to Vandiperiyar (₹25) every 30 minutes.

🛌 Sleeping

🛌 Inside the Park

The KTDC runs Periyar House, Aranya Nivas and the grand Lake Palace, all inside the reserve. Note that there's effectively a curfew at these hotels – guests are not permitted to roam the reserve after 6pm.

The Ecotourism Centre (p977) arranges tented accommodation within the reserve's buffer zone at the **Jungle Camp** (☑8547603066, 04869-22457; www.periyartiger reserve.org; d incl meals ₹5000), and has basic cottages at **Bamboo Grove** (r incl breakfast ₹1800) on the southwest edge of Kumily.

Lake Palace HOTEL $$$
(☑9400008589, 04869-223887; www.ktdc.com/lake-palace; Thekkady; r incl meals ₹16,000-32,000) There's a faint whiff of royalty at this restored KTDC-operated Travancore summer palace on Periyar Lake, accessible only by 20-minute boat ride. The six charismatic rooms are decorated with flair and antique furnishings. Though there's a 6pm curfew, staying inside the reserve gives you a good chance of seeing wildlife from your private terrace. Rates include a boat trip.

🛌 Kumily

Mickey Homestay HOMESTAY $
(☑04869-223196, 9447284160; www.mickey homestay.com; Bypass Rd; r ₹750-1000; 🛜) A genuine homestay with just five intimate,

Kumily & Periyar Tiger Reserve

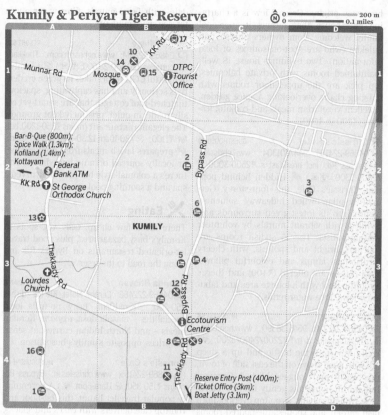

Kumily & Periyar Tiger Reserve

Sleeping
- 1 Bamboo Grove.....................................A4
- 2 Chrissie's Hotel B2
- 3 Claus Garden D2
- 4 El-Paradiso C3
- 5 Green View B3
- 6 Mickey Homestay C2
- 7 Spice Village B3
- 8 Thekkady Homestay B4

Eating
- 9 Ambadi C4
- 10 Ananda Bhavan B1
- Chrissie's Cafe .... (see 2)
- 11 French Restaurant & Bakery..............B4
- 12 Grandma's Cafe B3
- Spice Village .... (see 7)

Entertainment
- 13 Mudra Cultural Centre A3

Transport
- 14 Autorickshaw Stand B1
- 15 Kumily Bus Stand B1
- 16 Park Shuttle Bus Stop A4
- 17 Tamil Nadu Bus Stand B1
- Taxi & Jeep Stand .... (see 15)

fan-cooled rooms in a welcoming family house, with homely touches making them some of Kumily's cosiest budget picks. Balconies have rattan furniture and hanging bamboo seats and the whole place is fringed by greenery. The two cheapest rooms, with separate bathroom, can interconnect, and

home-cooked breakfasts are available (₹300 for two).

★ **Green View** GUESTHOUSE $$
(☎9447432008, 04869-224617; www.suresh greenview.com; Bypass Rd; r incl breakfast ₹750-2000; 🛜) 🍃 Grown from its humble

homestay origins, Green View is a charming guesthouse that retains its personal family welcome from owners Suresh and Sulekha (who are spot-on sources of local information). Two buildings house 18 well-maintained rooms with private balconies; top pick are the upper-floor rooms with hanging chairs overlooking a spice garden. Excellent vegetarian meals and cooking lessons (₹300 to ₹500).

★ **Chrissie's Hotel**　　　GUESTHOUSE $$
(☑ 04869-224155, 9447601304; www.chrissies. in; Bypass Rd; incl breakfast s ₹2500-3000, d ₹2800-3300; ☎ ≋) ◢ Hidden behind popular Chrissie's Cafe, this four-storey, German-Egyptian-owned hideaway somehow blends into its forest-green surrounds and is filled with vibrant murals by volunteer visiting artists. The 15 stylish rooms are spacious, bright and spotless, with cheery furnishings, lamps and colourful pillows. Yoga classes are offered (₹400) and there's a rooftop pool with a lounge area and fabulous views. Free water refills.

Claus Garden　　　HOMESTAY $$
(☑ 04869-222320, 9645138390; www.homestay. in; Thekkumkadu; d/tr/f ₹2200/2400/3200; ☎) Well away from the bustle and up a steep hill with good views on the east side of town, this warm and long-established German-Indian-run home has gently curving balconies, swinging chairs, a rooftop overlooking a lush garden, and spotless tile-floored rooms with attractive wooden furniture and splashes of art. Organic breakfasts include fresh-baked bread and homemade jams (₹300).

El-Paradiso　　　HOMESTAY $$
(☑ 7034337350, 04869-222350; www.elparadiso. in; Bypass Rd; r ₹1800; ☎) An immaculate and friendly family homestay with fresh, modern rooms, most opening onto a terrace overlooking greenery and featuring fun touches like elephants on wooden bedheads. The best four have balconies and hanging chairs. Cooking classes (₹600) are a speciality here, as is the coffee straight from the owners' farm.

Thekkady Homestay　　　HOMESTAY $$
(☑ 9446205008, 04869-224006; www.thekkady homestay.com; Puthenparambil House, Thekkady Rd; r ₹1500-1900; ☎) Murals of leopards, jungle landscapes and Periyar Lake line the stairs to this genial, characterful homestay, where a handful of rooms unfolds across the top floor above the family home on the road to the reserve. Rooms are spotless and up to date, with floral murals, filter water and a terrace space outdoors.

Spice Village　　　RESORT $$$
(☑ 04869-222314; www.cghearth.com; Thekkady Rd; cottages ₹20,600-28,600; ☎ ≋) ◢ Kumily's delightful CGH resort takes its green credentials seriously and has captivating, spacious thatched-roof cottages that are smart yet cosily rustic, in quiet, pristinely kept grounds. The elegant **restaurant** (mains ₹350-1200, buffet ₹1100; ⏱ 7.30-10am, 12.30-3pm & 7.30-10pm) ◢ prepares lavish meals from home-grown or locally sourced organic ingredients, and there's a colonial-style bar plus an ayurvedic spa and a soothing pool.

✗ Eating

There are a few cheap, tasty veg spots in Kumily's busy bazaar area, plus good traveller-oriented restaurants on Bypass Rd and along the road to the reserve.

Ananda Bhavan　　　INDIAN $
(☑ 04869-222466; Central Hotel, KK Rd; dishes ₹50-200; ⏱ 8am-10pm) Tasty, no-frills local specialities – masala dosa, *appam*, Keralan meals – and North Indian curries, at sensible prices, opposite Kumily's bus station.

Chrissie's Cafe　　　MULTICUISINE $$
(☑ 04869-224155; www.chrissies.in; Bypass Rd; mains ₹150-350; ⏱ 11am-6pm; ☎) A perennially popular traveller haunt, this 1st-floor and rooftop cafe delivers with cakes and snacks, excellent coffee, free water refills, well-prepared Continental faves like pastas and salads, and fabulous signature Middle Eastern meze platters and falafel wraps, served amid scattered pot plants.

Ambadi　　　INDIAN $$
(☑ 04869-222193; http://hotelambadi.com; Thekkady Rd; mains ₹100-300; ⏱ 7am-9.30pm; ☎) At the English-manor-style hotel of the same name, Ambadi feels more formal than most Kumily eateries, with an almost churchlike decor of carved wood and tiled floors. It's popular with locals and visitors alike for its well-executed, reasonably priced and extensive selection of North and South Indian favourites.

Grandma's Cafe　　　MULTICUISINE $$
(☑ 9995317261; Bypass Rd; mains ₹180-300; ⏱ 7am-11pm Nov-Mar, from noon Apr-Oct; ☎) Hidden down a few steps, this lively indoor-outdoor cafe-restaurant is all bamboo tables, good vibes and bright yellow walls scrawled

AYURVEDA

With its roots in Sanskrit, the word ayurveda comes from *ayu* (life) and *veda* (knowledge): the knowledge or science of life. Principles of ayurvedic medicine were first documented in the Vedas some 2000 years ago, but may have been practised centuries earlier, making this the most ancient known medical discipline.

Ayurveda sees the world as having an intrinsic order and balance. It argues that we possess three *doshas* (humours): *vata* (wind or air), *pitta* (fire) and *kapha* (water/earth), known together as the *tridoshas*. Most people have one or two dominant *doshas*, but deficiency or excess in any of them can lead to disease. An excess of *vata* may result in dizziness and debility; an increase in *pitta* may cause fever, inflammation and infection; *kapha* is essential for hydration.

Ayurvedic treatment, under the watch of university-trained doctors, aims to restore the balance, and hence good health, principally through two methods: *panchakarma* (internal purification) and herbal massage. *Panchakarma* is used to treat serious ailments, and is an intense detox regime, a combination of five types of different therapies to rid the body of built-up endotoxins. These include *vaman* (therapeutic vomiting), *virechan* (purgation), *vasti* (enemas), *nasya* (elimination of toxins through the nose) and *raktamoksha* (detoxification of the blood). Before *panchakarma* begins, the body is first prepared over several days with a special diet, oil massages *(snehana)* and herbal steambaths *(swedana)*. Although it may sound pretty grim, *panchakarma* purification might only use a few of these treatments at a time, with therapies like bloodletting and leeches only used in rare cases. But while yoga, meditation and ayurveda are all intertwined, this is still no spa holiday.

The herbs used in ayurveda grow in abundance in Kerala's humid climate – the monsoon is thought to be the best time of year for treatment, when there is less dust in the air and the pores are open – and every village has its own ayurvedic pharmacy.

with messages from past diners. Breakfasts wander the globe from French toast to Keralan veg curry with *appam,* while South Indian signatures (such as Chettinadu curries and masala-fried fish) mingle with noodles, biryanis and salads.

French Restaurant & Bakery   CAFE, BAKERY $$
(☑ 9961213107; Thekkady Rd; meals ₹100-280; ⊗ 8.30am-8pm) A shack-like, yellow-walled family operation just back from the park access road that's particularly good for breakfast or lunch – mainly for the fluffy tuna, veg or cheese baguettes baked on-site, but also for pasta, pizza, omelettes and noodle dishes.

★ Entertainment

Mudra Cultural Centre   LIVE PERFORMANCE
(☑ 9061263382; www.mudraculturalcentre.com; Thekkady Rd; tickets ₹200; ⊗ Kathakali 5pm & 7pm, kalarippayat 6pm & 7.15pm) Kathakali shows at this cultural centre are highly entertaining. Make-up and costume starts 30 minutes before each show. Arrive early for a good seat; use of cameras is free and welcome. There also two *kalarippayat* performances nightly. Schedules are usually reduced during the low season.

ⓘ Information

DTPC Tourist Office (☑ 04869-222620; www.dtpcidukki.com; off KK Rd; ⊗ 10am-5pm Mon-Sat)

Ecotourism Centre (☑ 04869-224571, 8547603066; www.periyartigerreserve.org; Thekkady Rd; ⊗ 6.30am-9pm)

ⓘ Getting There & Away

Kumily's **bus stand** (☑ 04869224242; KK Rd) is at the northeastern edge of town, with both private and KSRTC services:

Alleppey ₹140, 5½ hours, 5.15am, 7.40am, 10am, 1pm, 1.45pm

Bengaluru (Bangalore) ₹800 to ₹1050, 10 to 12 hours, 6pm, 7.15pm, 8pm, 9pm

Ernakulam (Kochi) ₹150 to ₹160, six hours, at least 20 daily

Kollam ₹150, 6½ hours, 10.50am, 11.45am

Kottayam ₹96 to ₹120, four hours, every 30 minutes

Munnar ₹120, five hours, 7am, 7.30am, 9.45am, noon

Trivandrum ₹200, six to eight hours, 3am, 8.45am, 10.15am, 3.40pm

Buses leave at 7.45pm and 9pm for Chennai (Madras; ₹900 to ₹1000, 10 hours) and every 30 minutes for Madurai (₹90, four hours) from the

SABARIMALA

Deep in the Western Ghats, 20km west of Gavi (which is 40km south of Kumily) and 50km east of Erumeli, Sabarimala is home to the Ayyappan Temple. It's said to be one of the world's most visited pilgrimage centres, with 40 to 60 million Hindu devotees trekking here each year. Followers believe the god Ayyappan (son of Shiva and Vishnu as his female incarnation Mohini) meditated at this spot.

Women aged 10 to 50 (ie of 'menstruating age') have traditionally only been allowed as far as the Pamba checkpoint, but, in September 2018, India's Supreme Court overturned the ban in a historic ruling, for the first time allowing women of any age to visit the temple. This led to large-scale, international-headline-hitting protests and some violent clashes between mobs of protesters (who disagreed with the Supreme Court's ruling, which they said, among other things, disregarded the wishes of the celibate god Ayyappan) and the police, media and several young women attempting the pilgrimage. Among the protesters were many women, though a countermovement in favour of the Supreme Court's verdict also emerged. Several thousand people were arrested for their roles in the 'protests' (which saw female journalists attacked). Two women of 'forbidden' age finally managed to access the temple in early January 2019, protected by a police escort, but, at the time of writing, the Supreme Court had agreed to reconsider its verdict and some of the few women who attempted the pilgrimage after the ban was lifted had been discriminated against upon returning home.

Tamil Nadu bus stand (KK Rd) just north over the border.

❶ Getting Around

It's 1.5km southeast from Kumily bus stand (p977) to the **main reserve entrance** (Thekkady Rd), and another 3km south from there to Periyar Lake. Private vehicles are no longer allowed on the main access road; you *can* still walk it, or hop on one of the frequent **official shuttle buses** (off Thekkady Rd) (₹20 return) from the car park on the southwest edge of Kumily.

Kumily town is small enough to explore on foot, though you can hire bicycles (₹200). **Autorickshaws** (KK Rd) charge ₹30 for short hops.

Munnar

📞 04865 / POP 38,500 / ELEV 1524M

The rolling hills around Munnar, South India's largest tea-growing region, are carpeted in emerald-green tea plantations, and the low Western Ghats scenery here is magnificent – you're often up above the clouds watching veils of mist clinging to mountaintops. Munnar itself is a scruffy, traffic-clogged administration hub, not unlike a North Indian hill station, but wander just a few kilometres out and you'll be engulfed in a thousand shades of green.

Once known as the High Range of Travancore, Munnar flourished as a tea-producing area from 1880 onwards. Today it's the commercial centre of some of the world's highest tea-growing estates, most operated by corporate giant Tata, with some overseen by local cooperative Kannan Devan Hills Plantation Company (KDHP); Harrisons Malayalam also owns a share.

Munnar and the surrounding Idukki district were badly hit by the 2018 floods (p968); tourism services were expected to be mostly back to normal by late 2019.

❂ Sights & Activities

Most travellers visit Munnar to explore the lush, tea-filled hillocks that surround it. Day trips to Top Station (p982), Eravikulam National Park (p983) and Chinnar Wildlife Sanctuary (p983) are especially popular, as are treks through the hills.

CSI Christ Church   CHURCH
(off AM Rd/NH85; ⊙9am-5pm) Constructed in neo-Gothic style in 1911, with granite imported from the UK, Munnar's oldest church contains a series of plaques commemorating prominent foreign tea planters laid to rest here.

Tea Museum   MUSEUM
(adult/child ₹125/40, camera ₹20; ⊙9am-5pm Tue-Sun) Around 1.5km northwest of town, this KDHP-owned museum is a demo model of a working tea factory, but still shows the basic process, along with a collection of relics from the British era including photographs and a 1905 tea-roller (skip the disappointingly bizarre factory demonstration). The walk to/from Munnar follows a busy

road with views across tea plantations; autorickshaws charge ₹25 from the bazaar.

★**Nimi's Lip Smacking Classes** COOKING
(☑9447330773; http://nimisrecipes.com; AM Rd/
NH85; class per person ₹3000; ◷3pm Mon-Fri,
2pm Sat & Sun) Award-winning food writer and cook Nimi Sunilkumar has earned a solid reputation for her Keralan cuisine, publishing her own cookbooks, website and blog, and offering popular hands-on classes in her home (next to Munnar's DTPC). You'll learn traditional Keralan recipes and take home a copy of her book *Lip Smacking Dishes of Kerala*.

Trekking

The best way to experience Munnar's beautiful hills is on a guided trek. Options range from half-day 'soft treks' around tea plantations (₹500 to ₹1000) to more arduous full-day mountain treks (from ₹1000), which open up stupendous views when the mist clears. Trekking guides are easily organised through your accommodation or the DTPC Tourist Office (p982). **Munnar Trekking** (☑04865-230940, 9447825447; www.munnartrek king.com; trek per person ₹650-1000) is a reputable operation run by Green View Inn (p979), while Green Valley Vista (p980) offers excellent trekking, too.

At the time of writing, the DTPC is also arranging overnight trekking trips (per person ₹3000) with camping in the Top Station area (p982).

Which areas are open for treks depends on current Forest Department regulations, which change roughly yearly. There are walks that you can do independently, but bear in mind that tea plantations are private property and trekking around them without a licensed guide is trespassing.

🗘 Tours

Taxis, jeeps and guesthouses charge ₹1200 to ₹1500 for a spin around the main local sights. The DTPC (p982) runs several fairly rushed but inexpensive full-day tours to points around Munnar. The **Sandal Valley Tour** (☑04865-231516; www.dtpcidukki.com; per person ₹400; ◷tour 9am-5pm) visits Eravikulam National Park (p983), several viewpoints, waterfalls, tea plantations and a sandalwood forest; the **Village Tour** (☑04865-231516; www. dtpcidukki.com; per person ₹400; ◷9am-5pm) covers a spice farm, Ponmudi Dam, and a few waterfalls and viewpoints. Note that the Tea Valley Tour includes elephant riding, which

Munnar

Lonely Planet does not recommend due to the serious animal-welfare concerns involved.

🛏 Sleeping

Munnar town has good budget options just south of the centre near the bus station. That said, the views and peace are out in the hills and valleys, where homestays and upmarket resorts make scenic bases; it can be quite a hike into town from some of these.

🛏 Munnar Town

Green View Inn GUESTHOUSE $
(☑04865-230940, 9447825447; www.greenview munnar.com; r ₹600-900; 🖥) Handily located near the main bus station, this popular guesthouse has fresh, clean budget rooms (the best on the upper floor), a friendly welcome, and reliable tours and treks. Young owner Deepak also runs Munnar Trekking and cosy nearby cafe Taste the Brews (p981), as well

as comfy, good-value **Greenwoods Cottage** (☑9447825447, 04865-230189; www.greenview munnar.com; Anachal; s/d ₹750/900; ☏), 12km southwest of town.

JJ Cottage GUESTHOUSE $

(☑04865-230104, 9447228599; jjcottagemnr@ gmail.com; r ₹500-1000; ☏) The charming family at this long-standing pink-walled spot 1.5km south of central Munnar (tucked into a lane just far enough from the main bus station) offers a varied and uncomplicated set of clean, bright and colourful great-value rooms with hot water. The top-floor deluxe has a separate sitting room and views across town.

Zina Cottage GUESTHOUSE $

(☑09496822163, 04865-230349; r ₹800-1200; ☏) If you want to be immersed in lush tea plantations but still close to town, Zina is the budget choice. While it looks slightly run-down, this fading, rose-pink, 50-year-old bungalow offers five clean, simple rooms, in a scenic location with rippling views and good hikes on its doorstep. It's 1km south of the main bus station (call for directions).

🛏 Munnar Hills

⭐ **Rosegardens** HOMESTAY $$

(☑04864-278243, 9447378524; www.munnar homestays.com; NH85, Karadipara; r incl breakfast ₹5000; ☏) 🌿 An award-winning, totally charming family homestay, peacefully located 12km southwest of Munnar, overlooking owner Tomy's exquisite nursery and organic spice and fruit plantation (complete with biogas plant!). The five spacious rooms are immaculate, with tea/coffee trays, solar-heated water and greenery-fringed balconies. Fuelled by own-grown ingredients, the home-cooked meals are a treat, from coconut-stuffed pancakes to delicately spiced Keralan dinners (₹300).

It's on the main road to Kochi, linked by regular buses, and also does free garden tours for guests and cooking classes (₹2000).

⭐ **Green Valley Vista** GUESTHOUSE $$

(☑04865-263261, 940004311; www.green valleyvista.com; Chithirapuram; r incl breakfast ₹2250-3850; ☏) 🌿 Green Valley's views are superb, its rooms smartly up to date, and its welcome warm. Rooms sprawl across three floors, all facing the valley, and have TVs, modern bathrooms, natural light, and private balconies with dreamy panoramas. There's an outdoor terrace, plus yoga mats, a restaurant and water refills, and staff organ-

ise trekking. It's 11km south of Munnar, with good bus connections.

Shade HOMESTAY $$

(☑9539103538, 9447825984; www.theshade. in; Chithirapuram; r incl breakfast ₹3000) Folded into a verdant valley, 13km south of Munnar, Santhosh and Maya's tranquil family home is encircled by palms, betel-nut trees and their own cardamom and fruit plantations. The four unfussy rooms are kept comfy and spotless; go for the corner room gazing out across the valley. Trekking and home-cooked dinners (₹200) are available.

Anna Homestay GUESTHOUSE $$

(☑8129980088, 8156980088; www.annahome stay.com; Chithirapuram; r incl breakfast with/ without AC ₹4500/2500; ❄☏) Near Anachal village, 12km southwest of Munnar, Anna is more of a cosy guesthouse than a homestay, with 11 very tidy modern rooms, spacious rooftop common areas, Keralan cooking and yoga classes on offer. Best are the colourful corner pads with balconies, such as room A, and there are two large air-con rooms.

Windermere Estate RESORT $$$

(☑0484-2425237; www.windermere-retreats. com; Bison Valley Rd, Pothamedu; r incl breakfast ₹13,440-27,520; ❄☏🏊) 🌿 An elegant boutique-meets-country retreat, 4km southeast of Munnar, where 18 supremely spacious garden- and valley-view rooms are sprinkled around serene grounds flanking an infinity pool with tea-garden panoramas. Top choice are the two suite-like 'Plantation Villas', surrounded by cardamom and coffee plantations and spectacular vistas. There's a cosy library above the country-inspired restaurant, which delivers Indian cuisine rooted in homegrown produce.

Tall Trees RESORT $$$

(☑04865-230641; www.ttr.in; Bison Valley Rd; r incl breakfast ₹11,500-17,000; ☏) The 26 smart, lemon-scented, contemporary-meets-classic-Keralan cottages at this shaded hillside resort are hidden away under a luxuriant *shola* (virgin forest) canopy, 6km southeast from Munnar, and come with balconies, kettle kits and filtered water. Activities on offer include tea tastings, campfires, ayurvedic massages and guided walks, while meals are served alfresco or in the glass-ceilinged restaurant.

🍴 Eating

Early-morning food stalls in the bazaar serve breakfast snacks and cheap meals and there

PARAMBIKULAM TIGER RESERVE

Possibly the most protected environment in South India (nestled behind three dams in a valley at 300m to 1440m, surrounded by Kerala and Tamil Nadu sanctuaries), **Parambikulam** (☑8300014873, 9442201691, 9442201690; https://parambikulam.org; Indian/foreigner ₹30/300; ⊙7am-6pm, last entry 3pm) constitutes 644 sq km of Kipling-storybook scenery and wildlife-spotting goodness, designated a tiger reserve in 2009. Far less touristed than Kerala's Periyar Tiger Reserve, it's home to elephants, leopards, sloths and around 26 tigers, though its gaur, sambar, chital and crocodiles, plus some of the largest and oldest teak trees in Asia, are more easily sighted.

Bookings for access to the park's buffer zones and Forest Department accommodation are *theoretically* done online up to six months ahead (though there were technical issues with this at the time of writing). Otherwise, contact the **reserve office** (☑9442201691, 9442201690; https://parambikulam.org; Anappady; ⊙7am-6pm), which *may* also have spots and accommodation available on the day. Activities include minibus safaris (₹200) and treks (Indian ₹1200 to ₹3600, foreigner ₹2400 to ₹6100).

Accommodation is in tented niches (Indian ₹6100 to ₹7300, foreigner ₹9700 to ₹12,100), treetop huts (Indian ₹3000 to ₹6100, foreigner ₹3600 to ₹9700) and an air-conditioned colonial-era bungalow (Indian ₹5000 to ₹6100, foreigner ₹7300 to ₹8500); rates are per room and cover meals plus trekking, rafting and wildlife-spotting minibus safaris.

Access to the reserve is via Pollachi (44km south of Coimbatore and 46km southeast of Palakkad) in Tamil Nadu, also the access point for Anamalai Tiger Reserve (p1093). There are three daily buses from Pollachi to Parambikulam (₹85, three hours) via Anamalai at 6am, 9.30am or 10am and 3.15pm. Taxis from Pollachi cost around ₹1700. The reserve sometimes closes due to fire risk in March and April, and is best avoided during the monsoon (June to August).

are some good affordable restaurants in Munnar town, but the region's best food is served at its homestays and resorts.

Rapsy Restaurant　　　　　INDIAN $
(☑04865-230456; Bazaar; dishes ₹50-200; ⊙7am-10pm) This spotless glass-fronted sanctuary in the bazaar is packed at lunchtime, with locals lining up for Rapsy's famous *paratha* (Indian-style flaky bread) or biryani. It's equally popular with travellers and makes a decent stab at North Indian curries and fancy international dishes like Spanish omelette and Israeli shakshuka (eggs with tomatoes and spices).

Taste the Brews　　　　　CAFE $
(dishes ₹20-90; ⊙hours vary) An easy-going traveller-oriented cafe, opposite the bus station, for Continental-style breakfasts (omelettes, fruit salads), fresh juices, carrot cake and tastings of local tea and coffee.

**Sree Mahaveer
Bhojanalaya**　　　　　NORTH INDIAN $$
(☑9633906581; Hotel SN Annex, Government Guesthouse Rd; thalis ₹90-320; ⊙7am-10pm) Friendly and well-dressed, this all-veg hit

at the northern end of Munnar keeps busy with families for its great range of thalis: pick from Rajasthani, Gujarati, Punjabi and more, plus a dazzling array of vegetarian rices and curries.

Ali Baba & 41 Dishes　　　　MULTICUISINE $$
(☑8078801666, 04865-233303; www.alibaba 41dishes.com; Mulakkada Jn, Lakshmi Rd; mains ₹130-300; ⊙11.30am-10.30pm; 🛜) A sizzling Indian-international menu of red-hot noodles, spiced seafood platters, paneer/chicken tikka, northern gravies and southern thalis draws locals and travellers to this halal restaurant with Munnar-themed murals on the walls, located near the bus station at the southern end of town.

☆ Entertainment

**Punarjani
Traditional Village**　　　　LIVE PERFORMANCE
(☑9895999701, 04865-263888; http://punarjani munnar.com; 2nd Mile, NH85, Pallivasal; ₹200-300; ⊙Kathakali 5pm, kalarippayat 6pm) Entertaining (though aimed at tourists) daily performances of Kathakali and *kalarippayat,* 7km southwest of Munnar. Same-day

WORTH A TRIP

THATTEKKAD BIRD SANCTUARY

A serene 25-sq-km park in the foothills of the Western Ghats, cut through by two rivers and two streams, **Thattekkad Bird Sanctuary** (☑ 04862-232271, 8547603194; www.thattekadbirdsanctuary.org; adult/child Indian ₹45/40, foreigner ₹190/40, camera/video ₹40/240; ☺ 7am-5pm) shelters around 300 fluttering species – unusual in that they are mostly forest rather than water birds – including Malabar grey hornbills, Jerdon's nightjars, grey drongos, darters, kingfishers, flycatchers, warblers, sunbirds, tiny 4g flowerpeckers and rarer species like the Sri Lankan frogmouth.

River boating (₹150 per person) and guided birdwatching trips (rates vary) are organised by the efficient reception office at the sanctuary's entrance; accommodation places also offer birdwatching. Local homestays make excellent bases; we recommend two-room **Bird Song Homestay** (☑ 8943894087, 9746248274; http://thattekadhomestay.com; Thattekkad Bird Sanctuary; r incl meals with/without AC ₹3500/3000; ❈ ☎), run by welcoming naturalist Vinod, and blue-walled **Jungle Bird Homestay** (☑ 9947506188, 0485-2588143; http://junglebirdhomestay.blogspot.com; Thattekkad Bird Sanctuary; r incl meals per person ₹1500, with AC d ₹3300-4000; ❈ ☎), both just inside the sanctuary. **Windermere Riverhouse** (☑ 0484-2425237; www.windermere-retreats.com; Neriamangalam Rd, Inchathotty; r incl breakfast & dinner ₹19,520; ❈ ☎ ☀) is a graceful, cream-coloured riverside bungalow in colonial-era tea-planter style, a 20km drive southeast of the sanctuary.

Thattekkad is on the Ernakulam–Munnar road. Buses from Ernakulam (₹40, two hours) and Munnar (₹60, two to three hours) run to Kothamangalam, from where you can catch an autorickshaw (₹150) or a bus (₹12, 25 minutes) for the final 12km northeast to Thattekkad.

tickets are usually available but for the best seats consider booking ahead.

❶ Information

DTPC Tourist Office (☑ 04865-231516; www.dtpcidukki.com; AM Rd/NH85; ☺ 8.30am-6.30pm)

Forest Information Centre (☑ 8547382391; ☺ 10am-5pm)

❶ Getting There & Away

Roads around Munnar are winding and often in poor condition following monsoon rains, so travel times may vary.

The main **KSRTC bus station** (AM Rd/NH85) is 1.5km south of the town centre, though all government buses also stop at one of several stands in Munnar town (from where private buses depart).

There are at least 18 daily buses to Ernakulam (Kochi; ₹115, five hours, 5.40am to 9.45pm); the 3pm is an air-con service. Government buses also run to Trivandrum (₹270 to ₹600, eight to nine hours, seven daily 4.50am to 9pm), Alleppey (₹150, five hours, four daily 6.20am to 4.30pm), Kumily (₹100, four to five hours, 6.30am) and Bengaluru (Bangalore; ₹800, 16 hours, 3.30pm) via Wayanad (₹500, 10 hours) and Mysuru (Mysore; ₹680, 13½ hours). Private buses go to Kumily (₹115, four to five hours) at 12.15pm and Madurai (₹110, five hours) at

12.30pm, 2.20pm and 5.30pm. There are separate stands for buses to Top Station (₹60, one hour, 8am, 9am and 9.30am) and Coimbatore (₹140, six hours, 3.30pm) via Chinnar Wildlife Sanctuary (₹60, one hour).

Taxis cost ₹2800 to Ernakulam, ₹3800 to Alleppey and ₹2400 to Kumily.

❶ Getting Around

Autorickshaws ply the hills around Munnar with bone-shuddering efficiency; short hops cost ₹20 to ₹50.

Gokulam Bike Hire (☑ 9447237165; per day ₹400-500; ☺ 9am-6pm) rents out motorbikes and scooters; call ahead.

Around Munnar

Top Station

High above Kerala's border with Tamil Nadu, Top Station (elevation 1880m) is popular for its spectacular views over the Western Ghats. From Munnar, three daily buses (₹60, 8am, 9am and 9.30am) make the 32km climb northeast past tea estates in around an hour, or take a return taxi or jeep (₹1200). You may see wild elephants on the way up.

Eravikulam National Park

Around 11km north of Munnar, the 97 sq km of grasslands and *shola* of **Eravikulam National Park** (☏04865-231587; www.eravi kulam.org; Indian/foreigner ₹120/400, camera/ video ₹40/400; ◷8am-4pm Apr-Jan) conceal the world's largest population (700 to 800) of endangered, but almost tame, Nilgiri tahr. Safari buses take you into the Rajamala tourist zone where the likelihood of sightings is high. The park also hosts Anamudi, South India's highest peak (2695m), though it was closed to climbers at the time of research, as were all Eravikulam treks (these may reopen). From Munnar, taxis cost ₹800 return.

CENTRAL KERALA

Kochi (Cochin)

☏0484 / POP 602,050

Set on a magnificent estuary, serene Kochi has been drawing traders, explorers and travellers to its shores for over 600 years. Nowhere else in India could you find such an intriguing mix: giant Chinese fishing nets, a 450-year-old synagogue, ancient mosques, Portuguese- and Dutch-era houses and the crumbling remains of the British Raj. The result is an unlikely blend of medieval Portugal and Holland and an English village grafted onto the tropical Malabar Coast. It's a delightful place to explore, laze in arty cafes and relax at some of India's finest homestays and heritage hotels. It's also an important centre for Keralan arts (traditional and contemporary) and a standout place to see Kathakali and *kalarippayat.*

Mainland Ernakulam is Kochi's hectic transport and cosmopolitan hub, while the historical towns of Fort Cochin and Mattancherry, though well ouristed, remain wonderfully atmospheric.

◉ Sights

◉ Fort Cochin

The historical European part of the city, Fort Cochin has a couple of small, sandy beaches, which are only really good for people-watching in the evening and gazing out at the incoming tankers. A popular promenade meanders from west-coast Mahatma Gandhi Beach to the Chinese fishing nets and fish market (p991).

Keep an eye out along the shore for the scant remains of Fort Immanuel, the 16th-century Portuguese fort from which the area takes its name.

Chinese Fishing Nets   LANDMARK
(Map p990) The unofficial emblems of the backwaters, and perhaps the most photographed, are the half-dozen giant cantilevered Chinese fishing nets on Fort Cochin's northeastern shore, known locally as *cheena vala*. A legacy of traders from the AD 1400 court of Kublai Khan, these spiderlike, 10m-tall contraptions rest on teak or bamboo poles and require five or six people to operate their counterweights at high tide.

St Francis Church   CHURCH
(Map p990; Church Rd; ◷8.30am-5pm) Constructed in 1503 by Portuguese Franciscan friars, this is believed to be India's oldest European-built church. The faded-yellow edifice that stands here today was built in the mid-16th century to replace the original wooden chapel, though it was later altered by both the Dutch and British. Explorer Vasco da Gama, who died in Cochin in 1524, was buried in this spot for 14 years before his remains were taken to Lisbon – you can still visit his tombstone in the church.

WORTH A TRIP

CHINNAR WILDLIFE SANCTUARY

This 90-sq-km **sanctuary** (☏04865-231587; www.chinnar.org; entry with 3hr trek Indian/foreigner ₹250/600; ◷8am-3pm), 50km northeast of Munnar, protects deer, leopards, elephants, gaur, langurs and endangered Nilgiri tahr and grizzled giant squirrels. Entry is by three-hour trek with tribal guides (two tribal groups live here). Tree-house (₹4000), mud-hut (₹5000) and log-house (₹4000) accommodation within the sanctuary are available; rates are per couple, including breakfast and dinner. For details contact Munnar's Forest Information Centre or DTPC.

Coimbatore- and Udumalpet-bound buses from Munnar stop at Chinnar (₹60, 1½ hours); return taxis cost ₹2000.

Kochi (Cochin)

Map labels: Ayur Dara (2km); Gundu Island (3km); Cherai Beach (25km); Vallarpadam Bridge; Bolgatty Island; Shanmugham Rd; Banerji Rd; ERNAKULAM; Kerala Bike Tours; Ernakulam Town Station; Vallarpadam Island; Mahatma Gandhi (MG) Rd; Park Ave; Vypeen Island; Bungalow Heritage Homestay & Neema's Kitchen; Vembanad Lake; Government of India Tourist Office; Embarkation Jetty; Ernakulam Junction Station; Mahatma Gandhi Beach; Customs Jetty; FORT COCHIN; MATTANCHERRY; See Fort Cochin Map (p990); See Mattancherry Map (p993); See Ernakulam Map (p988); Bazaar (Boat Jetty) Rd; Art of Bicycle Trips; Malabar Grills; Palace Rd; Green Woods Bethlehem; Beena Homestay; Reds Residency; KJ Herschel Rd; JEW TOWN; Willingdon Island; Terminus Jetty; Cochin Harbour Station; Navy Base; Shipyard; PERUMANOOR; Cocoa Tree; MG Rd; Bristow Rd; Kochi Naval Airport; 0 2 km; 0 1 miles

David Hall

GALLERY

(Map p990; www.davidhall.in; Church Rd; ⏱11am-9pm Tue-Sun, hours vary) Opposite the parade ground, this beautiful restored bungalow is all that remains of three 17th-century Dutch-era houses built using materials from demolished Portuguese churches. It's now an arts-and-culture centre, showcasing up-and-coming artists with performances and changing exhibitions.

Dutch Cemetery

CEMETERY

(Map p990; Beach Rd) Consecrated in 1724, this cemetery near Kochi's beach contains the worn and dilapidated graves of Dutch traders and soldiers. Its gates are normally locked but a caretaker might let you in, or ask at nearby St Francis Church (p983).

Santa Cruz Basilica

BASILICA

(Map p990; cnr Bastion St & KB Jacob Rd; ⏱9am-1pm & 2.30-5.30pm Mon-Sat, 10.30am-1pm Sun) Built on the site of an early-16th-century Portuguese church (demolished during the British Raj), Fort Cochin's imposing neoclassical Catholic basilica dates to 1902. In the striking pastel-coloured interior you'll find artefacts from the different historical eras in Kochi.

Kashi Art Gallery

GALLERY

(Map p990; ☑0484-2215769; www.kashiartgallery.com; Burgher St; ⏱8.30am-10pm) The pioneer of Fort Cochin's art revival, Kashi displays changing exhibitions of local artists in a creatively restored Dutch heritage house, attached to one of Kerala's most fabulous cafes (p991).

Indo-Portuguese Museum

MUSEUM

(Map p990; ☑0484-2215400; Bishop Kureethara Rd; adult/child ₹40/20; ⏱9am-1pm & 2-6pm Tue-Sun) The heritage of one of India's earliest Catholic communities – including vestments, silver processional crosses, altarpieces from the Kochi diocese and 19th-century sketches of Santa Cruz Basilica – is on show at this thoughtfully presented museum hidden in the tranquil garden of the Bishop's House. The basement contains remnants of the 16th-century Portuguese-built Fort Immanuel.

◉ Mattancherry & Jew Town

About 32.5km southeast of Fort Cochin, Mattancherry is the old bazaar district and centre of the spice trade. These days it's packed with spice shops and pricey Kashmiri-run emporiums that autorickshaw drivers will fall over backwards to take you to for a healthy commission – any offer of a cheap tour of the district will inevitably lead to a few shops. In the midst of this, Jew Town is a bustling port area with a fine synagogue. Scores of small firms huddle together in dilapidated old buildings and the air is filled with the biting aromas of ginger, cardamom, cumin, turmeric and cloves, though the lanes around Mattancherry Palace and the synagogue are packed with antique and tourist-curio shops rather than spices. Just south is Kochi's old Muslim quarter.

★ Mattancherry Palace   MUSEUM
(Dutch Palace; Map p993; Palace Rd, Mattancherry; adult/child ₹5/free; ⊙ 9am-5pm Sat-Thu) Mattancherry Palace was a generous gift presented to the Raja of Kochi, Veera Kerala Varma (1537–65), as a gesture of goodwill by the Portuguese in 1555. The Dutch renovated it in 1663, hence the alternative name, the Dutch Palace. The building combines European and Keralan styles, but the star attractions are the royal bedchamber's astonishingly preserved Hindu murals from the 17th to 19th centuries, which depict scenes from the Ramayana, Mahabharata and Puranic legends in intricate, colourful detail.

★ Pardesi Synagogue   SYNAGOGUE
(Map p993; Synagogue Lane, Mattancherry; ₹5; ⊙ 10am-1pm & 3-5pm Sun-Thu, 10am-1pm Fri, closed Sat & Jewish holidays) Originally built in 1568, Mattancherry's synagogue was partially destroyed by the Portuguese in 1662, and rebuilt two years later when the Dutch took Kochi. It features an ornate brass bema, elegant wooden benches, and elaborate hand-painted, willow-pattern floor tiles from Canton, China, added in 1762 during major remodelling under Ezekial Rahabi. It's magnificently illuminated by Belgian chandeliers and coloured-glass lamps. The graceful clock tower dates from 1760, with inscriptions in Malayalam, Hebrew, Roman and Arabic script.

The majority of Kochi's Pardesi Jews have emigrated, but the synagogue remains excellently preserved.

Jewish Cemetery   CEMETERY
(Map p993; AB Salem Rd, Mattancherry) Just southwest of Mattancherry's synagogue, the undisturbed Jewish Cemetery contains ancient tombstones marked with Hebrew script.

◉ Ernakulam & Around

Kerala Folklore Museum   MUSEUM
(☑ 0484-2665452; www.keralafolkloremuseum. org; Folklore Junction, Thevara; Indian/foreigner ₹100/200, camera ₹100; ⊙ 9am-6pm) Created in Kerala style from ancient temples and beautiful old houses collected by its owner, an antique dealer, the family-run folklore museum houses a priceless collection of over 5000 artefacts and covers three architectural styles: Malabar on the ground floor; Kochi/Portuguese on the 1st; and Travancore on the 2nd (top). The fine top-floor theatre has an 18th-century wood-carved ceiling depicting Hindu gods, as well as colourful Ramayana and Mahabharata murals. It's 4.5km south of Ernakulam Junction.

🏃 Activities

Popular South Indian cooking classes are held at **Neema's Kitchen** (☑ 9539300010; https:// neemaskitchen.co.in; Bungalow Heritage Homestay, Vypeen Island; classes per person ₹2000-2500; ⊙ 10.30am-1.30pm & 3.30-6.30pm) on Vypeen Island (just north of the jetty) and in Fort Cochin at Mrs Leelu Roy's **Cook & Eat** (Map p990; ☑ 0484-2215377, 9846055377; www.leelu homestay.com; 1/629 Quiros St, Fort Cochin; classes per person ₹1000; ⊙ 11am-1pm & 4-6pm Mon-Sat) and Green Woods Bethlehem (p987).

Ayurdara   AYURVEDA, YOGA
(☑ 9447721041; https://ayurdara.com; Murikkumpadam, Vypeen Island; per day ₹1650; ⊙ 9am-5.30pm) Run by third-generation ayurvedic practitioner Dr Subhash, this delightful, appointment-only waterside treatment centre specialises in personalised therapies of one to three weeks and also offers yoga (₹200). It's on Vypeen Island, 3km north of the Fort Cochin ferry jetty.

Loving Earth Yoga   YOGA
(Map p990; www.lovingearthyogacafe.com; 1/839 Quiros St, Fort Cochin; yoga ₹500; ⊙ cafe 8am-8pm Tue-Sun) Drop-in daily vinyasa, ashtanga, hatha and/or yin yoga classes on a breezy rooftop attached to an all-vegan cafe serving mezze platters, Buddha bowls and creative salads (₹200 to ₹300); see the website for current schedules.

🪁 Courses

The Kerala Kathakali Centre (p993) has short- and long-term courses in classical Kathakali dance, music and make-up as well as *kalarippayat* (from ₹650 per hour).

For a crash course in the martial art of *kalarippayat,* head to famed training centre Ens Kalari (p994), 6.5km southeast of Ernakulam, which offers intensive courses from one week to one month.

Tours

Ernakulam's knowledgeable Tourist Desk (p994) runs the popular full-day Great Water Valley Tour (₹1250, departs 8am, returns 6pm), by *shikara* and canoe, through backwater canals, villages and lagoons and vast Vembanad Lake; rates include lunch and some sections are by bus.

Art of Bicycle Trips CYCLING, WALKING
(☑8129945707; https://artofbicycletrips.com; KB Jacob Rd; 3hr/half-day tours ₹2250/4200; ☉9am-6pm Mon-Sat) Guided bicycle tours on quality mountain bikes with this India-wide operator include the three-hour Vasco Safari morning tour of the historic Fort area and a half-day ride around the backwaters. There are also evening walking food tours of Fort Cochin and Mattancherry (₹950).

Kerala Bike Tours TOURS
(☑9446492382, 9388476817; www.keralabike tours.com; 42/2252B St Benedict Road North, Kacheripady, Ernakulam) Organises multilingual Enfield Bullet tours around Kerala and the Western Ghats (six-day full-board trip per person including accommodation ₹109,000) and hires out touring-quality Enfields (from ₹12,000 per week) for serious riders with unlimited mileage, full insurance and free recovery/maintenance options.

Festivals & Events

Ernakulathappan Utsavam RELIGIOUS
(Shiva Temple, Ernakulam; ☉Jan/Feb) Eight days of festivities culminating in fireworks, music and a parade of 15 splendidly decorated elephants (which won't please everyone).

Kochi–Muziris Biennale ART
(☑0484-2215287; http://kochimuzirisbiennale. org; ₹100, free Mon; ☉Dec-Mar) Into its fourth edition (2018), this major contemporary biennial arts festival is one of the largest of its kind in Asia. Over 90 Indian and international artists bring their creativity to workshops, talks and exhibitions across Kochi, with heritage properties as venues.

Cochin Carnival CARNIVAL
(www.cochincarnival.org; ☉21 Dec) Fort Cochin's biggest bash, a 10-day festival culminating

on New Year's Eve. Street parades, colourful costumes, embellished elephants (which won't appeal to all), music, folk dancing and lots of fun.

Sleeping

Fort Cochin is the homestay capital of India – around 200! It's also home to some of Kerala's finest heritage accommodation, as well as contemporary-style hostels.

Ernakulam is cheaper and more convenient for onward travel, but the ambience and accommodation choices are less inspiring than in Fort Cochin.

Book ahead during the November-to-March high season, especially December and January.

Fort Cochin

Happy Camper HOSTEL $
(Map p990; ☑9742725668; www.facebook.com/ happycamperkochi; KB Jacob Rd; dm ₹500-600; ❀๑) ☞ Billing itself as a boutique hostel, Happy Camper is a relaxed place with three en suite, air-con dorms (for four or eight; lockers provided), a small kitchen, free water refills, vibrant wall art, an excellent little cafe and rooftop area, and friendly staff. Good location just south of the main tourist hub.

Zostel HOSTEL $
(Map p990; ☑011-39589007; www.zostel.com; 1/751A Njaliparambu Junction; dm ₹450, r ₹1270-1500; ❀๑) Zipped away down a small lane, Kochi's popular and sociable Zostel ticks all the right backpacker boxes. There are personal plugs, lights and lockers in the updated air-con dorms, which sleep four (mixed) or six (women only), along with three polished private doubles, and communal spaces adorned with lively cushions and murals.

Maritime HOSTEL $
(Map p990; ☑0484-2214785; https://thehostel crowd.com; 2/227 Calvathy Rd; dm ₹500, r ₹1200-1600; ❀๑) Behind a red-and-white facade, this branch of the Goan Hostel Crowd chain is just west of the Customs jetty. The nautical theme is a characterful touch; the en suite air-con dorms for four to six people have individual lockers and plugs; double rooms (with fan or air-con) are clean, compact and well kept; and there's a small kitchen plus a laundry and a library.

★ **Reds Residency** HOMESTAY **$$**
(☎9847030342, 9388643747; www.redsresidency.in; 11/372 A KJ Herschel Rd; r incl breakfast with AC from ₹1200, without AC ₹900-1200, AC rooftop cottage ₹1800; ❋ 🛜) ✔ Hotel-quality rooms come with solar-powered showers and a true family welcome from knowledgeable hosts Philip and Maryann at this delightful homestay. The five rooms – including a four-bed family room – are modern and immaculate, and there's a self-contained rooftop 'penthouse' cottage with a kitchen. Days begin with fabulous, lovingly prepared breakfasts. It's in a peaceful spot 1km south of central Fort Cochin.

★ **Green Woods Bethlehem** HOMESTAY **$$**
(☎0484-2216069, 9846014924; www.greenwoodsbethlehem.com; Kurisingal House; r incl breakfast with AC ₹1700-2000, without AC ₹1000-1500; ❋ 🛜) With a smile that brightens weary travellers, welcoming owner Sheeba looks ready to sign your adoption papers the minute you walk through the door. Down a quiet laneway, amid walled gardens thick with palms, this is one of Kochi's most serene homestays. The 10 humble but cosy rooms are scattered up rambling staircases; breakfast is served on the leafy rooftop.

Cooking classes/demonstrations (₹1000) happen daily. It's 1km south of central Fort Cochin.

Raintree Lodge HERITAGE HOTEL **$$**
(Map p990; ☎9747721091; www.fortcochin.com; 1/618 Peter Celli St; r incl breakfast ₹3300; ❋ 🛜) The five intimate, graceful and good-value rooms at this cheerful converted 18th-century house flirt with boutique-hotel status. Each mixes contemporary style with heritage carved-wood furniture; the two front upstairs rooms have gorgeous vine-covered Romeo-and-Juliet balconies. Breakfast is served at the wonderful Kashi Art Cafe (p991), run by the same team.

Beena Homestay HOMESTAY **$$**
(☎9447574579, 0484-2215458; www.homestaykochi.com; 11/359B Kadathanad; r incl breakfast & dinner with/without AC ₹3000/2500; ❋ 🛜) ✔ Beena has been feeding and sheltering travellers for years in the family homestay, just off Ponnoonjal Rd 1km south of central Fort Cochin, and maintains high standards with six spotless rooms, solar power, and home-cooked meals taken in the dining room.

Delight Home Stay HOMESTAY **$$**
(Map p990; ☎98461121421, 0484-2217658; www.delightfulhomestay.com; Post Office Rd; r incl breakfast ₹3000-4000; ❋ 🛜) One of Fort Cochin's original homestays, this charming white-washed house is adorned with elaborate woodwork and dangling terracotta plant pots, while the six custom-designed rooms are spacious and polished with heritage character. Good home-cooked food is served and there's a colourful garden.

Travellers Inn GUESTHOUSE **$$**
(Map p990; ☎9446332662, 0484-2215551; www.travelsinmind.com; 1/326B Princess St; r ₹1500-2500) In the heart of Fort Cochin, with a handy travel desk, this welcoming, efficiently operated Indian-Italian-run guesthouse has six unpretentious modern rooms, decorated with a single custom-made monochrome drawing of Kochi by a local artist. The two upper-floor front rooms come with small balconies.

★ **Old Harbour Hotel** HERITAGE HOTEL **$$$**
(Map p990; ☎0484-2218006; www.oldharbourhotel.com; 1/328 Tower Rd; r ₹15,000-27,000; ❋ 🏊) Overlooking a lush garden with lily ponds and a pool, the stylish Old Harbour is housed in a 300-year-old Dutch/Portuguese heritage building. The elegant mix of period and modern design lends it a more intimate feel than some of the more grandiose competition. The four garden-view rooms with balcony are divine; others have freestanding tubs or plant-filled, open-air bathrooms.

Brunton Boatyard LUXURY HOTEL **$$$**
(Map p990; ☎0484-2846500; www.cghearth.com; River Rd; r ₹28,160-56,320; ❋ 🛜 🏊) ✔ On the site of a Victorian-era shipyard, this grand CGH creation faithfully reproduces 16th-, 17th- and 18th-century Dutch, British and Portuguese architecture for an updated heritage look. Most rooms gaze out over the harbour, and have bathtubs and balconies with refreshing sea breezes. There are three excellent restaurants, complimentary yoga and bicycles, and a waterfront pool shaded by tangles of bougainvillea.

Malabar House BOUTIQUE HOTEL **$$$**
(Map p990; ☎0484-2216666; www.malabarhouse.com; 1/269 Parade Ground Rd; r incl breakfast €220-360; ❋ 🏊) What may just be one of the most romantic boutique hotels in Kerala, Malabar flaunts its chic blend of contemporary design and original 18th-century

Ernakulam

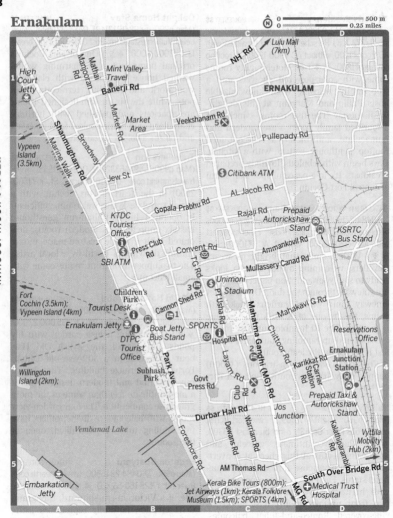

architecture like it's not even trying. Rooms are strung around a small pool; while suites are huge and lavishly appointed, standard rooms feel more snug. The award-winning Malabar Junction restaurant (p992) and Divine wine bar (p992) are top-notch.

Forte Kochi　　　　HERITAGE HOTEL **$$$**
(Map p990; ☑0484-2704800; www.fortekochi. in; Princess St; r incl breakfast ₹9600-22,400; ❄️🛜🏊) A chicly remodelled mango-yellow 1800s home with its origins dating back to the Portuguese-rule era, Forte Kochi is a welcome 2018 luxe arrival. Tiled floors and design-led bathrooms breathe fresh contem-

porary style into the 27 heritage-inspired rooms, which orbit an enticing pool, and there's an enormous suite with a freestanding claw-foot bath. Excellent location, good restaurant, charming staff.

Fort House Hotel HOTEL $$$
(Map p990; ☑0484-2217103, 9539375431; www.hotelforthouse.com; 2/6A Calvathy Rd; r incl breakfast ₹7500; ▣☎) Around 200m west of Fort Cochin's Customs jetty, this family-owned hideaway is one of the old core's few truly waterfront hotels, though the 16 smart, contemporary-Keralan rooms and well-regarded ayurvedic centre are tucked back in a lush garden, with the excellent restaurant (p992) taking prime lakeside position.

🛏 Mattancherry & Jew Town

Ginger House Museum Hotel HERITAGE HOTEL $$$
(Map p993; ☑0484-2213400; http://museumhotel.in; Ginger House Bldg, Mattancherry; r incl breakfast US$300-750; ▣☎☎) Above an astonishing private antiques collection, each of these eight exquisitely and individually themed design-meets-heritage rooms – with glossy contemporary bathrooms, personal coffee trays and beautiful period furnishings – feels like its own sumptuous little world. Expect a feast of carved teakwood, mirrored ceilings and baroque chandeliers. The rooftop has a small lake-view infinity pool, and there's an excellent waterfront restaurant (p993).

🛏 Ernakulam

John's Residency HOTEL $
(Map p988; ☑9995070834, 8281321395; TD Rd; r with AC ₹1600, s/d without AC ₹650/850; ▣@☎) A genuine backpacker place, efficiently run John's is your best budget bet for an overnight stop in Ernakulam, especially if John himself is in residence. It's 600m east of the boat jetty. Rooms are small (deluxes are bigger) but clean and decorated with flashes of colour and, for some, balconies, providing a welcoming feel for this price bracket.

Boat Jetty Bungalow HOTEL $$
(Map p988; ☑9746013198, 0484-2373211; www.boatjettybungalow.com; Cannon Shed Rd; s/d with AC ₹1350/1900, without AC ₹560/850; ▣) An 1891 former jetty-manager's house and ancestral home has been thoughtfully refurbished into budget-to-midrange accommodation, its palette of greys and compact,

impeccably kept rooms with bottled water offset by original wooden ceilings. It's 300m east of Ernakulam's jetty for Fort Cochin.

Grand Hotel HOTEL $$
(Map p988; ☑0484-2382061, 9895721014; https://grandhotelkerala.com; MG Rd; s ₹3780-4100, d ₹4740-6260, all incl breakfast; ▣☎) This 1960s hotel, with its polished original art deco fittings, exudes the sort of retro glamour that contemporary hotels would love to re-create. The smart, spacious rooms have gleaming parquet floors, tea/coffee trays and large modern bathrooms with hairdryers. Also here are good global-cuisine restaurant **Grand Pavilion** (☑0484-2382061, 9895721014; mains ₹245-480; ⊙7.30-10.30am, noon-3.30pm & 7-10pm) and Ernakulam's most sophisticated bar, **Couchyn** (⊙11am-11pm).

🛏 Around Kochi

Bungalow Heritage Homestay HOMESTAY $$
(☑9846302347; https://thebungalow.co.in; Vypeen Island; r incl breakfast with AC ₹5100-6600, without AC ₹4500-6000; ▣☎) Just 300m north from Vypeen Island's ferry dock, this beautiful 1930 Keralan heritage house is a delight, with two large connecting rooms featuring quaint furnishings and grand wooden flooring on its Dutch-inspired upper floor. Owner Neema runs excellent cooking classes (p985) on the Portuguese-styled lower level. Minimum two-night stay.

Kallanchery Retreat HOMESTAY $$
(☑9847446683, 0484-2240564; www.kallancheryretreat.com; Panakkal House, Kumbalanghi; r & cottage incl breakfast ₹2000-3000; ▣☎) Escape the Kochi crowds at this peaceful waterside homestay and expansive garden in the village of Kumbalanghi, 13km south of Fort Cochin. Tidy rooms are either in the family home or in a lakefront cottage. Chinese fishing nets are on your doorstep, and boat trips, village tours, and home-cooked meals (₹350) courtesy of chef-owner Rockey are available.

🍴 Eating & Drinking

🍴 Fort Cochin

Some of Kochi's best cooking is served in Fort Cochin's homestays; also here are some of Kerala's finest cafes. Several top-end

KERALA FORT COCHIN

Fort Cochin

200 m
0.1 miles

N

Customs Jetty

Bazaar (Boat Jetty) Rd

Waterfront Granary (200m); Mattancherry (2km)

River (Calvathy) Rd

Venbanad Lake

Mahatma Gandhi Beach

Ferry to Vypeen Island

Kamalakadavu Jetty

Vypeen Island (300m)

Dispensary Rd

Fort Cochin Bus Stand

Rampath Rd

Tower Rd

Outdoor Cafes

Burgher St

Princess St

Rose St

Church Rd

Dutch Cemetery Rd

Parade Grounds

Parade Ground

Post Office Rd

Napier St

Parade Rd

Lily St

Elphinstone St

Quiros St

Peter Celli St

Bastion St

KB Jacob Rd

Fort Nagar

Fosse St

Amravathi Rd

New Rd

Kunnumpuram Junction

Amravathi Rd

Kit kat Rd

KB Jacob Rd

KL Bernard Rd

Sts Peter & Paul Church

SBI ATM

South India Bank ATM

FORT COCHIN

12
16
10
27
5
23
19
17
13
25
33
9 34
28
8
18
6
24
30
14
20
1
22
7
2
3
4
29
15
31
32
21
26
11

Fort Cochin

◉ Sights

1 Chinese Fishing Nets	B1
2 David Hall	A3
3 Dutch Cemetery	A3
4 Indo-Portuguese Museum	A4
5 Kashi Art Gallery	C2
6 Santa Cruz Basilica	C3
7 St Francis Church	B2

◎ Activities, Courses & Tours

8 Cook & Eat	B3
9 Loving Earth Yoga	B3

⬤ Sleeping

10 Brunton Boatyard	D1
11 Delight Home Stay	B3
12 Fort House Hotel	G1
13 Forte Kochi	C2
14 Happy Camper	C4
15 Malabar House	A3
16 Maritime	F1
17 Old Harbour Hotel	C2
18 Raintree Lodge	B3
19 Travellers Inn	C2
20 Zostel	B4

⊗ Eating

21 Dal Roti	A4
22 Drawing Room	B2
23 Fishmongers	C1
Fort House Restaurant	(see 12)
24 Fusion Bay	C3
Kashi Art Cafe	(see 5)
25 Loafers Corner	B2
Malabar Junction	(see 15)
26 Oceanos	A4
27 Qissa Cafe	D2
28 Teapot	B3

◎ Drinking & Nightlife

Clubb18	(see 27)
29 DiVine	A3

⊛ Entertainment

30 Kerala Kathakali Centre	C3

◉ Shopping

31 Anokhi	A3
32 Fabindia	A4
33 Idiom Bookshop	B2
34 Niraamaya	B3

KERALA KOCHI (COCHIN)

hotels have excellent restaurants, too. Only a few places serve alcohol with meals.

Behind the Chinese fishing nets are a handful of **fishmongers** (Map p990; River Rd; ⊙restaurants 8am-9pm), from whom you can buy the day's catch then have it cooked at one of the simple restaurants on nearby Tower Rd (for an additional charge); a fillet of kingfish costs around ₹400.

★ **Kashi Art Cafe** CAFE $$
(Map p990; Burgher St; dishes ₹150-350; ⊙8.30am-10pm; 🖗) ⌖ Fort Cochin's original (and best) art cafe, this fashionable, natural-light-filled space has a Zen vibe, a creeping vertical garden and stylish wood tables spreading out into a courtyard dotted with contemporary artwork. The coffee is strong, organic ingredients are used wherever possible, and the luscious breakfasts and lunches are excellent (French toast, home-baked cakes, creative salads).

★ **Dal Roti** INDIAN $$
(Map p990; 🕿9746459244; 1/293 Lily St; mains ₹170-350; ⊙noon-3pm & 6.30-10pm Wed-Mon) Always-busy Dal Roti is one of Fort Cochin's most-loved restaurants. The knowledgeable owner Ramesh will hold your hand through his expansive North Indian menu (with its own glossary!) and help you dive into a delicious world of vegetarian, eggetarian

and nonvegetarian options. From *kati* rolls (filled *paratha* fried with a coating of egg) and stuffed *paratha* to seven thali types, you won't go hungry.

Fusion Bay SEAFOOD $$
(Map p990; 🕿9995105110; KB Jacob Rd; mains ₹150-450; ⊙12.30-11pm) This unassuming little family restaurant in central Fort Cochin is renowned locally for its imaginative Kerala Syrian fish delicacies cooked in the *pollichathu* style (masala spiced and grilled in a banana leaf), and assorted seafood dishes such as spicy fish *pappas,* coconut-fried prawns and fish in mango curry. There are a few veg choices too.

Loafers Corner CAFE $$
(Map p990; 🕿0484-2215351; www.facebook.com/loaferscornercafe; 1/351 Princess St; dishes ₹170-200; ⊙9am-10pm; 🖗) A stylishly restored 200-year-old Dutch-Portuguese-style building, Loafers is all reclaimed wood, minimalist design, cosy window booths and delicate murals. It's a good, relaxed spot for a coffee, a fresh juice, breakfast or a light meal, with a bistro-style menu of sandwiches, wraps, pancakes, pastas and homemade cakes.

Drawing Room INTERNATIONAL, INDIAN $$
(Map p990; www.facebook.com/thedrawingroomkochi; Church Rd; mains ₹150-450; ⊙11am-11pm) Set in the grand Cochin Club, this stylish

cafe-restaurant enjoys a wonderful garden location with large windows facing out to the water, and is jazzed up by freehand murals that weave together classic Kerala scenes with musical elements. The lightly creative menu, based on family recipes, features salads, pastas, soups and fish or prawn curries. There's regular live music in season.

Fort House Restaurant   SEAFOOD, INDIAN **$$**
(Map p990; ☑ 9539375431, 0484-2217103; www.hotelforthouse.com; 2/6A Calvathy Rd; mains ₹170-900; ⊙ 7.30am-10.30pm) The waterside restaurant at the family-owned Fort House Hotel (p988) is a prime choice for a leisurely lunch, fringed by hot-pink bougainvillea and plants overflowing from earthy-red pots. The signatures are the seafood dishes (including Keralan-style fish curry), though the flavoursome veg dishes pack a punch too. Dine at tables overlooking the water or in the calm covered garden.

Qissa Cafe   CAFE **$$**
(Map p990; ☑ 0484-2215769; www.facebook.com/QissaCafe; No 18 Hotel, Rampath Rd; dishes ₹180-300; ⊙ 7.30am-10pm; ☎) Usually packed with fashionable Kochiites, Qissa channels a cosmopolitan scene with its mismatched pastel-painted chairs, outdoor garden and buzzy atmosphere. Come for the homemade cakes, brunch-type snacks (avocado toast has arrived!), stuffed omelettes, heartier creations like lemon-pesto pasta, and chilled fresh juices and lemonades presented in jam jars. Good coffee and tea too.

Teapot   CAFE **$$**
(Map p990; Peter Celli St; dishes ₹180-300; ⊙ 8.30am-9pm) Behind an ivy-covered facade, this atmospheric cafe is perfect for 'high tea', with an impressive choice of brews, sandwiches and cakes turned out in airy, heritage-style rooms amid canary yellow walls and wood-beamed ceilings. Witty tea-themed accents include antique teapots, tea chests for tables and a gnarled, tea-tree-based glass table. Snacks include omelettes, grilled sandwiches and a veggie stew with *appam*.

Oceanos   SEAFOOD **$$**
(Map p990; ☑ 9633713653; Elphinstone St; mains ₹180-600; ⊙ 12.30-10pm) Gloriously fresh seafood is the thing at this smart, locally popular restaurant with turquoise table runners and touches of greenery. Fish is served in spicy *pollichathu* style, in mango curry or

perhaps grilled with a coconut sauce. There are also Goan-Portuguese seafood classics like *peixe recheado* (grilled spice-stuffed fish) and some South and North Indian veg and nonveg favourites.

Malabar Grills   INDIAN **$$**
(☑ 9061800042; www.facebook.com/malabargrillskochi; Kokers Junction, Amaravathi Rd; mains ₹110-350; ⊙ 9am-11pm; ☎) Join feasting Indian families at this sprawling modern restaurant fronted by a barbecue just southeast of Fort Cochin's tourist centre. Breakfasts (₹30 to ₹80) are classic South India: *puttu, iddiyappam* (a rice noodle dish), dosa, *idli* with *sambar* (soupy lentil dish with vegetables). Later, the focus turns to thalis (₹90 to ₹140), biryanis and, especially, grilled meats and seafood.

★**Malabar Junction**   INTERNATIONAL **$$$**
(Map p990; ☑ 0484-2216666; www.malabarhouse.com; Parade Ground Rd; mains ₹450-800, tasting menus ₹2500; ⊙ 7am-11pm) Set in an open-sided pavilion or at candlelit poolside tables, this outstanding restaurant at Malabar House (p987) is (almost) Bollywood-star glam. The ambitious East-meets-West menu creatively fuses local and European flavours – the signature dish is the seafood platter (₹3200), or try an elegant 'trilogy' of Indian curries. An impressive choice of Indian wines (Sula, Fratelli, Grover Zampa) accompanies meals.

Upstairs, the **DiVine wine bar** (⊙ 11am-11pm) serves upmarket tapas-style snacks and wines by the glass.

Clubb18   CLUB, BAR
(Map p990; www.no18.co.in; No 18 Hotel, Rampath Rd; ⊙ 11.30am-midnight) Hands down Fort Cochin's liveliest after-dark hang-out, this moodily lit muralled club-bar spills out onto a poolside terrace, serving cool Kingfishers (₹200), cocktails (₹500) and Indian wines (₹400 to ₹800) to a trendy local crowd. Busy from 9pm, with DJs Friday to Sunday.

✕ Mattancherry & Jew Town

Kayees Ramathula Hotel   INDIAN **$**
(Map p993; Kayees Junction, Mattancherry; biryani ₹130-170; ⊙ noon-2pm) This no-frills spot is legendary among Kochi locals for its lunchtime chicken, mutton and seafood biryanis – get here early or miss out. Don't confuse it with the lime-green biryani place on the corner – Kayees is next door.

Mattancherry

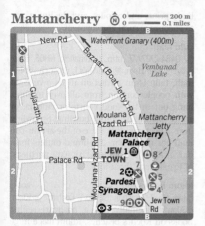

New Rd · Waterfront Granary (400m)

Bazaar (Boat Jetty) Rd
Vembanad Lake
Gujarathi Rd
Moulana Azad Rd · Mattancherry Jetty
Mattancherry Palace
JEW 1 · TOWN
Palace Rd
2 **Pardesi Synagogue**
Moulana Azad Rd
Jew Town Rd
3

KERALA KOCHI (COCHIN)

Mocha Art Cafe
CAFE $$

(Map p993; ☎0484-2224357; www.facebook.com/themochaartcafe; Synagogue Lane, Mattancherry; dishes ₹150-450; ☺9am-9pm) This gorgeous, multiroom, 300-year-old spice warehouse, built in Dutch style, was once lived in by the rabbis of Mattancherry's synagogue, which you can admire from a snug original window booth. Open-brick walls, vertical gardens and local art add a contemporary touch. Cooking here is a skilful blend of Keralan curries, omelettes and wholewheat sandwiches, and cakes from the on-site bakery.

Ginger House
INDIAN $$$

(Map p993; ☎0484-2213400; http://museumhotel.in; Jew Town Rd, Mattancherry; mains ₹230-800; ☺8am-8pm May-Oct, to midnight Nov-Apr) Hidden behind a massive antique-filled godown (warehouse) is this wonderful waterfront restaurant, where you can relax over fresh juices and punchy Indian dishes and snacks (including a deliciously creamy cashew-paneer curry). Walk through the priceless Heritage Arts showroom (check out the giant antique snake-boat canoe) to reach it.

✕ Ernakulam

Ernakulam's mega shopping malls provide food-court dining, and there are some reliable South Indian restaurants. Leafy Panampilly Nagar Ave, in a residential area 1.5km south of Ernakulam Junction train station, is lined with modern restaurants and cafes.

Frys Village Restaurant
KERALAN $

(Map p988; Chittoor Rd; mains ₹90-180; ☺noon-3.30pm & 7-10.30pm) This brightly decorated and breezy place with an arched ceiling is a great family restaurant with authentic Keralan food, especially seafood like *pollichathu* or crab roast. Fish and veg thalis are available for lunch.

Cocoa Tree
CAFE $$

(☎0484-4119529; www.facebook.com/cocoatreecafe; MG Rd, Panampilly Nagar, Avenue Regent; dishes ₹270-500; ☺11am-11pm; ☎) With trailing plants, gleaming fresh-cake displays and newspapers to flick through, this bright cafe makes a sophisticated, rustic-chic retreat from busy Ernakulam. Salads, sandwiches, burgers, omelettes and pastas fill the global-inspired menu, or just pop in for a coffee, a hot chocolate or a fresh juice. It's 1.5km south of Ernakulam Junction.

Chillies
ANDHRA $$

(Map p988; ☎0484-2354938; Layam Rd; mains ₹100-300; ☺11.30am-4pm & 7-11pm) A dark, buzzing 1st-floor restaurant, serving Kochi's best spicy Andhra cuisine on banana leaves, from biryanis to fish curry. Try a thali (₹170 to ₹190) for all-you-can-eat joy. Downstairs is a tandoori sister venture.

☆ Entertainment

There are several centres in Kochi where you can view Kathakali, the fast-paced traditional martial art of *kalarippayat* and performances of classical music and traditional *bharatanatyam* dance.

Kerala Kathakali Centre
LIVE PERFORMANCE

(Map p990; ☎9895534939, 0484-2217552; www.kathakalicentre.com; KB Jacob Rd, Fort Cochin; shows ₹300-350; ☺shows from 4pm) In an intimate, wood-lined theatre, this recommended long-running arts centre provides a useful introduction to Kathakali. It also hosts performances of *kalarippayat* (4pm), classical music (8pm to 9pm Sunday to Friday) and traditional dance (8pm Saturday), plus early-morning yoga (₹400) and meditation (₹250) sessions and a range of short- and long-term courses, including Kathakali (from ₹650 per hour).

Ens Kalari   LIVE PERFORMANCE
(☑0484-2700810; www.enskalari.org.in; Nettoor; entry by donation) To see real professionals practising *kalarippayat*, seek out this renowned 65-year-old training school 6.5km southeast of central Ernakulam. There are daily one-hour demonstrations (7.15pm; one day's notice required) or you can watch training sessions from 5.30pm daily except Sunday. The centre also runs intensive courses from one week (₹5000) to one month (₹19,500).

🛍 Shopping

Anokhi   FASHION & ACCESSORIES
(Map p990; ☑0484-2216275; www.anokhi.com; Lily St, Fort Cochin) Fabulous hand-block printed dresses, kurtas, skirts, bags and shirts in floaty fabrics blend Indian and European design at Anokhi, a Jaipur brand famous for its traditional-meets-contemporary fashion. You'll also find bedspreads, tablecloths and other home accessories in an alluring rainbow of colours.

Niraamaya   FASHION & ACCESSORIES
(Map p990; ☑0484-2217778; https://niraamaya. org; 1/605 Peter Celli St, Fort Cochin; ☺10am-5.30pm Mon-Sat) A world of soothing pinks, greys and oranges, Niraamaya sells 'ayurvedic' clothing, accessories, homewares and yoga mats – all made of organic cotton, coloured with natural herb dyes, or infused with ayurvedic oils, based on the ancient concept of *ayurvastra* (healthy fabrics). There's another **branch** (Map p993; 6/217 AB Salem Rd; ☺10am-5.30pm) in Mattancherry.

Fabindia   CLOTHING, HOMEWARES
(Map p990; ☑0484-2217077; www.fabindia.com; 1/281 Napier St, Fort Cochin; ☺9.30am-9pm) This renowned fair-trade Indian brand has fine Indian textiles, fabrics, clothes, homewares, ceramics and natural beauty products, created using traditional techniques by village craftspeople across the country. The style is modern Indian, with silks and cottons in lively prints and colours, and the line works to encourage rural employment.

Lulu Mall   MALL
(☑0484-2727777; http://lulumall.in; NH66, Edappally; ☺9am-11pm; 🅿) India's largest shopping mall, Lulu is an attraction in its own right with people coming from all over to shop, hang out in the food courts or cinema, or go ice skating or tenpin bowling. Sprawling over 7 hectares, this state-of-the-art air-con mall has more than 215 brand outlets from Calvin Klein to Fabindia. It's 9km northeast of Ernakulam's boat jetty.

Idiom Bookshop   BOOKS
(Map p990; Bastion St, Fort Cochin; ☺10am-6.30pm) Originally just a pushcart selling books on Kochi's beaches, Idiom has a huge range of quality new and used tomes, including India-focused literature. There's another **branch** (Map p993; Bazaar Rd, Mattancherry; ☺10am-5pm) in Mattancherry.

ℹ Information

MEDICAL SERVICES

Lakeshore Hospital (☑emergency 9961630000; www.vpslakeshorehospital.com; NH Bypass, Marudu) Modern hospital 8km southeast of central Ernakulam.

Medical Trust (Map p988; ☑0484-2358001; www.medicaltrusthospital.com; MG Rd, Ernakulam; ☺24hr)

MONEY

ATMs in Fort Cochin cluster around Kunnumpuram Junction.

Unimoni (UAE Exchange; Map p988; ☑0484-4392416; www.unimoni.com; Chettupuzha Towers, PT Usha Rd, Ernakulam; ☺9.30am-6pm Mon-Fri, to 2pm Sat) has a foreign exchange.

TOURIST INFORMATION

DTPC Tourist Office (Map p988; ☑0484-2350300; Ernakulam Jetty, Ernakulam; ☺10am-5pm Mon-Sat)

Government of India Tourist Office (☑0484-2669125; www.incredibleindia.org; Willingdon Island; ☺9am-6pm Mon-Fri)

KTDC Tourist Office (Map p988; ☑0484-2353234; www.ktdc.com; Shanmugham Rd, Ernakulam; ☺8am-6.30pm) Just north of Ernakulam's main jetty.

Tourist Desk (Map p988; ☑9847044688, 0484-2371761; touristdesk1990@gmail.com; Ferry Jetty, Ernakulam; ☺8am-6pm) This private tour agency is extremely knowledgeable and helpful about Kochi and beyond, and runs a good backwaters tour. It also provides maps, ferry schedules and self-guided walking tours entitled *Historical Places in Fort Cochin*.

ⓘ Getting There & Away

AIR

Cochin International Airport (☑ 0484-2610115; http://cial.aero; Nedumbassery), 30km northeast of Ernakulam, is a popular hub, with international flights to/from the Gulf States, Sri Lanka, the Maldives, Malaysia, Bangkok and Singapore.

On domestic routes, Jet Airways (p1210), Air India (p1208), IndiGo (p1210), SpiceJet (p1210), Vistara (p1210) and/or GoAir (p1210) fly direct to Chennai, Mumbai, Bengaluru (Bangalore), Hyderabad, Delhi, Goa and Trivandrum. Air India flies daily to Agatti in Lakshadweep.

BUS

All long-distance services operate from Ernakulam's **KSRTC bus stand** (Map p988; ☑ 0484-2372033; Ernakulam; ⊙ reservations 6am-10pm) or the massive **Vyttila Mobility Hub** (☑ 0484-2306611; www.vyttilamobility hub.com; Vyttila), a state-of-the-art transport terminal 4km east of Ernakulam Junction train station. Numerous private bus companies have superdeluxe, air-con, video and Volvo buses to long-distance destinations, such as Bengaluru

(Bangalore), Chennai, Mangaluru (Mangalore), Trivandrum and Coimbatore; prices vary depending on the standard. Agents in Ernakulam and Fort Cochin sell tickets. Private buses use Vyttila as well as **Kaloor bus stand** (Kaloor), 3km north of Ernakulam Junction.

TRAIN

Ernakulam has two train stations, Ernakulam Junction and Ernakulam Town. There's a **reservations office** (Map p988; Ernakulam Junction, Ernakulam; ⊙ 8am-8pm Mon-Sat, to 1pm Sun) for both at Ernakulam Junction, but it's easier to book online or through a travel agent.

There are frequent local and express trains to Trivandrum (2nd class/sleeper/3AC ₹95/165/490, four to five hours), via Alleppey (₹50/140/495, 1½ hours) or Kottayam (₹50/140/495, one to two hours), and to Thrissur (2nd class/AC chair ₹60/260, 1½ hours). There are also 10 daily trains to Calicut (2nd class/sleeper/3AC ₹90/140/495, four to five hours) and Kannur (₹115/190/495, five to 6½ hours).

ⓘ Getting Around

TO/FROM THE AIRPORT

Bright-orange AC buses run between the airport and Fort Cochin (₹88, 1¾ hours, at least 16

MAJOR BUSES FROM ERNAKULAM

Buses to the following destinations operate from the KSRTC Bus Stand and/or Vyttila Mobility Hub. In addition, private buses operate on long-haul routes.

DESTINATION	FARE (₹)	DURATION (HR)	FREQUENCY
Alleppey	60-110	1½	every 10-30min
Bengaluru	790-1270	12	11 daily
Calicut	360	5	hourly
Chennai*	1533	16-18	4.30pm
Coimbatore	185-200	5	14 daily
Kalpetta (for Wayanad)	300	7	5 daily
Kannur	300-385	8	5 daily
Kanyakumari*	280	8	2.30pm
Kollam	135-250	4	every 10-20min
Kottayam	70-135	2	every 10min 3.45am-10pm
Kumily (for Periyar)	220	5	15 daily
Madurai*	450	10	8pm, 8.15pm, 8.30pm
Mangaluru*	400	11	6.30pm, 8.35pm, 10.30pm
Munnar*	125	4½	10 daily
Mysuru*	740-850	10	6pm, 7pm, 8pm, 10.50pm
Puducherry*	675	18	4pm
Thrissur	70	2	every 10-20min
Trivandrum	185-380	5-7	every 20-30min

* Departs only from KSRTC bus stand

daily) via Ernakulam's MG Rd or the Vyttila Mobility Hub. There are 24-hour prepaid taxi stands at the domestic and international terminals: ₹880 to Ernakulam, ₹1250 to Fort Cochin. Uber and Ola taxis charge around ₹700 and ₹1000 respectively.

AUTORICKSHAW & TAXI

Autorickshaw trips shouldn't cost more than ₹30 around Fort Cochin, ₹50 around Ernakulam or ₹80 from Fort Cochin to Mattancherry.

Prepaid autorickshaws from Vyttila cost ₹86 to Ernakulam Jetty, ₹110 to Ernakulam Junction and ₹214 to Fort Cochin; from prepaid autorickshaw stands at the **KSRTC bus stand** (Map p988; KSRTC bus stand, Ernakulam; ☉ 6.30am-11pm) or Ernakulam Junction (p996) it's ₹30 to the jetty and ₹180 to Fort Cochin. To get from Ernakulam to Fort Cochin after ferries (and buses) stop running you'll need a taxi or an autorickshaw.

Uber (www.uber.com) and Ola Cabs (www.olacabs.com) drivers are a popular alternative to **taxis** (Map p990; River Rd, Fort Cochin) for trips around Kochi; short hops cost around ₹60. In Ernakulam, there's a **prepaid taxi stand** (Map p988; Ernakulam Junction, Ernakulam; ☉ 24hr) at Ernakulam Junction.

BOAT

Ferries are the fastest and most enjoyable form of transport between Fort Cochin and the mainland. The main stop at Fort Cochin is **Customs Jetty** (Map p990; Bazaar Rd, Fort Cochin); some ferries also use Fort Cochin's **Kamalakadavu Jetty** (Map p990; River Rd, Fort Cochin). **Mattancherry Jetty** (Map p993; Bazaar Rd, Mattancherry), near the palace and synagogue, was closed indefinitely at research time, but may resume services to Willingdon Island. The jetty on the eastern side of Willingdon Island is **Embarkation** (Map p988; Willingdon Island); the west one, opposite Mattancherry, is **Terminus** (Willingdon Island). One-way fares are ₹3 or ₹4.

Ferries run to Vypeen Island from **Ernakulam Jetty** (Map p988; Park Ave, Ernakulam) and **Fort Cochin** (Map p990; River Rd, Fort Cochin).

Ferries to Bolgatty Island depart from **High Court Jetty** (Map p988; Shanmugham Rd, Ernakulam).

Fort Cochin

Ferries go from Fort Cochin's Customs Jetty to Ernakulam Jetty (20 minutes) every 10 to 25 minutes from 5.55am to 9.50pm. There's also a new high-speed ferry from Kamalakadavu Jetty to Ernakulam (with/without air-con ₹20/10, 12 minutes, six daily). Ferries also hop between Customs and Willingdon Island 24 times a day.

Roll-on, roll-off car and passenger ferries go every 20 minutes from Fort Cochin to Vypeen Island between 6.40am and 9.30pm (five minutes).

Ernakulam

Ferries run from Ernakulam Jetty to Fort Cochin's Customs Jetty (20 minutes) every 15 to 20 minutes from 4.40am to 9.10pm, some via Willingdon Island (10 minutes). Ernakulam Jetty has ferries to Vypeen Island (25 minutes) every 25 to 35 minutes from 6am to 9.30pm, also via Willingdon; return ferries run from 6.25am to 10pm.

BUS

Airport buses and local buses from Ernakulam use the central **Fort Cochin bus stand** (Map p990; River Rd, Fort Cochin). There are no regular buses between Fort Cochin and Mattancherry Palace, but it's an enjoyable 2km (30-minute) walk (or a quick cycle) through the busy warehouse area along Bazaar Rd.

BICYCLE & MOTORCYCLE

Bicycles (from ₹150) and scooters (₹400 per day) or Enfields (from ₹1300 per day) can be hired from agents in Fort Cochin.

METRO

Partly inaugurated in mid-2017, Kochi's elevated metro (https://kochimetro.org) will eventually connect Kochi's bus and train stations, additional suburbs and the airport, though at the time of writing wasn't yet very useful to travellers.

MAJOR LONG-DISTANCE TRAINS FROM ERNAKULAM

DESTINATION	TRAIN NO & NAME	FARES (₹; SLEEPER/ 3AC/2AC)	DURATION (HR)	DEPARTURE (DAILY)
Bengaluru	16525 Bangalore Exp (A)	345/945/1355	11½	6.05pm
Chennai	12624 Chennai Mail (A)	395/1050/1490	12	7.30pm
Delhi	12625 Kerala Exp (B)	885/2300/3415	46	3.50pm
Goa (Madgaon)	16346 Netravathi Exp (A)	415/1135/1640	14½	2.05pm
Mumbai	16346 Netravathi Exp (A)	615/1655/2430	27	2.05pm

Trains: (A) departs from Ernakulam Junction; (B) departs from Ernakulam Town

Around Kochi

Cherai Beach

On Vypeen Island, 25km north of Fort Cochin, golden 3km-long Cherai Beach makes a fun day trip or getaway from Kochi, especially if you hire a scooter or a motorbike in Fort Cochin. The main beach entrance can get busy, but with kilometres of lazy backwaters just a few hundred metres from the seafront and a smattering of quiet fishing villages to explore, this unhurried area is becoming increasingly appealing to travellers.

🛏 Sleeping & Eating

Les 3 Elephants   RESORT $$$

(☑ 0484-2480005, 9946012040; www.3elephants.in; Convent St, Cherai Beach; cottages incl breakfast with AC ₹8020-13,770, without AC ₹5070-8850; ❄ 🛜 🌊) Hidden from the beach but with the backwaters on your doorstep, Les 3 Elephants is a soothing French-Indian-owned resort with boutique flair. The beautifully and uniquely designed cottages have private sit-outs and lovely backwater views across gardens to Chinese fishing nets. There's yoga and meditation plus an ayurvedic spa (massage ₹1500), and the restaurant serves excellent home-cooked French-Indian fare (mains ₹200 to ₹500). Guests can use the pool at a neighbouring property, while nearby Mini Elephant rooms offer a more budget-friendly experience (₹1000).

La Dame Rouge   HERITAGE HOTEL $$$

(☑ 0484-2481062, 9496016599; www.ladamerouge.com; Manapilly, Ayyampally; r incl breakfast & dinner €80-180; 🛜) Wrapped in greenery, 4.5km southeast of Cherai Beach, this bluewashed 250-year-old house makes an intimate, character-filled escape. French owner Marco has five thoughtfully styled, all-different heritage-chic rooms; one is a massive split-level suite with its own massage room. The food, served at a communal table, is a tasty fusion of French, Indian and fresh seafood. Ask locally for 'Marco's house'.

Chilliout Cafe   CAFE $$

(☑ 9744138387; www.facebook.com/chillioutcafe; Cherai Beach; mains ₹180-550; ⊙ noon-9pm Thu-Tue; 🛜) A breezy, open-sided, French-Portuguese-Indian-run hang-out for sea views, relaxed vibes and authentically good European-style comfort food right by the beach. Delicious burgers, pizzas, pastas, crepes, fresh juices, home-cooked fries and barbecue dishes are all carefully prepared by a charming team.

CHENNAMANGALAM'S HANDLOOM WEAVERS

The Chennamangalam area is known for its traditional handloom weaving industry, which was devastated by the 2018 Kerala floods, with the livelihoods of its 600 weavers (mostly women) suddenly at immense risk. The flood damage to the five handloom cooperative societies here is estimated to have hit a staggering 150 million rupees. A high-profile campaign spearheaded by Kochi designers has since been working to get this female-powered industry back on its feet – its *chekkutty* dolls, made using ruined saris, have become a symbol of the weavers' (and Kerala's) resilience.

ℹ Getting There & Away

To get here from Fort Cochin, catch the roll-on roll-off vehicle ferry (p996) to Vypeen Island (per person ₹3, two-wheeler ₹9, car ₹50), then either take an autorickshaw from the jetty (₹500 to ₹600) or catch one of the frequent northbound buses (₹20, one hour) to Cherai village, 1.5km east of the beach. Buses also run every 10 minutes from Ernakulam's **Boat Jetty bus stand** (Map p988; Ernakulam Boat Jetty, Ernakulam) to North Paravur (₹20, one hour; 6km east of Cherai Beach).

North Paravur & Chennamangalam

Nowhere is the tightly woven religious cloth that is India more apparent than in North Paravur and Chennamangalam, 30km north of Kochi, home to one of the oldest synagogues (p998) in Kerala. Also here are a Jesuit church and the ruins of a Jesuit college (the Jesuits first arrived in Chennamangalam in 1577), a Hindu temple on a hill overlooking the Periyar River, a 16th-century mosque, and Muslim and Jewish burial grounds. In North Paravur town, you'll find the *agraharam* (place of Brahmins), a small street of closely packed and brightly coloured houses originally settled by Tamil Brahmins.

Travel agencies in Fort Cochin organise tours to both places.

Buses serve North Paravur every 10 minutes from Ernakulam's Boat Jetty bus stand (p997; ₹20, one hour). The area is also easily reached by local bus from Cherai Beach (only 6km west).

Around 5km northeast of North Paravur, the beautifully restored **Chennamangalam Synagogue** (admission ₹2, camera ₹10; ⊙10am-4.30pm Tue-Sun) is one of Kerala's most ancient, established in 1420 (though rebuilt in 1614 following a fire). The interior is awash with door and ceiling wood-reliefs in dazzling colours, while just outside lies one of the oldest tombstones in India – inscribed with the Hebrew date corresponding to 1269.

Thrissur (Trichur)

☑ 0487 / POP 315,960

While the rest of Kerala has its fair share of celebrations, untouristed, slightly chaotic Thrissur is the cultural cherry on the festival cake, with a seemingly endless list of energetic festivities. Centred around a large park (known as the 'Round') and a Hindu temple complex, Thrissur worked as a second capital for the Cochin royal family during the 16th century, and is also home to a Nestorian Christian community whose denomination dates to the 3rd century AD.

⊙ Sights

Thrissur is renowned for its central temple, as well as for its impressive churches, including the massive whitewashed **Our Lady of Lourdes Cathedral** (St Thomas College Rd; ⊙dawn-dusk), the splendid neo-Gothic 1925 **Basilica of Our Lady of Dolours** (Puttanpalli Church, New Church; High Rd; ⊙dawn-dusk), and the 1814 **Marth Mariam Church** (Chaldean Church, Nestorian Church; www.churchoftheeast india.org; High Rd; ⊙dawn-dusk), headquarters of India's Chaldean Syrian community.

Archaeology Museum   MUSEUM
(☑0487-2333056; Thrissur-Shornur Rd; adult/child ₹20/5; ⊙9.30am-1pm & 2-4.30pm Tue-Sun) The refurbished Archaeology Museum is housed in the wonderful 200-year-old Sakthan Thampuran Palace, built in Keralan-Dutch style. Its mix of artefacts includes 12th-century Keralan bronze sculptures and giant earthenware pots, weaponry, coins and a lovely carved chessboard. To the side is a shady heritage garden.

Vadakkunathan Kshetram Temple   HINDU TEMPLE
(Round; ⊙5-10am & 5-8pm) Finished in classic Keralan architecture, one of the oldest Hindu temples in the state crowns the low hill at the heart of Thrissur. It's dedicated to Shiva and though its present form dates from the 16th to 17th centuries, it has its roots in the 9th century. Only Hindus are allowed inside, though the intricate wood carvings on the main gate are worth admiring and the surrounding park is a popular spot to linger.

✳ Festivals & Events

Thrissur Pooram   RELIGIOUS
(www.thrissurpooramfestival.com; ⊙Apr/May) The largest and most colourful of Kerala's temple festivals, with huge processions of caparisoned elephants around the Vadakkunathan Kshetram Temple.

Animal-rights campaigns against Thrissur Pooram have started to gain momentum in recent years, as concerns have grown over the welfare of the captive temple elephants.

🛏 Sleeping & Eating

Gurukripa Heritage   HERITAGE HOTEL $
(☑0487-2421895; http://gurukripaheritage.in; Chembottil Lane; r with AC ₹1600-1900, without AC ₹900; ❄🖥) Almost a century old but now neatly refurbished, Gurukripa is a fine budget heritage hotel with more charm than most, in a quietish spot set back from the road just south of the Round. Simple rooms are unpretentious but clean, with heavy wooden doors, though some of the cheapest air-con ones are a tad musty.

Hotel Luciya Palace   HOTEL $$
(☑0487-2424731; www.hotelluciyapalace.com; Marar Rd; s ₹3250-3780, d ₹4070-7670; ❄🖥) In a cream-coloured, colonial-style building, this is Thrissur's most characterful midranger, and its spacious, modern rooms are great value (desks, hairdryers, tea/coffee trays, even shower curtains!). It's tucked into a quiet cul-de-sac just 200m southwest of the Round, and has a good all-day multicuisine restaurant (mains ₹150 to ₹360).

Clayfingers Pottery   GUESTHOUSE $$
(☑0480-2792234; www.clayfingerspottery.com; Kadalassery; r incl breakfast ₹4750; ❄🖥) For something uniquely creative, seek out these four palm-fringed 'art cottages' attached to an artisan pottery warehouse, which occupies a reincarnated 1950s brick-and-tile factory 13km south of Thrissur. Terracot-

Thrissur (Trichur)

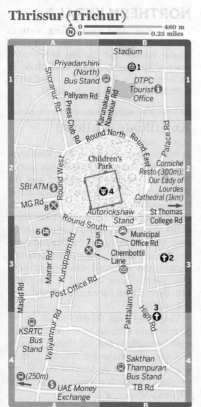

Thrissur (Trichur)

⊚ Sights
1 Archaeology Museum B1
2 Basilica of Our Lady of Dolours B3
3 Marth Mariam Church......................... B4
4 Vadakkunathan Kshetram Temple ... B2

⊜ Sleeping
5 Gurukripa Heritage A3
6 Hotel Luciya Palace A3

⊗ Eating
7 Hotel Bharath..................................... A3
8 Navaratna Restaurant.........................A2

laced omelettes, and there are freshly squeezed juices. It's 500m east of the Round.

Navaratna Restaurant   MULTICUISINE $$
(☑ 0484-7241994; Round West; mains ₹130-210; ☉10am-11pm) Dark, intimate and air-con-cooled, this is one of the classier dining experiences in the city centre, with marble-effect floors and seating at check-cloth tables on raised platforms. Downstairs is veg and upstairs is nonveg, highlighting lots of North Indian specialities and a few Chinese and Keralan dishes.

ⓘ Getting There & Around

Hundreds of **autorickshaws** (Round South) gather at the Round and usually use the meter; short trips cost ₹20.

BUS

From Thrissur's **KSRTC bus stand** (☑ 0487-2421150; RS Rd) buses leave every 20 to 30 minutes for Trivandrum (₹250, seven hours), Ernakulam (Kochi; ₹72, 3½ hours), Calicut (₹102, four hours), Palakkad (₹60, three hours) and Kottayam (₹124, four hours). Hourly buses go to Kannur (₹130, six hours). There's a noon bus to Coimbatore (₹100, three hours); otherwise change at Palakkad. Buses also serve Mysuru (Mysore; ₹600, eight hours, 2.30pm, 9pm and 10pm) and Bengaluru (Bangalore; ₹700 to ₹1000, nine hours, 8pm and 9pm).

Frequent local services chug along to Guru-vayur (₹35, one hour), Irinjalakuda (₹32, 50 minutes) and Cheruthuruthy (₹40, 1½ hours). Two private bus stands – **Sakthan Thampuran** (Pattalam Rd) and **Priyadarshini (North)** (Thrissur-Shornur Rd) – have more buses to these destinations, though the chaos involved in navigating the two hardly makes using them worthwhile.

TRAIN

The train station is 1.5km southwest of the Round, with regular services to Ernakulam (2nd class/

ta floors, stylish bathrooms, wooden bed frames and subtle wall art embellish the rooms, and the on-the-ball team also runs a terrace cafe. Guests can join resident artists for clay-pottery workshops.

★**Hotel Bharath**   SOUTH INDIAN $
(☑ 0487-2421720;   hotelbharathtcr@gmail.com; Chembottil Lane; mains ₹90-150; ☉ 6.30am-10pm) Spotless, air-conditioned Bharath is widely regarded as the best veg restaurant in town and *the* place for a lunchtime thali (₹86 to ₹165), a Keralan breakfast or a spicy curry.

Corniche Resto   INTERNATIONAL $$
(☑ 819733448; www.facebook.com/cornicheresto; 1st fl, PIK Tower, St Thomas College Rd; dishes ₹90-360; ☉ 11.30am-11pm; 🛜) Indian flavours infuse the global-inspired menu at this fashionable hang-out furnished with cosy booths, suspended lamps and coffee paraphernalia. Spicy-pumpkin pastas and paneer-masala wraps meet chicken-tikka burgers and spice-

MAHÉ

On the Malabar Coast about 10km south of Thalasseri (formerly Tellicherry), riverside Mahé is surrounded by, but not actually part of, Kerala – it's part of the Union Territory of Puducherry (Pondicherry), formerly under French India. It was occupied by the French in 1721, and finally returned to India in 1954 (though some inhabitants opted for French citizenship). Apart from the riverfront promenade with its Parisian-style street lamps, the province is similar to other towns along Kerala's coast, and Malayalam and English are the main languages. The other obvious difference is that there is no restriction on the sale of alcohol here (unlike in Kerala) and sales tax is low.

sleeper/3AC ₹60/140/495, 1½ to 2½ hours), Calicut (₹70/140/495, three hours), Coimbatore (₹90/140/495, three hours) and Trivandrum (₹110/195/495, six to 7½ hours).

Around Thrissur

The Thrissur region supports several institutions that are nursing the dying classical Keralan performing arts back to health, while Guruvayur, 25km northwest of Thrissur, is home to the celebrated **Shri Krishna Temple** (Guruvayur; ⊙ 3am-1pm & 4.30-10pm), closed to non-Hindus.

Frequent local buses from Thrissur's KSRTC bus stand (p999) serve Guruvayur (₹35, one hour), Irinjalakuda (₹32, 50 minutes) and Cheruthuruthy (₹40, 1½ hours), or take a taxi.

Kerala Kalamandalam   CULTURAL PROGRAMS
(☑ 0488-4262418;   www.kalamandalam.org;
Cheruthuruthy; courses per month ₹600; ⊙ Jun-Mar) Using an ancient Gurukula system of learning, students undergo intensive study in Kathakali, *mohiniyattam* (dance of the enchantress), Kootiattam, percussion, voice and violin. A Day with the Masters (Indian/foreigner ₹1000/1400) is a morning program allowing visitors to tour the theatre and classes and see various art and cultural presentations; book ahead by email. It's 30km north of Thrissur.

NORTHERN KERALA

The Malabar Coast from Calicut north to the Karnataka border features a string of coastal villages and dazzling honey-toned beaches far less touristed than those in southern Kerala. The region is famed for its enthralling *theyyam* rituals (p1172).

Kozhikode (Calicut)

☑ 0495 / POP 431,560

Northern Kerala's largest city, Kozhikode (still widely known as Calicut) has been a prosperous trading town since at least the 14th century and was once the capital of the formidable Zamorin dynasty. Vasco da Gama first landed at Kappad, 15km north of the city, in 1498, on his way to snatch a share of the subcontinent for king and country (Portugal that is) – though the Zamorins resisted and remained independent until Tipu Sultan's army invaded in the 1760s, with the city then falling under British control in 1792.

These days trade depends mostly on exporting Indian labour to the Middle East, while agriculture and the timber industry are economic mainstays. Though Calicut is also famous for its Malabar cuisine, for travellers it's mainly a jumping-off point for Wayanad, Mysuru or Bengaluru.

⊙ Sights

At the heart of the city, Mananchira Sq, the former courtyard of the Zamorins, preserves its original spring-fed tank and a leafy park. The central **Church of South India** (Bank Rd; ⊙ dawn-dusk), with its unique European-Keralan architecture and three-tiered tower, was established in 1842 by Swiss missionaries. About 1km west of Mananchira Sq is Calicut Beach – not much for swimming but good enough for a sunset stroll along the promenade.

Around 2km southwest of the city centre sits the 14th-century wooden **Miskhal Masjid** (Kuttichira Mosque; Kuttichira; ⊙ dawn-dusk), an attractive, four-storey aquamarine mosque supported by impressive wooden pillars and with traditional sloping tiled roofs.

Kozhikode (Calicut)

Map scale: 0 — 500 m / 0 — 0.25 miles

Map labels:
- Harivihar (1km)
- KSRTC Bus Stand
- Mavoor (Indira Gandhi) Rd
- Corporation Rd
- Beach Rd
- Bank Rd
- RC Rd
- 8
- SBI ATM
- 2 DTPC Tourist Office
- Convent Rd
- 7
- 10
- Cherooty Rd
- AG Rd
- Tank
- 3 Ansari Park
- Pavamani Rd
- Stadium Rd
- Taluk Rd
- 6 11
- Arabian Sea
- Court Rd
- Town Hall Rd
- SM Rd
- GH Rd
- MM Ali Rd
- 5
- MP Rd
- Big Bazaar Rd
- Palayam Rd
- Railway Station Rd
- Train Station
- Autorickshaw Stand
- Beypore (10km)
- (24km)
- Tali Temple
- 4
- 9

🛏 Sleeping & Eating

Famous for its Malabar cuisine, Calicut is regarded as the food capital of northern Kerala. With its large student population, it's also easily northern Kerala's liveliest nightlife spot (mostly within five-star hotels).

Beach Hotel   HERITAGE HOTEL **$$**
(☏9745062055, 0495-2762055; www.beach heritage.com; Beach Rd; r incl breakfast ₹4130-4720; ❄🛜) Built in 1890 to house the Malabar British Club, this slightly worn but quite charming six-room hotel has more character than most other Calicut accommodation (though the service underwhelms). Upstairs rooms come with indoor lounges, soaring ceilings, sea views and original polished-wood floors; those on the ground floor have tucked-away garden-facing terraces and tiled flooring.

On-site **Salkaram** (☏9745062055, 0495-2762055; mains ₹150-300; ⊙7am-10.30pm) turns out tasty pan-Indian cooking, while the bamboo **Hut** (⊙11am-11pm) bar-restaurant is popular for beers and snacks.

Alakapuri   HOTEL **$$**
(☏0495-2723451; www.hotelalakapuri.com; MM Ali Rd; with AC s ₹1300, d ₹1850-3150; without AC s ₹600-800, d ₹1750- 3050; ❄🛜) Set back from a busy market area, friendly in-demand Alakapuri is built motel-style around a green lawn (complete with fountain!). Various rooms are a little scuffed, but reasonable value, and there's a restaurant plus bar.

★ Harivihar   HOMESTAY **$**
(☏0495-2765865, 9847072203; www.hariv| com; Bilathikulam; s/d incl meals €100/125; ┊ northern Calicut, the restored 1850 '

the Kadathanadu royal family is as serene as it gets – a traditional family compound with pristine lawns, constructed around the architectural principles of Kerala Vastu. The six large rooms are beautifully furnished with dark-wood antiques. It's primarily an ayurvedic, yoga and meditation retreat, with vegetarian meals and various packages.

Zains SOUTH INDIAN $
(☑0495-2366311; Convent Cross Rd; dishes ₹40-180; ☺noon-10pm) A local favourite for its Malabar dishes, biryanis and snacks, with a small terrace out the front, three-decades-old Zains is run by the entrepreneurial Zainabi Noor and is usually busy in the afternoons and evenings. It's also known for its *meen pathiri* (rice-based bread with fried fish) and *unnakai* (a boiled-banana sweet).

★ **Paragon Restaurant** INDIAN $$
(☑0495-2767020; www.paragonrestaurant.net; Kannur Rd; dishes ₹170-370; ☺6am-midnight) Join the inevitably long queue out the door at this always-packed restaurant, founded in 1939. The overwhelming menu is famous for its legendary chicken biryani and fish dishes – such as *pollichathu* or *molee* (fish pieces in coconut sauce). Also has an aircon room (from noon only).

The team also runs busy-busy **Salkara** (☑0495-2300042; http://salkara.com; Platform 1, dishes ₹45-180; ☺5.30am-2.30pm & 3.30-11pm) at the train station.

Adam's Teashop SOUTH INDIAN $$
(Adaminde Chayakkada; ☑0495-2365800; www.ackd.in; Beach Rd; mains ₹80-400; ☺noon-midnight) Distressed-wood shutters, vibrant paintwork and old-school radios create a retro-style scene at this wildly popular restaurant near the beach, where classic Malabari dishes are given a creative makeover.

Biryanis come wrapped in banana leaves; there are jazzed-up chicken, beef or prawn tiffin boxes; or try the *pachakkari* or fish *pollichathu*.

❶ Getting There & Away

AIR
Kozhikode International Airport (www.kozhikodeairport.com; Karipur), 25km southeast of the city, serves major domestic destinations as well as the Gulf.

SpiceJet (p1210) and IndiGo (p1210) have the best domestic connections, with direct flights to Bengaluru (Bangalore), Chennai, Delhi, Mumbai and/or Hyderabad. Jet Airways (p1210) flies to Mumbai and Air India (p1208) to Trivandrum.

BUS
Government buses operate from the enormous but orderly **KSRTC bus stand** (☑0495-2723796; Mavoor Rd). For Wayanad district, buses go to Sultanbatheri (₹80 to ₹200, three to four hours, every 15 minutes), Kalpetta (₹60 to ₹160, three hours, every 10 minutes) and Mananthavadi (₹90, three hours, every 20 to 30 minutes).

TRAIN
The train station is 1km south of Mananchira Sq, with frequent trains to Kannur (2nd class/sleeper/3AC ₹60/140/495, two hours), Mangaluru (sleeper/3AC/2AC ₹165/495/700, 3¾ to five hours), Ernakulam (₹170/495/745, 3½ to five hours) and Trivandrum (₹240/710/1000, 10 hours).

Heading southeast, eight daily trains go to Coimbatore (sleeper/3AC/2AC ₹140/495/700, four to five hours), via Palakkad (₹140/495/700, 2½ hours).

❶ Getting Around
Calicut has a glut of **autorickshaws** (MM Ali Rd) and most use the meter, with short hops costing ₹20 to ₹40; it's around ₹40 from the city centre

BUSES FROM CALICUT'S KSRTC BUS STAND

DESTINATION	FARE (₹)	DURATION (HR)	FREQUENCY
Bengaluru	336-1000	9	7 daily
Ernakulam (Kochi)	370	6	hourly 5am-10pm, midnight, 12.25am, 1.15am, 1.30am
Kannur	90	3	every 30min
Mangaluru	430	6-7	11.58pm
Mysuru	204-370	5	11 daily
Ooty	380	5½	hourly 4am-10pm
Trissur	121	3½	every 10min
Trivandrum	389-693	10	16 daily

to the train station. Taxis charge around ₹800 to the airport, which has a prepaid-taxi counter.

Wayanad Region

☑ 04935 & 04936 / POP 817,420 / ELEV 760M (MANANTHAVADI)

Many Keralites rate the northern elevated Wayanad region, which rises to between 700m and 2100m northeast from Calicut, as the most beautiful part of their state. Encompassing part of the Western Ghats' Nilgiri Biosphere Reserve (p972), which spills into Tamil Nadu and Karnataka, Wayanad's landscape combines mountain scenery, rice paddies of ludicrous green, skinny betel nut trees, bamboo, red earth, spiky ginger fields, slender eucalyptuses, and rubber, cardamom and coffee plantations. It's an excellent place to spot wild elephants. Foreign travellers stop here between Mysuru (Mysore), Bengaluru (Bangalore) or Ooty (Udhagamandalam) and Kerala, and Wayanad is a popular escape for city-based Indians – yet it remains fantastically unspoilt and satisfyingly secluded.

The 345-sq-km sanctuary has two pockets: Muthanga (east) bordering Tamil Nadu, Tholpetty (north) bordering Karnataka. The district's three main towns make good transport hubs – Kalpetta (south), Sultanbatheri (Sultan Battery; east) and Mananthavadi (northwest) – but the best accommodation is scattered across Wayanad.

◉ Sights & Activities

Rafting, kayaking, zip-lining and other adventure activities have sprung up in recent years.

★ Wayanad

Wildlife Sanctuary   NATURE RESERVE
(☑ 04936-271013, 04935-250853; www.wayanad sanctuary.org; entry to each part Indian/foreigner ₹115/310, camera/video ₹40/240; ⊙7-10am & 3-5pm mid-Apr–mid-Mar) Wayanad's ethereal 345-sq-km sanctuary is accessible only by two-hour jeep safari (₹680), on which you might spot langurs, chital deer, sambar, peacocks, wild boar or wild elephants; the odd tiger and leopard wanders through, though you'd be incredibly lucky to spot one. Jeeps are arranged at either of the sanctuary's two entrances, **Tholpetty** (Tholpetty–Coorg Rd; Indian/foreigner ₹115/310, camera/video ₹40/240, jeep ₹680; ⊙7-10am & 3-5pm mid-Apr–mid-Mar) and **Muthanga** (NH766; Indian/foreigner ₹115/310, camera/video ₹40/240, jeep ₹680; ⊙7-10am & 3-5pm mid-Apr–mid-Mar); during the November-to-March high season, arrive

Wayanad Region

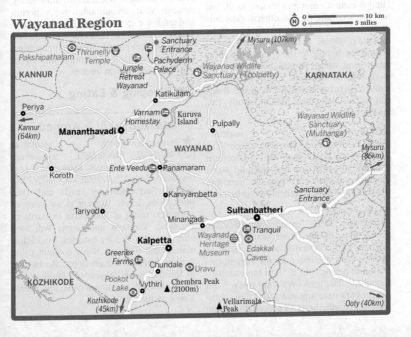

NAGARHOLE NATIONAL PARK

South India's much-loved Nagarhole National Park (p886), in neighbouring Karnataka, is within day-tripping reach from northern Wayanad (just 18km north of Tholpetty).

at least an hour before the morning or afternoon openings to register and secure a vehicle.

Whether you go to Tholpetty or Muthanga essentially depends on whether you're staying in the north or south of Wayanad, as there's no difference in the chances of spotting wildlife or the visiting arrangements. Both Tholpetty and Muthanga close from mid-March to mid-April, but remain open during the monsoon. There are a limited number of guides and jeeps permitted in the park at one time, and trekking is not permitted.

Thirunelly Temple
HINDU TEMPLE

(http://thirunellitemple.com; ⊙5.30am-noon & 5.30-8pm) Thought to be one of the oldest temples on the subcontinent, Thirunelly Temple huddles beneath the Brahmagiri Hills 15km southwest of Tholpetty. Non-Hindus cannot enter the temple itself, but it's worth visiting for the otherworldly mix of ancient and intricate pillars backed by mountain views. Follow the path uphill behind the temple to the stream known as Papanasini, where Hindus believe you can wash away all your sins; a trail branches off halfway up to an ancient Shiva shrine. Buses run to Thirunelly from Mananthavadi (₹35, 1½ hours).

Jain Temple
JAIN TEMPLE

(NH766, Sultanbatheri; ⊙8am-noon & 2-6pm) The 13th-century Jain temple on the western edge of Sultanbatheri has splendid stone carvings and is an important monument to the region's strong historical Jain presence.

Edakkal Caves
CAVE

(adult/child ₹30/20, camera/video ₹50/200; ⊙8am-4pm Tue-Sun) These remote hilltop 'caves' – more accurately a small series of caverns – are celebrated for the ancient collection of petroglyphs in their top chamber, thought to date back over 3000 years. From the car park near Ambalavayal (12km southwest of Sultanbatheri) it's a steep 20-minute

walk up a winding road to the ticket window, then another steep climb up to the light-filled top cave.

Wayanad Heritage Museum
MUSEUM

(Ambalavayal; adult/child ₹20/10, camera/video ₹20/150; ⊙9am-5.30pm) In the village of Ambalavayal, 12km southwest from Sultanbatheri near the Edakkal Caves, this small but fascinating museum exhibits tools, weapons, pottery, carvings and other artefacts dating back to the 9th century, shedding light on Wayanad's significant Adivasi population. Displays of note include Neolithic axes, 13th-to 14th-century hero stones and a fine stone-carved Rama from the Vijayanagar era.

Trekking

There's some good trekking around the district (though not in the wildlife sanctuary itself), but it's tightly controlled by the Forest Department and various trekking areas open and close depending on current environmental concerns. Kalpetta's DTPC Tourist Office (p1006) can advise on which treks are available. At the time of research, three treks were open: Chembra Peak (2100m; but only to the midway point); Banasura Hills in the south; and Brahmagiri Hills in the north. Permits and guides are mandatory and can be arranged at forest offices in south or north Wayanad or, more easily, through your accommodation. A permit and guide for up to five people costs around ₹1500 for Chembra, ₹2950 for Banasura and ₹2000 for Brahmagiri. Weather permitting, trekking is available year-round, though beware the rainy-season leeches.

🛌 Sleeping & Eating

🛌 Mananthavadi & Around

⭐ Varnam Homestay
HOMESTAY $$

(☏9745745860, 9400055873; www.varnamhomestay.com; Kurukanmoola, Kattikulam; s/d incl breakfast & dinner ₹1500/2500, villa ₹2000/3000; ❀🛜🛌) Surrounded by jungle and spice plantations, lovely Varnam is an oasis of calm 3km south of Katikulam in northern Wayanad. Varghese and Beena will look after you with Wayanad stories, local information and delicious home cooking using organic farm-fresh ingredients. Rooms are in the traditional 50-year-old family home or an elevated 'tree-house' villa, and there's a pool on the way.

Jungle Retreat Wayanad   GUESTHOUSE $$

(9742565333; www.jungleretreatwayanad.com; Thirunelly; per person incl meals from ₹3250; ☎) The handful of rooms at this welcoming jungle guesthouse are comfortably appealing, but the standout factor is the fabulous location on the sanctuary boundary (13km southwest of Tholpetty). Best are the rustic cottages with terraces facing the reserve, beyond a watering hole frequented by local wildlife. Rates include a wildlife-spotting walk, and a host of activities can be arranged (₹350).

Ente Veedu   HOMESTAY $$

(9446834834, 9847511437; www.enteveedu. co.in; Panamaram–Sultanbatheri Rd, Panamaram; r incl breakfast with AC ₹3500-4500, without AC ₹2500-3000; ☀☎) Secluded and on an 80-year-old estate overlooking banana plantations, ginger crops and rice paddies, this charming homestay (which translates as My Own Home) 15km southeast of Mananthavadi is definitely worth seeking out. Large, simply styled rooms – some interconnecting – are split between a modern house and a bamboo block (with details crafted by local artisans), and there's a colourful wicker-strewn lounge.

Kalpetta & Around

Hibernest Chembra   HOSTEL $

(9846642171; www.hibernest.com; APJLP School Rd, Kunnambetta; dm ₹1000; ☀☎) Chembra Peak looms high above this peacefully positioned, red-brick, colonial-era bungalow turned boutiqueish hostel, set in leafy gardens 6km south of Kalpetta. Four-person en suite dorms (mixed or women-only) are equipped with personal lockers, plugs, lights and curtained bunks, while facilities include a communal kitchen. There's another branch just west of Kalpetta.

Greenex Farms   RESORT $$

(8606818555, 9645091512; http://greenex-farms.com; Chundale Estate Rd, Moovatty; incl breakfast dm ₹1460, r ₹3070-5780; ☎☀) A beautifully remote-feeling resort fringed by spice, coffee and tea plantations, 8km southwest of Kalpetta. Each of the private cottages is individually designed, most with a separate lounge, bathroom, balcony and superb views; there's also tree-house accommodation, as well as a bunker-style 12-bed dorm. There are also restaurants, a campfire, walks, activities and a swimming pond.

Sultanbatheri & Around

Mint Flower Residency   HOTEL $$

(04936-222206, 9745222206; www.mintflower residency.com; Chungam, Sultanbatheri; s/d with AC from ₹1230/1790, without AC ₹850/1570) Immediately north of central Sultanbatheri, the efficiently operated budget annexe of Mint Flower Hotel is in great condition. It's no frills, but the surprisingly contemporary rooms are spotless and come with colour feature walls (though no hot showers).

★ Tranquil   RESORT $$$

(04936-220244; www.tranquilresort.com; Kuppamudi Coffee Estate, Kolagapara; r incl breakfast ₹11,770-17,600, tree house ₹18,430-23,000; ☉closed Easter; ☎☀) With a warm family welcome, this wonderfully peaceful and exclusive resort is pocketed away on an incredibly lush 1.5 sq km of working pepper, coffee, vanilla and cardamom plantations. The elegant eight-room house has sweeping verandahs filled with plants and handsome furniture, and there are also two custom-designed tree houses that may be Kerala's finest (complete with French-press coffee grown on-site).

A network of 11 marked walking trails meanders around the plantation, and you'll also enjoy a bar, a lounge area and a pool. It's 7km southwest of Sultanbatheri, but feels a world away.

Amaryllis   HOMESTAY $$$

(9847865824, 9847180244; http://amarylliskerala.com; Narikund; r incl meals ₹13,340-32,000; ☎☀) Amid coffee, fruit and spice plantations with sweeping reservoir panoramas, Amaryllis elevates the humble Kerala homestay into a luxury-boutique affair. Personally designed by welcoming, well-travelled owners Victor and Jini, the nine inviting rooms include a wood-walled cottage, a suite with a lake-view bath, and two stylish polished-bamboo tree houses with terraces and glassed-in showers. Breakfast happens on the verandah overlooking the pool.

 BOOKING BUSES

Some Kerala buses can be prebooked online via www.keralartc.in or www. kurtcbooking.com (though foreign cards aren't always accepted).

ⓘ Information

DTPC Tourist Office (☏ 04936-202134, 9446072134; http://wayanadtourism.org; Kalpetta; ⊗ 9.30am-5pm Mon-Sat) Also has offices at Kalpetta's new bus stand (p1006) and seasonally at Lakkidi (southern Wayanad) and Katikulam (northern Wayanad).

ⓘ Getting There & Away

WITHIN KERALA

Buses brave the winding roads – including a series of nine spectacular hairpin bends – between Calicut and Kalpetta (₹60 to ₹160, three hours) every 10 minutes; Calicut buses also run to/from Sultanbatheri (Pulpally Rd, Sultanbatheri; ₹80 to ₹200, three to four hours, every 15 minutes) and Mananthavadi (Kozhikode Rd; 73 to ₹90, three hours, every 20 to 30 minutes). Buses operate roughly hourly during daylight hours between Kannur and Mananthavadi (₹73, three hours). Kalpetta also has eight daily buses to Trivandrum (₹490, 23 hours) via Ernakulam (Kochi; ₹300, six hours). All Kalpetta buses stop at its **New bus stand** (Main Rd, Kalpetta).

TO/FROM TAMIL NADU & KARNATAKA

From Sultanbatheri's KSRTC bus stand (p1006), buses go to Ooty (Udhagamandalam; ₹200, three hours) at 8am and 12.45pm. From Mananthavadi's Municipal bus stand (p1006), there are buses to Ooty (₹150, 4½ hours) at 11am and midnight.

Buses run from Kalpetta to Bengaluru (Bangalore; ₹390, 6½ hours) via Mysuru (Mysore; ₹167, 3½ hours) every 30 minutes, most of them stopping in Sultanbatheri; note that the border gate here on the NH766 is closed between 9pm and 6am. There are buses from Mananthavadi to Mysuru (₹85, three hours) at 9.30am, 11.30am, 12.30pm, 2pm and 4.30pm, via the alternative northern (Kutta–Gonikoppal) route, whose border is open 24 hours.

ⓘ Getting Around

The Wayanad district is quite spread out but buses link Mananthavadi, Kalpetta and Sultanbatheri every 10 to 30 minutes during daylight hours (₹22 to ₹35, one to two hours). From Mananthavadi, buses head to Tholpetty (₹28, one hour) every 30 minutes from 6.30am to 9.30pm. From Sultanbatheri, private buses serve Muthanga (₹20 minutes, one hour) every 10 minutes from 6am to 7pm. Taxis tour the region for ₹1500 to ₹2000 per day.

Kannur & Around

☏ 0497 / POP 56,820

Under the Kolathiri rajas, Kannur (formerly Cannanore) was a major port bristling with international trade. Since then, the usual colonial suspects, including the Portuguese, Dutch and British, have had a go at exerting their influence on the region, leaving behind the odd fort. Today Kannur, 80km north of Calicut, is an unexciting, though agreeable, town known mostly for its weaving industry and cashew trade. For travellers, this area's appeal lies in its entrancing *theyyam* rituals and untouristed golden beaches.

This is a predominantly Muslim part of Kerala, so local sensibilities should be kept in mind: wear a sarong over your bikini on the beach.

⦿ Sights & Activities

The Kannur region is the best place in Kerala to see the spirit-possession ritual called *theyyam* (p1172); on most nights of the year between November and April there should be a *theyyam* ritual on at a village temple somewhere in the vicinity. Ask at your hotel/guesthouse or contact Kurien at Costa Malabari.

Fort St Angelo FORT
(Fort Rd; ⊗ 9am-6pm) **FREE** One of the earliest Portuguese settlements in India (constructed with permission from Kannur's rulers), the 1505 St Angelo Fort looms tall on a promontory 3km south of town, displaying a fusion of Portuguese, Dutch and British architecture. Wander the well-preserved walls and gardens within.

Arakkal Museum MUSEUM
(Ayikkara Hospital Rd; adult/child ₹20/10, camera ₹25; ⊗ 10am-5pm Tue-Sun) Housed in part of the royal palace of the Arakkal family, a powerful Kannur dynasty with its roots dating to the 12th century, this harbourfront museum features antiques, furniture, weapons, silver and portraits, between tiled roofs, white walls and shuttered windows. It's a fascinating look into the life of Kerala's only Muslim royal family.

Thottada Beach BEACH
Framed by low palm-sprinkled headlands and a shallow lagoon, this beautiful powdery gold-sand expanse, 8km southeast of Kannur centre, is home to the area's most

charming homestays. It's wonderfully secluded, though the sea can get rough.

🛏 Sleeping & Eating

Although there are plenty of hotels in Kannur town, the best places to stay are the homestays dotted around near the beach at Thottada (8km southeast).

Blue Mermaid Homestay
HOMESTAY $$

(📞9497300234; www.bluemermaid.in; Thottada Beach; r incl breakfast & dinner with/without AC ₹4000/3000, cottage ₹4000; ❄🛜) 🍴 In a prime spot among palms, frangipanis and oleanders, facing northern Thottada Beach, charming Blue Mermaid has two immaculate rooms in a traditional home, eight bright air-con rooms occupying a modern mint-green building, and a whimsical stilted 'honeymoon cottage'. Friendly owners Indu and Parveen serve fine Kerala meals using garden-fresh ingredients and home-grown Wayanad coffee (plus free water refills).

Waves Beach Resort
GUESTHOUSE $$

(📞9447173889, 9495050850; www.wavesbeachresort.co.in; Thottada Beach, Adikadalayi; r incl meals ₹3000-3500; 🛜) Crashing waves will lull you to sleep at these four simply styled, very cute hexagonal laterite huts and adjacent four-room cottage above a semiprivate little cove, just north of Thottada Beach. The welcoming owners, Seema and Arun, have extra high-season rooms at another neighbouring property.

Costa Malabari
GUESTHOUSE $$

(📞9447775691; ps_kurian@rediffmail.com; Thottada Beach, Adikadalayi; r incl meals ₹3000-4000; ❄🛜) Costa Malabari pioneered tourism in this area and consists of three lovely homestay-style properties just back from Thottada Beach. Costa Malabari 1 has spotless, spacious rooms in an old hand-loom factory; there are more rooms in two other nearby bungalows, and all serve home-cooked Keralan food on banana leaves. Manager Kurien is an expert on *theyyam* and arranges visits.

Kannur Beach House
HOMESTAY $$

(📞9847186330; www.kannurbeachhouse.com; Thottada Beach; s/d incl breakfast & dinner ₹2600/3600; ☺Sep-Apr) A century-old traditional Keralan building with handsome wooden shutters, hidden beneath coconut palms and separated from Thottada Beach by a small lagoon – this is an original seafront homestay. The five rooms are simply done, but you can enjoy sensational ocean sunsets from your porch or balcony and dig into home-cooked Malabar meals. Yoga and trips to see *theyyam* are offered.

Ezhara Beach House
HOMESTAY $$

(📞9846424723, 0497-2835022; www.ezharabeachhouse.com; Ezhara Kadappuram; r from ₹950; 🛜) Under the watch of welcoming Hyacinth, this character-filled heritage home fronts unspoilt, palm-fringed Ezhara Beach, 9.5km southeast of Kannur. Rooms are simple but functional, a world of activities can be arranged (from market visits to trekking), and guests rave about the homemade Keralan and Continental meals.

KK Heritage Home
HOMESTAY $$

(📞9446677254, 9447486020; www.kkheritage.com; Thottada Beach; r incl meals ₹2600-3100; ☺Sep-May; ❄🛜) Slightly back from Thottada Beach in the palm groves, this long-established two-storey home pleases with its six spotless rooms, good food, deckchair-laden terraces and cheerful welcome. There's a ₹500 air-con surcharge, and owner Sreeranj can advise on *theyyam* performances.

Hotel Odhen's
INDIAN $

(Onden Rd; mains ₹30-100; ☺noon-4pm) Kannur's must-try restaurant, in the market area, is usually packed at lunchtime. The speciality is Malabar cuisine, specifically the banana-leaf thalis with a dazzling range of spicy extras including masala-fried fish.

❶ Getting There & Away

AIR

The much-anticipated **Kannur International Airport** (www.kannurairport.in; Mattannur), 27km east of Kannur, opened in December 2018. At the time of writing, GoAir (p1210) flies to Bengaluru (Bangalore) and Hyderabad; IndiGo (p1210) to Bengaluru, Chennai, Goa and Hyderabad; and Air India (p1208) to Gulf destinations including Abu Dhabi and Doha.

BUS

Kannur's enormous (one of the largest in Kerala) but orderly **Central bus stand** (New bus stand; Thavakkara), 1km southeast of the town-centre train station, is used by private and some government buses, but most long-distance state buses still operate from the **KSRTC bus stand** (Caltex Junction), 1.5km northeast of the train station.

KERALA BEKAL & AROUND

VALIYAPARAMBA BACKWATERS & THEJASWINI RIVER

Unfolding just inland from the coast halfway between Kannur and Kasaragod, Kerala's 'northern backwaters' offer a more peaceful alternative to the better-known waterways down south. Valiyaparamba's large body of water is fed by five rivers, including the Thejaswini, and fringed by ludicrously green groves of nodding palms.

Houseboat trips in this region tend to be day cruises, popular with domestic tourists. Based near the mouth of the Thejaswini, **Bekal Ripples** (📞7025488222; www.bekal ripples.com; Thejaswini River) is one of a few local operators offering houseboat trips here, with options from 5½-hour daytime jaunts (₹1500 per person) to overnight stays for two (₹14,000); book ahead. Neeleshwar Hermitage (p1009), meanwhile, offers overnight trips aboard one of Kerala's most luxurious houseboats, the two-room Lotus (from ₹22,500; www.thelotuskerala.com).

Alternatively, with advance planning, it's possible to explore the northern backwaters using the region's public State Water Transport Department ferries (www.swtd.kerala. gov.in). From Kotti (500m west of the train station at Payyanur, which is 38km northwest of Kannur and 45km southeast of Bekal), ferries run at 6.30am to Ori (17km northwest; ₹20, 2¾ hours), via surrounding islands. You can hop off along the way at, take a later ferry to or start from Ayitti Jetty (9km northwest of Kotti), which has at least three daily ferries to/from Kotti (₹10, 1½ hours).

For accommodation on land, stay at **V Retreat** (📞9845022056; www.vretreat.in; Kadapuram Rd, Valiyaparamba; r incl breakfast ₹3500; ❋ 🛜), a secluded homestay with three simple rooms and local-style meals (₹250 to ₹300), perched between the backwaters and an almost-deserted golden beach; it's 10km northwest of Payyanur and 5km southwest of Ayitti Jetty.

The KSRTC bus stand has buses to Mananthavadi in Wayanad (₹90, three hours, every 30 minutes 5am to 10pm); Ooty (Udhagamandalam; via Wayanad; ₹220, nine hours, 7.30am and 10pm); Ernakulam (Kochi; ₹300 to ₹350, seven hours, 11 daily) via Thrissur (₹200, six hours); Calicut (₹90, two to three hours, every 10 minutes); Kasaragod (for Bekal; ₹75, 2½ hours, every 10 minutes); and Bengaluru (Bangalore; ₹450, nine hours, six daily) via Mysuru (Mysore; ₹250, six hours).

There are also buses to Mananthavadi (₹90, three hours, eight daily 8.20am to 2.45pm) from the Central bus stand.

TRAIN

There are frequent trains to Thalasseri (2nd class/sleeper ₹60/140, 20 minutes, 21 daily), Calicut (sleeper/3AC/2AC ₹140/495/700, 1½ hours, 20 daily), Thrissur (₹190/540/745, four hours, 10 daily), Ernakulam (₹190/495/700, five to 6½ hours, eight daily) and Alleppey (₹245/630/880, five daily).

Heading north, trains run to Mangaluru (Mangalore; sleeper/3AC/2AC ₹140/495/700, three hours, 14 daily) via Bekal Fort (₹140/495/700, 1½ hours, four daily), and up to Goa (₹320/870/1300, eight hours, three daily).

ℹ️ Getting Around

For Thottada Beach, take bus 29 (₹10, 20 minutes) from Plaza Junction opposite the train station and get off at Adikadalayi village temple, 1km north of the beach. Autorickshaws charge ₹200.

Bekal & Around

📞 0467 / POP 54,170 (KASARAGOD)

Bordering Karnataka in Kerala's far north, Kasaragod district is known for the long, unspoilt, honey-gold beaches at Bekal and nearby Palakunnu and Udma (just north) and Nileshwar (just southeast), as well as for the enormous 17th-century Bekal Fort – all of which are begging for DIY exploration.

Kannur lies 76km southeast of Bekal while Mangaluru (Karnataka) sits 70km north, and you'll probably hear Kannada and Tulu just as much as Malayalam on the streets here. This area is gradually being colonised by glitzy five-star resorts, but it's still worth the trip for off-the-beaten-track adventurers. Bearing in mind the sensibilities of the local Hindu and Muslim population, it's best to cover up with a sarong on the beach.

☉ Sights & Activities

Bekal Fort   FORT
(Bekal; Indian/foreigner ₹25/300; ☉8am-5pm)
The huge laterite-brick Bekal Fort, built between 1645 and 1660, is the largest in Kerala
and sits on Bekal's rocky headland with fine
views. It passed into British hands in 1792,
having originally been seized from the Ik-
keri Nayaks by Hyder Ali in 1763.

Kappil Beach   BEACH
Isolated Kappil Beach, 6km north of Bekal,
is a beautiful, lonely stretch of fine gold-
hued sand with calm water, but beware
of shifting sandbars. Autorickshaws from
Bekal cost around ₹100.

Nileshwar Beach   BEACH
Around 18km southeast of Bekal, Nileshwar's gorgeous beach is a tranquil, palm-bor-
dered expanse of blonde sand that fades into
the hazy distance; there are a couple of lovely resorts here.

🛏 Sleeping & Eating

The five-star hotels are the most popular
places to stay in the Bekal area, but there
are also a couple of homestays and cheap,
average-quality hotels between Kanhangad
(10km south) and Kasaragod (16km north).

★Neeleshwar Hermitage   RESORT $$$
(☑0467-2287510; www.neeleshwarhermitage.com;
Ozhinhavalappu, Nileshwar; s ₹16,910-33,540, d
₹19,590-40,070; ☉closed Jul; ☀☎🏊) ⚐ This
fabulous, plastic-free beachfront ecoresort
consists of 18 sleekly designed thatch-roof
cottages inspired by Kerala fishers' huts,
with voguish touches like pre-loaded iPods
and stylish indoor-outdoor bathrooms (two
with plunge pools). Built according to Kerala Vastu, the Hermitage has a beachfront
infinity pool, lush gardens fragrant with
frangipani, superb organic food, a luxurious
houseboat (www.thelotuskerala.com), and
yoga, meditation and ayurveda.

Taj Bekal Resort & Spa   RESORT $$$
(☑0467-6616612; www.tajhotels.com; Kappil
Beach, Udma West; r ₹12,160-30,340; ☀☎🏊)
An elegant blend of Balinese and Keralan
architecture infuses Bekal's opulent Taj, on
secluded southern Kappil Beach 6km north
of town. The pool overlooks the backwaters
(go kayaking or rafting), and there are three
restaurants, a bar and a stunning 2-hectare
spa. All 66 rooms are sumptuously styled,
with tubs and hanging outdoor beds; the
stars are the exquisite private-pool villas.

Kanan Beach Resort   RESORT $$$
(☑0467-2288880, 8606208880; http://kanan
beachresort.com; Nileshwar; cottages incl breakfast ₹12,800-15,360; ☀☎🏊) Comfortable
whitewashed cottages with terraces and
traditional Mangaluru-tile roofs surround a
pool amid shady grounds of palms and hibiscus at this warm, French-founded resort
fronting Nileshwar's beautiful beach (18km
southeast of Bekal). The friendly team organises yoga, kayaking, ayurvedic treatments and other activities.

❶ Getting There & Away

AIR
Bekal is easily accessible from both Kannur's
new airport (p1007) in Kerala and Karnataka's
Mangaluru International Airport (p894).

BUS
Frequent buses run from the main NH66 through
Bekal to both Kanhangad (₹12, 20 minutes) and
Kasaragod (₹15, 20 minutes), from where you
can pick up trains to Mangaluru, Goa or Kochi.

TRAIN
Kanhangad, 10km south of Bekal, and Kasaragod, 16km north of Bekal, are major train hubs.
Tiny Bekal Fort station, right on Bekal's beach,
has trains to/from Mangaluru (Mangalore;
sleeper/3AC/2AC ₹140/495/700, two hours,
five daily), Kannur (₹140/495/700, two hours,
four daily), Calicut (₹140/495/700, three
hours, three daily) and Ernakulam (Kochi;
₹220/595/880, eight hours, one daily).

LAKSHADWEEP
POP 64,470
Comprising a string of 36 palm-covered,
white-sand-skirted coral islands 300km
off the Kerala coast, Lakshadweep (India's
smallest Union Territory) is as stunning as
it is isolated. Only 10 of these islands are
inhabited, mostly by Sunni Muslim fishers.
With fishing and coir production the main
sources of income, local life here remains
highly traditional, and a caste system divides islanders between Koya (land owners),
Malmi (sailors) and Melachery (farmers).
The archipelago's administrative centre is
Kavaratti island, and most islanders speak a
dialect of Malayalam.

KERALA LAKSHADWEEP

At the time of writing, foreigners were only allowed to stay on a few islands: Kadmat, Kavaratti, Bangaram, Thinnakara, Agatti and Minicoy, effectively from mid-September to mid-May. During monsoon months, while most resorts remain open, transport can be difficult.

Lakshadweep's real attraction lies underwater: the 4200 sq km of pristine archipelago lagoons, unspoilt coral reefs and warm waters are a magnet for scuba divers and snorkellers.

Lakshadweep can only be visited on a prearranged package trip. At the time of research, resorts on Kadmat, Minicoy, Kavaratti, Agatti and Bangaram islands were open to tourists – though some trips are boat-based packages that include a cruise from Kochi, island visits, water sports, diving and nights on board the boat. At research time foreigners were permitted to stay on Agatti Island, but most people just fly to Agatti airport and take a boat transfer to other islands. Packages include permits and in some cases meals, and can be arranged though Kochi-based **SPORTS** (Society for the Promotion of Recreational Tourism & Sports; Map p988; ☑ 0484-2355387, 9495984001; http://lakshadweeptourism.com; Anzaz Arcade, Hospital Rd, Ernakulam; ⊗ 10am-5pm Mon-Fri).

🛏 Sleeping & Eating

Accommodation in Lakshadweep is limited; it's best to book this before arranging flights and permits, via Kochi-based SPORTS or an authorised private tour operator (SPORTS has a list of these).

There are some basic **cottages** (☑ 0484-2355387; http://lakshadweeptourism.com; s/d ₹10,000/15,000) and the more upmarket **Bangaram Island Resort** (☑ 8547703595; http://bangaramislandresort.in; s/d ₹10,700/15,960) on otherwise uninhabited Bangaram Island, reached by one-hour boat from Agatti. On nearby Thinnakara Island, also an hour away from Agatti by boat, you can sleep in tents (single/double ₹8000/10,000).

Kavaratti Island has beachfront huts (single/double ₹5250/9450) accessed by boat from Agatti (two hours); these are available as part of the four- to five-day SPORTS Taratashi package.

Kadmat Island Resort (☑ 0484-4011134, 0484-2397550; www.kadmat.com; Kadmat; 2 night s/d incl meals with AC ₹13,450/20,210, without AC ₹11,450/16,030; ❄) on Kadmat offers 28 modern cottages overlooking the beach, some air-conditioned; get here by overnight boat from Kochi or boat transfer from Agatti (two hours).

On the remote island of Minicoy, Lakshadweep's second-largest and southernmost island, you can stay in beachside rooms and cottages at **Minicoy Island Resort** (☑ 0484-2355387; http://lakshadweeptourism.com; Minicoy; s ₹5250-6330, d ₹7350-9450; ❄); bookings are through the six- or seven-day SPORTS Swaying Palms cruise package (₹5250 to ₹10,500).

❶ Information

PERMITS

All visits require a special permit, which can be organised by tour operators or SPORTS in Kochi and is readily available for travellers who have confirmed accommodation bookings in Lakshadweep.

TOURIST INFORMATION

Mint Valley Travel (Map p988; ☑ 0484-2397550; www.mintvalley.com/travel; 5th fl, Metro Plaza Bdg, Market Road Junction, Ernakulam; ⊗ 10am-5pm Mon-Fri, to 2pm Sat) Reliable private tour operator.

SPORTS is the main organisation for tourist information and package tours, based in Kochi.

❶ Getting There & Away

Air India (p1208) flies between Kochi and Agatti Island daily; flights must be booked independently from tour packages. Boat transfers from Agatti airport to Bangaram, Thinnakara, Kadmat and Kavaratti cost ₹1000 to ₹4000 per person, though are often included in packages. During monsoon season, boats to Kavaratti, Bangaram and Kadmat may be replaced by helicopters.

Six passenger ships travel between Kochi and Lakshadweep, taking 14 to 18 hours, though obtaining tickets for these can be tricky; contact SPORTS (p1010). Cruise packages include the five-day, three-island Samudram trip (adult/child ₹32,030/23,100). See the tour packages section of https://lakshadweeptourism.com for details.

Tamil Nadu

POP 80.8 MILLION

Best Places to Eat

➡ Villa Shanti (p1049)

➡ Dreaming Tree (p1041)

➡ Bangala (p1066)

➡ Murugan Idli Shop (p1070)

➡ La Belle Vie (p1085)

➡ Annalakshmi (p1024)

Best Places to Stay

➡ Saratha Vilas (p1066)

➡ La Maison (p1086)

➡ Jungle Hut (p1093)

➡ Villa Shanti (p1047)

➡ Svatma (p1059)

➡ Surf Turf (p1032)

Why Go?

Tamil Nadu is the homeland of one of humanity's living classical civilisations, stretching back uninterrupted for two millennia and very much alive today in the Tamils' language, dance, poetry and forms of Hinduism.

Some of the temples here are among India's finest, from the sculpted stonework at Thanjavur (Tanjore) to the sprawling halls at Madurai. Across the state, pulsing urban centres rise like concrete islands amid a landscape of palm and banana plantations, rice fields and rugged sandstone scarps. Among them you'll find yoga and meditation retreats, ancient forts and bohemian B&Bs.

When the hot chaos of Tamil temple towns overwhelms, escape to the southernmost tip of India where three seas mingle; to the splendid mansions sprinkled across arid Chettinadu; or to the cool, forest-clad, wildlife-prowled Western Ghats. Tamil Nadu is welcoming but remains proudly distinct from the rest of India.

When to Go
Chennai

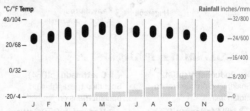

Jan–Mar The weather is at its (relative) coolest and the monsoon is over.

Jul–Sep Hit the hill stations after the crowded 'season' but while the weather is still good.

Nov–Dec The full-moon festival of lights.

Tamil Nadu Highlights

1 Puducherry (p1042)
Soaking up unique Franco-Indian flair.

2 Hill Stations (p1076)
Escaping the heat at Kodaikanal or Ooty.

3 Thanjavur (p1057)
Admiring the crowning glory of Chola temple architecture, the Brihadishwara Temple.

4 Chettinadu (p1064)
Spending the night in an opulent mansion.

5 Madurai (p1067) Getting lost in the colourful chaos of Tamil temple life.

6 Mamallapuram (p1033)
Enjoying a beachy vibe amid remarkable temples and carvings.

7 Chennai (p1013) Exploring Tamil Nadu's traditional but cosmopolitan capital.

8 Kanyakumari (p1073)
Standing on the wave-swept tip of the subcontinent.

9 Mudumalai Tiger Reserve (p1092) Tracking down rare exotic wildlife in majestic mountains.

History

While some would have you believe that the uniting feature among South Indian states is a preference for rice over roti, their ancient cultural connection is perhaps most profoundly rooted in language. Tamil (of Tamil Nadu), Malayalam (of Kerala), Telugu (Telangana and Andhra Pradesh) and Kannada (Karnataka) are all Dravidian tongues – and their speakers trace their cultural and religious identity back in an unbroken line to classical antiquity, long before the Aryan people arrived on the subcontinent from the north. Tamils consider themselves the standard bearers of Dravidian civilisation, with a considerable amount of pride.

The Tamil language was well established in Tamil Nadu by the 3rd century BC, the approximate start of the Sangam Age, when Tamil poets produced the body of classical literature known as Sangam literature. The Sangam period lasted until about AD 300, with three main Tamil dynasties arising in different parts of Tamil Nadu ('Tamil Country'): the early Cholas in the centre, the Cheras in the west and the Pandyas in the south.

By the 7th century the Pallavas, also Tamil, established an empire based at Kanchipuram, extending from Tamil Nadu north into Andhra Pradesh. They take credit for the great stone carvings of Mamallapuram (Mahabalipuram) and constructed the region's first free-standing temples.

Next in power were the medieval Cholas (whose connection with the early Cholas is hazy). Based in the Cauvery Valley of central Tamil Nadu, at their peak the Cholas ruled Sri Lanka and the Maldives plus much of South India, and extended their influence to Southeast Asia, spreading Tamil ideas of reincarnation, karma and yogic practice.

The Cholas raised Dravidian architecture to new heights with the magnificent towered temples at Thanjavur and Gangaikondacholapuram, and carried the art of bronze image casting to its peak, especially in their images of Shiva as Nataraja, the cosmic dancer. *Gopurams,* the tall temple gate towers characteristic of Tamil Nadu, made their appearance in late Chola times.

By the late 14th century much of Tamil Nadu was under the sway of the Vijayanagar empire based at Hampi (Karnataka). As the Vijayanagar state weakened in the 16th century, some of their local governors, the Nayaks, set up strong independent kingdoms, notably at Madurai and Thanjavur. Vijayanagar and Nayak sculptors carved wonderfully detailed temple statues and reliefs.

Europeans first landed on Tamil shores in the 16th century, when the Portuguese settled at San Thome. The Dutch, British, French and Danes followed in the 17th century, striking deals with local rulers to set up coastal trading colonies. Eventually it came down to the British, based at Chennai (then Madras), against the French, based at Puducherry (then Pondicherry). The British won out in the three Carnatic Wars, fought between 1744 and 1763. By the end of the 18th century British dominance over most Tamil lands was assured.

The area governed by the British from Madras, the Madras Presidency, included parts of Andhra Pradesh, Kerala and Karnataka, an arrangement that continued as Madras State after Indian Independence in 1947, until Kerala, Karnataka, Andhra Pradesh and present-day Tamil Nadu (130,058 sq km) were created on linguistic lines in the 1950s. It wasn't until 1968 that the current state (population 80 million) was officially named Tamil Nadu.

Tamil Nadu's political parties are often headed up by former film stars, most prominent among them controversial former chief minister and AIADMK (All India Anna Dravida Munnetra Kazhagam) leader Jayalalithaa Jayaram. Known as Amma (Mother), Jayalalithaa was worshipped with almost deitylike status across the state until her death on 5 December 2016. You're sure to see her face – round and benevolent – on posters and billboards throughout the state, conferring blessings from beyond on current political candidates.

CHENNAI (MADRAS)

♪044 / POP 10.4 MILLION

If you have time to explore Chennai (formerly Madras), this 400-sq-km conglomerate of urban villages and diverse neighbourhoods making up Tamil Nadu's capital will pleasantly surprise you. Its role is as keeper of South Indian artistic, religious and culinary traditions.

With its sweltering southern heat, roaring traffic and lack of outstanding sights, Chennai has often been seen as the dowdier sibling among India's four biggest cities. But it's well worth poking around its museums and temples, savouring deliciously authentic

TOP STATE FESTIVALS

International Yoga Festival (Puducherry/Pondicherry; ⊘ 4-7 Jan) Workshops, demonstrations and competitions, attracting experts from across India and beyond.

Pongal (statewide; ⊘ mid-Jan) Marks the end of the harvest season and is one of Tamil Nadu's most important festivals.

Thyagaraja Aradhana (Thiruvaiyaru; www.thiruvaiyaruthyagarajaaradhana.org; ⊘ Jan) This important five-day Carnatic music festival honours the saint and composer Thyagaraja.

Teppam Festival (Float Festival; Madurai; ⊘ Jan/Feb) Meenakshi Amman Temple deities are paraded around town in elaborate procession and floated in a brightly lit 'minitemple'.

Natyanjali Dance Festival (Chidambaram ; www.natyanjalichidambaram.com; ⊘ Feb) This five-day dance festival attracts 300 to 400 classical dancers from all over India.

Chithirai Festival (Madurai; ⊘ Apr/May) A two-week celebration/reenactment of the marriage of Meenakshi to Sundareswarar (Shiva).

Karthikai Deepam Festival (statewide; ⊘ Nov/Dec) Festival of lights, best seen at Tiruvannamalai, where the legend began.

Chennai Festival of Music & Dance (Madras Music & Dance Season; Chennai; ⊘ mid-Dec–mid-Jan) One of the largest of its type in the world, this festival celebrates South Indian music and dance.

Mamallapuram Dance Festival (Mamallapuram; ⊘ Dec-Jan) Showcasing classical and folk dances from all over India, with many performances on an open-air stage.

Covelong Point Surf, Music & Yoga Festival (Covelong/Kovalam; www.covelongpoint.com; ⊘ Aug) Expect kayak races, volleyball tournaments, group yoga and plenty of surfing.

South Indian delicacies or taking a sunset saunter along Marina Beach – the world's second-longest urban beach.

Among Chennai's greatest assets are its people, infectiously enthusiastic about their home town; they won't hit you with a lot of hustle and hassle. Recent years have thrown in a new layer of cosmopolitan glamour: luxe hotels, sparkling boutiques, quirky cafes, and smart contemporary restaurants – but the best of Chennai remains its old soul.

History

The southern neighbourhood of Mylapore is Chennai's Ur-settlement; in ancient times it traded with Roman, Chinese and Greek merchants. In 1523 the Portuguese established their nearby coastal enclave, San Thome. Another century passed before Francis Day and the British East India Company rocked up in 1639, searching for a good southeast-Indian trading base, and struck a deal with the local Vijayanagar ruler to set up a fort-cum-trading-post at Madraspatnam fishing village. This was Fort St George, built from 1640 to 1653.

The three Carnatic Wars between 1744 and 1763 saw Britain and its colonialist rival France allying with competing South Indian princes in their efforts to get the upper hand over local rulers – and each other. The French occupied Fort St George from 1746 to 1749 but the British eventually triumphed, and the French withdrew to Pondicherry (today Puducherry).

As capital of the Madras Presidency, one of the four major divisions of British-era India, Madras grew into an important naval and commercial centre. After Independence, it became capital of Madras State and then of its successor, Tamil Nadu. The city was renamed Chennai in 1996. Today it's a major IT hub and is often called 'the Detroit of India' for its booming motor-vehicle industry.

◉ Sights

★ **Government Museum**   MUSEUM
(Map p1022; www.chennaimuseum.org; Pantheon Rd, Egmore; Indian/foreigner ₹15/250, camera/video ₹200/500; ⊘ 9.30am-5pm Sat-Thu) Housed across from the striking British-built Pantheon Complex, this excellent museum is Chennai's best. The big highlight is building 3, the Bronze Gallery, with a superb collection of South Indian bronzes from the 7th-century Pallava era through to modern times (and English-language explanatory material).

It was from the 9th to 11th centuries, in the Chola period, that bronze sculpture peaked. Among the Bronze Gallery's impressive pieces are many of Shiva as Nataraja, the cosmic dancer, and an outstanding Chola bronze of Ardhanarishvara, the androgynous incarnation of Shiva and Parvati.

The main Archaeological Galleries (building 1) represent all the major South Indian periods from 2nd-century BC Buddhist sculptures to 16th-century Vijayanagar work, with rooms devoted to Hindu, Buddhist and Jain sculpture. Building 2, the Anthropology Galleries, traces South Indian human history back to prehistoric times, displaying tribal artefacts from across the region; outside it is a tiger-head cannon captured from Tipu Sultan's army in 1799 upon his defeat at Srirangapatnam.

The museum also includes the National Art Gallery, Contemporary Art Gallery and Children's Museum, on the same ticket. Some sections may be closed for renovation.

★**Kapaleeshwarar Temple**   HINDU TEMPLE
(Map p1016; Ponnambala Vathiar St, Mylapore; ⊙6am-noon & 4-9.30pm) Mylapore is one of Chennai's most characterful and traditional neighbourhoods; it predated colonial Madras by several centuries. Its Kapaleeshwarar Temple is Chennai's most active and impressive, and is believed to have been built after the Portuguese destroyed the seaside original in 1566. It displays the main architectural elements of many a Tamil Nadu temple – a rainbow-coloured *gopuram*, pillared *mandapas* (pavilions) and a huge tank – and is dedicated to the state's most popular deity, Shiva.

Legend tells that in an angry fit Shiva turned his consort Parvati into a peacock, and commanded her to worship him here to regain her normal form. Parvati supposedly did so at a spot just outside the northeast corner of the temple's central block, where a shrine commemorates the event. Hence the name Mylapore, 'town of peacocks'. The story is depicted at the west end of the inner courtyard, on the exterior of the main sanctum.

The temple's colourful **Brahmotsavam festival** (⊙Mar/Apr) sees the deities paraded around Mylapore's streets.

St Thomas Mount   RELIGIOUS SITE
(Parangi Malai; off Lawrence Rd, Guindy; ⊙6am-8pm) FREE The reputed site of St Thomas' martyrdom in AD 72 rises in the southwest of Chennai, 2.5km north of St Thomas

Mount train station. The Church of Our Lady of Expectation, built atop the 'mount' by the Portuguese in 1523, contains what are supposedly a fragment of Thomas' finger bone and the 'Bleeding Cross' he carved. The city and airport views are wonderful. Take the metro to the Nanganullar Rd stop and catch an autorickshaw there.

Tara Books   GALLERY
(☎044-24426696; www.tarabooks.com; ⊙10am-7pm) Producers of beautiful hand-printed books, this publishing company is based in southern Chennai. Visit its **Book Building** (☎044-24426696; www.tarabooks.com; Plot 9, CGE Colony, Kuppam Beach Rd, Thiruvanmiyur; ⊙10am-7.30pm Mon-Sat) FREE showroom, where you can browse, buy and maybe catch a talk by an author or artist. You can also check out the printing shop, **AMM Screens** (☎9962525740; 1 Elim Nagar, Perungudi; ⊙10am-1pm & 2-6pm), and watch pages being silk-screened and hand-bound into finished volumes. The Book Building is conveniently visited together with the nearby Kalakshetra Foundation (p1019), just 700m north. The print shop is about a 10-minute autorickshaw ride southwest.

Vivekananda House   MUSEUM
(Vivekanandar Illam, Ice House; Map p1016; www.vivekanandahouse.org; Kamarajar Salai; adult/child ₹20/10; ⊙10am-12.30pm & 3-7.15pm Tue-Sat) The marshmallow-pink Vivekananda House is interesting not only for its displays on the famous 'wandering monk', Swami Vivekananda, but also for its semicircular form, built in 1842 to store ice imported from the USA. Vivekananda stayed here briefly in 1897, preaching his ascetic Hindu philosophy to adoring crowds. Displays include a photo exhibition on the swami's life, a 3D reproduction of Vivekananda's celebrated 1893 Chicago World's Parliament of Religions speech, and the room where he stayed, now used for meditation.

San Thome Cathedral   CATHEDRAL
(Map p1016; Santhome High Rd, Mylapore; ⊙5.30am-8.30pm) This soaring Roman Catholic cathedral, a stone's throw from the beach, was founded by the Portuguese in 1523, then rebuilt by the British in neo-Gothic style in 1896, and is said to mark the final resting place of St Thomas the Apostle. It's believed 'Doubting Thomas' brought Christianity to the subcontinent in AD 52 and was killed at St Thomas Mount (p1015), Chennai, in AD 72. Behind the cathedral is the **tomb**

Chennai (Madras)

TAMIL NADU

2 km
1 mile

Andaman Shipping Office
Ticketing Counter (350m)
Rajaji Salai (North Beach Rd)
Beach Train Station
Parry's Corner
High Court
Armenian St
GEORGE TOWN
Elephant Gate
Mint St
NSC Bose Rd
Rattan Bazaar Rd
54 Court
55
VOC Rd (Wall Tax Rd)
32
28

Fort St George Entrance
Fort St George
Rajaji Salai
Esplanade Rd
Fort Train Station
GH Rd

Nehru Stadium
Sydenham's Rd
VEPERY
Vepery High Rd
Central Train Station
33
EVK Sampath Salai
Perambur Barracks Rd
Ritherdon Rd
Poonamallee High Rd (EVR Periyar Salai)

Park Town Train Station
Park Train Station
Chintadripet Train Station
West Kuvam River Rd
Langs Garden Rd
Cooum River
Anna Salai (Mount Rd)
Swami Sivananda Salai
Island Grounds

CHEPAUK
Chepauk Train Station
Chepauk Stadium
Wallajah Rd
30
Bells Rd
Anna Sq

Ellis Rd
Triplicane High Rd (Quaide-Millath Rd)
Bharathi Salai (Pycroft's Rd)
Anna Salai (Mount Rd)

EGMORE
Adinathar Rd
Rajarathinam Stadium
Binny Rd
Egmore Train Station
Gandhi Irwin Rd
Halls Rd
Casa Major Rd
Pantheon Rd
College Rd
PUDUPET
Ethiraj Salai
Anderson Rd
Haddows Rd
Greams Rd
THOUSAND LIGHTS

Purusavakkam High Rd

See Anna Salai, Egmore & Triplicane Map (p1022)

NUNGAMBAKKAM
Khader Nawaz Khan Rd
Valluvar Kottam High Rd
Chetpet Train Station
Harrington Rd
Sterling Rd
Tank Bund Rd
51

CHETPET
Pachaiyappa's College
Kilpauk Garden Rd
New Avadi Rd
Shenoy Nagar
CMBT (3km);
Omni Bus Stand (3.5km)
Sahodaran (100m)
Nelson Manickam Rd
Nungambakkam Train Station

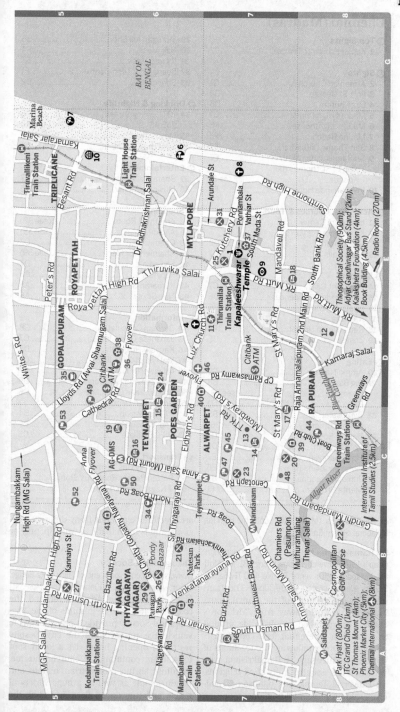

TAMIL NADU

Chennai (Madras)

of St Thomas (Map p1016; Santhome High Rd, Mylapore; ⊙9am-8pm) FREE.

Sri Ramakrishna Math   RELIGIOUS SITE
(Map p1016; www.chennaimath.org; 31 RK Mutt Rd, Mylapore; ⊙Universal Temple 4.30-11.45am & 3-9pm, evening prayers 6.30-7.30pm) The tranquil, flowery grounds of the Ramakrishna Math are a world away from Mylapore's chaos. Orange-robed monks glide around and there's a reverential feel. The Math is a monastic order following the teachings of the 19th-century sage Sri Ramakrishna, who preached the essential unity of all religions. Its Universal Temple is a handsome, modern, salmon-pink building incorporating architectural elements from different religions, and is open to all, to worship, pray or meditate.

Theosophical Society   GARDENS
(www.ts-adyar.org; south end of Thiru Vi Ka Bridge, Adyar; ⊙grounds 8.30-10am & 2-4pm Mon-Sat) FREE Between the Adyar River and the coast, the 100-hectare grounds of the Theosophical Society provide a peaceful, green, vehicle-free retreat from the city. Despite restricted opening hours, it's a lovely spot to wander, containing a church, mosque, Buddhist shrine, Zoroastrian temple and Hindu temple as well as a huge variety of native and introduced flora, including the

offshoots of a 450-year-old banyan tree severely damaged by a storm in the 1980s.

Marina Beach
BEACH

(Map p1016) Take an early morning or
evening stroll (you don't want to roast
here at any other time) along the 3km-long
main stretch of Marina Beach and you'll
pass cricket matches, flying kites, fortune-
tellers, fish markets, corn-roasters and
families enjoying the sea breeze. But don't
swim: strong rips make it dangerous. At
the southern end, the ridiculously popular
Madras Lighthouse (Map p1016; Indian/for-
eigner ₹20/50, camera ₹25; ⊙10am-1pm & 3-6pm
Tue-Sun) is India's only lighthouse with a
lift; the panoramic city and beach views are
fabulous.

Kalakshetra Foundation
ARTS CENTRE

(☑044-24521169; www.kalakshetra.in; Muthu-
lakshmi St, Thiruvanmiyur; ⊙campus 8.30-11.30am
Mon-Fri Jul-Feb, craft centre 9am-1pm & 2-5pm Mon-
Sat, all closed 2nd & 4th Sat of month) Founded
in 1936, Kalakshetra is a large serious
school of Tamil classical dance and music
(sponsoring many students from disadvantaged backgrounds), set in beautiful, shady
grounds in south Chennai. During morning
class times visitors can (quietly) wander the
complex. Across the road is the **Kalakshetra Craft Centre** (Indian/foreigner ₹100/500),
where you can see Kanchipuram-style handloom weaving, textile block-printing and
the fascinating, rare art of *kalamkari*
(hand-painting on textiles with vegetable
dyes); if you're feeling inspired, there are
courses too. For upcoming performances,
check the website.

Madras High Court
NOTABLE BUILDING

(Map p1016; Parry's Corner, George Town) Completed in 1892, this imposing red Indo-
Saracenic structure is said to be the world's
largest judicial building after the Courts
of London. The central tower was added
in 1912. At research time, visitors were not
permitted to wander the grounds, but if you
fancy trying, take your passport.

Fort St George
FORT

(Map p1016; Rajaji Salai; ⊙10am-5pm) `FREE`
Finished in 1653 by the British East India
Company, the fort has undergone many
facelifts. Inside the vast perimeter walls (the
ramparts are 18th-century replacements) is
now a precinct housing Tamil Nadu's Legislative Assembly & Secretariat, and a smattering of older buildings.

Valluvar Kottam
MONUMENT

(Map p1022; Valluvar Kottam High Rd, Nungambakkam; adult/child ₹3/2; ⊙8am-6pm) This 1976
memorial honours the Tamil poet Thiruvalluvar and his classic work, the 133-chapter
Thirukural. Its most striking element is
a 31m-high stone replica of Tamil Nadu's
largest temple chariot (from Thiruvarur),
pulled by two stone elephants and with giant wheels. In the adjacent auditorium, the
Thirukural's 1330 couplets are inscribed
on granite tablets. From the auditorium's
step-accessed roof, you can walk to the
foot of the shrine below the chariot's dome,
which holds a life-size seated Thiruvalluvar.

🏃 Activities

Isha Yoga Center
YOGA

(Map p1016; ☑044-24981185; www.ishayoga.org;
117 Luz Church Rd, Mylapore; ⊙7am-9pm) Offers
a variety of well-regarded yoga programs,
covering a range of mastery levels. Course
lengths vary.

Krishnamacharya Yoga Mandiram
YOGA, MEDITATION

(KYM; Map p1016; ☑044-24937998; www.kym.
org; 31 4th Cross St, RK Nagar; prices vary; ⊙8am-
7pm) Highly regarded, serious two-week and
month-long yoga courses, yoga therapy and
intensive teacher training. See the KYM
website for schedule and prices.

🥢 Courses

Kalakshetra Foundation
ART

(☑044-24525423; www.kalakshetra.in; Muthu-
lakshmi St, Thiruvanmiyur; per day ₹500) Kalakshetra's craft centre offers one-to two-
month courses in the intricate old art of *kalamkari* – hand-painting fabrics with natural vegetable dyes – which survives in only a
handful of places. Courses run 10am to 1pm
Monday to Friday.

International Institute of Tamil Studies
LANGUAGE

(☑9952448862; www.ulakaththamizh.org; CIT
Campus, 2nd Main Rd, Tharamani; 3-/6-month
course ₹5000/10,000) Intensive three-month
and six-month Tamil-language courses.

👉 Tours

★ Storytrails
WALKING

(Map p1016; ☑9940040215, 044-45010202; www.
storytrails.in; 21/2 1st Cross St, TTK Rd, Alwarpet;
from ₹1500) An excellent way to get a feel
for Chennai, these neighbourhood walking

CHENNAI'S OTHER CHURCHES

Armenian Church (Map p1016; Armenian St, George Town; ⊙9.30am-2.30pm, hours vary) A leafy, frangipani-scented haven in the midst of the George Town mayhem, the 18th-century Armenian Church is testament to the city's once-flourishing Armenian merchant community.

St Andrew's Church (St Andrew's Kirk; Map p1022; www.thekirk.in; 37 Poonamallee High Rd, Egmore; ⊙10am-5.30pm) This 1821 neoclassical Scottish Presbyterian church is one of India's most exquisite churches, rising up in leafy grounds in the middle of frenzied Egmore. Inspired by London's St Martin-in-the-Fields church, it has a grand columned portico.

Luz Church (Shrine of our Lady of Light; Map p1016; www.luzchurch.org; off Luz Church Rd, Mylapore; ⊙dawn-dusk) Styled with blue-and-white baroque elegance, pretty little palm-fringed Luz Church is Chennai's oldest European building, dating to 1516 – which also makes it one of India's oldest churches.

tours highlight themes like dance, temples, jewellery and bazaars. There are also popular food-tasting tours through George Town and in-house cooking classes. Most tours last 2½ hours. Calling is the best way to book; prices may vary depending on group size.

Royal Enfield Factory TOURS
(☏044-42230400; www.royalenfield.com; Tiruvottiyur High Rd, Tiruvottiyur; per person ₹600) The classic Enfield Bullet 350 motorcycle has been manufactured since 1955 in far northern Chennai. Two-hour tours run on the second and fourth Saturdays of each month at 10am. Bookings essential.

🛏 Sleeping

Hotels in Chennai are pricier than elsewhere in Tamil Nadu and not particularly good value. The Triplicane area is known for budget accommodation, but much of it is pretty gritty. Better cheapies are found in Egmore, and there are a couple of good hostels in other neighbourhoods. You'll find upper-midrange B&Bs in Nungambakkam, Poes Garden and Alwarpet. Top-end hotels are plentiful. Many hotels fill up by noon – book ahead!

Red Lollipop Hostel HOSTEL $
(Map p1016; ☏044-24629822; www.redlollipop.in; 129/68 RK Mutt Rd, Mandavelli; dm/s/d ₹650/1400/1680; ❄🕾) A boon for Chennai's budget travellers, Red Lollipop is a genuine, sociable hostel, 700m south of Mylapore's temple. Boldly colourful walls are scrawled with inspirational messages. Each of the spotless, locker-equipped six- to 10-bed dorms (one women-only) has its own bathroom. There's one private room, a rooftop

terrace, a shared kitchen, a lounge and very helpful staff.

Zostel HOSTEL $
(Map p1016; ☏011-39589002; www.zostel.com; 120/61 Ellaiamman Colony, 5th St, Teynampet; dm/r ₹600/1680; ❄🕾) Fresh on the Chennai scene, this branch of India's popular hostel chain is a success, with eight-bed dorms, a straightforward private room, a couple of spacious common areas, a shared kitchen and a washing machine. It's a five-minute walk from a metro stop in a quiet residential neighbourhood.

Paradise Guest House GUESTHOUSE $
(Map p1022; ☏044-28594252; www.paradiseguesthouse.co.in; 17/1 Vallabha Agraharam St, Triplicane; s/d ₹500/700, with AC ₹1000/1200; ❄🕾) Welcoming Paradise offers some of Triplicane's best-value digs: simple rooms with clean tiles, a breezy rooftop, friendly staff and hot water by the steaming bucket. It's basic, but unlike some other hotels in the neighborhood, it's not gritty and there are no dark vibes.

★ Footprint B&B B&B $$
(Map p1016; ☏9840037483; www.footprint.in; Gayatri Apts, 16 South St, Alwarpet; r incl breakfast ₹3400; ❄🕾) A beautifully comfortable, relaxed base on a quiet street in a leafy south Chennai neighbourhood. Three immaculate private rooms with king-size or wide twin beds share a thoughtfully arranged common area decorated with bowls of wild roses and old-Madras photos. Home-cooked breakfasts are generous, service is excellent, and the welcoming owners are full of Tamil Nadu tips. Book ahead.

Hanu Reddy Residences   GUESTHOUSE **$$**

(Map p1022; ☑044-43084563, 9176869926; www.hanureddyresidences.com; 6A/24 3rd St, Wallace Garden, Nungambakkam; incl breakfast s ₹3540-4130, d ₹4130-4720; ❋☎) Perfectly located on a quiet street just a block away from an international mix of restaurants, cafes and upscale shops. The 13 unpretentious rooms come with air-con, free wi-fi, tea/coffee sets, splashes of colourful artwork – and antimosquito racquets! Terraces have bamboo lounging chairs. Service hits that ideal personal-yet-professional balance. There's another **branch** (Map p1016; ☑044-24661021; 41/19 Poes Garden; r/ste incl breakfast ₹5900/10,240; ❋☎) in exclusive Poes Garden.

YWCA International Guest House   GUESTHOUSE **$$**

(Map p1022; ☑044-25324234; http://ywca madras.org/international-guest-house; 1086 Poonamallee High Rd; incl breakfast s ₹2065-2700, d ₹2600-3590, without AC s/d ₹1475/1890; ❋@☎) Chennai's YWCA guesthouse, set in shady grounds just north of Egmore station, offers a meticulously run property in a calm atmosphere. It has good-sized, brilliantly clean rooms, spacious common areas and solid-value meals (veg/nonveg ₹225/330). Lobby-only wi-fi costs ₹150 per day. In all, it's a fair value.

Hotel Victoria   HOTEL **$$**

(Map p1022; ☑044-28193638; www.empeehotels.com; 3 Kennet Lane, Egmore; incl breakfast s ₹2800-5075, d ₹3300-5550; ❋☎) Easily your smartest choice on hectic Kennet Lane. Rooms are clean and inviting, with kettles and flat-screen TVs, though not as exciting as the shiny lobby and cordial service suggest.

La Woods   HOTEL **$$**

(Map p1022; ☑044-28608040; www.lawoodshotel.com; 1 Woods Rd, Anna Salai; r incl breakfast ₹3540; ❋☎) Wonderfully erratic colour schemes throw fresh whites against lime greens and bright turquoises at this friendly, well-managed modern hotel. The shiny, spotless, contemporary rooms are perfectly comfy, with mountains of pillows, kettles, hairdryers and 'global' plug sockets. You can even plug your laptop or phone into the TV! On-site restaurant and futuristic-looking bar.

Hotel Chandra Park   HOTEL **$$**

(Map p1022; ☑044-40506060; www.hotelchandrapark.com; 9 Gandhi Irwin Rd, Egmore; incl breakfast s ₹1450-2900, d ₹1680-3540; ❋☎) Chandra Park's prices remain mysteriously lower than those at most similar establishments. 'Standard' rooms are smallish and a bit dated but have air-con, clean towels and tight, white sheets. Throw in polite service, 24-hour checkout and free wi-fi, and this is one of the best values in Chennai.

★**ITC Grand Chola**   HOTEL **$$$**

(☑044-22200000; www.itchotels.in; 63 Mount Rd, Guindy; r from ₹15,050; ❋☎≋) ❀ Chennai's most talked-about hotel is this ultraluxurious, 600-room, temple-inspired beauty in the city's southwest. A maze of sumptuous iPad-operated rooms, complete with soaking tubs and French press coffee kits, unfolds beyond the sweeping lantern-lit marble lobby. One corridor caters exclusively to women travellers. Also here are seven swish restaurants, two glitzy bars, three gyms, a spa and five pools. The hotel runs mostly on wind and solar power, and incorporates sustainable materials.

★**Ikhaya**   BOUTIQUE HOTEL **$$$**

(Map p1022; ☑7550120885; www.ikhaya.in; 6 Nawab Habibulah Ave, 1st St, Nungambakkam; r incl breakfast ₹4950-5900) A new iteration of a favourite old B&B, Ikhaya brilliantly brings together the best of heritage ambience and contemporary amenities. Rooms have carved wooden beds, throw rugs and modern bathrooms; some have balconies. The indoor dining area is a charming turquoise-and-white space, and there's an inner courtyard with tables, all part of the everything-made-from-scratch Mediterranean restaurant.

★**Raintree**   HOTEL **$$$**

(Map p1016; ☑044-42252525; www.raintree hotels.com; 120 St Mary's Rd, Alwarpet; r from ₹8730; ❋@☎≋) ❀ At this 'eco-sensitive' business-style hotel, floors are bamboo or rubber, water and electricity conservation hold pride of place, and AC-generated heat warms the bathroom water. Sleek, fresh, minimalist rooms are bright, comfy and stylish, with wonderful city vistas. A seaview infinity pool (doubling as insulation) and an open-air bar-restaurant grace the rooftop. Downstairs is excellent pan-Asian restaurant **Chap Chay** (mains ₹450-800, set menu ₹1900; ⏰noon-3pm & 7-11pm).

Taj Coromandel   HOTEL **$$$**

(Map p1022; ☑044-66002827; www.tajhotels.com; 37 Nungambakkam High Rd, Nungambakkam; r from ₹12,000; ❋☎≋) Luxurious without

Anna Salai, Egmore & Triplicane

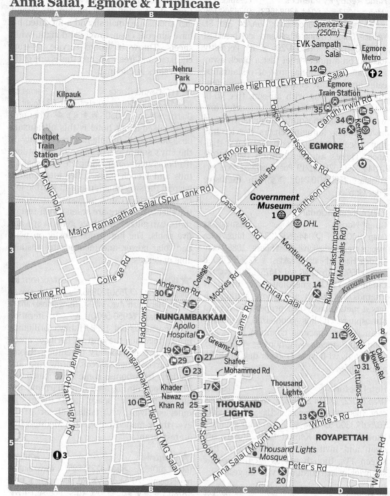

being overly ostentatious, the glittering Co-romandel offers a sensibly central top-end retreat from the city. Rooms flaunt a smart stripped-back style – with surround-sound speakers – and there's a lovely palm-shaded pool.

The marble-effect lobby hosts fine-dining South Indian restaurant **Southern Spice** (Map p1022; ☏044-66002827; mains ₹750-2100, thalis ₹1800-2200; ⊗12.30-2.45pm & 7-11pm), along with a busy cocktail bar.

Hyatt Regency   HOTEL **$$$**
(Map p1016; ☏044-61001234; http://chennai.regency.hyatt.com; 365 Anna Salai, Teynampet; r ₹10,000-11,950; ❄@🛜🛰) Smart, swish and bang up to date, this towering, triangular hotel is the most central of Chennai's newer top-end offerings. Contemporary art surrounds the sun-flooded atrium, local chefs head up three good restaurants and an insanely popular bar (p1026), and glossy rooms have walk-through bathrooms and fabulous sea/city panoramas through massive picture windows. Flowers fringe the pool and there's a luxury spa.

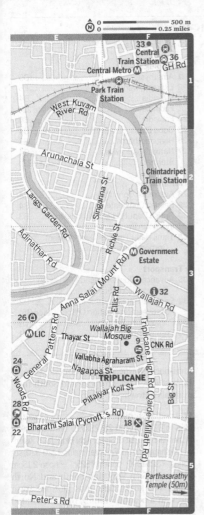

✖ Eating

Chennai is packed with inexpensive 'meals' joints ('messes') serving lunch and dinner thalis (all-you-can-eat meals) and tiffin (snacks) like *idli* (spongy, round fermented rice cakes), *vada* (doughnut-shaped deep-fried lentil savouries) and dosa (savoury crepes). Hotel Saravana Bhavan is always a quality veg choice. In the Muslim Triplicane High Rd area, you'll find great biryanis (fragrant, spiced steamed rice with meat and vegetables).

There's plenty of upmarket dining: classier Indian restaurants and international cuisines are on the rise.

Useful, well-stocked supermarkets include **Spencer's** (Map p1016; 15 EVK Sampath Salai, Vepery; ⏱7.45am-10pm), near Egmore and Central stations; Big Bazaar at **T Nagar** (Map p1016; 34 Sir Thyagaraya Rd, Pondy Bazaar, T Nagar; ⏱10.30am-9.30pm) and **Express Avenue mall** (Map p1022; Express Avenue, White's Rd; ⏱10am-9.30pm Mon-Fri, to 10pm Sat & Sun); **Nilgiri's** (Map p1022; 25 Shafee Mohammed Rd, Nungambakkam; ⏱9am-9.30pm) off Nungambakkam's Khader Nawaz Khan Rd; and **Amma Naana** (Map p1016; www.ammanaana.com; 82/100 Chamiers Rd; ⏱9am-9pm Mon-Sat) in Alwarpet.

Rayars Mess
SOUTH INDIAN **$**

(Map p1016; off Arundale St, Mylapore; dishes ₹10-45; ⏱7-10.30am & 3.30-6.30pm, hours vary) Down a dusty narrow alley off Arundale St, shoebox-sized Rayars has been pulling in ravenous crowds for over 70 years with its crispy evening *bonda* (mashed potato patties), *vada* and dosa. Breakfast at this family-run spot revolves around feathery *idli* and South Indian filter coffee.

Nair Mess
SOUTH INDIAN **$**

(Map p1016; 22 Mohammed Abdullah Sahib, 2nd St, Chepauk; meals ₹70; ⏱11.30am-3.30pm & 7-10pm) Big flavours are rustled up in a starkly simple setting at this no-nonsense, forever-busy spot, pocketed away in a lane opposite the Chepauk cricket stadium since 1961. Loaded banana-leaf thalis complemented by fish-fry dishes are the speciality.

Hotel Saravana Bhavan
INDIAN **$**

(Map p1022; ☎044-28192055; www.saravana bhavan.com; 21 Kennet Lane, Egmore; mains ₹125-250, thalis ₹125-155; ⏱6am-10.30pm) Dependably delish, Chennai's famous vegetarian chain doles out epically good South Indian thalis and breakfasts (*idli* and *vada* ₹45 to

Vivanta by Taj – Connemara
HERITAGE HOTEL **$$$**

(Map p1022; ☎044-66000000; www.vivantabytaj.com; Binny Rd, Anna Salai; r incl breakfast ₹11,990-14,390; ❋@🛜🏊) The top-end Taj Group has five hotels in and around Chennai, but this is the only one with historical ambience, built in the 1850s as the British governor's residence. Recently renovated throughout, tasteful luxury has been achieved in every detail. There's a beautiful pool in tropical gardens and the Chettinadu Raintree (p1025) restaurant is regarded as one of Chennai's best.

Anna Salai, Egmore & Triplicane

₹70, dosa ₹70 to ₹160), other Indian vegetarian fare and filter coffee. This branch is handy for Egmore station. Others include **Mylapore** (Map p1016; ☏044-24611177; 70 North Mada St; mains ₹125-250, thalis ₹125-155; ☺6am-10.30pm), **Pondy Bazaar** (Map p1016; ☏044-281576677; 102 Sir Thyagaraya Rd, T Nagar; mains ₹125-250, thalis ₹125-155; ☺6am-11pm) and, more upscale with a ₹320 buffet, **Thousand Lights** (Map p1022; ☏044-28353377; 293 Peter's Rd; mains ₹125-250, thalis ₹125-155; ☺8am-10.30pm), plus London, Paris and New York!

Ratna Café   SOUTH INDIAN $
(Map p1022; 255 Triplicane High Rd, Triplicane; dishes ₹35-85; ☺6am-11pm) Often crowded and cramped, Ratna is famous for its scrumptious *idli* accompanied by hearty doses of its signature *sambar* (soupy lentil dish with cubed vegetables). People have been gathering here since 1948. There are also North Indian mains, and an air-con room out the back.

Murugan Idli Shop   SOUTH INDIAN $
(Map p1016; http://muruganidlishop.com; 77 GN Chetty Rd, T Nagar; dishes ₹20-100; ☺7am-11.30pm) Those in the know generally agree that this particular branch of the small Ma-

durai-born Murugan chain serves some of the best *idli*, dosa, *uttapam* and South Indian meals in town.

★ **Annalakshmi**   INDIAN $$
(Map p1022; ☏044-28525109; www.annalakshmichennai.co.in; 1st fl, Sigapi Achi Bldg, 18/3 Rukmani Lakshmipathy Rd, Egmore; mains ₹220-320, set menus ₹825-1300, buffet ₹525; ☺noon-2.15pm & 7-9pm Tue-Sun) Very fine South and North Indian vegetarian fare, plus glorious fresh juices, in a beautiful dining room decorated with carvings and paintings, inside a high-rise behind the Air India building. Buffet lunches and dinners are served in another part of the same block. Annalakshmi is run by devotees of Swami Shanthanand Saraswathi; proceeds support medical programs for the poor.

Writer's Cafe   CAFE $$
(Map p1022; 127 Peter's Rd, Thousand Lights; mains ₹150-220; ☺9.15am-10pm) Half Higginbotham's bookshop, half casual cafe/restaurant, this is one of the best spots in Chennai for inexpensively priced, finely prepared, international food – from pastas to Thai curries and chicken with gravy and mash. There are plenty of tasty snacks, salads and pastries

too. Profits go to help victims of domestic violence.

Double Roti
BURGERS $$

(Map p1016; ☑044-30853732; http://doubleroti. in; 4/27 1st St, Cenotaph Rd, Teynampet; mains ₹215-650; ☺11am-11pm; 🕿) 'Double roti' refers to burger buns – the semi-open kitchen at this always-packed, super-casual, industrial-chic cafe plates them up with fun, flair and buckets of flavour. Lemonades and milkshakes are served in jars; burgers arrive in mini-frying pans; buckets come filled with masala fries; and witty slogans are chalked up on boards. There's plenty for vegetarians too, including fantastic spicy-falafel burgers.

Junior Kuppanna
SOUTH INDIAN $$

(Map p1016; ☑044-28340071; 4 Kannaiya St, North Usman Rd, T Nagar; mains ₹110-250, thalis ₹220; ☺noon-4pm & 6.30-11.30pm) From an impeccably clean kitchen (which you're welcome to tour) come limitless, flavour-packed lunchtime thalis, dished up traditional-style on banana leaves. This typical, frenzied Chennai 'mess' also has a full menu. Carnivores tiring of the pure-veg lifestyle can seek solace in specialities like mutton brains and pan-fried seer fish. Arrive early: it's incredibly popular. Branches across Chennai.

★Peshawri
NORTH INDIAN $$$

(☑044-22200000; www.itchotels.in; ITC Grand Chola, 63 Mount Rd, Guindy; mains ₹895-2450, set meals ₹3240-4140; ☺noon-3pm & 7-11.30pm) Perfect for a five-star splash-out, the ITC's signature Northwest Frontier restaurant serves inventive, flavour-popping creations at intimate booths alongside a glassed-in kitchen that gets you right in on the culinary action. Try huge hunks of pillowy chilli-grilled paneer, expertly spiced kebabs, or the deliciously rich house-special *dhal bukhara*, simmered overnight. There's an astounding international wine/cocktail list.

★Copper Chimney
NORTH INDIAN $$$

(Map p1016; ☑044-28115770; 74 Cathedral Rd, Gopalapuram; mains ₹265-750; ☺noon-3pm & 7-11.30pm) Meat-eaters will drool over the yummy North Indian tandoori dishes served in well-lit, stylishly minimalist surroundings, but the veg food here is fantastic too. Jain specialities mingle with biryanis, chicken kebabs, chargrilled prawns and fluffy-fresh naan. The *machchi* tikka – skewers of tandoori-baked fish – is superb, as is the spiced paneer kebab and grilled lamb.

★Amethyst
MULTICUISINE, CAFE $$$

(Wild Garden Cafe; Map p1022; ☑044-45991633; www.amethystchennai.com; White's Rd, Royapettah; mains ₹300-500; ☺10am-11pm; 🕿) Set in an exquisitely converted warehouse with a wraparound veranda from which tables spill out into lush gardens, Amethyst is a nostalgically posh haven that's outrageously popular with expats and well-off Chennaiites. Well-executed European-flavoured dishes range over quiches, pastas, sandwiches, crepes, creative salads, all-day breakfasts and afternoon teas. Fight for your table, then check out the stunning Indian couture boutique (p1027).

Enté Keralam
KERALAN $$$

(Map p1016; ☑7604915091; http://entekeralam. in; 1 Kasturi Estate, 1st St, Poes Garden; mains ₹290-575; ☺noon-3pm & 7-11pm) A calm ambience seeps through the four orange-toned, three-to four-table rooms of this elegant Keralan restaurant. Lightly spiced *pachakkari* vegetable stew is served with light, fluffy *appam* (rice pancake), the Alleppey curry is rich with mango, and there are plenty of fish dishes. Wind up with tender coconut ice cream. Set meals (veg/nonveg ₹945/1450) give a multi-dish miniformat taster.

Raintree
CHETTINADU $$$

(Map p1022; www.vivantabytaj.com; Vivanta by Taj – Connemara, Binny Rd, Anna Salai; mains ₹450-1000; ☺12.30-2.45pm & 7.30pm-midnight) This refined, wood-ceilinged restaurant is arguably Chennai's best place to savour the flavours of Tamil Nadu's Chettinadu region. Chettinadu cuisine is famously meat-heavy and superbly spicy without being chilli-laden, but veg dishes are good too. Dine outside in the leafy garden with water lilies.

Chamiers
MULTICUISINE, CAFE $$$

(Map p1016; ☑044-42030734; www.chamiershop. com; 106 Chamiers Rd, RA Puram; mains ₹300-500; ☺8.30am-11pm; 🕿) This bubbly 1st-floor cafe feels a continent away from Chennai, except that Chennaiites love it too. Flowery wallpaper, printed cushions, wicker chairs, wi-fi (per hour ₹100), wonderful carrot cake, croissants and cappuccino, English breakfasts, American pancakes, pastas, quiches, quesadillas, salads...

Ciclo Cafe
CAFE $$$

(Map p1016; ☑044-42048666; www.facebook. com/theciclocafe; 33/47 Gandhi Mandapam Rd, Kotturpuram; drinks ₹100-250, dishes ₹250-550; ☺11am-11pm daily, 7-10.30am Sat & Sun) Cycle-mad decor includes wheels on lamps,

DON'T MISS

CHENNAI STREET FOOD

Chennai may not have the same killer street-food reputation as Delhi or Mumbai, but there are some sensational South Indian street-side delicacies around, especially in Mylapore, George Town, Egmore and T Nagar, and along Marina Beach. If you'd like some guidance, Storytrails (p1019) runs fun story-themed food-tasting tours through George Town.

Mehta Brothers (Map p1016; 325 Mint St, George Town; dishes ₹20-40; ◷4-9pm Mon-Sat) Pulls in the crowds with the deep-fried delights of its signature Maharashtrian *vada pav* – spiced potato fritters in buns, doused in garlicky chutney.

Seena Bhai Tiffin Centre (Map p1016; 15/105 NSC Bose Rd, George Town; idlis & utta-pams ₹40; ◷7-11pm) Deliciously griddled, ghee-coated *idli* and *uttapam*.

Jannal Kadai (Ponnambala Vathiar St, Mylapore; items ₹20-30; ◷8-10am & 5-9.30pm Mon-Sat) Fast-and-furious hole-in-the-wall place famous for its hot crispy *bhajia* (vegetable fritters), *bonda* (battered potato balls) and *vada*.

chandeliers made from chains and bikes dangling in the window. But this place is more than just a gimmick: there's an extensive international menu, from Thai green curry to grilled Scottish salmon, plus a long list of sandwiches, burgers, and salads, all gigantic and delicious. Coffees, fresh juices and smoothies are also good.

Tuscana Pizzeria ITALIAN $$$
(Map p1022; ☏044-45038008; www.tuscana pizzeria.com; 19, 3rd St, Wallace Garden, Nungam-bakkam; mains ₹425-775; ◷noon-11.30pm) Tuscana turns out authentic thin-crust pizzas with toppings like prosciutto, mozzarella and sun-dried tomatoes, as well as more creative takes such as paneer tikka pizza, and tasty pastas, salads and topped breads. It even has whole-wheat and gluten-free pizzas. Eat in or takeaway.

🍸 Drinking & Nightlife

Chennai nightlife is on the up, with a smat-tering of lively new openings, but you'll need a full wallet for a night out here. Continen-tal-style cafes are growing in number, and, yes, Starbucks has arrived.

Bars and clubs in five-star hotels serve alcohol 24 hours a day, seven days a week, so that's where most of the after-dark fun happens. Solo guys ('stags') are often turned away, and there's usually a hefty admission charge for couples and men. Dress codes are strict: no shorts or sandals.

Other hotel bars, mostly male-dominated, generally close by midnight. If you're buy-ing your own alcohol, look for 'premium' or 'elite' government-run TASMAC liquor shops inside malls.

Radio Room BAR
(☏8500005672; www.radioroom.in; Somerset Greenways, 94 Sathyadev Ave, MRC Nagar, RA Puram; cocktails ₹450-600, dishes ₹200-300; ◷6-11.30pm Mon-Fri, 4-11.30pm Sat & Sun) From a keen young team comes this incredibly pop-ular radio-themed bar in southeast Chennai. It's all about mismatched furniture, a bar made of speakers and carefully mixed, in-spired cocktails and pitchers – some full of local flavour, like chai punch. Creative twists on Chennai's culinary favourites include mozzarella-stuffed *bhajias* (vegetable frit-ters) delivered in bicycle-shaped baskets.

365 AS LOUNGE, CLUB
(Map p1016; ☏044-61001234; https://chennai. regency.hyatt.com; Hyatt Regency, 365 Anna Salai, Teynampet; drinks ₹700; ◷3pm-2am) In the glamorous Hyatt Regency (p1022), Chen-nai's hottest party spot bursts into life on weekends, when wild DJ sets kick off on the terrace, playing pop music on Fridays and techno on Saturdays. Otherwise, it's a swish, sultry lounge serving carefully crafted cocktails alongside Indian and international wines, beers and spirits. Dress code is smart casual (for guys, trousers and closed shoes).

Flying Elephant BAR
(☏044-71771234; https://chennai.park.hyatt.com; Park Hyatt, 39 Velachery Rd, Guindy; drinks ₹300-575; ◷6pm-1am) Slickly contemporary and favoured by the elite, the high-energy, multi-level restaurant at the **Park Hyatt** (☏044-71771234; s/d incl breakfast from ₹14,880/15,520; ❋☏☎) morphs into a busy party spot from 11pm on Saturday. It's all very glam, with a sunken bar and garden-fresh herbs infusing

cocktails. The world-fusion food (₹650 to ₹2500), whipped up in five live kitchens, is good.

Sera the Tapas Bar
BAR

(Map p1016; ☑044-28111462; www.facebook.com/serathetapasbar; 71 Cathedral Rd, Gopalapuram; cocktails ₹275-500, tapas ₹235-325; ☉12.30pm-midnight) Where else in the world can you find DJs playing club music beneath bullfight posters next to TVs showing cricket? Sera is packed most nights with a young, fashionable crowd sipping sangria and cocktails. It's a good idea to book. Tapas include garlic prawns, fried calamari and aubergine dips; the *tortilla española* (potato omelette) is authentically good.

Lloyds Tea House
TEAHOUSE

(Map p1016; 179 Lloyds Rd, Gopalapuram; teas ₹70-180, dishes ₹150-320; ☉11am-11pm Mon-Fri, 8am-11pm Sat & Sun) Teas from across the globe collide in fabulously refreshing hot or iced concoctions at this soothing, contemporary teahouse. Pick from green teas, herbal infusions, Indian chais, Darjeeling offerings and Chinese Pu-erh teas. The Vietnamese 'Zen Garden' (iced, in a jar) is a fruity delight. Also does coffee, light meals and cakes.

10 Downing Street
PUB

(10D; Map p1016; www.10ds.in; 50 North Boag Rd, T Nagar; drinks ₹245-520, food ₹215-500; ☉11am-midnight) Casual British-themed pub (Big Ben on the wall, fish fingers on the menu, the Beatles and the Who on the sound system) with a small dance floor. It's popular with men and women, and the bar food is surprisingly good – try the Andhra 65 chicken.

☆ Entertainment

Classical Music & Dance

There's *bharatanatyam* (Tamil classical dance) and/or a Carnatic music concert going on in Chennai almost every evening. Check listings in the *Hindu* or *Times of India*.

The **Music Academy** (Map p1016; ☑044-28112231; www.musicacademymadras.in; 168/306 TTK Rd, Royapettah) is the most popular venue. The Kalakshetra Foundation (p1019) and **Bharatiya Vidya Bhavan** (Map p1016; ☑044-24643420; www.bhavanschennai.org; East Mada St, Mylapore) also stage many events, often free.

Cinema

Chennai has more than 100 cinemas, a reflection of the vibrant Tamil film industry ('Kollywood'). Most screen Tamil films, but the Phoenix Market City and Express Avenue (p1028) mall cinemas, among others, have regular English-language screenings. Tickets cost around ₹185.

🔒 Shopping

★ Nalli Silks
TEXTILES

(Map p1016; www.nallisilks.com; 9 Nageswaran Rd, T Nagar; ☉9am-9pm) Set up in 1928, the enormous, supercolourful granddaddy of Chennai silk shops sparkles with wedding saris and rainbows of Kanchipuram silks, as well as silk dhotis (long loincloths) for men.

★ Higginbothams
BOOKS

(Map p1022; higginbothams@vsnl.com; 116 Anna Salai, Anna Salai; ☉9am-8pm Mon-Sat, 10.30am-7.30pm Sun) Open since 1844, this grand white building is reckoned to be India's oldest bookshop. It has a brilliant English-language selection, including travel and fiction books, and a good range of maps.

Fabindia
CLOTHING, HANDICRAFTS

(Map p1016; www.fabindia.com; 390 TTK Rd, Alwarpet; ☉10.30am-8.30pm) 🍃 This fair-trade, nationwide chain sells stylishly contemporary village-made clothes and crafts. Perfect for picking up a kurta (long shirt with short/no collar) to throw over trousers. This branch is the brand new, two-storey flagship shop (opposite Kauvery Hospital), which has a top-floor cafe. Other branches are at **Woods Rd** (Map p1022; 3 Woods Rd, Anna Salai; ☉10.30am-8.30pm), **Express Ave** (Map p1022; 1st fl, Express Avenue Mall, White's Rd, Royapettah; ☉11.30am-9pm), **Nungambakkam** (Map p1022; 2nd fl, 9/15 Khader Nawaz Khan Rd; ☉10.30am-8.30pm), **T Nagar** (Map p1016; 44 GN Chetty Rd; ☉10.30am-8.30pm) 🍃 and **Besant Nagar** (T-25, 7th Ave, ☉10.30am-8.30pm).

Amethyst
FASHION & ACCESSORIES

(Map p1022; www.amethystchennai.com; White's Rd, Royapettah; ☉11am-7.30pm) Hidden away in a revamped warehouse surrounded by tropical greenery, Amethyst stocks luxury Indian fashion with ultracolourful contemporary flair. Downstairs, there's a dreamy flower shop and an insanely popular cafe (p1025).

Phoenix Market City
SHOPPING CENTRE

(www.phoenixmarketcity.com; 142 Velachery Main Rd, Velachery; ☉11am-10pm) Chennai's newest, most luxurious shopping mall hosts all the big-name Indian and international brands and chains, from Chanel and Zara to Bata, Lifestyle, and Global Desi (plus the city's original Starbucks). The multiplex cinema shows new release Tamil and Hollywood movies and has one IMAX screen.

Chamiers CLOTHING, HANDICRAFTS
(Map p1016; www.chamiershop.com; 106 Chamiers Rd, RA Puram; ⏱10.30am-7.30pm) On the ground floor of this popular cafe-and-boutique-complex, **Anokhi** (Map p1016; www.anokhi.com; 106 Chamiers Rd, RA Puram; ⏱10.30am-7.30pm) has wonderful, East-meets-West, hand-block-printed clothes, bedding, bags and accessories in floaty fabrics at good prices. Elegant **Amethyst Room** (Map p1016; www.amethystchennai.com; 106 Chamiers Rd, RA Puram; ⏱10.30am-7pm) next door takes things upmarket with beautiful Indian-design couture. Upstairs is **Chamiers for Men** (Map p1016; ⏱10.30am-7.30pm).

Naturally Auroville ARTS & CRAFTS
(Map p1022; www.naturallyaurovillechennai.com; 8 Khader Nawaz Khan Rd, Nungambakkam; ⏱10.15am-9pm) Colourful handicrafts and home-decor trinkets, including bedspreads, cushions, incense, scented candles and hand-made-paper notebooks, all from Auroville, near Puducherry.

Good Earth HOMEWARES
(Map p1022; www.goodearth.in; 3 Rutland Gate 4th St, Nungambakkam; ⏱11am-8pm) For the ultimate in India-chic interior design, glitzy Good Earth has everything from scented candles, gorgeously embroidered bedspreads and floral-stamped cushion covers to swanky tea-cups and delicately perfumed soaps. There's an air-conditioned cafe with cakes and pastries that are well worth your attention.

Starmark BOOKS
(www.starmark.in; 2nd fl, Phoenix Market City, Velachery; ⏱11am-9.30pm Mon-Fri, 10am-10pm Sat & Sun) Reliable modern bookshop stocking English-, Indian- and Tamil-language fiction and nonfiction, kids' books, magazines, Lonely Planet guides and other travel books. Also at **Express Avenue** (Map p1022; 2nd fl, Express Avenue, White's Rd, Royapettah; ⏱10.30am-9.30pm Mon-Fri, 10am-10pm Sat & Sun) mall.

Express Avenue MALL
(Map p1022; www.expressavenue.in; White's Rd, Royapettah; ⏱10am-10pm) This is one of Chennai's best and most central shopping malls, full of major international and Indian apparel chains. The top-floor food court is good for a quick bite.

Kumaran Silks TEXTILES
(Map p1016; www.kumaransilksonline.com; 12 Nageswaran Rd, T Nagar; ⏱9am-10pm) Housed in a beautiful building with an art deco facade and an interior of old-school wooden shelves, this is a classy place to browse saris (including 'budget saris') and plenty of Kanchipuram silk.

ⓘ Information

MEDICAL SERVICES

Apollo Hospital (Map p1022; ☏044-28290200, emergency 044-28293333; www.apollohospitals.com; 21 Greams Lane, Nungambakkam; ⏱24hr) State-of-the-art, expensive hospital, popular with 'medical tourists'.

Kauvery Hospital (Map p1016; ☏044-40006000; www.kauveryhospital.com; 199 Luz Church Rd, Mylapore; ⏱24hr) Good, private, general hospital.

MONEY

ATMs are everywhere, including at Central train station, the airport and the CMBT bus station.

Citibank (Map p1016; 50 CP Ramaswamy Rd, Alwarpet)

Citibank (Map p1016; Cathedral Rd, Teynampet)

POST

DHL (Map p1022; ☏044-42148886; www.dhl.com; 85 VVV Sq, Pantheon Rd, Egmore; ⏱9am-9pm) Secure international parcel delivery; branches around town.

Main Post Office (Map p1016; Rajaji Salai, George Town; ⏱8am-9pm Mon-Sat, 10am-4pm Sun)

Post Office (Map p1022; Kennet Lane, Egmore; ⏱10am-6pm Mon-Sat)

TOURIST INFORMATION

Indiatourism (Map p1022; ☏044-28460285, 044-28461459; www.incredibleindia.org; 154 Anna Salai, Anna Salai; ⏱9.15am-5.45pm Mon-Fri) Helpful on Chennai, plus other India destinations.

Tamil Nadu Tourism Development Corporation (TTDC; Map p1022; ☏044-25333333; www.tamilnadutourism.org; Tamil Nadu Tourism Complex, 2 Wallajah Rd, Triplicane; ⏱24hr) The state tourism body's main office takes bookings for its bus tours and answers questions. In the same building are state tourist offices from across India, mostly open 10am to 6pm. The TTDC also has a branch at Egmore train station.

TRAVEL AGENCIES

Milesworth Travel (Map p1016; ☏044-24338664; www.milesworth.com; RM Towers, 1st fl, 108 Chamiers Rd, Alwarpet; ⏱10am-6pm Mon-Fri, to 1.30pm Sat) Very professional,

BUSES FROM CHENNAI CMBT

DESTINATION	FARE (₹)	TIME (HR)	DEPARTURES
Bengaluru (Bangalore)	585-700	7-8	at least 50 daily
Coimbatore	570-600	11	15 daily
Ernakulam (Kochi)	1300	12-16	4.30pm
Hyderabad	845-1480	14	6.30pm, 7.30pm, 8.30pm
Kodaikanal	580	10-13	5pm
Madurai	500-1000	9-10	30 daily
Mamallapuram	40	2-2½	every 10min
Mysuru (Mysore)	670-1020	10	7pm, 7.45pm, 8.40pm, 10.05pm, 11.30pm
Ooty	600	12	4.30pm, 5pm, 7.15pm
Puducherry (Pondicherry)	250	4	every 15min
Thanjavur	380	8½	every 30min
Tirupati	200-350	4	every 15min
Trichy (Tiruchirappalli)	370	6½-7	every 30min
Trivandrum	1000	14	6 daily

welcoming agency that will help with all your travel needs.

ⓘ Getting There & Away

AIR

Chennai International Airport (☎044-22560551; Tirusulam) is in the far southwest of the city. The international terminal is 500m west of the domestic terminal; walkways link the two terminals.

BOAT

Passenger ships sail from George Town harbour direct to Port Blair in the Andaman Islands once or twice a month. There's no set schedule, so call for departure dates. The **Andaman Shipping Office Ticketing Counter** (☎044-25226873; www.andaman.gov.in; 2nd fl, Shipping Corporation of India, Jawahar Bldg, 17 Rajaji Salai, George Town; ☉10am-4pm Mon-Fri, to noon Sat) sells tickets – from ₹2825 for a bunk in an 80-bed dorm to ₹10,815 for a bed in a semiprivate room, with several categories in between – for the five-day trip. Book several days ahead, and take four copies each of your passport data page and Indian visa along with the originals. It can be a long process.

BUS
Government Buses

Most government buses operate from the large but surprisingly orderly **CMBT** (Chennai Mofussil Bus Terminus; Jawaharlal Nehru Rd, Koyambedu), 6km west of the centre. The most comfortable and expensive are the air-con buses (best of these are Volvo AC services), followed by the UD ('Ultra Deluxe'); these can generally be reserved in advance. You can book up to 60 days ahead at

the computerised reservation centre at the left end of the main hall, or online (www.tnstc.in).

The **Adyar Gandhinagar Bus Stand** (2nd Cross St, Adyar) is handy for bus 588 to Mamallapuram (₹40, 1½ hours, hourly 5am to 7.30pm).

Private Buses

Private buses generally offer greater comfort than non-AC government buses, at up to double the price. Their main terminal is the **Omni Bus Stand** (off Kaliamman Koil St, Koyambedu), 500m west of the CMBT, but some companies also pick up and drop off elsewhere in the city. Service information is at www.redbus.in; tickets can be booked through travel agencies.

Parveen Travels (Map p1022; ☎044-28192577; www.parveentravels.com; 11/5 Kennet Lane, Egmore) services to Bengaluru, Ernakulam (Kochi; Cochin), Kodaikanal, Madurai, Ooty (Udhagamandalam), Puducherry, Trichy and Thiruvananthapuram (Trivandrum) depart from its Egmore office.

TRAIN

Interstate trains and those heading west generally depart from Central station, while trains heading south mostly leave from Egmore. The **Advanced Reservation Office** (Map p1022; 1st fl, Chennai Central suburban station, Periyamet; ☉8am-2pm & 2.15-8pm Mon-Sat, 8am-2pm Sun), with its incredibly helpful Foreign Tourist Cell, is on the 1st floor in a separate 11-storey building just west of the main Central station building; go to counter 22. Bring photocopies of your passport visa and photo pages. Egmore station has its own **Passenger Reservation Office** (Map p1022; 1st fl, Egmore station, Egmore; ☉8am-2pm & 2.15-8pm Mon-Sat, 8am-2pm Sun).

🛈 Getting Around

TO/FROM THE AIRPORT
Bus

From the CMBT (p1029), city buses 70 and 170 to Tambaram stop on the highway across from the airport (₹12 to ₹15, 30 to 40 minutes).

Chennai Metro Rail

The Chennai Metro Rail system provides cheap, easy transport between the airport and some useful parts of the city, though its reach is limited. If you need to go somewhere along its route, it's worth taking (₹70 or less). The metro station is between the two airport terminals.

Taxi

Prepaid taxi kiosks outside the airport's international terminal charge ₹550/600 for a non-AC/AC cab to Egmore, and ₹450/500 to T Nagar. Rates are slightly lower at prepaid taxi kiosks outside the domestic terminal, and can be much lower by using Ola or Uber. Both terminals have Fast Track taxi booking counters, which can be good for long-distance trips.

Train

The cheapest airport transport option is suburban trains to/from Tirusulam station, opposite the domestic terminal parking areas, accessed via a signposted pedestrian subway under the highway. Trains run roughly every 15 minutes from 4.13am to midnight to/from Chennai Beach station (₹10, 40 minutes); stops include Nungambakkam, Egmore, Chennai Park and Chennai Fort.

AUTORICKSHAW

Most autorickshaw drivers refuse to use their meters and quote astronomical fares that come down quickly with some firm haggling. Avoid paying upfront, and always establish the price before getting into a rickshaw. Rates rise by up to 50% from 11pm to 5am.

There are prepaid autorickshaw booths outside the CMBT and 24-hour prepaid stands on the south side of Central station and outside the north and south exits of Egmore station.

Tempting offers of ₹50 autorickshaw 'city tours' sound too good to be true. They are. You'll spend the day being dragged from one shop to another.

MAJOR TRAINS FROM CHENNAI

DESTINATION	TRAIN NO & NAME	FARE (₹)	TIME (HR)	DEPARTURE
Agra	12615 Grand Trunk Express	745/1970/2880 (C)	31½	7.15pm CC
Bengaluru (Banglaore)	12007 Shatabdi Express*	775/1435 (A)	5	6am CC
	12609 Bangalore Express	150/545 (B)	6½	1.35pm CC
Coimbatore	12675 Kovai Express	180/665 (B)	7½	6.10am CC
	12671 Nilgiri Express	315/815/1150 (C)	7¾	8.55pm CC
Delhi	12621 Tamil Nadu Express	780/2050/3005 (C)	33	10pm CC
Goa	17311 Vasco Express (Friday only)	480/1310/1900 (C)	22	3pm CC
Hyderabad	12603 Hyderabad Express	405/1070/1520 (C)	13	4.45pm CC
Kochi	22639 Alleppey Express	400/1060/1505 (C)	11½	8.45pm CC
Kolkata	12842 Coromandel Express	665/1755/2555 (C)	27	8.45am CC
Madurai	12635 Vaigai Express	180/665 (B)	7¾	1.40pm CE
	12637 Pandian Express	315/815/1150 (C)	8	9.40pm CE
Mumbai	11042 Mumbai Express	540/1460/2125 (C)	25¼	12.20pm CC
Mysuru (Mysore)	12007 Shatabdi Express*	910/1815 (A)	7	6am CC
	16021 Kaveri Express	315/765/1100 (C)	9½	9.15pm CC
Tirupati	16053 Tirupathi Express	80/290 (B)	3½	2.15pm CC
Trichy (Tiruchirappalli)	12635 Vaigai Express	145/520 (B)	5	1.40pm CE
Trivandrum	12695 Trivandrum Express	470/1245/1785 (C)	16½	3.25pm CC

Departure Codes: CC – Chennai Central, CE – Chennai Egmore

*Daily except Wednesday

Fares: (A) chair/executive; (B) 2nd class/chair; (C) sleeper/3AC/2AC

CHENNAI BUS ROUTES

BUS NO	ROUTE
A1	Central–Anna Salai–RK Mutt Rd (Mylapore) –Theosophical Society–Thiruvanmiyur
1B	Parry's–Central–Anna Salai–Airport
10A	Parry's–Central–Egmore (S)–Pantheon Rd–T Nagar
11	Rattan–Central–Anna Salai–T Nagar
12	T Nagar–Pondy Bazaar–Eldham's Rd–Dr Radhakrishnan Salai–Vivekananda House
13	T Nagar–Royapettah–Triplicane
15B & 15F	Broadway–Central–CMBT
M27	CMBT–T Nagar
27B	CMBT–Egmore (S)–Bharathi Salai (Triplicane)
27D	Egmore (S)–Anna Salai–Cathedral Rd–Dr Radhakrishnan Salai–San Thome Cathedral
32A	Central–Vivekananda House
102	Broadway–Fort St George–Kamarajar Salai–San Thome Cathedral–Theosophical Society

Routes operate in both directions.

Broadway – **Broadway Bus Terminus** (Map p1016; George Town), George Town

Central – Central Station

Egmore (S) – Egmore station (south side)

Parry's – Parry's Corner

Rattan – **Rattan Bazaar Rd Bus Stop** (Map p1016; Rattan Bazaar Rd, George Town)

T Nagar – **T Nagar Bus Terminus** (Map p1016; South Usman Rd, T Nagar)

BUS

Chennai's city bus system is worth getting to know, although buses get packed to overflowing at busy times.

Fares are between ₹5 and ₹15 (up to double for express and deluxe services, and multiplied by five for Volvo AC services).

Route information is on www.mtcbus.org.

CHENNAI METRO RAIL

Chennai Metro Rail is an incredibly efficient way to get around the limited areas it serves – fortunately, stops include major transport hubs such as the airport, CMBT, and Egmore and Central railway stations. At the time of research, the system was nearly complete and travel was easy and uncrowded (but the Delhi metro was once like this too!). If you plan on using it more than once, get a metro card (₹50 refundable deposit) that you can preload with credit. Trains run from 5am to 10pm; trips cost ₹10 to ₹70.

TRAIN

Efficient, cheap suburban trains run from Beach station to Fort, Park (near Central station), Egmore, Chetpet, Nungambakkam, Kodambakkam, Mambalam, Saidapet, Guindy, St Thomas Mount, Tirusulam (for the airport), and on south to Tambaram. At Egmore station, the suburban platforms (10 and 11) and ticket office are on the station's north side. A second line branches south after Fort to Park Town, Chepauk, Tiruvallikeni (for Marina

Beach), Light House and Thirumailai (near the Kapaleeshwarar Temple). Trains run several times hourly from 4am to midnight, costing ₹10.

NORTHERN TAMIL NADU

East Coast Road

Chennai's sprawl peters out after an hour or so heading south on the East Coast Rd (ECR), at which point Tamil Nadu becomes red dirt, blue skies, palm trees and green fields, sprinkled with towns and villages (or, if you take the 'IT Expressway' inland, enormous new buildings).

There are several very worthwhile ECR stops if you're travelling between Chennai and Mamallapuram, 50km south. Among these is the low-key fishing-turned-surfing village of Kovalam (Covelong). Swimming along the coast is dangerous due to strong currents.

◉ Sights

★Cholamandal Artists' Village MUSEUM
(☏044-24490092; www.cholamandalartistsvillage. com; Injambakkam; museum Indian/foreigner ₹30/50; ⊙museum 9.30am-6.30pm) There's a

tropical bohemian groove floating around Injambakkam village, site of the Cholamandal Artists' Village, 10km south of Chennai's Adyar River. This 4-hectare artists' cooperative – founded in 1966 by artists of the Madras Movement, pioneers of modern art in South India – is a serene haven away from the world. Its fantastic art gallery features paintings and sculptures that blend tradition and postmodernity into provocative and moving expressions of imagination; it's one of the most worthwhile museums in Tamil Nadu.

DakshinaChitra   ARTS CENTRE

(☎044-27472603; www.dakshinachitra.net; East Coast Rd, Muttukadu; adult/student Indian ₹110/50, foreign ₹250/70; ☺10am-6pm Wed-Mon) DakshinaChitra, 22km south of Chennai's Adyar River, offers a fantastic insight into South India's traditional arts and crafts. Like a treasure chest of local art and architecture, this jumble of open-air museum, preserved village, artisan workshops (pottery, silk-weaving, basket-making) and galleries is strewn among an exquisite collection of real-deal traditional South Indian homes. You can see silk-weavers in action, have *mehndi* (ornate henna designs) applied and enjoy an array of shows.

Madras Crocodile Bank   ZOO

(☎044-27472447; www.madrascrocodilebank. org; Vadanemmeli; adult/child ₹40/20; ☺9-5pm Tue-Sun) Just 6km south of Kovalam, this incredible conservation and research trust is a fascinating peek into the reptile world. Founded by croc/snake-expert Romulus Whitaker, the bank has thousands of reptiles, including 17 of the world's 23 species of crocodilian (crocodiles and similar creatures), and does crucial work in maintaining genetic reserves of these animals, several of which are endangered. There's also a snake venom extraction centre (open 10am to 1pm and 2pm to 5pm), where you can watch scary serpents being milked.

Tiger Cave   HINDU SITE

(Saluvankuppam; ☺6am-6pm) FREE The Tiger Cave, 5km north of Mamallapuram, is an unfinished but impressive rock-cut shrine, dedicated to Durga (a form of Devi, Shiva's wife), probably dating from the 7th century. What's special is the 'necklace' of 11 monstrous tigerlike heads framing its central shrine-cavity, next to two carved elephant heads. At the north end of the parklike complex is a same-era rock-cut Shiva shrine. Beyond the fence lies the Subrahmanya Temple: an 8th-century granite shrine built over a brick, Sangam-era Murugan temple.

Kovalam (Covelong)

☎044 / POP 8120

This low-key fishing village, 30km south of Chennai and 20km north of Mamallapuram, has sprung into the spotlight for having probably the best surfing waves on the Tamil Nadu coast. It's now an increasingly popular travellers' hang-out, hosting a high-profile surfing/yoga festival and offering all kinds of water sports – everything from surfing and kayaking to blissful beachfront yoga.

Covelong Point Surf, Music & Yoga Festival (p1014) is a popular event in August.

For surf classes or surfing friends, head to 'social surfing school' **Covelong Point** (☎9840975916; www.covelongpoint.com; 10 Pearl Beach, Ansari Nagar; per hour board rental/surf classes ₹300/500; ☺hours vary), under the watch of Kovalam's original local surf pioneer Murthy. There are options for all levels, or try kayaking, diving, windsurfing and stand-up paddleboarding (SUP). The team also runs a lovely, relaxed **Surf Turf** (☎9884272572; www.surfturf.in; 10 Pearl Beach, Ansari Nagar; r incl breakfast ₹2065-5190, 2-person 'surf & stay' packages from ₹7000; ❄☎), a surf-mad B&B guesthouse with an unbelievably beautiful beachfront location.

Most buses travelling between Chennai and Mamallapuram will drop you at the ECR's Kovalam turnoff. Taxis to/from Mamallapuram or Chennai cost around ₹1000.

SURFING TAMIL NADU

The Tamil Nadu coast has become an increasingly popular destination for learning how to surf, windsurf, sea kayak and scuba dive. If you'd like to get on – or under – the water, check out these places (listed from north to south), some of which have great activity-and-accommodation packages:

➡ Kovalam: Covelong Point (p1032)

➡ Mamallapuram: Mumu Surf School (p1035)

➡ Puducherry: Kallialay Surf School (p1044)

➡ Rameswaram: Quest Academy (p1072)

Mamallapuram (Mahabalipuram)

📞 044 / POP 15,170

Mamallapuram, 50km south of Chennai, was the major seaport of the ancient Pallava kingdom based at Kanchipuram. A wander around the town's magnificent, World Heritage–listed temples and carvings inflames the imagination, especially at sunset.

In addition to ancient archaeological wonders, salty air and coastal beauty, there's also the traveller hub of Othavadai and Othavadai Cross Sts, where restaurants serve pasta, pizza and pancakes, and shops sell Tibetan trinkets. The town's buzzing, growing surf scene is another attraction.

'Mahabs', as most call it, is less than two hours by bus from Chennai, and many travellers make a beeline straight here. It's small and laid-back, and sights can be explored on foot or by bicycle.

◉ Sights

You can easily spend the better part of a day exploring Mamallapuram's marvellous temples, caves and rock carvings. Most were carved from the rock during the 7th-century reign of Pallava king Narasimhavarman I, whose nickname Mamalla (Great Wrestler) gave the town its name. Official Archaeological Survey of India guides can be hired at sites.

★ Arjuna's Penance   HINDU MONUMENT

(West Raja St; ⏰24hr) FREE The crowning masterpiece of Mamallapuram's stonework, this giant relief carving is one of India's greatest ancient artworks. Inscribed on two huge, adjacent boulders, the Penance bursts with scenes of Hindu myth and everyday South Indian life. In the centre, *nagas* (snakebeings) descend a once water-filled cleft, representing the Ganges. To the left Arjuna (hero of the Mahabharata) performs self-mortification (fasting on one leg), so that the four-armed Shiva will grant him his most powerful weapon, the god-slaying Pasupata.

Some scholars believe the carving actually shows the sage Bagiratha, who did severe penance to obtain Shiva's help in bringing the Ganges to earth. Shiva is attended by dwarves, and celestial beings fly across the carving's upper sections. Below Arjuna/Bagiratha is a temple to Vishnu (mythical ancestor of the Pallava kings), with sages, deer and

a lion. The many wonderfully carved animals include a herd of elephants and – humour amid the holy – a cat mimicking Arjuna's penance to a crowd of mice.

South along the road from Arjuna's Penance are the unfinished **Panch Pandava Mandapa** (West Raja St; ⏰6am-6pm) FREE cave temple; the **Krishna Mandapa** (West Raja St; ⏰6am-6pm) FREE, which famously depicts Krishna lifting Govardhana Hill to protect cows and villagers from a storm sent by Indra; an **unfinished relief carving** (West Raja St; ⏰24hr) FREE of similar size to Arjuna's Penance; and the empty **Dharmaraja Cave Temple** (Five Rathas Rd; ⏰6am-6pm) FREE.

★ Trimurti Cave Temple   HINDU TEMPLE

(Mamallapuram Hill; ⏰6am-6pm) FREE At the northern end of the Mamallapuram Hill compound, the Trimurti Cave Temple depicts the Hindu 'trinity' amid guardian figures: Brahma (left), Shiva (centre) and Vishnu (right). A fine carving of elephants adorns the back side of the rock.

Shore Temple   HINDU TEMPLE

(Beach Rd; combined 1-day ticket with Five Rathas Indian/foreigner ₹30/500, video ₹25; ⏰6am-6pm) Standing like a magnificent fist of rock-cut elegance overlooking the sea, surrounded by gardens and ruined courts, the two-towered Shore Temple symbolises the heights of Pallava architecture and the maritime ambitions of the Pallava kings. Its small size belies its excellent proportion and the supreme quality of the carvings, many now eroded into vaguely Impressionist embellishments. Built under Narasimhavarman II in the 8th century, it's the earliest significant free-standing stone temple in Tamil Nadu.

Five Rathas   HINDU TEMPLE

(Pancha Ratha; Five Rathas Rd; combined 1-day ticket with Shore Temple Indian/foreigner ₹30/500, video ₹25; ⏰6am-6pm) Huddled together at the southern end of Mamallapuram, the Five Rathas were, astonishingly, all carved from single large rocks. Each of these fine 7th-century temples was dedicated to a Hindu god and is now named after one or more of the Pandavas, the five hero-brothers of the epic Mahabharata, or their common wife, Draupadi. The *rathas* were hidden in the sand until excavated by the British 200 years ago.

Ratha is Sanskrit for 'chariot', and may refer to the temples' form or to their function as vehicles for the gods. It's thought that they

Mamallapuram (Mahabalipuram)

Mamallapuram (Mahabalipuram)

didn't originally serve as places of worship, but as architectural models.

The first *ratha* on the left after you enter is the Draupadi Ratha, in the form of a stylised South Indian hut. It's dedicated to the demon-fighting goddess Durga, who looks out from inside, standing on a lotus, and is depicted on the outside walls. Female guardians flank the entrance; a huge sculpted lion, Durga's mount, stands outside.

Next, on the same plinth, is the 'chariot' of the most important Pandava, the Arjuna Ratha, dedicated to Shiva. Its pilasters, miniature roof shrines and small octagonal dome make it a precursor of many later South Indian temples. A huge Nandi sits behind. Shiva (leaning on Nandi, south side) and other gods are depicted on the temple's outer walls.

The barrel-roofed Bhima Ratha was never completed, as evidenced by the missing north-side colonnade; inside is a shrine to Vishnu. The Dharmaraja Ratha, tallest of the temples, is similar to the Arjuna Ratha but one storey higher, with lion pillars. The carvings on its outer walls mostly represent gods, including the androgynous Ardhanarishvara (half Shiva, half Parvati) on the east side. King Narasimhavarman I appears at the west end of the south side.

The Nakula-Sahadeva Ratha (named after twin Pandavas) stands aside from the other four and is dedicated to Indra. The life-size stone elephant beside it is one of India's most famous sculpted elephants. Approaching from the gate to the north you see its back end first, hence its nickname Gajaprishthakara (elephant's backside).

Tour groups tend to arrive around 10am, so do yourself a favour and arrive earlier!

🏃 Activities

Numerous places in town offer massage (₹750 to ₹1500), yoga (per hour ₹300) and ayurvedic treatments, at similar rates. Ask fellow travellers, question therapists carefully and, if you have any misgivings, don't proceed.

Mumu Surf School SURFING
(📞9789844191; www.mumusurfindia.com; Othavadai St; 90min group/private classes ₹1100/1300; ⊗8am-6pm) Popular, well-organised school for all levels and board rental (per hour/day ₹250/1000); also runs beach clean-ups and the relaxed Sandy Bottom cafe.

Sri Durga AYURVEDA
(📞9840288280; sridurgaayurclinic@gmail.com; 35 Othavadai St; massages ₹750-1500, yoga per hour ₹300; ⊗7am-10pm) Massages and ayurvedic treatments (male therapists for men, female for women).

👉 Tours

Travel XS CYCLING, BIRDWATCHING
(📞044-27443260; www.travel-xs.com; 123 East Raja St; bicycle tours per person ₹800; ⊗9.30am-8pm Mon-Sat year-round, to 1pm Sun Nov-Mar) Runs half-day bicycle tours (minimum two people) to nearby villages, visiting local potters and observing *kolam* drawing (elaborate chalk, rice-paste or coloured powder designs, also called *rangoli*), and organises day trips, including to Kanchipuram and (seasonally) Vedanthangal Bird Sanctuary (📞044-22351471; adult/child ₹20/5, camera/video ₹25/150; ⊗6am-6pm Nov-Mar).

🛏 Sleeping

Budget-friendly backpacker guesthouses and a few midrange hotels are strung along Othavadai and Othavadai Cross Sts and the narrow village lanes off them. There are several top-end resorts on the northern edge of town. Prices rise on busy weekends and holidays.

Rajalakshmi Guesthouse GUESTHOUSE $
(📞9840545858; www.rajalakshmiguesthouse.in; 5 Othavadai Cross St; r ₹600-700, with AC ₹1200; ❄🛜) This friendly ochre-walled guesthouse has some of the best budget rooms in town. Those without AC are simple but well kept, while AC rooms are newer and perfectly comfortable. Hammocks hang on both floors and the in-house restaurant makes good food. Online discounts can bring AC room prices below ₹1000.

Silver Moon GUESTHOUSE $
(📞9952009952; silvermoonmahabs@gmail.com; 11 Othavadai Cross St; r ₹800-1500, with AC ₹1500-2000; ❄🛜) Conveniently attached to Joe's Cafe (p1036), the standard rooms here feel stylistically dated but are clean and in good shape. Deluxe rooms are spacious, with artistic wall murals and plenty of character for this price range. One of the better budget options in town.

Sri Harul Guest House GUESTHOUSE $
(📞9384620137; sriharul@gmail.com; 181 Bajanai Koil St, Fishermen's Colony; r ₹800, with AC

₹1000-1200;) The beach sits right below your balcony when you land one of the half-dozen sea-view rooms at Sri Harul, one of Mamallapuram's better seafront budget deals. Rooms are basic, medium-sized and quite clean.

Hotel Daphne
HOTEL $

(9894282876; www.moonrakersrestaurants.com; 24 Othavadai Cross St; r with/without AC ₹1700/900;) Non-AC rooms are perfectly acceptable and clean if nothing fancy, but the Daphne's seven air-con rooms are great value (especially top-floor rooms 13 and 14), most with four-poster beds, balconies and cane swing-chairs. The shaded, immaculate, fairy-lit courtyard, cordial staff and free wi-fi are other drawcards. Singles may get discounts if it's slow.

Hotel Mahabs
HOTEL $$

(044-27442645; www.hotelmahabs.com; 68 East Raja St; incl breakfast r ₹1625, with AC ₹2460-3775;) Friendly Mahabs is centred on a pretty mural-lined pool surrounded by lush gardens. Boring brown is the room theme, but they're very clean and comfy, with individual sit-out spaces. There's a decent in-house restaurant.

Radisson Blu Resort Temple Bay
RESORT $$$

(044-27443636; http://radissonblu.com/hotel-mamallapuram; 57 Kovalam Rd; r incl breakfast from ₹11,100;) The Radisson's luxurious chalets, villas and bungalows are strewn across manicured gardens stretching 500m to the beach. Somewhere in the middle is India's longest swimming pool (220m). Rooms range from large to enormous; the most expensive have private pools. The Radisson also offers Mamallapuram's finest (priciest) dining and a top-notch ayurvedic spa (massage ₹2500). It's ridiculously popular. Best rates online.

SLEEPING PRICE RANGES

Accommodation price ranges for a double room with private bathroom in Tamil Nadu:

₹ less than ₹1400

₹₹ ₹1400–₹4500

₹₹₹ more than ₹4500

Eating

Joe's Cafe
CAFE $

(Othavadai Cross St; snacks ₹45-130; 7.30am-8.30pm) A relaxed cafe with some 'sidewalk' seating, Joe's serves up crêpes, burgers and other snacks, along with good lassis, juices and coffee drinks. The iced cappuccino is perfect!

Mamalla Bhavan
SOUTH INDIAN $

(South Mada St; mains ₹55-90, meals ₹80-105; 7am-9.30pm) For an authentically good, wallet-friendly South Indian fill-up, swing by this simple, packed-out veg restaurant pumping out morning *idli, vada* and dosa, ₹20 filter coffee and banana-leaf lunchtime thalis. It's right beside the bus stand.

Gecko Restaurant
MULTICUISINE $$

(www.gecko-web.com; 37 Othavadai St; mains ₹180-380; 9am-10pm;) Two friendly brothers run this cute blue-and-yellow-walled spot sprinkled with colourful artwork and wood carvings, and with daily seafood specials chalked up on boards. The offerings and prices aren't that different from other tourist-oriented restaurants, but the personalised service and excellent cooking makes it worth a visit.

Le Yogi
MULTICUISINE $$

(8870944267, 9840706340; 19 Othavadai St; mains ₹190-450; 7.30am-11pm;) Some of Mamallapuram's best continental food. The pasta, pizza, sizzlers, crepes and *momos* (Tibetan dumplings) are genuine and tasty, service is exuberant, and the chilled-out setting, with bamboo posts, floor cushions and lamps dangling from a thatched roof, has a classic backpacker vibe.

Water's Edge Cafe
MULTICUISINE $$$

(044-27443636; www.radissonblu.com/hotel-mamallapuram; Radisson Blu Resort Temple Bay, 57 Kovalam Rd; mains ₹625-1150; 24hr) The Radisson's pool-side 'cafe' offers everything from American pancakes to grilled tofu, Indian veg dishes, pan-Asian cuisine and a fantastic breakfast buffet (₹1190). It's expensive, but smart and popular.

Shopping

The roar of electric stone-grinders has just about replaced the tink-tink of chisels in Mamallapuram's stone-carving workshops, enabling sculptors to turn out ever more granite sculptures (of varying quality), from

TAMIL NADU KANCHIPURAM

MAMALLAPURAM HILL

Many interesting monuments, mostly dating from the late 7th and early 8th centuries, are scattered across the rock-strewn hill on the west side of town. It takes about an hour to walk around the main ones. The hill is open from 6am to 6pm and has entrances on West Raja St and just off Five Rathas Rd.

Straight ahead inside the northernmost West Raja St entrance stands a huge, impossible-to-miss boulder with the inspired name of **Krishna's Butterball** (⊙6am-6pm) FREE, immovable but apparently balancing precariously. Beyond the rocks north of here is the Trimurti Cave Temple (p1033), honouring the Hindu 'trinity': Brahma (left), Shiva (centre) and Vishnu (right), flanked by guardians. On the back of this rock is a beautiful group of carved elephants.

South of Krishna's Butterball you reach the **Ganesh Ratha** (⊙6am-6pm) FREE, carved from a single rock, with lion-shaped pillar bases. Once a Shiva temple, it became a shrine to Ganesh (Shiva's elephant-headed son) after the original lingam was removed. Southwest of here, the **Varaha Mandapa** (⊙6am-6pm) FREE houses some of Mamallapuram's finest carvings, including columns with seated lions. The left panel shows Vishnu's boar avatar, Varaha, lifting the earth out of the oceans. The outward-facing panels show Vishnu's consort Lakshmi (washed by elephants) and Durga, while the right-hand panel has Vishnu in his eight-armed giant form, Trivikrama, overcoming the demon king Bali.

A little further south, then east (up to the left), is the 16th-century **Raya Gopura** (Olakkanatha Temple; ⊙6am-6pm) FREE, probably an unfinished *gopuram* (gateway tower). West just up the hill is the finely carved **Lion Throne** (⊙6am-6pm) FREE, depicted roaring. The main path continues south to the **Ramanuja Mandapa** (⊙6am-6pm) FREE and up to Mamallapuram's **lighthouse** (Indian/foreigner ₹10/25, camera/video ₹20/25; ⊙10am-5pm). Southwest of the lighthouse is the rock-carved **Mahishamardini Mandapa** (⊙6am-6pm) FREE, with excellent scenes from the Puranas (Sanskrit stories from the 5th century AD). The left-side panel shows Vishnu sleeping on the coils of a snake; on the right, Durga bestrides her lion vehicle while killing the demon-buffalo Mahisha. Inside the central shrine, Murugan sits between his parents, Shiva and Parvati.

₹100 pendants to person-sized Ganeshas (good luck getting one home!). There are also some decent art galleries, tailors and antique shops.

Apollo Books　　　　　　　BOOKS
(150 Fishermen's Colony; ⊙9.30am-9.30pm) Good collection of books in several languages, to sell and swap.

Southern Arts & Crafts　ANTIQUES, HANDICRAFTS
(☑044-27443675; 72 East Raja St; ⊙10.30am-10.30pm) Expensive but beautiful furniture, paintings, sculpture and carvings acquired from local homes, along with new quality sculpture.

❶ Information

Suradeep Hospital (☑044-27442448; 15 Thirukula St; ⊙24hr) Recommended by travellers.

Mamallapuram's **tourist office** (☑044-27442232; Kovalam Rd; ⊙10am-5.30pm Mon-Fri) is one of the most helpful in the entire state.

❶ Getting There & Away

From the **bus stand** (East Raja St), bus 599 heads to Chennai's Adyar/Gandhinagar Bus Terminus (₹45, 1½ hours) every 30 minutes from 6.50am to 8.30pm. Buses to Kanchipuram (₹50, two hours) leave at 8am, noon and 5.30pm.

Virtually all other useful buses to and from Mamallapuram stop at the ECR Bypass Rd Bus Stop, about 1km north of the town centre, including bus 118 to Chennai's CMBT (₹45, two hours) half-hourly, 4am to 8pm. (From there, the Chennai Metro connects to the airport, plus Central and Egmore railway stations.) Buses to Puducherry (₹150, two hours) stop roughly every 15 minutes.

Kanchipuram

☑044 / POP 165,000

Kanchipuram, 80km southwest of Chennai, was capital of the Pallava dynasty during the 6th to 8th centuries, when the Pallavas created the great stone monuments of Mamallapuram. Today a typically hectic modern

Kanchipuram

Indian town, it's famous for its numerous important and vibrant temples (and their colourful festivals), some dating from Pallava, Chola or Vijayanagar times. It's also known for its high-quality silk saris, woven on hand looms by thousands of families in the town and nearby villages. Silk and sari shops are strung along Gandhi Rd, southeast of the centre, though their wares are generally no cheaper than at Chennai silk shops.

Kanchipuram is easily visited in a day trip from Mamallapuram or Chennai, but it's worth seeing some of the temples after dark.

◉ Sights

All temples have free admission, though you may have to pay small amounts for shoe-keeping and/or cameras. Ignore claims that there's an entrance fee for non-Hindus.

Ekambareshwara Temple　　HINDU TEMPLE
(Ekambaranathar Temple; Ekambaranathar Sannidhi St; phone-camera/camera/video ₹10/20/100; ⊙6am-12.30pm & 4-8.30pm) Of South India's five Shiva temples associated with each of the five elements, this 12-hectare precinct is the shrine of earth. You enter beneath the 59m-high, unpainted south *gopuram*, whose lively carvings were chiselled in 1509 under Vijayanagar rule. Inside, a columned hall leads left into the central compound, which

Nandi faces from the right. The inner sanctum (Hindus only) contains a lingam made of earth and a mirror chamber where the central Shiva image is reflected in endless repetition.

Kamakshi Amman Temple　　HINDU TEMPLE
(Kamakshi Amman Sannidhi St; ⊙5.30am-noon & 4-8pm) This imposing temple, dedicated to Kamakshi/Parvati, is one of India's most important places of *shakti* (female energy/deities) worship, said to mark the spot where Parvati's midriff fell to earth. It's thought to have been founded by the Pallavas. The entire main building, with its gold-topped sanctuary, is off limits to non-Hindus, but the compound itself is beautiful, including a square tank with a shrine in the middle. It's wonderfully lit at night, making that the best time to visit.

Vaikunta Perumal Temple　　HINDU TEMPLE
(Vaikundaperumal Koil St; ⊙6am-noon & 4-8pm) This 1200-year-old Vishnu temple is a Pallava creation. The passage around the central shrine has lion pillars and a wealth of weathered but extremely detailed wall panels, some depicting historical events. The main shrine, uniquely spread over three levels and with jumping *yalis* (mythical lion creatures) on the exterior, contains images of Vishnu standing, sitting, reclining and riding his preferred mount, Garuda (half-eagle, half-man). It's well worth seeing.

Varadaraja
Perumal Temple　　HINDU TEMPLE
(Devarajaswami Temple; off Kanchipuram-Chengalpattu Rd, Little Kanchipuram; 100-pillared hall ₹1, camera/video ₹5/100; ⊙7.30am-12.30pm & 3.30-8pm) This enormous 11th-century Chola-built temple in southeast Kanchipuram is dedicated to Vishnu. Non-Hindus cannot enter the central compound, but the artistic

highlight is the 16th-century '100-pillared' marriage hall, just inside the (main) western entrance. Its pillars (actually 96) are superbly carved with animals, monsters, warriors and several erotic sculptures. *Yalis* frame its inner southern steps and at its corners hang four stone chains, each carved from a single rock.

Every 40 years the temple tank is drained, revealing a huge wooden statue of Vishnu that is worshipped for 48 days. After 2019's showing, the next is due in 2059.

Kailasanatha Temple   HINDU TEMPLE

(SVN Pillai St; ⊘6am-6.30pm, inner sanctum 6am-noon & 4-6.30pm) Kanchipuram's oldest temple is small, interesting mainly for its stonework. Dedicated to Shiva, it was built in the 8th century by Pallava king Narasimhavarman II (Rajasimha), who also created Mamallapuram's Shore Temple. Quieter than other temples in town, it has – sadly – been heavily restored, as the remaining older, eroded reliefs are much more evocative than the repaired ones.

🖝 Tours

RIDE   CULTURAL

(Rural Institute for Development Education; ✆044-27268223; www.rideindia.org; 48 Periyar Nagar, Little Kanchipuram; half-day tours incl lunch ₹1000) Kanchipuram's famous silk-weaving industry has traditionally depended heavily on child labour. This long-standing NGO helps reduce the industry's child-labour numbers, from over 40,000 in 1997 to under 4000 by 2007 (its own estimates), and empower the rural poor, especially women. It also runs some interesting tours that provide insights into the lives of people working in the industry.

🛏 Sleeping & Eating

RIDE   GUESTHOUSE $

(Rural Institute for Development Education; ✆044-27268223; www.rideindia.org; 48 Periyar Nagar,

Little Kanchipuram; per person ₹1000; ❋) This NGO offers simple, clean rooms at its base in a residential area, 5km southeast of central Kanchipuram. If things are quiet, the friendly owners put you up in their own colourful home next door. Home-cooked breakfast (₹150), lunch (₹250) and dinner (₹250) available. Book a day ahead. It's signposted 1km east of the Varadaraja Perumal Temple.

GRT Regency   HOTEL $$

(✆044-27225250; www.grthotels.com; 487 Gandhi Rd; r incl breakfast ₹2800; ❋🛜) The cleanest, comfiest and most stylish rooms in Kanchi, with marble floors, tea/coffee makers and glass-partitioned showers. The GRT's smart-ish Dakshin (mains ₹260-660; ⊘7am-11pm; 🛜) restaurant is overpriced, but offers a lengthy multicuisine menu of breakfast omelettes, South Indian favourites and tasty tandoori. Book online for discounts.

SSK Grand   HOTEL $$

(✆9443221774; www.hotelsskgrand.com; 70 Nellukara St; d incl breakfast ₹2230; ❋🛜) This brand new hotel has good-sized rooms with thick mattresses, couches, tea kettles and glassed-in showers. With online discounts that can knock ₹700 off the price, it's the best value in town.

Hotel Saravana Bhavan   SOUTH INDIAN $

(✆044-27226877; www.saravanabhavan.com; 66 Nellukara St; mains ₹80-250, meals ₹100-160; ⊘6am-10.30pm) A reliably good pure-veg restaurant with delicious dosa, a few North Indian surprises, a welcome air-con hall and thalis on the 1st floor. There's another (scruffier) branch (✆044-27222505; 504 Gandhi Rd; mains ₹80-250, meals ₹100-160; ⊘6am-10.30pm) just west of Gandhi Rd.

ℹ Getting There & Away

Suburban trains to Kanchipuram (₹25, 2½ hours) leave Chennai's Egmore station (platform 10 or 11) roughly hourly from 4.30am to 8.30pm.

BUSES FROM KANCHIPURAM

DESTINATION	FARE (₹)	TIME (HR)	DEPARTURES
Chennai	65-80	2	every 10min 3.30am-10.30pm
Mamallapuram	56	2	5.30am, 9.30am, 10.50am, 2.55pm, 4pm, 8pm
Puducherry (Pondicherry)	72	3	hourly 5.45am-9.20pm
Tiruvannamalai	110	3	every 30min 5.10am-9.30pm
Vellore	50	2	every 30min 3.30am-11pm

ℹ Getting Around

➔ **Bicycle hire** (Kamarajar St; per day ₹50; ⊙7.30am-8pm) is available at stalls outside the bus stand.

➔ An autorickshaw for a half-day tour of the five main temples (around ₹500) will inevitably involve stopping at a silk shop.

Tiruvannamalai

♪ 04175 / POP 145,280

There are temple towns, there are mountain towns, and then there are temple-mountain towns where God appears as a phallus of fire. Welcome to Tiruvannamalai, one of Tamil Nadu's holiest destinations.

Set below boulder-strewn Mt Arunachala, this is one of South India's five 'elemental' cities of Shiva; here the god is worshipped in his fire incarnation as Arunachaleshwar. At every full moon, 'Tiru' swells with thousands of pilgrims who circumnavigate Arunachala's base in a purifying ritual known as Girivalam; at any time you'll see Shaivite priests, sadhus (spiritual men) and devotees gathered around the Arunachaleshwar Temple.

Tiru's reputation for strong spiritual energies has produced numerous ashrams, and the town now attracts ever-growing numbers of spiritual-minded travellers.

◉ Sights

★ **Arunachaleshwar Temple**   HINDU TEMPLE
(Annamalaiyar Temple; www.arunachaleswarar temple.tnhrce.in; ⊙5.30am-12.30pm & 3.30-9.30pm) This 10-hectare temple is one of India's largest. Its oldest parts date to the 9th century, but the site was a place of worship long before that. Four huge, unpainted white gopurams mark the entrances; the main, 17th-century eastern one rises 13 storeys (an astonishing 66m), its sculpted passageway depicting dancers, dwarves and elephants. During festivals the Arunachaleshwar is awash with golden flames and the scent of burning ghee, as befits the fire incarnation of Shiva, Destroyer of the Universe.

Mt Arunachala   MOUNTAIN
This 800m-high extinct volcano dominates Tiruvannamalai – and local conceptions of the element of fire, which supposedly finds its sacred abode in Arunachala's heart. Devout barefoot pilgrims make the 14km (four-hour) circumambulation of the mountain, stopping at eight famous linga, especially on full-moon and festival days. The inner path is closed for the foreseeable future, but it's possible to circle around on the main road, or climb the hill past two caves where Sri Ramana Maharshi lived and meditated (1899–1922).

The hot ascent to the top opens up superb views of Tiruvannamalai, and takes five or six hours round trip: start early and take water. An unsigned path across the road from the northwest corner of the Arunachaleshwar Temple leads the way up past homes and the two caves, Virupaksha (about 20 minutes up) and Skandasramam (30 minutes). Women are advised not to hike alone, and it's suggested that no one go up after dark due to 'too many drunk boys'. Note that the trail to the top closes a month or two before the Deepam festival (p1014), but the caves remain accessible.

If you aren't that devoted, buy a Giripradakshina map (₹15) from the bookshop at Sri Ramana Ashram, hire a bicycle from a shop on the roadside 200m east of the ashram (per day ₹40) and ride around. Or make an autorickshaw circuit for about ₹400 (up to double at busy times).

🏃 Activities

Yoga, meditation and ayurveda sessions are advertised everywhere in the main ashram area.

Sri Ramana Ashram   MEDITATION
(Sri Ramanasramam; ♪04175-237200; www.sri ramanamaharshi.org; Chengam Rd; ⊙5am-9pm) This tranquil ashram, 2km southwest of Tiruvannamalai centre amid green, peacock-filled grounds, draws devotees of Sri Ramana Maharshi, one of the first Hindu gurus to gain an international following; he died here in 1950 after half a century in contemplation. Visitors can meditate and attend daily pujas (prayers) and chantings, mostly in the samadhi hall (closed 12.30pm to 2pm), where the guru's body is enshrined.

**Arunachala
Animal Sanctuary**   VOLUNTEERING
(♪9442246108; www.arunachalasanctuary.com; Chengam Rd; ⊙9am-5.30pm) ✎ Aimed at sterilisation, castration, rabies control, rehoming and affordable treatments, this nonprofit sanctuary, at the western end of Tiruvannamalai's ashram area, provides shelter to over 200 homeless and/or injured dogs, plus a few cats. Travellers may be able to help with bathing, feeding, applying creams or

simply playing with the animals – it's best to show up after 10.30am. Prepare to be deeply moved.

🛏 Sleeping & Eating

Rainbow Guest House   GUESTHOUSE $
(☎04175-236408, 9443886408; rainbowguest housetiru@gmail.com; 27/28 Lakshmanan Nagar, Perumbakkam Rd; s/d ₹600/1250; 🛜) A great-value, spick-and-span spot 800m southwest off Chengam Rd. Beyond the psychedelic exterior, wood-carved doors reveal simple, immaculate, fan-cooled rooms with hot wa-ter and tiled floors. Doubles are almost like suites: huge, some with small kitchens. Staff are gracious, cane chairs dangle along corri-dors and there are fantastic Mt Arunachala views from the spartan rooftop terrace.

Arunaalaya Residency   HOTEL $
(☎8098083062; www.arunaalaya.com; 120 Se-shatri Mada St; r ₹800, with AC ₹1960-3080; ❄) Though slightly overpriced if you want AC, Arunaalaya offers large, cool, clean-ish marble-floored rooms with colourful walls around two small garden patios, up a lane north off Chengam Rd. The non-AC rooms are good value. '

Sunshine Guest House   GUESTHOUSE $$
(☎04175-235335; www.sunshineguesthouseindia. com; 5 Annamalai Nagar, Perumbakkam Rd; s/d ₹1625/2350; ❄🛜) In a blissfully quiet spot 1km southwest of the main ashram area, this colourful guesthouse is fronted by gardens. Singles feel flimsy, like cheap mobile homes. Doubles are huge with plenty of character,

Hotel Arunachala   HOTEL $$
(Arunachala Inn; ☎04175-228300; www.hotel arunachala.com; 5 Vada Sannathi St; r ₹950, with AC s ₹1500, d ₹1680-2750; ❄) Right next to the Arunachaleshwar Temple's east entrance, Hotel Arunachala is clean and decent with pretensions to luxury in the marblesque floors, ugly furniture, keen management and lobby fish pond. Standard rooms feel halfway conceived; deluxe rooms are much better. Downstairs, pure-veg **Hotel Sri Arul Jothi** (dishes ₹40-80; ⊙5.30am-10.30pm) pro-vides good South Indian dishes (thalis ₹80 to ₹120).

Shanti Café   CAFE $
(www.facebook.com/shanticafetiru; 115A Chengam Rd; dishes ₹60-200, drinks ₹30-90; ⊙8.30am-8.30pm; 🛜) This popular and relaxed cafe with floor-cushion seating, up a lane off Chengam Rd, serves wonderful croissants, cakes, baguettes, pancakes, juices, coffees, teas, breakfasts and Indian meals with an extra-healthy twist. Omelettes are a good choice. It's run by a delightful team and there's an **internet cafe** (www.shantionline. com; per hour ₹25; ⊙8.30am-1.30pm & 3-7pm Mon-Sat) downstairs.

★Dreaming Tree   CAFE $$
(☎8870057753; www.dreamingtree.in; Ramana Nagar; mains ₹250-290; ⊙8.30am-10pm) 🖋 Super-chilled Dreaming Tree dishes out

TAMIL NADU TIRUVANNAMALAI

GINGEE FORT

With three separate hilltop citadels and a 6km perimeter of cliffs and thick walls, the ru-ins of enormous **Gingee Fort** (☎04145-222072; Gingee; Indian/foreigner ₹25/300; ⊙8am-5pm) rise out of the Tamil plain, 37km east of Tiruvannamalai, like castles misplaced by the Lord of the Rings. It was constructed mainly in the 16th century by the Vijayanagars and was later occupied by the Marathas, Mughals, French and British, then abandoned in the 19th century. The fort's sheer scale, dramatic beauty and peaceful setting make it a very worthwhile stop.

Today, few foreigners make it here, but Gingee is popular with domestic tourists for its starring role in various films. The main road linking Tiruvannamalai and Puducherry cuts between the fortified hills, just west of Gingee town. Of the three citadels, the easiest to reach, Krishnagiri, rises north of the road. To the south are the highest of the three, Rajagiri, and the most dismal and least interesting, Chakklidurg (which you can't climb). Ticket offices (with maps) are at the foot of Krishnagiri and Rajagiri.

Gingee is on the Tiruvannamalai–Puducherry bus route, with buses from Tiruvan-namalai (₹37, one hour) every 10 minutes. Hop off at the fort to save a trip back out from Gingee town. A taxi between Tiruvannamalai and Puducherry with a two- to three-hour stop at Gingee costs around ₹3000.

BUSES FROM TIRUVANNAMALAI

DESTINATION	FARE (₹)	TIME (HR)	DEPARTURES
Chennai	120-140	5	every 10min
Kanchipuram	63	3	hourly
Puducherry (Pondicherry)	63	3	hourly
Trichy (Tiruchirappalli)	123	5	every 45min
Vellore	37-50	2½	every 10min

huge portions of exquisite, health-focused veg fare, prepped with mostly organic ingredients, on a breezy thatched rooftop loaded with low-slung purple-cushioned booths. Expect fabulous 'hippie salads' and tofu stir-fries, luscious breakfasts, and all kinds of cakes, juices, lassis, lemonades and organic coffees. Signs lead the way (500m) across the road from Sri Ramana Ashram.

Tasty Café   CAFE $$
(Lakshmanan Nagar, Perumbakkam Rd; mains ₹100-240; ⊙7am-10pm) In a peaceful, shady courtyard of plastic chairs and wooden tables, friendly Tasty Café does well-prepared Indian and continental food, including pizza, pasta, pancakes and salads. It's 700m south-west off Chengam Rd. Try the daily specials.

Shopping

Shantimalai Handicrafts Development Society   ARTS & CRAFTS
(www.smhds.org; 83/1 Chengam Rd; ⊙9am-7pm Mon-Sat) Beautiful bedspreads, bags, incense, candles, oils, bangles, scarves and cards, all made by local village women.

ⓘ Getting There & Away

The **bus stand** (Polur Rd) is 800m north of the Arunachaleshwar Temple, and a ₹50 to ₹60 autorickshaw ride from the main ashram area. For Chennai, the best options are the hourly Ultra Deluxe services.

ⓘ Getting Around

Bike hire (per hour/day ₹10/40) is available opposite Sri Ramana Ashram (p1040), in the southwest part of town.

Puducherry (Pondicherry)

📞0413 / POP 1.3 MILLION

The union territory of Puducherry (formerly Pondicherry; generally known as 'Pondy') was under French rule until 1954. Some people here still speak French (and English with French accents). Hotels, restaurants and 'lifestyle' shops sell a seductive vision of the French-subcontinental aesthetic, enhanced by Gallic creative types and Indian artists and designers. The internationally famous Sri Aurobindo Ashram and its offshoot just north of town, Auroville, draw large numbers of spiritually minded visitors. Thus Pondy's vibe: less faded colonial-era *ville*, more bohemian-chic, New Age–meets–Old World hang-out on the international travel trail.

The older 'French' part of town (where you'll probably spend most of your time) is full of quiet, clean streets, lined with bougainvillea-draped colonial-style townhouses numbered in an almost logical manner. Newer Pondy is typically, hectically South Indian.

Enjoy fabulous shopping, French food (hello steak!), beer (*au revoir* Tamil Nadu alcohol taxes), and plenty of yoga and meditation.

⦿ Sights

Seafront   WATERFRONT
(Goubert Ave) Pondy is a seaside town, but that doesn't make it a beach destination; the city's sand is a thin strip of dirty brown that slurps into a seawall of jagged rocks. But Goubert Ave (Beach Rd) is a killer stroll, especially at dawn and dusk when half the town takes a romantic wander. In a stroke of genius, authorities have banned traffic here from 6pm to 7.30am.

Sri Aurobindo Ashram   ASHRAM
(📞0413-2233649; www.sriaurobindoashram.org; Marine St; ⊙8am-noon & 2-6pm) FREE Founded in 1926 by Sri Aurobindo and a French-born woman, 'the Mother', this famous spiritual community has about 2000 members in its many departments. Aurobindo's teachings focus on 'integral yoga' that sees devotees work in the world, rather than retreat from it. Visits to the main, grey-walled ashram building are cursory: you see the flower-festooned samadhi of Aurobindo and the Mother, then the bookshop. Ashram-

accommodation guests can access other areas and activities. Evening meditation around the samadhi is for everyone.

There are daily weekday ashram tours (per person ₹50), which begin at 8.30am with a film about Sri Aurobindo and the Mother and include visits to various ashram workshops where you can see batik work, hand-printing on saris, handloom weaving and more; enquire online (www.sri aurobindoautocare.com) or at the ashram's Bureau Central (p1050).

Puducherry Museum   MUSEUM
(http://art.puducherry.gov.in/museum.html; St Louis St; Indian/foreigner ₹10/50; ⊙9am-6.30pm Tue-Sun) Goodness knows how this convert-

ed late-18th-century villa keeps its artefacts from disintegrating, considering there's a whole floor of French-era furniture sitting in the South Indian humidity. On the ground floor look especially for Chola, Vijayanagar and Nayak bronzes, and pieces of ancient Greek and Spanish pottery and amphorae (storage vessels) excavated from Arikamedu, a once-major trading port just south of Puducherry. Upstairs is Governor Dupleix' bed.

**Institut Français
de Pondichéry**   LIBRARY
(☑0413-2231616; www.ifpindia.org; 11 St Louis St; ₹100; ⊙9am-6pm Mon-Fri) This grand 19th-century neoclassical building is also a flourishing research institution devoted to

TAMIL NADU TEMPLES

Tamil Nadu is home to some of India's most spectacular temple architecture and sculpture, and few parts of the country are as fervent in their worship of the Hindu gods. Its 5000-odd shrines are constantly abuzz with worshippers flocking in for *puja* (offering or prayer), and colourful temple festivals abound. More Tamil temples are dedicated to the various forms of Shiva than to any other deity, including his depiction as Nataraja, the cosmic dancer, who dances in a ring of fire with two of his four hands holding the flame of destruction and the drum of creation. Tamils also have a soft spot for Shiva's peacock-riding son Murugan (also Kartikeya or Skanda), who is intricately associated with their cultural identity.

The special significance of many Tamil temples makes them goals of countless Hindu pilgrims from all over India. The Pancha Sabhai Sthalangal are the five temples where Shiva is believed to have performed his cosmic dance (chief among them Chidambaram). Then there's the Pancha Bootha Sthalangal, the five temples where Shiva is worshipped as one of the five elements: Tiruvannamalai's Arunachaleshwar Temple (p1040), fire; Kanchipuram's Ekambareshwara Temple (p1038), earth; Chidambaram's Nataraja Temple (p1052), space; Trichy's Sri Jambukeshwara Temple (p1060), water; and, in Andhra Pradesh, Sri Kalahasteeswara Temple (www.srikalahasthitemple.com; off Sannidhi Rd; ⊙5.30am-9pm), air. Each of Kumbakonam's nine Navagraha temples is the abode of one of the nine celestial bodies of Hindu astronomy – key sites given the importance of astrology in Hindu faith. Architecturally, Brihadishwara Temple (p1057) in Thanjavur is a priceless gem.

Typical Tamil temple design features tall layered entrance towers *(gopurams)*, encrusted with often colourfully painted sculptures of gods and demons; halls of richly carved columns *(mandapas)*; a sacred water tank; and a series of compounds *(prakarams)*, one within the next, with the innermost containing the central sanctum where the temple's main deity resides. The earliest Tamil temples were small rock-cut shrines; the first free-standing temples were built in the 8th century AD; *gopurams* first appeared around the 12th century.

Admission to most temples is free, but non-Hindus are often not allowed inside inner sanctums. At other temples priests may invite you in and in no time you are doing *puja*, having an auspicious *tilak* mark daubed on your forehead and being hassled for a donation.

Temple touts can be a nuisance, but there are also many excellent guides; use your judgment and be on the lookout for badge-wearing official guides.

A South Indian Journey by Michael Wood and *Southern India: A Guide to Monuments, Sites & Museums* by George Michell are great reads if you're interested in Tamil temple culture. TempleNet (www.templenet.com) is one of the best online resources.

PUDUCHERRY'S CATHEDRALS

Pondy hosts one of India's best collections of over-the-top cathedrals. *Merci*, French missionaries. **Our Lady of Immaculate Conception Cathedral** (Mission St; ☺6am-noon & 3-7pm), completed in 1791, is a sky-blue, hot-yellow and cloud-white typically Jesuit edifice in a Goa-like Portuguese style. The brown-and-white grandiosity of the **Sacred Heart Basilica** (Subbaiah Salai; ☺5.30am-1pm & 6-8pm) is set off by beautifully restored stained glass and a Gothic sense of proportion. The twin towers and dome of the mellow-pink-and-yellow Notre Dame des Anges, built in the 1850s, look sublime in the late-afternoon light. Its smooth limestone interior was made using eggshell plaster; in the square opposite, there's a Joan of Arc statue.

Indian culture, history and ecology. Visitors can browse books in the beach-facing library.

Sri Manakula Vinayagar Temple
HINDU TEMPLE

(www.manakulavinayagartemple.com; Manakula Vinayagar Koil St; ☺5.45am-12.30pm & 4-9.30pm) Pondy may have more churches than most Indian towns, but the Hindu faith still reigns supreme. Pilgrims, tourists and the curious get a head pat from the temple elephant at this centuries-old temple dedicated to Ganesh, which contains around 40 skilfully painted friezes.

◉ French Quarter

Pocketed away just behind the seafront is a series of cobbled bougainvillea-wrapped streets and white-and-mustard buildings in various states of romantic *déshabillé*, otherwise known as Puducherry's French Quarter. A do-it-yourself heritage walk could start at the French consulate (p1197), near the north end of Goubert Ave, the seafront promenade (p1042). Head south, passing the 1836 **lighthouse** (Goubert Ave), then turn inland to shady, landscaped **Bharathi Park** (Compagnie St; ☺6am-7pm) FREE. The neoclassical governor's residence, **Raj Nivas** (Rangapillai St), faces the park's north side. Return to the seafront at the **Gandhi Memorial** (Goubert Ave), wander south past **Notre Dame des Anges** (Dumas St; ☺6-

10am & 4-7pm) church, and then potter south through the 'white town' – Dumas, Romain Rolland, Suffren and Labourdonnais Sts. Towards the southern end of Dumas St, pop in to the beautiful **École Française d'Extrême-Orient** (www.efeo.fr; 16-19 Dumas St; ☺8.30am-noon & 2-5.30pm Mon-Fri) FREE, with its extensive library of Indology.

A lot of restoration has been happening in this area: if you're interested in Pondy's architectural heritage, check out INTACH Pondicherry (www.intachpondicherry.org). The tourist office website (www.pondytourism.in) details heritage walks.

🏃 Activities

Yoganjali Natyalayam YOGA

(☏0413-2241561; www.icyer.com; 25 II Cross, Iyyanar Nagar; ☺9am-6pm) One-on-one, 10-lesson introductory yoga courses (₹7000) at the central-Pondy branch of the renowned International Centre for Yoga Education & Research. Contact the office at least a day before you'd like to begin.

Kallialay Surf School SURFING

(☏9442992874; www.surfschoolindia.com; Serenity Beach, Tandriankuppam; 1hr private classes ₹1800, board rental per 90min ₹400; ☺hours vary) Surfing continues to soar in popularity along Tamil Nadu's coast, and this long-standing, well-equipped, Spanish-run school, 5km north of Puducherry, offers everything from beginner sessions to intensive two-week courses.

La Casita CULTURAL PROGRAMS

(www.lacasitaindia.com; 147 Eshwaran Koil St; classes ₹250-350; ☺11am-3.30pm & 5.30-9pm Tue-Sun) A fun-filled Latino-inspired arts centre offering drop-in (and longer-term) yoga and Bollywood classes, along with tango, salsa, capoeira and Zumba. There's also a cosy rooftop travellers' cafe.

🎓 Courses

Sita CULTURAL PROGRAMS

(☏0413-4200718; www.pondicherry-arts.com; 22 Candappa Moudaliar St; classes ₹300-1200; ☺9am-1pm & 3-7pm Mon-Sat) This energetic Franco-Indian cultural centre runs a host of activities, open to visitors (even for a single session): Indian cooking, *bharatanatyam* or Bollywood dance, *kolam* making, *mehndi* (henna 'tattoos'), yoga, pilates, ayurveda and sari 'workshops', plus brilliant cycling and photography tours.

International Centre for Yoga Education & Research
YOGA

(Ananda Ashram; ☑0413-2622902; www.icyer. com; 16A Mettu St, Chinnamudaliarchavady, Kottukuppam; ☉10am-2pm) Rigorous six-month yoga-teacher-trainings are offered at Ananda Ashram, north of town, from October to March; fill out the application on the website and submit it well in advance.

👉 Tours

Storytrails
WALKING

(☑7339147770; www.storytrails.in; 551 Kamaraj Salai, 1st fl; tours per person ₹1100-6000; ☉7am-6.30pm) Chennai-born Storytrails runs terrific story-themed jaunts through the French Quarter – the perfect walking introduction to Pondy's historical and architectural delights.

🛏 Sleeping

If you've been saving for a splurge, this is the place: Puducherry's lodgings are as good as South India gets. Local heritage houses combine colonial-era romanticism with modern comfort and chic French-inspired styling, and there are some beautifully updated properties. Most of these rooms would cost five times as much in Europe. Book ahead for weekends, when some places raise prices.

Park Guest House
ASHRAM GUESTHOUSE $

(☑0413-2233644; parkgh@sriaurobindoashram. org; 1 Goubert Ave; r with/without AC ₹1500/950; ❋) Pondy's most sought-after ashram guesthouse, thanks to its wonderful seafront position, with the best-value air-con rooms around but no advance bookings. All front rooms face the sea and have a porch or balcony. There's a garden for yoga or meditation, plus vegetarian buffet lunches (₹150) and bicycle hire (per day ₹60).

International Guest House
ASHRAM GUESTHOUSE $

(INGH; ☑0413-233669; ingh@aurosociety.org; 47 NSC Bose St; s ₹450, d ₹550-700, s/d with AC ₹750/1680; ❋) The sparse, spotless rooms here, adorned with a single photo of the Mother, make for good-value ashram lodgings. It's very popular: book three weeks ahead.

Kailash Guest House
GUESTHOUSE $

(☑0413-2224485; http://kailashguesthouse.in; 43 Vysial St; s/d ₹1100/1500, with AC ₹1250/1750; ❋)

Good-value Kailash has simple, superclean rooms with well-mosquito-proofed windows, friendly management and a covered top-floor communal area. The lobby is a comfy but classy communal area. One of the best budget options in town.

⭐ Les Hibiscus
GUESTHOUSE $$

(☑0413-2227480, 9442066763; www.leshibiscus. in; 49 Suffren St; incl breakfast s ₹2000-2750, d ₹2250-3300; ❋@🛜) Mango-yellow Les Hibiscus has just a handful of fabulous high-ceilinged rooms with antique beds, coffee makers and a mix of quaint Indian art and old Pondy photos, at astoundingly reasonable prices. (The top-floor single room is a great deal.) The whole place is immaculately styled, fresh breakfasts are fantastic and management is genuinely friendly and helpful. Book well ahead.

Patricia Guest House
GUESTHOUSE $$

(☑0413-2335130; http://patriciaguesthouse.word press.com; 20/28 Francois Martin St; r ₹3300-4500; ❋🛜) A hot-orange (unsigned) heritage home has been lovingly transformed into a unique, relaxed, colour-bursting retreat in the northern French Quarter. Each of the seven rooms (some with separate bathrooms) surprises with individual character, and all are packed with South Indian art, printed fabrics and vibrant paintwork. The upper-floor 'cottage' opens on to its own thatched-roof terrace. Breakfast available (₹200).

Gratitude
GUESTHOUSE $$

(☑0413-2226029; www.gratitudeheritage.in; 52 Romain Rolland St; r incl breakfast ₹3540-7080; ❋🛜) A wonderfully tranquil 19th-century house (no shoes, no TVs, no children), sun-yellow Gratitude has been delightfully restored. Nine individually styled rooms sprawl across two floors around a tropically shaded courtyard; a couple of them could use another dose of refurbishment, so look at a few if you can. There's a roof terrace for yoga and massages. Breakfast is delicious.

Coloniale Heritage Guest House
GUESTHOUSE $$

(☑0413-2224720; http://colonialeheritage.com; 54 Romain Rolland St; r incl breakfast ₹2950-4700; ❋🛜) This leafy colonial-era haven with six comfy rooms (some up steep stairs) is crammed with character thanks to the owner's impressive collection of gem-studded Thanjavur paintings, Ravi Varma lithographs and other 19th- and 20th-century

Puducherry (Pondicherry)

South Indian art. One room has a swing, another its own balcony. Breakfast is laid out in the sunken garden-side patio.

Hotel de Pondichéry
HERITAGE HOTEL $$
(☏0413-2227409; www.hoteldepondichery.com; 38 Dumas St; incl breakfast s ₹2500, d ₹3000-5000; ❄❀❤) A colourful heritage spot with 14 comfy, quiet and spacious rooms, some sporting semi-open bathrooms, most with splashes of original modern art. A few are beginning to show some wear and tear, but most are in great shape. The excellent restaurant, Le Club (p1049), takes up the charming front courtyard and staff are lovely.

Red Lotus
BOUTIQUE HOTEL $$
(☏8870344334; www.redlotuspondicherry.com; 48-58 Nehru St; r ₹2465; ❄❤) Behind the flaming-red doors of a revamped merchant house, this glossy oriental-inspired guesthouse overlooks a busy street in the thick of Pondy's bazaar area. Cheery staff lead you to modish rooms decorated with witty wall slogans, floral murals, varnished wood and tea/coffee kits. The roof-terrace cafe-bar is full of aqua-cushioned sofas.

Nila Home Stay
GUESTHOUSE $$
(☏9443537209; www.nilahomestay.com; 18 Labourdonnais St; r ₹2800; ❄❤) A simple but

Puducherry (Pondicherry)

brilliantly characterful and well-kept French Quarter guesthouse run by welcoming hosts, with a range of fresh, colourful rooms (some with kitchens and/or terraces), handy communal kitchens and a low-key lounge area.

★ La Villa   BOUTIQUE HOTEL $$$
(☏0413-2338555; www.lavillapondicherry.com; 11 Surcouf St; r incl breakfast ₹13,300-20,500; ❉⊛≋) Queen of local boutique hotels is this intimate, six-room 19th-century beauty, sleekly updated by one of Pondy's top French-architect teams. From curved wooden bedheads to cocoonlike swing-chairs and abstract artwork, rooms blend white-on-white luxury with bold, contemporary design. It's impeccably styled, there's an upmarket patio restaurant, and you can breakfast overlooking the turquoise rooftop pool.

★ Villa Shanti   HERITAGE HOTEL $$$
(☏0413-4200028; www.lavillashanti.com; 14 Suffren St; r incl breakfast ₹8100-14,000; ❉⊛) Oc-

cupying a 100-year-old building revamped by two French architects, Villa Shanti puts an exquisitely contemporary twist on the French Quarter heritage hotel. Beautiful modern rooms combine superchic design with typically Tamil materials and colonial-style elegance: four-poster beds, Chettinadu tiles, walk-through bathrooms, Tamil-language murals. The sunken courtyard houses a hugely popular restaurant (p1049) and bar.

Villa Helena   HERITAGE HOTEL $$$
(☏0413-2226789; www.villa-helena-pondicherry.com; 13 Rue Bussy; incl breakfast s ₹2500-4500, d ₹4000-8000; ❉⊛) This gorgeous 19th-century French-run mansion is infused with contemporary character. Spread along plant-dotted galleries, immaculate, soft-toned rooms are done up in tasteful minimalist style, with stripy bedding, printed cushions, vintage furniture and stylish modern bathrooms. There's wonderful continental

cooking in the romantic courtyard restaurant.

Palais de Mahé
HERITAGE HOTEL $$$

(☎0413-2345611; www.cghearth.com; 4 Rue Bussy; r incl breakfast ₹23,000-28,100; ❄️🛜🏊) Three colonnaded floors of swish, soaring-ceilinged rooms with colonial-style wood furnishings and varnished-concrete floors rise around a seductive turquoise pool at this imposing heritage hotel. The first-rate rooftop restaurant serves impressive, creative fusion cuisine, including cooked-to-order breakfasts. From May through September rates drop by 30%.

Maison Perumal
HERITAGE HOTEL $$$

(☎0413-2227519; www.cghearth.com; 44 Perumal Koil St; r incl breakfast ₹13,300-14,850; ❄️🛜) Secluded rooms with colourful flourishes, antique beds and photos of the original owners surround two pillared patios at this renovated 130-year-old home, pocketed away in Pondy's less touristic Tamil Quarter. The excellent Tamil/French **restaurant** (☎0413-2227519; www.cghearth.com; 44 Perumal Koil St; lunch mains ₹350-550, dinner ₹1200; ⏰12.30-3pm & 7.30-9.30pm) cooks everything from market-fresh ingredients and gives culinary demonstrations. Heritage walking tours are offered and guests can use the pool at sister property Palais de Mahé.

Hotel de L'Orient
HERITAGE HOTEL $$$

(☎0413-2226111; www.dunewellnessgroup.com; 17 Romain Rolland St; r incl breakfast ₹7700-12,800; ❄️🛜) This grand restored 18th-century mansion has breezy verandas, keen staff and antique-filled old-world rooms in all shapes and sizes: some are cosy attics, others palatial, many have four-poster beds. A place to get that old Pondy feel while enjoying polished service and French, creole (French Indian) or South Indian food in the courtyard restaurant, Chez Francis (p1049).

Dune Mansion Calvé
HERITAGE HOTEL $$$

(☎0413-2970500; www.dunewellnessgroup.com; 36 Vysial St; r incl breakfast ₹6500-8850; ❄️🛜) 🏊
The old Tamil Quarter has almost as many mansions as the French Quarter but is off most tourists' radars. Reincarnated under environmentally friendly management, this 150-year-old heritage choice, on a quiet, tree-shaded street, mixes a soaring sense of space with a teak-columned atrium, Chettinadu-tiled floors, and 10 elegantly styled rooms featuring free-standing bathtubs and solar-powered hot-water systems.

Promenade
BOUTIQUE HOTEL $$$

(☎0413-2227750; www.sarovarhotels.com; 23 Goubert Ave; r incl breakfast ₹7670-9600; ❄️🛜) The Promenade is a flashy boutiquelike beachfront spot owned by the swish Hidesign group, with upscale, oriental-themed, (mostly) sea-facing rooms. If you're looking for modern and stylish, this is your hotel. The elegant rooftop restaurant serves good, pricey pan-Asian dishes and cocktails in a breezy, leafy, lantern-lit setting – you're forking out more for the location.

Eating

Puducherry is a culinary highlight of Tamil Nadu. You can get great South Indian cooking, well-prepped French and Italian cuisine, and delicious fusion food. If you've been missing cheese or have a craving for croissants, you're in luck, and *everyone* in the French Quarter does good brewed coffee and crêpes. There are some fabulous arty cafes too.

It's also worth exploring some of the options around nearby Auroville (p1051), especially in Kuilapalayam village.

Surguru Spot
SOUTH INDIAN $

(☎0413-4308084; www.hotelsurguru.com; 12 Nehru St; mains ₹115-140, thalis ₹150-220; ⏰6.30am-11pm) Fill up on crispy dosa and *vada,* pillowy *idli* and spicy lunchtime thalis in a smarter-than-average AC dining hall with yellow-washed pillars, just a couple of blocks from Sri Aurobindo Ashram. There's another **branch** (☎0413-4308083; 235 Mission St; mains ₹70-140, thalis ₹135-190; ⏰7am-10.40pm) in the Tamil Quarter.

Gelateria Montecatini Terme
ICE CREAM $

(GMT; Goubert Ave; ice creams ₹50-80; ⏰11am-11.30pm) Join the seafront crowds for creamy, authentic Italian gelato in tropical-tastic flavours like mango, watermelon and guava – or try something more exotic, like Himalaya salted caramel or Dubai Cream, with milk, chocolate, almonds and dates.

Baker Street
CAFE $

(123 Rue Bussy; dishes ₹40-200; ⏰7am-9pm; 🛜) A popular upmarket French-style bakery that does impressively delectable cakes, sandwiches, croissants and biscuits. The baguettes, brownies and quiches hold their own too. Eat in or takeaway.

★ **Café des Arts**   CAFE $$
(www.facebook.com/café-des-arts-155637583166;
10 Suffren St; dishes ₹140-370; ☺8.30am-6.30pm
Wed-Mon; 🛜) This bohemian cafe would look
perfectly at home in Europe, but this is Pon-
dy, so there's a cycle rickshaw in the garden.
Perfectly prepared dishes range from salads
to crêpes, baguettes, omelettes and toasties.
Coffees and fresh juices are great. The old
town-house setting is casual yet refined, with
low tables and lounge chairs arranged across
several rooms and an outdoor terrace.

Kasha Ki Aasha   CAFE $$
(www.kkapondy.com; 23 Surcouf St; mains ₹150-
295; ☺10am-8pm Thu-Tue; 🛜) A friendly all-
female team whips up great pancake breakfasts, lunches and cakes on the thatched
rooftop of this colonial-era-house-turned-
craft-shop-and-cafe, where the all-veg fusion
food includes 'European thalis' and 'Indian
enchiladas' (which feel a little overpriced for
what you get). The floaty fabrics and leather
sandals for sale downstairs come direct from
their makers. Live music Saturday night.

Le Café   CAFE $$
(☑0413-2334949; Goubert Ave; dishes ₹115-260;
☺24hr) Pondy's only seafront cafe is good for
croissants, cakes, salads, baguettes, break-
fasts and organic South Indian coffee (hot or
iced), plus welcome fresh breezes from the
Bay of Bengal. It's popular, so you often have
to wait for, or share, a table. But hey, it's all
about the location.

★ **Villa Helena**   CONTINENTAL, INDIAN $$$
(☑0413-4210806;   www.villa-helena-pondicherry.
com; 13 Rue Bussy; mains ₹340-720; ☺noon-3pm
& 7-10pm) One of Pondy's favourite culinary
teams heads up this fashionable continental-
Indian eatery, launched in 2016 in a dreamy,
lantern-lit patio engulfed by tropical gardens
and lined with white-columned corridors.
The menu leaps around the globe, delivering
luscious creative salads alongside beef fillets,
pastas, cheese boards, Indian classics and
the odd fusion invention.

★ **Villa Shanti**   CONTINENTAL, INDIAN $$$
(☑0413-4200028;   www.lavillashanti.com;   14
Suffren St; mains ₹250-780; ☺noon-2.30pm &
7.30-10.30pm) Smart candlelit tables in a
palm-dotted, pillared courtyard attached
to a colourful cocktail bar create a casually
fancy vibe at this packed-out hotel restau-
rant, one of Pondy's hottest dining spots.

The building's contemporary Franco-Indian
flair runs right through the North Indian/
European menu. While portions are small,
flavours are exquisite, and there are some
deliciously creative veg dishes. Open all day
for snacks and drinks.

Chez Francis   CREOLE, FRENCH $$$
(☑9159550341; 17 Romain Rolland St; mains ₹260-
590; ☺7.30-10am, 12.30-2.30pm & 7.30-10.30pm)
Fabulous French and creole cooking – such
as the fantastic prawn curry – is the order
of the day at this atmospheric courtyard restaurant at the heart of the Hotel de L'Orient.

Palais de Mahé   FUSION $$$
(☑0413-2345611; www.cghearth.com; 4 Rue Bussy;
mains ₹350-600; ☺12.30-3pm & 7-10.30pm) On a
magical roof terrace just back from Pondy's
seafront promenade, the Palais de Mahé's
superb restaurant specialises in ambitious,
beautifully presented fusion dishes, best
enjoyed alongside a signature Prohibition-
inspired cocktail. Seafood and steaks are per-
fectly prepared.

La Pasta World   ITALIAN $$$
(☑9994670282; www.facebook.com/lapastaworld;
55 Vysial St; mains ₹310-500; ☺5-10pm) Pasta lovers should make a pilgrimage to this
casual little Tamil Quarter spot with just a
few check-cloth tables. Run by Italians, sauces are authentically yummy and served over
perfect pasta in an open-plan kitchen as big
as the dining area. No alcohol: it's all about
the food.

Le Club   CONTINENTAL, INDIAN $$$
(☑0413-2227409; www.leclubraj.com; 38 Dumas
St; mains ₹370-550; ☺11.30am-3pm & 6.30-10pm)
The steaks (with sauces like blue cheese or
Béarnaise), pizzas, pastas and crêpes are all
top-class at this romantically lit garden res-
taurant. Tempting local-themed options in-
clude creole prawn curry, veg-paneer kebabs
and Malabar-style fish. Servings are large,
and there are plenty of wines, mojitos and
margaritas to wash it all down.

🍷 **Drinking & Nightlife**

Although Pondy is one of the better places
in Tamil Nadu to knock back beers, closing
time is a strictly enforced 11pm. Despite low
alcohol taxes, you'll only really find cheap
beer in 'liquor shops' and their darkened
bars. Hotel restaurants and bars make good
drinking spots.

L'e-Space BAR

(2 Labourdonnais St; cocktails ₹200, dishes ₹250-350; ⊙5-11pm daily & 10am-3pm Sat & Sun) A quirky little semi-open-air rooftop bar/cafe lounge that's friendly, laid-back and sociable, and which does good cocktails (assuming the bartender hasn't disappeared) and food.

🛍 Shopping

With all the yogis congregating here, Pondy specialises in boutique-chic-meets-Indian-bazaar fashion and souvenirs. There's some beautiful and original stuff, a lot of it produced by Sri Aurobindo Ashram or Auroville. Nehru St and MG Rd are the shopping hot spots; boutiques line the French Quarter.

★Kalki FASHION & ACCESSORIES

(134 Mission St; ⊙9.30am-8.30pm) Dazzling, jewel-coloured silk and cotton fashion, as well as accessories, incense, oils, scented candles, handmade-paper trinkets and more, mostly made at Auroville, where there's another **branch** (visitor centre; ⊙9.30am-6.30pm).

LivingArt Lifestyles FASHION & ACCESSORIES

(14 Rue Bazar St Laurent; ⊙10am-2pm & 3-8pm Tue-Sat) Breezy, boho-chic, block-printed dresses, skirts, trousers and crop-tops in fun-but-fashionable geometric patterns (all handmade at Auroville) sit side-by-side with beautifully crafted saris from across India.

Anokhi FASHION & ACCESSORIES

(www.anokhi.com; 1 Caserne St; ⊙10am-7.30pm) A sophisticated Jaipur-born boutique popular for its beautiful, bold block-printed garments with a traditional-turns-modern twist, and gorgeous colourful bedspreads, tablecloths, scarves, bags, homewares and accessories.

Auroshikha INCENSE

(www.auroshikha.com; 28 Marine St; ⊙9am-1pm & 3-7pm Tue-Sun) An endless array of incense, perfumed candles, essential oils and other scented trinkets, made by Sri Aurobindo Ashram.

Geethanjali ANTIQUES

(www.geethanjaliartifacts.com; 20 Rue Bussy; ⊙10am-8.30pm Mon-Sat, to 7.30pm Sun) The kind of place where Indiana Jones gets the sweats, this antique shop sells sculptures, carved doors, wooden chests, paintings and furniture sourced from Puducherry's colonial and even precolonial history. It ships to Europe for ₹20,000 per cu metre (check that your purchases aren't subject to export restrictions).

Fabindia CLOTHING, TEXTILES

(www.fabindia.com; 223 Mission St; ⊙10.30am-8.30pm) 🌿 Going strong since 1960, the Fabindia chain stocks stunning handmade, fair-trade products made by villagers using traditional craft techniques, and promotes rural employment. This branch has wonderful cotton and silk contemporary Indian clothing, along with high-quality fabrics, tablecloths, beauty products and furniture.

La Boutique d'Auroville FASHION & ACCESSORIES

(www.auroville.com; 38 Nehru St; ⊙9.30am-1pm & 2.30-8pm) Perfect for browsing through Auroville-made crafts: jewellery, pottery, clothing, shawls, handmade cards and herbal toiletries.

Hidesign FASHION & ACCESSORIES

(www.hidesign.com; 69 Nehru St; ⊙9am-9.30pm) Established in Pondy in 1978, Hidesign sells elegantly made designer leather bags, briefcases, purses, wallets and belts, at reasonable prices, and has outlets across the world.

Focus BOOKS

(204 Mission St; ⊙9.30am-1.30pm & 3-9pm Mon-Sat) Good collection of India-related and other English-language books (including Lonely Planet guides).

ⓘ Information

MEDICAL SERVICES

New Medical Centre (☎0413-2261200; www.nmcpondy.com; 470 Mahatma Gandhi Rd; ⊙24hr) Recommended private clinic and hospital.

TOURIST INFORMATION

Bureau Central (☎0413-2233604; bureau central@sriaurobindoashram.org; Ambour Salai; ⊙6am-noon & 4-6pm) Information on ashram-run accommodation, plus exhibitions on Sri Aurobindo and the Mother.

Tourist office (☎0413-2339497; www.pondy tourism.in; 40 Goubert Ave; ⊙9am-5pm) Has tours on its website. The office itself is pretty useless.

TRAVEL AGENCIES

Parveen Travels (☎0413-2201919; www. parveentravels.com; 288 Maraimalai Adigal Salai; ⊙24hr), near the bus stand, is a reliable option for private buses.

ⓘ Getting There & Away

AIR

Puducherry's airport is 6km northwest of the town centre. At the time of research, it was only

BUSES FROM PUDUCHERRY

The **bus stand** (Maraimalai Adigal Salai) is 2km west of the French Quarter, though buses to many major destinations run from Villupuram (₹35, one hour, every 15 minutes), 38km west of Puducherry.

Private bus companies, operating mostly overnight to various destinations, have offices along Maraimalai Adigal Salai west of the bus stand. Parveen Travels (p1050) is reliable.

DESTINATION	FARE (₹)	TIME (HR)	DEPARTURES
Bengaluru	270	8	10.30am, 7.30pm
Chennai	160 (Volvo AC 300)	4	every 10min; Volvo AC 6 daily
Chidambaram	80	2	every 30min
Kumbakonam	80	3	6.30am, 7.30am, 9.30am
Mamallapuram	72	2	every 10min
Tiruvannamalai	88	3	every 30min

being served by SpiceJet, with one daily flight to/from Bengaluru and another to/from Hyderabad.

TRAIN

Puducherry train station has just a few services. One daily train goes to Chennai Egmore at 5.35am, 2nd class only (₹90, four hours). Leave from Villupuram for many more services. The station has a computerised booking office for trains throughout India.

❶ Getting Around

➡ Pondy's flat streets are great for getting around by foot.

➡ Autorickshaws are plentiful, but drivers often quote absurdly high rates, so prepare to haggle before you get in. A trip from the bus stand to the French Quarter costs ₹100. From Pondy to Auroville costs ₹300.

➡ A good way to explore Pondy and Auroville is by rented bicycle or motorbike from **outlets** (Mission St; per day bicycle ₹100, scooter or motorbike ₹250-400) on northern Mission St, between Nehru and Vysial Sts.

Auroville

📞 0413 / POP 2953

Auroville, 'the City of Dawn', is a place that anyone with idealistic leanings will find compelling. It's an international community dedicated to peace, sustainability and 'divine consciousness', where people from across the globe, ignoring creed, colour and nationality, work together to build a universal, cash-free, nonreligious township. Some 12km northwest of Puducherry, Auroville was founded in 1968 by 'the Mother', cofounder of Puducherry's Sri Aurobindo Ashram (p1042).

Tucked into the jungle are more than 100 scattered settlements, with about 2500 residents of 52 nationalities – some 60% of Auro-

villians are foreign. Visiting offers a glimpse into this self-styled utopia, where you can bliss out on the peaceful setting, the oddly beautiful Matrimandir (p1052) and the easygoing friendliness. What's more, you'll find some excellent restaurants and cafes within Auroville and surrounding villages. The community benefits the area with a variety of projects, from schools and IT to organic farming, renewable energy and handicrafts production, employing 4000 to 5000 local villagers – but like most idealistic endeavours, it has a shadow, too, and some outsiders accuse Auroville's inhabitants of self-indulgent escapism.

◉ Sights

Auroville isn't directly geared for tourism – most inhabitants are just busy getting on with their lives – but it does have a good **visitor centre** (📞 0413-2622239; www.auroville.org; ☺ 9.30am-1pm & 1.30-5pm) with information desks, exhibitions and Auroville products. You can buy a handbook and map (₹20), and watch a 10-minute video. Free passes for external viewing of the Matrimandir (p1052), Auroville's 'soul', a 1km woodland walk away, are handed out here.

Visitors are free to wander Auroville's 10-sq-km network of roads and tracks. With two million trees planted since Auroville's foundation, it's a lovely shaded space. It's best explored by bicycle, with rentals available behind the visitor centre for ₹30 per half-day (with a ₹500 deposit).

If you're interested in getting to know Auroville, authorities recommend you stay at least 10 days and join an introduction and orientation program. To get properly involved, you'll need to come as a volunteer for six to 12 months. Contact the **Auroville**

Guest Service (☎0413-2622675; http://guest-service.auroville.org; Solar Kitchen Bldg; ⊙9.30am-12.30pm & 2-4pm Mon-Fri, 9.30am-12.30pm Sat) for advice on active participation.

Matrimandir   NOTABLE BUILDING
(⊙passes issued 9.30am-1pm & 1.30-4.45pm Mon-Sat, to 1pm Sun) `FREE` To some, the large, golden, almost spherical Matrimandir (Auroville's focal point), set amid red (cement) lotus petals and surrounded by pristine green parkland, evokes divine consciousness. To others, it looks like a giant golf ball or an alien spaceship. The main inner chamber, lined with white marble, houses a large glass crystal orb that suffuses a beam of sunlight around the space, conducive to deep meditation. To view it from outside, get a free pass from the visitor centre (p1051).

If you want to meditate inside, you must reserve one to six days ahead, in person, at Auroville's **Matrimandir Access Office** (☎0413-2622204; mmconcentration@auroville.org. in; visitor centre; ⊙10-11am & 2-3pm Wed-Mon).

🛏 Sleeping & Eating

Auroville has more than 80 guesthouses and homestays of hugely varied comfort levels and budgets, from ₹200 dorm beds to ₹5400 two-person cottages with pools.

Guest Accommodation Service (☎0413-2622704; http://guesthouses.auroville.org; visitor centre; ⊙9.30am-12.30pm & 2-5pm) offers advice on guesthouses in Auroville, but bookings are direct with each property. It's best to research and book through the website.

Dreamers Cafe   CAFE $
(visitor centre; snacks ₹80-150; ⊙8am-8pm) An open-air cafe featuring delicious pastries, sandwiches and other quick bites, along with top-notch coffee.

❶ Getting There & Away

➡ The main turning to Auroville from the East Coast Rd is at Periyar Mudaliarchavadi village,

6km north of Puducherry. From there it's 6km west to the visitor centre.

➡ A one-way autorickshaw to or from Puducherry costs ₹300. Otherwise, rent a bicycle or motorcycle from outlets (p1051) on northern Mission St in Puducherry.

CENTRAL TAMIL NADU

Chidambaram

☑04144 / POP 62,150

There's one reason to visit Chidambaram: the great temple complex of Nataraja (p1052), Shiva as the Dancer of the Universe. One of the holiest of all Shiva sites, this also happens to be a Dravidian architectural highlight. It's easily visited on a day trip from Puducherry, or en route between Puducherry and Tharangambadi or Kumbakonam.

Most accommodation is near the temple or the bus stand (500m southeast of the temple). The train station is 1km further southeast.

Opposite the bus stand, the busy, friendly **Saradharam** (☎04144-221336; 19 VGP St; r incl breakfast ₹1150, with AC ₹2000-2300; ❋🛜) is as good as it gets. It's a bit worn but comfortable enough, and a welcome respite from the town-centre frenzy.

◉ Sights

Nataraja Temple   HINDU TEMPLE
(East Car St; ⊙inner compound 6am-noon & 4.30-10pm) According to legend, Shiva and Kali got into a dance-off judged by Vishnu. Shiva dropped an earring and picked it up with his foot, a move that Kali could not duplicate, so Shiva won the title Nataraja (Lord of the Dance). It's in this form that endless streams of people come to worship him at this great temple. It was built during Chola times (Chidambaram was a Chola capital), but the main shrines date to at least the 6th century.

BUSES FROM CHIDAMBARAM

DESTINATION	FARE (₹)	TIME (HR)	DEPARTURES
Chennai	300	6	every 30min
Kumbakonam	60	3	hourly
Puducherry	75	2	every 30min
Thanjavur	120	3-4	hourly
Tharangambadi	40	2-3	every 30min

TRAINS FROM CHIDAMBARAM

DESTINATION	FARE (₹)	TIME (HR)	DEPARTURES
Chennai	300	6	every 30min
Kumbakonam	60	3	hourly
Puducherry	75	2	every 30min
Thanjavur	120	3-4	hourly
Tharangambadi	40	2-3	every 30min

The high-walled 22-hectare complex has four towering 12th-century *gopurams* decked out in ornate Dravidian stone and stucco work. The main entrance is through the east (oldest) *gopuram;* the 108 sacred positions of classical Tamil dance are carved in its passageway. To your right through the gopuram are the 1000-pillared 12th-century Raja Sabha (King's Hall; open only festival days), with carved elephants, and the large Sivaganga tank.

You enter the central compound (no cameras) from the east. In its southern part (left from the entrance) is the 13th-century Nritta Sabha (Dance Hall), shaped like a chariot with 56 finely carved pillars. Some say this is the spot where Shiva out-danced Kali.

North of the Nritta Sabha, through a door, you enter the inner courtyard, where most temple rituals are performed. Right in front are the attached hutlike, golden-roofed Kanaka Sabha and Chit Sabha (Wisdom Hall). The Chit Sabha, the innermost sanctum, holds the temple's central bronze image of Nataraja – Shiva the cosmic dancer, ending one cycle of creation, beginning another and uniting all opposites. Shiva's invisible 'space' form is also worshipped here.

At *puja* times devotees crowd into the encircling pavilion to witness rites performed by the temple's hereditary Brahmin priests, the Dikshithars, who shave off some of their hair but grow the rest of it long (thus representing both Shiva and Parvati) and tie it into topknots.

On the south side of the two inner shrines is the Govindaraja Shrine with a reclining Vishnu. Overlooking the tank from the west, the Shivakamasundari Shrine displays fine ochre-and-white 17th-century Nayak ceiling murals.

Priests may offer to guide you around the temple for ₹200 to ₹300. Unusually for Tamil Nadu, this magnificent temple is privately funded and managed, so you may wish to support it by hiring one, but there are no official guides.

🅘 Getting There & Away

BUS

Government buses depart from the **bus stand** (VGP St). **Universal Travels** (☑044-9842440926; VGP St; ☉9am-10pm), opposite the bus stand, runs Volvo AC buses to Chennai (₹500, five hours) at 8am and 4.30pm.

Destinations include those listed opposite.

Tharangambadi (Tranquebar)

☑04364 / POP 22,500

South of Chidambaram, the Cauvery River's many-armed delta stretches 180km along the coast and into the hinterland. The Cauvery is the beating heart of Tamil agriculture and its valley was the heartland of the Chola empire. Today the delta is one of Tamil Nadu's prettiest, poorest and most traditional areas.

The tiny seaside town of Tharangambadi, still known as Tranquebar, is easily the most appealing base. A great place to recharge from the crowded towns inland, this quiet former Danish colony is set right on a long sandy beach with delicious sea breezes and fishing boats. Denmark sold it to the British East India Company in 1845.

With its colonial-era buildings, the old part of town inside the 1792 Landporten Gate makes a brilliantly peaceful stroll, and has been significantly restored since the 2004 tsunami, which killed about 800 people here. INTACH Pondicherry (www.intachpondicherry.org) has a good downloadable map.

Notable buildings in town include the 1884 **post office** (Post Office St; ☉8.30am-6pm Mon-Sat), the 1718 **New Jerusalem Church** (Tamil Evangelical Lutheran Church; King's St; ☉dawn-dusk) and the tiny **Maritime Museum** (Queen's St; Indian/foreigner ₹5/50; ☉9.30am-2pm & 2.30-5pm, hours vary), with a display on the 2004 tsunami. The peach-hued seafront **Dansborg fort** (Parade Ground, King's St; Indian/foreigner ₹5/50, camera/video

₹30/100; ☉10am-5.45pm Sat-Thu) dates from 1624 and was occupied by the British in 1801. In its prime, it was the world's second-largest Danish castle.

🛏 Sleeping & Eating

Nippon Palace   HOTEL $
(☏9344440088; East Coast Rd; d ₹980-1200, with AC ₹1500-1700; @🛜) This newcomer is efficiently run by a manager fluent in English and helpful staff. Rooms are spacious and clean, delivering solid value. It's on the main road, about 300m from the bus stand.

★Bungalow on the Beach   HERITAGE HOTEL $$$
(☏04364-289036; www.neemranahotels.com; 24 King's St; r incl breakfast ₹8260-11,520; ❄🛜≋) Most Tranquebar accommodation is run by the sea-front Bungalow on the Beach, in the exquisitely restored 17th-century former residence of the British administrator. There are 17 beautiful old-world rooms in the main building and two other heritage locations in town. The main block has a cute multicuisine **restaurant** (☏04364-289036; mains ₹250-550; ☉7.30-9.30am, 12-3pm & 7.30-9.30pm), a dreamy swimming pool and a fantastic wraparound terrace. Book ahead.

❶ Getting There & Away

Buses in this region get incredibly crowded. Tharangambadi has regular connections with Chidambaram (₹75, two hours, hourly) and Karaikal (₹16, 30 minutes, half-hourly). From Karaikal buses go to Kumbakonam (₹55, two hours, half-hourly), Thanjavur (₹75, three hours, every hour) and Puducherry (₹115, four hours, half-hourly).

Kumbakonam

☏0435 / POP 170,000

At first glance Kumbakonam is just another chaotic Indian junction town, but then you notice the dozens of colourful *gopurams* pointing skyward from its 18 temples – a reminder that this was once a seat of medieval South Indian power. With another two magnificent World Heritage–listed Chola temples nearby, it's worth staying the night.

◉ Sights

Nageshwara Temple   HINDU TEMPLE
(Nageswaran Koil St; ☉6.30am-12.30pm & 4-8.30pm) Founded by the Cholas in 886, this is Kumbakonam's oldest temple, dedicated to

Shiva as Nagaraja, the serpent king. On three days of the year (in April or May) the sun's rays fall on the lingam. The elevated Nataraja shrine on the right in front of the inner sanctum is fashioned, in typical Chola style, like a horse-drawn chariot; colourful modern elephants stand beside it.

Kumbeshwara Temple   HINDU TEMPLE
(off Kumbeswarar East St; ☉6.30am-12.30pm & 4-8.30pm) Kumbeshwara Temple, entered via a nine-storey *gopuram,* a small bazaar and a long porticoed *mandapa,* is Kumbakonam's biggest Shiva temple. It dates from the 17th and 18th centuries and contains a lingam said to have been made by Shiva himself when he mixed the nectar of immortality with sand.

Mahamaham Tank   RELIGIOUS SITE
(LBS Rd) Surrounded by 16 pavilions, the huge Mahamaham Tank is one of Kumbakonam's most sacred sites. It's believed that every 12 years the waters of India's holiest rivers, including the Ganges, flow into it, and at this time a festival is held (next due: 2028). On the tank's north side, the **Kashivishvanatha Temple** (LBS Rd; ☉6.30am-12.30pm & 4-8.30pm) contains an intriguing trio of river goddesses, the central of which embodies the Cauvery River.

Sarangapani Temple   HINDU TEMPLE
(Sarangapani Koil Sannadhi St; ☉6.30am-12.30pm & 4-8.30pm) Sarangapani is Kumbakonam's largest Vishnu temple, with a 45m-high eastern *gopuram* embellished with low-level dancing panels as its main entrance. Past the temple cowshed (Krishna the cowherd is one of Vishnu's forms), another *gopuram* and a pillared hall, you reach the inner sanctuary, a 12th-century Chola creation styled like a chariot with big carved elephants, horses and wheels. Photography is not permitted inside.

Ramaswami Temple   HINDU TEMPLE
(Sarangapani 5th St; ☉6.30am-12.30pm & 4-8.30pm) Dating back to 1620, this temple at the southernmost end of Kumbakonam's main bazaar street has beautiful Nayak horse and *yali* carvings and fine frescoes.

🛏 Sleeping & Eating

Hotel Metro   HOTEL $
(☏0435-2403377; www.thehotelmetro.com; 19/11 Sarangapani Koil Sannadhi St; r ₹1300-1900; ❄🛜) Comfortable modern rooms with good beds make this the best value in Kumbakonam,

CHOLA TEMPLES NEAR KUMBAKONAM

Two of the three great monuments of Chola civilisation stand in villages just outside Kumbakonam: Darasuram's Airavatesvara Temple and the Gangaikondacholapuram Temple. Unlike the also World Heritage–listed Brihadishwara Temple (p1057) at Thanjavur, today these two temples receive relatively few worshippers (and visitors). They are wonderful both for their overall form (with pyramidal towers rising at the heart of rectangular walled compounds) and for the exquisite detail of their carved, unpainted stone.

Three kilometres west of Kumbakonam, the late-Chola Shiva **Airavatesvara Temple** (Darasuram; ⊙6am-8pm, inner shrine 6am-1pm & 4-8pm) was constructed by Raja Raja II (1146–73). The steps of Rajagambhira Hall are carved with vivid elephants and horses pulling chariots. This pavilion's 108 pillars, each unique, have marvellously detailed carvings, including dancers, acrobats and the five-in-one beast *yali* (elephant's head, lion's body, goat's horns, pig's ears and cow's backside). Inside the **main shrine** (flanked by guardians), you can honour the central lingam and get a *tilak* (auspicious forehead mark) for ₹10. On the outside of the shrine are several fine carved images of Shiva. Four *mandapas* frame the corners of the courtyardlike complex.

The temple at **Gangaikondacholapuram** (Brihadishwara Temple; ⊙6am-noon & 4-8pm) – 'City of the Chola who Conquered the Ganges' – 35km north of Kumbakonam, is dedicated to Shiva. It was built by Rajendra I in the 11th century when he moved the Chola capital here from Thanjavur, and has many similarities to Thanjavur's earlier Brihadishwara Temple. Its beautiful 49m-tall tower, however, has a slightly concave curve, making it the 'feminine' counterpart to the mildly convex Thanjavur one. Artistic highlights are the wonderfully graceful sculptures around the tower's exterior.

A massive Nandi (Shiva's vehicle) faces the temple from the tranquil surrounding gardens; a lion stands guard nearby. The main shrine, beneath the tower, contains a huge lingam and is approached through a long 17th-century hall. The fine carvings on the tower's exterior include: Shiva as the beggar Bhikshatana, immediately left of the southern steps; Ardhanarishvara (Shiva as half-man, half-woman) and Shiva as Nataraja, on the south side; Shiva with Ganga, Shiva emerging from the lingam, and Vishnu with Lakshmi and Bhudevi (the southernmost three images on the west side); and Shiva with Parvati (the northernmost image on the west side). Most famous is the masterful panel of Shiva garlanding the head of his follower, Chandesvara, beside the northern steps.

Most travellers visit the temples as a day trip from Kumbakonam. From Kumbakonam bus stand (p1056), buses to Gangaikondacholapuram (₹20, 1½ hours) run every 30 minutes. Returning, it can be quicker to catch a bus to Jayamkondan and transfer to Kumbakonam there. A half-day car trip to both temples, through Kumbakonam's reliable Hotel Raya's (p1055), costs ₹2400 (₹2700 with AC).

especially since discounts are offered if it isn't fully booked.

Hotel Raya's   HOTEL **$$**
(☎0435-2423170; www.hotelrayas.com; 18 Head Post Office Rd; r ₹1290, with AC ₹1515-1960; ❉) The Swiss-army knife of Kumbakonam hotels, Raya's has something for almost everyone, and can be busy. Service is friendly, but the lower-class rooms feel like they've been too neglected for too long. The **Hotel Raya's Annexe** (☎0435-2423270; 19 Head Post Office Rd; r ₹1850; ❉🛜) has the best, brightest rooms, but look at a few before settling on one if you can. The hotel's restaurant

Sathars Restaurant (☎0435-2423170; mains ₹140-240; ⊙11.30am-11.30pm) is popular for its veg and nonveg fare.

★**Mantra Koodam**   RESORT **$$$**
(☎0435-2462621; www.cghearth.com; 1 Bagavathapuram Main Rd Extension, Srisailapathipuram Village; incl breakfast s ₹8500-9720, d ₹9720-10,940; ❉🛜❄) 🅿 Lost in the riverside jungle, 10km northeast of Kumbakonam, this is a wonderful retreat from temple-town chaos. Comfy modern-rustic, Chettiar-style cottages are fronted by porches with rocking chairs, and have open-air showers and carved-teak doors. Cooking classes and trips to local

Kumbakonam

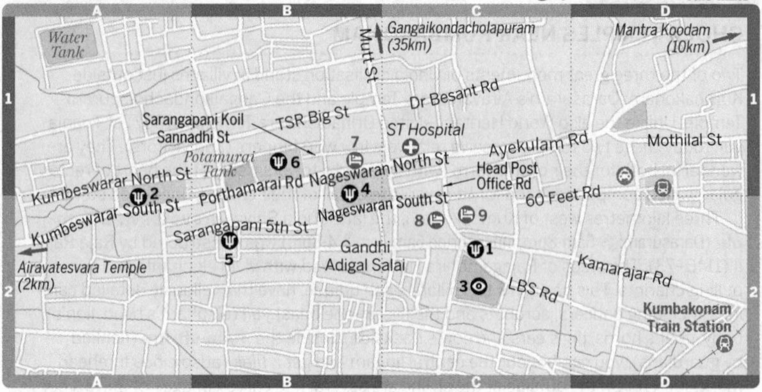

Map legend: N, scale 0–500 m / 0–0.25 miles

Map labels: Water Tank; Gangaikondacholapuram (35km); Mantra Koodam (10km); Mutt St; Dr Besant Rd; TSR Big St; ST Hospital; Ayekulam Rd; Mothilal St; Sarangapani Koil Sannadhi St; Potamurai Tank; 7; Nageswaran North St; Head Post Office Rd; 60 Feet Rd; Kumbeswarar North St; **6**; Porthamarai Rd; **4**; Kumbeswarar South St; **2**; Sarangapani 5th St; Nageswaran South St; 8; 9; Airavatesvara Temple (2km); **5**; Gandhi Adigal Salai; **1**; Kamarajar Rd; **3**; LBS Rd; Kumbakonam Train Station

Kumbakonam

◉ Sights
1	Kashivishvanatha Temple	C2
2	Kumbeshwara Temple	A2
3	Mahamaham Tank	C2
4	Nageshwara Temple	B1
5	Ramaswami Temple	B2
6	Sarangapani Temple	B1

⊟ Sleeping
7	Hotel Metro	B1
8	Hotel Raya's	C2
9	Hotel Raya's Annexe	C2

⊗ Eating
	Sathars Restaurant	(see 8)

silk weavers, traditional fabric painters and wax-casting sculptors are offered. The exquisite restaurant is Indian gourmet.

❶ Getting There & Away

BUS
Government buses depart from the **bus stand** (60 Feet Rd).

TRAIN
Five daily trains head to Thanjavur (2nd class/3AC/2AC ₹45/495/700, 30 minutes to one hour) and four to Trichy (₹60/495/700, 1½ to 2½ hours). Five daily trains to/from Chennai Egmore include the overnight Chennai Express/Train 16852 (sleeper/3AC/2AC/1AC ₹210/560/800/1335, 6½ hours) and the daytime Chennai Express/Train 16796 (₹210/555/795/1325, six to seven hours).

Thanjavur (Tanjore)

📞 04362 / POP 500,000

Here are the ochre foundation blocks of perhaps the most remarkable civilisation of Dravidian history, one of the few kingdoms to expand Hinduism beyond India, a bedrock for aesthetic styles that spread from Madurai to the Mekong. A dizzying historical legacy was forged from Thanjavur, capital of the great Chola empire during its heyday. Today Thanjavur is a crowded, hectic, modern Indian town – but the past is still very much present. Every day thousands of people worship at the Cholas' grand Brihadishwara Temple, and the city's labyrinthine royal palace preserves memories of other, later powerful dynasties.

BUSES FROM KUMBAKONAM

DESTINATION	FARE (₹)	TIME (HR)	DEPARTURES
Chennai (AC)	300	8	1.50pm
Chidambaram	50	2½-3	every 30min
Karaikal	40	2¼	every 15min
Thanjavur (Tanjore)	30	2	every 5min
Trichy (Tiruchirappalli)	60	4	every 5min

⊙ Sights

★ **Brihadishwara Temple** HINDU TEMPLE
(Big Temple; Big Temple St; ⊘6am-8.30pm, central shrine 8.30am-12.30pm & 4-8.30pm) Come here twice: in the morning, when the honey-hued granite begins to assert its dominance over the white dawn sunshine, and in the evening, when the rocks capture a hot palette of reds, oranges, yellows and pinks on the crowning glory of Chola temple architecture. The World Heritage–listed Brihadishwara Temple was built between 1003 and 1010 by Raja Raja I ('king of kings'). The outer fortifications were put up by Thanjavur's later Nayak and British regimes.

You enter through a Maratha-era gate, followed by two original *gopurams* with elaborate stucco sculptures. You might find the temple elephant under one of the *gopurams*. Several shrines are dotted around the extensive grassy areas of the walled temple compound, including one of India's largest statues of Nandi (Shiva's sacred bull), facing the main temple building. Cut from a single rock and framed by slim pillars, this 16th-century Nayak creation is 6m long. Don't miss the sublime sculptures at the shrine dedicated to Lakshmi, to the right of Nandi when entering the complex.

A long, columned assembly hall leads to the central shrine with its 4m-high Shiva lingam, beneath the superb 61m-high *vimana* (tower). The assembly hall's southern steps are flanked by two huge *dwarpals* (temple guardians). Many graceful deity images stand in niches around the *vimana's* lower outer levels, including Shiva emerging from the lingam (beside the southern steps); Shiva as the beggar Bhikshatana (first image, south side); Shiva as Nataraja, the cosmic dancer (west end of south wall); Harihara (half Shiva, half Vishnu) on the west wall; and Ardhanarishvara (Shiva as half-man, half-woman), leaning on Nandi, on the north side. Between the deity images are panels showing classical dance poses. On the *vimana's* upper east side is a later Maratha-period Shiva within three arches.

The compound also contains an interpretation centre along the south wall and, in the colonnade along the west and north walls, hundreds more linga. Both west and north walls are lined with exquisite lime-plaster Chola frescoes, for years buried under later Nayak-era murals. North of the temple compound, but still within the outer fortifications, are the 18th-century neoclassical Schwartz's Church (off Big Temple St; ⊘dawn-dusk) and a park containing the Sivaganga tank (off Big Temple St; ₹5, camera/video ₹10/25; ⊘dawn-dusk).

Official guides can be hired at the tourist information booth just outside the temple for 90-minute tours (₹500).

★ **Royal Palace** PALACE
(East Main St; Indian/foreigner ₹50/200, camera ₹30/100; ⊘9am-1pm & 1.30-5.30pm, art gallery 9.30am-1pm & 2-5pm) Thanjavur's royal palace is a mixed bag of ruin and renovation, superb art and random royal paraphernalia. The mazelike complex was constructed partly by the Nayaks who took over Thanjavur in 1535, and partly by a local Maratha dynasty that ruled from 1676 to 1855. The two don't-miss sections are the Saraswati Mahal Library Museum and the Art Gallery.

Seven different sections of the palace can be visited. 'Full' tickets include the Art Gallery and Saraswati Mahal Library Museum, along with the Mahratta Dharbar Hall, bell tower and Saarjah Madi; other sections require extra tickets. The main entrance is from the north, off East Main St. On the way in you'll come to the main ticket office, followed by the Maratha Palace complex.

Past the ticket office, a passage to the left leads to: first, the Royal Palace Museum (₹2), a small miscellany of sculptures, weaponry, elephant bells and rajas' headgear; second, the Maharaja Serfoji Memorial Hall (₹4), commemorating the enlightened Maratha scholar-king Serfoji II (1798–1832), with a better collection overlooking a once-splendid, now crumbling courtyard; and third, the Mahratta Dharbar Hall (⊘10am-5pm), where Maratha rulers gave audience in a grand but faded pavilion adorned with colourful murals (including their own portraits behind the dais) and sturdy pillars topped by arches filled with gods.

Exiting the passage, the fabulous Saraswati Mahal Library Museum is on your left, through a vibrant entranceway. Perhaps Serfoji II's greatest contribution to posterity, this is testimony both to the 19th-century obsession with knowledge accumulation and to an eclectic mind that collected prints of Chinese torture methods, Audubon-style paintings of Indian flora and fauna, world atlases, dictionaries and rare medieval books. Serfoji amassed more than 65,000 books and 50,000 palm-leaf paper manuscripts in Indian and European languages, though most aren't displayed. Hourly **audiovisual**

Thanjavur (Tanjore)

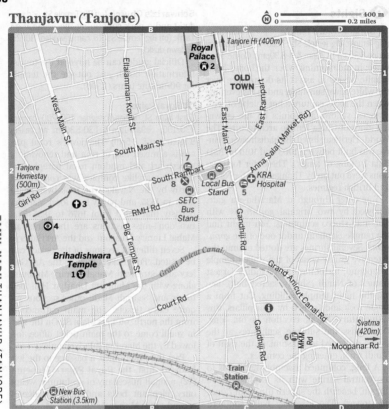

displays (⏱10.30am-4.30pm), highlight Thanjavur's sights, history and traditions in the attached cinema room.

Leaving the library, turn left for the Art Gallery, set around the Nayak Palace courtyard behind the bell tower. It contains a collection of stone carvings and superb, mainly Chola, bronzes, including some fabulous Natarajas in the New Visitors Hall; its main room, the 1600 Nayak Durbar Hall, has a statue of Serfoji II. From the courtyard, steps lead part the way up a large *gopuram*-like tower to a whale skeleton that washed up in Tharangambadi.

The renovated Saarjah Madi is best admired from East Main Rd for its ornate balconies.

💤 Sleeping

It's well worth staying in Thanjavur to see the 'Big' Temple at sunset. Central Thanjavur has a bunch of nondescript, cheap lodges opposite the SETC and local bus stands, a couple of decent midrange hotels, and a fabulous heritage option.

Kasi Inn   HOTEL $
(☎04362-231908; 1493 South Rampart Rd; s ₹1000, d₹1120-1650) Thanjavur's best value in the town centre has smallish but well-kept rooms with good mattresses and (sometimes) wi-fi. Plus, it's kitty-corner to an ice-cream shop!

Hotel Valli   HOTEL $
(☎04362-231584; 2948 MKM Rd; s/d ₹610/770, r with AC from ₹1090; ❄☎) Near the train station, green-painted Valli offers no-frills, spick-and-span rooms, friendly staff and a basic restaurant. It's in a reasonably peaceful leafy spot beyond a bunch of greasy backstreet workshops and a booze shop.

Tanjore Homestay   HOMESTAY $$
(☎9443157667; www.tanjorehomestay.blogspot.in; 64A Giri Rd, Srinivasa Puram; s/d incl breakfast ₹1800/2300; @☎) Under the watch of a wel-

Thanjavur (Tanjore)

coming Indian couple who serve tasty home-cooked meals, this low-key homestay offers four simple rooms with splashes of art. Breakfast is served in the pretty back garden and there's a rooftop terrace, plus hot water, air-con and wi-fi. It's in a residential area, 1.5km west of Thanjavur's main temple; no sign.

Hotel Gnanam   HOTEL **$$**
(📞04362-278501; www.hotelgnanam.com; Anna Salai; s/d incl breakfast ₹2700/3200; ❄🛜) One of the better values in town, the Gnanam has comfy, stylish rooms (some with balconies), with marble floors and polka-dot curtains. It's perfect for anyone needing modern amenities in Thanjavur's geographical centre. Its **Diana** (📞04362-278501; mains ₹125-350; ⏱11.30am-3.30pm & 6.30-10.30pm) and **Sahana** (📞04362-278501; mains ₹120-185; ⏱7am-10.30pm) restaurants are both good. Book ahead.

★ **Svatma**   HERITAGE HOTEL **$$$**
(📞04362-273222; www.svatma.in; 4/1116 Blake Higher Secondary School Rd, Maharnonbu Chavadi; r incl breakfast ₹13,440-22,400; ❄🛜🏊) This gorgeous boutique-heritage hotel has an elegant, uncluttered look inspired by and incorporating traditional local arts and crafts. Of the 38 rooms, those in the revamped heritage wing have the most character. Enjoy the dance shows, cooking classes, bronze-casting demonstrations – plus a spa and heavenly pool. It's 1.5km southeast of central Thanjavur.

Tanjore Hi   BOUTIQUE HOTEL **$$$**
(📞9487810301, 04362-252111; www.dunewellness group.com; 464 East Main St; r ₹4720; ❄🛜) 🏊 Just north of Thanjavur's palace, Tanjore Hi is a century-old, ecofriendly house refurbished with strikingly contemporary flair. Bold modern decor is all about deep blues, fresh whites, warm woods, wall murals and wildly illuminated ceilings. A staircase spirals up to the good, organic-fuelled, Indian-international rooftop restaurant.

🍽 Eating

Jigarthanda   ICE CREAM **$**
(South Rampart Rd; scoops ₹30; ⏱9.30am-10.30pm) Cool off here with the best ice cream in town – it's 'homemade in a factory', according to the workers.

Tanjore Hi   MULTICUISINE **$$**
(📞04362-252111; www.duneecogroup.com; 464 East Main St; mains ₹210-325; ⏱7.30-10am, 12.30-2.30pm & 7.30-10pm) 🏊 On a boutique-hotel rooftop, this industrial-chic restaurant is a welcome surprise in traditional Thanjavur. The world-wandering menu is fuelled by fresh, organic ingredients grown at the hotel's sister property in Kodaikanal. Dine at terrace tables outside or in the glassed-in air-con room.

Ideal River View Resort   MULTICUISINE **$$**
(📞04362-250533; www.idealresort.com; Vennar Bank, Palliagraharam; mains ₹200-450; ⏱7-9.30am, 12.30-2.30pm & 7.30-9.30pm) The good, semi-open-air Indian/Sri Lankan/Chinese restaurant at the jungle-fringed **Ideal River View Resort** (📞04362-250533; s/d incl breakfast ₹6500/7080; ❄🛜🏊) overlooks the river.

ℹ Information

Tourist office (📞04362-230984; Hotel Tamil Nadu, Gandhiji Rd; ⏱10am-5.45pm Mon-Fri) One of Tamil Nadu's more helpful offices.

ℹ Getting There & Away

BUS

The downtown **SETC Bus Stand** (RMH Rd) has hourly express buses to Chennai (₹420, 8¼ hours) from 7.30am to 12.30pm and 8pm to 11pm. Buses for most other cities leave from the **New Bus Station** (Trichy Main Rd), 5km southwest of the centre. Many arriving buses will drop you off in the city centre on the way out there. Services from the New Bus Station include: Chidambaram (₹100, four hours, hourly), Kumbakonam (₹40, 1½ hours, every five minutes),

Madurai (₹130, four hours, every 15 minutes) and Trichy (Tiruchirappalli; ₹43, 1½ hours, every five minutes)

TRAIN

The train station is at the southern end of Gandhiji Rd.

Chennai Four daily trains head to Chennai Egmore (seven hours) including the 11.20pm Chennai Express – train 16852 (sleeper/3AC/2AC/1AC ₹225/605/865/1450).

Kumbakonam Twelve daily trains – five with reserved seating (sleeper/3AC/2AC ₹45/495/700, 30 minutes to 1¼ hours).

Madurai Seventeen services per day (sleeper/3AC/2AC ₹160/495/700, four to five hours).

Trichy Nineteen daily trains – six have reserved seating (2nd class/3AC/2AC ₹45/495/700, 1½ hours), 13 are unreserved (₹15).

❶ Getting Around

Bus 74 (₹10) shuttles between the New Bus Station and the central **local bus stand** (South Rampart); autorickshaws cost ₹120.

Trichy (Tiruchirappalli)

📞 0431 / POP 847,390

Welcome to (more or less) the geographical centre of Tamil Nadu. Tiruchirappalli, universally called Trichy or Tiruchi, isn't just a travel junction: it also mixes up a heaving bazaar with some major temples. It's a huge, crowded, busy city, and the fact that most hotels are clumped together around the big bus station isn't exactly a plus point. But Trichy has a strong character and long history, and a way of overturning first impressions.

Trichy may have been a capital of the early Cholas in the 3rd century BC. It passed through the hands of the Pallavas, medieval Cholas, Pandyas, Delhi Sultanate and Vijayanagars before the Madurai Nayaks brought it to prominence, making it a capital in the 17th century and building its famous Rock Fort Temple (p1061). Under British control, it became an important railway hub known as Trichinopoly.

◉ Sights

⭐ **Sri Ranganathaswamy Temple**   HINDU TEMPLE

(Map p1061; Srirangam; camera/video ₹50/100; ◷6am-9.30pm) So large it feels like a self-enclosed city, Sri Ranganathaswamy is quite possibly India's biggest temple. It has 49 separate Vishnu shrines, and reaching the inner sanctum from the south, as most worshippers do, requires passing through seven *gopurams*. The first (southernmost), the **Rajagopuram** (Map p1061), was added in 1987, and is one of Asia's tallest temple towers at 73m high. Non-Hindus cannot pass the sixth *gopuram* so won't see the innermost sanctum, where Vishnu as Ranganatha reclines on a five-headed snake.

You pass through streets with shops, restaurants, motorbikes and cars until you reach the temple proper at the fourth *gopuram*. Inside on the left is an information counter selling tickets for the **roof viewpoint** (₹20), which affords semipanoramic views. Take no notice of would-be guides who spin stories to get hired. Also here, in the southwest corner, is the beautiful 16th-century Venugopal Shrine, adorned with superbly detailed Nayak-era carvings of preening *gopis* (milkmaids) and the flute-playing Krishna (Vishnu's eighth incarnation).

Turn right just before the fifth *gopuram* for the small **Art Museum** (Map p1061; ₹5; ◷9am-1pm & 2-6pm), displaying fine bronzes, tusks of bygone temple elephants, and a collection of exquisite 17th-century Nayak ivory figurines depicting gods, demons, and kings and queens (some in erotic poses). Continue left past the museum to the Sesha Mandapa, a 16th-century pillared hall with magnificently detailed monolithic Vijayanagar carvings of rearing battle horses and Vishnu's 10 incarnations sculpted on pillars. Immediately north is the 1000-pillared hall, whose recently unearthed lower base is carved into dance positions.

Inside the fifth gopuram is the Garuda Mandapa, containing an enormous shrine to Vishnu's man-eagle assistant, posed in semi-seated position to show that he's ever-ready to leap up and go to Vishnu the moment he is called to fly the god somewhere. Note, too, four remarkable sculptures of Nayak donors (with daggers on the hip).

Take bus 1 to/from the Central Bus Station or the Rock Fort stops just south of the Rajagopuram.

Sri Jambukeshwara Temple   HINDU TEMPLE

(Tiruvanaikoil, Srirangam; ◷5am-8pm) Of Tamil Nadu's five Shiva elemental temples, Sri Jambukeshwara is dedicated to Shiva, Parvati and the medium of water. The liquid theme is realised in the central shrine (closed to non-Hindus), whose Shiva lingam reputedly issues a nonstop trickle of water. In the north part of the complex is a shrine dedicated to Akilandeswari, Jambukeshwara's consort. A

Trichy (Tiruchirappalli)

Trichy (Tiruchirappalli)

good time to visit is around noon, when the temple elephant is involved in a procession between the two shrines.

If you're taking bus 1, ask for 'Tiruvanakoil'; the temple is 350m east of the main road.

★ Rock Fort Temple HINDU TEMPLE
(Map p1061; NSB Rd; camera/video ₹5/20; ⊙6am-8pm) The Rock Fort Temple, perched 83m high on a massive outcrop, lords over Trichy with stony arrogance. The ancient rock was first hewn by the Pallavas and Pandyas, who cut small cave temples on its south side, but it was the war-savvy Nayaks who later made

strategic use of the naturally fortified position. Reaching the top requires climbing over 400 stone-cut steps.

From NSB Rd on the south side, you pass between small shops and cross a street before entering the temple precinct itself, where there's a shoe stand. You might meet the temple elephant here. Then it's 180 steps up to the Thayumanaswamy Temple, the rock's biggest temple, on the left (closed to non-Hindus); a gold-topped tower rises over its sanctum. Further up, you pass the 6th-century Pallava upper cave temple on the left (usually railed off); on the left inside is a famous Gangadhara panel showing Shiva restraining the Ganges with a single strand of his hair. From here it's another 183 steps to the summit's small Uchipillaiyar Temple, dedicated to Ganesh. The views are wonderful, with eagles wheeling beneath and Trichy sprawling all around.

Back at the bottom, check out the 8th-century Pandya lower rock-cut cave temple, with particularly fine pillars (turn right as you exit the temple precinct, past five or six houses, then right again down a small lane).

The stone steps get scorching-hot in the midday sun and it's a barefoot climb, so time your visit carefully.

Railway Museum MUSEUM
(Map p1064; Bharatiyar Salai; adult/child ₹10/5, camera/video ₹20/40; ⊙9.30am-5.30pm Tue-Sun) Trichy's Railway Museum is a fascinating jumble of disused train-related equipment (phones, clocks, control boards), British-era railway construction photos, old train-line

maps (including a 1935 pre-Independence Indian Railway map) – and even modern-day London Underground tickets. It's 500m east of Trichy Junction.

St Joseph's College Museum
MUSEUM

(Map p1061; College Rd; ⊙10am-noon & 2-4pm Mon-Sat) FREE In the cool, green campus next to Lourdes Church (p1062), this dusty museum contains the creepy natural history collections of the Jesuit priests' Western Ghats excursions of the 1870s. Ask for access at reception on the left as you approach the museum. It was being renovated at the time of research.

St John's Church
CHURCH

(Map p1064; off Rockins Rd; ⊙dawn-dusk, hours vary) Adorned with original-period shuttered doors, elegant – and very white – St John's Church dates from the early 19th century.

Lourdes Church
CHURCH

(Map p1061; College Rd; ⊙6am-8.30pm) The hush of this 19th-century neo-Gothic church makes an interesting contrast to Trichy's frenetic Hindu temples. Note the cakelike pink-accented arches and the rose window at the eastern end.

🛏 Sleeping

Hotel Abbirami
HOTEL $

(Map p1064; ☑0431-2415001; 10 McDonald's Rd; r ₹750-850, with AC ₹1345-2360; ❄🛜) Despite the ground-floor bustle, this is the best deal in town. Even the cheapest AC rooms are appealing, with light wood, colourful glass panels and decent mattresses. Non-AC rooms are a bit worn, but still well kept.

Ashby Hotel
HOTEL $

(Map p1064; ☑0431-2460652; 17A Rockins Rd; s ₹650-900, d ₹750-950, with AC s ₹1120-1350, d ₹1680-1900; ❄) On the street between the train station and the Central Bus Station, this long-running budget spot greets you with elephant murals on its facade. Rooms are clearly due for some upgrades but are clean enough, though those with AC are overpriced. All are set around a shady, surprisingly quiet courtyard that manages to be almost charming.

Tranquility
GUESTHOUSE $$

(☑9443157667; www.tranquilitytrichy.com; Anakkarai, Melur, Srirangam; s/d incl breakfast ₹3200/4000; ❄🛜) This charming rustic-chic guesthouse sits in a gloriously rural setting 6km west of Sri Ranganathaswamy Temple.

Elegant, unfussy rooms are sprinkled with terracotta-horse statuettes, sparkly cushions, recycled wood-carved doors and custom-made furniture. Terrace swing-chairs overlook a sea of palms. Rates include bicycles and transfers. The knowledgable owners also offer a thatched-roof homestay room (p1062) just southwest of the temple's outermost wall.

Home with a View
HOMESTAY $$

(Map p1061; ☑9443157667; www.tranquilitytrichy. com; 43C Raghavendra Puram, opp Raghavendra Mutt; r incl breakfast ₹2000; 🛜) There's one tastefully simple thatched-roof room, with both a double and single bed, at this laid-back homestay just outside the Sri Ranganathaswamy Temple's seventh wall. Traditional homemade meals are a delight, as are the on-the-ball owners, who also run lovely countryside Tranquility, 6km west.

Grand Gardenia
HOTEL $$

(☑0431-4045000; www.grandgardenia.com; 22-25 Mannarpuram Junction; incl breakfast s ₹2950, d ₹3540-4720; ❄❄🛜) Elegant, modern rooms provide comfy beds and glassed-in showers at this corporate-style hotel, one of Trichy's smartest options. Nonveg Kannappa (☑0431-4045000; mains ₹120-220; ⊙11.30am-11.30pm) serves up excellent Chettinadu food; the rooftop terrace hosts a multicuisine restaurant (☑0431-4045000; mains ₹120-240; ⊙11.30am-3.30pm & 7-11pm). Comfort and amenities outweigh the uninspiring highway-side location, 1km south of Trichy Junction.

Breeze Residency
HOTEL $$

(Map p1064; ☑0431-2414414; www.breezeres idency.com; 3/14 McDonald's Rd; incl breakfast s ₹2075-3185, d ₹2250-3775; ❄@🛜❄) The Breeze is huge, aiming at upscale and in a relatively quiet, leafy location. The rooms are clean and comfortable, but feel institutional, with nothing special about them. Facilities include a gym, the buffet-only Madras Restaurant (Map p1064; ☑0431-4045333; lunch/dinner buffet from ₹350/450; ⊙noon-3pm & 7.30-11pm; ❄), a 24-hour coffee shop and a bizarre American Wild West–themed bar.

Ramyas Hotel
HOTEL $$

(Map p1064; ☑0431-2414646; www.ramyas.com; 13D/2 Williams Rd; incl breakfast s ₹2100-3250, d ₹2575-3850; ❄@🛜) Good service and facilities, plus comfortable rooms in shades of white, brown and copper, make this business-oriented hotel excellent value, though 'business-class' rooms are ironically small. Turquoise-clad **Meridian** (Map p1064; ☎0431-2414646; mains ₹130-250; ☺noon-3.30pm & 7-11.30pm) does tasty multicuisine fare, breakfast is a nice buffet and the breezy **Thendral** (Map p1064; ☎0431-2414646; mains ₹140-250; ☺7-10.30pm) roof-garden restaurant is brilliant.

Hotel Royal Sathyam   HOTEL **$$**
(Map p1061; ☎0431-4011414; www.sathyamgroup hotels.in; 42A Singarathope; incl breakfast s/d ₹1700/2000; ✳☎) The best option if you want to be close to the temple and market action. Rooms are small but smart enough, with a fresh wood-and-whitewash theme, and service is friendly.

✗ Eating

Shri Sangeetas   INDIAN **$**
(Map p1064; www.shrisangeetas.com; 2 VOC Rd; mains ₹95-130, thalis ₹85-150; ☺6am-12.30am) Don't let the behind-the-bus-station address put you off. Super-popular Sangeetas has tables in a buzzing, fairy-lit courtyard (or inside in air-con comfort) and a tantalising menu of pure-veg North and South Indian favourites – everything from *idli* and dosa to samosas, thalis and paneer tikka.

Vasanta Bhavan   INDIAN **$**
(Map p1061; 3 NSB Rd; mains ₹95-125, thalis ₹80-150; ☺6am-11pm) A great spot for a meal with views, near the Rock Fort. Tables on the outer gallery overlook the Teppakulam Tank, or there's an air-con hall. It's good for both North Indian veg food (of the paneer and naan genre) and South Indian. People

crowd in for lunchtime thalis. There's another **branch** (Map p1064; Rockins Rd; mains ₹95-125, thalis ₹80-150; ☺6am-11pm) in the Cantonment.

DiMora   MULTICUISINE **$$**
(Map p1061; ☎0431-4040056; www.dimora.co.in; 4th fl, Ambigai City Center, B29-30 Shastri Rd; mains ₹165-455; ☺noon-3.30pm & 7-11pm; ☎) Waiters in all-black take orders on mobile phones to a chart-toppers soundtrack that makes this smart, busy top-floor restaurant feel more Chennai than Trichy. The menu roams all over the world, but it's good for pastas, wood-fired pizzas, stir-fries and fresh juices, as well as tandoori and other Indian dishes.

🛍 Shopping

Saratha's   CLOTHING
(Map p1061; 45 NSB Rd; ☺9am-9.30pm) Bursting with clothing of every conceivable kind and colour, Saratha's claims to be (and might well be) the 'largest textile showroom in India'.

ℹ Information

Indian Panorama (☎0431-4226122; www.indianpanorama.in; 5 Annai Ave, Srirangam; ☺10am-6pm) Trichy-based and covering all of India, this professional, reliable travel agency/tour operator is run by an Indian–New Zealander couple.

Tourist Office (Map p1064; ☎0431-2460136; Williams Rd; ☺10am-5.45pm Mon-Fri)

ℹ Getting There & Away

Trichy is virtually in the geographical centre of Tamil Nadu and is well connected by air, bus and train.

GOVERNMENT BUSES FROM TRICHY

DESTINATION	FARE (₹)	TIME (HR)	DEPARTURES
Bengaluru (Bangalore)	450 (A)	8	20 UD daily
Chennai	245/340/460 (B)	6-7	15 UD, 2 AC daily
Coimbatore	215 (C)	4½-6	every 10min
Kodaikanal	400 (C)	5½	midnight
Madurai	120 (C)	2½	every 15min
Ooty	430 (A)	8½	UD 10.15pm
Rameswaram	185 (C)	6	hourly
Thanjavur (Tanjore)	45 (C)	1½	every 5min
Trivandrum	485 (A)	8	UD 8am, 7.30pm, 9.30pm, 10.30pm

Fares: (A) Ultra Deluxe (UD), (B) regular/UD/AC, (C) regular

For Kodaikanal, you can also take a bus to Dindigul (₹70, two hours, every 15 minutes) and change there.

Trichy Junction Area

Sangam Hotel (450m); Rock Fort Area (3km); Srirangam (7km)

KMC Speciality Hospital

Femina Travels

Guard's Park

Central Bus Station

CANTONMENT

McDonald's Rd

State Bank Rd

Flyover (under construction)

Grand Gardenia (1.3km); Tiruchirappalli International (5km)

Ola kiosk

Trichy Junction Train Station

Bharadiyar Salai (Madurai Rd)

Trichy Junction Area

◎ Sights
1 Railway Museum B2
2 St John's Church A3

⊜ Sleeping
3 Ashby Hotel A3
4 Breeze Residency B2
5 Hotel Abbirami A2
6 Ramyas Hotel A2

⊗ Eating
Madras Restaurant .... (see 4)
Meridian .... (see 6)
7 Shri Sangeetas A3
Thendral .... (see 6)
8 Vasanta Bhavan A2

ⓘ Transport
9 Parveen Travels A3

AIR

Trichy's airport is 6km southeast of Trichy Junction and the Central Bus Station.

BUS

Government buses use the busy but orderly **Central Bus Station** (Map p1064; Rockins Rd). The best services for longer trips are the UD ('Ultra Deluxe') buses; there's a booking office for these in the southwest corner of the station.

Private Buses

Private bus companies have offices near the Central Bus Station.

Parveen Travels (Map p1064; ☑9840962198; www.parveentravels.com; 12B Ashby Complex, Rockins Rd; ☺24hr) AC buses to Chennai (₹720, six hours, 12 daily), Trivandrum (₹1300, seven hours, 10pm and 11.30pm), and Kodaikanal (₹850, 4½ hours, 1.30am) plus non-AC semisleeper buses to Puducherry (₹550, four hours, 11.50pm) and Kodaikanal (₹550, 4½ hours, 2.15am).

TRAIN

Trichy Junction station is on the main Chennai–Madurai line. Of the 16 daily express services to Chennai, the best daytime option is the 9.05am Vaigai Express (2nd/chair class ₹145/520, 5½ hours). The overnight Pandian Express (sleeper/3AC/2AC/1AC ₹245/630/880/1470, 6¼ hours) leaves at 11.10pm.

Eleven daily trains to Madurai include the 7.05am Tirunelveli Express (2nd class/chair class ₹95/345, 2¼ hours) and the 1.35pm Guruvayur Express (2nd class/sleeper/3AC/2AC ₹80/140/495/700, 2¾ hours).

At least six daily trains head to Thanjavur (2nd class/sleeper/3AC ₹45/140/495, 40 minutes to 1½ hours).

TAXI

➤ Travel agencies and hotels provide cars with drivers.

➤ Reasonably priced **Femina Travels** (Map p1064; ☑0431-2418532; www.feminahotel. net; 109 Williams Rd; ☺6.30am-9pm) charges ₹2000 for up to eight hours and 100km (AC car).

➤ There's an **Ola kiosk** (Map p1064; ☺24hr) outside the railway station.

ⓘ Getting Around

➤ Bus 1 from Rockins Rd outside the Central Bus Station goes every few minutes to the Sri Ranganathaswamy Temple (₹10) and back, stopping near the Rock Fort Temple and Sri Jambukeshwara Temple en route.

➤ Autorickshaws from the Central Bus Station cost ₹200 to the Sri Ranganathaswamy Temple and ₹150 to the Rock Fort Temple.

SOUTHERN TAMIL NADU

Chettinadu

The Chettiars, a community of traders based around Karaikkudi (95km south of Trichy), hit the big time in the 19th century as financiers and entrepreneurs in colonial-era Sri Lanka and Southeast Asia. They lavished their fortunes on building 10,000 (maybe even 30,000) ridiculously opulent mansions in the 75 towns and villages of their arid rural homeland, Chettinadu. No expense was spared on finding the finest materials for these palatial homes: Burmese teak, Italian marble, Indian rosewood, English steel, and art and sculpture from everywhere.

After WWII, the Chettiars' businesses crashed. Many families left Chettinadu, and disused mansions decayed and were demolished or sold. Awareness of their value started to revive around the turn of the 21st century, with Chettinadu making it on to Unesco's tentative World Heritage list in 2014. Several mansions have now been converted into gorgeous heritage hotels that are some of Tamil Nadu's best.

◉ Sights & Activities

While there are a number of worthwhile sights scattered among Chettinadu's numerous villages, just being here is enough to make a stop rewarding. Aside from the main hubs of Pudukkottai and Karaikkudi, most towns are rural and peaceful, offering a unique combination of simple country life and impressive mansion architecture. The village of Kanadukathan is a great base from which to explore, and has a variety of accommodation and attractions – though nearby Kothamangalam, with the remarkable Saratha Vilas hotel, is also a choice place to stay. Other places worth visiting include Athangudi, with its famed mansion and tile makers, and Namunasamudram, with a unique religious shrine. To see the various sights in the area, it's easiest to hire a car or a rickshaw for full or half-day tours.

Vijayalaya Cholisvaram   HINDU TEMPLE
(Narthamalai; ⊙dawn-dusk) This small but stunning temple stands on a dramatically deserted rock slope 1km southwest of Narthamalai village (16km north of Pudukkottai). Reminiscent of the Shore Temple at Mamallapuram, without the crowds, it was probably built in the 8th or 9th century AD. Two (often locked) rock-cut shrines adorn the rock face behind, one with 12 impressively large reliefs of Vishnu. The Narthamalai turnoff is 7km south of Keeranur on the Trichy–Pudukkottai road; it's 2km west to Narthamalai itself.

Sittannavasal   JAIN TEMPLE
(Sittannavasal; Indian/foreigner ₹25/300, car ₹40; ⊙dawn-dusk) About 16km northwest of Pudukkottai, this small Jain cave temple conceals magnificent vegetable-oil frescoes, which you'll probably get to appreciate all by yourself. Note the Edenic garden paradise painted on the main ceiling, which includes fish, mythical sea monsters and beautiful water maidens. Or try making your 'Om' echo across an acoustic masterpiece of a meditation chamber, where statues of Jain saints sit cross-legged.

Pudukkottai Museum   MUSEUM
(Thirukokarnam, Pudukkottai; Indian/foreigner ₹5/100, camera/video ₹20/100; ⊙9.30am-5pm Sat-Thu) The relics of Chettinadu's bygone days are on display at this wonderful museum, 4km north of Pudukkottai train station. Its eclectic collection includes musical instruments, stamps, jewellery, megalithic burial artefacts, and some remarkable paintings, sculptures and miniatures.

Athangudi Palace Tiles   WORKSHOP
(☏9442229331; www.athangudipalacetiles.com; Athangudi Rd, Athangudi; ₹100; ⊙8am-6pm) Lusting after those exquisite handmade Chettinadu-mansion tiles? Then swing by this long-standing Athangudi workshop, where you can watch expert tile-makers displaying their technique. And of course, there are tiles for sale. Tile production starts each morning around 11am.

Sri Mahalakshmi
Handloom Weaving Centre   WORKSHOP
(19/6 KM St, Kanadukathan; ⊙9.30am-5.30pm) FREE Chettinadu is known for its handwoven, contrasting-colour silk-and-cotton Kandaangi saris (now increasingly hard to find). At this small weaving complex, you can watch weavers at work and browse racks of beautiful textiles.

🛏 Sleeping & Eating

To get a feel for the palatial life, book into one of Chettinadu's top-end hotels; they're pricey, but the experience is unique.

Chettinad Packer   HOSTEL $
(☏9786396414; www.facebook.com/Chettinad Packer; 30 AR St, Kanadukathan; per person ₹900; ❄🛜) Chettinadu's only backpacker-oriented accommodation features dorm rooms with bunk beds, plus one private room with four single beds. Simple but clean and well cared for, it's run by the same family that owns

CHETTINADU'S MANSIONS

Chettiar mansions are deeply traditional, privately owned family homes, with very limited visitor information. Several are open to the public, but opening hours can be erratic.

Athangudi Palace (Lakshmi House; Athangudi Rd, Athangudi; ₹100; ⊙9am-5pm) With perhaps the most exquisitely painted wood-carved ceilings in Chettinadu, Athangudi Palace is a popular film set. Take in the especially fine materials (Belgian marble, English iron), Chettiar history panels, chequered floors, and curious statues of British colonials and Hindu gods looming above the entrance.

CVCT and CVR House (CVRMCT St, Kanadukathan; ₹50; ⊙9am-5pm) Backed by the typical succession of pillar-lined courtyards, the impressive reception hall of this 'twin house' is shared by two branches of the same family. Don't miss the fabulous views over neighbouring mansions from the rooftop terrace.

VVR House (CVRMCT St, Kanadukathan; ⊙9am-5pm, hours vary) One of Chettinadu's oldest mansions, built in 1870 with distinctive egg-plaster walls, Burmese-teak columns, patterned tiled floors and intricate wood carvings. A ₹50 group 'donation' is expected.

Chettinadu Mansion. There's a shared kitchen and a pleasant, shaded outdoor garden space. If you're on a budget, stay here.

★ **Saratha Vilas**   BOUTIQUE HOTEL $$$
(☏9884936158, 9884203175; www.sarathavilas.com; 832 Main Rd, Kothamangalam; r incl breakfast ₹7200-12,100; ❄@🗋🐕) A different Chettiar charm inhabits this gorgeously renovated, French-run mansion from 1910, 6km east of Kanadukathan. Rooms combine the traditional and the contemporary with distinct French panache; the food is an exquisite mix of Chettiar and French; and there's a chic saltwater pool.

Most furnishings were personally designed by the knowledgable architect owners, hugely active players in the preservation of Chettinadu heritage.

They're also founders of local conservation NGO ArcHeS.

★ **Bangala**   HERITAGE HOTEL $$$
(☏04565-220221; www.thebangala.com; Devakottai Rd, Karaikudi; r incl breakfast ₹7640-8860; ❄🗋🐕) Chettinadu's original heritage hotel, this lovingly revamped, efficiently managed whitewashed 'bungalow' isn't a typical mansion but has all the requisite charm: colour-crammed rooms, antique furniture, old family photos and a beautiful tile-fringed pool. It's famous for its food: banana-leaf 'meals' (veg/nonveg ₹900/1000) are actually Chettiar wedding feasts (12.30pm to 2.30pm and 8pm to 10pm; book two hours ahead).

There are cooking 'masterclasses', yoga retreats, massage, and exclusive-access visits to local mansions.

★ **Visalam**   HERITAGE HOTEL $$$
(☏04565-273301; www.cghearth.com; Local Fund Rd, Kanadukathan; r incl breakfast from ₹8140; ❄@🗋🐕) Stunningly restored and professionally run by a Malayali hotel chain, Visalam is a relatively young Chettiar mansion, done in a fashionable 1930s art deco style. It's still decorated with the original owners' photos, furniture and paintings. The garden is exquisite, the 15 large rooms full of character, and the pool setting magical, with overflowing bougainvillea and a low-key restaurant alongside.

Chettinadu Court   HOTEL $$$
(☏9585594087; www.chettinadcourt.com; Raja's St, Kanadukathan; r incl breakfast from ₹4490; ❄🗋🐕) For a (relatively) economical Chettinadu sojourn, welcoming Chettinadu Court offers eight pleasant rooms sporting Athangudi tiles and a few heritage touches, along with a casual dining room that's really Kanadukathan's main tourist restaurant. The hotel shares an off-site pool with its nearby sister property Chettinadu Mansion.

Chettinadu Mansion   HERITAGE HOTEL $$$
(☏04565-273080; www.chettinadmansion.com; SARM House, 11 AR St, Kanadukathan; r incl breakfast from ₹6850; ❄🗋🐕) Friendly, well run and packed with character, this colourful century-old mansion is still owned (and lived in) by the original family. Of its 126 rooms, 12 are open to guests – all sizeable, with wacky colour schemes and private balconies gazing out over other mansions. The owners also run nearby Chettinadu Court, which has eight heritage-inspired rooms. The two share an off-site pool.

ⓘ Getting There & Away

Car is the best way to get to and around Chettinadu. Renting one with a driver from Trichy, Thanjavur or Madurai for two days costs around ₹7500. Or take a bus to whichever town you'd like to stay in – or as close to it as you can get – and hire a car there for day trips, for about ₹2500 per day.

From Trichy, buses run every five or 10 minutes to Pudukkottai (₹44, 1½ hours) and Karaikkudi (₹90, two hours); you can hop off and on along the way. From Madurai, buses run to Karaikkudi (₹95, two hours) every 30 minutes. There are also buses from Thanjavur and Rameswaram.

Three daily trains connect Chennai Egmore with Pudukkottai (sleeper/2AC/3AC ₹265/720/1035, six to eight hours) and Karaikkudi (₹280/775/1085, 6½ to 9½ hours). One train connects Chennai with Chettinad Station, for Kanadukathan (₹275/745/1070, nine hours).

Madurai

📞 0452 / POP 1.6 MILLION

Chennai may be the capital of Tamil Nadu, but Madurai claims its soul. Madurai is Tamil-born and Tamil-rooted, one of the oldest cities in India, a metropolis that traded with ancient Rome and was a great capital long before Chennai was even dreamed of.

Tourists, Indian and foreign, come here for the celebrated Meenakshi Amman Temple (p1067), a dazzling mazelike structure ranking among India's greatest temples. Otherwise, Madurai, perhaps appropriately given its age, captures many of India's glaring dichotomies: a centre dominated by a medieval temple and an economy increasingly driven by IT, all overlaid with the hustle, energy and excitement of a big Indian city and slotted into a much more manageable package than Chennai's sprawl.

History

Legend has it that Shiva showered drops of nectar *(madhuram)* from his locks on to the city, giving rise to the name Madurai – 'the City of Nectar'.

Ancient documents record the existence of Madurai from the 3rd century BC. It was a trading town, especially in spices, and according to legend was home to the third *sangam* (gathering of Tamil scholars and poets). Over the centuries Madurai came under the sway of the Cholas, Pandyas, local Muslim sultans, Hindu Vijayanagar kings and the Nayaks, who ruled until 1736 and set out the old city's lotus shape. The bulk of the Meenakshi Amman Temple was built under Tirumalai Nayak (1623–59), and Madurai became the hub of Tamil culture, playing an important role in the development of the Tamil language.

In 1840 the British East India Company razed Madurai's fort and filled in its moat. The four broad Veli streets were constructed on top and to this day define the old city's limits.

⊙ Sights

★ Meenakshi
Amman Temple   HINDU TEMPLE
(East Chitrai St; Indian/foreigner ₹5/50; ⊘5am-12.30pm & 3.30-10pm) The colourful abode of the triple-breasted warrior goddess Meenakshi ('fish-eyed' – an epithet for perfect eyes in classical Tamil poetry) is generally considered to be the peak of South Indian temple architecture, as vital to this region's aesthetic heritage as the Taj Mahal to North India. It's not so much a 17th-century temple as a 6-hectare complex with 12 tall *gopurams,* encrusted with a staggering array of gods, goddesses, demons and heroes (1511 on the 55m-high south *gopuram* alone).

According to legend, the beautiful Meenakshi (a version of Parvati) was born with three breasts and this prophecy: her superfluous breast would melt away when she met her husband. This happened when she met Shiva and took her place as his consort. The existing temple was mostly built during the 17th-century reign of Tirumalai Nayak, but its origins go back 2000 years to when Madurai was a Pandyan capital.

The four streets surrounding the temple are pedestrian-only. Temple dress codes and security are airport-strict: no shoulders or legs (of either gender) may be exposed, and no bags or cameras are allowed inside. Despite this, the temple has a happier atmosphere than some of Tamil Nadu's more solemn shrines, and is adorned with especially vibrant ceiling and wall paintings. Every evening at 9pm, a frenetic, incense-clouded procession carries an icon of Sundareswarar (Shiva) to Meenakshi's shrine to spend the night; visitors can follow along.

Before or after entering the temple, look around the **Pudhu Mandapa** (⊘dawn-dusk) **FREE**. The main temple entrance is through the eastern (oldest) *gopuram*. First, on the right, you'll come to the Thousand Pillared Hall, now housing the fascinating **Temple Art Museum** (Indian/foreigner ₹5/50, phone

TAMIL NADU MADURAI

Madurai

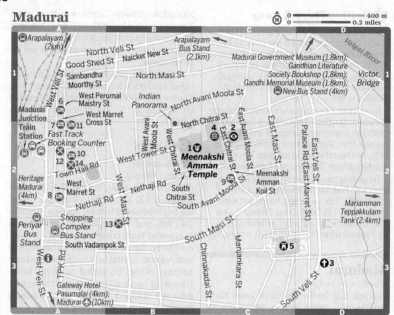

camera ₹50; ◷6am-2pm & 3-9pm). Moving on into the temple, you'll reach a Nandi shrine surrounded by more beautifully carved columns. Ahead is the main Shiva shrine, flanked on each side by massive *dwarpals*, and further ahead to the left in a separate enclosure is the main Meenakshi shrine, both off limits to non-Hindus. Anyone can, however, wander round the Golden Lotus Tank, where a small pavilion jutting out at the western end has ceiling murals depicting Sundareswarar and Meenakshi's marriage. Leave the temple via a hall of flower sellers and the arch-ceilinged Ashta Shakti Mandapa – lined with relief carvings of the goddess' eight attributes and displaying the loveliest of all the temple's elaborately painted ceilings; this is actually the temple entrance for most worshippers.

Gandhi Memorial Museum   MUSEUM
(www.gandhimmm.org; Gandhi Museum Rd; camera ₹50; ◷10am-1pm & 2-5.45pm) **FREE** Housed in a 17th-century Nayak queen's palace, this impressive museum contains a moving, comprehensive account of Gandhi's life and India's struggle for independence from 1757 to 1947; the English-language displays spare no detail about British rule. They include the blood-stained dhoti that Gandhi was wearing when he was assassinated in Delhi in 1948; it was here in Madurai, in 1921, that he first took up wearing the dhoti as a sign of native pride.

The small **Madurai Government Museum** (Gandhi Museum Rd; Indian/foreigner ₹5/100, camera ₹20; ◷9.30am-5pm Sat-Thu) is next door, and the Gandhian Literature Society Bookshop behind. Buses 3, 66, 75 and 700 from the **Periyar Bus Stand** (West Veli St) go to the Tamukkam bus stop on Alagarkoil Rd, 600m west of the museum.

Tirumalai Nayak Palace   PALACE
(Palace Rd; Indian/foreigner ₹10/50, camera/video ₹30/100; ◷9am-1pm & 1.30-5pm) What Madurai's Meenakshi Amman Temple is to Nayak religious architecture, Tirumalai Nayak's crumbling palace is to the secular. It's said to be only a quarter of its original size, but its massive scale and hybrid Dravidian Islamic style still testify to the lofty aspirations of its creator. From the east-side entrance, a large courtyard surrounded by tall, thick columns topped with fancy stucco work leads to the grand throne chamber with its 25m-high dome; two stone-carved horses frame the steps up.

Off the chamber's northwest corner is the Natakasala (Dance Hall), with a small archaeological collection.

Madurai

St Mary's Cathedral   CHURCH
(East Veli St; ⊙6am-6pm) This 20th-century
neo-Gothic construction's simple stained-
glass windows and bold-orange vaulting are
offset by a magnificent blue-and-white exterior with twirling spires.

It's just around the corner from the Tirumalai Nayak Palace.

⚡ Activities

Sivananda Vedanta Yoga Centre   YOGA
(☎0452-2521170; http://sivananda.org.in; 444 KK
Nagar, East 9th St; classes ₹400; ⊙6am-8.30pm
Mon-Sat, 6.30am-5.30pm Sun) Offers daily drop-
in yoga classes (book a day ahead) and 10-
day programs (₹6000). Also runs rigorous
extended courses at its ashram, 22km north
of Madurai.

⟳ Tours

Storytrails   WALKING
(☎7373675756; www.storytrails.in; 23 Park Ave, Old
Natham Rd; tours per person ₹1600-6000) This
Chennai-born organisation runs highly rated
story-based neighbourhood walking tours.
Prices depend on group size.

Foodies Day Out   FOOD & DRINK
(☎9840992340; www.foodiesdayout.com; 2nd fl,
393 Anna Nagar Main Rd; per person from ₹2500)
The best way to delve into Madurai's famous
foodie culture is on a fantastic evening tour
with these local culinary enthusiasts. Vegetarian and vegan options available.

🛏 Sleeping

TM Lodge   HOTEL $
(☎0452-2341651; 50 West Perumal Maistry St; s/d
₹680/980, with AC ₹1350-1570; ❋) The walls are
a bit scuffed, but the rooms are clean, mattresses are good, and TM is efficiently run.
Not bad at all for the price.

Treebo Berrys Boutique   HOTEL $$
(☎0452-2340256; www.berrysboutique.in; 25
West Perumal Maistry St; incl breakfast s/d from
₹1600/1900; ❋🛜) Berrys' 15 smart, con-
temporary, minimalist fruit-named rooms
are the most stylish on this hotel-packed
street. There's a soothing atmosphere, plus
a friendly welcome and an in-house restau-
rant. One of the best values in town – check
for online discounts.

Simap Residency   HOTEL $$
(☎0452-2350088; www.simapresidency.com;
12A/1 Meenakshi Amman Koil St; r incl breakfast
₹2500-2880; ❋🛜) Billing itself as a pilgrim
hotel open to all, the Simap is right in on
the temple action (and noise). Bare but
good-sized, modern rooms with tight white
sheets, AC and solar-heated water hide behind shiny wooden doors.

Madurai Residency   HOTEL $$
(☎0452-4380000; www.madurairesidency.com;
15 West Marret St; incl breakfast s ₹2950-3420, d
₹3300-3800; ❋🛜) The service is stellar and
the rooms are comfy and fresh at this win-
ner, which has a handy transport desk and
one of the the highest rooftop restaurants
in town. It's very popular, particularly with
Indian businessmen: book at least a day
ahead.

Hotel Park Plaza   HOTEL $$
(☎0452-4511111; www.hotelparkplaza.in; 114 West
Perumal Maistry St; s ₹2240-4800, d ₹2700-4800;
❋🛜) The Plaza's rooms are comfortable and
simply but smartly done up, with marble
floors, blue accent lighting and chunky mattresses; four have temple views. The (inap-
propriately named) Sky High Bar graces the
1st floor.

Hotel Supreme   HOTEL $$
(☎0452-2343151; www.hotelsupreme.in; 110 West
Perumal Maistry St; incl breakfast s ₹2450-3060, d
₹2700-3300; ❋🛜) A well-presented, slightly
faded hotel with friendly service; it's very
popular with domestic tourists. There's good
all-veg food at the rooftop Surya restaurant
(p1070).

TAMIL NADU MADURAI

★**Heritage Madurai**   HERITAGE HOTEL **$$$**
(☎9003043205;   www.heritagemadurai.com;
11 Melakkal Main Rd, Kochadai; r ₹6500-9600;
❄☎✿) This leafy haven, 4km northwest of
central Madurai, originally housed the old
Madurai Club. It's been impeccably tarted
up, with intricate Kerala-style woodwork,
a sultry sunken pool and airy, terracot-
ta-floored 'deluxe' rooms. Best are the 'villas'
featuring private plunge pools. There's a
good upscale North and South Indian res-
taurant (p1070), along with a spa, bar and
24-hour cafe.

**Gateway Hotel
Pasumalai**   HERITAGE HOTEL **$$$**
(☎0452-6633000; www.gateway.tajhotels.com; 40
TPK Rd, Pasumalai; r incl breakfast ₹8100-12,800;
@☎✿) A refreshing escape from the city
scramble, the Taj-group Gateway sprawls
across hilltop gardens 6km southwest of Madurai centre. The views, outdoor pool and
60 resident peacocks are wonderful, and
rooms are comfy and well equipped, with
glassed-in showers and do-it-yourself yoga
kits. The **Garden All Day** (☎0452-6633000;
www.gateway.tajhotels.com;   mains   ₹300-700;
☺6.30am-11pm) restaurant is excellent.

✕ Eating

★**Murugan Idli Shop**   SOUTH INDIAN **$**
(http://muruganidlishop.com; 196 West Masi St;
dishes ₹15-75; ☺7am-10.30pm) Though it now
has multiple Chennai branches, Murugan is
Madurai born and bred. Here you can put
the fluffy signature *idli* and chutneys to the
test, and feast on South Indian favourites
like dosa, *vada* and *uttapam*.

★**Sri Sabareesh**   INDIAN **$**
(49A West Perumal Maistry St; mains ₹65-90;
☺6am-11.30pm) Decked with old-Madurai
photos, Sri Sabareesh is a popular pure-veg
cheapie that rustles up good South Indian
thalis (₹90), dosa, *idli, uttapam* and *vada,*
plus sturdy mains.

Surya   MULTICUISINE **$**
(www.hotelsupreme.in; Hotel Supreme, 110 West
Perumal Maistry St; mains ₹80-160; ☺4pm-mid-
night) The Hotel Supreme's rooftop restaurant offers excellent service, good pure-veg
food and superb city and temple views. The
iced coffee might have been brewed by the
gods when you sip it on a hot, dusty day. The
downstairs AC restaurant is open from 7am.

Kumar Mess   SOUTH INDIAN **$$**
(96A West Perumal Maistry St; mains ₹140-280;
☺noon-4pm & 6.30-11pm) The nondescript fa-
cade leads into a casual dining space with
impeccable service, where a long list of meat
dishes is the main attraction. The chicken
dosa is fluffy and delicious!

Banyan Restaurant   INDIAN **$$$**
(☎0452-3244187; www.heritagemadurai.com; Her-
itage Madurai, 11 Melakkal Main Rd, Kochadai; mains
₹200-450; ☺7am-10.30pm) Set in the green-
clad Kerala-inspired grounds of the top-end
Heritage Madurai hotel (p1070), this elegant
eatery does beautifully spiced pan-Indian
dishes, along with popular lunchtime buffets. It's 4km northwest of central Madurai.

🛍 Shopping

Madurai teems with cloth stalls and tailors'
shops, as you might notice upon being approached by tailor touts. Drivers, guides
and touts will also be keen to lead you to
the craft shops in North and West Chitrai
Sts, offering to show you the rooftop temple
view – the views are good, and so is the inev-
itable sales pitch.

A great place for getting clothes made up
is the Pudhu Mandapa (p1067). Here you'll
find rows of tailors busily treadling away
and capable of whipping up a good replica
of whatever you're wearing in an hour or
two. A cotton top or shirt can cost ₹350.

ℹ Information

Indian Panorama (☎0452-2525821; www.
indianpanorama.in; North Chitrai St; ☺10am-
7pm Mon-Sat) Reliable South India–based
agency covering all of India.
Tourist office (☎0452-2334757; www.tamil-
nadutourism.org; 1 West Veli St; ☺10am-6pm
Mon-Fri) Also has branches at the airport and
train station.

ℹ Getting There & Away

AIR
➤ Madurai Airport is 12km south of town.
➤ SpiceJet (www.spicejet.com) flies once daily
to Colombo, Dubai and Hyderabad, and three
times daily to Chennai.
➤ Indigo (www.goindigo.in) flies five times a
day to Chennai and twice to Bengaluru and
Hyderabad.
➤ Jet Airways (www.jetairways.com) flies daily
to Chennai and Mumbai.

BUS

Most government buses arrive at and depart from the **New Bus Stand** (Melur Rd), 4km northeast of the centre. Services to Coimbatore, Kodaikanal, Ooty and Munnar go from the **Arapalayam Bus Stand** (Puttuthoppu Main Rd), 2km northwest of the old city. For Kanyakumari, take the bus to Nagercoil and change there. Tickets for more expensive (and more comfortable) private buses are sold by agencies on the south side of the **Shopping Complex Bus Stand** (btwn West Veli St & TPK Rd); most travel overnight.

TRAIN

From Madurai Junction station, 12 daily trains head to Trichy and 10 to Chennai; fastest is the 7am Vaigai Express (Trichy 2nd/chair class ₹95/345, two hours; Chennai ₹180/665, 7¾ hours). A good overnight Chennai train is the 8.40pm Pandian Express (sleeper/3AC/2AC/1AC ₹315/815/1150/1940, nine hours). To Kanyakumari the only daily train departs at 1.30am (sleeper/3AC/2AC/1AC ₹210/540/745/1245, five hours), but there are six daily trains to Nagercoil, near Kanyakumari.

Other destinations include the following (prices are for sleeper/3AC/2AC):

Bengaluru (two daily, ₹260/700/1000, 9½ hours)

Coimbatore (two daily, ₹235/595/830, 5½ hours)

Mumbai (Monday, Tuesday, Wednesday and Friday, ₹645/1705/2505, 34 hours)

Trivandrum (five daily, ₹205/550/780, seven hours)

❶ Getting Around

TO/FROM THE AIRPORT

Taxis cost ₹550 between the centre and the airport; Ola cars are closer to ₹400. Alternatively, bus 10 (₹15) runs to/from the Shopping Complex Bus Stand.

BUS

➡ From the New Bus Stand (p1071), buses 3, 48 and 700 shuttle into the city; an autorickshaw is ₹150.

➡ From Arapalayam Bus Stand (p1071), take a rickshaw to the centre for ₹100.

➡ Buses 3, 66, 75 and 700 from the central Periyar Bus Stand (p1068) run to the Gandhi Museum area.

TAXI

➡ There's a fixed-rate **taxi stand** (Madurai Junction) outside Madurai Junction train station, with fare boards (one day around Madurai ₹1400 to ₹1800).

➡ Fast Track also has a **taxi booking counter** (☏0452-2888999; Madurai Junction; ⊙24hr) here; rates are ₹90 for the first 3km, then ₹16 per kilometre.

Rameswaram

☏04573 / POP 45,000

Rameswaram was once the southernmost point of sacred India; leaving its boundaries meant abandoning caste and falling below the status of the lowliest skinner of sacred cows. Then Rama (incarnation of Vishnu, hero of the Ramayana) led a monkey-and-bear army across a monkey-built bridge to (Sri) Lanka, defeating the demon Ravana and rescuing his wife, Sita. Afterwards, prince and princess offered thanks to Shiva here. Today, millions of Hindus flock to the Ramanathaswamy Temple (p1072) to worship where a god worshipped a god.

GOVERNMENT BUSES FROM MADURAI

DESTINATION	FARE (₹)	TIME (HR)	DEPARTURES
Bengaluru (Bangalore)	515-700	9-10	8 buses 7pm-9.35pm
Chennai	635-975	9-10	every 30min, 5 AC buses 4pm-10pm
Kodaikanal	100	4	13 buses 1.30am-2.50pm, 5.50pm, 8.30pm
Coimbatore	170	5	every 10min
Ernakulam (Kochi)	325	9½	9am, 8pm, 9pm
Nagercoil	240	6	every 30min
Munnar	180	5	5.55am, 8am, 10.40am
Mysuru (Mysore)	375-490	9-12	4.35pm, 6pm, 8pm, 9pm
Ooty	300	8	7.15am, 9.15pm
Puducherry (Pondicherry)	240-260	7½	9.05pm, 9.30pm
Rameswaram	140	4-5	every 15min
Trichy (Tiruchirappalli)	90	2¼-3	every 5min

DHANUSHKODI

Pamban Island's promontory stretches 22km southeast from Rameswaram, narrowing to a thin strip of silky sand dunes halfway along. Near the southeastern-most tip stands the ghost town of Dhanushkodi. Once a thriving port, Dhanushkodi was washed away by a monster cyclone in 1964. The shells of its train station, church, post office and other ruins stand among a scattering of fishers' shacks; Adam's Bridge (Rama's Bridge), the chain of reefs, sandbanks and islets that almost connects India with Sri Lanka, stretches away to the east. For many, this is the final stop of a long pilgrimage. The atmosphere is at its most magical at sunrise, with pilgrims performing *pujas*.

In years past, reaching Dhanushkodi required an adventurous drive or walk across several kilometres of dunes. But a new tarmac road has made the trip a snap – and much more popular. The best way to go is by car (₹1200 round trip), which can be arranged by the reliable **Pavan Tours & Travels** (☑9952556605; www.pavantoursand travels.com; East Car St, Rameswaram). You can explore the ruins, watch teams of fishers pulling in their nets, and get as close as possible to Sri Lanka from the Indian mainland – with the sea on both sides of you.

Otherwise, Rameswaram is a small, scruffy fishing town on conch-shaped Pamban Island, connected to the mainland by 2km-long bridges. If you aren't a pilgrim, the temple alone barely merits the journey here. But the island's eastern tip, Dhanushkodi, only 30km from Sri Lanka, has a magical natural beauty that adds to Rameswaram's appeal. And for activity-loving travellers, the island's western edge is buzzing as a low-key water-sports destination.

⊙ Sights & Activities

Ramanathaswamy Temple HINDU TEMPLE
(East Car St; ◷6am-1pm & 3-8.30pm) Housing the world's most sacred sand mound (a lingam said to have been created by Rama's wife Sita, so he could worship Shiva), this temple is one of India's holiest shrines. Dating mainly from the 16th to 18th centuries, it's notable for its lengthy 1000-pillar halls and 22 *theertham* (temple tanks), in which pilgrims bathe before visiting the deity. Attendants tip pails of water over the (often fully dressed) faithful, who rush from *theertham* to *theertham*.

Quest Academy WATER SPORTS
(☑9820367412; www.quest-asia.com; Pirappan Valasai, off Madurai-Rameswaram Hwy) ⊘ Run by a team of Mumbaikar adventure-activity experts, this laid-back, ecofriendly water-sports centre offers kitesurfing, kayaking, windsurfing, snorkelling, SUP, sailing, camping, beach clean-ups and after-dark wildlife walks. See the website for prices. It's based on the mainland, 18km west of the Pamban Island bridge.

⫶ Sleeping & Eating

Kathadi South HUT $$
(☑9820367412; www.quest-asia.com; off Old Dhanushkodhi Rd, Pamban Island; s/d incl breakfast ₹2000/2750) ⊘ In calm palm-shaded grounds, Quest Academy offers three fuss-free thatched huts with shared bathrooms, along with a clutch of tents (single/double ₹1250/2200). There's solar power, home-cooked meals (₹350) and a shimmering white stretch of seafront sand just metres away. At the time of research, the camp was closed, and it was unknown whether it would reopen.

Kathadi North COTTAGE $$
(☑9820367412; www.quest-asia.com; Pirappan Valasai, off Madurai-Rameswaram Hwy; s/d incl breakfast ₹3500/4000; ⊛⌨) ⊘ Part of the wonderful Quest Academy water-sports centre, these four fan-cooled, beach-chic concrete huts with thatched roofs and open-air bathrooms huddle just inland from bleach-blond sands, on the mainland 18km west of Pamban Island. Rainwater is harvested, power is solar, doors are recycled and palm fences use on-site materials. The open kitchen dishes out communal meals (₹450 to ₹550).

Hotel Saara HOTEL $$
(☑9442700601; www.hotelsaara.com; 25 Mandi St; r ₹1680; ⊛⌨) This new hotel is probably the best bang for your buck in Rameswaram. Fresh rooms have tiled walls (no scuffed and hand-smudged paint!), in-room wi-fi and helpful management. It's on a relatively quiet side street near the temple.

Jiwan Residency
HOTEL $$

(☑04573-222207; www.jiwanresidency.com; Sangumal, Olaikuda Rd; r incl breakfast ₹3420-4110, ste ₹5400-5900; ⊛🌐) Towards the northeastern end of Rameswaram's seafront road, Jiwan is one of your best options: a fresh, neat business-styled hotel with bright, modern rooms in creams and beiges. Spacious 'superior' rooms have balconies; the two 'suites' enjoy ocean panoramas.

Daiwik Hotel
HOTEL $$

(☑04573-223222; www.daiwikhotels.com; Madurai–Rameswaram Hwy; r ₹4150-5000; ⊛🌐) Gleaming, comfy and welcoming, 'India's first four-star pilgrim hotel', 200m west of the bus station, is your classiest choice in Rameswaram. Airy rooms come smartly decked out with huge mirrors and local-life photos, there's a spa, and the pure-veg **Ahaan** (mains ₹160-270; ☺7am-10pm) restaurant is good.

Hotel Sri Saravana
HOTEL $$

(☑04573-223367; www.srisaravanahotel.com; 1/9A South Car St; r ₹1500-4500; ⊛🌐) The most popular of the town-centre hotels, Sri Saravana is friendly and clean enough, with decent service and spacious, erratically styled rooms. Higher-rated, huge rooms towards the top have sea views.

Hotel Annapoorna
INDIAN $

(West Car St; mains ₹70-120; ☺7am-10pm) A busy joint for south Indian breakfasts and thalis.

ⓘ Getting There & Away

Rameswaram's **bus stand** (Madurai-Rameswaram Hwy) is 2.5km west of town. Buses run to Madurai (₹150, four hours) every 10 minutes and to Trichy (₹250, seven hours) every 30 minutes. 'Ultra Deluxe' (UD) services are scheduled to Chennai (₹630, 13 hours) at 4.30pm and 5pm, plus one AC bus at 4pm (₹900). Other routes include Kanyakumari (₹300, eight hours) at 1.30pm and 5.55pm, and Bengaluru (₹7400, 12 hours) at 4.30pm, but these don't always run.

The train station is 1.5km southwest of the temple. Six daily trains to/from Madurai (₹35, four hours) have unreserved seating only. The Rameswaram–Chennai Express departs daily at 8.15pm (sleeper/3AC/2AC ₹360/950/1340, 11 hours) via Trichy (₹215/540/745, five hours). The Rameswaram–Kanyakumari Express leaves at 8.50pm Monday, Thursday and Saturday, reaching Kanyakumari (sleeper/3AC ₹275/710) at 4.10am.

Kanyakumari (Cape Comorin)

☑04652 / POP 22,450

This is it, the end of India. There's a sense of accomplishment on making it to the tip of the subcontinent's 'V', past the final dramatic flourish of the Western Ghats and the green fields, glinting rice paddies and slow-looping wind turbines of India's deep south. Kanyakumari can feel surreal; at certain times of year you'll see the sun set and the moon rise over three seas (Bay of Bengal, Arabian Sea, Indian Ocean) simultaneously. The Temple of the Virgin Sea Goddess, Swami Vivekananda's legacy and the 'Land's End' symbolism draw crowds of pilgrims and tourists to Kanyakumari, but it remains a small-scale, refreshing respite from the hectic Indian road.

◉ Sights

★ Padmanabhapuram Palace
PALACE

(☑04651-250255; Padmanabhapuram; Indian/foreigner ₹35/300, camera/video ₹50/2000; ☺9am-12.30pm & 2-4.30pm Tue-Sun) With a forest's worth of intricately carved rosewood ceilings and polished-teak beams, this labyrinthine palace, 35km northwest of Kanyakumari, near the Kerala border, is considered the finest example of traditional Keralan architecture today. Asia's largest wooden palace complex, it was once capital of Travancore, an unstable princely state taking in parts of both Tamil Nadu and Kerala. Under successive rulers it expanded into a magnificent conglomeration of corridors, courtyards, gabled roofs and 14 palaces. The oldest sections date to 1550.

Buses run every 20 minutes from Kanyakumari to Thuckalay (₹33, 1½ hours), from where it's an autorickshaw ride or 15-minute walk to the palace. Return taxis from Kanyakumari cost ₹1200.

From Thiruvananthapuram, take any bus towards Kanyakumari (₹80, three hours, four daily) and get off at Thuckalay. The Kerala Tourist Development Corporation (p949) runs full-day Kanyakumari tours from Thiruvananthapuram covering Padmanabhapuram (₹990, minimum four people, Tuesday to Sunday).

Vivekananda Memorial
MONUMENT

(₹20; ☺7.45am-4pm) Four hundred metres offshore is the rock where famous Hindu apostle Swami Vivekananda meditated from 25 to 27 December 1892, and decided to take his moral message beyond India's shores. A two-*mandapa* 1970 memorial to Vivekananda reflects temple architectural styles from across India. The lower *mandapa* contains what's believed to be goddess Kumari's footprint. With the constant tourist crowds this brings, Vivekananda would no doubt choose somewhere else to meditate today. Ferries shuttle out to the rock (₹50 return).

Vivekanandapuram ASHRAM
(☎04652-247012; www.vrmvk.org; Vivekanandapuram; ☺9am-8pm) Just 1km north of Kanyakumari, this peaceful ashram (offering a variety of yoga retreats) is the headquarters of spiritual organisation Vivekananda Kendra, devoted to carrying out Vivekananda's teachings. Its Vivekananda-focused 'Arise! Awake!' (₹10; ☺9am-1pm & 4-8pm Wed-Mon, 9am-1pm Tue) exhibition is worth a visit, as is the **Ramayana Darshanam** (₹30; ☺10am-1pm & 4-9pm), and you can stroll to the sea past a beautiful lotus-pool-lined memorial to the swami.

Thiruvalluvar Statue MONUMENT
(☺7.45am-4pm) FREE Looking like an Indian Colossus of Rhodes, the towering statue on the smaller island next to the Vivekananda Memorial (p1073) is of the ancient Tamil poet Thiruvalluvar. The work of more than 5000 sculptors, it was erected in 2000 and honours the poet's 133-chapter work *Thirukural* – hence its height of exactly 133ft (40.5m). Tides permitting, Vivekananda Memorial ferries (₹50 return) continue to Thiruvalluvar.

Kumari Amman Temple HINDU TEMPLE
(Sannathi St; ☺4.30am-noon & 4-8.30pm) The legends say the *kanya* (virgin) goddess Kumari, a manifestation of the Great Goddess Devi, single-handedly conquered demons and secured freedom for the world. At this temple on the tip of the subcontinent, pilgrims give her thanks in an intimately spaced, beautifully decorated temple, where the crash of waves from three seas can be heard beyond the twilight glow of oil fires clutched in vulva-shaped votive candles (referencing the sacred femininity of the goddess).

It's said that the temple's east-facing door stays locked to prevent the shimmer of the goddess' diamond nose-stud leading ships astray. From the main north-side gate, you'll be asked for a ₹20 donation to enter the 18th-century inner precinct, where men must remove their shirts, and cameras are forbidden.

The shoreline around the temple has a couple of tiny beaches, and bathing ghats where worshippers immerse themselves before visiting the temple. The *mandapa* just south of the temple is popular for sunset-watching and daytime shade.

**Swami Vivekananda
Wandering Monk Exhibition** MUSEUM
(Beach Rd; ₹10; ☺8am-noon & 4-8pm) In lovely leafy grounds, this excellent exhibition details Swami Vivekananda's wisdom, sayings, and encounters with the mighty and the lowly during his five years as a wandering monk around India from 1888 to 1893. Tickets also cover the Vivekananda-inspired 'Arise! Awake!' exhibition (p1074) in Vivekanandapuram, 1km north of town.

🛏 Sleeping

Hotel Narmadha HOTEL $
(☎04652-246365; Kovalam Rd; r ₹500-1000, with AC ₹1500; ❄︎🖥🗗) This long, colourful concrete block conceals friendly staff, a back-up generator and a range of budget rooms, with big steps up in quality the more you pay. The cheapest are bucket-water only, but the ₹1000 sea-view doubles with turquoise walls are good value.

Hotel Ocean Heritage HOTEL $$
(☎04652-247557; www.hoteloceanheritage.in; East Car St; s/d ₹1600/1800) Rupee for rupee perhaps the best value in Kanyakumari, this friendly hotel has comfortable beds, in-room wi-fi and 24-hour hot water. The best rooms have balconies with ocean glimpses, and the top floor restaurant makes a killer cold coffee.

Temple Citi HOTEL $$
(☎04652-246083; www.hoteltempleciti.com; West Car St; d from ₹1800; ❄︎🗗) Plain, gleaming, cream-clad rooms for two to six people, with AC, 24-hour hot water and spotless bathrooms, make this new-build block a popular choice and good value. Breakfast is included.

Hotel Sivamurugan HOTEL $$
(☎04652-246862; www.hotelsivamurugan.com; 2/93 North Car St; r ₹2600-3300; ❄︎🗗) A welcoming, well-appointed hotel, with spacious, spotless, marble-floored rooms and lobby-only wi-fi. 'Super-deluxes' have sea glimpses past a couple of buildings. Rates stay fixed year-round (a novelty for Kanyakumari) and there's 24-hour hot water.

Kanyakumari (Cape Comorin)

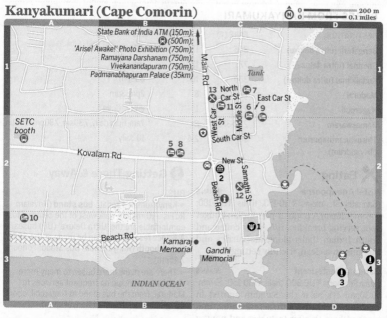

Kanyakumari (Cape Comorin)

⊙ Sights

1 Kumari Amman Temple....................C3
2 Swami Vivekananda Wandering
   Monk Exhibition...............................C2
3 Thiruvalluvar Statue.........................D3
4 Vivekananda Memorial.....................D3

🛏 Sleeping

5 Hotel Narmadha................................B2
6 Hotel Ocean Heritage.......................C1
7 Hotel Sivamurugan...........................C1

8 Hotel Tri Sea....................................B2
9 Seashore Hotel.................................C2
10 Sparsa Resort.................................A3
11 Temple Citi......................................C1

⊗ Eating

  Auroma....................................(see 10)
12 Hotel Annapoorna...........................C2
13 Sangam Restaurant.........................C1
  Seashore Hotel.......................(see 9)

Hotel Tri Sea   HOTEL $$
(☑04652-246586; www.hoteltrisea.in; Kovalam Rd; r ₹1000, with AC ₹1680-3200; ☀☞☐) You can't miss the high-rise Tri Sea, whose sea-view rooms are spacious, spotless and airy, with particularly hectic colour schemes. Cheaper rooms are smaller, but sometimes nicer, than pricier ones. Sunrise/sunset-viewing platforms and free in-room wi-fi are welcome bonuses, but the rooftop pool costs extra (₹200 per hour).

Sparsa Resort   RESORT $$$
(☑04652-247041; www.sparsaresorts.com; 6/112B Beach Rd; r incl breakfast ₹5300-7100; ☀☞☐) Away from the temple frenzy, on the west edge of town, elegant Sparsa is several notch-

es above Kanyakumari's other hotels. Fresh, orange-walled rooms with low dark-wood beds, lounge chairs and mood-lighting make for a contemporary-oriental vibe, and there's a lovely pool surrounded by palms, as well as good Indian cooking at Auroma (p1076).

Seashore Hotel   HOTEL $$$
(☑04652-246704; www.theseashorehotel.com; East Car St; r ₹4100-7700; ☀☞) The fanciest town-centre hotel has shiny, roomy chambers with golden curtains and cushions, glassed-in showers and kettles. It's lost its original sparkle, but all rooms except the cheapest offer panoramic sea views, and the 7th-floor restaurant (p1076) is one of Kanyakumari's best.

BUSES FROM KANYAKUMARI

DESTINATION	FARE (₹)	TIME (HR)	DEPARTURES
Bengaluru (ultra deluxe)	866	12-14	4.30pm, 5pm
Chennai (ultra deluxe)	775	12-14	5 daily
Kodaikanal (ultra deluxe)	360	10	8.15pm
Madurai	250	8	2pm, 3pm
Nagercoil	22	1	every 10min
Rameswaram	250-375	8	7am, 6pm daily, 7.30am, 7.30pm Fri-Sun
Thiruvananthapurum (Trivandrum)	90	2½	10 daily

✗ Eating

Hotel Annapoorna   INDIAN $

(Sannathi St; mains ₹110-150, thalis ₹120-180; ☺6am-9.30pm) A popular pan-Indian budget spot serving breakfast *idli*, filter coffee and South Indian thalis alongside curries and biryanis, in a clean, friendly setting.

Sangam Restaurant   INDIAN $

(Main Rd; mains ₹110-300, thalis ₹100-150; ☺7am-10.30pm) It's as if the Sangam started in Kashmir, trekked south across India, and stopped here to offer tasty veg and nonveg picks from every province along the way. The seats are soft and the food is good.

Seashore Hotel   MULTICUISINE $$

(www.theseashorehotel.com; East Car St; mains ₹190-360; ☺7-10am & 12.30-10.30pm; ﹡) Amazingly, this spruced-up 7th-floor hotel (p1075) restaurant is the only one in Kanyakumari with a proper sea view. There are plenty of Indian veg and nonveg choices, plus the odd continental creation. The Irani fish tikka is fantastic. Service is spot on, and it's a good breakfast bet (buffet ₹270).

Auroma   MULTICUISINE $$$

(www.sparsaresorts.com; Sparsa Resort, 6/112B Beach Rd; mains ₹200-700; ☺7-10am, noon-3pm, 7-11pm) Tucked away inside the stylish Sparsa Resort (p1075), 1km west of Kanyakumari's centre, lime-themed Auroma turns out tasty, refined tandoori and South Indian fare, plenty of seafood and decent breakfasts in fancy surrounds.

ⓘ Information

Tourist Office (☏04652-246276; Beach Rd; ☺10am-5.30pm Mon-Fri) Friendly but essentially useless.

ⓘ Getting There & Away

BUS

➤ Kanyakumari's sedate **bus stand** (Kovalam Rd) is a 10-minute walk west of the centre. Most comfortable are the 'Ultra Deluxe' (UD) buses. Advance reservations can be made at the **SETC ticket booth** (Kanyakumari Bus Stand; ☺noon-7.45pm).

➤ There are many more buses to many more destinations, including frequent services to Madurai, from the bus stand at Nagercoil, about 45 minutes northwest of Kanyakumari.

TRAIN

The train station is 800m north of Kanyakumari's centre. One daily northbound train, the Kanyakumari Express, departs at 5.20pm for Chennai (sleeper/3AC/2AC/1AC ₹415/1100/1565/2640, 13 hours) via Madurai (₹210/540/745/1245, 4½ hours) and Trichy (₹275/710/1000/1675, seven hours). Two daily express trains depart at 6.40am and 10am for Thiruvananthapurum (Trivandrum; sleeper/3AC/2AC ₹140/495/700, 2¼ hours), continuing to Kollam (Quilon; ₹140/495/700, 3½ hours) and Ernakulam (Kochi; ₹205/550/780, seven hours). More trains go from Nagercoil Junction, 20km northwest of Kanyakumari.

For real train buffs, the Vivek Express runs to Dibrugarh (Assam), 4236km and 80 hours away – India's longest single train ride. It departs Kanyakumari at 11pm Thursday (₹1085/2830/4265).

THE WESTERN GHATS

Welcome to the lush Western Ghats, some of the most precious heat relief in India. Rising like an impassable bulwark of evergreen and deciduous tangle, from north of Mumbai to the tip of Tamil Nadu, the World Heritage–listed Ghats (with an average elevation of 915m) contain 27% of India's flowering plant species and an incredible array of endemic wildlife. In Tamil Nadu they rise to over 2000m in the Palani Hills around Kodaikanal and the Nilgiris around Ooty. British influence lingers a little stronger up in these hills, where colonialists built 'hill stations' to escape the sweltering plains and covered slopes in neatly trimmed tea plantations. It's not just the air and (relative) lack of pollution that's refreshing – there's a certain acceptance of quirkiness and eccentricity here. Expect organic farms, handlebar-moustached trekking guides and leopard-print earmuffs.

Kodaikanal (Kodai)

🖉 04542 / POP 36,500 / ELEV 2100M

There are few more refreshing Tamil Nadu moments than leaving the heat-soaked plains for the sharp pinch of a Kodaikanal night or morning. This misty hill station, 120km northwest of Madurai in the protected Palani Hills, is more relaxed and intimate than its big sister Ooty (Kodai is the 'Princess of Hill Stations', Ooty the Queen). It's not all cold either; days feel more like deep spring than early winter.

Centred on a beautiful star-shaped lake, Kodai rambles up and down hillsides with patches of *shola* (virgin forest), unique to South India's Western Ghats, and evergreen broadleaf trees like magnolia, mahogany, myrtle and rhododendron. Another plant speciality is the *kurinji* shrub, whose lilac-blue blossoms appear every 12 years (next due 2030).

Kodai is popular with honeymooners and groups, who flock to its spectacular viewpoints and waterfalls. The renowned Kodaikanal International School provides some cosmopolitan flair. Visit midweek for peace and quiet.

👁 Sights

Berijam Lake   LAKE
(⏰9am-3pm) FREE Visiting forest-fringed Berijam Lake, 21km southwest of Kodaikanal, requires a Forest Department permit (₹250). Taxi drivers will organise this, if asked the day before, and do half-day 'forest tours' to Berijam, via other lookouts, for ₹2000.

**Sacred Heart Natural
Science Museum**   MUSEUM
(Kodaikanal Museum; Sacred Heart College, Law's Ghat Rd; adult/child ₹20/10, camera ₹20; ⏰9am-6pm) In the grounds of a former Jesuit seminary 4km downhill east of town, this museum has a ghoulishly intriguing miscellany of flora and fauna put together over more than 100 years by priests and trainees. Displays range over bottled snakes, human embryos (!), giant moths and stuffed animal carcasses. You can also see pressed famous *kurinji* flowers (*Strobilanthes kunthiana*).

Parks, Viewpoints & Waterfalls
Several natural beauty spots around Kodai (crowded with souvenir and snack stalls) are very popular with Indian tourists. They're best visited by taxi; drivers offer three-hour 12-stop tours for ₹1600 to ₹2000. On clear days, **Green Valley View** (⏰dawn-dusk) FREE, 6km from the centre, **Pillar Rocks** (₹5, camera ₹20; ⏰9am-4pm) FREE, 7km from the centre, and less-visited **Moir's Point** (₹10; ⏰10am-5pm), 13km from the centre, all along the same road west of town, have spectacular views to the plains below.

Other popular beauty spots include **Bryant Park** (off Lake Rd; adult/child ₹30/15, camera/video ₹50/100; ⏰9am-6pm), **Bear Shola Falls** and **Coaker's Walk** (₹10; ⏰7am-7pm).

🏃 Activities

The 5km Kodaikanal Lake circuit is lovely in the early morning before the crowds roll in. A walk along Lower Shola Rd takes you through the Bombay Shola, the nearest surviving patch of shola to central Kodai.

At the time of research, all hiking and trekking in the forests around Kodai was banned, following a forest fire in March 2018 in which 23 people died. To see if the situation has changed, contact the **District Forest Office** (🖉04542-241287; Muthaliarpuram; ⏰10am-5.45pm Mon-Fri); at the time of research they would not even offer a guess as to if or when the forests would reopen. Trails & Tracks (p1078) is your best local hiking resource, and Greenlands Youth Hostel (p1079) can also put you in touch with local guides (₹600 to ₹1000 per half-day) who can take you to places that are open.

Dolphin's Nose Walk   WALKING
This is a lovely walk of 4.5km (each way) from central Kodai, passing through budget-traveller hang-out Vattakanal to reach the Dolphin's Nose, a narrow rock lookout overhanging a precipitous drop. You might spot gaur (bison) or giant squirrels in the forested bits.

Kodaikanal (Kodai)

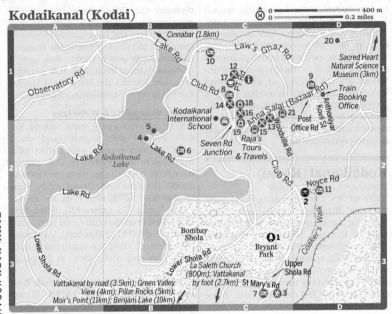

Trails & Tracks

TREKKING

(☎7598472791, 9965524279; thenaturetrails@
gmail.com; day walks per person per hour ₹100-500)
A reliable, well-established trekking outfit
run by very experienced local guide Vijay Kumar, offering day walks and overnight treks.
With the restrictions on hiking and camping
around Kodaikanal, he knows the best places that are still open, and operates multiday
trips overnighting in guesthouses. Book by
phone or email. Per-person price depends on
group size.

Boating & Cycling

If you're sappy in love like a bad Bollywood
song, the thing to do in Kodai is rent a pedal boat, rowing boat or Kashmiri *shikara*
(honeymoon boat) from the **Kodaikanal
Boat & Rowing Club** (Lake Rd; per 30min pedal
boat ₹100, shikara incl boater ₹490; ☉9am-6pm)
or **TTDC Boat House** (Lake Rd; per 30min
pedal boat ₹100, rowing boat/shikara incl boater
₹330/495; ☉9am-5.30pm).

Bicycle-rental (per hour ₹100) stands are
dotted around the lake.

🛏 Sleeping

Some hotels hike prices by up to 100% during the 'season' (April to June). There are
some gorgeous heritage places, and good-value midrange options if you can live without

colonial-era ambience. Most hotels have a
9am or 10am checkout April to June.

Sri Vignesh Guest House

GUESTHOUSE $

(☎9094972524; umaarkrishnan@gmail.com; Lake
Rd; r from ₹800; ☎) Up a steep driveway,
surrounded by neat flowery gardens with a
swing, this simple but characterful Raj-era
home is run by the kindly and interesting
Uma and Krishnan, who spent years in Africa for Krishnan's work as a humanitarian
doctor. Rooms are clean and very basic; you
have to schedule hot water as needed.

Snooze Inn

HOTEL $

(☎04542-240837; www.jayarajgroup.com; Anna
Salai; r ₹1000-1400; ☎) Rooms don't have quite
as much character as the exterior suggests,
but this is a decent-value budget choice
sporting clean bathrooms, plenty of blankets
and friendly staff.

★ Kodai Heaven

GUESTHOUSE $$

(☎8754707207, 9994116207; www.kodaiheaven.
com; 6 Dolphin's Nose Rd, Vattakanal; d ₹2800-
3800; ☎) This multilevel hillside guesthouse
will blow your mind with jaw-dropping
views that are far better than those offered
by any hotels in Kodaikanal proper. Rooms
are fun – some with wild murals inside and
out, others more subdued but still unique.
Most front on to terraces where you can sit

Kodaikanal (Kodai)

and gaze to your heart's content. Discounts are often available.

Altaf's Cafe GUESTHOUSE $$
(☎9487120846; www.altafscafe.com; Vattakanal; r ₹1500-3500) Popular little Middle Eastern–Italian Altaf's Cafe (p1081) runs a few sizeable doubles and three-bed rooms for six people (sometimes more!) with private bathroom, scattered across Vattakanal's hillside.

Mount Pleasant HOTEL $$
(☎9655126023, 04542-242023; www.kodaikanalheritage.com; 19/12-20 Observatory Rd; d incl breakfast ₹2250-2600; ☎) Despite being out on the fringes of Kodai's spaghetti-like street map, 2km west of the centre, Mount Pleasant is worth finding for its quiet setting, tasty food, and the welcoming Keralan owner's quirky

style (colourful wall weavings, coconut-wood beds, coir matting) – though the rooms feel a bit dowdy. Book ahead.

Greenlands Youth Hostel HOSTEL $$
(☎04542-240899; www.greenlandskodaikanal.com; St Mary's Rd; dm ₹600, d ₹1900-3000; ☎) This long-running, sociable budget favourite has moved into the midrange category, though many of its rooms don't reflect this. There's a pretty garden and wonderful views but the cheaper digs are basic. Hot water runs only from 8am to 10am. Dorms *may* be available, but are aimed at groups. Newer, comfier 'superdeluxes' are more modern, with colourful decor and balconies.

Hilltop Towers HOTEL $$
(☎04542-240413; www.hilltopgroup.in; Club Rd; incl breakfast d ₹2775-3150, ste ₹3600; ☎) Although it's bland on the outside, rustic flourishes like polished-teak floors, plus keen staff, in-room tea/coffee sets and a central location make the Hilltop a good-value midranger.

★Carlton HERITAGE HOTEL $$$
(☎04542-248555; www.carlton-kodaikanal.com; Lake Rd; r incl breakfast weekday/weekend from ₹8820/11,780; ☎) The cream of Kodai's hotels is a magnificent five-star colonial-era mansion overlooking the lake. Rooms are spacious with extra-comfy beds and, for some, huge private balconies. The grounds and common areas get the old hill-station ambience spot on: open-stone walls, billiards, evening bingo, fireplaces, a hot tub and a bar that immediately makes you want to demand a Scotch.

The good, buffet-focused restaurant (p1081) is Kodai's classiest.

Cinnabar HOMESTAY $$$
(☎9842145220; www.cinnabar.in; Chettiar Rd; r incl half-board ₹6000; ☎) ✎ Cinnabar's two elegant yet homey rooms offer a blissful escape, with 24-hour hot water, tea/coffee kits, glassed-in showers and lovely wooden floors and ceilings. Homemade cheese, bread, granola, jams and 'world' cuisine come courtesy of the clued-up owners, who recommend local hikes and source all ingredients from their organic fruit-and-veg garden out front. It's 2km north of town.

Elephant Valley FARMSTAY $$$
(☎9655439879; www.duneecogroup.com; Ganesh Puram, Pethupari; r incl breakfast with/without AC ₹9500/6500, ste from ₹15,350; ☎) ✎ Deep in

THE NILGIRIS & THEIR TRIBES

The forest-clothed, waterfall-threaded Nilgiris (Blue Mountains) rise abruptly from the surrounding plains between the lowland towns of Mettupalayam (southeast) and Gudalur (northwest). The upland territory, a jumble of valleys and hills with more than 20 peaks above 2000m, is a botanist's dream, with over 2300 flowering plant species, although much of the native *shola* forest and grasslands have been displaced by tea, coffee, eucalyptus and cattle.

Parts of the range are included in the Unesco-designated Nilgiri Biosphere Reserve, a 5520-sq-km area that arcs through Kerala, Tamil Nadu and Karnataka. One of the world's biodiversity hot spots, it contains several important tiger reserves, national parks and wildlife sanctuaries.

The Nilgiris' tribal inhabitants were left pretty much to themselves in this isolated homeland until the British arrived two centuries ago. Today, colonialism, migration, and Forest Department policies have reduced many tribal cultures to the point of collapse, and some have assimilated to the point of invisibility. Others, however, continue at least a semitraditional lifestyle.

Best known in Tamil Nadu's Western Ghats, thanks to their proximity to Ooty, are the Toda (around 1500). Some still inhabit tiny villages (*munds*) of traditional barrel-shaped huts made of bamboo, cane and grass. Toda women style their hair in long, shoulder-length ringlets, and are skilled embroiders; both sexes wear distinctive black-and-red-embroidered shawls. Central to Toda life is the water buffalo, which provides milk and ghee. Traditionally, it is only at funerals that the strictly vegetarian Toda kill a buffalo, to accompany the deceased.

Other tribes include the Kota (from around Kotagiri), Badaga, Irula, and Kurumba.

If you're interested in learning more about these communities, don't miss the Tribal Research Centre Museum (p1087), 10km southwest of Ooty. Organisations such as the Kotagiri-based Keystone Foundation (p1086) work to promote traditional crafts and activities.

the valley 22km northeast of Kodaikanal, off the Kodaikanal–Palani Rd, this ecofriendly French-run retreat sprawls across 48 hectares of mountain jungle and organic farm. Elephants, peacocks and bison wander through, and comfy local-material cottages, including a tree house, sit either side of a river. The French-Indian restaurant does wonderful meals packed with garden-fresh veg, and home-grown coffee. Wildlife spotting peaks April to July.

Cardamom House HOTEL $$$

(☑9360691793, 0451-2556765; www.cardamomhouse.com; near Athoor Village; r ₹4130-5550, with AC ₹5200-6500; ※☜⊠) 🌱 A beautiful hill-fringed hideaway, three hours' drive below Kodaikanal, seven-room Cardamom House overlooks bird-rich Lake Kamarajar (which you can admire from the pool). It's run with love by a retired Brit and local staff, and delicious meals (₹400 to ₹700) are made from locally sourced ingredients. Book well ahead. It's 5km west of Athoor Village, off the Dindigul–Batlagundu Rd.

Villa Retreat HOTEL $$$

(☑04542-240940; www.villaretreat.com; Club Rd; r incl breakfast ₹4250-7660; ☜) Take in the fantastic Coaker's Walk views from your garden breakfast table at this lovely old stone-built hotel, right next to the walk's northern end. It's a friendly place with comfy, good-sized rooms and, when it's cold, a roaring fire in the dining room. Prices are steep, but service is attentive. Morning nature walks are offered.

✗ Eating

★**Hotel Astoria** INDIAN $

(Anna Salai; mains ₹110-150, thalis ₹115-155; ⏱7am-10pm) This pure-veg restaurant is always packed with locals and tourists, especially at lunchtime when it serves fantastic all-you-can-eat thalis.

Pastry Corner BAKERY $

(3 Maratta Shopping Complex, Anna Salai; pastries from ₹80; ⏱10.30am-2pm & 3-6.30pm) Pick up oven-fresh muffins, croissants, cakes, cinnamon swirls and sandwiches at this popular

bakery, or squeeze on to the benches with a cuppa.

Tava
INDIAN $

(PT Rd; mains ₹70-140; ⏱11.30am-8.45pm Thu-Tue) Cheap, fast and clean, pure-veg Tava has a wide all-Indian menu; try the spicy, cauliflower-stuffed *gobi paratha* or *sev puri* (crisp, puffy fried bread with potato and chutney).

Ten Degrees
MULTICUISINE $$

(PT Rd; mains ₹260-480; ⏱noon-10pm) Honey-coloured wood and monochrome Kodai photos set the tone for tasty, elegantly prepared Indian and continental food. It does mouth-meltingly spicy wraps, homemade-bread sandwiches, burgers, salads, sizzlers, egg-based breakfasts and drinks served in jars.

Altaf's Cafe
MULTICUISINE $$

(☑9487120846; www.altafscafe.com; Vattakanal; dishes ₹70-200; ⏱8am-8.30pm) This open-sided cafe whips up soulful Italian, Indian and Middle Eastern dishes including breakfasts and *sabich* (Israeli aubergine-and-egg pita sandwiches), plus teas, coffees, juices and lassis, for hungry travellers in Vattakanal.

Muncheez
CONTINENTAL $$

(www.facebook.com/kodaimuncheez; PT Rd; mains ₹80-450; ⏱noon-9pm Fri-Wed) An always-busy hole-in-the-wall turned contemporary lounge with a signature-plastered bar, Muncheez is all about a short, simple menu of wraps, burgers, sandwiches and pizzas. Some fillings have delicious Indian twists, like *aloo jeera* (cumin potato) or red-hot paneer.

Carlton
MULTICUISINE $$$

(Lake Rd; buffet ₹950; ⏱7.30-10.30am, 1-3pm & 7.30-10pm) Definitely the place to come for a splash-out buffet-dinner fill-up: a huge variety of excellent Indian and continental dishes in limitless quantity. Lunch is à la carte.

Cloud Street
MULTICUISINE $$$

(www.cloudstreetcafe.com; PT Rd; mains ₹290-600; ⏱9-11am, 12.30-4pm & 6-9pm; 🛜) Why yes, that is a real Italian-style wood-fire pizza oven. And yes, that's hummus and falafel on the menu, along with oven-baked pasta and homemade cakes. It's all great food in a simple, relaxed, family-run setting with scattered candles and a crackling fire on cold nights. Live music every other Saturday.

🍷 Drinking & Nightlife

⭐Cafe Cariappa
CAFE

(www.facebook.com/cafecariappa; PT Rd; coffees ₹80-100; ⏱11am-6.30pm Tue-Sun; 🛜) A caffeine addict's dream, this rustic-chic wood-panelled shoebox of a cafe crafts fantastic brews from its own locally grown organic coffee. It also does homemade carrot cake, crêpes, sandwiches and fresh juices, and sells Kodai-made cheeses.

🛍 Shopping

Re Shop
ARTS & CRAFTS

(www.facebook.com/bluemangotrust; Seven Rd Junction; ⏱10am-1pm & 2-7pm Mon-Sat) 🧣 Stylish jewellery, fabrics, cards and more, at reasonable prices, made by and benefiting marginalised village women around Tamil Nadu.

Potter's Shed
CERAMICS

(PT Rd; ⏱11am-1pm & 2-6pm Mon-Sat) Perfect for pretty locally made mugs, bowls, plates and other pottery.

ℹ️ Information

Tourist office (☑04542-241675; PT Rd; ⏱10am-5.30pm Mon-Sat, to 2pm Sun) Doesn't look too promising at first glance but it's helpful enough.

ℹ️ Getting There & Away

BUS

For most destinations, it's quickest and easiest to take a bus from Kodai's **bus stand** (Anna Salai).

Private Buses

Raja's Tours & Travels (☑9842182851; http://rajastours.com; Anna Salai; ⏱8am-9pm) runs 20-seat minibuses with push-back seats to Ooty (₹500, eight hours, 7.30pm), plus overnight AC sleeper and semisleeper buses to Chennai (₹800 to ₹1200, 12 hours, 6.30pm) and Bengaluru (₹700 to ₹1000, 12 hours, 6.30pm). There are many other tour companies based at the bus stand.

TRAIN

The nearest train station is Kodai Rd, down in the plains 80km east of Kodaikanal. There are four daily trains to/from Chennai Egmore including the overnight Pandian Express (sleeper/3AC/2AC/1AC ₹295/765/1075/1815, 7½ hours), departing Chennai at 9.20pm and departing Kodai Rd northbound at 9.10pm. Kodai's post office has a **train booking office** (Post Office, Post Office Rd; ⏱9am-4pm Mon-Fri, to 2pm Sat).

Direct buses from Kodaikanal to Kodai Rd leave daily at 10.20am and 4.25pm (₹55, three hours);

GOVERNMENT BUSES FROM KODAIKANAL

DESTINATION	FARE (₹)	TIME (HR)	DEPARTURES
Bengaluru (Bangalore)	650	12	5.30pm
Chennai	600	12	6.30pm
Coimbatore	175	6	8.20am, 4.15pm
Madurai	120	4	15 daily
Trichy (Tiruchirappalli)	190	6	1.45pm, 3.30pm, 5.40pm, 6pm, 7pm

there are also plenty of buses between the train station and Batlagundu, on the Kodai–Madurai bus route. Taxis to/from the station cost ₹1200.

ℹ Getting Around

Central Kodaikanal is compact and easily walkable. There are no autorickshaws (believe it or not), but plenty of taxis. The minimum charge is ₹150 for up to 3km; to/from Vattakanal costs ₹400.

Bike rental is available around the lake (per hour ₹100).

Coimbatore

📞 0422 / POP 1.6 MILLION

This big business and junction city – Tamil Nadu's second largest, often known as the Manchester of India for its textile industry – is friendly enough and increasingly cosmopolitan, but the lack of interesting sights means that for most travellers it's just a stepping stone towards Ooty or Kerala. There are plenty of accommodation and eating options if you're staying overnight.

🏃 Activities

Isha Yoga Center YOGA, MEDITATION
(📞8300083111; www.ishafoundation.org; Poondi) This well-known ashram is 30km west of Coimbatore. Outside, there's a massive black sculpture of Shiva – claimed as the world's biggest bust-statue; inside are a series of artistically designed temples, including one housing the Dhyanalinga, believed to embody all seven chakras. Visitors are welcome for meditations; if you want to stay or take yoga courses, book ahead.

Direct buses to the ashram leave from Coimbatore's Town Bus Stand (Gandhipuram) – go to the website and click on Travel Information for timings and bus numbers.

🛏 Sleeping & Eating

iStay HOTEL $$
(www.hotelistay.com; Devi & Co Lane; s/d incl breakfast ₹2100/2600; ❄🛜) More modern, more comfortable and less noisy than some of its neighbours, iStay offers some of the best-value AC rooms across from the railway station – and in all of Coimbatore.

Corner Stay GUESTHOUSE $$
(📞9842220742; www.cornerstay.in; 4/1 Abdul Rahim Rd, opp DIG office; r ₹2000-3000; ❄🛜) On a quiet Racecourse-area lane, this homey guesthouse offers three impeccable, tastefully styled rooms with a communal lounge and balcony. Two share a kitchen, the other has its own, and there are home-cooked meals. It's 2km northeast of the train station.

Hotel ESS Grande HOTEL $$
(📞0422-2230271; www.hotelessgrande.com; 358-360 Nehru St; incl breakfast s/d from ₹2450/2900; ❄@) Handy for a few of Coimbatore's bus stands, friendly ESS has small but very clean, fresh rooms. Steep discounts are available on slow days. There are several other midrange and budget hotels on this street.

Residency Towers HOTEL $$$
(📞0422-2241414; www.theresidency.com; 1076 Avinashi Rd; s/d from ₹5200/5750; ❄@🛜🏊) Opening through a soaring lobby, the Residency is a top choice for its professional staff, well-equipped rooms, swimming pool, and excellent eating and drinking options, including great-value buffet meals at the Pavilion (buffet breakfast/lunch/dinner ₹650/1215/1330; ⏰7-10am, 12.30-3pm & 7-11pm). Check discounts online.

Junior Kuppanna SOUTH INDIAN $$
(📞0422-235773; www.hoteljuniorkuppanna.com; 177 Sarojini Rd, Ram Nagar; mains ₹140-200, thalis ₹140-180; ⏰noon-4pm & 6.30-11pm) Your favourite South Indian thalis come piled on to banana leaves with traditional flourish, and hungry carnivores will love the long menu of famously nonveg southern specialities, all from a perfectly spotless kitchen. Three branches across town.

Bird On Tree MULTICUISINE $$$
(📞9865831000; www.birdontree.com; 23 Kamaraj Rd; mains ₹275-550; ⏰noon-3pm & 7-10.30pm)

With a tiny terrace up in the trees and several indoor spaces, this fashionable restaurant plates up well-prepared dishes covering everything from Southeast Asian sizzlers and stir-fries to Indian clay-pot curries and continental pastas and salads. It's 3km northeast of Coimbatore Junction.

On The Go   MULTICUISINE $$$

(☑0422-4520116; www.onthegocbe.com; 167 Racecourse Rd; mains ₹275-560; ⊙12.30-2.45pm & 7.30-10.30pm) Colourful, contemporary, and filled with cartoons and turquoise sofas, this is a great place for tasty (if pricey) global fare, from Italian and Middle Eastern to Sri Lankan and North Indian.

❶ Getting There & Away

AIR

The airport is 10km east of town. Direct daily flights to domestic destinations include Bengaluru, Chennai, Delhi, Hyderabad and Mumbai on Air India (www.airindia.in), IndiGo (www.goindigo.in) and Jet Airways (www.jetairways.com). SilkAir (www.silkair.com) flies four times weekly to/from Singapore.

BUS
SETC Bus Stand

Express or superfast AC and Volvo government buses go from the **SETC Bus Stand** (Thiruvalluvar Bus Stand; Bharathiyar Rd), which is across the street from the **Town Bus Stand** (Gandhipuram Bus Stand; cnr Dr Nanjappa & Bharathiyar Rds).

Bengaluru non-AC/AC ₹460/740, nine hours, 12 daily

Chennai non-AC ₹510, AC ₹663-1020, 11 hours, eight buses 5.30pm to 10.30pm

Ernakulam non-AC ₹182, 5½ hours, eight daily

Mysuru non-AC/AC ₹190/420, six hours, 27 daily

Trivandrum non-AC/AC ₹355/725, 10½ hours, seven daily

Ooty Bus Stand

The **Ooty Bus Stand** (New Bus Stand; Mettupalayam Rd), 5km northwest of the train station, has services to Ooty (₹60, four hours) via Mettupalayam (₹20, one hour) and Coonoor (₹45, three hours) every 10 minutes, plus half-hourly buses to Kotagiri (₹34, three hours), 28 buses daily to Mysuru (₹188 to ₹420, six hours) and 11 to Bengaluru (₹460 to ₹740, nine hours). At busy times, you may wait up to two hours to board buses to Ooty/Coonoor.

Singanallur Bus Stand

From **Singanallur Bus Stand** (Kamaraj Rd), 6km east of the centre, buses go to Trichy (₹160, five hours), Thanjavur (₹200, 7¼ hours) and Madurai

Coimbatore

(₹170, five hours) every 10 minutes. Bus 140 (₹14) shuttles between here and the Town Bus Stand (p1083).

Ukkadam

Ukkadam Bus Stand (NH Rd), 1.5km southwest of the train station, has buses to southern destinations including Pollachi (₹33, 1¼ hours, every five minutes), Kodaikanal (₹144, six hours, 10am) and Munnar (₹157, 6½ hours, 8.15am).

Private Buses

Private buses to destinations such as Bengaluru, Chennai, Ernakulam, Puducherry, Trichy and Trivandrum start from the **Omni Bus Stand** (Sathy Rd), 500m north of the Town Bus Stand, or from ticket-selling agencies on Sathy Rd.

TAMIL NADU COIMBATORE

MAJOR TRAINS FROM COIMBATORE

DESTINATION	TRAIN NO & NAME	FARE (₹)	DURATION (HR)	DEPARTURES
Bengaluru (Bangalore)	16525 Bangalore Express	260/700/1000 (B)	8½	10.55pm
Chennai Central	12676 Kovai Express	180/665 (A)	7½	3.20pm
	22640 Chennai Express	315/815/1150 (B)	7½	10.10pm
Ernakulam (Kochi)	12677 Ernakulam Express	105/390 (A)	3¾	12.55pm
Madurai	16610 Nagercoil Express	235/595 (C)	5½	7.20pm
Thiruvananthapuram (Trivandrum)	12695 Trivandrum Express	285/735/1030 (B)	9	11.10pm

Fares: (A) 2nd class/AC chair; (B) sleeper/3AC/2AC; (C) sleeper/3AC

TAXI

Taxis up to Ooty (three hours) cost ₹2500; Ooty buses often get so crowded that a taxi is worth considering.

TRAIN

Coimbatore Junction is on the main line between Chennai and Ernakulam (Kochi, Kerala), with at least 13 daily trains in each direction. The 5.15am Nilgiri Express to Mettupalayam (sleeper/3AC/2AC ₹170/540/745, one hour) connects with the miniature railway departure from Mettupalayam to Ooty at 7.10am. The whole trip to Ooty takes seven hours.

ⓘ Getting Around

Many buses run between the train station and the Town Bus Stand (p1083).

Autorickshaws charge ₹80 from the train station to the Ukkadam Bus Station (p1083), ₹100 to the SETC (p1083) or Town Bus Stand (p1083) and ₹180 to the Ooty Bus Stand (p1083).

Coonoor

📞 0423 / POP 46,000 / ELEV 1720M

Coonoor is one of the three Nilgiri hill stations – Ooty, Kotagiri and Coonoor – that sit high above the southern plains. Smaller and quieter than Ooty (20km northwest), it has some fantastic heritage hotels and guesthouses, from which you can do exactly the same things (hike, visit tea plantations, marvel at mountain views) you would do from bigger, busier Ooty. From upper Coonoor, 1km to 3km northeast (uphill) from the town centre, you can look down over a sea of red-tile rooftops to the slopes beyond and soak up the cool climate, quiet environment and

beautiful scenery. But you get none of the above in lower (central) Coonoor, which is a bustling, honking mess.

◉ Sights

Highfield Tea Estate　　PLANTATION

(Walker's Hill Rd; ⊙9am-6pm) FREE Over 50 years old, this estate (2km northeast of upper Coonoor) is one of the few working Nilgiri tea factories open to visitors. Guides jump in quickly, but you're perfectly welcome to watch the full tea-making process independently. You can also, of course, taste and buy. The factory is closed Mondays, but the tea fields remain open.

Lamb's Rock　　VIEWPOINT

(Dolphin's Nose Rd; ₹10, camera/video ₹20/50; ⊙8.30am-6pm) A favourite picnic spot in a patch of monkey-patrolled forest, Lamb's Rock has incredible views past glimmering tea and coffee plantations to the hazy plains below. It's 6km east of upper Coonoor – walkable, if you like.

Dolphin's Nose　　VIEWPOINT

(Dolphin's Nose Rd; ₹10, camera/video ₹20/50; ⊙8.30am-6.30pm) About 10km west of town, this popular viewpoint exposes vast panoramas encompassing Catherine Falls (p1086) across the valley.

Sim's Park　　PARK

(Upper Coonoor; adult/child ₹30/15, camera/video ₹50/100; ⊙9am-5pm) Upper Coonoor's 12-hectare Sim's Park, established in 1874, is a peaceful oasis of sloping manicured lawns with more than 1000 plant species from several continents, including magnolia, tree ferns, roses and camellia. Kotagiri-bound buses drop you here.

🛏 Sleeping & Eating

Acres Wild
FARMSTAY $$

(📱9443232621; www.acres-wild.com; 571 Upper Meanjee Estate, Kanni Mariamman Kovil St; r incl breakfast ₹3775-4360; 📶) 🍴 This beautifully positioned farm on Coonoor's southeast edge is sustainably run with solar heating, rainwater harvesting and fresh cheeses from the milk of its own cows. Five large, stylish rooms, in three cottages, include kitchens and fireplaces. Your friendly host, Mansoor, is a great conversationalist and full of ideas for things to do away from the tourist crowds. Book ahead.

It also offers guests-only cheesemaking courses (from ₹8000).

YWCA Wyoming Guesthouse
GUESTHOUSE $$

(📱0423-2234426; http://ywcaagooty.com; Bedford; s/d ₹1200/1900) A ramshackle, 150-year-old gem, the good-value Wyoming is draughty and creaky but oozes colonial character, with wooden terraces and serene town views through trees. Rooms are good and clean, with geysers, and simple meals are available on request.

★180° McIver
HERITAGE HOTEL $$$

(📱0423-2233323; http://serendipityo.com; Orange Grove Rd, Upper Coonoor; r incl breakfast ₹4720-7080; 📶) A classic 1900s British bungalow at the top of town has been transformed into something special. The six handsome, airy rooms sport antique furniture, working fireplaces and big fresh bathrooms. Panoramas from the wraparound lawn (where you can dine) of the on-site restaurant La Belle Vie are fabulous.

Gateway
HERITAGE HOTEL $$$

(📱0423-2225400; www.tajhotels.com; Church Rd, Upper Coonoor; incl breakfast s from ₹6780, d/ste from ₹7375/13,400; 📶) A colonial-era priory turned gorgeous heritage hotel, the Taj-group Gateway has homey cream-coloured rooms immersed in greenery, most graced by working fireplaces. Garden view rooms open onto a grassy terrace with views. Evening bonfires are lit on the lawn, the good Gateway All Day restaurant overlooks the gardens, and there's free yoga along with Keralan ayurvedic massages.

Nilgiri's Supermarket
SUPERMARKET $

(Upper Coonoor; ⊗9am-9pm) Well-organised shelves are stocked with all of your self-catering needs, from fresh veggies to candy bars, plus tonnes of toiletries.

★La Belle Vie
MULTICUISINE $$$

(📱0423-2233323; http://serendipityo.com; 180° McIver, Orange Grove Rd, Upper Coonoor; mains ₹320-580; ⊗12.30-3.30pm & 7.30-10.30pm) With tables on the veranda of a beautifully revamped 19th-century bungalow, La Belle Vie has guests driving miles for its flavour-popping European-Indian food. Gazing out over the Nilgiris beyond a lovely lawn full of flower gardens, it's arguably Coonoor's most perfectly positioned restaurant.

Gateway All Day
MULTICUISINE $$$

(📱0423-2225400; www.tajhotels.com; Gateway Hotel, Church Rd, Upper Coonoor; mains ₹400-600, dinner buffet ₹1060; ⊗7.30-10.30am, 12.30-2.45pm & 7.30-10.30pm) Tucked between manicured gardens, this signature heritage-hotel restaurant is a lovely place for splurging on polished global cuisine and brilliant breakfast buffets. You'll feel like a Raj-era VIP, sipping Nilgiri-grown tea in the suitably characterful colonial-style setting of a 160-year-old converted priory.

🔒 Shopping

Green Shop
HANDICRAFTS, FOOD

(www.lastforest.in; Jograj Bldg, Bedford Circle; ⊗9.30am-7.30pm Mon-Sat) 🍴 Beautiful fair-trade local tribal crafts, clothes, fabrics and notebooks, plus organic wild honey, nuts, chocolates, soaps and teas.

ℹ Getting There & Away

Coonoor's **bus stand** (Lower Coonor) has frequent services to/from Ooty (₹16, one hour) and Kotagiri (₹20, 50 minutes).

Pick up buses to Coimbatore (₹45, three hours) at the **bus stop** (Coonoor Rd Roundabout) at the roundabout at the entrance to town, every 30 minutes.

Coonoor is on the miniature train line between Mettupalayam (1st/2nd class ₹185/25, 2¼ to 3¼ hours) and Ooty (₹150/25, 1¼ hours), with three daily trains just to/from Ooty, as well as the daily Mettupalayam–Ooty–Mettupalayam service.

Kotagiri

📱04266 / POP 28,200 / ELEV 1800M

The oldest and smallest of the three Nilgiri hill stations, Kotagiri is set in the most beautiful location of them all – 30km east of Ooty, beyond one of Tamil Nadu's highest passes. The forgettable town centre is surrounded

Nilgiri Hills

by plunging ridges sculpted with tea estates and dotted with pastel villages, framed by the high green walls of the Nilgiris.

Sights & Activities

A half-day taxi tour encompassing **Catherine Falls** (Kotagiri-Mettupalayam Rd) and **Kodanad Viewpoint** (Kodanad; ⏱dawn-dusk) costs around ₹1200.

Sullivan Memorial MUSEUM
(✆9488771571; Kannerimukku; adult/child ₹10/5; ⏱10am-5pm Thu-Tue) Just 2km north of Kotagiri centre, the house built in 1819 by Ooty founder John Sullivan has been refurbished in bright red and filled with fascinating photos, newspaper cuttings and artefacts related to local tribal groups, European settlement and icons like the miniature train. Also here is the Nilgiri Documentation Centre (www.nilgiridocumentation.com), dedicated to preserving the region's beauty and heritage.

Keystone Foundation VOLUNTEERING
(✆04266-272277; http://keystone-foundation.org; Groves Hill Rd) ✎ This Kotagiri-based NGO works to improve environmental conditions in the Nilgiris while involving, and improving living standards for, indigenous communities. Occasional openings for volunteers who are willing to stay at least one month.

Sleeping

★La Maison HERITAGE HOTEL $$$
(✆9585857732; www.lamaison.in; Hadatharai; s/d from ₹5625/6750; ☎) Flower-draped, French-owned La Maison is a beautifully renovated 1890s Scottish bungalow superbly situated on a hilltop surrounded by tea plantations, 5km southwest of Kotagiri. Casual yet stylish, here you'll find antique furniture, tribal handicrafts, old-Ooty paintings and two friendly dogs. Hike to waterfalls, visit tribal villages, savour home-cooked meals (₹900) or laze in the valley-facing hot tub. A special place!

Shopping

Green Shop FOOD, HANDICRAFTS
(http://lastforest.in; Johnstone Sq; ⏱9.30am-7pm) ✎ The ecofriendly Keystone Foundation's shop has goodies for picnics (local chocolates, wild honey) plus lovely tribal crafts.

Getting There & Away

Buses run half-hourly to/from Ooty (₹26, 1½ hours) and every 15 minutes to/from Coonoor (₹16, one hour) and Mettupalayam (₹25, 1½ hours). Buses to Coimbatore (₹60, 2½ hours) leave every 45 minutes.

Taxis to/from Ooty cost ₹1500.

Ooty (Udhagamandalam)

📞 0423 / POP 90,000 / ELEV 2240M

Ooty, 'Queen of Hill Stations', mixes Indian bustle and Hindu temples with beautiful gardens, an international school and charming Raj-era bungalows (which provide its most atmospheric accommodation). It may be a bit hectic, especially its messy centre, but it doesn't take long to escape into quieter, greener areas where tall pines rise above what could almost be English country lanes.

Memorably nicknamed 'Snooty Ooty', it was established by the British in the early 19th century as the summer headquarters of the Madras government. Development ploughed through a few decades ago, but old Ooty survives in patches – you just have to walk further out to find it.

The journey up here on the celebrated miniature train is romantic and the scenery stunning. Even the road up is impressive. During the April-to-June 'season', Ooty is a welcome relief from the steaming plains. Between October and March, overnight temperatures occasionally drop to 0°C.

⊙ Sights

Tribal Research Centre Museum   MUSEUM
(Muthorai Palada; Indian/foreigner ₹5/100; ⊙10am-1pm & 2-5pm Mon-Fri, hours vary) If you're interested in the Nilgiris' tribal communities you'll love this slightly scruffy, erratically open museum, with its fascinating exhibits on Nilgiri and other Tamil Nadu tribal groups (including model huts) and its fantastic artefacts (like the skulls of buffalo sacrificed at Toda funerals). Detailed English-language descriptions are good. It's just southwest of Muthorai Palada (M Palada), 10km southwest of Ooty en route to Avalanche and served by frequent buses.

Botanical Gardens   GARDENS
(www.ootygardens.com; Garden Rd; adult/child ₹30/15, camera/video ₹50/100; ⊙7am-6.30pm) Established in 1848, these pretty 22-hectare gardens are a living gallery of the Nilgiris' natural flora. Keep an eye out for a typical Toda *mund* (village), a fossilised tree trunk believed to be 20 million years old and, on busy days, around 20 million tourists.

St Thomas' Church   CHURCH
(St Thomas Rd; ⊙dawn-dusk) Set between trees at the eastern end of Ooty Lake, simple St Thomas' dates back to 1870.

Doddabetta   VIEWPOINT
(Ooty-Kotagiri Rd; ₹10, camera/video ₹10/50; ⊙8am-5pm) About 7km east of Ooty, Doddabetta is the highest point (2633m) in the Nilgiris. On clear days, it's one of the best viewpoints around; go early for a better chance of mist-free views. Kotagiri buses will drop you at the Doddabetta junction, then it's a steep 3km walk or a quick jeep ride. Taxis do return trips from Charring Cross (₹700).

Rose Garden   GARDENS
(Selbourne Rd; adult/child ₹30/15, camera/video ₹50/100; ⊙7.30am-6.30pm) With terraced lawns and over 20,000 rose bushes of more than 2000 varieties – best between May and July – the Rose Garden is a sweet place for a stroll, and has good Ooty views from its hillside location.

Nilgiri Library   LIBRARY
(📞0423-2441699; Hospital Rd; ⊙9.30am-1.30pm & 2.30-5.30pm) This quaint little haven in a crumbling, earthy-red 1867 building houses more than 30,000 books, including rare titles on the Nilgiris and hill tribes, and 19th-century British journals. Visitors can consult books in the reading room with a temporary one-month membership (₹500). Upstairs is a portrait of Queen Victoria presented to Ooty on her 1887 Golden Jubilee.

The library hosts the Ooty Literary Festival (www.ootylitfest.com) each September.

St Stephen's Church   CHURCH
(Church Hill Rd; ⊙9.30am-4.30pm Mon-Sat, 6.30am-1.30pm Sun) Perched above Ooty's centre, immaculate pale-yellow St Stephen's, built in 1829, is the Nilgiris' oldest church. It has lovely stained glass, huge wooden beams hauled by elephant from the palace of Tipu Sultan 120km away, and slabs and plaques donated by colonial-era churchgoers. In the overgrown cemetery you'll find headstones commemorating many an Ooty Brit, including Ooty founder John Sullivan's wife and daughter.

🏃 Activities

The best of Ooty is out in the beautiful Nilgiri Hills. Most hotels can put you in touch with local guides who do half-day hikes for around ₹600 per person. You'll normally drive out of town and walk through hills, tribal villages and tea plantations. The **Tourist Office** (📞0423-2443977; www.tamilnadu tourism.org; Wenlock Rd; ⊙10am-5pm) can also

Ooty (Udhagamandalam)

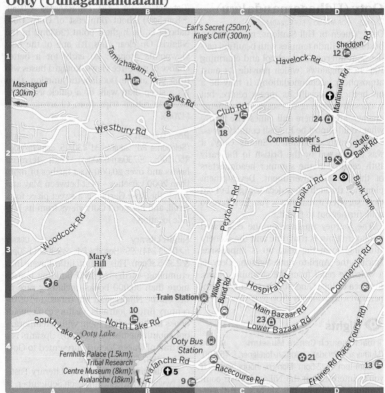

suggest some nice routes for do-it-yourself 'rural walks' between villages south of Ooty.

Overnight trekking in the forests around Ooty has been banned due to rising human–animal conflict in the region; a couple of foreigners have been trampled to death by elephants, and multiple tiger attacks on local villagers (some fatal) have occurred.

There are also concerns that unruly tourists are too disruptive in the forest at night. If you're interested in finding out if the policy has changed, contact the **Office of the Field Director** (☏0423-2445971; fdmtr@ tn.nic.in; Mt Stuart Hill; ☺10am-5.45pm Mon-Fri) for info.

Boathouse BOATING
(North Lake Rd; ₹13, camera/video ₹25/150; ☺9am-6pm) Rowing boats and pedal boats can be rented from the boathouse by Ooty Lake. Prices start from ₹85 per person (with a ₹180 deposit) for a two-seater pedal boat (30 minutes).

🛏 Sleeping

Ooty has some gorgeous colonial-era homes at the high end and some decent backpacker crashpads, but there isn't much in the lower midrange. During the 'season' (1 April to 15 June) hotels hike rates and checkout time is often 9am. Book well ahead for public holidays.

YWCA Anandagiri GUESTHOUSE $
(☏0423-2444262; www.ywcaagooty.com; Ettines Rd; dm ₹250, s ₹500-3300, d ₹1200-3300) This former brewery and sprawling complex of cottages is dotted with flower gardens. With clean, character-filled and freshly painted rooms, helpful staff, spacious common areas and a good restaurant (book ahead), you've got some excellent-value budget accommodation. The cheapest rooms have private bathrooms across the corridor. High ceilings can mean cold nights, but you can ask for extra blankets.

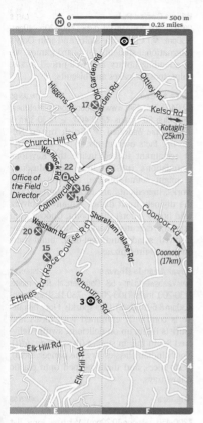

N
0 ——————— 500 m
0 ——————— 0.25 miles

Higgins Rd
Garden Rd
Ottley Rd
Old Garden Rd
Kelso Rd
Kotagiri (25km)
Church Hill Rd
Wenlock Rd
Commercial Rd
Office of the Field Director
Walsham Rd
Shoreham Palace Rd
Coonoor Rd
Coonoor (17km)
Ettines Rd (Race Course Rd)
Selbourne Rd
Elk Hill Rd

Ooty (Udhagamandalam)

⊙ Sights

1 Botanical Gardens F1
2 Nilgiri Library D2
3 Rose Garden E3
4 St Stephen's Church D1
5 St Thomas' Church B4

⊕ Activities, Courses & Tours

6 Boathouse A3

⊜ Sleeping

7 Hotel Welbeck Residency C2
8 Lymond House B2
9 Mount View Hotel B4
10 Reflections Guest House B4
11 Savoy B1
12 Wyoming D1
13 YWCA Anandagiri D4

⊗ Eating

14 Adyar Ananda Bhavan E2
15 Angaara E3
16 Junior Kuppana E2
17 Modern Stores E1
18 Place to Bee C2
    Savoy .... (see 11)
19 Shinkow's Chinese Restaurant D2
20 Willy's Coffee Pub E3

⊛ Entertainment

21 Ooty Racecourse D4

⊝ Shopping

    Green Shop .... (see 18)
22 Higginbothams E2
23 K Mahaveer Chand C4
24 Mohan's D2

TAMIL NADU OOTY (UDHAGAMANDALAM)

Reflections Guest House GUESTHOUSE $

(☏9843637974; reflectionsin@yahoo.co.in; 1B North Lake Rd; r ₹600-1600; ☏) A long-standing budget haunt, Reflections sits across the road from Ooty Lake. Most of its 12 spotless, good-value rooms have lake views; the best come with freshly updated bathrooms and open on to a grassy terrace. The super attentive owners serve snacks on request and can organise guided treks. Hot water is available anytime when requested.

Wyoming HERITAGE HOTEL $$

(☏0423-2452008; www.wyoming.in; 46 Sheddon Rd; r incl breakfast ₹3200-3800; ☏) Six simple, wonderfully spacious colonial-feel rooms open up to classic Nilgiri panoramas at this delightful sun-yellow heritage house high above Ooty. All have kettles, bottled water and pretty wood-panelled floors. It's well run by friendly hosts and you can enjoy breakfast in the table-dotted garden.

Lymond House HERITAGE HOTEL $$

(☏9843149490; www.serendipityo.com; Sylks Rd; r incl breakfast ₹4200-5470; ☏) This 1855 British bungalow has an edge over many of its peers. The cosy cottage features garden-fresh flowers, four-poster beds, working fireplaces and antique-lined lounges. The more expensive rooms are spacious and dramatic, while cheaper ones have less character and are perhaps showing wear around the edges. The cute restaurant serves good multicuisine food. Management is informal yet efficient.

Hotel Welbeck Residency HOTEL $$

(☏0423-2223300; www.welbeck.in; Welbeck Circle, Club Rd; r from ₹3650; ☏) An attractive older building that's been thoroughly spruced up with comfortable rooms, a touch of colonial-era class (a 1920 Austin saloon car at the front door!), a decent restaurant and very keen staff.

Mount View Hotel   HOTEL $$

(☑9566410117; www.mountviewheritage.com; Ettines Rd; r ₹1770-4130; ⊚) Perched on a quiet (bumpy) driveway handy for the bus and train stations, the nine enormous, high-ceilinged, wood-lined rooms in this old bungalow have been done up comfortably enough. The best have private terraces. Hot water is available in the morning and evening, and management is attentive. Look at a few rooms, as each is different.

Savoy   HERITAGE HOTEL $$$

(☑0423-2225500; www.gateway.tajhotels.com; 77 Sylks Rd; r incl breakfast from ₹6400; ⊚) The Savoy is one of Ooty's oldest hotels, with parts dating back to 1829. Cottages and swing-chairs are set around a charming lawn and garden. Colonial-style rooms have huge marble-clad bathrooms, log fires and bay windows. Welcome touches include a cocktail bar, an ayurveda centre and an excellent multicuisine dining room. Suites are much nicer than standard rooms.

King's Cliff   HERITAGE HOTEL $$$

(☑0423-2244000; www.littlearth.in; Havelock Rd; r incl breakfast ₹3275-9410; ⊚) Hidden away above Ooty on Strawberry Hill is this classic colonial-era house with wood panelling, antique furnishings, a snug lounge and good Indian/continental cooking at Earl's Secret, partly in a glassed-in conservatory. It's refined and comfortable. Cheaper rooms don't have the same old-world charm as the most expensive ones.

Fernhills Palace   HERITAGE HOTEL $$$

(☑0423-2443910; www.welcomheritagehotels.in; Fern Hill; r incl breakfast ₹12,160-38,400; ⊚) The Maharaja of Mysore's exquisite Anglo-Indian summer palace is full of totally over-the-top princely colonial style. All 19 rooms are gigantic suites, with antique furnishings, teak flourishes, tiled floors, fireplaces and hot tubs. Some are pristine, others need a paint job. You can play billiards, stroll the forest-fringed grounds and dine beneath wood-carved ceilings. The Maharaja himself stays here sometimes.

✖ Eating

Modern Stores   SUPERMARKET $

(144 Garden Rd; ⊙9.30am-8.30pm Wed-Mon, 11am-8.30pm Tue) Stocks all kinds of international foods, from muesli to marmalade, along with particularly good Western Ghats produce, such as breads, cheeses and chocolates.

Willy's Coffee Pub   CAFE $

(KCR Arcade, Walsham Rd; dishes ₹60-120; ⊙10am-9.30pm; ⊚) Climb the stairs and join Ooty's international students for board games, wi-fi, a lending library and well-priced pizzas, chips, toasties, cakes and biscuits.

Place to Bee   ITALIAN $$

(☑0423-2449464; www.facebook.com/placetObee; 176A Club Rd; mains ₹260-400; ⊙12.30-3pm & 6.30-9.30pm Wed-Mon) 🍴 Brush up on Nilgiri-bee facts over meals at this arty, fairy-lit restaurant tucked inside the Keystone Foundation's (p1086) little Bee Museum. It might sound bizarre, but the concept works, ingredients are locally sourced, and the divinely fresh dishes – many involving wild honey – don't disappoint. Choose from expertly executed pastas, Mediterranean-inspired salads and real-deal, build-your-own wood-fired pizzas.

Adyar Ananda Bhavan   INDIAN $$

(www.aabsweets.in; 58 Commercial Rd; mains ₹130-200, thalis ₹100-200; ⊙7.30-11.30am, noon-3.30pm & 6-10.30pm) This sparkly Ooty favourite is constantly crammed with locals and tourists filling up on delicious, swiftly delivered South Indian staples (dosa, *vada, idli*), North Indian classics (try the paneer tikka), fresh juices, and thalis heaped onto plastic yellow trays.

Angaara   INDIAN $$

(www.angaaraooty.com; 420 Ettines Rd; mains ₹200-450; ⊙noon-10.30pm) With a long list of nonveg tandoori and curry dishes, this is Ooty's best place to satisfy your meat craving. There's indoor/outdoor seating, and the decor is a weird mash-up of vintage and modern. There's also plenty here for vegetarians.

Junior Kuppana   SOUTH INDIAN $$

(www.hoteljuniorkuppanna.com; Commercial Rd; mains ₹150-220, thalis ₹160; ⊙8.30am-4.30pm & 6.30-10pm) Ooty's branch of the much-loved Tamil Nadu chain – known for its pristine kitchens and brilliantly fresh ingredients – delivers the South Indian goods with *idli*, dosa, *sambar*, chutneys, limitless thalis and plenty of meaty extras for carnivores.

Shinkow's Chinese Restaurant   CHINESE $$

(38/83 Commissioner's Rd; mains ₹180-350; ⊙noon-4pm & 6.30-10pm) Shinkow's is an Ooty institution. The simple, tasty chicken, pork, beef, seafood, veg, noodle and rice dishes are reliably good and quick to arrive at your chequer-print table. You'll leave full!

WORTH A TRIP

AVALANCHE VALLEY

The serene, protected Avalanche Valley – which extends towards Kerala from around 20km southwest of Ooty – provides the perfect antidote to Ooty's crowds. Rolling farmlands and twinkling tea plantations give way to hushed hills thick with orchids and native *shola* (virgin forest), where wildlife includes leopards, sloth bears, deer, langurs and the odd tiger (though you'd be lucky to spot them).

Access is restricted, so the only way to explore this blissfully peaceful area is by official two-hour forest department minibus **'ecotours'** (www.ootyavalanche.com; per person ₹150; ☺9.30am-3pm) or private-hire jeep trips (₹2000). There are several scenic stops along the way.

Minibuses depart from the southern side of Avalanche Lake – officially at 9.30am, 11.30am, 1.30pm and 3.30pm Monday to Friday, and about 30 minutes later on weekends. Timings, however, are inconsistent, as they leave when full, and if you miss a bus you may have to wait a long time for the next one.

Ooty taxi drivers charge ₹1600 for a return trip to the ecotour starting point, including waiting time.

Earl's Secret MULTICUISINE $$$
(☎0423-2452888; www.littlearth.in; King's Cliff, Havelock Rd; mains ₹350-550; ☺8-10am, noon-3pm & 7-10pm; ☎) You get a taste of everything at this elegant heritage-hotel restaurant up above Ooty. Half glassed-in conservatory, half tables scattered across Raj-era lounges with roaring winter fires, it does beautifully prepared Indian (mostly northern), continental and Southeast Asian dishes, including deliciously hot soups that are a godsend for chilly Ooty nights.

Savoy MULTICUISINE $$$
(☎0423-2225500; www.gateway.tajhotels.com; 77 Sylks Rd; mains ₹275-650; ☺7.30-10am, 12.30-3pm & 7.30-10.30pm) All wood walls, intimate lighting, live piano and plush orange velvets, the Savoy's candlelit dining room dishes up fabulous contemporary continental, Indian and pan-Asian cuisine – including all-day breakfasts, yummy salads, pastas and kebabs, and some unique tribal-inspired dishes.

☆ Entertainment

Ooty Racecourse HORSE RACING
(Ettines Rd; ₹100; ☺mid-Apr–mid-Jun) Ooty's racecourse dominates the valley between Charring Cross and the lake. Racing season runs from mid-April to mid-June, and on the two or three race days held each week the town is a hive of activity. Racing usually happens between 10am and 1pm, though this varies depending on participant numbers.

🛍 Shopping

K Mahaveer Chand JEWELLERY
(291 Main Bazaar Rd; ☺10am-8pm) K Mahaveer Chand has been selling particularly beautiful Toda tribal and silver jewellery for nearly 50 years.

Green Shop HANDICRAFTS, FOOD
(www.lastforest.in; Sargan Villa, off Club Rd; ☺9.30am-8.45pm) 🌿 Run by Kotagiri's Keystone Foundation (p1086), this fair-trade, organic-oriented shop sells gorgeous tribal crafts and clothes (including Toda embroidery), and wild honey harvested by local indigenous farmers.

Higginbothams BOOKS
(Commercial Rd; ☺9am-1pm & 3.30-7.30pm) A well-known chain with a good stash of English-language books.

Mohan's CLOTHING, ANTIQUES
(Commissioner's Rd; ☺10am-1.30pm & 3-8pm Fri-Wed) A curious assortment of antique telephones, radios and clocks, along with shawls, jewellery and warm clothes.

ⓘ Getting There & Away

The fun way to arrive in Ooty is on the miniature train from Mettupalayam. Buses also run regularly up and down the mountain from across Tamil Nadu, from Kerala, and from Mysuru and Bengaluru in Karnataka.

BUS

The Tamil Nadu and Karnataka state bus companies have reservation offices at Ooty's busy **bus**

BUSES FROM OOTY (UDHAGAMANDALAM)

DESTINATION	FARE (₹)	TIME (HR)	DEPARTURES
Bengaluru (Bangalore)	520-660	8	Volvo 7 daily
Chennai	650	14	4.30pm, 5.45pm, 6.30pm
Coimbatore	80	4	every 20min 5.50am-8.40pm
Coonoor	20	1	every 10min 5.30am-10pm
Kotagiri	26	1½	every 30min 6.30am-7pm, 7.40pm, 8.20pm
Mysuru (Mysore)	157-380	5	Express/Volvo 12/6 daily

station. For Kochi take a bus to Palakkad (₹96, six hours, 7am, 8am and 2pm) and change.

TRAIN

The miniature ('toy') train from Mettupalayam to Ooty – one of the Mountain Railways of India given World Heritage status by Unesco – is the best way to get here. The Nilgiri Mountain Railway requires special cog wheels on the locomotive, meshing with a third, 'toothed' rail on the ground, to manage the exceptionally steep gradients. There are wonderful forest, waterfall, mountainside and tea-plantation views along the way. The section between Mettupalayam and Coonoor uses steam engines, which push, rather than pull, the train up the hill.

For high season, book several weeks ahead; at other times a few days ahead is advisable (though not always essential). The train departs Mettupalayam for Ooty at 7.10am daily (1st/2nd class ₹205/30, 4¾ hours). From Ooty to Mettupalayam the train leaves at 2pm (3½ hours). There are also three daily trains each way just between Ooty and Coonoor (₹150/25, 1¼ hours). Departures and arrivals at Mettupalayam connect with the Nilgiri Express to/from Chennai Central (sleeper/3AC/2AC ₹340/895/1255, 9¼ hours).

Ooty is often listed as Udhagamandalam in train timetables. Mettupalayam is listed as Metupalaiyam (MTP).

TAXI

Taxis cluster at stands around town. Fixed one-way fares to many destinations include Coonoor (₹1200), Kotagiri (₹1500), Coimbatore (₹3000) and Mudumalai Tiger Reserve (₹1700). There are taxi stands at Charring Cross, Lower Bazaar Rd and Commercial Rd.

ⓘ Getting Around

Autorickshaws and taxis are everywhere. You'll find taxi fare charts at Charring Cross and outside the bus station. Autorickshaw fare charts are posted outside the bus station and botanical gardens and elsewhere. An autorickshaw from the train or bus station to Charring Cross costs ₹60.

There are jeep taxi stands near the bus station (Avalanche Rd) and municipal market (Hobert Park Cross Rd); expect to pay about 1½ times the local taxi fares.

Mudumalai Tiger Reserve

☑0423

In the Nilgiris' foothills, the newly enlarged 765-sq-km Mudumalai Tiger Reserve (☑0423-2445971; www.mudumalaitigerreserve.com; ₹400; ◷sometimes closed Apr, May or Jun) is like a classical Indian landscape painting given life: thin, spindly trees and light-slotted leaves conceal spotted chital deer and grunting wild boar. Also here are over 60 tigers, giving Mudumalai one of India's highest tiger population densities (though you'd be lucky to see one). Overall the reserve is Tamil Nadu's top wildlife-spotting place. You're most likely to see deer, peacocks, wild boar, langurs, jackals, Malabar giant squirrels, wild elephants (the park has several hundred) and gaur (Indian bison).

Mudumalai is one important link in an unbroken chain of wildlife sanctuaries known as the Nilgiri Biosphere Reserve, which spans parts of Kerala, Karnataka and Tamil Nadu, and is home to approximately 585 tigers – the world's single largest tiger population.

Mudumalai sometimes closes due to fire risk in April, May or June. Rainy July and August are the least favourable months for visiting.

◉ Sights & Activities

Hiking in the reserve is banned and private vehicles are only permitted on the main Ooty–Gudalur–Theppakadu–Mysuru road and the Theppakadu–Masinagudi and Masinagudi–Moyar River roads. The least expensive way to get inside the reserve is on an official minibus safari (☑0423-2445971; www.mudumalaitigerreserve.com; per person Indian/foreigner ₹340/2500, camera ₹53/500; ◷hourly 6.30-10am & 3-5pm), but the Gypsy/jeep safaris (☑0423-2445971; www.mudumalaitiger

reserve.com; per vehicle ₹4200, plus per passenger Indian/foreigner ₹130/400, camera ₹53/500; ⊙6.30-10am & 3-5pm) provide a much better experience. Some unlicensed operators offer hikes in the buffer zone but these are potentially dangerous with wild elephants wandering around.

Elephant Camp STABLES

(₹300; ⊙8.30-9am & 5.30-6pm) In mornings and evenings you can see the reserve's working elephants being fed at the elephant camp just east of the Mudumalai **reception centre** (🖉0423-2526235; www.mudumalaitigerreserve.com; Theppakadu; ⊙6.30am-6pm), where you'll need to buy tickets. Most elephants here are rescued from the timber trade and are unfit to return to the wild. (While Lonely Planet does not recommend or condone recreational elephant rides, the admission fee to elephant camp helps keep these animals fed.)

🛏 Sleeping & Eating

Sylvan Lodge LODGE $$
(🖉bookings 0423-2445971; www.mudumalaitigerreserve.com; Theppakadu; d ₹1700) Scruffy rooms straight out of a cheap hotel, but in a peaceful setting virtually right beside the Moyar River.

Theppakadu Log House LODGE $$
(🖉bookings 0423-2445971; www.mudumalaitigerreserve.com; Theppakadu; d ₹2600) The best of Theppakadu's reserve-owned accommodation: well-maintained wooden rooms with private bathrooms, but still pretty basic.

⭐**Jungle Hut** RESORT $$$
(🖉0423-2526463; www.junglehut.in; Bokkapuram; full board r ₹7310-9730; ❄🛜🏊) 🍴 Along with ecofriendly touches (solar power, rainwater harvesting), Jungle Hut has probably the best food in Bokkapuram (if you're visiting from another resort after dark, don't walk home alone!). Spacious, newly renovated rooms and luxury tents sprawl across large grounds at the foot of the soaring Nilgiris, where chital deer graze. Jeep safaris, treks and birdwatching can be arranged.

Bamboo Banks Farm LODGE $$$
(🖉9443373201; www.bamboobanks.com; Masinagudi; full board s/d ₹6570/7830; ❄🛜🏊) This family-run operation has seven simple, comfy cottages tucked into its own patch of unkempt jungle, 2km south of Masinagudi. Geese waddle around; there's a peaceful pool area with hammocks, swing-chairs and

a treetop viewing platform; meals are good Indian buffets; and the efficient owners organise biking and horse riding.

ℹ Getting There & Away

Small buses that can handle the Sighur Ghat road run from Ooty to Masinagudi (₹30, 1½ hours, 12 daily), from where there are jeeps and a few buses to Theppakadu.

Taxi day trips to Mudumalai from Ooty cost ₹2000, usually via the alternative Sighur Ghat road with its spectacular 36-hairpin-bend hill. (One-way trips cost the same.)

ℹ Getting Around

Slow local buses run a few times daily between Masinagudi and Theppakadu (₹5). Shared jeeps also ply this route for ₹15 per person (or you can have one to yourself for ₹150). Costs are similar for jeeps between Masinagudi and Bokkapuram.

Anamalai Tiger Reserve (Indira Gandhi Wildlife Sanctuary & National Park)

Well off most tourists' radar, **Anamalai Tiger Reserve** (Indira Gandhi Wildlife Sanctuary & National Park; www.atrpollachi.com; Indian/foreigner adult ₹30/300, child ₹20/200, camera/video ₹300/500; ⊙6am-4pm) is a pristine 958-sq-km reserve of tropical jungle, *shola* forest and grassland rising to 2400m and spilling over the Western Ghats into Kerala between Kodaikanal and Coimbatore. Declared a tiger reserve in 2007, it's home to all kinds of exotic endemic wildlife, much of it rare and endangered – including leopards and around 30 elusive tigers, though you're much more likely to see lion-tailed macaques, peacocks, langurs, spotted deer and elephants.

The reserve's bare-bones **Reception & Interpretation Centre** (🖉04259-238360; Topslip; ⊙7am-6pm), plus basic park accommodation, is at Topslip, 35km southwest of Pollachi (which is 40km south of Coimbatore). Questions are best referred to the **Pollachi Reception Office** (🖉9443435583, accommodation bookings 04259-238360; www.atrpollachi.com; 365/1 Meenkarai Rd, Pollachi; ⊙10am-5.45pm Mon-Fri), where you're more likely to reach an English speaker. Pollachi is also the nearest access point for Parambikulam Tiger Reserve (p981) in Kerala.

Tiny tea-plantation town Valparai, on the reserve's fringes 65km south from Pollachi and with one outstanding heritage hotel makes a more comfortable Anamalai base. Though it's surrounded by cultivated land, not jungle, you're just as likely to spot wildlife here.

From Topslip, there are 45-minute minibus jungle 'safaris' (☑9443435583; www.atrpollachi.com; Topslip; adult ₹200/2000, child ₹50/500; ☺7.30am-4.30pm), but rupee for rupee the guided treks (☑9443435583; www.atrpollachi.com; Topslip; treks per person 2km/4km/over 4km ₹200/500/1000; ☺7am-2pm) are much more worthwhile. The reserve also offers elephant rides; however, we recommend against riding elephants because of the harm that this causes to the animals.

🛏 Sleeping

Aditya Residency
HOTEL $

(☑04259-233093; adityaresidencypollachi@gmail.com; 27/1 S V V Naidu St; s/d ₹1000/1300; 🌐🛜) Helpful staff, clean air-conditioned rooms, and a quick walk to the bus stand make this a good overnight choice in Pollachi.

Forest Department Accommodation
GUESTHOUSE $$

(☑bookings 9443435583; www.atrpollachi.com; Topslip; r ₹1500-4000) Most people visit on day trips, but for those staying overnight, Topslip has simple Forest Department accommodation of varying comfort and cleanliness levels. Book several days ahead via the park's website.

★ Sinna Dorai's Bungalow
HERITAGE HOTEL $$$

(☑7094739309; www.sinnadorai.com; Valparai; incl full board s ₹7650-8650, d ₹9750-11,000; 🛜) Exquisitely located on a rambling tea estate, Sinna Dorai has just six huge rooms bursting with local early-20th-century history. A cosy library, wonderful homemade meals and charming service make you feel right at home. After-dark wildlife-spotting drives (you may see elephants, bison, lion-tailed macaques and leopards) run regularly, and experienced trekkers lead you out along local paths.

It's well signposted from central Valparai, 65km south of Pollachi.

ℹ Getting There & Away

The reserve's main access town is Pollachi. Buses connect Pollachi with Topslip (₹70, two hours, 6am, 10am, 11.15am and 3.15pm) and Valparai (₹65, three hours, half-hourly). Taxis cost ₹2000 to Topslip, ₹3000 to Valparai, whether you go one-way or return. From Coimbatore's Ukkadam Bus Stand (p1083), buses to Pollachi (₹39, one hour) run every five minutes, and there's one daily service to Valparai (₹65, four hours, 3pm). From Kodaikanal, most buses head to Pollachi via Palani. If you have to stay overnight in Pollachi, the Aditya Residency, near the bus stand, is a good choice.

Andaman Islands

Best Beaches

➜ Radhanagar (p1105)

➜ Ross & Smith Islands
(p1113)

➜ Butler Bay (p1114)

➜ Lalaji Bay (p1112)

➜ Merk Bay (p1113)

➜ Kalapathar (p1105)

Best Places to Stay

➜ Jalakara (p1107)

➜ Barefoot at Havelock
(p1107)

➜ Emerald Gecko (p1111)

➜ Taj Exotica (p1107)

➜ Ko Hee Homestay (p1116)

Why Go?

With shimmering turquoise waters fringed by primeval jungle, fantastic diving, and sugar-white, sun-toasted beaches melting under flame-and-purple sunsets, the far-flung Andaman Islands are the perfect Indian escape.

The population is a friendly mix of South and Southeast Asian settlers, as well as Negrito ethnic groups whose arrival here has anthropologists baffled. Adding to the islands' intrigue is their remoteness, 1370km east of the Indian mainland – but only 200km from Indonesia and 300km from Myanmar (Burma).

Of the archipelago's 572 islands, only 36 are inhabited and a small selection is open to travellers. With splendid beaches and diving, Havelock (Swaraj) is by far the most popular.

Permit requirements for the Andamans were eased in 2018; the effects of this on the islands' unspoilt state, not to mention the survival of their indigenous peoples, remains to be seen. To the south, the Nicobar Islands have, so far, been strictly off limits to tourists.

When to Go
Port Blair

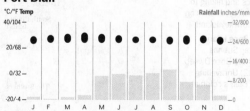

Dec–Mar Warm sunny days, turtles nesting and excellent diving conditions.

Oct–Dec & Mar–mid-May Mixed weather, but fewer crowds and lower costs.

Feb–Apr Pumping waves on Little Andaman for experienced surfers.

Andaman Islands Highlights

❶ Havelock Island
(Swaraj Dweep; p1104) Diving, snorkelling, sun-soaking, socialising, and feasting on fresh seafood on this dreamy, jungle-cloaked island.

❷ Neil Island
(Shaheed Dweep; p1109) Easing into a blissfully mellow pace of life and cycling between beaches and rice paddies.

❸ Kalipur (p1113)
Experiencing the wilds of North Andaman and seeing nesting turtles while island-hopping to pristine sands and coral reefs.

❹ Little Andaman
(p1114) Finding beautiful Butler Bay and a little piece of tropical paradise.

❺ Smith & Ross Islands (p1113)
Meeting this dazzling duo of northern islands, linked by a bleach-blonde sandbar.

❻ Long Island
(p1112) Going back to basics and hiking to sparkling beaches on this low-key island.

❼ Ross Island
(Netaji Subhas Chandra Bose Dweep; p1102) Unravelling Port Blair's colonial past.

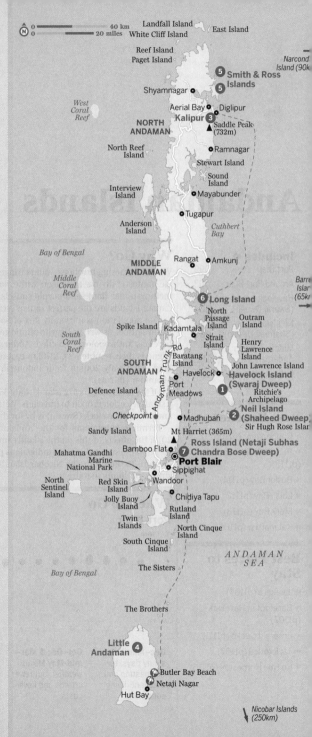

History

The date of initial human settlement on the Andamans and Nicobars is lost to history. Anthropologists say stone-tool crafters have lived here for around 2000 years, and scholars of human migration believe local indigenous tribes have roots in Negrito and Malay ethnic groups in Southeast Asia.

The Marathas started arriving in the late 17th century and, 200 years later, the British, used the Andamans as a penal colony for political dissidents following the 1857 First War of Independence (Indian Uprising). During WWII, some islanders greeted the invading Japanese as liberators, but the Japanese military proved to be harsh occupiers.

Following Indian Independence in 1947, the Andaman and Nicobar Islands were incorporated into the Indian Union, and became a Union Territory in 1956. With migration from the mainland (including Bengali refugees fleeing the chaos of partition), the population has grown from just a few thousand to more than 380,000. During the 20th-century influx, tribal land rights and environmental protection were often disregarded; while some conditions are now improving, indigenous tribes (p1115) remain largely in decline.

The islands were devastated by the 2004 Indian Ocean earthquake and the resulting tsunami, which caused more than 1000 fatalities. The Nicobars were especially hard hit; some estimate a fifth of the population was killed, while others were relocated to Port Blair. But by and large normalcy has returned, and tourism (especially domestic) has boomed in recent years, mostly on Havelock (Swaraj) and Neil (Shaheed) Islands.

Geography & Environment

Incredibly, the Andaman and Nicobar Islands form the peaks of the Arakan Yoma, a mountain range that begins in western Myanmar (Burma) and extends south into the Bay of Bengal and Andaman Sea, running all the way to Sumatra in Indonesia.

The isolation of the islands, separated from each other by the 150km-wide Ten Degree Channel, has led to the evolution of many endemic species. Of 62 identified mammals, 32 are unique to the islands, including the Andaman wild pig, crab-eating macaque, masked palm civet, and species of tree shrews and bats. Of the islands' 270 bird species, 18 are endemic, including ground-dwelling megapodes, *hawabills* (swiftlets) and the emerald Nicobar pigeon.

Climate

Sea breezes keep temperatures within the 23°C to 31°C range and the humidity at around 80% all year. It's very wet during the southwest (wet) monsoon between roughly mid-May and early October, while the northeast (dry) monsoon between November and December also has its fair share of rainy days.

ⓘ Information

Even though they are 1370km east of mainland India, the Andamans still run on Indian time. This means that it can be dark by 5pm and light by 4am; people here tend to be very early risers.

DANGERS & ANNOYANCES

Crocodiles are part of life in many parts of the Andamans, particularly Little Andaman, Wandoor, Corbyn's Cove, Baratang and North Andaman. An American tourist was killed by a saltwater crocodile while snorkelling off Havelock (Swaraj; at Neil's Cove) in 2010, as was a young Indian at Wandoor Beach in 2017. Reports suggest that human-crocodile conflict is on the rise: officially there have been six crocodile attacks since 2014, though the media suggests it's around 15. A high level of vigilance remains in place and swimming is banned at some beaches. It's important you keep informed, heed any warnings by authorities and avoid being in the water at dawn or dusk.

PERMITS

In a bid to boost tourism, the Indian government has overturned the requirement for foreigners to have a Restricted Area Permit (RAP) to visit 29 inhabited and 11 uninhabited islands in the Andamans.

The new list of RAP-free islands includes Havelock Island (Swaraj Dweep), Neil Island (Shaheed Dweep), Baratang Island, Long Island, North Andaman, South and Middle Andaman (including Port Blair but excluding tribal areas), North Passage, Interview Island, Smith Island and Little Andaman (excluding tribal areas), as well as Great Nicobar, Kamorta and Little Nicobar.

ANDAMAN NAME CHANGES

At the end of 2018, the Indian government announced that the names of several Andaman islands would be changed as part of a nationwide policy of 'decolonialisation'. Ross Island will henceforth be known as Netaji Subhas Chandra Bose Dweep, Neil Island has been renamed as Shaheed Dweep and Havelock Island has become Swaraj Dweep. As with other government-imposed name changes, expect the old names to remain in use on the ground for some time.

❶ SANDFLIES

Sandflies can be irksome, with these small biting insects sometimes causing havoc on the beach. Bring along hydrocortisone cream and calamine lotion for these bites. Seek medical assistance if it gets infected. To prevent bites, repellent containing DEET is your best bet, and avoid the beach at dawn and dusk.

Day visits without RAPs are now allowed to 11 uninhabited islands. At the time of writing, however, you still need additional permits for day trips to Jolly Buoy, Red Skin, North and South Cinque, Ross (north), Narcondam and Rutland Islands, as well as the Brothers and the Sisters. For most day permits, it's not the hassle that proves a barrier, but the cost; for Wandoor's Mahatma Gandhi Marine National Park, for example, permits cost ₹1000 for foreigners (₹75 for Indians).

The Nicobar Islands have long been off limits to all except Indian nationals engaged in approved research, government business or trade. With RAPs no longer required for Great Nicobar, Little Nicobar and Kamorta, what, if any, tourism impact will follow has yet to be seen.

❶ Getting There & Away

Ferry and flight services are often cancelled if conditions are too rough; build in a few days' buffer to avoid being marooned or missing your flight. These days, most travellers fly (rather than sail) to/from Port Blair.

AIR

Port Blair's Veer Savarkar International Airport has daily flights to/from Bengaluru (Bangalore), Chennai, Kolkata, Mumbai, Hyderabad and Delhi with Air India (p1208), IndiGo (p1210), GoAir (p1210), SpiceJet (p1210) and Vistara (p1210). At the time of writing, there were no international services, though direct flights to/from Southeast Asia were being talked about.

BOAT

Depending on who you ask, the infamous boat to Port Blair is either the only *real* way to get to the Andamans or a hassle and a half. The truth lies somewhere in between. Andaman Shipping Office (p1029) has boats from Chennai (₹2825 to ₹10,815, one to two monthly); Shipping Corporation of India (p482) departs from Kolkata (₹2776 to ₹10,766, scheduled monthly departs); and AV Bhanoji Rao, Garuda Pattabhiramayya & Co (p940) leaves from Visakhapatnam (₹2500 to ₹10,000, monthly). All arrive at Port Blair's Haddo Jetty (p1102).

Take sailing times with a large grain of salt. With hold-ups and variable weather and sea conditions, the trip can take a day or two more than the projected travel time.

You can organise your return ticket at the ferry booking office (p1102) at Port Blair's Phoenix Bay Jetty (p1102). Bring three passport photos, plus copies of your passport and visa. Updated schedules and fares can be found through the Shipping Corporation of India website (www.shipindia.com); otherwise enquire at Phoenix Bay's info office (p1102).

Classes vary slightly between boats, but the cheapest is bunk (₹2500), followed by 2nd class (six beds, ₹5000 to ₹6500), 1st class (four beds, ₹8000) and deluxe cabins (two beds, ₹10,000). Higher-end tickets cost as much as, if not more than, a plane ticket. If you go bunk, prepare for little privacy and unpleasant toilets. Food (tiffin snack for breakfast, meal-on-a-plate thalis for lunch and dinner) costs around ₹150/200 per day for bunk/cabin class, though bring extras. Some bedding is supplied, but if you're travelling bunk class bring a sleeping sheet.

There is no ferry between Port Blair and Thailand, but private yachts can usually get clearance. You can't legally get from the Andamans to Myanmar (Burma) by sea.

❶ Getting Around

AIR

At the time of writing, interisland sea planes were not operating and it was unlikely they would resume.

While the interisland helicopter service is generally reserved for islanders and VIPs, you

INTERNET ACCESS & MOBILE PHONES

Getting online in the Andamans continues to be a struggle. There are internet cafes in Port Blair and a few resorts with 'wi-fi' in Port Blair, and on Havelock (Swaraj) and Neil (Shaheed) Islands, but strong connections and smartphone data are rare. A new submarine optical fibre cable, which will link Chennai to Port Blair, Havelock, Little Andaman, Great Nicobar, Car Nicobar and Kamorta, is *scheduled* to be completed by the time you read this. Meanwhile, Jio, India's biggest 4G network, has been installing its services in the Port Blair area, with hopes of expanding across most popular islands in the near future.

All telephone numbers must include the ☑ 03192 area code, even when dialling locally. BSNL is the most reliable mobile-phone operator.

can chance your luck by applying one day before at the **Directorate of Civil Aviation office** (☑ 03192-233601; Port Blair Helipad, VIP Rd; ⊙ 8.30am-5pm Mon-Fri) at the helipad by the airport. However, the 5kg baggage limit and soaring price tag (for example ₹19,000 from Port Blair to Diglipur) precludes most tourists from using this service.

BOAT

Most islands can only be reached by water. Ferry ticket offices can be chaotic: expect hot waits (queues start hours in advance), slow service, queue-jumping and a rugby scrum to the ticket window; ladies' queues are a godsend, but they really only apply in Port Blair. Have your passport (for photo ID) and, if required, your ticket form handy. You may be able to buy tickets the day you travel by arriving at the appropriate jetty an hour beforehand, but this is risky; government ferry tickets are released one to three days ahead, so buy them as soon as possible. Hotels and travel agents can usually book ferry tickets for you.

There are regular boat services to Havelock (Swaraj) and Neil (Shaheed) Islands, as well as Rangat, Long Island, Mayabunder, Diglipur and Little Andaman. Ferry schedules are not currently available online; ask locally or check with Port Blair's Phoenix Bay Jetty ferry information office (p1102). All schedules are liable to change.

More comfortable (and more expensive) private ferry companies also run to Havelock and Neil Islands from Port Blair; tickets are usually available a month in advance online and in person, making these the easiest option for visitors. **Makruzz** (☑ 03192-236677; www.makruzz.com; 1st fl, TCI XPS Building, 100 JN Rd, Delaripur; ⊙ 9am-5.30pm) and **Green Ocean** (☑ 03192-230777; http://greenoceanseaways.com; 1st fl, Island Arcade, Junglighat; ⊙ 9am-1pm & 2-4pm Mon-Sat, 9am-1pm Sun) are the main operators.

BUS

The main island group – South, Middle and North Andaman – is connected by road, with ferry crossings and, increasingly, bridges. Buses run south from Port Blair to Wandoor and Chidiya Tapu, and north to Baratang, Rangat, Mayabunder and finally to Diglipur.

PRIVATE CAR

A car with driver costs ₹900 to ₹1100 per 35km, or around ₹11,250 for a return trip to Diglipur from Port Blair (including stopovers along the way). Due to restrictions in travel within tribal areas, foreigners are not permitted to drive their own vehicles to North and Middle Andaman.

Port Blair

POP 108,060

Surrounded by tropical forest and rugged coastline, the Andamans' lively provincial capital, Port Blair, is a vibrant mix of Indian Ocean inhabitants – Bengalis, Tamils, Telugus, Nicobarese and Myanmarese. Most travellers don't hang around any longer than necessary (usually one or two days while waiting to book onward travel in the islands, or returning for departure), but PB's fascinating history warrants exploration while you're in town. There are also some enticing day trips, such as to Mahatma Gandhi Marine National Park (p1103) and Chidiya Tapu (p1104).

⊙ Sights

★ **Cellular Jail**
National Memorial   HISTORIC BUILDING
(GB Pant Rd; Indian/foreigner ₹30/100, camera ₹200, sound-and-light show adult/child ₹50/25; ⊙ 8.45am-12.30pm & 1.30-4.45pm) A former British prison, the Cellular Jail now serves as a shrine to the political dissidents it once imprisoned. Construction began in 1896 and was completed in 1906 – the original seven wings (several of which were destroyed by the Japanese during WWII; only three now remain) contained 698 cells radiating from a central tower. Like many political prisons, it became something of a university for freedom fighters, who exchanged books, ideas and debates despite the walls and wardens.

Controversial Hindu freedom fighter Vinayak Damodar Savarkar was held here from 1914 to 1921 and his former cell is open to visitors.

Anthropological Museum   MUSEUM
(MG Rd; Indian/foreigner ₹20/150; ⊙ 9am-1pm & 1.30-4.30pm Tue-Sun) Port Blair's engaging anthropology museum provides a thorough and sympathetic portrait of the islands' indigenous tribal communities. The glass display cases may seem old school, but they don't feel anywhere near as ancient as the simple geometric patterns etched into a Jarawa chest guard, the skull left in a Sentinelese lean-to, the Andamanese shell waist girdle, or the totemic spirits represented by Nicobarese shamanic sculptures. No photography.

Samudrika Naval Marine Museum   MUSEUM
(Haddo Rd; adult/child ₹50/25; ⊙ 9am-12.30pm & 2-5pm Tue-Sun) Run by the Indian Navy, this diverse museum provides helpful insight into the islands' ecosystems, tribal communities, flora and fauna (including a small aquarium). On display are hawksbill turtle shells recovered from poachers and, outside, the skeleton of a young blue whale washed ashore on Kamorta Island in the Nicobars.

ANDAMAN ISLANDS PORT BLAIR

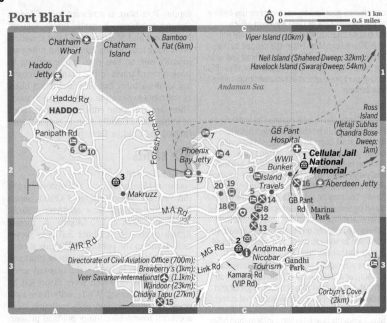

Port Blair

🛏 Sleeping

The tourist office (p1102) provides a list of approved homestays.

Aashiaanaa   GUESTHOUSE $
(📞 03192-234123; Marine Hill; r with AC ₹1700, without AC ₹850-950; ❄🛜) A reliable budget choice

under efficient management, Aashiaanaa has homely, well-kept rooms just 800m uphill from Phoenix Bay Jetty. Pricier rooms get you a balcony and air-con. Wi-fi is ₹60 per hour.

Amina Lodge   GUESTHOUSE $
(📞 9933258703, 9474275441; aminalodge@ymail.com; MA Rd, Aberdeen Bazaar; s ₹500, d ₹700-800;

⊙) Popular with budget travellers, friendly Amina offers four clean rooms with TV and an hour's free wi-fi, in a handy though somewhat-noisy location in the thick of Aberdeen Bazaar. Call ahead.

Lalaji Bay View GUESTHOUSE $
(⊙ 9476005820, 03192-236333; www.lalajibayview.com; RP Rd, Dignabad; r ₹800-1000, with AC ₹1400; ✲⊙) This popular backpacker spot keeps busy for its basic, sprucely maintained rooms, but it's the sociable rooftop Excel restaurant-bar that makes the place tick. Wi-fi costs ₹60 per hour.

Port Vista GUESTHOUSE $$
(⊙ 03192-241080, 8860427712; theportvista@gmail.com; 10 DP St, Haddo; r incl breakfast ₹2800-4000) At this friendly little guesthouse, oleanders and bougainvillea line the stairs to a terrace with wraparound views and just two colourful, pristine rooms with a dash more charm than most Port Blair offerings.

Andaman Homestay HOMESTAY $$
(⊙ 9474208233; www.andamanhomestay.com; Khushnaz Bungalow, 13 DP St, Haddo; r with AC ₹2500, s/d without AC ₹1000/1500, apt with/without AC ₹4000/2700; ✲⊙) A collection of spotless rooms and a split-level four-person apartment in a warm, mandarin-orange family home, just over 1km south of Haddo Jetty. The helpful Nobles also run popular kayaking trips from Port Blair and on Havelock Island (Swaraj Dweep).

Fortune Resort Bay Island HOTEL $$$
(⊙ 03192-234101; www.fortunehotels.in; Marine Hill; r incl breakfast from ₹12,800; ✲⊙⊠) One of PB's finest hotels, with panoramic sea views, pretty hillside gardens and elegant contemporary rooms with polished-wood floors; ask for one that's sea-facing. Relax over cocktails in Nico bar (p1102) and dine on refined global fare at the terrace restaurant.

J Hotel HOTEL $$$
(⊙ 03192-243700; www.jhotel.in; Aberdeen Bazaar; r incl breakfast ₹5900-7080; ✲⊙) A sleek, modern, professionally run find in the heart of Aberdeen Bazaar, with up-to-date, wood-floored, gold-and-cream rooms and a rooftop restaurant turning out multicuisine fare.

Sinclairs Bayview HOTEL $$$
(⊙ 03192-227824; www.sinclairshotels.com; South Point; incl breakfast d ₹12,800-17,920, q ₹17,920-25,600; ✲⊙⊠) Recently revamped, Sinclairs delivers some of Port Blair's smartest accommodation, with spacious, current rooms

looking out on the bay and seaside gardens, 2km southeast of town. There's a reliably good on-site multicuisine **restaurant** (mains ₹230-600; ⊙ 7.30-10.30am, 12.30-3.30pm & 7.30-10.30pm), plus a bar and spa.

✕ Eating & Drinking

★ **New Lighthouse Restaurant** INDIAN $$
(Marina Park; mains ₹130-360; ⊙ 11am-10.30pm) Fresh seafood grilled, steamed or barbecued to taste is the speciality at this unadorned favourite, but there's also punchy veg or prawn biryani and an impressive globe-trotting menu. The upstairs beer terrace (from 5pm) gets busy.

Excel Restaurant INTERNATIONAL $$
(⊙ 9476005820, 03192-236333; www.lalajibayview.com; RP Rd, Dignabad, Lalaji Bay View; mains ₹120-350; ⊙ 7.30am-10.30pm) The atmospheric bamboo restaurant atop Lalaji Bay View guesthouse brings a Havelock-style menu to the city, with grilled fish, burgers, *momos* (Tibetan dumplings) and more. A mellow, social place to chill out over a beer.

Annapurna Cafeteria INDIAN $$
(MG Rd; mains ₹170-250; ⊙ 6.30am-10.30pm) An excellent frills-free pure-veg option, reminiscent of a high-school cafeteria, that rustles up rich North Indian–style curries and delicious South Indian favourites, such as dosas (large savoury crêpe), *vadas* (doughnut-shaped deep-fried lentil savoury) and *uttapams* (thick, savoury South Indian rice pancake with finely chopped onions, green chillies, coriander and coconut).

Icy Spicy INDIAN $$
(⊙ 03192-329304, 03192-232704; Basement, Island Arcade, Junglighat; mains ₹150-215; ⊙ 11am-11.30pm) It doesn't look much from the outside, but buried away in this small mall is a busy, smartish pure-veg restaurant. It's often packed with visiting Indians, here for the tasty thalis (₹180 to ₹220), biryanis, North Indian gravies, and sugar-free goodies from the upstairs bakery.

Gagan Restaurant INDIAN $$
(Clock Tower, Aberdeen Bazaar; mains ₹150-200; ⊙ 7.30am-10pm) This locally loved and low-key Bengali hole-in-the-wall serves great food at good prices, including Nicobari fish, crab curries and paneer in a world of versions.

There's a samosa stand out front and the owners also run nearby restaurant **Ananda** (⊙ 03192-244041; Aberdeen Bazaar; mains ₹170-330; ⊙ 7am-10pm).

DON'T MISS

ROSS ISLAND (NETAJI SUBHAS CHANDRA BOSE DWEEP)

Renamed Netaji Subhas Chandra Bose Dweep in 2018 and just a 1.5km boat ride away from Port Blair, Ross Island (₹30; ⊘8.30am-2pm Thu-Tue) feels like a jungle-clad lost city, à la Angkor Wat, except here the ruins are Victorian English rather than ancient Khmer. The former British administrative headquarters in the Andamans, the island lost its vibrant social scene with the double whammy of a 1941 earthquake and invasion by the Japanese, but its ruined colonial-era architecture is still standing. In its day, Ross (not to be confused with its namesake island in North Andaman) was fondly called the 'Paris of the East' (along with Pondicherry, Saigon etc etc...). Landscaped paths criss-cross to dilapidated buildings, most of which are labelled (a church, a printing press). There's a herd of resident spotted deer, plus a small museum with historical displays.

Boats (₹320, 20 minutes) to Ross Island depart roughly hourly from Port Blair's Aberdeen Jetty between 8.30am and 2pm. Good sound-and-light shows (₹335 per person including return ferry) are often staged on the island; tickets are sold at Port Blair's tourist office.

Brewberry's
CAFE $$

(☑9679596637; MG Rd, Lamba Line; dishes ₹130-260; ⊘11am-10.30pm; ☜) Port Blair's only real contemporary, wi-fi-equipped hang-out cafe is opposite the airport, 2km south of the city centre. The chocolate-brown decor sets the tone for brownies, espresso, French-press coffee and well-executed wraps, pastas and other snacks.

Amaya
INTERNATIONAL $$$

(☑03192-242773; http://seashellhotels.net; Marine Hill, SeaShell Port Blair; mains ₹340-1000; ⊘11am-10.30pm; ☜) Amid palmtops, the SeaShell hotel's breezy and sophisticated rooftop lounge appeals for its sleek bar (cocktails ₹415), open-plan kitchen, high-season live music and views of Ross Island (Netaji Subhas Chandra Bose Dweep). Elegantly prepared dishes wander from fish tikka to spicy paneer (soft, unfermented milk-curd cheese) satay.

Nico Bar
BAR

(☑03192-234101; www.fortunehotels.in; Marine Hill, Fortune Resort Bay Island; ⊘11am-10.45pm) The closest you'll get to the Nicobars, the Fortune's bar is a classic for sea breezes and palm-spangled coastal views (the image on the old ₹20 note is based on this spot). A pleasant place to while away an afternoon or balmy evening with a frosty cocktail (₹300).

ℹ Information

Port Blair is the only place in the Andamans where you can reliably change cash and find enough ATMs, especially in Aberdeen Bazaar and MG Rd.

There are internet cafes with wi-fi and computer terminals in Aberdeen Bazaar near the clock tower, including **E-Cafe** (Ainternet & wi-fi per hour ₹40; ⊘9am-9.30pm Mon-Sat).

Andaman & Nicobar Tourism (☑03192-232694; www.andamantourism.gov.in; Kamaraj Rd; ⊘9am-1pm & 1.30-5pm Mon-Sat) The Andamans' main tourist office; books permits for restricted areas around Port Blair.

GB Pant Hospital (☑03192-233473, emergency 03192-232102; GB Pant Rd; ⊘24hr) Offers medical services.

Island Travels (☑03192-233358; www.islandtravelsandaman.com; MA Rd, Aberdeen Bazaar; ⊘9.30am-6.30pm Mon-Sat) Books hotels and transport.

ℹ Getting There & Away

BOAT

Most inter-island ferries depart from Phoenix Bay Jetty. Tickets can be purchased from its **ferry booking office** (⊘9am-1pm & 2-4pm Mon-Fri, to 12.45pm Sat) one to three days in advance; if they are sold out, you can chance your luck with a same-day ticket issued an hour before departure. There's a **ferry information office** (☑03192-245555; ⊘6am-7.30pm) inside the ticket office. New arrivals should make the jetty their first port of call to book tickets; hotels and travel agents can usually reserve ferries, too. Note that queues can start as early as 4am and tickets sell out fast, while ferry schedules may change.

Havelock (Swaraj) & Neil (Shaheed)

Given the challenges of securing government ferry tickets to reach Havelock Island (Swaraj Dweep) and Neil Island (Shaheed Dweep), most travellers use pricier private ferries, which run from Haddo Jetty and can be booked a month ahead.

Makruzz (p1099) has daily departures to Havelock (₹1407 to ₹3118, 1½ hours) at 8am and 1.30pm, plus a high-season-only ferry to Neil (₹1289 to ₹2802, one hour). Green Ocean (p1099) heads to Havelock (₹1050 to ₹1350, 2½ hours) at 6.30am, 7am and 12.30pm, returning at 9.30am and 3pm; from October to March, the 7am Havelock ferry continues to Neil (₹1850 to ₹2450, three hours).

Government ferries to Havelock (₹460 to ₹650, 2½ hours) depart daily at 6.20am and 2pm, returning at 9am and 4.30pm; ferries to Neil (₹460 to ₹650; two hours) leave at 6.30am and 11am, returning at 8.30am and 4pm. All these services book out fast.

Middle & North Andaman

There are at least two ferries a week to/from Diglipur (₹1050 to ₹1470, 17 hours) via Maya-bunder (₹840 to ₹1260, 10 hours), and three to four ferries a week to/from Long Island (₹630 to ₹1050, five hours) via Havelock and Neil.

Little Andaman

There are daily boats between Haddo Jetty and Little Andaman (₹500 to ₹1500, 5½ to eight hours), which regularly sell out.

BUS

Government buses run from the central **Mohan-pura Bus Terminus** (MA Rd, Aberdeen Bazaar). Andaman Trunk Rd (p1112) services can be booked up to nine days ahead.

Baratang ₹110, three hours, six daily 4am–12.15pm

Chidiya Tapu ₹24, one hour, nine daily 5.50am–8.10pm

Diglipur and Aerial Bay ₹280–₹290, 12 hours, 4am, 7am

Mayabunder ₹220, 10 hours, 4am, 9.45am

Rangat ₹160, seven hours, five daily 4am–12.15pm

Wandoor ₹24, one hour, hourly 6am–4.45pm

More comfortable, but pricier, private buses operate from a **bus stand** (off MA Rd) just north of the main bus station.

❶ Getting Around

TO/FROM THE AIRPORT

Taxis or autorickshaws from the airport to Ab-erdeen Bazaar cost around ₹150. Alternatively, jump on any bus (₹10 to ₹20) heading into Port Blair's main bus stand (p1103) from the main road outside the airport.

SLEEPING PRICE RANGES

The following price ranges refer to a double room with bathroom during high season (November to March) in the Andamans.

$ less than ₹1200

$$ ₹1200–₹4000

$$$ more than ₹4000

AUTORICKSHAW & MOTORCYCLE

Autorickshaws from Aberdeen Bazaar cost around ₹40 to Phoenix Bay Jetty and ₹60 to Haddo Jetty.

You can hire motorcycles for ₹500 per day, with outlets including the reliable **Saro Tours & Travels** (☑ 9933291466; Marine Rd, Aberdeen Bazaar; ⊙7am-7.30pm).

Around Port Blair

Wandoor

Wandoor, a tiny speck of a village with a pretty nearby beach 25km southwest of Port Blair, is a good spot to explore South Anda-man's lush interior. It's mostly known as a jumping-off point for Mahatma Gandhi Ma-rine National Park.

◉ Sights & Activities

Mahatma Gandhi
Marine National Park   NATIONAL PARK
(⊙Tue-Sun) 🏊 Comprising 15 islands of mangrove creeks, tropical rainforest and reefs supporting 50 types of coral and plen-ty of colourful fish, the 280-sq-km Mahatma Gandhi Marine National Park is ideal for snorkelling (gear rental ₹300). Three boats depart on half-day trips from Wandoor Jetty from 7.30am depending on demand, costing ₹885 in addition to the permit (Indian/for-eigner ₹75/1000) you'll need to prearrange from Port Blair's tourist office up to three days ahead. No plastics allowed. The marine park's snorkelling sites alternate every six months between Jolly Buoy and Red Skin, allowing the other to regenerate.

Wandoor Beach   BEACH
Wandoor has a lovely blonde beach, though at the time of writing swimming was prohib-ited due to a fatal crocodile attack in 2017.

ANET   VOLUNTEERING
(Andaman & Nicobar Environmental Team; ☑ 03192-280081; www.anetindia.org; North Wan-door) 🏊 Led by an inspiring team of dynam-ic Indian ecologists, this energetic research and conservation centre, founded in 1990, has occasional openings for specialised vol-unteers; check directly.

🍴 Sleeping & Eating

Sea Princess Beach Resort   RESORT **$$$**
(☑9609508000, 03192-280002; www.seaprincess andaman.com; Wandoor Beach; r incl breakfast ₹8260-12,800; ❀🛜🛋) Overlooking Wandoor's

WORTH A TRIP

CINQUE ISLAND

Surrounded by coral reefs, the uninhabited islands of North and South Cinque are connected by a sparkling-white sand-bar beach that disappears at high tide. They're among the most beautiful in the Andamans, with great snorkelling and diving. Only day visits are allowed, however, and unless you're on one of the day trips occasionally organised by local travel agencies, you'll need to get permission in advance by purchasing the Mahatma Gandhi Marine National Park permit (p1097) from Port Blair's tourist office (p1102) – and potentially an additional permit. By boat, the islands are 20km south (two hours) from Chidiya Tapu or 30km southeast (3½ hours) from Wandoor.

silky (though unswimmable) beach, this palm-studded resort provides a bar, a restaurant (meals ₹880) and well-equipped, wood-walled rooms dotted around a pool, with the spacious suites being the pick of the bunch.

❶ Getting There & Away

Buses from Port Blair run to Wandoor (₹24, one hour) hourly from 6am to 4.45pm; the latest return is at 8.15pm. Taxis charge ₹1000 to ₹1800 one way.

Chidiya Tapu

Chidiya Tapu, 25km south of Port Blair, is a tiny settlement fringed by beaches and mangroves, and famous for its celestial sunsets and silvery Munda Pahar Beach. It gets busy with day trippers from Port Blair.

◉ Sights & Activities

Chidiya Tapu–based Lacadives and Infinity Scuba run dive trips to local sites including Corruption Rock and a WWII British minesweeper wreck. They may also be able to organise trips to Cinque Island and Rutland Island.

Munda Pahar Beach BEACH
(◷ 9am-5pm) Loved for its fiery sunsets and wonderfully natural setting, this powdery silver-sand beach is popular with day trippers, although swimming was prohibited at research time due to crocodiles. A signposted 1km, 20-minute hike leads to a viewpoint.

Lacadives DIVING
(☏ 9531866304, 03192-281013; www.lacadives.com; single dive ₹3550; PADI Open Water course ₹29,500; ◷ Oct-May) ✦ A long-established, environmentally responsible dive company that also offers nature walks (₹250 to ₹1000).

Infinity Scuba DIVING
(☏ 03192-281183, 9474204508; www.infinityscubandamans.wordpress.com; Wild Grass Resort; 2-dive trip ₹4700, PADI Open Water course ₹25,960) Set up by ex-navy commander and expert Andamans diver Baath; offers diving and some snorkelling trips.

Reef Watch Marine Conservation VOLUNTEERING
(☏ 9476073291; www.reefwatchindia.org; Lacadives) ✦ This NGO with a focus on marine conservation accepts volunteers (minimum one week) to be involved in beach clean-ups, fish surveys and more. Contact the team to discuss opportunities that match your skills with their needs.

🛏 Sleeping & Eating

Wild Grass Resort RESORT $$$
(☏ 9474204508; www.wildgrassresorts.in; r incl breakfast ₹4500-6500; ❄) Set against a verdant jungle backdrop, 1.5km northwest of Chidiya Tapu village, Wild Grass' smart, modern cottages have an easygoing ambience; best are the two-storey bungalows with elevated terraces. It also has a recommended dive school, Infinity Scuba, and an atmospheric bamboo restaurant for beers and meals.

❶ Getting There & Away

Buses head from Port Blair to Chidiya Tapu (₹24, one hour) nine times daily from 5.50am to 8.10pm; the last return bus leaves at 6pm. Taxis charge ₹1250 to ₹1750 one way.

Havelock Island (Swaraj Dweep)

POP 5500

With sublime silken-blonde beaches, twinkling teal shallows and some of the best diving in South Asia, thickly forested Havelock (Swaraj) enjoys the well-deserved reputation of being a travellers' paradise. Indeed, for many, Havelock *is* the Andamans – it's what lures most visitors across the Bay of Bengal, many of them content to stay here for the entirety of their trip.

Havelock has been developing fast in recent years, with a rise in domestic tourism and concrete-clad resorts chasing away many of the original bamboo beach huts. But much of the island's 92 sq km (it's the largest in Ritchie's Archipelago) remains untouched, and the beaches and diving remain bewitching.

◉ Sights & Activities

Beaches

★ **Radhanagar Beach**   BEACH

(Beach 7) One of India's (and indeed Asia's) most fabulous and famous stretches of sand: a beautiful bleach-blonde curve of powdery sugar fronted by perfectly spiralled aqua waves, all fringed by lush native forest. It's on the northwest side of the island, 11km southwest of the jetty. Visit early morning to avoid the heat and crowds.

Beach 5   BEACH

On Havelock's eastern coast, palm-ringed Beach 5 has your classic tropical vibe with cream-coloured sand, cerulean sea, shady patches and few sandflies. Swimming can be difficult at low tide, when the water shallows out for kilometres.

Beach 3   BEACH

A slender strip of platinum east-coast beach, dotted with palms and a few fishing boats and overlooked by clumps of natural jungle. Beautiful, though not ideal for swimming as it's rocky. It's 3km southeast of the jetty.

Neil's Cove   BEACH

With its gorgeous teal 'lagoon', Neil's Cove is a gem of sheltered sand and crystalline water. Swimming is prohibited at dusk and dawn; take heed of warnings regarding crocodiles.

Kalapathar   BEACH

Pristine Kalapathar is a salt-white swathe of sand lapped by clear turquoise water. It's a favourite sunrise-gazing spot, and you may have to walk a bit to get away from the masses and souvenir shops.

Elephant Beach   BEACH

Along the island's northwest coastline, the alabaster sands of Elephant Beach, a popular snorkelling spot, are reached by a 40-minute, 1.8km walk through a muddy elephant logging trail. The path is well signposted off the cross-island road, 7.5km southwest of Havelock's jetty, but turns to bog if it's been raining. Head over around 6am for a better chance of having the place to yourself.

Diving & Snorkelling

With options for all levels, Havelock's diving scene is one of the Andamans' key attrac-

tions. Prices are around ₹6500 to ₹7500 for a two-tank dive, with options of Professional Association of Diving Instructors (PADI) or Scuba Schools International (SSI) introductory dives (₹4000 to ₹7000), open-water courses (four dives ₹26,000 to ₹31,000) and advanced courses (three to five dives ₹21,000 to ₹23,600).

Popular sites include Dixon's Pinnacle and Pilot Reef, with colourful soft coral; South Button for macro dives and rock formations; the Wall, for soft coral, pelagic fish and night dives; Jackson's Bar or Johnny's Gorge for deeper dives with schools of snapper, sharks, rays and turtles; and Minerva Ledge for a bit of everything. There are also wreck dives to SS Incheket, a 1950s cargo carrier, and MV *Mars*.

Snorkelling trips (₹2500 to ₹5000) can be booked through dive schools and hotels; most go to Elephant Beach.

Dive India   DIVING

(☑ 8001122205, 03192-214247; www.diveindia. com; Beach 3; 2-dive trip ₹7380, PADI Open Water course ₹30,680) The original PADI company on Havelock, and still one of the best, with basic beach-hut accommodation.

Barefoot Scuba   DIVING

(☑ 9474263120, 9566088560; www.barefoot scuba.in; Beach 3; 2-dive trip ₹6785, PADI Open Water course ₹29,740) Popular, long-established company with dive and accommodation packages (p1108) and snorkelling trips (₹2500 to ₹5000).

Ocean Tribe   DIVING

(☑ 9476012783, 9474240746, 03192-282255; http:// ocean-tribe.com; Beach 3; 2-dive trip ₹6490, SSI/ PADI Open Water course ₹21,500/24,500) Run by legendary local Karen divers Dixon, Jackson and Johnny, all of whom have dive sites named after them.

Andaman Bubbles   DIVING

(☑ 03192-282140, 8900936494; www.andaman bubbles.com; Beach 5; 2-dive trip ₹6785, SSI/PADI Open Water course ₹26,550/28,320) Quality outfit with professional, personable staff.

Other Activities

Some resorts organise guided jungle treks for keen walkers or birdwatchers. The rainforest is a spectacular, emerald-coloured hinterland cavern, and the birdwatching – especially on the forest fringes – is rewarding; look out for the blue-black greater racket-tailed drongo or black-naped oriole.

Yoga lessons may be available during high season at Flying Elephant (p1107).

Swaraj Dweep (Havelock Island)

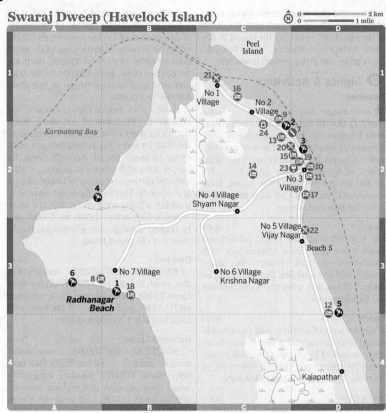

Peel Island

Karmatang Bay

No 1 Village

No 2 Village

No 4 Village
Shyam Nagar

No 3 Village

No 5 Village
Vijay Nagar

Beach 5

No 7 Village

No 6 Village
Krishna Nagar

Radhanagar
Beach

Kalapathar

ANDAMAN ISLANDS HAVELOCK ISLAND (SWARAJ DWEEP)

Andaman Kayak Tours   KAYAKING
(📱9476051158, 9933269653; www.andamanhome
stay.com; per person ₹3000-3500; ⊙Sep-May)
A popular activity operator that explores
Havelock's mangroves by sea kayak, runs
snorkel-and-kayak excursions, and organises memorable night trips to glide among
bioluminescence. Trips last 2½ hours.

🛏 Sleeping

Green Imperial   BUNGALOW $
(📱03192-282004, 9474206301; www.greenimperi
al.com; Beach 3; bungalows ₹800, r with AC ₹2500-
4000; ❄🐾) A favourite backpacker hang-
out, sprinkled across lush gardens of palms
and betel nuts just a few minutes' walk from
the beach. There are fan-cooled bamboo
bungalows with beds (not floor mattresses)
and private bathrooms, and plain, well-kept,
air-conditioned concrete cottages.

Coconut Grove Beach Resort   GUESTHOUSE $
(📱9538191748; http://coconutgrovebeachresort.
com; Beach 5; huts ₹1000-2200) Low-key Coconut Grove has a relaxed communal vibe
with no-frills, slightly-rough-around-the-
edges bamboo huts (some featuring open-
air showers, others sharing bathrooms)
arranged in a circular, palm-studded cluster.

Sea View Beach Resort   HUT $
(📱9531829129; http://ocean-tribe.com; Beach 3; r
₹1000-2000) Chilled-out thatched beach huts
with mosquito nets and concrete bathrooms,
plus slightly musty fan-cooled bungalows,
backing on to the Ocean Tribe (p1105) dive
shop, a bit away from the crowds.

Orient Legend Resort   GUESTHOUSE $
(📱9434291008, 03192-282389; www.havelock
beachresort.in; Beach 5; huts ₹500-600, r with AC
₹3000, without AC ₹1000-1500) This popular,
sprawling place covers most budgets, from
doghouse A-frame bamboo huts (the cheap-

Swaraj Dweep (Havelock Island)

est share bathrooms) to colourful concrete rooms offering a glimpse of the ocean.

Flying Elephant BUNGALOW $$
(☎8900920809, 9531861903; www.flying-elephant.in; Kalapathar; r incl breakfast ₹3980) Hidden away just inland from Kalapathar beach, among rice paddies, mango trees and betel palms, this warm, serene and efficiently run retreat has a yoga *shala* and simple, earthy bamboo bungalows (some duplexes) with landscaped outdoor stone-garden bathrooms.

Emerald Gecko BUNGALOW $$
(☎9531860527, 03192-233358; www.emerald-gecko.com; Beach 5; huts/bungalows/lodges ₹1890/3110/₹3760) 🌿 These double-storey, fan-cooled huts (with private shower but communal toilet) look to the water; the cosy bamboo bungalows have open-air bathrooms; and individual lodges, constructed from bamboo rafts that have drifted ashore from Myanmar (Burma), come with ambient lighting, private terraces and outdoor bathrooms. Free water refills.

★ **Jalakara** BOUTIQUE HOTEL $$$
(www.jalakara.info; No 4 Village; incl breakfast r ₹17,860-39,620, villas ₹35,800-63,950; ☺Oct-May;

✻☒) 🌿 Easily the chicest place to stay in the Andamans, this ecoconscious British-owned luxe-boutique hideaway is built into a banana-and-betel-nut plantation, 3.5km south of the jetty. It wows with its rainforest-view infinity pool, organic cooking, small spa, daily yoga, open-air bathrooms and seven highly original, design-led, tropical-life rooms, styled with antiques, earthy tones, polished concrete, and curtains crafted from saris.

★ **Barefoot at Havelock** RESORT $$$
(☎9731557551, 9840238042; www.barefoot-andaman.com; Radhanagar; tented cottages ₹10,500-13,000 cottages ₹14,500-21,500; ✻☎) 🌿 A thoughtfully designed, long-established, ecofriendly resort with elegantly comfortable timber, bamboo-thatched or tented cottages, just back from Radhanagar's sands. There's also a spa, a bar, a good restaurant, and seafood feasts served at private beach tables.

Taj Exotica LUXURY HOTEL $$$
(☎03192-283333; taj.tajhotels.com; Radhanagar; r incl breakfast ₹43,840-96,380; ✻☎☒) 🌿 Respecting (and replanting) the local rainforest, this much-anticipated Taj Group property brings contemporary luxury to Radhanagar. Glossy villas, inspired by Jarawa

tribe huts, are graced by enormous walk-through bathrooms, canvases of local marine life and, in some cases, private pools. You'll glimpse the glittering sea from the excellent restaurant overlooking a jungle-shrouded infinity pool.

Barefoot Scuba   BUNGALOW $$$
(📞9474263120; www.barefootscuba.in; Beach 3; cottages incl breakfast ₹5310-8260; ❄) 🍴 Smart, orange-walled, polished-wood cottages with terraces and a bit of style, in a knot of palms just steps from the beach. The most affordable 'cottages' are tentlike canvas constructions. Free water refills.

SeaShell Havelock   RESORT $$$
(📞9531907001, 03192-242773; www.seashellhotels.net; Beach 3; r incl breakfast ₹12,160-27,520; ❄ 🛜 🏊) One of Havelock's sleeker choices, featuring elegant all-wood cottages with tea-and-coffee kits, dotted around palm-shaded paths to an infinity pool with sea glimpses. There's beachfront yoga, a dive school and a smart cafe-pub for coffee and wi-fi.

Wild Orchid   RESORT $$$
(📞03192-282472; www.wildorchidandaman.com; Beach 5; r incl breakfast ₹8000-9000; ❄ 🛜) Well-established Wild Orchid's contemporary, wooden Andamanese-style cottages are strung around a tropical garden, the best of them vibrantly coloured and sporting half-canopied beds.

🍴 Eating & Drinking

There are *dhabas* (casual eateries, serving snacks and basic meals) near the jetty. The main bazaar (No 3 Village) has local meals, a market and a supermarket.

Alcohol is available from a **store** (🕐9am-noon & 3-8pm) near the ATMs at No 3 Village. Apart from a couple of bars and the wonderful jungle-shrouded club **Cicada** (Beach 5;

hours vary), due to reopen in 2019, Havelock nightlife is on the mellow beachy side.

Dakshin   SOUTH INDIAN $
(www.barefoot-andaman.com; No 1 Village; mains ₹80-270; 🕐6.30-10am & noon-3.30pm) Masala dosas, *uttapams* (thick, savoury rice pancake) and tasty thalis are swiftly served at this South Indian specialist, next to Havelock's jetty.

Fat Martin's   INDIAN $
(Beach 5; mains ₹70-140; 🕐11.30am-9pm) Popular open-air cafe with a good selection of Indian dishes and some particularly impressive dosas (paper-thin lentil-flour pancakes) including paneer tikka and Nutella.

★ Anju-Coco Resto   INTERNATIONAL $$
(www.facebook.com/pg/Anjucocoresto; Beach 5; mains ₹200-800; 🕐8am-10.30pm) One of Havelock's faves, down-to-earth roadside Anju-Coco offers a flavour-packed menu of zealously guarded Indian-international family recipes, with outstanding breakfasts, barbecue dishes, seafood and platters. Try a signature veg platter with charred paneer.

Rony's Restaurant   INDIAN $$
(Beach 5; mains ₹160-350; 🕐7am-10.30pm) A simple open-sided cafe with red plastic chairs and a few colourful murals, popular Rony's cooks up delish seafood curries, wood-fired pizzas, Israeli *sabich* (stuffed pita sandwich), breakfast pancakes and other backpacker favourites.

★ Full Moon Cafe   INTERNATIONAL $$$
(www.facebook.com/fullmoonandaman; Dive India, Beach 3; mains ₹140-550; 🕐7am-3.30pm & 6-10pm) 🍴 Run by an Irish-Indian couple, this mellow thatched-roof restaurant shares a sandy floored site with Dive India (p1105) and does fabulous seafood, salads, pastas, wraps, fresh juices, falafel platters, Indian

---

RAJAN: THE ANDAMANS' LAST SWIMMING ELEPHANT

In 2016 Havelock Island (Swaraj Dweep) lost one of its most celebrated, instantly recognisable and beloved residents: at the grand old age of 66, the Andamans' last swimming elephant, Rajan, passed away, and his 5-ton body was returned to the depths of the island.

Elephants were first brought to the Andaman Islands in the 1880s by the British to work in the logging industry fuelled by the lush local rainforests. The easiest way for them to travel between islands was by swimming, using their trunks as snorkels. But when logging was banned in 2000, the islands' 200 famous and often-spotted swimming elephants were mostly shipped off to mainland India. Rajan, however, fell into the care of the Barefoot at Havelock (p1107) resort on Havelock's Radhanagar Beach, starring in photo shoots and films, including Hollywood flick *The Fall* (2006), until he 'retired' here in 2014.

bites, and French-press coffee from South Indian beans. Free water refills, plus a book exchange.

B3 – Barefoot Bar & Brasserie
MULTICUISINE $$$

(www.barefoot-andaman.com; No 1 Village; mains ₹350-600; ⊙noon-9.30pm) Right by the jetty, with sea views, B3's breezy wooden deck makes a great place to wait for the ferry. Come for the scrumptious homemade pasta, the fresh-seafood specials and the best pizza on Havelock.

Red Snapper
INDIAN $$$

(☑ 03192-282472; www.wildorchidandaman.com; Beach 5, Wild Orchid; mains ₹250-800; ⊙8-10am, noon-2.30pm & 6-10.30pm) The thatched-roof, bamboo-clad Wild Orchid resort's restaurant exudes a romantic, candlelit island ambience, sizzling up lavish seafood platters, pepper-crust tuna, paneer or fish tikka (marinated in spices and dry-roasted) and other goodies. The mellow attached deck **bar** (⊙hours vary) is a good spot for a beer.

🛍 Shopping

Seven Heaven
FASHION & ACCESSORIES

(☑ 9531835632; No 3 Village; ⊙hours vary) A beach-chic 'island lifestyle' boutique filled with breezy dresses, kaftans and pants, plus beachwear, tribal-inspired jewellery and a few books.

ℹ Information

There are a couple of ATMs in No 3 Village. A handful of places have wi-fi, but it's *sloooow*.

Havelock Tourist Information Centre
(☑ 09474287741; Havelock Jetty, No 1 Village; ⊙8am-1pm & 2.30-5pm)

ℹ Getting There & Away

Government ferries run from **Havelock Jetty** (No 1 Village) in the island's north to Port Blair (₹650, 2½ hours) at 9am and 4.30pm, returning at 6.20am and 2pm. One ferry links Havelock (Swaraj Dweep) with Neil Island (Shaheed Dweep; ₹650, 1¼ hours) at 2.45pm, while three to four boats a week (9.30am on Monday, Wednesday, Friday and, sometimes, Saturday) head to Long Island (₹460, two hours) en route to Rangat, returning at 7am on Tuesday, Thursday and Sunday and 2pm on Friday. Tickets are available from the **ferry ticket office** (☑ 03192-245555; Havelock Jetty, No 1 Village; ⊙8am-1pm & 2-4pm Mon-Sat) one to three days in advance (most hotels arrange tickets for a fee). Schedules may change, and additional services might run during the November-to-April season.

Makruzz (☑ 03192-212355; www.makruzz.com; Havelock Jetty, No 1 Village; ⊙8am-4.30pm) runs at least once daily to Port Blair (₹1407 to ₹3118, 1½ hours) and Neil Island (₹1289 to ₹2882, one hour) and back. **Green Ocean** (☑ 03192-230777; http://greenocean seaways.com; Havelock Jetty, No 1 Village; ⊙8am-noon & 1-5pm) has two to three daily ferries to/from Port Blair (₹1171 to ₹1407, 2¼ hours) and one or two to Neil (₹876 to ₹994, 1¼ hours; returns may operate in high season). These can be booked online a month ahead.

At the time of writing, there were plans to introduce new express ferries between Port Blair and Havelock.

ℹ Getting Around

From 7am to 5.45pm, local buses run from the jetty to Kalapathar (₹12) via the east-coast villages every 1½ hours, and to Radhanagar hourly; the latest return buses are at 6.30pm. Autorickshaws from the jetty cost ₹50 to No 3 Village, ₹90 to No 5 and ₹500 to Radhanagar.

Otherwise, rent a scooter (per 24 hours ₹400 to ₹500) or bicycle (per day ₹100).

Neil Island (Shaheed Dweep)

Although its beaches are not as luxurious as those of its more famous island neighbour, Havelock (Swaraj Dweep), tranquil and wonderfully unhurried Neil (recently renamed Shaheed Dweep) has its own rustic charm, with a lusciously green landscape of rice paddies, fruit plantations and coconut palms. The main bazaar, at Neil Kendra in the centre of the island, has a mellow vibe; the jetty is 500m north of the bazaar.

Development has begun to creep in on Neil, however, and there's been a surge in domestic tourist activity near the jetty and along the north coast, especially on Beach 4.

◉ Sights & Activities

Beaches

Neil Island's five beaches all have their own personalities, though they aren't great for swimming due to shallow, rocky sea floors.

Beach 1
BEACH

(Lakshmanpur) A long sweep of sandy white coastline and mangroves wrapping around the northwest end of the island, 2km from the jetty, and gazing across to Havelock (Swaraj) Island's densely forested southern tip. There's a sunset viewpoint here, plus good snorkelling and snack stalls, and dugongs are sometimes spotted.

Beach 2
BEACH

On the southwest side of the island, signposted from Neil Kendra (1.5km), this rocky cove is famous for its striking Natural Bridge rock formation, accessible only at low tide.

Beach 3
BEACH

(Ramnagar Beach) This secluded rock-studded cove with powdery sand and good snorkelling sits on Neil's south coast and is one of the better beaches for lazing around.

Beach 4
BEACH

(Bharatpur) Neil Island's best swimming beach, though its proximity to the jetty (just west) is a turn-off, as is the rowdy day-trip scene packed with motorised boats, jet skis and banana-boat rides.

Beach 5
BEACH

On the far east of the island, 5km southeast of the jetty, Sitapur is a rugged sweep of silver-white sand, with small limestone caves accessible at low tide. It's popular for sunrise, and has some low-key accommodation.

Diving & Snorkelling

Neil offers some brilliant dive sites, with fish, large schools of jack, turtles, rays, reef sharks, soft and hard corals, and even the odd dugong. PADI Discover Scuba (₹7000 to ₹8000) and Open Water courses (₹28,300 to ₹30,700), among others, are available; two-dive trips cost around ₹6600 to ₹7400.

The island's best snorkelling is at the far (western) end of Beach 1 at high tide. Beach 3 also has good snorkelling. Gear hire costs around ₹200.

India Scuba Explorers
DIVING

(📞 9933271450; www.indiascubaexplorers.com; Beach 1; 2-dive trip ₹6600, PADI Open Water course ₹28,320) Neil's original dive shop, set up in 2007 by a husband-and-wife team, is popular for its personalised service and offers simple, clean budget rooms (₹700).

Dive India
DIVING

(📞 8001122205, 9679574266; www.diveindia. com; Neil Jetty; 2-dive trip ₹7380, PADI Open Water course ₹30,680) This professional and well-established Havelock Island (Swaraj Dweep) dive operator also has a Neil branch, just east of the jetty, with straightforward, modern accommodation (📞 9476007249; r ₹3500-5500; ❄).

ANDAMAN ISLANDS NEIL ISLAND (SHAHEED DWEEP)

DIVING IN THE ANDAMAN ISLANDS

Havelock Island (Swaraj Dweep; p1105) is the premier spot for diving in the Andamans, famed for its crystal-clear waters, deep-sea corals and kaleidoscopic marine life, including turtles, sharks and manta rays. There are also dive schools on Neil Island (Shaheed Dweep). The main dive season is November to April, with prime conditions from December, but trips run year-round, weather permitting. Diving is suitable for all levels.

While coral bleaching has been a major issue since 2010 (said to be linked to El Niño weather patterns) and an estimated 23% of corals off the coast of the Andaman and Nicobar Islands was lost to bleaching in 2016, diving remains world class. The shallows (where most of the bleaching happened) may not have particularly bright corals, but all the colourful fish are still here, and for depths beyond 16m, the corals remain as vivid as ever. The Andamans recovered from a similar bleaching in 1998, and today things are, likewise, slowly repairing themselves.

Keep an eye out for trips further afield such as to Barren Island, home to India's only active volcano, whose ash produces an eerie underwater spectacle for divers.

Protecting Marine Life

In general, you should only snorkel when it's high tide, as during low tide it's very easy to step on coral or sea sponges, which can irreparably damage them. In areas that have reefs with very shallow water, avoid wearing flippers – even the gentle sweep of a flipper-kick can damage decades' worth of growth. Divers need to be extra cautious about descents near reefs; colliding with the coral at a strong pace with full gear can be environmentally disastrous. Choose ecologically responsible dive operators and heed their advice.

Avoid touching marine life of any kind, including coral, as doing so may not only stress them and cause damage, but they could also be toxic. Finally, clear any rubbish you come across and refrain from taking souvenir shells or coral out of the ocean (it's ecologically detrimental but also potentially illegal).

🛏 Sleeping & Eating

There are cheap restaurants in the bazaar.

Kalapani
BUNGALOW $

(📞 9933225575; Beach 3; huts ₹200-600) Laid-back Kalapani has simple budget bungalows amid neat sandy gardens, the cheapest of which share communal bathrooms. Motorbikes, bicycles and snorkelling gear are available, and lovely owners Prakash and Bina are full of local tips.

Breakwater Beach Resort
BUNGALOW $

(📞 9933292654, 9531852332; neilbreakwater@gmail.com; Beach 3; huts ₹600-2000, bungalows with/without AC ₹4000/2800; 📶) An easy-going ambience, attractive gardens and a small restaurant (mains ₹140 to ₹250), with accommodation in basic thatched huts (some share bathrooms) and well-kept whitewashed concrete bungalows set back from Beach 3.

Sunrise Beach Resort
BUNGALOW $

(📞 9474202539; Beach 5; r ₹500-800) Simple turquoise-painted, fan-cooled concrete bungalows with hammocks sit 100m from Sitapur beach, and there's a cheerful welcome plus a sweet little restaurant among flowers. The cheapest rooms share bathrooms.

Sunset Garden
HUT $

(📞 9474220472, 9933294573; Beach 1; huts ₹300-800) Popular with foreign travellers, these basic sea-view bamboo huts (the most economical with communal bathrooms) enjoy a fairly secluded site, accessed via a 15-minute walk through rice fields (signposted) or round the back of Pearl Park Beach Resort.

★ Emerald Gecko
BUNGALOW $$

(📞 9020064604, 9820023416; www.emerald-gecko.com; Beach 5; r incl breakfast ₹2700-3700) 🌿 Ecofriendly boho bungalows, with ceiling fans, concrete bathrooms, mosquito nets, filtered water and hand-painted murals of local birds, set in a coconut plantation behind rice fields. Some rooms are split-level and there's a mellow cafe.

Silver Sand Beach Resort
RESORT $$$

(📞 03192-244914, 9476019332; http://silversandhotels.com; Neil Kendra; r incl breakfast ₹7260-12,800; 📶🏊) Arguably the island's most sophisticated resort: pool, restaurant, and cosy contemporary-style cottages done in earthy oranges and woods are dotted across a peaceful palm-shaded garden just a short wander from the water. It's 600m south of Neil Kendra.

SeaShell
RESORT $$$

(📞 9679587575; http://seashellhotels.net; Beach 1; r incl breakfast ₹8260-15,360; 📶) One of Neil's swishest stays, with an on-site dive school and smart bar-restaurant (mains ₹250 to ₹600). The elegantly contemporary rooms, featuring TVs and tea-and-coffee trays, trickle down to a mangrove-lined beach.

Garden View Restaurant
INDIAN $$

(dishes ₹80-300; ⏰6am-10pm, hours vary) Occupying a colourful garden pavilion, 1km west of Beach 5, this family-run operation is a relaxing little spot to knock back a Kingfisher or papaya lassi and tuck into thalis, biryanis, fish curries, prawn fried rice and much more.

Blue Sea
INDIAN $$

(📞 9476013330; Beach 3; mains ₹120-500; ⏰6am-10.30pm) A quirky shack-restaurant just back from Beach 3. Come for the unpretentious, chilled-out character, nearby beach and simple, well-prepared Indian and Continental fare, including fresh-seafood specials.

Chand Restaurant
INDIAN $$

(Neil Kendra; mains ₹130-250; ⏰7.30am-9pm) A blue-washed facade marks out this simple home-style restaurant in Neil's bazaar, where bread omelettes, steaming coffee and *paratha* (hotplate-cooked flaky bread with ghee) are whipped up.

There's also a jetty-side branch, **Sea View Chand** (Neil Jetty; dishes ₹60-300; ⏰hours vary).

ℹ Information

There are two ATMs in the main bazaar, but it's best to bring extra cash. Some accommodation has slow, patchy wi-fi.

ℹ Getting There & Away

Government ferries (Neil Jetty; ⏰6.30-8am & 10.30am-1pm) go to Port Blair (₹460 to ₹640, two hours) at 8.30am and 4pm; to Havelock (Swaraj; one hour) at 1pm; and to Long Island (₹700, five hours) at 8am on Monday, Wednesday and Saturday.

Makruzz (📞 9679536651, 9933265867; www.makruzz.com; Neil Jetty; ⏰8am-1pm & 2.30-4.30pm) has at least one daily ferry to/from Port Blair (₹1000 to ₹2300, one hour) and Havelock (₹900 to ₹2000, one hour). **Green Ocean** (📞 03192-230777; http://greenoceanseaways.com; Neil Jetty; ⏰8am-noon & 1-5pm) runs to Port Blair (₹1290 to ₹1640, two hours), then back via Havelock; there may be direct services to Havelock in high season. Schedules change seasonally.

ⓘ Getting Around

Roads are flat and distances short, so hiring a bicycle (per day ₹150) or scooter (per day ₹500) is the best way to get about; ask in the main bazaar or at your guesthouse. Autorickshaws charge ₹75 to ₹100 from the jetty to Beach 1 or 3.

Middle & North Andaman

Beyond the sun, sea and sand, the Andamans unfold into dense jungle that feels as primeval as the Jurassic, a green tangle of ancient forest that could have been birthed in Mother Nature's subconscious. This wild, antediluvian side of the islands can be seen on a long journey north from Port Blair to Middle and North Andaman. The loping, controversial Andaman Trunk Rd travels northwards, slicing through the homeland of the Jarawa tribe (p1115) and crossing tannin-red rivers prowled by saltwater crocodiles. The roll-on, roll-off ferries en route are slowly being replaced by bridges.

The first main stop of interest as you travel north is Baratang's limestone **caves** (Baratang; ⊙ trips 7.30am & 11am Tue-Sun), 90km north of Port Blair. After crossing from South Andaman to Baratang Island by vehicle ferry, it's a scenic 45-minute boat trip (return per person ₹700) from the jetty to the caves through mangrove forest. Free permits are required, organised at the jetty.

Rangat

Travelling north on the Andaman Trunk Rd (ATR), inland Rangat is the first main town in Middle Andaman after Baratang Island. It's primarily a transport hub, and most travellers just pass through en route to/from Long Island, Mayabunder or Diglipur.

ⓘ Getting There & Away

BOAT

Rangat Bay, 7.5km southeast of town, has ferries to Port Blair (₹630 to ₹1050, six hours) via Havelock (Swaraj), Neil (Shaheed) and Long Islands at 6.15am on Tuesday, Thursday and Sunday, returning at 6.15am on Monday, Wednesday and Saturday.

Ferries for Long Island (₹20, one hour) also depart from Yeratta Jetty, 12km southeast of Rangat (and accessed by local bus), at 9am and 3.30pm, returning at 7am and 2pm.

BUS

From Rangat's main bazaar, buses go to Port Blair (₹160 to ₹190, seven hours) at 4.30am, 5.45am, 9.15am and noon, and Diglipur (₹50 to ₹100, four hours) at 4.30am and 11.30am. Additional 'express' services to/from Port Blair and Diglipur pass through town. There are also hourly buses to Yeratta Jetty (₹10 to ₹20), for boats to Long Island.

Long Island

With its friendly island community, wooden homes left over from the logging industry and deliciously slow pace of life, Long Island is perfect for those seeking to dial life down a few more notches. Other than the odd motorcycle, there are no motorised vehicles on the island, and at certain times you'll be one of just a few tourists here. Long Island is off Middle Andaman, 10km south of Rangat.

Though there was no diving available at research time, there's good offshore snorkelling at Lalaji Bay and the beach near Blue

---

THE CONTROVERSIAL ANDAMAN TRUNK ROAD

Built in the 1970s, the Andaman Trunk Rd (ATR; NH4) from Port Blair to Diglipur cuts through the homeland of the Jarawa (p1115) and has brought the tribe into incessant contact with the outside world. Modern India and tribal life do not seem able to coexist – every time Jarawa and settlers interact, misunderstandings have led to friction, confusion and, at worst, violent attacks and death. Indian anthropologists and indigenous rights groups such as Survival International have called for the ATR to be closed; India's Supreme Court ordered it closed in 2002, but the closure was never implemented and its status continues to be under review.

At the time of writing, vehicles were permitted to travel only in convoys at set times from 6am to 3pm (though queues start from 4.30am). Photography is strictly prohibited, as is stopping or any other interaction with the Jarawa people, who are becoming increasingly reliant on handouts from passing traffic.

A ferry service, called the Alternate Sea Route, from Port Blair to Baratang was launched in 2017. An attempt to reduce traffic through South Andaman's Jarawa tribal reserve, it has so far failed to attract tourists.

Planet. You can also take a boat to North Passage Island for swimming and snorkelling at stunning Merk Bay (₹5000 to ₹6000 per small group), with its blinding-white sand and translucent waters. Blue Planet hires out snorkelling gear (around ₹150).

A 10km, 1½-hour trek through the jungle leads to secluded Lalaji Bay, a beautiful white-sand east-coast beach with good swimming and snorkelling; follow the arrows from the jetty, or arrange a guide (₹1000) through Blue Planet. Hiring a boat (₹5000 per small group) is also an option. You'll need a permit (free) from the Forest Office near the jetty.

Blue Planet (☑ 9474212180; www.blueplanet andamans.com; r ₹1680-2800, without bathroom ₹500) is a favourite place to stay, with its thatched bamboo rooms set around a Padauk tree, and is a 15-minute, 1.5km walk east from the jetty. There's good home-cooked food plus free filtered water, a low-key vibe, hammocks, and bamboo cottages (₹2200 to ₹3360) at a nearby location.

❶ Getting There & Away

There are three to four ferries a week from Port Blair (₹630 to ₹1050, five hours) to Long Island via Havelock (Swaraj) and Neil (Shaheed). Boats leave Port Blair at 6.15am on Monday, Wednesday, Friday and, usually, Saturday, returning at 7am on Tuesday, Thursday and Sunday and 2pm on Friday. From Yeratta Jetty, 12km southeast of Rangat, boats (₹20, one hour) cross to Long Island at 9am and 3.30pm, then back at 7am and 2pm. Hourly buses (₹10 to ₹20) go to Yeratta from Rangat.

Diglipur & Around

Those who make it as far as sparsely populated North Andaman are rewarded with some impressive natural attractions. The Diglipur area is a giant outdoor adventure playground, home to a world-famous turtle-nesting site, the Andamans' highest peak and a network of limestone caves, not to mention glorious snow-white beaches and some of the best snorkelling in the Andamans.

However, don't expect much of the sprawling, gritty bazaar town Diglipur itself (population 43,200), the Andamans' second-largest urban settlement, 80km north of Mayabunder. Instead, head straight for the tranquil coastal village of Kalipur (p1113), a 17km drive east of Diglipur.

There are rumblings of impending tourism development, with a bridge now linking North and Middle Andaman and plans for a public airport near Kalipur. But for now, the area remains satisfyingly remote.

◉ Sights & Activities

★ Ross & Smith Islands   BEACH

Like lovely tropical counterparts, the twin islands of Smith and Ross are connected by a slender, dazzlingly white sandbar, and are up there with the best in the Andamans for both swimming and snorkelling.

No permits are required for Smith, which is accessed by boat (₹5000 per boat, fits five people) from Aerial Bay, 4km southwest. Theoretically you need a permit for Ross (Indian/foreigner ₹75/1000) once you're on Smith, but as it's walkable from Smith, permits sometimes aren't checked.

Kalipur Beach   BEACH

Fringed by lush jungle and sparkling cerulean waves, the brown-sand beach at Kalipur, 17km east of Diglipur by road, is famous for its turtle nesting (p1114) from mid-December to April.

Craggy Island   ISLAND

A speck of an island off Kalipur Beach, Craggy is a good spot for snorkelling. Very strong swimmers can make it across, in good conditions only (flippers recommended); otherwise, a small motorised boat (₹3000 return) runs here from Aerial Bay, on the road from Diglipur to Kalipur.

Excelsior Island   ISLAND

North from Aerial Bay, Excelsior has beautiful, creamy white beaches, good snorkelling and resident spotted deer. Six-person boats from Aerial Bay cost ₹5000 to ₹6000, and you'll need a (free) permit; visiting arrangements may change, however, so it's best to ask locally.

Saddle Peak   TREKKING

(☑ Forest Office checkpoint 9679505917; permits Indian/foreigner ₹50/500) At 732m, Saddle Peak is the Andamans' highest point, opening up astounding archipelago views. You can trek through subtropical forest to the top and back (14km) from Lamiya Bay (just south of Kalipur) in six to seven hours. Permits must be procured on the day from the Forest Office checkpoint at the trailhead from 6.30am to noon; bring your passport.

It's a demanding trek, so start first thing and bring plenty of water (around 4L). For a local guide (₹500), contact the checkpoint after 2pm the day before. Otherwise, follow the blue arrows marked on the trees.

TURTLE NESTING AT KALIPUR

Reputedly the only beach in the world where leatherback, hawksbill, green and olive ridley marine turtles all nest along the same coastline, Kalipur is a fantastic place to observe this evening show from mid-December to March or April. Turtles can be seen most nights, and you may be able to assist with collecting eggs, or with the release of hatchlings. Ask locally.

🛏 Sleeping & Eating

Saddle Peak View Resort   RESORT $$
(📞 9434271731; www.facebook.com/saddle-peakviewresort; Kalipur Beach; r with/without AC ₹2500/2000; ❄) A small, simple, palm-dotted resort offering five well-kept, colour-walled rooms and home-cooked meals, just back from Kalipur Beach.

Pristine Beach Resort   GUESTHOUSE $$$
(📞 9474286787, 03192-271793; www.andaman pristineresorts.com; Kalipur Beach; r incl breakfast ₹2400-5900; ❄🐟🌐) Huddled among palms between paddy fields and the beach, this relaxing resort sleeps travellers in a range of immaculate wood or concrete rooms with kettles, air-con and hot water. There's a good multicuisine restaurant serving delicious fish Nicobari, and a pool may be in place by the time you read this.

ℹ Getting There & Away

From Diglipur's bazaar, buses run to Port Blair (₹250 to ₹410, 12 hours) via Rangat (₹65 to ₹150, 4½ hours) at 5am, 7am and 10pm or 10.30pm; some of these stop in Mayabunder (₹55 to ₹70, two hours). There are additional buses to Rangat via Mayabunder at 6.30am, 8.30am, 8.45am, 10am, 1.30pm and 5pm, and a 4.30am bus from Aerial Bay all the way south to Port Blair.

Ferries to Port Blair (₹1050 to ₹1470, 17 hours) via Mayabunder depart from Aerial Bay at 2pm on Tuesday and Sunday, returning at 9pm on Monday and Saturday.

ℹ Getting Around

Ferries arrive into Aerial Bay, 9km northeast of Diglipur and 9km northwest of Kalipur. Buses run every 30 to 45 minutes from Diglipur's bazaar to Kalipur (₹20, 45 minutes) via Aerial Bay (₹20, 25 minutes).

Little Andaman

As far south as you can go (for now) in the islands, Little Andaman, 130km south of Port Blair, has an appealing end-of-the-world feel. It's a gorgeous fist of mangroves, jungle and teal, ringed by fresh, sandy white beaches with fantastic surf. It rates highly as many travellers' favourite spot in the Andamans.

Badly hit by the 2004 tsunami, Little Andaman has slowly rebuilt itself. Much of the island is an off-limits 25-sq-km Onge tribal reserve. The main settlement is small, pleasant, southeast-coast Indira Bazaar, 2km west of Hut Bay Jetty. There are ATMs in Indira Bazaar and the village at Km16.

◉ Sights & Activities

Little Andaman Lighthouse   LIGHTHOUSE
Little Andaman's 41m-tall lighthouse makes for a worthwhile excursion, around 10km south of Hut Bay. Its 200 steps spiral up to magnificent views over the coastline and forest. The easiest way to get here is by jeep, motorcycle or a sweaty bicycle journey.

Beaches
Come prepared for sandflies (p1097); seek local advice as to where crocs may be currently congregating.

⭐ Butler Bay   BEACH
(Km14) Little Andaman's best beach: a spectacular, powder-soft golden-white sweep of sand, famed for having some of India's best surfing waves.

Kalapathar   BEACH
Kalapathar lagoon is a popular enclosed swimming area with shady patches of sand, around 12km north of Hut Bay. Look for the cave in the cliff face that you can scramble through for stunning ocean views.

Netaji Nagar   BEACH
The sprawling, rugged and blonde Netaji Nagar, stretching 8km to 12km north of Hut Bay, is the beach where most accommodation is located.

Surfing
Intrepid surfer travellers have been whispering about Little Andaman since it first opened to foreigners some years back. The reef breaks are legendary, but best suited to experienced surfers. The most accessible is Jarawa Point, a left reef break at the northern point of Butler Bay. Beginners should stick to beach breaks along Km8 to Km11. February to April generally bring the best waves. Some guesthouses rent surfboards for around ₹500/1000 per half-/full day and may be able to arrange classes (₹1500).

ISLAND INDIGENES

The Andaman and Nicobar Islands' indigenous peoples constitute 7.5% of the population and, in most cases, their numbers are decreasing. The Onge, Sentinelese, Andamanese and Jarawa are all of Negrito ethnicity, and share a strong resemblance to people from Africa. Tragically, numerous groups have become extinct over the past century. In 2010 the last speaker of the Great Andamanese Bo language passed away, bringing an end to a culture and language that originated 65,000 years ago. It's important to note that these tribal groups live in areas strictly off limits to foreigners – for their protection and dignity – and people have been arrested for trying to visit these regions.

Sentinelese

The self-sufficient hunter-gatherer Sentinelese, unlike the other tribes on these islands, have consistently repelled outside contact. For years, contact parties arrived on the beaches of North Sentinel Island, the last redoubt of the Sentinelese, with gifts of coconuts, bananas, pigs and plastic buckets, only to be showered with arrows, though some encounters have been a little less hostile. An estimated 150 Sentinelese remain. In late 2018 an American tourist/missionary was killed by arrows fired by the Sentinelese while attempting (illegally) to approach North Sentinel Island.

Jarawa

The 270 or so remaining Jarawa occupy a 1000-sq-km reserve on South and Middle Andaman Islands. In 1953 the chief commissioner requested that an armed seaplane bomb Jarawa settlements, and their territory has been consistently disrupted by the much-disputed Andaman Trunk Rd (p1112), forest clearance, and settler and tourist encroachment. In 2012 a video went viral showing an exchange between Jarawa and tourists, whereby a policeman orders them to dance in exchange for food. This resulted in a government inquest that saw the end of the so-called 'human safari' tours, but tourist traffic through their homeland continues to be a problem.

Onge

Two thirds of Little Andaman's Onge Island was taken over by the Forest Department and 'settled' in 1977. The 100 or so remaining members of the Onge tribe, traditionally hunters but now dependent on government handouts, live in a 25-sq-km reserve covering Dugong Creek and South Bay. When the 2004 tsunami struck, the Onge were able to interpret natural wind, sea and wildlife signs and survived by fleeing to higher, forested ground.

Andamanese

There were 7000 to 8000 Andamanese in the mid-19th century, living across South and Middle Andaman, but friendliness to colonisers was their undoing. By 1971, all but 19 of the population had been wiped out by measles, syphilis and influenza epidemics. Their population, on the brink of extinction, now numbers only 43 and has been resettled on tiny Strait Island – controversially, this is one of the islands now theoretically accessible for tourism without Restricted Area Permits (p1097).

Shompen

Only about 300 Shompen remain in the forests on Great Nicobar. Seminomadic hunter-gatherers who live along the riverbanks, they have resisted integration and avoid areas occupied by Indian immigrants.

Nicobarese

The 30,000 Nicobarese are the only indigenous people whose numbers are not decreasing. The majority have converted to Christianity and partly assimilated into contemporary Indian society. Mostly living in village units led by a headman, they probably descended from people of Malaysia and Myanmar (Burma), and inhabit a number of islands in the Nicobar group, centred on Car Nicobar, the region worst affected by the 2004 tsunami.

Waterfalls

Around 1km inland from Km5, the White Surf waterfalls offer a pleasant jungle experience for when you're done lazing on the beach. Meanwhile, the Whisper Wave waterfalls (inland from Kalapathar) involve a 4km forest trek, for which a guide is highly recommended; ask locally. You may be

MAYABUNDER & AROUND

In 'upper' Middle Andaman, 70km north of Rangat, the Mayabunder area is best known for its villages inhabited by Karen, members of a Burmese hill tribe who were relocated here during the British colonial period. It's a low-key destination that appeals to travellers looking for an experience away from the crowds. Seaside Mayabunder is the main hub, while a homestay scene is blossoming in Webi, the Andamans' original Karen settlement, founded in 1925, 7km southwest of town.

The highlight of this area's day trips is creepy Interview Island, inhabited by 35 wild elephants released after a logging company closed for business in the 1950s. Though closed to visitors at the time of writing, it's expected to reopen for day trips and was one of the islands for which Restricted Area Permits were removed (p1097) in 2018; ask locally. Other trips include to Rangat's **Dhaninallah Mangrove** (off NH4; ⊘6am-5pm) and to **Avis Island** (permit ₹250, boat hire ₹1000) for its snorkelling and cream-coloured beach.

Karen conservationist couple Saw John and Naw Doris have opened their traditional wood-and-palm home **Ko Hee Homestay** (☑9476090117, 9474215682; www.kohhee. wordpress.com; Webi; r without bathroom incl meals ₹1500) 🔗 to guests. It offers organic home-produce meals and three no-frills but comfy fan-cooled rooms and a cottage, all featuring Andaman redwood furniture, filtered water and shared bathroom. The setting, among Webi's electric-green rice fields, is beautifully serene.

The best place to stay in Mayabunder town is **Sea'n'Sand** (☑9531877578; NH4; r with AC ₹1200-1400, without AC ₹750; ❄). This pastel-pink guesthouse provides tasty meals, spick-and-span rooms with hot water by bucket, and tips from Karen hosts Titus and Elizabeth.

Mayabunder has daily buses (₹80 to ₹100, two hours) to Rangat and Diglipur at 5am, 9am, 1pm and 5pm. Buses trundle south to Port Blair at 4.30am, 6.30am and 7am (₹250 to ₹300, 10 hours). Port Blair–Diglipur ferries stop in Mayabunder (from Port Blair ₹840 to ₹1260, 10 hours), departing Port Blair at 9pm on Monday and Saturday and returning from Mayabunder at 9pm on Sunday and Tuesday.

tempted to swim in the rock pools, but beware of crocodiles.

🛏 Sleeping & Eating

Some accommodation closes outside the October-to-April high season. There are cheap and tasty thali places in Indira Bazaar.

Hawva Beach Resort   BUNGALOW $
(☑9775181290, Whatsapp 9474206130; Km8, Netaji Nagar; r ₹800) This laid-back family-run lodging has a handful of simple yellow-walled concrete cottages. It rents surfboards (₹500 for three hours) and cooks up flavoursome homemade meals (₹550 per day).

Rainbow Resort   BUNGALOW $
(☑9775274587, 9474204862; rainbowresort10km@ gmail.com; Km10, Netaji Nagar; r ₹300-600) A warm, family-run guesthouse with nine bungalows amid the palms. Rooms are unfussy, with the cheapest sharing bathrooms. Fresh Indian meals, surfboards and motorcycles can all be arranged.

Ieshika Resort   BUNGALOW $
(☑9531861060, Whatsapp 9474222951; Km8, Netaji Nagar; d/tr ₹800/1500) No-frills tin-roof concrete-and-bamboo cottages for two to three (some bunk-style), plus surfboard hire (₹1000 per day) and home-cooked meals (₹180).

❶ Getting There & Away

Boats sail to/from Port Blair daily, alternating between afternoon and evening departures on vessels ranging from big ferries with four- or two-bed rooms (six to 8½ hours) to faster 5½-hour government boats; all have air-con. Rates vary according to the class booked: seat (₹500), bunk (₹900), first class (₹1100), semideluxe (₹1300) or deluxe (₹1500). Ferries dock at Hut Bay Jetty; its ferry office is closed on Sunday.

Taxis/autorickshaws charge ₹700/100 between the jetty and Netaji Nagar.

❶ Getting Around

Frequent buses (₹17) to Netaji Nagar usually coincide with ferry arrivals; pricier shared jeeps (per person ₹140) are an alternative.

Motorbikes (₹500 per 24 hours) and bicycles (₹200) are popular for getting around. Otherwise, shared jeeps (₹20 to ₹30) and buses (₹17 to ₹30) are very handy.

Understand India

India Today

With such a diverse assortment of traditions, languages, religions and political views, what is striking about India is not the clash of divergent opinions and customs, but how well things work considering the manifold hurdles that arise. Despite challenges ranging from social welfare and caste politics to religious tensions and military squabbles with its neighbours, India continues to thrive as the most successful nation in South Asia and the largest democracy on Earth.

Best in Print

Midnight's Children (Salman Rushdie; 1981) Allegory about Independence and Partition.

A Fine Balance (Rohinton Mistry; 1995) Beautifully written, tragic tale set in Mumbai.

White Tiger (Aravind Adiga; 2008) Booker Prize–winning novel about class struggle in globalised India.

A Suitable Boy (Vikram Seth; 1993) More than 1300 pages of romance, heartbreak, family secrets and political intrigue.

Shantaram (Gregory David Roberts; 2003) Vivid impressions of Roberts' life in India. A traveller favourite!

Best on Film

Fire (1996), **Earth** (1998) and **Water** (2005) Trilogy directed by Deepa Mehta.

Pather Panchali (1955) Haunting masterpiece from Satyajit Ray.

Pyaasa (Thirst; 1957) and **Kaagaz Ke Phool** (Paper Flowers; 1959) For a taste of nostalgia.

Gandhi (1982) The classic.

Lagaan (2001) Written and directed by Ashutosh Gowariker.

The Political Landscape

Prime Minister Narendra Modi surged to power in the 2014 federal elections, when the Bharatiya Janata Party (BJP) scored a landslide victory over the ruling Indian National Congress (INC) and its leader Rahul Gandhi, great grandson of India's first prime minister, Jawaharlal Nehru. It repeated its success in the 2019 elections with an increased majority of seats in the Lok Sabha.

Modi vowed to boost the economy with reforms and campaigns such as 'Make in India', which set out to encourage foreign companies to manufacture and invest in the country. This appears to have yielded some positive results. According to the World Bank's 'Ease of Doing Business' ratings, India ranked at 77 among 190 global economies in 2018, up from 100th position in 2017 and 142nd in 2014. However, one of Modi's most daring fiscal moves, the demonetisation of ₹500 and ₹1000 banknotes in 2016 – to flush out black money – failed to achieve its objective, according to most analysts, and dampened economic growth following its announcement.

Although Modi has largely tried to keep the focus on developmental issues, his government has come under sharp criticism for failing to adequately curb brutal mob attacks – some resulting in death – on people (mainly Muslims) suspected of eating beef or transporting cows for slaughter. Cows are sacred to Hindus and cow slaughter is banned in many Indian states. Modi's government has also been criticised for not doing enough to alleviate the nation's agrarian crisis, which has seen numerous farmers commit suicide due to chronic financial stress.

Gender Equality

When it comes to gender equality, India was placed at 130 out of 189 countries in the UN's most recent Human Development Index (HDI). Despite successive governments making some progress on female empowerment, women in India remain considerably less socially, economically and politically empowered than men. Additionally, the current government hasn't succeeded in curtailing violence against women, with many crimes still going unreported due to family pressure, social stigma and lack of confidence in the justice system. More positively, in 2017 the government passed legislation prohibiting the practice of *talaq*, whereby Muslim men could divorce their wives by merely saying 'talaq' three times.

Plentiful People & Rocky Relations

India is emerging as a global superpower, but its greatest resource – its 1.35 billion people – is also perhaps its greatest challenge. The country regularly ranks as the world's fastest-growing economy, but almost a quarter of its vast population lives below the official poverty line, with less than US$1.90 of purchasing-power parity per day. With the population continuing to grow by around 1.2% – or 16.2 million people – per year, India faces an uphill struggle to ensure that the economic benefits of growth reach everyone.

India's growing power has also placed it in conflict with its neighbours. The traditional divide between China and India – the impregnable line of the Himalaya – is becoming increasingly porous as China expands its influence in Nepal and Pakistan to check Indian power in the region. China's ongoing supply of military equipment to Pakistan is a further bone of contention. In 2015, China embarked on an ambitious infrastructure project to create the China–Pakistan Economic Corridor (CPEC), which further cemented the impression that India is being hemmed in by its neighbour to the north. The US$60 billion CPEC project consists of a network of road and rail links and gas and oil pipelines that run through the Karakoram range to the Pakistan seaboard.

India–China relations have been further complicated by the Dalai Lama, the spiritual leader of Tibetan Buddhism, who lives in exile in Himachal Pradesh, along with members of the pre-1959 Tibetan government. Following the 1950 invasion by the Chinese People's Liberation Army, China claims all territory formerly administered by Tibet, and its government continues to dispute Indian ownership of parts of Arunachal Pradesh and Aksai Chin in Kashmir.

Chinese and Indian troops entered a tense stand-off in Aksai Chin in 2013, before politicians negotiated an end to the dispute. A subsequent incursion by Chinese forces into Arunachal Pradesh in 2016 revived fears that China nurtures ambitions to claim the region it refers to as South Tibet. Relations dipped again in mid-2017, when there was a military border standoff between India and China over the disputed region of Doklam (located near the Indian state of Sikkim), which is claimed by both China and India's ally, Bhutan. After weeks of deadlock, India

POPULATION: **1.35 BILLION**

GDP: **US$2.7 TRILLION (2018)**

UNEMPLOYMENT RATE: **3.5% (2018)**

LITERACY RATE: **65/82% (FEMALE/MALE)**

GENDER RATIO: **940/1000 (FEMALE/MALE)**

if India were 100 people

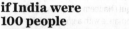

27 would be aged 0–14 years
18 would be aged 15–24 years
41 would be aged 25–54 years
8 would be aged 55–64 years
6 would be aged 65 years+

belief systems
(% of population)

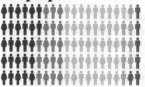

80 Hindu
14 Muslim
2 Christian

2 Sikh
1 Buddhist
1 Other

population per sq km

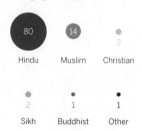

INDIA   CHINA   USA

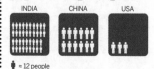

≈ 12 people

Best in Music

Taal Original Motion Picture Soundtrack (AR Rahman; 1999) A classic piece of feel-good *filmi* music.

Sajda (Jagjit Singh and Lata Mangeshkar; 1987) Haunting, beautiful *ghazal* devotional songs.

Music of the Deserts (Zakir Hussain; 1993) Indian classical music updated.

Ravi Shankar Live at the Monterey Pop Festival (Ravi Shankar; 1967) From India's most famous sitar maestro.

Aashiqui (Nadeem–Shravan; 1990) *Filmi* romance with a *ghazal* twist.

Dos & Don'ts

Dress modestly Avoid stares by avoiding tight, sheer and skimpy clothes.

Shoes It's polite to remove shoes before entering homes and places of worship.

Photos Best to ask before photographing people, ceremonies or sacred sites.

Bad vibes Avoid pointing soles of feet towards people or deities, or touching anyone with your feet.

and China agreed to withdraw troops, but tensions and distrust remain high.

The Pakistan Files

Decades of deadly border skirmishes between India and Pakistan over the disputed territory of Kashmir have long cast a shadow over the subcontinent. Contentious Kashmir has plagued India–Pakistan relations since Partition in 1947, and the predominantly Muslim Kashmir Valley is still claimed in its entirety by both countries, with a separate movement championing an independent state.

The dispute has sparked three India–Pakistan wars – in 1947, 1965 and 1971 – and a string of incursions and firing incidents across the Line of Control (LOC), which have killed tens of thousands of civilians on both sides of the divide. It's also cited as a motivation for many of the terrorist attacks carried out in India by Islamist militants. The government of Pakistan provides shelter – and, India alleges, financial, military and technical support – for armed groups that have carried out attacks in India, including raids on Indian Army barracks near the India–Pakistan border.

A lull in tensions in 2008 led to talks that might have created an autonomous region, but the situation deteriorated rapidly after terrorists killed at least 163 people during three days of coordinated bombings and shootings in Mumbai. The one sniper caught alive, a Pakistani, had ties to Lashkar-e-Taiba, a militant group that formed to assist the Pakistan Army in Kashmir in the 1990s and which has been implicated in dozens of attacks within India.

When former cricket legend Imran Khan became prime minister of Pakistan in 2018, there were indications that peace initiatives may resume afresh. However, relations soured after talks were abruptly cancelled by Prime Minister Modi, due to the killing of three Indian security personnel in Kashmir by suspected Pakistan-based militants. Delhi accused Islamabad of not being genuinely committed to halting cross-border terrorism, a charge that Prime Minister Khan vehemently denied. Progress over access for Sikhs to pilgrimage sites in Pakistan hinted at a thaw in relations, but a suicide bombing in February 2019 on the Jammu–Srinigar National Highway that killed more than 40 Indian soldiers has pushed things back to the brink.

History

Through invasions and empires, through the birth of religions and the collapse of civilisations, through bold leaps forward and countless cataclysms, India has proved itself to be, in the words of its first prime minister, Jawaharlal Nehru, 'a bundle of contradictions held together by strong but invisible threads'. India's history isn't just the history of a nation state, but the history of a legion of communities and cultures who, after centuries of strife, found greater strength bonded together than apart.

Indus Valley Civilisation

The Indus Valley, straddling the modern India–Pakistan border, is the cradle of civilisation on the Indian subcontinent. The first inhabitants of this region were nomadic tribes who cultivated land and kept domestic animals. Over thousands of years, an urban culture began to emerge from these tribes, and by 2500 BC large cities were well established, the focal points of what became known as the Harappan culture, which would flourish for more than 1000 years.

The great cities of the Mature Harappan period were Moenjodaro and Harappa in present-day Pakistan, but the city of Lothal near Ahmedabad, with its precise, carefully laid-out street plan, can still be visited. Harappan cities were astoundingly uniform, despite being spread across an enormous area. Even their brickwork and streets had a standard size. They often had a separate acropolis, suggesting a religious function, and great tanks, which may have been used for ritual bathing purposes. The major Harappan cities were also notable for their size – estimates put the population of Moenjodaro at some 50,000 at its peak.

By the middle of the 3rd millennium BC, the Indus Valley culture was arguably the equal of other great civilisations emerging at the time. The Harappans traded with Mesopotamia, and developed a system of weights and measures, along with highly developed art in the form of terracotta and bronze figurines. Recovered relics, including models of bullock carts and jewellery, offer the earliest evidence of a distinctive Indian culture. Indeed, many elements of Harappan culture would later become assimilated into Hinduism.

To learn more about the ancient Indus Valley civilisations, ramble around Harappa (www.harappa.com), which presents an accessible yet scholarly overview.

TIMELINE	10,000 BC	2600–1700 BC	1500 BC
	Stone Age paintings first made in the Bhimbetka rock shelters, in what is now Madhya Pradesh; the art continues here for many centuries. Settlements thought to exist across the subcontinent.	The heyday of the Indus Valley civilisation, spanning parts of Rajasthan, Gujarat and Sindh province in present-day Pakistan.	The Indo-Aryan civilisation takes root in the fertile plains of the Indo-Gangetic basin. Settlers speak an early form of Sanskrit, from which several Indian vernaculars, including Hindi, later evolve.

RK Narayan's 1973 *Ramayana* is a condensed and novelistic retelling of the 3rd-century BC classic. The renowned novelist took on the Mahabharata in 1978.

Clay figurines found at Harappan sites suggest worship of a mother goddess (later personified as Kali) and a male three-faced god (believed to be the historic Shiva) attended by four animals. Black stone pillars (associated with phallic worship of Shiva) and animal figures (the most prominent being the humped bull; later Shiva's mount, Nandi) have also been discovered. Now displayed in Delhi's National Museum, the 'dancing girl', a small bronze statuette of a young girl, whose insouciant gaze has endured over 4500 years, indicates a highly developed society, both in technical skills and in the pursuit of leisure as well as industry.

Early Invasions & the Rise of Religions

Harappan civilisation fell into decline from the beginning of the 2nd millennium BC. perhaps due to flooding or decreasing rainfall, which may have damaged the agriculture that its cities depended on. A more contentious theory – widely held in India despite a lack of archaeological evidence or written reports in ancient Indian texts – is that the Harappans were annihilated by Aryan tribes from the northwest. These invaders, so the theory goes, pushed the native Dravidian tribes of India south, explaining the ethnic differences between north and south today.

In fact, there's no clear evidence that the Aryans came from elsewhere, and it's even questionable whether the Aryans were a distinct race, so the 'invasion' could simply have been the import of new ideas from neighbouring cultures.

What is known is that Aryan peoples were responsible for the Sanskrit literary tradition. The Hindu sacred scriptures, the Vedas, were written during this period of transition (1500–1200 BC), and the caste system became formalised. These compositions are of seminal importance in terms of India's spirituality and history.

As Aryan culture spread across the Ganges plain in the late 7th century BC, its followers were absorbed into 16 major kingdoms, which were, in turn, amalgamated into four large states. Out of these states arose the Nanda dynasty, which came to power in 364 BC, ruling over huge swaths of North India.

During this period, the Indian heartland narrowly avoided two invasions from the west, which, if successful, could have significantly altered the path of Indian history. The first was by the Persian king Darius (521–486 BC), who annexed Punjab and Sindh (on either side of the modern India–Pakistan border). Alexander the Great advanced to India from Greece in 326 BC, an achievement in itself, but he turned back in Punjab, without ever extending his power deeper into India.

The period is also distinguished by the rise of two of India's most significant religions, Buddhism and Jainism, which arose around 500 BC in the northern plains. Both Buddha and Jainism's Mahavira questioned

1500–1200 BC	599–528 BC	563–483 BC	400–321 BC
The Rig-Veda, the first and longest of Hinduism's canonical texts, the Vedas, is written; three more books follow. Earliest forms of priestly Brahmanical Hinduism emerge.	The life of Mahavir, the 24th and last *tirthankar* (enlightened teacher) who established Jainism. Like Buddha, he preaches compassion and a path to enlightenment for all.	The life of Siddhartha Gautama. The prince is born in modern-day Nepal and attains enlightenment beneath the Bodhi Tree in Bodhgaya (Bihar), thereby transforming into Buddha (Awakened One).	Nanda dynasty evolves from the wealthy region of Magadha (roughly, today's Bihar) and grows to encompass a huge area, from Bengal to Punjab. It falls to Maurya in 321 BC.

the Vedas and were critical of the caste system, attracting many followers from the lower castes.

The Mauryan Empire & its Aftermath

If the Harappan culture was the cradle of Indian civilisation, Chandragupta Maurya was the founder of the first great Indian empire, probably the most extensive ever forged, stretching from Bengal to Afghanistan and Gujarat. He came to power in 321 BC, having seized control from the Nandas, and soon expanded the empire to include the Indus Valley previously conquered by Alexander the Great.

From its capital at Pataliputra (modern-day Patna), with its many-pillared palace, the Mauryan empire encompassed much of North India and reached as far south as modern-day Karnataka. There is much documentation of this period in contemporary Jain and Buddhist texts, plus the intensely detailed depiction of Indian statecraft in the ancient text known as the *Arthasastra*. The empire reached its peak under emperor Ashoka (p1125), who converted to Buddhism and spread the faith across the subcontinent. Such was Ashoka's power to lead and unite that after his death in 232 BC, no one could be found to hold the disparate elements of the Mauryan empire together. The empire rapidly disintegrated, collapsing altogether in 184 BC.

None of the empires that immediately followed could match the stability or enduring historical legacy of the Mauryans, but the Satavahanas came to control all of Maharashtra, Madhya Pradesh, Chhattisgarh, Karnataka and Andhra Pradesh. Under their rule, between 230 BC and AD 200, the arts, especially literature and philosophy, blossomed; Buddha's teaching thrived; and the subcontinent enjoyed a period of considerable prosperity. South India may have lacked vast and fertile agricultural plains on the scale of North India, but it compensated by building strategic trade links via the Indian Ocean, and overland with the Roman empire and China.

The Golden Age of the Guptas

The empires that followed the Mauryans may have claimed large areas of Indian territory as their own, but many secured only nominal power over their realms. Throughout the subcontinent, small tribes and kingdoms effectively controlled territory and dominated local affairs.

In AD 319, Chandragupta I, the third king of one of these tribes, the little-known Guptas, came to prominence by a fortuitous marriage to the daughter of one of the most powerful tribes in the north, the Liccavis. The Gupta empire grew rapidly and under Chandragupta II (r 375–413) achieved its greatest extent. The Chinese pilgrim Fa-hsien, visiting India

Mahavira and Buddha were contemporaries, and their teachings overlapped. Buddha lays out the discrepancies (and his critiques) in the *Sankha Sutta* and *Devadaha Sutta*, referring to Mahavira as Nigantha ('free from bonds') Nataputta. Read them at the Theravada resource, www.accesstoinsight.com.

Emperor Ashoka's ability to rule was assisted by a standing army consisting of roughly 9000 elephants, 30,000 cavalry and 600,000 infantry.

326 BC	321–185 BC	c 300 BC	1st Century BC
Alexander the Great invades India. He defeats King Porus in Punjab to enter the subcontinent, but a rebellion within his army keeps him from advancing beyond Punjab.	Rule of the Maurya kings. Founded by Chandragupta Maurya, this pan-Indian empire is ruled from Pataliputra (present-day Patna) and briefly adopts Buddhism during the reign of Emperor Ashoka.	Buddhism spreads across the subcontinent and beyond via Ashoka's monastic ambassadors: monks travel to Sri Lanka and Southeast Asia. Amaravathi, Sanchi and other stupas are erected.	The Pandayan Dynasty in Tamil Nadu sends emissaries to the ancient Greek and Roman empires.

Mauryan Remains

Junagadh (Gujarat)

Allahabad Fort (Uttar Pradesh)

Sarnath (Uttar Pradesh)

Sanchi (Madhya Pradesh)

Bodhgaya (Bihar)

Vaishali (Bihar)

Amaravathi (Andhra Pradesh)

at the time, described a people 'rich and contented', ruled over by enlightened and just kings.

Poetry, literature, astronomy, medicine and the arts flourished, with some of the finest work done at Ajanta, Ellora, Sanchi and Sarnath. The Guptas were tolerant of, and even supported, Buddhist practice and art. Towards the end of the Gupta period, Hinduism became the dominant religious force, however, and its revival eclipsed Jainism and Buddhism; the latter in particular went into decline in India with the Hun invasion and would never again be India's dominant tradition.

The invasions of the Huns at the beginning of the 6th century signalled the end of this era, and in 510 the Gupta army was defeated by the Hun leader Toramana. Power in North India again devolved to a number of separate Hindu kingdoms.

The Hindu South

Southern India has always laid claim to its own unique history. Insulated by distance from the political developments in the north, a separate set of powerful kingdoms emerged, among them the Satavahanas – who, though predominantly Hindu, probably also practised Buddhist meditation and patronised Buddhist art at Amaravathi and Sanchi – as well as the Kalingas and Vakatakas. But it was from the tribal territories on the fertile coastal plains that the greatest southern empires – the Cholas, Pandyas, Chalukyas, Cheras and Pallavas – came into their own.

The Chalukyas ruled mainly over the Deccan region of south-central India, although their power occasionally extended further north. In the far south, the Pallavas ruled from the 4th to 9th centuries and pioneered Dravidian architecture, with its exuberant, almost baroque, style. The surviving architectural high points of Pallava rule can be found across Tamil Nadu, including in the erstwhile Pallava capital at Kanchipuram and the seaport of Mamallapuram.

The south's prosperity was based on long-established trading links with other civilisations, among them the Egyptians and Romans. In return for spices, pearls, ivory and silk, the Indians received Roman gold. Indian merchants also extended their influence to Southeast Asia. In 850, the Cholas rose to power and superseded the Pallavas. They soon set about turning the south's far-reaching trade influence into territorial conquest. Under the reign of Rajaraja Chola I (985–1014), they controlled almost the whole of South India, the Deccan plateau, Sri Lanka, parts of the Malay peninsula and the Sumatra-based Srivijaya kingdom.

Not all of their attention was focused overseas, however, and the Cholas left behind some of the finest examples of Dravidian architecture, most notably the sublime Brihadishwara Temple in Thanjavur and Chidambaram's stunning Nataraja Temple. Both Thanjavur and Chid-

The concepts of zero and infinity are widely believed to have been devised by eminent Indian mathematicians during the reign of the Guptas.

AD 52	1st Century	319–510	4th–9th Centuries
Possible arrival of St Thomas the Apostle on the coast of Kerala. Christianity thought to have been introduced to India with his preaching in Kerala and Tamil Nadu.	International trade booms: the region's elaborate overland trade networks connect with ports linked to maritime routes. Trade to Africa, the Gulf, Socotra, Southeast Asia, China and even Rome thrives.	The golden era of the Gupta dynasty, the second of India's great empires after the Mauryas. The period is marked by a creative surge in literature and the arts.	The Pallavas, known for their temple architecture, enter the shifting landscape of southern power centres, establishing dominance from their base in Kanchipuram.

ambaram served as Chola capitals. Throughout this period, Hinduism remained the bedrock of South Indian culture.

The Muslim North

The first Muslims believed to reach India were some newly converted merchants crossing the Arabian Sea in the early 7th century, who established communities in various southern ports, and some small, pioneering Arabian forces in 663 from the north. Sporadic skirmishes occurred over the ensuing centuries, but no major confrontations took place until the late 10th century. But at this point, wave after wave of land assaults began convulsing the north.

At the vanguard of Islamic expansion was Mahmud of Ghazni. In the early 11th century, Mahmud turned Ghazni (in today's Afghanistan) into one of the world's most glorious capital cities, which he largely funded by plundering his neighbours' territories. From 1001 to 1025, Mahmud conducted 17 raids into India, most infamously on the famous Shiva Temple of Somnath in Gujarat. The Hindu force of 70,000 died trying to defend the temple, which eventually fell in early 1026. In the aftermath of his victory, Mahmud transported a massive haul of gold and other booty back to his capital.

Architecture of the Deccan Sultanates

Citadel, Golgumbaz, Ibrahim Rouza, Jama Masjid (Bijapur)

Fort, Bahmani Tombs (Bidar)

Golconda Fort, Qutab Shahi Tombs, Charminar (Hyderabad)

HISTORY THE MUSLIM NORTH

AN ENLIGHTENED EMPEROR

Apart from the Mughals and then the British many centuries later, no other power controlled more Indian territory than the Mauryan empire under Emperor Ashoka. His rule was characterised by flourishing art and sculpture, while his reputation as a philosopher-king was enhanced by the expressive rock-hewn edicts he used to instruct his people, express remorse at the human suffering resulting from his battles, and delineate the enormous span of his territory. Some of these moral teachings can still be seen, particularly the Ashokan Edicts at Junagadh in Gujarat.

Ashoka's reign also represented an undoubted historical high point for Buddhism: he embraced Buddha's teaching in 262 BC, declaring it the state religion and cutting a radical swath through the spiritual and social body of Hinduism. The emperor built thousands of stupas (spire-topped Buddhist monuments) and monasteries across the region, the extant highlights of which are visible at Sarnath in Uttar Pradesh – on the spot where Buddha delivered his first sermon expounding the Noble Eightfold Path – and Sanchi in Madhya Pradesh. Ashoka also sent missions abroad, and he is revered in Sri Lanka because he sent his son and daughter to carry Buddha's teaching to the island.

After his death, the empires disintegrated but Ashoka's legacy lives on, not least on the Indian national flag, which carries a symbol of the Ashoka Chakra, a wheel with 24 spokes.

500–600	8th Century	850	1192
The emergence of the Rajputs in Rajasthan. Hailing from three principal races supposedly of celestial origin, they form 36 clans, which spread across the region to secure their own kingdoms.	The first Parsi migrants make their way to India, fleeing persecution in their native Persia (modern-day Iran).	The Medieval Cholas, a Tamil dynasty, accrete power across South India, Sri Lanka and the Maldives in the 9th to 13th centuries.	Prithviraj Chauhan loses Delhi to Mohammed of Ghori. The defeat effectively ends Hindu supremacy in the region, exposing the subcontinent to subsequent Muslim rulers marching in from the northwest.

China still claims sections of India as part of its historic claim to all lands formerly ruled by Tibet, including Aksai Chin in Kashmir, western Arunachal Pradesh, and a tiny strip of land in northern Sikkim known as 'The Finger'.

Following Mahmud's death in 1033, Ghazni was seized by the Seljuqs and then fell to the Ghurs of western Afghanistan, who similarly had their eyes on the great Indian prize. In 1191, Mohammed of Ghur advanced into India in brutal fashion, before being defeated in a major battle against a confederacy of Hindu rulers. Undeterred, he returned the following year and routed his enemies. One of his generals, Qutab ud-din Aibak, captured Delhi and was appointed governor; it was during his reign that the renowned Delhi landmark, the Qutab Minar Complex, containing India's first mosque, was built. A separate Islamic empire was established in Bengal and, within a short time, almost the whole of North India was under Muslim control.

Following Mohammed's death in 1206, Qutab ud-din Aibak became the first sultan of Delhi. His successor, Iltutmish, brought Bengal back under central control and defended the empire from an attempted Mongol invasion. Ala-ud-din Khilji came to power in 1296 and pushed the borders of the empire inexorably south, while simultaneously fending off further attacks by Mongol hordes.

North Meets South

Ala-ud-din died in 1320, and Mohammed Tughlaq ascended the throne in 1324. In 1328, Tughlaq took the southern strongholds of the Hoysala empire, which had centres at Belur, Halebid and Somnathpur. However, while the empire of the pre-Mughal Muslims would achieve its greatest extent under Tughlaq's rule, his overreaching ambition also sowed the seeds of its disintegration.

After a series of successful campaigns Tughlaq decided to move the capital from Delhi to a more central location at Daulatabad near Aurangabad in Maharashtra, forcefully marching the entire population of Delhi 1100km south, with considerable loss of life. The megalomaniac ruler soon realised that this left the north undefended, and so the entire capital was marched north once again.

With the difficulties of keeping such a vast territory under central control, the days of the Ghur empire were numbered. The last of the great sultans of Delhi, Firoz Shah, died in 1388, and the fate of the sultanate was sealed when Timur (Tamerlane) made a devastating raid from Samarkand (in Central Asia) into India in 1398. Timur's sacking of Delhi was truly merciless; some accounts say his soldiers slaughtered every Hindu inhabitant.

After Tughlaq's withdrawal from the south, several splinter kingdoms arose. The two most significant were the Islamic Bahmani sultanate, which emerged in 1345 with its capital at Gulbarga, and later Bidar, and its bitter rival, the Hindu Vijayanagar empire, founded in 1336 with its capital at Hampi.

A History of South India from Prehistoric Times to the Fall of Vijayanagar by KA Nilakanta Sastri is arguably the most comprehensive (if heavy-going) history of this region.

13th Century	1321	1336	1345
The Pandyas, a Tamil dynasty dating to the 6th century BC, assumes control of Chola territory, expanding into Andhra Pradesh, Kalinga (Odisha) and Sri Lanka from their Madurai capital.	The Tughlaqs come to power in Delhi. Mohammed Tughlaq expands his empire but becomes known for inelegant schemes: moving the capital to Daulatabad and creating forgery-prone currency.	Foundation of the mighty Vijayanagar empire, named after its capital city, the ruins of which can be seen today in the vicinity of Hampi (in Karnataka).	Bahmani Sultanate is established in the Deccan following a revolt against the Tughlaqs of Delhi. The capital is set up at Gulbarga, in today's northern Karnataka, later shifting to Bidar.

The Mughals

Even as Vijayanagar was experiencing its last days, the next great Indian empire was being founded. The Mughal empire was massive, at its height covering almost the entire subcontinent. Its significance, however, lay not only in its size. Mughal emperors presided over a golden age of arts and literature and had a passion for building that resulted in some of the finest architecture in India, including Shah Jahan's Taj Mahal at Agra.

The founder of the Mughal line, Babur (r 1526–30), was a descendant of both Genghis Khan and Timur (Tamerlane). In 1525, he marched into Punjab from his capital at Kabul. With technological superiority brought by firearms, and consummate skill in simultaneously employing artillery and cavalry, Babur defeated the larger armies of the sultan of Delhi at the Battle of Panipat in 1526.

Despite this initial success, Babur's son, Humayun (r 1530–56), was defeated by a powerful ruler of eastern India, Sher Shah, in 1539 and forced to withdraw to Iran. Humayun spent much time outside India, a fact reflected in the design of his tomb in Delhi, which was created by Persian architects and influenced by Iranian style. Following Sher Shah's death in 1545, Humayun returned to claim his kingdom, eventually conquering Delhi in 1555. He died the following year and was succeeded by his young son Akbar (r 1556–1605), who, during his 49-year reign, managed to extend and consolidate the empire until he ruled over a mammoth area.

True to his name, Akbar (which means 'great' in Arabic) was probably the greatest of the Mughals: he not only had the military ability required of a ruler at that time, but was also widely regarded as a wise leader and a man of culture. He saw, as previous Muslim rulers had not, that the number of Hindus in India was too substantial to subjugate, and skilfully integrated Hindus into his empire, including them as advisers, generals and administrators.

Akbar also had a deep interest in religious matters; he spent many hours in discussion with religious experts of all persuasions, including Christians and Parsis, and abolished the punitive *jizya* tax imposed on non-Muslims as a condition of being allowed to continue their faith. Nevertheless, Akbar's tolerance of other cultures was relative – massacres of Hindus and other minorities were commonplace during his reign, most notoriously at Panipat and Chitrod.

Jehangir (r 1605–27) ascended the throne following Akbar's death and kept his father's empire intact, despite several challenges to his authority. In periods of stability, Jehangir spent time in his beloved Kashmir, eventually dying en route there in 1627. He was succeeded by his son, Shah Jahan (r 1627–58), who secured his position by executing all male relatives who stood in his way. During his reign, some of the most vivid

HISTORY THE MUGHALS

In its 800-year history, Delhi's Qutab Minar has been damaged by two lightning strikes and one earthquake, and has been repaired or built up by four sultans, one British major and one governor general.

Pallava Architecture in Tamil Nadu

Shore Temple, Mamallapuram

Five Rathas, Mamallapuram

Temples, Kanchipuram

Rock Fort Temple, Trichy (Tiruchirappalli)

**Good
History
Reads**
·····················
A Traveller's
History of India, by
SinhaRaja
Tammita-Delgoda

Empires of the
Indus, by Alice
Albinia
·····················
India: a History, by
John Keay

and permanent reminders of the Mughals' glory were constructed; in addition to the Taj Mahal, he oversaw the construction of Delhi's mighty Red Fort (Lal Qila) and converted the Agra Fort into a palace that would later become his prison.

The last of the great Mughals, Aurangzeb (r 1658–1707), imprisoned his father (Shah Jahan) and succeeded to the throne after a two-year struggle against his brothers. A religious zealot, Aurangzeb devoted his resources to extending the empire's boundaries, and thus fell into much the same trap as that of Mohammed Tughlaq some 300 years earlier. A combination of decaying court life and dissatisfaction among the Hindu population at inflated taxes and religious intolerance weakened the Mughal grip.

The empire was also facing serious challenges from the Marathas in central India and, more significantly, the British in Bengal. With Aurangzeb's death in 1707, the empire's fortunes rapidly declined, and Delhi was sacked by Persia's Nadir Shah in 1739. Mughal 'emperors' continued to rule right up until the First War of Independence (Indian Uprising) in 1857, but they were emperors without an empire.

The Rajputs & the Marathas

Throughout the Mughal period, there remained strong Hindu powers, most notably the Rajputs, hereditary rulers of Rajasthan. The Rajputs were a proud warrior caste with a passionate belief in the dictates of chivalry, both in battle and state affairs. The Rajputs opposed every foreign incursion into their territory, but they were never united. When they weren't battling foreign oppression, they squandered their energies fighting one another. This eventually led to their territories becoming vassal states of the Mughal empire. Their prowess in battle, however, was acknowledged, and some of the best military men in the Mughal armies were Rajputs.

The Marathas were less picaresque and ultimately more effective. They first rose to prominence under their great leader Shivaji, also known as Chhatrapati Shivaji Maharaj, who gathered popular support by championing the Hindu cause against the Muslim rulers. Between 1646 and 1680, Shivaji confronted the Mughals across most of central India before being captured and taken to Agra. Naturally, he managed to escape and continue his adventures. The larger-than-life war leader is a particular hero in Maharashtra, where many of his wildest exploits took place. He's also revered for the fact that, as a lower-caste Shudra, he showed that formidable leaders don't have to be of the Kshatriya (soldier) caste.

Shivaji's son was captured, blinded and executed by Aurangzeb, and his grandson wasn't made of the same sturdy stuff, so the Maratha empire continued under the Peshwas, hereditary government ministers

Persian was the official language of several empires, from Mahmud of Ghazni to the Delhi Sultanate to the Mughals. Urdu, which combines Persian, Arabic and indigenous languages, evolved over hundreds of years and came into its own during Mughal reign.

1526	1542–45	1600	1672
Babur becomes the first Mughal emperor after conquering Delhi. He stuns Rajasthan by routing its confederate force, gaining an edge with the introduction of matchlock muskets in his army.	St Francis Xavier's first mission to India. He preaches Catholicism in Goa, Tamil Nadu and Sri Lanka, returning in 1548–49 and 1552 in between travels in the Far East.	Britain's Queen Elizabeth I grants the first trading charter to the East India Company, with the maiden voyage taking place in 1601 under the command of Sir James Lancaster.	The French East India Company establishes an outpost at Pondicherry (Puducherry), which the French, Dutch and British fight over repeatedly in the coming century.

who became the real rulers. They gradually took over more of the weakening Mughal empire's powers.

The expansion of Maratha power came to an abrupt halt in 1761 at Panipat. In the town where Babur had won the battle that established the Mughal empire more than 200 years earlier, the Marathas were defeated by Ahmad Shah Durrani from Afghanistan. Maratha expansion to the west was halted, and although they consolidated their control over central India, they were to fall to India's final imperial power – the British.

The Rise of European Power

During the 15th century, the Portuguese sought a sea route to the Far East so they could trade directly in spices, hoping to also find the kingdom of legendary Christian ruler, Prester John, thought to contain the fountain of youth. Instead, they found lucrative trading opportunities on the Indian coast and, unexpectedly, a thriving Syrian Christian community, allegedly founded by St Thomas the Apostle.

White Mughals by William Dalrymple tells the true story of an East India Company soldier who married an Indian Muslim princess, a tragic love story interwoven with harem politics, intrigue and espionage.

HISTORY THE RISE OF EUROPEAN POWER

THE STRUGGLE FOR THE SOUL OF INDIA

Founded as an alliance of Hindu kingdoms banding together to counter the threat from the Muslims, the Vijayanagar empire rapidly grew into one of India's wealthiest and greatest Hindu empires. Under the rule of Bukka I (c 1343–79), the majority of South India was brought under its control.

The Vijayanagars and their arch enemy, the Bahmani sultanate, which was also based in South India, were evenly matched, but the atrocities committed by both sides almost defy belief. In 1366, Bukka I responded to a perceived slight by capturing the Muslim stronghold of Mudkal and slaughtering every inhabitant bar one, who managed to escape and carry news of the attack to Mohammad Shah, the sultan. Mohammad swore that he would not rest until he had killed 100,000 Hindus. Instead, according to the Muslim historian Firishtah, 500,000 'infidels' were killed in the ensuing campaign.

Yet somehow, Vijayanagar survived. In 1484, the Bahmani sultanate began to disintegrate, and five separate kingdoms – based on the major cities of Berar, Ahmadnagar, Bidar, Bijapur and Golconda – were formed. With little opposition from the north, the Hindu empire enjoyed a golden age of almost supreme power in the south. In 1520, the Vijayanagar king Krishnadevaraya even took Bijapur.

Like Bahmani, however, Vijayanagar's fault lines were soon laid bare. A series of uprisings divided the kingdom fatally, just at a time when the Muslim sultanates were beginning to form a new alliance. In 1565, Hampi was destroyed at the Battle of Talikota, and power passed to local Muslim rulers or Hindu chiefs once loyal to the Vijayanagar kings. One of India's grisliest periods came to an end when the Bahmani kingdoms fell to the Mughals.

1674	1707	1757	1801
Shivaji establishes the Maratha kingdom, spanning western India and parts of the Deccan and North India. He assumes the imperial title of Chhatrapati, which means 'Great Protector'.	Death of Aurangzeb, the last of the Mughal greats. His demise triggers the gradual collapse of the Mughal empire, as anarchy and rebellion erupt across the country.	British East India Company registers its first military victory on Indian soil. Siraj-ud-Daulah, nawab of Bengal, is defeated by Robert Clive in the Battle of Plassey.	Ranjit Singh becomes maharaja (great king) of the newly united Sikhs and forges a powerful kingdom from his capital in Lahore (in present-day Pakistan).

In 1498, Vasco da Gama arrived on the coast of modern-day Kerala, having sailed around the Cape of Good Hope. Pioneering this route gave the Portuguese a century-long monopoly over Indian and Far Eastern trade with Europe. In 1510, they captured Goa, followed by Diu in 1531; Goa was the last colony in India to be returned to the Indian people, following an Indian Army invasion in 1961. In its heyday, the trade flowing through 'Golden Goa' was said to rival that passing through Lisbon. However, the Portuguese didn't have the resources to maintain a world-wide empire and they were quickly eclipsed and isolated after the arrival of the British and French.

In 1600, Queen Elizabeth I granted a charter to a London trading company that gave it a monopoly on British trade with India. In 1613, representatives of the British East India Company established their first trading post at Surat in Gujarat. Further British trading posts, administered and governed by representatives of the company, were established at Madras (Chennai) in 1639, Bombay (Mumbai) in 1661 and Calcutta (Kolkata) in 1690. For nearly 250 years a commercial trading company, and not the British government, 'ruled' over British India.

By 1672, the French had established themselves at Pondicherry (Puducherry), an enclave they held even after the British departed and where architectural traces of the French era remain. The stage was set for more than a century of rivalry between the British and French for control of Indian trade. At one stage, the French appeared to hold the upper hand, even taking Madras in 1746. But they were outmanoeuvred by the British, and by the 1750s were no longer a serious force on the subcontinent.

Serious French aspirations effectively ended in 1750, when the directors of the French East India Company decided that their representatives were playing too much politics and doing too little trading. Key representatives were sacked, and a settlement designed to end all ongoing political disputes was made with the British. The decision effectively removed France as a serious influence on the subcontinent.

Britain's Surge to Power

The transformation of the British from traders to governors began almost by accident. Having been granted a licence to trade in Bengal by the Mughals, the Brits founded a new trading post at Calcutta in 1690, and business expanded rapidly. Under the apprehensive gaze of the nawab (local ruler), the British 'factories' and depots took on an increasingly permanent (and fortified) appearance.

Eventually the nawab decided that British power had grown large enough. In June 1756, he attacked Calcutta and, having taken the city, locked his British prisoners in a tiny cell, later immortalised as the 'black

Colonial-era Architecture

Colaba and Kala Ghoda, Mumbai (British)

BBD Bagh and environs, Kolkata (British)

Old Goa and Panjim, Goa (Portuguese)

Puducherry, Tamil Nadu (French)

1857	1858	1885	1919
The First War of Independence (Indian Uprising) against the British. With no national leader, freedom fighters coerce the Mughal king, Bahadur Shah Zafar, to proclaim himself emperor of India.	British government assumes control over India – with power officially transferred from the East India Company to the Crown – beginning the period known as the British Raj.	The Indian National Congress, India's first homegrown political organisation, is set up. It brings educated Indians together and plays a key role in India's enduring freedom struggle.	The massacre, on 13 April, of unarmed Indian protesters at Jallianwala Bagh in Amritsar (Punjab). Gandhi responds with his program of civil (nonviolent) disobedience against the British government.

hole of Calcutta'. The space was so cramped and airless that many were dead by the following morning.

Six months later, Robert Clive, an employee in the military service of the East India Company, led an expedition to retake Calcutta and entered into an agreement with one of the nawab's generals to overthrow the nawab himself at the Battle of Plassey (now called Palashi) in June 1757. With the British effectively in control of Bengal, the company's agents engaged in a period of unbridled profiteering. When a subsequent nawab finally took up arms to protect his own interests, he was defeated at the Battle of Baksar in 1764, a victory that confirmed the British as the paramount power in east India.

In 1771, Warren Hastings was made governor in Bengal. During his tenure, the company greatly expanded its control. He was aided by the fact that India was experiencing a power vacuum, created by the disintegration of the Mughal empire and the weakening of the Maratha Confederacy in Maharashtra. Hastings concluded a series of treaties with local rulers, and from 1784 onwards, the British government in London began to take a more direct role in supervising affairs in India, although the territory was still notionally administered by the East India Company until 1858.

In the south, the picture was confused by the strong British–French rivalry, and one ruler was played off against another. This was never clearer than in the series of Mysore Wars, in which Hyder Ali and his son, Tipu Sultan, waged a determined campaign against the British. In the Fourth Mysore War (1789–99), Tipu Sultan was killed at Srirangapatnam, and British power took another step forward. The long-running struggle with the Marathas was concluded a few years later, leaving only Punjab (held by the Sikhs) outside British control. Punjab finally fell in 1849 after the two Sikh Wars.

By the early 19th century, India was effectively under British control, although there remained a patchwork of states, many nominally independent and governed by their own rulers, the maharajas (or similarly titled princes) and nawabs. While these 'princely states' administered their own territories, a system of central government was developed. British bureaucratic models were replicated in the Indian government and civil service – a legacy that still exists today.

Trade and profit continued to be the main focus of British rule in India, with far-reaching effects. Iron and coal mining were developed, and tea, coffee and cotton became key crops. A start was made on the vast rail network that's still in use today, irrigation projects were undertaken, and the Mughal-era zamindar (landowner) system was encouraged, further contributing to the development of an impoverished and landless peasantry.

Amar Chitra Katha, a publisher of popular comic books about Indian folklore, mythology and history, has several books about Shivaji, including *Shivaji – The Great Maratha*, *Tales of Shivaji*, and *Tanaji, the Maratha Lion*, about Shivaji's close friend and fellow warrior.

HISTORY BRITAIN'S SURGE TO POWER

1930	1940	1942	1947
Salt satyagraha begins on 12 March. Gandhi embarks on this 24-day walk from his Sabarmati Ashram near Ahmedabad to the coastal village of Dandi to protest the British salt tax.	The Muslim League adopts its Lahore Resolution, which champions greater Muslim autonomy in India. Campaigns for the creation of a separate Islamic nation are spearheaded by Mohammed Ali Jinnah.	Mahatma Gandhi launches the Quit India campaign, demanding that the British leave India without delay and allow the country to get on with the business of self-governance.	India gains independence on 15 August. Pakistan is formed a day earlier. Partition is marked by a massive cross-border exodus and devastating intercommunal violence.

The British also imposed English as the local language of administration. For them, this was critical in a country with so many different languages, but it also kept the new rulers at arm's length from the Indian populace.

The Proudest Day – India's Long Road to Independence by Anthony Read and David Fisher is an engaging account of India's pre-Independence period.

The Road to Independence

Opposition to the British increased at the turn of the 20th century, spearheaded by the Indian National Congress, the country's oldest political party, also known as the Congress Party or Congress. It met for the first time in 1885 and soon began to push for participation in the government of India.

A highly unpopular attempt by the British to partition Bengal in 1905 resulted in mass demonstrations and brought to light Hindu opposition to the division. The Muslim community formed its own league and campaigned for protected rights in any future political settlement. As pressure rose, a split emerged in Hindu circles between moderates and radicals, the latter resorting to violence to publicise their aims.

With the outbreak of WWI, the political situation eased. India contributed hugely to the war: more than one million Indian volunteers were enlisted and sent overseas, suffering more than 100,000 casualties. However, rewards for this loyalty failed to materialise and disillusion followed. Disturbances were particularly persistent in Punjab, and in April 1919, following riots in Amritsar, a British Army contingent was sent to quell the unrest. Under direct orders of the officer in charge, they ruthlessly fired into a crowd of unarmed protesters at Jallianwala Bagh. News of the massacre spread rapidly throughout India, turning huge numbers of otherwise apolitical Indians into Congress supporters.

At this time, the Congress movement found a new leader in Mohandas Gandhi, a British-educated lawyer who suggested a new route to Indian self-governance through ahimsa – nonviolent resistance to British rule. Not everyone involved in the struggle agreed with or followed Gandhi's policy of nonviolence, yet the Congress Party and Gandhi remained at the forefront of the push for independence.

A Princess Remembers by Gayatri Devi and Santha Rama Rau is the captivating memoir of the former maharani of Jaipur, the glamorous Gayatri Devi (1919–2009).

As political power-sharing began to look more likely, and the mass movement led by Gandhi gained momentum, concerns grew amongst the Muslim community that an independent India would be dominated by Hindus who might not be sympathetic to other religious groups. By the 1930s, community leaders were openly raising the possibility of a separate Islamic state.

Political events were partially disrupted by WWII, when large numbers of Congress supporters were jailed to prevent disruption of the war effort.

1947–48	1948	1948	1948–56
First war between India and Pakistan takes place after the (procrastinating) maharaja of Kashmir signs the Instrument of Accession that cedes his state to India. Pakistan challenges the document's legality.	Mahatma Gandhi is assassinated in New Delhi by Nathuram Godse on 30 January. Godse and his co-conspirator, Narayan Apte, are later tried, convicted and executed (by hanging).	Operation Polo annexes Hyderabad into the Indian Union, bringing India's richest and most powerful princely state under central government control. Many are killed in the resulting communal violence.	Rajasthan takes shape, as the princely states form a beeline to sign the Instrument of Accession, giving up their territories, which are incorporated into the newly formed Republic of India.

Gandhi & the Quit India Movement

One of the great figures of the 20th century, Mohandas Karamchand Gandhi was born on 2 October 1869 in Porbandar, Gujarat. After studying in London (1888–91), he worked as a barrister in South Africa. Here, the young Gandhi became politicised, railing against the discrimination he encountered. He soon became the spokesperson for the Indian community and championed equality for all.

Gandhi returned to India in 1915 with the doctrine of ahimsa (nonviolence) central to his political plans, and committed to a simple and disciplined lifestyle. He set up the Sabarmati Ashram in Ahmedabad, which was innovative for its admission of the so-called caste-less Indians known as Untouchables.

Within a year, Gandhi had won his first victory, defending farmers in Bihar from exploitation. This was when it's said he first received the title 'Mahatma' (Great Soul) from an admirer. The passage of the

Gandhi, directed by Richard Attenborough, is one of the few movies that adeptly captures the grand canvas that is India while tracing the country's rocky road to Independence.

THE FIRST WAR OF INDEPENDENCE: THE INDIAN UPRISING

In 1857, half a century after establishing firm control of India, the British suffered a serious setback. To this day, the causes of the First War of Independence (also known as the Indian Uprising) are the subject of debate. Some blame an influx of cheap goods, such as textiles, from Britain that destroyed local livelihoods; others point to the dispossession of territories from Indian rulers, and taxes imposed on landowners.

However, the incident that's popularly held to have sparked the Indian Uprising took place at an army barracks in Meerut, Uttar Pradesh, on 10 May 1857. A rumour leaked out that a new type of bullet was greased with what Hindus claimed was fat from sacred cows, while Muslims maintained that it came from unclean pigs. Since loading a rifle involved biting the end off the waxed cartridge, these rumours provoked considerable unrest.

In Meerut, the situation was handled with a singular lack of judgement. The commanding officer lined up his soldiers and ordered them to bite off the ends of their issued bullets. Those who refused were immediately marched off to prison. The following morning, the soldiers of the garrison rebelled, shot their officers and marched to Delhi. Of the 74 Indian battalions of the Brits' Bengal Army, only seven (one of them Gurkhas) remained loyal to Britain. The soldiers and peasants rallied around the ageing Mughal emperor in Delhi, and besieged the British residency in Lucknow for five months before they were finally suppressed.

Almost immediately, the East India Company was wound up and direct control of the country was assumed by the British government, which announced its support for the existing rulers of the princely states, claiming they would not interfere in local matters as long as the states remained loyal to the British.

1950	1961	1962	1965
Drafted over two years, the Constitution goes into effect on 26 January, and India becomes a republic. The date commemorates the Declaration of Independence, put forth by the Indian National Congress in 1930.	Indian troops annex Goa in a campaign lasting just 48 hours. The era of European colonialism in India is over.	Border war (known as the Sino-Indian War) with China over the North-East Frontier Area and Ladakh. China successfully captures the disputed territory and ends the war with a unilateral ceasefire.	Skirmishes in Kashmir and Gujarat's disputed Rann of Kachchh (Kutch) flare into the Second India-Pakistan War, which involve the biggest tank battles since WWII. The war ends with a UN-mandated ceasefire.

discriminatory Rowlatt Acts in 1919, which allowed certain political cases to be tried without juries, spurred him to further action, and he organised a national hartal (strike). After the massacre of unarmed protesters in Amritsar, Gandhi, deeply shocked, began to organise his programme of civil (nonviolent) disobedience against the British.

By 1920 Gandhi was a key figure in the Indian National Congress, and he coordinated a national campaign of noncooperation or satyagraha (nonviolent protest) to British rule. In early 1930, Gandhi captured the imagination of the country, and the world, when he led a march of several thousand followers from Ahmedabad to Dandi on the coast of Gujarat, where he ceremoniously made salt by evaporating seawater, defying the much-hated salt tax; not for the first time, he was imprisoned. Released in 1931 to represent the Indian National Congress at the second Round Table Conference in London, he won the hearts of many British people, but failed to gain any real concessions from the government.

Disillusioned with politics, he resigned his parliamentary seat in 1934. He returned spectacularly to the fray in 1942 with the Quit India campaign, in which he urged the British to leave India immediately. His actions were deemed subversive, and he and most of the Congress leadership were imprisoned.

In the frantic independence bargaining that followed the end of WWII, Gandhi was largely excluded and watched helplessly as plans were made to partition the country. Gandhi stood almost alone in urging tolerance and the preservation of a single India, and his work on behalf of all communities drew resentment from some Hindu hardliners. On his way to a prayer meeting in Delhi on 30 January 1948, he was assassinated by a Hindu zealot, Nathuram Godse.

Independence & the Partition of India

The Labour Party victory in the British elections in July 1945 dramatically altered the political landscape. For the first time, Indian independence was accepted as a legitimate goal. This new goodwill did not, however, translate into any new wisdom as to how to reconcile the divergent wishes of the two major Indian parties. Mohammed Ali Jinnah, the leader of the Muslim League, championed a separate Islamic state, while the Congress Party, led by Jawaharlal Nehru, campaigned for an independent greater India.

In early 1946, a British mission failed to bring the two sides together – indeed, there was evidence that the British deliberately fostered resentment on both sides to discourage a unified resistance – and the country slid towards civil war. A 'Direct Action Day', called by the Muslim League in August 1946, led to the slaughter of Hindus in Calcutta, which prompted reprisals against Muslims. In February 1947, the nervous

Gandhian Sites

Raj Ghat, Delhi

Gandhi Smriti, Delhi

Anand Bhavan, Prayagraj (Allahabad)

Sabarmati Ashram, Ahmedabad

Kaba Gandhi No Delo, Rajkot

Mani Bhavan, Mumbai

Gandhi National Memorial, Pune

1971	1972	1974	1975
East Pakistan champions independence from West Pakistan. India gets involved, sparking the Third India-Pakistan War. West Pakistan surrenders, losing sovereignty of East Pakistan, which becomes Bangladesh.	The Simla Agreement between India and Pakistan attempts to normalise relations. The Kashmiri ceasefire line is formalised: the 'Line of Control' remains the de facto border between the two countries.	Fearing incursions from China and Pakistan, India initiates Operation Smiling Buddha, detonating an 8 kiloton nuclear weapon at a secret test site in the deserts of Rajasthan.	In a highly questionable move, Prime Minister Indira Gandhi declares a state of emergency under Article 352 of the Indian Constitution, in response to growing civil unrest and political opposition.

British government made the momentous decision that Independence would come by June 1948. In the meantime, the viceroy, Lord Archibald Wavell, was replaced by Lord Louis Mountbatten.

The new viceroy encouraged the rival factions to agree upon a united India, but to no avail. A decision was made to divide the country, with Gandhi the only staunch opponent. Faced with increasing civil violence, Mountbatten made the precipitous decision to bring forward Independence to 15 August 1947.

Dividing the country into separate Hindu and Muslim territories was immensely tricky; the dividing line proved almost impossible to draw. Some areas were clearly Hindu or Muslim, but others had evenly mixed populations, and there were 'islands' of communities in areas predominantly settled by other religions. Moreover, the two overwhelmingly Muslim regions were on opposite sides of the country and, therefore, Pakistan would inevitably have an eastern and western half divided by a hostile India.

An independent British referee was given the odious task of drawing the borders, well aware that the effects would be catastrophic for countless people. Calcutta, with its Hindu majority, port facilities and jute mills, was divided from East Bengal, which had a Muslim majority, large-scale jute production, no mills and no port facilities. One million Bengalis became refugees in the mass movement across the new border.

The problem was worse in Punjab, where tensions were already close to breaking point between the Muslim, Hindu and Sikh communities. The Sikhs had already campaigned unsuccessfully for their own state and now saw their homeland divided down the middle. Prior to Independence, Lahore's population of 1.2 million included approximately 500,000 Hindus and 100,000 Sikhs. When the dust had finally settled, roughly 1000 Hindus and Sikhs remained.

Punjab contained all the ingredients for an epic disaster, but the resulting bloodshed was far worse than anticipated. Huge population exchanges took place. Trains full of Muslims, fleeing westward, were held up and slaughtered by Hindu and Sikh mobs. Hindus and Sikhs fleeing to the east suffered the same fate at Muslim hands. The army that was sent to maintain order proved totally inadequate and, at times, all too ready to join the sectarian carnage. By the time the Punjab chaos had run its course, more than 10 million people had changed sides and at least 500,000 had been killed.

India and Pakistan became sovereign nations under the British Commonwealth in August 1947 as planned, but the violence, migrations and integration of a few states, especially Kashmir, continued. The Constitution of India was at last adopted in November 1949 and went into

The word Pakistan was originally an acronym thought of by a group of Cambridge Muslims to define a homeland consisting of P(unjab), A(fghania), K(ashmir), I(ran), S(ind), T(urkharistan), A(fghanistan) and (Baluchia)N. It also conflates the terms *pak*, a Persian word meaning pure/clean, and *sthāna*, an Indo-Aryan term meaning 'place'.

1984	1991	1999	2000
Indira Gandhi launches Operation Blue Star against Sikh separatists occupying the Golden Temple in Amritsar; four months later, she is assassinated by her Sikh bodyguards.	Former prime minister Rajiv Gandhi, son of Indira Gandhi, is killed in Tamil Nadu by a suicide bomber affiliated with the Liberation Tigers of Tamil Eelam (LTTE).	Conflict flares again between India and Pakistan along the Line of Control at Kargil in Jammu and Kashmir, the most serious clashes since Pakistan and India emerged as nuclear powers.	India marks the birth of its one billionth citizen, placing the country hot on the heels of China as the second most populous nation on earth.

THE KASHMIR CONFLICT

Kashmir is the most enduring symbol of the turbulent partition of India. In the lead-up to Independence, the delicate task of drawing the India–Pakistan border was complicated by the fact that India's 'princely states' were nominally independent. As part of the settlement process, local rulers were asked which country they wished to join. Kashmir was a predominantly Muslim state with a Hindu maharaja, Hari Singh, who delayed his decision. A ragtag Pashtun (Pakistani) army crossed the border, intent on racing to Srinagar and annexing Kashmir for Pakistan. The maharaja panicked and requested armed assistance from India. The Indian army arrived just in time to prevent the fall of Srinagar, and the maharaja signed the Instrument of Accession, tying Kashmir to India, in October 1947. The document's legality was disputed by Pakistan, and the two nations went to war, just two months after Independence.

In 1948, the fledgling UN Security Council called for a referendum (which remains a central plank of Pakistani policy) to decide the status of Kashmir, and a UN-brokered ceasefire in 1949 established a demarcation line between the two sides, called the Cease-Fire Line (later to become the Line of Control, or LOC). However, this did little to resolve the conflict. Two thirds of Kashmir fell on the Indian side, while the remainder was under Pakistani control, and both nations still claimed Kashmir in its entirety.

The Indian state of Jammu and Kashmir, as it has stood since that time, incorporates Ladakh (a Buddhist-majority region), Jammu (with a Hindu majority) and the 130km-long, 55km-wide Kashmir Valley (with a Muslim majority and most of the state's inhabitants). On the Pakistani side, over three million Kashmiris live in Azad (Free) Kashmir, known to Indians as Pakistan Occupied Kashmir (POK). Since the frontier was drawn, incursions across the LOC have occurred with dangerous regularity.

In 1989–90, the majority of Kashmiri Pandits (pandit means scholar, usually referring to a particular Hindu community of Brahmins) fled their homes following persecution and murder by extremists among the Muslim majority. Up to 170,000 left, many settling in refugee camps around Jammu.

effect on 26 January 1950 and, after untold struggles, independent India officially became a republic.

India Since Independence

Jawaharlal Nehru tried to steer India towards a policy of nonalignment, balancing cordial relations with Britain and Commonwealth membership with moves towards the former USSR. The latter was due partly to conflicts with China, and US support for its arch-enemy Pakistan.

The 1960s and 1970s were tumultuous times for India. A border war with China in what was then known as the North-East Frontier Area (NEFA; now the Northeast States) and Ladakh resulted in the loss of parts of Aksai Chin (Ladakh) and smaller NEFA areas. Wars with Paki-

2004	2005	2008	2009
The Congress Party's Manmohan Singh, renowned for liberalising the economy in the 1990s during his tenure as finance minister, is the first Sikh to become prime minister of India.	A huge 7.6 magnitude earthquake strikes near Muzaffarabad in Pakistan on 8 October, killing more than 86,000 in Indian- and Pakistan-administered Kashmir.	Coordinated attacks on tourist sites, hotels and religious sites in Mumbai by Pakistani militants kill 174 people in one of India's worst ever terrorist incidents.	The High Court in Delhi decriminalises gay sex, removing constraints on homosexuality imposed in colonial times. Four years later, the ruling is reversed.

stan in 1965 (over Kashmir) and 1971 (over Bangladesh) also contributed to a sense among many Indians of having enemies on all sides.

In the midst of it all, the popular Nehru died in 1964 and his daughter Indira Gandhi (no relation to Mahatma Gandhi) was elected as prime minister in 1966. Indira Gandhi, like Nehru before her, loomed large over the country, but India's first and only female leader was a controversial figure whose historical legacy remains hotly disputed.

In 1975, facing serious opposition and unrest, she declared a state of emergency (which later became known as the Emergency). Freed of parliamentary constraints, Gandhi was able to boost the economy, control inflation remarkably well and decisively increase efficiency. On the negative side, political opponents often found themselves in prison, India's judicial system was turned into a puppet theatre and the press was fettered.

Indira Gandhi's government was bundled out of office in the 1977 elections, but the 1980 election brought her back to power with a larger majority than ever before. She was assassinated in 1984 by her Sikh bodyguards after her decision to storm the Golden Temple in Amritsar, which was being occupied by fundamentalist Sikh preacher, Sant Jarnail Singh Bhindranwale.

Her son Rajiv took over, but in 1991 was assassinated in Tamil Nadu by a suicide bomber from a Sri Lankan militant group opposed to government actions against Tamil separatists based in India. Rajiv's widow, Italian-born Sonia, later became president, with Manmohan Singh as prime minister. However, the Congress party started losing popularity, largely due to a slowing economy and a slew of cronyism and corruption allegations.

The 2014 federal elections saw the Congress party suffer a thumping defeat under the shaky leadership of Rahul Gandhi, Indira's grandson. The BJP (Bharatiya Janata Party), headed by the confident and charismatic Narendra Modi, swept to power in a landslide victory, promising to clean up Indian politics and usher in a new era of economic development. Modi was formerly chief minister of Gujarat, which witnessed economic success during his tenure.

After coming to power, Modi launched a number of laudable campaigns – including 'Make in India' (to boost foreign investment); 'Beti Bachao, Beti Padhao' (to improve the plight of girls); and Swachh Bharat Abhiyan (to promote public cleanliness). However, they have received mixed reports vis-a-vis sustainable implementation and effectiveness.

One of Modi's boldest manoeuvres came on 8 November 2016, when the government, without warning, demonetised the nation's ₹500 and ₹1000 banknotes, a move intended to rein in tax-dodgers, corrupt officials and terrorism supporters, but which ultimately proved futile as most devalued bills eventually re-entered the financial system.

India's national anthem, *Jana Gana Mana* (Thou Art the Ruler of the Minds of All People), was written and composed by Bengali poet and Nobel Laureate Rabindranath Tagore.

HISTORY INDIA SINCE INDEPENDENCE

2014	2016	2018	2019
After a landslide election victory by the Bharatiya Janata Party (BJP), Gujarat-born Narendra Modi becomes India's prime minister.	The Modi government announces the sudden demonetisation of ₹500 and ₹1000 banknotes, aimed at stamping out tax evasion and corruption. Economic growth is dampened following the initiative's announcement.	India's Supreme Court votes unanimously to decriminalise homosexuality, removing criminal penalties for gay sex – imposed by the British in 1864 – from India's penal code.	The ruling BJP party, led by Modi, wins the 2019 country-wide elections and increases its majority in the Lok Sabha.

The Way of Life

Spirituality and family lie at the heart of Indian society, with these two tenets often intertwining in various ceremonies to celebrate auspicious occasions and life's milestones. Despite the growing number of nuclear families – primarily in the more cosmopolitan cities such as Mumbai, Bengaluru (Bangalore) and Delhi – the extended family remains a cornerstone of both urban and rural India, with males – usually the main breadwinners – generally considered the head of the household.

Marriage, Birth & Death

Different religions practise different traditions, but for all communities, marriage, birth and death are considered important and marked with ceremonies according to the relevant faith. Hindus are in the majority in India (around 80% of the population), while Muslims comprise the largest minority religion (about 14%).

Marriage is an exceptionally auspicious event for Indians. Although 'love marriages' have spiralled upwards in recent times (mainly in urban hubs), most Indian marriages are still arranged, be the family Hindu, Muslim, Sikh, Jain or Buddhist. Discreet enquiries are made within the community. If a suitable match is not found, the help of professional matchmakers might be sought, or advertisements may be placed in newspapers and/or on matrimonial websites. In Hindu families, the horoscopes of both potential partners are checked and, if propitious, there's a meeting between the two families.

Dowry, although illegal, is still a key issue in more than a few arranged marriages (mostly in conservative communities), with some families plunging into debt to raise the required cash and merchandise (from cars and computers to refrigerators and televisions). Health workers claim that India's high rate of abortion of female foetuses (sex-identification medical tests are banned in India, but they clandestinely occur in some clinics) is predominantly due to the financial burden of providing a daughter's dowry. Muslim grooms have to pay what is called a *mehr* to the bride.

The Hindu wedding ceremony is officiated by a priest and the marriage is formalised when the couple walk around a sacred fire seven times. Muslim ceremonies involve the reading of the Quran, and traditionally the husband and wife view each other via mirrors. Despite the existence of nuclear families, it's still the norm for a wife to live with her husband's family once married and assume the household duties usually outlined by her mother-in-law. Not surprisingly, the mother–daughter-in-law relationship can be a tricky one, as portrayed in various Indian TV soap operas.

Divorce and remarriage are becoming more common (primarily in bigger cities), but divorce is still not granted by courts as a matter of routine and is generally not looked upon very favourably by society. Among the higher castes, in more traditional areas, widows are expected to not remarry, to wear white and live pious, celibate lives.

Matchmaking has inevitably gone online, with popular sites including www.shaadi.com, www.bharatmatrimony.com and, in a sign of the times, www.secondshaadi.com – for those seeking a partner again.

Until recently, it was legal for Muslim males in India to obtain instant divorce according to sharia law (by uttering the word *talaq,* meaning 'divorce', three times). However, in 2017 the Modi government had the 'Muslim Women (Protection of Rights on Marriage)' bill passed in parliament, making instant divorce a criminal act, with offenders facing a fine and up to three years in jail.

The birth of a child is another momentous occasion, with its own set of special ceremonies, which take place at various auspicious times during the early years of childhood. For Hindus these include the casting of the child's first horoscope, name-giving, feeding the first solid food, and the first hair-cutting.

Hindus cremate their dead, and funeral ceremonies are designed to purify and console both the living and the deceased. An important aspect of the proceedings is the *sharadda,* paying respect to one's ancestors by offering water and rice cakes. It's an observance that's repeated at each anniversary of the death. After the cremation, the ashes are collected and, 13 days after the death (when blood relatives are deemed ritually pure), a member of the family usually scatters them in a holy river such as the Ganges or in the ocean. Sikhs similarly wash then cremate their dead. Muslims also prepare their dead carefully, but bury them, while the minority Zoroastrian Parsi community places its dead in 'Towers of Silence' (stone towers) to be devoured by birds.

The Caste System

Although the Indian Constitution does not recognise the caste system, caste can still wield considerable influence, especially in rural India, where the caste you are born into largely determines your social standing in the community. It can also influence your vocational and marriage prospects. Castes are further divided into thousands of *jati,* groups of 'families' or social communities, which are sometimes linked to occupation. Conservative Hindus will only marry someone of the same *jati,* and caste is often a criterion in matrimonial adverts: 'Mahar seeks Mahar' etc. In some very traditional families, young men and women who fall in love outside their caste have been murdered.

According to tradition, caste is the basic social structure of Hindu society. Living a righteous life and fulfilling your dharma (moral duty) raises your chances of being reborn into a higher caste and thus into better circumstances. Hindus are born into one of four varnas (castes): Brahmin (priests and scholars), Kshatriya (soldiers and administrators), Vaishya (merchants) and Shudra (labourers). The Brahmins are said to have emerged from the mouth of Lord Brahma at the moment of creation, Kshatriyas to have come from his arms, Vaishyas from his thighs and Shudras from his feet. Beneath the four main castes are the Dalits

MEHNDI

Mehndi is the traditional art of painting a woman's hands (and sometimes feet) with intricate henna designs for auspicious ceremonies, such as marriage. If quality henna is used, the design, which is orange-brown, can last up to one month.

In touristy areas, *mehndi*-wallahs are adept at applying henna tattoo 'bands' on the arms, legs and lower back. If you get *mehndi* applied, allow at least a few hours for the design process and required drying time (during drying you can't use your hennaed hands).

It's always wise to request the artist to do a 'test' spot on your arm before proceeding: some modern dyes contain chemicals that may cause allergies; be particularly cautious of 'black henna', which could include harmful chemicals. If good-quality henna is used, you should not feel any pain during or after the application.

If you want to learn more about India's caste system, these two books are a good start: *Interrogating Caste* by Dipankar Gupta and *Translating Caste*, edited by Tapan Basu.

(formerly known as Untouchables), who hold menial jobs such as sweepers and latrine cleaners. Many of India's complex codes of ritual purity were devised to prevent physical contact between people of higher castes and Dalits. A somewhat less rigid system exists in Islamic communities in India, with society divided into *ashraf* (high born), *ajlaf* (low born) and *arzal* (equivalent to the Dalits).

The word 'pariah' is derived from the name of a Tamil Dalit group, the Paraiyars. Some Dalit leaders, such as the renowned Dr BR Ambedkar (1891–1956), sought to change their status by adopting another faith; in his case it was Buddhism. At the bottom of the social heap are the Denotified Tribes. They were known as the Criminal Tribes until 1952, when a reforming law officially recognised 198 tribes and castes. Many are nomadic or seminomadic tribes, forced by the wider community to eke out a living on society's fringes.

To improve the Dalits' position, the government reserves a number of public-sector jobs, parliamentary seats and university places for them. Today these quotas account for almost 25% of government jobs and university student positions. The situation varies regionally, as different political leaders chase caste vote-banks by promising to include them in reservations. The reservation system, while generally regarded in a favourable light, has also been criticised for unfairly blocking tertiary and employment opportunities for those who would have otherwise got positions on merit. On the other hand, there are still examples of discrimination against Dalits in daily life – for example, higher castes denying them entry into certain temples.

Pilgrimage

Devout Hindus are expected to go on a *yatra* (pilgrimage) at least once a year. Pilgrimages are undertaken to implore the gods or goddesses to grant a wish, to take the ashes of a cremated relative to a holy river, or to gain spiritual merit. India has thousands of holy sites to which pilgrims travel; the elderly often make Varanasi their final one, as it's believed that dying in this sacred city releases a person from the cycle of rebirth. Sufi shrines in India attract thousands of Muslims to commemorate holy days, such as the birthday of a Sufi saint, while many Muslims also make the hajj to Mecca in Saudi Arabia.

KUMBH MELA

If crowds worry you, stay away. This one's big. Very big. Held four times every 12 years at four different locations across central and northern India, the Kumbh Mela is the largest religious congregation on the planet. This vast celebration attracts tens of millions of Hindu pilgrims, including mendicant *nagas* (naked sadhus, or holy men) from various Hindu monastic orders, who come together for a mass ceremonial dip in the sacred Ganges, Shipra or Godavari Rivers.

The origins of the festival go back to the battle for supremacy between good and evil. In the Hindu creation myths, the gods and demons fought a great battle for a *kumbh* (pitcher) containing the nectar of immortality. Vishnu got hold of the container and spirited it away, but in flight four drops fell on the earth – at Prayagraj (Allahabad), Haridwar, Nasik and Ujjain.

Celebrations last for around six weeks, but are centred on just a handful of auspicious bathing dates, normally six. The Prayagraj (Allahabad) event, known as the Maha (Great) Kumbh Mela, is even larger with even bigger crowds. Each location also holds an Ardh (Half) Mela every six years and a smaller, annual Magh Mela.

For detailed information (including exact dates and locations) of the Kumbh Mela, see www.kumbh.gov.in/en.

INDIAN ATTIRE

Widely worn by Indian women, the elegant sari comes in a single piece (between 5m and 9m long and 1m wide) and is ingeniously tucked and pleated into place without the need for pins or buttons. Worn with the sari is the choli (tight-fitting blouse) and a drawstring petticoat. The *palloo* is the part of the sari draped over the shoulder. Also commonly worn is the *salwar kameez*, a traditional dress-like tunic and trouser combination accompanied by a dupatta (long scarf). Saris and *salwar kameez* come in a spectacular range of fabrics, colours and designs.

Traditional attire for men includes the dhoti, and in the south, the lungi and the *mundu*. The dhoti is a loose, long loincloth pulled up between the legs. The lungi is more like a sarong, with its end usually sewn up like a tube. The *mundu* is like a lungi but is always white. A kurta (shirt) is a long tunic or shirt worn mainly by men, usually with no collar. Kurta pyjamas are a cotton shirt-and-trousers set, generally worn for relaxing or sleeping. *Churidar* are close-fitting trousers often worn under a kurta. A *sherwani* is a long coat-like men's garment.

There are regional and religious variations in costume – for example, you may see Muslim women wearing the all-enveloping burka.

Most festivals in India are rooted in religion and are thus a magnet for throngs of pilgrims. As many festivals are spiritual occasions – even those that have a carnivalesque sheen – it's important for tourists to behave respectfully. Also be aware that there have been deaths at festivals due to stampedes, so be extra cautious in large crowds.

Women in India

According to the most recent census, published in 2011, India's population includes 586 million women, with an estimated 68% of those working (mostly as labourers) in the agricultural sector.

Women in India are entitled to vote and own property. While the percentage of women in politics has risen over the past decade, they're still notably underrepresented in the national parliament, accounting for under 12% of parliamentary seats.

Although the professions are male dominated, women are steadily making inroads, especially in urban centres. Kerala was India's first state to break societal norms by recruiting female police officers in 1938. It was also the first state to establish an all-female police station (in 1973). For village women it's much more difficult to get ahead, but groups such as the Self-Employed Women's Association (SEWA) in Gujarat have shown what's possible, organising socially disadvantaged women into unions and offering micro-finance loans.

In low-income families especially, girls can be regarded as a serious financial liability, because at marriage a dowry might be demanded. For the urban middle-class woman, life is usually much more comfortable, but pressures still exist. Broadly speaking, she is far more likely to receive a tertiary education, but, once married, is often expected to 'fit in' with her in-laws and be a homemaker above all else. Like her village counterpart, if she fails to live up to expectations – even if it's just not being able to produce a grandson – the consequences can be dire. This is demonstrated by the extreme practice of 'bride burning', wherein a wife is doused with flammable liquid and set alight. A 2017 report indicated there were 21 dowry deaths registered each day across India, with just a 35% conviction rate.

Although the Constitution allows for divorcees (and widows) to remarry, few reportedly do so, simply because divorcees are traditionally considered outcasts from society, most evidently so outside the big cities. Divorce rates in India are among the world's lowest (around 14 in 1000)

India has the world's biggest diaspora population (pegged at around 16 million) according to a UN report, with the largest numbers in the UAE (United Arab Emirates) and USA.

Read more about India's Adivasis (tribal communities) at www.tribal.nic.in, a site maintained by the Indian government's Ministry of Tribal Affairs.

although they are rising. Most divorces take place in urban centres and are deemed less socially unacceptable among those occupying the upper echelons of society.

In October 2006, following women's civil rights campaigns, the Indian parliament passed a landmark bill (on top of existing legislation), giving women who are suffering domestic violence increased protection and rights. Prior to this legislation, although women could lodge police complaints against abusive spouses, they weren't automatically entitled to a share of the marital property or to ongoing financial support. Critics claim that many women, especially those outside India's larger cities, are still reluctant to seek legal protection because of the social stigma involved.

India remains a largely conservative and patriarchal society. Despite the sexualised images of women churned out in Bollywood movies (although prolonged kissing is still rarely seen on screen), many traditionally minded people consider a woman to be somehow wanton if she so much as goes out after dark or does not dress modestly.

According to India's National Crime Records Bureau (NCRB), reported incidences of rape have been increasing. It's believed that only a small percentage of sexual assaults are actually reported, largely due to family pressure and/or shame, especially if the perpetrator is known to the family – which is true in many cases.

Following the highly publicised gang-rape and murder of a 23-year-old Indian physiotherapy student in Delhi in December 2012, tens of thousands of people protested in the capital and beyond, demanding swift government action to address the country's escalating gender-based violence. It took a further year before legal amendments were made to existing laws to address the problem of sexual assault, including harsher punishments such as life imprisonment and the death penalty. Despite this, sexual violence against women remains rampant. According to the latest NCRB report, Delhi has the highest number of crimes against women – 13,803 out of a total of 41,761 cases registered in 19 major Indian cities. A considerable number of foreign female travellers to India have reported some form of sexual harassment.

The #MeToo movement swept India in 2018, resulting in a number of high-profile men in the media and entertainment industries losing their jobs and facing legal action due to sexual harassment allegations. It also saw a minister in the Modi government, MJ Akbar, resign after being accused of sexual misconduct by numerous women who worked with him during his tenure as a newspaper editor. The #MeToo movement has been widely praised for giving Indian women the collective confidence to speak out against sexual predators.

Adivasis

India's Adivasis (tribal communities; Adivasi translates to 'original inhabitant' in Sanskrit) have origins that precede the Vedic Aryans and the Dravidians of the south. These groups range from the Gondi of the central plains to the animist tribes of the Northeast States. Today, they constitute less than 10% of India's population and are comprised of more than 300 different tribal groups. The literacy rate for Adivasis is significantly below the national average.

Historically, contact between Adivasis and Hindu villagers on the plains rarely led to friction, as there was little or no competition for resources and land. However, in recent decades an increasing number of Adivasis have been dispossessed of their ancestral land and turned into impoverished labourers. Although they still have political representation thanks to a parliamentary quota system, the dispossession and exploita-

HIJRAS

India's most visible nonheterosexual group is the *hijras,* a caste of transvestites and eunuchs who dress in women's clothing. Some are gay, some are hermaphrodites and some were unfortunate enough to be kidnapped and castrated. *Hijras* have long had a place in Indian culture, and in 2014 the Indian Supreme Court recognised *hijras* as a third gender and a class entitled to reservation in education and jobs.

In the wider community, *hijras* work mainly as uninvited entertainers at weddings and celebrations of the birth of male children, and sometimes as prostitutes. In 2014, Padmini Prakash became India's first transgender daily TV news-show anchor, indicating a new level of acceptance.

Read more about *hijras* in *The Invisibles* by Zia Jaffrey and *Ardhanarishvara the Androgyne* by Dr Alka Pande.

tion of Adivasis has reportedly sometimes been with the connivance of officialdom.

Read more about Adivasis in *Archaeology and History: Early Settlements in the Andaman Islands* by Zarine Cooper, *The Tribals of India* by Sunil Janah and *Tribes of India: The Struggle for Survival* by Christoph von Fürer-Haimendorf.

Sport

Cricket has long been engraved on the nation's heart, with the first recorded match in 1721, and India's first test-match victory in 1952 in Chennai (then Madras) against England. It's not only a national sporting obsession, but a matter of enormous patriotism, especially evident whenever India plays against Pakistan. Matches between these South Asian neighbours – which have had rocky relations since Independence – attract especially passionate support, and the players of both sides are under immense pressure to do their respective countries proud. The most celebrated Indian cricketer of recent times is Sachin Tendulkar – fondly dubbed the 'Little Master' – who, in 2012, became the world's only player to score 100 international centuries, retiring on a high the following year.

Cricket – especially the Twenty20 format – is big business in India, attracting lucrative sponsorship deals and celebrity status for its players. The sport has not been without its murky side, though, with Indian cricketers among those embroiled in match-fixing scandals. International games are played at various centres – see Indian newspapers or check online for details about matches that coincide with your visit. Keep your finger on the cricketing pulse at www.espncricinfo.com and www.cricbuzz.com.

The launch of the Indian Super League (ISL; www.indiansuperleague.com) in 2013 has greatly helped promote football in the country. With games drawing huge crowds, and stints by international players such as the legendary Juventus footballer Alessandro Del Piero (who was signed for the Delhi Dynamos in 2014), the ISL has made global headlines. The first week of the ISL in 2014 had 170.6 million viewers – the figure for the first phase of the Indian Premier League cricket was 184 million, which gives a sense of football's growth in popularity. The I-League is the longer-running domestic league, but it has never attracted such media attention or funding.

Tennis has become increasingly popular, with Sania Mirza, Leander Paes and Mahesh Bhupathi being India's star performers in the international arena. For more information about Indian tennis see www.aitatennis.com.

India is known for its historical links to horse polo, which intermittently thrived on the subcontinent (especially among nobility) until

In 2018, Manipur-born mother-of-three Mary Kom became the world's most successful boxer, by winning a sixth gold medal in the Women's World Boxing Championships.

HOMOSEXUALITY IN INDIA

The British-era origins of Section 377 of the Indian Penal Code – which harks back to 1861 – makes homosexual sex legally punishable with up to 10 years imprisonment. However, in recent times, this law has seen an extraordinary series of legal twists and turns: homosexuality was decriminalised in 2009, only to be recriminalised in 2013 and then decriminalised (yet again) in 2018.

Although there's growing acceptance of homosexuality, especially among India's younger generation, it's still widely considered taboo in this largely conservative country. There are no reliable statistics regarding the number of homosexuals living in India, because many prefer to keep their identity concealed due to the ongoing social stigma.

Independence, after which patronage steeply declined due to dwindling funds. Today there's a renewed interest in polo thanks to beefed-up sponsorship and, although it remains an elite sport, it's attracting more attention from the country's burgeoning upper middle class. The origins of polo are not completely clear. Believed to have its roots in Persia and China around 2000 years ago, on the subcontinent it's thought to have first been played in Baltistan (in present-day Pakistan). Some say that Emperor Akbar (who reigned in India from 1556 to 1605) first introduced rules to the game, but that polo, as it's played today, was largely influenced by a British cavalry regiment stationed in India during the 1870s. A set of international rules was implemented after WWI. The world's oldest surviving polo club, established in 1862, is in Kolkata (Calcutta Polo Club; www.calcuttapolo.com). Polo takes place during the cooler winter months in major cities, including Delhi, Jaipur, Mumbai and Kolkata. It is also occasionally played in Ladakh and Manipur. Meanwhile, horse racing traces its roots back several hundred years, with India's first racecourse established in Chennai in 1777. Today, racing takes place in major cities including Mumbai, Kolkata, Delhi, Bengaluru (Bangalore) and Chennai.

Kabaddi is another noteworthy traditional sport in India. Two teams occupy two sides of a court; a raider runs to the opposing side, taking a breath and trying to tag one or more members of the opposite team. The raider chants 'kabaddi' repeatedly to show that they have not taken a breath, returning to the home half before exhaling.

Field hockey no longer enjoys the fervent following it once did. During its golden era, between 1928 and 1956, India won six consecutive Olympic gold medals in hockey; it later bagged two further Olympic gold medals, one in 1964 and the other in 1980. During the 2016 Olympics, in Rio, the team finished in eighth place. Recent initiatives to reignite interest in the game have had mixed results. Tap into India's hockey scene at Indian Hockey (www.indianhockey.com) and Indian Field Hockey (www.bharatiyahockey.org).

A record 117 Indian athletes competed in the 2016 Rio Summer Olympics, but the results were disappointing; India took home just one silver and one bronze medal, finishing 67th on the final medal tally. At these games, Sakshi Malik became the first Indian woman wrestler to win an Olympic medal (bronze in the women's freestyle 58kg category), while PV Sindhu (women's badminton) became the first Indian woman to win an Olympic silver.

Recommended books for cricket lovers include *The Illustrated History of Indian Cricket* by Boria Majumdar and *The States of Indian Cricket* by Ramachandra Guha.

Spiritual India

From elaborate city temples to simple village shrines, spirituality suffuses almost every facet of life in India. The nation's major faith, Hinduism, is practised by around 80% of the population and is one of the world's oldest extant religions, with roots extending beyond 1000 BC. Buddhism, Jainism and Zoroastrianism have a similarly historic pedigree and adherents of Islam form the country's largest religious minorities. Indeed, in a land that has long embraced the sacred, no matter where you travel spiritual India is bound to be a constant companion.

Hinduism

Hinduism has no founder or central authority and it isn't a proselytising religion. Essentially, Hindus believe in Brahman, who is eternal, uncreated and infinite. Everything that exists emanates from Brahman and will ultimately return to it. The multitude of gods and goddesses are just manifestations – knowable aspects of this formless phenomenon.

Hindus believe that earthly life is cyclical: you are born again and again (a process known as samsara), the quality of these rebirths being dependent upon your karma (conduct or action) in previous lives. Living a righteous life and fulfilling your dharma (moral code of behaviour; social duty) will enhance your chances of being born into a higher caste and better circumstances. Alternatively, if enough bad karma has accumulated, rebirth may take animal form. But it's only as a human that you can gain sufficient self-knowledge to escape the cycle of reincarnation and achieve moksha (liberation from samsara).

All Hindu deities are regarded as a manifestation of Brahman, who is often described as having three main representations, the Trimurti: Brahma, Vishnu and Shiva.

Brahman The One; the ultimate reality. Brahman is formless, eternal and the source of all existence. Brahman is *nirguna* (without attributes), as opposed to all the other gods and goddesses, who are manifestations of Brahman and therefore *saguna* (with attributes).

Brahma Only during the creation of the universe does Brahma play an active role. At other times he is in meditation. His consort is Saraswati, the goddess of learning, and his vehicle is a swan. He is sometimes shown sitting on a lotus that rises from Vishnu's navel, symbolising the interdependence of the gods. Brahma is generally depicted with four (crowned and bearded) heads, each turned towards a point of the compass. Worship of Brahma was gradually eclipsed by the rise of groups devoted to Shiva and Vishnu. Today, India has few Brahma temples.

Unravelling the basic tenets of Hinduism are two good books, both called *Hinduism: An Introduction* – one is by Shakunthala Jagannathan, the other by Dharam Vir Singh.

OM

The word 'Om' has significance for several religions, and is one of Hinduism's most venerated symbols. Pronounced 'aum', it's a highly propitious mantra (sacred word or syllable). The 'three' shape symbolises the creation, maintenance and destruction of the universe (and thus the holy Trimurti). The inverted *chandra* (crescent or half moon) represents the discursive mind and the *bindu* (dot) within it, Brahman. Buddhists believe that if 'Om' is intoned often enough with complete concentration, it will lead to a state of blissful emptiness.

The Hindu pantheon is said to have a staggering 330 million deities; those worshipped are a matter of personal choice or tradition.

Vishnu The preserver or sustainer, Vishnu is associated with 'right action'. He protects and sustains all that is good in the world. He is usually depicted with four arms, holding a lotus, a conch shell (it can be blown like a trumpet so symbolises the cosmic vibration from which existence emanates), a discus and a mace. His consort is Lakshmi, the goddess of wealth, and his vehicle is faithful Garuda, a fusion of man and bird. Said to emanate from the causal ocean, from which all physical things are created, the sacred River Ganges (Ganga) flows into the material world from Vishnu's feet, but is held back by the matted hair of Lord Shiva to prevent it destroying the earth.

Shiva Shiva is the destroyer – to deliver salvation at the end of each cycle of the universe – without whom creation of the new cycle couldn't occur. Shiva's creative role is phallically symbolised by his representation as the frequently worshipped lingam. With 1008 names, Shiva takes many forms, including Nataraja, lord of the *tandava* (cosmic victory dance), who paces out the creation and destruction of the cosmos. Sometimes Shiva has snakes draped around his neck and is shown holding a trident (representative of the Trimurti) as a weapon while riding Nandi, his bull. Nandi symbolises power and potency, justice and moral order. Shiva's consort, Parvati is capable of taking many forms, including the warlike goddesses Durga and Kali.

Other Prominent Deities

Elephant-headed Ganesh is the god of good fortune, remover of obstacles and patron of scribes. The broken tusk he holds was used to write sections of the Mahabharata, and his animal vehicle is Mooshak, a rat-like creature. How Ganesh came to have an elephant's head is a story with several variations. One legend says that Ganesh was born to Parvati in the absence of his father, Shiva, and so grew up not knowing him. One day, as Ganesh stood guard while his mother bathed, Shiva returned and asked to be let into Parvati's presence. Ganesh, who didn't recognise Shiva, refused. Enraged, Shiva lopped off Ganesh's head, only to later discover, much to his horror, that he had slaughtered his own son. He vowed to replace Ganesh's head with that of the first creature he came across, which happened to be an elephant.

Another prominent deity, Krishna is an incarnation of Vishnu, sent to earth to fight for good and combat evil. His dalliances with the *gopis* (milkmaids) and his love for Radha have inspired countless paintings and songs. Depicted with blue-hued skin, Krishna is often seen playing the flute.

Shiva is sometimes characterised as the lord of yoga, a Himalaya-dwelling ascetic with matted hair, an ash-smeared body and a third eye symbolising wisdom.

Hanuman is a hero of the Ramayana and loyal ally of Rama. He embodies the concept of bhakti (devotion). He's also the king of the monkeys, but is capable of taking on other forms.

Among Shaivites (followers of the Shiva movement), *shakti,* the divine creative power of women, is worshipped as a force in its own right. The concept of *shakti* is embodied in the ancient goddess Devi (divine mother), who is also manifested as Durga and, in a fiercer evil-destroying incarnation, Kali, both worshipped as aspects of Shiva's consort, Parvati. Other widely worshipped goddesses include Lakshmi, the goddess of wealth, and Saraswati, the goddess of learning.

THE SACRED SEVEN

The number seven has special significance in Hinduism. There are seven sacred Indian cities, which are all major pilgrimage centres: Varanasi, associated with Shiva; Haridwar, where the Ganges (Ganga) enters the plains from the Himalaya; Ayodhya, birthplace of Rama; Dwarka, with the legendary capital of Krishna thought to be off the Gujarat coast; Mathura, birthplace of Krishna; Kanchipuram, site of the historic Shiva temples; and Ujjain, venue of the Kumbh Mela every 12 years. There are also seven sacred rivers: the Ganges, Saraswati (thought to be underground), Yamuna, Indus, Narmada, Godavari and Cauvery.

TRIBAL RELIGIONS

A considerable number of tribal groups in India are animist. They believe that certain objects, animals or places are inhabited by spiritual entities. Religious ideas are closely intertwined with nature – a stone, river, tree or mountain etc may be deemed to have a spirit form. One example is the Mizos of northeast India who may walk around with large stones, believing them to be the abode of spiritual forces. Meanwhile, the Naga tribes of northeast India believe the earth was created out of water by a series of quakes triggered by an earthquake god. It is the sons of the earthquake god who have watched over the world ever since and delivered punishment to those who do wrong.

Also in the northeast exist tribes who follow Donyi-Polo (translated as 'Sun-Moon'), which is said to have emanated from Tibet's pre-Buddhist Bon religion. The sun and moon represent female and male energies – somewhat like the concept of Yin and Yang. Devotees believe in the oneness of all living creatures.

Sacred Texts

Hindu sacred texts fall into two categories: those believed to be the word of god (*shruti*, meaning 'heard') and those produced by people (*smriti*, meaning 'remembered'). The Vedas are regarded as *shruti* knowledge and considered the authoritative basis for Hinduism. The oldest of the Vedic texts, the Rig-Veda, was compiled over 3000 years ago. Within its 1028 verses are prayers for prosperity and longevity, as well as an explanation of the universe's origins. The Upanishads, the last parts of the Vedas, reflect on the mystery of death and emphasise the oneness of the universe. The oldest of the Vedic texts were written in Vedic Sanskrit (related to Old Persian). Later texts were composed in classical Sanskrit, but many have been translated into the vernacular.

The *smriti* texts comprise a collection of literature spanning centuries and include expositions on the proper performance of domestic ceremonies as well as the proper pursuit of government, economics and religious law. Among the well-known works are the Ramayana and Mahabharata, as well as the Puranas, which expand on the epics and promote the notion of the Trimurti. Unlike the Vedas, reading the Puranas is not restricted to initiated higher-caste males.

The Mahabharata

Thought to have been composed around 1000 BC, the Mahabharata focuses on the exploits of Krishna. By about 500 BC, the Mahabharata had evolved into a far more complex creation with substantial additions, including the Bhagavad Gita (in which Krishna proffers advice to Arjuna before a battle).

The story centres on conflict between the heroic gods (Pandavas) and the demons (Kauravas). Overseeing events is Krishna, who has taken on human form. Krishna acts as charioteer for the Pandava hero Arjuna, who eventually triumphs in a great battle against the Kauravas.

The Ramayana

Composed around the 3rd or 2nd century BC, the Ramayana is believed to be largely the work of one person, the poet Valmiki. Like the Mahabharata, it centres on conflict between the gods and the demons.

The story goes that Dasharatha, the childless king of Ayodhya, called upon the gods to provide him with a son. His wife duly gave birth to a boy. But this child, named Rama, was in fact an incarnation of Vishnu, who had assumed human form to overthrow the demon king of Lanka (now Sri Lanka), Ravana.

As an adult, Rama, who won the hand of the princess Sita in a competition, was chosen by his father to inherit his kingdom. At the last minute,

Two recommended publications containing English translations of holy Hindu texts are *The Bhagavad Gita* by S Radhakrishnan and *The Valmiki Ramayana* by Romesh Dutt.

Rama's stepmother intervened and demanded her son, Barathan, take Rama's place. Rama, Sita and Rama's brother, Lakshmana, were exiled and went off to the forests, where Rama and Lakshmana battled demons and other dark forces. Ravana's sister attempted to seduce Rama, but she was rejected and, in revenge, Ravana captured Sita and spirited her away to his palace in Lanka. Rama, assisted by an army of monkeys led by the loyal monkey god Hanuman, eventually found the palace, killed Ravana and rescued Sita. All returned victorious to Ayodhya, where Rama was welcomed and crowned king.

Sacred Flora & Fauna

Animals, particularly cows and snakes, have long been worshipped on the subcontinent. For Hindus, the cow represents fertility and nurturing, while snakes (especially cobras) are associated with fertility and welfare. Naga stones (snake stones) serve the dual purpose of protecting humans from snakes and appeasing snake gods.

Plants can also have sacred associations, such as the banyan tree, which symbolises the Trimurti, while mango trees are symbolic of love – Shiva is believed to have married Parvati under one. Meanwhile, the lotus flower is said to have emerged from the primeval waters and is connected to the mythical centre of the earth through its stem. Often found in the most polluted of waters, the lotus has the remarkable ability to blossom above murky depths. The centre of the lotus corresponds to the centre of the universe, the navel of the earth: all is held together by the stem and the eternal waters. The fragile yet resolute lotus is an embodiment of beauty and strength and a reminder to Hindus of how their own lives should be. So revered has the lotus become that today it's India's national flower. The Rudraksha (meaning 'Shiva's eye') tree is said to have sprung from Shiva's tears, and its seeds are used as prayer beads.

Worship

Worship and ritual play a paramount role in Hinduism. In Hindu homes you'll often find a dedicated worship area, where members of the family pray to the deities of their choice. Beyond the home, Hindus worship at temples. *Puja* is a focal point of worship and ranges from silent prayer to elaborate ceremonies. Devotees leave the temple with a handful of *prasad* (temple-blessed food), which is shared among others. Other forms of worship include *aarti* (the auspicious lighting of lamps or candles) and the playing of bhajans (devotional songs).

Islam

Islam is India's largest minority religion, followed by approximately 13.4% of the population. It's believed that Islam was introduced to northern India by Muslim conquerors (in the 16th and 17th centuries the Mughal empire controlled much of North India) and to the south by Arab traders.

Islam was founded in Arabia by the Prophet Mohammed in the 7th century AD. The Arabic term *islam* means to surrender, and believers (Muslims) undertake to surrender to the will of Allah (God), which is revealed in the scriptures, the Quran. In this monotheistic religion, God's word is conveyed through prophets (messengers), of whom Mohammed was the most recent.

Following Mohammed's death, a succession dispute split the movement, and the legacy today is the Sunnis and the Shiites. Most Muslims in India are Sunnis. The Sunnis emphasise the 'well-trodden' path or the orthodox way, while Shiites believe that only imams (exemplary leaders) can reveal the true meaning of the Quran. India also has a long tradition of Sufism, a mystical interpretation of Islam that dates back to the earliest days of the religion.

A sadhu is someone who has surrendered all material possessions in pursuit of spirituality through meditation, the study of sacred texts, self-mortification and pilgrimage. Learn more in *Sadhus: India's Mystic Holy Men* by Dolf Hartsuiker.

Muslims adhere to the 'five pillars' of Islam: profession of faith, ritual prayer five times a day, paying alms to the needy, fasting during the month of Ramadan and making the pilgrimage to Mecca.

All Muslims, however, share a belief in the Five Pillars of Islam: the shahada (declaration of faith: 'There is no God but Allah; Mohammed is his prophet'); prayer (ideally five times a day); the zakat (tax), in the form of a charitable donation; fasting (during Ramadan) for all except the sick, young children, pregnant women, the elderly and those undertaking arduous journeys; and the hajj (pilgrimage) to Mecca, which every Muslim aspires to do at least once.

To grasp the intricacies of Sikhism, read *Volume One* (1469–1839) and *Volume Two* (1839–2004) of *A History of the Sikhs* by Khushwant Singh.

Sikhism

Sikhism, founded in Punjab by Guru Nanak in the 15th century, began as a reaction against the caste system and Brahmin domination of ritual. Sikhs believe in one god and, although they reject the worship of idols, some keep pictures of their 10 gurus as a point of focus. The Sikhs' holy book, the Guru Granth Sahib, contains the teachings of the 10 Sikh gurus, several of whom were executed by the Mughals. Like Hindus and Buddhists, Sikhs believe in rebirth and karma. In Sikhism, there's no ascetic or monastic tradition ending the cycles of rebirth. Almost 2% of India's citizens are Sikhs, with most living in Punjab.

Born in present-day Pakistan, Guru Nanak (1469–1539) was largely dissatisfied with both Muslim and Hindu religious practices. He believed in family life and the value of hard work – he married, had two sons and worked as a farmer when not travelling around, preaching and singing self-composed *kirtan* (Sikh devotional songs) with his Muslim musician, Mardana. He is said to have performed miracles and he encouraged meditation on God's name as a prime path to enlightenment.

Nanak believed in equality centuries before it became socially fashionable and campaigned against the caste system. He was a practical guru, as in the principle of *kirat karni*: 'a person who makes an honest living and shares earnings with others recognises the way to God'. He appointed his most talented disciple, not one of his sons, to be his successor. His *kirtan* are still sung in gurdwaras (Sikh temples) today, and his picture is kept in millions of homes in and beyond the subcontinent.

Sikhs strive to follow the spiritual lead of the Khalsa, the five Sikh warriors anointed by Guru Gobind Singh as perfectly embodying the principles of the Sikh faith. Wearing a *dastar*, or turban, is mandatory for baptised Sikh men, and devout Sikhs uphold the 'Five Ks' – *kesh* (leaving

SPIRITUAL INDIA SIKHISM

RELIGIOUS ETIQUETTE

Whenever visiting a sacred site in India, dress and behave respectfully: don't wear shorts or sleeveless tops and refrain from smoking. Loud and intrusive behaviour isn't appreciated, and neither are public displays of affection or kidding around.

Before entering a holy place, remove your shoes (tip the shoe-minder a few rupees when retrieving them) and check if photography is allowed. You're permitted to wear socks in most places. Religious etiquette advises against touching locals on the head, or pointing the soles of your feet at a person, religious shrine or image of a deity. Protocol also advises against touching someone with your feet or touching a carving of a deity.

Head cover (for women and sometimes men) is required at some places of worship – especially gurdwaras (Sikh temples) and mosques – so carry a scarf. There are some sites that don't admit women and some that deny entry to nonadherents of their faith. Women may be required to sit apart from men. Jain temples request the removal of leather items you may be wearing or carrying and may also request that menstruating women not enter. When walking around any Buddhist sacred site go clockwise. Don't touch them with your left hand. Turn prayer wheels clockwise, with your right hand.

Taking photos inside a shrine, st a funeral ot religious ceremony, or of people taking a holy dip can be offensive. Flash photography may be prohibited in certain areas of a shrine, or may not be permitted at all.

Tibetan Buddhism's spiritual icon, the 14th Dalai Lama, resides in India, as does the 17th Karmapa (head of the Karma Kagyu sect).

hair uncut), *kanga* (carrying a wooden comb), *kara* (wearing an iron bracelet), *kacchera* (wearing cotton shorts) and *kirpan* (carrying a dagger or sword).

Buddhism

Despite its historical importance in India, less than 1% of the country's population is Buddhist today. Bodhgaya, in the state of Bihar, where Buddha achieved enlightenment, is one of Buddhism's most sacred sites, drawing pilgrims from across the world.

Scholars generally identify two predominant extant branches of Buddhism: Theravada (Doctrine of the Elders) and Mahayana (The Great Vehicle). Broadly speaking, followers of Theravada subscribe to the belief that attaining enlightenment – and thus liberating oneself from the cycle of birth and death – can be achieved by practising the Noble Eightfold Path (sometimes dubbed 'The Middle Way'). Theravada Buddhism focuses on the premise that self-effort is the path to enlightenment, with meditation playing a key role. Meanwhile, adherents of Mahayana believe Buddhahood (spiritual enlightenment as per Buddhist teachings)

INDIA'S BUDDHIST CIRCUIT

Northern Uttar Pradesh and Bihar are home to Buddhism's most sacred sites and thousands of Buddhists travel here every year to make a pilgrimage. This is the land where Buddha threw off his royal privilege, roamed as an ascetic, meditated for seven years, gained enlightenment, taught and set in motion the philosophy of Buddhism and its system.

There are several ways to visit the main sights. In terms of geography, it's easiest to come from Lumbini in Nepal, travel south to Kushinagar and Sarnath in Uttar Pradesh and then head east to Patna and Bodhgaya in Bihar.

In order of the events in Buddha's life, the major pilgrimage sites for Buddhists are:

Lumbini – Buddha's birthplace, just over the border in Nepal, though some remains from his royal kingdom of Kapilavastu are on the rival India site at Piprawha.

Bodhgaya (p525) – Buddha's enlightenment, underneath a bodhi tree; Dungeshwari Cave, where Buddha lived as an ascetic before renouncing his fast at nearby Sujata Stupa. There are dozens of monasteries here and several places to learn meditation.

Sarnath (p393) – Buddha's first sermon in the Deer Park, just outside Varanasi; a large stupa originally built by Emperor Ashoka and the famous lion-pillar capital that has become the symbol of India.

Kushinagar (p395) – Buddha's death, marked by a 5th-century statue of the reclining Buddha; see the stupa marking Buddha's cremation spot.

These sites boast dozens of modern monasteries built by Buddhist nations in their national architecture, many of which offer accommodation and are an attraction themselves.

Other significant places include the following sites in Bihar:

Vaishali (p522) – the remains of one of the stupas built to contain Buddha's ashes; there's also a stupa and Ashoka pillar marking the spot where Buddha spent several monsoons.

Rajgir (p529) – the cave where Buddha meditated and where the First Buddhist Council was held six months after his death.

Nalanda (p531) – the ruins of one of the ancient world's great universities.

Northern Bihar – Kesariya Stupa (p523), where the dying Buddha donated his begging bowl; Lauriya Nandangarh (p525), with a 2000-year-old stupa and nearby Ashoka pillar.

Many of the finest sculptures from these sites now reside in regional museums. The best are at Mathura (p410), Patna (p518) and Sarnath (p393). It was probably at Mathura (and Gandhara in modern-day Pakistan/Afghanistan) that the familiar image of the Buddha was developed for the first time.

can be attained via the bodhisattva path – a state in which one deliberately stays in the cycle of rebirth to help others achieve a state of awakening. Bodhisattvas are enlightened beings.

A sub-branch found in India is Tibetan Buddhism. Established in the 8th century AD, it incorporates teachings of Mahayana Buddhism as well as a range of rituals and spiritual practices (such as special mantras) derived from indigenous Tibetan religious beliefs such as the Bon religion. Supernatural beings are an important part of Tibetan Buddhism and come in the form of both benevolent and wrathful entities. India has notable Tibetan Buddhist communities, including Dharamsala (Himachal Pradesh), Tawang (Arunachal Pradesh), Rumtek (Sikkim) and Leh (Ladakh).

Buddhism emerged in the 6th century BC as a reaction against the strictures of Brahmanical Hinduism. Buddha (Awakened One) is believed to have lived from about 563 to 483 BC. Formerly a prince (Siddhartha Gautama) from the Nepali plains, Buddha, at the age of 29, embarked on a quest for emancipation from the world of suffering. He achieved nirvana (the state of full awareness) at Bodhgaya, aged 35. Critical of the caste system and the unthinking worship of gods, Buddha urged his disciples to seek truth within their own experiences.

Buddha taught that existence is based on Four Noble Truths: that life is rooted in suffering, that suffering is caused by craving, that one can find release from suffering by eliminating craving, and that the way to eliminate craving is by following the Noble Eightfold Path. This path consists of right understanding, right intention, right speech, right action, right livelihood, right effort, right awareness and right concentration. By successfully complying with these one can attain nirvana.

Buddhism had somewhat waned in parts of India by the turn of the 20th century. However, it saw a revival in the 1950s among intellectuals and Dalits who were disillusioned with the Hindu caste system, with nearly half a million people converting under the guidance of Dalit leader, BR Ambedkar. The number of followers has further increased with the influx of Tibetan refugees.

Jainism

Jainism arose in the 6th century BC as a reaction against the caste restraints and rituals of Hinduism. It was founded by Mahavira, a contemporary of Buddha.

Jains believe that liberation can be attained by achieving complete purity of the soul. Purity means shedding all *karman,* matter generated by one's actions that binds itself to the soul. By following various austerities (eg fasting and meditation), one can shed *karman* and purify the soul. Right conduct is essential, and fundamental to this is ahimsa (nonviolence) in thought and deed towards any living thing.

The religious disciplines of followers are less severe than for monks; some Jain monks go naked. The slightly less ascetic maintain a bare minimum of possessions, which include a broom to sweep the path before them to avoid stepping on any living creature, and a piece of cloth tied over their mouth to prevent the accidental inhalation of insects.

Today, around 0.4% of India's population is Jain, with the majority living in Gujarat and Mumbai. Some notable Jain holy sites include Sravanabelagola, Palitana, Ranakpur and the temples of Mt Abu.

Christianity

There are various theories circulating about Christ's link to the Indian subcontinent. Some, for instance, believe that Jesus spent his 'lost years' in India, while others say that Christianity came to South India with St Thomas the Apostle, who allegedly died in Chennai in the 1st century AD. However, many scholars attest that Christianity's arrival can

ANATOMY OF A GOMPA

Parts of India, such as Sikkim, Arunachal Pradesh, Himachal Pradesh and Ladakh, are known for their ornate, colourful gompas (Tibetan-style Buddhist monasteries). The focal point of a gompa is the *dukhang* (temple), where monks assemble to chant passages from the sacred scriptures; morning prayers are a particularly atmospheric time to visit gompas. The walls may be covered in vivid murals or *thangkas* (cloth paintings) of bodhisattvas (enlightened beings) and *dharmapalas* (protector deities). By the entrance to the *dukhang*, you'll usually find a mural depicting the Wheel of Life, a graphical representation of the core elements of Buddhist philosophy.

Most gompas hold *chaam* dances (ritual masked dances to celebrate the victory of good over evil) during major festivals. Dances to ward off evil feature masks of Mahakala, the Great Protector, usually dramatically adorned with a headdress of human skulls. The Durdag dance features skull masks depicting the Lords of the Cremation Grounds, while Shawa dancers wear masks of wild-eyed stags. These characters are often depicted with a third eye in the centre of their foreheads, signifying the need for inner reflection.

Another interesting activity at Buddhist monasteries is the production of butter sculptures, elaborate models made from coloured butter and dough. The sculptures are deliberately designed to decay, symbolising the impermanence of human existence. Many gompas also produce exquisite sand mandalas – geometric patterns made from sprinkled coloured sand, then destroyed to symbolise the futility of the physical plane.

be traced to around the 4th century, when a Syrian merchant, Thomas of Cana, set out for Kerala with around 400 families.

India's Christian community today stands at about 2.3% of the population, with the bulk residing in South India. Christianity is also widely practised in northeast India, with its origins believed to hark back to 1626, when two Jesuit missionaries visited this region. Today, the northeast has India's three Christian-majority states: 74.6% of the population are Christian in Meghalaya, 87% in Mizoram, and 88% in Nagaland. Manipur and Arunanchal Pradesh also have notable Christian communities at 41.3% and 30.3% respectively.

Catholicism established a strong presence in South India in the wake of Vasco da Gama's visit in 1498, and orders that have been active – if not always welcome – in the region include the Dominicans, Franciscans and Jesuits. Protestant missionaries are believed to have begun arriving – with a conversion agenda – from around the 18th century, particularly in India's tribal regions in the northeast.

Zoroastrianism

Zoroastrianism, founded by Zoroaster (Zarathustra), had its inception in Persia in the 6th century BC and is based on the concept of dualism, whereby good and evil are locked in a continuous battle. Zoroastrianism isn't quite monotheistic: good and evil entities coexist, although believers are urged to honour only the good. Both body and soul are united in this struggle of good versus evil. Although humanity is mortal, it has components that are timeless, such as the soul. On the day of judgement, the errant soul is not called to account for every misdemeanour – but a pleasant afterlife does depend on one's deeds, words and thoughts during earthly existence.

Zoroastrianism was eclipsed in Persia by the rise of Islam in the 7th century and its followers, many of whom openly resisted this, suffered persecution. Over the following centuries some immigrated to India, where they became known as Parsis. Historically, Parsis settled in Gujarat and became farmers; however, during British rule they moved into commerce, forming a prosperous community in Mumbai.

In recent decades the Parsi population has been spiralling downward; there are now believed to be less than 62,000 Parsis left in India, with most residing in Mumbai.

Delicious India

India's culinary terrain is deliciously diverse. From contemporary fusion dishes to traditional snacks, it's the sheer variety that makes eating your way through this country so rewarding. India has a particularly impressive array of vegetarian food, but carnivores won't be disappointed either, with plenty on offer – from hearty Mughal-inspired curries to succulent tandoori platters. Adding flair to the national smorgasbord are regional variations that make the most of locally sourced ingredients, be they native spices or fresh herbs.

A Culinary Carnival

India's culinary story is an ancient one, and the food you'll find here today reflects millennia of regional and global influences.

In fact, 'Indian food' is simply an umbrella term for a fantastically complex melting pot of regional cooking traditions, each different but all unified by a love of the spices that grow abundantly across the subcontinent. Every corner of the county has its own unique creations and its own unique cooking styles – Indian menus seen outside India are simply a collection of some of the best-known dishes.

Punjab is famous as the home of tandoori cooking, dhal makhani (black lentils and red kidney beans with cream and butter) and butter chicken, while Kerala is famed for its coconut-tinted curries and Bengal for its rich fish dishes. Mumbai is renowned for Persian-influenced Parsi food, while Lucknow and Hyderabad are legendary for meaty Mughal-inspired kebabs and biryani (steamed rice with meat or vegetables) dishes, and Gujarat serves some of India's most extravagant thalis (plate meals).

For most visitors, the easiest division to spot is between North Indian and South Indian cuisine. North Indian dishes are big on grilled meats, buttery sauces, rice and breads, while South Indian dishes are predominantly vegetarian, with lots of gram-flour-based fried snacks, and ferocious quantities of chilli.

Containing handy tips, including how to best store spices, Monisha Bharadwaj's *The Indian Spice Kitchen* is a terrific cookbook with more than 200 traditional recipes.

INDIAN-STYLE EATING

Traditionally, most people in India eat with their right hand. In the south, they use as much of the hand as is necessary, while elsewhere they use the tips of the fingers. The left hand is reserved for unsanitary actions such as removing shoes. You can use your left hand for holding drinks and serving yourself from a communal bowl, but it shouldn't be used for bringing food to your mouth. Before and after a meal, it's good manners to wash your hands.

Once your meal is served, mix the food with your fingers. If you are having dhal and *sabzi* (vegetables), only mix the dhal into your rice and have the *sabzi* in small scoops with each mouthful. If you are having fish or meat curry, mix the gravy into your rice. Scoop up lumps of the mix and, with your knuckles facing the dish, use your thumb to shovel the food into your mouth.

Land of Spices

Christopher Columbus was actually searching for the black pepper of Kerala's Malabar Coast when he stumbled upon America. The region still grows the finest quality of the world's favourite spice, and it's integral to most savoury Indian dishes.

Turmeric lends colour and flavour to the majority of Indian curries, but coriander seeds are the most widely used spice and add body to just about every dish. Indian 'wet' dishes – commonly known as curries in the West – usually begin with the crackle of cumin seeds in hot oil. Tamarind is sometimes known as the 'Indian date' and is a popular souring agent in the south. The green cardamom of Kerala's Western Ghats is commonly regarded as the world's best, and you'll find it in curries, desserts and warming chai (tea); the black variety stems from the northern hills. Saffron, the dried stigmas of crocus flowers grown in Kashmir, is so light it takes more than 1500 hand-plucked flowers to yield just one gram.

Spotlighting rice, *Finest Rice Recipes* by Sabina Sehgal Saikia shows just how versatile this humble grain is, with tempting creations such as rice-crusted crab cakes.

Fragrant Rice

Rice is a staple, especially in South India. Long-grain white-rice varieties are the most popular, served hot with just about any 'wet' cooked dish. From Assam's sticky rice in the far northeast to Kerala's red grains in the extreme south, you'll find countless regional varieties that locals will claim to be India's best, though this honour is usually conceded to basmati, a fragrant long-grain variety that is widely exported around the world. Rice is usually served after you have finished with the rotis (breads), often accompanied by curd to enrich the mix.

All Kinds of Bread

While rice is paramount in the south, wheat is the mainstay in the north. Roti, the generic term for Indian-style bread, is a name used interchangeably with chapati to describe the most common variety, an irresistible unleavened round bread made with whole-wheat flour and cooked on a *tawa* (hotplate). It may be smothered with ghee (clarified butter) or oil. In some places, rotis are bigger and thicker than chapatis and sometimes cooked in a tandoor oven. *Paratha* is a layered, pan-fried flatbread, which may also be stuffed, and makes for a hearty and popular breakfast. *Puri* – puffy fried-bread pillows – are another popular sauce soaker-upper. Naan is a larger, thicker bread, baked in a tandoor and usually eaten with meaty sauces or kebabs. In Punjab, look out for naan-like *kulcha*, flavoured with herbs and spices.

Thali means 'plate' in Hindi, and is the name of a complete meal, comprising a selection of dishes in small (usually metal) bowls served on a larger dish, plus roti, rice, chutneys and dessert. Unlimited thali means you get refills.

Dhal-icious!

The whole of India is united in its love for dhal (curried lentils or pulses). You may encounter up to 60 different pulses: the most common are *channa* (chickpeas); tiny yellow or green ovals called *moong* (mung beans); salmon-coloured *masoor* (red lentils); the ochre-coloured southern favourite, *tuvar* (yellow lentils; also known as *arhar*); *rajma* (kidney beans); *urad* (black gram or lentils); and *lobhia* (black-eyed peas).

DAIRY NATION

Milk and milk products make a huge contribution to Indian cuisine: *dahi* (curd/yoghurt) is commonly served with meals and is great for subduing heat; paneer is a godsend for the vegetarian majority; lassi is one in a host of nourishing sweet and savoury beverages; ghee is the traditional and pure cooking medium; and some of the finest *mithai* (Indian sweets) are made with milk.

SOUTHERN SPECIALITIES

Savoury dosas (also spelt dosai), a family of large, crispy, papery rice-flour crêpes, usually served with a bowl of hot *sambar* (soupy lentil dish) and another bowl of cooling coconut *chatni* (chutney), are a South Indian breakfast speciality that can be eaten at any time of day. The most popular is the masala dosa (stuffed with spiced potatoes), but there are also other fantastic dosa varieties: the *rava* dosa (batter made with semolina), the Mysuru dosa (like masala dosa but with more vegetables and chilli in the filling) and the *pessarettu* dosa (batter made with mung-bean dhal) from Andhra Pradesh. Nowadays, dosas are readily found in almost every corner of India, from Tamil Nadu to the Himalaya. Other southern treats to look for include *vada* (doughnut-shaped deep-fried lentil savoury) and *idli* (spongy, round, fermented rice cake), also served with *sambar* and *chatni*.

Meat Matters

Although India could well have more vegetarians than the rest of the world combined, it still has an extensive repertoire of excellent carnivorous fare. Chicken, lamb and mutton (sometimes actually goat) are the mainstays; religious taboos make beef forbidden to devout Hindus and pork to Muslims.

In northern India, you'll come across meat-dominated Mughlai cuisine, which includes rich curries, kebabs, koftas (meatballs) and biryanis. This spicy cuisine traces its history back to the (Islamic) Mughal empire that once reigned supreme. In the south, you'll find the meaty Chettinad cuisine of Tamil Nadu, which is beautifully spiced.

Tandoori meat dishes are another North Indian favourite, particularly in Punjab. The name is derived from the clay oven, or tandoor, in which the marinated meat is cooked. Also look out for the rich kebabs and biryanis of Awadhi (Lucknow) and Hyderabadi cuisine.

> Ghee is made by melting butter and removing the water and milk solids – ghee is the clear butter fat that remains. It's better for high-heat cooking than butter and keeps for longer.

Deep-Sea Delights

India has around 7500km of coastline, so it's no surprise that seafood is an important ingredient, especially on the west coast, from Mumbai down to Kerala. Kerala is the biggest fishing state, while Goa boasts particularly succulent prawns and fiery fish curries, and the fishing communities of the Konkan Coast – sandwiched between Goa and Mumbai – are renowned for their seafood recipes. Few main meals in Odisha (Orissa) exclude fish, and in West Bengal, puddled with ponds and lakes, fish is king. The far-flung Andaman Islands also won't disappoint seafood lovers, with the day's catch featuring on many menus.

Nature's Table

Vegetables are usually served at each main meal across India, and *sabzi* (vegetables) is a word recognised in every Indian vernacular. They're generally cooked *sukhi* (dry) or *tari* (in a sauce), and within these two categories they can be fried, roasted, curried, stuffed, baked, mashed and combined (made into koftas) or dipped in chickpea-flour batter to make a deep-fried *pakora* (fritter).

Potatoes are ubiquitous and popularly cooked with various masalas (spice mixes), with other vegetables, or mashed and fried for the street snack *aloo tikki* (mashed-potato patty). Onions are fried with other vegetables, ground into a paste for cooking with meats, and served raw as relishes, but are avoided by Jains. Heads of cauliflower are usually cooked dry on their own, with potatoes to make *aloo gobi* (potato-and-cauliflower curry), or with other vegetables such as carrots and beans. Fresh green peas turn up stir-fried with other vegetables in pilaus and biryanis and in one of North India's signature dishes, the magnificent *mattar paneer*

> Technically speaking, there's no such thing as an Indian 'curry' – the word, an Anglicised derivative of the Tamil word *kari* (sauce), was used by the British as a term for any spiced dish.

PAAN

Meals are often rounded off with *paan,* a fragrant mixture of betel nut (also called areca nut), lime paste, spices and condiments wrapped in an edible, silky *paan* leaf. Peddled by *paan*-wallahs, who are usually strategically positioned outside busy restaurants, *paan* is eaten as a digestive and mouth-freshener. The betel nut is mildly narcotic and some aficionados eat *paan* the same way heavy smokers consume cigarettes – over the years these people's teeth can become rotted red and black. Usually the gloopy red juice is spat out.

There are two basic types of *paan: mitha* (sweet) and *saadha* (with tobacco, which has similar health risks to other forms of tobacco use). A parcel of *mitha paan* is a splendid way to finish a meal. Pop the whole parcel in your mouth and chew slowly, allowing the juices to ooooooooze.

The Anger of Aubergines: Stories of Women and Food by Bulbul Sharma is an amusing culinary analysis of social relationships interspersed with enticing recipes.

(unfermented cheese and pea curry). *Baigan* (eggplant/aubergine) can be curried or sliced and deep-fried. Also popular is *saag* (a generic term for leafy greens), which can include mustard, spinach and fenugreek. Something a little more unusual is the bumpy-skinned *karela* (bitter gourd), which, like the delectable *bhindi* (okra), is commonly prepared dry with spices.

India's fruit basket is also bountiful. Along the southern coast are superluscious tropical fruits such as pineapples and papayas. Mangoes abound during summer (especially April and May), with India offering more than 500 varieties – the pick of the juicy bunch is the sweet Alphonso. Citrus fruit, such as oranges (often yellow-green in India), tangerines, pink and white grapefruits, kumquats and sweet limes, are widely grown. Himachal Pradesh produces crisp apples in autumn, while plump strawberries are especially good in Kashmir during summer. You'll find fruit inventively fashioned into a *chatni* (chutney) or pickle, and flavouring lassi, *kulfi* (flavoured firm-textured ice cream) and other sweet treats.

Pickles, Chutneys & Relishes

Pickles, chutneys and relishes are accompaniments that add extra zing to meals. A relish can be anything from a tiny pickled onion to a delicately crafted fusion of fruit, nuts and spices. One of the most popular side dishes is yoghurt-based raita, which makes a tongue-cooling counter to spicy food. *Chatnis* come in any number of varieties (sweet or savoury) and can be made from many different vegetables, fruits, herbs and spices.

Sweet Treats

India has a wildly colourful kaleidoscope of often-sticky and squishy *mithai* (Indian sweets), most of them supersugary. The main categories are *barfi* (a fudge-like milk-based sweet), soft *halwa* (made with vegetables, cereals, lentils, nuts or fruit), *ladoos* (sweet balls made with gram flour and semolina), and those made from *chhana* (unpressed paneer), such as *rasgullas*. There are also simpler – but equally scrumptious – offerings such as crunchy *jalebis* (coils of deep-fried batter dunked in sugar syrup; served hot) that you'll see all over the country.

The Book of Indian Sweets by Satarupa Banerjee contains a jolly jumble of regional sweet treats from Bengali rasgullas (cream-cheese balls flavoured with rose water) to Goan bebinca (sweet made from layers of sweet pancake).

Kheer (called *payasam* in the south) is one of the most popular after-meal desserts. It's a creamy rice pudding with a light, delicate flavour, enhanced with cardamom, saffron, pistachios, flaked almonds, chopped cashews or slivered dried fruit. Other favourites include hot *gulab jamuns* (deep-fried dough soaked in a rose-flavoured syrup) and refreshing *kulfi*. Each year, an estimated 15 tonnes of pure silver is converted into the edible foil that decorates many Indian sweets, especially during the Diwali festival.

Spiritual Sustenance

For many in India, food is considered just as critical for fine-tuning the spirit as it is for sustaining the body. Broadly speaking, Hindus traditionally avoid foods that are thought to inhibit physical and spiritual development, although there are few hard-and-fast rules. The taboo on eating beef (the cow is holy to Hindus) is the most rigid restriction.

Jains avoid foods such as garlic and onions, which, apart from harming insects in the ground when extracted, are thought to heat the blood and arouse sexual desire. You may come across vegetarian restaurants that make a point of advertising the absence of onion and garlic in their dishes for this reason. Devout Hindus may also avoid garlic and onions and these items may be banned from ashrams too.

Some foods, such as dairy products, are considered innately pure and are eaten to cleanse the body, mind and spirit. Ayurveda, the ancient science of life, health and longevity, also influences food customs.

Pork is taboo for Muslims and stimulants such as alcohol are avoided by the most devout. Halal is the term for all permitted foods, and *haram* for those prohibited. Fasting is considered an opportunity to earn the approval of Allah, to wipe the sin-slate clean and to understand the suffering of the poor.

Buddhists subscribe to the philosophy of ahimsa (nonviolence) and are mostly vegetarian. Jainism's central tenet is strict vegetarianism, and rigid restrictions are in place to avoid injury to any living creature. Vegetables that grow underground are considered *ananthkay* – one body containing many lives – and most Jains will avoid eating them because of the potential harm caused to insects during cultivation and harvesting.

India's Sikh, Christian and Parsi communities have few restrictions on what they can eat. At most Indian temples, blessed food known as *prasad* – often small sweets – is offered to devotees, but it isn't always hygienic to partake.

Where to Eat

You can eat well in India everywhere from ramshackle street *dhabas* (casual eateries, serving snacks and basic meals) and *bhojnalayas* (canteens serving vegetarian dishes and sweets) to plush five-star hotels and restaurants. Most midrange restaurants serve a few basic genres: South Indian (which usually means the vegetarian food of Tamil Nadu and Karnataka), North Indian (which largely comprises Punjabi/Mughlai fare) and possibly Indian interpretations of Chinese dishes. You'll also find the cuisines of neighbouring regions and states. Indians frequently migrate in search of work and these restaurants cater to the large communities seeking the familiar tastes of home.

Not to be confused with burger joints and pizzerias, restaurants in the south advertising 'fast food' are some of India's best. They serve the whole gamut of tiffin (snack) items and often have separate sweet counters. Many upmarket hotels have outstanding restaurants, usually with pan-Indian menus so you can explore various regional cuisines. Meanwhile, the independent restaurant dining scene keeps mushrooming in India's larger cities, with every kind of cuisine available, from Mexican and Mediterranean to Japanese and Korean.

Dhabas are oases to millions of truck drivers, bus passengers and sundry travellers going anywhere by road. The original *dhabas* dot the North Indian landscape, but you'll find versions of them throughout the country. The rough-and-ready but satisfying food served in these happy-go-lucky shacks has become a genre of its own, known as '*dhaba* food'.

The *Penguin Food Guide to India* by Charmaine O'Brien evocatively explores multiple regional cuisines from Goa to Uttarakhand.

Food that is first offered to deities at temples then shared among devotees is known as *prasad*. Indian sweets are the most common form of this holy offering.

DELICIOUS INDIA SPIRITUAL SUSTENANCE

STREET-FOOD TIPS

Tucking into street eats is a highlight of travelling in India. To help stave off tummy troubles, follow these tips:

➡ Give yourself a few days to adjust to the local cuisine, especially if you're unaccustomed to spicy food.

➡ If locals are avoiding a particular vendor, you probably should too. Any place popular with families is likely to be your safest bet.

➡ You may like to check how and where the vendor is cleaning the utensils, and how and where the food is covered. If the vendor is cooking in oil, take a peek to check it's clean. If the pots or surfaces are dirty, there are food scraps about or too many buzzing flies, don't be shy to make a hasty retreat.

➡ Don't be put off when you order some deep-fried snack and the cook throws it back into the wok. It's common practice to partly cook the snacks first and then finish them off once they've been ordered. Frying them hot again kills germs.

➡ Unless a place is reputable (and busy), it's advisable to avoid eating meat from the street.

➡ The hygiene standard at juice stalls varies, so exercise caution. Have the vendor press the juice in front of you and steer clear of anything stored in a jug or served in a glass (unless you're confident about the washing standards).

➡ Don't be tempted by glistening presliced melon and other fruit, which keeps its luscious veneer with regular dousing of often-unfiltered water.

Street Food

Whatever the time of day, street-food vendors are frying, boiling, roasting, peeling, simmering, mixing, juicing or baking different types of food and drink to lure peckish passers-by. Small operations usually have one special that they serve all day, while other vendors have different dishes for breakfast, lunch and dinner. The fare varies as you venture between neighbourhoods, towns and regions; it can be as simple as puffed rice or peanuts roasted in hot sand, or as complex as the riot of different flavours known as *chaat* (savoury snack). Fabulous cavalcades of taste include *chole bhature* (puffed bread served with spicy chickpeas and dipped in fragrant sauce) in North India; *aloo tikki* (spicy fried potato patties), which are renowned in Lucknow; *gol gappa/Panipuri/gup chup* (puffed spheres of bread with a spicy filling), all over India; and *idli sambar* (rice patties served with delectable sauce and chutney) in Chennai and the south.

Got the munchies? Grab *Street Foods of India* by Vimla and Deb Kumar Mukerji, which has recipes of much-loved Indian snacks, from samosas and *bhelpuri* (thin fried rounds of dough with rice, lentils, lemon juice, onion, herbs and chutney) to *jalebis* (orange-coloured coils of deep-fried batter dunked in sugar syrup; served hot) and *kulfi* (ice cream).

Vegetarians & Vegans

India excels when it comes to vegetarian fare. There's little understanding of veganism (the term 'pure vegetarian' means without eggs), and animal products such as milk, butter, ghee and curd are included in most Indian dishes. If you are vegan, your first problem is likely to be getting the cook to understand your requirements, though big hotels and larger cities are getting better at catering for vegans.

Cooking Classes

You might find yourself so inspired by Indian food that you'll want to take home a little Indian kitchen know-how, via a cooking course. Courses are most prevalent in tourist areas such as Goa, Rajasthan and Kerala. Some courses are professionally run, others are informal. Most require at least a few days' advance notice.

When to Eat

Three main meals a day is the norm in India. Breakfast is usually fairly light, traditionally *idli* (South Indian spongy fermented rice cake) and *sambar* (soupy lentil dish) in the south, and *parathas* in the north. Lunch can be substantial (perhaps an all-you-can-eat thali) or light, especially for time-strapped office workers. Dinner is usually the main meal of the day. It's generally comprised of a few different preparations – several curried vegetables (maybe also meat) dishes and dhal, accompanied by rice and/ or chapatis. Dishes are served all at once rather than as courses. Desserts are optional and most prevalent during festivals or other special occasions. Fruit may wrap up a meal. In many Indian homes, dinner can be a rather late affair (post-9pm) depending on personal preference and the season (eg late dinners during the warmer months). Restaurants usually spring to life after 9pm in the cities, but in smaller towns they're busy earlier.

Drinks Anyone?

Gujarat, Bihar, Nagaland and Lakshadweep are India's only dry states, though Kerala and other states have toyed with prohibition. There are drinking laws in place all over the country and each state may have regular dry days, when the sale of alcohol from liquor shops is banned. On Gandhi's birthday (2 October) alcohol restrictions widely apply. In Goa, alcohol taxes are lower and the drinking culture less restricted.

You'll find excellent watering holes in most big cities, especially Mumbai, Bengaluru (Bangalore; the craft-beer capital of India), Kolkata and Delhi, which are usually at their liveliest on weekends. The more upmarket bars serve an impressive selection of domestic and imported drinks, as well as draught beer. Many bars turn into music-thumping nightclubs anytime after 8pm, although there are quiet lounge-bars to be found in most large cities. In smaller towns, the bar scene can be a seedy, male-dominated affair – not the kind of place female travellers should venture into alone.

Wine drinking is steadily on the rise, despite the domestic wine-producing industry still being relatively new. The favourable climate and soil conditions in certain areas – such as parts of Maharashtra and Karnataka – have spawned some decent Indian wineries, such as those of the Grover and Sula Vineyards.

Stringent licensing laws and religious restrictions mean some restaurants won't serve alcohol. Places that depend on the tourist rupee may covertly serve you beer in teapots and disguised glasses – however, don't assume anything, at the risk of causing offence.

Very few vegetarian restaurants serve alcohol.

Local Spirits

An estimated three-quarters of India's drinking population quaffs 'country liquor', such as the notorious arak (liquor distilled from coconut-palm

---

For India-wide restaurant reviews and recommendations, one popular option is Zomato (zomato.com/ india), covering everywhere from Mumbai and Manali to Delhi and Darjeeling.

DELICIOUS INDIA WHEN TO EAT

Indian Recipes Online

Recipes Indian (www.recipes indian.com)

India Food Recipes (www.thokalath. com/cuisine)

Indian Food Forever (www.indian foodforever.com)

RAILWAY SNACK ATTACK

One of the thrills of travelling by rail in India is the culinary circus that greets you at almost every station. Roving vendors accost arriving trains, yelling and scampering up and down the carriages; fruit, *namkin* (savoury nibbles), omelettes, nuts and sweets are offered through the grills on the windows; and platform cooks try to lure you from the train with the sizzle of spicy goodies such as samosas. Frequent rail travellers know which station is famous for which food item: Lonavla station in Maharashtra is known for *chikki* (rock-hard toffee-like confectionery), Agra for *peitha* (square sweet made from pumpkin and glucose, usually flavoured with rose water, coconut or saffron) and Dhaund near Delhi for biryani.

Vegan Richa's Indian Kitchen: Traditional and Creative Recipes for the Home Cook by Richa Hingle has everything from tongue-tingling tempeh to cool saffron ice lollies.

sap, potatoes or rice) of the south. This is widely known as the poor-man's drink and millions are addicted to the stuff. Each year, many people are blinded or even killed by the methyl alcohol in illegal arak.

An interesting local drink is a clear spirit with a heady pungent flavour called *mahuwa,* distilled from the flower of the *mahuwa* tree. It's brewed in makeshift village stalls all over central India during March and April, when the trees bloom. *Mahuwa* is safe to drink as long as it comes from a trustworthy source. There have been cases of people being blinded after drinking *mahuwa* adulterated with methyl alcohol.

Rice beer is brewed all over east and northeast India, while in the Himalaya you'll find *tongba,* a warm beer prepared from millet, and a strong grain alcohol called *raksi,* which has a mild charcoal flavour and tastes vaguely like Scotch whisky.

Toddy, the sap from the palm tree, is drunk in coastal areas, especially Kerala, while feni is the primo Indian spirit, and the preserve of laid-back Goa. Coconut feni is light and rather unexceptional, but the more popular cashew feni – made from the fruit of the cashew tree – is worth a try.

Meanwhile, if you fancy sipping booze of the blue-blood ilk, traditional royal liqueurs of Rajasthan (once reserved for private consumption among nobility) are sold at some city liquor shops, especially in Delhi and Jaipur. Ingredients range from aniseed, cardamom and saffron to rose, dates and mint.

Non-Alcoholic Beverages

Chai (tea), the much-loved drink of the masses, is known for its generous use of milk and sugar. A glass of steaming, frothy chai is the perfect antidote to the vicissitudes of life on the Indian road; the disembodied voice droning '*garam* chai, *garam* chai' (hot tea, hot tea) is likely to become one of the most familiar and welcome sounds of your trip. Masala chai adds cardamom, ginger and other spices.

While chai is the traditional choice of most of the nation, South Indians have long shared their loyalty with coffee. In recent years the number of coffee-drinking North Indians has skyrocketed, with ever-multiplying branches of coffee chains and boutique cafes.

The subcontinent's wine industry is an ever-evolving one – take a cyber-sip of Indian wine at www.indianwines. info. Prime winemaking regions are found in the states of Maharashtra and Karnataka.

Masala soda is the quintessential Indian soft drink. It's a freshly opened bottle of fizzy soda, pepped up with lime, spices, salt and sugar. You can also opt for a plainer lime soda, which is soda with fresh lime, served sweet (with sugar) or salted as you prefer. Also refreshing is *jal jeera,* made of lime juice, cumin, mint and rock salt. Sweet and savoury lassi, a yoghurt-based drink, is especially popular nationwide and is another wonderfully cooling beverage.

Falooda is a rose-flavoured drink made with milk, cream, nuts and strands of vermicelli, while *badam* milk (served hot or cold) is flavoured with almonds and saffron.

Menu Decoder

achar	pickle
aloo	potato; also *alu*
aloo tikki	mashed-potato patty
appam	South Indian rice pancake
arak	liquor distilled from coconut milk, potatoes or rice
baigan	eggplant/aubergine; also known as brinjal
barfi	fudge-like sweet made from milk
bebinca	Goan 16-layer cake

besan	chickpea flour
betel	nut of the betel tree; also called areca nut
bhajia	vegetable fritters
bhang lassi	blend of lassi and bhang (a derivative of marijuana)
bhelpuri	thin fried rounds of dough with rice, lentils, lemon juice, onion, herbs and chutney
bhindi	okra
biryani	fragrant spiced steamed rice with meat or vegetables
bonda	mashed-potato patty
chaat	savoury snack, may be seasoned with chaat masala
chach	buttermilk beverage
chai	tea
channa	spiced chickpeas
chapati	round unleavened Indian-style bread; also known as roti
chawal	rice
cheiku	small, sweet brown fruit
dahi	curd/yoghurt
dhal	spiced lentil dish
dhal makhani	black lentils and red kidney beans with cream and butter
dhansak	Parsi dish; meat, usually chicken or lamb, with curried lentils, pumpkin or gourd, and rice
dosa	large South Indian savoury crêpe
falooda	rose-flavoured drink made with milk, cream, nuts and vermicelli
faluda	long chickpea-flour noodles
feni	Goan liquor distilled from coconut milk or cashews
ghee	clarified butter
gobi	cauliflower
gulab jamun	deep-fried balls of dough soaked in rose-flavoured syrup
halwa	soft sweet made with vegetables, lentils, nuts or fruit
idli	South Indian spongy, round, fermented rice cake
imli	tamarind
jaggery	hard, brown, sugar-like sweetener made from palm sap
jalebi	orange-coloured coils of deep-fried batter dunked in sugar syrup; served hot
karela	bitter gourd
keema	spiced minced meat
kheer	creamy rice pudding
khichdi	blend of lightly spiced rice and lentils; also *khichri*
kofta	minced vegetables or meat; often ball-shaped
korma	curry-like braised dish
kulcha	soft leavened Indian-style bread
kulfi	flavoured (often with pistachio) firm-textured ice cream
ladoo	sweet ball made with gram flour and semolina; also *ladu*
lassi	yoghurt-and-iced-water drink
malai kofta	paneer cooked in a creamy sauce of cashews and tomato
masala dosa	large South Indian savoury crêpe (dosa) stuffed with spiced potatoes

mattar paneer	unfermented cheese and pea curry
methi	fenugreek
mishti doi	Bengali sweet; curd sweetened with jaggery
mithai	Indian sweets
momo	savoury Tibetan dumpling
naan	tandoor-cooked flat bread
namak	salt
namkin	savoury nibbles
noon chai	salt tea (Kashmir)
pakora	bite-sized vegetable pieces in batter
palak paneer	unfermented cheese chunks in a puréed spinach gravy
paneer	soft, unfermented cheese made from milk curd
pani	water
pappadam	thin, crispy lentil or chickpea-flour circle-shaped wafer; also pappad
paratha/ parantha	flaky flatbread (thicker than chapati); often stuffed
phulka	a chapati that puffs up on an open flame
pilau	rice cooked in spiced stock; also pulau, pilao or pilaf
pudina	mint
puri	flat savoury dough that puffs up when deep-fried; also *poori*
raita	mildly spiced yoghurt, often containing shredded cucumber or diced pineapple
rasam	dhal-based broth flavoured with tamarind
rasgulla	cream-cheese balls flavoured with rose water
rogan josh	rich, spicy lamb curry
saag	leafy greens
sabzi	vegetables
sambar	South Indian soupy lentil dish with cubed vegetables
samosa	deep-fried pastry triangles filled with spiced vegetables (sometimes meat)
sonf	aniseed; used as a digestive and mouth-freshener; also *saunf*
tandoor	clay oven
tawa	flat hotplate/iron griddle
thali	all-you-can-eat meal; stainless steel (sometimes silver) compartmentalised plate
thukpa	Tibetan noodle soup
tiffin	snack; also refers to meal container often made of stainless steel
tikka	spiced, often marinated, chunks of chicken, paneer etc
toddy	alcoholic drink, tapped from palm trees
tsampa	Tibetan staple of roast-barley flour
upma	*rava* (semolina) cooked with onions, spices, chilli peppers and coconut
uttapam	thick savoury South Indian rice pancake with finely chopped onions, green chillies, coriander and coconut
vada	South Indian doughnut-shaped deep-fried lentil savoury
vindaloo	Goan dish; fiery curry in a marinade of vinegar and garlic
wazwan	traditional Kashmiri banquet

The Great Indian Bazaar

India's lively bazaars offer a treasure trove of goodies, from fabulously patterned textiles and silver ornaments to finely crafted woodwork and gemstone jewellery. There's an eclectic mix of village creations, with most regions having their own customs, some of them ancient. Indeed, village handicrafts are not only beautiful, they also provide employment at grass-roots level and encourage traditional manufacturing practices to prosper. Note that there is a ban (p1199) on the export of some antiques to help preserve the country's heritage.

Bronze Figures, Pottery, Stone Carving & Terracotta

In southern India and parts of the Himalaya, small images of deities are created by the age-old lost-wax process. A wax figure is made, a mould is formed around it, and the wax is melted, poured out and replaced with molten metal; the mould is then broken open to reveal the figure inside. Figures of Shiva as dancing Nataraja tend to be the most popular, but you can also find images of Buddha and numerous deities from the Hindu pantheon.

The West Bengalese also employ the lost-wax process to make Dokra tribal bell sculptures, while in Chhattisgarh's Bastar region, the Ghadwa Tribe has an interesting twist on the process: a fine wax thread covers the metal mould, leaving a latticelike design on the final product.

In Buddhist areas, you'll come across striking bronze statues of Buddha and the Tantric deities, finished off with exquisitely polished and painted faces.

In Mamallapuram (Mahabalipuram; Tamil Nadu), craftspeople using local granite and soapstone have revived the ancient artistry of the Pallava sculptors; souvenirs range from tiny stone elephants to enormous deity statues weighing half a tonne. Tamil Nadu is also known for bronzeware from Thanjavur and Trichy (Tiruchirappalli).

A number of places produce attractive terracotta items, ranging from bowls and decorative flowerpots to children's toys and images of deities. Outside temples across India you can often buy small clay or plaster effigies of Hindu deities.

Throughout India you can find finely crafted gold and silver rings, anklets, earrings, toe rings, necklaces and bangles, and pieces can often be made to order.

Carpets Carpets Carpets!

Carpet-making is a living craft in India, with workshops throughout producing top-notch wool and silk pieces. The finest carpets are produced in Kashmir, Ladakh, Himachal Pradesh, Sikkim and West Bengal, while you can find reproductions of tribal Turkmen and Afghan designs in states such as Uttar Pradesh. Carpet-making is also a major revenue earner for Tibetan refugees; most refugee settlements have cooperative carpet workshops. Antique carpets usually aren't antique – unless you buy from an internationally reputable dealer; stick to 'new' carpets.

The lost-wax technique for casting bronze has been used in the Indian subcontinent since at least 2500 BC, according to finds from Mohenjo-daro in modern-day Pakistan.

Cuttack in Odisha (Orissa) is famed for its lacelike silver-filigree ornaments known as *tarakasi*. A silver framework is made and then filled in with delicate curls and ribbons of silver.

In both Kashmir and Rajasthan, you'll find coarsely woven woollen *numdas* (or *namdas*), which are much cheaper than knotted carpets. Various regions manufacture flat-weave *dhurries* (kilim-like cotton rugs), including Kashmir, Himachal Pradesh, Rajasthan and Uttar Pradesh. Kashmiris also produce striking *gabbas* (rugs with appliqué), made from chain-stitched wool or silk.

Children have been employed as carpet weavers in the subcontinent for centuries. Child labour maintains a cycle of poverty, by driving down adult wages, reducing adult work opportunities and, importantly, depriving children of their education. The carpets produced by Tibetan refugee cooperatives are almost always made by adults; government emporiums and charitable cooperatives are usually the best places to buy.

Costs & Postage

The price of a carpet is determined by the number and the size of the hand-tied knots, the range of dyes and colours, the intricacy of the design and the material. Silk carpets cost more and look more luxurious, but wool carpets usually last longer. Expect to pay upwards of US$250 for a good-quality 90cm-by-1.5m (or 90cm by 1.8m, depending on the region) wool carpet, and around US$2000 for a similar-sized carpet in silk. Tibetan carpets are cheaper, reflecting the relative simplicity of the designs; many refugee cooperatives sell the same size for around US$100.

Some people buy carpets thinking that they can be sold for a profit back home, but unless you really know your carpets, you're better off just buying a carpet because you love it. Many places can ship carpets home for a fee – although it may be safest to send things independently to avoid scams – or you can carry them in the plane's hold (allow 5kg to 10kg of your baggage allowance for a 90cm-by-1.5m carpet, and check that your airline allows outsized baggage). Shipping to Europe for a carpet of this size costs around ₹4000.

Jewellery

Virtually every town in India has at least one bangle shop selling a wide variety, ranging from colourful plastic and glass to brass and silver.

Heavy folk-art silver jewellery can be bought in various parts of the country, particularly Rajasthan; Jaipur, Udaipur and Pushkar are good places to find silver jewellery pitched at foreign tastes. Jaipur is also renowned for its precious and semiprecious gems (and its gem scams). Chunky Tibetan jewellery made from silver (or white metal) and semiprecious stones is sold all over India. Many pieces feature Buddhist motifs and text in Tibetan script, including the famous mantra *Om Mani*

PUTTING YOUR MONEY WHERE IT COUNTS

Overall, a comparatively small proportion of the money brought to India by tourism is believed to reach people in rural areas. Travellers can make a greater contribution by shopping at community cooperatives set up to protect and promote traditional cottage industries and provide education, training and a sustainable livelihood at the grass-roots level. Many of these projects focus on refugees, low-caste women, tribal people and others living on society's fringes.

The quality of products sold at cooperatives is high and the prices are usually fixed, which means you won't have to haggle. A share of the sales revenue is channelled directly into social projects, such as schools, healthcare, training and advocacy programs for socially disadvantaged groups. Shopping at the national network of Khadi and Village Industries Commission emporiums will also contribute to rural communities.

Wherever you travel, keep your eyes peeled for fair-trade cooperatives.

Padme Hum (Hail to the Jewel in the Lotus). Some of the pieces sold in Tibetan centres, such as McLeod Ganj and Leh, are genuine antiques, but there's a huge industry in India, Nepal and China making artificially aged souvenirs. For creative types, loose beads of agate, turquoise, carnelian and silver are widely available. Buddhist meditation beaded strings made of gems or wood also make nice souvenirs.

Pearls are produced by most Indian seaside states, but they're a speciality of Hyderabad. You'll find them at most state emporiums across the country. Prices vary depending on the colour and shape: you pay more for pure white pearls or rare colours such as black, and perfectly round pearls are generally more expensive than misshapen or elongated pearls. A single strand of seeded pearls can cost as little as ₹600, but better-quality pearls are upwards of ₹1500.

Leatherwork

As cows are sacred in India, leatherwork is made from buffaloes, camels, goats or some other animal skin. Kanpur in Uttar Pradesh is the country's major leatherwork centre.

Most large cities offer a smart range of modern leather footwear at very reasonable prices, some stitched with zillions of sparkly sequins. The states of Punjab and Rajasthan (especially its capital, Jaipur) are famed for *jootis* (traditional, usually pointy toed slip-on shoes). *Chappals,* wonderful (often curly toed) leather sandals, are sold throughout India, but are especially good in the Maharashtrian cities of Kolhapur, Pune and Matheran.

In Bikaner (Rajasthan), artisans decorate camel hide with gold to produce lovely mirror frames, boxes and bottles, while in Indore (Madhya Pradesh), craftspeople stretch leather over wire-and-cloth frameworks to make toy animals.

Metal & Marble

You'll find copper and brassware throughout India – candleholders, trays, bowls, tankards, figurines and ashtrays are popular buys. In Rajasthan and Uttar Pradesh, the brass is often inlaid with exquisite designs in red, green and blue enamel.

Many Tibetan religious objects are created by inlaying silver in copper; prayer wheels, ceremonial horns and traditional document cases are all relatively inexpensive. Resist the urge to buy *kangling* (Tibetan horns) and *kapala* (ceremonial bowls) said to be made from inlaid human leg bones and skulls – they are illegal.

In all towns you can find *kadhai* (Indian woks, also known as *balti*) and other cookware for low prices. Beaten-brass pots are particularly attractive, while steel storage vessels, copper-bottomed cooking pans and steel thali trays are also popular souvenirs.

The people of Bastar in Chhattisgarh use an iron-smelting technique similar to the one discovered 35,000 years ago to create abstract sculptures of spindly animal and human figures. These are often also made into functional items such as lamp stands and coat racks.

A sizeable cottage industry has sprung up in Agra reproducing the ancient Mughal art form of pietra dura (inlaying marble with semiprecious stones).

Musical Instruments

The best range of Indian musical instruments is available in the larger cities, particularly Kolkata, Varanasi and Delhi. Prices vary according to the workmanship, degree of ornamentation and sound quality of the instrument.

Bidri, a method of damascening where silver wire is inlaid in gunmetal (a zinc alloy) and rubbed with soil from Bidar, Karnataka, is used to make jewellery, boxes and ornaments.

In Andhra Pradesh, intricately drawn, graphic cloth paintings called *kalamkari* depict deities and historic events. A centre for this ancient art is Sri Kalahasti.

Decent tabla sets (paired Indian-style drums), with a wooden tabla (tuned treble drum) and metal *dugi* or *bayan* (bass-tone drums), cost upwards of ₹5000. Cheaper sets are generally heavier and often sound inferior.

Sitars range anywhere from around ₹5000 to ₹25,000 (sometimes even more). The sound of each sitar will vary with the wood used and the shape of the gourd, so try a few. Note that some cheaper sitars can warp in colder or hotter climates. On any sitar, make sure the strings ring clearly and check the gourd carefully for damage. Spare string sets, sitar plectrums and a screw-in 'amplifier' gourd are sensible additions.

Other popular instruments include the *shehnai* (Indian flute), *sarod* (like an Indian lute), harmonium and *esraj* (similar to an upright violin). Conventional violins are good value – prices start at around ₹3500, while Kolkata is known for its quality acoustic guitars (from ₹3000).

Paintings

India is a major centre of contemporary art, and its larger cities are well stocked with independent galleries. Delhi, Mumbai, Bengaluru (Bangalore) and Kolkata are among the best places to look for shops and galleries selling contemporary paintings by local artists.

Miniatures

Reproductions of Indian miniature paintings are widely available, but the quality varies: the cheaper examples have less detail and are made with inferior materials. Udaipur and Bikaner in Rajasthan have a particularly good range of shops specialising in modern reproductions on paper and silk, or you can browse Delhi's numerous state emporiums.

In regions such as Kerala and Tamil Nadu, you'll come across miniature paintings on leaf skeletons that portray domestic life, rural scenes and deities.

Folk Art

In Andhra Pradesh, *cheriyal* paintings, in bright, primary colours, were originally made as scrolls for travelling storytellers.

The artists' community of Raghurajpur near Puri (Odisha) preserves the age-old art of *patachitra* (cloth) painting. Cotton or tassar (silk cloth) is covered with a mixture of gum and chalk; it's then polished, and images of deities and scenes from Hindu legends are painted on with exceedingly fine brushes. Odisha also produces *chitra pothi,* where images are etched onto dried palm-leaf sections with a fine stylus.

GANDHI'S CLOTH

More than 80 years ago, Mahatma Gandhi urged Indians to support the freedom movement by ditching their foreign-made clothing and turning to *khadi* – homespun cloth. *Khadi* became a symbol of Indian independence, and the fabric is still associated with politics. The government-run, nonprofit group Khadi and Village Industries Commission (www.kvic.org.in) serves to promote *khadi*, which is usually cotton, but can also be silk or wool.

Khadi outlets are simple, no-nonsense places, where you can pick up genuine Indian clothing such as kurta pyjamas (long shirt and loose-fitting trousers), scarves, saris and, at some branches, assorted handicrafts – you'll find them all over India. Prices are reasonable and are often discounted in the period around Gandhi's birthday (2 October). A number of outlets also have a tailoring service.

Bihar's unique folk art is Mithila (or Madhubani) painting, an ancient art form preserved by the women of Madhubani. These captivating paintings are most easily found in Patna, but are also sold in big city emporiums.

Thangkas

Superb *thangkas* (rectangular Tibetan paintings on cloth) of Tantric Buddhist deities and ceremonial mandalas are widely sold in Tibetan Buddhist areas, including Sikkim, parts of Himachal Pradesh and Ladakh. Some perfectly reproduce the glory of the murals in India's medieval gompas (Tibetan Buddhist monasteries); others are simpler. Prices vary, but bank on at least ₹4000 for a decent-quality *thangka* of A3 size, and a lot more (up to around ₹50,000) for large intricate *thangkas*. The selling of antique *thangkas* is illegal, and you would be unlikely to find the real thing anyway.

Textiles

Shawls

Indian shawls are famously warm and lightweight – quality pieces can often be better than the best down jackets. Shawls are made from all sorts of wool, and many are embroidered with intricate designs.

The undisputed capital of the Indian shawl is the Kullu Valley in Himachal Pradesh, with dozens of women's cooperatives producing fine woollen pieces. These may be made from wool (the cheapest, from around ₹700), angora (mohair – hair of the Angora rabbit) or *pashmina* (the downy hair of the pashmina goat). Avoid shahtoosh shawls, made from the hair of wild antelopes that are killed in the process.

Ladakh and Kashmir are major centres for *pashmina* production – you'll pay at least ₹6000 for the authentic article. Be aware that many so-called *pashminas* are actually made from a mixture of wool and silk; however, these 'fake' *pashminas* are still very beautiful, and a lot less expensive, costing around ₹1200.

Shawls from the Northeast States are known for their warmth, often with bold geometric designs. In Sikkim and West Bengal, you may also find fantastically embroidered Bhutanese shawls. Gujarat's Kutch region produces some particularly distinctive woollen shawls, patterned with subtle embroidery and mirror work. Handmade shawls and tweeds can also be found in Ranikhet and Almora in Uttarakhand.

Saris

Saris are found throughout India and come in a stunning array of textiles, colours and designs. Real silk saris are generally the most expensive, and the silk usually needs to be washed before it becomes soft. The 'silk capital' of India is Kanchipuram in Tamil Nadu (Kanchipuram silk is also commonly available in Chennai), but you can find fine silk saris in centres including Varanasi, Mysuru (Mysore) and Kolkata. Assam is renowned for its muga, endi and pat silks, produced by different species of silkworm and widely available in Guwahati. You'll pay upwards of ₹3000 for a quality embroidered silk sari.

Patan in Gujarat is the centre of the ancient and laborious craft of *patola*-making. Every thread in these fine silk saris is individually hand-dyed before weaving, and patterned borders are woven with real gold. Slightly less involved versions are produced in Rajkot. Gold thread is also used in the famous *kota doria* saris of Kota in Rajasthan.

Aurangabad, in Maharashtra, is the traditional centre for the production of *himroo* shawls, sheets and saris, made from a blend of cotton, silk and silver thread. Silk and gold-thread saris produced at Paithan (near

THE GREAT INDIAN BAZAAR TEXTILES

In towns with Buddhist communities, such as McLeod Ganj, Leh, Manali, Gangtok, Kalimpong, Darjeeling and Delhi, keep an eye out for 'Buddha shops' selling prayer flags, singing bowls and prayer wheels.

THE ART OF HAGGLING

Government emporiums, fair-trade cooperatives, department stores and modern shopping centres almost always charge fixed prices. Anywhere else, you may need to bargain as prices can be highly inflated – shopkeepers in many tourist hubs are accustomed to travellers with lots of money and little time to spend it, so you may end up being charged double or triple the going rate.

The first 'rule' to haggling is to never show too much interest in the item you've got your heart set on. Second, resist purchasing the first thing that takes your fancy. Wander around several shops and price items, but don't make it too obvious: if you return to the first shop, the vendor will know it's because they are the cheapest (resulting in less haggling leeway).

Decide how much you would be happy paying, and then express a casual interest in buying. If you have absolutely no idea of the going rate, a common approach is to start by slashing the price by half. The vendor will, most likely, look aghast, but you can now work up and down respectively in small increments until you reach a mutually agreeable price. You'll find that many shopkeepers lower their so-called 'final price' if you head out of the store saying you'll 'think about it'.

Haggling is a way of life in India and is usually taken in good spirit. It should never turn ugly. Always keep in mind how much a rupee is worth in your own country's currency, and how much you'd pay for the item back home, to put things in perspective. If you're not sure of the 'right' price for an item, think about how much it is worth to you. If a vendor seems to be charging an unreasonably high price, look elsewhere.

Aurangabad) are some of India's finest – prices range from around ₹7000 to a mind-blowing ₹300,000. Other regions famous for sari production include Madhya Pradesh, with its cotton Maheshwari saris (from Maheshwar) and silk Chanderi saris (from Chanderi), and West Bengal, for its *baluchari* saris from Bishnupur, which employ a traditional form of weaving with untwisted silk thread.

Khadi & Embroidery

Textile production is India's major industry and around 40% takes place at the village level, where it's known as *khadi* (homespun cloth) – hence the government-backed *khadi* emporiums around the country. These inexpensive superstores sell all sorts of items made from *khadi*, including the popular Nehru jackets and kurta pyjamas (long shirt and loose-fitting trousers), with sales benefitting rural communities. *Khadi* has become increasingly chic over recent years, with India's designers referencing the fabrics in their collections.

You'll find an amazing variety of weaving and embroidery techniques all over India. In tourist centres such as Goa, Rajasthan and Himachal Pradesh, textiles are stitched into popular items, including shoulder bags, wall hangings, cushion covers, bedspreads, clothes and much more. In Adivasi (tribal) areas of Gujarat and Rajasthan, small pieces of mirrored glass are embroidered onto fabric, creating eye-catching bags, vests, cushion covers and wall hangings. The region of Kutch (Gujarat) is particularly renowned for its embroidery.

Indian Textiles, by John Gillow and Nicholas Barnard, explores India's beautiful regional textiles and includes sections on tie-dye, weaving, beadwork, brocades and even camel girths.

Appliqué, Tie-Dye & Block-Print

Appliqué is an ancient art in India, with most states producing their own version, often featuring abstract or anthropomorphic patterns. The traditional lampshades and *pandals* (tents) used in weddings and festivals are usually produced using the same technique.

Gujarat has a diversity of textile traditions: Jamnagar is famous for its vibrant *bandhani* (tie-dye work) used for saris and scarves, among other things, and Vadodara is renowned for block-printed fabrics, used for bed-spreads and clothing. Ahmedabad is a good place to buy Gujarati textiles.

Block-printed and woven textiles are sold by fabric shops all over India: each region has its own speciality. The India-wide retail-chain stores Fabindia (www.fabindia.com), Anokhi (www.anokhi.com) and Soma (www.somashop.com) are striving to preserve traditional patterns and fabrics, transforming them into home-decor items and Indian- and Western-style fashions. Anokhi has the Anokhi Museum of Hand Printing (p130), which demonstrates the crafts.

Odisha has a reputation for bright appliqué and *ikat* (a Southeast Asian technique where thread is tie-dyed before weaving); the latter is also a speciality of Hyderabad. The town of Pipli, between Bhubaneswar and Puri, produces striking appliqué work. The techniques used to create *kalamkari* (cloth paintings) in Andhra Pradesh and Gujarat are also used to make lovely wall hangings and lampshades.

Be aware that it's illegal to buy shahtoosh shawls, as rare Tibetan antelopes are slaughtered to provide the wool. If you come across anyone selling these shawls, inform local authorities.

Woodcarving

Woodcarving is an ancient art form and today you'll find an impressive mix of traditional and contemporary designs. In Kashmir, walnut wood is used to make finely carved screens, tables, jewellery boxes and trays, often inspired by the decorative trim of houseboats. Willow cricket bats are another Kashmiri speciality.

Wood inlay is one of Bihar's oldest crafts – you'll find wooden wall hangings, tabletops, trays and boxes inlaid with metal and bone.

Sandalwood carvings of Hindu deities are one of Karnataka's specialities, but you'll pay a price for the real thing – a 10cm-high Ganesh costs around ₹3000 in sandalwood, compared to roughly ₹300 in kadamb wood. However, the sandalwood will release fragrance for years.

In Udaipur (Rajasthan), you can buy vividly painted figures of Hindu deities carved from mango wood. In many parts of Rajasthan you can also find fabric printing blocks carved from teak wood.

Buddhist woodcarvings are a speciality of Sikkim, Ladakh, Arunachal Pradesh and all Tibetan refugee areas. You'll find wall plaques of the eight lucky signs, dragons and *chaam* masks, used for ritual dances. Most of the masks are cheap reproductions, but you can sometimes find genuine *chaam* masks made from lightweight whitewood or papier mâché from around ₹3000.

Other Great Finds

It's little surprise that Indian spices are snapped up by tourists. All towns have shops selling locally made spices at great prices. Karnataka, Kerala, Uttar Pradesh, Rajasthan and Tamil Nadu produce most of the spices that go into garam masala (the 'hot mix' used to flavour Indian dishes), while the Northeast States and Sikkim are known for black cardamom and cinnamon bark. Note that some countries, such as Australia, have stringent rules regarding the import of animal and plant products. Check with your country's embassy for details.

Attar (essential oil, mostly made from flowers) shops can be found around the country. Mysuru (Mysore) is famous for its sandalwood oil, while Mumbai is a major centre for the trade of traditional fragrances, including valuable *oud,* made from a rare mould that grows on the bark of the agarwood tree. In Tamil Nadu, Ooty (Udhagamandalam) and Kodaikanal produce aromatic and medicinal oils from herbs, flowers and eucalyptus.

Indian incense is exported worldwide, with Bengaluru (Bangalore) and Mysuru, both in Karnataka, being major producers. Incense from Auroville in Tamil Nadu is also well regarded.

Be cautious when buying items that include international delivery, and avoid being led to shops by smooth-talking touts, but don't worry about too much else – except your luggage space!

A speciality of Goa is feni (liquor distilled from coconut milk or cashews): a head-spinning spirit that often comes in decorative bottles.

Quality Indian tea is sold in Darjeeling and Kalimpong (both in West Bengal), Assam and Sikkim, as well as parts of South India, such as Munnar in Kerala and the Ooty area in Tamil Nadu's Western Ghats. There are also top tea retailers in Delhi and other urban hubs.

In Bhopal in Madhya Pradesh, colourful *jari* shoulder bags, embroidered with beads, are a speciality. Also on the portables front, the Northeast States are noted for their beautiful handwoven baskets and wickerwork – each tribe has its own unique basket shape.

Jodhpur in Rajasthan, among other places, is famed for its antiques (though be aware that exporting antiques is prohibited).

Artisans in Jammu and Kashmir have been producing lacquered papier mâché for centuries, and papier mâché bowls, boxes, letter holders, coasters, trays and Christmas decorations are now sold across India, making inexpensive yet fabulous gifts (those with more intricate work command higher prices). In Rajasthan, look for colourful papier mâché puppets, typically sold as a pair and often depicting a husband and wife, and beautiful little temples, carved from mango wood and brightly painted with religious stories.

Fine-quality handmade paper – often fashioned into cards, boxes and notebooks – is worth seeking out. Puducherry (Pondicherry; Tamil Nadu), Delhi, Jaipur and Mumbai are good places to start.

Hats are also popular: the Assamese make decorated reed-pith sunhats, and Tibetan refugees produce woollen hats, gloves and scarves, sold nationwide. Traditional caps worn by men and women of Himalayan tribes are available in many Himachal Pradesh towns.

India has a phenomenal range of books at very competitive prices, including leather-bound titles. Big city bookshops offer the widest selections.

The Arts

India's magnificent artistic heritage is a reflection of the country's diverse ethnic groups and traditions. You'll encounter artful treasures around almost every corner, including the vivid body art of *mehndi* (henna), the soulful chants emanating from temples and the brightly decorated trucks rumbling along dusty roads. The wealth of creative expression is a highlight of travelling here, with many of today's artists fusing ancient and contemporary techniques to produce works that are as evocative as they are edgy.

Dance

The ancient Indian art of dance is traditionally linked to mythology and classical literature. Dance can be divided into two main forms: classical and folk. Classical dance is based on well-defined traditional disciplines. Following are some classical dance styles:

Indian Classical Dance by Leela Venkataraman and Avinash Pasricha is a lavishly illustrated book covering various Indian dance forms, including bharatanatyam, Odissi, Kuchipudi and Kathakali.

Bharatanatyam (also spelt Bharata Natyam) Originated in Tamil Nadu, and has been embraced throughout India.

Kathak Has Hindu and Islamic influences and was particularly popular with the Mughals. *Kathak* suffered a period of notoriety, when it moved from the courts into houses where *nautch* (dancing) girls tantalised audiences with renditions of the Krishna-and-Radha love story. It was restored as a serious art form in the early 20th century.

Kathakali Has its roots in Kerala; sometimes referred to as 'dance' but is essentially a kind of drama based on mythological subjects.

Kuchipudi A 17th-century dance-drama that originated in the Andhra Pradesh village from which it takes its name. The story centres on the envious wife of Krishna.

Odissi From Odisha (Orissa); thought to be India's oldest classical dance form. It was originally a temple art, and was later also performed at royal courts.

Manipuri Has a delicate, lyrical flavour; hails from Manipur. It attracted a wider audience in the 1920s, when acclaimed Bengali writer Rabindranath Tagore invited one of its most revered exponents to teach at Shantiniketan (West Bengal).

India's second major dance form, folk, is widespread and varied. It includes the high-spirited bhangra dance of Punjab, the theatrical dummy-horse dances of Karnataka and Tamil Nadu, and the graceful fishers' dance of Odisha. In Gujarat, the colourful group dance known as *garba* is performed during Navratri (Hindu festival held in September or October).

Pioneers of modern dance forms in India include Uday Shankar (older brother of the late sitar master Ravi), who once partnered with Russian ballerina Anna Pavlova. Rabindranath Tagore was another innovator; in 1901 he set up a school at Shantiniketan that promoted the arts, including dance.

The dance you'll probably most commonly see, though, is in films. Dance has featured in Indian movies since the dawn of 'talkies' and often combines traditional, folk and contemporary choreography.

Music

Indian classical music traces its roots back to Vedic times, when religious poems chanted by priests were first collated in an anthology called the Rig-Veda. Over the millennia, classical music has been shaped by many influences, and the legacy today is Carnatic (characteristic of South India) and Hindustani (the classical style of North India) music. With common origins, they share a number of features. Both use the raga (the melodic

TRADITIONAL KERALAN ARTS

Kathakali

The dance-drama art form of Kathakali is the dramatised presentation of a play, usually based on the Hindu epics the Ramayana, the Mahabharata and the Puranas.

Drummers and singers accompany the actors, who tell the story through their precise movements, particularly mudras (hand gestures) and facial expressions. Traditionally, all Kathakali performers are men, taking on both male and female roles (though there's now the occasional female Kathakali artist). Preparation for the performance is lengthy and disciplined. Paint, costumes, ornamental headpieces and meditation transform the actors both physically and mentally into the gods, heroes and demons they are about to play. Traditional performances can last for many hours, but you can see cut-down two-hour performances in tourist destinations.

Kalarippayat

Kalarippayat (or *kalari*) is an ancient tradition of martial-arts training and discipline, taught throughout Kerala. Some believe it is the forerunner of all martial arts and as ancient as 3000 years old. *Kalarippayat* peaked between the 13th and 16th centuries before declining during the British Raj. Masters of *kalarippayat,* called Gurukkal, teach their craft inside a special arena called a *kalari*. As well as open-hand combat and grappling, with techniques inspired by animal movements, the martial art is often associated with the use of weapons, including sword and shield *(valum parichayum),* short stick *(kurunthadi)* and long stick *(neduvadi).*

Theyyam

Theyyam refers both to the shape of the deity/hero portrayed, and to the actual ritual. There are around 450 different *theyyams,* each with a distinct costume, made up of face paint, bracelets, breastplates, skirts, garlands and exuberant, intricately crafted headdresses that can be up to 6m or 7m tall. Each protagonist loses his physical identity and speaks, moves and blesses the devotees as if he were that deity. Frenzied dancing and wild drumming create an atmosphere in which a deity indeed might, if it so desired, manifest itself in human form. *Theyyam* performers are male members of lower castes, treated with deep respect throughout the ritual.

The best place for visitors to see *theyyam* is in village temples in the Kannur region (p1006) of northern Kerala. Although tourists are welcome to attend, this is not a performance but a religious ritual, and the usual rules of temple behaviour apply: dress appropriately, avoid disturbing participants and villagers, refrain from displays of public affection.

shape of the music) and *tala* (the rhythmic meter characterised by the number of beats); *tintal,* for example, has a *tala* of 16 beats. The audience follows the *tala* by clapping at the appropriate beat, which in *tintal* is at beats one, five and 13. There's no clap at the beat of nine; that's the *khali* (empty section), which is indicated by a wave of the hand. Both the raga and the *tala* are used as a basis for composition and improvisation.

Both Carnatic and Hindustani music are performed by small ensembles, generally comprising three to six musicians, and both have many instruments in common. There's no fixed pitch, but there are differences between the two styles. Hindustani has been more heavily influenced by Persian musical conventions (a result of Mughal rule); Carnatic music, as it developed in South India, cleaves more closely to theory. The most striking difference, at least for those unfamiliar with India's classical forms, is Carnatic's greater use of voice.

To tune into the melodious world of Hindustani classical music, including a glossary of musical terms, get a copy of *Nād: Understanding Raga Music* by Sandeep Bagchee.

One of the best-known Indian instruments is the sitar (large stringed instrument), with which the soloist plays the raga. Other stringed instruments include the sarod (which is plucked) and the *sarangi* (which is played with a bow). Also popular is the tabla (twin drums), which provides the *tala.* The drone, which runs on two basic notes, is provided by the oboe-like *shehnai* or the stringed *tanpura* (also spelt tamboura). The hand-pumped keyboard harmonium is used as a secondary melody instrument for vocal music. Indian regional folk music is widespread and varied. Wandering musicians, magicians, snake charmers and storytellers often use song to entertain their audiences; the storyteller usually sings the tales from the great epics.

In North India you may come across *qawwali* (Sufi devotional singing), performed in mosques or at musical concerts. *Qawwali* concerts usually take the form of a *mehfil* (gathering) with a lead singer, a second singer, harmonium and tabla players, and a thunderous chorus of junior singers and clappers, all sitting cross-legged on the floor. The singers whip up the audience with lines of poetry, dramatic hand gestures and religious phrases as the two voices weave in and out, bouncing off each other to create an improvised, surging sound. On command the chorus dives in with a hypnotic and rhythmic refrain. Members of the audience often sway and shout out in ecstatic appreciation.

A completely different genre altogether, filmi (music from predominantly Bollywood films) includes modern, slower-paced love serenades, along with ebullient dance songs. Some of India's most timelessly iconic film music composers and singers include Kishore Kumar, RD Burman, Asha Bhosle and Lata Mangeshkar. Contemporary art-house music has filmi roots but is often more experimental. A composer and musical director who has won many accolades – including two Academy Awards – for his innovative style is Chennai-born AR Rahman. Films which feature his acclaimed musical scores include *Roja, Lagaan, Jodhaa Akbar, Slumdog Millionaire* and *127 Hours*. Rahman has excelled at integrating classical Indian music with world tunes, including electronic and orchestral fusion.

Painting

Around 1500 years ago artists covered the walls and ceilings of the Ajanta caves in Maharashtra, with scenes from Buddha's past lives. The figures are endowed with an unusual freedom and grace, and contrast with the next major style that emerged from this part of India in the 11th century.

India's Jain community created some particularly lavish temple art. However, after the conquest of Gujarat by the Delhi Sultanate in 1299, the Jains turned their attention to illustrated manuscripts, which could be hidden away. These manuscripts are the only known form of Indian painting that survived the Islamic conquest of North India.

The Indo-Persian style, characterised by geometric design coupled with flowing form, developed from Islamic royal courts, although the depiction of the elongated eye is one convention that seems to have been retained from indigenous sources. The Persian influence blossomed when artisans fled to India following the 1507 Uzbek attack on Herat (present-day Afghanistan), and with trade and gift-swapping between the Persian city of Shiraz, an established centre for miniature production, and Indian sultans.

The 1526 victory by Babur at the Battle of Panipat ushered in the era of the Mughals in India. Although Babur and his son Humayun were both patrons of the arts, Humayun's son Akbar is generally credited with developing the characteristic Mughal style. This painting style, often in colourful miniature form, largely depicts court life, architecture, nature, battle and hunting scenes, as well as detailed portraits. Akbar recruited artists from far and wide, and artistic endeavour first centred on the production of illustrated manuscripts, covering topics from history to mythology, but later broadened into portraiture and the glorification of everyday events. European painting styles influenced some artists, and this influence occasionally reveals itself in experiments with motifs and perspective.

Akbar's son Jehangir also patronised painting, but he preferred portraiture, and his fascination with natural science resulted in a vibrant legacy of paintings of flowers and animals. Under Jehangir's son Shah Jahan, the Mughal style became less fluid and, although the bright colouring was eye-catching, the paintings lacked the vigour of before.

Get arty with *Indian Art* by Roy C Craven, *Contemporary Indian Art: Other Realities,* edited by Yashodhara Dalmia, and *Indian Miniature Painting* by Dr Daljeet and Professor PC Jain.

THE ARTS PAINTING

Explore India's vibrant performing-arts scene – especially classical dance and music – at Art India (www.artindia.net), a detailed resource covering everything from Carnatic music to modern dance.

Miniature painting flourished first at the Mughal court in the 16th century, as well as the Deccan sultanates (Golconda, Bijapur, Bidar etc). As Mughal power and wealth declined, many artists moved to Rajasthan, where the Rajasthani school developed from the late 17th century. Later, artists from Rajasthan moved into the Himalayan foothills of Punjab, Himachal Pradesh and Uttarakhand, where the Pahari (Hill Country) school flourished in the 18th and early 19th centuries. The subject matter ranged from royal processions to shikhar (hunting expeditions), with many artists influenced by Mughal styles. The intense colours, still evident today in miniatures and frescoes in some Indian palaces, were often derived from crushed semiprecious stones, while the gold and silver colouring is finely pounded pure gold and silver leaf.

By the 19th century, painting in North India was notably influenced by Western styles (especially English watercolours), giving rise to what has been dubbed the Company School, which had its centre in Delhi. Meanwhile, in the south, painter Ravi Varma painted schmaltzy mythological scenes and portraits of women, which were hugely popular and gave Indian subjects a very Western treatment. Look out for the distinctive stylised works of Jamini Roy, depicting village life and culture.

Rabindranath Tagore, born in Kolkata in 1861, is especially famed for his contribution to literature, but he was also a gifted artist. With no formal art training, he began dabbling in painting in his 60s and created more than 2000 pieces. His individual style of melding classical Indian art traditions with uniquely modern (often simple and bold) flourishes attracted praise from art critics, especially in Europe. However, Tagore remained largely dismissive of his own artistic skills. Today, his paintings are widely lauded and feature in various exhibitions. India's National Gallery of Modern Art (http://ngmaindia.gov.in) lists 102 of Tagore's works.

The Madras Movement pioneered modern art in South India in the 1960s, while in the 21st century, paintings by contemporary Indian artists have been selling at record numbers (and prices) around the world. One very successful online art auction house is Saffronart (www.saffronart.com). The larger cities, especially Delhi and Mumbai, are India's contemporary-art centres, with a range of galleries in which to view and buy art.

Cinema

Encyclopedia of Indian Cinema by Ashish Rajadhyaksha and Paul Willemen chronicles India's dynamic cinematic history, spanning from 1897 to the 21st century.

India's film industry was born in the late 19th century – the first major Indian-made motion picture, Panorama of Calcutta, was screened in 1899. India's first real feature film, Raja Harishchandra, was made during the silent era in 1913, and it's ultimately from this film that Indian cinema traces its lineage.

Today, India's film industry is the biggest in the world – twice as big as Hollywood. Mumbai, the Hindi-language film capital, aka Bollywood (p767), is the biggest, but India's other major film-producing cities – Chennai (Kollywood), Hyderabad (Tollywood) and Bengaluru (Bangalore; Sandalwood) – also have a considerable output. A number of other centres produce films, in their own regional vernaculars too. Big-budget

---

RANGOLIS

Rangolis, the strikingly intricate chalk, rice-paste or coloured powder designs (also called kolams) that adorn thresholds, especially in South India, are both auspicious and symbolic. Rangolis are traditionally drawn at sunrise and are sometimes made of rice-flour paste, which may be eaten by little creatures – symbolising a reverence for even the smallest living things. Deities are deemed to be attracted to a beautiful rangoli, which may also signal to sadhus (ascetics) that they will be offered food at a particular house. Some people believe that rangolis protect against the evil eye.

films are often partly or entirely shot abroad, with some countries vigorously wooing Indian production companies because of the potential spin-off tourism revenue these films generate.

Broadly speaking, there are two categories of Indian films. Most prominent is the mainstream 'masala' movie – named for its 'spice mix' of elements. Designed to have something for every member of the family, the films encompass a blend of romance, action, slapstick humour and moral themes. Three hours and still running, these blockbusters are often tear-jerkers and are packed with dramatic twists interspersed with numerous song-and-dance performances. In Indian films made for the local market there is no explicit sex, and not even much kissing, although smooching has made its way into some Bollywood movies. However, lack of nudity is often compensated for by heroines dressed in skimpy or body-hugging attire, and the lack of overt eroticism is more than made up for with intense flirting and loaded innuendos.

The second Indian film genre is art house, which adopts Indian 'reality' as its base. Generally speaking, these films are socially and politically relevant. Usually made on infinitely smaller budgets than their commercial cousins, they are the ones that tend to win kudos at global film festivals and awards ceremonies. Bengali cinema, best represented by the work of Satyajit Ray, is particularly well regarded. In 2013, *Dabba* (Lunchbox), a non-Bollywood romantic comedy written and directed by Ritesh Batra, won the Grand Rail d'Or at Cannes International Critics' Week.

Indian films that have made it to the final nomination list of the Academy Awards (Best Foreign Language Film category) are *Mother India* (directed by Mehboob Khan, 1957), *Salaam Bombay!* (directed by Mira Nair, 1988) and *Lagaan* (directed by Ashutosh Gowariker, 2001).

Literature

India has a long tradition of Sanskrit literature, although works in the vernacular have contributed to a particularly rich legacy. In fact, it's claimed there are as many literary traditions as there are written languages.

Bengalis are traditionally credited with producing some of India's most celebrated literature, a movement often referred to as the Indian or Bengal Renaissance, which flourished from the 19th century with works by Bankim Chandra Chatterjee. But the man who to this day is mostly credited with first propelling India's cultural richness onto the world stage is the Bengali Rabindranath Tagore, with works such as *Gitanjali* (Song Offerings), *Gora* (Fair-Faced) and *Ghare-Baire* (The Home and the World).

One of the earliest Indian authors writing in English to receive an international audience, in the 1930s, was RK Narayan, whose deceptively simple writing about small-town life is subtly hilarious. Keralan Kamala Das (aka Kamala Suraiyya) wrote poetry, such as *Summer in Calcutta*, in English and her memoir, *My Story*, in Malayalam, which she later translated to English. Her frank approach to love and sexuality, especially in the 1960s and '70s, broke ground for women writers.

India has an ever-growing list of internationally acclaimed contemporary authors. Particularly prominent writers include Vikram Seth, best known for his epic novel *A Suitable Boy*, and Amitav Ghosh, who has won a number of accolades; his *Sea of Poppies* was shortlisted for the 2008 Man Booker Prize. A number of India-born authors have won the prestigious Man Booker, the most recent being Aravind Adiga, who won in 2008 for his debut novel, *The White Tiger*. The prize went to Kiran Desai in 2006 for *The Inheritance of Loss;* Desai is the daughter of the award-winning Indian novelist Anita Desai, who has thrice been a Booker Prize nominee. In 1997 Arundhati Roy won the Booker for her novel *The God of Small Things*, while Salman Rushdie took this coveted award in 1981 for *Midnight's Children*, which also won the Booker of Bookers prize in 1993.

THE ARTS LITERATURE

Bengali director Satyajit Ray (1921–92) is considered the father of Indian art films, winning global awards for movies such as *Pather Panchali* and *Aparajito*.

The acclaimed writer, poet and artist Rabindranath Tagore won the Nobel Prize in Literature in 1913 for *Gitanjali* (Song Offerings). For a varied taste of Tagore's work, read *Selected Short Stories*.

Sacred Architecture

India's remarkable assortment of historic and contemporary sacred architecture draws inspiration from an array of religious denominations. Although few of the wooden and occasionally brick temples built in early times have weathered the vagaries of nature, by the advent of the Guptas (4th to 6th centuries AD) of North India, sacred structures of a new type – better engineered to withstand the elements – were being constructed, and these largely set the standard for temples for several hundred years.

For Hindus, the square is a perfect shape, and complex rules govern the location, design and building of each temple, based on numerology, astrology, astronomy and religious principles. Essentially, a temple represents a map of the universe. At the centre is an unadorned space,

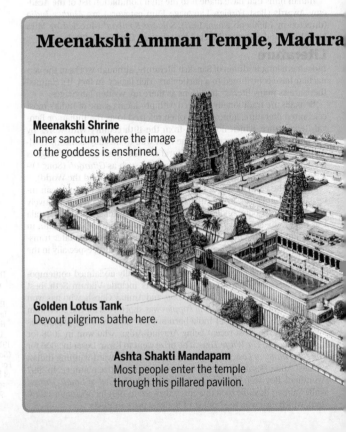

Meenakshi Amman Temple, Madura

Meenakshi Shrine
Inner sanctum where the image of the goddess is enshrined.

Golden Lotus Tank
Devout pilgrims bathe here.

Ashta Shakti Mandapam
Most people enter the temple through this pillared pavilion.

the *garbhagriha* (inner sanctum), which is symbolic of the 'womb-cave' from which the universe is believed to have emerged. This provides a residence for the deity to which the temple is dedicated.

Above a Hindu temple's shrine rises a tower superstructure known as a *vimana* in South India, and a *sikhara* in North India. The *sikhara* is curvilinear and topped with a grooved disk, on which sits a pot-shaped finial, while the *vimana* is stepped, with the grooved disk being replaced by a solid dome. Some temples have a *mandapa* (fore-chamber) connected to the sanctum by vestibules. The *mandapa* may also contain *vimanas* or *sikharas*.

A *gopuram* is a soaring pyramidal gateway tower of a Dravidian temple. The towering *gopurams* of various South Indian temple complexes, such as the nine-storey *gopurams* of Madurai's Sri Meenakshi Temple, take ornamentation and monumentalism to new levels.

Commonly used for ritual bathing and religious ceremonies, as well as adding aesthetic appeal, temple tanks have long been a focal point of temple activity. These often-vast, angular, engineered reservoirs of water, sometimes fed by rain, sometimes supplied – via a complicated drainage system – by rivers, serve both sacred and secular purposes. The waters of some temple tanks are believed to have healing properties, while others are said to have the power to wash away sins. Devotees (as well as travellers) may be required to wash their feet in a temple tank before entering a place of worship.

Discover more about India's diverse temple architecture at Temple Net (www.templenet. com), which has temple-related information from festival details to a glossary of terms.

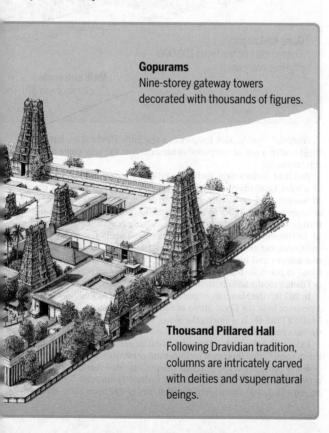

Gopurams
Nine-storey gateway towers decorated with thousands of figures.

Thousand Pillared Hall
Following Dravidian tradition, columns are intricately carved with deities and vsupernatural beings.

Golden Temple, Amristar

Pilgrim accommodation

Guru-ka-Langar
The temple kitchen feeds 100,000
pilgrims every day.

Main entrance
Clock tower and Sikh mu

From the outside, Jain temples can resemble Hindu ones, but inside they're often a riot of sculptural ornamentation, the very opposite of ascetic austerity.

Buddhist shrines have their own unique features. Stupas, composed of a solid hemisphere topped by a spire, characterise Buddhist places of worship and essentially evolved from burial mounds. They served as repositories for relics of Buddha and, later, other venerated souls. A further innovation is the addition of a *chaitya* (assembly hall) leading up to the stupa itself. Bodhgaya, where Siddhartha Gautama attained enlightenment and became Buddha, has a collection of notable Buddhist monasteries and temples. The gompas (Tibetan Buddhist monasteries) found in places such as Ladakh and Sikkim are characterised by distinctly Tibetan motifs and chortens, a more angular Tibetan style of stupa.

The focal point of a gompa (Tibetan Buddhist monastery) is the *dukhang* (temple), where monks assemble to chant passages from sacred scriptures.

In 262 BC, the Mauryan emperor Ashoka embraced Buddhism, and as a penance built the Great Stupa at Sanchi, in the central Indian state of Madhya Pradesh. It is among the oldest surviving Buddhist structures in the subcontinent.

India also has a rich collection of Islamic sacred sites, as its Muslim rulers contributed their own architectural conventions, including arched cloisters and domes. The Mughals uniquely melded Persian, Indian and provincial styles. Renowned examples include Humayun's Tomb in Delhi, Agra Fort, and the ancient fortified city of Fatehpur Sikri. Emperor

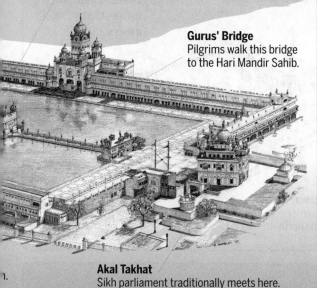

Hari Mandir Sahib
The most sacred part of the temple complex, with gold-plated dome and walls encrusted with semi-precious jewels.

Gurus' Bridge
Pilgrims walk this bridge to the Hari Mandir Sahib.

Akal Takhat
Sikh parliament traditionally meets here.

Shah Jahan was responsible for some of India's most spectacular architectural creations, most notably the Taj Mahal.

Islamic art eschews any hint of idolatry or portrayal of God, and it has evolved a vibrant heritage of calligraphic and decorative designs. In terms of mosque architecture, the basic design elements are similar worldwide. A large hall is dedicated to communal prayer and within the hall is a mihrab (niche) indicating the direction of Mecca. The faithful are called to prayer from minarets, placed at cardinal points. Delhi's formidable 17th-century Jama Masjid is India's biggest mosque, its courtyard able to hold 25,000 people.

The Sikh faith was founded by Guru Nanak, the first of 10 gurus, in the 15th century. Sikh temples, called gurdwaras, can usually be identified by their bud-like *gumbads* (domes) and *nishan sahib* (a flagpole flying a triangular flag with the Sikh insignia). Amritsar's stunning Golden Temple is Sikhism's holiest shrine.

Masterpieces of Traditional Indian Architecture by Satish Grover and The History of Architecture in India by Christopher Tadgell give interesting insights into temple architecture.

Jama Masjid, Delhi

Central Courtyard
Holds up to 25,000 people for Friday prayers.

Minaret
Tower from which the muezzin (crier) calls the faithful to worship.

Ablution Tank
Devotees wash here before entering the mosque.

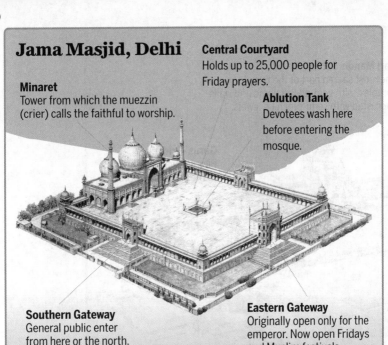

Southern Gateway
General public enter from here or the north.

Eastern Gateway
Originally open only for the emperor. Now open Fridays and Muslim festivals.

Sanchi

Great Stupa
Built by the emperor Ashoka in the 2nd century BC to enshrine relics of the Buddha.

Monastery Ruins
Accommodation surrounding a central courtyard.

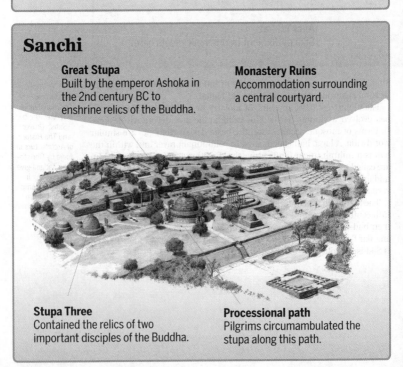

Stupa Three
Contained the relics of two important disciples of the Buddha.

Processional path
Pilgrims circumambulated the stupa along this path.

Wildlife & Parks

The wildlife of India comprises a vast array of animals from Europe, Asia and ancient Gondwanaland, all swirled together in a diverse mix of habitats from mangrove forests and jungles to deserts and alpine mountains. India is famous for its big, bold species – tigers, elephants, rhinos, leopards and bears. But there's much more, including a mesmerising collection of colourful birds and some of the world's most endangered and intriguing wildlife, such as the Ganges river dolphin and the Asiatic lion.

India's Iconic Species

Tigers, elephants and rhinos are among India's most renowned wildlife, all of which are scarce and in need of stringent protection.

Asian elephants – a completely different species to the larger African elephant – are revered in Hindu custom and were able to be domesticated and put to work. Fortunately, they've not been hunted into extinction (as they were in neighbouring China) and many still survive in the wild. Because they migrate long distances in search of food, these 3000kg animals require huge parks; interspecies conflicts often erupt when herds of elephants attempt to follow ancestral paths that are now occupied by villages and farms.

There are far fewer one-horned rhinos left and two thirds of the world's total population can be found in Assam's Kaziranga National Park, where they wander lush alluvial grasslands at the base of the Himalaya. A 2018 census revealed the number of one-horned rhinos in Kaziranga stood at 2413, an increase of 12 from the 2015 census. They may look sedate but rhinos are unpredictably dangerous – built like battering rams, covered in plates of armour-like skin, and using their sharp teeth to tear off chunks of flesh when they attack.

And then there's the mighty, majestic tiger. This iconic animal is critically endangered but can be seen, if you're lucky, at tiger reserves around

India's national animal is the tiger, its national bird is the peacock and its national flower is the lotus. The national emblem of India is a column topped by three Asiatic lions.

ANIMAL ATTACKS

Shrinking natural habitats and expanding human settlements are bringing humans and wildlife together as never before in India. Every year, new reports of tigers taking up residence in inhabited areas hit the press, alongside stories of urban leopards wandering around villages and even large towns. What is interesting is that the incomers are often tolerated by locals as a form of biological pest control, reducing the numbers of boar, deer and other wildlife that would otherwise graze on their crops. At the same time, the presence of humans may deter prowling male tigers, who might otherwise attack a female's cubs.

Nevertheless, authorities still advise caution in areas where humans and wildlife co-exist, with around 100 people reportedly killed or injured annually by wild jungle cats. While these attacks tend to get lots of press coverage and cause panic, it's actually rare for tigers to turn into true man-eaters; those that do are generally old, injured or both. In comparison, around 46,000 people in India die each year of snakebites, accounting for nearly half of the world's 100,000 annual snakebite deaths.

UNBEARABLY GOOD NEWS

In 2012 the Indian government announced that the dancing bear industry was extinct. After several centuries – and three decades after it was made illegal – this cultural tradition finally ended, with few lamenting its demise. In fact, the practice was bought out when the few remaining bear-handling communities, known as Kalandars, were redirected into more profitable enterprises.

Website Resources

Wildlife, conservation and environment awareness-raising at www.sanctuary asia.com

Wildlife Trust of India news at www. wti.org.in

Top birdwatching information and photo galleries at www.birding.in

the country – one of your best chances of spotting one is in Madhya Pradesh.

Tourism & Protection

Wildlife-watching has become one of India's prime tourist activities, and there are hundreds of national parks and wildlife sanctuaries offering opportunities to spot rare and unusual creatures. Your visit helps send a message to the government and local people that protecting endangered species and fragile ecosystems is important and of economic value.

Cats & Dogs

India is especially famed for its tigers, but is also home to 14 other species of wild cats. Hunting and human encroachment pose an ongoing threat to these animals.

Protection efforts have been successfully made on behalf of the Asiatic lion, a close relative of the more familiar African lion. A century ago there were only 20 of these lions left in the world, but their current population, an estimated 600 according to a 2018 census, indicates that they seem to be doing quite well in Gujarat's Sasan Gir National Park, the world's last surviving sanctuary of the Asiatic lion.

Up to 600 snow leopards are believed to exist in the alpine altitudes of Ladakh, Sikkim, Uttarakhand, Arunachal Pradesh and Himachal Pradesh – where it is the official state animal. This much-celebrated big cat is so elusive that many locals claim it can appear and disappear at will. Your chances of seeing one are small, but if you're really keen to seek this ghost-like feline, try Himachal Pradesh's Spiti region for starters.

Other wild cats include the clouded leopard and its smaller cousin, the marbled cat, both of which lurk in the jungles of the Northeast Region. They are strikingly marked with rosettes and rings for camouflage in the dappled light of their forest homes. India also has several species of primitive cat-like predators known as civets.

The country is also home to around 3000 wild Indian wolves, which can best be seen in Gujarat's Blackbuck National Park. The rare, and most ancient, breed – the Spitian Himalayan wolf – can be heard howling over the Spiti Valley. Jackals, foxes and dholes (wild dogs) can be spotted in enclaves around the country.

India's largest contiguous protected area is the Nanda Devi Biosphere Reserve, in Uttarakhand, covering 2237 sq km. It includes India's second-highest peak (Nanda Devi – 7817m) and the famous Valley of Flowers.

Indian Mammals

The most abundant forms of wildlife you'll see in India are deer (nine species), antelope (six species), goats and sheep (10 species), and primates (15 species). In the open grasslands of many parks look for the nilgai, India's largest antelope, or elegantly horned blackbucks. If you're heading for the mountains, keep your eyes open in the Himalaya for blue sheep – with partially curled horns – or the rare argali, with fully curled horns, found in Ladakh. The deserts of Rajasthan and Gujarat are home to arid land species such as chinkaras (Indian gazelles), while the mangrove swamps of the Sundarbans delta have chitals (spotted deer), who cope with their brackish environment by excreting salt from their nasal glands. Chitals are also the most prolific deer in central India's high-profile tiger reserves.

India's primates range from the extremely rare hoolock gibbon and golden langur of the northeast to species that are so common as to be regarded pests by some – notably the stocky and aggressive rhesus macaque and the slender grey langur. In the south, the cheeky monkeys that loiter around temples and tourist sites are bonnet macaques.

Endangered Species

Despite having amazing biodiversity, India faces a growing challenge from its burgeoning human population. Wildlife is severely threatened by poaching, human-wildlife conflict and habitat loss. One report suggested India had over 500 threatened species, including 247 species of plants, 53 species of mammals, 78 species of birds, 22 species of reptiles, 68 species of amphibians, 35 species of fish and 22 species of invertebrates.

Even well-resourced conservation projects, such as Project Tiger, face ongoing challenges. Every good news story seems to be followed by yet another story of poaching gangs or tiger or leopard attacks on villagers. All of India's wild cats, from snow leopards to panthers, are facing extinction from habitat loss and poaching for the lucrative trade in skins and body parts for Chinese medicine (a whole tiger carcass can fetch upwards of UK£32,000).

Even highly protected rhinos are poached for the medicine trade – rhino horn is highly valued as an aphrodisiac in China and as a material for making handles for daggers in the Gulf. Elephants are widely poached for ivory, and travellers can help by not buying ivory souvenirs.

Various species of deer are threatened by hunting for food and trophies, and the chiru, or Tibetan antelope, is nearly extinct because its hair is woven into wool for expensive shahtoosh shawls.

India's bear species remain under threat, although sloth bears are experiencing a reprieve with the demise of the dancing bear industry. In the rivers, India's famous freshwater dolphins are in dire straits from pollution, habitat alteration and direct human competition. The sea-turtle populations that nest on the Odisha coast also face environmental challenges.

Threatened primate species clinging on in rainforests in the south include lion-tailed macaques, glossy black Nilgiri langurs and the slender loris, an adept insect-catcher with huge eyes for nocturnal hunting.

India has 270 species of snake, of which 60 are poisonous. Of the various species of cobra, the king cobra is the world's largest venomous snake, reaching a length of 5m.

WILDLIFE & PARKS ENDANGERED SPECIES

Top Parks South

Mahatma Gandhi Marine National Park

Nagarhole National Park

Periyar Tiger Reserve

PROJECT TIGER

When naturalist Jim Corbett first raised the alarm in the 1930s, no one believed that tigers would ever be threatened. At the time, it was believed there were about 40,000 tigers in India, although no one had ever conducted a census. Then came Independence, which put guns into the hands of villagers, who pushed into formerly off-limits hunting reserves seeking highly profitable tiger skins. By the time an official count was made in 1972, there were only 1800 tigers left, and the international outcry partly prompted then Prime Minister Indira Gandhi to make the tiger the national symbol of India and set up Project Tiger (National Tiger Conservation Authority; http://projecttiger.nic.in). It has since established 50 tiger reserves totalling 71,027 sq km, which protect not only this top predator but all animals that share its habitat.

After some initial success against the practice, continuing poaching caused tiger numbers to plummet, from 3600 in 2002 to 1706 in 2011. Despite countless rupees and high-tech equipment devoted to saving this majestic animal, out of 63 wild tiger deaths in 2013, only one was from old age, while 48 were from poaching. Fortunately, the most recent tiger census results, published in January 2015, show an encouraging rise in India's tiger population, to 2226. This census revealed that the country's highest number of tigers, in the age group of 1½ years and over, are in Karnataka, which has a total of 408 tigers. Karnataka is followed by Uttarakhand with 340 tigers. Other states with more than 100 tigers are Madhya Pradesh, Tamil Nadu, Maharashtra, Assam, Kerala and Uttar Pradesh.

Birds

**Top Parks
North**

Corbett Tiger
Reserve

Kaziranga National
Park

Keoladeo National
Park

Ranthambhore
National Park

With more than 1200 species of birds, India is a fascinating destination for birdwatchers. Many birds are thinly spread over this vast country, but wherever critical habitat has been preserved in the midst of dense human activity, you might see phenomenal numbers of birds in one location. Winter can be a particularly good time, as wetlands throughout the country host northern migrants arriving to kick back in the lush subtropical warmth of the Indian peninsula. Throughout the year, wherever you may be travelling, look for colourful kingfishers, barbets, sunbirds, parakeets and magpies, or the blue flash of an Indian roller. Keen birdwatchers will take a special trip into the Himalaya in search of one of the world's most highly sought-after species, the enigmatic ibisbill.

Once considered the premier duck-hunting destination in the British empire, when royal hunting parties would shoot up to 4000 ducks in a single day, the seasonal wetlands of Rajasthan's Keoladeo were elevated to national park status in 1982, and the park is still rightly famous for its migratory avian visitors today.

Plants

Once almost entirely covered in forest, India's total forest cover is now 22.7%. Despite widespread clearing of native habitats, the country still boasts around 50,000 plant species, of which some 5200 are endemic. Species on the southern peninsula show Malaysian ancestry, while desert plants in Rajasthan are more clearly allied with the Middle East, and the conifer forests of the Himalaya derive from European and Siberian origins. The Forest Survey of India has set an optimistic target of returning to 33% cover.

Around 2000 plant species are described in texts on ayurveda (traditional Indian herbal medicine) and many are still widely used in the country.

Outside the mountain forests found in the Himalaya, nearly all the lowland forests of India are subtypes of tropical forest, with native sal forests forming the mainstay of the timber industry. Some of these tropical forests are true rainforest, staying green year-round – such as in the Western Ghats and in the northeast states – but most forests are deciduous; during the hot, dry months of April and May, many forests lose their canopies, as leaves wither and fall from the trees. This is often the best time to view wildlife, as the cover is thinner, and animals seek out scarce waterholes.

High-value trees, such as Indian rosewood, Malabar kino and teak, have been virtually cleared from the Western Ghats, and sandalwood is endangered across India due to illegal logging for the incense and woodcarving industries. A bigger threat to forested lands is firewood harvesting, often carried out by landless peasants who squat on gazetted government land.

Some trees have special religious significance in India, including the silk-cotton tree, a huge tree with spiny bark and large red flowers under which Pitamaha (Brahma), the god of creation, sat after his labours. Two well-known figs, the banyan and peepul, grow to immense size by dangling roots from their branches and fusing into massive jungles of trunks and stems – one giant is nearly 200m across. It is said that Buddha achieved enlightenment while sitting under a peepul (also known as the bodhi tree).

**Top Parks
Central**

Bandhavgarh
National Park

Kanha National
Park

Panna National
Park

Sundarbans Tiger
Reserve

The foothills and slopes of the Himalaya preserve classic montane species, including blue pine and deodar (Himalayan cedar), and deciduous forests of apple, chestnut, birch, plum and cinnamon. Above the snowline, hardy plants such as anemones, edelweiss and gentians can be prolific, and one fabulous place to see these flowers is at the Valley of Flowers National Park in Uttarakhand.

India's hot deserts have their own unique species – the khejri tree and various strains of scrub acacia. The hardy sea-buckthorn bush is the main fruiting shrub in the high-altitude deserts of the Himalaya.

PARKS & PEOPLE

While national parks and wildlife sanctuaries are crucial to protecting the habitats of India's endangered species, their creation has had some tragic consequences. When the Wildlife Protection Act of 1972 banned people from living in parks, about 1.6 million Adivasis and other forest-dwellers were evicted from their traditional lands. Many were resettled in villages and forced to abandon their age-old ways of life, resulting in profound personal suffering and irreplaceable cultural losses. Today, the Forest Rights Act of 2006 forbids the displacement of forest-dwellers from national parks (except in so-called 'critical wildlife habitat'), protecting the four million or so people who still live in them. However, the position of many forest-dwellers remains precarious – visit www.forestrightsact. com and www.traditionalculturesproject.org for the latest information.

National Parks & Wildlife Sanctuaries

Prior to 1972, India only had five national parks. The Wildlife Protection Act was introduced that year to set aside land for parks and stem the abuse of wildlife. The act was followed by a string of similar pieces of legislation with bold ambitions but few teeth with which to enforce them.

India now has 104 national parks and 543 wildlife sanctuaries, which constitute around 5% of India's territory. Additional parks have been authorised on paper but not yet implemented on the ground, or only implemented to varying degrees. There are also 18 biosphere reserves, overlapping many of the national parks and sanctuaries, providing safe migration channels for wildlife and allowing scientists to monitor biodiversity.

We highly recommend visiting at least one national park or sanctuary on your travels – the experience of coming face-to-face with a wild elephant, rhino or tiger will stay with you for a lifetime, while your visit adds momentum to efforts to protect India's natural resources. Wildlife reserves tend to be off the beaten track and infrastructure can be limited – book transport and accommodation in advance, and check opening times, permit requirements and entry fees before you visit. Many parks close to conduct a census of wildlife in the low season, and monsoon rains can make wildlife-viewing tracks inaccessible.

Almost all parks offer jeep or van tours, but you can also search for wildlife on guided treks and boat trips. Some parks may offer elephant-back safaris, but we don't recommend these due to the detrimental health implications for elephants, and because of the techniques used to train them to carry people. Due to increasing animal welfare concerns, some wildlife reserves have completely halted elephant-back safaris, while others may only allow tourists to walk alongside elephants, not ride them.

Rules introduced in 2012 put an end to 'tiger shows', whereby resting tigers became sitting ducks for tourists, who were taken off their jeep and put on elephants to get close to the, presumably peeved, tiger. Also, in many reserves, safari vehicle visits have been reduced and some tiger sanctuaries may be closed to safaris one day a week. These rules still are in flux, so do find out the latest situation before booking your safari.

Books About Wildlife

Mammals of India (Vivek Menon)

Treasures of Indian Wildlife (AS Kothari and BF Chhapgar)

The Maneaters of Kumaon (Jim Corbett)

For memorable wildlife shots, a camera with a long lens – at least 300mm – is essential.

The Landscape

India's topography is stunningly varied, with everything from steamy tropical jungles and coastal mangrove forests to windswept deserts and icy mountain peaks. At 3,287,263 sq km, it is the largest Asian country after China, and forms the vast bulk of the South Asian subcontinent.

The Lie of the Land

Look for the three major geographic features that define modern-day India: Himalayan peaks and hills along the northern borders; the alluvial floodplains of the Indus and Ganges (referred to locally as the Ganga) Rivers in the north; and the elevated Deccan Plateau that forms the core of India's triangular southern peninsula.

Recent World Health Organization (WHO) air pollution data revealed that a staggering 14 Indian cities (including Delhi) were among the world's 20 most polluted.

The Himalaya

Khangchendzonga, the highest peak in India reaches 8598m and forms part of the Himalaya mountain range that creates an almost impregnable boundary between India and its northern neighbours. These mountains formed when the Indian subcontinent broke away from Gondwanaland, a supercontinent in the southern hemisphere that included Africa, Antarctica, Australia and South America, and slammed with immense force into the Eurasian continent about 40 million years ago. This buckled the ancient sea floor upwards to form the Himalaya and associated ranges stretching 2500km from Afghanistan to Myanmar (Burma).

When the Himalaya reached its great heights during the Pleistocene (less than 150,000 years ago), it blocked and altered weather systems, creating the monsoon climate that dominates India today, as well as forming a dry rain-shadow to the north. Although it looks like a continuous range on a map, the Himalaya is actually a series of interlocking ridges, separated by countless valleys.

The Ganges Plain

Covering most of northern India, the vast alluvial plains of the sacred Ganges (Ganga) River drop a mere 200m between Delhi and the waterlogged wetlands of West Bengal, where the river joins forces with the Brahmaputra River and empties into the sea in Bangladesh. Vast quantities of eroded sediments from the highlands accumulate on the plains to a depth of nearly 2km, creating fertile, well-watered agricultural land.

Gujarat in the far west of India is separated from Sindh (Pakistan) by the Rann of Kutch, a brackish marshland that becomes a huge inland sea during the wet season. The waters recede in the dry season, leaving isolated islands perched on an expansive plain.

Get the inside track on Indian environmental issues at Down to Earth (www. downtoearth. org.in), an online magazine that explores stories often overlooked by mainstream media.

The Deccan Plateau

South of the Ganges plains, the land rises to the Deccan plateau, marking the divide between the erstwhile Mughal heartlands of North India and the Dravidian civilisations of the south. The Deccan is bound on either side by the densely forested Western and Eastern Ghats, which come together in their southern reaches to form the Nilgiri Hills in Tamil Nadu.

The Islands

Offshore from India are a series of island groups, politically part of India but geographically linked to the landmasses of Southeast Asia and islands of the Indian Ocean. The Andaman and Nicobar Islands lie far out in the Bay of Bengal, while the coral atolls of Lakshadweep (300km west of Kerala) are a northerly extension of the Maldive Islands, with a land area of just 32 sq km.

Environmental Issues

With well over a billion people, ever-expanding industrial and urban centres, and massive growth in chemical-intensive farming since the Green Revolution of the 1960s, India's environment is under considerable pressure. An estimated 65% of the land is degraded in some way, most of it seriously, and successive governments have consistently fallen short of most of their environmental protection goals.

Despite numerous laws, corruption has continued to exacerbate environmental degradation, particularly in the hydroelectricity and mining industries. Usually the people most affected are low-caste rural farmers and Adivasis (tribal people), who have limited political representation and few resources to fight big businesses.

Agricultural production has been reduced by soil degradation from over-farming, rising soil salinity, loss of tree cover and poor irrigation. The human cost is heartrending, and lurking behind all these problems is a basic Malthusian truth: there are far too many people for India to support.

As anywhere, tourists tread a fine line between providing an incentive for change and making the situation worse. Always consider your environmental impact while travelling, and look for options that will reduce your environmental footprint.

Climate Change

Changing climate patterns – linked to global carbon emissions – have been creating worrying extremes of weather in the country. While India's per-capita carbon emissions still rank behind those of the USA and Europe, the sheer size of its population makes it a major polluter.

It has been estimated that by 2030, India will see a 30% increase in the severity of its floods and droughts. In the mountain deserts of Ladakh, increased rainfall is changing time-honoured farming patterns, while glaciers on nearby peaks are melting at startling rates. Some of India's most devastating floods have occurred recently in Uttarakhand (in 2013), the Kashmir Valley (2014), Gujarat (2017) and most recently in Kerala in 2018, with each causing widespread loss of life and property.

Conversely, other areas of the country are experiencing reduced rainfall, causing drought and social upheaval over access to water. Meanwhile, islands in the Lakshadweep group, as well as the low-lying plains of the Ganges delta, are being inundated by rising sea levels, also linked to climate change.

Deforestation

Since Independence, more than 50,000 sq km of India's forests have been cleared for logging and farming, or destroyed by urban expansion, mining, industrialisation and river dams. Even in the well-funded, highly protected Project Tiger parks, the amount of forest cover classified as 'degraded' has tripled due to illegal logging. The number of mangrove forests has halved since the early 1990s, reducing the nursery grounds

A UN study predicts that by 2024 India will overtake China to become the world's most populous nation. It expects India's population to reach 1.5 billion by 2030.

THE LANDSCAPE ENVIRONMENTAL ISSUES

In 2016 the northeastern state of Sikkim became India's first fully organic state, with around 750 sq km being converted to certified organic land.

STRADDLING THE FUTURE

India is grappling with a growing dilemma: how to develop, modernise and expand economically, without destroying what's left of its environment, or adding to the global climate problem. The government has come under criticism for some conflicting stances. On one hand, Prime Minister Modi has made it his personal mission to clean up the Ganges River. In 2014 he launched the much publicised Swachh Bharat Mission (Clean India Mission) to provide universal sanitation and bring toilets to the people. Since then over 92,000,000 toilets have been built, with millions more on the way before October 2019, the mission's end date. Large-scale solar power generation, aiming to increase renewable capacity to 175 gigawatts by 2022 has also achieved impressive results.

But the government faces challenges when it comes to domestic coal mining (a major source of greenhouse gas emissions). India is the world's second-largest producer of coal, but for electricity generation, despite domestic production having risen in recent decades, the rate of growth is not meeting demand, making India increasingly reliant on imported coal.

Air quality is of great concern to citizens, especially in urban hubs such as Delhi, where crop burning in surrounding rural areas adds to the big city problems of traffic and industry emissions. Each winter, farmers in Delhi's neighbouring states burn over 30 million tonnes of crop stubble, with the smoke carried by wind to the landlocked capital city. The smoke contains a highly toxic mix of particulate matter, nitrogen dioxide, carbon dioxide and sulphur dioxide. The government has, so far, failed to take adequate measures to address root causes of the dire air pollution situation.

Noise pollution in major Indian cities has been measured at over 90 decibels – more than 1½ times the recognised 'safe' limit.

for the fish that stock the Indian Ocean and Bay of Bengal. According to news reports, from 2005 to 2007 India lost around 2206 sq km of dense forests; from 2015 to 2017 this increased to an estimated 6407 sq km.

India's first Five Year Plan in 1951 recognised the importance of forests for soil conservation, and various policies have been introduced to increase forest cover. This has yielded some success, but many regulations have been ignored by officials and illegal logging operations, as well as by ordinary people clearing forests for firewood and grazing. Try to seek out businesses that use more sustainable fuels in place of firewood.

Water Resources

Arguably the biggest threat to public health in India is inadequate access to clean drinking water and proper sanitation. With the population steadily marching upwards, agricultural, industrial and domestic water-usage levels are all expected to soar, despite government policies designed to control water use. The World Health Organization (WHO) estimates that less than a dozen Indian cities have adequate waste-water treatment facilities. Across India, untreated sewage and partially cremated bodies pour into river systems, while open defecation is a simple fact of life in most rural (and many urban) areas. It's reported that some 200,000 people die annually in India due to polluted water.

The Andaman and Nicobar Islands comprise 572 islands and are the peaks of a vast submerged mountain range extending almost 1000km between Myanmar (Burma) and Sumatra.

Rivers are also affected by run-off, industrial pollution and sewage contamination – the Sabarmati, Yamuna and Ganges are among the most polluted rivers on earth. At least 70% of the freshwater sources in India are now polluted in some way. Over recent years, drought has devastated parts of the subcontinent, particularly Rajasthan and Gujarat, and has been a driving force for rural-to-urban migration.

Water distribution is another volatile issue. Since 1947, an estimated 35 million people in India have been displaced by major dams, mostly built to provide hydroelectricity for an increasingly power-hungry nation, with limited compensation for those affected. Water disputes are also a bone of contention between India and Pakistan.

Survival Guide

Scams

India has an unfortunately deserved reputation for scams, both classic and newfangled. Of course, most can be avoided with some common sense and an appropriate amount of caution. They tend to be more of a problem in the major gateway cities (such as Delhi or Mumbai), or very touristy spots (such as Rajasthan). Chat with fellow travellers and check the India branch of Lonely Planet's Thorn Tree forum (www.lonelyplanet.com/thorntree) to keep abreast of the latest cons.

Contaminated Food & Drink

➡ Most bottled water is legit, but ensure that the seal is intact and the bottom of the bottle hasn't been tampered with.

➡ While in transit, try to carry packed food if possible, and politely decline offers of food or drink from locals on buses or trains; hygiene can be an issue and people have been drugged in the past.

➡ Though there have been no recent reports, the late 1990s saw a scam where travellers died after consuming food laced with dangerous bacteria from restaurants linked to dodgy medical clinics. In unrelated incidents, some clinics have given more treatment than necessary to procure larger

OTHER TOP SCAMS

➡ Gunk (dirt, paint, poo) suddenly appears on your shoes, only for a shoe cleaner to magically appear and offer to clean it off – for a price.

➡ Some shops are selling overpriced SIMs and not activating them; it's best to buy your SIM from an official outlet such as Airtel, Vodafone etc and check it works before leaving the area.

➡ Shops, restaurants or tour guides 'borrow' the name of their more successful and popular competitor.

➡ Touts claim to be 'government-approved' guides or agents, and sting you for large sums of cash. Enquire at the local tourist office about licensed guides and ask to see identification from guides themselves.

➡ 'Tourist offices' turn out to be dodgy travel agencies whose aim is to sell you overpriced tours, tickets and tourist services.

payments from insurance companies.

Credit-Card Cons

Be careful when paying for souvenirs with a credit card. While government shops are usually legitimate, private souvenir shops have been known to surreptitiously run off extra copies of the credit-card imprint slip and use them for phoney transactions later.

Ask the trader to process the transaction in front of you. Memorising the CVV/CVC2 number and scratching it off the card is also a good idea, to avoid misuse. If anyone asks for your PIN with

the intention of taking your credit card to the machine, insist on using the machine in person.

Druggings

Be extremely wary of accepting food or drink from strangers, even if you feel you're being rude. Women should be particularly circumspect. Occasionally, tourists (especially those travelling solo) have been drugged and robbed or even attacked. A spiked drink is the most common method, but snacks and even homemade meals have also been used.

Gem Scams

Don't be fooled by smooth-talking con artists who promise foolproof 'get rich quick' schemes. In this scam, travellers are asked to carry or mail gems home and then sell them to the trader's (nonexistent) overseas representatives at a profit. Without exception, the goods – if they arrive at all – are worth a fraction of what you paid, and the 'representatives' never materialise.

Travellers have reported this con happening in Agra, Delhi and Jaisalmer, but it's particularly prevalent in Jaipur. Carpets, curios and *pashmina* woollens are other favourites for this con.

Overpricing

Always agree on prices beforehand while using services that don't have regulated tariffs. This particularly applies to friendly neighbourhood guides, snack bars at touristy places, and autorickshaws and taxis without meters.

Photography

Ask for permission where possible while photographing people. If you don't have permission, you may be asked to pay a fee.

Theft

➡ Theft is a risk in India, as anywhere else. Keep your eye on your luggage at all times on public transport, and consider locking it, or even chaining it on overnight buses and trains. Remember that snatchings often occur when a train is pulling out of the station, as it's too late for you to give chase.

➡ Take extra care in dormitories and never leave your valuables unattended. Use safe deposit boxes where possible.

➡ Remember to lock your door at night; it is not unknown for thieves to take things from hotel rooms while occupants are sleeping.

Touts & Commission Agents

➡ Cabbies and autorickshaw drivers will often try to coerce you into staying at a hotel of their choice, only to collect a commission (added to your room tariff) afterward. Where possible, prearrange hotel bookings and request a hotel pick-up.

➡ You'll often hear stories about hotels of your choice being 'full' or 'closed' – check things out yourself and reconfirm and double-check your booking the day before you arrive.

➡ Be very sceptical of phrases like 'my brother's shop' and 'special deal at my friend's place'. Many fraudsters operate in collusion with souvenir stalls.

➡ Avoid friendly people and 'officials' in train and bus stations who offer unsolicited help, only to guide you to a commission-paying travel agent. Look confident, and if anyone asks if this is your first trip to India, say you've been here several times and that your onward travel is already booked.

Transport Scams

➡ Upon arriving at train stations and airports, if you haven't prearranged a pick-up, use public transport, or call an Uber or equivalent, or go to the prepaid taxi or airport shuttle-bus counters. Never choose a loitering cabbie who offers you a cheap ride into town, especially at night.

➡ While booking multiday sightseeing tours, research your own itinerary, and be extremely wary of anyone in Delhi offering houseboat tours to Kashmir – we've received many complaints over the years about dodgy deals.

➡ When buying a bus, train or plane ticket anywhere other than the registered office of the transport company, make sure you're getting the ticket class you paid for. Use official online booking facilities where possible.

➡ Train-station touts (even in uniform or with 'official' badges) may tell you that your intended train is cancelled/flooded/broken down or that your ticket is invalid or that you must pay to have your e-ticket validated on the platform. Do not respond to any approaches at train stations.

KEEPING SAFE

➡ A good travel-insurance policy is essential.

➡ Email copies of your passport identity page, visa and airline tickets to yourself, and keep copies on you.

➡ Keep your money and passport in a concealed money belt or a secure place under your shirt.

➡ Store at least US$100 separately from your main stash.

➡ Don't publicly display large wads of cash when paying.

➡ Consider using your own padlock at cheaper hotels.

➡ If you can't lock your hotel room securely from inside, stay elsewhere.

Women & Solo Travellers

Women Travellers

Reports of sexual assaults against women and girls are on the increase in India, despite tougher punishments being introduced after the notorious gang rape and murder of a female intern in Delhi in 2012. There have been several instances of sexual attacks on tourists over the last few years, though it's worth bearing in mind that the vast majority of visits are trouble free.

Unwanted Attention

Unwanted attention from men is a common problem.

➡ Being stared at is something you'll simply have to live with, so don't let it get the better of you.

➡ Be aware that men may try to take surreptitious photos with their phones – objecting loudly may discourage offenders.

➡ Refrain from returning male stares; this will be considered encouragement.

➡ Dark glasses, phones, books or electronic tablets are useful props for averting unwanted conversations.

➡ Wearing a wedding ring and saying you're due to meet your husband shortly can ward off unwanted interest.

Sexual Harassment

➡ Many women travellers have experienced provocative gestures, jeering, getting 'accidentally' bumped into and being followed, as well as more serious intrusions.

➡ Incidents are particularly common at exuberant (and crowded) public events such as the Holi festival. If a crowd gathers, find a less busy spot.

➡ Women travelling with a male partner will receive less hassle, but still be cautious.

Clothing

In big cities, you'll see local women dressing as they might in New York or London. Elsewhere women dress conservatively, and it pays to follow their lead.

➡ Avoid sleeveless tops, shorts, short skirts (ankle-length is recommended) and anything skimpy, see-through, tight-fitting or which reveals too much skin.

➡ Wearing Indian-style clothes such as the popular *salwar kameez* (traditional dress-like tunic and trousers) is viewed favourably.

➡ Drape a dupatta (long scarf) over your T-shirt to avoid stares – it also doubles as a head-covering for temple visits.

➡ Avoid going out in public wearing a choli (sari blouse) or a sari petticoat; it's like being half-dressed.

➡ Indian women tend to wear long shorts and a T-shirt when swimming; it's wise to wear a sarong from the beach to your hotel.

Staying Safe

The following tips will help you avoid uncomfortable or dangerous situations during your journey:

➡ Maintain a healthy level of vigilance, even if you've been in the country for a while. If something feels wrong, trust your instincts.

➡ Women have been drugged in the past so don't accept any food or drinks, even bottled water, from strangers.

➡ Keep conversations with unknown men short – being willing to chat can be misinterpreted.

➡ If you feel that a guy is encroaching on your space, he probably is. Protesting loudly enough to draw the attention of passers-by can stop unwelcome advances.

➡ The silent treatment can also be effective.

➡ Instead of shaking hands say *namaste* – the traditional, respectful Hindu greeting.

➡ Avoid wearing expensive-looking jewellery and carrying flashy accessories.

➡ Only go for massage or other treatments with female therapists, and go to cinemas with a companion.

➡ At hotels, keep your door locked, particularly at night; never let anyone you don't

SAFETY ON BUSES & TRAINS

➡ Don't organise your travel in such a way that it means you're hanging out at bus/train stations late at night.

➡ Solo women have reported less hassle by opting for the more expensive classes on trains, but try to avoid empty carriages.

➡ If you're travelling overnight by train, book an upper outer berth in 2AC; you're out of the way of wandering hands and the presence of fellow passengers is a deterrent to dodgy behaviour.

➡ On public transport, don't hesitate to return any errant limbs, put an item of luggage between you and others, be vocal (attracting public attention) or simply find a new spot.

know well into your hotel room.

➡ Avoid wandering alone in isolated areas – gallis (narrow lanes), deserted roads, beaches, ruins and forests.

➡ Use your smartphone's GPS maps to keep track of where you are; this will also alert you if a taxi/rickshaw is taking the wrong road.

➡ Try to look confident about where you are going in public; consult maps at your hotel (or at a restaurant) rather than on the street.

Taxis & Public Transport

Being female has some advantages; women can usually queue-jump for buses and trains without consequence and on trains and metros there are special ladies-only carriages. There are also women-only waiting rooms at some stations.

➡ Prearrange an airport pick-up from your hotel, particularly if you will arrive after dark.

➡ If travelling after dark, use a recommended, registered taxi service; travel with a companion where possible.

➡ Never hail a taxi in the street or accept a lift from a stranger.

➡ Never agree to have more than one man (the driver) in the car – ignore claims that this is 'just my brother' etc.

➡ Uber (www.uber.com) and Ola Cabs (www.olacabs.com)

are useful, as you get the driver's licence plate in advance; pass the details on to someone else as a precaution.

➡ When taking rickshaws alone, call/text someone, or pretend to, to indicate that someone knows where you are.

Sanitary Items

Sanitary pads are widely available, but tampons are usually restricted to pharmacies in some big cities and tourist towns.

Websites

Peruse personal experiences proffered by female travellers at www.journeywoman.com and www.wanderlustand lipstick.com. Blogs such as Breathe, Dream, Go (https://breathedreamgo.com) and Hippie in Heels (https://hippie-inheels.com) are also full of tips.

Solo Travellers

Travelling solo in India may be great, because local people are often so friendly, helpful and interested in meeting new people. You're more likely to be 'adopted' by families, especially if you're commuting together on a long rail journey. If you're keen to hook up with fellow travellers, try tourist hubs such as Delhi, Goa, Rajasthan, Kerala, Manali, McLeod Ganj, Leh, Agra and Varanasi, or browse the messages on Lonely Planet's Thorn Tree

forum (www.lonelyplanet.com/thorntree).

Cost

The most significant issue facing solo travellers is cost.

➡ Single-room accommodation rates are sometimes not much lower than double rates.

➡ Some midrange and top-end places don't even offer a single tariff.

➡ It's always worth trying to negotiate a lower rate for single occupancy.

➡ Ordering a *thali* (set-meal platter) at restaurants is an affordable way to try out a number of different dishes.

Safety

Most solo travellers experience no major problems in India, but, as anywhere else, it's wise to stay on your toes in unfamiliar surroundings.

➡ Some less honourable souls (locals and travellers alike) view lone tourists as an easy target for theft and sexual assault.

➡ Single men wandering around isolated areas have been mugged, even during the day.

Transport

➡ You'll save money if you find others to share taxis, autorickshaws, or a hired car and driver.

➡ Solo bus travellers may be able to get the 'co-pilot' seat beside the driver, handy if you've got a big bag.

Directory A–Z

Accessible Travel

If you have a physical disability or are vision impaired, the difficulties of travel in India can be exacerbated. If your mobility is considerably restricted, you may like to ease the stress by travelling with an able-bodied companion. One way that India makes it easier to travel with a disability is the access to employed assistance – you could hire an assistant, or a car and driver to get around, for example.

Accessibility Some restaurants and offices have ramps, but most tend to have at least one step. Staircases are often steep; lifts frequently stop at mezzanines between floors.

Accommodation Wheelchair-friendly hotels are almost exclusively top end. Make enquiries before travelling and book ground-floor rooms at hotels that lack adequate facilities.

Footpaths Where pavements exist, they can be riddled with holes, littered with debris and crowded. If using crutches, bring along spare rubber caps.

Transport Hiring a car with driver will make moving around a lot easier; if you use a wheelchair, make sure the car-hire company can provide an appropriate vehicle.

The following organisations may proffer further information:

Accessible Journeys (www.accessiblejourneys.com)

Disabled Holidays (www.disabledholidays.com)

Travel Eyes (www.traveleyes-international.com)

Enable Holidays (www.enableholidays.com)

Mobility International USA (www.miusa.org)

Download Lonely Planet's free Accessible Travel guide from http://lptravel.to/Accessible Travel.

Accommodation

Accommodation in India ranges from rustic village homestays to lavish heritage hotels in former palaces, and from dingy dives with bargain prices to modern hostels with the latest conveniences for travellers.

Reviews are listed first by price range, then by writer preference. Lonely Planet's price indicator icons refer to the cost of a double room, including a private bathroom, unless otherwise indicated. Note that each region has its own price ranges for accommodation.

Booking Services

Indian-based portals Goibibo (www.goibibo.com) and Oyo Rooms (www.oyorooms.com) offer big discounts on the midrange and top-end hotels that are registered with them. However, these can be of variable quality.

Indian Heritage Hotels Association (www.indianheritagehotels.com) Browse members of the association here.

Lonely Planet (www.lonelyplanet.com/india/hotels) Recommendations and bookings.

Reservations

Except during peak seasons in particular places, reservations are seldom essential. It's very rare to arrive in a town and not be able to find somewhere to stay; also, you usually get the cheapest price as a walk-in guest, particularly in budget accommodation.

Seasons

➔ High season usually coincides with the best weather for the area's sights and activities – normally spring and autumn (March to May and September

---

to November) in the mountains, and the cooler months (around November to mid-February) in the plains.

➡ In areas popular with foreign tourists, there's an additional peak period over Christmas and New Year; reserve well ahead at this time.

➡ Many temple towns have additional peak seasons around major festivals and pilgrimages.

➡ At other times significant discounts may be available; it's worth asking for one if your hotel seems quiet.

➡ Some hotels in places like Goa close during the monsoon period; hill stations such as Manali close in winter.

Taxes & Service Charges

A goods-and-services tax (GST) is usually calculated on top of the advertised rate for accommodation in India; its level varies according to the room price. Tax levels are as follows:

➡ Less than ₹1000: zero

➡ ₹1000–₹2499: 12%

➡ ₹2500–₹7499: 18%

➡ More than ₹7500: 28%

Rates quoted in listings include taxes.

Hotels
BUDGET & MIDRANGE HOTELS

➡ Shared bathrooms (often with squat toilets) are usually only found at the very cheapest lodgings.

➡ If you're staying in budget places, bring your own sleeping sheet or sleeping-bag liner, towel and soap.

➡ Insect repellent, a torch (flashlight) and padlock are handy accessories in many budget hotels.

➡ Midrange hotels tend to offer extras such as cable/satellite TV and air-conditioning.

➡ Noise pollution can be an issue (especially in urban hubs); pack earplugs and request a room that doesn't face a busy road.

➡ It's wise to keep your door locked at all times, as some staff (particularly in budget hotels) may knock and walk in without awaiting your permission.

➡ Note that some hotels lock their doors at night. Let the hotel know in advance if you'll be arriving late at night or leaving early in the morning.

➡ Away from tourist areas, cheaper hotels may not take foreigners because they don't have the necessary foreigner-registration forms.

TOP-END & HERITAGE HOTELS

India's top-end properties are stupendously fabulous, creating a cushioning bubble from the outside world, and ranging from wow-factor five-star chain hotels to historic palaces. In states such as Gujarat and Odisha (Orissa) there are increasing numbers of converted heritage properties.

Hostels & Dormitory Accommodation

There's an ever-increasing array of excellent hostels across India, offering such perks as air-con dorms, lockers and free wi-fi. Properties usually have mixed dorms, plus a female-only option. Impressive chains with branches dotted around India include Stops (www.gostops.com), Backpacker Panda (www.backpackerpanda.com), Moustache (www.moustachehostel.com) and Zostel (www.zostel.com).

More institutional dorm accommodation is offered by the hostels run by the YMCA, YWCA and Salvation Army or associated with Hostelling International (HI) or the Youth Hostels Association of India (YHAI). Some hotels have cheap dormitories, but these may be mixed gender and can be full of drunken men – not ideal conditions for women.

Homestays & Guesthouses

Homestays (family-run guesthouses) will appeal to those seeking a more personal setting with home-cooked meals. Options range from mud-and-stone village huts with hole-in-the-floor toilets to comfortable middle-class homes in cities. Contact the local tourist office for a list of local homestays and read up on your chosen place to see whether it's a genuine homestay, as some are more like budget hotels.

Camping

There are few official camping sites in India. On the other hand, wild camping is often the only accommodation option on trekking routes.

In some mountain or desert areas you'll also find summer-only tented camps, with accommodation in semi-permanent 'Swiss tents' with attached bathrooms.

Government Accommodation & Tourist Bungalows

The Indian government maintains a network of guesthouses for travelling officials and public workers, known variously as rest houses, dak (staging post) bungalows, circuit houses, Public Works

BOOK YOUR STAY ONLINE

For more accommodation reviews by Lonely Planet authors, check out http://lonelyplanet.com/hotels/. You'll find independent reviews, as well as recommendations on the best places to stay. Best of all, you can book online.

Department (PWD) bungalows and forest rest houses. These places may accept travellers if no government employees need the rooms, but permission is sometimes required from local officials.

'Tourist bungalows' are run by state governments – prices are usually midrange (though there are some cheap dorms), and rooms are usually spacious and clean.

Temple & Pilgrim's Rest Houses

Accommodation is available at some ashrams (spiritual retreats), gurdwaras (Sikh temples) and *dharamsalas* (pilgrims' guesthouses) for a donation or a nominal fee. Vegetarian meals are usually available at the refectories.

Note that these places have been established for genuine pilgrims, so abide by the house rules, which normally ban smoking and drinking alcohol on the premises.

Railway Retiring Rooms

Most large train stations have basic rooms for travellers holding an ongoing train ticket. Some are grim; others are surprisingly pleasant but almost all suffer from the noise of passengers and trains.

There's usually a choice between dormitories and private rooms (with 24-hour checkout), depending on the rail class you're travelling in.

Customs Regulations

You're supposed to declare Indian rupees in excess of ₹10,000, any amount of cash over US$5000, or a total amount of currency over US$10,000 on arrival.

You're also prohibited from importing more than one laptop, more than 2L of alcohol, more than 100 cigarettes or equivalent, or gifts and souvenirs worth over ₹8000.

Note also the restrictions on exporting antiques (p1199).

Embassies & Consulates

Most foreign diplomatic missions are based in Delhi, but there are various consulates in other Indian cities.

Australian: Delhi (☑011-41399900; www.india.high commission.gov.au; 1/50G Shantipath, Chanakyapuri; Ⓜ Lok Kalyan Marg), **Mumbai** (Map p756; ☑022-67574900; www.mumbai.consulate.gov. au; 10th fl, A Wing, Crescenzo Bldg, G Block, Plot C 38-39, Bandra Kurla Complex, Bandra East), **Chennai** (Map p1022; ☑044-45921300; www.chennai. consulate.gov.au; 9th fl, Express Chambers, Express Avenue Estate, White's Rd, Royapettah; ⊙9am-5pm Mon-Fri)

Bangladeshi: Delhi (☑011-24121394; www.bdhcdelhi.org; EP39 Dr Radakrishnan Marg, Chanakyapuri; Ⓜ Chanakyapuri), **Kolkata** (Map p466; ☑033-40127500; 9 Circus Ave; ⊙visas 9-11am Sat-Thu)

Belgian: Chennai (Map p1022; ☑044-40485500; http://india. diplomatie.belgium.be; Khader Nawaz Khan Rd, Nungambakkam; ⊙9.30am-12.30pm & 2.30-4.30pm)

Bhutanese: Delhi (☑011-26889230; www.mfa.gov.bt/ rbedelhi; Chandragupta Marg, Chanakyapuri; Ⓜ Chanakyapuri), **Kolkata** (Map p466; Tivoli Court, Ballygunge Circular Rd; ⊙10am-4pm Mon-Fri)

Electricity

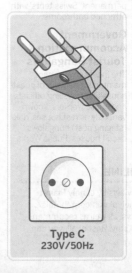

Type C
230V/50Hz

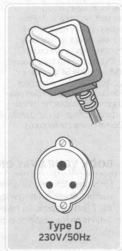

Type D
230V/50Hz

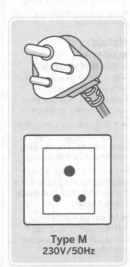

Type M
230V/50Hz

Canadian: Delhi (☎011-41782000; www.india.gc.ca; 7/8 Shantipath, Chanakyapuri; ⊙consular services 9am-noon Mon-Fri; MChanakyapuri), **Mumbai** (☎022-67494444; https://international.gc.ca/world-monde/india-inde/mumbai.aspx?lang=eng; 21st fl, Tower 2, Indiabulls Finance Centre, Senapati Bapat Marg, Elphinstone Rd West)

Chinese: Delhi (⊙consular 011-24677525, visas 011-30013601; http://in.china-embassy.org; 50-D Shantipath, Chanakyapuri; ⊙9am-12.30pm & 3-5.30pm Mon-Fri; MChanakyapuri)

French: Delhi (☎011-24196100; www.ambafrance-in.org; 2/50E Shantipath, Chanakyapuri; MChanakyapuri), **Mumbai** (Map p756;☎022-66694000; www.ambafrance-in.org/Consulate-in-Bombay; Wockhardt Towers, East Wing, 5th fl, Bandra Kurla Complex, Bandra East), **Puducherry** (Map p1046;☎0413-2231000; www.ambafrance-in.org; 2 Marine St; ⊙8am-1pm & 2.30-5pm Mon-Thu, to 1pm Fri)

German: Delhi (https://india.diplo.de; 6/50G Shantipath, Chanakyapuri; MChanakyapuri), **Kolkata** (Map p480;☎033-24791141; 1 Hastings Park Rd, Alipore), **Mumbai** (Map p752; ☎022-22832422; https://india.diplo.de/in-en/vertretungen/gkmumbai; 10th fl, Hoechst House, Nariman Point), **Chennai** (Map p1016;☎044-24301600; www.india.diplo.de; 9 Boat Club Rd, RA Puram; ⊙7.30am-3.30pm Mon-Thu, to 1.30pm Fri)

Irish: Delhi (☎011-24940 3200; www.dfa.ie/irish-embassy/india; C17 Malcha Marg, Chanakyapuri; ⊙9am-1.30pm & 2.30-5pm Mon-Fri; MChanakyapuri)

Israeli: Delhi (☎011-30414500, visas 011-30414538; www.embassies.gov.il/delhi; 3 Dr APJ Abdul Kalam Rd; ⊙9.30am-1pm Mon-Fri; MKhan Market), **Mumbai** (☎022-61600500; www.embassies.gov.il/mumbai; Marathon Futurex, 1301, A Wing, NM Joshi Marg, Lower Parel)

Japanese: Delhi (☎011-26876581; www.in.emb-japan.go.jp; 50G Shantipath, Chanakyapuri; ⊙9am-1pm & 2-5.30pm Mon-Fri; MChanakyapuri), **Mumbai** (Map p744; ☎022-23517101; www.mumbai.in.emb-japan.go.jp; 1 ML Dahanukar Marg, Cumballa Hill), **Chennai** (Map p1016;☎044-24323860; www.chennai.in.emb-japan.go.jp; 12/1 1st St, Cenotaph Rd, Teynampet; ⊙9am-5.45pm Mon-Fri)

Malaysian: Delhi (☎011-2415 9300; http://mw.kln.gov.my/web/ind_new-delhi/home; 50M Satya Marg, Chanakyapuri; ⊙8.30am-4.30pm Mon-Fri; MChanakyapuri), **Mumbai** (Map p756;☎022-26455751; www.kln.gov.my/web/ind_mumbai/home; 5th fl, Notan Classic Bldg, off Turner Rd, Bandra West), **Chennai** (Map p1016;☎044-24334434; www.kln.gov.my; 7 1st St, Cenotaph Rd, Teynampet; ⊙9am-5pm Mon-Fri)

Maldivian: Delhi (☎011-41435701; www.maldives embassy.in; C-3 Anand Niketan; MSir Vishveshwaraiah Moti Bagh)

Myanmar: Delhi (☎011-24678822; www.myanmedelhi.com; 3/50F Nyaya Marg; ⊙9.30am-4.30pm Mon-Fri; MLok Kalyan Marg), **Kolkata** (Map p480;☎033-24851658; 57K Ballygunge Circular Rd; ⊙visas 9am-noon Mon-Fri)

Nepali: Delhi (☎011-23476200; http://in.nepalembassy.gov.np; Mandi House, Barakhamba Rd; ⊙visa services 9am-1pm Mon-Fri; MMandi House), **Kolkata** (☎033-24561224; 1 National Library Ave, Alipore)

Netherlands: Delhi (☎011-24197600; www.netherlands worldwide.nl/countries/india; 6/50F Shantipath, Chanakyapuri; ⊙9am-5pm Mon-Fri; MChanakyapuri), **Mumbai** (Map p752;☎022-22194200; https://www.netherlands worldwide.nl/countries/india/about-us/consulate-general-in-mumbai; 1st fl, Forbes Bldg, Charanjit Rai Marg, Fort)

New Zealand: Delhi (☎011-46883170; www.nzembassy.com/india; Sir Edmund Hillary Marg, Chanakyapuri; ⊙8.30am-5pm Mon-Fri; MSir Vishveshwaraiah Moti Bagh), **Mumbai** (Map p756;☎022-61316666; www.mfat.govt.nz/en/countries-and-regions/south-asia/india/new-zealand-high-commission/new-zealand-consulate-general-mumbai; Level 2, Maker Maxity, 3 North Ave, Bandra Kurla Complex), **Chennai** (Map p1016;☎044-28112472; www.mfat.govt.nz; Rane Holdings Ltd, Maithri, 132 Cathedral Rd, Gopalapuram; ⊙8am-5.30pm Mon-Fri)

Pakistani: Delhi (☎011-26110601; www.mofa.gov.pk; 2/50G Shantipath, Chanakyapuri; MLok Kalyan Marg)

Singaporean: Delhi (☎011-46000915; www.mfa.gov.sg/newdelhi; E6 Chandragupta Marg, Chanakyapuri; ⊙9am-1pm & 1.30-5pm Mon-Fri; MChanakyapuri), **Mumbai** (☎022-22043205; www.mfa.gov.sg/content/mfa/overseas mission/mumbai.html; Maker Chambers IV, 14th fl, 222 Jamnalal Bajaj Rd, Nariman Point), **Chennai** (Map p1016; ☎044-28158207; www.mfa.gov.sg; 17A North Boag Rd, T Nagar; ⊙9am-5pm Mon-Fri)

Sri Lankan: Delhi (☎011-23010201; www.slhcindia.org; 27 Kautilya Marg, Chanakyapuri; ⊙8.45am-5pm Mon-Fri; MLok Kalyan Marg), **Mumbai** (Map p752;☎022-22045861; www.mumbai.mission.gov.lk; Mulla House, 34 Homi Modi St, Fort), **Chennai** (Map p1016;☎044-28241896; www.sldhcchennai.org; 56 Sterling Rd, Nungambakkam; ⊙9am-5.15pm)

Thai: Delhi (☎011-49774100; http://newdelhi.thaiembassy.org; D-1/3 Vasant Vihar; ⊙9am-5pm Mon-Fri; MVasant Vihar), **Kolkata** (Map p480;☎033-24407836; 18B Mandeville Gardens, Ballygunge), **Mumbai** (Map p752;☎022-22823535; www.thaiembassy.org/mumbai; 12th fl, Express Towers, Barrister Rajni Patel Marg, Nariman Point), **Chennai** (Map p1016;☎044-42300730; www.vfs-thailand.co.in; 3 1st Main Rd, Vidyodaya

Colony, T Nagar; ⏰8am-noon & 1-3pm Mon-Fri)

UK: Delhi (☎011-24192100; Shantipath, Chanakyapuri; ⏰9am-5pm Mon-Fri; Ⓜ️Lok Kalyan Marg), **Kolkata** (Map p466;☎033-22885172; 1A Ho Chi Minh Sarani), **Mumbai** (Map p756;☎022-66502222; www.gov.uk/government/world/organisations/british-deputy-high-commission-mumbai; Naman Chambers, C/32 G Block Bandra Kurla Complex, Bandra East), **Chennai** (Map p1022;☎044-42192151; www.gov.uk; 20 Anderson Rd, Nungambakkam; ⏰8.30am-4.30pm Mon-Thu, to 1.30pm Fri)

US: Delhi (☎011-24198000; https://in.usembassy.gov; Shantipath, Chanakyapuri; Ⓜ️Lok Kalyan Marg), **Kolkata** (Map p466;☎033-39842400; 5/1 Ho Chi Minh Sarani), **Mumbai** (Map p756;☎022-26724000; https://in.usembassy.gov/embassy-consulates/mumbai; C49, G Block, Bandra Kurla Complex, Bandra East), **Chennai** (Map p1016;☎044-28574000; http://in.usembassy.gov; 220 Anna Salai, Gemini Circle; ⏰9am-5pm Mon-Fri)

Insurance

➡ Comprehensive travel insurance to cover theft, loss and medical problems (as well as air evacuation) is strongly recommended.

➡ Some policies exclude potentially dangerous activities such as scuba diving, skiing, motorcycling, paragliding and even trekking; read the fine print.

➡ Some trekking agents may only accept customers who

EATING PRICE RANGES

Prices refer to the cost of a main course.

$ less than ₹150

$$ ₹150–₹300

$$$ more than ₹300

---

have cover for emergency helicopter evacuation.

➡ If you plan to hire a motorcycle in India, make sure that the rental policy includes at least third-party insurance.

➡ Check in advance whether your insurance policy will pay doctors and hospitals directly or reimburse you later (keep all documentation for your claim).

➡ It's crucial to get a police report in India if you've had anything stolen; insurance companies may refuse to reimburse you without one.

➡ Worldwide travel insurance is available at www.lonelyplanet.com/bookings. You can buy, extend and claim online anytime – even if you're already on the road.

Internet Access

There are few internet cafes these days, as wi-fi/3G/4G access is so widely available; wi-fi is usually free at your accommodation, but some places charge. Most restaurants, cafes and bars also offer free wi-fi, and there are a few public wi-fi hotspots in major cities.

Practicalities

➡ Charges, when they are applied, vary regionally; hourly rates range from ₹15 to ₹100 (or as high as ₹500 in five-star hotels). There's often a 15- to 30-minute minimum.

➡ The bandwidth load tends to be lowest in the early morning and early afternoon.

➡ Some places may ask to see your passport.

Security

Be cautious about using online banking on any nonsecure system. If you have no choice but to do this, consider changing your passwords afterwards as soon as you're on a secure connection.

Wireless Devices

➡ The simplest way to connect to the internet, when wi-fi is unavailable, is to use your smartphone as a personal wi-fi hotspot (use a local SIM to avoid roaming charges).

➡ Alternatively, companies that offer prepaid wireless 3G/4G modem sticks (dongles) include Reliance, Airtel, Tata Docomo and Vodafone. To connect you have to submit your proof of identity and address in India; check coverage as some providers only cover the state where you register, or charge higher fees for other states.

➡ Plug adapters are widely available throughout India, but bring spare plug fuses from home (local fuses will rarely fit).

Language Courses

There's a range of language courses across India, some requiring a minimum time commitment.

Delhi Hindu, Urdu and Sanskrit classes, among others, are available at Zabaan (www.zabaan.com).

Himachal Pradesh Three-month courses in Tibetan are offered at the **Library of Tibetan Works & Archives** (Map p325;☎9218422467; www.tibetanlibrary.org; Gangchen Kyishong; ⏰9am-1pm & 2-5pm Mon-Sat, closed 2nd & 4th Sat of the month), in McLeod Ganj. Several other places in McLeod Ganj offer courses in Tibetan and Hindi. The **Deer Park Institute** (☎01894-268508; www.deerpark.in; Tibetan Colony; course payment by donation; ⏰office 9am-noon & 2-6pm Mon-Sat) 🌿, in Bir, holds occasional courses in languages such as Pali, Sanskrit and Tibetan.

Mumbai Beginners' courses in Hindi, Marathi and Sanskrit at **Bharatiya Vidya Bhavan** (Map p744;☎022-23631261; www.bhavans.info; 2nd fl, cnr KM Munshi Marg & P Ramabai Marg,

Girgaum; language per hour ₹500, music per month ₹900; ⊙4-8pm).

Tamil Nadu Intensive three-month and six-month Tamil-language courses at the **International Institute of Tamil Studies** (☑9952448862; www.ulakaththamizh.org; CIT Campus, 2nd Main Rd, Tharamani; 3-/6-month course ₹5000/10,000) in Chennai.

Uttar Pradesh Hindi courses at **Pragati Hindi** (Map p386; ☑9335376488; www.pragati hindi.com; B-7/176 Harar Bagh) in Varanasi.

Uttarakhand Hindi courses at the well-regarded **Landour Language School** (☑0135-2631487; www.landourlanguage school.com; Landour; per hour group/private from ₹385/635; ⊙Feb–mid-Dec) in Mussoorie.

Legal Matters

If you're in a sticky legal situation, contact your embassy immediately. However, be aware that all your embassy may be able to do is monitor your treatment in custody and arrange a lawyer. In the Indian justice system, the burden of proof can often be on the accused and stints in prison before trial are not unheard of.

Antisocial Behaviour

➡ Smoking in public places is illegal, but this is rarely enforced; if caught you may be fined ₹200, which could rise to ₹500.

➡ People can smoke inside their homes and in most open spaces such as streets (heed any signs stating otherwise).

➡ Vaping (smoking e-cigarettes) is banned in Jammu, Kashmir, Karnataka, Punjab, Maharashtra and Kerala, and this is quite strongly enforced.

➡ Some Indian cities have banned spitting and littering, but this is enforced irregularly.

PROHIBITED EXPORTS

To protect India's cultural heritage, the export of certain antiques is prohibited – especially the export of those that are verifiably more than 100 years old. Reputable antique dealers know the laws and can make arrangements for an export-clearance certificate for old items that are OK to export. Detailed information on prohibited items can be found on the Archaeological Survey of India (ASI) website (http://asi.nic.in).

Under the Indian Wildlife Protection Act, the penalty for buying any product that endangers threatened species and habitats is a heavy fine or even imprisonment. Banned items include ivory; shahtoosh shawls (made from the down of rare Tibetan antelopes); and anything made from the fur, skin, horns or shell of any endangered species. Products made from certain rare plants are also banned.

Drugs

➡ Possession of any illegal drug is regarded as a criminal offence, which will result in a custodial sentence. This may be up to 10 years for possession, even for personal use, or 10 to 20 years if it's deemed that the purpose was sale or distribution. There's also usually a hefty fine.

➡ Cases can take months, even years, to appear before a court; the accused may have to await trial in prison.

➡ Be aware that travellers have been targeted in sting operations in Manali, Goa and other backpacker enclaves.

➡ Marijuana grows wild in various areas, but consuming it is still an offence, except in towns where bhang is legally sold for religious rituals.

➡ Police are particularly tough on foreigners who use drugs, so you should take this risk seriously.

➡ Pharmaceutical drugs that are restricted at home may be available over the counter or via prescription in India. Taking these without professional guidance can be dangerous.

Police

You should always carry your passport; police are entitled to ask you for identification at any time.

If you're arrested for an alleged offence and asked for a bribe, be aware that it is illegal to pay a bribe in India. Many people deal with an on-the-spot fine by just paying it, to avoid trumped-up charges. Corruption is rife, so the less you have to do with local police the better; try to avoid all potentially risky situations.

LGBT+ Travellers

In a landmark decision in 2018, India's Supreme Court ruled that gay sex in India was no longer a criminal offence. The ruling overturned a 2013 judgment that had upheld a colonial-era law under which gay sex was categorised as an 'unnatural offence'. The court also ruled that discrimination on the basis of sexual orientation is a fundamental violation of rights.

A 2014 ruling provided legal recognition of a third gender in India, a step towards increased acceptance of the large yet marginalised transgender (*hijra*) population.

Despite these rulings, India's LGBT+ scene remains relatively discreet, though less so in cities such as Delhi. The capital hosts the annual Queer Pride (www.facebook.com/delhiqueerpride) in November and also has a men-only gay guesthouse, Mister & Art House (www.misterandarthouse.com), in South Delhi. It's run by Delhi-based gay travel agency Indjapink (www.indjapink.co.in), which offers tailor-made tours. Founded by a well-known Indian fashion designer, the agency also has a guesthouse in Jaipur.

Serene Journeys (www.serenejourneys.co) is also recommended as a gay-friendly travel agency.

Nevertheless, LGBT+ visitors should be discreet in this conservative country. Public displays of affection are frowned upon for both homosexual and heterosexual couples.

Resources

Bombay Dost (http://bombaydost.co.in) Annual LGBTQ India magazine that's been running since 1990.

Gay Bombay (www.gaybombay.org) Lists gay events and offers support and advice.

Gaysi Zine (http://gaysifamily.com) Thoughtful monthly magazine and website featuring gay writing and issues.

Indian Dost (www.indiandost.com/gay.php) News and information, including contact groups in India.

Orinam (orinam.net) Has helpful, up-to-date info on LGBT+ support, events and pride marches in Chennai and Tamil Nadu.

Pink Pages (https://pink-pages.co.in) A national gay magazine that's been running for nearly 10 years.

Queer Azaadi Mumbai (http://queerazaadi.wordpress.com) Mumbai's queer-pride blog, with news.

Queer Ink (www.queer-ink.com) Online bookstore and multimedia platform for India's LGBT+ community.

Salvation Star (https://en-gb.facebook.com/SalvationStar)

An LGBT+ Facebook community in Mumbai that organises and promotes gay events and parties.

Maps

Most travellers will simply use Google Maps on their smartphone for travel around India. There's good GPS coverage in the main population centres. Most state-government tourist offices stock basic local maps, which are adequate for sightseeing.

The following are some of the better map series:

Eicher Various state maps showing rail and road networks.

Leomann Maps Useful trekking maps for Jammu and Kashmir, Himachal Pradesh and Uttarakhand.

Nelles (www.nelles-verlag.de)

Nest & Wings (www.nestwings.in)

Olizane Excellent topographic trekking maps of the Ladakh-Zanskar region at 1:150,000.

Survey of India (www.surveyofindia.gov.in)

TTK (www.ttkmaps.com)

Money

Most towns have ATMs, but it is wise to carry cash as backup. Mastercard and Visa are the most accepted cards. Travellers cheques are becoming harder and harder to change and are probably more hassle than they're worth.

Currency

The Indian rupee (₹) is divided into 100 paise, but only 50-paise coins are legal tender and these are rarely seen. Coins come in denominations of ₹1, ₹2, ₹5 and ₹10 (the 1s and 2s look almost identical); notes come in denominations of ₹5, ₹10, ₹20, ₹50, ₹100, ₹200, ₹500 and ₹2000.

The rupee is linked to a basket of currencies and has been subject to fluctuation in recent years.

ATMs & Eftpos

➜ ATMs are widespread.

➜ Visa, MasterCard, Cirrus and Maestro are the most commonly accepted cards.

➜ ATMs at Axis Bank, Citibank, HDFC, HSBC, ICICI and State Bank of India recognise foreign cards. Other banks may accept major cards (Visa, MasterCard etc).

➜ The limit you may withdraw in one transaction varies, from as low as ₹2000 up to a maximum of usually ₹10,000. A fee is almost always charged by the Indian bank for withdrawing money. It's a set fee (usually ₹150 to ₹300) rather than a percentage, so withdrawing more cash each time means you'll pay less in fees per unit.

➜ Before your trip, check whether your card can access banking networks in India and ask for details of charges.

➜ Notify your bank that you'll be using your card in India to avoid having it blocked; take along your bank's phone number just in case.

➜ Always keep the emergency lost-and-stolen numbers for your credit cards in a safe place, separate from your cards, and report any loss or theft immediately.

Credit & Debit Cards

➜ Credit cards and international debit cards are accepted at a growing number of shops, cafes, upmarket restaurants, and midrange and top-end guesthouses and hotels in bigger cities, and they can usually be used to pay for flights and train tickets.

➜ Cash advances on major credit cards are also possible at some banks.

➜ MasterCard and Visa are the most widely accepted cards.

→ Note that transaction fees can be high; however, some prepaid credit cards have no transaction fees.

Digital Wallets

PayTM (www.paytm.com) is India's major digital-wallet company. Local users pay for things through their smartphone, which is linked to their bank account. You can't link PayTM to a foreign bank account, and a loophole allowing foreign travellers to link and top up via a local SIM card was closed in 2018; check locally to see what the latest situation is.

Cash

→ Major currencies such as US dollars, pounds sterling and euros are easy to change throughout India.

→ Some banks also accept other currencies, such as Australian and Canadian dollars, and Swiss francs.

→ Private money changers deal with a wider range of currencies, but Pakistani, Nepali and Bangladeshi currency can be harder to change away from the border.

→ When travelling off the beaten track, always carry an adequate stock of rupees.

→ Whenever changing money, or receiving change, check every note. Don't accept any filthy, ripped or disintegrating notes, as others will refuse them when you try to spend them.

→ It can be tough getting change, so a stock of smaller currency (₹10, ₹20 and ₹50 notes) is invaluable.

→ You can change any leftover rupees back into foreign currency most easily at the airport. You may have to present encashment certificates or credit-card/ATM receipts, and show your passport and airline ticket.

ENCASHMENT CERTIFICATES

→ Indian law states that all foreign currency must be changed at official money changers or banks.

→ For every (official) foreign-exchange transaction you'll receive an encashment certificate (receipt), which will allow you to change rupees back into foreign

currency when departing India.

→ Encashment certificates should cover the rupee amount you intend to change back to foreign currency.

→ Printed receipts from ATMs are also accepted as evidence of an international transaction at most banks.

Money changers

Private money changers are usually open for longer hours than banks and are found almost everywhere (many also double as travel agents).

Hotels may also change money, but their rates are usually not as competitive.

Black Market

Black-market money changers exist, but legal money changers are so common that there's no reason to use illegal services, except perhaps to change small amounts of cash at land border crossings. If someone approaches you on the street and offers to change money, you're probably being set up for a scam.

Tipping

Bellhops and train/airport porters Tip ₹10 to ₹20.

Private drivers Tip ₹200 per day for good service.

Restaurants and hotels Service fees are sometimes added to bills automatically; otherwise, 10% is reasonable.

Taxis and rickshaws Not expected, but it's good to tip drivers/riders who are honest about the fare.

Trekking Per day: guides ₹350 to ₹500, porters ₹200 to ₹350.

Tour guides Tipping ₹200 to ₹350 per day is fair.

Opening Hours

The following are guidelines and may vary:

Banks (nationalised) 10am to 2pm/4pm Monday to Friday, to noon/1pm/4pm Saturday; closed second and fourth Saturday

---

PRACTICALITIES

Weights & Measures India uses the metric system. Additional units of measure you're likely to come across are lakh (one lakh equals 100,000) and crore (one crore equals 10 million).

Newspapers & Magazines English-language daily newsapers include the *Hindustan Times*, *Times of India*, *Indian Express*, *Hindu*, *Statesman*, *Telegraph*, *Daily News & Analysis* (DNA) and *Economic Times*. Current-affairs magazines include *Frontline*, *India Today*, *Week*, *Open*, *Tehelka*, *Outlook* and *Motherland*.

Radio The government-controlled All India Radio (AIR), India's national broadcaster, has more than 220 stations broadcasting local and international news. The multitude of FM stations includes Private FM, with music, current affairs, talkback and more, and Mirchi FM.

TV The national (government) TV broadcaster is Doordarshan. More people watch satellite and cable TV; English-language channels include the BBC, CNN, Star World, HBO, National Geographic and Discovery.

Bars and clubs Noon to 12.30am

Markets 10am to 7pm in major cities, with one closed day; rural markets once weekly, early morning to lunchtime

Museums/sights Often closed Monday

Post offices 9.30am to 5pm Monday to Saturday

Restaurants 8am to 10pm, or lunch (noon to 3pm) and dinner (7pm to 10/11pm)

Shops 10am to 7pm or 8pm, some closed Sunday

Photography

➸ Obtain permission when taking photos of people, especially women, who may find it offensive.

➸ India is touchy about anyone taking photographs of military installations – this can include train stations, bridges, airports, military sites and sensitive border regions.

➸ Avoid taking photos from planes taking off from (or landing in) airports actively shared by defence forces.

➸ Many places of worship – such as monasteries, temples and mosques – prohibit photography; it may also be inappropriate to take photos of public bathing, funerals and religious rituals.

➸ It's not uncommon for people in touristy areas to ask for a posing fee in return for being photographed. Ask first to avoid misunderstandings later.

Post

India Post (www.indiapost. gov.in) runs the most widely distributed postal service on earth, with 155,000 post offices. Mail and poste restante services are generally good, though the speed of delivery will depend on the efficiency of any given office. Airmail is faster and more reliable than sea mail, although it's best to use courier services (such as DHL and TNT) to send and re-

ceive items of value – expect to pay around ₹3500 per kilo for a parcel to Europe, Australia or the USA. Smaller private couriers are often cheaper, but goods may be repacked into large packages to cut costs and things sometimes go missing.

Sending Mail
LETTERS

➸ Posting airmail letters overseas costs around ₹25.

➸ International postcards cost around ₹15.

➸ For postcards, stick on the stamps before writing on them, as post offices can give you as many as four stamps per card.

➸ Sending a letter overseas by registered post costs an extra ₹70.

PARCELS

➸ Posting parcels can be either relatively straightforward or involve multiple counters and lots of queuing; get to the post office in the morning.

➸ All parcels sent through the government postal service must be packed up in white linen and the seams sealed with wax – agents near post offices usually offer this service for a small fee.

➸ An unregistered airmail package up to 250g costs ₹600 to ₹1000 to any country, plus ₹50 to ₹270 per additional 250g (up to a maximum of 2kg; different charges apply for higher weights).

➸ Parcel post has a maximum of 20kg to 30kg depending on the destination.

➸ Airmail takes one to three weeks, sea mail two to four months, and Surface Air-Lifted (SAL) – a hybrid where parcels travel by both air and sea – around one month.

➸ Express mail service (EMS; delivery within three days) costs around 30% more than the normal airmail price.

➸ Customs-declaration forms, available from the post office, must be stitched or pasted to the parcel. No duty is payable by the recipient for gifts under the value of ₹1000.

➸ Carry a permanent marker to write on the parcel any information requested by the desk.

➸ You can send printed matter via surface mail 'Bulk Bag' for ₹600 (maximum 5kg, plus ₹100 for each additional kilogram). Tailors can stitch the parcel with an opening so that it can be checked by customs.

➸ India Post (www.indiapost. gov.in) has an online calculator for domestic and international tariffs.

Receiving Mail

➸ To claim mail you'll need to show your passport.

➸ Ask senders to address letters to you with your surname in capital letters and underlined, followed by Poste Restante, GPO (main post office), and the city or town in question.

➸ Many 'lost' letters are simply misfiled under given/first names, so check under both your names and ask senders to provide a return address.

➸ Letters sent via poste restante are generally held for one to two months before being returned.

➸ It's best to have any parcels sent to you by registered post.

Public Holidays

There are three official national public holidays – Republic and Independence Days and Gandhi's birthday (Gandhi Jayanti) – plus a lot of other holidays celebrated nationally or locally, many of them marking important days in various religions and falling on variable dates.

The most important are the 'gazetted holidays' (listed), which are observed by central-government offices throughout India; see https://www.india.gov.in/calendar for the latest dates. On these days most businesses (offices, shops etc), banks and tourist sites close, but transport is usually unaffected. It's wise to make transport and hotel reservations well in advance if you intend to visit during major festivals.

Republic Day 26 January

Maha Shivaratri February/March

Holi February/March

Mahavir Jayanti March/April

Good Friday March/April

Buddha Purnima April/May

Eid al-Fitr May/June

Independence Day 15 August

Janmastami August/September

Eid al-Adha (Id ul-Zuha) July/August

Muharram August/September

Dussehra September/October

Gandhi Jayanti 2 October

Eid-Milad-un-Nabi October/November

Guru Nanak Jayanti November

Diwali October/November

Christmas Day 25 December

Safe Travel

➡ Travellers to India's major cities may fall prey to opportunistic crime, but many problems can be avoided with a bit of common sense and an appropriate amount of caution.

➡ Reports of sexual assaults have increased in recent years, so women should take care to avoid potentially risky situations.

➡ Browse advice from other travellers on the India branch of Lonely Planet's Thorn Tree forum (www.lonelyplanet.com/thorntree).

➡ Always check your government's travel-advisory warnings.

Rebel Violence

India has a number of dissident groups championing local causes who have employed the same tried-and-tested techniques of rebel groups everywhere: assassinations, and bomb attacks on government infrastructure, public transport, religious centres, tourist sites and markets. Curfews and strikes can close the roads (as well as banks, shops etc) for days on end in sensitive regions.

Certain areas are prone to insurgent violence – specifically Kashmir and remote tribal regions in Bihar, Jharkhand, Chhattisgarh, Odisha, Assam, Manipur and Nagaland. Check government travel advisory reports, and security websites such as www.satp.org, http://cdps

india.org and www.globalsecurity.org.

International terrorism is as much of a risk in Europe or the US, so this is no reason not to go to India, but it makes sense to check the local security situation carefully before travelling (especially in high-risk areas).

Smoking

➡ Smoking in public places is illegal, but this is rarely enforced; if caught you may be fined ₹200, which could rise to ₹500.

➡ People can smoke inside their homes and in most open spaces such as streets (heed any signs stating otherwise).

➡ Vaping (smoking e-cigarettes) is banned in Jammu, Kashmir, Karnataka, Punjab, Maharashtra and Kerala, and this is quite strongly enforced.

Telephone

There are few payphones in India (apart from in airports). Private STD/ISD/PCO booths offer inexpensive local, interstate and international calls, though they aren't as widespread as in the past. A meter displays how much the call is costing and usually provides a receipt when the call is finished.

➡ To call India from abroad, dial your country's international access code, then ✆91 (India's country code), then the area code (without the initial zero), then the local number. For mobile phones the area code and initial zero are not required.

➡ To call internationally from India, dial ✆00 (the international access code), then the country code of the country you're calling, then the area code (without the initial zero) and the local number.

WARNING: BHANG LASSI

Although it's rarely printed in menus, some restaurants in popular tourist centres will clandestinely whip up bhang lassi, a yoghurt and iced-water beverage laced with cannabis (and occasionally other narcotics). Commonly dubbed 'special lassi', this often potent concoction can cause varying degrees of ecstasy, drawn-out delirium, hallucination, nausea and paranoia. Some travellers have been ill for several days, robbed or hurt in accidents after drinking this fickle brew. A few towns have legal (controlled) bhang outlets. While these legal bhang sellers are happy to sell to foreigners, the bhang is intended for religious purposes. For travellers, buying from a legal shop is not a protection against being arrested for possession.

➡ Landline phone numbers have an area code followed by up to eight digits.

➡ Toll-free numbers begin with ☏1800.

➡ Mobile phone numbers usually have 10 digits, typically starting with an 8 or 9.

➡ To make interstate calls to a mobile phone, add 0 before the 10-digit number.

➡ To call a landline from a mobile phone, you always have to add the area code (with the initial zero).

➡ Some call-centre numbers might require the initial zero (eg calling an airline ticketing service based in Delhi from Karnataka).

➡ A Home Country Direct service, which gives you access to the international operator in your home country, exists for the US (☏000 117) and the UK (☏000 4417).

➡ To access an international operator elsewhere, dial ☏000 127. The operator can place an international call and assist you to make collect calls.

Mobile Phones

Roaming connections are excellent in urban areas, poor in the countryside and the Himalaya. Local prepaid SIMs are widely available. India operates on the GSM network at 900MHz, the world's most common; mobile phones from most countries will work on the subcontinent.

GETTING CONNECTED

➡ Indian mobile numbers usually have 10 digits, mostly beginning with 9 (but sometimes 6, 7 or 8).

➡ Getting connected involves some straight-forward paperwork and sometimes a wait of up to 24 hours for activation. Some regions require fiddlier processes than others.

➡ Mobiles bought in some countries may be locked to a particular network;

you'll have to get the phone unlocked, or buy a local phone (available from around ₹1000) to use an Indian SIM.

➡ It's easiest to obtain a local SIM in large cities and tourist centres – or, better yet, directly at airport booths when you land.

➡ Foreigners must supply between one and five passport photos, and photocopies of their passport identity and visa pages. Often mobile shops can arrange this for you, or you can ask your hotel to help.

➡ You must provide a residential address, which can be the address of your hotel, as well as a local reference (your hotel is generally fine for this too). Usually the phone company will call your hotel (warn the staff that a call will come through) any time up to 24 hours after your application to verify that you're staying there.

➡ It's a good idea to obtain the SIM in a place that you'll be for a day or two so that you can return to the vendor if there's any problem. To avoid scams, only obtain your SIM from a reputable branded phone shop.

➡ Prepaid mobile-phone packages are readily available for short-term visitors. SIMs often come free with a minimum data and call package. Industry newcomer Jio (the first mobile network to run entirely on 4G data technology; www.jio.com) has deals from ₹149 for 1.5GB of data per day to ₹509 for 4GB per day, both for 28 days. Airtel (www.airtel.in) charges ₹199 for 1.5GB per day for 28 days. It pays to shop around. Most large data packages are good for 28 days.

➡ More data is sold at stalls and shops (just look for phone-company logos). You pay the vendor and the

package/credit is deposited straight into your account.

CHARGES

➡ Calls within India are often included in prepaid packages along with the local SIM.

➡ International calls start at around ₹1 a minute. International outgoing messages cost ₹5. Incoming calls and messages are less than ₹1 and free respectively.

➡ Unreliable signals and problems with international texting (messages or replies not coming through or being delayed) are not uncommon.

➡ The leading service providers are Jio (part of Reliance), Airtel, Vodafone-Idea and BSNL. Coverage varies from region to region: Vodafone-Idea, Jio and Airtel have the widest coverage.

➡ BSNL and Airtel are best for the remote Andaman Islands, Jammu & Kashmir and the Northeast. Note that security in these regions is tight and you may need to leap through addition hoops – including providing a copy of the ID card of a local resident – to obtain a SIM.

Time

The subcontinent uses Indian Standard Time (GMT/UTC plus 5½ hours). India does not follow a daylight-saving system.

Toilets

Public toilets are best in major cities and tourist sites; the cleanest (usually with sit-down as well as squat facilities) are often at modern restaurants, shopping complexes and cinemas.

Beyond urban centres, toilets tend to be of the squat variety, and less well looked after. Toilet paper is almost never provided in public toilets, as locals tend to use water rather than paper to clean themselves. Modern toilets will have a bidet system attached, but most toilets outside urban centres will have a simple water tap and jug beside the toilet; the left hand is always used for toilet duties.

If you prefer to use paper, always carry your own with you. If there's a bin beside the toilet, that's where the paper should go. Otherwise, it's OK to throw/flush it down the toilet. It's also a good idea to carry hand sanitiser, as soap is rarely provided in public toilets.

Tourist Information

In addition to Government of India tourist offices (also known as 'India Tourism'), each state maintains its own network of tourist offices. These vary in quality – some are run by enthusiastic souls who go out of their way to help; others have an air of torpor and are little more than a means of drumming up business for State Tourism Development Corporation tours.

The nationwide tourism website of the Government of India is Incredible India (www.incredibleindia.org).

Visas

Apart from citizens of Nepal, Bhutan and the Maldives, who don't need visas for India unless they are arriving from mainland China, and citizens of Japan and South Korea, who can obtain a visa on arrival, everyone needs to apply for a visa before arriving in India. However, more than 150 nationalities can obtain the wonderfully hassle-free 60-day e-Visa.

There's also a six-month tourist visa, which is valid from the date of issue, not the date of arrival in India.

Entry Requirements

Visas are available at Indian missions worldwide, though in many countries applications are processed by a separate private company.

➡ Student and business visas have strict conditions (consult your Indian embassy for details).

➡ A standard 180-day tourist visa permits multiple entry for most nationalities.

➡ The 60-day e-Visa is usually a double-entry visa.

➡ Five- and 10-year tourist visas are available to US citizens *only* under a bilateral arrangement; however, you can still only stay in the country for up to 180 days continuously.

➡ Currently you are required to submit two digital photographs with your visa application (format jpeg 10kb–300kb), though only one for the e-Visa.

➡ An onward-travel ticket is a requirement for some visas, but this isn't always enforced (check in advance).

➡ Visas are priced in the local currency and may have an added service fee.

➡ Extended visas are possible for those of Indian origin (excluding those in Pakistan and Bangladesh) who hold a non-Indian passport and live abroad.

➡ If you need to register your visa (for stays of more than 180 days), or need a visa extension (only granted in exceptional cases) or a replacement for a lost passport (required before you can leave the country), then you should apply online at https://indianfrro.gov.in/eservices/home.jsp.

➡ If you need to see someone in person about your visa issue, then you should do so at the **Foreigners' Regional Registration Office** (FRRO; ☑ 011-26711443; https://boi.gov.in; 2nd fl, East Block 8, Sector 1, Rama Krishna Puram, Swami Vivekananda Marg; ☺9.30am-3pm Mon-Fri; Ⓜ Green Park) in Delhi.

➡ Check with the Indian embassy in your home country for any special conditions that may exist for your nationality.

E-TOURIST VISA

➡ Citizens from more than 150 countries can apply for an e-Visa (www.indianvisaonline.gov.in/evisa).

➡ You must apply a minimum of four days and a maximum of 120 days before you are due to arrive in India.

➡ The visa will be valid from your date of arrival in India.

➡ It's a double-entry visa that lasts for 60 days from your first date of entry.

➡ To apply, upload a photograph as well as a copy of your passport; have at

---

GOVERNMENT TRAVEL ADVICE

The following government websites offer travel advice and information on current hotspots.

Australian Department of Foreign Affairs (www.smartraveller.gov.au)

British Foreign Office (www.gov.uk/foreign-travel-advice)

Canadian Department of Foreign Affairs (www.voyage.gc.ca)

German Foreign Office (www.auswaertiges-amt.de)

Japanese Ministry of Foreign Affairs (www.mofa.go.jp)

New Zealand Ministry of Foreign Affairs & Trade (safetravel.govt.nz/health-and-travel)

US State Department (http://travel.state.gov)

least 180 days' validity in your passport and at least two blank pages.

➡ If your application is approved, you will receive an attachment to an email within 72 hours (though normally much sooner), which you'll need to print out and take with you to the airport. You'll then have the e-Visa stamped into your passport on arrival in India.

➡ Note that the e-Visa is also sometimes referred to as a 'visa on arrival', though you need to apply for it before you arrive.

➡ E-Visas are only valid for entry through 26 designated airports: Ahmedabad, Amritsar, Bagdogra, Bengaluru (Bangalore), Chennai, Chandigarh, Coimbatore, Delhi, Gaya, Goa, Guwahati, Hyderabad, Jaipur, Kochi (Cochin), Kolkata, Kozhikode (Calicut), Lucknow, Madurai, Mangaluru (Mangalore), Mumbai, Nagpur, Pune, Trichy (Tiruchirappalli), Thiruvananthapuram (Trivandrum), Varanasi and Visakhapatnam.

➡ They are also valid for arrival at five designated seaports: Kochi, Goa, Mangaluru, Mumbai and Chennai.

➡ E-Visa holders can, however, leave India from any authorised immigration checkpoint.

RE-ENTRY REQUIREMENTS

The previous rule of no re-entry on the same visa for two months after leaving India no longer applies to foreign nationals (except nationals of Afghanistan, China, Iran, Pakistan, Iraq, Sudan and Bangladesh, foreigners of Pakistani and Bangladeshi origin, and stateless persons). E-Visas

can now be used for double entry into India.

VISA EXTENSIONS

India is extremely stringent with visa extensions. At the time of writing, the government was granting extensions only in circumstances such as medical emergencies or theft of passport just before the applicant planned to leave the country (at the end of their visa).

If you do need to extend your visa due to any such exigency, you should first apply online at e-FRRO (https://indianfrro.gov.in/eservices/home.jsp), which also deals with replacements for lost/stolen passports (required before you can leave the country).

If you need to see someone in person, or are called in for an interview, the place to go is the **Foreigners' Regional Registration Office** (FRRO; ☑ 011-26711443; https://boi.gov.in; 2nd fl, East Block 8, Sector 1, Rama Krishna Puram, Swami Vivekananda Marg; ⏰ 9.30am-3pm Mon-Fri; Ⓜ Green Park) in Delhi. There are also some regional FRROs, but these are even less likely to grant an extension.

Assuming you meet the stringent criteria, the FRRO is permitted to issue an extension of 14 days (free for nationals of most countries; enquire on application). You must bring one passport photo (take more, just in case), your passport (or emergency travel document, if your passport is missing), and a letter from the hospital where you're having treatment if it's a medical emergency. Note that this system is designed to get you out of the country promptly with the correct official stamps, not to give you two extra weeks of travel and leisure.

TRAVEL PERMITS

Access to certain parts of India – particularly disputed border areas – is controlled by a system of permits that applies mostly to foreigners but also to Indian citizens in some areas.

Permits are required to visit Arunachal Pradesh, Sikkim and certain parts of Himachal Pradesh, Ladakh and Uttarakhand that lie close to the disputed border with China/Tibet. A permit is also necessary for travel to the Lakshadweep Islands and to some parts of the Andaman Islands.

In Odisha, permission is no longer required to visit tribal regions, and there's nothing to stop tourists from taking a bus or taxi to visit regional markets, but some villages are off limits to visitors (due to potential Maoist activity), so seek local advice before setting out.

Obtaining a permit is usually a formality, but travel agents must apply on your behalf for certain areas, including many trekking routes passing close to national borders.

Work

India's economy is growing, and there's plenty of potential in the thriving job market. Websites where you can look at opportunities include Transitions Abroad (www.transitionsabroad.com), Go Abroad (jobs.goabroad.com) and job portals such as Naukri (www.naukri.com). There are also opportunities to teach English as a foreign language; see TEFL (www.tefl.org.uk). To work in India you'll need to apply for an employment visa. Employment visas are usually granted for one year, or the term of the contract, and can be extended in India.

Transport

GETTING THERE & AWAY

Plenty of international airlines service India, and overland routes to/from Nepal, Bangladesh and Bhutan are all open. Flights, tours and other tickets can be booked online at www.lonelyplanet.com/bookings.

Entering the Country

Entering India by air or land is relatively straightforward, with standard immigration and customs procedures. A previously frustrating law barring re-entry into India within two months of the previous date of departure has been done away with (except for citizens of some Asian countries), thus allowing most travellers to combine their India tour with side trips to neighbouring countries.

Passports

To enter India you need a valid passport and an onward/return ticket, and a visa. Note that your passport needs to be valid for at least 180 days after your entry into India, and should have at least two blank pages. If your passport is lost or stolen, immediately contact your country's representative. Keep digital photos or photocopies of your airline ticket and the identity and visa pages of your passport in case of emergency.

Air

India is well served by international airlines and has an excellent range of budget domestic flights. You are required to show a copy of your ticket and your passport in order to enter the airport, whether flying internationally or within India. A digital copy on your smartphone is usually sufficient.

Airports & Airlines

India has four main gateways for international flights: Delhi, Mumbai, Chennai and Bengaluru (Bangalore). A number of other cities also service international carriers, including Hyderabad, Kochi (Cochin), Kolkata, Lucknow, Amritsar, Thiruvananthapuram (Trivandrum) and Kannur.

Amritsar (Sri Guru Ram Dass Jee International Airport; www.amritsarairport.com; Ajnala Rd, Rajasansi)

Bengaluru (☑1800 4254425; www.bengaluruairport.com)

Chennai (☑044-22560551; Tirusulam)

Delhi (☑01243376000; www.newdelhiairport.in; Ⓜ IGI Airport)

Hyderabad (☑040-66546370; http://hyderabad.aero; Shamshabad)

Kochi (☑0484-2610115; http://cial.aero; Nedumbassery)

Kolkata (NSCBIA (CCU); www.calcuttaairport.com)

CLIMATE CHANGE & TRAVEL

Every form of transport that relies on carbon-based fuel generates CO_2, the main cause of human-induced climate change. Modern travel is dependent on aeroplanes, which might use less fuel per kilometre per person than most cars but travel much greater distances. The altitude at which aircraft emit gases (including CO_2) and particles also contributes to their climate change impact. Many websites offer 'carbon calculators' that allow people to estimate the carbon emissions generated by their journey and, for those who wish to do so, to offset the impact of the greenhouse gases emitted with contributions to portfolios of climate-friendly initiatives throughout the world. Lonely Planet offsets the carbon footprint of all staff and author travel.

Kannur (www.kannurairport.in; Mattannur)

Lucknow (☎0522-2435404; www.lucknowairport.com)

Mumbai (Map p756;☎022-66851010; www.csia.in; Santa Cruz East) ✈

India's national carrier is **Air India** (☎1860-2331407, 011-24667473; www.airindia.com), which operates international and domestic flights. Air travel in India has had a decent safety record in recent years.

Departure Tax

Departure tax and other charges are included in airline tickets.

Land

Although most visitors fly into India, it is possible to travel overland between India and Bangladesh, Bhutan, Nepal, Pakistan and Myanmar (Burma). The overland route from Nepal is the most popular. For more on these routes, check for up-to-date information on Lonely Planet's Thorn Tree forum (www.lonelyplanet.com/thorntree) or see the Man in Seat 61 (www.seat61.com) go to the Train Travel in India page and click on the Europe to India overland link.

Border Crossings

If you enter India by bus or train, you'll be required to disembark at the border for standard immigration and customs checks.

You *must* have a valid Indian visa in advance, as no visas are available at the border. Note that Indian e-Visas (p1205) are not valid at land borders; they are valid only at designated airports and seaports.

Drivers of cars and motorbikes will need the vehicle's registration papers, liability insurance and an international driver's permit in addition to their domestic licence. You'll also need a Carnet de Passage en Douane (a customs document), which acts as a temporary waiver of import duty on the vehicle.

For travellers wishing to visit Tibet from India, the only way to do so is to exit to Nepal and then enter Tibet through the border crossing at Kodari as part of an organised tour. Alternately, you could fly to Lhasa from Kathmandu.

For the latest paperwork requirements and other important driving information, contact your local automobile association.

BANGLADESH

There are four main land crossings where foreigners can cross between Bangladesh and India, all in West Bengal or the Northeast States.

Heading from Bangladesh to India, you have to prepay the exit tax, which can be done at a Sonali Bank branch (in Dhaka, in another big city or at the closest branch to the border).

Exiting Bangladesh overland is complicated by red tape – if you enter the country by air, you'll require a road permit (or 'change of route' permit) to leave by land.

To apply for visa extensions and change-of-route permits you'll need to visit the **Immigration and Passport Office** (☎02-815 9525; www.dip.gov.bd; Passport Bhaban, E-7 Agargaon, Sher-e-Bangla Nagar; ☺Sun-Thu 10am-1pm) in Dhaka.

Some travellers have reported problems exiting Bangladesh overland with the visa issued on arrival at Dhaka airport.

BHUTAN

Phuentsholing is the main entry and exit point between India and Bhutan, although the eastern checkpoint at Samdrup Jongkhar is also used. You can also cross from Assam to Gelephu in Bhutan, though it's a remote crossing.

As entry requirements need advance planning, it's best to consult a travel agent or Bhutanese Embassy for up-to-the-minute details. Travellers need to organise a tour with a Bhutanese travel

OVERLAND TO/FROM BANGLADESH

ROUTE/BORDER TOWNS	TRANSPORT	VISAS
Kolkata–Dhaka/Petrapole (India) & Benapole (Bangladesh)	Regular daily Kolkata–Dhaka buses; twice-weekly train via Darsana border post.	Obtain in advance. To buy a train ticket, Darsana must be marked on your Bangladeshi visa.
Siliguri–Rangpur/Chengrabandha (India) & Burimari (Bangladesh)	Regular Siliguri–Chengrabandha buses, then bus to Rangpur, Bogra & Dhaka. Also direct daily Siliguri–Dhaka buses.	Obtain in advance.
Shillong–Sylhet/Dawki (India) & Tamabil (Bangladesh)	Jeeps run from Shillong to Dawki. From Dawki, walk (1.5km) or take a taxi to Tamabil bus station for regular buses to Sylhet.	Obtain in advance.
Agartala–Dhaka/Agartala, 3km from border (India) & Akhaura, 5km from border (Bangladesh)	Akhaura is on the Dhaka–Comilla and Dhaka–Sylhet train lines. There are 3 weekly buses from Agartala to Dhaka.	Obtain in advance.

OVERLAND TO/FROM NEPAL

ROUTE/BORDER TOWNS	TRANSPORT	VISAS
Sunauli (India)–Bhairawa/ Siddharthanagar (Nepal)	Trains from Delhi to Gorakhpur, then half-hourly buses to border. One direct AC bus from Varanasi to Kathmandu via Sunauli (₹1370, 10pm). Buses & jeeps from Bhairawa (Siddharthanagar) to Pokhara, Kathmandu & central Nepal.	Nepali visas available at border (6am-10pm)
Raxaul Bazaar (India)– Birganj (Nepal)	Daily buses from Patna & Kolkata to Raxaul Bazaar. Mithila Express train daily from Kolkata. Regular day/ night buses from Birganj to Kathmandu & Pokhara.	As above (6am-6pm)
Panitanki (India)– Kakarbhitta (Nepal)	Buses &/or jeeps run to Panitanki from Siliguri, Darjeeling & Kalimpong. Regular buses from Kakarbhitta to Kathmandu (13 hours) & other destinations. Bhadrapur airport (23km away) has flights to Kathmandu.	As above (7am-7pm)
Rupaidiha Bazaar/ Jamunaha (India)– Nepalganj (Nepal)	Slow buses from Lucknow to Rupaidiha Bazaar, then rickshaw to Jamunaha. Nepalganj has buses to Kathmandu & Pokhara, flights to Kathmandu.	As above
Banbassa (India)– Bhimdatta/Mahendranagar (Nepal)	Buses from Haldwani & Pithoragarh to Banbassa, then rickshaw to border. From Bhimdatta (Mahendranagar) there are daily buses to Kathmandu and one daily service to Pokhara.	As above (6am-6pm)
Gauriphanta (India)– Dhangadhi (Nepal)	Daily buses run from Lucknow to Gauriphanta. Dhangadhi is served by buses & flights from Kathmandu.	As above (8am-5pm)

agent and pay a fixed daily fee in order to obtain a Bhutanese visa. Also see www.tourism.gov.bt and Lonely Planet's *Bhutan*.

A Bhutan government–operated bus to Phuentsholing (₹600, 15 hours) leaves at 7pm daily, except Sunday, from the walled northeastern yard of Kolkata's Esplanade bus station, where there are two special **ticket booths** (Map p474; Esplanade bus station; ☾9.30am-1pm & 2-6pm Mon-Sat). It's faster and more comfortable, however, to take the 13149 Kanchankanya Express (sleeper/3AC/2AC ₹370/1010/1455, 14 hours, 8.30pm) from Sealdah train station to Hasimara, and then travel the last 18km by local bus or taxi to Phuentsholing. Note that you may have to camp a night at this border town for your Bhutanese visa to be processed.

MYANMAR
Two remote crossings between India's Northeast States and northwestern Myanmar are open to foreigners – at Zokhawthar/Rihkhawdar in Mizoram, and at Moreh/Tamu in Manipur. You'll need to obtain a Myanmar visa in advance (see http://evisa.moip.gov.mm) to cross.

Crossing from Mizoram, jeeps run from Aizawl or Champhai to Zokhawthar/Rihkhawdar, with onward transport to Tiddim & Kalaymyo (Kalay) in Myanmar. Crossing from Manipur, shared taxis, buses and helicopter run from Imphal to Moreh/Tamu, with onward transport to Kalaymyo or Mandalay in Myanmar.

NEPAL
Weather conditions and flooding permitting, there are six land border crossings between India and Nepal.

Multiple-entry visas (15/30/90 days US$25/40/100 – US-dollar cash is preferred, though you can sometimes pay in Indian rupees) are available at the Nepali immigration post (you need two passport photos). Note that it can be a hassle getting an Indian visa in Nepal. It's much easier to travel with a multiple-entry Indian visa

if you plan to go from India to Nepal and then return to India.

Most people cross into India at the Sunauli border, then take an onward bus or train from there, though it's faster and more comfortable to take a taxi to Gorakhpur and get a train or bus from there.

Travel agents in Varanasi often try to sell tourists 'through' tickets to Kathmandu. In reality only the Nepali-run Shree Manjushree Bus Sewa Samiti has direct overnight AC buses to Kathmandu (₹1300, 17 hours, 10pm), running irregularly according to demand. Book tickets at the bus stand in Varanasi.

From Bihar, the busy border crossing between Raxaul and Birganj is the most direct route to Kathmandu and eastern Nepal. The border at Raxaul (p523) is open from 6am to 10pm.

PAKISTAN
Given the rocky relationship between India and Pakistan, crossing by land depends on the current state of relations

OVERLAND TO/FROM PAKISTAN

Assuming that the border is open, a daily bus departs from Delhi's Ambedkar Stadium Bus Stand (p106) (₹2400, 12 hours, 6am) for Lahore; the journey involves four stops. Book your tickets in advance from a window at the bus stand.

For security reasons, current government advice warns foreigners against using trains within Pakistan. There are twice-weekly trains between Lahore and Attari (on the Indian side of the border), where there's a customs-and-immigration stop. There are frequent buses from Amritsar to the Wagah border (just beyond Attari). Check that the border is open before you leave; usual hours are 8.30am to 2.30pm mid-April to mid-October, and 9.30am to 3pm mid-October to mid-April; arrive at least an hour before closure. From Wagah there are buses and taxis on to Lahore.

The Thar Express, a weekly train service between Jodhpur and Karachi, is only open to Indian or Pakistani nationals. Trains leave Jodhpur (Bhagat Ki Kothi station, about 4km from the main station) every Saturday (Friday in the opposite direction). Customs/immigration is at Munabao (at the Indian border), where you physically change trains. Expect extremely tight security.

between the two countries – check locally.

If the crossings are open, you can reach Pakistan from Delhi, Amritsar (Punjab) and Rajasthan by bus or train. The 'Karvan-e-Aman' (Caravan of Peace) bus route from Srinagar to Pakistan-administered Kashmir is only open to Indian citizens.

You must have a visa to enter Pakistan. It's easiest to obtain this from the Pakistani mission in your home country. At the time of writing, the **Pakistani High Commission** (☑011-26110601; www.mofa.gov.pk; 2/50G Shantipath, Chanakyapuri; M Lok Kalyan Marg) in Delhi was not issuing tourist visas for most nationalities, but this could change.

Sea

There are no international passenger ferries to or from India, but you may be able to secure a place on a cargo ship. See www.cargoship voyages.com for options.

GETTING AROUND

Air

Domestic air travel is booming in India, and there are several national and regional airlines serving all corners of the country, including some budget carriers.

Airlines in India

Transporting vast numbers of passengers annually, India's domestic airline industry is very competitive. Major carriers include:

Air India (☑1860-2331407, 011-24667473; www.airindia.com)

AirAsia (☑Delhi office 011-26303939, customer care 80-46662222; www.airasia.com)

GoAir (☑18602-100999; www.goair.in)

IndiGo (☑011-43513200; www.goindigo.in)

Jet Airways (☑91-39893333; www.jetairways.com)

SpiceJet (☑0987-1803333; www.spicejet.com)

Vistara (☑9289-228888; www.airvistara.com)

Apart from airline sites, bookings can be made through portals such as Cleartrip (www.cleartrip.com), Make My Trip (www.makemytrip.com) and Yatra (www.yatra.com).

Security norms require you to produce your ticket and passport when you enter an airport; a digital ticket on your smartphone is usually sufficient. Every item of cabin baggage needs a label, which must be stamped as part of the security check (collect tags at the check-in counter). Flights to sensitive destinations, such as Srinagar and Ladakh, have extra security restrictions. Spot checks of cabin baggage may take place on the tarmac before you board.

Keeping peak-hour congestion in mind, the recommended check-in time for domestic flights is two hours before departure, even though check-in actually closes 45 minutes before departure. The usual baggage allowance is 15kg (10kg for smaller aircraft) in economy class, though Air India allows 25kg.

Bicycle

There are no restrictions on bringing a bicycle into the country. However, bicycles sent by sea can take a few weeks to clear customs in India, so it's better to fly them in. It may be cheaper – and less hassle – to hire or buy a bicycle locally. Read up on bicycle touring before you travel: Neil and Harriet Pike's excellent *Adventure Cycle-Touring Handbook* (2015), Laura Stone's *Himalaya by Bike* (2008) and Rob Van Der Plas' *Bicycle Touring Manual* (1998) are good places to start.

Hire

➡ Tourist centres and traveller hang-outs are the easiest spots to find bicycles for hire – enquire locally.

➤ Prices vary: a roadworthy Indian-made bicycle costs around ₹40 to ₹150 per day; mountain bikes, where available, are more like ₹400 to ₹800 per day.

➤ Hire places may require a cash security deposit (it may be stating the obvious, but avoid leaving your airline ticket or passport).

➤ Bike-share schemes have been unveiled in cities such as Delhi, Hyderabad and Mumbai, though for now you can only sign up for them with a local ID.

Practicalities

➤ Mountain bikes with off-road tyres give the best protection against India's puncture-inducing roads.

➤ Roadside cycle mechanics abound, but you should still bring spare tyres, brake cables, lubricating oil, a chain-repair kit and plenty of puncture-repair patches.

➤ Bikes can often be carried for free, or for a small luggage fee, on the roof of public buses – handy for uphill stretches.

➤ Contact your airline for information about transporting your bike and customs formalities in your home country.

➤ Be conservative about the distance you expect to cover – an experienced cyclist can manage around 60km to 100km a day on the plains, 40km to 60km on all-weather mountain roads and 40km or less on dirt roads.

Buying a Bike

➤ Delhi's ragtag **Jhandewalan Cycle Market** (Map p68; ⊙11am-8pm; Ⓜ Jhandewalan) has imported and domestic new and secondhand bikes, and spare parts.

➤ Mountain bikes with reputable brands that include Hero and Atlas generally start at around ₹6000.

➤ Reselling is usually fairly easy – ask at local cycle shops or put up an advert on travel noticeboards. If you purchased a new bike and it's still in reasonable condition, you should be able to recoup around 50% of what you originally paid.

Road Rules

➤ Vehicles drive on the left in India, but otherwise road rules are not generally followed.

➤ Cities and national highways can be hazardous places to cycle, so, where possible, stick to back roads.

Transporting Bikes

For long hauls, transporting your bike by train can be convenient. Buy a standard train ticket for the journey, then take your bike to the station parcel office with your passport, registration papers, driver's licence and insurance documents. Packing-wallahs will wrap your bike in protective sacking for ₹100 to ₹200, and you must fill out several forms and pay the shipping fee, which varies according to the route and train type – plus an insurance fee of 1% of the declared value of the bike. Bring the same paperwork to collect your bike from the goods office at the other end. If the bike is left waiting at the destination for more than 24 hours, you'll pay a storage fee of around ₹100 per day.

Some locals hang their bikes from their handlebars outside the window of the carriage – don't do this.

Boat

➤ A new overnight cruise ship, **Angriya Cruise** (☑8314810440; www.angriyacruises.com; Victoria Docks 15, Purple Gate, off Ferry Wharf, Mazagão; d with/without window from ₹6800/5300), between Mumbai and Goa was launched in late 2018; it runs three times a week from either end.

➤ Scheduled but infrequent ferries connect mainland India to the Andaman Islands, with departures once or twice a month to Port Blair from Chennai, Kolkata and Visakhapatnam; see www.andamans.gov.in.

➤ From mid-September to mid-May, ferries travel from Kochi (Cochin; Kerala) to the islands of Lakshadweep, though tickets for these can be tricky to obtain and are almost exclusively available through package tours.

➤ There are also numerous shorter ferry services across rivers, from chain pontoons to coracles and various boat cruises.

Bus

Buses go almost everywhere in India and are the only way to get around many mountainous areas. They tend to be the cheapest way to travel. Services are fast and frequent, and rarely need to be booked in advance.

Roads in mountainous or curvy terrain can be perilous; buses are often driven with wilful abandon, and accidents are possible on any route.

Avoid night buses unless there's no alternative: driving conditions are more hazardous and drivers may be inebriated or overtired.

All buses make snack and toilet stops (some more frequently than others), providing a break but possibly adding hours to journey times.

Shared jeeps complement the bus service in many mountain areas.

Classes

State-owned and private bus companies each offer several types of bus, graded loosely as 'ordinary' or 'local', 'semi-deluxe', 'deluxe' or 'super deluxe'. These classes are usually open to interpretation, and the exact grade of luxury offered in a particular class varies.

Ordinary buses tend to be ageing rattletraps, while the deluxe grades range from less decrepit versions of ordinary buses to flashy Volvo coaches with air-con and reclining seating.

There's rarely any need, and nor is it usually possible, to pre-book seats on ordinary 'local' buses. More deluxe AC buses, though, are less frequent, so pre-booking is a good idea – doing so from the departure station the day before you travel normally suffices.

Buses run by the state government are usually more reliable (if there's a breakdown, another bus will be sent to pick up passengers), and seats can usually be booked up to a month ahead. Many state governments now operate super-deluxe buses.

Travel agencies in many tourist towns offer relatively expensive private two-by-two buses, which tend to leave and terminate at conveniently central stops.

On any bus, try to sit up the front to minimise the bumpy effect of potholes. Never sit directly above the wheels. Earplugs are invaluable on long-distance trips.

Luggage

Luggage is stored in compartments underneath the bus (sometimes for a small fee) or carried on the roof.

If you've pre-booked your bus, arrive at least an hour before the departure time – some buses cover roof-stored bags with a canvas sheet, making last-minute additions inconvenient or impossible.

If your bags go on the roof, make sure they're securely locked, and tied to the metal baggage rack – unsecured bags can fall off on rough roads.

Theft is a (minor) risk: watch your bags at snack and toilet stops. Never leave day-packs or valuables unattended inside the bus.

Reservations

Most deluxe buses can be booked in advance at the bus station, through travel agencies and online at portals such as Cleartrip (www. cleartrip.com), Makemytrip

(www.makemytrip.com) and **Redbus** (☎011-39412345; www.redbus.in).

Reservations are rarely possible on ordinary 'local' buses; just turn up at the bus station and hop on the next available bus. Note: you won't always get a seat, but you'll always be allowed on board.

On very busy routes, one way to secure a seat is by sending a travelling companion ahead to claim some space. Another is to pass a book or article of clothing through an open window to bag an empty seat.

If you board a bus midway through its journey, you may have to stand until a seat becomes free.

Many buses only depart when full – passengers might suddenly leave yours to join one that looks nearer to departing.

Many bus stations have a separate women's queue (not always obvious when signs are in Hindi and men join the melee), and women also have an unspoken right to elbow their way to the front of any bus queue.

Costs

The cheapest buses are ordinary 'local' government buses, but prices vary from state to state. Expect to pay around ₹100 for a typical two- to three-hour journey.

Add around 50% to the ordinary fare for deluxe services, double the fare for air-conditioning, and triple or quadruple the fare for a two-by-two super-deluxe service.

Rajasthan Roadways offers discounts for female travellers.

Car

Few people bother with self-drive car hire – not only because of the hair-raising driving conditions but also because hiring a car with driver is comparatively affordable in India, particularly if several people share the cost. Hertz (www.hertz.com) is one of the

few international companies with representatives in India.

Hiring a Car & Driver

Most towns have taxi stands or car-hire companies where you can arrange short or long tours.

Not all hire cars are licensed to travel beyond their home state. Those that are will pay extra state taxes, which are added to the hire charge.

Ask for a driver who speaks some English and knows the region you intend to visit. Try to see the car and meet the driver before paying anything.

A wide range of cars now operate as taxis. From a proletarian Tata Indica hatchback to a comfy Toyota Innova SUV, there's a model to suit every budget.

Hire charges for multiday trips cover the driver's meals and accommodation – drivers should make their own sleeping and eating arrangements. Many hotels have inexpensive rooms specifically set aside for drivers.

It's essential to set the ground rules from day one: to avoid difficulties later, politely but firmly let the driver know that you're in charge.

Costs

Car-hire costs depend on the distance and the terrain (driving on mountain roads uses more petrol, hence the higher cost).

One-way trips usually cost the same as return ones (to cover the petrol and driver charges for getting back).

Hire charges vary from state to state. Some taxi unions set a maximum time limit or a maximum kilometre distance for day trips – if you go over, you'll have to pay extra. Prices also vary according to the make and model of the taxi.

To avoid misunderstandings, get *in writing* what you've been promised (quotes should include petrol, sightseeing stops, all your chosen destinations, and meals and accommodation for the driver). If a driver asks you for money for petrol en route because he is short of cash, get receipts for reimbursement later. If you're travelling by the kilometre, check the odometer reading before you set out so as to avoid confusion later.

For sightseeing day trips around a single city, expect to pay upwards of ₹1400/1800 for a non-AC/AC car with an eight-hour, 80km limit per day (extra charges apply for longer trips). For multiday trips, operators usually peg a 250km minimum running distance per day and charge around ₹8/10 per kilometre for a non-AC/AC car for anything over this.

A tip is customary at the end of your journey; around ₹200 per day is fair.

Hitching

Hitching is never entirely safe, and not recommended, particularly for female travellers. Those who do hitch should understand that they are taking a small but serious risk, as there have been robberies and worse in the past. However, for a negotiable fee, truck drivers supplement the bus service in some remote areas. As drivers rarely speak English, you may have difficulty explaining where you wish to go and working out a fair price to pay. Be aware that truck drivers have a reputation for driving under the influence of alcohol; always trust your instincts.

Local Transport

Buses, cycle-rickshaws, autorickshaws, e-rickshaws, tempos (big, brutal-looking autorickshaws), taxis, boats, tongas (horse-drawn carts), metros and urban trains provide transport around India's cities.

Costs for public transport vary from town to town.

For any transport without a fixed fare, agree on the price *before* you start your journey and make sure that it covers your luggage and every passenger.

Even where meters exist, drivers may refuse to use them, demanding an elevated 'fixed' fare; bargain hard. Fares usually increase at night (by up to 100%) and some drivers charge a few rupees extra for luggage.

Carry plenty of small bills for taxi and rickshaw fares, as drivers may struggle to find change for you.

In some places taxi/ autorickshaw drivers are involved in commission rackets (p1191).

App-based taxis such as Uber and Ola Cabs mean you can call a taxi or autorickshaw and the fare will be electronically calculated – no arguments, and cheaper than ordinary taxis, though the whole procedure tends to be more time-consuming than simply hailing an auto.

Autorickshaw

Similar to the tuk-tuks of Southeast Asia, the Indian autorickshaw is a three-wheeled motorised contraption with a tin or canvas roof and sides, usually with room for two passengers (although you'll often see many more squeezed in) and limited luggage.

They are also referred to as autos, scooters and riks.

Autorickshaws are mostly cheaper than taxis (typically around half the price) and usually have a meter, although getting it turned on can be a challenge. You can call autos via the Ola Cabs Auto app (www.olacabs. com), which electronically calculates your fare when you finish the journey – no more haggling!

Travelling by auto is great fun, but – thanks to the open windows – it can be noisy (and chilly in winter).

In some cities there are larger, more environmentally friendly e-rickshaws (electric rickshaws), some of which (though not all) are shared and thus cheaper, but you'll have to be going in the same direction as the other passengers. In the Northeast States these e-rickshaws are known as *totos*.

Boat

Various kinds of local boats offer transport across and down rivers in India, from big car ferries to wooden canoes and wicker coracles. Most of the larger boats carry bicycles and motorcycles for a fee.

Bus

Urban buses range from fume-belching, human-stuffed mechanical monsters that travel at breakneck speed to sanitised air-conditioned vehicles with comfortable seating and smoother ride quality. In any case, it's usually far more convenient to opt for an autorickshaw or taxi, as they're quicker and more frequent (though more expensive).

Cycle-Rickshaw

A cycle-rickshaw is a pedal cycle with two rear wheels, supporting a bench seat for passengers. Most have a canopy that can be raised in wet weather or blazing sunshine but lowered to provide extra space for luggage.

Fares must be agreed in advance – speak to locals to get an idea of a fair price for the distance you intend to travel.

Kolkata is the last bastion of the hand-pulled rickshaw, known as the *tana* rickshaw. This is a hand-cart on two wheels pulled directly by the rickshaw-wallah.

Metro

Metro systems have transformed urban transport in India's biggest cities and are expanding each year. Cities with metros include Delhi (which has one of the world's largest), Mumbai, Kolkata, Chennai, Bengaluru, Hyderabad, Kochi and Jaipur.

Taxi

Most towns have taxis, and these are usually metered; however, getting drivers to use the meter can be a hassle. To avoid fare-setting shenanigans, use prepaid taxis where possible. Apps such as Uber and Ola, or radio cabs, are sometimes a more efficient option in larger cities.

PREPAID TAXIS

Major Indian airports and train stations have prepaid-taxi and radio-cab booths. Here you can book a taxi, even long distance, for a fixed price (which will include baggage) and thus avoid commission scams. Hold onto your receipt until you're sure you've reached your destination, then give it to your driver. The driver won't get paid without it.

Radio cabs cost marginally more than prepaid taxis but are air-conditioned and staffed by the company's chauffeurs. Cabs have electronic, receipt-generating fare meters and are fitted with GPS units, so the company can monitor the vehicle's movements around town. This minimises the chances of errant driving or unreasonable demands for extra cash by the driver afterwards.

Smaller airports and stations may have prepaid-autorickshaw booths instead of or as well as prepaid-taxi booths.

Tempo & Vikram

Vikrams and the more brutal-looking tempos are outsized autorickshaws with room for more passengers, shuttling on fixed routes for a fixed fare.

In country areas you may also see the fearsome-looking 'three-wheeler' –

a crude tractor-like tempo with a front wheel on an articulated arm – or the Magic, a cute minivan that can carry up to a dozen passengers.

Other Local Transport

In some towns, *tongas* (horse-drawn two-wheelers) and *victorias* (horse-drawn carriages) still operate. Kolkata has a tram network, and Mumbai, Delhi, Kolkata and Chennai, among other centres, have suburban trains.

Motorcycle

Long-distance motorcycle touring is hugely popular in India. However, it can be quite an undertaking; there are tours (p1216) for those who don't want the rigmarole of going it alone.

The most common starting point for tours is Delhi, though Manali is another possible hub, and the most frequently visited destinations include Rajasthan, South India and Ladakh. Weather is an important factor: check for the best times to visit different areas. To cross from neighbouring countries, confirm the latest requirements with the relevant diplomatic mission.

Driving Licence

Technically, to hire a motorcycle in India you must have a valid international driver's permit in addition to your domestic licence. Some places in tourist areas may rent out a motorcycle without asking for a driving permit/licence, but you won't be covered by insurance in the event of an

accident, and you may also face a fine if you're stopped by police.

Hire

The classic way to motorcycle around India is on a Royal Enfield, built to both vintage and modern specs. Fully manual, these are easy to repair (parts can be found almost everywhere in India). On the other hand, Enfields are heavy and often less reliable than many of the newer, Japanese-designed bikes.

Plenty of places rent out motorcycles for local trips and longer tours. Japanese- and Indian-made bikes in the 100cc to 150cc range are cheaper than the big 350cc to 500cc Enfields.

As security, you'll need to leave a large cash deposit (ensure you get a receipt that stipulates the refundable amount) and show your passport/air ticket. Do not leave these documents, in particular your passport, which you'll need for hotel check-ins and if stopped by the police.

Prices range from region to region and depend on the quality of the bike. **Kerala Bike Tours** (☑9446492382, 9388476817; www.keralabiketours.com; 42/2252B St Benedict Road North, Kacheripady) in Ernakulam, for example, hires out touring-quality Enfields from ₹12,000 per week, including unlimited mileage, full insurance and free recovery/maintenance options. **Lalli Motorbike Exports** (☑011-28750869, mobile 09811140161; www.lallisinghadventures.com; 1740-A/55 Hari Singh Nalwa St, Abdul Aziz Rd; ☺10am-7pm Tue-Sun; ℳKarol Bagh), in Delhi, rents quality Enfields for ₹700 to ₹1350 per day.

Helmets are available for ₹1000 to ₹5500, with the best Indian-brand 'Studs' coming in many models. Extras (panniers, luggage racks, protection bars, rear-view mirrors, lockable fuel caps, petrol filters, extra tools) are also easy to come by.

Reputable hire agencies include:

MANNING THE METER

Getting a metered ride is only half the battle. Meters are almost always outdated, so fares are calculated using a combination of the meter reading and a complicated 'fare-adjustment card'. Predictably, this system is open to abuse. It's usually better to simply agree a fare beforehand. To get a rough estimate of fares in advance, try the portal www.taxiautofare.com. Better still, ask a local for advice.

Allibhai Premji Tyrewalla
(Map p744; ☑9867964163,
022-23099313; www.premjis.
com; 205 Dr D Bhadkamkar
(Lamington) Marg, Mumbai;
☺10am-7pm Mon-Sat)

Anu Auto Works (Royal
Moto Touring; Map p322;
☑9816163378; www.royalmoto
touring.com; Vashisht Rd,
Manali; ☺office 9am-9pm
Jun-Sep)

Kerala Bike Tours
(☑9446492382, 9388476817;
www.keralabiketours.com;
42/2252B St Benedict Road
North, Kacheripady, Ernakulam)

Lalli Motorbike Exports
(☑011-28750869, mobile
09811140161; www.lallisingh
adventures.com; 1740-A/55
Hari Singh Nalwa St, Abdul Aziz
Rd, Delhi; ☺10am-7pm Tue-
Sun; Ⓜ Karol Bagh)

Rajasthan Auto Centre (Map
p112; ☑9829188064, 0141-
2568074; www.royalenfield
salim.com; Sanganeri Gate,
Sanjay Bazaar, Jaipur; ☺10am-
8pm Mon-Sat, to 2pm Sun)

Purchase

For longer tours, purchasing
a new motorcycle may sound
like a great idea. However,
selling motor vehicles to
foreigners comes with reams
of complicated paperwork;
foreigners are not allowed
to register vehicles in their
name; and in many situa-
tions procuring a motorcycle
might not be possible or
feasible at all.

Secondhand bikes are
widely available, though, and
paperwork is simpler than
for a new machine. All privately owned vehicles over
15 years old are banned from
Delhi roads.

To find a secondhand
motorcycle, check travellers'
noticeboards and ask motorcycle mechanics and other
bikers. A well-looked-after
secondhand 350cc Enfield
costs ₹65,000 to ₹115,000.
A good-condition 500cc
with UCI engine ranges from
₹95,000 to ₹140,000.
You'll also have to pay for
insurance.

THE POETIC SIGNAGE OF THE BRO

In Ladakh, Himachal Pradesh, Arunachal Pradesh and
Sikkim, the Border Roads Organisation (BRO) builds
'roads in the sky', including some of the world's highest
passes accessible by car. Risking life and limb to keep
the roads open, the BRO has a bewitching turn of phrase
when it comes to driver warnings, including:

➡ Life is short, don't make it shorter.

➡ It is not a rally, enjoy the valley.

➡ After whisky, driving risky.

➡ Be gentle on my curves.

➡ Better to be late than to be the late Mr.

OWNERSHIP PAPERS

There's plenty of paperwork
associated with owning a
motorcycle. The process is
complicated and time-
consuming, so it's wise to
seek advice from the agent
selling the bike.

Registration papers are
signed by the local registration authority when the bike
is first sold; you'll need these
when you buy a secondhand
bike.

Foreign nationals cannot
change the name on the
registration, but you must
fill out forms for change of
ownership and transfer of
insurance.

A new registration lasts
for 15 years, after which it
may be renewed for ₹5000
for five years; make absolutely sure that it states
the 'roadworthiness' of the
vehicle, and that there are no
outstanding debts or criminal
proceedings associated with
the bike. The office of the
state transport department
where the bike was registered
can provide this information.

Insurance

Only hire a bike that has insurance – if you hit someone
without insurance the consequences will be very costly.
Reputable companies will
include third-party cover in
their policies; those that don't
probably aren't trustworthy.

You must also arrange
insurance if you buy a motorcycle (usually you can organ-

ise this through the person
selling the bike).

Comprehensive insurance
for a new Royal Enfield can
cost ₹4000 to ₹5000 per
year. Insurance for a secondhand Royal Enfield may cost
₹800 to ₹4000, depending
on the age of the vehicle.

Fuel, Spare
Parts & Extras

Petrol and engine oil are
widely available in the plains,
but petrol stations are rarer
in the mountains. If travelling
to remote regions, carry
enough extra fuel (seek local
advice about fuel availability
before setting off). At the
time of writing, petrol costs
around ₹68 per litre in Delhi,
but it can cost up to ₹85 per
litre in some regions.

Get your machine (par-
ticularly older ones) serviced
regularly. Indian roads and
engine vibration work things
loose quite quickly.

Check the engine and
gearbox oil level regularly
(at least every 500km) and
clean the oil filter every few
thousand kilometres.

Given the road conditions,
the chances are that you'll
make at least a couple of
visits to a puncture-wallah
– start your trip with new
tyres and carry spanners to
remove your own wheels.

It's a good idea to bring
your own protective equipment (jackets, gloves etc).

Motorbikes can be trans-
ported by train (p1211) in the

same way as bicycles. Empty the fuel tank first.

Road Conditions

Given the varied road conditions, India can be challenging for novice riders. Hazards range from cows and chickens crossing the carriageway to broken-down trucks, unruly traffic, pedestrians on the road, and ubiquitous potholes and unmarked speed humps. Rural roads sometimes have grain crops strewn across them to be threshed by passing vehicles – a serious sliding hazard for bikers.

Try not to cover too much territory in one day: on busy national highways, expect to average 40km/h to 50km/h without stops; on winding back roads and dirt tracks this can drop to 10km/h.

Never ride in the dark – many vehicles drive without lights, and dynamo-powered motorcycle headlamps are useless at low revs while negotiating around potholes.

Organised Motorcycle Tours

Dozens of companies offer motorcycle tours around India with support vehicle, mechanic and guide. Here are a few well-established companies:

Blazing Trails (www.blazingtrailstours.com)

H-C Travel (www.hctravel.com)

Himalayan Roadrunners (www.ridehigh.com)

Indian Motorcycle Adventures (www.indianmotorcycleadventures.com)

Lalli Mobike Adventures (www.lallisinghadventures.com)

Moto Discovery (www.motodiscovery.com)

World on Wheels (www.worldonwheels.tours)

Shared Jeep

In mountain areas shared jeeps supplement the bus services, charging similar fixed fares.

Although nominally designed for five to six passengers, most shared jeeps squeeze in more. The seats beside and immediately behind the driver are more expensive than the cramped bench seats at the rear.

Jeeps only leave when full; people often bail out of a half-full jeep and pile into one with more passengers that's ready to depart. Drivers will leave immediately if you pay for all of the empty seats and 'reserve' a vehicle for yourself.

Jeeps run from jeep stands and 'passenger stations' at the junctions of major roads; ask locals to point you in the right direction.

In some states, jeeps are known as 'sumos' after the Tata Sumo, a popular vehicle.

Travel sickness, particularly on winding mountain roads, may mean you are asked to give up your window seat to queasy fellow passengers.

Train

Travelling by train is a quintessential Indian experience. Trains offer more space and a smoother ride than buses and are especially recommended for long journeys that include overnight travel. India's rail network is one of the largest and busiest in the world, and Indian Railways is the world's eighth-largest employer on earth, with roughly 1.3 million workers. There are more than 7000 train stations across the country.

Useful trains are listed here, but there are hundreds more. The best way of sourcing updated information, including fares, is online, through sites such as Indian Railways (www.indianrailways.gov.in/railwayboard), Erail (https://erail.in) and the very useful Seat 61 (www.seat61.com/india).

If you can't get online, there's also the long-running, comprehensive timetable booklet *Trains at a Glance* (₹70), available at many station bookstands and better bookshops/news stands, and published annually.

You may have to show your passport as ID onboard, but usually showing a digital copy of your reservation (rather than a printout) is enough.

Trains can be delayed at any stage of the journey; to avoid stress, factor some leeway into your plans.

EXPRESS TRAIN FARES BY DISTANCE

DISTANCE (KM)	1AC* (₹)	2AC* (₹)	3AC* (₹)	AC CHAIR (CC)** (₹)	SLEEPER (SL)** (₹)	2ND CLASS (II)** (₹)
100	1203	706	498	205	77	47
500	2054	1209	846	577	276	151
1000	3362	1949	1352	931	446	258
1500	4320	2498	1708	1189	573	334
2000	5272	3025	2057	1443	698	412

* Rajdhani/Duronto Trains ** Mail/Express Trains

Booking Tickets in India

You can book through a travel agency or hotel (for a commission), in person at the train station or online (p39).

Refunds are available on any ticket, even after departure, with a penalty – rules are complicated, so check when you book.

AT THE STATION

Get a reservation slip from the information window, fill in the name of the departure station, the destination station, the class you want to travel in and the name and number of the train. Join the (long) queue for the ticket window, where your ticket will be printed. Women should take advantage of the separate women's queue – if there isn't one, go to the front of the regular queue.

Stations in larger cities, including Delhi, Mumbai and Chennai, have dedicated ticket counters for foreigners (usually as part of a separate office called the International Tourist Bureau, which sells tourist-quota seats on certain classes of train). This makes buying tickets in person much easier.

Reservations

Most long-distance services have 'general' (2nd-class) compartments with unreserved seating, and more comfortable reserved compartments, plus sleeper berths for overnight journeys.

Shatabdi Express trains are same-day services with seating only; Rajdhani Express trains are long-distance overnight services between Delhi and state capitals with a choice of 1AC, 2AC, 3AC and 2nd-class seats; Duronto Express trains cover similar routes in less time.

You must make a reservation for AC chair (CC), AC executive chair (ECC), sleeper (SL), 1AC, 2AC and 3AC carriages. Book well ahead for any overnight journeys, and all travel during holidays and festivals.

TOURIST QUOTA

As well as the regular general quota (GN), a special (albeit small) tourist quota is set aside for foreign tourists travelling between popular stations.

These seats can now be booked up to 365 days ahead through the IRCTC (p39; www.irctc.co.in) or at Tourist Reservation Bureaus in large cities; you'll need to show your passport and visa as ID, and payment is either with a card (some bureaus accept international cards) or in rupees (sometimes they'll ask for ATM receipts), UK pounds or US dollars.

Online, there's a ₹200 service charge per ticket, plus a ₹100 registration fee, and you can book only 1AC, 2AC or ECC (AC executive chair) tickets. In person, there's no service charge and you can book cheaper train classes such as sleeper (SL) too.

TAKTAL TICKETS

Indian Railways holds back a limited number of tickets on key trains and releases them at 10am (AC) and 11am (non-AC) one day before the train is due to depart. A charge of ₹100 to ₹500 is added to the price of each ticket.

RESERVATION AGAINST CANCELLATION (RAC)

Even when a train is fully booked, Indian Railways sells a handful of seats in each class as 'Reservation Against Cancellation' (RAC). This means that if you have an RAC ticket and someone cancels before the departure date, you will get that seat (or berth). You'll have to check the reservation list at the station on the day of travel to see if you've been allocated a confirmed seat/berth. Even if no one cancels, you can still board the train as an RAC ticket holder and travel without a seat.

WAITLIST (WL)

Trains are frequently overbooked, but many passengers cancel and there are regular no-shows. So if you buy a ticket on the waiting list you're quite likely to get a seat, even if there are a number of people ahead of you on the list. Check your booking status at www.indianrail.gov.in/pnr_enq.html by entering your ticket's PNR number. A refund is available if you fail to get a seat – ask the ticket office about your chances.

Costs

➡ Fares are calculated by distance and class (p1218) of travel; Rajdhani and Shatabdi trains (p1218) are slightly more expensive, but the price includes meals. Most air-conditioned carriages have a catering service (meals are brought to your seat). In unreserved classes it's a good idea to carry your own snacks.

➡ Children under the age of five travel free, while those aged between five and 12 are charged half-price if they do not have their own berth (but full price if they do).

➡ Senior discounts (40% and 50% off for men over 60 and women over 58, respectively) only apply to Indian citizens.

Tours

Tours are widely available, run by tourist offices, local transport companies and travel agencies. Organised tours can be an inexpensive way to see several places in one trip, but they can be rushed. If you arrange a tailor-made tour, you'll have more freedom about where you go and how long you stay.

Drivers may double as guides, or you can hire a qualified local guide for a fee. In tourist towns, be wary of touts claiming to be professional guides.

Health

There is huge geographical variation in India, so in different areas heat, cold and altitude can cause health problems. Hygiene is poor in most regions, so food- and water-borne illnesses are common. A number of insect-borne diseases are present, particularly in tropical areas. Medical care is basic in various areas (especially beyond the larger cities), so it's essential to be well prepared.

Pre-existing medical conditions and accidental injury (especially traffic accidents) account for most life-threatening problems. Becoming ill in some way, however, is common. Fortunately, most travellers' illnesses can be prevented with some common-sense behaviour or treated with a well-stocked travellers' medical kit. However, never hesitate to consult a doctor while on the road, as self-diagnosis can be hazardous.

BEFORE YOU GO

You can buy many medications over the counter in India without a doctor's prescription, but it can be difficult to find some of the newer drugs, particularly the latest antidepressant drugs, blood-pressure medications and contraceptive pills. Be circumspect about self-medicating, as travellers mixing the wrong drugs or overdosing have on occasion ended in tragedy. Bring the following:

➡ medications in their original, labelled containers

➡ a signed, dated letter from your physician describing your medical conditions and medications, including generic medication names

➡ a physician's letter documenting the medical necessity of any syringes you bring

➡ if you have a heart condition, a copy of your ECG taken just prior to travelling

➡ any regular medication (double your ordinary needs).

Insurance

Don't travel without health/travel insurance. Emergency evacuation is expensive. There are various factors to consider when choosing insurance. Read the small print.

➡ You may require extra cover for adventure activities such as rock climbing and scuba diving.

➡ In India, doctors usually require immediate payment in cash. Your insurance plan may make payments directly to providers or it will reimburse you later for overseas health expenditures. If you do have to claim later, make sure you keep all relevant documentation.

➡ Some policies ask that you telephone back (reverse charges) to a centre in your home country, where an immediate assessment of your problem will be made.

Vaccinations

Specialised travel-medicine clinics are your best source of up-to-date information; they stock all available vaccines and can give specific recommendations for your trip. Most vaccines don't give immunity until *at least* two weeks after they're given, so visit a doctor well before departure. Ask your doctor for an International Certificate of Vaccination (sometimes known as the 'yellow booklet'), which will list all the vaccinations you've received.

Required & Recommended Vaccinations

The only vaccine required by international regulations is that for yellow fever. Proof of vaccination will only be required if you have visited a country in the yellow-fever zone within the six days prior to entering India. If you are travelling to India from Africa or South America, you should check to see if you require proof of vaccination.

The World Health Organization (WHO) recommends

VACCINATIONS FOR LONG STAYS

The following immunisations are recommended for long-term travellers (more than one month) or those at special risk (seek further advice from your doctor):

Japanese B encephalitis Three injections in all. Booster recommended after two years. Sore arm and headache are the most common side effects. In rare cases an allergic reaction comprising hives and swelling can occur up to 10 days after any of the three doses.

Meningitis Single injection. There are two types of vaccination: the quadravalent vaccine gives two to three years' protection; the meningitis group C vaccine gives around 10 years' protection. Recommended for long-term backpackers aged under 25.

Rabies Three injections in all. A booster after one year will then provide 10 years' protection. Side effects are rare – occasionally headache and sore arm.

Tuberculosis (TB) A complex issue. Adult long-term travellers are usually advised to have a TB skin test before and after travel, rather than vaccination. Only one vaccine is given in a lifetime.

the following vaccinations for travellers going to India (as well as being up to date with measles, mumps and rubella vaccinations). Note that there is no vaccine for malaria (p1220), so prophylaxis is used instead.

Adult diphtheria and tetanus Single booster recommended if none in the previous 10 years. Side effects include sore arm and fever.

Hepatitis A Provides almost 100% protection for up to a year; a booster after 12 months provides at least another 20 years' protection. Mild side effects such as headache and sore arm occur in 5% to 10% of people.

Hepatitis B Now considered routine for most travellers. Given as three shots over six months. A rapid schedule is also available, as is a combined vaccination with hepatitis A. Side effects are mild and uncommon, usually headache and a sore arm. In 95% of people lifetime protection results.

Polio Only one booster is required as an adult for lifetime protection. Inactivated polio vaccine is safe during pregnancy.

Typhoid Recommended for all travellers to India, even those only visiting urban areas. The vaccine offers around 70% protection, lasts for two to three years and comes as a single shot. Tablets are also available,

but the injection is usually recommended as it has fewer side effects. Sore arm and fever may occur.

Varicella If you haven't had chickenpox, discuss this vaccination with your doctor.

Medical Checklist

Recommended items for a personal medical kit include:

→ Antibacterial cream, eg mupirocin

→ Antibiotic for skin infections, eg amoxicillin/ clavulanate or cephalexin

→ Antifungal cream, eg clotrimazole

→ Antihistamine – there are many options, eg cetirizine for daytime and promethazine for night

→ Antiseptic, eg Betadine

→ Antispasmodic for stomach cramps, eg Buscopam

→ Contraceptive

→ Decongestant, eg pseudoephedrine

→ DEET-based insect repellent

→ Diarrhoea medication – consider an oral rehydration solution (eg Gastrolyte), diarrhoea

'stopper' (eg loperamide) and antinausea medication (eg prochlorperazine); antibiotics for diarrhoea include ciprofloxacin; for bacterial diarrhoea azithromycin; for giardia or amoebic dysentery tinidazole

→ First-aid items such as scissors, elastoplasts, bandages, gauze, thermometer (but not mercury), sterile needles and syringes, safety pins and tweezers

→ Ibuprofen or another anti-inflammatory

→ Iodine tablets (unless you are pregnant or have a thyroid problem) to purify water

→ Migraine medication if you suffer from migraines

→ Paracetamol

→ Pyrethrin to impregnate clothing and mosquito nets

→ Steroid cream for allergic or itchy rashes, eg 1% to 2% hydrocortisone

→ Sunscreen (with a high SPF)

→ Throat lozenges

→ Thrush (vaginal yeast infection) treatment, eg clotrimazole pessaries or Diflucan tablet

→ Ural or equivalent if prone to urinary-tract infections

Websites

There's a wealth of travel-health advice on the internet; www.lonelyplanet.com is a good place to start. It's a good idea to consult your government's travel-advisory website (p1205) to see if there are any specific health risks to be aware of.

Further Reading

Recommended references include *Travellers' Health* by Dr Richard Dawood and *Travelling Well* by Dr Deborah Mills, which is now also available as an app; check out the website (www.travellingwell.com.au) too.

IN INDIA

Availability & Cost of Healthcare

Medical care is hugely variable in India. Some cities now have clinics catering specifically to travellers and expatriates; these clinics are usually more expensive than local medical facilities, and offer a higher standard of care. Additionally, the staff members know the local system, including reputable hospitals and specialists. They may also liaise with insurance companies should you require evacuation. It's usually difficult to find reliable medical care in rural areas.

Self-treatment may be appropriate if your problem is minor (eg traveller's diarrhoea), you are carrying the relevant medication, and you cannot attend a recommended clinic. If you suspect a serious disease, especially malaria, travel to the nearest quality facility.

Before buying medication over the counter, check the use-by date, and ensure that the packet is sealed and properly stored (eg not exposed to the sunshine).

Infectious Diseases

Malaria

This is a serious and potentially deadly disease. Before you travel, seek expert advice according to your itinerary (rural areas are especially risky) and on medication and side effects.

Malaria is caused by a parasite transmitted by the bite of an infected mosquito. The most important symptom of malaria is fever, but general symptoms, such as headache, diarrhoea, cough or chills, may also occur. Diagnosis can only be properly made by taking a blood sample.

Two strategies should be combined to prevent malaria: mosquito avoidance and antimalarial medications. Most people who catch malaria are taking inadequate or no antimalarial medication.

Travellers are advised to prevent mosquito bites by taking these steps:

➡ Use a DEET-based insect repellent on exposed skin. Wash this off at night – as long as you are sleeping under a mosquito net. Natural repellents such as citronella can be effective but must be applied more frequently than products containing DEET.

➡ Sleep under a mosquito net impregnated with pyrethrin.

➡ Choose accommodation with proper screens and fans (if not air-conditioned).

➡ Impregnate clothing with pyrethrin in high-risk areas.

➡ Wear long sleeves and trousers in light colours.

➡ Use mosquito coils.

➡ Spray your room with insect repellent before going out for your evening meal. A variety of medications are available:

Chloroquine and Paludrine combination Limited effectiveness in many parts of South Asia. Common side effects include nausea (40% of people) and mouth ulcers.

Doxycycline (daily tablet) A broad-spectrum antibiotic that helps prevent a variety of tropical diseases, including leptospirosis, tick-borne disease and typhus. Potential side effects include photosensitivity (a tendency to sunburn), thrush (in women), indigestion, heartburn, nausea and interference with the contraceptive pill. More serious side effects include ulceration of the oesophagus – take your tablet with a meal and a large glass of water, and never lie down within half an hour of taking it. It must be taken for four weeks after leaving the risk area.

Lariam (mefloquine) This weekly tablet suits many people. Serious side effects can be an issue with this drug, though, and include depression, anxiety, psychosis and seizures. Unusually vivid nightmares that last months after use of the drug are not uncommon. Anyone with a history of depression, anxiety, other psychological disorders or epilepsy should not take Lariam. It is considered safe in the second and third trimesters of pregnancy. Tablets must be taken for four weeks after leaving the risk area.

Malarone A combination of atovaquone and proguanil. Side effects are uncommon and mild, most commonly nausea and headache. It is the best tablet for scuba divers and for those on short trips to high-risk areas. It must be taken for one week after leaving the risk area.

Traveller's Diarrhoea

This is by far the most common problem affecting travellers in India – between 30% and 70% of people will suffer from it within two weeks of starting their trip. It's usually caused by bacteria, and thus responds promptly to treatment with antibiotics.

Traveller's diarrhoea is defined as the passage of more than three watery

DRINKING WATER

➡ Never drink tap water.

➡ Bottled water is generally safe – check that the seal is intact at purchase.

➡ Avoid ice unless you know it has been made without tap water.

➡ Be careful of fresh juices served at street stalls in particular – they're likely to have been watered down with tap water or may be served in jugs/glasses that have been rinsed in tap water.

➡ Avoid fruit that you don't peel yourself, as it will likely have been rinsed in tap water. Alternatively, rinse fruit yourself in mineral water before you eat it.

➡ Boiling water is usually the most efficient method of purifying it.

➡ The best chemical purifier is iodine. It should not be used by pregnant women or those with thyroid problems.

➡ Water filters should also filter out most viruses. Ensure your filter has a chemical barrier such as iodine and a small pore size (less than four microns).

➡ In tourist areas, some guesthouses, cafes and restaurants use water filters; use your own judgment as to whether you think this water will be safe to drink.

bowel actions within 24 hours, plus at least one other symptom, such as fever, cramps, nausea, vomiting or feeling generally unwell.

Treatment consists of staying well hydrated; rehydration solutions like Gastrolyte are the best for this. Antibiotics such as ciprofloxacin or azithromycin should kill the bacteria quickly. Seek medical attention quickly if you do not respond to an appropriate antibiotic.

Loperamide is just a 'stopper' and doesn't get to the cause of the problem. It can be helpful, though (eg if you have to go on a long bus ride). Don't take loperamide if you have a fever or blood in your stools.

Amoebic dysentery Amoebic dysentery is very rare in travellers but is quite often misdiagnosed by poor-quality labs. Symptoms are similar to bacterial diarrhoea: fever, bloody diarrhoea and generally feeling unwell. You should always seek reliable medical care if you have blood in your diarrhoea. Treatment involves two drugs: tinidazole or metronidazole to kill the parasite in your gut and then a second drug to kill the cysts. If left untreated, complications such as liver or gut abscesses can occur.

Giardiasis Giardia is a parasite that is relatively common in travellers. Symptoms include nausea, bloating, excess gas, fatigue and intermittent diarrhoea. The parasite will eventually go away if left untreated, but this can take months; the best advice is to seek medical treatment. The treatment of choice is tinidazole, with metronidazole a second-line option.

Other Diseases

Avian flu 'Bird flu' or Influenza A (H5N1) is a subtype of the type A influenza virus. Contact with dead or sick birds is the principal source of infection and bird-to-human transmission does not easily occur. Symptoms include high fever and flu-like symptoms with rapid deterioration, leading to respiratory failure and death in many cases. Immediate medical care should be sought if bird flu is suspected. Check www.who.int/en.

Cholera There are occasional outbreaks of cholera in India. This acute gastrointestinal infection is transmitted through contaminated water and food, including raw or undercooked fish and shellfish. Cases are rare among travellers, but those who are travelling to an area of active transmission should consult with their health-care practitioner regarding vaccination.

Dengue fever This mosquito-to-borne disease is becomingly increasingly problematic, especially in the cities. As there is no vaccine available it can only be prevented by avoiding mosquito bites at all times. Symptoms include high fever, severe headache and body ache and sometimes a rash and diarrhoea. Treatment is rest and paracetamol – do not take aspirin or ibuprofen, as these increase the likelihood of haemorrhage. Make sure you see a doctor to be diagnosed and monitored.

Hepatitis A This food- and water-borne virus infects the liver, causing jaundice (yellow skin and eyes), nausea and lethargy. There is no specific treatment for hepatitis A; you just need to allow time for the liver to heal. All travellers to India should be vaccinated against hepatitis A.

Hepatitis B This sexually transmitted disease is spread by body fluids and can be prevented by vaccination. The long-term consequences can include liver cancer and cirrhosis.

Hepatitis E Transmitted through contaminated food and water, hepatitis E has similar symptoms to hepatitis A but is far less common. It is a severe problem in pregnant women and can result in the death of both mother and baby. There is no commercially available vaccine, and prevention is by following safe eating and drinking guidelines.

HIV Spread via contaminated body fluids. Avoid unprotected sex, unsterile needles (including in medical facilities) and procedures such as tattoos. The growth rate of HIV in India is one of the highest in the world.

Influenza Present year-round in the tropics, influenza (flu) symptoms include fever, muscle aches, a runny nose, cough and sore throat. It can be severe in people over the age of 65 or in those with medical conditions such as heart disease or diabetes – vaccination is recommended for these individuals. There is no specific treatment, just rest and paracetamol.

Japanese B encephalitis This viral disease is transmitted by mosquitoes and is rare in travellers. Most cases occur in rural areas and vaccination is recommended for travellers spending more than a month outside cities. There is no treatment, and the virus may result in permanent brain damage or death. Ask your doctor for further details.

Rabies This fatal disease is spread by the bite, scratch or, if you already have an open wound, possibly even the lick of an infected animal – most commonly a dog or monkey. Rabies is almost always fatal once symptoms appear, but treatment before this is very effective. You should seek medical advice immediately after any animal bite and commence postexposure treatment. Having pretravel vaccination means that postbite treatment is greatly simplified. If an animal bites you, immediately wash the wound with soap and water for several minutes, and apply iodine-based antiseptic. If you are not prevaccinated you will need to receive rabies immunoglobulin as soon as possible, ideally within a few hours. If travelling with a child, make sure they're aware of the dangers and that they know to tell you if they've been bitten, scratched or licked by an animal.

Tuberculosis While TB is rare in travellers, those who have significant contact with the local population (such as medical and aid workers and long-term travellers) should take precautions. Vaccination is usually only given to children under the age of five, but adults at risk are advised to have pre- and posttravel TB testing. The main symptoms are fever, cough, weight loss, night sweats and fatigue.

Typhoid This serious bacterial infection is also spread via food and water. It causes a high and slowly progressive fever and headache, and may be accompanied by a dry cough and stomach pain. It is diagnosed by blood tests and treated with antibiotics. Vaccination is recommended for all travellers who are spending more than a week in India. Be aware that vaccination is not 100% effective, so you must still be careful with what you eat and drink.

Zika At the time of writing, most of India had been categorised as having a moderate risk of Zika virus (except for Rajasthan, which had a high risk, especially Jaipur), though there have been recent cases in Tamil Nadu and Ahmedabad. Check online for current updates.

Environmental Hazards

Air Pollution

Air pollution is a huge problem in India. According the World Health Organization (WHO), Delhi is the most polluted major city in the world. The next six most polluted cities are also in North India. If you have severe respiratory problems, speak with your doctor before travelling to India. All travellers are advised to listen to advisories on pollution levels from the Indian press or government officials. It's worth taking a properly fitted face mask if you are affected by air quality. In North India air pollution is at its worst during the cooler winter months (November and December particularly), partly due to the stubble-burning of crops in rural regions surrounding the big cities, and not helped by all the firecrackers let off during Diwali.

Short-term exposure can lead to a sore throat, sore eyes, itchy skin and a runny nose. As well as face masks, throat lozenges can help, as can frequently rinsing your face, hands and hair. Long-term exposure is, obviously, more serious.

Diving & Surfing

Divers and surfers should seek specialised advice before they travel to ensure that their medical kit contains treatment for coral cuts and tropical ear infections. Divers should ensure that their insurance covers them for decompression illness – get specialised diving insurance through an organisation such as Divers Alert Network (www.danasiapacific.org). Certain medical conditions are incompatible with diving; check with your doctor.

Food

Dining out brings with it the possibility of contracting diarrhoea. Ways to help avoid food-related illness:

➡ avoid tap water, and food rinsed in it

➡ eat only freshly cooked food

➡ avoid shellfish and buffets

➡ peel fruit

➡ cook vegetables

➡ soak salads in iodine water for at least 20 minutes

➡ eat in busy restaurants with a high turnover of customers.

Heat

Many parts of India, especially down south, are hot and humid throughout the year. For most visitors it takes around two weeks to comfortably adapt to the hot climate. Swelling of the feet and ankles is common, as are muscle cramps caused by excessive sweating. Prevent these by avoiding dehydration and excessive activity in the heat. Don't eat salt tablets (they aggravate the gut); drinking rehydration solution or eating salty food helps. Treat cramps by resting, rehydrating with double-strength rehydration solution and gently stretching.

Dehydration is the main contributor to heat exhaustion. Recovery is usually rapid and it is common to feel weak for some days afterwards. Symptoms include the following:

➡ feeling weak

➡ headache

➡ irritability

➡ nausea or vomiting

➡ sweaty skin

➡ a fast, weak pulse

➡ normal or slightly elevated body temperature.

Treatments include:

➡ getting out of the heat

➡ fanning the sufferer

➡ applying cool, wet cloths to the skin

➡ laying the sufferer flat with their legs raised

➡ rehydrating with water containing a quarter of a teaspoon of salt per litre.

Heatstroke is a serious medical emergency requiring urgent attention. Symptoms include the following:

➡ weakness

➡ nausea

➡ a hot, dry body

➡ temperature of over 41°C

➡ dizziness

➡ confusion

➡ loss of coordination

➡ seizures

➡ eventual collapse.

Treatment:

➡ get out of the heat

➡ fan the sufferer

➡ apply cool, wet cloths to the skin or ice to the body, especially to the groin and armpits.

Prickly heat is a common skin rash in the tropics, caused by sweat trapped under the skin. Treat it by moving out of the heat for a few hours and by having cool showers. Creams and ointments clog the skin so they should be avoided. Locally bought prickly-heat powder can be helpful.

Altitude Sickness

If you're going to altitudes above 3000m, acute mountain sickness (AMS) is an issue. The biggest risk factor is going too high too quickly – follow a conservative acclimatisation schedule found in good trekking guides, and *never* go to a higher altitude when you have any symptoms that could be altitude related. There is no way to predict who will get altitude sickness, and it is quite often the younger, fitter members of a group who succumb.

Symptoms usually develop during the first 24 hours at altitude but may be delayed up to three weeks. Mild symptoms include the following:

➡ headache

➡ lethargy

➡ dizziness

➡ difficulty sleeping

➡ loss of appetite.

AMS may become more severe without warning and can be fatal. Severe symptoms include the following:

➡ breathlessness

➡ a dry, irritative cough (which may progress to the production of pink, frothy sputum)

➡ severe headache

➡ lack of coordination and balance

➡ confusion

➡ irrational behaviour

➡ vomiting

➡ drowsiness

➡ loss of consciousness.

Treat mild symptoms by resting at the same altitude

or lower until recovery, which usually takes a day or two. Paracetamol or aspirin can be taken for headaches. If symptoms persist or become worse, immediate descent is necessary; even 500m can help. Drug treatments should never be used to avoid descent or to enable further ascent.

The drugs acetazolamide (Diamox) and dexamethasone are recommended by some doctors for the prevention of AMS; however, their use is controversial. They can reduce the symptoms, but they may also mask warning signs; severe and fatal AMS has occurred in people taking these drugs.

To prevent AMS, carry out the following steps:

➡ ascend slowly – have frequent rest days, spending two to three nights at each rise of 1000m

➡ sleep at a lower altitude than the greatest height reached during the day, if possible. Above 3000m, don't increase sleeping altitude by more than 300m daily

➡ drink extra fluids

➡ eat light, high-carbohydrate meals

➡ avoid alcohol and sedatives.

Insect Bites & Stings

Bedbugs Don't carry disease, but their bites can be itchy. You can treat the itch with an antihistamine.

Lice Most commonly appear on the head and pubic areas. You may need numerous applications of an antilice shampoo such as pyrethrin.

Ticks Contracted while walking in rural areas. Ticks are commonly found behind the ears, on the belly and in armpits, and bites can lead to serious infections such as Kyasanur forest disease. If you have had a tick bite and have a rash at the site of the bite or elsewhere, fever or muscle aches, see a doctor.

CARBON MONOXIDE POISONING

Some mountain areas rely on charcoal burners for warmth, but these should be avoided due to the risk of fatal carbon-monoxide poisoning. The thick, mattress-like blankets used in many mountain areas are amazingly warm once you get beneath the covers. If you're still cold, improvise a hot-water bottle by filling your drinking-water bottle with boiled water and covering it with a sock.

Doxycycline prevents tick-borne diseases.

Leeches Found in humid rainforest areas. They don't transmit any disease, but their bites are often itchy for weeks and can easily become infected. Apply an iodine-based antiseptic to any leech bite to help prevent infection.

Bee and wasp stings Anyone with a serious bee or wasp allergy should carry an injection of adrenaline (eg an Epipen).

Skin Problems

Fungal rashes There are two common fungal rashes that affect travellers. The first occurs in moist areas of the body, such as the groin, the armpits and between the toes. It starts as a red patch that slowly spreads and is usually itchy. Treatment involves keeping the skin dry, avoiding chafing and using an antifungal cream such as clotrimazole or Lamisil. The second, *Tinea versicolor*, causes light-coloured patches, most commonly on the back, chest and shoulders. Consult a doctor.

Cuts and scratches These become easily infected in humid climates. Immediately wash all wounds in clean water and apply antiseptic. If you develop signs of infection (increasing pain and redness), see a doctor.

Sunburn

Even on a cloudy day sunburn can occur rapidly.

➡ Use a strong sunscreen (factor 30) and reapply after a swim.

➡ Wear a wide-brimmed hat and sunglasses.

➡ Avoid lying in the sun during the hottest part of the day (10am to 2pm).

➡ Be vigilant above 3000m – you can get burnt very easily at altitude.

If you become sunburnt, stay out of the sun until you have recovered, apply cool compresses and, if necessary, take painkillers for the discomfort. One per cent hydrocortisone cream applied twice daily is also helpful.

Women's Health

For gynaecological health issues, seek out a female doctor.

Birth control Bring adequate supplies of your own form of contraception.

Thrush Heat, humidity and antibiotics can all contribute to thrush. Treatment is with antifungal creams and pessaries such as clotrimazole. A practical alternative is a single tablet of fluconazole (Diflucan).

Urinary-tract infections These can be precipitated by dehydration or long bus journeys without toilet stops; bring suitable antibiotics.

Language

The number of languages spoken in India helps explain why English is still widely spoken here, and why it's still in official use. Another 22 languages are recognised in the constitution, and more than 1600 minor languages are spoken throughout the country.

Major efforts have been made to promote Hindi as the national language of India and to gradually phase out English. However, English remains popular, and while Hindi is the predominant language in the north, it bears little relation to the Dravidian languages of the south such as Tamil. Consequently, very few people in the south speak Hindi.

Many educated Indians speak English as virtually their first language and for a large number of Indians it's their second tongue. Although you'll find it easy to get around India with English, it's always good to know a little of the local language.

HINDI

Hindi has about 600 million speakers worldwide, of which 180 million are in India. It developed from Classical Sanskrit, and is written in the Devanagari script. In 1947 it was granted official status along with English.

Most Hindi sounds are similar to their English counterparts. The main difference is that Hindi has both 'aspirated' consonants (pronounced with a puff of air, like saying 'h' after the sound) and unaspirated ones, as well as 'retroflex' (pronounced with the tongue bent

backwards) and nonretroflex consonants. Our simplified pronunciation guides don't include these distinctions – read them as if they were English and you'll be understood.

Pronouncing the vowels correctly is important, especially their length (eg a and aa). The consonant combination ng after a vowel indicates nasalisation (ie the vowel is pronounced 'through the nose'). Note also that au is pronounced as the 'ow' in 'how'. Word stress is very light – we've indicated the stressed syllables with italics.

Basics

Hindi verbs change form depending on the gender of the speaker (or the subject of the sentence in general), so it's the verbs, not the pronouns 'he' or 'she' (as is the case in English) which show whether the subject of the sentence is masculine or feminine. In these phrases we include the options for male and female speakers, marked 'm' and 'f' respectively.

Hello./Goodbye.	नमस्ते ।	na·ma·*ste*
Yes.	जी हाँ ।	jee haang
No.	जी नहीं ।	jee na·*heeng*
Excuse me.	सुनिये ।	su·ni·ye
Sorry.	माफ़ कीजिये ।	maaf *kee*·ji·ye
Please ...	कृपया ...	kri·pa·*yaa* ...
Thank you.	थैंक्यू ।	thayn·kyoo
You're welcome.	कोई बात नहीं ।	*ko*·ee baat na·*heeng*

| How are you? | आप कैसे/कैसी हैं? | aap *kay*·se/*kay*·see hayng (m/f) |
| Fine. And you? | मैं ठीक हूँ । आप सुनाइये । | mayng teek hoong aap su·*naa*·i·ye |

WANT MORE?

For in-depth language information and handy phrases, check out Lonely Planet's *Hindi, Urdu & Bengali Phrasebook* and *India Phrasebook*. You'll find them at **shop.lonelyplanet.com**, or you can buy Lonely Planet's iPhone phrasebooks at the Apple App Store.

NUMBERS – HINDI

1	१	एक	ek
2	२	दो	do
3	३	तीन	teen
4	४	चार	chaar
5	५	पाँच	paanch
6	६	छह	chay
7	७	सात	saat
8	८	आठ	aat
9	९	नौ	nau
10	१०	दस	das
20	२०	बीस	bees
30	३०	तीस	tees
40	४०	चालीस	chaa·lees
50	५०	पचास	pa·chaas
60	६०	साठ	saat
70	७०	सत्तर	sat·tar
80	८०	अस्सी	as·see
90	९०	नब्बे	nab·be
100	१००	सौ	sau
1000	१०००	एक हज़ार	ek ha·zaar

What's your name?
आप का नाम क्या है? aap kaa naam kyaa hay

My name is ...
मेरा नाम ... है। me·raa naam ... hay

Do you speak English?
क्या आपको अंग्रेज़ी kyaa aap ko an·gre·zee
आती है? aa·tee hay

I don't understand.
मैं नहीं समझा/ mayng na·heeng sam·jaa/
समझी। sam·jee (m/f)

Accommodation

Where's a ...? ... कहाँ है? ... ka·haang hay
  guesthouse गेस्ट हाउस gest haa·us
  hotel होटल ho·tal
  youth hostel यूथ हास्टल yoot haas·tal

Do you have क्या ... कमरा kyaa ... kam·raa
a ... room? है? hay
  single सिंगल sin·gal
  double डबल da·bal

How much is ... के लिये ... ke li·ye
it per ...? कितने पैसे kit·ne pay·se
  लगते हैं? lag·te hayng

night एक रात ek raat
person हर व्यक्ति har vyak·ti

air-con ए० सी० e see
bathroom बाथरूम baat·room
hot water गर्म पानी garm paa·nee
mosquito net मसहरी mas·ha·ree
washerman धोबी do·bee
window खिड़की kir·kee

Directions

Where's ...?
... कहाँ है? ... ka·haang hay

How far is it?
वह कितनी दूर है? voh kit·nee door hay

What's the address?
पता क्या है? pa·taa kyaa hay

Can you show me (on the map)?
(नक्शे में) दिखा (nak·she meng) di·kaa
सकते है? sak·te hayng

Turn left/right.
लेफ्ट/राइट मुड़िये। left/raa·it mu·ri·ye

at the corner कोने पर ko·ne par
at the traffic सिगनल पर sig·nal par
lights
behind ... ... के पीछे ... ke pee·che
in front of ... ... के सामन ... ke saam·ne
near ... ... के पास ... ke paas
opposite ... ... के सामने ... ke saam·ne
straight ahead सीधे see·de

Eating & Drinking

What would you recommend?
आपके ख्याल में aap ke kyaal meng
क्या अच्छा होगा? kyaa ach·chaa ho·gaa

Do you have vegetarian food?
क्या आप का खाना kyaa aap kaa kaa·naa
शाकाहारी है? shaa·kaa·haa·ree hay

I don't eat (meat).
मैं (गोश्त) नहीं mayng (gosht) na·heeng
खाता/खाती। kaa·taa/kaa·tee (m/f)

I'll have ...
मुझे ... दीजिये। mu·je ... dee·ji·ye

That was delicious.
बहुत मज़ेदार हुआ। ba·hut ma·ze·daar hu·aa

Please bring the menu/bill.
मेन्यू/बिल लाइये। men·yoo/bil laa·i·ye

Key Words

bottle	बोतल	bo·tal
bowl	कटोरी	ka·to·ree
breakfast	नाश्ता	naash·taa
dessert	मीठा	mee·taa
dinner	रात का खाना	raat kaa kaa·naa
drinks	पीने की चीज़ें	pee·ne kee chee·zeng
food	खाना	kaa·naa
fork	काँटा	kaan·taa
glass	गिलास	glaas
knife	चाकू	chaa·koo
local eatery	ढाबा	daa·baa
lunch	दिन का खाना	din kaa kaa·naa
market	बाज़ार	baa·zaar
plate	प्लेट	plet
restaurant	रेस्टोरेंट	res·to·rent
set meal	थाली	taa·lee
snack	नाश्ता	naash·taa
spoon	चम्मच	cham·mach

Meat & Fish

beef	गाय का गोश्त	gaai kaa gosht
chicken	मुर्गी	mur·gee
duck	बतख़	ba·tak
fish	मछली	mach·lee
goat	बकरा	bak·raa
lobster	बड़ी झींगा	ba·ree jeeng·gaa
meat	गोश्त	gosht
meatballs	कोफ़्ता	kof·taa
pork	सुअर का गोश्त	su·ar kaa gosht
prawn	झींगी मछली	jeeng·gee mach·lee
seafood	मछली	mach·lee

Fruit & Vegetables

apple	सेब	seb
apricot	खुबानी	ku·baa·nee
banana	केला	ke·laa
capsicum	मिर्च	mirch
carrot	गाजर	gaa·jar
cauliflower	फूल गोभी	pool go·bee
corn	मक्का	mak·kaa
cucumber	ककड़ी	kak·ree
date	खजूर	ka·joor
eggplant	बैंगन	bayng·gan
fruit	फल	pal
garlic	लहसुन	leh·sun
grape	अंगूर	an·goor
grapefruit	चकोतरा	cha·kot·raa

lemon	निम्बू	nim·boo
lentils	दाल	daal
mandarin	सन्तरा	san·ta·raa
mango	आम	aam
mushroom	खुम्भी	kum·bee
nuts	मेवे	me·ve
orange	नारंगी	naa·ran·gee
papaya	पपीता	pa·pee·taa
peach	आड़ू	aa·roo
peas	मटर	ma·tar
pineapple	अनन्नास	a·nan·naas
potato	आलू	aa·loo
pumpkin	कद्दू	kad·doo
spinach	पालक	paa·lak
vegetables	सब्ज़ी	sab·zee
watermelon	तरबूज़	tar·booz

Other

bread	चपाती/ नान/रोटी	cha·paa·tee/ naan/ro·tee
butter	मक्खन	mak·kan
chilli	मिर्च	mirch
chutney	चटनी	chat·nee
egg	अंडे	an·de
honey	मधु	ma·dhu
ice	बर्फ़	barf
ice cream	कुल्फ़ी	kul·fee
pappadams	पपड़	pa·par
pepper	काली मिर्च	kaa·lee mirch
relish	अचार	a·chaar
rice	चावल	chaa·val
salt	नमक	na·mak
spices	मिर्च मसाला	mirch ma·saa·laa
sugar	चीनी	chee·nee
tofu	टोफू	to·foo

Drinks

beer	बियर	bi·yar
coffee	कॉफ़ी	kaa·fee
(sugarcane) juice	(गन्ने का) रस	(gan·ne kaa) ras
milk	दूध	dood
red wine	लाल शराब	laal sha·raab
sweet fruit drink	शरबत	shar·bat
tea	चाय	chaai
water	पानी	paa·nee
white wine	सफ़ेद शराब	sa·fed sha·raab
yoghurt	लस्सी	las·see

Emergencies

Help!
मदद कीजिये!   ma·dad kee·ji·ye

Go away!
जाओ!   jaa·o

I'm lost.
मैं रास्ता भूल
गया/गयी हूँ।   mayng raas·taa bool ga·yaa/ga·yee hoong (m/f)

Call a doctor!
डॉक्टर को बुलाओ!   daak·tar ko bu·laa·o

Call the police!
पुलिस को बुलाओ!   pu·lis ko bu·laa·o

I'm ill.
मैं बीमार हूँ।   mayng bee·maar hoong

Where is the toilet?
टॉइलेट कहाँ है?   taa·i·let ka·haang hay

Shopping & Services

I'd like to buy ...
मुझे ... चाहिये।   mu·je ... chaa·hi·ye

I'm just looking.
सिर्फ़ देखने आया/
आयी हूँ।   sirf dek·ne aa·yaa/ aa·yee hoong (m/f)

Can I look at it?
दिखाइये।   di·kaa·i·ye

How much is it?
कितने का है?   kit·ne kaa hay

It's too expensive.
यह बहुत महंगा/
महंगी है।   yeh ba·hut ma·han·gaa/ ma·han·gee hay (m/f)

There's a mistake in the bill.
बिल में गलती है।   bil meng gal·tee hay

bank	बैंक	baynk
post office	डाक ख़ाना	daak kaa·naa
public phone	सार्वजनिक फ़ोन	saar·va·ja·nik fon
tourist office	पर्यटन ऑफ़िस	par·ya·tan aa·fis

Time & Dates

What time is it?
टाइम क्या है?   taa·im kyaa hay

It's (10) o'clock.
(दस) बजे हैं।   (das) ba·je hayng

Half past (10).
साढ़े (दस)।   saa·re (das)

morning	सुबह	su·bah
afternoon	दोपहर	do·pa·har
evening	शाम	shaam
Monday	सोमवार	som·vaar
Tuesday	मंगलवार	man·gal·vaar
Wednesday	बुधवार	bud·vaar
Thursday	गुरुवार	gu·ru·vaar
Friday	शुक्रवार	shuk·ra·vaar
Saturday	शनिवार	sha·ni·vaar
Sunday	रविवार	ra·vi·vaar

Transport

When's the ... (bus)?	... (बस) कब जाती है?	... (bas) kab jaa·tee hay
first	पहली	peh·lee
last	आख़िरी	aa·ki·ree
bicycle	साइकिल	saa·i·kil
rickshaw	रिक्शा	rik·shaa
boat	जहाज़	ja·haaz
bus	बस	bas
plane	हवाई जहाज़	ha·vaa·ee ja·haaz
train	ट्रेन	tren
a ... ticket	के लिये ... टिकट दीजिये।	ke li·ye ... ti·kat dee·ji·ye
one-way	एक तरफ़ा	ek ta·ra·faa
return	आने जाने का	aa·ne jaa·ne kaa
bus stop	बस स्टॉप	bas is·taap
ticket office	टिकटघर	ti·kat·gar
timetable	समय सारणी	sa·mai saa·ra·nee
train station	स्टेशन	ste·shan

Does it stop at ...?
क्या ... में रुकती है?   kyaa ... meng ruk·tee hay

Please tell me when we get to ...
जब ... आता है,
मुझे बताइये।   jab ... aa·taa hay mu·je ba·taa·i·ye

Please go straight to this address.
इसी जगह को
फ़ौरन जाइए।   is·ee ja·gah ko fau·ran jaa·i·ye

Please stop here.
यहाँ रुकिये।   ya·haang ru·ki·ye

TAMIL

Tamil is the official language in the South Indian state of Tamil Nadu. It's one of the major Dravidian languages of South India, with records of its existence going back more than 2000 years. Tamil has about 62 million speakers in India.

Like Hindi, the Tamil sound system includes a number of 'retroflex' consonants (pronounced with the tongue bent backwards). Unlike Hindi, however, Tamil has no 'aspirated' sounds (pronounced with a puff of air). Our simplified pronunciation guides don't distinguish the retroflex consonants from their nonretroflex counterparts – just read the guides as if they were English and you'll be understood. Note that aw is pronounced as in 'law' and ow as in 'how'. The stressed syllables are indicated with italics.

NUMBERS – TAMIL

1	ஒன்று	on·dru
2	இரண்டு	i·ran·tu
3	மூன்று	moon·dru
4	நான்கு	naan·ku
5	ஐந்து	ain·tu
6	ஆறு	aa·ru
7	ஏழு	ey·zu
8	எட்டு	et·tu
9	ஒன்பது	on·pa·tu
10	பத்து	pat·tu
20	இருபது	i·ru·pa·tu
30	முப்பது	mup·pa·tu
40	நாற்பது	naar·pa·tu
50	ஐம்பது	aim·pa·tu
60	அறுபது	a·ru·pa·tu
70	எழுபது	e·zu·pa·tu
80	எண்பது	en·pa·tu
90	தொன்னூறு	ton·noo·ru
100	நூறு	noo·ru
1000	ஓராயிரம்	aw·raa·yi·ram

Basics

Hello.	வணக்கம்.	va·nak·kam
Goodbye.	போய் வருகிறேன்.	po·i va·ru·ki·reyn
Yes./No.	ஆமாம்./இல்லை.	aa·maam/il·lai
Excuse me.	தயவு செய்து	ta·ya·vu sei·du
Sorry.	மன்னிக்கவும்.	man·nik·ka·vum
Please.	தயவு செய்து.	ta·ya·vu chey·tu
Thank you.	நன்றி.	nan·dri

Do you speak English?

நீங்கள் ஆங்கிலம் பேசுவீர்களா? — neeng·kal aang·ki·lam pey·chu·veer·ka·la

I don't understand.

எனக்கு விளங்கவில்லை. — e·nak·ku vi·lang·ka·vil·lai

Accommodation

Where's a ... nearby?	அருகே ஒரு ... எங்கே உள்ளது?	a·ru·ke o·ru ... eng·ke ul·la·tu
guesthouse	விருந்தினர் இல்லம	vi·run·ti·nar il·lam
hotel	ஹோட்டல	hot·tal

Do you have a ... room?	உங்களிடம் ஓர் ... அறை உள்ளதா?	ung·ka·li·tam awr ... a·rai ul·la·taa
single	தன	ta·ni
double	இரட்டை	i·rat·tai

How much is it per ...?	ஓர் ... என்னவிலை?	awr ... en·na·vi·lai
night	இரவுக்கு	i·ra·vuk·ku
person	ஒருவருக்கு	o·ru·va·ruk·ku

air-conditioned	குளிர்சாதன வசதியுடையது	ku·lir·chaa·ta·na va·cha·ti·yu·tai·ya·tu
bathroom	குளியலறை	ku·li·ya·la·rai
bed	படுக்கை	pa·tuk·kai
window	சன்னல	chan·nal

Eating & Drinking

Can you recommend a ...?	நீங்கள் ஒரு ... பரிந்துரைக்க முடியுமா?	neeng·kal o·ru ... pa·rin·tu·raik·ka mu·ti·yu·maa
bar	பார்	paar
dish	உணவு வகை	u·na·vu va·kai
place to eat	உணவகம்	u·na·va·ham

I'd like (a/the) ..., please.	எனக்கு தயவு செய்து ... கொடுங்கள்.	e·nak·ku ta·ya·vu chey·tu ... ko·tung·kal
bill	விலைச்சீட்டு	vi·laich·cheet·tu
menu	உணவுப்– பட்டியல்	u·na·vup·pat·ti·yal
that dish	அந்த உணவு வகை	an·ta u·na·vu va·hai

Do you have vegetarian food?

உங்களிடம சைவ உணவு உள்ளதா? — ung·ka·li·tam chai·va u·na·vu ul·la·taa

Emergencies

Help!	உதவு!	u·ta·vi
Go away!	போய் வீடு!	pow·i vi·tu

Call a doctor!		
ஐ அழைக்கவும்		i a·zai·ka·vum
ஒரு மருத்துவர்!		o·ru ma·rut·tu·var

Call the police!		
ஐ அழைக்கவும்		i a·zai·ka·vum
போலீஸ்!		pow·lees

I'm lost.		
நான் வழி தவறி		naan va·zi ta·va·ri
போய்வீட்டேன்.		pow·i·vit·teyn

Where are the toilets?		
கழிவறைகள் எங்கே?		ka·zi·va·rai·kal eng·key

Shopping & Services

Where's the market?		
எங்கே சந்தை		eng·key chan·tai
இருக்கிறது?		i·ruk·ki·ra·tu

Can I look at it?		
நான் இதைப்		naan i·taip
பார்க்கலாமா?		paark·ka·laa·maa

How much is it?		
இது என்ன வீலை?		i·tu en·na vi·lai

That's too expensive.		
அது அதிக வீலையாக		a·tu a·ti·ka vi·lai·yaa·ka
இருக்கிறது.		i·ruk·ki·ra·tu

bank	வங்கி	vang·ki
internet	இணையம்	i·nai·yam
post office	தபால்	ta·paal
	நிலையம்	ni·lai·yam
tourist office	சுற்றுப்பயண	chut·rup·pa·ya·na
	அலுவலகம்	a·lu·va·la·kam

Time & Dates

What time is it?		
மணி என்ன?		ma·ni en·na

It's (two) o'clock.		
மணி (இரண்டு)		ma·ni (i·ran·tu)

Half past (two).		
(இரண்டு) முப்பது.		(i·ran·tu) mup·pa·tu

yesterday	நேற்று	neyt·tru
today	இன்று	in·dru
tomorrow	நாளை	naa·lai
morning	காலை	kaa·lai
evening	மாலை	maa·lai
night	இரவு	i·ra·vu

Monday	திங்கள்	ting·kal
Tuesday	செவ்வாய்	chev·vai
Wednesday	புதன்	pu·tan
Thursday	வீயாழன்	vi·yaa·zan
Friday	வெள்ளி	vel·li
Saturday	சனி	cha·ni
Sunday	ஞாயிறு	nyaa·yi·ru

Transport & Directions

Where's the ...?		
... எங்கே இருக்கிறது?		... eng·key i·ruk·ki·ra·tu

What's the address?		
வீலாசம் என்ன?		vi·laa·cham en·na

Can you show me (on the map)?		
எனக்கு (வரைபடத்தில்)		e·nak·ku (va·rai·pa·tat·til)
காட்ட முடியுமா?		kaat·ta mu·ti·yu·maa

Is this the ... to (New Delhi)?	இது தானா (புது–டில்லிக்குப்) புறப்படும் ...?	i·tu taa·naa (pu·tu til·lik·kup) pu·rap·pa·tum ...
bus	பஸ்	pas
plane	வீமானம்	vi·maa·nam
train	இரயில்	i·ra·yil

One ... ticket (to Madurai), please.	(மதுரைக்கு) தபவு செய்து ... டிக்கட் கொடுங்கள்.	(ma·tu·raik·ku) ta·ya·vu chey·tu ... tik·kat ko·tung·kal
one-way	ஒரு வழிப்பயண	o·ru va·zip·pa·ya·na
return	இரு வழிப்பயண	i·ru va·zip·pa·ya·na
bicycle	சைக்கிள்	chaik·kil
boat	படகு	pa·ta·ku
bus stop	பஸ் நிறுத்தும்	pas ni·rut·tum
economy class	சிக்கன வகுப்பு	chik·ka·na va·kup·pu
first class	முதல் வகுப்பு	mu·tal va·kup·pu
motorcycle	மோட்டார் சைக்கிள்	mowt·taar chaik·kil
train station	நிலையம்	ni·lai·yam

What time's the first/last bus?		
எத்தனை மணிக்கு		et·ta·nai ma·nik·ku
முதல்/இறுதி		mu·tal/i·ru·ti
பஸ் வரும்?		pas va·rum

How long does the trip take?		
பயணம் எவ்வளவு		pa·ya·nam ev·va·la·vu
நேரம் எடுக்கும்?		ney·ram e·tuk·kum

GLOSSARY

Adivasis – tribal people

Ardhanarishvara – *Shiva*'s half-male, half-female form

Arjuna – Mahabharata hero and military commander; he had the *Bhagavad Gita* related to him by *Krishna*.

Aryan – Sanskrit for 'noble'; those who migrated from Persia and settled in northern India

ashram – spiritual community or retreat

ASI – Archaeological Survey of India; an organisation involved in monument preservation

autorickshaw – noisy, three-wheeled, motorised contraption for transporting passengers, livestock etc for short distances; found throughout the country, they are cheaper than taxis

Avalokitesvara – in Mahayana Buddhism, the *bodhisattva* of compassion

avatar – incarnation, usually of a deity

ayurveda – ancient and complex science of Indian herbal medicine and holistic healing

azad – Urdu for 'free', as in Azad Jammu and Kashmir

Baba – religious master or father; term of respect

bagh – garden

bahadur – brave or chivalrous; an honorific title

baksheesh – tip, donation (alms) or bribe

banyan – Indian fig tree; spiritual to many Indians

baoli – see *baori*

baori – well, particularly a step-well with landings and galleries; in Gujarat it is more commonly referred to as a *baoli*

barasingha – deer

basti – slum

bearer – like a butler

Bhagavad Gita – Hindu Song of the Divine One; Krishna's lessons to *Arjuna*, the main thrust of which was to emphasise the philosophy of *bhakti*; it is part of the Mahabharata

bhajan – devotional song

bhakti – surrendering to the gods; faith, devotion

bhang – dried leaves and flowering shoots of the marijuana plant

bhangra – rhythmic Punjabi music/dance

Bharat – Hindi for India

bhavan – house, building; also spelt bhawan

Bhima – Mahabharata hero; the brother of Hanuman, husband of Hadimba, father of Ghatotkach, and renowned for his great strength

bindi – forehead mark (often dot-shaped) made from *kumkum*, worn by women

BJP – Bharatiya Janata Party

Bodhi Tree – tree under which *Buddha* sat when he attained enlightenment

bodhisattva – enlightened beings

Bollywood – India's answer to Hollywood; the film industry of Mumbai (Bombay)

Brahma – Hindu god; worshipped as the creator in the Trimurti

Brahmanism – early form of Hinduism that evolved from Vedism (see *Vedas*); named after *Brahmin* priests and *Brahma*

Brahmin – member of the priest/scholar caste, the highest Hindu caste

Buddha – Awakened One; the originator of *Buddhism*; also regarded by Hindus as the ninth incarnation of *Vishnu*

Buddhism – see *Early Buddhism*

cantonment – administrative and military area of a Raj-era town

Carnatic music – classical music of South India

caste – a Hindu's hereditary station (social standing) in life; there are four main castes: Brahmin, Kshatriya, Vaishya and Shudra

chaam – ritual masked dance performed by some Buddhist monks in gompas to celebrate the victory of good over evil and of Buddhism over preexisting religions

chaitya – prayer room; assembly hall

chakra – focus of one's spiritual power; disc-like weapon of *Vishnu*

Chamunda – form of Durga; armed with a scimitar, noose and mace, and clothed in elephant hide, her mission was to kill the demons Chanda and Munda

chandra – moon, or the moon as a god

Chandragupta – Indian ruler in the 3rd century BC

chappals – sandals or leather thonglike footwear; flip-flops

char dham – four pilgrimage destinations of Badrinath, Kedarnath, Yamunotri and Gangotri

charas – resin of the marijuana plant; also referred to as hashish

charbagh – formal Persian garden, divided into quarters (literally 'four gardens')

chedi – see *chaitya*

chhatri – cenotaph (literally 'umbrella'), or pavilion

chikan – embroidered cloth (speciality of Lucknow)

chillum – pipe of a hookah; commonly used to describe the pipes used for smoking ganja (marijuana)

chinkara – gazelle

chital – spotted deer

chogyal – king

choli – sari blouse

chorten – Tibetan for stupa

choultry – pilgrim's rest house; also called dharamsala

chowk – town square, intersection or marketplace

Cong (I) – Congress Party of India; also known as Congress (I)

coracle – a small, traditional keel-less boat, often round or oval in shape, comprising a wickerwork or lath frame over which greased cloth or hide is stretched

dagoba – see *stupa*

Dalit – preferred term for India's Untouchable caste; see also *Harijan*

dargah – shrine or place of burial of a Muslim saint

darshan – offering or audience with a deity

deul – temple sanctuary

Devi – *Shiva*'s wife; goddess

dhaba – basic restaurant or snack bar

dham – holiest pilgrimage places of India

dharamsala – pilgrim's rest house

dharma – for Hindus, the moral code of behaviour or social duty; for Buddhists, following the law of nature, or path, as taught by Buddha

dhobi – person who washes clothes; commonly referred to as dhobi-wallah

dhobi ghat – place where clothes are washed

dhoti – long loincloth worn by men; like a lungi, but the ankle-length cloth is then pulled up between the legs

Digambara – 'Sky-Clad'; Jain group that demonstrates disdain for worldly goods by going naked

diwan – principal officer in a princely state; royal court or council

Diwan-i-Am – hall of public audience

Diwan-i-Khas – hall of private audience

dowry – money and/or goods given by a bride's parents to their son-in-law's family; it's illegal but still widely exists in many arranged marriages

Draupadi – wife of the five Pandava princes in the *Mahabharata*

Dravidian – general term for the cultures and languages of the deep south of India, including Tamil, Malayalam, Telugu and Kannada

dukhang – Tibetan prayer hall

dun – valley

dupatta – long scarf for women often worn with the *salwar kameez*

durbar – royal court; also a government

Durga – the Inaccessible; a form of *Shiva*'s wife, Devi, a beautiful, fierce woman riding a tiger/lion; a major goddess of the *Shakti* order

Early Buddhism – any of the schools of Buddhism established directly after Buddha's death and before the advent of Mahayana; a modern form is the Theravada (Teaching of the Elders) practised in Sri Lanka and Southeast Asia; Early Buddhism differed from the Mahayana in that it did not teach the *bodhisattva* ideal

gabba – appliquéd Kashmiri rug

gali – lane or alleyway

Ganesh – Hindu god of good fortune; elephant-headed son of *Shiva* and Parvati, he is also known as Ganpati and his vehicle is Mooshak (a ratlike creature)

Ganga – Hindu goddess representing the sacred Ganges River; said to flow from *Vishnu*'s toe

ganj – market

gaon – village

garh – fort

Garuda – man-bird vehicle of *Vishnu*

gaur – Indian bison

Gayatri – sacred verse of Rig-Veda repeated mentally by Brahmins twice a day

geyser – hot-water unit found in many bathrooms

ghat – steps or landing on a river; a range of hills or a road up hills

giri – hill

gompa – Tibetan Buddhist monastery

Gopala – see *Govinda*

gopi – milkmaid; Krishna was fond of them

gopuram – soaring pyramidal gateway tower of Dravidian temples

Govinda – Krishna as a cowherd; also just cowherd

gumbad – dome on an Islamic tomb or mosque

gurdwara – Sikh temple

guru – holy teacher; in Sanskrit literally 'goe' (darkness) and 'roe' (to dispel)

Guru Granth Sahib – Sikh holy book

haat – village market

haj – Muslim pilgrimage to Mecca

haji – Muslim who has made the haj

hammam – Turkish bath; public bathhouse

Hanuman – Hindu monkey god, prominent in the Ramayana, and a follower of Rama

Hari – another name for *Vishnu*

Harijan – name (no longer considered acceptable) given by Mahatma Gandhi to India's Untouchable caste, meaning 'children of god'

hashish – see *charas*

hathi – elephant

haveli – traditional, often ornately decorated, residences, particularly those found in Rajasthan and Gujarat

hijab – headscarf used by Muslim women

hijra – eunuch, transvestite

hookah – water pipe used for smoking marijuana or strong tobacco

howdah – seat for carrying people on an elephant's back

ikat – fabric made with thread which is tie-dyed before weaving

imam – Muslim religious leader

imambara – tomb dedicated to a Shiite Muslim holy man

Indo-Saracenic – style of colonial architecture that integrated Western designs with Islamic, Hindu and Jain influences

Indra – significant and prestigious Vedic god; god of rain, thunder, lightning and war

jagamohan – assembly hall

Jagannath – Lord of the Universe; a form of Krishna

jali – carved lattice (often marble) screen; also refers to the holes or spaces produced through carving timber or stone

Jataka – tale from Buddha's various lives

jauhar – ritual mass suicide by immolation, traditionally performed by Rajput women at times of military defeat to avoid being dishonoured by their captors

jhula – bridge

ji – honorific that can be added to the end of almost anything as

LANGUAGE GLOSSARY

a form of respect; thus 'Babaji', 'Gandhiji'

jooti – traditional, often pointy-toed, slip-in shoes; commonly found in North India

juggernaut – huge, extravagantly decorated temple 'car' dragged through the streets during certain Hindu festivals

jyoti linga – naturally occurring lingam believed to derive currents of *Shakti*

kabaddi – traditional game (similar to tag)

Kailasa – sacred Himalayan mountain; home of *Shiva*

Kali – ominous-looking evil-destroying form of Devi; commonly depicted with dark skin, dripping with blood, and wearing a necklace of skulls

Kama – Hindu god of love

Kama Sutra – ancient Sanskrit text largely covering the subjects of love and sexuality

kameez – woman's shirtlike tunic; see also *salwar kameez*

karma – Hindu, Buddhist and Sikh principle of retributive justice for past deeds

khadi – homespun cloth; Mahatma Gandhi encouraged people to spin this rather than buy English cloth

Khalsa – Sikh brotherhood

Khan – Muslim honorific title

khur – Asiatic wild ass

kirtan – Sikh devotional singing

koil – Hindu temple

kolam – see *rangoli*

kot – fort

kothi – residence or mansion

kotwali – police station

Krishna – *Vishnu*'s eighth incarnation, often coloured blue; he revealed the *Bhagavad Gita* to *Arjuna*

kumkum – coloured powder used for *bindi* dots

kund – lake or tank; Toda village

kurta – long shirt with either short collar or no collar

Lakshmana – half-brother and aide of Rama in the Ramayana

Lakshmi – *Vishnu*'s consort, Hindu goddess of wealth; she

sprang forth from the ocean holding a lotus

lama – Tibetan Buddhist priest or monk

Laxmi – see *Lakshmi*

lingam – phallic symbol; auspicious symbol of *Shiva*; plural 'linga'

lok – people

Lok Sabha – lower house in the Indian parliament (House of the People)

Losar – Tibetan New Year

lungi – worn by men, this loose, coloured garment (similar to a sarong) is pleated by the wearer at the waist to fit

madrasa – Islamic seminary

maha – prefix meaning 'great'

Mahabharata – Great Hindu Vedic epic poem of the Bharata dynasty; containing approximately 10,000 verses describing the battle between the Pandavas and the Kauravas

Mahakala – Great Time; *Shiva* and one of 12 jyoti linga (sacred shrines)

mahal – house or palace

maharaja – literally 'great king'; princely ruler

maharana – see *maharaja*

maharani – wife of a princely ruler or a ruler in her own right

maharao – see *maharaja*

maharawal – see *maharaja*

mahatma – literally 'great soul'

Mahavir – last tirthankar

Mahayana – the 'greater-vehicle' of Buddhism; a later adaptation of the teaching that lays emphasis on the *bodhisattva* ideal, teaching the renunciation of nirvana in order to help other beings along the way to enlightenment

maidan – open (often grassed) area; parade ground

Maitreya – future Buddha

mandal – shrine

mandala – circle; symbol used in Hindu and Buddhist art to symbolise the universe

mandapa – pillared pavilion, temple forechamber

mandi – market

mandir – temple

mani stone – stone carved with the Tibetan-Buddhist mantra 'Om mani padme hum' ('Hail the jewel in the lotus')

mani walls – Tibetan stone walls with sacred inscriptions

mantra – sacred word or syllable used by Buddhists and Hindus to aid concentration; metrical psalms of praise found in the *Vedas*

Maratha – central Indian people who controlled much of India at various times and fought the Mughals and Rajputs

marg – road

masjid – mosque

mata – mother

math – monastery

maya – illusion

mehndi – henna; ornate henna designs on women's hands (and often feet), traditionally for certain festivals or ceremonies (eg marriage)

mela – fair or festival

mithuna – pairs of men and women; often seen in temple sculpture

Moghul – see *Mughal*

monsoon – rainy season

muezzin – one who calls Muslims to prayer, traditionally from the minaret of a mosque

Mughal – Muslim dynasty of subcontinental emperors from Babur to Aurangzeb

Mumbaikar – resident of Mumbai (Bombay)

namaste – traditional Hindu greeting (hello or goodbye), often accompanied by a respectful small bow with the hands together at the chest or head level

Nanda – cowherd who raised Krishna

Nandi – bull, vehicle of *Shiva*

Narayan – incarnation of *Vishnu* the creator

Nataraja – *Shiva* as the cosmic dancer

nawab – Muslim ruling prince or powerful landowner

Naxalites – ultra-leftist political movement begun in West Bengal as a peasant rebellion; characterised by violence

nilgai – antelope

nirvana – ultimate aim of Buddhists and the final release from the cycle of existence

niwas – house, building

nizam – hereditary title of the rulers of Hyderabad

nullah – ditch or small stream

Om – sacred invocation representing the essence of the divine principle; for Buddhists, if repeated often enough with complete concentration, it leads to a state of emptiness

Osho – the late Bhagwan Shree Rajneesh, a popular, controversial guru

paan – mixture of betel nut and leaves for chewing

padma – lotus; another name for the Hindu goddess Lakshmi

pagoda – see *stupa*

paise – the Indian rupee is divided into 100 paise

palanquin – boxlike enclosure carried on poles on four bearer's shoulders; the occupant sits inside on a seat

Pali – the language, related to Sanskrit, in which the Buddhist scriptures were recorded; scholars still refer to the original Pali texts

pandal – marquee; temple shrine

Parsi – adherent of the Zoroastrian faith

Partition – formal division of British India in 1947 into two separate countries, India and Pakistan

Parvati – another form of Devi

pashmina – fine woollen shawl

PCO – Public Call Office, from where you can make local, interstate and international phone calls

peepul – fig tree, especially a bo tree

peon – lowest-grade clerical worker

pietra dura – marble inlay work characteristic of the Taj Mahal

pradesh – state

pranayama – study of breath control; meditative practice

prasad – temple-blessed food offering

puja – literally 'respect'; offering or prayers

pukka – proper; a Raj-era term

punka – cloth fan, swung by pulling a cord

Puranas – set of 18 encyclopaedic Sanskrit stories, written in verse, relating to the three gods, dating from the 5th century AD

purdah – custom among some conservative Muslims (also adopted by some Hindus, especially the Rajputs) of keeping women in seclusion; veiled

Purnima – full moon; considered to be an auspicious time

qawwali – Islamic devotional singing

qila – fort

Quran – the holy book of Islam, also spelt Koran

Radha – Krishna's consort and the most revered of the gopis

raga – any of several conventional patterns of melody and rhythm that form the basis for freely interpreted compositions

railhead – station or town at the end of a railway line; termination point

raj – rule or sovereignty; British Raj (sometimes just Raj) refers to British rule

raja – king; sometimes rana

rajkumar – prince

Rajput – Hindu warrior caste, former rulers of northwestern India

Rama – seventh incarnation of *Vishnu*

Ramadan – Islamic holy month of sunrise-to-sunset fasting (no eating, drinking or smoking); also referred to as Ramazan

Ramayana – story of Rama and Sita and their conflict with Ravana; one of India's best-known epics

rana – king; sometimes raja

rangoli – elaborate chalk, rice-paste or coloured powder design; also known as kolam

rani – female ruler or wife of a king

ranns – deserts

rath – temple chariot or car used in religious festivals

rathas – rock-cut Dravidian temples

Ravana – demon king of Lanka who abducted Sita; the titanic battle between him and Rama is told in the Ramayana

rickshaw – small, two- or three-wheeled passenger vehicle

Rig-Veda – original and longest of the four main *Vedas*

rishi – any poet, philosopher, saint or sage; originally a sage to whom the hymns of the *Vedas* were revealed

Road – railway town that serves as a communication point to a larger town off the line, eg Mt Abu and Abu Road

Rukmani – wife of Krishna; died on his funeral pyre

sadar – main

sadhu – ascetic, holy person, one who is trying to achieve enlightenment; often addressed as 'swamiji' or 'babaji'

sagar – lake, reservoir

sahib – respectful title applied to a gentleman

salai – road

salwar – trousers usually worn with a kameez

salwar kameez – traditional dresslike tunic and trouser combination for women

samadhi – in Hinduism, ecstatic state, sometimes defined as 'ecstasy, trance, communion with God'; in Buddhism, concentration; also a place where a holy man has been cremated/buried, usually venerated as a shrine

sambar – deer

samsara – Buddhists, Hindus and Sikhs believe earthly life is cyclical; you are born again and again, the quality of these rebirths being dependent upon your karma in previous lives

sangha – community of Buddhist monks and nuns

Saraswati – wife of Brahma, goddess of learning; sits on a white swan, holding a veena (a type of string instrument)

Sat Sri Akal – Sikh greeting

Sati – wife of *Shiva*; became a sati ('honourable woman') by immolating herself; although banned more than a century ago, the act of sati is still (very) occasionally performed

satra – Hindu Vaishnavaite monastery and centre for art

satyagraha – nonviolent protest involving a hunger strike, popularised by Mahatma Gandhi; from Sanskrit, literally meaning 'insistence on truth'

Scheduled Castes – official term used for the Untouchable or Dalit caste

Shaivism – worship of *Shiva*

Shaivite – follower of *Shiva*

shakti – creative energies perceived as female deities; devotees follow Shaktism order

sheesha – see *hookah*

shikara – gondola-like boat used on lakes in Srinagar (Kashmir)

shikhar – hunting expedition

Shiva – Destroyer; also the Creator, in which form he is worshipped as a lingam

shola – virgin forest

shree – see *shri*

shri – honorific male prefix; Indian equivalent of 'Respected Sir'

Shudra – caste of labourers

sikhara – Hindu temple-spire or temple

Singh – literally 'lion'; a surname adopted by Sikhs

Sita – Hindu goddess of agriculture; more commonly associated with the Ramayana

sitar – Indian stringed instrument

Siva – see *Shiva*

sree – see *shri*

sri – see *shri*

stupa – Buddhist religious monument composed of a solid hemisphere topped by a spire, containing relics of Buddha; also known as a *dagoba* or *pagoda*

Subhadra – Krishna's incestuous sister

Sufi – Muslim mystic

Sufism – Islamic mysticism

Surya – the sun; a major deity in the *Vedas*

sutra – string; list of rules expressed in verse

swami – title of respect meaning 'lord of the self'; given to initiated Hindu monks

tabla – twin drums

tal – lake

tank – reservoir; pool or large receptacle of holy water found at some temples

tantric Buddhism – Tibetan Buddhism with strong sexual and occult overtones

tempo – noisy three-wheeler public transport vehicle, bigger than an *autorickshaw*; see *Vikram*

thakur – nobleman

thangka – Tibetan cloth painting

theertham – temple tank

Theravada – orthodox form of Buddhism practised in Sri Lanka and Southeast Asia that is characterised by its adherence to the Pali canon; literally 'dwelling'

tikka – mark Hindus put on their foreheads

tirthankars – the 24 great Jain teachers

tonga – two-wheeled horse or pony carriage

torana – architrave over a temple entrance

trekkers – jeeps; hikers

Trimurti – triple form or three-faced; the Hindu triad of *Brahma*, *Shiva* and *Vishnu*

Untouchable – lowest caste or 'casteless', for whom the most menial tasks are reserved; the name derives from the belief that higher castes risk defilement if they touch one; formerly known as *Harijan*, now *Dalit*

Upanishads – esoteric doctrine; ancient texts forming part of the *Vedas*; delving into weighty matters such as the nature of the universe and soul

urs – death anniversary of a revered Muslim; festival in memory of a Muslim saint

Valmiki – author of the Ramayana

Vedas – Hindu sacred books; collection of hymns composed in preclassical Sanskrit during the second millennium BC and divided into four books: Rig-Veda, Yajur-Veda, Sama-Veda and Atharva-Veda

vihara – Buddhist monastery, generally with central court or hall off which open residential cells, usually with a Buddha shrine at one end; resting place

vikram – tempo or a larger version of the standard tempo

vimana – principal part of Hindu temple; a tower over the sanctum

vipassana – insight meditation technique of Theravada Buddhism in which mind and body are closely examined as changing phenomena

Vishnu – part of the Trimurti; Vishnu is the Preserver and Restorer who so far has nine *avatars*: the fish Matsya; the tortoise Kurma; the wild boar Naraha; Narasimha; Vamana; Parasurama; Rama; Krishna; and Buddha

wallah – man; added onto almost anything, eg dhobi-wallah, chai-wallah, taxi-wallah

yakshi – maiden

yali – mythical lion creature

yatra – pilgrimage

yatri – pilgrim

yogini – female goddess attendants

yoni – female fertility symbol; female genitalia

zenana – area of an upperclass home where women are secluded; women's quarters

Behind the Scenes

SEND US YOUR FEEDBACK

We love to hear from travellers – your comments keep us on our toes and help make our books better. Our well-travelled team reads every word on what you loved or loathed about this book. Although we cannot reply individually to your submissions, we always guarantee that your feedback goes straight to the appropriate authors, in time for the next edition. Each person who sends us information is thanked in the next edition – the most useful submissions are rewarded with a selection of digital PDF chapters.

Visit **lonelyplanet.com/contact** to submit your updates and suggestions or to ask for help. Our award-winning website also features inspirational travel stories, news and discussions.

Note: We may edit, reproduce and incorporate your comments in Lonely Planet products such as guidebooks, websites and digital products, so let us know if you don't want your comments reproduced or your name acknowledged. For a copy of our privacy policy visit lonelyplanet.com/privacy.

OUR READERS

Many thanks to the travellers who used the last edition and wrote to us with helpful hints, useful advice and interesting anecdotes:

A Abhishek Kumar, Ajinkya shinde, Alban Fraval, Alexandre Bernuit, Angus Murray, Annie Ward-Amble, Arlo Adams, Arzu Unel-Cleary **B** Barney Smith, Bev Missing **C** Carl Strid, Carole Corthesy, Charles Clark, Coline Carime, Cristiana Tavares **D** David Koppers, David Patrickcampbell, Denise Couzens, Dermilly Renaud, Diego Riveiro Lasheras, Dor Shaim **E** Elisabeth Carrier-Deziel, Ernst Lessan, Eyal Barel **F** Fabio Cambi, Franziska Hammerl **G** Garnier Etienne, Giovanni Rossi, Girish Yogiraj, Gregory Gapsis, Guy Manno **H** Henrik Nielsen, Hitesh Geel **I** Iggy Vandycke **J** Jacob Webber, Jayde Imber, Jeremy Frewer, Jerome Camier, Jessica Raynal, John Osman, John Smith, Jonathan Ng Wei Xiang, Juan Naballas, Juan Pont, Judith Frazer, Judy Kitcher **K** Keith Freeman, Krista Vaillancourt **L** Laura Maria, Leona Lynen, Lindsay Lueptow **M** Maarten Golterman, Mackenzie Dalton, Madelaine King, Mai Dolang, Marjan Geertsema, Matthew Hudson, Michal Rudziecki, Michele Walton **N** Nancy Erwin, Nigel Crosscombe, Noel Bristow, Noémie Comeau **O** Olivia Gray, Ollie Townley **P** Penny Kisby, Peter Jordan, Praful Kapadia, Praniith Selvaranjan **Q** Quentin Thwaites **R** Raj K Gupta, Ramon Queiroz, Rasmus Krath, Ricardo Alcalde, Richard Jenkins, Rosemary Holland, Ryan Harding **S** Saeed Ghinai, Sam Cooper, Sharon Smith, Shiva Krishnan, Sophia Herrmann, Stefano Montali, Steven Sacco **T** Ted Moore, Troy Mithrush **V** Vanessa Woerner **Z** Zac Hudson

WRITERS' THANKS

Lindsay Brown

Thanks to all the folks who assisted me throughout my travels in Rajasthan. I am very grateful to Satinder, Ritu, Raj, Dicky and Kavita in Jaipur; Anoop and Bunty in Pushkar; Nikhil and Atush in Jodhpur; Ravindra in Ranthambhore; Harsh in Bikaner; Vikram in Jaisalmer; and Keshav and Manish in Bundi. Special thanks to Jenny.

Paul Harding

Thanks must go to the many friends I reconnected with in Goa and the new people I met on this trip. Big thanks to Jack, Ajit and family in Panaji; Ravi in Vagator; John, Jack and Kate in Palolem; and Joanna and Xavi in Patnem. Thanks also to friends in Kochi and Alleppey, Philip, Maryann, Johnson, Shibu and Niaz, and to Joe at Lonely Planet for entrusting me with Goa. Biggest thanks goes to my travelling companions, Hannah and Layla.

Anirban Mahapatra

My sincere thanks to the many friendly and helpful people I met on the road during my research trip. To Soumen in Bhubaneswar, Debjit and Jitendra in Dhenkanal, Bubu in Puri and Iftekhar in Kolkata for sharing valuable information along the way, and to drivers Dinesh, Dukhan and Umesh for driving me several hundred kilometres through the great Indian countryside. And finally, to the fabulous Lonely Planet *India* team for coming together to produce yet another edition of this awesome title.

Daniel McCrohan

Love, hugs and kisses to my amazingly patient wife, Taotao, and two incredible children, Dudu and Yoyo; and to mum for helping out so much. At LP, huge thanks to Joe for trusting in me, and to my fellow writers, especially Abi, Isabella, John, Bradley, Mark and Kevin. In Delhi, a big thank you to Pradeep, Shahadutt, Pash, Catriona and Paula (amessing!), and of course to Nick, and to Dilip and his beautiful family, for being such wonderful hosts.

Isabella Noble

Huge thanks in Kerala: Paul, John, Roy, Lee, Kumar, Mariann and Philip, Johnson, Daniel, Roy Joseph, Dileep and Tomy, Beena and Varghese, Ajay, Suresh and Sulekha, Debra, Joseph, Yazer, the French yogis, and Mr Babu at Kochi's Vyttila Mobility Hub. Cheers to Norbu and Sangay in Darjeeling; and to Samit, Ashish, Sanjay, Rahul, Mark, Atalanta, Pawan, Jocelyn, Abnash and Shakti in the Andamans. Extra grateful to my fabulous *India* cowriters, and, at home, to Jack, Dan, Andrew and Paps.

Michael Benanav

I'd like to thank Isabella Noble – one of LP's own South India experts – for all of her Tamil Nadu advice. And as always, thanks to Luke and Kelly for their patience and understanding while I'm away.

Stuart Butler

Thank you to my wife, Heather, and children, Jake and Grace, for their patience and for joining me for part of my research. And a special note for Jake and Grace: thank you for helping me to see the wonder of India through new eyes! In India thank you to Shaikh 'Johnny' Mukarram, Salim A Chhipa, Nirdos, Jehan and Katie, Sheema and Jhampan, Manav, Dr Raghu Chundawat and Joanna. Finally, thank you to all the Indians who helped make this hands down my most enjoyable trip to India ever.

Mark Elliott

First and foremost, my thanks, love and endless admiration to Sally Cobham. On the road, a great big thank you to hundreds of kind souls who helped me so much, including Rakesh Sharma (Shimla), Tony and Jackie Nelson, Iris and Eelke, Trent and Nick, Mohan, Ashok, Suresh (Rampur), Dave, Ed, Maddy, Ros and Geoff (Sarahan), Bitu Negi and Rana (my salvation at Karcham), Ashish (Katra), Chewang and Dependra (Nako), Vaneet Rana, Mark and Noam, Kishor Nakwa, Sonam, unhappy Jason, Deepak and the gang at Bikki's Dhaba (Purthi), Ajay and Dij (Premnagar temple), Rocky and the bikers, Rashmi and Abhilash (Dalhousie), Tsering Bhutia, Ranjita, John and the Wongden family (Mangan), Atul Sharma, Gokul Butail (Palampur), Lalit, Bupender Thakur and BS Rana (Jibhi), Sanju, Veena and Pragati (Kullu), Eva (Naggar) and Gotham (Manali).

Trent Holden

Foremost I'd like to thank Joe Bindloss for giving me the amazing opportunity to head up north to cover the pristine, impossibly beautiful state of Uttarakhand. Thanks also to my fellow writers on this book, and to the inhouse production team for putting this book together. A massive shout out to Padam who helped me with getting around for a significant chunk of the trip, and Red Chilli from Rishikesh for arranging such a relaxed, capable driver. Also a big send out to all the trekking companies in Joshimath, most notably Dinesh from Eskimo Adventures and Ajay from Himalayan Snow Runner for all their help and advice on the road. Finally, lots of love to my fiancée Kate, and to all my family and friends.

Bradley Mayhew

Thanks to Rouf in Rinagar; Anil and Ramesh Wadhwa in Agra; Zaheer Bagh in Kargil; Juma Malik and Tashi of Hidden North in Leh; Harish and Michael Schmid in Varanasi. Thanks to Carolyn for keeping me company in Varanasi.

John Noble

Thanks to hundreds of people in India for answering my thousands of questions and all sorts of other help. Above all: Swalehul Islam, Sushma Chetri, Krishno Dey, Sukanya Ray, Kanak Chandra, Norbu and Sangay Dekeva, Norden and Thinlay Pempahishey, Oken Tayeng, PK Baruah, Sangay Bhutia, Kevichulie Meyase and James Perry. Extra special thanks to Isabella Noble for sharing the entire experience! Thanks to Joe and the rest of the team for constant good fellowship. And to Jack, Dan and Sarah for supplying those missing words in the last few days.

Kevin Raub

Thanks to Joe Bindloss and all my fellow partners in crime at LP. On the road, Anil Whadwa and Bagpacker Travels, Pankil Shaw, Jas Charanjiva, Khaki Tours, Priyanka Jacob, Roxanne Bamboat, Sanil Kapse, Sudakshina Banerjee, Ashok Tours & Travels, Sakshi Chari, Sheetal Waradkar, Chirag Rupani, Zaid Purkars and Amrut and Aditya Dhanwatay.

Sarina Singh

Gratitude to the many readers who wrote to us with their feedback and travel experiences. At Lonely Planet, thanks to Joe for being such a delightful editor; to my fellow cowriters; and to everyone involved in this book's production. Finally, warm thanks to my parents for always being so fantastic.

Iain Stewart

Thanks to Jonty in Hyderabad for her insight and helpful tips. I was greatly aided by Prakash in Bengaluru (Bangalore), whose expertise of the craft beer scene and emerging restos is quite something. In Mysuru (Mysore) the folk from Gully Tours proved excellent company, as did the thousands of Hindu pilgrims I accompanied on the Tirumula trek. And thanks to all at LP, including Joe Bindloss and my fellow Team *India* writers.

ACKNOWLEDGEMENTS

Climate map data adapted from Peel MC, Finlayson BL & McMahon TA (2007) 'Updated World Map of the Köppen-Geiger Climate Classification', *Hydrology and Earth System Sciences*, 11, 1633–44.

Cover photograph: City Palace, Jaipur, Rajasthan; Pikoso.kz/Shutterstock ©

Illustrations pp1176-7, pp1178-9 and p1180 by Kelli Hamblet; pp374-5 and pp876-7 by Michael Weldon; pp66-7, pp358-9 and pp638-9 by Javier Zarracina.

THIS BOOK

This 18th edition of Lonely Planet's *India* guidebook was curated by Joe Bindloss, Lindsay Brown, Paul Harding, Anirban Mahapatra, Daniel McCrohan, Isabella Noble and John Noble. This guide was researched and written by Joe, Lindsay, Paul, Anirban, Daniel, Isabella and John, along with Michael Benanav, Stuart Butler, Mark Elliott, Trent Holden, Bradley Mayhew, Kevin Raub, Sarina Singh and Iain Stewart. The previous edition was also written by Lindsay, Anirban, Isabella, John, Kevin, Sarina, Michael, Mark, Paul, Bradley

and Iain, along with Abigail Blasi and Anna Kaminski. This guidebook was produced by the following:

Destination Editor Joe Bindloss

Senior Product Editor Kate Chapman

Senior Cartographer Valentina Kremenchutskaya

Product Editor Amanda Williamson

Book Designer Mazzy Prinsep

Assisting Editors Sarah Bailey, James Bainbridge, Judith Bamber, Imogen Bannister, Katie Connolly, Michelle Coxall, Kate Daly, Andrea Dobbin, Samantha

Forge, Emma Gibbs, Carly Hall, Kate James, Kellie Langdon, Jodie Martire, Alison Morris, Lauren O'Connell, Kristin Odijk, Charlotte Orr, Monique Perrin, Christopher Pitts, Simon Williamson

Assisting Cartographers Anita Banh, James Leversha

Cover Researcher Naomi Parker

Thanks to Will Allen, Jennifer Carey, Katie Connelly, Grace Dobell, Bailey Freeman, Evan Godt, Gemma Graham, Shona Gray, Andi Jones, Sandie Kestell, Anne Mason, Kate Mathews, Claire Naylor, Karyn Noble, Niamh O'Brien, Matt Phillips, Kathryn Rowan

Index

Map Legend

Sights

- Beach
- Bird Sanctuary
- Buddhist
- Castle/Palace
- Christian
- Confucian
- Hindu
- Islamic
- Jain
- Jewish
- Monument
- Museum/Gallery/Historic Building
- Ruin
- Shinto
- Sikh
- Taoist
- Winery/Vineyard
- Zoo/Wildlife Sanctuary
- Other Sight

Activities, Courses & Tours

- Bodysurfing
- Diving
- Canoeing/Kayaking
- Course/Tour
- Sento Hot Baths/Onsen
- Skiing
- Snorkelling
- Surfing
- Swimming/Pool
- Walking
- Windsurfing
- Other Activity

Sleeping

- Sleeping
- Camping
- Hut/Shelter

Eating

- Eating

Drinking & Nightlife

- Drinking & Nightlife
- Cafe

Entertainment

- Entertainment

Shopping

- Shopping

Information

- Bank
- Embassy/Consulate
- Hospital/Medical
- @ Internet
- Police
- Post Office
- Telephone
- Toilet
- Tourist Information
- Other Information

Geographic

- Beach
- Gate
- Hut/Shelter
- Lighthouse
- Lookout
- Mountain/Volcano
- Oasis
- Park
- Pass
- Picnic Area
- Waterfall

Population

- Capital (National)
- Capital (State/Province)
- City/Large Town
- Town/Village

Transport

- Airport
- Border crossing
- Bus
- Cable car/Funicular
- Cycling
- Ferry
- Metro/MRT/MTR station
- Monorail
- Parking
- Petrol station
- Skytrain/Subway station
- Taxi
- Train station/Railway
- Tram
- Underground station
- Other Transport

Routes

- Tollway
- Freeway
- Primary
- Secondary
- Tertiary
- Lane
- Unsealed road
- Road under construction
- Plaza/Mall
- Steps
- Tunnel
- Pedestrian overpass
- Walking Tour
- Walking Tour detour
- Path/Walking Trail

Boundaries

- International
- State/Province
- Disputed
- Regional/Suburb
- Marine Park
- Cliff
- Wall

Hydrography

- River, Creek
- Intermittent River
- Canal
- Water
- Dry/Salt/Intermittent Lake
- Reef

Areas

- Airport/Runway
- Beach/Desert
- Cemetery (Christian)
- Cemetery (Other)
- Glacier
- Mudflat
- Park/Forest
- Sight (Building)
- Sportsground
- Swamp/Mangrove

Note: Not all symbols displayed above appear on the maps in this book

Trent Holden

Uttarakhand A Geelong-based writer, located just outside Melbourne, Trent has worked for Lonely Planet since 2005. He's covered 30-plus guidebooks across Asia, Africa and Australia. With a penchant for megacities, Trent's in his element when assigned to cover a nation's capital – the more chaotic the better – to unearth cool bars, art, street food and underground subculture. On the flipside he also writes books to idyllic tropical islands across Asia, in between going on safari to national parks in Africa and the subcontinent. When not travelling, Trent works as a freelance editor, reviewer and spending all his money catching live gigs. You can catch him on Twitter @hombreholden.

Bradley Mayhew

Kashmir & Ladakh; Agra & the Taj Mahal; Uttar Pradesh Bradley has been writing guidebooks for 20 years now. He started travelling while studying Chinese at Oxford University, and has since focused his expertise on China, Tibet, the Himalaya and Central Asia. He is the cowriter of Lonely Planet guides Tibet, Nepal, Trekking in the Nepal Himalaya, Bhutan, Central Asia and many others. Bradley has also fronted two TV series for Arte and SWR, one retracing the route of Marco Polo via Turkey, Iran, Afghanistan, Central Asia and China, and the other trekking Europe's 10 most scenic long-distance trails. Bradley has also worked on guides to Mongolia, Jordan, Morocco, India and the Indian Himalaya; written for Rough Guides; contributed chapters to Silk Road: Monks, Warriors & Merchants and is a cowriter of Insight Guide's Silk Road.

Kevin Raub

Mumbai; Maharashtra Atlanta native Kevin started his career as a music journalist in New York, until he ditched the rock 'n' roll lifestyle for travel writing. He has since written more than 70 Lonely Planet guides, focused mainly on Brazil, Chile, Colombia, USA, India, the Caribbean and Portugal. Kevin also contributes to a variety of travel magazines in both the USA and UK. Along the way, the self-confessed hophead is in constant search of wildly high IBUs in local beers, and continues pounding the world's pavements with one goal in mind: membership in the Travelers' Century Club before the age of 50. His country count currently stands at 93. Follow him on Twitter and Instagram @RaubOnTheRoad.

Sarina Singh

After finishing her business degree Sarina bought a one-way ticket to India, where she met an aspiring photographer who requested her to write a paragraph for one of his photos in the hope he could get it published. The magazine asked Singh to turn her 100 word 'caption' into a 3000 word feature, and so began her accidental writing career. After five years in India she returned to her home town of Melbourne to pursue postgraduate studies at one of Australia's top journalism universities. Sarina has written for 50 Lonely Planet titles, including more than 10 editions of India; four editions of Rajasthan and three editions of South India. She has also written for dozens of other international publications such as UK's Sunday Times and USA's National Geographic Traveler. Find her on Twitter @sarina_singh and www.sarinasingh.com. Sarina wrote the Plan Your Trip, Understand and Survival Guide sections.

Iain Stewart

Karnataka; Telangana & Andhra Pradesh Iain trained as journalist in the 1990s and then worked as a news reporter and a restaurant critic in London. He started writing travel guides in 1997 and has since penned more than 60 books for destinations as diverse as Ibiza and Cambodia. Iain's contributed to Lonely Planet titles including Mexico, Indonesia, Central America, Croatia, Vietnam, Bali & Lombok and South-East Asia. He also writes regularly for the Independent, Observer and Daily Telegraph and tweets at @iaintravel. He'll consider working anywhere there's a palm tree or two and a beach of a generally sandy persuasion. Iain lives in Brighton (UK) within firing range of the city's wonderful south-facing horizon.